The Great Scots Musicography

The Complete Guide to Scotland's Music Makers

Martin C. Strong

Illustrations by Stuart Murray

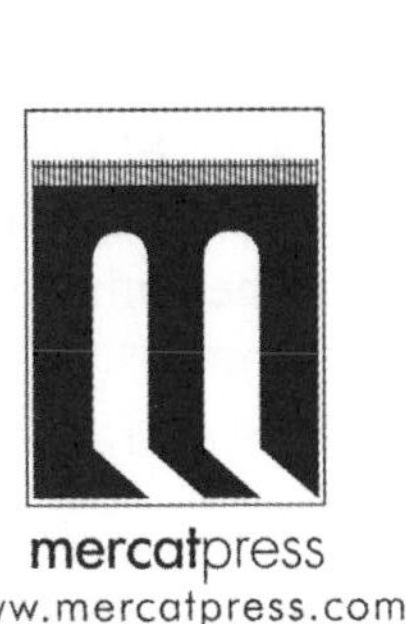

mercatpress
www.mercatpress.com

This book is dedicated to ...

my mother JEAN FOTHERINGHAM
(born: 6th of January 1929,
died of cancer: 31st of August 1985)

Still missing you
and thanks for still
guiding me through all
the hard times.

my dad GERRY/GEOFF STRONG
(born: 28th of July 1930,
died of a heart attack: 20th October 1998)

Will miss you always.
You were also a great friend, inspiration
and someone who could make me laugh.

Hope you're both getting on up there.
If only ...

* * *

First published in 2002 by Mercat Press,
10 Coates Crescent, Edinburgh EH3 7AL

ISBN 1 84183 041 0

Typeset by TexturAL, Dundee

Printed and bound in Scotland by Bell & Bain, Glasgow

Contents

Acknowledgements

I'd like to thank contributors BRENDON GRIFFIN, ADAM STAFFORD, ALAN Y. LAWSON, VIC GALLOWAY, JAMIE WATSON, GRANT MACNAMARA, JOHN HUTCHISON, TERRY HOUNSOME, BRUCE FINDLAY, and illustrator STUART MURRAY..

Also my friends and acquaintances ALLAN and ELAINE BREWSTER, VIC ZDZIEBLO, DAWN FORD (+ family), DOUGIE NIVEN, MIKEY KINNAIRD, IAN 'HARRY' HARRISON, ANDY RISK, SANDY and CAROLINE McCRAE, PETER McGUCKIN, EILEEN SCOTT-MONCRIEFF (+ family), ELAINE BROWN, KIP HANNAN, TONY HUGHES, PAUL HUGHES, TAM MORRISON, MICHAEL FLETCHER, HAMISH BRUCE + everyone at Alex SMITH's bar in Falkirk, PAUL KLEMM, BILL FISHER, BRIAN McLAUGHLIN, JIM + BETTY, JOHN McARDLE, LAURIE DOOLAN, BARNEY MIERS, BILLY and ANN ROSS, CAROLINE and ARCHIE, JIM + ANN CONNAL, MARIE + STEPH, ROBERT FAUX, CARRIE DRUMMOND, BARRY MOORE, ALLAN 'EAGY' EAGLESHAM + LEONA, GIZMO, GRANT BAILEY, JIM BEATTIE, JOE SIMPSON, KIRSTEN ROSE, TONY WEIR, MARTIN McDERMOTT, PAUL BAAS, STEVEN HUGHES, IAIN McLEAN, DAVIE GALLOWAY, MARTIN "No.7" MULLAN, ANDREANA + TONY, ALEC GRAY, BRUCE FINDLAY, RICHARD MIDNIGHT HATSIZE SNYDER (ex-Captain Beefheart & The Magic Band), HAMISH McLEOD PRENTICE, BRIAN VAUSE, RUSSELL MAYES, ROY JACK, SHUG MACKIE, STEVIE CANAVAN, TOM COCHRANE, IAIN SUTHERLAND, JOHN + TRACY, GEORGE MAIN, RAY NOTLEY, DEREK IRVINE + ELIZABETH BARCLAY, DAVIE BLAIR, LES O'CONNOR (deceased), CHRIS REID (deceased), GEORDIE YOUNG (deceased), BUFF, TED MOCHAR, DAVIE SEATH, GRAHAM MINTO, DAVID FLETCHER, RAY MORTON, DAVID BLUE, HUNTER WATT, DEREK CLARKIN, STEVEN and JOANNE HAGGERTY, GYLLA-FIONA SIMPSON, ANDY MILNER, BOB PARR, STEWART CRUICKSHANK, LINDSAY HUTTON, MALCOLM STEWART (of Jimpress fanzine), the Hebrides pub guys DAVIE BISSETT, MALCOLM YORK, ANDY SUTHERLAND (+ TINA) and JOHN BISSETT, WILLIE LIDDLE, MICK QUINN, ARTHUR JACK, EWAN (of Europa Records, Friar Street, Stirling; a brilliant shop for every type of music buff), STEVE + KATEY + staff at GILDED CAGE, Falkirk, everyone at MERCAT PRESS and CANONGATE BOOKS (they know who they are), DEREK KILLAH and all the staff who helped me at the Falkirk Library. If I've forgotten anyone I'm sorry as I've just moved house and papers are all over the place.

A very special mention to my daughters SUZANNE and SHIRLEY, my grandson IVOR, my auntie JOYCE, my cousins PAUL, STEPHEN (+ NINA), BRIAN (+ JEANETTE), KEVIN (+ KAREN) and MAUREEN McELROY, AVRIL and JACKIE, uncle FRANK in Australia, ISOBEL and DANNY BUCHANNAN, JENNIFER and DANIEL.

The books which helped greatly were:– THE HISTORY OF SCOTTISH ROCK AND POP: ALL THAT EVER MATTERED (by Brian Hogg), ROCKIN' AROUND BRITAIN (Pete Frame), RECORD COLLECTOR RARE RECORD PRICE GUIDE, GUINNESS BRITISH HIT SINGLES & ALBUMS, DAZZLING STRANGER (by Colin Harper), SINGLES FILE (Terry Hounsome), THE GUINNESS WHO'S WHO OF . . . (Colin Larkin), FIT LIKE, NEW YORK? (Pete Innes), THE TAPESTRY OF DELIGHTS (Borderline Productions), ROCK LPs (Tilch), THE INTERNATIONAL DISCOGRAPHY OF THE NEW WAVE (B George & Martha DeFoe), ROBERT BURNS – PRIDE & PASSION (Gavin Sprott) and of course THE GREAT ROCK DISCOGRAPHY (by . . . er, me!). Also please note the brilliant official/unofficial band/record-label websites on the internet, including ALL MUSIC GUIDE, GRACENOTE, AMAZON, etc. Other weekly/monthly music journos I read and thank are the NME, LASERLOG/R.E.D., RECORD COLLECTOR, MUSIC WEEK, BILLBOARD and KERRANG!

* * * * *

Foreword

To be asked to do a foreword for a book is certainly an honour, a surprise and something that seriously bolsters the ego. Any book! However this is not just 'any book' – it's a Martin C. Strong book and therefore a work of meticulous research, painstaking accuracy and, to be quite frank, slightly unhealthy obsession!

If you've ever had the chance to leaf through one of Martin's 'Magna Opi' (my Latin's not what it used to be!), you'll know the level of dedication he has and the minute detail he goes into. The man is on a mission. For example, when meeting in an Edinburgh pub to discuss this book, I arrived sporting a T-shirt with a new Scottish band's logo emblazoned on the front. His initial smile and friendly handshake were hastily withdrawn as he scrambled about in a pocket for a pen and scrap of paper to jot down their name and any details I had about them – "Oh No, Vic. I havenae got them in the book" – this was before we'd even bought a pint!

You must understand then, that 'The Great Scots Musicography' continues in this maniacal tradition and follows his previous scholarly works in style. In fact, it could be Martin's finest offering to date, or at least closest to the Falkirk man's heart. It's a book that plots and documents every detail (to my knowledge anyway) of the rich tapestry of musical heritage that continues to live and breathe in our wee country regardless of trends, fashions or economic and political change. I mean, what other land could have produced the likes of Lonnie Donegan, The Rezillos, Alex Harvey, Tommy Smith, Travis, Jimmy Shand and The Jesus and Mary Chain? And what other book could include facts and figures about both The Krankies and Mogwai? (Surely we can get these two into a studio to do an album together?!). From Evelyn Glennie to Idlewild; Billy Connolly to the Bay City Rollers; Sydney Devine to The Skids; as well as record labels and clubs – this has them all and is sure to astound and enhance a million musical minds.

What also deserves the utmost respect is the inclusion of chapters concerning minor artists and MP3 bands (with a frighteningly large piece on a certain beat-combo called 'Huckleberry'. . . ahem). This is an almost impossible task and could probably warrant a complete book all to itself, requiring continual monitoring of the Internet and the day-to-day discovery of new and unheard artists. However, I don't know anyone more suited to the job.

If you're a lover of Scottish music past, present and future, this book has to be seen as a benchmark. It may simply be a starting place for some or confirmation for others. One thing's for sure, it's going to teach me a thing or two about a myriad of artists I've only ever heard of, and help me recount all the useful (and useless) pieces of information I can't store in my tiny little brain.

So dig in and enjoy, get inspired, continue our great legacy and give Martin a never-ending series of re-editions to work on.

Vic Galloway

(Broadcaster and Rock'n'Roll Mercenary!)

Introduction

MC Strong – Musicography

Born: MARTIN CHARLES STRONG, 8th September 1960, Musselburgh, nr. Edinburgh. Raised in Falkirk by his divorced mother from the age of seven(-ish), fitba' crazy Martin took his interest in music after listening to DJs Alan Freeman and John Peel on Radio 1; Top Of The Pops (and a little later) The Old Grey Whistle Test were to also give him inspiration when his mother finally bought a telly.

While visiting his dad Gerry (and Hibernian FC) in Edinburgh every fortnight, Martin would also listen to his cousin's (the McELROYS from Portobello) record collection which included the likes of Scottish acts The CORRIES, The INCREDIBLE STRING BAND and DONOVAN; it made a change from 'Sabbath and 'Purple. A headbanger in every sense of the word, Martin would be caught out by his mother, er, performing in front of the mirror. His mother Jean would subsequently buy him an electric guitar (+ 0–11 amp), although after listening to his rendition of "Smoke On The Water" over and over (and over!) again, she decided to sell one of them off. Luckily, the local rag (The Falkirk Herald) wouldn't take unruly children but they did have a section to sell unwanted second-hand goods; this is why MC hates it when people say he has to play an instrument to be able to write about music.

A top fan of (The SENSATIONAL) ALEX HARVEY (BAND) until Punk and New Wave came onto the music scene, the tall, lean and hairy High School dropout – he's still tall but forget the lean and hairy! – went from job to job in search of anything really that would let him keep his headphones on; he still grunts about not getting that place behind the counter at his local record shop. A labourer, er, a footballer?, a salesman and er, a labourer (again and again), the man with only two O-Levels (Art & Arithmetic) counted down the days until he found his niche – and it wasn't painting by numbers. STRONG would re-invent the Discography but not the Wheel (that would come later in Falkirk). Since 1982 – incidentally and poignantly at the same time as SIMPLE MINDS' "Promised You A Miracle" was high in the charts – Martin worked on his own style of easy-to-read Discographies although it would be another twelve years and a lotta, lotta heartache and hair loss before its publication in December 1994 – his promise to the pub(lic) was fulfilled.

. . . And Now For Something Completely Serious!

The Book(s): Martin has come a long way since The GREAT ROCK DISCOGRAPHY hit the shops. In fact, his 829-page First Edition nearly didn't reach the shops at all, when, only a fortnight before it was supposed to do so (September 1994), his publishers Canongate Press went to the receivers. However, along came young Mr. Byng (Jamie, to you!), who helped buy out the company . . . and the rest – as they say – was history. Thankfully, for an enthusiastic but well-worn Mr. Strong (Martin, to anybody!), the man from down south kept his book on. Along with other offshoots (Psychedelic, Metal (2), Alternative & Indie and Wee discographies), the GRD has now sold in excess of 150,000 copies worldwide and is now in its 6th Edition (published by Canongate Books in September 2002); counting that tome, 12 books in all.

Well over two years ago, at the turn of the new millennium, Strong (with encouragement of freelance typesetter Alan Lawson and a few biographers – see acknowledgements) took on the task of detailing the facts about Scottish outfits not already tackled in previous editions. Little did the naive Bairn from Falkirk know how many Discographies/Biographies were needed. Strong had never really established a good database that included such giant genres as Folk, Traditional, Comedy/Entertainers, Jazz, Classical, etc; his field was more Rock, Pop & Indie. In fact, he might just have got away with the latter three genres in a book on their own, but his vision was to include every Scottish artist that ever recorded, no matter what music they performed. In May/June 2001, the book was ready.

Sadly (and unwisely in many people's opinions), Canongate decided to reject a (nearly completed) typeset draft of Martin's THE GREAT SCOTS MUSICOGRAPHY on grounds that it wouldn't sell more than a couple of thousand copies. Not ever a man to waste his time, the hurt (but yet slightly proud and angry) Strong took it to three further so-called Scottish publishers, who – after what seemed a long-drawn-out period – also politely decided to give it a miss.

Just when he thought it was safe to get back in the murky waters of publishing books – although he was now concentrating on another Canongate tome, THE GREAT METAL DISCOGRAPHY II – his new agent, David Fletcher, found yet another publisher, this time the proudly Scottish and thankfully ambitious MERCAT PRESS.

However, things weren't bricks and mortar quite yet, as on the day of Martin's Mercat interview, parent company and major book retailer, James Thin, were on the TV news and in danger of folding. Strong – as previously mentioned – had seen it nearly happen to him and his book before several years ago with Canongate. He still attended the Mercat meeting and was given assurances by a worthy trio of Seán Costello, Tom Johnstone and Catherine Read, that once everything was resolved – although "it could take months" – the book would hit the shops. Meanwhile, in the first half of 2002, Martin completed the GRD VI for Canongate – he was fulfilling his contract but not yet his dream.

In July 2002, Strong woke up, bought a new flat and took up the task to complete his Scottish tome. When he finally finished the Musicography (incidentally, a non-dictionary word between Discography and Biography) that September, "The Man Who" . . . finally found meaning to the TRAVIS album of that title and his own music-filled life.

Who's Included, and Why

Well, what's in the book then? Apart from the obvious that there's only Scottish recording artists in this book, what marks it out as different from my usual run-of-the-mill Discography tomes? Well, for one, it goes further to being up to date (around 9 months ahead of the recently published GREAT ROCK DISCOGRAPHY 6th edition). I've been allowed to take the Scots book releases up to September 2002 while – because of the scale and size of the project – the aforementioned GRD can only go as far as the end of 2001.

I've also omitted 'Album Rating' – basically I didn't want to compare LENA ZAVARONI with say LULU or ANNIE LENNOX. The title of the book suggests that every artist included is "great" – you decide if you think otherwise.

This illustrated Scots book (complete with Contents & Index pages) is also the first of its kind to feature record-label biographies/discographies; yes, 'Temple' and 'Greentrax' to 'Zoom' and 'Chemikal Underground'. Note also that you can differentiate between Scottish and foreign acts, as the latter are in italics not bold. Most of the label discographies also incorporate potted biographies of the associated Scottish acts.

Could Section 10 on mp3 (internet) groups be the future of the music industry? Personally, I hope not.

How do I ascertain who's worthy and who's not? My definition of a Scot is a person who was born here (obviously!), has made Scotland their home or who has been brought up a Scot – no matter where in the world that be. This book has left out many prejudices where they should be – in the bin.

The world is now – and has been for some time – an easier place to access, commute and settle down in, therefore many Scots-born people have flown the nest to warmer and more prosperous climates such as America, Australia and even England. Earlier this year I thought seriously about moving to Los Angeles. Would that have made me less of a Scot? – I've stayed here for 42 years. I didn't do the deed anyway, but one day I might. There are hundreds of Scots-born musicians who, for one reason or another and sometimes outwith their control (e.g. their parents emigrated), have crossed the border or the water to further their career. Future 'Talking Heads' frontman DAVID BYRNE was only a toddler when his parents went to Baltimore via Canada. Others too have left these shores at a very young age:– IAN ANDERSON (Jethro Tull) who now fish-farms up north, BON SCOTT, ANGUS and MALCOLM YOUNG (all AC/DC), JIMMY BARNES (Cold Chisel), MARK KNOPFLER (Dire Straits), DR ROBERT (Blow Monkeys) and solo artist FINLEY QUAYE.

Others to vacate our wee perimeters to make a name for themselves were LONNIE DONEGAN, KARL DENVER, JACK BRUCE (Cream), BRIAN CONNOLLY (Sweet), EVE GRAHAM (New Seekers), AL STEWART, DONOVAN, ANNIE LENNOX (Tourists & Eurythmics), FISH (Marillion; he still stays here though), folkie ERIC BOGLE, JIMMY SOMERVILLE (Bronski Beat), ALAN FREW (Glass Tiger), Creation boss ALAN McGEE (who took The JESUS & MARY CHAIN and PRIMAL SCREAM with him), The SHAMEN and ex-GOODBYE MR MACKENZIE girl SHIRLEY MANSON (Garbage); there is also an arms-length list of jazzmen who understandably took off to London to be near the scene.

Others to depart "AFTER" they made a name for themselves were Bellshill lassie SHEENA EASTON (complete with "rich" Californian accent), LULU (with "rich" borderline accent to suit anywhere and anything she's doing), ex-SLIK man MIDGE URE (to Ultravox; Glaswegian accent still in tow), Grangemouth duo the COCTEAU TWINS (to London) and not forgetting comedian/actor BILLY CONNOLLY (now a part-time Scot who'd like to live a lotto the time here but only if the price was right).

Don't be too judgemental on these ex-pats: some of us/you would probably do the same (i.e. if we married a foreigner and had lots of dosh to spread around). Remember, all the major music labels and celebrity people are based in London and America and although it only takes a few hours (or several) to jump on a plane and get to work, you couldn't do it every day.

I've talked about our exports and that brings us nicely to our imports. Many people have talked to me about why I would include some artists who weren't born in Scotland. Do they (or you) really want me to exclude Manchester-born EWAN MacCOLL, Surrey-born JOHN MARTYN, Calcutta-born HAMISH IMLACH, Leicester-born DAVEY GRAHAM, Irish-born OWEN HAND, most of whom have a Scots accent that could strip wallpaper? Others to have come to these shores a little later than birth have been KLF man BILL DRUMMOND (born South Africa), jazz saxophonist TOMMY SMITH (born Luton), jazz guitarist MARTIN TAYLOR (born Harlow), ambient folkie MARTYN BENNETT (born Newfoundland) and a whole group IONA (from south of the border) who settled and named themselves after the island.

Of course, the most controversial inclusion was always going to be London-born ROD STEWART. The tartan troubadour and surely honorary Scot (if ever there was one) supports Scotland's football team (even now!), has been known to sing about Scotland and virtually shags for Scotland! If Rod The Mod was excluded (as he was in Brian Hogg's "History Of Scottish Rock & Pop" several years back!) then what of the whole of BIG COUNTRY (although raised in Dunfermline, STUART ADAMSON – sadly now deceased – was actually born in Manchester!). In fact the question of what defines Scottishness could, and might just, provide a book's worth of conjecture. The ever expanding Scottish diaspora throws up yet more dilemmas as the world becomes a much smaller place. Getting back to ROD, who after all, could have had a professional footballing career, it's obvious where his soccer sympathies lie. Having Scottish parentage (like several of today's English-born fitba'-playing professionals!), STEWART would be eligible to play for Scotland and indeed only a few years ago (2000), he pulled on a dark blue jersey for a celebrity match against the "Auld Enemy". Prime Minister Tony Blair on the other hand, prefers to shout for England (no matter what the sport; the recent bid for The Ryder Cup being an example) despite going to school north of the border. Then again, maybe the debate should be put on hold until ROD actually decides to live in the country he's so keen on. Scotland has such a wide spread of musical talent ranging from the great bards to folk and traditional country dance music, classical and jazz, rock, pop, indie and modern dance music. What other country (bar the USA, possibly?!) could fill this wide and varied spectrum – oh yes, and we have SALSA CELTICA too.

To end the introduction – I do go on, don't I? – Mercat Press and myself invite ANY reader to come up with their Top 10, 20 or 30 albums from Scottish artists and the same for singles/tracks; do not list an Ultravox or Eurythmics set please, as selections must appear in this book. My personal favourites/playlist over the years have been:- The SENSATIONAL ALEX HARVEY BAND, MOGWAI, The INCREDIBLE STRING BAND, COCTEAU TWINS, The BETA BAND, DONOVAN, ASSOCIATES, The BLUE NILE, ARAB STRAP, TRAVIS, BOARDS OF CANADA, MALINKY, MARTYN BENNETT, IVOR CUTLER, DAVEY GRAHAM, BERT JANSCH, SHOOGLENIFTY, SPARE SNARE, BELLE & SEBASTIAN and more recently the unsigned LADY MIDNIGHT and SULA BASANA / Y'ALL FANTASY ISLAND.

All above written by Me, Myself & I on the 27th & 30th of September 2002. I hope the whole of Scotland (and beyond) love this book . . . for ever.

Martin C. Strong
Falkirk, September 2002

How to Read the Book

If you're struggling in any way how to comprehend some of the more complex parts of each discography, here are some examples to make it easier. Read below for around 10 minutes, taking a step at a time. The final lines/examples you see will give you a good guide before you proceed with the actual chronological discographies. However, I think that once you've read your own favourites you'll have a good idea.

GROUP / ARTIST

Formed/Born: Where/When ... biography including style/analysis, songwriters, cover versions, trivia, etc.

SINGER (born; b. day/month/year, town/city) – vocals, whatever (ex-GROUP; if any) / **MUSICIAN** (b. BIRTH NAME, 8 Sep'60, Musselburgh) – instruments / **OTHER MUSICIANS** – other instruments, vocals, etc.

UK Label US Label

UK date. (single, ep or album) *(UK cat.no.)* *<US cat.no.>* **THE TITLE** [ ] [ ] US date

note:- UK label – might be another country's label if not released in UK.
also:- Labels only appear when the group signs to a new one.
note:- UK date – might be foreign, <even American at times>, if not initially issued in Britain.
note:- (UK catalogue number; in curved brackets) <US cat.no.; in angle brackets>
note:- chart positions, UK + US, are in the boxes below labels.
also:- the boxes in the above example have been left blank, thus they did not hit either UK or US charts.
note:- US date after the boxes indicates a variation from its UK counterpart.
also:- Any other info on the right of the boxes (e.g. German) indicates it was not issued in the US.

UK date. (7") *(UK cat.no.)* **A-SIDE. / B-SIDE** [ ] [-]
US date. (7") *<US cat.no.>* **A-SIDE. / DIFFERENT B-SIDE** [-] [ ]

note:- The two examples above show that the UK + US release did not have an identical A-side & B-side, thus the chart boxes are marked with a – to indicate it was not released in either the UK or the US.

UK date. (7"/c-s) *(CATNO 1/+C)* **A-SIDE. / B-SIDE** [ ] [-]

note:- above had two formats with the same tracks (i.e. 7"/c-s). However, catalogue numbers will always vary among different formats – often only slightly (e.g. CATNO 1/+C). Each cat.no. would read thus:- (7")=*(CATNO 1)* and (c-s)=*(CATNO 1C)*. To save space the (/) slash comes into effect. The (/) means "or" and in this case it is prefixed with a + sign for the equivalent cassette (c-s).

UKdate. (7"/c-s) *(example same as above)* **SEE ABOVE** [ ] [-]
(12"+=/cd-s+=) *(CATNO 1-12/1-CD)* – Extra tracks.

note:- If there are more formats with extra or different tracks, a new line would be used. Obviously there would also be alternative catalogue numbers utilising the "(/)" as before. Extra tracks would therefore mean the addition of the sign "(+=)" to each format.

UK date. (lp/c/cd) *(CATNO 200/+MC/CD)* *<US catno 4509>* **ALBUM TITLE** [ ] [ ]

– Track listing / Track 2 / And so on. *(re-issued = re-iss. A later date, and other 'Label' mentioned, if different from original; new cat.no.) (could be re-iss. many times and if "(+=)" sign occurs there will be extra tracks from the original) <could also apply to the US release if in pointed brackets>*

note:- Album above released in 3 formats, thus 3 catalogue numbers are necessary. The "long-player" lp *(CATNO 200)* is obvious. The "cassette" c = +MC *(CATNO 200MC)* or "compact disc" CD *(CATNO 200CD)*. The US *<cat.no.>* will normally be just one set of numbers (or see further below for other details).

UK date. (cd/c/lp) *(CD/TC+/CATNO+200)* *<UScatno 4509>*
ALBUM TITLE [ ] [ ] US date

note:- This time a prefix is used instead of a suffix, hence the difference before the standard lp catalogue number. For instance, the cd would read as *(CDCATNO 200)*.

Jun 97. (cd/c/lp) *<(5557 49860-2/-4/-1)>* **ALBUM TITLE** [1] [1] May 97

note:- Some catalogue numbers don't include any letters, but instead consist of a number sequence followed by one digit which universally corresponds with the format (i.e. 2 = cd / 4 = c / 1 = lp).
also:- If the US numbers are identical, there would be no need to list them separately, i.e. *<(the numbers)>*
note:- I've also marked down an actual date of release and its variant in the US (you'll find this fictitious album also hit No.1 in both charts "and ah've no even heard it yet, man!")

— **NEW MUSICIAN/SINGER** (b.whenever, etc.) – instruments (ex-GROUP(s) replaced = repl. DEPARTING MUSICIAN/SINGER, who joined whatever
note:- Above denotes a line-up change.

GROUP or ARTIST with major change of name

note:- above would always be in grey.

UK Label US Label

Jun 97. (cd/c/lp; GROUP or ARTIST with minor change of name) *<(5557 49860)>* **ALBUM TITLE** [1] [1] May 97

– compilations, etc. –

UKdate. (cd) *compilation Label only; (cat.no.)* **ALBUM TITLE** [100] [-]
– Track listing would be selective, only included if the release was deemed essential.

Formats & Abbreviations

VINYL (black-coloured unless stated)

(lp) = The (LONG PLAYER) record ... circular 12" plays at 33 1/3 r.p.m., and has photo or artwork sleeve. Approximate playing time ... 30–50 minutes with average 10 tracks. Introduced in the mid-50's on mono until stereo took over in the mid-60's. Quadrophonic had a spell in the 70's, but only on mainly best-selling lp's, that had been previously released. Because of higher costs to the manufacturer and buyer, the quad sunk around 1978. Also note that around the mid-50's, some albums were released on 10 inch. Note:– average cost to the customer as of now = £9.00 (new). Collectors can pay anything from £1 to over £500, depending on the quality of the recording. Very scratched records can be worthless, but unplayed mint deletions are worth a small fortune to the right person. Auctions and record fairs can be the place to find that long lost recording that's eluded you. This applies to all other vinyl below.

(d-lp) = The (DOUBLE-LONG PLAYER) record ... as before. Playing time 50–90 minutes on 4 sides, with

average 17 tracks. Introduced to rock/pop world in the late 60's, to complement compilations, concept & concert (aka live) albums.
Compilations:– are a selection of greatest hits or rare tracks, demos, etc.
Concepts:– are near-uninterrupted pieces of music, based around a theme.
Note that normal lp's could also be compilations, live or concept. Some record companies through the wishes of their artists, released double lp's at the price of one lp. If not, price new would be around £15.

(t-1p) = The (TRIPLE-LONG PLAYER) record ... as before. Playing time over 100 minutes with normally over 20 tracks. Because of the cost to the consumer, most artists steered clear of this format. Depending on the artwork on the sleeve, these cost over £17.50. (See its replacement, the CD.)

(4-1p-box) = The (BOXED-LONG PLAYER) record (could be between 4 and 10 in each boxed-set). As the triple album would deal with live, concept or compilation sides, the boxed-set would be mostly re-issues of all the artist's album material, with probably a bonus lp thrown in, to make it collectable. Could be very pricey, due to lavish outlay in packaging. They cost over £25 new.

(m-lp) = The (MINI-LONG PLAYER) record ... playing time between 20 and 30 minutes and containing on average 7 tracks. Introduced for early 80's independent market, and cost around £5.
= Note:– This could be confused at times with the extended-play 12" single.

(pic-1p) = The (PICTURE DISC-LONG PLAYER) record.. . as before but with album artwork/ design on the vinyl-grooves. Mainly for the collector because of the slightly inferior sound quality. If unplayed, these can fetch between £10 and £250.

(coloured lp) = The (COLOURED-LONG PLAYER) record; can be in a variety of colours including ... white / blue / red / clear / purple / green / pink / gold / silver.

(red-1p) = The (RED VINYL-LONG PLAYER) record would be an example of this.

(7") = The (7-INCH SINGLE). Arrived in the late 50's, and plays at 45 r.p.m. Before this its equivalent was the 10" on 78 r.p.m. Playing time now averages 4 minutes per side, but during the late 50's up to mid-60's, each side averaged $2^{1/2}$ minutes. Punk rock/new wave in 1977/78 resurrected this idea. In the 80's, some disco releases increased playing time. Another idea that was resurrected in 1977 was the picture sleeve. This had been introduced in the 60's, but mostly only in the States.
Note:– cost in mid-2002 averaged £2.50; second-hand rarities can cost between 25p and £200, depending again on their condition. These might also contain limited freebies/gifts (i.e. posters, patches, stickers, badges, etc). Due to the confusion this would cause, I have omitted this information, and kept to the vinyl aspect in this book. Another omission has been DJ promos, demos, acetates, magazine freebies, various artists' compilations, etc. Only official shop releases get a mention.

(7" m) = The (7-INCH MAXI-SINGLE). Named so because of the extra track, usually on the B-side. Introduced widely during the early 70's; one being ROCKET MAN by ELTON JOHN.

(7" ep) = The (7-INCH EXTENDED PLAY SINGLE). Plays mostly at $33^{1/3}$ r.p.m., with average playing time 10–15 minutes and 4 tracks. Introduced in the late 50's as compilations for people to sample their albums. These had a *title* and were also re-introduced from 1977 onwards, but this time for punk groups' new songs.

(d7") = The (DOUBLE 7-INCH SINGLE). Basically just two singles combined ... 4 tracks. Introduced in the late 70's for the "new wave/romantics", and would cost slightly more than normal equivalent.

(7" pic-d) = The (7-INCH PICTURE-DISC SINGLE). This was vinyl that had a picture on the grooves, which could be viewed through a see-through plastic cover.

(7" sha-pic-d) = The (7-INCH SHAPED-PICTURE-DISC SINGLE). Vinyl as above but with shape (i.e. gun, mask, group) around the edge of the groove. Awkward because it would not fit into the collector's singles box. Initially limited, and this can still be obtained at record fairs for over £3. Note:– However, in the book the type of shape has not been mentioned, to save space.

(7" coloured) = The (7-INCH COLOURED SINGLE). Vinyl that is not black (i.e. any other colour:– red, yellow, etc). Note:– (7" multi) would be a combination of two or more colours (i.e. pink/purple).

(7" flexi) = The (7-INCH FLEXIBLE SINGLE). One-sided freebies, mostly given away by magazines, at concerts or as mentioned here; free with single or lp. Worth keeping in mint condition and well protected.

(12") = The (12-INCH SINGLE). Plays at 45 r.p.m., and can have extended or extra tracks to its 7" counterpart (+=) or (++=). B-side's playing speed could be at 33 r.p.m. Playing time could be between 8 and 15 minutes. Introduced in 1977 with the advent of new wave and punk. They were again a must for collectors for the new wave of British heavy metal scene.

(12"ep) = The (12-INCH EXTENDED PLAY SINGLE). Virtually same as above but *titled* like the 7" ep. Playing time over 12 minutes, and could have between 3 and 5 tracks.

(d12")	=	The (DOUBLE 12-INCH SINGLE). See double 7". Can become very collectable and would cost new as normal 12", £4.50.
(12" pic-d)	=	The (12-INCH PICTURE-DISC SINGLE). As with 7" equivalent ... see above.
(12" sha-pic-d)	=	The (12-INCH SHAPED-PICTURE-DISC SINGLE). See above 7" equivalent.
(12" colrd)	=	The (12-INCH COLOURED SINGLE). Not black vinyl ... see above 7" equivalent.
(10")	=	The (10-INCH SINGLE). Plays at 45 r.p.m. and, like the 12", can have extra tracks (+=). Very collectable, it surfaced in its newer form around the early 80's, and can be obtained in shops at £4.50. Note:– also (10" ep) / (d10") / (10" coloured) / (10" pic-d) / (10" sha-pic-d).

CASSETTES

(c)	=	The (CASSETTE) album ... size in case $4^{1/2}$ inches high. Playing-time same as lp album, although after the mid-80's cd revolution, some were released with extra tracks. Introduced in the late 60's, to compete with the much bulkier lp. Until the 80's, most cassettes were lacking in group info, lyric sheets, and freebies. Note:– cost to the consumer as of now = £10–£11 new. But for a few exceptions, most do not increase in price, and can be bought second-hand or budget-priced for around £5.
(d-c)	=	The (DOUBLE-CASSETTE) album ... as above, and would hold same tracks as d-lp or even t-1p. Price between £12 and £16.
(c-s)	=	The (CASSETTE-SINGLE). Now released mostly with same two tracks as 7" equivalent. The other side played the same 2 or 3 tracks. Introduced unsuccessfully in the US around the late 60's. Re-introduced there and in Britain in the mid-80's. In the States, it and its cd counterpart have replaced the charting 7" single for the 90's. Cost new is around £1.99–£2.99, and might well become quite collectable.
(c-ep)	=	The (CASSETTE-EXTENDED PLAY SINGLE). Same as above but *titled* as 12".

COMPACT DISCS

(cd)	=	The (COMPACT DISC) album. All 5" circular and mostly silver on its playing side. Perspex casing also includes lyrics & info, etc. Introduced late in 1982, and widely the following year (even earlier for classical music). Initially for top recording artists, but now in 2002 nearly every release is in cd format. Playing time normally over 50 minutes with some containing extra tracks or mixes. Possible playing time is just over 75 minutes. Marketed as unscratchable, although if they go uncleaned, they will stick just as vinyl. Average price now is £15, and will become collectable if, contrary to most gloomy predictions, they do not deteriorate with time.
(d-cd)	=	The (DOUBLE-COMPACT DISC) album ... same as above although very pricey, between £20 and £25.
(cd-s)	=	The (COMPACT DISC-SINGLE). Mainly all 5" (but some 3" cd-s could only be played with a compatible gadget inside the normal cd player). Playing time over 15 minutes to average 25 minutes, containing 4 or 5 tracks. Introduced in 1986 to compete with the 12" ep or cassette. 99% contained extra tracks to normal formats. Cost new: £2.99 to £4.99.
(pic-cd-s)	=	The (PICTURE-COMPACT DISC-SINGLE). Has picture on disc, which gives it its collectability. Also on (pic-cd-ep).
(vid-pic-s)	=	The (VIDEO-COMPACT DISC-SINGLE). A video cd, which can be played through stereo onto normal compatible TV screen. Very costly procedure, but still might be the format of the future. Promo videos can be seen on pub jukeboxes, which has made redundant the returning Wurlitzer style.

DIGITAL AUDIO TAPE

(dat)	=	The (DIGITAL AUDIO TAPE) album. Introduced in the mid-80's and, except for Japan and the rich yuppie, are not widely issued. It is a smaller version of the cassette, with the quality of the cd.

Another format (which I have not included) is the CARTRIDGE, which was available at the same time as the cassette. When the cassette finally won the battle in the early 80's, the cartridge became redundant. All car-owners of the world were happy when thieves made them replace the stolen cartridge player with the resurrected cassette. You can still buy these second-hand, but remember you'll have to obtain a second-hand 25-year-old player, with parts possibly not available.

Other abbreviations: repl. = replaced / comp. = compilation / re-iss. = re-issued / re-dist. = re-distributed

1
The Great Scots Musical Heritage

Where else would you start this overview of Scotland's musical good and great than with the country's greatest ambassador, just over 200 years dead though he may be. The man in question is ROBERT BURNS, otherwise known as RABBIE BURNS, Scotland's national Bard or even the "Ploughman Poet", the latter title referring to his upbringing as the son of a poor tenant farmer. His songs continue to be performed by many of our current musicians.

* * *

Robert BURNS

was born in Alloway in Ayrshire on the 25th January 1759. Despite his family's poverty, the young RABBIE benefitted from a personal tutor (John Murdoch) and developed a taste for literature at a relatively young age. At the tender age of 15, the budding poet put pen to paper for the very first time. The result was 'My Handsome Nell', the first but certainly not the last BURNS poem to celebrate the earthly pleasures of whisky and women.

The man certainly had more luck with the ladies than he did with agriculture, his father's death in 1784 prompting an abortive farming venture with his brother. Although he was still in the fields upon the publication in 1786 of his first poetry volume, 'Poems – Chiefly In The Scottish Dialect', his literary ambitions and wandering spirit were to eventually take him to Edinburgh. By the point, the amorous wordsmith had already "sired" several weans to various women including his wife-to-be, Jean Armour; thankfully for the promiscuous poet the CSA were but a twinkle in the government's eye.

ROBERT was finally given his critical due in Auld Reekie where he became the toast of the bohemian bourgeoisie. Unfortunately this newfound fame didn't translate to financial reward and he was obliged to take up the undesirable position of tax collector (a subject which inspired one of his best works, 'The Deil's Awa Wi' The Exciseman'). A creatively fertile period for the Bard, BURNS made a major contribution to both James Johnson's 'Scots Musical Museum' (from 1787 . . .) and George Thomson's 'Select Collection of Original Scottish Airs' (from 1793 . . .), although he officially received scant recompense for his efforts. In fact, RABBIE's muse matured like a fine malt – a metaphor the great man would no doubt approve of – and much of his most revered verse was written in his twilight years (although he'd barely scraped into middle-age by the time of his death). As well as women, his favourite subjects were politics, religion and the Grim Reaper, BURNS' radical views reflecting his working class roots. A measure of his popularity was the turnout (in excess of 10,000) at his funeral in Dumfries on the 25th of July 1796, the great man having gone to meet his maker four days earlier as a result of endocarditis (inflammation of the lining membrane of the heart).

His musical legacy remains staggering, both in terms of quality and quantity. A detailed outline of his entire catalogue would fill a book in itself (there have been many – try for example Gavin Sprott's ' . . . Pride and Passion') but among his most famous pieces are, in no particular order, 'Auld Lang Syne', 'A Red, Red Rose', 'Tam O' Shanter', 'Green Grow The Rashes, O', 'Ye Banks And Braes o' Bonnie Doon', 'Such A Parcel Of Rogues In A Nation', 'Ae Fond Kiss', 'A Man's A Man For A' That', 'Ca' The Yowes', 'John Anderson My Jo', 'To A Mouse', 'The Lea Rig', 'Tam Lin', 'The Flowers Of The Desert' and 'The Twa Dogs'; the list could go on forever. BURNS' fame, both at home and abroad, seems to grow with each passing year. The annual ritual to celebrate his birth, The Burns Supper, attracts millions to various locations all over the globe and there can be few Scotsmen (native or adopted) who haven't raised a glass to Ayrshire's most famous son. His influence on the Folk artists of today is incalculable and everyone from JEAN REDPATH to EDDI READER have interpreted his songs. Even modern leftfield artists such as APPENDIX OUT have sung BURNS in their own obscure wee way.

Famous Fiddlers Three

If there were only three other pre-disc, pre-war musicians I could pick, then I couldn't go wrong with the following fiddlers. NIEL GOW, ROBERT TANNAHILL and J. SCOTT SKINNER – who've been mentioned time and time again in the Folk section – were over a century apart: **NIEL GOW** born near Dunkeld in Inver, Strathbraan on the 22 March, 1727 (died 1st March, 1807) and **JAMES SCOTT SKINNER** born in Banchory on the 15th of August 1843 (died on the 17th March 1927 in Aberdeen). Both virtuosos of the folk fiddle, the former had a 'Collection of Strathspey Reels' published in Edinburgh in 1784, while the latter "Strathspey King" composed over 600 tunes in the Scots idiom. Squeezed in time between these folk legends was **ROBERT TANNAHILL** (b. 1774, Paisley), a flautist, poet and songwriter who was inspired by Burns. Prone to bouts of depression, TANNAHILL drowned himself in a canal in 1810. Many would follow but few would gain the respect these three artists earned.

* * *

2
Folk Music

Oor Ain Folk: While every country in the world can boast its own indigenous folk music, few traditions have encompassed and celebrated culture and history as vividly and as passionately as Scotland. Obviously, Scots people have been writing, singing, blazing their fiddles and playing the pipes for generations yet the relatively short history of recorded folk music, to all intents and purposes, began after the Second World War.

The story really begins in the mid-50's with EWAN MacCOLL who, having met legendary folklorist Alan Lomax, set about unearthing and recording the huge legacy of British folk song. Although many people were under the impression that MacCOLL was indeed Scottish, it was later revealed that the man was born and bred in Manchester. He nevertheless warrants inclusion in this book for the pivotal part he played in reviving Scottish folk and bringing it to the nation's attention. Another major player in the native folk resurgence was Glasgow-born ALEX CAMPBELL, a well-travelled troubadour who carried on the itinerant singing tradition, if not the politics, of Woody Guthrie and Pete Seeger (whose half-sister Peggy tied the knot with CAMPBELL in order to remain with MacCOLL in the UK).

Yet if anybody can lay claim to the excavation and re-discovery of Scotland's folk heritage, it is the late, great HAMISH HENDERSON. Amongst many other achievements, HENDERSON tracked down ageing "source" singers such as JEANNIE ROBERTSON, JIMMY MacBEATH, DAVY STEWART and BELLE STEWART. These were people who had inherited centuries-old oral traditions yet had never ventured into a proper studio. HENDERSON initially made field recordings before supervising bonafide sessions. Just as importantly, he introduced them to the eager young folk-revivalists of the day. Thus the likes of ROBIN HALL & JIMMIE MacGREGOR, IAN CAMPBELL, DAVY GRAHAM, HAMISH IMLACH, The FISHER FAMILY (ARCHIE et al) and BERT JANSCH were given fresh inspiration from singers/performers who were the living embodiment of Scots tradition. To put things into context, the flourishing Edinburgh scene was mirrored by the activity in Glasgow (where, ironically, a few of the aforementioned were raised), London and of course Greenwich Village, New York, where Bob Dylan, Joan Baez and Phil Ochs were packing out the coffee houses. Also appearing in the Village's hipper establishments was one JEAN REDPATH, a Fifer born and bred, and an ambassador for Scottish song (especially the works of ROBERT BURNS). At the other end of the spectrum was Dylan-wannabe DONOVAN, the Glasgow-born pop star taking folk-inspired music into the charts for the very first time (thus his inclusion in the early Pop & Rock section).

Less hip but certainly no less traditional than the likes of REDPATH, The CORRIES – who for the bulk of their career comprised ROY WILLIAMSON and RONNIE BROWNE – represented the most identifiably Scottish face of folk. While not taking the tartan'n'shortbread factor to the extremes of say, The ALEXANDER BROTHERS (see another section), The CORRIES stirred the hearts of the masses with self-penned classics such as 'FLOWER OF SCOTLAND'; this has since become the National Anthem, with everyone from The McCALMANS to the Scottish football and rugby squads paying homage.

Flower-power was also the driving factor behind The INCREDIBLE STRING BAND, a wildly experimental outfit based on folk but heavily influenced by psychedelia. Multi-talented core members, ROBIN WILLIAMSON and MIKE HERON gravitated more towards the traditional side of folk in their latter-day solo careers. On the other hand, Glaswegians AL STEWART and JOHN MARTYN started out as folkies but soon evolved their own unique, hugely popular singer-songwriter style (as detailed in the early Pop &Rock section).

Also hailing from Glasgow were The HUMBLEBUMS, an easy-going folk outfit who originally comprised BILLY CONNOLLY and TAM HARVEY before GERRY RAFFERTY came on board. Like many Scottish folk revivalists, the group were on the roster of London-based 'Transatlantic' records, although CONNOLLY and RAFFERTY were both to go on to bigger and better things as solo artists. In fact by the early 70's the Scottish folk revival had run out of steam (Pentangle featuring JANSCH, Steeleye Span and Fairport Convention were just three of many still cutting it down south) and it was left to Shetland fiddler ALY BAIN and hard-hitting Glasgow songwriter DICK GAUGHAN to produce some credible folk music.

A new wave of young Scottish folk bands coalesced from the early 70's, although they spent a number of years treading the boards before venturing into the studio. The TANNAHILL WEAVERS (featuring DOUGIE MACLEAN and HUDSON SWAN), BATTLEFIELD BAND (with BRIAN McNEILL, ALAN REID, etc), SILLY WIZARD (the CUNNINGHAM brothers PHIL and JOHNNY passed through the ranks) and OSSIAN (spearheaded by the JACKSON clan of whom WILLIAM garnered most plaudits) were all bands, with perhaps the exception of BATTLEFIELD BAND, whose multi-talented individual members achieved greater recognition outwith the groups themselves.

While many of these musicians launched their solo careers towards the end of the decade, a lesser-known quantity began to makes waves around the same time. An ex-pat living in Australia, ERIC BOGLE was already pretty famous down

under by the time songs such as 'NO MAN'S LAND' (aka 'THE GREEN FIELDS OF FRANCE') and 'THE BAND PLAYED WALTZING MATILDA' reached the ears of British audiences.

Back in the Highlands and Islands, the more traditional Gaelic elements of folk music were being rediscovered and remoulded by folk-rock bands like RUNRIG (fronted by DONNIE MUNRO) and the more meditative CAPERCAILLIE (featuring KAREN MATHESON). The innovative folk fusions pursued by both acts would finally make mainstream critics (even south of the border) sit up and take note. Of course this would only happen er, 'ONCE IN A LIFETIME' as RUNRIG stormed the UK album charts in the late 80's despite much of the material being sung in Gaelic. CAPERCAILLIE's chart success was a bit longer in coming but no less deserved as the dancefloor-inflected 'COISICH, A' RUIN' hit the Top 40 in 1992. The band's willingness to experiment with electronic textures arguably opened the floodgates for a plethora of Nu-folk artists who once again put Scotland on the cutting edge.

With less emphasis on dogged tradition (excepting the likes of WOLFSTONE and er, The OLD BLIND DOGS) and more on originality and humour, folk music finally became sexy. The likes of The TARTAN AMOEBAS, SHOOGLENIFTY, DEAF SHEPHERD (all three on the sharp-eyed 'Greentrax' imprint) and Newfoundland-born MARTYN BENNETT, all remade folk music in their own respective idiosyncratic image. With the rise and rise of Glasgow's annual Celtic Connections Festival, the scene is in ruder health than perhaps any time in its history.

* * * * *

Joe AITKEN (see under ⇒ Springthyme records)

ALBA (see under ⇒ JSD BAND)

ALBANY (see under ⇒ ANDERSON, Billy or MacLEOD, Margaret)

ANAM

Formed: Dublin . . . Autumn 1992 by singer/songwriter BRIAN O hEADRA (aka O'HARA), who'd previously lived in Newfoundland, Canada as a child. Having soaked up a wealth of Celtic music influences, he began writing songs as a teenager and went on to study Irish Folklore and English literature.

Characterised by their adherence to Gaelic language singing, ANAM scooped a best band award at Brittany's L'Orient Interceltic Festival in 1993. A return visit to the festival in 1994 led to a meeting with AIMEE LEONARD, an Orcadian (Orkney Isles) vocalist/multi-instrumentalist who became part of ANAM prior to the recording of an eponymous debut album on their own 'Ceirnini Anam' label later that year. This was closely followed by 'SAOIRSE' (1995) while another new recruit arrived in the shape of Dublin-born accordionist TREASA HARKIN, who'd previously played button accordion with Comhaltas Ceoltair Fireann (Association of Irish Musicians) and worked in Dublin's Irish Traditional Music Archive. A subsequent major label deal with the Japanese 'JVC/Victor' company resulted in the 'FIRST FOOTING' album, released the same year ANAM upped sticks and moved to Edinburgh.

At home in the city's thriving folk scene, the group welcomed the addition of Cornish mandolin/bouzouki player, NEIL DAVEY, who made his debut on the group's 1998 album, 'RIPTIDE'. Produced by CALUM MALCOLM and featuring an array of native talent (TANNAHILL WEAVERS, SHOOGLENIFTY, RORY McLEOD etc), the record comprised a set of tunes composed largely by O HEADHRA and brought to life by LEONARD's ringing vocal harmonies. Yet the singer was to leave later that year, her replacement coming in the shape of FIONA MACKENZIE. A Gaelic vocalist from the Isle Of Lewis who'd previously recorded with both MACKENZIE (a trio featuring her sisters EILIDH and GILLIAN) and SEELYHOO, FIONA made her debut on ANAM's millennial release, 'TINE GHEAL – BRIGHT FIRE'. Also making her debut was Edinburgh-born fiddler ANNA-WENDY STEVENSON, a ubiquitous figure on the local folk scene who'd already worked with the ANNA MURRAY BAND, SAVOURNA STEVENSON and CALLUNA. With youth on their side and worldwide licensing and distribution deals, the newly Scots-dominated band look set to go from stength to strength.

BRIAN O hEADHRA – vocals, acoustic guitar, bodhran / with various personnel

Ceirnini / not iss.

1994. (cd) **ANAM** [-] [-] Irish

— added **AIMEE LEONARD** (b. Orkney Islands) – bodhran, tin whistle, keyboards, recorder, oboe, djembe, etc

Feb 95. (cd) **SAOIRSE** [-] [-] Irish

— added **TREASA HARKIN** – accordion (ex-COMHALTAS CEOLTAIR FIREANN) / guests incl. MYLES FARRELL – bouzouki + GERRY O'BEIRNE – guitars, etc

J.V.C. / J.V.C.

May 97. (cd) *(JVC 9011-2) <3504>* **FIRST FOOTING** [ ] [ ] Jun97
– Mylie's revenge – The piper's wedding (reels) / Take this moment / Siul, a ruin (Walk my love) / The last pint – Trim the velvet (reels) / The next market day – the market square (waltz) / Planxty Joe Burke / Lovely Joan / Dan Amhairgin (Amhairgin's poem) / Shetlag (jig) / Sally free and easy / The sweet flowers of Milltown (jig) – The sweet flowers of Milltown (reel) – Paddy's trip to Lake Arthur / The liberty. *(re-iss. Mar00 on 'Linn'; CKD 135)*

— added **NEIL DAVEY** (b. Newquay, Cornwall) – mandolin, bouzouki (of DALLA) / guests inc. SHOOGLENIFTY, JOHN MARTIN (of TANNAHILL WEAVERS) / RORY McLEOD, etc

J.V.C. / Green Linnet

May 98. (cd) *(JVC 90342) <GLCD 3121>* **RIPTIDE** [ ] [ ] Jun98
– Riptide (reels) / This time / Kjetil's song / An blew Treghys (Cornish gavotte) / Mo chaillin donn (My brown haired girl) / Mary and the soldier / The long night (slip jigs) / House on the hill (reels) / Westlin' winds / Fourteen days / Belgarth waltz / Aird a chuamhain / The way is clear. *(re-iss. Mar00 on 'Linn'; CKD 134)*

— when AIMEE left, she was repl. by **FIONA MacKENZIE** (b. Isle of Lewis) – vocals, bodhran (ex-SEELYHOO, ex-MacKENZIE) + **ANNA-WENDY STEVENSON** (b. Edinburgh) – fiddle (of CALLUNA) / guests again from SHOOGLENIFTY

Linn / Linn

Feb 00. (cd) *(<CKD 121>)* **TINE GHEAL – BRIGHT FIRE** [ ] [ ]
– Tine gheal – Bright fire / The conundrum / In O / Will you break my heart? / Heb dewa / Mhurchaidh bhig a chinn a' chonais / Father Tim / S' gann gun dirich mi chaoidh / The seagull / North Americay / Tane an gove / Nan's song / Ta an oiche seo dorcha.

— BRIAN has since recorded his first solo album . . .

Tom ANDERSON (see under ⇒ BAIN, Aly)

Davey ARTHUR

Born: Edinburgh, 24 Sep'54. In his late teens, ARTHUR formed the The BUSKERS with two errant brothers from The FUREYS folk clan, namely PAUL and GEORGE. News of a road accident involving The BUSKERS led to FINBAR and EDDIE returning to the UK (where they'd been on tour) and the subsequent formation of TAM LINN, an outfit which featured DAVEY, PAUL, FINBAR and EDDIE. A successful performance at the Cambridge Folk Festival and the eventual addition of GEORGE preceded a name change to THE FUREYS & DAVEY ARTHUR.

A more commercial strain of crossover folk saw the group break into the UK Top 20 in 1981 with the single, 'When You Were Sweet Sixteen'. While follow-up, 'I Will Love You (Every Time When We Are Gone)' failed to repeat this success, mid-80's 'K-Tel'-released albums such as 'Golden Days' (1984) and 'At The End Of A Perfect Day' (1985) appealed to the easy listening end of the folk market and sold fairly respectably, notching up Top 20 and Top 40 positions respectively. A plethora of compilation sets kept ARTHUR's/THE FUREYS' name in the public consciousness and the band continued to pull in the crowds at their live gigs. DAVEY subsequently returned to being a solo entertainer, releasing 'CELTIC SIDE SADDLE' (1994) and 'CUT TO THE CHASE' (1997).

• **Note:** not to be confused with English duo DAVE & TONI ARTHUR, who released LP's in the 60's for 'Transatlantic', 'Topic' and 'Trailer'.

DAVEY ARTHUR – vocals, acoustic guitar / with session people

Park / not iss.

Aug 94. (cd/c) *(PRK CD/MC 26)* **CELTIC SIDE SADDLE** [ ] [-]
– Celtic side saddle / Hail Mary full of grace / Galway farmer / Fair city set / Emigrant / Over the ocean / Slip 'n' slides / Euston Station / Mad lady and me / Walk / Sit you down / Ness pipers / Sister Marcella.

Blue Bowl / not iss.

Oct 97. (cd; as DAVEY ARTHUR & CO.) *(BLUE 31)* **CUT TO THE CHASE** [ ] [-]
– The blue stack set / When another domino falls / A New York miracle / A small drop on the side / Cut to the chase / A song for yesterday / Na cailini – Girls / The singing tap set / A nobleman's wedding / Seamus Alfonsus set / She loves to dance / Na cailini – Girls.

AVALON (see under ⇒ Lismor records)

B

BACHUE

Formed: Edinburgh . . . 1995 as BACHUE CAFE, a cooler than yer fridge jazz-folk duo consisting of vocalist/harpist CORRINA HEWAT and jazz pianist and guitarist DAVID MILLIGAN. After their eponymous debut in 1996, CORRINA (also of SEANNACHE) subsequently worked with CHANTAN, while MILLIGAN appeared on sets by CATRIONA MACDONALD, CAROL KIDD, SUZANNE BONNAR and KEVIN MACKENZIE's SWIRLER. Although they abandoned the CAFE element of their moniker, there was still a bit of CAFE in their music – PENGUIN CAFE ORCHESTRA, that is, albeit with more of a traditionally Scottish twist. In 1998, MILLIGAN was commissioned to play a suite for 2 pianos at the Celtic Connections under the 'Lifting The Lid' banner. Signing to ALASDAIR FRASER's US-based 'Culburnie' records, BACHUE (pronounced "bash-ooey") turned on the style with 1999's follow-up 'A CERTAIN SMILE', converting the traditional 'JOHNNY WAS A SHOEMAKER' into a double-bass-driven, EBTG-like near dancefloor groover. Elsewhere, HEWAT worked wonders with her harp, manipulating harmony and space to mesmerising effect. Despite these attempts at comparison and pigeonholing, BACHUE's strange musical brew consistently defies any successful categorisation. CORRINA and DAVID are currently working as the BIG BASHOOEY (for another Celtic Connections 2001 – they did 1996) roping in six other top musicians/singers CLARE McLAUGHLIN (fiddle), JULIAN ARGUELLES (saxophone, whistle), COLIN STEELE (trumpet), ALYTH McCORMACK (vocals), JOHN SPIERS (bass) and DONALD HAY (drums, percussion). 2001 will also see the pair work with DAVE GRAY on the experimental WAKING GIANTS, while CORRINA is recording with MARY MacMASTER (of SILEAS, POOZIES, La BOUM and POLLEN) and ALYTH McCORMACK in the all-female trio SHINE.

CORRINA HEWAT – vocals, harp / **DAVID MILLIGAN** (b.1970 Galashiels) – piano, guitar / with **BRIAN SHIELS** – bass / **DAVY CATTANACH** – percussion / **IAIN FRASER** – fiddle / **MAIRI CAMPBELL** – viola

Highlander not iss.

Mar 96. (cd/c; as BACHUE CAFE) *(HRM CD/C 001)* **BACHUE CAFE** [ ] [-]
– Morrison's jig – The ale is dear – Caitlin na aodha – Monaghan's jig / Intermediate fiddler / Lassie lie near me / Roslin Castle – The ewie with the crooked horn – The hag with the money / Waltzing for dreamers / Jig for D.G. / Auchindoon / Jade's cat – The artist – Jimmy on the moor / Are you sleeping, Maggie? / Caroline's dance – The rolling waves – The Brig o' Perth / Icarus / Brenda Stubbert's reel – Cutting bracken – Song of the chanter – G minor reel.

— **PHIL BANCROFT** – saxophones; repl. FRASER

— **HORSE McDONALD** – harmony vocals (+ solo artist) repl. CAMPBELL

Culburnie Culburnie

Jan 99. (cd) *(<CUL 114D>)* **A CERTAIN SMILE** [ ] [ ]
– A certain smile / Walk: Gravel walk – Kissin' is the best of a' – Robert the minnow / My Johnny was a shoemaker / Disnae: Sgian dubh – Disnae waltz / The Phrayes / Ballad of the sad young men / Marsaili Stewart Skinner / If I were a blackbird / The music box: Colin's – The humours of Barrack Street – Charlie Hunters jig / Plums: Lyndsay Grace Johnson – This is just to say / The birken tree / Set to rights: The warlock – The Arras fisherman – The rights of man / Fiddle-idle / Loving Hannah / The beaten track – A certain smile.

— DAVID continued to work with CAROL KIDD and has own trio with TOM LYNE (bass) and TOM BANCROFT (drums); he also arranged COLIN STEELE's album, 'Twilight Dreams'.

BADENOCH

Formed: 1998 by members of The PICTS or CUTTING EDGE (half each). CUTTING EDGE were formed in the mid-90's with PAUL ANDERSON, GEORGE CRAMICHAEL, ANGUS WARES, DERYK MITCHELSON and JAMES GORGON, while The PICTS were made up from DOUGLAS McQUEEN HUNTER, DOUGLAS BALLANTYNE, JEREMY STIRLING, STUART LAW, STUART 'NICO' GLASGOW and TONY HIGGINS. While CUTTING EDGE were lighter in their free-flowing folk (example debut album, 'TURNING THE TIDE' (1995), The PICTS were like WOLFSTONE fused with accordion player SANDY BRECHIN (see BURACH). Having plied their traditional thumping reels and jigs at numerous ceilidhs and Scottish dances, The PICTS were ready to take their wares to the recording studio. 'THE ISLAND' was released early in '99 and showed them at their swinging best. Later in the year, BADENOCH were finally out on record, the confusingly-titled 'CALEDON' (there was another Scots act by this name!) was a mini-CD also released on the 'Pict' label. CUTTING EDGE were back in full-flow in 2002 via second set, 'FREE FALL', while The PICTS – with newcomer RUARIDH CAMPBELL replacing BALLANTYNE – delivered their sophomore set, 'MOVING SANDS' that summer.

CUTTING EDGE

PAUL ANDERSON – fiddle / **GEORGE CARMICHAEL** – accordion / **ANGUS WARES** – guitars / **DERYCK MITCHELSON** – keyboards / **JAMES GORGON** – drums

Ninegates not iss.

Feb 95. (c/cd) *(NG/+CD 1007)* **TURNING THE TIDE** [ ] [-]
– Turning the tide / Seagate salsa / Beechgrove / Jig of slurs / When she sleeps / Sniffer's delight / The ass in the graveyard / The silver spire / O'Keefe's No.7 / Ceilidh Dave / Miss Rowan Davies / Shandon bells / Gorgon's "ola" / Rudy's reggae / Lily the pict.

— note: a different CUTTING EDGE released an eponymous set in '99

Highlander not iss.

Mar 02. (cd) *(TORT 01000)* **FREE FALL** [ ] [-]
– Free fall / How much / Skunk / Here I go / The seven year itch / Trains and tears / Gravel's bolero / Borranchero et Antiguo El Paso / Wild mountain thyme / Pride.

the PICTS

DOUGLAS McQUEEN HUNTER – vocals, guitar / **DOUGLAS BALLANTYNE** – fiddle / **STUART LAW** – accordion / **JEREMY STIRLING** – keyboards / **STUART 'NICO' GLASGOW** – bass / **TONY HIGGINS** – drums, percussion

Pict not iss.

Feb 99. (cd) *(PICT 002CD)* **THE ISLAND** [ ] [-]
– The peak: Martin Martin hits the beach – The Glasgow reel – Charlie's last peak / The shearin' / Glenshee / Lament for Archie Findlater / The federals: Waiting for the federals – Grandfather mountain – The reconcilliation reel – Banjo breakdown / Baby Rachel grooves / Three spalpeans: The three spalpeans – Calipoe house – The Atholl Highlanders / Pacific waves / Elephant jam / The reelflexologist: Jenny dang the weaver – Wing Commander – Donald MacKenzie's reel – The woman I never forgot – Cottage in the grove / The island / Castlebay T party. *(re-iss. Sep00; same)* *<US-iss.Jun02 on 'Orchard'; 802117>*

— **RUARIDH CAMPBELL** – fiddle; repl. BALLANTYNE

Jul 02. (cd) *(PICT 004CD)* **MOVING SANDS** [ ] [-]
– Daybreak / Spring / The bear dance / Record with shades on: Fosgail an dorus – Trip to Lyon – The break for freedom – The ceilidh / Wonder of love / Moving sands: Moving sands – Roddy Gourley's reel – Morag's reel – Extract / Dusk / The blackberry bush: The blackberry bush – Jaffa dance – MacArthur road / Kirsty's tune / Long wave – The brolum / A winter's night / Thunderhead: Tipsy sailor – The boys of Ballymost – Thunderhead – The unknown.

BADENOCH

— CUTTING EDGE + BADENOCH members

Pict not iss.

Oct 99. (m-cd) *(PICT 003CD)* **CALEDON** [ ] [-]
– Caledon & the tree shanty jig / Colleen / World of green / Galway & the reel Miss Fit / Freetime.

BAG O' CATS (see under ⇒ Greentrax records)

Aly BAIN

Born: 15 May'46, Lerwick, Shetland Isles. One of the most well known and respected fiddle players in the world, ALY BAIN is a talented ambassador for not only his chosen instrument but also his country.

Learning to play in his early teens, BAIN initially made a name for himself locally before moving to Glasgow and meeting singer/guitarist MIKE WHELLANS at the Falkirk Folk Festival in 1971. The pair recorded and released an eponymous album together the same year on the Bill Leader's 'Trailer' label; they both would join the ranks of The BOYS OF THE LOUGH (BAIN until 2001). Another inspiration for ALY was TOM ANDERSON with whom he cut a couple of sets for 'Topic' in the mid-late 70's: 'THE SILVER BOW' (1976) and 'SHETLAND FOLK FIDDLING VOL.2' (1978). The latter album was rumoured to have been seen by some Sassenachs as an admission by the Islanders that they weren't paying their taxes.

ALY's solo recording life began at 40 (well, almost) with an eponymous debut album in 1985 on the 'Whirlie' label. Following another dalliance with the BOYS ('Farewell and Remember Me' and 'Sweet Rural Shade'), BAIN hooked up with Louisiana natives QUEEN IDA & THE BONTEMPS ZYDECO BAND for the 1988 album, 'ALY MEETS THE CAJUNS'. The Americans also appeared on 'ALY BAIN & FRIENDS' (1989), a hugely popular hoedown which gathered together the likes of PHIL CUNNINGHAM, CAPERCAILLIE, CLIVE GREGSON & CHRISTINE COLLISTER and HAMISH MOORE.

1990's 'ALY BAIN WITH YOUNG CHAMPIONS', again found him sharing the spotlight, this time with the cream of Scotland's young fiddle talent. Following 1992's 'LONELY BIRD' solo set, BAIN began a long standing association with PHIL CUNNINGHAM, the pair appearing together on 'THE PEARL' (1994) and 'THE RUBY' (1997). The Shetlander's most famous partnership came in 1995 when he cut an album with The BT SCOTTISH ENSEMBLE entitled 'FOLLOW THE MOONSTONE'. The appropriately titled 'ANOTHER GEM' (2000) saw ALY and CUNNINGHAM into the new millennium in fine style, the pair augmented by MALCOLM STITT, COLIN MacFARLANE and STUART NISBET, who collectively added a bit of American country roots-style twang to proceedings.

BAIN's exploration of transatlantic folk forms has been an ongoing preoccupation throughout his career, examining the development of traditional music via the Celtic diaspora in Ireland, Canada, Brittany and beyond through both his albums and various TV series ('Down Home', 'Push The Boat Out' and 'The Shetland Set'). Sadly, his inspiration for many a note, Dr. TOM ANDERSON, died before the new millennium had begun. Late in 2001, BAIN was back (this time with Danish/Norwegian-raised Swede ALE MOLLER) on a Celtic-Nordic project, 'FULLY RIGGED'.

ALY BAIN – fiddle / with various guests

Leader | not iss.

1971. (lp; MIKE WHELLANS & ALY BAIN) *(LER 2022)* **MIKE WHELLANS & ALY BAIN** ☐ -

— after a spell with The BOYS OF THE LOUGH (until 1972), WHELLANS went on to release a couple of Blues albums

Topic | not iss.

1976. (lp; by TOM ANDERSON and ALY BAIN) *(12TS 281)* **THE SILVER BOW: The Fiddle Music of Shetland** ☐ -
(c-iss.Feb85; KTSC 281) (<cd-iss. Nov93; TSCD 469>)

1978. (lp; by ALY BAIN and TOM ANDERSON) *(12TS 379)* **SHETLAND FOLK FIDDLING VOL.2** ☐ -
(c-iss.Feb85; KTSC 379)

Whirlie | not iss.

Mar 85. (lp/c) *(WHIRLIE 1/+C)* **ALY BAIN** ☐ -
– Margaret's waltz – Peter Davidson – Jessica's tune – Barrowburn reel / Louis' waltz – Le grande chaine – The newly weds' reel / Waiting for the federals / Dr. James Donaldson – The anvil reel / The auld noost / The barmaid – The carpenter – The reconcilliation / The hangman's reel / Calum Donaldson – The scholar – Maid in a box / Kevin McCann's – Munster grass – Barclays / Margaret's waltz / Blaydon flats – Alamootie – Dodd's farewell to Shetland / Da braaken baa – Violet Tulloch's hornpipe / Shack's farewell to the workman's club – Glen Farquhar – Reested mutton. *(cd-iss. Dec93; WHIRLIE 1CD)*

— ALY would subsequently join Irish contingent, BOYS OF THE LOUGH

Mar 89. (cd/c/lp) *(CD/C+/TRAX 026)* **ALY BAIN & FRIENDS** (ALY BAIN recorded with Various Artists) ☐ -
– Waiting for the federals / Donald MacLean's farewell to Oban / Dean cadalan samhach / Kerryman's daughter / Maiden's prayer / Jimmy Mann's reel / It's all just talk / The pearl / The floggin' / Waiting for the federals / Chimes at midnight / Humours of Tulla / New road under my wheels / Anne's tune / Love of the islands / Bonjour tristesse.

— ALY BAIN & FRIENDS was performed with PHIL CUNNINGHAM, VIOLET TULLOCH, JUNIOR DAUGHERTY, WILLIE HUNTER, WILLIE JOHNSON, ALLAN TAYLOR, MARTIN O'CONNOR and also featured solo spots by CAPERCAILLIE, BOYS OF THE LOUGH, CLIVE GREGSON & CHRISTINE COLLISTER, HAMISH MOORE & DICK LEE plus all the way from Louisiana QUEEN IDA & THE BONTEMPS ZYDECO BAND.

Lismor | not iss.

Dec 88. (lp/c) *(LIF L/C 7017)* **ALY MEETS THE CAJUNS** (recorded with Various 'Cajun' Artists) ☐ -
(cd-iss. Feb89; LCOM 9009)

Apr 90. (cd) *(LCOM 9027)* **DOWN HOME (ALY BAIN'S LEGENDARY RECORDINGS)** (collection) ☐ -

Springthyme | not iss.

May 90. (cd/c) *(SPR CD/C 1032)* **ALY BAIN WITH YOUNG CHAMPIONS** (with Various 'young' Artists) ☐ -

Whirlie | Green Linnet

Oct 92. (c/cd) *(WHIRLIE 2/+CD)* *<GLCD 3105>* **LONELY BIRD** ☐ ☐ Jan96
– Gillian's reel – Charles Sutherland – Donald Stewart the piper / Mrs Jamieson's favourite / Rosemary Brown / Spey in spate – Pottinger's reel – Dowd's reel / The beauty of the north – The pirates hornpipe / Midnight on the water – Bonaparte's retreat / Herr Roloff's farewell / Aly's waltz / Annalese Bain – Phil Cunningham's reel – Andy Brown's reel / Lonely bird / Weindia Little – Da fashion o da lassies – Da black hat / Junior's waltz / Captain Campbell – Earl Grey – Largo's fairy dance.

— next with **PHIL CUNNINGHAM** – accordion, cittern, keyboards, mandolin, whistles, etc

Oct 94. (c/cd; by ALY BAIN & PHIL CUNNINGHAM) *(WHIRLIE 3/+CD)* *<GLCD 3107>* **THE PEARL** ☐ ☐ Oct95
– Megan's wedding – The Herra boys – The Barrowburn reel / Bonnie Nancy / Devant ta porte – Mamou two step / The jig Runrig – The Swedish jig / Queendale Bay / The waltz of the little girls / The shores of Loch Bee – The headlands – The floggin' reel / The music of Spey / Seud nan ceud Bliadhna – Memories of Father McDonnell – The braes of Dunvegan march / Belle Mere's waltz / The auld fiddler – Bb tune / The pearl.

Oct 95. (c/cd; as ALY BAIN & The B.T. SCOTTISH ENSEMBLE) *(WHIRLIE 4/+CD)* **FOLLOW THE MOONSTONE** ☐ -
– Till far / Julverset / Vib ad lib / Salme / Eklundapolska nr 3 / Da auld foula reel / Winyadepla / The day dawn / Doon ra rooth / Minnie a shirva's cradle song / Papa stour sword dance / Captain Campbell / John Roy Lyall / Beauty of the north / The hurricane / Herr Roloff's farewell.

Sep 97. (c/cd; by ALY BAIN & PHIL CUNNINGHAM) *(WHIRLIE/+CD 5)* *<GLCD 3123>* **THE RUBY** ☐ ☐ Aug98
– Estonian waltz – La vie est pas donne – La bastringue / Violet Tulloch Queen of Lerwick / Flett from Flotta – Sabhal Iain ig uisdean – The drampire – Aly's soond / Logan water / The wee bells of tak-ma-doon road – Glencoe village hall – Lady Mary Ramsay's reel / Sarah's song / Bonaparte's retreat / Sunset over Foula – Isles of Gletness – Starry night in Shetland / La ronfleuse gobel – La grande ghaine – Gallop de Malbaie / The ruby.

— the duo were augmented by **MALCOLM STITT** – guitar, bouzouki / **COLIN MacFARLANE + STUART NISBET** – dobro

Whirlie | Compass

Aug 00. (c/cd; by ALY BAIN & PHIL CUNNINGHAM) *(WHIRLIE/+CD 8)* *<4312>* **ANOTHER GEM** ☐ ☐ May01
– My Lily / The sweetness of Mary / Hughie Jim Paul's reel / The Lake Charles waltz / The reel de la liberation / The reel du voyageur / Reel traditionnelle de Quebec / Cliff and Viv's homecoming waltz / A waltz for Aly / Charlie Hunter's jig / The mouse in the cupboard / Rosewood / Tonder. . . the eternal friendship / Cathkin braes / The feis rois reel / Bob McQuillen's reel / Sophie's dancing feet / Sophie's lullaby.

Whirlie | NorthSide

Nov 01. (cd; by ALY BAIN & ALE MOLLER) *(WHIRLIECD 7)* *<6064>* **FULLY RIGGED** ☐ ☐ Jan02
– The fully rigged ship – The new rigged ship / Da day dawn – Joskvarnleken (the Jos mill tune) – Da auld foula reel – Winyadepla / Da trowie burn / Tame her when da sna comes – Da dykes o'Voe – Sailor o'er da rough trees / The Unst bridal march – Maggie O'Ham – Da foula reel / Bjornvalser fran Skane (bear waltzes from Skane) / Bonaparte's retreat / Da bride's a bonnie ting (the bride's a bonnie thing) / Hallingar fran dalsand (hallings from Dalsland) – Da bonnie isle o'Whalsay – Da fashion o' da Delting lassies / Jims vals (Jim's waltz) / Da silver bow – Marsh fran Fryksdalen (march from Fryksdalen) / Hangman's reel / Papa stour sword dance – Svardsdans polska (sword dance polska) / The great silkie of Sule Skerry.

– compilations, etc. –

Sep 99. (cd) *Highlander; (HRMCD 006)* **ROAD TO THE ISLES** ☐ -

BANNAL (see under ⇒ Greentrax records)

Freeland BARBOUR

Born: c.early 1950's, Glasgow. Having been a member of the legendary SILLY WIZARD in the mid-70's, accordion-player FREELAND released a one-off solo set for 'R.E.L.' records, 'FIRE IN THE HEARTH' (1977). After his departure from the group, he joined the WALLACHMOR CEILIDH BAND, alongside NEIL MacMILLAN and GUS MILLAR, the three teaming up once again with 90's outfit, The OCCASIONALS (from Perthshire, Skye and Edinburgh). In between times, two further sets 'NO LONG FAREWELL' and 'KILLIEKRANKIE' were released on 'Lapwing' towards the end of the 80's.

The OCCASIONALS – augmented by banjo/mandolin expert KEVIN MacLEOD, guitarists MALCOLM JONES and BRIAN MILLAR, fiddlers JIM BARRIE and CHARLIE SOANE and drummers ALLY MacINTYRE and GUS MILLAR – kicked off their musical account for 'Iona' records with the release of 'FOOTNOTES' (1993), an uplifting and emotional set of Scottish country dance tunes. The following year, FREELAND collaborated with fiddler IAIN FRASER on 'NORTHLINS', before the accordionist signed a deal with 'Greentrax'. An OCCASIONALS sophomore set, 'BACK IN STEP', by mid '96; NEIL MacMILLAN (piano & bass) and MAIRI CAMPBELL (fiddle/viola) were now augmenting BARBOUR, MacLEOD, MILLAR and JONES.

Three years on (and after a solo sojourn by MacLEOD, 'Springwell' and a FREELAND appearance on a GHILLIES album), The OCCASIONALS were hopping mad once again, fiddler IAN HARDIE lining up for the concert set, 'LIVE AT ABERDEEN MUSIC HALL' (1999).

FREELAND BARBOUR – accordion

R.E.L. | not iss.

1977. (lp/c) *(REL/REC 462)* **FIRE IN THE HEARTH** ☐ -

Lapwing | not iss.

Dec 88. (lp/c) *(LAP 105/+C)* **NO LONG FAREWELL** ☐ -

Dec 89. (lp/c/cd) *(LAP 126/+C/CD)* **KILLIEKRANKIE** ☐ -
– Glorious revolution / White rose / House of Stewart / Bluidy clavers / Cameronians march / Lands beyond Forth / Tremble false whigs / The band at distance (Bonnie Dundee) / Dudhope / Green field of Dalcomera / Blair Castle / Braes of Glen Roy / Murray's siege / Mackay's advance / Men from Lochaber / Am feasgair samhraidh (the summer evening) / Alit Girnaig / Thickets of Raon Ruaraidh / Battle of Killiecrankie / MacBean's chase / Fight and pursuit / Urrard House / South to Dunkeld / Firy cross / Battle of Dunkeld / Thanksgiving / There is no enemy in sight / Old Blair / Killiecrankie.

— now with **IAIN FRASER** – fiddle / plus guests **JIM WALKER, KEVIN MacLEOD + CORRINA HEWAT**

Iona | not iss.

Aug 94. (cd; as FREELAND BARBOUR & IAIN FRASER) *(IRCD 027)* **NORTHLINS** ☐ -
– Old Fincastle / Northlins / Pride of the north / Blue bonnets / Devil in the kitchen / Golden mile / Walnut grove / Valparaiso / The loup / Tummelside / Drummossie moor / The north wall / Farewell to whisky / Am balachan siubhlach / The merry making / Last light.

OCCASIONALS

FREELAND BARBOUR – accordion / **MALCOLM JONES** – guitar, dobro / **KEVIN MacLEOD** – banjo, mandolin / **JIM BARRIE + CHARLIE SOANE** – fiddles / **MALCOLM JONES** – guitar / **BRIAN MILLAR** – guitar / **GUS MILLAR** – drums / **ALLY MacINTYRE** – drums

Iona not iss.

Jan 93. (cd/c) *(IRCD/IRC 021)* **FOOTNOTES: THE COMPLETE SCOTTISH CEILIDH DANCE**

— **MAIRI CAMPBELL** – fiddle, viola; repl. BARRIE + SOANE

— **NEIL MacMILLAN** – piano, bass; repl. BRIAN + ALLY

Greentrax Greentrax

Jul 96. (cd/c) *(CD/C TRAX 107)* **BACK IN STEP**

— **FREELAND, KEVIN + GUS** were joined by **IAN HARDIE** – fiddle

Nov 99. (cd) *(CDTRAX 184)* **LIVE AT ABERDEEN MUSIC HALL (live)**

Bill BARCLAY (see ⇒ Section 4: Celebrity Corner)

Jim and Sylvia BARNES (see under ⇒ KENTIGERN)

BATTLEFIELD BAND

Formed: Glasgow . . . 1969 by Falkirk-born fiddler BRIAN McNEILL and singer/guitarist ALAN REID. One of Scotland's premier folk-revival outfits, the BATTLEFIELD BAND have been a constant presence on the traditional music scene for over three decades now. Through a continually evolving personnel, McNEILL and REID initially formed the core of the band, joined on 1977's eponymous debut album by JAMIE McMENEMY and JOHN GAHAGAN. 1980's 'PREVIEW' EP and 'HOME IS WHERE THE VAN IS' album marked the beginning of a twenty year (and counting) association with the Midlothian-based 'Temple' label, the latter's title a humorous testament to the band's hard-touring ethos.

Although BATTLEFIELD BAND were dealt a potentially fatal blow in the mid 80's with the departure of founder McNEILL (for a solo career), Geordie ALISTAIR RUSSELL proved himself a worthy successor. The mid to late 80's saw a couple of collaborative projects with distinguished harper, ALISON KINNAIRD, namely 'MUSIC IN TRUST – VOL.1' (1986) and 'MUSIC IN TRUST – VOL.2' (1988).

Come the 90's, the veteran troupe were as fighting fit as ever, enthused by the injection of new blood in the shape of ex-OSSIAN piper/vocalist, IAN MacDONALD and youthful multi-instrumentalist JOHN McCUSKER (who also worked with country-rockers The RADIO SWEETHEARTS). The appropriately titled 'NEW SPRING' (1991) saw the new-look group recording together for the first time, MacDONALD subsequently taking a major writing role in BATTLEFIELD BAND's established mix of reels, ballads and adaptations of traditional tunes. 1995's 'THREADS' set featured a tribute to Yorkshire folk singer KATE RUSBY and a fiddle tune dedicated to 'XESUS AND FELISA', two Galicians the group met on their travels.

As well as the Celtic outposts of Europe, the band are hugely popular in the USA where they've had their records intermittently released by the Chicago-based 'Flying Fish' label, 'Temple' taking over in the mid-90's. A real live American, MIKE KATZ, joined up for 1998's 'RAIN, HAIL OR SHINE', along with esteemed Scots songwriter and versatile instrumentalist DAVY STEELE, both men having come from the ranks of CEOLBEG.

Throughout the latter stages of their career, BATTLEFIELD BAND have been credited with subtly updating their traditional sound via the use of electric keyboards, one of the first folk outfits to do so. The group were still going strong in '99, that year's 'LEAVING FRIDAY HARBOUR' exploring their favoured lyrical terrain of loss, regret and separation. In March 2001, with the celebrated Banknock-born vocalist KARINE POLWART (of MALINKY) in their ever-evolving ranks, The BATTLEFIELD BAND unleashed their umpteenth set, 'HAPPY DAZE'. On a sadder note, former member DAVY STEELE died of cancer on the 11th of April the same year. The BATTLEFIELD BAND (REID, KATZ, KILBRIDE and newcomer ALASDAIR WHITE) returned in September 2002 with a fresh batch of tunes under the title of 'TIME & TIDE'.

BRIAN McNEILL (b. 6 Apr'50, Falkirk) – vocals, fiddle, mandolin, bouzouki, cittern, concertina, etc. / **ALAN REID** (b. 2 May'50) – vocals, organ, guitar / **JAMIE McMENEMY** – vocals, cittern, guitarra / **JOHN GAHAGAN** – whistle, concertina

Topic not iss.

1977. (lp) *(12TS 313)* **THE BATTLEFIELD BAND**
– Silver spear – Humours of Tulla / The shipyard apprentice / Crossing the Minch / Minnie Hynd / Glasgow Gaelic club / The brisk young lad / Birnie bouzle / Compliments of the band (Sir David Davidson of Cantray – A Cameron's Strathspey – Scott Skinner's compliments to Dr.MacDonald) / Bonnie Jean / Paddy Fahey's reel / Joseph's fancy / The hog's reel / It was all for our rightful king / The Inverness gathering / Marquis of Huntly's Strathspey / John MacNeil's reel / Miss Margaret Brown's favourite / Deserts of Tulloch / The cruel brother. *(re-iss. 1981; same) (re-iss. Aug94 on 'Temple' cd/c; TP 55 CD/C)*

— **PAT KILBRIDE** (b. Ireland) – vocals, guitar, cittern, bodhran; repl. GAHAGAN + RICKY STARRS

1978. (lp) *(12TS 381)* **AT THE FRONT (BATTLEFIELD BAND 2)**
– Lady Carmichael / South of the Grampians / Mickie Ainsworth / The bachelor / Ge do theid mi do m'leabraidh / The battle of Harlaw / Jenny Nettles – The Grays of Tongside / Tae the beggin' / The tamosher / The blackbird and the thrush – The Moray club / Lang Johnnie Moir / The brown milkmaid – Dunnottar Castle – Maid of Glengarrysdale – Disused railway / The Lady Leroy / Stirling Castle / Earl of Mansfield. *(re-iss. 1981; same) (cd-iss. Sep93; MWCD 4004) (re-iss. Feb94 on 'Temple' cd/c; TP 56 CD/C)*

— **JENNY CLARK** – vocals + **DUNCAN McGILLIVRAY** – pipes + guest ALEC DUDGEON – side drum; repl. KILBRIDE + McMENEMY

1979. (lp) *(12TS 404)* **STAND EASY**
– Miss Drummond of Perth – Fiddler's joy / Traditional reel – The Shetland fiddler / Seven braw gowns / Miss Drummond of Perth's favourite Scotch measure / Miss MacLeod's minuet / My last farewell to Stirling – Cuidich'n righ / I hae laid a herrin' in salt – My wife's a wanton wee thing / The Banks of the Allan / The battle of Falkirk Muir / John D.Burgess / The Braemar gathering / I hae nae with I hae nae kin / Miss Lyall / Small coals for nailers / Bleaton Gardens / Christ has my hart ay / Joe McGann's fiddle – Center's bonnet. *(re-iss. 1981; same) (re-iss. Feb94 on 'Temple' cd+=/c+=; COMD2/CTP 052)* – PREVIEW

— **SYLVIA BARNES** – dulcimer, bodhran + **JIM BARNES** – guitar; repl. JENNY

Temple Flying Fish

1980. (12"ep) *(ETP 10)* **PREVIEW**

— **GED FOLEY** – guitar, mandolin, vocals + **MARTIN COLLEDGE** – banjo, guitar + **ROBIN MORTON** – bodhran; repl. SYLVIA + JIM BARNES

1980. (lp/c) *(TP/CTP 005) <FF 250>* **HOME IS WHERE THE VAN IS**
– Major Malley's march and reel / Malcolm Currie bonny Barbry-O / Look across the water – Misses – Garden of Troup – The keelman ower land / Braw lads of Galla water / Up and waur them a' Willie / Joseph McDonald's jig / The snuff wife – Thief of Lochaber / Cockle Geordie – Miss Graham – Miss Thompson / The boar and the fox / Blackhall rocks / Lads o' the fair / The Cowal gathering the iron man – Dancing feet – Dick Gossip's reel / 6 Mary Cassidy. *(cd-iss. Feb89; COMD 2006)*

1982. (lp/c) *(TP/CTP 007) <FF 274>* **THE STORY SO FAR** (compilation)
– 74th Highlander's farewell to Edinburgh – A cup of tea / The shipyard apprentice / Johnny Armstrong / Captain Ross / The Atholl gathering / Miss Drummond of Perth's favourite Scotch measure / Miss McLeod's minuet / Rantin' rovin' Robin / Joseph McDonald's jig / The snuff wife / Thief of Lochaber / Ge do theid mi do m'leabaidh / Wae's me for Prince Charlie / Miss Margaret Brown's favourite / Deserts of Tulloch / Seven braw gowns / Lady Madeleine Sinclair / The Spey in spate / The Duke Of Perth / The bachelor / Lord Huntley's cave / Lady in the bottle / Stewart Chisholm's walkabout.

— **DOUGIE PINCOCK** (b. 7 Jul'61, Glasgow) – pipes, flute, saxophone, percussion; repl. most recent newcomers (see above)

Dec 82. (lp/c) *(TP/CTP 010)* **THERE'S A BUZZ**
– Bessie McIntyre – Johnny McDonald's reel – Roddy McDonald's fancy / Shining clear / Sir Sidney Smith's march / A chance as good as any – Reid's rant / Lord Haddo's favourite / Tending the steer – Sandy Thompson – The Calrossie cattle wife / The Presbytarian hornpipe – The watchmaker's daughter – The hurricane / The battle of Waterloo – Kilcoy's march – The Quaker / One miner's life – The image of God / Kantara to el 'Arish – Christmas carousal – Willie Roy's loomhouse / The green plaid. *(cd-iss. Feb94; COMD 2007)*

— **ALISTAIR RUSSELL** (b.15 Feb'51, Newcastle) – guitar, vocals; repl. McNEILL who continued solo

Jun 84. (lp/c) *(TP 015/+C)* **ANTHEM FOR THE COMMON MAN**
– The tide's out – James McLellan's favourite – Dougie's decision – The ferryman – Lady doll Sinclair (the four minute warning) / Ina MacKenzie – The braes of Mellinish – Troy's wedding / The old changing way / The hook of Holland – Dominic MacGowan / The snows of France and Holland / Anthem / The Yew tree / The port of call / Miners' wives / I am the common man / McHugh's other foot – The man with two women (Sauchiehall salsa). *(cd-iss. Feb89; COMD 2008)*

Mar 86. (lp/c) *(TP/CTP 021)* **ON THE RISE**
– The pilgrim's march – Scarley & black – The struggle – Struny lodge / The clumsy lover – The unmade bed Knopogue / The gale warning – The anchor stream reel – The farmer's daughter / After hours – The green gates – The ship in full sail / John MacKenzie's fancy / The train journey north / Montrose / She's late but she's timely / Bad moon rising – The rising moon reel / The dear green place / Island Earth no more – Flight of the eaglets. *(cd-iss. Feb89; COMD 2009)*

Sep 86. (lp/c; as the BATTLEFIELD BAND with ALISON KINNAIRD) *(TP/CTP 022)* **MUSIC IN TRUST – VOL.1**
– The sweet maid of Mull – MacLeod of Mull / Frideray / Cro cinnt-saile – The Kilbarchan weaver / Lady Haddo / The silver darlin's / The Duchess of Gordon / The St. Kilda girls lament – The St.Kilda wedding march / Anst'er market – The east neuk of Fife / Brodick Castle / Dunkeld steeple – Killekrankie / Mo rungael og / Glenfinnan highland gathering – Lady MacKenzie of Gairloch – The five sisters / Held in trust. *(cd-iss. Feb94; COMD 2010)*

Nov 87. (lp/c)(cd) *(TP/CTP 027)(COMD 2002)* **CELTIC HOTEL**
– Conway's farewell – Andy Renwick's ferret – Shortcoated Mary / Seacoalers / Return to Kashmagiro – The cuddy with the wooden leg / Jock the can / The rovin' dies hard / Muineira sul sacrato della chiesa / The Celtic Hotel / The left-handed fiddler / The floating crowbar – The ships are sailing – Lucy Campbell – June apple / We work the black seam / The tail o' the bank.

Oct 88. (lp/c)(cd; as the BATTLEFIELD BAND with ALISON KINNAIRD) *(TP/CTP 029)(COMD 2004)* **MUSIC IN TRUST – VOL.2** ☐ ☐-
– The laird of Brodie – Danzig Willie – The merchants jig / A'chlach uaine (the green stone) / I ha'e a wife – The tarbolton jig – Tarbolton lodge / The massacre of Glencoe / Falkland Palace / Lawer's loup – Miss Jane Fraser – Mrs Maule's reel / Goat fell / Farewell to Glenshalloch / The fruiting branch – Gledstanes' march / Pitmedden / The mote of Mark – The grey mare's tail / Held in trust – Peace and plenty / Fingal's weeping – The maids of Kintail / Hill house – The philosopher's chair.

— **IAIN MacDONALD** (b.28 Jul'60, Inverness) – bagpipes, flute, whistle, vocals (ex-OSSIAN) repl. PINCOCK who went into session work and later went solo in '94

Oct 89. (lp/c/cd) *(TP/CTP/COMD2 034)* **HOME GROUND LIVE FROM SCOTLAND (live)** ☐ ☐
– Home ground / The Yew tree / After hours / Pincock's pleasure / The dear green place / Fare thee well whisky / The hornpipes / The rovin' dies hard / Bad Moon rising / Farewell Johnny Minedr / Band of a thousand chances / Peace and plenty.

— **JOHN McCUSKER** (b.15 May'73) – fiddle, piano, whistle, accordion, cittern, mandolin (ex-PARCEL OF ROGUES) repl. McLEAN

— line-up **ALAN REID, ALISTAIR RUSSELL, IAIN MacDONALD + McCUSKER**

Jun 91. (cd/c/lp) *(COMD2/CTP/TP 045)* **NEW SPRING** ☐ ☐
– Inveraray Castle – Calum Beag – Lucy Cassidy / The green and the blue / Seann bhriogais aig uilleam – Lady Margaret Stewart / Cearcall a' chuain – The Kaimes lassies – The night we had goats / Calum Fhionnlaigh / Working away – The toastie jig / The Prince of Wales – Angst agus Angus – Let there be dreams / Darien / Miss Sarah MacManus – The appropriate dipstick – Cape Breton fiddlers' welcome to Shetland / The Devil uisge beatha / The golden eagle – O'er the moor to Maggie – The highland man kissed his grannie – Wissahickon drive / Farewell to Ravenscraig My night out with big Iain / I feel like going home / Farewell my love – Auchindoun – Tom Paine's Strathspey – The sands of Loch Bee – The handshaker – Cailleach an dudain.

Mar 93. (cd/c) *(COMD2/CTP 050)* **QUIET DAYS** ☐ ☐
– Captain Lachlan MacPhail of Tiree – Peter McKinnon of Skeabost – The blackberry bush / The river / Dalnabreac – The bishop's son – Miss Sharon McCusker / From here to there : Jack broke the prison door – Toss the feathers – The easy club reel / The St. Louis stagger – The ass in the graveyrad – Sandy's new chanter / Captain Campbell – Stranger at the gate – John Keith Laing / Hold back the tide / Blistered fingers: The Cumbernauld perennials – The keep left sign – Taking the soup / Bonnie George Campbell – Mo dhachaidh – The Loch Ness monster / Curstaidh's farewell / The Hoodie craw / Col. MacLean of Ardgour – Pipe Major Jimmy MacGregor – Rocking the baby / How will I ever be simple again?: Dawn song.

Temple Temple

Sep 95. (cd/c) *(<COMD2/CTP 062>)* **THREADS** ☐ ☐ Nov95
– In and out the harbour – The top tier – Sleepy Maggie – Molly Rankin / The Arran convict / Snow on the hills – Xesus and Felisa / Tramps and hawkers / My home town – Kalabakan / The weary whaling ground / Miss Kate Rusby / The same old story / Simon Thoumire's jig – Shake a leg – Ril gan Ainm / MacPherson's lament / Tam Bain's lum – The price of the pig – Isabelle Blackley / The Indian lass.

Jan 97. (cd/c) *(<COMD2/CTP 065>)* **ACROSS THE BORDERS (live)** ☐ ☐ Feb97
– Miss Sarah MacManus – Appropriate dipstick – Cafe Breton fiddlers welcome to Shetland / Tramps and hawkers / Snow on the hills – Xesus and Felisa / Concert reel – Green mountain / Arran convict / My home town – Kalabakan / Tuireadh Iain Ruaidh / Trimdon Grange explosion / Simon Thoumire's jig – Shake a leg – Rul gan ainm / Miss Kate Rusby / The green and the blue / Donnie MacGregor – Clumsy lover / Woe be gone – Bubba's reel – Frank's reel / Six days on the road / In and out of the harbour – The top tier – Sleepy Maggie – Molly Rankin.

— **REID + McCUSKER** enlisted **MIKE KATZ** – bagpipes, bass, guitar, etc + **DAVY STEELE** (b. Preston Pans, nr. Edinburgh) – bouzouki, guitar, vocals, etc (ex-DRINKERS DROUTH, ex-GAEL FORCE, ex-CLAN ALBA, ex-CEOLBEG, ex-CALEDON)

Apr 98. (cd/c) *(<COMD2/CTP 074>)* **RAIN, HAIL OR SHINE** ☐ ☐
– Bodachan a gharaidh (the jolly old General MacDonald – Craig an fhithich) / Heave ya ho / Margaret Ann – Manor Park – Trip to the Bronx / Jenny o' the braes / Magheracloone – Norland winde – Royal Scottish pipers society – Garden loo – Donald MacLean / The beaches of St. Valery / Elizabeth Clare / Wee Michael's march – Oot b'est da vong / The lass o' Glencoe / The Canongate twitch – Steamboat to Detroit – Twenty pounds of gin – Break yer bass drone.

Aug 99. (cd) *(<COMD 2080>)* **LEAVING FRIDAY HARBOR** ☐ ☐ Sep99
– Clan Coco – The road to Benderloch – Fifteen stubbies to Warragul / The last trip home – The Luckenbooth / It's nice to be nice – The auld Toon band – McCabe's reel / The straw man / Leaving Friday harbor / The 24th guards brigade at Anzio – The Melbourne sleeper – MacRae's of Linnie / One more chorus – The mason's apron – The mountain road / The pleasure will be mine / Something for Jamie / The sister's reel – Marion & Donald – The lassie with the yellow petticoat – Jesse "the body" Ventura's reel / Logie O'Buchan – Logie's waltz.

— sadly, the departing STEELE died of cancer on the 11th of April 2001

— added guest **KARINE POLWART** – vocals (of MALINKY)

Mar 01. (cd) *(<COMD 2085>)* **HAPPY DAZE** ☐ ☐
– The Devil's courtship – An dro / Medium man – Floating candles – Nighean cailleach nan cearc (the hen wife's daughter) / The banks of red roses / Tiny wee vin – The road to the aisle / The Riccarton tollman's daughter / Shepherd lad / The merry Macs – Dr. Iain MacAonghais (Dr John MacInnes) – Fonn air cailleach an T-siosalaich (Mrs Chisholm's delight) / Happy days / Whaur will ye gang? – March of the Ceili man / A mile down the road – Johnny's jig – Boys of the puddle / Start it all over again.

— added **ALASDAIR WHITE** – fiddle, whistles, bouzouki

Sep 02. (cd) *(<COMD 2090>)* **TIME & TIDE** ☐ ☐
– Chuir i gluin air a bhodach – DJ MacLeod's – The Ness pipers – The Earl of space / Nancy's whisky / If Cadillac made tractors – Happy birthday Fiona – MacFarlane's rant / Camden town / James Cameron – Fosgail an doras – The skylark's ascension / Time & tide / The bonnie Jeannie Deans / The walking nightmare – Drive home from mainlanders – The mill house / Rothesay bay / Banais choinnich / Eileen MacDonald – Welcome the piper / Sunset / Whiskey from the field – Volcanic organic.

– compilations, etc. –

1982. (lp) *Stoof; (MU 7475)* **WINTERFOLK '80** ☐ ☐-

May 88. (cd) *Temple; (COMD 2001)* **AFTER HOURS** ☐ ☐-
– After hours – The green gates – The ship in full sail / Frideray / A chance as good as any – Reid's rant / Anthem / The dear green place / Look across the water – Mrs Garden of Troup – The Keelman ower land / The green plaid / Mary Cassidy / I am the common man / The St. Kilda girl's lament – The St. Kilda wedding march / The lads o' the fair / The Sauchiehall Street salsa / The boar and the fox / The battle of Waterloo – Kilcoy's march – The Quaker / The snows of France and Holland / Bad moon rising – The rising moon reel.

Oct 93. (cd) *Topic; (TSCD 468)* **OPENING MOVES** (1977-79) ☐ ☐-
– Silver spear – Humours of Tulla / Shipyard apprentice / Cruel brother / Ge do theid mi do m'leabradh / Battle of Harlaw / Jenny Nettles / Grays of Tongside / Tae the beggin / Tamosher / Blackbird and the thrush – Moray club / Lang Johnnie More / Brown milkmaid – Dunnottar Castle / Maid of Glengarrysdale / Disused railway / Lady Leroy / Miss Drummond of Perth – Fiddler's joy / Traditional reel – Shetland fiddler / My last farewell to Stirling – Cuidich n' right / I hae laid a herrin' in salt – My wife's a wanton wee thing / Banks of the Allan / The battle of Falkirk muir / Joe McGann's fiddle – Centre's bonnet.

May 96. (cd) *Escalibur; (CD 802)* **FAREWELL TO NOVA SCOTIA** ☐ ☐-

Feb 98. (cd) *Munich; (MRCD 188)* **LIVE CELTIC FOLK MUSIC (live)** ☐ ☐-

ALAN REID

Temple Temple

Feb 98. (cd/c) *(<COMD2/CTP 072>)* **THE SUNLIT EYE** ☐ ☐
– Iolair na mara (The sea eagle) / The sleeping warrior / What can a lassie dae? / Just a boy / The million dollar sweetie – Feiger's warning / Rantin' rovin' robin / Five bridges to cross / Cumberland house – Pinky, Porky and Jim / Renaldo the rebounder / Love no more / The Wilton Street dawdle / Norman MacAskill of Lochinver / Mary Morison.

Mar 01. (c) *(BK 010)* **MARTYRS, ROGUES & WORTHIES** ☐ ☐-

JOHN McCUSKER

Temple Temple

Apr 95. (cd/c) *(<COMD2/CTP 059>)* **JOHN McCUSKER** ☐ ☐
– Tommy People's reel – Frank's reel / Biodag aig MacThomais – Mulqueen's reel / Brigid's waltz / Bobby – Bag of plums / Rosin the beau / The rose in the heather – Does this train go to Bellshill? – Trip to Kilkenny / Craigcullen / St. Bride's way – The bouncing Czech / Radio sweethearts' waltz – Sandy Hall – The camel's hump / Air for Jakes / John Daly's hornpipe – Bubba's reel – McFadden's handsome daughter.

Jul 00. (cd) *(<COMD 2083>)* **YELLA HOOSE** ☐ ☐ Aug00
– The boys of the puddle – Sean Og Potts / Shetland molecule – For all the cows / Sailing through the narrows – Kev goes to Brittany – Pur the orangutan / Ann MacGuire's silver wedding – 30 year jig / Wee Michael's march – Joe's tuxedo – Pacific avenue / Blue bonnets over the border – Khazi / Rod Cameron's uncle – Xesus and Felicia / Al's big day / Night visiting song / Emma and Jamie's wedding / Carrickmacross – Yella hoose – Trip to the phone.

Alex BEATON (see under ⇒ CUMBERLAND THREE)

Jack BECK (see under ⇒ HERITAGE)

BEGGARS MANTLE

Formed: Kirkcaldy, Fife ... 1983 by BRUCE DAVIES and BILL McARTHUR, borrowing the moniker from JOHN WATT's old ceilidh outfit, the BEGGARS MANTLE BAND. The contemporary/trad folk duo's first visit to the studio was in the mid-80's when they issued two sets for 'Lochshore', 'MILESTONE' (1984 – and originally on their own imprint) and 'HOME THAT I LOVE' (1985). After their split in 1989, DAVIES (who'd turned professional in '86) went solo. Influenced by a number of folk artists such as TAM PAXTON, JOHN DENVER, DOUGIE MacLEAN, The McCALMANS and The CORRIES (to mention but a handful), DAVIES recorded a plethora of albums (his latest being 2000's 'O'ER THE BORDER') mostly for his mail-order Rothes Recordings and often tours the States. In 1995, BRUCE won the prestigious Edinburgh Folk Club Songwriting Contest.

BRUCE DAVIES (b.25 Nov'55, Kirkcaldy) – vocals, acoustic guitar / **BILL McARTHUR** – vocals, acoustic guitar

Milestone not iss.

1984. (lp/c) *(MS/CMS 001)* **MILESTONE** ☐ [-]
– Barnyards of Delgaty / The massacre of Glencoe / Roses of Prince Charlie / Jock o' Hazeldean / Wee china pig / Loch Lomond / The wee Scots lad / Aye waulkin' O / The braes o' Mar / No man's land / Mingulay boat song. *(re-iss. Apr85 on 'Lochshore' lp/c; LOCLP/ZCLOC 1015)*

Lochshore not iss.

Oct 85. (lp/c) *(LOCLP/ZCLOC 1036)* **HOME THAT I LOVE** ☐ [-]
– Home that I love / Gentle Annie / All God's creatures (a place in the choir) / Broom o' the Cowdenknowes / Friends of mine / The Carrick hills / Beggars mantle / Whiskey on a Sunday / Rantin' rovin' Robin / Love's the rising sun / Rolling hills of the borders / Will ye no' come back again.

Scotdisc not iss.

Feb 87. (c) *(CITV 436)* **GOING PLACES** ☐ [-]
– Hills of Caithness / Sonny's dream / The Crinian canal / Glasgow lullaby / Skye boat song / Leaving Nancy / The city of Chicago / All my lovin' / Tramps & hawkers / Silver darlings / Hello Patsy Fagan / Ye banks & braes / Road to Bavaria.

— next with guests **WENDY WEATHERBY** – cello, vocals / **GORDON YOUNG** – accordion / **IAIN ANDERSON** – narration

Scottish Tourist Board not iss.

1988. (c) *(none)* **THE QUEST FOR SCOTLAND** (some instrumentals) ☐ [-]
– Scots wha' hae / The battle of Bannockburn / Flo'ers o' the forest / The Queen's Mary's (WENDY) / Charlie is my darlin' / Skye boat song / I will go / Smile in your sleep / The wark o' the weavers / The boatie rows / Instrumental medley:- Dark island – Westering home – Northern lights / Bonnie Gallowa' – Loch Lomond – I belong to Glasgow (GORDON) / The Sunday driver / Flo'ers o' Edinburgh / Fitba' crazy / Atholl Highlanders / Listen to the teacher / Ann Elizabeth polka / Doon in the wee room.

— the duo split some time in 1989

BRUCE DAVIES

— **BRUCE** – vocals, guitars, banjo, mandolin, mouth organ, keyboards / with various session people

Rothes Recordings not iss.

1990. (lp) *(RR 001)* **CALEDONIA** ☐ [-]
1990. (lp; as BRUCE DAVIES with MARK KENNETH) *(RR 002)* **THE CALEDONIAN COLLECTION** ☐ [-]
1991. (lp) *(RR 003)* **IN CONCERT (live)** ☐ [-]
1992. (lp/cd) *(RR 004/+CD)* **BY REQUEST** ☐ [-]
1994. (lp) *(RR 005)* **TROUBADOUR** ☐ [-]
1994. (lp) *(RR 006)* **ANTHOLOGY** (compilation) ☐ [-]
1995. (lp/cd) *(RR 007/+CD)* **WI' LICHTSOME HE'RT** (compilation & new) ☐ [-]
– Scots wha ha'e / Wee china pig / The water is wide / I ha'e seen the Hielan's / Smile in your sleep / My love is like a red, red rose / Ye banks and braes / Smuggler / Jeely piece song / Loch Lomond / Yellow on the broom / Skye boat song / Annie Laurie / The new teacher / Ae fond kiss / Auld lang syne.
1996. (lp/cd) *(RR 008/+CD)* **FROM A DISTANCE** (compilation) ☐ [-]
– From a distance / The massacre of Glencoe / Charlie in the meadow / Old man river / Forty five years / Fields of Athenrye / It doesn't matter anymore / You've got a friend / The midges / Annie's song / Margarita / I'll never find another you / Leaving Nancy / Always on my mind / Ballad of St. Anne's reel / Wind beneath my wings.
1997. (lp/cd) *(RR 009/+CD)* **LIFE BEGINS** ☐ [-]
– Santa somethin' / A wish for me / The best is you / Home / Flowers are red / It'll happen soon to you (the zig zaggy song) / Give yourself to love / Only the memory / Travelin' troubadour / Maybe he needs you / The hug song / A night at home / I'm in love / Life begins.
1998. (lp/cd) *(RR 010/+CD)* **THE BEST OF TOMORROWS** ☐ [-]
– Beautiful river / You touched me / Golden, golden / Whatever happened / On the road with you / When two hearts combine / I'm not sayin' (Dave & Amy's song) / Coffee in bed / For fathers and sons / Take a little time / Lies / Another time, another place / The best of tomorrows / Beautiful river (reprise).
1999. (lp/cd) *(RR 011/+CD)* **O'ER THE BORDER** ☐ [-]
– Jock Tamson's bairns / Rolling hills of the border / Coulter's candy / Jock o' Hazeldean / Generations of change / Scarborough settlers' lament (Canadian exile song) / Home that I love / A kiss from Wishaw Cross / The hills of Caithness / The dark island / Granny Fraser's flittin' / Caledonia / Green grow the rashes / Address to the haggis (incl. pipe tunes – A man's a man – Corn rigs) / Auld lang syne / My bonnie Mary (gae bring tae me a pint o' wine).

– compilations, others, etc. –

2000. (cd) *Medium Rare; <MR 001>* **WILL YE NO' COME BACK AGAIN** [-] [-] mail-o

BENACHALLY CEILIDH BAND

Formed: based around rural Scotland ... by JAKE DONNELLY and JIM LEIGHTON (no, not the goalkeeper!), two former members of AN TEALLACH CEILIDH BAND (a few albums on 'Lismor' exist from the first half of the 90's:- 'CATCHING THE SUN RISE' and 'A SHIP IN FULL SAIL'). Joined by equally seasoned campaigners PETE CLARK (from HERITAGE and SMEDDUM), MARTIN MacLEOD (ex-CAPERCAILLIE), MARTIN HADDEN (ex-SILLY WIZARD) and third 'Martin', MARTIN DIBBS (ex-DOUGIE MacLEAN BAND), the 40-something superfolkgroup took to the road for a series of tours.

JAKE DONNELLY – caller, banjo, mandolin / **JIM LEIGHTON** – midi accordion, piano / **PETE CLARK** – fiddle / **MARTIN MacLEOD** (b. Oban) – fiddle / **MARTIN HADDEN** (b.23 May'57, Aberdeen) – guitar, bass / **MARTIN DIBBS** – drums

Smiddy Made not iss.

Dec 97. (c/cd) *(C+/SMD 610)* **HAPPY FEET** ☐ [-]
– Gay Gordons / Dashing white sergeant / Old time waltz / Strip the willow / Slow foxtrot / St. Bernard's waltz / Highland Scottische / Cumberland square eight / Eva three step / Duke of Perth / Pride of Erin waltz / Virginia reel / Military two step / Canadian barn dance / Orcadian strip the willow / Last dance.

PETE CLARK

May 98. (c/cd) *(C+/SMD 615)* **EVEN NOW – THE MUSIC OF NIEL GOW** ☐ [-]

Margaret BENNETT (see under ⇒ Tartan Tapes records)

Martyn BENNETT

Born: 1971, Newfoundland, Nova Scotia, Canada. Like many natives of Northern Canada, BENNETT was descended from Celtic ancestry and as a child was immersed in Gaelic Scots song. He developed his interest in traditional music after his family relocated to Scotland in the mid-70's, winning a place in a prestigious Edinburgh music school and going on to study at the Royal Scottish Academy Of Music And Drama in Glasgow. Here he underwent classical training in piano and violin while playing folk sessions in pubs by night.

To his wide ranging instrumental mastery (including the Ceol Mor Highland Bagpipe tradition) and knowledge of both traditional and classical forms, BENNETT was to subsequently add a love of dance music, discovered during Glasgow's heady year of culture in 1990. He was soon in demand as a composer for theatrical productions, scoring music for the Tom McGrath adaptation of 'Kidnapped' and David Harrower's 'Knives In Hens' amongst others. This led to work in TV and film and in turn to live performance, BENNETT completing a US tour with WOLFSTONE and playing at the Stirling Castle Premiere for 'Braveheart'.

With various guest slots under his belt, the piping prodigy finally went into the studio in his own right for 1996's 'MARTYN BENNETT'. Released on native label 'Eclectic', the album laid down the blueprint for his unique brand of bang(in') up to date urban folk. The formula was expanded further on 1997's landmark 'BOTHY CULTURE', an electro-soup soundclash of colliding musical cultures. Chaperoned by a collage of ever shifting dancefloor moods (four to the floor beats, rattling drum'n'bass snares and squelching synths all present and correct), BENNETT flirted successfully with ethnic traditions from as far afield as Turkey, India and Scandinavia without compromising the essentially Scottish folk context. Most intriguing was 'HALLAIG', a vaguely unsettling monologue by the late Gaelic poet Sorley Maclean, set to a suitably haunting soundtrack. Another, 'AYE?', was used for a Scots Porridge Oats TV ad; his violin reminiscent of the MAHAVISHNU ORCHESTRA in the mid-70's.

During this prolific spell for the multi-talented BENNETT, he also contributed violin to FISH's 'Sunsets On Empire' set. More recently, the Pied Piping Pixie has collaborated on one set, 'HARDLAND VOL.1' (2000) with MARTIN LOW. Now on the roster of SIMON THOUMIRE's 'Footstompin'' imprint, MARTYN delivered yet another inspiring set. 'GLEN LYON' (2002) was a song cycle of ancestral Gaelic field songs that were often performed by his mother, MARGARET. They had been passed down from generation to generation, stopping off probably once and for all at MARTYN's atmospheric fantasy soundscapes.

MARTYN BENNETT – pipes, bagpipes, violin, keyboards

Eclectic not iss.

Mar 96. (cd) *(ECLCD 9614)* **MARTYN BENNETT** ☐ [-]
– Swallowtail / Erin / Cuillin (part 1) / Cuillin (part 2) / Deoch an dorus (part 1) / Deoch an dorus (part 2) / Floret silva undique / Jacobite bebop / 3 sheeps 2 the wind (part 1) / 3 sheeps to the wind (part 2) / Stream.

Rykodisc Rykodisc

Oct 97. (cd) *(<RCD 10381>)* **BOTHY CULTURE** ☐ ☐ Jan98
– Tongues of Kali / Aye? / Shputnik in Glenshiel / Hallaig / Ud the Doudouk / 4 notes / Joik / Yer man from Athlone / Waltz for Hector.

Cuillin not iss.

Aug 00. (cd; as MARTYN BENNETT & MARTIN LOW) *(CUILCD 01)* **HARDLAND VOL.1** ☐ [-]
– Love is here (intro) / Love machine / Spree / Threadbare / How it got there / Harry's in Heaven / Handshaker / Snipe shadow / Rasta plan / This guy thunders / Distortion pipe / PLAY.

Footstompin' not iss.

Mar 02. (cd) *(CDFSR 1714)* **GLEN LYON – A SONG CYCLE** ☐ [-]
– Peter Stewart, 1910 / Buain a'choirce (Reaping song) / Suid mar chuir mi'n geamhradh tharram (Night visiting song) / Uamh an oir (Cave of gold) / A fhleasgaich uir, leanainn thu (Young man, I'd follow you) / Ho rinn O (Unrequited love song) / A thearlaich oig (Oh young Charles Stewart) / Cumha iain gairby (Lament for John MacLeod of Raasay) / Hiuraibh o, ghraidh an tig thu? (Will you return, my love?) / Dh' eirich mi moch maduinn cheutain (Waulking song) / Air bhith dhomsha (In praise of brothers, happy) / Cumha mhic criomain (MacCrimmon's lament) / Oran nam mogaisean (Indian moccasin song) / Fhir a'leadain thlath (Lad with the smooth tresses) / Griogal cridhe (Glen Lyon's lament).

Ian F. BENZIE (see under ⇒ OLD BLIND DOGS)

BIG SKY (see under ⇒ CAPERCAILLIE)

Bill BLACK & His Scottish Dance Band (see under ⇒ Springthyme records)

Donald BLACK (see under ⇒ Greentrax records)

BLACKEYED BIDDY (see under ⇒ Greentrax records)

BLACK WATCH (Pipes & Drums of the 1st Battalion) (see under ⇒ Greentrax records)

Bob BLAIR (see under ⇒ Springthyme records)

BLAZIN' FIDDLES

Formed: Highlands & Islands of Scotland . . . summer 1998 initially for a one-off Highland Festival concert by six of the hottest, young – but nevertheless veteran – solo fiddlers:- CATRIONA MACDONALD (from the Shetlands), ALLAN HENDERSON (from Mallaig), BRUCE MACGREGOR (from Inverness), IAIN MACFARLANE (from Glenfinnan) and AIDAN O'ROURKE (from Oban); DUNCAN CHISHOLM was also an integral part of the formation. Accompanied by ANDY THORBURN and MARC CLEMENT on piano and guitar respectively, The BLAZIN' FIDDLES were ready to set audiences alight all over the world. Their debut album, 'FIRE ON!' (2000), garnered rave reviews, one even going as far as to say that they were "the Led Zeppelin of Folk". After ringing in the bells for BBC1's Hogmanay show, The BLAZIN' FIDDLES were back with an even sweeter instrumental set, 'THE OLD STYLE' (2002); great prospects for them and the whole of Scottish folk music are surely ahead.

CATRIONA MACDONALD – fiddle / **ALLAN HENDERSON** – fiddle / **DUNCAN CHISHOLM** – fiddle / **BRUCE MACGREGOR** – fiddle / **AIDAN O'ROURKE** – fiddle / **IAIN MACFARLANE** – fiddle / with **ANDY THORBURN** – piano + **MARC CLEMENT** – guitar

Blazin' not iss.

Jun 00. (cd) *(BRCD 001)* **FIRE ON!** ☐ [-]
– The heights of Casino – Donald, Willie and his dog – The Kilbrandon / Dolina MacKay – The little cascade – The banshee / The Greenland man's tune – Sister Jean / Bodaich bheaga abriachan – Loch Gorm – Colin Clachair – Johnny Finlay / Ho da lo la lo – Ghoid lad mo bhean an raoir – Ugi's na mo thriall dhachaidh / The Glenfinnan midge factory – Ciaran tourish – The waves of rush – Carol-Anne's / Marnie Swanson of the grey coast / Kenny MacDonald's – Garster's dream – The grey buck – Ho ro mo bhobain an dram / The Lochaber gathering – In and out the harbour – Barney's Balmoral / Mrs Robertson of Greshornish – Stirling Castle – Donnie MacGregor – The rambler / Farquhar and Hettie's – My Cape Breton home / The mouseskin shoe – Siobhan O'Donnell's – Peter MacKinnon of Skeabost – Bonnie Mulligan.

— now without CHISHOLM who had other commitments

Aug 02. (cd) *(BRCD 002)* **THE OLD STYLE** ☐ [-]
– Bullocks / Flora / Sir James / Catalina / Athole brose / Three steps / Dancing on the Moon / Strathmarches / Sheiling / Swedish / Eejit.

Eric BOGLE

Born: 1944, Peebles. At the age of 25, BOGLE, like so many Scots before him, emigrated to Australia where he initially lived in Canberra. After a period working as an accountant, he eventually took up singing/writing/performing full-time, releasing 'NOW I'M EASY' as his domestic debut album in 1980. This contained both 'NO MAN'S LAND' (better known as 'GREEN FIELDS OF FRANCE' when recorded by The MEN THEY COULDN'T HANG amongst others) and 'THE BAND PLAYED WALTZING MATILDA', a biting anti-war commentary adapted from a traditional Australian folk song.

Although it remains his most famous work and signature tune, BOGLE has consistently followed a songwriting agenda centering on political and humanitarian issues, especially anti-war themes. Which isn't to say he lacks a sense of humour, far from it, as a cursory listen to any of his live efforts will attest. A concert set recorded in 1977, 'ERIC BOGLE LIVE IN PERSON', marked the man's first UK release in 1982 while 'Topic' issued 'WHEN THE WIND BLOWS' three years later as BOGLE's first readily available studio set. The title track of 1987's 'SINGING THE SPIRIT HOME' album was a harrowing yet uplifting true story about a black prisoner's execution in South Africa. 1993's 'MIRRORS' set, meanwhile, railed against both the modern day horrors of Brazil's murdered street children and the ghosts of Nazi Germany.

Double live set, 'I WROTE THIS WEE SONG . . .' (1994) is as good a starting point as any for BOGLE beginners, featuring a clutch of his most enduring songs and a heavy dose of between-song banter. A folk protest singer in the mould of WOODY GUTHRIE, PHIL OCHS etc., rather than a folk traditionalist, BOGLE rarely relies on anything other than an acoustic guitar for accompaniment although he regularly performs and records with longstanding friends JOHN MUNRO and BRENT MILLER. Virtually all of BOGLE's 90's recordings were released in the UK via Scots label, 'Greentrax', the most recent being 'THE EMIGRANT & THE EXILE' (1997), 'SMALL MIRACLES' (1997) and 'ENDANGERED SPECIES' (2000).

ERIC BOGLE – vocals, acoustic guitar / with **JOHN MUNRO** – guitar, mandolin, vocals / plus others

Larrikin not iss.

1980. (lp) *(LRF 041)* **NOW I'M EASY** [-] [-] Austra
– Now I'm easy / Leaving Nancy / I hate wogs / No man's land / Leaving in the morning / Since Nancy died / War correspondent / Song of the whale / Front row cowboy / The band played Waltzing Matilda. *(UK-iss.1988 on 'Plant Life'; PLR 042) (re-iss. Mar89 on 'Larrikin' cd/lp; CD+/LRF 041) <(US cd-iss. Dec97 on 'Celtic'; CMCD 004)>*

1981. (lp; by ERIC BOGLE featuring JOHN MUNRO & BRENT MILLER) **PLAIN AND SIMPLE** [-] [-] Austra
– Lady from Bendigo / Dan / The Aussie bar-b-q / Glasgow lullaby / Belle of Broughton / Mary and me / No man's land / Queensland whalers / No use for him / Bloody rotten audience / Gentle Annie. *(UK-iss.1988 on 'Plant Life'; PLR 033) (<cd-iss. Nov97 on 'Greentrax'; CDTRAX 147>)*

1981. (lp) *(LRF 104)* **SCRAPS OF PAPER** [-] [-] Austra
– Scraps of paper / No man's land / Front row cowboy / A reason for it all / He's nobody's moggy now / And the band played Waltzing Matilda / Now I'm easy / Just not coping / The ballad of Henry Holloway / If wishes were fishes. *(UK-iss.1988 on 'Plant Life'; PLR 046) (re-iss. Oct88; same as Australian) <US-iss.Mar89 on 'Flying Fish' lp/c/cd; FF/+90/70 311> (re-iss. Jun94 on 'Larrikin' cd/c; LARR CD/C 104) (cd re-iss. Mar97 on 'Flying Fish'; same)*

Autogram not iss.

1982. (lp) *(ALLP 211)* **ERIC BOGLE LIVE IN PERSON (live in 1977)** ☐ [-]
– Now I'm easy / The band played Waltzing Matilda / Belle of Broughton / Glasgow lullaby / Mansion hoose on the hill / Leavin' Nancy / No man's land / Mary and me / No use for him / Traditional folksinger's lament / The hero's return (Belfast song).

1982. (lp) *(ALLP 220)* **ERIC BOGLE, DOWN UNDER** [-] [-] bootleg
– Shining river / Poor wee Billy MacMahon / She's be right / For king and country / No man's land / Homeless man / Wee pot stove / Queensland whalers / Owd zither / Island in the river / Death of Ben Hall.

1982. (lp) *(ALLP 253)* **ERIC BOGLE PURE** [-] [-] bootleg
– Seasons / Simple man's love song / Leavin' in the morning / Little fishy / Ice queen / My little darling / Sandt is a soldier / Why should I care / Suffer the children / Whisky-wine / I hate wogs (Oriental gentleman) / Belfast song.

Topic not iss.

Mar 85. (lp; by ERIC BOGLE with JOHN MUNRO & BRENT MILLER) *(12TS 437)* **WHEN THE WIND BLOWS** ☐ ☐
– When the wind blows / Hard hard times / Birds of a feather / Lock keeper / Soldier soldier / Bushfire / Shining river / The enigma / Little Gomez / Safe in the harbour. *<US-iss.Mar89 on 'Flying Fish' lp/cd; FF/+90 354> (re-iss. Jun94 on 'Larrikin' cd/c; LARR CD/C 144)*

Larrikin not iss.

Jan 86. (d-lp/d-c) *(LRF/TC-LRF 160)* **IN CONCERT (live)** -

Sonet Flying Fish

Apr 87. (7") *(SON 2320)* **SINGING THE SPIRIT HOME. / AUSTRALIAN THROUGH AND THROUGH** -

Jun 87. (lp) *(SNTF 983)* *<FF 447>* **SINGING THE SPIRIT HOME**
– An old song / Lifetime / Singing the spirit home / Twenty years ago / All the fine young men / Leaving the land / Australian through and through / Lancelot and Guinevere / Silo / Shelter. *(Aus-iss.1988 on 'Larrikin' cd/c/lp; CD/TC+/LRF 220)*

Sonet Philo

Sep 88. (cd/lp) *(SNT CD/F 1004)* *<CD+/PH 1125>* **SOMETHING OF VALUE**
– Something of value / Katie and the dreamtime land / Harry's wife / A change in the weather / Poor bugger Charlie / Rosie / Going back to Dublin / Them old songwritin' blues / Two strong arms / Across the hills of home (Jimmy's song). *(re-iss. 1988 on 'Larrikin' cd/lp; CD+/LRF 220)*

Greentrax Alcazar

Apr 91. (cd/c) *(CD/C TRAX 040)* *<115>* **VOICES IN THE WILDERNESS**
– Peace has broken out / The lily and the poppy / Blues for Alex / What kind of man / Wilderness / Feed the children / Amazon / Silly slang song / Fences and walls / It's only Tuesday / The gift of years.

Greentrax Larrikin

Nov 93. (cd/c) *(CD/C TRAX 068)* *<CD/TC LRF 282>* **MIRRORS**
– Refugee / One small life / Plastic Paddy / Welcome home / Flat stony broke waltz / Vanya / Don't you worry about that / Mirrors / The song / Short white blues / At risk / Never again – Remember / Somewhere in America / Wouldn't be dead for quids / Wishing is free.

Nov 94. (d-cd/d-c) *(CD/C TRAX 082D)* **I WROTE THIS WEE SONG . . . (live)** -
– Sound of singing / Leaving the land / Silly slang song / Mirrors / A reason for it all / Flying finger filler / Vanya / Don't you worry about that / Somewhere in America / Them old songwriting blues / Rosie // Feed the children / Singing the spirit home / Leaving Nancy / Now I'm easy / Plastic Paddy / No mans land / Never again – Remember / Short white blues / Welcome home / Daniel smiling / Eric and the informers / Shelter / The gift of years.

Greentrax Greentrax

Feb 97. (cd/c; by ERIC BOGLE & JOHN MUNRO) *(<CD/C TRAX 121>)* **THE EMIGRANT & THE EXILE**
– Poacher's moon / Were you there? / The strangers / World Cup fever / The ballad of Charles Devonport / Progress / Marking time / Campbell's daughter / One small star / Listen to the old ones / The end of an auld song / Cuddy river reverie / Kissing English arses talking blues / Standing in the light.

Jun 97. (cd) *(<CDTRAX 130>)* **SMALL MIRACLES** Oct98
– Small miracles / The diggers' legacy / Dedication day / Ekka's silver jubille song / Always back to you / The blessing / Here in the green / Sayonara Australia / The golden city / Somebody's daughter / Keeper of the flame / Romeo and Juliet in Sarajevo / The red heart / Troy's song / Unsung hero / Heart of the land / One small star.

Jul 00. (cd) *(<CDTRAX 196>)* **ENDANGERED SPECIES**
– Our national pride / The sign / Just here for the money / Jingle jangle / No gods at all / Robin's rant – Tom O'Neill's tantrum / The road to El Dorado / You've got nothing I need / Journeys / Turning circles / Beam me up, Scotty / Endangered species / The Waltzing Matilda waltz / Jimmy Dancer / The river of time.

– compilations, etc. –

Aug 89. (cd/c/lp) *Greentrax; (<CD/C+/TRAX 028>)* **THE ERIC BOGLE SONGBOOK**
– A reason for it all / Nobody's moggy now / Hard hard times / Scraps of paper / If wishes were fishes / Front row cowboy / And the band played Waltzing Matilda / Little Gomez / The Aussie bar-b-q / When the wind blows.

May 92. (cd/c) *Greentrax; (<CD/C TRAX 051>)* **THE ERIC BOGLE SONGBOOK VOLUME 2** 1994
– Now I'm easy / Glasgow lullaby / No man's land / Do you know any Bob Dylan? / My youngest son came home today / Belle of Broughton / Leaving Nancy / Singing the spirit home / Wee china pig / Leaving the land / Rosie / All the fine young men / Across the hills of home (Jimmy's song).

Jan 94. (cd) *Wundertute; (TUT 72162CD)* *<55222>* **HARD HARD TIMES** Mar97
– Lady from Bendigo / Glasgow lullaby / Hard hard times / A reason for it all / Shining river / Song of the whale / Mary and me / Twenty years ago / When the wind blows / Never again / Belle of Broughton / Safe in the harbour.

1990's. (c; as ERIC BOGLE, REDGUM) *Larrikin; (LARRC 203)* **NEVER UNDERESTIMATE THE POWER OF SONG** -

Mar 01. (cd) *(<CDTRAX 210>)* **BY REQUEST**
– (selections from THE ERIC BOGLE SONGBOOKS)

BONGSHANG

Formed: Shetland Isles . . . 1991 by frontman and banjo wizard JJ JAMIESON (formerly of HEXOLOGY and SWAMPTRASH) along with star-pupil drummer CHRISTOPHER ANDERSON (from Dougie Johnston's Master Dance Band!), teenage bassman BRYAN PETERSON, guitarist NEIL PRESHAW and fiddler LEONARD SCOLLAY. Another crew of Celtic folk-fusion meisters to emerge from the fertile Shetland scene, BONGSHANG built up a fervent local following with their high-octane brew of furious fiddling, ballistic banjo and dancefloor groove.

Their unique musical appeal also extended to Europe where a series of festival and TV appearances (including a support slot to the late guitar hero RORY GALLAGHER) raised their profile among foreign fans. Spurred on by such a promising start to their career, the quartet released a self-financed debut album, 'CRUDE', in late 1993. Demand was such that the resources of a professional record label soon became imperative and BONGSHANG subsequently joined the eclectic roster of 'Iona' records, home to the likes of spiritual brethren, The HUMPFF FAMILY. The label duly remastered and re-issued 'CRUDE' to an enthusiastic reception in late '95, following on from the band's incendiary performance at Glasgow's annual Celtic Connections Festival earlier that year. Although a sophomore effort – tentatively titled 'LEWD' and recorded in the group's home studio – was due for release in early '96, the new recording (now as 'THE HURRICANE JUNGLE') didn't see light of day until '97; SCOLLAY and HOOK had by now been replaced by former 'Young Composer Of The Year' and! 'Shetland Fiddler Of The Year', PETER GEAR.

Towards the end of the millennium, BONGSHANG delivered their third set, 'VL-LO-FONE' (1999).

JJ JAMIESON – vocals, banjo (ex-HEXOLOGY, ex-SWAMPTRASH) / **NEIL PRESHAW** – guitar / **BRYAN PETERSON** – bass / **CHRISTOPHER ANDERSON** – drums (ex-DOUGIE JOHNSON band) / **LEONARD SCOLLAY** – fiddle / plus **STEVIE HOOK** – sound

Doovf not iss.

Oct 94. (cd) *(doovfcd 1)* **CRUDE** -
– Le introducement / Things to come / The floggin set / If & when / Lee Highway blues / Phosphene – Tamlinn / The hangmans reel / Dig a hole / Scotland – Frosty morning / A.K.A. crude / Wedding row / Reprise. *(re-iss. Nov95 on 'Iona' cd/c; IRCD/IRC 032)*

— **PETER GEAR** – fiddle; repl. SCOLLAY + HOOK

Dec 95. (c-ep) *(doovf 1.5)* **CHUG** -
– Probleme / Meatball / Dubweiser / D-drone.

— added **JOANNA REDMAN** – backing vocals

May 97. (cd) *(doovfcd 2)* **THE HURRICANE JUNGLE** -
– D/drone / All that hate / Probleme / Tackhead / Dubweiser / Tangled flies / Abandon motion / The honeyshroud / Hurrican jungle.

— BONGSHANG split in 1997 but re-formed a few years later

— **JAMIESON + ANDERSON** recruited **GORDON TULLOCH** – guitar, vocals (of FILSKA) + **ANDREW GRAY** – bass + the returning **SCOLLAY**

Dec 99. (cd) *(doovfcd 3)* **VL-LO-FONE** -
– Intro / Myrakle / Launderette / Grass widow / Longer / Superfresco / Cassini / Grass orphan / Wisdom / Kalifornia.

BONNIE SCOTS

Formed: Hamilton/Blantyre, Lanarkshire . . . late 60's by the tartan duo of MICK MADDEN (a Catholic) and JACKIE DIXON (a Protestant), who entertained the audience with some good humoured jibes about their religious divide. Backed by SULLIVAN'S GYPSIES, the pair made only one LP, 'LAUGH AND CRY', in 1969. However, both took off to Canada, JACKIE ending up in Huntsville, Ontario and MICK in Vancouver.

MICK MADDEN – vocals / **JACKIE DIXON** – vocals / with SULLIVAN'S GYPSIES: **FERGUS O'BYRNE** – banjo, organ / **DERMOT O'REILLY** – guitars, mandolin / **MERRILL MILLS** – bass / **TOM HENDERSON** – drums

Birchmount not iss.

1969. (lp) *(BM 543)* **LAUGH AND CRY** -
– This land is your land / The drunken man / Jeanie McCall / Northern lights of Aberdeen / Scotland ra brave / Coulter's candy / Lonely prison cell / Dundee weaver / The Billy and the Sally / Lizzie Lindsay.

— split when DIXON emigrated to Canada; MADDEN also relocated there

Gill BOWMAN

Born: Edinburgh. An elegant traditional/Celtic vocalist who has worked with an array of well-known folk musicians, GILL began her recording career with 1991's 'CITY LOVE' album. This was followed by 1994's 'PERFECT LOVER', a fine collection of traditional and contemporary material once again co-written with WENDY STEWART. A veritable authority on RABBIE BURNS and his wealth of songs, poems and ballads, GILL released 'TOASTING THE LASSIES' later that year in celebration of the bard's bicentennial, having already won widespread critical acclaim for her Edinburgh Fringe show of the same name.

During a song workshop run by Edinburgh's Adult Learning Project, BOWMAN first came into contact with KARINE POLWART, future lead singer of both BATTLEFIELD BAND and MALINKY. After subsequently hearing her wow an audience in the back room of The Oxford Bar, GILL approached her about working together. The end result was 'HIGHWIRED', an excellent mix of country and folk, traditional and modern, released to critical acclaim in summer 2000 under the banner of MacALIAS. Produced by RAB NOAKES and featuring the likes of DUNCAN CHISHOLM and DAVID VERNON, the album showcased the pair's contrasting vocal styles and ringing harmonies. POLWART – tipped as one of the most promising young Scottish singers to emerge in years – provided the country twang and a rootsy edge, giving EMMYLOU HARRIS a run for her money on opener 'ALL THE WAY BACK HOME'. BOWMAN, meanwhile provided the BURNS interpretations (together with fascinating background notes on each song) and haunting original compositions such as 'WINTER SUN', inspired by the heartbreaking conditions endured by female miners in 18th century Fife. The pair even arranged a murder ballad NICK CAVE would've been proud of, 'FINE FLOWERS IN THE VALLEY'.

GILL BOWMAN – vocals, acoustic guitar / with **WENDY STEWART** – co-writer, electric harp, concertina

Fellside / not iss.

Feb 91. (lp/c/cd) *(FE 080/+C/CD)* **CITY LOVE** [ ] [-]
– Your average woman / A very good year / Verses / The ballad of the four Mary's / Make it good / City love / Psychics in America / Story today / Lang-a-growing / Different game / If I didn't love you.

— now with also JACK EVANS – bass / MILTON CAMPBELL – viola / CHRISTINE KYDD – backing vocals / JIM MALCOLM – harmonica, vocals

Greentrax / Greentrax

Sep 94. (cd/c) *(<CD/C TRAX 081>)* **PERFECT LOVER** [ ] [ ] Jan95
– Take me home / Walking away / Sweet Tibbie Dunbar – Rantin' dog / Dear friend / Comin' thro' the rye / This time / To be like you / Ae fond kiss / Dream Angus / Making friends / Somebody's baby.

Feb 95. (cd/c) *(<CD/C TRAX 085>)* **TOASTING THE LASSIES** [ ] [ ] Mar95
– Green grow the rashes / Now westlin winds / Banks o' Doon / Sweet Tibbie Dunbar – Rantin' dog / Sweet Afton / Comin' thro' the rye / Ae fond kiss / Deli's awa' wi' th' exciseman / Lea-rig / Rose bud, by my early walk / O, this is no my ain lassie / Auld lang syne.

MacALIAS

— **GILL BOWMAN + KARINE POLWART** – vocals (of MALINKY, of BATTLEFIELD BAND) / with also **DUNCAN CHISHOLM** – fiddle / **COLIN McFARLANE** – guitars, mandolin / **DAVIE PATON** – bass / **DAVID VERNON** – accordion / **FRASER SPIERS** – harmonica / **JIM McDERMOTT** – drums

Jun 00. (cd) *(<CDTRAX 199>)* **HIGHWIRED** [ ] [ ]
– Winter song / I don't think she'll stay / All the way back home / Take me in your arms / Rantin' dog / Gowden locks o' Anna / Fine flowers – Bonnie at morn / John C Clarke / Violet and the rose / Wild west romance.

BOYS OF THE LOUGH

Formed: 1967 . . . by Irish-born CATHAL McCONNELL, ROBIN MORTON and TOMMY GUNN; the latter subsequently leaving the remaining duo to issue the collaborative 'AN IRISH JUBILEE' (1969). The Scottish connection came about when the pair met up with Lerwick-born fiddler ALY BAIN (see BAIN's own entry) and his singer/guitarist friend MIKE WHELLANS (see WHELLANS own entry) at the Falkirk Folk Festival. In 1972, WHELLANS dropped out and was substituted by another Scot, Glasgow-born DICK GAUGHAN (see GAUGHAN's own entry), the quartet issuing their eponymous set later in the year. However, by the following year, GAUGHAN was a free agent once again, pursuing a successful solo career from then on. DAVE RICHARDSON from Northumberland in England was drafted in to complete further several 70's albums. Founder MORTON was to leave towards the end of that decade (became head of 'Temple' records in Scotland), although tragically his replacement TICH RICHARDSON (brother of DAVE) was killed in a road accident in September '84.

Together with his busy solo schedule, ALY has continued to be a mainstay with The BOYS OF THE LOUGH. From 1985's 'TO WELCOME PADDY HOME' album to 1992's 'THE FAIR HILLS OF IRELAND', this line-up of 2 Irish (McCONNELL and mid-80's newcomer CHRISTY O'LEARY), 2 English (RICHARDSON and newest member CHRIS NEWMAN) plus the solitary Scotsman ALY BAIN, have made up this folk outfit and folk legend. Of late, Scotsman MALCOLM STITT (of TANNAS) has replaced NEWMAN in the late 90's, while O'LEARY and then BAIN (the latter in 2001) have also departed.

BREAD, LOVE AND DREAMS (see ⇒ Section 7: Rock & Pop)

Sandy BRECHIN (see under ⇒ BURACH)

Stuart (& Duncan) BROWN

Born: 7 May'56, Springburn, Glasgow. Having mastered recorder, bouzouki and whistle, STUART became part of Welsh folk outfit MABSANT who evolved from the pubs and clubs of Cardiff in 1978. For the next decade or so (with STUART's double bass-playing older brother DUNCAN joining in 1980), MABSANT delivered several Celtic-styled long-players – from 'Cwlwm Pedwar' in '82 to 'Ton Gron' in 1990 – and performed a great set at the Inverness Folk Festival of 1982.

Ronnie BROWNE (see under ⇒ CORRIES)

Ian BRUCE

Born: 21 Jan'56, Rutherglen, Glasgow. IAN initiated his folk career under the watchful eye of his older brother FRASER who already had a couple of solo albums under his belt ('Shamrock And Heather' and 'Farewell Tae Tarwathie'). The pair cut a trio of albums together for the 'Lochshore' label, namely the charmingly titled 'MRS. BRUCE'S BOYS VOL.1' (1981), 'VEIL OF THE AGES' (1982) and the equally charmingly titled 'MRS. BRUCE'S BOYS VOL.2' (1984).

Mrs Bruce's boys then went their respective ways, IAN initially forming the short-lived SCOTLAND YARD with MARILYN MIDDLETON POLLOCK and SANDY STANAGE; the trio's album, 'Wishing For Friday', never saw the light of day. IAN's solo career began in earnest in 1988 with the 'TOO FAR FROM SHE' album, a record that secured him a deal with the English Borders 'Fellside' label. 'BLOWDEN'S DREAM' (1990) found favour with fans of gentle singer/songwriter fare while BRUCE went on to undertake a kind of mini-tour of Scottish labels, recording 'FREE AGENT' (1994) for 'Iona', 'HODDEN GREY' (1998) for 'Greentrax' (an album that found him working with weel kent folk faces DOUGIE PINCOCK and MALCOLM STITT) and finally, 'ALLOWAY TALES' for Eaglesham-based hi-fi manufacturer 'Linn' in 1999.

IAN's traditionally flavoured material has also proved popular abroad and he has toured in Ireland, Europe and the USA. • **Note:** The album, 'Gospel Accordion' by IAN & MAY BRUCE was not from this IAN.

FRASER & IAN BRUCE

FRASER BRUCE (b.13 Jan'47, Fulham, London) – vocals, acoustic guitar / **IAN BRUCE** – vocals, acoustic guitar (former solo artist with two albums on 'Nevis', 'SHAMROCK AND HEATHER' and 'FAREWELL TAE TARWATHIE')

Lochshore / not iss.

May 81. (lp/c) *(LOCLP/ZCLOC 1007)* **MRS. BRUCE'S BOYS VOL.1** [ ] [-]
– Ryebuck shearers / Leaving the dales / The king's shilling / Rise up Jack / Ring a Rosie / Cape Ann / The walking song / The new railroad / Isle of Haut / Down where the drunkards roll / The Gadie rins.

Oct 82. (lp/c) *(LOCLP/ZCLOC 1018)* **VEIL OF THE AGES** [ ] [-]
– Nostradamus / John o' dreams / I don't belong to Glasgow / Can ye saw cushions / Grey funnel line / The hagged man / Sally Wheatley / Roll on the day / Roseville fair / Stumpy / Farewell to gold / Aye's the boy.

Oct 84. (lp/c) *(LOCLP/ZCLOC 1028)* **MRS. BRUCE'S BOYS VOL.2** [ ] [-]
– The idiot / Western boat / A man you don't meet every day / Catch me if you can / Tatties and herring / Edinburgh / Mrs. McDonald's lament / Waiting for the lark / Deportees / Bonny Susie Cleland / The wedding / Tak' a dram.

— IAN formed the short-lived outfit SCOTLAND YARD with MARILYN MIDDLETON POLLOCK + SANDY STANAGE; the album 'WISHING FOR FRIDAY' was withdrawn before release

IAN BRUCE

Ruglen / not iss.

1988. (lp) *(LUMS 0101)* **TOO FAR FROM SHE** [ ] [-]

Fellside / not iss.

Mar 90. (cd) *(FECD 076)* **BLODWEN'S DREAM** [ ] [-]
– John / Factory life / Eldorado / Classical music / Ghost of a chair / Farewell deep blue / No noise / This peaceful evening / I can play you anything / Black fog / Blodwen's dream. *(re-iss. Nov95 cd/c; FE 076 CD/C)*

Iona — not iss.

Jul 92. (cd/c) *(FE 085 CD/C)* **OUT OF OFFICE** ☐ [-]

Jul 94. (cd) *(IRCD 026)* **FREE AGENT** ☐ [-]
– Scarborough settlers lament / Bizzie Lizzie / Hearts of Ohio / Find out who your friends are / Please be here / Out of sight / Corners / No satisfaction / Bad bet / Anchor line / Dawn of a brand new day / Free agents / Ladioes left behind / Find out who your friends are (reprise).

Wild Goose — not iss.

Nov 96. (cd) *(WGS 277CD)* **KIND AND GENTLE NATURE** ☐ [-]

Greentrax — Greentrax

Mar 98. (cd) *(<CDTRAX 156>)* **HODDEN GREY** ☐ ☐ Jun98
– The stoutest man in the forty TWA / Trumpet sounds / Jute mill song / Will ye go tae Flanders / She was a rum one / Diamond ship / List Bonnie laddie / Johnny Gallacher / Gi'e me a lass wi' a lump o' land / Kiss the children for me Mary / Tatties an' herrin' / Yella haired laddie / Forfar souger / Bleächer lassie o' Kelvinhaugh / Slippy stane.

Linn — Linn

Aug 99. (cd) *(<CKD 112>)* **ALLOWAY TALES** ☐ ☐ Feb00
– Ye Jacobites by name / Lassie wi the lintwhite locks / Galloway Tam / Ye banks and braes o' bonnie Doon / Soldier's return / Such a parcel of rogues in a nation / Man's a man for a that / Auld man's winter thought / Craigieburn-Wood / Auld lang syne / O, when she cam ben, she bobbed – O Malley's meek / Now westlin winds and slaught'ring guns / Ca' the yowes / Thames flows proudly to the sea.

Jul 01. (cd; as IAN BRUCE BAND) *(AKD 173)* **JIGS, JIVES AND JACOBITES (recorded live at the Riverside club, Glasgow)** ☐ [-]
– Where should I go / Sweet fallen angels / Dark Lochnagar / Bob Parson strathspey / Pearls before swine / Jigs / Namenoia / How do you feel / My matin and my motorbike / Pets and Myra's wedding / Mellow.

Norman BUCHAN

Born: Rutherglen. Although very little was recorded by the man himself, he will be noted in history as a fine contributor of Scottish traditional songs and teaching. As an English teacher at Rutherglen Academy, NORMAN tutored the likes of ARCHIE FISHER, GORDEANNA McCULLOCH, BOBBY CAMPBELL and JOSH MacCRAE, EWAN McVICAR and ANNE NEILSON during the 1960's folk boom; the foundation of subsequent recordings by these artists was his wee red songbook entitled, '101 Scottish Songs'. NORMAN became an MP for Labour, winning Renfrewshire West in '64 and Paisley South in '83, rising to the heights of Shadow Minister for the Arts (he resigned due to his Socialist principles); his wife Janey took over his quest three after his death in 1990.

BULLY WEE BAND

Formed: Glasgow ... early 70's by Fifer brothers JOHN and JIM YARDLEY along with Irishman FRANK SIMON and the classically-trained IAN CUTLER. Spiritual cousins to the likes of SILLY WIZARD, BULLY WEE (as they were originally known) incorporated rock into traditional folk idioms, releasing their eponymous debut album in 1975. SIMON subsequently departed and was to be replaced by Irish cellist/mandolin player FERGUS FEELY on 1976's 'ENCHANTED LADY' album. Following 1978's 'SILVERMINES' album, COLIN REECE was added to the fold and he featured on the traditionally-flavoured 'THE MADMAN OF GOTHAM' (1981). Although this album (which didn't feature JOHN YARDLEY) effectively marked the end of the road for the band, most of the various members remained in the folk scene. REECE subsequently formed a duo with CUTLER and the pair released the 'FACE TO FACE' album in 1982 before REECE went solo and cut the 'WELL KEPT SECRET' set in 1985. He then moved into cabaret and stand-up comedy, backing JIM DAVIDSON amongst others, while CUTLER continued to make a living on the ceilidh circuit. FEELY, meanwhile, joined The STEVE ASHLEY BAND and later the American cajun outfit, LE RUE. Latter day BULLY member MARTIN ALLCOCK went on to work with bigger names such as FAIRPORT CONVENTION and JETHRO TULL. The man who started it all, JIM YARDLEY, undertook a solo tour of Norway.

JOHN YARDLEY (b. 7 Jan'46, Dunfermline) – vocals, guitar, bodhran / **JIM YARDLEY** (b.23 Oct'44, Dunfermline) – vocals, guitar, mandolin / **FRANK SIMON** (b. Boyle, County Roscommon, Ireland) – guitar, whistles, vocals / **IAN CUTLER** (b.22 Dec'53, London) – violin, viola, organ, etc

Folksound — not iss.

1975. (lp; as BULLY WEE) *(FS 102)* **BULLY WEE** ☐ [-]
– Trooper and the maid / The friar's bitches – The road to Boyle / The beggar wench / From the north / Up and down again – The kid on the mountain / Highland Harry / The jolly tinker – Rolling in the rye grass / The road to Dundee / Arthur McBride / The three healths / The lark in the morning – Morrison's jig / Three gypsies.

— **FERGUS FEELY** (b. Jul'53, Dundalk, Ireland) – cello-mandolin, vocals; repl. SIMON

Red Rag — not iss.

1976. (lp; as BULLY WEE) *(RRR 007)* **ENCHANTED LADY** ☐ [-]
– Kinkora jig – Behind the haystack – Willie Coleman's jig / The Cowdenknowes / The trumpet hornpipe – The Mointeach reel / The jolly beggar – The meadow / Martin Wynns No.2 / Enchanted lady – Boys o' the lough – Green fields of Ross Beigh / Cold haily windy night / The banks of the Suir – Cortes gardens / The snows.

1978. (lp) *(RRR 017)* **SILVERMINES** ☐ [-]
– The Kielder hunt / Strike the gay harp – The Blarney pilgrim / The hills of Ardmorn / Leitrim town – The master Crowley – Kitty's wedding / Open the door / The silvermines – Lady Anne Montgomery / The road to Dundee / Arrival – Donnybrook fair / Leaboy's lassie.

— **COLIN REECE** (b.28 Sep'47, London) – vocals, guitar + **PHIL MOORE** – piano; repl. JOHN

Jigsaw — not iss.

May 81. (lp) *(SAW 1)* **THE MADMAN OF GOTHAM** ☐ [-]
– The madman of Gotham / Girl that broke my heart / Tibbie Dunbar / Cheapside / Margaret's waltz / Patrick the fabulous magician / Way below the tide / Wedding at Stanton Drew / Geiranger – Gallaghers.

— added **MARTIN ALCOCK** (b. 5 Jan'57, Manchester) – guitar, bouzouki, bass, mandolin, keyboards; repl. CUTLER + REECE who issued their own album in '82, 'FACE TO FACE'; REECE would go solo releasing 'WELL KEPT SECRET' in 1985 and was recently backing comedian JIM DAVIDSON while CUTLER is in ALBION MORRIS and other ceilidh bands. ALCOCK joined FAIRPORT CONVENTION (after a brief spell as duo with FEELY) and later JETHRO TULL, while the remaining Scotsman JIM YARDLEY went solo and toured Norway.

BURACH

Formed: Edinburgh ... mid-90's by ALISON CHERRY, DOUG ANDERSON, SANDY BRECHIN and former IRON HORSE fiddler GAVIN MARWICK; also augmented by MALCOLM STITT on the writing front. Coasting on the wave of renewed interest in Scottish traditional roots music, BURACH scooped first place in the annual Belhaven Brewery Folk Group competition (1994/95) before releasing a debut album, 'THE WEIRD SET' (1995), on the 'Greentrax' label.

The band's passionate and magnetic take on nu-folk translated particularly well to the live environment and through time, the quartet were to take their unique sound further afield than the usual round of European festivals. The unique sound in question was fuelled in no small part by accordionist extraordinaire SANDY BRECHIN, one of Scotland's most talented musicians and also a member of SEELYHOO, among others. The man's wonderfully titled debut solo album, 'OUT OF HIS BOX', appeared in 1996 on his own label ('Brechin All Records'), a disc that featured in many end of year polls. BURACH themselves followed up with a sophomore effort, 'BORN TIRED', in 1997, before opting to go full-time in late '99. If the reception of 'DEEPER' (2000) was anything to go by, the decision had been an auspicious one and the band celebrated with a sterling Celtic Connections appearance in the company of SHARON SHANNON.

The new millennium also saw the group broadening their geographical horizons in line with their musical explorations. Audiences in South America (where they performed on the same bill as Cuba's COMPANY SEGUNDO), the Arabian Gulf and Eastern Europe were treated to Scottish musical hospitality BURACH style, a number of concerts orgnanised in tandem with the British Council. Back home, the schedule was no less hectic and engagements included a Princes Street Gardens appearance in front of Prince Charles.

• **Covered:** Richard Thompson's 'VINCENT BLACK LIGHTNING 1952'.

ALISON CHERRY – vocals / **DOUG ANDERSON** – guitars, mandolin, banjo / **SANDY BRECHIN** – accordion, vocals (of SEELYHOO) / **GAVIN MARWICK** – fiddle (of IRON HORSE)

Greentrax — Greentrax

Jul 95. (cd/c) *(<CD/C TRAX 093>)* **THE WEIRD SET** ☐ ☐ Oct95
– All I ask – Boiling black kettle / The curve / The weird set: Post-conscious modernisation of space – The candlelight reel – The jar o' lentils / Zombie song / Three reels: Return to Milltown – Tarbolton lodge – Oni Bucharesti / Green loch / Vincent black lightning 1952 / Rest of your life / January the 8th / Concertina set: Dick gossips – Earl's chair / Half wat round – Walking the line / What shall we drink to tonight?

Jul 97. (cd) *(<CDTRAX 136>)* **BORN TIRED** ☐ ☐ Sep97
– How on earth? / Funky fat challenge / Nothing left to say / Highfield set / Drop my body / Born tired / Ring around the Moon / Antidote / Sleep of the dead / Smuggler's skull & crossed bones / You're not the only one / Destitution / Lullaby.

May 00. (cd) *(<CDTRAX 189>)* **DEEPER** ☐ ☐ Jun00
– And still there / Birds set / Beautiful blues / Keep on shining / Sweet thing / Turn up for the books / Shadow of the night / Life and times of Johnny Hattersfield / Flora whistle a Scandinavian tune / Left unsaid / Heart of gold / Knot quite Silverstone . . .

SANDY BRECHIN

— with **AARON JONES** – bass / **COLIN McFARLANE** – guitars, mandolin, lapsteel, keyboards / **JIM WALKER** – drums

Brechin All | not iss.

Apr 96. (cd/c) *(CD/C BAR 6001)* **OUT OF HIS BOX** ☐ ☐
– The Gay Gordon's set: Hangin' out the windows – Smoke in the air / The drink's set: Buckfast at Tiffany's – Apricot brandy – The ensign / Things with strings: The bouzouki reel – Brechin wind – The Tazmanian devil / Colin's set: Charlie Stuart's jig – The dirt detective – Dunara / A strathspey and two reels: Roddy's last trip – Highly strung – Sonically justified / Out of his box: The drunken tattie howker – Your drunken fumbling fingers / Tha meudial is maighear's mo ghraidh / It's accordion music Jim, but not as we know it: Tommy Peoples – Sloppy bellows – Massochist waltz / The gas set: Three good fellows – Charlie's dance – Cape Breton mouth music / Timepieces: Nice hands, shame about the face – Tune for a new found watch / The jaunty set: The crapper – The Tongadale – Cameron Alexander Stewart Low / The bassplayer's set: Dusty windowsill – Pete Brady's chubby cheeks – The long water / Metamorphosis: Admirals on the bow – Butter(fly) fingers / The last St. Bernard's waltz: The last waltz.

Greentrax | Greentrax

Mar 99. (cd) *(<CDTRAX 169>)* **OUT OF HIS TREE** ☐ ☐ May99
– Turtles, dogs & fine Highland cheese set: Green mutant ninja turtle blood – The Tain cheese factory – It's a dogs life / Canadian barn dance: Song of the chanter – Willie's brogues – The bonk band / Out of his tree set: Photocopies to the famous – The pinkie-wrestler – The jelly river / East winds / Millennium set: Alasdair James Allan – The Scottish parliament – Eurotrash / Strange Strathspey's: John Currie's infra-red scanner – The bouncing bridge – Campbell's red cords / The fishing set: The broken reel – The tickled trout / The seafarers set: The rollin' stone – The 40-ouncer – A l'eau, c'est l'heure / Time enough for a waltz set: The waltz in time – Kate Jorgensen's waltz / Exhausted set: The canny repair – The dwarf / Two fours set: Walter Gilchrist's pipe organ – Alastair McCallum of Caindow / The Skye stromash set: Oliver the otter killer – Tape me to the bannister – The long jumpers / Aberdour set: Roger McAndrew's 50th fling – Kate McAndrew's gin sling / Lost in Guingamp.

C

CALASAIG

Formed: Highlands . . . 1998 by KEITH JOHNSTON, KEITH EASDALE and KIRSTEN EASDALE. Pooling the talents and considerable experience of CALASAIG's various members, debut set 'UNTIL THEN' (1998) revealed a rich collage of traditional folk influences stretching the length and breadth of the British Isles. 'MAKING FOR THE SHORE' (2000) was another memorable collection which retained the vitality and depth of its predecessor while chief songwriter JOHNSTON released his debut solo set the same year. The well received 'NO STRANGER TO THIS KIND OF GAME' reflected both the man's musical background and wide ranging tastes, an enjoyable detour from the relatively narrow musical confines of traditional folk. JOHNSTON was helped in his endeavours by fellow CALASAIG members KEITH and KIRSTEN, both of whom also possess impressive CV's.

Multi-instrumentalist KEITH EASDALE has previously played with the likes of WILLIAM JACKSON, ALISTAIR HULETT and The SCOTTISH FIDDLE ORCHESTRA, appearing on the latter's 1997 set, 'Live In Toronto'. His sister KIRSTEN has previously sung with WHISKY FINGERS amongst other bands, putting her vocal knowledge to good use in various community based singing workshops. The lady has also contributed to volume IX of the Linn label's 'Robert Burns – The Complete Songs', released in 2001.

CALASAIG themselves were back in 2002 with a third album, 'NEAR & FAR', many of the tracks aired at that year's Celtic Connections festival in Glasgow. Meanwhile, the spiritually motivated KIRSTEN delivered her solo set, 'BE NOT AFRAID' (2002), a record which was inspired by the 6th Century and more modern times.

KEITH JOHNSON – guitar, washboard, bodhran, cello, vocals, etc / **KEITH EASDALE** – pipes, fiddle, flute, piano, mouthorgan, etc / **KIRSTEN EASDALE** – viola, fiddle, bodhran, vocals / with also **JOHN KING** – accordion / **DAVID SCOTT** – organ

Bellcraig | not iss.

Mar 99. (cd) *(BKDCD 101)* **UNTIL THEN** ☐ ☐
– Kenny Gillies of Portnalong, Skye – Paddy's leather breeches – The snuff wife / I once loved a lass / Whistle o'er the lave 'ot / Kate Whitten's – Beathag's / Tha mi sgith / Dance with me / Stirling Brig / The debatable land – Waste of time / Cockle Geordie / King fareweel / Ae fond kiss / The drunken landlady – The kid on the mountain – Hardimann the fiddler / Because.

— added **ROD MORISON** – guitars, bouzouki, etc / guests + KING + **MAGGIE MacINNES** – clarsach / **TONY O'DOIBHAILEIN** – percussion

May 00. (cd) *(BKDCD 103)* **MAKING FOR THE SHORE** ☐ ☐
– The dancer – Philip Begg's conundrum – John Murray's / My son John – Miss Thomson / Farewell to Benavie – Dae you love an apple / My home town – The crags of Tumbledown mountain / Sally gardens / The fourth of July – Making for the shore / Travelling west / Balshare / Farewell to whisky / Ramsden's rant – Laura Beaton's reel – Cough up the Donal / The Spanish cloak – The shepherd's wife / Eine kleine nachtmusik – The horn concerto – Jimmy Ward's – Out on the ocean / How can my poor heart / Avonhaugh.

— the **EASDALE**'s + **JOHNSON** added **ANDY WEBSTER** – guitar / **CELINE DONOGHUE** – fiddle, banjo, bodhran, vocals / and guest **DEREK WILLIAMSON** – vocals, guitar / plus 6th member **JOHN WETHERBY**

Jun 02. (cd) *(BKDCD 105)* **NEAR AND FAR** ☐ ☐
– Humours of whisky – Thief of Lochaber / The five Carlins / Indiana / Heights of Casino – Foxhunters' – The alien piper / Banks of the Lea / Jimmy Ward's – Hardimann the fiddler / Waes me for Prince Charlie / The parting – Major Mally's march & reel / In almost every circumstance / Thig am bata / The bucks of Oranmore – The Limerick lassies / In friendship's name / Listening at Montgomery's Tavern – The MacKenzie rebellion – Return to the Holy Loch – Hog town.

KEITH JOHNSTON

— actually featured the **EASDALE**'s

Sep 00. (cd) *(BKDCD 019)* **NO STRANGER TO THIS KIND OF GAME** ☐ ☐

KIRSTEN EASDALE

— with her brother + **MORISON**

R2 | not iss.

Jan 02. (cd) *(R2CD 2008)* **BE NOT AFRAID** ☐ ☐
– Bright blue rose / Columba's hymn / Be thou my vision / Mallaig sprinkling song / Light of light / My ain countrie / Abide with me / Lord of the dance / Be not afraid / I know that my redeemer lives / Christ has my heart ay / The sacred heart / Carol of the bagpipes / The Lord's prayer.

CALEDON

Formed: Edinburgh . . . late 90's by a 7-piece super trad-folk outfit consisting of RORY CAMPBELL, MARY McMASTER, PATSY SEDDON, EILIDH SHAW, DAVY STEELE, MIKE TRAVIS and GREG BORLAND, all mostly solo artists and veterans of over a dozen groups. Their one and only album to date, 'THE NOBLE TROUSERS' (2000), was a well-crafted piece of work that set out their musical stall. As previously mentioned all members had their own projects:- piper RORY was a solo artist (plus duo with MALCOLM STITT), GREG with BURACH, MARY and PATSY with The POOZIES and SILEAS, EILIDH was also solo (one album for 'Greentrax', 'HEEPIRUMBO') and MIKE with CEOLBEG. Prestonpans-born singer/musician DAVY STEELE was a former player with CEOLBEG, CLAN ALBA and The BATTLEFIELD BAND; he also issued two albums, 'SUMMERLEE' in '94 and 'CHASING SHADOWS' in '98. Sadly, DAVY was to die of cancer on the 11th of April, 2001. His legacy is that his songs have been used by everyone from The McCALMANS to IAIN MacKINTOSH. A tribute set, 'DRINKERS DROUTH WITH DAVY STEELE' was delivered posthumously.

RORY CAMPBELL – bagpipes, whistles, vocals / **GREG BORLAND** – bass, fiddle, vocals / **MARY McMASTER** – harps, Gaelic/English vocals, percussion / **PATSY SEDDON** – harp, vocals / **EILIDH SHAW** – fiddle, vocals / **DAVY STEELE** – guitar, bouzouki, vocals / **MIKE TRAVIS** – drums, vocals

Hypertension | not iss.

Mar 00. (cd) *(HYCD 297169)* **THE NOBLE TROUSERS** ☐ ☐
– The noble trousers set: The noble trousers – Gavotten a menez – The Ness pipers / The weeping streets set: Weeping streets of Paris – Strathconnan – The lads o' Mull – Drive home the mainland na Goisidich / Highland laddie – The road to recovery / MacLeod's set: Janet of Perth – Kenneth J. MacLeod – Faca tu saor an t-Sabhaidh – Amusons nous I filles / The old woman's set: The old woman's reel – The Fionnlagh ag innearadh – Am buachaille dubh – Patti / The Lowlands of Holland – Rory's wee tune / Raigmore set: Raigmore – Arthur Gillies – Inspector Donald Campbell of Ness – Lord Dunsmore – Rory MacLeod / Gu de niste ni mise – Rinn mi moch eirigh / The exile song – Lament for the children.

DAVY STEELE

Celtic Music | not iss.

Apr 94. (cd) *(CMCD 046)* **SUMMERLEE** ☐ ☐
– we're no gonna leave here / Eyes of child / The Lea Rig / Quitly sing you to sleep / Jenny's story / Johnny Moat / Part time friendship / Lost in the long grass / The rose o' summerlee / The ballad of Jimmy Steele.

— now with various members of CALEDON

Temple Temple

Feb 98. (cd) *(<TMS 2073>)* **CHASING SHADOWS**
– Kishmul's diary / Brand new day / Ioch Tay boat song / Jimmy Waddell – Iochanside / Long hellos short goodbyes / Tam Glen – Dancing in Dinan / Tibby Dunbar / The brothers reconciliation / Calton weaver / Leave her Johnny, leave her / Chasing shadows / Scotland yet.
(re-iss. Mar00 on 'Hypertension'; HYCD 297171)

EILIDH SHAW

— with various folk musicians

Greentrax Greentrax

Nov 97. (cd/c) *(<CD/C TRAX 131>)* **HEEPIRUMBO** Jan98
– My dad Paddy / Just for Gordon / 70th year / Simon's waltz / Bowjob / Highland jigs / Scottie dance band heaven / Liz Carroll's / Inveran / Finisher.

CALLUNA (see under ⇒ Mill records)

Alex CAMPBELL

Born: 1925, Glasgow. A kind of Scottish equivalent to WOODY GUTHRIE, CAMPBELL has often been credited as being the inspiration behind the romanticised troubadour lifestyle embraced by the 60's folk revival. He endured a tough upbringing even by pre-war Glasgow's grim standards, his whole family dying of TB in the same year. He was subsequently raised by his grandmother and developed an interest in folk song through his Boy Scout activities. As well as giving young ALEX an appetite for travel, the movement's connection to the military brought him into contact with servicemen from all over the world, some of whom taught him folk songs from their respective countries.

In the mid-50's, following a spell in the civil service, he decamped to Paris where poverty eventually forced him into busking. During a near four year residency at La Contrescarpe, CAMPBELL honed his performing skills and became a central figure in the city's cafe scene. He inevitably came into contact with young bucks like DAVEY GRAHAM and WIZZ JONES which encouraged him to make reconnaisance trips back to London. He eventually moved there at the turn of the decade, by which time he'd already cut an impressive number of records for various French labels.

Back in Britain, ALEX encountered a folk scene dominated by the presence of EWAN MacCOLL. Although he played in MacCOLL's famous Ballads & Blues club, CAMPBELL was none too keen on MacCOLL's strict, heavily politicised approach and the pair were known to have a frosty relationship. This despite the fact that ALEX married MacCOLL's girlfriend PEGGY SEEGER so she could legally stay in Britain. Yet while MacCOLL was regarded as an authority on folk, CAMPBELL had a reputation as a magnanimous supporter of the scene and was pivotal in the growth of folk clubs all over the country as well as being consistently supportive of young talent. Although he never stayed in the one place for long, he was always in the right place at the right time, his sentimental style, outrageous sense of humour and generosity of spirit endearing him to most people he met.

While he's famously rumoured to have released over one hundred albums (most on European labels), CAMPBELL apparently never took recording seriously and the actual records sold poorly. The man's first UK release came as late as 1964, when 'Transatlantic' licensed his 'FOLK SESSION' album from the legendary American 'Folkways' label, releasing it at budget price on their new 'Xtra' imprint. Although ALEX wasn't known for original material, the self-penned 'BEEN ON THE ROAD SO LONG' certainly made its mark. Released as a rare 7" on 'Transatlantic' in 1965, the track found its way into the repertoire of many 60's performers, The SPINNERS and BERT JANSCH included.

The mid-60's marked the height of CAMPBELL's fame and for a long time he was the most formidable draw on the scene despite his dearth of record sales. In 1967, he teamed up with SANDY DENNY, JOHNNY SILVO and CLIFF AUNGIER to record the album, 'ALEX CAMPBELL AND HIS FRIENDS'; probably his best known release to date. The 70's saw him moving first to Germany and then on to Denmark where he was to see out his final years. The odd album did appear on British shelves, most notably 1981's 'CRM', a collaboration with ALAN ROBERTS and DOUGIE MACLEAN, CAMPBELL working with young talent right up until the end. Many have testified to ALEX's desire to leave the relentless grind of the travelling folk singer, the man himself only too aware that his hard-drinking lifestyle was slowly killing him. Sadly, he was never able to make the break and finally succumbed to an alcohol-related death in Denmark, January, 1987.

ALEX CAMPBELL – vocals, guitar, harmonica

unknown not iss.

1958. (7"ep) **CHANSONS POPULAIRES DES ETATS-UNIS** - - French
1958. (7"ep) **CHANSONS POPULAIRES DES ETATS-UNIS 2** - - French
1958. (7"ep) **BAHAMA'S SONGS** - - French
1959. (7"ep) **LA CONTRESCARPE** - - French
1959. (7"ep) **AMERICAN'S SQUARE DANCE** - - French
1960. (7"ep) **LET'S SING WHILE WE WORK AND PLAY** - - French
1960. (7"ep) **SONGS AND STORIES OF THE WEST** - - French
1960. (7"ep) **LET'S LISTEN AND SING TO AMERICAN FOLKSONGS** - - French
1960. (7"ep) **LET'S VISIT GREAT BRITAIN** - - French

— next with **GERRY COCHRANE + DAVID LAIBMAN**

Arc not iss.

1963. (7"ep) *(ARC 36)* **WAY OUT WEST WITH ALEX CAMPBELL** -
– The wabash canonball / The streets of Laredo / The old Chisholm trail / Jesse James. *(re-iss. 1963 on 'Society'; SOC 912)*

Society not iss.

1963. (lp) *(SOC 936)* **BEST LOVED SONGS OF BONNIE SCOTLAND** -
– The nut brown maiden / Wi' a hundred pipers / The Skye boat song / The bluebells of Scotland / Ye banks and braes / Johnny Cope / Come o'er the stream, Charlie / Will ye no come back again / The Dundee weaver / Twa heids are better than yin / The piper o' Dundee / The land o' the leal / Gin I were where the gaudie rins / The wark o' the weavers / Lezzie Lindsay / The wee cooper o' Fife.

1964. (lp) *(SOC 960)* **. . .SINGS FOLK** -
– Johnny lad / The gentleman soldier / The bonny ship the Diamond / The Gresford disaster / Tae the beggin' I will go / Engine 143 / Turra merket / Captain Kidd / Will ye go, lassie, go / Willie More / The Calton weaver / Tramps and hawkin' lads / I wished I was a rock / Drinkin' ower risky. *(re-iss. 1964 on 'Fidelity'; FID 2171)*

1964. (7"ep) **THE 'WAAG' INTERNATIONAL** - - Europe
1964. (7"ep) **MY OLD GIBSON GUITAR** - - Europe
1964. (7"ep) **ALEX CAMPBELL** - - Europe

Xtra not iss.

1964. (lp) *(XTRA 1064)* **ALEX CAMPBELL** -
(above featured MARTIN CARTHY)

Transatla. not iss.

Feb 65. (7") *(TRASP 4)* **BEEN ON THE ROAD SO LONG. / THE NIGHT VISITING SONG** -

— next credited to **ALEX CAMPBELL and his Folk Group with PETER MAYNARD (bass) and Ian McCann (guitar, banjo and mandolin)**

Presto not iss.

1965. (lp) *(PRE 676)* **FAVOURITE SONGS OF BONNIE SCOTLAND** -
– The piper o' Dundee / Bluebells of Scotland / Marie Hamilton / Ye banks and braes / Rothesay-o / Leezie Lindsay / Highland laddie / Will ye no come back again / Gin I were where the gaudie rins / My love is like a red red rose / The round tree / Wi' a hundred pipers.

— next credited **ALEX CAMPBELL, COLIN WILKIE & SHIRLEY HART**

1965. (lp) *(PRE 648)* **SING FOLK** -
– The bonnie ship the Diamond / The Blarney stone / Johnny lad / The buffalo skinners / Drinker's ower risky / Tae the beggin' I will go / The gallows tree / Pleasant and delightful / The Calton weaver / Johnny Harg / The gentleman soldier.

Storyville not iss.

1965. (lp) *(623 035)* **ALEX CAMPBELL IN COPENHAGEN** - - Danish

— next with **SANDY DENNY, The JOHNNY SILVO FOLK GROUP (JOHNNY SILVIO, DAVID MOSES, ROGER EVANS) + CLIFF AUNGIER & PAUL McNEILL**

Saga not iss.

1967. (lp) *(ERO 8021)* **ALEX CAMPBELL & HIS FRIENDS** -
– Down in the mine (dark as a dungeon) / Midnight special / Corn, bread, peas and black molasses / Freight train / The false bride / Don't think twice / Chilly winds / Blue sleeves / Dick Derby / You never wanted me / Been on the road so long / Dinks song / This train / Tell old Bill / Freedom.

Apr 68. (7") *(OPP 2)* **VICTORIA DINES ALONE. / PACK UP YOUR SORROWS** -

1968. (lp) *(EROS 8028)* **ALEX CAMPBELL 'LIVE'** -
– Et maintenant / Wild rover / Victoria dines alone / The nightingale / The Durham lockout / New York gals / Pack up your sorrows / All for me grog / Hold on to me babe The blackbird / The heavenly shore / The coal-owner & the pitman's wife / Pleasant and delightful.

Ad-Rhythm/Tepee not iss.

1971. (ltd-lp) *(ARPS-1)* **THIS IS ALEX CAMPBELL VOL.1** -
1971. (ltd-lp) *(ARPS-2)* **THIS IS ALEX CAMPBELL VOL.2** -
(above sets re-iss. 1987 as 'WITH THE GREATEST RESPECT' on 'Sundown' d-lp; SDLP 2048)
– Soldiers joy / Richmond cotillion / Mrs. McLeod's reel / Cherry tree carol / One summer's evening / Chicago fire tragedy / Dreadful memories / Farewell to Tarwathie / Drinkin' o'er risky / Naomi wise / Jimmy Brown the news boy / Pretty Boy Floyd / Wars o' high Gairmany / My love is like a red red rose / San Francisco Bay blues / Gloryland / Railroad song / Stranger blues / Roll on buddy / Pretty Polly / Pay me my money down / Long gone from home / The pig song / East Virginia blues / Pretty Saro / I'll fly away.

— now with **WERNER LAEMMERHIRT** – guitar / **DIETHART HESS** – bass / **WOLFGANG FLOREY** – cello

Plane / not iss.

1972. (lp) *(S11 F100)* **LIFE IS JUST THAT WAY** [-] [-] German
– Joe Turner's blues / Cocaine blues / Grey funnel line / Marie's wedding / Life is just that way / Martin Luther King's dream / Thirsty boots / Portland town / Been on the road so long / But I don't care (I'm going home).

— next with **TOM LUKE** – guitar, etc / **JENS RUGSTED** – bass

Reca / not iss.

1976. (lp) *(RLP 5004)* **GOODBYE BOOZE** [-] [-] German
– Goodbye booze / Little Maggie / The penny whistle / The banjo man / Och, I'll lay ye doon, love / Won't get drunk no more / Farewell to Glasgow city / Tie the ruck wi' me / Matt Highland / Freight train blues / Jock O'Hazeldean / Sean O'Brien / The band played Waltzing Mathilda.

— next with **the TANNAHILL WEAVERS: DOUGIE MacLEAN, MICHAEL REINHARDT, ROY GULLANE, HUDSON SWAN + PHIL SMILLIE)**

Antagon / not iss.

1976. (lp) *(LP 3206)* **BIG DADDY OF FOLK MUSIC** [-] [-] German
– Declaration of Arbroath – The flooers o' the forest / Blackwaterside / The rigs o' rye / A man's a man for a' that / Bogie's bonnie belle / The flooer o' Northumberland / Open your door softly / Robbie dear / The shearin's no for you / Mrs McGraw updated / Instrumental medley.

— next featured ROGER SUTCLIFFE, NICK STRUTT, DAVE TOWNSEND, GORDON TYRELL + TOM McCANVILLE

Golcar / not iss.

1976. (lp) *(LKLP 6043)* **NO REGRETS** [ ] [-]

— next with **PHIL BEER, PAUL DOWNES + DEREK SMITH**

Sweet Folk All / not iss.

1977. (lp) *(SFA 095)* **TRADITIONAL BALLADS OF SCOTLAND** [ ] [-]
– The battle of Otterbourne / The twa corbies / Bonnie James Campbell / Wae's me for Chairlie / King fareweel / I will go / Bonnie Bessie Logan / The gypsy laddie / Bonnie Glenshee / Lord Gregory / Fareweel, fareweel / A Scottish settler's lament.

S.T.U.K. / not iss.

1979. (lp) **DET ER GODT AT SE DIG** (IT'S GOOD TO SEE YOU) [-] [-] Europe

Happy Bird / not iss.

1979. (d-lp) *(90031)* **LIVE AND STUDIO** [ ] [-]
– Wild rover / Henry my son / The roving Irishman / Dink's song / Tail toddle / Roll on buddy roll on / What's the life of a man / Everybody loves Saturday night / One day we'll see them / Killiecrankie // (studio lp=) GOODBYE BOOZE.

Burlington / not iss.

Dec 79. (lp; ALEX CAMPBELL – ALAN ROBERTS – DOUGIE MACLEAN) *(BURL 002)* **C R M** [ ] [-]
– The trooper and the maid / I lo'ed nae a lassie but ane / The jute mill song / Her fa la la lo / Whar widne fecht for Charlie / Leis an lurgainn / Bonnie Mary / Rattlin' roarin' Willie / John Anderson my Jo / Miss Elizabeth Campbell / Alick C. MacGregor / Jock Stewart / Little song.

C.C.C. / not iss.

Feb 82. (lp) *(CCC 811)* **LIVE IN BELGIUM (live)** [ ] [-]

— in January '87, ALEX in Denmark died of drink-related causes.

– compilations, etc. –

1968. (lp) *Hallmark; (HM 573)* **THE SCOTTISH BREAKAWAY** [ ] [-]
– Scottish breakaway (instrumental) / Scotland the brave / Wee magic stane / Jute mill song / Jeannie MacPherson / Blantyre explosion / Jolly beggarman / Freedom come all ye (or 'Weary life') / Maid to the mill / Weel may the keel row / MacPherson's rant / Rob Roy MacGregor.

1969. (lp) *Transatlantic; (TRA SAM 6)* **ALEX CAMPBELL SAMPLER** [ ] [-]
– Been on the road so long / I'm a rover / The Overgate / Round Cape Horn / Plane wreck at Los Gatos / My old Gibson guitar / Love is teasing / Glesca Peggy / John Gordon / Kissing in the dark / My singing bird / Why o why / Don't you put me down.

1972. (lp) *Boulevard; (4073)* **. . .AT HIS BEST** [ ] [-]
– The girl in Tennessee / Highland laddie / Rail roading & rambling / Rothesay O / Marie Hamilton / Advertised in Boston / Daddy fox / Skye boat song / Bluebells of Scotland / The whale fishers farewell / Railroad Bill / John Hardy.

Dec 87. (lp) *Sundown;* **WITH THE GREATEST RESPECT** [-] [ ]

Ian CAMPBELL

Born: 10 Jun'33, Aberdeen. In his early teens, CAMPBELL and his family moved to Birmingham where he became hooked on the 50's skiffle boom and subsequently formed The CLARION SKIFFLE GROUP in 1956. Two years on, a slight change in musical tack saw them become The IAN CAMPBELL FOLK GROUP, initially comprising a line-up of IAN, his sister LORNA, banjo player GORDON McCULLOCH and guitarist DAVE PHILLIPS. By the time of the group's 1962 debut EP release, 'SONGS OF PROTEST' (the first live folk session to be released on vinyl), fiddle maestro DAVE SWARBRICK had joined the ranks while multi-instrumentalist JOHN DUNKERLEY had replaced McCULLOCH.

CAMPBELL and Co were one of the many acts to appear on the seminal 'Edinburgh Folk Festival' albums, a project organised by future 'Transatlantic' men Nat Joseph and Bill Leader. Nat in particular was impressed by the group and their socially conscious approach, signing them up as the label's flagship folk act via 1963's 'THIS IS THE IAN CAMPBELL FOLK GROUP'. Part-time up until this point, 1963 was also the year the group turned professional as exposure on ITV's 'Hullaballo' show and appearances at the Edinburgh Festival boosted their profile. The band were to enjoy a fruitful relationship with 'Transatlantic' right up until the late 60's, their commercial appeal allowing the label to take risks with more left-field artists like BERT JANSCH. Albums such as 'THE CONTEMPORARY CAMPBELLS' (1966) and 'NEW IMPRESSIONS OF THE IAN CAMPBELL FOLK GROUP' (1967) sold respectably and they even came within a whisker of the Top 40 with a 1965 cover of Bob Dylan's 'THE TIMES THEY ARE A-CHANGIN' (incredibly, IAN CAMPBELL's crew were the first British folkies – but certainly not the last – to cover a Dylan song). They were also a prototype for the folk-rock groups – and even supergroups – of the late 60's and early 70's, FAIRPORT CONVENTION for example, with whom SWARBRICK took up after leaving CAMPBELL in 1966.

From this point on the group went through numerous personnel changes, recording sporadically until the mid 70's when the departure and subsequent death of DUNKERLEY (from Hodgkin's Disease) dealt a blow to the band's future. Although IAN and LORNA soldiered on, IAN's decision to become a mature student necessitated the recruitment of various session players to fulfil live commitments.

On the recording front, it'd be almost 20 years before the group re-emerged, releasing 'AND ANOTHER THING' for the Yorkshire-based 'Celtic' label in late '97. More prominent in the 80's and 90's were IAN's sons, ALI and ROBIN, who formed chart-topping pop-reggae outfit, UB40, their earliest, politically-inclined material echoing their father's left-wing sentiments of old. • **Covered:** THE JUTE MILL SONG (Mary Brooksbank) / ACROSS THE HILLS + DO YOU REMEMBER? (Leon Rosselson) / I KNOW MY LOVE (McPeake Family) / DIRTY OLD TOWN + THIRTY FOOT TRAILER + NET HAULING SONG + THE IRON ROAD (Ewan MacColl) / MY DONAL (Owen Hand) / THE D-DAY DODGERS (Hamish Henderson) / LIVERPOOL LULLABY + FOUR POUNDS A DAY (Stan Kelly) / BATTLE OF THE SOMME (PM Robertson) / THE CIRCLE GAME + DOCTOR JUNK (Joni Mitchell) / I'M NOT SAYING (Gordon Lightfoot) / ON THE M1 (Harvey Andrews) / I THINK IT'S GOING TO RAIN TODAY (Randy Newman) / THE LADY CAME FROM BALTIMORE (Tim Hardin) / PRIVATE HAROLD HARRIS (David Morgan) / etc. • **Note:** not to be confused with other artiste IAIN CAMPBELL.

IAN CAMPBELL FOLK GROUP

IAN CAMPBELL – vocals, guitar / **LORNA CAMPBELL** (b.1939, Aberdeen) – vocals / **JOHN DUNKERLEY** (b.1942) – banjo, mandolin, accordion, guitar; repl. GORDON McCULLOCH / **DAVE SWARBRICK** (b. 5 Apr'41, London) – fiddle, mandolin / with **DAVE PHILLIPS** – guitar + **BRIAN BROCKLEHURST** – bass

Topic / not iss.

1962. (7"ep) *(TOP 82)* **SONGS OF PROTEST** [ ] [-]
– Viva la Quince brigade / We will overcome / The boys of Wexford / The peat bog soldiers / Domovina / The Cutty Wren.

1963. (7") *(STOP 102)* **THE SUN IS BURNING. / THE CROW ON THE CRADLE** [ ] [-]

— **BRIAN CLARK** – guitar, vocals; repl. PHILLIPS

Transatla. / Elektra

1963. (lp) *(TRA 110)* **THIS IS THE IAN CAMPBELL FOLK GROUP** [ ] [ ]
– Twa recruiting sergeants / The keel row / The unquiet grave / To hear the nightingale sing / The drover's dream / Traditional medley (instrumental) / Rocking the cradle / The jute mill song / Johnny lad / Blow boys blow / Down in the coal mine / Garton mother's lullaby / The bells of rhymney / The apprentice's song / Rocky road to Dublin – Drops of brandy (instrumental) / Homeward bound / The water of Tyne / The wee cooper o' Fife. *(re-iss. 1969; TRA SAM 9) (re-iss. Jul73 as 'PRESENTING THE . . .' on 'Contour'; 2870 314)*

1964. (lp) *(TRA 118)* **ACROSS THE HILLS** [ ] [-]
– Across the hills / Come kiss me love / The blind man / I know my love / The derby ram / Mary mild / Remember me / The cockfight / The gypsy rover / Cho cho Losa / The keeper / Instrumental medley / Collier laddie / We're nae awa' to bide awa'.

Jan 65. (7") *(TRASP 2)* **KELLY FROM KILLANE. / BOYS FROM WEXFORD (with Boys From Wexford)** [ ] [-]

Mar 65. (7") *(TRASP 5)* **THE TIMES THEY ARE A-CHANGIN'. / ACROSS THE HILLS** [42] [-]

1965. (7"ep) *(TRAEP 128)* **SAMPLER EP** [ ] [-]

1965. (lp) *(TRA 137)* **CONTEMPORARY CAMPBELLS** <US-title 'RIGHTS OF MAN'> [ ] [ ] 1966
– Marilyn Monroe / Dirty old town / Thirty foot trailer / My Donal / Battle of the Somme / Hard life on the cut / Net hauling song / Death come easy / Rights of man /

Liverpool lullaby / Four pounds a day / The dove / Bloody Orkney / The D-day dodgers / Lord of the dance.
1966. (7") *(TRASP 6)* **COME KISS ME. / THE FIRST TIME EVER I SAW YOUR FACE**
1966. (7") *(TRASP 7)* **GUANTANAMERA. / MARY ANNE**
— **GEORGE WATTS** – flute, piccolo, clarinet; repl. SWARBRICK who later joined FAIRPORT CONVENTION, etc.
1966. (7"; as IAN CAMPBELL) *(TRASP 10)* **ONE EYED REILLY. / SNOW IS FALLING**
1966. (lp) *(TRA 151)* **NEW IMPRESSIONS OF . . .**
– Lord of the dance / Berwick brose (Come to Berwick Johnnie – Brose and butter) / The snow is falling / The bold Benjamin / New York gals / The shoemaker / Baron O'Brackley / Aye wauking o' / Lover let me in / Greensleeves / Can ye sew cushions / Farewell to Tarwathy / Gulls of Invergordon / Laird o' the windy city / Card song.
1967. (7"; as the IAN CAMPBELL FOUR) *(BIG 103)* **LOVER LET ME IN. / PRIVATE HAROLD HARRIS**
(above actually leased to subsidiary, 'Big T')
— added **DAVE PEGG** – contrabass, mandola
1968. (lp) *(TRA 163)* **THE CIRCLE GAME**
– The iron road / Private Harold Harris / The circle game / The lady came from Baltimore / The old man's song / Wooed and married / North Sea holes / Paddy lay back / Do you remember? / Willie's gone / I'm not saying / I think it's going to rain today / Doctor Junk / On the M1.

Xtra — not iss.

1968. (lp; by IAN CAMPBELL & JOHN DUNKERLEY) *(XTRA 1074)* **TAM O'SHANTER**
— **ANDY SMITH** – banjo, mandolin, guitar, fiddle; repl. temp. MANSELL DAVIES who emigrated to Canada and became a festival organiser
— added **DAVE SWARBRICK**

Music For Pleasure — not iss.

1969. (lp) *(SMFP 1349)* **IAN CAMPBELL AND THE IAN CAMPBELL FOLK GROUP WITH DAVE SWARBRICK**
– Beggin' I will go / Sugar candy / Wild colonial boy / Sleepytoon / Here come the navvies / The jolly herring / The fireman's song / The praties they grow small / The Kerry recruit / The barrin' o' the door / Eight shillings a week / The coast of Peru.

Major Minor — not iss.

Oct 69. (7"; as IAN CAMPBELL) *(MM 639)* **BREAK MY MIND. / GOVAN CROSS SPECIAL**
— (1971) **MIKE HADLEY** – bass; repl. SMITH

Argo — not iss.

Apr 71. (lp) *(ZFB 13)* **THE SUN IS BURNING – THE SONGS OF IAN CAMPBELL**
– Come kiss me, love / The snow is falling / Old man's tale / I don't know / Alexander Somerville / Dragoon / The sun is burning / Lover, let me in / A hard life on the cut / I just can't wait / The man in black / Apprentice's song / Talking blackbird.
— **CAMPBELL** with **LORNA + + DAVE + JOHN + BRIAN / + SPIKE HEATLEY** – double bass / **DEREK CRAFT** – flute, piccolo

Pye — not iss.

Jun 72. (lp) *(PKL 5506)* **SOMETHING TO SING ABOUT**
– The apprentice's song / The haymakers / The greasy wheel / The Iron horse / The Durham lockout / The Sheffield grinder / The testimony of Patience Kershaw / Medley of children's street songs / The flash frigate / Ask a p'liceman / Rigs of London town / No courage in him / The girl I left behind me / The Cutty wren / Leave them a flower. *(<cd-iss. Oct97 & Oct98 on 'Wooden Hill'; HILLCD 21>)*
— (1976) DUNKERLEY left through ill health and sadly died a year later from Hodgkinson's Disease
— (1978) **IAN + LORNA** continued after she divorced the exiting BRIAN CLARK; they recruited on session **AIDEN FORD** (b.1960) – banjo, mandola / **COLIN TOMMIS** (b.1960) – guitar – they left around 1984

Celtic — not iss.

Dec 97. (cd) *(CMCD 070)* **AND ANOTHER THING**

– compilations, others, etc. –

Jan 64. (7") *Decca; (F 11802)* **MARILYN MONROE. / THE BELLS OF RHYMNEY**
1964. (7"ep) *Decca; (DFE 8592)* **IAN CAMPBELL FOLK GROUP**
1969. (lp) *Transatlantic; (TRA SAM 4)* **THE IAN CAMPBELL GROUP SAMPLER**
1969. (lp; as IAN CAMPBELL FOLK FOUR) *Transatlantic; (TRA SAM 12)* **SAMPLER 2**
1981. (lp; as The CAMPBELL FAMILY) *Topic; (12T 120)* **THE SINGING CAMPBELLS** (rec.1965)
(re-iss. Aug94 on 'Ossian' cd/c; OSS 97 CD/C)
(above was IAN, LORNA, sister WINNIE with their parents DAVE + BETTY plus friend BOB COONEY)
May 86. (lp) *Storyville; (SLP 900)* **LIVE**
Jan 96. (cd) *Essential; (<ESMCD 357>)* **THIS IS THE IAN CAMPBELL FOLK GROUP! / ACROSS THE HILLS** Mar96
Nov 97. (cd) *Essential; (<ESMCD 523>)* **THE CONTEMPORARY CAMPBELLS / NEW IMPRESSIONS OF THE IAN CAMPBELL FOLK GROUP**

Kenna CAMPBELL (see under ⇒ Macmeanmna records)

Roddy CAMPBELL (see under ⇒ Greentrax records)

Rory CAMPBELL (see under ⇒ Lochshore records)

CANNACH (see under ⇒ Lochshore records)

CANTYCHIELS (see under ⇒ Greentrax records)

CAPERCAILLIE

Formed: Taynuilt, Argyllshire . . . 1984 by high school friends KAREN MATHESON, DONALD SHAW and MARC DUFF together with SHAUN CRAIG, MARTIN McLEOD and JOAN MacLACHLAN. Young traditionalists with a sterling pedigree (MATHESON was the grandaughter of Scots singer ELIZABETH MacNEILL while SHAW picked up the All Britain Accordion Championship in 1984) and a creative brief to carry indigenous Gaelic music into the 20th century, CAPERCAILLIE launched their career with the self-financed 'CASCADE' (1984).

Although the band initially recorded traditional songs and reels (arrangements by SHAW and CRAIG) with all-Gaelic vocals, their characteristic crossover sound began to gel on late 80's albums 'CROSSWINDS' (1987) and 'SIDEWAULK' (1989). By this stage, CRAIG had made way for talented Irishman, MANUS LUNNY (brother of DONAL), while fiddler extraordinaire CHARLIE McKERRON had replaced MacLACHLAN. In addition, JOHN SAICH had joined on bass following the departure of MARTIN McLEOD.

The new look CAPERCAILLIE quickly made their mark in 1989 with 'THE BLOOD IS STRONG', a commissioned soundtrack for a Channel 4 documentary on the history of Scotland's Gaelic population. The record sold upwards of 100,000 copies, paving the way for 1991's groundbreaking 'DELIRIUM'. Released on the 'B.M.G.'-affiliated 'Survival' imprint and produced by DONAL LUNNY, the album invested CAPERCAILLIE's traditional influences with a sophisticated contemporary sheen. Nowhere was this more evident than on 'COISICH A' RUIN', a radical interpretation of a 400 year old Gaelic song featuring funk-plucking bass, itchy percussive rhythms and stabbing synths. Star of the show as ever was MATHESON, whose dreamy, evocative tonsils even moved Sir Sean (Connery) to comment that her throat must have been touched by God!

CAPERCAILLIE surely improved their own grounds for Knighthood in 1992 after 'COISICH . . .' was used as the theme tune to 'A Prince Among Islands', a documentary charting Prince Charles' journey to the Outer Hebridean island of Berneray. The band's soundtrack EP of the same name gave them their first Top 40 entry in early summer '92 (the first Scots Gaelic material to reach the chart!) while 'GET OUT', a mixture of live tracks and remixes, was released later the same year. 1993's 'SECRET PEOPLE' was another Top 40 entry, featuring the anthemic 'FOUR STONE WALLS' and paving the way for the experimentation of 'CAPERCAILLIE' (1994). Despite its eponymous title, the album wasn't a return to their roots, rather a trip into uncharted territory as WILL MOWAT (SOUL II SOUL) remixed a selection of 'SECRET PEOPLE' tracks in a world music meets dancefloor stylee (funk'n'fling, a new genre anyone?). Obviously this wasn't to purist tastes and the group catered more to longtime fans with 1995's classy 'TO THE MOON' album, tracks such as the traditional 'Ailein Duinn' (originally recorded for the 'Rob Roy' soundtrack) possessing sufficient atmospherics to warrant a Scottish CLANNAD tag.

Following on from KAREN's 1996 solo set, 'THE DREAMING SEA' (featuring contributions from TOMMY SMITH and songwriter JAMES GRANT, ex-LOVE AND MONEY), CAPERCAILLIE once again pushed the musical envelope with 'BEAUTIFUL WASTELAND' (1997), incorporating real live vocalists from Equatorial Guinea ('INEXILE') and reincarnating the traditional 'TREE' into a whirling dervish of uillean pipes and club-orientated beats. 1998's 'DUSK TILL DAWN' retrospective comprised most of their essential tracks, a stop-gap before 'NADURRA' (2000) took CAPERCAILLIE into the new millennium.

Meanwhile, McKERRON and SAICH were carving out their more traditional type folk outfit, 'BIG SKY' (2000), augmented by SHAW and vocalist LAURA McKERRON. In May 2002, both CAPERCAILLIE and KAREN released two further sets, the former with 'LIVE IN CONCERT', the latter with 'TIME TO FALL'; another to feature JAMES GRANT.
• **Trivia:** A Capercaillie is a rare, near extinct breed of Highland Wood Grouse. The track 'BREISTEACH' was used as the title tune for Scottish Television's Gaelic soap opera, 'Machair'.

KAREN MATHESON (b.11 Feb'63) – vocals / **SHAUN CRAIG** – guitar, bazouki / **JOAN MacLACHLAN** – fiddle, vocals / **DONALD SHAW** – accordion, keyboards, vocals / **MARC DUFF** – recorder, whistles, etc.

S.R.T. / not iss.

1984. (lp) *(SRT4KL 178)* **CASCADE** [ ] [-]
– The little cascade / An eala bhan / Marc's set:- (a) Mhair, bhan og, (b) Slip jig, (c) Ridhie mo nighean donn / Milleadh nam braith rean / The ale is dear:- (a) The ale is dear, (b) Da bush below da garden, (c) Da bonnie Isle of Whalsary, (d) The moving cloud / An T-iarla dimrach / Troy's wedding:- (a) Troy's wedding, (b) The earl's chair, (c) The highland reel / Eilean a'cheo / Maighdeanan na h-airidh / Maggie's megaset:- (a) Bargenny bowling green, (b) Dick's gossip reel, (c) Trip to Windsor, (d) Sleepy Maggie. *(re-iss. Jun86; same)*

— **MANUS LUNNY** – bazouki, guitar; repl. SHAUN CRAIG

— **CHARLIE McKERRON** – fiddle; repl. JOAN

— added **MARTIN MacLEOD** – bass, fiddle

Green Linnet / not iss.

Jul 87. (lp/c) *(SIF/CSIF 1077)* **CROSSWINDS** [ ] [-]
– Puirt-a-beul / Soraidh bhuam gu barraidh / Glenorchy / Am buachaille ban / Haggis / Brenda's Stubbert's set / Ma theid mise tuilleagh / David Glen's / Umaigh a 'bhan-thigreach / My lagan love / Fox on the town / An ribhinn donn. *(<US + cd-iss. May92; GLCD 1077>)*

— **JOHN SAICH** – bass; repl. MARTIN who later joined BENACHALLY CEILIDH BAND

Feb 89. (lp/c/cd) *(SIF 1094/+C/CD)* **SIDEWAULK** [ ] [-]
– Alasdair mhic cholla ghasda / Balindore / Fisherman's dream / Sidewaulk reels / Iain chlim 'cuaich / Rosgail an dorus – Nighean bluidh rhuadh / The turnpike / Both sides the Tweed / The weasel / Oh mo dhuthaich. *<US cd-iss. 1993 on 'Green Linnet'; GLCD 1094>*

Celtic Music / not iss.

Apr 89. (lp/c) *(GNP/+C 1001)* **THE BLOOD IS STRONG** [ ] [-]
– Aignish / Arrival theme / Iona / Calum's road / Fear a' bhata (My boatman) / Dean cadalan samhach (Sleep softly my darling) / Grandfather mountain / An atairreachd ard / S fhada leam an eidhche gheamhraidh / The Hebrides / Lordship of the Isles / Arrival reprise / Colum eille / Downtown Toronto. *(re-iss. Sep91 on 'Survival-RCA' lp/c; ZL/ZK 74993) (cd-iss. Jun94; ZD 74993) (re-iss. Jul95 on 'Survival' cd/c; SUR CD/MC 014) <US cd-iss. Mar97 on 'Wanderlute'; 55422>*

Survival-R.C.A. / not iss.

Nov 91. (cd/c/lp) *(ZD/ZK/ZL 73113)* **DELIRIUM** [ ] [-]
– Rann na Mona / Waiting for the wheel to turn / Aodann srath bhain / Cape Breton song / You will rise again / Dr. McPhail's reel / Coisich, a' ruin / Kenny McDonald's jigs / Heart of the highland / Breisteach / Servant to the slave. *(cd+=/c+=)* – Dean saor an spiorad / Islay ranter's reels. *(re-is.May95 on 'Survival' cd/c/lp; SUR CD/MC/LP 015) <US cd-iss. Jan96 on 'Green Linnet'; GLCD 3108>*

Nov 91. (7"/c-s) **WAITING FOR THE WHEEL TO TURN. / BREISLEACH** [ ] [-]
(cd-s+=) – ('A'extended) / Dr. McPhail's reel.
(cd-s) – ('A'side) / Kenny McDonald's jig medley, feat. Unnamed jig.

— now with **JAMES MacKINTOSH** – drums, percussion

May 92. (7"ep/12"ep/cd-ep) *(ZB/ZT/ZD 45393)* **A PRINCE AMONG THE ISLANDS** [39] [-]
– Coisich, a' ruin (Walk, my beloved) / Fagail Bhearnaraidh (Leaving Bernaray) / The Lorn theme / Gun teanm mirus na ruin tha seo (Remembrance).

Survival – Arista / Arista

Oct 92. (cd/c) *(74321 11588-2/-4)* **GET OUT** (live & remixes) [ ] [-]
– Waiting for the wheel to turn / Pige ruadh (The brown whisky jar) / (a) Dean cadalan samhach, (b) Servant to the slave / Silver spear reels / Outlaws / Coisich a' ruin / Fear a' bhata / Dr. McPhail's trance. *(re-iss. May95 & May99 on 'Survival' cd/c; SUR CD/MC 016) <US cd-iss. Jan96 on 'Green Linnet'; GLCD 3110>*

Sep 93. (cd/c/lp) *(74321 16274-2/-4)* **SECRET PEOPLE** [40] [-]
– Bonaparte / Grace and pride / Tobar Mhoire / Four stone walls / Crime and passion / The Whimney Hills jigs / An eala bhan / Seice ruairidh / Stinging rain / Hi rim bo / The miracle of being / The Harley ashtray / Oran. *(cd+=)* – Black fields. *(re-iss. May95 on 'Survival' cd/c/lp; SUR CD/MC/LP 017) <Us cd-iss. Jan96 on 'Green Linnet'; GLCD 3104>*

Aug 94. (12"/c-s/cd-s) *(74321 22180-1/-4/-2)* **WHEN YOU RETURN. / DISTANT HILL** [ ] [ ]
(cd-s+=) *(74321 22505-2)* – (2-'A'mixes).

Sep 94. (cd/c) *(74321 22911-2/-4) <15123>* **CAPERCAILLIE** [61] [ ] 1995
– Miracle of being / When you return / Grace and pride / Tobermory / Take the floor / Stinging rain / Alasdair mhic cholla ghasda / Crime of passion / Bonaparte / When you return (wide screen mix). *(re-iss. May95 + Jul01 on 'Survival' cd/c; SUR CD/MC 018)*

Nov 94. (c-s) *(74321 25119-4)* **MIRACLE OF BEING / ('A'mix)** [ ] [ ]
(c-s+=/cd-s+=) *(74321 25053-4/-2)* – (3-'A'mixes).

Survival / Green Linnet

Jun 95. (c-s) *(SURMC 55)* **AILEIN DUINN (DARK ALAN) / AILEIN DUINN** [65] [ ]
(cd-s+=) *(SURCD 55)* – Gaelic psalm theme / The Laurel House theme.

Oct 95. (cd/c) *(SUR CD/MC 019) <GLCD 3117>* **TO THE MOON** [41] [ ] Jan96
– To the moon / Claire in Heaven / The wanderer / Price of fire / Rob Roy reels / Ailean Duinn / Nil si / Crooked mountain / God's alabi / Collector's daughter / Only you.

— now a 7-piece **MATHESON, McKERRON, LUNNY, SAICH, SHAW + WILF TAYLOR** – drums / **CHIMP** – percussion, berenbow

Survival / Rykodisc

Sep 97. (cd/c) *(SUR CD/MC 021) <10441>* **BEAUTIFUL WASTELAND** [55] [ ]
– M'ionam / Inexile / The tree / Am mur gorm (The blue rampart) / Beautiful wasteland / Co ni mire rium (Who will flirt with me?) / Shelter / Hebridean hale-bopp / Kepplehall – 25KTS / Thiocfadh leat fanacht / Finlay's / Sardinia.

— **MARC DUFF** – whistle, bodhran, Yamaha EW1; repl. WILF + CHIMP

Survival / Valley

Oct 98. (cd/c) *(SUR CD/MC 023) <15121>* **DUSK TILL DAWN – THE BEST OF CAPERCAILLIE** (compilation) [ ] [ ] Aug00
– Coisich a ruin / Miracle of being (Youth remix) / The tree / Aileen duinn / Grace and pride / The Whinney hills jigs / Claire in Heaven / Outlaws / Inexile (1998 remix) / Seice ruairidh / Kepplehall – 25KTS / Tobermory / Waiting for the wheel to turn / Nil si I nGra / Four stone walls / Dr. MacPhail's reel / Breisleach (live).

Nov 98. (cd-ep) *(CAP 5)* **DUSK TILL DAWN EP** [ ] [-]
– Miracle of being (Youth radio mix) / Inexile ('98 radio mix) / Coisich a ruin.

Sep 00. (cd/c) *(SUR CD/MC 025) <15131>* **NADURRA** [ ] [ ]
– Chuir m'athair / Mo chailin / Argyll lassies (slipjigs) / Hope springs eternal / Truth calling / Hoireann O / The hollybush / Tighinn air a'mhuir / Rapture / Michael's matches / Gaol troimh aimsirean / The cockerel in the creel.

May 02. (cd) *(SURCD 027)* **LIVE IN CONCERT (live)** [ ] [-]
– Mo chailin dileas donn / Finlays / Kepplehall: Kepplehall – The Osmosis reel / Nil si I ngra / The miracle of being / Dr MacPhails reel – Cape Breton song / The weasel set: Granny hold the candle – The weasel in the dyke – MacLeod's farewell / Inexile / Iain ghlinn cuaich / Bonaparte / The Rob Roy reels: The road to Rio – Bulgarian red – Shetland reel – The gesto reel – Kiss the maid behind the barrel – The Rob Roy reel / Coisich a ruin / Crime of passion / The tree.

– compilations, etc. –

Oct 98. (cd) *Eureka; (EURCD 700)* **WAULKROOTS (dance mixes)** [ ] [-]

Nov 01. (cd) *Camden-RCA; (74321 89579-2)* **HEART OF THE HIGHLAND** [ ] [-]

KAREN MATHESON

with **TOMMY SMITH** – saxophone / **JAMES GRANT** – steel guitar, vocals (ex-LOVE AND MONEY) / + The BT SCOTTISH ENSEMBLE

Survival / Survival

Oct 96. (cd/c) *(<SUR CD/MC 020>)* **THE DREAMING SEA** [ ] [ ]
– There's always Sunday / Rithill aill / The dreaming sea / Mi le m'uilinn / Early morning grey / Ic Iain ic sheumais / One more chance / Fac thu na feidh / An frideag airgid / At the end of the night, move on / Calbharaigh, Evangeline. *(re-iss. May98; same)*

Vertical / Sanctuary

May 02. (cd) *(VRTCD 002) <84560>* **TIME TO FALL** [ ] [ ] Jul02
– All the flowers of the bough / Morning / Time to fall / My whispered reason / Bonnie Jean / Goodbye Phoebe / An ataireachd ard (The surge of the sea) / Speed of love / Moonchild / Moch di luain / Hoping for you / World stood still.

BIG SKY

CHARLIE McKERRON – fiddle, guitar, keyboards, programming vocals / **JOHN SAICH** – bass, guitar, keyboards, vocals, programming / **LAURA McKERRON** – vocals / with also **MICHAEL McGOLDRICK** – flute, whistle / **MARC DUFF** – synthesizer, whistle, bodhran / **DONALD SHAW** – accordion / **JAMES MACKINTOSH** – drums / **PHIL BANCROFT** – sax / **EILIDH SHAW** – fiddle / **SIMON BRADLEY** – fiddle / **TOM BANCROFT** – drums / **DAVID 'CHIMP' ROBERTSON** – percussion / **FRASER SPIERS** – harmonica / **GARY FINLAYSON** – banjo / **IAIN McLEOD** – mandolin / **CHRIS STOUT** – fiddles / **SANDRA MACKAY + DAVY SCOTT + BRIAN McALPINE** – backing vocals

Survival / Valley

Oct 99. (cd) *(SURCD 024) <15129>* **VOLUME 1: THE SOURCE** [ ] [ ] Sep00
– Golden hair / Las temporadas / Millennium girl / Angel / Delicious / New Sardinia / Fly so high / Biro Guiro / Ambient beach.

Aileen CARR (see under ⇒ Greentrax records)

the CAST: Mairi Campbell & Dave Francis

Formed: Edinburgh . . . 1991 by trad/Celtic-folk duo DAVE FRANCIS and MAIRI CAMPBELL. Not to be confused with Scouse retro popsters CAST, this duo are an altogether more traditional proposition. A native of Edinburgh, CAMPBELL studied at London's Guildhall School Of Music before returning to Auld Reekie and its burgeoning folk scene. FRANCIS, meanwhile, honed his skills in the village halls of the North East before touring the USA and finally settling in the 'Burgh.

The pair released their debut album, 'THE WINNOWING', in 1995 on the 'Culburnie' label, impressing critics with their exquisite harmonies and intuitive, graceful approach to Scotland's rich musical heritage. Follow-up set, 'COLOURS OF LICHEN' (1996) was equally well received, released the same year that FRANCIS was appointed director of the Edinburgh Folk Festival. The following year he took up the post of Traditional Music Co-ordinator with the Scottish Arts Council, balancing his responsibilities with the demands of The CAST.

In addition to regular broadcasting work for Radio Scotland, the duo have performed on TV and radio both in Europe and the USA, even playing to an audience that included President Bill Clinton and his wife Hilary at the Kennedy Center Honors ceremony. They've also been closely involved in teaching and traditional Scottish country dancing workshops, forming part of BELLA MacNAB's DANCE BAND alongside various members of SALSA CELTICA, JOCK TAMSON'S BAIRNS and ANAM.

• **Covered:** LULLABYE FOR A VERY NEW BABY (Peggy Seeger) / + other trad from Burns, etc

MAIRI CAMPBELL – vocals, viola, fiddle / **DAVE FRANCIS** – vocals, guitar / with **BRIAN SHIELS** – double bass

Culburnie Culburnie

Oct 95. (cd/c) *(<CUL 104 CD/C>)* **THE WINNOWING** [ ] [ ] May96
– Auld lang syne / Scots Callan o' bonnie Dundee / Archie Campbell – Marjorie Campbell – Miss Lyall's strathspey – Miss Lyall's reel – The St Kilda wedding / The step-dancing song / Flowers o' the forest / Green grow the rashes / Bright fields of England – Crossing to Ireland / Kilkelly / Ye banks and braes / Royal visit.

Jul 96. (cd/c) *(<CUL 109 CD/C>)* **COLOURS OF LICHEN** [ ] [ ] Nov96
– Giant / Broom o' the Cowdenknowes – Tha mi tinn / Aviemore – Ca' the stirks frae oot the corn – The drummer – The Argyle bowling green / Hall of mirrors / Lullabye for a very new baby / Memories of Father Angus McDonnell / The duke of Gordon's birthday – The London lasses – Da eye wifie / The fyrish reel / The piper and the maker / Eventide / Basker's delight – Mrs McGhee – The black hoe / The auld refrain / John Anderson, my Jo.

Dec 99. (cd-s) *(CUL 201D)* **AULD LANG SYNE** [ ] [-]

Davy CATTANACH (see under ⇒ OLD BLIND DOGS)

CAULD BLAST ORCHESTRA (see under ⇒ EASY CLUB)

CEOLBEG

Formed: Dundee . . . early 80's by flautist PETER BOOND with vocalist AILEEN CARR and fiddler STUART MORISON feature attractions. CEOLBEG Mk.II were formed by BOOND in 1988, this time around himself and fellow musicians/ singers KATIE HARRIGAN, ANDY THORBURN, GARY WEST, DAVY STEELE and ADIE BOLTON. Their debut set, 'NOT THE BUNNY HOP' was released on their own imprint in 1990, produced by PHIL CUNNINGHAM (ex-SILLY WIZARD); the record was re-issued for 'Greentrax' in the Spring of '92. Their debut for the label, the DICK GAUGHAN-produced 'SEEDS TO THE WIND' (1991), saw a change in personnel, BOOND, STEELE, WEST and BOLTON remaining while THORBURN and HARRIGAN had been replaced by COLIN MATHESON and WENDY STEWART respectively. Canadian pipe band drummer JIM WALKER was brought into the fold after the sophomore's release, providing a sound rhythmic structure to the band's fluid, evocative sound.

Taken literally, their moniker refers to the Gaelic term for "small music" as opposed to Ceol Mor which denotes "big music" i.e. pibroch. Yet CEOLBEG put an original spin on the traditional "small music" of reels and jigs, embellishing an industrious back line of guitar, cittern and bouzouki with a whirling, melange of pipes, harp and flute. Critics were also quick to applaud the finely tuned balance of instrumentals and songs, STEELE's rich, couthy vocals demonstrating why he was regarded as one of the finest singers – not to mention contemporary songwriters – in Scotland.

Following 1993's 'UNFAIR DANCE', WEST was briefly replaced by Californian piper, MIKE KATZ (whose skirl has oft been heard on Edinburgh's Princes Street). His tenure was brief, however, and after a North American tour, he left to join The BATTLEFIELD BAND along with STEELE in 1995, veteran ROD PATERSON brought in as lead vocalist for 1996's 'CEOLBEG FIVE'.

What with a slew of side projects and increasing family commitments, it was to be a further four years before the CEOLBEG crew entered the studio again for the millennial 'CAIRN WATER' (2000) – they disbanded in 2002.

• **Songwriters:** Mostly traditional songs except SHOALS OF HERRING (Ewan MacColl) / HERALD OF BORES (Andy Hornby) / OH, WERE I ON PARNASSUS' HILL (words; Burns) / TO EACH AND EVERY ONE OF YOU (Gerry Rafferty) / LIKE ANOTHER ROLLING STONE (Michael Marra) / etc.

PETER BOOND – flutes, whistles, cittern / **DAVY STEELE** (b. Prestonpans) – vocals, bouzouki, guitar, bodhran / **GARY WEST** – pipes, whistles, vocals / **ANDY THORBURN** – keyboards, vocals / **KATIE HARRIGAN** – harps, vocals / **ADIE BOLTON** – sound man (+ fully-fledged member)

own label not iss.

1990. (cd) *(none)* **NOT THE BUNNY HOP** [ ] [-]
– Tam Billy's jig – Archie Beag and Callum Mor – Miss Donella Beaton / It was long ago – The three-wheeled rabbit – My lass has a lovely red schleppack / The soft horse reel – Pumpkin's fancy / Snug in a blanket – / Otago river – Iain Ghlinn Cualch – The shores of Loch Bea / The big parcel – Not the bunny hop / Queen of Argyll / The high and the mighty / Arthur Gillies / Farewell to the haven / The De'il's awa wi the exciseman – The seagull. *(re-iss. Apr92 on 'Greentrax' cd/c; CD/C TRAX 053)*

— **COLIN MATHESON** (b. Kilmarnock) – keyboards, guitar, accordion, vocals; repl. THORBURN who later went solo / **WENDY STEWART** – vocals, electric harp, concertina, clarsach; repl. HARRIGAN

Greentrax Greentrax

Dec 91. (cd/c) *(CD/C TRAX 048)* **SEEDS TO THE WIND** [ ] [-]
– Mazurka set: Mazurka du Morvan – Hip / Senorita Ana Rocio – Seeds to the wind / The coupit yowe set: Alan MacPherson of . . .. / Glenlivet / A' the airts / Here's a health tae the sauters – Cajun two-step / Johnnie Cope / See the people run / Lord Galloway's lamentation.

— added **JIM WALKER** (b. Saskatoon, Canada) – drums, percussion

Aug 93. (cd/c) *(<CD/C TRAX 058>)* **AN UNFAIR DANCE** [ ] [ ]
– Zito the bubbleman / Galicia revisited / The jolly beggar / Gale warning / The collier's way / Stand together / Wild West waltz / Ceol beag / Seton's lassie / Train journey north / My love is like a red red rose / The sleeping tune.

— **MIKE KATZ** (b. California, USA) – pipes, bass; repl. WEST

— **ROD PATERSON** – vocals, guitar (ex-Solo artist, ex-CHORDA, ex-JOCK TAMSON'S BAIRNS, ex-EASY CLUB, of the PICTS) repl. STEELE, who, with KATZ joined The BATTLEFIELD BAND

Apr 96. (cd/c) *(<CD/C TRAX 100>)* **CEOLBEG FIVE** [ ] [ ] May96
– Mother Farquhar – A skate in the hand is . . . – Gillie's favourite / Willie Wastle / Chow man – Catriona Og / Cadal cha / Cockerel in the creel – Duncan Finlay's – Black cocks of Berriedale / The presence – The old maid's dream / Borderline – Les freres Denis / India / The nodding song – Guide'en tae ye kimmer – The Skye Bridge dance / Duncan Cla's – Dr. Iain MacAonghais – Finlay . . .. / Gaberlunzie man.

— **MIKE TRAVIS** – drums, percussion, vocals; repl. WALKER who had already joined SEELYHOO

— + joined **MATHESON, STEWART, PATERSON + WEST**

Jan 00. (cd) *(<CDTRAX 188>)* **CAIRN WATER** [ ] [ ] Apr00
– Cantabrian jig – Billy Forsyth's dancing shoes / Shoals of herring / Cairn water / Working shifts / The Scottish branle – Herals of bores / Eppie Moray / Oh, were I on Parnassus' hill / Drumchorrie / Return of the bunny: Archie Mackenzie of Dumbarton – Not the bunnyhop / To each and every one of you / Reels: The congress reel – Elizabeth's big coat – The champion of the sea – Jack Daniels / Like another rolling stone.

WENDY STEWART

she's helped out on both sets by JIM WALKER (percussion), COLIN MATHESON (keyboards & guitar) and GARY WEST (whistle & small pipes).

Jan 93. (cd/c) *(<CD/C TRAX 059>)* **ABOUT TIME** [ ] [ ]
– Hip hip bouree – Pheasant feathers / Bonawe Highlanders – Stirling Castle – Rachel Rae / Harp song of the Dane woman / Love lie near me / The burning bing / Petronella / Polska from Ormunga / Silent rains / Roslin Castle – Miss Gordon of Gight / St. Bride's coracle / The streams of Abernethy – Puinneagan cail / William Joseph Gumpy – The king's house / Wild west waltz.

Mar 97. (cd/c) *(<CD/C TRAX 126>)* **ABOUT TIME 2** [ ] [ ]
– MacLeod of Mull – The kitchen piper / The January man / Rachael Rae / Fish feis / Probabobably – Maggie's pancakes – Breal yer bass drone / Fotheringay – Pavane / Barbara Grigor – The little cascade / Dances with friends / The dusty miller – Love and whisky – Bobbing Joan / An caiora – Carolan's welcome / Drummond Castle.

CHANTAN (see under ⇒ KYDD, Christine)

Duncan CHISHOLM (see under ⇒ WOLFSTONE)

the CLAN (see under ⇒ WE FREE KINGS; Section 8: Rock, Pop & Indie)

CLAN ALBA (see under ⇒ GAUGHAN, Dick)

CLIAR (see under ⇒ Macmeanmna records)

CLUTHA

Formed: Glasgow . . . early 70's by traditional folk vocalist GORDEANNA McCULLOCH (who'd first appeared on 'Topic' V/A EP, 'New Voices From Scotland' in 1965) and fellow chanters/musicians RONNIE ALEXANDER, JOHN EAGLESHAM and ERLEND VOY. GORDEANNA had made the grade in the 60's at Rutherglen Academy Ballads Club courtesy of her English teacher turned Scottish traditional voice tutor, NORMAN BUCHAN. As CLUTHA (meaning lodge or piece of ground – used in NZ quite a lot), GORDEANNA and Co released two sets for 'Topic' records (c.mid-70's), 'SCOTS BALLADS SONGS & DANCE TUNES' and 'BONNIE MILLE DAMS'.

Having sung abroad with this popular outfit, the clear-voiced McCULLOCH subsequently delivered her own eponymous LP. In 1991, she teamed up with Blairgowrie's AILEEN CARR, Fife's CHRIS MILES and Dundee's MAUREEN JELKS to form all-female trad/folk harmony quartet, PALAVER, a performance at the Ballyshannon Festival going down a storm. However, she departed from the aforementioned group to concentrate on solo work; although she still performs the odd concert duo with CHRIS. In 1997, GORDEANNA's long-awaited solo return was complete, 'Greentrax' releasing 'IN FREENSHIP'S NAME', for which she was backed up by WILLIAM JACKSON, DOUGIE PINCOCK, STUART MORRISON, BRIAN MILLER and CHARLIE SOANE. A few years on, she released another set, this time for 'Fellside', 'SHEATH & KNIFE' (2000).

• **Note:** CHRIS MILES and MAUREEN JELKS released their own albums, 'NOT BEFORE TIME' and 'FIRST TIME EVER', respectively.

GORDEANNA McCULLOCH – vocals / **RONNIE ALEXANDER** – vocals, guitar / **JOHN EAGLESHAM** – vocals, concertina / **CALLUM ALLAN** – fiddle / **ERLEND VOY** – vocals, fiddle, concertina

Topic not iss.

1974. (lp) *(12TS 242)* **SCOTS BALLADS SONGS & DANCE TUNES** ☐ -
– The soor milk cairt / Donald Blue / Mount and go / Deil in the lum / Jigs: The Moudiewort – The Caledonian hunt's delight – The shepherd's wife / Andro and his cutty gun / The rigs o' rye / The dark island – Battle of the Somne – Greenwoodside – Campbell's farewell to Redcastle – Invercauld gathering – Paddy's leather breeches / Johnny Sangster / Wha's fu / Andrew Ross / Corn rigs – Soldier's joy – Mrs McLeod / The Gaberlunzie man.

1977. (lp) *(12TS 330)* **BONNIE MILLE DAMS** ☐ -
– My apron / Bonnie Susie / Fareweel tae Kemper – Kilworth hills / High Jeanie, high / Braes o' Lochie / The terrible twins / Banks o' the Allan / Ochiltree walls / Binnorie-o / Logan water / Niel Gow – Captain MacDuff's reel / Among the blue flowers and the yellow / The false bride / Maids o' the black glen / Back o' the moon – Donald Willie and his dog – I laid a herrin' in saut – Mossie and his mare.

GORDEANNA McCULLOCH

1978. (lp) *(12TS 370)* **GORDEANNA McCULLOCH** ☐ -
– Yowie wi the crookit horn / There's a herrin' in the pan / Sheath and knife / Jock since I ever saw yer face / Chevy chase / Captain Wedderburn / The gallant weaver / Eence upon a time / Caw the yowes / Bawbie Allan / The Hielan laddie / Be kind tae yer nainsel. *(cd-iss. Oct00 as 'SHEATH & KNIFE' on 'Fellside'+=; FECD 117)* – Kirk o' Birnie Bouzle / Dowie dens o' Yarrow / Lichtbob's lassie / Will ye gang love / Bleacher lassie o' Kelvinhaugh.

Greentrax not iss.

Jun 97. (c/cd) *(C/CD TRAX 123)* **IN FREENSHIP'S NAME** ☐ ☐
– The shuttle rins / The bawbee birlin / Johnny, my lad / The laird o' the Dainty Dounby / My bonnie laddie's lang a' growing / The shepherd's wife / Skippin' barfit thro' the heather / Tam Bowie / The laird o' Warriston / Tail toddle / The plooman laddies / Willie's droon'd in Yarrow / The laird o' Drum / In freenship's name.

CLYDESIDERS

Formed: Clyde . . . early 70's by SANDY KELSO, DUNCAN McCRONE, CHRIS STOUT, JOHN GRAHAM and DUNCAN MacDONALD; they named themselves after a mid 1920's Socialist political movement. For thirty years now, The CLYDESIDERS have performed their blend of old and new with their own traditional aplomb. One of Scotland's most respected and entertaining groups, The CLYDESIDERS have also delivered a plethora of LP's, beginning with er . . . 'THE CLYDESIDERS ALBUM' for 'Lismor' in 1979. Worth mentioning too that vocalist GORDEANNA McCULLOCH also performed with them early on. In November 1996, while they had another set 'CROSSING THE BORDERS' in the can, The CLYDESIDERS and a film crew toured the isle of Lindisfarne (Holy Island) alongside fellow folkies, LINDISFARNE to commemorate the death of their frontman, Alan Hull. The CLYDESIDERS guitarist, DUNCAN McCRONE has recently issued his own solo set, 'JUST A BOY' (2001), a mixture of contemporary songs and downbeat instrumentals.

SANDY KELSO – vocals / **CHRIS STOUT** – fiddle, keyboards, vocals / **JOHN GRAHAM** – guitar, mandolin, vocals / **DUNCAN MacDONALD** – bass / added in 1979; **DUNCAN McCRONE** – guitar, vocals (ex-HOT TODDY, ex-DAPPLEGRIM)

Lismor not iss.

1979. (lp/c) *(LILP/LICS 5095)* **THE CLYDESIDERS ALBUM** ☐ -
– The Waverley polka / All the good times / Kelty chippie / Mormond braes / The wee room / Annie's song / Johnny's fancy / Spanish ladies / Pack up your sorrows / The sludge boat song / Rollin' in my sweet baby's arms / Rigs o' rye / Fitba referee / Closing time.

Lochshore not iss.

Apr 81. (7") *(LOCH 601)* **SCOTLAND'S JIM WATT. /** ☐ -

Apr 81. (lp/c) *(LOCLP/ZCLOC 1001)* **A TOUCH OF THE CLYDESIDERS** ☐ -
– McPherson's rant / The land I loved so well / Fiddler's choice / Loch Lomond / Wee china pig / Paddy Kelly's brew / Home boys home / The wee Kirkcudbright centipede / I hae seen the Heilans / Ramblin' boy / Ballad of Jesse James / Always Argyll / Mirsheen durkin / Scotland's Jim Watt.

Jul 82. (7") *(LOCH 604)* **SAILING HOME. / THE LAND I HAVE LEFT** ☐ -

Jul 82. (lp/c) *(LOCLP/ZCLOC 1010)* **SAILING HOME** ☐ -
– Killiecrankie / Can't help but wonder where I'm bound / Dashing white sergeant / Breakdown / Leaving Nancy / All God's creature / Goodbye America / Sailing home / Switch out the sun / The land I have left / The Athole Highlanders – Soldiers joy – Fairie dance / Hills of Connemara / Will ye no come back again.

Klub not iss.

May 83. (7") *(KLUB 39)* **MY LOVE IS LIKE A RED RED ROSE. / HILLS OF CONNEMARA** ☐ -

Nov 83. (7") *(KLUB 42)* **WILD MOUNTAIN THYME. / HOME TO THE KYLES** ☐ -

Nov 83. (lp/c) *(KLP/ZCKLP 41)* **WILD MOUNTAIN THYME** ☐ -
– Wild mountain thyme / Glasgow lullaby / There was a lad / Silver darlings / A little suite (Dr Finlay's casebook) / Para Handy polka / Sponge (Beechgrove Garden) / Trumpet hornpipe (Captain Pugwash) / Welcome home to Glasgow / My love is like a red red rose / Home to the Kyles / Lowlands low / Burnie boozie / If wishes were fishes / Barren rocks of Aden / La russe / Cadder woods / River / Corn rigs.

Sep 84. (7") *(KLUB 46)* **WE'VE LIVED IN A DREAM. / ISLAND OF ARRAN** ☐ -

Oct 84. (lp/c) *(KLP/ZCKLP 47)* **THINKING OF HOME** ☐ -
– We've lived in a dream / Turn a deaf ear / Take the high road / Banks and braes / Tenpenny piece – Rakes of Kildare – Blackthorn stick / Just my old lady / Island of Arran / Ukelele lady / Thinking of home / Bogman's pig / Goodnight Irene / Catfish / When you were sweet sixteen / Wild mountain thyme / Glasgow lullaby.

Nov 85. (7") *(KLUB 51)* **MAYBE SOMEDAY. / SLOOP JOHN B** ☐ -

Nov 85. (lp/c) *(KLP/ZCKLP 54)* **IT'S GOOD TO SEE YOU** ☐ -
– Maybe someday / Morning glory / The Skye boat song / Dill pickle rag / Come by the hills / Till you return to me / It's good to see you / Sloop John B / Mountains of Mourne / The primrose / You took advantage of me / With friends like you.

— retired from the studio for a while

Lochshore not iss.

Sep 91. (cd/c) *(CD/ZC LOC 1062)* **TIME FOR A CHANGE** ☐ -
– The surf and the silver fishes / The soor milk cairt / Where is the Glasgow / I belong to Glasgow / Paddy's leather breeches / Jog o' slur / Big John McNeil / McGinty's meal and ale / The rose of Allandale / Vote for me / Fiddler's green / Work o' the weavers / Agnes in A / The Boston stomp / The four o'clock in the morning tune / Enchanted island / I wish I was hunting / Dolina McKay / Farewell to Nova Scotia. *(cd+=)* – Goodnight and joy be with ye all.

R.E.L. not iss.

Apr 96. (cd/c) *(RE CD/CS 502)* **CROSSING THE BORDERS** ☐ -
– Highland Harry / Tae the beggin' / Surf and the silver fishes / Sonny's dream / Pig set / Land o' the leal / Band o' shearers / Albion heart / My old man / Kate's wedding / Rowan tree / I once loved a lass / Stay young.

- compilations, others, etc. -

Mar 87. (c) *Lochshore; (ZCCLS 712)* **THE LEGENDS OF SCOTLAND** [ ] [-]
Nov 01. (cd) *Downtown; (TOWN 1001)* **THE WAVERLEY COLLECTION** [ ] [-]

DUNCAN McCRONE

with **CHRIS STOUT, CY JACK, BILLY ROSS, JIM YULE, STEVE LAWRENCE + RAY LAIDLAW**

Downtown not iss.

Oct 01. (cd) *(TOWN 1002)* **JUST A BOY** [ ] [-]

COINNEACH (see under ⇒ Lochshore records)

COLOUR OF MEMORY

Formed: Western Isles . . . 1992. Comprising the talented trio of ALASDAIR JOSS, JULIA DOW and ALYTH McCORMACK, The COLOUR OF MEMORY drew on the various members' diverse musical skills for their 1994 debut album, 'THE OLD MAN & THE SEA'. Bringing consistent comparisons with the likes of CLANNAD and ENYA, the record featured JOSS's Celtic New Age-style synth atmospherics blended with the part-Gaelic vocals of DOW and McCORMACK, both singers true to their Western Isles upbringing (Arran and Stornoway, to be exact).

Coming from an acting background, DOW was more inclined towards jazz while the classically trained McCORMACK went on to win a gold medal at the National Gaelic Mod in 1997. She also went on to record her own solo Jim Sutherland-produced album, 'AN IOMALL – THE EDGE' (2000), featuring traditional Gaelic songs tempered by jazz and world influences. Prior to this she appeared on the BBC TV programme 'Celtic Electric' as well as touring with the 'Rhythms Of The Celts' show and working with PHIL CUNNINGHAM.

ALASDAIR JOSS – keyboards, bass, programmer / **JULIA DOW** – vocals / **ALYTH McCORMACK** – vocals / augmented by IAIN McDONALD, ALLISON McLEOD, DOUGIE PINCOCK, ALI MacLEOD, CALUM MALCOLM, ROBERT PURSE, ALAN EMSLIE, LYNSEY JOSS + RHONA MacKAY

Iona Mesa-Atlantic

Dec 94. (cd/c) *(IRCD/IRC 028) <92547>* **THE OLD MAN & THE SEA** [ ] [ ]
– Grace / Rigmarole / An emotional fish / Changed days / Into my own / Always with me / Days on end / Sun fire majestic / Old man and the sea.

— they've been conspicuous by their absence

ALYTH McCORMACK

Vertical not iss.

Mar 01. (cd) *(VERTCD 054)* **AN IOMALL – THE EDGE** [ ] [-]
– Hi horo / A mhairead og / MacCrimmon / Mo thruaigh / MhicShiridh / O mo dhuthaich / Selkie / The mulaidh / Bothan / Fhleasgaich oig / Mar a tha / Dheannain sugradh.

Billy CONNOLLY (see ⇒ Section 4: Celebrity Corner)

CONTRABAND (see under ⇒ OSSIAN)

Arthur CORMACK (see under ⇒ MAC-TALLA)

CORRIES

Formed: Edinburgh . . . 1962 as The CORRIE FOLK TRIO by former architect and skiffle man BILL SMITH, who brought together bearded ex-art teachers RONNIE BROWNE (a one-time rugby player from the Lowlands) and ROY WILLIAMSON (from the North-East and education via Gordonstoun). After meeting at Edinburgh's College Of Art, the trio performed at folk clubs around the capital before expanding the line-up with the addition of Belfast-born female singer PADDIE BELL in 1963 – the voice of an angel. Billed as The CORRIE FOLK TRIO WITH PADDIE BELL, this early incarnation of The CORRIES released a handful of albums on the 'Waverley' label before BELL departed to have a child in 1965. SMITH also departed the following year after the 'BONNET, BELT AND SWORD' album, leaving a core duo of WILLIAMSON and BROWNE.

The pair duly changed their name to The CORRIES and increasingly combined their staple Scottish traditional fare with stirring original compositions from the pen of WILLIAMSON. One such composition, 'FLOWER OF SCOTLAND', has recently been adopted as Scotland's national anthem after years of unofficial anthem status among football and rugby fans. The track was featured on 'THE CORRIES IN CONCERT' (1969), a hugely popular set that helped establish their name. Overtly nationalistic, the duo were at their most effective singing Jacobite rebel songs such as 'WHA WADNA FECHT FOR CHARLIE' and 'SOUND THE PIBROCH', appealing both to native folk fans and the worldwide Scots diaspora. As well as being a skilled songsmith, WILLIAMSON also hand-built many of his own instruments including the combolin. This consisted of two guitar-like instruments, WILLIAMSON's featuring a normal guitar fingerboard with attached bandurria while BROWNE's incorporated a mandolin and four bass strings into a guitar structure. This independent approach extended to the duo's business affairs as they set up their own 'Pan Audio' label and recording studio.

While not to everyone's taste, the group's brand of bawdy, suggestive humour was an integral part of their appeal and The CORRIES' huge fanbase ensured the success of their STV series, 'The Corries & Other Folk'. In 1983 the duo received an International Film and Television Festival award for the programme, just one of the many they both hosted and appeared on throughout their career. They even ventured into film with BROWNE taking a role in the film, 'The Bruce', which also featured a rendition of 'FLOWER..'.

Sadly, the pair's musical partnership finally came to an end in 1990 when WILLIAMSON died from a brain tumour although BROWNE made the decision to carry on in a solo capacity.

CORRIE FOLK TRIO

BILL SMITH – acoustic guitar, some vocals / **RONNIE BROWNE** – vocals, acoustic guitar / **ROY WILLIAMSON** – concertina, bodhran, mandolin, harmonica, kazoo, some vocals

Waverley not iss.

1963. (7"ep) *(ELP 129)* **CORRIE FOLK TRIO** [ ] [-]
1963. (7"ep) *(ELP 131)* **YON FOLK SONGS IS FOR THE BURDS** [ ] [-]

— added **PADDIE BELL** (b. Belfast, N. Ireland) – vocals, banjo

1964. (lp) *(ZLP 2042)* **CORRIE FOLK TRIO and PADDIE BELL** [ ] [-]
– The singing games (medley: The windy city – Call on the one you love – 1 2 3 O'Leary – I'm no goin' tae Barry's trip) / Lock the door, Lariston / Jock o' Braidislee / Doodle let me go / The lass o' Fyvie / The itinerant cobbler / Lord Gregory / McPherson's farewell / Coorie doon / Greenland fisheries.
1965. (lp) *(ZLP 2050)* **THE PROMISE OF THE DAY . . .** [ ] [-]
– My love she's but a lassie yet / Shoals o' herrin' / The trooper and the maid / Whistling gypsy / Queen Mary / The leaving of Liverpool / Uist tramping song / Johnnie lad / Roddy McCorly / Verdant braes o' screen / Around Cape Horn / Fear a bhata / Killiecrankie / Jock Hawk's adventures in Glasgow. *(re-iss. 1965 on 'Music For Pleasure'; MfP 50154)*

— PADDIE went off to go solo

Fontana not iss.

1966. (lp) *(STL 5337)* **THOSE WILD CORRIES** [ ] [-]
– Maid of Amsterdam / There are no pubs in Kirkintilloch / Quiet lands of Erin / Gentlemen soldier / Lammas tide / Galway races / Lowlands low / Riever's galley / Kerry recruit / I'm a rover / Cam ye by Atholl.
1966. (7") *(H 738)* **OCTOBER SONG. / HOW SHALL I GET THERE?** [ ] [-]

the CORRIES

— now without SMITH

1967. (lp) *(STL 5401)* **BONNET, BELT & SWORD** [ ] [-]
– Hot asphalt / Cam ye o'er frae France / Joy of my heart / The jolly beggar / Bring back my granny to me / Glenlyon lament / Johnny Cope / Gaberlunzie king / Haughs of Corndale / Banks of Newfoundland / Parcel o' rogues / North sea holes / Katie Bairdie / Oor wee school / I once loved a lass / Blow ye winds / My brother Bill's a fireman. *(re-iss. Jul84 on 'Mercury' lp/c; PRICE/PRIMC 67) (cd-iss. Mar95 on 'Beat Goes On'; BGOCD 271)*
1968. (lp) *(STL 5465)* **KISHMUL'S GALLEY** [ ] [-]
– Kismuil's galley / Roving journeyman / Lewis bridal song / Spanish shawl / Cruel brother / Gallus bloke / Highland lament / Twa corbies / Night visitor's song / Doran's favourite / Toon o' Kelso / October song / Shamrock and the thistle.
Nov 69. (7") *(H 1064)* **KISHMUL'S GALLEY. / LORD OF THE DANCE** [ ] [-]
1969. (lp) *(STL 5484)* **IN CONCERT (live)** [ ] [-]
– Johnny lad / Lord of the dance / Flower of Scotland / Wild mountain thyme / Ca' the yowes / Bonnie lass o' Fyvie / Skye boat song / Wild rover / Kid songs / Hills of Ardmorn. *(c-iss.Sep78 on 'Mercury'; 7108 050)*
Apr 70. (lp) *(6309 004)* **SCOTTISH LOVE SONGS** [46] [-]
– Tiree love song / Annie Laurie / Ae fond kiss / Nut brown maiden / Sally free and easy / Liverpool Judies / Granny's in the cellar / Road to Dundee / Hunting tower / Lowlands of Holland.

Columbia not iss.

Jan 71. (lp) *(SCX 6442)* **STRINGS AND THINGS** [ ] [-]
– Garten mother's lullaby / Heiland Harry / The heidless cross / Rattlin' roarin' Wullie / Jock o' Hazeldean / Flood Garry / Kiss the children for me, Mary / I will go / Three Shetland tunes:- (a) The hen's march, (b) Peerie hoose ahint the burn, (c) Norwick wedding / The dowie dens o' Yarrow.

Aug 71. (d-lp) *(SCX 6467)* **LIVE AT THE ROYAL LYCEUM THEATRE, EDINBURGH (live)** [ ] [-]
– Wha wadna fecht for Charlie / Liberty / Side by side / Tramps and hawkers / The great silkie / Lyceum blues / Ye Jacobites by name / Lowlands away / Abigail / The old triangle / Dream Angus / Maids when you're young / Bonnie Dundee. *(re-iss. Oct76 on 'Note-EMI'; NTS 109)*

Sep 72. (lp) *(SCX 6511)* **SOUND THE PIBROCH** [39] [-]
– A man's a man / Kate Darymple / Petronella / Farewell tab tarwathie / Sound the pibroch / Scots wha hae / Peggy Gordon / Bluebells of Scotland / I know my love / Lark in the morning / Where two hawks fly / Westering home.

Dara — not iss.

1973. (c) *(SPA 001)* **A LITTLE OF WHAT YOU FANCY** [ ] [-]
– The black Douglas / The castle of Drumore / The collier laddie / Bogie's bonnie belle / The boys of Bluehill – Derry hornpipe / The news from Moidart / The rose of Allendale / The river / The Isle of Skye / Helen of Kirkonnel / Sherrifmuir / Derwentwater's farewell.

1974. (c) *(SPA 002)* **LIVE FROM SCOTLAND VOLUME 1 (live)** [ ] [-]
– Falladly / Mingulay boat song / Lads among the heather / A Scottish holiday / Hugh the Graeme / Maggie Lauder / The roses of Prince Charlie / Dark Lochnagar / Loch Tay boat song / The m,hm song / Flower of Scotland. *(cd-iss. Oct96; CDPA 002)*

1974. (7") *(SPA 003)* **FLOWER OF SCOTLAND. / THE ROSES OF PRINCE CHARLIE** [ ] [-]

1975. (c) *(CPA 008)* **LIVE FROM SCOTLAND VOLUME 2 (live)** [ ] [-]
– Lock the door, Lariston / Sunday driver / Come o'er the stream Charlie / King Fareweel / Yur losin' them / Ettrick lady / Nancy whisky / Sae will we yet / Lord Yester / Reivers galley / La-di-dum / Johnny ra / MacPherson's rant.

1975. (c) *(CPA 015)* **LIVE FROM SCOTLAND VOLUME 3 (live)** [ ] [-]
– The Portree kid / The Sherramuir fight / Jamie Raeburn / Chevalier's muster roll / Shoals o' herring / The massacre of Glencoe / The Friday game / The battle of Prestonpans / Weep ye by Atholl / The rattling bog.

E.M.I. — not iss.

Apr 76. (7") *(EMI 2447)* **WHA WADNA FECHT FOR CHARLIE. / DERWENTWATER'S FAREWELL** [ ] [-]

Dara — not iss.

Jan 78. (c) **PEAT FIRE FLAME** [ ] [-]
– Leezie Lindsay / Braw braw lads / The peat fire flame / Mormond braes / Come by the hills / The white cockade / The barge of Gorrie Crovan / Turn ye tae me / Eriskay love lilt / The wee cooper o' Fife / Lord Gregory / The poacher.

1980. (c) *(CPA 036)* **STOVIES** [ ] [-]
– The bloody sarks / The bonnie moorhen / Birnie boozle / Country western medley / The broom o' the Cowdenknowes / The bantam cock / Dumbarton's drums / The standard on the braes o' Mar / (Ye picked a fine time to leave me) Lucille / Arkinholm / The blackbird / The bricklayer's song / Welcome royal Charlie.

1982. (c) *(SPA 040)* **THE DAWNING OF THE DAY** [ ] [-]
– The dawning of the day / Bloody Waterloo / Big Nellie May / Turn ye tae me / The lammas tide / The blue bonnets / The green fields of France / The widow and the fairy / The Queen's Maries / Blow ye winds / Bothwell Castle / The silver tassie.

Jul 85. (c) *(CPA 066)* **SCOTLAND WILL FLOURISH** [ ] [-]
– All God's creatures / The wee grey finch / The birth of the Corries' blues / The wedding of Lachie McGraw / Ballenmuir cottage / My bonnie laddie's lang a-growin' / The news from Moidart / Scotland will flourish / Kids on the range / The banks of Newfoundland / Haul away Rosie / The Highlander's farewell / A man's a man.

Feb 86. (c; w-drawn) *(CPA 070)* **THE CORRIES** [-] [-]

Nov 87. (lp/c) *(PA/CPA 083)* **BARRETT'S PRIVATEERS** [ ] [-]
– North Sea shoals / Jock o' Braidislee / The tortoise / Rise rise / Loch Lomond / Dashing arts / Twa racruitins sergeants / The Walter o' Tyne / The folker / Barrett's privateers / Strangest dream / Rosin the beau.

Dec 88. (c) *(CPA 090)* **THE BONNIE BLUE (live)** [ ] [-]
– The bonnie blue / Oh dear me / The clingfilm wrapper blues / A Tiree love song / Tramps and hawkers / The garten mother's lullaby / Who'll take the ball from Maggie Thatcher? / The winter it is passed / Er fa la la lo / Bonnie Gallowa' / The Hieland house hunter / Lowlands awa'.

— when WILLIAMSON died of cancer (12th August 1990), BROWNE went solo

- compilations, others, etc. -

1970. (lp) *Talisman; (STAL 5005)* **IN RETROSPECT** [ ] [-]
– (above features PADDIE BELL on some tracks)

Nov 71. (lp) *Philips; (6382 025)* **THESE ARE . . . THE CORRIES** [ ] [-]

1973. (7"; as the CORRIE FOLK TRIO) *Waverley; (SLP 530)* **LOVE IS TEASIN'. / WALLY WALLY** [ ] [-]

1974. (lp) *Fontana; (6382 059)* **THESE ARE . . . THE CORRIES VOL.2 - THE SKYE BOAT SONG** [ ] [-]

Dec 74. (lp) *Philips; (6382 083)* **CAM YE BY ATHOLL** [ ] [-]

Oct 77. (d-lp) *Philips; (6625 035)* **SPOTLIGHT ON THE CORRIES** [ ] [-]

Apr 79. (lp/c) *Glen; (GLN/TC-GLN 1005)* **16 SCOTTISH FAVOURITES** [ ] [-]

Apr 80. (c) *Ideal Tapes; (TC-IDL 8)* **A MAN'S A MAN** [ ] [-]

Jun 86. (c) *Lochshore; (ZCLLS 707)* **LEGENDS OF SCOTLAND** [ ] [-]

Mar 87. (lp/c: *Music For Pleasure; (MFP/TC-MFP 50478)* **BEST OF THE CORRIES** [ ] [-]

Mar 88. (cd) *Lismor; (LCOM 9006)* **THE COMPACT COLLECTION** [ ] [-]

May 90. (cd) *Compacts Of Pleasure; (CDB 792193-2)* **THE VERY BEST OF THE CORRIES** [ ] [-]
(re-iss. Feb97 on 'EMI Gold' cd/c; CDSL/TCSL 8285)

Oct 90. (cd/c/lp) *B.B.C.; (BBCCD/ZCF/REB 820)* **FLOWER OF SCOTLAND** [ ] [-]
(re-iss. Jun94 & Jun99 on 'Moidart' cd/c; MOI CD/MC 002)

Feb 91. (cd/c) *Ideal; CD/TC IDL 101)* **THE CORRIES** [ ] [-]

Apr 91. (cd/c) *Pickwick; (PWK S/MC 4054P)* **BEST OF THE CORRIES** [ ] [-]

Jun 93. (cd/c) *Moidart; (MOI CD/MC 005)* **THE SILVER COLLECTION** [ ] [-]
(re-iss. Jun99; same)

Dec 93. (cd/c; as the CORRIES and RONNIE BROWNE) *Moidart; (MOI CD/MC 009)* **SCOTS WHA HAE** [ ] [-]

1990's. (cd) *HMV Easy; (HMV 522234-2)* **THE CORRIES COLLECTION** [ ] [-]

Feb 95. (cd/c) *Beat Goes On; (BGO CD/MC 267)* **IN CONCERT / SCOTTISH LOVE SONGS** [ ] [-]

Sep 96. (cd) *Beat Goes On; (BGOCD 326)* **THOSE WILD CORRIES / KISHMUL'S GALLEY** [ ] [-]

Apr 97. (cd/c) *Moidart; (MOI CD/MC 013)* **CORRIE FOLK TRIO and PADDIE BELL / THE PROMISE OF THE DAY . . .** [ ] [-]
(cd re-iss. Oct00 on 'Beat Goes On'; BGOCD 519)

May 98. (cd-ep) *Moidart; (MOISN 001)* **FLOWER OF SCOTLAND** [ ] [-]
– Flower of Scotland / The massacre of Glencoe / The roses of Prince Charlie / Scotland will flourish.

Oct 98. (d-cd) *Beat Goes On; (BGOCD 419)* **A LITTLE BIT OF WHAT YOU FANCY / STRINGS AND THINGS** [ ] [-]

Jan 99. (d-cd) *Beat Goes On; (BGOCD 437)* **LIVE AT THE ROYAL LYCEUM THEATRE, EDINBURGH / SOUND THE PIBROCH** [ ] [-]

Jun 99. (cd/c) *Moidart; (MOI CD/MC 014)* **STRINGS AND THINGS / LIVE AT THE ROYAL LYCEUM THEATRE, EDINBURGH** [ ] [-]

Jun 99. (cd/c) *Moidart; (MOI CD/MC 015)* **SOUND THE PIBROCH / A LITTLE BIT OF WHAT YOU FANCY** [ ] [-]

Jul 00. (d-cd) *Moidart; (MOICD 018)* **PEAT FIRE FLAME / STOVIES** [ ] [-]

Jan 01. (d-cd) *Moidart; (MOICD 020)* **LIVE FROM SCOTLAND VOL.1 & 2** [ ] [-]

Jul 01. (cd) *EMI Plus; (576272-2)* **HERITAGE** [ ] [-]

Mar 02. (d-cd) *Moidart; (MOICD 022)* **LIVE FROM SCOTLAND VOL.3 & 4** [ ] [-]

RONNIE BROWNE

Greentrax — not iss.

May 90. (12"; as RONNIE BROWNE & SCOTTISH RUGBY TEAM / BORDERS POLICE PIPE BAND) *(STRAX 1001)* **FLOWER OF SCOTLAND. / FLOWER OF SCOTLAND (instrumental)** [ ] [-]

Reekie — not iss.

1992. (cd) *(REEMCD 101)* **THE FIRST TIME** [ ] [-]
– Donald McGillavry / The Hielan' man / Afton water / Black is the colour of my true love's hair / The effen bee / No more wild rover / Scotland is the place for me / The first time ever I saw your face / Blackwaterside / A Scottish holiday / Flower of Scotland / we're no' awa' tae bide awa' / The wild mountain thyme.

Karussell-A&M — not iss.

1995. (cd) **THE KISSING GATE** [ ] [-]

Scotdisc — Scotdisc

Oct 95. (cd/c/video) *(<CD/K/V ITV 602>)* **SCOTTISH LOVE SONGS** [ ] [ ] Jan96
– Dumbarton's drums / My love is like a red, red rose / Come all ye fair and tender maidens / The touch and the go / The bonnie lass o' Fyvie / Loch Lomond / The bonnie Earl o' Moray / The canvas of my life / Kate Darymple / The massacre of Glencoe / Mary Hamilton – The Queen Maries / Leezie Lindsay / Gin I were a baron's heir / Willie's gan tae Melville Castle / The parting glass.

Jun 96. (cd/c) *(<CD/K ITV 618>)* **BATTLE SONGS & BATTLES** [ ] [ ]
– Rise! rise! lowland and highland man / The bonnie wells o' Wearie / Stirlin' Brig / Such a parcel o' rogues in a nation / The floo'ers o' the forest / Where two hawks fly / Cam' ye by Atholl / I once loved a lass / Lochnagar / Helen of Kirkconnel / The chevalier's muster roll / My faithful fond one / Kishmul's galley / Ye Jacobites by name / Roses of Prince Charlie / Ae fond kiss.

ROY WILLIAMSON

Moidart — not iss.

Oct 91. (cd/c) *(MOI CD/MC 001)* **THE LONG JOURNEY SOUTH** [ ] [-]
– The long journey south / Laggan love / The Skye boat song / Donald Og / Peggy Gordon / Nicky's theme / Number one / Tuscan / The long journey south (reprise). *(re-iss. Jun99; same)*

PADDIE BELL

Alauda — not iss.

1993. (c) *(ALAMC 101)* **THE DAWN OF A BRAND NEW DAY** [ ] [-]
– The dawn of a brand new day / Far away in Australia / The flight of Earls / Pretoria / My dear and only love / Ulysees / A trip over the mountain / Song for the fox / The dowie dens o' Yarrow / 1999 / The Isle Of Eigg / The rigs o' rye / Freewheeling now.

Mar 97. (cd/c) *(ALA CD/MC 102)* **MAKE ME WANT TO STAY** [ ] [-]
– Make me want to stay / If I were a blackbird / Trying to get over you / 6000 lonely miles / Peace must come / Raglan road / Who is he – who am I / The verdant braes of Skreen / Somewhere in America / Every time / Jamie Foyers / Johnnie Faa / The meeting of the waters / Ten thousand candles.

Sep 98. (cd; by PADDIE BELL & SEAN PUGH) *(ALACD 103)*
AN IRISH KISS [ ] [-]
– Come to light / The Queen's Maries / My ain countrie / Down by the Sally Gardens / Willie Archer / The night visiting song / Wings of the sphinx / Joys of love / Highland lullaby / Sailing through the sky / An Irish kiss / Reconciliation.

Nov 01. (cd; by PADDIE BELL / FINBAR & EDDIE FUREY) *(ALACD 104)* **I KNOW WHERE I'M GOING** [ ] [-]

COTTERS

Formed: Edinburgh . . . late 60's by ALISTAIR WATSON and ALEX SUTHERLAND after meeting in a folk club. The duo were soon residents at another folk club at the Amber Mile in Royal Terrace, where they performed alongside the likes of The DOOBRIES (BILL BARCLAY and JIMMY McKINLAY). In 1969, The COTTERS released their only recording, 'SCOTTISH FOLK', although they subsequently took work cutting a TV ad for Carling Black Label in Canada. ALEX returned to be a piano-tuner but died of cancer around the mid 80's. ALI, meanwhile, left Scotland and emigrated to Western Australia, although he too was to die of cancer in 2001.

ALISTAIR WATSON – vocals / **ALEX SUTHERLAND** – vocals, acoustic guitar

Page One not iss.

1969. (lp) *(FORS 030)* **SCOTTISH FOLK** [ ] [-]
– Mingulay boat song / Killicrankie / Lowlands low / Ye Jacobites / Charlie's lament / McPherson's farewell / Tramps and hawkers / Bonnie ship the Diamond / Wild flying dove / Standard on the braes o' Mar / Fair and tender ladies / Night errant.

Elspeth COWIE

Born: Lanark, Ayrshire. Regarded as one of Scotland's finest traditional singers, ELSPETH began her recording career back in 1988 as a member of popular trad folk outfit SEANNACHIE. As lead singer and bodhran player she featured on the albums 'Take Note' (1988) and 'Devil's Delight' (1992), the various members leaving to do their own thing not long after the release of the latter set.

As a singer capable of bringing traditional material to life, she became noted as a leading folk vocalist in her own right and appeared on many collections including the 'Ceilidh House Sessions' (1995), 'Scottish Love Songs' (1998) and 'The Flowers Of Edinburgh' (1999) as well as on the 'Linn' label.

In 1997, ELSPETH teamed up with CORRINA HEWAT and CHRISTINE KIDD as the vocal "supertrio" CHANTAN, recording the 'Primary Colours' album. Also of note was her vocal contribution to SIMON THOUMIRE's 'Music For A New Parliament', an amalgam of folk and jazz composed to celebrate the reopening of the Scottish Parliament in 1999.

Finally, in 2001, ELSPETH released her solo debut album, 'NAKED VOICE' (the first for the 'Scotfolk' imprint), a combination of classic Scottish ballads, lullabies and more modern folk material. A guardian of the musical heritage she loves, this well respected singer was currently national organiser of the Traditional Music & Song Association of Scotland and also organises the Piping Centre programme for Glasgow's annual Celtic Connections festival.

ELSPETH COWIE – vocals, bodhran

Scotfolk not iss.

Mar 00. (cd) *(SFCD 01)* **NAKED VOICE** [ ] [-]
– Cruel mither / Twa sisters / The great silkie / Alison Cross / MacCrimmon / The laird o' Elfin / Dream Angus / Guns & drums / Auld maid in a garret / Green grow the laurel / Fisherman's wife / A sailor's life / Glenlyon lament / Fotheringay.

Jim CRAWFORD (see under ⇒ Springthyme records)

CROFT NO. FIVE (see under ⇒ Tartan Tapes records)

Tony CUFFE

Born: Greenock, 1954. 'When First I Went to Caledonia' is the lone testament to Tony Cuffe's solo talents. He took up guitar at thirteen and went on to join the nucleus of musicians who shaped Scottish traditional music in the 1970s and 1980s, the tunings and fingerstyle techniques he developed for playing Scottish and Irish tunes becoming a major influence on guitarists including the now world-renowned Tony McManus.

After studying English at Glasgow University, Cuffe moved to Edinburgh to teach but was soon sidetracked by the music scene that grew up around Sandy Bell's pub. He joined ALBA, whose sole album was released on Rubber Records, and then helped form JOCK TAMSON'S BAIRNS, their determination to present Scottish music acoustically in the canny rhythms intended contradicting the prevailing Irish frenzy.

After contributing vocals, guitar, whistles and songs "Cuffe-temised" from archival trawls to the Bairns' first album, Jock Tamson's Bairns ('Temple'), in 1980 Cuffe replaced Billy Ross in the similarly inclined OSSIAN and remained central to their rich, beautifully controlled sound throughout the decade, touring widely and recording albums including Seal Song and Dove Across the Water. In 1981, he reunited with Bairns, Norman Chalmers, Derek Hoy and Rod Paterson, to record the revered Fergusson's Auld Reikie in tribute to poet Robert Fergusson, with Billy Kay reading Fergusson's vivid evocations of 1770s Edinburgh.

Having visited America regularly with Ossian, in 1988 Cuffe decided to settle in Boston, where the bustling Irish music scene embraced him to the extent that he twice joined the White House's St Patrick's Day celebrations. He taught at music festivals, continued to tour with Ossian colleague Billy Jackson and had just begun recording a second solo album when he was found to have cancer. It's a mark of his stature and the respect fellow musicians held him in that those joining in fund-raising concerts to pay for his treatment included uilleann piping legend Paddy Keenan and accordion icon Joe Derrane. Having watched a video of a fundraiser held back home in Portobello, Cuffe lapsed into unconsciousness and died on December 18, 2001.

TONY CUFFE – vocals, guitar, whistle

Iona not iss.

Jun 88. (lp/c) *(IR/+C 011)* **TONY CUFFE – When First I Went To Caledonia** [ ] [-]
– When first I went to Caledonia / Miss Wharton Duff – The mare / The iron horse / Caledonia / Dr. MacInnes' fancy – Jim Tweedie's sea legs / The Buchan turnpike / The lass o' Patie's mill / The weary pund o' tow / Paddy Kelly's – The humours of Tulla / Otterburn / The Scalloway lasses – Miss Forrester. *(cd-iss. Feb94; IRCD 011)*

CUMBERLAND THREE

Formed: Glasgow . . . late 50's by schoolfriends ALEX BEATON, BRIAN FOGARTY and LEONARD STURROCK, all three also members of a skiffle group. After leaving school, singers BRIAN and LEONARD met up with an unknown German student who introduced them to Folk music. Regrouping with ALEX, they formed The CUMBERLAND THREE (nothing whatsoever to do with a US outfit featuring John Stewart) and by 1963 they were playing a residency at Glasgow's premier jazz joint, 'The Royal Garden'. Performing alongside the likes of JOSH McRAE and the duo of ROBIN HALL & JIMMIE MacGREGOR, the trio decided that London would be a better stamping ground for their type of traditional folk. Inking a deal with 'Parlophone', ALEX and Co released what was to become their one and only LP, 'INTRODUCING . . .' (1964), although they split-up soon afterwards. Of the three, only New York resident BEATON was to be heard of again. In 1968, he began a lengthy singing career that encompassed popular and traditional Celtic songs in a country style that the Americans just loved; he has since released a barrowload of albums/CD's.

ALEX BEATON – vocals, acoustic guitar / **BRIAN FOGARTY** – vocals / **LEONARD STURROCK** – vocals / with **PETE SAYERS** – banjo

Parlophone not iss.

1964. (7") *(R 5113)* **THE CUMBERLAND CREW. / CHILLY WINDS** [ ] [-]

1964. (lp) *(PMC 1233)* **INTRODUCING . . .** [ ] [-]
– Blow ye winds / Wild mountain thyme / The Cumberland crew / Whisky in the jar / Banua / Sur la route de Dijon / Whip jamboree / The river is wide / When I was young / Chilly winds / Had a girl (but she left me) / New land / Goin' away for to leave you / San Miguel / Autumn to May.

— broke up in 1965; **ALEX BEATON** uprooted to New York, releasing a plethora of easy-listening traditional cassettes for his own 'Glenfinnan' label:- 'SCOTLAND FOREVER', 'LAPD PIPE BAND', 'THE SCOTSMAN', 'I HAVE SEEN THE HIGHLANDS', cd's 'DAFT DITTIES', 'HALFWAY HOME', 'A DREAM OF ARRAN', 'SONGS OF PRAISE – PIPES OF PEACE', 'THE ROAD TO THE ISLES', 'BEATON'S BEST', 'IN THE SCOTTISH TRADITION', 'CHRISTMAS CLASSICS', 'THE WATER IS WIDE', 'KIDDING AROUND' and 'OVER THE BORDER'.

Johnny & Phil CUNNINGHAM

Born: JOHNNY:- 27 Aug'57, Portobello, Edinburgh + brother PHIL:- 27 Jan'60, Portobello. While the adolescent PHIL was still studying accordion and playing classical violin in the school orchestra, 14-year-old JOHNNY was cutting a rug with early 70's folk traditionalists SILLY WIZARD. Upon leaving school, PHIL also joined the band, playing alongside his big brother through the period 1976-1983. By this point the siblings had already recorded their own album together, 'AGAINST THE STORM' (1980), a record which had presented PHIL with the opportunity to work on the original compositions he'd increasingly been contributing to SILLY WIZARD albums.

Throughout the 80's, both JOHNNY and PHIL released solo material, the former showcasing his nimble fingered fiddling on 'THOUGHTS FROM ANOTHER WORLD' (1980) and 'FAIR WARNING' (1988), while the latter released 'AIRS & GRACES' (1984) as well as recording 'Fire In The Glen' (1986) as a collaboration with ANDY M. STEWART and MANUS LUNNY. The pair were reunited in RELATIVITY, a mid-80's Celtic "supergroup" which also featured Irish ex-BOTHY BAND siblings MICHAEL O DOMHNAILL and TRIONA NI DOMHNAILL. Particularly well received in the USA – where the majority of its personnel were based – the band released a couple of albums in 1987, namely the eponymous 'RELATIVITY' and 'GATHERING PACE'. The following year saw the start of PHIL's illustrious career as a record producer with MAIRI MacINNES' 'Causeway'. He's since gone on to twiddle the knobs for the likes of DOLORES KEANE, ALTAN, WOLFSTONE, CONNIE DOVER and even ISLA ST. CLAIR.

1988 was also the year PHIL began his long standing association with Shetland fiddler ALY BAIN, the pair initially working together on a series of TV shows for Channel 4 (they also subsequently recorded together, releasing 'The Pearl' in 1994). 1990 saw PHIL expand his talents into the world of theatre, taking the position of Music Director for Bill Bryden's production, 'The Ship'. He also wrote the instrumental music for the show which enjoyed a sell-out run during Glasgow's year as European City Of Culture. This led on to a spate of TV work for BBC Scotland through the early-mid-90's including directorial roles in both the Gaelic music series 'Tall a'Bhaile' and New Year's hoedown 'Hogmanay Live'.

Perhaps the most ambitious project of his career, the 'Highlands And Islands Suite' was a highly successful attempt to fuse traditional Scottish music with classical. The piece received its premiere at the 1997 Celtic Connections Festival in Glasgow, featuring a cast of 150 plus musicians including a fiddle and concert orchestra.

JOHNNY CUNNINGHAM's career took a slightly different – if no less ambitious – turn, working and living in the States where he toured alongside the likes of BONNIE RAITT, BILL MORRISSEY and even HALL & OATES. He also spent four years with experimental 'Windham Hill' group, NIGHTNOISE (one 1995 album, 'A DIFFERENT SHORE' exists), before following his brother into the world of theatre. Working with New York company, 'Mabou Mines', he wrote and arranged the music for 'Peter & Wendy', a production based on JM Barrie's 'Peter Pan'. The show itself enjoyed a number of sell-out runs while the award winning soundtrack was released on American indie label, 'Alula'.

• **Note:** There was another JOHN CUNNINGHAM who released records on 'La-Di-Da' in the late 80's-90's.

JOHNNY CUNNINGHAM – fiddle, mandolin / with **PHIL CUNNINGHAM** – keyboards, accordion

Highway not iss.

1980. (lp) *(SHY 7011)* **AGAINST THE STORM** [ ] [-]
(re-iss. 1988 on 'Shanachie'; SH 79017)

JOHN CUNNINGHAM

1981. (lp) *(SHY 7013)* **THOUGHTS FROM ANOTHER WORLD** [ ] [-]
(re-iss. 1988 as 'JOHN CUNNINGHAM' on 'Shanachie'; SH 79029)

Green Linnet Green Linnet

Oct 88. (lp/c) *(<SIF/CSIF 1047>)* **FAIR WARNING** [ ] [ ]
– Celtic society's quickstep – 42nd Highlander's farewell / Archibald MacDonald of Keppoch / Planxty Drew – Planxty Wilkinson / Sad is my fate (is br-nac mo cineamuin) / Lord Drummond – Lady Margaret Stewart – Crarae / Logan water / The Drovers lads (Gillan an Drover) – The mug of brown ale / Waulkin' o' the fauld / Fair warning: Blair Atholl – The Cairdin' o't – Lexy McAskill. *(cd-iss. 1990; GLCD 1047)*

— JOHNNY wrote/played fiddle/sang on next play; augmented by **SUSAN McKEOWN** – vocals / **SEAMUS EGAN** – flute, whistles, bodhran / **JAY ANSILL** – Celtic harp, mandolin / **LARRY CAMPBELL** – guitar / **JAMSHIED SHARIFI** – keyboards, percussion / **CHARLIE GIORDANO + MICK McAULEY** – accordion / **BEN WITTMAN** – percussion / **KAREN KANDEL** – vocals, narration

Alula Alula

Sep 99. (cd) *(<ALU 1006>)* **PETER & WENDY** [ ] [ ] Nov98
– Two is the beginning of the end (instrumental) – On these magic shores / Nana's walkabout / Memories to bed / Darling's waltz / Star lullaby / Shadow dance / Stories to tell / The flight / The landing / Pirates! / The crocodile tango / The Wendy house / The wolves of Neverland / Mermaids / Neverbird / Tinkerbell's warning / Light that beauteous flame / The duel / Lost boys lament / Two is the beginning of the end.

PHIL CUNNINGHAM

R.E.L. not iss.

Dec 84. (lp/c) *(REL/REC 474)* **AIRS AND GRACES** [ ] [-]
– Andy M. Stewart's reel – The harsh February / The house in Rose valley / Miss Rowan Davies / Jackson's No.2 – Jean's reel – Moving cloud / Flodigarry island – The wee man from Skye / Joey's tune / The log splitter jig – You'll have a dram? / Margaret MacKinnon of Digg / Farewell to Ireland – Hogties reel. *(<re-iss. 1989 on 'Green Linnet' lp/c; SIF/CSIF 3032>) (cd-iss. Nov93; GLCD 3032)*

— In 1986, PHIL teamed up with ANDY M. STEWART and MANUS LUNNY on the album, 'FIRE IN THE GLEN'

— next with **FINLAY M MacRAE, FOSS PATERSON, NEIL HAY, DAVEY GARRETT, KOOS KOOS McKAFFERTY, FRED CORSIE + ALY BAIN**

Green Linnet Green Linnet

Feb 90. (lp/c) *(<SIF/CSIF 1102>)* **THE PALOMINO WALTZ** [ ] [ ]
– The bombardier beetle – Webbs wonderful / The Ross memorial hospital / The Palomino waltz – Donna's waltz / The four stroke reel – Martin O'Connor's flying clog – The four stroke reel / Leaving Glen Affric / Ceilidh funk / The wedding / Violet Tulloch's welcome to the crask of Aigas – The laird of Drumblair / Ciara McCarthy's lullaby. *(cd-iss. Nov92; GLCD 1102)*

May 94. (d-cd) *(GLCD 200)* **REBOX** (collection) [ ] [ ]

— In Oct'94, PHIL collaborated with ALY BAIN on the album, 'THE PEARL'

RELATIVITY

JOHNNY & PHIL CUNNINGHAM with Irish-born musicians living in America **TRIONA NI DHOMHNAIL** – vocals, keyboards / **MICHAEL O DHOMHNAIL** – vocals, guitar

Green Linnet Green Linnet

Mar 87. (lp/c; as PHIL & JOHNNY CUNNINGHAM / M. O DHOMHNAIL / T. NI DHOMHNAIL) *(<SIF/CSIF 1059>)*
RELATIVITY [ ] [ ]
– Hut on Staffin Island / Sandy MacLeod of Garafad / Soft horse reel / There was a lady / Gile Mear / Gracelands / When Barney flew over the hills / Leaving Brittany / Pernod waltz / An seanduine doite / John Cunningham's return to Edinburgh / Heather bells – Bell reel / Limerick lasses / Ur-chill an-chreagain. *(<cd-iss. Feb88; GLCD 1059>)*

Aug 87. (lp/c) *(<SIF/CSIF 1076>)* **GATHERING PACE** [ ] [ ]
– Blackwell court / Gathering pace / Rose catha na mumhan / Miss Tara Macadam / Me theid tu unaonaugh / Siun ni dhuibhir / When she sleeps / The Monday morning reel / Ceol Anna. *(cd-iss. May88; GLCD 1076)*

CUTTING EDGE (see under ⇒ BADENOCH)

D

DAIMH

Formed: West Coast of Scotland . . . late 90's by ANGUS MacKENZIE, ROSS MARTIN (also a member of TABACHE), COLM O'RUA, GABE MacVARISH and JAMES BREMNER. With the various members hailing from different parts of the Celtic world, i.e. Scotland, Ireland, Cape Breton and erm, California (!?), DAIMH follow a heavily Gaelic-influenced musical agenda. This much was evident from their debut album, 'MOIDART TO MABOU' (2000), featuring a combination of English and Gaelic-language compositions drawing from traditional and original sources. Produced by former BATTLEFIELD BAND piper IAIN MacDONALD, the album also featured ANNE MARTIN, INGRID HENDERSON and JOHN PURSER.

ANGUS MacKENZIE – pipes / **ROSS MARTIN** – guitar / **COLM O'RUA** – banjo, mandola / **GABE McVARISH** – fiddle / **JAMES BREMNER** – bodhran / with also **IAIN MacDONALD** – pipes, flutes, whistles, jews harp (of BATTLEFIELD BAND) / **ANNE MARTIN** – vocals / **INGRID HENDERSON** – piano / **JOHN PURSER** – cello

G.I.M. not iss.

Oct 00. (cd) *(GIMCD 001)* **MOIDART TO MABOU** [ ] [-]
– Welcome to Scotsville / Go Jerry! / Oran Eile do'n phrionnsa / Goat island / Nighean donn a' chuailein riomhaich / Strathspeys and reels / The king / The brown one / Nighean bhan ghrulainn / Polkas / Wise maid.

DALRIADA

Formed: Western Isles . . . early 90's by COLIN KENNEDY, CLARK SORLEY and ROBBIE DALE, the former two being left as a duo after their debut set, 'ALL IS FAIR', was delivered in 1991 for 'Iona'. The moniker stems from Dal Riada, a Western Isles colony (on Alba and Erin) set up by invading Gaels from Ulster (sometime between 350 and 500 A.D.). The aforementioned debut contained re-worked Scottish ballads, re-interpreted for quite possibly rock/pop-loving youngsters to appreciate more. After a seven-year itch, DALRIADA returned with their long-awaited follow-up piece, 'SOPHISTRY AND ILLUSION' (1998), a beautiful-crafted concept CD marking them out to be one of Celtic music's most promising acts.

COLIN KENNEDY – vocals, guitars / **CLARK SORLEY** – keyboards, bass/rhythm programming / **ROBBIE DALE** –

Iona not iss.

Nov 91. (cd/c) *(IRCD/IRC 015)* **ALL IS FAIR** [ ] [-]
– The Haughs of Cromdale / Scots wha ha'e / Green grow the rashes O / Jock o' Hazeldean / Ye Jacobites by name / Will ye no' come back again / Johnnie Cope / Loch Lomond / MacPherson's farewell / Ae fond kiss / Caledonia / The grey man.

— the duo added guests EILIDH SHAW, ALASTAIR McDONALD, SIMON THOUMIRE, SANDY BRECHIN, DOUGIE PINCOCK, ROBBIE DALE, RAB HANDLEIGH, LORRAQINE JORDAN, MIKE LAWRENCE, ANDY McGLASSON, etc.

Qudisc not iss.

Oct 98. (cd) *(QUCD 001)* **SOPHISTRY AND ILLUSION** [ ] [-]
– Innocent / Sleeping child / In the blood / Break the chain / Oh to be so innocent / This land / Good enough / Walls / Trickster / Let life begin / Everlasting / Ploughman's loop / Lying's rampant / Greenlands / Bonnie Doon / Free at last. *(<re-iss. Jul01 on 'Strathan'; 8019130001-1>)*

Bruce DAVIES (see under ⇒ BEGGARS MANTLE)

DEAF HEIGHTS CAJUN ACES (see ⇒ Section 8: Rock, Pop & Indie)

DEAF SHEPHERD

Formed: based- Edinburgh . . . 1993; by the mid-90's the line-up had solidified around JOHN MORRAN, RORY CAMPBELL, MARIANNE CURRAN, CLARE McLAUGHLIN and MALCOLM STITT, the individual members' varied geographical roots bringing together both Gaelic, Highland and Lowland folk traditions. Unlike most of the young folk-inspired bands in Edinburgh, Shetland and beyond, DEAF SHEPHERD don't cross-pollinate the genre with contemporary rock, pop and dance styles. Instead, they bring a youthful enthusiasm and consummate musicianship to timeless jigs, reels, airs and ballads as well as interpreting more modern folk compositions.

Utilising such traditional instrumentation as bagpipes, whistles, bouzouki, fiddle and bodhran, the group made their recording debut with 1996's 'AE SPARK O NATURE'S FIRE' album. The record arrived soon after their debut performance at Glasgow's Celtic Connections festival, the show going down so well the band were invited back almost every year thereafter. Since the mid-90's, they've also been a ubiquitous presence on the European folk festival scene, from Shetland, Orkney and Aberdeen to the French Alps, Galicia and Portugal.

1997 saw the release of sophomore effort, 'SYNERGY', a record that drew widespread critical acclaim as DEAF SHEPHERD were hailed as one of Scotland's most exciting and powerful exponents of traditional Celtic-influenced music. An Irish twist was subsequently added in the shape of percussionist MARK McGUIRE while RORY went on to lend a hand to OLD BLIND DOGS. MARIANNE (also involved in Greentrax outfit, CANTYCHIELS), meanwhile, joined McLAUGHLIN and guitarist GAVIN RALSTON in side project CMc, releasing the 'SNAP AND ROLL' album in 2000. JOHN MORRAN, meanwhile, featured solo on volumes 5, 6 and 7 of the Complete Songs Of Robert Burns.

DEAF SHEPHERD were back early in 2002, their self-financed 'EVEN IN THE RAIN', featuring SAM BROWN on the closing song ('LOST FOR WORDS AT SEA').

JOHN MORRAN – vocals, guitar / **RORY CAMPBELL** – bagpipes, whistles, vocals / **MARIANNE CURRAN** (now CAMPBELL) – fiddle, vocals / **CLARE McLAUGHLIN** – fiddle / **MALCOLM STITT** – bouzouki, bagpipes, guitar, vocals, bass pedals

Greentrax Greentrax

Mar 96. (cd/c) *(<CD/C TRAX 104>)* **AE SPARK O NATURE'S FIRE** [ ] [ ]
– Gie's a drink / The Glen house – Mrs Jean Campbell / The minister's set / Logan braes / New pa / Finbarr / Ah surely / Peggy Gordon / Double pipe set / Lost for words at sea / The foreign set.

Dec 97. (cd) *(<CDTRAX 143>)* **SYNERGY** [ ] [ ]
– Jean Carignan / The ewe wi' the crookit horn / The Devil in the kitchen / The boys of Malin / Alistair's reel / Winter o' life / First light / Pawkie Paiterson / Father John / Weepers I shall wear / Reverend's revenge / Huntin' the buntin' / Clanranald / The coarncraik / Keys money fags.

— RORY joined the OLD BLIND DOGS and CALEDON, although he remained with 'SHEPHERD

— added **MARK MAGUIRE** – bodhran, percussion

Deaf Shepherd not iss.

Jan 02. (cd) *(DEAFSHEPHERD 1)* **EVEN IN THE RAIN** [ ] [-]
– Millennium village / The bonnie lass o Wellwid ha' / Mince / Chessmen / Yestreen I had a pint o wine / Poilin ni lionsaigh / Braemar gathering / I coft a stane haslock woo – Ben Wyviss / Jimmy Lothian's / The mermaid sang / Even in the rain: Even in the rain – The Quebec breakdown – Unknown – Gregor Lowrey's / Lost for words at sea (featuring vocals by SAM BROWN).

CMc: CLARE McLAUGHLIN & MARIANNE CAMPBELL

— with **GAVIN RALSTON** – guitar

Snap not iss.

Apr 00. (cd) *(SNAP 001)* **SNAP AND ROLL** [ ] [-]
– Julia's / Smokey lum / At work on the land / Miser's purse / Tune for Roddy / Mad Turk / MacLeod of Mull / Flowers of Edinburgh / Trip to Galicia / New claret / Tambo's.

Karl DENVER (see ⇒ Section 7: Rock & Pop)

Barbara DICKSON (see ⇒ Section 7: Rock & Pop)

Lonnie DONEGAN (see ⇒ Section 7: Rock & Pop)

DONOVAN (see ⇒ Section 7: Rock & Pop)

Blair DOUGLAS (see under ⇒ MAC-TALLA)

DRAMBUIE KIRKLISTON PIPE BAND (see under ⇒ Greentrax records)

Ivan DREVER

Born: Isle Of Sanday, Orkney. Although his first love was country, DREVER became increasingly involved in traditional music, forming KNOWE O'DEIL in 1984 with IAN COOPER. The pair released several albums, 'Knowe O'Deil' (1986), 'Orkney Anthem' (1986) and 'The Viking's Bride' (1987) in this incarnation before DREVER hooked up with DICK CLARKE for collaborative set, 'OCTOBER BRIDGE' (1988).

A belated solo album, 'HOMELAND', arrived in 1990, presaging the man's relocation to mainland Scotland and a position as lead vocalist, multi-instrumentalist and chief songwriter with Inverness-based folk-rockers WOLFSTONE. Despite the band's hard-gigging schedule, DREVER's extra-curricular activities were numerous. Keeping it in the musical family, so to speak, he worked with band member STRUAN EAGLESHAM on 'BACK TO BACK' (1994) and other WOLFSTONE stalwart, DUNCAN CHISHOLM on the acclaimed 'THE LEWIS BLUE' (1998). With PHIL CUNNINGHAM also lending a hand, the latter was a largely self-penned affair taking a mellow acoustic approach and drawing comparisons with WOLFSTONE's 'This Strange Place', a DREVER solo project in all but name.

The man's other solo albums include 'EVERY BREAKING HEART' (1992) and 'FOUR WALLS' (1996) while his sizeable canon of original song has been utilised by the likes of The DUBLINERS and DAVEY ARTHUR.

IVAN DREVER – vocals, guitar (of WOLFSTONE) / initially with the KNOWE O'DEIL: **IAN COOPER**

Attic not iss.

1986. (lp; by The KNOWE O'DEIL) *(ATC 002)* **KNOWE O'DEIL** [ ] [-]
1986. (lp; by The KNOWE O'DEIL) *(ATC 008)* **ORKNEY ANTHEM** [ ] [-]
Apr 87. (lp) *(ATC 011)* **CHILDREN'S FOLK TALES FROM ORKNEY** [ ] [-]
Sep 87. (lp; by The KNOWE O'DEIL) *(ATC 015)* **THE VIKING'S BRIDE** [ ] [-]

Mar 88. (lp) *(ATC 021)* **OCTOBER BRIDGE** □ -
May 90. (lp) *(ATC 023)* **HOMELAND** □ -

— IVAN also joined WOLFSTONE at this point

— his solo album was augmented by **DUNCAN CHISHOLM** – fiddle (of WOLFSTONE) / **STRUAN EAGLESHAM** – keyboards, bodhran (of WOLFSTONE) / **ALLAN WILSON** – small pipes / **MICKY AUSTIN** – banjo

Mar 92. (lp) *(ATC 030)* **EVERY BREAKING HEART** □ -
– I am the night / President Garfield / Here's to you / Planxty Hewlett / A new day / The little ones / For you / High level hornpipe / On my land / Tir aluinn / King's own herbacious borderers / Maggie's song / Rowan Drever / To leave you / The Bonar built piper / Road to Mount Tinnierun / Dinner's dangerous river jacket / Has she been aye / Fair Fiona's hand / Farewell to Orkney. *(cd-iss. Dec97; ATCD 030)*

1990's. (cd) **ISLES NE'ER FORGOTTEN** □ -

May 94. (c/cd; by IVAN DREVER and STRUAN EAGLESHAM) *(AT/+CD 036)* **BACK TO BACK** □ -
– Know way of knowing / Mary Eaglesham / Nae dish Donaldson / Irma's song / No tie ups / Roddy McCourt / No place for sorrow / Reasons / The fisherman / It doesn't seem quite right / Andrew Hunter's Evanton hat dance / The streets of Evanton. *(cd re-iss. Dec97; same)*

Iona not iss.

Jul 96. (cd/c) *(IRCD/IRC 037)* **FOUR WALLS** □ -
– The ballad of Jimmy Fry / Catching the dream / Timmer the tartar – Colonel Sir Neil MacRae of Howden End / How far / Called to fire / Chrissy Jane Drever / We sometimes hurt too / Kinnairdie's awa' wi' the geese – John Boocock's reel / Brave souls / Brae's o' Glenniffer.

— next with **DUNCAN CHISHOLM** – fiddle / plus **PHIL CUNNINGHAM** – keyboards, accordion, mandolin, whistles + **BRIAN McNEILL**

Oct 98. (cd/c; as IVAN DREVER and DUNCAN CHISHOLM) *(IRCD/IRC 062)* **THE LEWIS BLUE** □ -
– The flower of Kristiansand / Snowdrops in the rain / Fiddle reels: Maggie's pancakes – The little cascade / Leaving the harbour / Night in that land / Three jigs: Sonny Brogan's – Burke's – Trip to Leverkusen / The battle of Falkirk / Bonnie Lindsay / Warm embrace / Two reels: The ramnee ceilidh – The torn curtains / The Lewis blue.

— also with **CHISHOLM** plus **ANDY SIMMERS** – keyboards

Orcadian not iss.

Jun 00. (cd) *(ORCCD 01)* **BLACK WHITE AND BLUE** □ -
– Glasgow rain / Annie Laurie / Fiona Halloway's / Dashing white spirit / The north side / Charlie's hame / Stevie sings the blues / Moira McCrossan / Where I'm going to be / Paul Haigh's last bus / Kye Goodmans / Brothers in arms.

– compilations, etc. –

May 98. (cd/c) *Attic; (ATCD/ATC 051)* **THE ORKNEY YEARS VOL.1 (1986-1992)** □ -
– The hard road / Dick Head's delight / Betty Corrigall / Which way / 15 jars of rhubarb jam rag / Orkney anthem / Day of the drover / Dominic McGowan / The sea king / The road home / Bonar built piper / Farewell to Orkney.

DRINKERS DROUTH

Formed: Glasgow . . . 1974 with the line-up of JACK AITKEN, DAVE BLACK and brothers BRIAN and TONY DOUGAN. They performed their folk harmonies and traditional songs for the rest of the 70's and in 1981 they teamed up with soon-to-be fifth member, DAVY STEELE. For the next five years, the quintet toured Scotland and all over Europe, even managing to release a few low-key albums, 'WHEN THE KYE COMES HAME' (1982) and 'BOUND TO GO' (1984). DAVY of course, went on to sing and play with numerous outfits including CEOLBEG, CLAN ALBA, The BATTLEFIELD BAND and CALEDON. He also released a few solo albums in this hectic 90's period, but sadly the new millennium lost a much-loved character when he died of cancer on the 11th of April, 2001; DRINKERS DROUTH and 'Greentrax' records paid him respect by releasing 'A TRIBUTE' set later in the year.

BRIAN DOUGAN – vocals, mouth organ / **TONY DOUGAN** – guitar, vocals / **JACK AITKEN** – guitar, vocals, bouzouki, autoharp / **DAVE BLACK** – mandolin, vocals, fiddle, bouzouki / **DAVY STEELE** – vocals, guitar, 5-string banjo, whistle

Drouth not iss.

1982. (lp) *(DD 01)* **WHEN THE KYE COMES HAME** □ -
– Let me in this ae nicht – Merrily kissed the Quaker / Dream Angus / Birnie bouzle / Heave ya ho / When the kye comes hame / The prickly bush / Cam ye o'er frae France – The store cheque / Wha'll dreg a buckie-o / Tiree love song / Gospel ship.

1984. (lp) *(DD 02)* **BOUND TO GO** □ -
– The exile song / Johnny Sangster / The bonnie light horseman / When Charlie tae the Hielands came / Lord Marlborough / The Soutar's o' Selkirk – The deid cat / The sodger's return / Private William Coffey / I'se the bye / The ploughman / Bound to go.

— after their split (though they still perform live), DAVY went on to play for various bands (see above for details)

– compilations, etc. –

Nov 01. (cd) *Greentrax; (CDTRAX 223)* **A TRIBUTE** □ -
– (all but 2 tracks of above LP's)

DROP THE BOX

Formed: Shetlands . . . 1992 as NATIVE SONS by first-year Aberdeen University students, JAMES L HENRY (writer and throaty singer), INGE THOMSON (with sweeter larynx), and three folk musicians MICHAEL FERRIE, FRASER MOUAT and AKY GILLILAND. Currently putting a different, if no less compelling, spin on the increasingly popular traditonal-meets-contemporary genre, DROP THE BOX nevertheless began life as an all-acoustic affair. An eponymous debut album appeared on the indigenous 'Lochshore' label in October '95 although its release was overshadowed by the news that talented fiddle player FERRIE was suffering from cancer. He was to die in February of the following year, aged just 21.

Despite such a devastating blow so early on in their career, the band found the strength to carry on, performing a comeback gig at the Shetland Folk Festival later that year. 1998's 'HONEYTRAP' was a confident step forward, often skilfully combining funky drumming (check the MASSIVE ATTACK-style backbeat to 'DANCING'), chunky basslines, full-on fiddling and chicken scratch guitar and occasionally going for instrumental intensity ('WINGS') or indie swooning ('MOLASSES'). A common thread of Celtic melancholy connected the disparate elements while the vocal contrast between the resigned HENRY and the candyfloss-voiced THOMSON made for interesting listening. The band even explored themes of homosexuality, gender and identity on 'SEXUALITY', hardly conventional lyrical terrain for a roots-centered act.

In addition to shows in Canada, France and Scandinavia, DROP THE BOX have performed at Glasgow's Celtic Connections, Edinburgh's Festival Fringe and Aberdeen's (now sadly defunct) Alternative Festival, giving notice that they're not about to drop the folk-fusion torch anytime soon. With HENRY and THOMSON recruiting names such as EILIDH SHAW, RUSSELL GAIR and JONATHAN RITCH, it wasn't surprising that their third rousing set, 'LOVEDAY', was much anticipated in Spring 2001.

JAMES L. HENRY – vocals, guitar / **INGE THOMSON** – vocals, accordion, flute, percussion / **MICHAEL FERRIE** (b. 1975) – fiddle / **FRASER MOUAT** – bass / **AKY GILLILAND** – drums

Lochshore Lochshore

Oct 95. (cd) *(<CDLDL 1234>)* **DROP THE BOX** □ □ Apr97
– Edge of the world / Dr Love / Da mushroom house / His intention / Now becomes today / Not the love / One kiss Nancy / Saved / Not coming your way / Tamlin / Straight from the heart.

— **KEVIN HENDERSON** – fiddle; repl. FERRIE who died of cancer in February 1996 (aged only 21)

May 98. (cd) *(<CDLDL 1268>)* **HONEYTRAP** □ □ Feb00
– Run dry / Dancing / Silver fox: a) Foxy chique – b) Silver fox reel – c) Milligarth madness / Honeytrap: a) Honeytrap – b) Hogties / Bigger things / Red bee: a) Red bee – b) Tune for a lost harmonica / Molasses / Sexuality / Wings / Here with me / Bigger things (reprise).

— **HENRY + THOMSON** recruited **EILIDH SHAW** – fiddle, vocals (solo artist & ex-CALEDON) / **JONATHAN RITCH** – bass / **RUSSELL GAIR** – drums

Brightest Spark not iss.

Mar 01. (cd) *(BRIGHTCD 0209)* **LOVEDAY** □ -
– More than this / Cloudburst / Silence / Bit part / Bubblebox / Quoy brae / Follow me / Spinning / Look thru me / Raining / Dubset.

Gordon DUNCAN (see under ⇒ Greentrax records)

Jock DUNCAN (see under ⇒ Springthyme records)

E

Kirsten EASDALE (see under ⇒ CALASAIG)

EASY CLUB

Formed: Edinburgh . . . 1983 by Welsh-born JACK EVANS and former fellow JOCK TAMSON'S BAIRNS guy ROD PATERSON; future TANNAHILL WEAVERS member JOHN MARTIN and JIM SUTHERLAND were also present. After a handful of albums, 'THE EASY CLUB' (1984), 'CHANCE OR DESIGN' (1985) and 'SKIRLIE BEAT' (1987), the players went their separate ways once again.

EVANS continued to work for various theatre companies and contributed session work on TV; EVANS even provided production for the theatre show in 1990, funnily enough entitled 'A' Jock Tamson's Bairns'.

The CAULD BLAST ORCHESTRA (an eight-piece stage band featured in the show) stayed together as a group, completing a debut album, 'SAVAGE DANCE', not long afterwards. While an EASY CLUB collection was in the shops, so was the CBO follow-up, 'DURGA'S FEAST' (1996), its strength relying on the band's unique and eclectic instrumental presentation. In between all this, JACK curated the Edinburgh Folk Festival (1993-96) and continued to work in production.

In 1999, having already set up another weird but wonderful Folk/ceilidh ensemble, KELTIK ELEKTRIK, he produced the celebration to Scotland's Parliament, 'A Clear Day's Dawnin' (released on 'Greentrax' records). Alongside MIKE KATZ (of the BATTLEFIELD BAND), SIMON THOUMIRE and TONY McMANUS, EVANS completed a second 'ELEKTRIK set, sub-titled 'JUST WHEN YOU THOUGHT IT WAS SAFE TO SIT DOWN' (2000). The following year, the ever versatile guitarist (etc!), sidelined with SPRINGWELL, a trio also featuring McMANUS and KEVIN MacLEOD. From the mid 90's, JIM SUTHERLAND produced the first two SHOOGLENIFTY albums and was to have released his first solo set for 'Eclectic' records in '96 – you can listen to the excellent track 'FLICK IT UP AND KICK IT' if you find the V/A set, 'Folk 'n' Hell'.

ROD PATERSON – vocals, guitar, mandola (ex-JOCK TAMSON'S BAIRNS) / **JACK EVANS** (b. Cardiff) – guitar, mandolin, moothie, piano, etc / **JOHN MARTIN** – fiddle, cello / **JIM SUTHERLAND** – bodhran, cittern, percussion, bass

Abbeyhill not iss.

Nov 84. (lp) *(ABB 1001)* **THE EASY CLUB** . ☐ [-]
– The Easy Club reel – Janine's reel / Dirty old town / Waltzes: The innocent railway – Daphne's trousers – A bruxa / The auld toon shuffle / The Arnish light – The ostrich / The train journey north / The Midlothian mining song / The radical road – Murdo MacKenzie of Torridon / Fause, fause hae ye been / Ms. Lyall – John McNeill's reel. *(cd-iss. Apr01 on 'Greentrax'; CDTRAX 205)*

R.E.L. not iss.

Oct 85. (lp/c) *(RELS/RECS 479)* **CHANCE OR DESIGN** ☐ [-]
– Black is the colour / The North Sea Chinaman the liguist / This for that / Neal Slessor Thomson – The desert march / The Eyemouth disaster / The quiet man – Erse for Alba / Isle of Ewe – The Dhu hill – The 40 p.c. rule – Auld Wattie / The diamond / West Pilton circus – The Pumpherston hornpipe / Chance or design / The long distance runner – Bodhran solo.

May 87. (lp/c) *(RELS/RECS 483)* **SKIRLIE BEAT** ☐ [-]
– Auchengeich / Euphemia / To India / Skirlie beat / The Hielanman's umbrella / The first time ever I saw your face / Doon in the wee room / Song of the Clyde / The shipyard.

— added **NORMAN CHAMBERS** – concertina, percussion, whistle (ex-JOCK TAMSON'S BAIRNS)

— JACK mainly went into session and production work and later formed the CAULD BLAST ORCHESTRA and KELTIK ELEKTRIK

– compilations, etc. –

1992. (cd/c) *Eclectic; (ECL CD/TC 9103)* **ESSENTIAL** ☐ [-]
– The Easy Club reel – Janine's reel / Dirty old town / The diamond / Euphemia / The train journey north / Black is the colour of my true love's hair – The little cascade / The quiet man – Erse for Alba / Fause, fause hae ye been / Skirlie beat / The auld toon shuffle / The road to Gerenish – Bodhran solo / The innocent railway – Daphne's trousers – A bruxa / Auchengeich / The North Sea Chinaman – The linguist / Neal Slessor Thomson – The desert march / This for that / Murdo MacKenzie of Torridon – Loch Carron – The radical road – Dr MacInnes' fancy / The collier's 8-hour day / The Arnish light – The ostrich / The Eyemouth disaster / The Easy Club reel. *(re-iss. Jan96; same)*

CAULD BLAST ORCHESTRA

— with **JACK EVANS** plus seven other musicians

Eclectic not iss.

1990. (cd/c) *(ECL CD/TC 9002)* **SAVAGE DANCE** ☐ [-]
– Reels within wheels / Tower of Babel stomp / Cauld blast / Savage dance / The oyster wives' dance / Tarbolton lodge / Railyard band / Rantin' reel / Green shutters / Bottle hymn of the republic / Quaich. *(re-iss. Jan96; same)*

Jan 96. (cd/c) *(ECL CD/TC 9410)* **DURGA'S FEAST** ☐ [-]
– Mixed blood / The black rock / March of the undecided / Belvedere / Tango for a drowning man / The last gift / Silver silber / Sleep of the innocent / Symphony of the Mammon.

KELTIK ELEKTRIK

JACK EVANS and his crew; **MIKE KATZ** – pipes (of BATTLEFIELD BAND) / **TONY McMANUS** – guitar (Solo artist, etc) / **KATHRYN NICOL** – fiddle / **SIMON THOUMIRE** – concertina (Solo Artist, of KEEP IT UP)

G2 not iss.

Nov 98. (cd) *(G2CD 7003)* **EDINBURGH HOGMANAY PARTY MIX** ☐ [-]
– Clumsy lover / Alehouse / Ale is dear / Caledonia / Lexy MacAskill / Blue Dalzell / New mullindhu / Wild mountain thyme / Jigtime / Flower of Scotland / Amazing grace / Donald's little cascade / Auld lang syne / Reels.

Nov 00. (cd) *(G2CD 7006)* **KELTIK ELEKTRIK 2: JUST WHEN YOU THOUGHT IT WAS SAFE TO SIT DOWN** ☐ [-]
– The long note / Caber feidh / The fair maid of Takla Makan / The braes o' Balquidder / The Oyster wives' rant / You're welcome home / Grainne / Oranmore / Caledfwich / The old pipe reel.

JACK EVANS

below credited (on the sleeve) **MAIRI CAMPBELL & JERRY GARDNER**

Greentrax Greentrax

Mar 00. (cd) *(<CDTRAX 192>)* **ONCE UPON A TIME IN THE NORTH** ☐ ☐ May00
– Walk right in – Brave Lewie Roy – O'er bogie / MacGregor the roarer – Angus G. MacLeod – Once upon a time in the north / A' bhirlinn bharrach – The Atholl and breadalbane highlanders / Early mornin' train / Sandiag / Tarbolton / Ballad of Joe Meek / Lass of Glenshee / Fugitives from Urjaz / Two minutes' pandemonium.

— JACK subsequently worked with TONY McMANUS and RORY MacLEOD

ECLIPSE FIRST (see under ⇒ Iona records)

ELECTRICS (see ⇒ Section 8: Rock, Pop & Indie)

ENTER THE HAGGIS

Formed: Toronto, Canada . . . March 1995 by piper/singer/songwriter CRAIG DOWNIE, who pieces together a band to support traditional Irish outfit TIP SPLINTER at the Ultrasound venue. Towards the end of the year, Scots-mad DOWNIE bumps into (hic!) bass player ROBERT McCRADY (known as RODENT to cool cats in the neighbourhood!) and the pair set about finding new 'HAGGIS members. The New Year (hic!) saw barman/drummer KEN HORNE join, and shortly afterwards guitarist TEEMIE PATERSON and fiddler/guitarist DONALD QUAN; although the latter was superseded by DUNCAN CAMERON after leaving for England.

With several of their own compositions under their sporran, CRAIG and the boys delivered their debut CD-album, 'LET THE WIND BLOW HIGH', in the summer of '98 (lifted from a famous line on Andy Stewart's 'DONALD WHERE'S YER TROOSERS?', which the trad quintet folked up with anarchic ease). The following year saw the record issued on Edinburgh-based 'R.E.L.', although personnel changes led to only CRAIG and RODENT remaining – newcomers MIKEY PALLETT, TREVOR LEWINGTON and JAMES CAMPBELL were in place for a powerful Regina Highland Games appearance. Gigs as far away as San Francisco (at O'Neill's Irish pub in San Mateo) were one of the highlights of the new millennium – Scotland and the rest of the world would have to wait a little longer.

CRAIG DOWNIE – bagpipes, vocals, tin whistle, acoustic guitar / **RODENT** (b. ROBERT McCRADY) – bass, acoustic guitar, vocals / **TEEMIE PATERSON** (b. TOM) – guitars, vocals / **DUNCAN CAMERON** – fiddle, vocals, acoustic guitar, bouzouki, mandolin, uilleann bagpipe, bodhran, banjo / **KEN HORNE** – drums, darbuka, percussion

not iss. Indie Pool

Jun 98. (cd) **LET THE WIND BLOW HIGH** [-] ☐ Canada
– Enter . . . / Where will ye go? / Donald where's yer troosers? / The train / Skyswimmer / Bagpipes on Mars / Home / The three little jigs / Widow's walk / Ride my monster / The Mexican Scotsman. *(UK-iss.Jul99 on 'R.E.L.'; RECD 529)*

— **MIKEY PALLETT** – fiddle, keyboards, vocals; repl. CAMERON

— **TREVOR LEWINGTON** – guitar, vocals; repl. PATERSON

— **JAMES CAMPBELL** – drums, percussion; repl. HORNE

Jack EVANS (see under ⇒ EASY CLUB)

EXILES

Formed: Glasgow . . . mid-60's by the folk-rock vocal trio of ENOCH KENT, PAUL LENIHAN and GORDON McCULLOCH; their first set 'FREEDOM, COME ALL YE' also featured fiddler BOBBY CAMPBELL. The latter had served his apprenticeship in the late 50's under the wing of Renfrewshire Academy English teacher music voice tutor, NORMAN BUCHAN. In this time, CAMPBELL befriended JOSH MacRAE and a host of others (including GORDON McCULLOCH), meeting in such auspicious places as The Glasgow Folksong Club (run by BUCHAN). Part of the "Broomhill Bums" team of singers and musicians, BOBBY soon found solace in the quartet, The EXILES. This group managed to release a couple of LP's in the mid-60's for the legendary 'Topic' label, 'FREEDOM, COME ALL YE' (1966) and 'THE HALE AND THE HANGED' (1967).

ENOCH KENT – vocals, whistle, guitar / **BOBBY CAMPBELL** – fiddle, vocals, mandolin, guitar / **GORDON McCULLOCH** – vocals, guitar, banjo, harmonica / with **PAUL LENIHAN** – (some) vocals

Topic not iss.

1966. (lp) *(12T 143)* **FREEDOM, COME ALL YE** ☐ -
– The ballad of accounting / The moving on song / We're only over here for exploration / Thank Christ for Christmas / The pigeon / The pound a week rise / Freedom, come all ye / For a' that and a' that / Arthur MacBride / Willie Brennan / Wae's me for Prince Charlie / La pique / Van Diemen's land / Twa recruiting sergeants.

1967. (lp) *(12T 164)* **THE HALE AND THE HANGED** ☐ -
– The jolly beggar / The fair flower of Northumberland / Reels: The corner house / The Sally gardens The laird o' the windy wa' / Dainty Davie / Le reel du pendu / Queen Eleanor's confession / The plooman laddie / The shoals of herring / Airs slip jig and reel – The coolin / I walked up to her / Rocky road to Dublin / The wee weaver / The battle of Harlaw / I will lay ye doon, love / Planxty Davis.

— the group split up after above

F

FIDDLERS' BID (see under ⇒ Greentrax records)

FIDDLER'S FIVE (see under ⇒ Temple records)

FILSKA

Formed: Quarff, Shetlands . . . 1994, the brainwave of fiddler JOYCE REID, who invited her daughters HENNA and BETHANY alongside her longtime former schoolfriend GEMMA WILSON; both siblings soon won awards at Shetland's Annual Young Fiddler Of The Year. With sales of their debut set 'HARVEST HOME' (1996) doing well, they made their first TV appearance on Grampian's 'Ceol na Fidhle' the following year. With London-based guitarist/vocalist ANDREW TULLOCH (son of VIOLET) on board – initially as a guest – FILSKA recorded their sophomore set, 'TIME AND TIDE' (1998). Subsequent tours of over 60 countries, noteably the Forde and Falun Festivals in Norway and Sweden, preceded the Lorient Festival 2000 in France. Early in 2002, the quartet played the prestigious Celtic Connections, described as "tight as the proverbial drum" by The Scotsman.

JOYCE REID – fiddle / **HENNA REID** – fiddle, piano / **BETHANY REID** – fiddle, accordion / with also **GEMMA WILSON** – fiddle

Attic not iss.

May 96. (cd) *(ATCD 044)* **HARVEST HOME** ☐ -
– The Quarff lassies – Lay Dee at Dee – Miss Spence's reel alive – Sail her ower da Raftrees – Deil stick da minister / Jigs; The wee copper o' Fife – The jig of slurs – The Glenorchy / Irish air; Planxty fanny power / Kevin's reel; Pottinger's reel / Jigs; Hamilton house – Kenny Gillies of Portnalor / Pauline's country / Jigs; Donald Willie and his dog – The curlew / Largo's fairy dance – Xmas in the morning – Theme from BBC TV's Para Handy / Reels; Susan's broken ankle – Maggie's reel / The hen's march o'er the middle / The love o' the Isles – Bill Black's button box / Reels; Drowsy Maggie – Liz's reel / Reels; Alex Muir, Northlands / Afton water – Harvest home / The Deil's awa wi' the exciseman / The fiddler from Santa Barbara – Laxo burn – Joanne Elizabeth Jamieson's favourite.

— added **ANDREW TULLOCH** – guitar, vocals (ex-HOM BRU)

Highlander not iss.

Dec 98. (cd) *(HRMCD 005)* **TIME AND TIDE** ☐ -
– Bunjie's dilemma / Lexie McAskill / Tom's lost the keys / The one inch trowel / Multitimber jig / Lady Montague / Guzzle together / Song for Paul / Troy's wedding / Monday morning / Brenda Stubbert's reel / Dunns dings aa / The water is wide.

— awaiting their third album later in 2002

FINDASK

Formed: Glasgow . . . early 70's by WILLIE LINDSAY and STUART CAMPBELL. After meeting at the city's University Of Strathclyde, the duo began making a name for themselves in local folk clubs and student unions, duly advancing to support act for the likes of FAIRPORT CONVENTION. The lads plugged away for nigh on a decade before the Midlothian-based 'Temple' label signed them up for a belated debut album, 'BETWEEN THE WHITE LINES' (1984). A follow-up, 'WAITING FOR A MIRACLE', was released in 1987 although CAMPBELL subsequently suffered from an extended period of illness, the pernicious anaemia with which he was afflicted seriously affecting his ability to carry on with the band.

WILLIE LINDSAY (b.24 Jan'52) – vocals, guitar, harmonica, flute, whistles / **STUART CAMPBELL** (b.16 Mar'51) – bouzouki, cittern, guitar, mandolin, vocals

Temple not iss.

May 84. (lp) *(TP 014)* **BETWEEN THE WHITE LINES** ☐ -
May 88. (lp/c) *(TP/CTP 026)* **WAITING FOR A MIRACLE** ☐ -
(c re-iss. Feb94; same)

— at this point CAMPBELL became extremely ill and the duo could only occasionally perform

FINE FRIDAY (see under ⇒ Tartan Tapes records)

FINN MACCUIL

Formed: Glasgow . . . 1977 by TONY IRELAND, JOHN WILSON, NICK KEIR and main vocalist MADELAINE TAYLOR. Traditional folk but with some arrangements from the band members KEIR and WILSON, finn maccuil issued only one set, 'SINK YE SWIM YE' (1978). After their split, IRELAND delivered a couple of solo LP's and relocated to Germany with his German wife. NICK, meanwhile, joined the ranks of The McCALMANS in September '82 and has been an integral part of the folk giants for 20 years.

MADELAINE TAYLOR – vocals, guitar, spoons / **TONY IRELAND** – guitar, dulcimer, vocals / **JOHN WILSON** – bass, guitar, vocals / **NICK KEIR** – mandolin, vocals, recorder, whistle

R.E.L. not iss.

1978. (lp) *(REL 460)* **SINK YE SWIM YE** ☐ -
– Birnie Bouzle / Newry town / Mary Hamilton / The friar well fitted / The shearing / New jigs / The minstrel / The little drummer / The Gaberlunzie man / The poachers / The dancers of Ruhendorf.

— after their split, KEIR joined the McCALMANS (of which IRELAND was the arranger)

TONY IRELAND

mult-instrumentalist

Peak not iss.

1983. (lp) *(3581)* **JOHNNY O'COCKLEY'S WELL** ☐ -
– The recruited collier / Lanigan's ball / Over the borders – St Kilda wedding – Connaught man's rambles / Jock Stewart / Lord Yester / Cam ye o'er frae France? / Johnny O'Cockley's well / Corn rigs / The bonny Gateshead lassie / Down by the Salley gardens / Come under my plaidie – The Duke of Perth – The Deil among the tailors.

— next with **NICK KEIR, BRIAN McNEILL, DEREK MOFFAT + IAN McCALMAN**

Ireland not iss.

1987. (lp) *(IR 2001)* **THE CHAMPION** ☐ -
– Tae the beggin' / The Turkish girl – Hannah on the mountain – Miss Catherine Jane Spree's / My bonnie Mary / Greenland haul away – The faeries' hornpipe – The Cameronian reel / My love's in Germany / What you do with what you've got / Alan Reid's fancy – O'Carolan's draught / Traveller's moon / The champion.

Archie FISHER

Born: 23 Oct'39, Glasgow, son of an Isle Of Barra speaker/singer and a local police inspector who also sang opera, music hall, etc. The FISHER FAMILY (ARCHIE, RAY, CINDY, JOYCE, AUDREY and CILLA) became quite popular all over Scotland, releasing a few recordings on 'Topic' during the 60's. ARCHIE, meanwhile, had learned his trade from the late, great NORMAN BUCHAN at the Renfrewshire Academy and was school pals with HAMISH IMLACH. Influenced by PETE SEEGER, BROWNIE McGHEE and SONNY TERRY, ARCHIE offered up his own blend of folk-blues, although little was released until the mid-60's.

As well as playing guitar on his sister CILLA's records, ARCHIE finally issued a couple of his own over the period 1968-1970: 'ARCHIE FISHER' and 'ORFEO' (both worth a wee bit of cash). He also released the album 'WILL YE GANG, LOVE', in the late 70's as well as collaborating with BARBARA DICKSON on 'THE FATE O' CHARLIE'. A fount of knowledge on all things folky, Archie has been hosting Radio Scotland's Travelling Folk programme since 1983. ARCHIE and GARNET ROGERS issued two sets 'SUNSETS I'VE GALLOPED INTO . . .' (1988) and 'OFF THE MAP' (1992), his style reminiscent of DICK GAUGHAN or MARTIN CARTHY.

FISHER FAMILY

ARCHIE, RAY, CINDY, JOYCE, AUDREY + (PRIS)CILLA

Topic — not iss.

1961. (7"ep; RAY & ARCHIE FISHER) *(TOP 67)* **FAR OVER THE FORTH** ☐ ☐
– The night visiting song / Far over the Forth / The twa corbies / Kilbogie.

1966. (lp) *(12T 137)* **THE FISHER FAMILY** ☐ ☐
– Come all ye Fisher lassies / Schooldays over / Rigs o' rye / Donalogue / For our lang biding here / Joy of my heart / Hey ca'through / What's poor Mary weeping for / Bonny lass o' Ballochmvie / I am a miller tae ma trade / Birkin tree / I am a freeborn man / Aince upon a time. *(re-iss. May81; same)*

— sister CILLA would team up with ARTIE TREZISE and later become the SINGING KETTLE

ARCHIE FISHER

ARCHIE – vocals, guitar, dulcimer, concertina, sitar / with **JOHN MacKINNON** – violin, mandolin / **JOHN DOONAN** – piccolo

Xtra — not iss.

1968. (lp) *(XTRA 1070)* **ARCHIE FISHER** ☐ ☐
– Open the door softly / Reynardine / The terror time / The three gypsies / The Kilder hunt / The trooper and the maid / The child on the road / The beggar wench / Bogie's bonnie belle / Matt Highland / Farewell she / The snows. *(re-iss. 1982 on 'Celtic Music'; CM 007) (cd-iss. Dec97; CMCD 007)*

Trailer — not iss.

1969. (lp; ARCHIE FISHER – BARBARA DICKSON – JOHN MacKINNON) *(LER 3002)* **THE FATE O' CHARLIE** ☐ ☐
– Cam ye o'er frae France / The three healths / Wha wadna fecht for Charlie / The white cockade / My bonnie Heiland laddie / The Highland widow's lament / The battle of Prestonpans / Killiecrankie / O'er the water to Charlie / Prince Charlie / Highland Harry / The fate o' Chatlie / The Highlander's lament / O'er the water / The flowers o' the forest.

Decca — not iss.

Aug 70. (lp; as BARBARA DICKSON & ARCHIE FISHER) *(SKL 5041)* **THRO' THE RECENT YEARS** ☐ ☐
– The January man / You like the sun / Morning / Tears of rage / Friends and lovers / Somebody counts on me / Frolicsome alcoholic mermaid / If I'd stayed around / Lullaby for father / I am the great sun / First of the few / Fiddler's green / Together forever / Through the recent years.

Dec 70. (lp; w-drawn) *(SKL 5057)* **ORFEO** ☐ ☐

— next with **WENDY GROSSMAN** – concertina, banjo, dulcimer / **KATHY WESTRA** – cello / **ANNIE MAYO MUIR** – flute / **LANI HERMANN** – fiddle

Folk Legacy — not iss.

1976. (lp) *(FSS 61)* **THE MAN WITH A RHYME** ☐ ☐
– Twa bonnie maidens / Welcome Royal Charlie / Dark eyed Molly / Queen among the heather / Jock Stewart / The witch of the West-mer-lands / The echo mocks the corncrake / Western island / Upstairs, downstairs / Mount and go / The wounded whale / The cruel brother / Coshieville / South wind. *(<cd/c-iss.Mar98; FLEG 61 CD/C>)*

— next with **JOHN TAMS** – melodion / **ALAN BARTY** – fiddle

Topic — not iss.

1976. (lp) *(12TS 277)* **WILL YE GANG, LOVE** ☐ ☐
– O Charlie, o Charlie / Lindsay / The broom o' the Cowdenknowes / Mally Lee / Will ye gang, love / The flower of France and England, o / The laird o' windy wa's / Men o' worth / Looly, looly / Dreg song / Adam Cameron / Blackbirds and thrushes / The gallant ninety two / The rovin' ploughboy. *(cd-iss. May93 on 'Green Linnet'; GLCD 3076)*

— next with **GARNET ROGERS** – synthesizer, flute, guitar, violin / **DAVE WOODHEAD** – bass, piano

Greentrax — not iss.

Aug 88. (lp/c) *(TRAX/CTRAX 020)* **SUNSETS I'VE GALLOPED INTO** ☐ ☐
– Ashfields and brine / Yonder banks – The shipyard apprentice / The cuillins of home / Southside blues / Silver coin / The presence / Gunsmoke and whisky / Bill Hosie / I wandered by a brookside / Merry England / The great north road / Eastfield / The black horse / All that you ask. *(<cd-iss. Apr92; CDTRAX 020>)*

Snow Company — not iss.

1992. (c; by ARCHIE FISHER & GARNET ROGERS) *(SGS 1112)* **OFF THE MAP** ☐ ☐

RAY FISHER

she featured on V/A set, 'The Iron Muse' (1963 Topic'; 12T 86)

— ARCHIE's sister also delivered a few sets

Leader — not iss.

1972. (lp) *(LER 2038)* **THE BONNIE BIRDY** ☐ ☐
– Johnny Sangster / Mill o' Tifty's Annie / Botty at morn / The Forfar sodger / The pride of Glencoe / The silkie of Sulskerry / The bonnie birdie. *(re-iss. May81; same)*

— next with **JOHNNY CUNNINGHAM** – fiddle

Folk Legacy — not iss.

1982. (lp) *(FSS 91)* **WILLIE'S LADY** ☐ ☐
– The pressers / The bonnie wee lassie that never said no / The red-haired man's wife / The kye have come hame / Willie's lady / Are ye sleepin' Maggie / Miller tae my trade / The wearie cutters / Betsy Bell / Over yonder banks / When fortune turns the wheel.

— with COLIN ROSS, MARTIN CARTHY & JOHN KIRKPATRICK

Saydisc — not iss.

1990. (cd) *(CDSDL 391)* **TRADITIONAL SONGS OF SCOTLAND** ☐ ☐
– Night visiting song / Wark o' the weavers / Lady Keith's lament / The Gallowa hills / Coulter's candy / Willie's fatal visit / Twa recruiting sergeants / Floo'ers o' the forest / MacGinty's meal and ale / Baron o' Brackley / Gipsy laddies / Lang biding here / Jute mill son.

Cilla FISHER & Artie TREZISE

Born: 26 Sep'52, Glasgow & 3 Apr'47, St. Andrews, Fife. The wee-est wean of the FISHER clan, CILLA cut her musical teeth singing alongside her siblings ARCHIE and RAY and even sang on the radio before she'd reached her teens. TREZISE, meanwhile, was a relative veteran of the folk scene at the time he hooked up with CILLA, having performed with the likes of The GREAT FIFE ROAD SHOW.

The pair first got together in the mid-70's, enlisting the help of ARCHIE and fiddler ALLAN BARRY for their eponymous debut album in 1976. The multi-instrumentalist/vocal duo recorded 'BALCANQUHAL' as a follow-up set the following year. Again released on Bill Leader's self-titled label, the record went on to win a Melody Maker folk award.

CILLA and ARTIE initiated their own label, 'Kettle', for 1979's 'FOR FOUL DAY AND FAIR' while 1980's 'CILLA & ARTIE' was released on the 'Topic' label. The early 80's saw the pair turn their attention towards the chidren's market with The SINGING KETTLE, an educational show that toured the UK and resulted in a number of spin-off TV series.

CILLA FISHER – vocals / **ARTIE TREZISE** – vocals / with **ARCHIE FISHER** – guitar (also a solo artist) / **ALLAN BARRY** – fiddle

Autogram — not iss.

1976. (lp) *(ALLP 206)* **CILLA FISHER & ARTIE TREZISE** ☐ ☐
– Hieland whisky / When I was noo but sweet sixteen / The Gaugers / Hirslin Kate / Baron o' Brackley / Guise o' Tough / Bunch of Thyme / Work of the weavers / Birnie bouzle / Tae the beggin' / Jamie Raeburn / The good looking widow / The keech in the creel. *(re-iss. May88; same)*

— next with **ARCHIE FISHER** – guitar / **ALLAN BARTY** – fiddle, mandola / **PETE SHEPHEARD** – melodeon

Leader — not iss.

1977. (lp) *(LER 2100)* **BALCANQHAL** ☐ ☐
– Hash o' Benagoak / Leaboy's lassie / Wheel of fortune / Miller o' Dron / Nancy Bell / Jock Stewart / Love and freedom / Magdale green / Spinner's wedding / Rare's hill / Aikey brae.

Kettle — not iss.

1978. (lp) *(KAC 1)* **FOR FOUL DAY AND FAIR** ☐ ☐
– Sodger laddie / Rhynie / Feein' time / The bothy lads / The jolly beggar / Billy Taylor / Laird o' the dainty Doonby / The first time / The shepherd lad / Twa recruitin' sergeants / False lover won back / The miller / The maid gaed tae the mill / The final trawl.

Topic not iss.

1980. (lp) *(12TS 405)* **CILLA & ARTIE** ☐ ☐
– Norland wind / The beggar man / What can a young lassie / Fisher lassies / Generations of change / Fair maid of London Town / The wicked wife / The gypsy laddies / Blue bleezin' blind drunk / John grumlie / The Jeannie C. *(cd-iss. May98 on 'Greentrax'; CDTRAX 9050)*

— they virtually took the moniker of the SINGING KETTLE, except . . .

Kettle not iss.

Oct 83. (lp; by CILLA FISHER) *(KOP 11)* **SONGS OF THE FISHING** ☐ ☐
– The boatie rows / Caller herrin' / Dance tae yer daddie / Dreg song / Eyemouth disaster / The final trawl / The fisherman's wife / Fisherrow / Hushaba ma bairnie / The isle of May / The prosperity / Tatties and herrin' / Whaur will we gang.
above with **CAROL JAMIESON** – piano + **DAVY TULLOCH** – fiddle
below with **GARY COUPLAND** – keyboards / **BRIAN McNEILL** – concertina, fiddle, viola / **BRIAN MILLER** – guitar / **STUART ANDERSON** – accordion / **RON SHAW** – cello / **HAMISH MOORE** – pipes / **CATHAL MacCONNELL** – whistle

Oct 86. (lp/c) *(KOP/+C 17)* **REACHING OUT** ☐ ☐
– The tinkerman's daughter / The old simplicity / Yellow on the broom (music of the Spey) / A miner's lullaby (coorie doon) / Some hae meat / John Anderson my Jo / The Fisher lass / Tale of '81 (land of hope and glory) / Hunted on the hillside / Logie o' Buchan.

— CILLA + ARTIE carried on with The SINGING KETTLE

Ray FISHER (see under ⇒ FISHER, Archie)

5 HAND REEL

Formed: Glasgow . . . 1975 by ex-BOYS OF THE LOUGH guitarist DICK GAUGHAN, CHUCK FLEMING (subsequently replaced by BOBBY EAGLESHAM), TOM HICKLAND, Leeds-born BARRY LYONS (ex-TREES and ex-MR.FOX) and DAVE TULLOCH. What with the presence of former JSD BAND fiddle maestro FLEMING, comparisons to that band were unavoidable although FIVE HAND REEL never quite managed the same crossover success. Following an independently released 1977 debut single, 'REEL REGGAE', the band signed to 'R.C.A.' and completed an eponymous debut album the same year. After a further two sets, 'FOR A' THAT' (1977) and 'EARL O'MORAY' (1978), GAUGHAN struck out for a solo career and was replaced by another Englishman, SAM BRUCKEN. In fact, the band only lasted one more album, 'A BUNCH OF FIVES' (1979) before splitting in the early 80's. TULLOCH reunited with GAUGHAN in the musical conglomerate CLAN ALBA in '95.

DICK GAUGHAN (b. RICHARD PETER GAUGHAN, 17 May'48) – vocals, guitar (ex-BOYS OF THE LOUGH) / CHUCK FLEMING (ex-TREES, ex-J.S.D. BAND) departed (later was part of SYNCOPACE and FIDDLERS FIVE) and was repl. by **BOBBY EAGLESHAM** – vocals, guitar, mandolin, dulcimer / **TOM HICKLAND** – keyboards, fiddle, vocals / **BARRY LYONS** (b. Leeds) – bass, keyboards, percussion (ex-TREES, ex-MR.FOX) / **DAVE TULLOCH** – drums, percussion

Rubber not iss.

Apr 76. (7") *(ADUB 7)* **REEL REGGAE. / THE KNIGHT AND THE SHEPHERD'S DAUGHTER** ☐ ☐

Mar 77. (lp/c) *(RUB 019)* **5 HAND REEL** ☐ ☐
– Both sides of the Forth / Death of Argyll / Kempy's hat / The knight and the shepherd's daughter / Sliave gallion braes / Wee wee German lairdy / The maid of Listowel / When a man's in love / Frankie's dog. *(re-iss. Mar77 on 'R.C.A.' lp/c; PL/PK 25065) (re-iss. Jun88 on 'Black Crow'; CRO/+C 211)*

R.C.A. not iss.

May 77. (lp/c) *(PL/PK 25066)* **FOR A' THAT** ☐ ☐
– Bratach bana / Pinch of snuff / A man's a man for a' that / Haugh's o' Cromdale / Ae fond kiss / P stands for Paddy – Paddy Fahey's reel / The cruel brother / Carrickfergus / Lochanside – The jig of slurs / Linda Brechin's / The Marquis of Tullybardine. *(re-iss. Jun88 on 'Black Crow'; CRO 212)*

Apr 78. (7") *(PB 5082)* **MY LOVE IS LIKE A RED RED ROSE. / PINCH OF SNUFF** ☐ ☐

May 78. (lp/c) *(PL/PK 25150)* **EARL O' MORAY** ☐ ☐
– My love is like a red, red rose / Sheriffmuir / The child on the road / The bonnie Earl o' Moray / The trooper and the maid / The beef- can close / Jackson and Jane / Freedom come-all-ye.

— **SAM BRUCKEN** (b. England) – vocals, guitar (ex-THERAPY) repl. GAUGHAN whose daughter took ill; he subsequently went solo and rejoined The BOYS FROM THE LOUGH for a short-time

Topic not iss.

1979. (lp) *(12TS 406)* **A BUNCH OF FIVES** ☐ ☐
– I'll lay you down / Man from God knows where / Maggie Lauder / Satan will appear / House of Airlie / Paddy's green shamrock shore / The land of Leal.

— split in the early 80's

– compilations, etc. –

Sep 80. (lp) *R.C.A.; (PL 25267)* **NOTHING BUT THE BEST** ☐ ☐
– The bonnie Earl o' Moray / Bratach bana / P stands for Paddy / Both sides of the Forth / Carrickfergus / My love is like a red red rose / Freedom come-all-ye / The knight and the shepherd's daughter / Sheriff Muir / Frankie's dog.

FOLLOW THAT CAMEL (see under ⇒ Iona records)

Jennifer FORREST . . . (see under ⇒ Macmeanmna records)

FOUNDRY BAR BAND (see under ⇒ Springthyme records)

Allie FOX (see under ⇒ Vixen records)

Gillian FRAME & BACK OF THE MOON (see under ⇒ Tartan Tapes records)

Alasdair FRASER

Born: 14 May'55, Clackmannan. Widely versed in Scotland's fiddling tradition, ALASDAIR FRASER is renowned as not only a consummate recording and performing artist but a respected fiddle teacher. His recording career began in 1983 with the 'PORTRAIT OF A SCOTTISH FIDDLER' album, FRASER subsequently setting up the 'Culburnie' label both as an outlet for his own work and as a showcase for native talent.

The first release was a collaborative album with longtime US-born associate PAUL MACHLIS entitled 'SKYEDANCE' (1987), a moniker FRASER would later adopt for his millennial Celtic supergroup. The early 90's saw him teaming up with guitarist JODY STECHER on 'THE DRIVEN BOW' as well as completing another project with MACHLIS entitled 'THE ROAD NORTH'. Equally adept at atmospheric Gaelic laments and classically-styled airs as fiery reels, FRASER has had his compositions featured on a variety of Celtic/New Age compilation albums and has contributed solo violin to the soundtracks of such Hollywood blockbusters as 'Last Of The Mohicans' and 'Titanic'.

1995 saw the release of his 'DAWN DANCE' opus, an entirely self-composed album which combined folk, baroque, rock and medieval influences and was awarded the NAIRD Indie Award for best Celtic album in 1996. The record's success encouraged FRASER to form SKYEDANCE along with piper ERIC RIGLER (who himself has recorded with the likes of MIKE OLDFIELD and TRACY CHAPMAN and performed on the 'Braveheart' soundtrack) and bassist MICK LINDEN, the 6-piece recording 'WAY OUT TO HOPE STREET' in 1997.

Following on from a collaboration with top Scots guitarist TONY McMANUS, 'RETURN TO KINTAIL' (1999), FRASER marshalled his SKYEDANCE troops for 'LABYRINTH' (2000), an album which combined traditional Scottish fare with various strands of world music. The new millennium also saw ALASDAIR (in tandem with MACHLIS) returning to his fiddle roots with 'LEGACY OF THE SCOTTISH FIDDLE: VOLUME 1' (2001), the first in a new series aiming to explore Scotland's rich fiddle heritage. In addition to these albums, his Californian-based label, 'Culburnie' (www.culburnie.com), is home to such talented artists as CHRISTINE KYDD, CHANTAN, The CAST, BACHUE, ABBY NEWTON (a New York-born cellist who has worked with FRASER himself, PAUL MACHLIS, JEAN REDPATH, KATE McGARRIGLE and TOM ANDERSON as well as performing in many chamber and symphony orchestras), ANDY SHANKS and JIM RUSSELL. In 2002, SKYEDANCE returned to the recording front via an exotic set of adrenaline-fuelled tunes, 'LIVE IN SPAIN'; it boasted the aid of Galician, Asturian and Basque singers and musicians:- MERCEDES PEON, HEVIA, JOSE MANUEL TEJEDOR, KEPA JUNKERA, MIKEL LABOA, JOXAN GOIKOETXEA and OREKA TX.

ALASDAIR FRASER – fiddle, viola / with guests

Ross not iss.

Nov 83. (lp/c) *(WGR/CWGR 063)* **PORTRAIT OF A SCOTTISH FIDDLER** ☐ ☐
– Sands of Murness / Auld Willie Hunter / The acrobat / The Shelburne reel – Ganam (hornpipe & reel medley) / Tog orm mo phiob (lift to me my pipes) – Braigh Loch Iall (the braes of Loch Eil) – Miss Brady (lament, air & reel medley) / Mrs. E.M. Ross's welcome to Kiltarlity cottage – The Kirrie Kebbuck – Culburnie cottage (March, Strathspey & reel medley) / The weeping birches of Kilmorack (slow air) / Miss MacPherson Grant – Miss Wharton Duff – MacCrimmon's lament (lament) / J.F. Dickie's delight – J.F. Dickie's reel (slow Strathspey & reel medley) / Allan's

reel – Acheson – Fiddler's whim – Kiley's reel (reel, jig & reel medley) / The nameless lassie (slow air) / The braes of Castle Grant – Captain Horne – Morning music, the apple tree (March, Strathspey & reel medley) / The vale (pastoral) / The mathematician – Sir David Davidson of Cantray (hornpipe & reel medley). *(re-iss. Jul95 on 'Culburnie' cd/c; CUL 109 CD/C)*

Culburnie Culburnie

Feb 87. (lp/c; by ALASDAIR FRASER & PAUL MACHLIS)
(CUL/+C 101) **SKYEDANCE** [ ] [-]
– The scolding wives of Abertaff / I'll break your head for you / Catch and kiss the romp / The haggis / Eilean beag donn a' chuain / Slip jig / Skye dance / Nighean donn a' chuailein riomhaich / Ruileadh cailleach sheatadh cailleach / The bird's nest / Harris dance / The "J.B." reel / The shepherdess / The "J.B." reel / Harris dance / Skye dance / Locheil's awa' to France / A nochd gur faoin mo chadal dhomh. *(cd-iss. Oct95; CUL 101CD)*

— next with **JODY STECHER** – guitar

1992. (cd/c; by ALASDAIR FRASER & JODY STECHER)
(CUL CD/C 102) **THE DRIVEN BOW** [ ] [ ]
– Lady Louisa Gordon / Mrs. Garden of Troup / The fisher's wedding / Lady Harriet Hope / The mill of Laggan / Blue bonnets over the border / There was an old woman tossed up in a blanket 17 times as high as the Moon / The rock and the wee pickle tow / Jessie Smith / The braes of Mar / Jenny Dang the weaver / Pretty Peggy / Domhnall dubh / The nine pint coggie / Ladar mor a' chogain / Calum Findlay / Father John MacMillan of Barra / The devil in the kitchen / Miss Drummond of Perth / Mackinnon's rant / Traditional reel / Margaree reel / The conundrum / The sprig of Ivy / Captain Campbell / Calum Breugach / King George IV / The king's reel / Old time wedding reels / The Cape Breton symphony's welcome to the Shetland Isles / Father Francis Cameron / Sandy McIntyre's trip to Boston / The Lea rig / The McNeils of Ugadale / Dr. Angus and Emily MacDonald's trip to San Francisco. *(re-iss. Jul95; same)*

— in the 90's, he also collaborated with pianist PAUL MACHLIS on the album, 'THE ROAD NORTH', issued on 'Sona Gaia'

Jul 95. (cd/c) *(<CUL 106 D/C>)* **DAWN DANCE** [ ] [ ]
– First light – Dawn rant / Dawn dance / Wooden whale – Leaps & bounds – Skye barbeque / Stratherrick / Funky 105 / Rain on Rannoch / Common ground / Eilidh's frolic / Sally mo ghradh / Independence trail – Galen's arrival / Pamela Rose Grant / Free rein / Theme for Scotland.

below **SKYEDANCE** were **FRASER, RIGLER, MACHLIS, CHRIS NORMAN, MICK LINDEN + PETER MAUND**

Sep 97. (cd/c; by SKYEDANCE) *(<CUL 111 CD/C>)* **WAY OUT TO HOPE STREET** [ ] [ ]
– Way out to Hope Street / Walking the plank / Donostia / Year's turning / Midnight on Raasay – The Braemar cappuccino / Dizzy / Stoney run / The lupine / Dark jewel / Tathaich nam fonn (A song-haunted place) / The Skyedance reels: Ruilleadh cailleach – The bird's nest – Harris dance / Skerray / Reel de Flores / Bannockburn.

— next with **TONY McMANUS** – guitar

Jun 99. (cd; by ALASDAIR FRASER & TONY McMANUS)
(<CUL 113D>) **RETURN TO KINTAIL** [ ] [ ]
– Bidh clann Ulaidh (Men of Ulster) / Ross' reel no.4 – Reichswall Forest / Roslin castle – Miss Gordon of Gight / The marquis of Huntly – The ewie wi' the crooked horn – John Cheap the Chapman – Peerie weerie – West Mabou reel / Calum Sgaire / Donald Willie and his dog – Alex MacDonald – Chloe's passion / Lady Louisa Gordon's Strathspey – The Highlands of Banffshire – The merrymaking / Seathan – Na goisidich (The gossips) / Sitting in the stern of a boat / A mhaighdean mhara (The mermaid) / Lieutenant Maguire's jig – The curlew – Sleepy Maggie – Tail toddle / The sweetness of Mary – Devil in the kitchen – Willie Davie – The sound of Mull – The high road to Linton / Theidh mi dhachaigh (Return to Kintail).

— **FRASER, RIGLER, LINDEN, MACHLIS + CHRIS NORMAN**

Feb 00. (cd; as SKYEDANCE) *(<CUL 116CD>)* **LABYRINTH** [ ] [ ]
– The spark / La gallega / Till October / Cat in a bag / Fite fuaite / The iron ring – The boxwood reel / The other side of sorrow / Inside the shadows / When she drives / Into the labyrinth / Ariadne's thread / The Pentz road / Evensong.

Jan 01. (cd; as ALASDAIR FRASER & PAUL MACHLIS) *(<CUL 118CD>)* **LEGACY OF THE SCOTTISH FIDDLE – Volume 1** [ ] [ ]
– Miss Dumbreck – Miss Cameron of Balvenie (Marshall) – Clydeside lassies / The auld brig o' Don / The beauty of the north (Mais' an Taobh Tuath) / Madame Neruda / Chapel Keithack – Belmont / Earl Haig / Earl Grey – The left handed fiddler / Rose-acre / Craigellachie Brig – Largo's fairy dance / The ancient barons of Kilravock (Barain Chulrabhaig) / Mrs. McPherson of Gibton – The novelty (Nuaghalachd) / Lady Charlotte Campbell's new strathspey (Robert Mackintosh) – Lady Charlotte Campbell's reel / Miss Hannah of Elgin – Sir George Clark of Penicuik / Major L. Stewart of the island of Java reel / Mrs. Jamieson's favourite Charles Grant / The rose-bud of Allenvale / Seann triubhais uilleachain (Willie's auld trews) / Da forfeit o' da ship – Da grocer – Jack is yet alive / Mr.A.Q. Wilken's favourite – Jenny Hardie's reel / Mrs. Major L. Stewart of the island of Java / The iron man – The Smith's a gallant fireman – The Forth-Bridge reel Williamson Blyth – Gillan's reel Peter Milne – The auld wheel / Niel Gow's lament for the death of his second wife.

— added **PETER MAUND** – percussion

May 02. (cd; by SKYEDANCE) *(<CUL 119>)* **LIVE IN SPAIN (live)** [ ] [ ]
– Harris dance / Dizzy / Marabilla / Dinkey's medley / Cries and shrieks of woe / A stor mo chroi / Stoney run / The spark / Way out to Hope Street / Theme for Scotland / Donostia / Txoria txori / The other side of sorrow / Galen's medley / Tail toddle finale.

– others, etc. –

Mar 98. (cd; by ALASDAIR FRASER & PAUL MACHLIS)
Narada; (24384553920) **THE ROAD NORTH** [ ] [-]

Iain FRASER (see under ⇒ BARBOUR, Freeland)

Gregor FULLARTON (see ⇒ End Folk 2)

GABERLUNZIE (see under ⇒ Lochshore records)

GAUGERS

Formed: North East Scotland . . . mid-70's by ARTHUR WATSON, TOM SPIERS and PETER HALL, all fine vocalists and musicians of the traditional Scottish folk ilk. In the mid-70's the GAUGERS surfaced on the legendary 'Topic' label, whilst later releases were on 'Springthyme' and c/o Aberdeen Council Libraries.

ARTHUR WATSON – vocals, whistle / **TOM SPIERS** – vocals, fiddle, viola / **PETER HALL** – vocals, concertina, melodeon, keyboards

Topic not iss.

1976. (lp) *(12TS 284)* **BEWARE OF THE ABERDONIAN** [ ] [-]
– Young Jackie / The cruel brother / Monymusk lads / The keys to the cellar – Go to Berwick, Johnnie / The lass o' Moorland hills / The bonnie lass o' Anglesey / Sleep sound in the morning – Donald Blue / The Aberdonian / Lochaber no more / The minister's sheep / Bogie's bonnie belle / The ewe wi' the crookit horn – The jolly shepherd – Polly Stewart / The scranky black farmer. *(cd-iss. Mar01 on 'Sleepytown'; SLPYCD 008)*

Springthyme not iss.

Feb 90. (c) *(SPRC 1031)* **THE FIGHTING SCOT** [ ] [-]
– Banks of Sicily / Johnnie Gallagher / Battle of Harlaw / Pretty Polly / List bonnie lassie / The trumpet sounds / Charles Edward Stewart's welcome – Killiecrankie / Martinmas time / Haughs o' Cromdale / Will ye go tae Flanders / Scots wha ha'e / The Forfar sodger / Pills of white mercury / Ower the water – Three good fellows – Sherriffmuir / The baron o' Brackley / The deadly wars. *(cd-iss. Jun94 on 'City Arts'; SLPYCD 002)*

City Arts not iss.

Jun 94. (cd) *(CACD 101)* **AWA WI' THE ROVIN' SAILOR** [ ] [-]
– Come a' ye fisher lassies / Herrin' is the king of the sea / Ogilvie's boat / Grey selchie of Sule Skerry / Lovely Nancy – Far from home / The Boddammers hinged the monkey / The diamond ship / The handsome cabin boy / Will your anchor hold? / Tatties & herrin' / Haul away the bowline / The bold Princess Royal / Barnacle waltz – Steamboat waltz / Farewell tae Tarwaithie / The Gauger / The sweet kumadee / Rolling home.

– compilations, etc. –

Mar 01. (cd) *Sleepytown; (SLPYCD 009)* **NO MORE FOREVER**
(outtakes, demos, live & rare tracks) [ ] [-]
– Monymusk lads / Mains o' Culsh / Bonnie Udny / The Maskin rung / The gypsy laddies / Absence / Mulnabeeny / Tae the beggin' / Fair Ellen / The merchant's son / The cuckoo's nest / The jolly beggar / The bleached mute / The present time is ours.

Dick GAUGHAN

Born: RICHARD PETER GAUGHAN, 17 May'48, Glasgow. Raised in Leith, Edinburgh since he was a toddler, the teenage GAUGHAN was influenced by local heroes of the folk revival such as BERT JANSCH, HAMISH IMLACH and ARCHIE FISHER. His own recording career began in 1972 with the Bill Leader-produced 'NO MORE FOREVER' album, the same year DICK was to become a member of Scots-Irish troupe BOYS OF THE LOUGH. His tenure was brief, however, as he subsequently helped found folk-rock group FIVE HAND REEL, featuring on 'Five Hand Reel' (1976), 'For A' That' (1977) and 'Earl O' Moray' (1978).

Having already recorded a follow-up solo set with 1977's 'KIST O' GOLD', DICK struck out on his own once more with 'COPPERS AND BRASS' (1978) featuring guitar interpretations of traditional Scots/Irish jigs and reels. 1981's 'HANDFUL OF EARTH' album finally established him as a voice on the modern folk scene, the man's staunch Socialist views espoused in the likes of 'THE WORKER'S SONG'. Indeed, the following year's 'SONGS

OF EWAN MacCOLL' was a tribute to one of GAUGHAN's equally hard line political antecedents. 1983's 'PARALLEL LINES' was a collaboration with London-Irish folk veteran ANDY IRVINE while GAUGHAN was to work with none other than BERT JANSCH – as well as RAB NOAKES and RORY McLEOD – on 1988's 'WOODY LIVES', a one-off tribute to another legendary musical/political agitator, WOODY GUTHRIE.

Although he wasn't quite so prolific in the 90's, DICK continued to interpret traditional Scottish music in his own unique, striking and often innovative style, cutting a couple of albums for the native 'Greentrax' label. The more recent of these, the reflective 'REDWOOD CATHEDRAL' (1998), featured interesting renditions of Townes Van Zandt's 'PANCHO & LEFTY' and The Byrds' 'Turn, Turn, Turn', demonstrating GAUGHAN's original approach to contemporary folk. His session work has included DAVY SPILLANE's 'Summerlee' set and BILLY BRAGG's 'The Internationale'; he also guested on 'The Back O' The North Wind' by BRIAN McNEILL.

In November 2001, GAUGHAN issued the hushed and beautiful 'OUTLAWS AND DREAMERS', a part folksy/part contemporay collection of tracks with minimal production values, and virtually just himself plucking the guitar. Accompaniment came from former BATTLEFIELD BAND fiddler BRIAN McNEILL (who joined GAUGHAN after working with him on the aforementioned '. . .North Wind' set), and added that melancholic tenderness that was sometimes missing from his earlier work. The set, overall, produced an earthy, Celtic atmosphere that did justice to GAUGHAN's dreamy and gentle songwriting.

• **Covered:** LAND OF THE NORTH WIND (Allan Taylor) / RUBY TUESDAY (Rolling Stones) / WAIST DEEP IN THE BIG MUDDY (Pete Seeger) / GERONIMO'S CADILLAC (Michael J. Murphy & Charles Quattro) / 1952 VINCENT BLACK LIGHTNING (Richard Thompson) and some lyrics by HAMISH HENDERSON / MUIR AND THE MASTER BUILDER + EWEN AND THE GOLD (Brian McNeill) / GONE, GONNA RISE AGAIN (Si Kahn) / RECONCILLIATION (Ron Kavana) / THOMAS MUIR OF HUNTERSHILL (Adam McNaughtan) / OCTOBER SONG (Robin Williamson) / LET IT BE ME (Becaud, Delanoe & Curtis) / FINE HORSEMEN (Lal Waterson).

DICK GAUGHAN – vocals, guitars / with various friends inc. **ALY BAIN** – fiddle

Leader not iss.

1972. (lp) *(LER 2072)* **NO MORE FOREVER** -
– Rattlin' roarin' Willie – The friar's britches / MacCrimmon's lament – Mistress Jamieson's favourite / Jock o' Hazeldean / Cam ye ower frae France / The bonnie banks o' Fordie / The thatchers o' Glenrae / The fair flower of Northumberland / The teatotaller – Da tushker / The three healths / The John MacLean march / The green linnet. *(re-iss. Jun91 lp/c/cd; LER/+C/CD 2072) (cd re-iss. Dec97; same)*

— DICK joined BOYS OF THE LOUGH then FIVE HAND REEL before going solo again

1977. (lp) *(LER 2103)* **KIST O' GOLD** -
– The Earl of Errol / The Granemore hare / Rigs o' Rye / The gipsy laddies / Lord Randal / Maggie Lauder – Cathaoir an Iarla (The Earl's chair) / Banks of green willow / 51st Highland Division's farewell to Sicily / The city of Savannah – Ril gan ainm / Raglan road / Johnny miner / The ballad of accounting. *(re-iss. Sep85; same)*

— with **TOM HICKLAND** – piano (of FIVE HAND REEL)

Topic not iss.

1978. (lp) *(12TS 315)* **COPPERS AND BRASS: SCOTS & IRISH DANCE MUSIC ON GUITAR** -
– Jigs: Coppers and brass – The gander in the pratie hole / Reels: O'Keefe's – The foxhunter's / Hornpipes: The flowing tide – The fairies' hornpipe / Reels: The oak tree – The music in the glen / Planxty Johnson / Slip jig: Gurty's frolics / Reels: The spey in spate – The hurricane / 6/8 marches: Alan MacPherson of Mosspark – The jig of slurs / Reels: The thrush in the storm – The flogging reel / 12-8 jig and reels: Ask my father – Lads of Laoise – The Connaught heifers / Reels: The bird in the bush – The boy in the gap – MacMahon's reel / Jigs: Strike the gay harp – The shores of Lough Gowna / Shetland reels: Jack broke da prison door – Donald blue – Wha'll dance wi' Wattie. *(c-iss.Nov88 on 'Ossian'; OSS 41C) (<cd-iss. Dec92 on 'Green Linnet'; GLCD 3064>)*

— with **BARRY LYONS** – bass (of FIVE HAND REEL, ex-TREES, ex-MR.FOX)

1978. (lp) *(12TS 384)* **GAUGHAN** -
– Bonnie Jeannie o' Belthelnie / Bonnie lass amang the heather / Crooked Jack / The recruited collier / The pound a week rise / My Donald / Willie o' Winsbury / Such a parcel o' rogues in a nation / Gillie Mhor. *(cd-iss. Nov90 +=; TSCD 384)*Bonnie woodha' / The Auchengeich disaster / 6-8 marches: Alan MacPherson of Mosspark – The jig of slurs / 12-8 jig and reels: Ask my father – Lads of Laoise – The Connaught heifers / Jigs: Strike the gay harp – Shores of Lough Gowna / Shetland reels: Jack broke the prison door – Donald blue – Wha'll dance wi' Wattie.

— next with **BRIAN McNEILL, PHIL CUNNINGHAM + STEWART ISBISTER**

1981. (lp) *(12TS 419)* **HANDFUL OF EARTH** -
– Erin-go-bragh / Now westlin winds / Craigie hill / World turned upside down / The snows they smelt the soonest / Lough Erne – First kiss at parting / Scojun waltz – Randers hopsa / A song for Ireland / The worker's song / Both sides of the Tweed. *(cd-iss. Oct89; TSCD 419) (c-iss.Nov90; KTSC 419) <US cd-iss. 1990's on 'Green Linnet'; GLCD 3062>*

Rubber not iss.

Jun 82. (lp; by DICK GAUGHAN, DAVE BURLAND & TONY CAPSTICK) *(RUB 027)* **SONGS OF EWAN MacCOLL** (rec. 1978) -
– Ballad of accounting / Moving-on song / Jamie Foyers / Freeborn man / The Manchester rambler / Schooldays end / Thirty-foot trailer / The big hewer / The first time ever I saw your face / Sweet Thames flow softly / Shoals of herring. *(re-iss. Jun88 on 'Black Crow' lp/c; CRO/+C 215) (cd-iss. Jul97; CROCD 215)*

— next with **ANDY IRVINE** – bouzouki, mandolin, harmonica, vocals / **BOB LENOX** – piano / **MARTIN BUSCHMANN** – sax / **NOLLAIGH NI CATHASAIGH** – fiddle / **JUDITH JAENICKE** – flute

Folk Freak not iss.

1983. (lp; as DICK GAUGHAN & ANDY IRVINE) *(FF 4007)* **PARALLEL LINES** -
– The Creggan white hare / The lads o' the fair – Leith docks / At twenty-one / My back pages – Afterthoughts / The dodgers song / Captain Thunderbolt / Captain Colston / Floo'ers o' the forest. *(cd-iss. Oct89 on 'Wundertuter'; CDTUT72 4007) <US cd-iss. 1990 on 'Green Linnet'; SIF 3201>*

— with **DAVE TULLOCH** – percussion / **DAVE PEGG** – bass / **WILL LINDFORS** – drums, percussion / **LENOX / ALAN TALL** – sax + **JUDY SWEENEY**

Celtic Music not iss.

Sep 84. (lp/c) *(CM/+C 017)* **A DIFFERENT KIND OF LOVE SONG** -
– A different kind of love song / Revolution / Prisoner 562 / Song of choice / The father's song / Think again / As I walked on the road / Stand up for Judas / By the people / Games people play. *(cd-iss. Dec97; CMCD 017) (cd-iss. Nov97 on 'Appleseed'; APRCD 1018)*

Dec 84. (7") *(CMS 300)* **GAMES PEOPLE PLAY. / A DIFFERENT KIND OF LOVE SONG** -

1985. (lp) *(CM 030)* **LIVE IN EDINBURGH (live)** -
– Revolution / Now westlin' winds / Which side are you on? / Victor Jara of Chile / Companeros / Workers song / Your daughters and your sons / Four green fields / Ballad of accounting / Jamie Foyers / Glenlogie / World turned upsidedown. *(cd/c-iss.Dec97; CMCD/CMC 030)*

— next with **CLARKE SORLEY, ALLAN TALL, JIM SUTHERLAND + BILLY JACKSON**

S.T.U.C. not iss.

1986. (lp) *(STUC 2)* **TRUE AND BOLD: SONGS OF THE SCOTTISH MINERS** -
– Miner's life is like a sailor's / Schoolday's end / Farewell to 'Cotia / Auchengeich disaster / Pund a week rise / Collier laddie / Which side are you on? / Drunk rent collector / Blantyre explosion / One miner's life / Ballad of '84. *(cd-iss. Dec97; STUCCD 2)*

Folk Freak not iss.

1988. (lp; by DICK GAUGHAN & LEON ROSSELSON) *(FF 4010)* **SONGS FOR PEACE** -

— In Jun'88, GAUGHAN featured on 4 tracks from the 'WOODY LIVES' Various Artists compilation for 'Black Crow' *(CRO/+C/CD 217)*

Celtic Music not iss.

Oct 89. (lp) *(CM 041)* **CALL IT FREEDOM** -
– Bulmer's fancy – The silver spire / Shipwreck / What you do with what you've got / Ludlow massacre / That's the way the river flows / Amandial / Call it freedom / When I'm gone / Seven good soldiers / Fifty years from now – Yardheads.

Impetus not iss.

1990. (lp; by DICK GAUGHAN & KEN HYDER) *(IMP 18506)* **FANFARE FOR TOMORROW** (rec. March 1985) -
– Sharpeville / Liberation / Fanfare for tomorrow / Political prisoners / Salute to Pitheid & Clachan / News from nowhere. *(cd-iss. Aug98; IMPCD 18506)*

Greentrax Greentrax

Jun 96. (cd/c) *(<CD/C TRAX 109>)* **SAIL ON**
– Land of the north wind / Son of man / Ruby Tuesday / Waist deep in the big muddy / No cause for alarm / The sist (Highland) Division's farewell to Sicily / No gods & precious few heroes / Geronimo's cadillac / 1952 Vincent Black lightning / Sail on / The freedom come-all-ye.

Greentrax Appleseed

Nov 98. (cd) *(CDTRAX 158) <1027>* **REDWOOD CATHEDRAL**
– Muir & the master builder / Gone, gonna rise again / Reconciliation / Why old men cry / Thomas Muir of Huntershill / October song / Ewen & the gold / Let it be me / All the king's horses / Pancho & Lefty / Turn, turn, turn (to everything there is a season) / Fine horseman.

Oct 01. (cd) *(CDTRAX 222) <1058>* **OUTLAWS AND DREAMERS** Nov01
– The yew tree / Florence in Florence / Dowie dens o' Yarrow / Tom Joad / Outlaws and dreamers / When I'm gone / John Harrison's hands / What you do with what you've got / Tom Paine's bones / Strong women rule us all / Wild roses.

Sep 02. (d-cd) *(CDTRAX 236D)* **PRENTICE PIECE (THE FIRST THREE DECADES)** (compilation)
– Sail on / Florence in Florence / The Auchengeich disaster / Land of the north wind / The wind that shakes the barley / Games people play / Muir and the master builder / Willie o' Winsbury / Both sides the Tweed / The father's song / Strike the gay harp – Shores of Loch Gowna / The cruel brother / October song / Lassie, lie near me / The

pound a week rise / Why old men cry / The yew tree / Floo'ers o' the forest / 51st (Highland) Division's farewell to Sicily / Scojun waltz – Randers hospa / Outlaws and dreamers.

CLAN ALBA

DICK GAUGHAN, MARY MacMASTER, BRIAN McNEILL, FRED MORRISON, PATSY SEDDON, DAVY STEELE, MIKE TRAVIS + DAVE TULLOCH

Clan Alba not iss.

1995. (d-cd) *(CLANCD 001)* **CLAN ALBA** ☐ [-]
– Five to six / Dressed to kill (incl. The scarlet coat) / Harpset: Hopscotch with Jenny – Trip to Gorthleck – The girl with the flowing arms – Travis's fancy / Oran na cloiche (The song of the stone) / Lark and the bowman / Cam ye owre frae France / True Thomas / Fred's jigs (incl. Alex MacDonald) // Bye, bye, big blue / Air a' ghille tha mo run (I love the boy) / Clan Alba: Clan Alba march – Lexy MacAskill – Latha siubhal beinne dhomh – Hawk hornpipe / No gonnae leave here / Growing wings / Canan nan gaidheal (The language of the Gael) / Tar the house: Tar the house – Lament for Ronald MacDonald of Morar the traditional / Childhood's end.

GHILLIES (see under ⇒ Greentrax records)

Phamie GOW (see under ⇒ Greentrax records)

Davey GRAHAM

Born: 22 Nov'40, Leicester. Born to a Scottish father and a Guyanese mother, DAVY was brought up in London's 'Notting Hill', a cauldron of racial ferment in the 50's. By all accounts, the young DAVY was a withdrawn and enigmatic figure, characteristics which would mark him out from the majority of 50's/60's folkies and which would forever cast him in the role of the revival's shadowy outsider. He was nevertheless an innovator and regarded by many as the founder of the folk guitar instrumental.

After leaving school in 1958, he was one of the first of the new generation of young folk players to hit the beatnik trail to Paris and then on to Morocco where he absorbed exotic tunings and Arabic modal styles. In summer '59, GRAHAM's technical virtuosity was exposed to the nation via a BBC documentary, 'Hound Dogs and Bach Addicts'; in the company of LONNIE DONEGAN, BERT WEEDON etc, DAVY proceeded to thrill viewers with a revelatory blues/fingerstyle arrangement of 'CRY ME A RIVER', a song featured on his debut album, 'THE GUITAR PLAYER' (1961). Prior to this, GRAHAM had issued a split EP with ALEXIS KORNER, '3/4 A.D.', which included perhaps his most famous track, 'ANGI', a pioneering concoction of baroque, folk, blues and jazz later covered by BERT JANSCH and PAUL SIMON amongst others. KORNER was something of a mentor for GRAHAM and though he was to eventually follow a folk rather than blues path, he did appear briefly in the line-up of KORNER's BLUES INCORPORATED (and later in JOHN MAYALL'S BLUESBREAKERS).

In 1965, GRAHAM released 'FOLK, BLUES & BEYOND . . .' on 'Decca', a pivotal record for the new breed of young folk musicians and a platform for his jazz-influenced, oriental-inspired, alternately tuned artistry. The 'FOLK ROOTS, NEW ROUTES' album, released just a month later, was equally influential, an unlikely collaboration with Sussex traditional singer, 'SHIRLEY COLLINS' which had begun as a one-off concert. Yet around this time, GRAHAM followed in the footsteps of his jazz heroes by cultivating a heroin habit. A combination of the drugs and frequent trips abroad conspired to keep him as elusive a figure as ever and, with the advent of The BEATLES, THE BYRDS, etc, all experimenting with Eastern influences, GRAHAM had serious competition. He also had competition from the likes of BERT JANSCH, who developed a more accessible brand of guitar experimentation. While DAVY was still a massive draw and hypnotic performer at hip Soho clubs like Les Cousins, the awkward uncommerciality of his music didn't help him sell albums.

He recorded only sporadically throughout the 70's (a couple with his wife HOLLY GWINN in 1970) and not at all during the 80's, ill health curtailing much of his activities. A familiar face on the Edinburgh/Glasgow axis of the folk revival, DAVEY GRAHAM (as he was preferrably billed since the mid-70's) subsequently returned to Scotland where he taught guitar and occasionally performed – he's now back in London
. • **Note:** His 60's LP's are worth a tidy sum – mint.

DAVEY GRAHAM

DAVEY GRAHAM – vocals, acoustic guitar

Golden Guinea not iss.

1961. (lp) *(GGL 0224)* **THE GUITAR PLAYER** ☐ [-]
– Don't stop the carnival / Sermonette / Take five / How long, how long blues / Sunset eyes / Cry me a river / The ruby and the pearl Buffalo / Exodus theme / Yellow bird / Blues for Betty / Hallelujah, I love her so. *(cd-iss. Jun92 on 'See For Miles'+=; SEECD 351)* – Angle / 3/4 a.d. / Davy's train blues.

Topic not iss.

1962. (7"ep; as DAVEY GRAHAM & ALEXIS KORNER) *(TOP 70)* **3/4 A.D.** ☐ [-]
– 3/4 A.D. / Angle / (+ 2 others by ALEXIS KORNER).

Decca London

1963. (7"ep; shared w/ THAMESIDERS) *(DFE 8538)* **FROM A LONDON HOOTENANNY** ☐ [-]

1965. (lp) *(LK 4649)* **FOLK, BLUES AND BEYOND** ☐ [-]
– Leavin' blues / Cocaine / Sally free and easy / Black is the colour of true love's hair / Rock me baby / Seven gypsies / Ballad of the sad young men / Play-out piece / Moanin / Skillet / Ain't nobody's business if I do / Maajun / I can't keep from crying sometimes / Don't think twice, it's all right / My babe / Goin' down slow / Better git it in your soul. *(cd-iss. Oct91 on 'Deram'; 820988-2)* *(<cd re-iss. Jul99 on 'Topic'; TSCD 820>)*

1965. (lp; by SHIRLEY COLLINS / DAVEY GRAHAM) *(LK 4652)* **FOLK ROOTS, NEW ROUTES** ☐ [-]
– Nottamun town / Proud Maisrie / The cherry tree carol / Blue monk / Hares on the mountain / Reynardine / Pretty Saro / Rif mountain / Jane, Jane / Love is pleasin' / Boll Weevil, holler / Hori horo / Bad cgirl / Lord Gregory / Grooveyard / Dearest dear. *(re-iss. 1981 on 'Righteous'; GDC 001)*

Jul 66. (lp) *(LK 4780)* **MIDNIGHT MAN** ☐ [-]
– No preacher blues / The fakir / I'm looking through you / Hummingbird / Watermelon man / Stormy Monday / Money honey / Walking the dog / Fire in my soul / Lost lover blues / Neighbour, neighbour / Jubilation / Bags any old iron / Jelly roll baker.

Oct 68. (7") *(F 12841)* **BOTH SIDES NOW. / TRISTANO** ☐ [-]

Jan 69. (lp; mono/stereo) *(LK/SKL 4969)* *<PS 552>* **LARGE AS LIFE AND TWICE AS NATURAL** ☐ ☐
– Both sides now / Bad boy blues / Tristano / Babe, it ain't no lie / Bruton town / Sunshine raga / Freight train blues / Jenra / Electric chair / Good morning blues / Beautiful city / Blue raga.

Nov 69. (lp; mono/stereo) *(LK/SKL 5011)* **HAT** ☐ [-]
– Getting better / Lotus blossom / I'm ready / Buhaina chant / Homeward bound / Love is pleasing / Hornpipe for harpsichord played upon guitar / Down along the cove / Hoochie coochie man / Stan's guitar / Pretty Polly / Bulgarian dance / I am a rock / Oliver.

1970. (lp) *(SKL 5056)* **THE HOLLY KALEIDOSCOPE** ☐ [-]
– Flowers never bend with the rainfall / Wilt thou unkind / Blackbird / Blues at Gino's / Since I fell for you / Sunny moon for two / Fingerbuster / Here, there and everywhere / Ramblin' sailor / Mary, open the door / I know my love / Charlie / Bridge over troubled water / Little man you've had a busy day.

—— next with his wife **HOLLY** – vocals / **KESHAV SATHE** – tabla, tambura / **EDDIE TRIPP** – bass / **TONY KINSEY** – drums

President not iss.

1970. (lp; as DAVEY GRAHAM & HOLLY) *(PTLS 1039)* **GODINGTON BOUNDRY** [ ] [-]
– I'm a freeborn man (of the travelling people) / Preacher / All of me / Afta / On Green Dolphin Street / Dallas rag / Round midnight / Worksong / Joe Joe the cannibal kid / Everything's fine right now / Mighty fortress is our god (eine festeburg is unser gott) / Mother nature's son / Grooveyard / Forty ton parachute / Nadu silma. *(re-iss. May88; same) (cd-iss. May99 & May02 on 'See For Miles'; SEECD 693)*

DAVEY GRAHAM

— was now preferred as his christian name

— **ROGER BUNN** – bass; repl. TRIPP + KINSEY

Eron not iss.

1976. (lp) *(ERON 007)* **ALL THAT MOODY** [ ] [-]
– Fingerbuster / Smooth one / To find the sun / Tristano, etc. / Anji / Travelling man / Sunshine raga / Kim / La morena / Preacher blues. *(re-iss. Sep85 lp/c; ERON 007 LP/CA) (re-iss. Nov98 on 'Rollercoaster'; ROLL 2023) (cd-iss. Jul99 +=; RCCD 3022)* – Travellin' man / Blue raga / All of me / Suite in D-minor / Happy meeting in glory / Jenra / Gold ring / For a princess.

Kicking Mule Kicking Mule

Jan 78. (lp) *(SNKF 138)* **THE COMPLETE GUITARIST** [ ] [-]
– Lord Mayo – Lord Inchiquin / Lashtail's room / Ein feste burg (a mighty fortress in our God) / The road to Lisdoonvarna (jig & reel) / Renaissance piece / Hardiman the fiddler / Sarah / Frieze britches / Blues for Gino / The hunter's purse / Prelude from the suite in D minor / Fairies hornpipe Forty-ton parachute / The gold ring / Down Ampney / Banish misfortune. *(<cd-iss. Jul99 +=; KMCD 3914>)* – Dance for two people / Bloody fields of France / Happy meeting in glory / Farewell to the creeks.

— in Sep'78, GRAHAM featured on the LP, 'IRISH REELS, JIGS, HORNPIPES & AIRS' on 'Kicking Mule' *(SNKF 153)*

Nov 79. (lp) *(SNKF 158) <KM 161>* **DANCE FOR TWO PEOPLE** [ ] [ ]
– Dance for two people / Bloody fields of Flanders / Indian piece / Lute prelude / She moved through the bizarre / Minuets I & II / Reng / Breath on me breath of God / El cafe de Chinitas / Happy meeting in glory / Farewell to the creeks / Yemeni tagism / Mna na Heireann / Kim / Lady Hunsdon's puffe / Wash nha home / Two hymns / Uskudar. *(re-iss. Mar89; same as US)*

Crackin' Up not iss.

Apr 93. (cd/c) *(CRACKPROBE CD/CASS 034)* **PLAYING IN TRAFFIC** [ ] [-]
– Jinaco / Amalia / Joy of my heart (eilean mo chridh) / Majuun / Aydede / Sita ram / Arioso / Rain and snow / Kitty's rambles / Bury my body / The ram in the thicket / Don't let your deal go down / Buhaina chant / The preacher / Somethin' / The King of Denmark's galliard / Guardame Las Vacas / Capricho Arabe / Hesamalo / Jenra / Ramkali.

– compilations, etc. –

Aug 86. (lp) *See For Miles; (SEE 48)* **FOLK BLUES AND ALL POINTS IN BETWEEN** [ ] [-]
– Leaving blues / Cocaine / Rock me baby / Moanin' / Skillet / Ain't nobody's business if I do / Maajun(a) taste of Tangier / I can't keep from crying sometimes / Going down slow / Better git it in your soul / Freight train blues / Both sides now / No preacher blues / Bad boy blues / I'm ready / Hoochie coochie man / Blue raga. *(cd-iss. May90; SEECD 48)*

Nov 98. (10"lp) *Rollercoaster; (ROLL 2022)* **AFTER HOURS (live at Hull University)** [ ] [-]
– She moved thru' the bizarre – Blue raga / Bouree in E minor / Buffalo / Jubilation / Cocaine / Grooveyard / Gavotte or bouree / How long blues / Miserlou.

May 99. (cd) *Topic; (TSCD 818)* **FIRE IN THE SOUL** [ ] [-]
– No preacher blues / The fakir / Watermelon man / Money honey / Fire in my soul / Neighbour, neighbour / Jubilation / Angi / Bad boy blues / Tristano / Babe, it ain't no lie / Bruton town / Jenra / I'm ready / Buhaina chant / Hornpipe for harpsichord played upon guitar / Down along the cove / Stan's guitar / Pretty Polly / Bulgarian dance / Oliver / Blues at Gino's / Sunny moon for two / Charlie / Ramblin' sailor.

Angus GRANT (see under ⇒ Springthyme records)

Robin GRAY (see under ⇒ MACLENNAN, Dolina . . .)

GREEN (see under ⇒ Lochshore records)

Gordon GUNN Band (see under ⇒ Greentrax records)

H

Robin HALL & Jimmie MACGREGOR

Born: 27 Jun'37, Edinburgh & 10 Mar'30, Springburn, Glasgow. Although both men studied in Glasgow and each subsequently gravitated to the London folk scene, it took a chance meeting at the 1959 World Youth Festival in Vienna to provide the impetus for their musical partnership. Prior to this, MACGREGOR, a familiar face at EWAN MacCOLL's Ballads & Blues club, had briefly played with both CHAS McDEVITT and the CITY RAMBLERS. HALL, meanwhile, had also been making something of a name for himself as a folk singer on the London coffee bar scene, releasing an album of child ballads, 'LAST LEAVES OF TRADITIONAL BALLADS' (1959). Encouraged by the support of American opera singer PAUL ROBESON, the pair returned from Vienna thoroughly enthused with their new venture.

Although JIMMIE was actually a member of The STEVE BENBOW FOLK FOUR at the time, a fortuitous spot on the 'Tonight' TV show – singing 'FOOTBALL CRAZY' – cemented their partnership and ensured they became the folk revival's first TV stars. This appearance subsequently led to a deal with 'Decca', the pair's debut album, 'SCOTTISH CHOICE' (1961) notable as being the first collection of unadulterated Scottish songs released on a major label. As well as becoming familiar faces on 'Tonight' and another English folk showcase, 'Hullabaloo', they began hosting their own, hugely popular Scottish TV variety show, 'The White Heather Club'. This ran for five years and covered the more traditional side of the Scottish music scene, featuring the likes of MOIRA ANDERSON, ANDY STEWART and JIMMY SHAND. While better known for their TV work, the duo maintained a fairly prolific release schedule throughout the 60's and 70's, occasionally recording as The GAILLARDS (LEON ROSSELSON, etc).

When they finally went their separate ways at the dawn of the 80's, HALL concentrated on broadcast journalism, having already picked up awards for a 1977 Radio Clyde documentary, 'The Sing Song Streets'. MACGREGOR went on to compile a series of folk song books before initiating his highly successful West Highland Way series. Viewers were treated to the genial Glaswegian trekking the famous route, stopping off for banter and the occasional song. This project led to a number of spin-off outdoors programmes which he worked on in tandem with his long running 'MacGregor's Gathering' show on Radio Scotland. Sadly, ROBIN was to die in 1998.

ROBIN HALL – vocals, guitar / **JIMMIE MACGREGOR** – vocals, guitar, mandolin

Collector not iss.

1959. (lp; by ROBIN HALL) **LAST LEAVES OF TRADITIONAL BALLADS** [ ] [-]

1959. (7"ep) *(JES 5)* **GLASGOW STREET SONGS volume two** [ ] [-]
– The Wee Magic Stane: a. Three craw – b. If you will marry me – c. Duke Street jail . . . You canna shove your granny off a bus – The world must be coming to an end / The Wee Magic Stane: a. Johnnie lad – b. The wee magic stane.

1960. (7"ep; by ROBIN HALL) *(JES 6)* **THE BONNIE LASS O' FYVIE** [ ] [-]

1960. (7"ep; by ROBIN HALL) *(JES 7)* **MACPHERSON'S RANT** [ ] [-]

1960. (7") *(JDS 3)* **FOOTBALL CRAZY. / ROSIN THE BEAU** [ ] [-]
(re-iss. Aug60 on 'Decca'; F 11266)

1961. (7"ep) *(JES 9)* **GLASGOW STREET SONGS VOL.3** [ ] [-]

Topic not iss.

1960. (7"; as The GAILLARDS) *(STOP 101)* **BLACK AND WHITE. / BAHNUAH** [ ] [-]

Decca not iss.

Mar 61. (7") *(F 11340)* **THE MONSTER OF LOCH NESS. / SINNER MAN** [ ] [-]

Ace Of Clubs not iss.

1961. (lp) *(ACL 1065)* **SCOTTISH CHOICE** [ ] [-]
– Tramps and hawkers / Brochan lom, tana lom – Bodachan a' Mhirein / The day we went to Rothesay / The craw killed the pussie / The stoutest man in the Forty Ttwa / Highland fairy lullaby / My love she's but a lassie yet / Mingulay boat song / Nicky Tams / The piper o' Dundee / The bonnie Earl o' Moray / Mormond braes / Coulters candy / The rovin ploughboy – with the GAILLARDS (aka SHIRLEY BLAND & LEON ROSSELSON). *(re-iss. 1971 on 'Decca-Eclipse' lp/c; ECS/KECC 2074)*

H.M.V. not iss.

1962. (lp) *(CLP 1646)* **TONIGHT AND EVERY NIGHT** [ ] [-]
– Johnnie lad / Hares on the mountain / Inverey / Scottish medley (the 42nd – My love's she but a lassie yet – Mormond braes) / Twa heids are better than yin / Cuttie's

waddin' / Ye banks and braes / Glasgow street song medley / Mick Maguire / Davey Faa / The recruiting sergeant / The wild mountain thyme / Gin I were where the gaudie rins / The old triangle (Brendan Behan) / Ca' the yowes to the knowes / Three craws. *(re-iss. Jul82 as 'TWA HEIDS ARE BETTER THAN YIN' on 'Bulldog'; BDL 1019)*

— next 2 with **ROSSELSON** – guitar, etc / **JOHN JOBSON** – bass

Philips / not iss.

1964. (lp; as The GAILLARDS) **THE NEXT TONIGHT WILL BE – ROBIN HALL AND JIMMIE MacGREGOR** □ -
– Dig my grave / Villancico / Go tell Aunt Rhody / My love is like a red red rose / Asikatali / A bold young farmer / When I first came to this land / Johnny I hardly knew you / Lamidbar / Up among the heather / Ksekina mia psarapoula / A bucketful of mountain dew / The Overgate / Lowlands / Time for man go home. *(re-iss. 1973 as 'A ROVIN'' on 'Decca-Eclipse'; ECS 2126)*

1964. (lp) *(6382 124)* **BY PUBLIC DEMAND** □ -
– Enniskillen Dragoon / Sinner man / Love's a teasing / The frog and the mouse / Lullaby for a mucky kid / Haunted single end / Tapuach hineni / Donald Don / The Gallowa hills / Times are getting hard / Drinking gourd / Fal-o-ro, we're sailing / Corrie doon / Dirty old town / Roddy McCorley.

Fontana / not iss.

1965. (7") *(H 624)* **I WILL GO. / LULLABY FOR A MUCKY KID** □ -
1966. (lp) **THE RED YO-YO** □ -
1967. (lp) **SONGS OF GRIEF AND GLORY** □ -

znow with **JACK EMBLOW** – accordion / **BILL SUTCLIFFE** + **BRIAN BROCKLEHURST** – bass / **LISA TURNER** – banjo

Decca Eclipse / not iss.

1969. (lp) *(ECM 2024)* **SCOTCH AND IRISH** □ -
– The 42nd / Rosin the beau / If you will marry me / Brian O'Lynn / Baloo Baleerie / The holy ground / Whisky you're the devil / The Queen's four Marys / The hot ashfelt / The Calton weaver / Bonnie lass o' Fyvie / The parting glass. *(re-iss. 1970 on 'Decca-Eclipse'; ECS 2024)*

— with the **JIM JOHNSTON BAND** plus **ANGUS CAMERON** – fiddle / **IAIN McAFFIE** – guitar / **HERBIE McTAGGART** – flute

Mercury / not iss.

1969. (lp) *(SMCL 20169)* **ONE OVER THE EIGHT** □ -
– Charlie is my darling / Tatties and herring / Johnny has gone for a soldier / As I came doon the Canongate / The whisky chorus / The bonny broom / Heil-ya-ho, boys / One over the eight / Ludgin' wi' big Aggie / The auld sang / Tha tighinn fodham Eiridh (Rise and follow Charlie) / The sweet nightingale / The dundee weaver.

Dec 69. (7") *(TF 1066)* **LITTLE CHURCH BELLS. / HERE'S TO THE YEAR THAT'S AWA'** □ -

— with **BOBBY CAMPBELL** – fiddle / **ALASTAIR McDONALD** – banjo / **BRIAN BROCKLEHURST** – contra bass

Fontana Special / not iss.

1970. (lp) *(6438 033)* **WE BELONG TO GLASGOW** □ -
– The barras / Two heids / All-bally-bee / Ma wee gallus bloke / There is a happy land – Ye canny shove yer granny – I sent her for breid / The Govan billiard hall song / I'll no marry you / Nancy Whisky / Kelvin haugh / Three craws.

— now with **McDONALD** + **CAREY WILSON** – fiddle / **IAIN CAMPBELL** – bass / **HERBIE McTAGGART** – wind / **BOBBY ORR** – drums

Nevis / not iss.

1972. (lp; as ROBIN & JIMMIE) *(NEVR 003)* **HIGHLANDS & LOWLANDS** □ -
– Rattlin' roarin' Wullie / As I came doon the Overgate / Fetlar lullaby / On the banks of Loch Lomond / If you ever come to London / Bonny hills o' Gallawa' Jock McGraw / Ho-van gorry 0-go / Birlinn ghoraidth chrobhain / Toddlin' hame / Rory Murphy.

Eclipse / not iss.

Oct 74. (lp) *(ECS 2161)* **KIDS STUFF** □ -
– Candlelight fisherman / England forever / Glasgow medley / Three craws / etc.

— now with **SEAN O'ROURKE, ALEX HUTTON, RICKI FERNANDEZ** + **BILLY THOM**

Beltona / not iss.

Dec 75. (lp/c) *(SBE/KSBC 181)* **SCOTLAND'S BEST** □ -
– Rattlin' roarin' / Wullie / Fail-oro, we're sailing / Ca' the yowes / Scotland's dawn / Why should the cockle-gatherers / The new 'Football crazy' / Fishing & trawling / Busk & go / The gaudie / Let Glasgow flourish / The dark island – The master of Ballantrae / Guid-nicht and joy be wi' you.

Dec 77. (lp) *(SBE 190)* **SONGS FOR SCOTLAND** □ -
– The land of MacLeod / Where is the Glasgow I used to know? / The field of Bannockburn / Fetlar lullaby / The wee magic stane / Pack your tools and go / England forever / The freedom come all ye / St. Andrew / The miner's lullaby / The John MacLean march / Scottish tradition / Is there for honest poverty (a man's a man for a' that).

— went their separate ways; MacGREGOR worked on radio, HALL died in '98

– (ROBIN HALL) others, etc. –

1964. (7"ep) *Collector; (JES 12)* **ROBIN HALL** □ -
1964. (7"ep) *Collector; (JES 13)* **ROBIN HALL SINGS AGAIN** □ -
1970. (lp) *Hallmark; (SHM 698)* **GLASGOW STREET SONGS** □ -

Owen HAND

Born: c.1939, Colnes, County Monaghan, Ireland. Raised in Edinburgh, the young OWEN was a wanderer at heart, making his living by turns as a coal miner, hot-dog vendor, whaler and amateur boxer (with the 432nd Light Artillery Regiment of the T.A.). A regular at The Howff folk club in Edinburgh's Royal Mile, the bearded hopeful was taken under the wing of guitar tutor LEN PARTRIDGE. A contemporary of BERT JANSCH (who championed OWEN's rendition of 'THE GARDENER') during the early to mid 60's Folk revival, HAND relocated to London where BILL LEADER briefly paired him up with radical songwriter, LEON ROSSELSON, in the group the THREE CITY FOUR.

Due to family commitments (i.e. a wife and a young daughter), HAND was forced to spend a lot of his time in Edinburgh with the result that the aforementioned quartet never came to much. Nevertheless, the Irishman did eventually end up living in London full-time, regularly performing at Les Cousins in Soho and recording a couple of trad-type solo sets for 'Transatlantic', 'SOMETHING NEW' (1965) and 'I LOVED A LASS' (1966); these LP's are now worth a tidy sum. Prior to the latter's release, OWEN took off to a Kibbutz in Israel and on his return – due to troubles in the Middle East – he found that the album had been overdubbed without his permission. He has never recorded since.

Despite being such a key figure in both the Edinburgh and London Folk scenes, OWEN's legacy is slim, only a handful of modern artistes (the pairing of JANET RUSSELL & CHRISTINE KYDD among them) acknowledging his influence.

OWEN HAND – vocals, acoustic guitar

Transatla. / not iss.

1965. (lp) *(TRA 127)* **SOMETHING NEW** □ -
– Sally free and easy / Last thing on my mind / Acre of girl to a foot of ground / My Donal / She likes it / Morning train / One day old / The Ogie man / Take a look / Jimmy Wilson / You, like the sun / Rambling boy.

1966. (lp) *(TRA 138)* **I LOVED A LASS** □ -
– The barley tree / Cam' ye o'er frae France / Keishmul's galley / Jock Hawk / Musselburgh / Jenny Nettles / Inveray (the baron of Brackley) / The gardener / Ye Jacobites by name / I loved a lass / Kilbogie / The cuckoo's nest / The beggar wench / Bogie's bonny belle.

— OWEN virtually retired from the music biz after above

– compilations, etc. –

Mar 99. (cd) *Pier; (PIERCD 502)* **SOMETHING NEW / I LOVED A LASS** □ -

Ian HARDIE (see under ⇒ JOCK TAMSON'S BAIRNS)

Jonny HARDIE & Gavin MARWICK (see under ⇒ OLD BLIND DOGS)

Jean HART (see under ⇒ Wee Folk of the 60s)

Allan HENDERSON (see under ⇒ Lochshore records)

Hamish HENDERSON

Born: 11 November 1919, Blairgowrie, Perthshire. With the fertile, berry-picking environs of HENDERSON's home town serving as both a nexus for travelling people and a gateway to the Highlands, the youngster was exposed to a rich tradition of folk song and balladry from an early age. Although his family subsequently moved to Devon, HAMISH's interest in folklore remained and he went on to study at London's Dulwich College. There, he came into contact with the works of poet Hugh MacDiarmid whom he would later befriend and maintain a well documented correspondence.

Bizarrely enough, HENDERSON's first real career move was as an undercover agent in pre-war Nazi Germany, a post he'd been picked out for while studying at Cambridge on a scholarship. Throughout the Second World War he worked in intelligence with the Highland Division, his experiences abroad inspiring both 'ELEGIES FOR THE DEAD IN CYRENAICA' and 'THE HIGHLAND DIVISION'S FAREWELL TO SICILY', a song later recorded by ROBIN HALL and JIMMY MacGREGOR amongst others. After the war, HAMISH finished his studies at Cambridge before completing the aforementioned war verse. Eventually published in 1948, 'ELEGIES . . .' won the Somerset Maughan award although HENDERSON was to increasingly forego poetry for song. It was an interest further piqued by meetings with folksong collectors John Lorne Campbell (Laird Of Canna), Seamus Ennis and Calum Maclean (brother of Sorley) as well as pioneering American musicologist Alan Lomax.

After assisting Lomax in his collection of Scottish songs, HAMISH carried on with his own research in the employ of Edinburgh University's School of Scottish Studies. Thus began the most rewarding phase of his career as he proceeded to "discover" many 'source' singers from the furthest flung corners of the land, attempting to bring their rich oral heritage to the wider population. This heritage was especially rich among the travelling people, many of whom were descended from clans defeated at the Battle of Culloden. JEANNIE ROBERTSON in particular was a key "find", her incredible repertoire of song along with that of other travellers presented for public consumption at the zenith of the 60's 'Folk Revival'.

The first seeds of the revival were sown in the early 50's when the 'People's Festival' was set up as a more culturally inclusive alternative to the highbrow perspective of the recently inaugurated Edinburgh International Festival. The 'People's Festival' included a ceilidh which featured singers from all over Scotland – including many rooted out by HENDERSON – and set the stage for a grass roots resurgence in folksong. HAMISH's key role in the rediscovery of Scotland's heritage was further underlined with his various TV and radio appearances over the years while his own songwriting achievements included the anti-apartheid anthem 'FREE MANDELA' and the internationalist anthem in Scots, 'FREEDOM CAME AA YE'. Sadly, HAMISH was to die on the 8th of March, 2002.

Ingrid & Allan HENDERSON

Formed: Fort William . . . early 90's. The teenage sister and brother duo were from a musical family who toured the West Coast, the 1990 BBC Radio 2 Young Tradition award winner INGRID on clarsach and piano, and ALLAN a fiddler who was a graduate from RSAMD. INGRID had accompanied such recently established names as Gaelic outfit CLIAR and Skye vocalist ANNE MARTIN, while ALLAN had performed for BLAZIN' FIDDLES on their album, 'Fire On'. Signed to 'Lochshore' records, the pair issued two albums, 'LIGHT OF THE MOUNTAIN' (1993) and 'THE PERPETUAL HORSESHOE' (1994). Since then, the pair have gone on to greater things as already mentioned, ALLAN has also released his own trio set, 'TURNING PHRASES' (1997).

INGRID HENDERSON – clarsach, piano / **ALLAN HENDERSON** – fiddle

Lochshore not iss.

May 93. (cd/c) *(CD/ZC LDL 1204)* **LIGHT OF THE MOUNTAIN (SOLUS A BHEINNE)** [ ] [-]
– Highland road / Sound of sleat:- Lass of Paties mill – Lorna Mitchell's 18th birthday – Half hour crossing – Twentieth century fox – Sound of sleat / Air for Alex Henderson / Heights of casino:- Heights of casino – Hull's reel / Parson's farewell – Donnie Caolis of Burnbank / Strop the razor:- Strop the razor – Curlew – Kesh jig – Rocking the baby – Kate MacPherson's rant / Oran America / Solus a bheinne (light of the mountain):- Solus a bheinne – Monoghan's jig / Irish jigs:- Eighlin ni Riordain's slide – Caitlin ni chathasaigh – The sport of the chase.

Jun 94. (cd/c) *(CD/ZC LDL 1216)* **THE PERPETUAL HORSESHOE** [ ] [-]
– The fair hills of Moidart – The eagle's whistle / The China jig – The perpetual horseshoe / Nimbus / MacLean of Penny Cross – Angus Grant's march / Sitting in the stern of a boat / The wee fiddler's reel – The rough bounds reel – Craig's pipes reel / The loss of Iolaire / Blue orchid / Tom Clark's trip to Russia / Coilsfield house / The Quirang pipers – Jig run jig – Barney from Kilarney – The '45 jig – McKenna's jig.

the ALLAN HENDERSON TRIO

Hypertension not iss.

Feb 97. (cd) *(HYCD 297170)* **TURNING PHRASES** [ ] [-]
– 6-8 marches / Strathspeys and reels / An t-eilean mulleach / Bush set / 2-4 marches / Pipe set / Oran airsaig / Waltzes / Turning phases / Tam lin / Reels / Slow air and reel.

HERITAGE

Formed: Dunfermline, Fife . . . 1976 by JACK BECK, jew's-harp player LINDSAY PORTEOUS and GEORGE HAIG, along with MIKE WARD, DAVIE LOCKGART and JIM DUNN. In the early 80's, HERITAGE released two sets, 'SOME RANTIN ROVIN FUN' (1980) and 'WHEN THE DANCIN' IT'S A' DONE' (1981), for the 'No Bad' (once indie home to The SKIDS!). Signing to Ian Green's 'Greentrax' imprint, the traditional HERITAGE issued their one and only set for the label, 'FIFE AND A' THE LANDS ABOUT IT' (1989). LINDSAY and JACK both released their own solo efforts around the same time, although it would be another four years before 'Temple' records delivered their follow-up, 'TELL TAE ME' (1993). JACK BECK has since become highly regarded in trad/folk circles, his 'O LASSIE, LASSIE' (1989), builds a bridge between auld rural Scotland and the new urban folk (as Archie Fisher described it). • **Note:** not to be confused with the mid-90's metal act who issued 'Remorse Code' (1996).

JACK BECK – vocals, guitar / **LINDSAY PORTEOUS** – bodhran, percussion, jews harp / **GEORGE HAIG** – banjo, autoharp / **DAVIE LOCKHART** – fiddle / **JIM DUNN** – accordion / **MIKE WARD** – synthesizer, whistle, smallpipes, dulcimer

No Bad not iss.

Feb 80. (lp) *(NBLP 1)* **SOME RANTIN' ROVIN' FUN** [ ] [-]
– The blackthorn stick – The rakes of Kildare – Drowsie Maggie / Sleepytoon – The haughs o' Cromdale / The Reverend Archie Beaton – Cherish the ladies – The penpenny bit – The frost is all over / The band o' shearers / The reel of Tulloch / The Atholl Highlanders / Gordon's favourite – Viellafjord – The peerie hoose a'hint the burn / Dunfermline feein' mercat / Fanny power / Londsay's reel – Flogging reel / The jig o' slurs – The hare in the corn – Hartigan's fancy / Hishie ba' / Julia Delaney – The foxhunter jig.

Feb 81. (lp) *(NBLP 2)* **WHEN THE DANCIN' IT'S A' DONE** [ ] [-]
– Over the water wi' Charlie – The key of the cellar – Bonnie Prince Charlie / Tattie time / Niel Gow's lament for his second wife / Lochiel's welcome to Glasgow – Jig o' slurs / Bogie's bonnie bell / Boulavogue – The Munster cloak / Farewell tae Tarwathie / Hills of Glenorchy – Hare in the corn – Hartigan's fancy – Athole Highlanders / Fordell ball / Salmon tails up the water – The rose tree / The rock and the wee pickle tow / Haste to the wedding – Charlie Hunter – Drops of brandy / The plaidie awa' – Maggie's foot / Ae fond kiss – I'll ay ca' in by yon toon – My love she's but a lassie yet.

— **BECK + PORTEOUS + HAIG** recruited **ALISTAIR MARSHALL** – flute, whistle, musette / **PETE CLARK** – fiddle (also of BENACHALLY CEILIDH BAND) plus **ALAN MacDONALD** – mandolin / **DOMINIQUE LaLAURIE** – melodeon

Feb 89. (c/lp) *(C+/TRAX 024)* **FIFE AND A' THE LANDS ABOUT IT** [ ] [-]
– Haughs o' Cromdale / Flooers o' Edinburgh / High road to Linton (reels) / Dainty Davy / Jocky said to Jenny / Jinglin' John / Drops o' brandy / The Lea rig / Fisherrow / Flett from Flotta / Fife and a' the lands about it / Occitan polkas / Coorie doon / The mill, mill o' / Rowantree march / Spootaskerry / Colonel Fraser / Willafjord / Twa corbies / Jennie's black e'e / The iron man / Bottom o' the punchbowl.

Temple Temple

Nov 93. (cd/c) *(COMD2/CTP 051)* **TELL TAE ME** [ ] [ ]
– The acrobat – The echo / April waltz – Okkpik waltz – Calum Crubach – Sandy MacIntyre's trip to Boston – The king's reel / Bonny Glenshee / The Duke of Fife's welcome to Deeside – Campbell's farewell to Redcastle / Jig O'Connor – Carolan's draught – Planxty Mrs. O'Connor / Scottischa de la Montanha Negra – Scottische a servant – Scottische l'Italuenne / Valse de Vertoujit – Valse a bargoin / Bonny Undy / The apple tree – John Keith Laing – Bill Powrie / Fornethy House / Tell tae me / Calabrian pastorale.

— split up after above

LINDSAY PORTEOUS & FRIENDS

Tron Workshop not iss.

1987. (c) *(TWO 1)* **A WORLD OF MY OWN** [ ] [-]
8- Nurgle's fancy / French medley / The John MacLean march / Lindsay's trump hora / Derry hornpipe / Go to Berwick Johnnie / Fair and tender ladies / The fox hunt / The braes of Tulimet / Chanters song / Weavers – Drops of brandy / Torryburn lassies / Marquis of Huntly's / Da south end – My darling asleep – The maid in the meadow / Merrily kiss the Quaker – Dingle regatta – Fairy reel – Hangman's reel / Un, deux, trois (French medley) / Elsie Marley / Connaught man's ramble / La mariposa (The butterfly) / Sally Goodin / The musical priest / Tmour the tartar / Bonaparte's retreat / Dorset four hand reel / Athol Highlanders / Tripping upstairs / Job of journeywork / The black mountain.

Jan 89. (c) *(CTRAX 022)* **PORTRAIT OF A JEW'S HARP PLAYER** [ ] [-]
– Reel of Tulloch – Duke of Perth's reel / Cuttie's waddin' / Duke of Fife's welcome to Deeside – The banks hornpipe farewell to the creeks (Planxty Hamish) / Athole Highlanders – The fairy reel / Bratach bana / Beeswing hornpipe / Freedom come all ye / The merry blacksmith – Willafjord – Sleep soond Ida morning / Braes of Tullymet – The Inverness gathering – Plaidie awa' – White cockade / The flower's of Edinburgh / Soldier's joy / Timour the tartar I'll aye ca' in by yon toon / Drops of brandy / Tail toddle / Hens march tae the midden – Speed the plough – The Spey in Spate – The ale is dear.

JACK BECK

with **GARY COUPLAND, PETE CLARK, MIKE WARD, DAVY LOCKHART, LINDSAY PORTEOUS, CHIS MILES, ANDY HUNTER, GEORGE HAIG, COLIN STUART + ALISTAIR MARSHALL**

Greentrax — not iss.

Aug 89. (c/lp) *(C+/TRAX 027)* **O LASSIE, LASSIE**
– Birnie boozle / Matt Hyland / Twa corbies / Kilbowie hill / The bleacher lass o' Kelvinhaugh / Bound to be a row / Ned of the hill / The jolly beggar / Love is teasing / The merchant's son. *(cd-iss. May02; CDTRAX 027)*

Living Tradition — not iss.

Oct 01. (cd) *(LTCD 1006)* **HALF OWER HALF OWER TAE ABERDOUR**

Mike HERON

Born: 12 Dec'42, Glasgow. From 1965, multi-instrumentalist HERON was an integral part of psychedelic folk legends, The INCREDIBLE STRING BAND. For the next several years or so, this trio, duo or group (ROBIN WILLIAMSON was its other mainstay) hit the mark with top sets such as 'The 5,000 Spirits . . .' (1967), 'The Hangman's Beautiful Daughter' (1968) and 'Liquid Acrobat . . .' (1971). However, they bowed out in 1974 after their final set, 'Hard Rope & Silken Twine', failed to generate much interest outside their ever decreasing fanbase. Having already delivered a one-off solo LP, 'SMILING MEN WITH BAD REPUTATIONS' in 1971 (with members of FAIRPORT CONVENTION, The WHO and JOHN CALE), MIKE formed his own outfit under the banner of his second set, 'MIKE HERON'S REPUTATION' (1975). In 1977, HERON – as he was now monikered – issued his best and most commercial work to date, 'DIAMONDS OF DREAMS', a record that contained the excellent 'DON'T KILL IT CAROL' (later a hit for MANFRED MANN'S EARTH BAND). A low-key set, 'MIKE HERON' (for the US 'Casablanca' imprint), was neglected by British labels, and it would be some time – early 1988 – before we would hear from the man again, albeit demo tracks on 3 volumes of 'THE GLENROW TAPES'. In 1996, MIKE resurfaced once again with his long-awaited fifth album, 'WHERE THE MYSTICS SWIM', a folk/roots record that suggested he wasn't ready to pack it in just yet. In fact, it would be to every proper music fan's delight that the "live" reformation of the mighty INCREDIBLE STRING BAND happened shortly afterwards; a Celtic Connections concert in Glasgow on the 26th of January 2001 was indeed the highlight of the festival.

MIKE HERON – vocals, multi / incl. members of **FAIRPORT CONVENTION** plus **GERARD DOTT**

Island — Elektra

Apr 71. (7") *(WIP 6101)* **CALL ME DIAMOND. / LADY WONDER**

Apr 71. (lp) *(ILPS 9146)* <EKS 74093> **SMILING MEN WITH BAD REPUTATIONS**
– Call me Diamond / Flowers of the forest / Audrey / Brindaban / Feast of Stephen / Spirit beautiful / Warm heart pastry / No turning back / Beautiful stranger. *(cd-iss. Aug91; IMCD 129)*

May 71. (7") <45739> **CALL ME DIAMOND. / BRINDABAN**

MIKE HERON'S REPUTATION

N'bourhood — N'bourhood

1975. (lp) *(<NBH 80637>)* **MIKE HERON'S REPUTATION**
– Down on my knees / Easy Street / Evie / Residential boy / Without love / Born to gone / Angels in disguise / Wine of his song / Meanwhile the rain / One of the finest / Singing the dolphin. *(cd-iss. Jun96 & Apr98 on 'Unique Gravity'; UGCD 5606)*

1975. (7") *(NBH 3109)* **EVIE. / DOWN ON MY KNEES, AFTER MEMPHIS**

HERON

Bronze — not iss.

May 77. (7") **DO IT YOURSELF (DESERT SONG). / DON'T KILL IT CAROL**

May 77. (lp) *(ILPS 9460)* **DIAMOND OF DREAMS**
– Are you going to hear the music / Don't kill it Carol / Do it yourself (desert song) / Redbone / Turn up your love light / Draw back the veil / Stranded in Iowa / Diamond of dreams / Baby goodnight.

MIKE HERON

Zoom — not iss.

Aug 78. (7") *(ZUM 5)* **SOLD ON YOUR LOVE. / PORTLAND ROSE**

not iss. — Casablanca

1980. (lp) <7186> **MIKE HERON**
– Brooklyn miracle / Mexican girl / Treat your woman like a star / Blackfoot side / Tale of the miracle / Lonely never win / Beginner's guide to past lives / Gaugin in the South Seas / Child in your eyes / Tearproof days. *(<cd-iss. Mar02 on 'Unique Gravity'; UGCD 5209>)*

Demon — not iss.

Feb 96. (cd) *(FIENDCD 776)* **WHERE THE MYSTICS SWIM**
– Tom & Alexei / Always / Mexican girl / 1968 / Killing the dragon / Dry all my rain / A song for Robert Johnson / Leaning on my heart / 29 words / Baby goodnight. *(cd re-mixed.Mar01 on 'Unique Gravity'; UGCD 5008)*

— MIKE also reunited with ROBIN on 'BLOOMSBURY 1997' set (see below)

Unique Gravity — Unique Gravity

Apr 98. (cd) *(<UGCD 5607>)* **CONFLICT OF EMOTIONS** — Sep98
– Torch song / Belinda / It takes my breath away yet / Jane / Maker of islands / Transiberian express / Squeeze the minutes / Winter in China / Savage moon.

– his compilations, etc. –

Jan 88. (c/lp) *Glenrow; (MH/+LP 001)* **THE GLENROW TAPES**
(cd-iss. Jun93 on 'Voiceprint'; VP 140CD)

Jan 88. (c/lp) *Glenrow; (MH/+LP 002)* **THE GLENROW TAPES VOL.2**

Jan 88. (c/lp) *Glenrow; (MH/+LP 003)* **THE GLENROW TAPES VOL.3**

Heather HEYWOOD (see under ⇒ Greentrax records & Springthyme records)

Lizzie HIGGINS

Born: c.1939, Aberdeen, daughter of the great JEANNIE ROBERTSON and piper DONALD HIGGINS, who taught her many of the travelling songs in her repertoire. Having been brought up on the road, the family finally settled in a house on the outskirts of the Granite City. LIZZIE subsequently became one of the unsung heroines of traditional folk/ballad singing, recording a number of unaccompanied songs which found a home at the legendary 'Topic' records. In 1985, she cut her final release for 'Lismor', appropriately entitled 'WHAT A VOICE'.

LIZZIE HIGGINS – vocals

Topic — not iss.

1970's. (lp) *(12TS 185)* **PRINCESS OF THE THISTLE**
– Wha's at the windy / Lovely Molly / Fair of Ballnafannin / Young Emsley / Bonnie Udny / Far over the Forth / Laird of Dainty Downby / Seasons / Davy Faa / Red roses / Young but growing / Lass o' Glenshea. *(c-iss.Oct90 on 'Springthyme'; SPRC 1021)*

1975. (lp) *(12TS 260)* **UP AND AWA' WI' THE LAVEROCK**
– Up and awa' wi' the laverock / Lord Lovat / Soo sewin' silk / Lady Mary Ann / MacDonald of Glencoe / Forester / Tammy Toddles / Aul' rogue gray / Twa brothers / Cruel mother / Lassie gathering nuts.

Lismor — not iss.

Jun 85. (lp/c) *(LIF L/C 7004)* **WHAT A VOICE**
– What a voice, what a voice / Willie's ghost / MacPhee / Glenlogie / Tammy Toddles / An old maid in a garret / Tak the buckles fae your shin / MacCrimmon's lament / Cindy / Beggar, a beggar / Allison Cross / Mankind.

— LIZZIE retired from the folk scene after above

HIGHLAND CONNECTION (see under ⇒ Greentrax records)

HIGHLANDER (see under ⇒ Lochshore records)

Tom HOY

Born: 5 Feb'50, Glasgow. From the mid 70's to the late 70's, HOY provided backing (guitar and vocals) to the ever-evolving folk-rock outfit, MAGNA CARTA; they had once featured the talents of another Scots guitarist, DAVEY JOHNSTONE (of Elton John fame). By the turn of the decade, TOM and Newcastle-born ROBIN THYNE (also of MAGNA CARTA and the NATURAL ACOUSTIC BAND), departed acrimoniously to form offshoot duo, NOVA CARTA.

John HUBAND (see under ⇒ Springthyme records)

Tom HUGHES & His Border Fiddle (see under ⇒ Springthyme records)

Alistair HULETT

Born: 1953, Glasgow. By the time a teenaged ALISTAIR HULETT moved to New Zealand, like many Scots before him, he'd already developed a serious taste for folk music. He made a natural progression from fan to performer, subsequently relocating to Australia where he honed his skills on the folk club circuit. By the time punk had made its way down under in 1979, the ex-pat Scot had already begun to exercise his own songwriting talent and eventually married his love of both punk and folk in ROARING JACK. Formed in the early 80's, the band eventually released their debut set, 'Street Celtability', in 1986, topping the Aussie indie chart and setting the pace for other young bands of their ilk. The Celtic connection central to their music found HULETT and Co supporting Blighty brethren such as The POGUES while a sophomore set, 'The Cat Among The Pigeons' (1988), was nominated for the Australian equivalent of a Brit award. Despite similar plaudits for a third set, 'Through The Smoke of Innocence' (1989), the band called it a day towards the end of the decade and ALISTAIR resumed the solo career he'd begun in his teens. Unsurprisingly perhaps, the singer-songwriter gravitated back towards more traditional folk with his acclaimed debut album, 'DANCE OF THE UNDERCLASS' (1991). In contrast, 'IN THE BACKSTREETS OF PARADISE' was a harder hitting (at least musically) affair comprising songs originally penned for a fourth ROARING JACK album and recorded by HULETT's newly formed HOOLIGANS. Although the Scotsman proceeded to tour the record's harder material with this acoustic outfit, he simultaneously maintained a concert schedule geared towards the purists. Although orginally intended as a solo venture, 'SATURDAY JOHNNY AND JIMMY THE RAT' (1995) ended up as a collaboration with another (then) ex-pat, English folk veteran DAVE SWARBRICK. A tribute to the original folk revival, the record revealed a natural chemistry that also translated to the stage. A hugely popular Australian tour was followed by long awaited UK gigs while the duo went on to cut a second set together, 1998's 'THE COLD, GREY LIGHT OF DAWN'. The whole experience eventually led to ALISTAIR once again residing in Glasgow where of late he's been creating a series of politically motivated workshop projects concentrating on popular protest.

ALISTAIR HULETT – vocals, guitars

Red Rattler / not iss.

1991. (cd) *(RATCD 001)* **DANCE OF THE UNDERCLASS** - / - Austra
– Among Proddy dogs & Papes / Yuppietown / After the smoke cleared / Destitution road / He fades away / Suicide town / No half measures / Farewell to whisky / The swaggies have all waltzed Matilda away / Plains of Maralinga / Dictatorship of capital / The internationale.

1994. (cd) *(RATCD 002)* **IN THE BACK STREETS OF PARADISE** - / - Austra
– New age of the fist / Everyone I know / Militant red / She's got no conscience / John McLean's march / Good morning Bouganville / Victor Jara of Chile / Almost unintentional / Out in the danger zone / Kick it over.

ALISTAIR HULETT & DAVE SWARBRICK

1996. (cd) *(RATCD 003)* **SATURDAY JOHNNY AND JIMMY THE RAT** - / - Austra
– Saturday Johnny and Jimmy the rat / In the days of '49 / An bunan buidhe (The yellow bittern) / Blue murder / The earl of Errol / The tattie howkin' / A migrant's lullabye / Ways of a rover / The Forfar sodger / Behind barbed wire / The old divide and rule.

Apr 98. (cd) *(MFCD 513)* **THE COLD GREY LIGHT OF DAWN** / -
– The siege of Union Street / Chylde Owlett / Among Proddy dogs and Papes / Sons of liberty / Suicide town / The days that the boys came down / The merchant's son / When the wee birds start leaving / Harold's best men / The swaggies have all waltzed away.
(above issued on 'Musikfolk' UK)

2002. (cd) *(RATCD 005)* **RED CLYDESIDE** - / - Austra
– The Red Clydesiders / The lassies of Neilston / Mrs. Barbour's army / Don't sign up for war / The granite cage / When Johnny came hame tae Glesga / Around George Square / John Maclean and Agnes Wood / The ghosts of Red Clyde.

HUMBLEBUMS

Formed: Glasgow . . . 1968 by BILLY CONNOLLY and TAM HARVEY. A showcase for the banjo'n'banter of future stand-up guru CONNOLLY, the duo proved hugely popular on the thriving folk scene. Their debut album, 'FIRST COLLECTION OF MERRY MELODIES', appeared on 'Transatlantic' in early '69 prior to the arrival of former FIFTH COLUMN man GERRY RAFFERTY later the same year. Introduced to the group by his friend DANNY KYLE, RAFFERTY brought his not inconsiderable gift for McCARTNEY-esque melodicism to both 'THE NEW HUMBLEBUMS' (1969) and especially 'OPEN UP THE DOOR' (1970). This newfound professionalism sat somewhat uncomfortably alongside BILLY's irreverent approach and when the question of touring came up things eventually came to a head (by this point the trio had already been trimmed to a duo with the departure of HARVEY). Although the group were still performing at folk clubs, attempts to play the newer material proved a headache – 'OPEN UP . . .' had employed many session musicians – and 'Transatlantic' suggested taking a backing band on the road. Hardly comfortable in the role of pop/rock star, this was the point where CONNOLLY bailed out and returned to the intimacy of the folk circuit. RAFFERTY meanwhile, went on to release a debut solo album, 'Can I Have My Money Back' (1971) before forming STEALER'S WHEEL. • **Covered:** GOOD-BYE-EE! (Weston/Lee) / MY SINGING BIRD (trad.).

BILLY CONNOLLY (b.24 Nov'42, Anderston, Glasgow) – vocals, banjo, guitar / **TAM HARVEY** – guitar, mandolin, vocals

Transatla. / not iss.

Jan 69. (lp) *(TRA 186)* **FIRST COLLECTION OF MERRY MELODIES** / -
– Why don't they come back to Dunoon / My dixie darling / Now I feel so old / Give me a little of your time / Victory rag / Will you follow me / Little blue lady / Travel away / Come and drink my wine / Cripple creek / Close your eyes / Windy and warm.

— added **GERRY RAFFERTY** (b.16 Apr'46, Paisley) – vocals, guitar, bass (ex-FIFTH COLUMN)

Jun 69. (7") *(BIG 122)* **SATURDAY ROUND ABOUT SUNDAY. / BED OF MOSSY GREEN** / -

Jul 69. (lp) *(TRA 201)* **THE NEW HUMBLEBUMS** / -
– Look over the hill and far away / Saturday round about Sunday / Patrick / Everybody knows that / Rick rack / Her father didn't like me anyway / Please sing a song for us / Joe Dempsey / Blood and glory / Coconut tree / Solk pyjamas / Good-bye-ee!

Sep 69. (7") *(BIG 127)* **COCONUT TREE. / HER FATHER DIDN'T LIKE ME ANYWAY** / -

May 70. (7") *(BIG 130)* **SHOESHINE BOY. / MY APARTMENT** / -

Jun 70. (lp) *(TRA 218)* **OPEN UP THE DOOR** / -
– My apartment / I can't stop now / Open up the door / Mary of the mountains / All the best people do it / Steamboat row / Mother / Shoeshine boy / Cruisin' / Keep it to yourself / Oh no / Song for Simon / Harry / My singing bird.

— (HARVEY had departed by now) + both CONNOLLY and RAFFERTY went solo, the latter also forming STEALER'S WHEEL

– compilations, etc. –

Oct 74. (t-lp) *Transatlantic; (TRA 288)* **THE COMPLETE HUMBLEBUMS** / -

Jun 81. (lp/c) *Transatlantic; (TRS/KTRS 107)* **THE HUMBLEBUMS** / -
(cd-iss. Nov89 on 'Line'; TACD 900551)

Apr 84. (d-lp/d-c) *Cambra; (CR/+T 134)* **THE HUMBLEBUMS (BILLY CONNOLLY & GERRY RAFFERTY)** / -

Aug 96. (cd) *Castle Pulse; (PDSCD 542)* **THE BEST OF THE HUMBLEBUMS** / -

Apr 97. (cd) *Essential; (ESMCD 498)* **THE NEW HUMBLEBUMS / OPEN UP THE DOOR** / -

HUMPFF FAMILY (see ⇒ section 8: Rock, Pop & Indie)

Jim HUNTER

Born: Edinburgh. As a young child, HUNTER learned to play the Highland pipes, although by his early teens he had moved on to guitar. Inspired by Delta blues singers/musicians, JIM developed a near unique style of bottle-neck and slide guitar, fusing both blues and folk. Together with his band of locals, he released two self-financed cassettes towards the end of the 80's; a compilation of these gave him his debut album proper, 'UPHILL SLIDE', for 'Temple' in 1990. A few years later, HUNTER delivered his follow-up long-player, 'FINGERNAIL MOON' (1992). Subsequently signing to 'Watercolour' records, the rugged and gifted veteran awoke again, this time with 'CRACK O' NOON CLUB' (1996). A low-key 4th set, 'TURNING THE TIDE' (2001), was finally released after his spell with the SONGHUNTER project (alongside ANDY THORBURN); an album, 'SPIRIT OF THE HUNTER' was issued in '98.

JIM HUNTER – vocals, bottle-neck guitar / with band

Temple / Temple

Sep 90. (cd/c; as The JIM HUNTER BAND) *(<COMD2/CTP 040>)* **UPHILL SLIDE**
– Way of the white cloud / When you leave / Don't want you to see me this way / A good bad woman / Burnt out in the snow / Waste the paint / Unfinished business / Love on the line / Strength to carry on / Sleep dearie sleep – Raeberry Street. *(re-iss. Feb94; same)*

Jul 92. (cd/c) *(<COMD2/CTP 047>)* **FINGERNAIL MOON** / 1993
– When the geese fly over / Irish girl – Hunter's jig / Man in a crisis / Joanna / Cold

winter's night / Long walk in the rain / The hungry I / Words I might have said / Midnight train / Limbo ships / Angels. *(re-iss. Feb94; same)*

Watercolour not iss.

Mar 96. (cd/c) *(CRA CD/C 014)* **CRACK O' NOON CLUB** ☐ -
– Big man with the beard / Howling at the moon / Walking all over / I will take you home / Crazy dreams / Thirty four miles / Waterfall / Miss Fiona MacLeod / Closer to the truth / Little Martha / Big old diesel motor / Bitter sweet / I will take you home (reprise).

— in 1998/99, JIM teamed up with ANDY THORBURN and ANDREW MURRAY (among others) to release the SONGHUNTER project, 'SPIRIT OF THE LAND'

Sep 01. (cd) *(SCOTCD 022)* **TURNING THE TIDE** ☐ -

— there was a Netherlands collection, 'SPARKS IN FLIGHT'

Jimmy HUTCHISON (see under ⇒ Springthyme records)

I

Hamish IMLACH

Born: 10 Feb'40, Calcutta, India. An honorary Scot by dint of his contributions to the 60's Scottish folk revival, HAMISH IMLACH wasn't exactly a prolific artist or a master musician in his own right but a major player in the development of the Edinburgh/Glasgow scene. His father was a folk guitarist who'd earned the name 'Ragtime Cowboy Joe' due to his stage banter, regaling audiences with tales of Butch Cassidy & The Sundance Kid; the IMLACH clan had apparently once had interests in a Bolivian silver mine where they employed the outlaws during their legendary but mysterious South American phase (see Bruce Chatwin's brilliant 'In Patagonia' for further reading on this matter). HAMISH's mother, meanwhile, owned a hairdressing business in Calcutta, the couple divorcing during the Second World War.

After a stint in Australia, the family moved to Broomhill, Glasgow in 1953. Here, the teenage IMLACH was to meet ARCHIE FISHER, his future folk brother in arms. The pair shared a love of skiffle, jazz and blues, although the portly HAMISH was more concerned with the partying opportunities such pastimes could present. His mother absent, IMLACH had free reign of the family boarding house, playing host to a gang of Glasgow folkies informally known as The Broomhill Bums. One of his soirees was even graced by the presence of visiting American luminaries SONNY TERRY and BROWNIE McGHEE, the pair so impressed by the Scottish scene they'd return many times.

HAMISH himself began performing in his early 20's, teaching guitar (a young JOHN MARTYN was one of his more famous pupils) at Andrew Moyes's Folksong club by day and singing by night. The early 60's also saw him make his recording debut, cutting a series of Irish rebel songs for 'Decca' under the aegis of The EMMETONES, a front for the anonymous studio trio of IMLACH, JOSH MACRAE and BOBBY CAMPBELL. As well as making the scene in Glasgow, IMLACH was a famous face in Edinburgh's burgeoning folk crowd and regularly appeared at the pivotal 'Howff' on the Royal Mile. Indeed, his next appearance on vinyl was 'The Edinburgh Folk Festival', a two-volume set recorded in the capital by future 'Transatlantic – Xtra' men, Nat Joseph and Bill Leader.

The latter label was among the first to issue HAMISH's own recordings during the latter half of the 1960's, releasing a rare 7" single, 'I'M THE BOY TO FREEZE 'EM' and the eponymous 'HAMISH IMLACH' (1966); there were four more in quick succession, 'LIVE!' (1967), 'BEFORE . . . AND AFTER' (1967), 'THE TWO SIDES OF . . .' (1968) and 'BALLADS OF BOOZE' (1969), all testaments to his famous sense of humour. Like his father before him, he performed as both singer and raconteur, never happier than when delighting audiences with tall tales and waggish gags. Many of these were recounted in 'Cod Liver Oil And The Orange Juice – Reminiscences Of A Fat Folk Singer', the self-deprecating title of his 1992 autobiography (co-written with former "Broomhill Bum" Ewan McVicar), the title itself taken from 1985's 'SONNY'S DREAM' album.

1993 saw the screening of 'Acoustic Routes', a one-off documentary tracing the history of the folk revival and featuring a reunion of HAMISH, ARCHIE FISHER, ANNE BRIGGS and BERT JANSCH at the former premises of The Howff. Yet by this point, IMLACH's health was in serious decline; after years of illness, one of the folk revival's most fondly remembered fathers finally passed away on the 1st of January 1996.

HAMISH IMLACH – vocals, acoustic guitar

Transatla. not iss.

1966. (7") *(TRASP 11)* **I'M THE BOY TO FREEZE 'EM. / SCOTTISH BREAKAWAY** ☐ -

Xtra not iss.

1966. (lp) *(XTRA 1039)* **HAMISH IMLACH** ☐ -
– Johnny O' Breadislee / Men of Knoydart / The zoological gardens / Street songs / Cod liver oil and orange juice / The gaudie / If it wasn't for the union / The Cumbie boys / Erin go bragh / The soldier's prayer / Black is the colour / Foggy dew. *(re-iss. Mar77; TRA SAM 43)*

1967. (lp) *(XTRA 1050)* **LIVE! (live)** ☐ -
– I was a gay spark in my time / Whisky you're the Devil / Early morning blues / The ballad of Timothy Evans / It's better in the dark / Campbell / Castlereagh / The wind blew the bonnie lassie's plaidie awa' / Paddy lay back.

— next added **BOBBY CAMPBELL** – fiddle / **OSCAR ST CYR** – mandola, concertina

1967. (lp) *(XTRA 1059)* **BEFORE . . . AND AFTER** ☐ -
– Tall tale / Let Ramensky go / Copper's song / The klan / McPherson's farewell / Candy man / The 37 bus / I am a miller / The castle of Drumboe / The Dundee cat I / Sporting life.

— next with **CLIVE PALMER, ARCHIE FISHER, RAY WARLEIGH, JOHN MacKINNON + MARTIN FREY**

1968. (lp) *(XTRA 1068)* **THE TWO SIDES OF HAMISH IMLACH** ☐ -
– Jean Harlow (died the other day) / Clapped out motorcar / I got fooled / Bourgeois blues / The horny bull / The happiest day / The McGreggors / Anthony Riley / History of football / The priest and the minister / Clive's song.

— next with **JOHN MacKINNON, TOM HARVEY, IAIN MacKINTOSH, DARYL RUNSWICK + MIKE WHELLANS**

1969. (lp) *(XTRA 1094)* **BALLADS OF BOOZE** ☐ -
– Beer is best / The mountain dew / Little Maggie / Scottish sabbath / Maids when you're young / As usual / Good bye booze / Drunk / Drunk again / Twelve and a tanner a bottle / Whisky seller / The moonshiner / The Calton weaver / The poor beasts.

— next w/ **MacKINTOSH, FISHER, WHELLANS + ALLAN BARTY, TOM McGRATH**

1972. (lp) *(XTRA 1128)* **FINE OLD ENGLISH TORY TIMES** ☐ -
– Forty pence butter / One day old / Base details / If you want to see the general / Downtrodden landlord / Automation (fascination) / Twelve pence ain't a shilling / Pie in the sky / Whisky / Dialogue / Five eyes / Fine old English Tory times.

— next w/ **HARVEY, MacKINTOSH, RUNSWICK, WHELLANS + MIKCK MOLONEY**

Feb 74. (lp) Xtra; *(XTRA 1131)* **MURDERED BALLADS** ☐ -
– Cornflakes sugar teardrops / Bluebird / Baldheaded woman / People upstairs / Coulters candy / Daddy what if? / Tableau at twilight / Jenny Jenkins / The whale / The mermaid / The rabbit / Traveling rhythm / Murdered ballad / The lion / The night squad / That terrible terrible night.

— augmented now by **IAIN MacKINTOSH**

Autogram not iss.

1976. (lp) *(ALLP 209)* **SCOTTISH SABBATH** ☐ -
– Scottish sabbath / Downtrodden landlord / Kelty clippie / Better in the dark / The gaudie / The Kerry recruit / Whisky and women / Men of Knoydart / The general / Pretty little horses / If it wasn't for the unions / The oyster girl / The band played Waltzing Mathilda / Goodbye booze. *(re-iss. May88; same)*

1978. (lp; by HAMISH IMLACH & IAIN MACKINTOSH)
(ALLP 215) **A MAN'S A MAN** ☐ -
– A man's a man for a' that / Jamie Foyers / D-day dodgers / Parcel of rogues / The roving ploughboy / Wae's me for Prince Charlie / McPherson's rant / Skye boat song / Betsy Bell / The can o' tea / I am a miller / Freedom come all ye / The flooers o' the forest / Baron of Brackley / Johnny Cope. *(re-iss. May88; same)*

Kettle not iss.

1979. (lp) *(KOP 3)* **THE SPORTING LIFE** ☐ -
– Castlereagh / Timothy Evans / Sure to be a row / Sporting life / Western cowboy / Wagoner's lad / Whisky and women / No mans land / Smoker's song / Black is the colour. *(re-iss. Apr95 on German 'MusiKiste'; 26-6-250)*

Lismor not iss.

Jun 85. (lp/c) *(LIF L/C 7006)* **SONNY'S DREAM** ☐ -
– Cod liver oil and the orange juice / The ballad of William Brown / Mary Anne / The reprobate's lament / Salonika / Kisses sweeter than wine / The smokers song / If it wasn't for the union / The parcel o' rogues / I didn't raise my son to be a soldier / Goodbye booze / D-day dodgers / Seven men of Knoydart. *(cd-iss. May95; LCOM 7006)*

MusiKiste not iss.

1986. (cd; by HAMISH IMLACH & IAIN MACKINTOSH)
(26-6-358) **LIVE IN HAMBURG (live)** - - German
– Johnny Cope / Skye boat song / The general / Weary life / Dance band on the Titanic / Rollin' / Susie / Paddy lay back / Tramps and hawkers / The new restaurant / Lily the pink / My friends / All the tunes in the world (encore). *(re-iss. Apr95; same)*

1989. (cd) *(26-6-359)* **PORTRAIT (live)** ☐ -
– I wish they'd do it now / Chemical worker's song / Hokey Smoky – Take the children and run / Deep elm blues / The coalowner and the poor pitman's wife / Marilyn / He's in the jailhouse now / Clive's song / One day old / The dove / Dark as a dungeon / Johnny, I hardly knew you / Ghost army of Korea parade / Ain't playin' me fair. *(re-iss. Apr95; same)*

— HAMISH died on the 1st of January, 1996 – below were posthumous

Lochshore Lochshore

Mar 96. (cd/c; by HAMISH IMLACH, MURIEL GRAVES & KATE KRAMER) *(<CD/ZC LDL 1238>)* **MORE AND MERRIER**
– Castlereagh / Mary Alice Jones / Black is the colour / I like beer / She moved through the fair / Shit I've forgotten the words / Mary Anne / Hills of Lorne / Pub with no beer / Amazing grace / Wiilowy gardens / Aunt Clara / Jock of Bredeslie / If you go away / If it wasnae for the unions.

Vindaloo not iss.

Dec 97. (cd; HAMISH IMLACH & MURIEL GRAVES) *(CURRYCD 001)* **TWO'S COMPANY** (rec. 1993) -
– Boozin' / The nobleman / Makin' whoopee / Ballad of the carpenter / Cigarettes and whisky / The bunch of thyme / Dead puppies / Solid gone / I can play anything / Whistle daughter whistle / Donal Og / Salvation Army song / Irish ballad / Maxwell's silver hammer / The wagoner's lad.

– compilations, etc. –

1969. (lp) *Transatlantic; (TRA SAM 9)* **SAMPLER 1** -
Nov 69. (lp) *Xtra; (XTRA 1121)* **ODD RARITY** -
1973. (lp) *Transatlantic; (TRA SAM 31)* **ALL ROUND ENTERTAINER 2** -
Nov 97. (cd) *Essential; (ESMCD 522)* **THE DEFINITIVE TRANSATLANTIC COLLECTION** -
– It's better in the dark / Cod liver oil and the orange juice / Johnny O'Breadislee / Erin go bragh / If it wasn't for the union / The foggy dew / The copper's song / McPherson's farewell / 37 bus medley / Jean Harlow (died the other day) / Clapped out motorcar / McGreggors / Anthony Riley / Beer is best / Little Maggie / Goodbye booze / Calton weaver / Clive's song / Cuckoo / Kilbogie / Bluebird / Jenny Jenkins / Travelling rhythm.

INCREDIBLE STRING BAND

Formed: Glasgow . . . early 1966 by ROBIN WILLIAMSON, London-born CLIVE PALMER and MIKE HERON. From the early 60's, WILLIAMSON had played London gigs alongside BERT JANSCH (future PENTANGLE), before he returned to Glasgow. In the early 60's, ROBIN formed a duo with Englishman PALMER, although they found it difficult to establish themselves, that is, until 1965 when PALMER set up the 'Incredible' folk club in Sauchiehall Street. That same year, the pair performed at the Edinburgh Folk Festival, catching the eye of Nathan Joseph of 'Transatlantic' records who recorded them for the concert's Various Artists compilation. After their folk club was shut down by the police, they became a trio, adding MIKE HERON to become The INCREDIBLE STRING BAND.

After months tracking them down, American producer JOE BOYD finally found them and duly signed them to 'Elektra'. He subsequently took them to London, where they recorded their eponymous debut album (summer '66). With this well-received record under their belt, PALMER departed for Afghanistan. When he returned he declined to re-join the act, who were now broke but under the management of BOYD. Upon ROBIN's return from Morocco, the duo (augmented by some friends), played an 'Elektra' records package alongside TOM PAXTON and JUDY COLLINS, at The Royal Albert Hall. It helped promote their second album, '5,000 SPIRITS OR THE LAYERS OF THE ONION', which made the UK Top 30 in 1967. Their underground blend of psychedelic folk was crystallised on such charming tracks as, 'CHINESE WHITE', 'FIRST GIRL I LOVED' and 'PAINTING BOX'.

In Spring '68, they surprisingly crashed into the UK Top 5 with their third set, 'THE HANGMAN'S BEAUTIFUL DAUGHTER'. The album's witty lyrics (alternately penned by HERON or WILLIAMSON) and ethnic multi-instrumentation was embellished with the vocals of the duo's girlfriends, LICORICE and ROSE. The highlights of this album, arguably the group's finest hour, were 'A VERY CELLULAR SONG', 'THE MINOTAUR'S SONG' and 'KOEEOADDI THERE'. Late that year, they issued 2 single lp's as a double-set, 'WEE TAM' & 'THE BIG HUGE'. However, this brilliant but confused package failed to sell. Over the next two years, they released three UK Top 40 albums ('I LOOKED UP', a collection of baroque eclecticism – 'U' verging on pantomine), but after a move to 'Island' in 1971, they soon faded from the commercial limelight. Nevertheless, the second 'Island' album, 'LIQUID ACROBAT AS REGARDS THE AIR', hit the Top 50, boasting the spine-tingling melancholy of the 11-minute 'DARLING BELLE'.

HERON and WILLIAMSON went their separate ways in the mid-70's, the former writing 'DON'T KILL IT CAROL' (later a hit for MANFRED MANN'S EARTH BAND), the latter becoming something of a self-styled cosmic folk storyteller (complete with harp). ROBIN released his first solo set, 'MYRRH', in 1972 while still a member of the legendary folk-hippies. After the group's split in 1974, he relocated to California where he immersed himself in Celtic folklore while keeping a toe in musical waters via the FAR CRY CEILIDH BAND. Although the latter project never actually made it to vinyl, the harp-based ROBIN WILLIAMSON & HIS MERRY MEN was a more concrete proposition featuring CHRIS CASWELL, SYLVIA WOOD, JERRY McMILLAN, DIRK DALTON, STU BROTMAN and LOUIS KILLEN. The group released a trio of albums at the tail end of the 70's, namely 'JOURNEY'S EDGE' (1977), 'AMERICAN STONEHENGE' (1978) and 'A GLINT AT THE KINDLING' (1979).

ROBIN went solo in the early 80's, kicking off a series of albums for the American 'Flying Fish' label with 1981's 'SONGS OF LOVE & PARTING'. Although the bulk of the early 80's was taken up by a series of mail order (from Ireland's 'Claddagh' label) spoken word cassettes firmly in the bardic tradition, 'LEGACY OF THE SCOTTISH HARPERS' (1984) was the first in a two-volume exploration of Scotland's rich clarsach tradition while 'SONGS FOR CHILDREN OF ALL AGES' was a music-based foray into the children's market.

Come the 90's, ROBIN was once again resident in the UK where he occasionally appeared on the festival circuit with his idiosyncratic combination of Celtic storytelling and song. Following on from 1993's collaboration with JOHN RENBOURN ('WHEEL OF FORTUNE'), the mystic troubadour enjoyed an impressively prolific mid-late 90's period, the highlight of which was 'BLOOMSBURY 1997', a live recording of his much publicised reunion concert with former ISB partner MIKE HERON.

Although HERON hasn't been quite as visible since the ISB's split, he has surfaced with the occasional solo set, harking back to an ISB-style sound on 1996's 'WHERE THE MYSTICS SWIM'. Another old ISB face cropped up in 1999 as ROBIN recorded 'AT THE PURE FOUNTAIN' with CLIVE PALMER, the pair completing a second set, 'JUST LIKE THE IVY', the following year. The big news, however, was a full INCREDIBLE STRING BAND reunion at the 2001 Celtic Connections Festival in Glasgow, messrs WILLIAMSON, HERON, PALMER plus newcomers LAWSON DANDO and BINA WILLIAMSON (ROBIN's wife) putting in an acclaimed performance which more than justified the hype and boded well for the future.

ROBIN WILLIAMSON (b.24 Nov'43, Edinburgh) – vocals, guitars, etc. / **CLIVE PALMER** (b. 1943, Edmonton, London) – guitar, banjo, vocals / **MIKE HERON** (b.12 Dec'42, Glasgow) – vocals, rhythm guitar, sitar, etc.

Elektra Elektra

Jun 66. (lp) *(EUK 254) <EKS 7322>* **THE INCREDIBLE STRING BAND**
– Maybe someday / October song / When the music starts to play / Schaeffer's jig / Womankind / The tree / Whistle tune / Dandelion blues / How happy am I / Empty pocket blues / Smoke shovelling song / Can't keep me here / Good as gone / Footsteps of the heron / Niggertown / Everything's fine right now. *(re-iss. Jul68; EKL 254); hit No.34) (cd-iss. Jul93; 7559 61547-2) (cd re-iss. Jun94 on 'Hannibal'; HNCD 4437)*

— now a duo when PALMER went to abroad; he later formed FAMOUS JUG BAND

— added **CHRISTINA 'LICORICE' McKENNA** – some vocals, organ (a guest on below) plus guests **DANNY THOMPSON** – double bass (of PENTANGLE) / **JOHN HOPKINS** – piano

Jul 67. (lp; mono/stereo) *(EUK/+S7 257) <EKS 74010>* **THE 5,000 SPIRITS OR THE LAYERS OF THE ONION** 26
– Chinese white / No sleep blues / Painting box / The Mad Hatter's song / Little cloud / The eyes of fate / Blues for the muse / The hedgehog's song / First girl I loved / You know that you could be / My name is death / Gently tender / Way back in the 1960's. *(re-iss. 1968; EKS 7257) (re-iss. Jan73 + 1976; K 42001) (cd-iss. Mar92; 7559 60913-2) (cd re-iss. Jun94 on 'Hannibal'; HNCD 4438)*

Mar 68. (7") *(EKSN 45028)* **PAINTING BOX. / NO SLEEP BLUES** -

Mar 68. (lp; mono/stereo) *(EUK/+S7 258) <EKS 74021>* **THE HANGMAN'S BEAUTIFUL DAUGHTER** 5 Jun68
– Koeeoaddi there / The minotaur's song / Witches hat / A very cellular song / Mercy I cry city / Waltz of the new Moon / The water song / There is a green crown / Swift as the wind / Nightfall. *(re-iss. Jan73 + 1976; K 42002) (cd-iss. Mar92; 7559 60835-2) (cd re-iss. Jun94 on 'Hannibal'; HNCD 4437)*

— **MIKE, ROBIN** and his girlfriend **LICORICE** introduced MIKE'S girlfriend **ROSE SIMPSON** – some vocals, bass, percussion, violin

Oct 68. (d-lp; mono/stereo) *(EKL/EKS7 4036-7)* **WEE TAM / THE BIG HUGE** -
(d-cd-iss. Nov94 on 'Hannibal'; HNCD 4802)

Oct 68. (lp; mono/stereo) *(EKL/<EKS7 4036>)* **WEE TAM** Mar69
– Job's tears / Puppies / Beyond the see / The yellow snake / Log cabin home in the sky / You get brighter / The half-remarkable question / Air / Ducks on a pond. *(re-iss. Jan73 + 1976; K 42021) (cd-iss. Feb92; 7559 60914-2) (<cd re-iss. Nov94 on 'Hannibal'; HNCD 4802>)*

Oct 68. (lp; mono/stereo) *(EKL/<EKS7 4037>)* **THE BIG HUGE** Mar69
– Maya / Greatest friend / The son of Noah's brother / Lordly nightshade / The mountain of God / Cousin caterpillar / The iron stone / Douglas Traherne Harding / The circle is unbroken. *(re-iss. Jan73 + 1976; K 42022) (cd-iss. Jul93; 7559 61548-2)*

— LICORICE was now a full-time member

Oct 69. (7") *(EKSN 45074)* **BIG TED. / ALL WRIT DOWN** -

Nov 69. (lp) *(<EKS 74057>)* **CHANGING HORSES** 30
– Big Ted / White bird / Dust be diamonds / Sleepers, awake! / Mr. & Mrs. /

Creation. *(cd-iss. Jul93 & May01; 7559 61549-2) (cd-iss. Dec94 on 'Hannibal'; HNCD 4439)*

— added guest **DAVE MATTACKS** – drums of FAIRPORT CONVENTION

Apr 70. (lp) *(<EKS 7401>)* **I LOOKED UP** 30 Jul70
– Black Jack Davy / The letter / Pictures in a mirror / This moment / When you find out who you are / Fair as you. *(re-prom.1970; 2469 002) (cd-iss. Dec94 on 'Hannibal'; HNCD 4440) (cd re-iss. Jul02; 7559 62760-2)*

Apr 70. (7") *(2101 003)* **THIS MOMENT. / BLACK JACK DAVY** -

May 70. (7") *<45696>* **THIS MOMENT. / BIG TED** -

— augmented by **JANET SHANKMAN** – b.vocals (ROBIN married her Dec70) **PETE GRANT** – banjo / **GREG HART** – sitar (of STONE MONKEY) plus guest **MALCOLM LE MAISTRE** – keyboards, bass (of EXPLODING GALAXY)

Oct 70. (d-lp) *(2665 001) <7E 2002>* **"U"** 34 Jan71
– El wool suite / The juggler's song / Time / Bad Sadie Lee / Queen of love / Partial belated overture / Light in the time of darkness – Glad to see you / Walking along with you / Hirem pawn Itof – Fairies' hornpipe / Bridge theme / Bridge song / Astral plane theme / Invocation / Robot blues / Puppet song / Cutting the strings / I know you / Rainbow. *(re-iss. Jan73; K 62002) (d-cd-iss. Jul02; 7559 62761-2)*

— Back to basic duo of **ROBIN + MIKE** plus **LICORICE + ROSE**

Island Elektra

Apr 71. (lp) *(ILPS 9140)* **BE GLAD FOR THE SONG HAS NO ENDING** -
– Come with me / All writ down / Vishangro / See all the people / Waiting for you / (Be glad for) The song has no ending. *(cd-iss. Jun98 on 'Edsel'; EDCD 564)*

— **MALCOLM LE MAISTRE** – keyboards, bass, vocals returned to repl. ROSE

Oct 71. (lp) *(ILPS 9172) <74112>* **LIQUID ACROBAT AS REGARDS THE AIR** 46 Feb72
– Talking of the end / Dear old battlefield / Cosmic boy / Worlds they rise and fall / Evloution rag / Painted chariot / Adam and Eve / Red hair / Here till here is there / Tree / Jigs: Eyes like leaves – Sunday is my wedding day – Drops of whiskey – Grumbling old men / Darling Belle. *(re-iss. Aug91 cd)(c; IMCD 130)(ICM 9172)*

— added **GERARD DOTT** – clarinet, saxophone (he played on HERON's 1972 solo album) and guest on one **STUART GORDON** – viola

Oct 72. (lp) *(ILPS 9211)* **EARTH SPAN** -
– My father was a lighthouse keeper / Antoine / Restless night / Sunday song / Black Jack David / Banks of sweet Italy / The actor / Moon hang low / The sailor and the dancer / Seagull. *(cd-iss. Dec92 on 'Edsel'; EDCD 360)*

Nov 72. (7") *(WIP 6145)* **BLACK JACK DAVID. / MOON HANG LOW** -

— **STAN LEE** – bass repl. LICORICE who joined WOODY WOODMANSEY Band **JACK INGRAM** – drums (added to ROBIN, MIKE, MALCOLM, GERARD and STAN)

Island Reprise

Feb 73. (7") *(WIP 6158)* **AT THE LIGHTHOUSE DANCE. / JIGS** -

Feb 73. (lp) *(ILPS 9229) <2139>* **NO RUINOUS FEUD**
– Explorer / Down before Cathy / Saturday maybe / Jigs / Old Buccaneer / At the lighthouse dance / Second fiddle / Circus girl / Turquoise blue / My blue tears / Weather the storm / Little girl. *(cd-iss. Nov92 on 'Edsel'; EDCD 367)*

— **GRAHAM FORBES** – electric guitar (ex-POWERHOUSE) repl. GERARD / **JOHN GILSTON** – drums repl. INGRAM

Mar 74. (lp) *(ILPS 9270) <2198>* **HARD ROPE & SILKEN TWINE**
– Maker of islands / Cold February / Glancing love / Dreams of no return / Dumb Kate / Ithkos. *(cd-iss. Feb93 on 'Edsel'; EDCD 368)*

— WILLIAMSON + HERON went on to solo careers; the pair re-formed late 1999 with PALMER, LAWSON DANDO + BINA WILLIAMSON

Pig's Whisker Pig's Whisker

Aug 01. (cd) *(<PWMD 5024>)* **BLOOMSBURY 2000 (live)** Nov01
– Maker of islands / Ducks on a pond / Air / The storm is on the ocean / Big city blues / Waltz of the new moon / Goodbye / You know what you could be / October song.

– compilations etc. –

Mar 71. (lp) *Elektra; (EKS 74065) / Reprise; <7E 2004>* **RELICS OF THE INCREDIBLE STRING BAND**

Nov 76. (d-lp) *Island; (ISLD 9)* **SEASONS THEY CHANGE – BEST OF THE INCREDIBLE STRING BAND** -
– Black Jack David / Blues for the muse / Nightfall / Puppies / Cold days of February / Worlds they rise and fall / Chinese white / Empty pocket blues / When the music starts to play / Saturday maybe / Red hair / The circle is unbroken / First girl I loved / Cosmic boy / Darling Belle / My father was a lighthouse keeper / Queen Juanita and her fisherman lover.

Oct 91. (cd/lp) *Band Of Joy; (BOJ CD/LP 004)* **ON AIR (live)** -

Nov 92. (cd) *Windsong; (WINCD 029)* **BBC RADIO 1 LIVE IN CONCERT** -

Jun 97. (cd) *Blueprint; (PWMD 5003)* **CHELSEA SESSIONS 1967** -
(<re-iss. Mar98 on 'Pig's Whisker'; PWCD 5003)> (re-iss. Jul00; PWCD 5023)

Aug 98. (cd) *Mooncrest; (<CRESTCD 002>)* **FIRST GIRL I LOVED (live)**
– Cousin caterpillar / I know that man / The circle is unbroken / Wild cat blues / The first girl I loved / Everything's fine right now / Old buccaneer / Catwalk rag / Giles crocodile / Turquoise blue / My father was a lighthouse keeper / Black Jack David / Ithkos.

May 01. (cd) *Island; (IMCD 280)* **HERE TILL THERE IS HERE (AN INTRODUCTION TO THE INCREDIBLE STRING BAND)** -

Jul 01. (cd) *Warner ESP; (9548 39803-2)* **THE BEST OF THE INCREDIBLE STRING BAND 1966-1970** -

— HERON and WILLIAMSON also released solo albums before their split. HERON = 'SMILING MEN WITH BAD REPUTATIONS' and WILLIAMSON = 'MYRRH'.

— they went on to solo careers in 1975

IOLAIR

Formed: Aberdeen . . . mid-late 70's by man and wife NORMAN STEWART and JANICE CLARK. Greatly encouraged by her aunt, Lindy Cheyne (who was a founder member of the Aberdeen Folk Song Club), JANICE was brought up listening to traditional Folk/Source singers such as JEANNIE ROBERTSON, JIMMY MacBEATH and LIZZIE HIGGINS. Meanwhile, Easter Ross-born chanter NORMAN, cut his teeth on Gaelic music and was a frequent visitor to Sandy Bell's pub in Edinburgh where he struck up a friendship with folklore legend/songwriter, HAMISH HENDERSON. After only one eponymous LP in 1980, little or nothing was heard from the couple. • **Note:** JANICE's younger sister JENNY augmented The BATTLEFIELD BAND in the 80's; her other sister KATHLEEN also sang a fair bit.

JANICE CLARK – vocals / **NORMAN STEWART** – vocals / with **CHRISTINE MARTIN** – fiddle

Celtic Music not iss.

1980. (lp) *(CM 003)* **IOLAIR** -
– The kings command / Gaudie rins / Sitting in the stern of a boat / Shirra dam / Glasgow Gaelic club – The blackberry bush / Sandwood down to Kyle / Laddie lie near me / Ciaora – The wee man from Skye / Cirichree / As I went into Inverness-shire / The poachers / Yellow haired laddie / John MacMillan of Barra – MacLeod of Mull / Fisherman's wife.

— split musically after above

IONA

Formed: Iona ... 1988 by multi-instrumentalists Englishman DAVID FITZGERALD (a former member of the ADRIAN SNELL group) and DAVE BAINBRIDGE alongside doctor turned singer, JOANNE HOGG. The trio named themselves after the island of Iona off Scotland's west coast where FITZGERALD originally came up with his vision of the band during a Christian retreat. Aiming to spread the gospel of the early Christian faith which St. Columba first brought to the island in 563 a.d., IONA released their eponymous debut album in 1988. In presenting their religious message, the band created a musical backdrop of soft jazz-fusion, prog-rock, ambient keyboard washes and Celtic melodies that brought comparisons with the likes of CLANNAD, ENYA, KATE BUSH, YES and GENESIS.

By 1992's follow-up set, 'BOOK OF KELLS', the trio had expanded to a quintet with the addition of former KAJAGOOGOO man (no, really!) NICK BEGGS and drummer TERRY BRYANT. The latter album was a concept set based around The Book Of Kells, an 8th Century Christian manuscript thought to originate from the island. Following the record's release, founding member FITZGERALD left to undertake a music degree and was subsequently replaced by MIKE HAUGHTON. The sax man made his debut on 1994's 'BEYOND THESE SHORES', another concept set inspired by St. Brendan's Voyage wherein the Irish monk sailed across the Atlantic in a wood and leather boat. ROBERT FRIPP even made a guest appearance on the album, the ex-KING CRIMSON man also lending his talents to 1996's 'JOURNEY INTO THE MORN', a record that featured new faces TROY DONOCKLEY and TIM HARRIES (the latter a replacement for BEGGS) and shifted the emphasis from instrumental passages to the haunting Gaelic vocals (from original 8th Century text) of JOANNE HOGG.

Regarded by many fans and commentators as best sampled in a live environment, IONA finally recorded 'IONA LIVE: HEAVEN'S BRIGHT SUN' for posterity in 1997, a mammoth two-disc set straddling the prog/folk-rock divide which they've made their own. After a late 90's sabbatical, the group returned with a slightly modified line-up (BAINBRIDGE, DONOCKLEY, HOGG, PHIL BARKER and FRANK VAN ESSEN) on 'WOVEN CORD' (1999), a document of a live collaboration with the ALL SOULS ORCHESTRA recorded at London's Royal Festival Hall in Spring '99. DAVID FITZGERALD meanwhile, made a brief return to the recording scene in 1995 with solo set, 'COLUMCILLE'.
• **Note:** not to be confused with the IONA of the late 70's who released the 'CUCKOO' LP for 'Silver Scales'.

DAVE BAINBRIDGE – keyboards, guitars / **JOANNE HOGG** – vocals, acoustic guitar / **DAVID FITZGERALD** – saxophone, wind (ex-BRYN HAWORTH)

Celtic Music / Fore Front

Nov 88. (lp)<cd> *(CM 001) <CDO 2700>* **IONA** [ ] [ ] 1990
– Turning tide / Flight of the wild goose / The island / White sands / Dancing on the wall / A'mhachair – the plain / Vision of Naran / Beijing / Iona – mother of Lindisfarne / Trilogy / Here I stand / Columcille. *(cd/c-iss.1990 & May95 on 'What'; WHAD/WHAC 1266)*

— added **NICK BEGGS** (b.15 Dec'61, Hertfordshire) – chapman stick, bass (ex-KAJAGOOGOO) + **TERL BRYANT** – drums, percussion

What / not iss.

1992. (cd/c) *(WHAD/WHAC 1287)* **THE BOOK OF KELLS** [ ] [-]
– Kells opening theme / Revelation / Matthew – the man / Chi-rho / Mark – the lion / The river flows / Luke – the calf / Virgin and child / Temptation / The arrest – Gethsemane / Trinity – The godhead / John – The eagle / Kells / Eternity – no beginning no end. *(re-iss. May95; same)*

— (Sep'92) **MIKE HAUGHTON** – sax, flute, recorder, vocals (ex-CLIFF RICHARD) repl. FITZGERALD who went on a full-time degree

Nov 93. (cd/c) *(WHA 1300 CD/C)* **BEYOND THESE SHORES** [ ] [-]
– Prayer on the mountain / Treasure / Brendan's voyage (navigato) / Edge of the world / Today / View of the islands / Bird of Heaven / Murlough Bay / Burning like fire / Adrift / Beachy Head / Machrie moor / Healing / Brendan's return / Beyond these shores. *(cd re-iss. Jul96l WHAD 1300)*

— **TIM HARRIES** – bass + **TROY DONOCKLEY** – whistles, percussion, pipes; repl. BEGGS

Alliance / Forefront

Oct 95. (cd/c) *(ALCD/ALC 050) <25142>* **JOURNEY INTO THE MORN** [ ] [ ] Feb96
– Bi-se I mo shuil, pt.1 / Irish day / Wisdom / Everything changes / Inside my heart / Encircling / Journey into the morn / Lindisfarne / No heart beats / The search / Divine presence / Heaven's bright sun / Bi-se I mo shuil, pt.2 / When I survey. *(c re-iss. Sep96; CORDCD 1)*

3-Cord / 3-Cord

Apr 96. (c-s/cd-s) *(CA/CD CORD 1)* **IRISH DAY** [ ] [-]
Jun 96. (c-s/cd-s) *(CA/CD CORD 2)* **WISDOM** [ ] [-]

— **PHIL BARKER** – bass; repl. HARRIES

Jul 97. (d-cd/d-c) *(CORD CD/MC 2) <25178>* **HEAVEN'S BRIGHT SUN** [ ] [ ]
– Turning tide / Treasure / Flight of the wild goose / Today / Irish day / Luke / Inside my heart / Trilogy / I will give my love an apple // The island / Iona / Columcille / Heaven's bright sun / Chi-rho / Bi-se I mo shuil part 2 / Kells theme / Reels / When I survey.

— (5-piece) **BAINBRIDGE, HOGG, BARKER + DONOCKLEY** added **FRANK VAN ESSEN** – drums, percussion (without HAUGHTON + BRYANT; the latter issued a few solo sets, 'PSALM' 1995 and 'BEAUTY AS FAR AS THE EYE CAN SEE' 1997)

Alliance / not iss.

Oct 99. (cd/c; as IONA & the ALL SOULS ORCHESTRA) *(190180-2/-4)* **WOVEN CORD** [ ] [-]
– Overture:- Bi-se I mo shuil / Man / White sands / Murlough Bay / Dancing on the wall / Encircling / Lindisfarne / Revelation / Woven cord / Beyond these shores.
May 00. (cd/c) *(190177-2/-4)* **OPEN SKY** [ ] [-]
– Woven cord / Wave after wave / Open sky / Castlerigg / A million stars / Light reflected / Hinba / Songs of ascent (parts 1-3).

– compilations, etc. –

Dec 96. (cd/c) *What; (WHAD/WHAC 1303)* **THE VERY BEST – TREASURES** [ ] [ ]
– Treasure / The island / Flight of the wild goose / Chi-rho / Burning like fire / Iona / Revelation / Columcille / Dancing on the wall / Kells / Today / Here I stand. *(cd re-iss. Apr02; same)*

Tony IRELAND (see under ⇒ FINN MacCUIL)

IRON HORSE (see under ⇒ Lochshore records)

ISLANDERS

Formed: Mount Florida, Glasgow . . . 1964 by university lecturer JIM and NANCY CRAIG. Their humble beginnings started out at a concert party run by Charlie Sweeney at Pollok Community Centre. The quartet at the time also consisted of IAIN MACKINTOSH and JOHN NOBLE, the former getting his bass to gigs by Mini; apparently his girlfriend was relegated to the back seat. In 1965, 'THE ISLANDERS' LP was released on Edinburgh's 'Waverley' records, a BBC TV series 'The Making Of America' previewing a few soundbites. Now without MACKINTOSH, who made a name for himself on the solo circuit, The ISLANDERS recorded a second eponymous set, this time for 'R.C.A.' in 1968; ALEX HUTTON had also been a member prior to this release. Writing several of their own numbers, the CRAIGs also chose the songs of Dylan, Ochs, Lightfoot, Paxton, Guthrie and Hamish Henderson as well as trad numbers. Another three years passed by until the appearance of their third and final effort, 'THE PATTERNS OF FOLK' (1971), on which the pair were joined by EDDIE POLLARD and NOEL EADIE.

JIM CRAIG – vocals / **NANCY CRAIG** – tambourine, vocals / **IAIN MacKINTOSH** – bass / **JOHN NOBLE** – guitar / with guest **IAN BROWN** – bass

Waverley / not iss.

Apr 65. (lp) *(ZLP 2049)* **THE ISLANDERS** [ ] [-]
– The hour that the ship comes in / Polly wolly doodle / Four strong winds / The pawn song / Mary don't you weep / Spanish is a loving tongue / John Henry / The dark island / Red yo-yo / No Irish need apply / Golden river / Jolly roving tars / Banks o' Sicily.

— **JIM + NANCY** recruited **EDDIE POLLARD** – guitar + **PETE** – bass; repl. ALEX HUTTON (MacKINTOSH was later to go solo)

RCA Victor / not iss.

1968. (lp) *(RD 7950)* **THE ISLANDERS** [ ] [-]
– I ain't marchin' any more / Early in the morning / Last class seaman / Hush little babe / No more words / The Gallowa' hills / John Reilly / Steel rail blues / Going to the zoo / Gypsy boy / Pride of man / Yes, yes, yes / Wild flying dove / Twa recruitin' sergeants / Freedom come-all-ye / That's my song.

— the **CRAIG's + ED** were joined by **NOEL EADIE**

Waverley / not iss.

Apr 71. (lp) *(SZLP 2124)* **THE PATTERNS OF FOLK** [ ] [-]
– If I had a hammer / Before I met you / Jeely-piece song / Song for a winter's night / I can't help but wonder (where I'm bound) / I never will marry / Wild rover / The orange and the green / Children of the mist / Farewell to Fuinary / Rivers of Texas / Song of the city / The sergeants / Freedom come-all-ye / Strangest dream / Wild colonial boy.

— The ISLANDERS split after above

J

George JACKSON & Maggie MacINNES (see under ⇒ OSSIAN)

William JACKSON (see under ⇒ OSSIAN + Mill records)

Bert JANSCH

Born: 3 Nov'43, Glasgow. Another of Scotland's unsung musical heroes, acoustic guitarist BERT JANSCH was highly influential in not only the development of the 60's Brit-folk revival but on the style and technique of rock players such as NEIL YOUNG and JIMMY PAGE.

Unlike most musicians, JANSCH didn't really discover his talent until he was a bit older. After a spell working as a gardener for Glasgow council, JANSCH headed for Edinburgh where he became immersed in the thriving folk scene. Kipping down in the flat of ARCHIE FISHER (one of the scene's main players), he began forging his distinctive guitar-picking style. This period also marked his first encounter with obscure, semi-legendary folkie ANNE BRIGGS, with whom he was to strike up a lasting, if loose, musical/personal bond.

The pair were to subsequently share a London flat through the winter of '62/'63, co-writing a batch of songs (one of which, 'WISHING WELL', was later recorded by BERT on his 1968 album, 'BIRTHDAY BLUES') wherein BRIGGS' more traditional style combined well with JANSCH's complex but soulful finger-picking. The very fact that JANSCH wrote his own material was significant in itself at a time when most artists were relying largely on traditional material. Signed to 'Transatlantic', the Scots troubadour released his eponymous debut album in 1965, a groundbreaking work featuring classic compositions such as 'STROLLING DOWN THE HIGHWAY' and 'NEEDLE OF DEATH' (inspired – if that's the right word – by a friend's drug-related death). In its striking originality, the record set the tone for what was to come; following on from sophomore effort, 'IT DON'T BOTHER ME' (1965), JANSCH held the folk scene in thrall yet again with the open-tuned innovation of 'JACK ORION' (1966). Subtly powerful, darkly ruminating and always compelling, the album resounded to echoes of BRIGGS' influence and

indeed the traditional 'BLACKWATER SIDE' had originally come to BERT's attention via his wandering minstrel mate. This version of the song is also rumoured to have inspired LED ZEPPELIN's 'Black Mountain Side', thereby drawing as direct a link as any between JANSCH's mid-60's experiments and rock's subsequent development.

Having previously guested on BERT's recordings, close friend and fellow folkie JOHN RENBOURN took a full half-share of the work on 1966's 'BERT AND JOHN' while the pair would go on to work together in folk supergroup PENTANGLE (alongside JACQUI McSHEE, DANNY THOMPSON and TERRY COX). JANSCH was a pivotal member of this project and although he continued to release impressive solo sets like 'NICOLA' (1967) and 'BIRTHDAY BLUES' (1968), the bulk of the late 60's/early 70's period was taken up by group activities.

Following PENTANGLE's demise in 1973, BERT cut a one-off set for 'Reprise' entitled 'MOONSHINE' before signing to 'Charisma' for a clutch of albums through the mid-late 70's. Rarely straying from his unique amalgam of Scots-Irish folk and blues, he has continued to record and perform into the 80's and 90's without ever troubling the mainstream. Content to plough his own niche and record on a variety of independent labels (most recently 'Cooking Vinyl', for whom he cut 1995's 'WHEN THE CIRCUS COMES TO TOWN'), JANSCH commands a loyal following among both fans and musicians while critics rarely have a bad word to say about him. Yet still it seems somehow unjust that this "Godfather Of Folk" doesn't have a higher profile.

BERT JANSCH – vocals, acoustic guitar

Transatla. Vanguard

1965. (lp) *(TRA 125)* **BERT JANSCH** [ ] [-]
– Strolling down the highway / Smokey river / Oh how your love is strong / I have no time / Finches / Rambling's going to be the death of me / Veronica / Needle of death / Do you hear me now? / Alice's wonderland / Running from home / Courting blues / Casbah / Dreams of love / Angie. *(re-iss. 1980 + Jan88; TRS 117) (re-iss. Jun88 on 'Transatlantic'/'Demon'; TRANDEM 1) (cd-iss. Jun01 on 'Castle'; CMRCD 204)*

Dec 65. (lp) *(TRA 132)* **IT DON'T BOTHER ME** [ ] [-]
– Oh my babe / Ring-a-ding bird / Tinker's blues / Anti apartheid / The wheel / A man I'd rather be / My lover / It don't bother me / Harvest your thoughts of love / Lucky thirteen / As the day grows longer now / So long (been on the road so long) / Want my daddy now / 900 miles. *(re-iss. Jul76 as 'EARLY BERT' on 'Xtra'; XTRA 1163) (cd-iss. Oct93 on 'Transatlantic'-'Demon'+=; TDEMCD 16)* – The times has come / Soho / In this game / Dissatisfied blues. *(cd re-iss. Jul96 on 'Essential'; ESMCD 407) (cd re-iss. Jun01 on 'Castle'; CMRCD 205)*

1966. (lp) *(TRA 143)* **JACK ORION** [ ] [-]
– The waggoner's lad / The first time ever I saw your face / Jack Orion / The gardener / Nottamun town / Henry Martin / Blackwaterside / Pretty Polly. *(re-iss. Jul76 as 'EARLY BERT VOL. 2' on 'Xtra'; XTRA 1164) (cd-iss. Aug01 on 'Castle'; CMRCD 304)*

1966. (lp; BERT JANSCH & JOHN RENBOURN) *(TRA 144)*
BERT AND JOHN [ ] [-]
– East wind / Piano time / Goodbye pork pie hat / Soho / Tie tocative / Orlando / Red's favourite / No exit / Along the way / The time has come / Stepping stones / After the dance. *(cd-iss. Oct98 on 'Wooded Hill'+=; HILLCD 8)* – Wagoner's lad / Lucky thirteen / In this game / Dissatisfied blues / Hole in the cole / Bells. *(cd re-iss. Aug01 on 'Castle'; CMRCD 203)*

1966. (7"ep) *(TRA EP 145)* **NEEDLE OF DEATH** [ ] [-]
– Running from home / Tinker's blues / Needle of death / The wheel.

Transatla. Reprise

Jun 67. (7") *(BIG 102)* **LIFE DEPENDS ON LOVE. / A LITTLE SWEET SUNSHINE** [ ] [-]

Jul 67. (lp) *(TRA 157)* **NICOLA** [ ] [-]
– Go your way my love / Woe is love my dear / Nicola / Come back baby / A little sweet sunshine / Love is teasing / Rabbit run / Life depends on love / Weeping willow blues / Box of love / Wish my baby was here / If the world isn't there. *(re-iss. Jul76 as 'EARLY BERT VOL.3' on 'Xtra'+=; XTRA 1165)* – Come sing me a happy song to prove we can all get along the lumpy, bumpy road.

Dec 68. (lp) *(TRA 179)* <6343> **BIRTHDAY BLUES** [ ] [ ]
– Come and sing me a happy song / To prove / The bright new year / Tree song / Poison / Miss Heather / Rosemary Sewell / I've got a woman / A woman like you / I'm lonely / Promised land / Birthday blues / Wishing well blues.

Jun 71. (lp) *(TRA 235)* <6455> **ROSEMARY LANE** [ ] [ ]
– Tell me what is true love / Rosemary Lane / M'lady Nancy / A dream, a dream, a dream / Alman / Wayward child / Nobody's bar / Reynardine / Silly women / Peregrinations / Sylvie / Sarabanda / Bird song. *(re-iss. Jan77 as 'EARLY BERT VOL. 4' on 'Xtra'; XTRA 1170) (cd-iss. Sep94 on 'Transatlantic'/'Line'; TACD 9.007840) (cd re-iss. Oct98 on 'Wooded Hill'; HILLCD 2)*

Reprise Reprise

Feb 73. (lp) *(K 14234)* <2129> **MOONSHINE** [ ] [ ]
– Yarrow / Brought with the rain / January man / Night time blues / Moonshine / First time ever I saw your face / Rambleaway / Twa corbies / Oh my father. *(cd-iss. Sep95 on 'Jansch'; BJ 001CD) (cd re-iss. Jan01 on 'Castle'; CMRCD 112)*

Mar 73. (7") *(K 14234)* **OH MY FATHER. / THE FIRST TIME EVER I SAW YOUR FACE** [ ] [-]

Charisma Kicking Mule

Sep 74. (lp) *(CAS 1090)* **L.A. TURNAROUND** [ ] [ ]
– Fresh as a sweet Sunday morning / Chambertin / One for Jo / Travelling man / Open up the Watergate (let the sunshine in) / Stone monkey / Of love and lullaby / Needle of death / Lady nothing / There comes a time / Cluck old hen / The blacksmith.

Nov 74. (7") *(CB 240)* **IN THE BLEAK MIDWINTER. / ONE FOR JO** [ ] [ ]

Nov 75. (lp) *(CAS 1107)* **SANTA BARBARA HONEYMOON** [ ] [ ]
– Love a new / Mary and Joseph / Be my friend / Baby blue / Dance lady dance / You are my sunshine / Lost and gone / Blues run the game / Built another band / When the teardrops fell / Dynamite / Buckrabbit.

Nov 75. (7") *(CB 267)* **DANCE LADY DANCE. / BUILD ANOTHER BAND** [ ] [ ]

May 77. (lp) *(CAS 1127)* <202> **A RARE CONUNDRUM** [ ] [ ]
– Daybreak / One to a hundred / Pretty Saro / Doctor, doctor / 3 a.m. / The Curragh of Kildare / Instrumentally Irish / St.Flacre / If you see my love / Looking for a home / Poor mouth / Cat and mouse / Three chord trick / Lost love. *(cd-iss. Jun97; CASCD 1127)*

— In 1978 he appeared on CONUNDRUM & RICHARD HARVEY single, 'Black Birds of Brittany'.

Feb 79. (lp) *(CLASS 6)* **AVOCET** [ ] [ ]
– Avocet / Bittern / Kingfisher / Kittiwake / Lapwing / Osprey.

Sonet Kicking Mule

Apr 80. (7") *(SCK 44)* **TIME AND TIME. / UNA LINEA DI DOLCEZZA** [ ] [-]

Jul 80. (lp' by BERT JANSCH & CONUNDRUM) *(SNTF 162)*
<309> **13 DOWN** [ ] [ ]
– Una linea di dolcezza / Let me sing / Down river / Nightfall / If I had a lover / Time and time / In my mind / Sovay / Where did my life go / Single Nose / Ask your daddy / Sweet mother Earth / Bridge. *(cd-iss. Sep98 on 'Kicking Mule'; KMCD 3909)*

Logo Kicking Mule

Feb 82. (lp) *(GOL 1035)* **HEARTBREAK** [ ] [ ]
– Is it real? / Up to the stars / Give me the time / If I were a carpenter / Wild mountain thyme / Heartbreak hotel / Sit down beside me / No rhyme nor reason / Blackwater side / And not a word was said. *(re-iss. May89 on 'Hannibal'; HNBL 1312) (cd-iss. Jul93; HNCD 1312)*

Feb 82. (7") *(GO 409)* **HEARTBREAK HOTEL. / UP TO THE STARS** [ ] [ ]

Mausoleum not iss.

Sep 85. (lp) *(KOMA 788006)* **FROM THE OUTSIDE** [ ] [-]
– Sweet rose in the garden / Black bird in the morning / Read all about it / Change the song / Shout / From the outside / If you're thinking 'bout me / Silver raindrops / Why me? / Get out of my life / Time is an old friend. *(cd-iss. Aug93 on 'Hypertension' +=; HYCD 200128)* – River running /

High emotion / From the inside. *(cd re-iss. Mar01 on 'Castle'; CMRCD 170)*

Black Crow — not iss.

Mar 88. (lp/c/cd; BERT JANSCH & ROD CLEMENTS) *(CRO 218)* **LEATHER LAUNDERETTE**
– Strolling down the highway / Sweet Rose / Brafferton / Ain't no more cane / Why me? / Sundown station / Knight's move / Brownsville / Bogie's bonny belle / Leather launderette / Been on the road so long.

— his backers now **PETER KIRTLEY** – guitar, b.vocals, percussion / **DANNY THOMPSON** – double bass, percussion, chimes / **STEVE BAKER** – blues harp / **STEFAN WULFF** – percussion / **FRANK WULFF** – percussion, alto-flute, etc.

Temple — Hypertension

Nov 90. (cd/c/lp) *(COMD2/CTP/TP 035)* **SKETCHES**
– Ring-a-ding bird / One for Jo / Poison / The old routine / Needle of death / Oh my father / Running, running from home / Afterwards / Can't hide love / Moonshine / A woman like you / A windy day. *(cd+=)* – As the day grows longer now. *(cd/c re-iss. Feb94; same)*

Run River — Capitol

Nov 90. (lp/c/cd) *(RRA/+MC/CD 0012)* *<71365>* **THE ORNAMENT TREE** 1991
– The ornament tree / Banks o' Sicily / Rambling boys of pleasure / Rock road to Dublin / Three dreamers / Mountain streams / Blackbird of Mullamore / Ladyfair / Road tae Dundee / Tramps and hawkers / January man / Dobbins flower vale. *(cd re-iss. Jan01 on 'Castle'; CMRCD 111)*

Cooking Vinyl — not iss.

Sep 95. (cd) *(COOKCD 092)* **WHEN THE CIRCUS COMES TO TOWN**
– Walk quietly by / Open road / Back home / No-one around / Step back / When the circus comes to town / Summer heat / Just a dream / The lady doctor from Ashington / Stealing the night away / Honey don't you understand / Born with the blues / Morning brings peace of mind / Living in the shadows.

Cooking Vinyl — True North

Mar 98. (cd) *(COOKCD 138)* *<TN 165>* **TOY BALLOON** Sep98
– Carnival / She moves through the fair / All I got / Bett's dance / Toy balloon / Waitin' and wonderin' / Hey Doc / Sweet talking lady / Paper houses / Born and bred in old Ireland / How it all came down / Just a simple song.

When — Castle

Jun 00. (d-cd) *(WENCD 211)* *<683>* **CRIMSON MOON** Aug00
– Caledonia / Going home / Crimson moon / Down under / October song / Looking for love / Fool's mate / Riverbank / Omie wise / My Donald / Neptune's daughter / Singing the blues // Strolling down the highway / Needle of death / It don't bother me / Lucky thirteen / Blackwaterslide / The first time ever I saw your face / Rabbit run / Woe is love my dear / Nobody's bar / Rosemary lane. *(cd No.1 re-iss. Oct00; WENCD 211X)*

– compilations, etc. –

on 'Transatlantic' unless mentioned otherwise

1966. (lp) *Vanguard; (VSD 97212)* **LUCKY THIRTEEN**
1969. (lp) *Vanguard; <VMD 6506>* **STEPPING STONES**
Nov 69. (lp) *(TRANSAM 10)* **THE BERT JANSCH SAMPLER**
Dec 72. (lp) *(TRANSAM 27)* **BOX OF LOVE – THE BERT JANSCH SAMPLER VOL. 2**
– Oh how your love is strong / In this game / The gardener / Soho / I am lonely / Renegrinations / Casbah / Dissatisfied blues / As the day grows longer now / Box of love / Birthday blues / Nobody's bar.
Mar 78. (lp) *(MTRA 2007)* **ANTHOLOGY**
1980. (lp) *(TRA 333)* **THE BEST OF BERT JANSCH**
Jul 87. (cd) *(TRA 604/TRACD 604)* **THE ESSENTIAL COLLECTION VOL.1**
Sep 87. (cd) *(TRA 607/TRACD 607)* **THE ESSENTIAL COLLECTION VOL.2**
Jun 92. (cd) *Shanachie; <SHANCD 99004>* **THE BEST OF BERT JANSCH**
Jul 92. (cd) *Transatlantic-Demon; (TDEMCD 9)* **THE GARDENER: THE ESSENTIAL BERT JANSCH 1965-1971**
– The gardener / Alice's wonderland / Running from home / Tinker's blues / It don't bother me / The waggoner's lad / The first ever I saw your face / Go your way my love / My lover / Woe is love my dear / Black waterside / Rabbit run / A woman like you (studio) / Market song / A woman like you (live) / Wishing well / Rosemary Lane / Peregrinations / Poison / Miss Heather Rosemary Sewell / Reynardine / Bird song / When I get home / I am lonely.
Dec 92. (cd; as BERT JANSCH / JOHN RENBOURN) *Shanachie; <SHANCD 99006>* **AFTER THE DANCE**
Jul 93. (cd) *(TDEMCD 16)* **BERT JANSCH / JACK ORION**
Jul 93. (cd) *Virgin; (CDVM 9024)* **THREE CHORD TRICK** (74-79 material)
Sep 93. (cd) *Windsong; (WINCD 039)* **BBC RADIO 1 LIVE IN CONCERT (live 1980-82 with CONUNDRUM)**
Dec 93. (cd) *(TDEMCD 17)* **NICOLA / BIRTHDAY BLUES**
Jul 96. (cd) *Essential; (ESMCD 407)* **BERT JANSCH / IT DON'T BOTHER ME**
Aug 96. (cd) *Jansch; (BJ 002CD)* **LIVE AT 12 BAR**
– Summer heat / Curragh of Kildare / Walk quietly by / Come back baby / Backwaterslide / Fresh as a sweet Sunday morning / Morning brings peace of mind / Lily of the west / Kingfisher / Trouble in mind / Just a dream / Blues run the game / Let me sing / Strolling down the highway / Woman like you / Instrumental. *(re-iss. Aug00 on 'Essential'; ESMCD 921)*
Jan 97. (cd) *Essential; (ESMCD 459)* **JACK ORION / NICOLA**
Jul 97. (cd) *Essential; (ESMCD 519)* **BIRTHDAY BLUES / ROSEMARY LANE**
Jun 98. (d-cd) *Recall; <153>* **BLACKWATER SIDE**
Dec 98. (cd) *Big Beat; (CDWIKD 182)* **YOUNG MAN BLUES – LIVE IN GLASGOW – 1962-1964**
Sep 00. (d-cd) *Essential; (CMEDD 009)* **DAZZLING STRANGER: ANTHOLOGY**
– Strolling down the highway / Angi / Running from home / Needle of death / It don't bother me / Lucky thirteen / Blackwaterside / The first time ever I saw your face / Soho / Rabbit run / Woe is love my dear / Bells / Wishing well / Poison / I am lonely / Train song / Nobody's bar / January man / Reynardine / Rosemary lane / When I get home / Oh my father moonshine / Fresh as a sweet Sunday / Lost and gone / Blacksmith / Chambertin / You are my sunshine / Blues run the game / One to a hundred / Sweet Mother Earth / Where did my life go / Blackbird in the morning / Playing the game / Is it real / Lady fair / Old routine / Three dreamers / The ornament tree / Summer heat / Morning brings peace of mind / Carnival / Toy balloon / Looking for love / October song.
Jan 01. (cd) *Castle; (CMRCD 022)* **LIVE IN AUSTRALIA**
Apr 02. (cd) *Castle Pie; (PIESD 270)* **AN INTRODUCTION TO BERT JANSCH**

Maureen JELKS (see under ⇒ Springthyme records)

JOCK TAMSON'S BAIRNS

Formed: Edinburgh . . . late 70's by Burns aficionado/singer ROD PATERSON, Kelso solicitor and fiddler IAN HARDIE, JOHN CROALL and NORMAN CHALMERS (the latter once a part of NOT THE FULL SHILLIN alongside TONY CUFFE, BRIAN McNEILL, etc). DEREK HOY joined the JTB team following the release of their 1980 eponymous debut album, a record that enjoys the prestige of featuring in RICHARD THOMPSON's all-time Top 10. Although the group hooked up with OSSIAN's TONY CUFFE on the 'Iona' album, 'Fergusson's Auld Reekie' (1981), their brief career came to an end with 'THE LASSES' FASHION' (1982), after which the various members occupied themselves with other projects (see below).

Nigh on two decades after the latter set's release, a line-up of PATERSON, CROALL, HARDIE, HOY and CHALMERS recorded a brand new JTB album, 'MAY YE NEVER LACK A SCONE' (2001) and performed to a packed house at Glasgow's Celtic Connections Festival.

ROD PATERSON – vocals, guitar, mandola (ex-CHORDA CLEICH) / **JOHN CROALL** – vocals, bodhran, whistle (ex-CHORDA CLEICH) / **IAN HARDIE** – fiddle, vocals / **NORMAN CHALMERS** – concertina, percussion, whistles / plus **JACK EVANS** (b. Cardiff) – guitar

Temple — not iss.

1980. (lp) *(TP 002)* **A' JOCK TAMSON'S BAIRNS**
– Arthur Bignold of Lochrosque / Hugh MacDonald / Sandy Duff / Birken tree / Hieland soldier / Mullindhu / The Skyeman's jig / Jenny Dang the weaver / Brave Lewie Roy / Wantoness / Caithkin braes / Clarke Saunders / Miss Grace Hay's / The shepherdess / In dispraise of whisky / The hills of Perth / Mrs. MacDougall / Sae will we yet. *(re-iss. Jan83; same)*

— (1981) added **DEREK HOY** – fiddle

Topic — not iss.

1982. (lp) *(12TS 424)* **THE LASSES' FASHION**
– The lasses' fashion / The robin / The merry nicht under the Tummel brig / The braes o' Balquhidder / Greig's Strathspey / Miss Wharton Duff / Lady Keith's lament / The gates of Edinburgh / O'er bogie / Mrs. Gordon of Uvie / Tibbie Fowler / Strathspey – The Shetland fiddler's society / Grant's reel / Gladstone's reel / The laird o' Drum / Kempy Kaye / Donald Willie & his dog / Peter MacKinnon of Skeabost.

— in 1981, the group teamed up with OSSIAN's TONY CUFFE on the album, 'FERGUSSON'S AULD REIKIE' on 'Iona' records

— split for a decade or so while the each went into other projects:- CHALMERS joined OSSIAN, The EASY CLUB (with ROD) and the CAULD BLAST ORCHESTRA, HARDIE went solo and joined the HIGHLAND CONNECTION (now in The GHILLIES), HOY is now part of the BELLA McNABB CEILIDH BAND, while PATERSON is now solo (part-time with The PICTS) and a member of CEOLBEG. JTB re-formed in 2000:- **PATERSON, CROALL, HARDIE, HOY + CHALMERS**

Greentrax — Greentrax

Feb 01. (cd) *(<CDTRAX 206>)* **MAY YE NEVER LACK A SCONE**
– Gude claret – Wee Highland laddie / Prince Charlie's march – Joy gae wi' my love – Ho ho chaileagan / Braes o' Gleniffer / MacGregor of Ruara – The king's house / Bogie's bonnie belle / The back of the Change House – Miss Girdle – The bristly beard – Barney's Balmoral / Woo'd and married and ' / Loch Etive side – South Uist golf club – The country girl and the Hungarian fiddler – Mrs Willie Wassle / Dusty Miller – Wee Willie Gray / Duncan McNeill's farewell to Melfort / Boc liath nan

ghobar (The grey duck) – The rock and the wee pickle tow / Johnny Sangster / The unreel – Les trois grande Luthiers / Donal Don – Piper's cave.

– compilations, etc. –

Feb 94. (c) *Temple; (<CTP 004>)* **TRADITIONAL MUSIC AND SONG FROM SCOTLAND** ☐ ☐ Apr95

Apr 96. (cd) *Greentrax; (<CDTRAX 112>)* **JOCK TAMSON'S BAIRNS** (two early albums) ☐ ☐ May96

IAN HARDIE

Greentrax Greentrax

Oct 86. (lp/c) *(TRAX/CTRAX 001)* **A BREATH OF FRESH AIRS** ☐ -
– Cheviot blast / The poetic milkman / Kelsae brig / The bull ring / The omnibus / The tuneless clock / The junction pool / The Duke's dyke / The eight sided square / The damside / Bowmont water / Border worthies' Burns club / Pipe Major Rev. Joe Brown / The cleek / The floaded goat / Catch-a-penny fox / The red herring / Venchen circle / Old bean waltz / Hospital wood / Auchope caim / North to England / Hoselaw chapel / The black hag / Schoolroom pipers / Yetholm haugh / Tobermory wedding / The late white swan / The leg-up / Tanner's swee / The hen hole / Mabon of Torwoodlee.

Feb 92. (cd/c) *(<CD/C TRAX 049>)* **A BREATH OF FRESHER AIRS** ☐ ☐ 1994
– Mrs Elspeth Hardie – The goat in the boat – Fiona's jig – The new 19th / Mellerstan house – The knock of Braemoray – Andrew James Hardie / Cawdor Wood – The palpitation reel – Mrs Wullie Wastle / The 'compose yourself' waltz – Segs hornpipe – The Macbeaths of Tulloch Castle / The Invernairn two-step / Lochindorb – The Lochdhu waltz / The grand slam – Horsburgh castle / Vivianae – Helsinki harbour – Lethen bar – White in the heather / The sutors' waltz – The bonnie lass o' Wark – The lights of Balintore / Dulsie Bridge – The locked bucket / Shifting sands / Esther Stephenson of Embleton / Chatterin' teeth – The Nigg rigs jig – The oystercatcher / Drumochter sun – The crown knot / Snow on the ben – The up an' doon reel / The The lost village of Culbin – Tarbat Ness light / Drummossie muir.

— in 1994, HARDIE featured on V/A comp 'Ecosse: A Breath Of Scotland Volume 1', released on 'Playasound'

— in Jan'95, the HIGHLAND CONNECTION (featuring HARDIE, with J. CLARK & D. GORDON) issued the album 'GAINING GROUND' *(CD/C TRAX 087)*

— next with **ANDY THORBURN** – piano, keyboards

Mar 98. (cd; by IAN HARDIE & ANDY THORBURN) *(<CDTRAX 152>)* **SPIDER'S WEB** ☐ ☐ May98
– Tweedledee reel / My compliments to the biochemist / The Brackla waltz / Jig of the Clan Beag / The last farewell / Glenkinchie's compliments to the lord and lady MacFarlane of Bearsden / Lime hill / The camembert waltz / The setting sun / Streens / The 31 steps / The Gallowhill reel / Torgarrow.

ROD PATERSON

Greentrax Greentrax

Mar 87. (lp/c) *(TRAX/CTRAX 004)* **TWO HATS** ☐ -
– My funny valentine / Every time we say goodbye / Willie Wassle / My nannie / Pierre le Bateau / Wrong joke again / I do it for your love / Steggie / Bleacher lass o' Kelvinhaugh. *(c re-iss. Sep94; same)*

Apr 88. (lp/c) *(TRAX/CTRAX 016)* **SMILING WAVED GOODBYE** ☐ -
– Roll that boulder away / Le carcon malheureux / Lord Gordon's kitchen boy / Flting up to London / You / Smiling waved goodbye / Earl Richard / The Dowie dens of Yarrow / A wee flingette. *(c re-iss. Sep94; same)*

— in the 90's, ROD would join top folk act, CEOLBEG – >

Nov 96. (cd/c) *(<CD/C TRAX 117>)* **SONGS FROM THE BOTTOM DRAWER: ROD PATERSON SINGS BURNS** ☐ ☐ Dec96
– Mary Morrison / Ye banks and braes / Wert thou in the cauld blast / Waukrife Minnie / Gray twins / Parcel of rogues in a nation / Gae bring tae me a pint o' wine / Guidwife coont the lawin' – The coggie's revenge / Red red rose / Gloomy December / A man's a man / Ochone for somebody / Auld lang syne.

Jul 00. (cd) *(<CDTRAX 197>)* **UP TO DATE** (compilation) ☐ ☐ Aug00
– Bleacher lass of Kelvin haugh / My funny valentine / Every time we say goodbye / Willie Wassle / My nannie O / Pierre le Bateau / Wrong joke again / I do it for your love / Steggie / Roll that boulder away / La garcon malheureux / Lord Gordon's kitchen boy / Smiling waved goodbye / Earl Richard / Dowie dens of Yarrow / Wee flingette (instrumental).

Keith JOHNSTON (see under ⇒ CALASAIG)

J.S.D. BAND

Formed: Glasgow . . . 1969 by fiddle player CHUCK FLEMING along with DES COFFIELD, SEAN O'ROURKE, JIM DIVERS and COLIN FINN. Initially part of the thriving Glasgow/Edinburgh folk scene, the J.S.D. BAND cut their teeth alongside the likes of BILLY CONNOLLY, GERRY RAFFERTY, HAMISH IMLACH, RAB NOAKES, etc. Their debut album, 'COUNTRY OF THE BLIND' (1971), offered up an enticing selection of electrified folk-rock from around the British Isles and precipitated comparisons with contemporaries like STEELEYE SPAN and LINDISFARNE. It also caught the attention of John Peel who became something of a patron, giving the band airplay on his show and penning sleevenotes for their next two albums.

By the release of 1972's 'THE J.S.D. BAND', the lads had already relocated to London where they played to sell-out audiences at such esteemed venues as the Albert Hall, the Royal Festival Hall and the Queen Elizabeth Hall as well as supporting DAVID BOWIE on the first Ziggy Stardust tour. In fact, throughout their short career, the band shared top billing with the likes of STATUS QUO, JOHNNY WINTER, LOU REED and even SLY & THE FAMILY STONE (!) while legendary acts such as The AVERAGE WHITE BAND and fellow Scots The SENSATIONAL ALEX HARVEY BAND actually supported the JSD BAND.

Yet while the band were a live force to be reckoned with, the pressures of constant touring together with musical differences and family commitments eventually led to the JSD's demise. 'TRAVELLING DAYS' (1973) served as the group's swansong album although they released a further couple of singles ('SUNSHINE LIFE FOR ME' and 'HAYES AND HARLINGTON BLUES') before disbanding in mid-'74.

A gap of twenty years ensued before the JSD BAND resumed business in the mid-90's with an all-original line-up and a brand new album, 'FOR THE RECORD' (1997). Consisting of acoustic re-interpretations of material from the group's early 70's heyday, the album was in contrast to 'PASTURES OF PLENTY' (2000), a return to the amplified folk-rock sound which originally made them famous.

DES COFFIELD – vocals, mandolin, guitars, accordion, piano / **SEAN O'ROURKE** – banjo, guitar, fiddle, flute, vocals / **CHUCK FLEMING** – fiddle, mandolin / **JIM DIVERS** – bass, cello, vocals / **COLIN FINN** – drums, percussion

Regal Zonophone not iss.

Jul 71. (lp) *(SRLZ 1018)* **COUNTRY OF THE BLIND** ☐ -
– Country of the blind / Cooleys / Childhood memories / Sarah Jane / Old time heartaches / Nancy / Jenny pickling cockles / Don't think twice, it's all right / Darling Corey / Morning dew / Cousin caterpillar / Over and over / Hope / Wonders of nature.

Cube not iss.

Nov 72. (lp) *(HIFLY 11)* **THE J.S.D. BAND** ☐ -
– Open road / As I roved out / Betsy / Barney / Brallaghan / Johnny O'Breadislea / Going down / Dusty road / Sylvie / Irish girl / Honey babe / Groundhog. *(cd-iss. Oct99 & Oct00 on 'Eclipse'+=; ECCD 1)* – Sarah Jane / Paddy stacks / Fishing blues / Sarah Jane (stereo mix).

Mar 73. (7") *(BUG 29)* **SARAH JANE. / PADDY STACKS** ☐ -

Jun 73. (lp) *(HIFLY 14)* **TRAVELLING DAYS** ☐ -
– The Galway races / Fishin' blues / Sarah Jane / Travelling days / King's favourite / The cuckoo / Dowie dens of Yarrow / Down the road / Young waters / Green fields (of America).

Apr 74. (7") *(BUG 40)* **SUNSHINE LIFE FOR ME. / REEL COOL** ☐ -

Jul 74. (7") *(BUG 49)* **HAYES AND HARLINGTON BLUES. / THE CUCKOO** ☐ -

— disbanded when most members departed; **IAIN LYON** (ex-MY DEAR WATSON) contributed to the short-lived NEW JSD BAND

— however, the JSD BAND were in full-swing once more around 1996 (O'ROURKE formed ALBA – one eponymous album in 1982 for 'Rubber' records – and in the 90's moonlighted with his own jazz-folk outfit, The KELTZ)

— **FLEMING, COFFIELD, O'ROURKE, DIVERS + FINN** plus **ROB MAIRS** – 5-string banjo, dobro

Lochshore K.R.L.

May 97. (cd) *(<CDLDL 1256>)* **FOR THE RECORD** (acoustic set) ☐ ☐
– Sarah Jane / As I roved out / Cuckoo / Irish girl – The musical priest / Groundhog: Johnny O'Breadislea / The sunshine hornpipe – The mountain road / Darlin' Corey / The Galway races / Goin' down the road / Don't think twice / Down the road / Morrison's jig – Cooley's reel / Over and over.

May 98. (cd) *(<CDLDL 1274>)* **PASTURES OF PLENTY** ☐ ☐ Feb00
– The bonny lass of Albany / Unknown polka – The dancing master's reel – As I went out upon the ice / Pastures of plenty / The downfall of Paris – The chanter's tune / Shake loose the border / Seamus's jig – Unknown – The Monaghan jig – Unknown / Patrick's island / The gypsy laddie / The Sligo maid – The humours of Tulla – St. Anne's reel – The green fields of Rossbeigh – O'Rourke's reel / Shady cove / Rodney's glory – An spalpeen fanach / The Spanish lady.

KEEP IT UP (see under ⇒ Tartan Tapes records)

KELTIK ELEKTRIK (see under ⇒ EASY CLUB)

KELTZ / ALMANAC (see ⇒ Section 5: Jazz

Mary Ann KENNEDY & Charlotte PETERSEN (see under ⇒ Macmeanmna records)

Ross KENNEDY & Archie McALLISTER (see under ⇒ Lochshore records)

KENTIGERN

Formed: Glasgow area . . . late 70's by former members of TINKLER MAIDGIE and The INVERNESKY FIREMEN. Piper/flautist DOUGIE PINCOCK, JOHN GAHAGAN, JIMMY McGUIRE and SANDY STANAGE were joined by JIM and SYLVIA BARNES and it would be this line-up that recorded their eponymous set for 'Topic' in 1979. However, with half the group augmenting The BATTLEFIELD BAND at various times it was inevitable that KENTIGERN would disband. In the mid-80's, the BARNES family re-emerged as SCOTCH MEASURE, a trio with ANDY LAVERY in tow. Keeping up with all things traditional and folk, IAN & SYLVIA BARNES would once again reunite in the studio for a 1991 release, 'MUNGO JUMBO'.

JIM BARNES – guitar, cittern, vocals / **SYLVIA BARNES** – vocals, dulcimer, guitar / **JOHN GAHAGAN + JIMMY McGUIRE + SANDY STANAGE + DOUGIE PINCOCK**

Topic not iss.

1979. (lp) *(12TS 394)* **KENTIGERN** ☐ -
– Cullen Bay – Jig of slurs – Seagull / The corncake / Breton tunes – Greenwoodside / The weary farmers / Pipe Major Donald McLean of Lewis – The weavers of Newly – Kail and pudding – Loch Roag / The iron horse / The last o' tinkler / Rathven market – The conundrum / Gin I were shot o' her / Hebridean air – The braes of Tulimet – The braes of Mellinish / Wild roving no more / Put me in the great chest – The three peaks of South Uist – South Uist.

— after their split PINCOCK would carve out a solo career and join The BATTLEFIELD BAND; SYLVIA and IAN were also members at some period

SCOTCH MEASURE

SYLVIA + JIM BARNES / + ANDY LAVERY – keyboards, vocals

Topic not iss.

1985. (lp) *(12TS 426)* **SCOTCH MEASURE** ☐ -
– Ythanside / For a' that / The brewer laddie / Wild rovin' / The bonnie lad that handles the plough / The swallow / The laird of Dainty Dounby / The Calton weaver / The hadweaver and the factory maid / The twa magicians.

JIM AND SYLVIA BARNES

with **LAVERY** + **ERICA SCOTT** – flute / **ANDY CHEYNE** – bass / **JEZ LOWE** – harmonica

Cerberus not iss.

1991. (cd) *(CS 002)* **MUNGO JUMBO** ☐ -
– Kishmul's gallery / False hae ye been Mrs Greig / Lady Diamond / Lichtbob's lassie / This is no' my plaid / Willie brewed a peck o' maut / Galloways / Rural courtship / Young Allan / I wonder / The forester.

Moira KERR

Born: c.1950's, Glasgow. As well as exercising her vocals chords (from toddler age onwards), MOIRA's other childhood love was athletics and as a teenager, she scored successive Scottish titles in the shot-putt until a back injury caused her early retirement. Turning her attention to music, MOIRA got off to a good start by winning a talent contest while her recording career was initiated in 1981 with 'BEST OF BOTH WORLDS' on the 'Ross' label.

The singer subsequently set up her own label, 'Mayker', for 1983's 'GLEN NEVIS' set, following this with a series of cassette-only releases throughout the 80's. Largely self-penned (she also composes the music), her lyrical songs deal in themes of Scotland's historical and cultural heritage in the spirit – if not the language – of its ancient Gaelic traditions. Boasting a warm, clear vocal style and an accessible, easy listening sound, MOIRA appeals to a wide cross section of music fans as opposed to a narrow niche in the folk market.

Following 1989's 'BBC' release, 'MACIAIN OF GLENCOE' (featured on BBC TV Scotland's 'Eagle's Eye View Of Glencoe'- she also composed music for another BBC TV programme 'Where Eagles Fly'), KERR again took up the theme of the haunting glen in 1995's 'GLENCOE – THE GLEN OF WEEPING'. More recently, MOIRA released the 'TIME AND TIDE' (2000) album, launched with the singer performing her version of 'SAILING' as the tall ships set sail from Greenock. As well as an arrangement by CAPERCAILLIE's DONALD SHAW and contributions from other talented names in the folk scene, the record featured a guest spot from the Scottish netball squad(!).

MOIRA KERR – vocals, acoustic guitar / with session people, etc

Ross not iss.

Sep 81. (lp/c) *(WGR/CWGR 014)* **BEST OF BOTH WORLDS** ☐ -
– Don't you ever fall in love with me / Pride goes before a fall / Walk right back / Let me love you once before you go / I'll never forget yesterday / I only want to be with you / I know you're gonna sing that love song / Killing me softly with his song / Blue angel eyes / Say goodbye to your daddy / If / Bye bye love.

Mayker not iss.

1983. (c) *(CMAYK 2)* **GLEN NEVIS** ☐ -
– Glen Nevis / Whiskey in the jar / Coulter's candy / Wee laddie / The bonnie lass o' Fyvie / Thyme / Scotland I miss you tonight / Gallowa' hills / Scotland again / Wild mountain thyme / Crofters ceilidh / Dark island.

1983. (c) *(CMAYK 3)* **COTTAGE ON THE HILL** ☐ -
– The cottage on the hill / The Queen's four Mary's / The jeely piece song / Highland fairy lullaby / My lad is fair / Scotland again / Jock o' Hazeldean / The auld maid in the garret / I'll be back there / I know a lad / Flower of Scotland.

Nov 83. (7") *(MAYK 4)* **THE MINGULAY BOAT SONG. / THE WATER IS WIDE** ☐ -

1985. (c) *(CMAYK 5)* **SCOTLAND I'M YOURS** ☐ -

B.B.C. not iss.

Jan 89. (7") *(RESL 231)* **MACAIN OF GLENCOE. /** ☐ -

Aug 89. (lp/c/cd) *(REN/ZCN/BBCCD 734)* **MACIAIN OF GLENCOE** ☐ -
– MacIain of Glencoe / The dark island / Charles Edward Stuart / The Skye boat song / The island of Tiree / Always Argyle / I once loved a lad / Ca' the ewes / The Mingulay boat song / Farewell to Tarwathie / Loch Lomond / A sense of belonging. *(re-iss. Apr92 & Jun99 on 'Moidart' cd/c; MOI CD/MC 003) (cd re-iss. Mar01 on 'Moidart'; MIDCD 009)*

Feb 91. (cd/c) *(BBCCD/ZCF 771)* **WHERE EAGLES FLY** ☐ -
(re-iss. Apr92 on 'Moidart' cd/c; MOI CD/MC 004) (video-iss.Mar98 on 'West Five'; WES 8N)

Tangmere not iss.

Sep 94. (cd/c) *(CFTM CD/CC 01)* **BE THOU MY VISION** ☐ -
– Be thou my vision / Who would true valour see / I vow to thee my country / Holy, holy, holy / Teach me, my God and King / O thou camest from above / By cool Siloam's shady rill / Stand up stand up for Jesus / Dear Lord and father of mankind / Immortal, invisible, God only wise / Forty days and forty nights / Breathe on me breath of God / Alleluya, sing to Jesus / Jerusalem.

Mayker not iss.

Jan 95. (cd)(c) *(CDMAYK 1)(CMAYK 7)* **GLENCOE – THE GLEN OF WEEPING** (orig. 1992) ☐ -
– Closer to Heaven / This child / Oban bay / Loch Lomond hills / Three months of the year / The glen of weeping / Gleann bhaille chaoil / When I dream / The Curragh of Kildare / Isle of Innesfree / Arran the island I love / You'll be there / The glen of weeping (instrumental reprise). *(re-iss. Sep99 cd/c; CD/C MAYK 1)*

Sep 95. (cd/c) *(CD/C MAYK 9)* **BRAVEST HEART** ☐ -
– Bravest heart / Corryvreckan / She moved through the fair / Only a woman's heart / Islands in the mist / The Queen's four Mary's / Fear a bhata / For justice and honour / Long black veil / House carpenter / Safely ashore / Highlanders.

May 97. (cd/c) *(CD/C MAYK 10)* **CELTIC SOUL** ☐ -
– MacIain of Glencoe / Will ye go lassie go / Where eagles fly / Sands of time / Corryvreckan / The Skye boat song / Bravest heart / Loch Lomond / Island of Tiree / Flower of Scotland / Highlanders / Mingulay / The dark island / Farewell to Tarwathie / Skye high / Drifting away. *(re-iss. Sep99; same)*

Sep 99. (cd/c) *(CD/C MAYK 14)* **TIME AND TIDE** ☐ -
– Sailing / Together / Dumbarton drums / Highland Harry / Ae fond kiss / This is my world / Kismul's galley / Banquo's walk / Eshaness / Alba mo graidh / When the pipers play / The thief of life.

– compilations, others, etc. –

Nov 96. (cd/c) *Moidart; (MOI CD/MC 010)* **ALL THE BEST** ☐ -
– MacIain of Glencoe / Where eagles fly / The Skye boat song / Loch Lomond / The dark island / Banquo's walk / Sands of time / Drifting away / The Mingulay boat song / Everlasting visions / Paradise for two / Cuillin. *(re-iss. Jun99; same)*

KERRIES (see under ⇒ Wee Folk of the 60s)

Alison KINNAIRD (see under ⇒ MAC-TALLA)

KINNELL (see under ⇒ Lochshore records)

KRYSIA (see under ⇒ NATURAL ACOUSTIC BAND)

Christine KYDD

Born: 13 Dec'57, Glasgow. Renowned as a singer, songwriter and guitarist, CHRISTINE KYDD has made her name in the field of traditional Scots song as both a harmony singer and a solo performer. Over the years she has worked with an impressive list of collaborators including ALASDAIR FRASER, SILEAS, ANDY THORBURN, JACK EVANS, NORMAN CHALMERS, FRANKIE ARMSTRONG, WENDY WEATHERBY as well as members of SHOOGLENIFTY, MOUTH MUSIC and The CAULD BLAST ORCHESTRA. One of her most well known partnerships was with Fife-born traditional singer JANET RUSSELL, the pair appearing together on BBC Radio 2's 'Folk On 2' programme and recording an eponymous collaborative album for 'Greentrax' in 1988.

Performing live, KYDD has shared a stage with folk heavyweights such as CAPERCAILLIE, CHRISTY MOORE and The TANNAHILL WEAVERS. Prior to its recent demise, CHRISTINE held the position of Artist In Residence at the Aberdeen Alternative Festival, her teaching credentials evidenced by the high demand for her voice workshops in Britain, Europe and the USA.

More recently, CHRISTINE has formed one third of CHANTAN alongside ELSPETH COWIE (of SEANNACHIE) and CORRINA HEWAT (of BACHUE), a "supertrio" aiming to inject a bit of fresh creative blood into traditional music by combining folk, blues and jazz with harmony and acappella singing. The all-female trio made their debut in 1997 with the 'PRIMARY COLOURS' album, a varied collection of traditional songs and lesser known BURNS compositions set to fresh, original arrangements.

On the solo front, CHRISTINE released the 'DARK PEARLS' album (1999), like CHANTAN's set issued on ALASDAIR FRASER's 'Culburnie' imprint.

CHRISTINE KYDD – vocals, acoustic guitar / with **STEAFAN HANNIGAN** – bouzouki, banjo, uilleann pipes, bodhran, whistles / **FIONA LARCOMBE** – fiddle / **MARY McLAUGHLIN + JACKI SUMMERS** – backing vocals

Fellside not iss.

Oct 93. (cd) *(FE 093CD)* **HEADING HOME** □ [-]
– The sailor laddie / Can ye sew cushions – On children / My darling ploughman boy / Tiored o' workin' / The lonesome rovin' wolves / The snows they melt the soonest / The weekend song / Cotton mill girls / I know moonlight / The old man's mare's dead / Letter to Syracuse / Gloomy December. *(re-iss. Oct00; same)*

— in 1994, RUSSELL and KYDD released their follow-up collaboration album, 'DANCIN' CHANTIN' for 'Greentrax'

Culburnie Culburnie

Dec 99. (cd) *(<CUL 115CD>)* **DARK PEARLS** □ □
– Lord Gregory / King's shillin' / Jenny Nettles / Fause, fause / Sheath and knife / Greenwoodside / Plooman laddies / The rovin' ploughboy / The twa brithers / Fisherrow – The song of the fishgutters / Capernaum / Sailor laddie / Bonnie laddie I gan bye ye.

CHANTAN

CHRISTINE KYDD plus **ELSPETH COWIE** – vocals, percussion (also a Solo Artist, ex-SEANNACHIE) / **CORRINA HEWAT** – vocals, Scottish harp (of BACHUE, ex-SEANNACHIE)

Culburnie Culburnie

Jan 97. (cd/c) *(<CUL 108 CD/C>)* **PRIMARY COLOURS** □ □
– Gloomy winter's noo awa' / John Anderson / Slave's lament / Darn that dream / The collier laddie / Donal Og / The witches' reel / The dowie dens o' Yarrow / If I had a ribbon bow / Wha'll mow me now / The braes o' Killiekrankie O – The lea-rig / Boser girls / Hishey bah / Down in the jungle.

Danny KYLE (see under ⇒ Iona records)

L

Robin LAING

Born: Edinburgh. Up until the mid-90's, LAING held down the demanding job of director of a mental health charity, working part-time on his singing/songwriting. His 1989 debut album, 'EDINBURGH SKYLINE', brought admiration from many on the folk scene, critics noting his debt to 60's folkies like PAUL SIMON and RALPH McTELL. With a gentle, often melancholy vocal style and careful, finger-picking acoustic guitar accompaniment, LAING's combination of self-penned material and interpretations of traditional ballads and ROBERT BURNS songs has seen him build up a loyal grassroots following.

1994's 'WALKING IN TIME' brought further plaudits and in 1996 LAING took the plunge and devoted himself to music full-time. That year also saw the inclusion of his wistful Bonnie Prince Charlie ballad, 'THE SUMMER OF '46', on 'The Music & Song Of Greentrax', the East Lothian label for which he continues to record.

'THE ANGEL'S SHARE' (1997) was based around a one-man theatre piece exploring the demon drink or more specifically, Scotch whisky. More prolific than ever, LAING released a fourth set, 'IMAGINARY LINES', in October '99. He also continues to involve himself in community work, taking song classes in Lanarkshire – where he's currently based – and holding down the post of convener of the New Makar's Trust, a non-profit organisation dedicated to the promotion of native songwriting talent.

ROBIN LAING – vocals, acoustic/Spanish guitar / with cellist RON SHAW, JIM SUTHERLAND, NICK KEIR + COLIN RAMAGE

Greentrax Greentrax

Mar 89. (c/lp) *(C+/TRAX 021)* **EDINBURGH SKYLINE** □ [-]
– Edinburgh skyline / Burke & Hare / Love is born / The Union canal / Leaving today / Icarus / Ulysses / Isle of Eigg / Day by day / Andrew Lammie / Spring song / Passing time. *(<US + cd-iss. Sep94 & Feb98; CDTRAX 021>)*

— he retained SHAW + found BRIAN McNEILL, DOUGIE PINCOCK, IAIN JOHNSTONE, JASON DOVE + MARCUS WATT

Apr 94. (cd/c) *(CD/C TRAX 072)* **WALKING IN TIME** □ [-]
– The soldier maid / Kilbowie hill / The summer of '46 / Punters / The unquiet grave / The lass o' Paties mill / El punado de centeno – Jamie Foyers / Billy Taylor / The Forth Bridge song / The loose noose – Deacon Brodie / When two hearts combine / Lament on the death of hid second wife / Calypso's island / Experience.

— now with JAMES MALCOLM, JOHN MARTIN, WENDY WEATHERBY, HAMISH BAYNE + NICK WEIR

Jul 97. (cd/c) *(<CD/C TRAX 137>)* **THE ANGEL'S SHARE** □ □ Sep97
– More than just a dram / Our glens / Piper MacNeil / Willie brewed a pack o' maut / The parish o' Dunkeld / Tak' aff your dram / Twelve and a tanner a bottle / Whiskey and women / Nancy's whisky / The De'il's awa' wi' the exciseman / A bottle o' the best / John Barleycorn / Tongue discipline / Tall tale / Whisky you're the devil / Tak' a dram / A wee deoch an' dorus.

— now with **DAVID SCOTT, JIM GASH, BRIAN McALPINE, WENDY WEATHERBY, AMY GEDDES, TOM McNIVEN + Mr. DEREK STAR**

Oct 99. (cd) *(<CDTRAX 185>)* **IMAGINARY LINES** □ □ Dec99
– Where did the morning go? / The wife of Ushers Well / Cyclops / A nation's heart / Carmichael hill / Watershed / Closer to Heaven / Pittsburg, Pa. / Michigan skies / Heavy horses / Born in the wrong time / Venezuela / Black clothes / The secret song of time.

Steve LAWRENCE & Hudson SWAN (see under ⇒ Lochshore records)

Jackie LEVEN (see ⇒ Section 8: Rock, Pop & Indie)

LIVINGSTONES

Formed: Hamilton/Blantyre, Lanarkshire ... 1964. Frontman FRANK McKAY and his versatile and multi-talented brother KEN had graduated from Glasgow University. There, they met up with fellow graduate DAVID McCABE, regarded highly as one of the best (Burns-inspired) folk singers of his generation and who also played a mean chanter. A fourth member, JOHN DEMPSEY, subsequently joined up in 1965 for a folk boat tour between Glasgow and Rothesay; a TV appearance in France soon followed. In 1968, they finally recorded their debut album, an 'IN CONCERT' set performed at Hamilton's Town Hall. Little was heard from the quartet thereafter, although FRANK became a history teacher, running his school's folk club part-time.

FRANK McKAY – vocals / **KEN McKAY** – guitars, banjo, mandolin, whistle, dulcimer, balalaika / **DAVID McCABE** – vocals, chanter / **JOHN DEMPSEY** – vocals

Waverley not iss.

1968. (lp) *(SZLP 2105)* **. . .IN CONCERT (live)** ☐ [-]
– Ye Jacobites by name / The buroo song / The wild rover / What'll be king but Charlie / The first time / The yellow haired laddie / Bonnie Dundee / High Dunn / My Johnny is a shoemaker / Tramps and hawkers / San Miguel / The Irish rover.

Living Tradition label (see under ⇒ Springthyme records)

the LORELEI (see under ⇒ Lochshore records)

Mac/Mc

MacALIAS (see under ⇒ BOWMAN, Gill)

Ishbel MacASKILL

Born: Point, Isle Of Lewis. Despite being born into one of the few non-singing families in Point – a village renowned for its Gaelic singing tradition – ISHBEL began exercising her vocal chords not long after learning her first words. Although she sang occasionally in the school choir, her talent remained overlooked and it took encouragement from the likes of ROBIN HALL and JIMMIE McGREGOR to persuade MacASKILL she had a future in the folk world.

Her first professional performance came at the Mod fringe in 1979 and she's since gone on to become one of the most respected traditional Scottish singers in the world. She's also one of the most recognisable, with her melancholy, soulful, unaccompanied style seeing her dubbed as the 'Aretha Franklin Of Gaelic Singing'. If that's just too much to get your head around, then hear the evidence for yourself on any one of the three albums she's recorded over her long career, 'BELOVED LEWIS' (1988) and 'SIODA' (1994). The most recent of these, 'ESSENTIALLY ISHBEL' (2000) was released on her own-named imprint.

Over the years, ISHBEL had made countless TV and radio appearances as well as captivating audiences in France, Spain, Israel, the USA and beyond, consolidating her position as a leading ambassador for Scotland's Gaelic music and culture.

ISHBEL MacASKILL – vocals / with various backers

Lapwing not iss.

Mar 88. (lp/c) *(LAP 117/+C)* **BELOVED LEWIS** ☐ [-]
– Would that you have been / Young girl of the fair hair / The high swell of the sea / I cannot sleep / The deer are on the Uig slope / Beloved Lewis / The brother's killing / The lament for John Roy / Near Loch an duin / I'll make a verse / A lament for Donnie Ferguson.

— next with **WENDY STEWART** – harp, concertina / **BILLY ROSS** – guitar, dulcimer / **BLAIR DOUGLAS** – keyboards, accordion / **IAIN MacINNES** – pipes, whistles / **CHAZ STEWART** – guitar / **DICK DRAKE** – drums / plus guests **MICHAEL MARRA, ARTHUR CORMACK, GILLIAN MacKENZIE, AMANDA MILLEN + FIONA MacKENZIE**

Skye not iss.

1994. (cd) *(SKYECD 06)* **SIODA (SILK)** ☐ [-]
– Thig an smeorach as t-Earrach / Chi mi'n toman / Aignis / Tha mo spiorad cianail / Bha mi latha Samhraidh an Steornabhagh – The conundrum / 'S daor a cheannaich mi'n t-iasgach / Ho ro chan eil cadal orm / Gradh geal mo chridh' / Gur muladach sgith mi / Braigh Loch Iall / Oran na maighdinn-mhara.

— next with **CORRINA HEWAT** – harp, backing vocals / **LEO McCANN** – accordion / **TONY McMANUS** – guitar / **DUNCAN McGILLIVRAY** – pipes, guitar, mouth-organ / **ALYTH McCORMACK + AMANDA MILLEN** – backing vocals

MacAskill not iss.

Jun 00. (cd) *(IMCD 001)* **ESSENTIALLY ISHBEL** ☐ [-]
– An teid thu leam a mhairi / An innis aigh / Waulking set / Canan nan gaidheal / Piobaireachd dhomhnuill dhuibh / Soraidh leis an alt / An ataireachd ard / Mor a' cheannaich / Bidh clann Ulaidh air do Bhanais / Fair and tender lasses / Griogal cridhe / Puirt a beul / Nighean nan geug.

Jimmy MacBEATH

Born: 1894, Portsoy. Claiming – rightly or wrongly – he was a descendant of MacBeth (King of Scotland!), JIMMY was a major inspiration to many 60's folkies. A source and bothy ballad singer of renowned distinction (much in the mould of DAVIE STEWART), the cloth-capped farmer also worked with contemporary BERT JANSCH. MacBEATH released two LP's for 'Topic', 'WILD ROVER NO MORE' (1967) and 'BOUND TO BE A ROW' (1972), before he died on the 7th January, 1972 in Aberdeenshire. His legacy was an Alan Lomax (Portrait series) collection for 'Rounder', 'TRAMPS & HAWKERS', released early in 2002.

JIMMY MacBEATH – vocals

Topic not iss.

1967. (lp) *(12T 173)* **WILD ROVER NO MORE** ☐ [-]
– Bold English navvy / Come a' ye tramps an' hawkers / Johnny McIndoe / Wind blew the bonnie lassie's plaidie awa' / Merchant and the beggar maid / Nicky Tams / Barnyards of Delgaty / I'm a stranger in this country / Moss o' Burreldale / Highlandman's ball / McPherson's rant / Grat for gruel / Drumdelgie / Wild rover no more. *(c-iss.Nov88 on 'Springthyme'; SPRC 1020)*

1972. (lp) *(12T 303)* **BOUND TO BE A ROW** ☐ [-]
– There's bound to be a row / Banks of Inverurie / Ythanside / Erin go bragh / Bogie's bonnie belle / Cow wi' the iron tail / Arlin's fine braes / Bonnie lass o' Fyvie / Pittenweem Jo / Ye canna pit it on tae Sandy / Boston smuggler / Highland Rorie's wedding / Magdalene green / Marin fair / Roving baker. *(re-iss. 1981; same)*

– compilations, others, etc. –

Apr 88. (c) *Folktracks; (60-058)* **TRAMPS AND HAWKERS** ☐ [-]
– Tramps and hawkers / Next pudden Ken / Moss o' Burreldale / Muckin' o' Geordie's byre / The dowie dens of Yarrow / Hawick common riding song / Day we went to Rothsay-o / John Anderson, my Jo / Forfar soldier / Down by the maudlin green.

Apr 88. (c) *Folktracks; (60-059)* **HORSEMAN'S WORD** ☐ [-]
– Jim the carter lad / The farmer, the ploughboy and the dairymaid / Come all ye lonely lovers / Bogie's bonnie belle / Drumdelgie / Mormond braes / Auld quarry knowes / Barnyards of Delgaty.

Apr 88. (c) *Folktracks; (60-060)* **McBEATH, McCAFFREY AND McPHERSON** ☐ [-]
– Wind blew the bonnie lassie's plaidie awa' / Hey, jump and on you go / Awa' tae the scrap i' the morning / Tobacco pipes and porter / Smith's a gallant fireman / When the boat comes in / Skippin' barfit' through the heather / Van Dieman's land / McCallum the poacher / He widna want his gruel / Rich girl and robbers / The gallant forty-twa / Eppie Morrie / Devil of of Portsoy / Torn a ripit, torn a goon / Trooper lad.

Jan 02. (cd) *Rounder; (<ROUCD 1834>)* **TRAMPS & HAWKERS** ☐ ☐
– Tramps and hawkers / Drumdelgie / The jolly Carter lad / A dash good drink from the farm servants (interview) / The moss of Burreldale / The muckin O Geordie's byre / MacPherson's lament / It always beats up in ten minutes yet (interview) / Mormond braes / Bonny Portsoy, you're ae ma ain (interview & story) / The dowie dens o' Yarrow / A threed O blue song (interview) / John Anderson, my Jo / Fined five pounds (interview) / Teribus / Pirns O thread an needles an packets o preens (interview) / The gallant forty-twa / Too verocious, like they were hot in the blood (interview) / McCafferty was a great soldier (interview) / McCafferty / I'd get shot (interview) / I wasn't so far advanced as get tied up (interview) / Down by the Magdalene green / The auld quarry knowe / Bogie's bonny belle / Neeps tae pluck / Tramps and hawkers.

Craig McCALLUM Scottish Country Dance Band (see under ⇒ Greentrax records)

McCALMANS

Formed: Edinburgh . . . August 1964 as the IAN McCALMAN FOLK GROUP by IAN McCALMAN, Dundee-born/Fife-raised DEREK MOFFAT and the African-born HAMISH BAYNE. Having met at Edinburgh's School Of Art, the trio became 'weel kent' faces in the capital's pubs and clubs where they developed their three-part vocal harmony folk style. Combining influences from the 60's American folk revival with traditional Scottish song, the group appealed to a wide ranging audience, even securing their own TV show on BBC Scotland in 1970.

By this point they already had a major label debut album – 'ALL IN ONE' (1967) – under their belt as well as a couple of sets for the independent 'One-Up' label. A golden era for the band, the early 70's saw them releasing a further three major label long players, 'TURN AGAIN' (1971) on 'C.B.S.', 'NO STRINGS ATTACHED' (1972) and 'AN AUDIENCE WITH THE McCALMANS' (1973), both on 'R.C.A.'. The latter half of the decade was marked by a series of recordings for London-based folk label, 'Transatlantic' while 1986's 'PEACE AND PLENTY' began a long association with esteemed East Lothian folk bastion, 'Greentrax'.

Come the 90's, The McCALMANS were still going strong, recording an album of contemporary Scottish works in the shape of 'FLAMES ON THE WATER' (1990) and hosting their own show on Radio 2. 1995 saw the release of 'IN HARMONY', a compilation album celebrating the group's 30th anniversary. Remarkably, in all those years the group had only undergone one change in line-up, NICK KEIR having replaced founding member HAMISH BAYNE back in the early 80's.

The line-up's last album, 'KEEPERS' (1999) was another satisfying combination of old, new, borrowed and blue, its title track a lament for the Scottish lighthouse keepers of old. Sadly, DEREK MOFFAT was to die of lung cancer in October 2001. His replacement, STEPHEN QUIGG, was to feature on their return set, 'WHERE THE SKY MEETS THE SEA' (2002).

IAN McCALMAN (b. 1 Sep'46) – vocals, guitar / **DEREK MOFFAT** (b.29 Jun'48 Dundee) – vocals, guitar, mandolin, bodhran / **HAMISH BAYNE** (b. Nairobi, Kenya) – vocals, mandolin, concertina

E.M.I. not iss.

1967. (lp) **ALL IN ONE MIND** ☐ ☐

One-Up not iss.

1968. (lp) *(OU 2161)* **McCALMANS FOLK** ☐ ☐
– Santiago / Off to sea / North country farmer / Bold tenant farmer / Pains of Waterloo / Homeward bound / Pace egging song / Sally free and easy / Gala water / Quaheri / Farewell to Funiary / Cocaine blues / Doo-me-ama / Do let me go.

1969. (lp) **SINGERS THREE** ☐ ☐

C.B.S. not iss.

1971. (lp) *(CBS 64145)* **TURN AGAIN** ☐ ☐
– What would happen if I'd stayed around / Broom / Widow of Glencoe / Without me, just with you / Balena / East Neuk misfortune / Turn a deaf ear / Second mariner's song / Loving Hannah / Captain's lament / ad gypsy / Streets of London.

R.C.A. not iss.

1972. (lp) *(PL 25086)* **NO STRINGS ATTACHED** ☐ ☐
– The women are a' gane wud / The weaving song / A carrion crow / A kangaroo / Rise and follow Charlie / The chief's return from war / Windmills / The tailor / Busk, busk / Far fairer she / The execution of Montrose / Veronica. *(re-iss. Jul77; same)*

1973. (lp) *(LSA 3179)* **AN AUDIENCE WITH THE McCALMANS** ☐ ☐
– Bonnie Dundee / The trawling trade / My Johnny is a shoemaker / Charles in France / The love bug will bite you (if you don't watch out) / The burning / Kilgannon mountain / Mingulay boat song / Auburn maid / All around my hat / Bread and fishes / Sweet senorita / Good night and joy.

Transatla. not iss.

1975. (lp) *(54001)* **SMUGGLER** ☐ ☐ German
– Smuggler / If mother should die / Gardens / Hornpipe – reels / Mount and go / The boatie rows – The Carls o' Dysart / The flower o' the forest / The barnyards o' Delgaty / Bar-room / No churchman am I / The silkie of Sule Skerry / A man's a man for a' that / Nagasaki / Johnnie Cope / Skye boat song / Tammy Traddlefeet – The rising.

1976. (lp) *(XTRA 1166)* **HOUSE FULL (live)** ☐ ☐
– Ye Jacobites by name / Coasts of Barbary / It's the boy / Kora / Mine / Awa whigs awa / Dingle regatta / A little village / Farewell the Faroes / Sweeter than sugar / Alkie braes / Diamond / Boat song / Proposal & acceptance / Tim McGuire.

Mar 77. (7") *(BIG 563)* **ROMEO & JULIET. / SMUGGLER** ☐ ☐

Apr 77. (lp) **SIDE BY SIDE BY SIDE** ☐ ☐
–

Sep 78. (lp) *(TRA 357)* **BURN THE WITCH** ☐ ☐
– Fare ye well ye Mormond braes / The lion (Edinburgh Castle) / Jennie Lasswade / Farewell to Nova Scotia / She had to go and lose it all at the Astor / Aye waulkin O / Gin I were where the gaudie rins / Veronica / Burn the witch / Bonnie lass o' Gala water / Jock Stewart / March of the Cameron men / Phantom whistler – Random jig / Doon in the wee room / Recruiting service drum / Song of heroes.

1980. (lp) **McCALMANS LIVE (live)** ☐ ☐

Greenwich Village not iss.

May 81. (lp) *(GVR 209)* **THE ETTRICK SHEPHERD – THE WORKS OF JAMES HOGG** ☐ ☐
– McLean's welcome / Donald MacDonald / The witch of Fife / Bonnie Prince Charlie / King Willie / I ha'e naebody now / The Highlander's farewell / Sir Morgan O'Doherty's farewell to Scotland / Reply to Sir Morgan O'Doherty's farewell to Scotland / The moon was a-waning / Ladies' evening song / Rise! rise! Lowland and Highland men / Good night and joy. *(c-iss.Sep91 on 'Greentrax'; CTRAX 046)*

Gundog not iss.

1981. (7") *(GUNS 005)* **GOD BLESS THE BIRTHDAY BOY. / SEAGULL CRY** ☐ ☐

1982. (lp) **BONNIE NANDS AGAIN** ☐ ☐

—— (Sep'82) **NICK KEIR** (b.14 Mar'53, Edinburgh) – vocals, guitars, banjo, mandolin, whistles, recorder (ex-FINN MACCUIL) repl. BAYNE

Greentrax Greentrax

Nov 86. (lp/c) *(TRAX/CTRAX 002)* **PEACE AND PLENTY** ☐ ☐
– Song of the plough / The colliery gate / No you won't get me down in your mines / The black bear – The drover's lad – The top house / South Australia – Esikibo river – Blood red roses – Little Sally Rackett / Up and rin awa' Geordie / Mothers, daughters, wives / The Highland road / Barratt's privateers / Men of the sea / Song for Europe / Tae the weavers gin ye gang / Leave her Johnny / Tullochgoran / Bells of the town. *(cd-iss. Oct90 +=; CDTRAX 002)* – Scotland / Falkirk tryste. *<US cd-iss. Sep94; same as US>*

Aug 88. (cd/c/lp) *(CD/C+/TRAX 019)* **LISTEN TO THE HEAT – LIVE** ☐ ☐
– I have seen the Highlands / Town of Kiandra / Mount & go / Sister Josephine / 23rd June / Prisoner's song / The song song / Rambling rover / Rory Murphy / First Christmas / Lakewood / Thriemuir hornpipe / Royal Belfast / The president's men / Air ta la la la lo / Sickening thank you song. *<US-iss.Sep94; same as UK>*

Nov 88. (cd/c/lp) *(CD/C+/TRAX 023)* **ANCESTRAL MANOEUVRES** ☐ ☐
– Ancestral manoeuvres / 10,000 miles away / Avalon / Aberlady bay / Skye air, etc / Ghoulies & ghosties / Scotland / Falkirk tryste / Da song o'da papa men / Sidmouth folk festival blues / Rolling hills of the borders / Loves the rising sun / Goodnight sweetheart. *<US-iss.Sep94; same as UK>*

Jul 90. (cd/c) *(CD/C TRAX 036)* **FLAMES ON THE WATER** ☐ ☐
– Ah'm e man at muffed it / Isle of Eigg / Devolution anthem / Farewell tae the haven / Sounding / Hawks and eagles / The siege / Who pays the piper / Festival lights / Shian road / Men o' worth / Curtain call. *<US-iss.Sep94; same as UK>*

Jul 91. (cd/c) *(CD/C TRAX 045)* **SONGS FROM SCOTLAND** ☐ ☐
– The boys that broke the ground – The Tiree love song – Who put the mush – Highland laddie – All the tunes in the world – The most amazing thing of all – I will go / Widow Mackay – April waltz – The lark in the morning – Ainster harbour – Twa recruitin' sergeants – Rolling home / Roll the woodpile down / Up and awa' wi' the Laverock / Scarece o' tatties / A hundred years ago – Westering home – The last session. *<US-iss.Sep94; same as UK>*

Sep 93. (cd/c) *(CD/C TRAC 067)* **HONEST POVERTY** ☐ ☐
– Kelvin's grove – Paddy's leather britches – Behind the haystack / A man's a man for a' that / Single handed sailor / Your daighters and your sons / Niel Gow's apprentice / The children are running away / War outside – The white collar holler / I feel like Buddy Holly / Parade / Portnahaven / The 8-3-0 / Wha'll be king but Charlie / Father Mallory's dance / The New Year's Eve song / Hermless. *<US-iss.Sep94; same as UK>*

Jan 95. (cd/c) *(CD/C TRAX 086)* **IN HARMONY – 30th ANNIVERSARY COMPILATION ALBUM** ☐ ☐
– Pace egging song / The sun rises bright in France / The broom / Windmills / My Johnny is a shoemaker / Smuggler / Ye Jacobites by name / Farewell to Sicily / Burn the witch / The ladies' evening song / Kelty clippie / Bonnie maid of Fife / Scotland / Bonnie lass o' Gala water / Mothers, daughtrs, wives / Rambling rover / Farewell tae the haven / The last session – All the tunes in the world / A man's a man for a' that / Bound to go.

Nov 95. (cd/c) *(<CD/C TRAX 097>)* **FESTIVAL LIGHTS – LIVE** ☐ ☐
– Don't call me early in the morning / Pills / Far down the line / The Highland road / Some hae meat / Tearing our industry down / Golden arches / Shanties / The bonnie barque / The Bergen / The barnyards of Delgaty / Goodnight sweetheart / Festival lights.

Aug 97. (cd/c) *(<CD/C TRAX 138>)* **HIGH GROUND** ☐ ☐ Oct97
– Don't waste ma time / Cancel Marie's wedding / Lochs of the Tay / Don't sit on my Jimmy Shands / They sent a wumman / Five o'clock in the morning / Instrumental medley: Alas that I came o'er / No-one left but me / Take her in your arms / Upstairs, doonstairs / High ground – Vogrie / Wrecked again / White horses / Cholesterol / Libertas Ragusta.

Jun 99. (cd) *(<CDTRAX 174>)* **KEEPERS** ☐ ☐ Jul99
– Keepers / The back of the north wind / (Leave us) Our glens / Strong women rule us all with their tears / The back o' the aisler / Nowhere else to go / Yellow on the broom / Birnie bouzle / The birks of Invermay / Star o' the bar / Here's a health tae the sauters / Battle of Waterloo / The soor milk cairt / Let us drink and go hame.

—— **STEPHEN QUIGG** (b. 1960, Adrossan, Ayrshire) – guitar, bodhran, mouth organ (solo artist) repl. MOFFAT who died in October 2001

May 02. (cd) *(CDTRAX 232)* **WHERE THE SKY MEETS THE SEA** ☐ ☐
– Farm auction / The last leviathan / The fishing days / Galway to Graceland / Women o' Dundee / Ae fond kiss / Voice of my island / Applecross bay / Laerke's tune / Rise rise / Gallant Murray / The Highlands tomorrow / Wild old tune / Running home / Spinner's wedding.

– compilations, etc. –

1979. (lp) *;* **THE BEST OF THE McCALMANS** ☐ ☐
(cd-iss. Nov00 on 'PlayaSound'; PS 65238)

Dec 86. (lp/c) *Ross; (WGR/CWGR 092)* **SCOTTISH SONGS** ☐ ☐
– Johnnie Cope / The bonnie maid of Fife / The Mingulay boat song / Gin I were the gadie rins / Come a' ye tramps and hawker lads / Willie's gan tae Melville castle / Fare ye weel ye Mormond braes / Coshieville / Bonnie lass o' Gala water / The lion Wallace saw / Fareweel tae Tarwathie / Smuggler. *(re-iss. Jul93 cd/c; CDGR/CWGR 092)*

Apr 97. (cd) *Essential; (<ESMCD 521>)* **SMUGGLER / BURN THE WITCH** ☐ ☐

Ewan MacCOLL

Born: JIMMIE MILLER, 25th January 1915, Salford, Manchester. Despite his contrary origins, MacCOLL actually grew up influenced by his Scottish parents, developing his staunch communist views as a direct result of the Depression and its effect on his father, William Miller (also a singer, as was his Auchterarder-born, Gaelic speaking mother, Betsy Hendry) and the working men of his neighbourhood. Resolving to make a change through the arts, EWAN became actively involved in Left Wing street theatre as a teenager. This eventually led on to the co-founding of the Theatre Workshop (with Joan Littlewood, who was to become his first wife), a touring project dedicated to awakening political consciousness in the provincial working classes. As playwright, actor, director and singer, MacCOLL doggedly pursued his cause for nigh on ten years, eventually losing interest in the Workshop in the mid-50's after it had secured a permanent base in Stratford.

A meeting with legendary blues/folk musicologist/folklorist ALAN LOMAX planted the seeds of a new mission for MacCOLL, to systematically revive the wealth of traditional British folk song as a political tool in the advance of the Socialist cause. Along with a coterie of sympathetic comrades (including DOMINIC BEHAN, BERT LLOYD, ISLA CAMERON, RORY McEWAN, ISOBEL SUTHERLAND, SHIRLEY COLLINS, MALCOLM NIXON, ERIC WINTER and KARL DALLAS), he set the groundwork for the huge upsurge in interest which traditonal music enjoyed from the mid-50's to the late 60's. WINTER and DALLAS were both journalists whose increasing column inches in Melody Maker gave MacCOLL's activities exposure. LLOYD, meanwhile, was the head honcho at 'Topic' records, a label originally under the aegis of the Workers Music Association which, incidentally, numbered both MacCOLL and ALAN LOMAX among its membership.

'Topic' was to become a folk bastion throughout the revival and MacCOLL released his first recording, 'ENGLISH/SCOTTISH POPULAR BALLADS', through the label in 1956. This, a collaboration with LLOYD, was a characteristically ambitious 9-volume set attempting a representative sampling of Professor Francis James Child's huge canon of songs. Subsequent albums found MacCOLL working with American banjo player PEGGY SEEGER, the half-sister of PETE SEEGER and by 1959, MacCOLL's long-term partner; the pair had first met in 1956 although it'd taken an arranged marriage with Glaswegian folk singer ALEX CAMPBELL to furnish PEGGY with UK citizenship and thus allow her to stay in the country.

While MacCOLL was to maintain a prolific release schedule for 'Topic' (mostly collaborating with either LLOYD or SEEGER), it was his celebrated late 50's BBC radio series, 'Radio Ballads', that was to really prove inspirational. This began with 'The Ballad Of John Axon', a programme documenting the history of the British railway network and its workers. A further seven instalments explored the lives of genuine working people through their own eyes and against a musical backdrop of specially written traditional song. The series' forerunner was 'Ballads & Blues', a winning combination of British and American folk song which subsequently lent its name and concept to MacCOLL's club.

Opening its doors in the late 50's, The Ballad And Blues Club played host to the cream of the UK's folk singers as well as visiting US legends like BIG BILL BROONZY. More importantly, it created a blueprint for folk clubs up and down the country, even though MacCOLL was to fall out with organiser Malcolm Nixon (who retained the name) and subsequently start another venture, the Singers Club.

While MacCOLL was the undisputed Godfather of the scene and wielded an often intimidating authority, many found his intense, unpredictable temperament hard to bear (the rift between MacCOLL and ALEX CAMPBELL was especially prominent). What's more, the man's earnest, dour, almost puritanical approach to folk music created a schism as the revival gathered pace. Some accused MacCOLL of being a fake and derided what they perceived as an elitist, intellectual clique in his self-styled Critics Group, set up in 1964 to impart the knowledge of MacCOLL and Company to up and coming youngsters via a series of records, books and research projects. Nevertheless, there was no denying the man's groundbreaking influence, his continuing domination of a large part of the London scene and his early work in the provinces and Scotland ensuring his every pronouncement (usually controversial, critical and outspoken) was pored over.

He provided a platform for ANNE BRIGGS, who made her recording debut singing a couple of songs on 'THE IRON MUSE', a LLOYD/MacCOLL quasi concept set exploring the history of folksong in relation to industrial heritage. Unsurprisingly, MacCOLL also played a major hand in the Centre 42 project of the early 60's, another touring initiative aimed at bringing culture to the working classes outwith the confines of London. Although the Critics Group disintegrated in 1970, MacCOLL continued his relatively prolific work rate through the decade when the shock waves from the 60's revival were still being felt.

Although he fathered two children (one of whom, KIRSTY, was to subsequently carve out a successful musical career of her own before being tragically drowned on a holiday in Mexico in 2000) to a second wife Jean Newlove, PEGGY remained his constant musical companion right up until his death in 1989. Together the pair formed the 'Blackthorne' label in the late 70's, continued to perform regularly and were heavily invloved in the miners' strike of 1984 (MacCOLL was a vociferous critic of Thatcher's government).

As well as the incredible wealth of traditional song he unearthed and interpreted in his lifetime, a number of his self-penned pieces have reached the realms of pop music, notably the heart-rending 'THE FIRST TIME EVER I SAW YOUR FACE' (most famously via ROBERTA FLACK) and 'DIRTY OLD TOWN', a classic The POGUES made their own.

EWAN MacCOLL – vocals, acoustic guitar

Topic not iss.

1957. (10"lp; as EWAN MacCOLL & PEGGY SEEGER) *(10T 13)* **SHUTTLE AND CAGE**

1958. (10"lp) *(10T 26)* **BARRACK ROOM BALLADS**

1958. (10"lp; as EWAN MacCOLL & A.L. LLOYD) *(10T 36)* **BOLD SPORTSMEN ALL**

1959. (lp; as EWAN MacCOLL & DOMINIC BEHAN) *(12T 41)* **STREETS OF SONG**

1960. (10"lp; as EWAN MacCOLL & ISLA CAMERON) *(10T 50)* **STILL I LOVE HIM**

1960. (lp; as EWAN MacCOLL & PEGGY SEEGER) *(12T 61)* **CHORUS FROM THE GALLOWS**
– Derek Bentley / The black velvet band / Jamie Raeburn's farewell / Johnny O'Breadiesley / Hughie the Graeme / Minorie / The treadmill song / Turpin hero / The crafty farmer / McKafferty / Jimmie Wilson / The lag's song / Van Dieman's land / Go down ye murderers. *(cd-iss. Nov98; TSCD 502)*

1962. (lp; as EWAN MacCOLL & PEGGY SEEGER) *(exist)* **HAUL ON THE BOWLIN'**

1962. (lp) *(12T 79)* **SONGS OF JACOBITE REBELLIONS**
– Ye Jacobites by name / Such a parcel of rogues in a nation / Will ye go to Sherriffmuir / Wae's me for Prince Charlie / Charlie is my darling / The haughs of Cromdale / The bonnie moorhen / Johnnie Cope / Came ye o'er frae France / There's three brave loyal fellows / This is no my ain house / The piper o' Dundee / Donald MacGillavry / MacLean's welcome / Will ye no come back again. *(cd/c-iss.Apr94 on 'Ossian'; OSS 103 CD/C)*

1963. (lp) *(exist)* **OFF TO SEA ONCE MORE**

1963. (lp) *(exist)* **FOURPENCE A DAY – BRITISH INDUSTRIAL FOLK SONGS**

1964. (lp; as EWAN MacCOLL & A.L. LLOYD) *(12T 103)* **ENGLISH AND SCOTTISH FOLK BALLADS**

1964. (lp; as EWAN MacCOLL & PEGGY SEEGER) *(12T 104)* **STEAM WHISTLE BALLADS**
– The wark of the weavers / Droylsden wakes / The four loom weaver / The Calton weaver / Oh dear me / The coal owner and the pitman's wife / Four pence a day / The Gresford disaster / Will Caird / The iron horse / Poor Paddy works on the railway / Cannily cannily / The song of the iron road / The Blantyre explosion / The collier laddie / Moses of the mail.

— next with **PEGGY SEEGER** – banjo, guitar (as usual) / **JIMMIE MacGREGOR** – guitar / **JOHN COLE** – harmonica

1966. (lp) *(12T 130)* **BUNDOOK BALLADS**
– Any complaints / The fortress song / Farewell to Sicily / The ballad of Wadi Maktilla / The dying soldier / The ghost army of Korea / Browned off / When this ruddy war is over / Join the British army / On the move tonight / The second front song / Seven years in the sand / Hand me down petticoat / The young trooper cut down in his prime / Bless 'em all.

EWAN MacCOLL & PEGGY SEEGER

1966. (lp) *(12T 147)* **THE MANCHESTER ANGEL**
– We poor labouring man / Georgie / Barbara Allen / Sheepcrook and black dog / Bramble briar (strawberry town) / One night as I lay on my bed / The grey cock / Of the begging I will go / The sheep-stealer (I am a brisk lad) / The Manchester angel / The bold Richard / The press gang / Round Cape Horn / Through Moorfields / Homeward bound.

Xtra not iss.

1967. (lp; as EWAN MacCOLL & A.L. LLOYD) *(XTRA 1052)* **BLOW BOYS, BLOW**
(cd-iss. Aug96 on 'Tradition'; TCD 1024)

1967. (lp) *(XTRA 1054)* **CLASSIC SCOTS BALLADS**

1967. (lp) *(XTRA 5013)* **A SAILOR'S GARLAND**

Argo not iss.

1966. (lp) *(DA 66)* **THE LONG HARVEST 1**

1967. (lp) *(DA 67)* **THE LONG HARVEST 2**

1967. (lp; as EWAN MacCOLL, CHARLES PARKER & PEGGY SEEGER) *(RG 502)* **SINGING THE FISHING**

1967. (lp; by EWAN MacCOLL, PEGGY SEEGER, CHARLES PARKER) *(DA 140)* **THE BIG HEWER – A RADIO BALLAD . . .** (documentary & music)

1968. (lp) *(DA 83)* **THE AMOROUS MUSE**
(re-iss. Jun72; ZFB 66)

1968. (lp) *(DA 84)* **THE ANGRY MUSE**
(re-iss. May72; ZFB 65)

1968. (lp; by EWAN MacCOLL) *(DA 85)* **THE WANTON MUSE**
– Ballad of trades / The shepherd lad / The wanton seed / Bonnie lassie's plaidie / The coachman and his whip / The thrashing machine / Maid of Australia / The cuckoo's nest / The gairdener chylde / The vintner / Andrew and his cutty gun / All fours / The cobbler / The mowdiewark / The furze field / Long peggin' awl / The maid gaed to the mill / The bird in the bush / She was a rum one. *(re-iss. Jun72; ZFB 67)*

1968. (lp) *(DA 68)* **THE LONG HARVEST 3**

1969. (lp) *(DA 69)* **THE LONG HARVEST 4**

Mar 69. (lp) *(DA 98)* **THE PAPER STAGE 1** ☐ ☐
Mar 69. (lp) *(DA 99)* **THE PAPER STAGE 2** ☐ ☐
1970. (lp; by EWAN MacCOLL & CHARLES PARKER) *(DA 133)* **THE TRAVELLING PEOPLE** ☐ ☐
1970. (lp) *(DA 70)* **THE LONG HARVEST 5** ☐ ☐
Jan 71. (lp) *(DA 136)* **ON THE EDGE** ☐ ☐
1971. (lp) *(DA 141)* **THE FIGHT GAME** ☐ ☐
1971. (lp) *(DA 71)* **THE LONG HARVEST 6** ☐ ☐
1972. (lp) *(DA 72)* **THE LONG HARVEST 7** ☐ ☐
1973. (lp) *(DA 73)* **THE LONG HARVEST 8** ☐ ☐
1974. (lp) *(DA 74)* **THE LONG HARVEST 9** ☐ ☐
1975. (lp) *(DA 75)* **THE LONG HARVEST 10** ☐ ☐

Blackthorne not iss.

1977. (lp) *(BR 1055)* **SATURDAY NIGHT AT THE BULL AND MOUTH** ☐ ☐
1977. (lp) *(BR 1057)* **COLD SNAP** ☐ ☐
1978. (lp) *(BR 1059)* **HOT BLAST** ☐ ☐
1980. (lp) *(BR 1063)* **KILROY WAS HERE** ☐ ☐
1980. (lp) *(ESB 79)* **BLOOD AND ROSES** ☐ ☐
1981. (lp) *(ESB 80)* **BLOOD AND ROSES 2** ☐ ☐
1982. (lp) *(ESB 81)* **BLOOD AND ROSES 3** ☐ ☐
1982. (lp) *(ESB 82)* **BLOOD AND ROSES 4** ☐ ☐
1983. (lp) *(ESB 83)* **BLOOD AND ROSES 5** ☐ ☐
1985. (c; by EWAN MacCOLL) *(BS 1)* **DADDY, WHAT DID YOU DO IN THE STRIKE?** ☐ ☐
1985. (lp) *(BR 1065)* **FREEBORN MAN** ☐ ☐
<US-iss.1988 on 'Rounder' lp/c; ROU/+C 3080>
1986. (lp) *(BR 1067)* **ITEMS OF NEWS** ☐ ☐

Rounder Rounder

1988. (lp; as PEGGY SEEGER & EWAN MacCOLL) *(<ROU 4003>)* **AT THE PRESENT MOMENT** ☐ ☐

—— sadly, EWAN was to die in 1989; below was a posthumous collaboration

Cooking Vinyl not iss.

May 90. (lp/c/cd) *(COOK/+C/CD 036)* **NAMING OF NAMES** ☐ ☐
– Economic miracle / Just the tax for me / The grocer / Not going to give it back / Sellafield child / Bring the summer home / Maggie went green / Nuclear means jobs / Hose hungry blues / Dracumag / Rogue's gallery / The island / We remember (naming of names).

- compilations, others, etc. -

1961. (lp) *PRE; (13004)* **THE BEST OF EWAN MacCOLL** ☐ ☐
1965. (lp; as EWAN MacCOLL & CHARLES PARKER) *Argo; (RG 474)* **THE BALLAD OF JOHN AXON** (rec. 1958) ☐ ☐
1960's. (7"; as EWAN MacCOLL & PEGGY SEEGER) *AUEW; (AUEW 1)* **WE ARE THE ENGINEERS. / I'M GONNA BE AN ENGINEER** ☐ ☐
1970. (lp; as EWAN MacCOLL & PEGGY SEEGER) *Decca; (SPA 102)* **THE WORLD OF EWAN MacCOLL & PEGGY SEEGER** ☐ ☐
1972. (lp; as EWAN MacCOLL & PEGGY SEEGER) *Decca; (SPA 216)* **THE WORLD OF EWAN MacCOLL & PEGGY SEEGER** ☐ ☐
Dec 72. (lp) *Argo; (ZFB 12)* **SOLO FLIGHT** ☐ ☐
– The bonnie bunch of roses / The tunnel tigers / A roving hielan man / The iron-moulder's wedding / The bold poachers / Ye hae lien wrang lassie / The fowler / The maid of Reigate / Sheath and knife / Alan Tyne o' Harrow / Roseberry / The molecatcher / James Herries / The penny wager / The tattie-lifting song / Lament for the death of a nobody. *(cd-iss. May00; TSCD 810)*
Nov 74. (lp) *Tradition; (TLP 1015)* **CLASSIC SCOTS BALLADS** ☐ ☐
Sep 90. (lp/c/cd) *Cooking Vinyl; (COOK/+C/CD 038)* **BLACK AND WHITE – THE DEFINITIVE EWAN MacCOLL COLLECTION** ☐ ☐
– Ballad of accounting / The driver's song / My old man / Dirty old town / Black and white / Brother did you weep / The press gang / The shoals of herring / The Manchester rambler / Sheath and knife / Highland muster roll / Cam ye o'er frae France / The maid gaed tae the mill / The moving on song / Nobody knew she was there / Looking for a job / Kilroy was here / The first time ever I saw your face / The foggy dew / The joy of living. *(cd re-iss. Feb95; same)*
1992. (c; as EWAN MacCOLL & PEGGY SEEGER) *Blackthorne; (BSC 2)* **WHITE WIND AND BLACK TIDE** ☐ ☐
1992. (lp; as EWAN MacCOLL & PEGGY SEEGER) *Blackthorne; (BR 8732)* **THE NEW BRITON GAZETTE** ☐ ☐
May 93. (cd) *Topic; (<TSCD 463>)* **THE REAL MACCOLL** (rec.1959-1966) ☐ ☐
– Ye Jacobites by name / Johnny Cope / Cam ye o'er frae France / Haughs o' Cromdale / Such a parcel o' rogues in a nation / Farewell to Sicily / Derek Bentley / Johnny O'Breadislee / Go down ye murderers / Van Diemen's land / Minorie / Sheep crook and black dog / The bramble briar / One night as I lay on my bed / The grey cock / The Blantyre explosion / The Gresford disaster / Four loom weaver / Song of the iron road / Dirty old town.
Apr 94. (cd/c) *Ossian; (OSS 101 CD/C)* **BOTHY BALLADS** ☐ ☐
Apr 94. (cd/c) *Ossian; (OSS 102 CD/C)* **SONGS OF ROBERT BURNS** ☐ ☐
Apr 94. (cd/c) *Ossian; (OSS 104 CD/C)* **TRADITIONAL SONGS AND BALLADS** ☐ ☐
Apr 94. (cd/c) *Ossian; (OSS 105 CD/C)* **SCOTTISH POPULAR SONGS** ☐ ☐
Jun 95. (cd) *Nectar; (NTMCD 502)* **THE LEGEND OF EWAN MacCOLL** ☐ ☐
(re-iss. Feb98 on 'Reactive'; REMCD 514)
Jun 96. (cd) *Cooking Vinyl; (MASHCD 002)* **EFDSS & 70th BIRTHDAY CONCERTS (live)** ☐ ☐
Jul 97. (cd; as EWAN MacCOLL & PEGGY SEEGER) *Tradition; (<TCD 1051>)* **CLASSIC SCOTS BALLADS** ☐ ☐
Aug 98. (d-cd) *Snapper; (SMDCD 149)* **ANTIQUITIES** ☐ ☐
Sep 98. (cd; as EWAN MacCOLL & A.L. LLOYD) *Topic; (TSCD 495)* **BOLD SPORTSMEN ALL (GAMBLERS AND SPORTING BLADES)** ☐ ☐
(below 8 releases with CHARLES PARKER & PEGGY SEEGER)
May 99. (cd) *Topic; (TSCD 801)* **RADIO BALLADS VOL.1** ☐ ☐
May 99. (cd) *Topic; (TSCD 802)* **RADIO BALLADS VOL.2** ☐ ☐
May 99. (cd) *Topic; (TSCD 803)* **RADIO BALLADS VOL.3** ☐ ☐
May 99. (cd) *Topic; (TSCD 804)* **RADIO BALLADS VOL.4** ☐ ☐
May 99. (cd) *Topic; (TSCD 805)* **RADIO BALLADS VOL.5** ☐ ☐
May 99. (cd) *Topic; (TSCD 806)* **RADIO BALLADS VOL.6** ☐ ☐
May 99. (cd) *Topic; (TSCD 807)* **RADIO BALLADS VOL.7** ☐ ☐
May 99. (cd) *Topic; (TSCD 808)* **RADIO BALLADS VOL.8** ☐ ☐

Alyth McCORMACK (see under ⇒ COLOUR OF MEMORY)

Duncan McCRONE (see under ⇒ CLYDESIDERS)

Alasdair MacCUISH & The BLACK ROSE CEILIDH BAND (see under ⇒ Macmeanmna records)

Gordeanna McCULLOCH (see under ⇒ CLUTHA)

John McCUSKER (see under ⇒ BATTLEFIELD BAND)

Chas McDEVITT (see ⇒ Section 7: Rock & Pop)

Alastair McDONALD

Born: 1941, Glasgow. At the age of eight, he emigrated with his family to Australia, although he would return to Scotland as a teenager and with a large interest in music; American folk, jazz and pop in particular. The 50's were now in full swing and ALASTAIR wanted to be part of it in any way he could. He performed at churches, ceilidhs, hospitals and anywhere that would take him, honing his plucky banjo-picking with each successive gig. By 1962, ALASTAIR had earned an award as Best Banjo Player at the Elgin Festival, he was indeed leader of his field at this particular point. Although his whimsical vocal chords were a little lighter than his peers (such as JANSCH, GAUGHAN and MARTYN), he still managed to pull off some fine renditions of traditional Scots songs on his 1969 major label debut set, 'BATTLE BALLADS'. He broadened his horizons even more in 1973 when he was asked to co-host (with PETER MORRISON) a new TV show, 'Songs Of Scotland'; it was around this time that his tribute cassettes to BONNIE PRINCE CHARLIE and ROBERT BURNS filtered through from 'Nevis' records. Viewing figures soared around the country ensuring that the programme would be repeated year after year. His versitality knew no bounds as he moved into pantomime, children's TV and variety, although this proved to be a sticking point for those of the purist folk ideals. His range of music styles also gave him work abroad (North America, Europe, East Africa and Israel), although he would always return to his beloved Scotland to play to enthusiastic crowds. On the recording front, ALASTAIR has amassed over 30 releases for 'Corban' records, although he must have been proud when folk giants, 'Greentrax', issued his best set to date, 'VELVET AND STEEL' (1995).

ALASTAIR McDONALD – vocals, acoustic guitar

Major Minor not iss.

1969. (lp) *(MMLP 51)* **BATTLE BALLADS** ☐ ☐
– Stirling Brig / The Wallace / Bannockburn / Horo chall eile / Harlaw / Parcel of rogues / The wee wee German lairdie / The shores of Sutherland / The fire raisers / Hush hush / Henny Monro / John MacLean. *(re-iss. Jan80 on 'Nevis' lp/c; NEV LP/C 014)*

Nevis not iss.

1970's. (lp/c) *(NEV LP/C 002)* **SCOTLAND IN SONG** ☐ ☐
– Over the sea to Skye / Rantin' rovin' Robin / Loch Lomond / Mouth music / The barras / Silver darlings / Glencoe / The cooper o' Fife / Bonnie Gallaway / Mary Jane. *(re-iss. May81; same)*
1970's. (c) *(NEVC 101)* **BONNIE PRINCE CHARLIE** ☐ ☐

1970's. (c) *(NEVC 108)* **SCOTLAND FIRST** [ ] [-]
1970's. (lp/c) *(NEV LP/C 112)* **ALASTAIR McDONALD SINGS ROBERT BURNS** [ ] [-]
(re-iss. May77; same) (re-iss. Mar96 on 'Lochshore' c/cd; LBP 2020/+CD)

Polydor | not iss.

Sep 76. (7") *(2058 775)* **LET'S FOOT IT OUT TOGETHER. / BARON'S HEIR** [ ] [-]
Oct 76. (lp) *(2383 404)* **ALASTAIR McDONALD** [ ] [-]
– MacNeil's galley / Galloa hills / The Shetland oil song / The bonnie Earl o' Moray / The monster of Loch Ness / Bruce at Bannockburn / The Uist tramping song / A baron's heir / The wee Kirkcudbright centipede / Abu chuille / Football crazy / Follow me up to Carlow / Tramps and hawkers.

Emerald | not iss.

Apr 78. (7") *(MD 1205)* **THE EARLY MORNING WORKER. / RORY MOR'S LAMENT** [ ] [-]
May 78. (lp/c) *(GES/KGES 1178)* **MUSIC OF THE HIGHLANDS** [ ] [-]
– The gypsy laddie / The early morning worker / Jamie Raeburn / Melville castle / The sylkie (the seal) / Music of the Highlands / Bonnie ship the diamond / Get up, get out / The exile song / Kirsteen / Perfervidum / Street songs / Rory Mor's lament. *(re-iss. Oct81; same) (re-iss. Nov84 lp/c; BER/KBER 005)*
1979. (lp/c) *(GES/KGES 1206)* **THE WEE KIRKCUDBRIGHT CENTIPEDE** [ ] [-]
– Blantyre explosion / Leave them a flower / Highland lullaby / Queen Mary / A mockin' bird / The tramcar / The tod / Kelvin Grove / Aitken drum / The height starvation song / Yuri Gagarin / The Eskimo republic / Ribeanan / Riobhach / The wee Kirkcudbright centipede. *(re-iss. Oct81; same)*

McCoochley Street | not iss.

Apr 82. (7") *(MS 9)* **WE'VE BEEN INVITED. / BRUCE'S ADDRESS** [ ] [-]

Corban | not iss.

Sep 83. (lp) *(CBN 001)* **WHITE WINGS** [ ] [-]
– The puffer / Loch Tay / Bruce's address / Shoals o' herrin' / Over the mountain / No comin' oot / Lament for McCrimmon / Wee Jock sparra / Smile in your sleep / Cam' ye by Atholl / White wings. *(re-iss. Apr89; same)*
Oct 83. (7") *(CBN 002)* **COLOMBE SHALOM. / WHITE WINGS** [ ] [-]
1985. (lp) *(CBN 003)* **GLENCOE** [ ] [-]
– The bonnie ship of Diamond / Ten wee wimmin / Silver darlings / Kismuil's galley / Hie Johnny Cope / Glencoe / The wee Kirkcudbright centipede / Jamie Raeburn / Abu chuile / A baron's heir / Sing me a song (requiem). *(cd-iss. Apr89; CDNCD 003)*

Lismor | not iss.

Dec 88. (lp/c) *(LILP/LICS 5173)* **AT THE JAZZ BAND BALL** [ ] [-]
– Will the circle be unbroken / Up above my head / Your feet's too big / At the jazz band ball (Mr. Wu) / Just a closer walk with thee / 'Taint no sin / Chinese laundry blues / Down by the riverside (with BENNY WATERS) / Frankie and Johnny / My bucket's got a hole in it / Marching through Georgia / Corn bread, peas and black molasses / Ballin' the jack / Mississippi mud.

Greentrax | not iss.

Mar 95. (cd/c) *(CD/C TRAX 078)* **VELVET AND STEEL** [ ] [-]
– Jamie Foyers / The Bruce / Bonnie Earl o' Moray / Harlaw / The seer / Lock the door / Haugh o' Cromdale / Killiecrankie / My bonnie Mary / Blue bonnets / Flodden – Flooers o' the forest / Culloden's harvest / Fyvie / Sheep and stag remain.

– compilations, others, etc. –

on 'Corban' records unless mentioned otherwise
Jan 78. (c) *V.F.M.; (VCA 035)* **SCOTTISH FOLK SONGS** [ ] [-]
Nov 85. (c) *Ross; (CWGR 088)* **THE SURGE OF THE SEA** [ ] [-]
Sep 87. (lp/c) *Emerald; (GES/KGES 1236)* **THE BEST OF ALASTAIR McDONALD** [ ] [-]
Apr 89. (c) *(CBNC 004)* **JOURNEY THROUGH SCOTLAND** [ ] [-]
Apr 89. (lp; as ALASTAIR McDONALD & PETER MORRISON) *(CBN 006)* **SING A SONG OF SCOTLAND** [ ] [-]
(re-iss. Jun99; same)
Apr 89. (c) *(CBNC 007)* **JOURNEY THROUGH SCOTLAND, VOL.2** [ ] [-]
Apr 89. (lp) *(CBN 010)* **SONGS OF LIFE, LIBERTY AND LAUGHTER** [ ] [-]
1990. (c) *(CBNC 011)* **BEARS, CROWS & CENTIPEDES** [ ] [-]
(cd-iss. 1999; CBNCD 021)
1991. (c) *(CBNC 013)* **O'ER MOUNTAIN & MOOR** [ ] [-]
1992. (c) *(CBNC 014)* **LEANING** [ ] [-]
1993. (c) *(CBNC 015)* **SCOTFREE** [ ] [-]
Sep 91. (cd/c) *Scotdisc; (CD/K ITV 547)* **SONGS GRETNA TO GLENCOE** [ ] [-]
May 93. (c) *Scotdisc; (SCOT 100C)* **THE SONGS OF SCOTLAND** [ ] [-]
Mar 94. (c) *(CBNC 016)* **SINGS OF HEROES & LEGENDS** [ ] [-]
Nov 94. (c) *(CBNC 017)* **SCOTTISH HEARTBEAT** [ ] [-]
Feb 96. (cd/c) *Lismor; (LCOM/LICS 5250)* **HONEST POVERTY** [ ] [-]
Sep 96. (cd/c) *(CBN CD/C 019)* **HEROES AND LEGENDS OF SCOTLAND** [ ] [-]
Jun 98. (cd/c) *(CBN CD/C 022)* **SCOTTISH LAUGHLINES** [ ] [-]
1999. (cd) *(CBNCD 024)* **THROUGH SCOTLAND IN SONG** [ ] [-]
Feb 00. (cd/c) *(CBN CD/C 027)* **HOUSE OF MACDONALD** [ ] [-]
– (tracks from 'GLENCOE & OTHER REQUESTS')
Mar 01. (cd) *Corban; (CBNCD 029)* **PATRIOT'S HEART** [ ] [-]

Catriona MACDONALD

Born: 9 Dec'68, Shetland Isles. The Shetland lass first picked up the fiddle as a child, beginning professional tuition with the late fiddle master Dr TOM ANDERSON. One of his most gifted pupils, CATRIONA soon scooped the Shetland Folk Society's Young Fiddler of the Year award and became closely involved in Shetland's Young Heritage, a group set up by ANDERSON to nurture the Islands' fiddle tradition.

She went on to win the BBC Radio 2 Young Tradition Award (in 1991) and study at London's Royal College of Music where she met future collaborator, IAN LOWTHIAN. The piano accordionist was to join musical forces with CATRIONA for a debut album, 'OPUS BLUE' (1994), acclaimed by one MARK KNOPFLER amongst many others. Her talent attracted the cream of Scotland's new young traditionalists such as CONRAD IVITSKY and DAVID MILLIGAN. A former member of SWAMPTRASH, IVITSKY played bass for Edinburgh folk guerillas SHOOGLENIFTY while pianist MILLIGAN is closely involved in the Scottish jazz scene. Both appeared on CATRIONA's second album, 'BOLD' (2000), alongside top guitarist TONY McMANUS, percussionist extrordinare JAMES MACKINTOSH (SHOOGLENIFTY/CAPERCAILLIE/AFRO-CELT SOUND SYSTEM), Norwegian church organist IVER KLEIVE and of course IAN LOWTHIAN. The record saw her blossoming as a solo talent, inspired and energised by the high pedigree of musicians backing her up.

Her talent as a composer was also in evidence, CATRIONA's original tunes informed by her beloved Shetland heritage while simultaneously exploring new possibilities and interspersed with both traditional tunes and material from LOWTHIAN. The CD also came with fascinating little sleeve notes explaining each song, penned by 'The Shetland Fiddle Diva' herself.

As well as appearing on the IAN BRUCE albums, 'Hodden Grey' (1998) and 'Alloway Tales' (2000), CATRIONA also initiated the STRING SISTERS, a project featuring six of the world's most talented fiddlers: Americans LIZ CARROLL and LIZ KNOWLES, Norwegian ANNBJORG LIEN, Canadian NATALIE MacMASTER and ALTAN's MAIREAD NI MHAONAIGH. After making their acclaimed debut at the millennial Celtic Connections festival in Glasgow, the group made a second appearance in 2001 due to much popular demand.

In addition to her music biz activities, the Shetland prodigy is also closely involved in teaching and had her own fiddle school in Vementry, Shetland.

CATRIONA MACDONALD – fiddle / with **IAN LOWTHIAN** – piano accordion

Acoustic Radio | not iss.

May 94. (cd/c; by CATRIONA MacDONALD & IAN LOWTHIAN) *(ARAD CD/C 103)* **OPUS BLUE** [ ] [-]
– Islay rant – Farewell to Chernobyl – Tam Lin / Emma / The day dawn – The grouse's revenge – Up da strouds da sailor goes / Sister Jean / The crazy flautist – The hangover p** – The dram shell / Christmas day Ida mournin' – Myra's jog – Da Scallowa lasses / Tha mi linn leis a' ghaol (I am sick with love) / Millie O'Godger / Brudmarsch efter byss-call – Roddare I basark.

— the pair added **DAVID MILLIGAN** – piano / **CONRAD IVITSKY** – double bass / **TONY McMANUS** – guitar / **JAMES MacKINTOSH** – drums, percussion / **IVER KLEIVE** – church organ

Peerie Angel | Compass

Feb 00. (cd) *(PAP 001)* <4294> **BOLD** [ ] [ ] Jun00
– Andy's saltire – Maggie's pancakes / Shetland reels / Michael's mazurka / The Shetland fiddle diva – Purfy / Eilidh's trip in Germany – The Monday morning reel – Land ta Lea / The Tuddal troll / Freddie's tune / Return to the Stewartry – Slanttigart – Tame her when da snaw comes / The lost ponytail – Dennis' tune / Da silver bow – The joy of it!

Finlay MacDONALD (see under ⇒ Tartan Tapes records)

Iain MacDONALD (see under ⇒ Greentrax records)

John MacDONALD

Born: 1905, Pitgaveny, Elgin, Morayshire. A traditional folk singer for many years, JOHN cut the odd track for Folktracks in the early to late 50's. He worked as a gamekeeper/molecatcher by day and night, singing Burns ballads to keep himself amused his daughter ENA was also present at a few of these recording sessions. JOHN's best material came from the 1975 set, 'THE SINGING MOLECATCHER OF MORAYSHIRE' (Topic; 12TS 265) and it was later re-issued on to CD by 'Greentrax' in '98.

Scott MacDONALD (see ⇒ Section 7: Rock & Pop)

Shelagh McDONALD (see ⇒ Section 7: Rock & Pop)

Sarah McFADYEN and Kris DREVER (see under ⇒ Tartan Tapes records)

Kirk MacGEACHY

Born: Edinburgh. At an early age, KIRK moved across the Atlantic to Canada, although his roots led him to front New Age Celtic outfit, OREALIS. In the first half of the 90's, the septet/sextet/whatever (including Portobello-born fiddler JOHNNY CUNNINGHAM on production) released two innovative and well-received sets for 'Green Linnet', 'CELTIC MUSIC – MUSIQUE CELTIQUE' (1990) and 'NIGHT VISIONS' (1995) – the first with dreamy chanter ALLISON MacGEACHY, the second with FIONA MacGEACHY.

Matt McGINN

Born: 17 Jan'28, Gallowgate, Glasgow. Together with his mother, father, five sisters and three brothers in a pokey two-roomed flat, he learned fast about the hardships of life; when MATT was only three an older brother died of pneumonia. From Irish stock, MATT (but under protest!) was sent to a Roman Catholic school and had his first communion in 1935. At the outbreak of the Second World War, MATT was separated from his family and went to live on the Broom Estate in Newton Mearns. MATT subsequently took to the life of petty crime and in the Autumn of 1940, he was sent to an Approved School for over a year. On his release, MATT the lad was no more and he set about earning a crust as a vanboy, a blacksmith's assistant and anything else available. Shortly after the war and inspired by socialist/anarchist speakers, MATT joined the Communist Party (c.1949) and began to speak his own mind on a soapbox in Brunswick Street and the Barras.

The 50's saw MATT fall for fellow campaigner Jeanette and after the usual time of courtship, he married her. The couple would move to Rutherglen then Fernhill once their first son was born and when daughters Eleanor and Shonagh arrived they flitted to a bigger house in Spittal. However, MATT's Communist Party leanings were wearing thin and arguments were aplenty. He decided enough was enough in 1956.

The latter half of the 50's took a dramatic upturn when he was elected as a shop steward after he organised a strike; he would earn a scholarship to Ruskin College (through the T&GWU) and progressed to Oxford University (diploma in Economics and Political Science). Now training to become a teacher at Huddersfield Training College (c.1960), the fresh-faced MATT won a local newspaper competition for a 'Folk' song and embarked on a new career in music.

MATT subsequently tried his hand at writing and performing his own (hit or miss) songs and with an innate sense of timing to compensate for his croaky vocals, he found he could command a good audience. MATT could protest alright, he had been doing so for his fellow workers for several years now and when it came to putting it down on paper it was, as they say, a doddle. His joke-telling and singing pre-dated BILLY CONNOLLY; the Big Yin was surely inspired by MATT – they were also on the same 'Transatlantic' label. Not exactly politically correct (listen to 'GALLOWGATE CALYPSO') – and who minded in those days when you were allowed to laugh without thinking too hard about it – MATT delivered his patter throughout halls, clubs and other Folk-orientated venues. His songs such as 'THE DUNDEE GHOST' and 'THE FOOTBA' REFEREE' were loved by everyone fortunate to hear them – two early sets 'HONESTY IS OUT OF THE FASHION' and 'LITTLE TICKS OF TIME' only sold moderately.

Always a conscientious demonstrator and speaker for the Socialist movement in Scotland, he was always against bigotry, even if his songs appeared to take one side ('THE BOYS OF LISBON') over another. Celebration was indeed a word MATT (who became the bard to the Scottish Daily News) would be synonymous with all his life. After unfruitful spells on other labels during the first half of the 70's, MATT was to die on the 6th January, 1977, of smoke inhalation after falling asleep with a lighted cigarette in his hand. There have been a handful of McGINN faithful during his time, including foreign acts such as The WEAVERS, PETE SEEGER and The BRANDYWINE SINGERS, while Scots folk acts The McCALMANS, BLACKEYED BIDDY and NORTH SEA GAS have all covered his songs.

Matt McGinn

MATT McGINN – vocals / with a few people on backing

— he appeared on the 'The Iron Muse' V/A collection in 1963

— another V/A set, 'To-night At The Attic' featured his tracks plus that of DANNY KYLE, JOSH MacRAE and DAVY SPIERS

Xtra – Transatla. / not iss.

1966. (lp) *(XTRA 1045)* **MATT McGINN** ☐ -
– The red yo yo / Willie Macnamara / Old Johnny Bull / Big Sammy / The footba' referee / Ban the Beatles / The heilan' man / The first man on the Moon / Manura manyar / Gallowgate calypso / Lots of little soldiers / Unner alow the ground. *(re-iss. Mar77 on 'Transatlantic'; TRA SAM 41)*

Transatla. / not iss.

1967. (7") *(TRASP 15)* **THE BOYS FROM LISBON. / I'M LOOKING FOR A JOB** ☐ -

1967. (7") *(TRASP 18)* **I HAVE SEEN THE HIGHLANDS. / I'LL BE COMING HOME TO GLASGOW** ☐ -

1967. (lp) *(XTRA 1057)* **MATT McGINN AGAIN** ☐ -
– Rob Roy MacGregor / Mambo / The rolling hills o' the border / Moaning / We'll all be angels / On the road to Aldomaster / I/O/U. / The ballad of John McLean / Three nights & a Sunday / The king & the key / Rosy Anna / I'm looking for a job / Big Willie's blues. *(re-iss. May77 on 'Transatlantic'; TRA SAM 43)*

1968. (lp; as MATT McGINN and his friends) *(XTRA 1071)* **HONESTY IS OUT OF THE FASHION** ☐ -
– Honesty is out of the fashion / The Pekinese dog / The sash – Kevin Barry / The Dundee ghost / The ballad of the Q4 / Biddie McGrath / The leaving of Liverpool / Ros in the bow / Two foot tall / The sequel to the Dundee weaver / No nay never / The big orange whale / The pill / Coorie doon.

1969. (lp) *(XTRA 1078)* **LITTLE TICKS OF TIME** ☐ -

RCA INt. / not iss.

1971. (lp) *(INTS 1240)* **TAKE ME BACK TO THE JUNGLE** ☐ -
– Take me back to the jungle / With fire and with sword / Tony Capaldi / Cead mile failte / The little carpenter / The wurram and the sparra / Hi Jack / Life is a fountain / Have a banana / The man they could not hang / Tell me what the tea leaves tell me / On the beach at Portobello.

1972. (lp) *(INTS 1368)* **TINNY CAN ON MY TAIL** [ ] [-]
– Tinny can on my tail / The gay liberation / I've packed up my bags / Skull and crossbones / Lady Chat / Wi' Jimmy Reid and Airlie / Troubled waters in my soul / Yes, yes, U.C.S. / In a neat little town / Rich man's paradise / Get up, get out / The Ibrox disaster.

Gem not iss.

1973. (lp) *(GES 1079)* **THE TWO HEIDED MAN** [ ] [-]
– (introduction by David Scougall) / Height starvation song / The two heided man – Ra dug frae ra port – The Prime Minister – Timbuktu / The depth of my ego / The silver screw / St. Colomba and the Masons / The big Glasgow polis / The big effen bee / The foreman O'Rourke / The philosophy of frun / Farrer and murrer / The black velvet hand / Snowball / Ra murrer of five – My farrer – The Tay – There are two teams in Glasgow – The one legged man.

Jul 74. (lp) *(GES 1120)* **THE TWO HEIDED MAN STRIKES AGAIN** [ ] [-]
– Benny Lynch / Billy Davidson's twins / The big shike / The sugary cake and candy man / The buckin' bronco / A tribute to McGonnegal / The bonnie broon haired lassie / The royal infirmary / Janetta / Five million Scotsmen will call / I woke up with the dawning / Frankie Vaughan / The magic shadow show / Samson / The teuchter / Wally Brodie / We ain't gonna dig no more / I was born 10,000 years ago.

Pye not iss.

Oct 75. (lp) *(PKL 5527)* **SCREWTOPS ARE FALLING ON MY HEAD** [ ] [-]
– (introduction by Matt McGinn Jnr.) / Granda / The cradle of civilization: selection of stories & jokes. song: Cider wi' yer ma' my darlin' is a Charlie, I got it my way / My wee Auntie Sarah / Crofter story / Suzie: Screwtops incl. leaving a police van / Gaelic joke / Heiderum hauderum / Maggie might / Glaswegians would / Two wee germs story / Somebody's wean / The Schmitt family story / Nelly may.

Dec 75. (7") *(7N 45555)* **MY WEE AUNTIE SARAH. / GRANDA** [ ] [-]

—— McGINN died after a fire on the 6th January, 1977

– compilations, etc. –

1960's. (lp) *Transatlantic; (TRA SAM 8)* **SAMPLER** [ ] [-]

Nov 88. (c) *Scotdisc; (KITV 454)* **THE PORTRAIT** [ ] [-]
– The footba' referee / The Dundee cat / The red yo yo / Willie Macnamara / Skinny ma linky long legs / The Dundee ghost / Tra la la tweet / Cor wee wean / Loch Lomond / Rob Roy MacGregor / Moaning / I owe you / Three nights & a Sunday / I'm looking for a job / Polly had a poodle / Manura Manya / No nay never.

Aug 00. (cd) *Essential; (ESMCD 930)* **THE BEST OF . . .** [ ] [-]
– The Dundee ghost / The footba' referee / Gallowgate calypso / Honesty is out of the fashion / Little ticks of time / Coorie doon / The ballad of John McLean / Willie Macnamara / Rosy Anna / The boys of Lisbon / The red yo yo / The ballad of Q4 / On the road to Aldomaster / Rob Roy MacGregor / Lots of little soldiers / The pill / Bingo Bella / I'm looking for a job / Big Sammy / The rolling hills of the border / Morning Elanora / The heilan' man / Three nights & a Sunday / I have seen the Highlands / Eternity will soon be over.

Mar 01. (cd) *R.E.L.; (RECD 538)* **THE RETURN OF THE TWO HEIDED MAN (live)** [ ] [-]

Bruce MacGREGOR (see under ⇒ Macmeanmna records)

Jimmie MacGREGOR (see under ⇒ HALL, Robin . . .)

Iain MacINNES (see under ⇒ OSSIAN)

Mairi MacINNES (see under ⇒ Greentrax records)

Iain MacKAY (see under ⇒ Macmeanmna records)

Mae McKENNA (see ⇒ Section 7: Rock & Pop)

MacKENZIE (see under ⇒ SEELYHOO)

Andy MACKENZIE and John MacPHAIL

Formed: Falkirk/Slamannan, Stirlingshire area . . . late 70's. The traditional folk duo regularly performed stints during the tourist season – mainly in Ullapool (the 'Mercury Motor Inn' to be exact). ANDY was said to be the one with a bit flair, his tartan attire adding finesse to his tenor banjo-playing, while he also drove to gigs in a 3-wheeled Reliant Regal Supervan. JASON is said to be still performing at hotels in Fort William.

ANDY MACKENZIE – tenor banjo, mandolin, guitar, bodhran, pipes / **JOHN MacPHAIL** – vocals, acoustic guitar

Loudon not iss.

1980. (lp) *(LDN 460)* **ANDY MACKENZIE AND JOHN MacPHAIL** [ ] [-]
– Skye boat song / Bread and fishes / Flowers of Edinburgh – Soldier's joy / Massacre of Glencoe / Sound the pibroch / Highland Harry / MacPherson's rant / Helen of Kirkconnel / The life of a rover / Ye Jacobites by name / A man's a man / Scotland the brave.

Eilidh MacKENZIE (see under ⇒ MAC-TALLA)

Talitha MacKENZIE

Born: 1959, New York City, New York, USA. Perhaps not truly Scottish in the sense that she wasn't born 'n bred, TALITHA MacKENZIE's contribution to Afro-celtic music (from the mid 80's to the present day) has been as important to our musical heritage as Alan Lomax and his travelling Library of Congress was to America's deep south. MacKENZIE taught herself Gaelic at the age of sixteen, due to her insatiable fascination with Scottish roots music. She was an accomplished pianist, and set up her own "Structure and Form in Music and Movement" course at Harvard and Boston University between 1982-84. She founded the world music ensemble SEDENKA in 1985 and issued a collaboration with Celtic group ST. JAMES GATE in the same year. She also toured Scotland, making field recordings of traditional songs as well as releasing her own self-financed set 'SHANTYTOWN' in 1986. The album, which was made up from traditional bothy ballads, dirges and sea shanties, all displayed MacKENZIE's soft and gentle harmonies, as well as her ability to translate traditional songs in such a beautiful way. She moved to Scotland the same year and became a full-time member of staff at Edinburgh University, as well as a contributing member to incoming Scottish legends MOUTH MUSIC. After the release of their eponymous debut album in 1991, MacKENZIE concentrated on her own solo work, issuing the highly acclaimed 'SOLAS' in 1994, followed by the more pop-orientated 'SPIORAD' (1996) which fused her Celt eclecticism with jazzy overtones, resulting in something truly original, yet something firmly rooted in the past.

TALITHA MacKENZIE – vocals / with various musicians

not iss. own label

1986. (lp) *(none)* **SHANTYMAN** [-] [ ]

—— TALITHA studied at Edinburgh Uni and joined MOUTH MUSIC late 80's

Riverboat Shanachie

Mar 94. (cd) *(TUGCD 1007)* *<SHANCD 79084>* **SOLAS** [ ] [ ]
– Hoireann / Sheatadh cailleach (the old woman's reel) / 'S muladach mi's mi air m'aineoi (mournful am I) / Seinn O! (sing!) / Uamh an oir (the cave of gold) / Owen's boat (O seallaibh curaigh eoghainn) / CH mi na morbheanna – JFK (mist-covered mountains) / Rol hol III Leo / Funky bird medley: Bann de ribinnean – Dannsa nan Tunnagan (band of Ribbo) / Theid mi dhachaigh (the MacKenzie lullaby). *(re-iss. Feb99 on 'Shanachie'; same)*

Sep 96. (cd) *<SHANCD 78003>* **SPIORAD** [-] [ ]
– Fill lu O / 3 things / Fionnaghuala (fair shoulders) / Hopa! / Ajde jano / Fear a bhata / Saor an t-sabhaidh / Changerais-tu? / Spiorad (spirit) / Griogari (Gregor) / A fhleasgaich oig (O most gentle youth).

—— TALITHA featured on a 1997 V/A compilation, 'Celtic Mouth Music'

Rob MacKILLOP (see under ⇒ Greentrax records)

Maeve MacKINNON (see under ⇒ Macmeanmna records)

Iain MacKINTOSH

Born: 20 July 1932, Mount Florida, Glasgow. It was 1964 when the youthful ISLANDERS member drove his mini to gigs; the front seat of the car had to be removed to fit his bass therefore relegating his girlfriend to the back seat. Having recorded one eponymous LP (for 'Waverley' in 1965) with the quartet, IAIN decided it was time for him to branch out. However, it wouldn't be until 1973 and the LP, 'BY REQUEST' (featuring songs by TOM PAXTON, GALLAGHER & LYLE, EWAN MacCOLL, BOB DYLAN, ADAM McNAUGHTAN and JAKE THACKERAY), that his solo career would finally begin. More LP's were to follow, a collaboration with HAMISH IMLACH in '78 and several sets for 'Kettle' records quickly went unnoticed. Playing contemporary folk music (a lot from the pen of HARRY CHAPIN and ERIC BOGLE) through a plethora of instruments and of course the banjo, it wasn't until he teamed up with 'Greentrax' stalwarts BRIAN McNEILL and ALAN REID (the latter still with The BATTLEFIELD BAND) that his career started to flourish. 1988's 'GENTLE PERSUASION' was the imprint's fourteenth release and paved the way for MacKINTOSH to gain the respect he richly deserves. On two subsequent sets, 'RISKS AND ROSES' (1991) and 'STAGE BY STAGE' (1995 – with McNEILL once again!), he covered the odd tune by such US luminaries as Lyle Lovett and Harry Chapin.

IAIN MacKINTOSH – vocals, guitar, etc. / w/ various sessioners

Autogram not iss.

1973. (lp) *(ALLP 196)* **BY REQUEST** [ ] [-]
– John McLean's march / Concertina medley: The sea maiden – Holyrood house / Annie's song / Spanish fandango / Bantam cock / Mrs Canatelli / Pipe medley: The dark island – The bugle horn / Old man's song / Chickens / Jimmy Clay / The terror time / Who killed Davy Moore / International / Saturday night / The Glasgow that I used to know / Wildwood flower / Three men from Carntyne.

1975. (lp) *(MPA 010)* **ENCORE** [ ] [-]
– B.A.C.O.N. and E.G.G.s / The ballad of Penny Evans / Nae luck about the hoose / Ballad of Joe Hill / Mary Mack's mother / The capitalist dream / I wish I was a rock – Darkies dream / The Fairfield crane / My sweet lady / Pipe selection: Massacre of Glencoe – Brocham lom / Farewell to Glasgow / And the band played Waltzing Mathilda.
(above issued on 'Dara' records)

1978. (lp; by HAMISH IMLACH & IAIN MacKINTOSH) *(ALLP 215)* **A MAN'S A MAN** [ ] [-]
– A man's a man for a' that / Jamie Foyers / D-day dodgers / Parcel of rogues / The roving ploughboy / Wae's me for Prince Charlie / McPherson's rant / Skye boat song / Betsy bell / The can o' tea / I am a miller / Freedom come all ye / The flooers o' the forest / Baron of Brackley / Johnny Cope.

Verlag . . . Bauernhaus not iss.

1979. (lp) *(PL 513)* **STRAIGHT TO THE POINT** [-] [-] German
– No use for him / Sam Stone / Hero's return / Roslin Castle / The writing of Tipperary / Blood upon the grass / Whose garden was this / Prisoner 562 / Flowers are red / For a' that – For all dat – Trotz alledem.

Kettle not iss.

1979. (lp) *(KOP 2)* **LIVE IN GLASGOW (live)** [ ] [-]
– The cat's in the cradle / I'm my own grandpa / No man's land / A poor old man / Song of unrequited love / Quo' the idealist / The writing of Tipperary / Granny Fraser's flittin' / Flowers are red / Scrumpy / No use for him / Liz / Unaccomanied song / Paddy and the bricks / Put another log on the fire / The oldest swinger in town.

1981. (lp) *(KOP 6)* **SINGING FROM THE INSIDE (live)** [ ] [-]
– An honest working man / A sweet song of yesterday / William / Annie Brown / Armstrong / Tomorrow / Why do the little girls grow crooked / I'm going back on my bicycle / Wars o' Germany / For the special friends / The food-a-holic / The Glasgow mother's lullaby / The traditional folk singer's lament / We sell everything / You are the only song.

1984. (lp) *(KOP 14)* **HOME FOR A WHILE** [ ] [-]
– Some kind of love / The long road to perfection / A wild Utopian dream / Whatever you say, say nothing / I'll stick on the stamp / The rolling hills o' the borders / Take the children and run / The ballad of Jimmy Steele / Protect and survive / I'm quiet / Young Paul / Pearl-handled pocket knife / All used up / The Greenland whales / Call me the whale.

1986. (lp) *(KOP 16)* **STANDING ROOM ONLY** [ ] [-]
– How can it end / Fifty pence / Margarita / Message from Mother Earth / The songs that Harry wrote / For all the good people / Oor Hamlet / Love song / Hands off the old town / Mary Cecelia Brown / You don't need a dog / Sing for the song.

— in 1986, IAIN and HAMISH IMLACH released another collaborative set, 'LIVE IN HAMBURG' for German 'MusiKiste' (26-6-356)

Greentrax Greentrax

Apr 88. (c/lp; by IAIN MacKINTOSH with BRIAN McNEILL & ALAN REID) *(C+/TRAX 014)* **GENTLE PERSUASION** [ ] [-]
– Tomorrow, you're gone / Uncle Walter / Run the film backwards / My old man / It's so easy to dream / When I'm gone / January man / The farm auction / Wheelchair talking blues / Song of the pineapple rag / First you lose the rhyming / Waltzing around in the nude / Five ways to kill a man. *<(US + cd-iss. Feb97; same)>*

Feb 01. (cd/c) *(CD/C TRAX 043)* **RISKS AND ROSES** [ ] [-]
– If I had a boat / Remember when the music / I wish I was in Glasgow / The rats are winning / The king of Rome / Flowers are red / My home town / Roses from the wrong man / Acceptable risks / Dill pickle rag / Annie McKelvie / Kilkelly / The hug song / Cheeky young lad.

Nov 91. (cd) *(34-6-098)* **JUST MY CUP OF TEA** [-] [-] German
– The horse / 1913 massacre / Tunes of glory / Poor boy on the road / A man you meet every day / Sure sounds like society to me / The last stand / The activity room / Old men and children / Strong women rule the world / The high-low song / I can't touch the sun / Newfoundland.
(above issued on 'MusiKiste')

Nov 95. (cd/c; by IAIN MacKINTOSH & BRIAN McNEILL) *(<CD/C TRAX 101>)* **STAGE BY STAGE** [ ] [ ]
– The plainstanes – The Glasgow magistrate / The wind and rain / The sea maiden – The Balkan hills / Bonny wee lass who never said no / Holyrood house / Generations of change / Dallas domestic / Smoky mokes / Beautiful dreamer – Traveller's moon / Summer of love / Recruited collier – The tank – Cronin's / The fisherman's lilt – What you do with what you've got – The black swan / Roslin Castle – You can't take it with you when you go.

Iain McLACHLAN (see under ⇒ Springthyme records)

Duncan McLAUCHLAN

Born: 1951, Dunfermline, Fife. Born to a multi-instrumentalist musical father who'd played with Fife's accordion legend JIMMY SHAND, DUNCAN took up guitar and piano at the ages of 11 and 12 respectively and began writing his own songs in his early teens. He was soon a schoolboy regular at Dunfermline Folk Club where he got the chance to play alongside the likes of TOMMY MAKEM and HAMISH IMLACH. Although he was to spend a few years in various local rock outfits, his career was to be characterised by a nomadic life of worldwide travel working for a multinational electronics firm.

In 1996, DUNCAN made a permanent move to the USA where he rekindled his interest in folk music and initially played in the Milwaukee-based band FREE WHISKI (sic). After subsequently marrying a Brazilian woman, the Fife exile relocated to Atlanta in 1999 where he now performs with his wife, a bodhran player with a degree in classical music. Finally, in 1999, he unveiled his debut solo album, 'ROAD TO DESTINY'. Written, sung, played and produced by the multi-talented McLAUCHLAN and recorded entirely in his own home studio, the album – which enjoyed substantial specialist airplay throughout the USA – was inpsired both by the man's wandering lifestyle and his memories of Scotland. Readers interested in obtaining a copy can pick one up via the Internet at MusicScotland or Folkweb.

DUNCAN McLAUCHLAN – vocals, guitar

Netreal Netreal

1999. (cd) *(<NMS 20946>)* **THE ROAD TO DESTINY** [ ] [ ]
– The road to destiny / The callin' o' your name / A place called home / The Buckie bronco / A trace of fear / From father to son / Fairy dance / Bonnie is her name / Little green card / Retreat from the Buchaille (traditional) / Rachel / The time for peace is here.

Dougie MACLEAN

Born: 27 Sep'54, Dunblane, Perthshire. Arguably, no other song save maybe 'Flower Of Scotland' has served to galvanise Scotland's collective national identity as successfully as 'CALEDONIA'. While the song's fame possibly eclipses that of its author, the name of DOUGIE MACLEAN has become synonymous with quality Scottish roots music both at home and (especially) abroad. Born to folk-loving parents (his mother played mandolin and his father fiddle), MACLEAN began his own musical career with PUDDOCK'S WELL alongside ANDY M. STEWART and MARTIN HADDEN (later of SILLY WIZARD). MACLEAN's next venture was with The TANNAHILL WEAVERS, an accomplished Scottish folk outfit. The band headhunted DOUGIE after hearing him busk in uptown Kinross and although he only served a relatively short apprenticeship with them he did appear on their 1976 debut set, 'Are Ye Sleeping Maggie'.

His next move was to hook up with ALAN ROBERTS, another Scots folkie with whom he toured Europe and recorded 1979's 'CALEDONIA' album. Released on the 'Plant Life' label, the record was met with an enthusiastic critical reception while the reverberations of its homesick title track would be felt throughout DOUGIE's career. Around the same time, the pair cut the 'CRM' album with ALEX CAMPBELL, the veteran Scots folkie and European busker extrordinaire who's rumoured to have cut around 100 albums(!).

DOUGIE wasn't quite as prolific but he got his solo career off to a fine start in the early 80's with albums such as 'SNAIGOW' (1980), 'ON A WING AND A PRAYER' (1981) and 'CRAIGIE DHU' (1982). 1980 had also seen him put in a brief stint with Scots band SILLY WIZARD, the connection going back to his teenage years when he'd played with future members ANDY M. STEWART and MARTIN HADDEN.

In 1983, DOUGIE and his wife JENNIFER founded their own 'Dunkeld' label and recording studio at their home base in Perthshire. The label's first release was a re-issued 'CRAIGIE DHU' followed by new material in the shape of 1984's 'FIDDLE' and 1985's 'SINGING LAND'. In addition, MACLEAN used the facilities to record and release music by a host of indigenous artists including SHEENA WELLINGTON, HAMISH MOORE and GORDON DUNCAN. The latter half of the 80's saw DOUGIE's star rising as 'Dunkeld' became one of the UK's most important independent folk labels. A subsequent link-up with US National Public Radio show, 'Thistle & Shamrock', saw DOUGIE undertake a successful tour of the States alongside other artists on the 'Dunkeld' roster. By the turn of the decade the operation had expanded to encompass a publishing wing and retail outlet, MACLEAN's recordings finally hitting the chainstore shelves in Scotland and also achieving distribution in the States. Albums such as 'REAL ESTATE' (1988), 'WHITEWASH' (1990) and 'INDIGENOUS' (1991) enjoyed unprecedented critical acclaim and soaring sales.

Yet what really put the name of DOUGIE MACLEAN on the lips of Scotland's man in the street was a re-issued 'CALEDONIA'. Ironically and quite possibly fittingly, the track achieved Scots Mythic Anthem status after being used in a beer commercial. Sung by the gravel-throated FRANKIE MILLER, the song reached No.1 on the Scottish chart in 1992 and was subsequently adopted as an unofficial theme tune by patriotically minded Scots everywhere. Its unashamed nostalgia was perfect for the SNP (Scottish National Party) who used it as their theme for the elections to the newly inaugurated Scottish Parliament in 1997. A mark of MACLEAN's newfound popularity among the masses was an invitation to perform in front of 30,000 rugby fans at Edinburgh's Murrayfield Stadium the same year.

Longtime folk fans, meanwhile, lapped up 'SUNSET SONG' (1994) and 'RIOF' (1997) as well as sold-out concerts at the annual Celtic Connections festival in Glasgow. Scotland's famous diaspora also ensured that MACLEAN could command full-houses in places like New Zealand and especially the USA where he's performed with longtime friend, country singer KATHY MATTEA. More surprising was the airing of the MACLEAN-penned 'THE GAEL' by the massed military bands at the 1998 Festival Of Remembrance held in London's Royal Albert Hall. Even more surprising (and amusing) was a techno version of the latter track which made the Spanish and German Top 10 in 1999.

A man of many talents, DOUGIE has also completed theatre, (musical director of TAG's 'A Scot's Quair' in 1993), television and soundtrack work ('The Last Of The Mohicans') while his songs have been covered by some of the world's leading roots artists. His most recent recording was 'PERTHSHIRE AMBER', an extended four-part composition initially premiered at Perth Festival Of The Arts in 1999 and released on disc the following year. His record company can be found at (www.dunkeld.com or co.uk or www.dougiemaclean.com – under construction). He now owns a hotel in Dunkeld and a coffee-shop in Edinburgh – needless to say, both specialise in the best of folk music.

DOUGIE MACLEAN – vocals, guitar, keyboards, fiddle, bass, etc (ex-TANNAHILL WEAVERS, ex-SILLY WIZARD, ex-MOSAIC) / with various friends/musicians

1978. (lp; as ALAN ROBERTS & DOUGIE MACLEAN) *(PLR 012)* **CALEDONIA** ☐ [-]

Burlington / not iss.

Dec 79. (lp; ALEX CAMPBELL – ALAN ROBERTS – DOUGIE MACLEAN) *(BURL 002)* **C R M** ☐ [-]
– The trooper and the maid / I lo'ed nae a lassie but ane / The jute mill song / Her fa la la lo / Whar widne fecht for Charlie / Leis an lurgainn / Bonnie Mary / Rattlin' roarin' Willie / John Anderson my Jo / Miss Elizabeth Campbell / Alick C. MacGregor / Jock Stewart / Little song.

Plant Life / not iss.

Nov 80. (lp) *(PLR 022)* **SNAIGOW** ☐ [-]
– Rolling home / King's command / Mill brae / Lassie's trust in providence / Bonnie Isle of Whalsay / Nothern cowboy / Back to the island / Silently sad Hieland Harry / Ye banks and braes of Bonny Doon / John McColl's reel / Alex Campbell's reel / Loch Tay boat song.

Nov 81. (lp) *(PLR 034)* **ON A WING AND A PRAYER** ☐ [-]

Dunkeld / not iss.

1983. (lp/c) *(DUN/+C 001)* **CRAIGIE DHU** ☐ [-]
– Gin I were a baron's heir / Ready for the storm / It was a' for our rightfu' king / High flying seagull / Edmondton airbus / Craigie Dhu / Bonnie Bessie Logan / Seannair's song / It fascinates me / Tullochgorum / Caledonia. *(cd-iss. Jan92; DUNCD 001) <Us cd-iss. 1999 on 'Blix Street'; 10054>*

1984. (lp/c) **(DUN/+C 002) FIDDLE** ☐ [-]
– The osprey / Bob MacIntosh / Atholl Arms / Ku-ring-gal chase / Farewell to Craigie Dhu / The tattie ball / When are you coming over? / Mr. & Mrs. MacLean of Snaigow / Roy Ashby's / Buckny burn – One summer's morning / The ferry – Spoutwell's / Riechip / Leduckie / The centre. *(cd-iss. Nov93; DUNCD 002)*

1985. (lp/c) *(DUN/+C 004)* **SINGING LAND** ☐ [-]
– Singing land / Bonnie woods o' Hatton / Desperate man / The other side / This love will carry / Tumbling down / Kelphope Glen / Guillotine's glory / Another story / Goodnight and joy. *(cd-iss. Nov93; DUNCD 004)*

1988. (lp/c) *(DUN/+C 008)* **REAL ESTATE** ☐ [-]
– Solid ground / Restless fool / Buffalo jump / Garden valley / The emmigrant / Green grow the rushes / Homeland / The Mhairi bhan / Are ye sleeping Maggie? / She loves me (when I try). *(cd-iss. Nov93; DINCD 008)*

Jul 90. (lp/c/cd; as DOUGIE MACLEAN & KATHY MATTEA) *(DUN/+C/CD 010)* **WHITEWASH** ☐ [-]
– Trail of the survivor / Gloomy winter / No no no / Rescue me / Dolina / Family of the mountains / Shame / No nighean don / Until we meet again / Little ones walk on.

Nov 90. (lp/c/cd) *(DUN/+C/CD 011)* **THE SEARCH** ☐ [-]
– The search / The abyssal / Thermocline / The origin / Sixties vigil / The gael / The underwater vigil / Loch Ness.

Jan 92. (cd/c) *(DUN CD/C 015)* **INDIGENOUS** ☐ [-]
– Rite of passage / Rank & roses / War / Slave's lament / Turning away / Let her go / This line is broken / Ae fond kiss / Thundering in / Eternity. *<US cd-iss. 1999 on 'Blix Street'; 10060>*

Aug 93. (cd/c) *(DUN CD/C 017)* **SUNSET SONG** ☐ [-]
– Sunset song / The burning of Peesie's knapp / The Kinraddie song / Cloud Howe / Cirrus / The eviction / The bridge incident / The Kaimes / Grey granite / Distress.

Jun 94. (cd/c) *(DUN CD/C 019)* **MARCHING MYSTERY** ☐ [-]
– Deepest part of me / It belongs to us / All together / Holding back / Hearts can never hide / Broken wings / The land / When the people speak / Expectation.

Nov 95. (cd/c) *(DUN CD/C 020)* **TRIBUTE (A TRIBUTE TO ROBERT BURNS. NIEL GOW & ROBERT TANNAHILL)** (traditional) ☐ [-]
– Ca' the yowes / Are ye sleepin' Maggie? / Scots wha' hae / Neil Gow's lament / The slave's lament / Ye banks and braes / For a' that / Gloomy winter / Rattlin' roarin' Willie / Auld lang syne / Farewell to whisky. *<US cd-iss. 1999 on 'Blix Street'; 10063>*

Dunkeld / Blix Street

Aug 97. (cd/c) *(DUN CD/C 021) <10064>* **RIOF** ☐ ☐ 1999
– Stepping stones / Stolen / Scythe song / Feel so near / Gneiss wind / Sfhada leam / An oidche ghemraidh / She will find me / Big river / Fragments from a mug's game / Distant son.

Jan 00. (cd) *(DUNCD 023) <10065>* **PERTHSHIRE AMBER** ☐ ☐ May00
– First movement . . . Perthshire amber / Second movement . . . Crannog – Castle Menzies / Third movement . . . The fair city / Fourth movement . . . Rannoch – The butterstone . . . . / S. Mr. & Mrs. MacLean of Snaigow / The search / The Kaimes / Enhanced track (dub).

– compilations, others, etc. –

1989. (lp) *Dambuster; (DAM 002)* **BUTTERSTONE** (rec.1983) ☐ [-]
(cd-iss. Dec97; DAMCD 002)

Feb 96. (cd) *Osmosys; (<OSMOCD 004>)* **DOUGIE MACLEAN'S CALEDONIA (THE PLANT LIFE YEARS)** ☐ ☐ Jan97
– Plooboy laddies / Johnny teasie weasle / Over my mountain / Mistress McKinley's breakfast surreals / Northern cowboy / I lo'e nae a lassie but ane / Rattlin' roarin' Willie / Mormond braes / Caledonia / Jock Stewart / Leis a lurighan / Rolling home / Mill brae / Lassies trust in providence / Bonnie isle o' Whalsay / Ye banks and braes o' bonnie doon.

Jan 97. (cd) *Putumayo; (<M 117-2>)* **THE DOUGIE MACLEAN COLLECTION** ☐ ☐ 1995
– Rite of passage / Singing land / Solid ground / Broken wings / Marching mystery / The search / Turning away / Caledonia / Ready for the storm / Trail of the survivor / This love will carry. *(re-iss. Feb01; PUTU 1102)*

Dolina MACLENNAN (& Robin GRAY)

Born: c.1940, Isle Of Lewis. Steeped in the art of traditional Gaelic song since childhood, DOLINA first performed in public after moving down to Edinburgh in 1958. There she had a residency at the Waverley Bar in St.Mary's Street – just round the corner from the famous World's End – alongside guitarist ROBIN GRAY, the pair's pioneering weekend club nights developing in tandem with the legendary Howff in the Royal Mile (369 High Street). Although holding down a teaching job across the water in Fife, DOLINA became a favourite at the Howff at the dawn of the 60's along with the likes of LEN PARTRIDGE and sisters, LIZ and MAGGIE CRUICKSHANK.

In 1961, she and GRAY ventured to London where they toured the hotspots of the capital's burgeoning scene, subsequently returning to Edinburgh and a Sunday night residency at the Howff. Towards the end of the year, they issued a debut EP, 'BY MORLAND BRAES' on 'Topic' and performed at the opening night of the Dunfermline Howff, a club modelled on the soon-to-close Auld Reekie institution.

After giving up her teaching job, DOLINA moved into a friend's flat near Edinburgh University, which rapidly became a crash pad for all and sundry on the folk scene. In fact, the flat was used to record the various artists – DOLINA included – that made up the 2 volumes of 'Edinburgh Folk Festival', the seminal recording that prefigured 'Transatlantic' records.

DOLINA MacLENNAN – vocals / **ROBIN GRAY** – acoustic guitar

Topic / not iss.

1961. (7"ep) *(TOP 68)* **BY MORMOND BRAES** ☐ [-]

—— both DOLINA and ROBIN still toured but eventually retired

Donnie M. MacLEOD (see under ⇒ Macmeanmna records)

Kevin MacLEOD (see under ⇒ Iona records)

Tony McMANUS

Born: 1965, Paisley. Raised on a diet of traditional Scots and Irish music, McMANUS developed his unique acoustic guitar style in an almost wholly self-taught capacity. Signed to 'Greentrax', he made his solo recording debut in 1996 with the eponymous 'TONY McMANUS', garnering widespread acclaim from folk circles and beyond. The man's incredibly nimble-fingered picking technique brought admiration and respect from all quarters of the traditional music scene, engendering a huge list of guest recording appearances for the likes of BRIAN McNEILL, WILLIAM JACKSON and KATE RUSBY amongst many others.

His musical knowledge extends to overseas outposts of the Celtic tradition including Brittany, Galicia, Cape Breton and Quebec, McMANUS's follow-up set, 'POURQUOI QUEBEC?' (1998), being recorded in the French-Canadian province and featuring the fretless bass playing of ALAIN GENTY and the pieds magique (foot tapping!) of ANDRE MARCHAND.

1998 also found TONY taking the stage as a touring replacement for SOIG SIBERIL in fiddle-based folk supergroup, CELTIC FIDDLE FESTIVAL, a collective comprising KEVIN BURKE, JOHNNY CUNNINGHAM and CHRISTIAN LEMAITRE. The following year McMANUS recorded 'RETURN TO KINTAIL' (1999) with ALASDAIR FRASER while his startling talent was finally availed to novices via a couple of instructional videos released on STEFAN GROSSMAN's 'Guitar Workshop' imprint. Recognised as a contemporary of Scottish six-string wizards like ALAN NEAVE and MARTIN TAYLOR, McMANUS' talent has seen him embraced by both Scotland's jazz and classical communities. A third set, 'CEOL MORE' (a pun for "big music") was issued early 2002 and featured EWEN VERNAL (from CAPERCAILLIE) and GUY NICOLSON (from SALSA CELTICA), a mixed batch of trad and jazz with renditions of Robert Burns' 'YE BANKS AND BRAES' and Charlie Mingus' 'GOODBYE PORK PIE HAT'.

TONY McMANUS – acoustic guitar, mandolin / with **BRIAN McNEILL** – fiddle, producer / **JIM RUSSELL** – bodhran / **MIKE TRAVIS** – percussion / **PATSY SEDDON** – harp

Greentrax Greentrax

Dec 95. (cd/c) *(<CD/C TRAX 096>)* **TONY McMANUS** ☐ ☐ Jan96
– Doherty's – Return to Milltown – Tommy Peoples / The sweetness of Mary – The piper's bonnet / The emigrant's farewell / The Flanagan brothers jig – Dermot Byrnes – Miss Sarah McFayden / Jackie Coleman's – The millener's daughter – Rakish Paddy – Connor Dunn's / Breizh – The duck – The seagull / The humours of Barrack Street – The letterkenny blacksmith / Ar bhurach na laoi / The snowy path – The harper's chair / Gavotte de Marcel – Dans Fisel / Hector the hero – The girl's of Martinfield / The Johnstown reel / What a wonderful world – Charlie Hunter's – The humours of Tulla.

— next with **ALAIN GENTY** (b. France) – fretless bass / **DENIS FRECHETTE** – piano

Feb 98. (cd) *(<CDTRAX 151>)* **POURQUOIS QUEBEC?** ☐ ☐ Apr98
– Tha biodag aig MacThomais / A tune for Frankie – An phis fluich / Mornings at bonny doon – Janine's reel / Port na bPucai – The crooked road / The 70th year / Irene Meldrum's welcome to Bon Accord / Catherine Kelly's – The sunset / Sean O duibhir a ghleanna / The dance of Suleiman / The maid behind (MacGlinchey's) bar / Annan waters.

— in 1999, McMANUS collaborated with ALASDAIR FRASER on the album, 'RETURN TO KINTAIL'.

— next with **EWEN VERNAL** – bass (of CAPERCAILLIE) / **GUY NICOLSON** – tablas (of SALSA CELTICA)

Feb 02. (cd) *(<CDTRAX 226>)* **CEOL MORE** ☐ ☐
– Lady Ann Montgomery's reel – Eilish Brogan – Paddy Fahey's / The lament of the viscount of Dundee – Dr MacPhail's reel / Sliabh gheal gCua na feile – Kishor's tune / Ye banks and braes / Goodbye pork pie hat / The king of the pipers / Exile – La reve du Queteux Tremblay – Pierre's right arm / An drochaid bheag – The chandelier / Suite de ridees / The old bush / Shalom aleichem.

Alison McMORLAND

Born: 12 Nov'40, Clarkston, Renfrewshire. From an early age, after her family moved to Strathaven, she was weaned on the Scottish tradition/source singers of the North East. Having spent time in the 60's living in Helston, Cornwall, ALISON decided to take up folk singing on a full-time basis. Subsequent work included a time producing a teaching manual for Washington's famous Smithsonian Institute; she would find this time essential to her need to put source singing back at the forefront of Scottish folk music. In 1970 she sang her first gig at the Irvine Festival (she also won the women's traditional trophy at Kinross Folk Festival a year later), while the rest of the decade was kept busy by researching folk records from all over the globe.

Having collected a number of children's songs and games, she put it to good use by presenting BBC Radio's 'Listen With Mother' for a number of years. Her initial recordings would be of children's folklore, while she also sang guest spots for The Albion Band and instigated a workshop with Frankie Armstrong.

In 1977, she delivered her magnum opus, 'BELT WI' COLOURS THREE', an album of absorbing passion that won her a fresh audience with traditional Scots folk record buyers; fiddler ALY BAIN and piper RAB WALLACE would accompany the ground-breaking set. McMORLAND had also published many books, one of them 'Memories' – a retrospective of Humberside's older community – was in the shops around the mid-80's.

In 1990, she worked for Strathclyde Regional Council as the Traditional Folk Arts Lecturer, her employment also taking her all around the world. Early in 2001, she finally returned to the fore with a fresh set of songs, 'CLOUDBERRY DAY' (on Living Tradition's 'The Tradition Bearers' series), a recording augmented by veteran folkies NORMAN CHALMERS and DEREK HOY (of JOCK TAMSON'S BAIRNS). That same year she performed side by side with her Glasgow-born, songwriting husband, GEORDIE McINTYRE, at the 20th Orkney Folk Festival. ALISON is probably one of Scotland's finest chanters, it's been said many times over that she has kept the source singing tradition alive. "She has a voice that shines like the dawn of a new day" was another quote.

ALISON McMORLAND – vocals, banjo / with various session people

unknown not iss.

1975. (lp; with Various Artists) **SCOTS SONGS AND MUSIC – LIVE FROM KINROSS (live)** ☐ -

1977. (lp) **SONGS AND RHYMES FROM LISTEN WITH MOTHER** ☐ -

Tangent not iss.

1977. (lp) *(TGS 125)* **BELT WI' COLOURS THREE – TRADITIONAL SCOTS SONGS** ☐ -

Big Ben not iss.

1977. (lp/c) *(BBX/+MC 504)* **ALISON McMORLAND PRESENTS THE FUNNY FAMILY – SONGS, RHYMES AND GAMES FOR CHILDREN** ☐ -

— during this period, ALISON featured on two V/A sets, 'Freedom Come All Ye – Poems And Songs Of Hamish Henderson' (1977) and 'The Good Old Way – The Best Of British Folk' (1977)

Topic not iss.

1980. (lp) *(12TS 403)* **ALISON McMORLAND & PETA WEBB** ☐ -
– Two pretty boys / What can a young lassie? / Jogging up the Claudy / In London so fair / Convict's song / Sailing's a weary life / Factory girl / May morning dew / Green banks of Yarrow / Dowie dens of Yarrow / Our ship is ready.

— also in 1980, ALISON featured on an album, 'MY SONG IS MY OWN – SONGS FROM WOMEN', alongside FRANKIE ARMSTRONG, KATHY HENDERSON and SANDRA KERR. The following year and 1990, V/A sets 'Nuclear Power No Thanks!' and 'Glasgow Horizons', hit the small retail shops

— next with **NORMAN CHALMERS** – concertina, imbira / **DEREK HOY** – fiddles / and **KIRSTY POTTS** – vocals (on 1)

Living Tradition not iss.

Jan 01. (cd) *(LTCD 1003)* **CLOUDBERRY DAY** ☐ -
– Traivellers joy / Sailin's a weary life / Edom o' Gordon / Be guid tae me / The twa sisters / Twa years ower young / Hap and row / The flyting o' life and daith / The American stranger / Skippin' bar'fot through the heather / Belt wi' colours three / Pullin hard against the stream / Cloudberry day.

John McNAIRN (see ⇒ End Folk 2)

Adam McNAUGHTAN (see under ⇒ Greentrax records)

McNAUGHTON'S VALE OF ATHOLL PIPE BAND (see under ⇒ Greentrax records)

Brian McNEILL

Born: 6 Apr'50, Falkirk. A talented vocalist and multi-instrumentalist, McNEILL was a founder and core member of BATTLEFIELD BAND from their inception right up until 1989 when he decided to concentrate on his own development as a songwriter and solo performer. He'd already begun his solo recording career back in 1978 when he released 'MONKSGATE', a collection of traditional music from Scotland, Ireland, Wales and Northern England. Three years later he teamed up with fellow BB founder ALAN REID for the 'SIDETRACKS' album on 'Topic', his final moonlighting effort being 1985's 'UNSTRUNG HERO' set.

The expert fiddler launched his solo career proper in 1990 with 'THE BUSKER AND THE DEVIL'S ONLY DAUGHTER' (featuring both BATTLEFIELD BAND and CILLA FISHER), subsequently signing to East Lothian label, 'Greentrax', with whom he was to enjoy a fruitful relationship throughout the 90's. 'THE BACK O' THE NORTH WIND' (1991) was followed by a further couple of collaborative albums, 1994's 'HORSE FOR

COURSES' with Irishman TOM McDONAGH and 1995's 'STAGE BY STAGE' with IAIN MACKINTOSH. Never a man to shy away from overt social comment, McNEILL was as defiant as ever on 1995's 'NO GODS', its title track a lament for Scotland's lost opportunities and misplaced nationalistic pride. Skirling pipes aside, the track's rampant guitars, brass and drums mark it out as perhaps the most un-folky track McNEILL has yet penned.

The 90's also saw BRIAN extending his talents into production (ERIC BOGLE & JOHN MUNRO's 'Emigrant & The Exile') and novel writing, the man currently working on his third book. Regarded as one of Scotland's most accomplished contemporary songwriters in the folk sphere, McNEILL has had his songs performed by the likes of DICK GAUGHAN, JEAN REDPATH, SHARON SHANNON and The McCALMANS.

BRIAN McNEILL – vocals, multi-instruments (ex-BATTLEFIELD BAND)

Escalibur not iss.

1978. (lp) *(BUR 001)* **MONKSGATE – Traditional music from Scotland, Ireland, Wales & Northumbria** [ ] [-]
– Queen of sluts – Willie is a bonny lad / The flowers of the thorn / The oyster girl – The centenary – Shane's fancy / Master Crowley's reel – Bobby Casey's reel / The Duke of Fife's welcome to Deeside – Belladrum house – The witch of the wave / Rowley burn – Roxburg Castle / Planxty Charles Coote – Planxty Hugh O'Donnell / The bag of potatoes – The little pig lamenting the empty trought – Brian O'Laimhin / Monksgate / The hag at the spinning wheel / The eclipse – The mathematician / Modest Miss France – The marchioness of Huntly – Miss Shepherd – Pretty Peg. *(cd/c-iss.May93 on 'Greentrax'; CD/C TRAX 062)*

Topic not iss.

Jun 81. (lp; by ALAN REID & BRIAN McNEILL) *(12TS 417)* **SIDETRACKS** [ ] [-]

Temple Temple

Mar 85. (lp) *(TP 017)* **UNSTRUNG HERO** [ ] [-]
– Lift your glass to the landlady – Peter Alver's favourite – The steeple reel / The butterfly chain / Angela Morrison's pavanne – The white dress – The foggy banks of Haines / The boys that broke the ground – Ortiguera / The tall ships in their prime / The ivory reel – Miss Susan Feddersen – The quill / Belle-ile / Crookhill / The Laverock sang / The heron / Molly's roses – Hamish Henderson's refusal / Blue jay and a cardinal / Bothkennar / Down the road to Galloway – Catherine Jane's polka. *(c-iss.Feb94; CTP 017) (cd-iss. Oct97; COMD2 017)*

Oct 90. (cd/c) *(<COMD2/CTP 042>)* **THE BUSKER AND THE DEVIL'S ONLY DAUGHTER** [ ] [ ]
– The sidewalk reels:- Cold frosty morning – Yankee dollar – The trip to Marblehead / High Handenhold / Lady Glasgow / The golden ox – The silver waltz / The gilded shadow / The Devil's only daughter / The busker / The pavement jigs:- Salt the pot – Miss Catherine Jane Spree's – The perfect pitch / Miss Hamilton / Greenland's icy waters / The owl waltz / McNeill's favourite:- Captain O'Kane – Jamie Allen – The mason's apron. *(re-iss. Feb94; same)*

Greentrax Greentrax

Sep 91. (cd/c) *(<CD/C TRAX 047>)* **THE BACK O' THE NORTH WIND** [ ] [ ]
– The back o' the north wind / The entail / Strong women rule us with their tears / The rock & the tide / Destitution road / Muir & the master builder / The Atlantic reels / The best o' the barley / Ewen & the gold / Drive the golden spike / Lang Johnny Moir / Steel man / The bridal boat.

Mar 94. (cd/c; by BRIAN McNEILL & TOM McDONAGH) *(CD/C TRAX 071)* **HORSES FOR COURSES** [ ] [ ]
– Horses for courses – The rank outsider – The black mare – Neck and neck / Miss Grant's jig – Danzig Willie – Sonny's mazukka / Tripping down the stairs – The convenience reel – Bleaton gardens / Mrs. Crotty's reel – The shoemaker's reel – Return to Camden Town / Sunday on the jar / The dark island / Johnny Gallagher – Jimmy Ward's jig / The snows of France and Holland / The clergyman's lamentation – The last adder / Mary and the soldier – The A.L.M.A. / Black water side.

—— in Sep'95, he teamed up with IAIN MACKINTOSH on the album, 'STAGE BY STAGE' *(CD/C TRAX 101)*

Dec 95. (cd/c) *(<CD/C TRAX 098>)* **NO GODS** [ ] [ ]
– No gods and precious few heroes / Miss Michison regrets / Any Mick'll do / The drover's road – Breton wedding march / Trains and my grandfather / Tommy Sheridan's – Annie Lawson – Jocky's treble tops – Assynt crofters / Montrose / Inside the whale – Princess Augusta / Fighter / Alison Hargreaves – Veillion's young Master Haigh / Steady as she goes / Bring back the wolf.

Catherine-Ann MacPHEE
(see under ⇒ Greentrax records)

Josh MacRAE

Born: IAN MacRAE, c.1939, Glasgow. Having studied under the watchful eye of Renfrewshire Academy tutor NORMAN BUCHAN, JOSH went on to become a member of The REIVERS (alongside BUCHAN and – it was thought – EWAN MacCOLL) in the late 50's. Described at the time as Scotland's answer to The WEAVERS, they appeared on STV's 'Jigtime' and released a couple of 45's, 'THE WEE MAGIC STANE' and 'DOWN IN THE MINES' around the same period. Now a local celebrity of sorts, MacRAE started out on his own solo sojourn, 'TALKIN' ARMY BLUES' being the first (but only one for 'Pan Scottish') of many singles released during the early 60's. JOSH was an acquaintance of many up and coming folk/blues artists including JIMMIE MacGREGOR (a friend from his Glasgow School Of Art days) and JAMIE McEWAN (from his time in the National Service). The aforementioned singles for 'Pye' records such as 'TALKIN' SOUTHERN BLUES', 'LET RAMENSKY GO', 'WILD SIDE OF LIFE' and 'MESSING ABOUT ON THE RIVER', all bombed desperately outside of Scotland, although a self-titled set for 'Transatlantic' in 1966 gave him back some street cred. Sadly, MacRAE gave his last interview in 1976 with AILEE MUNRO. In it he announced that "there's more in common between a celt and a cowboy than a celt and an Englishman".

REIVERS

JOSH MacRAE / NORMAN BUCHAN / EWAN MacCOLL

Top Rank not iss.

Oct 59. (7") *(JAR 244)* **THE WEE MAGIC STANE. / THE WRECK OF THE JOHN B** [ ] [-]
Jan 60. (7") *(JAR 283)* **DOWN IN THE MINES. / GOVAN IS A BUSY PLACE** [ ] [-]

JOSH MacRAE

Pan Scottish not iss.

Jan 60. (7") *(PAN 6)* **TALKIN' ARMY BLUES. / (instrumental)** [ ] [-]

Top Rank not iss.

Feb 60. (7") *(JAR 290)* **TALKIN' ARMY BLUES. / TALKIN' GUITAR BLUES** [ ] [-]

Pye not iss.

Apr 60. (7") *(7N 15306)* **TALKIN' SOUTHERN BLUES (original TALKIN' BLUES). / TALKING THRO' THE MILL** [ ] [-]
May 60. (7") *(7N 15307)* **LET RAMENSKY GO. / SKY HIGH JOE** [ ] [-]
Jun 60. (7") *(7N 15308)* **WILD SIDE OF LIFE. / DEAR JOHN** [ ] [-]
Jan 61. (7") *(7N 15319)* **MESSING ABOUT ON THE RIVER. / HIGH CLASS FEELING** [ ] [-]
May 61. (7") *(7N 15360)* **ARKANSAS RAMBLER. / NEVER NEVER MAN** [ ] [-]
Aug 61. (7") *(7N 15384)* **DO IT YOURSELF. / SPECIAL PLACE OF YORN** [ ] [-]
Aug 65. (7") *(7N 15926)* **BARON JAMES McPHAIT. / THE WEE FERRY** [ ] [-]

Transatla. not iss.

1966. (lp) *(TRA 150)* **JOSH MacRAE** [ ] [-]

—— MacRAE retired from the music biz after above only to re-surface with Irish folkie, NICK JONES (as IAN MacRAE) on the 1981 tribute single, 'BALLAD OF LADY DI' / 'THREE MINUTES OF SILENCE' on 'Stiff' *(WED 1)*

– compilations, etc. –

1960. (7"ep) *Pye; (NEP 24131)* **WALKIN', TALKIN' SINGIN'** [ ] [-]
1960. (7"ep) *Top Rank; (JKP 2061)* **JOSH MacRAE** [ ] [-]
1966. (lp) *Golden Guinea; (GGL 0335)* **MESSING ABOUT ON THE RIVER** [ ] [-]

MAC-TALLA

Formed: Isle Of Lewis, Skye . . . 1993 by producer ROBIN MORTON, who employed the services of seasoned Gaelic-singers CHRISTINE PRIMROSE, EILIDH MacKENZIE and ARTHUR CORMACK and the fine musicianship of harpist/cellist ALISON KINNAIRD and ex-RUNRIG accordion-player BLAIR DOUGLAS (also on keyboards). Taking their moniker from the Gaelic for Echo, the group managed to get together for live outings and a splendid one-off set, ' . . .MAIRIDH GAOL IS CEOL' (1994). Mostly all the players were always around as soloists, KINNAIRD with several albums to her credit as well as four books and an MBE in 1997. PRIMROSE, meanwhile, issued her own solo sets, as did the other members of this exciting folk supergroup.

CHRISTINE PRIMROSE (b.17 Feb'52) – vocals / **EILIDH MacKENZIE** – vocals / **ARTHUR CORMACK** – vocals / **ALISON KINNAIRD** (b.30 Apr'49) – harp, cello / **BLAIR DOUGLAS** – accordion, keyboards (ex-RUNRIG)

Temple not iss.

Feb 94. (cd/c) *(COMD2/CTP 054)* **. . .MAIRIDH GAOL IS CEOL** [ ] [-]
– Illean bithibh sunndach (Boys be happy) / Seann oran seilge (Old hunting song) / Griogal cridhe (Beloved Gregor) / Puirt-a-beul (Mouth music): Eadaraibh a huinn o – Domhnall dubh an Domhnallaich – Nighean rudh bha(n – Meal do bhrogan – Ciamar a ni mi an dannsa direach) / Crodh an tailleir (The tailor's dowry) / Barcelona / Ailean Duinn (Brown haired Alan) / Mrs. Jamieson's favourite / Puirt-a-beul (Mouth music): (Dh'fhaibhainn sgiobalta – Fhuair mi nead a ghurra-gug – Fear a bhios fada

phosadh – Ruidhlidh na coillich dhubha) / A chailin aluinn (The beautiful girl) / Togail curs air leodhas (Setting a course for Lewis) / Braigh Uige (Uig brae).

ALISON KINNAIRD

Mulligan not iss.

1978. (c) *(CSH 001)* **THE HARP KEY** ☐ ☐
– Rory Dall's port / Princess Augusta / Caoineadh rioghail (the royal lament) / Glenlivet – Castle Drummond / Balquhidder / Fluich an oidhche – Heman dubh / Port Atholl / Killiecrankie / Cumha crann nan teud (the lament for the harp key) / The kid on the mountain / Fuath nam fidhleirean (contempt for fiddlers) / Chapel Keithack / Granton-on-Spey (biale nan granndach) / Port Patrick / The rymer / The duchess of Buccleuch's favourite – The earl of Haddington – Miss Charlotte Brodie's jig. *(re-iss. Sep80 on 'Milligan'; LUN 029) (re-iss. Jan83 on 'Temple' lp/c; SH/CSH 001) (cd-iss. Apr96; COMD1 001)*

Temple not iss.

1980. (lp/c) *(TP/CTP 003)* **THE HARPER'S GALLERY** ☐ ☐

— during the mid-late 80's, ALISON recorded two volumes of 'MUSIC IN TRUST' with The BATTLEFIELD BAND

1983. (lp/c; as ANN HEYMANN & ALISON KINNAIRD)
(TP/CTP 013) **THE HARPER'S LAND** ☐ ☐
– The harper's land / Ellen's dreams / Lady Iveagh / The Braidwood waits / Rory Dall Morison's jig – Far-fuadach 'a chlarsair (The harper's dismissal) / The Granard tunes:- Carraic na t-uaine – The market house – John Dungan's return – The canon's cup / Bas alastruim – McAllistruim's march / Miss Hamilton / Cum easbig barraghaal (Bishop of Argyle's lament) / Baltiorum – Charlie's fancy / Blar siabh an t-siorradh – The battle of Sheriffmuir / The bells of Cork City – The dusty miller / Clarsach na cloiche (The harp of stones) / Airs by Fingal / Leslie's march. *(cd-iss. Feb94; COMD2 012)*

1988. (c) *(BK 003)* **HARP TUTOR** ☐ ☐

Dec 88. (cd) *(COMC2 005)* **THE SCOTTISH HARP** ☐ ☐
– Rory's Dall's port / Granton-on-Spey (biale nan granndach) / Bas Alastruim (the death of Alasdair) / Ellen's dreams / Carrill's lament / The Deiking glasse / The Braidwood waits / The kid on the mountain / McLoud's salute / Cumh easbig earraghaal (the bishop of Argyle's lament) / Port Atholl / Cro cinn t-saile the Kilbarchan weaver / The conundrum / Lady Livingston – Dunkeld steeple / Balfour village – Shapinsay polka / Ring of crystal, ring of stone. *(re-iss. Feb94; same)*

CHRISTINE PRIMROSE

1982. (lp/c) *(TP/CTP 006)* **AITE MO GHAOIL (PLACE OF MY HEART)** ☐ ☐
– Ceann loch an duin / Curstaidh brus / Duanag a' chiobair / Carlobhagh / Strath ban / Coille an fhasaich / Greas ort dhachaidh a dh'eilean a'fhraoich / Si Morag 'si Morag / Nuair a chi thu caileag bholdheach / Calum sgaire / Nan caedaicheadh an tide dhomh / Nan tigheadh tu idir / Comunn uibhist's bharraidh / N teid thu leam mo higran donn / A fhleasgaigh oig bi furachail. *(cd-iss. Apr93; COMD2 003)*

1987. (lp/c) *(TP/CTP 024)* **'S TU NAM CHUIMNHE** ☐ ☐
– Th m'eudail is m'aighear 's mo ghradh (My treasure my delight, my love) / Coinnichidh mi an gleann an fhraoich (When the evening mist comes swirling near) / Togail curs air Leodhas (Setting a course for Lewis) / La dhomh 's mi'm beinn a'cheathaich (One day on the misty mountain) / Fadachd an t-seoladair (The sailor's longing) / Cumha ruairidh mhoir (Ruairidh mor's lament) / Taladh (The clan MacCulloch) / 'S daor a cheannaich mi'n t-iasgach (Dearly have I paid for fishing) / O'n dh'fhag thu mi 's mulad orm (Since you've left me, I'm sad) / Gad 'ionndrainn (Missing you) / Tom an t-searraich (The foal's hillock) / 'N ath bhanais bhois agam (The next wedding I go to). *(c-iss.Feb94; CTP 024) (cd-iss. Apr95; COMD2 024)*

ALISON KINNAIRD & CHRISTINE PRIMROSE

Temple not iss.

Oct 90. (cd/c) *(COMD2/CTP 041)* **THE QUIET TRADITION** ☐ ☐
– Oran do Mhac Leoid dhun Bheagain (Song to the MacLeod of Dunvegan) / O'n chuir mo leannan culaibh rium – Do chrochadh a thoill thu (Since my darling turned from me – You deserve to be hanged) / Da mihi manum (Give me your hand) / Tha mi fo churam (I am full of care) / Cailleach an dudain (The old woman of the mill-dust) / O 's toil 's gu ro thoil learn (O I like, I do like) / Cumha crann nan teud (The lament for the harp key) / Tha thide agam elrigh (It is time for me to rise) / The crags of Ailsa – Staffa's shore / An smeorach (The thrush) – The song-thrush – The mistle-thrush / Tha na h-uain air an tulaich (The lambs are on the hillock) / Port Lennox / Bean mhic a' mhaoir (The wife of the bailif's son) / Sneached Heisgeir (The snows of Heiskeir) – Sleepy Maggie / Mo ghaol oigfhear (My dear young man).

BLAIR DOUGLAS

Redburn not iss.

Dec 84. (lp) *(RED 1)* **CELTOLOGY** ☐ ☐
– Failte (do'n ghaidhealtachd) / Eisd (ris an oigridh) / Mhairead / Err in peace – Roison dubh / Donald, Willie and his dog / Range games / Eilean Uibhist mo ruin (Uist my love), Irene Meldrum's welcome to Bon Accord, Iain R. Douglas / Dark island / Step dancing / Alex MacEachern's strathspey – Beverley in Barra / Gu tir (Landward) / Alan MacPherson of Mosspark – Crossing the Minch – Brolum / So'nam shineadh air an t-sliabh (Tears on the tide). *(c-iss.Jan92 on 'Macmeanmna'; SKYE 03)*

Macmeanmnanot iss.

Dec 90. (c/cd) *(SKYE/+CD 02)* **BENEATH THE BERET** ☐ ☐
– Braigh Uige (Braes of Uig) / Iain Ghlinn cuaich / Solus m'aigh / Kate Martin's waltz / Celtic jive / Blair's got a wah-wah pedal (and he's gonna use it) / Ghost of Glasgow / Growing up / Mardi Gras music / Glove game (Benny Lynch) / Irish eyes / King is king.

Oct 96. (c/cd) *(SKYE/+CD 09)* **A SUMMER IN SKYE** ☐ ☐
– A summer in Skye / The Skye glen waltz / The second sight / The landlord's walk / A' bhean ionmhainn (The beloved wife) / Iain Angus Douglas's welcome to the big wide world – The woodworker – An corran glas / The gugahunter / NicMhathain's thank you / An cocaire beag (The little chef) / Skye at last! / Fear beag a' chridhe mhoir (Little one of the big heart) / Nelson Mandela's welcome to the city of Glasgow / Ora nam buadh (Hymn of the graces) / Miss Ina MacLellan's air.

ARTHUR CORMACK

1984. (lp/c) *(TP/CTP 016)* **NUAIR BHA MI OG** ☐ ☐
– Failte do'n Eilean Sgiathanach (Hail to the Isle of Skye) / An t-aodann ban (Edinbaine) / Nuair bha mi og (When I was young) / Puirt a beul (Mouth music) / Gruagach og an fhuilt bhain (The young fair haired maiden) / 'S e mo bheachd ort a' bhais (My opinions of death) / Thoir mo shoraidh thar an t-saile (Convey my farewell across the sea) / Gilean ghleann-dail (The sons of Glendale) / Eilean a' cheo (The misty isle) / Carn air a' mhonadh (The cairn on the moor) / Cumha Alasdair dhuinn (Lament for brown-haired Alasdair) / Ho ro 'illean na bithemaid tursach (Ho ro boys, let's not be sad) / Mo nighean donn nan gobhar (My brown-haired goat-herder) / An gaol a thug mi og (The love of my young days) / Nach gorach mi gad chaoineadh (How foolish of me to cry for you) / Oran eile air an aobhar cheudna (Another song on the same theme) / Mo ghaol an te nach diobhair mi (My love who would not forsake me). *(re-iss. Jul92 cd/c; COMD2/CTP 016)*

1989. (cd/c) *(COMD2/CTP 032)* **RUITH NA GAOITH (CHASING THE WIND)** ☐ ☐
– Ruith na gaoith (Chasing the wind) / O Mhairi e Mhairi (O Mary) / 'S mor mo churam 's mi ga stiuireadh (great is my sorrow as I steer the boat) / 'S truagh nach do dh'fhuirich mi tioram air tir (What a pity I never stayed on dry land) / Tionnaidh am bat' (Turn the boat) / A' choille ghruamach (The gloomy forest) / Gad chuimhneacchadh (Remembering you) / Gradh geal mo chridh (Fair love of my heart) / Oran an t-saighdear (The soldier's song) / Mairi ruadh a' dannsa an nochd (Red-haired Mary will be dancing tonight) / A nigheanag a' ghraidh (My beloved girl) / Fhir a shiubhlas na frithe (A Culloden lament) / Loch na h-ob (Loch na h-Ob) / An cluinn thu mi mo nighean donn (Do you hear me my brown-haired girl).

EILIDH MacKENZIE

Nov 92. (cd/c) *(COMD2/CTP 048)* **ELDEADH NA SGEULACHD (THE RAIMENT OF THE TABLE)** ☐ ☐

— EILIDH subsequently became part of her sisters' group, MacKENZIE

CHRISTINE PRIMROSE

Temple Temple

Jul 01. (cd) *(COMD2 086)* **GUN SIREADH GUN LARRAIDH (WITHOUT SEEKING, WITHOUT ASKING)** ☐ ☐
– Ceann traigh ghuinneart – Fraoch a Ronaigh / An gille dubh ciar-dhubh / A mhairead og / Bean a' chotain ruaidh / An till mise chaoidh / Oganaich an or-fhuit bhuidhe / Oran mu'n ghuragaich / Dheanainn sugradh ris an nigh'n dubh / Soraidh bho granger / Do ghaidheil shiatail / Nach truagh leat mi's tu'n eirinn / So nam shineadh air t-sliabh.

MAC UMBA (see under ⇒ Greentrax records)

Ewan McVICAR

Born: Glasgow. Although rarely getting to the stage of recording one album or single, McVICAR would be best remembered for his songwriting and storytelling prowess during the late 50's and early 60's. He studied music and verse under the watchful eye of tutor, NORMAN BUCHAN, building up a friendship which lasted for years to come. In fact, the pair met up constantly at NORMAN's Scottish Folk Club in the city's Trongate (a place of merryment and frequented by EWAN MacCOLL, JOSH MacRAE and HAMISH IMLACH). One of the "Broomhill Bums" (as they were kindly regarded), EWAN continued to write and tell stories. He has since published a handful of books that include 'One Singer, One Song' (1990), 'Streets, Schemes And Stages' (1991 with Mary McCabe) and the children's book, 'Brownies And Fairies And Lang-legged Beasties'. There is also available a book and 37-track CD by KATHERINE CAMPBELL and EWAN entitled 'Traditional Scottish Songs And Music' (New Holland Publishers).

Jim/James MALCOLM (see under ⇒ OLD BLIND DOGS)

MALINKY

Formed: Edinburgh-based. MALINKY were 1999's Celtic Connections "Open Stage" winners and consisted of Edinburgh-based folk, KARINE POLWART, STEVE BYRNE, Irishman MARK DUNLOP and Englishman KIT PATTERSON. KARINE, who was also part of The BATTLEFIELD BAND subsequently teamed up with GILL BOWMAN to form MacALIAS.

However, it was via her own group MALINKY that the Banknock-born songstress really flowered as a masterful interpreter of traditional Scots Folk ballads. Arguably one of the finest releases in the Greentrax catalogue, 'LAST LEAVES', garnered widespread critical acclaim, its title a defiant reference to the 1925 Greig-Keith collection 'Last Leaves Of Traditional Ballads And Ballad Airs' which predicted the death-knell for the centuries old oral tradition. Although STEVE BYRNE was impressive throughout, KARINE's wonderfully earthy tone and passionate Scots dialect stole the show on such timeless tracks as 'ALISON CROSS', 'THE BEGGAR MAN', 'THE DREADFUL END OF MARIANNA FOR SORCERY' and 'DIMNA JUDA'.

Unlike many modern Folk acts, MALINKY somehow manage to sound lost in the Highland mist of time yet thoroughly contemporary as most who witnessed their Celtic Connections 2001 show would no doubt attest. Now without PATTERSON (newcomers were LEO McCANN and JON BEWS), MALINKY delivered their sophomore set, '3 RAVENS', in August 2002, festival spots at Cambridge, Sidmouth, Brittany and Tonder (Denmark) followed.

KARINE POLWART – vocals (of BATTLEFIELD BAND) / **STEVE BYRNE** – vocals, bouzouki, guitars, etc / **MARK DUNLOP** – bodhran, whistle / **KIT PATTERSON** – fiddle, guitar, mandolin

Greentrax Greentrax

Jan 00. (cd) *(<CDTRAX 190>)* **LAST LEAVES**
– Whaur dae ye lie? / Strathmartine mains (love and freedom) – Banish misfortune / The hills of Ardmorn / The light dragoon / The dreadful end of Marianna for sorcery / Thomas Elvogue's No.2 – Rocky road to Dublin – Merrily kissed the Quaker – Cathal McConnell's slip jig / The beggar man / Dimna Juda / Alison Cross / The bonnie lass of Fyvie – The silver spear / Jimmy Waddell – The battle of the Somme / The green wedding – Bill Harte's jig.

— **MALINKY** were now **POLWART, BYRNE + DUNLOP** with additions **LEO McCANN** (button box, whistle) + **JON BEWS** (vocals, fiddle)

Aug 02. (cd) *(<CDTRAX 233>)* **3 RAVENS**
– Billy Taylor / The lang road doon / Thaney / Leaving Rum / The roving ploughboy / The trawlin' trade / Three ravens / Yorkston Athletic / I dreamed last night of my true love / The false lover won back / Gone to the bower / The sound of a tear not cried / Follow the heron / Tail end of the tour.

Michael MARRA (see ⇒ Section 8: Rock, Pop & Indie)

John MARTYN (see ⇒ Section 7: Rock & Pop)

Karen MATHESON (see under ⇒ CAPERCAILLIE)

Ed MILLER (see under ⇒ Greentrax records)

MIRK (see under ⇒ Springthyme records)

Hamish MOORE

Born: c. early 50's, South Uist. After completing a veterinary degree in the mid-70's, HAMISH worked as a vet for more than a decade before retiring and devoting himself wholly to music. Having played the Highland bagpipes since childhood, he discovered the smaller, bellows-blown pipes in 1980, a relatively obscure instrument up until that point. With a mission to bring the sound of the Scottish small pipes to a wider audience, HAMISH began manufacturing them to order, modelling them on an old 19th century set he'd chanced upon.

His own recording career began in the mid-80's with a couple of albums for DOUGIE MACLEAN's 'Dunkeld' label, namely 'CAULD WIND PIPES' (1985) and 'OPEN ENDED' (1987). As the principal tutor of small pipes at Cape Breton's Gaelic College over the period 1992-6, MOORE became immersed in the music of this Celtic-Canadian outpost and recorded an album there in 1994, 'DANNSA' AIR AN DROCHAID (STEPPING ON THE BRIDGE)'.

His dedication to reviving the Gaelic tradition has also seen him set up a number of piping schools, both in Scotland and the USA, while he's currently the musical director of the Ceolas summer school on the Hebridean island of South Uist.

East Lothian label, 'Greentrax', recently re-issued 'THE BEES KNEES', an album HAMISH originally recorded in the early 90's with jazzman DICK LEE.

HAMISH MOORE – the bagpipes, smallpipes, etc

Dunkeld not iss.

Jan 85. (lp) *(DUN 003)* **CAULD WIND PIPES** -
– Calanish high over Bunachton / Got to Berwick Johnny / Jocky said to . . . / Old bean waltz / Thinkan and daean (Mary's tune) / Sailor's lass / Mrs. Isabella Sutherland / Country dance / Euphemia / Low of Gavalry / Roslin Castle / Campbelltown kiltie ball / MacCrimmon's lament / The mill, mill-o.

1988. (lp) *(DUN 006)* **OPEN ENDED** -
– Lark in the morning / Moving cloud / Torment / Ellis Kelly's delight / Back man / Maggie Lauder / Spey / Galician jigs.

— next with **DICK LEE** – saxes, clarinets, co-writer / next two also with **ANNE EVANS, JOHN KENNY, JIM SUTHERLAND, MICHAEL MARRA, RICK BAMFORD, GRAHAM ROBB, TOM BANCROFT, STUART SMITH + JOHN RAE**

Harbourtown Green Linnet

Nov 90. (cd/c; by HAMISH MOORE / DICK LEE) *(HAR CD/MC 014) <GLCD 3056>* **THE BEES KNESS** 1991
– Thunderhead – The Easy Club reel / The rumblin' brig – Boatman Bill – Iain McGee's Romanian boot / Nighean dubh Alainn – The teapot hig / The rock and the wee pickle tow – Bannocks of Bermeal – Song for Julie – Nail aihan thugam – Jenny's chickens – Jenny dang the weaver / Maggie's reel – The Slippit bar – Paddy in Sauna / The slow hare – The mongoose in the byre – The bees kness / Staten Island – Trip to Pakistan / Anne's tune – Buccleuch Street – The famous Ballymoate. *(cd re-iss. Sep00 on 'Greentrax'; CDTRAX 202)*

Greentrax Greentrax

Sep 93. (cd/c; by HAMISH MOORE & DICK LEE) *(<CD/C TRAX 063>)* **FAREWELL TO DECORUM** Sep94
– Third movement of a concerto for bagpipe & jazz orchestra / Autumn returns / Galician jigs / The cat's pyjamas – The mental blockade / Farewell to Nigg / Resolution No.9 / Ye banks and braes – Malts on the optics – Farewell to decorum / Round dawn / Forest lodge – Primrose lass – Miss Girdle / The monster / 12.12.92 (a march for democracy) – Freedom come all ye.

— next with Scottish & Cape Breton musicians incl. **ROD PATERSON, IAN HARDIE, WENDY WEATHERBY, JERRY HOLLAND, PAUL MacDONALD + HILDA CHAISSON**

Jul 94. (cd/c) *(<CD/C TRAX 073>)* **STEPPING ON THE BRIDGE**
– King George IV Strathspey – The king's reel / Blue bonnets – Larach Alasdair – Margaret MacLachlan / The back of the Change House – Lucy Campbell's – Yetts of Muckhart – Go immediately – High road to Linton / Father John MacMillan of Barra – Sprig of ivy / St. Joseph's – Crossing of the Minch / MacGregor's search / Cameron's Strathspey – The crippled boy – The Devil in the kitchen – Lady Margaret Stewart – Tail toddle – Sleepy Maggie / Helen Black of Inveran – Dainahasaig – Auld Reekie – The glen where the deer is – Spark's rant / O' a' the aits the wind can blaw / Battle of Waterloo – Wee Highland laddie – The 8th Argyll's farewell to the 116th regiment de Ligne – The boy's lament for his dragon / Brose & butter – Up wi' Eli Eli – Souter's o' Selkirk – Go to Berwick Johnny – Lochaber dance / Stumpie: Stumpie / Mrs. Hamilton of Pitcaithland / Molly Rankin's / Brenda Stubbert's – Jack Daniel's.

Paul MOUNSEY

Born: Ayrshire. Brought up Ross-shire in the Highlands, MOUNSEY studied at Trinity College in London and subsequently lectured at the capital's Goldsmith's College. A job offer from Brazilian commercial music company, Play It Again, led him to the megalopolis of Sao Paulo where he began composing for TV and advertising. As well as providing music for top directors such as Tony Scott and Dariusz Wolski, MOUNSEY's blossoming reputation found him working with the likes of MICHAEL NYMAN and ETTA JAMES as well as native legends like CHICO BUARQUE, OLODUM and ANTONIO CARLOS JOBIM. His own recording career began in 1994 with 'NAHOO', a self confessed "attempt to present this folk tradition using contemporary pop styles other than conventional rock". The folk tradition he was on about was that of his own country and more specifically the Gaelic tradition, while the styles he referred to ran the gamut from hip-hop, samba, native chanting and techno to anthemic guitar histrionics, MORRICONE-style orchestration and new age keyboard ambience. A cover of Runrig's 'ALBA' and various archive samples sourced from Edinburgh's School Of Scottish Studies demonstrated where he was coming from although the end product was far too successful a cultural cross-breed to ever be filed under the convenient folk-crossover pigeonhole. Released in the UK on Scottish label 'Iona', the record was given a resounding worldwide critical thumbs up, spurring MOUNSEY on for a follow-up, 'NAHOO TOO' (1997). Rather than simply tweaking the established formula, the record found MOUNSEY conjuring up ever more inventive ways to interpret his native tradition in a truly groundbreaking, cosmopolitan fashion. Again the critical reaction was ecstatic and in 1999, MOUNSEY released the final part of his trilogy, 'NAHOO 3: NOTES FROM THE REPUBLIC'. Hailed as one of Scotland's most talented expatriate sons, his skills as a composer, arranger and musician are beyond doubt. To these he can add lecturer and critic, the man in Brazil an authority on film music and a regular contributor to 'Bravo' magazine.

PAUL MOUNSEY – keyboards, vocals, electronics / with various foreign/Brazilian musicians

Iona — Mesa-Atlantic

Oct 94. (cd/c) *(IRCD/IRC 029)* <92506> **NAHOO** — 1995
– Passing away / Alba / Robert Campbell's lament / Journeyman / Dalmore / Stranger in a strange land / As terras baixas da Holanda / From ebb to flood / I will go / My faithful fond one / Illusion.

— <in the US-only, the album was cred. to NAHOO featuring PAUL MOUNSEY>

Feb 98. (cd) *(IRCD 050)* **NAHOO TOO** — -
– Remembrance / Wherever you go / North / Infinite contempt / Another clearance / Kaiwa farewell / Psalm / Turned on the dog / Nahoo / The fields of Robert John / Fall / A Mhairead Og (I) / A Mhairead Og (II) / Red river / Hope you're not guilty / Nahoo reprise / Lullaby.

Nov 99. (cd) *(IRCD 068)* **NAHOO 3 – NOTES FROM THE REPUBLIC** — -
– Nahoo nation / Independence blues / The keening / Notes from the republic / Unfinished business / Don Roberto's sabbath / Night falls / Mad litany / Carver Agnus with bites / The first time ever I saw your face / Reel slow / Taking leave (beir soraidh bhuam) / Fiunary / Last thoughts.

MOUTH MUSIC

Formed: Edinburgh . . . late 80's by Sheffield-born composer MARTIN SWAN and American-born vocalist TALITHA MacKENZIE, the pair getting together after SWAN witnessed TALITHA singing traditional Gaelic airs in a village hall on the island of South Uist. Back in the capital – where TALITHA was studying Gaelic culture – they set to work on a fusion of customised puirt-a-beul (the Gaelic "mouth music" tradition after which the band were named), folk multi-instrumentation, Afro-centric percussion and synth ambience. The resulting 'MOUTH MUSIC' (1990) album was in many respects ahead of its time; if BRIAN ENO and DAVID BYRNE had already begun their ethnomusicological experimentation, the likes of CAPERCAILLIE, MARTYN BENNETT and AFRO CELT SOUND SYSTEM were yet to release their definitive works.

1992's 'BLUE DOOR GREEN DOOR' EP was a further step forward with the whirling 'SEINN O' (used in Scotland on the Drambuie TV ad) proving that Caledonian tradition and club dancefloor weren't mutually exclusive. With TALITHA then going off for a solo career, SWAN brought in JACKIE JOYCE and MICHAELA ROWAN for sophomore album, 'MO-DI' (1993). This branched out even further into cosmopolitan fusion as JOYCE's Ghanian roots lent a Franco-African air to proceedings and SWAN's own compositions balanced the Gaelic numbers.

In fact, 1995's 'SHORELIFE' was made up almost wholly of original JOYCE/SWAN compositions, losing a bit of the Gaelic mystery in the process. It also proved to be the group's final release and while the various members had since remained by and large out of the spotlight. Six years later, however, the group reformed and issued their comeback album 'SEAFARING MAN' (2001), a beautiful ode to the sea, with original and traditional songs thrown into the salt-water mix. Mandolins, plucky guitars and fiddles set sail for the opening title track, while Gaelic ballad 'MANITOBA' settled the dust and had the listener wondering why this suberb ensemble had been on the back-burner for so long.

MARTIN SWAN – multi-instruments / **TALITHA MacKENZIE** – vocals / with 7-piece backing band incl. **JEREMY BLACK** – bongos / **JAMES MACKINTOSH** – drums, tabla / **GEORGE McDONALD** – sax / **QUEE MACARTHUR** – bass

Triple Earth — Rykodisc

Aug 90. (lp/c/cd) *(TERRA/+C/CD 109)* <RCD/RACS 10196> **MOUTH MUSIC** — Jan91
– Bratach bana / Mor a' cheannaich / Chi mi na morbheanna / Mile marbh'aisg a' ghaol / Froach a rpnaigh / Co ni mire rium / Martin Martin / I bhi a da / Air fail a lail o. *(cd re-iss. Apr93; TRECD 109)*

Jan 92. (cd-ep) *(TERRACDEP 209)* <1023> **BLUE DOOR GREEN DOOR EP**
– 'S Muladach / The 45 revolution / Seinn O. *(re-iss. Jul98; same)*

— **JACKIE JOYCE** – vocals, (some) mandolin + **MICHAELA ROWAN** – vocals, (some bass); repl. TALITHA who went solo

Feb 93. (cd/c) *(TRE CD/C 111)* <RCD/RACS 10242> **MO-DI**
– Birnam / He Mandu / Hoireann O / Milking the cow / Waiting / Crathadh 't 'Aodaich & Zbadba / Maudit / So step off. *(cd+=)* – He Mandu (version) / Crathadh 't 'Aodaich & Zbadba (version). *(re-iss. Feb95; same)*

May 93. (12") *(TEMN 3-12)* **HE MANDU. / SO STEP OFF** — -

Oct 94. (m-cd/m-c) *(TREM CD/C 113)* <RCD/RACS 10309> **SHORELIFE** — Feb95
– Move on / Tomorrow / The world is for all / Time / Ruler of the tides / Make it real / Forever to travel / Infinity / Colour of my love.

— disbanded in 1995; TALITHA featured on a V/A compilation in '97, 'Celtic Mouth Music' – **SWAN** re-formed MOUTH MUSIC yet again

Jul 98. (cd-ep) *(TEMCD 113)* **MOVE ON (radio) / MOVE ON (go to mix) / COLOUR OF MY LOVE / HERE AND BLOWN AWAY** — -

— **SWAN** recruited **ISHBEL MacASKILL + KAELA ROWAN** – vocals + **MARTIN FUREY**

Skiteesh — not iss.

Apr 01. (cd) *(SKIT 200101)* **SEAFARING MAN** — -
– Seafaring man / Whaling ship / Milleadh nam braithrean / Manitoba / Month of July / Inveralligin / Thoir a nail ailean thugam / Snowgatherer.

Donnie MUNRO

Born: 2 Aug'53, Uig, Isle Of Skye. A key member of top nationalistic folk/pop act RUNRIG, DONNIE helped guide the band from his early twenties onwards. The impassioned frontman enjoyed a string of album successes with the band over the course of a decade, 'Once In A Lifetime' probably being their best loved anthem. With RUNRIG's lyrics often possessing a political sub-text, it came as little surprise when DONNIE succumbed to the real world of politics. After first taking up the post of elected Glasgow University rector, the outspoken singer became a candidate for the New Labour Party in 1997's landslide victory. Somehow balancing the careers of politician and solo artist, MUNRO gathered together a sterling cast of native musicians/singers (see below) and recorded a debut solo album, 'ON THE WEST SIDE' (1999). As well as cutting a couple of Gaelic-language tracks, DONNIE took it upon himself to cover Donovan's 'CATCH THE WIND' and Steve Earle's 'NOTHING BUT A CHILD'. An ill-advised 'LIVE' set was delivered as the follow-up, although fans far and wide caught the man at his best again via studio LP, 'ACROSS THE CITY AND THE WORLD'. • **Trivia:** DONNIE also guested on a FIONA KENNEDY single, 'Follow Me'.

DONNIE MUNRO – vocals / with numerous co-vocalists plus co-writer **ALLAN CUTHBERTSON** – keyboards / **SANDRA CIANCO** – percussion, drums / **EWEN VERNAL** – bass / **ROBERT WALLACE** – pipes / **BRIAN KELLOCK** – pianoforte / **DUNCAN CHISHOLM** – violin / **SANDY BRECHIN** – accordion / + guests KAREN MATHESON

Vital Spark — Hypertension

Aug 99. (cd) *(VITALCD 03)* <HYP 0194> **ON THE WEST SIDE**
– On the west side / Chi mi'n tir / Morning light / Catch the wind / Fields of the young / Nuair bha mi og / Dark eyes / Nothing but a child / Georgie / The garden boy. *(re-iss. Jun01 & Nov01 on 'Hypertension'; HYP 0194)*

Nov 99. (cd-s; by DONNIE MUNRO & HOLLY THOMAS) *(VITAL 05CD)* **WILL YOU WALK ON BY** — -

Hypertension — not iss.

Jan 01. (cd) *(HYP 1203)* **DONNIE MUNRO (live)** — -
– On the west side / City of lights / Morning light / Dark eyes / Harvest moon / Irene / Always the winner / Chi mi'n geamradh / My back pages / Only the brave / Garden boy / Walk on by / The greatest flame. *(re-dist.Nov01)*

Feb 02. (cd-ep) *(HYPS 2312)* **SHE KNOWS LOVE / QUEEN OF THE HILL / NOTHING BUT A CHILD / FIELDS OF THE YOUNG** — -

Mar 02. (cd) *(HYP 2212)* **ACROSS THE CITY AND THE WORLD** — -
– Sweetness on the wind / Queen of the hill / You're the rose / Weaver of grass / Irene / She knows love / The greatest gift / Amazon / Highland heart / Calum Sgaire. *(re-dist.Jul02)*

Anna MURRAY (see under ⇒ Lochshore records)

N

Peter NARDINI

Born: 1949, Largs, Ayrshire. A graduate from the Glasgow School Of Art (1970-1975), painter NARDINI tried his hand at poetry and songwriting. His recording career began in 1981/82 when Scottish 'Kettle' records released 45's, 'THINK YOU'RE GREAT' and 'WE JUST MIGHT WIN'. A debut LP, 'IS THERE ANYBODY OUT THERE?', was issued by 'Temple' towards the end of '85, the artist showing he was capable of writing sone catchy tunes. His sharp brogue tongue and wit fused JACQUES BREL or LOUDON WAINWRIGHT III acidic humour with BILLY BRAGG-style politics; best examples being the Protestant versus Catholic cut, 'THE BALLAD OF LAWRENCE AND EUGENE GREEN' and the Thatcher-baiting 'WHY SINK THE BELGRANO?'. NARDINI continued to establish himself as a painter and only returned to the recording studio for one more album, 'SCREAMS & KISSES' (1993). This was a fitting return for the Glaswegian minstrel, we were indeed "in the presence of a man who can paint stories and sing pictures" – as reviewer Donny O'Rourke gracefully put it. NARDINI was principal art teacher at a Lanarkshire secondary school until he recently took early retirement and his superb paintings can be viewed and bought on many sites on the internet.

PETER NARDINI – vocals, acoustic guitar, keyboards

Kettle / not iss.

Dec 81. (7") *(KS 701)* **THINK YOU'RE GREAT. /** ☐ [-]

May 82. (7") *(KS 702)* **WE JUST MIGHT WIN. / STOP IT I LIKE IT** ☐ [-]

Temple / not iss.

Dec 85. (lp/c) *(TP/CTP 020)* **IS THERE ANYBODY OUT THERE?** ☐ [-]
– Who is that? / Is there anybody out there? / It'll no' happen again / White heat / Why sink the Belgrano? / God rules ok! / The ballad of Lawrence Orange and Eugene Green / As I speak / I'll no' let you doon / Name droppin' / Michael / Now that Hitler's back in style / Rosary beads / Glasgow cathedral. *(c re-iss. Feb94; same) (cd-iss. Oct00+=; COMCD 2020)* – Hogmanay – Atholl highlanders / Why did you let me go out fishing / Lanarkshire girls / Deo gratlas.
above extra tracks with **JOHN McCUSKER** – fiddle, accordion / **STEWART FORBES** – sax / **GAVIN LIVINGSTONE** – guitar

Eclectic / not iss.

1993. (cd/c) *(ECL CD/TC 9307)* **SCREAMS & KISSES** ☐ [-]
– A don't know / Light up the sky / A wid become an astronaut / And I will fly / She said 'o, is that right! / A kiss from Wishaw Cross / Another star / Zak Anderson / Doubletake / You're like a rock / Don't shut the door ma / A river without you. *(re-iss. Jan96; same)*

NATURAL ACOUSTIC BAND

Formed: Milngavie, Glasgow . . . 1969 by TOM HOY, Geordie-born and bred ROBIN THYNE and KRYSIA KOCJAN (pronounced 'kotsyan'). The latter Scots-born singer was of Polish/Flemish descent and talented enough to share the billing at several gigs. Opening their live account on Guy Fawkes night (1969) at the Alloa Working Men's Club, The NATURAL ACOUSTIC BAND plied their wares all over the country and beyond before landing a contract with 'R.C.A.'. Two albums, 'LEARNING TO LIVE' and 'BRANCHING OUT', were delivered in quick succession, although none gave the folk-buying public much to rave about; STEELEYE SPAN, The STRAWBS and FAIRPORT CONVENTION were all making it big time. KRYSIA then bailed out leaving the remaining pair to recruit JOANNA CARLIN, although when she also left to pursue a solo career (as MELANIE HARROLD), HOY teamed up with MAGNA CARTA; two years later in '77, THYNE took the same route and eventually formed their own version, NOVA CARTA (one LP for 'C.B.S.' in 1979, 'ROADWORKS'). During all this personnel turmoil, KRYSIA delivered her own self-titled set in 1974 – she now teaches voice techniques in the USA.

TOM HOY (b. 5 Feb'50, Glasgow) – guitar, vocals / **ROBIN THYNE** (b. 1 Nov'50, Newcastle Upon Tyne) – guitar, vocals / **KRYSIA KOCJAN** (b.10 Aug'53, Craigendoran) – vocals / with also **AYMIN MOHAMMED** – bass + **GRAHAM MORGAN** – drums

R.C.A. / not iss.

Jul 72. (lp) *(SF 8272)* **LEARNING TO LIVE** ☐ [-]
– Learning to live / Sometimes I could believe in you / Subway Cinderella / Free / Tom / February feeling / Maybe it was the sunshine / Midnight study / All I want is your love / Waiting for the rain / Dying bird / High in my head.

Oct 72. (lp) *(SF 8314)* **BRANCHING IN** ☐ [-]
– Running into changes / Schoes / Money / Follow your love / Road to the sun / Is it true blue (there's nothing unnatural about electricity) / First boy / I'll carry you / Little leaf / Moontime writer / Travellers on the road.

Feb 73. (7") *(RCA 2324)* **ECHOES. / IS IT TRUE BLUE** ☐ [-]

— KOCJAN left in early '73 (see below) while HOY and THYNE continued for a few years (initially with new vocalist **JOANNA CARLIN**) until they joined MAGNA CARTA before splintering into NOVA CARTA

KRYSIA

with a plethora of folk backers **JERRY DONAHUE, DAVE MATTACKS, DAVE PEGG** plus **JOHN RABBIT BUNDRICK, RAY COOPER + RAY COOPER**

1974. (lp) *(LPL1 5052)* **KRYSIA** ☐ [-]
– Good morning holiday / Leaf must fall / So passes life / La belle dame sans merci / Mr. Physician / Lady of the mountains / Wet Tuesday / Another song / Sweet William / You should have been a painter.

Aug 74. (7") *(RCA 2445)* **ANOTHER SONG. / WET TUESDAY** ☐ [-]

— KRYSIA subsequently did loads of session work – she lives in London.

NEW CELESTE

Formed: Glasgow . . . late 70's by IAIN FERGUS alongside GRAEME DUFFIN, IAIN BAYNE and Falkirk-born IAN TELFER. Taking the idea of fusion one step further, the group set out to combine the jazz-rock idiom with traditional Celtic music over such albums as 'HIGH SANDS AND THE LIQUID LAKE' (1978), 'ON THE LINE' (1979) and 'NEW CELESTE LIVE' (1981). Following their split in the early 80's, the various members went on to bigger – if not necessarily better – things: DUFFIN went on to session for popsters WET WET WET, BAYNE joined the massed ranks of RUNRIG and TELFER became part of English-based folkies The OYSTER BAND.

This wasn't the end of the story though as 1990 saw FERGUS re-invent NEW CELESTE with an all-new cast of STEVE REID, ROD DOROTHY, WILLIE LOGAN, JERRY SOFFE and IAN COPELAND. The revamped group recorded an acclaimed album for 'Lismor' records entitled 'THE CELTIC CONNECTION' (from which Glasgow's celebrated annual hoedown later took its name) while subsequent live gigs and festivals were sufficiently well-received to warrant a follow-up set. 'IT'S A NEW DAY' arrived in 1996 on the 'Iona' imprint, critics praising the band's masterful blend of jazz, rock, Celtic and world influences while namechecking the likes of MOVING HEARTS and even The ALLMAN BROTHERS.

IAIN FERGUS – acoustic guitar, vocals / **GRAEME DUFFIN** – guitar / **IAN TELFER** (b.28 May'48, Falkirk) – fiddle / **STEWART GRESTY SMITH** – bass, synthesizer, piano / **IAIN BAYNE** – drums

Arfolk / not iss.

1978. (lp) *(SB 372)* **HIGH SANDS AND THE LIQUID LAKE** [-] [-] Dutch

— **ROD DOROTHY** – violin + **RONNIE GERRARD** – violin, mandolin; repl. TELFER who joined OYSTER BAND (he later became a session man for EWAN MacCOLL and LEON ROSSELSON / **CHRISTIAN EVANS** – drums; filled in for BAYNE who later joined RUNRIG (in 1985)

Hansa / not iss.

1979. (lp) *(200402)* **ON THE LINE** [-] [-] German
– P stands for Paddy / Johnny / Winter brings a melody / Nova Scotia / My keepers / On the line / Ploughmen (two brethren) / Building a motorway / Morrison's jig. *(UK-iss.1988 on 'Escalibur'; BUR 803)*

1981. (lp) **NEW CELESTE LIVE (live)** [-] [-] French

— split until 1990 when **IAIN FERGUS** re-formed them as a 6-piece:- **STEVE REID** – guitars / **WILLIE LOGAN** – guitars, keyboards, vocals / **ROD DOROTHY** – violin, vocals / **JERRY SOFFE** – fretless bass / **IAN COPELAND** – drums

Lismor / not iss.

Oct 90. (cd)(c) *(LCOM 9036)(LIFC 7019)* **THE CELTIC CONNECTION** ☐ [-]
– Music for a found harmonium / I once loved a lass / Wiggly jig / When a man's in love / Don't think about me – Banks of the Bann – Bann air / The Celtic connection suite: East of the Tisza – Celtic connection – Rocky road to Dublin – Out jig / Julie – Glen Moriston – Reel ale – Irish stew / Fare thee well sweet Mally.

Iona / not iss.

Jul 96. (cd/c) *(IRCD/IRC 033)* **IT'S A NEW DAY** ☐ [-]
– The banks of Ayr / Stumblin' & stottin' / The lasher / The posie – The Scottish brawl / Reconnected / It's a new day / 70 years – The caber / Polkadotty / Davie and Jeannie / Dance of Los / The randan / Prove yourself, yourself.

— after they split REID joined PIPEDOWN (one set for 'Greentrax')

Watt NICOLL

Born: late 30's, Glasgow; his formative years having been spent between Glasgow and Dundee. WATT was a man of many talents, including a child prodigy bagpipe player (he was entered for competitions), a speedway biker for the Glasgow Tigers and a leader of a traditional jazz band for five years. Having played the folk circuit as a singer-songwriter, NICOLL signed a deal with 'Transatlantic' offshoot imprint, 'Xtra' (also home to HAMISH IMLACH and MATT McGINN among others). His debut LP, 'THE BALLAD OF THE BOG', was released in 1968, and showed a tongue-in-cheek sleeve depicting the bearded NICOLL outside a Gents (a "bog" to the uninitiated). The early 70's saw three further albums, 'WATTcha!' (1970), 'NICE TO BE NICE' (1971) and 'WATT'S ON' (1972), although his whimsical wit was beginning to wane. 'WATT NICOLL'S WEE CARRY OUT', was his swansong to the record buying public, although the man himself appeared on TV as the "pet man", having set out his stall as a zoological columnist in a national newspaper. A recent claim to fame – if you forget that he was also a Miss Scotland publicity agent! – was in 1999 when England football manager, Kevin Keegan, hired NICOLL to motivate his team to beat Poland in a qualifier 3-1. 'THE BALLAD OF THE BOG' comes to mind again – but for different reasons.

WATT NICOLL – vocals, penny whistle, ocarina / with various session players

Xtra — not iss.

1968. (lp) *(XTRA 1062)* **THE BALLAD OF THE BOG** [ ] [-]
– Remote control / Factory horn / Wee wains / Scriptures / Idle welder / Just made it legal / Greenfields of Dundee / The Fifie / Craftsmen of old / Swandown girl / Whisky drinkers / The pipe / Ballad of the bog.

1970. (lp) *(XTRA 1108)* **WATTcha!** [ ] [-]
– Early in the morning / Weathermen / Berryfields of Blair / Farewell to Dundee / The whistling duke / Old King Cole / The fiddler and the dancer / Paraffin lamp seller / Morning of the dawn seque / Pendulum song / Tribute to Burns / Wild mountain thyme.

1971. (lp) *(XTRA 1122)* **NICE TO BE NICE** [ ] [-]
– Song of the car / Love's over / Willow twig artist / El Condor pasa / Ach, ah dinna ken / Border lands / Today is the first day / Ca the ewes / Dodi's boys (lodging in the cold ground – Kate Dalrymple – Reel o' Stumpie O) / Home town / The hour glass song.

1972. (lp; with DOREEN) *(XTRA 1129)* **WATT'S ON** [ ] [-]
– Looking back through the years / Queen of the border / King of the castle / March of the Cameron men / McCrimmon / Evening bright / Letters that I write / Swandown girl / Baratza / One man and a double whisky / Unfinished lullaby.

Grampian — not iss.

1976. (lp) *(MOR 4027)* **WATT NICOLL'S "WEE CARRY OUT"** [ ] [-]
– Annie Laurie / The Scottish cowboy / The other side of me / Home town / The Scottish working man's blues / Auld Scots songs medley: Roaming in the gloaming – Ye banks and braes – My ain folk / Flower of Scotland / Liberty / Pipe selection: Heilan laddie – Morning has broken – No awa to bide awa.

— WATT retired from the biz

Rab NOAKES (see ⇒ Section 7: Rock & Pop)

NORFOLK & JOY

Formed: Edinburgh ... mid-70's. NORFOLK and JOY were the amalgamation of two traditional folk acts; NORFOLK consisting of singer/guitarist LES RUSSELL, bassist DICK WALINCK and fiddler BILLY CRANSTON, while JOY was actually JOY GREIG (or GRIEGS as it is mistakenly depicted on their LP sleevenotes), a friend and part-time singer with the group who had served her time in outfits such as The JOYLINS (with LINDA WYMAN) and BUZZARD. The quartet performed at the capital's 'Amber Mile' folk night outlets (aka hotels on the Royal Terrace) and released one set in 1979, 'SCOTSOUNDS'. After their split, CRANSTON uprooted to Holland with his Dutch wife and daughter. However, he was to be killed in a car crash in 1984.

LES RUSSELL – vocals, guitar / **BILLY CRANSTON** – fiddle, whistle, mandolin / **DICK WALINCK** – bass, double bass / **JOY GREIG** – vocals

Dara — not iss.

1979. (lp) *(MPA 031)* **SCOTSOUNDS** [ ] [-]
– Mason's apron / Peggy Gordon / Dainty Davie / Braes of Mar / Glencoe massacre / Rattlin' roarin' Willie / Hen's march / Leezie Linzay / Lowlands away / Bonnie Dundee / John Anderson my Jo / Come by the hills.

NYAH FEARTIES (see ⇒ Section 8: Rock, Pop & Indie)

OCCASIONALS (see under ⇒ BARBOUR, Freeland)

OLD BLIND DOGS

Formed: Aberdeen . . . 1990 by Granite city folk veterans IAN F. BENZIE, BUZZBY McMILLAN and JONNY HARDIE. While BENZIE's pedigree stretched back to the heady days of the late 50's/early 60's folk revival, HARDIE was a classically trained viola player who'd become fixated on the fiddle after travelling around the British Isles. Upon his return to the North East, he'd hooked up with multi-instrumentalist McMILLAN as a busking duo although the pair also played in various bands before forming a trio with BENZIE. By the time percussionist DAVY CATTANACH (also a veteran of the live music scene who had previously played with McMILLAN in an array of blues, rock and reggae outfits) joined up in 1992, OLD BLIND DOGS were beginning to make a name for themselves as purveyors of an enticing folk/contemporary fusion.

With the man's conga-playing adding a bit of exotic spice to proceedings, the group initiated a long association with the 'Lochshore' label via 1992's debut set, 'NEW TRICKS'. The canny canines' distinctive melange of traditional Scottish fare, hypnotic rhythms and progressive arrangements brought widespread acclaim for albums such as 'CLOSE TO THE BONE' (1993), 'TALL TAILS' (1994) and 'LEGACY' (1995) while the addition of piper/woodwind player FRASER FIFIELD put a new spin on the band's sound prior to 1997's 'FIVE'. The ensuing two years witnessed a period of major upheaval as first CATTANACH departed (to be replaced by WOLFSTONE drummer/percussionist GRAEME 'MOP' YOUNGSON) and then BENZIE finally quit the band after a 1998 US tour.

In keeping with tradition, though, HARDIE and McMILLAN just couldn't let sleeping dogs lie, the pair subsequently fashioning a new line-up of PAUL JENNINGS, JIM MALCOLM and DEAF SHEPHERD man, RORY CAMPBELL. The newcomers made their debut on 1999's 'THE WORLD'S ROOM', a record that once again put OLD BLIND DOGS' folk/worldbeat policy back on the international Celtic roots agenda. HARDIE, meanwhile, had been moonlighting with Edinburgh sidekick and IRON HORSE man, GAVIN MARWICK since 1995, the pair recording 'UP IN THE AIR' (1995) and 'THE BLUE LAMP' (1999). A busy year for HARDIE, 1999 also saw him partying with ALYTH McCORMACK and RORY CAMPBELL on 'THE CAPTAIN'S COLLECTION'.

Despite being newly installed as OLD BLIND DOGS' lead vocalist, JIM MALCOLM is a highly regarded folk singer/songwriter who plays a multitude of instruments. His voice is melancholy with husky overtones, his traditionally-inspired lyrics/songs are both thought-provoking and modern day. Two albums for the label, 'SCONEWARD' and 'ROHALLION' (see further below) were well-received in every quarter, while his most recent, 'RESONANCE' (2000) gave him an even higher profile.

IAN F. BENZIE – vocals, guitar / **BUZZBY McMILLAN** – bass, cittern, etc / **JONNY HARDIE** – fiddle, vocals, mandolin / **DAVY CATTANACH** – percussion

own label — not iss.

1990. (c) *(none)* **OLD BLIND DOGS** [ ] [-]

1991. (c) *(none)* **OLD BLIND DOGS 2** [ ] [-]

Lochshore — not iss.

Sep 92. (cd/c) *(CD/ZC LOC 1068)* **NEW TRICKS** [ ] [-]
– Bennachie / The Garnethill – Miss Mairi MacPhail of Laxdale / The bonnie banks o' Fordie / J & B reel – The bonawe highlanders / The wee wee German lairdie / Monaghan's jig / The bonnie lass o' Fyvie / Song for Autumn / Gala water / The ferret sea / Bedlam boys – The rights of man. *(re-iss. Jul94 cd/c; LOC 1068 CD/C)*

Oct 93. (cd/c) *(LDL CD/C 1209)* **CLOSE TO THE BONE** [ ] [-]
– Kilboogie / Linden rise / The cruel sister / The honeymoon reel – Kings – The Clayslaps reel / The twa corbies / The universal hall – The nuptial knot – The Barlinnie highlander / MacPherson's rant – The winging / Seonaidh mor – The fall – Dick gossops / Margaret Cromar / The trooper and the maid or the trumpet sounds at Burreldales / The broken pledge – Claggy's dilemma – Hamilton's jig / Jean O'Bethelnie (Glenlogie). <*US-iss.Apr97; same as UK*>

Sep 94. (cd/c) *(CD/ZC LDL 1220)* **TALL TAILS** [ ] [-]
– The barnyards o' Delgaty / The burn o' Craigie – The moon coin jig – Miss Isobel Blackley / The banks o' Sicily / The sportsman's haunt – Mrs Bailey of Redcastle – Sherlock's fancy / A wife in every port / Boondock skank / The pills of white mercury / Miss Sheperd – Sandy Grant – The hurricane / Lay ye doon love / Willie's aul' trews – The auld reel 1 / The auld reel 2 / P stands for Paddy / The buzzard. <*US-iss.Feb00; same as UK*>

Oct 95. (cd/c) *(CD/ZC LDL 1233)* **LEGACY**
– Mormond braes – Charles Sutherland / Malcolm Ferguson – Finbar Saunders / The Lancashire lads / There were twa bonnie maidens / The rose and the Lindsey O' / Hollis Brown / The bonnie Earl o' Moray / The salmon leap – Rip the calico / Jenny tied the bonnet tight – The crooks of the kingdom / The snows they melt the soonest / The Birken tree / The £5 flute – Donald McLennan's exercise – What pain I have endured since last year / Tibbie Fowler – Breton dance tune. <*US-iss.Apr97; same as UK)*

— added **FRASER FIFIELD** – pipes, woodwind

Oct 97. (cd) *(CDLDL 1264)* **FIVE**
– Glen Kabul – Trip to Pakistan – The fourth floor / The battle of Harlaw / Lord MacDonald's march to Harlaw – The mither tap – The cauldron / Parcel o' rogues / The walking nightmare – The shopgirl – Croix rousse / Janine's reel – In and out the harbour – The hawk / The lowlands of Holland / Johnny o' Braidislee / Leaving Lochboisdale / Summerside – Mouy'ton mayo / Andros 2 / Andros 3.

— CATTANACH + FIFIELD then BENZIE departed in 1998 (the former and the latter had already gone solo)

— **HARDIE + McMILLAN** recruited **RORY CAMPBELL** – Border pipes, vocals, etc (ex-DEAF SHEPHERD + solo artist) / **PAUL JENNINGS** – percussion / **JIM MALCOLM** – guitar, harmonica, vocals (also a solo artist)

Green Linnet | Green Linnet

Oct 99. (cd) <*GLCD 1201*> **THE WORLD'S ROOM**
– To the beggin' I will go / The branie: The auld ranters – The branie / The Forfar sodger / Mill o' tifty / Bannockburn road / Battle of Waterloo / Soup of the day / Roslin castle / Edward / The ritual: The ritual – The leap year – Johnnie MacDonald's reel.

May 01. (cd) *(<GLCD 1214>)* **FIT?**
– Is there for honest poverty / Come a' ye Kincardine lads / Much better now / Tramps and hawkers / Country girl / Sky city / Reres hill / The rejected suitor / Awa' whigs awa' / Cuilfhionn / Black-haired lad / Tatties and herrin'.

– compilations, etc. –

Nov 99. (cd) *Lochshore; (<CDLDL 1294>)* **LIVE (live)** Dec99
– The twa corbies / The salmon leap: The salmon leap – Rip the calico – Jenny tied the bonnet tight – The crooks of the kingdom / The bonnie Earl o' Moray / Malcolm Ferguson – Finbar Saunders / Bedlam boys – The rights of man / The pills of white mercury / Lay ye doon love / The barnyards o' Delgaty / The buzzard / MacPherson's rant – Winging / The cruel sister / Bennachie (gin I whaur the Gaudie Rins).

JONNY HARDIE & GAVIN MARWICK

— MARWICK was of the IRON HORSE

— (first with DAVY CATTANACH as third collaborator)

Lochshore | Lochshore

Jan 95. (cd/c) *(LDL CD/C 1226)* **UP IN THE AIR**
– The rejected lover / Willie's auld trews – Keep it up – Dogs bite Chapmen / Rob Roy MacGregor – Prince Charles – Charles Sutherland / The McNeils of Ugadale – Jig brest St Marc – Lads of Tain – Mrs MacInroy of Lude / Andy M Stewart's / Lady Mary Stopford – The blackhaired lad / Kissing is the best of a' / A Breton march – An Irish reel – Hatton burn / The hills of Glenorchy – Neil Gow's wife / Captain Keeler – Will you marry me / Mrs Forbes, Leith – Hamish's reel – The periwig – Carnie's canter / A Breton jig – Isobel Blackley – Dougie's decision / The dancing bear – Ril bheara / Jenny dang the weaver – J.F. Dickie – Athol brose / Indo para isorg (A Galician waltz) / Gur mis tha gu craigteadh o'n uiridh / John Stephen of Chance Inn. <*US-iss.Feb00 on 'KRL'; 1226*>

— next with guests **ANDY THORBURN + ARRON JONES**

Jun 99. (cd) *(<CDLDL 1287>)* **THE BLUE LAMP**
– The quiet man – The solstice – The silver spire / Podoloy hora – The good drying / The blue lamp suite, parts 1-4 / Marni Swanson of the grey coast / The factory smoke – Fishers rant – The search / Goa way – Suite des ridees de Pontivy – The siege of Delhi / The kings favourite – McGuire's jig / Roderick Dhu / Princess Beatrice – President Garfield – The Saratoga hornpipe – The high level / The snuff wife – Snug in a blanket – The duck.

Greentrax | Greentrax

Dec 99. (cd; as JONNY HARDIE & ALYTH McCORMACK with RORY CAMPBELL) *(CDTRAX 187)* **THE CAPTAIN'S COLLECTION**
– MacLeod of MacLeod's chorus song / Lovat's restoration / Battle of Kinloch Lochy / Nuptial knot / Braes of Lochiel / Ferintosh / Mary young and fair / Keep it up / Place true love thine arms around me / Niel Gow's style / My love today is hertofore / Sean Trews.

IAN F. BENZIE

Lochshore | not iss.

May 95. (cd/c) *(CD/ZC LDL 1228)* **SO FAR**
– The laird o' Drum / Hold on to me babe / Wantoness / John Anderson my Jo / Silver dagger / Rue / Willie more / The braes o' Gight / Johnson Carrickfergus / Cold blow and the rainy night / Are ye sleepin' Maggie / The deadly wars / Can ye dance / May we go now. <*US cd-iss. Feb00; same as UK*>

DAVY CATTANACH

Lochshore | not iss.

Sep 97. (cd) *(CDLDL 1252)* **DANCING IN THE SHADOWS**
– Everyday / Been & gone / Do you need me / Prince of the winding road / Cold heart / Closing eyes / Black eyed smoke / Manmade / I mean you / Lady angel / Who needs rhythm / Chameleon man. <*US-iss.Feb00; same as UK*>

JIM MALCOLM

Greentrax | Greentrax

Mar 95. (cd/c; as JAMES MALCOLM) *(<CD/C TRAX 083>)* **SCONEWARD**
– Scotch blues / Neptune / Losin' auld Reekie / Wild geese / Scotlandshire / Achiltibuie / Lochs of the Tay / Wisest fool / Up the Noran water / Barren lands / Grandfathers / Party / Flowers of Edinburgh.

Apr 98. (cd) *(<CDTRAX 150>)* **ROHALLION**
– Battle of the Waterloo / Amulree / Gorbals melody / Skye cuckoo rag / Sierra whoosh (hitching out of Oban) / Vinney den / Tam O'Shanter (pt.1) / Dream / Cycles / Billy won't come back to Edinburgh.

— next with also **PAUL JENNINGS** – percussion

Beltan | not iss.

Aug 00. (cd) *(BELTANCD 101)* **RESONANCE**
– Weepers I shall wear / Nae gentle dames tho ne'er sae fair / Jimmy's gone to Flanders / New Parliament rag / Lochanside / The workers' song / Huntin' the buntin' / In the land / Rohallion / Cruel sister / Tam O' Shanter (part 2) / There grows a bonny brier bush / Duncan Grey.

OSSIAN

Formed: Glasgow . . . 1976 by BILLY JACKSON, GEORGE JACKSON, JOHN MARTIN and BILLY ROSS, naming themselves after a 3rd century Celtic bard (all bar ROSS had previously played together on CONTRABAND's 1974 eponymous album with singer MAE McKENNA). One of OSSIAN's first assignments was the provision of musical backing for a Jura-based theatre company, this work leading to further commissions including 'Clanna Cheo', a play inspired by the legend of Rob Roy which enjoyed a run in London.

A combination of jigs, reels, Gaelic airs and traditional Scots songs, the eponymous 'OSSIAN' album marked the group's debut for 'Springthyme' in 1977. Celtic folk revivalists influenced by such diverse artists as The INCREDIBLE STRING BAND, The CORRIES and even ALISTAIR McLEOD, the group formed the 'Iona' label in 1979 via 'ST. KILDA WEDDING'. Through this imprint, the band released albums such as 'SEAL SONG' (1981), 'DOVE ACROSS THE WATER' (1982), 'BORDERS' (1985) and 'LIGHT ON A DISTANT SHORE' (1986) as well as new member TONY CUFFE's 1982 collaboration with JOCK TAMSON'S BAIRNS, 'FERGUSSON'S AULD REIKIE'.

Having already recorded a side project set with ROSS in 1984 ('MISTY MOUNTAIN'), BILLY JACKSON – with help from GEORGE – initiated his solo career in 1988 with 'MUSIC FOR THE CELTIC HARP'. Prior to this the talented harpist/multi-instrumentalist had already been commissioned to compose 'The Wellpark Suite' for the 1985 Glasgow Mayfest, an ambitious project combining traditional and contemporary music styles. Now going under the more distinguished title of WILLIAM JACKSON, he celebrated Glasgow's 1990 year of culture by releasing 'ST. MUNGO: A CELTIC SUITE FOR GLASGOW', a piece which saw him working with The Scottish Orchestra Of New Music. 1992's 'CELTIC TRANQUILITY' album highlighted the man's subtle artistry on the clarsach, his talent for evocative soundscapes leading to TV work including a doumentary on The History Channel ('Battle Of The Clans') and a series on National Trust properties for STV.

While JACKSON's solo recording schedule has become increasingly prolific with the likes of 'INCHCOLM' (1995), 'ANCIENT HARP OF SCOTLAND' (1998) and 'SCOTTISH ISLAND' (1998), he's also extended his talents into record production, overseeing albums by BILLY ROSS (2000's 'SHORE STREET'), IAIN MacINNES and CALLUNA. A mark of the man's standing came in summer '99 as his composition 'LAND OF LIGHT' (1999) was performed at Edinburgh Castle to mark the 100th birthday celebrations of the Queen Mother. In addition to teaching clarsach (Scottish harp), JACKSON is also a trained music therapist, helping children with cerebral palsy and autism.

JACKSON, ROSS and new to the fold IAIN MacINNES and STUART MORISON were OSSIAN's new line-up who recorded the splendid comeback set, 'THE CARRYING STREAM' (1997) for 'Greentrax'; the latter three made up the one-off SMALLTALK who'd released a self-titled album a few years previously, while both MacINNES and ROSS had delivered solo sets

('TRYST' and 'SHORE STREET' respectively) for 'Greentrax' at the turn of the century.

• **Songwriters:** Group & mainly borrowed traditional Scots/Gaelic tunes:- AE FOND KISS + GALA WATER (Rabbie Burns) / SITTING IN THE STERN OF A BOAT (MacLeod) / O MO DHUTHAICH (MacPhee) / SIMON'S WART (W. Hunter snr.) / MUSIC OF SPEY (Skinner) / SPOOTASKERRY (Ian Burns) / DEAN CADALAN SAMHACH (Iain MacMhurchaidh) / 'S GANN GUN DIRICH (Norman Nicolson) / FAREWELL TO WHISKY (Niel Gow) / etc.

CONTRABAND

MAE McKENNA – vocals / **BILLY JACKSON** – Celtic harp, Uillean pipes, whistles, vocals, acoustic bass / **GEORGE JACKSON** – mandolin, fiddle, whistle, flute, guitar, vocals / **JOHN MARTIN** – fiddle, mandolin, cello, vocals / **PETER CAIRNEY** – guitar / **ALEC BAIRD** – drums

Transatla. not iss.

1974. (lp) *(TRA 278)* **CONTRABAND** -
– Rattlin' roarin' Willie / The black rogue – Sir Philip McHugh – Alice Cooper's favourite / Lady for today / The Devil's fiddle / On the road / The Spanish cloak – Pea-pod McGinley – The youngest daughter / Alec's interlude / Stainforth blues / Come up smiling / The banks of Claudy / Edward Sayers' brass band.

— MAE subsequently went solo

OSSIAN

BILLY + GEORGE JACKSON + JOHN MARTIN + BILLY ROSS – vocals, guitar, dulcimer, whistle

Springthyme not iss.

1977. (lp/c) *(SPR/+C 1004)* **OSSIAN** -
– The corncrake (song) – I hae a wife o ma ain (jig) / Sitting in the stern of a boat (Mi'm shuidh' an deireadh bata) (slow air) / Ma rovin eye / O mo dhuthaich (oh my country) (Gaelic song) – Ossian's lament / The 72nd Highlanders farewell tae Aberdeen (pipe march) – The favourite dram / Ae fond kiss (song) / Brose and butter (song) – Monaghan jig – Jackson's bottle of brandy (jig) / Music of Spey (slow air) / Let me in this ae nicht (song) / Spootaskerry (Shetland reels) – The willow kishie – Simon's wart / Oidche mhath leibh (goodnight to you) (Gaelic song). *(re-iss. 1983 lp/c; same) (cd-iss. Apr97; SPRCD 1004)*

Iona not iss.

Mar 79. (lp) *(IR 001)* **ST. KILDA WEDDING** -
– The St. Kilda wedding, Perrie Werrie (reel) – The honourable Mrs.Moll's reel / Gie me a lass wi a lump o'land (song) / Iomramh eadar il' a's Uist (rowing from Islay to Uist), the source of Spey / Dean Cadalan Samhach (Gaelic song) / Gala water (song), Major David Manson (reel) / 'S gann gunn Dirich mi chaoidh (Gaelic song) / Farewell to whisky (slow air) / My love is the fair lad (march) – The Forth Bridge (Strathspey) – Pretty Pegg (reel) / The braes o' Strathblane (song) / More grog coming, Tilley Plump, da Foostra (reels). *(re-iss. 1988 & Oct91 cd/c; IRCD/IRC 001)*

— **TONY CUFFE** – vox, guitar, tiple (ex-ALBA) repl. ROSS

Jul 81. (lp) *(IR 002)* **SEAL SONG** -
– a) The sound of sleat, b) Aandowin' at the bow, c) The old reel / To pad the road wi me / Coilsfield House / The Hielandmen cam' doon the hill – The Thornton jig / Aye waukin-o / Corn rigs / Lude's supper / The road to Drumleman / A fisherman's song for attracting seals – Lieutenant MacGuire – Walking the floor / Mull of the mountains. *(re-iss. 1988 & Oct91 cd/c; IRCD/IRC 002)*

— In 1981/2, TONY CUFFE and members of JOCK TAMSON'S BAIRNS celebrated the work of 18th Century Scots poet ROBERT FERGUSSON by releasing the 'FERGUSSON'S AULD REIKIE' set *(IR 004)*

— added **IAIN McDONALD** (b.28 Jul'60, Inverness) – Highland pipes, flute, whistle

1982. (lp) *(IR 004)* **DOVE ACROSS THE WATER** -
– a) Duncan Johnstone, b) The duck, c) The curlew / Braw sailin on the sea / Drunk at night, dry in the morning / Will ye go to Flanders? / Tae the beggin / Mile Marbhaisg / Dove across the water (I) Iona theme, (II) March the cunning workmen, (III) Columba, (IV) Iona theme reprise. *(re-iss. Jan88; c/cd-iss. Oct88 & Oct91; IRC/+D 004)*

Jan 85. (lp/c) *(IR/+C 007)* **BORDERS** -
– Troy's wedding – Biddy from Slicp / Rory Dall's sister's lament / Charlie, oh, Charlie / I will set my ship in order / John McDonald's – The sandpit / Bide ye yet / Neath the gloamin' star at e'en / The new house in St.Peters – The gew wi the crookit horn – Willie Murray's. *(cd-iss. 1988 & Oct91; IRCD 007)*

Oct 85. (lp; BILLY JACKSON with OSSIAN & FRIENDS) *(IR 008)* **THE WELLPARK SUITE** -
– Glasgow, 1885: The dear green place changed / Life in the city – The march of the workers / Molendinar: The spring / The brewing / Fermentation / A Glasgow celebration. *(was iss.on 'Mill' lp/c; MR 001/MRC 001) (re-iss. Jan88/ c/cd iss.Oct88 & Oct91; IRC/+D 008)*

1986. (lp) *(IR 009)* **LIGHT ON A DISTANT SHORE** -
– a) Johnny Todd, b) Far from home / It was all for our rightful king (song) – La chanson des liurges (inst.) – The Sun rises bright in France (song) / a) Mrs.Stewart of Grantully, b) Be sud an gille truagh, c) Calum Johnston's, d) Harris dance / a) Jamie Raeburn, b) The broomielaw / Light on a distant shore, (i) Arrival, (ii) New York harbour, (iii) At work on the land, (iv) In the new world. *(re-iss. Jan88/ c/cd iss.Oct88 & Oct91; IRC/+D 009)*

— OSSIAN split after above; McDONALD joined BATTLEFIELD BAND; although OSSIAN did re-form for a set in '97:- **BILLY ROSS + BILLY JACKSON** with **STUART MORISON** – fiddle, mandolin, cittern, vocals + **IAIN MacINNES** – pipes, etc

Greentrax Greentrax

Sep 97. (cd/c) *(<CD/C TRAX 127>)* **THE CARRYING STREAM** Nov97
– Fisherrow – Noose and the ghillies / Black crags – Barney's Balmoral – Mrs. Webster – Duke of Hamilton / Logan water – Pennan den / Working man / Mo chaillin dileas donn / Port Lennox / Blustering home – Flora MacDonald – David Glen's jig / Flower of France and England / Maighdeanan na h'airidh / Alick Cameron – Joe McGann's fiddle – Jenny's jig.

- compilations, etc. -

Apr 94. (cd/c) *Iona; (IRCD/IRC 023)* **THE BEST OF OSSIAN** -
– a) The St. Kilda wedding, b) Perrie Werrie reel, c) The honourable Mrs. Moll's reel / 'S gann gunn dirich mi chaoidh / The road to Drumleman / a) The sound of sleat, b) Aandowin' at the bow, c) The old reel / a) Will ye go to Flanders?, b) Lord Lovat's lament / a) Duncan Johnstone, b) The duck, c) The curlew / Drunk at night, dry in the morning / I will set my ship in order / Rory Dall's sister's lament / a) Johnny Todd, b) Far from home / a) Jamie Raeburn, b) The broomielaw / a) Mrs. Stewart of Grantully, b) Be sud an' gille truagh, c) Calum Johnston's, d) Harris dance.

SMALLTALK

BILLY ROSS, IAIN MacINNES + STUART MORISON

Greentrax Greentrax

Oct 94. (cd/c) *(<CD/C TRAX 079>)* **SMALLTALK**
– Colonel Fraser / Mary Ann MacInnes / The famous bridge / Kail & pudding / Cumha coire a' cheathaich / Jock Hawk / New claret / The low country dance / The arvasar blacksmith / The black haired lad / The Shetland fiddler / Over the sea to Nova Scotia / Rose Anderson / Les vielles bottines / The heights of Cassino / 'S truagh nach do dh'fhuirich / The Fhorton jig / James Byrne's jig / Duncan McKillop / The bee in the knickers / Fil o ro.

BILLY JACKSON & BILLY ROSS

Iona not iss.

Nov 84. (lp/c) *(IR/+C 005)* **MISTY MOUNTAIN** -
– Beinn a' cheataich / Landfall / Glen of Copeswood / Lass o' Glenshee / Boyne water / Guidnicht and joy be wi' ye a' / Country girl and the Hungarian fiddler / Tar the house / Little cascade / Geil mill / First step / Trusdar bodaich drochaid luideach / Na'm faighinn gille ri cheannach / For our lang bidin' here / Meudail is m'aighear s'mo ghradh. *(cd-iss. 1988 & Oct91; IRCD 005)*

GEORGE JACKSON & MAGGIE MacINNES

Jan 85. (lp/c) *(IR/+C)* **CAIRISTONA** -
– The dairyman's daughter / Bhi a ta / Ruidhle mo nighean donn / Fath mo mhulaid a bhith ann / Lovely Annie / Medley / The parting / The little cascade / The burning of Auchindoun / Lachlann dubh / Medley / Faca sibh raghail na ailein / Making for the shore / Cairistona. *(cd-iss. 1988; IRCD 006)*

WILLIAM JACKSON

with also GEORGE JACKSON

Jan 88. (lp/c/cd) *(IR/+C/CD 010)* **MUSIC FOR THE CELTIC HARP** -
– Lady Amelia Murray's Strathspey / Breton march / Waulking o' the faulds / Port Lennox / Strike the young harp / John MacLean of Lewis / Paradise alley / Angel's ascent / Threefold flame / Air by Fingal / Emigrant peak / St. Kilda dance / Fair shoemaker / Rose without rue. *(re-iss. Oct91 as 'HEART MUSIC' cd/c; IR CD/C 010)*

below with The Scottish Orchestra Of New Music

Greentrax not iss.

Dec 90. (cd/c) *(CD/C TRAX 041)* **ST. MUNGO: A CELTIC SUITE FOR GLASGOW** -
– St. Mungo's blessing / The bird / The tree / The bell / The fish.

Iona not iss.

Jun 92. (cd/c) *(IR CD/C 016)* **CELTIC TRANQUILITY** -
– Light on a distant shore / Arrival / New York harbour / At work on the land / Harvest of the fallen / Glasgow 1885 the dear green place / Molendinar / Fermentation / Paradise valley / Landfall / Fish.

Linn Honest

Mar 95. (cd/c) *(AKD 037 CD/C) <5037>* **INCHCOLM** 1996
– Corryvreckan / In the northeast kingdom / New road / Waterfall / Pure land / Gardyne Castle / Salve splendor / Abbey Craig / Columcille / Lover's call. *(cd re-iss. Oct00 on 'Mill'; MRCD 013)*

Linn not iss.

1998. (cd) *(AKD 082)* **CELTIC EXPERIENCE 2** -
1999. (cd) *(AKD 108)* **CELTIC EXPERIENCE 3** -

Mill not iss.

Oct 98. (cd) *(MRCD 010)* **THE ANCIENT HARP OF SCOTLAND** -
Oct 98. (cd) *(MRCD 011)* **A SCOTTISH ISLAND** -
Apr 99. (cd) *(MRCD 016)* **LAND OF LIGHT** -
– Land of light (main instrumental – choral – Gaelic) / Glasgow jigs / Molendinar / Tree / Corrywrecken / Columcille / Mary Scott / Iona / Jura.

— In Jun'01, JACKSON teamed up with MacKENZIE on the album, 'CELTIC' for 'Linn' records *(AKD 145)*

– (his) compilations, etc. –

Aug 99. (cd) *Mill; (MRCD 012)* **THE CELTIC SUITES** ☐ -
– (THE WELLPARK + ST. MUNGO) *(re-iss. Nov99 on 'Linn'; LINCD 001)*

Jul 00. (3xcd-box) *Linn; (AKD 127)* **THE CELTIC EXPERIENCE VOL.1-3** ☐ -

BILLY ROSS & JOHN MARTIN

Springthyme not iss.

Feb 90. (c) *(SPRC 1029)* **BRAES OF LOCHIEL** ☐ -
– Hut on Staffin Island – Lone bush / Smith's a gallant fireman / The battle of Sheriffmuir / Dheannainn sugradh / Lass from Erin's Isle / Dr. MacInnes' fancy – Lexy MacAskill / Avondale / Scandinavian polkas / Bold navvy man / Braes of Lochiel / Jenny Dang the weaver – Malcolm the tailor / Auld meal mill. *(cd-iss. Feb94; SPRCD 1029)*

BILLY ROSS

— with basically the current line-up of OSSIAN (minus JACKSON)

Greentrax Greentrax

Aug 00. (cd) *(<CDTRAX 198>)* **SHORE STREET** ☐ ☐
– Highland soldier / Collier laddie / Fiolleagan / Lady Mary Anne / Adam Cameron / Mill of Tifty's Annie / Up in the morning / S'daor a cheannaich mi' n t'lasgach / Rashie Moor / Gloomy winter / Matty groves / Th m'fheudail is m' aighear's mo ghradh.

IAIN MacINNES

with **MAIRI CAMPBELL, WILLIAM JACKSON, IAIN MacLEOD, JAMES MacKINTOSH, AIDEN O'ROURKE + TONY McMANUS**

Greentrax Greentrax

Dec 99. (cd) *(<CDTRAX 182>)* **TRYST** ☐ ☐
– Eliza Ross: Eliza Ross's reel – Gilbert of the Antartic – James MacLellan's favourite / The fair lad: My love is the fair lad – The man from Glengarry – Johnnie McDonald / Quicksteps: Celtic society's quickstep – Capt. Grant – Murray's welcome – 72nd High Street, Aberdeen / Victoria Ross: Miss Victoria Ross – Lady Doll Sinclair – A' chunhag – McFarlane's / Vatersay Bay / Highland lassie: Going to the fair – The hen's march – The snuff wife / Jamie MacInnis of Cape Breton – The Portree men / Miss Ferguson: Miss Ferguson of Reith – Invergordon Castle – Lady Loudon – Lord MacDonald Cameron / Lowlands: My home town – Brose & butter – Drops of brandy / Highland brigade: Highland brigadeat Waterloo – Glasgow Gaelic club – Duncan M Steward / Dr. McInnes fancy: Angus Ramsay's lullaby – Dr. McInnes fancy – Peter MacKinnon of Skeabost.

P

PARCEL O' ROGUES (see under ⇒ Temple records)

Rod PATERSON (see under ⇒ JOCK TAMSON'S BAIRNS)

Davie PATON (see under ⇒ PILOT; Section 7: Rock & Pop)

Rod PAUL (see under ⇒ Greentrax records)

PEATBOG FAERIES (see under ⇒ Greentrax records)

Michael PHILIP Ceilidh Band (see under ⇒ Springthyme records)

PICTS (see under ⇒ BADENOCH)

Dougie PINCOCK (see under ⇒ Greentrax records)

PIPEDOWN (see under ⇒ Greentrax records)

Karine POLWART (see under ⇒ MacALIAS)

POOZIES (see under ⇒ SILEAS)

Lindsay PORTEOUS (see under ⇒ HERITAGE)

Christine PRIMROSE (see under ⇒ MAC-TALLA)

PROCLAIMERS (see ⇒ Section 8: Rock, Pop & Indie)

R

Iain RANKIN / RANKIN FILE (see under ⇒ Greentrax records)

Jean REDPATH

Born: 28 Apr'37, Fife. Godmother and guardian of traditional Scottish song, JEAN REDPATH has devoted her professional life to the interpretation of Caledonia's rich songwriting/oral history in tandem with a scholarly approach to that history's rediscovery and preservation. Like thousands before her, REDPATH gleaned a knowledge of ancient song from her mother who passed it down in the time-honoured source tradition, JEAN subsequently delving further into her native folk culture while reading Scottish Studies at Edinburgh University.

A move to the USA precipitated her early career as a folk singer in the coffeehouses of New York's hip Greenwich Village. Despite her more genteel approach, she was embraced by the same audiences that revered protest heroes like BOB DYLAN and PHIL OCHS, people impressed not only by her soaring mezzo-soprano but by her extensive, intuitive knowledge of Scotland's vocal tradition. After performing at the city's School Of Social Research, JEAN took up the offer of a deal from 'Elektra' and released her debut album, 'SCOTTISH BALLAD BOOK' (1964). She had actually recorded an album's worth of songs – 'SKIPPING BAREFOOT THROUGH THE HEATHER' – for the 'Prestige' label in 1963 although this wasn't released unitl '65. These, of course, were US-only affairs, the singer making her UK debut in 1966 with 'SONGS OF LOVE, LILT AND LAUGHTER'. Ironically, the latter was to be her only record available domestically in Scotland for more than a decade.

In 1975 she began a long association with the Vermont-based 'Philo' label, where she began the massive undertaking of recording the complete works of ROBERT BURNS. Although the first volume appeared in 1976, the next five were released consecutively through the early-mid 1980's, none, bizarrely enough, enjoying a release in the great bard's native land. The project was briefly put on ice in the mid-80's as REDPATH hooked up with longtime collaborator, US-born cellist ABBY NEWTON. The pair completed 'LADY NAIRNE' (1986) – a tribute to early 19th Century composer CAROLINE OLIPHANT – before enlisting violinist ALISTAIR HARDIE for 'MUSIC AND SONGS OF THE SCOTTISH FIDDLE' (1986).

'Greentrax' picked up the thread of the ROBERT BURNS project in 1987 with VOL.6 although sadly the series was abandoned completely at the turn of the decade following the death of producer Serge Hovey. Happier news for JEAN was when she was awarded the MBE in 1987 for her services towards Scottish traditional music. 1990 saw the release of JEAN's next album, 'LEAVING THE LAND'. Although her recording days were put on hold, JEAN continued to lecture at Stirling University, having begun her academic lecturing career in the 70's at Weslyan University in Connecticut.

In recognition of her contribution to the knowledge and appreciation of Scotland's rich cultural legacy, the First Lady of folk was awarded an MBE; a few years later, her comeback set 'SUMMER OF MY DREAMS' (2000) reunited her with 'Greentrax'.

JEAN REDPATH – vocals, acoustic guitar

not iss. Elektra

1964. (lp) *<EKN 7214>* **SCOTTISH BALLAD BOOK** - ☐
– Barbary Allan / She moved through the fair / Lassie wi' the yellow coatie / Rantin' laddie / Johnnie lad / Nicky Tams / Wee cooper o' Fife / Johnnie Cope / The ploughboy, o / Kirk Swaree / Tae the weavers.

not iss. Prestige

1965. (lp) **SKIPPING BAREFOOT THROUGH THE HEATHER** (rec.1963) - ☐

Bounty not iss.

1966. (lp) *(BY 6004)* **SONGS OF LOVE, LILT AND LAUGHTER** ☐ -
(re-iss. Feb69 on 'Clan'; 233004)

not iss. Elektra

1967. (lp) *<EKN 7274>* **LADDIE LIE NEAR ME**
– Crookit bawbee / Wae's me for Prince Charlie / Dainty Davy / Gin I were a baron's heir / Gypsy laddie / Inverey / Caller o'u / The day we went tae Rothesay, o / O wert thou in the cauld blast / Quiet land of Erin / Clark Saunders.

not iss. Folk Legacy

1973. (lp) *<49>* **FRAE MY AIN COUNTRY**

— next with **ABBY NEWTON** – cello / + others

not iss. Philo

1975. (lp/c) *<PH/CPH 2015>* **JEAN REDPATH**
– Rambleaway / I live not where I love / Lagan love / My faithful Johnny / Captain Wedderburn's courtship / The terror time / Dancing at Whitsun / Blackwater side / The grey silkie / Ned of the hill / Lady Dysie / MacCrimmon's lament. *(<UK + re-iss. Oct88; same>) (<cd-iss. 1990; CDPH 2015>)*

1976. (lp/c) *<PH/CPH 1037>* **THE SONGS OF ROBERT BURNS VOL.1**
– Cauld kail in Aberdeen / To the weaver's gin ye go / Wantonness / My tocher's the jewel / Charlie he's my darling / Lady Mary Ann / Amang the trees / Country lassie / The De'il's awa wi' th' exciseman / Johnie Blunt / Winter it is past / Red, red rose / Logan water / Corn rigs. *(UK-iss.Jun88 on 'Greentrax' lp/c; TRAX/CTRAX 017) (<UK + re-iss. Oct88; same>)*

Leader not iss.

Jan 77. (lp) *(LER 2106)* **THERE WERE MINSTRELS**
– Dumbarton's drums / Rattlin' roarin' Willie / My love she's but a lassie yet / Robin Shure in hairst / West Virginia mine disaster / Gilderoy / Sheath and knife / Yellow yorlin / Rob Roy / No, sir / Clerk cloven / Caroline of Edinburgh town / Dave & Jeannie.

B.B.C. not iss.

Dec 77. (lp) *(ZCM 293)* **JEAN REDPATH WITH GUESTS**

— next with **JAY UNGAR** – guitar

Philo Philo

1977. (lp/c) *<PH/CPH 1048>* **THE SONGS OF ROBERT BURNS VOL.2**
– Had I the wyte / Nine inch will please a lady / Beware o' bonnie Ann / Cooper o' cuddy / Sweetest May / A parcel of rogues in a nation / Auld lang syne / Hey now Johnnie lad / Mary Porison / Dusty Miller / Steer her up / It was a' for our rightfu' king / Sae flaxen were her ringlets. *(UK-iss.Jun88 on 'Greentrax' lp/c; TRAX/CTRAX 018) (<UK + re-iss. Oct88; same>)*

Nov 78. (lp/c) *<PH/CPH 1054>* **SONG OF THE SEALS**
– Davy Faa / Poor rovin' lassie / Mili o' tifty Annie / Highland Harry / Polwarth on the green / Song of the seals / The dowie dens o' Yarrow / Logie o' Buchan / College boy / Mockin' o' Geordie's byre / Birnie bouzle – Johnny lad / Johnny my man. *(<UK + re-iss. Oct88; same>)*

Sep 79. (lp) *(<PH 1061>)* **FATHER ADAM**
– Willie's rare / Highland laddie / Sir Patrick Spens / Rigs o' rye / Roy's wife of Aldivalloch / Bonnie Susie Cleland / Father Adam / The twa brothers / The shearin's no for you / The trooper and the maid / Jock o' Hazeldean / A slee one. *(<c re-iss. Oct88; same>)*

Sep 80. (lp; by JEAN REDPATH & ABBY NEWTON) *(<PH 1066>)* **LOWLANDS**
– Wee bird cam' tae my apron / Faraway Tom / Who shall count for thee / Lichtbob's lassie / Lassie wi' the yellow coatie / Clerk Saunders / Mary Hamilton / Bonny at morn / Gallowa' hills / Riddles wisely expounded / Rose of Allandale / Lowlands. *(<re-iss. Oct88; same>) (<cd-iss. Aug94; PH 1066CD>)*

Nov 80. (lp; by JEAN REDPATH & LISA NEUSTADT) *<PH 1068>* **SHOUT FOR JOY**
– O little town of Bethlehem / Green street / Go tell it on the mountain / Away in a manger / The holly bears a berry / The flower of Jesse / The Christ-child's lullaby / Still the night / Joy to the world / Shout for joy / Sherburne C.M. / Shepherds arise / Adeste fideles / Rorate coeli desuper / It came upon a midnight clear.

1982. (lp/c) *<PH 1071/+C>* **THE SONGS OF ROBERT BURNS VOL.3**
– The lass o' Ecclefecken / The banks o' Doon / Slave's lament / O fare ye weel my auld wife / The belles of Mauchline / Duncan Davidson / The ploughman / Phillis the fair / The deuk's dang o'er my daddie / Will ye go tae the Indies, my Mary / Song, composed in August / The reel o' Stumpie / Green grow the rushes-o. *(UK-iss.Jun87 on 'Greentrax' lp/c; TRAX/CTRAX 006) (<re-iss. Oct88; same>)*

1983. (lp/c) *<PH 1072/+C>* **THE SONGS OF ROBERT BURNS VOL.4**
– Wha is that at my bower door? / Address to the woodlark / There grows a bonie brier-bush / The Taylor fell thro' the bed / Here's his health in water / Behold, my love / Rattlin' roarin' Willie / Tam glen / Thou hast left me ever / Jamie / I'll ay ca' in by yon toun / The lea rig / My collier laddie / O, this is no my ain lassie / O can ye labor lea / A long winter night. *(UK-iss.Jun87 on 'Greentrax' lp/c; TRAX/CTRAX 007) (<re-iss. Oct88; same>)*

1984. (lp/c; by JEAN REDPATH / ABBY NEWTON / DAVID GURAKOV / JONATHAN FELDMAN) *<PH 1082/+C>* **HAYDN: SCOTTISH SONGS**
(<UK + re-iss. Oct88; same>)

Jul 86. (lp/c; by JEAN REDPATH & ABBY NEWTON) *(<PH 1087/+C>)* **LADY NAIRNE**
– Auld house / Strathearn / The lammie / Lament of the covenanter's widow / The lass o' Livingstone / Will ye no' come back again / Lass o' Gowrie / The rowan tree / Caller herrin' / Charlie's landing / The laird o' Cockpen / The regalia / The white roses of June / Land o' the Leal.

1986. (lp/c) *<PH 1093/+C>* **THE SONGS OF ROBERT BURNS VOL.5**
– The Lea-rig / My collier laddie / O, this is no my ain lassie / My Nanie, o / Fragment / Posie / Mill, mill O / O, were I on Parnassus hill / German lairdie / The battle of Sherra-moor / Lament of Mary Queen of Scots / You're welcome, Willie Stewart. *(re-iss. Jun87 on 'Greentrax' lp/c; TRAX/CTRAX 008) (<re-iss. Oct88; same>)*

— next with **ALISTAIR HARDIE** – fiddle / **ABBY NEWTON** – cello

Lismor not iss.

Dec 86. (lp/c) *(LIF L/C 7009)* **MUSIC AND SONGS OF THE SCOTTISH FIDDLE**
– The cradle song / Gow's lamentation for Abercarny / The lowlands of Holland / Through the wood, laddie / Nathaniel Gow's lament for the death of his brother / Willie Duncan / Mrs. Dundas of Arniston / I'm a doun for lack o' Johnnie / Caledonia's wail for Niel Gow her favourite minstrel and Niel Gow's style / The heiress / A wee bird cam' to our ha' door / Highland Harry / The flower o' the quern / Niel Gow's lament for the death of his second wife / The Birks of Aberfeldy. *(re-iss. Feb97; LCOM/LIFC 7009)*

Greentrax Philo

Jan 87. (lp/c) *(TRAX/CTRAX 005) <PH 1114/+C>* **THE SONGS OF ROBERT BURNS VOL.6**
– Killiecrankie / Galloway Tam / Strathalan's lament / The fornicator / Here's to thy health / Last May a braw woo'er / Gloomy December / Jamie, come try me / The white cockade / The cardin' o't / Sandy and Jockie / Hey ca' thro'. *(<re-iss. Oct88; same as US>)*

1987. (lp/c) *<PH 1110/+C>* **A FINE SONG FOR SINGING**
– I will make you brooches / Up the Noran water / Captive song of Mary Stuart / Wild geese / Capernaum / Now the die is cast / South wind / Song of wandering aengus / Rohallion / The tryst / John o' dreams / Broom o' the Cowdenknowes / Annie Laurie / Broken brook. *(<UK + re-iss. Oct88; same>) (cd-iss. Feb90 on 'Greentrax'; CDTRAX 032)*

below also featured numerous members of The ANGEL BAND

not iss. Fretless

1988. (lp; by JEAN REDPATH & LISA NEUSTADT) *<FR 138>* **ANGELS HOVERING 'ROUND**
– Where the soul never dies / Land where we'll never grow old / There are angels hovering 'round / Dry bones / Lighthouse / Precious memories / The world is not my home / Angel band / Harbour bells / Down on my knees / Jesus won't you come by here / Give me your hand / Have thine own way.

1988. (lp; by JEAN REDPATH & LISA NEUSTADT) *<FR 154>* **ANYWHERE IS HOME**

B.B.C. not iss.

Jan 90. (lp/c; by JEAN REDPATH & ROD PATERSON) *(REH/ZCR 737)* **MILLER'S REEL**
– The mill, mill-o / My ain kind dearie / This is no my ain lassie / Green grow the rushes-o / O can ye labour lea / My love is like a red, red rose / The ploughman lad / Corn rigs / Jamie, come try me / The lass o' Ecclefechen / The collier laddie / Laddie lie near me / Bonnie brier-bush / O steer her up / My nanie o / My love is like a red, red rose / Here's his health in water / Thou has left me ever, Jamie / Wantonness / The mill, mill-o (instrumental).

Greentrax Philo

Nov 90. (cd/c/lp) *(CD/C+/TRAX 029) <CD/C+/PH 1126>* **THE SONGS OF ROBERT BURNS VOL.7**
– The Mauchline lady / O, merry hae I been / The gallant weaver / The young Highland rover / Cauld is the e'enin blast / My father was a farmer / My love she's but a lassie yet / Ode to Spring / O, guild ale comes / The bonnie lass of Albanie / O for ane-and-twenty, Tam / Where are the joys.

Dec 90. (cd/c/lp) *(CD/C+/TRAX 039) <CD/C+/PH 1131>* **LEAVING THE LAND**
– Leaving the land / Miss Admiral Gordon's Strathspey – Scarborough settler's lament / Un Canadien errant / Last minstrel show / Snow goose / Next time round / Sonny's dream / Maggie / Hallowe'en / Leaving Lerwick harbour / Now I'm easy / The wild lass.

— accompanied by **ALASDAIR FRASER** – fiddle / **ABBY NEWTON** – cello / **JACQUELINE SCHWAB** – piano

Dec 00. (cd) *(CDTRAX 208)* **SUMMER OF MY DREAMS**
– Summer of my dreams / Come by the hills / Sailor's sweetheart / Dark eyed Molly / Yellow on the broom / Gypsy lass / Bonnie Bessie Logan / Maggie Lauder / Parlez moi d'amour / Alas poor Queen / Andy's gone with the cattle / Wallie's gone to Melville Castle – Mally Lee / Dumbarton's drums / Sweet Thames flow softly / Blackbird / Farm auction.

– compilations, others, etc. –

Jul 90. (lp/cd) *Rounder; (<ROU/+CD 11556>)* **FIRST FLIGHT** ('Elektra' recordings)

1994. (cd,c) *JPR; <JR 101>* **LOVE IS TEASIN'**

1995. (cd,c) *JPR; <JR 102>* **SUMMER OF MY DREAMS**

1995. (cd) *JPR; <JR 103>* **THE SONGS OF ROBERT BURNS**

1995. (cd) *JPR; <JR 104>* **THE SONGS OF ROBERT BURNS VOL.2**

Feb 96. (cd) *Greentrax; (<CDTRAX 114>)* **THE SONGS OF ROBERT BURNS VOLS 1 & 2**

Feb 96. (cd) *Greentrax; (<CDTRAX 115>)* **THE SONGS OF ROBERT BURNS VOLS 3 & 4**

Feb 96. (cd) *Greentrax; (<CDTRAX 116>)* **THE SONGS OF ROBERT BURNS VOLS 5 & 6**
1997. (cd) *JPR; <JR 105>* **THE SONGS OF ROBERT BURNS VOL.3**
1997. (cd) *JPR; <JR 106>* **THE MOON'S SILVER CRADLE**
1997. (cd) *JPR; <JR 107>* **A WOMAN OF HER TIME**
1998. (cd) *JPR; <JR 108>* **THINK ON ME**
1999. (cd) *JPR; <JR 109>* **STILL THE NIGHT**
1999. (cd) *JPR; <JR 110>* **NOW & THEN**
2001. (d-cd) *JPR; <JR 111>* **JEAN REDPATH LIVE (live 1998)**

Alan REID (see under ⇒ BATTLEFIELD BAND)

Jim REID (see under ⇒ Springthyme records)

REIVERS (see under ⇒ MacRAE, Josh)

RELATIVITY (see under ⇒ Johnny & Phil CUNNINGHAM)

ROBERT FISH BAND (see under ⇒ Tartan Tapes records)

Alan ROBERTS (see under ⇒ MACLEAN, Dougie)

Jeannie ROBERTSON

Born: REGINA ROBERTSON, 1908, Aberdeen, daughter to a large tinker (gypsy) family based around the North East of Scotland (although her father, Donald, died soon after her birth). Her clan's annual summer travels through the north-eastern Highlands exposed wee JEANNIE to a wealth of songs and stories which she'd subsequently incorporate into her repertoire. Her travels also introduced her to her future husband, DONALD HIGGINS, an itinerant piper of whom her family disapproved.

The greatest of the 'source' singers, JEANNIE was invited by folklorist HAMISH HENDERSON to the Edinburgh Festival, and, alongside JIMMY MacBEATH, Irishman DOMINIC BEHAN and HAMISH himself, played an unforgettable session. In 1953, she recorded with producer PETER KENNEDY (around the same time as ISABEL SUTHERLAND), inspired by her mother and recited in her usual broad Scots a cappella. Later the same year (November, to be exact), she travelled down to London at the request of ALAN LOMAX, the Texas-born producer pulling out the best of JEANNIE as she floated gracefully unaccompanied through trad gems such as 'SON DAVID', 'THE BATTLE OF HARLAW' and the epic 'BONNIE ANNIE AND ANDREW LAMMIE'; the posthumous CD 'THE QUEEN AMONG THE HEATHER' was testament to this.

Subsequently signed to the pivotal 'Topic' label, she recorded two inspirational sets, the 10" 'I KEN WHERE I'M GOING' and the eponymous 'JEANNIE ROBERTSON', towards the end of the 50's. Early the following decade, she was back among the folk fraternity (DOLINA MacLENNAN and JIMMIE MacBEATH), performing at Edinburgh's legendary Howff venue. Among the many singers schooled by JEANNIE was female ballad singer RAY FISHER, while her own daughter LIZZIE HIGGINS followed in her mother's footsteps, recording for 'Topic' in the mid-70's.

Considered by many as one of the most original and influential singers of World Folk music, JEAN HIGGINS (under her married name) was awarded the MBE in 1968 for her services to Scottish music. Sadly, having lost her husband a few years earlier, JEANNIE died at her Aberdeen home on the 13th March, 1975.

JEANNIE ROBERTSON – vocals

Topic / not iss.

1959. (10"lp) *(10T 52)* **I KEN WHERE I'M GOING**
1959. (lp) *(12T 96)* **JEANNIE ROBERTSON**
– The bonnie wee lass who never said no / What a voice / My plaidie's awa' / The gypsy laddies / When I was no' but sweet sixteen / MacCrimmon's lament / Roy's wife of Aldivalloch / Lord Lovat. *(re-iss. Aug94 on 'Ossian' cd/c; (OSS 92 CD/C)*

Collector / not iss.

1960. (lp) *(JFS 4001)* **LORD DONALD**
—— she died on the 13th of March 1975

– compilations, others, etc. –

1984. (lp/c) *Lismor; (LIF L/C 7001)* **UP THE DEE AND DOON THE DON: A MONUMENTAL FIGURE OF WORLD FOLKSONG (1908-1975)**
– The overgate / The battle of Harlaw / Busk bonnie lassie / The laird o' the windy wa' / The jolly beggar / I saw my own bonnie lass / Ten o'clock is ringing / For I will lay you doon / Twa' recruitin' sergeants / Busk and go (Cuttie's wedding) / A dottered auld Carle / Far over the Forth / Eenst upon a time / An auld man cam courtin' me / Gallowa' hills / My son David / Bonnie lass come over the burn / Jeannie my dear / The braes o' Killecrankie.
Apr 88. (c) *Folktracks; (60-067)* **WHAT A VOICE**
– Loch o' Shallin / Never wed an auld man / Go away from my window / The old witch woman / A blin' drunk / Bonny lassie-o / Maggie / Rub-a-dub-dub / Flashy dashy petticoats / Eenst upon a time / Crooked house / Eenty peenty / My daddy wouldna / The cuckoo's nest / Bonny wee Highland man / Susan Pyatt / The overgate / Braes of Balquidder / The four Maries / Lord Lovatt / The moon shined on my bed last night.
1990. (c) *Folktracks; (60-186)* **THE GYPSY LADY**
– Davey fae Dentidoonbye / The lassie who never said no / Brenan on the moor / Handsome cabin boy / When I was no' but sweet sixteen / The jolly beggar / The laird o' Drum / Lord McDonald / Twa brothers.
1990. (c) *Folktracks; (60-187)* **SILLY JOHN AND THE FACTOR**
Nov 90. (c) *Springthyme; (SPRC 1025)* **GREAT SCOTS BALLAD SINGER**
Sep 98. (cd) *Rounder; (<ROUCD 1720>)* **THE QUEEN AMONG THE HEATHER**
– The reel of Tullochgorum / When my apron hung low / She'd a lot of old songs / Son David / It's a true song / The battle of Harlaw / Wi' my rovin' eye / Never wed an old man / The moon shined on my bed last night / The laird of the Dentidoonbye / The handsome cabin boy / I doubt she could have been a good girl! / She was a rum one / Lord Lovatt / (introduction to) . . . / Bonnie Annie and Andrew Lammie / (. . .commentary on) / The queen among the heather.

ROCK SALT & NAILS

Foremed: Shetland Isles . . . 1990 by guitarist PAUL JOHNSTON and drummer JOHN CLARK. JOHNSTON had already cut his teeth in Edinburgh's live scene where he worked a day job as an architect, his subsequent relocation to the Northern Isles concurrent with his interest in traditonal music. A stable line-up subsequently formed around JOHNSTON, his wife FIONA, fiddler MAGNUS JOHNSTON (no relation) and the rhythm section of CLARK and RUSSELL GAIR.

After a few years of dedicated touring, the band signed to 'Iona' and released the 'WAVES' album as their debut in 1994. Along with Shetland compatriots like DROP THE BOX, JOHNSTON and Co. were intent on developing the cross-fertilisation possibilities presented by the Isles' musical heritage. Despite the hard-core folk sensibilities suggested by their moniker, ROCK SALT & NAILS' musical recipe was a more easy-going amalgam of acoustic-strummed pop/rock, piano and fiddle interspersed with the odd ballad and rocking reel, PAUL not sounding too dissimilar to a younger RICKY ROSS at times.

A prolific work rate of one album a year through the mid-90's – 'MORE AND MORE' (1995), '4,6,2,1' (1996), 'STAND YOUR GROUND' (1997) – saw the band picking up increasing amounts of press column inches while an appearance at the Aberdeen Alternative Festival went down a storm. 1999's 'BOXED' album was another strong effort, highlighting their dynamic approach and even attempting to make folk music sexy by naming a song suite 'EMMA'S G-SPOT' . . .

PAUL JOHNSTON – guitar, strumstix, vocals / **MAGNUS JOHNSTON** – fiddle / **FIONA JOHNSTON** – keyboards, vocals / **JOHN JAMES CLARK** – bass / **RUSSELL GAIR** – drums

Iona / not iss.

Jan 94. (cd/c) *(IR CD/C 025)* **WAVES**
– The man who ate mountains / Stockit light – Waiting for the federals / Happy to be here / Jack broke da prison door / Faroe rum / Oliver Jack / Willafjord / Iron horse / Arkansas traveller / Welcome / Central house / Square da Mizzen / Doon hingin' tie / Waves / Hut on Staffin Island / Barmaid / Music for a found harmonium.
May 95. (cd/c) *(IR CD/C 030)* **MORE AND MORE**
– Don't know about you – Friday card school / Saomeday / Jack broke da prison door / Life / Lucy Bain / More and more / Uneasy ride / Tilly plump set / Grandmother's eyes / Forced to return – Spootiskerry / Lucy Bain reprise.

Forth / not iss.

Jul 96. (cd) *(FORCD 39)* **4,6,2,1**
– The chocolate biscuit set / I'm looking through you / Breakdown / Well, well, well / Sister / That's just me / Laxoburn / Never apologise / Dance / Shaggy's sexy Shetland set. *(re-iss. Mar99; same)*
Oct 97. (cd) *(FORCD 50)* **STAND YOUR GROUND**
– Flight / Landing light / P.V.S. / Little bird / Wrong day / Well Wynde suite / Sad and lonely day / Shadows on the wall / History / Dumpy's set. *(re-iss. Mar99; same)*
—— band were at this stage **PAUL JOHNSTON, FIONA JOHNSTON + JOHN JAMES CLARK** plus **PAUL ANDERSON** – fiddles / **DAVID JAMIESON** – drums, percussion, vocals / **EMMA JOHNSTON** – fiddles, piano, vocals

— added guests **RON KAVANA** (b. Ireland) – 'bazooka', guitar, mandolin, vocals + **PETER WOOD** – accordion

Iona / not iss.

Apr 99. (cd) *(IRCD 065)* **BOXED** [ ] [-]
– Speed / Butterflies / Bad weather / Maas / Just around the corner / Romancing and dancing: a) I don't feel like dancing, b) Dancing tonight / You & me / Emma's G-spot: a) Come again you're welcome, b) The hurricane, c) The grocer / Rye-grass.

Billy ROSS (see under ⇒ OSSIAN)

RUA

Formed: New Zealand . . . early 90's by Scots ex-pats including piper JIMMY YOUNG and a group of multi-instrumentalists, mainly DENNY STANWAY, JAMES WILKINSON, JON HOOKER, JAMES MacKINTOSH and MIKE CONSIDINE. RUA released a number of studio sets in their adopted country, the compilation 'HOMELAND' (1993) was as issued as their UK debut for 'Greentrax'; MATTHEW LAWRENCE replaced MacKINTOSH thereafter. Relatively big in France, their sophomore set 'AO-TEA-ROA' (1995), was just as imaginative and creative as their first. Leader JIMMY YOUNG went solo towards the end of the millennium, 1999's 'PIPEWORKS' album – with a host of Scottish musicians including IAIN MacINNES and IAIN MacDONALD – contained a musical tribute to Greenpeace vessel, Rainbow Warrior.

JIMMY YOUNG – Northumbrian pipes, etc / **DENNY STANWAY** – vocals, multi / **JAMES WILKINSON** – acoustic guitar, bass, vocals, multi / **JON HOOKER** – guitars / **JAMES MacKINTOSH** – drums, congas / **MIKE CONSIDINE** – bouzouki / with also **CHIC MacAULAY** – acoustic guitar, cittern / **DAVY STEWART** – guitar, mandola, vocals, etc

Greentrax / Greentrax

Mar 93. (cd/c) *(CD/C TRAX 061)* **HOMELAND: THE RUA COLLECTION** (compilation) [ ] [-]
– The Commonwealth suite: The parting glass – Setting sail – The storm / Ao-tea-roa / Hoea ra – Dawn of a new age – Te Rua / Jock o' Hazeldean / Homeland – The last battle / Kyle brack rambler – Idle reel – Chili reel / The Diamontina drover / The millworker / Simple song / Dublin reel – Sean sa cheo / The first time ever / The java jive – Jimmy Ward's jig / Jungle Johnny – The red haired rafter – Maurice Spence's / Molloy's / Sailing into Walpole's marsh.

MATTHEW LAWRENCE – percussion, drums; repl. MacKINTOSH

Sep 95. (cd) *(<CDTRAX 103>)* **AO-TEA-ROA (live)** [ ] [ ] Nov95
– Music from the jungles of Caledonia – Bri o' Locheil / The raider / Jeltic music: Breton air – The plain tree / The Moon & St. Christopher / Caribbean Celts / Allelujah / Hayfever: Lisheen slide – Hayfever / The college boy / Bannd on the run: Banks of the Bann – Allaghery County / Eleanor Rigby / Waltzurka: Sir William Hardie's waltzurka – Warrior jig / Winter's rage / Arrival in Auckland: Arrival in Auckland – The Pacific reel / Highland cream: Bri o' Lochiel. *<re-iss. Feb96 as 'HARBOUR LIGHTS' on 'Manu'; 1495>*

— STEWART + MacAULEY appeared only on some tracks above

– others, etc. –

Jul 94. (cd) *Ode; (CDODE 1391)* **LIVE IN THE CATHEDRAL (live)** [ ] [-]

JIMMY YOUNG

with most members of RUA + a plethora of Scots music people including **IAIN MacDONALD & IAIN MacINNES**

Aug 99. (cd) *(<CDTRAX 171>)* **PIPEWORKS** [ ] [ ] Sep99
– The warrior's reel: Rip the calico / Sir William Hardie's waltzurka / Full rigged: The warrior's jig – The celebration reel / The exodus / Pacific crossing: Plain sailing – Pacific crossing / The arrival: Out of the mist – Pacific fling – The arrival / End of the rainbow: Burial at sea – Resurrection / Who knows where the time goes / Last hoedown at Tron / The braes, the braes / Denny's air. *(re-iss. Jun00; same)*

RUBY BLUE (see ⇒ Section 8: Rock, Pop & Indie)

RUNRIG

Formed: North Uist . . . 1973 as The RUN-RIG DANCE BAND, by brothers RORY and CALUM McDONALD plus BLAIR DOUGLAS. Following local gigs on the islands, the band found encouraging support from the gaelic media, subsequently travelling to mainland Scotland and playing a gig at the Kelvin Hall in Glasgow. Schoolfriend DONNIE MUNRO joined the following year as a lead vocalist while DOUGLAS was replaced by ROBERT McDONALD on accordion.

This line-up remained steady through the band's debut album, 'PLAY GAELIC' (1978), released on the independent 'Neptune' label (and subsequently re-issued in 1995 on 'Lismor'). As the title suggested, this was a steadfastly indigenous release with no English language tracks although it was well received in folk circles and encouraged the group to set up their own label, 'Ridge'. Amid further line-up changes, RUNRIG released a follow-up, 'HIGHLAND CONNECTION' (1979), the record featuring a mix of Gaelic and English language tracks including 'LOCH LOMOND', a traditional song which would become a firm favourite with their growing fanbase.

It was to be a further five years before the release of 'RECOVERY' (1984), the band having toured heavily, embellishing their sound with the relative exotica of keyboards (played by, gasp, an Englishman!, RICHARD CHERNS). As a result, the album proffered a more accessible brand of Celtic-rock (described as a cross between BIG COUNTRY, The CHIEFTAINS and HORSLIPS), a sound that crystallised with 'HEARTLAND' (1986) on the likes of 'DANCE CALLED AMERICA' (dealing with the tragedy of the highland clearances). With a growing number of admirers in both America and Europe, it seemed that the only place which failed to understand the group was, funnily enough, England. Nevertheless, the band were signed by London-based major, 'Chrysalis' in 1988, following the successful 'CUTTER AND THE CLAN' (1987) album, a collection which numbered such enduring RUNRIG favourites as 'ROCKET TO THE MOON' and 'PROTECT AND SURVIVE'.

Their major label debut, the live 'ONCE IN A LIFETIME', was released the same year and dented the lower region of the UK chart. This marked the beginning of RUNRIG's most commercially successful period, the band almost making the Top 10 with the 'SEARCHLIGHT' album in 1989. An appearance on Scottish TV caused a considerable surge in interest, 'THE BIG WHEEL' (1991) making the UK Top 5. Its success caught many people off guard, and it was a testament to the support of native fans, the album once again selling negligibly south of the border. Soon after the record's release the band played an open air concert, fittingly, at Loch Lomond, before 45,000 fans.

Successive releases like 'AMAZING THINGS' (1993), a near No.1 album, and 'MARA' have consolidated the band's standing as one of Scotland's premier exports alongside whisky and PRIMAL SCREAM. While they sometimes tend to overdo the bombastic Braveheart shenanigans, they have to be applauded in their brave efforts to keep the gaelic langauge alive, often in the face of apathetic indifference or even outright hostility.

However, the band's success seemed to be on hold as they searched for a replacement for the politicised DONNIE MUNRO. In 1998/99, all was revealed when Canadian (MUNRO-soundalike!) BRUCE GUTHRO filled his boots for fresh set, 'IN SEARCH OF ANGELS'. In the summer of 2001, 'THE STAMPING GROUND' was released to subdued press reviews and a brief UK Top 75 placing.

• **Trivia:** Due to their religious beliefs they never play live on a Sunday.
• **Note:** (for discography, see Section 8: Rock, Pop & Indie)

RUNT O' THE LITTER (see under ⇒ Iona records)

Janet RUSSELL

Born: 11 Jan'58, Buckhaven, Fife. After beginning her career in Edinburgh's folk clubs and Festival Fringes, RUSSELL hooked up with CHRISTINE KYDD in what was to become a fruitful and long running partnership. The pair's contrasting vocal styles made for haunting harmony singing, as evidenced on their eponymous debut album. Released on 'Greentrax' in 1988, the record paved the way for JANET's solo debut proper, 'GATHERING THE FRAGMENTS', the same year. In '89, RUSSELL joined a plethora of folkies on LES BARKER's 'The Stones Of Callanish', subsequently putting her solo work on the backburner as she concentrated on giving birth to her first child.

She re-emerged in the early 90's as part of SISTERS UNLIMITED alongside three other females, the project releasing live set (recorded at the Purcell Room on London's South Bank), 'NO LIMITS' (1991). After taking more time out to have a second child, JANET released a belated follow-up solo effort in the shape of 'BRIGHT SHINING MORNING?' (1993). The latter's often heavily political slant was eschewed for a more traditional approach on 'DANCIN' CHANTIN' (1994), JANET's second collaborative effort with CHRISTINE KYDD. 1995, meanwhile, found her back with a second set from SISTERS UNLIMITED entitled 'NO BED OF ROSES'.

JANET RUSSELL – vocals, etc / with various help

Greentrax / not iss.

Feb 88. (lp/c; by JANET RUSSELL AND CHRISTINE KYDD) *(C+/TRAX 011)* **JANET RUSSELL AND CHRISTINE KYDD** [ ] [-]
– Buy brooms besoms / Dainty Davy / Up wi' the Carls o' Dysart / The De'ils awa' wi' th' exciseman / Deja mal Mariee / Bonny at morn / Children of Africa / My Donald – Ode to big blue / Tae the weavers gin ye gang / Old and strong – Mountain song / Do you love an apple / Last carol / Stand up, fight for your

rights – Everyone 'neath a vine and fig tree. *(re-iss. Aug93 cd/c; CD/C TRAX 011)*

Harbour Town / not iss.

1988. (lp/c) *(HAR 003/+C)* **GATHERING THE FRAGMENTS** [ ] [-]
– Old woman is watching / The children are running / The blude red rose / The band of shearers – The musical priest – The wind that shakes the barley / The hills of Ardmorn / All the tunes in the world / The secretary's song / Sanctuary / Fast bright nights / Choices / Land of the leal / Curtain call.

— the following year, she and a plethora of folk people appeared on LES BARKER's 'The Stones Of Callanish'

Oct 93. (cd/c) *(HAR CD/C 026)* **BRIGHT SHINING MORNING?** [ ] [-]
– Bright shining morning? / Ettrick / Childminder's song / Can't hug you / Fly away / Sheath and knife / Garten mother's lullaby / Mouth music / Jeannie Jenkins / Song for a seafarer / Soweto / Accidents / Bury my heart / St. Peters fields / I know love / The bluebell polka.

Greentrax / not iss.

Sep 94. (cd/c; by JANET RUSSELL & CHRISTINE KYDD)
(CD/C TRAX 077) **DANCIN' CHANTIN'** [ ] [-]
– Les filles des forges – Maire Nighean Alastair – Up and awa' wi the laverock / Lady Mary Anne – Reel o' stumpie – Tail toddle / Rattling roaring Willie / The fisherman's wife / Logan water / Duncan Gray / Terror time / Strathmartine braes / Clerk Saunders / La caille / Pride's awa' / The bluebell polka / The parting glass / Jock since ever.

SISTERS UNLIMITED

JANET RUSSELL with 3 others

Harbour Town / not iss.

Nov 91. (lp/c/cd) *(HAR 013/+C/CD)* **NO LIMITS** [ ] [-]
– No going back / Promises / Breastfeeding baby in the park / Tomorrow / Mouth music / My better years / Working girl blues / Dance / Old and strong / My true love once / When I was single / On children / No man's momma / Forgive and forget / We were there.

Fellside / not iss.

Jun 95. (cd/c) *(FE 104 CD/C)* **NO BED OF ROSES** [ ] [-]
– Voices / More than a paycheck / The collier's lassie / Love-lar-i / A stor mo chroi / Dance to your daddy – Cockle gatherers – Tail toddle / My rebellious adolescent / Chipko / Mother I feel you under my feet – Sun wind and water / Women o' Dundee / Keep your nose out of mama's business / Dancing on the gravel / Mrs Jones Lias / Childbirth shanty (no bed of roses) / Sleep well / Your cheating heart.

Jim RUSSELL (see under ⇒ SHANKS, Andy . . .)

S

SALSA CELTICA (see ⇒ Section 5: Jazz)

SANGSTERS (see under ⇒ Greentrax records)

SCOTCH MEASURE (see under ⇒ KENTIGERN)

Elfrida SCOTT (see under ⇒ Greentrax records)

Mike SCOTT (see under ⇒ WATERBOYS; Section 8: Rock, Pop & Indie)

Willie SCOTT

Born: 1897, Canonbie, Dumfriesshire. Brought up in the exposed hill terrain on the border between Scotland and England, WILLIE attended school near Brampton in Cumberland. He went on to follow the family sheep farming tradition at Stobbs, Roxburghshire, later tending flocks in Fife and Berwickshire. By the time SCOTT released his first LP, 'THE SHEPHERD'S SONG – BORDER BALLADS' for 'Topic' in 1968, he'd amassed an extensive repertoire of Borders songs and ballads, sung unaccompanied with a unique intonation which no doubt stemmed from his simultaneous knowledge of the English dialect. In addition to his farming and singing talents, WILLIE was also an expert crook-maker. Sadly, in 1989, at the ripe old age of 92, WILLIE went to the great sheep farm in the sky. Towards the end of the century, those meticulous people at 'Greentrax' gave the record an overdue CD re-issue, complete with a great cover shot of the man at work courtesy of Farmer's Weekly.

WILLIE SCOTT – vocals

Topic / not iss.

1968. (lp) *(12T 183)* **THE SHEPHERD'S SONG – BORDER BALLADS** [ ] [-]
– The shepherd's song / Piper MacNeil / The Kielder hunt / Jamie Raeburn / Bonnie wee lass trampin' lass / Bloody Waterloo / Jock Geddes / The Dowie dens of Yarrow / Herd laddie o' the glen / The lads that were reared amang heather. *(cd-iss. Oct98 on 'Greentrax'; CDTRAX 9054)*

— WILLIE died in 1989

SCOTTISH GAS CALEDONIAN PIPE BAND (see under ⇒ Greentrax records)

SCOTTISH STEPDANCE COMPANY (see under ⇒ Tartan Tapes records)

SEANNACHIE

Formed: Edinburgh . . . 1987 by SIMON THOUMIRE, DONALD GORMAN, DEREK HARKINS and JOHN BORLAND; singer/bodhran player ELSPETH COWIE was added after their debut set, 'WITHIN THE FIRE' (1987). Through varying line-ups – which at one time or another have included JONATHAN SIMONS, ALEX YELLOWLEES, PENNY CALLOW, the aforementioned DEREK HARKINS, SEAMUS HAYES, CORRINA HEWATT and DAVE MILLIGAN – the group became a firm fixture on the Scottish folk circuit and recorded a trio of albums: 'WITHIN THE FIRE' (1987), 'TAKE NOTE' (1988), 'THE DEVIL'S DELIGHT' (1991). The latter set featured a line-up of BORLAND, DONALD GORMAN, ELSPETH COWIE, NICK BRENNAN and SIMON THOUMIRE, a concertina ace who subsequently re-released the album on his own 'Tartan Tapes/Foot Stompin' Records' label in 2000. Although the band briefly regrouped in the late 90's for a European jaunt, the various members are currently committed to other projects, not least the ubiquitous THOUMIRE.

SIMON THOUMIRE – concertina, keyboards, whistles / **DONALD GORMAN** – fiddle / **JOHN BORLAND** – bouzouki / **DEREK HARKINS** – guitar / added **ELSPETH COWIE** (b. Lanark) – vocals, bodhran

Raven / not iss.

1987. (lp/c) *(RR/+C 001)* **WITHIN THE FIRE** [ ] [-]
1988. (lp/c) *(RR/+C 002)* **TAKE NOTE** [ ] [-]

— **NICK BRENNAN** – guitar; repl. HARKINS

Nov 91. (cd/c) *(RR CD/C 003)* **THE DEVIL'S DELIGHT** [ ] [-]
– German lairdie – Trip to Roscoff / Alan McPherson of Mosspark – Thomas Bankhead's – The green pastures – The mason's other apron / Barbara Allen / Tullochgorum – The flagon reel – The Devil's dream / Lord Franklin / Lady Dorothea Stewart Murray – Captain Carswell – Finlay's people – The big skerry / Albert Ross – La Grenouille – Mary Joe's / Anthem for Ireland / Good wife admit the wanderer / The Earl of Errol / The sutrika – Things to come – Pottinger's reel / John Anderson.

— SIMON subsequently formed his own named outfit and folk supergroup KEEP IT UP, ELSPETH went into session work, joined female trio CHANTAN and finally went solo

SEELYHOO

Formed: Edinburgh-based . . . mid-90's by Orkney-born twins the WRIGLEY SISTERS (HAZEL and JENNIFER), Gaelic singer FIONA MacKENZIE, accordionist SANDY BRECHIN, percussionist JIM WALKER and bouzouki player AARON JONES. SEELYHOO is an old Scots word for a membrane normally found in a new born baby's head; it apparently signifies good luck.

Recording both traditional and contemporary material, SEELYHOO made their debut with 'THE FIRST CAUL' (1996) on 'Greentrax', an acclaimed set of nu-Folk with an occasionally quirky edge. 1998's 'LEETERA' meanwhile, was another competent combination of Gaelic airs and spirited reels, MacKENZIE sounding not unlike a folkier Scottish cousin of DOLORES O'RIORDAN (of the CRANBERRIES).

From the onset of the 90's, JENNIFER & HAZEL WRIGLEY have maintained their own partnership while ace box-player BRECHIN formed his own band for the albums 'OUT OF HIS BOX' (1996) and 'OUT OF HIS TREE' (1999).

FIONA MacKENZIE – vocals, whistle / **HAZEL WRIGLEY** (b.1974) – guitar, mandolin, keyboards / **JENNIFER WRIGLEY** (b.1974) – fiddles / **SANDY BRECHIN** – accordion (also of BURACH) / **JIM WALKER** – percussion, drums / **AARON JONES** – bouzouki, bass, vocals

Greentrax Greentrax

Jan 96. (cd/c) *(<CD/C TRAX 102>)* **THE FIRST CAUL**
– Miss Sarah MacFadyen – Farewell to the rock o' Cleary / Mick's knitted triplets – Brumely brae – Jenny's chickens / Air sgiathan na h-oidhche / The first leg – The last leg / Mhurchaidh bhig a chinn a chonnais – Dairmaid's reel / Sometimes it doesn't work – The lucky cap – The potato tree / Hoy's dark and lofty isle / Superwasp – Along the coast of Norway – Neckbuster / Sean McGuire – Bear island – Drever's reel / Cuin a chi mi thusa luaidh / The Stronsay weaver – Trip to California / Dh'iomain mam bo / The lost job – The old copperplate – The diesel accordion / The walk – Miss Lyall's / The fly to Rousay – Porto the rat – Dale's place.

— **NIALL MUIR** – bass, backing vocals; repl. JONES

Aug 98. (cd) *(<CDTRAX 160>)* **LEETERA**
– Na spioradan briste – Grace Brechin / Hoy high – hoy low / Bidh clann Ulaidh / The Marquis of Huntly's farewell – Ashley's Strathspey / Cait na dh'fhag thu'n fhichead gini? – Fornethy house / Ghiulain sinn / Torpedo supper – Billy & Mackay – The brides cog / Dheanainn sugradh ris an nighinn duibh – Haggis fondue / Tor breac / Tir nan og / Cheese peace – The slip'in / Restoration day / Aj's – The nippy sweet – The custard pie gang / Bha dathan a' danns – The red tin roof.

— FIONA joined Edinburgh-based/Irish-founded outfit, ANAM; SANDY continued with BURACH and released his second solo set, 'OUT OF HIS TREE' (1999)

JENNIFER and HAZEL WRIGLEY

Attic not iss.

1991. (cd) *(AT 026)* **DANCING FINGERS**
– Bachelor's reel – The Shelburne reel / Jenny dang the weaver – Glass of beer – Mick's knitted triplets / The fly to Rousay – The trip to Rousay / Star of County Down / Listen to the mockingbird / The Hinderayre waltz – Speaking fingers / Grey eagle / Martin Wynne's No.2 – Ril gin ainm / Ale is dear – Sleepy moggy – All the ships are sailing / South Nevi / Clarke's favourite – Drever's reel / Cincinnati rag / The chappet nail – Burning strings / Tide at the Taing – The strawzelnut.

Jan 95. (cd/c) *(AT 038 CD/C)* **THE WATCH STONE**

— with **JIM WALKER** – percussion, snare drums / **BRIAN SHEILS** – bass / **NEIL DAVEY** – mandolin (of ANAM) / **EAMON COYNE** – banjo

Greentrax Greentrax

Nov 97. (cd/c) *(<CD/C TRAX 148>)* **HULDRELAND** Jan98
– Eynhallow soond – The Halloween flit / Rohan – Keenan's welcome – Peedie Sophie / Meg's hornpipe – Reel o' Colster / The giant party – Stoned giants / Hills of Hoy / Shannandah falls / Barbara's wedding – Irene's reel / Ingi / Light fight – Chi cha / The Whistlebinkies ghost – Dougal's sustain / Horse of Copinsay / Orkney Isles hornpipe – Toe Reid / The ba' rag / Huldreland.

Nov 99. (cd/c) *(<CD/C TRAX 183>)* **MITHER O' THE SEA** Feb00
– Swelkie / Brae o' Scorne / Mrs Violet Eunson / Shaninsay polka / Compliments to the Orkney Norway friendship association / Running the lee / Adelaide / Trip to Orkney waltz / Whal's rost / Way oot west / Duchess of Gordon / R Aim's compliments to J Craigie / Teran / JF Dickie / Jimmy o' the Bu's polka / Master ship / Fiotta dash / Phantom flight / Bessie Millie's sixpence / Scotification / Holm band tune.

below featured storyteller **DAVID CAMPBELL**

Attic not iss.

Jan 01. (cd; as JENNIFER & HAZEL WRIGLEY with DAVID CAMPBELL) *(ATCD 057)* **ORKNEY AFTER SUNSET**
– Go good my songs / The ring of Brodgar / The standing stones of Stenness / Thor's hammer / Magnus and Hakon / The sandy lamb polka / The beachcomber / The old polka / Betty Corrigal / The Sabistons / Elegy.

Geosound not iss.

Nov 01. (cd; as the WRIGLEY SISTERS) *(GSCD 001)* **SKYRAN**
– Orcadia / Orkneyites / Newark bay / Broonie o' Copinsay / Sleepy laddie / Dingeshowe dancers / Miss Eilidh Shaw / Thoumire's trendy treads / Utiseta / Stronsay waltz / North ron' reel / South ron' reel / Auld bow / Deerness mermaid / Watchman's polka / Whorf reel / Fairy ring / Trowie dart / Hen pen dirio / Orca.

MacKENZIE

sisters **FIONA, GILLIAN + EILIDH** (the latter also of MAC-TALLA and a solo artist)

Macmeanmnanot iss.

Dec 97. (c/cd) *(SKYE/+CD 10)* **CAMHANACH**
– Sheila Gordon of Weem / Tha fadachd cian do ghaoil orm (Long have I missed your love) / 'S truagh nach d'rugadh dall mi (Alas that I was not born blind), hai-o eadaraibh o / Ho-ro's toigh leam fhin thu (How I love you) / Waulking song set / Buaidh na bardachd (The muse) / A' fagail Ghriais (Leaving Gress) / Haghaidh o, haghaidh o / Chi mi thallad (See yonder) / Is e cho priseil dhomh (So precious to me) / A' fighe le feur (Knitting grass) / Leabaidh naoimh aula (The of Saint Aula).

Linn not iss.

Jul 01. (cd; as MacKENZIE & WILLIAM JACKSON) *(AKD 145)*
NOTES FROM A HERBIDEAN ISLAND
– Anna bheag / MacPhee's reel / Marion and Donald / Tall toddle / Ba mo leanabh / Barbara's jig / Kenny MacDonald's jig / Fisherman's song for attracting seals / Blue ribbon Scottish measure / Battle of Waterloo / The wee Highland laddie / Skye dance / Harris dance / Mermaid's song / Chaidh mi'n traigh a deanamh maoraich / Rory Dall's sister's lament / Iain ruaidh lament / Looking south over the border.

SETANTA (see under ⇒ WALKER, Ian)

Andy SHANKS & Jim RUSSELL

Formed: Kirkcaldy, Fife . . . mid-90's when the two singer-songwriters went around schools and clubs promoting the work of Burns. Guitarist/singer SHANKS mixes contemporary with a folk-rock sound, while the multi-instrumentalist RUSSELL has been writing songs since he left school. In 1996, after JIM won the Jack Stewart Memorial Songwriting competition (with the song 'ST ANDREW IN THE WINDOW') and ANDY won the Edinburgh Folk Songwriting Competition (with 'THIRTY YEAR MAN'), the duo were invited by fiddler, ALASDAIR FRASER, to record an album. Produced by DAVID SCOTT and BILL WELLS, 'DIAMONDS IN THE NIGHT' (1997), collated all of their work to date plus a few covers stemming from the pens of cult folkies June Tabor and The Sangsters.

ANDY SHANKS – vocals, guitar / **JIM RUSSELL** – multi-instrumentalist / with **JOHN BURGESS** – tenor sax / **LINDSAY COOPER** – double bass (ex-HENRY COW) / **DAVID SCOTT + BRIAN McALPINE** – keyboards, etc (ex-PEARLFISHERS) / plus **WENDY WEATHERBY** – cello / **WILF TAYLOR** – percussion (of CAPERCAILLIE) / + the TORRIDON STRING QUARTET

Culburnie Culburnie

Jun 97. (cd/c) *(<CUL 112 D/C>)* **DIAMONDS IN THE NIGHT**
– Balgonie bairn / Thirty year man / Ash pirates / Rags and days / Street dances / Money guns and the green forest / St Andrew in the window / Compass heart / The road here / Diamonds in the night / Midnight city buses / Mogadishi / The fiddler / The wake.

Eilidh SHAW (see under ⇒ CALEDON)

SHOOGLENIFTY

Formed: Cockenzie, East Lothian . . . 1993 by IAN MACLEOD, ANGUS R. GRANT, GARRY FINLAYSON, MALCOLM CROSBIE, CONRAD IVITSKY and JAMES MACKINTOSH. A beast of strange beauty, SHOOGLENIFTY have been injecting a bit of rock glamour and eastern promise into folk's often genteel musical environs for nigh on a decade. An all-instrumental outfit, these plucky Scots first unveiled their unique barrage of violins and dancefloor banjo grooves (described as "Acid Croft" by the boys themselves) via 1994's brilliantly titled 'VENUS IN TWEEDS' album. Released on the local 'Greentrax' label, the record was a shot in the arm for the folk crossover scene, mixing up funky drumming, exotic atmospherics and the duelling "Deliverance"-styled banjos of MACLEOD and FINLAYSON.

'A WHISKY KISS' followed in 1996, by which time they'd built up quite a reputation for their unhinged live show, both at home and increasingly abroad. A mark of their standing in world music circles came in 1996 with the release of concert set, 'LIVE AT SELWYN HALL', on PETER GABRIEL's prestigious 'Womad' label. In late '97, the band headlined the Commonwealth Heads Of Government Concert in Edinburgh where the likes of "Bonnie" Prince Charlie (the English version), Robin Cook and Nelson Mandela looked on and quite possibly even tapped their feet. The following year, SHOOGLENIFTY played to a packed Sydney Opera House in Australia, heralding an unprecedented stage invasion and much Antipodean revelry.

They finally returned to the studio in 2000 for new label, 'Vertical', their third album proper 'SOLAR SHEARS' showing the band were progressing into Folk music's finest rockers. • **Songwriters:** MacLEOD, GRANT or FINLAYSON, except HOPTSOI (Kari Reiman) / FAREWELL TO NIGG (D. Johnstone).

IAIN MACLEOD (b. 4 Apr'62, Strathy Point) – mandolin, tenor banjo / **ANGUS R. GRANT** (b.14 Feb'67, Fort William) – fiddle / **GARRY FINLAYSON** (b.24 Sep'52, Kirkwall) – banjo, banjax / **MALCOLM CROSBIE** (b.25 May'60, Edinburgh) – guitars, whistling / **CONRAD IVITSKY** (b.28 Nov'68, Edinburgh) – bass / **JAMES MACKINTOSH** (b.11 Aug'66, Fort William) – drums, percussion, piano

Greentrax Greentrax

Aug 94. (cd/c) *(<CD/C TRAX 076>)* **VENUS IN TWEED**
– Pipe tunes / Horace / The point road / Venus in tweeds / Waiting for Conrad / Two fifty to Vigo / Paranoia / Buying a blanket / The Tammienorrie / The point road (Joiner's mix).

Jun 96. (cd/c) *(<CD/C TRAX 106>)* **A WHISKY KISS**
– Da eye wifey / She's in the attic / A song for Susie / A whisky kiss / Good drying / Hoptsoi / The price of a pig / Farewell to Nigg.

Womad not iss.

Aug 96. (cd) *(WS 008CD)* **LIVE AT SELWYN HALL (live)**
– The pipe tunes / The radical road / Two fifty to Vigo / Hoptsoi / Venus in tweeds / Waiting for Conrad / Good drying / Da eye wifie / The Tammienorrie.

Vertical not iss.

Nov 00. (cd) *(VERTCD 053)* **SOLAR SHEARS** [ ] [-]
– The hijab / Schuman's leap / Igor's / August / Delighted / Maggie Ann of Clachnabrochan / Rod's doorway / 29 steps / Kinky Haroosh / Bjork's chauffeur.

SHOORMAL

Formed: Quarff, Shetlands . . . 1997 by an 8-piece consisting of JOYCE McDILL, FREDA LEASK, DONNA SMITH, TREVOR SMITH, GREGG ARTHUR, MAY GAIR, EMMA JOHNSTON and CHRISTOPHER ANDERSON. A Shetland supergroup of sorts, SHOORMAL featured many musicians who'd already made their mark in the tight-knit Islands music scene and beyond. ANDERSON, for example, was already a weel kent face as the beat behind folk-rockers BONGSHANG while JOHNSTON's fiddle was an integral part of ROCK SALT & NAILS. Although the vocal trio of LEASK, McDILL and SMITH had been hitherto more obscure, the press fell over themselves to praise the ladies' unmistakable three-part harmonies on debut album, 'INDIGO SKIES' (2000). Produced by BONGSHANG man JJ JAMIESON, the record's beguiling Americana via Lerwick rootsiness and irresistible vocal panache saw it swoon its way into the heart of many a critic.

FREDA LEASK – vocals / **JOYCE McDILL** – vocals / **DONNA SMITH** – vocals / **TREVOR SMITH** – guitar / **GREGG ARTHUR** – piano, acoordion / **EMMA JOHNSON** – fiddle / **MAY GAIR** – double bass / **CHRISTOPHER ANDERSON** – drums (of BONGSHANG)

Shetland not iss.

Dec 00. (cd) **INDIGO SKIES** [ ] [-]
– Shoormal / Dancing in different times / Distant star / Wild wind / Maggie Reid / Rosewood / Tell me / Indigo skies / When God dips his pen of love in my heart / Catch da tide / Prodigal / Hymn.

SILEAS

Formed: Edinburgh . . . 1985 by PATSY SEDDON and MARY MacMASTER. Both had previously been members of all female 7-piece outfit SPRANGEEN who recorded a one-off eponymous album for 'Springthyme' records in 1984. Both were also well versed in Gaelic history and culture (the name SILEAS – pronounced "SHEELIS" – was in honour of 17th century Gaelic bard, Sileas Na Ceapaich), having studied the subject to degree level.

The duo's mutual love of the harp brought them together for 1986's debut album, 'DELIGHTED WITH HARPS', following it up with the acclaimed 'BEATING HARPS' two years later. Critics praised the pair's inventive approach to the harp (or clarsach in Gaelic), MARY's wire-strung model complementing SEDDON's gut-strung harp and melding with the vocals (part Gaelic/part English) to mesmerising effect.

Following 1990's 'HARPBREAKERS' set, SEDDON and MacMASTER teamed up with KAREN TWEED and SALLY BARKER to form The POOZIES. The early 90's also saw the girls joining folk veterans DICK GAUGHAN, BRIAN McNEILL and DAVY STEELE amongst others in the CLAN ALBA project wherein they played electric harp. These diversions, as well as guest slots on recordings by the likes of JUNE TABOR and MADDY PRIOR, led to a gap of almost eight years before another SILEAS album hit the shelves, the belated (and much anticipated) 'PLAY ON LIGHT' finally released in 1996. MARY and PATSY were also part of the 7-piece, CALEDON, who released one set, 'THE NOBLE TROUSERS' (2000). The former is now a member of Scottish trad trio, SHINE, alongside ALYTH McCORMACK and CORRINA HEWAT.

SPRANGEEN

PATSY SEDDON (b.12 Jan'61, Edinburgh) – vocals, clarsach, fiddle / **MARY MacMASTER** (b.22 Nov'55, Glasgow) – vocals, clarsach, temple bells, whistle / **KATHLEEN KING** – double bass, fiddle / **MARTA McGLYNN** – concertina / **ROSA MICHAELSON** – fiddle, triangle, duck-call / **VAL PEEK** – fiddle / **ANN WARD** – concertina, flute

Springthyme not iss.

1984. (lp/c) *(SPR/+C 1013)* **SPRANGEEN** [ ] [-]
– Sally Hunter – Off she goes – Lads of Dunse / Miss Sine Flemington – The ale is dear / In dispraise of whisky – The favourite dram / Alasdair MacColla / O'Carolan's draught / Gypsy's warning – Flora MacDonald – Sweet Molly / Miss Shepherd – Jenny Nettles – Mrs MacLeod of Raasay / Braes of Strathblane – Sgian dubh – Hills of Glenorchy / Lovely Molly / Braigh Loch Iall – Miss Lyall – Loch Leven castle / Ciamar a ni mi an dannsa direach – Paddy's leather breeches / Atholl Highlanders. *(re-iss. Oct86; same)*

— after they split, ROSA formed the LOOSE MOOSE CEILIDH BAND, releasing one eponymous album in 1992 for 'Lomoco' records

SILEAS

MARY + PATSY

Lapwing not iss.

Jul 86. (lp/c) *(LAP 113/+C)* **DELIGHTED WITH HARPS** [ ] [-]
– The Brigs / Cadal chan fhaigh mi (I can get no sleep) / Reels: Millbrae – The Spey in spate / Eppie Morrie / Air and reel – The chanter's tune – Marry me now / Da day dawn / The little cascade / Tha mulad / 'S coltach mi ri craobh gun duilleag – Feadan glan a'phiobair / John Anderson my Jo / The judges dilemma – The Inverness gathering. *(cd-iss. Dec86 & Dec98; LAPCD 113) <US cd-iss. 1998 on 'Green Linnet'; GLCD 3039)*

Green Linnet not iss.

Apr 88. (lp/c) *(SIF/CSIF 1089)* **BEATING HARPS** [ ] [-]
– The pipers / The silver whistle / Oh wee white rose of Scotland / The solos / Miss Gordon of Gight / Puirt-a-beul / The shore of Gruinard / Ca' the yowes / The dogs / Beating harps. *(re-iss. Oct93 cd/c; GL CD/C 1089)*

— the pair joined CLAN ALBA with DICK GAUGHAN, etc

Oct 96. (cd/c) *(<CD/C TRAX 118>)* **PLAY ON LIGHT** [ ] [ ]
– Buain a'choirce / May Colvin / Cumba easbuig earraghaidheal / Laill leathag / Cameron MacFadyen – Dr. Cameron's casebook – Miss Kirsten Lindsay Morrison / Mo dhomhnullan fhein / Planxty crockery – Domhnall dubh / Pi li li liu / Dr. Florence Campbell of Jammalamadugu – Duncan Johnstone / The Castlebay scrap – Stuarts rant / Ain't no sunshine – The flawless juggler / Miss Ann Cameron of Balvenie – Amy's rollerskates – Paddy's leather breeches / Tha sior chaoineadh.

– compilations, others, etc. –

Oct 98. (cd) *Lapwing; (LAPCD 127)* **HARPBREAKERS** [ ] [-]

POOZIES

— **PATSY + MARY** now with **SALLY BARKER** (b. Barrow-upon-Soar, Leicestershire) – vocals, guitar, percussion (also a Solo Artist) + **KAREN TWEED** (raised from England/Ireland stock) – piano, accordion, piano, vocals (ex-KATHRYN TICKELL BAND)

Hypertension not iss.

Aug 93. (cd/c) *(HYCD/HYMC 132)* **CHANTOOZIES** [ ] [-]
– We built fires / Mountaineer's sect / Les femmes chaussses / Willie's old trousers / Honesty / Foggy mountain top / Crazy raven / Waking up in a wonderful wark / Dheanainn sugradh / Love on a farmboy's wages / Another train. *(cd re-iss. Mar95; HYCD 200132)*

Jan 95. (cd/c) *(HYCD/HYMC 150)* **DANSOOZIES** [ ] [-]
– Hey now my Johnny lad / Two fifty to Vigo / Company of women / Cotton mill girls / The bay tree set / Static on my radio / The polkas / In between the lines / Poncho and Lefty / Beinn' a' cheathaich / Hoagies – Porsche / Ship of love / In another life. *(re-iss. May95 cd/c; HYCD/HYMC 200150)*

— **KATE RUSBY** – vocals, guitar, fiddle (Solo Artist) repl. BARKER

Pure not iss.

1997. (cd-ep) *(POOZ 01)* **COME RAISE YOUR HEAD** [ ] [-]
– The widow – Charlie's cap / Mr. Grapes – Heidi Hendi / Lonesome road / The bay tree waltz – Faca sibh – Jig jazz (live versions).

1999. (cd) *(PRCD 03)* **INFINITE BLUE** [ ] [-]
– Come all ye lonely lovers / Hogties reel / Si Morag / Lasses fashion / Neptune / Crrooked rain to Dublin / Tack till Thomas / Ma plaid / Freya dances / Sorrows away / Maja's brudvals / Tanteeka / Lost in fishponds / Shepherd's wife / Andrew Carr / Mill house / Rabbit stew / Freddie's reel / Maid of Llanwellyn / Emma and Jamie's wedding.

— around the same time, KAREN collaborated on a few albums with IAN CARR, 'SHHH' (1995) and 'FYACE' (1997)

— now without KATE

Compass not iss.

Oct 00. (cd) *(COMCD 4290)* **RAISE YOUR HEAD: A RETROSPECTIVE** (compilation) [ ] [-]
– The widow / Mr. Grapes / We built fires / The mountaineer's set / Honesty / Willie's old trousers / Another train / Hey now my Johnny lad / The Baytree set / Company of women / Poncho and Lefty / Ma plaid – Freya dances / Maid of Llanwellyn – Emma and Jamie's wedding / In another life.

SILENCERS (see ⇒ Section 8: Rock, Pop & Indie)

SILLY WIZARD

Formed: Edinburgh . . . 1972 by BOB THOMAS, CHRIS PRITCHARD and the English-born GORDON JONES. The first in a bewildering series of personnel changes came almost immediately as PRITCHARD departed and both JOHN CUNNINGHAM and MADELAINE TAYLOR joined up. The band's first few years were characterised by instability as frontwoman TAYLOR left to join WITCHES PROMISE, new members came and went, and an album's worth of material was abandoned. In 1976, a line-up of THOMAS, JONES, CUNNINGHAM and ANDY M. STEWART (NOT the White Heather man, thus the 'M') recorded an eponymous debut album for Transatlantic offshoot 'Xtra' with the help of future REZILLOS man, ALASDAIR DONALDSON and future WALLACHMORE CEILIDH BAND member, FREELAND BARBOUR. Later the same year, JOHN's ace accordion-playing brother PHIL became a fully fledged WIZARD as did MARTIN HADDEN, an old mate of STEWART's with whom he'd played in high school band PUDDOCK'S WELL.

1979 proved another busy year what with a couple of albums for 'Highway' – 'CALEDONIA'S HARDY SONS' and 'SO MANY PARTINGS' – and the temporary addition of another erstwhile PUDDOCK'S man, DOUGIE MACLEAN. 1980 saw SILLY WIZARD cut the theme tune for the original version of Scottish soap opera, 'Take The High Road', while their growing popularity in the USA led to many commentators citing them as one of Scotland's finest exporters of traditional and contemporary sounds, narrative ballads and dance music. 1985's 'LIVE IN AMERICA' reflected their transatlantic appeal and fittingly, the group played their farewell gig in New York three years later.

While THOMAS and JONES subsequently formed their own 'Harbourtown' label, STEWART collaborated with Irishman MANUS LUNNY, HADDEN formed a band with ALLEN CARR and JANE ROTHFIELD, and PHIL CUNNINGHAM became an ever more ubiquitous figure on the Scottish folk scene in both a production and instrumental capacity.

GORDON JONES (b.21 Nov'47, Birkenhead, Liverpool) – guitar, mandolin / **BOB THOMAS** (b.28 Jul'50, Robroyston, Glasgow) – guitar / **JOHN CUNNINGHAM** (b.27 Aug'57, Edinburgh) – fidle, mandolin / **MADELAINE TAYLOR** (b. Perth) – vocals, guitar, bodhran, spoons; repl. CHRIS PRITCHARD

— **ANDY M. STEWART** (b. ANDREW McGREGOR STEWART, 8 Sep'52, Alyth, Perthshire) – banjo, vocals (ex-PUDDOCK'S WELL) – was added, then – repl. NEIL ADAMS (MADELAINE TAYLOR had already left to form WITCHES PROMISE)

— the four were augmented around 1975 by short-stay members **ALASDAIR DONALDSON** – bass (he would join The REZILLOS) + **FREELAND BARBOUR** – accordion (he joined WALLOCHMORE CEILIDH BAND)

Xtra / not iss.

1976. (lp) *(XTRA 1158)* **SILLY WIZARD** [ ] [-]
– Pibroch / Jenny Gray's whiskey / Wind that shakes the barley – The ale is dear / Carlisle wall / My loves in Germany / Election jig / The Heron election ballad No.4 / Atholl braes – The drunken piper / The shearing / The fairy dance / Land o' the Leal. *(re-iss. 1983 as 'FIRST ALBUM' on 'Highway'; SHY 7022)*

— (late '76) added **PHIL CUNNINGHAM** (b.27 Jan'60, Edinburgh) – keyboards / **MARTIN 'Mame' HADDEN** (b.23 May'57, Aberdeen) – bass, vocals (ex-PUDDOCK'S WELL)

Highway / not iss.

1978. (lp) *(SHY 7004)* **CALEDONIA'S HARDY SONS** [ ] [-]
– Mo Chuachag laghach (My kindly sweetheart) / The Isla waters / The twa brithers / The auld pipe reel – The brolum / Glasgow Peggy / Monymusk lads / The ferryland sealer / Fhear a bhata (The boatman) / Jack Cunningham's farewell to Benbecula – Sweet Molly / Broom o' the Cowdenknowes. *(re-iss. 1988 on 'Shanachie'; SH 79015)*

1979. (lp) *(SHY 7010)* **SO MANY PARTINGS** [ ] [-]
– A scare o' tatties – Lyndhurst / The valley of Strathmore / Bridget O'Malley / A.A. Cameron's Strathspey – Mrs. Martha Knowles – The Pitnacree ferryman / The new shillin' / Donald McGillavry – O'Neill's cavalry march / The highland clearances / Miss Catherin Brosnan / Wi' ma dog and gun / Miss Shepherd – Sweeney's buttermilk / McGlinchey's reels. *(re-iss. 1988 on 'Shanachie'; SH 79016)*

— JOHN took off to join US-based outfit, RAINDOGS, although he always maintained a dual partnership with brother PHIL

— added **DOUGIE MACLEAN** (b.27 Sep'54, Dunblane) – guitar, fiddle, vocals (ex-PUDDOCK'S WELL)

— added **RON ASHBY** – drums

Oct 80. (7") *(SHY 100)* **TAKE THE HIGH ROAD. / DONALD McGILLAVRY** [ ] [-]

1981. (lp) *(SHY 7016)* **WILD & BEAUTIFUL** [ ] [-]
– If I was a blackbird / Pipe Major Donald Campbell – The orphan – The kestrel – Come up alang (jigs) / The pearl / The fisherman's song – Lament for the fisherman's wife / Hame, hame, hame – Tha mi sgith (I am tiered) / Tha mi sgith (I am tiered) – Eck Stewart's march – MacKenzie's fancy (marches) / Miss Patricia Meagher – Laura Lynn Cunningham / A.B. Corsie (the lad from Orkney) – Ril bheara – Richard Dwyer's (reels). *(re-iss. 1988 on 'Shanachie'; SH 79028)*

— now without DOUGIE who was already a solo artist

— SILLY WIZARD featured on the V/A set, 'Winterfolk' in 1982

Nov 83. (lp/c) *(SHY/SHC 7025)* **KISS THE TEARS AWAY** [ ] [-]
– The queen of Argyll / Golden golden / Finlay M. MacRae / The banks of the Lee / Sweet Dublin bay / Monighean Donn, gradh mo chridhe / Banks of the Bann / The greenfields of Glentown / The Loch Tay boat song. *(re-iss. 1988 on 'Shanachie'; SH 79037) (cd-iss. Apr88; SHANCD 79037)*

— **JOHNNY** returned; **BOB THOMAS** – guitar; repl. ASHBY

R.E.L. / not iss.

Jun 85. (lp/c) *(RELS/RECS 476)* **LIVE IN AMERICA (live)** [ ] [-]
– Reels: The green fields of Glentown – The Galtee reel – Bobby Casey's number two – A.B. Corsie the lad from Orkney / The queen of Argyll – The valley of Strathmore / The parish of Dunkeld – The curlew / The ramblin rover / The banks of the Lee / John & Phil – reels: The humours of Tulla – Toss the feathers – Saint Anne's reel – Lexy MacAskill – The Limerick lasses – Jean's real – The musical priest / Reels: Mrs. Martha Knowles – The Pitnacree ferryman – The new bob.

Oct 85. (lp/c) *(RELS/RECS 478)* **GOLDEN, GOLDEN** (compilation) [ ] [-]
(c re-iss. Oct93 on 'Green Linnet'; CSIF 3037)

— final line-up **ANDY, JOHNNY, PHIL, MARTIN, GORDON + KATHY STEWART**

Green Linnet / Green Linnet

Feb 87. (lp/c) *(<SIF/CSIF 1070>)* **A GLINT OF SILVER** [ ] [ ]
– Roarin' Donald – The man who shot the windmill – A glint of silver / The secret portrait – Wha'll be king but Cherlie / Lover's heart / When summer ends / The chill eastern winds / Willie Archer / Simon MacKenzie's welcome to his twin sisters – Farewell to "the heb" / The blackbird of sweet Avondale. *(cd-iss. Apr88; GLCD 1070)*

— split after a farewell gig in New York, 1988; JONES and THOMAS formed 'Harbourtown' records, STEWART worked with MANUS LUNNY, HADDEN was part of HADDEN, (JANE) ROTHFIELD and (ALLAN) CARR – he later joined The BENACHALLY CEILIDH BAND – while PHIL went solo and formed RELATIVITY with brother JOHNNY

– compilations, etc. –

1985. (lp) *Shanachie; (SHAN 79048)* **THE BEST OF SILLY WIZARD** [ ] [-]
– Valley of Strathmore / Donald McGillavry – O'Neill's cavalry march / A.A. Cameron Strathspey – Mrs Martha Knowles – The Pitnacree ferryman – The new shillin' / Fisherman's song / Queen of Argyll / Finlay M. MacCrae / The pearl / Isla waters / Mo chuachag laglach (My kindly sweetheart) / Broom o' the Cowdenknowes / Green fields of Glentown – The Galtee reel – Bobby Casey's numbere two – Wing Commander Donald MacKenzie's reel. *(cd-iss. Nov98; SHANCD 79048)*

Oct 93. (d-cd) *Green Linnet; (<GLCD 3036-7>)* **LIVE WIZARDRY** (live Sanders theater, Cambridge, Massachusetts, USA) [ ] [ ]
– The green fields of Glentown – The Galtee reel – Bobby Casey's No.2 / A.B. Corsie, the lad from Orkney / The queen of Argyll / The valley of Strathmore / The parish of Dunkeld / The ramblin' rover / The banks of the Lee / The humours of Tulla – Toss the feathers – Saint Anne's reel – Lexy MacAskill / The Limerick lasses – Jean's reel – The musical priest / Mrs. Martha Knowles – The Pitnacree ferryman – The new Bob – Miss Shepherd – Sweeney's buttermilk – McGlinchey's reels / Donald McGillavry / The blackbird / Scarce o' tatties – Lyndhurst / Golden, golden / Mae's fancy – The cliffs of Moher – The rose of red hill – Clootie dumplings / The laird o' Drumblair – Sleepy Maggie / The broom o' the Cowdenknowes.

Dec 97. (cd) *Lapwing; (LAPCD 130)* **THE EARLY YEARS** [ ] [-]

Rod SINCLAIR (see under ⇒ Springthyme records)

SISTERS UNLIMITED (see under ⇒ RUSSELL, Janet)

SKYEDANCE (see under ⇒ FRASER, Alasdair)

SMALLTALK (see under ⇒ OSSIAN)

SONGHUNTER (see under ⇒ THORBURN, Andy)

SPRANGEEN (see under ⇒ SILEAS)

STAIRHEID GOSSIP (see under ⇒ Greentrax records)

Isla ST. CLAIR

Born: 1952, Aberdeenshire. The daughter of noted songwriter ZETTA ST. CLAIR, ISLA started singing and composing before she'd even reached her teens. Her early career as a folk singer saw her signing to 'Decca' in 1979, releasing the 'ISLA' album and a further clutch of flop singles in the early 80's. More successful was her subsequent move into TV work as BBC producers picked her out for the role of assistant to Larry "Shut That Door" Grayson on legendary Saturday night game show, 'The Generation Game'.

After leaving the show, ISLA founded her own production company specialising in traditional music and film. Targeting an international audience, ISLA released a series of albums centering on various historical themes including 'MURDER & MAYHEM', 'ROYAL LOVERS & SCANDALS' and 'CELTIC LEGENDS', the latter a soundtrack to the award winning video series, 'The Powerful Story Of The Great Highland Bagpipes'. Also included in this series was the acclaimed 'When The Pipers Play, a video/CD celebrating both the Scottish and Irish bagpipes. Among the record's many highlights was the rousing title track, featuring ISLA backed by both a grand string section and a troupe of 100 pipers at Edinburgh's Holyrood Palace. The singer has also made occasional forays into TV and radio, most famously on the award winning BBC TV series, 'The Song And The Story'.

ISLA ST. CLAIR – vocals / with various backing

Decca not iss.

Nov 79. (7") *(FR 13881)* **CHILD IN A MANGER. / NATIVITY** ☐ -
Nov 79. (lp) *(SKL 5317)* **ISLA** ☐ -

Ariola not iss.

Oct 80. (7") *(AHA 566)* **SONGBIRD. / YURI** ☐ -

Tangent not iss.

Apr 81. (lp/c) *(TGS/+MC 112)* **SINGS TRADITIONAL SCOTTISH SONGS** ☐ -

Clare not iss.

Jul 81. (lp) *(ISLA 1)* **THE SONG AND THE STORY** ☐ -

Stiletto not iss.

Nov 82. (7") *(STL 4)* **CHRISTMAS DREAM. / THE WAY IT USED TO BE** ☐ -

Dingles not iss.

1983. (7") *(SID 36)* **STILL NO SIGN OF THE LIFEBOATS. / EVERYTHING'S TURNED OUT FINE** ☐ -

— ISLA took a long sabbatical from recording until . . .

— next with **ALLEN PARK** – keyboards, arranger, etc / **BENNY GALLAGHER** – accordion

Moidart not iss.

Jun 93. (cd/c) *(MOI CD/MC 008)* **INHERITANCE** ☐ -
– The flowers of the forest / Ye Jacobites by name / Smile in your sleep / Fareweel to Tarwathie / Fear a' bhata / MacCrimmon's lament / The 51st Highland Division's farewell to Sicily / Come ye o'er frae France / Hush ye noo / The Norland wind / Freedom come-all-ye / The hills of Ardmorn. *<US cd-iss. Jun97; same as UK>* *(re-iss. Jun99; same)*

— next with **IAN HARDIE** – fiddle, double bass / **PHIL CUNNINGHAM** – multi / **TONY McMANUS + BOB THOMAS** – acoustic guitars

Greentrax Greentrax

Oct 96. (cd/c) *(<CD/C TRAX 119>)* **SCENES OF SCOTLAND** ☐ ☐ Nov96
– Lest we forget (poem) / Queen Edinbro' / Couthy Cullen / Ballachulish / Call tae arms (poem) / Lament for the commandos – Dunkirk / Lullin' the littlin' / Toast to Stornaway / The lifeboat / Spinning wheel / Glen Isla – Green ruby waltz / Glencoe / The bonnie boats o' Buckie / Poet and lover (poem).

Oct 97. (cd/c) *(<CD/C TRAX 145>)* **TATTIES & HERRIN' – THE LAND** ☐ ☐ Dec97
– Tatties & herrin' / The plooman laddies / Wi' my rovin' eye / Arlin's fine braes / Up the Noran water / Bogie's bonnie belle / Kirk o' Birnieboozle / Drumdelgie / Chairlie o' Chairlie / Band o' shearers / Johnny Sangster / Guise o' tough / Barnyeards o' Delgaty / Nicky Tams / The dying ploughboy / Twa recruitin' sergeants / Emigrants farewell to Donside / Hilly's man / Tatties & herrin'.

Oct 97. (cd/c) *(<CD/C TRAX 146>)* **TATTIES & HERRIN' – THE SEA** ☐ ☐ Dec97
– Tatties & herrin' / Song of the fishgutters / Skippin barfit / Lullin the littlin' / Children's nonsense songs / Bonnie fisher lass / Fisherman's lassie / Shoals of herring / Greenland whale / Fareweel tae Tarwathie / Mermaid / Bonnie boats o' Buckie / Herrin's heid / Johnny my man / Will your anchor hold? / Lifeboat / Song of the fisherman's wife / Couthy Cullen / Tatties & herrin'.

R.E.L. not iss.

Oct 98. (cd) *(RECD 528)* **WHEN THE PIPERS PLAY** ☐ -
– When the pipers play / Ticonderoga / Teady O'Neale / The piper at the Alamo / Flowers of the forest / American piper / French king's bodyguard / Mouth music / Irish dance / Twa recruiting sergeants / Muir of Culloden / A hundred pipers.

— with **JOE O'DONNELL** – fiddle / **DANNY PRENDERGAST** – guitar

May 00. (cd) *(REHCD 533)* **MURDER & MAYHEM** ☐ -
– Baron of Brackley / Battle of Harlaw / Barthams dirge / Twa corbies / Banks of sweet Dundee / Helen of Kirkconnell / Eppie Morrie / Reynardine / Lammikin.

Jun 00. (cd) *(REHCD 532)* **ROYAL LOVERS AND SCANDALS** ☐ -
– Barbara Allen / Earl of Errol / Matty Groves / Marie Hamilton / Gaberlunzie man / Queen Jane / Bonnie Earl of Moray / Bonnie house of Airlie.

Davy STEELE (see under ⇒ CALEDON)

Savourna STEVENSON

Born: Of Scottish & English parentage, although she currently lives in Scotland. One of the country's most accomplished small harp players, SAVOURNA has made the instrument her own by exploring its possibilities in the contexts of world music, blues and jazz as well as its more familiar folk setting. Her recording career began back in 1984 with the release of 'TICKLED PINK', an album which not only showcased her talents as an arranger of traditional works but unveiled a few of her own compositions.

Her increasingly experimental approach was evident in 1990's 'TWEED JOURNEY', a long awaited sophomore effort which found STEVENSON's harp at the forefront of a 7-piece ensemble comprising major players from Scotland's rock and jazz scenes. 'CUTTING THE CHORD' (1993) meanwhile, saw her team up with veteran folk/jazz double-bassist DANNY THOMPSON, a man who brought the midas touch to JOHN MARTYN's classic 70's albums and a former PENTANGLE member. In the mid-90's SAVOURNA appeared alongside a raft of stars (including THOMPSON, fiddle maestro ALY BAIN and ubiquitous Irishman DONAL LUNNY) in the TV series, 'Transatlantic Sessions'. She also wrote the music for a BBC TV documentary on the life and times of Scottish novelist Robert Louis Stevenson, released on CD as 'TUSITALA, TELLER OF TALES' (1995).

Following on from a successful tour together, STEVENSON, THOMPSON and JUNE TABOR recorded 1996 collaborative set, 'SINGING THE STORM', a collection of songs both commissioned for, and initially performed at the 1995 Borders Festival. More recently, STEVENSON worked with former MOVING HEARTS man, DAVY SPILLANE on the 'CALMAN THE DOVE' album (1998), while another solo set, 'TOUCH ME LIKE THE SUN' (2000) featured EDDI READER and WENDY WEATHERBY.

SAVOURNA STEVENSON – harp / with **ALY BAIN** – fiddle

Springthyme not iss.

1985. (lp/c) *(SPR/+C 1016)* **TICKLED PINK** ☐ -

Eclectic not iss.

Dec 90. (cd/c) *(ECL 9001 CD/TC)* **TWEED JOURNEY** ☐ -
– Aeolian / Basse Breton rhapsody / Cutting the chord / Harplands / Blues in 10. *(re-iss. Jan96; same)*

— next with **DANNY THOMPSON** – double bass (ex-PENTANGLE)

Jul 93. (cd/c) *(ECL 9308 CD/TC)* **CUTTING THE CHORD** ☐ -
– The source / Fording the Tweed / Waulk from the Tweed / Lost bells / Trows & Cowdieknowes / Percussion solo / Forest flowers / Tweed journey. *(re-iss. Jan96; same)*

1995. (cd/c) *(ECL CD/TC 9412)* **TUSITALA, TELLER OF TALES** ☐ -
– Tusitala, teller of tales / Jeckyll & Hyde / Clyde to Sandy Hook / Across the plains / Mexican Monterey / Silverado squatters / La solitude / Modestine / Treasure Island & Long John Silver / Road of the loving heart / Child's garden & the kidnapped reel / Island seas / Molokai. *(re-iss. Jan96; same)*

— next with Irishman **DAVY SPILLANE** – whistles, Uilleann pipes / **ANNE WOOD** – fiddle

Cooking Vinyl Cooking Vinyl

— in May'96, SAVOURNA was credited on the CD album, 'SINGING THE STORM' w/ JUNE TABOR and DANNY THOMPSON for 'Cooking Vinyl'; *COOKCD 102)*

Jan 98. (cd; by SAVOURNA STEVENSON & DAVY SPILLANE) *(<COOKCD 137>)* **CALMAN THE DOVE** ☐ ☐
– Calman the wolf / The white swan / An buachaille / Calman the dove / Where there's women there's trouble / I mo chridh / Mesmerising Nessy / The bell ringer / Sith as a Ghaillionn.

— next with guests **WENDY WEATHERBY** – cello / **MAIRI CAMPBELL** – violin, viola / **EDDI READER** – vocals

Mar 00. (cd) *(<COOKCD 192>)* **TOUCH ME LIKE THE SUN** ☐ ☐
– Emily's calling / Touch me like the sun / Fording the Tweed / Blue orchard / Come try me / No false love / A thousand curses / Dug's lugs / Tickled blue.

Al STEWART (see ⇒ Section 7: Rock & Pop)

Andy M. STEWART

Born: ANDREW McGREGOR STEWART, 8 Sep'52, Alyth, Perthshire. Brought up amidst traditional Scottish song and poetry by his music loving parents, ANDY's own stage career began with PUDDOCK'S WELL, a high school band also numbering a young DOUGIE MACLEAN. The group made quite a name for themselves locally, landing a residence at Blairgowrie Folk Club and even supporting top Scots folk-rock outfit, SILLY WIZARD. They were so impressed with STEWART they recruited him themselves following the subsequent demise of PUDDOCK'S WELL.

From the mid-70's through to the band's final years in the mid-80's, ANDY was an integral part of SILLY WIZARD, recording eight albums and touring worldwide, especially in the States. He launched his own solo recording career with 1982's well received 'BY THE HUSH' album, a combination of traditional pieces and self-penned material. 'FIRE IN THE GLEN' (1986), meanwhile, passed strong social comment on the Highland Clearances as ANDY shared the billing – and songwriting duties – with PHIL CUNNINGHAM and MANUS LUNNY. STEWART and the Irish born LUNNY subsequently extended their partnership to a further two albums, namely 'DUBLIN LADY' (1988) and 'AT IT AGAIN' (1988), initiating STEWART's long standing deal with the 'Green Linnet' label of Ireland.

As the 90's saw LUNNY become increasingly involved with CAPERCAILLIE, STEWART teamed up with another Irishman, GERRY O'BEIRNE, who both produced, played on and and co-wrote his 'MAN

IN THE MOON' (1994) album. 'DONEGAL RAIN' followed in 1997, STEWART increasingly dividing his time between music and freelance technician work for TV and film companies.

ANDY M. STEWART – vocals, banjo, etc (ex-PUDDOCK'S WELL, ex-SILLY WIZARD) / with various friends

Highway not iss.

1982. (m-lp) *(SHY 7018)* **BY THE HUSH** – Haud your tongue dear Sally / The ramblin rover / By the hush / The orphans' wedding / Patrick Sheehan / The parish of Dunkeld – The curlew / They wounded old Ireland / I'd cross the wild Atlantic. *(re-iss. Apr86; same) (cd-iss. Oct89 on 'Wundertute'; CDTUT 72138) (re-iss. Oct93 on 'Green Linnet' cd/c; GLCD/CSIF 3030)*

— teamed up with Edinburgh-born **PHIL CUNNINGHAM** and **MANUS LUNNY** (b. 8 Feb'62, Dublin) – bouzouki, guitar, vocals

Topic not iss.

Nov 86. (lp; by ANDY M. STEWART, PHIL CUNNINGHAM & MANUS LUNNY) *(12TS 443)* **FIRE IN THE GLEN** – Treorachadh – I mourn for the islands / The gold claddagh ring / Fire in the glen / The spare shillin' – The Viszla's rambles – The lying dew – Nil so I nGra (She's not in love) / Watkins' wee red whiskers – All hail to Mevagissey – The girls at Martinfields / Young Jimmy in Flanders / Brighidin ban mo store / Ferry me over . *(cd-iss. 1989 on 'Wundertute'; CDTUT 72153) (cd re-iss. Oct89 on 'Shanachie'; SHAN 79062CD)*

Green Linnet Green Linnet

Apr 88. (lp/c; by ANDY M. STEWART & MANUS LUNNY) *(<SIF/CSIF 1083>)* **DUBLIN LADY** – Take her in your arms / Where are you (tonight I wonder) / Dublin lady / Freedom is like gold / Bogle's bonnie belle / Dinny the piper – Amhran na tae (song of the tea) / Heart of the home / The humours of whiskey / Tak' it, man, tak' it. *(<cd-iss. Feb92; GLCD 1083>)*

— next collaboration with also **RONAN BROWNE, DAMIEN QUINN, CHARLIE McKERRON + DONALD SHAW**

Nov 88. (lp/c; by ANDY M. STEWART & MANUS LUNNY) *(<SIF/CSIF 1107>)* **AT IT AGAIN** – At it again / My heart it belongs to she / The Haughs of Cromdale / The exile of Erin air – I mo sheasamh ar an tra (as I stand on the beach) / Tae the weaver's gin ye go / If I never spent a morning without you / Monday morning / Brid og ni mhaille – Bridgit O'Malley / Mary Mheaigi's (reel) – Frank Mors (hornpipe) – The trip to Lerwick (jig). *(<cd-iss. Feb92; GLCD 1107>)*

— with **GERRY O'BEIRNE** – guitars, keyboards, etc / **PHIL CUNNINGHAM** – accordion, keyboards, etc / **KATHY STEWART** – vocals / + others

Apr 94. (cd/c) *(<GLCD/GLC 1140>)* **MAN IN THE MOON** – The echo mocks the corncrake / Island of sorrows / The Gaberlunzieman / The man in the moon / Kathy-Anne's waltz / Listen to the people / Sweet king William town / The errant apprentice / MacGregor's gathering / The lakes of Pontchartrain / The land o' the Leal.

Nov 97. (cd) *(<GLCD 1183>)* **DONEGAL RAIN** – Ramblin' Irishman / Matt Hyland / Gallant Murray (gathering of Athole) – White rose / Queen amongst the heather / Tibbie Fowler o' the glen / Reckless affection / Irish stranger / Mary and the hielan' sodger / Banks of sweet Dundee / When you took your love / Donegal rain.

– compilations, others, etc. –

1988. (cd) *Wundertute; (TUT 72.140)* **THE SONGS OF ROBERT BURNS** - - Germany – Rantin' rovin Robin / Ca' the yowes to the knowes / Is there for honest poverty (for a' that) / Green grow the rashes, O / Ae fond kiss / Hey, ca' thro' / Hey how Johnie lad / The lea-rig / It was a' for our rightfu' king / A red, red rose / To the weaver's gin ye go. *(re-iss. 1992 & May94 on 'Green Linnet' cd/c; GLCD/CSIF 3059)*

— ANDY M. STEWART also featured on many an Irish V/A compilation set including 'THE CELTS RISE AGAIN' with LUNNY.

Belle STEWART (and Family)

Born: 18th July, 1906, Caputh, nr. Blairgowrie, a direct descendent of 'tinker' families and clans who scattered after the battle of Culloden, 1746. A member of the proud STEWART family – highly regarded as one of the most authentic bearers of the oral tradition in Europe – BELLE was first brought to the folk community's attention by School of Scottish Studies researcher Maurice Fleming who discovered BELLE and her family working at the Blairgowrie berry harvest. This piqued the interest of A.L. LLOYD at the 'Topic' label who released 'THE STEWARTS OF BLAIR' (1972) and 'THE TRAVELLING STEWARTS' (1973) under the The STEWART FAMILY banner. In 1977, the same imprint furnished BELLE (now nearing pensionable age!) with her first and only solo LP, 'QUEEN AMONG THE HEATHER'. Following her death in September 1997, 'Greentrax' paid tribute to her legacy by re-releasing the latter set on CD.

BELLE STEWART – vocals / with her family; **CATHY, SHEILA + ALEX**

Topic not iss.

1972. (lp; by The STEWART FAMILY) *(12T 138)* **THE STEWARTS OF BLAIR** – Huntingtower / Caroline of Edinburgh town / In London's fair city / Queen amang the heather / The dowie dens o' Yarrow / The lakes o' Shillin / Over yon hills there lives a lassie / The convict's song / Young Jamie Foyers / The concrake amang the Whinney / Busk, busk bonnie lassie / March, Strathspey & reel: Leaving Lismore – The 74th farewell to Edinburgh – The shepherd's crook – Miss Proud. *(cd-iss. 1994 as 'ALEX, BELLE, CATHY & SHEILA' on 'Ossian'; OSSCD 96)*

1973. (lp; by The STEWART FAMILY) *(12T 179)* **THE TRAVELLING STEWARTS** – Johnnie my man / Willie's fatal visit / The battle o'er / Scotland the brave / The 51st Division in Egypt / Bogie's bonnie belle / McGinty's meal and ale / My bonnie Tammy / McPherson's lament / Drunken piper / Brig o' Perth / The reel of Tulloch / Loch Dhui / Dawning of the day / Donald's return to Glencoe.

1977. (lp) *(12TS 307)* **QUEEN AMONG THE HEATHER** – Queen among the heather / Here's a health to all true lovers / Betsy belle / The berryfields of Blair / The soft country chiel (the toon o' Dalry) / Whistlin' at the ploo' / Bonnie wee lassie frae Gourock / The overgate / Blooming Caroline o' Edinburgh toon / Busk, busk, bonnie lassie (Bonnie Glenshee) / Late last night / The twa brothers / Leezie Lindsay. *(cd-iss. Oct98 on 'Greentrax'; CDTRAX 9055)*

Folktrax not iss.

Nov 79. (c; by BELLE STEWART & FAMILY) *(60182)* **THE BONNY HOOSE O' BLAIR** – Betsy belle / Burning sands of Egypt / Two pretty boys / Muckin' o' Geordie's byre / Twa heids are better than yin / The dowie dens o' Yarrow / Lass o' Bon Accord / Ramblin' Irishman / Mist covered mountain / Bonnie wee Jeannie Mackay / De'il in the kitchen / London society / Galway maid behind the bar / Happy ol' days / Step dance / Three gallant sons / Loch Dhui / Nobleman's wedding / Gay Gordons.

Lismor not iss.

Jul 85. (lp/c; by BELLE STEWART & FAMILY) *(LIF L/C 7010)* **THE STEWARTS O' BLAIR** – Come a' ye jolly ploomen / Lakes of Shillin / Bonnie hoose o' Airlie / Moving on song / A nobleman / Jock Stewart / Inverness-shire / Banks of the Lee / Betsy belle / Dawning of the day / My dog and gun / The Berryfields o' Blair / I'm no coming oot the noo / Mickey's warning / Hatton woods / The parting song / Canntaireachd. *(cd/c-iss.Aug94 on 'Ossian'; OSS 96 CD/C)*

— BELLE died in September, 1997.

Chaz STEWART (see under ⇒ Macmeanmna records)

Davey STEWART (see under ⇒ Springthyme records)

Davie STEWART

Born: 1901, Dundee. DAVIE was the cloth-capped, street busking button-accordion player and vocalist who released several cassettes ('SCOTS BALLADS', 'TWO SCOTS TINKERS TALES' and 'LIFE TRAVELLING ROADS') in the 50's & 60's. He died in October 1972. Alongside friend JIMMY MacBEATH and JOHN STRACHAN, he would be sadly missed by folklore giants ALAN LOMAX and HAMISH HENDERSON.

His posthumous 1978 LP for 'Topic' records finally gained enough respect for IAN GREEN at 'Greentrax' to give it a CD re-issue 20 years on. Tracks such as 'I'M OFTEN DRUNK AND I'M SELDOM SOBER' and 'THE DAFT PIPER' were typical of a man who's sold thousands of records worldwide. His rendition of 'MacPHERSON'S RANT' was definitely the most unique version I've ever heard, IVOR CUTLER must've taken note. DAVIE perhaps took inspiration from Native Indian war cries for his novel cantering interpretation of 'THE 74th HIGHLANDERS' FAREWELL TO EDINBURGH' and 'DOWIE DENS O' YARROW', an unintentionally thigh-slapping treat for anyone not familiar with this surreal, nonsensical (at least to unschooled modern ears) style of song.

DAVIE STEWART – vocals, squeezebox

Topic not iss.

1978. (lp) *(12T 293)* **DAVIE STEWART** – MacPherson's rant / The jolly beggar / Cantering: The 74th Highlanders farewell to Edinburgh – The piper's bonnet – Mrs MacLeod of Raasay / I'm often drunk and I'm seldom / Jigs: Taghter Jack Walsh – The Connaughtman's ramble / The overgate / The merchant's son / The daft piper / Boolavogue / Hornpipe" Harvest home / The Dowie dens o' Yarrow. *(cd-iss. Jul98 on 'Greentrax'; CDTRAX 9052)*

– compilations, others, etc. –

Nov 79. (c) *Folktracks; (60-180)* **THE DOWIE DENS O' YARROW** -
Nov 79. (c) *Folktracks; (60-462)* **THE TINKER'S TALE** -
Jun 99. (cd) *Smith Mearns; (SMR 081CD)* **DAVIE STEWART ENTERTAINS YOU** -
Jan 00. (cd) *Smith Mearns; (SMR 101CD)* **CEILIDH AND OLD-TIME DANCING** -

Jan 02. (cd) *Rounder; (<ROUCD 1833>)* **GO ON, SING ANOTHER SONG**
– The Tarves rant / The hash O Bennagoak / Last night I was in the Granzie / Onything at all for a few coppers (interview) / Mormond braes / Go on, sing another song (interview) / Tramps and hawkers / A wagon of their own, maybe three or four ponies (interview) / McGinty's meal and ale / The first song that I ever learned (interview) / MacPherson's rant / (Auld Jock) Bruce of the fornet / Nicky Tams / The Highland tinker / Maggie the milkmaid / The dying ploughboy / Jamie Raeburn / Bing avree, dilly (interview) / The dowie dens of Yarrow.

Lucy STEWART (see under ⇒ Greentrax records)

Margaret STEWART & Allan MacDONALD (see under ⇒ Greentrax records)

John STRACHAN

Born: 1875, Crichie, Aberdeenshire. Another farmer (like JIMMY MacBEATH and DAVIE STEWART) to come from the hills and glens of Aberdeenshire, STRACHAN (who was now over 75!) sat down in front of folklorist, Alan Lomax to record ballads and conversation. His gritty Scots brogue was finally heard many years after his death (on the 2nd of November, 1958) when 'Rounder' records issued the Lomax sessions as 'SONGS FROM ABERDEENSHIRE' (2002).

JOHN STRACHAN – vocals

- compilations, etc. -

Jan 02. (cd) *Rounder; (<ROUCD 1835>)* **SONGS FROM ABERDEENSHIRE**
– The hairst of Rettie / The miller of Straloch / Glenlogie / The beggar man / Rhynie / The merchant's son / The minister's daughters they were three / Fin the bed began tae heat / Binnorie, o Binnorie / The knight and the shepherd's daughter / The stootest man in the forty twa / Bonny Udny / The bonny lass of Fyvie / Cylde's water / The laird of Drum / Robin Hood / MacPherson's rant / Johnnie O Braidislie / The guise of tough / The bogheid crew / Harrowing time / Where the gadie rins / Lang Johnnie more / I had some far better verses than that.

STRAMASH (see under ⇒ Greentrax records)

STRAVAIG (see under ⇒ Greentrax records)

Isabel SUTHERLAND

Born: 1921, Edinburgh, daughter of an antique dealer father and singer mother from Tannochside in Lanarkshire. In the mid-50's, ISABEL began singing alongside her friends SIMON and ELLA WARD, although it would be in London (at the "Good Earth Club" in Soho in 1954) that she would gain vital experience. In December 1959, she went into the recording studio with producer PETER KENNEDY, the results being released some time later by 'Folktracks'. Described as playing "mouth music" (port-a-beul) mostly unaccompanied on "big" sounding traditional Scottish ballads. Of course, she was better known for her association with folk legend EWAN MacCOLL and his group of friends believed to be part of the Communist Party. Her recordings were to say the least, sparse, only two releases have managed to hit the independent shops, 'VAGRANT SONGS OF SCOTLAND' and the aforementioned '59 recording 'THE LICHT BOB'S LASSIE', er, not what you might think. ISABEL passed away in 1988.

ISABEL SUTHERLAND – vocals / some with **STEVE BENBOW** – guitar / **JOHN COLE** – harmonica

Topic / not iss.

1960. (lp) *(12T 151)* **VAGRANT SONGS OF SCOTLAND** [-]

—— ISABEL died in 1988

- compilations, others, etc. -

Apr 88. (c) *Folktracks; (FTX-062)* **THE LICHT BOB'S LASSIE** [-]
– The licht Bob's lassie / 'S'ann an Ile (It was in Isla) / The forlorn lover (or) False bride / The roving ploughboy / The lady o' the Denty doon-by / The two brothers (child #49) / The auld maid in the garret / Down by the Greenwood side-i-o (The cruel mother) / Lord Lovat / I'm a young bonny lassie / The beggar-man / The overgate / The bonny lad is lang a-growing / The bleacher lassie of Kelvin haugh / Reel of Tullochgorum – I lost my love and I care not / The moon shined on the bed last night / O love is teasin' / The four Maries.

SWAMPTRASH (see ⇒ Section 8: Rock, Pop & Indie)

Hudson SWAN (see under ⇒ Lochshore records)

TABACHE (see under ⇒ Lochshore records)

T

TANNAHILL WEAVERS

Formed: Paisley ... 1968. After honing their skills in the folk clubs of Glasgow, Edinburgh and beyond, the group signed to the 'Plant Life' label in the mid-70's. By this point, the line-up had evolved to comprise a completely new cast of musicians, namely ROY GULLANE, HUDSON SWAN, PHIL SMILLIE and DOUGIE MACLEAN, the latter having been plucked from busking obscurity in Kinross. MACLEAN stayed with The 'WEAVERS for their first two albums, 'ARE YE SLEEPING, MAGGIE?' (1976) and 'THE OLD WOMAN'S DANCE' (1978) before going off to a hugely successful solo career.

Following on from a further two (eponymous) sets for the 'Plant Life' label either side of 1980, it'd be the middle of the decade before they signed their long standing deal with US imprint 'Green Linnet'. A core of GULLANE and SMILLIE remained steady in a regularly changing line-up, shaping the music policy over albums such as 'PASSAGE' (1984), 'LAND OF LIGHT' (1987), 'CULLEN BAY' (1991) and 'CAPERNAUM' (1994).

Regarded by many as Scotland's finest purveyors of traditional folk, the group's patented combination of acoustic guitars, fiddle, flute, bagpipes and bouzouki is often impassioned and compelling. In contrast to the likes of CAPERCAILLIE and RUNRIG, The TANNAHILL WEAVERS are rooted in a Lowland Scots tradition with the majority of their harmony-rich, immaculately arranged traditional ballads/songs sung in broad Scots as opposed to Gaelic. Hardly surprising then, that they've been known to reel off the odd RABBIE BURNS tune, most recently 'CRAIGIEBURN WOOD' and 'WESTLIN' WINDS' on 1998's excellent 'EPONA' album.

The WEAVERS' original material is also worthy of praise, chief songwriter GULLANE turning out a fine couple of politically-orientated numbers on the latter set in the shape of 'GREAT SHIPS' and 'RICH MAN'S SILVER'. More than three decades on from their inception, the band are still going strong, entering the new millennium with 'ALCHEMY' (2000).

DOUGIE MACLEAN (b.27 Sep'54, Dunblane) – fiddle, guitar, vocals / **ROY GULLANE** (b. Maryhill, Glasgow) – vocals, guitar, tenor banjo (from 1969) / **HUDSON SWAN** (b.31 Aug'54, Paisley) – fiddle, guitar, bouzouki (from 1972) / **PHIL SMILLIE** (b.22 Dec'55, Kelvin Hall, Glasgow) – flute, bodhran, vocals (from 1975) basically replaced originals JOHN CASSIDY (vocals, guitar, flute, whistles) / STUART McKAY (guitar, vocals) / DAVIE SHAW (bass, guitar) / GORDON DUNCAN (bagpipes)

Plant Life / not iss.

1976. (lp) *(PLR 001)* **ARE YE SLEEPING, MAGGIE** [-]
– Are ye sleeping, Maggie / Ferrickside / Galley of Lorne / Birnie Bouzle / Cam ye by Atholl / Hugaibh oirbh / The gypsy laddie / My love's in Germany / The overgate / Can ye yowes.

1978. (lp) *(PLR 010)* **THE OLD WOMAN'S DANCE** [-]
– Gloomy winter's now awa' / Wha'll dance wi Wattie / Traditional pipe major George Allan / The McGregors / Bonnie was yon Rosie Briar / The laird of Cockpen / The Irish washerwoman / The cook in the kitchen / Miss Girdle.

—— now without DOUGIE MACLEAN who went solo

1979. (lp) *(PLR 017)* **THE TANNAHILL WEAVERS** [-]
– The geese in the bog / the jig of slurs / Jock Stewart / Tae the weavers gin ye gang / The blackberry bush / Willie Cummings / The red speckled hen / Dalena McKay / The merchant's son / Doctor Ross' 50th welcome to the Argyllshire gathering / Ned of the hills / The gypsy laddie / Lady Mary / The De'il's awa' wi' the exciseman / Cam ye o'er frae France / Cameron McFadgen / The humours of Cork / The Skyeman's jig.

1981. (lp) *(PLR 028)* **TANNAHILL WEAVERS 4** [-]
– Johnnie Cope / The Athole highlanders / The trooper and the maid / The sound of sleat / I once loved a lass / Paddy O'Rafferty / Sandy Duff / Auld lang syne / Captain Carswell / Susan MacLeod / The cabar feidh / The Gaberlunzie man / Mrs. MacLeod of Raasay / The terror time / The birken tree / Lieutenant Maguire / Donald MacLean.

—— **LES WILSON** – bouzouki, keyboards (joined for a year in '82)

Green Linnet / Green Linnet

1984. (lp) *(SIF 3031)* **PASSAGE** [-]
– Roddie MacDonald's favourite / Jamie Raeburn's farewell / Harris and the mare / Duntroon – Trip to Alaska / The Highland laddie / At the end of a pointed gun /

Lady Dysie / The coach house reel – Marie Christinie – The coach house reel / Phuktiphano – John MacKenzie's fancy / Drink a round. *(<re-iss. Oct93 cd/c; GLCD/CSIF 3031>)*

Feb 87. (lp/c) *(SIF/CSIF 1067)* **LAND OF LIGHT** ☐ ☐
– Lucy Cassidy – The bletherskate – The Smith of Chilliechassie / The Scottish settler's lament / Donald MacLean's farewell to Oban – Dunrobin castle – The wise maid – Iain's jig / The rovin' heilandman / The yellow haired laddie – Dream Angus / Land of light / The queen amang the heather – Mairi Anne MacInnes / Bustles and bonnets / The American stranger / Conon bridge – Macbeth's Strathspey – Major David Manson – Mrs. MacPherson of Inveran. *(<cd-iss. Jun88; GLCD 1067>)*

— **ROY GULLANE + PHIL SMILLIE** / plus **ROSS KENNEDY** – bouzouki, bass pedals, vocals / **STUART MORRISON** – fiddles, guitars / **IAIN MacINNES** – bagpipes, etc (SWAN formed his own named band)

Apr 88. (lp/c) *(<SIF/CSIF 1081>)* **DANCING FEET** ☐ ☐ 1990
– Turf lodge – The Cape Breton fiddlers' – Welcome to the Shetland Isles – Lady Margaret Stewart – The flaggon / Tranent Muir / Isabeaux s'y promene banais mairead / Fisher row – Newmarket house / Wild mountain thyme / Maggie Lauder / The smokey lum – Maggie's pancakes – Dancing feet – The mason's apron / Mary Morrison / The Campbelltown kiltie ball – The back of the moon – Kelsae brig / Put me in the great chest – Sergeant MacDonald's reel / The final trawl.

— **LES WILSON** – vocals, bouzouki, keyboards (returned) + **JOHN MARTIN** – fiddle, cello, vocals; repl. KENNEDY (who formed a duo with ARCHIE McALLISTER) + MORRISON

Mar 91. (cd/c) *(<GLCD/CSIF 1108>)* **CULLEN BAY** ☐ ☐
– The standard on the braes o' Mar – The haughs o' Cromdale / The fiddler – The fiddler's jig – Jenny dang the weaver – The reel of Tulloch / Joy of my heart / Aikendrum / Samuel the weaver – The panda – Thunderhead – The Cannongate twitch – Allan MacDonald's reel / Kintail / A night visitor's song / Cullen Bay Dalnahassaig – S'Ionadh riud a chunnaic mi – Alick C. MacGregor / Braw burn the bridges.

— **KENNY FORSYTH** – bagpipes, whistles; repl. MacINNES

Nov 92. (cd) *(<GLCD 1121>)* **THE MERMAID'S SONG** ☐ ☐
– Greenwood side – Highland laddie – Pattie / Logie o' Buchan / Elspeth Campbell – Kenny Gilles of Portnalong, Skye – Malcolm Johnstone – Thornton jig / The cuillins of Rhum / The mermaid's song – The Herra boys – The fourth floor / Are ye sleeping Maggie? – The noose and the ghillie / A bruxa – Unknown / Come under my plaidie / Welcome Royal Charlie – Campbell's farewell to Redcastle / Flashmarket close – MacArther – Colonel Fraser – The swallow's tale / The ass in the graveyard.

Oct 94. (cd) *(<GLCD 1146>)* **CAPERNAUM** ☐ ☐
– The blackbird set: Blackley of Hillsdale – The blackbird – The hankie dance – Jack Daniel's reel – The farmer's daughter / Capernaum / The plooboy laddies – John Murray of Lochee / The unicorn set: The unicorn – Trip to Pakistan – An andro / The braes o' Balquhidder / The hieland sodger / The Carls o' Dysart / The log splitter set: Caradale bay – The log splitter – Calibachan – Drochaid luideach / The sound of Taransay / The brewer laddie – Cathkin braes / The Bergen / Gray Bob's set: Gray Bob – Cutty's wedding – Loch Carron – Gray Bob / Captain Ward – The streaker / Hame.

— **DUNCAN J. NICHOLSON** – bagpipes, whistles; repl. FORSYTH

Nov 96. (cd) *(<GLCD 1176>)* **LEAVING ST. KILDA** ☐ ☐
– Good drying set / Hieland Harry / The rigs o' rye / The Anthol gathering / St. Kilda set / The shearin's no for you / The three healths / Crann Tara set / The wars o' Germany / Islay Charms set / Last May a braw wooer / Fareweel you silver darlin's.

Sep 98. (cd) *(<GLCD 1193>)* **EPONA** ☐ ☐
– Interceltic set / When the kye come hame / Lord Drummond / The braes o' Gleniffer / The great ships / Carronside set / Rich man's silver / McGregor of Rora set / Craigieburn wood / Loch Tayside set / Westlin' winds / Robin Tamson's smiddy.

— **GED GRIMES** – bass, percussion; repl. FORSYTH

Oct 00. (cd) *(<GLCD 1210>)* **ALCHEMY** ☐ ☐
– The fair maid of Oban set / It was all for our rightful king / One for the road set / The gallant shearers / The Breton connection / Ower the moor amang the heather / For aye / The silver whistle set / Malley Leigh / Hebridean dream / Helen of Kirkconnell – Les Wilson's welcome to Lewis / The wagtail set.

– compilations, etc. –

Jul 92. (cd/c) *Green Linnet; (GLCD/CSIF 1100)* **THE BEST OF THE TANNAHILL WEAVERS 1979-1989** ☐ ☐
– The geese in the bog – Jog of slurs / Auld lang syne / Tranent muir / The Highland laddie / Lucy Cassidy – The bletherskate – The Smith of Chilliechassie / Farewell to Flunary – Heather island / Roddie MacDonald's favourite / The gypsy laddie / Jamie Raeburn's farewell / Johnnie Cope – The Atholl Highlanders / I once loved a lass / Turf lodge – The Cape Breton fiddlers / Welcome to the Shetland Isles – Lady Margaret Stewart – The flaggon.

Oct 97. (cd) *Green Linnet; (GLCD 1182)* **THE TANNAHILL WEAVERS COLLECTION - CHOICE CUTS 1987-1996** ☐ ☐
– The blackbird set / Wild mountain thyme / Capernaum / Crann Tara set / Joy of my heart – Kintail / The Carls o' Dysart – The log splinter set / Hieland Harry / The braes o' Balquhidder / Are ye sleeping Maggie? / Campbelltown kiltie ball / The cuillins of Rhum / The plooboy laddies – John Murray of Lochee / The good drying set / Braw burn the bridges.

TANNAS (see under ⇒ Lochshore records)

TARRAS

Formed: Borders, Scotland/England ... 1994 by JOSS CLAPP and ROB ARMSTRONG, two young teenagers inspired by Celtic/Brit-Folk and Blues, while also taking both genres into experimentation (they were noted to like JJ CALE and The PRODIGY!). They then added accordionist BEN MURRAY (son of North-East musician Phil Murray) and multi-instrumentalist JON REDFERN. Fiddler EMMA HANCOCK completed the line-up who signed to the re-actified 'Topic' label. The Spring of 1999 finally saw their more than promising debut set 'RISING' hitting the shops. Rootsy and energetic, it opened with the traditional song, 'PARSONS GREEN', while most of the others were self-penned numbers, highlights being 'MAGPIE'S REVENGE' and the polka-friendly 'MEN SHOULD WEAR THEIR LONG HAIR DOWN'. Towards the end of that summer, Roots label 'Rounder' thought it worthy of a US release, it seemed the band could be going a long way; Paul Birchall (noted for his work with M-PEOPLE) re-mixed a few of their subsequent tracks. At the start of 2001, a sophomore set 'WALKING DOWN MAIN STREET' (produced by Richard Evans), was well-received by the likes of Mojo, although the band had trimmed down to a trio of CLAPP, REDFERN and MURRAY; ARMSTRONG and others still augmented.

JOSS CLAPP – vocals, guitar, bass, mandolin / **BEN MURRAY** – vocals, accordion / **JON REDFERN** – vocals, percussion, guitar / **ROB ARMSTRONG** – cittern, vocals / **EMMA HANCOCK** – violin, whistle, vocals

Topic Rounder

Apr 99. (cd) *(TSCD 506) <617029>* **RISING** ☐ ☐ Sep99
– Parsons green / Whisky town / Magnadoodle / Oakey strike evictions / Da fields o 'Foula – My love is a fair lad / Captain Grant / Rising / Be real / The happy salmon / Magpie's revenge / So tired / Men should wear their long hair down / The long road home.

— now the basic trio of **CLAPP, MURRAY + REDFERN** with **ROB ARMSTRONG** plus **THEO CLAPP** – kit, keyboards / **MANNY ELIAS** – percussion / **JAMES PINNOCK + RORY FRANCIS** – djembe / **LUKE MURRAY** – soprano sax / **LOUISE PEACOCK** – violin / **SWEET NOTHINGS** – backing vocals

Apr 01. (cd) *(TSCD 524)* **WALKING DOWN MAIN STREET** ☐ ☐
– Arizona / The Russian & the radio / Fires / Los Troyas / Only one / The seige / Ye mariners – Cajun Malaysian / Calico / Dark eyed sailor / Bagels.

TARTAN AMOEBAS

Formed: Edinburgh-based ... 1992 by fiddle maestro and songwriting dynamo FRASER McNAUGHTON, who brought together various personnel for each album (in fact the word amoeba denotes "a single celled organism whose shape is perpetually changing"). Although they started out playing ceilidhs, the group's innovative approach soon created a demand for conventional live gigs and in 1993 they released their eponymous debut album on the independent 'Kaya'.

Native label, 'Iona' were suitably impressed by the band's cosmopolitan sound and snapped them up for 1995's 'IMAGINARY TARTAN MENAGERIE' (try saying that after a few drams). With pipes, guitar and brass bolstering their gung-ho musical approach, they galvanised audiences from the Edinburgh fringe to the Braveheart Premier's after-show party in Stirling. Younger and funkier than the likes of CAPERCAILLIE, The TARTAN AMOEBAS successfully flirted with a raft of exotic jazz, world and latin influences without compromising their traditional folk roots.

'EVOLUTION' (1997) was another bold step forward, demonstrating a reluctance to relinquish their ubiquitous funky backbeat and creating perhaps the first "Scotsploitation" track on record with the soundtrack chase-style 'GROOVY WEAN'. They also came up with what was very possibly the first ANANDA SHANKAR meets The ROYAL SCOTS DRAGOON GUARDS moment in pop history with 'TRANSCENDENTAL BRU'. Made, of course, in Scotland, by The TARTAN AMOEBAS.

1999's 'GIANT' opus was even better, a more mature and focused effort with a more convincing fusion of trumpet, bagpipes and violin in the likes of 'NEW DAY DAWNING'. 'RESCUE' and 'DAN' introduced haunting vocals courtesy of JULIE FOWLIS, while 'STRANGE DAYS' featured some spooky Twilight Zone-style theramin. The jazzy 'JEELY PIECE', meanwhile, stands as possibly their most realised funk'n'fling effort to date and bodes well for the future.

FRASER McNAUGHTON – fiddle, highland pipes / **GEORGE MacCALLUM** – trumpet / **BOB CARTER** – guitar / **ALEX FIENNES** – bass / **EUAN TURNER** – drums / **GUY NICOLSON** – percussion

Kaya / not iss.

Sep 93. (cd) *(KAYACD 1)* **TARTAN AMOEBAS** [ ] [-]
– Pinch of snuff / Reels of Tulloch / Lark in the morning / Miss Stewart / Loch Leven castle / Funky pipes / Dubh / Alex's reels / Johnnie Cope / Kwela. *(<re-iss. Jun97 on 'Greentrax'; CDTRAX 133>)*

— **FRASER** now with **BOB CARTER, JERRY HEPBURN, GUY NICOLSON, EUAN TURNER + the AMOEBAS HORNS**

Iona / not iss.

Nov 95. (cd/c) *(IRCD/IRC 034)* **IMAGINARY TARTAN MENAGERIE** [ ] [-]
– Ska-reggae / Sub Heaven / Penguin blues / Road rage / New pipe order / Briefcase shuffle / Claverhouse / I close my eyes / Adios amoebas.

— **FRASER** now with **BOBBY PINKMAN** – pipes / **SCOTT MONCRIEFF** – guitars / **MARK WOTHERSPOON** – drums / **JASON WOTHERSPOON** – bass / **TOM DALZELL + J. SIMON VAN DER WALT + STEVE KETTLEY** – horns

Aug 97. (cd) *(IRCD 058)* **EVOLUTION** [ ] [-]
– He ro ho ro hi / The watergaw / Transcendental bru / Face to face / Infinite snack mode / Big sky / Once / Putting up shelves / Changing light / A study in scarlet / Easy peasy / The groovy wean / Reggalypso.

— **FRASER + JASON + TOM + SCOTT** added **JULIE FOWLIS** – vocals, highland bagpipes / **PATRICK DEVLIN** – trumpet

— **GAVIN RUTLEDGE** – drums; repl. MARK

Jun 99. (cd) *(IRCD 066)* **GIANT** [ ] [-]
– New day dawning / Rescue / Giant / The vision / Dan / Head in the clouds / Strange days / Paper boats / Jeely piece / A last jig.

an TEALLACH CEILIDH BAND / BENACHALLY . . . Pete CLARK (see under ⇒ Springthyme records)

TEQUILA MOCKINGBIRD

Formed: Edinburgh ... 2000 by MARK DALZIEL, ROY HUNTER, GAIL GRAVES and lead singer SOOZINIZ. Along with several guest players, including accordion giant PHIL CUNNINGHAM, the excellently-named TEQUILA MOCKINGBIRD finally got around to releasing their folk-rock debut, 'AGORA MESMO', early in 2001. • **Trivia:** The website www.tequilamockingbird.com is not theirs but a US-based studio/group.

SOOZINIZ – vocals, guitar, fiddle / **MARK DALZIEL** – guitars, sitar, poetry, vocals / **ROY HUNTER** – bass, drums, vocals / **GAIL GRAVES** – percussion, vocals / plus guests **NIGEL BAILLIE** – flugel horn / **RONAN BRESLIN** – organ, trombone / **ALAN CRUIKSHANK** – drums / **PHIL CUNNINGHAM** – accordion / **SANDY NELSON** – mandolin / **BRIAN MacNEILL** – organ, synths / **GILL RISI + YSLA ROBERTSON** – violins

Tequila Mockingbird / not iss.

Feb 01. (cd) *(HICK 01)* **AGORA MESMO** [ ] [-]
– In her mind / Don't hold me down / Somewhere in between / Here and now / River / It's true, I do / Mesmo / Time and again / Almost home / Organised mess / Song No.7 / The ohmm.

Andy THORBURN

Born: Evanton, Ross-shire. A classically trained pianist, a composer, a teacher and a ubiquitous presence on the Scottish folk scene, the name of ANDY THORBURN has become increasingly synonymous with quality as the late 90's have given way to the new millennium. Included on the man's extensive CV are keyboard/accordion stints with The GHILLIES, The PEATBOG FAERIES, CEOLBEG, MOUTH MUSIC, SALSA CELTICA (on 2000's'The Great Scottish Latin Adventure') and WOLFSTONE (as well as The VAST MAJORITY, a side project involving the latter outfit's DUNCAN CHISHOLM and IVAN DREVER). As director and arranger, he also played a chief role in the SONGHUNTER project album, 'SPIRIT OF THE LAND' (1999), alongside JIM HUNTER, ANDREW MURRAY, GRAEME FLETT and HEATHER MacLEOD.

More recently, THORBURN has worked with BLAZIN' FIDDLES, DAVID MILLIGAN, JOHNNY HARDIE & GAVIN MARWICK, AZITIZ, BEN WYVIS and The LOVEBOAT BIG BAND. ANDY's talents extend to music publishing and have seen him typesetting a book of bagpipe tunes for RORY CAMPBELL and the complete works of RUNRIG amongst others.

In his own right, ANDY completed his Celtic Connections-commissioned first solo set, 'TUATH GU DEAS – NORTH TO SOUTH', early in the year 2000, having already completed a joint effort, 'SPIDER'S WEB', with IAN HARDIE back in 1998. He even branched into small screen work with the Celtic TV series 'Sruth Na Maoile', for which he took the role of musical advisor.

SONGHUNTER

ANDY THORBURN with **JIM HUNTER** – acoustic guitar, vocals / **ANDREW MURRAY** – guitars, vocals / **GRAHAM FLETT** – bass / **HEATHER MacLEOD** – vocals

G2 / G2

Feb 99. (cd) *(<G2CD 7004>)* **SPIRIT OF THE LAND** [ ] [ ] Mar99
– Spirits of the land / If wishes were horses / Jamestown / Gaol ghlinn oirinn / Red roses and razor blades / Manager / Diminished dreams / Falling leaves / Comfortable lie / Place of welcome / Hebridean island morning / Snow in Bordeaux / Close our eyes and sleep / Dover to Calais / Highland line.

ANDY THORBURN

ANDY THORBURN – keyboards, concertina

— in 1998, he teamed up with IAN HARDIE (ex-JOCK TAMSON'S BAIRNS) to release 'SPIDER'S WEB'

— next with **RORY CAMPBELL, ELSPETH COWIE, CHRISTINE KYDD, LINDSAY BLACK, MARY ANN KENNEDY, CHARLIE MacLEOD, HEATHER MacLEOD, MARY McMASTER, CORRINA HEWAT, JIM MALCOLM, ALYTH McCORMACK + ROD PATERSON**

Andy Thorburn / not iss.

Jan 00. (cd) *(ATMUFCD 1)* **TUATH GU DEAS – NORTH TO SOUTH** [ ] [-]
– An cuan / The tides / Calgacus / Solitudinem / Pacem appellant / From Dyneiddin / Trycant Eurdorch / 300 men / Nyt Atcorsant / Catraeth / Gospel according to / Arbroath rap / Statues of Iona / Shift Owre / Pacem appellant / There's Deils / Chi mi le mo / B'e anDolair / Eil thu deas / Watch us spin / Solitudinem faciunt / Fagail / Gaidhlig. Canan / The Deil aye taks / When the fight's / Sea mise mi.

— ANDY has since joined SALSA CELTICA

Simon THOUMIRE

Born: 11 Jul'70, Edinburgh. THOUMIRE made his first mark in the music world by winning the coveted BBC Radio 2 Young Tradition Award in his early teens. By his mid-20's, he'd become a respected composer, performer and producer, having notched up several TV and radio appearances including The Shetland Sessions and The Transatlantic Sessions alongside the likes of ALY BAIN and PHIL CUNNINGHAM. THOUMIRE's technical virtuosity on the concertina has found him in demand as not only a performer but a music teacher in both Britain and the USA.

On the recording front, he made his debut in 1990 with the critically acclaimed 'HOOTZ', a collaboration with guitarist IAN CARR (not the veteran jazz-fusionist). 1992's 'DEVIL'S DELIGHT' album was another collaborative effort, this time with roots act SEANNACHIE. In 1993, the multi-talented Scot formed his own trio, The SIMON THOUMIRE THREE alongside jazz musicians KEVIN MacKENZIE and BRIAN SHIELS. Formed with the aim of taking native traditional music into uncharted musical waters, the group have released two albums to date, 'WALTZES FOR PLAYBOYS' (1994) and 'MARCH, STRATHSPEY AND SURREAL' (1996). In addition, THOUMIRE has had two of his compositions aired at the annual Celtic Connections Festival in Glasgow: the 'Celtic Connections Suite' (a specially commissioned piece which was subsequently issued on CD – 1998) and 'Scottish Requiem' for strings brass and choir, a piece featuring Latin text translated into Scots. Since the mid-90's, he has also taken a major part in Yehudi Menuhin's 'Live Music Now!' project, writing a special piece for the organisation's 20th birthday which he subsequently performed alongside JENNIFER and HAZEL WRIGLEY at The Barbican in London.

In 1995, SIMON recorded the 'EXHIBIT A' album, alongside keyboard player FERGUS MACKENZIE, an experimental project aiming to combine folk music and contemporary dancefloor rhythms. Supergroup KEEP IT UP meanwhile, were THOUMIRE's seasoned but youthful traditionalists in both Scottish folk and jazz, SIMON, KEVIN MACKENZIE, EILIDH SHAW and MALCOLM STITT delivered their eponymous debut album towards the end of 1998 and saw it premiered at Denmark's Tonder Festival in summer 2000 – cool! From 1997, THOUMIRE has been the main man behind two joint record outlets, 'Tartan Tapes' and 'Foot Stompin' – for more see under Tartan Tapes.

SIMON THOUMIRE – concertina, pipes, bodhran, etc

Black Crow / not iss.

Oct 90. (lp/c; by SIMON THOUMIRE & IAN CARR) *(CRO 225/+MC)* **HOOTZ!** [ ] [-]

— at this stage, SIMON was also part of SEANNACHIE (two albums previously:- 'WITHIN THE FIRE' and 'TAKE NOTE'), who delivered another album in 1992, 'DEVIL'S DELIGHT'

— SIMON was next joined by **KEVIN MacKENZIE** – guitar / **BRIAN SHIELS**

Acoustic Radio | not iss.

Mar 94. (cd/c; as the SIMON THOUMIRE THREE) *(ARAD CD/C 102)* **WALTZES FOR PLAYBOYS** [ ] [-]

— next with **FERGUS MACKENZIE** – keyboards, percussion

Iona | not iss.

May 95. (cd/c; by SIMON THOUMIRE & FERGUS MACKENZIE) *(IRCD/IRC 031)* **EXHIBIT A** [ ] [-]
– By the right / Green man / Interaction / Topless / Totally tropical / Experience the real / Starjumping / 7 down / Overcast / Art of non-resistance.

Green Linnet | not iss.

Aug 96. (cd/c; as the SIMON THOUMIRE THREE) *(GLCD/GLC 1171)* **MARCH, STRATHSPEY & SURREAL** [ ] [-]
– John's got school tomorrow – The North Sea Chinaman – Bus spotter reel / Overcast / Bridge of Don / Mrs. Meddle's march, Strathspey, and surreal / Montropolis – Jig for Nina – The green pastures / Eddy Kelly's / Jim's jig – The snuff wife – Eileen MacDonald / Spare parts / Gloomy-go-round – Merry-go-round / Miss Laura Thoumire / Bob McQuillan's reel – Major role / Martin Wynne's No.1 – John McCusker's roof – Woof Vicky woof.

Tartan Tapes | not iss.

Nov 98. (cd; as the SIMON THOUMIRE ORCHESTRA) *(CDTT 1005)* **CELTIC CONNECTIONS SUITE** [ ] [-]
– Celtic connections club / Fiesta in the Highlands / World bagpipe championships / Gravy waltz / John Thoumire's castle / Reels.

Aug 99. (cd; as the SIMON THOUMIRE ORCHESTRA) *(CDTT 1007)* **MUSIC FOR A NEW SCOTTISH PARLIAMENT** [ ] [-]
– Doom no boom / Reflections 1 / Discussion begins / Reflections 2 / Your eyes are shut / Reflections 3 / Debate continues / All together again / Yes yes / Ceilidh for everyone / Views 1 (two people) / Views 2 (four people) / Counting canons / And freedom be our guide / The future's bright.

White Label | not iss.

1999. (cd) *(CDWH 1)* **SOLO1** [ ] [-]
– Swedish polska – 21 piece suite – Flowers of Edinburgh – Da new rigged ship – Trip to Windsor / 79th farewell to Gibraltar / Jim's jig – Thomas's jig – Haste to the wedding / Slow air / Maire's reel – Irish traditional reel – Scones of Bocgty / March for a new Scottish parliament – Prince Charles welcome to Simon Thoumire's concertina / Granton fish bowl / Ponyjigg / John Keith Lang – Julia Delaney – Charlie Lennon No.1.

THULBION (see under ⇒ Greentrax records)

TONIGHT AT NOON (see ⇒ Section 8: Rock, Pop & Indie)

Artie TREZISE (see under ⇒ FISHER, Cilla . . .)

Violet TULLOCH (see under ⇒ Greentrax records)

Jane TURRIFF (see under ⇒ Springthyme records)

Ian WALKER

Born: 27 Apr'48, Govanhill, Glasgow. Influenced by the local music scene of the 60's, IAN went one further by performing at the Glasgow Folk Centre where he developed a reputation. However, for various reasons, he took a hiatus from the live scene until the mid-70's. Returning to the fold at the turn of the decade, WALKER reapplied himself around the folk festival and club circuits and finally found a record label via Cumbrian-based, 'Fellside'. In 1988, his debut set, 'FLYING HIGH' was issued, opening track 'ROSES IN DECEMBER' and others such as 'SING ME A SONG MR BLOOM' and 'HAWKS AND EAGLES FLY LIKE DOVES' (the latter recorded by The McCALMANS and DICK GAUGHAN), a must for all would-be fans. Subsequent albums, 'SHADOWS IN TIME' (1989) and 1993's 'CROSSING THE BORDERLINES' (the latter with Lanarkshire-based traditional band SETANTA), were also pleasing to the ear.

Around this period, WALKER also worked abroad (Ireland, Germany and the States!) with folk supergroup, BLUE ROOSTER; also in line-up IAN BRUCE, IAN MURRAY and DEZ WALTERS. In 1994, he teamed up with Bo'ness singer, JIMMY SCOTT, the VANGEL duo debuting at East Lothian's annual Carberry Festival; an appearance alongside PADDIE BELL (ex-CORRIE FOLK TRIO) also marked them out at that year's Edinburgh Fringe Festival. VANGEL delivered their one and only (mail-order/net) long-player, 'BRAND NEW', late in 1998; WALKER and SCOTT continue to perform their own brand of gospel-folk.

IAN WALKER – vocals, acoustic guitar, banjo, autoharp

Fellside | not iss.

May 88. (lp/c) *(FE 060/+C)* **FLYING HIGH** [ ] [-]
– Roses in December / Sing me a song Mr Bloom / Beats of the heart / Too far from she / Don't turn the key / Some hae meat / Hawks and eagles fly like doves / Child on the green / Do you see my face / The greatest thrill / Amazing satellite picture show / Catch a rainbow.

Aug 89. (lp/c) *(FE 073/+C)* **SHADOWS IN TIME** [ ] [-]
– Shadows in time / Ladder of life / Portrait of a woman / Sun / Let me hear you smile / Ghost train / Dancing on the sun / When the bough breaks / Mountain boy / Blodwen's dream / Rising of the green / Million city lights.

May 93. (cd/c; by IAN WALKER & SETANTA) *(FE 088 CD/C)* **CROSSING THE BORDERLINES** [ ] [-]
– Polkas / Whatever you think / Slaibh gallion braes / Ring around the Moon / Ponte Isabella – The man of the house – The bucks of Oranmore / The healing touch / Remember Solferino / The soldiers return / The merry blacksmith – Miss Susan Cooper – Willafjord / St. Paul's song / An comhra donn – The Galtee rangers – The foxhunters / The anchor line.

— in 1998, he and JIMMY SCOTT issued the collaborative, 'BRAND NEW'

WATERBOYS (see ⇒ Section 8: Rock, Pop & Indie)

John WATT (see under ⇒ Springthyme records)

WE FREE KINGS (see ⇒ Section 8: Rock, Pop & Indie)

Sheena WELLINGTON

Born: c.1940's, Dundee. Born into a family steeped in folksinging, SHEENA seemed destined to carry on the tradition sooner or later. As it turned out, her full-scale involvement in the folk scene came later, after both she and her husband Malcolm had completed their respective stints in the Royal Navy. The couple bought a guest house in St. Andrews, Fife, where SHEENA became a resident singer and compere at the local folk club. Inspired by source singers BELLE STEWART and JEANNIE ROBERTSON, she also began hosting a traditional music show on Dundee's Radio Tay, initiating a fruitful broadcasting career that'd see her working for the BBC in both a TV and radio capacity.

Her recording career began in 1986 with the 'KERELAW' album on DOUGIE MACLEAN's 'Dunkeld' label, attracting widespread critical acclaim both at home and abroad. Follow-up 'CLEARSONG' was equally well received and though it'd be almost a decade before she released another album, her hectic schedule of writing, lecturing, teaching and performing kept her more than busy. In addition to her myriad Scottish appearances (including the Edinburgh Festival), SHEENA has toured successfully throughout Europe as well as the USA and Canada. A mark of her authority on matters traditional was her appointment to the Music Committee of the Scottish Arts Council in 1992, the first traditional musician to be granted such an honour.

A much anticipated live album, 'STRONG WOMEN', was released on 'Greentrax' in 1995, its moving BRIAN McNEILL-penned title track demonstrating the ringing, East Coast-accented purity of SHEENA's voice. She was the toast of the Glasgow's Celtic Connections Festival in 1996, although her most famous performance to date came three years later at the official reconvening of the Scottish Parliament. SHEENA's rendition of Robert Burns' 'A MAN'S A MAN FOR A' THAT' was deemed by many to be the highlight of the day, summing up the mood of a country once again in command of its own destiny.

Since 1997, SHEENA has also held the post Traditional Arts Development Officer for Fife Council, working ceaselessly to promote traditional music and dance throughout the area.

SHEENA WELLINGTON – vocals / with various backing

Dunkeld | not iss.

1986. (lp/c) *(DUN/+C 005)* **KERELAW** [ ] [-]
– Derwentwater's farewell / Newport braes / The death of Queen Jane / The Irish boy / The last leviathan / Bunch of thyme / Nicky Tams / Aileen Aroon / Eh'll bide a wiver O / Sheath and knife. *(cd-iss. Jul99; DUNCD 005)*

Jul 87. (lp/c) *(DUN/+C 012)* **CLEARSONG** [ ] [-]
– Women o Dundee / Beirut / Christ child's lullaby (Taladh Chriosa) / Yellow on the broom / My ain countrie / Where are ye now? / There was a lad / The Dandy & the Beano / Willie's fatal visit / Julia's song. *(<US + cd-iss. Jul94; DUNCD 012>)*

— next with **SIMON THOUMIRE** – concertina

Greentrax Greentrax

Oct 95. (cd/c) *(<CD/C TRAX 094>)* **STRONG WOMEN**
– Strong women rule us with their tears / Dark eyed Molly / Address the haggis / Mill O'Tifty's Annie / Tryst / Flase bride / Glasgow councillor / Slaves lament / Seattle / Great silkie O'Sule Skerrie / Shearin' / Waulkrife Minnie / Silver tassie / My luv's like a red red rose / Little Sunday school.

Mick WEST (see under ⇒ Lochshore records)

Mike WHELLANS

Born: c.1945, Galashiels, the Borders. Son of jazz drummer BOBBY WHELLANS, MIKE picked up his father's sticks by the time he was attending primary school; by the time he was 14 he was performing for local dance bands at weddings and functions. It would be during this period that MIKE turned his quicks hands to the guitar. Towards the end of the 60's, he decided to turn pro and teamed up with Shetland fiddler ALY BAIN (for one collaborative LP in '71). BAIN also invited him into the ranks of Irish-Scots folk outfit, The BOYS OF THE LOUGH, although WHELLANS only stayed until 1972 when he was superseded by DICK GAUGHAN. Influenced by the likes of JIMMY REED and WILLIE DIXON, it was inevitable that MIKE and his flat-picking guitar skills would turn to the blues; a solo set, 'DIRT WATER FOX' (1976), was proof in the pudding. To earn a crust, MIKE toured abroad and finally found an audience in Denmark where he settled in the late 80's. However, 'Temple' records boss ROBIN MORTON (also ex-BOYS OF THE LOUGH) tempted him back to cut what was to be his last studio outing, 'SWING TIME JOHNNY RED' (1990). A gutsy piece of live in the studio songwriting, Chicago was indeed, transported to the shores of Bonnie Scotland. Throughout the 90's MIKE continued to play festivals all around Europe, although his new home in Denmark (and Scandinavia) seemed to be his favourite haunt.

MIKE WHELLANS – vocals, guitar, mouth harp

Leader not iss.

1971. (lp; by MIKE WHELLANS & ALY BAIN) *(LER 2022)* **MIKE WHELLANS AND ALY BAIN** [ ] [-]

— next with **CILLA FISHER** – vocals / **COLIN BLAINE** – guitar / **BILLY JACKSON & THE CITIZEN'S BAND** – bass

Dara not iss.

Oct 76. (lp) *(MPA 016)* **DIRT WATER FOX** [ ] [-]

Temple Temple

Jul 90. (cd/c/lp) *(<COMD2/CTP/TP 036>)* **SWING TIME JOHNNY RED** [ ] [ ]
– Living in a nightmare / Sweet little Jenny / Same sweet thing / Down and outa hand / Movers and shakers / Howling for my baby / Swing time Johnny Red / Thinking about you baby / Too close for comfort / Sweet suspicion / Chicago and Southside / Desperate desire. *(cd/c re-iss. Feb94; same)*

WHIRLIGIG (see under ⇒ Lochshore records)

Nancy WHISKEY (see under ⇒ McDEVITT, Chas; Section 7: Rock & Pop)

WHISTLEBINKIES

Formed: Glasgow-based . . . late 60's by JIM DALY, GEORDIE McGOVERN, MICHAEL BRODERICK and SEANE McGEE. The WHISTLEBINKIES or "The Scottish Chieftans" as they are sometimes referred to, were spurred on in their formation by the Britain-wide 60's folk revival although unsurprisingly they chose to revive their own Scots/Celtic traditions. More specifically they pioneered the renewed interest in instruments such as the bellows-blown bagpipes.

While their eponymous 1971 debut set employed a familiar fiddle/mandolin/banjo set-up, 1977's 'THE WHISTLEBINKIES' (a second eponymous set but this time for 'Claddagh') utilised a more innovative combination of clarsach, pipes, fiddle and flute. While the emphasis remained on traditional material, the line-up had changed considerably with only BRODERICK surviving from the original line-up alongside newcomers EDDIE McGUIRE, RAB WALLACE and RAE SIDDALL. As well as featuring a memorable version of the late Hamish Henderson's 'FREEDOM COME ALL YE', 'WHISTLEBINKIES 2' (1980) revealed the previously unheard writing talents of WALLACE as well as the vocals of new harpist RHONA MacKAY. Presumably preferring to concentrate on the music rather then album titles, the group celebrated ten years of recording with 1981's 'THE WHISTLEBINKIES 3', welcoming new members MARK HAYWARD and STUART EYDMANN. The latter was to make a significant songwriting contribution to 1985's 'THE WHISTLEBINKIES 4' (at least LED ZEPPELIN had alternative titles!), an album that saw JUDITH PEACOCK take over from MacKAY. A fifth volume offered up more of the same in 1988, longtime fans knowing pretty much what to expect but anticipating a new album all the same.

Like many Scottish folk acts, The WHISTLEBINKIES spread the word far and wide, largely in Europe. Unlike many Scottish folk acts, however, the group toured in China, their 1991 visit earning them a place in the record books as the first Caledonian crew to do so. That year also saw the release of the 'INNER SOUND' album, the group subsequently going on to sign a deal with the thriving 'Greentrax' label. With folk more popular than ever in the 90's, 'A WANTON FLING' (1996) proved they could work up a sweat as easily as any of the young bucks, as did 1999's 'TIMBER TIMBRE'.

The band's CV also proves they're more than just a veteran folk act, a list of collaborators as varied as DAVID ESSEX, YEHUDI MENHUIN, CAPELLA NOVA and The SCOTTISH CHAMBER ORCHESTRA attesting to their versatility and innovative spirit.

MICHAEL BRODERICK – vocals, effects / **JIM DALY** – fiddle / **GEORDIE McGOVERN** – banjo, mandolin / **SEANE McGEE** – guitar

Deacon not iss.

1971. (lp) *(DEA 1053)* **THE WHISTLEBINKIES** [ ] [-]
– Twa recruiting sergeants / Sherrif Muir / Cradle song / James Conolly / Home boys home / Banks of the roses / Admiral Benbow / Sullivan John / Mormon braes / The Boston burglar.

— they recorded an album in East Germany (1975) – it's very obscure

— sole survivor **BRODERICK** recruited **RAB WALLACE** – pipes / **EDDIE McGUIRE** – fiddle, piccolo, clarsach / **RAE SIDDALL** – fiddle / plus **PETER ANDERSON** – side drum, bongos, bodhran + **CHARLES GUARD** – clarsach

Claddagh not iss.

1977. (lp/c) *(CC/4CC 22)* **THE WHISTLEBINKIES** [ ] [-]
– Alena MacAskill – MacDonald's exercise – Jig of slurs / Haughs o' Cromdale / Farewell to Nigg / Mrs MacLeod of Raasay – Mrs McGuire – Staten Island – Peat fire flame – Reel of Tulloch – High road to Linton / The battle of Sherriffmuir / March of Brian Boru – Eileen Aroon – O'Keefe's – Morrison's jig / Donald MacGillivray / Gillie Callum – The barn dance – Sleepy Maggie – The blacksmith's reel / The Royal Scottish pipers – The harper – The traditional reel / The Ness pipers.

— **BRODERICK, McGUIRE, WALLACE + ANDERSON** recruited **RHONA MacKAY** – clarsach, vocals + **BOB NELSON** – fiddle

1980. (lp/c) *(CC/4CC 31)* **THE WHISTLEBINKIES 2** [ ] [-]
– The linen cap – Ghlass ault – The Kilearn reel – Waulkin' o' the fauld – The weaving reel / The bonnie moorhen / Duncan Johnstone's strathspey – John MacKechnie – Mrs MacPherson of Inveran / The Marquis of Huntly's strathspey – Sir Ronald MacDonald's reel – The penny wedding / Phiutharag 'sa phiuthar (Sister, oh sister) / Andrew Wallace – Broderick's bodhran / Great is the cause of my sorrow / John MacDonald of Glencoe / Mrs MacDonald of Dunach / Gealach nan Eilean (Island moon) / The fossil grove – Sir John Henderson – Miss Hannah's jig – The sailor's wife / Freedom come all ye.

— **STUART EYDMANN** – fiddle, concertina, vocals; repl. NELSON

— added **MARK HAYWARD** – fiddle

1981. (lp/c) *(CC/4CC 34)* **THE WHISTLEBINKIES 3** [ ] [-]
– The Lewis jig – Duncan MacKillop – Granny MacLeod / The taw corbies / The ladies hornpipe – Lowe's – Duncan Johnstone / Nathaniel Gow's lament for the death of his brother – Glenlivet – The three peaks of South Uist / Ane ground / The sheepwife / Clean please strae – The Keel row – The Bowmore reel (or Miss Girdle) – The Whistlebinkies' reel – Devonshire Terrace / There'll never be peace until Jamie comes hame / The hare in the corn – The road to Lisdoonvarna – Ar Eirinn ni Neosfainn ce hi (for Ireland I'll not tell her name) / The Kilarney boys of pleasure – Jackie Coleman's reel – Farewell to Erin / MacBeth.

— **JUDITH PEACOCK** – clarsach, vocals; repl. RHONA

1985. (lp/c) *(CC/4CC 43)* **THE WHISTLEBINKIES 4** [ ] [-]
– The low country jig – The lads o' Dunse – Woo'ed an married an' a' – I hae a wife o' my ain – Follow her o'er the border / Sir John Fenwick / An cota ruadh (The Redcoat) – Reel of Bogie – The fiddler – Miss Victoria Ross – Bellamy's brush – Mairin ni dhubhain – The straits of Corfu / Pipe Major Calum Campbell / Ailein Duinn (Brown-haired Alan) / MacDonald of the Isles / Highland river – The Rubic cube / Gwerz an ene reiz – Person Plouergat – An dro / Dr Hugh Alexander Low of Tiree – Father John MacMillan of Barra / For a' that and a' that.

— PEACOCK left; guests were MARY ANN KENNEDY + JO MILLER

1988. (lp/c) *(CC/4CC 50)* **THE WHISTLEBINKIES 5** [ ] [-]
– Auntie Cairistion – The stool of repentance – Cailleach dudain / A Mhairead og (Young Margaret) – Dominic McGowan / The motley crew – The black Maria – Barlinnie Highlander / Jock ' Hazledean / The foxhunter's jig – Rattlin' roarin' Willie – Athol Highlanders / John Roy Stuart – The Marquis of Tweedale's reel – Miss Margaret Graham of Gartmore's favourite – The feetwashing / The farewell's farewell / The winter is past / The boys of Ballinahinch – Matt Molloy's – The humours of Tulla – An ancient clan march – Maidin domhnaight (On Sunday morning) / Rolling home to Caledonia / The dogs among the bushes.

Lochshore not iss.

Oct 91. (cd/c) *(CD/ZC LOC 1063)* **INNER SOUND** ☐ [-]
– Inner sound: MacLeod of Mull – Bonny at morn / The Christening piece / A reel, Strathspey and reel: The lost boys – The Montrose 500 – Miss Valerie Wallace – Peter MacLeod's reel – The Boston cuffes / Beloved Gregor (Griogal cridhe) / Oran mor *[cd-only]* / Isle of Barra march / The tryst / The piper's controversy / Theme from Etain / Bright love of my heart (Gradh geal mo cridhe) *[cd-only]* / Quicksteps: Follow my Highland soldier – 72nd farewell to Aberdeen – Campbell's farewell to Redcastle – Barren rocks of Aden. *<US cd-iss. Feb00; same as UK>*

Greentrax Greentrax

Feb 96. (cd/c) *(<CDTRAX 095>)* **A WANTON FLING** ☐ ☐ Mar96
– The pipers' jig / Ay waulkin O / The Whistlebinkies jig / Ho-ro mo chauchag / Dunkeld bridge / Cam ye o'er frae France? / Taladh / Farewell to Muirhead's / Deireadh leave, 1940 / The wee Eddie reel: Keltan's reel – Loch an duin – MacFarlane's reel – A' bhanals ghaidhealach (the Highland wedding) – Willie Davie / A wanton fling / A 'bhaisa mu dheireadh.

— **McGUIRE, ANDERSON, EYDMANN, WALLACE, HAYWARD** + the returning **PEACOCK** added **ANNALIESE DAGG** – viola, fiddle / plus 8th member **JAMES MacMILLAN** – vocals, whistle

Mar 99. (cd) *(<CDTRAX 159>)* **TIMBER TIMBRE** ☐ ☐ May99
– Nuair a bha mi og (When I was young) / The sailor's wife / Eilean scalpaigh na hearadh / John Roy Stewart / Tha mulad, tha mulad / Achmore loch / The tryst / The mason's apron / A china set / My wife's a drunkard / Moran's return.

– compilations, etc. –

Jan 92. (cd)(c) *Claddagh; (CC 54CD)(4CC 54)* **ANNIVERSARY** ☐ [-]
– Farewell to Nigg / The piper, the harper, the fiddler / Great is the cause of my sorrow / The fiddle Strathspey and reel / Macbeth / The island jigs / The Whistlebinkies' reel / Ane ground / Sir John Fenwick / Allein Duinn / MacDonald of the isles / Dominic McGowan / The fiddlers' farewell / The winter it is past / Dogs among the bushes / Rattling roaring Willie / Barlinnie Highlander / A change of tune.

WILDERNESS CHILDREN
(see ⇒ Section 8: Rock, Pop & Indie)

Duncan WILLIAMSON
(see under ⇒ Springthyme records)

Robin WILLIAMSON

Born: 24 Nov'43, Edinburgh. ROBIN, of course, was the legendary multi-instrumentalist from The INCREDIBLE STRING BAND, who – with musical compadre MIKE HERON – ruled the psychedelic folk world from 1966 to 1974. ROBIN released his first solo set, 'MYRRH', in 1972 while still a member of the legendary folk-hippies. After the group's split in 1974, he relocated to California where he immersed himself in Celtic folklore while keeping a toe in musical waters via the FAR CRY CEILIDH BAND. Although the latter project never actually made it to vinyl, the harp-based

ROBIN WILLIAMSON & HIS MERRY MEN was a more concrete proposition featuring CHRIS CASWELL, SYLVIA WOOD, JERRY McMILLAN, DIRK DALTON, STU BROTMAN and LOUIS KILLEN. The group released a trio of albums at the tail end of the 70's, namely 'JOURNEY'S EDGE' (1977), 'AMERICAN STONEHENGE' (1978) and 'A GLINT AT THE KINDLING' (1979). ROBIN went solo in the early 80's, kicking off a series of albums for the American 'Flying Fish' label with 1981's 'SONGS OF LOVE & PARTING'. Although the bulk of the early 80's was taken up by a series of mail order (from Ireland's 'Claddagh' label) spoken word cassettes firmly in the bardic tradition, 'LEGACY OF THE SCOTTISH HARPERS' (1984) was the first in a two volume exploration of Scotland's rich clarsach tradition while 'SONGS FOR CHILDREN OF ALL AGES' was a music based foray into the children's market. Come the 90's, ROBIN was once again resident in the UK where he occasionally appeared on the festival circuit with his idiosyncratic combination of Celtic storytelling and song.

Following on from 1993's collaboration with JOHN RENBOURN ('WHEEL OF FORTUNE'), the mystic troubadour enjoyed an impressively prolific mid-late 90's period, the highlight of which was 'BLOOMSBURY 1997', a live recording of his much publicised reunion concert with former ISB partner MIKE HERON. ROBIN recorded 'AT THE PURE FOUNTAIN' with CLIVE PALMER, the pair completing a second set, 'JUST LIKE THE IVY', the following year. The big news, however, was a full INCREDIBLE STRING BAND reunion at the 2001 Celtic Connections Festival in Glasgow, messrs WILLIAMSON, HERON, PALMER plus newcomers LAWSON DANDO and BINA WILLIAMSON (ROBIN's wife) putting in an acclaimed performance which more than justified the hype and boded well for the future.

ROBIN WILLIAMSON – vocals, multi / with guest **DAVID CAMPBELL** – viola

Island-Help not iss.

Apr 72. (lp) *(HELP 2)* **MYRRH** ☐ [-]
– Strings in the earth and air / Rends moi-demain / The dancing of the Lord of Weir / Will we open the heavens / Through the horned clouds / Sandy islands / Cold harbour / Dark eyed lady / Dark dance / I see us all get home. *(cd-iss. Nov92 on 'Edsel'; EDCD 366)*

ROBIN WILLIAMSON with his MERRY MEN

with **CHRIS CASWELL** – wind / **SYLVIA WOODS** – harp / **JERRY McMILLAN** – strings / **PETE GRANT** – dobro, banjo / **DIRK DALTON + STU BROTMAN** – bass / **LOUIS KILLEN** – concertina

not iss. Flying Fish

1977. (lp) *<FF 033>* **JOURNEY'S EDGE** [-] ☐
– Border tango / The tune I hear so well / Red eye blues / Tomorrow / Mystic times / Lullaby for a rainy day / Wrap city phapsody / The Maharajah of Magador / The bells / Voices of the Barbary Coast / Out on the water. *(re-iss. Mar89; same) (cd-iss. Jun93 on 'Edsel'; EDCD 374)*

Criminal Flying Fish

1978. (lp) *(STEAL 4) <FF 062>* **AMERICAN STONEHENGE** ☐ ☐
– Port London early / Pacheco / Keepsake / Zoo blues / These islands green / The man in the van / Sands in the glass / Her scattered gold / When evening shadows fall / Rab's last woollen testament. *<re-iss. Mar89; same> (cd-iss. Jul94 on 'Edsel'; EDCD 389)*

Jun 79. (lp) *(STEAL 6) <FF 096>* **A GLINT AT THE KINDLING** ☐ ☐
– The road the gypsies go / Me and the mad girl / Lough Foyle / The woodcutter's song / By weary well / Boyhood of Henry Morgan the Pooka / Five denials on Merlin's grave / The poacher's song / Song of Mabon. *(re-iss. Jun86 on 'Awareness' lp/c; AWL/WAT 1006) <US re-iss. Mar89; same> (cd-iss. Jan96 with 'SELECTED WRITINGS 80-83' on 'Music Corporation'; TMC 9201)*

ROBIN WILLIAMSON

Claddagh Flying Fish

1981. (lp) *(CCF 5) <FF 257>* **SONGS OF LOVE & PARTING** ☐ ☐
– Verses in Stewart Street / For Mr. Thomas / Fare thee well Sweet Mally / Return no more / Tarry wool / For three of us / Sigil / Flower of the briar / The forming of Blodeuwedd / Gwydion's dream / Verses at Balwearie tower / A night at Ardpatrick / The parting glass. *(re-iss. Sep84; same) (<cd-iss. Jan96 with 'FIVE BARDIC MYSTERIES' on 'Music Corporation'; TMC 9403>)*

1983. (lp) *(CCF 10)* **MUSIC FOR THE MABINOGI** ☐ ☐
<US-iss.Jun88 as 'SONGS FOR THE MABINOGI' on 'Flying Fish'; FF 340>

Nov 84. (lp/c) *(CCF/4CCF 12) <FF 358>* **LEGACY OF THE SCOTTISH HARPERS** ☐ ☐
– Scotch cap / Scotland / Flowers of the forest – Cromlet's lilt – Chevy Chase / Weel hoddled lucky – Lochmaben harper / Gilderoy – Cow the gowan / MacGregor's lament – MacGregor's search / Kilt thy coat Maggie – Three sheepskins / Lord Dundee's lamentation – Braes o' Killiecrankie / I'll mek ye fain to follow me / Lady Cassilis' lilt – Auld Jew – Broom o' Cowdenknowes / MacDonald of the isles salutation / Rushes – Birk and green hollin / Soor plooms / Jockey went to the wood / Babks of Helicon – The De'il tak the wars. *(cd-iss. 1986; CCF 12CD)*

1986. (lp/c) *(CCF/4CCF 16) <FF 390>* **LEGACY OF THE SCOTTISH HARPERS VOL.2** ☐ ☐

Towerbell not iss.

Feb 85. (lp/c) *(TVLP/ZCTV 1)* **THE DRAGON HAS TWO TONGUES** (TV film soundtrack) ☐ [-]
(re-iss. Aug87 on 'T.E.R.' lp/c; TER/ZCTER 1133)

Plant Life Flying Fish

Sep 87. (lp/c) *(PLR/PLC 075) <FF 407>* **WINTER'S TURNING** ☐ ☐
– Drive the cold winter away – Cold and raw / Avant de s'en aller / Pastime with good company – Somerset wassail / Greensleeves morris – Green groweth the holly / Eagle's whistle / Past 1 o'clock – Great Tom's cast / Sheep under the snow – Welsh morris / Praetorius' courante CLXXIX / Drive the cold / Blow blow thou winter wynd – Vivaldi's winter largo / Carolan's quarrel with the landlady – Christmas eve / Hunting the wren / Corelli's sonato (a violino E violino O) – Scottish country dance / Polka du Tapis. *(<cd-iss. Dec94 & Mar97 on 'Flying Fish'; FF 70407>)*

May 88. (lp/c) *(CCF/4CCF 19)* **SONGS FOR CHILDREN OF ALL AGES** ☐ [-]
– Witches hat / Herring song / Three men went a hunting / Fool's song / Horses dance / Brian O'Linn / Butter / Water song / Raggle taggle gipsies / Froggy would a wooing go / Liberty – Old Dan Tucker / Ivy sing Ivy / Back of Burnie's hill – Over the hills and far away / Gartan lullaby.
(above issued for 'Claddagh' records)

Nov 88. (lp/c/cd) *(PLR/PLC/PLCD 081) <FF 448>* **TEN OF SONGS** ☐ ☐
– Ancient song / Lammas / Political lies / Scotland yet / Skull and nettlework / The barley / Here to burn / Verses at Ellesmere / Innocent love / Verses at Powls. *(<cd-iss. Dec94 & Mar97 on 'Flying Fish'; FF 70448>)*

— Late in 1993, WILLIAMSON and JOHN RENBOURN (ex-PENTANGLE) released CD-album 'WHEEL OF FORTUNE'; *(Demon; FIENDCD 746)*

Eclectic not iss.

Feb 96. (cd) *(<TMC 9504>)* **THE ISLAND OF THE STRONG DOOR** ☐ [-]
– Love letter to my wife Bina / Scadian / Billy & the scrapper / If wishes were horses / In four quarters of the world / Bless this kiss / I pray to God in God's absence / Late in the evening / Daughter's dance (Vashti) / The island of the strong door.

Greentrax Greentrax

Jun 97. (cd) *(<CDTRAX 134>)* **CELTIC HARP AIRS & DANCE TUNES** Aug97
– Lude's supper – The lark in the morning / Meggie's fou / Mwynen mon / Galway rambler / Port Atholl – The brae of Tulliemet / Rock of pleasure / Scholar / Glan medd dod mwyn / Old frieze britches / Blackbird – Downfall of Paris / Kimiad – The mountain road.

Pig's Whisker Pig's Whisker

Mar 98. (cd; by ROBIN WILLIAMSON & MIKE HERON)
(<PWMD 5006>) **BLOOMSBURY 1997 (live)** Aug98
– Everything's fine right now / Scotland yet / Red hair / October song / Maya / Favourite sins / Love letter to my wife Bina / Mexican girl / North sea beaches – Koeeoaddi there / 1968 / Feast of Stephen / Every time I hear the sweet birds singing / Log cabin home in the sky / You've been a friend to me.

Apr 98. (cd) *(<PWMD 5008>)* **RING DANCE** Aug98
– Ring dance / Veshengro / Back in Paris / My enemy is listening / Gaol for sure / Fine fingered hands / At Waverley station / Lady with the book / Take a heed of me sometimes / Invocation / Lights of sweet St. Anne / I see us cross great waters.

Oct 98. (cd) *(<PWMD 5010>)* **A JOB OF JOURNEY WORK**
– The banks of Bunclody / Hard times in old England – Monie musk / Geordie Gordon / The black horse / William Taylor / Nottamun town / The May morning dew / Bold Riley-O / These old shoes – Miss MacLeod's reel / Riding down to Portsmouth / Ye've lain wrang / A job of journey work / The streams of lovely Nancy / Brown skin girl / Hughie the Graham / Toderoday / Don't let your deal go down / Rothesay Bay.

Jun 99. (cd) *(<PWCD 5015>)* **THE OLD FANGLED TONE**
– Paddy Green's shamrock shore / Jordan is a hard road / Black is the colour / Captain Ward / Bonny Kells water / South coast / Battleship of Maine / Will ye go to Flanders / The wild colonial boy / 10/9 / Erin gu bragh / Down by the salley gardens / Whisky you're the Devil / Ye banks and braes. *(re-iss. Mar01; same)*

Jul 99. (cd) *(PWCD 5016)* **MUSIC FROM MACBETH** -

Jul 99. (cd; by ROBIN WILLIAMSON & CLIVE PALMER)
(<PWMD 5017>) **AT THE PURE FOUNTAIN**
– Come a ye tramps and hawkers / Pretty fair maid / Paris / For far soldier / (I can't help it if I'm) Still in love with you / Relax your mind / Cam ye o'er frae France / Rise when the rooster crows / A la belle etoile / Bless you (for being an angel) / Sally Ann / Green grow the laurels / The show must go on / Wae's me for Prince Charlie / Salty dog / The night of the ragmen's ball.

Apr 00. (cd; by ROBIN WILLIAMSON & CLIVE PALMER)
(<PWMD 5021>) **JUST LIKE THE IVY**
– You've been a friend to me / Going across the sea / Planxty Irwin – Spanish is a loving tongue / Boston burglar / Downtown dandies / Blind fiddler / Just like the ivy / Bonny Cragside – Neil Gow's wife / The storm is on the ocean / Empty pocket blues / Salty dog / Bonny doon / Rambling boy / Side by side.

– compilations, etc –

on 'Pig's Whisker' unless mentioned otherwise

Aug 86. (lp/c; ROBIN WILLIAMSON & HIS MERRY MEN)
Awareness; (AWL/AWT 1005) **SONGS AND MUSIC 1977** -

Apr 97. (cd) *(<PWMD 5001>)* **THE MERRY BAND'S FAREWELL CONCERT AT McCABE'S (live 14 December, 1979)** Oct97
– Wassail / Her scattered gold / By weary well / The woodcutter's song / Flower of the briar / The legend / Five denials on Merlin's grave / Cadgers on the Cannongate.

May 97. (d-cd) *(PWCD 5002)* **THE MIRROR MAN SEQUENCIES 1961-1966** -
– Mirror man's sequencies / Oh Marie / Sheepish / Beef gadjies / Run run run / Kerrera / Flat foot skiffle / Ironstone bit / Behold the Indian unicorn / Orion arc / To unmake demons / On the job / Hand of Fatima.

Mar 98. (cd) *(PWMD 5004)* **DREAM JOURNALS 1966-1976** -
– Dream journals foreword / There was no snow / Carefully folding my wings / On the way to the cathedral / On our holidays / Charlie the taxi driver / Turn again / These are dreams / Out with McClachan / Snah eer / From Odin's tree / Welsh pavanes.

Sep 98. (cd) *(<PWMD 5007>)* **GEMS OF CELTIC STORIES – ONE**
– Tale of Culhwch and Olwen / Aden Ffwynach.

Sep 98. (cd) *(<PWMD 5009>)* **GEMS OF CELTIC STORY – TWO**
– Dialogue of the two sages / Voyage of Mael Duinn / Birth of Lugh / Wooing of Findabair.

Nov 99. (cd) *(<PWMD 5019>)* **SONGS FOR CHILDREN OF ALL AGES / WINTER'S TURNING**

Mar 02. (cd) *(<PWMD 5023>)* **GEMS OF CELTIC STORIES – THREE** Jul02

below are non-chronological; spoken word with some instrumentation (mainly mail order on 'Claddagh' Ireland)

1981. (c) **THE FISHERMAN'S SON AND THE GRUGACH OF TRICK** - -

1982. (c) **PRINCE DOUGIE AND THE SWAN MAIDEN** - -

1982. (c) **RORY MOR AND THE GRUGACH GAIR** - -

1983. (c) **FIVE HUMOROUS TALES OF SCOTLAND** - -

1984. (c) **SELECTED WRITINGS** - -
– The fair / The fair dance / Edinburgh / Lammas.

1984. (c) **FIVE HUMOUROUS TALES OF SCOTLAND AND IRELAND** - -

1985. (c) **FIVE CELTIC TALES OF ENLIGHTENMENT** - -

1985. (c) **FIVE BARDIC TALES** - -
– The spoils of Annwn / The battle of the trees / The dialogue of the two sages / The voyage of the Bran, son of Febal / Three Celtic nature poems.

1985. (c) **FIVE LEGENDARY HISTORIES OF BRITAIN** - -

1985. (c) **FIVE CELTIC TALES OF PRODIGIES AND MARVELS** - -

1985. (c) **FIVE TALES OF ENCHANTMENT** - -

1991. (cd/c) **MUSIC FOR THE NEWBORN** -

Roy WILLIAMSON (see under ⇒ CORRIES)

WOLFSTONE

Formed: Inverness . . . mid-80's by mean fiddler DUNCAN CHISHOLM and rock musician DAVID FOSTER – not to be confused with Irish political outfit, the WOLFTONES. Combining traditional Scots folk with progressive rock, WOLFSTONE's eponymous debut album – released in 1988 – created a new genre: prog-folk, or perhaps metallic ceilidh?! Whatever their intentions, the end result made for interesting, if retrospectively somewhat dated listening. With a supporting cast of ROGER NIVEN, IAIN MACDONALD and STUART & STRUAN EAGLESHAM, the record jigged and weaved through the likes of 'RECONCILIATION' and 'TATTIES', underlaying the fiddles and whistles with MIKE OLDFIELD-style electric guitar. 'READY FOR THE STORM', meanwhile, was a more typically moody 80's synth-rock piece while the haunting synth atmospherics of 'CAVE' conjured up an unlikely meeting of KRAFTWERK and CLANNAD.

Following on from sophomore effort, 'WOLFSTONE 2' (1989), the group entered the new decade with a major upheaval in personnel, ANDY MURRAY, IVAN DREVER and ALLAN WILSON replacing NIVEN, FOSTER and MACDONALD respectively. A new deal with the native 'Iona' label was also in the offing, leading to the release of 'UNLEASHED' (1991), another helping of kilt-whipping reels alongside more adventurous material. 'THE CHASE' followed in 1992, presaging another line-up reshuffle and change of label: a new rhythm section of WAYNE MACKENZIE and MOP YOUNGSON was in place for 'YEAR OF THE DOG' (1994), the first of a trio of albums for 'Green Linnet'. Featuring erstwhile SILLY WIZARD man, PHIL CUNNINGHAM, in both a production and playing capacity, the record was a strong, confident, if slightly over-polished effort ('THE SEA KING' veered too close to American AOR for comfort) featuring a clutch of stirring politically-minded anthems. 'THE BRAVE FOOT SOLDIERS' commemorated a trans-Scotland STUC march while 'WHITE GOWN' was a defiant lyrical stand against American racists, The Ku Klux Klan. Closer to home, if distant in memory, the Highland Clearances was the subject of 'THE BRAES OF SUTHERLAND', a first person narrative recounting the anguish of impending emigration.

Despite the band's continuing development in both songwriting and musicianship, they haven't quite managed to raise their profile in line with the likes of CAPERCAILLIE and RUNRIG. Nevertheless, WOLFSTONE command a loyal following, both at home and in the USA/Canada, a further three albums, 'THE HALF TAIL' (1996), 'THIS STRANGE PLACE' (1998) and 'SEVEN' (1999) consolidating their niche as solid purveyors of Celtic-rock. After clocking up another few thousand miles on the road, the group returned to the studio for 'ALMOST AN ISLAND' (2002), a more reflective effort inspired by their highland home of Inverness.

DUNCAN CHISHOLM – fiddle, sequencer / **DAVID FOSTER** – bass, drums, sequencer / **STUART EAGLESHAM** – rhythm guitar, vocals / **STRUAN EAGLESHAM** – piano, keyboards / **ROGER NIVEN** – guitars / **IAIN MACDONALD** – pipes, whistle, flute

unknown not iss.

1988. (lp) **WOLFSTONE** -
– Reconciliation / Tatties (Scarce of tatties – Pet of the pipers – Corner house jig) / Ready for the storm / Banjo (Annie MacDonald's piano – Banjo breakdown – Jig of slurs) / Cave / Brolum (Brolum – Lexy Macaskill – Jeannie dang the weaver) / How long / Paddys (P M Donald MacLean's farewell to Lewis – Humours of Glendart – Paddys leather breeches) / Rocky 5 (Cape Breton symphony – Gravil walks to granie – Jackie Coleman's – Andy Renwick's ferret – Rock mountain road). *(re-iss. Apr94 on 'Celtic Music' c/cd; CMC/+D 072)*

1989. (lp) **WOLFSTONE II** -
– The Flying Scotsman / Homeland / Red hot polkas / When she sleeps / Battle / JC tunes / Race with the Devil / A stor moi chroi / Mingulay boat song.

— **ANDY MURRAY** – guitar; repl. NIVEN

— **IVAN DREVER** (b. Sanday, Orkneys) – vocals, guitar (Solo Artist) repl. FOSTER

— **ALLAN WILSON** – pipes, whistle, flute; repl. MACDONALD

Iona not iss.

Nov 91. (c/cd) *(IR/+CD 014)* **UNLEASHED** -
– Cleveland park: (a) Cleveland park, (b) The banks of the Allan, (c) Kenny Gillies of Portnalong / Song for yesterday / The silver spear: (a) Paddy Fehey's, (b) The silver spear / Sleepy toon / Hector the hero / The howl: (a) The Louis reel, (b) Morrison's jig, (c) Shoe polishers jig / Here is where the heart is: (a) Lily the Pict, (b) Here is where the heart is / Hard heart / Erin: (a) The coast of Austria, (b) Toss the feathers, (c) Farewell to Erin, (d) Captain Lachlan MacPhail of Tiree.

— now without WILSON; guests incl. **NEIL HAY** – bass / **JOHN HENDERSON** – drums / **DOUGIE PINCOCK** – pipes, flute, whistle

Aug 92. (c/cd) *(IR/+CD 018)* **"THE CHASE"** □ [-]
– Tinnie run (The road to Mount Tinnie run – The boys of Ballymoat – Alan MacPherson of Mosspark) / Glass and the can / The prophet / The appropriate dipstick (Lori Connor – The appropriate dipstick – John Leith Laing) / Flames and hearts / The £10 float (Kinnaird House – The cottage in the grove) / Close it down (Close it down – Duncan Johnstone) / Jake's tune / The early mist / Cannot lay me down (Cannot lay me down – The lady of Ardross).

Sep 93. (c-ep/cd-ep) *(IMCS/ICDS 801)* **BURNING HORIZONS / BATTLE / THE PROPHET** □ [-]

— **WAYNE MACKENZIE** – bass + **MOP YOUNGSON** – drums; repl. MURRAY; guests now **GORDON DUNCAN** – bagpipes / **PHIL CUNNINGHAM** – accordion, whistles / **TAJ WYZGOWSKI** – electric guitars

Green Linnet | Green Linnet

Jul 94. (cd/c) *(<GL 1145 CD/C>)* **YEAR OF THE DOG** □ □
– Holy ground / Ballavanich (The boys of Ballavanich – Mrs Crehan's) / The sea king / The brave foot soldiers / The double rise set (Gingerhog's No.2 – The double rise – Crossing the mince – Give us a drink of water) / White gown / Morag's set (Morag's reel – Laura Lynn Cunningham – The harsh February – Miss Lyall) / The braes of Sutherland / Dinner's set (Dinner's dangerous river jacket – Richard Dwyer's reel – Sandy MacLeod of Garafad).

— added **STEVIE SAINT** – pipes / plus guests

Aug 96. (cd/c) *(<GLCD/GLC 1172>)* **THE HALF TAIL** □ □
– Zeto / Tall ships / Gillies / Heart and soul / Granny Hogg's enormous wallet / Bonnie ship the Diamond / Glenglass / Clueless / No tie ups.

— now without TAJ + MOP

Mar 98. (cd/c) *(<CD/C TRAX 1188>)* **THIS STRANGE PLACE** □ □
– Harlequin: The harlequin – Pipe Major Stevie Saint / This girl / Let them sing / Banks of the Ness / This strange place / Stevie's set: The wild monkey dance – Black eyed jam / Till I sleep / The Arab set: An Arab in the court of Kintail – The Redwood reel / Reluctant journey / Kazakhstan: Thief in the night – The hills of Kazakhstan.

— **DUNCAN, STUART, WAYNE + STEVIE** enlisted **ANDY SIMMERS** – piano, keyboards + **TONY SOAVE** – drums

Jun 99. (cd) *(<GLCD 1198>)* **SEVEN** □ □
– Psycho woman / Brave boys / Jen's tune / Black dog / Quinie fae Ryhnie / John Simmers / J-time / Wild and the free / Crowfeathers / Maggie's / Fingal's cave.

— added **BRIAN McNEILL** – keyboards / **MARC CLEMENT** – guitar / + **COLLETTE O'LEARY** – vocals

Once Bitten | not iss.

Apr 01. (cd) *(OBRCD 01)* **LIVE – NOT ENOUGH SHOUTING** □ [-]
– Psycho woman / Brave boys / Quinie / Balivanich / Crowfeathers / Black dog / John Simmers / J-time / Wild & the free / Clueless / Prophet / Tinny run / Gillies / Maggies.

— line-up now **CHISHOLM, STUART EAGLESHAM, STEPHEN SAINT + WAYNE MacKENZIE** (bass, vocals)

May 02. (cd) *(OBRCD 002)* **ALMOST AN ISLAND** □ [-]
– The piper and the shrew / Elav the terrible / Where the summers go / La grand nuit du Port de Peche / The queen of Argyll – The Knockard elf / 5-4 madness / Davie's last reel / Jericho / All our dreams / The panda.

– compilations, etc. –

Jul 97. (cd/c) *Iona; (IRCD/IRC 056)* **PICK OF THE LITTER: THE BEST OF WOLFSTONE** □ [-]
– The battle / Tall ships / Glass & the can / Cleveland Park / Heart and soul / The howl / White gown / Glenglass / Brave foot soldiers / Dinner's set / Sleepy toon / The 10 pound float / Holy ground / Clueless / No tie ups.

DUNCAN CHISHOLM

with **PHIL CUNNINGHAM, IVAN DREVER, STUART EAGLESHAM, ANDY THORBURN + GRAHAM WILLOUGHBY**

Copperfish | not iss.

Mar 98. (cd) *(CPF 001CD)* **REDPOINT** □ [-]
– The rose of St. Magnus / The congress set / Lady Ramsay / Asleep at the wheel / Leaving Stoer / Kirkhill / Moonlight at Loch Ness / Marnie Swanson set / The lady of Ardross.

John WRIGHT (see under ⇒ Greentrax records)

Jennifer & Hazel WRIGLEY (see under ⇒ SEELYHOO)

Jimmy YOUNG (see under ⇒ RUA)

Young Pipers Of Scotland (see under ⇒ Greentrax records)

* * *

wee folk notes

The following artists/groups don't merit a full entry, but warrant a wee mention. . .

The **BRAELANDERS :** Orkney-based, and played Hawaiian ceilidh around the pubs and clubs. They released one album, 'MUSIC AND SONG' for 'Mariner Music' in September '99.

Meanwhile, around the same period, Scots drovers and cowboys, **CEILIDH MENAGE** delivered their one and only set, 'PLAIDS & BANDANAS' in 1998 – yeehaw!

Inverness singer/songwriter, **Gregor FULLARTON** issued an eclectic batch of traditional and contemporary songs (for 'Black Dog Audio') under the cheeky title of 'AWAY TO FOLK' (1999).

Jean HART was from Edinburgh and circulated around the Burns Howff Club. She was one of the many Scottish folk artists to sign for 'Transatlantic', although only one eponymous LP (TRA 111) was issued in 1963.

The **KERRIES** folk-pop group released a couple of records in the 60s for 'Major Minor': 'COULTER'S CANDY. / GALLON OF WHISKY AND A BARREL OF BEER', and 'THE KERRIES'.

Borders balladeer/folk singer **John McNAIRN** released his solo set, 'BORDERLAND' for 'OffBeat Scotland' in 1999.

The PORTOBELLO CEILIDH BAND, a fivesome whose performances have included Embra's Hogmanay bash, released a CD in 2001 called 'Spider Stomp' – a rattling good set of dancing music plus a couple of songs from heid-bummer Roy Henderson.

Paisley-born singer/songwriter, **Neil THOMSON** plied his trade around the turn of the decade/millennium, issuing one CD for 'Ardura': 'PEOPLE OF THE PAST' (2000).

folk labels

Foot Stompin' records (see under ⇒ Tartan Tapes records)

Greentrax records

Founded: Cockenzie, East Lothian . . . 1986 by retired police inspector IAN D. GREEN, who had run the local police folk-club, affectionately known as "Fuzz-Folk". A lover of traditional Scottish folk music since he was a teenager, IAN brought together some of the finest singers and musicians from around the length and breadth of Scotland, including a few from further afield (mainly Cape Breton/Canada). The first Greentrax release came in the shape of fiddler IAN HARDIE's 'A Breath Of Fresh Airs' in October '86, the former Kelso solicitor and member of JOCK TAMSON'S BAIRNS staying on with the label throughout his long career. At the beginning of 2001, the Greentrax imprint had delivered more than 200 releases (including offshoot 'G2'), everyone from JEAN REDPATH to ex-pat ERIC BOGLE to rising ambient folkies SHOOGLENIFTY. You can contact them at:- Cockenzie Business Centre, Edinburgh Road, Cockenzie, East Lothian, EH32 0HL, or telephone 01875 814 155, or at www.greentrax.com. For beginners to try out the music you couldn't go far wrong with: 'THE MUSIC & SONG OF GREENTRAX: The Best of Scottish Music' (two CD's for the price of one).

note:- most of the below releases were also available in the US

Oct 86. (c/lp) *(C+/TRAX 001)* **IAN HARDIE – A Breath of Fresh Airs**
Oct 86. (c/lp) *(C+/TRAX 002)* **McCALMANS – Peace And Plenty**

• **IAIN MacDONALD** was born in Stornoway, although he would subsequently move east to Insch in Aberdeenshire. A singer-songwriter in the vocal/acoustic tradition and regarded highly by noneother than folk legend DICK GAUGHAN, IAIN delivered his solo debut below. Developing his political lyrical skills even stronger, IAIN issued a second set, 'THIS LAND WAS ONCE FREE' in 1989 and was also part of the DESPERATE DANZ BAND who issued one LP that October, 'SEND THREE AND FOURPENCE WE'RE GOING TO A DANCE', on 'Happas' *(HAPPAS 1)*

Oct 86. (c/lp) *(C+/TRAX 003)* **IAIN MacDONALD – Beneath Still Waters**
– Coldest night of the year / Maid of Islay / Do you think it's right / The Iolaire / Santiago stadium / No fun city / Free Nelson Mandela / Ask questions later? / All our dreams / Bed of shifting stone.

Feb 87. (c/lp) *(C+/TRAX 004)* **ROD PATERSON – Two Hats**
Jun 87. (c) *(CTRAX 005)* **JEAN REDPATH – The Songs Of Robert Burns Volume 6**
Jun 87. (c) *(CTRAX 006)* **JEAN REDPATH – The Songs Of Robert Burns Volume 3**
Jun 87. (c) *(CTRAX 007)* **JEAN REDPATH – The Songs Of Robert Burns Volume 4**
Jun 87. (c) *(CTRAX 008)* **JEAN REDPATH – The Songs Of Robert Burns Volume 5**

• **CATHERINE-ANN MacPHEE** is originally from the island of Barra off the West Coast of Scotland. In the early 80's, she became well-known for her "7.84" theatre/production work in Edinburgh (acting and singing) and was soon regarded as one of the best Gaelic singers around having spent time in Cape Breton, Toronto, Tbilisi, Leningrad and Moscow. Her first album (with members of OSSIAN on backing) was a mixture of traditional protest/folk songs plucked from various sources and regions throughout the Highlands. Her second, 'CHI MI'N GEAMHRADH (I SEE WINTER)' in 1991, featured among others JACK EVANS, SAVOURNA STEVENSON and ALLAN MacDONALD. Singing from the heart once more, CATHERINE-ANN's third long-player 'SINGS MAIRI MHOR' (1994) – augmented this time by BANNAL, OSSIAN and clarsach player MARY ANN KENNEDY – was arguably her best work to date. The highlight for the beginner was definitely 'NUAIR BHA MI OG (When I Was Young)'.

Dec 87. (c/lp) *(C+/TRAX 009)* **CATHERINE-ANN MacPHEE – Canan Nan Gaidheal (The Language Of The Gael)**
– Hi ro ri o ra ill o / A nighean nan geug taladh / Puirt-a-beul / Soiridh leis a' bhreacan ur / Iomair thusa, choinnich chrindhe / Canan nan gaidheal / 'S fliuch an oidhche / Onan an "Iolaire" / Cearcall a' chuain / An ataireachd ard. *(re-iss. May93 cd/c; CD/C TRAX 009)*

• **HEATHER HEYWOOD** was born and raised in Irvine, Ayrshire. Having sung from a very early age, her first public performance was in 1970 at her local folk club. A year later at the Irvine Marymass festival/competition of traditional singing, HEATHER was awarded runners-up prize, one of the judges was noneother than JEAN REDPATH. For the next decade or so, HEATHER shy'd away from the spotlight, although she was present – either as a judge or a guest singer – at many a folk festival. Reluctant to enter a studio, it took time and plenty of encouragement before she finally recorded her Greentrax debut below. Augmented by viola/fiddler BRIAN McNEILL (among others), the album made HEATHER a trad/folk star overnight. However, it would be five long years before a follow-up. Around the New Year of '93, HEATHER's sophomore set, 'BY YON CASTLE WA', gave her the title of the singer's singer. Opening track, 'THE SANDS O' THE SHORE' (arranged by McNEILL and piper DOUGIE PINCOCK), was a beautifully sung traditional shanty tale of lost love. She has since moved on to 'Living Tradition' records.

Nov 87. (c/lp) *(C+/TRAX 010)* **HEATHER HEYWOOD – Some Kind Of Love**
– The sally Gardens / Lord Lovat / A song for Ireland / Some kind of love / Let no man steal your thyme / Bonnie laddie ye gang by me / My bonnie moorhen / The cruel mother. *(re-iss. Oct94 cd/c+=; CD/C TRAX 010)* – Wid ye gang love.

Feb 88. (c) *(CTRAX 011)* **JANET RUSSELL AND CHRISTINE KYDD – Janet Russell & Christine Kydd**

• **ADAM McNAUGHTAN** was born in Glasgow just prior to the 2nd World War. His witty songs (own words over mostly traditional tunes) were of the comic-folk variety and sung with little accompaniment. ADAM released two albums for Greentrax back to back in the early part of '88, the first 'THE GLASGOW THAT I USED TO KNOW' was actually recorded and released in 1975 (with guitar/vocals provided by LESLEY HALE) and mainly inspired by his life in Dennistoun. You'll recognise the opening track, 'THE JEELY PIECE SONG', from a recent TV advert, while others are either hit or miss. 'WORDS, WORDS, WORDS' was an album of fresh cuts including a rendition of hero MATT McGINN's 'RAP TAP TAP'. Eight years later, McNAUGHTAN was in town for another stab at the witty rant, his 'LAST STAND AT MOUNT FLORIDA' (1996) said it all. ADAM is certainly not as serious as he looks (grey hair and beard). After re-issuing the aforesaid debut albums as one double CD package in April 2000, the singer featured at the following year's Celtic Connections in Glasgow.

Feb 88. (c) *(CTRAX 012)* **ADAM McNAUGHTAN – The Glasgow That I Used To Know**
– The jeely piece song / School songs / Dance noo laddie / They're pullin' doon the buildin' next tae oors / Mammie songs / Old Annie Annie Brown / Jail songs / Ludgin' wi' big Aggie / A wee drappie o't / The Glasgow that I used to know / Music hall fragments / The transportation ballad / Football songs / The Derry & Cumberland boys / Bonnie wee country lass / Street songs / Haddie in the pan / Now that you're gone.

Feb 88. (c) *(CTRAX 013)* **ADAM McNAUGHTAN – Words, Words, Words**
– The Glasgow that I used to know / Rap tap tap – The coming of the wee Malkies – Chinese songs – Lament for the lost dinner-ticket – The teacher's rant / Airn John / The West End perk serenade / Nursing feathers / The haill week o' the fair / The Glasgow Sunday school / The yellow on the broom / The Glasgow courtship / Robin Tamson's smiddy / Fitba' crazy / Blood upon the grass / The lion & the glove / We will not have a motorway / Oor hamlet.

Apr 88. (c/lp) *(C+/TRAX 014)* **IAIN MacKINTOSH with BRIAN McNEILL & ALAN REID – Gentle Persuasion**
Mar 88. (c) *(CTRAX 015)* **Various Artists – Sandy Bell's Ceilidh**
Apr 88. (c/lp) *(C+/TRAX 016)* **ROD PATERSON – Smiling Waved Goodbye**
Jun 88. (c/lp) *(C+/TRAX 017)* **JEAN REDPATH – The Songs Of Robert Burns Volume 1**
Jun 88. (c/lp) *(C+/TRAX 018)* **JEAN REDPATH – The Songs Of Robert Burns Volume 2**
Aug 88. (cd/c/lp) *(CD/C+/TRAX 019)* **McCALMANS – Listen To The Heat – Live**
Aug 88. (lp/c) *(TRAX/CTRAX 020)* **ARCHIE FISHER & GARNET ROGERS – Sunsets I've Galloped Into**
Mar 89. (c/lp) *(C+/TRAX 021)* **ROBIN LAING – Edinburgh Skyline**
Jan 89. (c) *(CTRAX 022)* **LINDSAY PORTEOUS & FRIENDS – Portrait Of A Jew's-Harp Player**
Jun 88. (c/lp) *(C+/TRAX 023)* **McCALMANS – Ancestral Manoeuvres**
Feb 89. (c/lp) *(C+/TRAX 024)* **HERITAGE – Fife And A' The Lands About It**
Aug 89. (c/lp) *(C+/TRAX 025)* **IAIN MacDONALD – This Land Was Once Free**
– Another package deal / Comrades in the dark / This land was once free / Was it on the fields of Flanders / Heaven is / The last mystery / I never wondered why / In secret gardens / That quiet place.
Mar 89. (cd/c) *(CD/C TRAX 026)* **ALY BAIN (& Various Artists) – Aly Bain & Friends**
Aug 89. (c/lp) *(C+/TRAX 027)* **JACK BECK – O Lassie, Lassie**
(cd-iss. May02; CDTRAX 027)
Aug 89. (cd/c/lp) *(CD/C+/TRAX 028)* **ERIC BOGLE – The Eric Bogle Songbook**
Nov 89. (cd/c) *(CD/C TRAX 029)* **JEAN REDPATH – Leaving The Land**
Dec 89. (cd/c) *(CD/C TRAX 030)* **Various Artists – The Music & Song Of Scotland**

• **LUCY STEWART** was another trad/folk singer, this time from the North East, this time from the well-respected STEWART clan.

Feb 90. (c) *(CTRAX 031)* **LUCY STEWART – Traditional Singer From Aberdeenshire, Scotland Vol.1**
– The battle o' Harlaw / Two pretty boys / Tifty's Annie / The Laird o' Drum / Doon by the Greenwood sidie O / The beggar king / The bonnie hoose o' Airlie / Barbary Allen / The swan swims so bonnie O.

Feb 90. (c/lp) *(C+/TRAX 032)* **JEAN REDPATH – A Fine Song For Singing**
Jan 90. (c) *(CTRAX 033)* **Various Artists – Revival In Britain**

• **STRAMASH** attributed their one and only cassette album to Glasgow folkie MATT McGINN, although little was known about the band.

Mar 90. (c) *(CTRAX 034)* **STRAMASH – McGinn Of The Carlton: The Songs And Stories of Matt McGinn**

– The magic shadow show / The Dundee ghost / Rob Roy MacGregor-o / Benny has been / The pill / Janetta / The foreman O'Rourke / Get up get out / If it wisnae for the union / Can o' tea / I'm looking for a job / Three nights and a Sunday / We'll have a may-day / The magic shadow show (instrumental) / Jeannie Gallagher / The red yo-yo / Coorie doon / The Gallowgate calypso / Troubled waters in my soul / Bingo Bella / I love you / Manura Manya / Depth of my ego / Skin.

Mar 90. (c/lp) *(C+/TRAX 035)* **BILL BARCLAY – The Very Best Of Bill Barclay**
May 90. (12") *(STRAX 1001)* **RONNIE BROWNE & SCOTTISH RUGBY TEAM / BRODERS POLICE PIPE BAND – Flower Of Scotland / (instrumental)**
Jul 90. (cd/c) *(CD/C TRAX 036)* **McCALMANS – Flames On The Water**

• **CRAIG McCALLUM** leads his Scottish Dance Band into the usual trad reels, polkas. His group included fellow accordion-player GILLIES CRICHTON, fiddler ALISON SMITH, on keyboards RICHARD CURRIE, bassist BILLY CRAIB and drummer GORDON SMITH. After a one-off for Greentrax, McCALLUM and Co returned to the fold in '98 with the CD '75th ANNIVERSARY DANCES' *(Royal Scottish Country Dance Society; RSCDSCD 010)*

Oct 90. (cd/c) *(CD/C TRAX 037)* **THE CRAIG McCALLUM SCOTTISH DANCE BAND – In A Different Light**

Apr 91. (cd/c) *(CD/C TRAX 038)* **CATHERINE-ANN McPHEE – Chi Mi'n Geamhradh (I See Winter)**
– Chi mi'n geamhradh (I see winter) / Chaidh mo Dhunnchadh dha'n bheinn (My Duncan went to the hill) / O hi ri lean (A spinning song) / Bidh clann Ulaidh (Ulster men) / Mile marbhphaisg air a' Ghaol (Thousand curses upon a love) / Seathan (A waulking song) / Bu deonach leam tilleadh (I would willingly return) / 'S muladachi mi's mi air m' aineol (I am sad here among strangers) / Bothan airigh am braigh Rainneach (Shieling in Brae Rannoch) / Tha na h-uain air an tulaich (The lambs are on the hills) / Na libh o ho I.
Nov 90. (7") *(STRAX 1002)* **BILL BARCLAY – The Twelve Days Of Christmas / Polly Had A Poodle**
Nov 90. (cd/c) *(CD/C TRAX 039)* **JEAN REDPATH – The Songs Of Robert Burns Volume 7**
Apr 91. (cd/c) *(CD/C TRAX 040)* **ERIC BOGLE – Voices In The Wilderness**
Dec 90. (cd/c) *(CD/C TRAX 041)* **WILLIAM JACKSON – Celtic Suite For Glasgow**

• **ELFRIDA SCOTT** is a Gaelic singer who had already released one solo cassette in 1986, 'BY YON CASTLE WA' *(Ross; CWGR 101)*
Jan 91. (cd/c) *(CD/C TRAX 042)* **ELFRIDA SCOTT – Burns Songs In Gaelic**

Feb 91. (cd/c) *(CD/C TRAX 043)* **IAIN MacKINTOSH – Risks And Roses**
Jul 91. (cd/c) *(CD/C TRAX 045)* **McCALMANS – Songs From Scotland**
Sep 91. (cd/c) *(CD/C TRAX 046)* **McCALMANS – The Ettrick Shepherd**
Sep 91. (cd/c) *(CD/C TRAX 047)* **BRIAN McNEILL – The Back O' The North Wind**
Dec 91. (cd/c) *(CD/C TRAX 048)* **CEOLBEG – Seeds To The Wind**
Jan 92. (cd/c) *(CD/C TRAX 049)* **IAN HARDIE – A Breath Of Fresher Airs**
Mar 92. (cd) *(CDTRAX 050) JUDY SMALL – Word Of Mouth: The Best Of Judy Small* (JUDY is an Australian lady)
Apr 92. (cd/c) *(CD/C TRAX 051)* **ERIC BOGLE – The Eric Bogle Songbook Vol.2**
May 92. (cd/c) *(CD/C TRAX 052) NIAMH PARSONS – Loosely Connected* (NIAMH is Irish)
Feb 93. (cd/c) *(CD/C TRAX 053)* **CEOLBEG – Not The Bunny Hop**
Dec 92. (cd/c) *(CD/C TRAX 054)* **HEATHER HEYWOOD – By Yon Castle Wa'**
– The sands o' the shore / Far over the Forth / For a new baby / False false ha'e ya been / I ha'e but son – The wandering piper / Jamie / The wife of Ushers Well / Mistress Heywood's fancy / The dowie dens o' Yarrow / Some people cry / MacCrimmon's lament – MacCrimmon's sweetheart / The corncrake amang the Whinny Knowes / Aye wakin O / Young Watters / Paul's song.
Aug 92. (cd/c) *(CD/C TRAX 055) PAUL HERRON – Different Worlds* (PAUL is another Irish artist)

• **BLACKEYED BIDDY** were formed around the mid-80's by leader LIONEL McCLELLAND. A contemporary folk outfit reinterpreting some trad or RABBIE BURNS songs with McCLELLAND's own material, BLACKEYED BIDDY delivered a couple of fine LP's 'GUID NEIBOURS' *(Birnock; BNK/+C 1)* and 'HIGH SPIRITS' *(Dunkeld; DUN/+C/CD 014)* – both 1988 – before finally issuing their one and only set for Greentrax. The opening track was an old MATT McGINN number.
May 93. (cd/c) *(CD/C TRAX 056)* **BLACKEYED BIDDY – Peace, Enjoyment, Love & Pleasure**
– Rolling hills of the borders / Too small a word / Silent majority / Monday morning / Ailsa Ann Anderson / Bonnie ship the Diamond / Right to be free / The Swedish waltz – The lonesome boatman / Ae fond kiss / Farewell tae the haven / Little cascade – Keir's tune.

• **RANKIN FILE** were an early 70's country-folk trio of Scots-born, Canadian-raised singer/songwriter IAIN RANKIN (vocals, guitar), TONY MITCHELL (guitar, vocals) and RICK NICKERSON (bass, vocals). They recorded two low-key albums between 1971 and 1973 (the eponymous 'RANKIN FILE' and 'MR. SAX'; *Folk Heritage; FHR 048)*, before all went into retirement. IAN GREEN released a collection of this work below, while the now bespectacled, silver-haired RANKIN contemplated releasing his solo effort. With musicians such as COLIN MacFARLANE, IAIN BRUCE, FRASER SPIERS, KEITH BURNS, ALY BAIN, IAIN JOHNSTONE, GINA RAE all helping out, the appropriately-titled 'OUT OF NOWHERE' (with IAIN sounding more than a little like HARRY NILSSON!) did reasonably well.
Dec 92. (cd/c) *(CD/C TRAX 057)* **RANKIN FILE – For The Record**
– Call on me / Sense of kind / Words & the wisdom / Canadian railroad trilogy / Leaving home / Whispy / Leaving is the story of my life / Carefully / Lost it on the road / Met her on the shap / Drank his son to death / The circle turns again / Mrs. Mann & me / Mr. Sax.

Jul 93. (cd/c) *(CD/C TRAX 058)* **CEOLBEG – An Unfair Dance**
Jan 93. (cd/c) *(CD/C TRAX 059)* **WENDY STEWART – About Time**
Dec 92. (cd/c) *(CD/C TRAX 060)* **Various Artists: Scotland Now Vol.2 (The Music & The Song)**
Mar 93. (cd/c) *(CD/C TRAX 061)* **RUA – The Rua Collection: Homeland**
May 93. (cd/c) *(CD/C TRAX 062)* **BRIAN McNEILL – Monksgate**
Sep 93. (cd/c) *(CD/C TRAX 063)* **HAMISH MOORE & DICK LEE – Farewell To Decorum**

• the **SCOTTISH GAS CALEDONIAN PIPE BAND** were a stunning ensemble of traditional pipers (for ceilidh/dance) by F. MacLEOD.
Nov 93. (cd/c) *(CD/C TRAX 064)* **SCOTTISH GAS CALEDONIAN PIPE BAND – Out Of The Blue**

• The **SANGSTERS** were formed in Kirkcaldy . . . early 90's by three vocalists ANNE COMBE, FIONA FORBES and SCOTT MURRAY (the latter also played guitar). Borrowing some of their material from likely sources such as BURNS and BOGLE (they also covered songs by IRVING BERLIN, PHIL COULTER and ANDY M. STEWART), this harmony-fuelled traditional folk trio released a solitary album for 'Greentrax' in 1993, 'BEGIN' – listen to the tracks 'SILENCE AND TEARS' and 'SHEATH AND KNIFE' (the latter about incest and murder!) and you'll think The SEEKERS have come back, although their tongue-in-cheek 'C-RAP' spoils what might've been an otherwise flawless first attempt. A 7-year hiatus (in which ANNE was awarded the MBE!) was finally overcome when the the trio plus fourth member JOHN BLACKWOOD (on bouzouki & guitar) returned with a follow-up set, 'SHARP AND SWEET' (2000).
Jul 93. (cd/c) *(CD/C TRAX 065)* **SANGSTERS – Begin**
– Jesse / Feed the children / Heart like a wheel / Chorus song / The Lea-rig / The white cockade / Sheath and knife / C-rap / Some kind of love / Will ye gang love / Steal away / Helen of Kirkconnel / Simple melody / Golden golden / Silence and tears / The quiet comes in.

• **STEPHEN QUIGG** is a Scottish folk singer/guitarist (also banjo & bodhran) of the contemporary style. In 1985, a cassette of traditional/own compositions was issued as 'CATCH ME IF YOU CAN' *(scotdisc; KITV 386)*. Working with mandolin/mouth-organ player NICK KEIR, he managed to deliver a long-awaited follow-up album. He joined The McCALMANS in 2001.
Jul 93. (cd/c) *(CD/C TRAX 066)* **STEPHEN QUIGG – Voice Of My Island**
– Steal away / The gallant Murray / Voice of my land / Almost every circumstance / Strong women rule us with all their tears / Freewheeling now / The work of the weavers / Come by the hills / Whatever you say, say nothing / Annie McKelvie / Willie's gang tae Melville Castle / The last leviathan.

Sep 93. (cd/c) *(CD/C TRAX 067)* **McCALMANS – Honest Poverty**
Nov 93. (cd/c) *(CD/C TRAX 068)* **ERIC BOGLE – Mirrors**
Dec 93. (cd/c) *(CD/C TRAX 069)* **IAIN RANKIN – Out Of Nowhere**
– Teardrop in the ocean / 30 storeys high / We're still here / Out of nowhere / Go to Hell but turn right / Daddy was a miner / McGingle's violin / Make love to me / Old friend / One step forward and two steps back / Next time you talk to Heaven / Wild horses / Let's do it all over again.
Jun 94. (cd/c) *(CD/C TRAX 070)* **CATHERINE-ANN MacPHEE – sings Mairi Mhor**
– Nuair bha mi og / Coinneamh nan croitearan / Eilean a cheo / Soraidh leis an nollaig uir / Soraidh le Eilean a' cheo / Oran beinn-li / Camanach Glaschu / Oran sarachaidh / Clach Agus Mairi / Luchd na beurla / Mar a tha / Faistneachd agus – Beannach do na gaidheal.
Mar 94. (cd/c) *(CD/C TRAX 071)* **BRIAN McNEILL – Horses For Courses**
May 94. (cd/c) *(CD/C TRAX 072)* **ROBIN LAING – Walking In Time**
Jul 94. (cd/c) *(CD/C TRAX 073)* **HAMISH MOORE – Stepping On The Bridge**

• **STRAVAIG** are four Scots women vocalists, MOIRA GREENWOOD, SUSIE KELLY, JEAN McMONIES and PHYLLIS MARTIN, who at times surrounded themselves with excellent Greentrax stable musicians including FRED MORRISON (pipes, whistles), producer DAVY STEELE (bodhran, bouzouki & percussion), EILIDH SHAW (drums), PATSY SEDDON (electric harp), and engineer ROY ASHBY (bass drum). Their one and only set for the label featured an acappella rendition of Ewan MacColl's 'SONG OF THE FISHGUTTERS'.
Jul 94. (cd/c) *(CD/C TRAX 074)* **STRAVAIG – Movin' On**
– The Birken tree / Back home again in Indiana / Song of the fishgutters / The terror time / The pressers / Dumfries hiring fair / The Dundee weaver / The bonnie wee lassie's answer / My ain countrie / Miller tae ma trade / Davey faa' / Bonnie lass come ower the burn / Another clearing time / Di nanina.

• **GORDON DUNCAN** has fast become the young man's piper. He has shifted piping into the 21st century due to his insight to bring drum'n'bass'n'bouzouki! backing (provided by JIM SUTHERLAND 'n' CONRAD MOLLESON 'n' ROSS KENNEDY) to his innovative bagpipe playing. After an enterprising and delightful solo debut below, he took a breather (well, not really!) in 'Greentrax' stable outfit, The HIGHLAND CONNECTION'. He marked his solo comeback in 1997 with awe-inspiring 'THE CIRCULAR BREATH'; he was augmented this time by IAN CARR (guitar), RANALD SUTHERLAND (bass), ANDY COOK (Ugandan harp), GERRY O'CONNOR (banjo), DONALD HAY (drums) and not forgetting SUTHERLAND on exotic percussion.

Aug 94. (cd/c) *(CD/C TRAX 075)* **GORDON DUNCAN – Just For Seumas**
– Hornpipe & jig: Jim Tweedie's sea-legs – John Paterson's mare / 4 Strathspeys and 3 reels: Brig o' Perth – Rusty gun – Stirling Castle – Duke of Gordon's birthday – Ramnee ceilidh – Susan Lazel's – Ness pipers / 204 marches: Duchess of Edinburgh – Lonach gathering / 3 Jigs: Moonlight on the heather – The millstead – Biddy from Sligo / Selection: Showacho – Bu deonach leam tilleach – Hector MacLean – Cape Breton fiddler's welcome to Shetland – The sister's reel / Air: Loch Broom bay / Jigs: Nora Crionna – Unknown – Port Sean Seosahm – Red Ken's – Brady's / 3 Strathspeys & 3 reels: Ewe wi' the crookit horn – John Roy Stewart – Dora MacLeod – John Morrison of Assynt House – The Smith of Chilliechassie – Miss Proud / Slow air & 4 reels: Donal Og – Wild Irishman – Rakish Paddy – Madame Bonaparte – Richard Dwyers / 3 jigs: Callach an Dudain – Tatter Jack Walsh – Donald Cameron's powderhorn / Jig and 3 reels: The last tango in Harris – The Ballivanich reel – McPherson's – Good drying / Piobaireachd: The massacre of Glencoe / Just for Seumas set: Just for Seumas – The thin man – Lament for Mary MacLeod – Break yer bass drone.

Aug 94. (cd/c) *(CD/C TRAX 076)* **SHOOGLENIFTY – Venus In Tweeds**
Sep 94. (cd/c) *(CD/C TRAX 077)* **JANET RUSSELL & CHRISTINE KYDD – Dancin' Chantin'**
Mar 95. (cd/c) *(CD/C TRAX 078)* **ALASTAIR McDONALD – Velvet And Steel**
Oct 94. (cd/c) *(CD/C TRAX 079)* **SMALLTALK – Smalltalk**

• **DOUGIE PINCOCK** was of course the original bagpiper of BATTLEFIELD BAND and a session man for a plethora of trad-folk outfits. His solitary album (which included guitarist MALCOLM JONES) was mostly self-penned, DOUGIE augmenting his usual display of pipe playing with saxophones, flute and bodhran. Two years on, DOUGIE collaborated with JOHN YOUNG on the album, 'WATER OF LIFE' *(Kilmahew; ADL CD/MC 01)*.

Nov 94. (cd/c) *(CD/C TRAX 080)* **DOUGIE PINCOCK – Something Blew**
– The gem so small – The piper's piper – Eric Bigstone's leaky boat / Douglas Adam's fancy – The fastest gasman – The video kid / Miss Cara Spencer – Return to Kashmagiro / The Balnain household – Tanks for the memories / MacCrimmon's sweetheart / The rest – The unrest / The twins / The January girl – The handyman's legacy – The Rogart refusal / Song for Chris / The piper's bonnet – Blair Drummond – Charlie's welcome – Pretty Marion / Deireadh an rathaid fhada / The gem so small.

Sep 94. (cd/c) *(CD/C TRAX 081)* **GILL BOWMAN – Perfect Lover**
Jan 95. (d-cd/d-c) *(CD/C TRAX 082D)* **ERIC BOGLE – I Wrote This Wee Song**
Mar 95. (cd/c) *(CD/C TRAX 083)* **JAMES MALCOLM – Sconeward**

• the **DRAMBUIE KIRKLISTON PIPE BAND** were self-explanatory pipers from er, Kirkliston, who were both rousing and innovative (in trad circles at least).

Apr 95. (cd/c) *(CD/C TRAX 084)* **DRAMBUIE KIRKLISTON PIPE BAND – A Link With The '45**
– The king has landed in Moidart / Glenfinnan Highland gathering / March of the Cameron men / Johnnie Cope / Southward bound / Wae's me for Prince Charlie / The '45 revolution / A link with the '45 / The young pretender / White rose of Culloden / Skye boat song / The fugitive / Tribute to the lost souls / Will ye no come back again.

Feb 95. (cd/c) *(CD/C TRAX 085)* **GILL BOWMAN – Toasting The Lassies**
Jan 95. (cd/c) *(CD/C TRAX 086)* **McCALMANS – In Harmony: 30th Anniversary Compilation Album**

• **HIGHLAND CONNECTION** were three of Greentrax's finest instrumentalists, IAN HARDIE (also a soloist and ex-member of JOCK TAMSON'S BAIRNS), JANICE CLARK and DAGGER GORDON.

Jan 95. (cd/c) *(CD/C TRAX 087)* **HIGHLAND CONNECTION – Gaining Ground**
– Cam na gaillich – The Knockdhu (reel) – Helsinki harbour / Mrs. Maj. L. Stewart of the island of Java – The bog of Gight – The Duke of Gordon's / Mrs. Gordon Uvie / Roy's wife of Aldivalloch – J.F. MacKenzie – Roy's wife reel / The gathering – The welcome – The dance – The past – The pipes – The present (part 1) – The present (part 2) – The farewell (A Ross & Cromarty welcome to Scotland's music (suite) / My tochter's the jewel / Haud yer tongue dear Sally / Campbell's roup – Seven seas hornpipe / Losing ground.

• **THULBION** are yet more Shetland-based musicians with their own distinctive feel. The pairings of IAN and JUDI NICOLSON (on accordion and fiddle) and ANDREW and VIOLET TULLOCH (on guitar and piano), were quality players on their one-off for the label.

Jan 95. (cd/c) *(CD/C TRAX 088)* **THULBION – Twilight Bound**
– King's reel – The perfect host – Boys of Portaferry / Trad reel / Twilight / St. Gilbert's hornpipe – The fiddler's wife – Chromatic hornpipe / Annie / John D. Burgess – Major Nickerson's fancy / Dick Gossip's reel / James F. Dickie – J.F. Dickie's delight / Sheilis / Branden's centennial waltz – Waltz for Mary Ann – Raemona / Gravel walk – Andy Renwick's ferret – Old mountain road / Time for thought / Theodore Napier – The Laird of Mackintosh – The Earl of Lauderdale / Little Daisy – North King Street – Lady on the island / Killavil reel – Far from home – Paddy on the turnpike / Loretta / Frankie & Maureen Robb – Grew's hill – Duncan Black's hornpipe – The doon hingin' tie / Eeles' dream.

• **ED MILLER** is a traditional folk singer/guitarist/whistler from Edinburgh, his voice both rich and accented although he's stayed in the States for some time. His first long-player for Greentrax (below) was compiled from three recordings from 1989-1993 and featured ex-pats such as fiddlers ALASDAIR FRASER and ISLA ROSS. Retaining the BROTHERTON siblings RICH and KATHY, MILLER (now a part-time radio DJ in Texas), recorded his follow-up set, appropriately-titled 'THE EDINBURGH RAMBLER' (1997).

Jul 95. (cd/c) *(CD/C TRAX 089)* **ED MILLER – At Home With The Exiles**
– Pittenween Jo / Darling Alfie / John MacLean march / Blood upon the grass / Bottle o' the best / Mistress / Yellow on the broom / Jute mill song / Crooked Jack / Broom o' the Cowdenknowes / Generations of change / A man's man / At home with the exiles / Tak a dram.

Apr 95. (cd/c) *(CD/C TRAX 090)* **Various Artists – The Music & Song Of Edinburgh**

• **DONALD BLACK** is regarded as the finest and fastest mouthorgan player in the country. With the help of DOUGIE PINCOCK (pipes), NAN MacIVER (piano), MARTIN McHUGH (bodhran) and MALCOLM JONES (guitar), DONALD released his only solo set to date – both original and unconventional although with an air of grace. DONALD BLACK and MALCOLM JONES (of RUNRIG) subsequently – September 2000 – released their own collaborative set for 'MacMeanmna', 'CLOSE TO HOME'.

Jul 95. (cd/c) *(CD/C TRAX 091)* **DONALD BLACK – Westwinds**
– Pipe jigs: Paddy's leather breeches – Kenny Gillies of Portnalong – Wee Todd / J Scott Skinner slow airs / Cape Breton set / Slow air / Welcome Christmas morning / Shetland reels / Pipe slow air – 6-8 march – 2-4 march / Hebridean duet / Shores of Loch Linnhe / Slow air – 2/4 pipe marches / Touch of the Irish / Lewis danns a rathad.

• **MAIRI MacINNES** is a fine Gaelic singer who'd already released one album for 'Lismor', 'CAUSEWAY, in 1989. This was produced by PHIL CUNNINGHAM with other musicians being MALCOLM JONES, JIM SUTHERLAND, ROD PATERSON, MARTIN O'CONNOR and ANDY MUNRO. Her comeback Greentrax set saw her utilise the skills of WILLIAM JACKSON, FOSS PATERSON, WENDY WEATHERBY, FRED MORRISON, TONY McMANUS and JAMES MacKINTOSH.

Jul 95. (cd/c) *(CD/C TRAX 092)* **MAIRI MACINNES – This Feeling Inside**
– Puirt-a-beul / Follow the light / Cum ar 'naire / Come back to me / Neanhnaid gheal dochais / Sit at my table / Fraoch a Ronaidh / Far from home / Fear a bhata / Precious days / Mile marphaisg air a Ghaol / Eilean m' araich / Puirt-a-beul / This feeling inside.

Jul 95. (cd/c) *(CD/C TRAX 093)* **BURACH – The Weird Set**
Oct 95. (cd/c) *(CD/C TRAX 094)* **SHEENA WELLINGTON – Strong Women**
Feb 96. (cd/c) *(CD/C TRAX 095)* **WHISTLEBINKIES – A Wanton Fling**
Dec 95. (cd/c) *(CD/C TRAX 096)* **TONY McMANUS – Tony McManus**
Oct 95. (cd/c) *(CD/C TRAX 097)* **McCALMANS – Festival Lights**
Mar 96. (cd/c) *(CD/C TRAX 098)* **BRIAN McNEILL – No Goods**

• **BANNAL** were formed in the Highlands around the mid-90's as a conglomorate of weaver women soloists singing in Gaelic. MAIRI MacARTHUR, MAEVE MacKINNON and MARY C MacLEAN were the main protagonists, although a single big drum beat was always constant. The highlight on their one and only set was the traditional folk tune, 'CHAIDH MI 'NA GHLEANNAN AS T-FHOGHAR'.

Feb 96. (cd/c) *(CD/C TRAX 099)* **BANNAL – Waulking Songs**
– Nhean ud thall, gu de th' orr' Aire? – 'S muladach mi's air aineol – 'S I tir mo ruin sa ghaidheallacha / He mandu / Latha dhomh's mi 'm beinn a' Cheathaich / Dh'eirich moch maduinn cheltein / Beir soiridh bhuam / Thug mi 'n oidhche ge b'fhad I / Chan eil mi gun mhulad orm / Clo mhicllemhicheil / Gura mi tha trom duilich / Chunnaic mise 'n t-og uasal – Mile marbhphaisg air a' ghaol / Mhurchaidh bhig / He mo leannan, ho mo leannan – Mo nighean donn ho gu / Chaidh mi 'na ghleannan as t-fhoghar / An long Eirannach.

Apr 96. (cd/c) *(CD/C TRAX 100)* **CEOLBEG – Five**
Nov 95. (cd/c) *(CD/C TRAX 101)* **IAIN MacKINTOSH & BRIAN McNEILL – Stage By Stage**
Jan 96. (cd) *(CDTRAX 102)* **SEELYHOO – The First Caul**
Nov 95. (cd) *(CDTRAX 103)* **RUA – Ao-tea-roa**
Mar 96. (cd/c) *(CD/C TRAX 104)* **DEAF SHEPHERD – A Spark O' Nature's Fire**

• **WILLIE HUNTER** was a veteran Shetland fiddle player whose only recording of note (until his time with Greentrax!) was an LP entitled '1982' *(Celtic Music; CM 010)*. His accomplice on his first two Greentrax albums were pianist **VIOLET TULLOCH**, while his final Ceilidh/dance recordings brought together the **CULLIVOE BAND** (IVOR SCOLLAY, GORDON JAMIESON, MARGARET COUPER, ALAN SCOLLAY, VICTOR JAMIESON and IAN TULLOCH).

Apr 96. (cd/c) *(CD/C TRAX 105)* **WILLIE HUNTER – Leaving Lerwick Harbour**

Jun 96. (cd/c) *(CD/C TRAX 106)* **SHOOGLENIFTY – A Whisky Kiss**
Jul 96. (cd/c) *(CD/C TRAX 107)* **OCCASIONALS – Back In Step**
Apr 96. (cd/c) *(CD/C TRAX 108) KEVIN MITCHELL – I Sang The Sweet Refrain* (KEVIN is another Irishman)
Jun 96. (cd/c) *(CD/C TRAX 109)* **DICK GAUGHAN – Sail On**
Jun 96. (cd/c) *(CD/C TRAX 110)* **Various Artists – Grand Concert Of Scottish Piping**
– (with GORDON MOONEY, ANGUS D. MacCOLL, MARTYN BENNETT, GORDON DUNCAN, IAIN MacINNES and ALLAN MacDONALD)

- **McNAUGHTON'S VALE OF ATHOLL PIPE BAND** were led by IAN DUNCAN (pipe major) and JAMES KING (drum major), with augmentation coming from soloists MARY-ANN MacKINNON and ANDREW WRIGHT; a concert outfit of high traditional standard.

Jul 96. (cd/c) *(CD/C TRAX 111)* **McNAUGHTON'S VALE OF ATHOLL PIPE BAND – Live 'N' Well**

Apr 96. (cd) *(CDTRAX 112)* **JOCK TAMSON'S BAIRNS – Jock Tamson's Bairns** (re-issue)

- **MAC UMBA** were formed after several drumming workshops at the Glasgow School Of Art in 1994. The Batucada (all-drumming!) delivery began to take in more conventional instruments such as guitars, bass, flutes and voices, but it wasn't until they were asked to play at the football World Cup in France, that MAC UMBA found their niche. JOHN GILMOUR and JOHNNY BEAVER, along with GERI B, KENNY WELSH, TINA CLARKE (the latter a percussionist and singer!), were joined by bagpipers JAMIE AITKEN, ANDY GRANT and KENNY SUTHERLAND, Scotland were now side by side with the Brazilian rhythm (instead of playing against them!). Dancers CHRISTELLE, THAISSA and LARA topped off their frantic live/street set which was now taken all around the world. MAC UMBA's debut album was a best seller for the label in Austin, Texas!, their second (see further below) – which took a year in the making – was much like a good dram. Exotic, dynamic and visually stunning, were all well used words to describe MAC UMBA's colourful festive spirit and unique Folk sound.

May 96. (cd/c) *(CD/C TRAX 113)* **MAC UMBA – Don't Hold Your Breath**
– Moonshine / Mo chuachag laghach thu / The selkie / 6-8 / Itapuan / Son de meglomania / Cullen Bay / Heaven scent / MacCrimmon's lament / Fairy glen / Lochanside / Sandy's new chanter / Just five more minutes / Loch Roag / A man's a man / Damp carpet / Ruby Grant meglomania.

Mar 96. (cd) *(CDTRAX 114)* **JEAN REDPATH – The Songs Of Robert Burns Volumes 1 & 2**
Mar 96. (cd) *(CDTRAX 115)* **JEAN REDPATH – The Songs Of Robert Burns Volumes 3 & 4**
Mar 96. (cd) *(CDTRAX 116)* **JEAN REDPATH – The Songs Of Robert Burns Volumes 5 & 6**
Nov 96. (cd/c) *(CD/C TRAX 117)* **ROD PATERSON – Songs From The Bottom Drawer**
Oct 96. (cd/c) *(CD/C TRAX 118)* **SILEAS – Play On Light**
Oct 96. (cd/c) *(CD/C TRAX 119)* **ISLA ST. CLAIR – Scenes Of Scotland**
Sep 96. (cd/c) *(CD/C TRAX 120)* **ADAM McNAUGHTAN – Last Stand At Mount Florida**
– The dear green place / Cholesterol / You've got to get your folios done / The Scottish song / The soor mulk cairt / The shy lover / Old man Noah / The green belongs to Glasgow folk / The weaver's lament / Coming hame – My grandfather's socks / Thomas Muir of Huntershill / Erchie Cathcart / The twin towered stand.
Feb 97. (cd/c) *(CD/C TRAX 121)* **ERIC BOGLE & JOHN MUNRO – The Emigrant & The Exile**
Mar 97. (cd/c) *(CD/C TRAX 122)* **GORDON DUNCAN – The Circular Breath**
– MacDonald's: Mrs. MacDonald, Glenuig – Isabell MacDonald / The high drive / Jolly tinker – Tain in the rain – Ash city / Clan meets tribe / Contradiction / Donald MacLennan's tuning phrase – Unknown – I laid a herring in salt – John MacDougall's exercise / The circular breath: Pressed for time – Earl of Seaforth's salute / Shepherd's crook – Nadia MacIsaac – Loch Loskin – Inveraray Castle – John McKechnie – Mrs. MacPherson of Inveran – The sheepwife / Galacian jig – Blow my chanter – The famous Baravan / Craig's pipes – Woman of the house – Trip to Sligo – MacFadden's reel / MacDougall's gathering.
Jun 97. (cd/c) *(CD/C TRAX 123)* **GORDEANNA McCULLOCH – In Freenship's Name**

- **PEATBOG FAERIES** formed in the Isle Of Skye . . . 1994 by piper PETER MORRISON (not that one!), guitarist ALI PENTLAND (also keyboards), fiddler BEN IVITSKY, bass & bodhran man INNES HUTTON, drummer IAIN COPELAND and keyboard-player NURUDIN. One of the most sophisticated purveyors of the ever burgeoning Celtic-fusion thang, PEATBOG FAERIES concentrate their not inconsiderable energies on reconciling traditional Scottish folk with all manner of global exotica and a healthy dose of dancefloor rhythm to boot. Signed to 'Greentrax', the band's 1996 debut album, 'MELLOWOSITY' unveiled their crossover sound that'd previously been the sole preserve of punters lucky enough to have caught them live. Fiddles, guitar and bagpipes wrestled behind dub reggae basslines and pulsing funk/techno workouts, while haunting siren-like Eastern European melodies flowed serenely through the mix. The band went from strength to strength in the late 90's, widening their touring horizons by playing at the 1999 Glastonbury Festival as well as undertaking dates in Spain. By late 2000, and after the 'FAERIES were more conspicuous by their absence, guitarist TOM SALTER (ex-ALI FARKA TOURE) replaced ALI whose wife was having a baby. However, in Spring the following year, fans were more than happy when a sophomore set, 'FAERIE STORIES', was giving them plenty to shout about. This time it fused reggae, hip-hip, jazz, soca and some tunes borrowed from Macedonia; what more could you want?

Dec 96. (cd/c) *(CD/C TRAX 124)* **PEATBOG FAERIES – Mellowosity**
– Lexy MacAskill / Eigman / Manili beetle / Macedonian woman's rant / Angus Mackinnon / Leaving the road / Weary we've been – Dancing feet / Maids of Mount Cisco / Mellowosity.

Mar 97. (cd/c) *(CD/C TRAX 125)* **Various Artists – Young Pipers Of Scotland**
Mar 97. (cd/c) *(CD/C TRAX 126)* **WENDY STEWART – About Time 2**

- The **GHILLIES** (meaning a hunting guide) were formed as a superfolkgroup conglomerate of traditional Scots musicians/writers who contributed some tracks and their time (under the banner of the TMSA – the Traditional Music & Song Association of Scotland) to this one-off set. Fiddler IAN HARDIE, pianist ANDY THORBURN, accordionist FREELAND BARBOUR, guitarist JACK EVANS (also on whistle) and piper DUNCAN McGILLIVRAY were all at the forefront of the sessions which also included PHIL CUNNINGHAM, GORDON DUNCAN, WILLIAM JACKSON, JIM SUTHERLAND and MARTIN BENNETT.

Feb 97. (cd/c) *(CD/C TRAX 5006)* **GHILLIES – The Nineties Collection, Volume Two**
– The passive drinker – Sir James of the bings / Leith central – Forfar reel – W.J. More – Salvation reel / Creag an righ / Dance of the roag salmon – Campbell's heels – March for Morven May / Wild west waltz – The first snow – Astryd's waltz / Song for Chris – Port Allan o'g – Assynt crofters – Maggie's reel / Jig of the Clan Beag – Willie Gillingham R.M. – Fiddle cushion / Da Bouster boy – Clark's cases – Nan of the Strath / Trees of North Uist – Tom MacGregor / Da eye wife – Living by the sea – Reel for Eilidh Shaw – Pinewoods auction – Mr. & Mrs. MacLean of Snaigow / The dingwall jig – The jig Runrig / Circle of darkness – Duncan Johnstone's – Sheep running about / Fuaran – T.C. Humbley's – Skye barbeque.

Sep 97. (cd/c) *(CD/C TRAX 127)* **OSSIAN – The Carrying Stream**
Sep 97. (cd/c) *(CD/C TRAX 128)* **Various Artists – Second Grand Concert Of Piping**
– (with ST LAURENCE O'TOOLE PIPE BAND QUARTET, PATRICK MOLARD, FRANCO MELIS & ORLANDA MASCIA, JOHN MacLEAN and MALCOLM ROBERTSON)
Sep 97. (cd/c) *(CD/C TRAX 129)* **FERGIE MacDONALD – the 21st album**
Jun 97. (cd) *(CDTRAX 130)* **ERIC BOGLE – Small Miracles**
Nov 97. (cd/c) *(CD/C TRAX 131)* **EILIDH SHAW – Heepirumbo**

- **MARGARET STEWART & ALLAN MacDONALD** (both Gaelic speaking Scots) teamed up for a one-off set to highlight both MARGARET's crystal clear singing and ALLAN's pibroch bagpipes playing. The pairing also had a common interest in historical or mythical stories surrounding the legends of Northern Scotland, i.e. the track 'UAMH AN OIR' ('Caves Of Gold') which also featured clarsach/harp player INGRID HENDERSON. A second set, 'COLLA MO RUN' was issued towards the end of 2001.

Feb 98. (cd/c) *(CD/C TRAX 132)* **MARGARET STEWART & ALLAN MacDONALD – Fhuair Mi Pog**
– Fhuair mi pog a laimh righ / Bha caileag as t-earrach / Cille pheadair / Dol dhan taigh bhuan leat / O Mhairi 's tu mo Mhairi / I ho ro 's na hug oro eile / He na milibhig / Slainte bhon t-seann duthaich / Ochion a righ, gur tinn an galair an gradh / Cro chinn t-saile – A' bhanais a bha'n ciostal odhar – Siuthadaibh bhalachaibh / Cumba mhic an toisich / Ruidhlichean pioba (pipe reels) / Uamh an oir – Cumha an t-seana chlaidheimh / 'S olc an obair do theachdairean cadal / Port na bPuacai.

May 97. (cd) *(CDTRAX 133)* **TARTAN AMOEBAS – Tartan Amoebas**
Jun 97. (cd) *(CDTRAX 134)* **ROBIN WILLIAMSON – Celtic Harp Airs And Dance Tunes**
Jun 97. (cd) *(CDTRAX 135) BRENDAN POWER – Riverdance Distilled* (BRENDAN is an Irish artist)
Jul 97. (cd) *(CDTRAX 136)* **BURACH – Born Tired**
Jul 97. (cd/c) *(CD/C TRAX 137)* **ROBIN LAING – The Angel's Share**
Aug 97. (cd/c) *(CD/C TRAX 138)* **McCALMANS – High Ground**
Aug 97. (cd) *(CDTRAX 139) BRENDA STUBBERT – In Jig Time* (BRENDA is from Cape Breton)
Jul 97. (cd) *(CDTRAX 140) NATALIE MacMASTER – A Compilation* (NATALIE is Canadian)
Jul 97. (cd) *(CDTRAX 141) NATALIE MacMASTER – Fit As A fiddle*
Aug 97. (cd) *(CDTRAX 142) NATALIE MacMASTER – No Boundaries*
Dec 97. (cd) *(CDTRAX 143)* **DEAF SHEPHERD – Synergy**
Oct 97. (cd/c) *(CD/C TRAX 144)* **WILLIE HUNTER & VIOLET TULLOCH – The Willie Hunter Sessions** (see above antry)
Oct 97. (cd/c) *(CD/C TRAX 145)* **ISLA ST. CLAIR – Tatties & Herrin' – The Land**
Oct 97. (cd/c) *(CD/C TRAX 146)* **ISLA ST. CLAIR – Tatties & Herrin' – The Sea**
Nov 97. (cd) *(CDTRAX 147)* **ERIC BOGLE – Plain And Simple**
Nov 97. (cd/c) *(CD/C TRAX 148)* **JENNIFER & HAZEL WRIGLEY – Huldreland**
Dec 97. (cd) *(CDTRAX 149) ALEX FRANCIS MacKAY – A Lifelong Home* (ALEX is from Cape Breton)
Apr 98. (cd) *(CDTRAX 150)* **JIM MALCOLM – Rohallion**
Feb 98. (cd) *(CDTRAX 151)* **TONY McMANUS – Pourquois Quebec?**
Mar 98. (cd) *(CDTRAX 152)* **IAN HARDIE & ANDY THORBURN – Spider's Web**
Feb 98. (cd) *(CDTRAX 153)* **ROBERT BROWN & ROBERT NICOL – Masters Of The Pibaireachd Vol.1** (instructional)
Mar 98. (cd) *(CDTRAX 154)* **Various Artists – Scottish Fiddle Rally (Concert Highlights 1985-1995)**

- **ROB MacKILLOP** plays an 18th century wire-strung guittar (yes, with two T's!) and brings back days of yore in a New-Age/folkie/medieval type way. He also looks the part with his colourful bandana and 'save our trees' attitude. Once a member of the similar ROWALLAN CONSORT with wire-strung clarsach plucker WILLIAM TAYLOR (one 1995 album exists, 'NOTES OF JOY', for 'Temple' *COMD2/CTP 058)*, MacKillop is also a university lecturer on both lute and guitar. ROB's one and only set for Greentrax was probably the label's most unique offering to date; ROB and WILLIAM also contributed a track, 'SCOTS LAMENT FOR MR OSWALD – OVER THE WATER TO CHARLIE', to the 'SCOTTISH HARPS' compilation.

Jun 98. (cd) *(CDTRAX 155)* **ROB MacKILLOP – Flowers Of The Forest**
– Chancellours: Five pieces from the Balcarres manuscript (11 couse lute):- If thy were myne own thing – Lord Aboin's aire or welcome home from London – No charme above her – Peggie I must love thee – Remember me at evening / Five pieces

from the Skene manuscript (Mandour):- I serve a worthie ladie – Flowers of the forest – Canaries – I will not go to bed till I suld die – Andrew Dundee / Six untitled pieces from the millar – McAlman manuscript / Port: Five ports from the Straloch manuscript (Ten course lute):- Port Jean Lindsay – Port Rorie Dall – Port priest / I love my love in secret (pieces for the wire-strung 18th century guittar from various sources):- Reel / Up we't Eli Eli – Tweed side – Secret kiss – Lady lie neir mee / Three pieces from the Wemyess manuscript (11 course lute):- Aur last good night – Lilt milne / Lament for the luters (one piece from the MacKillop manuscript).

Mar 98. (cd) *(CDTRAX 156)* **IAN BRUCE – Hodden Grey**
Mar 99. (cd) *(CDTRAX 157) MARGO CARRUTHERS – The Talent Of The Bard: Gaelic Songs From Cape Breton* (MARGO is Canadian)
Nov 98. (cd) *(CDTRAX 158)* **DICK GAUGHAN – Redwood Cathedral**
Mar 99. (cd) *(CDTRAX 159)* **WHISTLEBINKIES – Timber Timbre**
Aug 98. (cd) *(CDTRAX 160)* **SEELYHOO – Leetera**
Jul 99. (cd/c) *(CD/C TRAX 161)* **MAC UMBA – Bruhahaho**
– Glenmalambo / Gale warning / Asa Branca / Gordon's / Springtime cha cha / Brenda's / Jamie's request (solo) / Dinky's / Mildew mayhem / Steam train.

• the **Pipes & Drums Of the 1st Battalion The BLACK WATCH** had been making other records for 'MfP' and 'Summit', before getting around to recording their blazing set for Greentrax.

Oct 98. (cd/c) *(CD/C TRAX 162)* **the Pipes & Drums Of The 1st Battalion The BLACK WATCH – The Ladies From Hell**

Jun 98. (cd) *(CDTRAX 163) NATALIE MacMASTER – My Roots Are Showing*
Jun 98. (cd) *(CDTRAX 164)* **ED MILLER – The Edinburgh Rambler** (see above entry)
– Home away from home / Rigs o' the rye / Manchester (Edinburgh) rambler / Muir the master builder / Room for us all in the dance / Freewheelin' now / Same old story / Shearin' no for you / Silver darlins / I hae laid a herrin' in saut / Scots wha hae / Teacher's rant / The green and the blue / The Devil made Texas / Irish washerwoman / Lads o' Duns / Duns dings a'.
Sep 98. (cd) *(CDTRAX 165) JIMMY CROWLEY – Uncorked* (JIMMY is from er, Cork!)
Nov 98. (cd) *(CDTRAX 166) EILEEN McGANN – Heritage* (EILEEN is Canadian)

• **FIDDLERS' BID** are a Shetland-based septet featuring the fiddles of CHRISTOPHER STOUT (fiddle, viola), ANDREW GIFFORD (fiddle, guitar), KEVIN HENDERSON (fiddle) and MAURICE HENDERSON (fiddle), along with guitarist STEVE YARRINGTON (acoustic guitar), DAVID COLES (bass) and CATRIONA McKAY (Scottish harp, piano). Groundbreaking (quite literally!) trad-folk and if you like your music lively and full of it, this is for you. A second set, 'DA FARDER BEN DA WELCOMER' was delivered towards the end of 2001 after a tour of Tasmania!

Nov 98. (cd/c) *(CD/C TRAX 167)* **FIDDLERS' BID – Hamnataing**
– Da sneck o' da smaalie / Yellow stockings / Hamnataing / Da sabbit prawn / Seagull / African set / Insheer / Skye barbeque / Michael's mazurka / Isle of Aigas / Trows / Da tief upon da lum.

Dec 98. (cd) *(CDTRAX 168)* **Various Artists – Folkal Point: Edinburgh, Traditional Music From A New Generation**
Mar 99. (cd) *(CDTRAX 169)* **SANDY BRECHIN – Out Of His Tree**
Apr 99. (cd) *(CDTRAX 170)* **BRIAN McNEILL – To Answer The Peacock**
Aug 99. (cd) *(CDTRAX 171)* **JIMMY YOUNG – Pipeworks**
Jun 99. (cd/c) *(CD/C TRAX 172)* **Various Artists – Gaelic Women: Ar Canan 's ar ceol**

• **AILEEN CARR** was born in Coupar Angus and raised by her musical/singing family. After hearing BELLE STEWART at a festival in Blairgowrie (c. 1967), AILEEN decided to become a singer herself. In 1973, while at teacher training college, she was handed a copy of the 1973 'Scottish Folksinger' (written by PETER HALL and NORMAN BUCHAN). When her family moved south to Goole in Yorkshire, she became a floor singer in a club in Hull. On her return to Scotland, she gained a residency at a folk club in St. Andrews, also doing a turn at the Kinross Festival. The 80's saw AILEEN join up with CEOLBEG for a short spell, although she subsequently turned to acappella folk outfit, PALAVER. By 1995, the confident balladeer was shining at the Edinburgh Festival, rave reviews led her to go full-blooded into solo work. Just as the millennium was approaching, AILEEN finally got to work on her debut album. Augmented by the likes of TONY McMANUS, STUART MORISON, IAIN MacINNES, BRIAN KELLOCK and MAUREEN JELKS, the CD was released in the summer 2000, AILEEN's powerful and eclectic vocal style winning over the fans.

Aug 00. (cd) *(CDTRAX 173)* **AILEEN CARR – Green Yarrow**
– Mormond braes / Silken snood / The cuckoo's nest / The banks of green Yarrow / When these shores were new / The shepherd lad o' Rhynie / The Forfar sodger / This is no' my plaid / The cuckoo / Love is teasing / The baron o' Brackley.

Jun 99. (cd) *(CDTRAX 174)* **McCALMANS – Keepers**

• **CANTYCHIELS** was yet another of piper RORY CAMPBELL's outfits (he of DEAF SHEPHERD, CALEDON and the OLD BLIND DOGS). Along with BRIAN McALPINE (keyboards, accordion, etc), ANDY HARRISON (vocals, guitar), DAVE CANTWELL (percussion, drums), GREGOR LOWREY (accordion), MARIANNE CAMPBELL (fiddle), BRIAN W. McFIE and HARRY SULLIVAN (guitars), this contemporary trad-folk group wrote mostly all their material; BURNS' song 'RED RED ROSE' was thrown in for good measure.

Jun 99. (cd) *(CDTRAX 175)* **CANTYCHIELS – Cantychiels**
– Still – Fruit for thought – Still (reprise) / Red red rose / The cauldron / The train / 6 ft of snow / Arlene's waltz / Fireman Sam – Chalet fever / Loch Tay / Annag nic iain – Cheques in the fire / Learning the game.

Jun 99. (cd) *(CDTRAX 176)* **Various Artists – A Clear Day's Dawnin': A Thousand Years Of Scotland's Music To Welcome A New Parliament**

— note for below: JOHN WRIGHT was born in the south of England and raised in Manchester. In 1980, he became a shepherd in the Scottish borders and turned his hand to singing folk-styled ballads. He has released a handful of sets for Cumbrian-based imprint 'Fellside' as well as three for 'Greentrax'; fiddler STEWART HARDIE and guitarist KENNY SPIERS make up his BAND.

Jul 99. (cd) *(CDTRAX 177) JOHN WRIGHT BAND – Pages Turning*
Jun 99. (cd) *(CDTRAX 178)* **KEVIN MacLEOD – Springwell**

• **ROD PAUL** was an ex-IRON HORSE musician. He was augmented here by FRASER FIFIELD, ARCHIE McALLISTER, KEN GARDEN, LEE AGNEW and LYNN MORRISON.

Sep 99. (cd) *(CDTRAX 179)* **ROD PAUL – Birlinn**
– Birlinn reel / Aberuchill / Wildcat: Spout rolla – Neish's island – Earthquake house – Wildcat / Millennium bug / Open door / Loch Voil / Deil's cauldron: The sprite's Strathspey – On a clear day – Broken banks – Twenty shilling wood – The Deil's cauldron / Piper-eels: The Ross bridge – Shaky brig – Fort of the fist / The old Drove Road – Captain Correlli's – The painted rock / The Comrie jigs: Empty carriage – Joys of barley – Carlton Place – Comrie cancer club / Bird's nest.

Jun 99. (cd) *(CDTRAX 180) NATALIE MacMASTER – In My Hands*
Aug 99. (cd) *(CDTRAX 181)* **ROBERT BROWN & ROBERT NICOL – Master Of Piobaireachd Vol.2** (instructional)
Sep 99. (cd) *(CDTRAX 182)* **IAIN MacINNES – Tryst**
Oct 99. (cd/c) *(CD/C TRAX 183)* **JENNIFER & HAZEL WRIGLEY – Mither O' The Sea**
Nov 99. (cd) *(CDTRAX 184)* **OCCASIONALS – Live At Aberdeen Music Hall**
Oct 99. (cd) *(CDTRAX 185)* **ROBIN LAING – Imaginary Lines**
Nov 99. (cd/c) *(CD/C TRAX 186)* **WILLIE HUNTER with the CULLIVOE BAND – Willie's Last Session** (see above entry)

• JONNY is of OLD BLIND DOGS, ALYTH – COLOUR OF MEMORY and RORY CAMPBELL is ex-DEAF SHEPHERD and now with OLD BLIND DOGS

Dec 99. (cd) *(CDTRAX 187)* **JONNY HARDIE & ALYTH McCORMACK / RORY CAMPBELL – The Captain's Collection**

Jan 00. (cd) *(CDTRAX 188)* **CEOLBEG – Cairn Water**
May 00. (cd) *(CDTRAX 189)* **BURACH – Deeper**
Jan 00. (cd) *(CDTRAX 190)* **MALINKY – Last Leaves**

• **RODDY CAMPBELL** is the younger brother of 'Lochshore' artist, RORY, who incidentally produced and played on this one and only Gaelic/traditional set. RODDY is a vocalist and pipes man who plays guitar and whistle, while MALCOLM STITT also provided some guitar work. Harpist MARY McMASTER also features, other instrumentation via ANGUS GRANT and MARIANNE CAMPBELL (fiddle), DONALD HAY (percussion) and PADDY SHAW (accordion).

Mar 00. (cd) *(CDTRAX 191)* **RODDY CAMPBELL – Tarruinn Anmoch – Late Cull**
– Fagail bharraigh / Domhnullan dannsair / Seonaid / Mo run a' chruinneag / Barn dance: Tam Bain's lum – Lucy Cassidy / Fonn mo leannain / An gille ruadh / Cairistiona / Fionaghalla / Na bodachain / Bhean ud thall / Oran na cloiche / Cha d'fhuair mi'n cadal / Na bodachain.

Mar 00. (cd) *(CDTRAX 192)* **JACK EVANS – Once Upon A Time In The North**

• **BAG O' CATS** are jazz-folk musician DICK LEE (formerly a collaborator & sax/clarinet player with HAMISH MOORE), RICK BAMFORD (percussion), RICK STANDLEY (double bass, electric bass), FRASER FIFIELD (smallpipes, whistles, saxophone) and NIGEL RICHARD (cittern, pipes). Their much-delayed mixed-bag debut effort of Worldly reels/ragas/etc finally hit the shops via the Himalayas and the Cairngorms!

Feb 01. (cd) *(CDTRAX 193)* **BAG O' CATS – Out Of The Bag**
– Rainstick / Raven / Inverleith Park / Glen Kabul / Making hay / Popocatepetl / King of Laois / Itsno reel / Moody Rudi / Halkidiki / Basant muchari.

Jun 00. (cd) *(CDTRAX 194) JOHN WRIGHT – A Few Short Lines*
Apr 00. (d-cd) *(CDTRAX 195D)* **ADAM McNAUGHTAN – The Words That I Used To Know** (compilation)
Jul 00. (cd) *(CDTRAX 196)* **ERIC BOGLE – Endangered Species**
Jul 00. (cd) *(CDTRAX 197)* **ROD PATERSON – Up To Date**
Aug 00. (cd) *(CDTRAX 198)* **BILLY ROSS – Shore Street**
Jun 00. (cd) *(CDTRAX 199)* **MacALIAS – Highwired**

• the next CD was a competition dedicated to the work of the late Stornoway teacher of bagpipes DONALD MacLEOD MBE, who died in 1984

Sep 00. (cd) *(CDTRAX 200)* **Various Artists – World Masters Of Piping**

Nov 00. (cd) *(CDTRAX 201) JOHN WRIGHT BAND – Language Of The Heart*
Sep 00. (cd) *(CDTRAX 202)* **HAMISH MOORE / DICK LEE – The Bees Knees** (re-issue)

Oct 00. (cd) *(CDTRAX 203) BUDDY MacMASTER – The Judique Flyer* (BUDDY is a Cape Breton fiddler)

• the **GORDON GUNN BAND** are made up of its leader on fiddle, PHIL ANDERSON (on guitar, bass, keyboards & percussion) and BILLY PEACE (on keyboards, accordion & percussion). They fuse together Scottish traditional styles with jazz and country music. GORDON was a member of RUBY RENDALL'S BAND and ADDIE HARPER & THE WICK BAND/TRIO (who released a handful of cassettes in the early 80's:- 'PRIDE OF THE NORTH' and 'ON THE ROAD BY THE RIVER', which were collected together in 1998 as CD 'THE MAGNETIC STARS OF THE NORTH'), while BILLY and PHIL played in the RUBY RENDALL BAND (two sets for 'Ross' records:- STRAIGHT FROM THE HEART' 1984 and 'NEVER LOOK BACK' 1986).

Nov 00. (cd) *(CDTRAX 204)* **GORDON GUNN BAND – Shoreside**
– Mulvihill's – The Galway rambler – Bobby Casey's No.2 – Wing Commander Donald MacKenzie's reel / J.D Peace of Shoreside – Ton & Mima's golden wedding – The dragon / Dna Bourrees – Montgomery Bell waltz / La gigue a M.Lasante – Le reel des quatre fers en l'air / Reel Beatrice / Orkney / Derrane's reel – Dublin porter – The missing sign post – Andy Brown's reel / Castlebay scrap – Mouth of the Tobique – Mittens breakdown / Return to the brandy wine / The Barrowburn reel – Walking on the moon – Elliot's fancy – John Keith Laing / Slow air for Margaret / Hogties reel – The wooden whale / Nancy Finlayson / Salton de Candamu – Dos salees – Donald MacLean's jig / The fair dancer reel – The mason's apron.

Feb 01. (cd) *(CDTRAX 206)* **JOCK TAMSON'S BAIRNS – May Ye Never Lack a Scone**
Dec 00. (cd) *(CDTRAX 207)* **SANGSTERS – Sharp & Sweet**
– The fause bride / My bonnie Mary / Willie brewed a peck o' maut / Beware o' bonnie Ann / O that I had ne'er been married / Lover's heart / Lassie think lang / Refuse and perfume / The mill, mill o / Wert thou in the cauld blast / Parcel o' rogues / Guiding light, evening star / Barbara Allan / Tail toddle / Away ye broken heart / Hallowe'en / Duncan Gray / Lady Mary Ann / A dyker's compliments to her neighbours / Somewhere along the road.
Dec 00. (cd) *(CDTRAX 208)* **JEAN REDPATH – Summer Of My Dreams**
Aug 01. (cd) *(CDTRAX 209)* **MAIRI MacINNES – Orosay**
– Uibhist nam beann arda / Orra bhonna Bhonnagan / Nighean chruinn donn / An aisling / Orain luaidh – An fhleasgaich ur leannain thu / Orosay / Laoidh an iasgair / Puirt a beul / Fagail bhomaia / Oran na cloiche / Gran uibhist / Carry me across the ocean.
Mar 01. (cd) *(CDTRAX 210)* **ERIC BOGLE – By Request** (collection)
Oct 01. (cd) *(CDTRAX 213)* **Various Artists – Scots Women; Live From Celtic Connections 2001**
Jun 01. (cd) *(CDTRAX 214)* **PEATBOG FAERIES – Faerie Stories**
– Martin Roachford's – The oyster woman's rant / The folk police / Captain Coull's parrot / Namedropper – The little cascade / Faerie stories / Cameronian rant / Get yer frets off, Mr Problematic / Caberdrone / Weirdness / Alexander MacAskill of Bernera / Harris.
Aug 01. (cd) *(CDTRAX 215)* **Various Artists – The Best Of Scottish Music Music Vol.2; Greentrax Recordings 15th Anniversary**
– MacUMBA – Gale warning / MALINKY – Strathmartine mains / NATALIE MacMASTER – Boys of the lake set / DICK GAUGHAN – Muir and the master builder / KEVIN MacLEOD – Pipe and fiddle reels / JACK EVANS – Tarbolton / AILEEN CARR – Mormond braes / OSSIAN – Logan water / MARGARET STEWART & ALLAN MacDONALD – O mhairi 's to mo mhairi / GORDON GUNN BAND – Orkney / BILLY ROSS – Gloomy winter / JENNIFER & HAZEL WRIGLEY – Meg's hornpipe set / macALIAS – All the way back home / ROD PAUL – Birlinn reel / JOCK TAMSON'S BAIRNS – Gude claret / ROB MacKILLOP – Chancellours farewell / FIDDLER'S BID – Da sabbit prawn set / JOHN WRIGHT BAND – Time for leaving / IAIN MacINNES – Eliza Ross set / SALSA CELTICA – Yo me voy – Maggie's pancakes.
Apr 01. (cd) *(CDTRAX 216)* **ROBERT BROWN & ROBERT NICOL – Masters Of Piobaireachd Vol.3**
Nov 01. (cd) *(CDTRAX 217)* **MARGARET STEWART and ALLAN MacDONALD – Colla Mo Run**
– The flagon / Road to Loch nam Bearnas / Cutty's wedding / Rothiemurchus rant / Lochiel's away to France / The flagon / Theid is gun teid e leam / Rinn thu eudail mo Mhealladh / We're a case the bunch of us / Angela / Seudan a'chuain / Sean duine cha ghabh mi idir / Tha soir coineadh am beinn dobhrain / Aig baile / Oran fear ghlinne-cuaich / Hug oreann o ro gur toigh leam fhin thu / Oran talaidh an eich-uisge / Colla mo run / Hi ho leagain / Katie Ness of Kinnyside / Glen Lyon / Cameronian's rant / General MacDonald / Tha sinn a' falbh / Na h-Eilhirich.
Dec 01. (cd) *(CDTRAX 218)* **FIDDLERS' BID – Da Farder Ben Da Welcomer**
– Yarmin Yowes return / Uyea isle / Zander the sander / Leaving Lerwick harbour / Da shaalds / Du's bun lang awa an I'm tocht lang to see dee / On the wings of a skorie / Christine / The sneug water waltz / Da farder ben da welcomer / The pumping bass / The swan.
Jun 01. (cd) *(CDTRAX 219) SLAINTE MHATH – Slainte Mhath*
—— (note: SLAINTE MHATH are from Cape Breton)

• **PIPEDOWN** were formed in '98 by County Tyrone-born piper LES MOORE (also of the DAVID URQUHART TRAVEL PIPES AND DRUMS), Isle Of Harris-born mandolin-player AXEL CAMPBELL, guitarist and Fifer STEVE REID (ex-NEW CELESTE) and Denny-born percussionist STEVE FIVEY. Without the latter, they played at Glasgow's Celtic Connections 2001 and won the Danny Kyle Open Stage Award. A dynamic live outfit, they took their sources on their debut set, 'THE FIRST MEASURE' (2002), from Scotland and Ireland, also encompassing a wide range of sounds stemming from Cape Breton and Bulgaria.

Feb 02. (cd) *(CDTRAX 220)* **PIPEDOWN – The First Measure**
– The rebel / The boys of Balivanich / Reels / The old hag / The ass in the graveyard / In with the bricks / Hornpipes / Conrad the Bulgarian / The spice of life / The ivy leaf / The silver mower / Ian McGee's Romanian boots.

Oct 01. (cd) *(CDTRAX 222)* **DICK GAUGHAN – Outlaws And Dreamers**
Nov 01. (cd) *(CDTRAX 223)* **DRINKERS DROUTH with DAVY STEELE – A Tribute**

• **PHAMIE GOW** was raised in the foothills of the Lammermuirs in the Scottish Borders. Having graduated from the Royal Scottish Academy of Music and Drama (RSAMD), she received several commissions for film and theatre. PHAMIE (on vocals, piano & clarsach) recruited a backing band that comprised fiddler ALASDAIR FRASER, vocalists PATSY SEDDON and MAIRI CAMPBELL, cellist MIKE GHIA, piano and accordion player JAMES ROSS, oboe player AMANDA DAVIS and Uillean pipes man ERIC RIGLER. They performed her 'LAMMERMUIR' set live at the Glasgow Royal Concert Hall for the Celtic Connections 2000, although the album itself took a little longer to release. Her talent for atmospheric songwriting was well showcased here and everyone from musical director and producer Dr. Fred Freeman to musician and composer Eddie McGuire to Rob Adams of The Herald, thought it worthy of the highest praises.

Jan 02. (cd) *(CDTRAX 224)* **PHAMIE GOW – Lammermuir**
– Dawning day / Lammermuir / Oh wild and stormy Lammermuir / Thackie hirsel / The kale pot / My ladies meadows / The herring road / Bells / The bride / The popping stone / In memorium of Lady John Scott / Lammentation / Reflections / Lucia / Ride o'er Lammermuir / On the black hill / The fading day / The night fold.

Mar 02. (cd) *(CDTRAX 225) BARRA MACNEILS – Racket In The Attic*
—— (note: the BARRA MACNEILS are from Cape Breton, Nova Scotia)
Feb 02. (cd) *(CDTRAX 226)* **TONY McMANUS – Ceol More**
Apr 02. (cd) *(CDTRAX 227)* **ROB MacKILLOP – The Healing**
– Niel Gow's lament for the death of his second wife / Port Atholl / I love my love in secret / Lady Buccleugh's lament / Auld lang syne / A Scots lament / Joy to the personne of my love / Till I lulled beyond thee / The laydie Louthians lilte / The Isle of Rea / Sueit smyling Katie loues me / She rouid me in her aprone / John come kiss me noue / The lowlands of Holland / Alace I lie my alon I'm lik to die auld / Aderneis lilt / Lady Cassilles lilt / Blew breiks / Port Joan Morrison / MacKillop's rant / Nine / The healing (pibroch for the lute).
Mar 02. (cd) *(CDTRAX 228) COLCANNON – Covering Our Tracks*
—— (note: COLCANNON are from Adelaide in South Australia)
Jun 02. (cd) *(CDTRAX 229) SLAINTE MHATH – VA*

• **STAIRHEID GOSSIP** are a 5-piece a capella group of women (EILEEN PENMAN, CLAIRE LAMOND, REBECCA McKINNEY, ELAINE WALLACE and SYLVIA McGOWAN) from the Lowlands of Scotland.

Apr 02. (cd) *(CDTRAX 230)* **STAIRHEID GOSSIP – Stirrin' It Up**
– The burning of Auchendoon / Bahele bonke / King of the castle / Rantin' dog / Harriet Tubman / High Germany / Women o' Dundee / Johnny I hardly knew you / Don't leave nobody but the baby / Baron o' Brackley / Igami lama / You can't put me down / Aye waukin' O / Cotton mill girls / Bone upon stone / Both sides of the Tweed / Wagoner's lad / The twa corbies.

Jun 02. (cd) *(CDTRAX 231)* **Various Artists – Masters Of Piobaireachd Vol.4: Robert U Brown & Robert Nicol**
May 02. (cd) *(CDTRAX 232)* **McCALMANS – Where The Sky Meets The Sea**
Aug 02. (cd) *(CDTRAX 233)* **MALINKY – 3 Ravens**
Aug 02. (cd) *(CDTRAX 234)* **Various Artists – The King Has Landed; Songs Of The Jacobite Risings**
Sep 02. (d-cd) *(CDTRAX 236D)* **DICK GAUGHAN – Prentice Piece**

– other Greentrax albums (mainly older recordings)

the first batch (No.'s 9001-9018) are sets entitled 'Scottish Tradition Series from The School Of Scottish Studies Archives'

May 93. (cd/c) *(CD/C TRAX 9001)* **Bothy Ballads: music from the North-East** (1971)
– (with JOHN MacDONALD, JAMIE TAYLOR, JIMMY MacBEATH, CHARLIE MURRAY)
Nov 92. (cd/c) *(CD/C TRAX 9002)* **Music From The Western Isles** (1971)
Jan 94. (cd/c) *(CD/C TRAX 9003)* **Waulking Songs From Barra** (1972)
Jan 94. (cd/c) *(CD/C TRAX 9004)* **Shetland Fiddle Music** (1973)
– (with WILLIE HENDERSON & BOBBY JAMIESON, TOM ANDERSON, BOBBY PETERSON, JIMMY JOHNSTON with PAT SUTHERLAND, RONALD COOPER, WILLIE HUNTER and The CULLIVOE TRADITIONAL FIDDLE BAND)
Nov 92. (cd/c) *(CD/C TRAX 9005)* **The Muckle Sangs** (1975)
– (with JEANNIE ROBERTSON, LIZZIE HIGGINS, BETSY WHYTE, JOHN STRACHAN, JANE TURIFF, JIMMY MacBEATH, etc)
Aug 94. (cd/c) *(CD/C TRAX 9006)* **Gaelic Psalms From Lewis** (1975)

• **CALUM RUADH** was born at the start of the last century and became Skye's leading bard/poet until he died on the 25th February, 1978; this album was first issued around the same time.

Mar 95. (c) *(CTRAX 9007)* **CALUM RUADH – The Bard Of Skye** (1978)

Mar 95. (c) *(CTRAX 9008)* **JAMES CAMPBELL OF KINTAIL – Gaelic Songs** (1984)
May 93. (cd/c) *(CD/C TRAX 9009)* **The Fiddler And His Art** (1988)
– (artists incl. PAT SHEARER, ANDREW POLESON, HUGH INKSTER, DONALD MacDONNELL and HECTOR MacANDREW)
Jul 95. (c) *(CTRAX 9010)* **PIPE MAJOR WILLIAM MacLEAN – Pibroch** (1976)
Nov 95. (c) *(CTRAX 9011)* **PIPE MAJOR ROBERT BROWN – Pibroch** (1977)
Nov 95. (c) *(CTRAX 9012)* **PIPE MAJOR ROBERT NICOL – Pibroch** (1977)
Nov 95. (c) *(CTRAX 9013)* **CALUM & ANNIE JOHNSTON – Songs, Stories & Piping From Barra** (1981)
Nov 95. (c) *(CTRAX 9014)* **Gaelic Stories told by Peter Morrison** (1979)
Nov 95. (c) *(CTRAX 9015)* **GEORGE MOSS – Pibroch** (1982)

- the Rev **WILLIAM MATHESON** was the former head (lecturer and reader) with the University of Edinburgh Department of Celtic Studies. With help from the Scottish Arts Council, the double-cassette was made available in March 2001 for the first time on double-CD. WILLIAM recorded the songs in Gaelic Iorram and half in Amhran; his days working as a consultant/folklorist had certainly paid off.

Dec 93. (d-c) *(CTRAX 9016D)* **WILLIAM MATHESON – Gaelic Bards & Minstrels** *(d-cd-iss. Mar01; CDTRAX 9016D)*

May 00. (d-cd) *(CDTRAX 9017D)* **Scottish Traditional Tales**
Oct 98. (c) *(CTRAX 9018)* **Clo Dubh Clo Donn**
Apr 99. (cd/c) *(CD/C TRAX 9019)* **JOAN MACKENZIE – Seonag Niccoinnich**
May 94. (cd/c) *(CD/C TRAX 5002)* **Various Artists – Ceilidh House Sessions**
Nov 95. (cd) *(CDTRAX 5003)* **Various Artists – Folk Songs Of North East Scotland**
Oct 95. (cd/c) *(CD/C TRAX 5004)* **Various Artists – The Nineties Collection**
Jul 96. (cd) *(CDTRAX 8696)* **Various Artists – The Music & Song Of Greentrax: The Best Of Scottish Music**
Feb 97. (cd/c) *(CD/C TRAX 5005)* **Various Artists – S.T.U.C. Centenary Album (If It Wisnae For The Unions)**
Sep 97. (cd) *(CDTRAX 5007)* **Various Artists – Scottish Harps**
Jul 97. (video) *(TRAXV 2002) NATALIE MacMASTER – A Fiddle Lesson* (Cape Breton fiddler)
Feb 98. (video) *(TRAXV 2003) TRACEY DARES – A' Chording to the Tunes* (A Cape Breton piano accompaniment lesson)
May 98. (cd) *(CDTRAX 9050)* **CILLA FISHER & ARTIE TRESIZE – Cilla & Artie**
May 98. (cd) *(CDTRAX 9051)* **Various Artists – The Caledonian Companion** (first issued 1975)
Jul 98. (cd) *(CDTRAX 9052)* **DAVIE STEWART – Davie Stewart**
Jul 98. (cd) *(CDTRAX 9053)* **JOHN MacDONALD – The Singing Molecatcher Of Moray**
Oct 98. (cd) *(CDTRAX 9054)* **WILLIE SCOTT – The Shepherd's Song**
Oct 98. (cd) *(CDTRAX 9055)* **BELLE STEWART – Queen Among The Heather**
Jun 99. (cd/c) *(CD/C TRAX 5008)* **Various Artists – Orain Nan Gaidheal**
Apr 00. (cd) *(CDTRAX 5009)* **Various Artists – Ceol Na Pioba/Ceol Mor**

— Greentrax also released albums by artists from other countries – including *MAKVIRAG* (of Hungary) – Bekesseg *(CTRAX 5001)*

Greentrax 'G2' offshoot

Jul 98. (cd) *(G2CD 7001)* **FELSONS – Glad**
Aug 98. (cd) *(G2CD 7002)* **TAM WHITE'S SHOESTRING – The Real Deal**
Nov 98. (cd) *(G2CD 7003)* **KELTIK ELEKTRIK – Edinburgh Hogmanay Party Mix**
Mar 99. (cd) *(G2CD 7004)* **SONGHUNTER – Spirit Of The Land**
Jun 00. (cd) *(G2CD 7005)* **SALSA CELTICA – The Great Scottish Latin Adventure**
Nov 00. (cd) *(G2CD 7006)* **KELTIK ELEKTRIK – Just When You Thought It Was Safe To Sit Down**

— - the Celtic Connections Various Artists series (Vols.1-6) –
Oct 00. (cd) *(CDGMP 8001)* **Songs Of Scotland**
Oct 00. (cd) *(CDGMP 8002)* **Songs Of Robert Burns**
Oct 00. (cd) *(CDGMP 8003)* **Ceilidh Band Music Of Scotland**
Oct 00. (cd) *(CDGMP 8004)* **Bagpipes Of Scotland**
Oct 00. (cd) *(CDGMP 8005)* **Fiddles Of Scotland**
Oct 00. (cd) *(CDGMP 8006)* **Celtic Sounds Of Scotland**

Iona records

Founded: Glasgow – this is the new folk section of Lismor.
(see biography under parent label, 'Lismor' records)

- Iona discography -

Mar 79. (lp) *(IR 001)* **OSSIAN – St. Kilda Wedding**
Jul 81. (lp) *(IR 002)* **OSSIAN – Seal Song**

- **FERGUSSON'S AULD REIKIE** featured BILLY KAY (reading the great bard's 18th Century poetry) along with Folk musicians TONY CUFFE (of OSSIAN), ROD PATERSON, NORMAN CHALMERS and DEREK HOY (all of JOCK TAMSON'S BAIRNS). The re-issue on CD in 2000 was part of the celebrations for the 250th anniversary of Fergusson's birth, when Auld Reekie was again performed in Embra by the same personnel.

Dec 81. (lp) *(IR 003)* **FERGUSSON'S AULD REIKIE – Fergusson's Auld Reekie**
– The flowers o' Edinburgh / Auld Reikie / Mallie Leigh / Cauler water / The yellow-haired laddie / Leith races / Duncan MacCallipin / Hallow fair / Hunting the hare / Caller oysters / The daft days / Tullochgorum / Torry burn / Elegy on the death of Scots music / The Birks of Invermay / The ghaists / The new game of 41 / Such a parcel of rogues in a nation / Canongate cadgers / Lassies o' the Canongate / The caller shades / The gates o' Edinburgh. *(cd-iss. Aug00 on 'Smiddy Made'; SMD 617)*

1982. (lp) *(IR 004)* **OSSIAN – Dove Across The Water**
Nov 84. (lp/c) *(IR/+C 005)* **BILLY JACKSON & BILLY ROSS – Misty Mountain**
Jan 85. (lp/c) *(IR/+C 006)* **GEORGE JACKSON & MAGGIE MacINNES – Cairistona**
Jan 85. (lp/c) *(IR/+C 007)* **OSSIAN – Borders**
Oct 85. (lp/c) *(IR/+C 008)* **BILLY JACKSON & FRIENDS – The Wellpark Suite**
1986. (lp/c) *(IR/+C 009)* **OSSIAN – Light On A Distant Shore**
Jan 88. (lp/c/cd) *(IR/+C/CD 010)* **WILLIAM JACKSON – Heart Music – Music For The Celtic Harp**
Jun 88. (lp/c) *(IR/+C 011)* **TONY CUFFE – When First I Went To Caledonia**

- **ECLIPSE FIRST** were IAN KIRKPATRICK (accordion), MAGGIE MacINNES (clarsach), MARTIN HUGHES (whistles), STEWART MacISAAC (bouzouki), GEORGE JACKSON (guitar), CHRIS MILLER (fiddle) and of course, The SCOTRAIL VALE OF ATHOLL PIPE BAND. This just might have been the first serious attempt to put a Scots trad-folk group/ensemble and a pipe band together under the one roof, or recording.

Oct 90. (cd/c) *(IR CD/C 012)* **ECLIPSE FIRST – Eclipse First** (this album was probably shelved and then issued as below)
Sep 91. (cd/c) *(IR CD/C 013)* **ECLIPSE FIRST & SCOTRAIL VALE OF ATHOLL PIPE BAND – Names And Places**
– Breizh / Landing at Roscoff / West wind / Isle de Groix / La grande nuit du Port de Peche / Scotia / The games / The road to Copshie / The Oban inn / The Victoria bar / Craigdarroch arms / Gaeltacht / Glen Mhor / The loom house / The Creagorry ceilidh / The boys of Ballivanich / Common ground / Addie MacLean / Lachie Robertson / Yehed mad / The road home.

Nov 91. (c/cd) *(IR/+CD 014)* **WOLFSTONE – Unleashed**
Nov 91. (cd/c) *(IR CD/C 015)* **DALRIADA – All Is Fair**
Jun 92. (cd/c) *(IR CD/C 016)* **WILLIAM JACKSON – Celtic Tranquility**

— AVALON had already issued two albums for mother label, 'Lismor'.
Aug 92. (cd/c) *(IR CD/C 017)* **AVALON – Higher Ground**
– The lion of the north / The sons of the sea / The last gasp medley / Into the mists / A soldier's dream / The Barloch reels / Palais de dance / Stretch the bow / The wild cherry tree / Ellis Isle.
Aug 92. (c/cd) *(IR/+CD 018)* **WOLFSTONE – "The Chase"**
Oct 92. (c/cd) *(IR/+CD 019)* **HUMPFF FAMILY – Mother's**
Oct 92. (c/cd) *(IR/+CD 020)* **CAROL LAULA – Still**
Dec 92. (cd/c) *(IRCD/IRC 021)* **OCCASIONALS – Footnotes**

— The concept of this fund-raiser (for the Highland Hospice in Inverness) was designated to noneother than local fish farmer, IAN ANDERSON. Not knowing that Mr. ANDERSON was in fact the Scots-born leader of JETHRO TULL, Iona records warned him of all the legal pitfalls of such a musical venture – JETHRO TULL were at the same time celebrating their 25th Anniversary! – oops. Anyway, with a host of Scottish singers/players including a surprise for English! guitar legend ERIC CLAPTON on a JACK BRUCE track, the project sold quite well.

Mar 94. (cd/c) *(IR CD/C 022)* **Various Artists – Heart Of The Lion**
– WOLFSTONE – Prophet / TONIGHT AT NOON – John MacLean march / BATTLEFIELD BAND – Conways farewell / ALISON KINNAIRD & CHRISTINE PRIMROSE – Cailleach an dudain / JACK BRUCE with MAGGIE REILLY & ERIC CLAPTON – Ships in the night / PHIL CUNNINGHAM – Andy M. Stewart reel / CAPERCAILLIE – Fear a'Bhata / JETHRO TULL – Warm sporran / BATTLEFIELD BAND – Green and the blue / JETHRO TULL – Broadsword / ALISON KINNAIRD – Sneachd heisgeir / DALRIADA – Haughs of Cromdale / WOLFSTONE – Erin / PHIL CUNNINGHAM – Farewell to Ireland / CAPERCAILLIE – Coisich a'Ruin / JETHRO TULL – Cheerio.

Apr 94. (cd/c) *(IR CD/C 023)* **OSSIAN – The Best Of Ossian**
Nov 93. (cd/c) *(IR CD/C 024)* **KELTZ – Prince Of Peace**
Jan 94. (cd/c) *(IR CD/C 025)* **ROCK, SALT & NAILS – Waves**
Jul 94. (cd) *(IRCD 026)* **IAN BRUCE – Free Agent**
Aug 94. (cd/c) *(IR CD/C 027)* **FREELAND BARBOUR & IAIN FRASER – Northlins**
Dec 94. (cd/c) *(IR CD/C 028)* **COLOUR OF MEMORY – The Old Man & The Sea**
Oct 94. (cd/c) *(IR CD/C 029)* **PAUL MOUNSEY – Nahoo**
May 95. (cd/c) *(IR CD/C 030)* **ROCK, SALT & NAILS – More And More**
May 95. (cd/c) *(IR CD/C 031)* **SIMON THOUMIRE & FERGUS MacKENZIE – Exhibit A**
Nov 95. (cd/c) *(IR CD/C 032)* **BONGSHANG – Crude**
Jul 96. (cd/c) *(IR CD/C 033)* **NEW CELESTE – It's A New Day**
Nov 95. (cd/c) *(IR CD/C 034)* **TARTAN AMOEBAS – Imaginary Tartan Menagerie**

— the Various Artists in question here were basically GILL BOWMAN, DAVY STEELE, ROBIN LAING, FIONA FORBES, TICH FRIER and SCOTT MURRAY. The album below is a ROBERT BURNS tribute, albeit with foul language and sexual connotations.

Jul 96. (cd/c) *(IR CD/C 035)* **Various Artists – The Merry Muses**
– Yellow yellow Yorlin / My girl she's airy she's buxom & gay / Nich inch will please a lady / Logan water / Ye haelien wrang lassie / Bonniest lass / As I cam o'er the Cairneymount / O gie the lass her fairin lad / Cuddie the cooper / Wad ye do that / Ye jovial boys who loved the joys / Dainty Davie / Muirland Meg / How can I keep

my maidenhead / Nae hair on't / In Edinburgh town they've made a law / There was a jolly gauger a gauging he did ride / Duncan Gray / Duncan MacLeerie.

Jul 96. (cd/c) *(IR CD/C 036) WAYNE TOUPS & ZYDECAJUN – Back To Bagoa* (WAYNE TOUPS . . . is a Canadian outfit)
Jul 96. (cd/c) *(IR CD/C 037)* **IVAN DREVER – Four Walls**

• **RUNT O' THE LITTER** were a Scottish good-time ceilidh/folk sextet consisting of MANDY McCLELLAND (vocals & percussion), RITA MURRAY (fiddle & vocals), COLIN MODERATE (bagpipes & whistles), ALAN BROWN (guitar & mandolin), STEVE DOWLING (guitar) and COLIN JOHNSTON (banjo). Sounding more Irish/DUBLINERS or American than Scots, the RUNT delivered their old-time trad (RABBIE BURNS, WALTER SCOTT, etc) tunes and for the most part, it worked.

Aug 96. (cd/c) *(IR CD/C 038)* **RUNT O' THE LITTER – Knot The Metrognome**
– Cricklewood set: Rakish Paddy – Cricklewood – The boy in the gap / Song & reel: Jock Stewart – The blackberry bush / Morrison's jig / The bowlegged tailor set: The boys of Killybegs – The bowlegged tailor – The maid behind the bar / Song: Coming down in the rain / Song & reel: The roving gambler – Off to California / Pipe on the hob / Song: Nancy Spain / Song: The summer sent you / The reconciliation set: Fermoy lasses – The reconciliation – The girl who broke my heart – The reconciliation / The contradiction set: Paddy Fahey – The contradiction – Three little birds – The contradiction / Song & reel: The twa corbies – The new mown hay / Song & jig: Ae fond kiss – Banish misfortune.

Mar 97. (cd/c) *(IR CD/C 039) OLIVER SCHROER – Jigzup* (OLIVER is from Ontarion, Canada)
Aug 96. (cd/c) *(IR CD/C 040) MAD PUDDING – Dirt And Stone* (yet another from Canada!)
Nov 96. (cd/c) *(IR CD/C 041) J.P. CORMIER & FRIENDS – Return To The Cape (aka fiddler JOHN PAUL CORMIER from Cape Breton)*
Feb 97. (cd) *(IRCD 042) RICHARD WOOD – The Celtic Touch* (also Canadian)
Mar 97. (cd) *(IRCD 043) BARRA MacNEILS – Timespan* (are from the Maritimes)
Jan 97. (cd) *(IRCD 044) JAMIE MacINNES & PAUL MacNEIL – Fosgail An Dorus*
Mar 97. (cd/c) *(IR CD/C 045) MARY JANE LAMOND – Bho Thir Nan Craobh* (a Gaelic singer from Cape Breton)
Mar 97. (cd) *(IRCD 046) LLAN DE CUBEL – IV* (this outfit are from Asturias in Northern Spain!)
Mar 97. (cd/c) *(IR CD/C 047) BARRA MacNEILS – The Traditional Album*
May 97. (cd) *(IRCD 048) BARACHOIS – Acadian Music From Prince Edward Island* (they are French-speaking from Acadien / Maritimes)
May 97. (cd) *(IRCD 049) LORETTO REID & BRIAN TAHENY – Celtic Mettle* (this duo are Canadian)
Feb 98. (cd) *(IRCD 050)* **PAUL MOUNSEY – Nahoo Too**
May 97. (cd) *(IRCD 051) JOHN ALLAN CAMERON – Glencoe Station* (this man's French-Canadian)
May 97. (cd) *(IRCD 052)* **ANNE LORNE GILLIES – O Mo Dhuthaich (Oh My Land)**
May 97. (cd) *(IRCD 053) RITA & MARY RANKIN – Lantern Burn* (these sisters are from Cape Breton)
Jun 97. (cd) *(IRCD 054)* **Various Artists – Indigenous Tribes**
Jul 97. (cd) *(IRCD 055) MAD PUDDING – Rattle Of The Stovepipe*
Jul 97. (cd/c) *(IR CD/C 056)* **WOLFSTONE – Pick Of The Litter: The Best Of Wolfstone**
Feb 98. (cd/c) *(IR CD/C 057) J.P. CORMIER – Another Morning*
Feb 98. (cd) *(IRCD 058) JIM FIDLER – Gypsy* (JIM is from Newfoundland)
Sep 97. (cd) *(IRCD 059)* **TARTAN AMOEBAS – Evolution**
Feb 98. (cd/c) *(IR CD/C 060) RICHARD WOOD – Fire Dance*

• **DANNY KYLE** was born in Paisley in 1940. His inspirations came from JOSH MacRAE, ELVIS and a wry sense of humour plucked deep from the political heart of his hometown. With help from folk veterans BRIAN McNEILL, ANDY THORBURN, DOUGIE PINCOCK, FRASER SPIERS, RAB MAIRS and TOMAS LYNCH, DANNY's paean to his heroes and friends ("soft targets"), came in the shape of his one and only set below – sadly, it was released just a few months after he passed away.

Feb 98. (cd) *(IRCD 061)* **DANNY KYLE – Heroes And Soft Targets**
– Music of the loom / Galway to Graceland suite:- Galway Bay – Galway to Graceland – Are you lonesome tonight / Messing about on the river – Perfect day / Shift and spin / Midnight special / Keek-a-boo / The lament for the Gordons / Sacco's message to his son / Hermless / Glasgow farewell – Weary hobo / The Glasgow pub bus – Run to Ballyshannon / Yawning man.

Oct 98. (cd/c) *(IR CD/C 062)* **IVAN DREVER & DUNCAN CHISHOLM – The Lewis Blue**
Nov 98. (cd) *(IRCD 063) Various Artists – Transatlantic Sessions Volume 1*
Nov 98. (cd) *(IRCD 064) Various Artists – Transatlantic Sessions Volume 2*
Apr 99. (cd) *(IRCD 065)* **ROCK, SALT & NAILS – Boxed**
Jun 99. (cd) *(IRCD 066)* **TARTAN AMOEBAS – Giant**
Nov 99. (cd) *(IRCD 067)* **FOLLOW THAT CAMEL – Alba Vinyl**
Nov 99. (cd) *(IRCD 068)* **PAUL MOUNSEY – Nahoo 3: Notes From The Republic**

Lismor records

Founded: As Scotland's premier purveyor of traditional sounds, Lismor records have been guardians of the nation's musical heritage for nigh on three decades. Also boasting a sister label, 'Iona', which has both charted folk music's coming of age and realised Lismor's long held maxim, "Taking Traditional Music Towards 2000", Glasgow's Celtic bastion has entered the new millennium on a surer footing than ever.

Back in 1973, Lismor began trading from the back room of a Glasgow record shop, catering to the musical demands of displaced Highlands and Islanders who'd migrated south looking for work. From four releases in their first year, the label's schedule had expanded to twenty-seven albums by 1976. 1978 saw the release of RUNRIG's debut set, 'Play Gaelic', still one of Lismor's best selling recordings. Running the gamut of Scottish traditional fare and beyond, the label has catered for the a cappella strains of Gaelic song, unaccompanied harp and fiddle, Scottish country dance music, the song and poetry of Robert Burns and of course the stirring sound of the Highland bagpipe. A highlight of the label's many bagpipe recordings is 'Live In Ireland' by Canadian world champions, The 78th FRASER HIGHLANDERS PIPE BAND, while solo piping has been covered in depth by the 'World's Greatest Pipers' series.

Fiddle maestro ALY BAIN was the star of both 'Down Home' and 'Meets The Cajuns' in the late 80's, documenting the acclaimed TV series. He also featured prominently on volumes 1 & 2 of 'The Shetland Sessions' alongside the likes of The POOZIES, PHIL CUNNINGHAM, EDDIE LE JEUNE and SIMON THOUMIRE. Sister label 'Iona' was founded in 1978 as a vehicle for OSSIAN, the pioneering Glasgow folk act headed by WILLIAM JACKSON.

Under new ownership since 1990, the company sought to showcase younger artists putting a contemporary spin on traditional music. These artists have included WOLFSTONE, The HUMPFF FAMILY, CAROL LAULA, ROCK, SALT & NAILS, JAMES GRANT, The KELTZ and TARTAN AMOEBAS amongst others with 'Iona' going for quality rather than quantity. The label's development has been in tandem with the explosion of worldbeat/folk fusion that has seen traditionally-rooted hybrid sounds spring up everywhere from Nova Scotia to Galicia.

Taken as a whole, the Lismor and Iona labels have made a pivotal contribution to the preservation and advancement of Scottish music, an achievement recognised by the Scottish Music Industry Association. In total, the latter organisation have awarded the labels 55 silver discs, 21 gold and 12 platinum in recognition of sales. Now online – at www.lismor.com – and transforming itself into a truly global concern, Lismor/Iona is primed to take advantage of the growing worldwide interest in Celtic-based music. (See also Lismor in section 3 (Traditional), and Iona in section 8 (Rock, Pop & Indie).)

– folk discography –

1984. (lp/c) *(LIF L/C 7001)* **JEANNIE ROBERTSON – A Monumental Figure Of World Folksong (1908-1975)**
1984. (lp/c) *(LIF L/C 7002)* **ANDY HUNTER – King Fareweel**
1984. (lp/c) *(LIF L/C 7003)* **IDEAL BAND – A Measure Of Freedom**
Jun 85. (lp/c) *(LIF L/C 7004)* **LIZZIE HIGGINS – What A Voice**
Jun 85. (lp/c) *(LIF L/C 7006)* **HAMISH IMLACH – Sonny's Dream**
Jun 85. (lp/c) *(LIF L/C 7007)* **ATHUR JOHNSTONE – Generations Of Change**
Dec 86. (lp/c) *(LIF L/C 7009)* **JEAN REDPATH with ALASTAIR HARDIE & ABBY NEWTON – The Music And Songs Of The Scottish Fiddle**
Jul 85. (lp/c) *(LIF L/C 7010)* **BELLE STEWART & FAMILY – Stewarts O' Blair**
May 86. (lp/c) *(LIF L/C 7011)* **Various Artists – Down Home Vol.1: Fiddle Music**
May 86. (lp/c) *(LIF L/C 7011)* **Various Artists – Down Home Vol.2: Fiddle Music**
(cd-iss. 1990's as 'DOWN HOME RECORDINGS'; LCOM 9027)

• **AVALON** were a riotous Celtic folk-rock venture from Edinburgh and heavily influenced by Irish outfit, HORSLIPS. Their vocal 5-piece line-up featured ERNE PARKIN (vocals & guitar), LES COCKBURN (fiddle, mandolin, guitar, banjo, whistles & vocals), STEVE MOSS (guitars), ROY MARTIN (bass & piano) and BILLY MILNE (drums & percussion).

May 86. (lp/c) *(LIF L/C 7013)* **Rocky Roads**
– Overture / Jack in irons / Traveller's tale / Greenpeace / Leith Walk / Bruntsfield link / Leith link / Open roads / Ballrooms of romance / Another encore / Blue highways / Road to Dingwall / Arran more.
May 87. (lp/c) *(LIF L/C 7015)* **Heavy Hearts**
– Litany / Anton the fox / Heavy hearts / On the field of broken dreams / Candy row / Sea link / The Knerbs of Bettar Mully: Sound of Mull – Flotterstone jig – Dode's reel / So still the scene / Silver and steel / Just between friends / Sandgate lass.

—— a subsequent 1992 set appeared on 'Iona' records

May 86. (lp/c) *(LIF L/C 7014)* **TWILIGHT – Modern Folk Arrangements**
Dec 88. (lp/c) *(LIF L/C 7016)* **TONIGHT AT NOON – Down To The Devils** *(cd-iss. Nov90; LCOM 9041)*
Dec 88. (lp/c) *(LIF L/C 7017)* **ALY BAIN & Various Artists – Aly Meets The Cajuns**

(cd-iss. Oct92; LCOM 9009)
Aug 90. (lp/c) *(LIF L/C 7018)* **Various Artists – Glasgow Horizons**
Oct 90. (cd) *(LCOM 7019)* **NEW CELESTE – The Celtic Connection**
Apr 91. (c)(cd) *(LIFC 7020)(LCOM 9039)* **ARTHUR JOHNSTONE – North By North**
Mar 92. (cd) *(LCOM 7021)* **Various Artists – The Shetland Sessions Vol.1**
Mar 92. (cd) *(LCOM 7022)* **Various Artists – The Shetland Sessions Vol.2**

Lochshore records

Founded: Glasgow . . . 1981 out of 'Klub' (KRL) records. Klub Records Limited was the brainchild of Gus MacDonald and Isobel Waugh who originally went into business as cassette tape retailers in the early 70's. With years of industry experience behind him (at 'C.B.S.'), MacDonald took the plunge and kickstarted the KRL label in 1977 with a recording of veteran Scots comedian HECTOR NICOL (see celebrity pages).

When fellow Glaswegian ANDY CAMERON had a major UK hit with 'ALLY'S TARTAN ARMY' in '78, it marked a major coup for the fledgling KRL. Buoyed by this success, the label decided to enter a song in the Eurovision song contest, winning the UK heats with RIKKI PEEBLES' 'Only The Light'. Less glamourous was the staple product of the company, tourist-trapping tartan shortbread fare such as The CLYDESIDERS, The TARTAN LADS and GABERLUNZIE under the Klub/Igus billing. The latter were passionate patriots and easy-listening folk guitarists/singers GORDON MENZIES and ROBIN WATSON, who had been performing together since the early 70's. Having recorded for 'Klub' and then 'Lochshore', the duo were also popular abroad (Europe, North America and the Middle East.

Meanwhile, back at the ranch, in an attempt to corner a niche market, MacDonald moved into recording pipe bands and solo pipers, establishing the 'Monarch' imprint as a vehicle for the new venture. The operation was an unqualified success and for the past 6 years the label has recorded the World Pipe Band Championships. 'Lochshore' re-launched properly in '92 with an album by new signings HIGHLANDER and IRON HORSE, the imprint having since become recognised as a bastion of innovative folk music.

Inspired by his next signing OLD BLIND DOGS, MacDonald went on a mission to record the cream of Scotland's folk renaissance. The likes of IRON HORSE, Welsh-born LORRAINE JORDAN and TANNAS all helped establish Lochshore's reputation while cutting edge acts like The KELTZ, KHARTOUM HEROES, DROP THE BOX and SKUOBUIE DUBH ORCHESTRA have lent the label credibility in the worldbeat/Celtic fusion scene.

MacDonald also set up sister project Lochshore Video and produced a series of acclaimed programmes (for Grampian TV) featuring Lochshore artists. More recently, KRL/Lochshore released 'A Musical Celebration Of 550 Years Of The University Of Glasgow', as part of the famous institution's 2001 anniversary year.

– folk discography –

- **HIGHLANDER** were fronted by easy-listening Scots singer JEFF LEYTON, who subsequently turned to the classics and sang the lead in 'Phantom Of The Opera'.

Feb 92. (cd) *(CDLDL 1201)* **HIGHLANDER – Born To Be A Warrior**
– Born to be a warrior / The journey south / Into battle / First time / I heard them cry / Run like the wind / Only one road / Homecoming / 1328 / Homeland.

- **IRON HORSE** were from the central belt and consisted of ROSS KENNEDY (vocals, guitar), LYNN MORRISON (vocals, keyboards), ROD PAUL (mandolin, banjo, whistles), GAVIN MARWICK (fiddles) and ANNIE GRACE (whistles, vocals). A strong, rootsy, acoustic-folk eponymous debut was delivered in 1992, although the following year's 'THRO' WATER, EARTH & STONE' saw STEVE LAWRENCE (bouzouki, guitars, percussion, etc) replace KENNEDY who teamed up with ALISTAIR McALLISTER; they subsequently lost MARWICK on 'FIVE HANDS HIGH' (1994) who teamed up with JONNY HARDIE of the OLD BLIND DOGS. In 1995, MARWICK returned to the fold for 'VOICE OF THE LAND', the tracks lifted from the documentary series 'The Gamekeeper'. Now consisting of ANNIE, LYNN, ROD and GAVIN, plus BRIAN McALPINE (keyboards, guitars, accordion, vocals) and LEE AGNEW (drums & mouth percussion), the ever-developing IRON HORSE issued their final set for 'Lochshore', entitled 'DEMONS & LOVERS' (1997).

Sep 92. (cd/c) *(LDL 1202 CD/C)* **IRON HORSE – The Iron Horse**
– Aonoch mor gondola – Annie's wean – Glasgow express / Wha'll be king but Charlie – Thro' the heather / The Lea rig / The burning of Auchindoun – Turn again / The Cape Breton fiddlers' welcome to the Shetland Isles – Morag's No.2 – The lintie / The antique dealer – The parting of the hare / The travelling people / Miss Lynn Morrison / The iron horse – The Glendale festival / When she cam' ben she bobbit – The anvil – Duncan Johnstone.

May 93. (cd/c) *(LDL 1204 CD/C)* **INGRID & ALLAN HENDERSON – Light Of The Mountain**
May 93. (cd/c) *(LDL CD/C 1205) LORRAINE JORDAN – Inspiration* (LJ was born in Wales of Irish parents, but now lives in Scotland!)
May 93. (cd/c) *(LDL CD/C 1206)* **IRON HORSE – Thro' Water, Earth & Stone**
– The unknown reel: The peacock's feather – The bell reel – Tam's grey mare / For a' that: The goatherd – The major's maggot – James McLellan's favourite – Duncan the gauger / The piper's bonnet / Till Jamie comes hame / The poachers: Assynt reclaimed – The poachers / The cabbage town reel: The jellyfish – The Blantyre reel – Portuguese train / The Earl of Moray: The gift – The conclusion – J.F. Dickie's delight – Weights and measures – Andy White's reel – Molly Rankin's – The repeal of the union / The hen's march: The iron horse jig – The tipsy sailor – The judge's dilemma / Mother martyr.
Feb 97. (cd) *(CDLDL 1207) TRAIN JOURNEY NORTH – First Tracks*
Oct 93. (cd/c) *(LDL CD/C 1208) BOOGALUSA – Careless Angels And Crazy Cajuns*
Oct 93. (cd/c) *(LDL CD/C 1209)* **OLD BLIND DOGS – Close To The Bone**
Jul 94. (cd) *(LDL 1210CD) SKUOBHIE DUBH ORCHESTRA – Spike's 23 Collection*
Mar 94. (cd/c) *(LDL CD/C 1211) DAVID ALLISON – Guitar Gi-tar*
Mar 94. (cd/c) *(LDL 1212 CD/C) LORRAINE JORDAN – Crazy Guessing Games*

- **the LORELEI** were formed in Aberdeenshire, 1993 by Celtic-Rock inspired MARTIN WATSON (vocals, guitar), KEITH 'Beefy' ALLARDYCE (guitar), JONNY PALMER (bass), KEITH GRANT (drums, harmonica), WILLIAM 'Flossie' LEYS (fiddle, mandolin, banjo) and DIANE BEATTIE (viola).

Jun 94. (cd/c) *(CD/ZC LDL 1213)* **the LORELEI – Headstrong**
– Wendy frenzy / Perfect world / Humour / Last leviathan / Hold / Mediocre / Perricardium / Lara / Tie-dyed / Headstrong / Greed / Goat / Donny / Nails.

Jul 94. (cd/c) *(CD/ZC LDL 1214)* **IRON HORSE – Five Hands High**
– The 8 step waltz / A'bhean ladaich / This is no' my plaid / Stobieside lodge / The rubber man / Glasgow Peggy / The linguist / Inheritence / Lowlands of Holland / The sheepwife / The heiress / Fragment / Northern cross rising.
Jul 94. (cd/c) *(CD/ZC LDL 1215) CRAOBH RUA – The More That's Said The Less The Better* (Belfast-based outfit)
Jun 94. (cd/c) *(LDL 1216 CD/C)* **INGRID & ALLAN HENDERSON – Perpetual Horseshoe**

- **TANNAS** were a Gaelic-singing trad-folk supergroup consisting of DONALD SHAW (accordion, keyboards, vocals), MALCOLM STITT (guitar), CHARLIE McKERRON (fiddle), FRED MORRISON (pipes, whistles), IAN MURRAY (percussion, drums) and SANDY MACKAY (vocals). By the time they had delivered their debut set, 'OIGHREACHD' in '94, TANNAS had built up a strong following due to concerts all over Europe, including France, Spain, Austria and especially Italy. A Top 5 Folk album in Q magazine, they also won the Interceltic Folk Group Competition at L'Orient in '95. Ethereal, ambient and a tad like MOUTH MUSIC, TANNAS were fast becoming a worthy act to follow, more so with the release of their award-winning sophomore set, 'RU-RU' (1995). However, it would be four long years before the eclectic TANNAS would bounce back. 'SUILEAN DUBH' (1999), chalked-marked nu-folk for the 21st Century, textured, cool and timeless, were all words used so easily to describe this great band.

Nov 94. (cd/c) *(CD/ZC LDL 1217)* **TANNAS – Oighreachd (Heritage)**
– Ca'nan nan gaidheal / Sabhal Ia'nt'Ic uisdean / Abu chuibhl' / Look behind you / Tuireadh Iain ruaidh / The battle of Waterloo / The session set / Eilean beag donn a' chuain / A fhleasaich oig bi furachail / Bodachan cha phos mi / Cearcall AO chuain / Cha te'id Fionnlagh a Dh'Eige.

- **ROSS KENNEDY & ARCHIE McALLISTER** met in the West Coast of Scotland . . . 1993 by former TANNAHILL WEAVERS and IRON HORSE bouzouki plucker ROSS KENNEDY and his fiddle-playing chum ARCHIE McALLISTER. From slow airs to uptempo reels, both men show why they have quickly established themselves among the country's most formidable partnerships in modern traditional folk music. Three albums on 'Lochshore', 'TWISTED FINGERS' (1994), 'GATHERING STORMS' (1996) and 'THE WHITE SWAN' (1999), have been received well, and not only north of the border.

Oct 94. (cd) *(CDLDL 1218)* **ROSS KENNEDY & ARCHIE McALLISTER – Twisted Fingers**
– Mhari MacLean – Morag's reel – The Devil's delight / Can of tea / Ingleside / Kenny Gilles – Bobby MacLeod's – The general gathering 1745 – The curlew / Bonnie Jean / Forbes Morrison – The nine pint coggie – The brig o' Dee / Barbara Allan / John Barleycorn – On Galway Bay / Fiunary / The auld wheel – Lads of Laois – Hey ho my bonnie lass – Twisted fingers / Cluny castle / North Sea shoals – Sweet Molly / The black hoe – The man from North Connel – The drawing of Effie's letter.

- **ANNA MURRAY** was born on the Isle Of Lewis. A native Gaelic speaker, MURRAY was immersed in the world of Gaelic song from an early age and began learning the highland bagpipes before she'd reached her teens. She picked up a number of awards at the annual Mod Gaelic music festivals, appeared on local TV and was much in demand at ceilidhs throughout the Western Isles. Subsequently signed to Lochshore, ANNA made her recording debut with the 'OUT OF THE BLUE' album in 1994, wherein she displayed her virtuosity on the pipes and her ability to bring a fresh, modern approach to Gaelic song. This was followed in 1997 by 'INTO INDIGO', a record that had critics praising her original arrangements and contemporary spin on the often cobwebbed world of piping. It even beat off stiff competition to secure a placing in the Mojo magazine Top 10 Folk Albums of 1997, (incredibly but perhaps predictably) being the only Scottish release included. She then worked as composer and musical director for Iain Crichton Smith's Traverse Theatre production of 'Lazy Bed'. A much anticipated third album, 'TRI NITHEAN – THREE THINGS' was released in early 2000, timed to coincide with her appearance at the millennial instalment of the ever popular Celtic Connections festival in Glasgow.

Oct 94. (cd/c) *(CD/ZC LDL 1219)* **ANNA MURRAY – Out Of The Blue**

– An drochaid chluiteach – Swallow's tail – MacFadden's reel / Cadal cha dean mi (I can get no sleep) / Malcolm Ferguson – John MacLean / Mo chridhe trom (My heavy heart) / Chase the train – The Piobreachd club / Caoidh mo dhochais (Mourning my lost hopes) / Little cascade / Doctor MacInnes' fancy – The high level / Am breacan uallach (The heavy plaid) / Slieve Russel – Donald Cameron's powder horn / Seagull – Donald MacLean – Chloe's passion / Tir nan Og (Land of the ever-young).

Sep 95. (cd) *(CDLDL 1222)* **KHARTOUM HEROES – Khartoum Heroes**
Feb 95. (cd/c) *(CD/ZC LDL 1223) BOOGALUSA – Boogalusa*
Oct 95. (cd/c) *(CD/ZC LDL 1224)* **GABERLUNZIE – For Auld Lang Syne**
– I will go / Dirty old town / Deid fish and diesel / Teuchat storm / Caledonia / Saddle the pony / Humours of Glendart / Let the eagle live / The west wind / Nancy Whisky / 5 o'clock in the morning / Sailors hornpipe / Trumpet hornpipe / Brahan seer / Auld lang syne.
Jan 95. (cd/c) *(LDL CD/C 1225) OIGE – Live* (they're Irish)
Jan 95. (cd) *(CDLDL 1226)* **JONNY HARDIE & GAVIN MARWICK – Up In The Air**

• **WHIRLIGIG** were initiated in Glasgow . . . 1994 (at the city festival) by classically-trained violinist twin sisters FIONA and JENNIFER CUTHILL, alongside former IRON HORSE guitarist/percussionist STEVE LAWRENCE. Not to be confused with the similarly Celtic-orientated US WHIRLYGIG, this Baroque/renaissance outfit went on to release another fine set, 'WHAT IF A DAY . . .' in 1997 (featuring ANNE CHAURAND on lute and guitar).

Mar 95. (cd/c) *(CD/ZC LDL 1227)* **WHIRLIGIG – Celtic Dawn**
– Roslin Castle / The harper – Lady Catherine Ogle / Border spirit / Miss Lynn Morrison / Corn rigs / Aisleag ur / Pipe jigs / When she cam ben / I serve a worthy lady / The suidh / Mary Scott / The flower of Yarrow / Celtic dawn.

May 95. (cd/c) *(CD/ZC LDL 1228)* **IAN F. BENZIE – So Far**

• **MICK WEST** is a piper from the west of Scotland. His solo album, 'FINE FLOWERS . . .' was delivered for '95, while he also in-house sessioned for piper RORY CAMPBELL on his 1997 set, 'Magaid A Phipir'. The same year, WEST's 4-piece band released 'RIGHT SIDE O' THE PEOPLE'.

Jul 95. (cd/c) *(CD/ZC LDL 1229)* **MICK WEST – Fine Flowers And Foolish Glances**
– Bonnie Jean Cameron / Lassie lie near me / Chester city / The seasons / Fine flowers in the valley / The mission hall / Braw sailin on the sea / Medley: Twa bonnie boys – Rip the calico – Sean O'Dhuibhir a' Gleanna / The Blantyre explosion / Farewell to the gold.

Jul 95. (c/cd) *(LDL 1229/1230 C)* **HOM BRU – Rowin Foula Doon**
Oct 95. (cd/c) *(CD/ZC LDL 1231)* **TANNAS – Ru-Ra**
– Mairead nan cuiread – The Bob Parsons Strathspey / O ho na ribeannan – Sean triubas – Faca tu saor an t-sabhaidh / The old hags set: Lucy Cassidy – Ruidhleadh cailleach / An drochaid chluiteach – The Smith of Killiechassie / Nach fhreagair thu, Cairistona / Cumt'Ur gealladh / T'si Morag / Coill' an fhasaich / T'n uair bha mi na mo Mhaighdinn – B'fhearr mar a bha mi'n uiridh / Mrs Mary Stitt / Caillte a chaoidh.
Sep 95. (cd/c) *(CD/ZC LDL 1232)* **IRON HORSE – Voice Of The Land**
– Voice of the land (original) / Stray peas / The 8-step waltz / The rumbling bridge / Raindance / Leannan sith / The white mountains / Voice of the land (instrumental) / Requiem – Fox's glove / Beyond the river / Black crows and ravens / Glen tilt / The sheepwife / Voice of the land (Acid-croft mix).
Oct 95. (cd/c) *(CD/ZC LDL 1233)* **OLD BLIND DOGS – Legacy**
Oct 95. (cd) *(CDLDL 1234)* **DROP THE BOX – Drop The Box**
Nov 95. (cd) *(CDLDL 1235) JOURNEYMEN – Wanderlust*
Nov 95. (cd/c) *(CD/ZC LDL 1236)* **the LORELEI – Progression**
– Hello / Bike / Fluffy cabbage / Sweet Suzi summertime / Run from me / Buy / Float across the sky / Evil Homer / Bullshit / Bag of dreams / Dehydration.
Mar 96. (cd/c) *(CD/ZC LDL 1237) CRAOBH RUA – No Matter How Cold & Wet You Are As Long As You're Warm & Dry*
Mar 96. (cd/c) *(CD/ZC LDL 1238)* **HAMISH IMLACH, MURIEL GRAVES & KATE KRAMER – More And Merrier**

• **HUDSON SWAN** was born 31st August '54, Paisley. A former fiddler & guitarist of The TANNAHILL WEAVERS from 1972 to 1987, HUDSON re-emerged in the mid-90's with his self-named band. In 1998, HUDSON and STEVE LAWRENCE delivered their own set, 'AMALGAMATION'.

Jun 96. (c/cd) *(LDL/+CD 1239)* **HUDSON SWAN BAND – Prospect Lane**
– Do-li-a / My collier laddie / Beinn chabhair / The reluctant pirate – Barney Brallaghan / The ballad of cursed Anna / Miss Elizabeth Tannahill Stark / O'er the ocean / Cannily, cannily / The corncrake – Paddy Keenan's / Peerie's air / The Indian lass / My Johnny was a shoemaker / Epilogue.

Jun 96. (cd) *(CDLDL 1240)* **JURA CEILIDH BAND – Jura Ceilidh Band**
Jun 96. (cd/c) *(CD/ZC LDL 1241) OIGE – Bang On*
Jul 96. (cd) *(CDLDL 1242) ALBANATCHIE – Natives*
Aug 96. (cd) *(CDLDL 1243)* **ROSS KENNEDY & ARCHIE McALLISTER – Gathering Storms**
– The milltimber jig – Priscillas – Donald MacLean / The braes o' Bedlay / The doctor's reel – The spinning wheel – Sullivan's – Johnny lad – The Jura music festival reel / Ossian / The lark in the morning – The gathering storms – The lowland of Scotland – Feadan glan a' phiobair / The water is wide / The rock on the Clyde – Kissed yestreen – Miss Campbell of Sheerness – The skylark's ascension / The bonnie ship the diamond / Happy we are aw the gither / The bride's reel – The white crow – Southwest Bridge reel – The auld fiddler – Fag a phiob bhochd.

• **TABACHE** were formed in the Isle Of Seil (off the coast south of Oban) late 1994 by fiddle whizzkid AIDAN O'ROURKE and English singer/fiddler/flautist CLAIRE MANN (from Newcastle-upon-Tyne). O'ROURKE incorporated his mixed Scottish/Irish heritage into a compelling style of fiddle playing that has seen him pick up a plethora of awards over the years. Having begun learning the instrument at the age of nine, he went on to claim two national titles and was subsequently the subject of a BBC documentary. While still a teenager he toured North America with the Caledonia Ramblers and has since performed live around Britain and Europe with DEAF SHEPHERD, TANNAS and even CAPERCAILLIE. MANN, meanwhile, has won even more awards, netting a staggering eighty medals in Fleadh Cheolis over a six year period as well as winning the All-Ireland flute championships two years running in 1993/94. Her CV also includes touring duties with Edinburgh bands, The FINDLAYS and ARUN as well as a stint with COMHALTAS CEOLTOIRI EIREANN. Prior to the recording of the 'ARE YOU WILLING?' album, the TABACHE line-up was completed by ROSS MARTIN, an accomplished guitarist who's also worked with the likes of DEAF SHEPHERD and DAIMH as well as piper FRED MORRISON. The aforementioned album and their 1999 released sophomore set, 'WAVES OF RUSH', combined traditional material with original compositions (from the pen of MARTIN), the use of double bass and percussion lending the record a modern edge.

Nov 96. (cd) *(CDLDL 1244)* **TABACHE – Are You Willing?**
– Obsessive island / Marches / Lily of the west / Jigs of brown ale / The knight on the road / Punch in the face / Gregg's pipes set / Slow air / The road to Clady / Promised rain / The Galway Bay set.

Nov 96. (cd/c) *(CD/ZC LOC 1099)* **VALERIE DUNBAR – The Best Of**
Mar 97. (cd) *(CDLDL 1245) CYTHARA – Cythara*
Jan 97. (cd) *(CDLDL 1246) DEIRDRE CUNNINGHAM – City Of Tribes*
Jan 97. (cd) *(CDLDL 1247)* **KELTZ – The Mystery Of Amergin**
Feb 97. (cd) *(CDLDL 1201)* **HIGHLANDER – Born To Be Warrior**
Sep 97. (cd) *(CDLDL 1248)* **WHIRLIGIG – What If A Day . . .**
– Breton set / Simon Brodie / My lord of Marchie Pavan / What if a day . . . / A toye / Wilson's wilde / Coranto / Les poulez houpes galliard / Watkin's ale / Frog galliard / Fayne would I wed / Giles Farnaby's dream / Lord Lovat's lament / Quartre bransles / Scotch tunes / Scots canaries / Sanz Canarios / Longmynd.
Mar 97. (cd) *(CDLDL 1249)* **ANNA MURRAY – Into Indigo**
– Finbarr Saunders – Gaol na h-oige / Na goisidich – Tar the house – The Ness pipers / Saoil a'mhor / The hazy day – Zeto the bubbleman – The last tango in Harris / An ribhinn bhoidheach / Southpark house – Tarruing teann an crois – Kevin's celtic chasm / Mairead nan cuiread / Dolina MacKay – The Ballivanich – Brown haired maid / An deidh's mo mhealladh / Braigh Loch-Tail – Miss Campbell of Sheerness – The Atlantic bridge / A ghaoil saoil am faigh mi thu? – Hacking windows / Crann Tara – Alasdair Oig mhic'ic neacail / Gad Ionndrainn.

• **RORY CAMPBELL** is one Scotland's finest pipers (he also plays whistle and sings). The much in-demand session player's first solo set featured an array of trad-folk superstars including DONALD SHAW, MALCOLM STITT, BRIAN McALPINE, MICK WEST, WILF TAYLOR, MARC DUFF and MARIANNE CURRAN. RORY's second (a collaboration with the aforementioned MALCOLM STITT), 'FIELD OF BELLS' (1999), was another to knock the cockles off their shells; this time JIM SUTHERLAND and NEIL HARLAND provided the rhythm.

Mar 97. (cd/c) *(CD/ZC LDL 1250)* **RORY CAMPBELL – Magaid A Phipir (The Piper's Whim)**
– Asturian set:- Lachie and the tractor – Careau Llaniscu – Cutting down the privet hedge – Donachd Head – An Islay melody – Margaret McCall / Hornpipes: The wee man from Skye – The Barlinnie Highlander – Arthur Gillies / Jig groove: Bannockburn reel – Asturias jig / Shepherd's crook set: Bat' an taillear – Shepherd's crook / Mirren's pyjamas – Calum fighader agus Calum taillear – Mo shuiridhach bi suigartach – Trad. reel – Linlithgow Palace / The dreams of old Pa Fogerty / Breton set: Torre de Hercules – Breton Andro – Paul McIver / Nine eights set: The Girvan ceilidh – I ha'e a wife o' my ain – Tending the cattle with a heavy heart – Donald, Willie and his dog / Strathspeys & reels: Morag McNeil, Tangasdale – Tha dinan brog, Donnachadh dubh – Magaid a phiper – Trad. jig – An gun's t-apron / Gur milis Morag / Wedding set: Barbara and Andy's wedding – The oiseanbeag reel – Slow jig – Clementina – An 'nighan, ponn bheadarach / M.S.& R.: Traigh a' ghoirtein – Hecla – Dolina McKay / Tangasdale beach.

Mar 97. (cd) *(CDLDL 1251) CHILDE ROLANDE – Foreign Land*
Sep 97. (cd) *(CDLDL 1252)* **DAVY CATTANACH – Dancing In The Shadows**
Sep 97. (cd) *(CDLDL 1253) CYTHARA – Pluckin' Hammered*

• **COINNEACH** were from the Highlands and formed by Celtic fiddler DEBBIE SWANSON. Both Lochshore sets delve into the mystical Pict era with superb musicianship.

Mar 97. (cd) *(CDLDL 1254)* **COINNEACH – Life In A Scottish Greenhouse**
– How many battles / (Life in a) Scottish greenhouse / The rhythm method / No time to cry / Gloomy summer / Energy rising / Coinneach / Sound of the sound / The animal song / The phantom fiddler.

Apr 97. (cd) *(CDLDL 1255)* **Various Artists – Northern Lights**
May 97. (cd) *(CDLDL 1256)* **J.S.D. BAND – For The Record**
May 97. (cd/c) *(CD/ZC LDL 1257)* **DAVIE PATON – Fragments**

• **LOOKING EAST** were formed in Scotland mid-90's by MICHAEL MAGG (flutes, bansuri), GRAHAM HIGH (guitars) and their Indian-born/ancestry tabla-player and percussionist VIJAY KANGUTKAR; tanpura player CHIARA SCHILSKA guested. Exhilarating classical jazz-rock music bringing Scotland a rightful piece of World music at one eponymous swoop.

Sep 97. (cd) *(CDLDL 1258)* **LOOKING EAST – Looking East**
– African scherzo / Reunion / Todi / Beneath the canopy / Dedication / Seven eight / Looking east / Adagio / Canary.

Mar 97. (cd) *(CDLDL 1259) CRAOBH RUA – Soh It Is*
May 97. (cd/c) *(CD/ZC LDL 1260)* **GABERLUNZIE – Twa Corbies**
– Twa corbies / The Loch Tay boat song / Flower in the snow / Born beyond the border / Slow goin' easy / MacPherson's rant / The Wallace / The old Balgedie road / Margaret's waltz medley / Jute mill song / Lonely in the bothy.
Jun 97. (cd/c) *(CD/ZC LOC 1102)* **HECTOR SCOTT & NEIL McFARLANE with FIONA CAMPBELL – Breath O' June**
Jul 97. (cd) *(CDLDL 1261)* **HOT TODDY CEILIDH BAND – Three Sheets To The Wind**
Dec 97. (cd) *(CDLDL 1262)* **MICK WEST BAND – Right Side O' The People**
– Young Munro / Shift and spin / The Highland muster roll / Ballad of John McLean / Jamie Foyers / The propeller song / The battle of Waterloo / The braes of Melinish / Martin Ainsborough's / Road to Dundee / The January man / Lord Randall / MacCrimmons lament / The little cascade / Freedom come ye all.
Dec 97. (cd) *(CDLDL 1263)* **CANNACH – The Moons Of Glenloy**
Oct 97. (cd) *(CDLDL 1264)* **OLD BLIND DOGS – Five**
Dec 97. (cd/c) *(CD/ZC LDL 1265)* **IRON HORSE – Demons & Lovers**
– The steampacket: The steampacket – The false alarm – The siren / Auchindoun – Real Ecosse / Park No.1: The Lee rug – Sylvia – Park No.1 / The Luthier: Davidson the Luthier – Feis rois – The Luthier jig – The half gill / The traveller / Anathea / Glazgo – Tommy's No.2 – Upstairs at the wheel – Faith healer / The elphin knight – The enchantment / The demon lover – Eastland breeze / Caleo / The sleeping warrior.
Dec 97. (cd) *(CDLDL 1266) WENDY MacISAAC – That's What You Get* (she's a Cape Breton fiddler)

• **GREEN** were formed around Argyll and the islands . . . mid-90's by trad folkies (mainly a duo plus friends) who also ventured into theatre/dance productions – nothing whatsoever to do with that SCRITTI POLITTI bloke. Having supported the likes of STEELEYE SPAN, SHARON SHANNON and CAPERCAILLIE – while also touring Africa and Russia! – GREEN finally delivered their originally composed debut 'FOUND ON THE WAVE'. It found them trying out everything from blues, country, classical, jazz and of course, Scottish ceilidh/dance.

Dec 97. (cd) *(CDLDL 1267)* **GREEN – Found On The Wave**
– Leaving Carolina / Found on the wave / High and low / Jamie Gow's farewell to methadone / The Marie Celeste / Squaddie's lament / Oh Jonnie my man / A baroque daydream / Prayer for tomorrow / Rattlin' roarin' Willie / Grandads song / The fulmer.

May 98. (cd) *(CDLDL 1268)* **DROP THE BOX – Honeytrap**
Dec 97. (cd) *(CDLDL 1269)* **JCB** *with JERRY HOLLAND – A Trip To Cape Breton*
Dec 97. (cd) *(CDLDL 1270)* **Various Artists – The Piping Concert: Celtic Connections**
Dec 97. (cd) *(CDLDL 1271)* **CHRIS ARMSTRONG – Notes In Ma Heid**
Mar 98. (cd) *(CDLDL 1272)* **ELISE MacLELLAN – Kiss ON The Wind**

• **STEVE LAWRENCE** was a member of IRON HORSE (four years) before he teamed up with fellow multi-instrumentalist and session man HUDSON SWAN for a one-off set. Augmented by guest musicians ANNA MURRAY, TIM BREWSTER, IAN CHALMERS, JOHN SAUNDERS, DUNCAN LIGHT, FIONA CUTHILL and LINDSEY HUNT, the 'AMALGAMATION' record showed the duo were not past it by any means. LAWRENCE-SWAN are an instrumental folk-pop duo with a TV theme-like feel.

Mar 98. (cd) *(CDLDL 1273)* **STEVE LAWRENCE & HUDSON SWAN – Amalgamation**
– Miss Thomson / Spirit of the glen / Swinging the cat / a) The psycho magnet – b) Crocodile / a) Bill Stark's fiddle – b) The cottage at Camus Crois – c) The claypit reel / The little cascade / Kaivonkansi / Four thirty in the morning / a) The amalgamation – b) High ground jig / Bourees / Secret games / Seven hearts.

May 98. (cd) *(CDLDL 1274)* **J.S.D. BAND – Pastures Of Plenty**
Jul 98. (cd) *(CDLDL 1275)* **TOMMY F. COUPAR – The Piper's Muse**
May 98. (cd) *(CDLDL 1276) CARLENE ANGLIM & ALLISTER GITTENS – Mellow Frenzy* (an Irish duo)
Aug 98. (cd) *(CDLDL 1277) DEIRDRE CUNNINGHAM – A Cry From The Heart*
Feb 99. (cd) *(CDLDL 1278)* **HUDSON SWAN BAND – Flyte Of Fancy**
– Brave Wolfe / Slaggan boy / The barleycorn – Jug of brown ale / The drummer boy for Waterloo / Flyte of fancy / The nag's head / Are you going to leave me / The fledgling / The Oakey strike eviction / Black fox / Greenstone point – Braigh Lock Iall / Danny Dannielle / Johnny O'Braidislea – Beyond the river.
Jun 99. (cd) *(CDLDL 1279)* **KELTZ – The Seas Are Deep**
Aug 98. (cd) *(CDLDL 1280)* **COINNEACH – Ice, Trees And Lullabies**
– Ice, trees and lullabies / Town that I love "in the rain" / Black is the colour / Still November / Rain in my heart / The black room / Strong sense of something / Holding out for freedom / Springtime / Ships / Blow away.

— COINNEACH subsequently (early 2000) issued their own '2000 TEARS EP' – 2000 tears / Highland jail / Scottish greenhouse 2000.

Jan 99. (cd) *(CDLDL 1281) CEOL NA gCAPALL – Breath Of Fresh Air* (an outfit from N.Ireland)
Feb 99. (cd) *(CDLDL 1283)* **TABACHE – Waves Of Rush**
– Waves of rush – The Duke of Fife's welcome to Deeside – Touching cloth / Castle Grant: Braes of Castle Grant – J.S. Skinner (Strathspey) – J.S. Skinner (reel) – Loch Glassie – Up downy / Helen of Kirkconnel / Jack's christening: The blacksmith's reel – Hamish Moores' – Jack's christening – Traditional Irish jig / The quiet place / Slipslide: Frank Mor's – Nelly Mahony's – Matt Daly's slide – Poirt an deorai – Super Scot / The Bay of Biscay / Machrivanish: Ca' the ewes – The Slovenian chicken – Iain MacPherson's – Machrivanish / The Newry highwayman / The sound of Seil: Norman Holmes' – The best day of my life – Sound of Seil – Bobby Casey's.
Nov 99. (cd) *(CDLDL 1284)* **FRED MORRISON – The Sound Of The Sun**
Jun 99. (cd) *(CDLDL 1285)* **RORY CAMPBELL & MALCOLM STITT – Field Of Bells**
– Opinions: Opinions 1 – Irish traditional – Annag nic Iain – The giraffe – Opinions 2 / MacLean's: MacLean of Pennycross – No panteloni / Airmail / John Griffin's / Guti: Fred & Anna's strathspey – The interviewee – Guti / The spree / Field of bells / Low country: Marchmy – A low country dance / Ranters: An t ord gallach – Don Manson's reel – Paul's apple tree – The Islay rantewrs – Tae the house / Braze: Wild berries – The braes of Mellinish.
Nov 99. (cd) *(CDLDL 1286)* **ROSS KENNEDY & ARCHIE McALLISTER – The White Swan**
– The Lakewind reels: Joey Beatons – The perlwig – Peter Davidsons – The Doune of Invernochty – Sean Maguires / The Dowie dens o' Yarrow / The white swan: The heather ale jig – Tipsy sailor – The white swan – The road to Kintyre / The hills of Lorne / The lang awa ship / Jerry Holland's reels: Dave MacDonalds wedding reel – Iggy and Squiggle – Mutts favourite – Harry Bradshaws / Lachlan dubh / The dark island / The blaw jigs: Glencoe hall – Roll out the snake – Harvey's fancy – The barbar shop – Blaw jig / For my mother dear / Boy of storms / Reels: Farquhar Mathieson – Kerry McAllisters / Slow air: Gun bhris mo chridh' o'n dh'fhalbh / Kilbowie hill / The Java reels: The Java reel – Wolfes reel – The Arran ceilidh – Birlin in Brittany.
Jun 99. (cd) *(CDLDL 1287)* **JONNY HARDIE & GAVIN MARWICK – The Blue Lamp**
Nov 99. (cd) *(CDLDL 1988) ANN GRAY – Shouting At Magpies* (ANN's from Nova Scotia)
Sep 99. (cd) *(CDLDL 1289)* **TANNAS – Suilean Dubh (Dark Eyes)**
– Suilean dubh / Seallaibh curaigh eoghainn – The Lochaber badger / Andy's saltire – Fear a bhios fada gun phosadh / Illean a I / Bi falbh o'n uinneig / 'S toigh leam cruinneag dhonn nam bo (tribute to Na H-oganaich) / Catharis – Haighhaidh – Lexy Macaskill / Air a' ghille tha mo run / Caitlin / Thoir dhomh do lamh / Ruidhleadh na coilich dhubha / Buain na rainich.

• **KINNELL** were formed in Glasgow, 1997 by ex-DEAF SHEPHERD fiddler GAVIN PENNYCOOK, ex-TANNAS flautist/whistler FRANCES MORTON and Dublin-born bouzouki player TONY CAMPBELL (ex-SETANTA, ex-GAROID O'LEARY). They played traditional songs except for a few supplied by the group.

Sep 99. (cd) *(CDLDL 1290)* **KINNELL – Donald's Dog**
– Gooseberry: The gooseberry bush – The drunken flautist – Trip to Nenagh / Finnish polkkas: The Laihian polkka – Kuortaneen polkka / Dans Loudeac: Dans Loudeac – Get up old maid and shake yourself – The humming drummer / The duck: Bill Harte's – Miss Campbell of Sheerness – The duck / Tralalavalsen: Tralalavalsen – Tarantella / Scahill's: Unknown – Unknown – Dolina MacKay – Silver spear / Slow air: Irish traditional / Countdown: Polka d'ouest bretagne – Haughs of Cromdale / Cleveland Park: Cleveland Park – Thief of Lochaber / Ekelundapolska / The salvation: The salvation reel – Unknown / And his dog: The Earl of Home – Munera – Donald, Willie and his dog / Wing commander: Wing commander Donald McKenzie – Bulgarian red – Father O'Grady's trip to Bocca.

Nov 99. (cd) *(CDLDL 1291) BOWHOUSE QUINTET – Live In Ennis* (an Irish outfit)
Nov 99. (cd) *(CDLDL 1292) GIBB TODD – Connected*
Jan 00. (cd) *(CDLDL 1293)* **ANNA MURRAY – Tri Nithean: Three Things**
– Strathspey & reels: Chuir i gluin air a' bhodaich – Thoir a-null Ailean Thugan – Untitled reel – In and out the harbour / 'S fhada leam an oidhche gheamhraidh ruidhleadh: Ruidhleadh mo nighean donn – Thoir a-null Ailean Thugam – Bothan a bh'aig Fionnghala / Ailean duinn / Reels: Mhor as' whaler cuidich mi – The grey Bob – The cockerel in the creek / O co thogas: O co thogas dhiom an fhadachd? / Hornpipes: The pipers controversy – Duncan Johnston / Nighean mo ghaoil: Nighean mo ghaoil an Nighean donn Og / 6-8 marches: Donald MacLean of Lewis – Ben Gullion – MacLeod of Mull / Tha mo run: Tha mo run air a' ghille / Jigs: Lady in the bottle – Old hag you have killed me – Price of the pig / Bean a' chotain ruaidh / Doctor Finlay's chord book / Puirt a beul: I blu ada – Fear am beinn an t-slochdan duibh – Cuir nan gobhar as a' chreig – Buachaille dubh Fionnghala / Traditional reels: Traditional – Wedding reel.
Nov 99. (cd) *(CDLDL 1294)* **OLD BLIND DOGS – Live**
Apr 00. (cd) *(CDLDL 1295)* **CHRIS ARMSTRONG – Quantum Leap**
May 00. (cd) *(CDLDL 1296) CRAOBH RUA – If Ida Been Here, Ida Been There*
May 00. (cd) *(CDLDL 1297)* **GABERLUNZIE – Rolling Home: Live Frae The Briggs**
– Road to the isles / Park bar song / Hickory wind / Cape Breton waltz – Sarah Menzies of Carnbo / Katie / 1320 / Coulter's candy / Back o' the north wind / Medly / Nut brown maiden / Wintergreen / The Moon / Rolling home / Will ye no come back again.
Jun 00. (cd) *(CDLDL 1298) ASTURIANA MINING COMPANY – Patrimonia (Heritage)* (American natives)
Nov 00. (cd) *(CDLDL 1300)* **Various Artists – Piping Up**
Jul 01. (cd) *(CDLDL 1302)* **WHIRLIGIG – First Frost**
– Thou were my ain thing / Never love the more / Morrison's jig / Flemish wedding march / Willow song / First frost / Man in a brown hat / Dance of the washerwoman / Fantinel / Fancy / Callanish / Kemp's jig / William Kimber's schottiche / Elziza / Smyling / Kate / Adieu France / Salterrello.

Macmeanmna records

Founded: Gladstone Buildings, Quay Brae, Portree, Isle Of Skye . . . late 80's by ARTHUR CORMACK, BLAIR DOUGLAS, CAILEAN MacLEAN and SHONA CORMACK, all four featuring on the label's debut release as MACMEANMNA – 'The Island' (1990). BLAIR went on to release a handful of albums on his own, while the quartet signed on a plethora of Scottish-based acts during the rest of the 90's (see below). One of the more recent releases, 'LASAIR DHE' (Flame Of God), was a V/A set (CLIAR and friends, basically) recorded live at Glasgow Cathedral and the Queen's Hall in Edinburgh in March 2001. The songs – commissioned by the Highland Festival in '99 where they won a Saltire award – were new pieces of music based on Gaelic psalms, performed spiritually by the MACMEANMNA team and 200 choral singers from around the country.

– discography –

Jun 90. (c) *(SKYE 01)* **MACMEANMNA – Skye: the Island**
Dec 90. (c/cd) *(SKYE/+CD 02)* **BLAIR DOUGLAS – Beneath The Beret**
Jan 92. (c) *(SKYE 03)* **BLAIR DOUGLAS – Celtology** (re-issue)
— note: there is no SKYE 04

• **MARY ANN KENNEDY & CHARLOTTE PETERSEN** have performed together since 1989. MARY ANN was born and bred in Glasgow, although her family comes from Skye and Tiree. Having begun playing piano and harp from an early age, KENNEDY went on to win gold medals at the Traditional (1987) National Mod (1988) and studied at the Royal Academy of Music and Drama in Glasgow where she won the Governor's Recital Prize. In 1989, she again won the International Celtic Harp Competition at Lorient in Brittany. Danish-born CHARLOTTE – who was brought up in Scotland since she was a young child – has also won a plethora of prizes including a Fraser Harp Scholarship at the RAMD where she graduated with a B.A. Music Performance. This is definitely harp-playing at its very best.

Oct 94. (c/cd) *(SKYE/+CD 05)* **Strings Attached**
– Oganaich an or-fhuilt bhuidhe / The sailor's wife – Morrison's jig – The tenpenny bit – Kate Martin's waltz / The harper's farewell to Bushmills / An coire riabhach / Canon in D / One hump or two? / An eal' air a' chuan / The musical priest / Eilean a' cheo / Ailean duinn – Discovery – Peter Davidson's reel / An t-Iarla diurach / An honest man / Bho'n chuir mo leannan culthaobh rium – Dh'fhalhainn sgiobalta – Meal do bhrogan – Nead na lach as a luachair / Take five – Willa fjord.

Jan 95. (c/cd) *(SKYE/+CD 06)* **ISHBEL MacASKILL – Sioda**

• The Isle Of Lewis singer **IAIN MacKAY** chose to stay on the island rather than take up his music elsewhere. A popular traditional folk singer, IAIN won the Gold Medal at the National Mod in Inverness way back in 1972 and went on to become the winner of Seann Nos at Killarney's Pan-Celtic Festival. An album, 'VOICE OF THE HEBRIDES' was issued by 'Lismor' in 1976, although he had previously recorded one for 'Gaelfonn'. He is happily married with five children (four girls and a boy).

Sep 95. (c/cd) *(SKYE/+CD 07)* **Seoladh**
– M'eudail air do shuilean donna – Larach do thacaidean / Och nan och tha mi fo mhulad / Mo nighean donn 's toigh leam thu / 'S e siabost as boidhche leam / Mairi mhin mheall-shuileach / Eilean beag Leodhais / Banais mor chamshroin / Ceann loch an duin / Ochoin a righ gur e mi tha muladach / Mor nighean a' ghibearlain / Bu tu mo chruinneag bhoidheach / Direadh nam beann arda.

• **MAEVE MacKINNON** was a great friend of contemporary folk singer MICHAEL MARRA, whom she met and worked with while sheltering at Saint Chrissie MacPhee at Leth Mheadhanach. At first, MARRA thought she was a fortune teller until she revealed exactly what was a Gaelic-medium. From Ullapool, the shy MAEVE's vocal chords are sincere and uplifting; pity it's her only set so far.

Mar 96. (c/cd) *(SKYE/+CD 08)* **Fo Smuain**
– Oran chaluim sgaire / Ailean Duinn / Fath mo mhulaid a bhith ann / Soraidh bhuam gu Eilean Bharraigh / Puirt a beul / Mo thruaigh leir thu ille bhuidhe / Sheol mo run / Co ni mire rium? / Oran do Eilean mhiughlaidh / Disathuirne ghabh mi mulad / Ochoin a righ gur e mi tha muladach / 'S toigh leam an ciobair / Gur e mis' tha gu tinn.

Oct 96. (c/cd) *(SKYE/+CD 09)* **BLAIR DOUGLAS – A Summer In Skye**
1997. (c-s) *(SKYE 701)* **BLAIR DOUGLAS – Kate Martin's Waltz**
Dec 96. (vid) *(SKYEV 01)* **ARTHUR CORMACK & BLAIR DOUGLAS – Skye**
Dec 97. (c/cd) *(SKYE/+CD 10)* **MacKENZIE – Camhanach**

Sep 98. (c/cd) *(SKYE/+CD 11)* **JENNIFER FORREST & HER SCOTTISH DANCE BAND – The Skye Connection**

• **KENNA CAMPBELL** had already released one CD-album, 'CURAIDH SINTE' in Dec'96 for 'WhiteWave'; *WHFP 0001)*, before she signed to 'Macmeanmna'. Her excellent set (partly taken from earlier BBC sessions) showed her beautiful dreamy voice matched by her songs of long lost loves.

Apr 99. (c/cd) *(SKYE/+CD 12)* **Guth A Shniomhas**
– Nuair bha mi og / Oran Beinn-Li / Chuir ni chas mhor (BBC 1976) / Tha'n t-uisg', tha'n ceo / Rannan breugach (BBC 1976) / Laoidh fhraoich (BBC 1995) / As an doimhneachd / Dearrsadh gealaich air Loch Hostadh (BBC 1983) / A' racan a a bh' againne (BBC 1972) / O, 's ann tha mo ghaol-sa thall (BBC 1983) / Bothan airigh am braigh rainneach / Alasdair a gleanna garadh (BBC 1995) / Tha biodag aig MacThomais – Siud a' rud a thogadh fonn – Alasdair Gorm (BBC 1995) / Am maraiche 's a leannan (BBC 1983) / Fac thu na feidh? – Chuirinn mo bhalachan (BBC 1976) / Cumha Iain ghairbh (BBC 1977) / A' chlach agus Mairi / Chaidh mo dhonnachadh na bheinn (BBC 1977) / Bha buachaillean an duthaich shear / Mo bho dhubh mhor – Tiugainn leam 'ille dhuibh – Tha fear am beinn ruidhleadh mo nighean donn.

• **CLIAR** were formed in 1998 by established folk musicians ARTHUR CORMACK (vocals), MARY ANN KENNEDY (vocals & clarsach), BRUCE MacGREGOR (fiddle), INGRID HENDERSON (piano & clarsach) – who replaced BLAIR DOUGLAS, MAGGIE MacDONALD (vocals) and CHAZ STEWART (guitar). Taking both their name and inspiration from their itinerant Gaelic forefathers, CLIAR released their eponymous debut album below. The record was recorded exclusively in Gaelic, featuring many traditional love songs, a set of mouth music tunes from KENNEDY and MacDONALD and a tribute by MacGREGOR to the hardships endured by his own clan. Hailed by a BBC Scotland presenter as "album of the year so far", the record looks set to confirm CLIAR's growing reputation as Scotland's newest Celtic "supergroup". INGRID has also released CD's for 'Lochshore' with her brother ALLAN HENDERSON.

Jun 00. (c/cd) *(SKYE/+CD 13)* **Cliar**
– Clo mhic ille Mhicheil – Blue bonnets / A fhleasgaich oig as ceanalta / The DT's set / Mo chailin dileas donn / Puirt a beul / Domhnall nan domhnall / The nameless clan / Cumha coire cheathaich / Bha ma leannan Ann / The Para Handy set / Ghraidh an tig thu? / The harpie set / S truagh nach d'rugadh dall mi.

• **DONNIE M. MacLEOD** comes from Stornoway on the Isle of Lewis. In 1996, the Gaelic singer won the prestigious Traditional Gold Medal at the National Mod in Blairgowrie. Produced by MARY ANN KENNEDY, DONNIE's album was full of tradition and grace respecting the old source singers from past generations.

Apr 00. (c/cd) *(SKYE/+CD 14)* **Sguab Is Dloth**
– O's toil 's gu ro thoil leam (Oh I like, I do like) / Dh'fhalbh m'inntinn (My mind went away) / Tha sneachd' air druim Uachdair (There is snow on Drumochter) / Am maraiche 's a leannan (The sailor and his sweetheart) / Cuir a chinn dilis (Faithful one) / Tha mise fo mhulad san am (I am sad at this time) / Nuair a rainig mi 'n doras (When I reached the door) / Smeorach Chlann raghnaill (MacDonald of Clanranald's thrush) / 'S mi air m'uilinn sa' leabaidh (On my elbow in bed) / Mairi nighean Alasdair – Gaol na h-Oige (Mary, Alasdair's daughter) / Ri fuaim an taibh (At the ocean's sound) / Air feasgar soilleir samhraidh (On a bright summer's evening) / A chailin duinn a chuailein reidh (Brown-haired girl with the smooth locks) / Uamh an oir (The cave of gold).

Sep 00. (cd) *(SKYECD 15)* **DONALD BLACK & MALCOLM JONES – Close To Home**
– Close to home / Pipe jigs / Eilean Scalpaidh na Hearadh / Jim Christie / Pipe reels / Eilean / Irish set / The Lawrie drivers / Pipes 6-8 / Sheiling / MSR / Harper set / The Ballachullish stomp / Kintail / Danns an t-Sabhail / Close to home pipes.

• Ballachulish-based **CHAZ STEWART** (b. 6 Nov'58, Milton-of-Campsie, Stirlingshire) has become one of Scotland's leading guitar pluckers. Having picked up the guitar at age 10, CHAZ developed his technique through playing HENDRIX, ZEPPELIN and PASTORIUS numbers. Aged around 19, he relocated to Glasgow, where he performed with local rock bands before finding session work. In the mid-80's, STEWART sessioned on BLAIR DOUGLAS' 'Beneath The Beret' set, and it was through the former RUNRIG man, that he took up the acoustic guitar after discovering Gaelic music. In the 90's, he was invited to join CLIAR (see above) and, more surprisingly, DONNIE MUNRO's band. During this hectic period, CHAZ still managed to record a solo set and work with BURACH on their 2000/2001 world tour. CHAZ was augmented on his swinging jazz/folk solo set by BLAIR DOUGLAS (accordion & organ), MARY ANN KENNEDY (harp & backing vocals), ANDY ALLAN (bass), NICK TURNER (drums & programming) and EILEEN HESTER (backing vocals).

Jun 01. (cd) *(SKYECD 16)* **The Angel Falls**
– Return to Whiplash gulch / Castaway / This is where I am / A day in the rain / The games we play / Amazon / Scotia Nova / While you were asleep / Wasted time / Whatever you say / Farewell to the mill / The timekeeper.

• **BRUCE MacGREGOR** as mentioned previously, the fiddler of CLIAR and BLAZIN' FIDDLES. Taught by the late, DONALD RIDDELL, BRUCE displays adventurous techniques all giving refreshed passion to traditional music. On this set, he is joined by PHIL CUNNINGHAM, JONNIE HARDIE, INGRID HENDERSON, KRIS DREVER, ARTHUR CORMACK, MARC CLEMENT, PAUL JENNINGS, FINLAY MacDONALD, CHRISTINE HASSON, LIZA MULHOLLAND, CHAZ STEWART, MARY ANN KENNEDY and MAGGIE MacDONALD.

Jun 01. (cd) *(SKYECD 17)* **101 Reasons To Do Nothing**
– The Highlanders revenge / Cambridge caravan catastrophe / Liza Mulholland / Sir Henri Laphroig Dinoir of Cluthiebootle / Grindaboo / Cajan Chaz / 101 reasons / Cianalach / The promotion jig / The miser / Peggy Mulholland / Bill and Sandy / Falls of Lora / Cropey's lament for King George V.

• **ALASDAIR MacCUISH & THE BLACK ROSE CEILIDH BAND** were formed in Glasgow in the early 90's as a traditional Scottish dance outfit with more than a hint of contemporary styles thrown in.

Mar 02. (cd) *(SKYECD 18)* **Stepping Out**

– Ceilidh cascade / Hebridean Schottische / Gaelic waltz / The panda / Gay Gordons / Postie's jig / The swan / Highland barn dance / Pipe jigs / A flying trip / St Bernard's waltz / Britannia two step / The seagull / Captain Stretch's mandolin / Strip the willow / Dunoon barn dance / The banshee / Take it easy.

Mar 02. (cd) *(SKYECD 19)* **Various Artists – Lasair Dhe (Flame Of God)**
Jul 02. (cd) *(SKYECD 20)* **Various Artists – A Highland Fiddler – The Clunes Collection Of Donald Riddell**
– tracks by DUNCAN CHISHOLM, IAIN MacFARLANE, BRUCE MacGREGOR & guests)
Jul 02. (cd) *(SKYECD 21)* **CLIAR – Gun Tamh**
– Strathspeys and reels / Domhnall an duin / Nighean donn a' chuaillein riomhaich / Ingy's jigs / An gille dubh ciar dubh / Cailleach an airgid – Rachainn a shuiridh' air oighrig / Bruce's reels / A' chailin mhaiseach dhonn / Puirt a-beul / Am buachaille ban / Shona MacDonald / O thoir a nall am botul.

Mill records

Founded: by WILLIAM JACKSON, founding member of folk group OSSIAN. He subsequently established himself as one of Scotland's finest contemporary composers with the likes of 'THE WELLPARK SUITE', 'ST. MUNGO' and 'INCHCOLM', incorporating elements from his traditional background into a classical framework. Latterly, 'Mill' has served as a platform for JACKSON's own work with the release of 'The Ancient Harp Of Scotland' in 1998 and the re-issue of 'A Scottish Island' the same year. His aforementioned earlier works, meanwhile, were re-issued and repackaged on 'Mill' in 1999 as 'The Celtic Suites'. The imprint's 5th release came courtesy of MAE McKENNA, an old colleague of JACKSON's from way back in the days of OSSIAN forerunners, CONTRABAND (who recorded one set for 'Transatlantic' in '74). Her angelic larynx obviously still impressed Mr. JACKSON who decided MAE would be the first artiste he'd sign (apart from himself, of course). Her 'SHORE TO SHORE' (1999) album – don't be fooled by the out of sync catalogue number – arguably outstripped anything she'd recorded previously.

– discography –

Oct 98. (cd) *(MRCD 010)* **WILLIAM JACKSON – The Ancient Harp Of Scotland** (re-issue)
Oct 98. (cd) *(MRCD 011)* **WILLIAM JACKSON – A Scottish Island** (re-issue)
Aug 99. (cd) *(MRCD 012)* **WILLIAM JACKSON – The Celtic Suites: The Wellpark / St. Mungo** (re-issue)
Oct 00. (cd) *(MRCD 013)* **WILLIAM JACKSON – Inchcolm** (re-issue)
Oct 00. (cd) *(MRCD 014)* **MAE McKENNA – Mirage & Reality** (re-issue)
May 99. (cd) *(MRCD 015)* **MAE McKENNA – Shore To Shore**
Apr 99. (cd) *(MRCD 016)* **WILLIAM JACKSON – Land Of Light**

- **CALLUNA** are based in Edinburgh and comprise of four very talented females who met at the Royal Scottish Academy of Music and Drama. CHARLOTTE PETERSON was born in Denmark but has lived most of her life in Scotland. She studied with fellow clarsach player SAVOURNA STEVENSON and got her degree at the RSAMD; CHARLOTTE's now both a teacher and a composer and has featured on MARY ANNE KENNEDY's 'Strings Attached' set. ANNA WENDY STEVENSON is also known as the fiddler with ANAM and has played the instrument from a very early age. She studied classical music (won a scholarship to the USA) and works freelance for TV/media; she's also composed for the likes of ANNA MURRAY, JOHN RAE'S CELTIC FEET and the aforementioned SAVOURNA. REBECCA KNORR is of American origin but has lived in Scotland since the mid-80's. A teacher of the wooden flute at the RSAMD, she has also worked with TONY McMANUS, SHOOGLENIFTY and BOYS OF THE LOUGH. Last but not least, WENDY WEATHERBY, is probably the best known of the four. She is a respected cellist and vocalist, having recorded with WILLIAM JACKSON on his 'Celtic Suites'; her own solo set, 'A BREATH ON THE COLD GLASS' was issued in 1999 on 'Watercolour Music'. CALLUNA featured on the V/A compliation 'Folkal Point', before delivering their spirited eponymous debut album, a record that combined Scottish traditional/dance songs, airs and of course, grace.

Sep 00. (cd) *(MRCD 017)* **CALLUNA – Calluna**
– Kevin Ryan's / Toothy's / Alfred E Milne / Fine floo'ers / Calgary reel / Bump in the night / Fause, fause hae ye been / Skelp the lugs / The Johnstown reel / The bonnie labouring boy / Blowing hat and cold / Donald MacLeod's.

Springthyme records

Founded: Cupar, Fife . . . mid-70's by PETER SHEPHEARD. 'Springthyme' was the stamping ground for the now legendary traditional folk outfit, OSSIAN, while other various source, ceilidh, group recordings have emerged from this timeless imprint. You could try for more info by e-mailing:- music@springthyme.co.uk / or at website www.springthyme.co.uk

'Living Tradition' was an offshoot of 'Springthyme' founded in Kilmarnock in 1997 by PETE HEYWOOD (all the necessary artist info is documented below).

– discography –

— next with ALY BAIN, TOM ANDERSON and The SHETLAND FIDDLERS, etc
1974. (lp/c) *(SPR/+C 1001)* **Various Artists – Scots Songs And Music: Live At Kinross Festival 1973**

- This pairing from the Kingdom of Fife were backed by the local ceilidh outfit the BEGGARS MANTLE BAND (aka ROBIN McKIDD, BRIAN MILLAR and JOCK MULLEN), songs like 'KELTY CLIPPIE' and 'PITTENWEEM JO' trademark Scottish standards; DAVEY was not the DAVIE STEWART, accordion traveller born in the early 1900's.

1975. (lp/c) *(SPR/+C 1002)* **JOHN WATT & DAVEY STEWART with The BEGGARS MANTLE BAND – Shores Of The Forth**
– Fife's got eveything including blue skies / Farewell to the ferries / The poacher / The new toon hall / Bobby Muldoon / Schooldays over / Eany meany / Kelty clippie / Eyemouth disaster / Annabelle Rosabelle / The boatie rows / My wee dog / Pittenweem Jo / Dunfermline linen / Fisher's hornpipe / The shores of the Forth / Lochaber gathering – Tam Bain's lum.

1976. (lp/c) *(SPR/+C 1003)* **Various Artists – Scots Songs And Music Volume 2: Live At Kinross Festival 1974 & 1975**
1977. (lp/c) *(SPR/+C 1004)* **OSSIAN – Ossian**
(cd-iss. Apr97; SPRCD 1004)

- **TOM HUGHES** was a Jedburgh-born fiddler who began playing at the age of seven, taught by his father THOMAS – TOM's fiddle-maker grandfather HENRY was also a renowned bowman, while his uncles (family circle et al) performed locally at Borders ceilidhs. At the ripe old age of 70, the er, young HUGHES released his debut set (this was a unique feat at the time – see further on).

1983. (lp/c) *(SPR/+C 1005)* **TOM HUGHES AND HIS BORDER FIDDLE – Tom Hughes And His Border Fiddle**
– Braes o' Mar / Tam's old love song / Banks of Kale water / Marquis of Lorne's hornpipe / Henry Hughes' favourite / Sidlaw hills / The wife she brewed it / Faudenside polka / Auld Robin Gray / Flouers o' Edinburgh / East neuk of Fife / Lady Mary Ramsay / Orange and blue / Millicent's favourite / Tam's untitled hornpipe / Farewell to whiskey / Roxburgh castle / Kelso hiring fair / Old rustic bridge / Morpeth rant / Auld garden kirn.

Aug 83. (7") *(SP 002)* **JOHN WATT & DAVEY STEWART – Kelty Clippie**

- The **FOUNDRY BAR BAND** were formed in Arbroath around the summer of 1976 after Dundee-born singer/player JIM REID plucked a handful of fiddlers, accordionists, etc from his local Foundry Bar and entered the Kinross Folk Festival. An inspired move indeed, REID and the group duly won the competition and decided to carry on as a band (others were GEORDIE ANDERSON – fiddle, JIM THOMSON, JIM BROWN and HARRY SCOTT – accordion, CHRISTINE STEWART – guitar, SANDY BEATTIE – bass and MARSHALL RAE – 'sticks').

1983. (lp/c) *(SPR/+C 1007)* **FOUNDRY BAR BAND – The Foundry Bar Band**
– Auchmithie / Hot punch / O nach aghmhor / The guise o' tough / Out on the ocean / Roxburgh castle / Mrs. H.L. MacDonald of Dunach / Grant Farquharson of Inveravon / Catherine Street / The Rhodesian regiment / Tramps and hawkers / Wee Tod.

- **BILL BLACK** was of course, nothing to do with the ELVIS associate/solo artist from the Memphis c.late 50's/early 60's. BILL BLACK & HIS SCOTTISH DANCE BAND were definitely one of the country's leading purveyors of dance music, delivering three sets for the label.

1983. (lp/c) *(SPR/+C 1008)* **BILL BLACK & HIS SCOTTISH DANCE BAND – The Shepherd's Choice**

- **MIRK** were a traditional ballad outfit who'd already delivered one LP in 1979, 'MODDANS BOWER' for 'Mother Earth'; *(MUM 1205)*. It now fetches upwards of £60, while the 'Springthyme' follow-up 'TAK A DRAM', could get half that. It featured songs from MARGIE SINCLAIR, 'GLENLOGIE', 'CAIRN-O-MOUNT' and the title track 'TAK A DRAM'.

1983. (lp/c) *(SPR/+C 1009)* **MIRK – Tak A Dram**
– Why should I / The Dowie dens of Yarrow / Lady Charlotte Durham / Bonnie wee lassie's answer / Och hey Johnnie lad / PM George Ross' farewell to the Blackwatch / Glenlogie / Cairn-o-mount / Farewell to Cape Helles / Glasgow Caithness centenary gathering / Eighth Blackwatch on Passchendale ridge / John Keith Laing / Bill Powrie (marches and reels) / Tak a dram.

1983. (lp/c) *(SPR/+C 1010)* **BORDER STRATHSPEY AND REEL SOCIETY – Ringing Strings Of The Border**

- **KONTRABAND** were mainly Danish musicians (bar St. Andrews-born, ROD SINCLAIR) giving Celtic Folk music a new twist. They had formed in 1974 and played the annual Tonder Festival (reunion in 1999), while SINCLAIR offered up a few solo releases, 'BREAKS & BONDS' and the cassette-only 'WHEN THE COCK CROWS'.

1983. (lp/c) *(SPR/+C 1011) KONTRABAND – North Star*

1984. (lp/c) *(SPR/+C 1012)* **FOUNDRY BAR BAND – On the Road With . . .**
1984. (lp/c) *(SPR/+C 1013)* **SPRANGEEN – Sprangeen**
1985. (lp/c) *(SPR/+C 1014)* **Various Artists – Bothy Greats**
– (recorded live at the Elgin Bothy Ballad Championship)

• **JIM REID** (of The FOUNDRY BAR BAND) is a renowned Dundonian singer and songwriter ('VINNEY DEN' and 'THE SPARK AMONG THE HEATHER' are excellent), a guitarist, mouth harpist and concertina player. Poet VIOLET JACOB was the inspiration for the track, 'THE WILD GEESE'; it has since become a standard. Another, 'UP THE NORAN WATER', was taken from HELEN CRUICKSHANK's poem 'Shy Geordie'. In the early 90's, JIM teamed up with accordionist JOHN HUBAND (also from Dundee) to collaborate on the album, 'FREEWHEELING NOW', the self-penned title track a prince among picturesque trad tunes.

Jul 85. (lp/c) *(SPR/+C 1015)* **JIM REID – I Saw The Wild Geese Flee**
– The wild geese / Norland wind / Lassie wi' the yellow coatie / The shearin's no for you / Stobbie parliament picnic / Upon the moss o' Burreldale / Up the Noran water / Bogie's bonnie belle / Flower of Northumberland / Foundry bar / Busk busk bonnie lassie / Spark among the heather / Rowan tree / Vinney den / Rohallion. *(cd-iss. Feb97; SPRCD 1015)*

Oct 85. (lp/c) *(SPR/+C 1016)* **SAVOURNA STEVENSON – Tickled Pink**
Feb 86. (lp/c) *(SPR/+C 1017)* **Various Artists – Coorse And Fine: Songs And Ballads Of Dundee**
– (feat. JIM REID, CHARLIE LAMB, ANNIE WATKINS, LOWLAND FOLK, etc)

• **AN TEALLACH CEILIDH BAND** were formed (between Keith to Sligo and Kerry to Tonder!) by banjo-player/caller JAKE DONNELLY and included midi accordionist JIM LEIGHTON who was also a member of The LOOSE MOOSE CEILIDH BAND. Their venture with Springthyme brought forth two sets before they signed to 'Lismor' for the album 'CATCHING THE SUN RISE' (1991). The aforementioned pair subsequently founded The BENACHALLY CEILIDH BAND along with fiddler PETE CLARK (a solo artist with a few CD's under his belt, including 'EVEN NOW'), Oban fiddler MARTIN MacLEOD (ex-CAPERCAILLIE), guitarist/bassist MARTIN HADDEN (ex-SILLY WIZARD) and drummer MARTIN TIBBS (ex-DOUGIE MacLEAN BAND). This sextet delivered their one and only CD album, 'HAPPY FEET', towards the end of the 90's.

Oct 88. (lp/c) *(SPR/+C 1018)* **AN TEALLACH CEILIDH BAND – The Plough And The Stars**

• **DUNCAN WILLIAMSON** is a traditional storyteller and balladeer who subsequently released another cassette in 1994, 'PUT ANOTHER LOG ON THE FIRE' for 'Veteran Tapes' *(VT 128)*

Nov 88. (c) *(SPRC 1019)* **DUNCAN WILLIAMSON – Mary And The Seal**

Nov 88. (c) *(SPRC 1020)* **JIMMY McBEATH – Wild Rover No More** (re-issue)
Oct 90. (c) *(SPRC 1021)* **LIZZIE HIGGINS – Princess Of The Thistle** (re-issue)

• **IAIN McLACHLAN** was born and raised on the Outer Herbridean island of Benbecula. The button-key accordionist wrote his own tunes, one of them 'THE DARK ISLAND' was best described as being as fresh as the sea breezes wafting over the Uist machair. IAIN also contributed fiddle and melodeon to his 'Springthyme' set and was accompanied by Bayhead/North Uist's CALUM IAIN MacCORQUODALE on fiddle and accordion plus Balivanich's CALUM CAMPBELL on goose and jaws harp – Jesus, I know it gets lonely up there, but come on eh! – I've notified the proper authorities.

Nov 90. (c) *(SPRC 1022)* **IAIN McLACHLAN – An Island Heritage**

Jun 88. (c) *(SPRC 1023)* **BILL BLACK & HIS SCOTTISH DANCE BAND – Coast To Coast**

• **ANGUS GRANT** is from the West Highlands and a top class exponent of the fiddle. His 70's set for 'Topic' *(12TS 347)* was eventually issued by Springthyme.

Nov 90. (c) *(SPRC 1024)* **ANGUS GRANT – Highland Fiddle**
– Pipe Major Sam Scott / Portree Bay / Flower o' the quern / Mrs. H.L. MacDonald of Dunach / J.F. MacKenzie / Captain MacDiarmid / Mo mhathair / Laura Andrews / The goatherd / The curlew / Millicent's favourite hornpipe / Harvest home / Stirling Castle / MacKinnon's reel / Dargai / Kilworth hills / Loch Maree / Niel Gow's lament for his second wife / Marquis of Huntly's farewell / Marquis of Tullibardine / Marquis of Lorne / The monstrel's favourite hornpipe / Iain Ghlinn cuaich / Seann Drochaid / Miss Addy / Lady Montgomerie / Da mirrie boys of Greenland / Leveneep head / Willafjord / Forneth House / Clan MacColl / Cameron's got his wife again / Jock Wilson's ball.

Nov 90. (c) *(SPRC 1025)* **JEANNIE ROBERTSON – The Great Scots Ballad Singer**
Dec 88. (cd/c) *(SPR CD/C 1026)* **FOUNDRY BAR BAND – Rolling Home**

• **JOE AITKEN** is a berry farmer from Kirriemuir who works by day and sings traditional North-East bothy ballads by night.

Dec 88. (c) *(SPRC 1027)* **JOE AITKEN – If Ye've Never Been Tae Kirrie**

Jan 90. (cd/c) *(SPR CD/C 1028)* **AN TEALLACH CEILIDH BAND – Drops Of Brandy**
Feb 90. (cd/c) *(SPR CD/C 1029)* **BILLY ROSS & JOHN MARTIN – Braes Of Lochiel**
Mar 90. (c) *(SPRC 1030)* **JIM REID & JOHN HUBAND – Freewheeling Now**
– Hey Donald / Whar the dichty rins / Queer fowk / Cruachan Ben / O gin I were a baron's heir / The great storm is over / Music on his mind / Back in Scotland / The Balaena / An t-Eilean muileach / The lassie o' the morning / The moothie man / Oh dear me / Scattered / There's no indispensable man / The auld Beech tree / Freewheeling now. *(cd-iss. Dec93; SPRCD 1030)*
Feb 90. (c) *(SPRC 1031)* **GAUGERS – The Fighting Scot**
May 90. (c) *(SPRC 1032)* **ALY BAIN – & Young Champions**
1990. (c) *(SPRC 1033)* **BILL BLACK & HIS SCOTTISH DANCE BAND – A Reel Cracker**

• **JIM CRAWFORD** was a master of the melodeon (a two row Hohner Double-Ray!) and at 77 when this was recorded, he was entitled to be.

Feb 90. (c) *(SPRC 1034)* **JIM CRAWFORD – On The Melodeon**

• **MICHAEL PHILIP CEILIDH BAND** were undeniably the fastest dance band in town (The Riverside Club – where they recorded their set – is in Glasgow). The line-up featured MICHAEL PHILIP and ROBERT ROSS on accordion, PAUL CLANCY on keyboards, SUZANNE GRAY on bass and GORDON ROBERTSON on drums – quite a conventional set-up really. If you like your 'DASHING WHITE SERGEANT' more dashing and your 'GAY GORDONS' more . . . er, jolly, then you'll love this.

Nov 90. (c) *(SPRC 1035)* **MICHAEL PHILIP CEILIDH BAND – At The Riverside** (cd-iss. May93; *SPRCD 1035)*

• The **LEDA TRIO** were renaissance players PETER CAMPBELL-KELLY (violin), KATHERINE THOMSON (harpsicord) and KEVIN McCRAE (cello). Inspired by 18th Century Edinburgh and the beautiful melodies written at the time (by composer to George III, JAMES OSWALD, and the ill-fated, poverty-stricken DAVID FOULIS), the trio issued their Classical-meets-the 20th Century album in '94.

May 94. (cd/c) *(SPR CD/C 1036)* **LEDA TRIO – Airs For All Seasons**
– Sonata III in E major: Allegro – Largo – Allegro non troppo / The lilac: Largo – Gavotte – Jog / The nightshade: Aria – Sostenuto – Hornpipe / Sonata V in A major: adagio – Allegro – Allegro non troppo / The lily: Aria – Allegro – Adagio – Amoroso / The sneezewort: Amoroso – Pastoralle / The narcissus: Air – Jig / Sonata II in F major: Non troppo allegro – Adagio – Allegro moderato.

May 96. (cd/c) *(SPR CD/C 1037)* **BILL BLACK & HIS SCOTTISH DANCE BAND – The Dawning**

• **JANE TURRIFF** was born 1915 in Aberdeen, the eldest child to Highland/Celtic travellers Donald and Christina Stewart – in fact, her mother's brother was noneother than singer DAVIE STEWART. Nearing her fortieth birthday in 1955, folklorist/producer HAMISH HENDERSON decided it was time to record JANE at her home in Fetterangus. Complete with accordion and her powerful traditional voice (and yodel!), she continued to record the odd track or two (over a hundred to be exact!) for the North East Folklore Archive. While the rest of the country/nation/world was boppin' to the sound of Rock'n'Roll, JANE was giving concerts in her ain wee hoose. In 1995, her best recitations were released on CD. Entitled 'SINGIN IS MA LIFE', it described JANE's unsung history to a tee. She now lives and performs at her home in Mintlaw.

Apr 96. (cd/c) *(SPR CD/C 1038)* **JANE TURRIFF – Singin Is Ma Life**
– A sailor lad an a tailor lad / The bonnie blue hankie / Dowie dens o Yarrow / The wings of a swallow / My wee doggie / The cobbler / Rigs o rye / The derby ram / No one to welcome you home / Down by the green bushes / Poor little Joe / The Boston smuggler / Mill o Tifty's Annie / Wi his grey baird / The ring your mother wore / Empty saddles / Barbara Allen / What can a young lassie / A braw young sailor lad / Will the angels / Bonnie Udny / The rovin ploughboy.

• **JOCK DUNCAN** was born 1925 in New Deer, Aberdeenshire, the son of a folk music loving family steeped in the Scottish traditional heritage and er, farming. At fourteen and with Britain at war, JOCK listened intensely to his newly acquired radio, although by day he was content to work on the Fyvie farm. Inspired by a 1931 'Beltona' recording of GEORGE MORRIS singing 'Hash O' Benagoak', while his brother took fiddle lessons from the legendary J.F. DICKIE, the young JOCK formed his own Scottish dance bands, the FYVIE LOONS and the QUINES. Having served his time in the RAF, DUNCAN found work at the Hydro Board in Caithness and Pitlochry but continued to sing at local halls and competitions; he apparently won eight trophies in succession!). His Doric (North-East) tongue was always at the fore of every song, his rich vocal tones warming the heart of every person lucky enough to witness his unaccompanied bothy ballads. Augmented by BRIAN McNEILL (yes, the Falkirk fiddler) and others of the same ilk, the 70-year cloth-capped singer recorded his debut! album, 'YE SHINE WHAR YE STAN!' (1997). His rendition of traditional tunes such as 'CRUEL MOTHER', 'GLENLOGIE' and 'THE TRADESMEN'S PLOOIN' MATCH', drew plaudits from every quarter (especially The Herald) when he subsequently appeared at the Edinburgh Festival and the Celtic Connections Festival. He still performs regularly and helps school workshops

Feb 97. (cd/c) *(SPR CD/C 1039)* **JOCK DUNCAN – Ye Shine Whar Ye Stan!**
– Gruel / Rhynie / Lothian hairst / Haister's reel / Cruel mother / Hash o' Benagoak / Bogie's bonnie belle / Glenlogie / Bonnie Udny / Bonnie lass o' Fyvie / Sleepytoon / Mormond braes / Hairst o' Rettle / MacFarlan o' the Sprotts / Plouboy lads /

Drumdelgie / Battle of Harlaw / Desperate battle / Banks of Inverurie / Barnyards o' Delgaty.

1997. (c) *(SPRC 1040)* **Various Artists – North East Tradition 1** (feat. JANE TURRIFF, ELIZABETH STEWART, ROBERT LOVIE, JOCK DUNCAN, etc)

– Living Tradition discography –

- **BOB BLAIR** was a singer/guitarist and concertina player and the first in the Living Tradition series 'The Tradition Bearers'. Augmented by fiddler FINLAY ALLISON, he started off the label in fine oral style.

Mar 00. (cd) *(LTCD 1001)* **BOB BLAIR – Reaching For The High, High Lands** – Kissin's nae sin / Cairn o' mount / Bonny Peggy / A wee drap o't / Waly, Waly / Duncan Gray / It was in the toon o' Kelso / O gin my love were a pickle o' wheat / The collier laddie / The grey silkie of Sule Skerry / Johnny lad / Ye hae lien wrang / The bonnie lassie o' the mornin'.

- **JIMMY HUTCHISON** was born in Frobost in the Isle of Uist (he looks about 80 years-old on the album cover!). Another Source/folk singer, he was augmented by fiddler TOM SPIERS, guitarist BRIAN MILLER and IAN McCALMAN on mouth organ.

Mar 00. (cd) *(LTCD 1002)* **JIMMY HUTCHISON – Corachree** – Erin-go-bragh / She was a rum one / Matty Groves / The overgate / The beggarman / I'll lay ye doon love / Phiege a grath / Corachree / False lover won back / Spanish lady / Lord Donald / D-day dodgers.

- **MAUREEN JELKS** was born in Dundee and having cut her teeth as a member of PALAVER, JELKS was ready to go into the recording studio; at this point she was augmented by fiddler TOM SPIERS and whistle man ARTHUR WATSON. Inspired by such Source singing luminaries as BELLE STEWART, the sadly overlooked MARY BROOKSBANK and GORDEANNA McCULLOCH (whom she'd heard while attending the Kinross Folk Festival and subsequently replaced in PALAVER), MAUREEN's love of old-time Folk music was obvious in her interpretations of Scots traditional songs. 'EENCE UPON A TIME' (2001) was her long-time coming debut release for 'Living Tradition', a record that also showed MAUREEN's sense of tongue-in-cheek fun.

Jan 01. (cd) *(LTCD 1004)* **MAUREEN JELKS – Eence Upon A Time** – Eence upon a time / Mary mild / Black waterside / The bonnie hoose o' Airlie / Fair Rosie-Anne / The wimmen o' Dundee / Why should I / Johnnie my man / Donal Ogg / Silken snood / The cruel mother / Eh'm a Dundee lassie / Rue and thyme / The rantin' laddie.

- **HEATHER HEYWOOD** had already released two albums for 'Greentrax' before she finally got around to making a third for Living Tradition.

Sep 00. (cd) *(LTCD 1007)* **HEATHER HEYWOOD – Lassies Fair & Laddies Braw** – Up and awa' wi' the Laverock / Two bonny boys / Logie o' Buchan / The bonny wee lassie who never said no / Queen among the heather / Birnie Bouzle / Jamie Raeburn / The Auchengeich disaster / The lowlands of Holland / The baron o' Brackley / The terror time / The Lichtbob's lassie / Farewell to whisky.

- **JOHN WATT** was born in Dunfermline and recorded in the 70's/80's for 'Springthyme' (mainly with DAVEY STEWART). Since then his work has been recorded by artistes from Canada to Denmark – The kingdom of Fife loves this man. On this 'HEROES' set, he is joined by RAB NOAKES, JACK BECK, PETE CLARK, ERIK KNUSSEN, NEIL PATERSON, FRASER SPIERS, COLIN MacFARLANE, DAVID VERNON, KEN MUIR and even ginger football commentator ARCHIE MacPHERSON! – I never thought the latter would ever get into a music book.

Sep 00. (cd) *(LTCD 3001)* **JOHN WATT – Heroes** – The day that Billy Cody played the auld grey toon / Big Neil / Pittenweem Jo / Charlie Dickson / Herzogin Cecile / Kentucky Saturday night / It's fine to keep in wi' the gaffer – Bonnie Dundee / Ode to Joe Currie / I don't like Dundee / The Kelty clippie / John Thomson – Flowers o' the forest / Set of tunes / Jocky's incredible flight / Owt for nowt – Avanti polo / No snow falls today / Wild West show / Sweet Sue.

Tartan Tapes

Founded: via SIMON THOUMIRE, JOHN THOUMIRE and ELIZABETH HEPBURN at 17 Redford Drive, Edinburgh, EH13 OBL. Already well established as a main player in Scotland's traditional music scene, THOUMIRE's concertina wizardry previously won him a BBC Young Tradition Award while his CV includes collaborations with guitarist IAN CARR and long running folk outfit SEANNACHIE.

Set up to present the most essential Scots/Irish traditional and contemporary music currently available, the label was launched with 'Trip To Scotland' by HAMISH MacGREGOR and The BLUE BONNETS. The MacGREGOR in question was actually THOUMIRE himself in pseudonymous disguise while the BLUE BONNETS were actually noted folkies JENNIFER and HAZEL WRIGLEY together with JULIA LEGGE. The album was unusual in that the 30 tracks all featured Scottish place names in the title, showcasing the varying styles of folk music within Scotland's borders. MacGREGOR subsequently issued a follow-up entitled 'Love Songs' wherein six of the nation's finest trad singers (SHEENA WELLINGTON, CORRINA HEWATT, TAM WHITE etc) were backed up by the likes of EILIDH SHAW, PHIL BANCROFT and of course, THOUMIRE himself. Sandwiched between these releases was 'Dances With Fish' by the ROBERT FISH BAND, a good time ceilidh outfit from Edinburgh.

'Tartan Tapes' furthered their reputation with the 'Heat The Hoose' album, a document of Edinburgh's annual fiddle festival featuring the likes of ALASDAIR FRASER, the aforementioned SHAW and Donegal crew CONNAILLAIGH (featuring LIZ DOHERTY) amongst others. Proof – if any was needed – that Edinburgh is now Scotland's (if not Britain's) traditional music epicentre was amply provided on 'Flowers Of Edinburgh', an overview of the Capital's fertile scene with contributions from the likes of SANDY BRECHIN, ELSPETH COWIE, TALITHA MacKENZIE, IAN McLEOD and many more.

In fact, with so much exciting talent about it was hardly surprising that THOUMIRE initiated a sister imprint, 'Foot Stompin' Records'. Stompin' their way into the review columns were 'Birlin' Fiddles' (a joint effort with fiddlers JENNIFER WRIGLEY, ALLAN HENDERSON and JULIA LEGGE accompanied by guitarist SANDY WRIGHT), 'Blazin' Fiddles' (another all-star fiddle extravaganza), a second volume of 'Heat The Hoose', 'In The Sunny Long Ago' by folk scholar MARGARET BENNETT (mother of MARTYN) and an eponymous debut set by gifted piper FINLAY MacDONALD. As well as producing most of the above albums, there's no doubt that THOUMIRE has kept a tight rein on the quality control.

Forthcoming releases from his Celtic mini-empire include 'Attention All Personnel' by CROFT No FIVE, a relatively new group formed in 1998 with the aim of adapting traditional music to the rhythms of the club dancefloor. Also in the offing is 'Soul Music' by SCOTTISH STEPDANCE COMPANY (a duo hailing from the Isle of Skye and intent on promoting the art of traditional Stepdance) and a debut album by GILLIAN FRAME, winner of the Young Scottish Traditional Musician 2001 Award and one of Scotland's brightest young fiddle hopes.

– discography –

- **HAMISH MacGREGOR (AND THE BLUE BONNETS)** was indeed the pseudonym of THOUMIRE, the BLUE BONNETS were fiddlers JULIA LEGGE and JENNIFER WRIGLEY, plus HAZEL WRIGLEY (on guitar & keyboards). Under this guise, the talented SIMON and his crew produced some toe-tapping numbers set to historical sites around our beautiful land.

Jul 97. (cd/c) *(CD/MC TT 1001)* **Trip To Scotland** – Flowers of Edinburgh – The St Kilda wedding / Loch Lomond – Loch Ruan – Loch Maree / Pennan den / Stones of Stenness (Orkney) – Killiecrankie / Arniston Castle – Inver lassies / Dark Lochnagar / Roslin Castle – Stirling Castle – Roxburgh Castle / Kelso races – Miss Ann Cameron of Balvenie – Hoddorn Castle / The banks of Loch Ness – Ben Nevis / Ye banks and braes of Bonnie Doon – Farewell to Fuinary – The road and miles to Dundee – Morag of Dunvegan / Glasgow hornpipe – Inverness gathering – Perth assembly / Skye boat song / Spootiskerry (Shetland) – Da Scallowa lassies – Bonnie isle of Wallasay.

- The 'Burgh's **ROBERT FISH BAND** are a 6-piece ceilidh-type outfit made up of two fiddlers VERNON GALLOWAY and SARAH NORTHCOTT, a guitarist ROY CARBARNS, STAN REEVES on accordion & whistle, COLIN WHITE on bass and DAVE COOPER on drums & percussion (what, no ROBERT FISH); The moniker ROBERT FISH stems from a Robert Burns-era bard who maintained the great one himself plagiarised his 'Tae A Pint' poem to 'Tae A Haggis'. The ROBERT FISH BAND played at the Labour Party Conference and under the wing of producer/mentor SIMON THOUMIRE, delivered this rousing set of 2/4 marches and Cape Breton-influenced sounds.

Dec 97. (cd/c) *(CD/MC TT 1002)* **Dances With Fish** – Funky fjord (based on the Shetland reel Willafjord) / 2/4 marches (Gay Gordons): Campbell's farewell to Redcastle – Corriechollies welcome to the northern meeting – The drunken piper / Johnny's polka's (dashing white sergeant): Troopers lane – Isle of glass – The trampoline – Father is my shirt you have washed / Irish jigs (strip the willow): My darling asleep – O'Sullivan's march – Ne'er shall wean her – The rambling pitchfork / Strathspeys (Highland Scottishe): The burning of the piper's hut – Captain Campbell / Thomas Leixlip: Lanachree and Megram – The laird's guid brither / 6/8 march (Boston two step): Murdo Mackenzie of Torridon / Lucifer Polka's (dashing white sergeant): Lucy Farr's I – Lucy Farr's II – Glenside II / French Canadian waltzes (St Bernard's waltz): Black Jock – Valse du coq – Gullimetre's waltz clog / Cape Breton reels (foursome or reel of Tulloch): Geordie McLeish – Jenny Nettles – Cape Breton symphony's welcome to the Shetland Isles – Molly Rankin's / Moran's return / Stan's jigs (Shetland strip the willow): The boys of Ballymote – The cliffs of Moher – The 50p table – Gangin up frae Hawksland – Difrigg lassies.

- **HAMISH MacGREGOR** was this time THOUMIRE himself (on concertina, lowland pipes and bodhran), along with musicians EILIDH SHAW (fiddle), SANDY WRIGHT (guitar), KEVIN MacKENZIE (guitar), ROD PATERSON (guitar) and PHIL BANCROFT (saxophone) – for singers see below.

Apr 98. (cd/c) *(CD/MC TT 1003)* **Scottish Love Songs**
– The bleacher lassie (ALAN REID) / Banks o' red roses (CORRINA HEWAT) / I loved a lass (ROD PATERSON) / Partans in the creel (SHEENA WELLINGTON) / Ae fond kiss (CORRINA HEWAT) / Amang the stepping stanes (TAM WHITE) / The leaboy's lassie (ELSPETH COWIE) / The lassie o' bonnie Glencoe (ALAN REID) / My love is like a red red rose (SHEENA WELLINGTON) / Just like another rolling stone (ROD PATERSON) / Ca' the yowes (ELSPETH COWIE) / Will ye no come back again? (CORRINA HEWAT).

Jul 98. (cd) *(CDTT 1004)* **Various Artists – Heat The Hoose**
– ALASDAIR FRASER + TONY McMANUS: Lochaber no more – Calliope house – The cowboy jig / CONNAILLAIGH: Gravel walks to grannie / CLARE MANN & AIDAN O'ROURKE: Obsessive island – Clare's jig – Dennis Langton's – Calum Findlay / PAUL ANDERSON: Fyvie Castle – J.F. Dickie's delight / ALASDAIR WHITE: Eilean beag donn a' chuain / KAREN STEVEN: Calum Breugach – Mrs. J. Forbes – Unknown – Johnny Sullivan's / CONNAILLAIGH: The silver spire / PAUL ANDERSON: Valley of silence / CLARE McLAUGHLIN: Drive the golden spike – O'Donnell's / AIDAN O'ROURKE: Traditional reel – Barney's Balmoral – The morning star / EILIDH SHAW + KEVIN MacKENZIE: The seventieth year / AMY GEDDES: Colin Campbell's – The Isla rant – Millfire / CHRIS STOUT: Aly's soond – Da Scalloway lasses – Cape Breton welcome to Shetland.

Nov 98. (cd) *(CDTT 1005)* **SIMON THOUMIRE ORCHESTRA – Celtic Connections Suite**

Jun 99. (cd) *(CDTT 1006)* **Various Artists – Flowers Of Edinburgh**
– cMc with JOHN MORAN: James & Lara's wedding – The lassies of Stewarton – Sully's No.6 / JIM MALCOLM, DAVE WATT & IAIN MacFADYEN: Battle of Waterloo / MAIRI CAMPBELL & IAIN MacINNES: Sporting Jamie – Calum Crubach – Lady Louden – Lady Doll Sinclair – A cuachag – The black haired lad / TALITHA MACKENZIE: Adje Jano / JOHN MORAN & CHARLOTTE PEDERSON: She's like the swallow / JIM SUTHERLAND, IAIN MacLEOD & SIMON BRADLEY: Simon Bradley's march – Major Campbell Green – Anna-Wendy's – White line fever – Bjork's chauffeur – Hurley's house / RUSSELL HUNTER, EILIDH SHAW, SIMON BRADLEY & ANGUS GRANT: Scott Skinner's compliments to Dr. MacDonald – Stirling Castle – Pretty Peggy – Albarada Asturiana / MAY SHAW & TONY MITCHELL: The water is wide / SANDY BRECHIN: The canny repair – The dwarf / EILIDH SHAW, ROSS MARTIN and LEO McCANN: Cameron Highlanders – Miss Campbell of Sheerness – Last tango in Harris – Good dryin' / ELSPETH COWIE: German lairdie / SIMON THOUMIRE & JIM SUTHERLAND: Calliope house – Saddle the pony – The drunken sailor – Itchy fingers / 'THE FLOWERS OF EDINBURGH'.

Aug 99. (cd) *(CDTT 1007)* **SIMON THOUMIRE ORCHESTRA – Music For A New Scottish Parliament**

– Foot Stompin' discography –

— **KEEP IT UP** are SIMON THOUMIRE, jazz guitarist KEVIN MacKENZIE (also of SWIRLER), fiddler/vocalist EILIDH SHAW (of HIGHFIELD BAND, of POWER TROUT, of POOZIES, ex-CALEDON, etc) and bouzouki/piper MALCOLM STITT (of DEAF SHEPHERD, of TANNAS, of BOYS OF THE LOUGH). Reflecting the vitality of the current traditional folk scene, this latest project from the ubiquitous THOUMIRE involves a cast of musicians seasoned in their respective fields yet all relatively youthful. One of my personal favourites from their accomplished eponymous debut was 'THE CANONGATE TWITCH', an affliction I've been subject to on more than one occasion . . .

Nov 98. (cd) *(CDFSR 1701)* **Keep It Up**
– Charlie Hunter's jig – Miss Ann Cameron of Balvennie – The duck – unknown / Men of Argyll – Captain Horn – Struy lodge / Lango Lee – The bee sting – Donald, Willie and his dog / Just for Gordon – Willie Murray – Duntroon Castle – Alan Henderson's reel / Barbara's jig – Old woman's dance – The St. Kilda wedding / Mo chaoin challin (My gentle girl) / Simon Bradley's Strathspey – Alec C. MacGregor / Tail toddle – The Canongate twitch – Jock Wilson's ball – Captain Lachlan McPhail of Tiree / Battle of Waterloo / Carron side.

Aug 99. (cd) *(CDFSR 1702) LIZ DOHERTY – Last Orders*

Feb 00. (cd) *(CDFSR 1703)* **Various Artists – Birlin' Fiddles with JENNIFER, ALLAN HENDERSON, JULIA LEGGE and SANDY WRIGHT**
– The fashion o' the lassies – St. Kilda wedding / MacDonald's march – Miss Hutcheon o' the manse – Dougal's sustain / The rose among the heather – Colum Beag – Illean bithibh sunndach / The horse of Copinsay – The sound of sleat – Highland reel – John Keith Lang / Traditional jig – Andy de Jarlie – Isobel Blackley / My Cape Breton home / Barbara's wedding – Ashley's strathspey – Carol-Ann's reel / Rohan – Inspector Donald Cameron of Ness – Ruidhle cailleach / John Pottinger's compliments to Ronald Cooper – Roddy MacDonald's fancy / Fali o ro / Fiddler's cramp – The smith's a gallant fireman – AJ's / The hills of Glen Orchy – Cailleach an Duardain.

Feb 00. (cd) *(CDFSR 1704) LIZ DOHERTY & FIDDLESTICKS – Racket In The Rectory*

Jul 00. (cd) *(CDFSR 1705)* **Various Artists – Fast And Furious (Trad Music For A Modern Generation)**
– FINLAY MacDONALD: The plagiarist – The day we had the goat / LIZ DOHERTY & FIDDLESTICKS: Krapulakatrilli / SIMON THOUMIRE ORCHESTRA: The future is bright / LIZ DOHERTY: Monce in a basket – The third flight home – Andy Broon's reel / SIMON THOUMIRE: Fast & furious / JENNIFER WRIGLEY, ALLAN HENDERSON, JULIA LEGGE, SANDY WRIGHT (BIRLIN' FIDDLES): Da fashion o da lassies – St. Kilda wedding / LIZ DOHERTY & FIDDLESTICKS: Untitled – Untitled – Cataroni / SIMON THOUMIRE ORCHESTRA: Ceilidh for everyone / KEEP IT UP: Tail toddle – The Canongate twitch – Jock Wilson's ball – Captain Lachlan MacPhail of Tyree / RUSSELL HUNTER, EILIDH SHAW, SIMON BRADLEY, ANGUS GRANT: Scott Skinner's compliments to Dr. MacDonald – Stirling Castle – Pretty Peggy – Albarada Asturiana / BIRLIN' FIDDLES: Traditional jig – Andy de Jarlie – Isobel Blackley / CONNAILLAIGH: Gravel walks to Grannie / cMc: James and Lara's wedding – The lassies of Stewarton – Sully's No.6.

• **FINLAY MacDONALD** was brought up by a bagpipe playing father and went on to graduate from the Royal Scottish Academy of Music and Dance with a degree in Traditional Music. The piping prodigy subsequently lent his musical talent to various folk-orientated outfits including the BATTLEFIELD BAND, OLD BLIND DOGS, KINLOCHARD CEILIDH BAND and the NEILSTON and DISTRICT PIPE BAND, enjoying touring engagements which took him all over the world. He finally released his own eponymous debut album late in 2000, a combination of self-penned and traditional material (as well as a couple of tunes written by fellow piper ALLAN MacDONALD) featuring a stellar cast of Edinburgh musicians including KEVIN MacKENZIE, BRIAN KELLOCK and JOHN RAE. Fiddler CHRIS STOUT and singer FINDLAY NAPIER also featured on the record, both members of the group The LOOP alongside MacDONALD himself.

Nov 00. (cd) *(CDFSR 1706)* **Finlay MacDonald**
– The plagiarist – The night we had the goats / Angus Sutherland – The mountain dairymaid / Jox the box (jig & reel) – Trad reel / Captain McKerrell's – Nigel Richards' / The road to Loch Nam Bearnish – Major Forbes – Nameless – Lord William / Miss Gow – The Cameronian rant – The flaggon / Lake Orchid / Waulking song – Greek street / The rusty gun – A.A. Cameron's – The Meechans / The Humpback whale / I would have preferred thee at first, but not now sir – Donald of the sun – Welcome to Jo McAuley's / My old man is long a' dying – An t-Ord gallach – Sugar merchant / Cowden hall.

Jan 01. (cd) *(CDFSR 1707)* **Various Artists – Heat The Hoose 2**
– AIDAN O'ROURKE with MALCOLM STITT: George O'Hardy – Miller O'Drone – The rejected lover – Hazy hill / SARAH MacFADYEN with KRIS DREVER: Starter for twelve / LIZ DOHERTY: Donegal tune – The tartar frigate – The waves of rush / KENNY FRASER: Beautiful Lake Ainslie / CLAIRE MANN with AARON JONES: Tune for Frankie – Mutt's favourite – Ril ghearoid ui chroinin / JOHN McCUSKER with IAN CARR and IAIN MacDONALD: Boys of the puddle – The scullion's wife / EILIDH SHAW with RUSSELL HUNTER: Ola Blackstrom's tune / MAEVE and ORNA GILCHRIST: Maeve's tune – Rannie MacLellan – My kindly sweetheart – The ale is dear / GILLIAN BOUCHER with EWAN MacPHERSON: Seamus Connely's – Humours of Lisadell – Reel of Rio / ANNA WENDY STEVENSON with MALCOLM STITT: Jean Mauchline – Tune for Nuala / SIMON BRADLEY with XEL PEREDA: Shelley's reel – Untitled – Major Campbell Graham MBE / JENNIFER WRIGLEY with HAZEL WRIGLEY: The princess' polka – Unknown – Sean McGuire's / DEREK and SARAH HOY with DAVE FRANCIS: Missinyersel – The olympian – Andy Coogan's jig / RUSSELL HUNTER with SANDY WRIGHT: Annie Laurie / CLARE McLAUGHLIN with KRIS DREVER: The gates of Mullagh – Stasia's reel – The dark horse reel / MARIANNE CAMPBELL with DOUGLAS CASKIE: The beard and bees'knees.

• **MARGARET BENNETT** ; After growing up in the Western Isles surrounded by the rich oral ballad tradition, MARGARET emigrated to Newfoundland, Canada where the folksong tradition was perhaps even more entrenched. While abroad she gave birth to her son MARTYN, now an acclaimed nu-folk artist in his own right. Upon returning to Scotland in the mid-70's, she concentrated on her studies, gaining a post-graduate MA in Folklore and a Phd in Ethnology; she currently holds an honorary Research Fellowship at Glasgow University's School of Scottish and Celtic Studies and is regarded as a world authority on Scottish folklore. In addition to her academic and literary talents (she's also the prizewinning author of several books), MARGARET is a resepected folksinger in her own right, having appeared at many festivals throughout the Western world and even performing at the 2000 Holyrood Palace Garden Party. She has also made numerous appearances on TV and radio. She was awarded the Master Music Maker Award in recognition of her lifelong commitment to musicianship and teaching. MARGARET finally made it into CD with 'IN THE SUNNY LONG AGO' (2001), an album recorded in Tobermory, Isle of Mull and produced by her son MARTYN. Released on THOUMIRE's 'Foot Stompin' imprint, the record featured such up and coming folk names as GILLIAN FRAME and brothers FINDLAY and HAMISH NAPIER.

Apr 01. (cd) *(CDFSR 1708)* **In The Sunny Long Ago**
– Go and leave / Sweet forget-me-nots / Sonny's dream / An t-oighre Og / Pat Murphy's meadow / Rocks of Merasheen / Ailein, Ailein / Aye waulkin / Connemara / Plooman laddies / Jock o Hazeldean / Oran Chaluim sqaire / Bonnie bunch o thyme.

• **CROFT NO. FIVE** are a vibrant, high-octane and funky quintet led by JOHN SOMMERVILLE, an accordionist with the feel-good energy of PHIL CUNNINGHAM. Melodic with fiddles, bass, guitars, drums and accordions, the CROFT also used samples and effects.

Sep 01. (cd) *(CDFSR 1709)* **Attention All Personnel**
– Cutting the cake: Cutting the cake – Trio to JJ's / Release da hounds: The Ramnee ceilidh – Release da hounds / Phat jigs: Thorb the robot – Agent Raj / Half inch: The half inch incident / Legless: The legless barman – Stuck in a life / Lanark: Last train

from Lanark – Boogie woogie waltz / Knightmare: Heidi – The walking nightmare – The Harris dance – Road to Errogie / Rancid maidens: The rancid maidens of Shmo – Rigo's rant / Track 1: The plagiarist / Gambrinus: The man of Arran / 4ForePlay / Dave's white Astra: Bowl of flakes – Dave's white Astra / Escape from Alvie.

• **SCOTTISH STEPDANCE COMPANY** are indeed four stepdancers backed by fiddle, bagpipes, etc (unknown). If you loved RIVERDANCE, you'll probably love this feisty, toetapping (or even 'Footstompin'') collection of traditional strathspeys, reels and jigs.

Sep 01. (cd) *(CDFSR 1710)* **Sole Music**
– High road / Errogie / Alison's solo / Tacsi / Clan Beag / Thig am bata / Waterloo / John's solo / Sienn O / Nightmare / Gloomy / Angus G / Sgathach / Finale.

• **GILLIAN FRAME** & BACK OF THE MOON were fresh-faced outfit from Arran comprising fiddler and singer, GILLIAN FRAME (b. 1980), her brothers FINDLAY (piano) and HAMISH NAPIER (guitar), plus SIMON McKERRELL (on uilleann and border pipes). Winner of the Young Scottish Traditional Musician of the year, she and the guys set about recording their eponymous debut set taking their love of the Shetlands, Ireland and Cape Breton as their template.

Sep 01. (cd) *(CDFSR 1711)* **Gillian & Back Of The Moon**
– Kitten on the lane – The undertow – Paddy Fahens / Sands of the shore / Eric's march – The jubille jig / O'er bogie – Sister's reel – Bonnie Isle of Whalsay / Will ye gang love / The rolling hills of the borders / Blarney pilgram – Miss Campbell of Shearness – Sonny's Brogan / Gin I were a baron's heir / Shuibhail le mi's ceanntirre – Warlocks – Captain Ross's / Am buachaille ban / The Greenland whale fisheries / Fingal's weeping – An t-ord Geallach – Back of the moon.

Sep 01. (cd) *(CDFSR 1712) CLAIRE MANN – Claire Mann*
• (CLAIRE is Newcastle-born flautist/fiddler; the album features SIMON)

Nov 01. (cd) *(CDFSR 1713)* **SIMON THOUMIRE & DAVID MILLIGAN – The Big Day In**
– The tipsy sailor – The future is bright – J.F. Dickie / Joseph's jig – Bessie Brown / Tumble in Loch Tummel – Big Bertha – Stasia's reel / Love comes quietly – Forsaken / Highland – Kiss the lass ye like the most – Billy McGuire's box / Hasiera – Artikutza / Hirplin' Danny – Mrs Maule of Paumure's favourite / The sand pitt – Mrs Grace Tait – Trip to Windsor / Invercauld's reel – Miss Admiral Gordon's reel / The auld wheel – David Adams / March for a new Scottish parliament – Queen of the Highlands – The Celtic nymph / 1 2 3 4 / Roddy Campbell's favourite / Keep it up / Corrina's touch.

Mar 02. (cd) *(CDFSR 1714)* **MARTYN BENNETT – Glen Lyon – A Song Cycle**

• **FINE FRIDAY** are three young musicians from the Edinburgh circuit; a longstanding residency at Sandy Bell's saw them evolve as the most promising trio for some time. Guitarist/singer KRIS DREVER (from Orkney), fiddler ANNA-WENDY STEVENSON (from Edinburgh) and flautist NUALA KENNEDY (from Dundalk in Ireland) fused jigs and reels with a neat blend of Scottish, Irish and Scandinavian material; they also covered Boo Hewerdine's 'HUMMINGBIRD' and Steve Tilston's 'SLIP JIGS AND REELS'.

Apr 02. (cd) *(CDFSR 1715)* **Gone Dancing**
– Cold blow / The humours of Westport – Julia Delaney's / Andy Broons / Jean Mauchline – Tune for Nuala / Selkie / Rosie Martin's – Miss Anne Cameron of Balvenie – Lord Lovat's / Gamaldans – Vossavalsen – Reinlenter / Hummingbird / Compliments to Sean Maguire – Compliments to Hugh Hughson of Newcastle / Alison's lament – Hanna Luers / Slip jigs and reels / Lacy's jig – Grogan's jig – Winnie Hayes jig / Gerry Cromane's – Ceapaval – The duchess of Percy / Funeray.

– White Label output –

1999. (cd) *(CDWH 1)* **SIMON THOUMIRE – Solo1**

• **SARAH McFADYEN + KRIS DREVER** are from the Orkney Islands and have a varied musical pedigree. Fiddler SARAH was taught by veteran (but still youthful) folk celebrity JENNIFER WRIGLEY, while vocalist/guitarist KRIS (also on banjo) was the son of the legendary WOLFSTONE man IVAN DREVER. Their renditions of some trad songs are a hit as far as Europe and Cape Breton; KRIS is also featuring in a ceilidh dance show touring America's West Coast and Chile.

2000. (cd) *(CDWH 2)* **SARAH McFADYEN AND KRIS DREVER – Sarah McFadyen And Kris Drever**
– Starter for 12 / Union Street session / The Selkie / The glen road to Carrick / Reels and strathspey / Cauld blaw the rainy night / Sisters reel / Jenny Wrigley's / Panic sets in / King of the pipers / Traditional air.

Temple records

Founded: 1978 in the village of Temple, Midlothian, Temple Records have carved out a significant niche for themselves as suppliers of high quality traditional music from Scotland and – to a lesser extent – Ireland. Operating from their home base of a converted church, the label has consistently released acclaimed material regardless of the vagaries of musical fashion.

The man behind it all is County Armagh folk veteran ROBIN MORTON, whose bumper CV includes a couple of published collections of Ulster folksong, a handful of recordings for 'Topic' and a lengthy stint in Irish legends BOYS OF THE LOUGH, a band he helped found back in 1967 alongside TOMMY GUNN and CATHAL McCONNELL. He first came to Scotland in 1969 to work on a PhD at Edinburgh University although band activities occupied most of his time up until the late 70's when he set up Temple. With a brief to release material overlooked by other labels, the company kicked things off with ALISON KINNAIRD's 'The Harp Key' (1978) and unwittingly sparked off a small harp revival. A similar situation occurred with CHRISTINE PRIMROSE's 'Aite Mo Ghaoil' (1982), one of the first Gaelic language recordings in a market which is fast becoming saturated.

In the mid-80's, MORTON set up an American branch, Temple US, in response to growing international demand for the label's recordings. Unlike many other labels, Temple are keen to differentiate between Scottish and Irish music (PAT KILBRIDE, part of the latter) rather than lumping them together under the increasingly popular banner of Celtic music. In fact, the label's dedication to quality has meant that their roster and back catalogue remains relatively modest in size, displaying a selective A&R policy. In addition to the aforementioned artists, the label has released material by the likes of The BATTLEFIELD BAND (whom MORTON has been managing since 1980).

As well as holding down the position of Edinburgh Folk Festival director for 3 years, MORTON has expanded Temple's reach by setting up a publishing wing (Kinmore Music) and a video production company.

– albums discography –

1978. (lp/c) *(TP/CTP 001)* **ALISON KINNAIRD – The Harp Key**
1979. (lp/c) *(TP/CTP 002)* **FLORA MacNEIL – Craobh Nan Ubhal**
1980. (lp/c) *(TP/CTP 003)* **ALISON KINNAIRD – The Harper's Gallery**
1980. (lp/c) *(TP/CTP 004) PAT KILBRIDE – Rock And Roses*
1980. (lp/c) *(TP/CTP 005)* **BATTLEFIELD BAND – Home Is Where The Van Is**
1982. (lp/c) *(TP/CTP 006)* **CHRISTINE PRIMROSE – Aite Mo Ghaoil (Place Of My Heart)**
1982. (lp/c) *(TP/CTP 007)* **BATTLEFIELD BAND – The Story So Far**
1982. (lp/c) *(TP/CTP 008)* **Various Artists – A Controversy Of Pipers**
Dec 82. (lp/c) *(TP/CTP 009)* **FINLAY McNEIL – Fonn Is Furan**
Dec 82. (lp/c) *(TP/CTP 010)* **BATTLEFIELD BAND – There's A Buzz**
1983. (lp/c) *(TP/CTP 013) ANN HEYMANN &* **ALISON KINNAIRD – The Harper's Land**
Jun 84. (lp/c) *(TP/CTP 015)* **BATTLEFIELD BAND – Anthem For The Common Man**
1984. (lp/c) *(TP/CTP 016)* **ARTHUR CORMACK – Nuair Bha Mi Og**
Mar 85. (lp/c) *(TP/CTP 017)* **BRIAN McNEILL – Unstrung Hero**
Oct 85. (lp/c) *(TP/CTP 018)* **IAIN MACFADYEN – Ceol Mor-Ceol Beag**
Dec 85. (lp/c) *(TP/CTP 019) MAIRE NI CHATHASAIGH – The Living Wood*
Jan 86. (lp/c) *(TP/CTP 020)* **PETER NARDINI – Is There Anybody Out There?**
Mar 86. (lp/c) *(TP/CTP 021)* **BATTLEFIELD BAND – On The Rise**
Sep 86. (lp/c) *(TP/CTP 022)* **BATTLEFIELD BAND with ALISON KINNAIRD – Music In Trust – Vol.1**
1987. (lp/c) *(TP/CTP 024)* **CHRISTINE PRIMROSE – 'S Tu Nam Chuimnhe**
Jul 87. (lp/c) *(TP/CTP 025)* **DEAF HEIGHTS CAJUN ACES – Les Flammes D'enfer**
Oct 88. (lp/c) *(TP/CTP 028)* **Various Artists – A Celebration Of Scottish Music**
Oct 88. (lp/c) *(TP/CTP 029)* **ALISON KINNAIRD & THE BATTLEFIELD BAND – Music In Trust, Vol.2**
Jan 90. (lp/c) *(TP/CTP 031)* **GORDON MOONEY – Over The Border**
Dec 88. (cd/c) *(COMD2/CTP 032)* **ARTHUR CORMACK – Ruith Na Gaoith (Chasing The Wind)**

• **PARCEL O' ROGUES** were a young trad folk quartet including future BATTLEFIELD BAND musician, JOHN McCUSKER.

Sep 89. (lp/c/cd) *(TP/CTP/COMD2 033)* **PARCEL O' ROGUES – Parcel O' Rogues**
– MacDonald's fancy – Conlon's 2 – The sponge – Conlon's 1 / Such a parcel o' rogues / Bridie's hornpipe – Peggy's jig / Songs of rage / Your daughters and your sons / Grappelli's dream / Harvey's workhouse – Harvey's home / The ballad of Sam Stone / The blackbird / What you do with what you've got – Far from home / Small deeds for big words / Loch Fyne hotel – The bairn's last dram.

Oct 89. (lp/c/cd) *(TP/CTP/COMD2 034)* **BATTLEFIELD BAND – Home Ground Live From Scotland**
Nov 90. (cd/c) *(COMD2/CTP 035)* **BERT JANSCH – Sketches**
Jul 90. (cd/c) *(COMD2/CTP 036)* **MIKE WHELLANS – Swing Time Johnny Red**
Aug 90. (cd/c) *(COMD2/CTP 037)* **SHOTTS & DYKEHEAD CALEDONIA PIPE BAND – Another Quiet Sunday**
Sep 90. (cd/c) *(COMD2/CTP 040)* **JIM HUNTER BAND – Uphill Slide**
Oct 90. (cd/c) *(COMD2/CTP 041)* **ALISON KINNAIRD & CHRISTINE PRIMROSE – The Quiet Tradition**
Oct 90. (cd/c) *(COMD2/CTP 042)* **BRIAN McNEILL – The Busker And The Devil's Only Daughter**
Jan 91. (cd/c) *(COMD2/CTP 043)* **Dr. ANGUS MacDONALD – A' Sireadh Spors**
Apr 91. (cd/c) *(COMD2/CTP 044)* **FIDDLERS 5 – Fiddlers 5**
Jun 91. (cd/c/lp) *(COMD2/CTP/TP 045)* **BATTLEFIELD BAND – New Spring**
Jul 92. (cd/c) *(COMD2/CTP 047)* **JIM HUNTER – Fingernail Moon**
Nov 92. (cd/c) *(COMD2/CTP 048)* **EILIDH MacKENZIE – Eldeadh Na Sgeulachd (The Raiment Of The Table)**
Dec 92. (cd/c) *(COMD2/CTP 049)* **Various Artists – Temple Sampler**

May 93. (cd/c) *(COMD2/CTP 050)* **BATTLEFIELD BAND – Quiet Days**
Dec 93. (cd/c) *(COMD2/CTP 051)* **HERITAGE – Tell Tae Me**
Jan 94. (cd/c) *(COMD2/CTP 053)* **DYSART & DUNDONALD PIPE BAND – In Concert, Ballymena 1983**
Feb 94. (cd/c) *(COMD2/CTP 054)* **MAC-TALLA – Mairidh Gaol Is Ceol**
1994?. (cd-s) *(TMS 555)* **DYSART & DUNDONALD PIPE BAND – Peace In Our Time / Scots Wha Hae – The Lea Rig – The Auld Hoose / Highland Cathedral**
Oct 94. (cd/c) *(COMD2/CTP 057) ANN HEYMANN – Queen Of Harps*
Feb 95. (cd/c) *(COMD2/CTP 058)* **ROWALLAN CONSORT – Notes Of Joy**
Apr 95. (cd/c) *(COMD2/CTP 059)* **JOHN McCUSKER – John McCusker**
Jul 95. (cd/c) *(COMD2/CTP 060)* **WILLIAM McCALLUM – Hailey's Song**
Oct 95. (cd/c) *(COMD2/CTP 061)* **as above**
Nov 96. (cd) *(COMD2 062)* **Various Artists – Magic & Mystery**
Mar 97. (cd) *(COMD2 063) SEAMUS TANSEY – Easter Snow*
Jul 97. (cd/c) *(COMD2/CTP 064)* **JACK LEE & ALASDAIR GILLIES – The Piping Centre 1996 Recital Series, Vol.I**
Dec 97. (cd/c) *(COMD2/CTP 066)* **Various Artists – The Band Room Masters Solo Drumming Championship 1997**
– JIM KILPATRICK / ERIC WARD / JOHN SCULLION / GORDON BROWN / PAUL TURNER / JAMES KING / JIM COLLINS / JACKIE HOULDEN / BARRY WILSON / ALLAN CRAIG / NEIL CRANSTON / ARTHUR COOK.
Aug 97. (cd/c) *(COMD2/CTP 067)* **JOHN D. BURGESS & DONALD MacPHERSON – The Piping Centre 1996 Recital Series, Vol.II**
Oct 97. (cd/c) *(COMD2/CTP 070)* **WILLIAM MORRISON & Dr. ANGUS MacDONALD – The Piping Centre 1996 Recital Series, Vol.III**
Mar 98. (cd/c) *(COMD2/CTP 071)* **DAVY STEELE – Chasing Shadows**
Feb 98. (cd/c) *(COMD2/CTP 072)* **ALAN REID – The Sunlit Eye**
Feb 98. (cd/c) *(COMD2/CTP 073)* **ANGUS MacCOLL & GORDON DUNCAN – The Piping Centre 1996 Recital Series, Vol.IV**
Apr 98. (cd/c) *(COMD2/CTP 074)* **BATTLEFIELD BAND – Rain, Hail Or Shine**
Sep 97. (cd) *(COMD2 075)* **WILLIAM McCALLUM & BOB WORRALL – The Piping Centre 1997 Recital Series, Vol.I**
Sep 97. (cd) *(COMD2 076)* **JOHN PATRICK & STUART LIDDELL – The Piping Centre 1997 Recital Series, Vol.II**
Sep 97. (cd) **(COMD2 077) ALASDAIR GILLIES & MAJOR GAVIN STODDART – The Piping Centre 1997 Recital Series, Vol.III**
Sep 97. (cd) *(COMD2 078)* **IAN DUNCAN & RODDY MacLEOD – The Piping Centre 1997 Recital Series, Vol.IV**
Jul 99. (cd) *(COMD2 079) Various Artists – Irish Traditional Music: Played On Uillean Pipes / Hammer Dulcimer / Flute & Fiddle*
Aug 99. (cd) *(COMD2 080)* **BATTLEFIELD BAND – Leaving Friday Harbour**
Mar 00. (cd) *(COMD2 081)* **FLORA MacNEIL – Orain Floraidh**
May 00. (cd) *(COMD2 082)* **Various Artists – Harps, Pipes & Fiddles**
Jul 00. (cd) *(COMD2 083)* **JOHN McCUSKER – Yella Hoose**
Feb 01. (cd) *(COMD2 085)* **BATTLEFIELD BAND – Happy Daze**
Jul 01. (cd) *(COMD2 086)* **CHRISTINE PRIMROSE – Gun Sireadh, Gun Iarraidh**
Aug 01. (cd) *(COMD2 087)* **BRIAN LAMOND & RICHARD PARKES – The Piping Centre; 3rd Recital Series – Volume 1**
Aug 01. (cd) *(COMD2 088)* **ALLAN MacDONALD & GORDON WALKER – The Piping Centre; 3rd Recital Series – Volume 2**
Apr 02. (cd) *(COMD2 089) PAT KILBRIDE – Nightingale Lane*
Sep 02. (cd) *(COMD2 090)* **BATTLEFIELD BAND – Time & Tide**

– CD re-issues, etc –

Feb 94. (cd) *(COMD1 006)* **CHRISTINE PRIMROSE – Aite Mo Ghaoil**
Feb 94. (cd) *(COMD1 008)* **Various Artists – A Controversy Of Pipers**
Feb 94. (cd) *(COMD1 009)* **FINLAY MacNEILL – Fonn Is Furan**
Feb 94. (cd) *(COMD2 001)* **BATTLEFIELD BAND – After Hours**
Feb 94. (cd) *(COMD2 002)* **BATTLEFIELD BAND – Celtic Hotel**
Feb 94. (cd) *(COMD2 003)* **Various Artists – A Celebration Of Scottish Music**
Feb 94. (cd) *(COMD2 004)* **ALISON KINNAIRD & THE BATTLEFIELD BAND – Music In Trust, Vol.2**
Feb 94. (cd) *(COMD2 005)* **ALISON KINNAIRD – The Scottish Harp**
Feb 94. (cd) *(COMD2 006)* **BATTLEFIELD BAND – Home Is Where The Van Is**
Feb 94. (cd) *(COMD2 007)* **BATTLEFIELD BAND – There's A Buzz**
Feb 94. (cd) *(COMD2 008)* **BATTLEFIELD BAND – Anthem For The Common Man**
Feb 94. (cd) *(COMD2 009)* **BATTLEFIELD BAND – On The Rise**
Feb 94. (cd) *(COMD2 010)* **ALISON KINNAIRD & THE BATTLEFIELD BAND – Music In Trust**
Feb 94. (cd) *(COMD2 012) ANN HEYMANN &* **ALISON KINNAIRD – The Harper's Land**
Feb 94. (cd) *(COMD2 017)* **BRIAN McNEILL – Unstrung Hero**
Feb 94. (cd) *(COMD2 018)* **IAIN MACFADYEN – Ceol Mor-Ceol Beag**
Feb 94. (cd) *(COMD2 020)* **PETER NARDINI – Is There Anybody Out There?**
Feb 94. (cd) *(COMD2 031)* **GORDON MOONEY – Over The Border**

– books or cassettes, etc. –

1988. (-) *(BK 001)* **ALISON KINNAIRD – The Harp Key**
1988. (-) *(BK 002)* **BATTLEFIELD BAND – Forward With Scotland's Past**
1988. (-) *(BK 003)* **ALISON KINNAIRD – The Small Harp Tutor**
1990's. (-) *(BK 004PB)* **KEITH SANGER & ALISON KINNAIRD – Tree Of Strings**
1990's. (-) *(BK 005)* **DOUGIE PINCOCK – The Gem So Small**
1990's. (-) *(BK 006)* **The ABC Of Highland Dancing & Games Directory**
1990's. (-) *(BK 007)* **ROBERT PHILLIPS – Music For The Lute In Scotland**
1990's. (-) *(BK 008)* **ALISON KINNAIRD – The Lothian Collection**
1990's. (-) *(BK 009)* **JOHN McCUSKER – Bothwell Boy**
Mar 01. (-) *(BK 010)* **ALAN REID – Martyrs, Rogues And Worthies**

Vixen records

Formed: Late 1999 . . . by singer/songriter ALLIE FOX at 14 Hillside Terrace, Selkirk. Born to a Scottish father and an English mother, ALLIE is a veteran of the British folk scene although she only moved permanently to the Borders in 1993. There, she began teaching guitar and voice as well as setting up the The String Jam Club, a folk venue in Galashiels which has been running since 1997. The year 2000 found ALLIE setting up 'Vixen' primarily as a vehicle for the release of her debut album, 'DIVING FOR PEARLS'. Recorded at Edinburgh's Offbeat Scotland studios and produced by Iain McKinna (whose previous credits include MIKE HERON's 'Where The Mystics Swim' and TALITHA McKENZIE's 'Solas'), the album featured a host of top Scottish session players including JOHN RUTHERFORD, GAVIN DICKIE and RON SHAW. It also received widespread critical acclaim that saw reviewers drawing comparison with the likes of JONI MITCHELL, SANDY DENNY etc, and consistently praising FOX's strong, emotive vocal style, the album's Spanish tinges and its tribute to Afro-American boxing legend Joe Louis, 'JOE LOUIS BLUES'.

ALLIE FOX

ALLIE FOX – vocals, acoustic guitar / with **JOHN RUTHERFORD** – guitar (of MIKE HERON BAND) / **DAVE** – percussion (of FISH, CAPERCAILLIE) / **GAVIN DICKIE** – fretless bass (of ECLECTIC SHOCK, of The NAT KINGS, of JOHN WRIGHT BAND) / **RON SHAW** – cello (of BOYS OF THE LOUGH, CAULD BLAST ORCHESTRA) / **JIMI McRAE** – piper (from 'Braveheart' movie) / + the CAPRICCIO STRING QUARTET

Oct 00. (cd) *(VIX 002)* **ALLIE FOX – Diving For Pearls**
– Out of the blue / Backstreet girl / Rise and shine / Birdwoman / Marguerita / I was wrong / The meaning of love / The moon above the rooftops / Diving for pearls / Joe Louis blues.

3

Traditional Performers

The Kilted Story. . . Traditional tartan-bearers and Ceilidh/Dance: Aaah, hark back to the days dressed in school-shorts, blazer and cap (no, it wasn't yesterday, mister!) – aye, ANDY STEWART's "Donald, Where's Your Troosers?" was very appropriate way back then. Listening to JIMMY SHAND on the wireless, that radiogram on the sideboard in the corner next to your ma's best china; filling the cups with Scotland's national drink, Irn Bru, would earn you a slap around the lugs. Reading the Oor Wullie annual you just got for Christmas and knowing it would soon be the New Year and another hogmanay party for the grown-ups who'd "dance the buckles off their shoes" while a guy called Cameron Brig would always get a slurred mention for no' being a whisky. You'd ask yer ma if it was haggis and neeps for tea and she'd answer yes and I've got you a treat son: shortbread. You'd get a row for drinking too much ginger (juice), although saturated sugar-coated shortbread was somehow okay for your teeth (see under 'dentist, a').

Anyway, I think you've got the picture of our wee life north of the border, well at least before the trendy 60s & 70s came along. It was a great divide between the generations in they days, we loved Pink Floyd and Neil Young, they loved The ALEXANDER BROTHERS and SYDNEY DEVINE. Nowadays, we still love Pink Floyd and Neil Young while another generation craves for TRAVIS and DARIUS.

You certainly have to respect these aforementioned tartan-bearers of Scottish tradition and culture (and don't forget KENNETH McKELLAR, MOIRA ANDERSON, CALUM KENNEDY, and all Jock Tamson's bairns), who have kept their roots and singing standards throughout the years to give pleasure to millions, and not just in Scotland, but throughout the world, where our culture is not mocked but admired; just look at the tourists in Edinburgh city centre (and beyond!) lapping up our pipers and our street musicians/theatre, especially in August during the festival period.

Here is a (sort of) chronological list of these entertainers; discographies have been relegated to future editions and/or the internet.

* * *

Jimmy SHAND

was born on 28th January 1908, in East Wemyss, Fife. A true Scottish – not to mention Fife – institution, JIMMY SHAND's nimble fingered accordion-playing has brought pleasure to generations of Scots over the last half century. One of nine children, JIMMY began his working life in the local coal mines before the 1926 General Strike forced him to find alternative employment. It proved to be a blessing in diguise as JIMMY's new job in a music shop led to him signing a recording contract. The owner of the shop had been bowled over by JIMMY's accordion playing, helping him land the deal in 1933.

A series of sessions for the BBC followed and in 1945, he formed the JIMMY SHAND BAND. Over the period 1953-65, he released a staggering number of 7" singles for 'Parlophone', largely reels, waltzes, hornpipes and basically any form of accordion-based Scottish Country dance music worth shaking a leg to. His most famous tune from the period was undoubtedly 'BLUEBELL POLKA', a national Top 20 hit that featured on the chart for nearly the whole of 1956. He and his band were also a regular fixture on TV and radio, often appearing on the BBC's hugely popular White Heather Club alongside the likes of ANDY STEWART and MOIRA ANDERSON. While America had ELVIS and England/Britain had the BEATLES, Scotland had JIMMY SHAND – 20,000 screaming (mostly female!) fans at an open-air concert in Aberdeen couldn't be wrong.

Such were his musical services to the nation, JIMMY was awarded an MBE in 1962 while Eammon Andrews got out the big red book for him on This Is Your Life in 1978. Still dedicated to the miners' cause, JIMMY played benefit gigs around the country during the 1984 strike (58 years since the last one!). In 1994, a JIMMY SHAND video was an unlikely runaway success, no doubt ensuring that the octogenarian broke the record for the oldest artist ever to make the Top 10 music video chart. In fact, JIMMY reached the grand old age of 91 before he died at his home in Auchtermuchty in December 2000. A BBC tribute to the great man screened in January 2001.

His son Jimmy SHAND Jnr. carried on the tradition; his band released recordings for 'Emerald' in the 70's.

Will STARR

was born in 1922, in Banknock (or Croy), Stirlingshire. An accordion player in the mould of JIMMY SHAND, WILL first came to the attention of the music world via a Scottish Half Hour programme during the war (November 1943). The wee man toured the Lowlands and Highlands with singer ROBERT WILSON and subsequently landed a deal with 'Parlophone' records in 1955; he was also a part of The White Heather Club around this time. During a three-year spell with the label, STARR delivered a handful of 45's from 'EIGHTSOME REELS' to 'IRISH WASHERWOMAN'. After a one-off single, 'CROY HILL' for 'H.M.V.' in 1959, WILL retired from the industry, although several compilations filtered out. Of the more recent, 'KING OF THE SCOTTISH ACCORDIONISTS' Volumes 1 and 2 were released by 'Sleepytown' in July 2002.

Robert WILSON

was another Scottish singer born in the 20's to grace the White Heather Club and his recordings (for 'H.M.V.') go back to 1952. From that year's 'AFTON WATER' to 1959's 'SONG OF THE CLYDE' (with GORDON MacKENZIE) to 'ONE HUNDRED THOUSAND WELCOMES' in '62, WILSON's warm personality and friendly smile made him the darling of many who snuggled indoors to watch their black & white TV. He was indeed succeeded on the WHC by . . .

Andy STEWART

who was born on the 20th of December 1933 in Glasgow. The son of a teacher, ANDY spent his childhood and schooldays further north in Arbroath before making his stage debut at Leith's Gaiety Theatre in his teens. Intent on a career in showbusiness, STEWART got his big break when he replaced a sick Harry Gordon in a production of Dick Whittington's Cat. During the Rock'n'Roll era of the mid-late 50's, wee ANDY was honing his skills as a much-loved all-round entertainer through hosting tartan TV knees-up, 'The White Heather Club' as well as his jaunts around the world as a headlining variety performer.

The kilted ANDY moved into the Pop world in 1960, releasing a debut single, 'DONALD WHERE'S YOUR TROOSERS?' (backed by the WHITE HEATHER CLUB). The song was a self-deprecating novelty number detailing the trials of a naive Highland lad finding himself in the big city, no doubt containing just a shred of truth. It wasn't just the Scots who found the song funny, the Americans buying it in sufficient numbers to put it in the Hot 100; perhaps the ELVIS impersonation helped swing it. A more rousing follow-up, 'A SCOTTISH SOLDIER' (with a melody dating back to the Crimean War!), finally made him a UK-wide household name as it hovered around the national Top 20/30 for nigh on a year; again the Yanks lapped it up. Unfortunately ANDY's musical diet of shortbread and whisky proved a mite too twee for the populace during his 60's 'H.M.V.' years. Nevertheless, his high profile status as a family showman (singer/songwriter/comedian/host) kept him in the money as he presented his own TV series, The Andy Stewart Show, while radio shows such as 17 Sauchie Street and Scotch Corner maintained his popularity. The Tartan Trouper even turned his hand to acting by appearing in a 1963 US Sci-Fi B-movie, 'Battle Beyond The Sun', quite possibly scaring the aliens with the threat of some kilt-lifting.

ANDY was finally given Royal recognition in 1976 when he was awarded an MBE, Princess Margaret no doubt sympathising with the sentiments of 'CAMPBELLTOWN LOCH'. Having been granted the freedom of Angus (the Scottish district where he was raised) in 1987, STEWART was given the proverbial freedom of the charts at Xmas '89 when a dusted-down version of 'DONALD . . .' hit the UK Top 5; at the grand old age of 56, the veteran teuchter became a pop star all over again. Sadly, only a handful of years later and after a long illness, ANDY passed away in his Arbroath home on the 11th of October 1993.

Kenneth McKELLAR

was born in Paisley, 1927, son of a greengrocer. After leaving school he studied forestry at Aberdeen University and gained a B.Sc. KENNETH began broadcasting from 1947 at Aberdeen then Glasgow and subsequently won the Sir James Caird Scholarship in 1949; around the same time he entered the Royal College of Music, London. His operatic and oratario larynx also found favour, when, in 1953, he toured with the Carl Rosa Company. A few years later, he signed a record contract with 'Decca', although his traditional ballads/songs (including debut, 'SCOTLAND THE BRAVE', MY LOVE IS LIKE A RED, RED ROSE' and 'SKYE BOAT SONG') only found interest north of the border. However, with the eligibility of the EP charts in 1960, McKELLAR found he had not been forgotten; ' . . .SINGS HANDEL', 'HANDEL'S ARIAS', 'KENNETH McKELLAR No.2' and 'ROAD TO THE ISLES' were all listed; in '64 he appeared on stage with the 'Kismet' operatic production.

1966 was not a good year for McKELLAR (and I suppose for many Scots in one way or another!). An institution in his own right, McKELLAR was astonishingly hand-picked by the BBC to represent the United Kingdom in another, the dreaded Eurovision Song Contest. The TV viewers were offered the opportunity to choose one of six McKELLAR ballads (a new system from the ten acts they used to pick from!) and they selected 'A MAN WITHOUT LOVE'. It goes without saying that in a world that was musically into the Swinging 60's (folk, psychedelia and garage), even Europe wasn't ready for Britain's new angle on pop. With the single only managing to scrape into the charts at No.30, the BBC wished they'd never set eyes on the Scotsman (thankfully, Scots lass LULU, saved our red faces by winning in 1969).

Surprisingly, McKELLAR managed to have another chart entry when budget collection 'THE WORLD OF KENNETH McKELLAR' hit No.27 in the summer of '69; noticeable was the absence of the aforementioned flop. A year later, the man was back again, this time with Top 50 (No.45) album, 'ECCO DE NAPOLI'; he managed to release numerous albums and singles well into the 80's and 90's. The well-respected and much-loved McKELLAR continued to boom his fantastic voice around the world and on British TV appearances alongside the likes of MOIRA ANDERSON, etc.

Sydney DEVINE

was born 1942 in Cleland, Lanarkshire. He entered the world of showbusiness at the tender age of 13 (around 1955) and spent the next decade or so trying to emulate his idol ANDY STEWART. A one-off single for 'Top Rank' (with the WHITE HEATHER GROUP), 'WEE JEAN FRAE AULD ABERDEEN', was issued in 1959, although it sold very moderately, even in Scotland.

DEVINE abandoned his rock'n'roll meets traditional style of the 60's for a fresh country & western approach in the 70's and this seemed to please the punters in social clubs, etc. After a period on Irish label, 'Emerald' in the early 70's, yer man SYDNEY signed a deal with 'Philips', and it was at this time he had his most fruitful period. In the spring of 1976, he was in the UK Top 20 (No.14) with a double-set, 'DOUBLY DEVINE', while another long-player, 'DEVINE TIME', also made the Top 50 before Xmas; mothers and grannies from Wick to the Borders were proud to say they had SYDNEY in their house. His clean-cut, Cheshire-cat smile and honky-tonk attire were to the blue-rinse brigade a diversion from Scotland's other acts at the time, The BAY CITY ROLLERS, NAZARETH and The SENSATIONAL ALEX HARVEY BAND (Alex was about seven years older than him!).

To coincide with Scotland's national football team going to Argentina to play in the World Cup finals of 1978, SYDNEY released his tribute single, 'SCOTLAND FOREVER', and duly hit the Top 50 (No.48); comedian ANDY CAMERON surpassed him somewhat (Top 10, in fact) with 'Ally's Tartan Army'. DEVINE subsequently captured the hearts of a growing female fanbase even more so in the 80's – the north of England was also a favourite haunt – with album after album after album, mainly released on tartan traditional label, 'Scotdisc'.

In the mid 90's, SYD ventured into line-dancing and successfully cornered the market in the selling of records and videos in this field – so take your pardners and dream of the Wild West – of Glasgow!?

If the White Heather Club had one more patron then . . .

Joe GORDON

would have to be acknowledged. There were several singles by 'H.M.V.' released as JOE GORDON FOLK FOUR (JOE GORDON GROUP SIX was also thought of – sic!). Between 1959's debut 'BARNYARDS O' DELGATY' to 1963's swansong 'GRANNIE FRASER'S FLITTIN', JOE made his mark as a novelty traditional crooner. Away from the madding crowds and the quiet tranquillity of Scotland's Highlands once more and you have the smooth . . .

Calum KENNEDY

Born in the mid-late 1930's in the north east of Scotland, he was truly the voice of Scotland after winning the National Mod gold medal in 1955. In between the odd single for 'Beltona' records – including Gaelic-speaking debut 'RIBHINN A BHEIL CUIMHN' AGAD', 'O MHAIRI E MHAIRI', 'THE ROAD TO DUNDEE' and 'HASTE YE BACK' – KENNEDY won the World Championship Gold Medal in Moscow (c.1957). Popular around the world especially North America and Australasia, CALUM soon became oor grannie's darling (yet again!) via Grampian TV's 'Calum's Ceilidh'. The stout and proud CALUM subsequently married ANNE GILLIES and they had five daughters FIONA, KIRSTEEN, MORAG, MORVEN and DEIRDRE (all contributors to the LP, 'ROUND AT CALUM'S' in 1969). His oldest, FIONA, went on to be a traditional folk singer in her own right, 1995's 'MAIDEN HEAVEN' being produced by PHIL CUNNINGHAM.

Glen DALY

was born in Glasgow (c.1940's) of Irish parentage; a cabaret singer/comedian, he delivered a handful of 45's for 'Piccadilly' in the early 60's. Moving to 'Beltona' records, he concentrated on the Irish market having been a staunch Celtic supporter from er, birth. Celtic F.C. even managed to crop up on most of his subsequent recordings (mainly for 'Pye') – 'HAIL, HAIL, CELTIC' coming out at a time (1967) when the buoys were kings of Europe, having been the first British team to win the coveted European Cup. His success around the circuit (mainly as a resident at Glasgow's Ashfield Club run at the time by Jimmy Donald) didn't go further afield than Scotland, although he did breach the UK charts (at No.28) with a budget-LP, 'A GLASGOW NIGHT OUT', towards the end of 1971.

Larry MARSHALL

was another Scots trad-crooner and became famous for having compered the One O'clock Show. He appears to have only released two singles, 'OLD SCOTCH MOTHER' (for 'Parlophone' in 1960) and 'CALLING YOU AGAIN TO BONNIE SCOTLAND' (for 'Pye' in 1964).

the ALEXANDER BROTHERS

(kilted accordionists and singers, Cambusnethan (Lanarkshire)-born brothers TOM – b.25 Jun'34 – and JACK – b.11 Nov'35) had released a plethora of 7" singles on 'Piccadilly' and 'Pye' from 1962 onwards. Traditional songs such as 'BONNIE WEE JEANNIE McCALL', 'NOBODY'S CHILD', 'WILD SIDE OF LIFE', 'THE NORTHERN LIGHTS OF OLD ABERDEEN' and 'THESE ARE MY MOUNTAINS' graced the homes of many a Scottish music lover although none charted in Britain. However, a budget LP named after the latter of the aforementioned platters hit the Top 30 towards the end of '66 – note that some of these releases were produced by the legendary Tony Hatch (he of New Faces panel fame!) who whisked them and long-standing (to this day!) manager ROSS BOWIE down to London. Both siblings are still going strong after over forty years in the business, and a tribute to 'JIMMY SHAND (THE LEGEND)' was issued for 'Scotdisc' (as many others were) in October 2001. Forthcoming releases include a tribute to ANDY STEWART. Having performed at such prestigious venues as New York's Carnegie Hall and the Sydney Opera House, both brothers now live in and around Glasgow, TOM in Bearsden and JACK in Prestwick; O.B.E.'s should be in the post come 2003.

Moira ANDERSON

was born in Kirkintilloch, East Dunbartonshire on the 5th of June 1940. Formerly a pupil of Ayr Academy, soprano singer MOIRA drew her inspiration from traditional Scottish folk songs although she reinterpreted each with her own MOR aplomb. 'THESE ARE MY MOUNTAINS' (for 'Fontana' records) and 'CHARLIE IS MY DARLING' (for 'Pye') kick-started her musical career in 1966, although it would three further years (and a move to 'Decca') until she had her inaugural UK Top 50 entry via 'THE HOLY CITY'. The album, 'THESE ARE MY SONGS' (1970), also graced the charts the following year, albeit one week at No.50. Her repertoire over the years has included operatic standards from the pens of such old-time luminaries as Gilbert & Sullivan (to name only two); arrangements at times courtesy of conducter, Peter Knight.

Along with the likes of ANDY STEWART, PETER MORRISON, STUART GILLIES, etc., MOIRA became an integral part of STV's kilt, haggis and shortbread culture. A long-time devout Christian, she subsequently became a long-standing compere for ITV's 'Songs Of Praise', releasing her religious and spiritual albums for this record market. Having received an OBE for her services to music, she took a final curtain call with a few recordings for 'Lismor' in the late 80's; 'MY SCOTLAND – A LAND FOR ALL SEASONS' and '20 SCOTTISH FAVOURITES' – pass me ma whisky!

Other singers who graced our TV sets and sometimes our parents' rickety gramophone players were . . .

Bill McCUE

who sang Scottish ballads (mainly from the pen of ROBERT BURNS) on many an LP from 1970 onwards. From the late 80's onwards, one-time Lanarkshire miner BILL was a recording artist for 'Scotdisc'; 'A' THE BEST FROM BILL McCUE' (CDITV 587) being issued in 1996. BILL subsequently received his gong (OBE), but sadly he was to pass away later in the 90's.

The Pipes and Drums and Military Band of the Royal Scots Dragoon Guards

(phew, what a mouthful). For five weeks from April 1972, this ensemble held the No.1 spot in the UK charts. Due to BBC Radio 2 listeners demanding its release, 'AMAZING GRACE' – a traditional tune which had also been a massive 45 for folk singer Judy Collins – became the first of three bagpipe hits in '72, the other two being 'HEYKENS SERENADE' and 'LITTLE DRUMMER BOY'; the RSDG still release records to this day.

Alasdair GILLIES

is one our top bagpipers; in fact he is the World Champion and releases recordings for 'Lochshore' and 'Lismor'.

Peter MORRISON

was all over our TV screens during the 70's, his appearances from the success he had in 1973 when co-hosting 'Songs Of Scotland' with singer/banjo-player ALASTAIR McDONALD. An Arts & Law graduate at Glasgow University, well-groomed PETER was definitely a favourite of every housewife around the country. In the 80's, he compered a host of Hogmanay shows and starred in 'The Magic Of Musicals' (for Grampian television), 'Once Upon A Song' (for STV) and 'Top C's & Tiaras' (for Channel 4). On the recording front, the youthful looking MORRISON issued a string of albums for 'Lismor' (he now records at 'Corban'), while his live work kept him busy all over the world; in 1996 he completed a 16-date tour of America. His work with ROBERT BURNS material (a theatre production of 'Rantin, Rovin, Robin' in particular) and on Radio 2 has given PETER much clout around the traditional fraternity.

Anne Lorne GILLIES

was born in 1944 on the Western Isles. Taking up singing at an early age, she has since become the No.1 exponent of the Gaelic traditional/contemporary voice. In fact, she has since voiced her opinion on many occasions as the SNP candidate for her local Western Isles constituency. From the 70's until her signing for 'Lochshore' in the 80's, ANNE's inspired renaissance vocal tones were best measured up on LP's such as 'THE HILLS OF LORNE' (also a single in '82) and 'SINGS . . . THE SONGS OF THE GAEL' (1982).

Marie GORDON-PRICE

was in the STV limelight for most of the 70's, the vocalist managing to release only one single (in 1973) for 'Pye', 'I LOVE HOW YOU LOVE ME'.

Valerie DUNBAR

is a traditional singer with a plethora of releases on a variety of labels, noteably 'Lochshore' offshoot 'Klub'.

Mary SANDEMAN

was another young lady to sing traditional ballads, but she made it big time under another moniker, ANEKA (see ⇒ Section 8 : Rock, Pop & Indie).

Ann WILLIAMSON

was born in Bo'ness (c. 1960) and has released discs since the early 80's. A handful of singles including 'WHEN YOU AND I WERE YOUNG MAGGIE' and 'LIKE STRANGERS' were issued in 1982/83 for 'Emerald' records. More recently in the 90's, she has appeared on the 'Scotdisc' imprint with spiritual country albums, 'FLOWER OF SCOTLAND' (1994) and 'AMAZING GRACE' (1995). She now lives in Wallacestone, Stirlingshire under her married name Ann Hogg.

Fergie MacDONALD

was an early exponent of button-key accordion playing, FERGIE has since become an institution/legend of the ceilidh/dance fraternity. For over 30 years now, the innovative pioneer of the traditional Scottish box has released a barrel load of long-players including 'FERGIE MacDONALD & HIS HIGHLAND DANCE BAND' (1972), 'SWING YOUR PARTNERS' (1976) and 'THERE'S IRISH ON THE ISLANDS' (1981). Having spent most of the 80's as a publican, gamekeeper/clay-pigeon champion, psychotherapist!, etc, FERGIE revealed his comeback album for 'Lismor', 'AGUS NA MUIDEARTAICH', in 1993. Four years later and now on the books of the 'Greentrax' stable (run by IAN GREEN and augmented by protégé producer PHIL CUNNINGHAM), MacDONALD released the poignantly-titled 'THE 21st ALBUM' (1997) – also his first release in the US. Not content with sitting back or lying down (it can happen sometime after several drams of the hard stuff!), FERGIE got up to date by releasing the timely 'MILLENNIUM STRIP THE WILLOW' early in 2000.

Ah! well, something had to spoil it. . .

FRAN & ANNA

were the Scottish singing sisters from make-up, get-up, hair-do hell, the joke of the Central Belt, the Highlands, the Lowlands and the world. Cringeworthy but loved – in a fashion! – by your great, great grannies and girning grandads!. F&A released two sing-a-long LP's in 1977/78, 'LOVE FROM FRAN & ANNA' (no thanks!) and 'THE INCREDIBLE FRAN AND ANNA' (incredible?!). This pair of pantomime twins made the KRANKIES look like a real father and son comedy duo! A subsequent tribute single in '82, 'IT'S SCOTLAND FOREVER', might well have been taken to Spain by our World Cup Squad and possibly the best excuse for why we came back home so early – AGAIN! In 2001, FRAN & ANNA were awarded O.B.E.'s for their contribution to Scottish music. It makes you wonder if The Society For the Deaf made this remarkable presentation.

In recent years, country man

David WILKIE

(with his band COWBOY CELTIC) delivered the eponymous 'COWBOY CELTIC' (1996) and 'COWBOY CEILIDH' (1998) on 'Red House'.

Bill ALEXANDER

Fife-born country singer **BILL ALEXANDER** released his only album to date, 'DREAMS', in 1999 on 'Mariner Music'.

traditional labels

Lismor records

are Scotland's premier purveyor of traditional sounds and have been guardians of the nation's musical heritage for nigh on three decades. Also boasting a sister label, 'Iona', which has both charted folk music's coming of age and realised Lismor's long held maxim, "Taking Traditional Music Towards 2000", Glasgow's celtic bastion has entered the new millennium on a surer footing than ever.

Back in 1973, Lismor began trading from the back room of a Glasgow record shop, catering to the musical demands of displaced Highlands and Islanders who'd migrated south looking for work. From four releases in their first year, the label's schedule had expanded to twenty-seven albums by 1976 (including a few by STUART ANDERSON – 'Welcome' and 'On Top Of The World'). 1978 saw the release of RUNRIG's debut set, 'Play Gaelic', still one of Lismor's best selling recordings. Running the gamut of Scottish traditional fare and beyond, the label has catered for the a cappella strains of Gaelic song, unaccompanied harp and fiddle, Scottish country dance music, the songs and poetry of Robert Burns, and of course the stirring sound of the Highland bagpipe. A highlight of the label's many bagpipe recordings is 'Live In Ireland' by Canadian world champions, The 78th FRASER HIGHLANDERS PIPE BAND, while solo piping has been covered in depth by the 'World's Greatest Pipers' series.

Fiddle maestro ALY BAIN was the star of both 'Down Home' and 'Meets The Cajuns' in the late 80's, documenting the acclaimed TV series. He also featured prominently on volumes 1 & 2 of 'The Shetland Sessions' alongside the likes of The POOZIES, PHIL CUNNINGHAM, EDDIE LE JEUNE and SIMON THOUMIRE. Sister label 'Iona' was founded in 1978 as a vehicle for OSSIAN, the pioneering Glasgow folk act headed by WILLIAM JACKSON.

Under new ownership since 1990, the company sought to showcase younger artists putting a contemporary spin on traditional music. These artists have included WOLFSTONE, The HUMPFF FAMILY, CAROL LAULA, TARTAN AMOEBAS, JAMES GRANT, The KELTZ and ROCK SALT & NAILS (amongst others) with 'Iona' going for quality rather than quantity. The label's development has been in tandem with the explosion of worldbeat/folk fusion that has seen traditionally-rooted hybrid sounds spring up everywhere from Nova Scotia to Galicia.

Taken as a whole, the Lismor and Iona labels have made a pivotal contribution to the preservation and advancement of Scottish music, an achievement recognised by the Scottish Music Industry Association. In total, the latter organisation have awarded the labels 55 silver discs, 21 gold and 12 platinum in recognition of sales. Now online – at www.lismor.com – and transforming itself into a truly global concern, Lismor/Iona is primed to take advantage of the growing worldwide interest in celtic-based music. (see also Lismor in folk section)

– traditional discography –

Nov 73. (lp) *(LILP 5004)* **PETER MORRISON – Scotland The Brave**
Jun 74. (lp) *(LILP 5006)* **Various Artists – Ceud Mile Failte (Gaelic Ceilidh)**
Jun 74. (lp) *(LILP 5007)* **LOCHIES – Lewis Folk**
Nov 74. (lp) *(LILP 5012)* **DRIFTERFOLK – Reflections**
Apr 75. (lp) *(LILP 5017)* **RON GONNELLA – Fiddlers Fancy**
1987. (lp) *(LILP 5022)* **Various Artists – Better Class Of Folk**
Sep 75. (lp/c) *(LILP/LICS 5025)* **IAIN MacKAY – Voice Of The Hebrides**
Sep 75. (lp/c) *(LILP/LICS 5027)* **TARTAN LADS – By the Lochside**
Sep 75. (lp/c) *(LILP/LICS 5028)* **LOCHIES – Home To Lewis**
Nov 75. (lp) *(LILP 5032)* **JOE GORDON & SALLY LOGAN – Joe Gordon & Sally Logan**
Nov 76. (lp) *(LILP 5037)* **STUART ANDERSON – Stuart Anderson's Welcome**
Nov 76. (lp) *(LILP 5041)* **SEAMUS MacNEIL – Purely Piobaireachd**
Nov 76. (lp/c) *(LILP/LICS 5043)* **LOMOND FOLK – Blended Scotch**
Nov 76. (lp/c) *(LILP/LICS 5044)* **RON GONNELLA – Fiddle Gems**
nov 76. (lp/c) *(LILP/LICS 5049)* **TARTAN LADS – Scotland Yet**
Nov 76. (lp/c) *(LILP/LICS 5053)* **JOE GORDON & SALLY LOGAN – Together**
Nov 76. (lp/c) *(LILP/LICS 5054)* **DRIFTERFOLK – All Kinds Of Folk**
Nov 76. (lp/c) *(LILP/LICS 5057)* **LOCHIES – North By North-West**

Nov 76. (lp/c) *(LILP/LICS 5060)* **GLASGOW CALEDONIAN STRATHSPEY & REEL SOCIETY – Fiddles Galore**
Nov 76. (lp/c) *(LILP/LICS 5061)* **FERGIE MacDONALD – Swing Your Partners**
Jun 77. (lp/c) *(LILP/LICS 5069)* **Various Artists – Bonnie Scotland Show**
Jul 77. (lp/c) *(LILP/LICS 5070)* **RON GONNELLA – Burn's Night**
Jul 77. (lp/c) *(LILP/LICS 5072)* **DONALD MacLEOD – Pipe Tunes For Highland Dances**
Jul 77. (lp/c) *(LILP/LICS 5080)* **STUART ANDERSON – On Top Of The World**
Jul 77. (lp/c) *(LILP/LICS 5082)* **GLASGOW & STRATHCLYDE UNIVERSITY OTC PIPE BAND – same**
Nov 77. (lp/c) *(LILP/LICS 5083)* **JOHN CARMICHAEL'S CEILIDH BAND – John Carmichael's Ceilidh Band**
Jun 78. (lp/c) *(LILP/LICS 5085)* **RON GONNELLA – Tribute To Niel Gow**
Jun 78. (lp/c) *(LILP/LICS 5088)* **LOCHIES – Slainte Mhaith (Good Health)**
Jul 78. (lp/c) *(LILP/LICS 5089)* **DONALD MacLEOD – Positively Piobaireachd**
Jan 78. (lp/c) *(LILP/LICS 5092)* **Various Artists – Robert Burns Songbook**
Jul 80. (lp/c) *(LILP/LICS 5099)* **RON GONNELLA – Scottish Fiddle Master**
Jul 80. (lp/c) *(LILP/LICS 5100)* **Various Artists – All The Best From Scotland – Vol.1**
Oct 81. (lp/c) *(LILP/LICS 5113)* **Various Artists – Treasures Of Scotland**
Nov 81. (lp/c) *(LILP/LICS 5115)* **Various Artists – Best Of Accordion & Fiddle**
Jan 82. (lp/c) *(LILP/LICS 5116)* **Various Artists – Best Of Dance Bands & Dances Of Scotland**
Dec 82. (lp/c) *(LILP/LICS 5117)* **Various Artists – Popular Songs Of Scotland**
Nov 82. (lp/c) *(LILP/LICS 5120)* **JOHN ELLIS & HIS HIGHLAND COUNTRY BAND – A Reel Kick**
Sep 83. (lp/c) *(LILP/LICS 5123)* **JAMES NICOL – Last Rose Of Summer**
Nov 83. (lp/c) *(LILP/LICS 5125)* **PIPE MAJOR JOHN D. BURGESS – Plays The Great Highland Bagpipe**
Dec 83. (lp/c) *(LILP/LICS 5126)* **FERGIE MacDONALD – There's Irish On The Islands**
Jan 84. (lp/c) *(LILP/LICS 5127)* **BOBBY MacLEOD AND HIS MUSIC – The Genuine Article**
May 84. (lp/c) *(LILP/LICS 5130)* **RHONA MacKAY – Sings And Plays The Music Of The Harp**
Dec 83. (lp/c) *(LILP/LICS 5132)* **DONALD MacLEOD – Farewell My Love**
Jul 84. (lp/c) *(LILP/LICS 5134)* **Various Artists – Grant's Piping Championship (Ceol Mor – Piobaireachda)**
Jul 84. (lp/c) *(LILP/LICS 5135)* **Various Artists – Grant's Piping Championship (March, Strathspey & Reel)**
Oct 84. (lp/c) *(LILP/LICS 5136)* **JACOBITES – Ye Jacobites By Name**
Oct 84. (lp/c) *(LILP/LICS 5137)* **GLASGOW CALEDONIAN STRATHSPEY & REEL SOCIETY – In Concert**
Nov 84. (lp/c) *(LILP/LICS 5138)* **BOX & BANJO BAND – Go Dancing**
(cd-iss. Jan90; LCOM 9020)
Nov 85. (lp/c) *(LILP/LICS 5143)* **PIPE MAJOR ANGUS MacDONALD – The World's Greatest Pipers Vol.1**
Nov 85. (lp/c) *(LILP/LICS 5144)* **BOX & BANJO BAND – Great Scottish Singalong**
Jul 86. (lp/c) *(LILP/LICS 5147)* **HUGH A. MacCALLUM – The World's Greatest Pipers Vol.2**
Jul 86. (lp/c) *(LILP/LICS 5148)* **JAMES NICOL – Scotland Again**
Dec 86. (lp/c) *(LILP/LICS 5149)* **Various Artists – The World Pipe Band Championship 1986**
Jan 87. (lp/c) *(LILP/LICS 5151)* **PIPE MAJOR G.N.M. STODDART B.E.M. – The World's Greatest Pipers Volume 3**
Feb 87. (lp/c) *(LILP/LICS 5153)* **GAELFORCE ORCHESTRA – Play The Melodies Of Scotland**
(cd-iss. Jul89; LCOM 9010)
Mar 87. (lp/c) *(LILP/LICS 5154)* **BOX & BANJO BAND – At The Movies**
Mar 87. (lp/c) *(LILP/LICS 5155)* **BOX & BANJO BAND – Bouncing In The Ballroom**
Jul 87. (lp/c) *(LILP/LICS 5158)* **JOHN ELLIS & HIS HIGHLAND COUNTRY BAND – Fire In The Kilt**
Jul 87. (lp/c) *(LILP/LICS 5159)* **MURRAY HENDERSON – The World's Greatest Pipers Volume 4**
(cd-iss. May96; LCOM 5159)
Apr 87. (lp/c) *(LILP/LICS 5160)* **FERGIE MacDONALD & IAIN McLACHLAN – Kings Of The Button Keyed Box**
Jul 87. (lp/c) *(LILP/LICS 5161)* **Various Artists – Scotland: The Pipes And Drums**
Jul 87. (lp/c) *(LILP/LICS 5162)* **Various Artists – Scotland: The Singers And The Songs**
(cd-iss. Aug87; LCOM 9002)
Jul 87. (lp/c) *(LILP/LICS 5163)* **Various Artists – Scotland: The Dances And The Dance Bands**
(cd-iss. Aug87; LCOM 9003)
Jul 87. (lp/c) *(LILP/LICS 5164)* **Various Artists – Scotland: The Music Of A Nation**
(cd-iss. Aug87; LCOM 9004)
Feb 88. (lp/c) *(LILP/LICS 5168)* **BOX & BANJO BAND – Could I Have This Dance**
Feb 88. (lp/c) *(LILP/LICS 5169)* **GAELFORCE ORCHESTRA – Scotland Again**
Mar 88. (cd/c) *(LCOM/LICS 5170)* **JOHN WILSON – The World's Greatest Pipers Volume 5**
Apr 88. (cd/c) *(LCOM/LICS 5171)* **PIPE MAJOR ROBERT MATHIESON – Grace Notes**
Jun 88. (lp/c) *(LILP/LICS 5172)* **BOX & BANJO BAND – A Hundred Thousand Welcomes**
Dec 88. (lp/c) *(LILP/LICS 5173)* **ALASTAIR McDONALD – At The Jazz Band Ball**
Jul 89. (lp/c) *(LILP/LICS 5174)* **Various Artists – Drummers Fanfare**
Jul 88. (lp/c) *(LILP/LICS 5175)* **Various Artists – Dancing Strings Of Scotland**
Dec 88. (lp/c) *(LILP/LICS 5176)* **BOX & BANJO BAND – Christmas Crackers**
Jul 89. (lp/c) *(LILP/LICS 5177)* **RODERICK J MacLEOD – The World's Greatest Pipers Vol.6**
Jan 90. (lp/c) *(LILP/LICS 5179)* **GAELFORCE ORCHESTRA – Scotland Forever**
Jan 90. (lp/c) *(LILP/LICS 5180)* **IAIN McFADYEN – The World's Greatest Pipers Vol.7**
Apr 90. (c)(cd) *(LICS 5182)(LCOM 9026)* **RUNRIG – Play Gaelic**
Jan 90. (lp/c) *(LILP/LICS 5183)* **JOHN ELLIS – Birlin Sporrans**
Jan 90. (lp/c)(cd) *(LILP/LICS 5185)(LCOM 9013)* **DONALD MacPHERSON – The Master Piper**
Jan 90. (lp/c)(cd) *(LILP/LICS 5186)(LCOM 9021)* **BOX & BANJO BAND – Go Sequence Dancing**
Aug 90. (lp/c) *(LILP/LICS 5189)* **JOHN McDOUGALL – The World's Greatest Pipers Vol.8**
Aug 90. (lp/c/cd) *(LILP/LICS/LCOM 5190)* **AULD REEKIE DANCE BAND – Capital Reels**
Sep 90. (lp/c)(cd) *(LILP/LICS 5191)(LCOM 9025)* **GAELFORCE ORCHESTRA – From Highlands To Lowlands**
Oct 90. (lp)(cd) *(LILP 5192)(LCOM 9038)* **PIPE MAJOR ROBERT MATHIESON – Ebb-Tide**
Nov 90. (lp/c)(cd) *(LILP/LICS 5193)(LCOM 9037)* **GLASGOW GAELIC MUSICAL ASSOCIATION – Gaelic Galore**
Apr 91. (c)(cd) *(LICS 5196)(LCOM 9035)* **RIVERSIDE CEILIDH BAND – Horses For Courses**
Jul 91. (c)(cd) *(LICS 5197)(LCOM 9045)* **PIPE MAJOR BILL LIVINGSTONE – The World's Greatest Pipers Volume 9**
Jul 91. (c)(cd) *(LICS 5198)(LCOM 9046)* **BOBBY ABBOTT – Welcome To Glensharragh**
Aug 91. (c)(cd) *(LICS 5199)(LCOM 9047)* **DUNDEE STRATHSPEY & REEL SOCIETY – Fiddle Me Jig**
Nov 91. (cd) *(LCOM 5204)* **JOHN WALSH – Time To Spare**
Nov 91. (cd) *(LCOM 5205)* **Various Artists – The Grand Gaelic Concert**
Mar 92. (cd) *(LCOM 5206)* **JOHN MacLEOD – MacLeod Of Dunvegan**
Nov 91. (cd) *(LCOM 5207)* **CHARLIE COWIE – Unsquare Dance**
Dec 91. (cd) *(LCOM 5208)* **AN TEALLACH CEILIDH BAND – Catching The Sun Rise**
May 92. (cd/c) *(LCOM/LICS 5209)* **BOX & BANJO BAND – Dancing Party**
Mar 92. (cd/c) *(LCOM/LIFC 5210)* **JOHN ELLIS & HIS HIGHLAND COUNTRY BAND – Dancin' Wi' Claymores**
Apr 93. (c) *(LIFC 5211)* **Various Artists – Amazing Grace And Other Scottish Anthems**
Oct 91. (cd/c) *(LCOM/LICS 5215)* **GAELFORCE ORCHESTRA – Skye High**
Oct 90. (cd) *(LCOM 5216)* **JAMES McGILLIVRAY – The World's Greatest Pipers Volume 10**
Sep 94. (cd/c) *(LCOM/LIDC 5217)* **MICHAEL GREY – Composers' Series Vol.1**
Jan 93. (cd) *(LCOM 5218)* **Various Artists – The International Ceilidh Band Championship**
Jan 93. (cd) *(LCOM 5219)* **COLIN MacLELLAN – The World's Greatest Pipers Volume 11**
Jun 93. (cd) *(LCOM 5220)* **GLASGOW GAELIC MUSICAL ASSOCIATION – A Centenary Selection**
Oct 93. (cd/c) *(LCOM/LICS 5222)* **FERGIE MacDONALD – Agus Na Muideartaich**
Sep 93. (cd) *(LCOM 5223)* **FRED MORRISON – The Broken Chanter**
Oct 93. (cd) *(LCOM 5224) CROOKED JACK – Tomorrow Must Wait*
Oct 93. (cd) *(LCOM 5225)* **Dancing Strings Of Scotland: Encore**
Jan 94. (cd) *(LCOM 5226)* **Various Artists – Wild Conserves: The Flavours Of Scotland (In Aid Of Scottish Wildlife Trust)**
Apr 94. (cd) *(LCOM 5228)* **Various Artists – Lismor 21st Anniversary Album**
Oct 93. (cd/c) *(LCOM/LICS 5230)* **GAELFORCE ORCHESTRA – Abide With Me**
Jul 94. (cd) *(LCOM 5231)* **PIPE MAJOR ALASDAIR GILLIES – The World's Greatest Pipers Vol.12**
May 94. (cd) *(LCOM 5232)* **SIR HARRY LAUDER – Sir Harry Lauder**
May 94. (cd) *(LCOM 5233)* **MASTER JOE PETERSEN – The Phenomenal Boy Singer**
May 94. (cd) *(LCOM 5234)* **WILL FYFFE – Will Fyffe**
May 94. (cd) *(LCOM 5235)* **WILLIAM MacEWAN – The Original Glasgow Street Singer/Evangelist**
Sep 94. (cd) *(LCOM 5237)* **AN TEALLACH CEILIDH BAND – A Ship In Full Sail**
Jan 95. (cd) *(LCOM 5240)* **HOOLEY GANZBAND – Noo! That's Whit Ah Ca' Ceilidh Vol.1**
Jan 95. (cd) *(LCOM 5241)* **RIVERSIDE CEILIDH BAND – First Footing**
Mar 95. (cd) *(LCOM 5242)* **BRUCE GANDY – Composers' Series**
May 95. (cd/c) *(LCOM/LICS 5243)* **Various Artists – Scottish Gold: In The Piping Tradition**
May 95. (cd/c) *(LCOM/LICS 5244)* **Various Artists – Scottish Gold: In The Popular Song**
May 95. (cd/c) *(LCOM/LICS 5245)* **Various Artists – Scottish Gold: In The Celtic Tradition**
May 95. (cd/c) *(LCOM/LICS 5246)* **Various Artists – Scottish Gold: In The Ceilidh & Dance Tradition**
Aug 95. (cd/c) *(LCOM/LICS 5248)* **ROYAL SCOTS DRAGOON GUARDS – Second To None**
Feb 96. (cd/c) *(LCOM/LICS 5251) BOBBY BROWN & THE CAPE BRETON FIDDLERS – The Cape Breton Fiddle Company*
Aug 96. (cd/c) *(LCOM/LICS 5252)* **PIPE SERGEANT GORDON J. WALKER – The World's Greatest Pipers Volume 13**
Aug 96. (cd/c) *(LCOM/LICS 5253)* **ROBERT WALLACE – Breakout**
Oct 96. (cd/c) *(LCOM/LICS 5254)* **WILLIAM McCALLUM – The World's Greatest Pipers Volume 14**
Nov 96. (cd/c) *(LCOM/LICS 5255)* **ANGUS MacCOLL – The Clan MacColl**
Oct 96. (cd) *(LCOM 5256)* **NOO! 2 – That's Whit Ah Ca' Ceilidh**
Nov 96. (cd/c) *(LCOM/LICS 5257)* **PIPE MAJOR IAIN MORRISON & IAIN MORRISON Jnr. – Back To Back**
Nov 96. (cd/c) *(LCOM/LICS 5258)* **COILA – Get Reel**
Jan 97. (cd) *(LCOM 5260)* **AULD REEKIE SCOTTISH DANCE BAND – More Capital Reels**
Jun 97. (cd) *(LCOM 5261)* **MICHAEL GREY – Cuts From Traditional Cloth**
Feb 98. (cd/c) *(LCOM/LICS 5262)* **ROBERT MATHIESON – The Big Girl**
May 98. (cd) *(LCOM 5264)* **ANN GRAY – A Twist In The Tale**
Dec 98. (cd) *(LCOM 5269)* **Various Artists – A Piping Hot Christmas**

Nov 99. (cd) *(LCOM 5282)* **JOHN ELLIS & HIS HIGHLAND COUNTRY BAND – Thistle & The Shamrock**
Jul 02. (cd) *(LCOM 5290)* **WILLIAM BOYLE – Bagpipe Virtuoso**
Jul 02. (cd) *(LCOM 5294)* **BOX & BANJO BAND – 60 Magic Minutes**

– others, etc. –

Jul 78. (lp/c) *(LIB S/C 4001)* **Various Artists – Sounds Of Scotland**
Dec 79. (lp) *(LIDL 6001)* **Various Artists – Grant's Whisky Piping Championship Vol.1**
Dec 79. (lp) *(LIDL 6002)* **Various Artists – Grant's Whisky Piping Championship Vol.2**
Nov 79. (lp/c) *(LID L/C 6003)* **PETER MORRISON – Son Of The Homeland**
Nov 81. (lp/c) *(LID L/C 6005)* **PETER MORRISON – Memories**
Nov 82. (lp/c) *(LID L/C 6007)* **ALEXANDER BROTHERS – Scotland For Me**
Sep 83. (lp/c) *(LID L/C 6008)* **ANDY STEWART – Come In, Come In**
Jan 84. (lp/c) *(LID L/C 6009)* **KENNETH McKELLAR – In Scotland**
Nov 84. (lp/c) *(LID L/C 6011)* **ALEXANDER BROTHERS – Collection**
Nov 85. (lp/c) *(LID L/C 6012)* **KENNETH McKELLAR – Highland Journey**
Jul 86. (lp/c) *(LID L/C 6015)* **PETER MORRISON – A Toast To The Music Of Scotland**
(cd-iss. Aug96; LCOM 6015)
Dec 86. (lp/c) *(LID L/C 6016)* **ALEXANDER BROTHERS – Sincerely Yours**
— PETER also issued cassette, 'GAELIC STORIES' for 'Tangent' in 1989; previously in '79, 'Decca' had released d-lp 'FOCUS ON' *(FOS 63/4)*
— (see also 'Ross' records in 1996 for 'LAND OF THE EAGLE')
1987. (lp/c) *(LID L/C 6018)* **GLASGOW PHOENIX CHOIR – Glasgow Phoenix Choir**
1987. (lp/c) *(LID L/C 6019)* **KENNETH McKELLAR – To Robert Burns, A Tribute**
1988. (lp/c) *(LID L/C 6020)* **Various Artists – The Patter, The Album**
1988. (lp/c) *(LID L/C 6021)* **ANDY STEWART – Back In The Bothy**
1988. (lp/c) *(LID L/C 6022)* **MOIRA ANDERSON – A Land For All Seasons (My Scotland)**
Nov 88. (lp/c) *(LID L/C 6023)* **ALEXANDER BROTHERS – My Island Too**
Dec 88. (lp/c) *(LID L/C 6024)* **KENNETH McKELLAR – Today**
(cd-iss. Jul89; LCOM 9011)
Jan 89. (lp/c) *(LID L/C 6025)* **MAY HAROLD – Introducing May Harold**
Jan 89. (lp/c) *(LID L/C 6026)* **MAIRI MacINNES – Causeway**
(cd-iss. Oct92; LCOM 9018)
Jan 90. (lp/c) *(LID L/C 6029)* **MAY HAROLD – Flying On My Own**
Aug 90. (cd)(c) *(LIDC 6030)(LCOM 9024)* **GLASGOW PHOENIX CHOIR – With Voices Rising**
Apr 91. (c)(cd) *(LIDC 6033)(LCOM 9043)* **SCOTTISH PHILHARMONIC SINGERS – Scottish Philharmonic Singers**
Sep 92. (cd) *(LCOM 6035)* **ALEXANDER BROTHERS – A Toast To Absent Friends**

– even more releases –

Dec 87. (cd)(d-lp/d-c) *(LCOM 9005)(LDDL/LCDM 8002)* **Various Artists – The World Pipe Band Championship 1987**
Jul 88. (d-lp/d-c) *(LDD L/C 8004)* **PIPE MAJOR DONALD MacLEOD M.B.E. – The New York Recordings 1967**
Dec 88. (d-lp/d-c/d-cd) *(LDDL/LDDC/LCOM 8005)* **ROB GORDON & HIS BAND – The Complete Caledonian Ball**
Dec 88. (d-lp/d-c) *(LDDL/LDDC 8007)* **Various Artists – World Pipe Band Championship 1988**
1989. (c)(cd) *(LICS 8008)(LCOM 9014)* **ROB GORDON & HIS BAND – Old Time & Sequence Ball**
Sep 95. (cd) *(LCOM 9017)* **BOX & BANJO BAND – Singalonga Scotland**
Dec 89. (cd)(c) *(LCOM 9019)(LIDL 8009)* **Various Artists – World Pipe Championship 1989**
Aug 90. (cd)(c) *(LCOM 9023)(LIDC 8010)* **ALEXANDER BROTHERS – Now**
Aug 90. (cd) *(LCOM 9027)* **ALY BAIN – Down Home**
Aug 90. (cd) *(LCOM 9031)* **ALEX BEATON – 20 Hits Of Scotland**
Sep 87. (lp/c) *(LRI R/C 3001)* **GAELFORCE ORCHESTRA – Play The Melodies Of Ireland**
Nov 90. (lp/c)(cd) *(LIL P/C 3004)(LOCM 9029)* **GAELFORCE ORCHESTRA – From The Green Island To The Land Of The Eagle**
Nov 90. (lp/c)(cd) *(LIL P/C 3005)(LOCM 9030) MEG DAVIS – The Claddagh Walk*

– singles, etc. –

Nov 86. (7") *(LISP 2009)* **ALEXANDER BROTHERS – Farewell My Love**
Nov 86. (7") *(LISP 2010)* **ALEXANDER BROTHERS – Gentle Annie**
Nov 86. (7") *(LISP 2011)* **GAELFORCE ORCHESTRA – Dumbarton's Drum / Old Rustic Bridge**

Scotdisc records was founded by BGS Productions Ltd., Newtown Street, Kilsyth, Glasgow, Scotland, G65 0JX.
www.scotdisc.co.uk

– discography –
– (with videos) –

— offshoot 'Prism' is only briefly mentioned
1980's. (c) *(KITV 200)* **JIM MacLEOD & HIS BAND – Caledonian Ceilidh**
1980's. (c) *(KITV 201)* **JIM MacLEOD & HIS BAND – Anniversary Collection**
1980's. (c) *(KITV 202)* **JIM MacLEOD & HIS BAND – Encore**
Jun 84. (c/vid) *(PLA C/TV 329)* **Various Artists – Scottish Karaoke**
Jun 84. (c/cd) *(K/CD ITV 354)* **Various Artists – This Is Scotland**
Aug 84. (c) *(KITV 362)* **TOMMY SCOTT – Pipes & Strings Of Scotland led by Pipe Majoe Willie Cochrane Vol.1**
Sep 84. (c/lp) *(K+/ITV 365)* **ALASDAIR GILLIES – Silver And Gold**
Sep 84. (c/vid) *(PLATV 370)* **Various Artists – Reflections Of Scotland**
Aug 84. (7") *(ITV7S 371)* **TOMMY SCOTT – Going Home**
Sep 84. (c) *(KITV 373)* **SYDNEY DEVINE – From Scotland With Love**
Dec 85. (c/lp) *(K+/ITV 385)* **DENNY & DUNIPACE PIPE BAND – Plays Scotlands Best**
(cd-iss. May87; CDITV 385)
Dec 86. (cd/lp) *(CD+/ITV 394)* **TOMMY SCOTT – Pipes & Strings Of Scotland led by Pipe Major Willie Cochrane Vol.2**
Dec 86. (cd/c/lp) *(CD/K+/ITV 411)* **TOMMY SCOTT – Scotland With Bill Garden**
Dec 86. (cd/c/lp) *(CD/K+/ITV 416)* **ALASDAIR GILLIES – Among My Souvenirs**
Dec 86. (c) *(KITV 418)* **STUART ANDERSON – Plays Scottish Favourites**
Dec 86. (c) *(KITV 420)* **PREMIER ACCORDION BAND – Go Country Western**
Dec 86. (c) *(KITV 421)* **VALERIE DUNBAR – Sings Sacred**
Dec 86. (c/cd) *(K/CD ITV 422)* **JIM MacLEOD – Dance Party Favourites**
Dec 86. (cd/c/vid) *(CD/K/V ITV 423)* **BILL GARDEN & HIS HIGHLAND FIDDLE ORCHESTRA – Sailing**
Jun 87. (cd/c/lp) *(CD/K+/ITV 426)* **TOMMY SCOTT'S ROYAL HIGHLAND SHOWBAND – . . . Starring Pipe Major Willie Cochrane**
Dec 87. (c) *(KITV 430)* **SYDNEY DEVINE – Always And Forever**
Nov 87. (cd/c/lp) *(CD/K+/ITV 431)* **TOMMY SCOTT – Collection**
Sep 87. (c) *(KITV 433)* **NORTH SEA GAS – Live From Edinburgh: North Sea Gas In Concert**
Dec 87. (c) *(KITV 436)* **BEGGARS MANTLE – Going Places**
Dec 87. (c) *(KITV 438) IRISH ROVERS – Wasn't That A Party*
Dec 87. (c/cd) *(K/CD ITV 444)* **JIM MacLEOD – Hogmanay Party**
Nov 87. (c) *(KITV 445)* **BANCHORY STRATHSPEY & REEL SOCIETY – In Crathe's Castle Vol.2**
Nov 87. (c) *(KITV 447)* **LOU GRANT – Glasgow Sings Along**
Dec 87. (c) *(KITV 449)* **Various Artists – Discover Scotland**
Dec 87. (c/lp) *(K+/ITV 450)* **MARY CAMERON – A Pride Of Bonnie Scotland**
Aug 88. (c) *(KITV 453)* **RON GONNELLA – International Friendship Fiddle**
Jul 89. (c/cd) *(K/CD ITV 455)* **ROYAL SCOTS DRAGOON GUARDS – Scottish Salute**
Aug 89. (cd/c/lp) *(CD/K+/ITV 456)* **TOMMY SCOTT – Pipes & Strings Of Scotland Vol.3**
Sep 88. (7") *(ITV 459)* **MARY CAMERON – Durisdeer / Dumbarton's Drums**
Oct 88. (c/cd) *(K/CD ITV 460)* **KENNETH MacDONALD – The Sound Of Kintail**
Dec 88. (c/cd) *(K/CD ITV 461)* **JIM MacLEOD – Welcome To My World**
Dec 88. (c) *(KITV 462)* **AYRSHIRE FIDDLE ORCHESTRA – Fiddlers Gathering**
Dec 88. (c) *(KITV 463)* **PREMIER ACCORDION BAND – Go Hawaiian**
Dec 88. (c) *(KITV 464)* **VALERIE DUNBAR – Calling Me Home**
Dec 88. (c/cd) *(K/CD ITV 467)* **BILL McCUE – Count Your Blessings**
Dec 88. (c/lp) *(K+/ITV 468)* **LOU GRANT – Presents Party Time In Scotland**
Dec 88. (c) *(KITV 469) IRISH ROVERS – Have Another Party*
Dec 88. (c) *(KITV 475)* **CHESTERS PEACE – Songs Of Friendship**
Dec 88. (c) *(KITV 476) PHILOMENA BEGLEY – Country Scots'n'Irish*
Dec 88. (c/cd) *(K/CD ITV 478)* **TOMMY SCOTT – Pipes & Dixie Banjo Band**
Dec 88. (cd) *(CDITV 480)* **Various Artists – Scotland The Brave**
May 89. (7") *(ITV7S 481)* **STUART ANDERSON Jnr. – Bonnie Wee Jeannie McCall**
Jul 89. (cd/c) *(CD/K ITV 483)* **NORTH SEA GAS – Caledonian Connection**
Jul 89. (cd/c) *(CD/K ITV 484)* **BILL McCUE – Lucky White Heather**
Nov 89. (c) *(KITV 486)* **LAURIE ACCORDION ORCHESTRA – Laurie Accordion Orchestra**
Nov 89. (c) *(KITV 488)* **HELEN RANDELL – The Best Of**
Oct 89. (c) *(KITV 489)* **CLANSMEN – Flying Scotsmen**
Oct 89. (cd/c) *(CD/K ITV 491)* **JIM MacLEOD & HIS BAND – play Selected Scottish Country Dances**
Nov 89. (c) *(KITV 501)* **FIONNA DUNCAN – McJazz Allstars**
Nov 89. (cd/c/lp) *(CD/K+/ITV 502)* **STUART ANDERSON Jnr. – Stuart Anderson's Party**
Oct 89. (7") *(ITV7S 504)* **JOHN MacLEOD – Steel Away / Slow Waltz – Ballad Of Glencoe / Wee Ladies**
Nov 89. (c) *(KITV 506)* **AYRSHIRE FIDDLE ORCHESTRA – Bowing The Strings**
Nov 89. (c) *(KITV 507)* **CHESTERS PEACE – Every Face Tells A story**
Nov 89. (c) *(KITV 508) IRISH ROVERS – Tall Ships & Salty Dogs*
Oct 90. (c) *(KITV 510)* **RON GONNELLA – Fiddle And Pipe Favourites**
Oct 90. (cd/c) *(CD/K ITV 511)* **TOMMY SCOTT – The Scottish Fiddle Concept**
Oct 90. (cd/c) *(CD/K ITV 512) PADDY NEARY – Musical Jems*
Jul 90. (cd/c/vid) *(CD/K/V ITV 514)* **BILL GARDEN FIDDLE ORCHESTRA – Iolaire: The West islands**
Aug 90. (cd/c) *(CD/K ITV 515)* **CALEDONIAN HERITAGE PIPES & DRUMS – Amazing Grace**
Sep 90. (cd/c) *(CD/K ITV 516)* **STUART LIDDELL – The Competing Highland Dancer**
Oct 90. (c) *(KITV 519)* **WILLIE COCHRANE – Pipe Major**
Nov 90. (c) *(KITV 520)* **Various Artists – Forth Bridge Centenary**
Nov 90. (cd/c) *(CD/K ITV 521)* **TOMMY SCOTT – Pipes And Dixie Bands**
Dec 90. (vid) *(VITV 524)* **SYDNEY DEVINE – Country Vol.1**
Dec 90. (vid) *(VITV 525)* **STUART ANDERSON Jnr. – In The Country**
Dec 90. (re-vid) *(VITV 526)* **JIM MacLEOD – Hogmanay Party**
Dec 90. (cd/c/lp) *(CD/K+/ITV 528)* **TOMMY SCOTT – Hopscotch Ceilidh Party**
Dec 90. (c) *(KITV 529)* **TOMMY TRUESDALE – A Tree In The Meadow**
Dec 90. (cd/c) *(CD/K ITV 530)* **SYDNEY DEVINE – The Green Grass Of Home**
Apr 91. (c) *(KITV 536)* **STUART ANDERSON – Caledonian Party**
Apr 91. (c) *(KITV 537)* **LAURIE ACCORDION ORCHESTRA – Laurie Accordion Orchestra Vol.2**

Jul 91. (cd/c) *(CD/K ITV 538) TOM KILPATRICK – Fifty Shades Of Green*
Aug 91. (c) *(KITV 539)* **WES SHEPPARD – Introducing . . .**
May 91. (cd/c) *(CD/K ITV 540)* **TARTAN LADS – . . . Of Bonnie Scotland**
Sep 91. (cd/c) *(CD/K ITV 541)* **NORTH SEA GAS – Keltic Heritage**
Apr 92. (cd/c) *(CD/K ITV 542)* **LENA MARTELL – Sometimes When I'm Dreaming**
May 92. (cd/c) *(CD/K ITV 543)* **CULTURE CEILIDH BAND – After The Ceilidh**
May 92. (cd/c) *(CD/K ITV 544)* **JIM MacLEOD – Dance Dance Dance One More Time**
Sep 91. (cd/c) *(CD/K ITV 545)* **TOMMY SCOTT – Scotland Forever**
Jun 92. (cd/c/vid) *(CD/K/V ITV 546)* **CALEDONIAN HERITAGE PIPES & DRUMS – Auld Lang Syne**
Sep 91. (cd/c) *(CD/K ITV 547)* **ALISTAIR McDONALD – Songs Gretna To Glencoe**
Aug 91. (cd/c/vid) *(CD/K/V ITV 548)* **JIM MacLEOD & HIS BAND – The Land Of MacLeod**
Nov 91. (cd/c/vid) *(CD/K/V ITV 549)* **Various Artists – The White Heather Tour Of Scotland**
Jul 92. (cd/c/vid) *(CD/K/V ITV 551)* **STUART ANDERSON Snr. – Takes The High Road**
Aug 94. (cd/c) *(CD/K ITV 552)* **BILL McCUE & KINLOCHARD CEILIDH BAND – Rob Roy Country: The Heart Of Scotland**
Aug 92. (c) *(KITV 553)* **AYRSHIRE FIDDLE ORCHESTRA – Fiddle De De**
Sep 92. (cd/c) *(CD/K ITV 554)* **TOMMY SCOTT – Hop Scotch 2**
Oct 92. (cd/c/vid) *(CD/K/V ITV 556)* **Various Artists – Amazing Grace (A Real Highland Fling)**
Oct 92. (cd/c/vid) *(CD/K/V ITV 559)* **STUART ANDERSON Jnr. – Acts Naturally**
Sep 92. (cd/c) *(CD/K ITV 560) TOM KILPATRICK – The Shamrock Strand*
Apr 93. (c/cd) *(IRVC 562/+CD)* **CAMPBELLS – Castlebay**
May 93. (cd/c/vid) *(CD/K/V ITV 563)* **WES SHEPPARD – Scotland**
Oct 92. (cd/c/vid) *(CD/K/V ITV 564)* **TOMMY SCOTT – Going Home**
May 93. (c) *(SCOT 100C)* **ALISTAIR McDONALD – Songs Of Scotland**
Aug 93. (cd/c/vid) *(CD/K/V ITV 565)* **JIM MacLEOD & HIS BAND – A Scottish Tour**
May 93. (cd/c/vid) *(CD/K/V ITV 567)* **BILL GARDEN FIDDLE ORCHESTRA – Travel The Firth Of Clyde**
May 93. (cd/c/vid) *(CD/K/V ITV 568)* **ALEXANDER BROTHERS – Song Of The Clyde**
May 94. (cd/c) *(CD/K ITV 569)* **TOMMY SCOTT – Scots Country**
Nov 93. (cd/c/vid) *(CD/K/V ITV 572)* **Various Artits – Christmas In Scotland**
Sep 93. (cd/c/vid) *(CD/K/V 573)* **WES SHEPPARD – Andy's Scottish Party**
Oct 93. (cd/c/vid) *(CD/K/V 574)* **ANN WILLIAMSON – A portrait Of Scotland**
Nov 93. (cd/c/vid) *(CD/K/V 576)* **ALEXANDER BROTHERS – Friendly Folk From Edinburgh To The Borders**
Sep 94. (cd/c) *(CD/K ITV 577)* **BILL GARDEN FIDDLE ORCHESTRA – Travel The Lake District**
Nov 94. (cd) *(CDITV 578)* **BANCHORY STRATHSPEY & REEL SOCIETY – A Tribute To Scott Skinner**
Sep 94. (cd/c) *(CD/K ITV 580)* **TOMMY SCOTT – Best Of Hopscotch**
Aug 94. (cd/c) *(CD/K ITV 581) BRASS PENNIES – Pride Of England*
Aug 94. (cd/c/vid) *(CD/K/V ITV 583)* **JIM MacLEOD – Take The Road And Miles**
Sep 94. (cd/c) *(CD/K ITV 585)* **NORTH SEA GAS – Scottish Destiny**
Oct 94. (cd/c/vid) *(CD/K/V ITV 587)* **BILL McCUE – A' The Best From . . .**
Sep 94. (c) *(KITV 588)* **AYRSHIRE FIDDLE ORCHESTRA – Ayr's & Graces**
Sep 94. (cd/c) *(CD/K ITV 589)* **CHRIS YOUNG – Sings The Great Songs**
Aug 94. (cd/c) *(CD/K ITV 590)* **ANN WILLIAMSON – Flower Of Scotland**
Oct 94. (cd/c/vid) *(CD/K/V ITV 591)* **CITY OF GLASGOW PHILHARMONIC ORCHESTRA – Flower Of Scotland**
Nov 94. (cd/c/vid) *(CD/K/V ITV 592)* **BILL GARDEN'S ORCHESTRA – North Wales Land Of Song**
Nov 94. (cd/c) *(CD/K ITV 593)* **ALEXANDER BROTHERS – The Glorious North**
Jun 95. (cd/c/vid) *(CD/K/V ITV 594)* **BILL McCUE – Scotland's Royal Highland Show**
Dec 94. (c) *(KITV 595)* **JACKIE NELSON – Sail Away**
Nov 94. (cd/c/vid) *(CD/K/V ITV 596)* **VALERIE DUNBAR – Argyll**
Nov 94. (cd/c/vid) *(CD/K/V ITV 597)* **TOMMY SCOTT – Hail Hail Caledonia**
Nov 94. (cd/c) *(CD/K ITV 598)* **SYDNEY DEVINE – Norfolk Country**
Mar 95. (cd/c/vid) *(CD/K/V ITV 600)* **ANN WILLIAMSON – Amazing Grace**
Mar 95. (cd/c) *(CD/K ITV 601)* **KINLOCHARD CEILIDH BAND – Slainte**
Oct 95. (cd/c/vid) *(CD/K/V ITV 602)* **RONNIE BROWNE – Scottish Love Songs**
Oct 95. (cd/c/vid) *(CD/K/V ITV 604)* **JIM MacLEOD – Ceilidh**
Aug 95. (cd/c) *(CD/K ITV 605)* **BANCHORY STRATHSPEY & REEL SOCIETY – Geol Na Fidhle**
Nov 95. (cd/c/vid) *(CD/K/V ITV 606)* **TOMMY SCOTT – Highland Holiday**
Oct 95. (cd/c) *(CD/K ITV 607)* **NORTH SEA GAS – The Power Of Scotland**
Feb 96. (cd/c/vid) *(CD/K/V ITV 608)* **TOMMY SCOTT – Scots Wha Hae Wi' Wallace**
Mar 96. (cd/c/lp) *(CD/K/V ITV 610)* **TOMMY SCOTT – Holiday In Ireland**
May 96. (cd/c) *(CD/K ITV 611)* **QUEEN VICTORIA SCHOOL, DUNBLANE – Tunes Of Scotland**
Oct 96. (cd/c/vid) *(CD/K/V ITV 613)* **BILL GARDEN'S ORCHESTRA – Visions Of Caledonia**
Oct 96. (cd/c/vid) *(CD/K/V ITV 614)* **BILL GARDEN'S ORCHESTRA – The Uilleann Pipes Of Ireland Featuring Eric Rigler**
Oct 96. (cd/c/vid) *(CD/K/V ITV 615)* **JIM MacLEOD'S ALL STAR SCOTTISH DANCE BAND – . . . All Star Scottish Dance Band**
Oct 96. (CD-Rom) *(ITVR 616)* **The Multimedia Adventure From The World Of Bagpipes!**
Oct 95. (cd/c/vid) *(CD/K/V ITV 617)* **Various Artists – Tommy Scott's Street Party**
Nov 96. (cd/c/vid) *(CD/K/V ITV 618)* **RONNIE BROWNE – Battle Songs And Ballads**
Dec 96. (cd/c) *(CD/K ITV 620)* **SYDNEY DEVINE – The Big Country Line Dance Party Vol.1**
Dec 96. (cd/c/vid) *(CD/K/V ITV 621)* **Various Artists – Scottish Family Christmas**
Mar 97. (cd/c) *(CD/K ITV 622)* **KINLOCHARD CEILIDH BAND – Spirit Of Freedom**
Jun 97. (cd/c) *(CD/K ITV 623)* **LOWLAND BAND – The Spirit Of Scotland**
Nov 97. (cd/c/vid) *(CD/K/V 625)* **SYDNEY DEVINE – The Big Country Line Dance Party Vol.2 (20 Non Stop Line Dances)**
Nov 97. (cd/c) *(CD/K ITV 627)* **ANN WILLIAMSON – Songs For The Country Line Dancer**
Nov 97. (vid) *(VITV 627)* **HARLEY MARSHALL – The Big Country Line Dancing Club**
Oct 97. (cd/c) *(CD/K ITV 629)* **NORTH SEA GAS – Schiehallion**
Nov 97. (cd/c/vid) *(CD/K/V ITV 630)* **TOMMY SCOTT – Scotland**
Nov 97. (vid) *(VITV 631)* **ALISTAIR McDONALD – Velvet And Steel**
Jan 00. (cd/c/vid) *(CD/K/V ITV 632)* **JIM MacLEOD – The Big Scottish Ceilidh Dance Party**
Sep 97. (cd/c) *(CD/K ITV 633)* **TOMMY SCOTT – Country Ceilidh Party**
Nov 97. (cd/c) *(CD/K ITV 634)* **GLASGOW PHOENIX CHOIR – Highland Cathedral**
Jan 98. (cd/c) *(CD/K ITV 635)* **Various Artists – Ceilidh In The Park**
Apr 98. (cd/c) *(CD/K ITV 637)* **BILL GARDEN – Reflections Of Scotland**
Sep 98. (cd/c) *(CD/K ITV 638)* **TOMMY SCOTT – Dream: The Classic Country Collection**
Jun 98. (cd/c/vid) *(CD/K/V ITV 639)* **LONE PIPERS OF THE SCOTTISH REGIMENTS – same**
Jul 98. (cd/c) *(CD/K ITV 640)* **Band & Bugles of the LIGHT DIVISION – The Best Of British**
Aug 98. (cd/c) *(CD/K ITV 641)* **BANCHORY STRATHSPEY & REEL SOCIETY – A Tune For Bill**
Sep 98. (cd/c) *(CD/K ITV 642)* **ROYAL SCOTS DRAGOON GUARDS – Highland Cathedral**
Dec 98. (cd/c) *(CD/K ITV 643)* **GLASGOW PHOENIX CHOIR – Caledonian Christmas**
Jun 99. (cd/c) *(CD/K ITV 644)* **Pipes & Drums Of The 1st Battalion ARGYLL & SUTHERLAND HIGHLANDERS – Salute From Stirling Castle**
Jun 99. (cd/c/vid) *(CD/K/V ITV 645)* **JIM MacLEOD – Non-Stop Ceilidh Dancing**
Jun 99. (vid) *(VITV 646)* **TOMMY SCOTT – World**
Jun 99. (cd/c) *(CD/K ITV 647)* **LENA MARTELL – Inspirations**
Jun 99. (cd/c) *(CD/K ITV 648)* **Various Artists – Ceilidh In The Park 2**
Jun 99. (cd/c) *(CD/K ITV 649)* **Pipe Major JIM MOTHERWELL – The Queen's Piper**
Jun 99. (cd/c) *(CD/K ITV 650)* **ERISKAY LILT – Just A Little Bit**
Jun 99. (cd/c) *(CD/K ITV 651)* **TOMMY TRUESDALE – Favourites**
Jun 99. (cd/c/vid) *(CD/K/V ITV 653)* **TOMMY SCOTT – Nearer To Thee**
Jun 99. (cd/c) *(CD/K ITV 654)* **GLASGOW PHOENIX CHOIR – Scotland Land Of Praise**
Jan 00. (cd) *(CDITV 655)* **Pipes & Drums Of The 1st Battalion BLACK WATCH – Majestic Scotland**
Jan 00. (cd/c) *(CD/K ITV 656)* **KINLOCHARD CEILIDH BAND – Strip The Willow**
Jan 00. (cd/c/vid) *(CD/K/V ITV 657)* **JIM MacLEOD – Hogmanay Party At Blair Castle**
May 00. (cd/c) *(CD/K ITV 658)* **GLASGOW PHOENIX CHOIR – Titanic**
Jun 00. (cd/c) *(CD/K ITV 659)* **LOWLAND BAND OF THE SCOTTISH DIVISION – Flowers Of The Forest**
Jul 00. (CD-Rom) *(ITVRPC 660)* **An Interactive CD-Rom Postcard From Scotland**
Aug 00. (cd/c) *(CD/K ITV 661)* **BAND OF HER MAJESTY'S SCOTS GUARDS – Into The 21st Century**
Oct 00. (cd/c) *(CD/K ITV 663)* **NORTH SEA GAS – Spirit Of Scotland**
Oct 00. (cd/c) *(CD/K ITV 664)* **TOMMY SCOTT – Songs Of Praise**
Oct 00. (cd/c) *(CD/K ITV 667)* **TOMMY SCOTT – The Special Requests**
Nov 00. (cd/c) *(CD/K ITV 668)* **JIM MacLEOD – Welcome To Dunblane**
Aug 01. (cd/c) *(CD/K ITV 672) The Band Of Bugles Of The ROYAL IRISH REGIMENT – Last Of The Great Whales*
Aug 01. (cd/c) *(CD/K ITV 673)* **Various Artists – In Search Of Scotland**
Aug 01. (cd/c) *(CD/K ITV 674)* **Various Artists – The Royal Stewart Tartan Music Collection**
Aug 01. (d-cd/d-c) *(LCD/LK ITV 675)* **TOMMY SCOTT – Double Hop Scotch Party Collection; Sing And Dance To 101 Great Songs**
Aug 01. (cd-s) *(CDITV45 676)* **ROYAL SCOTS DRAGOON GUARDS – Highland Cathedral**
Nov 01. (cd/c) *(CD/K ITV 677)* **GLASGOW PHOENIX CHOIR – Auld Lang Syne**
Nov 01. (cd/c) *(CD/K ITV 678)* **ALEXANDER BROTHERS – Favourite Memories**
Nov 01. (cd/c) *(CD/K ITV 679)* **TOMMY SCOTT – Christmas Sing-a-long Party**
Oct 01. (cd-s) *(CDITV45 680)* **ALEXANDER BROTHERS – Jimmy Shand The Legend**
Nov 01. (cd/c) *(CD/K ITV 681)* **JIM MacLEOD – High Days And Holidays**

—— JIM received an MBE in 2001 and was awarded it at Buckingham Palace on the 20th of February, 2002

Nov 01. (cd-s) *(CDITV45 682)* **LEIGH GARDEN – Highland Cathedral**

(more traditional imprints)

Overview: When 'Waverley' (owned by Geo. Jeffrey Ltd. at 23 Earl Grey Street in Edinburgh) started out with some 78's, who would've thought that over 50 years later we'd still be listening to them. Without going too deeply into these but giving them a mention nevertheless, these were the main imprints for this genre:- 'Norco', 'Nevis', 'Bonspiel', 'Grange', 'Ross', 'R.E.L.', 'Scotdisc', 'Moidart', 'Thule' and 'Sleepytown'. The lists from these labels are far too big (and probably monotonous) to include in this book, but most have their own websites.

4

Celebrity Corner

(actors, comedians, and child entertainers)

The Story: Although better known for their endeavours in other areas of the Arts (i.e. music hall, stage/theatre, film/TV, comedy, etc), a great number of weel-kent Scottish faces entered the studio for the odd (occasionally very odd) recording or two. What follows is a potted history of these variety performers, from the stand-up (JIMMY LOGAN) to the comic (BILLY CONNOLLY) to the ridiculous (SCOTLAND WORLD CUP SQUAD).

The story unfolds in approximately chronological order. . .

* * * * *

The pre-War Music Hall entertainers . . .

Sir Harry LAUDER

HARRY will be best remembered as a rousing singer and even cannier songwriter. Born in the seaside town of Portobello in 1870, he began his professional life as a blarney-talking comedian on the thriving turn of the century Music Hall scene. Complete with full Highland dress, the tartan troubadour began incorporating an extensive song repertoire that included such musical standards as 'ROAMIN' IN THE GLOAMIN', 'I LOVE A LASSIE' and 'STOP YOUR TICKLIN' JOCK'. Surprisingly, this went down a storm in London (where the haggis-chasing caricature survives to this day) and abroad. The man was eventually awarded a knighthood in recognition of his musical services to the troops during the First World War. As an actor he also appeared in a handful of films in his later years ('The End Of the Road', etc), Sir HARRY finally going to that great Music Hall in the sky in 1950. The cream of his work can be heard on a re-mastered CD collection, 'THE ROAD TO THE ISLES'; (Flapper; PASTCD 7834).

Around at roughly the same time – although born 20 years earlier – was Helensburgh-born . . .

Jack BUCHANAN

JACK left Scotland at a young age for the bright lights of London. In the pre-war years, JACK made a name for himself in theatre before making his big screen debut in 1917's 'Auld Lang Syne'. After a number of British films, BUCHANAN's sophisticated, Anglicised image led him to Hollywood where he starred opposite the likes of Irene Bordoni and Jeanette MacDonald. Upon his return to Blighty in the early 30's, the top-hat and tailed actor-turned-director featured in musicals such as 'Yes, Mr.Brown' and 'That's A Good Girl'. Having built up an extensive CV by the close of the Second World War, he took a break in the post-war years, only to return in 1953 alongside Fred Astaire and Nanette Fabray in the acclaimed 'The Band Wagon'. If spontaneously breaking into song at the slightest excuse is your bag then his career highlights can be found on 'JACK BUCHANAN' (Flapper; PASTCD 9763).

There must've been something in the Helensburgh water; the very same year that JACKIE boy was lording it up with ASTAIRE and Co . . .

Deborah KERR

(also born in that self-same west coast town) was nominated for two Academy Awards in recognition of her performances in 'Edward My Son' (1953) and 'From Here To Eternity' (1953). She was subsequently nominated for roles in four other films including the 1956 musical, 'The King And I' alongside Yul Brynner. The latter of these recordings was released on soundtrack and hit US No.1.

Another contemporary of the era was comic genius . . .

Will FYFFE

Born in 1883, WILL was, by popular consent, the funniest Music Hall character of the day. Unlike the debonair BUCHANAN, FYFFE left it rather late in life to begin his movie career. From his first starring role in 1934's 'Happy', WILL had them rolling in the aisles right through the 30's and during the Second World War. Songs such as 'Twelve And A Tanner A Bottle', 'It Isn't The Hen That Cackles The Most' and 'I Belong To Glasgow', were recorded for posterity (he died in 1947) and can now be heard on shiny CD via 'WILL FYFFE (LEGENDARY SCOTTISH SINGER . . .)' *(Lismor; LCOM 5234)*

Scotland's music halls would once again pack in the punters when the war dust had finally settled and ration coupons were finally consigned to history. Foremost among the new breed of entertainers was Glaswegian. . .

Later Performers . . .

Jimmy LOGAN

(born JAMES SHORT, 1928) was a traditional Music Hall man who, along with his parents (JACK SHORT and MAY DALZIEL) and siblings was part of the LOGAN FAMILY. After establishing himself in the post-war pantomime scene, the versatile performer made his name with 'The Five Past Eight Show' at Glasgow's Alhambra theatre and later dabbled in film ('The Fuller Brush Man' and 'Floodtide').

In 1964, LOGAN snapped up the Metropole Theatre which he ran for almost a decade. Of course one of his many talents was singing and the man occasionally entered the studio for the odd novelty 45 (see below). In the early 70's, he became a guest member of the 'Carry On' team, starring in such calamitous classics as 'Carry On Girls' and 'Carry On Abroad'. Having briefly followed in the footsteps of his hero, HARRY LAUDER, by starring in a London stage show ('The Mating Game'), JIMMY paid tribute to the Music Hall pioneer with his own 1976 show, 'Lauder'.

In the twilight of his career, the comic took on more demanding stage work and appeared in 1984's 'The Entertainer', '89's 'Brighton Beach Memoirs' and 'The Comedians' from 1991. JIMMY subsequently masterminded 'The Fabulous Fifties' for the 1993 Edinburgh Festival and was awarded the London critics' choice for his trouble. In 1996, after years of service to the showbusiness industry, he was awarded the OBE, although by this point he was battling with cancer of the oesophagus. A mere month before his death on the 13th of April 2001, the redoubtable stage trouper performed a charity benefit, raising around £30,000 for cancer victims and their families.

– JIMMY LOGAN discography –

		H.M.V.	not iss.
1961.	(7") *(POP 974)* **MacFARLANE. / THE HEART OF SCOTLAND**		-
		R.C.A.	not iss.
Aug 68.	(7") *(RCA 1739)* **I HAVE DREAMED. / THE ROAD TO DUNDEE**		-
Nov 68.	(7") *(RCA 1774)* **NEW YEAR BELLS. / HOUSE & AIRLIE**		-

The same generation who grew up with the laughter of JIMMY LOGAN ringing in their ears also loved the likes of STANLEY BAXTER and LEX McLEAN (not forgetting his sister UNA), although sadly – for this book at least – none of them made it to vinyl. A pair who did – and a right pair rey wir – were . . .

FRANCIE & JOSIE

(aka Glaswegians JACK MILROY and RIKKI FULTON). The latter was another to get his initial break on the aforementioned 'Five Past Eight' show, going on to win the nation's heart with his New Year 'Scotch & Wry' specials featuring FULTON himself as the unforgettable Reverend I.M. Jolly. His partner in comical crime MILROY (a "desert rat" in World War II), meanwhile, worked a similar passage through the Glasgow footlights although he didn't achieve quite the same solo fame as FULTON. Sadly, JACK (who was actually born JAMES CRUDEN, 28th December, 1915 in Govanhill) would die in hospital on the 1st February, 2001, having recently received his M.B.E. Playing gormless teddy boys, the FRANCIE & JOSIE stand-up act harked back to the Vaudeville era with added Glasgow banter. The inimitable pair were finally recorded for posterity in 1981 on an eponymous 'Lochshore' LP. RIKKI (b. 1924, Dennistoun) – the youngest son of a shopkeeper – also starred in several mid-80's films including 'Local Hero', 'Comfort And Joy', 'Gorky Park' and the TV comedy return of 'The Tales Of Para Handy' in 1995.

Curiously enough, there are few women down on celebrity corner but keeping the side up for the girls was . . .

Molly WEIR

(b. 1920) a native Glaswegian and younger sister of broadcaster and naturalist TOM WEIR. She made her name in 50's radio via the likes of 'ITMA' and 'The McFlannels'. Her one moment of vinyl madness came with the 1957 single, 'GLASGOW' ('Parlophone'; R 4340), after which she moved into films ('The Prime Of Miss Jean Brodie'), theatre/radio ('Life With The Lions'), TV ('Rentaghost') and general minor celebrity fame, even writing her own newspaper column. She now bides just outside London, in Pinner.

John CAIRNEY

was born in Glasgow, 1930. He was one of the country's leading supporting actors (from 'Miracle in Soho' and 'Lucky Jim' onwards) and he also released a few 45's . . .

		H.M.V.	not iss.
1957.	(7") *(POP 424)* **TWO STRANGERS. / A CERTAIN GIRL I KNOW**		-
		Waverley	not iss.
1974.	(7") *(SLP 543)* **PLEASE. / DEEP PURPLE**		-

— CAIRNEY has since recorded a spoken-word CD for 'R.E.L.' dramatising 'The Robert Burns Story'.

Believe it or not, Scotland's über-star/actor (and former Mr. Universe) . . .

Sean CONNERY

(b. 25 Aug '30, Fountainbridge, Edinburgh), even made it to vinyl via a Pre-BOND collaborative 7"/78 with co-star JANET MUNRO entitled 'PRETTY IRISH GIRL' (from the film 'Darby O'Gill And The Little People'). I think we know how many films Sir Sean has made – he now resides in Spain although he jets back to Scotland, Britain and America from time to time.

Another Scots actor (and soon-to-be double agent!) who came in from the cold was . . .

David McCALLUM

(b.19 Sep'33, Glasgow). Son of a concert violinist father and cellist-playing mother (who incidentally were also members of the London Philharmonic Orchestra), McCALLUM aspired to following in his parents' footsteps after time served in the Royal West African Frontier Force. In complete contrast to his grandiose intentions, DAVID joined RADA to study acting and by 1957, had entered the glitzy showbiz world of movies. Starring roles duly arrived thick and fast for the debonair, fair-haired brainbox and through late 50's British-made films, 'Robbery Under Arms', 'Violent Playground', 'A Night To Remember', 'The Secret Place' and 'Hell Drivers', the young man established himself very quickly. The early 60's were equally fruitful, 'The Long And The Short And The Tall' and 'Freud' (in which he played a post-'Psycho' mother-obsessed mental patient!) led him to be picked for the all-star classic war movie, 'The Great Escape', in 1963.

Having worked for American television on several 'Outer Limits' episodes, McCALLUM progressed to being the Russian secret-agent, Ilya Kuryakin (alongside Robert Vaughn) in the long-running cult TV series, 'The Man From U.N.C.L.E.'. It was during this spell between 1964 and 1967, that DAVID took the opportunity to try his hand at conducting, emerging from 'Capitol' records studio early 1966 with an LP, 'MUSIC – A PART OF ME'. Surprisingly enough, his classical interpretations of such standards as 'YESTERDAY', '(I CAN'T GET NO) SATISFACTION' and 'DOWNTOWN', were cool and groovy enough to reach the US Top 30 . . . Almost identical in formulaic approach and hot on the heels of the record was another US Top 100 breaker, 'MUSIC, A BIT MORE OF ME' (1966), while the man sang opposite the beautiful NANCY SINATRA on one of the 'U.N.C.L.E.' TV episodes (he was also married to actress Jill Ireland at the time, but re-married in '67 to Katherine Carpenter). It was inevitable that the Caledonian teenage pin-up would be typecast as a spy and many suchlike made-for-TV roles in 'The Spy With My Face', 'One Spy Too Many' and 'One Of Our Spies Is Missing', came his way. In 1967, he composed, acted and starred in the film, 'Three Bites Of The Apple', although the critics were not forthcoming with their praise.

By the late 60's, McCALLUM wanted a new challenge and put aside his musical aspirations to concentrate on serious acting, his most memorable roles coming in the shape of the excellent UK TV series 'Colditz' (in 1971), 'Frankenstein: The True Story' movie (in '73) and 'The Invisible Man' (in '75). For the next two decades or so, "The Man From G.L.A.S.G.O.W.", was hardly ever away from appearing on our TV sets, further work included 'The Watcher In The Woods', 'Behind Enemy Lines', 'Hear My Song' (about singer JOSEF LOCKE) and the more recent 'Cherry' in 1999. Three years earlier, cult 'Creation' label off-shoot, 'Rev-Ola', opened up old musical wounds by releasing his 'OPEN CHANNEL D' CD-album.

– DAVID McCALLUM discography –

		Capitol	Capitol
Feb 66.	(lp; stereo/mono) *(<S+/T 2432>)* **MUSIC – A PART OF ME**		27
	– One, two, three / Turn, turn, turn / The "in" crowd / A taste of honey / Yesterday / I can't get no satisfaction / We gotta get out of this place / Downtown / The far side of the moon / Louise / Insomnia / The sugar cane.		
Apr 66.	(7") *(CL 15439)* **COMMUNICATION. / MY CAROUSEL**	32	
Jun 66.	(lp; stereo/mono) *(<S+/T 2498>)* **MUSIC: A BIT MORE OF ME**		79
	– Uptight (everything's alright) / Michelle / Batman theme / Call me / Isn't it wonderful / My world is empty without you / 5 o'clock world / Shadow of your smile (love theme from 'The Sandpiper') / It won't be wrong / Far away blue / The edge / Final.		
Nov 66.	(7") *(CL 15474)* **IN THE GARDEN. / THE HOUSE ON BRECKENRIDGE LANE**		-
1967.	(lp) **McCALLUM**	-	
	– 98.6 / I'm a believer / Mellow yellow / Penny Lane / 59th Street Bridge song / Strawberry fields forever / California dreaming / Mercy mercy mercy / White daisies / Oh my.		

— thankfully, DAVID returned to the world of acting

– compilations, etc. –

Sep 96.	(cd) *Creation – Rev-ola; (CREV 43CD)* **OPEN CHANNEL D**		-
Jul 01.	(cd) *EMI; (533131-2)* **MUSIC IS A PART OF ME**		
	– MUSIC – A PART OF ME / MUSIC: A BIT MORE OF ME)		

Not quite as dashing as McCALLUM, and certainly not as tall, the diminutive

Ronnie CORBETT

(b.1930, Edinburgh) first appeared on our television screens in the company of David Frost ('That Was The Week That Was', etc) in the mid-late 60's. While working with Frost he first came into contact with hefty English funnyman, Ronnie Barker, whom he would subsequently partner in the hugely popular comedy duo, The Two Ronnies. Prior to the duo's 1971 TV debut, the bespectacled wee RONNIE both starred in the BOND-spoof movie, 'Casino Royale', and issued a couple of 45's (see below). Unsurprisingly, pop stardom didn't beckon and it was as one half of the Two Ronnies that CORBETT would become a household name.

– Ronnie CORBETT discography –

		UK	US
		Columbia	not iss.
Dec 68.	(7") *(DB 8512)* **BIG MAN. / FANCY YOU FANCYING ME**	☐	-
		Philips	not iss.
Nov 70.	(7") *(6006 070)* **IT'S ALL GOING UP, UP, UP. / PUT ON A HAPPY FACE**	☐	-
		Decca	not iss.
Oct 74.	(7") *(FR 13554)* **FANNY. / TO GET A LAUGH**	☐	-

— there were of course, BBC recordings of 'The Two Ronnies' TV series

Billy CONNOLLY

was born (24 Nov'42) in Anderston, Glasgow. Possibly Scotland's most famous and best loved entertainment export after Sean Connery, BILLY CONNOLLY has plied many trades in his time although it's his unique style of expletive-filled stand-up comedy that made the man what he is today. After an unstable childhood (which has nevertheless provided many a hilarious tale for his audiences) during which he lived with his two aunts, the young BILLY began a welding apprenticeship in the shipyards of Govan. This hard-bitten working class world of piss-taking and general "Glesga Banter" has often been cited by the man as a formative environment in his development as a comedian and his shipyard days have also proved a rich source of material over the years. Although his apprenticeship was interrupted by a spell in the army, he later completed it and briefly worked in Nigeria.

Upon his return to Glasgow, he became involved in the city's thriving folk scene, playing banjo in a string of bands before forming The HUMBLEBUMS with TAM HARVEY. Signed to the 'Transatlantic' label, the duo made their vinyl debut in early 1969 with 'FIRST COLLECTION OF MERRY MELODIES'. Expanding to a trio shortly after following the addition of GERRY RAFFERTY, the group released a speedy follow-up in the shape of 'THE NEW HUMBLEBUMS' (1969). Live, their combination of irreverent, banjo-picking folk and impromptu humour went down a storm yet CONNOLLY's increasing share of the limelight eventually led to a split in the ranks. Following a final album, 'OPEN UP THE DOOR' (1970), RAFFERTY went off to form the more rock-orientated STEALERS WHEEL while CONNOLLY worked on his stand-up act.

He was soon playing to packed out houses up and down the country and in 1974 hit the UK Top 10 with his 'SOLO CONCERT' set. A follow-up, 'COP YER WHACK OF THIS' (1974), also made the Top 10 and spawned his first solo single, 'THE WELLY BOOT SONG'. Sadly, this didn't make the chart, although a mere six months later he was sitting pretty at UK No.1 with his cheeky rendition of Tammy Wynette's 'D.I.V.O.R.C.E.'. While the bulk of CONNOLLY's albums comprised rip-roaring stand-up sketches, the man's sporadic contributions to rock'n'roll shouldn't be overlooked... 'IN THE BROWNIES' for instance, a send-up of the Village People which cracked the Top 40 in 1979 and no doubt had the girl guide movement dancing in their tents.

By the 1980's, BILLY's hard-drinking lifestyle was catching up with him as he struggled to cope with the pressures of fame and an impending d.i.v.o.r.c.e. Thankfully, the strife had no long-term effect on his wayward sense of humour and in 1987 he released the massive selling 'BILLY AND ALBERT', featuring highlights of his sell-out run at London's Albert Hall. Having made his film debut back in 1979 with 'Absolution', CONNOLLY's big screen profile received a significant boost in 1990 when he starred with Liam Neeson in 'The Big Man'. The late 80's/early 90's also saw him starring in American TV sitcoms, 'Head Of The Class' and 'Billy', while a subsequent decision to live in the USA (with new wife, actress/comedienne Pamela Stephenson) led to predictable stick from the Scottish press.

1993 saw him back in Glasgow to film the award-winning 'Down Among The Big Boys', an engaging crime comedy/drama premiered at that year's Edinburgh Festival. Another high profile film role came in 1997 when he starred opposite Dame Judy Dench in 'Mrs Brown', a biopic of Queen Victoria. The 90's have also seen the "Big Yin" work on a number of hugely popular BBC TV series including his 'Musical Tour Of Scotland' and a jaunt 'round Australia, scooping up a BAFTA award in the process. Always careful in his choice of parts, he recently served up another brilliant performance (as an Edwardian artist-turned-nude photographer opposite fellow Scot Douglas Henshall) in 'Gentlemen's Relish', a BBC TV drama aired over the 2000 festive period.

Blessed with that rare ability to make people laugh about any and every mundanity life can throw up, BILLY CONNOLLY is surely a national treasure. We may never see his like again, or at least as mad a head of hair and beard.

• **Songwriters:** CONNOLLY except several revamped (comic-wise) standards.

• **Filmography:** ABSOLUTION (1979) / BULLSHOT CRUMMOND (1983) / BLUE MONEY (1984) / WATER (1985) / THE RETURN OF THE MUSKATEERS (1989) / THE BIG MAN – aka CROSSING THE LINE (1990) / HEAD OF THE CLASS and BILLY (American TV; early 1990's) / INDECENT PROPOSAL (cameo 1993) / DOWN AMONG THE BIG BOYS (TV; 1993) / MUPPET TREASURE ISLAND (1996) / DEACON BRODIE (TV; 1997) / MIDDLETON'S CHANGELING (1997) / MRS. BROWN (1997) / STILL CRAZY (1998) / THE IMPOSTERS (1998) / THE DEBT COLLECTOR (1999) / BOONDOCK SAINTS (2000).

BILLY CONNOLLY – vocals, banjo, etc

		UK	US
		Transatla.	not iss.
Nov 72.	(lp) *(TRA 258)* **LIVE!**	☐	-

– Stainless steel wellies / Song for a small man / The donkey / Telling lies / Glasgow Central / Good love / A little of your time / Near you / Winchburgh Junction / Oh dear / McGinty. *(re-iss. Feb81 lp/c; TRS/KTRS 103) (c-iss.Mar95 on 'Castle'; CCCMC 104)*

May 74. (lp) *(TRA 279)* **SOLO CONCERT** [8] [-]
– Glasgow accents . . . Nine and a half guitars / Marie's wedding (musical arrangement) / Harry Campbell and the heavies / Nobody's child / A life in the day of . . . / The jobbie wheecha . . . / The short haired police cadet / Leo McGuire's song / The crucifixion. *(c-iss.Mar95 on 'Castle'; CCCMC 105)*

Polydor not iss.

Dec 74. (lp) *(2383 310)* **COP YER WHACK OF THIS** [10] [-]
– Last train to San Fernando / Three men from Carntyne / Help me make it through the night / Lucky Uncle Freddie / Tam the bam / What's in a name / Constantine-Tyrone / Talkin' blues / Late call / Funny thing religion / The afternoon after the morning after the night before / Cripple creek / George, my faithful roadie / Sergeant, where's mine / Scottish Highland national dress – The welly boot song.

Mar 75. (7") *(2058 558)* **WELLY BOOT SONG. / SERGEANT, WHERE'S MINE** [ ] [-]

Oct 75. (7") *(2058 652)* **D.I.V.O.R.C.E. / CUCKOO** [1] [-]

Nov 75. (lp) *(2383 368)* **GET RIGHT INTAE HIM** [6] [-]
– "Wellies" on / A wee swearie / A four letter word / D.I.V.O.R.C.E. / Weekend soldier / Join the army and . . . / Coat of many colours / Wellies / Willies / Schooldays / The janny song / Ivan the terrible / No place like home / The Queen's Christmas party / Leather breeches / Back to school / Oh! no! / "Wellies" off.

Jul 76. (7") *(2058 748)* **NO CHANCE (NO CHARGE). / IT'S NO GOTTA NAME** [24] [-]

Dec 76. (lp/c) *(2383/3170 368)* **ATLANTIC BRIDGE** [20] [-]
– Dunfermalino – Stars on Sunday / The Orient express / The two Laplanders / Rentalaugh – The vaseline salesmen / Rodney & Cynthia / My grandfathers clock / A Partick lullabye / The shitkickers waltz / Half-stoned cowboy / The optician / They'll never put this on a record / Death / Hot time in the old town / Japanese doctor / The American welly boot song.

Jan 78. (lp/c) *(2383/3170 463)* **RAW MEAT FOR THE BALCONY** [57] [-]
– Isn't it a shame / Pain in my ass / The walker . . . the parachutist / As usual / Have you ever thought about being a pervert / Football violence / John Stonehouse went swimming / Gandhi's revenge / Two little boys in blue / The death of Robin Hood / The Scottish fighting man / Closin' time (Cryin' time) / The welly boot song.

Jan 79. (7") *(POSP 21)* **I COULDN'T SPELL ****. / COUNTRY & WESTERN SUPER SONG** [ ] [-]

1979. (7") *(POSP 89)* **THE WELLY BOOTS. / IN THE BROWNIES** [ ] [-]

Aug 79. (7") *(2059 160)* **IN THE BROWNIES. / WOKE UP THIS MORNING** [38] [-]

Oct 79. (lp/c) *(2383/3170 543)* **RIOTOUS ASSEMBLY** [ ] [-]
– In the brownies / When in Rome / Teenage parties / Marvo and the lovely Doreen / Old-fashioned Tennessee waltz / Welly blues / Doctor . . . the optician / Glasgow high court / Sexy Sadie and lovely Raquel / In appreciation (welly boot march).

Nov 80. (7") *(POSP 201)* **TELL LAURA I LOVE HER. / YOOTHA'S SONG** [ ] [-]

Jun 83. (7") *(POSP 549)* **YOU TAKE MY PHOTOGRAPH (I BREAK YOUR FACE). / OZ MOZ** [ ] [-]

Jul 83. (lp/c) *(POLD/+C 5077)* **A CHANGE IS AS GOOD AS ARREST** [ ] [-]
– Jesus Christ, I'm nearly 40 / Bram Stoker sucks / Hey Dolores / Jock's rap / You take my photograph (I break your face) / A day in the country / Oz moz / Goodbye Wranglers, hello Calvin Klein / The half bottle / How rotten for Daphne / I wish I was in Glasgow.

Stiff not iss.

Mar 85. (7") *(BUY 218)* **SUPER GRAN. / YOOTHA'S SONG** [32] [-]
(one-side-7"sha-pic-d) *(DBUY 218)* – ('A'side).

Audiotrax not iss.

Jun 85. (7"; as BILLY CONNOLLY with CHRIS TUMMINGS & SINGING REBELS BAND) *(ATX 10)* **FREEDOM. / Jimmy Helms: CELEBRATION** [ ] [-]

(above featured GEORGE HARRISON, RINGO STARR and ERIC CLAPTON)

10-Virgin not iss.

Nov 87. (lp/c/cd) *(DIX/CDIX/DIXCD 65)* **BILLY AND ALBERT** [81] [-]
– President of America / The Pope / Australian talent show / Edinburgh festival / Learning the banjo / Dachshund / Nuclear / Jey lag / Box of chocolates / Hotel room in Perth / Condoms / Variety theatre / Childhood songs / Visiting Scotland / Wee brown dogs / Neck lumps / The casual vomit / Driving the porcelain truck / Something has to give. *(re-iss. Oct94 on 'Virgin' cd/c; VCC CD/MC 006)*

— In Oct'90, BILLY featured on 'THE DREAMSTONE' TV series/album released on 'Adventure' *(ADVT CD/TC/LP)*

Virgin not iss.

Oct 91. (cd/c) *(CDV/TCV 2678)* **LIVE – AT THE ODEON HAMMERSMITH, LONDON** [ ] [-]
– Doomsday / Parliament / Pitt bulls / Sheep dogs / Doggy sex / Multiple orgasms / Longevity of sex / Algebra / Chatting up woman / Crimplene suits / Underpants / Tweed trousers / Scottish holidays / Don't drink the water / Sunny Spain / Fresh air fortnight / Army beds / Swimming in the North Sea / Sumo wrestlers / We don't belong, in there / I laughed / It goes away.

Polygram TV Tickety-Boo

Dec 95. (cd/c) *(529 036-2/-4)* <529 816-2> **MUSICAL TOUR OF SCOTLAND** [ ] [ ]
– Banjoland / The islands theme / The waltzing fool / Tangle of the isles theme / Glasgow / Flower of Scotland theme / Campbell's farewell / Will ye go / From here to Claire / The islands / Waltz of the waves / Tangle of the isles / Barges / Flower of Scotland / Glasgow theme / Will ye go theme / Irish heartbeat.

– compilations, others, etc. –

Sep 75. (lp) *Transatlantic; (TRA SAM 32)* **WORDS AND MUSIC** [34] [-]
– If it was'nae for your wellies / Everybody knows that / Saltcoats at the fair / Silk pyjamas / Harry Campbell and the heavies / Leo McGuire's song / Stainless steel wellies / Little blue lady / Give me a little of your time / The music teacher – Marie's wedding.

Oct 76. (d-lp) *Transatlantic; (GAR 1)* **THE CONNOLLY GOLDEN GIFT BOX** [ ] [-]
– (LIVE! + SOLO CONCERT).

Aug 77. (lp) *Hallmark; (SHM 927)* **BILLY CONNOLLY** [ ] [-]

Feb 78. (d-lp/c) *Pickwick; (PDA/PDC 035)* **THE BILLY CONNOLLY COLLECTION** [ ] [-]

Jul 78. (lp/c) *Xtra; (MTRA/KMTRA 2008)* **ANTHOLOGY** [ ] [-]

1979. (lp) *Transatlantic; (TRA SAM 38)* **THE BIG YIN; MORE WORDS AND MUSIC FROM BILLY CONNOLLY** [ ] [-]

Nov 81. (lp/c) *Polydor; (POL TV/VM 15)* **THE PICK OF BILLY CONNOLLY** [23] [-]

(re-iss. Nov83 lp/c; SPE LP/MC 57) (re-iss. May93 on 'Spectrum' cd/c; 550 036-2/-4)

Feb 83. (lp/c) *Spot; (SPR/SPC 8530)* **BILLY CONNOLLY IN CONCERT** [ ] [-]

Apr 84. (d-lp/d-c) *Cambra; (CR/+T 133)* **A BIG YIN DOUBLE HELPING** [ ] [-]

Dec 85. (lp/c) *Philips; (PHH/+C 2)* **WRECK ON TOUR** [ ] [-]

Feb 89. (cd/c/lp) *Scotdisc; (CD/K+/ITV 451)* **THE PORTRAIT** [ ] [-]

Sep 89. (d-lp/c/cd) *Castle; (CCS LP/MC/CD 218)* **THE COLLECTION: ON TOUR WITH THE BIG YIN** [ ] [-]

Jun 95. (cd/c) *Truetrax; (TRT CD/MC 176)* **LIVE – IN CONCERT** [ ] [-]

Jun 98. (cd) *Recall; (194)* **DAY IN THE LIFE OF** [ ] [-]

Aug 99. (cd) *Castle Pie; (PIESD 021)* **COMEDY AND SONGS** [ ] [-]
– Glasgow accents – nine and a half guitars / Marie's wedding (musical appreciation) / The jobbie weecha / Short haired police cadet / Harry Campbell and the heavies / Leo McGuire's story / Life in the day of / Stainless steel wellies / Telling lies.

Another comedian/singer born on the other side of Scotland was . . .

Bill BARCLAY

(b.22 Feb'43, South Lorne Place, Leith, Edinburgh). After leaving Norton Park secondary, young football-daft BILL took up many a job including an apprentice joiner, a dining car waiter and his most long-serving (four years) as an operating theatre technician at Edinburgh's Western General Hospital. During these times, BILL turned his hand to singing and joined a skiffle band playing washboard and the tea-chest bass.

In the early 60's, aged only eighteen, BARCLAY formed his own folk group, The DOOBRIES (no brothers involved!). They included co-founder JIMMY McKINLAY and Canadian IAIN JARDINE McINTYRE who replaced original banjo player MARTIN SINCLAIR. After a few years playing the local toilet circuits, the band gradually fell by the wayside leaving BILL to sing all the songs. Like CONNOLLY at the time, BARCLAY began interspersing his folk-orientated songs with jokes and one-liners; as BILL has commented, "the jokes were going down better than the songs".

He eventually packed in his hospital job and went professional in the early 70's, gigs at festivals and folk clubs had his comic reputation growing with each week. In 1974, BILL received his first major break came when he supported ROD STEWART on his UK tour; a debut single, the hilarious 'THE TWELVE DAYS OF CHRISTMAS' was released soon afterwards. The following year, he was the warm-up support act to ELTON JOHN at one-off concert at the Playhouse; a gig with rock'n'roll giant BILL HALEY at the Apollo, Glasgow was also a claim to fame. BARCLAY subsequently travelled down south to London's Theatre Royal, where he performed three nights with DUSTY SPRINGFIELD (the only man to do so, me thinks?); rock festivals at Reading, White City and Lincoln spread him over a larger audience which helped boost sales of his albums, 'ALMOST LIVE' (1975) and 'VIVA DUNBAR' (1977).

Much in the same way as CONNOLLY again, but without the same media praise and success, BILL took to acting. He has appeared in many a major Scottish-production TV play, including 'Sense Of Freedom', 'Down Where The Buffalo Roam', 'Shoot For The Gun', 'Gunfight At The Joey Kaye Coral', 'Down Among The Big Boys' (as the police sergeant opposite CONNOLLY) and 'Taking Over The Asylum'; more police character work has come via 'Taggart', 'Rab C. Nesbitt' and 'Take The High Road'. From the early 80's until now, BILL has presented/compered for Radio Forth on their lunchtime shows.

In 1990, the gigantic folk/trad imprint, 'Greentrax', released his greatest moments, 'THE VERY BEST OF . . .', although his proudest moments have been giving laughs to his fanclub abroad in Iraq and the Middle East, Hong Kong and Germany. (Thanks to BILL for the e-mail.)

BILL BARCLAY – vocals, acoustic guitar

G.M. not iss.

Nov 74. (7") *(GMS 31)* **THE TWELVE DAYS OF CHRISTMAS. / DOES YOUR HAIR HANG LOW?** ☐ -

(re-iss. Nov77; GMS 9041)

1975. (lp) *(GML 1016)* **ALMOST LIVE** ☐ -
– (introduction) / Railway porter / American tour '72 / Camp in the country / The bookie / Epsom races / Mr. Sax / Does your hair hang low? / Language barrier / Edinburgh / Jeely piece song / Two wee hard men / The twelve days of Christmas / In which Bill Barclay bids farewell.

1975. (7") *(GMS 35)* **AIN'T GONNA DRINK NO MORE. / PASSING SHOW** ☐ -

Pye not iss.

Jan 77. (lp) *(PKL 5555)* **VIVA DUNBAR** ☐ -
– (Wayne Marshall introduces Bill Barclay) / Ah, bisto – Bill and Ben – Siamese twins / Viva Dunbar / Fokkers / Five foot two, eyes of blue / Dishes in the sink / Glass knickers / Doctor's surgery / Rooster / Bee sting – Irishman / Tall tale / Barnyards of Delgaty / (band introduction) / Scottish knock – Neighbours / D-day dodgers / Doctor and the girl / Polly had a poodle / Concert in the rain – Hebridean evening / Bye bye blackbird.

Safari not iss.

Jun 78. (7") *(NIL 1)* **HOAT PIES FOR US ARGENTINA. / MY OLD MAN LAYS CARPETS** ☐ -

Nov 78. (7") *(SAFE 12)* **BURNS NIGHT FEVER. / GUINNESS BOOK OF RECORDS** ☐ -

Nov 79. (7") *(SAFE 20)* **HEY JIMMY. / I'M GOING TO SEE A . . . .** ☐ -

Nov 79. (lp) *(BOOB 1)* **HALF ALIVE** ☐ -

Greentrax not iss.

Mar 90. (c/lp) *(C+/TRAX 035)* **THE VERY BEST OF BILL BARCLAY** ☐ -
– Ghost train – The Falkland Islands / Blood bats / A plague of moths / Does your hair hang low? / Rock'n'yule / My old man lays carpets / The sports section / The travel agent / The Scottish G.I. / Polly had a poodle / Chapati junction – The polis / The twelves days of Christmas.

Nov 90. (7") *(STRAX 1002)* **THE TWELVES DAYS OF CHRISTMAS. / POLLY HAD A POODLE** ☐ -

Another more cerebral comedian hailing from the east coast was . . .

Graeme GARDEN

(b.18 Feb'43, Aberdeen). Along with fellow English-born Cambridge University graduates, BILL ODDIE and TIM BROOKE-TAYLOR, GRAEME progressed from the Footlights Revue of the early 60's to the pioneering and oft hilarious BBC Radio show, 'I'm Sorry I'll Read That Again'; in fact, GRAEME superseded GRAHAM CHAPMAN who went on to become part of the rival Monty Python team. While TV work beckoned for song/skit-writer ODDIE and the equally talented BROOKE-TAYLOR, the bespectacled Mr. GARDEN had become a qualified doctor after serving his time at King's College Hospital in London.

In 1970, and with the 'Python team on our screens every week, the witty pranksters got together again for a pilot TV show premiered that November as The GOODIES. This was the start of several series for the Beeb, with GRAEME usually playing the laid-back, straight-laced guy trying to calm things down between the manic BILL and TIM. Towards the end of 1974, The GOODIES even entered the singles chart with 'The In Betweenies', backed by the festive 'Father Christmas Do Not Touch Me'. Indeed, the novelty trio – with mainly the experienced ODDIE as lyricist – had four further pokes into the pop charts (all in the space of a year!):- 'Funky Gibbon', 'Black Pudding Bertha (The Queen Of Northern Soul)', 'Nappy Love / Wild Thing' and 'Make A Daft Noise For Christmas'. However, by the early 80's the joke had run a bit thin and the trio went their separate ways; ODDIE became a TV presenter on the rather unlikely subject of ornithology, BROOKE-TAYLOR tried out his hand at acting in sit-coms, while the brainy GG worked as the compere on radio/TV quiz shows, etc.

Although there were several top Scots DJ's around (STUART HENRY and TONY MEEHAN were probably the most famous), only one got around to actually releasing a record/7". Glasgow's

TIGER TIM

(wearer of hideous "tiger" attire!) was a short, cheeky presenter who also presented various children's show for TV around the mid-late 70's.

– TIGER's discography –

G.T.O. not iss.

May 75. (7") *(GT 22)* **STARGIRL. / YES I WILL** ☐ -

President not iss.

Dec 75. (7") *(PT 445)* **MERRY CHRISTMAS MR. CHRISTMAS. / MOVING ON** ☐ -

The immortal words "Hey, Budgie" (in a mandatory, gravel-voiced Glaswegian accent) came from the throat of

Iain CUTHBERTSON

A lasting gift to popular culture, the Scots-born actor having played the hard-man gangster, CHARLIE ENDELL in the 70's cult TV series 'Budgie' (starring former pop star, ADAM FAITH). CUTHBERTSON's own bid for pop stardom came in the shape of 'MACK THE KNIFE' (Decca; F 13326), a growling rendition of the crooning standard released under his screen character.

The 70's heralded a golden era of Scottish stand-up spearheaded by the surprise success of the aforementioned BILLY CONNOLLY (and to a lesser extent, BILL BARCLAY), a long-haired, bearded renegade from the folk revival who won the hearts and minds of the nation (England included) with his expletive filled tall tales of hard-bitten Glasgow life; both have their own discographical entries in the book's Folk section. In the wake of CONNOLLY's massive popularity, Glasgow comedians such as JOHNNY BEATTIE, HECTOR NICOL and ANDY CAMERON became relatively famous and made the obligatory singles/albums (see entry for 'Klub' below).

Also from that neck of the woods (Greenock, to be exact), eccentric veteran genius of the one-liners,

Chic MURRAY

(b. CHARLES THOMAS McKINNON MURRAY, 1919), left his mark on the world via his own cabaret stage act 'The Chic Murray Show', a string of film appearances ('Casino Royale' and 'Gregory's Girl') and a one-off football song. A man ahead of his time (especially with that ubiquitous bunnet), CHIC was commemorated in 'The Chic Murray Story', a play performed at the 1997 Edinburgh Festival twelve years after his untimely death. The aforementioned football song was recorded during Scotland's 1974 campaign . . .

An avalanche of vinyl was unleashed in the name of the

SCOTLAND WORLD CUP SQUAD

It all began in 1974 when we actually qualified for the first time in living memory (mine's at least!). With England kicking off the football theme song craze four years previous (forgetting Glasgow-born LONNIE DONEGAN's 'World Cup Willie' in '66) via the chart-topping 'Back Home', the Scotland squad entered the studio to record their very own 'EASY EASY'. Although the song did pretty well and even made the national Top 20, Scotland, as per usual, caught an early flight home from West Germany. Heading that year's list of unofficial entries to football's equivalent of the Eurovision Song Contest was the aforementioned comedian CHIC MURRAY with 'IT'S A' SCOTLAND' – released on 'Waverley' (SLP 549) – followed by SYDNEY DEVINE's tribute to manager Willie Ormond ('Oor Wee Willie') and The ALEXANDER BROTHERS with 'Bonnie Scotland Evermore'. It goes without saying of course, that the vast majority of the players (including gap-toothed Joe Jordan, big Jim Holton and wee Billy Bremner) were better suited to shouting obscenities on the park rather than singing in tune on vinyl.

Four years later in 1978, 'Ally's Tartan Army' was ready to take on the world once more, well at least ANDY CAMERON was. Despite the disastrous Argentina campaign, at least this song remained for posterity as probably the finest example of a much-maligned genre. Well, certainly compared to that year's official World Cup Squad anthem where the players were accompanied by adopted Scot, ROD STEWART on 'OLE OLA'; as if short-lived manager Ally McLeod didn't have enough on his plate! The same old musical faces (bar JOHNNY BEATTIE) were trundled out again in '78 with their own "inspirational gems" i.e. SYDNEY DEVINE (this time with a minor hit, 'Scotland Forever') and The ALEXANDER BROTHERS ('Scotland Scotland'); the SCOTLAND SONS also released 'Hey Argentina' / 'Flower Of Scotland'.

With the concept of a World Cup song now as familiar as the obligatory first stage exit, the "tunes" came thick and fast during the 80's and 90's as Scotland incredibly qualified for six finals out of a possible seven (1994 being the annus horribilis). Among the chart highlights were 1982's 'WE HAVE A DREAM' (and it stayed just that) and 1990's 'SAY IT WITH PRIDE', the latter featuring a host of Scottish celebs. Although 1994 was a fallow year for the Scottish team, compensation was forthcoming via qualification (the first time ever!) for the European Championship Finals (Euro '96). Going head to head in the UK Top 20 were the official ROD STEWART's 'PURPLE HEATHER' and PRIMAL SCREAM's infinitely superior 'The Big Man And The Scream Team Meet The Barmy Army Uptown'. Despite getting stuffed by the Auld Enemy twice in succession (in the aforementioned Euro campaign and then again in a two-leg play-off for Euro 2000), Scotland again qualified for the World Cup Finals in 1998. From 1974's boastful 'EASY EASY', DEL AMITRI were now begging the team 'Don't Come Home Too Soon' (enough said) . . .

– discography –

	Polydor	not iss.
May 74. (lp) *(2383 282)* **EASY EASY**	3	-
Jun 74. (7") *(2058 452)* **EASY EASY. / SCOTLAND SCOTLAND**	20	-
	Riva	not iss.
May 78. (7"; as ROD STEWART featuring The SCOTTISH WORLD CUP FOOTBALL SQUAD) *(Riva 15)* **OLE OLA (MULHER BRASILEIRA). / I'D WALK A MILLION MILES FOR ONE**	4	-
	Klub	not iss.
Jun 78. (lp) *(KLP 8)* **ARGENTINA '78**		-

— now credited to the **SCOTTISH WORLD CUP SQUAD**

	WEA	not iss.
Apr 82. (7") *(K 19145)* **WE HAVE A DREAM. / WRAP UP THE CUP**	5	-
	Columbia	not iss.
Apr 86. (7") *(DB 9130)* **BIG TRIP TO MEXICO. / CARRY THE HOPES OF SCOTLAND**		-
	R.C.A.	not iss.
Jun 90. (7") *(PB 43791)* **SAY IT WITH PRIDE. / ('A'version)**	45	-

(12"+=/cd-s+=) *(PT/PD 43791)* – ('A'extended).

	Warners	not iss.
Jun 96. (cd-s; by ROD STEWART with The SCOTTISH EURO '96 SQUAD) *(W 0354CD)* **PURPLE HEATHER**	16	-

— in 1998, DEL AMITRI scored a Top 20 hit (alongside the Scotland squad) with the pleading 'Don't Come Home Too Soon'.

— Note: Apologies to anyone looking for singles/songs by Scotland's domestic teams (they know who they are) but this wee footballing extraganza is strictly a one-off and a bit of neccessary fun.

Klub records, for whom the SCOTLAND squad recorded in 1978, also hosted three of Glasgow's best loved comedians. The imprint's first and only major hit came via well-known blue-nose joke-teller

Andy CAMERON

Scotland had gone to the World Cup Finals with insanely high hopes after beating a rampant path through the qualifying rounds. Their early exit went down in the history books for all the wrong reasons but at least one aspect of the campaign is worth remembering: the theme song. 'ALLY'S TARTAN ARMY' (as in Ally McLeod, Scotland's optimistic manager!), surely ranks as the all-time greatest World Cup anthem and certainly CAMERON's fifteen (nae, three) minutes of fame. A die-hard Rangers supporter, CAMERON has er, graced our TV screens for the last several years courtesy of long-running Scottish soap, 'High Road'.

Preceding this hit by a year (or so), was a side-splitting debut LP by the notorious

Hector NICOL

a blue comic who held a 5-year residency at the infamous Ashfield Club; one of his subsequent albums, 'BRAVO JULIET' (a play on words of the TV female cop, 'Juliet Bravo') even made the Top 100. However, it would be as an actor that HECTOR would arguably make his most memorable performance. Few would forget his appearance in the Peter McDougall play, 'Just A Boy's Game', when he hissed the death-bed line, "see you son, A've never liked you" to character grandson and fellow performer turned actor FRANKIE MILLER.

Last but not least was. . .

Johnny BEATTIE

a comedian of the old school who recorded a couple of low-key efforts (including 'Snookeroo') in the mid-80's (for 'Klub' singers, see under Lochshore records).

– Klub records discography (comedians only) –

Jun 77. (lp) *(KLP 2)* **HECTOR NICOL – Laffin Room Only**

(above was originally issued on 'New Key' records (NKR 900L/P))

Jan 78. (lp) *(KLP 3)* **HECTOR NICOL – The Lady And The Champ**		
Feb 78. (7") *(Klub 3)* **ANDY CAMERON – Ally's Tartan Army / I Want To Be A Punk Rocker**	6	
Apr 78. (lp) *(KLP 5)* **ANDY CAMERON – Andy's Tartan Album**		
May 78. (7") *(Klub 6)* **ANDY CAMERON – We'll Be There Over There / Don't Cry For Us Argentina**		
May 78. (lp) *(KLP 7)* **HECTOR NICOL – Scotch And Full Of It**		
Nov 79. (lp/c) *(KLP/ZCKLP 17)* **HECTOR NICOL – Cop Of The North**		
Nov 80. (lp/c) *(KLP/ZCKLP 24)* **HECTOR NICOL – The Hobo Sexual**		
Mar 82. (7") *(Klub 33)* **ANDY CAMERON – We're On The March Again / Scotland**		
Nov 82. (lp/c) *(KLP/ZCKLP 37)* **HECTOR NICOL – I'm A Country Member (Brand X)**		
Nov 83. (7") *(Klub 44)* **JOHNNY BEATTIE – Glasgow Rap / The B Rap**		
Apr 84. (lp/c) *(KLP/ZCKLP 42)* **HECTOR NICOL – Bravo Juliet**	92	-
Nov 85. (7") *(Klub 56)* **JOHNNY BEATTIE – Snooker / The Wee Cock Sparrer**		
Nov 88. (lp/c) *(KLP/ZCKLP 67)* **JOHNNY BEATTIE – Tribute To The Kings Of Scottish Comedy**		

The election of MAGGIE THATCHER in 1979 heralded major political and culture change (usually for the worse) but more importantly, provided unprecedented material for budding comedians/impersonators. One of the most accurate impersonators of Mrs.T was Scotland's own

Janet BROWN

who ventured onto vinyl that fateful year with the 'IRON LADY' single.

Preceding JANET by a few years was all-round entertainer. . .

Allan STEWART

who also tried his hand at impersonating celebs as well as singing and stand-up comedy. He would go on to host his own TV variety show, although little was heard from him after the early 80's dawn of Alternative comedy.

– discography ALLAN STEWART –

	Penny Farthing	not iss.
May 74. (7") *(PEN 838)* **BRAVE NEW WORLD. / TOMORROW IS THE FIRST DAY**		-
Aug 74. (7") *(PEN 848)* **HOLD ME. / HE'S GOT THE WHOLE WORLD IN HIS HAND**		-
Aug 75. (7") *(PEN 887)* **WHO TURNED THE LIGHT OUT ON MY LIFE. / BRAVE NEW WORLD**		-
	Rampage	not iss.
Apr 78. (7") *(RAM 3)* **OPENING NIGHT. / BRAVE NEW WORLD**		-
Aug 78. (7") *(RAM 9)* **HEAVEN ABOVE. / HOW I SEE MY LOVE**		-

Two Scots doing the Alternative thing in their own inimitable way were ROBBIE COLTRANE and RORY BREMNER. The larger than life

Robbie COLTRANE

(b. ROBERT MacMILLAN, 1950, Rutherglen) trod the boards for the likes of the Traverse Theatre before making his name with 'Comic Strip Presents . . .' alongside Rik Mayall, Ade Edmundson, Nigel Planer, French & Saunders, Keith Allen, etc. One of the biggest successes of his career however, came with John Byrne's gritty TV black comedy, 'Tutti Frutti', in 1987; COLTRANE played a beer-swilling frontman for a hard-touring C&W-inspired combo. He's never been out of work since, starring in major 90's films including 'Nuns On The Run', 'Peter's Friends' and 'Goldeneye'.

Rory BREMNER

(b.1951, Morningside, Edinburgh), meanwhile, made his mark on the satirical 80's puppet-fest, 'Spitting Image', making his way (albeit in the background) to No.1 via 'The Chicken Song'. I'm not sure, but wasn't he the man behind a spoof version of Paul Hardcastle's 'N-N-Nineteen'.

If confrontation was your comedy bag, then Glasgow-born

Craig FERGUSON

(aka BING HITLER) was your man. A bonafide manic street preacher, BING mercilessly taunted his audiences into submission with a series of verbal assaults all in the name of comedy. Arguably Scotland's funniest comedian during the 80's, CRAIG subsequently killed off his alter-ego and successfully turned his hand to acting in the 90's. Having taken a lead role in the stage productions of 'The Rocky Horror Show' and 'The Odd Couple', he relocated to the States where he eventually found fame as Mr.Wick on 'The Drew Carey Show'. Of late, Hollywood has taken FERGUSON to its glamorous bosom with the man playing a camp Scottish hairdresser in the movie, 'The Big Tease'.

– discography –

Jammy / not iss.

Oct 86. (lp/c) *(JR LP/CP 861)* **BING HITLER LIVE AT THE TRON (live)** ☐ -

Polydor / not iss.

Nov 88. (7") *(PO 26)* **SCOTLAND (HOOCH OCH AYE). / BITE / HOOCH OCH AYE (live)** ☐ -

Nov 88. (lp/c) *(837643-1/-4)* **MENTAL . . . BING HITLER IS DEAD?** ☐ -
– Thor / Scandinavians / Turkey in the Eurovision Song Contest / Explorers / Philosophers and sex / Advertising and sex / Wrestling round 1 / Scotland hooch och aye / Wrestling round 2 / Meaningless songs / The compendium of games / Scary television / Bite.

A camp double act . . .

VICTOR & BARRY

were equal parts STANLEY BAXTER and HINGE & BRACKETT. Sporting Kelvinside accents and dandy attire to boot, the pair supposedly emerged from deepest Glasgow before first hitting stage and screen in the late 80's. The alter-egos of Angus-born ALAN CUMMING and Falkirk-born FORBES MASSON, VICTOR & BARRY minced their way onto vinyl in 1988 with the tongue-up-cheek 'GLASGOW' single. They subsequently graced the small screen as flight attendants in the semi-successful 'The High Life'. Nowadays, CUMMING makes his living as a film actor (and theatre in the US), while his former sidekick MASSON recently took a serious role in Eastenders.

– discography –

Jammy / not iss.

Dec 88. (7") *(JRS 881)* **GLASGOW. /** ☐ -

Dec 88. (c) *(JRCP 881)* **HEAR VICTOR & BARRY AND FAINT** ☐ -
– Kelvinside men / Marks & Spencers / Recipe of life / A smile costs nothing / Glasgow / The Proclaimers song / It's hard being a celebrity / Why isn't things the way they used to be / Dreams can come true.

An oddity of the Scottish comedy scene,

ST. ANDREW & THE WOOLLEN MILL

were a mid-80's Dundee crew that at various times numbered the likes of newsreader JACKIE BIRD and singer/songwriter MICHAEL MARRA among the ranks; their repertoire included renditions of MARRA's 'Baps And Pastel', 'Hermless' and 'Zorro'. The mysterious man known as ST. ANDREW usually sported a pair of green wellies, which curious readers can see for themselves on their one and only video.

– discography –

Dark Side Of The . . . / not iss.

Jul 86. (7") *(DHS 001)* **PINBALL WIZARD. / THE SKYE BOAT SONG** ☐ -

1980's. (cd) **THE WOOLLEN MILL STORY** ☐ -

Probably the most successful sit-com of the 90's was 'One Foot In The Grave', introducing . . .

Richard WILSON

as possibly the most grouchy old man on TV, VICTOR MELDREW. The bane of actress ANNETTE CROSBIE's screen life, VICTOR/RICHARD also featured on the show's theme tune, released as a collaborative Top 50 single (with ERIC IDLE) towards the end of '94.

Surely SEAN's shuccessor (sic!) to Scotland's thespian throne . . .

Ewan McGREGOR

(b.31 Mar'71, Crieff, Perthshire) put a face to Irvine Welsh's seminal novel 'Trainspotting'. After leaving school, McGREGOR became part of the Perth Repertory Theatre which led to a place at the Guildhall School of Music and Drama; he'd previously picked up awards for his French horn playing at high school. From there, the boyish actor landed a part in Dennis Potter's TV musical/drama, 'Lipstick On Your Collar' (screened 1993). Noteable roles in 'Scarlet & Black' and Bill Forsyth's 'Being Human', paved the way for a starring role in the Scots-made 1994 (Danny Boyle-directed) movie, 'Shallow Grave'. Boyle once again offered EWAN a major starring role, this time as drug-addict, Mark Renton, in the cult 1996 movie, 'Trainspotting' – truly one of the all-time classics and possibly *the* film of the 90's. His celluloid dialogue/voiceover was utilised by dance duo, PF PROJECT (aka JAMIE WHITE and MOOSE), late in '97, the track 'CHOOSE LIFE' earning the co-credited EWAN and the group an unusual UK Top 10 hit (No.6); it could also be heard on the soundtrack of 'Trainspotting #2'. He subsequently learned how to play some banjo from the master himself, BILLY CONNOLLY. Starring and singing in the musical, 'Moulin Rouge', EWAN (with co-star Nicole Kidman) even managed to hit the UK No.27 in September 2001 courtesy of the single, 'COME WHAT MAY'.

Filmography: Lipstick On Your Collar (TV; 1993) / Scarlet & Black (TV; 1993) / Shallow Grave (1994) / Blue Juice (1995) / Trainspotting (1996) / Brassed Off (1996) / The Pillow Book (1996) / A Life Less Ordinary (1997) / The Serpent's Kiss (1997) / Rogue Trader (1998) / Little Voice (1998) / Velvet Goldmine (1998; he played IGGY POP) / Nightwatch (1998) / Eye Of The Beholder (1999) / Star Wars: Episode 1 – The Phantom Menace (1999) / Nora (2000) / Moulin Rouge (2001).

Dean PARK

the fresh-faced comedian/singer issued a few singles; in Nov'01 he released 'IN CONCERT' for the 'Robert C Kelly' imprint; earlier that year saw the EP 'WEE ANDY WEBBER'S SCOTTISH MEDLEY'.

* * * * *

Child Entertainers

A wee history: By the early 70's, the days when children were seen and not heard was unfortunately over. While America had previously enthused over teeny stars such as SHIRLEY TEMPLE, MICKEY ROONEY and JUDY GARLAND back in the pre-war showbiz boom, Scotland made up for lost time with a vengeance as the likes of NEIL REID and LENA ZAVARONI terrorised Top Of The Pops during the spangly 70's. Forget DONNY OSMOND's 'Puppy Love' and MICHAEL JACKSON's 'Rockin' Robin', Scotland had to contend with NEIL REID's 'Mother Of Mine' and LENA ZAVARONI's 'Ma, He's Making Eyes At Me'. If the 70's were hard to take, then the 80's were a damn sight worse; we're talking Bonnie Langford and The KRANKIES here. Thankfully the 90's have been a bit subdued on the child front as Scots kids presumably spend most of their time playing with their Gameboys while Welsh choirmeisters ALED JONES and CHARLOTTE CHURCH rake in the dosh.

* * * * *

Neil REID

was born in 1960, Motherwell, Lanarkshire. Before NEIL was even into double figures, the young schoolboy was singing in local working men's clubs, augmenting his keyboard-playing uncle. At the age of eleven, his parents and teacher helped him enter Hughie Green's 'Opportunity Knocks', a TV talent competition that he won no less than three times. At the break of '72 and with a contract on 'Decca', the baby-faced NEIL was all the rage as his tearjerking pop ballad 'MOTHER OF MINE' (penned by BILL PARKINSON of pop group, P.A.T.C.H.) nearly hit the coveted No.1 spot. However, the grannies and easy-listening brigade up and down the country hit the shops in droves when his eponymous debut LP was released. It subsequently topped the chart for three weeks, knocking off T.REX's 'Electric Warrior' in the process – a 20th Century Boy, indeed.

NEIL's glory days were numbered though and after a follow-up 45, 'THAT'S WHAT I WANT TO BE', failed to crack the Top 50, it seemed NEIL's musical career was over before his 12th birthday. While the teenyboppers bought The OSMONDS and The JACKSONS, NEIL suffered flop after flop, although foreign tours and a conversion to Christianity kept his profile in the spotlight. Having put up with producers wanting him to sound "young", the teenager retired from the biz and worked in burger joints and other jobs to support himself. Performing only occasionally for relatives and friends, NEIL ended up being a successful salesman while taking up residence in Blackpool with his new family.

- discography -

		Decca	not iss.
Dec 71.	(7") *(F 13264)* **MOTHER OF MINE. / IF I COULD WRITE A SONG**	2	
Jan 72.	(lp) *(SKL 5122)* **NEIL REID**	1	-
Mar 72.	(7") *(F 13300)* **THAT'S WHAT I WANT TO BE. / IF WISHES WERE SHIPS**	45	-
Aug 72.	(lp) *(SKL 5136)* **SMILE**	47	-
Jun 73.	(7") *(F 13410)* **END OF THE WORLD. / JOANNA, MARRY ME**		-
Jul 73.	(lp) **I'LL WALK WITH GOD**		-
		Philips	not iss.
1974.	(7") *(6006 389)* **HAZEL EYES. / YOU'RE THE WINE IN MY LIFE**		-

— NEIL retired in the mid-70's only to briefly return in the early 80's

- compilations, others, etc. -

Sep 85.	(7") *Old Gold; (OG 9538)* **MOTHER OF MINE. / ALL KINDS OF EVERYTHING**		-

Lena ZAVARONI

was born on 4 Nov'63, Rothesay, Isle of Bute. A pre-pubescent star, little LENA got her first break on TV talent contest, Opportunity Knocks, before she'd reached her 10th birthday. Younger even than previous winner NEIL REID, the pint-sized singer possessed a rasping yell that even put LULU to shame. The winning song in question, 'MA, HE'S MAKING EYES AT ME' (an old Johnny Otis number), became her debut single, a subsequent UK Top 10 early in '74. However, the formula was wearing a little thin even by the release of follow-up, 'PERSONALITY' (another revamped R&B chestnut, this time by Lloyd Price), a minor Top 40 hit. During this brief heyday, LENA also shared a stage with FRANK SINATRA and even performed for then US President, Gerald Ford.

Tragically, her talent proved her undoing as the youngster struggled to cope with homesickness while attending an exclusive stage school in London. At the age of only 13, LENA was diagnosed as suffering from anorexia, a condition she struggled with for over two decades amid a number of unsuccessful comeback attempts. As a last resort, she underwent a tricky brain operation even though her weight was under five stone. She never recovered and died at the age of only 35. In many respects, she could well have been the JUDY GARLAND of her day had the ever growing scourge of anorexia not taken hold.

- discography -

		Philips	not iss.
Jan 74.	(7") *(6006 367)* **MA, HE'S MAKING EYES AT ME. / ROCK-A-BYE YOUR BABY WITH A DIXIE MELODY**	10	-
Mar 74.	(lp) *(6308 201)* **MA, HE'S MAKING EYES AT ME** – *(re-iss. Nov76 on 'Hallmark'; SHM 891)*	8	-
May 74.	(7") *(6006 391)* **PERSONALITY. / SCHOOLS OUT**	33	-
Jan 75.	(lp) *(9109 200)* **IF MY FRIENDS COULD SEE ME NOW** *(re-iss. Nov76 on 'Hallmark' lp)(c; SHM 901)(HSC 277)*		-
Feb 75.	(7") *(6006 445)* **YOU'RE BREAKING MY HEART. / YOU'RE NEVER TOO OLD TO BE YOUNG**		-
Jun 75.	(7") *(6006 462)* **SMILE. / HEY, HEY, WHAT DO YOU SAY**		-
		B.B.C.	not iss.
Mar 76.	(7") *(BEEB 13)* **SOME OF THESE DAYS. / SOMETHING ABOUT YOU BABY**		-
		Galaxy	not iss.
1976.	(7") *(GX 50)* **I SHOULD'VE LISTENED TO MAMA. / OUT OF YOUR HEAD**		-
Feb 77.	(7") *(GY 114)* **AIR LOVE. / PINCH ME AM I DREAMING**		-
Mar 77.	(lp/c) *(GAL/+C 6012)* **PRESENTING LENA ZAVARONI** – Whole world in his hands / Won't somebody dance with me / Napony / As usual / Rose, Rose / Mama Tembu's wedding / Speak to me pretty / If it wasn't for you, dear / Air love / Can we make it go away / Say, has anybody seen my sweet Gypsy Rose / Pinch me, am I dreaming.		-
Apr 78.	(lp/c) *(GAL/+C 6020)* **SONGS ARE SUCH GOOD THINGS** –		-
Jul 79.	(lp/c) *(GAL/+4 6022)* **LENA ZAVARONI & HER MUSIC** – I am / You keep me dancing / Until the night / Back in time / Then again you're gonna wake up / Somebody should have told me / Dancing free / Dancing all night / I don't need a doctor / Spotlight.		-
1980.	(7") *(GX 160)* **SOMEWHERE SOUTH OF MACON. / LITTLE THINGS MEAN A LOT** *(re-iss. Sep81 on 'President'; PTZ 496)*		-
May 80.	(7") *(GY 163)* **JUMP DOWN JIMMY. / READY FOR . . .**		-
Nov 80.	(7") *(GY 177)* **WILL HE KISS ME TONIGHT? / DREAM COME TRUE**		-
		President	not iss.
Mar 81.	(7") *(PT 492)* **ROSES AND RAINBOWS. / RESERVE ME**		-
		B.B.C.	not iss.
May 82.	(lp/c) *(REB/ZCF 443)* **HOLD TIGHT, IT'S LENA** – Hold tight / I'll see you in my dreams / Ain't she sweet / The very thought of you / T'ain't what you do / Meet me in St. Louis, Louis / Sing sing sing / CC rider / Penny Lane / You needed me / It's a miracle / A certain smile / Bridge over troubled water.		-
Jun 82.	(7") *(RESL 117)* **HOLD TIGHT (WANT SOME SEAFOOD MAMA). / AIN'T SHE SWEET**		-

— she retired from the music business after her career was blighted by anorexia nervosa; she was to die weighing in at 5 stone in 1999

Wee Stuart ANDERSON

(son of accordion-player STUART ANDERSON) was another child singer to gain attention from winning the TV show, 'Opportunity Knocks'; the 6 year-old sang the traditional Scottish standard, 'BONNIE WEE JEANNIE MacCALL'. Lately, not so wee but still kitted out in his kilt, he collaborated with his dad on an album, 'Scotland Our Home'.

KRANKIES

were formed in Glasgow . . . mid-70's by pint-sized cheeky schoolboy JIMMY KRANKIE (actually a woman named JEANETTE) and his school chum; strangely, in real life the pair were a married couple. From stage and panto work, the dastardly duo made it to the small screen where they delighted kids and tortured adults with their catchphrase, "fan'dabi'dozi". Incredibly, a single inspired by the ubiquitous catchphrase entered the UK Top 50 early in '81 but thankfully their paeon to Scotland's Spanish World Cup campaign hit a bum note. The pair dressed up for celebrity TV shows and the annual pantomime season, even securing their own children's TV series.

- discography -

		Rubber	not iss.
Mar 76.	(7") *(ADUB 5)* **WHERE'S ME MUM. / BUT YOU LOVE ME DADDY**		-
		Polydor	not iss.
May 79.	(7") *(2059 128)* **CHARLIE BROWN. / SPEEDY GONZALES**		-
		Monarch	not iss.
Jan 81.	(7") *(MON 21)* **FAN'DABI'DOZI. / WEE JIMMY KRANKIE**	46	-
		R.C.A.	not iss.
Sep 81.	(7") *(RCA 119)* **JIMMY'S GANG. / WE'RE GOING TO SPAIN**		-

Dec 81. (lp/c) *(RCA LP/K 3052)* **IT'S FAN'DABI'DOZI** -

(re-iss. Nov84 lp/c; NL/NK 70494)
Feb 82. (7") *(RCA 192)* **HUBBA DUBBA DOOBY. / THE KRANKIES ROCK** -
Apr 82. (7") *(RCA 217)* **WE'RE GOING TO SPAIN. / THE HAGGIS SONG** -

Mawson & Wareham not iss.

Jun 82. (lp) *(MWM 1012)* **TWO SIDES OF THE KRANKIES** -

Relax not iss.

Oct 84. (lp/c) *(LAX LP/C 100)* **THE KRANKIES GO TO HOLLYWOOD** -
Nov 84. (7") *(LAX 2)* **HAND IN HAND AT CHRISTMAS. / GRANNIE KRANKIE MEETS THE MEN FROM MARS** -

— the KRANKIES continued with the odd TV show and appearances

- others, etc. -

1980's. (c) *V.F.M.; (VCA 627)* **KRANKIES VOL.1** -
1980's. (c) *V.F.M.; (VCA 628)* **KRANKIES VOL.2** -
1980's. (c) *V.F.M.; (VCA 629)* **KRANKIES VOL.3** -

the SINGING KETTLE

were actually CILLA FISHER and ARTIE TREZISE, formerly a much respected folk duo who made a permanent move into toddler's/children's entertainment during the early 80's. Having already released a couple of 'SINGING KETTLE'-titled cassettes, CILLA and ARTIE (and multi-instrumentalist GARY COUPLAND) adopted the name from the mid-80's onwards, enrapturing hordes of youngsters and producing a series of top selling videos. During the 90's, the 'KETTLE posse were joined by CILLA's daughter JANE and newest member KEVIN MacLEOD, with their ITV series going stronger than ever. Towards the end of the millennium, FISHER, TREZISE and COUPLAND all received an MBE in recognition of their contribution to children's entertainment. JANE departed recently to join her boyfriend's techno-punk outfit, MOTORMARK – a cross between Kraftwerk and the Sex Pistols! We await the results.

- discography -

1982. (c) *(KOPC 10)* **SINGING KETTLE 1** -
1985. (c) *(KOPC 15)* **SINGING KETTLE 2** -
Oct 88. (lp/c) *(KOP/+C 18)* **SCOTCH BROTH** -
1989. (c) *(KOPC 19)* **SINGING KETTLE 3** -
1990. (c) *(KOPC 21)* **SINGING KETTLE 4** -
1991. (c) *(KOPC 22)* **THE BIG GREEN PLANET** -
Jul 93. (c) *(KOP 24C)* **WILD WEST SHOW** -
Jul 93. (c) *(KOP 25C)* **WORLD TOUR** -
Aug 95. (cd/c) *(KOP 27 CD/C)* **GREATEST HITS VOL.1** -
Aug 95. (c) *(KOP 28C)* **PIRATES** -
May 99. (c) *(KOPC 31)* **FUNNY FARM** -
Nov 99. (c) *(KOPC 32)* **MILLENNIUM CHRISTMAS PARTY** -
Mar 00. (c/v) *(KOP 33C/KOP 34V)* **HOMEMADE BAND** -
Nov 01. (c) *(KOP 38C)* **WINTER WONDERLAND** -
Mar 02. (c/v) *(KOP 39C/KOP 40V)* **JUNGLE PARTY** -

HAPPY GANG

are a trio of colourful, over-enthusiastic adults from Edinburgh who should know better (ach well, somebody's got to do it and it is for the kids). SPATZ, NICKY and MR P have made several recordings or "goodies" as they call them on their website; the cassettes 'PING' and 'WOW' should be self-explanatory while 'SPLOOSH' is their latest.

CHICKEN SHED THEATRE

were formed in Falkirk as a youth stage production collective specialising in family entertainment. Unusually for such a project, CST released a one-off single for a major label (see below) which was even tipped to make Christmas '97 No.1 – St.Winifred's Choir please come back, all is forgiven.

- discography -

Columbia not iss.

Dec 97. (c-s/cd-s) *(665417-4/-2)* **I AM IN LOVE WITH THE WORLD / DON'T KNOW IF I BELIEVE IN CHRISTMAS / LITTLE TOMMY** 15 -

5
Jazz

All That Jazz An' That: Taken as a whole, jazz never quite captured the British popular imagination in the same way as rock'n'roll, blues and soul. Scotland was obviously no different in this respect although a relatively small coterie of musicians have always interpreted this Stateside export in unique and interesting ways. While New Orleans gave birth to the genre during the post-slavery era, Scotland didn't really start swinging to the likes of Glenn Miller, Duke Ellington and Tommy Dorsey until the Second World War was underway. A combination of radio, import singles and resident GIs ensured that jazz reached a wider British/Scottish audience than it had done in the 30's. A fair number of people were enthused enough to have a go themselves, especially when forming a Big Band with your fellow conscripts offered a welcome diversion from the ordeals of war.

The Squadronaires was one such outfit, a loose ensemble of RAF colleagues that numbered at least two Scotsmen, trombonist GEORGE CHISHOLM and trumpeter TOMMY McQUATER. Both had already cut their teeth in Glasgow, the latter lucky enough to blow for Benny Carter when he arrived on British soil in the mid-30's. After the war, CHISHOLM went on to work with the likes of Fats Waller and Louis Armstrong, while McQUATER (like CHISHOLM) subsequently worked closely with Jack Parnell. Although there was a small scene in Scotland, ambitious jazzmen took the train down south or travelled even further afield. Fifer JOE TEMPERLEY for example, initially played with Parnell before carving out a fruitful career in New York, the saxophonist subsequently appearing on a number of Broadway soundtracks. With little or no music business infrastructure in Scotland at the time, homegrown artists such as SANDY BROWN, TOMMY WHITTLE, JIMMY DEUCHAR, ALEX WELSH, The CLYDE VALLEY STOMPERS, AL FAIRWEATHER and TOMMY SAMPSON were obliged to release records mainly for London-based labels.

In fact the capital was witnessing the heyday of British Trad jazz with 50's stars like Chris Barber, Ken Colyer and Cyril Davies grooming many talented young musicians. Another famous Scot LONNIE DONEGAN passed through the ranks of Barber and Colyer's band before going on to single-handedly invent the skiffle movement and take the pop charts by storm with 'Rock Island Line'. Glasgow-born CHAS McDEVITT followed a similar if not quite so successful path (for both artists refer to Pop/Rock section part 1).

Yet by its very nature, jazz remained by and large the province of beatniks, purists and connoisseurs. By the late 60's, Trad jazz had long since fallen out of fashion, although the experimentalism of the era eventually led to the cross-fertilization of jazz and rock. While John Coltrane had blazed the trail of free-form jazz, Miles Davis ripped up the rule book with his trippy, groundbreaking fusions of jazz, funk and rock. Scotland's most noted exponent of fusion was Dumfries-born IAN CARR, who had served his time on the scene with the likes of Don Rendell, before forming cult jazz-rock act, Nucleus; guitarist JIM MULLEN also explored various avenues in this vein, notably alongside Dick Morrissey.

Pivotal to the development of the Scottish scene was undoubtedly the mid-70's formation of Edinburgh's 'Hep' records. While initially the company functioned purely as a jazz importer, it subsequently began signing its own acts including native pioneers like the aforementioned TEMPERLEY and DEUCHAR, as well as up-and-coming talent BOBBY WELLINS and MARTIN TAYLOR. Heavily influenced by Django Reinhardt, the latter guitarist made a major mark in the mainstream jazz world during the 80's and 90's as did saxophonist TOMMY SMITH. From Edinburgh's once infamous Wester Hailes to the prestigious Berklee School of Music in Boston and eventually on to the legendary 'Blue Note' imprint, it's fair to say that SMITH (a former HUE AND CRY sessioner) is the closest Scotland has come to boasting of a bonafide international jazz star.

Today, both Edinburgh and Glasgow are home to fertile jazz scenes with indigenous veterans such as CAROL KIDD, BRIAN KELLOCK and NIGEL CLARK continuing to fly the flag for Scottish jazz. Both cities also play host to major jazz festivals which attract top drawer talent from all over the globe. Most importantly perhaps, Scotland now boasts a raft of jazz/jazz-friendly labels with the likes of the aforementioned 'Hep' (still going strong), 'Linn' and 'Caber', providing an alternative to the London hegemony. In fact, the Scottish jazz scene appears healthier than ever, if only by its sheer diversity. Whether it's the sub-tropical stramash of SALSA CELTICA or the wayward wiles of BILL WELLS (his avant-garde meanderings are dealt with in the Pop/Rock section part 2), Jock Jazz has entered the new millennium with all trumpets blowing. Nice . . .

* * * * *

ALMANAC (see under ⇒ KELTZ)

B

BACHUE (see ⇒ section on Jazz)

Phil BANCROFT (see under ⇒ Caber Music)

Tom BANCROFT (see under ⇒ Caber Music)

Sandy BROWN

Born: 25 Feb'29, Izatnagar, India. How someone born in the Far East and educated at Edinburgh's Royal High School should wind up sounding like a singer and musician brought up on a Mississippi levee is part of the mystery and charm of Sandy Brown. Brown wasn't a copyist, although he recorded songs and tunes by Tennesseean blues singer Leroy Carr and Louis Armstrong: the music of New Orleans in particular and America's southern states in general was simply inside him. As was the High Life style that Brown embraced on Go Ghana, years before the term World Music was coined and African music became an everyday sound.

It was the music of New Orleans that snared the teenaged Brown when he formed his first band at the Royal High School, and there were no approximations either – the music had to be just so. When no drummers capable of meeting Brown's stringent standards could be found, pianist Stan Grieg, who had the required feel, was switched to the kit. And yet, Brown wasn't a deaf-to-all-else purist. As well as Armstrong and Carr, he recorded tunes by Charles Mingus, Woody Herman and Johnny Mandel and enthused about the exciting, earthy qualities of early records arriving in Britain on the Tamla Motown label. He did, however, demand – and project – the true spirit of blues and jazz in his music.

Arriving in London in 1954 with fellow RHS alumni, trumpeter Al Fairweather and Greig, he quickly established the Fairweather-Brown All-Stars as the hottest new band on the scene and his own architect's business as the leading authority on acoustics (Sandy Brown Associates designed hundreds of studios for the BBC and clients worldwide). From an early passion for revivalist playing in the Armstrong mould, he moved to a more sophisticated, mainstream style, always sounding like himself alone, as his 'McJAZZ' and 'DR McJAZZ' albums from the 1950s confirm. His band of the 1960s, featuring saxophonist Tony Coe, trombonist Tony Milliner, and pianist Brian Lemon alongside Fairweather, took this style to its peak, but growing business commitments ultimately lessened Brown's musical availabity. Even so, when he did get to exercise his musical creativity, on recordings such as Hair at Its Hairiest with George Chisholm and Kenny Wheeler and a final recording with Brian Lemon's trio, 'IN THE EVENING', he always found top form. Sadly, his health began to deteriorate in his forties and, on March 15th 1975, he died while watching Scotland's Rugby team lose to England in the Calcutta Cup match. His inventive spirit, however, lives on in his music and his writings, The McJazz Manuscripts.

SANDY BROWN'S JAZZ BAND

SANDY BROWN – clarinet, vocals / with at times **AL FAIRWEATHER** – trumpet

Esquire — not iss.

1953. (10"lp; with BOBBY MICKLEBURGH) *(20-022)* **SANDY BROWN** ☐ -

1953. (7"ep) *(EP 28)* **SANDY BROWN'S JAZZ BAND** ☐ -

Tempo — not iss.

1955. (7"ep) *(EXA 13)* **SANDY BROWN'S JAZZ BAND** ☐ -

1955. (7"ep) *(EXA 33)* **SANDY BROWN'S JAZZ BAND** ☐ -

1956. (lp) *(TAP 3)* **SANDY'S SIDEMEN PLAYING COMPOSITIONS BY AL FAIRWEATHER** ☐ -

1956. (7"ep) *(EXA 49)* **TRADITIONAL JAZZ SCENE '56** ☐ -

Nixa — not iss.

Mar 57. (lp) *(NJL 9)* **McJAZZ** ☐ -
(re-iss. May86 on 'Dormouse'; DM 6)

1957. (7"ep) *(NJE 1054)* **BLUE McJAZZ** ☐ -

1957. (7"ep) *(NJE 1056)* **AFRO McJAZZ** ☐ -

Tempo — not iss.

1958. (7"; as SANDY BROWN'S JAZZ BAND) *(A 124)* **AFRICAN QUEEN. / SPECIAL DELIVERY** ☐ -

Columbia — not iss.

1964. (7"; as SANDY & THE TEACHERS) *(DB 7244)* **LISTEN WITH MAMMY. / REAL SWEET** ☐ -

Fontana — not iss.

1968. (lp) *(TE1 7473)* **SANDY BROWN ALL STARS** ☐ -

1969. (lp; as SANDY BROWN & HIS GENTLEMEN FRIENDS) *(SFJL 921)* **HAIR AT ITS HAIRIEST** ☐ -

SANDY BROWN with the BRIAN LEMON TRIO

aka **BRIAN LEMON** – piano / **TONY ARCHER** – bass / **BOBBY ORR** – drums

77 — not iss.

Dec 71. (lp) *(SEU 12/49)* **IN THE EVENING** (live in London, 16th May, 1971) ☐ -
– Ole Miss / Oxford Brown / In the evening / Ebun / Eight / Legal Pete / The badger / True love's heart / Lucky Schiz and the big dealer / Minstrel song / Louis. *(re-iss. Mar84 on 'Hep Jazz'; HEP 2017) (cd-iss. Jan98 on 'Hep'+=; HEPCD 2017)* – Strike up the band / I'm coming Virginia / Sandy's blues / Gentlemen of the bar.

— SANDY died on the 15th March 1975

– compilations, etc. –

May 83. (lp) *Spotlite; (SPJ 901)* **SPLANKY** (rec.March 1966) ☐ -
– Splanky / In the evening / Roll 'em Pete / I got it bad (and that ain't good) / Royal Garden blues.

Feb 96. (cd) *Lake; (LACD 58)* **McJAZZ & FRIENDS** ☐ -

Apr 98. (cd) *Lake; (LACD 94)* **THE HISTORIC USHER HALL CONCERT 1952 (live)** ☐ -

Sep 00. (cd) *Lake; (LACD 133)* **SANDY'S SIDEMEN** ☐ -
– Everybody loves Saturday night / Too bad / Something blue / Tree top tall papa / African queen / Special delivery / Nothing blues / Africa blues / Black six blues / Blues stampede / Fifty fifty blues / Nobody met the train / Stay / Swiss Kriss / High time / Look the other way / Candy stripes / Mouse party / My neck of the woods.

Feb 02. (cd) *Lake; (LACD 160)* **WORK SONG** ☐ -
– Goosey gander / Morning chorus / Wednesday night prayer meeting / Royal garden blues / Stompin' at the Savoy / Lover for sale / Work song / Ain't got no / Aquarius / Black boys / Easy to be hard / Where do I go / Hare Krishna / Where do I go / Machester England / Air / Electric blues.

1988. (lp) *CSA; (CLPS 1009)* **CLARINET OPENING** ☐ -

BURT / MacDONALD QUARTET

Formed: Falkirk-based . . . mid-80's and headed by guitarist GEORGE BURT and saxophonist RAYMOND MacDONALD, the rhythm section being GEORGE LYLE (on bass) and ALLAN PENDREIGH (on drums); NICOLA MacDONALD (on vocals) was the 5th member. All four (or five – NICOLA ran the Glasgow-based 'Big Sky' imprint) had considerable experience, BURT with folkies ANDY SHANKS & JIM RUSSELL and has collaborated with The HIGH SOCIETY JAZZ BAND and long-time friend BILL WELLS. MacDONALD also leaned to the Rock avant-garde side while working with MOUNT VERNON ARTS LAB and FUTURE PILOT AKA; the Artistic Director for film and television also moonlighted with Scotland's only sax group, HUNG DRAWN QUARTET, a Be-Bop outfit who also comprised GRAHAM WILSON, ALLON BEAUVOISIN and KEITH EDWARDS (two albums, 'A TRAIN IN THE DISTANCE' and 'HEY THERE YOU HOSERS!' appeared in 1995 and 2001 respectively). LYLE is a member of the GREEN ROOM TRIO (alongside CHICK LYALL) and PENDREIGH was a veteran of Stan Tracey, Don Rendall and Art Themen groups; the latter is currently with BRIAN KELLOCK and JOHN BURGESS projects.

With this long and distinguished pedigree, it wasn't surprising the BURT MacDONALD QUARTET (who also cut two sets with Lol Coxhill) were described by The List as "one of the most inventive outfits on the Scottish scene" when presented with the revue of their low-key set, 'OH HELLO' (1998); a second set, 'BIG BROTHERS' was delivered in October 2000. More recently, two other BURT/McDONALD4 LOL COXHILL sets were issued: 'TSUNAMI' (2001) and 'COXHILL STREET' (2002) – both on the 'F.M.R.' label.

GEORGE BURT – guitar / **RAYMOND MacDONALD** – saxophone / **GEORGE LYLE** – bass / **ALLAN PENDREIGH** – drums / with **NICOLA MacDONALD** – vocals, melodica, whistle own label / not iss.

Sep 98. (cd) *(CD 001)* **OH HELLO** ☐ ☐
– Still life boogie woogie / Down by the Sally Gardens / Smooth day? / Cozy street / The northern Pannonica / Moon! stars! clouds! / Love & kisses / Tea time calypso / Melody intelligence / Streetlights through the windscreen.

B.M.A. / not iss.

Oct 00. (cd) *(BMACD 002)* **BIG BROTHERS** ☐ ☐
– Fibonacci's blues / The candid friend / Mercury lullaby / The sleevenotes / A foggy bay (near Lundin Links) / Noises from the roof / Hedonism / One note swinger / 601 halcyon days / The new Eyetalian half step / Mugs & poles.

HUNG DRAWN QUARTET

— see line-up in biog

H.D.Q. / not iss.

1995. (cd) *(CD 001)* **A TRAIN IN THE DISTANCE** ☐ ☐
– Indecision – Pretty eyes / McGonagle abroad / Drastic measures / Morning smile / Take one in the morning / The rent / Red hot teapot / Crazy dog theme – On the Beach Boys bus / Miss Otis regrets / Remember fun.

2001. (cd) *(HDQCD 002)* **HEY THERE YOU HOSERS** ☐ ☐
– Flying visit / Hey there you hosers / Just the job / 601 halcyon days / Little wave / Up late / Another Sunday / T-time calypso / Doctor Don / The sleeve notes / Still life boogie woogie / Paw prints.

C

Ian CARR

Born: 21 Apr'33, Dumfries. IAN CARR has been a central figure on the experimental edge of the jazz spectrum for nigh on four decades, an achievement recognised by Wire magazine who presented him with an award in 1987.

Despite his Northern birthplace, CARR was raised in the north of England (South Shields in Durham, to be exact) and went on to study English Literature at King's College in Newcastle. Following a spell in the army in the late 50's, he formed EMCEE FIVE with his English-born younger brother MIKE and future guitar virtuoso JOHN McLAUGHLIN. A self-taught trumpeter, CARR's early years also found him playing with The NEW JAZZ ORCHESTRA, The JOE HARRIOT QUARTET and, together with saxophonist DON RENDELL, The RENDELL – CARR QUINTET. The latter outfit cut seven – now all highly collectable – albums for 'Columbia' during the 60's, namely 'SHADES OF BLUE', 'PHASE III', 'LIVE', 'CHANGE IS 1', 'CHANGE IS 2', 'DUSK FIRE' and 'GREEK VARIATIONS'.

In 1969, CARR formed pioneering jazz-rock fusion outfit NUCLEUS alongside CHRIS SPEDDING, KARL JENKINS, JOHN MARSHALL, JEFF CLYNE and BRIAN SMITH. Signed to 'Vertigo' the group made their debut in 1970 with the 'ELASTIC ROCK' album, venturing into similar territory to SOFT MACHINE (to whom more than a few former members would gravitate) and surprisingly making a brief sojourn into the UK Top 50. Occasionally recording as IAN CARR'S NUCLEUS and utilising a revolving cast of musicians, CARR led the band right into the 80's, maintaining an ever prolific release schedule.

He continued to undertake occasional live work with NUCLEUS up until 1989. He left to tour with American composer GEORGE RUSSELL's DRUMSTICK. Solo set, 'OLD HEARTLAND' (1988) was recorded with the help of the KREISLER STRING ORCHESTRA while the 90's saw further collaborations with the likes of JOHN TAYLOR, 'SOUNDS AND SWEET AIRS' (1992).

In addition to his musical pursuits, CARR has written widely on jazz and jazz musicians, completing biographies on both MILES DAVIS and KEITH JARRETT and contributing a weekly column to BBC Music Magazine. He is also associate professor at London's Guildhall School Of Music And Dance, lecturing weekly on jazz history.

• **Note** Albums just credited to NUCLEUS are not included.

IAN CARR – trumpet / with various back-up

Vertigo / Core

Jul 72. (lp) *(6360 076)* **BELLADONNA** ☐ ☐
– Belladonna / Summer rain / Rema Dione / Mayday / Suspension / Hector's house.

Mar 76. (lp; as IAN CARR NUCLEUS) *(9286 019)* **DIRECT HITS** (compilation) ☐ ☐
– Bull dance / Crude blues / Roots / Sarsparilla / Song for the bearded lady / Suspension / A taste of sarsparilla / Torso.

Capitol / Capitol

Jul 78. (lp; by IAN CARR NUCLEUS) *(<EST 11771>)* **IN FRAGRANTE DELICTO** ☐ ☐
– Gestalt / Mysteries / Heyday / In fragrane delicto.

Feb 79. (lp; by IAN CARR NUCLEUS) *(<EST 11916>)* **OUT OF THE LONG DARK** ☐ ☐
– Gone with the weed / Lady bountiful / Solar wind / Selina / Out of the long dark / Sassy (American girl) / Simply this (the human condition) / Black ballad / For Liam.

M.M.C. / M.M.C.

Oct 88. (cd/c/lp) *(<CD/TC+/MMC 1016>)* **OLD HEARTLAND** ☐ ☐
– Open country / Interiors / Disjunctive boogie / Spirit of place / Full fathom five / Old heartland / Things past.

Celestial Harmonies / Celestial Harmonies

May 96. (cd; by IAN CARR & JOHN TAYLOR) *(<13064>)* **SOUNDS AND SWEET AIRS** ☐ ☐
(re-iss. Nov98; same)

– others, etc. –

Oct 98. (cd) *Beat Goes On; (BGOCD 420)* **OLD HEARTLANDS / OUT OF THE LONG DARK** ☐ ☐

Sep 02. (cd) *Beat Goes On; (BGOCD 566)* **SOLAR PLEXUS / BELLADONNA** ☐ ☐

George CHISHOLM

Born: 29 Mar'15, Glasgow. One of Britains's greatest and earliest exponents of the trombone. His early recordings in London from 1936 onwards (not including work with FATS WALLER) were fine examples of British trad-jazz and featured among others TOMMY McQUATER on trumpet, BENNY WINSTONE on clarinet and ANDY McDEVITT on tenor sax. After wartime service in the RAF during which he played for the SQUADRONAIRES), CHISHOLM branched out into other work, mainly for the BBC Show Band in the early 50's (onwards) who backed the manic comedy radio programme, The Goons (he remained a friend of SPIKE MILLIGAN until he died).

From there, GEORGE went on to work with LOUIS ARMSTRONG plus The Black & White Minstrel Show, the latter a family entertainment show which might not have been seen in a proper light today because of its political incorrectness. His singer wife CAROLE CHISHOLM also appeared on several later releases, while he himself contributed his own style of showboating vocals. In the early 60's, the now distinguished GEORGE went into acting and made dozens of TV appearances, while the film 'The Mouse On The Moon' was premiered in 1963. A few years later, a second more successful movie, 'The Knack . . . And How To Get It' (1965) was followed by the odd guest spot on the Morecambe & Wise Show; he'd later turn up in 'Superman III'.

Having counted JIMMY SHAND as one of his favourite artists, GEORGE also sessioned for a plethora of jazz and pop stars including everyone from BENNY BAKER to LONG JOHN BALDRY to ANDY FAIRWEATHER LOW. Sadly, in 1997, at the age of 82, GEORGE died. In early 2000, a host of jazz artistes paid him tribute via the album, 'George Chisholm's Gentlemen Of Jazz'.

GEORGE CHISHOLM – trombone, vocals

Beltona / not iss.

1956. (7"/78; as GEORGE CHISHOLM & BLUENOTES with BERT WEEDON) *(BL/BE 2671)* **HONKY TONK. / D.R. ROCK** ☐ ☐

Decca / not iss.

1959. (lp) *(LK 4147)* **CHIS** ☐ ☐

Philips / not iss.

1961. (7") *(BF 1141)* **THAT'S A PLENTY. / JAZZING ON A SCALE** ☐ ☐
1962. (7") *(326531)* **IN A PERSIAN MARKET. / THE GLOW-WORM** ☐ ☐
1962. (lp) *(SBBL 612)* **TRAD TREAT** ☐ ☐
1963. (lp) *(BL 7694)* **MUSIC FOR ROMANTICS** ☐ ☐

Wing / not iss.

1964. (lp) *(WL 1043)* **TRAD SPECIAL** ☐ ☐

Columbia / not iss.

1969. (lp) *(SCX 6195)* **THE MAGNIFICENT SEVEN** ☐ ☐

Gold Star / not iss.

1973. (lp) *(1500001)* **GEORGE CHISHOLM** ☐ ☐

Velvet / not iss.

1973. (lp) *(VELP 1002)* **IN A MELLOW MOOD** ☐ ☐

Line / not iss.

1975. (lp) *(L 2030)* **TROMBONE SHOWCASE** ☐ ☐

77 — not iss.

1977. (lp; as GEORGE CHISHOLM ALL STARS) *(SEU 12/43)* **ALONG THE CHISHOLM TRAIL** [ ] [-]
(re-iss. Jul88; same)

Fellside — not iss.

Apr 81. (lp) *(FE 016)* **THE GATEWAY JAZZ BAND WITH GEORGE CHISHOLM** [ ] [-]

Flutegrove — not iss.

Jul 82. (lp) *(HJ 107)* **GEORGE CHISHOLM, KEITH SMITH AND HEFTY JAZZ** [ ] [-]

Zodiac — not iss.

Jul 86. (lp; as GEORGE CHISHOLM JAZZ GIANTS) *(ZR 1025)* **THAT'S A PLENTY** [ ] [-]
Oct 86. (lp) *(ZR 1026)* **THE SWINGING MR.C** [ ] [-]

C.M.J. — not iss.

Mar 90. (cd/c) *(CMJ CD/MC 011)* **GEORGE CHISHOLM WITH MAXINE DANIELS & THE JOHN PETTERS BAND** [ ] [-]

— in 1997, GEORGE died

- compilations, others, etc. -

Apr 98. (cd) *Timeless; (CBC 1044)* **EARLY DAYS 1935-1944** [ ] [-]
Dec 98. (cd) *Lake; (<LACD 108>)* **IN A MELLOW TONE** [ ] [ ]

Nigel CLARK

Born: Glasgow. An integral member of Glaswegian sophisti-jazz popsters HUE AND CRY, CLARK went on to exercise his not inconsiderable guitar and arranging skills in a solo capacity after leaving the band in 1992. Indulging his love of jazz, he formed The NIGEL CLARK QUINTET, drawing much press acclaim for both his live work and debut album, 'WORLDWIDE SOUND' (1996), featuring the likes of Edinburgh keyboard wizard BRIAN KELLOCK and sax maestro TIM GARLAND. CLARK's impressive CV also includes a recording collaboration with CLANNAD's MAIRE BRENNAN as well as three albums with Scotland's very own jazz singer CAROL KIDD with whom he has performed in such far flung corners of the globe as China and Indonesia. In addition, NIGEL has performed alongside Dutch guitar legend JAN AKKERMAN, both at the 1997 Midem trade fair at Cannes (where CLARK represented the Glasgow International Jazz Festival) and the 1997 North Sea Jazz Festival. The QUINTET's second album was based on a series of pieces commissioned by the Scottish Arts Council. In 2001, CLARK (now a member of S.G.Q.) led his own trio, releasing the 'GRAND HOTEL EUROPA' for New York-based label, 'Arkadia'.

NIGEL CLARK – guitars / **BRIAN KELLOCK** – piano, keyboards / **TIM GARLAND** – saxophones (of LAMMAS) / **EWEN VERNAL** – bass (ex-DEACON BLUE) / **MIKE BRADLEY** – drums (ex-GANG OF THREE, ex-CO-MOTION, ex-BRIAN KELLOCK TRIO)

Sienna — not iss.

1996. (cd; as NIGEL CLARK QUINTET) *(SNA 1001)* **WORLDWIDE SOUND** [ ] [-]
– Batfunk: The worldwide sound feat. T.N.T. / 2,000 giraffes / Over the moon / No romance / Ice / 26th samba / Only a dream / The high wire / E.C.T.

Arkadia — Arkadia

Aug 01. (cd) *(<ARKADIA 70451>)* **GRAND HOTEL EUROPA** [ ] [ ] Oct01
– East of the sun / Grand hotel Europa / Dolphin dance / Sakura samba / Once I loved / In another moment / Island dance / Caso de Verao / How deep is the ocean / You are too beautiful.

CLYDE VALLEY STOMPERS

Formed: Glasgow . . . early 50's initially as The CLYDE VALLEY JAZZ BAND by bandleader ALEX WELSH and a crew of neatly-suited, all-male Big Band musicians. From their first single in 1956 for 'Beltona' records, 'UIST TRAMPING SONG', to a plethora of others for 'Decca' and 'Pye Jazz', The CLYDE VALLEY STOMPERS (with IAN MENZIES now in tow) became very popular with traditional jazz fans north of the border; Glaswegian MALCOLM NIXON was their agent/manager. In summer 1962, now on 'Parlophone' records, the 'STOMPERS hit the UK Top 30 with their edited version of Prokofiev's 'PETER AND THE WOLF'. Following the failure of their follow-up, 'ISTANBUL' in '63, the group decided to call it a day; the advent of new labelmates, The BEATLES, didn't help their cause. In 1981, The CLYDE VALLEY STOMPERS returned to the fold with a new set, 'REUNION '81', another in '85 'FIDGETY FEET' also failed to bring back the good old days.

ALEX WELSH – bandleader / **IAN MENZIES** –

Beltona — not iss.

1956. (78) *(BL 2648)* **UIST TRAMPING SONG. / KEEP RIGHT ON TO THE END OF THE ROAD** [ ] [-]
1956. (78) *(BL 2649)* **I LOVE A LASSIE. / OLD RUSTIC BRIDGE BY THE MILL** [ ] [-]
1956. (78) *(BL 2650)* **OLD TIME RELIGION. / PEARLY GATES** [ ] [-]

Decca — not iss.

May 57. (7",78; with MARY McGOWAN) *(F 10897)* **BILL BAILEY WON'T YOU PLEASE COME HOME. / MILENBERG JOYS** [ ] [-]

— the band broke into two factions; the other being IAN MENZIES'

Pye Jazz — not iss.

1958. (7"/78; as IAN MENZIES with his NEW STOMPERS) *(7+/NJ 2027)* **POLLY WOLLY DOODLE. / IN A PERSIAN MARKET** [ ] [-]
1958. (7"/78; as IAN MENZIES & the CLYDE VALLEY STOMPERS) *(7+/NJ 2028)* **BILL BAILEY WON'T YOU PLEASE COME HOME. / HOT TIME IN THE OLD TOWN TONIGHT** [ ] [-]
1958. (7"ep; as IAN MENZIES) *(NJE 1049)* **MELODY MAKER ALL STARS** [ ] [-]
1959. (7"; as IAN MENZIES & the CLYDE VALLEY STOMPERS) *(7NJ 2031)* **THE FISH MAN. / SALTY DOG** [ ] [-]
1960. (lp) *(NJL 23)* **HAVE TARTAN – WILL TRAD** [ ] [-]
1960. (lp) *(NJL 26)* **IAN MENZIES AND HIS CLYDE VALLEY STOMPERS** [ ] [-]
1961. (7"; as IAN MENZIES & the CLYDE VALLEY STOMPERS) *(7NJ 2041)* **BLACK ANGUS. / THE BIG MAN** [ ] [-]
1961. (7"; as IAN MENZIES & the CLYDE VALLEY STOMPERS) *(7NJ 2044)* **PLAY TO ME GYPSY. / TROMBONES TO THE FORE** [ ] [-]
1961. (7"; as IAN MENZIES & the CLYDE VALLEY STOMPERS) *(7NJ 2046)* **AUF WIEDERSEH'N. / TABOO** [ ] [-]

— IAN MENZIES also issued a solo single, 'ROYAL GARDEN BLUES' b/w 'ROOM WITH A VIEW' on 'P.R.T.'

Parlophone — not iss.

Jul 62. (7") *(R 4928)* **PETER AND THE WOLF. / LOCH LOMOND** [25] [-]
1963. (7") *(R 5043)* **ISTANBUL. / CASBAR** [ ] [-]

— recorded little for the rest of the 60's and the whole of the 70's

Country House — not iss.

Dec 81. (lp/c) *(BGC/KBGC 300)* **REUNION '81** [ ] [-]
– Hindustan / Old rugged cross / Sister Kate / High society / Bourbon street parade / Old tyme religion / Savoy blues / Bill Bailey.

Jul 85. (lp/c) *(BGC/KBGC 351)* **FIDGETY FEET** [ ] [-]
– At the jazz band ball / Isle of Capri / When my dreamboat comes home / Fidgety feet / Salty dog / Creole love call / Tiger rag / My mother's eyes / Hiawatha rag / Goodnight, my sweet prince / When the saints go marching in / I can't stop loving you.

— the 'STOMPERS retired from the studio after above

- compilations, etc. -

Apr 97. (cd) *Lake; (LACD 79)* **IAN MENZIES & HIS CLYDE VALLEY STOMPERS 1959-60: GREAT BRITISH TRADITIONAL JAZZBANDS VOL.9** [ ] [-]
– Roses of Picardy / Beale St. blues / Gettysburg march / Swinging Seamus / Ace in the hole / Sailing down Chesapeake bay / In a Persian market / There'll be a hot time in the old town tonight / Mack the knife / The world is waiting for the sunrise / Tres moutarde / Just a closer walk with thee / Yellow dog blues / Irish black bottom / Royal garden blues / The fish man / Salty dog / Scotland the brave.

CONCERTO CALEDONIA (see under ⇒ Linn records)

Lonnie DONEGAN (see under ⇒ Section 7: Rock & Pop)

Jimmy DEUCHAR

Born: JAMES DEUCHAR, 26 Jun'30, Dundee. The trumpet playing son of a Dundee saxophonist and bandleader, Deuchar was doing his National Service in the RAF when, on one of the visits he made as often as possible to London's Club Eleven jazz HQ, he plucked up the courage to ask if he could sit in with John Dankworth's band. Dankworth agreed, reluctantly – only to find that the 19 year-old Deuchar was already a player of covetable skill. As soon as Deuchar's two years' RAF service was up, Dankworth hired him and, in 1953, Deuchar joined what was to become a landmark in British modern jazz, Ronnie Scott's nine-piece orchestra.

By this time Deuchar was recognised not only as one of Britain's leading trumpeters, through playing recording sessions with Jack Parnell as well as Dankworth, but was also developing into a composer and arranger of rare gifts. Vibraphonist Lionel Hampton recognised these qualities and whisked Deuchar off the US, where Deuchar also toured with Scott before moving to Cologne to join Kurt Edelhagen's radio orchestra. Back in London in 1960 (after issuing the now very rare 'PAL JIMMY' in '58), he rejoined Scott for two years, then teamed up with the outstanding saxophonist/vibist Tubby Hayes to create some of the greatest jazz of the era in Hayes' still revered big band. Edelhagen took him back to Germany as soloist and staff arranger in 1966 and as the 1960s swung towards the 1970s, the Kenny Clarke-Francey Boland Big Band also called on Deuchar's cultured musicianship and visionary arranging talents. A much repeated – and true – story of these times has Deuchar sketching out band arrangements on a cigarette packet at the back of the band bus en route to the next gig.

In the early 1970s Deuchar returned to Dundee, where he worked on arrangements for various contacts, including the BBC Radio Orchestra, and played a regular Sunday lunchtime gig at The Sands in Broughty Ferry. One Sunday, an elegant American admired Deuchar's playing and after playing piano during the band break, pooh-poohed reciprocated praise, saying that his sons were the musicians in the family – they were Randy and Michael, the Brecker Brothers. The Scots Connection, recorded for Edinburgh-based Hep Records around this time, shows what stirred Old Man Brecker's enthusiasm and why jazz musicians visiting Dundee would always ask if Jimmy Deuchar would be coming along to the gig.

Throughout the 1980s and into the 1990s Deuchar continued to write, notably for the Jack Sharpe Big Band with whom he made a special hometown appearance at the local jazz festival, and for expatriate American saxophonist Spike Robinson, for whose Gershwin Collection album Deuchar provided beautifully understated string arrangements. Shortly before he died, Deuchar was commissioned by Alastair Robertson of 'Hep' records to write a jazz suite for an eleven piece band led by Lochgelly-born baritone saxophonist Joe Temperley, a long time resident of New York and veteran of the big bands of Woody Herman, Buddy Rich and Wynton Marsalis. Sadly, Deuchar never heard what was to be his last musical statement performed. He handed over the charts and counted out tempos to Robertson on a hospital visit, and died a week later (on the 9th of September). The result, 'CONCERTO FOR JOE', was released on 'Hep' in 1995 and is lasting testimony to a brilliant musician, composer and arranger.

JIMMY DEUCHAR – trumpet, flugelhorn / with various sessioners

		Esquire	not iss.
1954.	(10"lp) *(20-059)* **DIG DEUCHAR, DON'T DANCE**		-
1956.	(7"ep) *(EP 93)* **JIMMY DEUCHAR QUARTET**		-
1956.	(7"ep) *(EP 103)* **JIMMY DEUCHAR QUARTET**		-
		Tempo	not iss.
1955.	(10"lp) *(LAP 2)* **JIMMY DEUCHAR ENSEMBLE**		-
1955.	(7"ep) *(EXA 18)* **PUB CRAWLING WITH JIMMY DEUCHAR**		-
1956.	(lp) *(TAP 4)* **TOP TRUMPETS**		-
1958.	(lp) *(TAP 20)* **PAL JIMMY** – Swingin' in studio two / Heather mist / Jak-Jak / Pal Jimmy / Split second / My funny valentine / I didn't know what time it was / Bewitched, bothered and bewildered / I could write a book. *(cd-iss. Dec01 on 'Jasmine'; JASCD 624)*		-
1958.	(7",78; as JIMMY DEUCHAR & HIS PALS) *(A 167)* **BEWITCHED, BOTHERED AND BEWILDERED / MY FUNNY VALENTINE**		-
1958.	(7"ep; as The JIMMY DEUCHAR SEXTET) *(EXA 79)* **OPUS DE FUNK**		-
1958.	(7"ep) *(EXA 81)* **SWINGIN' IN STUDIO TWO**		-
1959.	(7"ep; with The VICTOR FELDMAN QUINTET) *(EXA 88)* **WAIL**		-
		Hep Jazz	not iss.
Apr 81.	(lp; as the JIMMY DEUCHAR QUINTET) *(HEP 2008)* **THE SCOTS CONNECTION**		-

— JIMMY died on the 9th of September 1993

– compilations, etc. –

1956.	(lp) *Vogue; (LDE)* **SHOWCASE** (rec.1953) – Climbin' the bush / Stormy weather / Early / Spain / Time was / Magoo / Someone to watch over me / Toot sweet. *(cd-iss. Mar01 on 'Jasmine'+=; JASCD 616)* – PUB CRAWLING WITH JIMMY DEUCHAR EP – Treble gold / Bass house / I.P.A. special / Final selection.		-
Jul 87.	(lp; as JIMMY DEUCHAR / ALAN CLARE / VICTOR FELDMAN / TONY KINSEY) *Esquire; (ESQ 330)* **THOU SWELL**		-
Aug 01.	(cd) *Jasmine; (JASCD 621)* **OPUS DE FUNK** – E / Colne Springs / Four X / Red barrel / I'll take romance / Speak low / Between the Devil and the deep blue sea / Opus de funk / Lullaby in rhythm / How long has this been going on / Milestones.		-

Jim DOUGLAS

Born: May 13, 1942, Gifford, East Lothian. An elegant guitarist whose style impressed many visiting American musicians during his time with the ALEX WELSH BAND, DOUGLAS played with THE CLYDE VALLEY STOMPERS prior to joining Welsh in 1964. He remained with Welsh until the bandleader's death in 1982, playing banjo as well as guitar and recording with pianist Earl Hines and cornettist Ruby Braff, among others. Following the Welsh Band's demise, he worked with trumpeter ALAN ELSDON's band and was a pivotal figure when the Alex Welsh Memorial Band formed in tribute to the former leader of what Chicagoan tenor saxophonist Bud Freeman once referred to as 'the best small band of its kind in the world'.

Fionna DUNCAN

Born: 1938, Gairlochhead; she attended Rutherglen Academy. Growing up in a musical family, FIONNA gravitated towards singing as a counterpoint to her piano playing siblings. Early exposure via both Radio Scotland and Glasgow's Snug Club paved the way for a mid-50's stint with the ubiquitous CLYDE VALLEY STOMPERS. After initially performing between London and Glasgow, the singer moved to the Old Smoke on a permanent basis and worked in cabaret. Yet DUNCAN was to abruptly leave the music business in the early 70's after a nasty accident in Turkey, subsequently working as a hairdresser for most of the decade. Yet with a voice as gutsy, lived-in and timed to perfection as any jazz singer Britain has produced (influences include Louis Armstrong and Bessie Smith), it was only a matter of time before FIONNA was back on stage where she belonged. After a long and colourful career the singer decided she wanted to give something back, to pass on her rich knowledge of song, self-expression and performance. This she achieved by a series of highly regarded workshops in Edinburgh and Glasgow, the likes of CATHIE RAE and NIKKI KING benefitting from her wealth of experience. More recently, she and co-tutor SOPHIE BANCROFT took their expertise to the Islay Jazz Festival. Also worth noting is that she released a couple of LP's including 1982's 'FIONNA'S FELLAS' and 1985's 'COME AND GET IT', the latter featuring Eggy Ley's Hot Shots.

F

Al FAIRWEATHER

Born: Edinburgh. trumpeter. AL worked with ART HODES BLUE FIVE.

AL FAIRWEATHER – trumpet / + at times credited with **SANDY BROWN** – clarinet, vocals

		Columbia	not iss.
1957.	(7"ep) *(SEG 7653)* **AL FAIRWEATHER'S JAZZ BAND**		-
1960.	(lp) *(33SX 1159)* **AL AND SANDY**		-
1960.	(lp) *(33SX 1221)* **AL'S PALS**		-
1961.	(lp) *(33SX 1306)* **DOCTOR McJAZZ**		-
1963.	(lp; with SANDY BROWN'S ALL STARS) *(33SX 1509)* **THE INCREDIBLE McJAZZ**		-
1960's.	(7"ep) *(SEG 8157)* **STUDY IN BROWN**		-
1960's.	(7"ep) *(SEG 8181)* **GROOVER WAILIN'**		-

– others, etc. –

1958.	(7"ep) *Tempo; (EXA 63)* **AL FAIRWEATHER'S JAZZMEN**		-
1958.	(lp) *Nixa; (NJT 511)* **FAIRWEATHER FRIENDS**		-
Mar 97.	(cd) *Lake; (LACD 75)* **MADE TO MEASURE** (rec.1959) – By the fireside / Music goes 'round and around / Sue's blues / Exactly like you / Goody goody / Easy to love / Sometimes I'm happy / Tin roof blues / I can't give you anything but love / Red for go / September in the rain / If I had you / Coe pilot / Grapevine / Doin' the racoon.		-

— in Jul'97, AL FAIRWEATHER featured on a CD by 'Lake' artists GROOVE JUICE SPECIAL & SWEET SUBSTITUTE (LACD 83)

G

Jim GALLOWAY

Born: JAMES BRAIDIE GALLOWAY, 28 Jul'36, Kilwinning, Initially performing on clarinet and alto sax, GALLOWAY took up the soprano sax after relocating to Canada in 1965. By 1968 he was leading The METRO STOMPERS and subsequently went on to form The WEE BIG BAND in the late 70's. 'THREE IS COMPANY' – a live date from 22nd September, 1973 – was released on vinyl in 1979 as GALLOWAY's debut album, featuring the man leading stride pianist DICK WELLSTOOD and sticksman PETE MAGADINI through a set of classic jazz and swing standards. 1983's 'THOU SWELL' saw him teaming up with veteran pianist JAY McSHANN, a favourite collaborator with whom he also recorded 1992 Xmas set, 'JIM AND JAY'S CHRISTMAS'. The cream of GALLOWAY's work was released in 2001 as 'MUSIC IS MY LIFE', a double CD of New Orleans-influenced material featuring collaborations with WELLSTOOD, McSHANN and English trad jazz revivalist HUMPHREY LYTTELTON.

JIM GALLOWAY – saxophones / with **DICK WELLSTOOD** – piano / **PETE MAGADINI** – drums / **JAY McSHANN** – piano / **JAKE HANNA** – drums / with **FRASER MacPHERSON** – sax

Sackville Sackville

Apr 79. (lp) *(<2007>)* **THREE IS COMPANY** (recorded 22nd September, 1973)
– Minor drag / Lulu's back in town / Broken windmill / Sunday morning / Blues alley bump / After you've gone / Buddy Bolden's blues / I'd climb the higheat mountain / Let's get away from it all / Everything I've got.

Apr 81. (lp) *(<4002>)* **METRO STOMPERS**

–

May 83. (lp; as JIM GALLOWAY QUARTET & JAY McSHANN) *(<4011>)* **THOU SWELL**
– Thou swell / Someone to watch over me / Wrap your troubles in dreams / Black butterfly / Sweet Sue / I've got the world on a string / Just a gigolo / Humoresque / I only have eyes for you.

Dec 92. (cd; by JIM GALLOWAY & JAY McSHANN) *<SACKCD 3054>* **JIM AND JAY'S CHRISTMAS** –

Jun 93. (cd) *<SACKCD 3057>* **WEE BIG BAND** –

1990's. (cd; as JIM GALLOWAY & RALPH SUTTON) *(<SACKCD 3038>)* **XMAS SPECIAL**

Jul 96. (cd) *(<SKCD 3057>)* **KANSAS CITY NIGHTS**

–

Dec 98. (cd; as RALPH SUTTON & JIM GALLOWAY) *<(SKCD 23062)>* **POCKETFUL OF DREAMS**

– others, etc. –

Mar 81. (lp) *Hep Jazz; (HEP 2008)* **BOJANGLES**

Feb 99. (cd; by ED POLCER & THE JIM GALLOWAY BIG FIVE) *Jazzology; <(JCD 293)>* **AT THE BALL**

Apr 00. (cd; by ALLAN VACHE & JIM GALLOWAY) *Nagel Hayer; <(NHCD 054)>* **RAISIN' THE ROOF**

Jan 01. (d-cd) *Sackville; <SACKCD 5006>* **MUSIC IS MY LIFE** –

— Sep'88, JIM and ART HODES released 'LIVE AT TORONTO'S CAFE DES COPAINS'

Ron GEESIN (see ⇒ Section 7: Rock & Pop)

John GOLDIE (see under ⇒ Caber music)

GREEN ROOM (see under ⇒ LYALL, Chick)

Stan GREIG

Born: STANLEY MACKAY GREIG, 12 Aug'30, Edinburgh. His first real taste of performing live was when he joined Sandy Brown's band at the Royal High School in Edinburgh in 1945. Originally a pianist, he took up drums while working with Brown's band as no local drummers met Brown's exacting standards and when he joined New Orleans traditionalist Ken Colyer's band, having moved to London in 1954, it was as a drummer. The following year he joined Humphrey Lyttelton, again on drums, before going on to play piano with the Al Fairweather-Sandy Brown All-Stars (1956-60) and Acker Bilk (1960-68). From 1969 he led his own trio and quintet, including trumpeter Colin Smith and saxophonist Al Gay, and in 1975 he formed the London Jazz Big Band. Despite excellent arrangements, by Greig himself, band members Al Fairweather, John Picard and others, and top ranking musicians, the band failed to receive due recognition and was never recorded. After a spell with George Melly, he rejoined Humphrey Lyttelton, as pianist this time, in 1985. He subsequently left "Humph" but remains a highly respected member of Britain's senior jazz community, and is particularly revered for his show-stopping boogie-woogie features.

STAN GREIG'S JAZZ BAND

STAN GREIG – vocals, piano, + drums / with **JOHNNY HAWKSWORTH** – bass / **RICHIE BRYANT** – drums

Tempo not iss.

1959. (7"ep) *(EXA 90)* **STAN GREIG'S JAZZ BAND** –

Rediffusion not iss.

1971. (lp) *(ZS 116)* **BOOGIE WOOGIE** –

Calligraph not iss.

1985. (lp) *(CLGLP 004)* **BLUES EVERY TIME** –

Lake not iss.

Aug 98. (cd; as STAN GREIG) *(LACD 97)* **BOOGIE WOOGIE** (rec. 1971 & 1997) –
– Yancey special / Shout for joy / Honky tonk train blues / Tell 'em about Yancey / Big fish boogie / Roll 'em Pete / Six wheel chaser / Death ray boogie / Monday struggle / Boogie at the Ken / Last order blues / Boogie woogie / Night train boogie / Luxemboogie.

Jul 00. (cd; by RACHAEL PENNELL & STAN GREIG SEXTET) *(LACD 129)* **PAPA SAID . . .** –
– It's wonderful / Mean to me / Little sugar in my bowl / I got a right to sing the blues / Don't explain / Honeysuckle rose / Is you is or is you ain't my baby / I ain't got nothing but the blues / Loverman / Somebody loves me / Baby won't you please come home / Alright OK you win / Just squeeze me / What a little moonlight can do / Love me or leave me / Miss Otis regrets.

MacJazz not iss.

May 02. (cd; by WALLY FAWKES & STAN GREIG) *(MACCD 003)* **JAZZ JURASSICS** –
– Lucky duck / Autumn in Tufnell Park / in the shade of the old apple tree / Comes love / Day dream / Revolutionary blues / La Rosita / Nearness of you / Where folly walks / Very thought of you / Bechet's wedding day / Buddy's bolden blues / Wabash blues / How long how long blues / When I grow too old to dream.

Steve HAMILTON

Born: 1973, Aberdeen. Born into a musical family – his father, Laurie, was the house guitarist for Grampian Television for many years, Steve Hamilton began his musical career with two unhappy years of classical piano lessons at primary school. It was to be some time before he put finger to keyboard again, but at the age of thirteen or fourteen he stumbled into music again inspired by Chick Corea's Mad Hatter album, particularly the weird and wonderful synthesiser sounds he heard on it.

An unsuccessful attempt to turn professional on leaving school brought the advice from friend and mentor Tommy Smith to go to Berklee College of Music in Boston, where Smith had studied. With a scholarship and much generosity from well-wishers, including a donation from Phil Collins, Hamilton left for the States and returned four years later with his diploma. He spent the next five years living and working in London, adding to his CV an impressively varied list of musicians which includes the legendary Ray Charles, trumpeters Freddie Hubbard and Eddie Henderson, guitarists Martin Taylor and Jim Mullen, alto saxophonist Bobby Watson, vibists Gary Burton and Bobby Hutcherson, and soul singers Percy Sledge and Sam Moore (of Sam & Dave). He also featured on Smith's brilliant but demanding Glasgow Jazz Festival commission and album, Beasts of Scotland, and thereafter joined former Yes and King Crimson drummer, Bill Bruford's jazz group, EARTHWORKS, contributing piano, keyboards and compositions to the albums A Part, and Yet Apart and Footloose and Fancy Free.

HAMILTON relocated to Edinburgh in 2001, since when he has continued to work with Earthworks, worked with the Scottish National Jazz Orchestra, toured with James Brown's former funky horn section, Pee Wee Ellis and Fred Wesley, and formed a duo, SMILING SCHOOL, with guitarist Don Paterson.

Paul HARRISON (see under ⇒ Caber music)

Jimmy HASTINGS

Born: 1930s, in Aberdeen. One of the most respected saxophonists on the British jazz and session musician scene, HASTINGS grew up in Tomintoul and played accordion in a local dance band in his early teens. Then, inspired by Gerry Mulligan and the great Count Basie tenorist Eddie 'Lockjaw' Davis, he took up the saxophone and later the clarinet and flute. After serving his saxophone apprenticeship in the Aberdeen Beach Ballroom band, he moved to London in the late 1950s and, in 1957, he auditioned for Humphrey Lyttelton's band but lost out to Tony Coe.

Thirty-five years later he finally joined the LYTTELTON band, where he remains, but in the meantime he had acquired vast experience, working with Sarah Vaughan, Frank Sinatra, Benny Carter, Michael Garrick, John Dankworth and in Rolling Stone Charlie Watts' Big Band. He also worked in sessions and many West End shows, and enjoyed a long stint with the BBC Radio Orchestra. A very classy and adaptable player, his session credits include records with Canterbury prog rockers Caravan (Pye Hastings, Caravan's guitarist/singer is Jimmy's younger brother) and with 1970s prog rock/jazzers Hatfield & the North.

HUE AND CRY (see ⇒ Section 8: Rock, Pop & Indie)

Ken HYDER

Born: 29 Jun'46, Dundee. One of the pioneers of the European folk-jazz movement, Hyder took up the drums as a Harris Academy fourth-year pupil in Dundee, although his interest in music had been stirred as a youngster by his grandmother's singing of Scots songs. The spirit of these songs and Hyder's affection for bagpipe music, particularly by the great pibroch specialist John D Burgess, conjoined with the free-ranging jazz improvisation of John Coltrane and Albert Ayler when, having moved to London in his job as a journalist, Hyder formed Celtic jazz band Talisker in 1969. The group was among the first signings to Virgin Records' Caroline subsidiary, releasing the rugged Dreaming of Glenisla, and over the next fifteen years went on to record four further albums, including 'LAND OF STONE' (for ECM Records' JAPO imprint) and its final and most accessible record, 'HUMANITY'. Its personnel included, at various times, Scotsman Lindsay Cooper and the mighty Paul Rodgers on bass, former King Crimson violinist David Cross, and Dundonian guitarist, Don Paterson.

During this time Hyder had also formed several side projects, including the short-lived Big Team (whose Under the Influence album boasted hometown references such as the mill-rhythmed Jute's Oot and Hipsters, Flipsters and Soapy Souter's Sisters) and long-lasting duos with former Henry Cow saxophonist Tim Hodgkinson and Edinburgh-born singer Maggie Nicols. Nicols, a veteran of the Spontaneous Music Ensemble, Keith Tippett's mammoth Centipede and the improvising vocal quartet Voice, which also included Julie Tippetts (nee Driscoll), is an extraordinary performer whose singing conjures up fragments of Scots song, Billie Holiday, Aretha Franklin, John Coltrane and spontaneously created lines and chants drawing on her mother's North African ancestry. Her work with Hyder in Hoots and Roots is consistently fascinating. With Hodgkinson, Hyder has ventured widely, including trips to Siberia, where Hyder studied Tuvan throat singing and shamanic drumming as well as collaborating with Tuvan rockers Yat Ha.

Hyder's other musical adventures have included extensive work with former Soft Machine saxophonist Elton Dean, a long-running duo with bagpiper Dave Brooks, the Bardo State Orchestra (with American trumpeter Jim Dvorak, Brazilian bassist Marcio Mattos and, on occasions, four Tibetan monks) and collaborations with Scottish singer-guitarist Dick Gaughan, uilleann piper Tomas Lynch, and singers Valentina Ponomareva, Phil Minton and Frankie Armstrong. His 2002 release, 'BEAR BONES' with Celtic-Anglo-Siberian trio K-Space, includes a photo of the young Hyder at about the time he began to appreciate his grandmother's singing. Aw.

KEN HYDER – drums, percussion, vocals

Impetus / not iss.

1990. (lp; by DICK GAUGHAN & KEN HYDER) *(IMP 18506)* **FANFARE FOR TOMORROW** [ ] [-]
(cd-iss. Aug98; (IMPCD 18506)

— KEN (with The BIG TEAM) previously issued 'Under The Influence'

1990. (lp; by TALISKER) *(IMP 18508)* **HUMANITY** [ ] [-]
(cd-iss. Aug98; IMPCD 18508)

— other previous TALISKER sets (80's), 'DREAMING OF GLENISLA', 'LAND OF STONE', 'THE LAST BATTLE' and 'THE WHITE LIGHT'; all on German labels

1991. (lp; by TIM HODGKINSON & KEN HYDER) *(IMP 18616)* **SHAMS** [ ] [-]
(cd-iss. Aug98; IMPCD 18616)

Woof / Megaphone

1990's. (cd; by HODGKINSON / HYDER / PONOMAREVA) **THE GOOSE** [ ] [ ]

Silly Boy Lemon / not iss.

1990's. (cd; by DAVE BROOKS / KEN HYDER) **PIPING HOT** [ ] [-]

— also around this time he worked with piper TOMAS LYNCH, Russian VLADIMIR REZITSKY, CHANTER, BING SELFISH, TSHISA! and NORTHERN LIGHTS

Impetus / not iss.

Aug 98. (cd; by BARDO STATE ORCHESTRA) *(IMPCD 19425)* **THE ULTIMATE GIFT** [ ] [-]

Aug 98. (cd; by BARDO STATE ORCHESTRA) *(IMPCD 19527)* **WHEELS WITHIN WHEELS** [ ] [-]

Dec 98. (cd; by KEN STONE & DAVE BROOKS / MAGGIE NICOLS) *(IMPCD 19732)* **THE KNOWN IS IN THE STONE** [ ] [-]

Slam / not iss.

Jul 01. (cd; by SHAMS – TIM HODGKINSON / KEN HYDER) *(SLAMCD 238)* **BURGHAN INTERFERENCE** [ ] [-]

2002. (cd; by K-SPACE – TIM HODGKINSON / KEN HYDER / GENDOS CHAMZYRYN) **BEAR BONES** [ ] [-]

MAGGIE NICOLS

33Jazz / not iss.

Jun 00. (cd) *(33WM 111)* **LIFE (LOVERLY)** [ ] [-]

— she also collaborated with PINGUIN MOSCHNER and JOE SACHSE on the album, 'NEVERGREENS'

Brian KELLOCK

Born: 1962, Edinburgh. Having crafted his piano-playing technique over the course of more than a decade (he worked with TAM WHITE and others), the pianist took up the post in JAMES MORRISON's jazz group; they toured the world in the 90's. BRIAN subsequently acquired session work for the likes of HUE AND CRY, TOMMY SMITH and AILEEN CARR. Throughout the late 80's to the late 90's, KELLOCK collaborated with foreign-based jazz giants, JANUSZ CARMELLO (on his 'A Portrait' set in '89 – orchestrated by JIMMY DEUCHAR), SPIKE ROBINSON (on his 1991 set, 'Stairway To The Stars') and HERB GELLER (on the album, 'Hollywood Portraits'). The last of these was recorded in 1999, although BK had already found time to form his own BRIAN KELLOCK TRIO with KENNY ELLIS on bass and JOHN RAE on drums. Their debut set, 'SOMETHING'S GOT TO GIVE' (1999) – a tribute record to Fred Astaire – was somewhat overlooked by some of the trendier journals. Towards the end of '99, KELLOCK once again collaborated, this time with veteran Scottish bluesman TAM WHITE on the album, 'THE CROSSING'. In 2002, KELLOCK won the BBC Jazz Award for Best Album, 'LIVE AT HENRY'S', this stylish virtuoso of the piano had now come of age and who knows if life really does begin at forty.

Spike Robinson & BRIAN KELLOCK

Hep Jazz / not iss.

Oct 91. (cd) *(HEPCD 2049)* **STAIRWAY TO THE STARS** [ ] [-]
– Gone with the wind / Beautiful love / Gypsy sweetheart / It's always you / It's a blue world / Summer thing / From herte to eternity / Stairway to the stars / It should happen to you.

BRIAN KELLOCK TRIO

BRIAN KELLOCK – piano / **KENNY ELLIS** – bass / **JOHN RAE** – drums

Caber not iss.

Jan 99. (cd) *(Caber 003)* **SOMETHING'S GOT TO GIVE: A TRIBUTE TO FRED ASTAIRE** ☐ -
– They can't take that away from me / The way you look tonight / I won't dance / I concentrate on you / The continental / Fred's revenge (part one) / Isn't this a lovely day / Change partners / Fred's revenge (part two) / Something's got to give.

Oct 99. (cd; by TAM WHITE & BRIAN KELLOCK) *(Caber 009)* **THE CROSSING** ☐ -

Jul 01. (cd) *(Caber 020)* **LIVE AT HENRY'S (live)** ☐ -
– Introduction / TP in NYC / Chant / Conception / Lennies pennies / Three for Doreen / 317 East 32nd Street / Sho'nuff / Horace-scope / The peacocks – Ezzthetic.

– compilations, others, etc. –

Mar 00. (cd; by Herb Geller & BRIAN KELLOCK) *Hep Jazz; (<HEPCD 2078>)* **HOLLYWOOD PORTRAITS** (rec. 1999) ☐ ☐ Jul00
– Carole Lombard / Marlene Dietrich / Rita Hayworth / Ginger Rogers / Audrey Hepburn / Claudette Colbert / Joan Crawford / Mae West / Judy Garland / Bette Davis / Judy Holiday / Gloria Swanson / Grace Kelly / Elinor Powell / Marilyn Monroe / Ingrid Bergman / Betty Grable / Vivien Leigh / Greta Garbo / Lana Turner.

Jan 01. (3xcd-box) *Caber; (Caber 017)* **BOXED SET** ☐ -

KELTZ

Formed: Glasgow . . . early 90's by SEAN O'ROURKE together with guitarist PAUL HENDERSON and Indian percussion player VIJAY KANGUTKAR. A veteran session player and founder member of both the JSD BAND and ALBA, O'ROURKE came up with the concept of The KELTZ, a highly original and striking fusion of Indian classical music and Scottish folk. He duly recruited jazz guitarist HENDERSON and Indian Classical maestro KANGUTKAR, the latter having studied under distinguished teacher PUNDIT TARANATH RAO before coming to Glasgow and working in TV and theatre.

Aware of the similarities between Indian and Celtic music in terms of rhythm and scales, O'ROURKE realised a unique east-meets-west vision of improvised folk fusion with the release of debut album, 'THE PRINCE OF PEACE' (1993). Issued on the 'Iona' label, the record combined layers of tabla-dominated Indian percussion with whistle, bodhran, flute and jazz-inflected guitar to create a curiously hypnotic and mystical listening experience. Follow-up sets, 'THE MYSTERY OF AMERGIN' (1997) and 'THE SEAS ARE DEEP' (1999), both appeared on the 'Lochshore' label, also home to the likes of OLD BLIND DOGS and SKUOBHIE DUBH ORCHESTRA. In 1997, PAUL moonlighted with his own Glasgow-based cosmopolitan jazz outfit, ALMANAC (others in the band were GREGOR CLARK, GUY RICARBY, Dublin-born BRIAN BYRNE and Philippino HERMIE LONGALONG), who released the album, 'JAZZERS & GROOVERS'.

SEAN O'ROURKE – flute, sax, acoustic guitar, bouzouki, bass, whistle, bodhran (ex-JSD BAND, ex-ALBA) / **PAUL HENDERSON** – guitar / **VIJAY KANGUTKAR** (b. Bombay, India) – percussion (of LOOKING EAST)

Iona not iss.

Nov 93. (cd/c) *(IRCD/IRC 024)* **PRINCE OF PEACE** ☐ -
– The gate / The Siyah-chal / The mountains of Sulaymanlyyih / The exile / The garden of Ridvan / The reel of revelation / The release jig / The ascension.

Lochshore Lochshore

Jan 97. (cd) *(CDLDL 1247)* **THE MYSTERY OF AMERGIN** ☐ -
– Mystery of Amergin / Sineads reel / Vijay's / Tune for Aidan Leons jig / Little firey one part 1 / Little firey one part two / Garten mather's lullaby / Ginepo leer / The oak tree / Reel for Farzanch / Logan water / The blackbird. *<US-iss.Feb00; same as UK>*

Jun 99. (cd) *(<CDLDL 1279>)* **THE SEAS ARE DEEP** ☐ ☐ Jul99
– O'Carolan's dream / The lads of Mull / The seas are deep / The dam busters' jig / Mama's pet / Untitled march / Tull's jig / Untitled polka / Lexy McAskill / Tom Bigby / Castle Kelly / The maids of Mount Cisco / Salutaris hostia / The ale is dear.

ALMANAC

PAUL HENDERSON – guitar / plus **HERMIE LONGALONG** – saxophones, flute, wind synths / **GREGOR CLARK** – trumpet, flugelhorn / **BRIAN BYRNE** – piano, keyboards / **GUY RICARBY** – drums

OK-Lochshore not iss.

Apr 99. (cd) *(CDOK 3010)* **JAZZERS & GROOVERS** ☐ -
– Hit it / Festive frolics / Mmmh nice / Don & Walt / Mr Ben / Jazzers and groovers / Joe / Wwweb lust / Sunshine / The blues.

Carol KIDD

Born: 1945, Glasgow. By 1961 at the age of 15, the young CAROL became part of a trad-jazz combo and even managed to marry the trombone player a few years later. However, she found herself ill at ease with the pop world (LULU, etc), her renditions of popular jazz standards only finding an audience through the residency at Ronnie Scott's and nearer home, the Edinburgh Jazz Festival. Finally signing a contract with 'Linn' records (also home to the BLUE NILE), the talented singer released her eponymous debut set in 1984.

Although this was followed by 'ALL MY TOMORROWS' in 1986 and 'NICE WORK (IF YOU CAN GET IT)' a year later, KIDD only took up singing as her full-time professional occupation in 1990 after appearing alongside FRANK SINATRA at Glasgow's Ibrox Stadium. With both her confidence and profile given a significant boost, she finally gave up the day job (as a hotelier) and set her sights on catering to jazz fans instead. The same year, CAROL netted her first award as 'THE NIGHT WE CALLED IT A DAY' (1990) was voted Best Jazz Recording by UK music retailers. As well as being named Best Performer at the Edinburgh Jazz Festival, she subsequently picked up a Best Vocalist award in France at the Cannes International Jazz Awards.

The 90's also saw her touring outwith Europe for the first time while on the recording front, CAROL released another couple of well received albums, 'I'M GLAD WE MET' (1991) and 'THAT'S ME' (1995). In 1992, Beirut hostage Terry Waite featured on BBC Radio's 'Desert Island Discs' choosing CAROL's version of 'WHEN I DREAM'; an album of the same name donated royalties to Terry's favourite causes. She has since become very popular in the Far East, while the aforementioned 'WHEN I DREAM' has become a hit courtesy of its inclusion in Asian film, 'Shiri'. CAROL was even awarded an MBE in 1998 for her services to Jazz while more recently (March 2001), she delivered her tenth album proper, 'A PLACE IN MY HEART'.

CAROL KIDD – vocals / with session people

Aloi – Linn Linn

Aug 84. (lp/c) *(AKH/AKC 003)* **CAROL KIDD** ☐ -
– Then I'll be tired of you / We'll be together / You go to my head / It isn't so good it couldn't be better / The more I see you – I've grown accustomed to her face / Yes, I know when I've had it / Waltz for Debbie / Never let me go / Like someone in love / Trouble is a man / I'm shadowing you / Spring can really hang you up the most / I like to recognise the tune. *(cd-iss. Aug90; AKHCD 003) <US cd-iss. May98; same>*

Jan 86. (lp/c) *(AKH/AKC 005)* **ALL MY TOMORROWS** ☐ -
– Don't worry 'bout me / I'm all smiles / Autumn in New York / My funny valentine / Round midnight / Dat dere / Angel eyes / When I dream / I thought about you / Folks who live on the hill / Haven't we met / All my tomorrows. *(cd-iss. Aug90; AKHCD 005) (cd re-iss. Aug97; AKD 068) <US cd-iss. Jun98; same>*

Jun 87. (lp/c) *(AKH/AKC 006)* **NICE WORK (IF YOU CAN GET IT)** ☐ -
– Nice work if you can get it / Havin' myself a time / Isn't it a pity / Bidin' my time / Sing for your supper / Daydream / I'll take romance / New York on Sunday / What is there to say / Mean to me / I guess I'll have to change my plan / Starting tomorrow / Confessions. *(cd-iss. Aug90; AKHCD 006) <US cd-iss. Jun98; same>*

Sep 90. (lp/c/cd) *(<AKH/+CS/CD 007>)* **THE NIGHT WE CALLED IT A DAY** ☐ ☐
– How little it matters, how little we know / Where or when / I fall in love too easily / I loved him / The night we called it a day / Where are you / The glory of you / I could have told you so / I think it's going to rain today / Gloomy Sunday.

Nov 91. (cd/c/lp) *(<AKD/AKC/AKH 017>)* **I'M GLAD WE MET** ☐ ☐
– Lean baby / Don't go to strangers / Bad bad Leroy Brown / I guess I'll hang my tears out to dry / Georgia on my mind / You're cheating yourself / I wish I'd met you / You're awful / Don't take your love from me / I'm a fool to want you / Please don't talk about me when I'm gone / Sometimes (not often).

Apr 94. (cd/c/lp) *(AKD/AKC/AKH 026)* **CRAZY FOR GERSHWIN** ☐ -
– I got plenty of nuthin / I've got a crush on you / Ain't necessarily so / Someone to watch over me / Little jazz bird / Do it again / Stormy weather / Summertime / Sometimes not often / Is you is my baby / Smile / Porgy / Drifting / Rockabye your baby. *<US-iss.Jun00; same>*

Aug 95. (cd) *(<AKD 042>)* **THE BEST OF CAROL KIDD VOL.1** (compilation) ☐ ☐ Nov98
– I got plenty of nuthin / Georgia on my mind / Sing for your supper / Then I'll be tired of you / I wish I'd met you / I'm shadowing you / Haven't we met / The night we called it a day / Autumn in New York – My funny valentine / You're cheatin' yourself / Where or when / How little we know / We'll be together again / Don't worry about me / Never let me go / I'll take romance / Lean baby / Don't take your love from me / Nice work if you can get it.

Aug 95. (cd) *(AKD 043)* **THE BEST OF CAROL KIDD VOL.2** (compilation) ☐ -
– New York on Sunday / When I dream / Sometimes (not often) / I'm all smiles / Bad, bad Leroy Brown / Ain't neccessarily so / I could have told you so / I'm a fool to want you / Starting tomorrow / I'll guess I'll have to change my plan / I fall in love too easily / Round midnight / It isn't so bad / Don't go to strangers / Where are you / The more I see you – I've grown accustomed to your face / Trouble is a man / Bidin' my time / Dat dere / Please don't talk about me when I'm gone.

Sep 95. (cd/c/lp) *(AKD/AKC/AKH 044)* **THAT'S ME** ☐ -
– You don't bring me flowers / Send in the clowns / When the world was young /

Round midnight / I can't get started (with you) / I'm always chasing rainbows / Let me sing and I'm happy / This bitter earth / Somewhere over the rainbow / The trolley song / That's me.

Mar 01. (cd) *(AKD 146)* **A PLACE IN MY HEART** [ ] [-]
– Little girl blue / Pennies from Heaven / The charm of you / I've got you under my skin / Put your dreams away / The very thought of you / The sunny side of the street / If you are but a dream / I'll never smile again / I get a kick out of you / I get along without you very well / Bewitched, bothered and bewildered.

– compilations, etc. –

Nov 92. (cd/c/lp) *The Hit Label; (AHL CD/MC/LP 5)* **WHEN I DREAM** [ ] [-]
– When I dream / Bad bad Leroy Brown / Cinderella / I guess I'll have to change my plan / Sweet chariot / Sunday in New York / Georgia on my mind / The more I see you – I've grown accustomed to her face / With a little help from my friends / He moves through the fair / Sometimes (not often).

Nov 99. (3xcd-box) *Linn; (<AKD 116>)* **THE LINN BOX 2** [ ] [ ]
– (CAROL KIDD / ALL MY TOMORROWS / NICE WORK IF YOU CAN GET IT).

Bill KYLE

Born: 1940s, Dunfermline. KYLE first came to prominence as the drummer in 1970s Scottish jazz/rock group HEAD, which won the Dunkirk Jazz Festival award for new groups and recorded three albums, including its final work, Blackpool Cool, before the quintet went their seperate ways in the early 1980s. Following that, Kyle co-led the KYLE–KEDDIE SEXTET with trombonist Brian Keddie and took a guiding interest in the early career of saxophonist Tommy Smith, financing one of Smith's pre-Berklee albums and including him in his own groups. While working in the computer industry in America in the 1970s he had lessons with ex-Miles Davis drummer Tony Williams and made contacts with musicians with whom he would later tour the UK in his NEW YORK JAZZ and ATLANTIC BRIDGE groups. Flamboyant New York vibes player Joe Locke, saxophonist Dave O'Higgins, pianist Steve Hamilton and Tommy Smith all appeared in one or other of these.

As well as continuing to play jazz in various bands, Kyle has long been an enthusiastic and hard-working champion of the music. In the early 1970s he was instrumental in setting up PLATFORM, the Scottish Arts Council-funded organisation responsible for promoting jazz in Scotland, and enjoyed a long association with the organisation, latterly as a director of the company, until its demise in 1988.

Bill and former Head bassist, Graham Robb, reconvened in 2001 with HEAD2HEAD and have been playing a few gigs with top young Scottish musicians in the front line; they also have a CD, called Head2Head.

KYLE has been involved in various other jazz promotion initiatives and in April 2002 he opened THE BRIDGE Jazz Bar, a dedicated, live-jazz-seven-nights-a-week venue, in South Bridge, Edinburgh. Officially opened by Joe Locke, the Bridge offers regular performance opportunities to Scottish musicians and has featured visiting American musicians including Los Angeles-based saxophonist Bob Sheppard and star bassist Buster Williams' Quartet, featuring drummer Lenny White.

L

Carol LAULA (see ⇒ Section 8: Rock, Pop & Indie)

LOOKING EAST (see under ⇒ Lochshore records; Section 2: Folk)

Chick LYALL

Born: 1958, Edinburgh. During the early 90's, pianist/composer LYALL formed The GREEN ROOM, alongside DAVID GARRETT and DAVID BAIRD. CHICK was the most experienced having recorded an album ('TILTING GROUND') in the 80's with Norwegian saxophonist TORE BRUNBORG. However, this went mainly unheard – due to the fall of record label, 'Watercourse' – until 1999 when LYALL delivered the folk-tinged jazz set on his own imprint. Released around the same time was CHICK's lone set, 'SOLO' (1999), which was described as more introspective and adventurous (lend an ear to 'SOLITARY DANCE'), much like Keith Jarrett before him. If you loved your jazz on the quiet side of avant-garde, GREEN ROOM had supplied two ultimate coffee-table relaxers in the shape of 'HIDDEN MUSIC' in '94 and 'LIVE TRAJECTORIES' in '96.

GREEN ROOM

CHICK LYALL – keyboards, flute, bamboo percussion / **DAVID GARRETT** – percussion, dulcimer, piano / **DAVID BAIRD** – cello, voices, Chapman stick, tape loops

Leo not iss.

Jul 94. (cd) *(LABCD 007)* **HIDDEN MUSIC** [ ] [-]
– Rotations / Fable / Bone / Big foot / Totem / Flux / Mosquito / Fracture / Embryo / Satellites.

Feb 96. (cd) *(LABCD 025)* **LIVE TRAJECTORIES** [ ] [-]
– Trajectories / Hieroglyph / Biomorph / Divertimento / Flux II / Arabesque / Amazon / Endgame. *(re-iss. Aug98; same)*

— now a duo of **LYALL + GARRETT**

— not to be confused with the US jazz outfit on 'Mo' Funk' 2000; the album 'Connect'.

CHICK LYALL

— solo keyboards & synthesizer

Caber not iss.

Jan 99. (cd) *(CABER 005)* **SOLITARY DANCE** [ ] [-]
– Flow river flow / Solitary dance / First epigram / First object of contemplation / Sam song / Second epigram / Dusk / Blow wind blow / Third epigram / Second object of contemplation.

CHICK LYALL and TORE BRUNBORG

CHICK LYALL with **TORE BRUNBORG** – saxophones

Chick not iss.

1999. (cd) *(CArch 001)* **TILTING GROUND** [ ] [-]
– The tilting ground / Pulse song / Perhaps hand / Voiceover, parts I-IV.

Mac / Mc

Chas McDEVITT (see ⇒ Section 7: Rock & Pop)

Laura MacDONALD

Born: 1975, Glasgow. LAURA embarked on her musical career at the tender age of 16 when she joined the Strathclyde Youth Jazz Orchestra. This enabled the saxophonist to gain a scholarship into the Berklee College in 1995. A year later, the young LAURA was nominated for "the most Outstanding Performer" at the Glasgow International Jazz Festival. In 1997, she progressed to become the first winner of the Scottish Young Jazz Musician award which led her to work with the likes of VICTOR LEWIS, CARLA BLEY, TOMMY SMITH and the SCOTTISH NATIONAL JAZZ ORCHESTRA. SMITH signed her to 'Spartacus' records towards the end of the millennium and an album, 'LAURA' (recorded in New York with the aid of JEFF 'TAIN' WATTS, DAVID BUDWAY and JAMES GENUS), was delivered in the summer 2001. Half originals, half cover versions (including Pat Metheny's 'ALWAYS & FOREVER', Charles Mingus' 'SLOP', Rodgers & Hart's 'HAVE YOU MET MISS JONES' and Nat Simon's 'POINCIANA'). She had certainly come a long way in such a short time.

LAURA MacDONALD – saxophone / with **JEFF 'TAIN' WATTS** – drums / **JAMES GENUS** – bass / **DAVID BUDWAY** – piano

Spartacus not iss.

Aug 01. (cd) *(STS 002)* **LAURA** [ ] [-]
– The hex / Always & forever / Slop / Have you met Miss Jones? / Unknown quantities / Poinciana / Last confession / Can you hear me thinking?

John McLEVY

Born: Jan 2, 1927, Dundee. Regarded by his peers as a trumpet and flugelhorn player of great style and economy, McLEVY worked in hotel bands when he first arrived in London in the 1950s. Then, after a spell at the BBC with Cyril Stapleton, he became prominent on the London jazz scene during the 1960s. His humorous, hard-swinging style attracted the attention of US trumpeter

Bobby Hackett, who recommended McLevy to BENNY GOODMAN for a British big band that Goodman led on a European tour in 1970, an outing in whose success McLevy played no little part. He also played in Goodman's small group with Hank Jones, Slam Stewart, Bucky Pizzarelli and George Masso before moving into studio work, recording no fewer than twenty-one albums with singer Max Bygraves. He didn't allow session work to blunt his creative edge or dull his enthusiasm for blowing jazz and he co-led a very popular group with accordionist Jack Emblow for many years before settling into retirement in the late 1990s.

Tommy McQUATER

Born: 4 September 1914, Maybole, Ayrshire. One of the first British jazz trumpeters, McQUATER began playing cornet at the age of eleven in the Maybole Brass Band and while still in his teens joined LOUIS FREEMAN's band at Green's Playhouse in Glasgow. He moved to London with Freeman in 1933 and the following year joined Jack Payne's Orchestra, subsequently moving to Lew Stone and then Ambrose's band, where he and trombonist George Chisholm formed a partnership that developed into a long-lasting friendship and, later, a comedy team.

These bandleaders were all household names at the time although they played for dancing and only allowed McQuater to play his explosive style occasionally: when American saxophonist BENNY CARTER arrived in Britain in the mid 1930s, McQuater and Chisholm were first choices for his British band. In 1939, MCQUATER formed the HERALDS OF SWING, whose immediate impact was halted by the outbreak of World War II. McQuater joined the RAF band, the SQUADRONAIRES, playing lead trumpet, and after peace was declared he freelanced with the BBC Showband, in studios and as a jazz soloist.

He and Chisholm worked together frequently as a musical and comical double act and the 1960s found McQuater still busy, working with Jack Parnell at the London Palladium, playing lead trumpet in Elstree Film Studio's orchestra and making jazz club appearances. During the 1970s and 1980s, he continued to do studio work and played at Bill McGuffie's Niner Club, often with fellow Scottish trumpeter John McLevy. He also taught several prominent trumpeters, including Ian Carr, Alan Elsdon and Digby Fairweather, and remains one of the great characters of the early days of British jazz.

Ron MATHEWSON

Born: Feb 19, 1944, Lerwick, Shetland Isles. One of the great double bassists in European jazz, MATHEWSON comes from a musical family in an area where, although fiddle music reigns supreme, swing jazz has long had an impact through musicians such as the hugely influential guitarist, Peerie Willie Johnson. Mathewson's own musical career began at the age of eight with piano lessons. He took up bass at fifteen and within three years had moved to London, quickly immersing himself in the Soho jazz scene. Following a tour of Germany with a Dixieland band and sundry freelance gigs, he joined the great British saxophonist and vibist, TUBBY HAYES, working with him from 1966 until 1973, when Hayes died tragically young. He also worked with Stan Getz, Oscar Peterson, Ben Webster, Bill Evans, and Phil Woods, among many, many others, and led his own groups including THE RON MATHEWSON SIX PIECE, featuring saxophonists Alan Skidmore and Stan Sulzmann, into the 1970s.

He then became a regular member of Ronnie Scott's group and also worked with guitarist Jim Mullen's quartet and in Our Band (Mullen and saxophonist Dick Morrissey's straightahead band, as opposed to their Morrissey-Mullen jazz/funk group). During the 1980s, due to personal problems, MATHEWSON withdrew from gigging, but gradually he returned and by 2002 he was back, his magnificent tone and agile technique once again to the fore. His far from overcrowded discography includes albums with Tubby Hayes, including Mexican Green (1967), and Ronnie Scott, and the collaborative Seven Steps to Evans (1979) with Gordon Beck, Kenny Wheeler, Stan Sulzmann and Tony Oxley.

Ken MATHIESON

Born: 30 Jun'42, Uddingston, Glasgow. The young KEN began playing traditional jazz while still at school and went on to make his mark on the local scene during the 1960's. Over the period 1970-71, he relocated to the sprawling Brazilian metropolis of Sao Paulo where he played some gigs and got a permanent taste for the many and varied kinds of "musica Brasileira". Returning to Scotland, he made a living as a freelance session drummer for theatre, TV, radio etc. During the 70's he also began a long running residency at Milngavie's Black Bull Jazz Club where he worked with visiting legends like BENNY CARTER, BUD FREEMAN and SONNY STITT.

In 1987, following the demise of the Black Bull, KEN inaugurated the Glasgow International Jazz Festival with a raft of talent including SARAH VAUGHAN, DIZZY GILLESPIE and CHICK COREA. While the festival became a regular fixture in Scotland's musical calender, MATHIESON immersed himself in the musical side of things, touring with FAT SAM'S BAND. He subsequently formed, arranged and led no less than three bands of his own to cater for his wide ranging tastes: PICANTE (a meeting of bebop and Brazilian styles), JAZZ ECOSSE ALL-STARS (trad Dixieland featuring vocalist FIONNA DUNCAN) and THE CELEBRITIES OF JAZZ (a septet concentrating on the small-group style of BUCK CLAYTON and BUDDY TATE). He's since founded a further two outfits, GROOVEBUSTERS and BRAZILLIANCE. A man of many talents, KEN has also researched and presented a show on Radio Scotland and is due to begin work on a biography of 1940's jazz drummer BIG SID CATLETT.

In 1995, KEN set up his own JAZZ CELEBRITIES outfit to play classic mainstream sounds; they consisted of trumpeter BILLY HUNTER and saxophonist JOCK GRAHAM (both ex-TOMMY SAMPSON ORCHESTRA), trombonist JOHN McGUFF (ex-CLYDE VALLEY STOMPERS), pianist TOM FINLAY (ex-FAT SAM'S), bassist LINDSAY COOPER (ex-BOB WALLIS'S STORYVILLE JAZZMEN) and sax/clarinet man JACK DUFF (a soloist); sadly, the latter two have since died.

Ian MENZIES (see under ⇒ CLYDE VALLEY STOMPERS)

Jim MULLEN

Born: 26 Nov'45, Glasgow. Like many city-based Scottish musicians of his generation, Mullen's first gigs were at church hall dances, having acquired his first guitar at the age of ten and 'going public' within a year. In his mid teens, by this time a committed jazz fan and working with American singer Billy Daniels and Glasgow band leader Andy Park's ambitious, Gil Evans-influenced ten-piece, he was playing double bass, an instrument that played a big part in fashioning Mullen's idiosyncratic guitar style. A left hander, Mullen didn't bother to change the bass strings round. He played it right-handed and when he switched back to guitar – after watching his bass's neck and body part company while he tried to hold it together and finish a gig, it felt natural to continue playing right-handed, with his fingers – or more accurately – his thumb like one idol, Wes Montgomery, while leading a guitar-vibes-bass trio like another idol, Tal Farlow.

After leaving Park's band, he also led Jim Mullen & Co, featuring future members of the Average White Band, before moving to London in 1968. There he worked with Cream lyricist, Pete Brown before joining Dundee-born drummer Robbie McIntosh in organist and now acid jazz god Brian Auger's nascent Oblivion Express in 1970. After three albums with Auger – ranging from the tear it up jazz fusion of the first Oblivion Express album to the more groove-based Second Wind – Mullen left to join Vinegar Joe (featuring Elkie Brooks and Robert Palmer) then soul choir Kokomo.

While touring the US with Kokomo he decided to stay on – his friends in the Average White Band were doing rather well, after all. He played with flautist Herbie Mann and then began a residency in New York with British saxophonist Dick Morrissey. Their audiences were stuffed with New York players, who loved Mullen's bluesy directness and Morrissey's classy invention, and Atlantic Records commissioned the Average White Band to record 'UP', which became the first Morrissey–Mullen album. Back in London, the Morrissey–Mullen Band became hugely popular on the jazz scene, selling out gigs the length and breadth of the UK and releasing a string of albums which, while classy, didn't quite convey the steaminess of the band's live performances. Morrissey-Mullen made several more, 'CAPE WRATH' (1979), 'BADNESS' (1981), 'LIFE ON THE WIRE' (1982) – the last two both making the UK Top 50 – and 'IT'S ABOUT TIME' (1983). Morrissey–Mullen split in 1985 after 'THIS MUST BE THE PLACE', although the two musicians remained friends and played together occasionally afterwards in more straight ahead settings, including an album with blues singer Jimmy Witherspoon, until Morrissey's untimely death in 2000. Mullen went on to lead the similarly groove-based MEANTIME and tour with fellow Scot, saxophonist Bobby Wellins, and during the 1990s he released a series of albums varying from the state-of-the-art fusion of 'INTO THE NINETIES' to the Blue Note-styled 'WE GO BACK'.

He also worked with singers Claire Martin and Tam White, and when Chigaco folk-soul legend Terry Callier rebooted his career, Mullen was his guitarist of choice. Subsequently, in addition to partnering former AWB singer-guitarist Hamish Stuart in the supergroovy JimJam, Mullen has recorded an album of Robert Burns songs (making Burns not only the first singer-songwriter but a writer of jazz standards predating Gershwin, Porter et al by a good 150 years), an album of his favourite cartoon themes, Animation, and a typically exciting session with his Organ Trio.

Brilliant spontaneity, forged from a lifetime's dedication to studying, absorbing and most of all playing great music, is what Mullen listeners have come to expect from one of jazz's true originals. The Jim Mullen Burns title might equally apply to his heat seeking style which includes crisp, clear phrasing, a penchant for mischievously quoting other tunes during solos (he once even managed to quote Miles Davis's Jean-Pierre in a thirty-second Yellow Pages television commercial), the ability to create excitement from the most commonplace melody (yes, including the Perry Como hit 'It's Impossible' on his Organ Trio CD), and the passion that made one critic describe Mullen's right thumb as "the best blues singer Glasgow has ever produced."

JIM MULLEN – guitar, bass / with session people

Coda not iss.

Oct 84. (lp/cd) *(CODA 4/+CD)* **THUMBS UP**
– Blue Montreux / Fall / As if you read my mind / Crepescule / Thumbs up / Herbal scent / Friends / Beauty and the beast.

Castle not iss.

Oct 90. (cd/c/lp) *(SAP CD/MC/LP 101)* **INTO THE 90's**
– Houdini / Safe haven / Breathless / 606 theme / Contraflow / Risky business / Absent friends / Hip-hoperation.

Phantom not iss.

Jul 94. (cd) *(EFZ 1003)* **SOUNDBITES**
– Don't ask / Famous last words / Mr. Fonebone / Soundbites / Strayhorn / Raspberries / Three wishes / Straight and narrow / Fingerprint / Evidence. *(re-iss. Sep01 on 'Jazzprint'; JPVP 106CD)*

May 95. (cd) *(EFZ 1012)* **RULE OF THUMB**
– Rule of thumb / Shelflife / Speed of sound / Nova Scotia / Spare change / Best before / Say no more / Skid / Power of three / Foureyes. *(re-iss. Feb02 on 'Jazzprint'; JPVP 104CD)*

Black Box Jazz Black Box Jazz

Aug 00. (cd; as JIM MULLEN QUARTET) *(<BBJ 2016>)* **BURNS** Nov00
– Count the lawin' / Banks and braes / Bonnie wee thing / Comin' through the rye / Willie Gray / The Lea rig / Sweet Afton / For the sake o' somebody / Lassie lie near me / A man's a man / Red, red rose.

Jazzprint not iss.

Jun 01. (cd) *(JPVP 103CD)* **LIVE IN GLASGOW (live)**
– Peace / Embraceable you / At the Mambo Inn / My ideal / Things ain't what they used to be / Medication.

Feb 02. (cd) *(JPVP 105CD)* **WE GO BACK**
– Born to be blue / Ritha / My foolish heart / Medication / I fall in love too easily / Paris eyes / Darn that dream / Outeractive / Smart money / One finger snap.

Black Box Jazz not iss.

Jan 02. (cd) *(BBJ 2022)* **ANIMATION**
– One song / Ev'rybody wants to be a cat / Dream is a wish your heart makes / I've got no strings / Second star to the right / I'm wishing / Baby mine / Give a little whistle / You can fly / With a smile and a song / When you wish upon a star.

d.s. MURRAY QUARTET

Formed: Glasgow . . . late 1996 by MURRAY and his crew ALLAN WYLIE, RICK STANDLEY and TASOS BOBBOS. Initiated as a vehicle for the original compositions of MURRAY, the group's music uses an improvisational framework rooted in classic jazz but inspired and informed by modern dancefloor styles such as drum'n'bass and hip-hop. A series of 12" singles complete with state-of-the-art club remixes signalled the group's crossover ambitions while their acclaimed live shows appealed to both hardened jazz buffs and dance fans alike. A debut album, 'HOME MOVIES' (1999), was released on Scottish label Lochshore's subsidiary, 'OK Jazz', receiving high praise from more adventurous critics.

D.S. MURRAY – guitar / **ALLAN WYLIE** – trumpet / **RICK STANDLEY** – bass / **TASOS BOBBOS** – drums

OK Jazz not iss.

1999. (cd) *(CDOK 3011)* **HOME MOVIES**
– Space cadets / Lust for life / John Holmes / Sweetmeat / Waltz Disney / Ecstasy / Paranoia / Acid jazz / Jungle bunnies are go.

David NEWTON

Born: 2 Feb'58, Glasgow. DAVID NEWTON is a consistently bright talent, a pianist, accompanist and composer who's worked with jazz greats such as BENNY CARTER, HUMPHREY LYTTELTON and many others including MARTIN TAYLOR and TINA MAY. He began his musical career (c.1978) in a Bradford trio while studying at Leeds College of Music. He subsequently returned to Scotland, Edinburgh to be exact and worked with several touring American musicians, while also being part of the BUDDY DE FRANCO combo; NEWTON delivered his first solo release, 'GIVEN TIME', in 1988. CAROL KIDD's musical director and pianist until 1994, the now London-based NEWTON released his first album for Linn in 1991. Entitled 'Victim Of Circumstance', the record's laidback piano, bass and drums trio sound brought widespread critical acclaim as did its follow-up, 'EYE WITNESS' (1991); both included renditions of two MATT DENNIS standards alongside his own compositions. He completed a trio of releases for the label in 1994 with 'RETURN JOURNEY', a solo piano odyssey. NEWTON also made guest appearances on KIDD's 'I'm Glad We Met' and MARTIN TAYLOR's 'Change Of Heart' and 'Kiss And Tell' while more recently (1998), he released a Hoagy Carmichael tribute in collaboration with BRIAN LEMON.

DAVID NEWTON – piano / with various session people

G.F.M. not iss.

1988. (lp) *(GFMLP 8003)* **GIVEN TIME**
– Someday my prince will come / There will never be another you / Given time / How deep is the ocean / I've never been in love before / Katy's song / Prelude to a kiss / The days of wine and roses / Last drop blues.

— next with **ALEC DANKWORTH** – bass / **CLARK TRACEY** – drums

Linn Linn

Feb 91. (cd/c/lp) *(AKD/AKC/AKH 013)* **VICTIM OF CIRCUMSTANCE**
– Wishful thinking / The night we called it a day / Katy's song / It never entered my mind / Victim of circumstance / One and only / Please come home / The way you look tonight. *<US cd-iss. Nov98; same as UK>*

— now with **DAVE GREEN + ALAN GANLEY** (of CAROL KIDD's band)

Nov 91. (cd/c/lp) *(AKD/AKC/AKH 015)* **EYE WITNESS**
– Ol' blue eyes / Bedroom eyes / Angel eyes / Eye witness / Soul eyes / Stars in my eyes / Eye of the hurricane / My mother's eyes. *<US cd-iss. Jun98; same as UK>*

Apr 94. (cd/c/lp) *(AKD/AKC/AKH 025) <5025>* **RETURN JOURNEY** Oct95
– Stolen time / Only passing through / While you're away / On the horizon / Home from home / On my own / On the road / Into somewhere / Gone forever.

— later in '94, NEWTON collaborated with ALAN BARNES on the album, 'LIKE MINDS' for 'Fret' (FJCD 105)

Candid Candid

Nov 95. (cd; as DAVID NEWTON TRIO) *(<CCD 79714>)* **IN GOOD COMPANY** (rec. Sept'94)
– Get lost / Bleesed land / Teach me tonight / June time / My romance / There's a small hotel / Sugar cake / The remark you made / Older and wiser / When I see you cry. *(re-iss. Feb97; same)*

Mar 96. (cd) *(<CCD 79728>)* **12th OF THE 12th: A JAZZ PORTRAIT OF FRANK SINATRA** Apr96
– My kind of town (Chicago is) / I've got the world on a string / I fall in love too easily / Witchcraft / The lady is a tramp / This is all I ask / It's nice to go trav'ling / Violets for your furs / All over nothing at all / You make me feel so young / All the way / Twelfth of the twelfth / Only the lonely – Saturday night is the loneliest night of the week / In the wee small hours of the morning. *(re-iss. Feb97; same)*

Oct 97. (cd) *(CCD 79742)* **DNA**
– DNA / Julia / Highwire / Where is the one / Feet on the ground / Garden of dreams / Ablution / Scribe / We'll be together again.

Impetus Blue Note

Sep 98. (cd; by the NEWTON-TRACEY BAND) *(ASCCD 23) <07777 8069621>* **BOOTLEG ERIC**
– What you will / Faith in Alec / Bootleg Eric / College groove / Springs eternal / Blue trinity.

not iss. Zephyr

Oct 98. (cd; by DAVID NEWTON & BRIAN LEMON) *(<ZECD 20>)* **DAVID NEWTON MEETS BRIAN LEMON TO PLAY HOAGY CARMICHAEL** ☐ ☐
– Riverboat shuffle / Nearness of you / Rockin' chair / Two sleepy people / Georgia on my mind / My resistance is low / Skylark / Up a lazy river / Stardust / Small fry / One morning in May / Blues for Hoagy.

Concorde Jazz not iss.

Aug 98. (cd; by ALAN BARNES & the DAVID NEWTON TRIO) *(CCDEU 48422)* **BELOW ZERO** ☐ -
– Woodville / Song for Strayhorn / Below zero / Estate / College groove / The flower is a wonderful thing / K4 Pacific / Lady's vanity / Waltz for Debbie / Blessed land / Mambo koyama.

Feb 00. (cd) *(CCDEU 48802)* **HALFWAY TO DAWN** ☐ -
– Dreamsville / I wish / Halfway to dawn / Tricotism / Scotch blues / Bright new day / Last night when we were young / You do something to me / Kiss and tell.

Jun 00. (cd; by ALAN BARNES & DAVID NEWTON) *(CCDEU 49052)* **SUMMERTIME** ☐ -
– Art's oregano / Summertime / Freeman of London / Di's waltz / Bluebird of Delhi / Tico Tico / Street of dreams / Black and tan fantasy / Don't be that way / Early Autumn / Hawk / Autumn nocturne / Charlie the chulo / Haunted melody / Zoot.

Maggie NICOLS (see under ⇒ HYDER, Ken)

ORIGINAL DOWNTOWN SYNCOPATORS (see under ⇒ GEESIN, Ron; Section 7: Rock & Pop)

P

Don PATERSON

Born: 1963, Dundee. A guitarist, poet and playwright, PATERSON took up music at school and was soon immersed in learning from John Martyn, John Abercrombie and Ralph Towner. He gained his early work experience in covers bands playing around Dundee social clubs and with his father, Russ, a country-folk styled singer-guitarist; in the early 1980s he led a trio which included Nico Bruce (nephew of Jack) on bass guitar, playing mainly original compositions.

Having played a few dates around Scotland with drummer Ken Hyder in a short-lived free improvising group called Restless Natives, he moved to London in 1984 to join Hyder's TALISKER, working alongside former King Crimson violinist David Cross and recording Humanity (Impetus Records, 1986). In 1990, Talisker having split, he formed Celtic-jazz band LAMMAS with saxophonist Tim Garland. The group, described by one admiring critic as "the intersection of Steps Ahead, Oregon and Moving Hearts" and featuring Mark Fletcher (drums), uilleann pipesmeister and bodhran player, Steafan Hannigan, and singer Christine Tobin alongside Paterson's six- and twelve-string guitars and Garland's flutes, whistles, saxes and synths, went on to receive considerable acclaim for albums including its debut, Lammas, which not only featured star trumpeter Kenny Wheeler but also boasted a tune called Skitters. After five albums, the group split in 1999.

By now also a highly respected poet (collections including Nil Nil for faber & faber), PATERSON returned to Scotland and briefly had a duo with pianist David Milligan before teaming up with keyboardist Steve Hamilton. Busy with writing work, including poetry, plays, teaching creative writing, poetry readings, he remains a musician of considerable imagination and flair – and one of the few members of the Musicians' Union to have worked on the Commando comics (during a brief immediately post-school "proper job" flirtation).

Cathie RAE (see ⇒ section 8: Rock, Pop & Indie)

John RAE (see under ⇒ Caber music)

Ronnie RAE

Born: 1938, Edinburgh. A bassist of huge experience and father to a veritable Scottish jazz clan (drummer John; pianist Ronnie Jnr; and singers Cathie, Sylvia and Gina), RONNIE began his career in 1965 with the ALEX WELSH BAND, where he recorded with such giants as saxophonists Ben Webster, Eddie 'Lockjaw' Davis and Bud Freeman, pianist Earl Hines and cornettist Ruby Braff. After leaving Welsh he became THE bassist for hire in Scotland and may well be the only jazz bassist whose CV includes shows with Harry Worth, Tommy Cooper and Ronnie Corbett.

A random selection of the many, many internationally recognised jazz names he has worked with in the music's time-honoured "with local rhythm section" scenario includes alto saxophonists Bobby Watson and Lee Konitz, tenorists Spike Robinson and Bobby Wellins, trumpeter Jimmy Deuchar, cornettist Warren Vache, guitarist Louis Stewart, and singer Carol Kidd. The list is almost endless but it's some measure of the regard that he is rightly held in that, when Red Norvo & Tal Farlow regrouped their vibes-guitar-bass trio for a UK tour in the 1980s, Ronnie slotted in with ease. (Norvo & Farlow had a trio with Charles Mingus on bass in the 1950s, so there's following in daunting footsteps for you.)

At the age of sixty, RONNIE finally stepped out of the rhythm section shadows to form his own group, SCOTIA NOSTRA, playing his own music with a team of younger players, including son John on drums. He is also heard regularly with singer Fionna Duncan and daughter Cathie's group and took great pride in appearing on debut recordings by daughters, Cathie (Time Out – own label) and Sylvia (Close Enough – Caber), which were launched almost simultaneously in September 2002.

S

SALSA CELTICA

Formed: Edinburgh . . . 1996 by the Cuban-inspired collective of GALO CERON-CARRASCO, TOBY SHIPPEY, ANDREW BARNETT, STEVE KETTLEY, ALEX HUDSON, DAVID 'DEMUS' DONNELLY, DOUG HUDSON, GUY NICOLSON and DAVID 'CHIMPO' ROBERTSON, all members of various bands based in Scotland including CAPERCAILLIE, TARTAN AMOEBAS, FRED MORRISON'S CEOLAS, MOUTH MUSIC, WOLFSTONE, OLD BLIND DOGS, BAG O' CATS, BLACKANIZED, BLAZIN' FIDDLES, DEMUSPHERE, CAULD BLAST ORCHESTRA, LATINO 2000, COMMITMENTS, NIGHTMARES ON WAX, AZITIZ, FINLEY QUAYE, MATT BIANCO, ROBERTO PIA, LOS TRES FENOMENOS and LIAM HARNEY'S CELTIC FUSION.

Proof that gringos really can raise the salsa temperature with the best of them, 1997's hugely impressive 'MONSTRUOS Y DEMONIOS ANGELS AND LOVERS' album was a revelation to Scotland's indie-dominated music scene. Recorded after a trip to Cuba itself, the record's vitality, diversity and incredible fluidity suggested that SALSA CELTICA had bottled the spirit of Fidel Castro's Caribbean island and brought it back with them. Despite only numbering one bonafide Latino in the line-up, the Edinburgh hispanophiles conjured up an exotic array of tropical moods via stabbing brass, acoustic guitar, dreamy flute, elastic percussion and sultry, haunting female backing vocals. In fact, the album left for dead most of the so called "Salsa" increasingly clogging up record shop shelves and compilation albums in the wake of the Buena Vista-inspired Cuban renaissance.

SALSA CELTICA have since become a regular fixture on the Edinburgh live scene, playing alongside the capital's resident Venezuelan star, CARLOS PENA and representing one of the highlights of the city's 1998 Hogmanay celebrations. In 1999, the band were invited back to Cuba to work with CONJUNTO FOLKLORICO DE CUTUMBA while the new millennium saw the release of their hotly anticipated follow-up album, 'THE GREAT SCOTTISH LATIN ADVENTURE'.

GALO CERON-CARRASCO – guitar, Colombian tiple / **TOBY SHIPPEY** – trumpet, percussion / **ANDREW BARNETT** – saxes / **DAVID 'EL CHIMPO' ROBERTSON** – bongos, percussion / **DOUGIE 'EL PULPO' HUDSON** – congas / **GUY NICOLSON** – timbales / **DAVID 'DEMUS' DONNELLY** – bass / **STEVE KETTLEY** – sax, flute, jaw's harp / **ALEX HUDSON CRAUFORD** – piano

Eclectic not iss.

Aug 97. (cd) *(ECLCD 9717)* **MONSTRUOS Y DEMONIOS ANGELS AND LOVERS** ☐ -
– Salsa Celtica / La reina rumbera / Guajira del sol / Osain / Paisa / No hay Olvido, Pablito / La batea / KouKou / Frente a frente / El cometa bop / Escorpion / Loco a loco / Kulu.

— **KENNY FRASER** – fiddle, bagpipes; repl. GALO

— **FRASER FIFIELD** – pipes, whistles, sax; repl. BARNETT

— **DAVID PATRICK** – piano; repl. CRAUFORD

— added guests **ANDY THORBURN** – accordion / **LENO ROCHO** – vocals / **MARIO CARIBE** – bass / **SIMON VAN DER WALT** + **RYAN QUIGLEY** – trumpets

G2 not iss.

Jun 00. (cd) *(G2CD 7005)* **THE GREAT SCOTTISH LATIN ADVENTURE** ☐ -
– Rumba Escocia / Malacon / Milonga for Iona / Yo me voy / Maggie's pancakes / Flaquita / Fuerte confuego ardiente / Vampiras / Carnoustie albatross / Leonardo capanga / Estrelita Celta / El capitan.

Tommy SAMPSON

Born: 1918. If, at one time, Tommy Sampson appeared to be everywhere, that's probably because he was, or at least his band was. At ballroom dancing's peak, there were four Tommy Sampson bands, all playing Sampson's arrangements and bearing his name – mostly in his absence – working in Perth, Inverness, Ayr and Aberdeen.

Sampson got his musical training and early experience as a youngster in the Salvation Army and led his first band as a prisoner of war following his capture at the Battle of Tobruk. Following repatriation in 1945, he led the Scottish Command Dance Orchestra until his army discharge in 1946. The following year he formed his own band, beginning a long career as both bandleader and talent spotter. His first band, regarded generally as the best and most swinging big band in Britain in the 1940s, included Lochgelly-born baritone saxophonist Joe Temperley, who went on to join Buddy Rich – as did a later Sampsonite, fellow Fifer and baritone player, Jay Craig. Subsequent bands included singers Rosemary Squires and Danny Street, saxophonists Bill Skeat, Danny Moss and Alan Skidmore, and trombonist Johnny Keating, who later moved to Hollywood where he scored films including Arthur Haley's Hotel.

When the big band era came to a close, Sampson worked as a song plugger/arranger with London-based music publishers and sang with the George Mitchell Choir, which led to him becoming musical director of (Falkirk-born) Mitchell's long-running Black & White Minstrels television show. Returning to Scotland, he formed a band for dancing – one band grew into four – and has remained active ever since.

Even the arrival of disco music in the 1970s didn't put him out of business, as it did many others – an early, and costly, lesson learned when he refused to play commercially showing Sampson the importance of being flexible. "I wasn't going to be left behind," he recalled. "So I had my bands play pop."

Still in demand in his 80s as an arranger, for artists including Edinburgh crooner Craig McMurdo, Sampson celebrated fifty years as a bandleader – the celebration was a little overdue – in a special Edinburgh International Jazz & Blues Festival concert in 2002 with special guests, Sampson band old boys, drummer Eric Delaney and saxophonist Danny Moss.

• **Note:** The aforementioned GEORGE MITCHELL died late August 2002 at a nursing home in Albrighton, Shropshire.

TOMMY SAMPSON – with orchestra

Melodisc not iss.

Feb 58. (7",78; as TOMMY SAMPSON & HIS STRONGMEN) *(MEL 1411)* **ROCKIN'. / ROCK'N'ROLL THOSE BIG BROWN EYES** ☐ -

Parlophone not iss.

Jul 58. (7",78; as TOMMY SAMPSON ORCHESTRA) *(R 4458)* **LAZY TRAIN. / SMOOTH MOOD** ☐ -

— SAMPSON retired from solo studio work but still performed live

SCOTTISH GUITAR QUARTET (see under ⇒ Caber music)

(see under ⇒ Caber music)

George SCOTT-WOOD

Born: 1903, Glasgow. During the 30's and 40's, the popular jazzman and virtuoso accordion player led The SIX SWINGERS who cut a few (very rare) tracks for 'Zonophone' before the war; SAM BROWNE provided vocals. Sadly, GEORGE was to die in 1978.

Eddie SEVERN (see under ⇒ Caber music)

SHINE (see under ⇒ BACHUE)

Tommy SMITH

Born: 27 Apr'67, Luton, England, but brought up in Edinburgh's Wester Hailes estate, he first picked up the tenor saxophone at the age of 12. SMITH's precocious talent saw him win a scholarship to the famous Berklee School Of Music in Boston, USA when he was only seventeen. During his first year at the college, SMITH and his group FORWARD MOTION released a debut album, 'THE BERKLEE TAPES' (1984).

While cutting his musical teeth alongside GARY BURTON, the heavily JOHN COLTRANE-influenced SMITH released 'GIANT STRIDES' as his first solo album in 1983. Later he was snapped up by 'Blue Note', cutting 'STEP BY STEP' (1989) and the BURTON-produced 'PEEPING TOM' (1990). After breathing new life into a string of dusty classics on 1991's 'STANDARDS', SMITH signed with the burgeoning 'Linn' label (home to The BLUE NILE and CAROL KIDD amongst others). 1994's 'REMINISCENCE' resurrected his FORWARD MOTION band while 'MISTY MORNING AND NO TIME' (1995) was a unique tribute to Scots poet Norman MacCaig, using SMITH's increasingly individual post-bop style to translate the poet's words into music.

'BEASTS OF SCOTLAND' (1996) was a tad different, each track named after, and presumably expressing the nature of, Scotland's creatures, from the magnificent Golden Eagle to the humble (yet bloody exasparating!) Highland Midge. 1998's 'THE SOUND OF LOVE' was more straightforward, a tribute to the balladry of DUKE ELLINGTON and BILLY STRAYHORN. The following year saw the ever prolific sax maestro release two collaborative sets, 'GYMNOPEDIE' with MURRAY McLACHLAN, and 'BLUE SMITH" with JOHN SCOFIELD. Working in New York with JAMES GENUS, KENNY BARRON and CLARENCE PENN, SMITH returned on his new label, naming his next set, 'SPARTACUS' (2001), after the imprint. A follow-up CD, 'INTO SILENCE' (2002) – recorded in the Hamilton Mausoleum (a strange place with a 15-second reverberation) – was the third for the imprint, the second being new signing, LAURA MacDONALD. Noteworthy is SMITH's work in founding The Scottish National Jazz Orchestra, in which he operates as instigator, motivator, player, conductor, compere! He is also just about to start a Scottish Youth Jazz Orchestra – busy is TOMMY's middle name.

TOMMY SMITH – saxophone

not iss. H.E.P.

Nov 84. (lp; by FORWARD MOTION) *<2026>* **THE BERKLEE TAPES** - ☐

— now with **ALAN TAYLOR** – bass + **JOHN RAE** – drums

G.F.M. not iss.

Feb 87. (lp) *(GFMLP 8001)* **GIANT STRIDES** ☐ -

Blue Note Blue Note – Capitol

Mar 89. (cd/c/lp) *(CD/TC+/BLT 1001) <91930>* **STEP BY STEP** ☐ ☐
– Ally the wallygator / Step by step / Ghosts / Pillow talk / Time piece / Springtime / Freetime / Ever never land.

May 90. (cd/c/lp) *(CD/TC+/BLT 1002) <94335>* **PEEPING TOM** ☐ ☐
– The new road / Follow your heart / Merry go round / Slip of the tongue / Interval time *[cd-only]* / Simple pleasures *[cd-only]* / Peeping Tom / Quiet picnic *[cd-only]* / Affairs, please / Harlequin / Boats and boxes *[cd-only]* / Biting at the apple / Baked air *[cd-only]*.

May 91. (cd/c/lp) *(CD/TC+/BLT 1003) <96452>* **STANDARDS** ☐ ☐ Jan91
– Star eyes / Speak low / Skylark / September song / Blacken blue / Mildew / You've changed / My secret love / Night and day / My old flame / Julia / Lover / Dreamscapes pt.1 / Silent but deadly (dreamscapes pt.4).

Oct 92. (cd/c/lp) *(CD/TC+/BLT 1005)* **PARIS (live)** ☐ -
– Dischord / True sobriety / Reflections / Day light / Ping pong / Children play / Phraseology / Tear / Birth / Lost / Fragments / Occidentalism.

Linn Linn

Feb 94. (cd/c/lp; by TOMMY SMITH & FORWARD MOTION) *(<AKD/AKC/AKH 024>)* **REMINISCENCE** [ ] [ ] Jul94
– Hope / Memoir / On the ocean floor / Old times / Folk song / Emancipation of dissonance / Day dreams / Ally / Is really this it / Reminiscence.

May 95. (cd/c/lp) *(<AKD/AKC/AKH 040>)* **MISTY MORNING AND NO TIME** [ ] [ ]
– Intrusion / Estuary / Incident / Memorial / The root of it / You went away / Dipper / Rag and bone / Sounds of the day / Country dance / Misty morning and no time / Day break / Two friends / Trapped.

Aug 96. (cd) *<AKD 054>* **BEASTS OF SCOTLAND** [-] [ ]
– Golden eagle / Salmon / Midge / Wolf / Red deer / Gannet / Conger eel / Spider / Seal / Wildcat.

May 97. (cd) *(<AKD 059>)* **AZURE** [ ] [ ]
– Gold of the Azue / Escape ladder / Siesta / Smile of the flamboyant wings / Vowel song / Constellation – The morning star / Calculation / Dancer / Dialogue of the insects / Blue.

Feb 98. (cd) *(<AKD 084>)* **THE SOUND OF LOVE (The Ballads Of Duke Ellington & Billy Strayhorn)** [ ] [ ]
– Johnny come lately / Star-crossed lovers / In a sentimental mood / The flower is a lovesome thing / Chelsea bridge / Isfahan / Duke Ellington's sound of love / Sophisticated lady / Passion flower / Solitude / Prelude to a kiss / Cottontail.

May 99. (cd; by TOMMY SMITH & MURRAY McLACHLAN) *(AKD 103)* **GYMNOPEDIE** [ ] [-]
– Gymnopedie / Bagpipe music / Gnossienne No.1 / Children's song No.7 / Arietta / Children's song No.6 / Notturno / Bulgarian rhythm / Gnossienne No.3 / Je te veux / Hall of mirrors (sonata No.1) / Dreaming with eyes wide open (sonata No.1).

Nov 99. (cd) *(<AKD 110>)* **BLUE SMITH** [ ] [ ]
– El Nino / Hubba hubba / Rain dance / Dr Sco / Touch your toes / Amazing Grace / Bracken blue / Blues blew blue / Eany meany miny mo / The miracle / Dr Smith.

Spartacus not iss.

Mar 01. (cd) *(STS 001)* **SPARTACUS** [ ] [-]
– The peacocks / I want to be happy / Emily / Bye bye blackbird / It never entered my mind / The lady is a tramp / When I'm all alone / Spartacus / I loves you Porgy.

Feb 02. (cd) *(STS 003)* **INTO SILENCE** [ ] [-]
– The scream / Oran na politician / Naima / Libra / Capella / Ad te levavi / Deneb / My romance / Orlon / Aquila / Phoenix / Tibi, Christe, splendour patris / Cassiopeia / My one & only love / Perseus / Ursa minor / 'S ann aig Port Taigh na h-airigh / Cetus / Lynx / Indus / Vela / Gradual / Draco / Alleluia / Collect.

– compilations, etc. –

Mar 00. (3xcd-box) *Linn; (AKD 124)* **THE LINN BOX VOL.4** [ ] [-]
– (REMINISCENCE / MISTY MORNING AND NO TIME / AZURE).

Colin STEELE (see under ⇒ Caber music)

Ian STEWART (see ⇒ Section 7: Rock & Pop)

T

Martin TAYLOR

Born: 1956, Harlow, Essex, England, although he now resides in Ayr. The son of jazz bassist, BUCK TAYLOR, MARTIN was only four when he first got his hands on a guitar. While not poring over VAL DOONICAN and his Cifford Essex model, he was much impressed by Gypsy guitar hero, DJANGO REINHARDT as well as jazz pianists like ART TATUM. The influence of the latter artist was pivotal during the formative years of TAYLOR's musical development as he began laying the foundations for his characteristic solo technique.

The 'TAYLOR MADE' album marked his vinyl debut in 1979, its release precipitating a plunge into the jazz spotlight as STEPHANE GRAPPELLI plucked TAYLOR from obscurity for a series of concerts in his native France. The collaboration was a roaring success and the pair subsequently travelled to the States for a series of high profile dates, initiating a decade plus partnership which extended to over 20 albums. During this period, TAYLOR worked with some of the most legendary names in the business inluding YEHUDI MENUHIN, NELSON RIDDLE and PEGGY LEE. Following on from 1981's 'SKYE BOAT', the nimble-fingered Scot picked up his own solo career again in 1987 with the acclaimed 'SARABANDA' album, a mix of slick jazz and classic swing that even included a Gaelic title ('EILEN DHU').

Yet he only really began concentrating on his solo work after signing a deal with Eaglesham label, 'Linn' (also home to The BLUE NILE and CAROL KIDD) at the turn of the decade. 1990's 'DON'T FRET' kicked things off, followed a year later by 'CHANGE OF HEART' (1991) and the top selling 'ARTISTRY' (1993), an album which sat atop the British jazz charts for more than a month. 1993 also saw him hooking up with GRAPPELLI once more for the 'REUNION' album and a BBC TV documentary. Tribute set, 'SPIRIT OF DJANGO' (1994) found TAYLOR paying homage to his late hero via a combination of creative REINHARDT interpretations and new material composed in the Gypsy's groundbreaking spirit. Again, the record made No.1 in the jazz charts and was even nominated for best album at the UK jazz awards. 1995's 'PORTRAITS' took a different tack, MARTIN working in Nashville with six-string country wizard CHET ATKINS.

His heavy touring schedule also took him to Australia in 1997 where he cut 'TWO'S COMPANY', an album of duets with a raft of native talent largely unknown in Britain. The record was eventually released in 1999, a year that not only saw a dual set, 'I'M BEGINNING TO SEE THE LIGHT', with mandolin maestro DAVID GRISMAN (they had met in 1980 through the 'TONE POEMS I & II' collaborations) but found TAYLOR signing a major label deal with 'Sony', the first UK jazz artist to do so in 30 years. 'KISS & TELL' (1999) represented the first fruits of the new deal, a laid back offering flitting between smooth jazz, bossa nova, a funky cover of 'MIDNIGHT AT THE OASIS' and even a reworking of 'HAWAII FIVE-O', all performed with his characteristic fluidity and attention to detail.

The new millennium found MARTIN as busy as ever, receiving an Honorary doctorate from the University Of Paisley, releasing his autobiography (also entitled 'Kiss & Tell') and cutting his first live album, 'GYPSY' (1998), a release in the spirit of his earlier REINHARDT tribute and utilising the same band. More recently (January 2001), TAYLOR appeared on the Esther Rantzen daytime show, performing alongside French easy-listening legend SACHA DISTEL.

• **Note:** While TAYLOR's work is usually the preserve of jazz fans, the wider public were unwittingly exposed to his talent via the hugely popular "Nicole-Papa" Renault Clio TV ads.

• **Songwriters:** Covered a multitude of jazz standards incl. ON GREEN DOLPHIN STREET (B. Kaper) / EMILY (Johhny Mandel & Johnny Mercer) / MINOR TRUTH + LADY BE GOOD (Harold Ousley) / ST. THOMAS (Sonny Rollins) / MY LATIN BROTHER (George Benson) / TEACH ME TONIGHT (Sammy Cahn – Gene De Paul) / WATCH WHAT HAPPENS (Michael LeGrand – Gimbel) / SCRAPPLE FROM THE APPLE (Charlie Parker) / SENOR MOUSE + WINDOWS (Chick Corea) / BRIGHT SIZE LIFE (Pat Metheny) / WAITING (Peter Ind) / + loads more in the 90's.

MARTIN TAYLOR – guitar / with **PETER IND** – bass / **JOHN RICHARDSON** – drums

Wave / not iss.

1979. (lp; as MARTIN TAYLOR with JOHN RICHARDSON & PETER IND) *(WAVE 17)* **TAYLOR MADE** [ ] [-]
– On Green Dolphin Street / Emily / Minor truth / Lady be good / St. Thomas / My Latin brother / Teach me tonight / Watch what happens / Scrapple from the apple. *(cd-iss. Jul98' WAVE 17CD)*

1981. (lp; as MARTIN TAYLOR & PETER IND) *(WAVE 24)* **TRIPLE LIBRA** [ ] [-]
– Manhattan tea party / Senor mouse / Ginger / Triple libra / Windows / Bright size life / Waiting / Green eyes. *(cd-iss. Jul98; WAVE 24CD)*

Concord Jazz / not iss.

Jun 82. (lp) *(CJ 184)* **SKYE BOAT** [ ] [-]
– Mouse's spinney / Check it out / St. Thomas / Falling in love with love / Body and soul / Billie's bounce / Stompin' at the Savoy.

Hep Jazz / not iss.

Nov 86. (lp) *(HEP 2032)* **TRIBUTE TO ART TATUM** [ ] [-]

Dec 88. (lp; with BUDDY DE FRANCO) *(HEP 2039)* **GARDEN OF DREAMS** [ ] [-]

— now with **JOHN PATITUCCI** + **DAVID HUNGATE** – bass (of TOTO) / **MIKE WOFFORD** – piano / **RALPH HUMPHREY** – drums / **PAULINHO DA COSTA** – percussion / **SAL MARQUEZ** – trumpet / and guest **STEPHANE GRAPPELLI** – violin

Gaia / Gaia

Feb 89. (lp/c/cd) *(<139018-1/-4/-2>)* **SARABANDA** [ ] [ ] Nov87
– Mornin' / Call to Sarabanda / They can't take that away from me / Jenna / Cherokee ridge / Holiday for two / I remember Clifford / Deja vu / Don't blame me / I got rhythm / Eilen dhu (The dark island).

— now with **DAVID NEWTON** – piano, synthesizer / **DAVE GREEN** – bass / **ALLAN GANLEY** – drums

Linn / Linn

Dec 90. (cd/c/lp) *(<AKD/AKC/AKH 014>)* **DON'T FRET** [ ] [ ]
– I love you / Blue in green / I'm old fashioned / Laverne walk / Moonlight in Vermont / Mugavero / Don't fret / You know it's true.

— **BRIAN SHIELS** – bass + **JOHN RAE** – drums; repl. GREEN + GANLEY

Nov 91. (cd/c/lp) *(<AKD/AKC/AKH 016>)* **CHANGE OF HEART** [ ] [ ]
– 73 Berkeley Street / The gypsy / You don't know me / After hours / Change of heart / I get along without you very well / Angel's camp.

Feb 93. (cd/c/lp) *(<AKD/AKC/AKH 020>)* **ARTISTRY** [ ] [ ]
– Polka dots and moonbeams / Stella by starlight / Teach me tonight / The dolphin / Georgia on my mind / They can't take that away from me / Here there and everywhere – Day tripper / Just squeeze me / Gentle rain / Cherokee / Certain smile.

— next with **STEPHANE GRAPPELLI** – violin

Oct 93. (cd; as STEPHANE GRAPPELLI & MARTIN TAYLOR) *(AKD 022)* **REUNION** [ ] [-]
– Jive at five / Willow weep for me / Drop me off at Harlem / Miraval / Jenna / Reunion / Emily / Hotel Splendid / La dame du lac / I thought about you / It's only a paper moon.

Oct 94. (cd/c) *(<AKD/AKC 030>)* **SPIRIT OF DJANGO** [ ] [ ]
– Chez Fernand / Minor swing / Night and day / Nuages / James / Double top / Django's dream / Swing 42 / Lady be good / Honeysuckle rose / Johnny and Mary.

— with **CHET ATKINS** – guitar

Mar 96. (cd/c) *(<AKD/AKC 048>)* **PORTRAITS** [ ] [ ]
– Shiny stockings / Like someone in love / Sweet Lorraine / I got rhythm / Why did I choose you? / My funny valentine / Do you know what it means to miss New Orleans? / I remember Clifford / Ol' man river / Here, there & everywhere / In a mellow tone / My one and only love / Kiko / Very early.

— now with **JACK EMBLOW** – accordions / **DAVE O'HIGGINS** – saxophones / **TERRY GREGORY** – bass / **JOHN GOLDIE** – rhythm guitar

Feb 97. (cd) *(AKD 058)* **YEARS APART** [ ] [-]
– Sweet Sue, just you / Going home again / Undecided / Musette for a magpie / I can't give you anything but love / Czardas / Hi Lily, hi lo / Dinah / Years apart / The gypsy / Chicago / Manoir de mes reves.

Jun 98. (cd; as MARTIN TAYLOR'S SPIRIT OF DJANGO) *(<AKD 090>)* **GYPSY (live)** [ ] [ ] Feb00
– Gypsy medley: Cold winds – The tipsy gypsy – Czardas / My vardo / Chicago / Chez Fernand / Tears / Kushti / Nuages / I can't give you anything but love / Dreaming of you / Sweet Sue, just you / Musette for a magpie / Chillin with Oscar / Squid kid.

Apr 99. (cd) *<AKD 081>* **TWO'S COMPANY** (live in Australia October 1997) [-] [ ]
– I thought about you / I'll never be the same again / I've never been in love before / Triste / You're my everything / I'm beginning to see the light / Skylark / Billie's bounce / Bewitched / Royal garden blues / You stepped out of a dream / When I fall in love / Gone with the wind / Everything happens to me / Willow weep for me / Don't blame me / My foolish heart.

– compilations, others, etc. –

Jun 88. (lp/c; as LOUIS STEWART & MARTIN TAYLOR) *Livia; (LRLP/LRCS 7)* **ACOUSTIC GUITAR DUETS** (live in Dublin, July 1985) [ ] [-]
– Pick yourself up / Morning of the carnival / Jive at five / Coming through the rye / Cherokee / Stompin' at the Savoy / Darn that dream / Farewell to Erin.

Sep 91. (cd/c; as GORDON GILTRAP & MARTIN TAYLOR) *Prestige; (CDS/CASS GP 007)* **MATTER OF TIME** [ ] [-]

Nov 97. (cd) *Linn; (AKD 064)* **GOLD** [-] [-] Scots
– Johnny & Mary / Sweet Sue, just you / Sweet Lorraine / I'm old fashioned / Minor swing / It's only a paper moon / Undecided / In a mellow tone / I love you / Nuages / The gypsy / I get along without you very well / Angel's camp / I got rhythm.

Apr 98. (cd; as STEPHANE GRAPPELLI & MARTIN TAYLOR) *Linn; (AKD 094)* **CELEBRATING GRAPPELLI** (tracks from 'YEARS APART' & 'REUNION') [ ] [-]

— next with **JIM KERWIN** – bass / **GEORGE MARSH** – drums

Aug 99. (cd; as MARTIN TAYLOR & DAVE GRISMAN JAZZ QUARTET) *Acoustic Disc; (<ACD 36>)* **I'M BEGINNING TO SEE THE LIGHT** [ ] [ ]
– I'm beginning to see the light / Autumn leaves / Do you know what it means to miss New Orleans / East of the sun / Autumn in New York / Makin' whoopee / Lover man / Exactly like you / Willow weep for me / Foggy day / Cheek to cheek / Bewitched, bothered and bewildered.

Sep 99. (3xcd-box) *Linn; (AKD 115)* **THE LINN BOX, VOL.1** [ ] [-]
– (DON'T FRET / CHANGE OF HEART / ARTISTRY).

— next with **RANDY BRECKER, EDDIE GOMEZ, KIRK WHALUM, AL FOSTER, JAY ASHBY + GEORGE GARZONE**

Oct 99. (cd) *Sony Jazz; (<495387-2>)* **KISS AND TELL** (rec. 1992) [ ] [ ]
– Kiss and tell / You've changed / Odd couple / Garden of dreams / What a friend we have in Jesus / Midnight at the oasis / Mona Lisa / Five-O / Sunstep / Ginger / Midnight voyage / Nearness of you.

Sep 00. (cd) *Linn; (<AKD 144>)* **STEPPING STONES** [ ] [ ] Nov00
– Johnny & Mary / Double top / You know it's true / Hotel Splendid / I got rhythm / My Vardo / Undecided / Chez Fernand / Why did I choose you? / Georgia on my mind / Sweet Sue, just you / The dolphin / I get along without you very well.

Apr 01. (cd) *Milestone; (<MCD 9306-2>)* **IN CONCERT** (live 1998 in Manchester) [-] [ ] Aug00
– They can't take that away from me / Why did I choose you? / In a mellow tone / Georgia on my mind / I got rhythm / I'm old fashioned / The dolphin / Sweet Lorraine / Stella by starlight / Lulu's back in town / I remember Clifford / Taking a chance on love.

Jul 01. (cd) *Sony Jazz; (503321-2)* **NITELIFE** [ ] [ ]
– Chaff & grain / Doctor spin / That's the way of the world / Deja vu / Hymne a l'amour / Nitelife / Green lady / Beboptimism / Across the pond / I get along without you very well.

Joe TEMPERLEY

Born: 20 Sep'29, Lochgelly, Fife. Not the likeliest of vocations for a son of such a hard bitten location as Lochgelly, jazz musician no doubt seemed a far more attractive job description than coal miner when a young JOE TEMPERLEY was considering his career options. Encouraged by his family, the budding saxophonist gained early experience locally before heading to London where, over the course of the 1950's, he blew tenor sax with the likes of JACK PARNELL, HARRY PARRY and TONY CROMBIE, graduating to baritone with Scots-born TOMMY WHITTLE and HUMPHREY LYTTELTON.

TEMPERLEY's tenure with LYTTELTON stretched from 1958 through to 1965, a crucial apprenticeship which readied him for a mid-60's move to New York. Perseverence paid off and the Fifer found himself playing alongside such jazz luminaries as WOODY HERMAN, BUDDY RICH, THAD JONES and DUKE PEARSON. Session work in Broadway show orchestras paid the bills (JOE subsequently appeared on soundtracks to 'Sophisticated Ladies', 'Cotton Club' and 'Biloxi Blues' amongst others) although an undoubted career highlight came in 1974 when he took up the vacancy left by HARRY CARNEY in the DUKE ELLINGTON ORCHESTRA (TEMPERLEY subsequently released a tribute set to the great man on the centennial of his birth in 1999).

Three years later, TEMPERLEY reached another career milestone when he released what was, to all intents and purposes, his debut album, a collaborative set with KATHY STOBART, 'SAXPLOITATION' (1977). His next record, 'JUST FRIENDS' (1981), was a dual effort with JIMMY KNEPPER issued by veteran Scottish jazz label, 'Hep', as was 'SPECIAL RELATIONSHIP' (1982) with BOBBY WELLINS and 'WHEN YOU'RE SMILING' (1982), the latter an impromptu set recorded during the 1980 Edinburgh Festival. TEMPERLEY's long standing membership of the WYNTON MARSALIS-directed LINCOLN CENTER JAZZ ORCHESTRA began in 1990 while the following year saw the release of his acclaimed 'NIGHTINGALE' album. 1994's 'CONCERTO FOR JOE', meanwhile, documented six orchestral pieces specially composed by Scotsman JIMMY DEUCHAR and performed at that year's Glasgow Jazz Festival. The baritone maestro's intuitive grace informed much of 1998's 'WITH EVERY BREATH . . .', a record that also showcased TEMPERLEY's ability on soprano sax and clarinet.

Come the new millennium, the septuagenarian's talents remained undimmed on 'EASY TO REMEMBER' (2001), an adventurous outing featuring the likes of arranger FRANK GRIFFITH and long time sparring partner TONY COE. 'SUNBEAM AND THUNDERCLOUD', recorded with pianist DAVE McKENNA, followed in 2002. While TEMPERLEY's illustrious (and, it has to be said, often unsung) career has seen him hobnob with the jazz elite, the man has never forgotten his roots, co-founding the Fife Youth Jazz Orchestra to encourage musical talent in Scotland at grass roots level.

JOE TEMPERLEY – baritone saxophone

Spotlight | not iss.

May 77. (lp; by JOE TEMPERLEY & KATHY STOBART) *(LP 503)* **SAXPLOITATION** ☐ -

Hep Jazz | Hep Jazz

Apr 81. (lp; by JOE TEMPERLEY & JIMMY KNEPPER) *(HEP 2003)* **JUST FRIENDS** ☐ -

Dec 82. (lp; with JIMMY KNEPPER & BOBBY WELLINS) *Hep; (HEP 2012)* **SPECIAL RELATIONSHIP** (rec.1979-80) ☐ -
(<cd-iss. Jul02; HEPCD 2012>)

Mar 92. (cd) *(<HEPCD 2052>)* **NIGHTINGALE** ☐ ☐
– Raincheck / Body and soul / Indian summer / Sunset and a mockingbird / Petite fleur / Nightingale / It's you or no one / Creole love / Action / My love is like a red red rose.

Mar 95. (cd) *(<HEPCD 2062>)* **CONCERTO FOR JOE (live)** ☐ ☐
– Hackensack / Snibor / Sentimental mood / Blues for Nat / East of the sun and west of the moon / Single petal of a rose / Cotton tail / Awright already / The blues / Slow for Joe / A day at a time / Sixes and sevens.

— in 1996, JOE teamed up with DAVE McKENNA on collaborative set, 'SUNBEAM AND THUNDERCLOUD'.

Aug 98. (cd) *(<HEPCD 2073>)* **WITH EVERY BREATH . . .** ☐ ☐ Oct98
– Three little words / When lights are low / Skylark / Riverside drive / Close to you / Blue monk / Long ago (and far away) / The very thought of you / Skye boat song / In a sentimental mood / With every breath I take / Smoke gets in your eyes / Ow! / I hear the shadows dancing.

— in Jul'99, he and MICHAEL HASHIM released 'MULTI COLOURED BLUE', also for 'Hep Jazz'

Naxos Jazz | Naxos Jazz

Jun 99. (cd) *(<86032-2>)* **DOUBLE DUKE** ☐ ☐
– Rain check / Creole love call / Tricotism / Black and tan fantasy / Double Duke (Rubber bottom – Cottontail) / Try a little tenderness / Elsa / Fascinating rhythm / Danny boy.

Hep | Hep

Oct 01. (cd) *(<HEPCD 2083>)* **EASY TO REMEMBER** ☐ ☐
– That old feeling / The very thought of you / I let a song go out my heart / Easy to remember / East of the sun / Warm valley / Just friends / How little we know / Someone to watch over me / Things ain't what they used to be / Ask me now / Torpedo / Heilan' laddie.

Simon THOUMIRE (see ⇒ Section 2: Folk)

TRIO AAB (see under ⇒ Caber music)

W

Bobby WELLINS

Born: ROBERT COULL WELLINS, 24 Jan'36, Glasgow. Bobby was born into a showbiz family – his father played saxophone and clarinet with the Sammy Miller Showband and his mother sang with the band, although they also worked as a duo – and a career in music was what his father intended for young Bobby when dad began giving him alto saxophone lessons at the age of 12. The jobbing musician's "weddings, bar miztvahs . . ." joke, to denote do-anything availability, soon became the teenager's workload around Glasgow's Jewish community and after graduating from Chichester College of Further Education and the RAF School of Music in Uxbridge, there were more functions to be played with showband veterans Malcolm Mitchell and Vic Lewis.

The latter afforded Wellins the thrill of meeting his idol when, on an ocean liner engagement that took Lewis' band to the Big Apple, Wellins met the great tenor saxophonist Lester Young on a New York street. Something in this meeting must have stirred Wellins because on his return to London, in 1956, he joined Buddy Featherstonhaugh's quintet alongside trumpeter Kenny Wheeler and began concentrating on the tenor saxophone. One of jazz's truly distinctive sounds – and an influence on many players, including Tommy Smith – was born.

In the early 1960s Wellins joined drummer Tony Crombie's band, where he met and formed a lasting association with pianist Stan Tracey. Wellins' work on Tracey's 1965 homage to Dylan Thomas, the Under Milk Wood suite, a haunting, once heard never forgotten sound, was to become one of the great milestones of British jazz, although it had actually been preceded the year before by Wellins' equally haunting but cruelly overlooked (and now hen's teeth rare) Culloden Moor Suite. As well as working with Tracey on two further albums, during the 1960s Wellins played and recorded with, amongst others, John Dankworth and Tubby Hayes before personal problems put a halt to activities for almost a decade. Having moved to Bognor Regis to escape the jazz life's temptations, he returned in great form in the mid 1970s, releasing the splendid Dreams are Free and the appropriately titled, if rather spoiled by an out of tune piano, Live Jubilation with a quartet including long-time associate, pianist Peter "Southend Pierre" Jacobsen.

A superior session with former Charles Mingus trombonist Jimmy Knepper for Edinburgh-based Hep Records in 1980 confirmed Wellins' place as one of jazz's great originals, his spare, measured elegance and sometimes austere, lonely tone carrying the essence of bluesy expression. Live work was sporadic and Wellins filled in by teaching but in 1982, he reunited with Tracey for a splendid tribute to the then recently deceased Thelonious Monk and the following year, bizarrely, Wellins' quartet appeared at a promotional shindig for the Erco lighting company, an occasion for which Wellins composed six new pieces. The performance was recorded and distributed among the company's staff and only received an official release, by Hep Records, in 1997. Touring and recording with The Rolling Stones' drummer's orchestral sideline, infamously known as Charlie Watts' Big Bar, followed before Wellins teamed up with fellow Glaswegian, guitarist Jim Mullen, to fulfil one of these 'we've always meant to do this' ideas.

During the 1990s Wellins continued to teach on various courses, recorded Nomad with special guest, singer Claire Martin, toured and recorded with the now sadly deceased Spike Robinson's Tenor Madness. He also reconvened with Tracey for a special performance of Starless and Bible Black from Under Milk Wood at Glasgow International Jazz Festival, marking Tracey's 70th birthday in 1996, and fulfilled another long-held ambition when he recorded The Satin Album, his tenor saxophone assuming the Billie Holiday role in a remake of Holiday's classic Lady in Satin album.

BOBBY WELLINS QUARTET

BOBBY WELLINS – tenor sax / with 70's quartet **PETER JACOBSON** – piano / **ADRIAN KENYON** – bass / **SPIKE WELLS** – drums

Vortex | not iss.

Sep 78. (lp) *(VS 1)* **LIVE . . . JUBILATION (live)** ☐ -
– Jubilation / Nomad / What's happening? / Spider.

May 79. (lp) *(VS 2)* **DREAMS ARE FREE** ☐ -
– Dreams are free / Love dance / Aura / Conundrums / What is the truth? / Ba-loos.

Hep Jazz not iss.

Jul 82. (lp; by JIMMY KNEPPER & BOBBY WELLINS) *(HEP 2011)* **PRIMROSE PATH** (rec.Nov'80) [ ] [-]
– Primrose path / What is there to say? / Song for Keith (piano solo) / Gnome on the range / 'Round about midnight / Latterday saint.

— later in '82, KNEPPER and WELLINS augmented JOE TEMPERLEY on another 'Hep Jazz' set, 'Special Relationship' (recorded 1978)

Sungai not iss.

Jun 90. (lp; as BOBBY WELLINS) *(BW 11)* **BIRDS OF BRAZIL** [ ] [-]
– Birds of Brazil: I – II – III / Angel eyes / Moonray / In walked Bud. *(cd-iss. Nov00; BW 11CD)*

Hot House not iss.

May 95. (cd; as BOBBY WELLINS featuring Claire Martin) *(HHCD 1008)* **NOMAD** (rec. April 1992) [ ] [-]
– Cucb / Be my love / Nomad / Sandu / Love for sale / Willow weep for me / Remember me / This I dig of you / Little rootie tootie / Silent love / This here / Cabin in the sky.

— In 1994, he recorded with TERRY SEABROOK's CUBANA BOP on the set, 'Can't Stop Now'.

Jazzizit not iss.

Feb 97. (cd; as BOBBY WELLINS) *(JITCD 9607)* **THE SATIN ALBUM** [ ] [-]
– I'm a fool to want you / For heaven's sake / You don't know what love is / I get along without you very well / For all we know / Violets for your furs / You've changed / It's easy to remember / But beautiful / Glad to be unhappy / I'll be around / The end of a love affair.

Jan 99. (cd; by STAN TRACEY & BOBBY WELLINS) *(JITCD 9816)* **COMME d'HABITUDE** [ ] [-]
– Comme d'Habitude / Nice work if you can get it / Bewitched / I get a kick out of you / The lady is a tramp / Night and day / Angel eyes / Guess I'll hang my tears out to dry / What's new / Poor butterfly / I've got the world on a string / Nice 'n' easy.

Feb 01. (cd) *(JITCD 0024)* **THE BEST IS YET TO COME** [ ] [-]
– Good life / When Joanna loved me / I wanna be around / Fascinating rhythm / Stranger in paradise / San Francisco / When the sun comes out / Quiet nights / Taking a chance on love / You must believe in spring / The best is yet to come.

– compilations, etc. –

Aug 97. (cd) *(<HEPCD 2070>)* **MAKING LIGHT WORK** (rec. 1 October 1983) [ ] [ ] Jul02
– Erco makes light work / Visionaire / Bossa oseris / Logotec logarhythm / Sound / Downright downlight / Take the A train / Just friends – I'm beginning to see the light.

Sep 97. (cd) *Cadillac; (SGCCD 05)* **DON'T WORRY 'BOUT ME** [ ] [-]
– I concentrate on you / My old flame / In your sweet way / Lover man / I'm wishing / Don't worry 'bout me / How deep is the ocean / Tracery.

Bill WELLS (see ⇒ Section 8: Rock, Pop & Indie)

Alex WELSH

Born: 9 Jul'29, Leith, Edinburgh. One of the most loved and respected musicians on the British jazz scene over the second half of the twentieth century, Welsh began playing cornet as a teenager in the Leith Silver Band. He was still at Broughton High School when the jazz bug bit. Hooked by the Chicago style of Dixieland that would be central to his style throughout his career, he acquired a trumpet and shortly afterwards joined clarinettist Archie Semple's Capital Jazz Band, playing both trumpet and cornet. In the early 1950's, determined to be a musician rather than work 9-to-5, he moved to London where he found work opportunities scarce until an agent advised him to form his own band. It wasn't to be just any band. Welsh hired the best musicians he could find, including former boss Semple, creating a disciplined, exciting unit and quickly made an impression, particularly following an early appearance at the Royal Festival Hall.

American players such as Jack Teagarden, Pee Wee Russell, Wild Bill Davison, Earl Hines and Ruby Braff, with whom the Welsh band later toured the U.S., were among those who showered praise on Welsh for his adherence to the hard-swinging Chicago style. Teagarden, in fact, once offered Welsh a job but was turned down. Like other bandleaders of the Trad. boom, Alex drew on a wide repertoire, including pop songs of the day, but without indulging in daft antics and fancy costumes: the music, full of vitality, excitement and enthusiasm, always came first. Welsh did reach the UK Top 50, with 'TANSY', in 1961 and his band also appeared on crooner Dickie Valentine recordings such as 'When the Red Red Robin Goes Bob Bob Bobbin' Along', but Welsh preferred to be – and was – accepted on his own terms.

When, in 1974, the long-running original Welsh band began to disintegrate, with the death of Archie Semple and trombonist Roy Crimmins' move abroad, he recruited saxophonist John Barnes and Roy Williams – who would go on to make their names on the mainstream jazz scene – as replacements and continued to tour all over the UK and Europe. On the 25th of June 1982, having played on through a long illness and weathering further changes in his band's personnel, Welsh died leaving a large gap in the British Traditional jazz scene.

In 2002, tribute act The Alex Welsh Legacy Band (featuring Roy Williams, Jim Douglas, John Barnes, Brian Lemon, Bobby Worth, Tom Saunders, Harvey Weston and Dave Shepherd) released 'The Sound Of Alex Volume One'.

ALEX WELSH & DIXIELANDERS

ALEX WELSH – cornet, trumpet / with others

Decca not iss.

Jun 55. (7") *(F 10538)* **I'LL BUILD A STAIRWAY TO PARADISE. / ECCENTRICS** [ ] [-]
Jul 55. (7") *(F 10557)* **BLUES MY NAUGHTY SWEETIE GIVES TO ME. / SHOE SHINER'S DRAG** [ ] [-]
Aug 55. (7"ep) *(DFE 6254)* **THE DIXIELANDERS AT THE RFH** [ ] [-]
Sep 55. (7") *(F 10607)* **AS LONG AS I LIVE. / NEW ORLEANS STOMP** [ ] [-]
Oct 55. (7"ep) *(DFE 6283)* **ALEX WELSH AND HIS DIXIELAND BAND** [ ] [-]
Nov 55. (7") *(F 10651)* **SUGAR. / SMILES** [ ] [-]
Nov 55. (7") *(F 10652)* **HARD-HEARTED HANNAH. / WHAT CAN I SAY AFTER I SAY I'M SORRY** [ ] [-]
Dec 55. (7"ep) *(DFE 6315)* **MUSIC FROM PETE KELLY** [ ] [-]

ALEX WELSH (Band)

— featured **BOY CRIMMINS** – trombone / **FRED HUNT** – piano / **ARCHIE SEMPLE** – clarinet / LENNY HASTINGS – drums

Nixa not iss.

1958. (lp) *(NJT 516)* **THE MELROSE FOLIO** [ ] [-]
– Kansas City stomp / Sidewalk blues / Tiajuana / Sugar babe / Dippermouth blues / Honey babe / King Porter stomp / Some day sweetheart.

Columbia not iss.

1959. (lp) *(33SX 1219)* **MUSIC OF THE MAUVE DECADE** [ ] [-]
– Charleston / Black bottom / Lonesome and sorry / I cover the waterfront / Shimma sha wabble / Don't leave me daddy / Nobody's sweetheart / Needle / Tell 'em about me / I cried for you / Mammy o' mine. *(cd-iss. Jun96 on 'Lake'+=; LACD 62)* – Down among sheltering palms / Please don't talk about me when I'm gone / Sleepy time gal / Bye bye blues.

Mar 61. (7") *(DB 4576)* **LAZY RIVER. / MONTMATRE** [ ] [-]
Jul 61. (7") *(DB 4686)* **TANSY. / MEMPHIS MARCH** [45] [-]
Aug 61. (lp) *(33SX 1322)* **IT'S RIGHT HERE FOR YOU** [ ] [-]
Oct 61. (7") *(DB 4727)* **ROSALIE. / YOU'LL CRY SOMEDAY** [ ] [-]
Feb 62. (7") *(DB 4792)* **I'M GONNA GO FISHIN'. / MY GAL SAL** [ ] [-]
1962. (lp) *(33SX 1429)* **ECHOES OF CHICAGO** [ ] [-]
1963. (7") *(DB 7074)* **THE UGLY BUG BALL. / ON THE FRONT PORCH** [ ] [-]

Strike not iss.

1966. (lp) *(JHL 102)* **STRIKE ONE** [ ] [-]
– Louisiana / I wished on the moon / Open country / Davenport blues / I got rhythm / Between the Devil and the deep blue sea / Bluesology / Oh baby / That old feeling / Strike one. *(cd-iss. Dec98 on 'Lake'+=; LACD 107)* – My blushing Rosie / When the midnight choo choo leaves for Alabam / Sunday / Broken doll.

1966. (7"ep) *(JHE 201)* **ALEX WELSH ENTERTAINS** [ ] [-]
1966. (7") *(JH 321)* **DAVENPORT BLUES. / STRIKE ONE** [ ] [-]

Columbia not iss.

1968. (lp) *(SX 6213)* **AT HOME WITH . . .** [ ] [-]
(re-iss. Sep87 on 'Dormouse'; DM 16)
1969. (lp) *(SX 6333)* **ALEX WELSH AND HIS BAND '69** [ ] [-]
1970. (lp) *(SCX 6376)* **DIXIELAND TO DUKE** [ ] [-]
– Mandy make your mind up / I'm coming Virginia / Queen Bess / Up jumped you with love / Winin' boy blues / Cornet chop suey / Ostrich walk / Buddy's habit. *(re-iss. Nov86 on 'Dormouse'; DM 7)*

Polydor not iss.

1971. (lp) *(2460 123)* **TRIBUTE TO LOUIS ARMSTRONG VOL.1** [ ] [-]
1971. (lp) *(2460 124)* **TRIBUTE TO LOUIS ARMSTRONG VOL.2** [ ] [-]
1971. (lp) *(2460 125)* **TRIBUTE TO LOUIS ARMSTRONG VOL.3** [ ] [-]

— his band incl. **ROY WILLIAMS** (trombone) + **JOHNNY BARNES** (reeds)

Black Lion not iss.

1972. (lp) *(BLP 12109)* **IF I HAD A TALKING PICTURE** [ ] [-]
– If I had a talking picture of you / Lazy river / Breezin' along with the breeze / Dapper Dan / Love is just around the corner / By the time I get to Phoenix / Splanky / Blueberry hill / Opus one. *(cd-iss. Nov97; BLC 760521)*

Aug 72. (lp) *(BLP 12112)* **AN EVENING WITH . . . VOL.1** [ ] [-]
Aug 72. (lp) *(BLP 12113)* **AN EVENING WITH . . . VOL.2** [ ] [-]
Dec 72. (d-lp) *(BLP 12115-6)* **IN CONCERT (live)** [ ] [-]

— ARCHIE SEMPLE died in 1974; **JOHN BARNES + BOY** were now his backing band

1975. (lp) *(BLP 12120)* **BAND SHOWCASE VOL.1** [ ] [-]

1976. (lp) *(BLP 12121)* **BAND SHOWCASE VOL.2**
1976. (lp) *(BLP 12131)* **DIXIELAND PARTY**
1976. (d-lp) *(BLPX 12161-2)* **SALUTE TO SATCHMO**
(above also feat. HUMPHREY LYTTLETON, BRUCE TURNER + GEORGE CHISHOLM)

One-Up not iss.

Nov 77. (lp) *(OU 2196)* **IN A PARTY MOOD**

— ALEX died on 25th June 1982

- compilations, etc. -

Apr 88. (lp/c) *Lake; (LA 5008/+C)* **LIVE AT THE ROYAL FESTIVAL HALL VOL.1 1954-1955**
(cd-iss. Oct00; LACD 8)
Oct 90. (cd/c) *Black Lion; (BLCD/BLC 76053)* **CLASSIC CONCERT**
– Chinatown, my Chinatown / I want a little girl / Dapper Dan / Oh! baby / Dippermouth blues / Maple leaf rag / Sleepy time down south / Tangerine / St. Louis blues / If I had a talking picture of you / 9.20 special.
May 93. (cd) *Black Lion; (BLCD 760510)* **DOGGIN' AROUND**
Nov 95. (cd) *Black Lion; (BLCD 760515)* **LOUIS ARMSTRONG MEMORIAL CONCERT**
Apr 98. (cd) *Lake; (LACD 92)* **DIXIELAND TO DUKE / THE MELROSE FOLIO**
May 00. (cd) *Jazzology;* **VINTAGE ALEX WELSH**
Feb 01. (cd) *Lake; (LACD 145)* **IT HAS TO BE**
Oct 01. (cd) *Upbeat Jazz; (UPCD 175)* **OH! BABY**
– As long as I live / Sweeping the blues away / Jelly roll / Blue and sentimental / Oh, baby / As long as I live (2) / Confessin' / It don't mean a thing (if it ain't got that swing) / Just one more chance / Doggin' around.
Feb 02. (cd) *Lake; (LACD 157)* **PEE WEE RUSSELL WITH ALEX WELSH & HIS BAND**

Tam WHITE (see ⇒ Section 7: Rock & Pop)

Tommy WHITTLE

Born: 13 Oct'26, Grangemouth. Described by Jazz FM's Campbell Burnap as "a stylish weaver of dreams to rank with all the legendary Americans", Tommy Whittle (on either sax, clarinet or flute) showed the promise to live up to such estimations when he joined the legendary Ted Heath Orchestra at the age of twenty. He had served his early musical apprenticeship in Kent with Claude Giddings's band (which also included drummer Ronnie Verrell and pianist Ralph Sharon, who was later to become singer Tony Bennett's long-time accompanist), John Claes' Clay Pigeons, Lew Stone, Carl Barriteau and Harry Hayes. The six years he spent with Heath not only established his name among jazz listeners, it also prepared him for leading his own groups. He also worked with Tony Kinsey's Trio and as featured soloist with the BBC Show Band, winning the Melody Maker and New Musical Express polls as a result.

In 1956, Whittle was chosen for an exchange trip to the US which saw Sidney Bechet tour the UK and the following year he took a quartet over to America in exchange for Gerry Mulligan's group. Then, after three years as musical director for the Dorchester Hotel in the early 1960s, he joined Jack Parnell's ATV orchestra, beginning a durable career in TV and record sessions which has included dates with Bing Crosby, Peggy Lee, Barbara Streisand, Georgie Fame, Paul McCartney and rock band Caravan, among many others.

The antithesis of the faceless studio musician, Whittle has always kept his jazz edge sharp with regular appearances at jazz clubs up and down the country, often with his wife, singer Barbara Jay, and in all-star bands such as the Jazz Journal All-Stars, with whom he appeared at Nice Jazz Festival in France, and the Pizza Express All-Stars.

TOMMY WHITTLE – tenor saxophone, clarinet, flute

Esquire not iss.

1954. (78) *(10-408)* **MARTINI. / YESTERDAYS**
1954. (lp) *(20-028)* **WAXING WITH WHITTLE**
(re-iss. Apr79; ESQ 305)
1955. (lp) *(20-048)* **TOMMY WHITTLE QUINTET**
1956. (7"ep) *(EP 37)* **TOMMY WHITTLE QUINTET**
1956. (78) *(10-468)* **HOW HIGH THE MOON. / LESTER LEAPS IN**
1956. (lp) *(20-061)* **SPOTLIGHTING TOMMY WHITTLE**
1956. (lp) *(20-068)* **LULLABY AND RHYTHM**

H.M.V. not iss.

1957. (7"; as TOMMY WHITTLE & HIS QUARTET) *(POP 379)* **THE FINISHER. / CABIN IN THE SKY**
1958. (7"ep) *(7EG 8325)* **TOMMY WHITTLE QUARTET**

Tempo not iss.

1960. (lp) *(TAP 27)* **NEW HORIZONS**

Alamo J.A.M.

Apr 79. (lp; by TOMMY WHITTLE QUARTET) *<JAM 648>* **WHY NOT**
Jun 79. (lp; by TOMMY WHITTLE QUARTET) *(AJ 4501)* **JIG SAW**

Miles Music not iss.

May 86. (lp; by TOMMY WHITTLE & ALAN BARNES) *(MM 001)* **STRAIGHT EIGHT**
– Straight eight / Con Alma / Joking / Peppercorn / Note 8.7 / Goodbye / That's all / Early / Stablemates.

Teejay not iss.

Nov 92. (cd/c; as TOMMY WHITTLE QUARTET) *(TEEJAY 103/+C)* **WARM GLOW**

Sine not iss.

Dec 98. (cd; as TOMMY WHITTLE & THE BOB HUDSON TRIO) *(SND 0077)* **ENCORE!**
– Flamingo / Darn that dream / Sweet and lovely / Trotting / It never entered my mind / Wave / My foolish heart / Teejay blues / Night and day / On Green Dolphin Street / My romance.

- compilations, etc. -

1960's. (lp) *Ember; (EMB 3305)* **EASY LISTENING**
Dec 87. (lp) *Esquire; (ESQ 334)* **MORE WAXING WITH WHITTLE**
– Archer's treat / Pyramid / Willow weep for me / Crazy rhythm / Ten-bar gait / The finisher / Someone to atchover me / Harry's blues / Flamingo / (I don't stand) A ghost of a chance (wits you) / I'll remember April / You've done something to my heart / Stars fell on labama.

jazz labels

Caber music

Founded: Haddington, nr. Edinburgh . . . 1997 by TOM BANCROFT and SUZY MELHUISH, although they shifted base to 47b Bridge Street, Musselburgh. A man of many talents but essentially a jazz drummer/composer, BANCROFT set up the 'Caber' label after receiving funding from the National Lottery.

With a brief to release "all the great music going on in Scotland", he initiated the release schedule via his own TOM BANCROFT ORCHESTRA and the 'Pieology' album. Next up was a re-issued of a 1980's set by the JOHN RAE COLLECTIVE ('The Big If Smiles Again') and The BRIAN KELLOCK TRIO with their FRED ASTAIRE tribute, 'Something's Got To Give'. Through '98/'99, CHICK LYALL, PHIL BANCROFT TRIO (TOM's brother), SWIRLER (cutting edge jazz meets dancefloor project featuring TOM and PHIL together with KEVIN McKENZIE, DAVE MILLIGAN and JOHN SPEIRS), TRIO AAB (TOM, PHIL and KEVIN) and TAM WHITE AND BRIAN KELLOCK all released acclaimed sets, the latter collaboration scooping a Scotsman "Pick Of The Bunch for 1999" award. Yet while the plaudits for creative distribution came thick and fast, there was criticism of Caber's CDR release policy. In order to counter rumours that CDR's had a limited lifespan, the label introduced a lifetime guarantee on all their releases as well as a scratch replacement scheme (if your disc gets scratched they'll replace for a nominal fee), surely a first for any record company! The label's current catalogue of over 25 releases also includes a number of non-Caber artists such as SUZANNE BONNAR ('Empty Tables'), JOHN BURGESS ('The Beautiful Never'), NIGEL CLARK QUINTET ('World-Wide-Sound'), VIOLET LEIGHTON ('Speak Low'), the BURT MACDONALD QUARTET ('Oh Hello') and CRAIG McMURDO & THE SWING KINGS ('Singin' and Swingin').

Being a company with an emphasis on the use of new technology and improvisation, Caber conceived PROJECTS 1/2/3 in 1999 as an innovative new recording venture. The plan was to take three composers working in different musical arenas and ask them to each record an album. After their initial release, the respective albums would be continually re-mixed and re-shaped, creating a constantly evolving recording that would be sold in limited edition instalments after each reworking. At the end of 18 months a new composer would then take up where the original one left off, carrying on the process indefinitely.

For fans of more conventional CD releases, the 1999/2000 schedule included sets by CHICK LYALL & TORE BRUNBORG (actually another re-issue), the EDDIE SEVERN QUARTET and TOM and PHIL BANCROFT amongst others as well as a Scottish Jazz Vocal collection. Note:- www.caber-records.com is an American bagpipe/recording company run by SCOTT CAWTHON (his outfit, WEAVERS OF THE TARTAN, released Pipin' Hot in 1984).

– discography –

- **TOM BANCROFT** is a Cambridge graduate and qualified medical doctor and has been closely involved with the Scottish jazz scene since the 1980's. The former husband of GINA RAE (of the jazz-crazy RAE family), he became a teacher of jazz drumming, improvisation (which he strives to make a universal skill) and composition, and worked at Napier University in Edinburgh. In a drumming capacity, his CV includes a host of high profile employers/collaborators (TOMMY SMITH, MARTYN BENNETT and even the late great SUN RA amongst others) while his compositional skills have seen him writing for TV, film, dance and small/big bands as well as penning a children's musical. He has also conceived many one-off projects such as his multi-media performance 'Multi-Story Karma Park' for 1997's Glasgow Jazz Festival.

Jan 99. (cd) *(Caber 001)* **TOM BANCROFT ORCHESTRA – Pieology: The First Six Years Of The Tom Bancroft Orchestra**
– Cat 'n' mouse / Pieology / Scottish heart / The piano is a dark horse / The battle of Algiers / Sleepy head / Coal & logs.

Jan 99. (cd) *(Caber 003)* **BRIAN KELLOCK TRIO – Something's Got To Give: A Tribute To Fred Astaire**

- **TRIO AAB** are, in fact, twins PHIL and TOM BANCROFT, together with guitarist KEVIN MACKENZIE. Well known on the Scottish scene as musicians in their own right (sax/drums/guitar respectively), the individual talents which make up TRIO AAB are also successful composers and the meeting of minds that was 'COLD FUSION' resulted in considerable critical acclaim. Their debut album and one of the 'Caber' label's first releases, the record's adventurous melding of jazz, folk, drum'n'bass, house and hip-hop together with its wildly creative improvisational approach saw it lauded as one of the top albums of 1999 by Radio 3's 'Jazz On Three' programme. The trio were also named as best band of the Bath International Festival Jazz Weekend (2000) by The Times, who reserved particular praise for the 'DARK DRILLER' piece wherein TOM incorporated a set of power tools into his percussive armoury. In 2001, the TRIO AAB released another set, 'WHEREVER I LAY MY HOME THAT'S MY HAT'.

Jan 99. (cd) *(Caber 004)* **TRIO AAB – Cold Fusion**
– Gotta decide / Untitled / Jiggle / Bees niece / Sprog landscapes / When will the blues ever leave / Abstract / Open jungle / I ain't mad at cha.

Jan 99. (cd) *(Caber 005)* **CHICK LYALL – Solitary Dance**

- **SWIRLER** comprises of KEVIN MacKENZIE (guitar), DAVE MILLIGAN (keyboards), TOM BANCROFT (drums), PHIL BANCROFT (sax) and JOHN SPIERS (bass), all making their their mark worldwide as Scotland's leading jazz fusionists. They featured on the BBC's 'Be-Bop To Hip-Hop' programme and sold out at both the Edinburgh and Glasgow Jazz Festivals in 1998. GINA RAE makes a welcome guest appearance on two tracks from their eponymous debut, 'EZ4U' and 'IN YOUR ARMS', both cool and funky – yeh!

Jan 99. (cd) *(Caber 006)* **SWIRLER – Swirler**
– EZ4U / Mythology / Tblisi haze / In your arms / Switch.

- **PHIL BANCROFT** is the equally talented twin brother of ubiquitous jazz drummer/composer/label boss TOM. PHIL has studied with the likes of George Galzone and Dave Liebman. In addition to a number of big name rock/pop/folk stars featuring on his CV (i.e. RICKY ROSS, HUE AND CRY, CAPERCAILLIE), his acclaimed tenor saxophone playing has graced such diverse jazz-based projects as the EDDIE SEVERN QUINTET, JOHN RAE'S CELTIC FEET, SWIRLER and TRIO AAB. Like his brother, PHIL has successfully dabbled in composing, writing scores for film and dance and netting the 1998 Herald Angel award for his work with the 'Fresh Mess' dance company. As well as performing/recording with the various aforementioned artists, he released a 1998/'99 CD by his own PHIL BANCROFT TRIO (with drummer MARCELLO PELITTERI and bassist STEVE WATTS) entitled 'SWINGS AND ROUNDABOUTS'.

Jan 99. (cd) *(Caber 007)* **PHIL BANCROFT TRIO – Swings And Roundabouts**
– Jiggle / Space buffie 1999 / B's niece / Rock house / Hubert and cowboy Pete / Free / I got it bad / Swings and roundabouts / Love gone- wrong.

Oct 99. (cd) *(Caber 008)* **Various Artists – Caber Compilation #1**
– SWIRLER – EZ4U / BRIAN KELLOCK TRIO – The continental / PHIL BANCROFT TRIO – Jiggle / CHICK LYALL – Flow river flow / TRIO AAB – Gotta decide / TAM WHITE & BRIAN KELLOCK – The water is wide / TOM BANCROFT ORCHESTRA – The piano is a dark horse / SWIRLER – Wrinkle / TRIO AAB – Abstract / BRIAN KELLOCK TRIO – Something's got to give.

Oct 99. (cd) *(Caber 009)* **TAM WHITE & BRIAN KELLOCK – The Crossing**

- **JOHN RAE** (while also a drummer with The Scottish National Jazz Orchestra) is a member of the capital's famous jazz-playing RAE family. JOHN made his recording debut at the age of 16 with the local prodigy TOMMY SMITH. Since then, he's gone on to work with a raft of jazz talent including TAL FARLOW, ART FARMER and MARTIN TAYLOR amongst many others. When he's not drumming with the Scottish National Jazz Orchestra or the BRIAN KELLOCK TRIO, RAE can be found leading his own outfits: The POWER OF SCOTLAND BIG BAND and JOHN RAE's CELTIC FEET. As The JOHN RAE COLLECTIVE, 'Caber' re-issued 'THE BIG IF SMILES AGAIN' (in 1998) as one of the first releases on the label while his CELTIC FEET project was conceived as a vehicle for incorporating Celtic folk elements (RAE has studied the fiddle for more than ten years) into a jazz framework. Initiated in 1998 with funding from the Scottish Arts Council, the band (completed by MARIO CARIBE, BRIAN KELLOCK, EILIDH SHAW, PHIL BANCROFT and SIMON THOUMIRE) released their eponymous debut album in summer '99 and a follow-up, 'BEWARE THE FEET' (2001). A founding member of the Scottish Composer's Jazz Ensemble, RAE's writing skills are equally as important to his various projects as his drumming talents and he's also composed for TV, radio, ensembles, etc.

Oct 99. (cd) *(Caber 010)* **JOHN RAE'S CELTIC FEET – John Rae's Celtic Feet**
– The Napier stride / May 7th / Power of the radge / The boy / Under the kilt / Celtic feet / MacAlgo / MacKulu / Now's the time and now's the hour / Blow / Slumber Jack.

- Pianist **PAUL HARRISON** (winner of the prestigious Scottish Young Jazz Musician of 1998 and 1999). The PAUL HARRISON TRIO (with credits to bassist MARIO LIMA CARIBE and youthful Scots drummer PADDY FLAHERTY on the sleeve), made their mark almost immediately backing the likes of foreign players, BOBBY WATSON, DAVID SANCHEZ and INGRID JENSEN.

Jun 00. (cd) *(Caber 013)* **PAUL HARRISON TRIO – Nemesis**
– Six down / Song / Foot in the door / Rhythm's changing / alse / Nemesis / For the day after / Tricks / Small moves.

Nov 00. (cd) *(Caber 015)* **Various Artists – Yuletide Log #1: Xmas Jazz Compilation**
– (festive songs by JOHN RAE'S CELTIC FEET / COLIN STEELE & DAVE MILLIGAN / TRIO AAB / SUZANNE BONNAR & MARIO CARIBE / BRIAN KELLOCK TRIO / PHIL BANCROFT & CHICK LYALL / GINA RAE / FIONNA DUNCAN / CABER ALLSTARS / SYLVIA RAE)

- **EDDIE SEVERN** has been hard at work over the past few years. A lead trumpet player with the Scottish National Jazz Orchestra (with TOMMY SMITH and Co), SEVERN has played with such jazz giants as JOHN DANKWORTH & CLEO LAINE and JOE TEMPERLEY. His eclectic credits even stretch to the world of pop-C&W via performing on stage with KENNY ROGERS, CONNIE FRANCIS and the late, great TAMMY WYNETTE. His compositions have been used by The SCOTTISH COMPOSERS JAZZ ENSEMBLE and the Scottish Arts Council, while others have been worked on by fellow trumpeter KENNY WHEELER.

Jun 01. (cd) *(Caber 016)* **EDDIE SEVERN – Moments In Time**

Jan 01. (3xcd-box) *(Caber 017)* **BRIAN KELLOCK – Boxed Set**
Aug 01. (cd) *(Caber 018)* **JOHN RAE CELTIC FEET – Beware The Feet**
Jun 01. (cd) *(Caber 019)* **Various Artists – Caber Compilation #2**
– JOHN RAE'S CELTIC FEET – The Napier stride / PAUL HARRISON TRIO – Six down / CHICK LYALL – Voice over / JOHN BURGESS QUARTET – Once upon a long ago / TAM WHITE – Broadway Rose / CABER KIDS – Raspberry song / PHIL & TOM BANCROFT – Demo / JOHN RAE'S CELTIC FEET – Under the kilt / JOHN BURGESS QUARTET – The north beach hi-life / CABER KIDS – Alien saga.
Jul 01. (cd) *(Caber 020)* **BRIAN KELLOCK TRIO – Live At Henry's**
Nov 01. (cd) *(Caber 021)* **TRIO AAB – Wherever I Lay My Home That's My Hat**

- **SCOTTISH GUITAR QUARTET** feature MALCOLM McFARLANE, NIGEL CLARK, KEVIN MacKENZIE and GED BROCKIE; influences ROBERT FRIPP (eh!)

Apr 02. (cd) *(Caber 023)* **SCOTTISH GUITAR QUARTET – Near The Circle**
– Near the circle / One more day / Denial / Ice / This is just to say / Forget me not / Silver hills / Pools in sunlight / Reaching forth / Wes / Twisted to the floor / New beginnings / Near the circle / Ice (alternate take).

- Edinburgh-born **COLIN STEELE** has been a professional trumpet player since his days sessioning for the likes of HUE AND CRY. However, the world of pop music was not for COL, who took off to France before studying jazz at London's Guildhall School Of Music. Occasionally returning to Scotland, he joined The JOHN RAE COLLECTIVE and after finishing college he moved back to Edinburgh. With jazz and funk a very big part of his musical repertoire, STEELE set up his own live music club, Midnight Blue, a venue which ran for over two years at the Cafe Graffiti; around this time (1999) he and singer CATHIE RAE developed their own show, 'A Tribute To Chet Baker' (his inspiration) for the Edinburgh Festival. The album, 'TWILIGHT DREAMS' (2002) was dedicated to the late Cristina Alfo, the mother of his daughter; he is currently in jazz collective MELTING POT, alongside BRIAN SHIELS, MARTIN KERSHAW, DAVE MILLIGAN, ROSS MILLIGAN and PAUL MILLS.

Mar 02. (cd) *(Caber 024)* **COLIN STEELE – Twilight Dreams**

- Airdrie-man **JOHN GOLDIE** played with MARTIN TAYLOR, his guitar virtuoso and band leadership second to none. GOLDIE's first album 'TURN & TWIST' features drummer JIM DRUMMOND and bassman EWEN VERNAL on a mixture of standards and originals.

Jonjo not iss.

1997. (cd) *(JONJO 001CD)* **JOHN GOLDIE – Turn & Twist**

Hep (Jazz) records

Founded: Now based in the picturesque Perthshire town of Pitlochry, Hep Jazz was founded by ALASTAIR ROBERTSON, a school teacher and fan of big band jazz from its mid-1940s heyday. At first Hep specialised in recordings from this era, drawn from acetates and radio transcriptions and featuring many well-known musicians, including Tommy Dorsey, Ted Heath, Harry James, Kay Starr and most notably Slim Gaillard, the inventor of a language known as "Vout", whose jive talking style might reasonably be claimed as a humorous forerunner of rap. Pianist and guitarist Gaillard had been extremely popular in the 1940s due to an American radio show and his double act with bassist Slam Stewart (Slim 'n' Slam); his re-emergence in 1982 at Robertson's behest, on an album recorded with Charlie Parker's former employer, pianist Jay McShann, illustrates Robertson's knack of using old contacts to find worthwhile new ventures. Gaillard's career went on to enjoy a lengthy Indian summer, as have several other Hep artists'.

In 1978, having established the 1000 Series of remasters - the list including vibist Red Norvo, the Dorsey Brothers and Claude Thornhill - alongside the Metronome catalogue, Robertson launched a further series concentrating on modern and mainstream musicians from the USA, UK and Europe. Initial successes came via pianist Eddie Thompson and tenorists Tony Coe and Spike Robinson – another American artist whose career Robertson helped to re-launch. Robinson had served in the US Navy in Britain during World War II before going into the aviation industry (he worked with Nasa at Cape Canaveral), but had made such an impression in the 1940s that a group of enthusiasts in London located him and brought him over to play some gigs. He eventually retired from his day job, returned to music full-time and settled in Essex.

Other such Robertson "revamps" include saxophonists Don Lanphere, a former Woody Herman and Artie Shaw sideman who made a spectacular return from narcotics abuse via Hep in 1982, and Herb Geller, a West Coast styled altoist long domiciled in Germany who played his first gig in Scotland in many years during the 1990s and recorded with the great Scottish pianist Brian Kellock on Hollywood Portraits.

While Hep can claim other American "finds" such as the Chicago trumpeter Robert Mazurek, whose band became familiar to Edinburgh Fringe audiences in the mid-1990s, and pianist Jessica Williams, now an international hot property, as well as adventurous additions such as idiosyncratic New Yorkers, East Down Septet, Robertson's commitment to Scottish musicians has paid artistic dividends. Indeed, long before the arrival of labels such as Linn and Caber, Hep was documenting Scottish jazz musicians alongside their American counterparts. Sandy Brown, Jimmy Deuchar, Bobby Wellins – including a recording with former Charles Mingus trombonist Jimmy Knepper – Joe Temperley, and (following a recording with Temperley in 1997) guitarist Jim Mullen all have valuable recordings in the 2000 Series... and in the case of Temperley and Mullen, ongoing relationships with Robertson, whose enthusiasm and dedication continues unabated in his retirement from the chalk face.

Address: PO Box 50, Edinburgh EH7 5DA. www.hepjazz.com

- discography - (the 2000 series)

Apr 79. (lp) *(HEP 2001) HOWARD McGHEE ORCHESTRA – Cookin' Time*
Apr 81. (lp) *(HEP 2002) EDDIE THOMPSON & SPIKE ROBINSON – Ain't She Sweet*
(cd-iss. Apr98; HEPCD 2002)
Apr 81. (lp) *(HEP 2003)* **JOE TEMPERLEY & JIMMY KNEPPER – Just Friends**
Apr 81. (lp) *(HEP 2004) NAT PIERCE QUINTET – 5400 North*
(cd-iss. Sep96; HEPCD 2004)
Apr 81. (lp) *(HEP 2006) SLIM GAILLARD – Legendary McVoutie*
(cd-iss. Jul90; HEPCD 2006)
Apr 81. (lp) *(HEP 2007) EDDIE THOMPSON TRIO & ROY WILLIAMS – When The Lights Are Low*
(cd-iss. Jan97; HEPCD 2007)
Apr 81. (lp) *(HEP 2008)* **JIMMY DEUCHAR QUINTET – The Scots Connection**
Feb 82. (lp) *(HEP 2009) NAT PIERCE ORCHESTRA – The Ballad Of Jazz Street*
(cd-iss. Apr97; HEPCD 2009)
Jun 82. (lp) *(HEP 2010) BENNY WATERS with* **JOE TEMPERLEY** & ROY WILLIAMS – When You're Smiling
(cd-iss. Aug97; HEPCD 2010)
Jul 82. (lp) *(HEP 2011) JIMMY KNEPPER &* **BOBBY WELLINS** – Primrose Path
Dec 82. (lp) *(HEP 2012)* **JOE TEMPERLEY** with JIMMY KNEPPER & **BOBBY WELLINS – Special Relationship**
(cd-iss. Mar94 & Jul02; HEPCD 2012)
Apr 82. (lp) *(HEP 2013) NAT PIERCE – Boston Bustout*
(cd-iss. Nov95; HEPCD 2013)
Dec 82. (lp) *(HEP 2014) BUDDY DE FRANCO – Live Buenos Aires*
(cd-iss. Nov95; HEPCD 2014)
Oct 83. (lp) *(HEP 2015) ROY WILLIAMS with EDDIE THOMPSON – Something Wonderful*
(cd-iss. Jul96; HEPCD 2015)
Nov 83. (lp) *(HEP 2016) DIGBY FAIRWEATHER (with John Barnes, Bruce Turner, Tony Coe &* **Sandy Brown**) – Songs For Sandy
(cd-iss. Jul98; HEPCD 2016)
Mar 84. (lp) *(HEP 2017)* **SANDY BROWN / BRIAN LEMON TRIO – In The Evening**
(cd-iss. Jan98; HEPCD 2017)
Dec 83. (lp) *(HEP 2018) BUDDY DE FRANCO – Mood Indigo*
Aug 83. (lp) *(HEP 2019) DON LANPHERE QUINTET – Out Of Nowhere*
May 83. (lp) *(HEP 2020) SLIM GAILLARD – Anytime, Anyplace*
(cd-iss. Mar96; HEPCD 2020)
Jul 84. (lp) *(HEP 2021) EDDIE THOMPSON TRIO & SPIKE ROBINSON – Memories Of You*
(cd-iss. Aug94; HEPCD 2021)
Mar 84. (lp) *(HEP 2022) DON LANPHERE QUINTET – Into Somewhere*
Apr 84. (lp) *(HEP 2023) BUDDY DE FRANCO QUINTET – On Tour UK*
Apr 84. (lp) *(HEP 2024) SLIM GAILLARD – At Birdland 1951*
(cd-iss. Jan96; HEPCD 2024)
Aug 85. (lp) *(HEP 2027) DON LANPHERE – Don Loves Midge*
(cd-iss. Sep93; HEPCD 2027)
Aug 85. (lp) *(HEP 2028) SPIKE ROBINSON & EDDIE THOMPSON TRIO – At Chesters Vol.1*
(cd-iss. Jan92; HEPCD 2028)
Nov 85. (lp) *(HEP 2029) SLIM GAILLARD – The Voutest*
(cd-iss. Sep98; HEPCD 2029)
Apr 86. (lp) *(HEP 2030) BUDDY DE FRANCO QUINTET – Grooving*
Jan 87. (lp) *(HEP 2031) SPIKE ROBINSON & EDDIE THOMPSON TRIO – At Chesters Vol.2*
(cd-iss. Jun94; HEPCD 2031)
Nov 86. (lp) *(HEP 2032)* **MARTIN TAYLOR – Tribute To Art Tatum**
Mar 87. (lp) *(HEP 2034) DON LANPHERE – Stop*
(cd-iss. Apr99; HEPCD 2034)
Sep 87. (lp) *(HEP 2035) SPIKE ROBINSON with ELAINE DELMAR – In Town*
(cd-iss. Jun93; HEPCD 2035)
Nov 88. (lp) *(HEP 2037) TONY COE – Some Other Autumn*
(cd-iss. Jan96; HEPCD 2037)
Dec 88. (lp) *(HEP 2039) BUDDY DE FRANCO /* **MARTIN TAYLOR – Garden Of Dreams**
Dec 88. (lp/cd) *(HEP/+CD 2040) DON LANPHERE SEXTET – Go Again*
(cd-iss. Jul90; HEPCD 2040)
Apr 90. (lp/cd) *(HEP/+CD 2041) DANISH RADIO BIG BAND – Crackdown*
Feb 89. (lp/cd) *(HEP/+CD 2042) SPIKE ROBINSON – Plays Gershwin*
Feb 89. (cd) *(HEPCD 2043) SHADES OF KENTON – Round Midnight Concert*
Oct 89. (lp) *(HEP 2044) JANUSZ CARMELLO – A Portrait*
(cd-iss. Sep90; HEPCD 2044)
Oct 89. (lp) *(HEP 2045) SPIKE ROBINSON & LOUIS STEWART & JANUSZ CARMELLO – Three For The Road*
(cd-iss. Oct90; HEPCD 2045)
Jan 90. (lp) *(HEP 2046) JAY CLAYTON & DON LANPHERE – Live At Jazz Alley: The Jazz Alley Tapes*
(cd-iss. Sep92; HEPCD 2046)
Oct 90. (cd) *(HEPCD 2047) RICHARD DAVIS & FRIENDS – One For Frederick (Live At Sweet Basil)*
Dec 90. (cd) *(HEPCD 2048) DON LANPHERE & LARRY CORYELL – Lanphere / Coryell*
Oct 91. (cd) *(HEPCD 2049) SPIKE ROBINSON with* **The BRIAN KELLOCK TRIO** – Stairway To The Stars
May 92. (cd) *(HEPCD 2051) DANISH RADIO BIG BAND – Suite For Jazz Band*
Mar 92. (cd) *(HEPCD 2052)* **JOE TEMPERLEY – Nightingale**
Oct 92. (cd) *(HEPCD 2053) SPIKE ROBINSON & GEORGE MASSO – Plays Arlen*
Sep 93. (cd) *(HEPCD 2054) JESSICA WILLIAMS – The Next Step*
Jun 94. (cd) *(HEPCD 2055) JESSICA WILLIAMS – In The Pocket*
Oct 94. (cd) *(HEPCD 2056) SPIKE ROBINSON – Plays Henry Warren*
Aug 94. (cd) *(HEPCD 2057) LOUIS STEWART – Overdrive*
Sep 94. (cd) *(HEPCD 2058) DON LANPHERE & BUD SHANK & DENNY GOODHEW – Lopin'*
Sep 94. (cd) *(HEPCD 2059) ROBERT MAZUREK – Man Facing East*
Feb 95. (cd) *(HEPCD 2060) JAY THOMAS – 360 Degrees*
Mar 95. (cd) *(HEPCD 2061) JESSICA WILLIAMS – A Song That I Heard*
Mar 95. (cd) *(HEPCD 2062)* **JOE TEMPERLEY – Concerto For Joe**
Jun 95. (cd) *(HEPCD 2063) EAST DOWN SEPTET – Out Of Gridlock*
Jun 95. (cd) *(HEPCD 2064) TRINITY ORCHESTRA – Trinity Fair*
Jun 95. (cd) *(HEPCD 2065) ROBERT MAZUREK / ERIC ALEXANDER – Badlands*
Mar 96. (cd) *(HEPCD 2066) HERB GELLER – Plays The Al Cohn Songbook*
Jan 97. (cd) *(HEPCD 2067) ROBERT MAZUREK & ERIC ALEXANDER – Blue Green*
Nov 96. (cd) *(HEPCD 2068) MICHAEL HASHIM with Claudio Roditi – Keep A Song In Your Soul: Plays Fats Waller*
Mar 97. (cd) *(HEPCD 2069) EAST DOWN SEPTET – Channel Surfin'*
Aug 97. (cd) *(HEPCD 2070)* **BOBBY WELLINS – Making Light Work**
Aug 97. (cd) *(HEPCD 2071) SPIKE ROBINSON & GENE DiNOVI – At The Stables*
Jan 98. (cd) *(HEPCD 2072) DON LANPHERE & JOHN PUGH – Don Still Loves Midge*
Aug 98. (cd) *(HEPCD 2073)* **JOE TEMPERLEY – With Every Breath..**
Dec 98. (cd) *(HEPCD 2074) HERB GELLER QUARTET – I'll Be Back*
Aug 99. (cd) *(HEPCD 2075) MICHAEL HASHIM /* **JOE TEMPERLEY** – Multi Coloured Blue
Oct 99. (cd) *(HEPCD 2076) GENE DiNOVI – Souvenir: Plays The Music Of Benny Carter*
Feb 00. (cd) *(HEPCD 2077) FRANK GRIFFITH – The Suspect*
Mar 00. (cd) *(HEPCD 2078) HERB GELLER &* **BRIAN KELLOCK** – Hollywood Portraits
Sep 01. (cd) *(HEPCD 2079) MICHAEL HASHIM – Plays Kurt Weill*
Jan 01. (cd) *(HEPCD 2080) FRANK GRIFFITH NONET – Ealing Jazz Festival 2000*
Apr 01. (cd) *(HEPCD 2081) JOHN HART TRIO – Scenes From A Song*
Jun 01. (cd) *(HEPCD 2082) JESSICA WILLIAMS – I Let A Song Go Out Of My Heart*

Oct 01. (cd) *(HEPCD 2083)* **JOE TEMPERLEY – Easy To Remember**
Mar 02. (cd) *(HEPCD 2084) HERB GELLER – To Benny And Johnny With Love*
2002. (cd) *(HEPCD 2085)* **JIM MULLEN – Somewhere in the Hills**

Linn records

Founded: Eaglesham, Renfrewshire . . . 1984 as the recording arm of Hi-Fi manufacturers Linn Products. With a brief to release music recorded to the highest possible specifications – in line with the company's audio expertise – Linn began life in 1984 when they released The BLUE NILE's debut album, 'A Walk Across The Rooftops'. Having used the album as a demonstration tape for their Hi-fi equipment, the company were sufficiently impressed to make it their first official release (in conjunction with 'Virgin').

Maintaining tight quality control over their A&R policy, the label nurtured a sophisticated catalogue consisting largely of jazz (CAROL KIDD, TOMMY SMITH, MARTIN TAYLOR, HUE AND CRY, TIM GARLAND etc) and classical (LENINGRAD SYMPHONY ORCHESTRA, PALLADIAN ENSEMBLE, POLISH CHAMBER ORCHESTRA, MAGNIFICAT, CATHERINE KING & JACOB HERINGMAN etc.) with a few folk artists (ANAM, ANDREW WHITE, IAN BRUCE, The McCLUSKEY BROTHERS, WILLIAM JACKSON) and a couple of Bluesy rock acts (JON STRONG and The STEVE GIBBONS BAND).

Among the lesser known talents on the Linn roster was JEFF LEYTON, an actor/singer who made quite a name for himself in London's West End. The uncle of jazz saxophonist TOMMY SMITH, LEYTON has consistently won critical plaudits over the course of the 90's for his lead role in various versions of the hugely popular French musical, 'Les Miserables'. His first solo album, 'The Music Of The Night', was released on 'Linn' in 1998 to coincide with that year's tour of the ever popular 'Les Mis..'. Featuring songs from hit shows such as 'West Side Story' and 'Jesus Christ Superstar', the album was conceived and produced by his more famous (in Scotland at least) nephew.

On the classical side of things, cellist WILLIAM CONWAY and pianist PETER EVANS got together in (1990) for the collaborative 'DEBUSSY, MARTIN, POULENC' album. A native of Glasgow, CONWAY had previously studied at the Royal Scottish Academy of Music and Drama where his talents won him various scholarships and where he now teaches. A former Principal Cellist with the Scottish Chamber Orchestra, he now holds a similar position with the Goldberg Ensemble, the Chamber Orchestra of Europe and the Hebrides Ensemble. EVANS, meanwhile, studied piano at Edinburgh University and the Vienna Hochschule before going on to perform around the world. In addition to his work with CONWAY he's also collaborated with cellist STEVEN ISSERLIS, works regularly with the SCO and co-directs the Hebridean Ensemble alongside CONWAY.

One of Linn's biggest classical signings was the BT SCOTTISH ENSEMBLE, a group of 12 string players directed by violinist CLIO GOULD. The ensemble began life back in 1969 as the SCOTTISH BAROQUE ENSEMBLE under the guidance of violinist LEONARD FRIEDMAN, taking on the BT sponsorship in 1993. The 90's have seen the group put in acclaimed performances all over Britain and abroad, commissioning works by native composers such as CRAIG ARMSTRONG and JUDITH WEIR as well as playing the works of MENDELSSOHN, TCHAIKOVSKY etc. In 1994, the ensemble performed 'Seven Last Words From The Cross' on BBC TV (alongside CAPPELLA NOVA), a JAMES MacMILLAN commission. More recently, they released their debut recording for Linn, 'TEARS OF THE ANGELS' (1998), a collection of pieces commissioned from contemporary composer JOHN TAVENER. A less well known composer, JAMES OSWALD, was the inspiration behind 'COLIN'S KISSES' (1999), a much acclaimed album by Scots early music afficionados CONCERTO CALEDONIA. Born in the sleepy East Neuk village of Crail in 1710, OSWALD's Scottish folk-influenced baroque style saw him eventually become King George III's chamber composer. Taking its title from an OSWALD song cycle (possibly one of the earliest cycles composed), the aforementioned album also featured interpretations of the man's airs, instrumental works and miniatures.

Another Linn act worthy of mention are The WALLACE COLLECTION, a groundbreaking brass quintet featuring band leader/trumpeter JOHN WALLACE, trumpeter JOHN MILLER, horn player PAUL GARDHAM, trombonist SIMON GUNTON and tuba player ROBIN HAGGART. Their highly original approach has been witnessed by audiences in literally ever corner of the globe, from Madrid to Sierra Leone and even Kazakhstan. Having read music at King's College Cambridge, JOHN became principal trumpeter for the Philharmonic Orchestra. Gained classical credibility by featuring on numerous recordings by past and present composers (VERDI, HOLST, MUSSORGSKY, BACH, VIVALDI, SHOSTAKOVICH, HANDEL, HAYDN, MENDELSSOHN, AARON COPELAND – need I go on!). In 1993, WALLACE premiered the religious piece, 'Epiclesis', at the Edinburgh Festival; modern day Scots composer/fellow-trumpeter JAMES MacMILLAN slightly altered the work five years later and invited his good friend to play on the album, 'Epiclesis – Ninian'. WALLACE progressed to become head of the brass faculty at the Royal Academy Of Music and also worked for the London Sinfonietta. He is now head of the RSAMD in Glasgow.

For more information about Linn records, their address is 257 Drakemire Drive, Castlemilk, Glasgow, G45 9SZ and (www.linnrecords.co.uk).

– discography –

Apr 84. (lp/c) *(LKH/+C 1)* **BLUE NILE – A Walk Across The Rooftops**
Oct 89. (lp/c/cd) *(LKH/+C/CD 2)* **BLUE NILE – Hats**
— for further BLUE NILE singles, info, see their discography
Aug 84. (lp/c) *(AKH/AKC 003)* **CAROL KIDD – Carol Kidd**
Jan 86. (lp/c) *(AKH/AKC 005)* **CAROL KIDD – All My Tomorrows**
Jun 87. (lp/c) *(AKH/AKC 006)* **CAROL KIDD – Nice Work (If You Can Get It)**
Sep 90. (lp/c/cd) *(AKH/+CD/CD 007)* **CAROL KIDD – The Night We Called It A Day**
Sep 90. (cd) *(CKD 002)* **Debussy, Martin, Poulenc**

— here's a list of Linn's mostly English/foreign classical CD's
1990. (cd) *(CKD 001) POLISH CHAMBER ORCHESTRA – Live: Mozart, Vivaldi, Bach, Bartok & Elgar*
1990. (cd) *(CKD 003) ENGLISH CLASSICAL PLAYERS – Mozart Symphony No.40*
1991. (cd) *(CKD 004) LENINGRAD SYMPHONY ORCHESTRA – Dmitri Shostakovich: Symphony No.5 in D Minor Op.*
1991. (cd) *(CKD 005) JILL FELDMAN & NIGEL NORTH – Udite Amanti: 13th Century Italian Love Songs*
1991. (cd) *(CKD 006) NIGEL NORTH – Baroque Lute*
1992. (cd) *(CKD 007) NEW LONDON CONSORT – Music From The Time Of Columbus*
1992. (d-cd) *(CKD 008)* **Various Artists – Scotland's Music**
1992. (cd) *(CKD 009)* **WILLIAM CONWAY & PETER EVANS – Rachmaninov**
1993. (cd) *(CKD 010) PALLADIAN ENSEMBLE – An Excess Of Pleasure*
1993. (cd) *(CKD 011) NEW LONDON CONSORT – Elizabethan & Jacobean Consort Music*
1993. (cd) *(CKD 012) MUSICA DE CAMERA – Albinoni & Pachalbel*
1994. (cd) *(CKD 013) NIGEL NORTH – Bach On The Lute Vol.1*
1994. (cd) *(CKD 015) PALLADIAN ENSEMBLE – The Winged Lion*

— Linn records now continues releasing combined genres
Feb 91. (cd/c) *(AKD/AKC 013)* **DAVID NEWTON – Victim Of Circumstance**
Dec 90. (cd/c) *(AKD/AKC 014)* **MARTIN TAYLOR – Don't Fret**
Nov 91. (cd/c) *(AKD/AKC 015)* **DAVID NEWTON – Eye Witness**
Nov 91. (cd/c) *(AKD/AKC 016)* **MARTIN TAYLOR – Change Of Heart**
Nov 91. (cd/c) *(AKD/AKC 017)* **CAROL KIDD – I'm Glad We Met**
Mar 92. (cd/c) *(AKD/AKC 018) CLAIRE MARTIN – The Waiting Game* (CLAIRE was born in South London)
Apr 93. (cd/c) *(AKD/AKC 019) STEVE GIBBONS BAND – Birmingham To Memphis* (Steve's a blues singer from Birmingham, England)
Feb 93. (cd/c) *(AKD/AKC 020)* **MARTIN TAYLOR – Artistry**
Apr 93. (cd/c) *(AKD/AKC 021) CLAIRE MARTIN – Devil May Care*
Oct 93. (cd) *(AKD 022) STEPHANE GRAPPELLI &* **MARTIN TAYLOR – Reunion**
Oct 93. (cd/c) *(AKD/AKC 023) JON STRONG – Follow Me* (Jon is not from Scotland – not with a surname like that! – what'ma sayin'?)
Feb 94. (cd/c) *(AKD/AKC 024)* **TOMMY SMITH & FORWARD MOTION – Reminiscence**
Apr 94. (cd/c) *(AKD/AKC 025)* **DAVID NEWTON – Return Journey**
Apr 94. (cd/c) *(AKD/AKC 026)* **CAROL KIDD – Crazy For Gershwin**
Sep 94. (cd/c) *(AKD/AKC 028) CLAIRE MARTIN – Old Boyfriends*
Oct 94. (cd) *(CKD 029) NIGEL NORTH – Bach On The Lute Vol.2*
Oct 94. (cd/c) *(AKD/AKC 030)* **MARTIN TAYLOR – Spirit Of Django**
Feb 95. (cd) *(CKD 031) PHILIP PICKETT – Alchemist*
Mar 95. (cd) *(AKD 034) RAY GELATO GIANTS – The Full Flavour* (RAY's from England)
1995. (cd) *(CKD 035) PURCELL SIMFONY – Henry Purcell: The Indian Ocean*
1995. (cd) *(CKD 036) PALLADIAN ENSEMBLE – Bach Trio Sonatas*
Mar 95. (cd/c) *(AKD/AKC 037)* **WILLIAM JACKSON – Inchcolm**
May 95. (cd) *(CKD 039) NEW LONDON CONSORT – Ars Subtilior*
May 95. (cd/c) *(AKD/AKC 040)* **TOMMY SMITH – Misty Morning And No Time**
Jul 95. (cd) *(CKD 041) PALLADIAN ENSEMBLE – A Choice Collection: Music Of Purcell's London*
Aug 95. (cd) *(AKD 042)* **CAROL KIDD – The Best Of . . . Vol.1**
Aug 95. (cd) *(AKD 043)* **CAROL KIDD – The Best Of . . . Vol.2**
Sep 95. (cd/c) *(AKD/AKC 044)* **CAROL KIDD – That's Me**
Nov 95. (cd/c) *(AKD/AKC 046) CLAIRE MARTIN – Offbeat*
Dec 95. (cd) *(CKD 047)* **Various Artists – The Complete Songs Of Robert Burns Volume 1**
Mar 96. (cd/c) *(AKD/AKC 048)* **MARTIN TAYLOR – Portraits**
Mar 96. (cd) *(CKD 049) NIGEL NORTH – Bach On The Lute Vol.3*
1997. (cd) *(CKD 050) PALLADIAN ENSEMBLE – Trios For 4*

Feb 96. (cd) *(CKD 051)* **Various Artists – The Complete Songs Of Robert Burns Volume 2**
1996. (cd) *(CKD 052) MAGNIFICAT – The Golden Age Volume 1: Europe* (Magnificat are an English classical ensemble)
Oct 96. (cd) *(AKD 054)* **TOMMY SMITH – Beasts Of Scotland**
Oct 96. (cd) *(CKD 055) NIGEL NORTH – Bach On The Lute Vol.4*
Oct 96. (cd/c) *(AKD/AKC 057)* **HUE AND CRY – Jazz Not Jazz**
Feb 97. (cd) *(AKD 058)* **MARTIN TAYLOR – Years Apart**
May 97. (cd) *(AKD 059)* **TOMMY SMITH – Azure**
1996. (cd) *(CKD 060) MAGNIFICAT – Tomas Luis de Victoria: Officium Defunctorum*
1997. (cd) *(CKD 062)* **Various Artists – The Complete Songs Of Robert Burns Volume 3**
1997. (cd) *(AKD 063) PERFECT HOUSEPLANTS – Snap Clatter (are from London)*
1997. (cd) *(AKD 064)* **MARTIN TAYLOR – Gold**
1997. (cd) *(CKD 065) SCHIDLOF QUARTET – Shostakovich*
Mar 97. (cd) *(AKD 066) CLAIRE MARTIN – Make This City Ours*
1997. (cd) *(CKD 067) ENSEMBLE DUMONT – Henri Dumont: Les Litanies De La Vierge*
Oct 00. (cd) *(AKD 069) GERARD PRESENCER – The Optimist (was born in London)*
1998. (cd) *(CKD 070) PALLADIAN ENSEMBLE – Les Saisons Amusantes*
1998. (cd) *(CKD 071) MUSICA SECRETA – Lucrezia Vizzana Componimenti Musicali (1623)*
1997. (cd) *(CKD 073)* **BT SCOTTISH ENSEMBLE – The Celtic**
– Violin concerto:- The Celtic; i. Ceilidh – ii. Lament for Collessie – iii. The copper of Clapham / Celtic air (from 'The Four Elements') / Flute concerto:- The Connemara / The four elements: Earth / Water / Fire.
1997. (cd) *(AKD 074) TIM GARLAND – Enter The Fire*
May 00. (cd) *(CKD 075) MAGNIFICAT – Spem In Alium*
Mar 98. (cd) *(CKD 076) ORLANDO CONSORT & PERFECT HOUSEPLANTS – Extempore*
Feb 98. (cd) *(AKD 078) JACK JONES – New Jack Swing* (JJ is that US crooner; all on his own again)
Aug 98. (cd) *(AKD 079) GERARD PRESENCER – Platypus*
Dec 97. (cd) *(AKD 080)* **Various Artists – Celtic Experience 1**
Apr 99. (cd; imp) *(AKD 081)* **MARTIN TAYLOR – Two's Company**
1998. (cd) *(AKD 082)* **WILLIAM JACKSON – Celtic Experience 2**
1998. (cd) *(CKD 083)* **Various Artists – The Complete Songs Of Robert Burns Volume 4**
Feb 98. (cd) *(AKD 084)* **TOMMY SMITH – The Sound Of Love**
1998. (cd) *(CKD 085)* **BT SCOTTISH ENSEMBLE – Tears Of The Angels**
– . . . Depart in peace / My gaze is ever upon you / Tears of the angels.
1998. (cd) *(CKD 086)* **Various Artists – The Complete Songs Of Robert Burns Volume 5**
1998. (cd) *(AKD 087)* **Various Artists – All Night Jazz**
1999. (cd) *(CKD 088)* **Various Artists – Auld Lang Syne**
1999. (cd) *(CKD 089) CATHERINE KING & JACOB HERINGMAN – Airs De Cour*
Jun 98. (cd) *(AKD 090)* **MARTIN TAYLOR – Gypsy (The Spirit Of Django)**
1999. (cd) *(CKD 092)* **THE WALLACE COLLECTION – The Golden Section**
Feb 99. (cd) *(AKD 093) CLAIRE MARTIN – Take My Heart*
Apr 98. (cd) *(AKD 094) STEPHANE GRAPPELLI &* **MARTIN TAYLOR – Celebrating Grappelli**
2000. (cd) *(CKD 095)* **BT SCOTTISH ENSEMBLE – Shostakovich**
– Chamber symphony in C minor, Op, 110a:- i. Largo – ii. Allegro molto – iii. Allegretto – iv. Largo – v. Largo – vi. Piano concerto No.1 in C minor, Op 35:- i. Allegro moderato – ii. Lento – iii. Moderato – iv. Allegro con Brio / Two pieces for string octet, Op.11: Prelude – adagio / Scherzo – Allegro molto.
1999. (cd) *(CKD 096) SCHIDLOF QUARTET – Dvorak*
1999. (cd) *(CKD 097) NIGEL NORTH – A Variete Of Lute Lessons*
Nov 98. (cd) *(AKD 098)* **JEFF LEYTON – The Music Of The Night**
– If I can't love her / Maria / Pity the child / My heart will go on / The rose / Music of the night / Gethsemane / Bring hime home / This is the moment / Father and son / Long ago / Against all odds / Gliding / Somewhere / Last night of the world / My love's like a red, red rose.
1999. (cd) *(CKD 099)* **Various Artists – The Complete Songs Of Robert Burns Volume 6**
Nov 99. (cd) *(CKD 100) PALLADIAN ENSEMBLE – The Sun King's Paradise*
Sep 99. (cd) *(CKD 101)* **CONCERTO CALEDONIA – Colin's Kisses**
Jun 99. (cd) *(AKD 102)* **HUE AND CRY – Next Move**
May 99. (cd) *(AKD 103)* **TOMMY SMITH & MURRAY McLACHLAN – Gymnopedie**
Mar 99. (cd) *(AKD 104) JACK JONES – . . . Pays A Tribute To Tony Bennett*
Apr 99. (cd) *(CKD 105) NIGEL NORTH – English Ayres By Thomas Campion*
Apr 99. (cd) *(AKD 106) ANDREW WHITE – Guitarra Celtic* (Andrew is from Newcastle-Upon-Tyne)
2000. (cd) *(CKD 107)* **Various Artists – The Complete Songs Of Robert Burns Volume 7**
1999. (cd) *(AKD 108)* **WILLIAM JACKSON – Celtic Experience 3**
1999. (cd) *(CKD 109) MAGNIFICAT – Philippe Rogier: Missa Ego Sum Qui Sum*
Nov 99. (cd) *(AKD 110)* **TOMMY SMITH – Blue Smith**
2000. (cd) *(CKD 111) ELENA RIU – Piano Icons For The 21st Century* (Elena's an Hispanic-American)
Aug 99. (cd) *(CKD 112)* **IAN BRUCE – Alloway Tales**
2001. (cd) *(CKD 113) MUSICA SECRETA – Dialogues With Heaven*
Sep 99. (3xcd-box) *(AKD 115)* **MARTIN TAYLOR – The Linn Box 1**
Nov 99. (3xcd-box) *(AKD 116)* **CAROL KIDD – The Linn Box 2**
Feb 01. (cd) *(CKD 117) DUNEDIN CONSORT – In The Beginning*
2000. (cd) *(CKD 118) The SIXTEEN – A Choral Pilgrimage*
May 00. (cd) *(AKD 120)* **McCLUSKEY BROTHERS – Housewives' Choice**
Feb 00. (cd) *(CKD 121)* **ANAM – Tine Gheal / Bright Fire**
Apr 00. (cd) *(AKD 122) CLAIRE MARTIN – Perfect Alibi*
Feb 00. (3xcd-box) *(AKD 123) CLAIRE MARTIN – The Linn Box 3*
Mar 00. (3xcd-box) *(AKD 124)* **TOMMY SMITH – The Linn Box 4**
2001. (cd) *(CKD 125) JOHN TOLL – Orlando Gibbons: The Woods So Wild*
2000. (cd) *(CKD 126) PALLADIAN ENSEMBLE – Held By The Ears*
Jul 00. (3xcd-box) *(AKD 127)* **WILLIAM JACKSON & Various Artists – The Celtic Experience Vol.1-3**
2000. (cd) *(CKD 128) NIGEL NORTH – Bach On The Lute Box Set*
2000. (cd) *(AKD 129) BARB JUNGR – Chanson: The Space In Between* (Barb's a female born in Europe but living in Britain)
Feb 01. (cd) *(AKD 130) PERFECT HOUSEPLANTS – New Folk Songs*
2001. (cd) *(CKD 132) SCHIDLOF QUARTET – Schumann*
Mar 00. (cd) *(AKD 133)* **JEFF LEYTON – Songs From The Show**
Mar 00. (cd) *(CKD 134)* **ANAM – Riptide** (re-issue)
Mar 00. (cd) *(CKD 135)* **ANAM – First Footing** (re-issue)
2001. (cd) *(CKD 140)* **CONCERTO CALEDONIA – Mungrel Stuff**
2001. (cd) *(CKD 141) The SIXTEEN – Buxtehude: Membra Jesu Nostri*
2000. (cd) *(CKD 142) CATHERINE KING & JACOB HERINGMAN – A Renaissance Songbook*
2001. (cd) *(CKD 143)* **Various Artists – The Complete Songs Of Robert Burns Volume 8**
Sep 00. (cd) *(AKD 144)* **MARTIN TAYLOR – Stepping Stones**
Jul 01. (cd) *(AKD 145)* **MacKENZIE & WILLIAM JACKSON – Notes From A Hebridean Island**
Mar 01. (cd) *(AKD 146)* **CAROL KIDD – A Place In My Heart**
Nov 00. (cd) *(CKD 148) The SIXTEEN – In Honore JS Bach*
Nov 00. (cd) *(CKD 151) ORCHESTRA OF THE AGE OF ENLIGHTENMENT – Vivaldi Concerti*
Feb 01. (cd) *(CKD 152) AMERICAN BOYCHOIR – Mass And Vespors For The Feast Of Holy Innocents*
2001. (cd) *(CKD 153) FITZWILLIAM STRING QUARTET – The Seven Last Words*
2001. (cd) *(CKD 154) ENSEMBLE DUMONT – La Messe Du Roi*
2002. (cd) *(CKD 158) CATHERINE KING & THE NORWEGIAN BAROQUE ORCHESTRA – Alto Arias*
Mar 02. (cd) *(CKD 162)* **THE WALLACE COLLECTION – Hammered Brass**
2002. (cd) *(CKD 164) CLARA SANABRAS – The New Irish Girl . . .*
2001. (cd) *(CKD 168) PALLADIAN ENSEMBLE – Held By The Ears*
2002. (cd) *(CKD 169) MUSICA SECRETA – Dangerous Graces*
2001. (cd) *(CKD 170) PASSACAGLIA – Telemann: Chamber Music*
2001. (cd) *(CKD 174) MAGNIFICAT – Giovanni Pierluigi da Palestrina*
2001. (cd) *(CKD 178) GILLIAN WEIR . . . – Concerto For Organ*
2002. (cd) *(CKD 179) DAVID PAUL JONES – Something There*
2002. (cd) *(CKD 180) GILLIAN WEIR . . . – Concerto For Organ SACD*
2001. (cd) *(CKD 181) NORWEGIAN BAROQUE ORCHESTRA – Bach Orchestral Suites & Harpsichord Concerto*
2002. (cd) *(CKD 183) PAMELA THORBY with SONNERIE – Baroque Recorder Concertos*
2002. (cd) *(AKD 190) WILLARD WHITE – The Paul Robeson Legacy*

6
Classical

Classical Caledonian Composers: With the likes of JAMES MACMILLAN, JAMES DILLON and EVELYN GLENNIE taking up reams of column inches in the national press, the state of Scottish classical contemporary music has rarely been healthier. Although classical music has been documented in depth elsewhere, no book claiming to cover the sphere of Scottish music in all its glorious diversity would be complete without at least a cursory glance at both Scotland's rich classical heritage and its modern-day practitioners. Due to the complexity of chronicling this genre in the usual discographical format, it was decided to restrict this section to purely biographical information. The one exception to this is EVELYN GLENNIE who gets a full discography in view of her many Pop/Rock collaborations.

Our pre-20th century musicians are covered briefly here in chronological order

It might surprise the casual reader to know that Scotland's classical pedigree goes right back to the 1500's when composers **ROBERT CARVER** (born c.1490–c.1560) and **ROBERT JOHNSON** (born Duns, Berwickshire, c.1500–c.1560) were setting down choral pieces on some of the earliest surviving manuscripts. The cream of their work has been recorded by early music aficionados CAPPELLA NOVA, while anyone interested in CARVER's original manuscripts can find them at the National Library of Scotland.

Moving on a couple of hundred years to the 18th Century, two other composers emerged north of the border, namely **Sir JOHN CLERK** of Penicuik (1676–1755) and **WILLIAM McGIBBON** (1695–1756). The former was educated at both Glasgow and Leiden (Netherlands) Universities before going on to Rome where he studied composition under CORELLI. The latter was an Edinburgh-born violinist composing sonatas during the Baroque era, becoming one of the first classical composers to interpret Scottish folk music.

Although not born in Scotland, the world famous **EDVARD GRIEG** (1843–1907) was actually born to Scottish parents (in Bergen, Norway), the ROD STEWART of his day you might say. While quite probably not wont to strut around in a tartan scarf, GRIEG did his mother country proud by penning the revered 'Peer Gynt Suite' in 1875 (probably better known to non-classical buffs as that one on the Nescafe ad!).

A plethora of native composers were born in the 19th Century: **Sir ALEXANDER CAMPBELL MACKENZIE** (1847–1935) was born in Edinburgh but underwent his musical schooling in Germany and London (at the Royal Academy Of Music). After his late 1800's composing heyday ('RHAPSODIE ECOSSAISE', 'COLUMBA', 'THE ROSE OF SHARON', 'PIBROCH', etc), he spent the latter half of his life as the Royal Academy's principal.

JAMES A. MOONIE (1853–1923) meanwhile, remained in the city of Edinburgh where he was born, conducting and composing for a variety of choirs.

Greenock-born **WILLIAM WALLACE** (1860–1940) also headed south to the Royal Academy in London, where he was presumably treated better than his Braveheart namesake. The former medical student nevertheless composed a symphonic poem to the latter, 'SIR WILLIAM WALLACE', while also writing 'THE MASSACRE OF THE MACPHERSONS' and 'IN PRAISE OF SCOTTISH POESIE'.

Another Scotsman to study at the Royal Academy was **LEARMONT DRYSDALE** (1866–1909), an Edinburgh-born former architect who scored operas such as 'THE KELPIE' and 'RED SPIDER' as well as an 'OVERTURE TO TAM O'SHANTER'.

Hawick-born **JOHN BLACKWOOD McEWEN** (1868–1948) was another RAM graduate who took over the reins as principal from the aforementioned MACKENZIE in 1923/4, making a lasting contribution to the creation of chamber music between the wars.

A composer to make a significant mark south of the border was **HAMISH MacCUNN** (1868–1916). The Greenock-born son of a rich shipping merchant, he won a scholarship to the newly established Royal College Of Music in London at the age of 15. Something of a classical prodigy, MacCUNN first came to the attention of London's musical elite after the noted conductor Sir August Manns featured HAMISH's 'CIOR MHOR' in one of his concerts. The young MacCUNN then composed his most famous overture, 'THE LAND OF THE MOUNTAIN AND THE FLOOD', at the age of only 19. Despite his youth he was subsequently appointed Professor of Harmony at the capital's Royal Academy of Music, a position he held for six years before taking up a similar post at the Guildhall. During this time he continued to compose Scottish-influenced overtures such as 'THE DOWIE DENS OF YARROW' and 'THE SHIP O' THE FIEND' as well as choral pieces and numerous songs. The multi-talented MacCUNN also moved successfully into opera, composing 'JEANIE DEANS' (based on Scott's novel, 'Heart Of

Midlothian') and the Celtic-inspired 'DIARMID', the latter partly performed in Balmoral Castle at the request of Queen Victoria. In his 30's, MacCUNN increasingly turned from composition to conducting and was a fervent fan of Wagner as translated into English. He died young at the age of only 48 after being struck down with throat cancer. The BBC Scottish Symphony Orchestra helped raise MacCUNN's profile by recently recording a series of the largely forgotten composer's works including excerpts from his operas.

More obscure was **DAVID STEPHEN** (1869–1946), a self-taught Dundonian organist who went from playing in his local church to composing the symphonies 'CONCERT OVERTURE' and 'HEBRIDES OVERTURE'.

The Edinburgh-born **CHARLES MacPHERSON** (1870–1927) was also an organist although he eventually held the top spot in the more salubrious surrounds of St. Paul's. After moving down south at an early age, he was initially a chorister at the cathedral before going on to study at the RAM. While his later compositions were focused on the church, his earlier work included the 'CRIDHE AN GHAIDHIL' overture and 'THREE GAELIC MELODIES'.

FRANCIS GEORGE SCOTT (1880–1958) was born in the border town of Hawick and educated at both Edinburgh University and Moray House. After carving out a career as a music teacher/lecturer, the patriotic SCOTT composed a number of pieces based on the works of ROBERT BURNS and HUGH MacDIARMID.

Son of the aforementioned JAMES MOONIE, the Peeblesshire-born **W.B. MOONIE** (1883–1961) undertook his education at Edinburgh University before going on to Hoch Conservatoire (Frankfurt, Germany). After the death of his father in 1923, he returned to the 'Burgh where he conducted various choirs and composed several choral works including 'CALEDONIA' (1911), 'GLENARA' (1913), as well as an opera, 'THE WEIRD OF COLBAR'.

Balancing out the Edinburgh contingent was Glasgow's own **JAMES FRISKIN** (1886–1967), a Royal College of Music graduate who emigrated to New York in his late twenties. There, he taught at both the Institute of Musical Arts and the Juilliard Graduate School. His works include 'PIANO QUINTET' and 'CONCERT OVERTURE'.

- 20th Century Classical Composers

Unusually, among the first composers to emerge in the 20th Century were female, no easy occupation in the male dominated bastion of classical music. **ISOBEL DUNLOP** (1901–1975) studied in Vienna and Malta as well as Edinburgh University. Although she composed many choral and instrumental pieces as well as an opera ('THE SILHOUETTE' – 1969) she was more famous for co-founding the Saltire Music Group and the Saltire Singers. **MARIE DARE** (1902–1976) meanwhile, hailed from Newport-On-Tay in north Fife. She was educated at London's Guildhall School of Music before going on to study in Paris. After spending the early part of her career performing in Europe she returned to Edinburgh after the Second World War where she was appointed principal cellist in the Reid Orchestra.

From here on, composers are listed in alphabetical rather than chronological order. . .

Colin BROOM

Born: 1973, Glasgow. At the age of 8, the young COLIN began playing tenor horn in The Salvation Army before teaching himself piano from the age of 11 onwards. By his mid-20's, BROOM had gained a BA in Applied Music from the University Of Strathclyde and had also become a competent percussionist. In 1996 he composed 'GEOMETRIC FANFARE' for the 21st Conference of the Association of Teachers and Education in Europe, his improvisational contemporary classical style subsequently given an outlet via the INVENTION ENSEMBLE, a 10-strong outfit of likeminded musicians (including J. SIMON VAN DER WALT) formed in late '97. Apparently he has a penchant for the literature of Herman Hesse, author of one of the finest religious/philosophical works of the past century, 'Siddhartha'.

Erik CHISHOLM

Born: 4 January 1904, Cathcart, Glasgow. Although his formal education was minimal – he left school at the age of 13 – he did study piano under Philip Halstead and organ with Herbert Walton (he was apparently giving Cathedral recitals before he reached his teens), while his precocious compositional ability eventually led to tutelage from Russian pianist LEFF POUISHNOFF.

At 22, CHISHOLM decamped to Nova Scotia where he took on the responsibilities of organist and choirmaster at Westminster Presbyterian Church and Director of Music at Picton Academy. In his mid-20's, he returned home for an extended period of study during which he gained both a Bachelor of Music degree and a Doctorate in music from Edinburgh University. While still a student in 1929, CHISHOLM co-founded the 'Active Society For The Propagation Of Contemporary Music', helping to bring some of Europe's most famous composers to Glasgow; the likes of SORABJI, ALFREDO CASELLA, SZYMANOWSKI, BELA BARTOK, JOHN IRELAND and CYRIL SCOTT all made the trip north. ERIK also became a distinguished conductor, marshalling the Glasgow Grand Opera Society over the period 1930–39 and conducting the Celtic Ballet in 1938/39; his interest in the form had already led him to establish the Scottish Ballet Society. During the war, he conducted both the Carl Rosa Opera Company and The Anglo-Polish Ballet before being posted to Singapore in 1943 with a brief to set up and conduct The Singapore Symphony Orchestra.

In 1946, the man's career entered a new phase when he was appointed Professor Of Music at Cape Town University in South Africa. As well as improving the range and quality of degrees on offer, he founded the SA National Music Press as an outlet for native composers. In 1951, ERIK founded the Opera School with a similar aim, putting on the premier of JOHN JOUBERT's 'Silas Marner' and thus helping put the composer's name on the map; other productions included his own 'DARK SONNET' and 'MURDER IN THREE KEYS' trilogy as well as BARTOK's 'Bluebeard Castle'. The Opera gained an international reputation via its touring productions, CHISHOLM further enhancing his cosmopolitan outlook with trips to both India and Russia. The Indian trip inspired one of his most notable works, 'SECOND PIANO CONCERTO (ON HINDUSTANI THEMES)', Scots soloist AGNES WALKER subsequently performing the concerto all over Europe.

Although his travels spanned the globe, he remained in South Africa until his death in the early 70's. In his time, ERIK CHISHOLM composed more than a hundred works, largely orchestral, piano and song, but also choral, ballet and opera. While few were actually published, he did complete a book entitled 'Celtic Folk Songs', featuring piano arrangements of traditional songs from the Scottish Highlands and Islands.

Martin DALBY

Born: 1942, Aberdeen. After attending Aberdeen Grammar School, he won a scholarship to the Royal College of Music in London in 1960, studying composition under Herbert Howells and viola under Frederick Riddle. A subsequent scholarship travel award saw him spend two years in Italy where he played viola in a small chamber orchestra.

Upon his return, DALBY took up the post of producer at the recently inaugurated Radio 3 where he worked until 1971. A year out as the Cramb Research Fellow in Composition at Glasgow University was followed by a return to the BBC – albeit BBC Scotland – where he was promoted to Head Of Music. As a composer he's been commissioned by various orchestras and ensembles – including the Royal Scottish National Orchestra for whom he recently wrote 'THE MARY BEAN' – as well as the Edinburgh Festival and smaller festivals in Cheltenham, Orkney etc. His works include choral pieces, songs, song-cycles and most notably, chamber music. In 1993 he gave up his BBC responsibilities and devoted himself to composing full-time, increasingly concentrating on his home city where he composed 'THE WHITE MAN' for The Scottish Chamber Orchestra in celebration of Union Street's 200th anniversary. DALBY also composed a string quartet piece to mark Aberdeen University's 500th birthday.

His 'FIRST THURSDAY IN MAY' celebrated the re-establishment of the Scottish Parliament in 1999 while his production of Radio Scotland's 'Scotland's Music' documentary netted him a Sony Gold Award. He is currently working on an orchestral suite aiming to reinterpret the musical legacy of Scots fiddler/composer, J. SCOTT SKINNER.

Peter Maxwell DAVIES

Born: 1934, Salford, Manchester. Although born in England and having attended both the Royal Manchester College of Music and Manchester University, DAVIES relocated to Hoy on the Orkney Isles in 1970. He's lived and worked there ever since, setting up the St.Magnus Festival in 1977 and drawing inspiration from both Orkney's natural environment and native authors such as George Mackay Brown. His extensive output includes operas such as 'THE DOCTOR OF MYDDFAI', 'TAVERNER' and 'THE LIGHTHOUSE', ballets (including 'SALOME'), choral works, orchestral pieces, an acclaimed symphonic cycle and children's music-theatre. Sir Peter is also an accomplished conductor, currently holding the positions of Associate Conductor/Composer with London's Royal Philharmonic Orchestra and Conductor/Composer with Manchester's BBC Philharmonic as well as Composer Laureate of the Scottish Chamber Orchestra.

James DILLON

Born: 29 Oct'50, Glasgow. After originally honing his musical skills in traditional pipe bands and rock groups, he began working in the classical sphere despite having no formal compositional training. Relatively experimental in nature, his music has found a more welcoming audience abroad than in Scotland with a raft of ensembles – including the BBCSO, BBCSSO, the London Sinfonietta, Musikfabrik, Ensemble Recherche and Ensemble Inter-Contemporain – airing his work at festivals in Brussels, Paris, Strasbourg, Vienna and Sydney as well as Glasgow, Edinburgh and London. On the recording front, a handful of his compositions have been released on the NMC and Montaigne/Auvidis labels. The man's TRAMWERK BOOK 1 (1995) netted the 1997 Royal Philharmonic Society Award for chamber-scale composition while his most recent piece, 'RESIDUE' was exclusively aired at the Witten New Music Days festival in April '99. The following year, the bushy-haired DILLON completed his 'Nine Rivers' cycle by releasing La coupure for percussion and electronics, while he also composed a violin concerto at the BBC Proms.

Patrick DOYLE

Born: 1953, nr.Glasgow. Brought up in a family environment which encouraged his tuba and piano playing, DOYLE went on to study at the Royal Scottish Academy of Music and Drama. After graduating in 1974 he found work as a piano teacher although his sights were set on bigger things i.e. composing and acting. Appearances in both John Byrne's production of 'The Slab Boys' and the 1978 Edinburgh Festival comedy revue, 'Glasvegas' (for which he also wrote the score) initiated a long career in TV, theatre and latterly, film. As well as composing for STV's 'Charlie Endell' and the BBC's 'The Butterfly's Hoof' he secured parts in television dramas such as 'The Monocled Mutineer' and the award winning 'Tutti Frutti'. He also won a bit part in the acclaimed 'Chariots Of Fire' although it'd be another ten years before his film composition career really took off.

In 1987, a musical commission for Kenneth Branagh's Renaissance Theatre Company led to the full-time position(s) of composer/musical director. DOYLE subsequently composed the music for a host of Renaissance productions including 'Much Ado About Nothing', 'King Lear' and 'Midsummer's Night's Dream'. It was also through Branagh that DOYLE began his career in composing film scores, the thespian don inviting him to pen the score for his new film version of Shakespeare's 'Henry V' in 1989. This in turn led on to an incredibly prolific decade during which PATRICK scored soundtracks for the likes of 'Carlito's Way' (1993), 'Mary Shelley's Frankenstein' (1994), 'A Little Princess' (1995), 'Sense and Sensibility' (1995), 'Hamlet' (1996), 'Donnie Brasco' (1997), 'Romeo and Juliet' (1997) and 'Great Expectations' (1998) amongst others. DOYLE's fame has even seen him commissioned by the Prince Of Wales no less, for 'THE THISTLE AND THE ROSE', a song cycle for soprano and chorus written to commemorate the Queen Mother's 90th birthday back at the dawn of the 90's. He also composed 1998's 'THE FACE IN THE LAKE', a short concert piece for a children's story narrated by the scrumptious Kate Winslet. This work was included on the Grammy Award winning CD, 'Listen To The Storyteller' (1998).

Tommy FOWLER

Born: 1948, Aberdeenshire. After initially holding down a career as a journalist/broadcaster during the 70's/80's, FOWLER became a mature student at Glasgow University where he graduated with a BMH in composition. His works have been performed by the Scottish Chamber Orchestra, the Royal Scottish National Orchestra and Cappella Nova amongst others, including pieces for film, concert and theatre. TOMMY is currently undertaking part-time composition research for a PhD which he combines with commissioned work.

Bruce FRASER

Born: 1947, India. Although he was born on the subcontinent, FRASER was educated in Scotland and went on to study at the Royal Scottish Academy Of Music and the Guildhall School of Music. While he initially made his living as a freelance trombonist and a music teacher, his talents as a composer – largely for wind band, brass band and educational material for schools – eventually led to him setting up his own publishing company, 'Lomond Music' in 1982. Concerned largely with works for teaching purposes, the company's catalogue has grown to almost 200 titles. He had also composed for string, woodwind and brass as well as choral and orchestral works (including 'THE VISIT', performed by Anstruther Philharmonic Society in 1992). His 'MAGNIFICAT' for Soprano, Baritone, Choir and Orchestra – composed in memory of his daughter – was performed by Dunfermline Choral Union in 1996.

Paul GALBRAITH

Born: Edinburgh. An internationally acclaimed classical guitarist, GALBRAITH received his big break at the tender age of 17 when he won a silver medal in the Segovia International Guitar Competition. This in turn led to performances with the likes of the Scottish Chamber Orchestra, the Scottish Symphony Orchestra, the Royal Philharmonic and the Chamber Orchestra of Europe amongst others. Initially signed to Edinburgh's 'Eclectic' records, he utilised the familiar 6-string guitar on 1990's 'MUSIC FOR SOLO GUITAR BY MANUEL M. PONCE' before moving on to his more famous customised 8-string model with 1996's 'INTRODUCING THE BRAHMS GUITAR'. PAUL resided for a time in Greece (homeland of pianist/conductor/philosopher George Hadjinikos, PAUL's longtime tutor), later relocating to Brazil's sprawling metropolis of Sao Paulo where he co-founded the Brazilian Guitar Quartet.

His specially designed guitar has come to be regarded as a pivotal innovation in the classical world, as has his unique approach to the instrument. It's an approach which saw him nominated for an American Grammy Award, courtesy of his 1998 album of Bach Sonatas & Partitas for unaccompanied violin. GALBRAITH has become particularly popular in the States where he toured with the Moscow Chamber Orchestra and where his New York performances have garnered impressive reviews. Other recent recordings include 'PLAYS HAYDN KEYBOARD SONATAS' (1999), 'ESSENCIA DO BRASIL' (1999; Brazilian Guitar Quartet), 'LUTE SUITES OF J.S. BACH' (2000) and 'IN EVERY LAKE THE MOON SHINES FULL' (2001), the latter set taking its name from a poem by Portuguese poet Fernando Pessoa and featuring a cosmopolitan mix of folk songs from Spain, Greece, Hungary and GALBRAITH's native Scotland.

Evelyn GLENNIE

Born: 1965, Aberdeenshire, Scotland. The world's only full-time solo percussionist, EVELYN GLENNIE has consistently pushed the boundaries of the form and is recognised as not only one of the most talented musicians Scotland has ever produced but one of the most talented in the world. The youngest of three children, EVELYN was raised on a farm some 25 miles north of Aberdeen, a rural upbringing characterised by an immersion in both traditional Scottish song and the indigenous Doric dialect. Her interest in percussion subsequently developed in her earliest years at high school, around the same time that EVELYN was rendered almost completely deaf by a mysterious illness. Fascinated by the range of percussion instruments and their inherent possibilities, she re-taught herself to sense percussive vibrations and so master her chosen endeavour in her own way.

In 1982, the teenage EVELYN won a scholarship to the Royal Academy Of Music in London and went on to make her headline-grabbing professional debut in the mid-80's. An incredibly prolific career ensued as she not only performed with most of the world's most esteemed classical ensembles – repositioning the role of orchestral percussion in the process – but went on to commission over ninety new works for solo percussion. GLENNIE's own recording career began in 1988 with a Grammy-winning interpretation of Bartok's Sonata For Two Pianos And Percussion, a heady start that led on to a series of albums for 'R.C.A.' running the gamut of her stylistic diversity and beyond. The most recent of these, 'SHADOW BEHIND THE IRON SUN' (2000), was a leap into free improvisation overseen by veteran US studio whizz Michael Brauer. Inspired by her love of composers such as JOHN CAGE and reflecting her motivational drive of constant experimentation, the record found EVELYN drawing sound from such unlikely sources as a set of customised car exhaust pipes and children's music boxes. No stranger to cross-fertilisation, she's also worked with the similarly adventurous BJORK, the Kodo Japanese drummers (who recently toured Scotland), Balinese gamelan ensembles and Brazilian samba schools among many other traditional musicians the world over.

A respected ethnomusicologist in her own right, GLENNIE is the proud owner of an extensive collection of ethnic instruments and is a fund of knowledge on native folk traditions. Her wealth of talent also extends to TV and film soundtrack work, largely composed in collaboration with her husband GREG MALCANGI. EVELYN appeared at the 2001 Celtic Connections festival in Glasgow where she teamed up with ubiquitous ex-SILLY WIZARD man, PHIL CUNNINGHAM for CEILIDH, a percussion-based folk extravaganza featuring The BLAZIN' FIDDLES and the RSNO.

– EVELYN GLENNIE discography –

RCA Red Seal / R.C.A.

Apr 90. (cd/c/lp) *(RD/RK/RL 60242)* **RHYTHM SONG** ☐ ☐
– Etude in C, op.6, No.10 / Robbin' Harry / Rhythm song / Berceuse / The flight of the bumble bee / Czardas / Mexican dance for marimba No.1 / Mexican dance for marimba No.2 / Maple leaf rag / A little prayer / Black key study / Michi / Capriccioso, op.28 (introduction & rondo).

Oct 91. (cd) *(RD 60557)* **LIGHT IN DARKNESS** ☐ ☐
– Eldorado / Dream of the cherry blossoms / The song of Dionysius / Marimba dance (1-3) / Marimba spiritual / Light in darkness / Two movements for Marimba (1-2).

Oct 91. (cd/c) *(RD/RK 60870)* **DANCIN'** ☐ ☐
– Slaughter on tenth avenue / Clog dance / Strauss medley / The swan / Astaire-Rogers medley / Can can / Bolero / Hoe down / Invitation to the dance / Heyre kati / Valse brilliante taps in tempo.

Catalyst / Catalyst

Nov 92. (cd) *(09026 61277-2)* **REBOUNDS: CONCERTOS FOR PERCUSSION** ☐ ☐
– Concerto pour batterie et petit orchestre / Concerto for solo percussion and chamber orchestra:- I. Molto vivo – II. Presto – III. Interlude (moderato) – IV. Con brio / Concerto para marimba e orquestra de cordas:- I. Saudacao – II. Lamento – III. Danca / Despedida / Concerto pour marimba et ensembles a cordes.

Sep 93. (cd) *(09026 61916-2)* **VENI, VENI, EMMANUEL** ☐ ☐
– Veni, veni, Emmanuel (8 parts) / After the tryst / " . . .As others see us . . ." (6 parts) / Three dawn rituals (3 parts) / Untold.

Oct 95. (cd) *(09026 68193-2)* **WIND IN THE BAMBOO GROVE** ☐ ☐
– Michi for marimba / Divertimento / Wind in the bamboo grove / "Rhapsody" / Variations on Japanese children's songs / Marimba spiritual.

Apr 96. (cd) *(09026 68195-2)* **DRUMMING** ☐ ☐
– Entrances / Halasana / Sorbet No.1: Latin American interlude / Bongo-O / Sorbet No.2: Chinese cymbals / Prim / Sorbet No.3: UDU trail / The anvil chorus / Sorbet No.4: Woodblocks and falling instruments / To the earth / Sorbet No.5: Wood and metal chimes / Pezzo da concerto No.1, op.15, for snare drum / Sorbet No.6: Simtak debut / Matre's dance / Exits / Sorbet No.7: Hi-hat playout.

RCA Red Seal / R.C.A.

Oct 98. (cd/c; as EVELYN GLENNIE & BLACK DYKE BAND)
(09026 63234-2/-4) **REFLECTED IN BRASS** ☐ ☐
– Yorkshire ballad / Gypsy virtuoso / Taps in tempo / Gymnopedie No.1 / Green triplets / Xylophone classics medley / Whirlwind / Cartoon music / Rudy's rambles / Hitten 'em up / Tween heather and sea / Golden age of the xylophone / Danny boy / Slavische fantasie / Gee whizz.

Jul 00. (cd) *(09026 63406-2)* **SHADOW BEHIND THE IRON SUN** ☐ ☐
– First contact / Shadow behind the iron sun / Attack of the glow worm / Land of vendom / Icefall / Thunder caves / Council / Warrior's chant / Battle cry / Wind horse / Crossing the bridge / Last contact / Battle cry (bonus mix).

— now cred. w/ JOHN HARTE, PHILIP SMITH & LONDON PHILHARMONIC ORCHESTRA

Black Box / not iss.

Oct 00. (cd) *(BBM 1051)* **AFRICAN SUNRISE – MANHATTAN RAVE** ☐ [-]

– compilations, etc. –

May 97. (d-cd/d-c) *RCA Victor; (74321 47629-2/-4)* **GREATEST HITS** ☐ ☐
– Entrances / Halasana / Sorbet No.1 / Rhythm song / My spine / Slaughter on 10th Avenue / Sorbet No.5 / Little prayer / Eldorado / Sorbet No.7 / Black key study / Divertimento / Taps in tempo / Born to be wild / Michi for marimba / Sorbet No.4 / Light in darkness / Anvil chorus / Rhapsody / The swan / Sorbet No.3.

Iain HAMILTON

Born: 6 Jun'22, Glasgow. Upon winning a scholarship to the Royal Academy Of Music, HAMILTON gave up his burgeoning engineering career and dedicated himself to music full-time. A series of awards and a Bachelor of Music degree from London University ensued as did an honorary degree from the University of Glasgow. Although a key figure in London's classical music world (chairman of the Composers' Guild, member of the BBC's Music Advisory Panel etc), HAMILTON relocated to New York in 1961 where he lectured as Professor of Music at Duke University. He nevertheless continued to spend time in London where he was elected a Fellow Of The Royal Academy, finally returning to the city for good in 1981.

The highlights of his many orchestral works include 1971's 'AMPHION: CONCERTO No.2', 1975's 'AURORA FOR ORCHESTRA' (premiered by the Scottish National Orchestra at New York's Carnegie Hall) and 1977's 'CLEOPATRA FOR SOPRANO AND ORCHESTRA'. HAMILTON has also been closely involved with stage productions during his career, 'THE CATILINE CONSPIRACY' commissioned and premiered by Scottish Opera in 1974. 1976's 'TABURLAINE' was commisioned by the BBC while 1978's 'ANNA KARENINA' was commissioned and premiered by The English National Opera. His bulging CV additionally includes a number of chorale commissions such as 'THE REQUIEM', 'PROMETHEUS' and 'THE ST. MARK PASSION'. More recently, the veteran composer has enjoyed premieres of his 'SECOND PIANO CONCERTO' and 'VERS APPOLINAIRE' courtesy of The BBC Scottish Symphony Orchestra' while his aforementioned 70's piece 'AURORA' was toured by the Royal Scottish National Orchestra.

John HEARNE

Born: 1937, Reading, England. Born to Welsh parentage, HEARNE extended his Celtic connection by permanently relocating to Scotland in 1970. Having studied at St.Luke's College in Exeter and the University College of Wales, Aberystwyth, he briefly taught music in Iceland before beginning a 17-year stint as a lecturer at Aberdeen College of Education. In 1985 his suite for brass and percussion, 'THE FOUR HORSEMEN' was voted the best new work premiered at that year's Edinburgh Festival Fringe. Now a freelance composer, singer and conductor based in Inverurie, his latest works include the 'DE PROFUNDIS' overture for Aberdeen's 500th anniversary in 1995 and 1998's 'SOLEMN AND STRANGE MUSIC' for piano duet. The latter resulted in a second Gregynog Composers' Award Of Wales for HEARNE after he first scooped the prize in 1992 with choral piece, 'LAETATUS SUM'.

Alistair JUSTICE

Born: 30 Sep'74, Birmingham, England. Having previously studied under Steve Martland and Dr Sadie Harrison at Goldsmiths College, London, ALISTAIR now lives in Edinburgh where he's currently studying for a PhD in Composition. His works have been performed by various orchestras including Ensemble Alpeh, The University of Edinburgh Medics Orchestra, The Goldsmiths Sinfonia and The Goldsmiths College Windband. He has also worked as a conductor and trombonist in a freelance capacity with the University Of Stirling Orchestral Society and The Stockbridge and New Town Community Orchestra. Work in progress includes a theatrical collaboration with The Co-Opera-Tive while a performance of 'THE FEAR OF STRANGERS' by the JEFFERSON JUSTICE ENSEMBLE is set for the near future.

Kenneth LEIGHTON

Born: 2 Oct'29, Wakefield, England. Before he'd even left school, LEIGHTON completed a diploma in piano performance and went on to study Classics and music at Oxford. In 1951, the same year he graduated, the talented musician won a travel scholarship which took him to Rome and a course of study with Petrassi. Lecturing posts at both the Royal Naval School Of Music and Leeds University were followed by a ten year teaching stint at Edinburgh University. In 1970 he was appointed as the university's Reid Professor of Music, a post he held up until his death in 1988. Among his many compositions are concertos, choral works, instrumental and vocal pieces and a couple of symphonies. He even composed an opera, 'COLUMBA', which was premiered in 1981. The late pianist also committed much of his work to vinyl, recording mainly for the British Music Society.

Malcolm LINDSAY

Born: early 1960's, Fife. In the 80's, LINDSAY worked with RICKY ROSS in a very early incarnation of DEACON BLUE although he's since become famous as an electro-acoustic composer with a CV of more than 80 performed works to his name. Among the many and varied organisations which have commissioned work from him are the Scottish Arts Council, Fife Regional Council, Glasgow City Council, Fotofeis and the Scottish Chamber Orchestra while his many collaborations have involved the likes of cult Scots writer Janice Galloway, ex-SKIDS frontman RICHARD JOBSON and poet Ronnie Kerr. In 1995, he formed The MOORS with Carol Moore and Stuart Duffin, releasing a CD entitled 'MOOR FIRE BURN'. The poems of the aforementioned Kerr were the inspiration behind LINDSAY's 'SOLITARY CITIZEN' for string quartet, recorded by the Scottish Chamber Orchestra quartet QUARTZ and released on disc in 1997. Another SCO quartet, Mr McFall's Chamber, performed a series of the Fifer's compositions at the Greenbelt '99 arts festival as well as a live rendition of 'SOLITARY..' for BBC Radio Scotland and a performance of 'THE HOMELANDS SUITE' at Edinburgh's Bongo Club in Spring 2000. Also in the summer of '99, LINDSAY wrote 'THE LIGHTHOUSE SUITE' in response to a commission for the opening of that new building in Glasgow; the suite was performed at the building's grand opening by the BT Scottish Ensemble and is due for a CD release.

John McLEOD

Born: 1934, Aberdeen. After studying at the Royal Academy Of Music under the tutelage of Sir Lennox Berkeley, McLEOD went on to become one of Scotland's most celebrated composers. As well as amassing an extensive recorded catalogue of orchestral works, concertos, chamber pieces, choral works, symphonies and more, he has completed commissions for the likes of RAIMUND GILVAN, BENJAMIN LUXON, EVELYN GLENNIE and PETER DONOHOE. Through the 80's and 90's, he moved into composing for TV and film and over the period 1991–97 held the post of Head Of Composing for Film and Television at the London College Of Music. He also taught as a Visiting Lecturer at the Royal Academy Of Music where he was elected a Fellow in 1989. He has even conducted many performances of his own compositions by such noted orchestras as the Royal Scottish National Orchestra, the BBC Scottish Symphony Orchestra, the Scottish Chamber Orchestra and even The Polish Radio and TV Symphony Orchestra of Krakow. Among his most recent works to be premiered are 'MACHAR – PORTRAIT OF A SAINT' (commissioned by Aberdeen Sinfonietta) and 'THE SUN DANCES' (commissioned by the National Youth Orchestra Of Scotland). McLEOD was made a Fellow Of The Royal Society Of Arts in 1994 and is currently serving on the Board of The Society For The Promotion Of New Music.

James MACMILLAN

Born: 16 Jul'59, Kilwinning, Ayrshire. Educated at both Edinburgh and Durham universties, trumpeter MACMILLAN went on to become one of the most esteemed composers of the modern era. A devout Catholic, many of his works have dealt in religious and associated themes; 'THE CONFESSION OF ISOBEL GOWDIE' (1990) centered on a medieval witch hunt and received considerable critical acclaim upon its premiere at the BBC Proms. Through the late 80's and 90's, MACMILLAN's prolific output included 1989's 'THE EXORCISM OF RIO SUMPUL' for chamber orchestra, 1992's hugely popular 'VENI, VENI, EMMANUEL' percussion concerto, 1993's 'SEVEN LAST WORDS FROM THE CROSS' for choir and string orchestra, 1995's 'ADAM'S RIB' for brass quintet, 1996's opera, 'INES DE CASTRO' and 1998's 'AFTER THE TRYST' for violin and piano. He's worked with the London Symphony Orchestra, the New York Philharmonic Orchestra and the Los Angeles Philharmonic Orchestra while the likes of EVELYN GLENNIE, Sir COLIN DAVIS and Sir ANDREW DAVIS have all performed/conducted his work. He is currently working on a series of commissions for the BBC Philharmonic.

Muir MATHIESON

Born: 24 January 1911, Stirling. The cousin of composer CEDRIC THORPE DAVIE, he graduated from London's Royal College Of Music, and his contribution was mainly to the British film industry. From Alexander Korda's 'Catherine The Great' in 1934, right through to 'Henry V' (1945) and 'Hamlet' (1948), the composer/musical director became accomplished in a career that spanned over five decades; he was also nominated for a Best Score Oscar via the movie 'Genevieve' in 1954. In 1961, he even achieved a US Top 50 album with a re-working of 'GONE WITH THE WIND'. That same year, MATHIESON landed the lucrative job as director of Grampian television and even found time to compose its theme. On August 2nd, 1975 (aged 64), MUIR died at his home in London.

Thea MUSGRAVE

Born: 27 May'28, Scotland. Having studied at both Edinburgh University and the Conservatoire in Paris, THEA became the first British Composer to win the Lili Boulanger prize in 1952. Her early works were performed by the Saltire Singers whom she later tutored. She subsequently became Guest Professor at the University Of California, Santa Barbara, in 1970. Two years later she took up permanent residence in the USA after securing a position as Distinguished Professor at Queen's College of the City University of New York. A winner of both the Koussevitsky Award and two Guggenheim fellowships, THEA composed the groundbreaking 'SPACE PLAY' in 1974. An intense interest in the dramatic possibilites inherent in music led her to compose her first opera in 1973, 'THE VOICE OF ARIADNE', following it up with 1977's 'MARY, QUEEN OF SCOTS'.

MUSGRAVE went on to explore the use of electronics in opera works such as 'GOLDEN ECHO 1' for horn and 'NARCISSUS' for flute/clarinet. Continuing her predeliction for mythical/historical thematic figures, THEA chose the legendary South American liberator Simon Bolivar (after which Bolivia took its name) as the inspiration behind her acclaimed 1995 opera commissioned by the Los Angeles Music Center Opera. 1995 was also the year she received an Honorary Doctorate from Glasgow University. Recent works such as 'AUTUMN SONATA', 'WILD WINTER' and 'A MEDIEVAL SUMMER' reflect her increasing preoccupation with seasonal cylces and the transience of life while 'SONGS FOR A WINTER'S EVENING' was based on the poems of ROBERT BURNS. Other recent commissions include 'PHOENIX RISING' (for the BBC Symphony Orchestra), premiered at the Royal Festival Hall in 1998 and 'THREE WOMEN – QUEEN, SLAVE, MISTRESS', premiered by the Women's Philharmonic in San Francisco in 1999.

Having begun her career in an era when the classical sphere was still a largely male-dominated bastion, THEA has gone on to win considerable respect as both a composer and conductor.

Jeremy S RANDALLS

Born: 1959, Scotland. After studying the flute at both the Royal Scottish Academy Of Music and Drama and London's Royal College Of Music, RANDALLS (who also plays whistle, bouzouki and banjo) formed folk outfit FLUMGUMMERY in 1981 alongside EWAN ROBERTSON. The duo released a lone eponymous album in 1984, the same year he formed The BLAKE ENSEMBLE and premiered the William Blake-inspired 'Little Vagabond' at the Edinburgh Festival. The early-mid 80's also saw him develop a close working relationship with Rumanian musicologist Viorel Cosma, a series of RANDALLS' works – including 'SONATA FOR SOLO CELLO' (1980), 'BRASS TRIO' (1981) and 'DUET FOR FLUTE AND VIOLA' (1985) – subsequently broadcast in the poverty-stricken Eastern Bloc country. Over the period 1986-7, RANDALLS held the position of musical director with Scotland's 7:84 Theatre Company while a number of Scottish Arts Council-backed commissions included 1988's 'DUO SONATA' for flute and piano and 1990's 'LE TOMBEAU DE MARTINU'. During the 1980's, RANDALL also taught music at a variety of Scottish state and private schools including a 2-year stint at the RSAMD.

1992 saw him complete the 'LATIN AMERICAN SKETCHES', a commission for Australian Flautist Alison Mitchell and Scots guitarist ALLAN NEAVE. Winnie The Pooh of all people was the inspiration behind 'HUMS OF POOH', premiered in 1993 by The Walton Ensemble (commissioned with the kind permission of the A.A. Milne Foundation). The Royal Scottish National Orchestra also commissioned RANDALLS for 'CEILIDH' for the Scottish Proms in Glasgow's Royal Concert Hall. The latter half of the 90's saw him concentrating much of his energies in Palermo, Italy where he gave a series of pre-Opera lectures and where his work, 'Caliban' was premiered in 1996. The multi-talented composer even plays in a Dixieland jazz band in the Sicilian capital!

Magnus ROBB

Born: 1970, Edinburgh. As a viola player on tour with the National Youth Orchestra of Scotland, ROBB met the composer JOHN McLEOD with whom he subsequently studied composition. One of his first works was 'THE GYRES' for solo piano, premiered during the 1998 Edinburgh Festival. He went on to study at the University Of York under David Blake during which time he composed his 'DELPHI' for chamber orchestra as well as 'LIOS MOR', a work inspired by the island of Lismore. The former piece was later aired by the Nederlands Radio Kamerorkest at the 1991 Gaudeamus International Music Week. MAGNUS duly relocated to the Netherlands – after a year at London's Guildhall School Of Music And Drama – where he spent three years studying at the Royal Conservatory in The Hague.

Both his 'SKYN' for solo viola and 'THE ANCIENT LANGUAGE OF THE BIRDS' were composed around this time with the latter premiered in 1995 by vocalist Linda Hirst and the Chamber Group Of Scotland. Hirst also performed the premiere of his solo mezzo-soprano piece, 'SUMMONING DAWN – THE RUBYTHROAT DREAMING', a BBC commission inspired by ROBB's summer '95 trip to Tuva in southern Siberia. As well as experiencing first hand the area's Khoomei singing style, MAGNUS made numerous birdsong recordings from the steppes. 1995 also saw a further commission from the BBC, 'BLOOD FOLIAGE', a work premiered at that year's Edinburgh Festival by Aberdeen's Yggdrasil Quartet. Now residing in Amsterdam, ROBB is currently hard at work on a vocal composition (with financial support from the Scottish Arts Council) and a commission for the Royal Philharmonic Orchestra.

William SWEENEY

Born: 1950, Glasgow. Following his schooling at Knightswood Secondary, SWEENEY studied music at the Royal Scottish Academy Of Music and Drama with WT Clucas and Frank Spedding before heading south to London's Royal Academy of Music where he studied under Alan Hacker and Harrison Birtwistle. Inspired by jazz, world music and traditional Scottish folk, he has been commissioned by a variety of organisations including the BBC, RSAMD, STUC, Glasgow's Mayfest, Cappella Nova and Glasgow University. As well as composing for his preferred instrument, the clarinet, SWEENEY has completed a variety of instrumental and vocal works, his most recent being 'THE WOODS OF RAASAY', a reworking of Gaelic poet Sorley Maclean's famous poem for soprano, bass and orchestra.

Marc YEATS

Born: 1962, London, England. YEATS began composing after attending one of PETER MAXWELL DAVIES' summer schools in Hoy, Orkney in 1994. Now based on the Isle Of Skye, this painter-turned composer used his background in art to inform his musical works by translating his perceptions of colour, texture and form into sound. His many compositions include piano, orchestral and choral works which have been performed by the BBC Philharmonic Orchestra, the Tokyo City Philharmonic Orchestra and the Scottish Chamber Orchestra amongst others. One of his most recent orchestral pieces, 'THE ROUND AND SQUARE ART OF MEMORY' was commissioned by the BBC for the BBC Philharmonic and pianist Kathryn Stott.

– other (short-takes) –

Bryan ANDERSON

Born: 1957, Glasgow. • **Educated:** Glasgow University, Sussex University, Massachusetts Institute of Technology. • **Selected Works:** 'CURVES OF A REFLECTED LIGHT', 'STRING QUARTET', 'CHAMBER CONCERTO'. • **Died:** 1985 in a hill walking accident on Ben Nevis.

Jennifer BARKER

Born: 1965, Stirlingshire. • **Educated:** Glasgow University, Syracuse University (New York), Pennsylvania University (Philadelphia). • **Selected Works:** 'THREE HIGHBROWS WE' • **Currently:** Professor of Theory/Composition at Virginia's Christopher Newport University.

George BARRONS

Born: 1925, Kirkcaldy, Fife. • **Educated:** Edinburgh University, Zurich Univerity. • **Selected Works:** 'TEN MINIATURES FOR PIANO', 'COOPERCEILIDH'. • **Died:** 1999.

Rory BOYLE

Born: 1950, Ayr. • **Educated:** Royal Scottish Academy of Music and Drama. • **Selected Works:** 'MARIMBA CONCERTO', 'SONATA FOR CELLO' • **Recently:** Completed commission from National Youth Orchestra Of Scotland.

Edward J BROWN

Born: 1929, Cowdenbeath, Fife. • **Educated:** Royal College Of Music, London. • **Selected Works:** 'IMMORTAL CHARMS' • **Currently:** Retired in Ontario, Canada where he still performs as an assistant organist.

Ronald CENTER

Born: Aberdeen, 1913. • **Educated:** Studied piano with Julien Rosetti and organ with William Swainson. • **Selected Works:** 'THE COMING OF CUCHULAIN', 'DIVERTIMENTO'. • **Died:** 1973.

James CLAPPERTON

Born: Aberdeen, 1968. • **Educated:** Royal Northern College of Music, Freiburg Musikochschule (Germany), Buffalo University (New York). • **Selected Works:** 'ERLICH FANTASYSIS', 'THE FIRMAMENT SERENE'.

Robert CRAWFORD

Born: 1925, Edinburgh. • **Educated:** Guildhall School Of Music. • **Selected Works:** 'SYMPHONIC STUDY: LUNULA' • **Currently:** Retired but still composing.

Peter DAVIDSON

Born: 1957, Glasgow. • **Educated:** Cambridge University, York University. • **Selected Works:** 'HET DERDE LAND', 'THE GHOST AT AULABY' • **Currently:** Lecturer at Warwick University.

Kenneth DEMPSTER

Born: 1962, Edinburgh. • **Education:** Napier University (Edinburgh), Royal Academy of Music (London), Yale University (USA). • **Selected Works:** 'MODERN ATHENIANS', 'SCOTTISH SPIRITS', 'CLAN RANALD'S DAUGHTER'. • **Currently:** Lectures at Napier University.

David DORWARD

Born: 1933, Dundee. • **Educated:** St.Andrews University, Royal Academy of Music (London). • **Selected Works:** 'TONIGHT, MRS MORRISON', 'AMAZONIAN MOONFLOWER', 'SYMPHONY No.2'. • **Currently:** Retired and living in Edinburgh.

Isobel DUNLOP

Born: 1901, Scotland. • **Educated:** Edinburgh University. • **Selected Works:** 'THE SILHOUETTE', 'FANTASY QUARTET'. • **Died:** 1975.

John Maxwell GEDDES

Born: 1941, Glasgow. • **Educated:** Royal Scottish Academy of Music. • **Selected Works:** 'OMBRE', 'VOYAGER', 'OBOE CONCERTO'.

Janetta GOULD

Born: 1926, Kilsyth. • **Educated:** Glasgow University. • **Selected Works:** 'THREE SOLEMN MELODIES' • **Currently:** Working on her long term project of writing accompaniments to the songs of Robert Burns.

David HORNE

Born: Stirling, 1970. • **Educated:** St.Mary's Music School (Edinburgh). • **Selected Works:** 'SPLINTERED UNISONS', 'REACHING OUT', 'TEVELLERS'. • **Currently:** Studying composition at Harvard University in California.

David JOHNSON

Born: Edinburgh, 1942. • **Educated:** Aberdeen University, Cambridge University. • **Selected Works:** 'THOMAS THE RHYMER', 'THE MORTAL MEMORY'.

David Paul JONES

Born: 1969. • **Educated:** Royal Scottish Academy of Music and Drama. • **Selected Works:** 'MACBETH', 'PARALLEL LINES', 'FROM THE EDGE OF THE WORLD'.

John LUNN

Born: Glasgow, 1956. • **Educated:** Glasgow University, Royal Scottish Academy of Music and Drama, Massachusetts Institute of Technology • **Selected Works:** 'LE VOYAGE'.

Stuart MacCRAE

Born: 1976, Inverness. • **Educated:** Durham University. • **Selected Works:** 'BORERAIG' • **Currently:** Working on a commission from the BBC Philharmonic.

Edward McGUIRE

Born: 1948, Glasgow. • **Educated:** Royal Academy of Music (London). • **Selected Works:** 'PETER PAN', 'A GLASGOW SYMPHONY', 'THE LOVING OF ETAIN'.

George MacILLWHAM

Born: 1926, Glasgow. • **Educated:** Royal Scottish Academy of Music, Royal Academy of Music (London). • **Selected Works:** 'CIR MHOR', 'DALRIADA OVERUTRE', 'ALBA'.

Gordon MacPHERSON

Born: 1965, Dundee. • Educated: York University. • **Selected Works:** 'IMPERSONAL STEREO', 'LAME GOD', 'ON E'. • **Currently:** Composer in residence at the Royal Scottish Academy of Music and Drama.

Kevin MAYO

Born: 1964, Stirling. • **Educated:** Edinburgh University, Royal College of Music (London) • **Selected Works:** 'DAYDREAMS IN DARKNESS', 'WALKING ON A MOBIUS STRIP'. • **Currently:** Completing a chamber piece for the BBC Scottish Symphony Orchestra.

Peter NELSON

Born: 1951, Glasgow. • **Education:** Edinburgh University, Glasgow University, Massachusetts Institute of Technology. • **Selected Works:** 'GROSS CONCERTO', 'GAMES'. • **Currently:** Working as a senior music lecturer at Edinburgh University.

Alasdair NICOLSON

Born: 1961, Inverness. • **Educated:** Edinburgh University • **Selected Works:** 'TREE OF STRINGS', 'BREAKDANCE'. • **Currently:** Involved in educational work for schools.

Buxton ORR

Born: 1924, Glasgow. • **Education:** Composition under Benjamin Frankel, conducting with Aylmer Buesset. • **Selected Works:** 'THE WAGER', 'RING IN THE NEW'.

Robin ORR

Born: 1909, Brechin. • **Education:** Royal College of Music (London), Pembroke College (Cambridge) • **Selected Works:** 'FULL CIRCLE', 'ON THE RAZZLE', 'SINFONIETTA HELVETICA'. • **Currently:** Retired.

John PURSER

Born: 1942, Glasgow. • **Educated:** Fettes College, Royal Scottish Academy of Music and Drama. • **Selected Works:** 'THE UNDERTAKER', 'THE BELL'.

Thomas WILSON

Born: 1927, Colorado, USA. • **Educated:** Glasgow University. • **Selected Works:** 'THE CONFESSIONS OF A JUSTIFIED SINNER', 'SYMPHONY No.5' • **Currently:** Fellow of the Royal Scottish Academy of Music and Drama.

7

Rock & Pop

(pre-punk era)

Great Scots In Rock & Pop: As ELVIS was raising the blood pressures of teenage kids across the Atlantic, Britain (in fact, Scotland) already had its own rock'n'roll revolutionary courtesy of Skiffle King, LONNIE DONEGAN. Even before 'Heartbreak Hotel' had shook up the charts, yer man LONNIE had smashed both the UK and US Top 10's with his folk/jazz-cum-skiffle version of Leadbelly's 'ROCK ISLAND LINE'. Of course, historical tomes will tell us (including this book!) that Glasgow-born DONEGAN went on to have a plethora of hits including three chart-toppers, 'CUMBERLAND GAP', 'GAMBLIN' MAN' and the novelty 'MY OLD MAN'S A DUSTMAN'. The Skiffle genre had another Scots innovator (however brief) in CHAS McDEVITT, who had a UK Top 5 hit in 1957 with 'FREIGHT TRAIN'.

When the music was about to take its last breath, Scotland and her unusual brand of R'n'R provided another British No.1 via the arrival of LORD ROCKINGHAM'S XI (aka HARRY ROBINSON) and their jazzy jig, 'HOOTS MON' (recently resurrected on a wine gums TV ad with mad Highlander for good measure).

Escaping the kilted performances of JACKIE DENNIS, JIMMY SHAND and ANDY STEWART (the latter two have already been documented in the Traditional Performers section), and preceding the advent of The Beatles, next on the gravy train of Glasgow-born hitmakers was KARL DENVER. From 1961 to 1962, he had no fewer than four consecutive UK Top 10 hits including the high-pitched, yodel-laden 'WIMOWEH' (better known as 'The Lion Sleeps Tonight').

The sixties were already swinging come the arrival of Scotland's newest prodigy, MARIE LAWRIE. In spring 1964, 15-year-old LULU (as she was better known) and THE LUVVERS screeched their way into the UK Top 10 with the ear-bashing stomp, 'SHOUT!'. This proved to be a great introduction to the wee lass from Lennoxtown who went on to have an abundance of hits (including a US No.1 'TO SIR WITH LOVE'), marry a Bee Gee (Maurice Gibb) and win the 1969 Eurovision Song Contest (with 'BOOM BANG-A-BANG). Revamping her career in the nineties with the hit 'INDEPENDENCE', she famously guested alongside Britain's best-loved boyband Take That on their massive 1993 No.1, 'Relight My Fire' as well as youthfully(!) co-presenting The National Lottery.

With the Folk revival already underway here in the UK (and on the East Coast of the USA via GUTHRIE, DYLAN, BAEZ, PAXTON etc), it was inevitable that British equivalent DONOVAN made his break for stardom. Early in 1965, the Maryhill-born teenager with the blue-corded cap whispered his way into the ears of audiences on both sides of the Atlantic via 'CATCH THE WIND'. This paved the way for subsequent ear-candy for the tripped-out hippie-folk generation; five classics from the era were undoubtably 'SUNSHINE SUPERMAN', 'MELLOW YELLOW', 'THERE IS A MOUNTAIN', 'JENNIFER JUNIPER' and 'HURDY GURDY MAN'.

The Folk and Blues revival were as immense in Scotland as anywhere else around Britain and beyond. In the way of Folk there was of course the eclectic talents of The INCREDIBLE STRING BAND (featuring the multi-talented ROBIN WILLIAMSON and MIKE HERON), whose sophomore set in '67, '5,000 SPIRITS OR THE LAYERS OF THE ONION', introduced Folk music and its disciples to a new acid-rock/pop terrain. The duo (and their entourage at any given time) became more experimental without losing the core of their fanbase; 1968's 'THE HANGMAN'S BEAUTIFUL DAUGHTER' – although musically challenging – still making the Top 5. Moving folk music into bedsit singer-songwriter territory, AL STEWART and his contemporay counterpart JOHN MARTYN (both raised in Glasgow) were the next rising stars to cater predominantly for the LP buyer. In 1976, STEWART would outsell most of his British rivals with his magnum opus, 'YEAR OF THE CAT', while MARTYN knocked on the door of major chart stardom from the 70's to the 90's.

In the way of Blues – and when the majority of Scottish performers had to ply their trade down south for one reason or another – it wasn't any wonder that the cream of the crop would be snapped up. Talking of Cream, one of the supertrio's mainmen, JACK BRUCE, answered the call from Clapton and Baker and joined the heavy-rocking new Blues men from London. Mention 'I Feel Free', 'Sunshine Of Your Love' and 'White Room' in the company of ANY blues buff and you'll open the floodgates of nostalgia. These heady days of the mid sixties to the late sixties also pointed the way for another Scottish-born giant of the British Blues Boom. He was none other than Jethro Tull's IAN ANDERSON. He and his band of merry men from London were virtually "Living In The Past" (a JT hit in '69), with their OTT, eccentric ode to the 18th-century agriculturist whom they named the band after.

If any era was to be celebrated in terms of Scottish chart achievement, then this late sixties period for Caledonian pop was certainly it. We had them on toast, so to speak. Er, MARMALADE (out of mid-60's DEAN FORD & THE GAYLORDS) were at the forefront with several hits including the discarded Beatles 'White Album' cover version, 'OB-LA-DI, OB-LA-DA', a UK No.1 early in 1969 (the first for

a Scottish group). With former members of The POETS in tow, MARMALADE spread their wares even thicker with two further hits 'COUSIN NORMAN' and 'RADANCER' in '71/'72.

The pop world of 1971 also gave us the likes of MIDDLE OF THE ROAD (who had a No.1 with debut single, 'CHIRPY CHIRPY CHEEP CHEEP'), BRIAN CONNOLLY (with Sweet via their first of many glam-pop chartbusters, 'Co-Co') and EVE GRAHAM (whose nicer than nice New Seekers kicked off with 'Never Ending Song Of Love' and 'I'd Like To Teach The World To Sing').

In September 1971, another tartan flag-waver, ROD STEWART, hit No.1 with a double-A-sided 45, 'MAGGIE MAY' / 'REASON TO BELIEVE'. English born'n'bred ROD had previously failed to shake up the blues world in the 60's (via stints with London-based outfits, STEAMPACKET, SHOTGUN EXPRESS and The JEFF BECK GROUP), although the early 70's gave him some sort of street cred courtesy of two fine LP's, 'AN OLD RAINCOAT WON'T EVER LET YOU DOWN' (featuring Mike D'Abo's 'Handbags & Gladrags') and 'GASOLINE ALLEY'. It has taken many years (over thirty) for some "true Scots" to come to terms with why some "other Scots" accept Rod The Mod, but as he was brought up by his Scots parents, supports oor football team on every occasion (when he's not performing) and could theoretically have put on a navy blue jersey for us if his Brentford FC days had come to anything, I don't see the reason for him not being bonafide Scots.

Scotland was a breeding ground for Blues artists in the early to mid seventies – with our industries disintegrating – as artists/bands such as STONE THE CROWS, NAZARETH, The SENSATIONAL ALEX HARVEY BAND and FRANKIE MILLER would confirm.

From 1970, STONE THE CROWS (a quintet featuring the talents of MAGGIE BELL, JIM DEWAR and LES HARVEY) set out their musical stall courtesy of an eponymous LP, while the appropriately-monikered SENSATIONAL ALEX HARVEY BAND had been around and about for yonks. ALEX HARVEY (brother of the aforementioned LES), was a sixties crooner in the mould of Tommy Steele, and now it would be his turn to tear down the musical walls – quite literally! Late in 1973 – after a debut 'FRAMED' had bombed a year earlier – the enigmatic, ageing "Dennis The Menace of Rock" stormed out with 'NEXT . . .'. Controversial but funny with it, ALEX and his colourful bunch of ex-TEAR GAS men, walked up the plank of the charts in 1975 with a rasping version of 'DELILAH' (once property of Tom Jones) – sadly the Vambo man was to die in 1982 of a heart attack while returning from Zeebrugge.

Just prior to the second coming of HARVEY, Dunfermline's NAZARETH were high on the mountain top with 'BROKEN DOWN ANGEL'; who else could've given Joni Mitchell's 'THIS FLIGHT TONIGHT' the rawk treatment?

Quieter, at least on the performing side, FRANKIE MILLER was simmering away at the commercial music world; he didn't break commercially until 1977's 'BE GOOD TO YOURSELF' single. After being in the limelight once again in '92 with his version of DOUGIE MACLEAN's 'Caledonia', FRANKIE was to suffer a near fatal brain aneurysm in August 1994 – hopefully he'll last a while yet, if the man upstairs allows.

Returning to Folk once again, but on a lighter, easy-listening note, STEALER'S WHEEL (containing the cool and subsequently solo-bound GERRY RAFFERTY; 1978's 'BAKER STREET' needs no introduction except for the sax) were making their mark as the NAZ and SAHB were making theirs; monster hit, 'STUCK IN THE MIDDLE WITH YOU', getting the Tarantino treatment via 90's cult movie 'Reservoir Dogs'.

The AVERAGE WHITE BAND (or AWB) were a hybrid from all sources of Scottish pop music of the sixties, although this time around they chose funk and soul. Worldwide instrumental smash, 'PICK UP THE PIECES' (early '75), was certainly not typical of the 6-piece at the time; one of their most loved tunes was 'QUEEN OF MY SOUL' featuring HAMISH STUART on falsetto vocals.

In 1974, having had a one-off hit three years previously with 'SATURDAY NIGHT', Edinburgh's BAY CITY ROLLERS started the tartan-wearing revolution once again via Top 10 hit 'REMEMBER (SHA-LA-LA)'. A teenybop phenomenon on a Beatles scale, the 'ROLLERS continued on the pop bandwagon, reaching the top with 'BYE BYE BABY' and 'GIVE A LITTLE LOVE'; even the albums hit No.1.

A handful of bands were to come out of Scotland on the strength of the BAY CITY ROLLERS' success, PILOT having the biggest impression when 'JANUARY' made No.1 early 1975. SLIK and the world of MIDGE URE wouldn't be far away too – but that's another story . . .

* * * * *

"A Beat(en) Generation"

Introduction: The Scottish nearly-men (& women) of the post-Beatles, mid-late 60's era.

In addition to future top guns such as LULU, DEAN FORD (i.e. MARMALADE), ALEX HARVEY, The POETS, etc (who all have their own entries later in this section of the book), a number of quality Soul, R&B and Mod outfits were whipping up a storm north of Hadrian's Wall as the Beat craze took hold. In the wake of the BEATLES and The STONES, London-based record companies were scouring every major provincial city in England for any band with matching suits, winkle-pickers and three chords. Unfortunately, their itinerary – with the odd exception – didn't include Scotland.

Nevertheless, 'E.M.I./Columbia' eventually made it to Glasgow where a plethora of unsigned combos strutted their stuff in front of the bigwigs. The lucky winners were The GOLDEN CRUSADERS and DEAN FORD & THE GAYLORDS, both fairly unrepresentative of the Scottish scene in general. More authentic in terms of the music's Afro-American roots, The BOSTON DEXTERS (including a young TAM WHITE) were regarded highly enough north of the border although all their efforts to break into the London scene were in vain. Others to follow this ultimately futile path were The

ATHENIANS, The POOR SOULS, JOHNNY & THE COPYCATS (who later became psychedelic outfit MY DEAR WATSON) and The VIKINGS. Scuppered by lack of business acumen, manipulative A&R departments and miniscule promotional budgets, the Scottish contingent retreated to lick their wounds and try again.

As the Beat scene fragmented and evolved into Psychedelia and later Heavy and Progressive rock, many of these musicians/singers re-invented themselves and in some cases managed to play the London game and win!

- wee biogs & discogs -

ATHENIANS

— were formed in Edinburgh in 1963 by KEITH, CHARLES, ARTHUR and ALY BLACK. A smartly-dressed quartet who covered a variety of R&B classics (that were on reflection a bit lightweight), The ATHENIANS made their mark with a good rendition of the Shadows' 'THINKING OF OUR LOVE'. However, they split in 1966; ALY BLACK joined the BOSTON DEXTERS, while later member STUART TOSH subsequently joined PILOT.

		E.S.C.	not iss.
1964.	(7") *(1)* **YOU TELL ME. / LITTLE QUEENIE**	☐	-

— for the above label, the band also appeared on two EP's in '65 and '66 with the tracks, 'LOUIE LOUIE' and 'TEDDY BEARS PICNIC'

		Waverley	not iss.
1964.	(7") *(SLP 532)* **I'VE GOT LOVE IF YOU WANT IT. / I'M A LOVER NOT A FIGHTER**	☐	-
1965.	(7") *(SLP 533)* **THINKING OF OUR LOVE. / MERCY MERCY**	☐	-

BEACHCOMBERS

— were another outfit formed in the capital (1962). Unknown still to this day, The BEACHCOMBERS eventually took residency at the Top Storey Club in 1966, although by this time they had become The BOOTS.

		Columbia	not iss.
1963.	(7") *(DB 7124)* **MAD GOOSE. / YOU CAN'T SIT DOWN**	☐	-
1964.	(7") *(DB 7200)* **NIGHT TRAIN. / THE KEEL ROW**	☐	-

— **BOOTS** were actually The BEACHCOMBERS (w/ same unknown line-up)

		C.B.S.	not iss.
Jun 68.	(7") *(CBS 3350)* **THE ANIMAL IN ME. / EVEN THE BAD TIMES ARE GOOD**	☐	-
Nov 68.	(7") *(CBS 3833)* **KEEP YOUR LOVELIGHT BURNING. / GIVE ME ONE MORE CHANCE**	☐	-
		Youngblood	not iss.
1970.	(7") *(YB 1018)* **YOU BETTER RUN. / A TO DO**	☐	-

— unsure if above was actually their single

BLUES COUNCIL

— were formed in Glasgow around 1963 by former bandleader/saxophonist (at the Plaza Ballroom) BILL PATRICK. By 1964/65, BILL and his fresh-faced group (vocalist FRASER CALDER, lead guitarist LESLIE HARVEY, alto saxophonist LARRY QUINN, electric keyboard player JOHN McGINNIS, bassist JAMES GIFFEN and drummer BILLY ADAMSON) had shifted the music sound from blues and soul to a more Mod/dance-based style; they played the Scene Club in West Nile Street before trying their hand down south. Impressario and publisher Dick James (who later catered for Elton John on his own 'D.J.M.' imprint), almost immediately signed the band to 'Parlophone'. However, on the 12th of March 1965, while returning home in their van from an Edinburgh gig – and just prior to the release of their now very rare debut single, 'BABY DON'T LOOK DOWN' – FRASER and JAMES were tragically killed in a car crash. The remaining five, plus BOBBY PATRICK (ex-BIG SIX) and BOBBY WISHART (ex-SOUL BAND) carried on briefly before they disbanded; LES HARVEY (brother of the sensational ALEX HARVEY) later joined STONE THE CROWS but his life too was to be cut short when he was electrocuted on stage in 1972.

		Parlophone	not iss.
Apr 65.	(7") *(R 5264)* **BABY DON'T LOOK DOWN. / WHAT WILL I DO**	☐	-

Isabel BOND

— was born in Glasgow. She cut her musical teeth at the Top Ten Club in Hamburg (c.1963), working at its studios with in-house producer RICKY BARNES. Backed by the CRESCENDOES, the well-loved R&B singer performed with the likes of BILL PATRICK, GEORGE GALLAGHER, ALEX and LES HARVEY. After taking over from MAGGIE BELL at the Dennistoun Palais in '67, ISABEL finally got a deal via 'Major Minor' (see below).

		Major Minor	not iss.
1968.	(7") *(MM 566)* **CRY. / WHEN A WOMAN LOVES A MAN**	☐	-
1968.	(lp) *(MMLP 28)* **THE HEART AND SOUL OF ISABEL BOND**	☐	-
1969.	(7") *(MM 627)* **DON'T FORGET ABOUT ME. / YOU'LL NEVER GET THE CHANCE AGAIN**	☐	-

Sol BYRON & The IMPACTS

— BYRON was born BILLY LOCHART in Glasgow. The singer performed regularly at the Flamingo Ballroom, the venue even going as far as financing SOL BYRON & THE IMPACT's one and only 45, a cover of Marvin Gaye's 'PRIDE AND JOY' (now worth over £20). In 1966, after the IMPACTS split from BYRON, they formed The SENATE (see further on).

		Flamingo	not iss.
1964.	(7") *(PR 5027)* **PRIDE AND JOY. / YEAR AGO TONIGHT**	☐	-

EAST-WEST

— were formed in Edinburgh in 1962 by DAVID; surname unknown and the rest were equally mysterious although one of them joined THREE'S A CROWD (not sure which one).

		Decca	not iss.
Apr 63.	(7") *(F 11625)* **CHELSEA BOOTS. / SAMANTHA**	☐	-
Aug 63.	(7"; as DAVID & The EMBERS) *(F 11717)* **WHAT IS THIS. / TEDDY BEAR SPECIAL**	☐	-

FRANKIE & JOHNNY

— were formed in Glasgow . . . mid-60's by former (KINNING PARK) RAMBLERS vocalists, MAGGIE BELL and BOBBY KERR. Yes, this was the stamping ground for the young Miss BELL, who was inspired at an early age by Aretha Franklin and underrated blues queen Big Maybelle. After a couple of 45's in 1966 (the first of which is now worth over £100), F&J became the houseband at Dennistoun Palais, moving on to the troublesome Glasgow's Locarno and then Germany where they were joined by BILL and BOBBY PATRICK and LESLIE HARVEY. The latter guitarist built up a musical partnership with MAGGIE and when KERR went solo, they formed STONE THE CROWS. The rest is history, as they say.

		Decca	not iss.
Apr 66.	(7") *(F 22376)* **NEVER GONNA LEAVE YOU. / I'LL HOLD YOU** *(re-iss. May79 on 'Inferno'; HEAT 8)*	☐	-
		Parlophone	not iss.
Oct 66.	(7") *(R 5518)* **CLIMB EV'RY MOUNTAIN. / I WANNA MAKE YOU UNDERSTAND**	☐	-

James GAIT

— was born in Largs. A ballad singer with connections to GALLAGHER & LYLE who were his backing band.

		Pye	not iss.
1965.	(7") *(7N 15936)* **COMES THE DAWN. / MY OWN WAY**	☐	-
1966.	(7") *(7N 17021)* **WITH MY BABY. / MOST UNUSUAL FEELING**	☐	-

GIDIAN

— was born JAMES POLLOCK (probably Glasgow). Another balladeer, but this time he had a leg-up in the music world after being discovered by Liverpool comedian/singer Ken Dodd.

		Columbia	not iss.
Feb 66.	(7") *(DB 7826)* **TRY ME OUT. / THERE ISN'T ANYTHING**	☐	-
May 66.	(7") *(DB 7916)* **FIGHT FOR YOUR LOVE. / SEE IF SHE CARES**	☐	-
1966.	(7"; as GIDIAN and the UNIVERSALS) *(DB 8041)* **FEELING. / DON'T BE SENTIMENTAL**	☐	-
		U.P.C.	not iss.
1970.	(7") *(UPC 107)* **THAT'S LOVE. / WE ARE THE HAPPIEST**	☐	-

GOLDEN CRUSADERS

— were formed in Bathgate, West Lothian . . . 1960 out of The BLACKJACKS by DENNIS MURPHY (vocals), BRIAN SHERIDAN (vocals), BILL COLQUHOUN (lead guitar), JACK TAYLOR (sax), JACK LEE (drums) and brothers BRIAN (rhythm guitar) and ROBERT JOHNSON (bass). Deeply inspired by the Merseybeat scene (in 1963), The GOLDEN CRUSADERS were signed by Norrie

Paramor for a 'Columbia' debut, 'I'M IN LOVE WITH YOU'. Written by local trombonist and part-time member, ANDY DOOLAN, the single (and its two follow-ups, 'HEY GOOD LOOKING' and 'I DON'T CARE') didn't really do much in the sales front and the band split.

Columbia / not iss.

Feb 64. (7") *(DB 7232)* **I'M IN LOVE WITH YOU. / ALWAYS ON MY MIND** ☐ -
Sep 64. (7") *(DB 7357)* **HEY GOOD LOOKING. / COME ON COME ON** ☐ -
Feb 65. (7") *(DB 7485)* **I DON'T CARE. / THAT BROKEN HEART IS MINE** ☐ -

IRON CLAW

— were formed (a little later than the rest) in Dumfries . . . 1970. Vocalist WULLIE BROWN and bassist ALEX WILSON were two out of a mysterious quartet who also included future PILOT man BILLY LYALL. They managed to release only one cassette in their short span before they disbanded from the bedroom recording studio – 'DISMORPHOBIA' was the CD re-issue, I think!

own label / not iss.

1972. (ltd-c) *(none)* **IRON CLAW** ☐ -

– compilations, etc. –

Sep 98. (cd) *Audio Archive; (AACD 021)* **DISMORPHOBIA** ☐ -

MARK FIVE

— were formed in Dunfermline in 1963 as one of several outfits from the area. The following year and sickened by the lack of interest shown towards Scots acts during this boom Beat/Merseybeat period, guitarist MANNY CHARLTON and crew (including Edinburgh bass man BRIAN HENDERSON) put on their hiking boots and staged a massive publicity stunt by walking over five hundred miles to London to obtain a recording contract. Initially impressed by these desperate measures, 'Fontana' subsequently released a blistering (quite literally!) one-off 45, 'BABY WHAT'S WRONG', backed by a cover of the Isley Brothers' 'TANGO'. However, the single sold poorly and the MARK FIVE returned to Fife (by bus this time!); MANNY was to join the RED HAWKES before becoming well-known other locals, NAZARETH. • **Note:** their only single is now worth around £40.

Fontana / not iss.

Jan 65. (7") *(TF 513)* **BABY WHAT'S WRONG. / TANGO** ☐ -

— solo effort below featuring production by MARK WRITZ

Columbia / not iss.

1966. (7"; by BRIAN HENDERSON) *(DB 8006)* **FOLK'S IN A HURRY. / WHAT KIND OF WOMAN** ☐ -

— BRIAN would later resurface in NIRVANA (the 60's/70's outfit!)

McKINLEYS

— were formed in Edinburgh around 1963 by sisters SHEILA and JEANETTE McKINLEY. Egged-on by their musically-minded mother and father, these gifted part-time singers performed regularly at the Plaza and Palais ballrooms; the Scene in Portobello was also a favourite. On hearing a demo sent by their parents, The McKINLEYS were snapped up by the London-based production/songwriting team of John Carter and Ken Lewis. In 1964 'Columbia' records released two records in the space of three months, the Phil Spector-ish 'SOMEONE CARES FOR ME' and 'WHEN HE COMES ALONG'; the tartan-clad girls were also featured on TV shows 'Ready Steady Go' and 'Thank Your Lucky Stars'. The girls subsequently resurfaced in Hamburg (where else!) but by then the British Beat boom was fading fast.

Columbia / not iss.

Mar 64. (7") *(DB 7230)* **SOMEONE CARES FOR ME. / A MILLION MILES AWAY** ☐ -
(re-iss. 1973 on 'Spark'; SRL 1078)
Jun 64. (7") *(DB 7310)* **WHEN HE COMES ALONG. / THEN I'LL KNOW IT'S LOVE** ☐ -

Parlophone / not iss.

Nov 64. (7") *(R 5211)* **SWEET AND TENDER ROMANCE. / THAT LONELY FEELING** ☐ -

Columbia / not iss.

Jun 65. (7") *(DB 7583)* **GIVE HIM MY LOVE. / ONCE MORE** ☐ -

— split after a time in the Star Club, Hamburg

— **SHEILA McKINLEY**

1971. (7") *(DB 8768)* **AND WHEN THE WAR IS OVER. / LISTEN TO THE LITTLE CHILDREN** ☐ -

Rainbow / not iss.

1977. (7") *(RAIS 1002)* **GOODBYE MY LOVE. / (instrumental)** ☐ -

MISFITS

— were formed by Aberdeen unknowns around the mid-60's and who cut The Beatles' 'YOU WON'T SEE ME'; try the book 'Fit Like, New York' (about North East groups) although I couldn't find anything.

Aberdeen Student Charities / not iss.

1966. (7") *(PRI 101)* **YOU WON'T SEE ME. / HANGING AROUND** ☐ -

MOONRAKERS

— were formed in Edinburgh around 1963 as part of the capital's dance/Mod outfits. Their live set boasted renditions of various Kinks numbers including 'SITTIN' ON A SOFA', although it would be their novelty interpretation of the Hollywood Argyles' 'ALLEY OOP', that would set crowds alight. However, after the MOONRAKERS signed a deal with 'Polydor' in '66, trouble was to come their way when a gang of thugs beat up popular bassist, DEREK McDONALD. He sustained irreparable brain damage which sadly strained the band enough to let him go. Without him the MOONRAKERS were never the same and with the major deal going down the swanee, the band subsequently split having never made one single.

John O'HARA's PLAYBOYS

— were formed in Glasgow in the mid-60's by namesake singer/saxman JOHN O'HARA, with the help of BOBBY CAMPBELL (organ & vocals), BARRY HERD (lead guitar & vocals), BILL MATHIESON (bass), DAVE McHARG (drums) and other saxophonist PETER GREEN (no, not that one!). The band mainly played run-of-the-mill cover versions and released a plethora of patchy singles and a Mod-type LP, 'GET READY'. • **Note:** The JOHN O'HARA who released the 'Starsky And Hutch' theme as a single in 1977 was not the same guy.

Fontana / not iss.

Nov 66. (7") *(TF 763)* **START ALL OVER. / I'VE BEEN WONDERING** ☐ -
Mar 67. (7") *(TF 793)* **SPICKS AND SPECKS. / ONE FINE LADY** ☐ -
Jun 67. (7") *(TF 872)* **THE BALLAD OF THE SOON DEPARTED. / TELL ME WHY** ☐ -
Dec 67. (7") *(TF 893)* **ISLAND IN THE SUN. / HARRY** ☐ -
Apr 68. (7") *(TF 924)* **IN THE SHELTER OF MY HEART. / GOODNIGHT MR. NIGHTFALL** ☐ -
Jul 68. (7") *(TF 949)* **VOICES. / BLUE DOG** ☐ -
Sep 68. (7"; as JOHN O'HARA and the PLAYBOYS) *(TF 974)* **I STARTED A JOKE. / SHOW ME** ☐ -
1968. (lp) *(STL 5461)* **GET READY** ☐ -
– Funky Broadway / Respect / It's a wonder / Soul and inspiration / Harry / Gotta make a comeback / You don't know like I know / Island in the sun / Show me / It's a man's man's man's world / I was made to love her / Get ready / Sweet soul music / (I can't get no) Satisfaction.
1969. (7"; as JOHN O'HARA and the PLAYBOYS) *(TF 1043)* **MORE THAN JUST A WOMAN. / NO NO NO** ☐ -

— **JOHN O'HARA** went solo in the 70's

Polydor / not iss.

1970. (7") *(2001 074)* **TOGETHER WE CAN MAKE IT. / WHERE I BELONG** ☐ -

Spark / not iss.

1972. (7") *(SRL 1075)* **HAND ME DOWN MAN. / I AM THE CANDIDATE** ☐ -
1973. (7") *(SRL 1080)* **PROUD TO BE THE MAN I AM. / RASTUS RAVEL** ☐ -

— O'HARA retired from the music biz after above

ONE IN A MILLION

— were formed in Glasgow around the mid-60's out of The JAYGARS by brothers JIMMY (guitar) and JACK McCULLOCH (drums), BILLY FISHER (bass) and ALAN YOUNG (vocals & guitar). Early in '67, the uptempo beat outfit delivered their debut single for 'C.B.S.', 'USE YOUR IMAGINATION' (now worth nearly £100). However, it wasn't until exactly a year later that ONE IN A MILLION branched out into the psychedelic world with sophomore effort, 'FREDEREEK HERNANDO' (worth over £225!). Eclectic and described by many critics as one of the best psyched-out 7" records you'll ever hear, the band performed regularly at the Middle Earth venue. It was here that The Who's Pete Townshend noted them as worthy contenders for the Thunderclap Newman project. When the band split, JIMMY and JACK joined the aforementioned Thunderclap . . .; the former later joined JOHN MAYALL, STONE THE CROWS, then (PAUL McCARTNEY's) WINGS, while the latter formed WILD COUNTRY and ANDWELLA.

C.B.S. / not iss.

Jan 67. (7") *(202513)* **USE YOUR IMAGINATION. / HOLD ON** ☐ -

M.G.M. / not iss.

Jan 68. (7") *(MGM 1370)* **FREDEREEK HERNANDO. / DOUBLE SIGHT** ☐ -

Bobby PATRICK BIG SIX

— were formed in Edinburgh . . . 1963 by singer BOBBY PATRICK, older brother of 50's big band leader, BILL PATRICK. Virtually gatecrashed in London by producer RICKY BARNES, the group secured a record deal with 'Decca' and made appearances at Barnes' Hamburg residence, the Top Ten Club. They covered many a fine number including Major Lance's 'MONKEY TIME' and progressed to the famous Star Club in Hamburg. • **Note:** the singles are worth a wee sum especially the EP (over £100).

	Decca	not iss.
May 64. (7") *(F 11898)* **SHAKE IT EASY BABY. / WILDWOOD DAYS**		-
Nov 64. (7") *(F 12030)* **MONKEY TIME. / SWEET TALK ME BABY**		-
Dec 64. (7"ep) *(DFE 8570)* **TEENBEAT 3 (FROM STAR CLUB, HAMBURG)**		-

— the group shortened their name to BIG SIX although below was shelved

	Polydor	not iss.
1965. (7") **COMING HOME BABY. / STARLIGHT MELODY**		-

— BOBBY and his brother BILL joined The RAMBLERS

PHIL & THE FLINTSTONES

— were an unknown bunch of lads formed in Linlithgow, 1963. Desperate and frustrated to get a record deal, they manufactured their own limited-edition 7", a version of the Coasters' 'LOVE POTION No.9', which is now worth over £50.

	Bedrock	not iss.
1964. (7") *(PR 5371)* **LOVE POTION No.9. / HONEY DON'T**		-

POOR SOULS

— were formed in Dundee . . . 1964 out of the HI-FOUR by JOHNNY HUDSON (aka JOHNNY MORAN), main songwriter DOUG MARTIN and JOHN CASEY; CHICK TAYLOR would be added when they found their new moniker. The HI-FOUR played a few stints in Germany, tackling the likes of the Storyville Jazz Club in Cologne to the Top Ten Club in Hamburg; on their return they would support The Beatles at Dundee's Caird Hall. The POOR SOULS were not so much poor but they had soul, and lots of it. Signing to 'Decca', the quartet released their debut 45, 'WHEN MY BABY CRIES', a Drifter-esque type R&B number that helped them get work down south. Andy Lothian of 'Alp' records issued their next 7", 'LOVE ME', although it would be in Italy that they would try their luck just before they disbanded.

JOHNNY HUDSON/MORAN – vocals / **CHICK TAYLOR** – lead guitar / **DOUG MARTIN** – bass / **JOHN CASEY** – drums

	Decca	not iss.
Jun 65. (7") *(F 12183)* **WHEN MY BABY CRIES. / MY BABY SHE'S NOT THERE**		-
	Alp	**not iss.**
Jul 66. (7") *(595 004)* **LOVE ME. / PLEASE DON'T CHANGE YOUR MIND**		-

SCOTS OF ST. JAMES

— were formed in Glasgow around the mid-60's initially as short-lived The IN-CROWD by vocalist JIMMY OAKLEY, GRAHAM MAITLAND (guitar), MARMALADE-bound HUGHIE NICHOLSON (guitar); who was replaced by OWEN 'ONNIE' McINTYRE, ALAN KELLY (drums); who was replaced by NORRIE MacLEAN (ex-POETS) and DIEGO DANALAISE; who was replaced by STEWART FRANCIS. A minor supergroup of sorts, The SCOTS OF ST. JAMES were only around for a German tour and two low-key singles, 'GO' and 'TIMOTHY'. OAKLEY subsequently went solo and released the single, 'LITTLE GIRL' for 'United Artists' in 1968. HOPSCOTCH, meanwhile consisted of McINTYRE, MacLEAN, FRANCIS and KELLY, along with vocalist HAMISH STUART (ex-DREAM POLICE); MAITLAND would join FIVE DAY RAIN and later turned up in the FLEUR DE LYS and GLENCOE. Some of the HOPSCOTCH ended up in FOREVER MORE, HAMISH and ONNIE later formed the AVERAGE WHITE BAND.

	Go	not iss.
1966. (7") *(AJ 111404)* **GYPSY. / TIC TOC**		-
	Spot	**not iss.**
1967. (7") *(JW 1)* **TIMOTHY. / EIDERDOWN CLOWN**		-

SENATE

— were formed in Glasgow . . . 1966 by a band who had just quit as backers to SOL BYRON (as The IMPACTS). Former QUINTONES member and high-octane singer ALEX LIGERTWOOD (here as ALEX JACKSON) loved the R&B/soul sound of US singers RAY CHARLES, OTIS REDDING, MARVIN GAYE and CURTIS MAYFIELD; his natural vocal chords were always going to be in demand. The line-up also comprised DAVIE AGNEW (as MARK DAVID) on vocals and guitar, MIKE FRASER on bass (who replaced BRIAN JOHNSTON – ex-GOLDEN CRUSADERS – drummer ROBBIE MacINTOSH, trumpeter TONY RUTHERFORD (as TONY MIMMS) and BOB MATHER on saxophone. It was a pity that only one 45, 'CAN'T STOP' appeared, although The SENATE were one of the few bands mentioned in this section to release an LP, 'SOCK IT TO YOU ONE MORE TIME' (1968). The SENATE split while recording the aforementioned album, LIGERTWOOD, FRASER and MacINTOSH later resurfaced with the short-lived PRIMITIVES; MacINTOSH and LIGERTWOOD joined Brian Auger, while the latter also became part of the Jeff Beck Group, the AVERAGE WHITE BAND and a full-time member of Santana (he now lives in Southern California). Meanwhile, FRASER sessioned for ENNIO MORRICONE – a class act!

	Columbia	not iss.
1967. (7") *(DB 8110)* **CAN'T STOP. / AIN'T AS SWEET AS YOU**		-
	U.A.	**not iss.**
1968. (lp) *(SULP 1180)* **THE SENATE SOCK IT TO YOU ONE MORE TIME (live 1967)**		-

– Sock it to 'em J.B. / Summertime / Girls are out to get you / Love is after me / Sweet thing / Try a little tenderness / What is soul / Knock on wood / Intro 5 bars of 'Who's Afraid Of Virginia Woolf' / How sweet it is / You don't know like I know / Shake / Please stay / Can't stop / Invitation / Hold on I'm comin'. *(cd-iss. Apr92 on 'Line'; RTCD 901146)*

SOCIETIE

— were formed in Glasgow around the summer of 1966 out of A CERTAIN SOCIETY, by teenagers ROBBIE BURNS (vocals), DAVE DOUGALL (organ), DAVE STRUTHERS (bass & vocals) and er, SMILER FRAME (drums). One of the many psychedelic pop acts signed to 'Deram', the poshly-monikered SOCIETIE delivered only one solitary 45, 'BIRD HAS FLOWN', before taking off to obscurity; the rare single which was produced by ALLAN CLARKE (of The HOLLIES) can now fetch £25. However, both DOUGALL and STRUTHERS re-appeared in the early 70's, this time for the Irish/London-based jazzy Prog-rockers, ANDWELLA (the 'People's People' set in '71).

	Deram	not iss.
Nov 67. (7") *(DM 162)* **BIRD HAS FLOWN. / BREAKING DOWN**		-

Barry ST. JOHN

— was born BARBARA ST. JOHN, Glasgow. From the early to mid sixties, female singer BARRY was part of the British contingent who stormed Hamburg's Star Club in Germany. She scored a minor UK hit in 1965 (at the fifth attempt!) with a version of Tim Rose's 'COME AWAY MELINDA. A follow-up 6th single, 'EVERYTHING I TOUCH TURNS TO TEARS' has subsequently become very rare.

	Decca	not iss.
Jul 64. (7") *(F 11933)* **A LITTLE BIT OF SOAP. / THING OF THE PAST**		-
Sep 64. (7") *(F 11975)* **BREAD AND BUTTER. / CRY TO ME**		-
Mar 65. (7") *(F 12111)* **MIND HOW YOU GO. / DON'T YOU FEEL PROUD**		-
May 65. (7") *(F 12145)* **HEY BOY. / I'VE BEEN CRYING**		-
	Columbia	**not iss.**
Nov 65. (7") *(DB 7783)* **COME AWAY MELINDA. / GOTTA BRAND NEW MAN**	47	-
1966. (7") *(DB 7868)* **EVERYTHING I TOUCH TURNS TO TEARS. / SOUNDS LIKE MY BABY**		-
	Major Minor	**not iss.**
1968. (7") *(MM 587)* **CRY LIKE A BABY. / LONG AND LONELY NIGHT**		-
1969. (7") *(MM 604)* **BY THE TIME I GET TO PHOENIX. / TURN ON YOUR LOVELIGHT**		-
1969. (lp; mono/stereo) *(MMLP/SMLP 43)* **ACCORDING TO ST. JOHN**		-

– Love-eye-tis / Long and lonely night / Restless / Cheater man / Don't knock it / Tell mama / Turn on your lovelight / Cry like a baby / Fa fa fa / 98.6 / By the time I get to Phoenix / What's a matter baby.

	Decca	not iss.
Jul 74. (7") *(F 13529)* **MY MAN. / BRIGHT SHINES THE LIGHT**		-
	Bradley's	**not iss.**
Mar 75. (7") *(BRAD 7507)* **I WON'T BE A PARTY. / DO ME GOOD**		-

— ST. JOHN finally decided to retire from solo work after above

STOICS

— were formed in Glasgow . . . 1967 by guitarist/songwriter, JIMMY DORIS, along with JOHN WYNN (bass), JIM CASEY (drums) and HUGH McKENNA (keyboards). After a great debut 45, they added gruff singer FRANKIE MILLER (ex-WESTFARM COTTAGE) but they split soon after; DORIS became a songwriter for LULU, FRANKIE MILLER of course formed JUDE and later went solo. Meanwhile, McKENNA joined the DREAM POLICE and later The SENSATIONAL ALEX HARVEY BAND.

R.C.A. not iss.

Sep 68. (7") *(RCA 1745)* **SEARCH FOR THE SEA. / EARTH, FIRE, AIR AND WATER** ☐ -

STUDIO SIX

— were formed in Glasgow . . . 1966 by songwriter and guitarist NEIL GRIMSHAW, brother COLIN (vocals) and CHRIS McCLURE (rhythm guitar), RICKY KERRY (keyboards), GERRY TEDESHI (bass) and RON MILNE (drums). The latter was deposed by ex-POETS sticksman JIM BREAKEY just prior to the recording of their debut single, 'WHEN I SEE MY BABY', while we know that CHRIS went on to become cabaret star, CHRISTIAN.

Polydor not iss.

Dec 66. (7") *(BM 56131)* **WHEN I SEE MY BABY. / DON'T TELL LIES** ☐ -

Jul 67. (7") *(BM 56189)* **TIMES WERE WHEN. / I CAN'T SLEEP** ☐ -

Dec 67. (7") *(BM 56219)* **STRAWBERRY WINDOW. / FALLING LEAVES** ☐ -

1968. (7") *(BM 56361)* **BLESS MY SOUL (I'VE BEEN AND GONE AND DONE IT). / PEOPLE SAY** ☐ -

SYNANTHESIA

— were formed somewhere in Scotland (possibly Glasgow) . . . 1968 by three acid-folkies into Roman and Greek mythology. LESLIE COOK (vocals, mandolin, violin, percussion), DENNIS HOLMES (guitar, vibes, vocals) and JIMMY FRASER (saxophone, flute, vocals) created their own fusion of flowery pastel-rock over one solitary eponymous album in 1969 – it can now fetch up to £90.

RCA Victor not iss.

1969. (lp) *(SF 8058)* **SYNANTHESIA** ☐ -
– Minerva / Peek strangely and worried evening / Morpheus / Trafalgar Square / Fates / Tale of the spider and the fly / Vesta / Rolling and tumbling / Nnemoysne / Aurora / Just as the curtain finally falls.

THREE'S A CROWD

— were formed in Edinburgh around the mid-60's out of The EMBERS by vocalist/guitarist BOB 'SMIGGY' SMITH (also ex-BOSTON DEXTERS), drummer ALAN PRATT and guitarist JIMMY BAIN; frontman LINNIE PATTERSON would join the line-up in 1966. They only released one single, 'LOOK AROUND THE CORNER' before they disbanded. London-bound PRATT joined Prog-rockers The HOUSE OF LORDS and SMITH later turned up in WRITING ON THE WALL (with LINNIE); he would subsequently join BLUE. JIMMY BAIN would surface with RITCHIE BLACKMORE'S RAINBOW and WILD HORSES.

Fontana not iss.

1966. (7") *(TF 673)* **LOOK AROUND THE CORNER. / LIVING IN A DREAM** ☐ -

B&C not iss.

Oct 69. (7"; by HOUSE OF LORDS) *(CB 112)* **IN THE LAND OF DREAMS. / AIN'T GONNA WAIT FOREVER** ☐ -

So much for the wee bands (whose members mostly went on to greater things), now here's the rest that er, made it!

A

George ALEXANDER

Born: ALEX YOUNG, 28 Dec'46, Glasgow. Remaining in the UK as the rest of his family emigrated to Sydney, Australia, ALEX aka GEORGE ALEXANDER went on to form London-based bubblegum-pop combo, GRAPEFRUIT in 1967. While his brother GEORGE YOUNG found fame with The EASYBEATS, bassist/singer ALEXANDER staked his own claim to fame as JOHN LENNON christened the band as well as signing them on via the Beatles' 'Apple' records. Early in '68, the fruity popstars hovered just outside the UK Top 20 with the single 'DEAR DELILAH', while another hit 'C'MON MARIANNE' made up for a previous flop, 'ELEVATOR'. After a series of unsuccessful releases, GRAPEFRUIT's creative juices finally ran dry. Even a brief link up with brother GEORGE failed to resurrect their fortunes and a final split occurred in 1972.

Ian ANDERSON

Born: 10 Aug'47, Edinburgh. Having relocated over the border to Blackpool as a child, the young IAN discovered his love of music (especially the Blues) quite early on. In 1963, the singer formed his own outfit, The BLADES, along with school buddies JEFFREY HAMMOND-HAMMOND (on bass) and JOHN EVAN (on drums).

For the next four years, the group evolved and splintered with the aforementioned rhythm players forming the JOHN EVAN'S SMASH, while ANDERSON and his new chums (MICK ABRAHAMS, CLIVE BUNKER and GLENN CORNICK) took the group moniker JETHRO TULL. By mid-1968, the band were breaking through, a record contract from 'Island' being signed after a successful Sunbury Jazz & Blues Festival appearance. ANDERSON was of course the leader, a showman and stage extrovert par excellence, his shabby attire (tartan-plaid regalia, et al) and gruff vox sang through a mane of Fagan-istic long hair and beard, only topped by his erratic one-legged flute-playing; inspiration courtesy of jazz legend RAHSAAN ROLAND KIRK. The group's debut set, 'TIME WAS' entered the UK Top 10 towards the end of '68 and during the course of the next three years (and three further LP's 'STAND UP', 'BENEFIT' and 'AQUALUNG'), JETHRO TULL went massive all around the world – especially America.

However, come summer 1971, only ANDERSON remained from the original JETHRO TULL, although HAMMOND-HAMMOND and EVAN were now part of IAN's team. The Scots-born writer/singer was now undoubtably their commander-in-chief, his looking-glass lyrical banter often too heavy for the Pop world, especially his conceptual 'THICK AS A BRICK' and 'A PASSION PLAY' sets in '72 and '73 respectively. His dislike of the media and press were also rife at this point (and from then on in!). Sell-out tours around the world and Top 30 albums continued and by the late 70's, IAN/JETHRO TULL had turned into a folkie/acoustic-rock outfit – taking on old FAIRPORTS in the process.

Squeezed between two JETHRO TULL albums, 'THE BROADSWORD AND THE BEAST' (1982) and the technoid 'UNDER WRAPS' (1984), came his solo debut, 'WALK INTO LIGHT' (1983); the JT album 'A' – recorded with new musicians (bar long-termer, MARTIN BARRE) was scheduled to take this mantle until he thought better. Recorded with the help of JETHRO TULL newcomer PETER JOHN VITESSE, the patchy 'WALK INTO LIGHT' was both a critical and commercial disaster and it would take over a decade before ANDERSON would attempt another.

During this 10-year stretch, the now proud owner of a fish-farm in the north of Scotland continued to fit in the odd (very odd!) JETHRO TULL album. 'DIVINITIES: 12 DANCES WITH GOD', was indeed that difficult second album (not counting his twenty or so 'TULL sets!), ANDERSON now solely playing the flute while backing came via ANDREW GIDDINGS and a classical ensemble. Now New-Age and Musak-inspired, the serious IAN delivered a quick follow-up, 'THE SECRET LANGUAGE OF BIRDS' (2000) – maybe a talk with former "burd-lovin" footballer, Frank MacAvenney, would have come in handy.

IAN ANDERSON

— first augmented by **PETER JOHN VITESSE** – synth, keyboards

Chrysalis Chrysalis

Nov 83. (7") *(CHS 2746)* **FLY BY NIGHT. / END GAME** ☐ -

Nov 83. (lp/c) <(CDL/ZCDL 1443)> **WALK INTO LIGHT** 78 ☐
– Fly by night / Made in England / Walk into light / Trains / End game / Black and white television / Toad in the hole / Looking for Eden / User-friendly / Different Germany. *(cd-iss. 1988; CCD 1443) (cd re-iss. Jun97 on 'Beat Goes On'; BGOCD 350)*

— now with orchestra and strings & with ANDY GIDDINGS

E.M.I. E.M.I.

Sep 98. (cd) *(<CDC 555262-2>)* **DIVINITIES: 12 DANCES WITH GOD** ☐ ☐ May95
– In a stone circle / In sight of a minaret / In a black box / In the grip of stronger stuff / In material grace / In the moneylender's temple / At their father's knee / En Afrique / In the olive garden / In the pay of Spain / In times of India (Bombay valentine).

Papillion Varese

Mar 00. (cd) *(BTFLYCD 2000)* <061053> **THE SECRET LANGUAGE OF BIRDS** ☐ ☐
– The secret language of birds / Little flower girl / Montserrat / Postcard day / Water carrier / Set-aside / Better Moon / Sanctuary / Jasmine corridor / Habanero reel / Panama freighter / The secret language of birds, pt.2 / Boris dancing / Circular breathing / Stormont shuffle.

Miller ANDERSON

Born: 12 Apr'45, Johnstone, Refrewshire. In 1964, long after a move down to London, guitarist/singer MILLER cut his teeth with The ROYAL CRESTS, who evolved into KARL STUART & THE PROFILE.

The man would subsequently join The VOICE, who managed to release only one single, 'THE TRAIN TO DISASTER', before he was superseded by noneother than MICK RONSON. Remarkably, his next port of call was with the band that launched IAN HUNTER (future MOTT THE HOOPLE singer and mate of the aforementioned RONSON!). AT LAST THE 1958 ROCK'N'ROLL BAND (phew!), was also a short-lived venture, the Blues-loving MILLER finding work with the Prog-jazz outfit, The KEEF HARTLEY BAND. He stayed for a handful of sets including the mildly successful 'Halfbreed', while the man was also present for their 'Woodstock' 1969 appearance.

In the early 70's, the now solo ANDERSON signed to 'Deram', releasing his first full-set, 'BRIGHT CITY' (1971), a typically Progressive/Blues affair. HEMLOCK became MILLER's next project in 1973, although again, one album was the only thing to materialise. Short stints with SAVOY BROWN and BLOOD, SWEAT & TEARS were followed be an eponymous album reunion with HARTLEY under the DOG SOLDIER banner. Becoming a bit of a mercenary in the revolving door of the Rock session world, MILLER joined up with MARC BOLAN & T.REX in August 1976; work with DONOVAN followed after the Glam giant died. Towards the end of the 70's, the guitarist teamed up with former STONE THE CROWS musicians, RONNIE LEAHY and JIMMY McCULLOCH to form The DUKES, although they suffered a setback when McCULLOCH died. Undeterred, the group (which also included CHARLIE TUMAHAI) went on to secure a couple of minor hits, 'MYSTERY GIRL' and 'THANK YOU FOR THE PARTY'.

In 1982, ANDERSON was invited to join STAN WEBB's SPEEDWAY, which led to him playing bass for a re-united CHICKEN SHACK. However, unsurprisingly, this didn't last long and the man subsequently had positions in MOUNTAIN, SPENCER DAVIS and PETER YORK and SUPERBLUES. MILLER was now residing in Shoreham-On-Sea and was always in demand for the odd session. He also enjoyed periods with The GEMINI BAND (headed by JON LORD), and worked with COLIN HODGKINSON among others.

In 1998, the guitarist finally gave the people his long-awaited solo comeback (after 27 years!), 'CELTIC MOON', an acoustic-based record welcomed by many of his Blues-hardened fanbase.

VOICE

		Mercury	not iss.
1965.	(7") *(MF 905)* **THE TRAIN TO DISASTER. / TRUTH**	☐	-

AT LAST THE 1958 ROCK'N'ROLL SHOW

MILLER + IAN HUNTER – vocals +

		C.B.S.	not iss.
Mar 68.	(7") *(3349)* **I CAN'T DRIVE. / WORKING ON THE RAILROAD**	☐	-

— when HUNTER joined MOTT THE HOOPLE, ANDERSON began employment with KEEF HARTLEY BAND, but left in 1971 to go solo using most of said band

MILLER ANDERSON

— with **MICK WEAVER + PETER DINES** – keyboards / **NEIL HUBBARD** – guitar / **GARY THAIN** – bass / **ERIC DILLON** – drums / **HAROLD BECKETT** – flugelhorn / **LYNN DOBSON** – flute

		Deram	Deram
Aug 71.	(7") *(DM 337)* **BRIGHT CITY. / ANOTHER TIME, ANOTHER PLACE**	☐	-
Sep 71.	(7") *<85084>* **BRIGHT CITY. / GREY BROKEN MORNING**	-	☐
Oct 71.	(lp) *(SDL 3) <18062>* **BRIGHT CITY**	☐	☐

– Alice mercy / The age of progress / Nothing in this world / Bright city / Grey broken morning / High tide, high water / Shadow cross my wall.

HEMLOCK

ANDERSON / WEAVER / DINES / DILLON / + JAMES LEVERTON – bass / **CHRIS STEWART** – vocals / **CHRIS MERCER** – saxophones / **PETE WILLSHER** – steel guitar

		Deram	not iss.
Nov 73.	(lp) *(SML 1102)* **HEMLOCK**	☐	-

– Just an old friend / A lover's not a thief / Mister Horizontal / Ship to nowhere / Monopoly / Broken dream / Fool's gold / Garden of life / Young man's prayer.

— ANDERSON then regrouped with KEEF HARTLEY to form DOG SOLDIER. They released one eponymous lp for 'United Artists' (UAS 29769). After a period with T.REX, he became a session man for DONOVAN

the DUKES

MILLER ANDERSON with **RONNIE LEAHY** – keyboards (ex-STONE THE CROWS) / **JIMMY McCULLOCH** – guitar, vocals (ex-STONE THE CROWS) / **CHARLIE TUMAHAI** – bass, vocals (ex-BE-BOP DELUXE) / **STUART ELLIOTT + BARRY DE SOUZA** – drums / **MORRIS PERT** – percussion

		Warners	Warners
Aug 79.	(7") *(K 17453)* **HEART'S IN TROUBLE. / WHO'S GONNA TELL YOU**	☐	
Sep 79.	(lp) *(K 56710) <BSK 3376>* **THE DUKES**	☐	☐

– Heart's in trouble / Leavin' it all behind / All in a game / Billy Niles / Crazy fool / Who's gonna tell you / Turn on your side / I'll try to help / Heartbreaker.

Jan 80.	(7") *(K 17551)* **LEAVIN' IT ALL BEHIND. / I'LL TRY TO HELP**	☐	-

— **MICK GRABHAM** – guitar; repl. McCULLOCH who died in 1980

Sep 81.	(7") *(K 18867)* **MYSTERY GIRL. / MY SIMPLE HEART**	47	☐
Apr 82.	(7") *(K 19136)* **THANK YOU FOR THE PARTY. / LOVES FOOL**	53	☐
Aug 82.	(7") *(K 19252)* **I'M A SURVIVOR. / EVERY WOMAN IN THE WORLD**	☐	-

— the DUKES split and ANDERSON joined CHICKEN SHACK, etc

MILLER ANDERSON

— was solo again and now with **FRANK DIEZ** – guitar / **COLIN HODGKINSON** – bass / **WOLFGANG HAFFNER** – drums, percussion / **OLAF KUBLER** – sax / **JACKIE CARTER** – vocals

		In-Akustic	not iss.
Nov 98.	(cd) *(9046)* **CELTIC MOON**	-	- German

– Fog on the highway / Celtic moon / Two ships / Fools gold / Tame em up solid / Misplaced soul / Across the borderline / One gold coin / Shadow cross my wall / Boatman / Madonna of the street / High tec blues.

ARC

Formed: London, . . . 1970 by former SKIP BIFFERTY members JOHN TURNBULL and MICKEY GALLAGHER, both Scots-born musicians who were previously in another sixties group, Newcastle-based the CHOSEN FEW.

ARC were a basic Prog/Blues quartet completed by Australian TOM DUFFY and DAVE TRUDEX, the latter drummer being superseded by ROB TAIT then DAVE MONTGOMERY before they released their debut set, 'ARC . . . AT THIS' (1971) – it's now worth around £30. The record featured elements of poetry and harmony interspersed between some Progressive but heavy-duty rock. Both GALLAGHER and TURNBULL (with also TAIT and DUFFY) re-united with old SKIP BIFFERTY mate, GRAHAM BELL, to record one LP, 'Bell & Arc', (for 'Charisma') later in 1971.

JOHN TURNBULL – guitar, vocals / **MICKEY GALLAGHER** – keyboards / **TOM DUFFY** – bass, vocals / **DAVE MONTGOMERY** – drums, percussion; repl. ROB TAIT who repl. DAVE TRUDEX

		Decca	not iss.
Jan 71.	(lp) *(SKL-R 5077)* **ARC . . . AT THIS**	☐	-

– Let your love run through / It's gonna rain / Four times eight / An ear ago / Great lager street / Hello, hello, Monday / Perfectly happy man / Sophie's cat / You're in the garden.

— later in the year, TURNBULL + GALLAGHER joined up with GRAHAM BELL again to form the one-off collaboration, BELL & ARC; TURNBULL subsequently joined GLENCOE

ATHENIANS (see under ⇒ "A Beat(en) Generation")

AVERAGE WHITE BAND

Formed: Dundee/Glasgow . . . early 1972 by ALAN GORRIE and other noted session men, HAMISH STUART, ONNIE McINTYRE, ROBBIE McINTOSH, ROGER BALL and MALCOLM 'MOLLY' DUNCAN.

After supporting ERIC CLAPTON at his comeback Rainbow concert in '73, they gained enough attention to attract 'M.C.A.'. After one album, 'SHOW YOUR HAND', they moved to Los Angeles and signed to 'Atlantic', where the US audiences related more easily to their sound. Early in 1975, they scored a US No.1 with chant-orientated 'PICK UP THE PIECES', which was lifted from their self-titled top selling album. One of the few bands from Scotland (never mind Dundee!) to make it big in the States, what was even more ironic was that they didn't fit the usual Celtic musical stereotypes (i.e. folky, anthemic etc.), instead opting for a white funk/soul sound with top flight harmonies inspired by black artists of the 60's e.g. The ISLEY BROTHERS, MARVIN GAYE etc. The lock-tight rhythmic shuffle and classy horn stabs of the aforementioned 'PICK UP THE PIECES' assured the track a place in funk history, the record still being played out on dancefloors today.

Although celebrations were cut short with the shock heroin overdose of McINTOSH later that summer, AWB eventually found a replacement in STEVE FERRONE and began work on a follow-up set, 'CUT THE CAKE' (1975). Another sizeable Stateside success, the record's largely instrumental workouts weren't so enthusiastically embraced by a British audience. As the UK musical climate changed during the ensuing few years, AWB concentrated on America, their laidback, sun-kissed soul continuing to soundtrack Californian idyll. The creamy-rich 'QUEEN OF MY SOUL' was the group's last hit in Britain for almost five years, the band eventually storming back into the UK Top 20 in 1979 with the strong 'FEEL NO FRET' album, the evocative 'ATLANTIC AVENUE' another defining AWB moment.

After 'PICK UP THE PIECES', however, their most enduring track remains the yearning disco classic, 'LET'S GO ROUND AGAIN', only their second UK Top 20 hit. The accompanying album, 'SHINE' (1980) also went Top 20, although it marked a last stand of sorts, a subsequent effort, 'CUPID'S IN FASHION' (1982) seeing them floundering in tepid waters. Inevitably, they split the following year, while equally inevitably, perhaps, reforming at the end of the decade. A line-up of GORRIE, McINTYRE and BALL recruited ALEX LIGERTWOOD and a couple of session players, cutting a sole flop album, 'AFTERSHOCK' (1989).

Though they've since turned their backs on the studio, AWB continue to draw in the crowds every year with regular tours of the UK including a residency at London's Jazz Cafe. They continued to release the odd album, 'SOUL TATTOO' (1997) and the concert CD, 'FACE TO FACE LIVE' (1999). • **Songwriters:** GORRIE and STUART, except I HEARD IT THROUGH THE GRAPEVINE (Marvin Gaye) / IMAGINE (John Lennon) / WALK ON BY (Burt Bacharach) / etc. • **Trivia:** McINTYRE and McINTOSH sessioned on CHUCK BERRY's 'My Ding-A-Ling'.

HAMISH STUART (b. 8 Oct'49, Glasgow) – vocals, guitar / **ALAN GORRIE** (b.19 Jul'46, Perth) – vocals, bass / **ONNIE McINTYRE** (b.25 Sep'45, Lennoxtown) – lead guitar / **ROBBIE McINTOSH** (b. 1950) – drums / **ROGER BALL** (b. 4 Jun'44, Dundee) – saxophone / **MALCOLM 'MOLLY' DUNCAN** (b.24 Aug'44, Montrose) – tenor/soprano sax

M.C.A. M.C.A.

Apr 73. (7") *(MUS 1187)* **PUT IT WHERE YOU WANT IT. / REACH OUT** [ ] [-]
Jun 73. (7") *(MUS 1208)* **SHOW YOUR HAND. / THE JUGGLERS** [ ] [-]
Jun 73. (lp) *(MCF 2514)* <345> **SHOW YOUR HAND** [ ] [ ]
– The jugglers / This world has music / Twilight zone / Put it where you want it / Show your hand / How can you go home / Back in '67 / Reach out / T.L.C. *<US re-iss. Apr75 as 'PUT IT WHERE YOU WANT IT'; 475>* – hit No.39 *(UK re-iss. Feb82 under US title; MCL 1650) (re-iss. May83 on 'Fame' lp/c; FA/TC-FA 3062)*
Jul 73. (7") <40168> **THE JUGGLERS. / THIS WORLD HAS MUSIC** [-] [ ]
Jan 74. (7") *(MCA 86)* **HOW CAN YOU GO HOME. / TWILIGHT ZONE** [ ] [-]
(re-iss. May75; MCA 102)

Atlantic Atlantic

Jul 74. (lp/c) *(K/K4 50058)* <7308> **AVERAGE WHITE BAND** [6] [1] Sep74
– You got it / Got the love / Pick up the pieces / Person to person / Work to do / Nothing you can do / Just wanna love you tonight / Keepin' it to myself / I just can't give you up / There's always someone waiting. *(re-iss. Oct80 on 'RCA Int.'; INTS 5049) (re-iss. Jun86 on 'Fame' lp/c; FA/TC-FA 3157) (cd-iss. 1987; 781515-2) (cd re-iss. Oct96 as 'THE WHITE ALBUM' on 'Essential'; ESMCD 439) (cd re-iss. Jan02 on 'Hit'; AHLCD 020)*
Jul 74. (7") *(K 10489)* **PICK UP THE PIECES. / YOU GOT IT** [ ] [-]
(re-dist.Feb75, hit UK No.6)
Oct 74. (7") *(K 10498)* <3044> **NOTHING YOU CAN DO. / I JUST CAN'T GIVE YOU UP** [ ] [ ]
Nov 74. (7") <3229> **PICK UP THE PIECES. / WORK TO DO** [-] [1]

—— **STEVE FERRONE** (b.25 Apr'50, Brighton) – drums (ex-BRIAN AUGER) repl. ROBBIE who died of a heroin overdose 23rd Sep'74

Apr 75. (7") *(K 10605)* <3261> **CUT THE CAKE. / PERSON TO PERSON** [31] [10]
Jun 75. (lp/c) *(K/K4 50146)* <18140> **CUT THE CAKE** [28] [4]
– Cut the cake / School boy crush / It's a mystery / Groovin' the night away / If I ever lose this Heaven / Why? / High flyin' woman / Cloudy / How sweet can you get / When they bring down the curtain. *(cd-iss. Sep97 on 'Snapper'; SMMCD 508) (cd re-iss. Jan02 on 'Hit'; AHLCD 030)*
Aug 75. (7") *(K 10655)* <3285> **IF I EVER LOSE THIS HEAVEN. / HIGH FLYIN' WOMAN** [ ] [39]
Nov 75. (7") *(K 10701)* <3304> **SCHOOL BOY CRUSH. / GROOVIN' THE NIGHT AWAY** [ ] [33]
May 76. (7") *(K 10778)* **EVERYBODY'S DARLING. / WHY?** [ ] [ ]
Jul 76. (lp/c) *(K/K4 50272)* <18179> **SOUL SEARCHING** [60] [8]
– Overture / Love your life / I'm the one / A love of your own / Queen of my soul / Soul searching / Goin' home / Everybody's darling / Would you say / Sunny days (make me think of you) / Digging deeper. *(re-iss. Nov80 on 'RCA Int.' lp/c; INTS/INTK 5058)*
Aug 76. (7") *(K 10825)* <3354> **QUEEN OF MY SOUL. / WOULD YOU STAY** [23] [40]
Dec 76. (7") *(K 10880)* **A LOVE OF YOUR OWN. / SOUL SEARCHIN'** [ ] [-]
Jan 77. (d-lp/d-c) *(K/K4 60127)* <1002> **PERSON TO PERSON (live)** [ ] [28]
– Person to person / Cut the cake / If I ever lose this Heaven / Cloudy / T.L.C. / I'm the one / Pick up the pieces / Love your life / School boy crush / I heard it through the grapevine.
Mar 77. (7") *(K 10912)* **GOIN' HOME (live). / I'M THE ONE (live)** [ ] [-]
Mar 77. (7") <3388> **CLOUDY (live). / LOVE YOUR LIFE (live)** [-] [ ]

AVERAGE WHITE BAND / BEN E. KING

Jun 77. (7") <3402> **KEEPIN' IT TO MYSELF. / GET IT UP FOR LOVE** [-] [ ]
Jul 77. (lp/c) *(K/K4 50384)* <19162> **BENNY AND US** [ ] [33]
– Get it up for love / Fool for you anyway / A star in the ghetto / The message / What is soul / Someday we'll all be free / Imagine / Keepin' it to myself.
Jul 77. (7") *(K 10977)* **A STAR IN THE GHETTO. / KEEPIN' IT TO MYSELF** [ ] [-]
Aug 77. (7") <3427> **A STAR IN A GHETTO. / WHAT IS SOUL** [-] [ ]
Dec 77. (7") <3444> **FOOL FOR YOU ANYWAY. / THE MESSAGE** [-] [ ]

AVERAGE WHITE BAND

R.C.A. Atlantic

Jun 78. (lp/c) *(XL/XC 13053)* <19162> **WARMER COMMUNICATIONS** [ ] [28] Mar78
– Your love is a miracle / Same feeling, different song / Daddy's all gone / Big city lights / She's a dream / Sweet and sour / One look over my shoulder (is this really goodbye?). *(cd-iss. Jan02 on 'Hit'; AHLCD 029)*
Jun 78. (7") <3481> **ONE LOOK OVER MY SHOULDER. / LOVE IS A MIRACLE** [-] [ ]
Jun 78. (7"/7"colrd) *(XB/XC 9270)* **ONE LOOK OVER MY SHOULDER (IS THIS REALLY GOODBYE?). / BIG CITY LIGHTS** [ ] [-]
Aug 78. (7") <3500> **SHE'S A DREAM. / BIG CITY LIGHTS** [-] [ ]
Feb 79. (7") *(XB 1061)* **ATLANTIC AVENUE. / SHE'S A DREAM** [ ] [-]
Feb 79. (lp/c) *(XL/ZX 13063)* <19207> **FEEL NO FRET** [15] [32]
– When will you be mine / Please don't fall in love / Walk on by / Feel no fret / Stop the rain / Atlantic avenue / Ace of hearts / Too late to cry / Fire burning. *(re-iss. Sep81 lp/c; INTS/INTK 5140)*
Apr 79. (7"/7"colrd) *(XB/XC 1087)* <3563> **WALK ON BY. / TOO LATE TO CRY** [46] [92]
May 79. (7") <3581> **FEEL NO FRET. / FIRE BURNING** [-] [ ]
Jul 79. (7"/7"colrd) *(XB/XC 1096)* **WHEN WILL YOU BE MINE. / ACE OF HEARTS** [49] [ ]

R.C.A. Arista

Apr 80. (7"/12") *(AWB/+12 1)* **LET'S GO 'ROUND AGAIN. / (art 2)** [12] [-]
May 80. (lp/c) *(XL/XC 13123)* <9523> **SHINE** [14] [ ]
– Catch me / Let's go 'round again / Whatcha gonna do for me / Help is on the way / Shine / For you, for love / Into the night / Our time has come / If love only lasts for one night.
Jun 80. (7") <0515> **LET'S GO 'ROUND AGAIN. / SHINE** [-] [53]
Jul 80. (7"/12") *(AWB/+12 2)* **FOR YOU, FOR LOVE. / HELP IS ON THE WAY** [46] [-]
Jul 80. (7") <0553> **FOR YOU, FOR LOVE. / WHATCHA GONNA DO FOR ME** [-] [ ]
Jul 80. (7") <0580> **INTO THE NIGHT. /** [-] [ ]

—— added guest **RITCHIE STOTTS** – guitar (ex-PLASMATICS)

Jul 82. (7"/12") *(RCA/+T 250)* **YOU'RE MY NUMBER ONE. / THEATRE OF EXCESS** [ ] [-]
Sep 82. (lp/c) *(RCA LP/K 6052)* **CUPID'S IN FASHION** [ ] [ ]
– You're my number one / Easier said than done / You wanna belong / Cupid's in fashion / Theatre of excess / I believe / Is it love that you're running from? / Reach out I'll be there / Isn't it strange / Love's a heartache.
Sep 82. (7"/12") *(RCA/+T 274)* **I BELIEVE. / REACH OUT I'LL BE THERE** [ ] [-]

—— split 1983 but reformed in 1989 with **GORRIE, McINTYRE, BALL** recruited **ALEX LIGERTWOOD** (b.18 Dec'46, Glasgow) – guitar, vocals (ex-SANTANA, ex-BRIAN AUGER'S OBLIVION EXPRESS) / + on session **ELLIOT LEWIS** – keyboards / **TIGER McNEIL** – drums

—— HAMISH joined ERIC CLAPTON's band in 1990 and went solo

Polydor TRK

Aug 89. (lp/c/cd) *(839 466-1/-4/-2)* **AFTERSHOCK** [ ] [ ]
– The spirit of love / Aftershock / I'll get over you / Let's go all the way / Sticky situation / Love at first sight / Later we'll be greater / We're in too deep.
Oct 89. (7") *(PO 56)* **THE SPIRIT OF LOVE. / ('A'beat mix)** [ ] [-]
(12"/cd-s) *(PZ/+CD 56)* – ('A'dance) / ('A'-long beat) / ('A'-New York mix).

— In 1985, ALAN GORRIE released album **SLEEPLESS NIGHTS** for 'A&M-US', plus single; 'AGE OF STEAM / I CAN TAKE IT (after) / DIARY OF A FOOL / IN THE JUNGLE

— re-formed spring 1994 after the success of their compilation album

		Hit Label	not iss.
Mar 94.	(cd/c) *(AHL CD/MC 15)* **THE BEST OF THE AVERAGE WHITE BAND – LET'S GO ROUND AGAIN**	38	-
	(cd re-iss. Oct96 on 'Music Club'; MCCD 274) (cd re-iss. Jan02 on 'Red Bullet'; RB 6695)		
Mar 94.	(7"/c-s) *(HL/+C 5)* **LET'S GO ROUND AGAIN (the CCN mix). / ('A'mix)**	56	-
	(cd-s+=) *(HLCD 5)* – ('A'mixes).		

— **ALAN GORRIE, ONNIE McINTYRE, ROGER BALL** plus **ELIOT LEWIS** – vocals, keyboards, bass, guitar / **PETE ABBOTT** – drums, percussion

		Artful	Foundation
Feb 97.	(cd) *(ARTFULCD 7) <1601>* **SOUL TATTOO**		
	– Soul mine / Back to basics / Livin' on borrowed time / Every beat of my heart / Oh Maceo / Do ya really / I wanna be loved / No easy way to say goodbye / Love is the bottom line / Welcome to the real world / Window to your soul. *(re-iss. Feb02 on 'S.P.V.'; SPV 0763375-2)*		
		Millennium	**Millennium**
Jul 99.	(cd) *(<MMPCD 002>)* **FACE TO FACE LIVE (live)**		
	– Pick up the pieces / Let's go round again (pt.1) / Got the love / Love of your own / Work to do / Soul mine / Oh Maceo (dedicated to Maceo Parker) / Back to basics / Every beat of my heart.		

– compilations etc. –

Jul 81.	(7") *RCA-Gold; (GOLD 514)* **PICK UP THE PIECES. / CUT THE CAKE**		-
Sep 80.	(lp) *Atlantic; <19266>* **VOLUME VIII**	-	
Sep 81.	(lp) *R.C.A.; (RCA 5139)* **THE BEST OF THE AVERAGE WHITE BAND**		-
	– Pick up the pieces / Cut the cake / Queen of my soul / A love of your own / Person to person / I heard it through the grapevine / Walk on by / You got it / Cloudy / Work to do / Atlantic avenue / When will you be mine. *(re-iss. Aug84 lp/c; NL/NK 89091) (re-iss. May94 on 'Repertoire';)*		
Aug 94.	(cd) *Windsong; (WHISCD 005)* **LIVE ON THE TEST (live)**		-
Oct 96.	(cd) *Castle; (CCSCD 438)* **ABOVE AVERAGE**		-
Feb 97.	(cd) *Laserlight; (12891)* **THE VERY BEST OF THE AVERAGE WHITE BAND**		-
May 97.	(d-cd) *Snapper; (SMDCD 173)* **AVERAGE WHITE BAND**		-
Aug 97.	(cd-ep) *Club Classics; (CLCL 001)* **PICK UP THE PIECES / LET'S GO 'ROUND AGAIN / QUEEN OF MY SOUL**		-

B

BAY CITY ROLLERS

Formed: Edinburgh . . . 1967 by the LONGMUIR brothers, DEREK and ALAN, the pair finding NOBBY CLARKE and JOHN DEVINE after lengthy auditions. After a spell as SAXON they changed their moniker to The BAY CITY ROLLERS, found at random after pointing at Bay City, Michigan, on a map of the States.

Managed by Tam Paton, the group were signed to 'Bell' records in 1971, hitting the UK Top 10 soon after with a Jonathan King-produced cover of The Gentry's 'KEEP ON DANCING'. It proved a one-off, however, and it'd be 1974 before they graced the charts again. By the time 'REMEMBER (SHA-LA-LA)' had become a Top 10 hit, CLARKE and DEVINE had been replaced by frontman LES McKEOWN, STUART WOOD and ERIC FAULKNER, the line-up which would effect mid-70's chart domination and make tartan trendy into the bargain. With the help of songwriters Phil Coulter and Bill Martin, the Edinburgh lads couldn't put a foot wrong throughout that year, kicking up a teen storm with bubblegum pop anthems 'SHANG-A-LANG', 'SUMMERLOVE SENSATION' and 'ALL OF ME LOVES ALL OF YOU'.

Having started out as a BEATLES covers outfit, The BAY CITY ROLLERS at their height ironically provoked a level of knicker-wetting teen hysteria not witnessed since the Fab Four's heyday. Gracing Top Of The Pops with their trademark tartan flares, scarves and platform shoes, McKEOWN & Co. topped the UK charts twice in a row in 1975, first with a cover of The Four Seasons' 'BYE BYE BABY' followed by 'GIVE A LITTLE LOVE'. It was only a matter of time before the States could resist something so squeaky clean and identifiably Scottish at the same time, the boys hitting the US Top spot with 'SATURDAY NIGHT' (originally a UK flop two years previously!) towards the end of the year. Following the Top 5 success of 1976's 'LOVE ME LIKE I LOVE YOU', ALAN LONGMUIR departed for a short-lived solo career although he returned in 1978.

By then, the press knives were out for Rollermania and it wasn't long before the band's less than wholesome pedigree was exposed with revelations of drug use. On top of that, Paton was charged with indecency involving underage kids. Nevertheless, the ROLLERS kept rolling around the golden oldie circuit in various incarnations over the forthcoming decades while, for better or worse, they remain the biggest pop export Scotland has ever produced.

Amid the band's high-profile slot at Edinburgh's Hogmanay 2000 celebrations, yet more controversy reared its ugly and all too familiar head as former member DEREK LONGMUIR (now working as a hospital auxiliary!) was charged with possessing child porn.

GORDON 'NOBBY' CLARKE – vocals / **JOHN DEVINE** – guitar / **ALAN LONGMUIR** (b.20 Jun'53) – bass, accordion / **DEREK LONGMUIR** (b.19 Mar'52) – drums, percussion

		Bell	Bell
Jun 71.	(7") *(BLL 1164) <45169>* **KEEP ON DANCING. / ALRIGHT**	9	
Mar 72.	(7") *(BLL 1220)* **WE CAN MAKE MUSIC. / JENNY**		-

— (Jun'72) **ERIC FAULKNER** (b.21 Oct'54) – guitar; repl. DEVINE

Sep 72.	(7") *(BLL 1262) <45274>* **MANANA. / BECAUSE I LOVE YOU**		

— (Jan'73) **LES McKEOWN** (b.12 Nov'55) – vocals + **STUART WOOD** (b.25 Feb'57) – guitar, mandolin; repl. CLARKE

Jun 73.	(7") *(BLL 1319)* **SATURDAY NIGHT. / HEY C.B.**		-
Jan 74.	(7") *(BLL 1338)* **REMEMBER (SHA-LA-LA). / BYE BYE BARBARA**	6	-
Apr 74.	(7") *(BLL 1355) <45481>* **SHANG-A-LANG. / ARE YOU READY FOR THAT ROCK'N'ROLL**	2	
Jul 74.	(7") *(BLL 1369) <45607>* **SUMMERLOVE SENSATION. / BRINGING BACK THE GOOD TIMES**	3	

Oct 74. (7") *(BLL 1382) <45618>* **ALL OF ME LOVES ALL OF YOU. / THE BUMP** [4] [ ]
Oct 74. (lp) *(BELLS 244)* **ROLLIN'** [1] [-]
– Shang-a-lang / Give it to me now / Angel angel / Be my baby / Just a little love / Remember (sha-la-la) / Saturday night / Ain't it strange / Please stay / Jenny gotta dance / There goes my baby / Summerlove sensation.

Bell Arista

Mar 75. (7") *(BLL 1409) <0120>* **BYE BYE BABY. / IT'S FOR YOU** [1] [ ]
May 75. (lp) *(SYBEL 8001)* **ONCE UPON A STAR** [1] [-]
– Bye bye baby / The disco kid / La belle Jeane / When will you be mine / Angel baby / Keep on dancing / Once upon a star / Let's go / Marlina / My teenage heart / Rock and roll honeymoon / Hey! beautiful dreamer.
Jul 75. (7") *(BLL 1409)* **GIVE A LITTLE LOVE. / SHE'LL BE CRYING OVER YOU** [1] [-]
Sep 75. (7") *<0149>* **SATURDAY NIGHT. / MARLINA** [-] [1]
Sep 75. (lp) *<4049>* **BAY CITY ROLLERS** [-] [20]
– Bye bye baby / Give a little love / Be my baby / Summerlove sensation / Keep on dancing / Marlina / Shang-a-lang / Let's go (a huggin' and a kissin' in the moonlight) / My teenage heart / Remember (sha la la) / Saturday night.
Nov 75. (7") *(BLL 1461) <0170>* **MONEY HONEY. / MARYANNE** [3] [9] Jan76
Dec 75. (lp) *(SYBEL 8002)* **WOULDN'T YOU LIKE IT** [3] [-]
– I only wanna dance with you / Don't stop the music / Shanghai'd in love / Love is . . . / Maybe I'm a fool to rock'n'roll / Give a little love / Wouldn't you like it / Here comes that feeling again / Lovely to see you again / Eagles fly / Derek's end piece.
Mar 76. (lp) *<4071>* **ROCK N' ROLL LOVE LETTER** [-] [31]
– Money honey / La belle Jeane / Rock n' roll love letter / Maybe I'm a fool to love you / Wouldn't you like it / I only wanna dance with you / Shanghai'd in love / Don't stop the music / The disco kid / Eagles fly / Too young to rock & roll.
Apr 76. (7") *(BLL 1477)* **LOVE ME LIKE I LOVE YOU. / MAMA LI** [4] [-]
Apr 76. (7") *<0185>* **ROCK AND ROLL LOVE LETTER. / SHANGHAI'D IN LOVE** [-] [28]
Jun 76. (7") *<0193>* **DON'T STOP THE MUSIC. / DON'T STOP THE MUSIC (long)** [-] [ ]

— **IAN MITCHELL** (b.,22 Aug'58, Downpatrick, County Down, N. Ireland) – guitar; repl. ALAN LONGMUIR who tries a brief solo career

Aug 76. (7") *<0205>* **I ONLY WANT TO BE WITH YOU. / WRITE A LETTER** [-] [12]
Sep 76. (7") *(BLL 1493)* **I ONLY WANNA BE WITH YOU. / ROCK N' ROLLER** [4] [-]
Sep 76. (lp) *(SYBEL 8005) <4093>* **DEDICATION** [4] [26]
– Let's pretend / You're a woman / Rock 'n roller / Don't worry baby / Yesterday's hero / My Lisa / Money honey / Rock n' roll love letter / Write a letter / Dedication.
Nov 76. (7") *<0216>* **YESTERDAY'S HERO. / MY LISA** [-] [54]
Feb 77. (7") *<0233>* **DEDICATION. / ROCK N' ROLLER** [-] [60]

Arista Arista

May 77. (7") *(ARIST 108)* **IT'S A GAME. / DANCE DANCE DANCE** [16] [-]
May 77. (7") *<0256>* **YOU MADE ME BELIEVE IN MAGIC. / DANCE DANCE DANCE** [-] [10]
Jul 77. (7") *(ARIST 127)* **YOU MADE ME BELIEVE IN MAGIC. / ARE YOU CUCKOO / DEDICATION** [34] [-]
Aug 77. (lp) *(SPARTY 1009) <7004>* **IT'S A GAME** [18] [23] Jul77
– It's a game / You made me believe in magic / Don't let the music die / Love power / The way I feel tonight / Love fever / Sweet Virginia / Inside a broken dream / Dance dance dance / Rebel rebel.
Oct 77. (7") *(ARIST 144) <0272>* **THE WAY I FEEL TONIGHT. / LOVE POWER** [ ] [24]
Nov 77. (lp) *<4158>* **GREATEST HITS** (compilation) [-] [77]
– I only wanna be with you / Money honey / Rock and roll love letter / The way I feel tonight / Yesterday's hero / Dedication / Maybe I'm a fool to love you / You made me believe in magic / Don't stop the music / Saturday night.

— **PAT McGLYNN** (b.31 Mar'58) – guitar; repl. MITCHELL who formed ROSETTA STONE before formed his own named outfit who became LA ROX

— **ALAN LONGMUIR** returned to repl. McGLYNN

Oct 78. (7") *(ARIST 212)* **ALL OF THE WORLD IS FALLING IN LOVE. / IF YOU WERE MY WOMAN** [ ] [-]
Oct 78. (7") *<0363>* **WHERE WILL I BE NOW. / IF YOU WERE MY WOMAN** [-] [ ]
Oct 78. (lp) *(SPART 1075) <4194>* **STRANGERS IN THE WIND** [ ] [ ]
– Another rainy day in New York City / All of the world is falling in love / Where will I be now / Back on the street / Strangers in the wind / Love brought me such a magical thing / If you were my woman / Every tear I cry / Shoorah shoorah for Hollywood / When I say I love you (the pie).

ROLLERS

— **DUNCAN FAURE** – vocals, keyboards (ex-RABBIT) repl. McKEOWN who went solo (released 'ALL WASHED UP' in 1979 on the 'Egotrip' label)

May 79. (7") *(ARIST 259)* **TURN ON THE RADIO. / WASHINGTON'S BIRTHDAY** [ ] [-]
Jun 79. (lp) *(064-63136)* **ELEVATOR** [-] [-] German
– Stoned houses #1 / Elevator / Playing in a rock and roll band / Hello and welcome home / I was eleven / Stoned houses #2 / Turn on the radio / Instant relay / Tomorrow's just a day away / Who'll be my keeper / Back on the road again / Washington's birthday.
Jun 80. (lp) *(202204)* **VOXX** [-] [-] German
– God save rock & roll / Working for the people / Soho / The hero / '85 / Honey don't leave L.A. / New York / The jig / Only the young die old / Rebel rebel.

Epic not iss.

May 81. (7") *(EPC 1225)* **LIFE ON THE ROAD. / RICOCHET** [ ] [-]
Jul 81. (7") *(EPC 1402)* **NO DOUBT ABOUT IT. / SET THE FASHION** [ ] [-]
Aug 81. (lp/c) *(EPC/40 85004)* **RICOCHET** [ ] [-]
– Doors, bars, metal / Life on the radio / No doubt about it / Roxy lady / Ricochet / Won't you come home with me / Ride / Lay your love on the line / That's where the boys are / Set the fashion / This is your life.

— after they split, various BCR's play in versions of the band

– compilations, etc. –

Jun 92. (c/cd) *I.M.D.; (MC+/JHD 025)* **GREATEST HITS** [ ] [-]
Sep 92. (cd/c) *R.C.A.; (26/41 3001)* **COLLECTION** [ ] [-]
Dec 92. (cd/c) *Ariola Express; (2/4 95588)* **BAY CITY ROLLERS** [ ] [-]
Aug 95. (cd) *Arista; (<74321 26575-2>)* **ABSOLUTE ROLLERS** [ ] [ ]
– Saturday night / Shang-a-lang / Remember (sha-la-la) / Bye bye baby / I only want to be with you / All of me loves all of you / Give a little love / Summer love sensation / Rebel rebel / Money honey / Keep on dancing / Love me like I love you / Once upon a star / Be my baby / You made me believe in magic / The way I feel tonight / Another rainy day in New York City / It's a game / There goes my baby / Rock n' roll love letter / Bay City Rollers megamix.
May 96. (cd-s) *Old Gold; (126236367-2)* **BYE BYE BABY / GIVE A LITTLE LOVE** [ ] [-]
Nov 96. (cd) *Tring; (<QED 106>)* **BYE BYE BABY** [ ] [-]
Apr 97. (cd) *BR Music; (BM 1551)* **GREATEST HITS** [ ] [-]
May 97. (cd/c) *A-Play Collection; (10060-2/-4)* **THE VERY BEST OF THE BAY CITY ROLLERS** [ ] [-]
Mar 98. (cd) *RCA-Camden; (<74321 5696025>)* **SHANG-A-LANG** [ ] [ ] Dec99
Jul 98. (cd/c) *Hallmark; (<30906-2/-4>)* **THE VERY BEST OF THE BAY CITY ROLLERS** [ ] [ ] Dec99
Apr 99. (cd-box) *BMG Int.; <37045>* **THE COMPLETE ANTHOLOGY 1971-1980** [-] [ ]
Mar 00. (cd) *Delta; (CD 6203)* **THE BEST OF THE BAY CITY ROLLERS** [ ] [-]
Nov 01. (cd) *Metrodome; (METRO 296)* **ROLLERMANIA – THE VERY BEST OF THE BAY CITY ROLLERS** [ ] [-]

BEACHCOMBERS (see under ⇒ "A Beat(en) Generation")

BEATSTALKERS

Formed: Glasgow . . . 1962 by school friends DAVIE LENNOX, EDDIE CAMPBELL, ALAN MAIR and TUDGE WILLIAMSON; second guitar man RONNIE SMITH was added to boost the band's Mod/R&B sound.

Cutting their musical teeth playing weekends at Battlefield's Cooper Institute (fellow Glasgwegians The QUINTONES were in the next hall!) The BEATSTALKERS steadily picked up a healthy loyal following. Taking their material from listening to US imports such as DON COVAY, OTIS REDDING and The IMPRESSIONS (at Gloria's Record Bar!), the quintet were a hit on the dancehalls. However, in 1965, they were involved in a mighty fracas when an open-air gig in George Square (Glasgow) erupted with rival fans storming the dodgy stage. The police intervened many times and finally led the band out of the streets and into the tabloids the following day; accusations of a publicity set-up from rival bands were rife.

Later that year and now touted as the Scottish BEATLES, The BEATSTALKERS finally inked a deal with 'Decca', through MOODY BLUES manager, John Fenton, who was impressed by their energetic live set. Producer Denny Cordell was also present, although the man stunned the band when he chose not to release the band's versions of 'GIN HOUSE' or The Tams' 'HEY GIRL DON'T BOTHER ME'. Instead, he brought in relatively new-to-the-game songwriter, Tony Washington, who penned their debut 45, 'EV'RYBODY'S TALKING 'BOUT MY BABY'. To make things even worse CORDELL also produced another, altogether tamer version by (ex-CHEYNES singer) ROGER PEACOCK, and released it a few weeks prior to the band's version; a year and a half later 'GIN HOUSE' became a No.12 hit for AMEN CORNER. Another, and more disturbing groan was, that it sold tens of thousands during its initial release weeks – late '65 – and never charted because mostly all were bought in Scotland (a national British chart, indeed!); its B-side 'MR. DISAPPOINTED' summed up these days and became the group's unwanted anthem. Follow-up single, 'LEFT RIGHT LEFT' (penned by Glaswegian producer TOMMY SCOTT), also failed to sell in England, although its raucous Mod/Garage-esque version of Joe South/Tams' 'YOU BETTER GET A BETTER HOLD ON', rapidly became the fans' fave.

After the formulaic Holland/Dozier/Holland-penned third 45, 'A LOVE LIKE YOURS' also flopped (complete with instrumental TOMMY SCOTT B-side 'BASE LINE'), it was time for a change. 'C.B.S.' took the band on in 1967, although their first for the label, 'MY ONE CHANCE TO MAKE IT', was directionless at a time when flower-power was the rage. Subsequently taken under the wing of Kenneth Pitt – who also managed DAVID BOWIE! – The BEATSTALKERS delivered three further 45's, 'SILVER TREETOP SCHOOL FOR BOYS', 'EVERYTHING IS YOU' (actually a flip side of 'ROSE COLOURED GLASSES') and 'WHEN I'M FIVE' (A-side of REG KING's 'LITTLE BOY'), all, surprise, surprise, penned by the young "Starman" himself; they've become collector's items in the process, BOWIE even guesting on 'SILVER . . .'). On all of these recordings was new drummer JEFF ALLEN, who replaced TUDGE.

In 1969, things went from bad to worse. Having desperately attempted to pull back the Scottish fanbase (LENNOX's forced Englishness on the aforementioned 'SILVER . . .' didn't help!) with a mini-kilted promotion shot, the band were dealt a final blow when their gear was stolen from their van.

DAVIE LENNOX – vocals / **EDDIE CAMPBELL** – guitar / **RONNIE SMITH** – guitar, vocals / **ALAN MAIR** – bass / **TUDGE WILLIAMSON** – drums

		Decca	not iss.
Oct 65.	(7") *(F 12259)* **EV'RYBODY'S TALKING 'BOUT MY BABY. / MR. DISAPPOINTED**	☐	-
Mar 66.	(7") *(F 12352)* **LEFT RIGHT LEFT. / YOU'D BETTER GET A BETTER HOLD ON**	☐	-
Jul 66.	(7") *(F 12460)* **A LOVE LIKE YOURS. / BASE LINE**	☐	-
		C.B.S.	not iss.
May 67.	(7") *(CBS 2732)* **MY ONE CHANCE TO MAKE IT. / AIN'T NO SOUL (LEFT IN THESE SHOES)**	☐	-

— **JEFF ALLEN** – drums; repl. TUDGE

Dec 67.	(7") *(CBS 3105)* **SILVER TREETOP SCHOOL FOR BOYS. / SUGAR COATED MAN**	☐	-
Jun 68.	(7") *(CBS 3557)* **RAIN COLOURED ROSES. / EVERYTHING IS FOR YOU**	☐	-
Jan 69.	(7") *(CBS 3936)* **WHEN I'M FIVE. / LITTLE BOY**	☐	-

— disbanded when things just got too much to take (see above); JEFF ALLEN joined EAST OF EDEN while CAMPBELL appeared with pre-TEAR GAS outfit, MUSTARD

BEGGARS OPERA

Formed: Glasgow . . . late 60's originally as The SYSTEM by MARTIN GRIFFITH, RICKY GARDINER, ALAN PARK, MARSHALL ERSKINE and RAYMOND WILSON.

Early in 1971, and signed to the spiralling 'Vertigo' imprint through Inner City Entertainments agency, BEGGARS OPERA had a surprise hit single on the continent with 'SARABANDE', a post-psychedelic, non-LP cut. Around the same time, debut album 'ACT ONE' was released to limited reaction from the press, their flashy, classical-meets-Progressive stylings not to everyone's taste. Adding GORDON SELLAR and with co-lyricist VIRGINIA SCOTT always in tow, further albums 'WATERS OF CHANGE' (1971) and 'PATHFINDER' (1972) – the latter including a pomp-Rock cover of Jim Webb's 'MacARTHUR PARK' – met with similar muted critical response, accusations of pandering to YES and ELP fans were met with derision from BO's loyal following.

By the time of their fourth set, the West Coast-inspired 'GET YOUR DOG OFF ME!' (1973) album – complete with an OTT 'CLASSICAL GAS' – saw former WRITING ON THE WALL singer LINNIE PATTERSON in place. However, this piece of self-indulgence failed to make the grade, although subsequent BEGGARS OPERA formations found they had an audience in Prog-friendly Germany. RICKY GARDINER would find a piece of limelight once again when he joined DAVID BOWIE in 1976.

MARTIN GRIFFITHS – vocals / **RICKY GARDINER** – guitar, vocals / **ALAN PARK** – organ / **MARSHALL ERSKINE** – bass, flute / **RAYMOND WILSON** – drums / (also co-writer VIRGINIA SCOTT)

		Vertigo	Vertigo
Jan 71.	(7") *(6059 026)* **SARABANDE. / THINK**	☐	-
Jan 71.	(lp) *(6360 018) <5080>* **ACT ONE**	☐	☐

– Poet and peasant / Passacaglia / Memory / Raymond's road / Light cavalry.

— added **GORDON SELLAR** – bass, guitar, vocals / **VIRGINIA SCOTT** – keyboards, vocals

Nov 71.	(lp) *(6360 054)* **WATERS OF CHANGE**	☐	-

– Time machine / Lament / I've no idea / Nimbus / Festival / Silver peacock / Impromptu / The fox. *(cd-iss. Apr95 on 'Repertoire'; IMS 7029)*

— now w/out ERSKINE + SCOTT (although latter still co-writer on some)

Jun 72.	(7") *(6059 060)* **HOBO. / PATHFINDER**	☐	-
Aug 72.	(lp) *(6360 073)* **PATHFINDER**	☐	-

– Hobo / MacArthur Park / The witch / Pathfinder / From shark to haggis / Stretcher / Madame Doubtfire. *(cd-iss. 1989 on 'Line'; LICD 9.00728 0) (cd re-iss. Apr95 on 'Repertoire'; IMS 7028)*

— **LINNIE PATTERSON** – vocals (ex-WRITING ON THE WALL) + **COLIN FAIRLEY** – drums, percussion, vocals; repl. GRIFFITHS

Aug 73.	(lp) *(6360 090)* **GET YOUR DOG OFF ME!**	☐	-

– Get your dog off me! / Freestyle ladies / Open letter / Morning day / Requiem / Classical gas / Sweet blossom woman / Turn your money green / La-di-da / Working man.

Sep 73.	(7") *(6059 088)* **TWO TIMING WOMAN. / LADY OF HELL FIRE**	☐	-
Jul 74.	(7") *(6059 105)* **CLASSICAL GAS. / SWEET BLOSSOM WOMAN**	☐	-

— **RICKY GARDINER** brought back wife-to-be **VIRGINIA (SCOTT). PARK became CLIFF RICHARD's musical director.**

		Jupiter	not iss.
1974.	(lp) *(88907)* **SAGITTARY**	-	- German

– Sagittary / Something to lose / World crisis blues / Smiling in a summer dress / Freedom song / I'm the music man / Just twenty one / Jack the ripper / Love of my own / Simplicity.

— **PETE SCOTT** – vocals + **CLEM CATTINI** – drums; repl. FAIRLEY

1975.	(lp) *(27702)* **BEGGARS CAN'T BE CHOOSERS**	-	- German

– I'm a roadie / Beggars can't be choosers / Hungry man / You're not welcome / Young blood man / Union card / We must love / Keep climbing / Bar room pearl / Death.

— split when RICKY joined DAVID BOWIE on tour; reformed for below set

		Vertigo	not iss.
1979.	(lp) *(6350 060)* **LIFELINE**	-	- German

– Lifeline / I gave you love / You never believe I'm human / Showman in a showman / Yes I need someone / Lost in space / Now you're gone / Bad dreams / Four moons.

— folded for the last time

BILBO BAGGINS

Formed: Edinburgh . . . early 1974 by none other than TAM PATON, manager/etc of another Embra group The BAY CITY ROLLERS. In much the same way as the aforementioned 'ROLLERS, PATON handpicked these lads (JIMMY DEVLIN, BRIAN SPENCE, COLIN CHISHOLM and drummer GORDON LIDDLE) from lengthy auditions. With tartan already bulging everybody's wardrobe, the gimmick chosen for BILBO BAGGINS (the name taken from a character in 'The Lord Of The Rings' novel!) was American baseball wear.

There was space for one, maybe two successful pop groups from Scotland and these bandwagon(esque) jumpers were not welcome outside teenybop crazee Scotland. From their stab at the BCR'ers 'SATURDAY NIGHT' (their much hyped debut), single after single failed to breach the national charts. By Spring 1976 (and with new fifth member GORDON McINTOSH), their record label, 'Polydor' had had enough as the group (now BILBO) hit the UK Top 50 with 'Lightning'-released 'SHE'S GONNA WIN'.

As the band failed to emulate this brief liaison with the charts, DEVLIN worked his way up to MD (managing director!) of 'Polydor'. However, the most surprising occurrence was when LIDDLE (without a single O-grade!) subsequently graduated in Law in 1984 and is currently (from 1998) a sheriff in Edinburgh – complete with wig and gown.

JIMMY DEVLIN – vocals / **COLIN CHISHOLM** – guitar / **BRIAN SPENCE** – bass / **GORDON LIDDLE** – drums

		Polydor	not iss.
Jun 74.	(7") *(2058 479)* **SATURDAY NIGHT. / MONDAY MORNING BLUES**	☐	-
Nov 74.	(7") *(2058 530)* **SHA NA NA NA SONG. / RUN WITH THE DEVIL**	☐	-
Apr 75.	(7") *(2058 575)* **HOLD ME. / DANCE TO THE BAND**	☐	-
Jan 76.	(7") *(2058 667)* **BACK HOME. / WHAT'S GOIN' ON**	☐	-
Mar 76.	(7") *(2058 707)* **IT'S A SHAME. / PLEASE SIR**	☐	-

— added **GORDON McINTOSH** – keyboards

		Lightning	not iss.
Mar 78.	(7") *(LIG 521)* **I CAN FEEL MAD. / DOLE QUEUE BLUES**	☐	-
Aug 78.	(7"; as BILBO) *(LIG 548)* **SHE'S GONNA WIN. / YOU WANNA BE YOUR LOVER**	42	-
Nov 78.	(7"; as BILBO) *(LIG 551)* **DON'T BLAME IT ON ME. / (version)**	☐	-
Feb 79.	(7"; as BILBO) *(GIL 56)* **AMERICA. / HE MUSTN'T NOW**	☐	-

— disbanded soon after above

BLUE

Formed: Glasgow . . . 1972 by former members of the POETS, HUGH NICHOLSON and IAN MacMILLAN along with English-born ex-WHITE TRASH drummer, TIMMY DONALD. If melodic, easy-on-the-ear pop-rock was master, then BLUE were its servants, frontman NICHOLSON having recently served some time with fellow Glaswegian popsters, MARMALADE. Things looked bright for the trio early in '73, when the Robert Stigwood Organisation (R.S.O.) signed them up on a worldwide deal. However, after two patchy sets, 'BLUE' (1973) and 'LIFE IN THE NAVY' (1974) – the latter with German-born addition SMIGGY – the group petered out in 1975. A year or two later, NICHOLSON and MacMILLAN regrouped with newcomers DAVID NICHOLSON (HUGH's brother) and CHARLIE SMITH, this line-up promising enough to give ELTON JOHN's label 'Rocket' the impetus to take over the reins; Blue Moves, indeed. In Spring '77, BLUE notched up their first UK Top 20 hit (Top 100 US) courtesy of the single 'GONNA CAPTURE YOUR HEART', although the accompanying long-player, ANOTHER NIGHT TIME FLIGHT' (1977), bombed. Further attempts to enter the hit parade fell on deaf ears and one more dull set, 'FOOL'S PARTY' (1979), was their last before they disbanded.

• **Note:** the mid-80's outfit (on 'Zuma'), the early 90's one (on 'Mercury') and mid-90's BLUE (on 'Sabres Of Paradise'), were in fact three entirely different groups.

HUGH NICHOLSON (b.30 Jul'49, Rutherglen) – vocals, guitar (ex-POETS, ex-MARMALADE) / **IAN MacMILLAN** (b.16 Oct'47, Paisley) – bass, vocals (ex-POETS) / **TIMMY DONALD** (b.29 Sep'46, Bristol) – drums

		R.S.O.	R.S.O.
May 73.	(7") *(2090 109)* **RED LIGHT SONG. / LOOK AROUND**	□	-
Jul 73.	(7") *(2090 114)* <405> **LITTLE JODY. / THE WAY THINGS ARE**	□	□
Aug 73.	(lp) *(2394 105)* <873> **BLUE**	□	□

– Red light song / Look around / Someone / Sunset regret / Timi's black arrow / Sitting on a fence / Little Jody / Let me know / I wish I could fly / Skye banana boat song / The way things are / Sunshine or falling rain. *(cd-iss. Nov99 on 'The Record Label'; SPINCD 2007)*

—— added **SMIGGY** (b. ROBERT SMITH, 30 Mar'46, Kiel, Germany) – guitar, vocals

May 74.	(7") *(2090 130)* **LONESOME. / MAX BYGRAVES**	□	-
Jul 74.	(lp) *(2394 133)* **LIFE IN THE NAVY**	□	-

– Sweet memories / Lonesome / Sad Sunday / Atlantic Ocean / Love / Max Bygraves / You give me love / Big bold love / Mr. Moon / Let's talk it over. *(cd-iss. Nov99 on 'The Record Label'; SPINCD 2008)*

Feb 75.	(7") *(2090 154)* <508> **TOO MANY COOKIES IN THE JAR. / DON'T LET THIS FEELING GO**	□	□
Jun 75.	(7") *(2090 163)* **ROUND AND ROUND. / I KNOW HOW IT FEELS**	□	-

—— **NICHOLSON + MacMILLAN** recruited **DAVID NICHOLSON** – bass, guitar, keyboards + **CHARLIE SMITH** – drums

		Rocket	Rocket-MCA
Apr 77.	(7") *(ROKN 522)* <40706> **GONNA CAPTURE YOUR HEART. / THE SHEPHERD**	18	88
May 77.	(lp) *(ROLL 7)* <2290> **ANOTHER NIGHT TIME FLIGHT**	□	□

– Another night time flight / Fantasy woman / The shepherd / Strange thing / Bring back the love / I'm alone / Tired of loving you / Capture your heart / I understand. *(cd-iss. Nov99 on 'The Record Label'; SPINCD 2001)*

Jul 77.	(7") *(ROKN 527)* **ANOTHER NIGHT TIME FLIGHT. / FALLING**	□	-
Aug 77.	(7") <40762> **ANOTHER NIGHT TIME FLIGHT. / I'M ALONE**	-	□
Sep 77.	(7") *(ROKN 531)* **BRING BACK THE LOVE. / TIRED OF LOVING YOU**	□	-
Oct 77.	(7") <40801> **BRING BACK THE LOVE. / FALLING**	-	□
Nov 77.	(7") *(ROKN 534)* **WOMEN. / I'M ALONE**	□	-
Feb 79.	(7") *(XPRES 8)* **STRANGEST TOWN. / CHANGE IN THE WEATHER**	□	-
Mar 79.	(lp) *(TRAIN 4)* **FOOL'S PARTY**	□	-

– Strangest town / Danger sign / Mexico / Mona / I don't want to leave her / Victim / Blue nights / Love sings / Fool's party / Without you / Long enough / How beautiful. *(cd-iss. Oct99 on 'The Record Label'; SPINCD 2002)*

Apr 79.	(7") *(XPRES 10)* **LOVE SINGS. / I'LL GET YOU BACK**	□	-
May 79.	(7") *(XPRES 16)* **DANGER SIGN. / CELLAR FLOOR**	□	-

—— BLUE sadly split up after above

– compilations, others, etc. –

1987.	(7") *Old Gold; (OG 9699)* **GONNA CAPTURE YOUR HEART. /**	□	-
Oct 99.	(cd) *The Record Label; (SPINCD 2004)* **THE L.A. SESSIONS**	□	-
Oct 99.	(cd) *The Record Label; (SPINCD 2006)* **COUNTRY BLUE**	□	-

BLUES COUNCIL (see under ⇒ "A Beat(en) Generation")

BODKIN

Formed: Falkirk, Stirlingshire . . . early 70's by Prog-rockers ZEIK HUME, MICK RIDDEL, DOUG ROME, BILL ANDERSON and DICK SNEDDON.

After a few years of touring the toilet circuits of Scotland, BODKIN – which apparently means a small blunt instrument used in craft/needlework – "progressed" to the final of the National Rock Band Contest Of Great Britain. Hosted by the NME, BODKIN came in second and might've won had they not been forced to use standard toned-down equipment instead of their own Fenders, Hammonds and Marshalls. With a heavy bias towards SABBATH-meets-ELP type guitar riffs and crashing keyboards, BODKIN were determined to release their own album.

In 1972, local record producer Jim West helped them achieve their ambition and recorded (at local Central Studios!) their one and only eponymous LP which was sold at gigs. Dark, mystical and indeed heavy, the players decided to concentrate on their day jobs. Highly collectable and subsequently worth over £300, the master tapes were obtained by a German collector who finally found an outlet in Italy ('Akarma' records) to release it on CD. With a new fold-out cross sleeve and occult artwork courtesy of Giorgius Mangora, the five-track album hit a few independent shops late 2000.

ZEIK HUME (b.1950) – vocals / **MICK RIDDEL** (b.1946) – lead guitar / **DOUG ROME** (b.1950) – keyboards / **BILL ANDERSON** (b.1943) – bass / **DICK SNEDDON** (b.1950) – drums

		West	not iss.
1972.	(lp) *(CSA 104)* **BODKIN**	□	-

– Three days after death pt.1 / Three days after death pt.2 / Aunty Mary's trashcan / After your lumber / Plastic man. *(re-iss. Oct00 on 'Akarma' lp/cd; AK 125/+CD)*

—— never released anything else and split almost immediately

Isabel BOND (see under ⇒ "A Beat(en) Generation")

BOOTS (see under ⇒ "A Beat(en) Generation" – BEACHCOMBERS)

BOSTON DEXTERS (see under ⇒ WHITE, Tam)

BO WEEVILS (see under ⇒ TEAR GAS)

BREAD, LOVE AND DREAMS

Formed: Edinburgh . . . 1968 by pastel folkies, DAVID McNIVEN and ANGIE REW, the pair completing the line-up with CAROLYN DAVIS and session men from PENTANGLE, TERRY COX and DANNY THOMPSON.

With the aforementioned PENTANGLE (complete with BERT JANSCH) and INCREDIBLE STRING BAND all the rage, BREAD, LOVE AND DREAMS designed their version of flower-power folk-rock possibly a little too late to obtain any real credibility. Nonetheless, three albums (all very collectable now – the third over £200!), were released by 'Decca' over the course of a few years. Their eponymous debut in '69 – which featured their one and only 45, 'VIRGIN KISS' – was followed by 'THE STRANGE TALE OF CAPTAIN SHANNON AND THE HUNCHBACK FROM GIGHA' (1970) and 'AMARYLLIS' (1971), the latter showcasing the lengthy title track on one side; very Progressive and adventurous for a so-called Folk act.

DAVID McNIVEN – vocals, keyboards, guitar / **ANGIE REW** – vocals, flute / with **CAROLYN DAVIS** – guitar, vocals / plus **TERRY COX + DANNY THOMPSON** (of PENTANGLE) on rhythm

		Decca	not iss.
Aug 69.	(7") *(F 12958)* **VIRGIN KISS. / SWITCH OUT THE SUN**	□	-
Sep 69.	(lp; mono/stereo) *(LK/SKL 5008)* **BREAD, LOVE AND DREAMS**	□	-

– Switch out the sun / Virgin kiss / Least said / Falling out backwards / Lady of the night / Main street / Artificial light / Until she needs you / Mirrors / Poet's song / Yellowbellied redback / 95 octane gravy. *(cd-iss. Sep01 on 'Hugo Montes'; HMPCD 006)*

Sep 70.	(lp; mono/stereo) *(LK/SKL 5048)* **THE STRANGE TALE OF CAPTAIN SHANNON AND THE HUNCHBACK FROM GIGHA**	□	-

– Hymn for Sylvia / Masquerade / Sucking on a cigarette / He who knows all / Lobster quadrille / Butterfly land / Purple hazy melancholy / Sing me a song / The strange tale of Captain Shannon and the hunchback from Gigha.

Jun 71.	(lp) *(SKL 5081)* **AMARYLLIS**	□	-

– Amaryllis, part 1 – Out of the darkness, into the light, part 2 – Zoroaster's prophecy, part 3 – Light / Time's the thief / My staircupboard at 3 a.m. / Brother John / Circle of the night.

— prior to the above set, CAROLYN was already working with The LOOKING GLASS, who released one single, 'CAN YOU BELIEVE' / 'FREEDOM IN OUR TIME' for Philips (BF 1837) in 1970. Meanwhile, DAVID played clarinet for The HUMAN BEAST on their collectable set, 'INSTINCT' and apparently is still working inside the music scene (c.1990's).

Jack BRUCE

Born: JOHN SYMON ASHER BRUCE, 14 May'43, Bishopbriggs. At 17 he won a scholarship to R.S.A. of music although the prodigiously talented teenager joined local band JIM McHARG'S SCOTSVILLE JAZZBAND, before moving to London and playing in BLUES INCORPORATED with ALEXIS KORNER.

In 1963 he became a member of GRAHAM BOND ORGANISATION, joining JOHN MAYALL'S BLUESBREAKERS a couple of years later. He also released a one-off debut solo 45 around the same time and after a six month spell with MANFRED MANN, he made his greatest ever career move, co-forming legendary power trio, CREAM, alongside ERIC CLAPTON and GINGER BAKER. One of the greatest bass players of all time, his hard hitting style and booming vocals were an integral part of the CREAM sound, his technique mimicked by countless heavy rock bands in the years that followed.

After the band's demise in late 1968, he went solo, remaining with 'Polydor'. Recorded with a backing band including DICK HECKSTALL-SMITH and CHRIS SPEDDING, his debut album, 'SONGS FOR A TAILOR' (1969) hit the UK Top 10 despite its ambitious, idiosyncratic blend of jazz-fusion (the track 'THEME FOR AN IMAGINARY WESTERN' subsequently becoming a hit for MOUNTAIN). This was his only commercial success though, and subsequent albums such as 'HARMONY ROW' (1971) and 'OUT OF THE STORM' (1974) failed to chart. Featuring MICK TAYLOR on guitar, the latter set was a more straightforward hard rock effort, while the 1977 set, 'HOW'S TRICKS' was recorded under the JACK BRUCE BAND moniker.

1980 saw him team up with DAVID SANCIOUS, DAVE CLEMPSON and BILLY COBHAM as JACK BRUCE & FRIENDS, releasing an album for 'Epic'. He then teamed up with another veteran guitarist, ROBIN TROWER, for an album on 'Chrysalis', although throughout much of the ensuing decade he focused on his drug and alcohol problems.

The 90's saw BRUCE reunited with old mucker GINGER BAKER for the ethnic flavoured 'A QUESTION OF TIME', the pair subsequently forming BBM along with GARY MOORE and enjoying Top 10 success with 'AROUND THE NEXT DREAM'. Sadly for JACK, his son and member of the AFRO CELT SOUND SYSTEM died in October, 1997.

In the summer of 2001, JACK was back with a fresh set of recordings, 'SHADOWS IN THE AIR' complemented by appearances by old chums CLAPTON, MOORE and DR. JOHN.

• **Trivia:** During 1970, he was also part of US jazz-rock outfit TONY WILLIAMS' LIFETIME, releasing album of same name.

JACK BRUCE – vocals, bass (ex-BLUES INCORPORATED, ex-GRAHAM BOND ORGANISATION) with session people

Polydor Atco

Dec 65. (7") *(BM 56036)* **I'M GETTIN' TIRED (OF DRINKING AND GAMBLING). / ROOTIN' TOOTIN'** [ ] [-]

— (see above for details between 1966 and 1968.) He brought in friends **JON HISEMAN** – drums / **DICK HECKSTALL-SMITH** – sax / **CHRIS SPEDDING** – guitar / etc.

Sep 69. (lp) *(583 058)* <33306> **SONGS FOR A TAILOR** [6] [55]
– Never tell your mother she's out of tune / Theme for an imaginary western / Tickets to water falls / Weird of Hermiston / Rope ladder to the Moon / The ministry of bag / He the Richmond / Boston ball game, 1967 / To Isengard / The clearout. *(re-iss. May84; 2459 360) (cd-iss. May88 & Apr97; 835 242-2)*

— **JOHN McLAUGHLIN** – guitar (solo artist), repl. SPEDDING

Jan 71. (lp) *(2343 033)* <33349> **THINGS WE LIKE** [ ] [ ]
– Over the cliff / Statues / Sam enchanted Dick (medley:- Sam's back / Rill's thrills) / Born to be blue / Hchhh blues / Ballad of Arthur / Things we like. *(re-iss. Apr71; 2310 070)*

— retained some past musicians, bringing in **LARRY COYRELL** – guitar / **MIKE MANDEL** – keyboards / **MITCH MITCHELL** – drums

Sep 71. (lp) *(2310 107)* <33365> **HARMONY ROW** [ ] [ ]
– Can you follow? / Escape to the Royal wood (on ice) / You burned the tables on me / There's a forest / Morning story / Folk song / Smiles and grins / Post war / Letter of thanks / Victoria sage / The consul at sunset. *(cd-iss. 1980's;)*

Oct 71. (7") *(2058 153)* **THE CONSUL AT SUNSET. / LETTER OF THANKS** [ ] [ ]

— In 1972/73, he became part of WEST, BRUCE & LAING (see; MOUNTAIN) He also collaborated on lp ESCALATOR OVER THE HILL with PAUL HAINES and CARLA.

— now with **MICK TAYLOR** – guitar / **CARLA BLEY** – piano / **RONNIE LEAHY** – keyboards / **BRUCE GARY** – drums

R.S.O. R.S.O.

Oct 74. (7") *(2090 141)* **KEEP IT DOWN. / GOLDEN DAYS** [ ] [-]

Nov 74. (lp) *(2394 143)* <4805> **OUT OF THE STORM** [ ] [ ]
– Pieces of mind / Golden days / Running through our hands / Keep on wondering / Keep it down / Into the storm / One / Timeslip. *(cd-iss.)*

— now with **SIMON PHILIPS** – drums / **HUGH BURNS** – guitar / **TONY HYMAS** – keyboards

Mar 77. (lp; as JACK BRUCE BAND) *(2394 180)* <1-3021> **HOW'S TRICKS** [ ] [ ]
– Without a word / Johnny B '77 / Times / Baby Jane / Lost inside a song / How's tricks / Madhouse / Waiting for the call / Outsiders / Something to live for.

— Friends: **DAVID SANCIOUS** – guitar, keyboards / **DAVE CLEMPSON** – guitar / **BILLY COBHAM** – drums

Epic Epic

Dec 80. (lp; as JACK BRUCE & FRIENDS) *(84672)* <JE 36827> **I'VE ALWAYS WANTED TO DO THIS** [ ] [ ]
– Hit and run / Running back / Facelift 318 / In this way / Mickey the fiddler / Dancing on air / Livin' without ja / Wind and the sea / Out to lunch / Bird alone.

— In 1981 he teamed up with BILL LORDAN and ROBIN TROWER to release lp 'B.L.T.' Early the following year he and ROBIN TROWER released 'TRUCE' album on 'Chrysalis'; *CHR/ZCHR 1352).* He returned to solo work after below 45 was featured on TV car advert.

Virgin Virgin

Jun 86. (7"/12") *(VS 875/+12)* **I FEEL FREE. / MAKE LOVE** [ ] [ ]

President Intercord

Jan 87. (lp/c) *(PTLS/PTLC 1082)* **AUTOMATIC** [ ] [ ]
– A boogie / Uptown breakdown / Travelling child / New world / Make love (part 2) / Green and blue / The swarm / Encore / Automatic pilot.

— next with **ANTON FIER** – drums (ex-PERE UBU) / **KENJI SUZUKI** – guitar

Epic Epic

Jan 88. (lp/c/cd; JACK BRUCE, ANTON FIER & KENJI SUZUKI) **INAZUMA SUPER SESSION – ABSOLUTELY LIVE (live)** [ ] [ ]
– Generation breakdown / White room / Out into the field / Working harder / Sittin' on top of the world / Sunshine of your love / Crossroads / Spoonful – Beat of rock.

— now with **VERNON REID, NICKY HOPKINS, ALLAN HOLDSWORTH, GINGER BAKER**

Jan 90. (cd/c/lp) *(465 692-2/-4/-1)* <45729> **A QUESTION OF TIME** [ ] [ ]
– Life on Earth / Make love / No surrender! / Flying / Hey now princess / Blues you can't lose / Obsession / Kwela / Let me be / Only playing games / A question of time. *(re-iss. Feb91;)*

— with **PETE BROWN** still lyricist / plus **ERIC CLAPTON** – lead guitar / **STUART ELLIOT** – drums / **PETER WIEHE** – rhythm guitar / **MAGGIE REILLY** – b.vocals / **CLEM CLEMPSON** – rhythm guitar, etc / **TRILOK GURTU** – percussion / and guests on 1 each **DICK HECKSTALL-SMITH + DAVID LIEBMAN** – saxophones

C.M.P. C.M.P.

Mar 93. (cd/c/lp) *(CMP CD/MC/LP 1001)* **SOMETHIN ELS** [ ] [-]
– Waiting on a word / Willpower / Ships in the night / Peace of the East / Close enough for love / G.B. dawn blues / Criminality / Childsong / F.M.

— with **GARY MOORE** – guitar, vocals / **MAGGIE REILLY** – vocals / **GARY 'Mudbone' COOPER** – vocals, percussion / **CLEM CLEMPSON** – guitars / **DICK HECKSTALL-SMITH** – saxophone / **BERNIE WORRELL** – keyboards / **PETE BROWN** – vocals, percussion / **GINGER BAKER + SIMON PHILLIPS + GARY HUSBAND** – drums / **FRANCOIS GARNY** – bass / **MALCOLM BRUCE** – acoustic guitar, keyboards / **JONAS BRUCE** – keyboards / **ART THEMIN** – saxophone / **HENRY LOWTHER** – trumpet / **JOHN MUMFORD** – trombone / + **KIP HANRAHAN**

Mar 94. (d-cd/d-c) *(CMP CD/MC 1005)* **CITIES OF THE HEART (live)** [ ] [ ]
– Can you follow? / Running thro' our hands / Over the cliff / Statues / First time I met the blues / Smiles & grins / Bird alone / Neighbor, neighbor / Born under a bad sign // Ships in the night / Never tell your mother she's out of tune / Theme for an imaginary western / Golden days / Life on Earth / NSU / Sitting on top of the world / Politician / Spoonful / Sunshine of your love. *(cd re-iss. Aug94 + Nov94 + Mar96 + Apr98; CMPCD 1005)*

BBM

(aka GINGER BAKER, JACK BRUCE & GARY MOORE) A near reformation of CREAM with MOORE taking the place of CLAPTON.

Virgin Capitol

Jun 94. (cd/c/lp) *(CD/TC+/V 2745)* <39728> **AROUND THE NEXT DREAM** [9] [ ]
– Waiting in the wings / City of gold / Where in the world / Can't fool the blues / High cost of living / Glory days / Why does love (have to go wrong) / Naked flame / I wonder (why are you so mean to me?) / Wrong side of town.

Jul 94. (7"/c-s) *(VS/+C 1495)* **WHERE IN THE WORLD. / DANGER ZONE** [57] [ ]
(cd-s+=) *(VSCDG 1495)* – The world keeps on turnin'.
(cd-s) *(VSCDX 1495)* – ('A'side) / Sittin' on top of the world / I wonder (why are you so mean to me?).

JACK BRUCE

Sep 95.	(cd) *(CMPCD 1010)* **MONKJACK**		-

– Third degree / The boy / Shouldn't we / David's harp / Know one blues / Time repairs / Laughing on music / Street / Folksong / Weird of Hermiston / Tightrope / The food / Immoral ninth.

		Sanctuary	Sanctuary
Jul 01.	(cd) *(SANCD 84) <84511>* **SHADOWS IN THE AIR**		

– Out into the fields / 52nd Street / Heart quake / Boston ball game 1967 / This anger's a liar / Sunshine of your love / Directions home / Milonga / Dancing on air / Windowless rooms / Dark heart / Mr. Flesh / He the Richmond / White room / Surge.

– compilations, others, etc. –

on 'Polydor' UK unless mentioned otherwise

1974.	(d-lp) *(2659 024) / R.S.O.; <PD 3505>* **AT HIS BEST**		1972
Nov 80.	(d-lp)(d-c) *(2658 137)(3524 218)* **GREATEST HITS**		
Jul 89.	(d-lp/c/cd) *(837 806-1/-4/-2)* **WILLPOWER** *(cd re-iss. Apr95; same)*		
May 92.	(cd/c) *Castle; (CCS CD/MC 326)* **THE COLLECTION**		-
Nov 92.	(cd; JACK BRUCE & FRIENDS) *Traditional Line; (TL 1324)* **LIVE AT THE BOTTOM LINE (live)**		-
May 94.	(cd; by DICK HECKSTALL-SMITH, JACK BRUCE & JOHN STEVENS) *Atonal; (EFA 11956-2)* **THIS THAT**		-
Sep 95.	(cd) *Windsong; (WINCD 076)* **BBC LIVE IN CONCERT** *(re-iss. Jul98 on 'Strange Fruit'; SFRSCD 067)*		-
Aug 96.	(cd) *C.M.P.; (CMPCD 1013)* **THE COLLECTORS EDITION** *(re-iss. May98; same)*		-
Mar 98.	(cd) *Strange Fruit; (WHISCD 010)* **LIVE ON THE TEST**		-
Nov 99.	(cd) *Ranch Life; (CRANCH 15)* **CONCERT CLASSICS**		-
Sep 01.	(d-cd) *Burning Airlines; (<PILOT 125>)* **DOING THIS . . . ON ICE! (live in 1980)**		Oct01
Aug 02.	(d-cd) *Superior; (SU 29501)* **JACK BRUCE AND FRIENDS IN CONCERT (live)**		-

BUZZ (see under ⇒ WHITE, Tam)

Sol BYRON & THE IMPACTS (see under ⇒ "A Beat(en) Generation")

C

Junior CAMPBELL

Born: WILLIAM CAMPBELL, 31 May'47, Glasgow. Once the lead singer/guitarist of MARMALADE (and its embryonic predecessor DEAN FORD & THE GAYLORDS; '63-'70), JUNIOR launched his solo career in 1971 and signed to 'Deram' records. However, his prosperous time with "Ob-La-Di, Ob-La-Da" chart-toppers MARMALADE didn't guarantee a hit single, not at first anyway as his maiden solo effort, 'GOODBYE BABY JANE' flopped.

The following Autumn, CAMPBELL resurrected his musical Soul and armed with some gospel harmonics, the man had his first UK Top 10 hit via 'HALLELUJAH FREEDOM'. Waiting for the right moment to strike again, CAMPBELL's patience paid off when another single, 'SWEET ILLUSION', reached the Top 20. Subsequent singles all failed miserably to get the man back into chart action, and when his album, 'SECOND TIME AROUND' (1974), floundered, he should have just called it a day; the record was also noteable for containing over-produced covers of the Beatles' 'DRIVE MY CAR' and Dylan's 'POSITIVELY 4th STREET'. Luckily for him but unfortunately for punters, JUNIOR secured a new deal with ELTON JOHN's imprint, 'Rocket' in 1975. Yet after only five singles (two of them for 'Private Stock') and an AWOL sophomore LP, he plummeted even further.

After a spell at the production desk in the late 70's/early 80's, CAMPBELL subsequently penned the theme tune to the popular UK children's animation, 'Thomas The Tank Engine' (and 'Tugs'); well, at least old JUNIOR finally got to work alongside 'Thomas . . .' narrator RINGO STARR.

JUNIOR CAMPBELL – vocals, guitar, keyboards, harmonica (ex-MARMALADE) / with **PETE ZORN** – sax, flute / **RICK WEST** – bass / **RAYMOND DUFFY** – drums

		Deram	not iss.
Oct 71.	(7") *(DM 344)* **GOODBYE BABY JANE. / IF I CALL YOUR NAME**		-
Sep 72.	(7") *(DM 364)* **HALLELUJAH FREEDOM. / ALRIGHT WITH ME**	10	-
May 73.	(7") *(DM 387)* **SWEET ILLUSION. / ODE TO KAREN**	15	-
Oct 73.	(7") *(DM 403)* **(REACH OUT AN') HELP YOUR FELLOW MAN. / PRETTY BELINDA**		-
Feb 74.	(lp) *(SML 1106)* **SECOND TIME AROUND**		-

– (Reach out an') Help your fellow man / Drive my car / Carolina days / Wanderin' man / Somethin' deep in my soul / Pretty Belinda / Sweet illusion / Alone in my room / All gonna have a good time / Positively 4th Street / Hallelujah freedom.

Jun 74.	(7") *(DM 414)* **SWEET LADY LOVE. / IF I COULD BELIEVE YOU DARLIN'**		-
Oct 74.	(7") *(DM 421)* **OL' VIRGINIA. / WILLIE SINGS THE BLUES**		-

		Rocket	not iss.
Apr 76.	(7") *(ROKN 509)* **CARABINO LADY. / SOUTHERN MAN**		-
Sep 76.	(7") *(ROKN 514)* **HERE COMES THE BAND. / PICK UP**		-
Jan 77.	(7") *(ROKN 518)* **BABY HOLD ON. / PICK UP**		-

		Private Stock	not iss.
Mar 78.	(7") *(PVT 141)* **HIGHLAND GIRL. / CLIMB ON BOARD**		-
Sep 78.	(7") *(PVT 171)* **AMERICA. / RADIO MAN**		-

—— CAMPBELL moved into production and writing children's TV themes

– compilations, etc. –

Oct 83.	(7") *Old Gold; (OG 9358)* **HALLELUJAH FREEDOM. / SWEET ILLUSION**		-
Dec 01.	(d-cd) *Castle; (CMDDD 398)* **SECOND TIME AROUND** (all material)		-

Ian CARR (see ⇒ Section 5: Jazz)

CARTOONE

Formed: Glasgow . . . 1968 out of the largely unknown CHEVLONS. The line-up of bassist/vocalist DEREK CREIGON, guitarist MIKE ALLISON, guitarist MO TROWERS and drummer CHICK COFFILS, only managed to issue one 1966 flop single, 'TOO LONG ALONE', before they were posted missing. However, when a demo tape of the band (now called CARTOONE) filtered through to LULU agent for 'Atlantic', Mark London, things took a dramatic turn for the better. Supposedly signed to the aforementioned label on the same day as LED ZEPPELIN, CARTOONE duly spent time in the studio (with JIMMY PAGE on lead guitar!) perfecting their own brand of Caledonian Blues. Premiered by the single, 'KNICK KNACK MAN', their eponymous debut (released in Spring '69) bombed. To boost sales of the flagging set, CARTOONE were duly shipped off to tour North America, although MIKE's jitters got the better of him. Substituted at the last minute by local pal, LESLIE HARVEY (the brother of ALEX who was with POWER at the time) who temporarily filled his shoes.

Impressed by LESLIE's unique guitar style, Mark London tried to persuade him to stay with CARTOONE but the man wanted back to Glasgow, his girlfriend and POWER. Even 'ZEPPELIN manager/guru, Peter Grant, flew in from the States to see LES (and his group) playing at The Burns Howff but wasn't too disappointed with what he saw. Grant almost immediately signed HARVEY, BELL, DEWAR and McGINNIS, who became the soon-to-be legendary Blues giants STONE THE CROWS. Meanwhile, the unanimated CARTOONE disappeared for the very last time, leaving STC to take their place in Rock'n'Roll history.

CHEVLONS

DEREK CREIGON – vocals, bass / **MIKE ALLISON** – guitar / **MO TROWERS** – guitar / **CHICK COFFILS** – drums

		Pye	not iss.
1966.	(7") *(7N 17145)* **TOO LONG ALONE. / IT'S MY PROBLEM**		-

—— the group later changed their name to . . .

CARTOONE

		Atlantic	Atlantic
Jan 69.	(7") *(584 240)* **KNICK KNACK MAN. / A PENNY FOR THE SUN**		
Apr 69.	(lp) *(588 174) <SD 8219>* **CARTOONE**		

– Knick knack man / Withering wood / The sadness of Toby Jugg / A penny for the sun / I'll stay / Girl of yesterday / I can't walk back / Let me reassure you / Mr. Poor man / Ice cream dreams / Doing what mamma said / See me.

CHEVLONS (see under ⇒ CARTOONE)

CLOUDS

Formed: Edinburgh . . . 1968 by IAN ELLIS, HARRY HUGHES and BILLY RITCHIE. They had previously cut their teeth in R&B combo The PREMIERS, before forming underground act 1-2-3 (not to be confused with folk-pop act, ONE TWO & THREE) and making their debut at Falkirk's 'La Bamba' in November '66. The following year, they secured a deal with Brian Epstein's agency, although after his untimely death they were dropped.

However, as The CLOUDS, they signed to 'Island' with the help of impresario TERRY ELLIS, who brought in orchestra arranger DAVID PALMER (his past credits included JETHRO TULL). Their debut 45, 'MAKE NO BONES ABOUT IT', duly arrived in March '69, with their debut album following five months later. The aptly named 'SCRAPBOOK' was a directionless collection of ambitious, lyrically dour, group-penned songs, redeemed to a certain extent by sporadic bursts of humour. The title track was released as a second single although it was a further two years before they released the follow-up album, 'WATERCOLOUR DAYS'. The record attempted to blend together pop and progressive rock, again failing to strike a chord with the majority of the buying public. They played their final gig in October '71, with only IAN and HARRY re-showing on unheard demos of BOWIE's 'Hunky Dory'.

BILLY RITCHIE – keyboards, vocals, guitar / **IAN ELLIS** – guitar, vocals, bass / **HARRY HUGHES** – drums

		Island	Deram
Mar 69.	(7") *(WIP 6055)* **MAKE NO BONES ABOUT IT. / HERITAGE**		-
Aug 69.	(lp) *(ILPS 9100) <DES 18044>* **SCRAPBOOK** <US title 'UP ABOVE OUR HEADS'>		
	– Introduction – Scrapbook / The carpenter / The colours have run / I'll go girl / Grandad / Ladies and gentlemen / Humdrum / Union Jack / Old man / Waiter, there's something in my soup / Scrapbook.		
Sep 69.	(7") *(WIP 6067)* **SCRAPBOOK. / THE CARPENTER**		-
Dec 71.	(lp) *(ILPS 9151) <DES 18058>* **WATERCOLOUR DAYS**		
	– Watercolour days / Cold sweat / Lighthouse / Long time / Mind of a child / I know better than you / Leavin' / Get off my farm / I am the melody.		

—— split later in 1971, RITCHIE and group becoming anonymous once again

– compilations, etc. –

Jul 96.	(cd) *Beat Goes On; (BGOCD 317)* **SCRAPBOOK / WATERCOLOUR DAYS**		-

CODY (see under ⇒ TRASH)

Brian CONNOLLY

Born: 5 Oct'45, Hamilton, Lanarkshire. BRIAN was to find out in his late teens that he had actually been adopted; much later he discovered that the actor, Mark McManus, was in fact his half-brother.

Having left Scotland for the brights lights of London in the mid-60's, well Harrow to be exact, BRIAN filled the recently vacated (by noneother than IAN GILLAN) frontman position in local Beat combo, WAINWRIGHT'S GENTLEMEN. From here it was but a short step to the SWEETSHOP, the duo formed in early '68 by BRIAN and fellow former "GENTLEMAN", MICK TUCKER. By 1970, the classic SWEET line-up was in place with STEVE PRIEST and ANDY SCOTT completing the quartet. Hooking up with the Chinn-Chapman songwriting team, THE SWEET satiated the nation's appetite for sugary Glam-pop via an impressive string of massive-selling hits. From 1971's 'CO-CO' through 1973's 'BLOCKBUSTER' and 'BALLROOM BLITZ' and on to 1975's comeback of sorts 'FOX ON THE RUN', the platinum-mopped CONNOLLY was the band's heartthrob focal point, central to their OTT, wildly effeminate image.

However, the sex, drugs and rock'n'roll took its time-honoured toll, especially on CONNOLLY, whose heavy drinking only deteriorated when he left the band in '78. His recorded solo output amounted to a solitary single in 1982 for 'Carrere', 'HYPNOTIZED' / 'FADE AWAY', although his love of performing meant he was never far from the stage.

During the 80's, CONNOLLY's health became severely impaired as he suffered a series of heart attacks as well as a nervous disorder triggered by a bout of pneumonia. Although he'd given up drinking completely by the late 80's, BRIAN's fragile medical condition eventually led to death from renal failure on the 10th of February, 1997.

COPYCATS (see under ⇒ MY DEAR WATSON)

Ivor CUTLER

Born: 15 Jan'23, Govan, Glasgow. IVOR was brought up in the tenements of the largely industrial/docklands area of Glasgow and he was educated at Shawlands Academy. He subsequently worked for Rolls Royce and spent time in the RAF before he was dismissed. Having moved south to London in the early 50's, IVOR the poet/humourist/cartoonist began a career in teaching at A.S. Neill's Summerhill school.

In 1959, he featured on a Radio 4 special, entitled 'Monday Night At Home'. Early the following decade saw him forming his own comic trio, before he realised his own individual eccentric appeal and potential while working as a cartoonist for The Observer and Private Eye. In 1967, he took up the invitation to star as BUSTER BLOODVESSEL in The BEATLES' film 'Magical Mystery Tour'. By the mid-70's, after touring alongside SOFT MACHINE and ROBERT WYATT, etc (he had also become a regular on the John Peel radio show since 1969), IVOR signed to Richard Branson's (then) avant-garde label, 'Virgin'. This period brought forth the excellent albums 'DANDRUFF', 'VELVET DONKEY' & 'JAMMY SMEARS'.

In the 80's, he joined the 'Rough Trade' stable (home of ROBERT WYATT), and returned with the 'PRIVILEGE' album. He continued to write (i.e. children's book, poetry and one on philosophy 'Befriend A Bacterium') and in May '97, he surprisingly turned up on the now-famous 'Creation' label (home of OASIS, etc) with comeback 83-track album, 'A WET HANDLE', (also the name of his fourth series of Radio 3 night-time shows). Later that month, CUTLER took part in the 'Meltdown' festival at London's South Bank, alongside performance artist LAURIE ANDERSON and LOU REED. Of all people to even attempt an IVOR CUTLER song!, was American avant-gardist, JIM O'ROURKE, who virtually made 'WOMEN OF THE WORLD' his own.

CUTLER is both surreal and unhinged, a comic genius, aged, but down-to-earth and side-splittingly funny. An avant-garde artiste in every (non)sense of the word who prefers to listen to jazz legends KEITH JARRETT and THELONIUS MONK.

IVOR CUTLER TRIO

IVOR CUTLER – words, keyboards

Fontana not iss.

1959. (7"ep) *(TFE 17144)* **IVOR CUTLER OF Y'HUP** ☐ [-]
– Here's a health to Simon / Size 9 1/2 / Mary is a cow / Pickle your knees / Gravity begins at home / A cowpuncher and a bird / The Boo-Boo bird.

Decca not iss.

1961. (7"ep) *(DFE 6677)* **GET AWAY FROM THE WALL** ☐ [-]
– Stick out your chest / Turkish bath play / There's a turtle in my soup / Gruts for tea / Get away from the wall / The Tureen.

1961. (lp) *(LK 4405)* **WHO TORE YOUR TROUSERS?** ☐ [-]
– Steady job / The obliging fairy / First love / Who tore your trousers, James? / Are you alright, Jack? / A red flower / Do you ever feel lonely? / A warning to the flies / The market place / Grass seed / A tooth song / Egg meat / Muscular song / The handyman / As Chi.

Parlophone not iss.

Aug 67. (7") *(R 5624)* **I HAD A LITTLE BOAT. / A GREAT GREY GRASSHOPPER** ☐ [-]

1967. (lp) *(PCS 7040)* **LUDO** ☐ [-]
– Mud / A great grey grasshopper / Darling, will you marry me twice / A still, small fly / Deedle deedly, I pass / I had a little boat / Cockadoodledon't / Shoplifters / Mary's drawer / I'm happy / I'm going in a field / Go on, jump! / Flim flam flum / Good morning! how are you? shut up! / Last song / A suck of my thumb / The shapely balloon. *(cd-iss. Mar97 & Jun02 on 'Creation-Rev-ola'; CREV 049CD)*

Virgin not iss.

Oct 74. (lp) *(V 2021)* **DANDRUFF** ☐ [-]
– Hair grips / I believe in bugs / Fremsley / I'm walking to a farm / Baby sits / Life in a Scotch sitting room, Vol.12, Ep.1 / Vein girl / Five wise saws / Piano tuner song a.d. 2000 / An old Oak tree / My mother has two red lips / etc. *(re-iss. Mar84 lp/c; OVED/+C 33)*

Oct 75. (lp) *(V 2027)* **VELVET DONKEY** ☐ [-]
– If your breasts / I got no commonsense / Useful cat / Oh my eyes / The dirty dinner / Yellow fly / Mother's love / The meadow's go / Phonic poem / Life in a Scotch sitting room, Vol.2, Ep.2 / Birdswing / Nobody knows / Uneventful day / Little black buzzer / Bread and butter / A nuance / Go and sit upon the grass / The even keel / Pearly gleam / The best thing / Life in a Scotch sitting room, Vol.2, Ep.7 / Once upon a time / There's got to be something / The purposeful culinary instruments / Gee, amn't I lucky / The curse / I think very deeply / I slowly / Sleepy old snake / Titchy digits / The stranger. *(re-iss. Mar84 lp/c; OVED/+C 34)*

Sep 76. (lp) *(V 2065)* **JAMMY SMEARS** ☐ [-]
– Bicarbonate of chicken / Filcombe Cottage, Dorset / Squeeze bees / The turn / Life in a Scotch sitting room, Vol.2, Ep.11 / A linnet / Jumping and pecking / The other half / Beautiful cosmos / The path / Barabadabada / Big Jim / In the chestnut tree / Dust / Rubber toy / Unexpected join / Wooden tree / When I stand on an open cart / High is the wind / Surly buddy / Pearly-winged fly / Garden path at Filcombe / Paddington town / Cage of small birds / Life in a Scotch sitting room, Vol.2, Ep.6 / Irk / Lemon flower / Red Admiral / Everybody got / Wasted call. *(re-iss. Jul83 lp/c; OVED/+C 12)*

Harvest not iss.

Mar 78. (lp) *(SHSP 4084)* **LIFE IN A SCOTCH SITTING ROOM, VOL.2** ☐ [-]
– Episode 2 / Episode 3 / Episode 9 / Jungle tip – Owl, Ep.1 / Episode 11 / Jungle tip – Lion / Episode 5 / Episode 14 / Episode 7 / Episode 12 / Jungle tip – Leopard / Episode 8 / Episode 6 / Jungle tip – Boa / Episode 13. *(re-iss. Nov87 on 'Speakout' lp/c; SPOUT 2001/+C) (cd-iss. Apr02 on 'Rev-Ola'; CREV 1)*

Rough Trade not iss.

Jul 83. (7") *(RT 145)* **WOMAN OF THE WORLD. / COUNTING SONG** ☐ [-]

Jul 83. (lp; IVOR CUTLER & LINDA HIRST) *(ROUGH 59)* **PRIVILEGE** ☐ [-]
– Sit down / Use a brick / Home is the sailor / For practice / A doughnut in my hand / Fair's fair / Killer bee (jungle tip) / Whale badge / Blue bear / Creamy pumpkins / Counting song / My darling / Life in a Scotch sitting room (Vol.2, Episode 15) / Mostly tins / Tomato brain / Bad eye / Silent "S" / Halfway through / Look at the moon / Old black dog / The gathering doubt / Pussy on the mat / Large & puffy / People run to the edge / Country door / Piranhas (jungle trip) / Brenda / I love you but I don't know what I mean / Breathing regularly / Life in a Scotch sitting room (Vol.2, Episode 16) / Full of goods / Ok, I'll count to 8 / Secret drinker / Pass the ball Jim (for John Peel) / Over you go / Step it out lively, boys / Uncut moquette / Women of the world.

Apr 86. (lp) *(ROUGH 98)* **GRUTS** ☐ [-]

Nov 86. (d-lp) *(ROUGH 89)* **PRINCE IVOR** ☐ [-]

Strange Fruit not iss.

Feb 89. (12"ep) *(SFPS 068)* **PEEL SESSIONS** ☐ [-]

Creation not iss.

May 97. (cd/c) *(CRECD/C-CRE 217)* **A WET HANDLE** ☐ [-]
– Her tissues / An American drink / One day / Out of decency / My disposition / No. I won't / It's stupid / By the bush / The Thatcher generation / My vest / Goosie / When it wants / Her Zimmer / The farmer's wife / Bets / Just in time / The specific sundry / Just listen / The breaking point / Spring back / Hell / A man / The place / Hello explorer! / Not asking / His slow hand / Local creatures / Heptagon / Where's my razor? / One side / Singing to my foot / Ride off / A great albatross / A BERD / Half & half / Get off the road / A fine example / Faces of people / Stand well clear / Naughty Sydney / Perverse / The bargain / Space sandwich / Baked beetles / Taking hands / Entities / It / A kitchen knife / Not from hens / The carpet / Beyond / The way out / To take / Do you call that living? / On holiday / The taste of gunny / A blunt yashmak / The kiddies / I give up / My window box / A pain in the neck / Not even / Tablets / Flat thin chests / A good girl / He himself / Uncrossing her legs / Crete – Greece / Squeaky / Oddly comforting / An original sweet / The bridge / Butterfly / Snaps / Just / Hummed & hawed / Thursday / A cosy nest / A slice of seedcake / What a funny room / Heavy rock / The whole forest / Little Hetty.

Jun 98. (cd/c) *(CRECD/C-CRE 236)* **A FLAT MAN** ☐ [-]
– A bubble or two / A flat man / Jam / Alone / What have you got? / What? / Out with the light / I ate a lady's bun / One at a time / Living donkey / And so do I / Excitement / Questionaire / Bleeding shoes / A ball in a barrel / Blind / My next album / Aquarium / Flies / The dichotomy of love / Lemonade / Birdswing / Turn to the right / Empty house at Little Bedwyn / I built a house / Dumb dames / Jackfish / The bowling green / Patronage / One of the best / Search for Grace / A romantic man / True courage / Knocking at my door / Moist flier / Old boots / The long way / Your smell / Fish / Shoes / Deductive lepidopteron / Stubborn vassals / Filcombe cottage brook / Gorbals 1930 / British museum / Smack! / Ep.1. Doing the bathroom.

— in 1999, IVOR featured on V/A comp, 'Cute (h)ey?' on 'E.M.I.'

D

Jackie DENNIS

Born: 1942, Edinburgh. Young, free and kilted might well have described this updated, rock'n'roll version of SIR HARRY LAUDER. Early in 1958, JACKIE scored a UK Top 5 smash with his debut 45, 'LA DEE DAH', the tartan gimmick (also used by ANDY STEWART) was now set in place. What the Americans thought of young JACKIE when he was promoted on The Perry Como Show in America was anybody's guess. However, blushes were spared when his follow-up, 'MY DREAM', failed to register, although he did have one more chart success with a Top 30 cover of Sheb Wooley's 'PURPLE PEOPLE EATER'.

JACKIE DENNIS – vocals / with orchestra, etc

		Decca	not iss.
Feb 58.	(7",78) *(F 10992)* **LA DEE DAH. / YOU'RE THE GREATEST**	4	-
Apr 58.	(7",78) *(F 11011)* **MY DREAM. / MISS VALERIE**		-
Jun 58.	(7",78) *(F 11033)* **PURPLE PEOPLE EATER. / YOU-OO**	29	-
Sep 58.	(7",78) *(F 11060)* **MORE THAN EVER (COMA PRIMA). / LINTON ADDIE**		-
Nov 58.	(7",78) *(F 11090)* **LUCKY LADYBUG. / GINGERBREAD**		-
		Top Rank	not iss.
Jun 59.	(7",78) *(JAR 129)* **SUMMER SNOW. / NIGHT BIRD**		-

— JACKIE retired from the studio until . . .

		Special Request	not iss.
Apr 82.	(12") *(LR 5)* **ROCK YOUR LOVER. /**		-

– compilations, etc. –

1958.	(7"ep) *Decca; (DFE 6513)* **JACKIE DENNIS No.1** – La dee dah / You're the greatest / My dream / Miss Valerie.		-

Karl DENVER

Born: ANGUS McKENZIE, 16 Dec'34, Glasgow. A real oddity of the early 60's scene and perhaps a man ahead of his time in terms of world music, KARL DENVER was inspired by the exotic sounds he heard on his global travels in the merchant navy. His multi-octave vocal abilities and yodelling tendencies marked him out from many of his contemporaries while his clean-cut, pseudo C&W image projected him as a kind of bizarre Scots SLIM WHITMAN.

Over the course of 1961/'62, 'Decca' singles 'MARCHETA', 'MEXICALI ROSE' and 'NEVER GOODBYE' were all Top 10 hits while his Zulu chanting signature tune, 'WIMOWEH' – adapted from The TOKENS' hit, 'The Lion Sleeps Tonight' – reached the Top 5. Although he continued to score further minor hits up until the mid-60's, only a cover of Bill Anderson's 'STILL' threatened to trouble the Top 10 and KARL increasingly moved into cabaret.

Following 1974's lone 'SONNY BOY' single, he retired from the recording studio only to resurface more than a decade and a half later at the height of Manchester's baggy scene. Having lived in the city for years, DENVER was roped into a collaboration with infamous Madchester faves The HAPPY MONDAYS. The resulting 'LAZY ITIS – ONE ARMED BOXER' was a Top 50 hit during the summer of 1990 and the experience no doubt spurred him on to cut a new single, 'WON'T GIVE UP' and album, 'JUST LOVING YOU' (1993). Sadly, KARL was to die on 21st December 1998; a posthumous album, 'MOVIN' ON', was released the following year.

KARL DENVER – vocals, acoustic guitar

		Decca	unknown
Jun 61.	(7") *(F 11360)* **MARCHETA. / JOE SWEENEY**	8	
Oct 61.	(7") *(F 11395)* **MEXICALI ROSE. / BONNY SCOTLAND**	8	
Dec 61.	(lp) *(ACL 1098)* **WIMOWEH** (above issued on 'Ace Of Clubs') *(re-iss. Feb74 on 'Eclipse'; ECS 2139)*	7	-
Jan 62.	(7") *(F 11420)* **WIMOWEH. / GYPSY DAVY**	4	
Feb 62.	(7") *(F 11431)* **NEVER GOODBYE. / HIGHLAND FLING**	9	
May 62.	(7") *(F 11470)* **A LITTLE LOVE, A LITTLE KISS. / LONELY SAILOR**	19	
Sep 62.	(7") *(F 11505)* **BLUE WEEKEND. / MY MOTHER'S EYES**	33	
1962.	(lp) *(ACL 1131)* **KARL DENVER** *(above issued on 'Ace Of Clubs')*		-
Dec 62.	(7") *(F 11553)* **DRY TEARS. / PASTURES OF PLENTY**		-
Mar 63.	(7") *(F 11608)* **CAN YOU FORGIVE ME. / LOVE FROM A HEART OF GOLD**	32	
Jun 63.	(7") *(F 11674)* **INDIAN LOVE CALL. / MY MELANCHOLY BABY**	32	
1963.	(lp) *(LK 4540)* **LIVE AT THE YEW TREE (live)** –		-
Aug 63.	(7") *(F 11720)* **STILL. / MY CANARY HAS CIRCLES UNDER HIS EYES**	13	
Feb 64.	(7") *(F 11828)* **MY WORLD OF BLUE. / THE GREEN GRASS GROWS ALL AROUND**	29	
May 64.	(7") *(F 11905)* **LOVE ME WITH ALL YOUR HEART. / AM I THAT EASY TO FORGET?**	37	
1964.	(lp) *(LK 4596)* **WITH LOVE** –		-
Nov 64.	(7") *(F 12025)* **SALLY. / SWANEE RIVER**		-
		Mercury	not iss.
1965.	(7") *(MF 878)* **CRY A LITTLE SOMETIMES. / TODAY WILL BE YESTERDAY TOMORROW**		-
1965.	(7") *(MF 904)* **MARTA. / I'LL NEVER FORGET TO REMEMBER**		-
1965.	(7") *(MF 926)* **THE TIPS OF MY FINGERS. / I'M ALONE BECAUSE I LOVE YOU**		-
		Page One	not iss.
Apr 68.	(7"; as KARL DENVER TRIO) *(POF 063)* **YOU'VE STILL GOT A PLACE IN MY HEART. / I STILL MISS SOMEONE**		-
		Eclipse	not iss.
1970.	(lp) *(ECS 2013)* **KARL DENVER** – Canoe song / She moved thro' the fair / Careless love / Three lovely lassies from Bannion / Silver and gold / O'Brian the brave engineer / Walk on by / Sierra Sue / Moonlight becomes you / Weary blues / Far away / Highland fling.		-
		Emerald	not iss.
Nov 74.	(7") *(MD 1181)* **SONNY BOY. / CARELESS LOVE**		-

— he retired from the studio and lived in Manchester.

— in Jun'90, KARL collaborated on the HAPPY MONDAYS Top 50 hit, 'LAZYITIS – ONE ARMED BOXER'

		Plaza	not iss.
Aug 93.	(cd-s) *(PZA 074CD)* **WON'T GIVE UP /**		-
Oct 93.	(cd/c) *(PZA 004 CD/MC)* **JUST LOVING YOU** – From a jack to a king / Garden party / I can't stop loving you / San Fernando / King of the road / Just loving you / Song for Maria / Walk on by / Won't give up / Runaway / Voices of the Highlands / Little bitty tear / Travelling light / Answer to everything / Story of my life.		-

— sadly, KARL was to die on the 21st of December, 1998

Oct 99.	(cd/c) *(PZA CD/MC 014)* **MOVIN' ON** –		-

– compilations, etc. –

1962.	(7"ep) *Decca; (DFE 8501)* **BY A SLEEPY LAGOON**		-
1962.	(7"ep) *Decca; (DFE 8504)* **KARL DENVER HITS**		-
May 69.	(7") *Decca; (F 12928)* **WIMOWEH. / NEVER GOODBYE** *(re-iss. Sep85 on 'Old Gold'; OG 9535)*		-
1974.	(lp) *Eclipse; (ECS 2139)* **WIMOWEH** – Wimoweh / China doll / Open up dem pearly gates / Shin gan goo / Mexicali rose / Vella langra / Zimba / Rose Marie / Blue yodel / If I had my way / Marcheta / The peanut vendor.		-
Apr 85.	(c) *Autograph; (ASK 776)* **GREATEST HITS**		-
Feb 86.	(lp) *Decca; (TAB 90)* **THE VERY BEST OF KARL DENVER**		-
Feb 92.	(lp/c) *Pickwick; (PWKM/+C 4096P)* **NEVER GOODBYE – HIS VERY BEST** – Wimoweh / Still / Marcheta / Toodle-um-day / Eight times ten / If I had my way / Blue weekend / I can't help it / Mexicali rose / Love me with all your heart / Can you forgive me / Indian love call / My world of blue / O'Brian the brave engineer / My mother's eyes / Never goodbye.		-
Aug 99.	(cd) *Spectrum; (544126-2)* **THE BEST OF KARL DENVER** (all his hits) *(re-iss. Sep00 on 'Platinum'; PLATCD 580)*		-

Jim DIAMOND

Born: 28 Sep'51, Glasgow. JIM DIAMOND began his career as a club singer in Glasgow, performing in a band, JADE, that included future SENSATIONAL ALEX HARVEY BAND bassist CHRIS GLEN.

At the turn of the 70's, he was invited to join BLACK CAT BONES, which led him to Aberdeen-based group GULLY FOYLE. In 1975, JIM released an independent debut single, 'CLEAN UP THE CITY', before founding rock act BANDIT alongside JAMES LITHERLAND, DANNY McINTOSH, CLIFF WILLIAMS and GRAHAM BROAD. Despite a major label deal with 'Arista', the band's eponymous debut was a commercial clanger in 1977's punk-fired climate and although they went on to record a second album

('Partners In Crime'), JIM went his own way. After working with the late blues guru ALEXIS KORNER and producing ZOOT MONEY, he formed soul-pop act, PhD alongside classically-trained keys man, TONY HYMAS. Also featuring PHIL PALMER, SIMON PHILIPS, MARK CRANEY and STAN SULZMANN, the 'Warners'-signed group hit paydirt almost immediately as their synth-swooning debut single, 'I WON'T LET YOU DOWN', topped the UK chart. Although their eponymous debut album made the Top 40, subsequent singles bombed and DIAMOND was prevented from promoting sophomore effort, 'IS IT SAFE?' after contracting hepatitis.

He bounced back in late '84 with the tonsil-testing weepie, 'I SHOULD HAVE KNOWN BETTER', his second No.1 hit. Now signed to 'A&M' on a solo deal, DIAMOND scored a further major hit in 1986 with 'HI HO SILVER', the theme tune to TV drama series, 'Boon'. Again, he failed to capitalise on the success as a series of follow-up singles and an album, 'DESIRE FOR FREEDOM', met with poor sales.

Nevertheless, the man has remained a ubiquitous figure in the music industry, working with an array of artists both in a session and production capacity as well as performing live from time to time. 1993 found DIAMOND back in the charts as a 'Polygram TV' retrospective made the UK Top 20 while 1994 saw him recording again in his own right, releasing a couple of singles and an album, 'SUGAROLLY DAYS' for the independent 'Righteous' label. The latter was a combination of self-penned numbers (one written with GRAHAM LYLE) and traditional covers, 'COULTER'S CANDY (ALI BALI BE)', being an embarrassing example.

JIM DIAMOND

Bradley | not iss.

Apr 75. (7") *(BRAD 7511)* **CLEAN UP THE CITY. / BACK ON THE LINE** [ ] [-]

BANDIT

JIM DIAMOND – vocals / **JAMES LITHERLAND** – guitar (ex-MOGUL THRASH, etc) / **DANNY McINTOSH** – guitar, vocals / **CLIFF WILLIAMS** – bass, vocals / **GRAHAM BROAD** – drums, percussion

Arista | Arista

Feb 77. (lp) *(ARTY 149) <4113>* **BANDIT** [ ] [ ]
– Ohio / Hard on a loser / The leader of the pack / Dance when you boogie / Mr. James / Hung up on your love / Rocking my soul out / Pulling them punches / All coming back to me / Love and understanding.

Mar 77. (7") *(ARIST 89)* **OHIO. / ALL I CAN DO TO GET OVER IT** [ ] [ ]

Jun 77. (7") *(ARIST 115)* **LOVE AND UNDERSTANDING. / DANCE WHEN YOU BOOGIE** [ ] [-]

— BANDIT carried on for another album, 'Partners In Crime', without JIM, and, for that matter, without many of the others

PhD

JIM DIAMOND – vocals / **TONY HYMAS** (b. England) – keyboards, synthesizer / with also **PHIL PALMER** – guitar / **SIMON PHILLIPS + MARK CRANEY** – drums / **STAN SULZMANN** – sax

WEA | Warners

Feb 82. (7") *(K 79209)* **I WON'T LET YOU DOWN. / HIDEAWAY** [1] [ ]

Apr 82. (lp/c) *(K/K4 99150)* **PhD** [33] [ ]
– Little Suzie's on the up / War years / Oh Maria / Oo sha sha / I won't let you down / There's no answer to it / Poor city / Up down / Hollywood signs / Radio to on.

Jun 82. (7") *(K 79223)* **LITTLE SUZIE'S ON THE UP. / I'M GONNA TAKE YOU TO THE TOP** [ ] [-]

Apr 83. (7"/12") *(U 9996/+T)* **I DIDN'T KNOW. / THEME FOR JENNY** [ ] [-]

May 83. (lp) *(U 0050)* **IS IT SAFE?** [ ] [-]
– I don't know / Pretty ladies / Johnny / Shotgun romance / Changing partners / No right to be sad / Fifth of May / No happy endings / Beautiful day / New York City.

JIM DIAMOND

A&M | A&M

Oct 84. (7"/12") *(AM/+X 220)* **I SHOULD HAVE KNOWN BETTER. / THE IMPOSSIBLE DREAM** [1] [ ]

Jan 85. (7"/12") *(AM/+Y 229)* **I SLEEP ALONE AT NIGHT. / CALEDONIA** [72] [-]

May 85. (7") *(AM 247)* **REMEMBER I LOVE YOU. / ROCK'N'ROLL** [42] [-]

Jun 85. (lp/c/cd) *(AMA/AMC/CDA 5029)* **DOUBLE CROSSED** [ ] [ ]
– Double crossed / I sleep alone at night / After the fire / I should have known better / Stumblin' over / Remember I love you / New generation / Co-operation / She is woman / I'm yours / The impossible dream / Caledonia.

— in Sep'85, JIM DIAMOND and the song 'YOU CALL THIS VICTORY' appeared on a TONY BANKS ep.

Jan 86. (7"/12") *(AM/+Y 296)* **HI HO SILVER. / (instrumental)** [5] [ ]

Apr 86. (7"/12") *(AM/+Y 314)* **DESIRE. / TOGETHER** [ ] [-]

Jul 86. (7") *(AM 332)* **YOUNG LOVE (CARRY ME AWAY). / BLUE SONGS** [ ] [-]
(c-s+=) *(AMS 332)* – Young love / I should have known better / Remember I love you / Hi ho silver.

Sep 86. (lp/c/cd) *(AMA/AMC/CDA 5131)* **DESIRE FOR FREEDOM** [ ] [-]
– Desire / So strong / Young love (carry me away) / My weakness is you / I can't stop / Maybe one day / Hi ho silver / Judy's not that tough / You'll go crazy.

1987. (7") *(AM 367)* **SO STRONG. / YOU'LL GO CRAZY** [ ] [-]

Tembo | not iss.

Jun 87. (7"/12") *(TML/+X 126)* **SHOUT IT OUT. / THE MESSAGE OF CHILDWATCH** [ ] [-]

WEA | not iss.

Feb 89. (7") *(YZ 373)* **BROADWAY. / SECOND CHANCE** [ ] [-]

Polygram | not iss.

May 93. (cd/c) *(843847-2/-4)* **JIM DIAMOND** (compilation) [16] [-]
– Not man enough / Hi ho silver (theme from 'Boon') / I still love you / I won't let you down (PhD) / We dance the night away / I should have known better / It's true what they say / If you're gonna break my heart / Our love / Child's heart / Goodnight tonight.

Righteous | not iss.

May 94. (c-ep/cd-ep) *(JDS CD/TC 1)* **THE CALEDONIA E.P.** [ ] [-]
– Caledonia (heartland) / A red, red rose / Coulter's candy / Skye boat song.

Aug 94. (cd-s) *(JDSCD 2)* **SUGAROLLY MOUNTAINS** [ ] [-]

Sep 94. (cd/c) *(JDA CD/TC 1)* **SUGAROLLY DAYS** [ ] [-]
– Sugarolly mountains / The road to Dundee / One day without fear / Ae fond kiss / Coulter's candy (ali bali be) / The road to Flodigarry / Caledonia (heartland) / Wild mountain thyme (Will ye go lassie go) / Eastern promise / A red, red rose / The rowan tree / Skye boat song.

– compilations, etc. –

Oct 88. (7") *Old Gold; (OG 9813)* **I SHOULD HAVE KNOWN BETTER. / HI HO SILVER** [ ] [-]

Mar 99. (cd) *Spectrum; (554890-2)* **THE BEST OF JIM DIAMOND** [ ] [-]

Barbara DICKSON

Born: 27 Sep'47, Dunfermline, Fife. Something of a Scottish institution, BARBARA DICKSON has enjoyed a career spanning more than three decades during which time she's dabbled in a variety of musical genres and successfully negotiated both stage and screen.

Having left Woodmills High School at the age of 16/17, BARBARA moved to Edinburgh where she pursued her musical ambitions in the city's folk clubs while holding down a day job in the registry office. 'THE FATE O' CHARLIE' marked her vinyl debut in 1969, an independently released album which presaged a move to major label, 'Decca' at the turn of the decade. Continuing in a folk vein, BARBARA recorded 'THRO' THE RECENT YEARS' (1970) as a joint effort with ARCHIE FISHER while the albums 'DO RIGHT WOMAN' and 'FROM THE BEGGAR'S MANTLE FRINGED WITH GOLD' followed in '71 and '72 respectively. Throughout this period, the feisty Fifer worked with some of the roots scene's major players including GERRY RAFFERTY (who also worked with BILLY CONNOLLY in The HUMBLEBUMS) and DAVE MATTACKS, yet it was in the world of theatre that Babs was to find her true calling, or at least her big break. In 1974 she landed a high profile part in the BEATLES-inspired musical, 'John, Paul, George, Ringo . . . and Bert', performing at Liverpool's Everyman Theatre before the show began an extended run in London's West End. The soundtrack was released on the 'R.S.O.' label, with whom BARBARA also signed a solo contract.

Not coincidentally, she enjoyed her first chart success not long after when the title track from the 'ANSWER ME' (1976) album made the UK Top 10. Successive singles and albums further enhanced her position in the MOR/Adult contemporary market as she left her folk days far behind, going into the new decade on a high as 'THE BARBARA DICKSON ALBUM' (1980) went Top 10 and spawned one of her best known hits, 'JANUARY FEBRUARY'. 1982's compilation, 'ALL FOR A SONG', confirmed her popularity, remaining on the chart for nigh on a year and peaking at No.3. The early 80's also saw the multi-talented singer returning to the West End where she took an award-winning part in the musical 'Blood Brothers'. Another musical, 'Chess', was to furnish BARBARA with her biggest selling single to date in the shape of the 1984 chart topper, 'I KNOW HIM SO WELL', a tear-jerking duet with ELAINE PAIGE.

A series of compilation releases and solo sets kept her in the charts through the mid-late 80's while the 90's have seen further interesting developments in her career. Musically, she went back to her roots, releasing an album's worth of choice BOB DYLAN covers, 'DON'T THINK TWICE IT'S ALRIGHT' (1992). This was followed by a couple of back to basics efforts, 'PARCEL OF

ROGUES' (1994) and 'THE DARK END OF THE STREET' (1995), the latter album released on revamped roots label, 'Transatlantic'. In its choice of title track, the 1995 set also recalled her 'DO RIGHT WOMAN' album from way back in 1971, both songs of course, being Dan Penn/Spooner Oldham classics from the heyday of Southern country-soul. Like most of BARBARA's albums, these reached the Top 40 yet to most people the singer was more recognisable for her various TV roles including hard-bitten prostitution drama, 'Band Of Gold' and Scots detective series, 'Taggart'.

90's stage productions such as 'The 7 Ages Of Woman' and 'Spend, Spend, Spend' have seen BARBARA put in further award-winning performances and although her recording career has been put on the back burner, she continues to sell out concert halls around the country.

BARBARA DICKSON – vocals, piano / with session people

Trailer not iss.

1969. (lp; ARCHIE FISHER – BARBARA DICKSON – JOHN MacKINNON) *(LER 3002)* **THE FATE O' CHARLIE** [ ] [-]
– Cam ye o'er frae France / The three healths / Wha wadna fecht for Charlie / The white cockade / My bonnie Heiland laddie / The Highland widow's lament / The battle of Prestonpans / Killiecrankie / O'er the water to Charlie / Prince Charlie / Highland Harry / The fate o' Chatlie / The Highlander's lament / O'er the water / The flowers o' the forest.

Decca not iss.

Aug 70. (lp; as BARBARA DICKSON & ARCHIE FISHER) *(SKL 5041)* **THRO' THE RECENT YEARS** [ ] [-]
– The January man / You like the sun / Morning / Tears of rage / Friends and lovers / Somebody counts on me / Frolicsome alcoholic mermaid / If I'd stayed around / Lullaby for father / I am the great sun / First of the few / Fiddler's green / Together forever / Through the recent years.

Feb 71. (lp) *(SKL 5058)* **DO RIGHT WOMAN** [ ] [-]
– Easy to be hard / Turn a deaf ear / Something's wrong / The Garton mother's lullaby / Dainty Davy / Returning / Do right woman, do right man / The long and lonely winter / A lover's ghost / The blacksmith / Gloomy Sunday / And I will sing. *(cd/c re-iss. Aug92 on 'Deram'+=; 820959-2/-4)* – You like the sun / Thro' the recent years / Tears of rage / Fiddler's green.

Jun 72. (lp) *(SKL 5116)* **FROM THE BEGGAR'S MANTLE FRINGED WITH GOLD** [ ] [-]
– Witch of the Westmorlands / If I never, ever saw you again / The recruited collier / The morning lies heavy on me / Fine flowers in the valley / Lord Thomas of Winesberry and the king's daughter / The climb / The orange and the blue / Winter's song.

below also featured **GERRY RAFFERTY, JOE EGAN, KEVIN PEEK, DAVE MATTACKS, PETE ZORN**, etc

R.S.O. R.S.O.

1974. (lp) *(2394 141)* **JOHN, PAUL, GEORGE, RINGO AND BERT** (musical with the London Cast) [ ] [ ]
– I should have known better / Your mother should know / Ooee boppa / With a little help from my friends / Penny Lane / In the bleak midwinter / Here comes the sun / The long and winding road / Clap and cheer / Help! / Lucy in the sky with diamonds / You never give me your money – Carry that weight / We can work it out / I will be your love / A day in the life.

Nov 74. (7") *(2090 144)* **HERE COMES THE SUN. / THE LONG AND WINDING ROAD** [ ] [ ]

May 75. (7") *(2090 161)* **BLUESKIES. / FINE FEATHERS** [ ] [-]

Nov 75. (7") *(2090 174)* **ANSWER ME. / FROM NOW ON** [9] [ ]

Mar 76. (7") *(2090 186)* **PEOPLE GET READY. / GIVE ME SPACE** [ ] [-]

Jun 76. (7") *(2090 194)* **OUT OF LOVE WITH LOVE. / BOYS FROM THE MEN** [ ] [-]

Sep 76. (lp/c) *(2394/3216 167)* **ANSWER ME** [ ] [ ]
– People get ready / Boys from the men / My man / Lean on me / Goodbye dreamer / End of the world / Answer me / Goodbye to the cries / From the heart / Let it go / Judgement day / Driftaway. *(re-iss. 1985 on 'Polydor' lp/c; SPE LP/MC 5)*

Jan 77. (7") *(MCA 266)* **ANOTHER SUITCASE IN ANOTHER HALL. / REQUIEM FOR EVITA** [18] [ ]
(above issued on 'M.C.A.' and from 'Evita')

Apr 77. (7") *(2090 240)* **LOVER'S SERENADE. / HIGH TIDE** [ ] [-]

May 77. (lp/c) *(2394/3216 188)* **MORNING COMES QUICKLY** [58] [ ]
– Deep into my soul / Lover's serenade / Morning comes quickly / It makes me feel good / High tide / Who was it stole your heart away / When you touch me this way / I could fall / There's a party in my heart / Stolen love. *(re-iss. Mar85 on 'Polydor' lp/c; SPE LP/MC 91)*

Sep 77. (7") *(2090 258)* **I COULD FALL. / HE'S A FIREMAN** [ ] [-]

C.B.S. not iss.

Nov 78. (7") *(CBS 6825)* **CITY TO CITY. / BENNY GEE** [ ] [-]

Jan 79. (7") *(CBS 6977)* **FALLEN ANGEL. / LIGHT AS A FEATHER** [ ] [-]

Epic Epic

Aug 79. (7") *(EPC 7713)* **CAME BACK WITH THE SAME LOOK. / SWEET OASIS** [ ] [-]

Sep 79. (lp/c) *(EPC/40 83198)* **SWEET OASIS** [ ] [ ]
– Benny Gee / City to city / Fallen angel / Jesus train / Light as a feather / Magic man / Second sight / St. Joan / Talk to you / Sweet oasis. *(re-iss. Jun81 lp/c; EPC/40 32011)*

Dec 79. (7") *(EPC 8103)* **CARAVAN SONG. / CARAVANS ON THE MOVE** [41] [ ]

Feb 80. (7") *(EPC 8115)* **JANUARY FEBRUARY. / ISLAND IN THE SUN** [11] [ ]

Apr 80. (lp/c) *(EPC/40 84088)* **THE BARBARA DICKSON ALBUM** [7] [ ]
– January February / Any time / In the night / Hello stranger, goodbye my heart / Day and night / It's really you / Can't get by without you / I'll say it again / Now I don't know / Plane song. *(re-iss. Apr85 lp/c; EPC/40 32645) (cd-iss. Mar94 on 'Pickwick'; 982727-2)*

May 80. (7") *(EPC 8593)* **IN THE NIGHT. / NOW I DON'T KNOW** [48] [ ]

Jul 80. (7") *(EPC 8838)* **IT'S REALLY YOU. / PLANE SONG** [ ] [ ]

Mar 81. (7") *(EPCA 1058)* **ONLY SEVENTEEN. / YOU GOT ME** [ ] [ ]

May 81. (lp/c) *(EPC/40 84551)* **YOU KNOW IT'S ME** [39] [ ]
– Think it's over / Little by little in love / You know it's me / Hold on / We'll believe in lovin' / Only seventeen / You got me / I know you, you know me / I believe in you / My heart lies. *(re-iss. Sep93 on 'Spectrum' cd/c; 962982-2/-4)*

Jun 81. (7") *(EPCA 1293)* **MY HEART LIES. / YOU KNOW IT'S ME** [ ] [ ]

Nov 81. (7") *(EPCA 1858)* **RUN LIKE THE WIND. / FORGOTTEN TIME** [ ] [ ]

Jan 82. (lp/c) *(EPC/40 10030)* **ALL FOR A SONG** (compilation) [3] [ ]
– Run like the wind / Caravan song / Answer me / The long and winding road / Tonight / With a little help from my friends / January February / Will you love me tomorrow / Take good care / I believe in you / Another suitcase in another hall / Surrender to the sun. *(re-iss. Aug87; EPCBD 241) (re-iss. Nov88 lp/c/cd; 463002-1/-4/-2)*

Feb 82. (7") *(EPCA 1954)* **TAKE GOOD CARE. / TONIGHT** [ ] [ ]

Apr 82. (7") *(EPCA 2305)* **I BELIEVE IN YOU. / I KNOW YOU, YOU KNOW ME** [ ] [ ]

Oct 82. (7") *(EPCA 2882)* **HERE WE GO. / TONIGHT** [ ] [ ]

Nov 82. (lp/c) *(EPC/40 25086)* **HERE WE GO (LIVE ON TOUR)** [ ] [-]
– Caravan song / Answer me / Will you love me tomorrow / MacCrimmons lament / Stardust / January February / Drift away / Tonight / Come rain or come shine / Harden my heart / Here we go / Medley: Dancing in the street – He's a rebel – I only want to be with you – You keep me hangin' on.

Jan 83. (7") *(EPCA 3069)* **STOP IN THE NAME OF LOVE. / FIND A BETTER WAY** [ ] [-]

Aug 83. (7") *(EPCA 3684)* **TELL ME IT'S NOT TRUE. / TONIGHT** [ ] [-]

Sep 83. (m-lp) *(LLM 101)* **TELL ME IT'S NOT TRUE** [100] [-]
– Narration / Marilyn Monroe / My child / The Devil's got your number / Easy terms / Just a game / Sunday afternoon / My friend / Bright new day / One summer narration / Saying a word / Miss Jones (sign of the times) / Prison song / Light romance / There's a madman / Tell me it's not true. *(re-iss. Nov89 as 'BLOOD BROTHERS' lp/c/cd; LLM/+K/CD 3007)*
(above issued on 'Legacy' and from the musical 'BLOOD BROTHERS')

Mar 84. (7") *(EPCA 4191)* **KEEPING MY LOVE FOR YOU. / FIND A BETTER WAY** [ ] [-]

May 84. (7") *(EPCA 4413)* **I DON'T BELIEVE IN MIRACLES. / YOU DON'T KNOW WHAT YOU WANT** [ ] [ ]

Jun 84. (lp/c) *(EPC/40 25706)* **HEARTBEATS** [21] [ ]
– I don't believe in miracles / World without your love / Stop in the name of love / As time goes by / You don't know what you want / Tell me it's not true / We were never really out of love / One false move / The crying game / Keeping my love for you / Heartbeat's everything / MacCrimmon's lament.

— in Dec'84, ELAINE PAGE and BARBARA DICKSON had a UK No.1 hit with 'I KNOW HIM SO WELL', taken from the musical 'Chess' on 'R.C.A.'

M.C.A. not iss.

Mar 85. (7") *(MCA 955)* **STILL IN THE GAME. / PETER** [ ] [-]

Portrait not iss.

May 85. (7"/12") *(A/PRT 6169)* **CARAVAN SONG. / FORGOTTEN TIME** [ ] [-]

K-Tel not iss.

Nov 85. (lp/c/cd) *(ONE1/OCE2/ ONCD3 312)* **GOLD** [11] [-]
– I know him so well (with ELAINE PAIGE) / Missing you / Another good day for goodbye / Touch touch / Anyone who had a heart / A day in the life / You send me / What's love / Rivals / Soldiers / Rising water / Taking the next train home / If you're right. *(re-iss. Sep92 on 'Castle' cd/c; CLA CD/MC 297)*

Apr 86. (7") *(ONS 0008)* **IF YOU'RE RIGHT. / RIVALS** [ ] [-]

Sep 86. (7") *(BABS 1)* **TIME AFTER TIME. / SHE MOVES THRO' THE FAIR** [ ] [-]

Nov 86. (lp/c/cd) *(ONE1/OCE2/ONCD3 335)* **THE RIGHT MOMENT** [39] [-]
– The right moment / Tenderly / She moved thro' the fair / Time after time / Follow you, follow me / It's raining again today / Wouldn't it be good? / Boulder to Birmingham / Who are you anyway? / The vanishing days of love / Angie baby / Making history / Fine partly cloudy / If you go away. *(re-iss. Sep92 on 'Castle' cd/c; CLA CD/MC 310)*

Theobald Dickson not iss.

Oct 87. (lp/c/cd) *(TPD/+C/CD 001)* **AFTER DARK** [ ] [-]
– The right moment / Same day / Only a dream in Rio / Lush life / I don't believe in you / Caravan / Fortress in your heart / I think it's going to rain today / It's money that I love / Pride (in the name of love) / No milk today / I know him so well. *(re-iss. Aug92 on 'Castle' cd/c; CLA CD/MC 302)*

Feb 88. (7") *(TDPS 002)* **ONLY A DREAM IN RIO. / SAME SKY** [ ] [-]

Telstar not iss.

Apr 89. (lp/c/cd) *(STAR/STAC/TCD 2349)* **COMING ALIVE AGAIN** [30] [-]
– How long / It might be you / Precious cargo / Coming alive again / September

song / Dream of you / Every now and then / You're the voice / The letter / Give me one good reason / Song for Bernadette.

Valley not iss.

Apr 89. (7") *(VYL 1)* **COMING ALIVE AGAIN. /** [ ] [-]

Columbia not iss.

Aug 92. (cd/c) *(MOOD CD/C 25)* **DON'T THINK TWICE IT'S ALL RIGHT** [32] [-]
– Don't think twice, it's alright / With God on our side / When the ship comes in / Maggie's farm / Tears of rage / Oxford town / You ain't goin' nowhere / When I paint my masterpiece / The times they are a-changin' / Ring them bells / A hard rain's a-gonna fall / Blowin' in the wind.

Castle not iss.

Feb 94. (cd/c) *(CTV CD/MC 126)* **PARCEL OF ROGUES** [30] [-]
– Van Diemen's land / My lagan love / My Johnny was a shoemaker / Fine flowers in the valley / I once loved a lad / Jock o' Hazeldean / Sule skerry / Farewell to whisky / Lovely Joan / Donald Og / Geordie / Oh dear me / Parcel o' rogues.

Transatlatic not iss.

Nov 95. (cd/c) *(TRA CD/MC 117)* **THE DARK END OF THE STREET** [ ] [-]
– Young man cut down in his prime / The ballad of Springhill / Fine horseman / First time ever I saw your face / Brother, can you spare a dime / Love needs a heart / Who knows where the time goes / All the pretty little horses / The dark end of the street / Sandman's coming / Just one smile / Love hurts.

– compilations, etc. –

Jul 81. (lp) *Decca; (TAB 24)* **I WILL SING** [ ] [-]
Aug 82. (c-ep) *Epic; (EPCA40 2623)* **4 TRACK CASSETTE EP** [ ] [-]
– January February / Another suitcase in another hall / Answer me / Caravan song.
Oct 82. (lp/c) *Contour; (CN/+4 2058)* **BARBARA DICKSON** [ ] [-]
May 84. (7") *Old Gold; (OG 9420)* **ANOTHER SUITCASE IN ANOTHER HALL. / Julie Covington: Don't Cry For Me Argentina** [ ] [-]
Jan 85. (lp) *K-Tel; (NE 1287)* **THE BARBARA DICKSON SONGBOOK** [5] [-]
(cd-iss. Nov86; NCD 3287)
Oct 86. (lp/c) *Telstar; (STAR/STAC 2276)* **THE VERY BEST OF BARBARA DICKSON** [78] [-]
Jan 87. (7") *Old Gold; (OG 9664)* **JANUARY FEBRUARY. / CARAVAN SONG** [ ] [-]
Sep 87. (d-lp/c) *Castle; (CCS LP/MC 163)* **THE COLLECTION** [ ] [-]
(cd-iss. Apr90; CCSCD 163)
Jul 91. (cd/c) *Connoisseur; (VSOP CD/MC 166)* **NOW AND THEN** [ ] [-]
Nov 92. (cd/c; shared w/ ELAINE PAIGE) *Telstar; (TCD 2632)* **THE BEST OF ELAINE PAIGE AND BARBARA DICKSON** [22] [-]
Feb 96. (cd/c) *Columbia; (483796-2/-4)* **THE BEST OF BARBARA DICKSON** [ ] [-]
– Caravan song / January February / In the night / The crying game / Run like the wind / The long and winding road / Tonight / With a little help from my friends / Answer me (live) / Can't get by without you / Will you love me tomorrow / Stop in the name of love / As time goes by / Stardust / It's really you / I don't believe in miracles / Now I don't know / Tell me it's not true / I believe in you. *(re-iss. Jul98; same)*
May 96. (cd/c) *Spectrum; (552012-2/-4)* **THE WORLD OF BARBARA DICKSON** [ ] [-]
(re-iss. Nov98; same)

Lonnie DONEGAN

Born: ANTHONY JAMES DONEGAN, 29 Apr'31, Glasgow. The son of a classical violinist who played with the Scottish National Orchestra, DONEGAN began playing guitar in his teens. He was also an avid fan of folk, country, blues and jazz, immersing himself in the sounds of FRANK CRUMIT, JOSH WHITE, HANK WILLIAMS, LOUIS ARMSTRONG, LEADBELLY, WOODY GUTHRIE, etc.

His musical ambitions eventually led him to London where he auditioned for CHRIS BARBER's band; the pair hit it off immediately and became lifelong friends. Following a stint of national service in Europe (where he was introduced to the musical delights of the American Forces Radio Network), DONEGAN returned to form The KEN COLYER JAZZMEN with BARBER and KEN COLYER. Between sets, DONEGAN took the spotlight and began developing the frantic hybrid of blues, jazz, folk and country that would come to be known as 'Skiffle'. Named – by COLYER's brother – after an old blues combo, the DAN BURLEY SKIFFLE GROUP, this unique sound kicked off a musical revolution almost as far reaching as ELVIS PRESLEY's lip-curling cross of rockabilly, gospel and jump-blues.

When COLYER departed the group in 1954, BARBER took the helm and the band soon found themselves in the studio courtesy of 'Decca'. DONEGAN (who now took the stage name LONNIE after a compere confused him with guitarist LONNIE JOHNSON) persuaded the A&R man to let them cut a couple of tracks in his skiffle style, subsequently included on the 10" album, 'NEW ORLEANS JOY' (1955). One of them, 'ROCK ISLAND LINE' (a trad folk song cut by LEADBELLY amongst others), was released as a single – under the LONNIE DONEGAN SKIFFLE GROUP moniker – and proceeded to tear up the charts as well as the musical rule book; six months later it had sold an incredible three million copies, staying on the UK chart for 22 weeks and even making the US Top 10, a feat previously unheard of for a British act. Follow-up track, 'DIGGIN' MY POTATOES', was banned by the BBC for its suggestive title (hmmm . . .), giving old LONNIE (who duly signed to 'Pye') one of the first 'rebel' tags of the era. The ban only served to increase his popularity and over the next decade, an avalanche of hit singles buried the UK chart including No.1's 'CUMBERLAND GAP', 'PUTTING ON THE STYLE' (both 1957) and comic novelty track, 'MY OLD MAN'S A DUSTMAN' (1960). The latter track became the first ever single to go straight in at No.1, reflecting DONEGAN's 'King Of Skiffle' status. Imitators were ten a penny, utilising any DIY instruments they could lay their hands on i.e. washboards, soup spoons, etc. In fact, a young PAUL McCARTNEY was one particularly mad keen fan, an early incarnation of The BEATLES playing at one of DONEGAN's folk appreciation society gigs in 1958.

Ironically, though, the fab four's own adaptation of rock's roots steered the course of pop music in a different direction and skiffle mania was all but over by the early 60's. LONNIE's last Top 20 hit came in 1962 with 'PICK A BALE O' COTTON' and after 'THE FOLK ALBUM' (1965) failed to capture the imagination of the new folkies on the block, DONEGAN concentrated on production work for 'Pye'. 1970's flop 'LONNIEPOPS' album marked the end of his tenure with the label and he subsequently worked in Germany where there was a brief skiffle mini-revival.

The man's curious brand of humour was showcased once more in 1976 with a one-off single, 'I'VE LOST MY LITTLE WILLIE'. Unfortunately he suffered a heart attack the same year and relocated to California to recuperate in the West Coast sun. 1978 saw the release of 'PUTTING ON THE STYLE', an all-star skiffle affair featuring the likes of RINGO STARR, RON WOOD and ELTON JOHN, all long time fans. The album actually made the UK Top 60 although the C&W follow-up, 'SUNDOWN' (1979) made little headway. 1981, meanwhile found him teaming up with Scots group, SHAKIN' PYRAMIDS for a one-off single although continuing heart problems curtailed him for much of the early-mid 80's. A further one-off single, 'DONEGAN'S DANCING SUNSHINE BAND', appeared in summer '87.

In 1995, DONEGAN was presented with an Ivor Novello award, an occasion which saw him singing with longtime fan VAN MORRISON. The pair discussed cutting some tracks together, the results finally emerging in 1999 on 'MULESKINNER BLUES', an 'R.C.A.' set combining old and new material with contributions from the likes of ALBERT LEE, JACQUI McSHEE and even SAM BROWN. Standout tracks, though, were the two pairings with VAN the MAN, on the rabble-rousing title track and the brilliant remake of 'I'M ALABAMMY BOUND'. Clearly, DONEGAN (or VAN for that matter) hasn't reached the end of the rock island line just yet; he recently added Glastonbury to his already packed gig diary while his fans straddle both the generation gap and geographical boundaries (from Land's End to Falkirk, at least!). Basically DONEGAN IS SKIFFLE and we are not worthy.

LONNIE DONEGAN – vocals, guitar, banjo with his Skiffle Group: **DENNY WRIGHT** – lead guitar / **MICKY ASHMAN** – upright bass / **NICK NICHOLS** – drums

Decca London

Nov 55. (7"/78; as The LONNIE DONEGAN SKIFFLE GROUP) *(F/FJ 10647)* *<1650>* **ROCK ISLAND LINE. / JOHN HENRY** [8] [8] Feb56
Feb 56. (7"/78; as The LONNIE DONEGAN SKIFFLE GROUP) *(F/FJ 10695)* **DIGGIN' MY POTATOES. / BURY MY BODY** [ ] [-]

Pye Nixa Mercury

Apr 56. (7"/78) *(7N/N 15036)* *<70872>* **LOST JOHN. / STEWBALL** [2] [58] May56
Jun 56. (7"ep) *(NJE 1017)* **SKIFFLE SESSION EP** [20] [-]
– Railroad Bill / Stackalee / Ballad of Jessie James / Ol' Riley.
Aug 56. (7"/78) *(7N/N 15071)* **BRING A LITTLE WATER, SYLVIE. / DEAD OR ALIVE** [7] [ ]
(below lp hit the singles chart due to non-existence of UK lp chart)
Dec 56. (10"lp) *(NPT 19012)* **LONNIE DONEGAN SHOWCASE LP** [26] [-]
– Wabash cannonball / How long how long blues / Nobody's child / I shall not be moved / I'm Alabammy bound / I'm a rambling man / Wreck of the old '97 / Frankie and Johnny. *(re-iss. 1968 on 'Marble Arch'; MAL 797)*
Dec 56. (lp) *<M 920229>* **AN ENGLISHMAN SINGS AMERICAN FOLK SONGS** [-] [ ]
Jan 57. (7"/78) *(7N/N 15080)* **DON'T YOU ROCK ME, DADDY-O. / I'M ALABAMMY BOUND** [4] [ ]
Mar 57. (7"/78) *(7N/N 15087)* **CUMBERLAND GAP. / LOVE IS STRANGE** [1] [ ]
May 57. (7"/78) *(7N/N 15093)* **GAMBLIN' MAN. / PUTTING ON THE STYLE (live)** [1] [ ]
Sep 57. (7"/78) *(7N/N 15108)* **MY DIXIE DARLING. / I'M JUST A ROLLING STONE** [10] [ ]

Nov 57. (10"lp) *(NPT 19027)* **LONNIE** [ ] [-]
– Lonesome traveller / The sunshine of his love / Ain't no more cane on the Brazos / Ain't you glad you've got religion / Times are getting hard, boys / Lazy John / Light from the lighthouse / I've got my rocks in my bed / Long summer day. *(cd-iss. Feb00 on 'Sequel'+=; NEMCD 343)* – (extra tracks).

Dec 57. (7"/78) *(7N/N 15116)* **JACK O'DIAMONDS. / HAM 'N' EGGS** [14] [ ]

Apr 58. (7"/78) *(7N/N 15129)* **THE GRAND COOLEE DAM. / NOBODY LOVES LIKE AN IRISHMAN** [6] [ ]

Jun 58. (7"/78) *(7N/N 15148)* **SALLY, DON'T YOU GRIEVE. / BETTY, BETTY, BETTY** [11] [ ]

Sep 58. (7"/78) *(7N/N 15158)* **LONESOME TRAVELLER. / TIMES ARE GETTING HARD BOYS** [28] [ ]

Sep 58. (lp) *(NPL 18034)* **TOPS WITH LONNIE** [ ] [-]
– Don't you rock me, daddy-o / Putting on the style / Gamblin' man / My Dixie darling / Bring a little water, Sylvie / Cumberland gap / Grand Coulee Dam / Saly, don't you grieve / Nobody loves likes an Irishman / Lost John / Does your chewing gum lose it's flavour / Tom Dooley.

Nov 58. (7"/78) *(7N/N 15165)* **LONNIE'S SKIFFLE PARTY (medley part 1: LITTLE LIZA JANE – PUTTING ON THE STYLE – CAMPTOWN RACES – KNEES UP MOTHER BROWN. / (medley part 2: SO LONG – ON TOP OF OLD SMOKEY – DOWN IN THE VALLEY – SO LONG** [23] [-]

Nov 58. (7"/78) *(7N/N 15172)* **TOM DOOLEY. / ROCK O' MY SOUL** [3] [ ]

Pye-Nixa Dot

Dec 58. (lp) <*DLP 3159*> **LONNIE DONEGAN** [-] [ ]

Jan 59. (7"/78) *(7N/N 15181)* <*15911*> **DOES YOUR CHEWING GUM LOSE ITS FLAVOUR. / AUNT RILEY** [3] [ ] Feb59
<*US re-iss. Jul61; same*> – hit No.5

Apr 59. (7"/78) *(7N/N 15198)* **FORT WORTH JAIL. / WHOA BUCK** [14] [ ]

May 59. (lp) *(NPL 18043)* **LONNIE RIDES AGAIN** [ ] [ ]
– Fancy talking tinker / Miss Otis regrets / Jimmie Brown the newsboy / Mr. Froggy / Take this hammer / The gold rush is over / You pass me by / Talking guitar blues / John Hardy / House of the rising sun / San Miguel. *(re-iss. 1969 on 'Marble Arch'; MAL 1153) (cd-iss. Feb00 on 'Sequel'+=; NEMCD 344)* – (extra tracks).

Pye Atlantic

Jun 59. (7"/78) *(7N/N 15206)* **BATTLE OF NEW ORLEANS. / DARLING COREY** [2] [ ]

Aug 59. (7"/78; Irish-only) *(7N/N 15219)* **KEVIN BARRY. / MY LAGAN LOVE** [-] [-]

Sep 59. (7"/78) *(7N/N 15223)* **SAL'S GOT A SUGAR LIP. / CHESAPEAKE BAY** [13] [ ]

Nov 59. (7"/78) *(7N/N 15237)* **SAN MIGUEL. / TALKING GUITAR BLUES** [19] [ ]

Dec 59. (lp) <*8038*> **SKIFFLE FOLK MUSIC** [-] [ ]

Mar 60. (7"/78) *(7N/N 15256)* **MY OLD MAN'S A DUSTMAN. / THE GOLDEN VANITY** [1] [ ]

May 60. (7"/78) *(7N/N 15267)* **I WANNA GO HOME (THE WRECK THE THE JOHN). / JIMMY BROWN THE NEWSBOY** [5] [ ]

Aug 60. (7"/78) *(7N/N 15275)* **LORELEI. / IN ALL MY WILDEST DREAMS** [10] [ ]

Nov 60. (7") *(7N 15312)* **LIVELY. / BLACK CAT (CROSS MY PATH TODAY)** [13] [ ]

Dec 60. (7") *(7N 15315)* **VIRGIN MARY. / BEYOND THE SUNSET** [27] [ ]

Mar 61. (7") *(7N 15330)* **(BURY ME) BENEATH THE WILLOW. / LEAVE MY WOMAN ALONE** [ ] [ ]

Apr 61. (lp) *(NPL 18063)* **MORE! TOPS WITH LONNIE** [ ] [-]
– Battle of New Orleans / Lorelei / Lively! / Sal's got a sugar lip / I wanna go home / Leave my woman alone / My old man's a dustman / Fort Worth jail / Have a drink on me / (Bury me) Beneath the willow / Little Liza Jane / Puttin' on the style / Camptown races / Knees up, Mother Brown / On top of Old Smokey / Down in the valley / So long.

May 61. (7") *(7N 15354)* **HAVE A DRINK ON ME. / SEVEN DAFFODILS** [8] [ ]

Aug 61. (7") *(7N 15371)* **MICHAEL ROW THE BOAT. / LUMBERED** [6] [ ]

Jan 62. (7") *(7N 15410)* **THE COMMANCHEROS. / RAMBLIN' ROUND** [14] [ ]

Mar 62. (7") *(7N 15424)* **THE PARTY'S OVER. / OVER THE RAINBOW** [9] [ ]

Jun 62. (7") *(7N 15446)* **I'LL NEVER FALL IN LOVE AGAIN. / KEEP ON THE SUNNYSIDE** [ ] [-]

Aug 62. (7") *(7N 15455)* **PICK A BALE OF COTTON. / STEAL AWAY** [11] [ ]

Dec 62. (7") **THE MARKET SONG. / TIT-BITS (with MAX MILLER & The LONNIE DONEGAN GROUP)** [ ] [-]

Pye A.B.C.

Dec 62. (lp) *(NPL 18073)* **SING HALLELUJAH** [ ] [ ]
– Sing hallelujah / We shall walk through the valley / No hiding place / Good news, chariot's a-comin' / Noah found grace in the eyes of the Lord / Joshua fit the battle of Jericho / His eye is on the sparrow / Born in Bethlehem / This train / New burying ground / Steal away / Nobody knows the trouble I've seen. *(cd-iss. Feb00 on 'Sequel'+=; NEMCD 345)* – (extra tracks).

Apr 63. (7") *(7N 15514)* **LOSING BY A HAIR. / TRUMPET SOUNDS** [ ] [-]

Jun 63. (7") *(7N 15530)* **IT WAS A VERY GOOD YEAR. / RISE UP** [ ] [-]

Sep 63. (7") *(7N 15564)* **LEMON TREE. / I'VE GOTTA GIRL SO FINE** [ ] [-]

Nov 63. (7") *(7N 15579)* **500 MILES AWAY FROM HOME. / THIS TRAIN** [ ] [-]

Jul 64. (7") *(7N 15669)* **BEANS IN MY EARS. / IT'S A LONG ROAD TO TRAVEL** [ ] [-]

Sep 64. (7") *(7N 15679)* **FISHERMAN'S LUCK. / THERE'S A BIG WHEEL** [ ] [-]

Mar 65. (7") *(7N 15803)* **GET OUT OF MY LIFE. / WON'T YOU TELL ME** [ ] [-]

Jul 65. (7") *(7N 15893)* **LOUISIANA MAN. / BOUND FOR ZION** [ ] [-]

Aug 65. (lp) *(NPL 18126)* **THE LONNIE DONEGAN FOLK ALBUM** [ ] [-]
– I'm gonna be a bachelor / Interstate forty / After taxes / Where in the world are we going / Diamonds of dew / Bound for Zion / She was T-bone talking woman / Wedding bells / Reverend Mr. Black / The doctor's daughter / Blistered / Farewell. *(re-iss. 1967 on 'Golden Guinea'; GGL 0382) (cd-iss. Feb00 on 'Sequel'+=; NEMCD 346)* – (extra tracks).

Jan 66. (7") *(7N 15993)* **WORLD CUP WILLIE. / WHERE IN THIS WORLD ARE WE GOING** [ ] [-]

May 66. (7") *(7N 17109)* **I WANNA GO HOME. / BLACK CAT (CROSS MY PATH TODAY)** [ ] [-]

Jan 67. (7") *(7N 17232)* **AUNT MAGGIE'S REMEDY. / MY SWEET MARIE** [ ] [-]

Columbia not iss.

Mar 68. (7") *(DB 8371)* **TOYS. / RELAX YOUR MIND** [ ] [-]

Decca not iss.

Nov 69. (7") *(F 12984)* **MY LOVELY JUANITA. / WHO KNOWS WHERE THE TIME GOES** [ ] [-]

1970. (lp) *(SKL 5068)* **LONNIEPOPS – LONNIE DONEGAN TODAY** [ ] [-]
– Little green apples / Hey! hey! / First of May / Both sides now / If you go away / Love song to a princess / Who knows where the times goes / What the world needs now is love / My lovely Juanita / Windmills of your mind / Long haired lover from Liverpool / And you need me.

Pye not iss.

Nov 70. (7") *(7N 45009)* **BURNING BRIDGES. / I CAN'T TAKE IT ANY MORE** [ ] [-]

R.C.A. not iss.

Oct 71. (7") *(RCA 2128)* **COME TO AUSTRALIA. / DON'T BLAME THE CHILD** [ ] [-]

Pye not iss.

Oct 72. (7") *(7N 45184)* **SPEAK TO THE SKY. / GET OUT OF MY LIFE** [ ] [-]

Jun 73. (7"; by LONNIE DONEGAN & KENNY BALL) *(7N 45252)* **WHO'S GONNA PLAY THIS OLD PIANO. / SOUTH** [ ] [-]

Philips not iss.

1974. (lp) *(6305 227)* **LONNIE DONEGAN MEETS LEINEMANN** [-] [-] German
– Casey's last ride / Bottle of wine / Dixie darling / Frankie and Johnny / Tops at loving you / Gloryland / Leinemann's potatoes / Me and Bobby McGee / Does your chewing gum lose its flavour / Becky Deen / Jack o' diamonds.

1976. (lp) *(6305 288)* **COUNTRY ROADS** [-] [-] German
– Country roads / Rock island line / Keep on the sunny side / Dixie Lily / Louisiana man / Dead or alive / Midnight special / Muleskinner blues / Roll in my sweet baby's arms / Lost John / Have a drink on me / Dublin O'Shea.

Black Lion not iss.

Jul 76. (7") *(BSP 45105)* **LOST JOHN. / JENNY'S BALL** [ ] [-]

Decca not iss.

Aug 76. (7") *(FR 13669)* **I'VE LOST MY LITTLE WILLIE. / CENSORED** [ ] [-]

Chrysalis U.A.

Jan 78. (7") *(CHS 2205)* **ROCK ISLAND LINE. / HAM 'N' EGGS** [ ] [-]

Feb 78. (lp/c) *(CHR/ZCHR 1158)* <*UALA 827*> **PUTTIN' ON THE STYLE** [51] [ ]
– Rock Island line / Have a drink on me / Ham 'n' eggs / I wanna go home / Diggin' my potatoes / Nobody's child / Puttin' on the style / Frankie and Johnny / Drop down baby / Lost John.

Apr 78. (7") *(CHS 2211)* **PUTTIN' ON THE STYLE. / DROP DOWN BABY** [ ] [-]

May 79. (lp/c) *(CHR/ZCHR 1205)* **SUNDOWN** [ ] [-]
– I'm all out and down / Home / Streamline train / Sundown / Mama's got the know how / Morning light / Louisiana sun / The battle of New Orleans / Cajun / Dreaming my dreams with you.

Virgin not iss.

Nov 81. (7"ep; with the SHAKIN' PYRAMIDS) *(VS 460)* **CUMBERLAND GAP / WABASH CANNONBALL. / DON'T YOU ROCK ME DADDY-O / ONLY MY PILLOW / GRAB IT AND GROWL** [ ] [-]

— next with guests MONTY SUNSHINE, CHRIS BARBER, KEN COLYER, etc

Dakota not iss.

Dec 81. (d-lp/d-c) *(ICSD/ZCICSD 2001)* **JUBILEE CONCERT (live Autumn 1981)** [ ] [-]
– Ace in the hole / Isle Of Capri / Going home / Shine / Jenny's ball / One sweet letter from you / Hush-a-bye / Bugle call march / Ice cream / John Henry / Take this hammer / Railroad Bill / Tom Dooley / New burying ground / Grand Coulee Dam / New York town / Miss Otis Regrets / Does your chewing gum lose its flavour on the bedpost overnight / One night of love / Rock island line / Gloryland / Corrina Corrina / Goodnight Irene.

Rosie's Records — not iss.

Jul 87. (7"; with MONTY SUNSHINE) *(RR 015)* **DONEGAN'S DANCING SUNSHINE BAND. / LEAVING BLUES** -

— In 1987 he turned actor, noteably in TV series 'Rockcliffe's Babies'

— LONNIE returned with more stars as backing

Capo-RCA — Capo-RCA

Jan 99. (cd) *(<CAPO 501>)* **MULESKINNER BLUES**
– Muleskinner blues (with VAN MORRISON) / Please don't call me in the morning / Rock island line / When I get off this feeling / Fancy talking tinker / I'm Alabammy bound (with VAN MORRISON) / Stewball / Skiffle / Welfare line / All together now / I don't wanna lose you / Poker club / Spanish nights / Always from the heart.

— in Jan'2000, LONNIE hit the UK Top 20 (No.14) with VAN MORRISON and CHRIS BARBER on their album, 'THE SKIFFLE SESSIONS, LIVE IN BELFAST'

– compilations, others, etc. –

Jan 56. (78) *Nixa-Jazz; (NJS 2006)* **MIDNIGHT SPECIAL. / WHEN THE SUN GOES DOWN** -

1956. (7"ep) *Jazz Today; (JTE 107)* **BACKSTAIRS SESSION** -
– Midnight special / When the sun goes down / New burying ground / Worried man blues. *(re-iss. 1956 on 'Pye-Nixa'; NJE 1014)*

Nov 56. (78) *Oriole; (CB 1329)* **THE PASSING STRANGER. / (B-side by Tommy Reilly)** -

Dec 56. (7",78) *Columbia; (DB 3850)* **ON A CHRISTMAS DAY. / TAKE MY HAND PRECIOUS LORD** -

1957. (7"ep) *Pye-Nixa; (NEP 24031)* **HIT PARADE** -
– Lost John / Stewball / Bring a little water / Dead or alive.

1957. (7"ep) *Pye-Nixa; (NEP 24040)* **HIT PARADE VOL.2** -
– Cumberland gap / Love is strange / Don't you rock me, daddy-o / I'm Alabammy bound.

1958. (7"ep) *Pye-Nixa; (NEP 24067)* **HIT PARADE VOL.3** -
– Putting on the style / My Dixie darling / Gamblin' man / I'm just a rolling stone.

1958. (7"ep) *Pye-Nixa; (NEP 24075)* **DONEGAN ON STAGE (live)** -
– Mule skinner blues / Old Hannah / On a Monday / Glory.

1958. (7"ep) *Pye-Nixa; (NEP 24081)* **HIT PARADE VOL.4** -
– Grand Coolee Dam / Ham 'n' eggs / Nobody loves like an Irishman / Jack O'Diamonds.

1959. (7"ep) *Pye-Nixa; (NEP 24104)* **HIT PARADE VOL.5** -
– Tom Dooley / Rock o' my soul / Sally don't you grieve / Betty, Betty, Betty.

1959. (7"ep) *Pye-Nixa; (NEP 24107)* **RELAX WITH LONNIE** -
– Bewildered / Kevin Barry / It's no secret / My lagan love.

1959. (7"ep) *Pye-Nixa; (NEP 24114)* **HIT PARADE VOL.6** -
– The battle of New Orleans / Fort Worth jail / Does your chewing gum lose the flavour (on the bedpost overnight) / Darling Corey.

1960. (7"ep) *Pye-Nixa; (NEP 24127)* **YANKEE DOODLE DONEGAN** -
– Corrine Corrina / Junko partner / Nobody understands me / Sorry but I'm gonna have to pass.

1961. (7"ep) *Pye-Nixa; (NEP 24134)* **HIT PARADE VOL.7** -
– My old man's a dustman / The golden vanity / Sal's got a sugar lip / Talking guitar blues.

1961. (7"ep) *Pye-Nixa; (NEP 24149)* **HIT PARADE VOL.8** -
– Michael row the boat / I wanna go home / Lumbered / Have a drink on me.

Aug 62. (lp) *Golden Guinea; (GGL 0135)* **A GOLDEN AGE OF DONEGAN** 3 -
(re-iss. 1966 on 'Marble Arch'; MAL 636)

Jan 63. (lp) *Golden Guinea; (GGL 0170)* **A GOLDEN AGE OF DONEGAN VOL.2** 15 -
(re-iss. 1967 on 'Marble Arch'; MAL 698)

1970. (lp) *Hallmark; (HM 204)* **MY OLD MAN'S A DUSTMAN** -

1971. (lp/c) *Golden Hour; (GH/ZCGH 514)* **A GOLDEN HOUR OF LONNIE DONEGAN** -
(re-iss. Sep90 on 'Knight' cd/c; KGH CD/MC 129)

1973. (lp) *Golden Hour; (GH 565)* **A GOLDEN HOUR OF LONNIE DONEGAN VOL.2** -

1973. (lp) *Hallmark; (HMA 252)* **LONNIE DONEGAN** -

Jan 76. (7") *Pye; (7N 45548)* **BATTLE OF NEW ORLEANS. / PUTTIN' ON THE STYLE** -

1976. (lp) *Ronco; (RTL 2017)* **GREATEST HITS** -

1977. (12"ep) *Pye; (BD 108)* **DOES YOUR CHEWING GUM LOSE ITS FLAVOUR / MY OLD MAN'S A DUSTMAN. / BATTLE OF NEW ORLEANS / TOM DOOLEY** -

Nov 77. (d-lp/d-c) *Pye; (FILD/ZCFLD 011)* **THE LONNIE DONEGAN FILE** -

Jul 78. (7") *Pye; (7N 46096)* **MY OLD MAN'S A DUSTMAN. / I WANNA GO HOME** -

Jul 78. (7") *Pye; (7N 46107)* **TOM DOOLEY. / BATTLE OF NEW ORLEANS** -

Jul 78. (lp/c) *Music For Pleasure; (MFP 50389)* **THE HITS OF LONNIE DONEGAN** -

May 79. (7") *Flashback; (FBS 10)* **MY OLD MAN'S A DUSTMAN. / DOES YOUR CHEWING GUM LOSE ITS FLAVOUR** -

Feb 80. (c) *Bravo; (BRC 2530)* **GREATEST HITS** -

Jul 82. (7") *Old Gold; (OG 9131)* **GAMBLIN' MAN. / PUTTING ON THE STYLE** -

Mar 83. (lp) *Ditto; (DTO 10048)* **GREATEST HITS** -

Jun 85. (lp) *Bear Family; (BFX 15170)* **RARE AND UNISSUED GEMS** -

Oct 85. (lp/c) *Flashback; (FBLP/ZCFBL 8071)* **ROCK ISLAND LINE** -

Sep 87. (d-lp/d-c/d-cd) *P.R.T.; (PYL/PYM/PYC 7003)* **THE HIT SINGLES COLLECTION** -

Jan 89. (cd) *Pickwick; (PWK 076)* **THE BEST OF LONNIE DONEGAN** -

1989. (7") *Old Gold; (OG 9902)* **ROCK ISLAND LINE. / LAST TRAIN TO SAN FERNANDO** -

Sep 89. (lp/c/cd) *Castle; (CCS LP/MC/CD 223)* **LONNIE DONEGAN: THE COLLECTION** -

1991. (cd) *Music For Pleasure; (MFP 5917)* **LONNIE DONEGAN AND HIS SKIFFLE GROUP** -

Apr 92. (cd) *See For Miles; (SEECD 331)* **LONNIE DONEGAN – THE ORIGINALS** -

May 92. (cd/c) *See For Miles; (SEE CD/K 346)* **THE EP COLLECTION** -

Jul 92. (cd) *Kaz; (KAZCD 21)* **BEST OF LONNIE DONEGAN** -

Dec 92. (3xcd-box) *Sequel; (NXTCD 233)* **PUTTIN' ON THE STYLES** -

Oct 93. (cd) *See For Miles; (SEECD 382)* **THE EP COLLECTION VOL.2** -

Oct 93. (4xcd-box) *Bear Family; (BCD 15700)* **MORE THAN PIE IN THE SKY** -

May 94. (cd) *Disky; (GOLD 213)* **THE BEST OF LONNIE DONEGAN** -

1994. (d-cd) *Timeless; (CDTTD 586)* **40 YEARS JUBILEE** -

Mar 95. (cd/c) *Spectrum; (550761-2/-4)* **FAVOURITE FLAVOURS** -

Nov 95. (cd-s) *Old Gold; (12623 6343-2)* **DOES YOUR CHEWING GUM LOSE ITS FLAVOUR ON THE BEDPOST OVERNIGHT / CUMBERLAND GAP** -

Feb 96. (cd-s) *Old Gold; (12623 6343-2)* **GRAND COLUEE DAM / BRING A LITTLE WATER, SYLVIE** -

May 96. (cd-s) *Old Gold; (12623 6370-2)* **GAMBLIN' MAN / LOST JOHN** -

May 96. (cd-s) *Old Gold; (12623 6371-2)* **MY OLD MAN'S A DUSTMAN / PUTTING ON THE STYLE** -

Aug 96. (cd/c) *Autograph; (MAC CD/MC 165)* **KING OF SKIFFLE** -

Jul 97. (cd) *Laserlight; (21040)* **ROCK MY SOUL** -

Oct 98. (cd) *Castle Select; (SELCD 539)* **SKIFFLE SENSATION** -

Jun 99. (cd) *Zircon; (ZIRC 1002)* **LIVE 1957 – THE COMPLETE CONWAY HALL CONCERT (live)** -

Jun 99. (d-cd) *Jasmine; (JASCD 352/3)* **LONNIE DONEGAN MEETS LEINEMANN / COUNTRY ROADS** -

Aug 99. (cd) *Castle Pie; (PIESD 121)* **KING OF SKIFFLE** -

Sep 99. (d-cd) *Sequel; (NEECD 325)* **TALKING GUITAR BLUES – THE VERY BEST OF LONNIE DONEGAN** -
– Lost John / Stewball / Railroad Bill / Bring a little water, Sylvie / Dead or alive / Wabash cannonball / Nobody's child / Frankie and Johnny / Don't you rock me, daddy-o / Cumberland gap / Gamblin' man / Putting on the style / My Dixie darling / Jack O'Diamonds / On a Monday / Muleskinner blues / Grand Coulle Dam / Sally don't you grieve / Lonnie's skiffle (Little Liza Jane – Putting on the style – Camptown races – Little Liza Jane / Knees up mother Brown) / Tom Dooley / Does your chewing gum lose its flavour / Fort Worth jail / Battle of New Orleans / Sal's got a sugar lip / Take this hammer / You pass me by / San Miguel / Talking guitar blues / My old man's a dustman / I wanna go home / Lorelei / Sorry but I'm gonna have to pass / Lively / Virgin Mary / Have a drink on me / Michael row the boat ashore / Lumbered / The commancheros / The party's over / I'll never fall in love again / Pick a bale of cotton / This train / Noah found grace in the eyes of the Lord / Beans in my ears / She was T-bone talking woman / Farewell (fare thee well) / World Cup Willie.

Feb 00. (cd) *Sequel; (NEMCD 342)* **THE ORIGINAL ALBUMS REVISITED** -

Sep 00. (cd) *Delta; (47040)* **PUTTING ON THE STYLE** -

DONOVAN

Born: DONOVAN PHILIP LEITCH, 10 May'46, Maryhill, Glasgow. At the age of 10, his family moved to Hatfield (England). In 1964, while playing small gigs in Southend, he was spotted by Geoff Stephens and Peter Eden, who became his managers. Later that year, after performing on the 'Ready Steady Go!' pop show over three consecutive weeks, the denim-clad beatnik signed to 'Pye'.

His debut single, 'CATCH THE WIND' (issued the same time as DYLAN's 'The Times They Are A-Changin'), saw him break into the Top 5, later reaching Top 30 in America where he was enjoying the fruits of a burgeoning career. His follow-up, 'COLOURS', also made the Top 5 in the summer of '65, as did the debut album, 'WHAT'S BIN DID AND WHAT'S BIN HID'. Later in the year, the 'UNIVERSAL SOLDIER' EP saw DONOVAN begin to develop his uncompromising anti-war stance, a theme which he touched on with his second album, 'FAIRYTALE'. Initially heralded as Britain's answer to BOB DYLAN, he began to build on his folk/pop roots, progressing into flower-power with 'SUNSHINE SUPERMAN' in 1966. The album of the same name (issued only in the States) saw DONOVAN hit a creative high point and included the much revered, 'SEASON OF THE WITCH'. At the beginning of '67, the single 'MELLOW YELLOW' was riding high in the American hit parade, and 'EPISTLE TO DIPPY' soon followed suit. In the meantime, 'MELLOW YELLOW', was given a belated UK release (making Top 10), while its similarly titled parent album (again only issued in the US), hit No.14. 'SUNSHINE SUPERMAN', a UK compilation lp of both aforementioned albums, made the Top 30 in the middle of '67. His label, 'Pye', followed the same marketing strategy with his next UK album, the double 'A GIFT FROM A FLOWER TO A GARDEN', which was in actual fact, two US-only lp's in one.

During this highly prolific period, which saw him inspired by the transcendental meditation of guru Maharishi Mahesh Yogi, he released two sublime pieces of acid-pop in 'THERE IS A MOUNTAIN' and 'JENNIFER JUNIPER'. The momentum continued with, 'HURDY GURDY MAN', another classic sojourn into psychedelia which hit Top 5 on both sides of the Atlantic. In 1969, he collaborated with The JEFF BECK GROUP on 'GOO GOO BARABAJAGAL', although this was his final 45 to make a major chart appearance. An album, 'OPEN ROAD' (1970), named after his new band, surprised many by cracking the US & UK charts. In 1971, he recorded a double album of children's songs 'H.M.S. DONOVAN', which led to a critical backlash from the music press.

After a 3-year exile in Ireland for tax reasons, he set up home in California with his wife Linda Lawrence and daughters Astrella and Oriole. He has fathered two other children with his new American wife, Enid; DONOVAN LEITCH JNR. (star of the film 'Gas, Food, Lodging') and IONE SKYE, the latter said to be none too bothered about her famous father. DONOVAN enjoyed something of a renaissance in the early 90's when HAPPY MONDAYS' mainman SHAUN RYDER (now of BLACK GRAPE) sang his praises, leading to a comeback album, 'DONOVAN RISING'. He was still going strong in '96, releasing a well-received album, 'SUTRAS', for the RCA affiliated 'American' label.

• **Songwriters:** Self-penned except, UNIVERSAL SOLDIER (Buffy Sainte-Marie) / LONDON TOWN (Tim Hardin) / REMEMBER THE ALAMO (Jane Bowes) / CAR CAR (Woody Guthrie) / GOLDWATCH BLUES (Mick Softley) / DONNA DONNA (Kevess-Secunda-Secanta-Schwartz-Zeitlin) / OH DEED I DO+ DO YOU HEAR ME NOW (Bert Jansch) / CIRCUS OF SOUR (Paul Bernath) / LITTLE TIN SOLDIER (Shawn Phillips / LORD OF THE DANCE (Sydney Carter) / ROCK'N'ROLL WITH ME (David Bowie-Warren Peace) / MY SONG IS TRUE (Darell Adams) / NO MAN'S LAND (Eric Bogle) / WIND IN THE WILLOWS (Eddie Hardin) / NEWEST BATH GUIDE + MOIRA McCAVENDISH (John Betjeman) / THE SENSITIVE KIND (J. J. Cale) / traditional:- KEEP ON TRUCKIN' + YOU'RE GONNA NEED SOMEBODY + CANDY MAN + THE STAR + COULTER'S CANDY + HENRY MARTIN + THE HEIGHTS OF ALMA + YOUNG BUT GROWING + STEALIN'. He also put music to words/poetry by; William Shakespeare (UNDER THE GREENWOOD TREE) / Gypsy Dave (A SUNNY DAY) / Lewis Carroll (WALRUS AND THE CARPENTER + JABBERWOCKY) / Thora Stowell (THE SELLER OF STARS + THE LITTLE WHITE ROAD) / Fifida Wolfe (LOST TIME) / Lucy Diamond (THE ROAD) / Agnes Herbertson (THINGS TO WEAR) / Edward Lear (THE OWL AND THE PUSSYCAT) / Eugene Field (WYNKEN, BLYNKEN AND NOD) / W. B. Yeats (THE SONG OF WANDERING AENGUS) / Natalie Joan (A FUNNY MAN) / Thomas Hood (QUEEN MAB) / Astella Leitch (MEE MEE I LOVE YOU) / Warwick Embury (ONE NIGHT IN TIME) / Note; HURLEY GURLEY MAN originally had a verse by GEORGE HARRISON but this was not recorded and he only added this for live appearances.

• **Trivia:** DONOVAN sang co-lead on the title track from ALICE COOPER's 1973 lp 'Billion Dollar Babies'.

DONOVAN – vocals, acoustic guitar, harmonica with **BRIAN LOCKING** – bass / **SKIP ALLEN** – drums / **GYPSY DAVE** (b. DAVID MILLS) – kazoo, etc.

Pye Hickory

Mar 65. (7") *(7N 15801)* <1309> **CATCH THE WIND. / WHY DO YOU TREAT ME LIKE YOU DO** [4] [23] Apr65

May 65. (7") *(7N 15866)* <1324> **COLOURS. / TO SING FOR YOU** [4] [61] Jun65

May 65. (lp) *(NPL 18117)* <123> **WHAT'S BIN DID AND WHAT'S BIN HID** <US title 'CATCH THE WIND'> [3] [30]
– Josie / Catch the wind / Remember the Alamo / Cuttin' out / Car car * (riding in my car) / Keep on truckin' / Goldwatch blues / To sing for you / You're gonna need somebody on your bond / Tangerine puppet / Donna Donna * / Ramblin' boy *(re-iss. Jul68 on 'Marble Arch';)* – (omitted *)

Sep 65. (7") <1338> **UNIVERSAL SOLDIER. / DO YOU HEAR ME** [-] [53]

Sep 65. (7"ep) *(NEP 24219)* **THE UNIVERSAL SOLDIER EP** [13] [-]
– Universal soldier / The ballad of a crystal man / Do you hear me now* / The war drags on.

Oct 65. (lp) *(NPL 18128)* **FAIRYTALE** [20] [85] Dec 65
– Colours * / To try for the sun / Sunny Goodge street / Oh deed I do / Circus of sour / The summer day reflection song / Candy man / Jersey Thursday / Belated forgiveness plea / Ballad of a crystal man / Little tin soldier * / Ballad of Geraldine. *(re-iss. Mar69 on 'Marble Arch';)* – (omitted *). *(re-iss. Feb91 on 'Castle' cd/c; CLA CD/MC 226)*

Nov 65. (7") *(7N 15984)* **TURQUOISE. / HEY GYP (DIG THE SLOWNESS)** [30] [-]

Nov 65. (7") <1375> **YOU'RE GONNA NEED SOMEBODY ON YOUR BOND. / THE LITTLE TIN SOLDIER** [-] [ ]

Jan 66. (7") <1402> **TO TRY FOR THE SUN. / TURQUOISE** [-] [ ]

Feb 66. (7") *(7N 17067)* **JOSIE. / LITTLE TIN SOLDIER** [ ] [-]

Apr 66. (7") *(7N 17088)* **REMEMBER THE ALAMO. / THE BALLAD OF A CRYSTAL MAN** [ ] [-]

—— **DONOVAN** plus **JOHN CAMERON** – piano, harpsicord / **HAROLD McNAIR** – flute

Pye Epic

Jul 66. (7") *(7N 17241)* <10045> **SUNSHINE SUPERMAN. / THE TRIP** [2] [1] Jun66

Sep 66. (lp; mono<stereo) <*LN 24217*><*BN 26217*> **SUNSHINE SUPERMAN** [-] [11]
– Sunshine Superman / Legend of a girl child Linda / The observation / Guinevere / Celeste / Writer in the Sun / Season of the witch / Hampstead incident / Sand and foam / Young girl blues / Three kingfishers / Bert's blues. *(UK-iss.Feb91 on 'Beat Goes On' cd/c; BGO CD/MC 68) (cd re-iss. Oct96 on 'EMI Gold'; CDGOLD 1066)*

Nov 66. (7") <10098> **MELLOW YELLOW. / SUNNY SOUTH KENSINGTON** [-] [2]

Jan 67. (7") <10127> **EPISTLE TO DIPPY. / PREACHIN' LOVE** [-] [19]

Feb 67. (7") *(7N 17267)* **MELLOW YELLOW. / PREACHIN' LOVE** [8] [-]

Feb 67. (lp; mono><stereo) <*LN 24239*><*BN 26239*> **MELLOW YELLOW** [-] [14]
– Mellow yellow / Writer in the Sun / Sand and foam / The observation / Bleak city woman / House of Jansch / Young girl blues / Museum / Hampstead incident / Sunny South Kensington. *(cd-iss. Oct93 on 'Sony Europe';)*

Jun 67. (lp) *(NPL 18181)* **SUNSHINE SUPERMAN** [25] [-]
-(compilation of last 2 US albums)

Oct 67. (7") *(7N 17403)* <10212> **THERE IS A MOUNTAIN. / SAND AND FOAM** [8] [11] Sep67

—— **DONOVAN** retained **HAROLD** and in came **TONY CARR** – percussion / **CANDY JOHN CARR** – bongos **CLIFF BARTON** – bass / **KEITH WEBB** – drums / **MIKE O'NEIL** – keyboards / **MIKE CARR** – vibraphone / **ERIC LEESE** – electric guitar

Dec 67. (7") <10253> **WEAR YOUR LOVE LIKE HEAVEN. / OH GOSH** [-] [23]

Dec 67. (lp; mono><stereo) <*LN 24349*><*BN 26349*> **WEAR YOUR LOVE LIKE HEAVEN** [-] [60]
– Wear your love like Heaven / Mad John's escape / Skip-a-long Sam / Sun / There was a time / Oh gosh / Little boy in corduroy / Under the greenwood tree / The land of doesn't have to be / Someone's singing / Song of the naturalist's wife / The enchanted gypsy.

—— **KEN BALDOCK** – bass repl. BARTON, LEESE, WEBB, O'NEIL + MIKE CARR

Dec 67. (lp; mono><stereo) <*LN 24350*><*BN 26350*> **FOR LITTLE ONES** [-] [ ]
– Voyage into the golden screen / Isle of Islay / The mandolin man and his secret / Lay of the last tinker / The tinker and the crab / Widow with shawl (a portrait) / The lullaby of spring / The magpie / Starfish-on-the-toast / Epistle to Derroll.

Feb 68. (7") *(7N 17457)* <10300> **JENNIFER JUNIPER. / POOR COW** [5] [26]

Apr 68. (d-lp-box; mono/stereo) *(NPL/NSPL 20000)* <L2N6/B2N 171> **A GIFT FROM A FLOWER TO A GARDEN** [13] [19]
– (contains 2 US Dec67 albums boxed) *(cd-iss. Jul93 & Jun97 on 'Beat Goes On'; BGOCD 194)*

May 68. (7") *(7N 17537)* <10345> **HURDY GURDY MAN. / TEEN ANGEL** [4] [5]

Sep 68. (lp; mono/stereo) *(NPL/NSPL 18237)* <BN 26420> **DONOVAN IN CONCERT (live)** [ ] [18] Jul68
– Isle of Islay / Young girl blues / There is a mountain / Poor cow / Celeste / The fat angel / Guinevere / Widow with shawl (a portrait) / Preachin' love / The lullaby of Spring / Writer in the Sun / Rules and regulations / Pebble and the man / Mellow yellow. *(re-iss. May91 & Apr97 on 'Beat Goes On' cd/c/lp; BGO CD/MC/LP 90) (cd-iss. Nov94 on 'Start';) (re-iss. cd Jan96 on 'Happy Price'; HP 93432)*

Oct 68. (7") <10393> **LALENA. / AYE, MY LOVE** [-] [33]

Oct 68. (lp) <BN 26420> **HURDY GURDY MAN** [-] [20]
– Jennifer Juniper / Hurdy gurdy man / Hi, it's been a long time / Peregrine / The entertaining of a shy girl / Tangier / As I recall it / Get thy bearings / West Indian lady / Teas / The river song / The Sun is a very magic fellow / A sunny day.

Nov 68. (7") *(7N 17660)* **ATLANTIS. / I LOVE MY SHIRT** [23] [-]

Feb 69. (7") <10434> **ATLANTIS. / TO SUSAN ON THE WEST COAST WAITING** [-] [7] [35]

Mar 69. (lp) *(NPL/NSPL 18283)* <BXN 26439> **DONOVAN'S GREATEST HITS** (compilation) [ ] [4]
– Epistle to Dippy / Sunshine Superman / There is a mountain / Jennifer Juniper / Wear your love like Heaven / Season of the witch / Mellow yellow / Colours / Hurdy gurdy man / Catch the wind / Lalena. *<re-iss. 1972; PE 26439> <re-iss. 1973; BN 26836> (re-iss. Sep79 on 'CBS-Embassy' lp/c; CBS/40 31759) (cd-iss. Aug90 on 'Epic';)*

Jun 69. (7"; DONOVAN with The JEFF BECK GROUP) *(7N 17778)* **GOO GOO BARABAJAGAL (LOVE IS HOT). / BED WITH ME** [12] [-]

Sep 69. (7"; DONOVAN with The JEFF BECK GROUP) *<10510>*
GOO GOO BARABAJAGAL (LOVE IS HOT). / TRUDI [-] [36]

Sep 69. (lp; DONOVAN with The JEFF BECK GROUP) *<BN 26481>* **BARABAJAGAL** [-] [ ]
– Barabajagal / Superlungs my supergirl / I love my shirt / The love song / To Susan on the West Coast waiting / Atlantis / Trudi / Pamela Jo / Happiness runs. *(cd-iss. Oct93 on 'Sony Europe';)*

—— with **JOHN CARR** – drums, vocals / **MIKE THOMPSON** – bass, vocals / **MIKE O'NEILL** – piano

Dawn Epic

Sep 70. (lp) *(DNLS 3009) <30125>* **OPEN ROAD** [30] [16] Jul70
– Changes / Song for John / Curry land / Joe Bean's theme / People used to / Celtic rock / Riki tiki tavi / Clara clairvoyant / Roots of oak / Season of farewell / Poke at the Pope / New Year's resovolution. *(cd-iss. Sep00 on 'Repertoire'; REP 4880)*

Sep 70. (7"; DONOVAN with OPEN ROAD) *(DNS 1006) <10649>*
RIKI TIKI TAVI. / ROOTS OF OAK [ ] [55]

—— (DANNY – double bass)

Dec 70. (7"; DONOVAN with DANNY THOMPSON) *(DNA 1007)*
CELIA OF THE SEALS. / MR.WIND [ ] [-]

Feb 71. (7") *(10694>* **CELIA OF THE SEAS. / THE SONG OF THE WANDERING AENGUS** [-] [84]

Jul 71. (d-lp) *(DNLD 4001)* **H.M.S. DONOVAN** [ ] [-]
– The walrus and the carpenter / Jabberwocky / The seller of the stars / Lost time / The little white road / The star / Coulter's candy / The road / Things to wear / The owl and the pussycat / Homesickness / Fishes in love / Mr.Wind / Wynken, Bylnken and Nod / Celia of the seas / The pee song / The voyage to the Moon / The unicorn / Lord of dance / Little Ben / Can ye dance / In an old fashioned picture book / The song of the wandering Aengus / A funny man / Lord of the reedy river / Henry Martin / Queen Mab / La moor. *(cd-iss. Jan98 on 'Beat Goes On'; BGOCD 372)*

—— with guests **CHRIS SPEDDING** – guitar / **JOHN 'RABBIT' BUNDRICK** – keyboards / **JIM HORN** – bass / **COZY POWELL** – drums

Epic Epic

Mar 73. (lp) *(SEPC 65450) <32156>* **COSMIC WHEELS** [15] [25]
– Cosmic wheels / Earth sign man / Sleep / Maria Magenta / Wild witch lady / Sleep / The music makers / The intergallactic laxative / I like you / Only the blues / Appearances. *(cd-iss. Sep94 on 'Epic-Rewind'; 477378-2)*

Apr 73. (7") *(EPC 1471) <10983>* **I LIKE YOU. / EARTH SIGN MAN** [ ] [66]

Jun 73. (7") *(EPC 1644) <11023>* **MARIA MAGENTA. / THE INTERGALLACTIC LAXATIVE** [ ] [ ]

—— now with **STEVE MARRIOT, PETER FRAMPTON** and **NICKY HOPKINS**

Nov 73. (7") *(EPC 1960)* **SAILING HOMEWARD. / LAZY DAZE** [ ] [-]

Dec 73. (lp) *(SEPC 69050) <32800>* **ESSENCE TO ESSENCE** [ ] [ ]
– Operating manual for spaceship Earth / Lazy daze / Life goes on / There is an ocean / Dignity of man / Yellow star / Divine daze of deathless delight / Boy for every girl / Saint Valentine's angel / Life is a merry-go-round / Sailing homeward.

Jan 74. (7") *<11108>* **SAILING HOMEWARD. / YELLOW STAR** [-] [ ]

—— Mainly used session musicians from now on.

Sep 74. (7") *(EPC 2661) <50016>* **ROCK'N'ROLL WITH ME. / THE DIVINE DAZE OF DEATHLESS DELIGHT** [ ] [ ] Nov74

Nov 74. (lp) *(SEPC 69104) <33245>* **7-TEASE** [ ] [ ]
– Rock and roll souljer / Your broken heart / Salvation stomp / The ordinary family / Ride-a-mile / Sadness / Moon rok / Love of my life / The voice of protest / How silly / The great song of the sky / The quest.

Jan 75. (7") *<50077>* **ROCK AND ROLL SOULJER. / HOW SILLY** [-] [ ]

Feb 75. (7") *(EPC 3037)* **ROCK AND ROLL SOULJER. / LOVE OF MY LIFE** [ ] [-]

Jun 76. (lp) *(SEPC 86011) <33945>* **SLOW DOWN WORLD** [ ] [ ]
– Dark-eyed blue jean angel / Cryin' shame / The mountain / Children of the world / My love is true (love song) / A well known has-been / Black widow / Slow down world / Liberation rag.

Jun 76. (7") *<50237>* **A WELL-KNOWN HAS-BEEN. / DARK EYED BLUE JEAN ANGEL** [-] [ ]

Rak Arista

Aug 77. (7") *<0280>* **DARE TO BE DIFFERENT. / THE INTERNATIONAL MAN** [-] [ ]

Oct 77. (lp) *(SRAK 528)* **DONOVAN** [ ] [-]
– Brave new world / Local boy chops wood / Kalifornia kids / International man / Lady of the stars / Dare to be different / Mijah's dance / The light / Astral angel.

Nov 77. (7") *(RAK 265)* **THE LIGHT. / THE INTERNATIONAL MAN** [ ] [-]

Feb 78. (7") *(RAK 269)* **DARE TO BE DIFFERENT. / SING MY SONG** [ ] [-]

—— (note:- on above US singles [Jan 73, Jan 75, Jun 76, Aug 77] the 'B' side was mono version on 'A').

Luggage-R.C.A. Allegiance

Aug 80. (lp) *(PL 28429)* **NEUTRONICA** [ ] [-]
– Shipwreck / Only to be expected / Comin' to you / No hunger / Neutron / Mee Mee I love you / The heights of Alma / No man's land / We are one / Madrigalinda / Harmony. *(cd-iss. May01 on 'Burning Airlines'+=; PILOT 089)* – (acoustic versions +).

—— with **DANNY THOMPSON** – double bass / **JOHN STEPHENS** – drums / **TONY ROBERTS** – multi-wind instruments / and his 9 year-old daughter **ASTELLA** – dual vocals

Oct 81. (lp) *(PL 28472)* **LOVE IS ONLY FEELING** [ ] [-]
– Lady of the flowers / Lover o lover / The actor / Half Moon bay / The hills of Tuscany / Lay down Lassie / She / Johnny Tuff / Love is only feeling / Marjorie Margerine.

Oct 81. (7") *(7-LUG 03)* **LAY DOWN LASSIE. / LOVE IS ONLY FEELING** [ ] [-]

Jan 84. (lp) *(PL 70060) <72857>* **LADY OF THE STARS** [ ] [ ]
– Lady of the stars / I love you baby / Seasons of the witch / Bye bye girl / Every reason / Boy for every girl / Local boy chops wood / Sunshine superman / Til I see you again / Living for the lovelight.
After nearly 7 years in the wilderness, he returned on new label

Permanent Permanent

Nov 90. (cd/c/lp) *(PERM CD/MC/LP 2)* **DONOVAN RISING** [ ] [-]
– Jennifer Juniper / Catch the wind / The hurdy gurdy man / Sunshine superman / Sadness / Universal soldier / Cosmic wheels / Atlantis / Wear your love like heaven / Colours / To Susan on the west coast waiting / Young girl blues / Young but growing / Stealing / Sailing homeward / Love will find a way / Lalena. *(d-cd-iss. Jul00 on 'Burning Airlines'; PILOT 059)*

—— He had also credited on The SINGING CORNER's (Nov90) single version of his JENNIFER JUNIPER.

Silhouette not iss.

Apr 92. (cd-ep) *(MDCDKR 3)* **NEW BATH GUIDE / MOIRA McCAVENDISH / BROTHER SUN, SISTER MOON** [ ] [-]

American-RCA American

Oct 96. (cd) *(74321 39743-2)* **SUTRAS** [ ] [ ]
– Please don't bend / Give it all up / Sleep / Everlasting sea / High your love / The clear-browed one / The way / Deep peace / Nirvana / Eldorado / Be mine / Lady of the lamp / The evernow / Universe am I.

– compilations, others, etc. –

on 'Pye' UK / 'Hickory' (70's 'Epic') US unless otherwise mentioned

Dec 65. (7"ep) *(NEP 24229)* **COLOURS** [ ] [-]
– Catch the wind / Why do you treat me like you do / Colours / To sing for you.

Mar 66. (7"ep) *(NEP 24239)* **DONOVAN VOL.1** [ ] [-]
– Sunny Goodge Street / Oh deed I do / Jersey Thursday / Hey Gyp (dig the slowness).

Jul 66. (7") *<1417>* **HEY GYP (DIG THE SLOWNESS). / THE WAR DRAGS ON** [-] [ ]

Oct 66. (7") *<1470>* **SUNNY GOODGE STREET. / SUMMER DAY REFLECTION SONG** [-] [ ]

Sep 66. (lp) *<135>* **THE REAL DONOVAN** [-] [96]

Jan 67. (7") *<193>* **CATCH THE WIND. / UNIVERSAL SOLDIER** [-] [ ]

Oct 67. (lp) *Marble Arch; (MAL 718)* **UNIVERSAL SOLDIER** [5] [-]
(re-iss. Feb83 on 'Spot'; SPR/SPC 8514)

Feb 68. (7"ep) *(NEP 24287)* **CATCH THE WIND** [ ] [-]
– Catch the wind / Remember the Alamo / Josie / Rambling Rose.

Apr 68. (lp) *<143>* **LIKE IT IS, WAS AND EVERMORE SHALL BE** [-] [ ]

1968. (7") *<1492>* **DO YOU HEAR ME NOW. / WHY DO YOU TREAT ME LIKE YOU DO** [-] [ ]

Aug 68. (7"ep) *(NEP 24299)* **HURDY GURDY DONOVAN** [ ] [-]
– Jennifer juniper / Hurdy gurdy man / Mellow yellow / There is a mountain. *(re-iss. Nov71; PMM 104)*

Jun 69. (lp) *United Artists; (UAS 29044)* **IF IT'S TUESDAY IT MUST BE BELGUIM (Soundtrack)** [ ] [ ]

Nov 69. (lp) *(149>* **THE BEST OF DONOVAN** [-] [ ]

1970. (lp) *Marble Arch; (MAL 1168)* **THE WORLD OF DONOVAN** [ ] [-]

Oct 70. (7") *Janus; <A-501>* **COLORS. / JOSIE** [-] [ ]

Oct 70. (7") *Janus; <A-502>* **CATCH THE WIND. / WHY DO YOU TREAT ME LIKE YOU DO** [-] [ ]

Oct 70. (7") *Janus; <A-503>* **CANDY MAN. / HEY GYP (DIG THE SLOWNESS)** [-] [ ]

Nov 70. (d-lp) *Janus; <3022>* **DONOVAN P.LEITCH** (early work) [-] [ ]

1971. (lp) *Golden Hour; (GH 506)* **THE GOLDEN HOUR OF DONOVAN** [ ] [-]

1971. (lp) *Hallmark; (HMA 200)* **CATCH THE WIND** [ ] [-]
(re-iss. Apr86 on 'Showcase' lp/c; SH LP/TC 133)

1972. (lp) *Hallmark; (HMA 241)* **COLOURS** [ ] [-]
(re-iss. Oct87 on 'P.R.T.' lp/c/cd; PYL/PYM/PYC 7004)

1972. (7") *Memory Lane; <15-2251>* **SUNSHINE SUPERMAN. / MELLOW YELLOW** [-] [ ]

1972. (7") *Memory Lane; <15-2280>* **JENNIFER JUNIPER. / HURDY GURDY MAN** [-] [ ]

1973. (4xlp-set) *(11PP 102)* **FOUR SHADES OF DONOVAN / OPEN ROAD / DONOVAN'S GREATEST HITS/ / H.M.S. DONOVAN** [ ] [ ]

Nov 77. (d-lp/c) *(FILD/ZCFLD 004)* **THE DONOVAN FILE** [ ] [-]

Jul 78. (7") **COLOURS. / UNIVERSAL SOLDIER** [ ] [-]

Jul 80. (7"ep) *Flashback; (FBEP 107)* **EP** [ ] [-]
– Catch the wind / Turquoise / Colours / Universal soldier.

Oct 81. (lp/c) *P.R.T.; (SPOT/ZCSPT 1017)* **SPOTLIGHT ON DONOVAN** [ ] [-]

Jul 82. (7") *Old Gold; (OG 9134)* **CATCH THE WIND. / COLOURS** [ ] [-]

Jul 83. (10"lp/c) *P.R.T.; (DOW/ZCDOW 13)* **MINSTREL BOY**
Feb 85. (7") *EMI Gold; (G 4545)* **MELLOW YELLOW. / SUNSHINE SUPERMAN**
Aug 89. (7") *E.M.I.; (EM 98)* **SUNSHINE SUPERMAN. / JENNIFER JUNIPER**
(ext.12"+=) *(12EM 98)* – Wear your love like Heaven.
(cd-s++=) *(CDEM 98)* – Mellow yellow.
Sep 89. (cd)(c/lp) *E.M.I.; (CZ 193)(TC+/EMS 1333)* **GREATEST HITS AND MORE**
– Sunshine Superman / Wear your love like Heaven / Jennifer Juniper / Barabajagal (love is hot) / Hurdy gurdy man / Epistle to Dippy / To Susan on the West Coast waiting / Catch the wind / Mellow yellow / There is a mountain / Happiness runs / Season of the witch / Colours / Superlungs – My Supergirl / Lalena / Atlantis. *(cd+=)* – Preachin' love / Poor cow / Teen angel / Aye my love. *(lp re-iss. Dec99 on 'Simply Vinyl'; SVLP 155)*
1990. (cd) *Marble Arch;* **JOSIE**
(re-iss. Jul94 on 'Success')
Oct 90. (lp/c/cd) *See For Miles; (SEE/+K/CD 300)* **THE EP COLLECTION**
Dec 90. (cd/c) *Castle; (CCS CD/MC 276)* **THE COLLECTION**
Feb 91. (d-cd/d-c/d-lp) *E.M.I.; (CD/TC+/EM 1385)* **THE TRIP** (1964-1968 material)
Mar 91. (7") *Gulf Peace Team; (GPT 1)* **UNIVERSAL SOLDIER. / CATCH THE WIND**
(12"+=) *(GPT 001T)* – I'll try for the sun.
Jun 91. (cd/c) *Mammoth; (MMCD5/MMMC4 717)* **THE HITS**
Jul 91. (cd) *The Collection; (ORO 155)* **TILL I SEE YOU AGAIN**
(re-iss. Jul94 on 'Success')
Mar 93. (cd) *Dojo-Castle; (EARLD 13)* **THE EARLY YEARS**
Sep 93. (cd/c) *Remember; (RMB 7/4 5059)*
Dec 93. (cd) *Disky; (GOLD 206)* **GOLD: GREATEST HITS**
May 94. (cd) *Music DeLuxe; (MDCD 6)* **COLOURS**
Oct 94. (cd) *Charly; (CDCD 1206)* **SUNSHINE SUPERMAN**
Nov 94. (4xcd-box) *E.M.I.; (DONOVAN 1)* **ORIGINALS**
Jan 95. (cd/c) *Spectrum; (550 721-2/-4)* **UNIVERSAL SOLDIER**
Dec 95. (cd) *Javelin; (HADCD 197)* **SUNSHINE SUPERMAN**
Aug 96. (cd/c) *Hallmark; (30501-2/-4)* **SUNSHINE TROUBADOR**
Nov 96. (cd) *Experience; (EXP 013)* **DONOVAN**
Apr 97. (cd) *Artful; (ARTFULCD 5)* **THE VERY BEST OF**
May 97. (cd) *C.M.C.; (100082)* **SUNSHINE SUPERMAN**
Aug 97. (cd) *BR Music; (BM 1513)* **GREATEST HITS**
Jul 98. (cd) *Epic; (480552-2)* **THE DEFINITE COLLECTION**
Feb 00. (cd) *Castle Pie; (PIESCD 191)* **CATCH THE WIND**
Sep 00. (cd) *Metrodome; (METRO 441)* **SUNSHINE SUPERMAN**
May 01. (cd) *Music DeLuxe; (MDCD 006)* **COLOURS (live in concert)**

DREAM POLICE

Formed: Glasgow ... 1969 by vocalist DAVE BATCHELOR, TED McKENNA on keyboards, plus guitarists ONNIE McINTYRE and HAMISH STUART.

The DREAM POLICE moved to London and were soon spotted by 'Decca' records through the advice of JUNIOR CAMPBELL (then of MARMALADE); he would produce their debut in 1970, 'I'LL BE HOME', a mixture of orchestrated post quasi-psychedelia. In contrast, the flip-side, 'LIVING IS EASY', had more of a Prog-rock feel, although the 45 sold poorly, as did their follow-up, 'OUR SONG'. A third single, 'I'VE GOT NO CHOICE' – issued towards the end of the year – was slightly different and in a country-rock direction, a decision which split the band in two; BATCHELOR and McKENNA to TEAR GAS (and later ALEX HARVEY), McINTYRE and STUART re-uniting in the AVERAGE WHITE BAND.

DAVE BATCHELOR – vocals / **TED McKENNA** – keyboards / **ONNIE McINTYRE** – guitar, vocals (ex-SCOTS OF ST.JAMES) / **HAMISH STUART** – guitar, vocals

Decca Parrot

Mar 70. (7") *(F 12998) <3024>* **I'LL BE HOME (IN A DAY OR SO). / LIVING IS EASY**
Sep 70. (7") *(F 13079)* **OUR SONG. / MUCH TOO MUCH**
Nov 70. (7") *(F 13105)* **I'VE GOT NO CHOICE. / WHAT'S THE CURE FOR HAPPINESS**

— turned in their badges, when BATCHELOR and McKENNA joined TEAR GAS. They were soon to join The SENSATIONAL ALEX HARVEY BAND, BATCHELOR only as producer. They were replaced by JOE BREEN and MATT IRVING, who were later involved in session work, BREEN solo and IRVING for PAUL YOUNG. McINTYRE and STUART (after a spell with The BESERK CROCODILES) formed The AVERAGE WHITE BAND, the latter moving on to PAUL McCARTNEY in the 80's.

the DUKES (see under ⇒ ANDERSON, Miller)

E

Joe EGAN

Born: 1946, Paisley. Having cut his proverbial teeth with mid-60's folkies, the CENSORS (who became The MAVERICKS – no, not that one), EGAN expanding his horizons by forming the FIFTH COLUMN with GERRY RAFFERTY. The singing/songwriting pair managed to emerge with what was to become a rare and collectable one-off single, 'BENJAMIN DAY' for 'Columbia' in 1966. While EGAN went back to his daytime job, RAFFERTY joined The HUMBLEBUMS (with a new playing partner, BILLY CONNOLLY) and subsequently went solo.

In the early 70's, EGAN met up with RAFFERTY once again, although by this time GERRY had founded a new outfit, STEALER'S WHEEL (with RAB NOAKES). However, when RAB took off for a solo career in 1972, JOE fitted in nicely to the ever expanding embryonic line-up. With 'A&M' giving them a contract and producers Leiber & Stoller being called up to help them in the studio, all looked encouraging for the London-based outfit. Disillusioned by his experiences down south, RAFFERTY quit and returned home, unaware that the slow-burning eponymous STEALER'S WHEEL set of '73 was about to unearth one of the classic singles of all-time. 'Stuck In The Middle With You' hit paydirt both in Britain and America, although with an empty space in one of the performing stools, what were they going to do. RAFFERTY duly returned to the fold but not without threats by EGAN he'd quit if something wasn't sorted out (newcomer LUTHER GROSVENOR was in limbo!). The answer was to let go the rest of the band and continue STEALER'S WHEEL as a duo.

In 1974, RAFFERTY, EGAN and session men released the 'Ferguslie Park' set (named after a housing scheme in Paisley), but with no hit singles, it didn't exactly take the public by storm. After a third set in 1975, 'Right Or Wrong', the musical relationship with RAFFERTY and EGAN (not helped by management problems) teetered to a halt, the former subsequently becoming a top selling solo act after 'Baker Street' went Top 3.

Meanwhile, EGAN too carved out his solo career early in '79, although his attempts at the pop charts fell on deaf ears. 'OUT OF NOWHERE' (1979) and 'M.A.P.' (1981) did little to garner any support outside Scotland, even a guest spot for the successful GALLAGHER & LYLE duo on the former effort couldn't get EGAN back into the spotlight. Both RAFFERTY and himself were back in the studio a number of times sessioning for their old mucker, RAB NOAKES, although EGAN was to retire rather than exploit this further.

FIFTH COLUMN

JOE EGAN – vocals, guitar / **GERRY RAFFERTY** – vocals, guitar / **D. BELL** –

Columbia not iss.

1966. (7") *(DB 8068)* **BENJAMIN DAY. / THERE'S NOBODY THERE**

— went back to playing part-time until he joined STEALER'S WHEEL, which was of course more famous for including GERRY RAFFERTY. After they split, JOE EGAN went solo, at first augmented by GALLAGHER & LYLE

JOE EGAN

— with a plethora of session people

Ariola Ariola

Feb 79. (7") *(ARO 153)* **BACK ON THE ROAD. / MY MAMA TOLD ME**
May 79. (7") *(ARO 171)* **FREEZE. / PRIDE**
May 79. (lp) *(ARL 5021) <50064>* **OUT OF NOWHERE**
– Back on the road / Ask for no favours / Natural high / Why let it bother you / The last farewell / Freeze / Pride / No time for sorrow / Leavin' it all behind / Out of nowhere.
Sep 79. (7") *(ARO 187)* **THE LAST FAREWELL. / PRIDE**
Sep 80. (7") *(ARO 249)* **SURVIVOR. / HEART OF THE MOMENT**
Aug 81. (lp) *(ARL 5052)* **M.A.P.**
– Tell me all about it / Survivor / Stay as you are / Diamonds / Make on . . .

— EGAN retired from solo work after above

F

FIFTH COLUMN (see under ⇒ EGAN, Joe)

Neil FINLAY

Born: 1944, Huntly, Aberdeenshire. After leaving school at fifteen, NEIL worked at his father's music shop and quickly taught himself how to bang the drums; his first semi-pro work was for his dad's local dance outfit. In 1963, FINLAY turned professional by joining Coventry-based R&B/Mod combo, The SORROWS. His unique rolling drum patterns created the atmospheric backdrop to all their singles between 1965-67, including UK No.21 smash 'TAKE A HEART', in summer 1965. Sandwiched inbetween the aforementioned platters was one solitary 1966 LP (also entitled 'TAKE A HEART'), a truly wonderful record that highlighted the unmistakeable drum pounding of NEIL.

Dave FLETT

Born: early 1950's, Aberdeen. After leaving school, the young guitarist debuted with the TREVOR HART band but left for the bright lights of London when it was clear he was going nowhere up north. In 1975, through an acquaintance and friend DAVE STROUD (ex-DADDY STOVE PIPE and now Aberdeen jeweller), DAVE auditioned for the vacant guitarist position with MANFRED MANN'S EARTH BAND. He stayed with the MANFRED's while they secured massive hits, 'Blinded By The Light' (from the 1976 album, 'The Roaring Silence') to 'Davey's On The Road Again' (from the album, 'Watch' in 1978). After his departure, the well-respected axeman had brief stints with his own SPECIAL BRANCH and in September 1979, he joined THIN LIZZY (alongside SCOTT GORHAM) for a Japanese tour. Due to nerves, food poisoning and other bad karma, the shy DAVE was seemingly not suited to the rigours of touring and after a Xmas gig he was replaced. After another, even shorter stint with ex-RORY GALLAGHER bassist GERRY McAVOY, DAVE took off to Miami, Florida; it's unclear if he still plays guitar.

Dean FORD & THE GAYLORDS (see under ⇒ MARMALADE)

FOREVER MORE

Formed: Dundee . . . late 60's out of HOPSCOTCH by ONNIE MAIR (aka OWEN McINTYRE), ALAN GORRIE, STEWART FRANCIS and Englishman MICK TRAVIS. HOPSCOTCH had released two singles for 'United Artists' in '68 and '69, before opting for a change in moniker and style. FOREVER MORE took inspiration from blues icons LEADBELLY and ROBERT JOHNSON, although the band incorporated folk, R&B and just about anything that was suitable in this ever-evolving, genre-twisting period. Complete with what they thought was a bonafide deal courtesy of experienced entrepreneurs and session men, RAY SINGER and SIMON NAPIER-BELL, they released a couple of albums ('YOURS FOREVER MORE' and 'WORDS ON BLACK PLASTIC') early in the 70's. However, when the scrupulous pair brought in session people and kept most of the money (allegedly over £15,000), FOREVER MORE chose to be no more. GORRIE and MAIR would eventually find their pot of gold in The AVERAGE WHITE BAND, while the other two formed GLENCOE way down south in London.

HOPSCOTCH

ONNIE MAIR (b. OWEN McINTYRE) – vocals, bass, guitar (ex-SCOTS OF ST. JAMES) / **HAMISH STUART** – vocals / **MICK TRAVIS** – guitar / **STEWART FRANCIS** – drums, vocals; repl. ALAN KELLY

U.A. not iss.

Jul 68. (7") *(UP 2231)* **LOOK AT THE LIGHTS GO UP. / SOME OLD FAT MAN** [ ] [-]

May 69. (7") *(UP 35022)* **LONG BLACK VEIL. / EASY TO FIND** [ ] [-]

FOREVER MORE

— **ALAN GORRIE** – piano, bass; repl. HAMISH who joined DREAM POLICE

R.C.A. R.C.A.

Mar 70. (lp) *(SF 8016) <LSP 4272>* **YOURS FOREVER MORE** [ ] [ ]
– Back in the States again / We sing / It's home / Home country blues / Good to me / Yours / Beautiful afternoon / 8 o'clock and all's well / Mean pappie blues / You too can have a body like mine / Sylvester's last voyage.

Jun 70. (7") *<0335>* **BEAUTIFUL AFTERNOON. / 1 O'CLOCK & ALL'S WELL** [-] [ ]

Nov 70. (7") *(RCA 2024)* **PUT YOUR MONEY ON A PONY. / YOURS** [ ] [-]

Jan 71. (lp) *(LSA 3015) <LSP 4425>* **WORDS ON BLACK PLASTIC** [ ] [ ]
– Promises of Spring / The wrong person / Last breakfast / Get behind me Satan / Put your money on a pony / Lookin' through the water / O'Brien's last stand / Angel of the Lord / What a lovely day.

— disbanded when McINTYRE and GORRIE formed AVERAGE WHITE BAND; FRANCIS and TRAVIS helped form GLENCOE, although the latter quit Spring '72

FRANKIE & JOHNNY (see under ⇒ "A Beat(en) Generation")

G

James GAIT (see under ⇒ "A Beat(en) Generation")

GALLAGHER & LYLE

Formed: Largs . . . 1964 by the songwriting duo of BENNY GALLAGHER and GRAHAM LYLE. Having both cut their teeth on the local beat group/R&B scene, the pair initially made their mark by penning DEAN FORD AND THE GAYLORDS' 1964 hit, 'Mr Heartbreak's Here Instead'.

PAUL McCARTNEY was quick to spot their collective talent and by 1967, G&L were holding down full-time staff writing jobs at 'Apple', the same year they made their recording debut with 'TREES', a one-off single for 'Polydor'. Among the fruits of their labour at 'Apple' was MARY HOPKIN's 'International' and 'Sparrow'. In 1969 the pair joined rootsy popsters McGUINNESS FLINT, for whom they penned two UK Top 5 hits, the classic 'WHEN I'M DEAD AND GONE' and 'MALT AND BARLEY BLUES'.

This success encouraged them to form their own recording group and together with a rhythm section of CHRIS STEWART and BRUCE ROWLAND, they released an eponymous debut album for 'Capitol' in 1972. A prolific couple of years ensued during which they not only cut a trio of albums for 'A&M' – 'WILLIE & THE LAP DOG' (1973), 'SEEDS' (1973) and 'THE LAST COWBOY' (1974) – but worked alongside RONNIE LANE in the first incarnation of his SLIM CHANCE band, appearing on the 1974 debut, 'Anyone For Anymore'. The Scots duo's easygoing MOR style and canny way with a harmony finally caught the nation's attention in 1976 when the disco-strings-enhanced 'I WANNA STAY WITH YOU', hit the Top 10 along with 'HEART ON MY SLEEVE'. Both were lifted from the 'BREAKAWAY' (1976) album, its title track having already furnished ART GARFUNKEL with the title of a 1975 solo album. Although 1977's 'LOVE IN THE AIRWAVES' album made the Top 20 and furnished ELKIE BROOKS with a minor hit (in the shape of 'RUNAWAY'), the duo's finely crafted pop fared badly as the late 70's New Wave scene took hold.

After a final couple of albums, 'SHOWDOWN' (1978) and 'LONESOME NO MORE' (1979), the pair went their separate ways, GALLAGHER into a production career and LYLE into a highly successful songwriting partnership with Terry Britten; among their clients were TINA TURNER ('What's Love Got To Do With It', 'We Don't Need Another Hero'), MICHAEL JACKSON ('Just Good Friends') and fellow Scot, JIM DIAMOND, for whom they penned the No.1 ballad, 'I SHOULD HAVE KNOWN BETTER'. LYLE once again teamed up with McGUINNESS (as McGUINNESS-LYLE), releasing the album, 'ACTING ON IMPULSE'.

BENNY GALLAGHER – vocals, guitar, mandolin, bass / **GRAHAM LYLE** – vocals, guitar, mandolin, banjo, bass

Polydor not iss.

Jul 67. (7"; as GALLAGHER-LYLE) *(BM 56170)* **TREES. / IN THE CROWD** [ ] [-]

— in 1969 they joined McGUINNESS FLINT and stayed for a few years

— now with new band **CHRIS STEWART** – bass / **BRUCE ROWLAND** – drums

Capitol Capitol

Jan 72. (7") *(CL 15710)* **DESIDERATA. / COMFORT AND JOY**

Mar 72. (lp) *(ST 21906) <11016>* **GALLAGHER & LYLE**
– Mrs. Vcantellis / City and suburban blues / Caledonia Steam Packet Co. / To Daid, Charlie and Ian / Broken wings / Coat for the Spring / Great Australian dream / Rock and roll hero / Greenfingers / Comfort and joy / Of a moment / Desiderata. *(re-iss. later 1972 on 'A&M'; AMLS 68125)*

— **HUGHIE FLINT** – drums (ex-McGUINNESS FLINT, ex-JOHN MAYALL) repl. CHRIS

A&M A&M

Jul 72. (7") *(AMS 7013)* **GIVE A BOY A BREAK. / JOIE DE VIVRE**

Mar 73. (7") *(AMS 7048)* **DAN. / HOME** -

Mar 73. (lp) *(AMLH 68142) <4384>* **WILLIE & THE LAP DOG**
– Willie / Home / Give a boy a break / Sittin' down music / Dan / Among the birks / Jesus save me / Hotel Constantine / The lap dog / Harmonium / Thoughts from a station.

May 73. (7") *(AMS 7063)* **JESUS SAVE ME. / AMONG THE BIRKS**

Aug 73. (7") *(AMS 7077)* **SITTIN' DOWN MUSIC. / S.S. MAN**

— **JIMMY JEWELL** – saxophone + **BRIAN ROGERS** – strings; repl. FLINT

Nov 73. (7") *(AMS 7087)* **SHINE A LIGHT. / ALL I WANT TO DO**

Dec 73. (lp) *(AMLS 68207) <4425>* **SEEDS**
– Country morning / Misspent youth / I believe in you / Sleepy head / Layna / The clearings / Remember then / Seeds of change / Shine a light / Randolf and me / Cape Cod houses / Seeds.

Feb 74. (7") *(AMS 7099)* **I BELIEVE IN YOU. / SEEDS**

— **BILL LIVSEY** – keyboards; repl. ROGERS

Oct 74. (lp) *(AMLS 68273) <3665>* **THE LAST COWBOY**
– Keep the candle burning / Song and dance man / Acne blues / I'm amazed / King of the silents / Rain / We / Mhairu / Villain of the peace / The last cowboy.

Nov 74. (7") *(AMS 7142)* **WE. / KING OF THE SILENTS**

— **RAY DUFFY** – drums / **ALAN HORNALL** – bass / **JOHN MUMFORD** – trombone; repl. ROWLAND

Jan 76. (lp/c) *(AMLH/CAM 68348) <4566>* **BREAKAWAY** 6
– Breakaway / Stay young / I wanna stay with you / Heart on my sleeve / Fifteen summers / Sign of the times / If I need someone / Storm in my soul / Rockwriter / Northern girl. *(re-iss. May84 on 'Spot' lp/c; SPR/SPC 8545) (re-iss. May93 on 'Spectrum' cd/c; 550064-2/-4)*

Feb 76. (7") *(AMS 7211) <1778>* **I WANNA STAY WITH YOU. / FIFTEEN SUMMERS** 6 49 Mar76

May 76. (7") *(AMS 7227) <1850>* **HEART ON MY SLEEVE. / NORTHERN GIRL** 6 67 Aug76

Aug 76. (7") *(AMS 7245)* **BREAKAWAY. / ROCKWRITER** 35

— **IAN RAE** – keyboards; repl. LIVESY

Jan 77. (7") *(AMS 7274)* **EVERY LITTLE TEARDROP. / STREET BOYS** 32

Jan 77. (lp/c) *(AMLH/CAM 68348) <4620>* **LOVE ON THE AIRWAVES** 19
– Love on the airwaves / The runaway / Every little teardrop / Had to fall in love / Street boys / Never give up on love / Dude in the dark / Head talk / Call for the captain / It only hurts when I laugh. *(re-iss. Feb81 on 'Music For Pleasure' lp/c; MFP/TCMFP 50497)*

Apr 77. (7") *(AMS 7282)* **THE RUNAWAY. / CALL OF THE CAPTAIN**

Jul 77. (7") *(AMS 7300)* **HAD TO FALL IN LOVE. / HEAD TALK**

— **BILL LIVSEY** – keyboards / **RAY COOPER** – percussion / **JIM HORN** – horns; repl. RAE + MUMFORD + JEWELL

Jan 78. (7") *(AMS 7332)* **SHOWDOWN. / GOLDEN BOY**

Jan 78. (lp/c) *(AMLH/CAM 68461) <4675>* **SHOWDOWN**
– Showdown / In your eyes / You're the one / Hurts to learn / It's over / Heartbreaker / Backstage / All grown up / Throw away heart / Next to you.

May 78. (7") *(AMS 7356)* **YOU'RE THE ONE. / BACKSTAGE**

Nov 78. (7") *(AMS 7396)* **MISSING YOU. / HEARTS DON'T BREAK** -

— **GALLAGHER & LYLE** plus **RAY DUFFY** now with guests **BAM KING** – guitar / **STEVE BINGHAM** – bass / **MEL COLLINS** – saxophone / **JULIEN DIGGLE** – percussion

Mercury Mercury

Aug 79. (7") *(6007 233)* **MISSING YOU. / SUNNY SIDE UP** -

Oct 79. (lp) *(9109 628)* **LONESOME NO MORE** -
– Believed in you / Concrete and steel / Deja vu / Diamonds / Fool for your love / Lay me down and die / Partners / Mexico / Let go / Wide wide world / Wheels / Missing you.

Aug 80. (7") *(MER 23)* **LIVING ON THE BREADLINE. / TAKE THE MONEY AND RUN** -

— went their separate ways in the early 80's. LYLE set up a songwriting partnership with TERRY BRITTEN writing hits for TINA TURNER, etc. He also released a solo single mid'83 'MARLEY'. / 'DOWN THE SUBWAY' on 'Red Bus'; *(RBUS 78)*

– compilations, others, etc. –

Feb 80. (lp/c) *Warwick; (WW/+4 5080)* **THE BEST OF GALLAGHER & LYLE** -

May 81. (d-c) *A&M; (CR 6)* **BREAKAWAY / SHOWDOWN** -

Jul 82. (7") *Old Gold; (OG 9150)* **I WANNA STAY WITH YOU. / HEART ON MY SLEEVE** -

Apr 88. (7") *A&M; (AM 443)* **YOU PUT THE HEART BACK IN THE CITY. / FIFTEEN SUMMERS** -
(12"+=) *(AMY 443)* – Heart on my sleeve.

Feb 91. (7") *A&M;* **HEART ON MY SLEEVE. /** -

Apr 91. (cd/c/lp) *A&M; (397123-2/-4/-1)* **HEART ON MY SLEEVE – THE VERY BEST OF GALLAGHER & LYLE** -
– Breakaway / I wanna stay with you / Every little teardrop / Heart on my sleeve / Stay young / Fifteen summers / Heart in New York / You put the heart back in the city / When I'm dead and gone / Malt and barley blues / Willie / Layna / We / Keep the handle burning / Runaway / I believe in you. *(re-iss. Oct92 cd/c; CD/C MID 172)*

Nov 95. (cd/c) *Spectrum; (551830-2/-4)* **THE BEST OF GALLAGHER & LYLE** -

Mar 99. (cd) *Strange Fruit; (SFRSCD 059)* **LIVE IN CONCERT (live)** -

Ron GEESIN

Born: 1943, Ayrshire. In 1961, he joined the Crawley-based jazz combo, The ORIGINAL DOWNTOWN SYNCOPATORS, who issued a few EP's as well as a very limited 10" album.

In 1965, he recorded a solo EP, before he started to write music for documentaries and TV commercials. Living in Notting Hill, London, he built up recording equipment for his next outing; the 1967 album 'A RAISE OF EYEBROWS'. The album highlighted GEESIN's eclectically experimental avant-garde jazz. In 1969, he toured alongside folkies ROY HARPER and RALPH McTELL, while he worked on his next project, 'THE BODY'. This was a collaboration with ROGER WATERS (of PINK FLOYD), who had previously invited RON to augment and co-write on PINK FLOYD's 'ATOM HEART MOTHER' album. In 1971/72, he sessioned and produced albums for BRIDGET ST. JOHN and ARMORY KANE respectively, 'Songs For The Gentle Man' and 'Just To Be There'. In 1973, he set up his own-named label, for which he issued three albums in the mid-70's. At the same time, he issued some library-only albums, although he was to drop out of the music scene in the late 70's and 80's. In 1990, after working on various BBC TV and radio productions, he surfaced once again with the cd-album, 'FUNNY FROWN'. RON now lives in Sussex.

• **Trivia:** In 1969, he appeared on lp 'JOHN PEEL PRESENTS TOP GEAR' with track 'Agitation In Anticipation Of Offspring, Parts W, X & Y'.

ORIGINAL DOWNTOWN SYNCOPATORS

RON GEESIN – piano / + ?

V.J.M. not iss.

1962. (7"ep) *(VEP 14)* **ORIGINAL DOWNTOWN SYNCOPATORS** -
– Sensation rag / Skeleton jangle / Mojo stomp / Indiana.

John R.T. Davis not iss.

1963. (10"lp) *(DAVLP 301-2)* **THE ORIGINAL DOWNTOWN SYNCOPATORS** -

Columbia not iss.

1964. (7"ep) *(SEG 8293)* **IT'S JASS** -

RON GEESIN

- vocals, keyboards, synthesizers, etc

no label not iss.

1965. (ltd-7"ep) *(RRG 319-320)* **RON GEESIN** -

Transatla. not iss.

Jun 67. (lp; stereo/mono) *(S+/TRA 161)* **A RAISE OF EYEBROWS** -
– A raise of eyebrows / Freedom for four voices and me / Psychedelia / Positives / It's all very new, you know / A female / Certainly random / The eye that nearly saw / Two fifteen string guitars for nice people / From an electric train / A world of too much sound / Another female / We're all going to Liverpool / Ha! ha! but reasonable.

— In 1970, he worked with PINK FLOYD on their album 'ATOM HEART MOTHER'. The group's main man returned the favour on below.

Harvest Harvest

Dec 70. (lp; by RON GEESIN & ROGER WATERS) *(SHSP 4008) <SW 751>* **MUSIC FROM THE BODY (soundtrack)**
– Our song / Sea shell and stone / Red staff writhe / Gentle breeze blew through life / Lick your partners / Bridge passage for three plastic teeth / Cain of life / Womb bit / Embryo thought / March past of the embryos / More than seven dwarfs in Penis land / Dance of the red corpuscles / Body transport / Breathe old folks ascension / Bedtime – Dream – Clime / Piddle in perspex / Embryonic womb talk / Mrs. Throat goes walking / Sea shell and soft stone / Give birth to a smile. *(cd-iss. 1989 on 'E.M.I.'; CDP7 92548-2) (cd re-iss. Feb96; CZ 178)*

Ron Geesin not iss.

May 73. (lp) *(RON 28)* **AS HE STANDS** -
– Roll 'em, bowl 'em-in three movements / Duet for two and a street market / On-through-out-up / Waiting for life / The middle of whose night? / Wrap a keyboard round a plant / Twist and knit for two guitars / Up above my heart / A cymbal and much electronics / To Roger Waters wherever you are / Mr. Pugeot's trot / Upon

compositions / Concrete line up / Rise up Sebastian! / Looming view / Can't you stop that thing.

1975. (lp) *(RON 31)* **PATRUNS** ☐ -
– B-wink / Octave creep / Double octave ripple / A, D & G black major throb / White note of calm / Dripped chromatic essence / Smoke hips (the time dance) / Grand E minor opening / E minor paint splash slap lash / E minor, lie down still / Pastrun spread / Platform twitch / Romanian rag tome shut / Chromatic trashers / Grand B major ending wink.

1977. (lp) *(RON 323)* **RIGHT THROUGH** ☐ -

Headscope | not iss.

1991. (cd) *(HEDCD 001)* **FUNNY FROWN** ☐ -
– Bell sigh / Driftbox / Vivaldi's Largo in D / Piano prance / Slink / Mad kite / Hot breath / Lonely park / Go! / Throat poise / The living city / Floating out / Ample sample / Ron's tune / Through leaves / Whistling heart / Fingal's grave.

1993. (cd) *(HEDCD 002)* **BLUEFUSE** ☐ -

– compilations, etc. –

on 'K.P.M.' unless mentioned otherwise

1972. (ltd-lp) *(KPM 1102)* **ELECTROSOUND** - - Library
1975. (ltd-lp) *(KPM 1154)* **ELECTROSOUND VOL.2** - - Library
1977. (ltd-lp) *(KPM 1201)* **ATMOSPHERES** - - Library
1988. (ltd-cd) *Themes Int.; (TIM 11CD)* **MAGNIFICENT MACHINES** - - Library

Mar 94. (cd) *Cherry Red; (CDBRED 110)* **HYSTERY (THE RON GEESIN STORY)** ☐ -
– Ron's address / Parallel bar / Throat sweat / Mental passage / Whistling heart / Go! / Foretease / Twisted pair / Big imp / Morecambe Bay / Sit down, mama / T'mith / Throb thencewards thrill / Smoked hips (the time dance) / Frenzy / Animal autos / Where daffodils do thrive / Upon composition / Can't you stop that thing? / Vocal chords / Syncopot / Song of the wire / Affections for string quartet / With a smile up his nose, they entered / Three vignettes / Certainly random / A raise of eyebrows / No.8 scalpel incision foxtrot.

Sep 95. (cd) *See For Miles; (SEECD 433)* **A RAISE OF EYEBROWS / AS HE STANDS** ☐ -

GIDIAN (see under ⇒ "A Beat(en) Generation")

GLENCOE

Formed: London . . . late 1971 by seasoned Scots campaigners GRAHAM MAITLAND, STEWART FRANCIS, MICK TRAVIS and Englishman NORMAN WATT-ROY. In April the following year, their acoustic folk sound was shelved when ex-SKIP BIFFERTY man, JOHN TURNBULL, was drafted in to replace college student TRAVIS. This bunch of intelligent, but gimmicky performers managed to secure a deal with 'Epic' records, who issued two patchy LP's, 'GLENCOE' (1972) and 'THE SPIRIT OF GLENCOE' (1973), before climbing down. The last of these was produced by BEN SIDRAN, a favourite with the West Coast brigade, while nearly all of the esteemed members re-united in IAN DURY & THE BLOCKHEADS.

GRAHAM MAITLAND – vocals, keyboards (ex-HOPSCOTCH, ex-FLEUR DE LYS, ex-FOLLOW THE BUFFALO) / **NORMAN WATT-ROY** – bass, vocals (ex-GREATEST SHOW ON EARTH) / **JOHN TURNBULL** – guitar, vocals (ex-SKIP BIFFERTY, ex-CHOSEN FEW, ex-ARC), repl. MICK TRAVIS / **STEWART FRANCIS** – percussion (ex-HOPSCOTCH, ex-FOREVER MORE)

Epic | Epic

Sep 72. (7") *(EPC 8383)* **LOOK ME IN THE EYE. / TELEPHONIA** ☐ -
Oct 72. (lp) *(EPC 65207) <31901>* **GLENCOE** ☐ ☐
– Airport / Look me in the eye / Lifeline / Telephonia / It's / Book me for the flight / Hay fever / Questions / Sinking down a well.
Jan 73. (7") *(EPC 1187)* **AIRPORT. / IT'S** ☐ -
Jun 73. (7") *(EPC 1597)* **FRIENDS OF MINE. / TO DEVINE MOTHER** ☐ -
Aug 73. (lp) *(EPC 65717) <32353>* **THE SPIRIT OF GLENCOE** ☐ ☐
– Friends of mine / Roll on blues / Strange circumstance / Nothing (is between us) / Is it you / Born in the city / Arctic madness / To divine mother / Song No.22 (om) / Two on an island (in search of a new world).
Nov 73. (7") *(EPC 1874)* **ROLL ON BLUES. / NOTHING (IS BETWEEN US)** ☐ -

— disbanded Apr'74; FRANCIS joined The SHARKS. NORMAN and JOHN teamed with MICKEY GALLAGHER – keyboards (ex-FRAMPTON'S CAMEL, ex-BELL & ARC, ex-SKIP BIFFERTY, ex-CHOSEN FEW) and Guyanian born session drummer CHARLEY CHARLES to form LOVING AWARENESS. They went to Palm Springs to record eponymous LP; released by 'More Love' in Aug76; *(ML 001)*. All members were then drafted into IAN DURY's backing band The BLOCKHEADS.

GOLDEN CRUSADERS (see under ⇒ "A Beat(en) Generation")

Eve GRAHAM

Born: 19 Apr'43, Perth. EVE EDEN, as she was then known, started out her singing career in Brummie band, The NOCTURNES. Along with four/five others including Mancunian LYN PETERS (aka LYN PAUL), the harmony-fuelled pop outfit released several flop singles and two albums for 'Columbia' between 1967/68.

At the turn of the decade, both brunette EVE and blonde LYN were duly invited by ex-SEEKERS/ex-NEW EDITION member turned manager, KEITH POTGER, to join the aptly-monikered NEW SEEKERS. Along with three equally starry-eyed males (MARTY KRISTIAN, PETER DOYLE and PAUL LAYTON), EVE and her new group found fame in the States, where a cover of Melanie's 'LOOK WHAT THEY'VE DONE TO MY SONG MA' climbed into the Top 20. MELANIE's songbook was also the source for two further minor hits, 'BEAUTIFUL PEOPLE' and 'NICKEL SONG', although these 45's achieved little or nothing back here in Blighty. However, things looked markedly brighter in summer '71, when the group hit UK No.2 with 'NEVER ENDING SONG OF LOVE'. Towards the end of the year, their sugary version of the Hillside Singers-penned 'I'D LIKE TO TEACH THE WORLD TO SING' (the Coca-Cola TV ad jingle) shot up to top the UK charts (and make Top 10 in the US). It was inevitable that their next step would involve the Eurovision Song Contest of April 1972. The song in question, 'BEG, STEAL OR BORROW', didn't quite win it for Britain, but it did provide them with another No.2 smash.

From then on, the hits just kept rolling off the production line, Harry Chapin's 'CIRCLES', Neil Young's 'DANCE, DANCE, DANCE' and the Fleetwood's 'COME SOFTLY TO ME' (as The NEW SEEKERS featuring MARTY KRISTIAN), were some of the inspired writing sources to beg, steal, or in fact, borrow from. The Who's 'PINBALL WIZARD – SEE ME FEEL ME' (from their 'Tommy' score) provided the group with yet another Top 20 smash, while not so inspiring was 'NEVERTHELESS' (from the pens of Eclection), a disappointing Top 40 flop credited to EVE GRAHAM and the NEW SEEKERS. Just when it looked all over for the pop-tastic 5-piece, they hit paydirt again, via their second chart-topper, 'YOU WON'T FIND ANOTHER FOOL LIKE ME'. However, only one further UK Top 5 hit, 'I GET A LITTLE SENTIMENTAL OVER YOU', graced the charts in Spring '74, the NEW SEEKERS bowing out after a long tour. A lucrative contract from 'C.B.S.' in 1976, ensured the group (without solo LYN) return to the music biz, although by '78 their dreams were well and truly over as EVE too left.

At the beginning of the 80's, EVE tried in vain to revive her career, a solitary album, 'WOMAN OF THE WORLD' (for er . . . 'Celebrity' records), only filling bargain bins.

EVE GRAHAM – vocals / with session people

Celebrity | not iss.

Feb 81. (7") *(ACS 3)* **YOUR LOVE. / FALLING IN LOVE AGAIN** ☐ -
Feb 81. (lp/c) *(AC LP/K 007)* **WOMAN OF THE WORLD** ☐ -
– All the money in the world / We got tonight / Give us time / Real to reel / Chanson pour les petits enfants / Woman of the world / Falling in love again / Just smile / Evergreen / Black widow spider / Leaving it all / Woman in love.

— EVE retired from show business soon after

H

Alex HARVEY

Born: 5 Feb'35, "the Gorbals" area, Glasgow. ALEX grew up in a politically aware, well-read family, taking his stance as a conscientious objector from his father. Following loads of jobs (36 to be exact, including a stint lion-taming!) he played in various skiffle groups and after winning a local talent contest in 1956, he was dubbed "The TOMMY STEELE Of Scotland".

In 1959, his BIG SOUL BAND backed touring American stars, EDDIE COCHRAN and GENE VINCENT, the former subsequently being killed in a car crash a few months later. By 1964, ALEX HARVEY AND HIS SOUL BAND were taking the well-trodden path to Hamburg, Germany, while back home LULU was capitalising on a hit version of 'Shout!', an ISLEY BROTHERS track which featured prominently in HARVEY's repertoire. During this heady mid-60's period, HARVEY himself released two LP's, the second of which 'THE BLUES' (1965) featured the precocious guitar playing of his younger brother LES. Travelling between London and Glasgow, ALEX

subsequently struggled on with his ever evolving musical vision, psychedelic GIANT MOTH backing him up during the flower-power era of '67.

After a run of flop singles, HARVEY joined the crew of the 'Hair' musical in London's West End, earning his crust by night (mainly as the guitarist but also contributing the occasional vocal) and continuing to write his own material by day. Towards the end of the decade, HARVEY released his first bonafide solo album, 'ROMAN WALL BLUES' (1969), backed up by his brother LES and some of the crew from the ROCK WORKSHOP ensemble in which ALEX was briefly involved.

Through a third party, ALEX was introduced to Glasgow band TEAR GAS (ZAL CLEMINSON, HUGH McKENNA, CHRIS GLEN and TED McKENNA), with whom he was so impressed he moved back to Scotland and secured them as his backing outfit. Early in 1972 they became The SENSATIONAL ALEX HARVEY BAND, and, after nationwide tours and a signature for 'Vertigo', released their debut album 'FRAMED'. 1972 was set to be an eventful, often traumatic year for ALEX, what with the tragic death of his brother LES (electrocuted while on stage with STONE THE CROWS) and a challenging support slot to Brummie chart-toppers SLADE. ALEX had his own way of approaching such a challenge, frequently goading audiences (especially if they happened to be from south of the border!) into a reaction, negative or otherwise – JOHNNY ROTTEN obviously took note. Visually, HARVEY was a larger than life JOHNNY KIDD-esque pirate figure with more than a hint of hidden menace. With his buccaneer attitude and dishevelled look, he was nothing less than a musical visionary, only matched by his clown-faced guitarist, ZAL CLEMINSON. Late in '73, SAHB issued the excellent 'NEXT . . .', promoting the album with an extensive tour which included of all places, Falkirk Town Hall. The unadulterated combination of European style seediness, OTT theatrics and futuristic comic book imagery came together in such classics as 'THE FAITH HEALER' (a 7 minute+ masterpiece), the self-explanatory 'GANG BANG' and Jacques Brel's 'NEXT'.

HARVEY was also a rather unlikely advocate of cleaning up the nation's streets, inventing the "Vambo" comic book character to push home his anti-vandal message. The track 'VAMBO MARBLE EYE', was the first and also the most memorable in a series of "Vambo" songs, urging fans "don't pish in your own water supply".

A year later, SAHB secured their first UK Top 20 album spot with 'THE IMPOSSIBLE DREAM' (1974), a more accessible effort which sacrificed some of its predecessor's grubby intensity although 'THE TOMAHAWK KID' and 'ANTHEM' kept the fans on HARVEY's alternative yellow brick road. The pinnacle of HARVEY and SAHB's colourful career came in 1975, a year that saw both a UK Top 10 album 'TOMORROW BELONGS TO ME' and a Top 10 rendition of Tom Jones' 'DELILAH' (from the 'LIVE' set), culminating in a series of three sold out Xmas shows at Glasgow's Apollo theatre. Gallus as ever, HARVEY entered the stage to the strains of Irving Berlin's 'CHEEK TO CHEEK', joined by a troupe of dancing girls who eventually turned their backs to the crowd and revealed their cheeky bare-ass attire; ALEX was so impressed he kissed each bum in turn before blessing each one with a rose . . . The aforementioned 'CHEEK . . .' featured on SAHB's next offering 'THE PENTHOUSE TAPES' (1976), a slightly disappointing covers set that led to the band signing a fresh deal with 'Mountain' records (also home to NAZARETH). Shortly afterwards, ALEX and the boys scored their second major UK hit, 'BOSTON TEA PARTY', although again the accompanying album 'SAHB STORIES' (1976), left most fans let down. While ALEX took off to Northern Scotland for a bizarre documentary album, ' . . .PRESENTS THE LOCH NESS MONSTER', SAHB WITHOUT ALEX (as they were briefly billed!) released their own set, 'FOURPLAY' (1977).

Even though ALEX had in some respects anticipated the advent of Punk Rock, SAHB were ill-equipped to compete in the brave new (wave) world. The 'ROCK DRILL' (1978) album was a final disappointing nail in the coffin while the death of HARVEY's mentor/manager BILL dealt him an emotional hammer blow. The band effectively came to an end when ALEX refused to board a plane for Stockholm, claiming that he'd seen a purple light and therefore couldn't cross water. Although his drinking and eccentric behaviour became more pronounced, he did subsequently form the not so sensational ALEX HARVEY BAND, returning to the recording studio with a new line-up for 1979's cult fave 'THE MAFIA STOLE MY GUITAR'. Years of hard living finally took its toll on ALEX as he succumbed to a heart attack on the 4th of February 1982, bizarrely enough just prior to boarding a return ferry from Belgium; he left behind wife Trudy and two sons.

• **Songwriters:** Most by himself and HUGH McKENNA, with additions from either ZAL or producer DAVE BATCHELOR. Covered; FRAMED (Leiber-Stoller) / I JUST WANT TO MAKE LOVE TO YOU (Willie Dixon) / GIDDY-UP-A-DING-DONG (Freddie Bell & The Bellboys) / THE IMPOSSIBLE DREAM (Leigh-Darion) / MONEY HONEY (. . . Stone) / RIVER OF LOVE (??) / TOMORROW BELONGS TO ME (Ebb-Kander) / DELILAH (hit; Tom Jones) / GAMBLIN' BAR ROOM BLUES (Alley-Rodgers) / CHEEK TO CHEEK (Irving Berlin) / LOVE STORY (Jethro Tull) / CRAZY HORSES (Osmonds) / SCHOOL'S OUT (Alice Cooper) / RUNAWAY (Del Shannon) / GOODNIGHT IRENE (Leadbelly) / SHAKIN' ALL OVER (Johnny Kidd).

• **Trivia:** HARVEY's 'LOCH NESS' lp, released unusually on 'K-Tel', featured only interviews from sightings of the monster.

ALEX HARVEY & HIS SOUL BAND

ALEX HARVEY – vocals / **RICKY BARNES** – saxophone, vocals / **ISOBEL BOND** – vocals / **GIBSON KEMP** – drums / **IAN HINDS** – organ / **BILL PATRICK** – guitar

		Polydor	not iss.
Jan 64.	(7"; as ALEX HARVEY) *(NH 52264)* **I JUST WANNA MAKE LOVE TO YOU. / LET THE GOOD TIMES ROLL**		-
Mar 64.	(lp) *(LPHM 46424)* **ALEX HARVEY AND HIS SOUL BAND (live)** – Framed / I ain't worrying baby / Backwater blues / Let the good times roll / Going home / I've got my mojo working / Teensville U.S.A. / New Orleans / Bo Diddley is a gunslinger / When I grow too old to rock / Evil hearted man / I just wanna make love to you / The blind man / Reeling and rocking. *(Germany re-iss. Oct87 lp/c; 831887-1/-4)*		-
Jun 64.	(7") *(NH 52907)* **GOT MY MOJO WORKING. / I AIN'T WORRIED BABY**		-

—— ALEX HARVEY brought in new soul band, (his brother **LES HARVEY** – guitar / **BOBBY THOMPSON** – bass / **GILSON KEMP** – drums)

Jul 65.	(7") *(BM 56017)* **AIN'T THAT JUST TOO BAD. / MY KIND OF LOVE**		-
Nov 65.	(lp) *(LPHM 46441)* **THE BLUES**		-

– Trouble in mind / Honey bee / I learned about woman / Danger zone / The riddle song / Waltzing Matilda / The blues / The big rock candy mountain / The Michegan massacre / No peace / Nobody knows you when you're down and out / St. James infirmary / Strange fruit / Kisses sweeter than wine / Good God almighty.

ALEX HARVEY

solo with session musicians.

Fontana not iss.

Sep 65. (7") *(TF 610)* **AGENT OO SOUL. / GO AWAY BABY** [-]

Nov 66. (7") *(TF 764)* **WORK SONG. / I CAN'T DO WITHOUT YOUR LOVE** [-]

— HARVEY now backed by **GIANT MOTH:- JIM CONDRON** – guitar, bass / **MOX** – flute / **GEORGE BUTLER** – drums

Decca not iss.

Jul 67. (7") *(F 12640)* **THE SUNDAY SONG. / HORIZON'S** [-]

Sep 67. (7") *(F 12660)* **MAYBE SOME DAY. / CURTAINS FOR MY BABY** [-]

— next with backing from ROCK WORKSHOP which incl. brother LES and loads of others. In 1970/71 for 'CBS', they released two lp's 'ROCK WORKSHOP' *(64075) & not with ALEX, a double 'THE VERY LAST TIME' (64394)*. Taken from first lp was 45; 'YOU TO LOSE'.

Fontana not iss.

Oct 69. (lp; stereo/mono) *(S+/TL 5534)* **ROMAN WALL BLUES** [-]
– Midnight Moses / Hello L.A., bye bye Birmingham / Broken hearted fairytale / Donna / Roman wall blues / Jumping Jack Flash / Hammer song / Let my bluebird sing / Maxine / Down at Bart's place / Candy. *(cd-iss. May02 on 'Red Bus'; RF 609)*

Nov 69. (7") *(TF 1063)* **MIDNIGHT MOSES. / ROMAN WALL BLUES** [-]

— ALEX then formed his trio (**IAN ELLIS** – bass, ex-CLOUDS, **DAVE DUFORT** – drums) This was broken up after the death, by stage electrocution, of his brother LES, who had been part of STONE THE CROWS since '69 (Aug72) **ALEX** recruited a whole band

— **TEAR GAS** who had already made two albums – Nov70 'PIGGY GO BETTER' on 'Famous', without the McKENNA brothers. Aug71. 'TEAR GAS' on 'Regal Zonophone', with all the members of below . . .

The SENSATIONAL ALEX HARVEY BAND

ALEX – vocals, guitar / **ZAL CLEMINSON** (b. 4 May'49) – guitar, vocals / **CHRIS GLEN** (b. 6 Nov'50) – bass / **HUGH McKENNA** (b.28 Nov'49) – keyboards / **TED McKENNA** (b.10 Mar'50) – drums

Vertigo Vertigo

Dec 72. (7") *(6059 070)* **THERE'S NO LIGHTS ON THE CHRISTMAS TREE, MOTHER, THEY'RE BURNING BIG LOUIE TONIGHT. / HARP** [-]

Jan 73. (lp) *(6360 081)* **FRAMED** [-]
– Framed / Hammer song / Midnight Moses / Isobel Goudie (part 1 – My lady of the night, part 2 – Coitus interruptus, part 3 – The virgin and the hunter) / Buff's bar blues / I just want to make love to you / Hole in her stocking / There's no lights on the Christmas tree, mother, they're burning big Louie tonight / St. Anthony. *(re-iss. Mar79 on 'Mountain';) (re-iss. Jul86 on 'Sahara' lp/c; (SAH 119/+TC) (cd-iss. 1986 on 'Samurai'+=; SAMRCD 00119)* – Smouldering / Chase it into the night.

Mar 73. (7") *(6059 075)* **JUNGLE JENNY. / BUFF'S BAR BLUES** [-]

Nov 73. (lp) *(6360 103) <1017>* **NEXT . . .**
– Swampsnake / Gang bang / The faith healer / Giddy up a ding dong / Next / Vambo marble eye / The last of the teenage idols (part I-III). *(re-iss. Mar79 on 'Mountain';) (re-iss. Nov84 on 'Sahara'; SAH 114) (pic-lp May86; SAH 114CD) (cd-iss. 1986 on 'Samurai'; SAMRCD 00114) (re-iss. Mar87 on 'Fame' lp/c; FA/TC-FA 3169)*

Feb 74. (7") *(6059 098)* **THE FAITH HEALER (edit). / ST. ANTHONY** [-]

Feb 74. (7") *<113>* **SWAMPSNAKE. / GANG BANG** [-]

Aug 74. (7") *(6059 106)* **SERGEANT FURY. / GANG BANG** [-]

Sep 74. (7") *<200>* **SERGEANT FURY. / TOMAHAWK KID** [-]

Sep 74. (lp)(c) *(6360 112) <2000>* **THE IMPOSSIBLE DREAM** [16]
– The hot city symphony; (part 1 – Vambo, part 2 – Man in the Jar) / River of love / Long hair music / Sergeant Fury / Weights made of lead / Money honey – The impossible dream / Tomahawk kid / Anthem. *(re-iss. Mar79 on 'Mountain';) (re-iss. Jul86 on 'Samurai' lp/c; SAH 116/+TC)*

Nov 74. (7") *(6059 112)* **ANTHEM. / ANTHEM (version)** [-]

Apr 75. (lp)(c) *(6360 120) <2004>* **TOMORROW BELONGS TO ME** [9]
– Action strasse / Snake bite / Soul in chains / The tale of the giant stoneater / Ribs and balls / Give my compliments to the chef / Sharks teeth / Ribs and balls / Shake that thing / Tomorrow belongs to me / To be continued . . . *(re-iss. Nov84 on 'Sahara'; SAH 111) (cd-iss. Jul86 on 'Samurai'+=; SAMRCD 00111)* – Big boy / Pick it up and kick it.

Vertigo Atlantic

Jul 75. (7") *(ALEX 001) <3293>* **DELILAH (live). / SOUL IN CHAINS (live)** [7]

Sep 75. (lp)(c) *(9102 007) <18184>* **THE SENSATIONAL ALEX HARVEY BAND "LIVE" (live)** [14] [100]
– Fanfare (justly, skillfully, magnanimously) / The faith healer / Tomahawk kid / Vambo / Give my compliments to the chef / Delilah / Framed. *(re-iss. Jul86 on 'Sahara' c/lp/pic-lp; TC+/SAH 117/+PD) (re-iss. Oct86 on 'Fame' lp/c; FA/TC-FA 3161) (cd-iss. 1986 on 'Samurai'; SAMRCD 00117)* – I wanna have you back / Jungle Jenny / Runaway / Love story / School's Out.

Nov 75. (7") *(ALEX 002)* **GAMBLIN' BAR ROOM BLUES. / SHAKE THAT THING** [38] [-]

Mar 76. (7") *(ALEX 003)* **RUNAWAY. / SNAKE BITE** [-]

Mar 76. (lp)(c) *(9102 007)* **PENTHOUSE TAPES** (old covers) [14] [-]
– I wanna have you back / Jungle Jenny / Runaway / Love story / School's out / Goodnight Irene / Say you're mine / Gamblin' bar room blues / Crazy horses / Cheek to cheek. *(re-iss. Mar79 on 'Mountain';) (re-iss. Nov84 on 'Sahara'; SAH 112) (cd-iss. Jul86 on 'Samurai'; SAMRCD 00112)*

Mountain not iss.

May 76. (7") *(TOP 12)* **BOSTON TEA PARTY. / SULTAN'S CHOICE** [13] [-]

Jul 76. (lp)(c) *(TOPS 112)* **SAHB STORIES** [11] [-]
– Boston Tea Party / Sultan's choice / $25 for a massage / Dogs of war / Dance to your daddy / Amos Moses / Jungle rub out / Sirocco. *(re-iss. Nov84 on 'Sahara'; SAH 115)*

Aug 76. (7") *(TOP 19)* **AMOS MOSES. / SATCHEL AND THE SCALP HUNTER** [-]

— now all 4 members without ALEX HARVEY. (HUGH on vocals)

Jan 77. (lp; SAHB WITHOUT ALEX) *(TOPC 5006)* **FOURPLAY** [-]
– Smouldering / Chase it into the night / Shake your way to Heaven / Outer boogie / Big boy / Pick it up and kick it / Love you for a lifetime / Too much American pie. *(re-iss. Nov84 on 'Sahara'; SAH 113)*

Jan 77. (7"; SAHB WITHOUT ALEX) **PICK IT UP AND KICK IT. / SMOULDERING** [-]

— In Apr'77, **ALEX HARVEY** released but withdrew, solo narrative lp 'PRESENTS THE LOCH NESS MONSTER' on 'K-Tel'; *NE 984)*

— re-formed **HARVEY, CLEMINSON, TED McKENNA and GLEN** recruited **TOMMY EYRE** – keyboards who repl. HUGH McKENNA

Aug 77. (7") *(TOP 32)* **MRS. BLACKHOUSE. / ENGINE ROOM BOOGIE** [-]

Mar 78. (lp)(c) *(TOPS 114)* **ROCK DRILL** [-]
– The rock drill suite: Rock drill – The dolphins – Rock and roll – King Kong / Booids / Who murdered sex / Nightmare city / Water beastie / Mrs. Blackhouse. *(re-iss. Nov84 on 'Sahara'; SAH 118)*

— (had already split late '77) CHRIS and TED joined ZAL in his own named band. ZAL later joined NAZARETH. TED later joined RORY GALLAGHER and then GREG LAKE BAND. TED and CHRIS later moved on to the MICHAEL SCHENKER GROUP.

ALEX HARVEY BAND

with **TOMMY EYRE** – keyboards / **MATTHEW CANG** – guitar / **GORDON SELLAR** – bass (ex-BEGGARS OPERA) / **SIMON CHATTERTON** – drums

R.C.A. not iss.

Oct 79. (7") *(PB 5199)* **SHAKIN' ALL OVER. / WAKE UP DAVIS** [-]

Nov 79. (lp/c) *(PL/PK 25257)* **THE MAFIA STOLE MY GUITAR** [-]
– Don's delight / Back in the depot / Wait for me mama / The Mafia stole my guitar / Shakin' all over / The whalers (thar she blows) / Oh Sparticus / Just a gigolo / I ain't got nobody. *(cd-iss. Sep91 on 'Mau Mau'; MAUCD 608) (cd re-iss. May98 on 'Edsel'; EDCD 562)*

May 80. (7") *(PB 5252)* **BIG TREE SMALL AXE. / THE WHALERS (THAR SHE BOWS)** [-]

— ALEX HARVEY died of a heart attack on the 4th of February 1982 while on a ferry from Belgium

– his posthumous releases –

Power Supply not iss.

Nov 83. (7") *(OHM 3)* **THE POET AND I. /** [-]

Nov 83. (c/lp) *(C+/AMP 2)* **SOLDIER ON THE WALL** [-]

SENSATIONAL ALEX HARVEY BAND

— actually re-formed for live gigs without ALEX!

Meantime not iss.

Apr 94. (cd/c) *(JIMBO/JIMMC 001)* **LIVE IN GLASGOW 1993 (live)** [-]
– The faith healer / St. Anthony / Framed / Gang bang / Amos Moses / Boston tea party / Midnight Moses / Vambo / Armed and dangerous / Delilah.

– SAHB compilations, etc. –

May 77. (lp) *Vertigo; (6360 147)* **BIG HITS AND CLOSE SHAVES** [-]
(re-iss. Apr79 on 'Mountain')

Jun 77. (7") *Vertigo; (6059 173)* **CHEEK TO CHEEK. / JUNGLE JENNY** [-]

Jul 80. (c/lp) *Mountain; (T+/TOPS 129)* **COLLECTOR'S ITEMS** [-]

Jul 80. (7"m) *Mountain; (HOT 2)* **DELILAH (live). / BOSTON TEA PARTY / THE FAITH HEALER** [-]

Aug 82. (d-lp/d-c) *R.C.A.; (RCA LP/K 9003)* **THE BEST OF THE SENSATIONAL ALEX HARVEY BAND** [-]
– Next / Framed / The faith healer / Tomahawk kid / The hot city symphony; part 1 – Vambo, part 2 – Man in the jar / Sergeant Fury / The tale of the giant stoneater / Action strasse / Delilah / Weights made of lead / Boston Tea Party / Anthem /

Runaway / Crazy horses / Big tree small axe / The Mafia stole my guitar / Gang bang / Tomorrow belongs to me. *(re-iss. May84 d-lp/d-c; PL/PK 70276)*

Nov 85. (lp/c) *Sahara; (SAH/+TC 041)* **LEGEND** ☐ -
(cd-iss. 1986 on 'Samurai'; SAMR 041CD)

Jan 86. (c) *Sahara; (SAH 041TC)* **ANTHOLOGY** ☐ -

Apr 86. (c) *Aura;* **DOCUMENT** ☐ -

Sep 86. (d-lp/c/cd) *Castle; (CCS LP/MC/CD 149)* **THE COLLECTION** ☐ -
– $25 for a massage / The tale of the giant stoneater / Action strasse / Gang bang / Next / Give my compliments to the chef / Framed / Tomorrow belongs to me / Dance to your daddy / Sgt.Fury / Sultan's choice / Delilah (live) / Soul in chains / The faith healer / Boston tea party / Vambo (part 1) / Dogs of war / There's no lights on the Christmas tree mother, they're burning big Louie tonight / Giddy up a ding dong.

Jul 87. (lp/c)(cd) *K-Tel; (NE1/CE2 368)(NCD 5139)* **THE BEST OF THE SENSATIONAL ALEX HARVEY BAND** ☐ -
– Delilah / The faith healer / Framed / Sergeant Fury / Jungle rub out / Love story / School's out / Boston Tea Party / Gamblin' bar room blues / Next / The man in the jar / Snake bite / Give my compliments to the chef / Cheek to cheek.

Sep 87. (lp/c/cd) *Start; (STF L/C/CD 1)* **PORTRAIT** ☐ -
(re-iss. Jan91 lp/c/cd; same)

Feb 91. (cd/c) *Music Club; (MC CD/TC 001)* **THE BEST OF THE SENSATIONAL ALEX HARVEY BAND** ☐ -
(re-iss. Jul94 on 'Success';)

Oct 91. (lp) *Windsong; (WINCD 002)* **BBC RADIO 1 LIVE IN CONCERT (live)** ☐ -

Jun 92. (cd/c) *Vertigo; (512 201-2/-4)* **ALL SENSATIONS** ☐ -

Nov 94. (cd) *Windsong; (WHISCD 004)* **LIVE ON THE TEST** ☐ -

Sep 94. (cd/c) *Spectrum; (550 663-2/-4)* **DELILAH** ☐ -

Feb 99. (lp) *Get Back; (GET 536)* **THE RISE AND FALL OF THE SENSATIONAL ALEX HARVEY BAND** ☐ -

May 99. (cd) *Bear Family; (<BCD 1630-2>)* **ALEX HARVEY AND HIS SOUL BAND** (not original LP) ☐ ☐

Feb 02. (cd) *Mercury; (586392-2)* **FAITH HEALER – AN INTRODUCTION TO THE SENSATIONAL ALEX HARVEY BAND** ☐ -

Apr 02. (d-cd) *Mercury; (586696-2)* **FRAMED / NEXT . . .** ☐ -

Apr 02. (d-cd) *Mercury; (586697-2)* **THE IMPOSSIBLE DREAM / TOMORROW BELONGS TO ME** ☐ -

Apr 02. (d-cd) *Mercury; (586698-2)* **THE PENTHOUSE TAPES / LIVE** ☐ -

Apr 02. (d-cd) *Mercury; (586699-2)* **ROCK DRILL / SAHB STORIES** ☐ -

Pye HASTINGS

Born: 21 Jan'47, Scotland, although he was raised in the Kent town of Lydden where he attended Pilgrims school. Abandoning his job as an insurance salesman, HASTINGS took off to Spain and Morocco before joining The WILDE FLOWERS. When they changed their moniker to CARAVAN in 1967, things began to take off for the Canterbury outfit (HASTINGS was also an integral part of this songwriting force). CARAVAN delivered a plethora of albums before splicing into other equally avant-Prog outfits like CAMEL, etc. HASTINGS never officially left CARAVAN and re-united the band for gigs in 1990. Since 1994 to now (2002), the group are still going strong; sample the PYE-penned 1995 set, 'THE BATTLE OF HASTINGS'.

HEMLOCK (see under ⇒ ANDERSON, Miller)

Brian HENDERSON (see under ⇒ "A Beat(en) Generation" – MARK FIVE)

Mike HERON (see ⇒ Section 2: Folk)

HI-FI'S (see under ⇒ Alp records)

HOPSCOTCH (see under ⇒ FOREVER MORE)

HOUSE OF LORDS (see under ⇒ "A Beat(en) Generation" – THREE'S A CROWD)

HUMAN BEAST

Formed: Edinburgh . . . late 60's initially as SKIN, by ED JONES, GILLIES BUCHAN and JOHN ROMSEY; the trio augmented by clarinet player DAVID McNIVEN (leader of BREAD, LOVE AND DREAMS). Opening with the mindblowing 'MYSTIC MAN' and followed by 'BRUSH WITH THE MIDNIGHT BUTTERFLY', all looked well for this grandiosely Eastern-inspired combo. Both heavy and psychedelic – US outfit BEACON STREET UNION come to mind – HUMAN BEAST were to become extinct shortly afterwards. However, the LP is very collectable and now changes hands for over 150 smackaroonies; we await its release onto CD.

ED(WARD) JONES – vocals, bass / **GILLIES BUCHAN** – guitar, vocals / **JOHN ROMSEY** – drums / plus **DAVID McNIVEN** – clarinet (of BREAD, LOVE AND DREAMS)

Decca not iss.

Nov 70. (lp; mono/stereo) *(LK/SKL 5053)* **HUMAN BEAST VOLUME ONE: INSTINCT** ☐ -
– Mystic man / Appearance is everything, style is a way of living / Brush with the midnight butterfly / Maybe someday / Reality presented as an alternative / Baked breakfast / Circle of the night.

— disappeared quickly from the music scene

I

INCREDIBLE STRING BAND

Formed: Glasgow . . . early 1966 by ROBIN WILLIAMSON, London-born CLIVE PALMER and MIKE HERON. From the early 60's, WILLIAMSON had played London gigs alongside BERT JANSCH (future PENTANGLE), before he returned to Glasgow. In April 1961, he formed a duo with Englishman PALMER, although they found it difficult to establish themselves, that is, until 1965 when PALMER set up the 'Incredible' folk club in Sauchiehall Street. That same year, the pair performed at the Edinburgh Folk Festival, catching the eye of Nathan Joseph of 'Transatlantic' records who recorded them for the concert's Various Artists compilation. After their folk club was shut down by the police, they became a trio, adding MIKE HERON to become The INCREDIBLE STRING BAND.

After months tracking them down, American producer JOE BOYD finally found them and duly signed them to 'Elektra'. He subsequently took them to London, where they recorded their eponymous debut album (summer '66). With this well-received record under their belt, PALMER departed for Afghanistan. When he returned he declined to re-join the act, who were now broke but under the management of BOYD. Upon ROBIN's return from Morocco, the duo (augmented by some friends), played an 'Elektra' records package alongside TOM PAXTON and JUDY COLLINS, at The Royal Albert Hall. It helped promote their second album, '5,000 SPIRITS OR THE LAYERS OF THE ONION', which made the UK Top 30 in 1967. Their underground blend of psychedelic folk was crystallised on such charming tracks as, 'CHINESE WHITE', 'FIRST GIRL I LOVED' and 'PAINTING BOX'. In Spring '68, they surprisingly crashed into the UK Top 5 with their third set, 'THE HANGMAN'S BEAUTIFUL DAUGHTER'. The album's witty lyrics (alternately penned by HERON or WILLIAMSON) and ethnic multi-instrumentation was embellished with the vocals of the duo's girlfriends, LICORICE and ROSE. The highlights of this album, arguably the group's finest hour, were 'A VERY CELLULAR SONG', 'THE MINOTAUR'S SONG' and 'KOEEOADDI THERE'. Late that year, they issued 2 single lp's as a double-set, 'WEE TAM' & 'THE BIG HUGE'. However, this brilliant but confused package failed to sell.

Over the next two years, they released three UK Top 40 albums ('I LOOKED UP', a collection of baroque eclecticism – 'U' verging on pantomine), but after a move to 'Island' in 1971, they soon faded from the commercial limelight. Nevertheless, the second 'Island' album, 'LIQUID ACROBAT AS REGARDS THE AIR', hit the Top 50, boasting the spine-tingling melancholy of the 11-minute 'DARLING BELLE'.

HERON and WILLIAMSON went their separate ways in the mid-70's, the former writing 'DON'T KILL IT CAROL' (later a hit for MANFRED MANN'S EARTH BAND), the latter becoming something of a self-styled cosmic folk storyteller (complete with harp). WILLIAMSON recorded a plethora of albums and poetry between 1977 and the present day, and even established his own imprint, 'Pig's Whisker'.

Although HERON hasn't been quite as visible since the ISB's split, he has surfaced with the occasional solo set, harking back to an ISB-style sound on 1996's 'WHERE THE MYSTICS SWIM'. Another old ISB face cropped up in 1999 as ROBIN recorded 'AT THE PURE FOUNTAIN' with CLIVE PALMER, the pair completing a second set, 'JUST LIKE THE IVY', the following year. The big news, however, was a full INCREDIBLE STRING

BAND reunion at the 2001 Celtic Connections Festival in Glasgow, messrs WILLIAMSON, HERON, PALMER plus newcomers LAWSON DANDO and BINA WILLIAMSON (ROBIN's wife) putting in an acclaimed performance which more than justified the hype and boded well for the future.

ROBIN WILLIAMSON (b.24 Nov'43, Edinburgh) – vocals, guitars, etc. / **CLIVE PALMER** (b. 1943, Edmonton, London) – guitar, banjo, vocals / **MIKE HERON** (b.12 Dec'42, Glasgow) – vocals, rhythm guitar, sitar, etc.

Elektra Elektra

Jun 66. (lp) *(EUK 254)* <*EKS 7322*> **THE INCREDIBLE STRING BAND** ☐ ☐
– Maybe someday / October song / When the music starts to play / Schaeffer's jig / Womankind / The tree / Whistle tune / Dandelion blues / How happy am I / Empty pocket blues / Smoke shovelling song / Can't keep me here / Good as gone / Footsteps of the heron / Niggertown / Everything's fine right now. *(re-iss. Jul68; EKL 254); hit No.34) (cd-iss. Jul93; 7559 61547-2) (cd re-iss. Jun94 on 'Hannibal'; HNCD 4437)*

—— now a duo when PALMER went to abroad; he later formed FAMOUS JUG BAND

—— added **CHRISTINA 'LICORICE' McKENNA** – some vocals, organ (a guest on below) plus guests **DANNY THOMPSON** – double bass (of PENTANGLE) / **JOHN HOPKINS** – piano

Jul 67. (lp; mono/stereo) *(EUK/+S7 257)* <*EKS 74010*> **THE 5,000 SPIRITS OR THE LAYERS OF THE ONION** 26 ☐
– Chinese white / No sleep blues / Painting box / The Mad Hatter's song / Little cloud / The eyes of fate / Blues for the muse / The hedgehog's song / First girl I loved / You know that you could be / My name is death / Gently tender / Way back in the 1960's. *(re-iss. 1968; EKS 7257) (re-iss. Jan73 + 1976; K 42001) (cd-iss. Mar92; 7559 60913-2) (cd re-iss. Jun94 on 'Hannibal'; HNCD 4438)*

Mar 68. (7") *(EKSN 45028)* **PAINTING BOX. / NO SLEEP BLUES** ☐ -

Mar 68. (lp; mono/stereo) *(EUK/+S7 258)* <*EKS 74021*> **THE HANGMAN'S BEAUTIFUL DAUGHTER** 5 ☐ Jun68
– Koeeoaddi there / The minotaur's song / Witches hat / A very cellular song / Mercy I cry city / Waltz of the new Moon / The water song / Three is a green crown / Swift as the wind / Nightfall. *(re-iss. Jan73 + 1976; K 42002) (cd-iss. Mar92; 7559 60835-2) (cd re-iss. Jun94 on 'Hannibal'; HNCD 4437)*

—— **MIKE, ROBIN** and his girlfriend **LICORICE** introduced MIKE'S girlfriend **ROSE SIMPSON** – some vocals, bass, percussion, violin

Oct 68. (d-lp; mono/stereo) *(EKL/EKS7 4036-7)* **WEE TAM / THE BIG HUGE** ☐ -
(d-cd-iss. Nov94 on 'Hannibal'; HNCD 4802)

Oct 68. (lp; mono/stereo) *(EKL/*<*EKS7 4036*>*)* **WEE TAM** ☐ ☐ Mar69
– Job's tears / Puppies / Beyond the see / The yellow snake / Log cabin home in the sky / You get brighter / The half-remarkable question / Air / Ducks on a pond. *(re-iss. Jan73 + 1976; K 42021) (cd-iss. Feb92; 7559 60914-2) (*<*cd re-iss. Nov94 on 'Hannibal'; HNCD 4802*>*)*

Oct 68. (lp; mono/stereo) *(EKL/*<*EKS7 4037*>*)* **THE BIG HUGE** ☐ ☐ Mar69
– Maya / Greatest friend / The son of Noah's brother / Lordly nightshade / The mountain of God / Cousin caterpillar / The iron stone / Douglas Traherne Harding / The circle is unbroken. *(re-iss. Jan73 + 1976; K 42022) (cd-iss. Jul93; 7559 61548-2)*

—— LICORICE was now a full-time member

Oct 69. (7") *(EKSN 45074)* **BIG TED. / ALL WRIT DOWN** ☐ -

Nov 69. (lp) *(*<*EKS 74057*>*)* **CHANGING HORSES** 30 ☐
– Big Ted / White bird / Dust be diamonds / Sleepers, awake! / Mr. & Mrs. / Creation. *(cd-iss. Jul93 & May01; 7559 61549-2) (cd-iss. Dec94 on 'Hannibal'; HNCD 4439)*

—— added guest **DAVE MATTACKS** – drums of FAIRPORT CONVENTION

Apr 70. (lp) *(*<*EKS 7401*>*)* **I LOOKED UP** 30 ☐ Jul70
– Black Jack Davy / Puppies / The letter / Pictures in a mirror / This moment / When you find out who you are / Fair as you. *(re-prom.1970; 2469 002) (cd-iss. Dec94 on 'Hannibal'; HNCD 4440) (cd re-iss. Jul02; 7559 62760-2)*

Apr 70. (7") *(2101 003)* **THIS MOMENT. / BLACK JACK DAVY** ☐ -

May 70. (7") <*45696*> **THIS MOMENT. / BIG TED** - ☐

—— augmented by **JANET SHANKMAN** – b.vocals (ROBIN married her Dec70) **PETE GRANT** – banjo / **GREG HART** – sitar (of STONE MONKEY) plus guest **MALCOLM LE MAISTRE** – keyboards, bass (of EXPLODING GALAXY)

Oct 70. (d-lp) *(2665 001)* <*7E 2002*> **"U"** 34 ☐ Jan71
– El wool suite / The juggler's song / Time / Bad Sadie Lee / Queen of love / Partial belated overture / Light in the time of darkness – Glad to see you / Walking along with you / Hirem pawn Itof – Fairies' hornpipe / Bridge theme / Bridge song / Astral plane theme / Invocation / Robot blues / Puppet song / Cutting the strings / I know you / Rainbow. *(re-iss. Jan73; K 62002) (cd-iss. Jul02; 7559 62761-2)*

—— Back to basic duo of **ROBIN + MIKE** plus **LICORICE + ROSE**

Island Elektra

Apr 71. (lp) *(ILPS 9140)* **BE GLAD FOR THE SONG HAS NO ENDING** ☐ -
– Come with me / All writ down / Vishangro / See all the people / Waiting for you / (Be glad for) The song has no ending. *(cd-iss. Jun98 on 'Edsel'; EDCD 564)*

—— **MALCOLM LE MAISTRE** – keyboards, bass, vocals returned to repl. ROSE

Oct 71. (lp) *(ILPS 9172)* <*74112*> **LIQUID ACROBAT AS REGARDS THE AIR** 46 ☐ Feb72
– Talking of the end / Dear old battlefield / Cosmic boy / Worlds they rise and fall / Evloution rag / Painted chariot / Adam and Eve / Red hair / Here till here is there / Tree / Jigs: Eyes like leaves – Sunday is my wedding day – Drops of whiskey – Grumbling old men / Darling Belle. *(re-iss. Aug91 cd)(c; IMCD 130)(ICM 9172)*

—— added **GERARD DOTT** – clarinet, saxophone (he played on HERON's 1972 solo album) and guest on one **STUART GORDON** – viola

Oct 72. (lp) *(ILPS 9211)* **EARTH SPAN** ☐ -
– My father was a lighthouse keeper / Antoine / Restless night / Sunday song / Black Jack David / Banks of sweet Italy / The actor / Moon hang low / The sailor and the dancer / Seagull. *(cd-iss. Dec92 on 'Edsel'; EDCD 360)*

Nov 72. (7") *(WIP 6145)* **BLACK JACK DAVID. / MOON HANG LOW** ☐ -

—— **STAN LEE** – bass repl. LICORICE who joined WOODY WOODMANSEY Band **JACK INGRAM** – drums (added to ROBIN, MIKE, MALCOLM, GERARD and STAN)

Island Reprise

Feb 73. (7") *(WIP 6158)* **AT THE LIGHTHOUSE DANCE. / JIGS** ☐ -

Feb 73. (lp) *(ILPS 9229)* <*2139*> **NO RUINOUS FEUD** ☐ ☐
– Explorer / Down before Cathy / Saturday maybe / Jigs / Old Buccaneer / At the lighthouse dance / Second fiddle / Circus girl / Turquoise blue / My blue tears / Weather the storm / Little girl. *(cd-iss. Nov92 on 'Edsel'; EDCD 367)*

—— **GRAHAM FORBES** – electric guitar (ex-POWERHOUSE) repl. GERARD / **JOHN GILSTON** – drums repl. INGRAM

Mar 74. (lp) *(ILPS 9270)* <*2198*> **HARD ROPE & SILKEN TWINE** ☐ ☐
– Maker of islands / Cold February / Glancing love / Dreams of no return / Dumb Kate / Ithkos. *(cd-iss. Feb93 on 'Edsel'; EDCD 368)*

—— WILLIAMSON + HERON went onto solo careers; the pair re-formed late 1999 with PALMER, LAWSON DANDO + BINA WILLIAMSON

Pig's Whisker Pig's Whisker

Aug 01. (cd) *(*<*PWMD 5024*>*)* **BLOOMSBURY 2000 (live)** ☐ ☐ Nov01
– Maker of islands / Ducks on a pond / Air / The storm is on the ocean / Big city blues / Waltz of the new moon / Goodbye / You know what you could be / October song.

– compilations etc. –

Mar 71. (lp) *Elektra; (EKS 74065) / Reprise;* <*7E 2004*> **RELICS OF THE INCREDIBLE STRING BAND** ☐ ☐

Nov 76. (d-lp) *Island; (ISLD 9)* **SEASONS THEY CHANGE – BEST OF THE INCREDIBLE STRING BAND** ☐ -
– Black Jack David / Blues for the muse / Nightfall / Puppies / Cold days of February / Worlds they rise and fall / Chinese white / Empty pocket blues / When the music starts to play / Saturday maybe / Red hair / The circle is unbroken / First girl I loved / Cosmic boy / Darling Belle / My father was a lighthouse keeper / Queen Juanita and her fisherman lover.

Oct 91. (cd/lp) *Band Of Joy; (BOJ CD/LP 004)* **ON AIR (live)** ☐ -

Nov 92. (cd) *Windsong; (WINCD 029)* **BBC RADIO 1 LIVE IN CONCERT** ☐ -

Jun 97. (cd) *Blueprint; (PWMD 5003)* **CHELSEA SESSIONS 1967** ☐ -
(<*re-iss. Mar98 on 'Pig's Whisker'; PWCD 5003)*> *(re-iss. Jul00; PWCD 5023)*

Aug 98. (cd) *Mooncrest; (*<*CRESTCD 002*>*)* **FIRST GIRL I LOVED (live)** ☐ ☐
– Cousin caterpillar / I know that man / The circle is unbroken / Wild cat blues / The first girl I loved / Everything's fine right now / Old buccaneer / Catwalk rag / Giles crocodile / Turquoise blue / My father was a lighthouse keeper / Black Jack David / Ithkos.

May 01. (cd) *Island; (IMCD 280)* **HERE TILL THERE IS HERE (AN INTRODUCTION TO THE INCREDIBLE STRING BAND)** ☐ -

Jul 01. (cd) *Warner ESP; (9548 39803-2)* **THE BEST OF THE INCREDIBLE STRING BAND 1966-1970** ☐ -

—— HERON and WILLIAMSON also released solo albums before their split. HERON = 'SMILING MEN WITH BAD REPUTATIONS' and WILLIAMSON = 'MYRRH'. Plus they went onto solo careers in 1975.

IRON CLAW (see under ⇒ "A Beat(en) Generation)

IRON VIRGIN

Formed: Edinburgh . . . 1973 initially as VIRGIN, although after auditions (my cousins PAUL and STEPHEN McELROY in attendance!) they – STUART HARPER, GORDON NICOL, MARSHALL BAIN, LAURIE RIVA and JOHN LOVATT – added the IRON. Fitting neatly into the NAZARETH meets SWEET bracket, IRON VIRGIN (complete with homemade American football regalia) were signed to 'Deram', for whom they released their Nick Tauber-produced debut single, a cover of Paul McCartney & Wings' 'JET'. Unfortunately, when the former Beatle and his band decided to release the 45, it flopped dismally. A follow-up single, 'REBELS RULE', was equally dismissed by the buying public outside of Scotland's central belt and the glam hard-rockers quickly disappeared.

STUART HARPER – vocals / **GORDON NICOL** – guitar / also **LAURIE RIVA, MARSHALL BAIN + JOHN LOVAT**

		Deram	not iss.
Feb 74.	(7") *(DM 408)* **JET. / MIDNIGHT HITCHER**		-
Jun 74.	(7") *(DM 416)* **REBELS RULE. / AIN'T NO CLOWN**		-

— disbanded after above

J

JAYGARS (see under ⇒ "A Beat(en) Generation – ONE IN A MILLION)

JOHNNY & THE COPYCATS (see under ⇒ MY DEAR WATSON)

Davey JOHNSTONE

Born: 6 May'51, Edinburgh. Raised in the Carrick Knowe and West Craigs areas of the city, DAVEY took up the guitar while at school. He later immersed himself in the local music scene and went on to play with both CARRICK FOLK and NOEL MURPHY'S DRAUGHT PORRIDGE.

In 1970, he was invited to join English folk newcomers MAGNA CARTA, playing on their 'Seasons' LP onwards. A fortuitous meeting with producer Gus Dudgeon subsequently led to JOHNSTONE backing up ELTON JOHN on his 'Madman Across The Water' album, an engagement which proved the first in a long line of big name sessions; amongst others JOAN ARMATRADING, KIKI DEE, and later ALICE COOPER, MEAT LOAF and LEO SAYER. He also found time to record a low key solo LP, 'SMILING FACE' (1973), although his professional relationship with ELTON took up the bulk of his schedule and even lasts to this day; he's currently EJ's musical director. In another twist of fate, JOHNSTONE was to date future ELTON collaborator KIKI DEE in a passionate romance which lasted four years.

Although he remained in the music business he was to settle down with new wife Kay in California through the 80's and 90's. Tragedy struck however, when on the 11th of May 2001, his nine year-old son Oliver died in a freak swimming pool accident at the family's L.A. home.

DAVEY JOHNSTONE – vocals, guitar / with various session people incl. BJ COLE, RAY COOPER, MOHAMMED AMIR, JOAN ARMATRADING, CHRIS LAURENCE, GRAHAM MORGAN + NIGEL OLSSON, DEE MURRAY, GUS DUDGEON, etc.

		Rocket	M.C.A.
1973.	(lp) *(ROLA 2) <MCA 340>* **SMILING FACE**		

– Keep right on / Janine / The boatman / Walking out / Our dear friend / Island / After the dance / You are – I am / Smiling face / Beautiful one / A lovely day / A lark in the morning with Mrs. McLeod.

— basically concentrated on session work and ELTON's band activities

		Ariola	not iss.
Jul 80.	(7") *(237)* **LOVE IS A CRAZY FEELING. / BURNIN'**		-

		not iss.	Solid Air
Feb 99.	(cd; as DAVEY JOHNSTONE & JOHN JORGENSON) *<9097>* **CROP CIRCLES**	-	

– 3rd neck from now / Crop circles / She's gonna cry soon / Reel it in / Exercise in fraternity / Bernadette's rose / Fat slag rag / Grooves and lands / Beyond ohm / Lavoya / Scarabride / Sacred path.

L

LIGHT OF DARKNESS (see under ⇒ REOCH, Mike . . .)

LORD ROCKINGHAM'S XI

Formed: London ... early 1958 by Elgin-born bandleader HARRY ROBINSON (real name HENRY), also a journalist with his local newspaper. This modern ensemble of 13 (not XI) became the resident band on ITV's popular music show, 'Oh Boy!'. The show's creator, Jack Good, dreamed up the inspired moniker of LORD ROCKINGHAM'S XI; incidentally named after a genuine historical figure. Their first single, 'FRIED ONIONS', was a surprise Top 100 entry in the US, although Britain was yet to be impressed. That was to change later in the year, when the band's follow-up, 'HOOTS MON' (based on the Scottish tune, 'ONE HUNDRED PIPERS'), stormed up the charts. Complete with trademark sax-laden backing (supplied by RED PRICE), this JOHNNY & THE HURRICANES-styled number hit the top of the British hit parade for three weeks that December. ROBINSON's unique Scottish dialect/voiceover ("hoots mon, there's a moose loose aboot this hoose") on the novelty instrumental was indeed its forte, although it was somewhat helped by exposure on the aforementioned 'Oh Boy!'; trivia fans take note that broadcaster, author and jazz "buff" BENNY GREEN anonymously played alto sax when the group appeared at a Royal Command Performance. LORD ROCKINGHAM'S XI faded into obscurity after a second hit 'WEE TOM' made the Top 20. This was probably due to the fact that lawyers were brought in to sort out a dispute on who owned the rights to LRXI – ROBINSON the leader, or GOOD its creator? Anyway, things were sort of resolved for a time when HARRY ROBINSON released further recordings under his own name; he also provided backing for Millie's No.1 hit, 'My Boy Lollipop' in 1964. In 1993, after a daft TV ad to sell of all things wine gums, 'HOOTS MON', stormed the charts again, er . . . at No.60.

HARRY ROBINSON – voice, etc / with **RED PRICE** – saxophone / **CHERRY WAINER** – organ / **BENNY GREEN** – alto sax / **RORY BLACKWELL** – drums / + others who remained anonymous

		Decca	London
May 58.	(7",78) *(F 11024) <1810>* **FRIED ONIONS. / THE SQUELCH**		96 Sep58
Oct 58.	(7",78) *(F 11059)* **HOOTS MON. / BLUE TRAIN** *(re-iss. Aug76; F 13663)*	1	
Jan 59.	(7",78) *(F 11104)* **WEE TOM. / LORD ROCKINGHAM I PRESSUME?**	16	
May 59.	(7",78) *(F 11139)* **RA-RA ROCKINGHAM. / FAREWELL TO ROCKINGHAM**		
Jun 60.	(7"; as HARRY ROBINSON "STRING SOUND") *(JAR 325)* **THE SKIRL. / WIMOWEH** (above issued on 'Top Rank')		-
Jan 61.	(7"; as HARRY ROBINSON'S XI) *(F 11319)* **HEAVY DATE. / SENTIMENTAL JOURNEY**		-
Jan 62.	(7") *(F 11426)* **NEWCASTLE TWIST. / ROCKINGHAM TWIST**		-

HARRY ROBINSON

		Fontana	not iss.
1962.	(7"; as HARRY ROBINSON CREW) *(H 376)* **SON OF TWIST. / WHISHT IT'S IN THE TWIST**		-
1960's.	(7"; as HARRY ROBINSON CREW) *(H 267230)* **BACKSCRATCHER. / SOME OTHER LOVE**		-
		Decca	**not iss.**
Feb 63.	(7") *(F 11591)* **WILDCAT. / LIKE YODEL**		-
Jul 63.	(7"; as the ROBINSON CREW) *(F 11706)* **TAXI (theme from the TV series). / STORMALONG**		-
		Columbia	**not iss.**
Dec 68.	(lp; as LORD ROCKINGHAM'S XI) *(SCX 6291)* **THE RETURN OF LORD ROCKINGHAM'S XI**		-
Apr 70.	(7"; as HARRY ROBINSON & HIS ORCHESTRA) *(DB 8677)* **AIRPORT (LOVE THEME). / SATURDAY IN THE KING'S ROAD**		-
		E.M.I.	**not iss.**
Apr 77.	(7" as HARRY ROBINSON & HIS STRINGS THAT SING) *(EMI 2602)* **ADAGIO ALBINONI. / DREAMER**		-

– compilations, etc. –

1958.	(7"ep) *Decca; (DFE 6555)* **OH BOY!**		-
Sep 93.	(7"/c-s/cd-s) *Decca; (882 098-7/-4/-2)* **HOOTS MON! / BLUE TRAIN / WEE TOM**	60	-

LULU

Born: MARIE LAWRIE, 3 Nov'48, Lennoxtown. Making her first public singing appearance before she even reached her teens, LAWRIE subsequently formed her own band The GLEN EAGLES. Soon renamed LULU & THE LUVVERS, they signed to 'Decca' and had a surprise UK Top 10 hit in 1964 with a frenetic cover of The Isley Brothers' 'SHOUT'. Its success made the diminutive LULU a schoolgirl star, her surprisingly soulful pubescent rasp blaring out of radios and TV sets across the country. This was followed into the charts by pop ballad 'LEAVE A LITTLE LOVE' although much of her mid-60's material consisted of rough'n'ready R&B covers such as The Rolling Stones' 'SURPRISE SURPRISE'; she even cut Bert Bern's 'HERE COMES THE NIGHT' before THEM/VAN MORRISON got their hands on it. She went solo in 1966 and was soon back in the UK Top 10 the following year with a cover of Neil Diamond's 'THE BOAT THAT I ROW'.

1967 also saw LULU make her critically acclaimed acting debut, co-starring alongside Sidney Poitier in the film, 'To Sir With Love'. The movie's title theme subsequently gave the Glaswegian a US No.1 and the success launched her into the ranks of the pop/rock aristocracy. She married BEE GEE, MAURICE GIBB in 1969, the same year she won the Eurovision song contest with the awful No.2 hit, 'BOOM BANG-A-BANG'. Juggling the opposing forces of TV showbiz personality and rock credibility, she made the obligatory pilgrimage to Muscle Shoals in 1970 for her blue-eyed soul effort, 'NEW ROUTES'. Released on 'Atlantic' and featuring the crack production team of Jerry Wexler, Tom Dowd and Arif Mardin', the record paired LULU with soul powerhouses like The DIXIE FLYERS and The MEMPHIS HORNS, spawning minor UK hit, 'OH ME OH MY (I'M A FOOL FOR YOU BABY)'.

1973/74 found her working with DAVID BOWIE on a cover of his own 'THE MAN WHO SOLD THE WORLD' (flipped with his 'WATCH THAT MAN'), her first UK Top 3 hit in nearly five years. For the remainder of the 70's and most of the 80's she was absent from the chart spotlight although she did score a couple of minor US hits in 1981 and made a brief UK Top 10 comeback in 1986 with a remake of 'SHOUT' (an exploitative re-release of the original version also went Top 10 at the same time).

A larger scale comeback/reinvention was effected early in 1993 with the club-influenced 'INDEPENDENCE' single (taken from the album of the same name), a near UK Top 10 hit. Later that year, she set the charts ablaze in tandem with TAKE THAT on a cover of Dan Hartman's 'RELIGHT MY FIRE', seeing her reach the British No.1 for the first time in her thirty year career. She continues to be one of Scotland's most high profile celebrities (in 1999/2000 she co-hosted the National Lottery Show) and incredibly, still looks like a spring chicken despite being in her 50's. Must be the Glasgow water . . .

LULU – vocals / + The LUVVERS:- **ROSS NELSON** – lead guitar / **JIM DEWAR** – rhythm guitar / **ALEC BELL** – keyboards / **JIMMY SMITH** – saxophone / **TONY TIERNEY** – bass / **DAVID MILLER** – drums

Decca | Parrot

Apr 64. (7"; as LULU AND THE LUVVERS) *(F 11884)* *<9678>* **SHOUT. / FORGET ME BABY** [7] [94] Jul64
(re-iss. Nov81; same)

Aug 64. (7") *(F 11965)* **CAN'T HEAR YOU NO MORE. / I AM IN LOVE** [ ] [-]

Oct 64. (7") *(F 12017)* **HERE COMES THE NIGHT. / THAT'S REALLY SOME GOOD** [50] [-]

Apr 65. (7") *(F 12128)* **SATISFIED. / SURPRISE SURPRISE** [ ] [-]

Jun 65. (7") *(F 12169)* **LEAVE A LITTLE LOVE. / HE DON'T WANT YOU NO MORE** [8] [ ]

Aug 65. (7") *(F 12214)* **TRY TO UNDERSTAND. / NOT IN THIS WHOLE WORLD** [25] [ ]

Sep 65. (lp) *(LK 4719)* **SOMETHING TO SHOUT ABOUT** [ ] [-]
– You touch me baby / You'll never leave her / I'll come running over / Not in this whole world / She will break your heart / Can I get a witness / Tell me like it is / Shout / Try to understand / Night time is the right time / Chocolate ice / So in love / The only one / Dream lover / He's sure the boy I love / Leave a little love. *(cd-iss. Apr89 on 'London'+=; 820618-2)* – (4 extra tracks).

Oct 65. (7") *(F 12254)* **TELL ME LIKE IT IS. / STOP FOOLING AROUND** [ ] [-]

Jan 66. (7") *(F 12326)* **CALL ME. / AFTER YOU** [ ] [-]

— The LUVVERS split with LULU in March and had their one and only ('Parlophone') single, 'The House On The Hill', a few months later.

Sep 66. (7") *(F 12491)* **OH WHAT A WONDERFUL FEELING. / TOSSIN' AND TURNIN'** [ ] [-]

Columbia | Epic

Mar 67. (7") *(DB 8169)* **THE BOAT THAT I ROW. / DREARY DAYS AND NIGHTS** [6] [ ]

Jun 67. (7") *(DB 8221)* **LET'S PRETEND. / TO SIR WITH LOVE** [11] [-]

Aug 67. (7") *<10187>* **TO SIR WITH LOVE. / THE BOAT THAT I ROW** [-] [1]
(above from the V/A soundtrack to the movie of the same name)

Oct 67. (7") *(DB 8295)* **LOVE LOVES TO LOVE LOVE. / YOU AND I** [32] [-]

Nov 67. (lp; stereo/mono) *(SCX/SX 6201)* *<26339>* **LOVE LOVES TO LOVE LULU** <US-title 'LULU SINGS . . . TO SIR WITH LOVE'> [ ] [24]
– To sir with love / Morning dew / You and I / Rattler / Day tripper / Love loves to love love / To love somebody / The boat that I row / Let's pretend / Take me in your arms and love me / Best of both worlds.

Dec 67. (7") *<10260>* **BEST OF BOTH WORLDS. / LOVE LOVE'S TO LOVE LOVE** [-] [32]

Feb 68. (7") *(DB 8358)* *<10302>* **ME, THE PEACEFUL HEART. / LOOK OUT** [9] [53]

May 68. (7") *(DB 8425)* **BOY. / SAD MEMORIES** [15] [ ]

Jul 68. (7") *<10367>* **MORNING DEW. / YOU AND I** [-] [52]

Oct 68. (7") *(DB 8500)* **I'M A TIGER. / WITHOUT HIM** [9] [ ]

Mar 69. (7") *(DB 8550)* **BOOM BANG-A-BANG. / MARCH** [2] [ ]

Aug 69. (lp; stereo/mono) *(SCX/SX 6265)* **LULU'S ALBUM** [ ] [-]
– Show me / Mighty Quinn / My ain folk / Where did you come from / Gimme some lovin' / I started a joke / Why did I choose you / The boy next door / Come September / A house is not a home / Cry like a baby.

— her backing band now were:- **DUANE ALLMAN + CORNELL DUPREE + EDDIE HINTON + JIMMY JOHNSON** – guitar / **BARRY BECKETT** – keyboards / **DAVID HOOD** – bass / **ROGER HAWKINS** – drums

Atlantic | Atco

Nov 69. (7") *(226 008)* *<6722>* **OH ME OH MY (I'M A FOOL FOR YOU BABY). / SWEEP AROUND YOUR OWN BACK DOOR** [47] [22] Dec69
(re-iss. Mar76; K 10726)

Jan 70. (lp) *(228 031)* *<310>* **NEW ROUTES** [ ] [88]
– Marley Purt drive / In the morning / People in love / After all (I live my life) / Feelin' alright / Dirty old man / Oh me oh my (I'm a fool for you baby) / Is that you love / Mr. Bojangles / Where's Eddie / Sweep around your own back door.

Apr 70. (7: as LULU with the DIXIE FLYERS) *<6749>* **HUM A SONG (FROM YOUR HEART). / WHERE'S EDDIE** [-] [54]

Jun 70. (7") *(2091 014)* **HUM A SONG (FROM YOUR HEART). / MR. BOJANGLES** [ ] [-]

Jul 70. (7") *<6761>* **GOOD DAY SUNSHINE. / AFTER THE FEELING IS GONE** [-] [ ]
Nov 70. (7") *<6774>* **MELODY FAIR. / TO THE OTHER WOMAN** [-] [ ]
Nov 70. (lp) *(2400 017)* **MELODY FAIR** [ ] [-]
– Good day sunshine / After the feeling is gone / I don't care anymore / Please stay / Melody fair / Take good care of yourself / Vine street / Move to my rhythm / To the other woman / Hum a song (from your heart) / Sweet memories / Saved.
Jan 71. (7") *(2091 049)* **GOT TO BELIEVE IN LOVE. / MOVE TO MY RHYTHM** [ ] [-]
Feb 71. (7") *<6819>* **EVERYBODY CLAP. / GOODBYE MY LOVE. GOODBYE** [-] [ ]
Apr 71. (7") *(2091 083)* **EVERYBODY CLAP. / AFTER THE FEELING IS GONE** [ ] [-]
Apr 72. (7") *<6885>* **IT TAKES A REAL MAN. / YOU AIN'T WRONG YOU JUST AIN'T RIGHT** [-] [ ]
Jul 72. (7") *(K 10185)* **EVEN IF I COULD CHANGE. / YOU AIN'T WRONG YOU JUST AIN'T RIGHT** [ ] [ ]

Polydor Polydor

Jan 74. (7") *(2001 490)* **THE MAN WHO SOLD THE WORLD. / WATCH THAT MAN** [3] [ ]

Chelsea Chelsea

1974. (lp) *<BCL1 0144>* **LULU** [-] [ ]
– Groovin' / Easy evil / I wish / A boy like you / Hold on to what you've got / Could it be forever / Funny how time slips away / Do right woman, do right man / Help me help you.
Nov 74. (7") *(2005 015)* **THE MAN WITH THE GOLDEN GUN. / A BOY LIKE YOU** [ ] [ ]
(above from the 'United Artists' V/A soundtrack album of the title)
Mar 75. (7") *(2005 022)* **TAKE YOUR MAMA FOR A RIDE (part 1). / (part 2)** [37] [ ]
Jul 75. (7") *(2005 031)* **BOY MEETS GIRL. / MAMA'S LITTLE CORNER OF THE WORLD** [ ] [ ]
Oct 75. (7") *(2005 048)* **HEAVEN AND EARTH AND THE STARS. / A BOY LIKE YOU** [ ] [ ]
1976. (lp) *(CHL 5002)* **HEAVEN AND EARTH AND THE STARS** [-] [-] German
– Heaven and Earth and the stars / Boy meets girl / Mama's little corner of the world / The man with the golden gun / Baby I don't care / Take your mama for a ride (part 1) / Honey you can't take it back / The man who sold the world / Watch that man / Old fashioned girl / Take your mama for a ride (part 2).

G.T.O. not iss.

Jan 78. (7") *(GT 116)* **YOUR LOVE IS EVERYWHERE. / THE GREATEST FEELIN' IN THE WORLD** [ ] [-]

Rocket Rocket

Oct 78. (7") *(XPRESS 3)* **DON'T TAKE LOVE FOR GRANTED. / LOVE IS THE SWEETEST MISTAKE** [ ] [ ]
Jun 79. (7") *(XPRESS 15)* **I LOVE TO BOOGIE. / DANCE TO THE FEELING IN YOUR HEART** [ ] [ ]
Jul 79. (lp/c) *(TRAIN/SHUNT 8)* **DON'T TAKE LOVE FOR GRANTED** [ ] [ ]
– I love to boogie / Don't take love for granted / Come see what love / Fool, fool / He's so in love / I could never miss you (more than I do) / Nice and slow / You are still a part of me / Bye bye now my sweet love / Love is the sweetest mistake.

Alfa-CBS Alfa-CBS

Oct 81. (7") *(A 1700) <7006>* **I COULD NEVER MISS YOU (MORE THAN I DO). / DANCE TO THE FEELING IN YOUR HEART** [62] [18] Jul81
Dec 81. (lp/c) *(ALF/40 85388) <11006>* **LULU** [ ] [ ] Sep81
– I could never miss you (more than I do) / The last time / If I were you / Loving you / Can't hold out on love / You win, I lose / Don't take love for granted / Who's foolin' who / You are still a part of me / If you're right.
Jan 82. (7") *(A 1892) <7011>* **IF I WERE YOU. / YOU WIN, I LOSE** [ ] [44] Nov81
May 82. (7") *(A 2423)* **I WILL DO IT FOR YOUR LOVE. / HOW CAN I BELIEVE YOU** [ ] [ ]
Jul 82. (7") *(A 2664)* **TAKE ME TO YOUR HEART AGAIN. / HOW CAN I BELIEVE YOU** [ ] [ ]
Jul 82. (lp/c) *(ALF/40 85628)* **TAKE ME TO YOUR HEART AGAIN** [ ] [-]
– I will do it for love / Nobody needs your love more than I do / You had to be there / Go now (before there's trouble) / I don't go shopping / Let her go / You're working nights now / If you steal my heart away / How can I believe you / Take me to your heart again.

Jive Jive

Jul 86. (7") *(LULU 1)* **SHOUT '86. / SHOUT (remix)** [8=] [ ]
(12") *(LULUT 1)* – ('A'remix) / ('A'-Harder mix) / You shout.
Jul 86. (7"; 'Decca' original) *(SHOUT 1)* **SHOUT. / FORGET ME BABY** [8=] [-]
(12"+=) *(SHOUX 1)* – Call me / Heatwave.
— (the above singles' sales were combined when both were released)
Nov 86. (7"/12"/d7"/s7") *(LULU/+T/D/X 2)* **MY BOY LOLLIPOP. / IT'S ONLY LOVE** [ ] [-]

Mercury not iss.

Apr 90. (7"/c-s) *(NEL/+MC 1)* **NELLIE THE ELEPHANT. / ('A'-sing a long)** [ ] [-]
(12"+=) *(NEL 1-12)* – ('A'extended).

Dome not iss.

Jan 93. (c-s/cd-s) *(C/CD DOME 1001)* **INDEPENDENCE / (mixes)** [11] [-]
Feb 93. (cd/c/lp) *(DOME CD/TC/LP 1)* **INDEPENDENCE** [67] [-]
– Independence / There has got to be a way / Restless moods / I'm back for more (with BOBBY WOMACK) / How 'bout us / Until I get over you / Let me wake up in your arms / You left me lonely / Rhythm of romance / I'm walking away / A place to fall.
Mar 93. (c-s/cd-s; LULU and BOBBY WOMACK) *(C/CD DOME 1002)* **I'M BACK FOR MORE / (mixes)** [27] [-]
Aug 93. (c-s/cd-s) *(C/CD DOME 1005)* **LET ME WAKE UP IN YOUR ARMS / (mixes)** [51] [-]
— In Oct'93, LULU finally hit UK No.1; albeit as a guest on TAKE THAT's 'Relight My Fire'.
Nov 93. (c-s/cd-s) *(C/CD DOME 1007)* **HOW 'BOUT US / (mixes)** [46] [-]
Aug 94. (c-s/cd-s) *(C/CD DOME 1011)* **GOODBYE BABY AND AMEN / (mixes)** [40] [-]
Nov 94. (c-s/cd-s) *(C/CD DOME 1013)* **EVERY WOMAN KNOWS / (mixes)** [44] [-]
Jul 97. (cd) *(DOMECD 11)* **ABSOLUTELY** (compilation) [ ] [-]
– Goodbye baby and amen / Every woman knows / There has got to be a way / This time baby / Independence / Some people / Save your soul / How 'bout us / Don't break my heart / Don't wanna fight / I'm back for more / Let me wake up in your arms / Every woman knows / Independence / Goodbye baby and amen / Relight my fire.

Mercury not iss.

May 99. (c-s) *(572612-4)* **HURT ME SO BAD / I DON'T WANNA FIGHT** [42] [-]
(cd-s+=) *(572613-2)* – ('A'mix).
(cd-s) *(572615-2)* – ('A'mixes).
Dec 99. (c-s) *(562585-4)* **BETTER GET READY / HURT ME SO BAD** [59] [-]
(cd-s+=) *(562585-2)* – ('A'mixes).
Mar 00. (c-s) *(156845-4)* **WHERE THE POOR BOYS DANCE / BETTER GET READY** [24] [-]
(cd-s+=) *(156845-2)* – Hurt me so bad.
May 02. (cd/c) *(063021-2/-4)* **TOGETHER** [4] [-]
– Teardrops (with ELTON JOHN) / SHAME SHAME SHAME (with ATOMIC KITTEN) / INSIDE THING (LET 'EM IN) (with PAUL McCARTNEY) / We've got tonight (with RONAN KEATING) / Sail on sailor (with STING) / Back at one (with WESTLIFE) / To sir with love (with SAMANTHA MUMBA) / With you I'm born again (with MARTI PELLOW) / The prayer (with RUSSELL WATSON) / Reunited (with CLIFF RICHARD) / I'm back for more (with BOBBY WOMACK) / Now that the magic has gone (with JOE COCKER) / Phunk phoolin (with KERPHUNK) / Relight my fire (with TAKE THAT).

– compilations, others, etc. –

1965. (7"ep) *Decca; (DFE 8597)* **LULU** [ ] [-]
– Heatwave / What's easy for two is hard for one / Nothing left to do but cry / Trouble with boys.
Aug 67. (lp) *Ace Of Clubs; (ACL 1232)* **LULU!** (material 1964-66) [ ] [-]
Nov 67. (7") *Parrot; <40021>* **SHOUT. / WHEN HE TOUCHES ME** [-] [96]
Dec 67. (lp) *Parrot; <71016>* **FROM LULU WITH LOVE** [-] [ ]
– Shout / Here comes the night / When he touches me / I'll come running / Call me / Surprise surprise / Leave a little love / She will break your heart / Lies / Take me as I am / Tossin' and turnin' / Tell it like it is.
1969. (lp; stereo/mono) *Decca; (S+/PA 8)* **THE WORLD OF LULU** [ ] [-]
Sep 70. (lp; stereo/mono) *Decca; (S+/PA 94)* **THE WORLD OF LULU VOL.2** [ ] [-]
Sep 71. (lp) *Music For Pleasure; (MFP 5215)* **THE MOST OF LULU** [15] [-]
– Let's pretend / I'm a tiger / Love loves to love love / You and I / To sir with love / March / The boat that I row / Boom bang-a-bang / Without him / Me, the peaceful heart / Boy / Dreary days and nights.
Nov 72. (lp) *Music For Pleasure; (MFP 5254)* **THE MOST OF LULU VOL.2** [ ] [-]
Oct 80. (lp/c) *Warwick; (WW/+4 5097)* **THE VERY BEST OF LULU** [ ] [-]
Jun 83. (lp/c) *Decca; (TAB/KTAB 70)* **SHOUT** [ ] [-]
Mar 84. (7") *Life Style; (LIFE 9)* **IS THAT SO? / (B-side by other artist)** [ ] [-]
Apr 84. (lp) *Life Style; (LEG 19)* **SHAPE UP AND DANCE WITH LULU** [ ] [-]
Jul 84. (7") *Old Gold; (OG 9393)* **SHOUT. / (B-side by Dave Berry)** [ ] [-]
Jan 89. (lp/c)(cd) *Music For Pleasure; (MFP/TC-MFP 5848)(CDMFP 6050)* **I'M A TIGER** [ ] [-]
Apr 89. (7") *Old Gold; (OG 9887)* **THE MAN WHO SOLD THE WORLD. / TAKE YOUR MAMA FOR A RIDE** [ ] [-]
May 89. (lp/c/cd) *Start; (CHEL V/C/D 1004)* **THE MAN WHO SOLD THE WORLD** [ ] [-]
Nov 94. (cd) *Rhino; <71815>* **FROM CRAYONS TO PERFUME: THE BEST OF LULU** [-] [ ]
Jan 95. (cd/c) *BR Music; (BR CD/MC 107)* **THE VERY BEST OF LULU** [ ] [-]
Mar 96. (cd/c) *EMI Gold; (CD/TC GOLD 1005)* **THE GOLD COLLECTION** [ ] [-]
(cd re-iss. Oct01; same)
May 96. (cd/c) *Spectrum; (551270-2/-4)* **THE WORLD OF LULU** [ ] [-]
Aug 96. (cd) *Disky; <(DC 86741-2)* **SHOUT** [ ] [ ]

Sep 96.	(cd) *See For Miles; (SEECD 452)* **THE EP COLLECTION** (*re-iss. Mar00; same*)		-
Nov 96.	(cd) *Laserlight; (16153)* **THE BEST OF LULU**		-
Feb 98.	(cd) *Disky; (<WB 88554-2>)* **THE BEST OF LULU** – Shout / To sir with love / Day tripper / Boom bang-a-bang / The man who sold the world / Take your mama for a ride / Independence / I'm back for more / Let me wake up in your arms / How 'bout us / I don't wanna fight / There has got to be a way / Restless moods / Until I get over you / You left me lonely / Place to fall / Don't break my heart / This time baby.		Jul98
May 99.	(cd) *Sequel; (NEMCD 423)* **THE MAN WHO SOLD THE WORLD**		-
Oct 99.	(cd) *Spectrum; (544130-2)* **THE BEST OF LULU**		-
Nov 99.	(d-cd) *Dome; (DOMECD 18)* **I'M BACK FOR MORE – THE VERY BEST OF HER 90's RECORDINGS** (*re-iss. Apr02; DOMECD 18X*)		-
Apr 02.	(cd) *E.M.I.; (538850-2)* **THE MOST OF LULU / LULU'S ALBUM**		-

LUVVERS (see under ⇒ LULU)

Mac/Mc

Chris McCLURE

Born: c.mid-40's, Glasgow. McCLURE began his showbiz life way back early in 1966 when he released a one-off single for 'Decca', 'THE DYING SWAN'. Safe and predictable pop, the well-groomed crooner attempted to crack the charts a few more times, and by 1969 he had even formed his own 5-piece band, The CHRIS McCLURE SECTION. However, after the appropriately-titled single 'YOU'RE ONLY WASTING TIME' bombed, McCLURE decided to reshape his career by altering his name to CHRISTIAN. Apart from an ever-increasing local fanbase, CHRISTIAN's solo sojourn only took off in clubs and halls around the country. It seemed he was destined to remain out of the national limelight when in 1976, modelling himself on LEO SAYER (even as much as singing the man's 'The Show Must Go On'), the permed afro-styled CHRISTIAN won ITV search-for-a-star show, 'New Faces'. However, the singer still never quite achieved that illusive chart hit, although he remains to this day a favourite with every easy-listening lover. In April 2002, his popularity was such that two shows, billed as 'The Chris McClure Story', were sell-outs at his favourite haunt, Glasgow's Pavilion Theatre; comic TV and radio sports presenter/columnist Tam Cowan was the compere.

CHRIS McCLURE – vocals (also of STUDIO SIX) / plus **SANDY NEWMAN** – guitar, keyboards / + three others

		Decca	not iss.
Feb 66.	(7") *(F 12346)* **THE DYING SWAN. / THE LAND OF THE GOLDEN TREE**		-
		Polydor	**not iss.**
Jan 68.	(7") *(BM 56227)* **HAZY PEOPLE. / I'M JUST A COUNTRY BOY**		-
May 68.	(7") *(BM 56259)* **ANSWER TO EVERYTHING. / MEDITATION**		-
		R.C.A.	**not iss.**
Jun 69.	(7") *(RCA 1849)* **OUR SONG OF LOVE. / WEATHER VANE**		-
		C.B.S.	**not iss.**
1969.	(7"; as the CHRIS McCLURE SECTION) *(CBS 7646)* **YOU'RE ONLY PASSING TIME. / SING OUR SONG**		-

—— the band split and McCLURE changed his name to . . .

CHRISTIAN

		Decca	not iss.
Mar 71.	(7") *(F 13137)* **OTHER SIDE OF LIFE. / SHE**		-
Jan 72.	(7") *(F 13275)* **NURSERY LANE. / DESPERATE DAN**		-
		Polydor	**not iss.**
Dec 76.	(lp) *(2384 091)* **THE FIRST CHRISTIAN** – The show must go on / I'm just a country boy / The answer to everything / Only the blues / Unchained melody / Happy birthday sweet sixteen / Crunchy grenola suite / (Don't go) Please stay / Saturday night at the movies / Jesus Christ superstar / Oh Carol.		-
Apr 78.	(7") *(2059 012)* **SHINE IT ON. / BRING BACK THE GOOD OLD OLD MELODIES**		-
May 78.	(lp) *(2383 500)* **SHINE IT ON** – Shine it on / Once upon a time / Sunday school to Broadway / The hungry years / Bad magic / Home / The little things / Too late to say goodbye / Holy Moses / Xarpenter, fisherman, prophet and physician.		-
Jul 78.	(7") *(2059 043)* **HOME. / HOLY MOSES**		-

		Gipsy	not iss.
1981.	(7") *(GIPSY 3)* **OH LITTLE MAMA. / (version)**		-
Nov 82.	(7"/12") *(GIPSY 8/+12)* **I'M STILL DANCING. / (version)**		-

—— CHRIS subsequently carried on in the cabaret world

Jimmy McCULLOCH (see under ⇒ STONE THE CROWS)

Chas McDEVITT

Born: 1935, Glasgow. Stints in both the CRANE RIVER JAZZ BAND and the CRANES SKIFFLE GROUP paved the way for the Scots banjo player/guitarist's own outfit, the CHAS McDEVITT SKIFFLE GROUP. Featuring a line-up of TONY KOHN, BILL BRANWELL (both from another skiffle act, the COTTON PICKERS), LENNIE HANSON and MARC SHARRATT, the band scooped first prize in a Radio Luxembourg talent contest where they also met their future lead singer NANCY WHISKEY.

A fellow Glaswegian, WHISKEY fronted McDEVITT's outfit on their 1957 debut single, 'FREIGHT TRAIN', a song that broke into both the UK Top 5 and the US Top 40 on the back of its performance (by the band themselves) in biopic 'The Tommy Steele Story'. Yet CHAS ran into legal problems over the song's copyright (it was originally composed by African-American folk singer ELIZABETH COTTEN) and although his third single release, 'GREENBACK DOLLAR', made the UK Top 30 later that summer, subsequent releases such as 'THE INTOXICATING MISS WHISKEY' and the 'CHAS AND NANCY EP' failed to chart.

While NANCY later embarked on a brief solo sojourn with The SKIFFLERS, McDEVITT found a replacement in the shape of Irish singer SHIRLEY DOUGLAS whom he went on to marry. Despite a series of 60's singles for 'H.M.V.' and 'Columbia', he couldn't replicate his earlier success and 'FREIGHT TRAIN' increasingly seemed like a musical albatross. The 70's found him recording sporadically, revisiting a host of old skiffle favourites on the 1976 set, 'TAKES YA BACK DON'T IT'.

CHAS McDEVITT SKIFFLE GROUP featuring NANCY WHISKEY

CHAS McDEVITT – vocals, guitar, banjo (ex-CRANE RIVER JAZZ BAND, ex-CRANES SKIFFLE GROUP) / **NANCY WHISKEY** (b.1937, Glasgow) – vocals / **TONY KOHN** – guitar / **BILL BRANWELL** – guitar (ex-COTTON PICKERS SKIFFLE GROUP) / **LENNIE HANSON** – bass / **MARC SHARRATT** – washboard

		Oriole	Chic
Apr 57.	(7",78) *(CB 1352) <1008>* **FREIGHT TRAIN. / THE COTTON SONG**	5	40 May57
May 57.	(7",78) *(CB 1357)* **IT TAKES A WORRIED MAN. / THE HOUSE OF THE RISING SUN**		-
Jun 57.	(7",78) *(CB 1371)* **GREENBACK DOLLAR. / I'M SATISFIED**	28	-
Aug 57.	(7",78) *(CB 1386)* **FACE IN THE RAIN. / SPORTING LIFE** (above also credited TONY KOHN)		-
Nov 57.	(10"lp) *(MG 10018)* **THE INTOXICATING MISS WHISKEY**		-
Nov 57.	(7"ep) *(EP 7002)* **CHAS AND NANCY EP**		-
Nov 57.	(7",78) *(CB 1395)* **SING, SING, SING. / MY OLD MAN**		-
1958.	(7",78) *(CB 1403)* **JOHNNY-O. / BAD MAN STACK-O-LEE**		-

—— NANCY formed her own SKIFFLERS and continued to work solo

CHAS McDEVITT & SHIRLEY DOUGLAS

—— **SHIRLEY DOUGLAS** (b. 1936, Belfast.)

1958.	(7",78) *(CB 1405)* **ACROSS THE BRIDGE. / DEEP DOWN**		-
1958.	(7",78) *(CB 1457)* **REAL LOVE. / JUKE-BOX JUMBLE**		-
1959.	(7",78) *(CB 1511)* **TEENAGE LETTER. / Shirley Douglas: SAD LITTLE GIRL**		-
		Top Rank	**not iss.**
Apr 60.	(7") *(JAR 338)* **FOREVER. / DREAM TALK**		-
		H.M.V.	**not iss.**
1961.	(7") *(POP 845)* **ONE LOVE. / CAN IT BE LOVE**		-
1961.	(7") *(POP 928)* **MOMMY OUT DE LIGHT. / I'VE GOT A THING ABOUT YOU**		-
1962.	(7") *(POP 999)* **HAPPY FAMILY. / THROWING PEBBLES IN A POOL**		-
		Columbia	**not iss.**
Jun 65.	(7") *(DB 7595)* **THE MOST OF WHAT IS LEAST. / DON'T BLAME ME**		-
1965.	(7") *(DB 7703)* **DON'T BELIEVE THEM. / WHERE AM I GOING**		-
1966.	(7") *(DB 7846)* **WHEN THE GOOD TIMES COME. / NEVER WED AN OLD MAN**		-

Fontana not iss.

Jul 68. (7") *(TF 957)* **CITY SMOKE. / ONE MAN BAND** [ ] [-]

Joy not iss.

Aug 72. (lp) *(JOYS 241)* **OLD, NEW, BORROWED AND BLUE** [ ] [-]

CHAS McDEVITT

President not iss.

Nov 73. (7") *(PT 410)* **A BOY CHILD IS BORN. / AMAZING GRACE** [ ] [-]

Joy not iss.

Jun 76. (lp/c) *(JOYS/TCJOYS 263)* **TAKES YA BACK DON'T IT** [ ] [-]
– Bloodshot eyes / Thirty days / Peggy Sue / La bamba / What a crazy world we're livin' in / Freight train / Walk right in / Cottonfields / San Francisco Bay / Rock island line / Tom Dooley / Wabash cannonball.

– compilations, etc. –

Nov 80. (7") *Old Gold; (OG 9052)* **GREENBACK DOLLAR. / FREIGHT TRAIN** [ ] [-]

Nov 93. (7"pic-d-ep; as the CHAS McDEVITT SKIFFLE GROUP featuring NANCY WHISKEY) *Rollercoaster; (RCEP 113)* **NANCY & CHAS EP** [ ] [-]
– Every day of the week / I saw the light / Ballad of the Titanic / Greenback dollar / Freight train.

Nov 93. (d-cd; as the CHAS McDEVITT SKIFFLE GROUP featuring NANCY WHISKEY & SHIRLEY DOUGLAS) *Rollercoaster; (RCCD 3007)* **FREIGHT TRAIN** [ ] [-]
– Freight train / Badman stack-o-lee / County jail / I'm satisfied / She moved through the fair / My old man / Poor Howard / Greenback dollar / Sing, sing, sing / BB blues / Deep down / Born to be with you / I want a little girl / Across the bridge / Come all ye fair and tender maidens / Sportin' life / Trottin' to the fair / Every day of the week / Face in the rain / Goin' home / Tom Hark / It makes no difference now / Good mornin' blues / Real love / Pop pouri / Everyday / I have the blues / I dig you baby / Ace in the hole / Tom Hark 2.

May 99. (cd) *Bear Family; (BCD 16156)* **THE CHAS McDEVITT SKIFFLE GROUP** [ ] [ ]

Dec 99. (cd) *Rollercoaster; (RCCD 6004)* **CHAS McDEVITT AND FRIENDS** [ ] [ ]

Robin McDONALD

Born: 18 Jul'43, Nairn. ROBIN came to prominence in 1962 as rhythm guitarist with Manchester hitmakers, BILLY J. KRAMER & THE DAKOTAS. For two years between May '63 until the summer of '65, the quintet notched up six major UK hits, starting with the Lennon & McCartney-penned 'DO YOU WANT TO KNOW A SECRET' (No.2) and two chart-toppers, 'BAD TO ME' and 'LITTLE CHILDREN'; ROBIN would subsequently become their bassist after ROY JONES departed. During their initiation period in 1963, the DAKOTAS also breached the Top 20 via 'THE CRUEL SEA', although ROBIN and his instrumentalists found it hard to emulate when BILLY J went solo in 1966.

Shelagh McDONALD

Born: Scotland. After featuring on a few V/A folk compilations, SHELAGH was one of the many singer/songwriter troubadours to sign for 'B&C'. There she cut an eponymous debut set in 1970, a fine mixture of her own compositions alongside some by Gerry Rafferty ('PEACOCK LADY'), the Byrds ('LET NO MAN STEAL AWAY YOUR THYME'), Keith Christmas and Andy Roberts (both of whom guested on the record). For her sophomore album, 'STARGAZER' (1971), SHELAGH showcased her excellent voice with a rendition of the traditional ballad, 'DOWIE DENS OF YARROW'. Sadly, SHELAGH has been conspicuous by her absence ever since.

SHELAGH McDONALD – vocals, acoustic guitar / with mainly **KEITH CHRISTMAS** – guitar / **PAT DONALDSON** – bass / **ROGER POWELL + GERRY CONWAY** – drums / **KEITH TIPPETT** – piano / **GORDON HUNTLEY** – steel guitar, dobro / **ANDY ROBERTS** – guitar

B&C not iss.

Dec 70. (lp) *(CAS 1019)* **THE SHELAGH McDONALD ALBUM** [ ] [-]
– Mirage / Look over the hill and far away / Crusoe / Waiting for the wind to rise / Ophelia's song / Richmond / Let no man steal away your thyme / Peacock lady / Silk and leather / You know you can't lose / Ophelia's song. *(cd-iss. Nov00 on 'Mooncrest'+=; CRESTCD 059)* – (some sessions from the next album).

Sep 71. (lp) *(CAS 1043)* **STARGAZER** [ ] [-]
–

—— she retired from the music business after above

Mae McKENNA

Born: c.1955, Coatbridge. Of Scottish/Irish stock, the young MAE was exposed to a wide cross-section of music that included everything from FRANK SINATRA and ART TATUM to JONI MITCHELL and JAMES TAYLOR.

At the tender age of 14 she joined the Lanarkshire youth orchestra as a viola player, the same instrument she played in high school gothic-folk band, DAY. An appearance at a local music festival resulted in MAE being headhunted and soon found the teenager making her professional debut on the folk scene fronting proto-Celtic rockers CONTRABAND, an early incarnation of OSSIAN also featuring JOHN MARTIN along with GEORGE and WILLIAM JACKSON. The group (completed by PETER CAIRNEY and ALEC BAIRD) recorded a one-off eponymous album in 1974, a record which featured MAE on violin, viola, piano and vocals. MAE subsequently went solo, making her debut for 'Transatlantic' the following year. The 'MAE McKENNA' set attempted to interpret pop nuggets such as Stevie Wonder's 'ALL IN LOVE IS FAIR', Gerry Rafferty's 'SONG FOR SIMON' and John Lennon's 'IMAGINE' in sumptuous orchestral fashion, aided and abetted by a cast of session players including pedal steel maestro BJ COLE. The likes of RONNIE LEAHY (ex-STONE THE CROWS), PAT DONALDSON and ISAAC GUILLORY lent a hand on the West Coast/Country-rock flavoured follow-up set, 'EVERYTHING THAT TOUCHES ME' (1976), MAE once again putting her own spin on contemporary favourites by the likes of RICHARD THOMPSON and JACKSON BROWNE. A third set, 'WALK ON WATER' (1977) saw appearances from COLIN BLUNSTONE and GERRY CONWAY as MAE tackled works by KIM CARNES and DAVID PAICH (the man behind TOTO's 'Hold The Line') as well as Motown chestnut, 'WHAT BECOMES OF THE BROKEN HEARTED'.

All this stood MAE in good stead for her subsequent career as a session singer, the Scots songstress appearing on records by artists as varied as ULTRAVOX, SCRITTI POLITTI and PETE TOWNSHEND. Bizarrely enough, she became a regular fixture at the STOCK/AITKEN/WATERMAN school of fluff and sang behind the likes of KYLIE, RICK ASTLEY, JASON DONOVAN et al. Her own solo career was back on track with 1988's 'NIGHTFALLERS', an album that anticipated the Celtic/New Age boom and featured the writing talents of former SENSATIONAL ALEX HARVEY BAND keyboard player HUGH McKENNA (actually her brother!). Released on 'Virgin' offshoot, 'Venture', the record also featured guest contributions from her old mate WILLIAM JACKSON. The talented songstress returned the favour by augmenting JACKSON on his 'Inchcolm' set as well as augmenting him on stage at both the Glasgow Folk Festival and Mayfest. MAE also guested alongside BILLY ROSS on his 'Ship To Shore' album.

Like many Scottish female folk singers, MAE has a soft spot for the works of Robert Burns, singing a trio of the bard's songs on a 'Linn' compilation. Her most recent album, the Nashville-recorded 'SHORE TO SHORE' (1999), boasted a haunting country roots edge which would no doubt appeal to fans of IRIS DEMENT, GILLIAN WELCH, etc.

MAE McKENNA – vocals, etc (ex-CONTRABAND) / with session people

Transatla. not iss.

1975. (lp) *(TRA 297)* **MAE McKENNA** [ ] [-]
– Dying to live / Once in the morning / All in love is fair / Other side of me / Song for Simon / Together we get by / Elderberry wine / How could we dare to be wrong / Imagine / Black-eyed Susan Brown / Said the major / Old man.

1976. (lp) *(TRA 321)* **EVERYTHING THAT TOUCHES ME** [ ] [-]
–

1977. (lp) *(TRA 345)* **WALK ON WATER** [ ] [-]
– Driven away / Love me tomorrow / There's been a mistake / What becomes of the broken-hearted / Sailin' / Love struck / He's a man after my own heart.

Feb 77. (7") *(BIG 553)* **I WANT TO BELIEVE IN YOU. / MY TOWN** [ ] [-]

—— next featured **WILLIAM JACKSON** – pipes, harp (of OSSIAN) / **HUGH McKENNA** – keyboards (ex-SAHB) / **JAMIE MOSES** – guitar / **GRAHAM WALKER** – drums/ etc

Venture Caroline

May 88. (cd/c/lp) *(CD/TC+/VE 18)* *<CAROL 1644-2>* **NIGHTFALLERS** [ ] [ ] 1992
– Nightfallers (intro) / Karisola / Moorings / Visions of time to come / Blue / Ochone / Sayonara / My lagan love / Fields of green / Manderley / Nightfallers.

Hypertension not iss.

Sep 93. (cd) *(HY 200121CD)* **MIRAGE & REALITY** [ ] [-]
– Dreamer / The chosen one / Dream lover / Heart to heart / Changes / In the circles / Too many promises / Flamenco / Time to go / Laoidh Chaluim Chille (St. Colomba's home). *(cd re-iss. Oct00 on 'Mill'; MRCD 014)*

Mill not iss.

May 99. (cd) *(MRCD 015)* **SHORE TO SHORE** [ ] [-]
– Footsteps of my father / Same old me / Where did it go? / Tonight (ce soir) / The Christ child lullaby / The sands of Tara's shore / New York harbour / The whistlin'

gypsy rover / Mo ghile mear / The spirit of love / On Heaven's shore / The world at our feet / The hick's farewell / Ca' the ewes.

McKINLEYS (see under ⇒ "A Beat(en) Generation")

MARK FIVE (see under ⇒ "A Beat(en) Generation")

MARMALADE

Formed: Shettleston, Glasgow . . . 1961 as The GAYLORDS, which numbered PAT FAIRLEY, WILLIE 'JUNIOR' CAMPBELL, BILL IRVINE RAYMOND DUFFY and singer THOMAS McALEESE; in 1963, the latter adopted a new name as they became DEAN FORD & THE GAYLORDS.

Initially inspired by the likes of CLIFF RICHARD & THE SHADOWS, their early live shows also complimented work of the American Motown and Stax labels. Having inked a deal with 'Columbia' records through Peter Walsh (also manager of BRIAN POOLE & THE TREMELOES), they featured on the BBC Scotland TV show, 'Come Thursday', while also performing regularly at Glasgow's top Picasso club. A rendition of Chubby Checker's 'TWENTY MILES' was chosen as their debut disc in April '64, although this and two subsequent follow-ups – an early Gallagher & Lyle-penned 'MR. HEARTBREAK'S HERE INSTEAD' and Shirley Ellis' 'THE NAME GAME' – failed to break them commercially. A slight reshuffle – GRAHAM KNIGHT substituting IRVING – led to the band briefly reverting to The GAYLORDS moniker for their fourth flop 45, 'HE'S A GOOD FACE (BUT HE'S DOWN AND OUT)'.

Later in '66 – and with English-born drummer ALAN WHITEHEAD replacing DUFFY – they took the name MARMALADE and relocated south to London; Archway to be exact. However, a further string of flops curtailed all hopes of the pop/soul 5-piece making it big time, although 1967's 'I SEE THE RAIN' did crack the Top 30 in the Netherlands. Chart attempt number five for MARMALADE, 'LOVIN' THINGS' (written by US bubblegummers, the GRASS ROOTS), finally got them out of a sticky mess and gave them their first UK Top 10 smash; their second Top 30 entry that year was 'WAIT FOR ME MARIANNE'.

Towards the end of '68, BEATLES publisher Dick James suggested a new Lennon/ McCartney number to the band, not knowing 'OB-LA-DI, OB-LA-DA' was scheduled for release on their forthcoming "White Album". Fortune was on MARMALADE's side however, when all parties concerned consented to the Caledonian popsters version; the jammy so-and-so's duly took it to No.1 for three weeks. After it departed from the hit parade, 'BABY MAKE IT SOON', also gave them another UK Top 10, although their final single for 'C.B.S.', 'BUTTERFLY' er . . . flapped. With a more favourable deal from the 'Decca' label, which gave the band complete freedom in the songwriting/arrangement departments, CAMPBELL and McALEESE penned the excellent 'REFLECTIONS OF MY LIFE', a record that took them into the UK Top 3 and for the first time, the US Top 10. The 1970 single, 'RAINBOW', was equally successful in Britain, although for some unknown reason, their sophomore album 'REFLECTIONS OF THE MARMALADE' (1970) failed – a feat the band would always emulate set after set. Early the following year, both CAMPBELL (for a semi-lucrative solo escapade) and WHITEHEAD toasted their farewell chart appearance via Top 20 effort, 'MY LITTLE ONE'. The incoming HUGHIE NICHOLSON and DOUGIE HENDERSON (both ex-POETS) staked their claim to fame when the Nicholson-penned single 'COUSIN NORMAN' peaked at No.6.

The aforementioned pair, alongside originals FORD and KNIGHT subsequently pressed on without FAIRLEY, who'd emigrated to the States; at the same time single 'RADANCER' was marking their 7th UK Top 10 entry, the Sunday tabloids exposed the band of having "groupie sex". Retreating to er . . . lick their wounds, MARMALADE (i.e. FORD, KNIGHT, HENDERSON, newcomer MIKE JAPP and basically session people) returned to the fold in 1973 and signed a new contract with 'E.M.I.', although a handful of harder-edged boogie singles all failed to make the grade. In 1975, the solo bound DEAN FORD made way for new vocalist/guitarist, SANDY NEWMAN (ex-CHRIS McCLURE SECTION), An appropriately-titled Top 10 single (and US Top 50), 'FALLING APART AT THE SEAMS', just about said it all the following year. MARMALADE (aka KNIGHT and NELSON) continued to release singles and albums throughout the latter half of the 70's and the 80's, while mainly working the cabaret circuit abroad with The TREMELOES.

DEAN FORD & THE GAYLORDS

DEAN FORD (b. THOMAS McALEESE, 5 Sep'46, Coatbridge) – vocals (ex-MONARCHS) / **PAT FAIRLEY** (b. 1 Apr'46) – lead guitar / **(WILLIE) JUNIOR CAMPBELL** (b.31 May'47) – rhythm guitar / **BILL IRVINE** – bass / **RAYMOND DUFFY** – drums

		Columbia	Columbia
Apr 64.	(7") *(DB 7264)* **TWENTY MILES. / WHAT'S THE MATTER WITH ME?**		-
Nov 64.	(7") *(DB 7402)* **MR. HEARTBREAK'S HERE INSTEAD. / I WON'T**		-
Jun 65.	(7") *(DB 7610)* **THE NAME GAME. / THAT LONELY FEELING**		-

— **GRAHAM KNIGHT** (b. 8 Dec'46) – bass; repl. IRVING

Jan 66.	(7"; as the GAYLORDS) *(DB 7805)* **HE'S A GOOD FACE (BUT HE'S DOWN AND OUT). / YOU KNOW IT TOO**		-

MARMALADE

— **ALAN WHITEHEAD** (b.24 Jul'46, Oswestry, Shropshire) – drums; repl. DUFFY (who later joined MATTHEWS' SOUTHERN COMFORT)

		C.B.S.	Columbia
Sep 66.	(7") *(202340)* **IT'S ALL LEADING UP TO SATURDAY NIGHT. / WAIT A MINUTE BABY**		-
Mar 67.	(7") *(202643)* **CAN'T STOP NOW. / THERE AIN'T NO USE IN HANGIN' ON**		-
Aug 67.	(7") *(2948)* **I SEE THE RAIN. / LAUGHING MAN**		-
Nov 67.	(7") *(3088)* **MAN IN A SHOP. / CRY (THE SHOOB DORORIE SONG)** *(re-iss. Jul71; 7200)*		-
May 68.	(7") *(3412)* **LOVIN' THINGS. / HEY JOE**	6	
Sep 68.	(7") *(3708)* **WAIT FOR ME MARIANNE. / MESS AROUND**	30	
Oct 68.	(lp) *(63414)* **THERE'S A LOT OF IT ABOUT**		

– Lovin' things / I see the rain / I shall be released / Summer in the city / Piece of my heart / There ain't no use in hanging on / Mr. Tambourine man / Wait for me Marianne / Mr. Lion / Station on 3rd Avenue / Chains / Hey Joe / Mess around Man in a shop.

Nov 68.	(7") *(3892)* **OB-LA-DI, OB-LA-DA. / CHAINS**	1	
May 69.	(7") *(4287)* **BABY MAKE IT SOON. / TIME IS ON MY SIDE**	9	
Oct 69.	(7") *(4615)* **BUTTERFLY. / I SHALL BE RELEASED**		-
		Decca	**London**
Dec 69.	(7") *(F 12982)* <20058> **REFLECTIONS OF MY LIFE. / ROLLIN' MY THING**	3	10 Feb70
Jun 70.	(lp) *(SKL 5047)* <575> **REFLECTIONS OF THE MARMALADE** <US-title 'REFLECTIONS OF MY LIFE'>		71

– Super clean Jean / Carolina in my mind / I'll be home (in a day or so) / And yours is piece of mine / Some other guy / Kaleidoscope / Dear John / Fight say the mighty / Reflections of my life / Life is. *(cd-iss. Jul88 & Jan93 on 'London'; 820 562-2)*

Jun 70.	(7") *(F 13035)* <20059> **RAINBOW. / THE BALLAD OF CHERRY FLAVOR**	3	51
Feb 71.	(7") *(F 13135)* **MY LITTLE ONE. / IS YOUR LIFE YOUR OWN**	15	

— **HUGHIE NICHOLSON** – guitar (ex-POETS) repl. CAMPBELL who went solo

— **DOUGIE HENDERSON** – drums (ex-POETS) repl. WHITEHEAD

Aug 71.	(7") *(F 13214)* **COUSIN NORMAN. / LONELY MAN**	6	
Nov 71.	(7") *(F 13251)* **BACK ON THE ROAD. / LOVE IS HARD TO RE-ARRANGE**	35	
Dec 71.	(lp) *(SKL 5111)* **SONGS**		

– Bad weather / Sarah / Mama / Back on the road / Lady of Catrine / Empty bottles / I've been around too long / Lovely nights / She wrote me a letter / Ride boy ride.

— now a quartet of **FORD, KNIGHT, NICHOLSON + HENDERSON** when FAIRLEY emigrated to the States

Mar 72.	(7"m) *(F 13297)* **RADANCER. / SARAH / JUST ONE WOMAN**	6	

— split when NICHOLSON joined CODY and then BLUE; MARMALADE re-formed almost immediately **(FORD, KNIGHT + HENDERSON)** + **MIKE JAPP** – guitar, keyboards, vocals / plus **JOE BREEN** – bass / **HOWIE CASEY** – drums / **ANDY BOWN** – organ

		E.M.I.	not iss.
Jun 73.	(7") *(EMI 2033)* **THE WISHING WELL. / ENGINE DRIVER**		-
Oct 73.	(7") *(EMI 2071)* **OUR HOUSE IS ROCKIN'. / HALLELUJAH FREEDOM BLUES**		-
Apr 74.	(7") *(EMI 2131)* **COME BACK JO. / THE WAY IT IS**		-
Oct 74.	(lp) *(EMC 3047)* **OUR HOUSE IS ROCKIN'**		-

– Come back Jo / The way it is / Our house is rockin' / Stuck on you / Mr. Heartbreaker / Love tale / Ole country rhythm / Douglas / Gypsy lady.

— **SANDY NEWMAN** – vocals, guitar, keyboards (ex-CHRIS McCLURE SECTION) repl. FORD who had already went solo (see below)

Target | Ariola

Jan 76. (7") *(TGT 105) <7619>* **FALLING APART AT THE SEAMS. / FLY FLY FLY** 9 | 49 Mar76
May 76. (7") *(TGT 110)* **WALKING A TIGHTROPE. / MY EVERYTHING**
Aug 76. (7") *(TGT 113)* **WHAT YOU NEED IS A MIRACLE. / THE RUSTY HANDS OF TIME**
Oct 76. (7") *(TGT 115)* **HELLO BABY. / SEAFARING MAN**

— **GARTH WATT-ROY** – vocals, keyboards (ex-GREATEST SHOW ON EARTH) repl. JAPP

Feb 77. (7") *(TGT 126)* **THE ONLY LIGHT ON MY HORIZON NOW. / LOUISIANA** | -
Mar 77. (lp) *(TGS 501)* **THE ONLY LIGHT ON MY HORIZON NOW** | -
– The only light on my horizon now / You steal the limelight / Living to feel the magic / Walking a tightrope / Louisianna / So sad / Hello baby / What you need is a miracle / The rusty hands of time / It's hard to understand / Rollin' on / Falling apart at the seams.

May 77. (7") *(TGT 128)* **HELLO BABY. / SENTIMENTAL VALUE** | -
Jul 77. (7") *(TGT 136)* **MYSTERY HAS GONE. / WASTING MY TIME** | -
Jan 78. (7") *(TGT 138)* **TALKING IN YOUR SLEEP. / MAKE IT REALLY EASY** | -

Sky | not iss.

Nov 78. (7") *(1010)* **HEAVENS ABOVE. / YOU'RE A LADY** | -
Jan 79. (lp) *(SKYLP 1)* **DOING IT ALL FOR YOU** | -
– Pepsey / Alright, O.K. / Fat Sally / You're a lady / Doing it all for you / Space pioneer / Make it real easy / Heavens above / Colour my world / So good to have you / Sentimental value.

— **ALAN HOLMES** – keyboards; repl. GARTH who joined the Q-TIPS

E.M.I. | not iss.

Oct 79. (7") *(EMI 5001)* **MADE IN GERMANY. / OOH BABY** | -

— **GLENN TAYLOR** – drums (ex-LOVE AFFAIR) repl. CHARLIE SMITH

Just Songs | Spectra

1982. (lp) *<SPA 3>* **HEARTBREAKER** - |
Jun 84. (7") *(JST 1)* **HEARTBREAKER. / I LISTEN TO MY HEART** | -

— (1989) **CHARLIE SMITH** returned to repl. TAYLOR

Hansa | not iss.

1989. (7"; as DAVE DEE & MARMALADE) *(imp.112712)* **SIROCCO. / I DON'T BELIEVE IN LOVE ANYMORE** - | - German

- compilations, others, etc. -

Dec 69. (lp) *C.B.S.; (SPR 36)* **THE BEST OF THE MARMALADE** | -
May 73. (7") *C.B.S.; (8205)* **OB-LA-DI, OB-LA-DA. / LOVIN' THINGS** | -
(re-iss. Feb78; CBS 5963) (re-iss. Jun82 on 'Old Gold'; OG 9195)
1973. (lp) *Embassy-CBS; (EMB 31032)* **OB-LA-DI, OB-LA-DA** | -
Jun 76. (lp) *Decca; (SPA 470)* **THE WORLD OF THE MARMALADE** | -
1979. (lp) *Queen; (1701278)* **HELLO BABY** | -
(re-iss. as 'HEAVENS ABOVE')
1980. (lp) *G&P; <GP 1001>* **MARMALADE** - |
Oct 80. (7"ep) *Decca; (F 13898)* **REFLECTIONS OF MY LIFE** | -
May 81. (lp) *Decca; (TAB 19)* **BACK ON THE ROAD** | -
Oct 83. (7") *Old Gold; (OG 9334)* **REFLECTIONS OF MY LIFE. / RAINBOW** | -
Aug 84. (7"ep/c-ep) *Scoop; (7SR/7SC 5045)* **6 TRACK HITS** | -
– Ob-la-di, ob-la-da / I shall be released / Summer in the city / Loving things / Wait for me / Baby make it soon.
Nov 84. (7"/12"; shared with the FORTUNES and MUNGO JERRY) *Record Shack; (HOC/T 8)* **HOOKED ON NUMBER ONES. / (part 2)** | -
Apr 85. (c) *Autograph; (ASK 777)* **OB-LA-DI, OB-LA-DA** | -
May 85. (lp/c) *Zuma; (ZOOM L/K 1)* **GREATEST HITS VOL.1** | -
Nov 85. (7") *E.M.I.; (MSSR 4)* **GOLDEN SHREDS. / (part 2)** | -
(12") *(MSSRT 4)* – ('A'side) / ('A'slow cut) / ('A'thick cut).
Mar 92. (cd) *C5; (C5CD 578)* **FALLING APART AT THE SEAMS . . . PLUS** | -
Apr 94. (cd) *Laserlight; (12275)* **HITS** | -
Nov 94. (cd) *Fairy Dust; (KLM 046)* **ALL THE HITS OF MARMALADE** | -
Apr 96. (cd) *Castle; (CCSCD 436)* **THE COLLECTION** | -
Nov 97. (cd) *Prestige; (CDSGP 0218)* **ALL THE HITS PLUS MORE** | -
– I see the rain / Lovin' things / Wait for me Mary Ann / Ob-la-di, ob-la-di / Baby make it soon / Reflections of my life / Rainbow / My little one / Cousin Norman / Back on the road / Radancer / Falling apart at the seams / Heavens above / I gave up / I listen to the heart / What are you gonna do / Best of my love / Good luck to you. *(re-iss. May00 & Oct00 & Feb02; same)*
Sep 99. (lp) *10th Planet; (TP 044)* **KALEIDOSCOPE** | -
Jan 00. (d-cd) *Sequel; (NEECD 335)* **RAINBOW (THE DECCA YEARS)** | -
(re-iss. Apr02 on 'Castle'; CMDDD 488)
Jan 00. (cd) *Sequel; (NEMCD 463)* **I SEE THE RAIN (THE C.B.S. YEARS 1966-1969)** | -
(re-iss. Mar02 on 'Castle'; CMRCD 487)
Apr 00. (cd) *Metrodome; (METRO 368)* **PURE GOLD** | -
Jan 01. (d-cd) *Castle; (CMDDD 146)* **MARMALADE vs. THE TREMELOES – A SWINGING 60's BATTLE OF THE BANDS** | -
Sep 01. (d-cd) *Castle; (CMEDD 281)* **REFLECTIONS OF THE MARMALADE – AN ANTHOLOGY** | -

DEAN FORD

— solo stuff after he left MARMALADE in 1975

E.M.I. | not iss.

Jun 75. (lp) *(EMC 3079)* **DEAN FORD** | -
Aug 75. (7") *(EMI 2333)* **HEY MY LOVE. / IF THE TIME IS RIGHT** | -
Nov 75. (7") *(EMI 2374)* **CRYING IN MY SLEEP. / CAPTAIN** | -
Nov 77. (7") *(EMI 2717)* **FEVER. / YOU ARE THE ONE** | -
1970's. (7") *(SPSR 382)* **CRYING IN MY SLEEP. / HEY MY LOVE** | -

Lena MARTELL

Born: 1949, Glasgow. LENA started out in the early 60's singing in pubs and clubs around the Barrowlands area of her home city. However, numerous attempts at the singles charts (for 'H.M.V.', 'Decca' and 'Pye') all failed to propel the easy-listening, contemporary cabaret singer into the spotlight. The Scottish public (the blue-rinse brigade, especially) all bought her country-styled spiritual albums by the barrow(land)load, two of them 'THAT WONDERFUL SOUND OF LENA MARTELL' (1974) and 'THE BEST OF LENA MARTELL' (1976), both reaching the UK charts – No.35 and No.13 respectively. With, once again, producer George Elrick in tow, LENA finally found the fame she dreamed of in October 1979. With a cover of Kris Kristofferson's 'ONE DAY AT A TIME', she topped the British charts for three weeks and became a darling overnight for BBC Radio 2 listeners; the song has since been adopted by Alcoholics Anonymous in the USA. An accompanying album, 'LENA'S MUSIC ALBUM' (1979), also hit paydirt (No.5), although bar a few hit albums in 1980, her singles success was nigh on over. She retired in the mid-80's and was last seen living in Bishopbriggs (c.1997).

LENA MARTELL – vocals / with various backing

H.M.V. | not iss.

1961. (7") *(POP 958)* **LOVE CAN BE. / THE NIGHT THE SKY FELL DOWN** | -
1962. (7") *(POP 1049)* **THE REASONS WHY. / TO THIS MAN** | -
1963. (7") *(POP 1152)* **LET THE MUSIC PLAY. / ONE BOY** | -
1964. (7") *(POP 1214)* **I WISH YOU WELL. / ARRIVERDERCI NOT ADDIO** | -

Decca | not iss.

Sep 64. (7") *(F 11978)* **I'M A FOOL TO WANT YOU. / ALL CRIED OUT** | -

Pye

1967. (7") *(7N 17276)* **POP GROUP SONG. / REFLECTIONS** | -
1967. (7") *(7N 17320)* **SOMEWHERE MY LOVE. / I WOULD MARRY SPRING** | -
1968. (7") *(7N 17458)* **IN TIME. / ONE OF THE CROWD** | -
1968. (7") *(7N 17609)* **COME SEPTEMBER. / YOU WANTED SOMEONE TO PLAY WITH** | -

Decca | not iss.

Jul 69. (7") *(F 12955)* **IT'S ANOTHER WORLD. / NOW** | -
Jan 70. (7") *(F 12993)* **LOVE YOU MADE A FOOL OF ME. / DON'T REMEMBER YOUR NAME** | -
May 70. (7") *(F 13024)* **FOR THE LOVE OF HIM. / I WOULD MARRY SPRING** | -
Sep 71. (7") *(F 13201)* **I'M GOING HOME. / THE WORLD OF THE CHILD** | -
Jan 72. (lp) *(SPA 246)* **THE WORLD OF LENA MARTELL** | -

Pye

May 72. (lp) *(NSPL 18378)* **PRESENTING LENA MARTELL** | -
Jan 73. (lp) *(NSPL 18414)* **THIS IS LENA MARTELL** | -
Jun 73. (7") *(7N 45250)* **WHILE WE'RE STILL YOUNG. / MIRACLES** | -
Sep 73. (7") *(7N 45280)* **FOUR & TWENTY HOURS. / MIRACLES** | -
Oct 73. (lp) *(NSPL 18385)* **A TOUCH OF LENA MARTELL** | -
Nov 73. (7") *(7N 45302)* **A SCOTTISH TRILOGY. / RICHES** | -
Apr 74. (7") *(7N 45338)* **BILLY. / THINK ABOUT IT BABY** | -
May 74. (lp) *(NSPL 18427)* **THAT WONDERFUL SOUND OF LENA MARTELL** 35 | -
Oct 74. (7") *(7N 45405)* **HASTA MANANA. / EVERYBODY WANTS TO BE LOVED** | -
Nov 74. (lp) *(NSPL 18447)* **SONGS** | -
Jan 75. (lp/c) *(NSPL/ZCP 18466)* **THE MAGIC OF LENA MARTELL** | -
Jul 75. (7") *(7N 45492)* **AFTER ALL IS SAID AND DONE. / PROUD TO BE A WOMAN** | -

Mar 76. (7") *(7N 45582)* **CALL COLLECT. / THE OLD RUGGED CROSS** [ ] [-]
Oct 76. (lp) *(NSPL/ZCP 18506)* **THE BEST OF LENA MARTELL** (compilation) [13] [ ]
Feb 77. (7") *(7N 45676)* **TIMES WERE. / I WOULD MARRY SPRING** [ ] [-]
Nov 77. (lp/c) *(NSPL/ZCP 18534)* **HELLO MISTY MORNING** [ ] [-]
Jan 78. (7") *(7N 46116)* **SOMEWHERE IN MY LIFETIME. / TIME TO SAY GOODBYE** [ ] [-]
Mar 79. (lp/c) *(NSPL/ZCP 18585)* **LENA MARTELL IN CONCERT AT THE ROYAL FESTIVAL HALL (live)** [ ] [-]
May 79. (lp) *(NSPL 18590)* **SOMEWHERE IN MY LIFETIME** [ ] [-]
Sep 79. (7") *(7N 46021)* **ONE DAY AT A TIME. / HELLO MISTY MORNING** [1] [ ]
Oct 79. (lp/c) *(N/ZCN 123)* **LENA'S MUSIC ALBUM** [5] [-]

P.R.T. not iss.

Jan 80. (7") *(7P 157)* **DON'T CRY FOR ME ARGENTINA. / DON'T REMEMBER YOUR NAME** [ ] [-]
Nov 80. (7") *(7P 209)* **WHY ME. / MELANCHOLY SUNDAY** [ ] [-]
Nov 81. (7") *(7P 225)* **PRAY WITH ME. / WHEN YOU WERE SWEET SIXTEEN** [ ] [-]

Country House not iss.

Sep 84. (lp/c) *(BGC/KBGC 376)* **LENA MARTELL TODAY** [ ] [-]
Nov 84. (7") *(BGC7S 379)* **YOU'RE MY HERO. / TIME TO GO** [ ] [-]

– compilations, etc. –

1970. (7") *Pye; (7N 45104)* **SOMEWHERE MY LOVE. / COME SEPTEMBER** [ ] [-]
1970. (7") *Pye; (7N 45140)* **IT'S TOO LATE NOW. / IN TIME** [ ] [-]
May 77. (lp/c) *Pye; (NSPL/ZCP 18513)* **VERY SPECIAL LOVE FROM LENA** [ ] [-]
May 78. (lp) *Ronco; (RTL 2028)* **THE LENA MARTELL COLLECTION** [12] [-]
May 79. (c) *Golden Hour; (ZCGH 668)* **THE GOLDEN HOUR OF . . .** [ ] [-]
1979. (c) *P.R.T.; (ZCP 11046)* **THE NIGHT AND THE MUSIC** [ ] [-]
Jan 80. (d-lp/d-c) *P.R.T.; (SPOT/ZCSPT 1004)* **SPOTLIGHT ON LENA MARTELL** [ ] [-]
Feb 80. (lp/c) *One Up; (OU/TC-OU 2229)* **LET THE MUSIC PLAY** [ ] [-]
Apr 80. (lp/c) *Ronco; (RTL/4CRTL 2046)* **BY REQUEST** [9] [-]
Sep 80. (lp/c) *Pickwick; (SSP/SSC 3072)* **LENA MARTELL** [ ] [-]
Nov 80. (lp/c) *Ronco; (RTL/4CRTL 2052)* **BEAUTIFUL SUNDAY** [23] [-]
Mar 81. (lp/c) *Hallmark; (SHM/HSC 3056)* **FEELINGS** [ ] [-]
(cd-iss. Jul91 on 'Pickwick'; PWKM 4069)
May 81. (lp/c) *Decca-Elite; (TAB/KTBC 20)* **SOMETHING SIMPLE** [ ] [-]
Jun 82. (c) *P.R.T.; (ZCTON 105)* **100 MINUTES OF . . .** [ ] [-]
Jul 82. (d-lp/d-c) *Ronco; (RTL/4CRTL 2078AB)* **SONGS OF LIFE / SONGS OF LIFE** [ ] [-]
Oct 82. (lp/c) *P.R.T.; (SPOT/ZCSPT 1025)* **SPOTLIGHT ON LENA MARTELL VOL.2** [ ] [-]
Apr 83. (7") *Old Gold; (OG 9295)* **ONE DAY AT A TIME / (other track by Brian & Michael)** [ ] [-]
Sep 83. (7"ep/c-ep) *Scoop; (7SR/7SC 5010)* **6 TRACK HITS** [ ] [-]
May 85. (lp/c) *Pickwick; (HSA/HSCM 263)* **THE LOVE ALBUM** [ ] [-]
1986. (lp/c) *P.R.T.; (NSPH/ZCP 18)* **COUNTRY STYLE** [ ] [-]
Jan 88. (lp/c) *P.R.T.; (PYL/PYC 6033)* **THE VERY BEST OF LENA MARTELL** [ ] [-]
1988. (cd) *Pickwick; (PWK 041)* **LOVE SONGS** [ ] [-]
May 89. (cd/c) *Pickwick; (GHCD/C90 9)* **LENA MARTELL** [ ] [-]
Sep 90. (cd/c) *Knight; (KGH Cd/MC 125)* **THE GOLDEN HOUR OF LENA MARTELL** [ ] [-]
May 92. (cd/c) *Scotdisc; (CD/K ITV 542)* **SOMETIMES WHEN I'M DREAMING** [ ] [-]
Dec 92. (cd/c) *Castle; (MAT CD/MC 220)* **THE BEST OF LENA MARTELL** [ ] [-]
Oct 94. (cd/c) *True Trax; (TRT CD/MC 131)* **FEELINGS – THE BEST OF LENA MARTELL** [ ] [-]
Mar 98. (cd/c) *Marble Arch; (MAC CD/MC 373)* **SONGS OF LIFE** [ ] [-]
Jun 99. (cd/c) *Scotdisc; (CD/K ITV 647)* **INSPIRATIONS** [ ] [-]
Aug 99. (cd) *Castle Pie; (PIESD 030)* **ONE DAY AT A TIME** [ ] [-]
Feb 00. (cd/c) *Castle Pulse; (PLS CD/MC 169)* <665> **THE BEST OF LENA MARTELL – ONE DAY AT A TIME** [ ] [Nov00]
– One day at a time / Movin' on / Until it's time for you to go / Pledging my love / Love letters / The first time ever I saw your face / Make the world go away / Running bear / Call collect / Old rugged cross / Danny come home / Six weeks every summer / Stay away from the apple tree / Everybody get together / Hillbilly hoedown / Feelings / Call / Four and twenty hours / Forever in blue jeans / I'm gonna be a country girl again / Help me make it through the night / It looks like I'll never fall in love again.

John MARTYN

Born: IAIN McGEACHY, 11 Sep'48, New Malden, Surrey (he was partly brought up on a houseboat by his English mother, the other six months of the year by his father in Glasgow after they separated just after he was born – his grandmother subsequently brought him up in Scotland). Having learned guitar techniques from folk singer HAMISH IMLACH, MARTYN moved to London in 1967 after being the first white solo artist to secure a deal with Chris Blackwell's 'Island' label.

His early albums, 'LONDON CONVERSATION' (1968) and 'THE TUMBLER' (1968) were competent folk sets, the latter revealing the first glimmers of MARTYN's nascent jazz/blues leanings, employing the services of respected flautist HAROLD McNAIR.

Following MARTYN's marriage to Coventry girl, BEVERLEY KUTNER, the pair began recording together in 1969, releasing two albums, 'STORMBRINGER' and 'THE ROAD TO RUIN' the following year. The latter set was the first of many MARTYN albums to feature the double bass work of friend (and then PENTANGLE member) DANNY THOMPSON, the only musical collaborator who would become a fairly permanent fixture in the singer's career.

Following the birth of the MARTYN's second child in 1971, JOHN resumed his solo career with 'BLESS THE WEATHER'. His most heavily jazz-influenced set to date, the record was a blueprint for much of MARTYN's subsequent work; here were the first signs of the singer's trademark lounge lizard slur (a defiantly unique hybrid of ERIC CLAPTON, LOWELL GEROGE and TOM WAITS) with which he'd dextrously negotiate the grey area where jazz, blues, folk and rock meet. With RICHARD THOMPSON on additional guitar (he also played on 'BLESS..') and a rhythm section courtesy of FAIRPORT CONVENTION (bassist DAVE PEGG and drummer DAVE MATTACKS), 'SOLID AIR' (1973) was the pivotal early MARTYN album. Pioneering use of acoustic guitar echo lent the album a uniquely haunting quality, the set featuring some of MARTYN's most affecting material. The title track was a drifting, twilight tribute to NICK DRAKE while among the more conventional, folk-ish numbers, 'OVER THE HILL' and lovely 'MAY YOU NEVER' (later covered by ERIC CLAPTON on his 'Slowhand' album) were soul stirring highlights.

The album considerably widened his large cult following which numbered musicians like STEVE WINWOOD, a collaborator on the follow-up, 'INSIDE OUT' (1973). The record traced the same nebulous path as its predecessor, as did 'SUNDAY'S CHILD' (1975), the latter employing the services of the late PAUL KOSSOFF (ex-FREE and latterly BACKSTREET CRAWLER).

In the two year gap prior to his next studio project, MARTYN released a limited (10,000) mail-order only (from his Sussex home) live album, the acclaimed 'LIVE AT LEEDS' (1975). The speed at which the pressing sold out indicated the extent of MARTYN's fanbase. Nevertheless, the singer was yet to make an overt attempt to turn his standing into commercial success; 'ONE WORLD' (1977) was as esoteric as ever. Extending his range of influences to include dub and oblique ambience, the record was another key release in MARTYN's career featuring both the gorgeous 'COULDN'T LOVE YOU MORE' and the sly, insidious skank of 'BIG MUFF', a collaboration with Jamaican legend LEE PERRY.

The ensuing three years saw MARTYN split with wife BEVERLEY, this harrowing period providing much of the impetus for 1980's 'GRACE AND DANGER'. While the album was a relatively sombre affair, the emergence of PHIL COLLINS (here contributing percussion, vocals and production) signalled a move towards a more mainstream sound. Inevitably, then, his 1981 album, 'GLORIOUS FOOL' (a political assault on newly elected US president Ronald Reagan) made the UK Top 30, the follow-up, 'WELL KEPT SECRET' (1982) reaching No.20. Since then, however, he's failed to consolidate this brief flurry of chart action, conceivably because MARTYN's albums rarely include any glaring hit singles.

Though the 80's were a fairly fallow period for MARTYN, he returned in fine style at the turn of the decade with 'THE APPRENTICE' (1990) and the sophisti-jazz of 'COOLTIDE' (1991). The latter set surfaced on 'Permanent' for whom he'd revisit a batch of old material on two studio sets and a live album over the course of the early-mid 90's. A surprise move to 'Go Discs!', resulted in his first Top 40 entry of the decade with 'AND' (1996). Upon the label's demise, MARTYN joined the new 'Independiente' stable (alongside TRAVIS!) and cut a low-key covers set, 'THE CHURCH WITH ONE BELL' (1998); he subsequently used the profits generated to help him procure the church pictured on the album sleeve(!). MARTYN's body of work remains unique, a rich seam of inspiration for the uninitiated; it's just a pity his talents aren't more widely acknowledged.

• **Covered:** COCAINE BLUES (trad.) / I'D RATHER BE THE DEVIL (Skip James) / JOHNNY TOO BAD (Slickers) / TIGHT CONNECTION TO MY HEART (Bob Dylan) / NEVER LET ME GO (Joe Scott) / HE'S GOT ALL THE WHISKEY (Bobby Charles) / GOD'S SONG (Randy Newman) / HOW FORTUNATE THE MAN WITH NONE (Dead Can Dance; words Bertholt Brecht) / SMALL TOWN TALK (Bobby Charles & Rick Danko) / EXCUSE ME MISTER (Ben Harper) / STRANGE FRUIT (Billie Holiday) / THE SKY

IS CRYING (Elmore James) / GLORY BOX (Portishead) / FEEL SO BAD (S. Hopkins) / DEATH DON'T HAVE NO MERCY (Reverend Gary Davis).
• **Trivia:** He has also guested on albums by CLAIRE HAMMILL, BURNING SPEAR and BACK STREET CRAWLER, to mention but a few.

JOHN MARTYN – vocals, acoustic guitar

Island Warners

Oct 67. (lp) *(ILP 952)* **LONDON CONVERSATION** [ ] [-]
– Fairy tale lullaby / Sandy grey / London conversation / Ballad of an elder woman / Cocaine blues / Run honey run / Back to stay / Rolling home / Who's grown up now / Golden girl / This time / Don't think twice. *(re-iss. Aug91 cd)(c; IMCD 134)(ICM 2074)*

— added **HAROLD McNAIR** – flute / **PAUL WHEELER** – guitar / **DAVE MOSES** – bass

Dec 68. (lp) *(ILPS 9091)* **THE TUMBLER** [ ] [-]
– Sing a song of summer / The river / Goin' down to Memphis / The gardeners / A day at the sea / Fishin' blues / Dusty / Hello train / Winding boy / Fly on home / Knuckledy crunch and slipp ledee slee song / Seven black roses. *(cd-iss. Apr94; IMCD 173)*

JOHN & BEVERLEY MARTYN

(as BEVERLEY, she recorded solo 45's) **BEVERLEY** nee KUTNER – vocals, with + **LEVON HELM** – drums (The BAND) / **PAUL HARRIS** – piano / **HARVEY BROOKS** – bass / **BIUX MUNDI** + **HERBIE LOVELL** – drums

Jan 70. (7") *(WIP 6076)* **JOHN THE BAPTIST. / THE OCEAN** [ ] [-]
Feb 70. (lp) *(ILPS 9113) <1854>* **STORMBRINGER** [ ] [ ]
– Go out and get it / Can't get the one I want / Stormbringer / Sweet honesty / Woodstock / John the baptist / The ocean / Traffic light lady / Tomorrow time / Would you believe me. *(re-iss. Aug91 cd)(c; IMCD 131)(ICM 9113)*
Apr 70. (7") **GO OUT AND GET IT. / CAN'T GET THE ONE I WANT** [-] [ ]

— with **DANNY THOMPSON** – bass (of PENTANGLE) / **WELLS KELLY** – drums, bass + **PAUL HARRIS**

Nov 70. (lp) *(ILPS 9133) <1882>* **THE ROAD TO RUIN** [ ] [ ]
– Primrose hill / Parcels / Auntie aviator / New day / Give us a ring / Sorry to be so long / Tree garden / Say what you can / The road to ruin. *(cd-iss. Mar93; IMCD 165)*

JOHN MARTYN

went solo again, with **DANNY THOMPSON** – double bass / **RICHARD THOMPSON** – guitar (solo artist) / **TONY REEVES** – (of COLOSSEUM) / **IAN WHITEMAN** and **ROGER POWELL** (of MIGHTY BABY)

Island Island

Nov 71. (lp) *(ILPS 9167) <9311>* **BLESS THE WEATHER** [ ] [ ]
– Go easy / Bless the weather / Sugar lump / Walk to the water / Just now / Head and heart / Let the good times come / Back down the river / Glistening Glyndebourne / Singing in the rain. *(re-iss. Aug91 cd)(c; IMCD 135)(ICM 9167)*

— retained **DANNY, RICHARD** and brought in **JOHN 'RABBIT' BUNDRICK** – keyboards / **DAVE PEGG** – bass / **DAVE MATTACKS** – drums / and **SPEEDY** (NEEMOI ACQUAYE) – congas / (all of FAIRPORT CONVENTION).

Nov 72. (7") *(WIP 6116)* **MAY YOU NEVER. / JUST NOW** [ ] [-]
Feb 73. (lp) *(ILPS 9226) <9325>* **SOLID AIR** [ ] [ ]
– Over the hill / Don't want to know / I'd rather be with the Devil / Go down easy / Dreams by the sea / May you never / The man in the station / Easy blues / Solid air. *(re-iss. Nov86 lp/c; ILPM/ICM 9226) (cd-iss. Feb87; CID 9226) (cd re-mast.Oct00; IMCD 274)*
Mar 73. (7") **MAY YOU NEVER. / DON'T WANT TO KNOW ABOUT EVIL** [-] [ ]

— retained **DANNY,** and brought in **BOBBY KEYES** and **REMI KABAKA** plus **STEVE WINWOOD** and **CHRIS WOOD** (both of TRAFFIC)

Oct 73. (lp) *(ILPS 9253) <9335>* **INSIDE OUT** [ ] [ ]
– Fine lines / Eibhli ghail ghiuin ni chearbhaill / Ain't no saint / Outside in / The glory of love / Look in / Beverley / Make no mistake / Ways to cry / So much in love with you. *(cd-iss. Apr94; IMCD 172)*

— with **DANNY THOMPSON / JOHN STEVENS** – drums / **PAUL KOSSOFF** – guitar (ex-FREE) and guests **BEVERLEY MARTYN** – vocals

Jan 75. (lp) *(ILPS 9296) <9396>* **SUNDAY'S CHILD** [ ] [ ]
– One day without you / Lay it all down / Root love / My baby girl / Sunday's child / Spencer the rover / Clutches / The message / Satisfied mind / You can discover / Call me crazy. *(cd-iss. Mar93; IMCD 163)*
Sep 75. (lp; ltd-mail order) *(ILPS 9343)* **LIVE AT LEEDS (live)** [-] [-]
– Outside in / Solid air / Make no mistake / Bless the weather / The man in the station / I'd rather be the Devil. *(re-iss. Jun87 on 'Cacophony'; SKELP 001) (cd-iss. May92 on 'Awareness'; AWCD 1036) (re-iss. cd Jul95 on 'Hypertension'; HYCD 200114) (cd re-iss. Aug98 on 'Blueprint'; OW 107CD)*
Feb 77. (7") *(WIP 6385)* **OVER THE HILL. / HEAD AND HEART** [ ] [-]
Mar 77. (lp) *(<ILPS 9484>)* **SO FAR SO GOOD** (compilation) [ ] [ ]
– May you never / Bless the weather / Head and heart / Over the hill / Spencer the rover / Glistening Glyndebourne / Solid air / One day without you / I'd rather be the Devil.

— with guests **STEVE WINWOOD** – keyboards / **MORRIS PERT** – percussion.

Nov 77. (lp/c) *(ILPS/ZCI 9492)* **ONE WORLD** [54] [-]
– Couldn't love you more / Certain surprise / Dancing / Small hours / Dealer / One world / Smiling stranger / Big Muff. *(re-iss. Sep86 lp/c/cd; ILPM/ICM/CID 9492)*
Jan 78. (7") *(WIP 6414)* **DANCING. / DEALER (version)** [ ] [-]

— with **PHIL COLLINS** – drums,vocals / **JOHN GIBLIN** – bass (both of BRAND X) / **TOMMY EYRE** – keyboards (GREASE BAND) / **DAVE LAWSON** – keyboards (ex-GREENSLADE).

Island not iss.

Oct 80. (lp/c) *(ILPS/ICT 9560)* **GRACE AND DANGER** [54] [-]
– Some people are crazy / Grace and danger / Lookin' on / Johnny too bad / Sweet little mystery/ Hurt in your heart / Baby please come home / Save some for me / Our love. *(cd-iss. May87; CID 9560)*
Oct 80. (7") *(WIP 6495)* **JOHNNY TOO BAD. / ('A'instrumental)** [ ] [-]
Mar 81. (7") *(WIP 6547)* **JOHNNY TOO BAD. / ('A'version)** [ ] [-]
(12") *(IPR 2046)* – ('A'ext. dub version) / Big Muff (ext.mix).
May 81. (7") *(WIP 6718)* **SWEET LITTLE MYSTERY. / JOHNNY TOO BAD** [ ] [-]

— with **PHIL COLLINS** – drums, vocals, producer / **ALAN THOMSON** – bass / **MAX MIDDLETON** – keyboards / **DANNY CUMMINGS** – percussion / **DICK CUTHELL** – horns 2.

WEA Duke

Aug 81. (7") *(K 79243)* **PLEASE FALL IN LOVE WITH ME. / DON'T YOU GO** [ ] [-]
Sep 81. (lp/c) *(K/K4 99178)* **GLORIOUS FOOL** [25] [-]
– Couldn't love you more / Amsterdam / Hold on my heart / Perfect hustler / Hearts and keys / Glorious fool / Never say never / Oascanel (get back home) / Didn't do that / Please fall in love with me / Don't you go.
Feb 82. (7") **COULDN'T LOVE YOU MORE. /** [-] [ ]

— with **DANNY** and **ALAN** plus **JEFFREY ALLEN** – drums / **JIM PRIME** – keyboards / **MEL COLLINS** – sax / **MARTIN DROVER** – trumpet / **LEE KOSMIN** and **STEVE LANGE** – harmony.

Aug 82. (lp/c) *(K/K4 99255)* **WELL KEPT SECRET** [20] [-]
– Could've been me / You might need a man / Hung up / Gun money / Never let me go / Love up / Changes her mind / Hiss on the tape / Back with a vengeance / Livin' alone.
Sep 82. (7") *(K 79336)* **HISS ON THE TAPE. / LIVIN' ALONE** [ ] [-]
Nov 82. (7") *(259987-7)* **GUN MONEY (US remix). / HISS ON THE TAPE (live)** [ ] [ ]

— touring line-up **ALAN THOMSON** – bass / **JEFFREY ALLEN** – drums / **DANNY CUMMINGS** – percussion / **RONNIE LEAHY** – keyboards

Body Swerve not iss.

Nov 83. (lp) *(JMLP 001)* **PHILENTHROPY (live)** [ ] [-]
– Sunday's child / Don't want to know / Johnny too bad / Make no mistake / Root love / Lookin' on / Hung up / Smiling stranger. *(re-iss. Mar86 on 'Dojo' lp/c/cd; DOJO LP/TC/CD 26)*

— **MARTYN** retained **JIM** and **ALAN** plus **BARRY REYNOLDS** add. guitar / **JACK WALDMAN** – keyboards / **ROBIN RANKIN** – keyboards / **JAMES HOOKER** – keyboards / **STEVEN STANLEY** – linn drums / **ANDY LYDEN** – linn drums / **UZZIAH 'STICKY' THOMPSON** – percussion / **COLIN TULLY** – saxophone / harmony by **MORWENNE LAIDLAW, TERRY NELSON** and **LORNA BROOKS**

Island Island

Oct 84. (7") *(IS 209)* **OVER THE RAINBOW. / ROPE SOUL'D** [ ] [-]
Nov 84. (lp/c) *(ILPS/ICT 9779)* **SAPPHIRE** [57] [ ]
– Sapphire / Over the rainbow / You know / Watching her eyes / Fisherman's dream / Acid rain / Mad dog days / Climb the walls / Coming in on time / Rope soul'd. *(cd-iss. Mar93; IMCD 164)*

— with **ALAN THOMSON** – fretless bass / **DANNY CUMMINGS** – percussion / **COLIN TULLY and FOSTER PATTERSON** – keyboards, vocals.

Feb 86. (lp/c/cd) *(ILPS/ICT/CID 9807)* **PIECE BY PIECE** [28] [-]
– Nightline / Lonely love / Angeline / One step too far / Piece by piece / Serendipity / Who believes in angels / Love of mine / John Wayne. *(cd+=)* – Tight connection to my heart / Solid air / One world / May you never.
Feb 86. (7") *(IS 265)* **ANGELINE. / TIGHT CONNECTION TO MY HEART** [ ] [-]
(12"+=) *(12IS 265)* – May you never / Certain surprise / One day without you.
(cd-ep+=) *(CID 265)* – May you never / Solid air / Glistening Glyndebourne.
May 86. (7") *(IS 272)* **LONELY LOVE. / SWEET LITTLE MYSTERY (live)** [ ] [-]
(12"+=) *(12IS 272)* – Fisherman's dream (live).

— **DAVID BALL** – bass repl. THOMPSON / added **ARRAN ABMUN** – drums + **JEFF CASTLE** – keyboards

Oct 87. (lp/c/cd) *(ILPS/ICT/CID 9884)* **FOUNDATIONS (live)** [ ] [-]
– Mad dog days / Angeline / The apprentice / May you never / Deny this love / Send me one line / John Wayne / Johnny too bad / Over the rainbow. *(re-iss. cd Apr94; IMCD 180)*

Permanent not iss.

Mar 90. (cd/c/lp) *(PERM CD/MC/LP 1)* **THE APPRENTICE** [ ] [-]
– Live on love / Look at that gun / Send me one line / Hold me / The apprentice / The river / Income town / Deny this love / UPO / Patterns in the rain. *(cd+=)* – The moment. *(cd re-iss. Apr98 on 'Indelible'; INDELCD 1)*
Aug 90. (7") *(PERM S12)* **DENY THIS LOVE (remix). / THE APPRENTICE (live)** [ ] [-]
(cd-s+=) *(CDPERM 1)* – ('A'-lp version).

Nov 91. (cd/c/lp) *(PERM CD/MC/LP 4)* **COOLTIDE** [ ] [-]
– Hole in the rain / Annie says / Jack the lad / Number nine / The cure / Same difference / Father Time / Call me / Cooltide.

Apr 92. (cd-s) *(CDPERM 3)* **JACK THE LAD / ?** [ ] [-]

Sep 92. (7") *(PERM 6)* **SWEET LITTLE MYSTERY. / HEAD AND HEART** [ ] [-]
(12"+=/cd-s+=) *(12/CD PERM 6)* – Never let me go.

Oct 92. (cd/c/lp) *(PERM CD/MC/LP 9)* **COULDN'T LOVE YOU MORE** [65] [-]
– Lonely love / Couldn't love you more / Sweet little mystery / Head & heart / Could've been me / One day without you / Over the hill / Fine lines / May you never / One world / Way's to cry / Angeline / Man in the station / Solid air / Never let me go.

Jan 93. (cd-s; w-drawn) **LONELY LOVE** [ ] [-]

— with on next album **SPENCER COZENS** or **CHRIS CAMERON** – keyboards / **GERRY CONWAY** or **WAYNE STEWART** – drums / **ALAN THOMPSON** or **JOHN GIBLIN** – bass / **MILES BOULD** or **MARK WALKER** – percussion / **DAVE GILMOUR** or **ALAN DARBY** or **BILL RUPERT** – guitar / **ANDY SHEPHERD** or **GERRY UNDERWOOD** – sax / **FRED NELSON** – piano / **LEVON HELM** – guest / and of course **PHIL COLLINS** – b.vocals, etc.

Jul 93. (cd/c) *(PERM CD/MC 14)* **NO LITTLE BOY** (old songs re-worked) [ ] [-]
– Solid air / Ways to cry / Could've been me / I don't wanna know / Just now / One day without you / Sweet little mystery / Pascanel / Sunday's child / Head and heart / Fine lines / Bless the weather / Man in the station / One world / Rock salt and nails / Hole in the rain.

— with **PHIL COLLINS, JOHN GIBLIN + ALAN THOMPSON, JERRY UNDERWOOD, SPENCER COZENS**, etc

Go! Discs | not iss.

Aug 96. (cd/c) *(828 798-2/-4)* **AND.** [32] [-]
– Sunshine's better / Suzanne / The downward pull of human nature / All in your favour / A little strange / Who are they? / Step it up / Carmine / She's a lover.

— now with **GIBLIN, COZENS / + ARRAN AHMUN** – drums, percussion

Blueprint | not iss.

Dec 97. (cd-ep) *(BP 276CD)* **SNOOO . . . / SHE'S A LOVER / ALL IN YOUR FAVOUR / STEP IT UP / A LITTLE STRANGE** [ ] [-]

Independiente | Thirsty Ear

Mar 98. (cd) *(ISOM 3CD)* <57053> **THE CHURCH WITH ONE BELL** [51] [ ]
– He's got all the whiskey / God's song / How fortunate the man with none / Small town talk / Excuse me mister / Strange fruit / The sky is crying / Glory box / Feel so sad / Death don't have no mercy.

Jun 98. (cd-s) *(ISOM 14MS)* **EXCUSE ME MISTER / GOD'S SONG (live) / ROCK, SALT AND NAIL (live) / JOHN WAYNE (live)** [ ] [-]

May 00. (cd) *(ISOM 15CD)* **GLASGOW WALKER** [66] [-]
– So sweet / Wildflower / The field of play / Cool in the life / Feel so good / Cry me a river / Mama T / Can't live without / The cat won't work tonight / You don't know what love is.

— in Mar'01, MARTYN was credited on the SISTER BLISS (of FAITHLESS) UK No.31 single, 'Deliver Me'

– compilations, etc. –

on 'Island' unless otherwise mentioned

Oct 82. (lp/c) *(ILPS/ICT 9715)* **THE ELECTRIC JOHN MARTYN** [ ] [ ]
(cd-iss. Apr88; CID 9715)

May 92. (cd) *Windsong; (WINCD 012)* **BBC RADIO 1 LIVE IN CONCERT (live)** [ ] [-]

Nov 92. (d-cd) *(ITSCD 2)* **SOLID AIR / ONE WORLD** [ ] [-]

Jun 94. (d-cd) *(CRNCD 4)* **SWEET LITTLE MYSTERIES – THE ISLAND ANTHOLOGY** [ ] [ ]

Jul 95. (d-cd/d-c) *Permanent; (PERM CD/MC 33) / Resurgent; <1122>* **LIVE (live at the Shaw Theatre, London, 31st March, 1990)** <US-title 'DIRTY, DOWN & LIVE'> [ ] [ ] Nov99
– Easy blues / May you never / Dealer / Outside in / Never let me go / Sapphire / Couldn't love you more / Deny this love / Fisherman's dream / Big Muff / Angeline / Sweet little mystery / The river / Income town / The apprentice / John Wayne / Look at the girl / Looking on / Johnny too bad / One world.

Mar 98. (cd) *Artful; (ARTFULCD 13)* **THE REST OF THE BEST** [ ] [-]

Mar 00. (d-cd) *Artful; (ARTFULCD 31)* **CLASSICS** [ ] [-]
(re-iss. Apr02; same)

Jul 00. (d-cd) *Eagle; (EDMCD 102)* **THE MASTERS (live '91)** [ ] [-]

Nov 00. (cd) *One World; (OW 113CD)* **THE NEW YORK SESSION** [ ] [-]

Apr 01. (cd) *Mooncrest; (<CRESTCD 065>)* **PATTERNS IN THE RAIN (some live)** [ ] [ ]

Jul 01. (cd; by JOHN MARTYN & DANNY THOMPSON) *One World; (OW 118CD)* **LIVE IN GERMANY 1986 (live)** [ ] [-]

Aug 01. (cd; by JOHN MARTYN & DANNY THOMPSON) *One World; (OW 115CD)* **LIVE AT THE BREWERY ARTS CENTRE KENDAL 1986 (live)** [ ] [-]

Aug 01. (cd) *One World; (OW 109CD)* **LIVE AT THE TOWN & COUNTRY CLUB 1986 (live)** [ ] [-]

Nov 01. (cd) *One World; (OW 116CD)* **LIVE AT THE BOTTOM LINE, NEW YORK 1983 (live)** [ ] [-]

Nov 01. (cd) *One World; (OW 119CD)* **SWEET CERTAIN SURPRISE (live)** [ ] [-]

May 02. (cd) *One World; (OW 117CD)* **LIVE IN MILAN (live)** [ ] [-]

Glen MASON

Born: 16 Sep'30, Stirling. A bit of a crooner and all-round entertainer, GLEN was a minor hitmaker and after one flop, 'HOT DIGGITY (DOG ZIGGITY BOOM)', he had two Top 30 hits towards the end of '56, 'GLENDORA' and 'GREEN DOOR'. Unfortunately, the latter was beaten back by FRANKIE VAUGHAN's version which hit No.2; "Glen Goes To Hollywood" was not to be. MASON was a bit of a mystery throughout his largely unfulfilled career and I think he spent most of his life in England.

GLEN MASON – vocals / with various people on session

Parlophone | not iss.

Jul 56. (7") *(R 4176)* **HOT DIGGITY (DOG ZIGGITY BOOM). / BABY GIRLS OF MINE** [ ] [-]

Sep 56. (7") *(R 4203)* **GLENDORA. / LOVE, LOVE, LOVE** [28] [-]

Nov 56. (7") *(R 4244)* **GREEN DOOR. / WHY MUST YOU GO, GO, GO** [24] [-]

Feb 57. (7") *(R 4271)* **DON'T FORBID ME. / AMORE** [ ] [-]

May 57. (7") *(R 4291)* **ROUND AND ROUND. / WALKING AND WHISTLING** [ ] [-]

Sep 57. (7") *(R 4334)* **CRYING MY HEART OUT FOR YOU. / WHY DON'T THEY UNDERSTAND** [ ] [-]

Nov 57. (7") *(R 4357)* **BY MY SIDE. / BY THE FIRESIDE** [ ] [-]

Jan 58. (7") *(R 4390)* **WHAT A BEAUTIFUL COMBINATION. / I'M ALONE BECAUSE I LOVE YOU** [ ] [-]

Mar 58. (7") *(R 4415)* **I MAY NEVER PASS THIS WAY AGAIN. / A MOMENT AGO** [ ] [-]

Jun 58. (7") *(R 4451)* **I KNOW WHERE I'M GOING. / AUTUMN SOUVENIR** [ ] [-]

Oct 58. (7") *(R 4485)* **THE END. / FALL IN LOVE** [ ] [-]

1959. (7") *(R 4562)* **THE BATTLE OF NEW ORLEANS. / I DON'T KNOW** [ ] [-]

1960. (7") *(R 4626)* **YOU GOT WHAT IT TAKES. / IF THERE'S SOMEONE** [ ] [-]

1960. (7") *(R 4723)* **I LIKE IT WHEN IT RAINS. / THAT'S WHAT I WANT** [ ] [-]

1961. (7") *(R 4834)* **SHADRACK. / DON'T MOVE** [ ] [-]

1962. (7") *(R 4900)* **ST. LOUIS BLUES. / THAT'S LIFE** [ ] [-]

Polydor | not iss.

1967. (7") *(BM 56155)* **TOO GOOD TO BE FORGOTTEN. / IT'S ALL OVER NOW** [ ] [-]

Feb 68. (7") *(BM 56232)* **LIFE'S GONE AND SLIPPED AWAY. / GO AWAY** [ ] [-]

— GLEN retired from the music business after above

MIDDLE OF THE ROAD

Formed: Glasgow . . . 1969 initially as PART FOUR by KEN ANDREW, IAN McCREDIE, ERIC McCREDIE and singer SALLY CARR. The following summer, the band used the moniker of LOS CARACAS to tour the sunny resorts of Italy and it was there that they stumbled upon a catchy little tune, 'CHIRPY CHIRPY CHEEP CHEEP' (an infectious precursor to 'The Birdie Song' perhaps!). With another new band name, MIDDLE OF THE ROAD, CARR and her cohorts signed a record deal with 'R.C.A.', who duly released the song as their debut single in May '71. For five weeks it topped the British charts and sold in countries all over Europe, although the US settled for MAC & KATIE KISSOON's Top 20 version.

For the next year or so, the yucky pop of MIDDLE OF THE ROAD littered the UK charts with four further, equally mind-numbing ditties, although thankfully each one ('TWEEDLE DEE TWEEDLE DUM', 'SOLEY SOLEY', 'SACRAMENTO' and 'SAMSON AND DELILAH') fared worse than its predecessor. In October, 1972, 'BOTTOMS UP', was given the thumbs down by their teenybop public, and it seemed MIDDLE OF THE ROAD's fifteen minutes was over.

The jetset lifestyle came crashing down to earth in such a short space of time, although thankfully SALLY CARR was eased back into circulation by her prophetic but understanding father; he had said, in not so many words, that, if the pop thing didn't work out she'd always be welcome back home. However, subsequent attempts at getting another hit failed time after time and eventually the 4-piece split. KEN ANDREW and IAN McCREDIE went on to produce

RUNRIG's debut set, 'Play Gaelic', while SALLY continued singing in local clubs and cabarets. In 1991, and always loved in Germany, MIDDLE OF THE ROAD turned up on a TV show. Around five years later and some more cabaret work behind them, the band re-recorded all their best tunes, releasing an eponymous comeback set in the process; they were also the subject of a TV series in 1999/2000.

SALLY CARR – vocals / **IAN McCREDIE** – guitar, flute, bagpipes / **ERIC McCREDIE** – bass, violin, keyboards, bagpipes / **KEN ANDREW** – drums, vibes, vocals

R.C.A. R.C.A.

May 71. (7") *(RCA 2047)* **CHIRPY CHIRPY CHEEP CHEEP. / RAININ' N' PAININ'** [1] [ ]

Aug 71. (7") *(RCA 2110)* **TWEEDLE DEE TWEEDLE DUM. / GIVE IT TIME** [2] [ ]

Nov 71. (7") *(RCA 2151)* **SOLEY SOLEY. / TO REMIND ME** [5] [ ]

Nov 71. (lp) *(8200)* **MIDDLE OF THE ROAD** [-] [-] German

Mar 72. (7") *(RCA 2184)* **SACRAMENTO. / LOVE SWEET LOVE** [23] [ ]

Jul 72. (7") *(RCA 2237)* **SAMSON AND DELILAH. / TRY A LITTLE UNDERSTANDING** [26] [ ]

Oct 72. (7") *(RCA 2264)* **BOTTOMS UP. / SEE THE SKY** [ ] [-]

Nov 72. (lp) *(LSP 10357)* **ACCELERATION** [-] [-] German
– Sacramento / On this land / Queen bee / Love sweet love / Then you'll know what love is for / Soley soley / The talk of the U.S.A. / Louise / Samson and Delilah / Try a little understanding / Medicine woman.

Mar 73. (7") *(RCA 2343)* **THE TALK OF THE U.S.A. / EVE** [ ] [-]

Apr 73. (lp) *(SF 8338)* **DRIVE ON** [ ] [-]
– Yellow boomerang / Universal man / See the sky / Wheel of the season / Blind detonation / Union silver / Honey no / Eve / On a westbound train / Bottoms up / Nothing can go wrong / Kailakee kalako.

Jun 73. (7") *(RCA 2388)* **UNION SILVER. / BLIND DETONATION** [ ] [-]

Ariola not iss.

1973. (lp) *(87260)* **MUSIC MUSIC** [-] [-] German
– Samba d'amour / Bloody Monday / Life's train / Don't send me roses / Queen of roses / Queen of rock and roll / Hard woman's comin' / I want for myself / Don't leave me now.

—— added **NEIL HENDERSON** – guitar, vocals

1974. (lp) *(87487)* **POSTCARD** [-] [-] German
– Jitter buggin' Jildy / Bad girl / One for the road / Do you wanna be with me / It's alright / Dry gluch Charlie / Bonjour ca va / Hang ups / Picture machine / Writing on the wall / Whisky and freedom / Thank you Lord.

—— reverted back to the basic 4-piece

1975. (lp) *(87897)* **YOU PAYS YER MONEY** [-] [-] German
– You pays yer money and you takes yer chance / Tell me / My story / Hang in there / Read between the lines / Country bus / Give it a try / Rockin' soul / Gone's the time / Shotgun mama / Gentle moments / Hooch wagon / You pays yer money and you takes yer chance.

Mar 75. (7") *(DJS 10361)* **HITCHIN' A RIDE IN THE MOONLIGHT. / DO YOU WANNA BE WITH ME** [ ] [-]
(above was issued in the UK by 'D.J.M.')

1975. (lp) *(89093)* **DICE** [-] [-] German
– Haven ground / Drive-in movies / Find the key / Far away / Look out the lover / Happy song / Hitchin' a ride in the moonlight / You got it coming to you / But tomorrow / It's the rain / Every day every night / D.J. song.

Pye not iss.

May 78. (7"; by SALLY CARR) *(7N 46074)* **PRETTY BOY BLUE. / MORNING** [ ] [-]

O.K. not iss.

Oct 80. (7") *(OK 002)* **STEAL A PIECE OF MY HEART. / LONELY** [ ] [-]

Pulsar not iss.

Jan 82. (7") *(PUS 103)* **PARTY TIME MEDLEY. / POSTCARD** [ ] [-]

—— concentrated on the cabaret/revival circuit, although they returned with

Koch Int. not iss.

Jun 97. (cd/c) *(3/2 99368)* **TODAY** [ ] [-]
– Midnight blue / Samson and Delilah / Love takes prisoners / Sacramento / Dance with me / South America / Soley soley / Turn on your radio / Chirpy chirpy cheep cheep / Tweedle dee tweedle dum / Kailakee kalako / Fall / One kiss.

– compilations, etc. –

1973. (lp) *R.C.A.; (SF 1433)* **CHIRPY CHIRPY CHEEP CHEEP** [ ] [-]

Dec 73. (lp) *R.C.A.; (LSP 10395)* **THE BEST OF . . .** [-] [-] German
– The talk of the U.S.A. / Samson and Delilah / Try a little understanding / louise / Chirpy chirpy cheep cheep / Soley soley / Medicone woman / Sacramento / Love sweet love / Queen bee / Tweedle dee tweedle dum.

Oct 74. (lp) *Camden; (CDS 1131)* **MIDDLE OF THE ROAD** [ ] [-]

Feb 75. (lp) *Camden; (CDS 1141)* **GREAT HITS** [ ] [-]

Sep 75. (7"m) *R.C.A.; (RCA 2602)* **CHIRPY CHIRPY CHEEP CHEEP. / TWEEDLE DEE TWEEDLE DUM / SOLEY SOLEY** [ ] [-]

May 82. (7") *RCA Golden Grooves; (GOLD 543)* **CHIRPY CHIRPY CHEEP CHEEP. / SOLEY SOLEY** [ ] [-]

Nov 86. (7") *Old Gold; (OG 9632)* **CHIRPY CHIRPY CHEEP CHEEP. / TWEEDLE DEE TWEEDLE DUM** [ ] [-]
(re-iss. Mar90; same)

Dec 92. (cd/c) *Ariola; (2/4 95594)* **MIDDLE OF THE ROAD** [ ] [-]

—— **SALLY + KEN** re-formed the group in 1991

Nov 97. (cd) *Prestige; (CDSGP 0357)* **ALL THE HITS PLUS MORE** [ ] [-]
– Chirpy chirpy cheep cheep / Sacramento / Tweedle dee tweedle dum / Kallakee kallakoe / Union silver / Soley soley / Bottoms up / Will you love me tomorrow / Talk of the U.S.A. / On this land / Samson and Delilah / Yellow boomerang / Tweedle dee tweedle dum / Chirpy chirpy cheep cheep. *(re-iss. Oct00 & Dec01; same)*

Nov 98. (cd) *Laserlight; (21323)* **MIDDLE OF THE ROAD** [ ] [-]

Jun 99. (cd-s) *Prestige; (CDSSGP 1013)* **CHIRPY CHIRPY CHEEP CHEEP (mixes) / DJ SONG** [ ] [-]

Sep 01. (cd) *Disky; (SI 64680-2)* **THE VERY BEST OF MIDDLE OF THE ROAD** [ ] [ ]

MIDNIGHT FLYER (see under ⇒ STONE THE CROWS)

Frankie MILLER

Born: 2 Nov'49, Bridgeton, Glasgow. After serving his musical apprenticeship in a series of pub outfits during the late 60's, MILLER relocated to London in mid '71. Newly installed in the capital, he formed JUDE alongside guitar maestro ROBIN TROWER and a rhythm section of JIM DEWAR and CLIVE BUNKER. The project proved short-lived, however, as TROWER went solo early the following year, taking DEWAR with him.

Teaming up with ex-members of the underrated BRINSLEY SCHWARZ (i.e. NICK LOWE, BOB ANDREWS, BILLY RANKIN and BRINSLEY SCHWARZ himself), MILLER proceeded to cut a debut solo album, 'ONCE IN A BLUE MOON' (1973) for 'Chrysalis'. The record failed to chart and the footloose singer-songwriter upped sticks for New Orleans where he hooked up with semi-legendary Crescent City soul guru, Allen Toussaint for the 'HIGHLIFE' (1974) album. Despite furnishing classic hits for Betty Wright ('SHOORAH SHOORAH') and Three Dog Night ('PLAY SOMETHING SWEET'), the album provided scant commercial pickings for MILLER himself.

Returning to the UK, he amassed a band consisting of HENRY McCULLOUGH, MICK WEAVER, CHRISSY STEWART and STU PERRY, cutting a third album, 'THE ROCK' (1975). Again sales were disappointing and it was 1977 before MILLER scored a rare Top 30 hit with 'BE GOOD TO YOURSELF', the lead track on that year's 'FULL HOUSE' album. Released under the moniker FRANKIE MILLER'S FULL HOUSE, the record was

recorded with a new band that lasted barely a year before MILLER again went solo. Augmented by such talents as PAUL CARRACK, 1978's 'DOUBLE TROUBLE' was another fine set of gravel-throated blues-rock that failed to notch up respectable sales. Retaining CARRACK and utilising a cast of session men, MILLER was finally rewarded for his efforts when the foot-tappin' parched-blues balladry of 'DARLIN' made the UK Top 10. Incredibly, the accompanying album 'FALLING IN LOVE . . . PERFECT FIT' (1979) still failed to chart, as did 1980's 'EASY MONEY' set, the latter representing his last release for 'Mercury'. Eventually picked up by 'Capitol', MILLER recorded 'STANDING ON THE EDGE' (1982) before cutting 'DANCING IN THE RAIN' (1986) for 'Vertigo' with a band that included such distinguished veterans as BRIAN ROBERTSON and SIMON KIRKE.

Having already begun an acting career in 1979 with Peter McDougall's TV play, 'Just A Boy's Game' (for which he also penned/sung the theme tune, 'Playin' The Game'), MILLER increasingly concentrated his energies on thespian matters as the 80's wore on. Despite a brief moment of fame in the early 90's when Tennent's Lager used his version of 'CALEDONIA' in a TV ad, MILLER's career has of late been severely curtailed by serious illness after he suffered a brain aneurysm on the 25th August, 1994; it has robbed him of his speech. One of Scottish music's great underrated performers, MILLER remains almost universally respected among rock's elder statesmen. On the 7th September 2002, a plethora of stars including Joe Walsh, paid tribute to the man at Glasgow's Barrowland; all proceeds went to the Drake Project, a music therapy charity.

FRANKIE MILLER – vocals (ex-JUDE) with ex-members of BRINSLEY SCHWARZ (aka NICK LOWE – bass / **BOB ANDREWS** – keyboards / **BRINSLEY SCHWARZ** – guitar / **BILLY RANKIN** – drums)

Chrysalis Chrysalis

Jan 73. (lp) *(<CHR 1036>)* **ONCE IN A BLUE MOON** [ ] [ ]
– You don't need to laugh (to be happy) / I can't change it / Candlelight sonata in f major / Ann Eliza Jane / It's all over / In no resistance / After all (I live my life) / Just like Tom Thumb's blues / Mail box / I'm ready. *(cd-iss. Oct98 on 'Repertoire'; REP 4725)*

— brought in a number of session men to replace last band

Jan 74. (lp) *(<CHR 1052>)* **HIGH LIFE** [ ] [ ]
– High life / Play something sweet (brickyard blues) / Trouble / A fool / Little angel / With you in mind / The devil gun / I'll take a melody / Just a song / Shoorah shoorah / I'm falling in love again. *(cd-iss. Mar94; CD25CR 04) (cd re-iss. Oct98 on 'Repertoire'; REP 4724)*

FRANKIE MILLER BAND

— with **HENRY McCULLOUGH** – guitar / **MICK WEAVER** – keyboards / **CHRISSY STEWART** – bass / **STU PERRY** – drums

Sep 75. (7") *(CHS 2074)* **A FOOL IN LOVE. / I KNOW WHY THE SUN DON'T SHINE** [ ] –
Dec 75. (lp) *(<CHR 1088>)* **THE ROCK** [ ] [ ]
– A fool in love / The heartbreak / The rock / I know why the sun don't shine / Hard on the levee / Ain't got no money / All my love to you / I'm old enough / Bridgeton / Drunken nights in the city. *(cd-iss. Oct98 on 'Repertoire'; REP 4726)*
Jul 76. (7") *(CHS 2095)* **THE ROCK. / THE HEARTBREAK** [ ] –
Oct 76. (7") *(CHS 2103)* **LOVING YOU IS SWEETER THAN EVER. / I'M OLD ENOUGH** [ ] –
May 77. (7") *(CHS 2147)* **BE GOOD TO YOURSELF. /** 27 –

FRANKIE MILLER'S FULL HOUSE

— with **RAY MINHINNIT** – guitar / **JAMES HALL** – keyboards / **CHARLIE HARRISON** – bass / **GRAHAM DEACON** – drums

Jun 77. (lp/c) *(<CHR/ZCHR 1128>)* **FULL HOUSE** [ ] [ ]
– Be good to yourself / The doodle song / Jealous guy / Searching / Love letters / Take good care of yourself / Down the Honky Tonk / The love of mine / Let the candlelight shine / (I'll never) Live in vain. *(cd-iss. Feb99 on 'Repertoire'; REP 4728)*
Jun 77. (7") *<CHS 2145>* **THE DOODLE SONG. / (I'LL NEVER) LIVE IN VAIN** – 71
Aug 77. (7") *(CHS 2166)* **LOVE LETTERS. / LET THE CANDLELIGHT SHINE** [ ] –
Nov 77. (7"ep) *(CHS 2184)* **ALVERIC'S ELFLAND JOURNEY EP** [ ] –
– Jealous guy / A fool in love / Brickyard blues / Sail away.

— went solo again, augmented by **PAUL CARRACK** – keyboards / **RAY RUSSELL** – guitar / **MARTIN DROVER** – trumpet / **CHRIS MERCER** – saxophone / **B.J. WILSON** – drums

Apr 78. (lp) *(<CHR 1174>)* **DOUBLE TROUBLE** [ ] [ ]
– Have you seen me lately Joan / Double heart trouble / The train / You'll be in my mind / Good time love / Love waves / (I can't) Breakaway / Stubborn kind of fellow / Love is all around / Goodnight sweetheart. *(cd-iss. Feb99 on 'Repertoire'; REP 4727)*
Jun 78. (7"colrd) *(CHS 2221)* **STUBBORN KIND OF FELLOW. / GOOD TIME LOVE** [ ] –

FRANKIE MILLER

— **FRANKIE** only retained **CARRACK**, and brought in **CHRIS HALL** – keyboards / **TIM RENWICK + STEVE SIMPSON + TERRY BRITTON** – guitar / **RON ASPERY** – horns / **TEX COMER + DAVE WINTOUR** – bass / **CHRIS SLADE + FRAN BYRNE** – drums

Oct 78. (7") *(CHS 2255)* **DARLIN'. / DRUNKEN NIGHTS IN THE CITY** 6 –
Jan 79. (7") *(CHS 2276)* **WHEN I'M AWAY FROM YOU. / AIN'T GOT NO MONEY** 42 –
Jan 79. (lp) *(CHR 1220)* **FALLING IN LOVE . . . PERFECT FIT** [ ] –
– When I'm away from you / Is this love / If I can love somebody / Darlin' / And it's your love / A woman to love / Falling in love with you / Everytime a teardrop falls / Pappa don't know / Good to see you. *(cd-iss. Feb99 on 'Repertoire'; REP 4729)*
Apr 79. (7") *(CHS 2299)* **GOOD TO SEE YOU. / COLD AND RAINY NIGHT** [ ] –

— his backing band were now **REGGIE YOUNG + BOBBY THOMPSON** – guitar / **JOE OSBOURNE** – bass / **LARRY LONDIN** – drums

Jun 80. (7") *(CHS 2436)* **SO YOUNG, SO YOUNG. / TEARS** [ ] –
Jul 80. (lp) *(<CHR 1268>)* **EASY MONEY** [ ] [ ]
– Easy money / The woman in you / Why don't you spend the night / So young so young / Forget about me / Heartbreak radio / Cheap . . .thrills / No chance / Gimme love / Tears. *(cd-iss. Jun99 on 'Repertoire'; REP 4731)*
Jul 80. (7") *(CHS CHS 2448)* **WHY DON'T YOU SPEND THE NIGHT. / HEARTBREAK RADIO** [ ] –

— now with **BARRY BECKETT** – keyboards, producer / **DAVID HOOD** – bass / **ROGER HAWKINS** – drums / **CHRIS SPEDDING** – guitar

Capitol Capitol

Jun 82. (7") *(CL 253) <5131>* **TO DREAM THE DREAM. / DON'T STOP** [ ] 62
Jun 82. (lp/c) *(<EST/TC-EST 12206>)* **STANDING ON THE EDGE** [ ] [ ]
– Danger danger / Standing on the edge / Zap zap / To dream the dream / Don't stop / Angels with dirty faces / Firin' line / Jealousy / It's all coming down tonight / On my way. *(cd-iss. Feb00 on 'Repertoire'; REP 4837)*
Aug 82. (7") *(CL 259)* **ANGELS WITH DIRTY FACES. / JEALOUSY** [ ] –
Sep 82. (7") **DANGER DANGER. / ON MY WAY** – [ ]

— brought in **BRIAN ROBERTSON** – lead guitar / **CHRISSIE STEWART** – bass / **SIMON KIRKE** – drums (ex-BAD COMPANY)

Vertigo not iss.

Mar 86. (7") *(VER 25)* **I'D LIE TO YOU FOR LOVE. / DANCING IN THE RAIN** [ ] –
(12"+=) *(VERX 25)* – Do it till we drop.
Apr 86. (lp/c)(cd) *(VERH/+C 34)(826647-2)* **DANCING IN THE RAIN** [ ] –
– I'd lie to you for love / Do it till we drop / That's how long my love is / How many tears can you hide / Dancing in the rain / Shakey ground / The boys and girls are doing it / Game of love / Gladly go blind / You're a puzzle I can't put down.

— FRANKIE concentrated more on acting in the mid 80's

M.C.S. not iss.

Mar 92. (7"/c-s/cd-s) *(MCS 2001/+C/CD)* **CALEDONIA. / I'LL NEVER BE THAT YOUNG AGAIN** 45 –

— since 1994, FRANKIE has suffered serious ill health due to a brain aneurysm

– compilations, etc. –

Feb 87. (7") *Old Gold; (OG 9688)* **DARLIN'. / BE GOOD TO YOURSELF** [ ] –
Mar 94. (cd/c) *Chrysalis; (CD/TC 1981)* **THE VERY BEST OF FRANKIE MILLER** [ ] –
– Darlin' When I'm away from you / Be good to yourself / I can't change it / High life / Brickyard blues / A fool in love / Have you seen me lately Joan / Love letters / Caledonia / Stubborn kind of fellow / Devil gun / Hard on the levee / Tears / I'm ready / Shoo-rah shoo-rah / Double heart trouble / So young, so young.
Apr 94. (cd) *Windsong; (WINDCD 54)* **BBC RADIO 1 LIVE IN CONCERT (live)** [ ] –
Mar 96. (cd) *Disky; (DC 86432-2)* **LOVE LETTERS** [ ] –

MISFITS (see under ⇒ "A Beat(en) Generation")

MOGUL THRASH

Formed: Dundee . . . September '69 as JAMES LITHERLAND'S BROTHERHOOD (aka The DUNDEE HORNS), the aforementioned ex-COLOSSEUM guitarist helped by MOLLY DUNCAN and ROGER BALL. The MOGUL THRASH moved to London (with BILL HARRISON and MIKE ROSEN in tow), found a new bass player in JOHN WETTON and quickly signed up to 'R.C.A.' where they made one brassy 45 and an eponymous, progressive jazz-rock album in '71. This was fairly popular in Europe, although only moderately successful on home shores. MOGUL THRASH subsequently broke up due to legal problems with their management, most members finding fame in other directions:- DUNCAN and BALL joined the AVERAGE WHITE BAND, LITHERLAND with BANDIT (alongside JIM DIAMOND).

JOHN WETTON (b.12 Jul'49, Derby) – vocals, bass / **JAMES LITHERLAND** – guitar (ex-COLOSSEUM) / **MOLLY DUNCAN** – saxophone / **ROGER BALL** – saxophone / **MIKE ROSEN** – trumpet / **BILL HARRISON** – drums

		R.C.A.	not iss.
Dec 70.	(7") *(RCA 2030)* **SLEEPING IN THE KITCHEN. / ST. PETER**		-
Jan 71.	(lp) *(SF 8156)* **MOGUL THRASH** – Something sad / Elegy / Dreams of glass and sand / Going north / Going west / St. Peter / What's this I hear. *(cd-iss. Aug99 on 'Voiceprint'+=; BP 300CD)* – Sleeping in the kitchen.		-

— split early 1971. WETTON joined FAMILY, then a string of bands; KING CRIMSON, ROXY MUSIC, URIAH HEEP, BRYAN FERRY, UK, ASIA, etc. Meanwhile, LITHERLAND formed BANDIT, while DUNCAN and BALL joined the AVERAGE WHITE BAND

MOONRAKERS (see under ⇒ "A Beat(en) Generation")

Neil MURRAY

Born: 27 Aug'50, Gattonside, nr. Galashiels. NEIL has been a renowned and seasoned "Rock" bass player for the likes of COLOSSEUM II (in the mid-70's), NATIONAL HEALTH (in 1977-78), WHITESNAKE (from 1978 to 1981), BERNIE MARSDEN (late 70's), GARY MOORE ('81 to '83), WHITESNAKE again (between 1984 to 1985), Jonathan King's disastrous NWOBHM "supergroup" GOGMAGOG in 85, PHENOMENA (1985-1987), Japanese! rockers VOW WOW (from 1987 to 1990), BLACK SABBATH (twice! 1990 and 1996) and the DAVE SHARMAN band (in the early 90's).

MY DEAR WATSON

Formed: Buckie, Morayshire . . . 1962 as The CIMMARONS by teenagers IAIN LYON and JOHNNY STEWART together with ROBERT LAWSON, BILLY CAMERON and ALISTAIR EWEN. The latter departed within the year and, trimmed to a 4-piece, the group took on the JOHNNY & The COPYCATS moniker. Influenced primarily by black American soul/R&B, they were quickly snapped up by local entrepreneur Albert Bonici and released their debut single, 'I'M A HOG FOR YOU BABY' on his 'Norco' label in 1964. A cover of the Lieber/Stoller-penned COASTERS hit, the record quickly sold out of its 1,000 pressing and buoyed the band up for a nationwide beat group talent contest. Despite making it to the final and pipping the likes of JOE BROWN to the winning post, LYON and Co were unable to accept their first prize of a recording contract as they were too young to sign.

This experience nevertheless persuaded them to go professional and they spent the next four years slogging it out on the German beat circuit. Over this period, The COPYCATS (as they were now billed) cut a couple of singles for German label, 'Cornet', namely 'ANGELA' and 'START THINKING ABOUT ME', both released in 1966. Back in Britain, the lads cut demos for both 'Pye' and 'Decca' before GEORGE YOUNG (of EASYBEATS fame) used his influence to secure a deal with 'Parlophone'. Unfortunately, the label insisted on a name change and Bonici made the strange choice of MY DEAR WATSON, kitting the band out in Victorian style gear for press photos. Undaunted, they made their major label debut with the YOUNG/VANDA-produced 'ELUSIVE FACE' single in 1968, following it up with 'STOP, STOP, I'LL BE THERE' later that year. They also took up a residency at London's Bag O'Nails club where they rubbed shoulders with the likes of GENO WASHINGTON and JIMI HENDRIX.

Although JOHNNY subsequently left due to marriage commitments, the band moved on to the 'DJM' label with new member ALEX ZIGGY SLATER. While they recorded an album's worth of material, only a solitary single, 'HAVE YOU SEEN YOUR SAVIOUR' saw the light of day in 1970. DJM were more concerned with pushing their session keyboardist REGGIE DWIGHT, soon to be renamed ELTON JOHN; ironically, ELTON had actually played on the still unreleased MY DEAR WATSON sessions. Exasperated with this state of affairs, the Scotsmen headed home and went their separate ways. LYON went on to play with a number of combos, most famously The JSD BAND, who, equally ironically, were another outfit to come so near yet so far. The COPYCATS debut single is worth £50, while MY DEAR WATSON vinyl is around £20.

JOHNNY & THE COPYCATS

JOHNNY STEWART – vocals, guitar / **IAIN LYON** – guitar / **BILLY CAMERON** – bass / **ROBERT CAMERON** – drums / + 1

		Norco	not iss.
1964.	(7") *(AB 102)* **I'M A HOG FOR YOU BABY. / I CAN NEVER SEE YOU**		-

— split for a while until they moved south and came up with a new name

COPYCATS

		Cornet	not iss.
1966.	(7") *(3005)* **ANGELA. / I'LL NEVER REGRET YOU**	-	- German
1966.	(7") *(5008)* **START THINKING ABOUT ME. / PAIN OF LOVE**	-	- German

MY DEAR WATSON

— **ALEX ALEXANDER** (aka ALEX YOUNG) – guitar (ex-TONY SHERIDAN) was a member circa 1967 until he joined GRAPEFRUIT and later The EASYBEATS

		Parlophone	not iss.
Apr 68.	(7") *(R 5687)* **ELUSIVE FACE. / THE SHAME JUST DRAINED**		-
Sep 68.	(7") *(R 5737)* **MAKE THIS DAY LAST. / STOP, STOP, I'LL BE THERE**		-
		D.J.M.	not iss.
Jun 70.	(7") *(DJS 224)* **HAVE YOU SEEN YOUR SAVIOUR. / WHITE LINE ROAD**		-

— when they split, LYON would later resurface with the NEW JSD BAND

N

NATURAL ACOUSTIC BAND (see ⇒ Section 2: Folk)

NAZARETH

Formed: Dunfermline . . . 1969 out of the ashes of The SHADETTES by DAN McCAFFERTY, PETE AGNEW and DARREL SWEET. With the addition of MANNY CHARLTON, the group turned pro and relocated to London, gaining a record contract with 'Pegasus' in the process. Already armed with a loyal homegrown support, the band released two earthy hard-rock albums for the label between late '71 and mid '72 before moving to 'Mooncrest'.

This was the band's turning point, NAZARETH hitting immediately with a Top 10 smash, 'BROKEN DOWN ANGEL'. An obvious focal point for the Caledonian rockers was the mean-looking McCAFFERTY, his whisky-throated wail coming to define the band's sound. Their acclaimed third album, 'RAZAMANAZ' followed soon after, narrowly missing the UK Top 10 but nevertheless spawning another top selling rock classic, 'BAD, BAD BOY'. With ROGER GLOVER (ex-DEEP PURPLE) at the production desk, NAZARETH re-invented Joni Mitchell's classic, 'THIS FLIGHT TONIGHT', the band virtually claiming it as their own with a re-working startling in its stratospheric melodic power. The accompanying, appropriately-named 'LOUD 'N' PROUD' album (also released in '73!), followed the established formula by combining excellent cover versions with original material, thus its Top 10 placing. However, by the following year, only their fifth album, 'RAMPANT' had achieved any degree of success.

America finally took NAZARETH to their hearts with the release of the much covered Boudleaux Bryant ballad, 'LOVE HURTS', the single making the US Top 10 in 1975 (JIM CAPALDI of Traffic had pipped them to the post in Britain). McCAFFERTY returned to the UK charts that year in fine fettle with yet another classy cover, Tomorrow's 'MY WHITE BICYCLE'. The frontman even found time to complete and release a full album's worth of covers, the big man and the band suffering a backlash from some of their more hardcore fans. Switching labels to 'Mountain' (home of The SENSATIONAL ALEX HARVEY BAND) late in 1975, the band suffered a dip in profile, although having signed to 'A&M' in America (in the heyday) they consolidated their earlier Stateside success. The ALEX HARVEY connection took another twist with the addition of the latter's clown-faced sidekick ZAL CLEMINSON on guitar. This helped to pull back some of NAZARETH's flagging support, the following JEFF 'Skunk' BAXTER (ex-DOOBIES)-produced set, 'MALICE IN WONDERLAND' hitting Top 30 in America. ZAL departed soon after, his surprising replacement being the American JOHN LOCKE, who in turn (after an album, 'THE FOOL CIRCLE' 1981) was superseded by Glaswegian BILLY RANKIN.

For the remainder of the 80's, NAZARETH churned out a plethora of reasonable albums, the band still retaining a North American fanbase while gaining a foothold in many parts of Europe. Founder member MANNY CHARLTON subsequently departed at the turn of the decade, RANKIN returning for their best album for ten years, 'NO JIVE' (1991). Surprisingly, after nearly 30 years in the business, NAZARETH are still plugging away, their most recent effort being 1995's 'MOVE ME'. A host of modern day hard-rockers such as AXL ROSE, MICHAEL MONROE, etc, claim to have been influenced by both McCAFFERTY and his three wise rockers, GUNS N' ROSES even covering 'HAIR OF THE DOG'. With McCAFFERTY, AGNEW and SWEET (plus newcomers JIMMY MURRISON and RONNIE LEAHY) carrying NAZARETH towards the 21st Century, their final album of the millennium was 'BOOGALOO' (1998). Sadly, DARRELL was to die in New Albany, Indiana, USA on the 30th of April, 1999.

• **Songwriters:** Group penned, except SHAPES OF THINGS (Yardbirds) / DOWN HOME GIRL (Leiber-Stoller) / I WANT TO DO EVERYTHING FOR YOU (Joe Tex) / TEENAGE NERVOUS BREAKDOWN (Little Feat) / THE BALLAD OF HOLLIS BROWN (Bob Dylan) / YOU'RE THE VIOLIN (Golden Earring) / WILD HONEY (Beach Boys) / SO YOU WANT TO BE A ROCK'N'ROLL STAR (Byrds) / I DON'T WANT TO GO ON WITHOUT YOU (Berns/Wexler). DAN McCAFFERTY solo covered OUT OF TIME (Rolling Stones) / WHATCHA GONNA DO ABOUT IT (Small Faces) / etc.

DAN McCAFFERTY – vocals / **MANNY CHARLTON** – guitar, vocals / **PETE AGNEW** (b.14 Sep'48) – bass / **DARRELL SWEET** (b.16 May'47, Bournemouth) – drums, percussion

Pegasus Warners

Nov 71. (lp) *(PEG 10) <BS 2615>* **NAZARETH** [ ] [ ] Feb73
– Witchdoctor woman / Dear John / Empty arms, empty heart / If I had a dream / Red light lady / Fat man / Country girl / Morning dew / King is dead. *(re-iss. Apr74 on 'Mooncrest'; CREST 10) (re-iss. Nov 75 & Apr80 on 'Mountain' lp/c; TOPC/TTOPC 5001) (cd-iss. May92 on 'Castle'; CLACD 286) (cd re-iss. Oct99 on 'Essential'; ESMCD 796) (cd re-iss. Jun02 on 'Eagle'; EAMCD 145)*

Jan 72. (7") *(PGS 2)* **DEAR JOHN. / FRIENDS** [ ] [-]

Jun 72. (7") *(PGS 4)* **MORNING DEW. / SPINNING TOP** [ ] [-]

Jun 72. (lp) *(PEG 14) <BS 2639>* **EXERCISES** [ ] [ ] Nov72
– I will not be led / Cat's eye, apple pie / In my time / Woke up this morning / Called her name / Fool about you / Love now you're gone / Madelaine / Sad song / 1692 (Glen Coe massacre). *(re-iss. Apr74 on 'Mooncrest'; CREST 14) (re-iss. Nov75 & Apr80 on 'Mountain' lp/c; TOPS/TTOPS 103) (re-iss. May85 on 'Sahara'; SAH 121) (cd-iss. Feb91 on 'Castle'; CLACD 220) (cd re-iss. Jun02 on 'Eagle'; EAMCD 146)*

Jul 72. (7") *<7599>* **MORNING DEW. / DEAR JOHN** [-] [ ]

Sep 72. (7") *(PGS 5)* **IF YOU SEE MY BABY. / HARD LIVING** [ ] [-]

Mooncrest A&M

Apr 73. (7") *(MOON 1)* **BROKEN DOWN ANGEL. / WITCHDOCTOR WOMAN** [9] [-]

May 73. (lp/c) *(CREST 1) <SP 4396>* **RAZAMANAZ** [11] [ ]
– Razamanaz / Alcatraz / Vigilante man / Woke up this morning / Night woman / Bad, bad boy / Sold my soul / Too bad, too sad / Broken down angel. *(re-iss. Nov75 & Apr80 on 'Mountain' lp/c; TOPS/TTOPS 104) (re-iss. Oct82 on 'NEMS' lp/c; NEL/NEC 6023) (re-iss. Dec89 on 'Castle' lp/cd; CLA LP/CD 173) (cd re-iss. Sep96 on 'Essential'; ESMCD 370) (cd re-iss. Sep01 on 'Eagle'; EAMCD 132)*

Jul 73. (7"m) *(MOON 9)* **BAD, BAD BOY. / HARD LIVING / SPINNING TOP** [10] [-]

Sep 73. (7") *<1453>* **BROKEN DOWN ANGEL. / HARD LIVING** [-] [ ]

Oct 73. (7") *(MOON 14)* **THIS FLIGHT TONIGHT. / CALLED HER NAME** [11] [-]

Nov 73. (lp/c) *(CREST 4) <3609>* **LOUD 'N' PROUD** [10] [ ]
– Go down fighting / Not faking it / Turn on your receiver / Teenage nervous breakdown / Freewheeler / This flight tonight / Child in the sun / The ballad of Hollis Brown. *(re-iss. Nov75 & Apr80 on 'Mountain' lp/c; TOPS/TTOPS 105) (re-iss. Dec89 on 'Castle' lp/cd; CLA LP/CD 174) (cd re-iss. Oct96 on 'Essential'; ESMCD 379) (cd re-iss. Sep01 on 'Eagle'; EAMCD 133)*

Nov 73. (7") *<1469>* **BAD, BAD BOY. / RAZAMANAZ** [-] [ ]

Feb 74. (7") *<1511>* **THIS FLIGHT TONIGHT. / GO DOWN FIGHTING** [-] [ ]

Mar 74. (7") *(MOON 22)* **SHANGHAI'D IN SHANGHAI. / LOVE, NOW YOU'RE GONE** [41] [ ]

May 74. (lp/c) *(CREST 15) <3641>* **RAMPANT** [13] [ ]
– Silver dollar forger (parts 1 & 2) / Glad when you're gone / Loved and lost / Shanghai'd in Shanghai / Jet lag / Light my way / Sunshine / a) Shapes of things – b) Space safari. *(re-iss. Nov75 & Apr80 on 'Mountain' lp/c; TOPS/TTOPS 106) (cd-iss. Sep92 on 'Castle'; CLACD 242) (cd re-iss. May97 on 'Essential'; ESMCD 551) (cd re-iss. Sep01 on 'Eagle'; EAMCD 134)*

Jul 74. (7") *<1548>* **SUNSHINE. / THIS FLIGHT TONIGHT** [-] [ ]

Nov 74. (7") *(MOON 37) <1671>* **LOVE HURTS. / DOWN** [ ] [8] Nov75

Mar 75. (7") *(MOON 44)* **HAIR OF THE DOG. / TOO BAD, TOO SAD** [ ] [-]

Apr 75. (lp/c) *(CREST 27) <4511>* **HAIR OF THE DOG** [ ] [17]
– Hair of the dog / Miss Misery / Guilty * / Changin' times / Beggars day / Rose in the heather / Whisky drinkin' woman / Please don't Judas me. *(In the US, track* repl. by 'Love hurts') (re-iss. Nov75 & Apr80 on 'Mountain' lp/c; TOPS/TTOPS 107) (re-iss. Oct82 on 'NEMS' lp/c; NEL/NEC 6024) (re-iss. May85 on 'Sahara'; SAH 124) (cd-iss. Feb92 on 'Castle'; CLACD 241) (cd re-iss. May97 on 'Essential'; ESMCD 550) (cd re-iss. Sep01 on 'Eagle'; EAMCD 127)*

May 75. (7") *<1671>* **HAIR OF THE DOG. / LOVE HURTS** [-] [ ]

May 75. (7") *(MOON 47)* **MY WHITE BICYCLE. / MISS MISERY** [14] [ ]
(re-iss. 1979 on 'Mountain'; NAZ 10)

Mountain A&M

Oct 75. (7") *(TOP 3)* **HOLY ROLLER. / RAILROAD BOY** [36] [-]

Nov 75. (lp/c) *(TOPS/TTOPS 108) <9020>* **GREATEST HITS** (compilation) [54] [ ]
– Razamanaz / Holy roller / Shanghai'd in Shanghai / Love hurts / Turn on your receiver / Bad bad boy / This flight tonight / Broken down angel / Hair of the dog / Sunshine / My white bicycle / Woke up this morning *(re-iss. Oct82 on 'NEMS' lp/c; NEL/NEC 6022) (re-iss. Apr89 on 'Castle' lp/c/cd; CLA LP/MC/CD 149)*

Feb 76. (7") *(TOP 8) <1819>* **CARRY OUT FEELINGS. / LIFT THE LID** [ ] [ ]

Mar 76. (lp/c) *(TOPS/TTOPS 109) <4562>* **CLOSE ENOUGH FOR ROCK'N'ROLL** [ ] [24]
– Telegram (part 1:- On your way / part 2:- So you want to be a rock'n'roll star / part 3:- Sound check / part 4:- Here we are again) / Vicki / Homesick again / Vancouver shakedown / Born under the wrong sign / Loretta / Carry out feelings / Lift the lid / You're the violin. *(re-iss. May85 on 'Sahara'; SAH 126) (re-iss. Jun90 on 'Castle' lp/c/cd; CLA LP/MC/CD 182) (cd re-iss. Feb02 on 'Eagle'; EAMCD 138)*

Jun 76. (7") *(TOP 14)* **YOU'RE THE VIOLIN. / LORETTA** [ ] [-]

Sep 76. (7") *<1854>* **LIFT THE LID. / LORETTA** [-] [ ]

Nov 76. (7") *(TOP 21)* **I DON'T WANT TO GO ON WITHOUT YOU. / GOOD LOVE** [ ] [-]

Nov 76. (lp/c) *(TOPS/TTOPS 113) <4610>* **PLAY 'N' THE GAME** [ ] [75]
– Somebody to roll / Down home girl / Flying / Waiting for the man / Born to love / I want to (do everything for you) / I don't want to go on without you / Wild honey / L.A. girls. *(re-iss. May85 on 'Sahara'; SAH 131) (cd-iss. Feb91 on 'Castle'; CLACD 219) (cd re-iss. Feb02 on 'Eagle'; EAMCD 139)*

Dec 76. (7") *<18??>* **I WANT TO (DO EVERYTHING FOR YOU). / BLACK CATS** [-] [ ]

Jan 77. (7") *(TOP 22)* **SOMEBODY TO ROLL. / VANCOUVER SHAKEDOWN** [ ] [ ]

Feb 77. (7") *<1895>* **I DON'T WANT TO GO ON WITHOUT YOU. / I WANT TO DO (EVERYTHING FOR YOU)** [-] [ ]

Apr 77. (7") *<1936>* **SOMEBODY TO ROLL. / THIS FLIGHT TONIGHT** [-] [ ]

Jun 77. (lp) *<4643>* **HOT TRACKS** (compilation) [-] [ ]

Sep 77. (7"ep) *(NAZ 1)* **HOT TRACKS** (compilation) [15] [-]
– Love hurts / This flight tonight / Broken down angel / Hair of the dog. *(re-iss. Jul80; HOT 1) (re-iss. Jan83 on 7"pic-ep on 'NEMS'; NEP 2)*

Nov 77. (lp/c) *(TOPS/TTOPS 115) <4666>* **EXPECT NO MERCY** [ ] [82]
– Expect no mercy / Gone dead train / Shot me down / Revenge is sweet / Gimme what's mine / Kentucky fried blues / New York broken toy / Busted / A place in your heart / All the king's horses. *(re-iss. May85 on 'Sahara'; SAH 123) (re-iss. Jun90 on 'Castle' cd/lp; CLA CD/LP 187) (re-iss. cd Sep93 on 'Elite'; ELITE 022CD) (cd re-iss. Feb02 on 'Eagle'; EAMCD 140)*

Jan 78. (7"m) *(NAZ 2)* **GONE DEAD TRAIN. / GREENS / DESOLATION ROAD** [49] [-]

Apr 78. (7") *(TOP 37)* **A PLACE IN YOUR HEART. / KENTUCKY FRIED BLUES** [70] [-]

Apr 78. (7") *<2009>* **SHOT ME DOWN. / KENTUCKY FRIED BLUES** [-] [ ]

Jul 78. (7") *<2029>* **GONE DEAD TRAIN. / KENTUCKY FRIED BLUES** [-] [ ]

—— added **ZAL CLEMINSON** (b. 4 May'49, Glasgow) – guitar, synth. (ex-SENSATIONAL ALEX HARVEY BAND)

Jan 79. (7") *(NAZ 3) <2116>* **MAY THE SUNSHINE. / EXPECT NO MERCY** [22] [ ]

Jan 79. (lp/c) *(TOPS/TTOPS 123) <4741>* **NO MEAN CITY** [34] [88]
– Just to get into it / May the sun shine / Simple solution (parts 1 & 2) / Star / Claim to fame / Whatever you want babe / What's in it for me / No mean city (parts 1 & 2). *(re-iss. May85 on 'Sahara'; SAH 120) (re-iss. May91 on 'Castle' lp/c/cd; CLA LP/MC/CD 213) (cd re-iss. Feb02 on 'Eagle'; EAMCD 135)*

Apr 79. (7",7"purple) *(NAZ 4) <2130>* **WHATEVER YOU WANT BABE. / TELEGRAM (PARTS 1, 2 & 3)** [ ] [ ]

Jul 79. (7") *<2158>* **STAR. / EXPECT NO MERCY** [-] [ ]

Jul 79. (7") *(TOP 45)* **STAR. / BORN TO LOVE** [54] [-]

Jan 80. (7") *(TOP 50) <2219>* **HOLIDAY. / SHIP OF DREAMS** [ ] [87]

Jan 80. (lp/c) *(TOPS/TTOPS 126) <4799>* **MALICE IN WONDERLAND** [ ] [41]
– Holiday / Showdown at the border / Talkin' to one of the boys / Heart's grown cold / Fast cars / Big boy / Talkin' 'bout love / Fallen angel / Ship of dreams / Turning a new leaf. *(re-iss. Sep90 on 'Castle' cd/lp; CLA CD/LP 181) (cd re-iss. Feb02 on 'Eagle'; EAMCD 136)*

Apr 80. (7") *<2231>* **SHIP OF DREAMS. / HEARTS GROWN COLD** [-] [ ]

NEMS A&M

Dec 80. (d7") *(BSD 1)* **NAZARETH LIVE (live)** [ ] [-]
– Hearts grown cold / Talkin' to one of the boys / Razamanaz / Hair of the dog.

—— added **JOHN LOCKE** (b.25 Sep'43, Los Angeles, Calif.) – keyboards (ex-SPIRIT)

Feb 81. (lp/c) *(NEL/NEC 6019) <4844>* **THE FOOL CIRCLE** [60] [70]
– Dressed to kill / Another year / Moonlight eyes / Pop the Silo / Let me be your leader / We are the people / Every young man's dream / Little part of you / Cocaine

(live) / Victoria. *(re-iss. Feb91 on 'Castle' cd/lp; CLA CD/LP 214) (cd re-iss. Feb02 on 'Eagle'; EAMCD 137)*

Mar 81. (7") *(NES 301) <2324>* **DRESSED TO KILL. / POP THE SILO** [ ] [ ]

— **BILLY RANKIN** (b. 25 Apr '59, Glasgow) – guitar; repl. ZAL who joined TANDOORI CASSETTE

Sep 81. (d-lp/c) *(NELD/NELC 102) <6703>* **'SNAZ (live)** [78] [83]
– Telegram (part 1:- On your way – part 2:- So you want to be a rock'n'roll star – part 3:- Sound check) / Razamanaz / I want to do everything for you / This flight tonight / Beggars day / Every young man's dream / Heart's grown cold / Java blues / Cocaine / Big boy / Holiday / Dressed to kill / Hair of the dog / Expect no mercy / Shape of things / Let me be your leader / Love hurts / Tush / Juicy Lucy / Morning dew. *(re-iss. Jan87 on 'Castle' lp/c/cd; CLA LP/MC/CD 130) (cd re-iss. May97 on 'Essential'; ESMCD 531) (cd re-iss. Sep01 on 'Eagle'; EAMCD 129)*

Sep 81. (7") *(NES 302) <2378>* **MORNING DEW (live). / JUICY LUCY (live)** [ ] [ ]

Dec 81. (7") *<2389>* **HAIR OF THE DOG (live). / HOLIDAY (live)** [-] [ ]

Jul 82. (7") *(NIS 101) <2421>* **LOVE LEADS TO MADNESS. / TAKE THE RAP** [ ] [ ]

Aug 82. (7") *<2444>* **DREAM ON. / TAKE THE RAP** [-] [ ]

— In 1982, RANKIN departed, and later released one US hit, 'BABY COME BACK' taken from the 1984 set, 'GROWIN' UP TOO FAST'.

Jan 83. (7") *(NIS 102)* **GAMES. / YOU LOVE ANOTHER** [ ] [-]

Feb 83. (lp/c) *(NIN 001) <4901>* **2XS** [ ] [ ] Jun82
– Love leads to madness / Boys in the band / You love another / Gatecrash / Games / Back to the trenches / Dream on / Lonely in the night / Preservation / Take the rap / Mexico. *(cd-iss. Feb91 on 'Castle'; CLACD 217) (cd re-iss. Feb02 on 'Eagle'; EAMCD 141)*

Jun 83. (7") *(NIS 103)* **DREAM ON. / JUICY LUCY** [ ] [-]

Vertigo | Capitol

Jun 83. (lp) *(812396-1)* **SOUND ELIXIR** [-] [ ] German
– All nite radio / Milk and honey / Whippin' boy / Rain on the window / Backroom boys / Why don't you read the book / I ran / Rags to riches / Local still / Where are you now. *(re-iss. Jul85 on 'Sahara'; SAH 130) (cd-iss. Feb91 on 'Castle'; CLACD 218) (cd re-iss. Jun02 on 'Eagle'; EAMCD 147)*

Jul 83. (7") *(812 544-7)* **WHERE ARE YOU NOW. / ON THE RUN** [-] [-] German

Sep 84. (lp/c) *(VERL/+C 20)* **THE CATCH** [ ] [ ]
– Party down / Ruby Tuesday / Last exit Brooklyn / Moondance / Love of freedom / This month's Messiah / You don't believe in us / Sweetheart tree / Road to nowhere. *(cd-iss. Feb02 on 'Eagle'; EAMCD 142)*

Sep 84. (7") *(VER 13)* **RUBY TUESDAY. / SWEETHEART TREE** [ ] [ ]
(12"+=) *(VERX 13)* – This month's messiah / Do you think about it.

Oct 84. (7"/12") *(880 085-1/+Q)* **PARTY DOWN. / DO YOU THINK ABOUT IT** [-] [-] German

1986. (lp/cd) *(830 300-1/-2)* **CINEMA** [-] [-] Europe
– Cinema / Juliet / Just another heartache / Other side of you / Hit the fan / One from the heart / Salty salty / White boy / A veterans song / Telegram / This flight tonight. *(cd-iss. Sep97 on 'Essential'; ESMCD 500) (cd re-iss. Aug01 on 'Eagle'; EAMCD 128)*

1986. (7") *(884 982-7)* **CINEMA. / THIS FLIGHT TONIGHT (live)** [-] [-] Europe
(12"+=) *(884 981-1)* – Telegram (live).

1989. (lp/cd) *(838 426-1/-2)* **SNAKES 'N' LADDERS** [-] [-] Europe
– We are animals / Lady luck / Hang on to a dream / Piece of my heart / Trouble / The key / Back to school / Girls / Donna – Get off that crack / See you, see you / Helpless. *(UK cd-iss. May97 on 'Essential'; ESMCD 501) (cd re-iss. Feb02 on 'Eagle'; EAMCD 143)*

1989. (cd-s) *(874 733-2)* **PIECE OF MY HEART / LADY LUCK / SEE YOU SEE ME** [-] [-] German

1989. (7") *(876 448-7)* **WINNER ON THE NIGHT. / TROUBLE** [-] [-] German
(12"+=/cd-s+=) *(876 448-1/-2)* – Woke up this morning (live) / Bad, bad boy (live).

— **BILLY RANKIN** – guitar; now totally repl. CHARLTON

Mausoleum | Griffin

Nov 91. (cd/c/lp) *(3670010.2/.4/.1) <3932>* **NO JIVE** [ ] [ ] 1993
– Hire and fire / Do you wanna play house / Right between the eyes / Every time it rains / Keeping our love alive / Thinkin' man's nightmare / Cover your heart / Lap of luxury / a.The Rowan tree (traditional) – b.Tell me that you love me / Cry wolf. *(cd+=)* – This flight tonight. *(cd re-iss. Sep97 on 'Essential'; ESMCD 502) (cd re-iss. Jun02 on 'Eagle'; EAMCD 148)*

Jan 92. (7") *(3670010.7)* **EVERY TIME IT RAINS / THIS FLIGHT TONIGHT 1991** [ ] [-]
(12"+=/cd-s+=) *(3670010.0/.3)* – Lap of Luxury.

Mar 92. (cd-ep) *(903005.3)* **TELL ME THAT YOU LOVE ME / RIGHT BETWEEN THE EYES / ROWAN TREE – TELL ME THAT YOU LOVE ME (extended)** [ ] [-]

Essential | Mayhem

May 97. (cd) *(ESMCD 503) <11076>* **MOVE ME** [ ] [ ] Oct95
– Let me be your dog / Can't shake these shakes / Crack me up / Move me / Steamroller / Stand by your beds / Rip it up / Demon alcohol / You had it comin' / Bring it on home to mama / Burning down. *(re-iss. Jun02 on 'Eagle'; EAMCD 149)*

— **McCAFFERTY, AGNEW + SWEET** added **JIMMY MURRISON** – guitar + **RONNIE LEAHY** – keyboards

S.P.V. | C.M.C.

Sep 98. (cd) *(SPV 0851850-2) <86263>* **BOOGALOO** [ ] [ ] Jan99
– Lights come down / Cheerleader / Loverman / Open up woman / Talk talk / Nothing so good / Party in the Kremlin / God save the South / Robber and the roadie / Waiting / May Heaven keep you. *(re-iss. Feb02; SPV 2301850-2)*

— on the 30th of April, 1999, DARRELL died

– compilations, others, etc. –

Jun 85. (d-lp) *Sahara; (SAH 137)* **20 GREATEST HITS** [ ] [-]

Jun 88. (d-lp/c/cd) *That's Original; (TFO LP/TC/CD 13)* **RAMPANT / HAIR OF THE DOG** [ ] [-]

Jul 88. (7") *Old Gold; (OG 9801)* **LOVE HURTS. / BAD BAD BOY** [ ] [-]

Jul 88. (7") *Old Gold; (OG 9803)* **THIS FLIGHT TONIGHT. / BROKEN DOWN ANGEL** [ ] [-]

Dec 88. (lp/c/cd) *Raw Power; (RAW LP/TC/CD 039)* **ANTHOLOGY** [ ] [-]

Jan 89. (cd-ep) *Special Edition; (CD3-17)* **THIS FLIGHT TONIGHT / BROKEN DOWN ANGEL / LOVE HURTS / BAD, BAD BOY** [ ] [-]

Jun 89. (cd) *Milestones; (MSSCD 102)* **MILESTONES** [ ] [-]

1990. (cd) *Ariola Express; (295969)* **BROKEN DOWN ANGEL** [ ] [-]

Jan 91. (cd/c/d-lp) *Castle; (CLA CD/MC/LP 280)* **THE SINGLES COLLECTION** [ ] [-]
– Broken down angel / Bad, bad boy / This flight tonight / Shanghai'd in Shanghai / Love hurts / Hair of the dog / My white bicycle / Holy roller / Carry out feelings / You're the violin / Somebody to roll / I don't want to go on without you / Gone dead train / A place in your heart / May the Sun shine / Star / Dressed to kill / Morning dew / Games / Love will lead to madness.

Oct 91. (3xcd-box) *Essential; (ESBCD 967)* **ANTHOLOGY** [ ] [-]

Nov 91. (cd) *Windsong; (WINDCD 005)* **BBC RADIO 1 LIVE IN CONCERT** [ ] [-]

Dec 91. (cd) *Dojo; (EARLCD 2)* **THE EARLY YEARS** [ ] [-]

Mar 92. (3xcd-box) *Castle; (CLABX 908)* **SNAZ / RAZAMANAZ / EXPECT NO MERCY** [ ] [-]

Apr 93. (cd) *Sequel; (NEMCD 639)* **FROM THE VAULTS** [ ] [-]

Jun 93. (cd/c) *Optima; (OPTM CD/C 009)* **ALIVE AND KICKING** [ ] [-]

Jun 94. (cd) *BR Music; (BRCD 1392)* **GREATEST HITS** [ ] [-]

Mar 96. (cd) *Disky; (CR 86711-2)* **CHAMPIONS OF ROCK** [ ] [-]

Oct 96. (cd) *Essential; (ESMCD 369)* **GREATEST HITS** [ ] [-]

Jul 98. (d-cd) *Reef; (SRDCD 707)* **LIVE AT THE BEEB** [ ] [-]
(d-cd re-iss. Feb00 on 'Snapper'; SMDCD 272)

Oct 98. (3xcd-box) *Essential; (ESMBX 308)* **RAZAMANAZ / LOUD 'N' PROUD / HAIR OF THE DOG** [ ] [-]

Apr 01. (d-cd)(t-lp) *Receiver; (RDPCD 016)(RRLT 009)* **BACK TO THE TRENCHES (live 1972-1984)** [ ] [-]

Aug 01. (cd) *Eagle; (EAGCD 141)* **THE VERY BEST OF NAZARETH** [ ] [-]

Jan 02. (d-cd) *Snapper; (SMDCD 387)* **NAZOLOGY** [ ] [-]

Mar 02. (cd) *Eagle; (EAGCD 204)* **HOMECOMING: GREATEST HITS LIVE IN GLASGOW (live)** [ ] [-]

Mar 02. (cd) *Music Club; (MCCD 486)* **LOVE HURTS – THE ROCK BALLADS** [ ] [-]

DAN McCAFFERTY

with some members of NAZARETH and SAHB

Mountain | A&M

Aug 75. (7") *(TOP 1) <1753>* **OUT OF TIME. / CINNAMON GIRL** [41] [ ]

Oct 75. (lp/c) *(TOPS/TTOPS 102)* **DAN McCAFFERTY** [ ] [ ]
– The honky tonk downstairs / Cinnamon girl / The great pretender / Boots of Spanish leather / Watcha gonna do about it / Out of time / You can't lie to a liar / Trouble / You got me hummin' / Stay with me baby. *(cd-iss. Jul94 on 'Sequel'; NEMCD 640)*

Nov 75. (7") *(TOP 5)* **WHATCHA GONNA DO ABOUT IT. / NIGHTINGALE** [ ] [-]

Mar 78. (7"m) *(DAN 1)* **STAY WITH ME, BABY. / OUT OF TIME / WATCHA GONNA DO ABOUT IT** [ ] [-]

Aug 78. (7") *(TOP 18)* **THE HONKY TONK DOWNSTAIRS. / TROUBLE** [ ] [-]

Aug 79. (7") *(TOP 47)* **BOOTS OF SPANISH LEATHER. / WATCHA GONNA DO ABOUT IT** [ ] [-]

— with German musicians + **PETE AGNEW** – bass

Mercury | not iss.

1987 (lp/cd) *(830 934-1/-2)* **INTO THE RING** [-] [-] German
– Into the ring / Backstage pass / Starry eyes / My sunny island / For a car / Caledonia / Headin' for South America / The departure (instrumental) / Southern Cross / Where the ocean ends we'll find a new born land / Sally Mary / Island in the Sun / Albatross / The last ones will be the first after all / Reprise.

1987. (7") *(888 397-7)* **STARRY EYES. / SUNNY ISLAND** [-] [-] German
(12"+=/cd-s+=) *(888 397-1/-2)* – Where the ocean ends, we'll find a new born land.

NEW GENERATION

(see under ⇒ SUTHERLAND BROTHERS)

Rab NOAKES

Born: c.late 40's, Fife. Brought up in Alloa, NOAKES was heavily influenced by Scottish folk revival players like ARCHIE FISHER, HAMISH IMLACH and BERT JANSCH. He followed the well-trodden path down south to London in 1966, frequenting the city's folk clubs and picking up tips from the stars of the day.

Subsequently securing a deal with 'Decca', he released 'DO YOU SEE THE LIGHTS' as his debut solo set in 1970. A brief spell in the original incarnation of STEALER'S WHEEL ensued and although RAB didn't appear on any of the band's albums he did guest on GERRY RAFFERTY's 1971 'Transatlantic' debut, 'Can I Have My Money Back'. RAFFERTY and JOE EGAN returned the favour on NOAKES' eponymous 1972 solo debut for 'A&M'. He also had major label muscle – not to mention the brassy punch of The MEMPHIS HORNS – behind the bluesy 'RED PUMP SPECIAL' (1974), the first of a couple of albums for 'Warners'. Unable to make any commercial headway, NOAKES seemed destined for cult critical appeal, despite a further major label ('M.C.A.') effort, 'RAB NOAKES', at the dawn of the 80's.

Following 1984's 'UNDER THE RAIN' album, he finally gave up recording in favour of production work for BBC Scotland. Nevertheless, he was involved in the 1988 WOODY GUTHRIE tribute set, 'Woody Lives' (alongside BERT JANSCH, DICK GAUGHAN and RORY McLEOD) and continues to be a popular figure on Scotland's folk circuit. More recently, RAB has returned to the contemporary music scene courtesy of two bluesy/country albums, 'STANDING UP' (1999) and the collaborative effort with mouthy man FRASER SPIERS, 'LIGHTS BACK ON' (2001) – the latter featuring MONICA QUEEN (ex-THRUM) and JAMES GRANT (ex-LOVE AND MONEY). Preceding this by several months was another joint effort, 'THROWING SHAPES' (2000), this time he was augmented by The VARAFLAMES.

• **Covered:** PSYCHO KILLER (Talking Heads) / DOWNTOWN LIGHTS (Blue Nile) / ABSOLUTELY SWEET MARIE (Bob Dylan) / etc (on latter two sets).

RAB NOAKES – vocals, guitar / with **ROBIN McKIDD** – guitar, vocals / **RONNIE RAE** – bass / **ALLAN TRAJAN** – keyboards / **BILL KEMP** – drums

Decca not iss.

1970. (lp) *(SKL 5061)* **DO YOU SEE THE LIGHTS** [ ] [-]
– Do you see the lights / Song for a pretty painter / On my own I built a bridge / Without me, just with you / Somewhere to stay / Together for ever / One more, one less / East Neuk misfortune / Question of travelling / Too old to die / Love story / Somebody counts on me.

— RAB was invited to join STEALER'S WHEEL and guested on GERRY RAFFERTY's 1971 LP, 'Can I Have My Money Back'

— **SID CAIRNS** – bass / **KARL HIMMEL** – drums / **JOE EGAN + GERRY RAFFERTY** – vocals; repl. RAE + KEMP + TRAJAN

A&M A&M

Sep 72. (7") *(AMS 7030)* **DRUNK AGAIN. / MILES AWAY** [ ] [-]
Oct 72. (lp) *(AMLH 68119)* **RAB NOAKES** [ ] [-]
– Drunk again / Jugglers / The way you know / Wait a minute / Goodnight loving trail / One bed, one purse / Just away / Half a mile from nowhere / Patter merchant / Everywhere you look / Hard on you / Travel sickness.
Nov 72. (7") *(AMS 7043)* **WAIT A MINUTE. / TRAVEL SICKNESS** [ ] [-]

— now with session people incl. the MEMPHIS HORNS

Warners Warners

Mar 74. (7") *(K 16361)* **CLEAR DAY. / WRONG JOKE AGAIN** [ ] [-]
Apr 74. (lp) *(K 46284)* <2777> **RED PUMP SPECIAL** [ ] [ ]
– Pass the time / As big as his size / Tomorrow is another day / The sketcher and the last train / Diamond ring / Branch / Wrong joke again / Sittin' in a corner blues / Clear day / Frisco depot.
Jul 74. (7") *(K 16431)* **BRANCH. / SITTING IN THE CORNER BLUES** [ ] [-]
Mar 75. (lp) *(K 56114)* **NEVER TOO LATE** [ ] [-]
– Stepping stone / Long time no see / Memories / Boy surely knew / Early morning friends / Turn a deaf ear / Slob / Never too late / Love letters / November afternoon / I'll be with you.
Mar 75. (7") *(K 16531)* **TURN A DEAF EAR. / I'LL BE WITH YOU** [ ] [-]

Ring-O not iss.

May 78. (7") *(2017 115)* **WAITING HERE FOR YOU. / RESTLESS** [ ] [-]
Jun 78. (lp) *(2339 201)* **RESTLESS** [ ] [-]
– She's all I see / Somebody counts on me / Long dark night / Waiting here for you / Restless / Get away from here / Don't stop now / I won't let you down / Fallen ones / Lonely boys tonight.
Jul 78. (7") *(2017 117)* **I WON'T LET YOU DOWN. / LONG AFTER DARK** [ ] [-]

M.C.A. M.C.A.

Aug 80. (7") *(MCA 641)* **I CAN'T GET ENOUGH OF YOU. / COME BACK HOME** [ ] [-]
Apr 81. (lp) *(MCF 3251)* <3082> **RAB NOAKES** [ ] [ ]
– I can't get enough of you / Don't let your heart break down / Feeling your way / Call it a day / Moment to moment / Come back home / Liberty's ledge / Memories / Shine a light / See me again.

— now back by the band GENE PITNEY'S BIRTHDAY, who featured **LORRAINE McINTOSH** – vocals (she later joined DEACON BLUE)

Black Crow not iss.

Mar 84. (lp/c) *(CRO/+C 207)* **UNDER THE RAIN** [ ] [-]
– Eden's flow / Take this letter / Don't keep passing me by / Stay awake / I feel I'm falling / How it started / Dublin take me / Silver hammer / The odd routine / How can I believe you / What kind of life is this.

— RAB retired from solo recording for a while . . . until

Moidart not iss.

Jun 99. (cd/c) *(MDMCD/MEMC 003)* **STANDING UP** [ ] [-]
– I've hardly started / I wish I was in England / What do you want the girl to do / Solid gone / Love is a gamble / Downtown lights / Gently does it / Blue dream / Psycho killer / Deep water / Open all night / Niel Gow's apprentice / Goodbye to all that / Lenny Bruce / When this bloody war is over / Remember my name / Absolutely sweet Marie.

— next with **FRASER SPIERS** – mouth harp / plus guests **COLIN McFARLANE** – guitar, bass / **JAMES GRANT + MONICA QUEEN** – backing vocals

Neon not iss.

Dec 00. (cd; as RAB NOAKES BAND & VARAFLAMES) *(NEONCD 001)* **THROWING SHAPES** [-] [-] w-drawn
Apr 01. (cd; by RAB NOAKES AND FRASER SPIERS) *(NEONCD 002)* **LIGHTS BACK ON** [ ] [-]
– Kill or cure / A love like yours / Devil's haircut / Round and bound / Billy / Wedding song / Lights / Spanish Harlem / Walking the dog / Turn a deaf ear / All gone wrong / Clear day / Fallen ones / Bring it on home / Long dark night.

NORTHWIND

Formed: Glasgow . . . early 70's by songwriters BRIAN YOUNG and HUGH BARR, along with TAM BRANNAN, COLIN SOMERVILLE and DAVE SCOTT (the latter had previously been The ELASTIC BAND, alongside future SWEET member ANDY SCOTT). Their one and only album, 'SISTER, BROTHER, LOVER . . ..' (for EMI's 'Regal Zonophone') was a gentle piece of "rural" Prog-acoustic rock, which now changes hands for over £150. The stand-out tracks were the mellow openers, 'HOME FOR FROZEN ROSES' and 'ACIMON AND NOIRAM' (a softer YES or WISHBONE ASH come to mind), while 'MANY TRIBESMEN' was dedicated to their time in Frankfurt, Germany. However, YOUNG and Co disappeared from the music biz, only YOUNG managing to claw his way back after he set up Ca Va recording studios.

BRIAN YOUNG – vocals, guitars / **HUGH BARR** – guitar / **COLIN SOMERVILLE** – organ, piano / **TAM BRANNAN** – bass, vocals / **DAVE SCOTT** – drums, percussion

Regal Zonophone not iss.

Aug 71. (lp) *(SLRZ 1020)* **SISTER, BROTHER, LOVER . . .** [ ] [-]
– Home for frozen roses / Acimon and Noiram / Castanettes / Sweet dope / Bystandin' / Guten abend / Peaceful / Many tribesmen / Quill. *(cd-iss. Apr98 on 'Audio Archive'; AACD 007)*

— split sometime in 1972

N.S.U.

Formed: Glasgow . . . 1968 by JOHN PETTIGREW, ERNIE REA, PETER NAGLE and 4th member BILLIE BROWN. Venturing south to London, this heavy Prog-rock trio/quartet managed to secure a gig at the Royal Albert Hall around the same time as they delivered their one and only set, 'TURN ON OR TURN ME DOWN' (1969) – if you have their rare LP it's worth over £125.

JOHN PETTIGREW – vocals / **ERNIE REA** – lead guitar / **PETER NAGLE** – bass, harmonica / **BILLIE BROWN** – drums

Stable not iss.

1969. (lp) *(SLE 8002)* **TURN ON OR TURN ME DOWN** [ ] [-]
– Turn on or turn me down / His town / You can't take it from my heart / Love talk / All aboard / Game / Stoned / Pettsie's blues / On the road.

— disbanded the following year

O

John O'HARA's PLAYBOYS (see under ⇒ "A Beat(en) Generation")

ONE IN A MILLION (see under ⇒ "A Beat(en) Generation")

1-2-3 (see under ⇒ CLOUDS)

P

PATHFINDERS (see under ⇒ TRASH)

Davie PATON (see under ⇒ PILOT)

Bobby PATRICK BIG SIX (see under ⇒ "A Beat(en) Generation")

Mike PATTO

Born: MICHAEL PATRICK McGRATH, 22 Sep'42, Glasgow. In 1966, he joined London outfit The BO STREET RUNNERS, debuting as MIKE "Too Much" PATTO on their (Beatles-penned) fourth single, 'DRIVE MY CAR'. He subsequently went on to do a short-lived stint with CHICAGO LINE (one single, 'JUMP BACK'), before joining the already formed Southport-based, psychedelic outfit, TIMEBOX. The outfit released a series of singles on 'Deram' (one of them, 'BEGGIN', was a FOUR SEASONS cover), before evolving into the more musically serious PATTO. His/their self-titled debut was an accomplished set of jazz-rock experimentation, which failed to achieve any commercial success. After a further two albums, PATTO joined SPOOKY TOOTH for their 'MIRROR' (1974) album, before forming the harder-edged BOXER – albums included the controversially-packaged 'BELOW THE BELT' (1976), 'BLOODLETTING' (1976) and 'ABSOLUTELY' (1977). Towards the end of '77, PATTO joined HINKLEY'S HEROES. Tragically, MIKE died of throat cancer on the 4th of March, 1979.

MIKE PATTO

Columbia / not iss.

Dec 66. (7") *(DB 8091)* **CAN'T STOP TALKING 'BOUT MY BABY. / LOVE** ☐ -

—— MIKE would join TIMEBOX in the middle of '67

PATTO

PATTO, HALSALL, GRIFFITHS + HALSEY

Vertigo / not iss.

Dec 70. (lp) *(6360 016)* **PATTO** ☐ -
– The man / Hold me back / Time to die / Red glow / San Antone / Government man / Money bag / Sittin' back easy. *(cd-iss. 1990's on 'Repertoire'; REP 4446) (re-iss. Jan02 on 'Akarma' lp/cd; AK 185/+CD)*

—— added briefly **BERNIE HOLLAND** – guitar (he left to join JODY GRIND)

Dec 71. (lp) *(6360 032)* **HOLD YOUR FIRE** ☐ -
– Hold your fire / You, you point your finger / How's your father / See you at the dance tonight / Give it all away / Air raid shelter / Tell me where you've been / Magic door. *(cd-iss. 1990's on 'Repertoire'; REP 4360) (lp re-iss. Feb02 on 'Akarma'; AK 190)*

Island / Island

Oct 72. (lp) *(ILPS 9210)* **ROLL 'EM SMOKE 'EM PUT ANOTHER LINE OUT** ☐ -
– Flat footed woman / Singing the blues on reds / Mummy / Loud green song / Turn turtle / I got rhythm / Peter Abraham / Cap'n P and the Atto's (sea biscuits part 1 & 2). *(cd-iss. Nov96 on 'Edsel'; EDCD 510)*

Dec 72. (7") *<1208>* **SINGING THE BLUES ON REDS. / MUMMY** - ☐

—— disbanded and HALSALL joined TEMPEST; PATTO joined SPOOKY TOOTH for one album 'THE MIRROR' (1974).

Good Ear / not iss.

Aug 74. (7"; by MIKE PATTO) *(EAR 106)* **SITTING IN THE PARK. / GET UP & DIG IT** ☐ -

—— MIKE would subsequently join another English-based band, BOXER

– PATTO compilations, etc. –

Oct 97. (cd) *Audio Archives; (AACD 008)* **MONKEY'S BUM** ☐ -
(re-iss. Apr02 on 'Akarma' lp/cd; AK 201/+CD)

—— PATTO split BOXER and joined HINKLEY'S HEROES, but sadly he was diagnosed with terminal throat cancer and died 4 March 1979.

PhD (see under ⇒ DIAMOND, Jim)

PHIL & THE FLINTSTONES (see under ⇒ "A Beat(en) Generation")

PILOT

Formed: Edinburgh . . . 1973 by DAVID PATON (also ex-BOOTS) and BILLY LYALL, both formerly of an embryonic BAY CITY ROLLERS; STUART TOSH was added soon afterwards. After laying down a number of demo tracks in London, the group emerged from the studios with a recording contract for 'E.M.I.' and a fourth member, guitarist IAN BAIRNSON.

Their witty and well-crafted teenybop style faltered initially when debut single, 'JUST A SMILE', didn't raise even a smirk. However, PILOT's course changed towards the end of 1974, when 'MAGIC' just failed to career into the UK Top 10; it later went Top 5 in America. At a time when the ROLLERS, the RUBETTES and MUD all ruled the pop charts, twee PILOT emerged as their more imaginative musical cousin. 'JANUARY' (released in er, January 1975), quickly flew up to the top of the hit parade and proved once again our wee Caledonian bands could compete with the best of them.

However, the changing climate towards pop took a dramatic turn (Punk-rock was just emerging) and after only a further two minor hits in '76, the band went into automatic pilot – numerous personnel changes dogged future stability. LYALL was no longer the co-PILOT, he would subsequently take up a largely unfruitful solo career while DOLLAR also took him under their wing; sadly, he was to die of an AIDS-related illness in '89. TOSH too, bailed out around 1977 and he re-emerged at first with 10cc. When PILOT finally split up in 1978, PATON and BAIRNSON fragmented to join the ALAN PARSONS PROJECT (he'd produced PILOT early on), with the former subsequently laying down session work for the likes of RICK WAKEMAN, CHRIS REA, MIDGE URE, etc. PATON went folkie and solo in the mid-90's (signing to 'Lochshore'!) and made a half self-penned/half BURNS-penned set, 'FRAGMENTS', in 1997.

DAVID PATON (b.29 Oct'51) – vocals, bass, guitar (ex-BOOTS) / **BILLY LYALL** (b.26 Mar'53) – synthesizer, piano, flute, vocals / **STUART TOSH** (b.26 Sep'51, Aberdeen) – drums / **IAIN BAIRNSON** (b. 3 Aug'53, Shetland Isles) – guitar (a session man until early 1975)

E.M.I. / E.M.I.

Jun 74. (7") *(EMI 2171)* **JUST A SMILE. / DON'T SPEAK LOUDLY** ☐ -

Oct 74. (7") *(EMI 2217) <3992>* **MAGIC. / JUST LET ME BE** 11 5 Mar75

Nov 74. (lp/c) *(EMC/TC-EMC 3045) <11368>* **FROM THE ALBUM OF THE SAME NAME** <US-title 'PILOT'> ☐ 82 May75
– Just a smile / Magic / Lucky for some / Girl next door / Lovely lady smile / Sooner or later / Don't speak loudly / Over the moon / Never give up / High into the sky / Auntie Iris / Sky blue. *(re-iss. Jan75 as 'PILOT'; same) (cd-iss. Jun91 on 'C5'; C5CD 567)*

Jan 75. (7") *(EMI 2255)* **JANUARY. / NEVER GIVE UP** 1 -

Apr 75. (7") *(EMI 2287)* **CALL ME ROUND. / DO ME GOOD** 34 -

May 75. (lp/c) *(EMC/TC-EMC 3075)* **SECOND FLIGHT** 48 -
– You're my No.1 / Love is / Call me round / Fifty-five degree north, three degree west / To you alone / Do me good / Heard it all before / Bad to me / You're devotion / January / Passion piece / Dear artist. *(cd-iss. Jun91 on 'C5'; C5CD 568)*

Sep 75. (7") *(EMI 2338)* **JUST A SMILE. / ARE YOU IN LOVE** 31 -

Sep 75. (7") *<4135>* **JUST A SMILE. / DON'T SPEAK LOUDLY** - 90

Jan 76. (7") *<4202>* **JANUARY. / DO ME GOOD** - 87

—— **PETER OXENDALE** – keyboards; repl. LYALL who went solo as WILLIAM LYALL and released a single in Sep'76, 'US' / 'MANIAC' *(EMI 2515)* and an accompanying album, 'SOLO CASTING' *(EMA 780)* which featured PILOT as back-up. He subsequently became part of pop duo DOLLAR but was to die of AIDS in December '89.

May 76. (7") *(EMI 2457)* **RUNNING WATER. / FIRST AFTER ME** ☐ ☐

Jun 76. (lp) *(EMA 779)* **MORIN HEIGHTS** ☐ -
– Hold on / Canada / First after me / Steps / The mover / Penny in my pocket / Lies and lies / Running water / Trembling / Maniac (come back) / Too many hopes. *(cd-iss. Jun91 on 'C5'; C5CD 569)*

Jun 76. (7"w-drawn; by DAVID PATON) *(EMI 2481)* **CANADA. / (version)** [ ] [-]
Jul 76. (7") *(EMI 2490)* **CANADA. / MOVER** [ ] [ ]
Oct 76. (7") *(EMI 2530)* **PENNY IN MY POCKET. / STEPS** [ ] [ ]

— **PATON + BAIRNSON** (TOSH joined 10cc) enlisted session people **STEVE SWINDELLS** – keyboards / **TREVOR SPENCER + HENRY SPINETTI** – drums

Arista Arista

Jul 77. (7") *(ARIST 111)* **GET UP AND GO. / BIG SCREEN KILL** [ ] [ ]
Aug 77. (lp) *(SPARTY 1014)* **TWO'S A CROWD** [ ] [-]
– Get up and go / Library door / Creeping round at midnight / One good reason why / There's a place / The other side / Monday, Tuesday / Ten foot tall / Evil eye / Mr. Do or die / Big screen kill.
Sep 77. (7") *(ARIST 139)* **MONDAY, TUESDAY. / EVIL EYE** [ ] [ ]
Nov 77. (7") *(ARIST 155)* **TEN FOOT TALL. / ONE GOOD REASON WHY** [ ] [ ]

— after they split, PATON and BAIRNSON joined KATE BUSH and later The ALAN PARSONS PROJECT (TOSH was also part of the latter outfit). In Apr'80, PATON issued a one-off 45, 'NO TIES NO STRINGS' / 'STOP AND LET GO' *(EMI 5063)*. PATON would also work with PAUL McCARTNEY, ELTON JOHN, RICK WAKEMAN, MIDGE URE, CHRIS REA, EDDI READER, etc

- compilations, etc. -

Oct 80. (lp/c) *EMI-Nut; (NUT/TC-NUT 29)* **THE BEST OF PILOT** [ ] [-]
– Sooner or later / Girl next door / Just a smile / You're my No.1 / Call me round / January / Magic / High in the sky / Passion piece / Penny in my pocket / Canada / Trembling / Never give up / Auntie Iris. *(re-iss. Jan91 on 'C5' lp/c/cd; C5/+K/CD 563)*
1987. (7") *Old Gold; (OG 9723)* **JANUARY. / MAGIC** [ ] [-]
Mar 97. (cd) *Disky; (DC 86579-2)* **MAGIC** [ ] [-]

DAVIE PATON

— with **PHIL CUNNINGHAM, MALCOLM STITT, JAMES MacKINTOSH**, etc

Lochshore not iss.

May 97. (cd/c) *(CD/TC LDL 1257)* **FRAGMENTS** [ ] [-]
– The bonnie blue bonnets / This honest land / Fallin' / For a' that / Ca' the yowes / Westlin' winds / Jock o' Hazeldean / Scots wha' hae / The holy fair / Loch Lomond.

POETS

Formed: Glasgow . . . 1961 by GEORGE GALLAGHER, JOHN DAWSON, TONY MYLES, HUME PATON and ALAN WEIR. They became residents at the Flamingo Ballroom prior to being discovered by ROLLING STONES' manager ANDREW LOOG OLDHAM, who subsequently signed them in 1964 to his management and production company.

Resplendent in their velvet suits and frilly shirts, their debut, 'NOW WE'RE THRU', just missed out on a Top 30 placing. Their blend of R&B songs (self-penned and covers), went some way towards breaking them outside of Scotland. They never had another hit, even when OLDHAM transferred them to his 'Immediate' label.

Their ever-changing line-ups didn't help matters, and by 1967 none of the originals remained, even FRASER WATSON (a member from a year past) bailing out. OLDHAM too lost interest, and without him, they signed a one-off deal with 'Decca', releasing 'WOODEN SPOON'. This was flipped over for the excellent Eastern psychedelic gem of a B-side, 'IN YOUR TOWER'. The A-side was written by their manager ERIC WOOLFSON and UNIT 4+2's TOMMY MOELLER. Their last two singles in 1971 were set up by DJ, TONY MEEHAN for a Strike Cola plug.

• **Trivia:** All 45's except their hit debut, are now worth over £25; the highest being 'WOODEN SPOON' at £80.

GEORGE GALLAGHER – vocals / **HUME PATON** – lead guitar, vocals / **TONY MYLES** – guitar / **JOHN DAWSON** – bass / **ALAN WEIR** – drums

Decca Dyno-vox

Oct 64. (7") *(F 11995)* <201> **NOW WE'RE THRU. / THERE ARE SOME** [31] [ ]
Feb 65. (7") *(F 12074)* **THAT'S THE WAY IT'S GOT TO BE. / I'LL CRY WITH THE MOON** [ ] [-]
Jul 65. (7") *(F 12195)* **I AM SO BLUE. / I LOVE HER STILL** [ ] [-]

— **FRASER WATSON** – guitar (ex-ARROWS), repl. MYLES

Immediate not iss.

Oct 65. (7") *(IM 006)* **CALL AGAIN. / SOME THINGS I CAN'T FORGET** [ ] [ ]
Jun 66. (7") *(IM 024)* **BABY DON'T YOU DO IT. / I'LL COME HOME** [ ] [ ]

— (late '66) no originals remaining just **FRASER** who recruited **ANDI MULVEY** – vocals / **IAN MacMILLAN** – guitar / **NORRIE McLEAN** – bass / **RAYMOND DUFFY** – drums

Decca not iss.

Feb 67. (7") *(F 12569)* **WOODEN SPOON. / IN YOUR TOWER** [ ] [ ]

— **DOUGIE HENDERSON** – drums; repl. JIM BREAKEY who repl. DUFFY

— **HUGHIE NICHOLSON** – guitar; repl. WATSON who joined PATHFINDERS

— **JOHNNY MARTIN** – organ; repl. MULVEY who joined MUSTARD

Pye not iss.

Dec 68. (7") *(7N 17668)* **LOCKED IN A ROOM. / ALONE AM I** [ ] [-]

Strike Cola not iss.

1971. (7") *(SC 1)* **HEYLA HOLA. / FUN BUGGY** [ ] [-]
1971. (7") *(SC 2)* **SHEW BLEW A GOOD THING. / OUT TO LUNCH** [ ] [-]
(re-iss. Nov71 on 'United Artists'; UP 35308)

— they finally disbanded the disjointed group. HUGHIE joined MARMALADE replacing JUNIOR CAMPBELL, and with McMILLAN, later formed BLUE after the former had been a part of CODY.

- compilations, etc. -

Jun 97. (cd) *Strike; (STRIKE 901)* **IN YOUR TOWER** [ ] [-]
Jan 02. (cd) *Distortions; (DYNOVOX 201)* **SCOTLAND'S 1** [ ] [-]
Apr 02. (lp) *Corduroy; (CORD 098)* **THE BEST OF THE POETS** [ ] [-]

POOR SOULS (see under ⇒ "A Beat(en) Generation")

Q

QUINTONES (see under ⇒ TRASH)

R

Gerry RAFFERTY

Born: 16 Apr'47, Paisley. In 1968, he joined The HUMBLEBUMS, alongside TAM HARVEY and future comedian, BILLY CONNOLLY. The trio signed up to folk label, 'Transatlantic', recording two albums, 'HUMBLEBUMS' (1969) & 'OPEN UP THE DOOR' (1970), together before parting ways.

RAFFERTY subsequently released a debut solo album, 'CAN I HAVE MY MONEY BACK', in 1971 before moving to London and forming STEALER'S WHEEL with RAB NOAKES and JOE EGAN. Signed to 'A&M', the band went through some major personnel upheaval prior to the release of their eponymous album in late '72, PAUL PILNICK, TONY WILLIAMS and ROB COOMBES replacing RAB NOAKES, IAN CAMPBELL and ROGER BROWN respectively. Overseen by veteran production duo, LEIBER & STOLLER, the album was characterised by gentle, folky harmonies and an unerring ear for pop melody, the haunting 'NEXT TO ME' resonating long after the first listen. Then of course, there was the 'Dylanesque' shuffle of 'STUCK IN THE MIDDLE OF YOU', a transatlantic Top 10 upon its original 1973 release and later an integral, ingeniously effective part of Quentin Tarantino's infamous 'Reservoir Dogs' movie. There was almost as much confusion surrounding the identity of the STEALER'S WHEEL line-up as there was among Tarantino's panicked criminal pros, RAFFERTY leaving for a couple of months before returning in time for a follow-up. By this point, all the original members (who themselves had been temporarily replaced!) were gone and the core duo of EGAN and RAFFERTY roped in a crew of session players to complete 'FERGUSLIE PARK' (1973). Another set of consummate folk-pop, the record was nevertheless a commercial disappointment save for a minor Top 30 hit, 'STAR'. Disillusioned, the pair completed one further set, the equally impressive 'RIGHT OR WRONG' (1975), before permanently parting company and embarking on respective solo careers.

After a number of years grappling with business problems, RAFFERTY emerged in early '78 with the 'CITY TO CITY' album. Changing tack to a more contemporary, MOR style, RAFFERTY scored a massive international hit (and a US No.1) with the 'BAKER STREET' single, RAPHAEL RAVENSCROFT's famous sax riff forming the basis of this world-weary classic. The track's success saw album sales go through the roof, RAFFERTY becoming something of a reluctant overnight superstar. Shunning the limelight and choosing not to promote the album in America (where it went platinum), RAFFERTY instead began work on a follow-up, 'NIGHT OWL' (1979). While failing to scale the commercial heights of its predecessor, the record was a sizeable success nonetheless, RAFFERTY's inimitably understated approach again delighting fans who put it into the UK Top 10. Subsequent albums such as 'SLEEPWALKING' (1982) and 'NORTH AND SOUTH' (1988) weren't quite as inspired, RAFFERTY taking a sabbatical during the mid-80's (although he did contribute to MARK KNOPFLER's 'Local Hero' soundtrack and produce The PROCLAIMERS' 1987 single, 'Letter From America').

He continued to record in the 90's, if sporadically, such seasoned hands as pedal steel player, B.J. COLE, lending their expertise to 1993's 'ON A WING AND A PRAYER', the record also featuring the backing vocal and co-writing talents of brother JIM.

• **Songwriters:** STEALER'S WHEEL was virtually a writing partnership for RAFFERTY and EGAN. GET OUT OF MY LIFE WOMAN (Allen Toussaint).

GERRY RAFFERTY – vocals, guitar (with session people including future STEALER'S WHEEL members)

Transatla. / Blue Thumb

1971. (lp) *(TRA 241)* <BTS 58> **CAN I HAVE MY MONEY BACK** [ ] [ ]
– New street blues / Didn't I / Mr. Universe / Mary Skeffington / Long way round / Can I have my money back / Sign on the dotted line / Make you break you / To each and everyone / One drink down / Don't count me out / Half a chance / Where I belong. *<US re-iss. 1978; 6031> (re-iss. Sep81 lp/c; TRS/KTRS 112) (re-iss. Apr85 on 'Autograph' c; ASK 769) (re-iss. cd+c Apr93 on 'Ariola Express') (cd re-iss. Oct98 on 'Wooded Hill'; HILLCD 3)*

Oct 71. (7") *(BIG 139)* **CAN I HAVE MY MONEY BACK. / SO SAD THINKING** [ ] [-]

Jan 72. (7") **CAN I HAVE MY MONEY BACK. / SIGN ON THE DOTTED LINE** [-] [ ]

STEALER'S WHEEL

GERRY with **JOE EGAN** – vocals, keyboards / **PAUL PILNICK** – guitar (ex-BIG THREE) repl. RAB NOAKES who went solo / **TONY WILLIAMS** – bass repl. IAN CAMPBELL / **ROD COOMBES** – drums repl. ROGER BROWN

A&M / A&M

Oct 72. (7") *(AMS 7033)* **LATE AGAIN. / I GET BY** [ ] [-]

Nov 72. (7") *(AMS 7036)* <1416> **STUCK IN THE MIDDLE WITH YOU. / JOSE** [ ] [6] Feb73
(re-dist.May73, hit UK No.8)

Dec 72. (lp) *(AMLH 68121)* <4377> **STEALER'S WHEEL** [ ] [50]
– Late again / Stuck in the middle with you / Another meaning / I get by / Outside looking in / Johnny's song / Next to me / Jose / Gets so lonely / You put something better inside of me.

Feb 73. (7") *(AMS 7046)* **YOU PUT SOMETHING BETTER INSIDE OF ME. / NEXT TO ME** [ ] [-]

— Group had disbanded when RAFFERTY had been replaced by **LUTHER GROSVENOR** (ex-SPOOKY TOOTH) for 2 months. **DELISLE HARPER** – bass repl. others

— By mid'73, they were a basic duo (**RAFFERTY & EGAN**) augmented by **BERNIE HOLLAND** – guitar / **CHRIS MERCER** – saxophone / **ANDREW STEELE** – drums / **CHRIS NEILL** – harmonica and loads more sessioners.

Aug 73. (7") *(AMS 7079)* **EVERYTHING'L TURN OUT FINE. / JOHNNY'S SONG** [33] [-]

Aug 73. (7") <1450> **EVERYONE'S AGREED THAT EVERYTHING WILL TURN OUT FINE. / NEXT TO ME** [-] [49]

Nov 73. (lp) *(AMLH 68209)* <4419> **FERGUSLIE PARK** [ ] [ ]
– Good businessman / Star / Wheelin' / Waltz (you know it makes sense!) / What more could you want / Over my head / Blind faith / Nothing's gonna change my mind / Steamboat row / Back on my feet again / Who cares / (Everyone's agreed that) Everything will turn out fine.

Dec 73. (7") *(AMS 7094)* <1483> **STAR. / WHAT MORE COULD I WANT** [25] [29]

Apr 74. (7") <1529> **WHEELIN'. / YOU PUT SOMETHING BETTER INSIDE OF ME** [-] [ ]

Feb 75. (7") *(AMS 7152)* **RIGHT OR WRONG. / THIS MORNING** [ ] [-]

Feb 75. (lp) *(AMLH 68293)* <4517> **RIGHT OR WRONG** [ ] [ ]
– Benediction / Found my way to you / This morning / Let yourself go / Home from home / Go as you please / Wishbone / Don't get me wrong / Monday morning / Right or wrong.

May 75. (7") *(AMS 7170)* **FOUND MY WAY TO YOU. / WISHBONE** [ ] [-]

May 75. (7") <1675> **FOUND MY WAY TO YOU. / THIS MORNING** [-] [ ]

— Broke up again later in the year. JOE EGAN went solo, as did GERRY.

– compilations, etc. –

Sep 78. (lp) *A&M; (AMLH 64708)* <4708> **THE BEST OF STEALER'S WHEEL** [ ] [ ]
– Stuck in the middle with you / Nothing's gonna change my mind / Star / This morning / Steamboat row / Next to me / Right or wrong / Go as you please / Benediction / Waltz (you know it makes sense!) / Blind faith / Late again / Wheelin' / Jose. *(re-iss. 1981 on 'Music For Pleasure'; MFP 50501) (cd/c-iss.Jun90 on 'Connoisseur'; CSAP CD/MC 106)*

Sep 78. (7") *A&M; <2075>* **(EVERYONE AGREED THAT) EVERYTHING'L TURN OUT FINE. / WHO CARES** [-] [ ]

Mar 82. (7") *Old Gold; (OG 9148)* **STUCK IN THE MIDDLE WITH YOU. / STAR** [ ] [-]

Sep 98. (cd) *Spectrum; (552496-2)* **STUCK IN THE MIDDLE** [ ] [-]

GERRY RAFFERTY

with many session people.

U.A. / U.A.

Oct 77. (7") *(UP 36278)* **CITY TO CITY. / MATTIE'S RAG** [ ] [ ]

Jan 78. (lp/c) *(UAS/TCK 30104)* <840> **CITY TO CITY** [6] [1]
– he ark / Baker Street / Right down the line / City to city / Stealin' time / Mattie's rag / Whatever's written in your heart / Home and dry / Island / Waiting for the day. *(re-iss. Mar85 on 'Fame' lp/c; FA/TC-FA 3119) (cd-iss. Jul89; CDFA 3119) (cd re-iss. Apr99 on 'D.C.C.'; GZS 1075)*

Feb 78. (7") *(UP 36346)* <1192> **BAKER STREET. / BIG CHANGE IN THE WEATHER** [3] [2] Apr78
above featured **RAPHAEL RAVENSCROFT** – saxophone

May 78. (7") *(UP 36403)* **WHATEVER'S WRITTEN IN YOUR HEART. / WAITING FOR THE DAY** [ ] [-]

Aug 78. (7") <1233> **RIGHT DOWN THE LINE. / WAITING FOR THE DAY** [-] [12]

Sep 78. (7") *(UP 36445)* **RIGHT DOWN THE LINE. / ISLAND** [ ] [-]

Nov 78. (7") <1266> **HOME AND DRY. / MATTIE'S RAG** [-] [28]

May 79. (7") *(UP 36512)* **NIGHT OWL. / WHY DON'T YOU TALK TO ME** [5] [-]

May 79. (lp/c) *(UAK/TCK 30238)* <958> **NIGHT OWL** [9] [29]
– Days gone down (still got the light in your eyes) / Night owl / The way that you do it / Why won't you talk to me / Get it right next time / Take the money and run / Family tree / Already gone / The tourist / It's gonna be a long night. *(re-iss. 1985 on 'Liberty' lp/c; ATAK/TC-ATAK 37) (re-iss. Jul86 on 'Fame' lp/c; FA/TC-FA 3147) (cd-iss. Jul89; CDFA 3147)*

May 79. (7") <1298> **DAYS GONE DOWN (STILL GOT THE LIGHT IN YOUR EYES). / WHY WON'T YOU TALK TO ME?** [-] [17]

Aug 79. (7") *(BP 301)* <1316> **GET IT RIGHT NEXT TIME. / IT'S GONNA BE A LONG NIGHT** [30] [21]

Mar 80. (7") *(BP 340)* **BRING IT ALL HOME. / IN TRANSIT** [54] [ ]

Mar 80. (lp/c) *(UAK/TCK 30298)* <1039> **SNAKES AND LADDERS** [15] [61]
– The Royal Mile / I was a boy scout / Welcome to Hollywood / Wastin' away / Look at the Moon / Bring it all home / The garden of England / Johnny's song / Didn't I / Syncopatin' Sandy / Cafe le Cabotin / Don't close the door. *(cd-iss. Mar89 on 'Liberty'; CZ 162)*

Oct 80. (7") *(BP 354)* <1366> **THE ROYAL MILE (SWEET DARLIN') . / WASTIN' AWAY** [67] [54] Jul80

Liberty / Liberty

Aug 82. (7") *(BP 413)* **SLEEPWALKING. / WHEN I REST** [ ] [ ]

Sep 82. (lp/c) *(LEG/TCG 30352)* <51132> **SLEEPWALKING** [39] [ ]
– Standing at the gates / Good intentions / A change of heart / On the way / Sleepwalking / Cat and mouse / The right moment / As wise as a serpent. *(re-iss. Sep84 on 'Fame' lp/c; FA/TC-FA 3113) (re-iss. Aug86 on 'E.M.I.' lp/c; ATAK/TC-ATAK 84) (cd-iss. Mar89; CZ 163) (cd re-iss. Feb01 on 'EMI Plus'; 576089-2)*

Nov 82. (7") *(BP 415)* **A CHANGE OF HEART. / GOOD INTENTIONS** [ ] [-]

Nov 82. (7") **STANDING AT THE GATES. / GOOD INTENTIONS** [-] [ ]

— he took some time off, although he did appear on MARK KNOPFLER's 'Local Hero' 1983 soundtrack and in 1987 produced 'Letter From America' by The PROCLAIMERS.

London / Polydor

Apr 88. (7") *(LON 170)* **SHIPYARD TOWN. / HEARTS DESIRE** [ ] [-]
(12"+=/cd-s+=) *(LON X/CD 170)* – ('A'lp version).

May 88. (lp/c)(cd) *(LON LP/C 55)(828089-2)* <835449> **NORTH AND SOUTH** [43] [ ] Jun88
– North and south / Moonlight and gold / Tired of talking / Hearts run dry / A dangerous age / Shipyard town / Winter's come / Nothing ever happens down here / On a night like this / Unselfish love. *(re-iss. Apr91; same)*

— now with **PAVEL ROSAK** – keyboards, drums, bass, percussion, programming / **HUGH BURNS** – electric guitars, co-producer / **MEL COLLINS** – sax / **B.J. COLE** – pedal steel / **ARRAN AHMUN** – percussion / **MO FOSTER** – bass / **BRYN HAWORTH** – bottleneck guitar / etc. Note: Brother **JIM RAFFERTY** also provided backing vocals & co-songwriting.

A&M / Avalanche

Nov 92. (7"/c-s/cd-s) **I COULD BE WRONG. / BAKER STREET / LIFE GOES ON** [ ] [-]

Feb 93. (cd/c) *(517495-2/-4)* <0016> **ON A WING & A PRAYER** [73] [ ]
– Time's caught up on you / I see red / It's easy to talk / I could be wrong / Don't

speak of my heart / Get out of my life woman / Don't give up on me / Hang on / Love and affection / Does he know what he's taken on / The light of love / Life goes on. *(cd re-iss. Jul02 on 'Spectrum'; 517238-2)*

		Polydor	Avalanche
Jun 95.	(cd) *(523599-2) <0017>* **OVER MY HEAD**	[ ]	[ ]

– Bajan moon / The waters of forgetfulness / Down and out / Over my head / The girl's got no confidence / Wrong thinking / Lonesome polecat / Right or wrong / Late again / Clear day / Out the blue / A new beginning / Her father didn't like me anyway.

– (his) compilations, others, etc. –

Apr 74.	(lp) *Transatlantic; (TRA 270)* **GERRY RAFFERTY REVISITED**	[ ]	[-]
Jul 87.	(cd) *Transatlantic; (TRACD 601)* **THE COLLECTION**	[ ]	[-]
Apr 78.	(7") *Logo; (GO 314)* **MARY SKEFFINGTON. / SHOESHINE BOY**	[ ]	[-]
Sep 78.	(lp) *Logo; (VISA 7006)* **GERRY RAFFERTY**	[ ]	[-]
Apr 84.	(lp/c) *Cambra; (CR/+T 132)* **THE FIRST CHAPTER**	[ ]	[-]
Jun 88.	(lp) *Demon; (TRANDEM 3)* **BLOOD AND GLORY**	[ ]	[-]
Nov 89.	(cd/c/lp) *E.M.I.; (CD/TC+/UAG 30333)* **RIGHT DOWN THE LINE – THE BEST OF GERRY RAFFERTY**	[ ]	[-]

– Baker Street / Whatever's written in your heart / Bring it all home / Right down the line / Get it right next time / Night owl / A dangerous age / Family tree / Shipyard town / The right moment / Look at the Moon. *(cd+=)* – The way that you do it / Tired of talking / The garden of England / Sleepwalking / As wise as a serpent.

Feb 90.	(7") *E.M.I.; (EM 132)* **BAKER STREET (remix). / NIGHT OWL (remix)**	[53]	[-]

(12"+=) *(12EM 132)* – ('A'extended).
(cd-s++=) *(CDEM 132)* – Bring it all home (remix).

Apr 95.	(cd) *Castle; (CCSCD 428)* **THE TRANSATLANTIC YEARS**	[ ]	[-]
Oct 95.	(cd/c) *Polygram TV; (529279-2/-4)* **ONE MORE DREAM – THE VERY BEST OF . . .**	[17]	[-]

– Get it right next time / The garden of England / Baker street / Moonlight and gold / Stuck in the middle with you / Night owl / Waiting for the day / Right down the line / Tired of talkin' / Bring it all home / The girl's got no confidence / Days gone down / Everyone's agreed that everything will turn out fine / Over my head / Shipyard town / Whatever's written in your heart.

Feb 96.	(cd/c) *True Trax; (TRT CD/MC 196)* **THE EARLY YEARS**	[ ]	[-]
Mar 97.	(d-cd) *Raven; <63>* **CLOWNS TO THE LEFT, JOKERS TO THE RIGHT: 1970-1982**	[-]	[ ]
Jun 98.	(cd) *EMI Gold; (494941-2)* **BAKER STREET**	[ ]	[-]
Oct 98.	(cd) *Castle Select; (SELCD 547) / Phantom; <21864-2>* **DON'T COUNT ME OUT: THE VERY BEST OF THE TRANSATLANTIC YEARS**	[-]	[ ]
Dec 99.	(cd) *Disky; <85442>* **BAKER STREET**	[-]	[ ]
May 00.	(cd) *Essential; (ESMCD 879)* **CAN I HAVE MY MONEY BACK – THE BEST OF GERRY RAFFERTY**	[ ]	[-]

RED HAWKES (see under ⇒ Alp records)

Mike REOCH and the TREMORS

Formed: Aberdeen . . . 1962 as The TREMORS by former skiffle-man TOMMY DENE who recruited bassist MIKE REOCH, guitarist BYRON GRANT, JOHN ROFT and DENNIS MORRISON; ROFT would leave in July 1963 to get married. DONALD STUART was subsequently drafted in as his replacement, as the combo became big hits around areas like Dundee; they were even voted North Of Scotland rock champions.

Entrepreneur and ALP records boss, ANDY LOTHIAN, became involved with the band in 1964 and in turn introduced them to legendary svengali pop producer, JOE MEEK. LOTHIAN ensured his protegees would get all the right treatment courtesy of STV pop slots alongside LULU & THE LUVVERS and a live set with ALEX HARVEY. With A&R men virtually crawling out of the woodwork to get to the much in-demand TREMORS, 'Decca' finally won out, although just when it seemed things were going great, they pulled out of a deal; TOMMY now left to pursue a solo career.

As MIKE REOCH & THE TREMORS, the band did stints in Germany and Denmark, but by 1966 and a couple of singles for German 'Fontana', they had returned to lick their wounds once again. Towards the end of the decade, REOCH and GRANT pulled their resources once again (with new vocalist JOHN LATIMER) and formed LIGHT OF DARKNESS. Based in Germany due to their German drummer MANFRED BEBERT, the band's output consisted of a sole self-titled album of raw garage rock that was notable primarily for the manic vocals of LATIMER. A cult classic, the album is highly sought after in its original form.

TOMMY DENE – vocals / **MIKE REOCH** – bass / **DONALD STUART** – rhythm guitar (ex-MIDNIGHTERS) repl. JOHN ROFT / **BYRON GRANT** (b. Brechin) – lead guitar / **DENNIS MORRISON** – drums

—— TOMMY DENE left for a solo career early in 1964

		Elite Special	not iss.
1964.	(lp) *(SOLPF 236)* **BEATEN AN INTERNATIONAL EVERGREENS**	[-]	[-] German

(above was probably a Various Artists set)

—— after their split REOCH and GRANT formed . . .

LIGHT OF DARKNESS

JOHN LATIMER – vocals, piano, organ, percussion / **BYRON GRANT** – guitars, fiddle / **MIKE REOCH** – bass, flute, piano, harmonica / **MANFRED BEBERT** – drums, percussion

		Philips	not iss.
Dec 70.	(lp) *(6305 062)* **LIGHT OF DARKNESS**	[-]	[-] German

– Movin' along / Love in your heart / Ain't no place where I belong / Soul Francisco / Freedom's fight / Time / Down out. *(re-iss. 1981 on 'ZYX') (re-iss. 1991 & Oct00 on 'Second Battle'; SB 019LP) (cd-iss. Jun97; SB 019)*

—— split after above

Harry ROBINSON (see under ⇒ LORD ROCKINGHAM'S XI)

S

SCOTS OF ST. JAMES (see under ⇒ "A Beat(en) Generation")

Tommy SCOTT

Born: Early 1940's, Glasgow. Balladeer TOMMY was known largely in the early to mid 60's courtesy of three flop singles for 'Decca', 'ANGELA' (in 1962), 'WHO WILL IT BE' and 'WRAP UP YOUR TROUBLES IN DREAMS' (both 1964). He subsequently teamed up with BILL MARTIN and attempted to write songs for the likes of The BOXTON DEXTERS (TAM WHITE's first outfit). Now a songsmith in his own right, TOMMY also moved into production, The BEATSTALKERS and THEM were part of his mid-60's Celtic entourage. The last heard of the man was when he worked in studios alongside MALCOLM NIXON.

TOMMY SCOTT – vocals / with orchestra, etc

		Decca	not iss.
1962.	(7"; as JAY & TOMMY SCOTT) *(F 11474)* **ANGELA. / DID YOU**	[ ]	[-]
Feb 64.	(7") *(F 11839)* **WHO WILL IT BE. / IF IT'S ME THAT YOU WANT**	[ ]	[-]
Jul 64.	(7") *(F 11942)* **WRAP UP YOUR TROUBLES IN DREAMS. / BLUEBERRY HILL**	[ ]	[-]

—— TOMMY went into the songwriting side

SENATE (see under ⇒ "A Beat(en) Generation")

SENSATIONAL ALEX HARVEY BAND (see under ⇒ HARVEY, Alex)

Derek / Phil SHULMAN

Born: 11 Feb'47 & 27 Aug'37, Glasgow. Raised in Portsmouth – along with third English-born younger brother RAY – the three siblings (DEREK on vocals, PHIL on sax and RAY on bass, guitar & vocals) formed a number of local outfits including The HOWLING WOLVES and The ROADRUNNERS; the latter evolved into SIMON DUPREE AND THE BIG SOUND.

In 1966, this psychedelic/R&B pop sextet gigged constantly around London and finally secured a contract with 'Parlophone'. After three flop singles, the band hit paydirt when the classic quasi-psychedelic 'KITES' (complemented by oriental vocal interlude) hit the UK Top 10. Unfortunately, this MOODY BLUES-esque number was their only major hit (follow-up, 'FOR WHOM THE BELL TOLLS' only reached No.43) and SD&tBS faded into obscurity once more. However, all was not lost as the brothers three formed the more fashionable and Prog-rock friendly GENTLE GIANT. Between 1970 and 1973, the 6-piece released four albums, 'GENTLE GIANT', 'ACQUIRING THE TASTE', 'THREE FRIENDS' and 'OCTOPUS', before PHIL decided it was time to leave. In 1974, after yet another set 'IN A GLASS HOUSE' (1973) failed to chart, the band finally made it big when sixth LP, 'THE POWER AND THE GLORY', cracked the US Top 100. The excellent 'FREE HAND' in '75 sold even better (US Top 50), audiences around the globe now appreciating their baroque'n'roll style; two of its highlights were undoubtably 'JUST THE SAME' and 'ON REFLECTION'.

With the advent of Punk rock in '76/'77, GENTLE GIANT petered out, leaving behind a further handful of mediocre albums, 'INTERVIEW' (1976), the live 'PLAYING THE FOOL' (1977), 'THE MISSING PIECE' (1977), 'GIANT FOR A DAY' (1978) and 'CIVILIAN' (1980). RAY subsequently took up the post at 'One Little Indian' where he signed The SUGARCUBES, while DEREK relocated to the Big Apple to become an A&R director with Polygram.

SOCIETIE (see under ⇒ "A Beat(en) Generation")

STEALER'S WHEEL (see under ⇒ RAFFERTY, Gerry)

Al STEWART

Born: 5 Sep'45, Glasgow. Moving to Bournemouth with his widowed mother as a toddler, STEWART later learned guitar alongside ROBERT FRIPP.

In the mid-60's, after briefly sharing a flat with fellow (then) budding singer/songwriter folkie, PAUL SIMON, he released a one-off '45, 'THE ELF', for 'Decca', one JIMMY PAGE (then a session musician) playing lead guitar. Signing to 'C.B.S.' in 1967, he debuted with the 'BED-SITTER IMAGES' album the same year, which if nothing else, helped invent the concept of the down-at-heel songwriter poring over angst-ridden ruminations in the safety of his room. STEWART's navel-gazing tales of doomed romance were given free rein on 'ZERO SHE FLIES' (1970) and 'ORANGE' (1972), punctuated by the odd track written from a more historical vein. 1973's quasi-concept affair, 'PAST, PRESENT & FUTURE', took the latter approach to its conclusion and in 'NOSTRADAMUS' featured one of STEWART's most compelling tracks.

Subsequently relocating to California, the singer's more Americanised latter 70's output saw him become a fairly major Stateside star. STEWART's first effort for 'R.C.A.', 'YEAR OF THE CAT' (1976) made the US Top 5 (UK Top 40) on the strength of the infectious title track, an American Top 10 hit in its own right. Produced by ALAN PARSONS, the record saw STEWART's fragile, understated style presented in a more accessible pop-folk framework, as did its (almost equally commercially fruitful) successor, 'TIME PASSAGES' (1978). 1980's '24 CARROTS' didn't perform quite so well, STEWART embroiled in business problems for much of the 80's. Comeback set, 'LAST DAYS OF THE CENTURY' (1988), was a synth-enhanced affair embracing STEWART's increasingly fanciful lyrical themes, the singer moving to 'E.M.I.', then 'Permanent' in the 90's for whom he continues to record consistent, if commercially limited material.

AL STEWART – vocals, guitar with orchestra

Decca / not iss.

Jul 66. (7") *(F 12467)* **THE ELF. / TURN INTO STONE** [ ] [-]

C.B.S. / Columbia

Sep 67. (7") *(CBS 3034)* **BEDSITTER IMAGES. / SWISS COTTAGE MANOEUVRES** [ ] [-]

Oct 67. (lp; stereo/mono) *(S+/BPG 63087)* **BED-SITTER IMAGES** [ ] [-]
– Bedsitter images / Swiss Cottage manoeuvres / Scandinavian girl * / Pretty golden hair * / Denise at 16 / Samuel, oh how you've changed! / Cleave to me * / A long way down from Stephanie / Ivich / Beleeka doodle day. *(re-iss. Jun70 as 'THE FIRST ALBUM (BED-SITTER IMAGES)'; CBS 64023)* – Lover man / Clifton in the rain. *(repl. * tracks)*

Jan 69. (lp; stereo/mono) *(S+/63460)* **LOVE CHRONICLES** [ ] [ ]
– In Brooklyn / Old Compton Street blues / Ballad of Mary Foster / Life and life only / You should've listened to Al / Love chronicles. *(re-iss.May82 on 'RCA International' lp/c; INT S/K 5120)*

Mar 70. (7") *(CBS 4843)* **ELECTRIC LOS ANGELES SUNSET. / MY ENEMIES HAVE SWEET VOICES** [ ] [-]

Mar 70. (lp) *(CBS 64023)* **ZERO SHE FLIES** [40] [-]
– My enemies have sweet voices / A small fruit song / Gethsemane again / Burbling / Electric Los Angeles sunset / Manuscript / Black hill / Anna / Room of roots / Zero she flies. *(re-iss. Oct85 on 'R.C.A.' lp/c; NL/NK 70874)*

Dec 71. (7") *(CBS 5351)* **THE NEWS FROM SPAIN. / ELVASTON PLACE** [ ] [-]

Feb 72. (7") *(CBS 7763)* **YOU DON'T EVEN KNOW ME. / I'M FALLING** [ ] [-]

Feb 72. (lp) *(CBS 64739)* **ORANGE** [ ] [-]
– You don't even know me / Amsterdam / Songs out of clay / The news from Spain / I don't believe you / Once an orange, always an orange / I'm falling / Night of the 4th of May. *(re-iss. Nov81 lp/c; CBS/40 32061) (cd-iss. Jul96 on 'Columbia'; 484441-2)*

Apr 72. (7") *(CBS 7992)* **AMSTERDAM. / SONGS OUT OF CLAY** [ ] [-]

C.B.S. / Janus

Sep 73. (7") *(CBS 1791)* **TERMINAL EYES. / LAST DAYS OF JUNE 1934** [ ] [-]

Oct 73. (lp) *(CBS 65726)* *<3063>* **PAST, PRESENT & FUTURE** [ ] [-] Jan74
– Old admirals / Warren Harding / Soho (needless to say) / Last days of June 1934 / Post World War Two blues / Roads to Moscow / Terminal eyes / Nostradamus. *(re-iss. Jun81 lp/c; CBS/40 32026) <US cd-iss. 1987 on 'Arista'; ARCD 8359> (cd-iss. Nov92 on 'Beat Goes On'; BGOCD 155)*

Apr 74. (7") *<243>* **NOSTRADAMUS. / TERMINAL EYES** [-] [ ]

— Around Spring'74, toured with backing band HOME

Jun 74. (7") *(CBS 2397)* **NOSTRADAMUS. / SWALLOW WIND** [ ] [-]

— backed w/ **GERRY CONWAY / SIMON NICOL / PAT DONALDSON & SIMON ROUSSEL**

Mar 75. (7") *<250>* **CAROL. / SIRENS OF TITAN** [-] [ ]

Apr 75. (7") *(CBS 3254)* **CAROL. / NEXT TIME** [ ] [-]

Apr 75. (lp/c) *(CBS/40 80477)* *<7012>* **MODERN TIMES** [ ] [30] Feb75
– Carol / Sirens of Titan / What's going on / Not the one / Next time / Apple cider / Re-constitution / The dark and rolling sea / Modern times. *(re-iss. Mar81 lp/c; CBS/40 32019) (cd-iss. Jan93 on 'Beat Goes On'; BGOCD 156)*

R.C.A. / Janus

Oct 76. (lp/c) *(RS/ 1082)* *<7022>* **YEAR OF THE CAT** [38] [5]
– Lord Grenville / On the border / Midas shadow / Sand in your shoes / If it doesn't come naturally, leave it / Flying sorcery / Broadway Hotel / One stage before / Year of the cat. *(re-iss. Sep81 lp/c; RCA LP/K 3015) (cd-iss. Nov84; ND 71493) (re-iss. Dec87 lp/c; NL/NK 71493) (re-iss. Apr91 on 'Fame' cd/c; CD/TC FA 3253) (cd re-mast.Sep01 on 'E.M.I.'; 535456-2)*

Jan 77. (7") *(RCA 2771)* *<266>* **YEAR OF THE CAT. / BROADWAY HOTEL** [31] [8] Nov76

Apr 77. (7") *(PB 5019)* *<267>* **ON THE BORDER. / FLYING SORCERY** [ ] [42]

R.C.A. / Arista

Sep 78. (lp/c) *(PL/PK 25173)* *<4190>* **TIME PASSAGES** [39] [10]
– Time passages / Valentina way / Life in dark water / A man for all seasons / Almost Lucy / Palace of Versailles / Timeless skies / Song on the radio / End of the day. *(re-iss. Sep81 lp/c; RCA LP/K 3026) (re-iss. Aug84 lp/c; PL/PK 70274) (cd-iss. Dec86; PD 70274) (cd re-iss. Oct91 on 'Fame'; CDFA 3312)*

Sep 78. (7") *<0362>* **TIME PASSAGES. / ALMOST LUCY** [-] [7]

Feb 79. (7") *(PB 5139)* *<0389>* **SONG ON THE RADIO. / A MAN FOR ALL SEASONS** [ ] [29] Jan79

Aug 80. (7") *(RCA 2)* **MONDO SINISTRO. / MERLIN'S TIME** [ ] [-]

Aug 80. (lp/c) *(PL/PK 25306)* *<9520>* **24 CARROTS** [55] [37]
– Running man / Midnight rocks / Constantinople / Merlin's time / Mondo sinistro / Murmansk run – Ellis Island / Rocks in the ocean / Paint by numbers / Optical illusion. *(re-iss. Sep81 lp/c; RCA LP/K 3042) (cd-iss. Aug92 on 'E.M.I.'; CZ 512)*

Aug 80. (7") *<0552>* **MIDNIGHT ROCKS. / CONSTANTINOPLE** [-] [24]

Nov 80. (7") *(RCA 17)* **PAINT BY NUMBERS. / OPTICAL ILLUSION** [ ] [ ]

Jan 81. (7") *<0585>* **RUNNING MAN. / MERLIN'S TIME** [-] [ ]

Oct 81. (7") *(RCA 149)* *<0639>* **INDIAN SUMMER. / PANDORA** [ ] [ ]

Nov 81. (d-lp/d-c) *(RCA LP/K 70257)* *<8607>* **LIVE – INDIAN SUMMER (live)** [ ] [ ]
– Here in Angola / Pandora / Indian summer / Princess Olivia / Running man / Time passages / Merlin's time / If it doesn't come naturally, leave it / Roads to Moscow / Nostradamus (part 1) – World goes to Riyadah – Nostradamus (part 2) / Soho (needless to say) / On the border / Valentina way / Clarence Frogman Henry / Year of the cat. *(re-iss. 1984 lp/c; PL/PK 70257)*

R.C.A. / Passport

May 84. (lp/c) *(PL/PK 70307)* **RUSSIANS AND AMERICANS** [83] [ ]
– Strange girl / Russians and Americans / Cafe society / One, two, three / The candidate / 1-2-3 / Lori, don't go right now * / Rumours of war / The gypsy and the rose * / Accident on 3rd Street. *<US repl. * track>* – The one that got away / Night meeting. *(cd-iss. Jul93 on 'E.M.I.'; CZ 523)*

Jun 84. (7") *(RCA 414)* **LORI, DON'T GO RIGHT NOW. / ACCIDENT ON 3rd STREET** [ ] [-]

May 85. (lp/c) *(PL/PK 70715)* **THE BEST OF AL STEWART** (compilation) [ ] [ ]
– Year of the cat / On the border / If it doesn't come naturally, leave it / Time passages / Almost lucky / Merlin's theme / Valentina way / Running man / Roads to Moscow / Here in Angola / Rumours of war. *<US cd 1988; ARCD 8433> (cd-iss. Feb97 on 'E.M.I.'; CTMCD 310)*

Enigma / Enigma

Sep 88. (lp/c/cd) *(ENVLP/TCENV/CDENV 505)* **LAST DAYS OF THE CENTURY** [ ] [ ]
– Last days of the century / Real and unreal / King of Portugal / Red toupee / Where are they now / Bad reputation / Josephine Baker / License to steal / Fields of France / Antartica / Ghostly horses of the plain. *(cd+=)* – Helen and Cassandra. *(re-iss. Jul90 cd/c/lp; 773 316-2/-4/-1)*

Oct 88. (7") *(ENV 4)* **KING OF PORTUGAL. / JOSEPHINE BAKER** [ ] [ ]
(12"+=) *(ENVT 4)* – Bad reputation.
(3"cd-s++=) *(ENVCD 4)* – ('A'-rock mix version).

E.M.I. Mesa

Feb 92. (cd/c/lp) *(CD/TC+/EMC 3613)* **RHYMES IN ROOMS (live)**
– Flying sorcery / Soho (needless to say) / Time passages / Josephine Baker / Nostradamus / On the border / Fields of France / Medley:- Clifton in the rain – A small fruit song / Broadway hotel / If it doesn't come naturally, leave it / Year of the cat. *(re-iss. cd Feb95 on 'Fame'; CDFA 3315)*

Mar 92. (7") **RHYMES IN ROOMS (live). / YEAR OF THE CAT (live)**
(cd-s+=) – Songs on the radio.

Permanent Mesa

Oct 93. (cd/c) *(PERM CD/MC 15)* **FAMOUS LAST WORDS** Feb94
– Feel like / Angels of mercy / Don't forget me / Peter on the white sea / Genie on a table top / Trespasser / Trains / Necromancer / Charlotte Corday / Hippo song / Night rolls on.

E.M.I. Mesa

Jun 95. (cd/c) *(CD/TC EMC 3710)* **BETWEEN THE WARS**
– Night train to Munich / The age of rhythm / Sampan / Lindy comes to town / Three mules / A league of notions / Between the wars / Betty Boop's birthday / Marion the Chatelaine / Joe the Georgian / Always the cause / Laughing into 1939 / The black Danube.

– compilations, etc. –

Apr 78. (lp/c) *R.C.A.; (PL/PK 25131) / Arista; <US-d-lp>* **THE EARLY YEARS** (1967-1970)
(re-iss. Oct81 lp/c; INT S/K 5156) (re-iss. Sep86 on 'Fame' lp/c; FA/TC-FA 3165)

1985. (7") *Arista;* **YEAR OF THE CAT / TIME PASSAGES** -

Nov 86. (7") *Old Gold; (OG 9642)* **THE YEAR OF THE CAT. / (other track by Climax Blues Band)** -

Jun 91. (cd/c) *E.M.I.; (CD/TC EMC 3590)* **CHRONICLES: THE BEST OF AL STEWART (1976-81)**
– Year of the cat / On the border / If it doesn't come naturally, leave it / Time passages / Almost Lucy / Song on the radio * / Running man * / Merlin's time / In Brooklyn / Soho (needless to say) * / A small fruit song / Manuscript / Roads to Moscow (live) / Nostradamus (part 1) – World goes to Riyadh – Nostradamus (part 2). *(cd+= *)*

Oct 93. (d-cd) *E.M.I.; (CDEM 1511)* **TO WHOM IT MAY CONCERN (1966-1970)**

Apr 97. (3xcd-box) *E.M.I.; (CDOMB 020)* **THE ORIGINALS**
– (YEAR OF THE CAT / TIME PASSAGES / RUSSIANS AND AMERICANS)

Ian STEWART

Born: 1938, Pittenweem, Fife. Raised from an early age in London, IAN became fascinated by the R&B scene, most notably Brit pioneer, ALEXIS KORNER. The pianist developed his skills (especially in the boogie-woogie style) and in the early 60's became part of an embryonic ROLLING STONES.

Early 1963, during a residency at Richmond's Crawdaddy club, the group was spotted by manager Andrew Loog Oldham, who offered them a contract. However, IAN was unceremoniously relegated to road manager and part-time piano-player after being told his persona/face/whatever didn't quite fit into Oldham's exacting band criteria. STU (as he was always known) took this knock-back hard although for subsequent years, he still remained the unrewarded "sixth ROLLING STONE". Early in 1965, The MONGRELS credited him on the B-side ('Stewball') of their second 45, 'My Love For You'. He contributed Chicago-styled piano playing to many STONES gems and outside session work came via HOWLIN' WOLF, LED ZEPPELIN ('Boogie With Stu') and of course, ALEXIS KORNER. IAN STEWART subsequently helped the 'STONES keep their Blues roots intact throughout their controversial and dynamic career; he was also an integral part of WATTS and WYMAN's R&B/jazz offshoot, ROCKET 88 (also featuring JACK BRUCE and ALEXIS), on their 1981 eponymous set. Sadly, STU was to die of a heart attack in a Harley Street clinic on the 12th of December, 1985, never forgotten by JAGGER, RICHARDS, WYMAN, WATTS and every 'STONE on Earth or Heaven. But for bad luck, the man might've had it all.

Rod STEWART

Born: RODERICK DAVID STEWART, 10 Jan'45, Highgate, London. Of Scottish parentage, STEWART remains a passionate Scotland supporter and considers himself an adopted Scot.

In addition to music, obviously, the singer's other passion is football, the young ROD initially biding his time as an apprentice for Brentford F.C. The lure of the itinerant lifestyle proved irresistible, however, and STEWART subsequently hooked up with folk singer, WIZZ JONES, busking/learning his trade around Europe before eventually being deported for vagrancy in 1963. Upon his return, STEWART threw himself headlong into the burgeoning Brit R&B scene as part of West Midlands group, JIMMY POWELL & The FIVE DIMENSIONS. He then took his feted harmonica blowing skills to London, playing on a live effort by JOHN BALDRY & THE HOOCHIE COOCHIE MEN. This in turn, led to ROD developing his vocal talents and releasing a one-off single for 'Decca' in 1964, 'GOOD MORNING LITTLE SCHOOLGIRL', before briefly joining BALDRY's new outfit (also featuring BRIAN AUGER, JULIE DRISCOLL and MICK WALLER, the latter a future STEWART collaborator), STEAMPACKET, the following year. After a dispute with BALDRY, STEWART then added a stint with SHOTGUN EXPRESS (alongside a star-studded line-up which boasted a young PETER GREEN and MICK FLEEETWOOD amongst others) to his increasingly impressive CV.

The big break finally came in 1967, when JEFF BECK recruited him as a lead singer, ROD's vocals gracing two albums, 'TRUTH' (1968) and 'BECK-OLA' (1969). While still a member of the JEFF BECK GROUP, STEWART signed a solo deal with 'Phonogram', debuting with 'AN OLD RAINCOAT WON'T EVER LET YOU DOWN' in early 1970 (US title, 'THE ROD STEWART ALBUM'). The record was a revelation, the years of practice finally coming together with STEWART rasping his way through a rootsy solo blueprint of folk, country, blues and R&B. Rapidly establishing himself as one of the finest white soul vocalists in the history of rock, STEWART's voice was a unique, compelling combination of bourbon-throated abrasiveness and blue-eyed crooning, equally at home on choice cover material (EWAN MacCOLL's 'Dirty Old Town' and MIKE D'ABO's 'Handbags And Gladrags') as his own brilliant originals, highlights being the gritty 'CINDY'S LAMENT' and the title track. Simultaneously, ROD had joined The FACES (formerly The SMALL FACES) along with RON WOOD, the pair forming the central writing core of the band as they grew from a laddish club act into stadium headliners, WOOD also becoming STEWART's right-hand writing partner through the pioneering early years of the singer's solo career. 'GASOLINE ALLEY' (1970) was a FACES album in all but name, if a bit more downbeat, WOOD, RONNIE LANE and KENNY JONES (IAN McLAGAN absent due to a 'bus strike', apparently!) all playing on a record which launched STEWART in the States (Top 30) and musically, was a companion piece to The FACES' acclaimed 'A Nod Is As Good As A Wink To A Blind Horse' (1971). Kicking in with the plaintive slide guitar moan and emotive reverie of the title track through a cover of ELTON JOHN's 'Country Comfort' and STEWART's own 'LADY DAY', the album also featured the first of his DYLAN cover versions, a sympathetic reading of 'ONLY A HOBO'. With the amplified acoustic double whammy of the 'MAGGIE MAY' / 'REASON TO BELIEVE' single in summer '71, ROD went from critical darling to international superstar overnight, the attendant transatlantic No.1 album, 'EVERY PICTURE TELLS A STORY' (1971) representing the creative pinnacle of his career. Featuring regular contributors such as guitarist, MARTIN QUITTENTON alongside the likes of DANNY THOMPSON and Scot, MAGGIE BELL, the album was a masterclass in roots rock boasting one of his most perfectly conceived originals in the lovely 'MANDOLIN WIND'. The choice of cover material was, as ever, impeccable, STEWART cutting a dash through ARTHUR CRUDUP's 'That's All Right' (a track originally made famous by ELVIS PRESLEY) and wringing a pathos from TIM HARDIN's aforementioned 'Reason To Believe' which even its doomed composer couldn't muster. 'NEVER A DULL MOMENT' (1972) was almost as good, the record taking STEWART's boisterous-lad-with-a-senstitive-side persona to its ultimate conclusion by interspersing a trio of worldly-wise rockers (including the classic 'TRUE BLUE') with a beautiful cover of BOB DYLAN's 'Mama You Been On My Mind', the record also spawning another UK No.1 single with 'YOU WEAR IT WELL'.

By 1974, The FACES were buckling under the pressure of STEWART's massive successful solo career although, ironically, this also began to slide inexorably downhill, creatively at least, with the disappointing 'SMILER' set. This was the sound of ROD going through the motions, only 'LOCHINVAR' and 'DIXIE TOOT' approaching previous standards. Worse was to come though, as STEWART jacked in London for America, hooking up with sex bomb actress, Britt Ekland and effecting one of the most extensive and needless musical turnarounds of the 70's. Many rock artists have been accused of 'selling-out' over the years but few managed it with such thoroughness and dearth of integrity. 'ATLANTIC CROSSING' (1975) and 'A NIGHT ON THE TOWN' (1976) had their moments (a cover of DANNY WHITTEN's 'I Don't Want To Talk About It' on the former and a definitive reading of CAT STEVEN's 'The First Cut Is The Deepest' on the latter), although danger signs were on the horizon. While the engaging ballad, 'THE KILLING OF GEORGIE' saw ROD acknowledging his sizeable gay following and the lilting 'TONIGHT'S THE NIGHT' (both major hits from 'A NIGHT . . .') proved ROD could still pen a decent love song, such tasteless nonsense as 'HOT LEGS' and 'D'YA THINK I'M SEXY' saw the singer living his sexist image up to the full as well as indulging his growing passion for pseudo-disco MOR. Predictably, by the release of 'BLONDES HAVE MORE FUN' (1978), STEWART was enjoying more success in America than his home country, the singer trawling a creative trough in the early 80's with the likes of 'FOOLISH BEHAVIOUR' and 'TONIGHT I'M YOURS'.

His sales figures remained relatively undiminished however, STEWART enjoying the life of the rock aristocrat, his string of relationships with high profile blondes never far from the gossip columns. Tellingly, the singer's best work of the decade came via a reunion with JEFF BECK, the pair getting together for a brilliant reworking of CURTIS MAYFIELD's 'People Get Ready' (Top 50).

The 90's saw STEWART regain at least some critical ground with 'VAGABOND HEART' (1991) while the obligatory 'UNPLUGGED . . . AND SEATED' (1993) saw an entertaining reunion with WOOD. Bizarrely enough, ROD has also exhibited a penchant for covering songs by arch weirdo, TOM WAITS, the latest of which, 'HANG ON ST. CHRISTOPHER', appeared on 'A SPANNER IN THE WORKS' (1995). While this alone signals that STEWART hasn't completely lost the musical plot, the prospect of him ever returning to the downhome brilliance of old looked slimmer with each passing year. However, 1998 saw Rod The Mod turn in a fine batch of covers (bar one of his own) under the title of 'WHEN WE WERE THE NEW BOYS'. At the tender age of 56, ROD crossed over to 'Atlantic' records although things didn't get off to a flyer when the single, 'RUN BACK INTO YOUR ARMS', flopped. However, 'I CAN'T DENY IT' restored the man to the Top 30 and secured a Top 10 spot for his umpteenth set, 'HUMAN' (2001). Moving to an Americanised blend of R&B-pop (BABYFACE and EN VOGUE might've been his template), ROD suffered a backlash of sorts from the critics who thought his previous set was a step forward.

• **Songwriters:** ROD's cover versions:- STREET FIGHTING MAN (Rolling Stones) + RUBY TUESDAY / SWEET SOUL MUSIC (Arthur Conley) / I KNOW I'M LOSING YOU (Temptations) / IT'S ALL OVER NOW (Valentinos) / MY WAY OF GIVING (Small Faces) / CUT ACROSS SHORTY (hit; Eddie Cochran) / ANGEL (Jimi Hendrix) / AMAZING GRACE (trad. / hit; Judy Collins) / I'D RATHER GO BLIND (Etta James) / ONLY A HOBO + SWEETHEART LIKE YOU (Bob Dylan) / TWISTIN' THE NIGHT AWAY + BRING IT ON HOME TO ME + YOU SEND ME + HAVING A PARTY + SOOTHE ME (Sam Cooke) / OH NO NOT MY BABY + PRETTY FLAMINGO (Manfred Mann) / COUNTRY COMFORTS + YOUR SONG (Elton John) / WHAT MADE MILWALKEE FAMOUS (hit; Jerry Lee Lewis) / SAILING (Sutherland Brothers) / THIS OLD HEART OF MINE (Isley Brothers) / GET BACK (Beatles) / YOU KEEP ME HANGIN' ON (Supremes) / I DON'T WANT TO TALK ABOUT IT (Crazy Horse member Danny Whitten) / SOME GUYS HAVE ALL THE LUCK (Robert Palmer) / HOW LONG (Ace) / SWEET LITTLE ROCK'N'ROLLER + LITTLE QUEENIE (Chuck Berry) / THE GREAT PRETENDER (Platters) / ALL RIGHT NOW (Free) / TRY A LITTLE TENDERNESS (Otis Redding) / THE MOTOWN SONG (L.J.McNally) / IT TAKES TWO (Marvin Gaye & Tammi Terrell) / DOWNTOWN TRAIN + TOM TRAUBERT'S BLUES (Tom Waits) / BROKEN ARROW (Robbie Robertson) / HAVE I TOLD YOU LATELY THAT I LOVE YOU (Van Morrison) / PEOPLE GET READY (Curtis Mayfield) / SHOTGUN WEDDING (Roy C) / WINDY TOWN (Chris Rea) / DOWNTOWN LIGHTS (Blue Nile) / LEAVE VIRGINIA ALONE (Tom Petty) / OOH LA LA (with The Faces) / CIGARETTES & ALCOHOL (Oasis) / ROCKS (Primal Scream) / SUPERSTAR (Superstar) / SECRET HEART (Ron Sexsmith) / HOTEL CHAMBERMAID (Graham Parker) / SHELLY MY LOVE (Nick Lowe) / WEAK (Skunk Anansie) / WHAT DO YOU WANT ME TO DO (Mike Scott). SIMON CLIMIE began writing for him from 1988. YOU'RE THE STAR single written by Livesey, Lyle & Miller.

• **Trivia/Blondeography:** BRITT EKLAND (marriage 5 Mar'75-1978) / ALANA HAMILTON (marriage 1979-1984) / KELLY EMBERG (1985-1990) / RACHEL HUNTER (marriage 1990-1999).

ROD STEWART – vocals with session people

Decca — Press

Oct 64. (7") *(F 11996)* **GOOD MORNING LITTLE SCHOOLGIRL. / I'M GONNA MOVE TO THE OUTSKIRTS OF TOWN** [ ] [ ]
(re-iss. Mar82)

—— in 1965, ROD joined STEAMPACKET but they issued no 45's; split Mar'66

Columbia — not iss.

Nov 65. (7") *(DB 7766)* **THE DAY WILL COME. / WHY DOES IT GO ON** [ ] [-]

Apr 66. (7") *(DB 7892)* **SHAKE. / I JUST GOT SOME** [ ] [-]

—— A month previous, he had joined SHOTGUN EXPRESS who released one 45, 'I COULD FEEL THE WHOLE WORLD TURN AROUND' Oct66 on 'Columbia'.

Immediate — not iss.

Nov 67. (7") *(IM 060)* **LITTLE MISS UNDERSTOOD. / SO MUCH TO SAY** [ ] [-]
(re-iss. Sep80 on 'Virgin') (re-iss. Feb83)

—— In 1968, he joined JEFF BECK GROUP, appearing on 2 albums; 'TRUTH' & 'BECK-OLA'. Similtaneously joined The FACES and returned to solo work 1969.

Vertigo — Mercury

Feb 70. (lp) *(VO 4) <61237>* **AN OLD RAINCOAT WON'T EVER LET YOU DOWN** <US-title 'THE ROD STEWART ALBUM'> [ ] [ ]
– Street fighting man / Man of constant sorrow / Blind prayer / Handbags and gladrags / An old raincoat won't ever let you down / I wouldn't ever change a thing / Cindy's lament / Dirty old town. *(re-iss. Aug83 on 'Mercury' lp/c; PRICE/PRIMC 27) (cd-iss. Nov87 & Sep95; 830 572-2) (cd re-iss. Aug98; 558058-2)*

Feb 70. (7") *<73009>* **AN OLD RAINCOAT WON'T LET YOU DOWN. / STREET FIGHTING MAN** [-] [ ]

May 70. (7") *(73031)* **HANDBAGS AND GLADRAGS. / MAN OF CONSTANT SORROW** [-] [ ]
<re-iss. Feb72; *73031*> – hit No.42.

Sep 70. (7") *(6086 002) <73095>* **IT'S ALL OVER NOW. / JO'S LAMENT** [ ] [ ]

Sep 70. (lp) *(6360 500) <61264>* **GASOLINE ALLEY** [62] [27] Jun70
– Gasoline alley / It's all over now / My way of giving / Country comfort / Cut across Shorty / Lady day / Jo's lament / I don't want to discuss it. *(re-iss. Aug83 on 'Mercury' lp/c; PRICE/PRIMC 28) (cd-iss. Oct84 + Sep95; 824 881-2) (cd re-iss. Aug98; 558059-2)*

Nov 70. (7") *<73115>* **GASOLINE ALLEY. / ONLY A HOBO** [-] [ ]

Jan 71. (7") *<73156>* **CUT ACROSS SHORTY. / GASOLINE ALLEY** [-] [ ]

Mar 71. (7") *<73175>* **MY WAY OF GIVING. /** [-] [ ]

May 71. (7") *<73196>* **COUNTRY COMFORT. / GASOLINE ALLEY** [-] [ ]

Mercury — Mercury

Jul 71. (7") *(6052 097) <73224>* **MAGGIE MAY. / REASON TO BELIEVE** [1] [1]
[19] [62]

—— (above was flipped over for BBC Radio One playlist. MAGGIE MAY was now the bigger played hit) *(re-iss. Oct84)*

Jul 71. (lp) *(6338 063) <609>* **EVERY PICTURE TELLS A STORY** [1] [1] Jun71
– Every picture tells a story / Seems like a long time / That's all right / Tomorrow is such a long time / Amazing Grace / Henry / Maggie May / Mandolin wind / (I know) I'm losing you / Reason to believe. *(re-iss. May83 lp/c; PRICE/PRIMC 15) (cd-iss. Nov87 & Sep95; 822 385-2) (cd re-iss. Aug98; 558060-2)*

Nov 71. (7") *<73244>* **(I KNOW) I'M LOSING YOU. / MANDOLIN WIND** [-] [24]

Jul 72. (lp) *(6499 153) <646>* **NEVER A DULL MOMENT** [1] [2]
– True blue / Lost Paraguayos / Mama you been on my mind / Italian girls / Angel / Interludings / You wear it well / I'd rather go blind / Twisting the night away. *(re-iss. May83 lp/c;) (cd-iss. Nov87 & Sep95; 826 263-2) (cd re-iss. Aug98; 558061-2)*

Aug 72. (7") *(6052 171)* **YOU WEAR IT WELL. / LOST PARAGUAYOS** [1] [-]

Aug 72. (7") *<73330>* **YOU WEAR IT WELL. / TRUE BLUE** [-] [13]

—— Sep72, a ROD STEWART early recording with PYTHON LEE JACKSON; 'In A Broken Dream' hits UK No.3 / US No.56.

Nov 72. (7") *(6052 198)* **ANGEL. / WHAT MADE MILWAUKEE FAMOUS (HAS MADE A LOSER OUT OF ME)** [4] [-]

Nov 72. (7") *<73344>* **ANGEL. / LOST PARAGUAYOS** [-] [40]

—— May73, older JEFF BECK & ROD STEWART recording 'I'VE BEEN DRINKIN' ' hit 27.

Aug 73. (7") *<73412>* **TWISTING THE NIGHT AWAY. / TRUE BLUE – LADY DAY** [-] [59]

Aug 73. (lp)(c) *(6499 484)(7142 183) <680>* **SING IT AGAIN ROD** (compilation of covers) [1] [31] Jul73
– Reason to believe / You wear it well / Mandolin wind / Country comforts / Maggie May / Handbags and gladrags / Street fighting man / Twisting the night away / Lost Paraguayos / (I know) I'm losing you / Pinball wizard / Gasoline alley. *(cd-iss. Oct84; 824882-2) (cd re-iss. Aug98; 558062-2)*

Aug 73. (7") *(6052 371) <73426>* **OH! NO NOT MY BABY. / JODIE** [6] [59] Oct73

Sep 74. (7") *(6167 033)* **FAREWELL. / BRING IT ON HOME TO ME – YOU SEND ME (Medley)** [7] [-]

Oct 74. (lp)(c) *(9104 001) <1017>* **SMILER** [1] [13]
– Sweet little rock'n'roller / Lochinvar / Farewell / Sailor / Bring it on home to me – You send me (medley) / Let me be your car / A natural man / A natural man / Dixie toot / Hard road / I've grown accustomed to her face / Girl of the North Country / Mine for me. *(cd-iss. Nov87 & Sep95; 832 056-2) (cd re-iss. Aug98; 558063-2)*

Nov 74. (7") *<73636>* **MINE FOR ME. / FAREWELL** [-] [91]

Jan 75. (7") *<73660>* **LET ME BE YOUR CAR. / SAILOR** [-] [ ]

Warners — Warners

Aug 75. (7") *(K 16600)* **SAILING. / STONE COLD SOBER** [1] [-]
(re-activated Sep76, hit UK No.3, re-iss. Jan84) (re-iss. Jun77 on 'Riva') (re-iss. Mar87 for Channel Ferry disaster fund, hit No.41)

Aug 75. (lp/c) *(K/K4 56151) <2875>* **ATLANTIC CROSSING** [1] [9]
– Three time loser / Alright for an hour / All in the name of rock'n'roll / Drift away / Stone cold sober / I don't want to talk about it / It's not the spotlight / This old heart of mine / Still love you / Sailing. *(re-iss. Jan78 on 'Riva' lp/c; RV LP/4 4) (cd-iss. Feb87; K2 56151) (blue-lp Jul77) (cd re-iss. Nov00 on 'WEA'; 9362 47729-2)*

Aug 75. (7") *<8146>* **SAILING. / ALL IN THE NAME OF ROCK'N'ROLL** [-] [58]

Riva Warners

Nov 75. (7") *(1)* **THIS OLD HEART OF MINE. / ALL IN THE NAME OF ROCK'N'ROLL** [4] [-]

Jan 76. (7") *<8170>* **THIS OLD HEART OF MINE. / STILL LOVE YOU** [-] [83]

May 76. (7") *(RIVA 3)* **TONIGHT'S THE NIGHT. / THE BALLTRAP** [5] [-]

Jun 76. (lp/c) *(RV LP/4 1) <2938>* **A NIGHT ON THE TOWN** [1] [2]
– Tonight's the night / The first cut is the deepest / Fool for you / The killing of Georgie (part 1 & 2) / The balltrap / Pretty flamingo / Big bayou / The wild side of life / Trade winds. *(re-iss. Jun83 on 'Warner Bros' lp/c; K/K4 56234) (cd-iss. 1989 on 'WEA'; K2 56234) (cd re-iss. Jun93; 7599 27339-2) (cd re-iss. Nov00 on 'WEA'; 9362 47730-2)*

Aug 76. (7") *(RIVA 4)* **THE KILLING OF GEORGIE. / FOOL FOR YOU** [2] [-]

Sep 76. (7") *<8262>* **TONIGHT'S THE NIGHT. / FOOL FOR YOU** [-] [1]

Nov 76. (7") *(RIVA 6)* **GET BACK. / TRADE WINDS** [11] [-]

Feb 77. (7") *<8321>* **THE FIRST CUT IS THE DEEPEST. / THE BALLTRAP** [-] [21]

Apr 77. (7") *(RIVA 7)* **THE FIRST CUT IS THE DEEPEST. / I DON'T WANT TO TALK ABOUT IT** [1] [-]

Apr 77. (7") *<8396>* **THE KILLING OF GEORGIE. / ROSIE** [-] [30]

Oct 77. (7") *(RIVA 11) <8476>* **YOU'RE IN MY HEART. / YOU GOT A NERVE** [3] [4]

Nov 77. (lp/c) *(RV LP/4 5) <3092>* **FOOT LOOSE AND FANCY FREE** [3] [2]
– Hot legs / You're insane / You're in my heart / Born loose / You keep me hangin' on / (If loving you is wrong) I don't want to be right / You got a nerve / I was only joking. *(re-iss. Jun83 on 'Warner Bros.' lp/c; K/K4 56423) (cd-iss. Jun89; K2 56423) (cd re-iss. Nov00 on 'WEA'; 9362 47731-2)*

Jan 78. (7") *(RIVA 10)* **HOT LEGS. / I WAS ONLY JOKING** [5] [-]

Feb 78. (7") *<8535>* **HOT LEGS. / YOU'RE INSANE** [-] [28]

Apr 78. (7") *<8568>* **I WAS ONLY JOKING. / BORN LOOSE** [-] [22]

May 78. (7"; by ROD STEWART with the SCOTLAND WORLD CUP SQUAD) *(RIVA 15)* **OLE OLA (MUHLER BRASILEIRA). / I'D WALK A MILLION MILES FOR ONE OF YOUR GOALS** [4] [-]

Nov 78. (7") *(RIVA 17)* **D'YA THINK I'M SEXY?. / DIRTY WEEKEND** [1] [-]

Dec 78. (7") *<8734>* **D'YA THINK I'M SEXY?. / SCARRED AND SCARED** [-] [1]

Dec 78. (lp/c)<US-pic-lp> *(RV LP/4 8) <3261>* **BLONDES HAVE MORE FUN** [3] [1]
– D'ya think I'm sexy / Dirty weekend / Ain't love a bitch / The best days of my life / Is that the thanks I get / Attractive female wanted / Blondes (have more fun) / Last summer / Standing in the shadows of love / Scarred and scared. *(re-iss. Jun83 on 'Warner Bros.' lp/c; K/K4 56572) (cd-iss. Jan91 on 'Warners'; 7599 27376-2) (cd re-iss. Nov00 on 'WEA'; 9362 47732-2)*

Jan 79. (7") *(RIVA 18)* **AIN'T LOVE A BITCH. / SCARRED AND SCARED** [11] [-]

Apr 79. (7") *<8810>* **AIN'T LOVE A BITCH. / LAST SUMMER** [-] [22]

Apr 79. (7") *(RIVA 19)* **BLONDES (HAVE MORE FUN). / THE BEST DAYS OF MY LIFE** [63] [-]

Nov 79. (lp/c) *(RODTV/+4 1) <3373>* **GREATEST HITS VOLUME 1** (compilation) [1] [22]
– Hot legs / Maggie May / a ya think I'm sexy / You're in my heart / Sailing / I don't want to talk about it / Tonight's the night / The killing of Georgie (parts 1 & 2) / Maggie May / The first cut is the deepest / I was only joking. *(re-iss. Jun83 lp/c; K/K4 56744) (cd-iss. Jan84 on 'Warner Bros.'; K2 56744)*

Dec 79. (7") *<49138>* **I DON'T WANT TO TALK ABOUT IT. / THE BEST DAYS OF MY LIFE** [-] [46]

May 80. (7") *(RIVA 23)* **IF LOVING YOU IS WRONG (I DON'T WANT TO BE RIGHT). / LAST SUMMER** [23] [-]

Nov 80. (7"/ext.12") *(RIVA 26/+T) <49617>* **PASSION. / BETTER OFF DEAD** [17] [5]

Nov 80. (lp/c) *(RV LP/4 11) <3485>* **FOOLISH BEHAVIOR** [4] [12]
– Better off dead / Foolish behaviour / My girl / She won't dance with me / Gi' me wings / So soon we change / Somebody special / Passion / Say it ain't true / Oh God, I wish I was home tonight. *(re-iss. Jun83 on 'Warner Bros.' lp/c; >)*

Dec 80. (7") *(RIVA 28)* **MY GIRL. / SHE WON'T DANCE WITH ME** [32] [-]

Mar 81. (7"/c-s) *(RIVA 29/+M)* **OH GOD, I WISH I WAS HOME TONIGHT. / SOMEBODY SPECIAL** [ ] [-]

Mar 81. (7") *<49686>* **SOMEBODY SPECIAL. / SHE WON'T DANCE WITH ME** [-] [71]

Oct 81. (7") *<49843>* **YOUNG TURKS. / SONNY** [-] [5]

Oct 81. (7") *(RIVA 33)* **TONIGHT I'M YOURS (DON'T HURT ME). / SONNY** [8] [-]

Nov 81. (lp/c) *(RV LP/4 14) <3602>* **TONIGHT I'M YOURS** [8] [11]
– Tonight I'm yours (don't hurt me) / Only a boy / Just like a woman / How long / Never give up on a dream / Jealous / Tora, Tora, Tora (out with the boys) / Young Turks / Tear it up / Sonny. *(re-iss. Jun83 lp/c; K/K4 56951) (cd-iss. Jun93 on 'Warners'; 7599 23602-2) (cd re-iss. Nov00 on 'WEA'; 9362 47717-2)*

Dec 81. (7") *(RIVA 34)* **YOUNG TURKS. / TORA, TORA, TORA (OUT WITH THE BOYS)** [11] [-]

Jan 82. (7") *<49886>* **TONIGHT I'M YOURS (DON'T HURT ME). / TORA, TORA, TORA (OUT WITH THE BOYS)** [-] [20]

Feb 82. (7") *(RIVA 35) <50051>* **HOW LONG. / JEALOUS** [41] [49] Apr82

Nov 82. (d-lp/d-c) *(RV LP/4 17) <23743>* **ABSOLUTELY LIVE (live)** [35] [46]
– The stripper / Tonight I'm yours / Sweet little rock'n'roller / Hot legs / Tonight's the night / The great pretender / Passion / She won't dance with me / Little Queenie / You're in my heart / Rock my plimsoul / Young Turks / Guess I'll always love you / Gasoline alley / Maggie May / Tear it up / D'ya think I'm sexy / Sailing / I don't want to talk about it / Stay with me. *(re-iss. Mar84 on 'Warner Bros.' d-lp/dc; 923743-1/-4) (cd-iss. Mar87; 923743-2)*

Nov 82. (7") *<29874>* **GUESS I'LL ALWAYS LOVE YOU (live). / ROCK MY PLIMSOUL (live)** [-] [ ]

Warners Warners

May 83. (7") *(W 9608) <29608>* **BABY JANE. / READY NOW** [1] [14]
(12"+=) *(W 9608T)* – If loving you is wrong (live).

Jun 83. (lp/c) *(K 923977-1/-4) <23877>* **BODY WISHES** [5] [30]
– Dancin' alone / Baby Jane / Move me / Body wishes / Sweet surrender / What am I gonna do / Ghetto blaster / Ready now / Strangers again / Satisfied. *(cd-iss. Jul84; K 923977-2)*

Aug 83. (7"/12") *(W 9564/+T) <29564>* **WHAT AM I GONNA DO?. / DANCIN' ALONE** [3] [35]

Dec 83. (7"/67"pic-d) *(W 9440/+P)* **SWEET SURRENDER. / GHETTO BLASTER** [23] [-]
(12"+=) *(W 9440T)* – Oh God I wish I was home tonight.

May 84. (7") *<29256>* **INFATUATION. / SHE WON'T DANCE WITH ME** [-] [6]

May 84. (7") *(W 9256)* **INFATUATION. / THREE TIME LOSER** [27] [-]
(12"+=) *(W 9256T)* – Tonight's the night.

Jun 84. (lp/c/cd) *(925095-1/-4/-4) <25095>* **CAMOUFLAGE** [8] [18]
– Infatuation / All right now / Some guys have all the luck / Can we still be friends / Bad for you / Heart is on the line / Camouflage / Trouble. *(free 1-sided 7"pic-d w.a.)* – INFATUATION / (interview).

Jul 84. (7") *(W 9204) <29215>* **SOME GUYS HAVE ALL THE LUCK. / I WAS ONLY JOKING** [15] [10]
(12"+=) *(W 9204T)* – The killing of Georgie.

Nov 84. (7") *(W 9115)* **TROUBLE. / TORA, TORA, TORA (OUT WITH THE BOYS)** [ ] [-]
(12"+=) *(W 9115T)* – This old heart of mine.

Dec 84. (7") *<29112>* **ALL RIGHT NOW. / DANCIN' ALONE** [-] [72]

— In 1985, he was credited on 45 'PEOPLE GET READY' by JEFF BECK.

Jun 86. (7") *(W 8668) <28668>* **LOVE TOUCH. / HEART IS ON THE LINE** [27] [6] May86
(12"pic-d+=) *(W 8668TP)* – Hard lesson to learn.

Jun 86. (lp/c)(cd) *(WX 53/+C)(925446-2) <25446>* **EVERY BEAT OF MY HEART** <US-title 'ROD STEWART'> [5] [28]
– Here to eternity / Another heartache / A night like this / Who's gonna take me home / Red hot in black / Love touch / In my own crazy way / Every beat of my heart / Ten days of rain / In my life. *(cd+=)* – Every beat of my heart (remix).

Jul 86. (7") *(W 8625) <28625>* **EVERY BEAT OF MY HEART. / TROUBLE** [2] [83] Nov86
(12"+=) *(W 8625)* – ('A'mix).
(12"pic-d+=) *(W 8625TE)* – Some guys have all the luck (live)

Sep 86. (7") *(W 8631) <28631>* **ANOTHER HEARTACHE. / YOU'RE IN MY HEART** [54] [52]
(12"+=) *(W 8631T)* – ('A'extended).

Jul 87. (7") *<28303>* **TWISTING THE NIGHT AWAY. / LET'S GET SMALL** [-] [80]
above was issued on 'Geffen' and on film 'Innerspace'.

May 88. (7")<US-c-s> *(W 7927) <27927>* **LOST IN YOU. / ALMOST ILLEGAL** [21] [12]
(12"+=/12"pic-d+=) *(W 7927 T/TP)* – ('A'extended).
(cd-s+=) *(W 7927CD)* – Baby Jane / Every beat of my heart.

May 88. (lp/c)(cd) *(WX 152/+C)(925684-2) <25684>* **OUT OF ORDER** [11] [20]
– Lost in you / The wild horse / Lethal dose of love / Forever young / My heart can't tell you no / Dynamite / Nobody loves you when you're down and out / Crazy about her / Try a little tenderness / When I was your man.

Jul 88. (7") *(W 7796) <27796>* **FOREVER YOUNG. / DAYS OF RAGE** [57] [12]
(12"+=) *(W 7796)* – ('A'extended).
(cd-s+=) *(W 7796CD)* – Every beat of my heart.

Jan 89. (7") **TRY A LITTLE TENDERNESS. / MY HEART CAN'T TELL YOU NO** [-] [ ]

Apr 89. (7") *(W 7729) <27729>* **MY HEART CAN'T TELL YOU NO. / THE WILD HORSE** [49] [4] Nov88
(12"+=/12"pic-d+=/cd-s+=) *(W 7729 T/TP/CD)* – Passion (live).

May 89. (7"/c-s) *<27657>* **CRAZY ABOUT HER. / DYNAMITE** [-] [11]

Nov 89. (7"/7"pic-d/c-s; with RONALD ISLEY) *(W 2686/+P) <19983>* **THIS OLD HEART OF MINE. / TONIGHT I'M YOURS (DON'T HURT ME)** [51] [-]
(12"+=/cd-s+=/12"pic-d+=) *(W 2686 T/TP/CD)* – Ain't love a bitch.

Nov 89. (d-lp/d-c/d-cd) *(925987-2/-4/-1) <25987>* **STORYTELLER – THE BEST OF ROD STEWART 1964-1990** (compilation) [3] [54]

— (was also issued UK on (7xlp)(4xc)(4xcd).

Jan 90. (7"/c-s) *(W 2647/+C) <22685>* **DOWNTOWN TRAIN. / THE KILLING OF GEORGIE (pt.1 & 2)** [10] [3] Nov89
(12"/cd-s) *(W 2647 T/CD)* – ('A'side) / Hot legs.

(12"+=) *(W 2647TE)* – ('A'side) / Cindy incidentally / To love somebody.
Mar 90. (7"; with RONALD ISLEY) *<19983>* **THIS OLD HEART OF MINE. / YOU'RE IN MY HEART** – 10
Mar 90. (cd/c) *<26158>* **DOWNTOWN TRAIN – SELECTIONS FROM STORYTELLER** (compilation) – 20
Nov 90. (7"/c-s; ROD STEWART & TINA TURNER) *(ROD 1/+C)* **IT TAKES TWO. / HOT LEGS (live)** 5
(12"+=/cd-s+=) *(ROD 1 T/CD)* – ('A'extended remix).
Mar 91. (7"/c-s) *(W 0017) <19366>* **RHYTHM OF MY HEART. / MOMENT OF GLORY** 3 5 Feb91
(12"+=/cd-s+=) *(W 0017 T/CD)* – I don't want to talk about it (re-recording).
Apr 91. (cd)(lp/c) *(<7599 26596-2>)(WX 408/+C)* **VAGABOND HEART** 2 10
– Rhythm of my heart / Rebel heart / Broken arrow / It takes two / When a man's in love / You are everything / The Motown song / Go out dancing / No holding back / Have I told you lately that I love you / Moment of glory / Downtown train / If only.
Jun 91. (7"/c-s) *(W 0030/+C) <19322>* **THE MOTOWN SONG. / SWEET SOUL MUSIC (live)** 10 10
(12"+=/cd-s+=) *(W 0030 T/CD)* – Try a little tenderness.
Aug 91. (7"/c-s) *(W 0059/+C)* **BROKEN ARROW. / I WAS ONLY JOKING** 54 –
(10"+=/cd-s+=) *(W 0059 T/CD)* – The killing of Georgie (parts 1 & 2).
Oct 91. (c-s,cd-s) *<19274>* **BROKEN ARROW / THE WILD HORSE** – 20
Apr 92. (c-s,cd-s) *<865944>* **YOUR SONG / MANDOLIN WIND** – 48
— <above issued on 'Polydor' US>
Apr 92. (7"/c-s) *(W 0104/+C)* **YOUR SONG. / BROKEN ARROW** 41 –
(12"+=/cd-s+=) *(W 0104 T/CD)* – Mandolin wind / The first cut is the deepest.
Nov 92. (7"/c-s) *(W 0104/+C)* **TOM TRAUBERT'S BLUES (WALTZING MATILDA). / NO HOLDING BACK** 6 –
(cd-s+=) *(W 0104CD)* – Downtown train.
(cd-s) *(W 0104CDX)* – ('A'side) / Sailing / I don't want to talk about it / Try a little tenderness.
Feb 93. (cd/c/lp) *(<9362 45258-2>)(WX 503/+C)* **ROD STEWART, LEAD VOCALIST** (part compilation) 3 –
– I ain't superstitious / Handbags & gladrags / Cindy incidentally / Stay with me / True blue / Sweet Mary lady / Hot legs / Stand back / Ruby Tuesday / Shotgun wedding / First I look at the purse / Tom Traubert's blues.
Feb 93. (7"/c-s) *(W 0158/+C)* **RUBY TUESDAY. / YOU'RE IN MY HEART** 11 –
(cd-s+=) *(W 0158CD)* – Out of order / Passion.
(cd-s+=) *(W 0158CDX)* – Crazy about her / Passion.
Apr 93. (7"/c-s) *(W 0171/+C)* **SHOTGUN WEDDING. / EVERY BEAT OF MY HEART** 21 –
(cd-s+=) *(W 0171CD)* – Sweet soul music (live).
(cd-s) *(W 0171CDX)* – ('A'side) / Memphis / Maybe I'm amazed / Had me a real goodtime (all 3 by ROD STEWART & THE FACES).
below with special guest **RONNIE WOOD** – guitar plus others **JEFF GOLUB** – guitar / **CARMINE ROJAS** – bass / **CHARLES KENTISS III** – piano, organ / **KEVIN SAVIGAR** – piano, organ & accordion / **JIM CREGAN** – guitar / **DON TESCHNER** – guitar, violin & mandolin / **PHIL PARLAPIANO** – accordion & mandolin / & backing singers
May 93. (cd/c/lp) *(<9362 45289-2/-4/-1>)* **UNPLUGGED . . . AND SEATED (live)** 2 2
– Hot legs / Tonight's the night / Handbags and gladrags / Cut across Shorty / Every picture tells a story / Maggie May / Reason to believe / People get ready / Have I told you lately / Tom Traubert's blues (waltzing Matilda) / The first cut is the deepest / Mandolin wind / Highgate shuffle / Stay with me / Having a party.
Jun 93. (7"/c-s) *(W 0185/+C) <18511>* **HAVE I TOLD YOU LATELY THAT I LOVE YOU? / GASOLINE ALLEY** 5 5 Apr93
(cd-s+=) *(W 0185CD)* –
(cd-s) *(W 0185CDX)* – ('A'side) / Love wars / One night.
Aug 93. (7"/c-s) *(W 0198/+C) <18427>* **REASON TO BELIEVE (unplugged). / IT'S ALL OVER NOW (unplugged)** 51 19
(cd-s+=) *(W 0198CD1)* – Love in the right hands.
(cd-s) *(W 0198CD2)* – ('A'side) / Cindy incidentally / Stay with me (both w / FACES).
— In Dec '93, ROD & STING, teamed up with BRYAN ADAMS on his US Top 5 hit 'All For Love'.
Dec 93. (7"/c-s) *(W 0226/+C)* **PEOPLE GET READY. / I WAS ONLY JOKING** 45 –
(cd-s) *(W 0226CD1)* – ('A'side) / Tonight's the night / If loving you is wrong (I don't want to be right).
(cd-s) *(W 0226CD2)* – ('A'side) / Da ya think I'm sexy / Sweet little rock'n'roller (live) / Baby Jane.
— Late '93, ROD, BRYAN ADAMS and STING teamed up on a song from 'The Three Musketeers' film; 'ALL FOR LOVE', which hit UK No.2 (early '94) + US No.1.
Dec 93. (c-s,cd-s; ROD STEWART with RONNIE WOOD) *<18427>* **HAVING A PARTY (live unplugged) / SWEET LITTLE ROCK AND ROLLER (live acoustic)** – 36
May 95. (c-s) *(W 0296C)* **YOU'RE THE STAR / SHOCK TO THE SYSTEM** 19 –
(cd-s+=) *(W 0296CD)* – Have I told you lately.
May 95. (cd/c/lp) *(<9362 45867-2/-4/-1>)* **A SPANNER IN THE WORKS** 4 35
– Windy town / Downtown lights / Leave Virginia alone / Sweetheart like you / This / Lady luck / You're the star / Muddy, Sam and Otis / Hang on St. Christopher / Delicious / Soothe me / Purple heather.
Jun 95. (c-s,cd-s) *<17847>* **LEAVE VIRGINIA ALONE / SHOCK TO THE SYSTEM** – 52
Aug 95. (c-s) *(W 0310C)* **LADY LUCK / HOT LEGS** 56 –
(cd-s+=) *(W 0310CD1)* – The groom still waiting at the altar / Young Turks.
(cd-s) *(W 0310CD2)* – ('A'side) / The killing of Georgie / Sailing / The first cut is the deepest.
Jun 96. (c-s/cd-s) *(W 0354 C/CD)* **PURPLE HEATHER / EVERY BEAT OF MY HEART** 16
— The official song for Scotland's Euro '96 football campaign. All proceeds were donated to the families of the Dunblane tragedy.
Nov 96. (cd/c) *(<9362 46467-2/-4>)* **IF WE FALL IN LOVE TONIGHT** 8 19
– If we fall in love tonight / Sometimes when we touch / I don't want to talk about it / For the first time / When I need you / Broken arrow / Have I told you lately / Tonight / Forever young / My heart can't tell you no / First cut is the deepest / Tonight's the night / You're in my heart.
Dec 96. (c-s) *(W 0380C) <17459>* **IF WE FALL IN LOVE TONIGHT / TOM TRAUBERT'S BLUES (WALTZING MATILDA)** 58 54 Nov96
(cd-s) *(W 0380CD)* – ('A'side) / So far away / I was only joking / Ten days of rain.
— N-TRANCE featured ROD on their version of 'DA YA THINK I'M SEXY?', which hit UK No.7 in Nov'97.
May 98. (c-s) *(W 0446C) <17195>* **OOH LA LA / A NIGHT LIKE THIS** 16 39 Jun98
(cd-s+=) *(W 0446CD)* – Ten days of rain.
Jun 98. (cd/c) *(<9362 46792-2/-4>)* **WHEN WE WERE THE NEW BOYS** 2 44
– Cigarettes and alcohol / Ooh la la / Rocks / Superstar / Secret heart / Hotel chambermaid / Shelly my love / When we were the new boys / Weak / What do you want me to do?
Aug 98. (c-s) *(W 0452C)* **ROCKS / STAY WITH ME (live)** 55 –
(cd-s+=) *(W 0452CD2)* – Maggie May (live).
(cd-s) *(W 0452CD1)* – ('A'side) / Hot legs (live) / Da ya think I'm sexy? (live).
Dec 98. (c-s/cd-s; w-drawn) *(W 465 C/CD)* **SUPERSTAR** – –

Universal **not iss.**

Apr 99. (c-s) *(UNC 56235)* **FAITH OF THE HEART / Mark Shainman: MAIN TITLE SCORE** 60 –
(cd-s+=) *(UND 56235)* – Front porch.

Atlantic **Atlantic**

Oct 00. (c-s) *(AT 0088C)* **RUN BACK INTO YOUR ARMS / WHEN WE WERE THE NEW BOYS** –
(cd-s+=) *(AT 0088CD)* – Red hot and black.
Mar 01. (c-s) *(AT 0096C) <85018>* **I CAN'T DENY IT / PEACH** 26 –
(cd-s+=) *(AT 0096CD)* – Do wah diddy.
Mar 01. (cd/c) *(<7567 83411-2/-4>)* **HUMAN** 9 50 Feb01
– Human / Smitten / Don't come around here / Soul on soul / Loveless / If I had you / Charlie Parker loves me / It was love that we needed / To be with you / Run back into your arms / I can't deny it. *(UK+=)* – Doo wah diddy (if you want me to go) / Peach.
May 01. (c-s; as ROD STEWART & HELICOPTER GIRL) *(AT 0104C)* **DON'T COME AROUND HERE / CUPID** –
(cd-s+=) *(AT 0104CD)* – Charlie Parker loves me.

– compilations, etc. –

Sep 72. (7"; by PYTHON LEE JACKSON) *Youngblood; (YB 1017) / GNP Crescendo; <449>* **IN A BROKEN DREAM. / THE BLUES** 3 56
(re-iss. Jul80 /12"+=) – Cloud 9. *(re-iss. Aug87 as "PYTHON LEE JACKSON / ROD STEWART" on 'Bold Reprieve')*
— PYTHON LEE JACKSON was in fact an Australian 5-piece of the late 60s, headed by keyboard player **DAVID BENTLEY**, who employed ROD to sing on 3 tracks from their lp 'IN A BROKEN DREAM'.
1979. (7") *Lightning;* **IN A BROKEN DREAM. / IF THE WORLD STOPS STILL TONIGHT** –
Below releases on 'Mercury' until otherwise mentioned.
Feb 76. (d-lp/c) *(6672 013)* **THE VINTAGE YEARS 1969-70**
Feb 76. (7") *(6086 02)* **IT'S ALL OVER NOW. / HANDBAGS AND GLADRAGS** –
1976. (7") **EVERY PICTURE TELLS A STORY. / WHAT MADE MILWAUKEE FAMOUS (HAS MADE A LOSER OUT OF ME)** –
Jul 76. (lp/c) **RECORDED HIGHLIGHTS AND ACTION REPLAYS**
Jun 77. (7"m) *(6160 007)* **MANDOLIN WIND. / GIRL FROM THE NORTH COUNTRY / SWEET LITTLE ROCK'N'ROLLER** –
Jun 77. (d-lp)(d-c) *(6643 030)(7599 141) <7507>* **THE BEST OF ROD STEWART** 18 90
(re-iss. Sep85 lp/c; PRID/+C 10)
Jul 77. (c) *(714506-1)* **THE MUSIC OF ROD STEWART (1970-71)** –
Aug 77. (d-lp/d-c) *(661903-1/-4)* **THE BEST OF ROD STEWART VOLUME 2**
Dec 78. (lp) *St.Michael;* **REASON TO BELIEVE** –
Nov 79. (7") *(6160 006)* **MAGGIE MAY. / YOU WEAR IT WELL** –
(re-iss. Apr88 on 'Old Gold';)

Sep 80. (lp) *(646306-1)* **HOT RODS** [ ] [-]
May 81. (lp) *(927913-2)* **BEST OF THE BEST** [ ] [-]
Sep 81. (lp/c) *Contour; (CN/+4 2045)* **MAGGIE MAY** [ ] [-]
(cd-iss. Jul90 on 'Pickwick'; PWKS 586)
Oct 82. (lp/c) *Contour; (CN/+4 2059)* **ROD STEWART** [ ] [-]
Jul 83. (d-c) *Cambra;* **ROD STEWART** [ ] [-]
Nov 83. (d-c) *Warners; (923955-2)* **ATLANTIC CROSSING / A NIGHT ON THE TOWN** [ ] [-]
Nov 84. (lp/c) *Astan; (2/4 0119)* **CAN I GET A WITNESS** [ ] [-]
Sep 85. (lp/c) *Contour; (CN/+4 2077)* **THE HITS OF ROD STEWART** [ ] [-]
Jan 87. (lp/c) *Contour; (CN/+4 2082)* **JUKE BOX HEAVEN (14 ROCK'N'ROLL GREATS)** [ ] [-]
Nov 87. (cd) *(925466-2)* **THE ROD STEWART ALBUM** [ ] [-]
Jul 88. (lp/c) *Knight; (KNLP/KNMC 10002)* **NIGHTRIDIN'** [ ] [-]
Feb 89. (c) *Venus; (VENUMC 3)* **THE MAGIC OF ROD STEWART** [ ] [-]
Jun 89. (lp/c/cd) *(830784-1/-4/-2)* **THE ROCK ALBUM** [ ] [-]
Jun 89. (cd) *(830785-2)* **THE BALLAD ALBUM** [ ] [-]
Oct 89. (lp/c/cd) *K-Tel;* **IN A BROKEN DREAM** [ ] [ ] 1988
Feb 91. (cd/c) *(846 988-2/-4)* **GASOLINE ALLEY / SMILER** [ ] [-]
Oct 92. (7"/c-s) **YOU WEAR IT WELL. / I WOULD RATHER GO BLIND** [ ] [ ]
(cd-s+=) – Angel.
Dec 92. (cd/c) *M Classics; (CJES D/C 2)* **JUST A LITTLE MISUNDERSTOOD** [ ] [-]
Feb 93. (cd; ROD STEWART & STEAMPACKET) *Charly;* **THE FIRST SUPER GROUP** [ ] [-]
Jul 93. (cd/c) *Telstar; (CDSR/TCSR 014)* **THE FACE OF THE SIXTIES** [ ] [-]
Jul 94. (cd/c) *Success;* **COME HOME BABY** [ ] [-]
Jan 95. (cd/c) *K-Tel; (ECD3/EMC2 109)* **THE EARLY YEARS** [ ] [-]
Aug 95. (cd/c) *Spectrum; (551110-2/-4)* **MAGGIE MAY – THE CLASSIC YEARS** [ ] [-]
(re-iss. Sep98; same)
Oct 95. (d-cd) *Mercury; (528 823-2)* **HANDBAGS AND GLADRAGS (The Mercury Recordings 1970-1974)** [ ] [-]
May 97. (cd) *Experience; (EXP 030)* **ROD STEWART** [ ] [-]
Jul 97. (cd) *Going For A Song; (GFS 061)* **ROD STEWART** [ ] [-]
Aug 98. (cd) *Mercury; (558873-2)* **THE VERY BEST OF ROD STEWART** [ ] [-]
Oct 99. (cd) *Spectrum; (544165-2)* **REASON TO BELIEVE** [ ] [-]
Jan 00. (cd) *Universal; (E 546836-2)* **UNIVERSAL MASTERS COLLECTION** [ ] [-]
Apr 00. (cd) *A.B.M.; (ABMMCD 1082)* **SHAKE** [ ] [-]
Jul 00. (d-cd+CD-rom) *Burning Airlines; (PILOT 044)* **ROD STEWART 1964-1969** [ ] [-]
(d-lp re-iss. Dec00 on 'Get Back'; GET 578) (re-iss. Nov01; same)
Oct 00. (d-cd) *Universal; (E 536421-2)* **EVERY PICTURE TELLS A STORY / GASOLINE ALLEY** [ ] [-]
Oct 00. (3xcd-box) *Universal; (E 546586-2)* **EVERY PICTURE TELLS A STORY / GASOLINE ALLEY / SMILER** [ ] [-]
Nov 01. (d-cd/d-c) *(8122 73581-2/-4) <78328>* **THE STORY SO FAR – THE VERY BEST OF** [7] [69]
Jun 02. (d-cd; shared w/ ERIC CLAPTON) *Delta Blue; (6305-2)* **WHITE BOY BLUES** [ ] [-]

Barry ST. JOHN (see under ⇒ "A Beat(en) Generation")

STOICS (see under ⇒ "A Beat(en) Generation")

STONE THE CROWS

Formed: Glasgow . . . 1969 as POWER by MAGGIE BELL (ex-FRANKIE & JOHNNY) and LES HARVEY, JOHN McGINNESS, JIM DEWAR and COLIN ALLEN completing the line-up.

The young MAGGIE began her career after getting up on stage to sing with ALEX HARVEY (brother of LES). She received 2 quid for her audacity, although she subsequently augmented (adopted Scot) ROD STEWART on his rasping LP title track, 'Every Picture Tells A Story'. Meanwhile, with legendary LED ZEPPELIN manager, Peter Grant, taking up the reins, the band were renamed STONE THE CROWS, securing a deal with ZEPPELIN's label, 'Atlantic' ('Polydor' in the UK). With the release of two highly acclaimed albums inside a year, 'STONE THE CROWS' and 'ODE TO JOHN LAW' (both 1970), BELL was touted as Scotland's answer to JANIS JOPLIN, her organic, bluesy vocals an essential ingredient in the band's soulful rock stew. Despite the encouraging reception, record sales were poor with both McGINNESS and DEWAR subsequently departing.

New recruits RONNIE LEAHY and STEVE THOMPSON were on board for the recording of 'TEENAGE LICKS' (1972), a record which seemed certain to furnish the band with the success they deserved. It wasn't to be though, the group's momentum stopped in its tracks following the electrocution of LES HARVEY during a live performance in Swansea later that year. JIMMY McCULLOCH was brought in to finish off the sessions for 'ONTINUOUS PERFORMANCE' (1972), an album that finally saw STONE THE CROWS making the UK Top 40. It was too little too late, however, and inevitably, the band packed it in, officially splitting in June '73 as McCULLOCH joined PAUL McCARTNEY & WINGS.

While ALLEN joined FOCUS, BELL released her debut solo set, the Jerry Wexler-produced 'QUEEN OF THE NIGHT', the following year. Despite the visceral power of her voice and the generally high standard of the songwriting, commercial recognition continued to elude her throughout the 70's. She did score a minor Top 40 hit with 'HAZELL', the theme tune from the TV series of the same name, while a one-off collaboration with fellow Scot, B.A. ROBERTSON, almost made the Top 10 with PJ Proby's 'HOLD ME' in 1981. The same year also saw the initiation of the MIDNIGHT FLYER project, an eponmyous album meeting with little success. A further series of singles met with little success, BELL has remained out of the limelight for the bulk of the past two decades.

• **Songwriters:** Group compositions, except DANGER ZONE (Curtis Mayfield) / DON'T THINK TWICE (Bob Dylan) / etc?. MAGGIE covered AFTER MIDNIGHT (JJ Cale) / WISHING WELL (Free) / I SAW HIM STANDING THERE (Beatles) / etc.

MAGGIE BELL (b.12 Jan'45) – vocals (ex-FRANKIE & JOHNNY) / **LES HARVEY** (b.1947) – guitar / **JOHN McGINNISS** – keyboards / **JIM DEWAR** (b.12 Oct'46) – bass / **COLIN ALLEN** – drums

Polydor Polydor

Mar 70. (lp) *(2425 017) <244019>* **STONE THE CROWS** [ ] [ ]
– The touch of your loving hand / Raining in your heart / Blind man / Foot on the hill / I saw America. *(cd-iss. Jan98 on 'Repertoire'; REP 4626)*
Oct 70. (lp) *(2425 042)* **ODE TO JOHN LAW** [ ] [-]
– Sad Mary / Friend / Love 74 / Mad dogs and Englishmen / Things are getting better / Ode to John Law / Danger zone. *(cd-iss. Jan98 on 'Repertoire'; REP 4624)*
Dec 70. (7") *(2066 060)* **MAD DOGS AND ENGLISHMEN. / SAD MARY** [ ] [-]

— **RONNIE LEAHY** – keyboards; repl. McGINNISS / **STEVE THOMPSON** – bass; repl. DEWAR who joined JUDE, then ROBIN TROWER

Jan 72. (lp) *(2425 701) <PD 5020>* **TEENAGE LICKS** [ ] [ ]
– Big Jim Salter / Faces / Mr. Wizard / Don't think twice / Keep on rollin' / Ailen Mochree / One five eight / I may be right I may be wrong / Seven lakes. *(cd-iss. Jan98 & Sep02 on 'Repertoire'; REP 4625)*

— halfway through recording, **JIMMY McCULLOCH** (b.13 Aug'53) – guitar (ex-THUNDERCLAP NEWMAN) repl. LES HARVEY who had been electrocuted by a live microphone on stage

Sep 72. (lp) *(2391 043) <PD 5037>* **'ONTINUOUS PERFORMANCE** [33] [ ]
– On the highway / One more chance / Penicillin blues / King Tut / Good time girl / Niagara / Sunset cowboy. *(cd-iss. Jan98 on 'Repertoire'; REP 4627)*
Oct 72. (7") *(2058 301)* **GOOD TIME GIRL. / ON THE HIGHWAY** [ ] [-]

— split in June '73 when McCULLOCH joined Paul McCARTNEY & WINGS; COLIN ALLEN joined FOCUS – McCULLOCH was to die of an overdose on the 27th of September, 1979; he had had a brief spell with MILLER ANDERSON and RONNIE LEAHY's group, The DUKES

– compilations, etc. –

Oct 76. (lp) *Polydor; (2482 279)* **STONE THE CROWS** [ ] [-]
– Big Jim Salter / Love 74 / Touch of your loving hand / Sad Mary / Good time girl / On the highway / Mr. Wizard / Sunset cowboy / Raining in your heart / Seven lakes. *(re-iss. Jun89 on 'Thunderbolt' lp/cd; THBL/CDTB 070)*
Feb 98. (cd) *Strange Fruit; (SFRSCD 049)* **BBC LIVE IN CONCERT (live)** [ ] [-]
Mar 98. (cd) *Strange Fruit; (SFRSCD 054)* **BBC SESSIONS VOL.1 1969-1970** [ ] [-]
Jul 98. (cd) *Strange Fruit; (SFRSCD 068)* **BBC SESSIONS VOL.2 1970-1971** [ ] [-]
Oct 99. (cd) *Global TV; (RADCD 145)* **THE VERY BEST OF MAGGIE BELL & STONE THE CROWS** [ ] [-]
May 02. (cd) *Angel Air; (SJPCD 116)* **LIVE IN MONTREUX 1972 (live)** [ ] [-]

MAGGIE BELL

— (solo) with session people

Polydor Atlantic

Dec 73. (lp) *(2383 239) <7293>* **QUEEN OF THE NIGHT** [ ] [ ]
– Cado queen / A woman left lonely / Souvenirs / After midnight / Queen of the night / Oh my my / As the years go passing by / Yesterday's music / We had it all / The other side / Trade winds. *(cd-iss. Mar00 on 'Repertoire'; REP 4661)*
Mar 74. (7") *(2058 447)* **OH MY MY. / AS THE YEARS GO PASSING BY** [ ] [-]

Apr 74. (7") **AFTER MIDNIGHT. / SOUVENIRS** [-] [ ]

Polydor Swan Song

Feb 75. (lp) *(2383 313) <SS 8412>* **SUICIDE SAL** [ ] [ ]
– Wishing well / Suicide Sal / I was in chains / If you don't know / What you got / In my life / Comin' on strong / Hold on / I saw him standing there / It's been so long. *(cd-iss. Mar00 & Sep02 on 'Repertoire'; REP 4663)*

Mar 75. (7") **WISHING WELL. / COMIN' ON STRONG** [-] [ ]

Swan Song not iss.

Mar 78. (7") *(K 19412)* **HAZELL. / NIGHT FLIGHTING** [37] [-]
(above from TV series of same name)

MIDNIGHT FLYER

MAGGIE BELL with **JOHN COOK** – keyboards / **ANTHONY GLYNNE** – guitar / **TONE STEVENS** – bass / **DAVID DOWLE** – drums

Swan Song Swan Song

Mar 81. (7") *(K 19423)* **ROUGH TRADE. / MIDNIGHT LOVE** [ ] [ ]
Mar 81. (lp/c) *(SSK/SK4 59412) <8509>* **MIDNIGHT FLYER** [ ] [ ]
– Hey boy / Love games / French kisses / In my eyes / Over and over / Last resort / Do you want my love / Sweet loving woman / Whatever I want / Midnight flyer / Rough trade.
Jun 81. (7") **IN MY EYES. /** [-] [ ]
Apr 82. (7") *(K 19426)* **WAITING FOR YOU. / ROCK'N'ROLL PARTY** [ ] [ ]

MAGGIE BELL

Oct 81. (7"; by B.A. ROBERTSON & MAGGIE BELL) *(BAM 1)* **HOLD ME. / SPRING GREEN** [11] [-]
Sep 82. (7") *(K 19428)* **GOOSE BUMPS. / KEY TO MY HEART** [ ] [ ]
Dec 82. (7") *(MB 1)* **CRAZY. / ALL I HAVE TO DO IS DREAM** [ ] [-]
Mar 83. (7"; as MAGGIE BELL & BOBBY WHITLOCK) **HERE, THERE & EVERYWHERE. / PUT ANGELS AROUND YOU** [-] [ ]

Cult not iss.

1989. (cd) *(2901200-2)* **CRIMES OF THE HEART** [-] [-] German
– Crimes of the heart / Love me stranger / Tonight / Burned out love affair / Endless night / I'm on the edge / Living a lie / Vision.

—— MAGGIE retired from the music business

– compilations, etc. –

Jan 02. (cd) *Angel Air; (SJPCD 100)* **LIVE AT THE RAINBOW 1974 (live)** [ ] [-]

JIMMY McCULLOCH & WHITE LINE

E.M.I. not iss.

Nov 76. (7") *(EMI 2560)* **CALL MY NAME. / TOO MANY LIES** [ ] [-]
below recordings were obviously posthumous
Feb 95. (cd) *Mouse; (MSCD 004)* **THE COMPLETE JIMMY McCULLOCH – WHITE LINE** [ ] [-]

STRING DRIVEN THING

Formed: Glasgow . . . mid-1968 by husband and wife team, CHRIS and PAULINE ADAMS. With percussionist JOHN MANNION in tow, they released a very limited eponymous album, followed by the 1970 single, 'ANOTHER NIGHT'. Moving away from their earlier harmony-driven sound, CHRIS and PAULINE enlisted the help of violinist GRAHAM SMITH and all-rounder COLIN WILSON, delivering another eponymous album in 1972. Now signed to 'Charisma' records, they issued an even better follow-up, 'THE MACHINE THAT CRIED' and lent a hit, 'IT'S A GAME', to tartan popstars The BAY CITY ROLLERS. Astonishingly, the ADAMS subsequently left the band they had formed, GRAHAM SMITH now taking up the reins, complemented by a host of musicians with whom he released a further couple of albums.

CHRIS ADAMS – guitar, vocals / **PAULINE ADAMS** – vocals / **JOHN MANNION** – percussion

Concord not iss.

1970. (ltd-lp) *(CON 1001)* **STRING DRIVEN THING** [ ] [-]
– July morning / Say what you like / Magic garden / Wonderful places / I don't wanna make up / City man / Another night in this old city / That's me lady / Catch as catch can / No more you and I / Lie back and let it happen / One of the lonely people.
Jun 70. (7") *(CON 7)* **ANOTHER NIGHT. / SAY WHAT YOU LIKE** [ ] [-]

—— split but the ADAMS' re-formed early in 1972

—— added **GRAHAM SMITH** – violin / **COLIN WILSON** – bass, guitar, banjo

Charisma Charisma

Sep 72. (lp) *(CAS 1062)* **STRING DRIVEN THING** [ ] [-]
– Circus / Fairground / Hooked on the road / Easy to be free / Jack Diamond / Let me down / Very last blue yodell / My real hero / Regent St incident / Where are you. *(re-iss. Aug76; same) (cd-iss. Aug92 on 'Worldwide';)*
Feb 73. (7") *(CB 203)* **CIRCUS. / MY REAL HERO** [ ] [-]

—— added **BILLY FAIRLEY** – drums, percussion

Sep 73. (7") *(CB 215)* **IT'S A GAME. / ARE YOU A ROCK'N'ROLLER** [ ] [-]
Sep 73. (lp) *(CAS 1070) <6063>* **THE MACHINE THAT CRIED** [ ] [ ]
– Heartfeeder / To see you / Night club / Sold down the river / Two timin' Rama / Travelling / People on the street / The house / The machine that cried / Going down. *(cd-iss. 1990's on 'Repertoire'; REP 4207) (cd re-iss. Jun97 on 'Ozit' official version; OZCD 00021)*
Mar 74. (7") *(CB 223)* **I'LL SING ONE FOR YOU. / TO SEE YOU** [ ] [-]

—— Amazingly the ADAMS' departed from their own group, alongside COLIN and BILLY. This left behind **GRAHAM SMITH** who recruited **ALUN ROBERTS** – guitar, vocals / **KIMBERLEY BEACON** – vocals / **JAMES EXELL** – bass, vocals / **COLIN FAIRLEY** – drums, vocals / **ALAN SKIDMORE** – saxophone / **KENNY ROWE + GRAHAM WHITE** – vocals

Charisma 20th Century

Nov 74. (7") *(CB 239)* **KEEP ON MOVING. / MRS. O'REILLY** [ ] [-]
Dec 74. (lp) *(CAS 1097) <470>* **PLEASE MIND YOUR HEAD** [ ] [ ]
– Overdrive / Without you / Josephine / Mrs. O'Reilly / Man of means / Black eyed queen / Keep on moving / Timpani for the Devil / To know you is to love you.
Feb 75. (7") *(CB 247) <2202>* **OVERDRIVE. / TIMPANI FOR THE DEVIL** [ ] [ ]

—— session man **COLIN WOOD** – piano, repl.SKIDMORE, ROWE + WHITE

Jan 76. (lp) *(CAS 1112) <503>* **KEEP YER 'AND ON IT** [ ] [ ]
– Starving in the tropics / Call out for mercy / Chains / Things we said today / But I do / Old friends / Ways of a woman / Part of it / Stand back in amazement.
Feb 76. (7") *(CB 276)* **BUT I DO. / STAND BACK IN AMAZEMENT** [ ] [-]
Sep 76. (7") *(CB 286)* **CRUEL TO FOOL. / JOSEPHINE** [ ] [-]
Oct 76. (7") *<2300>* **CRUEL TO FOOL. / SAIL AWAY** [-] [ ]

—— split after SMITH joined VAN DER GRAAF GENERATOR + PETER HAMMILL; he later emigrated to Iceland until a reformation in the mid-90's

Terrapin Truckin not iss.

Jul 95. (cd) *(TRUCKCD 023)* **SUICIDE LIVE BERLIN '94 (live)** [ ] [-]
– Let me down / Night club / Two timin' rama / Suicide / To see you / Dreams into dust / My real hero / Circus / Park circus / You miss me / The road goes on. *(cd-iss. Jun97 on 'Ozit'; OZCD 00018)*

– compilations, etc. –

Aug 92. (cd) *S.P.M.; (WWR 0038)* **DI$CHOTOMY – THE RARITIES 1971-1974** [ ] [-]
(re-iss. Mar02; same)
Apr 98. (cd) *Ozit; (OZITCD 0022)* **STUDIO 1972-1973 / LONDON 1995** [ ] [-]
Mar 02. (cd) *S.P.M.; (WWR 0069)* **LIVE IN MANCHESTER** [ ] [-]

Hamish STUART

Born: 8 Oct'49, Glasgow. A key member of Scots funksters The AVERAGE WHITE BAND, HAMISH provided that unmistakable falsetto which blessed such hits as 'Queen Of My Soul' and 'Let's Go Round Again'. He also made a major songwriting contribution and was a talented guitarist into the bargain, going on to work with some of the biggest names in soul including ARETHA FRANKLIN and DIANA ROSS. The Glaswegian's skill as a songsmith was also to benefit CHAKA KHAN who charted in the US (1981) with the STUART-penned 'WHAT CHA' GONNA DO FOR ME'.

Although he'd played alongside many different artists after AWB's 1982 split, it wasn't until 1987 that the man worked on his own pet project. A cosmopolitan supergroup of sorts, EASY PIECES was a collaborative effort with former AWB English drummer STEVE FERRONE, Chicago-born keyboard player DAVID "HAWK" WOLINSKI and Australian songstress RENEE GEYER, the quartet releasing a solo eponymous album. STUART's CV was further enhanced with an extended stint in PAUL McCARTNEY's band, the former BEATLES man enlisting HAMISH for the recording of his late 80's set, 'Flowers In The Dirt'.

STUART eventually got round to forming a solo band proper, becoming a perennially popular live act (especially in London where he established a sell-out residency) and releasing a belated solo set, 'SOONER OR LATER' (1999). Much like AWB themselves (whose late 80's reformation STUART was ironically absent from), the man continues to guarantee a sterling concert experience, more often than not with a little help from old friends.

HAMISH STUART – vocals, guitar / **STEVE PEARCE** – bass / **ADAM PHILIPS** – guitar, vocals / **ANDY WALLACE** – keyboards / **SNAKE DAVIS** – flute, saxophones / **IAN THOMAS** – drums / **JODY LINSCOTT** – percussion

Sulphur Compass

Jun 99. (cd) *(SUCCD 001) <4291>* **SOONER OR LATER** [ ] [ ] Apr00
– Sooner / Makin' it up / It is what it is / Care for you / I don't wanna be a rock / La land / Or / Reach you / New kind of fool / The same old moon / Once there was love / Midnight rush / Later / She is my lady.

STUDIO SIX (see under ⇒ "A Beat(en) Generation")

Stuart SUTCLIFFE

Born: 23 Jun'40, Edinburgh. STU, as he was known to his friends, is ensured a place in Rock'n'roll history as the mysterious 5th member of The BEATLES. For virtually the whole of 1960, SUTCLIFFE was on bass duties alongside LENNON, McCARTNEY, HARRISON and STARR (the latter replacing PETE BEST during this brief spell), as they played their famous Hamburg residency. After meeting and falling in love with a native art student, Astrid Kirchherr, he opted to quit the band and remain behind in Germany. Subsequently attending art college himself, STU had designs on becoming a serious painter; by all accounts he certainly had the potential, although he was cruelly struck down in his prime by a fatal brain haemorrhage. He died in his girlfriend's arms on the 10th of April, 1962, aged only 21.

Although many films were made about the Fab Four, there was little documentation about their early SUTCLIFFE-era career until 1994's 'Backbeat'. Completed partly as a result of the unprecedented interest in The BEATLES during the 90's, the film was accompanied by a book of the same name, co-authored by STU's sister, Pauline. She also collaborated with Kay Williams on an extensive pictorial and biographical compendium of STU's life entitled simply, 'Stuart'.

SUTHERLAND BROTHERS

Born: IAIN, c.1948, and GAVIN, c.1950, Peterhead, Aberdeenshire, sons of violinist GEORGE SUTHERLAND who was also leader of a jazz/swing dance band just after the second world war. In the late 50's, their dad uprooted the family to a town in Staffordshire, although the Scots lads were always encouraged to bring out their musical side.

The teenage brothers soon learned to play guitar and by the mid-60's, both were performing frequently in IAIN's school band. In 1967, the now multi-talented IAIN and GAVIN formed Midlands-based pop/rock quartet A NEW GENERATION who had a UK Top 40 hit in 1968 with 'SMOKEY BLUES AWAY'. In 1971, after making little headway, IAIN and GAVIN moved to London where they subsequently obtained a publishing deal from Chris Blackwell at 'Island' records. The SUTHERLAND BROTHERS (albeit complete with Island session men) were re-born into the music business via a self-penned, self-titled debut set early in '72, an easy-going harmony-friendly record that opening with single, 'THE PIE'. A second attempt at the pop charts surprisingly fell on deaf ears, their smooth version of 'SAILING' (later a massive No.1 for ROD STEWART) surely top of a large list of ones-that-got-away. Subsequently lifted from their second LP that year, 'LIFEBOAT', it marked the end of the SUTHERLAND BROTHERS Mk.1.

In 1973, the 'BROTHERS teamed up with London-based quartet, QUIVER (aka TIM RENWICK, BRUCE THOMAS, PETE WOODS and WILLIE WILSON), who'd already delivered a couple of albums for 'Warners'. The newly-billed SUTHERLAND BROTHERS AND QUIVER hit paydirt almost immediately, but not in Britain. The single '(I DON'T WANT TO LOVE YOU BUT) YOU GOT ME ANYWAY' reached the Top 50 in America, where a re-vamped 'LIFEBOAT' was promoted via a support slot to ELTON JOHN. Further albums for 'Island', 'DREAM KID' (1973) and 'BEAT OF THE STREET' (1974) were well-written affairs but did nothing to give the group their deserved UK breakthrough. An inspired move to 'C.B.S.' records in 1975 and plaudits for their contribution to ROD The Mod's Atlantic Crossing, gave the SUTHERLAND's some recognition, although that big hit still eluded them. This was put to right early in '76, when the smoochy 'ARMS OF MARY' hit the UK Top 5, a track taken from eventual Top 30 parent LP, 'REACH FOR THE SKY' (1975).

The following two years saw a few minor hits and two further SB&Q albums, 'SLIPSTREAM' (1976) and 'DOWN TO EARTH' (1977), but these were of little significance next to a population only buying Punk or Disco. It was inevitable that there would be a parting of the waves for QUIVER and the SUTHERLAND BROTHERS, although IAIN and GAVIN carried on with their AOR duo until the early 80's; the former would subsequently go solo.

A NEW GENERATION

IAIN SUTHERLAND – vocals, guitar, piano, harmonica / **GAVIN SUTHERLAND** – vocals, guitar, steel guitar, percussion / **CHRISTOPHER KEMP** – organ, vocals / **JOHN WRIGHT** – drums

Spark not iss.

Feb 68. (7") *(SRL 1000)* **SADIE AND HER MAGIC MISTER GARLAND. / DIGGER** [ ] [-]
May 68. (7") *(SRL 1007)* **SMOKEY BLUES AWAY. / SHE'S A SOLDIER BOY** [38] [-]
1970. (7") *(SRL 1019)* **POLICE IS HERE. / MISTER C** [ ] [-]

SUTHERLAND BROTHERS

IAIN + GAVIN recruited **KIM LUDMAN** – bass / **NEIL HOPWOOD** – drums, percussion

Island Island

Jan 72. (7") *(WIP 6120)* **THE PIE. / LONG LONG DAY** [ ] [-]
Feb 72. (lp) *(ILPS 9181) <9315>* **THE SUTHERLAND BROTHERS** [ ] [ ]
– The pie / Sleeping dog / Hallelujah / I was in chains / Medium wave / Big brother / War of roses / Midnight avenue / Sunny Street W14 / Where in the world / Long long day. *(re-iss. Nov77 on 'CBS'; 82297)*

— KIM + NEIL repl. by **JOHN 'RABBIT' BUNDRICK + JOHN HAWKEN + STEVE WINWOOD** – keyboards / **PAT DONALDSON + BOB RONGA** – bass / **DAVE MATTACKS** – drums

Aug 72. (7") *(WIP 6136)* **SAILING. / WHO'S CRYING NOW** [ ] [-]
Nov 72. (lp) *(ILPS 9212)* **LIFEBOAT** [ ] [-]
– Lady like you / Lifeboat / Where do we go wrong / Ireland / All I got is you / Space hymn / Change the wind / Sailing / Love is my religion / Real love. *(re-iss. Nov77 on 'CBS'; 82298)*
Nov 72. (7") *(WIP 6147)* **LADY LIKE YOU. / ANNIE** [ ] [-]

SUTHERLAND BROTHERS AND QUIVER

IAIN, GAVIN, TIM, WILLIE, BRUCE / + PETE WOOD – keyboards

Island Island

Feb 73. (7") *(WIP 6157)* **(I DON'T WANT TO LOVE YOU BUT) YOU GOT ME ANYWAY. / NOT FADE AWAY** [ ] [-]
Jul 73. (7") *<1217>* **(I DON'T WANT TO LOVE YOU BUT) YOU GOT ME ANYWAY. / ROCK AND ROLL SHOW** [-] [48]
Jul 73. (lp) *<9326>* **LIFEBOAT** [-] [77]
– (I don't want to love you but) You got me anyway / Lifeboat / Where do we go wrong / Space hymn / Change the wind / Sailing / Real love / Have you had a vision / Not fade away / Rock and roll show.
Dec 73. (lp) *(ILPS 9259) <9341>* **DREAM KID** [ ] [ ] Apr74
– You and me / I hear thunder / Flying down to Rio / Seagull – Lonely love / Champion the underdog / Bluesy world / Bad loser / Dream kid / Maker / Rollin' away – Rocky road – Saved by the angel.
Jan 74. (7") *(WIP 6182)* **DREAM KID. / DON'T MESS UP** [ ] [-]

— **TEX COMER** – bass, repl. BRUCE who later joined ELVIS COSTELLO

Nov 74. (7") *(WIP 6209)* **SAVIOUR IN THE RAIN. / SILVER SISTER** [ ] [-]
Dec 74. (lp) *(ILPS 9288)* **BEAT OF THE STREET** [ ] [-]
– World in action / Saviour in the rain / Devil are you satisfied / Bone dry / Beat of the street / Laid back in anger / Hi life music / Living in love / Annie / Last boy over the Moon. *(re-iss. Nov77 on 'CBS'; 82300)*

— now without WOOD + COMER

C.B.S. Columbia

Nov 75. (7") *(CBS 3769)* **AIN'T TOO PROUD. / MAD TRAIL** [ ] [-]
Nov 75. (lp/c) *(CBS/40 69191) <33982>* **REACH FOR THE SKY** [ ] [ ]
– When the train comes / Dirty city / Arms of Mary / Something special / Love on the Moon / Ain't too proud / Dr.Dancer / Reach for the sky / Moonlight lady / Mad trail. *(re-dist.May76 UK/US, hit UK No.26) (re-iss. Jun85 lp/c; CBS/40 32665) (cd-iss. Sep93 on 'Sony Collectors'; 983284-2) (cd re-iss. May95 on 'Columbia'; 480526-2)*
Mar 76. (7") *(CBS 4001) <10284>* **ARMS OF MARY. / WE GET ALONG** [5] [81]
Jun 76. (7") *(CBS 4336)* **WHEN THE TRAIN COMES. / LOVE ON THE MOON** [ ] [ ]

— added **ALBHY GALUTEN** – keyboards / **FLACO PADRON** – percussion

Sep 76. (lp/c) *(CBS/40 81593) <34376>* **SLIPSTREAM** [49] [ ]
– Slipstream / Wild love / Saturday night / If I could have your loving / Love on the side / Secrets / Dark powers / Something's burning / Sweet cousin / Midnight rendezvous / The prisoner / High nights.
Oct 76. (7") *(CBS 4668)* **SECRETS. / SOMETHING'S BURNING** [35] [ ]
Jan 77. (7") *(CBS 4934)* **IF I COULD HAVE YOUR LOVING. / MIDNIGHT RENDEZVOUS** [ ] [ ]

— **GALUTEN + PADRON** repl. by **MICK GRABHAM** – guitar / **ANDY PYLE + RICK WILLS** – bass / **JOHN SHEARER + BRIAN BENNETT** – percussion

Aug 77. (7") *(CBS 5563)* **ICE IN THE FIRE. / WHERE LIES YOUR SOUL** [ ] [-]
Sep 77. (lp) *(CBS 82255)* **DOWN TO EARTH** [ ] [-]
– Ice in the fire / Dark ship / Harbour light / Somebody's fool / Fun on the farm / Every tear I cry / Situations / Oh woman / Rock'n'roll people / Where lies your soul.
Nov 77. (7") *(CBS 5818)* **EVERY TEAR I CRY. / ROCK'N'ROLL PEOPLE** [ ] [-]

— the SUTHERLAND's split with QUIVER early 1978

SUTHERLAND BROTHERS

— now with **RITCHIE ZITO** – guitar / **WILLIAM D. SMITH** – keyboards / **BOB GLAUB** – bass / **MIKE BAIRD** – drums

Mar 78. (7") *(CBS 6226)* **ONE MORE NIGHT WITH YOU. / SUNBIRD** [ ] [-]
Jul 78. (7") *(CBS 6453)* **SOMEBODY'S FOOL. / SAILING** [ ] [-]
May 79. (7") *(CBS 7121)* **EASY COME EASY GO. / SHIP ON THE ROCKS** [50] [-]
May 79. (lp/c) *(CBS/40 83427)* **WHEN THE NIGHT COMES DOWN** [ ] [-]
– Natural thing / Have you ever been hurt / First love / Easy come easy go / As long as I've got you / I'm going home / When the night comes down / Dreams of you / Cruisin' / On the rocks / Crazy town.
Jul 79. (7") *(CBS 7746)* **AS LONG AS I'VE GOT YOU. / I'M GOING HOME** [ ] [-]
Oct 79. (7") *(CBS 7915)* **FIRST LOVE. / CRAZY TOWN** [ ] [-]

R.C.A. not iss.

Oct 81. (7") *(RCA 110)* **WHEN WILL I BE LOVED. / LOVE SICK** [ ] [-]

— split again after above

– compilations, etc. –

Jun 76. (lp) *Island; (ILPS 9358)* **SAILING** [ ] [-]
Apr 84. (7") *Old Gold; (OG 9402)* **ARMS OF MARY. / SECRETS** [ ] [-]
May 02. (cd) *Sony; (507709-2)* **THE VERY BEST OF THE SUTHERLAND BROTHERS** [ ] [-]
– The Pie / I was in chains / Real love / Sailing / You got me anyway / Lifeboat / Dream kid / Champion the underdog / Beat of the street / Laid back in anger / When the train comes / Arms of Mary / Dr. Dancer / Love on the moon / Moonlight lady / Slipstream / Secrets / Something's burning / When the night comes down / Easy come easy go.

IAIN SUTHERLAND

with **GAVIN / + DAVE MATTACKS** – drums / **PHIL PALMER** – guitar / **MICK WEAVER** – keyboards / **CHRIS STEWART** – bass / **ANDY RICHARDS** – synths / **JOHN EARL** – sax

Avatar not iss.

Sep 83. (lp) *(AVAL 4)* **MIXED EMOTIONS** [ ] [-]
– The wheel / Affairs of the heart / It coulda been Buddy Holly / Pictures of England / Night people / Lost and blind / Mixed emotions / New ways to kill the dragon / Waiting for the one / Blaze of glory.
Sep 83. (7") *(AVAT 5)* **IT COULDA BEEN BUDDY HOLLY. / DYNAMO** [ ] [-]
Feb 84. (7") *(AVAT 9)* **THE WHEEL. / FAITES VOS JEUX** [ ] [-]

— with **GAVIN + DAVE + TIM / + DAVE McGARRY** – keyboards / **DICK MORRISSEY** – sax

Metrognome not iss.

1985. (lp) *(827498-1)* **LEARNING TO DANCE** [-] [-] German
– Reunion / The last to know / The science of saying goodbye / Learning to dance / All my love is gone / Promised land / Love in a cold climate / She really makes the sparks fly / There goes another dream / Traveller.

GAVIN SUTHERLAND

Corazong not iss.

Mar 01. (cd) *(2000 005)* **DIAMONDS AND GOLD** [ ] [-]

SYNANTHESIA
(see under ⇒ "A Beat(en) Generation")

T

TEAR GAS

Formed: Glasgow . . . late 1968 out of the loud and soulful BO WEEVILS by guitarist ZAL CLEMINSON and bassist CHRIS GLEN.

Initially billing themselves MUSTARD, they also had in their ever-evolving ranks former POETS singer ANDI MULVEY, ex-MANDRAKE ROOT drummer WILLIE MONROE (who replaced brief-stay future SQUEEZE member, GILSON LAVIS) and ex-BEATSTALKERS keyboards player, EDDIE CAMPBELL. The latter would subsequently make way for another BO WEEVIL, DAVEY BATCHELOR when the quartet (without the departing MULVEY and CAMPBELL) changed to the more appropriate moniker, TEAR GAS. Aggressive and hostile were two of the adjectives best attributed to this psychedelic/prog-cum-heavy outfit, although trying to sound louder than DEEP PURPLE or LED ZEPPELIN was hard to do around the toilet circuits of Scotland's central belt.

However, it was at one of those aforementioned gigs that A&R man, Tony Calder (once sidekick of Andrew Loog Oldham), found them rocking the socks off their audience. Calder gave TEAR GAS the break they needed. He signed CLEMINSON and Co to his new 'Famous' label and took them south to London to record their debut set, 'PIGGY GO-BETTER' (1970). Shortly after its release however, around the same time as the band inked a major deal with 'Regal Zonophone', BATCHELOR bailed out; MUNROE too, would follow his path. The brothers McKENNA (HUGH on keyboards and TED on drums) were drafted in at short notice to complete their eponymous sophomore effort in late summer '71. Early the following year, 37 year-old Blues rocker/veteran, ALEX HARVEY, was introduced to the young TEAR GAS by his management. Within days, the Vambo man had invited all four to become part of his SENSATIONAL ALEX HARVEY BAND and the rest – as they say – was history.

DAVEY BATCHELOR – vocals, keyboards / **ZAL CLEMINSON** (b. ALASDAIR, 4 May'49) – guitar / **CHRIS GLEN** (b. 6 Nov'50, Paisley) – bass, vocals / **WILLIE MUNROE** – drums

Famous Paramount

Oct 70. (lp) *(SFMA 5751)* *<PAS 5029>* **PIGGY GO-BETTER** [ ] [ ]
– Lost awakening / Your woman's gone and left you / Night girl / Nothing can change your mind / Living for today / Big house / Mirrors of sorrow / Look what else is happenin' / I'm fallin' far behind / Witches come today.

— **TED McKENNA** (b.10 Mar'50) – drums, repl. MUNROE

— **HUGH McKENNA** (b.28 Nov'49) – keyboards, repl. BATCHELOR

Regal Zonophone not iss.

Aug 71. (lp) *(SLRZ 1021)* **TEAR GAS** [ ] [-]
– That's what's real / Love story / Lay it on me / Woman for sale / I'm glad / Where is my answer / Jailhouse rock / All shook up / First time.

— disbanded when they joined The SENSATIONAL ALEX HARVEY BAND

Dougie THOMSON

Born: 24 Mar'51, Glasgow. Cutting his teeth with the ALAN BOWN SET in the early 70's, bassman DOUGIE took up the vacant position (left by FRANK FARRELL) with top English outfit, SUPERTRAMP. In 1974, the much-lawded but previously unsuccessful group recorded and released the 'CRIME OF THE CENTURY' set. An excellent piece of work, it marked the turning point of SUPERTRAMP's career making both the British and American charts. 'CRISIS? WHAT CRISIS' (1975), 'EVEN IN THE QUIETEST MOMENTS' (1977) and the superb 'BREAKFAST IN AMERICA' (1979), all made the group a stack of cash, but by the late 80's SUPERTRAMP were finished. Mainman RICHARD DAVIES re-formed the band in the mid-90's, although he opted not to recall DOUGIE.

THREE'S A CROWD
(see under ⇒ "A Beat(en) Generation")

TRASH

Formed: Glasgow . . . mid-60's (out of the QUINTONES) as The PATHFINDERS by IAN CRAWFORD-CLEWS and NEIL McCORMACK. RONALD LEAHY, TIMI DONALD and COLIN HUNTER-MORRISON would add their weight to the Tamla-esque outfit (these PATHFINDERS were not to be confused with Merseyside namesakes on 'Decca' or indeed a Kent outfit on 'Hayton' records who issued a record each a year before this bunch took off).

In November '65 (and after ex-POETS man FRASER WATSON stepped in for the ill McCORMACK – he would become their manager!) the quintet released a one-off solo single, 'DON'T YOU BELIEVE IT', its failure to reach the British charts having little effect on their ever-growing teenage audience. However by 1967-68, Glasgow was becoming an increasing tribal war zone for local gangs such as the Tongs, the Bundy and the Toi, resulting in venues being shut down (some permanently!). A change was needed and after a brief spell as JASON'S FLOCK, the band ventured south to London via a proposition/deal with TONY MEEHAN (ex-SHADOWS). 'Apple' (the label founded by the BEATLES) took a liking to their version of Carole King's 'ROAD TO NOWHERE' and immediately instructed MEEHAN to release it, although one thing had to be changed and The PATHFINDERS became WHITE TRASH. However, this intervention backfired when the BBC shunned the aforementioned 7" (Enoch Powell's "river of blood" speech had just been aired early '69) and by the time the WHITE part had been omitted from the offending record, all momentum had been lost; CLEWSY's effective screeching over a barrage of sound ensuring this was certainly one-that-got-away.

However, the now hippie-like TRASH (without the departing COLIN) waited around for another opportunity and this arrived via press officer Derek Taylor, who had "borrowed" the BEATLES' acetate for their 'Abbey Road' album setting up some studio time to record 'GOLDEN SLUMBERS – CARRY THAT WEIGHT'. McCARTNEY and LENNON disagreed over its release and although it became a Top 40 hit, its sales were slightly affected by 'E.M.I.' (Apple's distributor!) issuing a version of the song by ORANGE BICYCLE. Lucky white heather was certainly never dished out to TRASH and after a spell backing US soul-rock singer MARSHA HUNT (at the Isle Of Wight festival in front of thousands!) the PATHFINDERS or (WHITE) TRASH were systematically binned by their label; LEAHY would be the only one to achieve a certain amount of Rock credibility when he joined STONE THE CROWS. An offshoot of TRASH were indeed CODY, who managed to release one countrified, CSN&Y-styled 45, 'I BELONG WITH YOU'.

PATHFINDERS

IAN CRAWFORD-CLEWS – vocals / **FRASER WATSON** – lead guitar (ex-POETS) repl. NEIL McCORMACK who became their manager after becoming ill / **RONALD LEAHY** – organ / **COLIN HUNTER-MORRISON** – bass / **TIMI DONALD** – drums

	Parlophone	not iss.
Nov 65. (7") *(R 5372)* **DON'T YOU BELIEVE IT. / CASTLE OF LOVE**		-

TRASH

— same line-up as The PATHFINDERS

	Apple	Apple
Feb 69. (7") *(APPLE 6)* **ROAD TO NOWHERE. / ILLUSIONS**		-
— (initially copies of above credited to WHITE TRASH)		
— now without HUNTER-MORRISON		
Oct 69. (7") *(APPLE 17)* **GOLDEN SLUMBERS – CARRY THAT WEIGHT. / TRASH CAN**	35	
— they changed their moniker in early 1970		

CODY

CLEWS, DONALD + LEAHY recruited **IAN McMILLAN + NORRIE McKENZIE**

	Polydor	not iss.
1970. (7") *(2058 100)* **I BELONG WITH YOU. / WANNA MAKE YOU HAPPY**		-

— after the group finally disbanded, LEAHY moved into production and joined STONE THE CROWS (subsequently with ALVIN LEE and JACK BRUCE) while DONALD joined BLUE – CLEWS went to work with horses in Arizona

Len TUCKEY

Born: 15 Dec'47, Aberdeen. Moving south to London, the tall and beefy guitarist joined the backing band of American glam star SUZI QUATRO in 1973 and during her most fruitful time – with smash hits such as 'CAN THE CAN', 'DEVILGATE DRIVE' and '48 CRASH' – married the petite singer. After raising a couple of children, Laura and Richard, they decided to divorce in the early 90's.

VIKINGS (see under ⇒ Alp records)

Gordon WALLER

Born: 4 Jun'45, Braemar. Sent to Westminster Boys public school, the privileged son of a doctor subsequently teamed up with former school chum PETER ASHER to form the aptly-titled pop duo PETER AND GORDON. The teenagers immediately established themselves in the Spring of 1964 when the PAUL McCARTNEY-penned 'A WORLD WITHOUT LOVE' topped the UK chart – PAUL was dating PETER's sister JANE at the time. Six more major hits completed a fruitful mid-60's period, the last of these being the novelty, 'LADY GODIVA' in Autumn '66. A split the following year led WALLER into solo work, although all his attempts – with singles 'ROSENCRANS BOULEVARD' etc – failed to get him back into the spotlight. In May '72, the singer/songwriter returned with a solo album on the spiralling cult imprint 'Vertigo' (once home to BLACK SABBATH!), although both critics and public alike shunned the work completely. Taking up farming, GORDON settled down to this new way of life, only briefly getting back into showbusiness via a short-lived stint (c.1976) in the musical, 'Joseph & His Amazing Technicolour Dreamcoat'.

GORDON WALLER – vocals, acoustic guitar (ex-PETER AND GORDON) / with session people

	Columbia	not iss.
Jan 68. (7") *(DB 8337)* **ROSENCRANS BOULEVARD. / RED, CREAM AND VELVET**		-
Jun 68. (7") *(DB 8440)* **EVERY DAY. / BECAUSE OF A WOMAN**		-
Dec 68. (7") *(DB 8518)* **WEEPING ANNALEAH. / THE SEVENTH HOUR**		-
	Bell	**not iss.**
Apr 69. (7") *(BLL 1059)* **I WAS A BOY WHEN YOU NEEDED A MAN. / LADY IN THE WINDOW**		-
May 70. (7") *(BLL 1106)* **YOU'RE GONNA HURT YOURSELF. / SUNSHINE**		-
	Vertigo	**A.B.C.**
May 72. (lp) *(6360 069)* <ABCX 749> **GORDON**		

– The saddest song / I won't be your ruin / At the end of the day / Before you go to sleep / Where this whole thing began / Rocky road to clear / Be careful, there's a baby in the house / Stranger with a black dove / Collection box.

— GORDON retired to his farm, although he did appear in the soundtrack the first production of 'Joseph And The Amazing Technicolour Dreamcoat'.

Andy WHITE

Born: 1930, Glasgow. Not the Irish folk troubadour of the mid-80's but the guy who stood in for a petrified RINGO STARR on the first BEATLES single, 'Love Me Do'. However, it was RINGO's drumming that finally featured on the 1962 hit, while ANDY's stickwork appeared on the 'Please Please Me' album version. Apparently, the session man was paid £11 for his troubles, while the BEATLES went on to make millions. WHITE subsequently worked for TOM JONES, BURT BACHARACH, HERMAN'S HERMITS and JIMMY PAGE. In 2000 he was a music teacher in a New Jersey police bagpipe band.

Tam WHITE

Born: July 1942, Edinburgh. A stonemason to trade, TAM first exercised his formidable vocal chords in The BOSTON DEXTERS, a mid-60's R&B/Soul outfit comprising TAM, JOHNNY TURNBULL, ALAN COVENTRY and TOTO McNAUGHTON. The band released a string of singles before disbanding in late '66, WHITE embarking on a solo career with a further string of singles for 'Decca' – his eponymous debut album for 'Middle Earth' was issued in 1970.

Unable to make a commercial breakthrough, he kept plugging away – occasionally recording under the more Anglo-friendly TOM WHITE – and finally made a bit of headway in the mid-70's with a rare Top 40 hit, 'WHAT IN THE WORLD'S COME OVER YOU'. The latter was released on Mickie Most's 'Rak' label, the famed producer picking WHITE up after judging in his favour in a TV talent contest. Sadly, this proved to be a one-off and after a couple of flop follow-up singles TAM took his leave of the recording studio for more than a decade.

Returning to Scotland, he built up a loyal following with his raw, impassioned blues performances, wowing audiences with a whisky 'n' razorblades voice that was part JOE COCKER, part ERIC CLAPTON and part FRANKIE MILLER. The late ALEXIS KORNER called him "The greatest undiscovered blues talent of our time", no mean praise from a blues curator who himself had a hand in the careers of everyone from The ROLLING STONES to JOHN RENBOURN.

1991 saw the release of 'KEEP IT UNDER YOUR HAT', a live show recorded at Ronnie Scott's in London. The 90's also saw TAM move into acting; he was the voice behind Robbie Coltrane's Big Jazza character in the BAFTA award-winning BBC TV series, 'Tutti Frutti' although a more high profile part came with the box-office blockbuster, 'Braveheart', in which he played a clan chief.

On the gig front, TAM subsequently developed two distinct units to cater to different live environments; TAM WHITE'S SHOESTRING BAND and TAM WHITE'S CELTIC GROOVE CONNECTION. The former comprised WHITE, NEIL WARDEN and FRASER SPIERS, an all-guitar/harmonica trio captured in full flight on 1998's 'REAL DEAL' album, a live set recorded during 1997's Commonwealth Heads Of Government Conference. The 'CONNECTION, meanwhile, is a jazzy big band affair featuring SPIERS, former BAD COMPANY man BOZ BURRELL (who, incidentally, has also worked with ALEXIS KORNER) and Scots jazz maestro BRIAN KELLOCK alongside a host of others. After making its debut at the 1997 Celtic Connections festival in Glasgow, this formation enjoyed a successful residency at the Spiegeltent on Princes Street during the 1998 Festival Fringe. More recently, TAM recorded 'THE CROSSING' (1999), a collaboration with KELLOCK.

• **Covered:** BORN UNDER A BAD SIGN (Booker T. Jones & William Bell) / THIS IS THE WAY WE MAKE A BROKEN HEART (John Hiatt) / EYESIGHT TO THE BLIND (Willie 'Sonny Boy' Williamson) / HOME IS WHERE THE HATRED IS (Gil Scott-Heron).

BOSTON DEXTERS

TAM WHITE – vocals / **JOHNNY TURNBULL** – guitar / **ALAN COVENTRY** – bass / **TOTO McNAUGHTON** – drums

Contemporary — not iss.

1964. (7") *(CR 101)* **LA BAMBA. / MATCHBOX** [ ] [-]
1964. (7") *(CR 102)* **YOU'VE BEEN TALKING ABOUT ME. / NOTHING'S GONNA CHANGE ME** [ ] [-]
1964. (7") *(CR 103)* **I'VE GOT TROUBLES OF MY OWN. / WHAT KIND OF GIRL ARE YOU** [ ] [-]

Columbia — not iss.

Mar 65. (7") *(DB 7498)* **I'VE GOT SOMETHING TO TELL YOU. / I BELIEVE TO MY SOUL** [ ] [-]
Jul 65. (7") *(DB 7641)* **TRY HARD. / NO MORE TEARS** [ ] [-]

—— **WHITE + TURNBULL** recruited **BRIAN HENDERSON** – bass + **MIKE TRAVIS** – drums (McNAUGHTON carried on with the BOSTON DEXTERS name for 9 months and brought in ex-ATHENIANS man ALY BLACK)

Mar 66. (7"; as BUZZ) *(DB 7887)* **YOU'RE HOLDING ME DOWN. / I'VE GOTTA BUZZ** [ ] [-]

—— disbanded late in '66

TAM WHITE

TAM WHITE – vocals, acoustic guitar / + session people

Decca — not iss.

Dec 67. (7"; w-drawn) *(F 12711)* **WORLD WITHOUT YOU. / SOMEONE YOU SHOULD KNOW** [-] [-]
Jan 68. (7") *(F 12723)* **DANCING OUT OF MY HEART. / I'LL STAY LOVING YOU** [ ] [-]
Jul 68. (7") *(F 12803)* **AMY. / BUILDING MY WORLD** [ ] [-]
Nov 68. (7") *(F 12849)* **GIRL WATCHER. / WAITING TILL THE NIGHT COMES ROUND** [ ] [-]
May 69. (7"; w-drawn as TOM WHITE) *(F 12934)* **THAT OLD SWEET ROLL. / DON'T MAKE PROMISES** [-] [-]

Deram — not iss.

Jun 69. (7") *(DM 261)* **THAT OLD SWEET ROLL. / DON'T MAKE PROMISES** [ ] [-]

Middle Earth — not iss.

Mar 70. (7") *(MDS 104)* **LEWIS CARROLL. / FUTURE THOUGHTS** [ ] [-]
Apr 70. (lp) *(MDLS 304)* **TAM WHITE** [ ] [-]
–

Pye — not iss.

Aug 74. (7"; as TOM WHITE) *(7N 45391)* **TAKE AWAY THE SUNSHINE. / WHERE DID ALL THE GOOD TIMES GO** [ ] [-]

Rak — not iss.

Jan 75. (7") *(RAK 193)* **WHAT IN THE WORLD'S COME OVER YOU. / AFTER ALL WE'VE BEEN THROUGH** [36] [-]
May 75. (7") *(RAK 203)* **PLEASE MR PLEASE. / RED EYE SPECIAL** [ ] [-]
Oct 75. (7") *(RAK 219)* **COOL WATER. / MISTER, I DON'T WANT YOUR DAUGHTER** [ ] [-]

—— returned to Edinburgh and the music scene in the 80's

Dexter — not iss.

Nov 86. (lp; as TAM WHITE & THE DEXTERS) *(DEX 2)* **LET THE GOOD TIMES ROLL** [ ] [-]

Jazz House — not iss.

Sep 91. (lp/c/cd; as The TAM WHITE BAND) *(JH R/MC/CD 018)* **KEEP IT UNDER YOUR HAT (live at Ronnie Scott's September 1990)** [ ] [-]
– More / The dream / Coupe de ville / Mad Sam / Good morning heartache *[cd-only]* / Street people / Stone-mason's blues / Sleep-late Louie's / Woman in love / Nature of the beast / 36th street mission blues *[cd-only]. (cd re-iss. Jan94 & Feb01; same)*

Expression — not iss.

Jun 92. (cd; as the TAM WHITE BAND) *(EXCD 1)* **BLUE ECCENTRICITY** [ ] [-]
– Coupe de Ville / Urban nomads / Mad Sam / Women in love / Nature of the beast / Piano player / Street people / Victim / Sleep late Louis / The dream.

Dick Bros. — not iss.

Oct 97. (cd) *(DDICK 23CD)* **MAN DANCIN'** [ ] [-]
– Pollution blues / Working class white boy / I've got that blue, blue feeling / Save me / King Cobra / Don't mess with the heart / Urban nomads / Man dancin' / Three time loser shoes / A long time comin' / Coupe de ville / The Ritz / Heartbreak hotel.

—— with **FRASER SPIERS** – harmonica / **NEIL WARDEN** – guitars

Duncans — not iss.

Aug 98. (cd; as TAM WHITE'S SHOESTRING) *(G2CD 7002)* **THE REAL DEAL (live)** [ ] [-]
– Pollution blues / Blue blue feeling / Born under a bad sign / This is the way we make a broken heart / Save me / Eyesight to the blind / Workin' class white boy / Home is where the hatred is / Stonemason's blues / Man dancin' / Long time comin'.

—— next with jazz pianist **BRIAN KELLOCK**

Caber — not iss.

Oct 99. (cd; by TAM WHITE & BRIAN KELLOCK) *(Caber 009)* **THE CROSSING** [ ] [-]
– Piano player / Careful man / Woman in love / Broadway rose / Me and the blues again / The dream / This love of mine – Nancy / Easy money / Hey mister / Fool / It should have been me / The water is wide.

WHITE TRASH (see under ⇒ TRASH)

WRITING ON THE WALL

Formed: Edinburgh . . . 1966 as The JURY, by JAKE SCOTT, BILL SCOTT, JIMMY HUSH and WILLY FINLAYSON. They found vocalist LINNIE PATTERSON, formerly part of mod/soul outfit The EMBERS (who released one single in 1963). LINNIE then joined THREE'S A CROWD, who issued the 45, 'LOOK AROUND THE CORNER', in '66.

The JURY were initially managed by TAM PATON (later boss of The BAY CITY ROLLERS, until London-born BRIAN WALDMAN took over). The name change came about in late '67 to match their influence by West Coast psychedelia. WALDMAN then opened a club in London, calling it MIDDLE EARTH. Using the same name, he also set up a label and issued a debut 45, 'CHILD ON A CROSSING', in late '69. An album, 'THE POWER OF THE PICTS', soon followed, but an offer from an American promoter was refused unwisely by WALDMAN, who wanted his complete roster taken on. The record was a heavy doom-laden, progressive rock effort, fusing CREAM / YARDBIRDS, ARTHUR BROWN, IRON BUTTERFLY and BLACK SABBATH. Late in 1970, they entered the studio with BOWIE, although the only fruits of these sessions were some rough demos.

Early the following year, after a John Peel session, LINNIE and SMIGGY left, although they did persuade FINLAYSON to return. In the summer of '72, they played in front of over 60,000 people at Brazil's Rio Song Festival, which was also televised for South American TV. Although the Brazilians hailed them as heroes, the band returned to London and obscurity. They released one more single, containing the excellent B-side, 'BUFFALO', but the "writing was on the wall" as they say, after their equipment and transport was stolen.

• **Songwriters:** Group with DONALD CAMERON (my former music teacher at Woodlands High, who died in the early 80's).

ROBERT 'Smiggy' SMITH – guitar (ex-EMBERS) repl. WILLY FINLAYSON (mid-69) / **BILL SCOTT** – keyboards / **JAKE SCOTT** – bass, vocals / **JIMMY HUSH** – drums / **LINNIE PATTERSON** – vocals

		Middle Earth	not iss.
Oct 69.	(7") *(MDS 101)* **CHILD ON A CROSSING. / LUCIFER'S CORPUS**		-
Nov 69.	(lp) *(MDLS 303)* **THE POWER OF THE PICTS**		-

– It came on a Sunday / Mrs. Coopers pie / Ladybird / Aries / Bogeyman / Shadow of man / Taskers successor / Hill of dreams / Virginia Water. *(cd-iss. 1991 'Repertoire'; REP 8002SP) (German cd on 'Green Tree'; GTR 001)(+=)* – Child on a crossing / Lucifer's corpus. *(UK re-iss. Aug00 on 'Repertoire'; REP 4854)*

— now without SMIGGY and LINNIE. They both teamed up with JIMMY BAIN to form STREETNOISE. LINNIE joined BEGGAR'S OPERA, while SMIGGY joined BLUE. They were both replaced by returning **WILLIE FINLAYSON**. In the mid-90's, LINNIE died of asbestosis.

		Pye	not iss.
Jun 73.	(7") *(7N 45251)* **MAN OF RENOWN. / BUFFALO**		-

— split when only JAKE SCOTT and JIMMY HUSH remained. FINLAYSON joined BEES MAKE HONEY, taking his song 'BURGHLEY ROAD'. He went on to form MEAL TICKET.

– compilations, etc. –

Oct 95.	(lp) *Tenth Planet; (TP 017)* **CRACKS IN THE ILLUSION OF LIFE: A HISTORY OF WRITING ON THE WALL**		-
Jul 96.	(lp) *Tenth Planet; (TP 018)* **BURGHLEY ROAD: THE BASEMENT SESSIONS**		-
Jun 97.	(lp) *Pie & Mash; (PAM 003)* **RARITIES FROM THE MIDDLE EARTH**		-

Y

George YOUNG

Born: 6 Nov'47, Glasgow. Having already inherited an interest in music from his older brothers STEVIE, ALEX and JOHN, GEORGE formed his first serious band upon emigrating with the remainder of his family to Sydney, Australia in 1963. Named The EASYBEATS, the band comprised another four ex-pat Europeans, one of whom, Dutchman HARRY VANDA, teamed up with GEORGE as his songwriting partner.

Following a series of extremely successful Australian-only singles and albums, the group relocated to London, having already inked a worldwide deal with 'United Artists'. The YOUNG-VANDA pairing proved their domestic popularity was no fluke as The EASYBEATS (or "the Australian Beatles" as they came to be known) strolled into the UK Top 10 in 1966 with the neo-psychedelic pop classic, 'FRIDAY ON MY MIND' (a Top 20 hit in the States six months later). Bar a solitary UK Top 20 hit in '68, 'HELLO, HOW ARE YOU?', the group failed to capitalise on their initial chart action.

Life became progressively more difficult for The EASYBEATS and they split in 1970, YOUNG retaining his partnership with VANDA through a series of short-lived studio projects. Although the likes of PAINTBOX, TRAMP, WHATWHAT, HAFFY'S WHISKY SOUR and the MARCUS HOOK ROLL BAND were doomed to obscurity, GEORGE spent a brief spell (c. 1972) in his brother GEORGE ALEXANDER's marginally successful GRAPEFRUIT outfit.

Having seemingly exhausted all his possibilies in England, YOUNG finally returned to Australia in 1974 to nurture the blossoming talents of his younger siblings, MALCOLM and ANGUS. After enjoying an extended period as AC/DC's production lynchpin (alongside VANDA), GEORGE returned to his pop roots towards the end of the decade with minor hitmakers, FLASH AND THE PAN (who scored a UK Top 10 in 1983 with 'WAITING FOR A TRAIN'). After working with other Australian acts (i.e. ROSE TATTOO, The SAINTS, etc), he resumed his position at the AC/DC production helm, seeing them into the new millennium with the 'Stiff Upper Lip' set.

John Paul YOUNG

Born: 21 Jun'50, Glasgow. Raised from an early age in Sydney, Australia, the pin-up pop songwriter (produced by HARRY VANDA and GEORGE YOUNG), made a name for himself via debut 45, 'DRIVE ME CRAZY' in 1972. However, it would take another three years before he tasted success on a wider scale courtesy of Stateside Top 50 hit, 'YESTERDAY'S HERO'. In 1978, complete with new backing group (which included part co-writer WARREN MORGAN), JOHN PAUL YOUNG was the toast of Australia when he scored a No.1 with 'LOVE IS IN THE AIR' (also Top 10 in the UK and US). However, each successive release seemed to take a nosedive and little was heard from him outside his adopted home. In 1992, the aforementioned 'LOVE IS IN THE AIR' hit the UK Top 50 again due to the track being used for that year's 'Strictly Ballroom' movie.

JOHN PAUL YOUNG – vocals, piano / with VANDA-YOUNG production

		Albert	not iss.
Mar 72.	(7") **PASADENA. / BETTER GO BACK TO BED**	-	- Austra
Feb 73.	(7") **DRIVE ME CRAZY. / FOR MY LOVE**	-	- Austra
Mar 74.	(7") **BAD TRIP. / IT'S ONLY LOVE**	-	- Austra
Mar 75.	(lp) **HERO**	-	- Austra

– Yesterday's hero / Bad trip / Things to do / The next time / Birmingham / St. Louis / Pasadena / Friends / Silver shoes & strawberry wine / The love game.

Aug 75.	(7") **THE LOVE GAME. / ST. LOUIS**	-	- Austra
Mar 76.	(7") **I HATE THE MUSIC. / MY NAME IS JACK**	-	- Austra

		Private Stock	Ariola America
Mar 76.	(7") *(PVT 49) <7607>* **YESTERDAY'S HERO. / THE NEXT TIME**		42 Nov75
Mar 76.	(lp) *(28161)* **J.P.Y.**	-	- German

– Keep on smilin' / Won't let this feeling go by / I hate the music / Standing in the rain / I still got you / If I could live my life again / St. Louis / Yesterday's hero / Friends / The love game / Pasadena / Birmingham.

Apr 76.	(7") **STANDING IN THE RAIN. / THE SAME OLD THING**	-	- Austra
Oct 76.	(7") **KEEP ON SMILIN'. / IF I COULD LIVE MY LIFE AGAIN**	-	- Austra
Feb 77.	(7") **I WANNA DO IT WITH YOU. / THE PAINTING**	-	- Austra
Feb 77.	(lp) **GREEN**	-	- Austra

– Gay time rock'n'roll / Just can't go / Down on my knees / Shake that thing / I wanna do it with you II / I know you / The same old thing / Here we go / Bring that bottle of wime over here / One of these times.

Sep 77.	(7") **WHERE THE ACTION IS. / DOWN ON MY KNEES**	-	- Austra
Jan 78.	(7") **HERE WE GO. / SHAKE THAT THING**	-	- Austra

— from now on we concentrate on US/UK releases only

		Ariola	Scotti Bro
Mar 78.	(7") *(ARO 117)* **LOVE IS IN THE AIR. / WON'T LET THIS FEELING GO BY**	5	-
Jun 78.	(7") *<402>* **LOVE IS IN THE AIR. / WHERE THE ACTION IS**	-	7
Sep 78.	(7") *(ARO 134)* **THE DAY THAT MY HEART CAUGHT FIRE. / LAZY DAYS**		-
Oct 78.	(lp/c) *(ARL/ZCARL 5011) <7101>* **LOVE IS IN THE AIR**		

– The day that my heart caught fire / Fool in love / Open doors / Lost in your love / Red hot ragtime band / 12 celsius / Lazy days / Love is in the air / Good, good, good / Lovin' in your soul.

Nov 78.	(7") *<405>* **LOST IN YOUR LOVE. / THE DAY THAT MY HEART CAUGHT FIRE**	-	55
Jan 79.	(7") *(ARO 142)* **LOST IN YOUR LOVE. / STANDING IN THE RAIN**		-
Sep 79.	(7") *(ARO 185)* **I CAN'T LET YOU OUT OF MY SYSTEM. / I DON'T WANNA LOSE YOU**		
Feb 80.	(7") *(ARO 210)* **LOVE YOU SO BAD IT HURTS. / I DON'T WANNA LOSE YOU**		
Feb 80.	(lp/c) *(ARL/ZCARL 5037)* **HEAVEN SENT**		-

– Heaven sent / Don't you walk that way / I don't wanna lose you / Love you so bad it hurts / Hot for you baby / Can't get you out of my system / I ain't ready for love / Bad side of the city.

— YOUNG retired from solo work after above

– compilations, others, etc. –

Jul 82.	(7") *Old Gold; (OG 9125)* **LOVE IS IN THE AIR. / LOVE YOU SO BAD IT HURTS**		-
Oct 92.	(7"/cd-s) *Columbia; (658769-7/-2)* **LOVE IS IN THE AIR (remix)**	49	-
1993.	(cd/c) *Laserlight; (1/7 2212)* **LOVE IS IN THE AIR**		-

record label

ALP records

Founded: In 1965 by ANDY LOTHIAN, promoter of the dancehall revues billed as the Clan Balls.

Having strong links with the then Pirate radio station, Radio Scotland, LOTHIAN set out to create a unique roster that reflected modern Soul & Pop tastes while still catering for the traditional Scottish market. Commercially, he also looked beyond native frontiers, striking a national distribution deal with major London label, 'Polydor'.

His first signings were Dunfermline's RED HAWKES, who included main songwriter and guitarist MANNY CHARLTON (formerly of MARK FIVE). Harking back to the showband era, the group's debut single, 'FRIDAY NIGHT', celebrated the heyday of Scotland's weekend dancehall culture; MANNY would subsequently resurface with hard-rock stadium fillers, NAZARETH.

Spearheading the tartan contingent within ALP Towers was accordionist JOHN HUBAND and his band SCOTTISH SOUND, who released two JIMMY SHAND-esque 45's in quick succession (there were soon to be others, LORNA FRASER, ANNE & CATHERINE BLACKMORE, etc).

Despite the excitement surrounding The POOR SOULS single 'Love Me', the track failed to fulfil its potential and the Dundee outfit (who'd already lost a deal with 'Decca') split shortly after.

This underwhelming episode also affected ALP who concentrated on more reliable fare before having another unsuccessful crack at the charts with Wishaw's HI-FI's (not the London bunch on 'Piccadilly'/'Pye'). ALP's tenth release, 'It's Gonna Be Working', failed to capture the band's soulful live spark. The label then pinned their hopes on Perth's VIKINGS. Formed in 1963 (out of The FALCONS) by guitarist DOUGIE WIGHTMAN and guitarist/vocalist ROY FLEMING, they were soon joined by bassist ALAN GORRIE and drummer GRAHAM DUNCAN (PETE HARTLEY left early in 1964). A succession of R&B-styled singers took the mic, IAN JACKSON, JOHNNY TAYLOR (aka JOHNNY LITTLE) and finally DREW LANG, although a subsequent festive fist fight (in '65) led to a scaled down line-up featuring the aforementioned LANG, GORRIE and WIGHTMAN. In the New Year, the three were joined by drummer DONNIE COUTTS and guitarist MIKE FRASER, the VIKINGS finally ready to record their first 45; Smokey Robinson's 'TRACKS OF MY TEARS' was mooted at the time. Instead, 'Polydor' suggested a cover of an obscure Paul Simon number, 'BAD NEWS FEELING', lack of interest making it worth a wee bit of cash today. A short-lived period as FANCY BRED was the last the public heard from these Northern challengers to UK soul, although GORRIE got his chance of fame when he became part of the AVERAGE WHITE BAND.

With this final failure, ALP was finally put to rest, another victim of London-centric business attitudes.

– discography –

Jan 66. (7") *(595 001)* **RED HAWKES – Friday Night / Lonely Boy**
Feb 66. (7") *(595 002)* **JOHN HUBAND & SCOTTISH SOUND – Radio Scotland Polka / Bella Flore**
May 66. (7") *(595 003)* **JOHN HUBAND & SCOTTISH SOUND – Scotland / Summer Road**
Jul 66. (7") *(595 004)* **POOR SOULS – Love Me / Please Don't Change Your Mind**
Jul 66. (7") *(595 005)* **LORNA FRASER – Loch Maree / My Love**
Jul 66. (7") *(595 007)* **ANNE & CATHERINE BLACKMORE – Scotland So Dear / Legend Of Scotland**
Sep 66. (7") *(595 010)* **HI-FI's – It's Gonna Be Working / I Wanna Hear You Say Yeah**
Oct 66. (7") *(595 011)* **VIKINGS – Bad News Feeling / What Can I Do**

8
Rock, Pop & Indie
(post new wave)

The Breakthroughs: While New Wave and Punk Rock was spreading like wildfire across the Atlantic from New York to London and beyond, Scotland's punk bands were finding it difficult to be part of the scene (although not necessarily the fashion). Young Scots into the Sex Pistols, The Damned and The Clash, were taking their time learning to play instruments and even mimic the foreign anarchists. However, three groups to finally break through (although not initially) were The REZILLOS, JOHNNY & THE SELF-ABUSERS and The SKIDS, who naturally stayed with the spirit of punk by issuing their debut 45's on DIY independent labels; respectively speaking 'CAN'T STAND MY BABY' (on Lawrie Love's 'Sensible' records in August '77), 'SAINTS AND SINNERS' (on English indie 'Chiswick' label in November '77) and 'CHARLES' (for 'No-Bad' records in March '78). All three were eventually snapped up by major record labels, The REZILLOS to 'Sire', SIMPLE MINDS (the new moniker for the SELF-ABUSERS) to 'Arista' and the SKIDS to 'Virgin'. Edinburgh's REZILLOS (led by FAY FIFE and EUGENE REYNOLDS), had the honour of being the first Scots post-punk act to play Top Of The Pops, the song in question being er, 'Top Of The Pops'. Dunfermline's the SKIDS (aka RICHARD JOBSON and STUART ADAMSON) subsequently followed the former's path of glory by entering the Top 10 with the anthemic 'INTO THE VALLEY'. Glasgow's SIMPLE MINDS were to achieve their "glittering prizes" a little later.

When Scotland was finally getting to grips with the Punk scene, we had already spawned – although unknown to the majority – a pivotal figure in the form of Dumbarton-born expatriate DAVID BYRNE who was achieving major success with Talking Heads in the aforementioned NY New Wave scene.

Ironically, other Scots expatriates living on foreign soil were leading their own individual groups to stardom. Frontman BON SCOTT, sibling guitarists ANGUS and MALCOLM YOUNG were 3/5ths of Australia's AC/DC who had already headbanged their way through a couple of LP's before they smashed into the UK Top 20 with 'Let There Be Rock' (1977). In the late 70's, gravel-voiced JIMMY BARNES was also making his mark down under, the Cowcaddens-born hard-rocker hitting the Australian charts with Cold Chisel; he would later hit the US charts as a solo artist. If it was cool guitar-picking you were after, then MARK KNOPFLER of (London-based) Dire Straits was yer man. Born in Glasgow and raised in Newcastle, he and his younger brother DAVID shook the music world by the neck when 'Sultans Of Swing' stormed the charts in 1979.

Another artist to stray down south to London was the popular singer/guitarist MIDGE URE (who'd initially had a No.1 in 1976 via SLIK's 'Forever And Ever'). Having survived the madness of the punk era, Glasgow-born URE (who had played part-time with Thin Lizzy) resurfaced at the turn of the decade as frontman of Ultravox. Having initially had a few hits, MIDGE and his new cohorts almost made it to the top of the charts with the video-friendly, 'Vienna'. MIDGE, of course, went on to carve out a successful solo career and is best remembered for his part in Band/Live Aid.

With the aforementioned MIDGE URE (with post-Punk PVC2) and SIMPLE MINDS both delivering 45's for Bruce Findlay's seminal 'Zoom' label in the late 70's, it would be Alan Horne's 'Postcard' imprint that would hone "the sound of young Scotland" in the early 80's. This enterprise was the musical playground for such artists as ORANGE JUICE, JOSEF K and AZTEC CAMERA, all to become major contributors to the country's fast-growing independent pop circle. All three mainmen, EDWYN COLLINS, PAUL HAIG and RODDY FRAME have subsequently enjoyed a certain degree of success as solo artists, while a fourth 'Postcard'-signed outfit, The BLUEBELLS, finally cracked it with 'YOUNG AT HEART' in 1984 (and No.1 in 1993!).

It wasn't just the men who were causing ripples in the world of music, Scots "sisters were doing it for themselves" around this era. A former fish-worker from Aberdeen, ANNIE LENNOX, had Top 10 successes as singer with The Tourists in 1979/80 ('I Only Want To Be With You' and 'So Good To Be Back Home Again'), while Bellshill lass SHEENA EASTON made it "big time" via Esther Rantzen's BBCTV show; quite literally she would never work '9 TO 5' (her debut smash in 1980) again! We can't of course forget the immense disco talent of KELLY MARIE or novelty one-hit wonder ANEKA (alias MARY SANDEMAN!), who both topped the charts with their unfashionable dancefloor-fillers ('FEELS LIKE I'M IN LOVE' and 'JAPANESE BOY' (un)respectively). Back to indie and the Peelie faves, his girls on top at the time were undoubtably CLARE GROGAN and ELIZABETH FRASER. CLARE and her ALTERED IMAGES (from Glasgow) soon shook off their indie-'DEAD POP STARS'-tag when the band celebrated a near chart-topper via 'HAPPY BIRTHDAY', in September '81; Grangemouth's industrial-goths the COCTEAU TWINS (alongside hubby-to-be ROBIN GUTHRIE) shattered the mould with the 'GARLANDS' LP a year later.

1982 was also a vintage year for two other bands:- The ASSOCIATES (from Dundee and featuring the soaring, passionate vocals of BILLY MACKENZIE and backer ALAN RANKINE) were on a different plain than most other Scottish acts around them. Having already delivered an album 'THE AFFECTIONATE PUNCH' in 1980 and an awe-inspiring

series of 12" singles the following year (released as 'FOURTH DRAWER DOWN'), the duo checked in to the pop motel courtesy of two excellent 45's, 'PARTY FEARS TWO' and 'CLUB COUNTRY' – BILLY MACKENZIE, R.I.P. 1997. Meanwhile, SIMPLE MINDS (now on 'Virgin' records) were finally reaping the benefits from an ever-growing fanbase who put 'PROMISED YOU A MIRACLE' into the UK Top 20. JIM KERR and his stadium-fillers inevitably broke through in the US when 'DON'T YOU (FORGET ABOUT ME)' hit the coveted No.1 spot in '85.

The 'MINDS were not the only Scots-based outfit to fill a stadium; there was also BIG COUNTRY, an anthemic bunch of Celtic-inspired musicians led by none other than Manchester-born, former SKIDS guitarist, STUART ADAMSON. In 1983, they set the charts ablaze with two hits, 'FIELDS OF FIRE (400 MILES)' and 'IN A BIG COUNTRY' (both from the platinum-selling album, 'THE CROSSING'). Regrettably, after a long career in music, ADAMSON committed suicide in Hawaii on the 16th of December, 2001.

Having been a part of The Eurythmics since the early 80's, ANNIE LENNOX's new outfit (with husband Dave Stewart) applied an electro-clash style to their romantically-themed, 'Sweet Dreams (Are Made Of This)' and 'Love Is A Stranger' (both Top 10 hits in the first half of '83). Ten years later, the chameleon-attired ANNIE was still at the top via her No.1 album, 'DIVA').

1983 also saw the rise of two other border-crossing chartbusters, FISH (of retro Prog-rockers, Marillion) and COLIN JAMES HAY (of Antipodean pop act, Men At Work). Marillion frontman and songwriter, FISH, stood out from the crowd – he was well over 6 foot – when his band hit the Top 20 with 'Garden Party' (from the album, 'Script For A Jester's Tear'), which secured his reputation come his solo career at the turn of the 90's. HAY, meanwhile, was certainly not beating around the bush after Men At Work had their worldwide chart-topper, appropriately-titled 'Down Under'.

The following year, Glaswegian Hi-NRG lads JIMMY SOMERVILLE and STEVE BRONSKI broke the mould with Hackney-based trio BRONSKI BEAT on a gender-questioning major hit 'SMALLTOWN BOY'. Chilling out completely were The BLUE NILE, who also emerged in 1984 with what was to become one of Scotland's best ever LPs 'A WALK ACROSS THE ROOFTOPS'; 'HATS' in 1989 wasn't too bad either.

Already making a name for himself was the Edinburgh-born MIKE SCOTT who scoured the country (England that is), for like-minded musicians who would ultimately make up The WATERBOYS. After their first single, 'A GIRL CALLED JOHNNY', remarkably failed to register a chart position in '83, the raggle-taggle wanderers subsequently hit the mark with the classy 'THE WHOLE OF THE MOON'.

The Caledonian indie scene was restored to the forefront thanks to an enterprising London-based young Scot, ALAN McGEE. He instigated the seminal 'Creation' imprint in '83, mainly at first to release his own BIFF BANG POW! records, although things would evolve quickly after the signing of three northern groups, The JASMINE MINKS (from Aberdeen), The PASTELS (from Glasgow) and The JESUS & MARY CHAIN (from East Kilbride) – McGEE would land Oasis a decade later. Brothers WILLIAM and JIM REID of the latter controversial and demonstrative Scots outfit debuted with 'UPSIDE DOWN' (their gigs were a bit topsy-turvy too!), their only 'Creation' release, having signed a lucrative contract with a major label and finding fresh-faced drum-kit basher, BOBBY GILLESPIE. 1985 produced three minor classic chart hits in the form of 'NEVER UNDERSTAND', 'YOU TRIP ME UP' and 'JUST LIKE HONEY', all eventually resting disconcertingly on their debut LP, 'PSYCHOCANDY'.

Spawned from this new slice of punk-psychedelia (and also on 'Creation') were PRIMAL SCREAM, with BOBBY GILLESPIE switching roles from the back of the stage to the front. It took them several attempts and a few genre twists for his band to finally come of age, with 1990's groundbreaking rave-inspired 'LOADED' (from 1991's 'SCREAMADELICA' massive set) being the catalyst for a whole new generation.

Meanwhile, back at the indie ranch somewhere between Bellshill and er, Bellshill, a number of associated outfits were being heard. The SOUP DRAGONS (with SEAN DICKSON and JIM McCULLOCH), The BMX BANDITS (DUGLAS STEWART and Co; with initially DICKSON and McCULLOCH, and later GORDON KEEN, FRANCIS MACDONALD, NORMAN BLAKE, etc), The VASELINES (EUGENE KELLY, FRANCES McKEE, JAMES SEENAN, etc) and TEENAGE FANCLUB (BLAKE, MACDONALD, GERARD LOVE, BRENDAN O'HARE, etc); note that 90's offshoot CAPTAIN AMERICA/EUGENIUS took in KELLY, KEEN, SEENAN, O'HARE, etc). Both The SOUP DRAGONS and The BMX BANDITS began their musical account in 1986, the former finally getting recognition in 1990 with a Top 5 cover of the Rolling Stones' 'I'M FREE', with the latter peddlars of twee Lo-Fi never quite getting free of the indie tag. The VASELINES' pre-grunge appeal spread further ashore, in fact to Aberdeen (not North but West to Seattle in the US of A) where a young Kurt Cobain somehow managed to get a hold of the rare vinyl; 'SON OF A GUN', 'MOLLY'S LIPS' and 'JESUS WANTS ME FOR A SUNBEAM', all became part of Nirvana's repertoire. Undoubtably the most influential and durable of this indie crop were TEENAGE FANCLUB. After defining too-cool-for-school slacker rock via a couple of minor hits and a few albums, the 'FANNIES tuned into the mainstream with 1991's melodic homage to the Beach Boys and Big Star, 'BANDWAGONESQUE' (McGEE and 'Creation' were at the helm yet again!).

From the mid to late 80's, Scotland produced a huge cluster of radio-friendly pop/soul fodder that invaded the British charts (and sometimes even the US lists) on many occasions. Names such as LOVE AND MONEY, The SILENCERS, DANNY WILSON, WET WET WET, HUE AND CRY, DEACON BLUE and GOODBYE MR MACKENZIE, all flew the flag on their own steam. The grinning MARTI PELLOW and his drookit crew first sailed into the charts in spring 1987 with 'WISHING I WAS LUCKY' and er, "Popped In & Souled Out" soon afterwards; their unmoveable and smooch-friendly 'LOVE IS ALL AROUND' was stuck at the top of the charts for 15 bloody weeks an' that. HUE AND CRY (aka brothers PAT and GREG KANE), meanwhile, were carving out their own soulful niche with the Top 10 single, 'LABOUR OF LOVE'; as the pair matured so did their jazz-orientated leanings. Real Gone Kids DEACON BLUE (fronted by RICKY ROSS) also fashioned their own blend of sophisti-pop, although it would take a little longer and a re-issue of that ship called 'DIGNITY' before the sextet made the grade. Who would've thought that minor hitmakers GOODBYE MR MACKENZIE (responsible for such gems as 'THE RATTLER', etc) would churn out such a rock chick icon in the shape of everybody's girl-next-door, SHIRLEY MANSON. Sadly, she had to say "Cheerio Mr MacScotland" and hello to America's Garbage (Butch Vig's band, that is!) in order to take on the transatlantic music world.

Talking of the States, but not distancing ourselves totally from this Atlantic crossing, we were posted a 'LETTER FROM AMERICA', sent by The PROCLAIMERS twins (CHARLIE and CRAIG). More of an ode to Scotland than America, the late 1987 Top 3 hit expressed disgruntlement over the closure of our industries; the similarly themed 'I'M GONNA BE (500 MILES)' also hit the Top 10, and funnily enough was exported to America five years later where it also cracked the Top 3. It's gotta be and it was definitely 'Perfect' for one-time bespectacled busker EDDI READER who was the main feature in English-based Fairground Attraction. Traditional folkies RUNRIG were also at their peak around the turn of the decade, but that's been mulled over in the Folk section.

At the other end of the spectrum, Glasgow's GUN and The ALMIGHTY were hacking a hole in the hard-rock scene. We'd already had our wee share of post-NWOBHM Scots outfits courtesy of HOLOCAUST, HEAVY PETTIN and PALLAS, but none had 'TAKEN ON THE WORLD' (a Top 50 debut) quite like GUN, who were eventually to hit paydirt with a Rawking cover of Cameo's 'WORD UP'. The ALMIGHTY, meanwhile, were another slow-burner, their debut set 'BLOOD, FIRE AND LOVE' (1989), 'CRANK'-ing up the volume past ten; later STILTSKIN would take us 'INSIDE' (1994) their post-Grunge minds and have a No.1 hit courtesy of a jeans ad.

Also towards the end of the decade, SHARLEEN SPITERI and her TEXAS troubadours (who took their cool cue from Ry Cooder and JJ Cale) scored a home run with their dustbowl debut, 'I DON'T WANT A LOVER'; the group re-invented themselves a few times to have a consistant string of hits and platinum-selling albums. DEL AMITRI (JUSTIN CURRIE, IAIN HARVIE and Co) were struggling for a while in the mid-80's, only to come up trumps in 1990 with that year's downbeat singalong, 'NOTHING EVER HAPPENS'.

The 90's started with a bang! (quite literally) for dancefloor music; its main rabble-rouser was undoubtedbly The SHAMEN. Having already a cult following from their indie-psychedelic roots in the last decade, original member COLIN ANGUS and relative newcomer WILL SINOTT helped to revolutionise the acid house scene (at least in Scotland). Sadly, the latter was to drown in May 1991, a few months before they had their first Top 5 entry, 'MOVE ANY MOUNTAIN', while the former was controversially (or allegedly) chanting "E's are good" or 'EBENEEZER GOODE' all the way to top spot just over a year later. A plethora of Scottish rave acts sprung up from all over the nation including THE TIME FREQUENCY, Q-TEX and SLAM, the latter (featuring ORDE MEIKLE and STUART McMILLAN) setting up their own massive independent dance imprint, 'Soma'.

'Chemikal Underground', meanwhile, might've confused the public to where their Glaswegian seeds lay, but they were certainly not of the dance lineage although you'd have been slightly forgiven after the release of 'DISCO NATION' by teeny-pop trio BIS. However, this was the label's second 7" released in summer '95, the first being feted NME Single Of The Week, 'MONICA WEBSTER' by C.U.'s C.E.O.'s The DELGADOS. BIS were to become the imprint's first big success when their EP, 'THE SECRET VAMPIRE SOUNDTRACK', bit into the Top 30. While juggling with their own output, The DELGADOS completed the signings of two other soon-to-be indie giants ARAB STRAP and MOGWAI. Falkirk act ARAB STRAP (fronted by AIDAN MOFFAT – a lover of all things spirit-ual and chemical) were indeed "Trainspotting for the music world" as their first releases 'THE FIRST BIG WEEKEND' (7") and 'THE WEEK NEVER STARTS ROUND HERE' (album) indicated. Perhaps Chemikal Underground's most pivotal signing was local lads, MOGWAI, a challenging modern-day bunch of 21st Century schizoid men who took elements of King Crimson, Slint and Sonic Youth and diverted each crescendo build-up with tranquil soundscapes.

Another group to emerge out of Glasgow's indie community were BELLE & SEBASTIAN, who fused twee bedsit angst with Nick Drake-esque spirit, which was evident on their college-financed debut, 'TIGERMILK' (1996). These publicity-shy upstarts subsequently managed to upset pop-guru Pete Waterman, after metaphorically stealing Best Newcomers prize from Steps at 1999's Brit Awards. It could've been worse if they had arrived at the gig with er, The Boys From The Arab Strap.

A 'GOOD FEELING' was in the air when TRAVIS hit the Top 10 with their aforementioned debut album in September '97. FRAN and Co went on to become Scotland's premier pop-rock outfit via two platinum-selling albums, 'THE MAN WHO' (1999) and 'THE INVISIBLE BAND' (2001). Putting aside charting soul brother from Edinburgh, FINLAY QUAYE, the other side of the coin dished out the likes of The BETA BAND and BOARDS OF CANADA. The former unleashed the now legendary 'THREE EPs' (did what it said on the tin!) towards the end of the 90's, while the latter sort of lectured by numbers that 'MUSIC HAS THE RIGHT TO CHILDREN' (1998). The kids were also involved in another way, as fans of Edinburgh's retro hard/punk rockers, IDLEWILD. However, RODDY WOOMBLE was having more of a Green Day than a bad day.

And then there was DARIUS. To be contined . . .

* * * * *

ABRAHAMS (see under ⇒ Fence records)

A.C. ACOUSTICS

Formed: Glasgow . . . 1992 by Kenmore-raised songwriter, PAUL CAMPION. Supporting the likes of MAZZY STAR and PJ HARVEY at Glasgow's Barrowlands, the band's initial line-up was completed by ROGER WARD, CAZ RILEY and DAVE GORMLEY. After an infamous gig at Glasgow's Garage supporting hard-core act NO MEANS NO, the boys were snapped up by respected indie label, 'Elemental'.

Their early indie-rock sound was crystallised on a handful of inspired, sporadic releases reminiscent of PAVEMENT or MERCURY REV, fuelling expectations for an album of skewed sonic brilliance. The band went to ground for a couple of years, resurfacing late in '96 with a new guitarist MARK RAINE and a single 'STUNT GIRL'. During their hiatus they recorded an album in Wales, which was deemed unacceptable for release. Their debut album proper, 'VICTORY PARTS' finally saw light of day in the summer of '97. In their absence, MOGWAI, URUSEI YATSURA, etc, had already found minor success after taking the lead from AC's early work. Much of this was evident come the release of 2000's epic 'UNDERSTANDING MUSIC', which took the atmospheric, chamber-rock format into new uncharted soundscapes.

'O' was issued two years later and enhanced this formula with CAMPION's vocals whispering away in a darkened corner to the rest of the group's sparse compositions. Tracks such as 'HOLD' and 'CLONE OF AL CAPONE' could've easily be credited to LEONARD COHEN, although the A.C. ACOUSTICS certainly managed to do justice to themselves by creating such a deep and offbeat album.

PAUL CAMPION – vocals / **ROGER WARD** – guitar / **CAZ RILEY** – bass / **DAVE GORMLEY** – drums

El'e'mental | Trance

Nov 93. (7"blue) *(ELM 16S)* **SWEATLODGE. / MV** [ ] [-]

Apr 94. (m-lp/m-cd) *(ELM 21 MLP/MCD) <31>* **ABLE TREASURY** [ ] [ ] Jan95
– Mother head sander / King Dick / Three / Leather buyer / Fat Abbey / Sister grab operator / Oregon pine washback / MV / Sweatlodge.

Nov 94. (12"ep/cd-ep) *(ELM 25 T/CD)* **HAND PASSES PLENTY EP** [ ] [-]
– Hand passes plenty / Love lies broken pieces / Love lies (Equamnemo mix) / Emily.

— **MARK RAINE** – guitar; repl. WARD

Nov 96. (7") *(ELM 30S)* **STUNT GIRL. / SHOKA** [ ] [-]
(cd-s+=) *(ELM 30CDS)* – Skeptic wrist eye / Sidenova.

Mar 97. (7") *(ELM 29S)* **I MESSIAH AM JAILER. / HIGH DIVERS** [ ] [-]
(7") *(ELM 29SX)* – ('A'side) / Violent peep.
(cd-s) *(ELM 29CDS)* – (all 3 tracks).

Jun 97. (cd/lp) *(ELM 31 CD/LP)* **VICTORY PARTS** [ ] [-]
– Hand passes empty / Stunt girl / Ex-quartermaster / Admirals all / Hammerhead / Kill Zane / Fast / Continuity freak / High divers / Absent luck liner / I messiah am jailer / Can't see anything / (Red not yellow).

Yoyo | not iss.

Nov 98. (7"ep/cd-ep) *(YO/+CD 3)* **LIKE RIBBONS EP** [ ] [-]
– Like ribbons / Lemon / Lunar page.

Feb 99. (7"ep) *(YO 4)* **SHE'S WITH STARS EP** [ ] [-]
– She's with stars / Dirty Paris / Lilo Lilo.
(cd-ep+=) *(YOCD 4)* – Stunt girl (the PmFf remix).

Cooking Vinyl | not iss.

Sep 00. (7") *(FRY 096)* **CRUSH. / LUKE ONE** [ ] [-]
(cd-s) *(FRYCD 096)* – ('A'side) / She kills for kicks (MC Sleazy remix) / Ridley rider (MC Sleazy remix).

Sep 00. (cd) *(COOKCD 201)* **UNDERSTANDING MUSIC** [ ] [-]
– Luke one / Chinese summer / Crush / Ridley rider / She kills for kicks / Dry salvage / Knot of knots / Super cup / B2 / Arcane action man / Flies / Parrot pine / Walter strains.

Feb 02. (cd) *(COOKCD 219)* **O** [ ] [-]
– Intro / Hold / A bell (of love rings out for you) / Clone of Al Capone / 16 4 2010 / Bright anchor (anchor me) / Interlude / Killed by fuck / Suck on silence / Conspicuously leaving (without saying goodbye) / Victoria / Poem / Outro.

ACID ANGELS (see under ⇒ JESUS & MARY CHAIN)

ACT (see under ⇒ LEER, Thomas)

ACTIVE FORCE (see under ⇒ Evolution records – Q-TEX)

ADULTERY (see ⇒ Section 9: wee post-punk groups)

ADVENTURES IN STEREO (see under ⇒ SPIREA X)

AEREOGRAMME (see under ⇒ FUKUYAMA)

AERIAL (see ⇒ Section 9: the 90s)

Dot ALLISON

Born: 1970, Edinburgh. The erstwhile ethereal-voiced chanteuse with early 90's ambient popsters ONE DOVE (who released a handful of mesmerising singles including 'White Love' and a fine album, 'Morning Dove White', without ever really fulfilling their potential), ALLISON disappeared from view following the band's demise in the mid-90's. A serious car accident further stalled her progress and it would be 1999 before she eventually resurfaced with a number of singles, occasional live appearances and collaborations with the likes of ARAB STRAP and DEATH IN VEGAS.

Her long awaited debut solo set, 'AFTERGLOW', was released that summer, a record that impressed both longstanding ONE DOVE fans as well as younger folks grooving to BETH ORTON and her ilk. Completely self-penned, the album also found DOT playing most of the instruments herself, her slow burning mood music combining elements from trip hop, orchestral pop, electronica and even folk.

It wasn't really surprising then, how similar ALLISON's second set 'WE ARE SCIENCE' (2002) sounded to GOLDFRAPP's lauded debut 'Felt Mountain'. Musically better than 'AFTERGLOW', the set focused more on her ability to create interesting soundscapes with pianos, strings and a whole load of weird sounding synths. The TWO LONE SWORDSMEN made a welcome appearance, as did DEATH IN VEGAS (she was dating RICHARD FEARLESS at the time) and selected members of MERCURY REV. 'MAKE IT HAPPEN' and 'I THINK I LOVE YOU' concentrated on ALLISON's bittersweet take-on of romance, whereas 'YOU CAN BE REPLACED' displayed her deep cynical views of relationships, matched with that of some dark psychedelia. Careful now!?

DOT ALLISON – vocals, guitar, keyboards, percussion, etc / with a plethora of session people & **MAGNUS FIENNES** – keyboards

Heavenly | Sub Pop

Feb 99. (7") *(HVN 81)* **TOMORROW NEVER COMES. / I WANNA FEEL THE CHILL (instrumental)** [ ] [-]

Mar 99. (7") *(HVN 87)* **MO' POP. / MELTED** [ ] [-]
(12"+=/cd-s+=) *(HVN 87 12/CD)* – Blind.

May 99. (7") *<SP 459>* **COLOUR ME. / TOMORROW NEVER COMES** [-] [ ]

Jun 99. (7") *(HVN 91)* **MESSAGE PERSONNEL. / TOMORROW NEVER COMES** [ ] [-]
(cd-s+=) *(HVN 91CD)* – ('A'-Arab Strap mix) / ('A'-Death In Vegas mix).

Heavenly | Deconstr.

Jul 99. (cd-ep) *<07822 17601-2>* **COLOUR ME / MESSAGE PERSONAL (Arab Strap long version) / TOMORROW NEVER COMES / MELTED (edit)** [-] [ ]

Oct 99. (12"/cd-s) *(HVN 93 12/CD) <70045>* **CLOSE YOUR EYES. / MR. VOYEUR / CLOSE YOUR EYES (Slam mixes)** [ ] [ ] Jan00

Oct 99. (cd/c) *(HVNLP 24 CD/MC) <16600>* **AFTERGLOW** [ ] [ ] Apr99
– Colour me / Tomorrow never comes / Close your eyes / Message personnel / I wanna feel the chill / Morning sun / Did I imagine you? / Mo' pop / Alpha female / In winter still.

Mantra | not iss.

Apr 02. (12"/cd-s) *(MNT 72 T/CD)* **SUBSTANCE / SUBSTANCE (Felix Da Housecat remix) / LO-FI LOVESONG** [ ] [-]

May 02. (cd/lp) *(MNT CD/LP 1028)* **WE ARE SCIENCE** [ ] [-]
– We're only science / Substance / You can be replaced / Performance / Wishing stone / Make it happen / Strung out / I think I love you / Hex / Lover.

Aug 02. (cd-s) *(MNT 74CD)* **STRUNG OUT / STOLEN KISSES / SWEET SURRENDER** [67] [-]
(12") *(MNT 74T)* – ('A'side) / ('A'-Radioactive man remix) / We're only science (Slam remix).
(cd-s) *(MNT 74CD2)* – ('A'side) / We're only science (Slam remix) / I think I love you (Tenniswood remix).

Tim ALLON (see ⇒ Section 9: the 90s)

ALMIGHTY

Formed: Glasgow . . . 1988 by RICKY WARWICK and STUMP MUNROE, who had evolved from 'FM Revolver'-signed band ROUGH CHARM, WARWICK also having served his time in NEW MODEL ARMY. At odds with most of the glam-metal of the day, the ALMIGHTY favoured warts'n'all, balls to the wall hard rock in the grand tradition of MOTORHEAD.

Signing to 'Polydor', the band released their debut, 'BLOOD, FIRE AND LOVE', late the following year. In keeping with the rather overblown title it was all very anthemic stuff, at times reminiscent of 'Electric'-era CULT with the likes of 'FULL FORCE LOVIN MACHINE' and 'WILD & WONDERFUL' highlights in their juggernaut of a live show. This was captured on the equally well received 'BLOOD, FIRE & LIVE', a concert set released in late 1990. 'SOUL DESTRUCTION' (1991) consolidated the band's success, the record (which included the sonic assault of the 'FREE'N'EASY' single) almost breaching the UK Top 20. With ex-ALICE COOPER axeman, PETER FRIESEN, replacing the departed TANTRUM, the band began work on 'POWERTRIPPIN', their most successful and accomplished work to date. The record reached No.5 upon its release in the Spring of 1993, a reflection of the sizable fanbase the band had built up through their relentless touring schedules.

Following a split with 'Polydor', the band signed with 'Chrysalis' in 1994, releasing the defiant 'CRANK' album later the same year. Two years on, they struggled to achieve significant sales on their 'JUST ADD LIFE' album, 'Raw Power' records subsequently taking over the reins of a band about to split. With NICK PARSONS coming into the fold to replace FRIESEN, The ALMIGHTY delivered an eponymous comeback set in 2000.

• **Songwriters:** Most penned by WARWICK, with some co-written with others. Covered; BODIES (Sex Pistols) / YOU AIN'T SEEN NOTHIN' YET (Bachman-Turner Overdrive) / IN A RUT (Ruts) / DO ANYTHING YOU WANNA DO (Rods) / etc.

• **Trivia:** They had meeting with Hell's Angels to discuss!? their similar group emblem/motif. ANDY CAIRNS of THERAPY? provided backing vox on 'CRANK' album.

RICKY WARWICK – vocals, rhythm & acoustic guitars / **TANTRUM** (b. McAVOY) – lead & rhythm guitars, vocals / **FLOYD LONDON** (b. FLOYD JAMES) – bass, acoustic guitar, vocals / **STUMP MUNROE** (b. JULIANS) – drums, percussion, vocals

Polydor M.C.A.

Jul 89. (7") *(PO 60)* **DESTROYED. / LOVE ME TO DEATH** [ ] [-]
(12"+=/12"s+=/cd-s+=) *(PZ/+P/CD 60)* – Blood, fire & love (metal version).

Oct 89. (lp/c/cd) *(841 347-1/-4/-2)* **BLOOD, FIRE & LOVE** [ ] [ ]
– Resurrection mutha / Destroyed / Wild and wonderful / Blood, fire & love / Gift horse / You've gone wild / Lay down the law / Power / Full force lovin' machine / Detroit. (c/cd+=) – New love sensation.

Jan 90. (7"ep/c-ep) *(PO/+CS 66)* **THE POWER EP** [ ] [ ]
– Power / Detroit / Wild and wonderful (live).
(12"clear-ep+=/12"pic-d-ep+=) *(PZF/PZP 66)* – ('A'-Killerwatt mix).
(cd-ep+=) *(PZCD 66)* – Lay down the law (live).

Jun 90. (7"/7"pic-d/c-s) *(PO/+P/CS 75)* **WILD & WONDERFUL. / THUNDERBIRD / GOOD GOD ALMIGHTY** [50] [ ]
(12"+=/12"pic-d+=) *(PZ/+P/CD 75)* – ('A'extended).

Oct 90. (m-cd/m-c/m-lp) *(847 107-2/-4/-1)* **BLOOD, FIRE & LIVE (live)** [62] [ ]
– Full force lovin' machine / You've gone wild / Lay down the law / Blood, fire & love / Destroyed / Wild and wonderful / Resurrection mutha / You ain't seen nothin' yet.

Feb 91. (7"/c-s) *(PO/+CS 127)* **FREE'N'EASY. / HELL TO PAY** [35] [ ]
(12"+=/cd-s+=) *(PZ/+CD 127)* – Bodies.

Mar 91. (cd/c/lp) *(847961-2/-4/-1)* **SOUL DESTRUCTION** [22] [ ]
– Crucify / Free'n'easy / Joy bang one time / Love religion / Bandaged knees / Praying to the red light / Sin against the light / Little lost sometimes / Devil's toy / What more do you want / Hell to pay / Loaded.

Apr 91. (7"/7"pic-d) *(PO/+P 144)* **DEVIL'S TOY. / BAD TEMPTATION** [36] [ ]
(12"+=/cd-s+=) *(PZ/+CD 144)* – ('A'extended).

Jun 91. (7") *(PO 151)* **LITTLE LOST SOMETIMES. / WILD ROAD TO SATISFACTION** [42] [ ]
(12"+=) *(PZ 151)* – Curiosity (live).
(pic-cd-s+=) *(PZCD 151)* – Detroit (live).

—— (Apr'92) **PETE FRIESEN** – lead guitar (ex-ALICE COOPER) repl. TANTRUM

Mar 93. (12"ep/cd-ep) *(PZ/+CD 261)* **ADDICTION. / ADDICTION (live) / SOUL DESTRUCTION (demo)** [38] [ ]

Apr 93. (cd/c/lp) *(519226-2/-4/-1)* **POWERTRIPPIN'** [5] [ ]
– Addiction / Possession / Over the edge / Jesus loves you . . . but I don't / Sick and wired / Powertrippin' / Taking hold / Out of season / Lifeblood / Instinct / Meathook / Eye to eye. *(cd w/ free live cd)* – Crucify / Full force loving machine / Love religion / Addiction / Sin against the light / Free 'n' easy / Wild and wonderful. *(re-iss. cd Apr95; 519104-2)*

May 93. (7"/c-s) *(PO/+P 266)* **OUT OF SEASON. / IN A RUT** [41] [ ]
(12"+=) *(PZ 266)* – Insomnia / Wild & wonderful (demo).
(cd-s+=) *(PZCD 266)* – Free'n'easy / Keep on rockin' in the free world.
(cd-s) *(PZCDX 266)* – ('A'side) / Fuckin' up / Out of season (demo) / Bodies.

Oct 93. (7"/c-s) *(PO/+CS 298)* **OVER THE EDGE. / TAKING HOLD (live)** [38] [ ]
(cd-s) *(PZCD 298)* – ('A'side) / Jesus loves you (but I don't) / Powertrippin' (live) / Blind.
(7"colrd) *(POP 298)* – ('A'side) / Lifeblood.

Chrysalis Chrysalis

Sep 94. (7"clear) *(CHS 5014)* **WRENCH. / SHITZOPHRENIC** [26] [ ]
(12"pic-d) *(12CHSPD 5014)* – ('A'side) / State of emergency / Hellelujah.
(cd-s) *(CDCHS 5014)* – ('A'side) / Do anything you wanna do / Give me fire.
(cd-s) *(CDCHSS 5014)* – ('A'side) / Thanks again, again / Knockin' on Joe.

Oct 94. (cd/c) *(CD/TC CHR 6086)* **CRANK** [15] [ ]
– Ultraviolent / Wrench / The unreal thing / Jonestown mind / Move right in / Crank and deceit / United state of apathy / Welcome to defiance / Way beyond belief / Crackdown / Sorry for nothing / Cheat. *(other cd+=; CDCHRZ 6086)* – Shitophrenic.

Jan 95. (7"pic-d) *(CHS 5017)* **JONESTOWN MIND. / ADDICTION (live) / CRANK (live) / DECEIT (live)** [26] [ ]
(12") *(12CHS 5017)* – ('A'side) / Jonestown dub / The unreal thing (live) / United state of apathy (live).
(cd-s) *(CDCHS 5017)* – ('A'side) / Wrench (live) / Move right in (live).
(cd-s) *(CDCHSS 5017)* – ('A'side) / Welcome to defiance (live) / Sorry for nothing (live).

Mar 96. (7"clear) *(CHS 5030)* **ALL SUSSED OUT. / EVERYBODY'S BURNING** [28] [ ]
(cd-s) *(CDCHS 5030)* – ('A'side) / Superpower / D.S.S. (Desperately Seeking Something).
(cd-s) *(CSCHSS 5030)* – ('A'side) / Tense nervous headshake / Canned Jesus.

Mar 96. (cd/c/lp) *(CD/TC+/CHR 6086)* **JUST ADD LIFE** [34] [ ]
– Ongoing and total / Do you understand / All sussed out / How real is real for you / Dead happy / Some kind of anything / Coalition star / 8 day depression / Look what happened tomorrow / 360 / Feel the need / Afraid of flying / Independent deterrent. *(cd re-iss. May96 w/ free live-cd 'JUST ADD LIVE'; RAWCD 118)* – Knockin' on Joe / Thanks again, again / Do anything you wanna do / State of emergency / Give me fire / Hellulajah / Jonestown mind (Therapy? & Ruts studio remixes). *(d-cd re-iss. Nov00 on 'Castle'; CMDDD 070)*

Raw Power not iss.

May 96. (cd-ep) *(RAWX 1022)* **DO YOU UNDERSTAND. / UNITED STATE OF APATHY (live) / OVER THE EDGE (live) / WILD & WONDERFUL (live)** [38] [-]
(cd-ep) *(RAWX 1023)* – ('A'side) / Crucify (live) / Jesus loves you (live) / I fought the law (live).
(cd-ep) *(RAWX 1024)* – ('A'-radio session) / Cheat (live) / Welcome to defiance (live) / Ultraviolent (live).

—— had already split by March, although they re-formed in 2000

—— **NICK PARSONS** – guitar, vocals; repl. FRIESEN

Sanctuary Sanctuary

Jun 00. (cd) *(SANC 003CD)* <4532> **THE ALMIGHTY** [ ] [ ]
– Broken machine / I'm in love (with revenge) / La chispa de la muerte / Big black automatic / For fuck's sake / Poison eyes / White anger comedown / TNT / Stop / USAK-47 / Alright / Barfly / Fat chance.

Sanctuary Pony Canyon

Oct 01. (cd) *(SANCD 101)* <1519> **PSYCHO-NARCO** [ ] [ ]
– Galvanize / 427 freak horsepower / Ruse / Soul on a roll / Begging / Hate the world / Waiting for earthquakes / If I knew what I wanted / 7x / Big idea idiot / Mondo balordo / Blowout kit for the underdog / Witness relocation programme / Million times nothing.

– compilations, etc. –

Apr 01. (cd) *Spectrum; (544390-2)* **WILD AND WONDERFUL** [ ] [-]
(re-iss. May02; same)

ALONE AGAIN OR (see under ⇒ SHAMEN)

ALTERED IMAGES

Formed: Glasgow . . . 1979 by JOHNNY McELHONE, TONY McDAID and MICHAEL 'TICH' ANDERSON, subsequently recruiting 'Gregory's Girl' bit actress, CLARE GROGAN, as a suitably kinetic frontwoman and second guitarist CAESAR. By mid 1980, they'd secured a support slot with SIOUXSIE & THE BANSHEES and following a promising John Peel session, were duly signed to 'Epic'.

Following minor chart success in early '81 with cult classic, 'DEAD POP STARS', CAESAR was replaced with JIM McKINVEN and the band released a second single, 'A DAY'S WAIT', to minimal reaction. It was a case of third time lucky, however, and the celebrations began in earnest with the release of 'HAPPY BIRTHDAY', a song which narrowly missed the top of the UK charts and came to define the band's kaleidoscopic pop sound. Bouncing about like a demented rag doll, GROGAN made for a compelling stage presence, her little-girl-on-helium vocals among the most disinctive in the new wave pack. 'HAPPY BIRTHDAY' the album spawned a further two major hits, namely 'I COULD BE HAPPY' and 'SEE THOSE EYES', although the band's popularity began to dip after the release of a second album, 'PINKY BLUE' (1982). ANDERSON and McINVEN subsequently departed (the latter would later reappear with ambient popsters ONE DOVE), STEPHEN LIRONI brought in as a replacement. A change in direction (or at least an altered image) resulted in a one-off Top 10 hit, 'DON'T TALK TO ME ABOUT LOVE', lifted from the accompanying album, 'BITE' (1983), although with GROGAN increasingly concentrating her full-time efforts on an acting career, the band ground to a halt later that year.

While LIRONI went on to form FLESH, McELHONE re-emerged initially with HIPSWAY, then TEXAS. Music wise, GROGAN released a lone 7" single, 'LOVE BOMB' in the mid-80's, later teaming up with LIRONI once more to form UNIVERSAL LOVE SCHOOL. Her cheeky grin can currently be witnessed on cable music channel, VH1, for whom GROGAN works as a presenter.

• **Songwriters:** McELHONE and group compositions / GROGAN lyrics. Also covered JEEPSTER (T.Rex) / SONG SUNG BLUE (Neil Diamond) / LITTLE TOWN FLIRT (Del Shannon).

• **Trivia:** STEVE SEVERIN (Siouxsie & The Banshees) produced debut 45, and MARTIN RUSHENT the debut album.

CLARE GROGAN (b. Mar'62) – vocals / **JOHNNY McELHONE** – guitar / **TONY McDAID** – bass / **MICHAEL 'Tich' ANDERSON** – drums / **CAESAR** – guitar

Epic / Portrait

Feb 81. (7") *(EPCA 1023)* **DEAD POP STARS. / SENTIMENTAL** [67] [ ]
(c-s+=) *(EPC40A 1023)* – Leave me alone.

— **JIM McKINVEN** – guitar (ex-BERLIN BLONDES) repl. CAESAR who joined The WAKE

May 81. (7") *(EPCA 1167)* **A DAY'S WAIT. / WHO CARES?** [ ] [ ]
Aug 81. (7") *(EPCA 1522)* **HAPPY BIRTHDAY. / SO WE GO WHISPERING** [2] [ ]
('A'dance mix-12"+=) *(EPCA13 1522)* – Jeepster.
Sep 81. (lp/c) *(EPC/40 84893)* **HAPPY BIRTHDAY** [26] [ ]
– (intro – Happy birthday) / Love and insects / Real toys / Idols / Legionaire / Faithless / Beckoning strings / Happy birthday / Midnight / A day's wait / Leave me alone / Insects / (outro – Happy birthday). *(re-iss. Sep83 lp/c; EPC/40 32355) (cd-iss. Sep91 & Jun95 on 'Columbia'; 480528-2) (re-iss. May93 on 'Sony Collectors'; 932944-2)*
Nov 81. (7"/7"pic-d) *(EPCA/+11 1834)* **I COULD BE HAPPY. / INSECTS** [7] [ ]
('A'dance mix-12"+=) *(EPCA13 1834)* – Disco pop stars.
Mar 82. (7"/7"pic-d) *(EPCA/+11 2198)* **SEE THOSE EYES. / HOW ABOUT THAT THEN (I MISSED MY TRAIN)** [11] [ ]
(12"+=) *(EPCA13 2198)* – ('A'extended).
Apr 82. (lp/c) *(EPC/40 85665)* **PINKY BLUE** [12] [ ]
– Pinky blue / See those eyes / Forgotten / Little brown head / See you later / Song sung blue / Funny funny me / Think that It might / I could be happy (version) / Jump jump / I could be happy (version) / Goodnight and I wish. *(cd-iss. Mar94 on 'Sony Collectors'; 983227-2)*
May 82. (7",7"pink) *(EPCA 2426)* **PINKY BLUE. / THINK THAT IT MIGHT (dance mix)** [35] [ ]
(12") *(EPCA13 2426)* – ('A'dance mix) / Jump jump – Think that it might (sequed dance mix).

— **STEPHEN LIRONI** – guitar, drums (ex-RESTRICTED CODE) repl. ANDERSON and McKINVEN The latter reappeared in the early 90s in ONE DOVE. Also used session people including **ANDY HAMILTON** – saxophone

Mar 83. (7"/7"pic-d/ext.12") *(EPCA/WA/EPCA13 3083)* **DON'T TALK TO ME ABOUT LOVE. / LAST GOODBYE** [7] [ ]
May 83. (7"/ext.12"/7"pic-d/ext.12"pic-d) *(EPCA/TA 3398)(WA/WTA 3398)* **BRING ME CLOSER. / SURPRISE ME** [29] [ ]
Jun 83. (lp/c) *(EPC/40 25413)* **BITE** [16] [ ]
– Bring me closer / Another lost look / Love to stay / Now that you're here / Don't talk to me about love / Stand so quiet / Change of heart / Thinking about you. *(c+=)* – Bring me closer (dance mix) / Don't talk to me about love (extended) / Surprise me / I don't want to know / Last goodbye.
Jul 83. (7"/ext.12") *(EPCA/TA 3582)* **LOVE TO STAY. / ANOTHER LOST LOOK (live)** [46] [ ]
Sep 83. (7") *(EPCA 3735)* **CHANGE OF HEART. / ANOTHER LOST LOOK** [ ] [ ]
(12"+=) *(TA 3735)* – Happy birthday / I could be happy.

— added on summer tour **DAVID WILD** – drums / **JIM PRIME** – keyboards

— the inevitable split came late '83. LIRONI formed FLESH and in the mid-90's returned to cult status when he formed The REVOLUTIONARY CORPS OF TEENAGE JESUS (with augmentation from – of all people – SUICIDE's ALAN VEGA). GROGAN had a brief solo career while McELHONE formed HIPSWAY and, later in 1989, formed TEXAS.

– compilations, others, etc. –

on 'Epic' unless mentioned otherwise

Mar 83. (7"ep/c-ep) *(EPCA/+40 2617)* **GREATEST ORIGINAL HITS** [ ] [-]
– Happy birthday / I could be happy / Dead pop stars / A day's wait.
May 84. (lp/c) *(EPC/40 25973)* **COLLECTED IMAGES** [ ] [-]
Jan 87. (7") *Old Gold; (OG 9663)* **HAPPY BIRTHDAY. / I COULD BE HAPPY** [ ] [-]
Jul 96. (cd) *(484339-2)* **REFLECTED IMAGES (THE BEST OF ALTERED IMAGES)** [ ] [-]
– Happy birthday (intro) / Dead pop stars / Happy birthday / Love and kisses / Real toys / I could be happy / See those eyes / Pinky blue / Forgotten / See you later / Don't talk to me about love / Bring me closer / Love to stay / Change of heart / Thinking about you / Happy birthday (12" mix) / Don't talk to me about love (12" mix) / Love to stay (12" mix) / Bring me closer (12" mix) / Last goodbye (don't talk to me about love) / Happy birthday (outro). *(re-iss. Aug00; same)*

FLESH

STEPHEN LIRONI – guitars (ex-ALTERED IMAGES)

London / not iss.

Sep 85. (7"/12") *(LON/+X 72)* **YOU CAN'T HELP. / SENTIMENTAL SUNDAY** [ ] [-]
Mar 86. (7"/12") *(LON/+X 87)* **THE 2ND CHOICE. / SELF YOURSELF** [ ] [-]

CLARE GROGAN

— revived her acting career, noteably in another Bill Forsyth movie 'Comfort And Joy', plus TV parts in 'Red Dwarf' & 'Blott On The Landscape'. Around this period (1986), she also went solo. Now with songwriters **DAVEY HENDERSON** (of WIN) and **HILARY MORRISON** (ex-FLOWERS)

London / not iss.

May 87. (7"/12") *(LON/+X 134)* **LOVE BOMB. / I LOVE THE WAY YOU BEG** [ ] [-]

— in 1989 she teamed up with LIRONI again to form UNIVERSAL LOVE SCHOOL

ALTERNATIVE

Formed: Dunfermline ... early 1980 by CRAIG NIZHO and ERIC BEVERIDGE, two sparring frontmen who were joined by other punk-minded geezers ROSNEY COMME, WOLF SUUMAN and JAMES MURPHY. Having made their vinyl debut on the infamous 'Bullshit Detector' compilation released by 'Crass', the ALTERNATIVE finally got around to issuing their own one-off single, 'IN NOMINE PATRE', in 1983.

CRAIG NIZHO – vocals / **ERIC BEVERIDGE** – vocals / **RODNEY COMME** – guitar / **WOLF SUUMAN** – bass / **JAMES MURPHY** – drums

Crass / not iss.

Mar 83. (7"ep) *(22-198/8)* **IN NOMINE PATRI EP** [ ] [-]

— disappeared after above single

AMATEUR GUITAR ANTI HEROES

(see under ⇒ Path records)

AMPHETAMEANIES

Formed: Glasgow . . . 1998 by 10-piece fronted by blonde JANE CHALMERS and skinhead STAN MILLAR, along with her musician chums HELEN LLOYD, JENNY (aka MISS DIVERSE) and LINDSEY WATSON, plus his pals RAT, ALEX HUNTLEY, MICK COOKE, GORDON DAVIDSON and JOEL GRAY (some of whom moonlighted with BELLE & SEBASTIAN, LUNGLEG and THE KARELIA). Ska-rawkers (in every sense of the paraphrase!), this cartoon-esque girl/boy outfit/ensemble released a handful of singles, the best of which was 'LAST NIGHT' and 'WHISKY'; the latter was delightfully influenced by The REZILLOS and SPLODGENESSABOUNDS. Live outings included a trip to Paris early in '99, while a riotous 'T In The Park' slot brought them a tidy earner. The following year, decade, century, whatever, saw the entourage deliver their schizoid debut set, 'RIGHT LINE IN NYLONS'.

JANE CHALMERS – vocals (of LUNGLEG) / **STAN MILLAR** – vocals / **HELEN LLOYD** – hammond organ, backing vocals / **RAT** – guitars / **ALEX HUNTLEY** – guitars, backing vocals, keyboards (of THE KARELIA) / **MISS DIVERSE** (b. JENNY) – saxophone, backing vocals, percussion / **LINDSEY WATSON** – trombone, backing vocals, big drum / **MICK COOKE** – trumpet, glockenspiel, backing vocals, big drum / **GORDON**

DAVIDSON – bass, percussion, backing vocals / **JOEL GRAY** – drums, percussion, very big drum

Flotsam & Jetsam / not iss.

Jul 98. (7") *(SHaG 13.09)* **Club Beatroot Part Nine** – Speed fever / VERA CRUISE: Wasted sounds. (above was released in conjunction with 'The 13th Note') [ ] [-]

Dec 98. (7") *(SHaG 021)* **AROUND THE WORLD IN 5 1/2 MINUTES** – Mo'ska / Tales of the Arizona highway patrol. [ ] [-]

Apr 99. (7"/cd-s) *(SHaG/+CD 024)* **LAST NIGHT. / SUSIETHEMUPPET** [ ] [-]

Oct 99. (7") *(SHaG 026)* **TREATY AT HARTHILL** – Whisky / NEWTOWN GRUNTS: Everywhere she goes. [ ] [-]

Jul 00. (cd) *(SHaG 027)* **RIGHT LINE IN NYLONS** [ ] [-]
– Last night / Bedroom holiday / Ghost bus / Speed fever / Prince Albert / Fiend or foe / Point blank / Whisky / The sun shines down / Theme from Radio Spytime / Driving home / Life without you / Susiethemuppet / 60 hours in Albuquerque.

ANALOGUE (see under ⇒ Evolution records – Q-TEX)

ANEKA

Born: MARY SANDEMAN, c.1955/56, Perthshire (I think) – yes, the mezzo soprano lady of the Highlands that sang traditional ballads on our TV sets in the late 70's; she also issued an LP, 'INTRODUCING MARY SANDEMAN' for 'R.E.L.' in 1980. As ANEKA – a name she pinned from a phonebook – and donning a kimono and a red shiny wig, she took the music world by surprise when her novelty debut single, 'JAPANESE BOY' (written by BOBBY HEATLIE) shot to No.1 in August 1981. However, apart from her follow-up 'LITTLE LADY' subsequently denting the Top 50, the name ANEKA was put into the one hit wonder file. Having been washed up – quite literally – ANEKA once again became MARY SANDEMAN and hosted her own TV show for the BBC in '82. A few years later, 'R.E.L' issued a second traditional LP, 'MARY SANDEMAN REQUESTS' (1985). MARY subsequently settled down to a family life but still popped up on the odd occasion for the Scottish Fiddle Orchestra and other Hogmanay-type things. I wonder if she still keeps her ANEKA gear?

ANEKA – vocals / with various backing

Ariola-Hansa / not iss.

Jul 81. (7") *(HANSA 5)* **JAPANESE BOY. / AE FOND KISS** [1] [-]

Oct 81. (7") *(HANSA 8)* **LITTLE LADY. / CHASING DREAMS** [50] [-]

Sep 82. (7") *(HANSA 13)* **OOH SHOOBY DOO DO LANG. / COULD IT LAST A LITTLE LONGER** [ ] [-]

Ariola / not iss.

Feb 83. (7") *(295)* **HEART TO BEAT. / STARSHINE** [ ] [-]

—— ANEKA returned to her proper name

– compilations, others, etc. –

1987. (7"; by ANEKA) *Old Gold; (OG 9710)* **JAPANESE BOY. / (track by other artist)** [ ] [-]

ANGELFISH (see under ⇒ GOODBYE MR MACKENZIE)

ANGELHEART (see ⇒ Section 9: Dance/Rave)

ANNIE CHRISTIAN

Formed: Leith, Edinburgh . . . Spring '97 by main songwriter, LARRY LEAN, CHRIS ADAMS, DAVID HUNTER and ANDREW HASTINGS (another member does the floating job!), all possessing a penchant for PRINCE and the late political comedian, BILL HICKS. Managed by Bruce Findlay (Radio DJ, famous for overseeing SIMPLE MINDS' rise to fame), the quartet delivered their debut, 'LOVE THIS LIFE', early the following year. They fitted neatly into the MANICS / STEREOPHONICS brand of rifferama rock, their gothic lyrics overpowering enough to set them apart. • **Covered:** TRANSMISSION (Joy Division).

LARRY LEAN – vocals, guitar / **CHRIS ADAMS** – guitar / **DAVID HUNTER** – bass / **ANDREW HASTINGS** – drums

Equipe Ecosse – V2 / Orchard

Mar 98. (7") *(EQE 500139-7)* **LOVE THIS LIFE. / THE SHATTERED BURLESQUE** [ ] [-]
(cd-s+=) *(EQE 500139-3)* – Satellites spin.

May 98. (7") *(EQE 500190-7)* **SOMEDAY MY PRINCE WILL COME AGAIN. / WHILE YOU SLEEP** [ ] [-]
(cd-s+=) *(EQE 500190-3)* – This world has no time for lovers.

Sep 98. (7") *(EQE 500253-7)* **THE OTHER WAY. / TRANSMISSION** [ ] [-]
(cd-s+=) *(EQE 500253-3)* – Drugs work.

Feb 99. (7") *(EQE 500516-7)* **KISS THE DAY GOODBYE. / GET IT ON** [ ] [-]
(cd-s+=) *(EQE 500516-3)* – 500 miles low.

Mar 99. (cd/lp) *(EQE 100214-2/-1)* *<6435>* **TWILIGHT** <US title 'SOFTCORE'> [ ] [ ] Jul00
– Love this life / Kiss the day goodbye / The other way / Secret and lies / Here is the news / Clearwater goldmine / Nothing is real / Ode to an Indian summer / The boy with the golden arm / Hicks (1961-1994) / Someday my prince will come again / Stupid thoughts / Twilight. *(CD-ROM tracks+=)* – The other way (video) / Kiss the day goodbye (video). *(cd re-iss. Dec00 as 'SOFTCORE' on 'Filthy Mouth'; FM 1)*

V2 / not iss.

Apr 99. (7") *(VVR 500674-7)* **LOVE THIS LIFE. / THE BOY WITH THE GOLDEN ARM (live)** [ ] [-]
(cd-s+=) *(VVR 500674-3)* – Clearwater goldmine (live).

ANOTHER PRETTY FACE (see under ⇒ WATERBOYS)

APB

Formed: Aberdeen . . . early 80's by IAIN SLATER, GLEN ROBERTS and GEORGE CHEYNE. Taking their inspiration from the bare-wired club sounds of New York, APB, funked their way from the Granite City to supporting their hero, JAMES BROWN, on a massive UK tour.

Having already completed five DIY singles on their own 'Oily' label, the group added a 5th member, MIKEY CRAIGHEAD, for extra percussive effect and released a one-off double-A 45, 'WHAT KIND OF GIRL' / 'DANCEABILITY' on 'Albion' in 1984. However, the group struggled from then on in and only a handful of singles and a much-delayed debut album, 'CURE FOR THE BLUES' (1986), surfaced before their demise. • **Note:** Not to be confused with the American A.P.B., whose 1982-83 line-up featured ARTIMUS PYLE (ex-LYNYRD SKYNYRD).

IAIN SLATER – vocals, bass / **GLEN ROBERTS** – guitar / **GEORGE CHEYNE** – drums

Oily / not iss.

Jul 81. (7") *(SLICK 6)* **CHAIN REACTION. / POWER CRISIS** [ ] [-]

Oct 81. (7") *(SLICK 7)* **(I'D LIKE TO) SHOOT YOU DOWN. / TALK TO ME** [ ] [-]

—— added **NEIL INNES** – keyboards (not the funnyman!)

Apr 82. (7") *(SLICK 8)* **PALACE FILLED WITH LOVE. / ALL YOUR LIFE WITH ME** [ ] [-]

Oct 82. (7") *(SLICK 9)* **RAINY DAY. / FROM YOU AND BACK TO YOU** [ ] [-]

Aug 83. (7"/12") *(SLICK/+12 10)* **ONE DAY. / HELP YOURSELF** [ ] [-]

—— added **MIKEY CRAIGHEAD** – percussion

Albion / not iss.

Mar 84. (12"ep) *(12ION 160)* **DANCEABILITY (parts 1 & 2). / CRAZY GREY / RAINY DAY / PALACE FILLED WITH LOVE** [ ] [-]

Jun 84. (7"/12") *(ION/12ION 170)* **WHAT KIND OF GIRL. / (2 versions)** [ ] [-]

Red River / Link

Jul 85. (7"/12") *(Ythan/+T 1)* **SUMMER LOVE. / IS THE MUSIC LOUD ENOUGH** [ ] [-]

Oct 85. (7") *(Ythan 2)* **SOMETHING TO BELIEVE IN. / SO MANY BROKEN HEARTS** [ ] [-]
(12"+=) *(YthanT 2)* – ('A'&'B'versions).

Apr 86. (7"/12") *(Ythan/+T 3)* **OPEN YOUR EYES. / SUNSET SONG** [ ] [-]

Apr 86. (lp) *(YthanLP 4)* **CURE FOR THE BLUES** [ ] [-]

–

Oct 87. (lp/cd) *(Ythan LP/CD 5)* **SOMETHING TO BELIEVE IN** (compilation) [ ] [ ]
– Shoot you down / Talk to me / Palace filled with love / Rainy day / One day / Summer love / Something to believe in / So many broken hearts / What kind of Girl? / Danceability (parts 1 & 2) / Chain reaction / Power crisis / All your life with me / From you & back to you / Help yourself / Is the music loud enough?

Oct 87. (7"ep) *(Ythan 6)* **MISSING YOU ALREADY. / BEST OF OUR LOVE / BOY, YOU'RE NOT SO GREAT** [ ] [-]
(12"-iss.Apr89; YthanT 6)

—— split some time in 1988, with some becoming . . .

LOVELESS

Embryo / not iss.

1988. (12"ep) *(EMB 001)* **FIELDS OF YELLOW / LOW DOWN SNEAK. / BIG FAT COW / HYPOCRITE** [ ] [-]

APPENDIX OUT

Formed: Glasgow . . . summer '94 by ALI ROBERTS and DAVE E. WHITE, inspired by a gig from country Lo-Fi'ers, PALACE. In fact it would be their leader, WILL OLDHAM, who released the first vinyl outing by APPENDIX OUT, entitled 'ICE AGE'.

Subsequently, the group of acoustic No-Fi troubadours enlisted the help of cellist LOUISE D and percussionist EVA PECK, the latter bringing sparse rhythm to the combo's folky weep-core. With the APPENDIX OUT line-up almost finalised, they donated material to the Up Records compilation CD '4x4' while split single 'WELL-LIT TONIGHT' was much sought after in some music quarters. This immediately caught the attention of eager-beaver labels planning to take folk/country screaming into the the 21st Century. But it was astonishingly US imprint 'Drag City' who came up trumphs when they signed the band in 1997 – adding them to a list of brilliant new generation songsmiths.

This prompted the release of the outfit's debut set, 'THE RYE BEARS A POISON' – a groundbreaking achievement for a "wee" band in '97 – most definitely a Sunday morning record, with its calming guitars, emotional vocals and splendid tranquillity reminiscent of NICK DRAKE's 'Pink Moon' era. Things could only get better for APPENDIX OUT. ROBERTS added guitarist-cum-percussionist GARETH EGGIE and flautist/keyboard-player EVA PECK to the cauldron of country karma who debuted on the band's second and most realised work, 'DAYLIGHT SAVING' (1999). Sticking with the WILL OLDHAM vs SMOG formula, the set was unique in its own right with songs such as opener 'FOUNDLING', leading the way to what should have blasted BELLE & SEBASTIAN out of the proverbial water. Of course, the troupe's style was very much American, but that's not to say APPENDIX OUT should not have been an asset to new Scottish music. Their softly spoken harmonies, mandolin breaks and acoustic set-ups were/are very much rooted in traditional folk (they even covered Anne Briggs 'LOWLANDS'), giving them the opportunity to shine where other bands would only sparkle.

'LIEDER FUR KASPER HAUSER', a 7" EP, was to be the group's next release late in '99. It featured the tracks 'EIN GRAUERSTAR IN DER KAVALLERIE' and the sombre instrumental 'AN DER NACHTIMMEL GEWOHNT', both of which helped inspire ROBERTS in his own traditional solo venture 'THE CROOK OF MY ARMS' (2001), which was recorded over a one-day period in Glasgow. He subsequently regrouped APPENDIX OUT to issue their fantasic folksy cover-pleaser EP 'A WARM AND YEASTY CORNER' (2002), which included a rendition of the Incredible String Band's 'A VERY CELLULAR SONG' and Ewan MacColl's 'THE FIRST TIME EVER I SAW YOUR FACE', to name two. Other tracks such as 'SALLY FREE AND EASY' and 'JOSEPHINE' were given the APPENDIX spin, with hushed flutes, pianos and a whole host of acoustic instruments adding to the outfit's sparse effect.

ALI ROBERTS (b. ALASDAIR, Callander) – vocals, guitar / **DAVE E. WHITE** – bass, violin, keyboards

Palace / Palace

Dec 96. (ltd-7") *(<PR 10>)* **ICE AGE. / PISSED WITH YOU** — Jan96

— added **EVA PECK** – drums / **LOUISE D** – cello

Creeping Bent / not iss.

Sep 97. (7") *(bent 027)* **WELL LIT TONIGHT. / (other track by the Leopards)** — -

Drag City / Drag City

Oct 97. (lp/cd) *(<DC 126/CD>)* **THE RYE BEARS A POISON**
– Our sea / Brazil / East Coast wedding / Many-legged boatmen / Frozen blight / Wild I lived in Flanders / Seagulls, belts / Lassie, lie near me / The harp key / Autumn.

Jun 98. (7") *(bent 034)* **LASSIE, LIE NEAR ME. / (other track by Policecat)** — -
(above issued on 'Creeping Bent', below on 'Liquefaction'/'Bad Jazz'>

Jul 98. (7"ep) *<Bebop 3>* **SECOND PERTHSHIRE HOUSE SONG / ROUND REEL OF EIGHT / TWELVE OF THEM / HAY BALE BLUES. / (others by Songs: Ohia)** -
(UK-iss.2000 on 'Bad Jazz'; same)

Jan 99. (7"ep) *(MILK 001)* **BOYHOOD / WILD LIVING. / (others by the MONGERS)** — -
(above issued on 'Galvani')

— **ALI ROBERTS** recruited **TOM CROSSLEY** – drums (of INTERNATIONAL AIRPORT) / **GARETH EGGIE** – guitar, percussion / **DAVE ELCOCK + KATE WRIGHT**

Jul 99. (lp/cd) *(<DC 152/+CD>)* **DAYLIGHT SAVING** — Apr99
– Foundling / The grey havens / Tangled hair / The scything / Little owl / Row upstream / Merchant city / Exile / Arcane lore. *(lp re-iss. Aug00; same)*

Nov 99. (7") *<WEST 007>* **LIEDER FUR KASPAR HAUSER** -
– Ein grauerstar in der kavallerie / An den nachtimmel gewohnt.
(above on 'Western Vinyl')

— added **MARK** (of DEN ALMA; with GARETH)

Mar 01. (cd) *(<DC 189CD>)* **THE NIGHT IS ADVANCING** — Apr01
– A path to our beds / The seven widows (the springs of night) / The groves of Lebanon / Golden tablets of the sun / Year waxing, year waning / Fortified jackdaw grove / The night is advancing / Cyclone's vernal retreat / (Bringing the yearlings) Home / Hexen in the anticyclone / Campfire's burning (round) / Organise a march.

Shingle Street / not iss.

Apr 02. (cd-ep) *(SHING 001)* **A WARM AND YEASTY CORNER** — -
– Window over the bay / Sally free and easy / The first time ever I saw your face / Josephine / A very cellular song.

ALASDAIR ROBERTS

not iss. / Secretly Canadian

Apr 01. (cd,lp) *<SC 48CD>* **THE CROOK OF MY ARM** -
– Lord Gregory / As I came in by Huntly town / Bonnie lass among the heather / The magpie's nest / Ploughboy lads / Lowlands / Master Kilby / Standing in yon flowe'ry garden / Ye banks and braes o' bonny Doon / The flase bride / The month of January / The wife of Ushers Well.

APPLES

Formed: Edinburgh . . . 1989 by lyricist/frontman CALLUM McNAIR, bass player IAN STODDART (straight from WIN) and SAMANTHA SWANSON (ex-HEY! ELASTICA).

With Indie, Rave and Madchester all the rage in the early 90's, The APPLES built up their street-cred by alienating some of the critical journos south of Watford who thought the core of the group's music was similar to EMF and JESUS JONES. 'Epic' records showed faith in the band, however, but only initially as their debut single, 'EYE WONDER', pierced the UK Top 75, at er . . . No.75. A follow-up, 'STAY PEOPLE CHILD', sold poorly and the accompanying album, 'HERE IS TOMORROW' was withdrawn, only to resurface once more in remixed form as 'PEOPLE' (1991).

The APPLES bore little fruit thereafter and were dropped unceremoniously from Epic; CALLUM was initially enthusiastic about his chances of making a comeback with the more adventurous CAPTAIN SHIFTY, but yet again his ambitions remained unrealised. It was a sore lesson for the APPLES who were unluckily short-changed by media/tabloid attention/hype for another fresh genre:- Grunge. If they had just been called APPLES AND PEARS . . .

CALLUM McNAIR – vocals (ex-SYNDICATE) / **IAN STODDART** - bass (ex-EVEREST THE HARD WAY, ex-WIN) / **SAMANTHA SWANSON** – vocals (ex-HEY! ELASTICA) / +1

Epic / not iss.

Feb 91. (7") *(656671-7)* **EYE WONDER. /** 75 -
(12"+=/cd-s+=) *(656671-6/-2)* –

Aug 91. (7") **STAY PEOPLE CHILD. /** — -
(cd-s+=) –

Sep 91. (cd/c/lp) *(468944-2/-4/-1)* **PEOPLE** — -
– Free / Stay people child / Colours / Eye wonder / Love on ya / Beautiful people / Here is tomorrow / Joy / Magic sign / All of the world.

1992. (7") **BEAUTIFUL PEOPLE. / LOVESIDEDOWNAROUND** — -
(12"+=/cd-s+=) – ('A'-Stereo guitar people) / ('A'mix).

— split soon after above; STODDART formed CAPTAIN SHIFTY who featured chanteuse NICKY KING on vocals (recorded for 'Different Class' in 1995); she's now a solo artist signed to 'Talkin' Loud'.

ARAB STRAP

Formed: Falkirk . . . 1995 by AIDAN MOFFAT and MALCOLM MIDDLETON. The former had already given up his day job at the local Sleeves record shop to team up with songwriter, JASON "JT" TAYLOR, in his outfit, BAY. This low-key band with drummer! AIDAN (augmented on their second release by RONNIE YOUNG, WILL HEGGIE – ex-COCTEAU TWINS – and ROSS BALLANY), released a couple of RED HOUSE PAINTERS-esque CD's, namely 'HAPPY BEING DIFFERENT' (1994) and 'ALISON RAE' (1995), the latter including a Lo-Fi cover of Roxy Music's 'IN EVERY DREAM HOME A HEARTACHE' and also coming free with an acoustic CD featuring a version of Nick Drake's 'WHICH WILL'.

AIDAN, meanwhile, was plotting his own breakaway group, ARAB STRAP

(named after a device used for horse-breeding and better known for something bought from a sex shop), re-establishing a friendship with MALCOLM while writing songs together in the latter's bedroom. A debut ARAB STRAP single, 'THE FIRST BIG WEEKEND', was warmly received by the music press in September '96, critics describing it as "trainspotting for the music world". AIDAN's drug/drink-fuelled life was portrayed in painful detail in a couple of the narrative songs from debut album, 'THE WEEK NEVER STARTS ROUND HERE' (incidentally the rhythm section was completed by GARY MILLER and DAVID GOW). His bittersweet, off-the-cuff, Scots-accented sagas of broken romance were squeezed between Lo-Fi mumblings of occasional pure genius – several of these provided by their equally wasted pal, JOHN MAUCHLINE. MALCOLM's guitar-plucking, meanwhile, came from the laid back school of cool, often played while literally lying on his back. The album was heralded by many (including John Peel) as the next big thing in exotic sound. It included seminal classics, 'THE CLEARING', 'COMING DOWN', 'I WORK IN A SALOON', 'WASTING' and 'DEEPER'. Their live set (including an early afternoon spot at Scotland's 'T In The Park' that added a host of singalong friends), was a mixture of apathy-in-concrete attitude with most people shouting for their favourite, 'THE FIRST BIG WEEKEND'; the track was subsequently used as the backing (with a new coherent talker!) on the Guinness ad (yes, that one that says about 38 per cent of all strippers were educated in a convent!).

A year on, with word of mouth cult status ensured, ARAB STRAP finally achieved minor chart glory when 'THE GIRLS OF SUMMER' EP dented the Top 75. Following on from a double header tour with drinking buddies, MOGWAI, the now bearded AIDAN and Co delivered a surprise Top 50 hit, 'HERE WE GO' (a double A-side with 'TRIPPY'), one of the many low-rent, X-rated classics on their Top 40 Spring 1998 follow-up, 'PHILOPHOBIA'. Having signed up with 'Go Beat' early in '99, ARAB STRAP proceeded to deliver a disappointing stop-gap limited-edition live set, 'MAD FOR SADNESS'. Four months later, the 'CHERUBS' EP made amends and was one of the highlights of their rush-released third studio album, the over commercialised 'ELEPHANT SHOE'.

However, after a two year vacation from the music scene, The 'STRAP returned in 2001 with their deeply poetic fourth outing 'THE RED THREAD'. Theme'd, as ever, around sex and love and drinking in the central belt of Scotland, the duo refused to change their style of song structure. But with single 'LOVE DETECTIVE' harking back to ARAB STRAP's earlier moments (thumping house beats, accompanied by MIDDLETON's sparse guitar playing) and closing track 'TURBULENCE' delivering a fine closure – if not conclusion – it's a wonder why this pair of talented musicians even strayed from their nest in the first place. Of late, AIDAN and a plethora of other, mainly Scottish musicians/singers, have got together for one set, 'Y'ALL GET SCARED NOW, YA HEAR' (2001) under the REINDEER SECTION banner. September 2002 was certainly an eventful month for MOFFAT and MIDDLETON with the release of both solo projects: the former with the LUCKY PIERRE minimalist instrumental set, 'HYPNOGOGIA', the latter with his solo effort, '5.14 FLUOXYTINE SEAGULL ALCOHOL JOHN NICOTINE' – the jury was certainly out on MOFFAT's noodlings.

AIDAN MOFFAT – vocals, keyboards / **MALCOLM MIDDLETON** – guitar / **GARY MILLER** – bass / **DAVID GOW** – drums

Chemikal Underground / Chemikal Underground

Sep 96. (7") *(CHEM 007)* **THE FIRST BIG WEEKEND. / GILDED** [ ] [-]

—— interruptions/tape narrative by **JOHN MAUCHLINE**

Nov 96. (lp/cd) *(<CHEM 010/+CD>)* **THE WEEK NEVER STARTS ROUND HERE** [ ] [ ] 1997
– Coming down / The clearing / Driving / Gourmet / I work in a saloon / Wasting / General plea to a girlfriend / The first big weekend / Kate Moss / Little girls / Phone me tonight / Blood / Deeper.

Mar 97. (12"/cd-s) *(CHEM 013/+CD)* **THE CLEARING (guest starring Isobel Campbell & Chris Geddes). / (remixed by Hungry Lions) (remixed by Iain Hanlon & Jonathan Hilditch)** [ ] [-]

Sep 97. (12"ep/cd-ep) *(CHEM 017/+CD)* **THE GIRLS OF SUMMER E.P.** [74] [-]
– Hey! fever / Girls of summer / The beautiful barmaids of Dundee / One day, after school.

Nov 97. (7"m) *(LISS 22)* **THE SMELL OF OUTDOOR COOKING. / THEME TUNE / BLACKSTAR** [ ] [-]
(above issued on 'Lissy's', below on 'Too Many Cooks')

1998. (7") *(BROTH 001)* **LIVE: PACKS OF THREE. / BLOOD** [ ] [-]

Chemikal Underground / Matador

Mar 98. (10"/cd-s) *(CHEM 20 T/CD)* **HERE WE GO. / TRIPPY** [48] [-]

Apr 98. (cd) *(CHEM 21CD) <OLE 315>* **PHILOPHOBIA** [37] [ ] May98
– Packs of three / Soaps / Here we go / New birds / One day, after school / Islands / The night before the funeral / Not quite a yes / Piglet / Afterwards / My favourite muse / I would've liked me a lot last night / The first time you're unfaithful.

Sep 98. (7") *(CHEM 27)* **(AFTERNOON) SOAPS. / PHONE ME TOMORROW** [74] [-]
(12"+=/cd-s+=) *(CHEM 27 T/CD)* – ('A'side) / Toy fights / Forest hills.

Go Beat / not iss.

May 99. (cd/lp) *(547387-2/-1)* **MAD FOR SADNESS (live)** [ ] [-]
– Intro – My favourite muse / Packs of three / New birds / Toy fights / Here we go / Phone me tomorrow / Girls of summer / Piglet / Blood / Afterwards. *<US cd-iss. Jul00 on 'Jetset'; 029>*

Aug 99. (12"ep/cd-ep) *(GOB X/CD 21 – 561263-1/-2)* **CHERUBS E.P.** [ ] [-]
– Cherubs / Motown answers / An eventful day / Pulled.

—— next with guests, CORA BISSETT, BARRY BURNS + ALAN WYLIE

Sep 99. (cd/lp) *(547805-2/-1)* **ELEPHANT SHOE** [ ] [-]
– Cherubs / One four seven one / Pyjamas / Autumnal / Lay the day free / Direction of strong man / Tanned / Aries the ram / The drinking eye / Pro-(your) life / Hello daylight. *<US cd-iss. Jun00 on 'Jetset'; 028>*

Chemikal Underground / Matador

Nov 00. (12"/cd-s) *(CHEM 048/+CD)* **FUKD ID VOL.2 EP** [ ] [-]
– Rocket, take your turn / Blackness.

Jan 01. (12"/cd-s) *(CHEM 049/+CD)* **LOVE DETECTIVE. / BULLSEYE / WE KNOW WHERE YOU LIVE** [66] [-]

Feb 01. (lp/cd) *(CHEM 050/+CD) <OLE 503>* **THE RED THREAD** [ ] [ ]
– Amor veneris / Last orders / Scenery / The Devil-tips / The long sea / Love detective / Infrared / Screaming in the trees / Haunt me / Turbulence.

May 01. (12"/cd-s) *(CHEM 051/+CD)* **TURBULENCE (mixes by BIS, ARAB STRAP & JASON FAMOUS)** [ ] [-]

LUCKY PIERRE

—— aka (French DJ) AIDAN MOFFAT with the FORCE

Lucky / not iss.

Feb 99. (7") *(LUCKY 001)* **PIERRE'S FINAL THOUGHT. / SOMETIMES I FEEL LIKE A MOTHERLESS CHILD** [ ] [-]

Jul 99. (12") *(LUCKY 02)* **BLANK FOR YOUR OWN MESSAGE** [ ] [-]

Melodic / not iss.

May 02. (12") **ANGELS ON YOUR BODY. / BOGEY ON MY SIX** [ ] [-]

Sep 02. (lp/cd) *(MELO 013/+CD)* **HYPNOGOGIA** [ ] [-]
– Angels of your body / Nurse flamingo / Shatterproof / Ghost two / The heart of all that is / The bit in the woods / Sometimes I feel like a motherless child / White Heaven in Hell / Ghost one / Bedwomb.

MALCOLM MIDDLETON

Chemikal Underground / not iss.

Sep 02. (cd) *(chem 062cd) 5.14 FLUOXYTINE SEAGULL ALCOHOL JOHN NICOTINE* [ ] [-]
– Crappo the clown / Wake up / The loneliest night of my life come calling / Best in me / Cold winter / Bring down (preprise) / Rotten heart / Speed on the M9 / 1, 2, 3, 4 / Birdwatcher / The king of bring / Devil and the angel.

BAY

JASON "JR" TAYLOR – vocals, guitar, bass / with **AIDAN MOFFAT** – drums!

Noise Annoys / Cargo

Nov 94. (m-cd) *(ANANCD 2)* **HAPPY BEING DIFFERENT** [ ] [-]
– Four miles / Spleen / Embossed and embellished / A shock in store for Piggsy / Kate / Your day out.

—— **JR** now with **AIDAN / + WILL HEGGIE** – bass (of LOWLIFE, ex-COCTEAU TWINS) / **ROSS BALLANY** – drums / **RONNIE YOUNG** – guitar

Oct 95. (cd) *(ANANCD 6)* **ALISON RAE** [ ] [-]
– Washington / Pure / Home / Dutch / Siamese / In every dream home a heartache / In Lisa's living room / Ruptured / Are you alone? / A great red shark / Surely someone somewhere. *(w/ free cd)* **ACOUSTIC** – Washington / Pure / Surely someone somewhere / Concrete lions / Spleen / Obligatory / Kate / Four years / Spaniard / Which will.

ARMOURY SHOW (see under ⇒ SKIDS)

Craig ARMSTRONG

Born: c.1963, Shettleston, Glasgow. ARMSTRONG's musical career got off to a flying start when he was named the UK's 'Young Jazz Musician Of The Year' in 1981, the teenage prodigy subsequently becoming an integral part of the mid-late 80's Scottish pop/rock scene. As well as putting in session work (mainly on keys) for the likes of HIPSWAY and TEXAS, ARMSTRONG also spent time as a fully-fledged member of The BIG DISH.

He was at the centre of things yet again in the 90's, working with superstars MADONNA, PASSENGERS (U2's side-project) and SUEDE. Perhaps his most credible work came via a collaboration with MASSIVE ATTACK, both playing piano and providing strings on 1994's 'Protection' set. His career took a dramatic turn in the middle of the decade as he was commissioned to write the scores for both 'Romeo & Juliet' and 'Mission Impossible'. U2's LARRY MULLEN and ADAM CLAYTON were also involved in the latter, while the former landed ARMSTRONG a well-deserved Ivor Novello award. Still very much the man behind the scenes, CRAIG finally delivered his very own solo album, 'THE SPACE BETWEEN US' in 1998. The record was released on MASSIVE ATTACK's 'Melankolic' label, a connection that extended to CRAIG re-working the Bristolians 'WEATHER STORM' as the album's opener. Elsewhere, the increasingly avant-garde composer covered the Blue Nile's 'LET'S GO OUT TONIGHT' (with the track's author PAUL BUCHANAN guesting) while the COCTEAU TWINS' LIZ FRASER turned up on 'THIS LOVE'. Prior to the latter's release as a single that summer, CRAIG had already experienced chart action (UK Top 30), partnering SHOLA AMA on 'SOMEDAY I'LL FIND YOU'.

The man took his introspective, widescreen sonic vision to a higher plane in 1999 with the soundtrack to 'PLUNKETT AND MACLEANE', combining his love of leftfield electronica with classically-inspired experimentation. A tad ENO-like in his pursuit of otherworldly sounds, CRAIG even managed to cover Talking Heads' 'HOUSES IN MOTION'. Advancing the field of soundtrack music, ARMSTRONG recruited EVAN DANDO, MOGWAI, BONO, STEVEN LINDSAY (of BIG DISH) and ALPHA who all made appearances on his third-set proper 'AS IF TO NOTHING' (2002), a swirling journey into the head of a talented technician. The MOGWAI track 'MIRACLE', was fantastic, as were cameos from DAVID McALMONT and PHOTEK. The weakest moment came from BONO himself who rehashed his vocals for 'FAR AWAY (SO CLOSE)', which was plainly unnecessary and probably just an excuse to receive some indie street-cred. Other highlights of the near UK Top 60 entry came from DANDO and WENDY STUBBS, but with all these guest spots one could almost forget about the scathing talent of ARMSTRONG, and, at times, the set did feel like a one big introverted, back-slapping vanity project.

CRAIG ARMSTRONG – keyboards, guitars, bass / with various . . .

Melankolic / Caroline

Feb 98. (cd/c/md) *(CDSAXX/SADMC/MDSAD 3) <9627>* **THE SPACE BETWEEN US** [ ] [ ]
– Weather storm / This love / Sly II / After the storm / Laura's theme / My father / Balcony scene (from 'Romeo & Juliet') / Rise / Glasgow / Let's go out tonight / Childhood / Hymn.

Jul 98. (c-s/cd-s) *(SAD C/D 3)* **THIS LOVE / RISE / 10 CANTO** [ ] [-]

Melankolic / Astralwerks

Mar 99. (cd) *(CDSAD 7) <6260>* **PLUNKETT AND MACLEANE** (original soundtrack) [ ] [ ]Jun99
– Hymn / Unseen / Ruby / Rebecca / Rochester / Robbery / Ball / Chance / Business: part 1 – part 2 – part 3 / Chances men / Revelations / Trouble / Duel / Love declared / Disaster / Hanging / Escape / Resolutions / Houses in motion / Childhood.

Apr 99. (12") *(SADT 4)* **HOUSES IN MOTION. / BALL** [ ] [-]
(cd-s+=) *(SADD 4)* – Rebecca.

Oct 01. (cd) *(CDVIR 152)* **KISS OF THE DRAGON (SYMPHONY FOR ISABELLE)** [ ] [-]
– As if you said nothing / Symphony for Isabelle (parts 2-19).
(above issued on 'Virgin')

Apr 02. (cd) *(CDSAD 13) <11907>* **AS IF TO NOTHING** [61] [ ]Feb02
– Ruthless gravity / Wake up in New York (with EVAN DANDO) / Miracle (with MOGWAI) / Amber / Finding beauty / Waltz (with ANTYE GREIE-FUCHS) / Inhaler / Hymn 2 (with PHOTEK) / Snow (with DAVID McALMONT) / Starless II / Stay (faraway, so close!) (with BONO) / Niente / Sea song (with WENDY STUBBS) / Let it be love (with STEVEN LINDSAY) / Choral ending.

May 02. (cd-s) *(SADD 14)* **WAKE UP IN NEW YORK / WALTZ (instrumental) / NATURE BOY (orchestral instrumental)** [ ] [-]

ASPIDISTRA

Formed: Perth . . . 1990 by teenagers vocalist/guitarist NEIL, guitarist IAN and drummer STUART, with bassist GOGS replacing the original second guitarist soon afterwards. Hardly accomplished musicians, and er proud of it, ASPIDISTRA (a tough evergreen indoor plant for the uninitiated!) were yet another shoegazing guitar-fuzzed outfit impressed by MY BLOODY VALENTINE or even KITCHENS OF DISTINCTION. Early in 1991, the quartet branched out with their debut EP, 'SUNRISE' (on Gateshead-based imprint 'Lust'), the best track from it being 'STUNNED'. Later the following year, the lads (without IAN) shot up once more with a few other 7" releases, 'GRIP' and 'CRADLE' (for the Loughborough-based label 'Fluff'), although they went to ground once again.

NEIL – vocals, guitar, bass / **IAN** – guitar / **GOGS** – bass / **STUART** – drums

Lust / not iss.

Apr 91. (7"ep) *(LUST 4)* **SUNRISE** [ ] [-]
– Sunrise / Stunned / Happy Sunday stories / Ignite.

—— now without IAN

Fluff / not iss.

Dec 91. (7") *(honey one)* **GRIP. / FRANCES** [ ] [-]

Nov 92. (7") *(honey five)* **CRADLE. / DEMAND BETTER PROTECTION** [ ] [-]

—— disbanded after above

ASSOCIATES

Formed: Dundee . . . 1979 by BILLY MACKENZIE and ALAN RANKINE, who had worked as a duo in 1976 (the ABSORBIC ONES). After a debut single on their own 'Double-Hip' label, they signed to Chris Parry's 'Fiction', a subsidiary of 'Polydor' records. Their glorious debut set, 'THE AFFECTIONATE PUNCH', was followed by a series of highly rated 45's for the independent 'Situation 2' label.

In 1982, they enjoyed their first taste of success when stylish 'PARTY FEARS TWO' and 'CLUB COUNTRY' both hit the UK Top 20. Energetic alternative dance rock, featuring high, passionate vocals of MACKENZIE, The ASSOCIATES inimitable, unclassifiable sound enjoyed only a very brief liaison with the pop charts. Now signed to 'Warners', the group's more accessible 'SULK' (1982) album made the UK Top 10, its lavish arrangements, white funk and stirring vocal histrionics going down well amid the craze for all things "New Romantic". Despite this belated recognition, the pair subsequently went their separate ways, losing their commercial momentum in the process.

When they finally got back together in 1984 (with a line-up of STEVE GOULDING, IAN McINTOSH, ROBERT SUAVE and L. HOWARD JONES), MACKENZIE and RANKINE recorded only one further single together, 'THOSE FIRST IMPRESSIONS', before the latter finally bowed out. The remaining members recorded the 'PERHAPS' (1985) album, a relative flop which saw a further set, 'THE GLAMOUR CHASE' shelved and MACKENZIE returned in 1990 with an album on the 'Circa' label, 'WILD AND LONELY', to little reaction. The ASSOCIATES name had seemingly been laid to rest when, a couple of years later, the singer released a solo set, 'OUTERNATIONAL'.

The next five years were quiet as MACKENZIE attended to his beloved greyhounds in his native Dundee. The music world was shocked, when, on the 22nd January '97, it was announced that he had taken his own life, reportedly depressed after the death of his mother a little earlier. Ironically, MACKENZIE had signed to the hip 'Nude' label (home of SUEDE), and had been working on new material at the time of his death. This material was posthumously released as 'BEYOND THE SUN', pundits and public alike mourning the death at 39 of one of music's forgotten geniuses.

• **Songwriters:** Lyrics / music by duo (until RANKINE's departure), except BOYS KEEP SWINGING (David Bowie) / LOVE HANGOVER (Diana Ross) / GOD BLESS THE CHILD (Billie Holiday) / HEART OF GLASS

(Blondie) / KITES (Simon Dupree & The Big Sound) / GROOVIN' WITH MR. BLOE (Mr. Bloe) / GREEN TAMBOURINE (Lemon Pipers) / I'M GONNA RUN AWAY FROM YOU (Tammi Lynn).

• **Trivia:** MACKENZIE featured on B.E.F.'s (HEAVEN 17) single 'IT'S OVER' circa '82.

BILLY MACKENZIE (b.27 Mar'57) – vocals / **ALAN RANKINE** – keyboards, guitar, etc

Double Hip | not iss.

Oct 79. (7") *(DHR 1)* **BOYS KEEP SWINGING. / MONA PROPERTY GIRL** [ ] [-]

(re-iss. Dec79 on 'M.C.A.'; MCA 537)

— added **NIGEL GLOCKER** – drums / guest **ROBERT SMITH** – guitar (of-CURE) who replaced unknown guitarist

Fiction | not iss.

Aug 80. (7") *(FICS 11)* **THE AFFECTIONATE PUNCH. / YOU WERE YOUNG** [ ] [-]

Aug 80. (lp/c) *(FIX/+C 5)* **THE AFFECTIONATE PUNCH** [ ] [-]

– The affectionate punch / Amused as always / Logan time / Paper house / Transport to Central / A matter of gender / Even dogs in the wild / Would I . . . bounce back / Deeply concerned / A. *(remixed & re-iss. Nov82; FIXD 5) (re-iss. Aug83 on 'Polydor' lp/c; SPE LP/MC 33)*

— **JOHN MURPHY** (b. Australia) – drums repl. GLOCKER (to TOYAH)

Situation 2 | not iss.

Apr 81. (7"/12") *(SIT 1/+12)* **TELL ME EASTER'S ON FRIDAY. / STRAW TOWELS** [ ] [-]

(re-iss. but w-drawn Nov82 on 'Beggars Banquet'; BEG 86)

Jun 81. (7") *(SIT 4)* **Q: QUARTERS. / KISSED** [ ] [-]

(12"+=) *(SIT 4T)* – Q: Quarters (original).

Aug 81. (7"/12") *(SIT 7/+T)* **KITCHEN PERSON. / AN EVEN WHITER CAR** [ ] [-]

Oct 81. (7"/12") *(SIT 10/+T)* **MESSAGE OBLIQUE SPEECH. / BLUE SOAP** [ ] [-]

Nov 81. (7"/12") *(SIT 11/+T)* **WHITE CAR IN GERMANY. / THE ASSOCIATE** [ ] [-]

Jan 82. (lp/c) *(SITU 2/+C)* **FOURTH DRAWER DOWN** [ ] [-]

– White car in Germany / A girl named Property / Kitchen person / Q; quarters / Tell me Easter's on Friday / The associate / Message oblique speech / An even whiter car. *(re-iss. Nov82 on 'Beggars Banquet' lp/c; BEGA/BEGC 43)*

R.S.O. | not iss.

1981. (7"/12"; as 39, LYON STREET) *(RSO/+X 78)* **KITES. / A GIRL NAMED POVERTY** [ ] [-]

— added **MICHAEL DEMPSEY** – bass (of CURE) / **MARTHA LADLY** – backing vocals (ex-MARTHA & THE MUFFINS)

Associates | WEA

Mar 82. (7"/12") *(ASC 1/+T)* **PARTY FEARS TWO. / IT'S BETTER THIS WAY** [9] [ ]

May 82. (7") *(ASC 2)* **CLUB COUNTRY. / IT'S YOU AGAIN** [13] [ ]

(12"+=) *(ASC 2T)* – Ulcragyceptemol.

Jun 82. (lp/c) *(ASCL/ASCC 1)* **SULK** [10] [ ]

– It's better this way / Party fears two / Club country / Love hangover / 18 carat love affair / Arrogance gave him up / No / Skipping / Nothing in something particular / Arrogance gave him up / White car in Germany / Gloomy Sunday / The associate. *(re-iss. Oct82 on 'WEA' lp/c; 240 005-1/-4) (cd-iss. Jul88 on 'WEA'; K 240005-2)*

Jul 82. (7") *(ASC 3)* **18 CARAT LOVE AFFAIR. / LOVE HANGOVER** [21] [ ]

(12"+=) *(ASC 3T)* – Voluntary wishes, swapit production.

— split & re-formed 1984 by **MACKENZIE + RANKINE** recruiting **STEVE GOULDING** – drums / **IAN McINTOSH** – rhythm guitar / **ROBERT SUAVE** – bass / **L. HOWARD JONES** – keyboards

WEA | WEA

May 84. (7"/ext.12") *(YZ 6/+T)* **THOSE FIRST IMPRESSIONS. / THIRTEEN FEELINGS** [43] [ ]

— **STEPHEN REID** – guitar; repl. RANKINE who joined PAUL HAIG. He also had a solo career between 1986-87, releasing two albums, 'THE WORLD BEGINS TO LOOK HER AGE' for 'Crepescule' and 'SHE LOVES ME NOT' for 'Virgin'

Aug 84. (7"/ext.12") *(YZ 16/+T)* **WAITING FOR THE LOVE BOAT. / SCHAMP OUT** [53] [ ]

Jan 85. (7"/7"pic-d) *(YZ 28/+P)* **BREAKFAST. / BREAKFAST ALONE** [49] [ ]

(12"+=) *(YZ 28T)* – Kites.

Feb 85. (lp/c) *(WX 9/+C)* **PERHAPS** [23] [ ]

– Those first impressions / Waiting for the love boat / Perhaps / Schampout / Helicopter helicopter / Breakfast / Thirteen feelings / The stranger in your voice / The best of you / Don't give me that I told you so look.

Oct 85. (7") *(YZ 47)* **TAKE ME TO THE GIRL. / PERHAPS** [ ] [-]

(ext.12"+=) *(YZ 47T)* – The girl that took me / ('A'instrumental).

(10"+=) *(YZ 47TE)* – God bless the child (live) / Even dogs in the wild (live) / The boy that Santa Claus forgot (live).

— The above 'A'side was later (in Mar88) covered by group/artist JIH.

— (early 1986) HUGHES and SUAVE joined PETE MURPHY

— **MACKENZIE** now used session people under The ASSOCIATES

Sep 88. (7") *(YZ 310)* **HEART OF GLASS. / HER ONLY WISH** [56] [ ]

(3"cd-s+=) *(YZ 310CD)* – Breakfast / Those first impressions.

('A'-Auchterhouse mix-12"+=) *(YZ 310T)* – ('A'-Auchterhouse instrumental).

(12"+=) *(YZ 310TX)* – ('A'-Temperamental mix) / Heavens blue.

Nov 88. (w-drawn lp/c)(cd) *(WX 222/+C)(244619-2)* **THE GLAMOUR CHASE** [-] [-]

Jan 89. (w-drawn 7") *(YZ 329)* **COUNTRY BOY. / JUST CAN'T SAY GOODBYE** [-] [-]

(w-drawn 12"+=) *(YZ 329T)* – Heart of glass (dub mix).

(w-drawn 3"cd-s++=) *(YZ 329CD)* – Take me to the girl.

Circa | Charisma

Mar 90. (c/cd/lp) *(CIRC/+D/A 11)* **WILD AND LONELY** [71] [ ]

– Fire to ice / Fever / People we meet / Just can't say goodbye / Calling all around the world / The glamour chase / Where there's love / Something's got to give / Strasbourg Square / Ever since that day / Wild and lonely / Fever in the shadows.

Apr 90. (7"/c-s) *(YR/+C 46)* **FEVER. / FEVER IN THE SHADOWS** [ ] [-]

(12"+=/s12"+=/3"cd-s+=/cd-s+=) *(YR T/TB/CD/CDT 46)* – Groovin' with Mr.Bloe.

Aug 90. (7"/c-s) *(YR/+C 49)* **FIRE TO ICE. / GREEN TAMBOURINE** [ ] [-]

(ext.12"+=) *(YRT 49)* – The glamour chase.

(10"++=/ext.cd-s++=) *(YR TX/CD 49)* – Groovin' with Mr.Bloe.

Sep 90. (12"ep) *<096448>* **FIRE TO ICE (mixes) / GREEN TAMBOURINE** [-] [ ]

Jan 91. (7"/c-s) *(YR/+C 56)* **JUST CAN'T SAY GOODBYE. / ONE TWO THREE** [ ] [-]

(12") *(YRT 56)* – ('A'-Time Unlimited mix) / ('A'-Time Unlimited instrumental) / ('A'-US mix).

(12") *(YRTX 56)* – ('A'-Time Unlimited mix) / ('A'-Time Unlimited instrumental) / ('A'-Karma mix).

(cd-s) *(YRCD 56)* – ('A'side) / ('A'-Time Unlimited piano mix) / ('A'-US version) / I'm gonna run away from you.

BILLY MACKENZIE

Jun 92. (7") *(YR 86)* **BABY. / SACRIFICE AND BE SACRIFICED (CH 8032 mix)** [ ] [-]

(cd-s+=) *(YRCD 86)* – Grooveature (D 1000 mix) / Colours will come (US 60659 mix).

(12") *(YRT 86)* – ('A'side) / Colours will come (Larry Heard remix) / Opal krush / Colours will come (Raw Stylus remix).

Aug 92. (7") *(YR 91)* **COLOURS WILL COME. / OPAL KRUSH** [ ] [-]

(12"+=/cd-s+=) *(YRT/YRCD 91)* – Look what you've done / Feels like the richtergroove.

Sep 92. (c/cd) *(CIRC/+D 22)* **OUTERNATIONAL** [ ] [-]
– Outernational / Feels like the richtergroove / Opal krusch / Colours wil come / Pastime paradise / Groovecture / Sacrifice and be sacrificed / Baby / What made me turn on the lights / Windows cell.

— In Jul'96, BILLY was featured on a single by LOOM, 'ANACOSTIA BAY'.

— Tragically on the 22nd January 1997, BILLY committed suicide in his father's garden shed; he had recently signed to 'Nude' records.

Nude | not iss.

Oct 97. (cd) *(NUDE 8CD)* **BEYOND THE SUN** [64] [-]
– Give me time / Winter academy / Blue it is / 14 mirrors / At the edge of the world / Beyond the sun / And this she knows / Sour jewel / 3 gypsies in a restaurant / Nocturne VII.

— early in 2000, a posthumous CD-album, 'MEMORY PALACE' (credited with PAUL HAIG) was released on 'Rhythm Of Life' *(ROL 003)*

Rhythm Of Life | not iss.

Mar 01. (cd; as BILLY MACKENZIE & STEVE AUNGLET) *(ROL 005)* **EUROCENTRIC** [ ] [-]
– Falling out with the future / Homophobic / 14th Century nightlife / Liberty lounge / When the world was young / Sing that song again / Soul that sighs / Wild is the wind / Mother Earth / Return to love.

– (ASSOCIATES) compilations, others, etc. –

Sep 81. (7"/12") *Fiction; (FICS/+X 13)* **A. / WOULD I . . . BOUNCE BACK** [ ] [-]

Nov 82. (7"/12") *Fiction; (FIXS/+X 16)* **A MATTER OF GENDER. / EVEN DOGS IN THE WILD** [ ] [-]

Oct 89. (12"ep/cd-ep) *Strange Fruit; (SFPS/+CD 075))* **THE PEEL SESSIONS** ('82) [ ] [-]
– It's better this way / Nude spoons / Me myself and the tragic story / Natural gender / Ulcragyceptemol.

Jan 91. (cd)(lp/c) *East West; (9031 72414-2)(WX 363/+C)* **POPERA** [ ] [-]
– Party fears two / Club country / 18 Carat love affair / Love hangover / Those first impressions / Waiting for the loveboat / Breakfast / Take me to the girl / Heart of glass / Country boy / The rhythm divine / Waiting for the loveboat (slight return) / Tell me Easter's on Friday / Q; quarters / Kitchen person / Message oblique speech / White car in Germany.

Jan 91. (7"/c-s) *East West; (YZ 534/+C)* **POPERETTA EP: WAITING FOR THE LOVEBOAT (Slight Return). / CLUB COUNTRY CLUB** [ ] [-]
(12"+=/cd-s+=) *(YZ 534 T/CD)* – Waiting for the loveboat (extended voyage) / Club country club (Time Unlimited).

Sep 94. (cd) *Nighttracks; (CDNT 006)* **THE RADIO ONE SESSION** [ ] [-]

May 02. (d-cd) *Warners; (8573 88496-2)* **THE GLAMOUR CHASE / PERHAPS** [ ] [-]

ASTRAL

Formed: Glasgow . . . early 1998 by a 5-piece headed by guitarist ROBERT McMAHON. Signed to 'Curveball' records by producer and Mushroom head, Rob Jefferson, this OASIS-meets-EMBRACE-esque outfit also hooked the listener in with spaced-out country. Two well-received singles into the deal, the ASTRAL lads finally set their full-length stall out by delivering their eponymous debut towards the end of '99.

ROBERT McMAHON – guitar / + 4

Curveball | not iss.

Oct 98. (7"orange/cd-s) *(CURVE 1/+CD)* **COME & GO** [ ] [-]

Sep 99. (cd-s) *(CURVE 8CD)* **FUTURE TIMES EP** [ ] [-]
– Future times / On & on / This road.

Oct 99. (cd) *(CURVE 9CD)* **ASTRAL** [ ] [-]
– Future times / Tranquilliser / Give me everything / Caribou / Come & go / Tonight / Fly back.

Last Episode | not iss.

Aug 00. (cd) *(5706520561CD)* **FILICETUM LUNARE** [ ] [-]

ASTRID

Formed: Stornoway, Isle Of Lewis . . . 1996 initially as KITE MONSTER by CHARLES CLARK, WILLIAM CAMPBELL and GARETH RUSSELL, the lads from the breezy Western Isles finding drummer, GARY THOM, while playing sporadic gigs in the city of Glasgow.

After fate shone down on this luscious pop sensation, the group were asked to support BELLE AND SEBASTIAN at a one-day festival in the aforementioned city. Scottish wannabe rock/indie-pop sensation EDWYN COLLINS was fortunate to hear their single on Sean Hughes' GLR show and almost immediately invited the band to record with him in his home studio. The result was the cutesy/sweet single 'IT'S TRUE', a hybrid collection of The BYRDS, TEENAGE FANCLUB and SUPERGRASS in their heyday. Following the single, was album 'STRANGE WEATHER LATELY' (1999), which was, again, produced and recorded by COLLINS. Its slight fault lay with the band's easy-flowing songs and styles evident on such tracks/singles as 'HIGH IN THE MORNING', 'REDGROUND' and 'BOY OR GIRL'; all flops. Chords jangled like nothing on earth and the set was awash with CLARK's cheerful and unintentionally menacing vocals; incidentally, three tracks were played on Jamie Oliver's BBC2's 'Naked Chef' cookery programme having already won an award at the Austin, Texas South By Southwest festival.

After issuing the summery pop single, 'IT NEVER HAPPENED' and playing an eagerly awaited performance at T In The Park, the group issued their sophomore set, 'PLAY DEAD' (2000), a sparkling, if not average indie pop record. This was followed by a feted session for John Peel and the release of the single 'TICK TOCK', which featured the fantasic B-side 'GLASTONBURY SONG'. A limited edition single (500 copies distributed) 'CHERRY CHERRY' was subsequently issued, although only on a first-come, first served basis for fans/record collectors et al. Lately, ASTRID members have moonlighted with Scottish/Irish collective, The REINDEER SECTION.

CHARLES CLARK – vocals, acoustic guitar / **WILLIAM CAMPBELL** – vocals, guitar / **GARETH RUSSELL** – bass / **GARY THOM** – drums

Fantastic Plastic | not iss.

Jun 97. (7"; as KITEMONSTER) *(FP 007)* **RUBBER DOLL. /** [ ] [-]

Apr 98. (ltd-cd-ep) *(FP 008)* **NO REASON / STANDING IN LINE / SEE THE SUN** [ ] [-]

Jul 98. (ltd-7"one-sided) *(FP7 011)* **WHAT TO SAY** [ ] [-]

Nov 98. (7"ep/cd-ep) *(FP/+7 012)* **HI-FI LO-FI EP** [ ] [-]
– Distance / I can see you / Can you feel it / 5 o'clock. *(cd-ep re-iss. Sep00; same)*

Mar 99. (ltd;cd-ep/7"ep) *(FP/+7 013)* **IT'S TRUE. / FOR YOUR GIRLFRIEND / BOSTON** [ ] [-]
(re-iss. Sep00; same)

Jul 99. (7") *(FP7 014)* **HIGH IN THE MORNING. / THE WAY I FEEL** [ ] [-]
(cd-s+=) *(FPS 014)* – God song.

Jul 99. (cd/lp) *(FP CD/LP 001)* **STRANGE WEATHER LATELY** [ ] [-]
– Kitchen T.V. / Plastic skull / High in the morning / Zoo / Standing in line / Bottle / Redground / Like a baby / Stop / Dusty / Boat song / Boy or girl / W.O.P.R.M. *(lp w/free 7") (cd re-iss. Sep00; same)*

Oct 99. (cd-ep/7"ep) *(FPS/FP7 016)* **REDGROUND. / COMPLAIN / WEIRD CLOUDS** [ ] [-]

Dec 99. (7"white) *(FP7 018)* **BOY OR GIRL. / SLEIGHRIDE** [ ] [-]

— **NEIL PAYNE** – drums (ex-SMILES) repl. THOM

Aug 00. (7"ep/cd-ep) *(FP7/FPS 020)* **MODES OF TRANSPORT EP** [ ] [-]
– Modes of transport / Tangle & tussle / Make heat / Starting to show.

Dec 00. (cd-s) *(FPS 024)* **CHERRY CHERRY / LONELY GIANT** [-] [-] mail-o

Feb 01. (7"ep/cd-ep) *(FP7/FPS 023)* **TICK TOCK EP** [ ] [-]
– Tick tock / Just yet / Glastonbury song.

Mar 01. (cd/purple-lp) *(FP CD/LP 003)* **PLAY DEAD** [ ] [-]
– It never happened / Tick tock / Wrong for you / Crying boy / Alas / Play dead / Fat girl / Just one name / Hard to be a person / Paper / Modes of transport / What you're thinking / Taken for granted / Horror movies.

May 01. (7") *(FP7 025)* **IT NEVER HAPPENED. / JIMMY** [ ] [-]
(cd-s+=) *(FPS 025)* – Turnaround.

ASTRID (see under ⇒ WILLIAMSON, Astrid)

ASTRO CHIMP (see under ⇒ VASELINES)

AURAL 4 PLAY (see under ⇒ Shoop records)

AVO-8

Formed: Edinburgh . . . mid 80's by JAN and STEVE HASTIE, CLAIRE and KENNY GOURLAY, GEORGE GLEN, the 8 being made up by KAREN, WILLIE and EDDIE. After a low-key 7" debut, 'GONE WRONG', the punky-pop AVO-8 resurfaced in 1988 with a Fast Forward-distributed single, 'IS THIS THE END?' (produced by Pete Haigh). The band subsequently inked a deal with 'Cherry Red' and released a couple more, 'BIG CAR' and 'OUT OF MY MIND'; if you can think an indie EURYTHMICS fused with DELTA 5 you'd be close.

JAN HASTIE – vocals / **CLAIRE GOURLAY** – vocals / **STEVE HASTIE** – guitars / **GEORGE GLEN** – bass / **KENNY GOURLAY** – drums / plus **KAREN, WILLIE + EDDIE**

Stroppo not iss.

1986. (7"m) *(STROP 1)* **GONE WRONG. / TARGET ONE / NO HESITATION** [ ] [-]

Avo Records not iss.

Feb 88. (12") *(AR-001)* **IS THIS THE END? / THINKING OF YOU / THE VOICE** [ ] [-]

Cherry Red not iss.

1989. (7") *(CHERRY 102)* **BIG CAR. / FAME** [ ] [-]
(12"+=) *(12CHERRY 102)* – It's a game.

1990. (7") *(CHERRY 105)* **OUT OF MY MIND. / SILVER LINING** [ ] [-]
(12"+=) *(12CHERRY 105)* –

— disbanded after above

AYR UNIT (see under ⇒ Mouthmoth records)

AZTEC CAMERA

Formed: East Kilbride . . . early 1980 by 15 year-old, RODDY FRAME, who released two independent 45's on ALAN HORNE's now semi-famous 'Postcard' label, before moving on to 'Rough Trade' in 1982.

The following year, RODDY and Co. hit the top of the indie charts (reached Top 30 nationally) with debut album, 'HIGH LAND, HARD RAIN', a largely acoustic-based affair combining folkish flights of fancy, Latin/jazz rhythms and an incisive lyrical flair with stunning results. The record's breezy lead track, 'OBLIVIOUS', was re-issued by new label 'Warners' later that year on the back of the album's success, one of the few AZTEC CAMERA singles to break the Top 20. FRAME brought in a new cast of musicians for 1984's MARK KNOPFLER-produced 'KNIFE' set, including seasoned Scots players CRAIG GANNON and MALCOLM ROSS. A more commercial offering, the record almost made the UK hit in 'ALL I NEED IS EVERYTHING'.

After a world tour, FRAME laid low for more than two years, penning material for 'LOVE' (1987), the most successful album of his career. Initially something of a non-starter, this over-produced yet affecting album eventually made the Top 10 almost a year after its release following the massive Top 5 success of the plaintive 'SOMEWHERE IN MY HEART' single. Despite courting the pop mainstream, FRAME's subsequent effort, 'STRAY' (1990) veered off into more eclectic territory, the Top 20 hit, 'GOOD MORNING BRITAIN', featuring MICK JONES of BIG AUDIO DYNAMITE / CLASH fame.

The 90's witnessed FRAME developing his earlier style, especially on the 1995 set, 'FRESTONIA'. Come 1998, the Scots veteran had signed to 'Independiente', releasing a minor hit, 'REASON FOR LIVING' which accompanied the relatively low-key pop-rock album, 'THE NORTH STAR'.

• **Covered:** JUMP (Van Halen) / DO I LOVE YOU (Cole Porter) / I THREW IT ALL AWAY (Bob Dylan) / BAD EDUCATION (Blue Orchids) / IF PARADISE WAS HALF AS NICE (Amen Corner).

• **Trivia:** In Autumn '83, while in the States supporting ELVIS COSTELLO, he lied about his age (19) to get into the country.

RODDY FRAME (b.29 Jan'64) – vocals, acoustic guitar / **DAVE MULHOLLAND** – drums / **CAMPBELL OWENS** – bass; who repl. ALAN WELSH late in 1980

Postcard not iss.

Mar 81. (7") *(81-3)* **JUST LIKE GOLD. / WE COULD SEND LETTERS** [ ] [-]

Jul 81. (7") *(81-8)* **MATTRESS OF WIRE. / LOOK OUTSIDE THE TUNNEL** [ ] [-]

Sep 81. (lp; w-drawn) *(81-13)* **GREEN JACKET GREY** [-] [-]

— (mid-'82) added temp. member **BERNIE CLARK** – keyboards / **DAVE RUFFY** – drums (ex-RUTS) repl. MULHOLLAND

Rough Trade Sire

Aug 82. (7"/7"pic-d) *(RT 112/+P)* **PILLAR TO POST. / QUEEN'S TATTOO** [ ] [-]

Jan 83. (7") *(RT 122)* **OBLIVIOUS. / ORCHARD GIRL** [47] [-]
(12"+=) *(RT 122T)* – Haywire.

Apr 83. (lp) *(ROUGH 47)* *<23899>* **HIGH LAND, HARD RAIN** [22] [ ] Aug83
– Oblivious / The boy wonders / Walk out to winter / The bugle sounds again / We could send letters / Pillar to post / Release / Lost outside the tunnel / Back on board / Down the dip. *(cd-iss. Feb87 +=; ROUGHCD 47)* – Haywire / Queen's tattoo / Orchard girl. *(re-iss. Sep93 on 'WEA' cd/c; 4509 92849-2/-4)*

May 83. (7"/12") *(RT/+T 132)* **WALK OUT TO WINTER. / SET THE KILLING FREE** [64] [ ]

WEA Sire

Oct 83. (d7") *(AZTEC 1)* **OBLIVIOUS. / ORCHARD GIRL // WE COULD SEND LETTERS (live). / BACK ON BOARD (live)** [18] [ ]

— **RODDY FRAME** retained **RUFFY** and brought into line-up:- **CRAIG GANNON** – bass (ex-BLUEBELLS) repl. OWENS / added **MALCOLM ROSS** – guitar (ex-ORANGE JUICE, ex-JOSEF K) / guest / **GUY FLETCHER** – keyboards

Aug 84. (7") *(AC 1)* **ALL I NEED IS EVERYTHING. / JUMP** [34] [ ]
(12") *(AC 1T)* – ('A'-Latin mix) / Jump (Loaded version).

Sep 84. (lp/c)(cd) *(WX 8/+C)(240 483-2)* *<25183>* **KNIFE** [14] [ ]
– Still on fire / Just like the U.S.A. / Head is happy (heart's insane) / The back door to Heaven / All I need is everything / Backwards and forwards / Birth of the true / Knife. *(cd-iss. Sep93; same) (cd re-iss. Jun02 on 'Wounded Bird'+=; WOU 5183)* – AZTEC CAMERA mini-lp tracks.

Nov 84. (7"/7"sha-pic-d) *(AC 2/+P)* **STILL ON FIRE. / WALK OUT TO WINTER** [ ] [ ]
(12"+=) *(AC 2T)* – Mattress of wire (live) / The boy wonders (live) / The bugle sounds again (live).

Apr 85. (10"m-lp) *<25285>* **AZTEC CAMERA (live)** [-] [ ]
– Birth of the true / Mattress of wire / Jump / The bugle sounds again / Backwards and forwards.

— **FRAME + RUFFY** alongside other session musicians **MARCUS MILLER** – bass / **DAVID FRANK** – keyboards (ex-SYSTEM) / **STEVE JORDAN** – guitar

Sep 87. (7"/ext-12") *(YZ 154/+T)* **DEEP AND WIDE AND TALL. / BAD EDUCATION** [ ] [ ]

Oct 87. (lp/c)(cd) *(WX 128/+C)(242 202-2)* *<25646>* **LOVE** [10] [ ]
– Deep and wide and tall / How men are / Everybody is a number one / More than a law / Somewhere in my heart / Working in a goldmine / One and one / Paradise / Killermont Street. *(cd-iss. Sep93; same)*

Jan 88. (7") *(YZ 168)* **HOW MEN ARE. / THE RED FLAG** [25] [ ]
(12"+=) *(YZ 168T)* – Killermont Street (live) / Pillar to post (live).
(cd-s+=) *(248 028-2)* – Oblivious / All I need is everything.

Apr 88. (7") *(YZ 181)* **SOMEWHERE IN MY HEART. / EVERYBODY IS A NUMBER ONE '86** [3] [ ]
(12"+=) *(YZ 181T)* – Down the dip / Jump.
(cd-s+=) *(YZ 181CD)* – Walk out to winter / Still on fire.

Jul 88. (7") *(YZ 199)* **WORKING IN A GOLDMINE. / I THREW IT ALL AWAY** [31] [ ]
(12"+=/12"s+=) *(YZ 199 T/W)* – ('A'version).
(cd-s++=) *(YZ 199CD)* – How men are.

Sep 88. (7") *(YZ 154)* **DEEP AND WIDE AND TALL. / BAD EDUCATION** [55] [ ]
(12"+=/cd-s+=) *(YZ 154 T/CD)* – More than a law.

— (live band '88: augmenting **FRAME + RUFFY**) **EDDIE KULAK** – keyboards / **GARY SANFORD** – guitar / **PAUL POWELL** – bass

— (by 1990, **FRAME** had lost RUFFY but retained **POWELL** / and new **GARY SANCTUARY** – keyboards / **FRANK TONTOH** – drums / guests **PAUL CARRACK, EDWYN COLLINS, MICKEY GALLAGHER & STEVE SI DELYNK.**

Jun 90. (cd)(lp/c) *(<9031 71694-2>)(WX 350/+C)* **STRAY** [22] [ ]
– Stray / The crying scene / Get outta London / Over my head / How it is / Good morning Britain (featuring MICK JONES) / The gentle kind / Notting Hill blues / Song for a friend. *(re-iss. cd+c Sep93)*

Jun 90. (7") *(YZ 492)* **THE CRYING SCENE. / TRUE COLOURS** [70] [ ]
(12"+=/cd-s+=) *(YZ 492 T/CD)* – Salvation.
(10"+=) *(YZ 492X)* – I threw it all away (live).

Sep 90. (7"/c-s; AZTEC CAMERA and MICK JONES) *(YZ 521/+C)* **GOOD MORNING BRITAIN. / ('A'live version)** [19] [ ]
(12"+=) *(YZ 521T)* – ('A'remix)
(cd-s+=) *(YZ 521CD)* – Consolation prize. (with EDWYN COLLINS)

Jul 92. (7"/c-s) *(YZ 688/+C)* **SPANISH HORSES. / JUST LIKE THE U.S.A. (live)** [52] [ ]
(cd-s) *(YZ 688CD1)* – ('A'side) / Killermont street (live) / The birth of the true (live) / Song for a friend (live).
(cd-s) *(YZ 688CD2)* – ('A'live version) / Stray (live) / The bugle sounds again (live) / Dolphins (live).

Apr 93. (7"/c-s) *(YZ 740/+C)* **DREAM SWEET DREAMS. / GOOD MORNING BRITAIN (live)** [67] [ ]
(cd-s+=) *(YZ 740CD1)* – Sister Anne (live) / How men are (live).
(cd-s) *(YZ 740CD2)* – ('A'side) / Mattress of wire (live) / Let your love decide (live) / Orchid girl (live).

May 93. (cd/c/lp) *(<4509 92492/-2/-4/-1>)* **DREAMLAND** [21] [ ]
– Birds / Safe in sorrow / Black Lucia / Let your love decide / Spanish horses / Dream sweet dreams / Piano's and clocks / Sister Ann / Vertigo / Valium Summer / Belle of the ball.

Jun 93. (7"/c-s) *(YZ 754/+C)* **BIRDS. / DEEP AND WIDE AND TALL** [ ] [ ]
(cd-s) *(YZ 754CD1)* – ('A'side) / Working in a goldmine / Knife.
(cd-s) *(YZ 754CD2)* – ('A'side) / Somewhere in my heart / Oblivious / Good morning Britain.

WEA Reprise

Oct 95. (c-s) *(WEA 007C)* **SUN / SUNSET** [ ] [ ]
(cd-s+=) *(WEA 007CD)* – The crying scene (live).
(cd-s) *(WEA 007CDX)* – ('A'side) / We could send letters (live) / Black Lucia (live) / The rainy season (live).

Nov 95. (cd/c) *(<0630 11929-2/-4>)* **FRESTONIA** [ ] [ ]
– The rainy season / Sun / Crazy / On the avenue / Imperfectly / Debutante / Beautiful girl / Phenomenal world / Method of love / Sunset.

– compilations, etc. –

Sep 90. (7") *Old Gold; (OG 9945)* **SOMEWHERE IN MY HEART. / OBLIVIOUS** ☐ -

— In Nov'90, 'DO I LOVE YOU?' appeared as the extra track on the 12" & cd-s of a Cole Porter tribute by The POGUES and KIRSTY MacCOLL

Oct 94. (cd) *Windsong; (WHISCD 006)* **LIVE ON THE TEST (live)** ☐ -

Jul 99. (cd/c) *WEA; (3984 28984-2/-4)* **THE BEST OF AZTEC CAMERA** 36 -
– Oblivious / Good morning Britain / Somewhere in my heart / Working in a goldmine / How men are / Birth of the true / Walk out to winter / Jump / All I need is everything / Deep & wide & tall / The crying scene / Killermont street / Spanish horses / Reason for living.

RODDY FRAME

Independiente Sony

Sep 98. (c-s) *(ISOM 18CS)* **REASON FOR LIVING / WINTER HAVEN HIGH** 45 ☐ Nov98
(cd-s) *(ISOM 18MS) <66231A>* – Rainy greys and blues.
(cd-s) *(ISOM 18SMS) <66231B>* – ('A'side) / Biba nova / The sea is wide.

Sep 98. (cd) *(ISOM 7CD) <120123>* **THE NORTH STAR** 55 ☐ Nov98
– Back to the one / The north star / Here comes the ocean / River of brightness / Strings / Bigger brighter better / Autumn flower / Reason for living / Sister shadow / Hymn to grace.

Redemption not iss.

Aug 02. (cd) *(RRUK 2)* **SURF** ☐ -
– Over you / Surf / Small world / I can't start now / Abloom / Tough / Big Ben / High class music / Turning the world around / Mixed up love / For what it was.

B

Howie B

Born: HOWARD BERNSTEIN, Glasgow. One of Scotland's more accomplished contributors to the world of dance music (in the widest sense of the term), BERNSTEIN actually began his music biz career in London as a DJ, subsequently working with Bristol production guru, NELLEE HOOPER.

He began releasing his own tracks under both HOWIE B and the OLD SCOTTISH alias for the likes of 'Mo Wax'. Inextricably linked with the mid-90's Bristol-based trip-hop scene, HOWIE produced for leading lights like TRICKY while also setting up the 'Pussyfoot' label for his own experimental breakbeat creations and other kindred spirits. The newly dancefloor-friendly BJORK also utilised his talents and as his reputation gathered pace he was even called into the production hotseat for U2 (becoming the 5th member in the process!).

1995 meanwhile, found him guesting with U.N.K.L.E., the much-hyped collaborative project by DJ SHADOW and JAMES LAVELLE. This in turn led to a major label deal with 'Polydor' and in 1996, the shaven-headed beats-boffin released his debut album, 'MUSIC FOR BABIES' to encouraging reviews. 1997's 'TURN THE DARK OFF' proved it was no fluke, a compelling melange of hurtling techno, abstract beats and slo-mo claustrophobia (check the haunting 'TAKE YOUR PARTNER BY THE HAND') that featured in many magazine's end of year polls. Although signed to a major, HOWIE still released stuff on his own label, namely 1998's 'HOWIE BE THY NAME' EP and 1999's 'JUGS FOR SALE'. The end of the millennium also saw the release of his third album, charmingly titled 'SNATCH'. Outwith his brief DADDYLONGLEGS project (alongside JEREMY SHAW and WILL O'DONOVAN), HOWIE B got back to grass roots on his comeback set, 'FOLK.' (2001), another eclectic recording and featuring this time, KARMEN WIYJNBERG, on some inspired vocals.

HOWIE B – vocals, samples, synthesizers

Pussyfoot not iss.

Dec 93. (12") *(Pussy 001)* **BREATHE IN** ☐ -

May 94. (12"; by DADDYLONGLEGS) *(Pussy 002)* **THE FOURTH WAY** ☐ -

May 94. (12") **FANFARE. / HAVE MERCY** ☐ -
(above issued on 'Mo Wax')

— in Dec'94, he collaborated with SKYLAB (MAT DUCASSE) on the '#1' set

Mar 95. (12"; w/ SIE) *(Pussy 003)* **BIRTH** ☐ -

May 95. (12") *(Pussy 004)* **GROOVE HARD SEX** ☐ -

Sep 95. (12") *(Pussy 006)* **AMBIDEXTROUS** ☐ -

Polydor not iss.

Mar 96. (cd/c/lp) *(529 464-2/-4/-1)* **MUSIC FOR BABIES** ☐ -
– Music for babies / Cry / Shag / Allergy / Away again / How to suckle / Here comes the tooth / On the way.

Sep 96. (12"ep/cd-ep) *(575187-1/-2)* **HOWIE B EP** ☐ -
– Butt meat / Chewin' bacco / Undercover.

Jun 97. (12"/cd-s) *(571 167-1/-2)* **ANGELS GO BALD: TOO. / TWO LONE SWORDSMEN (mixes)** 36 -
(cd-s) *(571 169-2)* – ('A'mixes).

Jun 97. (12"; as the CODFATHER with SIE & NAKED FUNK) *(Pussy 020)* **DEAD LEG – Pussy In My Robot** ☐ -
(above issued on 'Pussyfoot')

Jul 97. (cd/c/lp) *(537 934-2/-4/-1)* **TURN THE DARK OFF** 58 -
– Fizzy in my mouth – Your mouth / Hopscotch / Switch / Sore brown eyes / Take your partner by the hand: featuring Robbie Robertson / Limbo / Angels go bald: too / Who's got the bacon? / Baby sweetcorn (come here) / Butt meat.

Oct 97. (12"/cd-s) *(571 709-1/-2)* **SWITCH. / HOPSCOTCH** 62 -
(cd-s) *(571 711-2)* – ('A'mixes).

Mar 98. (12"/cd-s; HOWIE B featuring ROBBIE ROBERTSON) *(569 327-1/-2)* **TAKE YOUR PARTNER BY THE HAND (DJ Premier & Red Snapper remixes). / HOPSCOTCH (Wagon Christ & Dobie remixes)** 74 -
(cd-s) *(569 329-2)* – (other remixes).

Pussyfoot Palmskin

Oct 98. (12") *(Pussy 031)* **HOWIE BE THY NAME. /** ☐ -

Feb 99. (12") *(Pussy 032)* **JUGS FOR SALE. /** ☐ -

Mar 99. (cd/lp) *(Pussy cd/lp 011) <2010>* **SNATCH** ☐ ☐
– Gallway / Sniffer dog / Cook for you / Trust / Cotton high / Anniversary / To kiss you / Maniac melody / Black oak / I can sing but I don't want to / She called again.

DADDYLONGLEGS

HOWIE B + JEREMY SHAW (of NAKED FUNK) / with **WILL O'DONOVAN** – vocals

Oct 99. (lp/cd) *(Pussylp/+cd 016) <2035>* **HORSE** ☐ ☐
– Pony express / Giddy up / When Betty comes to town / Cobbler / Stallion / Don't milk ya hoss / Bareback / Black beauty / They shag horses don't they.

Jan 00. (12"/cd-s) *(PUSSY/+CD 038)* **WHEN BETTY COMES TO TOWN (mixes)** ☐ -

— in Apr'00, HOWIE B produced LES NEGRESSES VERTES set 'Trabendo'

HOWIE B

Azuli not iss.

Jul 01. (7") *(ALN7 02)* **UNDER THE BOARDWALK. /** ☐ -
(above from V/A set, 'Another Late Night'; *ALNCD 02)*

Go Beat not iss.

Sep 01. (cd/lp) *(549784-2/-1)* **FOLK.** ☐ -
– Making love on your side / All this means to me / Musical mayday / Touch / Dust / Watermelon sugar / Hey Jack / My wee cod piece / Tapdancer / Telephone.

— in Aug'02, HOWIE B mixed the 'Fabriclive Vol.5' CD-set

BABROO (see under ⇒ Limbo records)

BABY ASPIRIN (see under ⇒ Flotsam & Jetsam records)

BABY CHAOS

Formed: Stewarton, Ayrshire . . . 1992 by school-mates, CHRIS GORDON, GRANT McFARLANE, BOBBY DUNN and DAVY GREENWOOD. Discovered by former HAPPY MONDAYS manager turned A&R man, Nathan McGough, after an appearance on BBC2's 'Late Show', BABY CHAOS were promptly signed to 'East West' and initiated a series of singles starting with late 1993's 'SPERM'.

'BUZZ', 'GOLDEN TOOTH' and 'HELLO VICTIM' followed over the course of '94, a year which saw them play at the inaugural 'T In The Park' festival in Scotland and culminated in the release of their debut album, 'SAFE SEX DESIGNER DRUGS & THE DEATH OF ROCK'N'ROLL'. Described as Britain's answer to post-Seattle grunge rock with similarities to The WILDHEARTS and The MANICS, BABY CHAOS nevertheless had trouble with their musical identity; while the likes of Kerrang! tried to claim them for their own they were always more "Wean's Wild" than "Wayne's World". The band returned in the Spring of '96 with a follow-up, 'LOVE YOUR SELF ABUSE', hardly a departure from the debut but worthy of attention nonetheless.

CHRIS GORDON – vocals, guitar / **GRANT McFARLANE** – guitar / **BOBBY DUNN** – bass / **DAVY GREENWOOD** – drums

East West East West

Nov 93. (10"ep/cd-ep) *(YZ 792 TE/CD)* **SPERM. / SUPERPOWERED / TONGUE**

Feb 94. (7"/c-s) *(YZ 800/+C)* **BUZZ. / ETHER**
(12"+=/cd-s+=) *(YZ 800 T/CD)* – Coming clean.

May 94. (7"ep/12"ep/cd-ep) *(YZ 822/+T/CD)* **GOLDEN TOOTH E.P.**
– Golden tooth / Resurrected / No way / The Earth is dying, but never mind.

Oct 94. (7"/c-s) *(YZ 852/+C)* **HELLO VICTIM. / ROTTEN TO THE CORE**
(12"+=/cd-s+=) *(YZ 852 T/CD)* – Skinny.

Nov 94. (cd/lp) *(4509 98052-2/-1) <61821-2>* **SAFE SEX DESIGNER DRUGS & THE DEATH OF ROCK'N'ROLL**
– Sperm / Saliva / Go to hell / Breathe / Hello victim / Buzz / A bullet for the end / Camel / Golden tooth / Gazelle boy / Superpowered.

— (on tour only) **SIMON 'GEN' MATTHEWS** – drums (of JESUS JONES) repl. GREENWOOD due to nervous exhaustion

Apr 96. (7"/c-s) *(EW 036/+C)* **HELLO. / NEGATIVELY YOURS**
(cd-s+=) *(EW 036CD)* – Consider yourself.

Apr 96. (cd/c) *(<0630 14610-2/-4>)* **LOVE YOUR SELF ABUSE**
– Hello / She's in pain / Mental bruising for beginners / Ignoramus / Sensual art of suffocation / Confessions of a teenage pervert / Penny dropped / Pink / Love your self abuse.

Jun 96. (7"/c-s) *(EW 045/+C)* **IGNORAMUS. / FETCH**
(cd-s+=) *(EW 045CD)* – I don't want your friend.

— now without GREENWOOD who had a heart problem; they split soon after

BABY LEMONADE

Formed: Glasgow . . . 1986 by the 5-piece of JOAN, GRAHAM, GARY, MARK and MARTIN. Naming themselves after a SYD BARRETT track – and produced by DOUGLAS HART (of the JESUS & MARY CHAIN) – BABY LEMONADE signed to Eddie Connelly's 'Narodnik' imprint. In 1988, their debut LP, 'ONE THOUSAND SECRETS' featured TOM KANE who played keyboards on the track 'SUMMER HOUSE'.

JOAN – vocals, clarinet / **GARY** – guitar / **MARK** – guitar / **GRAHAM** – bass, tambourine / **MARTIN** – drums, vocals

Narodnik not iss.

May 87. (7") *(NRK 004)* **SECRET GOLDFISH. / REAL WORLD**

Sha La La not iss.

1987. (7"flexi) *(003)* **THE JIFFY NECKWARE CREATION. / Bachelor Pad: GIRL OF YOUR DREAMS**
(above was given free away with fanzine 'Are You Scared To Be Happy')

D.D.T. not iss.

Nov 88. (lp) *(DISPLP 22)* **ONE THOUSAND SECRETS**
– Summer house / etc

— the band split after above

BACHELOR PAD

Formed: Strathbungo, nr. Glasgow . . . 1987 out of the WEE CHERUBS by songwriters TOMMY CHERRY and MARTIN COTTER. The aforementioned minimalistic indie-pop outfit released a one-off single, 'DREAMING', in 1984 (its B-side a cover of the Velvet Underground's 'I'M WAITING FOR THE MAN') and duly disappeared for a few years. Up popped The BACHELOR PAD, a quintet comprising CHERRY (vocals & guitar), COTTER (guitar & vocals), music journo DAVE HARRIS (on keyboards), WILLIE BAIN (bass) and GRAHAM ADAM (drums).

In 1987, the Bachelor boys appeared on two flexi-discs, their own 'Simply Thrilled' fanzine-freebie 'ARE YOU SCARED TO GET HAPPY' and a shared effort, 'GIRL OF YOUR DREAMS', with fellow indie funsters BABY LEMONADE. Fusing quickfire retro-Punk, retro-Psyche and retro-Swinging Sixties, they delivered a handful of 45's for the 'Warhola Sound' imprint, including 'THE ALBUMS OF JACK', 'DO IT FOR FUN' and 'ALL HASH AND COCK'. Finally, in 1990, The BACHELOR PAD released their first long-player, 'TALES OF HOFMANN', for the neo-psychedelic friendly 'Imaginary' label (also home to the MOCK TURTLES). Their love of nonsensical lyrics, chemical gurus and pop icons, made for a rather schitzoid set of songs; 'COUNTRY PANCAKE' (which also featured on a CND video), the single-to-be 'SMOOTHIE' and a rendition of Bobby Freeman's 'DO YOU WANNA DANCE' (like the RAMONES on speed!) were as diverse as you could get.

After a handful of further 45's for Glasgow's 'Egg' label, The BACHELOR PAD players returned to their day jobs. The disillusioned HARRIS returned to journalism full-time and even interviewed a certain MC Strong – author of the Great Rock Discography first edition – via an article for The Sunday Times Scotland; coincidentally, he spotted an unfinished paper discography of The BACHELOR PAD. After seven years bad luck (the broken mirror lore and all that!?), here it is, DAVE – the curse is now lifted.

TOMMY CHERRY – vocals, guitar / **MARTIN COTTER** – guitar, vocals / **DAVE HARRIS** – keyboards / **WILLIE BAIN** – bass / **GRAHAM ADAM** – drums (probably not all WEE CHERUBS)

Bogaten not iss.

Sep 84. (7"; as the WEE CHERUBS) *(BOGATEN 2)* **DREAMING. / WAITING FOR THE MAN**

Sha La La not iss.

1987. (7"flexi) *(003)* **GIRL OF YOUR DREAMS. / (other track by BABY LEMONADE)**

Warhola Sound not iss.

Jul 87. (7") *(WS:3MINS)* **THE ALBUMS OF JACK. / JACK AND JULIAN**
(12"+=) *(WST:3MINS)* – Norwegian wood / (+2).

Feb 88. (7") *(WS:4MINS)* **DO IT FOR FUN. /**
(12"+=) *(WST:4MINS)* –

1988. (12") *(WST:5MINS)* **ALL HASH AND COCK. /**

Imaginary not iss.

May 90. (lp) *(ILLUSION 009)* **TALES OF HOFMANN**
– Prologue / I want to hold your head / Country pancake / Abu Nidal's bus / Life is hell / Stop me (buy another one) / Where is Lesley? / Eeek! / Smoothie / A taste of Sydney / Do you wanna dance / The coroner's wife / Garbagehead / Jack and Julian / Girl of your dreams / Fabulous Fanny / I feel sick / Sunshower sun / Tumble and fall / Epilogue.

— now without HARRIS

Egg not iss.

Jan 90. (7"ep) *(EGG 003)* **FRYING TONIGHT EP (live)**

Jan 91. (7") *(EGG 006)* **SMOOTHIE. / DO YOU WANNA DANCE**

May 91. (12") *(EGG 007)* **MEETING THE LOVELY JENNY BROWN. /**

— they split later in '91

BADGEWEARER

Formed: Castlemilk, Glasgow . . . 1990 by songwriter DAVID RANKIN, along with MITCHELL HODGE, TONY KENNEDY and ROSS MAIN. Taking music back to the early 80's heights of The BIRTHDAY PARTY or The MEMBRANES, this manic quartet self-financed, self-made and self-produced their debut LP, 'F.T.Q.' (1992); must mean something shocking as the Queen's photo is in the insert – for/fuck? delete as appropriate!). Tracks such as 'ROD STEWART'S PENIS', might well have alienated them from the establishment, had they been able to get their hands on a copy – of the record that is. Turning the heat up (eventually!) to maximum R&R-esque PERE UBU, BEEFHEART and The MINUTEMEN (well, their songs were just as short!), the group finally surfaced for 'Guided Missile' late in '94 with the EP, 'THIS IS NOT A DOOR'. A follow-up LP, 'A TOY GUN IN SAFE HANDS' (1995), went virtually unnoticed, although 3rd effort on CD!, 'THANK YOU FOR YOUR CUSTOM' (1996), picked up a review or two.

DAVID RANKIN – vocals / **MITCHELL HODGE** – guitar / **TONT KENNEDY** – bass / **ROSS MAIN** – drums

Gruff Wit not iss.

Feb 92. (lp) *(GRUFF 006)* **F.T.Q.**
– Inflexible expendable / N'alien head / Too much soap / We want your name / Moneylenders – Cumbernauld / Impersonal stereo / Karaoke casualty / Aftershock / Woolenhead and ears / Static / Rod Stewart's penis / Syndex / Satellite dish / Liquid cosh.

Guided Missile not iss.

Nov 94. (7"ep) *(GUIDE 2)* **THIS IS NOT A DOOR EP**

Oct 95. (lp) *(GUIDE 5LP)* **A TOY GUN IN SAFE HANDS**

Aug 96. (cd) *(GUIDE 7CD)* **THANK YOU FOR YOUR CUSTOM**
– The magic of the nightie / Touch pretend Angus / Victorian policeman / Jum / Terminal headboy / Equation / Vision gone true / Mr. & Mrs. / More land home / Bee park is cowboy yeehah (that's not my usual bourbon) burp howdy pardon / Accept the wheel / Ted Kennedy (chaps who quit it) / Bartrum – Tantrum / Cartoon Churchill with a real head / Living remnant / Animal martyr / Waterchute / Jewish Nazi / Underage balcony.

Apr 97. (lp) *(GUIDE 15LP)* **NOWNESS**

May 97. (7") *(GUIDE 16)* **CRITERION ADJOURNMENT SECRET COWBOY AGENDA. /**

— disbanded later in the year

BALAAM AND THE ANGEL

Formed: Cannock, Staffordshire . . . 1984 by Scottish born brothers JIM, MARK and DES MORRIS. They were encouraged at an early age by their father, who initiated their career by obtaining some cabaret gigs at Motherwell working mens clubs. Along with manager CRAIG JENNINGS, they founded the 'Chapter 22' label and soon found themselves supporting the likes of The CULT. Late in 1985, after releasing three indie hits, they moved onto 'Virgin', their debut for the label, 'SHE KNOWS', breaking them into the Top 75 in March '86. Five months later, the album, 'THE GREATEST STORY EVER TOLD' trod the same post-punk goth path. Two more albums followed until they were dropped by 'Virgin', obviously fans opting for their contemporaries The CULT and SISTERS OF MERCY. They re-emerged in 1990 as the heavier BALAAM, although little happened commercially, MARK nearly joining The CULT that year as the replacement for JAMIE STEWART.

MARK MORRIS (b.15 Jan'63, Motherwell) – vocals, bass / **JIM MORRIS** (b.25 Nov'60, Motherwell) – guitar, keyboards, recorder / **DES MORRIS** (b.27 Jun'64, Motherwell) – drums, percussion

Chapter 22 — not iss.

Nov 84. (12"ep) *(22-001)* **WORLD OF LIGHT / FOR MORE THAN A DAY. / THE DARKLANDS / A NEW DAWN** [ ] [-]

Mar 85. (12"ep) *(22-002)* **LOVE ME / THE THOUGHT BEHIND IT ALL. / FAMILY AND FRIENDS / 15th FLOOR** [ ] [-]

Sep 85. (7") *(CHAP 3-7)* **DAY AND NIGHT. / ISABELLA'S EYES** [ ] [-]
(12"+=) *(CHAP 3-73)* – Touch / Return again.

Virgin — Virgin

Mar 86. (7") *(VS 842)* **SHE KNOWS. / DREAMS WIDE AWAKE** [70] [-]
(d7"+=) *(VSD 842)* – Sister moon / Warm again.
(12"+=) *(VS 842-12)* – 2 into 1 / The darklands.

Jun 86. (7") *(VS 864)* **SLOW DOWN. / WALK AWAY** [ ] [-]
(12"+=) *(VS 864-12)* – Travel on / In the morning.

Aug 86. (lp/c) *(V/TCV 2377)* **THE GREATEST STORY EVER TOLD** [67] [ ]
– New kind of love / Don't look down / She knows / Burn me down / Light of the world / Slow down / The wave / Warm again / Never end / Nothing there at all. *(cd-iss. Jul87+=; CDV 2377)* – Walk away / Day and night. *(re-iss. 1989 lp/c; OVED/+C 250)*

Aug 86. (7") *(VS 890)* **LIGHT OF THE WORLD. / DAY AND NIGHT (live)** [ ] [-]
(12"+=) *(VS 890-12)* – She knows / Love.

Jul 87. (7") *(VS 970)* **(I'LL SHOW YOU) SOMETHING SPECIAL. / I FEEL LOVE** [ ] [-]
(12"+=) *(VS 970-12)* – Let it happen / You took my soul.

Sep 87. (7") *(VS 993)* **I LOVE THE THINGS YOU DO TO ME. / YOU'RE IN THE WAY OF MY DREAMS** [ ] [-]
(12"+=) *(VS 993-12)* – Things you know / As tears go by.

— added **IAN McKEAN** – guitar (ex-20 FLIGHT ROCKERS)

Jul 88. (7") <99340< **I LOVE THE THINGS YOU DO TO ME. / WARM AGAIN** [-] [ ]

Jul 88. (lp/c/cd) *(V/TCV/CDV 2476)* <90869> **LIVE FREE OR DIE** [ ] [ ] Apr88
– (I'll show you) Something special / I love the things you do to me / Big city fun time girl / On the run / Would I die for you / Live free or die / It goes on / Long time loving you / I won't be afraid / Running out of time. *(c+=)* – I feel love. *(cd++=)* – You took my soul / Let it happen / You're in my way of dreams / As tears go by.

Aug 88. (7") *(VS 1124)* **LIVE FREE OR DIE. / EAGLE** [ ] [-]
(12"+=) *(VST 1124)* – Complete control / ('A'-Texas Redbeard mix).

Sep 89. (7") *(VS 1213)* **I TOOK A LITTLE. / LONG TIME LOVIN' YOU** [ ] [-]
(12"+=/12"pic-d+=) *(VST/VSP 1213)* – Big city fun time girl / Would I die for you.
(12"+=/cd-s+=) *(VSTX/VSCD 1213)* – (remixes).

Nov 89. (lp/c/cd) *(V/TCV/CDV 2598)* **DAYS OF MADNESS** [ ] [ ]
– Don't want your love / I took a little / She really gets to me / Body and soul / Heartbreaker / The tenderloin / Two days of madness / Did you fall (or were you pushed?) / Goodbye forever / I'm the only one / Stop messin' round.

Feb 90. (7") *(VS 1229)* **LITTLE BIT OF LOVE. / DID YOU FALL (OR WERE YOU PUSHED?)** [ ] [-]
(12"+=/cd-s+=) *(VST 1229)* – She really gets to me (acoustic).

— split in the autumn of 1990 and now without McKEAN

Intense — not iss.

Oct 91. (m-lp/m-c/m-cd; as BALAAM) *(TENS 001/+MC/CD)* **NO MORE INNOCENCE** [ ] [-]
– Shame on you / Next to me / What love is / She's not you / Mr. Business / Just no good.

— next release took six from last and added five new ones

Bleeding Hearts — not iss.

Apr 93. (cd) *(CDBLEED 1)* **PRIME TIME** [ ] [-]
– Shame on you / Prime time / Next to me / What love is / Gathering dust / Eagle / She's not you / Mr. Business / Like a train / Burning / Just no good. *(re-iss. Feb98 on 'Darkend'; DARK 003CD)*

– compilations, etc. –

Oct 86. (lp) *Chapter 22; (CHAPLP 4)* **SUN FAMILY** [ ] [-]
(cd-iss. Jun02 on 'Anagram'; CDMGOTH 17)

BALLBOY

Formed: Edinburgh . . . late 90's by songwriter/guitarist and primary school teacher GORDON McINTYRE, a man more than a little influenced by the narrative doodlings of BELLE & SEBASTIAN.

Backed by student KATIE GRIFFITHS, nursery nurse NICK REYNOLDS and sound technician GARY MORGAN (who replaced an earlier line-up – see below), he unveiled his jangly, reflective muse on 1999's debut EP, 'SILVER SUITS FOR ASTRONAUTS'. With his slightly fey vocals, bittersweet twenty/thirty-something musings and pithy character sketches, comparisons with B&S's STUART DAVID were unavoidable. No bad thing though as McINTYRE carried it all off with more charm and grace than most indie hopefuls can muster, his voice imparting a rare authenticity. Summer 2000 follow-up, 'I HATE SCOTLAND.. EP', proved he wasn't scared of a bit of controversy, its scathing title track (dedicated to 'Keep Clause 28' "campaigner", Brian Souter) a flipside to Saltire-waving Caledonian romance while hidden track, 'THE SASH MY FATHER WORE', ironically exposed Scotland's "dirty secret" of religious bigotry. Although more musically adventurous than its predecessor, the record maintained acoustic strumming as BALLBOY's preferred field of play.

With a third EP in the can, the group sensibly issued a compilation album (a kind of "3 EPS" type thing) to an eager set of fans. 'CLUB ANTHEMS' (2002) was more social club than dance club, with the aforementioned 'I HATE SCOTLAND' making a brave appearance as the opening track. Other tracks (and the titles are great!) included 'SEX IS BORING', 'I'VE GOT PICTURES OF YOU IN YOUR UNDERWEAR' and, wait for it, 'ALL THE RECORDS ON THE RADIO ARE SHITE', which received an unfair lambasting by an NME hack (stick to The VINES, man, eh!).

GORDON McINTYRE – guitars, narration / **KATIE GRIFFITHS** – keyboards / **NICK REYNOLDS** – bass / **GARY MORGAN** – drums, percussion; repl. ALEXIS BEATTIE, CHRIS LOWRIE, JOHN McLEAN + ELIZABETH McLEAN

sl — Manifesto

Nov 99. (cd-ep) *(lone 06)* **SILVER SUITS FOR ASTRONAUTS – 4 SONGS** [ ] [-]
– Donald in the bushes with a bag of glue / A day in space / Dumper truck racing / Public park a.k.a dogs not kids.

Jul 00. (cd-ep) *(lone 08)* **I HATE SCOTLAND.. EP** [ ] [-]
– Essential wear for future trips to space / I hate Scotland.. / One sailor was waving / Olympic cyclist (acoustic version). *(hidden track+=)* – Donald Jr.; The sash my father wore.

Mar 01. (cd-ep) *(lone 10)* **GIRLS ARE BETTER THAN BOYS EP** [ ] [-]
– Leave the earth behind you and take a walk into the sunshine / I've got pictures of you in your underwear / Swim for health / They'll hang flags from cranes upon my wedding day.

Feb 02. (cd) *(lone 11)* <43301> **CLUB ANTHEMS** (compilation) [ ] [ ]
– Donald in the bushes with a bag of glue (new version) / A day in space (new version) / Dumper truck racing / Public park a.k.a. dogs not kids / Essential wear for future trips to space / I hate Scotland.. / One sailor was waving / Olympic cyclist (acoustic version) / Leave the earth behind you and take a walk into the sunshine / I've got pictures of you in your underwear / Swim for health / They'll hang flags from cranes upon my wedding day / Postcards from the beach / Sex is boring (acoustic version). *<US tracks in different order>*

Apr 02. (cd-ep/7"ep) *(lone 15/+5)* **ALL THE RECORDS ON THE RADIO ARE SHITE EP** [ ] [-]
– All the records on the radio are shite / Building for the future / Stars and stripes / Welcome to the New Year.

BAMBOO (see under ⇒ Hubba Hubba records)

BAMBULE (see under ⇒ CINdYTALK)

BANGTWISTER

Formed: Partick, Glasgow . . . 1996 by the trio of ALASDAIR MITCHELL (bass), GORDON 'Go-Go' BRADY (lead guitar) and KEITH BEACOM (drums); all share lead vocal duties. Once established on the local live front, BANGTWISTER released the 'Flotsam & Jetsam' one-off, 'AGONY AUNT', in April 1997. Described as a cross between hard-rock/metal and MC5, the whisky-drinking garage trio recalled the days when vinyl was demo-like and scratchy. This long-haired neo-psyche bunch were all the rage again after a second EP that year, entitled 'GROUNDED'. However, bar a BBC session, very little or nothing was heard from them thereafter, although a split tour 45, 'DOWNWARD SPIRAL' (along with the THANES, the GREASE MONKEYS and FIRESTONE: LEGEND OF THE HAWK) did see light in '98. A planned single for the 'Flycatcher' imprint was having technical difficulties getting released as of May 2001 and still is over a year later!

ALASDAIR MITCHELL – vocals, bass / **GORDON BRADY** – vocals, lead guitar / **KEITH BEACOM** – vocals, drums, percussion

Flotsam & Jetsam — not iss.

Apr 97. (7"m) *(SHaG 011)* **AGONY AUNT. / YOU'RE SO LOOSE / SHAKE IT!** [ ] [-]

BMB Music — not iss.

Dec 97. (cd-ep) *(BMBCD 1)* **GROUNDED e.p.** [ ] [-]
– Grounded / Happening in the back of my mind / Agony aunt / You're so loose / Shake it!

— continued to do the odd session for BBC, etc

— in '98, they also contributed 'DOWNWARD SPIRAL' to a 'Bronx Cheer' 7" EP, which featured The THANES, FIRESTONE: LEGEND OF THE HAWK and the GREASE MONKEYS

Trepanner — not iss.

May 01. (7") *(THC 003)* **WE'RE THE REACTION. / SOME KINDA REVOLUTION** [ ] [-]

Jimmy BARNES

Born: JAMES SWAN, 28 Apr'56, Cowcaddens, Glasgow – although raised in Adelaide, Australia since the age of four. Subsequently influenced by his older brother John's taste of music (i.e. The ROLLING STONES, The BEATLES and ROD STEWART) the gravel-throated BARNES formed hard rock/radio friendly outfit, COLD CHISEL in 1977, enlisting the help of IAN MOSS, IAN WALKER, PHIL SMALL and STEVEN PRESTWICH. With major label backing from the outset, COLD CHISEL became one of Australia's most consistent homegrown talents. 'BREAKFAST AT SWEETHEARTS' in '79, quickly became regarded as their best work, although a third set, 'EAST' made a minor impact in the States.

With several albums under their collective belt, BARNES opted for a solo career, releasing his first album, 'BODY SWERVE' in 1984. Eager to secure a substantial fanbase outside Australia, he signed a worldwide deal with 'Geffen', who in turn issued an eponymous album in 1986. Following the success of a minor US hit single, 'WORKING CLASS MAN', the album enjoyed an extended chart run, hovering on the fringes of the all important US Top 100. Utilizing the cream of the AOR set (i.e. DESMOND CHILD, JIM VALLANCE, NEAL SCHON, JONATHAN CAIN and MICK FLEETWOOD), he achieved similar success with the 'FREIGHT TRAIN HEART' opus in '88. Between these two releases, BARNES had his biggest hit to date, 'GOOD TIMES', although this shared credits with Antipodean allies, INXS.

Surprisingly dropped by 'Geffen', BARNES later moved to 'Atlantic' records, releasing the commercially disappointing 1990 set, 'TWO FIRES'. Throughout the 90's, BARNES continued to search for that elusive breakthrough (even re-forming COLD CHISEL in '97), although he remains one of Australian rock's most respected figures. Although Britain as a whole has lost touch, his Scottish fanbase have never wavered; he now lives a bit closer to his roots (due to tax problems), albeit in France.

JIMMY BARNES – vocals / with numerous session men

Mushroom — not iss.

1984. (lp) *(RML 53138)* **BODYSWERVE** [-] [-] Austra
– Vision / Daylight / Promise me you'll call / No second prize / Boys cry out for war / Paradise / A change is gonna come / Thick skinner / Piece of my heart / Fire / World's on fire.

1985. (d-lp) *(RML 53196-7)* **FOR THE WORKING CLASS MAN** [-] [-] Austra
– I'd die to be with you tonight / Ride the night away / American heartbeat / Working class man / Without your love / No second prize / Vision / Promise me you'll call / Boys cry out for war / Daylight / Thick skinned / Paradise.

— next with guests **JONATHAN CAIN, NEIL SCHON** (both BAD ENGLISH) + **MICK FLEETWOOD + DESMOND CHILD**

Geffen — Geffen

May 86. (lp/c) *(924089-1/-4) <24089>* **JIMMY BARNES** [ ] [ ] Mar86
– No second prize / I'd die to be with you tonight / Working class man / Promise me you'll call / Boys cry out for war / Paradise / Without your love / American heartbeat / Thick skinned / Ride the night away / Daylight.

May 86. (7"/12") *(GEF 3/+T) <28749>* **WORKING CLASS MAN (remix). / BOYS CRY OUT FOR WAR** [ ] [74] Mar86

— In Jun'87, BARNES and INXS hit the Top 50 with the single 'GOOD TIMES' on 'Atlantic' (89237)

May 88. (lp/c/cd) *(924146-1/-4/-2) <24146>* **FREIGHT TRAIN HEART** [ ] [ ]
– Driving wheels / Seven days / Too much ain't enough love / Lessons in love / Waitin' for the heartache / The last frontier / I'm still on your side / Do or die / I wanna get started with you / Walk on.

May 88. (7") *(GEF 38) <27920>* **TOO MUCH AIN'T ENOUGH LOVE. / DO OR DIE** [ ] [91] Jun88
(12"+=) *(GEF 38T)* – Working class man / Resurrection shuffle.

1988. (cd) *Mushroom; (D 24521-2)* **BARNESTORMING (live)** [-] [-] Austra
– Driving wheels / Good times / Too much ain't enough love / Lessons in love / Working class man / Waitin' for the heartache / Do or die / When a man loves a woman / Last frontier / Seven days / Temptation / No second prize / Walk on / Rising sun / Without your love / Paradise. *(UK-iss.May94; same)*

1989. (cd-s) **WAITIN' FOR THE HEARTACHE / SEVEN DAYS – 12" mix / GOING TO MEXICO** [-] [-] Austra

Sep 90. (cd/c/lp) *<(7567 82141-2/-4/-1)>* **TWO FIRES** [ ] [ ]
– Lay down your guns / Let's make it last all night long / Little darlin' / Love is enough / Hardline / One of a kind / Sister mercy / When your love is gone / Caught between two fires / Fade to black. *(cd+=)* – Hold on. *(cd re-iss. May94 on 'Mushroom'; TVD 93318)*

1991. (cd-s) **LAY DOWN YOUR GUNS / BROKEN HEARTS** [-] [-] Austra

Mushroom — Mushroom

1991. (cd) *(TVD 93344)* **SOUL DEEP** [-] [-] Austra
– I gotcha / (Your love keeps lifting me) Higher and higher / When something is wrong with my baby / Show me / Many rivers to cross / Reflections / Ain't no mountain high enough / I found a love / Signed sealed delivered (I'm yours) / Bring it on home to me / Here I am (come and take me) / River deep mountain high. *(UK-iss.Aug94; same)*

1991. (cd-s) **I GOTCHA / I GOTCHA (Tex mix)** [-] [-] Austra

1991. (cd-s) **WHEN SOMETHING IS WRONG WITH MY BABY / ALL I GOT** [-] [-] Austra

1992. (cd/c/lp) *(TVD/TVC/TVL 93372)* **HEAT** [ ] [ ]
– Sweat it out / Wheels in motion / Stand up / Burn baby burn / Something's got a hold / Love thing / Talking to you / Stone cold / Wait for me / Tears we cry / Right by your side / A little bit of love / I'd rather be blind / Not the loving kind / Knock me down / Catch your shadow. *(UK-iss.Jun93; same)*

1992. (cd-s) **SWEAT IT OUT / TELL ME THE TRUTH / SITTING AT THE BAR** [-] [-] Austra

Nov 93. (c-s/12"/cd-s) **STAND UP. /** [ ] [ ]

Nov 93. (cd) *(TVD 93390)* **FLESH & WOOD** [ ] [ ]
– It will be alright / The weight / Ride the night away / Guilty / You can't make love without soul / Hell of a time / Brother of mine / Fade to black / Flame trees / Still got a long way to go / Still on your side / Stone cold / Let it go / We could be gone / Love me tender. *(UK-iss.Dec94; same)*

— (last 2 albums also issued UK Feb94 d-cd/d-c; *D/C 45045)*

Feb 94. (cd-ep) *(D 11504)* **STONE COLD EP** [ ] [ ]
– Stone cold / Stand up (live) / Stone cold (live) / Catch your shadow (acoustic) / Stone cold (acoustic) / Working class man (acoustic).

1994. (cd-s) **THE WEIGHT / COLD COLD HEART** [-] [-] Austra

May 95. (c-s/cd-s) *(C/D 11980)* **CHANGE OF HEART / EDGEWOOD / THE OTHER SIDE** [ ] [-]
(cd-s) *(DX 11980)* – ('A'side) / Lay down your guns (live) / Come undone (acoustic) / You can't always get what you want (acoustic) / Many rivers to cross (acoustic).

Jun 95. (cd/c) *(TVD/TVC 93433)* **PSYCLONE** [ ] [ ]
– Used to be truth / Spend the night / Change of heart / Every beat / Come undone / Stumbling / Love and devotion / Mirror of your soul / Just a man / Fooling yourself / Tears / Going down alone / Because you wanted it.

1995. (cd-s) **COME UNDONE / BECAUSE YOU WANTED IT** [-] [-] Austra

Feb 00. (cd) *(MUSH 67CD)* **LOVE AND FEAR** [ ] [ ]
– Love and hate / Time will tell / By the grace of God / Thankful for the rain / Temptation / Love song / Do it to me / Love gone cold / Heart cries alone / Radio song / Blind can't lead the blind / Sorry.

2000. (cd-s) **THANKFUL FOR THE RAIN / HERE AND NOW / THANKFUL FOR THE RAIN (instrumental)** [-] [-] Austra

Epic — not iss.

Sep 00. (cd) *(857386194-2)* **SOUL DEEPER** (covers) [-] [-] Austra
– Land of a 1000 dances / Chain of fools / What becomes of the broken hearted / To love somebody / 634-5789 / Ain't too proud to beg / I put a spell on you / Money / Hold on I'm coming / Dancing in the street / All the young dudes / Respect.

Nov 00. (cd-s) *(857385642-2)* **CHAIN OF FOOLS** [-] [-] Austra

– compilations, etc. –

May 97. (d-cd) *Mushroom; (TVD 93465)* **THE BEST OF JIMMY BARNES** [ ] [ ]

1990's. (cd) *Mushroom; (IMPMUSH 32164)* **BARNES HITS ANTHOLOGY** [-] [-] Austra

1990's. (3xcd-box) *Mushroom; (MUSH 332742)* **JIMMY BARNES x 3** [-] [-] Austra
– (BODYSWERVE, TWO FIRES + CYCLONE)

Mike BARSON

Born: 21 Apr'58, Edinburgh. Exactly when this "Nutty Boy" moved down south to Camden (London) is unclear, although MIKE did attend local Gospel Oak school as a teenager. It was here the pianist/keyboard-player struck up a friendship with CHRIS FOREMAN and LEE THOMPSON, prior to becoming an art student (circa '75). All three subsequently formed their own Ska group, MORRIS AND THE MINORS (the moniker taken from the similarly-named small car, the Morris Minor) and evolved with the help of GRAHAM "Suggs" McPHERSON, MARK BEDFORD, CHAS SMASH and DAN WOODGATE into the (NORTH LONDON) INVADERS. When they became MADNESS in '79 and hit the Ska big-time courtesy of Top 20 hit, 'The Prince', BARSON was an intergral part of the Nutty 7-piece during the 80's and part of the 90's.

BASS BABY (see under ⇒ Clubscene records)

BASS REACTION (see under ⇒ Shoop records)

BASS X (see under ⇒ Shoop records)

BATHERS

Formed: Glasgow ... 1986 by former FRIENDS AGAIN frontman/songwriter, CHRIS THOMSON. After musical differences had put paid to FRIENDS AGAIN in the mid-80's, THOMSON was picked up by the ascendant 'Go! Discs' and together with DOUGLAS McINTYRE cut a debut BATHERS album, 'UNUSUAL PLACES TO DIE' (1987). Critics across the board hailed the album as a triumphant, modern interpretation of pop classicism yet its commercial potential was subsequently buried amid internal problems with the label. History repeated itself two years on as the similarly acclaimed 'SWEET DECEIT' (1990) fell victim to a period of instability at 'Island'.

THOMSON then took time out in the form of a side project, BLOOMSDAY, with two members of LLOYD COLE & THE COMMOTIONS. The trio cut a one-off album, 'Fortuny', before CHRIS resumed BATHERS duty with 1994's 'LAGOON BLUES' set. The first of a series of albums for the German 'Marina' label, the record bore all the hallmarks of THOMSON's passionate muse: orchestral strings, heart-tinkling ivories, lovingly crafted arrangements and a Europhile's vision of doomed romance. Having attracted a cult following of frothing critics and discerning fans, he didn't disappoint them with 1995's 'SUNPOWDER', LIZ FRASER (COCTEAU TWINS) guesting on an another set of elegantly lovelorn musings. 1997's 'KELVINGROVE BABY' was the final BATHERS set for 'Marina' before THOMSON inked a new deal with the London-based 'Wrasse' label (home to LADYSMITH BLACK MAMBAZO).

Featuring an expanded, experienced line-up of CALLUM McNAIR, HAZEL MORRISON, KEN McHUGH, DAVID CRICHTON, IAIN WHITE, PAUL LEONARD and ROBERT HENDERSON as well as contributions from BELLE & SEBASTIAN's ISOBEL CAMPBELL and RICHARD COLBURN, 1999's 'PANDEMONIA' again had the critics in rapture. Early TOM WAITS, Astral Weeks-period VAN MORRISON and indigenous mood merchants The BLUE NILE were all consistent comparisons. To this list you could probably add TINDERSTICKS, PORTISHEAD ('THE BELLE SISTERS') and in THOMSON's wracked vocals, vague hints of DAVID BOWIE. All high praise indeed but praise which is, by and large, merited. Although THOMSON's vocal/lyrical ruminations occasionally veer too close to pretension for comfort, The BATHERS' languid, atmospheric tapestries of strings, piano, guitar and occasional brass surely rank them as one of Scotland's most sophisticated pop purveyors.

CHRIS THOMSON – vocals, guitar, piano (ex-FRIENDS AGAIN) / **DOUGLAS McINTYRE** – guitar / plus a few others

Go! Discs — not iss.

Apr 87. (7") *(GOD 17)* **FANCY DRESS. / JU JU PEACH** [ ] [-]
(12"+=) *(GOD 18)* – Yellow buckskin.

Oct 87. (lp/c) *(A/Z GOLP 10)* **UNUSUAL PLACES TO DIE** [ ] [-]
– Perpetual adoration / Latta's dream / Fancy dress / Time regained / Take me back to the Brooklands / Candide / Ju ju peach / Unusual places to die / Isn't she shining? / Fortuny.

— **THOMSON** now with **JAMES LOCKE** – percussion / **SAM LOUP** – bass, organ / **GREER KITSON** – guitar, synths, etc / **FERMINA HAZE** – guitar, keyboards, percussion / **CAMPBELL OWENS** – bass

C.G.T. – Island — not iss.

Apr 90. (cd/c/lp) *(CGTI 2/4/1) – (CID/ICT/ILPS 9953)* **SWEET DECEIT** [ ] [-]
– The pursuit of an orchid / Two cats on the piano / Memory fever / For the delicious C / Desire regained / Get out of life / Pistol crazed / The wreck in the bay / Reason to feel / Memory fever (2) / The idylll off Crown Circus / Perpetual adoration / Sweet deceit / The honeysuckle rose / On the steps at Park Circus.

— now down to THOMSON solo again

Marina — not iss.

Apr 94. (cd/c) *(MA 2 – CD/MC 33962)* **LAGOON BLUES** [ ] [-]
– Lagoon blues pt.1 / Venice shoes / Gracefruit / Fermina fair / Sissoir / Never too late / The Ornella mutiny / Easter – for Edda Van Heemstra / Thru' the old Holmwood / Lolita / Via d'oro / Ave the leopards / Sweetheart sessions / Carnival / Easter Sorbonne / Lagoon blues pt.2

— with **KEN McHUGH** – bass / etc

May 95. (cd) *(MA 12)* **SUNPOWDER** [ ] [-]
– Danger in love / The Dutch Venus / The angel of Ruskin / Delft / Weem rock muse / Faithless / She's gone forever / Send me your halo / For Saskia / The night is young / Sunpowder. *(re-iss. Mar01 on 'Waddle-Marina'; MAC 4460-2)*

— now with **JAMES LOCKE** – co-producer, etc (ex-CHIMES, etc)

— also **KEN McHUGH, HAZEL MORRISON** (drums & percussion), **CARLO, COLIN, MARK + IAIN**

Feb 97. (cd) *(MA 22 – MACD 44682)* **KELVINGROVE BABY** [ ] [-]
– Thrive / Girlfriend / If love could last forever / East of East Delier / No risk no glory / Once upon a time on the Rapenburg / Kelvingrove baby / Girl from the Polders / Lost certainties / Dial / The fragrance remains insane / Hellespont in a storm / Twelve.

— **CHRIS** was now augmented mainly by **CALLUM McNAIR** – guitar, bass, vocals / **HAZEL + KEN** / plus others **IAIN WHITE + DAVY CRICHTON** – violin / **BARRY OVERSTREET** – sax / **ROBERT HENDERSON** – trumpet / *NEIL CAMERON* – double bass

Wrasse — not iss.

Sep 99. (cd) *(WRASS 015)* **PANDEMONIA** [-] [-] mail-o
– Twenty-two / Dreamless / Something precious has been destroyed (sleeper fragment I) / The Belle sisters / Tequila mockingbird / Sundown and longing / Trocadero girls / Huntly in love / The captives / Phantom sonata (sleeper fragment II) / Yellow crombie / Last night I loved you / Supernatural (sleeper fragment III) / Pandemonia.

— now with **PAUL LEONARD-MORGAN** – keyboards

– compilations, etc. –

Oct 01. (cd) *Wrasse; (WRASS 034)* **DESIRE REGAINED – THE BEST OF THE BATHERS** [ ] [-]
– Unusual places to drive / Perpetual adoration / Two cats on the piano / Are the leopards / Pandemonia / Girlfriend / For Saskia / Thrive / Belle sisters / Sunpowder / Angel on Ruskin / Last night I loved you / Pandemonia (part 2) / The night is young / Danger in love / Kelvin grove baby / Desire regained / Once upon a time on the Rapenburg / Twenty two / If love could last forever.

BLOOMSDAY

CHRIS THOMPSON + two members of the COMMOTIONS

Island — not iss.

Oct 90. (cd/c/lp) *(CID/ICT/ILPS 9972)* **FORTUNY** [ ] [-]
– The day the colours died / Patience / Just the same / Song of five / Blue poetry / Vitamin / Pablo's diary / I remain yours / Soft / Weight.

— checking above + below for correct track listing

1990. (cd-ep) **BLOOMSDAY EP** [ ] [-]
– Blush / Television / Tuesday to Thursday / Girl with a black dress / Suddenly June.

BAY (see under ⇒ ARAB STRAP)

BEAT FREAKS (see under ⇒ CHIMES)

BEAT POETS (see under ⇒ 53rd & 3rd records)

BEAUTY SCHOOL DROPOUT

Formed: Glasgow ... September 1995 by DAVE, RICHIE, BRAD and CRAIG; all Hawaiian-shirted converts from the ugly school dropout brigade of punks SCREECHING WEASEL and the DOUGHBOYS. Although they recorded what they described themselves as a shitty demo while generally fucking about trying to get a recording deal, BSD finally made the grade after a great gig in Falkirk c.1999 (alongside locals TURTLEHEAD). Spotted by an employee of 'Them's Good' records, they were snapped up to cut their debut album, 'TEASING THE FAT KIDS'; they were dumped from their roster soon afterwards and played their last gig at Nice'n'Sleazy's on the 21st of December 2001.

DAVE – vocals, guitar / **RICHIE** – guitar / **BRAD** – bass / **CRAIG** – drums

Them's Good | not iss.

Nov 99. (cd) *(Good 007cd)* **TEASING THE FAT KIDS LP** ☐ [-]
– Schizo girl / Just / Best kept secret / Safety net / Now you see me / Poison pen / Bad luck / Rain / Let you down / Hat thief / Square / Pass the buck.

Mar 00. (7") *(Good 011s)* **BEST KEPT SECRET. / BAD LUCK** ☐ [-]

Speedowax | not iss.

Dec 00. (7"ep) *(Atom 011)* **PASS THE BUCK / POISON PEN. / (other tracks by Discount)** ☐ [-]

— the band (who've now split) also featured on a handful of V/A sets

BE-ING (see ⇒ Section 9: Dance / Rave)

BELLE AND SEBASTIAN

Formed: Glasgow . . . early '96 by ex-choirboy/boxer!, STUART MURDOCH (the main songwriter) and ISOBEL CAMPBELL, who met and recruited additional members STUART DAVID, RICHARD COLBURN, STEVIE JACKSON and CHRIS GEDDES in a local cafe. They borrowed the group name from a popular 70's children's TV series (from France) about a young boy and his Pyrenees mountain dog.

Two months into their career, the expanded outfit released a very limited (1000 copies) college financed album, 'TIGERMILK', which gained sufficient airplay on national radio to ensure encroaching cult status. By the end of the year (and now with 7th member, SARAH MARTIN) they had unleashed their second set, 'IF YOU'RE FEELING SINISTER', which went on to sell in excess of 15,000 copies and gained much respect from end of the year critic polls.

Since then, BELLE AND SEBASTIAN have hit the singles chart three times with a series of highly desirable EP's, 'DOGS ON WHEELS', 'LAZY LINE PAINTER JANE' (with former THRUM larynx-basher MONICA QUEEN on excellent form) and culminating with their critically acclaimed Top 40 entry, '3.. 6.. 9 SECONDS OF LIGHT'. The fact that they've scaled such giddy heights of indie stardom with only a minimum of promotion and a handful of gigs speaks volumes for the quality of their vintage twee C-86-esque sound.

By late summer '98, expectations for a new album had reached fever pitch, critics unanimously hailing 'THE BOY WITH THE ARAB STRAP' as one of the year's finest (sadly, too late for esteemed Mercury Prize) and helped ease it into the Top 20. Their by now trademark combination of fey vocals, killer hooklines and avant-pop experimentalism resulted in some of B&S's most infectious tracks to date. With the spirit of NICK DRAKE ghosting in and out of focus (especially on 'SLEEP THE CLOCK AROUND' and 'A SUMMER WASTING'), this troupe of Glaswegian revivalists succeeded in putting the 60's and 70's through an 80's filter, incredibly coming up with something quintessentially 90's! The uninitiated should head straight for the holy trinity of tracks opening side two wherein BELLE & SEBASTIAN do an "ARAB STRAP" so to speak, the "Bairn"-like narrative of 'A SPACE BOY DREAM' complementing the BOLAN-esque stomp of the title track and sandwiching the brassy, BOO RADLEYS (but don't let that put you off!) style 'DIRTY DREAM NUMBER TWO'. Fans eager to get a glimpse of these elusive Scots shysters in the flesh should keep their eyes peeled, actual gigs are woefully few and far between.

Extra-curricular activities, meanwhile, included a US 'Sub Pop' 7" from STUART DAVID's spoken word/electro outfit, LOOPER (with also his wife, Wee KARN and his brother, RONNIE BLACK). They would continue as a unit early in 1999, releasing a debut album for 'Jeepster', while ISOBEL's side project, The GENTLE WAVES, also released a long-player on the same label. In July that year and due to demand from everybody bar possibly PETE WATERMAN and his STEPS (who were somewhat peeved about losing the recent Brit Newcomers award due to internet voting), BELLE & SEBASTIAN re-distributed their semi-quasi debut 'TIGERMILK'; this time it hit the UK Top 20.

After a two-year recording gap, B&S confidently returned with their fourth studio outing, the sublime, if not translucent 'FOLD YOUR HANDS CHILD, YOU WALK LIKE A PEASANT'. From its flaky opener, 'I FOUGHT IN THE WAR', listeners could detect that this album would be pale in comparison to the aforementioned 'BOY WITH THE . . .'. It seemed that, since the band had apparently broken into the mainstream of America, that their sound was becoming more MOR, more tweaked, more . . . STUART MURDOCH. With that in mind, however, MURDOCH did allow other band members to take the artistic reins: JACKSON and CAMPBELL sang on more songs than usual, slightly thwarting the ever-impending NICK DRAKE references. It could be just that B&S, like many other artists, followed a pivotal record with one that was weaker. Or maybe the group had simply lost their edge. On the eve of the release for this album they started doing press interviews – something that was frowned upon during their earlier years.

The band also covered uncharted territory by issuing the album 'STORYTELLING' (2002), the soundtrack to the Todd Solondz film of the same name. A bleak look into American suburbia, the movie was a follow-up to the highly controversial (and highly uncomfortable) work 'Happiness'. It eventually got edited so much by the producers that Solondz vowed never to make another movie again. Unfortunately, so was the B&S score, which didn't make the final cuts. And it's a shame really, because the group almost redeemed themselves by attempting to create proper film music. 'FREAK', 'FUCK THIS SHIT' and the humourously entitled 'BLACK AND WHITE UNITE' (believe it, you have to see the film to get the joke) all made for good soundtrack material. The only let down being the inclusion of 'sound-bites' from the film which were inter-spliced with the music. Unnecessary, and ultimately tiring, dialogue such as "Nigger, fuck me . . ." was hardly worthy of 'Pulp Fiction' proportions. Still, an interesting enough album to accompany an interesting enough film. ISOBEL, meanwhile, collaborated with celebrated Falkirk-born avant-jazz man, BILL WELLS, on the album 'GHOST OF YESTERDAY' (a take on the legendary BILLIE HOLIDAY).

STUART MURDOCH (b. 1967) – vocals, acoustic guitar / **ISOBEL CAMPBELL** – cello, vocals / **STEVIE JACKSON** – guitars, vocals / **STUART DAVID** – bass / **RICHARD COLBURN** – drums / **CHRIS GEDDES** – piano

Electric Honey | not iss.

May 96. (lp) *(EHRLP 5)* **TIGERMILK** ☐ [-]
– The state I am in / Expectations / She's losing it / You're just a baby / Electronic renaissance / I could be dreaming / We rule the school / My wandering days are over / I don't love anyone / Mary Jo. *(re-iss. Jul99 on 'Jeepster' cd/c/lp; JPR CD/MC/LP 007)* – hit No.13

— added **SARAH MARTIN** – violin, saxophone / and also extra member **MICK COOKE** – trumpet

Jeepster | Enclave-Capitol

Nov 96. (cd/c/lp) *(JPR CD/MC/LP 001)* *<56713>* **IF YOU'RE FEELING SINISTER** ☐ ☐ Feb97
– Stars of track and field / Seeing other people / Me and the Major / Like Dylan in the movies / The fox in the snow / Get me away from here, I'm dying / If you're feeling sinister / Mayfly / The boy done wrong again / Judy and the dream of horses.

May 97. (7") *(JPR7 001)* **DOG ON WHEELS. / THE STATE I AM IN (demo)** [59] [-]
(12"+=/cd-s+=) *(JPR 12/CDS 001)* – String bean Jean / Belle & Sebastian.

— guest on below, **MONICA QUEEN** – vocals (of THRUM)

Aug 97. (7") *(JPR7 002)* **LAZY LINE PAINTER JANE. / YOU MADE ME FORGET MY DREAMS** [41] [-]
(12"+=/cd-s+=) *(JPR 12/CDS 002)* – Photo Jenny / A century of Elvis.

Oct 97. (7"ep) *(JPR7 003)* **3.. 6.. 9 SECONDS OF LIGHT EP** [32] [-]
– A century of fakers / Le pastie de la bourgeoisie.
(12"ep+=/cd-ep+=) *(JPR 12/CDS 003)* – Beautiful / Put the book back on the shelf / *(hidden track-)* Songs for children.

— added guest **NEIL ROBERTSON** – bass

Jeepster | Matador

Sep 98. (cd/c) *(JPR CD/MC 003)* *<OLE 311>* **THE BOY WITH THE ARAB STRAP** [12] ☐
– It could have been a brilliant career / Sleep the clock around / Is it wicked not to care? / Ease your feet in the sea / A summer wasting / Seymour Stein / A space boy dream / Dirty dream number two / The boy with the arab strap / Chickfactor / Simple things / The rollercoaster ride.

Dec 98. (12"ep/cd-ep) *(JPR 12/CDS 009)* **THIS IS JUST A MODERN ROCK SONG / I KNOW WHERE THE SUMMER GOES. / THE GATE / SLOW GRAFFITI** [-] [-] -chart
below featured the MAISONETTES

May 00. (7") *(JPR7 018)* **LEGAL MAN. / WINTER WOOSKIE** [15] ☐
(cd-s+=) *(JPRCDS 018)* *<OLE 448>* – Judy is a dick slap.
(12") *(JPR12 018)* – ('A'side) / Judy is a dick slap (extended).

Jun 00. (cd/md/lp) *(JPR CD/MD/LP 010)* *<OLE 429>* **FOLD YOUR HANDS CHILD, YOU WALK LIKE A PEASANT** [10] [80]
– I fought in a war / The model / Beyond the sunrise / Waiting for the moon to rise / Don't leave the light on baby / The wrong girl / The chalet lines / Nice day for a sulk / Woman's realm / Family tree / There's too much love.

— STUART DAVID left after the recording of above

Jun 01. (7") *(JPR7 022)* **JONATHAN DAVID. / THE LONELINESS OF A MIDDLE DISTANCE RUNNER** [31] [-]
(12"+=/cd-s+=) *(JPR 12/CD 022)* – Take your carriage clock and shove it.

Nov 01. (7") *(JPR7 023)* **I'M WAKING UP TO US. / I LOVE MY CAR** [39] [-]
(12"+=/cd-s+=) *(JPRCDS 023)* – Marx and Engels.

Jun 02. (cd/lp) *(JPR CD/LP 014)* *<OLE 512>* **STORYTELLING** [26] ☐
– Fiction / Freak / Dialogue: Conan, early Letterman / Fuck this shit / Night walk / Dialogue: Jersey's where it's at / Black and white unite / Consuelo / Dialogue: Toby /

Storytelling / Dialogue: Class rank / I don't want to play football / Consuelo leaving / Wandering alone / Dialogue: Mandingo cliche / Scooby driver / Fiction (reprise) / Big John Shaft.

– compilations, etc. –

Mar 00. (cd) *Jeepster; (JPRBOX 001) / Matador; <OLE 313>* **LAZY LINE PAINTER JANE** (the first 3 EP's) — Oct00

the GENTLE WAVES

ISOBEL CAMPBELL with **RICHARD COLBURN, STUART MURDOCH, CHRIS GEDDES + STEVIE JACKSON**

Jeepster / Jeepster

Mar 99. (7") *(JPR7 011)* **WEATHERSHOW. / EVENSONG** — -

Apr 99. (cd/lp) *(JPR CD/LP 006) <4026>* **THE GREEN FIELDS OF FOREVERLAND . . .**
– Hangman in the shadow / Evensong / Renew & restore / Emmanuelle, skating on thin ice / Rose I love you / Enchanted place / Tree lullaby / Dirty snow for the broken ground / Weathershow / Chapter in the life of Matthew / To salt a scar.

Oct 00. (12"ep/cd-ep) *(JPR 12/CDS 019)* **FALLING FROM GRACE. /** — -
– Falling from grace / Going home / October's sky / Hold back a thousand hours.

Nov 00. (cd/lp) *(JPR CD/LP 011) <4051>* **SWANSONG FOR YOU**
– Let the good times begin / Partner in crime / Falling from grace / Loretta Young / Sister woman / Solace for pain / Flood / Pretty things / There is no greater gold / There was magic, then.

BELLES IN MONICA

Formed: Glasgow . . . early 1997 by rapper/producer KRUZE and guitarist RED. Things really got moving for this groovy hip hop act when they found the highly talented CHERELLE. Influenced mainly by ICE-T and 70's funk, KRUZE and his posse self-financed their debut 12", 'SWINGSTYLE'. The record was subsequently picked up by Glasgow's 'New Dawn', who immediately signed the group on a longer basis (a video was previewed on Cable TV's 'The Box'). With a live entourage of six players, BELLES IN MONICA performed all over Britain culminating at that year's MOBO awards ceremony in Manchester. Over the course of next few years, KRUZE and Co worked with Glasgow DJ DEMA and Urbanelite Productions (a subsidiary of 'New Dawn' records), although an album, 'RESISTANCE IS FUTILE' was still awaiting release as late as September 2002. However, a few well-received singles did surface in 2002, 'Y'ALL UNDER SURVEILLANCE' and 'MELTDOWN'; both pushing the barriers of hip hop a little further.

KRUZE – vocals, producer / **RED** – guitar / **CHERELLE** – vocals

own label / not iss.

Apr 98. (12"ep) *(none)* **SWINGSTYLE EP** — -

New Dawn / not iss.

Feb 02. (12")(cd-s) *(DAWN12 0001)(DAWNCD 0003)* **Y'ALL UNDER SURVEILLANCE (mixes)** — -

May 02. (12")(cd-s) *(DAWN12 0002)(DAWNCD 0004)* **MELTDOWN (mixes)** — -

BENDY TOY (see under ⇒ Starshaped records)

BERLIN BLONDES

Formed: Glasgow . . . late 70's by fresh-faced teenagers STEVEN BONOMI, ROBERT FARRELL, JIM SPENDER and NICK CLARKE; DANNY FRANKEL appeared to be their drummer! Creating a style reminiscent of ULTRAVOX!, NUMAN and even BILL NELSON, these black-lipstick'd futuristic New Romantics didn't quite appeal to the masses after their signing to 'E.M.I.'. The 'BLONDES opened their musical account very early in the 80's with the single 'SCIENCE' – not the most original title to get the ball rolling. An eponymous album released later in 1980 was very reliant on a cheap drum machine rhythm, bass lines and demure vox – typical bloody 80's. After the group's demise, SPENDER reverted to his real surname McKINVEN and joined ALTERED IMAGES.

STEVE BONOMI – vocals / **JIM SPENDER** (b. JAMES McKINVEN) – guitar / **ROBERT FARRELL** – keyboards / **NICK CLARKE** – bass / **DANNY FRANKEL** – drums

E.M.I. / not iss.

Jan 80. (7") *(EMI 5031)* **SCIENCE. / MANNEQUIN** — -

—— **PAUL SIMMONS** – (guest) drums; repl. DANNY

Oct 80. (lp) *(EMC 3346)* **BERLIN BLONDES**
– Framework / Astro / Science / Romance / Trail to Istanbul / Secret days / Mannequin / Neon probe / Zero song.

Feb 81. (7"/12") *(EMI/12EMI 5147)* **FRAMEWORK. / ZERO SONG** — -

—— SPENDER was to become McKINVEN and join ALTERED IMAGES when the BB's split after below

Scratch / not iss.

Aug 81. (7") *(SCR 005)* **MARSEILLES. / THE POET** — -

Guy BERRYMAN

Born: 1979, the Raith estate, Kirkcaldy, Fife. At the age of eleven (plucked from Seaview primary school), young GUY relocated to Kent with his parents, finding solace in funk and soul music although he also listened to indie. Although he went on to study engineering at the University of Central London, BERRYMAN subsequently quit to devote all his time to bass-playing/co-writing with indie crossover giants, COLDPLAY. Ironically, GUY was still paying off a student loan of around £8000 when the quartet's debut album, 'Parachutes' (2000), was sitting pretty at UK No.1.

BETA BAND

Formed: London . . . 1994 by ex-patriate Scotsman, STEVE MASON, the St. Andrews-born singer meeting up with Edinburgh University students, decksman JOHN MacLEAN, drummer ROBIN JONES and GORDON ANDERSON on a train down to the capital. There they worked at various day jobs while sharing a flat in Shepherd's Bush, although ill-health forced ANDERSON to return home in August '96. Portsmouth-born RICHARD GREENTREE, formerly bassist of SINISTER FOOTWEAR would become part of the zany quartet in early '97 after being introduced through mutual friends, PUSHERMAN. Discovered and subsequently produced by THE VERVE's NICK McCABE (who saw some potential in their psychedelic transcendental dub malarky), they were signed to 'Regal' records.

A pot-pourri of sound right enough (STONE ROSES or The MOONFLOWERS – remember them? – on a mantric mission!), the lads issued three EP's in the space of a year, 'CHAMPION VERSIONS', 'THE PATTY PATTY SOUND' and the excellent 'LOS AMIGOS DEL BETA BANDIDOS'. By popular demand (the vinyl was changing hands for upwards of £40 a time!) these were soon collected together on one shiny cd/album, simply titled 'THE THREE E.P.'S'. Lauded by the more discerning factions of the music press (the NME for one!), the bumbling art-rockers (by-passing the fashion stakes completely; safari suits, judo gear and horror of horrors, STEVE's "smart-arse" shell-suit being the disorder of the day) found themselves in the Top 40 by Autumn '98 with a long player that hung together surprisingly well. The sound of "baggy" ten years on, filtered through a kingsized bong, BETA standards such as 'DRY THE RAIN' ("It Will Be Alright"), 'INNER MEET ME', 'SHE'S THE ONE', 'DR. BAKER' and 'NEEDLES IN MY EYES' will surely come to be regarded as underground classics. To end the year, MASON moonlighted as KING BISCUIT TIME, releasing (to coincide with the latest edition of the band's zany in-house comic!) a bizarre EP of spaced-out drum'n'bass, '"SINGS" NELLY FOGGIT'S BLUES IN "ME AND THE PHARAOHS"'.

With expectation and hype rife about the recording schedules and rumoured double-disc set of their debut set proper, the band were finally ready to promote 'THE BETA BAND' long-player in June '99. However, delays due to an objection from JIM STEINMAN (for the sample/use of his BONNIE TYLER – 'Total Eclipse Of The Heart' collaboration) and the band's post-release qualms that it was "fucking awful" contributed to complete bewilderment within the press and its readers. At the end of June, the album shot into the Top 20 despite poor reviews stating over-production was its downfall (or was it just plain arsing about?). Opening with the self-explanatory 'THE BETA BAND RAP' (which might've been handled better by the BONZO's in the 60's!) and finishing with the baffling 'THE COW'S WRONG', the album shocked fans who thought the quartet were perhaps a tad over-indulgent. On reflection though, The BETA BAND's original stage interpretations of the tracks could not be faulted. It's just a pity that critical cohorts like the MANICS were beginning to be proved right.

As unfazed as ever, The BETA BAND shambled back into the fray with 'HOT SHOTS II' (2001; and a Top 20 hit!), the irony of the self-mocking title belying a half decent, occasionally brilliant set which certainly came closer to realising the promise of their early EP's. There was more focus, less sonic soup for the sake of it and more determined attempts at discernible songs. Which isn't to say they no longer walked that tightrope between endearingly wayward invention and rampant self-indulgence, the guiding hand of R&B producer C-Swing lending a contemporary edge to their urban meta-folk.

• **Covered:** ONE (Nilsson).
• **Trivia:** They guested on SPIRITUALIZED's 'Abbey Road' EP early '98.

STEVE MASON – vocals, percussion, drums, etc / **JOHN MacLEAN** – turntable, sampling / **RICHARD GREENTREE** – bass (ex-SINISTER FOOTWEAR) / **ROBIN JONES** – drums, percussion / GORDON ANDERSON departed before any recordings

Regal | Astralwerks

Jul 97. (12"ep) *(REG 16)* **CHAMPION VERSIONS** □ -
– Dry the rain / I know / B + A / Dogs got a bone.

Mar 98. (2x12"ep/cd-ep) *(REG 18/+CD)* **THE PATTY PATTY SOUND** □ -
– Inner meet me / The house song / The monolith / She's the one.

Jul 98. (cd-ep) *(REG 20CD)* **LOS AMIGOS DEL BETA BANDIDOS** □ -
– Push it out / It's over / Dr. Baker / Needles in my eyes.

Sep 98. (cd) *(7243 4 97385 2 2) <6252>* **THE THREE E.P.'S** (compilation) 35 □

Jun 99. (cd/d-lp) *(REG 30 CD/LP) <6268>* **THE BETA BAND** 18 □
– The Beta Band rap / It's not too beautiful / Simple boy / Round the bend / Dance o'er the border / Brokenupadingdong / Number 15 / Smiling / The hard one / The cow's wrong.

Jan 00. (12"/cd-s) *(REG 40/+CD)* **TO YOU ALONE. / SEQUINSIZER** □ -

Jul 01. (12"/cd-s) *(REG 60/+CD)* **BROKE. / WON / DANCE O'ER THE BORDER** 30 -

Jul 01. (d-lp/cd) *(REG 59/+CD) <10446>* **HOT SHOTS 2** 13 □
– Squares / Al Sharp / Humanbeing / Gone / Dragon / Broke / Quiet / Alleged / Life / Eclipse. *(bonus cd+=; REG 59CDL)* – Won.

Oct 01. (12"/cd-s) *(REG 65/+CD)* **HUMAN BEING. / UNKNOWN / THE HARD ONE** 57 -

Jan 02. (12"/cd-s) *(REG 69/+CD)* **SQUARES. / SQUARES (Bloah mix) / QUIET (acoustic – from 99X Atlanta session)** 42 -

KING BISCUIT TIME

aka **STEVE MASON** – vocals, etc

Regal | Astralwerks

Dec 98. (12"ep/cd-ep) *(REG 025/+CD)* **"SINGS" NELLY FOGGIT'S BLUES IN "ME AND THE PHARAOHS"** □ -
– Fatheriver / Niggling discrepancy / Little white / Eye o' the dug.

Jun 00. (12"ep/cd-ep) *(REG 049/+CD) <49657>* **NO STYLE EP** □ □ Jul00
– I walk the earth / Untitled / I love you / Time to get up.

BIFF BANG POW! (see under ⇒ McGEE, Alan)

BIFFY CLYRO

Formed: Glasgow . . . 1999 by the trio of SIMON NEIL, JAMES JOHNSTON and BEN JOHNSTON. Fusing an aggro-pop cocktail sound of NIRVANA and SOUNDGARDEN, they honed their youthful expertise with tours supporting the likes of the LLAMA FARMERS and SUNNA. The group began doing the toilet circuit before issuing a few independently produced singles, 'INAME' (for AEREOGRAMME's 'Babi Yaga' imprint) and 'THEKIDS . . .'. Their own brand of punk/emo rock was taken a step further early in 2001 when they were signed by 'Beggars Banquet', almost immediately issuing their impressive '27' single (a Kerrang! SOTW). 'JUSTBOY' and '57' (a Top 75 hit) followed hot on its heels, while their debut set, 'BLACKENED SKY' (2002) set out their stall to an already devoted fanbase. More MINOR THREAT than GREEN DAY, BIFFY CLYRO still managed to keep the whole fare melodic yet enduring with their tales of broken relationships, a million miles more meaningful than any current sports-clad punk, wrapped up in a clean, tight production sheen.

SIMON NEIL – vocals, guitar / **JAMES JOHNSTON** – bass, vocals / **BEN JOHNSTON** – drums, vocals

Babi Yaga | not iss.

2000. (cd-s) *(1cd)* **INAME / ALL THE WAY DOWN CHAPTER 2 / TRAVIS PERKINS** □ -

Electric Honey | not iss.

Oct 00. (cd-ep) **THEKIDSWHOPOPTODAYWILLROCKTOMORROW ep** □ -
– 27 / Hope for an angel / Justboy / Less the product.

Beggars Banquet | not iss.

Apr 01. (7"/cd-s) *(BBQ 352/+CD)* **27. / INSTRUCTIO4 / BREATHEHER** □ -

Oct 01. (7"/cd-s) *(BBQ 355/+CD)* **JUSTBOY. / BEING GABRIEL / UNSUBTLE** □ -

Feb 02. (7") *(BBQ 358)* **57. / KILL THE OLD TORTURE THEIR YOUNG (evening session)** 61 -
(cd-s) *(BBQ 358CD)* – ('A'side) / Hope for an angel (evening session) / Time is an imploding unit / Waiting for green.

Mar 02. (cd/lp) *(BBQ CD/LP 226)* **BLACKENED SKY** □ -
– Joy. discovery. invention / 27 / Justboy / Kill the old torture their young / Go slow / Christopher's river / Convex concave / 57 / Hero management / Solution devices / Stress on the sky / Scary Mary.

Jul 02. (7") *(BBQ 361)* **JOY. DISCOVERY. INVENTION. / ALL THE WAY DOWN** □ -
(cd-s) *(BBQ 361CD)* – ('A'side) / Toys toys toys choke toys toys toys / Houses of roofs.

BIG COUNTRY

Formed: Dunfermline . . . Autumn 1981 by STUART ADAMSON and BRUCE WATSON, following the former's departure from The SKIDS. They recruited brothers PETER (keyboards) and ALAN WISHART (bass) plus CLIVE PARKER (drums, ex-SPIZZ . . .) although by early 1982, the latter three had been replaced by the lynchpin rhythm section of MARK BRZEZICKI and TONY BUTLER.

After they turned down a contract with 'Ensign', the band signed to 'Mercury-Phonogram' in Spring '82, soon moving to London where they began work on a debut set, 'THE CROSSING' (1983). Previewed by the classic singles, 'FIELDS OF FIRE' & 'IN A BIG COUNTRY', the album traversed the charts in both Britain and America, introducing the famous (and, in certain quarters, much maligned) 'bagpipe' twin-guitar sound. Very much in the Celtic, stir-the-blood tradition, 'THE CROSSING' was a call to arms in a posturing, terminally pretentious early 80's music scene, its expansive, soaring sound transporting even the most smog-bound city dweller to the Scottish highlands. ADAMSON somehow managed to sing from the heart without sounding earnest, the chiming lament, 'CHANCE', displaying the raw emotive power this band once harnassed. Despite their straightforward approach, BIG COUNTRY were initially lauded by the press, even making something of a fashion statement with their trademark check shirts. With follow-up set, 'STEELTOWN' (1984), ADAMSON's voice of conscience examined Scottish industrial and economic decay; despite the subject matter, tracks such as the rousing 'FLAME OF THE WEST' burned with hope and optimism. Though the record entered the British chart at No.1, its less immediate appeal failed to translate into further Stateside success. This is where BIG COUNTRY began to lose their vision; although subsequent releases like 'THE SEER' (1986) and 'PEACE IN OUR TIME' (1988) continued to chart high and feature some inspired moments, creatively the band were merely treading water. The fact that the track 'ONE GREAT THING' was used on a Tennent's lager advert only seemed to underline its more pedestrian qualities.

Despite periods where the band came perilously close to splitting, BIG COUNTRY survived into the 90's, their albums never breaking the mould but eagerly received by the band's fiercely partisan fans. ADAMSON had always addressed social/political issues in a challenging and often sympathetic fashion, the band releasing a 1995 EP, 'NON!', in protest at France's nuclear testing programme. Signed to 'Transatlantic', however, the poor commercial showing of the band's last two albums, 'WHY THE LONG FACE?' (1995) and 'ECLECTIC' (1996), suggested that their appeal was waning.

Late in 1999, and thought to be because of his alcohol problems, STUART moved to Nashville, Tennessee. There, he formed The RAPHAELS, a roots country-orientated outfit who released one set, 'SUPERNATURAL' (2001). Sadly, this was to be ADAMSON's last outing. For nearly two months the man went AWOL and was subsequently found dead in a Hawaiian hotel room on the 16th of December, 2001. Scotland, and indeed the world of music, would mourn the death of such an enigmatic figure.

• **Songwriters:** Mostly ADAMSON / WATSON, except TRACKS OF MY TEARS (Smokey Robinson & The Miracles) / HONKY TONK WOMAN + RUBY TUESDAY (Rolling Stones) / AULD LANG SYNE (trad.) / ROCKIN' IN THE FREE WORLD (Neil Young) / FLY LIKE AN EAGLE (Steve Miller) / BLACK SKINNED BLUE EYED BOYS (Equals / Eddy Grant) / OH WELL (Fleetwood Mac) / (DON'T FEAR) THE REAPER (Blue Oyster Cult) / WOODSTOCK + BIG YELLOW TAXI (Joni Mitchell) / CRACKED ACTOR (David Bowie) / PARANOID (Black Sabbath) / SUMMERTIME (Gershwin – Du Bose Heyward) / ELEANOR RIGBY (Beatles) / SLING IT (Steve Harley) / I'M ON FIRE (Bruce Springsteen) / VICIOUS (Lou Reed) / I'M EIGHTEEN (Alice Cooper) / ON THE ROAD AGAIN (Canned Heat).

STUART ADAMSON (b.11 Apr'58, Manchester) – vocals, lead guitar, synthesizer (ex-SKIDS) / **BRUCE WATSON** (b.11 Mar'61, Timmins, Ontario, Canada) – guitar (ex-DELINX) / **TONY BUTLER** (b. 3 Feb'57, London) – bass (ex-ON THE AIR) / **MARK BRZEZICKI** (b.21 Jun'57, Slough, Bucks.) – drums (ex-ON THE AIR); the latter two repl. Scots-born brothers PETER and ALAN WISHART

Mercury | Mercury

Sep 82. (7") *(COUNT 1)* **HARVEST HOME. / BALCONY** □ □
(12"+=)(12"clear+=) *(COUNT 12)(COUNX 1)* – Flag of nations (swimming).

Feb 83. (7") *(COUNT 2) <811450>* **FIELDS OF FIRE. / ANGLE PARK** 10 52 Jan84
(12"+=/12"clear+=) *(COUN T/X 2-12)* – ('A'-alternative mix).
(7"sha-pic-d+=) *(COUP 2)* – Harvest home.

May 83. (7") *(COUNT 3) <814467>* **IN A BIG COUNTRY. / ALL OF US** [17] [17] Sep83
(12"+=) *(COUNT 3-12)* – ('A'-pure mix).
(12"++=) *(COUNT 313)* – Heart and soul.

Jun 83. (lp/c) *(MERH/+C 27) <812870>* **THE CROSSING** [3] [18] Jul83
– In a big country / Inwards / Chance / 1,000 stars / The storm / Harvest home / Lost patrol / Close action / Fields of fire / Porrohman. *(c+=)* – (4 remixes). *(re-dist.Mar84 lp/c; MERS/+C 27) (cd-iss. 1986; 812 870-2)*

Aug 83. (7") *(COUNT 4)* **CHANCE. / TRACKS OF MY TEARS (live)** [9] [ ]
(ext.12"+=)(ext.12"pic-d+=) *(COUNT 4-12)(COUP 4)* – The crossing.

Jan 84. (7") *(COUNT 5) <818834>* **WONDERLAND. / GIANT** [8] [86]
(12"+=) *(COUNT 5-12)* – ('A'extended).
(12"clear+=) *(COUNX 5)* – Lost patrol (live).
(d7"+=) *(COUNT 5-5)* – Lost patrol (live – parts one & two).

Apr 84 (m-lp) *<818835>* **WONDERLAND** [-] [65]
– Wonderland / Angle park / The crossing / All fall together.

Sep 84. (7"/7"w-poster) *(MER/+P 175)* **EAST OF EDEN. / PRAIRIE ROSE.** [17] [ ]
(12"+=/12"w-poster+=) *(MERX/+P 175)* – ('A'extended).

Oct 84. (lp/c) *(MERH/+C 49) <822831>* **STEELTOWN** [1] [70]
– Flame of the west / East of Eden / Steeltown / Where the rose is sown / Come back to me / Tall ships go / Girl with grey eyes / Rain dance / The great divide / Just a shadow. *(cd-iss. 1986; 822 831-2) (re-iss. May93 on 'Spectrum' cd/c)*

Nov 84. (7") *(MER 185)* **WHERE THE ROSE IS SOWN. / BELIEF IN THE SMALL MAN** [29] [ ]
(12"+=) *(MERX 185)* – ('A'extended remix) / Bass dance.
(d7"+=) *(MERD 185)* – Wonderland (live) / In a big country (live) / Auld Lang Syne (live).

Jan 85. (7") *(BCO 8)* **JUST A SHADOW. / WINTER SKY** [26] [ ]
(12"+=) *(BCO 8-12)* – ('A'extended remix).

Apr 86. (7"/7"sha-pic-d) *(BIGC/+P 1)* **LOOK AWAY. / RESTLESS NATIVES** [7] [ ]
(d7"+=) *(BIGCD 1)* – Margo's theme / Highland scenery.
(ext.12"+=) *(BIGCX 1-1)* – ('A'-Outlaw mix).
(12") *(BIG CX 1)* – ('A'extended) / Restless natives (soundtrack part one).

Jun 86. (7") *(BIGC 2)* **THE TEACHER. / HOME CAME THE ANGELS** [28] [ ]
(12") *(BIGCX 2)* – ('A'-Mystery mix) / Restless natives (soundtrack part two).

Jul 86. (lp/c/cd) *(MERH/+C 87)(826 844-2) <826 844>* **THE SEER** [2] [59]
– Look away / The seer / The teacher / I walk the hill / Eiledon / One great thing / Hold the heart / Remembrance day / The red fox / The sailor. *(re-iss. cd Aug94 on 'Vertigo')*

Sep 86. (7"/s7")('A'-Boston mix-12") *(BIGC/+G 3)(BIGCX 3-3)* **ONE GREAT THING. / SONG OF THE SOUTH** [19] [ ]
(d7"+=) *(BIGCD 3)* – Porrohman (live) / Chance (live).
(d7"+=) *(BIGCE 3)* – Wonderland (live) / Inwards (live).
('A'-Big Baad Country mix.c-s+=) *(BIGCM 3)* – In a big country (pure mix) / Fields of fire (live).
('A'-Big Baad Country mix.12"+=) *(BIGCR 3)* – Look away (outlaw mix).

Nov 86. (7"/remix-12") *(BIGC/+X 4)* **HOLD THE HEART. / HONKY TONK WOMAN (live)** [55] [ ]
(d12"+=) *(BIGCX 4-4)* – (interview parts one & two).

— added on tour **JOSS PHILIP-GORSE** – keyboards

Mercury Reprise

Aug 88. (7") *(BIGC 5)* **KING OF EMOTION. / THE TRAVELLERS** [16] [ ]
(12"+=) *(BIGC 5-12)* – Starred and Crossed.
(cd-s++=) *(BIGCD 5)* – Not waving but drowning.
(c-s+=) *(BIGMC 5)* – Starred and crossed / On the shore.

Sep 88. (7") **KING OF EMOTION. / IN A BIG COUNTRY** [-] [ ]

Sep 88. (lp/c)(cd) *(MERH/+C 130)(836 325-2) <25787>* **PEACE IN OUR TIME** [9] [ ]
– King of emotion / Broken heart (thirteen valleys) / Thousand yard stare / From here to eternity / Everything I need / Peace in our time / Time for leaving / River of hope / In this place / I could be happy here. *(cd+=)* – The travellers.

Oct 88. (7") *(BIGC 6)* **BROKEN HEART (THIRTEEN VALLEYS). / SOAPY SOUTAR STRIKES BACK** [47] [ ]
(12"+=/12"red+=) *(BIGC/+R 6-12)* – When a drum beats / On the shore.
(cd-s+=) *(BIGCD 6)* – Wonderland (12"mix).
(cd-s+=) *(BIGCDR 6)* – Made in Heaven / When a drum beats.

Jan 89. (7"/s7") *(BIGC/+P 7)* **PEACE IN OUR TIME. / PROMISED LAND** [39] [ ]
(12"+=) *(BIGC 7-12)* – Over the border / The longest day.
(12"+=) *(BIGCR 7-12)* – In a big country (live) / Chance (live).
(cd-s+=) *(BIGCD 7)* – Chance / The longest day.

— (Feb'90) **PAT AHERN – drums (ex-DAVE HOWARD SINGERS) repl. BRZEZICKI who joined PRETENDERS**

Apr 90. (7"/c-s) *(BIG C/MC 8)* **SAVE ME. / PASS ME BY** [41] [ ]
(12"+=) *(BIGC 8-12)* – Dead on arrival.
(cd-s+=) *(BIGCD 8)* – World on fire.
(cd-s+=) *(BIGCD 8-12)* – Wonderland (live) / Thousand yard stare (live).

May 90. (cd/c/lp) *(846 022-2/-4/-1)* **THROUGH A BIG COUNTRY – GREATEST HITS** (compilation) [2] [-]
– Save me / In a big country / Fields of fire / Chance / Wonderland / Where the rose is sown / Just a shadow / Look away / King of emotion / East of Eden / One great thing / The teacher / Broken heart (thirteen valleys) / Peace in our time. *(c+=/cd+=)* – Eiledon / The seer / Harvest home. *(re-iss. Feb93 cd/c)*

Jul 90. (7"/c-s) *(BIG C/MC 9)* **HEART OF THE WORLD. / BLACK SKINNED BLUE EYED BOYS** [50] [ ]
(12"+=) *(BIGC 9-12)* – Broken heart (thirteen valleys) (acoustic) / Peace in our time (acoustic).
(cd-s+=) *(BIGCD 9)* – Restless Natives.

Vertigo not iss.

Aug 91. (7") *(BIC 1)* **REPUBLICAN PARTY REPTILE. / COMES A TIME / YOU, ME AND THE TRUTH** [37] [-]
(10"ep+=/12"ep+=) *(BIC T/X 1)* – Comes a time.
(cd-ep) *(BIGCD 1)* – ('A'side) / Freedom song / Kiss the girl goodbye / I'm only waiting.

Sep 91. (cd/c/lp) *(510230-2/-4/-1)* **NO PLACE LIKE HOME** [28] [-]
– We're not in Kansas / Republican party reptile / Dynamic lady / Keep on dreaming / Beautiful people / The hostage speaks / Beat the Devil / Heap of faith / Ships / Into the fire. *(cd+=)* – You, me and the truth / Comes a time. *(re-iss. Aug94; same)*

Oct 91. (7"/c-s) *(BIC/+C 2)* **BEAUTIFUL PEOPLE. / RETURN OF THE TWO HEADED KING** [72] [-]
(12"pic-d+=) *(BICX 2)* – Fly like an eagle.
(cd-s+=) *(BICCD 2)* – Rockin' in the free world (live).

— **ADAMSON, BUTLER + WATSON** were joined by session men **SIMON PHILLIPS** – drums / **COLIN BERWICK** – keyboards

Compulsion Fox-RCA

Mar 93. (c-s/7") *(TC+/PULSS 4)* **ALONE. / NEVER TAKE YOUR PLACE** [24] [ ]
(12"pic-d+=) *(12PULSS 4)* – Winter sky / Look away.
(cd-s) *(CDPULSS 4)* – ('A'side) / Chance / Rockin' in the free world / Eastworld.

Mar 93. (cd/c/lp) *(CD/TC+/NOIS 2) <66294>* **THE BUFFALO SKINNERS** [25] [ ] Sep93
– Alone / Seven waves / What are you working for / The one I love / Long way home / The selling of America / We're not in Kansas / Ships / All go together / Winding wind / Pink marshmallow moon / Chester's farm. *(re-iss. Sep94; same) (cd re-iss. May02 on 'EMI Gold'; 321988-2)*

Apr 93. (c-s/7") *(TC+/PULSS 6)* **SHIPS (WHERE WERE YOU). / OH WELL** [29] [ ]
(12"+=/cd-s+=) *(12/CD PULSS 6)* – (Don't fear) The reaper / Woodstock.
(cd-s+=) *(CDXPULSS 6)* – The buffalo skinners / Cracked actor / Paranoid.

Jun 94. (cd/c/lp) *(CD/TC+/NOIS 5)* **WITHOUT THE AID OF A SAFETY NET (live)** [35] [-]
– Harvest home / Peace in our time / Just a shadow / Broken heart (thirteen valleys) / The storm / Chance / Look away / Steeltown / Ships / Wonderland / What are you working for / Long way home / In a big country / Lost patrol.

Transatla. Pure

May 95. (c-ep/cd-ep) *(TRAM/TRAX 1009)* **I'M NOT ASHAMED / ONE IN A MILLION (1st visit) / MONDAY TUESDAY GIRL / ('A'edit)** [69] [-]
(cd-ep) *(TRAX 1010)* – ('A'side) / Crazytimes / In a big country / Blue on a green planet.

Jun 95. (cd/c) *(TRA CD/MC/LP 109) <2200>* **WHY THE LONG FACE?** [48] [ ]
– You dreamer / Message of love / I'm not ashamed / ail into nothing / Thunder & lightning / Send you / One in a million / God's great mistake / Wild land in my heart / Thank you to the Moon / Far from me to you / Charlotte / Post nuclear talking blues / Blue on a green planet.

Aug 95. (12"ep/cd-ep) *(TRAT/TRAD 1012)* **YOU DREAMER EP** [ ] [-]
– You dreamer / Ice cream smile / Magic in your ice / Bianca.
(cd-ep) *(TRAX 1012)* – ('A'side) / I'm eighteen / Vicious / On the road again.

Nov 95. (cd-ep) *(TRAD 1013)* **NON!** [ ] [-]
– Post nuclear talking blues / Blue on a green planet / God's great mistake / All go together.
above was an action awareness record for Greenpeace.
below featured guests **BOBBY VALENTINO** – violin / **AARON EMERSON** – keyboards / **HOSSAM RAMZY + MOHAMMED TOUFIQ** – percussion / **CAROL LAULA + STEVE HARLEY + KYM MAZELLE** – vocals

Aug 96. (cd/c) *(TRA CD/MC 234)* **ECLECTIC** [41] [-]
– River of hope / King of emotion / Big yellow taxi / The buffalo skinners / Summertime / The night they drove old Dixie down / Eleanor Rigby / Winter sky / Sling it / I'm on fire / Where the rose is sown / Come back to me / Ruby Tuesday.

Track Record not iss.

Aug 99. (10"; BIG COUNTRY featuring EDDI READER) *(TRACK 0004C)* **FRAGILE THING. / I GET HURT / LOSERVILLE** [69] [-]
(cd-s) *(TRACK 0004A)* – (first & third tracks) / Dust on the road.
(cd-s) *(TRACK 0004B)* – (first two tracks) / John Wayne's dream.

Sep 99. (cd/c) *(TRK 1000 CD/CAS)* **DRIVING TO DAMASCUS** [ ] [-]
– Driving to Damascus / Dive in to me / See you / Perfect world / Somebody else / Fragile thing / The president slipped and fell / Devil in the eye / Trouble the waters / Bella / Your spirit to me / Grace. *(special cd+=; TRK 1000CDSP)* – Shattered cross / Too many ghosts.

Nov 99. (c-s) *(TRACK 0005C)* **SEE YOU / PERFECT WORLD** [ ] [-]
(cd-s+=) *(TRACK 0005A)* – This blood's for you.
(cd-s+=) *(TRACK 0005B)* – Camp Smedley's theme.

— STUART ADAMSON retired for a while – late in '99

Oct 00. (d-cd) *(TRK 1003CD)* **COME UP SCREAMING (live)** □ [-]
– Harvest home / King of emotion / Driving to Damascus / John Wayne's dream / The storm / Where the rose is sown / Come back to me / Somebody else / Look away / You dreamer / Your spirit to me / The president slipped and fell / Drive in to me / Lost patrol / 13 valleys inwards / Wonderland / We're not in Kansas / Porroh man / Chance / In a big country / Fields of fire.

– compilations, etc. –

Aug 94. (cd) *Nighttracks; (CDNT 007)* **RADIO 1 SESSIONS** □ [-]
Aug 94. (cd) *Legends In Music; (LECD 043)* **BIG COUNTRY** □ [-]
Aug 95. (cd) *Spectrum; (550 879-2)* **IN A BIG COUNTRY** □ [-]
Oct 95. (cd) *Windsong; (WINCD 075)* **BBC LIVE IN CONCERT (live)** □ [-]
Mar 01. (cd) *Big Country Tracks; (<BCRTRK 001>)* **UNDERCOVER** (cover versions) □ □ May01
Apr 01. (cd) *Big Country Tracks; (<BCRTRK 002>)* **RARITIES** □ □ May01
Jun 01. (cd) *Big Country Tracks; (BCRTRK 003) / Cleopatra; <71146>* **ONE IN A MILLION** □ □ Jul01
Aug 01. (cd) *Big Country Tracks; (<BCRTRK 005>)* **GREATEST 12" HITS VOL.1** □ □ Sep01
Oct 01. (cd) *Universal; (E 586314-2)* **UNIVERSAL MASTERS COLLECTION** □ [-]
May 02. (d-cd) *Universal TV; (586989-2)* **GREATEST HITS** (BIG COUNTRY & The SKIDS) [71] [-]
Jul 02. (6xcd-s-box) *Track; (TRKSP 001)* **THE SINGLES COLLECTION** □ [-]

RAPHAELS

ADAMSON plus **MARCUS HUMMON** – acoustic guitar / + others

Track Track

May 01. (cd) *(<TRK 0005CD>)* **SUPERNATURAL** □ □ Aug01
– Supernatural / Simple man / Private battlefield / Old country, country / Learning to row / Shattered cross / Toujour aimez / My only crime / Stand up / Too many ghosts / Blue rose / Mexican trout / Life is a church.

— ADAMSON was to die late 2001

BIG DISH

Formed: Airdrie . . . 1983, by songwriter STEVEN LINDSAY and RAYMOND DOHERTY, with MARK RYCE, JOHN HARPER and KEITH BURN being added shortly afterwards. Having graduated from Glasgow School Of Art, LINDSAY and Co subsequently took up residence in the "dear green place". Laid back stereotypical but intelligent Scots AOR in the mould of STEELY DAN or the BLUE NILE, The BIG DISH precipitated a glut of "Steely Niles" that threatened to engulf the Scottish music scene from the mid-80's onwards (i.e. DEL AMITRI, DANNY WILSON, DEACON BLUE, etc).

However, 'Virgin' (and 'Warners' US) deemed them worthy of a major record deal and proceeded to release a trio of memorable 45's, 'BIG NEW BEGINNING', 'PROSPECT STREET' and 'SLIDE' which helped boost sales of their debut album, 'SWIMMER' (1986). By this time, LINDSAY and DOHERTY had been joined by guitarist BRIAN McFIE, the trio subsequently expanding their sound with a team of sessioners including future soundtrack guru CRAIG ARMSTRONG. 1988 saw the release of sophomore set, 'CREEPING UP ON JESUS', a record obviously influenced by their Stateside travels. Again the album failed to take off in the way Virgin hoped and the BIG DISH subsequently jumped ship to the more sympathetic Atlantic offshoot 'East West'. ARMSTRONG, who'd now become a full-time member, briefly improved the band's fortunes by co-penning their first (and only) UK Top 40 hit, 'MISS AMERICA', as well as exerting his talented influence on the accompanying album, 'SATELLITES' (1991). However, after nigh on a decade as also-rans, the 'DISH threw in the towel.

STEVEN LINDSAY – vocals, guitar, keyboards / **RAYMOND DOHERTY** – bass / **MARK RYCE** – guitar / **JOHN HARPER** – keyboards / **KEITH BURN** – drums

Virgin Warners

Jun 85. (7") *(VS 776)* **BIG NEW BEGINNING. / JEALOUS** □ [-]
(12"+=) *(VS 776-12)* – I must be in love.
Oct 85. (7") *(VS 820)* **PROSPECT STREET. / SOMETHING FOR NOTHING** □ [-]
(12"+=) *(VS 820-12)* – Tours.

— now basic trio of **LINDSAY, DOHERTY + BRIAN McFIE** – guitars / augmented by **STEVEN CHEYNE** – keyboards / **RONNIE GURR** – drums

Aug 86. (7") *(VS 851)* **SLIDE. / REVEREND KILLER** □ □
(12"+=) *(VS 851-12)* – Presence.
Oct 86. (lp/c/cd) *(V/TCV/CDV 2374)* **SWIMMER** [85] □
– Prospect Street / Christina's world / Slide / Big new beginning / Another people's palace / Swimmer / The loneliest man in the world / Jealous / Her town / Beyond the pale / Second swimmer. *(re-iss. 1989 lp/c; OVED/+C 248)*
Oct 86. (7"/12") *(VS 913/+12)* **PROSPECT STREET. / FROM THE NEIGHBOURHOOD** □ □
Jan 87. (7") *(VS 928)* **CHRISTINA'S WORLD. / EVERLASTING FAITH** □ □
(12"+=) *(VS 928-12)* – She says nothing.
(cd-s++=) *(DISH 1)* – Slide / Reverend killer / Prospect street.

— trio now augmented by **CRAIG ARMSTRONG, WIX** – keyboards / **BLAIR CUNNINGHAM, CHARLIE MORGAN** – bass / **JOHN THIRKWELL, GARY BARNACLE, PETE THOMAS, TIM** – horns

Jun 88. (7") *(VS 1102)* **EUROPEAN RAIN. / VOODOO BABY** □ [-]
(10"+=) *(VSA 1102)* – Swimmer.
(12"+=) *(VST 1102)* – Time on your own.
(cd-s+=) *(VSCD 1102)* – Slide.
Aug 88. (lp/c/cd) *(V/TCV/CDV 2540)* **CREEPING UP ON JESUS** □ □
– Life / Waiting for the parade / Faith healer / Burn / Swansong / European rain / Jean / Monday / Wishing time / Where do you live? *(cd+=)* – Can't stand up. *(re-iss. Apr92 lp/c; OVED/+C 404)*
Sep 88. (7") *(VS 1136)* **FAITH HEALER. / BE MY FRIEND** □ [-]
(12"+=) *(VST 1136)* – Things fall into place.
(cd-s++=) *(VSCD 1136)* – Country song.
Oct 88. (7") **EUROPEAN RAIN. / LIFE** [-] □

— (late 1990 main group comprised **LINDSAY, McFIE, ARMSTRONG** and **WAYNE LIVESEY – programming /** with **RAYMOND DOHERTY, JOHN GIBLIN, PINO PALADINO** – bass / **TRACIE GILBERT** – tour bass / **GEOFF DUGMORE, MANU KATCHE, SKIP REID** – drums (latter also on tour)

East West Warners

Jan 91. (7") *(YZ 529)* **MISS AMERICA. / FROM THE MISSION BELL TO THE DEEP BLUE SEA** [37] □
(12"+=) *(YZT 529)* – The town celebrity.
(cd-s++=) *(YZCD 529)* – Roll down the flag.
Feb 91. (cd)(lp/c) *(9031 73314-2)(WX 400/+C)* **SATELLITES** [43] □
– Miss America / State of the union / Across the province / Give me some time / 25 years / Big town / Shipwrecked / Warning sign / Bonafide / Learn to love. *(re-iss. cd Nov93; same)*

— **COLIN BERWICK** – keyboards; repl. on tour ARMSTRONG who later went solo

Mar 91. (7"/c-s) **BIG TOWN. / GOOD WAY** □ [-]
(12"+=) – He stumbled on some magic.
(cd-s++=) – Medicine jar.
May 91. (7"/c-s) **25 YEARS. / SWIMMER** □ [-]
(12"+=/cd-s+=) – Jealous / Refugee.

— disbanded after above

– compilations, etc. –

Mar 94. (cd) *Virgin; (CDVM 9025)* **RICH MAN'S WARDROBE: A CONCISE HISTORY OF THE BIG DISH** □ [-]
– Christina's world / Wishing time / Swimmer / Life / Big new beginning / Jealous / Faith healer / Jean / Where do you live? / Waiting for the parade / European rain / The lonedliest man in the world / Voodoo baby / Slide / Prospect Street.

BIGSHOT (see under ⇒ Human Condition records)

BIKESHED (see under ⇒ MAGNETIC NORTH POLE)

BIOS (see ⇒ Section 9: Dance/Rave)

BIS

Formed: Glasgow . . . late 1994 by teenagers MANDA RIN and brothers SCI-FI STEVEN (who also became part of Kraut-rockers, GANGER) and JOHN DISKO. Initially gaining exposure through the tight-knit fanzine network, BIS were the first outfit to appear on The DELGADOS' now influential D.I.Y. label, 'Chemikal Underground', the release in question being the 7" maxi, 'DISCO NATION'.

In March '96, BIS also became the first bonafide indie band to play live on Top Of The Pops with a track, 'KANDY POP', from their Top 30 EP, 'THE SECRET VAMPIRE SOUNDTRACK'. Their blend of cutesy brat-pop – like ALTERED IMAGES meeting The SLITS – was developed over a further couple of low-key 45's before they finally signed on the dotted line for The BEASTIE BOYS' trendy 'Grand Royal' label (remaining independent in the UK through 'Wiiija') after turning down 50 major imprints. The trio subsequently forsook unappreciative Britain (where the press was increasingly turning against them after all the hype) to try Japan, where they soon became a top act, shifting 100,000 units of their 1997 debut album, 'THE NEW TRANSISTOR HEROES', in the space of only a few weeks. During this spell, BIS' imprint 'teen-c!' recordingz were still in operation, delivering releases by mates, LUGWORM, DICK JOHNSON and PINK KROSS, before winding up operations.

Returning to UK shores in 1998, they eventually hit the Top 40 again with 'EURODISCO', a taster from the accompanying second album proper 'SOCIAL DANCING' (1999). Produced by left-wing GANG OF FOUR member ANDY GILL, the album didn't do much to raise BIS' profile on the songwriting front. After second track 'I'M A SLUT', the cheesy chorus-lines and the shouty bubblegum pop lyrics made you want to cringe like you'd just witnessed a family member embarrassing themselves at karaoke. GILL's production became tiresome too; for a militant underground punk-rocker he spent too much time tweaking the album's production, so by the end it almost sounded as sugar-coated as a BRITNEY SPEARS record. Not good, not bad, just mindless shallow pop . . . there's nothing worse.

Things didn't get much better, with the release of the maturing 'MUSIC FOR A STRANGE WORLD' EP in 2000 and the Euro pop-tinged 'RETURN TO CENTRAL' (2001), which saw them add influences as diverse and as uncanny as NEW ORDER and CAN. Granted, this was a million miles away from the tooth-rotting 'KANDY POP', but the production still remained the same; staid, dull and polished to such a high sheen that even hard core fans of the band had forgotten their lo-fi indie roots.

A collaboration with Detroit's electro-clash heroes ADULT was soon to be delivered in the form of mini-album 'PLASTIQUE NOUVEAU' (2002), with the underground group providing a new spin on the BIS method, which by this time was beginning to sound like ERASURE and KRAFTWERK meeting in a Glaswegian indie disco. Big in Japan, apparently.

• **Songwriters:** SCI-FI or group, except THE BOY WITH THE THORN IN HIS SIDE (Smiths) / GERM FREE ADOLESCENTS (X-Ray Spex) / LOVE WILL TEAR US APART (Joy Division) / HURT (New Order) / SHACK UP (A Certain Ratio) / A VIEW FROM A HILL (Section 25) – 4 of the latter from the 'Factory' EP.

MANDA RIN (b. AMANDA MacKINNON, 22 Mar'77) – vocals, keyboards, recorder / **SCI-FI STEVEN** (b. STEVEN CLARK, 20 Mar'76) – vocals, synthesizers / **JOHN DISKO** (b. JOHN CLARK, 21 Aug'78) – guitar

Chemikal Underground | not iss.

Aug 95. (7"m) *(Chem 002)* **DISCO NATION. / PLASTIK PEOPLE / CONSPIRACY A GO-GO** [ ] [-]

Dec 95. (7"ep; various artists) *(che 47)* **ICKY-POO AIR-RAID** [ ] [-]
(above issued on 'Che')

Mar 96. (7"ep/cd-ep) *(Chem 003/+cd)* **THE SECRET VAMPIRE SOUNDTRACK** [25] [-]
– Kandy pop / Secret vampires / Teen-c power! / Diska.

teen-c! | not iss.

Jun 96. (7"ep/c-ep/cd-ep) *(SKETCH 001/+CS/CD)* **BIS VS. THE D.I.Y. CORPS** [45] [-]
– This is fake d.i.y. / Burn the suit / Dance to the disco beat.

Southern | K

Jun 96. (7") *(IPU 66)* **KEROLEEN. / ("Heavenly":- Trophy Girlfriend)** [ ] [ ]

Wiiija | Capitol

Oct 96. (7"ep/c-ep/cd-ep) *(WIJ 55/+MC/CD)* **ATOM POWERED ACTION! EP** [54] [-]
– Starbright boy / Wee love / Team theme / Cliquesuck.

Mar 97. (7") *(WIJ 67)* **SWEET SHOP AVENGERZ. / I'LL GET YOU BACK** [46] [-]
(7") *(WIJ 67X)* – ('A'side) / Rollerblade zero.
(cd-s+=) *(WIJ 67CD)* – Ninja hi skool.

Apr 97. (cd/c/lp) *(WIJ CD/MC/LP 1064) <56007>* **THE NEW TRANSISTOR HEROES** [55] [ ]
– Tell it to the kids / Sweet shop avengerz / Starbright boy / Popstar kill / Mr. Important / Antiseptic poetry / Popyura / Skinny tie sensurround / Poster parent / Monstarr / Everybody thinks that they're going to get theirs / Rebel soul / Photo shop / X-defect / Lie detector test / Dinosaur germs. *<US lp on 'Grand Royal'; GR 45>*

Apr 97. (7"ep; split w/ PINK KROSS VS LUGWORM) *(GUIDE 11)* **POP SONG / ROCCO NEGRO / (other two by LUGWORM)** [ ] [-]
(above issued on 'Guided Missile')

May 97. (7") *(WIJ 69)* **EVERYBODY THINKS THAT THEY'RE GOING TO GET THEIRS. / STATEMENT OF INTENT** [64] [ ]
(7") *(WIJ 69X)* – ('A'side) / Girl star.
(cd-s+=) *(WIJ 69CD)* – Cookie cutter kid.

Nov 98. (c-s) *(WIJ 086C)* **EURODISCO / LIKE ROBOTS** [37] [-]
(cd-s+=) *(WIJ 086CD)* – Cinema says.
(7") *(WIJ 086)* – ('A'side) / Stray cat blues.
(12") *(WIJ 086TR)* – ('A'mixes; Les Rhythmes Digitales / DJ Scissorkicks / Klute / original).

Feb 99. (7") *(WIJ 095)* **ACTION AND DRAMA. / GERM FREE ADOLESCENTS** [50] [ ]
(cd-s) *(WIJ 095CD)* – ('A'side) / Not even close / 17 hours.
(cd-s) *(WIJ 095CDX)* – ('A'side) / Eurodisco (Les Rhythmes Digitales mix) / Eurodisco (DJ Scissorkicks mix).

Mar 99. (cd/c/lp) *(WIJ CD/MC/LP 1088) <96439>* **SOCIAL DANCING** [ ] [ ] Aug99
– Making people normal / I'm a slut / Eurodisco / Action and drama / Theme from Tokyo / The hit girl / Am I loud enough / Shopaholic / Young alien types / Detour / Sale or return / It's all new / Listen up.

Jul 99. (7") *(WIJ 101)* **DETOUR. / KISS AND TELL** [ ] [-]
(cd-s+=) *(WIJ 101CD)* – Why don't we go home.

Wiiija | V2

Jun 00. (12"ep/cd-ep) *(WIJEP 116 T/CD) <81>* **MUSIC FOR A STRANGER WORLD** [ ] [ ]
– Dead wrestlers / Are you ready / How can we be strange / I want it all / Beats at the office / Punk rock points. *<US re-iss. 2001 on 'Lookout'; LK 263>*

Jul 00. (7") *(74489)* **POWERPUFF GIRLS. / (other track by APPLES IN STEREO)** [ ] [-]
(above issued on 'Rhino')

Chemikal Underground | not iss.

Oct 01. (12"ep/cd-ep) *(chem 058/+cd)* **FUKD ID VOL.5** [ ] [-]
– Brainclouds / European / Mamelodi sundown / Situation.

Artful | SpinArt

Jan 02. (cd) *(ARTFULCD 42) <SPART 98>* **RETURN TO CENTRAL** [ ] [ ] Sep01
– What you're afraid of / Silver spoon / Black pepper / The end starts today / Protection / Two million / Chicago / Metal box / We're complicated / Robotic / A portrait from space.

Oscarr | not iss.

May 02. (12"ep) *(OSC 004)* **FACT 2002 EP** [ ] [-]
– Love will tear us apart / Hurt / Shack up / A view from a hill.

SpinArt | SpinArt

Jul 02. (m-lp) *(<SPART 110>)* **PLASTIQUE 33** [ ] [ ]
– Protection / Robotic / Sound of sleet / Don't let the rain come down / The end starts today / Make it through / Brainclouds / Protection / The end starts today.

– compilations, etc. –

Dec 96. (cd-ep) **THIS IS TEEN-C POWER** [-] [ ]
– Kill yr boyfriend / School disco / Kandy pop / This is fake D.I.Y. / Burn the suit / Teen-c power.

Aug 98. (m-cd) *Grand Royal; (7581 480060-2) <GR 60>* **INTENDO** (demos & B-sides) [ ] [ ]
– Grand Royal with cheese / Girl star / Clockwork punk / Famous / Ninja hi skool / Kid cut / Automatic freestyle / I'll get you back / Cookie cutter kid / Grand Royal with cheese.

– other teen – c! recordingz –

Mar 97. (7") *(SKETCH 002)* **LUGWORM – Te Lo Dir'o! EP**
Aug 97. (7") *(SKETCH 003)* **PINK KROSS – Scumbag**
Dec 97. (7") *(SKETCH 004)* **DICK JOHNSON – Can't You Give Me Love**
Mar 98. (lp/cd) *(SKETCH 005 LP/CD)* **PINK KROSS – Chopper Chix From VP Hell**

KITCHEN

AMANDA plus **RYAN SEAGRIST** (b. Vero Beach, Florida) – guitar, vocals, etc (ex-DISCOUNT)

Damaged Goods | not iss.

Apr 01. (7"/cd-s) *(DAMGOOD 195/+CD)* **BETTER ON THE FLOOR. / AND HE LOVES IT / WE'RE JUST THE YOUTH** [ ] [-]

Jake BLACK

Born: Glasgow. Known simply as THE REVEREND Dr. D. WAYNE LOVE, he was one of the founders of the tongue-in-cheek acid-country outfit, ALABAMA 3. During the mid-90's, this ever-growing congregation of hick-looking ELVIS and HANK WILLIAMS fans toured the country (having formed in Brixton, London) and had a minor hit with 'AIN'T GOIN' TO GOA'. The cool, gospel-inspired track also featured on ALABAMA 3's riveting debut album, 'EXILE ON COLDHARBOUR LANE' (1997), alongside the HOWLIN' WOLF-sampled, 'WOKE UP THIS MORNING', recently a hit second time around (early in 2001) after the song popped up as the 'Sopranos' TV theme tune.

BLACKA'NIZED (see ⇒ Section 9: Dance/Rave)

BLIMP (see ⇒ Section 9: the 90s)

BLIND (see under ⇒ Evol records)

BLISTERS (see under ⇒ KARELIA)

BLOOD UNCLES

Formed: Edinburgh . . . mid-80's by former EXPLOITED and SQUARE PEG guitar-plucker, BIG JOHN DUNCAN, who somehow got introduced to ex-TWEETS (yes, the 'Birdie Song' outfit!) JON CARMICHAEL; making up the trio was bassman COLIN McGUIRE. Their debut EP, 'PETROL', showed no signs of "oi", just hard and brutal rock'n'roll. Signing to 'Virgin' late in 1986, the BLOOD UNCLES delivered a couple of decent singles, 'CRASH' and 'BEATHAG', before they bowed out courtesy of their one and only album, 'LIBERTINE' (1987).

BIG JOHN DUNCAN – guitar, vocals (ex-EXPLOITED, ex-SQUARE PEG) / **JON CARMICHAEL** – vocals / **COLIN McGUIRE** – bass

Drastic Plastic — not iss.

Apr 86. (12"ep) *(DRASTIC 1)* **PETROL EP** [ ] [-]

Virgin — not iss.

Apr 87. (7") *(VS 964)* **CRASH. / CARAVAN** [ ] [-]
(12"+=) *(VS 964-12)* – Never happy man.

Jul 87. (7") *(VS 980)* **BEATHAG. / GOD SAYS NO** [ ] [-]
(12"+=) *(VS 980-12)* – Broken town.

Aug 87. (lp/c/cd) *(V/TCV/CDV 2437)* **LIBERTINE** [ ] [-]
– Beathag / Let's go crazy / Under your heel / Crash / Danny's favourite game / Caravan / Shake / Scars in the morning / Never happy man / Breakdown express / Speaker. *(cd+=/c+=)* – Broken town. *(re-iss. 1989 lp/c/ OVED/+C 265)*

Oct 87. (12") *(VST 1015)* **LET'S GO CRAZY. / SHAKE** [ ] [-]

— split the following year, BIG JOHN joined GOODBYE MR MACKENZIE and later became a brief substitute for KURT COBAIN c/o NIRVANA!; in the late 90's he was a bouncer at Edinburgh music venues.

BLOOMSDAY (see under ⇒ BATHERS)

BLUEBELLS

Formed: Glasgow ... 1979 by BOBBY BLUEBELL and DAVE McCLUSKEY. After sending a demo tape to NICK HEYWARD, they secured a support slot with the man's teenybop sensations, HAIRCUT 100. The subsequent exposure led to a deal with 'London' records in the wake of an aborted debut single for hip Glaswegian label, 'Postcard'. By this stage the band boasted a line-up of BOBBY, KEN McCLUSKEY and his brother DAVID, RUSSELL IRVINE and LAWRENCE DONEGAN.

Following a string of also-ran singles (1982's 'FOREVER MORE', 1983's 'CATH' and 'SUGAR BRIDGE'), The BLUEBELLS' chart success finally flowered in 1984 when they narrowly missed the Top 10 with 'I'M FALLING'. Their defining moment (and musical albatross) came later that summer with the Top 10 'YOUNG AT HEART', an ebullient pop-folk hoedown co-written by SIOBHAN FAHEY of BANANARAMA (and later SHAKESPEARS SISTER) fame. Around this time CRAIG GANNON and NEAL BALDWIN replaced IRVINE and DONEGAN (who joined LLOYD COLE & The COMMOTIONS) respectively, both new recruits featuring on the band's Top 30 debut album, 'SISTERS' (1984). Despite this sudden upturn in their fortunes, a re-issued 'CATH' only just scraped the Top 40 and the band failed to emulate the longer term success of their more accomplished Glasgow brethren AZTEC CAMERA. GANNON actually went on to join the latter act (before deputising for ANDY ROURKE in the SMITHS) as The BLUBELLS finally withered in the mid-80's.

KEN and DAVE subsequently formed The McCLUSKEY BROTHERS alongside DAVIE DUNCAN, CHRIS MILLER, JAN WIGHTMAN, RAY DAVIDSON and BOBBY HENRY. Rooted in folk, the brothers' debut album, 'AWARE OF IT ALL' (1987) utilised such trad instrumentation as bodhran, uileann pipes, mandolin and even hurdy gurdy (eh?). While they went on to release a further trio of albums over the next decade and beyond – 'FAVOURITE COLOURS' (1993), 'WONDERFUL AFFAIR' (1996) and 'HOUSEWIVES' CHOICE' (2000) – their only brush with mainstream success came, rather ironically, via a brief BLUEBELLS chart resurgence. Following on from their Hogmanay 1990 reunion at Glasgow's 'Sub Club', the group were reunited once again in 1993 to perform on Top Of The Pops as 'YOUNG AT HEART' sat atop the UK chart. Almost ten years on from its original release, the single had been given a new lease of life after being used in a TV ad campaign.

BOBBY BLUEBELL (b. ROBERT HODGENS, 6 Jun'59) – rhythm guitar, vocals / **KEN McCLUSKEY** (b. 8 Feb'62) – vocals / **DAVID McCLUSKEY** (b.13 Jan'64) – drums with **RUSSELL IRVINE** – lead guitar / **LAWRENCE DONEGAN** – bass

Postcard — not iss.

Sep 81. (7"; w-drawn) *(81-12)* **EVERYBODY'S SOMEBODY'S FOOL. / OH DEAR!** [-] [-]

London — Sire

Oct 82. (7"/12") *(LON/+X 14)* **FOREVER MORE. / AIM IN LIFE** [ ] [-]
(with free 7"flexi; LYN 12361) – EVERYBODY'S SOMEBODY'S FOOL

Feb 83. (7"/12") *(LON/+X 20)* **CATH. / ALL I EVER SAID** [62] [-]

Jun 83. (d7"/12"ep) *(LON/+X 27)* **SUGAR BRIDGE (IT WILL STAND). / THE PATRIOT'S GAME // SOME SWEET GAME. / HAPPY BIRTHDAY** [72] [-]

Mar 84. (7"/12") *(LON/+X 45)* **I'M FALLING. / H.O.L.L.A.N.D.** [11] [ ]

Jun 84. (7",7"sha-pic-d/12") *(LON/+X 49)* **YOUNG AT HEART. / TENDER MERCY** [8] [ ]

— **CRAIG GANNON** – lead guitar; repl. IRVINE (both used on album) / **NEAL BALDWIN** – bass (ex-TV21) repl. DONEGAN who joined LLOYD COLE

Jul 84. (lp/c) *(LON LP/C 1)* **SISTERS** [22] [ ]
– Everybody's somebody's fool / Young at heart / I'm falling / Will she always be waiting / Cath / Red guitars / Syracuse university / Learn to love / The patriot's game / South Atlantic way.

Aug 84. (7") *(LON 54)* **CATH. / WILL SHE ALWAYS BE WAITING** [38] [ ]
(12"+=) *(LONX 54)* – Small town martyr / ('B'version).

Feb 85. (7") *(LON 58)* **ALL I AM (IS LOVING YOU). / THE BALLAD OF JOE HILL** [58] [-]
(12"+=) *(LONX 58)* – South Atlantic way.

— **ALISTAIR McLEOD** – guitar (ex-HIPSWAY) repl. GANNON who joined AZTEC CAMERA, SMITHS, etc.

— split some time in '85; HODGENS had a brief solo sojourn (he featured on a V/A sampler compilation, 'The Chain Gang') while the McCLUSKEY BROTHERS formed their own band. The BLUEBELLS re-formed when they had surprise hit in '93.

– compilations, others, etc. –

Apr 92. (7") *Old Gold;* **YOUNG AT HEART. / I'M FALLING** [ ] [-]

Jun 92. (cd/lp) *Vinyl Japan; (ASK CD/LP 12)* **SECOND** (the shelved 2nd lp) [ ] [-]
– Sweet Jesus / A thousand times / Scared / Orange County / God forgives you / Hey is it true / Mr. Joyce / Jimmy wonderful / Callander green / Any day now / Better days / Three sisters.

Mar 93. (c-s/cd-s) *London; (LON MC/CD 338)* **YOUNG AT HEART / I'M FALLING** [1] [ ]

Apr 93. (cd/c) *London; (828405/-2/-4)* **THE BLUEBELLS – THE SINGLES COLLECTION** [27] [ ]

Jun 93. (cd/c) *Optima; (OPTM CD/C 001)* **BLOOMIN' LIVE (live)** [ ] [-]

Nov 93. (cd) *Star; (ST 5005)* **YOUNG AT HEART** [ ] [-]

McCLUSKEY BROTHERS

were formed by **KEN & DAVE**(latter now guitar, banjo, vocals) **with DAVIE DUNCAN** – bodhran, snare / **CHRIS MILLER** – uileann, pipes, fiddle JAN WIGHTMAN – hurdy gurdy / **RAY DAVIDSON** – mandolin / **BOBBY HENRY** – piano, guitar

Thrush — not iss.

Jul 86. (12"ep) *(THRUSH 4)* **AWARE OF ALL. / HE'S ON THE BEACH / PLEASE GO TO SLEEP** [ ] [-]

Aug 87. (lp) **AWARE OF ALL** [ ] [-]
– On yer bike / Tell me truly / Street corner blues / Aware of all / Only our rivers / Take loving easy / Willie Lee / Searching for the bold young men / Union burying ground / John MacLean march / If I had a dream / Let the people free. *(cd-iss. Jun92 on 'Vinyl Japan'; ASKCD 13)*

— now a trio of the McCLUSKEY's plus **JIM SUTHERLAND** – percussion

D.D.T. — not iss.

Jan 88 (12"ep) *(DISP 15T)* **SHE SAID TO THE DRIVER. / UPSTREET DOWNFALL / SILENT JOURNEY** [ ] [-]

Kingfisher — not iss.

Jan 93. (cd) *(KF 001CD)* **FAVOURITE COLOURS** [ ] [-]
– Perfect afternoon / Lonely satellite / Favourite colours / She said to the driver / 1,000 years / Better days II / Cinder Street / When the loving comes / Slip away / Passport. *(re-iss. May93; same)*

Jun 96. (cd) *(KF 002)* **WONDERFUL AFFAIR** [ ] [-]
– Fever pitch / Wonderful affair / Release me / Pale horizon / 'Till the right thing comes / Twilight family / Busy city dreaming / Sooner or later / This is the night / Turn it over / It's not the end of the world.

Linn — not iss.

May 00. (cd) *(AKD 120)* **HOUSEWIVES' CHOICE** [ ] [-]

BLUE NILE

Formed: Glasgow ... 1981 by songwriter PAUL BUCHANAN, PAUL JOSEPH MOORE and ROBERT BELL. After a debut 45 on 'R.S.O.' (just prior to the label going belly up!), they were offered an unusual record contract by East Lothian label, 'Linn', the hi-fi manufacturer using their tape as a demo and subsequently being sufficiently impressed to sign the band up for their recently formed music business venture.

After an initial single, 'STAY', in Spring '84, the label issued the languorous debut album, 'A WALK ACROSS THE ROOFTOPS'. Garnering gushing reviews, this classic set of understated pop elegance created enough of a buzz for 'Virgin' to take over distribution. Its relatively lowly final chart position of No.80 belied the record's influence and impact, although it would be another five years before a follow-up as the trio locked themselves in the studio and diligently attempted to create another masterpiece. After a few false starts, they finally emerged in 1989 with 'HATS', a record which arguably topped their debut in the late night sophistication stakes, its moody atmospherics delicately caressed by PAUL BUCHANAN's silky croon (a singer who undoubtedly has the potential of being the next SINATRA). A UK Top 20 hit, the record's success saw The BLUE NILE leave their studio cocoon in the early 90's for a tour of America where they ended up working with such luminaries as ROBBIE ROBERTSON and RICKIE LEE JONES amongst others.

Now signed to 'Warners', it looked as if The BLUE NILE were finally destined to leave cultdom behind with a third set, 'PEACE AT LAST' (1996). Another classy effort, again the trio enjoyed critical plaudits and modest chart success while simultaneously failing to corner the wider pop market. Rumours are they are about to release their fourth set in not too distant future (another 7-year itch!).

PAUL BUCHANAN – vocals, guitar, synthesizer / **PAUL JOSEPH MOORE** – keyboards, synthesizer, etc. / **ROBERT BELL** – bass, synthesizer, etc.

R.S.O. / not iss.

Oct 81. (7") *(RSO 84)* **I LOVE THIS LIFE. / SECOND ACT** [ ] [-]

— added guests **CALUM MALCOLM** – keyboards, vocals (ex-BADGER, ex-HEADBOYS) / **NIGEL THOMAS** – drums

Linn-Virgin / A&M

Apr 84. (7"/12") *(LKS 1/+12)* **STAY. / SADDLE THE HORSES** [ ] [ ] 1985
(re-iss. Jan89 remixed 7"/12"/d7"+=; same/same/LKSD 1) – Tinseltown in the rain / Heatwave (instrumental).

Apr 84. (lp/c) *(LKH/+C 1)* **A WALK ACROSS THE ROOFTOPS** [80] [ ] 1985
– A walk across the rooftops / Tinseltown in the rain / From rags to riches / Stay / Easter parade / Heatwave / Automobile noise. *(cd-iss. Jan89; LKHCD 1)*

Jul 84. (7") *(LKS 2)* **TINSELTOWN IN THE RAIN. / HEATWAVE (instrumental)** [ ] [-]
('A'ext-12") *(LKS 2-12)* – Regret.

— now a basic trio plus session musicians.

Sep 89. (7") *(LKS 3)* **THE DOWNTOWN LIGHTS. / THE WIRES ARE DOWN** [67] [ ]
(12"+=/3"cd-s+=) *(LKS 3-12/CD3)* – Halfway to Paradise (TV theme).

Oct 89. (lp/c/cd) *(LKH/+C/CD 2)* *<5284>* **HATS** [12] [ ]
– Over the hillside / The downtown lights / Let's go out tonight / Headlights on the parade / From a late night train / Seven a.m. / Saturday night. *(re-iss. Apr92 on 'Virgin' cd/c; OVED CD/C 391)*

Sep 90. (7"/c-s) *(LKS/+C 4)* **HEADLIGHTS ON THE PARADE (Bob Clearmount mix). / ('A'-lp version)** [72] [ ]
(12"+=/cd-s+=) *(LKS 4-12/CD4)* – Easter parade (with RICKIE LEE JONES).

Jan 91. (7"/c-s) *(LKS/+C 5)* **SATURDAY NIGHT. / ('A'version)** [50] [ ]
(12"+=/cd-s+=) *(LKS 5-12/CD5)* – Seven a.m. (live in the U.S.) / or / Our lives.

Warners / Warners

Jun 96. (cd/c/lp) *(<9362 45848-2/-4/-1>)* **PEACE AT LAST** [13] [ ]
– Happiness / Tomorrow morning / Sentimental man / Love came down / Body and soul / Holy love / Family life / War is love / God bless you kid / Soon.

Sep 96. (c-ep/cd-ep) *(W 0373 C/CD2)* **HAPPINESS / NEW YORK MAN / WISH ME WELL** [ ] [ ]
(cd-ep) *(W 0373CD1)* – ('A'side) / War is love / O Lolita.

BLUES 'N' TROUBLE

Formed: Kirkcaldy, Fife ... early 80's by frontman – on vocals and mouth harp – TIM ELLIOTT, along with the brothers ALAN (known as SCOTTY) and SEAN SCOTT on rhythm, plus guitarists JOHN BRUCE and DAVE NEILL.

Plying the best rawking R&B this side of the Atlantic, B'N'T mixed their own cocktail of gutsy Blues. Inspired by American legends such as SONNY BOY WILLIAMSON I (they covered his 'GOOD MORNING LITTLE SCHOOLGIRL'), OTIS RUSH and ZZ TOP, main songwriters ELLIOTT and BRUCE showcased their songs all over the country – you must have seen them, they've been everywhere(!).

On the recording front, the band got going with two worthy 45's in '83/'84 and eventually their debut set in 1985, simply entitled 'BLUES 'N' TROUBLE'. From the opening track 'BORN IN CHICAGO' to the finale 'SPANK THE PLANK', the listener knew the band were taking no prisoners. The following years' sophomore set, 'NO MINOR KEYS', was another that pulled no punches, top 80's Blues star ROBERT CRAY and ROLLING STONES pianist IAN STEWART even lending a hand to the proceedings. Celebrations were indeed in order when classic 60's UK blues label, 'Blue Horizon' – complete with veteran producer MIKE VERNON and once home to FLEETWOOD MAC and CHICKEN SHACK – took them on for their third set, appropriately titled 'HAT TRICK' (1987). In the early 90's and after a few more LP's under their belt, they delivered a one-off set for 'Tramp' records, 'DOWN TO THE SHUFFLE' (1991).

For future releases they founded their own imprint, 'Barking Mad', and by 1993's 'POOR MOON', only ELLIOTT and SCOTTY had survived; the other accomplices were MIKE PARK, LOU MARTIN and LOX LOVELL. A LIVE! set in 1994, 'BAG FULL OF BOOGIE', was B'N'T's last recording for some time, although as they say up and down the country:- the band played on and on and on . . .

TIM ELLIOTT – vocals, mouthharp, guitar / **JOHN BRUCE** – guitar, dobro, vocals / **DAVE NEILL** – guitar, vocals / **ALAN 'SCOTTY' SCOTT** – bass, vocals / **SEAN SCOTT** – drums

Castle Rock / not iss.

Oct 83. (7") *(BNT 1)* **OLD TIME BOOGIE. /** [ ] [-]

Plus One / not iss.

Aug 84. (7") *(BNT 2)* **MYSTERY TRAIN. / C.T.** [ ] [-]

Ammunition / not iss.

Aug 85. (lp) *(BNTLP 1)* **BLUES 'N' TROUBLE** [ ] [-]
– Born in Chicago / Natural born lover / C.T. / Downtown Saturday night / Blues 'n' trouble / Sloppy drunk / Tearstains on my pillow / Mystery train / Wake up mama / Deep blue feeling / Spank the plank. *(cd-iss. 1989 & Oct94 as 'FIRST TROUBLE' on 'Line'; INCD 900326)*

Sep 85. (7") *(BNT 3)* **CADILLAC. / NATURAL BORN LOVER** [ ] [-]

Feb 86. (7") *(BNT 4)* **FINE, FINE, FINE. / FREE TO RIDE / RED HOT** [ ] [-]

May 86. (lp/c) *(BNT LP/C 2)* **NO MINOR KEYS** [ ] [-]
– Fine, fine, fine / All my love in vain / Clock on the wall / Honey pot / Tight 'n' juicy / Free to ride / You can run / Madison blues / Double trouble / Beautiful city.

Jul 87. (lp; w-drawn) *(BNTLP 3)* **THANK YOU AND GOODNIGHT** [-] [-]

Blue Horizon / not iss.

Aug 87. (lp) *(BLUH 001)* **HAT TRICK** [ ] [-]
– I got your number / Why / Cherry peaches / Travelling light / When the lights go down / Comin' home / What's the matter / Be mine tonight / Rockin' with you Jimmy / T.N.T. / See my baby shake it / Don't need no doctor. *(cd-iss. Nov87 & Oct94 on 'Line'; INCD 900397) (cd re-iss. Feb92; CDBLUH 001)*

Cacophony / not iss.

May 88. (lp/c) *(SKITE/+C 002)* **LIVE (live)** [ ] [-]
– Clock on the wall / Born in Chicago / Cherry peaches / Sugar coated love / BNT blues / What's the matter / Why / Travelling light / Honey pot / Driftin' blues / See my baby shake it / Madison blues / Lying on the kitchen floor. *(cd-iss. May99 on 'Line'; INCD 900572)*

Un-American Activities / not iss.

Dec 89. (lp) *(BRAVE 11)* **WITH FRIENDS LIKE THESE** [ ] [-]
– Wooly bully / Gotta keep control of myself / Sad, sad song / Boogie woogie Suzy Lee / It's a crime / Lone gone man / Nervous wreck / Sure hate being alone / I ain't living anymore / Feel like hell / Don't look at me like that / She's about a mover / Slippin' 'n' slidin'.

— **LOU MARTIN** – piano, organ; repl. NEILL

— **LOX LOVELL** – drums; repl. SEAN SCOTT

Tramp / not iss.

1991. (lp) **DOWN TO THE SHUFFLE** [ ] [-]
– Why why why / Tore up / Sleeping in the ground / Hooked on you / Statesboro blues / Emilia Jane / Papa Lou's boogie woogie / Stay with me / Fool no more / Bring it on home / Down to the shuffle / King Tut's Wah Wah Hut / You missed a good man / Rats crawlin' 'cross my face / Tribute to Kees.

— **MIKE PARK** – guitar; repl. BRUCE

Barking Mad / not iss.

Feb 93. (cd) *(BAMCD 1)* **POOR MOON** [ ] [-]
– Poor moon / Howling my life away / Breaking the ice / Please Mr. Postman / Po' boy / Living with my blues / Sweet little cutie / Looking for something / Pretty thing / Boogywalou / Twistin' on the moon / Gillian.

Jul 94. (cd) *(BAMCD 2)* **LIVE! - BAG FULL OF BOOGIE (live)** [ ] [-]
– Bag full of boogie / Riding in my cadillac / Deep blue feeling / You got me spinnin' / Blue because of you / Breaking the ice / Good morning little schoolgirl / Serenade for a wealthy widow / Slim's chance / Drugstore woman / Lookin' for my baby / Lowdown / Down in Dallas.

Road Goes On Forever — not iss.

May 00. (d-cd) *(RGFBNTDCD 011)* **BLUES GRAFFITI / RARE AND-OR LIVE – THE HAT TRICK ERA**
– Big city / Poorman's prison / Red wine boogaloo / Dames don't care / Drink till I die / Dr. Boogie / Little black engine / Louisiana blues / Dangerous curves / Another little drink / Can ladies kill? / Grim reaper blues / Hip shakin' mama (live jam) // Travelling light / When the lights go down / Comin' home / Rockin' with you Jimmy / T.N.T. / Don't need no doctor / Long gone man / Downtown Saturday night / Be mine tonight / What's the matter? / Why? / Cherry peaches / See my baby shake it / Sugar coated love / Lying on the kitchen floor / Madison blues.

– compilations, etc. –

Jun 94. (cd) *Line; (921211)* **FIRST TROUBLE / NO MINOR KEYS**
(d-cd-iss. Jun98 on 'Road Goes On Forever'+=; RGFBNTDCD 010) – Texas / What's the matter / Red hot / Wake up mama (original) // Let it rock / Slow down / Cadillac / Double trouble (original).

BMX BANDITS

Formed: Bellshill, Lanarkshire . . . summer 1985 by DUGLAS T. STEWART (ex-PRETTY FLOWERS) and future SOUP DRAGONS: SEAN DICKSON and JIM McCULLOCH. In 1986, they released a couple of 45's for Stephen Pastel's '53rd & 3rd' label, notably 'THE DAY BEFORE TOMORROW'. Later that year, DUGLAS was joined by drummer FRANCIS MACDONALD, although the pace slowed a little to let DUGLAS get out and support The SHOP ASSISTANTS (he was to mime Klaus Wunderlich on the organ and later host a night-time pop-TV show).

In 1989, The BMX BANDITS' return was complete with the release of a debut long-player, 'C86' (1990!). A year later, having signed to Tokyo-based 'Vinyl Japan', DUGLAS and Co (this time around boasting a beefed up sound courtesy of MACDONALD, EUGENE KELLY, GORDON KEEN and JOE McALINDEN) issued a more up to date jangle-pop follow-up, 'STARWARS' (1991). Subsequently signing to 'Creation' (who else!?), the 'BANDITS enjoyed cult success with 'SERIOUS DRUGS' and 'KYLIE'S GOT A CRUSH ON US' (the latter boasting of Miss MINOGUE's surprising patronage!); the latter was also performed by local friends and cohorts, TEENAGE FANCLUB.

During the mid-90's, this Bellshill pedal-(steel) powered supergroup delivered a further two sets of pleasant, harmony-fuelled retro-pop in 'GETTIN' DIRTY' (1995) and 'THEME PARK' (1996). In February '97, DUGLAS T. STEWART & COMPANY (i.e. NORMAN BLAKE) delivered what was to be a swansong set, 'FRANKENSTEIN'. • **Songwriters:** DUGLAS, until 1990 when he co-wrote with NORMAN BLAKE. Covered DON'T FIGHT IT, FEEL IT (Primal Scream) / C'EST LA VENT BETTY (Gabriel Yared) / GREEN GROW (Rabbie Burns; trad) / YO YO SONG (trad) / THINKIN' 'BOUT YOU BABY (Beach Boys) / GIRL AT THE BUS STOP (Television Personalities) / COME AND GET IT (Badfinger) / KYLIE'S GOT A CRUSH ON US (melody; Clydesmen) / LIKE A HURRICANE (Neil Young) / NAZI PUNKS FUCK OFF (Dead Kennedys) / CAST A SHADOW (Johnson-Lunsunda-Lewis) / I CAN'T STAY MAD AT YOU (Goffin-King) / THAT SUMMER FEELING (Jonathan Richman) / LITTLE RIVER OF SPRING (Okana-Takano). • **Trivia:** Took their name from children's bike film of the same name. 'KYLIE'S GOT A CRUSH ON US' was tongue-in-cheek humour about that lovely Australian singer!?

DUGLAS STEWART – vocals / with **SEAN DICKSON** – bass / **JIM McCULLOCH** – guitar (both of SOUP DRAGONS) / **BILLY & WILLIE** (of SHOP ASSISTANTS?)

53rd & 3rd — not iss.

Jul 86. (7") *(AGARR 003)* **SAD? / E102**
(12"+=) *(AGARR 003-12)* – The cat from outer space (live) / Strawberry Sunday (live) / Groovy good luck friend (live).

— now w /out SEAN (B-side only for JIM)

Jan 87. (7") *(AGARR 006)* **WHAT A WONDERFUL WORLD. / THE DAY BEFORE TOMORROW**
(12"+=) *(AGARR 006-12)* – Johnny Alucard / Sad? / Sandy's wallet.

— **DUGLAS** w / **FRANCIS MACDONALD** (b.11 Sep'70) – drums / + **GORDON KEEN** – guitar / + **NORMAN BLAKE** – guitar, vocals (of TEENAGE FANCLUB)

Jun 88. (7") *(AGARR 018)* **FIGURE 4. / STARDATE 21.11.70.**
(12"+=) *(AGARR 018T)* – In her hair / Bette Blue.

— now w / **NORMAN BLAKE + GERRY** (from TEENAGE FANCLUB)

Click — not iss.

Mar 90. (lp) *(LP 001)* **C86**
– Right across the street / Top Shop girl / Rimbaud and me / Yo yo song (1969) / Medley: Disco girl – Disco daze and disco knights / Your class / Disco girl II / Whirlpool / C86 / On somedays / But tonight / Let Mother Nature be your guide / Heaven's daughter. *(cd-iss. Nov92 as 'C86 AND MORE' on 'Vinyl Japan'+=; ASKCD 19)* – Stardate / Figure 4 / Strawberry sundae / C'est la vent Betty / Thinkin' 'bout you baby / Let Mother Nature be your guide (karaoke mix) / Your class. *(cd re-iss. Jul97 on 'Elefant'; ER 1048)*

Avalanche — not iss.

Dec 90. (cd/lp) *(ONLY CD/LP 007)* **TOTALLY GROOVY LIVE EXPERIENCE (live at Hattonrig Hotel)**
– Whirl pool / Girl at the bus stop / Your class / In her hair / E102 / Bongo brains / Disco girl / The day before tomorrow / Like a hurricane / Nazi punks fuck off.

— **DUGLAS** now w/ **EUGENE KELLY** (ex-VASELINES, of CAPTAIN AMERICA + EUGENIUS) + **GORDON KEEN / JOE McALINDEN** – guitar (of GROOVY LITTLE NUMBERS) / **FRANCIS MACDONALD** – drums

Vinyl Japan — not iss.

Oct 91. (cd/lp) *(ASK CD/LP 007)* **STARWARS**
– Come clean / Think tank / Smile for me / Green grow / Retitled / Life goes on / The sailor's song (pt.1) / Disguise / Studcats of life / Extraordinary / Do you really love me? / The sailor's song / Stars Wars.

Jan 92. (12"ep/cd-ep) *(TASK 12005/+CD)* **COME CLEAN / LET MOTHER NATURE BE YOUR GUIDE. / RETITLED / ('A'-funky train mix)**

Sunflower — not iss.

Aug 92. (red-lp) *(SUN 006)* **GORDON KEEN AND HIS BMX BANDITS**
– Kylie's got a crush on us / Come and get it / Girl at the bus stop / etc.

Creation — Tristar

Nov 92. (12"ep)(cd-ep) *(CRE 131T)(CRESCD 131)* **SERIOUS DRUGS / FUNNY FACE. / DON'T FIGHT IT FEEL IT (in concert) / SERIOUS DRUGS (demo)**

Jul 93. (7"/c-s) *(CRE/+CS 154)* **KYLIE'S GOT A CRUSH ON US. / HOLE IN MY HEART**
(12"+=)(cd-s+=) *(CRE 154T)(CRESCD 154)* – Thinkin' 'bout you baby / My generation.

Oct 93. (cd/lp) *(CRE CD/LP 133) <67207>* **LIFE GOES ON**
– Little hands / Serious drugs / Space girl / Scar / I'll keep on joking / Hole in my heart / Cast a shadow / Cats and dogs / Your dreams / My friend / It hasn't ended / Intermission (bathing beauties) / Kylie's got a crush on us.

Nov 93. (12"ep)(cd-ep) *(CRE 168T)(CRESCD 168)* **LITTLE HANDS / THE NEXT GIRL. / WITCHI TAI TO (home recording) / BUT TONIGHT (acoustic session)**

Apr 94. (7"ep/cd-ep) *(CRE/+SCD 181)* **SERIOUS DRUGS / LITTLE PONY. / I'LL KEEP ON JOKING / THE SAILOR'S SONG**

Creation — Creation

Mar 95. (7") *(CRE 192)* **GETTIN' DIRTY. / I CAN'T STAY MAD AT YOU**
(cd-s+=) *(CRESCD 192)* – Tiny fingers, tiny toes / This guy's in love with you.

May 95. (cd/lp) *(CRE CD/LP 174)* **GETTIN' DIRTY**
– Gettin' dirty / Hello again / Lost girl / Love, come to me / No future / Konnichiva #2 / On the road to Heaven / Little river of spring.
(below featured The MORLEY STRING QUARTET; b-side featured DAN PENN)

Aug 95. (7") *(CRE 207)* **LOVE, COME TO ME. / THAT SUMMER FEELING**
(cd-s+=) *(CRESCD 207)* – Come summer / Sunshine day.

Sep 96. (cd-ep) **WE'RE GONNA SHAKE YOU DOWN / LOVE AND MERCY (live) / LITTLE RIVER OF SPRING (live) / SERIOUS DRUGS (live)**

Oct 96. (cd) *(CRECD 202)* **THEME PARK**
– We're gonna shake you down / Girl nextdoor / Nuclear summertime / Teenage slaughtertime / This lonely guy / I wanna fall in love / One big heart / Opei mantra / Milky Way / Motorboat / Love makes the world go around / Before the blue moon / Lonely love / Evel Knievel / Ride the iron horse / In the afterglow / Sparkle finish / Our time has come.

— FRANCIS also teamed up with (his) 'Shoeshine' band SPEEDBOAT

Shoeshine — Elefant

Oct 96. (7") *(SHOE 002) <ER 173>* **HELP ME SOMEBODY. / GOLDEN TEARDROPS** — Jul97

— Mar'97, they turned up with idol KIM FOWLEY on his CD, 'HIDDEN AGENDA' on 'Receiver'; *RRCD 231)*

DUGLAS T. STEWART & COMPANY

with **NORMAN BLAKE** (of TEENAGE FANCLUB)

Vinyl Japan — not iss.

Feb 97. (cd) *(MASKCD 60)* **FRANKENSTEIN**
– Unbreakable heart / Hey little tomboy / Daddy daddy / Stupid / Tones / Airmail / Snow / Into the moon / Very / I'll be your baby tonight / Tones #2 / Gap (ten second of silence) / Frankenstein / And yes I'm still stupid.

BOARDS OF CANADA

Formed: Pentland Hills, nr. Edinburgh . . . 1995 by MICHAEL SANDISON and MARCUS EOIN. The group earned their acclaim after recording a ridiculous amount of tracks for experimental electronica label 'Skam' who signed the pair in 1996.

Hailed as 'Skam's greatest release to date, the 'TWOISM' EP set the ball rolling for the team in 1996 (now worth over £500). Audiences couldn't get enough of its catchy but simple, A-B-C (or L.F.O.) synth formats and melodies. References were, of course, made to The APHEX TWIN and JEGA, however 'HI SCORES' had a better twisted back-beat to it than, say, RICHARD D. JAMES' cult 'ANALOGUE BUBBLEBATH VOL.1'. It fooled listeners into thinking the band were American by its sheer 1992 hip-hop nostalgia and chilled out beach party vibes. This impressive debut was quickly followed up in late 1996 by a series of tracks for 'UMV' and 'Slam/Musik Aus Strom' side project label 'Mask', with 1998 witnessing the unfettering of the excellent "difficult" second release, 'MUSIC HAS THE RIGHT TO CHILDREN'. Cool as well as deeply serene, the album (distributed by 'Warp' and 'Matador') intensified that early 90's Miami trip-hop identity and added in a little scratching and sampling for good measure. A prime example of this was the single out-take, and the most famous track you'll hear from the album, 'ROYGBIV', which sounded like the Terminator doing slow motion break dancing in a crowded Beverly Hills house party.

1999 saw the latest from BOC, a PEEL SESSIONS EP, another triumph from the Peel acres and an entry into the 'Matador' 10th anniversary collection, 'Everything Is Nice'. The duo finally returned with a two track EP, 'A BEAUTIFUL PLACE IN THE COUNTRY', towards the end of 2000. The single was an unexpected trip into the psychedelic shenanigans that were about to be, once again, explored by The BOARDS OF CANADA.

In February 2002, their long-awaited sophomore album, 'GEOGADDI', was released to huge critical acclaim, which resulted in their first interview with the NME. For this they described the open Scottish wilderness as an inspiration for their hallucinogenic, spaced-out synth doodlings. They also declared that the meaning of their moniker was indeed (as older readers may recall!) lifted from an educational company whose films on science and nature had been shown while the pair had attended school. This reflected a lot of the new album; one track in question 'DANDELION' had a backwards moog drone accompanied by a man (actor Leslie Nielsen from 'Naked Gun' fame!) narrating a TV documentary about a diving team; this segued into the six and a half minute epic 'SUNSHINE RECORDER'. Track 16, 'THE DEVIL IN THE DETAILS', had a simple keyboard riff on a loop which played the insane shrills of a child and the voice of a distorted, disjointed telephone operator. 'GEODADDI' (a near Top 20 entry) was much darker and yet much more layered in terms of themes, music and ambience. For two guys living in the countryside this was quite a feat, a real slice of math-electronica that was both gentle and eerily sublime.

MICHAEL SANDISON (b. 14 Jul'71) – electronics / **MARCUS EOIN** (b.27 May'73) – electronics

Skam | not iss.

Dec 96. (m-lp) *(SKA 8)* **TWOISM** [ ] [-]
– Hi scores / Turquoise hexagon sun / Nlogax / June 9th / Seeya later / Everything you do is a balloon.

Jan 98. (7") *(KMAS 1)* **AQUARIUS. / CHINOOK** [ ] [-]

Warp - Skam | Matador

Mar 98. (10") *(WAP10 55)* **ROYGBIV. / TELEPHASIC WORKSHOP** [ ] [-]

Apr 98. (cd/d-lp) *(WARP CD/LP 55 – SKALD 1) <OLE 299-2/-1>* **MUSIC HAS THE RIGHT TO CHILDREN** [ ] [ ]
– Wildlife analysis / An eagle in your mind / The color of the fire / Telephasic workshop / Triangles & rhombuses / Sixtyten / Turquoise hexagon sun / Kaini industries / Bocuma / Roygbiv / Rue the whirl / Aquarius / Olson / Pete standing alone / Smokes quantity / Open the light / One very important thought. *(d-lp+=)* – Happy cycling.

Warp | Warp

Jan 99. (cd-ep) *(<WAP 114CD>)* **PEEL SESSIONS** [ ] [ ] Mar99
– Aquarius (version 3) / Happy cycling / Olson (version 3).

Nov 00. (12"/cd-s) *(<WAP 144/+CD>)* **IN A BEAUTIFUL PLACE OUT IN THE COUNTRY EP** [ ] [ ]
– Kid for today / Amo bishop Roden / In a beautiful place out in the country / Zoetrope.

Feb 02. (cd/t-lp) *(<WARP CD/LP 101>)* **GEOGADDI** [21] [ ]
– Ready let's go / Music is math / Beware the friendly stranger / Gyroscope / Dandelion / Sunshine recorder / In the annexe / Julie and Candy / The smallest weird number / 1969 / Energy warning / The beach at Redpoint / Opening the mouth / Alpha and Omega / I saw drones / The devil is in the details / A is to B as B is to C / Over the horizon radar / Dawn chorus / Diving station / You could feel the sky / Corsair / Magic window.

BOHN LEGION (see under ⇒ Stranded records)

BOOTS FOR DANCING

Formed: Edinburgh . . . late 1979 by the songwriting pair of DAVE CARSON and GRAHAM HIGH, who enlisted the rhythm section of DOUGIE BARRIE and STUART WRIGHT. Influenced by the quirky/manic dance-punk rhythms of GANG OF FOUR or The POP GROUP, BOOTS FOR DANCING enjoyed a bit of airplay on the John Peel Radio One show. The quartet signed to 'Pop Aural' (also the launching pad for The FIRE ENGINES) and released their debut platter, the eponymous 'BOOTS FOR DANCING' single in 1980. They were subsequently dogged by numerous personnel changes initiating with a brief stint from ex-REZILLOS man, ANGEL PATERSON, who left to join TV21 (two drummers/percussionists were introduced, JAMO STEWART and DICKIE FUSCO). HIGH was also to take off, his replacement being another REZILLOS ex, JO CALLIS who was joined by MIKE BARCLAY.

After a year long spell without a record, BFD were back with the follow-up, 'RAIN SONG', although this was certainly not as good as their debut. When CALLIS departed to take up a post in the HUMAN LEAGUE, the quintet were to release their third and last effort, 'OOH BOP SH'BAM', before CARSON became the only surviving original, he and BARCLAY having recruited SIMON TEMPLAR (another ex-REZILLOS and SHAKE member) and RONNIE TORRANCE (ex-JOSEF K).

DAVE CARSON – vocals / **GRAHAM HIGH** – guitar / **DOUGIE BARRIE** – bass / **STUART WRIGHT** – drums

Pop Aural | not iss.

Apr 80. (12"ep) *(POP 002)* **BOOTS FOR DANCING / PARACHUTE. / GUITARS / GIRL TROUBLE** [ ] [-]

— **JAMO STEWART** – drums + **DICKIE FUSCO** – percussion; repl. ANGEL PATERSON (ex-SHAKE, ex-REZILLOS) who repl. WRIGHT

— MIKE BARCLAY – guitar (ex-THURSDAYS) repl. HIGH who joined DELTA 5

— added **JO CALLIS** – guitar, vocals (ex-SHAKE, ex-REZILLOS)

Mar 81. (7") *(POP 006)* **RAIN SONG. / HESITATING** [ ] [-]

— trimmed to a quintet when CALLIS left to join HUMAN LEAGUE

Re-Pop X | not iss.

Feb 82. (7") *(WAY 100)* **OOH BOP SH'BAM. / MONEY IS THIN ON THE GROUND** [ ] [-]

— **SIMON TEMPLAR** (b. BLOOMFIELD) – bass (ex-FLOWERS, ex-SHAKE, ex-REZILLOS) repl. BARRIE

— **RONNIE TORRANCE** – drums (ex-JOSEF K) repl. FUSCO + STEWART (the latter formed The SYNDICATE

— hung up their footwear some time in '82.

BOTANY 5

Formed: Edinburgh . . . mid 80's by Stirling-born GORDON KERR and DAVID GALBRAITH. The former first came to attention of the music world in The JUGGERNAUTS, a band that also comprised JAMES LOCKE and the SLEVOR brother NIGEL and PAUL. They released one PAUL HAIG-produced 45, 'COME THROW YOURSELF UNDER THE MONSTROUS WHEELS OF THE ROCK'N'ROLL INDUSTRY AS IT APPROACHES DESTRUCTION' (phew!) in 1984, before the pair united as BOTANY 500 (taking the name from a type of jacket). Another funk'n'jazz flavoured slice of live string-enhanced ambience came out a few years later in the form of 'BULLY BEEF'.

Following the pair's parting of the ways in 1989, KERR retained the name, although he was forced to slightly alter it after an identically named American company threatened legal action. Subsequently signing to 'Virgin', KERR and newcomers STEVIE CHRISTIE and JASON ROBERTSON entered the studio with the BLUE NILE's CALLUM MALCOLM. The resulting 'INTO THE NIGHT' (1991), was preceded by two well-received singles, 'LOVE BOMB' and 'NATURE BOY', the group's mellow, meditative soundscapes bearing comparison with the likes of TALK TALK, The ORB and ANIMAL NIGHTLIFE. Before being lost forever to the music business jungle, the BOTANY 5 trio completed a series of acclaimed live shows aided and abetted by former ORANGE JUICE drummer, ZEKE MANYIKA.

GORDON KERR (b. Stirling) – vocals / **JAMES LOCKE** – guitar / **PAUL + NIGEL SLEVOR** – rhythm

Supreme Int. / not iss.

Nov 84. (7"; as JUGGERNAUTS) *(EDITION 84-2)* **COME THROW YOURSELF UNDER THE MONSTROUS WHEELS OF THE ROCK'N'ROLL INDUSTRY AS IT APPROACHES DESTRUCTION. / MY FIRST MILLION** -

— **KERR** now recruited **DAVID GALBRAITH** – keyboards, etc

1986. (12"ep; as BOTANY 500) *(EDITION 86-12)* **BULLY BEEF. / MY SILENT LOVE / CHILLSHAKE** -

— GALBRAITH was repl. by **JASON ROBERTSON** – guitar + **STEVIE CHRISTIE** – keyboards

Virgin / Virgin

Oct 90. (7") **LOVE BOMB. / SHADOWS AND DREAMS** -
(12"+=/cd-s+=) – ('A'-extended) / ('A'instrumental).

Jul 91. (12"/cd-s) **NATURE BOY. /** -

Aug 91. (cd/c/lp) *(CD/TC+/V 2664)* **INTO THE NIGHT**
–

Sep 91. (12"/cd-s) **ONLY ONE IN YOUR LIFE. /** -

— added for live appearances **ZEKE MANYIKA** – drums, vocals (ex-ORANGE JUICE + solo artist) / **CARMEL** – vocals (also solo artist)

— split some time in 1992

BOURGIE BOURGIE (see under ⇒ QUINN, Paul)

BOWS

Formed: Coupar Angus, Perthshire . . . 1998 by (black British singer) LUKE SUTHERLAND after the break-up of his indie-experimental band, LONG FIN KILLIE who had formed in the late 80's. Strange as it may seem, LFK began practising in his mother's – Lady Duncan of Jordanstone's – mansion. He made regular visits to her laundry room, where they spent their first three years pulling together enough material for debut set 'HOUDINI' (1995).

The quartet became a critically acclaimed folk/jazz fold who mixed primitive BETA BAND techniques with fiddle riffs and kazoo solos! After 1996's 'VALENTINO', the Scottish four were involved in a near fatal car accident which, arguably split the group (although it was said that they had nothing in common by that time), leaving enough space for recovery and a third release, 'AMELIA'; SUTHERLAND would, in turn go his own way. The troubled frontman began writing a book, 'Jelly Roll', inspired by his touring days with LFK, about the decent of a Scottish jazz band on the road. When released, the novel became an instant success, winning over critics and nominations for the Whitbread Book Of The Year.

SUTHERLAND established BOWS in '98 when he went into partnership with singer/songwriter SIGNE HOIRUP WILLE-JORGENSEN and ex-PhD student RUTH EDMOND. 'BLUSH' was issued the following year, becoming the catalyst for SUTHERLAND's second novel 'Sweet Meat'. His honest lyrics and MASSIVE ATTACK-like cool enabled him to pull off such gems as 'BIG WINGS' and 'IT'LL BE HALF TIME IN ENGLAND SOON', sending them into the darkest crevice of the human mind. Creepy backing tunes and orchestrated malevolance made this particular set float just above average.

LONG FIN KILLIE

LUKE SUTHERLAND – vocals / **PHIL** – guitar / **COLIN** – bass / **DAVEY** – drums

Too Pure / Warners

Oct 94. (12"yellow-ep/cd-ep) *(PURE 12/CD 39)* **BUTTERGUT EP** -
– The Lamberton lamplighter / Boy racer / Butterbelly.

— next featured **MARK E. SMITH** – vocals (of The FALL)

May 95. (7") *(PURE 44)* **HOLLYWOOD GEM. / THE HEADS OF DEAD SURFERS** -
(cd-s+=) *(PURECD 044)* – Flaccid tabloid / Stacked.

Jun 95. (cd) *(PURECD 47)* <43036> **HOUDINI** Jul95
– Man Ray / How I blew it with Houdini / Homo erectus / The heads of dead surfers / Montgomery / Love smothers allergy / Hollywood gem / The Lamberton lamplighter / Corngold / Idiot hormone / Rockethead on mandatory surveillance / Flower carrier / Unconscious gangs of men.

Apr 96. (cd-ep) *(PURECD 58)* **HANDS AND LIPS EP** -
– Hands and lips / Angel / Nation / Clinch.

May 96. (lp/cd) *(PURE/+CD 54)* <43076> **VALENTINO** Jul96
– Godiva / Pele / Kitten heels / A thousand wounded astronauts / Hands and lips / Valentino / Coward / Girlfriend / Matador / Cop / Cupid / Fresher.

Too Pure / Too Pure

Oct 97. (7") *(PURE 75)* **LIPSTICK. / CZ** -
(cd-s+=) *(PURE 75CDS)* – Love life.

Nov 97. (lp/cd) *(<PURE/+CD 74>)* **AMELIA** Apr98
– British summertime / Lipstick / Kismet / Resin / Sugar helping / Ringer / Chrysler / Bigger than England / Headlines / Gold swinger / Deep house / Yawning at comets.

— disbanded; DAVEY had already joined Dutch/English band, DONKEY

BOWS

— **LUKE SUTHERLAND** – vocals, multi / **SIGNE HOIRUP WILLE-JORGENSEN** – vocals / **RUTH EDMOND** – vocals

Mar 99. (cd-s) *(PURE 82CDS)* **BIG WINGS / SPEED MARINA / KING DELUXE / BIG WINGS (version)** -

May 99. (cd/lp) *(<PURE 90 CD/LP>)* **BLUSH** Aug99
– Big wings / Troy Polenta's big break / Blush / Overfor Kommer / King Deluxe / Speed marina / No.4 / Britannica / Aquavella / It'll be half time in England soon / Girls lips glitter / Sleepyhead / Rockets.

Jun 99. (7") *(PURE 97S)* **BLUSH. / ('A'-Ellis Island mix)** -
(cd-s+=) *(PURE 97CDS)* – Heart and two stars.

Oct 99. (7") *(PURE 88S)* **BRITANNICA. / TOTAL FUCKING MASSACRE** -
(cd-s+=) *(PURE 88CDS)* – ('A'-Scissorkicks mix) / ('A'-CD-Rom).

Mar 01. (cd-s) *(PURE 102CDS)* **PINK PUPPET (mixes; Mike Paradinas / Gonzales / Papa November / full reading of story)** -

Apr 01. (cd) *(PURE 104CD)* **CASSIDY** -
– Luftsang / Cuban welterweight rumbles hidden hitmen / Man fat / All 4 Onassis / Uniroyal / B boy blunt / Wonderland / DJ / Blue steeples / Hey Vegas / Sun electric / Ton ten all the way home.

BOYFRIEND

Formed: Glasgow . . . 1992 by STEPHEN JOLLIE, MARK McAVOY, DEREK McKEE and GEORGE WATSON. If you can imagine indie kings the TEENAGE FANCLUB in the same studio as ORANGE JUICE, the monotone and oft out-of-tune BOYFRIEND would be the love-child. Having said that, the quartet were a good band if not outstanding, probably the reason why ALAN McGEE's 'Creation' (home to friends TFC) thought it wise to sub-let the quartet to subsidiary 'August'.

BOYFRIEND's debut single, 'HEY BIG STAR', was a promising start to their indie-rock campaign, its driving seventies, NEIL YOUNG-esque guitars brooding side by side with more 'FANCLUB-styled vox. Parent album, 'HAIRY BANJO' (1993), set the band's stall out right from the start, although why they thought we needed another TFC was anybody's guess. However, 1993 was a prolific year for BOYFRIEND, a further single/EP 'LEATHERED' and a much-overlooked(!) mini-set 'RUBBER EAR', all hitting the indie shops; the latter's fitting finale was a squeaky, ill-advised cover of Paul McCartney & Wings' 'JET'. They took off to that great gig in the sky soon afterwards.

STEPHEN JOLLIE / MARK McAVOY / GEORGE WATSON / DEREK McKEE

August – Creation / not iss.

Feb 93. (12"ep/cd-ep) *(caug 002 t/cd)* **HEY BIG STAR / JAHLOPPEE. / GUITARIST NIPPLE / FLEW OUT** -

Mar 93. (cd/lp) *(rust 003 cd/lp)* **HAIRY BANJO**
– Hey big star / Summerthing / Kojak / Guitarist nipple / Rockwieller / Searching / Leathered / Two / Don't even try / Girl on my mind / Why should I pretend? / Air you breathe / Sunburnt.

Apr 93. (12"ep/cd-ep) *(caug 004 t/cd)* **LEATHERED EP** -
–

Oct 93. (m-cd) *(rust 006cd)* **RUBBER EAR**
– The ripple / Got a notion / The apple / Going out / Jet.

— disbanded in 1994

BOY HAIRDRESSERS (see under ⇒ TEENAGE FANCLUB)

BRAINSTORM (see under ⇒ MOUNT FLORIDA)

BRAVE CAPTAIN

Born: MARTIN CARR, 29 Nov'68, Thurso. Former guitarist with Liverpool outfit, The BOO RADLEYS, CARR quit after a soured relationship in 1996; he formed the enigmatic BRAVE CAPTAIN a few years later.

For anyone who'd heard the experimental indie-pop tinglings of CARR's original group, 'THE FINGERTIP SAINT SESSIONS VOL.1' was no let down for those expecting shimmering guitars, reminscent of late BEATLES or BRIAN WILSON (just before he lost his marbles – so to speak). Suffice to say that CARR had maintained his credibility as a songwriter throughout this mini-album, which was packed full of punches and surprises. For one, high-pitched SICE was pale in comparison to CARR's formal, if not experimental baritone musings which accompanied his fragile and graceful collection of modern pop songs. Examples of this could be found in the opening three minutes of 'RAINING STONES', and again on the epic closing track 'LITTLE BUDDAH', which clocked in at around 22 minutes.

Subsequently, the brave one issued his debut album proper on the post-Creation (DICK GREEN and MARK BOWEN) 'Wichita' imprint in 2000. Entitled 'GO WITH YOURSELF', this sophomore set acted as a sequel to CARR's aforementioned mini-set; a sort of 'FINGERTIP SAINT SESSIONS VOL 2', if it must be told. Along with the usual array of neo-melodies, CARR bravely employed the distant whispers of sadcore to his ever impending gleam. 'ASSEMBLY OF THE UNREPRESENTED' sounded like the sort of thing you would hear at a BOO RADLEY's reunion, while CARR's guitars and multi-instrumental accompaniment laid the solid foundations for one of indie's unsung protagonists. So, with everything good and well, BRAVE CAPTAIN ventured further into his musical field of unknown with the EP, 'BETTER LIVING THROUGH RECKLESS EXPERIMENTATION' (2001). Sporting a 'Rock-on' salute on the cover, the set generated column inches from hacks who had before ignored CARR and his ingenius incarnations. Cardiff's same, independently run 'Boobytrap' imprint issued BRAVE CAPTAIN's brilliant single 'CORPORATION MAN' in 2001, on a limited run. Those who were lucky enough to get their mits on the single knew that CARR had finally surpassed himself musically, with the title track employing the jumpy, guitar driven indie/punk that launched The SUPER FURRY ANIMALS into indie stardom. If perhaps, the single was given a bigger release the same might've just happened to the increasingly brilliant BRAVE CAPTAIN.

MARTIN CARR – vocals, guitar, bass, organ (ex-BOO RADLEYS) / with **GORWEL OWEN** – hammond, glockenspiel, minimoog, etc / **TONY ROBINSON + GARY ALESBROOK** – trumpet / **DAFYDD IEUAN** – drums / **MATT SIBLEY** – saxophone / etc

Wichita / Thirsty Ear

Aug 00. (m-cd/10"m-lp) *(WEBB 003/+LP)* **THE FINGERTIP SAINT SESSIONS VOL.1** □ -
– Raining stones / Big red control machine / Starfish / Third unattended bag on the right / The tragic story / Little buddah.

Oct 00. (cd/lp) *(WEBB 004/+LP)* **GO WITH YOURSELF** □ -
– The monk jumps over the wall / Assembly of the unrepresented / Tell her you want her / Where is my head / Ein Hoff Le / Hermit versus the world / Running off the ground / Reuben / Go with yourself.

Mar 01. (7"ep/cd-ep) *(WEBB 009S/+CD)* **BETTER LIVING THROUGH RECKLESS EXPERIMENTATION EP** □ -
– Better living through reckless experimentation / Canton hotel (these questions are very easy) / Me and you glue / Stronger.

Mar 01. (cd) *<57098>* **NOTHING LASTS HE SANG ONLY THE EARTH AND THE MOUNTAINS** - □
– The monk jumps over the wall / The tragic story / Tell her you want her / Big red control machine / Where is my head / Raining stones / Assembly of the unrepresented / Reuben / Ein Hoff le / Hermit versus the world / Third unattended bag on the right / Go with yourself.

Boobytrap / not iss.

Jun 01. (cd-s) *(BOOB 007CD)* **CORPORATION MAN** □ -

BREAD POULTICE & THE RUNNING SORES (see ⇒ Section 9: wee post-punk groups)

BREAKER (see under ⇒ STAFFORD, Baby)

Billy BREMNER

Born: c.1947, Aberdeen. One of the most unsung guitarists Scotland has ever produced, the self-taught BILLY began his career with local heroes The STRANGERS (as a replacement for the injured DEREK FREELAND) back in the early 60's. He then joined The TREMORS, another Aberdeen act who decamped to London where they struggled in bedsit misery trying in vain to land a decent record deal.

Remaining in the big smoke when the rest of the band returned north, BILLY landed a spot in The WALKER BROTHERS for a couple of years before recording a couple of singles with The LUVVERS (after LULU had departed) and serving brief spells in JOHNNY B GREAT and The QUOTATIONS. Although his contributions to NIRVANA's early material didn't make it to the final mix, BREMNER became a full-time session man and subsequently played on countless records by a variety of artists. Former QUIET FIVE man, KRIS IFE, recruited BILLY to publishing company 'Heath Levy Music' in the early 70's, where he worked on demos of writers' material.

Finally, the man released a solo single, 'DOWNTOWN HOEDOWN', in 1977 on 'Polydor', although the track was credited to BILLY MURRAY (to avoid confusion with the Leeds United and Scotland Captain of the same name). The following year, IFE was once again at the production helm for 'THE HEART AND THE STONE', BILLY's second single also under the MURRAY alias (and probably just as well given Scotland's footballing fiasco in Argentina that summer . . .). BILLY went on to become part of COMPASS alongside ROGER RETTIG and BRIAN HODGSON, the trio subsequently forming the core of the studio band responsible for The Rutland Weekend Songbook (the accompanying album for Rutland Weekend Television, itself the beat spoof brainchild of Eric Idle and Neil Innes).

BILLY added to an already exhaustive CV when he teamed up with NICK LOWE (and TERRY WILLIAMS) to form DAVE EDMUNDS backing band, ROCKPILE. Due to contractual problems, the group couldn't release any material under this moniker and their various albums were credited to either LOWE or EDMUNDS. A 1979 cover of ELVIS COSTELLO's 'Girls Talk', made the UK Top 5 (Top 75 in the USA), its Stateside success finally turning BILLY's career around and ensuring decent money after years of struggle.

Following ROCKPILE's demise in 1981, BILLY went on to cut a string of solo singles – under the BREMNER moniker this time – over the early to mid-80's including that year's 'Stiff' effort, 'LOUD MUSIC IN CARS'. 1982 saw the release of another 'Stiff' single, 'LAUGHTER TURNS TO TEARS' as well as a single for 'Demon' entitled 'MEEK POWER'. In 1984, he was back again with a couple of singles for 'Arista', namely 'SHATTERPROOF' and 'LOVE GOES TO SLEEP', although no doubt more punters were unwittingly exposed to BILLY's talent through BILLY CONNOLLY's 'Super Gran' . . .

The early 80's period also saw the highest profile role of BILLY's career, as a replacement for the recently deceased JAMES HONEYMAN-SCOTT in The PRETENDERS; as well as putting in a sterling performance on the classic hit, 'Back On The Chain Gang', the guitarist was to later work on the band's 'PACKED' (1990) album. When not putting in a turn on classic singles such as KIRSTY MacCOLL's 'There's A Guy Works Down The Chipshop Swears He's Elvis' and The BLUEBELLS' 'Young At Heart', BREMNER even found time for a belated solo album, 'BASH!' (1984).

In 1986, BILLY travelled to New York where he worked as the musical director on a theatre piece by Nicol Williamson. When the show's run ended, BILLY stayed on in the States, residing in California for six years before moving to country capital, Nashville. He continues to be major player in the Music City studio scene as well as fronting his own band, the chameleon-like Aberdonian exile even travelling to Sweden in the mid-90's where he played a series of dates with a local rockabilly band under the name BILLY & THE BJORNS . . .

BILLY BREMNER – vocals, guitar / with **DAVE KERR-CLEMENSON + JAMES ELLER** – bass / **BOBBY IRWIN + TERRY WILLIAMS** – drums / etc

Stiff / not iss.

Sep 81. (7") *(BUY 125)* **LOUD MUSIC IN CARS. / THE PRICE IS RIGHT** □ -

Feb 82. (7") *(BUY 143)* **LAUGHTER TURNS TO TEARS. / TIRED AND EMOTIONAL** □ -

Demon / not iss.

Aug 82. (7") *(D 1014)* **MEEK POWER. / YES PLEASE!** □ -

Arista / not iss.

Feb 84. (7") *(ARIST 557)* **SHATTERPROOF. / LOOK AT THAT CAR** □ -
(12"+=) *(ARIST12 557)* – Muscle bound.

Apr 84. (7") *(ARIST 566)* **WHEN LOVE GOES TO SLEEP. / FIRE IN THE POCKET** □ -
(12"+=) *(ARIST12 566)* – ('A'extended).

Jun 84. (lp) *(206.170)* **BASH!** □ -
– Fire in the pocket / Losing my touch / Shatterproof / Love is stranger than fiction / The perfect crime / Tired and emotional (and probably drunk) / Loud music in cars / Going steady with a heartache / When these shoes were new / The boat that's sunk a thousand ships / When love goes to sleep.

Rock City / not iss.

Feb 85. (7") *(RCR 6)* **ENDLESS SLEEP. / MONA LOTT** □ -

—— BILLY would join The PRETENDERS, etc. before embarking on another set

Hypertension / not iss.

Aug 98. (cd) *(HYCD 298178)* **GOOD WEEK'S WORK** □ -
– I get enough / I see it in your eyes / Green with envy / I can love you / Lookin' back thinkin' ahead / I thank them / Cover it up / Fine set of wheels / Pass this story 'round / Now is the time / Keep this house rockin' / You got to me.

BROCCOLI

Formed: Dundee . . . early '92 by singer/guitarist GRANT MILES (apparently a former nude model at an art college!), bassist BENNI ESPOSITO and drummer GRAEME GILMOUR – hardy vegetables indeed. Trash-punk/pop and strongly inspired by The DAMNED and LEATHERFACE, BROCCOLI sprung into action in '94 via a split EP with fellow Dundonians, MUPPET MULE (an off-shoot of SPARE SNARE). 1995 was indeed a prolific year for the perky trio, three further indie singles for as many labels shooting out, while tours with Americans J CHURCH proved tasty. The 'BROCCOLI' mini-set for 'Rugger Bugger' the following year, was however their last outing with Art College kid BENNI, who was superseded by former APPLEORCHARD guy SCOTT STEWART. Having been a fan of 70's/80's Mod band, The LAMBRETTAS, GRANT and the lads chose a cover of their 'DA-A-A-ANCE' for their next 45. While promoting their first full-set, 'HOME' (1998), BROCCOLI ("home" now in London's Gypsy Hill) toured alongside likeminded SNUFF, JUNE OF 44, LEATHERFACE and HOOTON 3 CAR, although basically these musical meatpackers were an out and out singles combo.

GRANT MILES – vocals, guitar / **BENNI ESPOSITI** – bass / **GRAEME GILMOUR** – drums

Chute | not iss.

1994. (ltd-7"ep) *(CHUTE 002)* **NEGLECT IT / WELTSCHMERTZ. / (other tracks by Muppet Mule)** [ ] [-]

Rooster | not iss.

Jan 95. (7"m) *(RSTR 002)* **BROKEN. / 10 JOURNEY TROUSERS / FIDO** [ ] [-]

Rumblestrip | not iss.

Jun 95. (7") **ALL SMILES. / PONDLIFE** [ ] [-]

Rugger Bugger | Snuffy Smile

Nov 95. (7") *(DUMP 030)* **RELENT. / 100 DAYS AND COUNTING** [ ] [-]
1996. (7"m) **LEAN. / SIDLEDOWN / PR EXORCISE** [ ] [-]
Aug 96. (m-lp/m-cd) *(SEEP 19/+CD)* **BROCCOLI** [ ] [-]
–

— **SCOTT STEWART** – bass, vocals (ex-APPLEORCHARD) repl. BENNI

1997. (7"ep) **DA-A-A-ANCE / SHORT STRAW FATE. / (other 2 by International Jet Set)** [ ] [-]
(above issued on 'Snuffy Smile')
May 98. (lp/cd) *(SEEP 23/+CD)* **HOME** [ ] [-]
– Constance / Chestnut road / I am a robot / R.S.V.P. / Sleep tight / Home / The tens / Tongue tied / Short straw fate / Well wishing.

Speedowax | not iss.

Jul 98. (7"ep) *(ATOM 006)* **LODGED / THE TENS. / (others by Pinto)** [ ] [-]

Solent | not iss.

Sep 98. (7"tour) *(SNT 01)* **DEFENCE. / Starfish: NEW EDITOR** [ ] [-]

Crackle | not iss.

Nov 98. (7"ep) *(VYM 021)* **CHESTNUT ROAD EP** [ ] [-]
– Chestnut Road / Television / Crackle song / Split up.

Speedowax | not iss.

Aug 99. (7",7"green) *(ATOM 012)* **LAST ONE. /** [ ] [-]

– compilations, etc. –

May 99. (cd) *Rugger Bugger; (SEEP 28CD)* **THE SINGLES 1993-1998** [ ] [-]
– Neglect it / Weltschmertz / Broken / 10 journey trousers / Fido / All smiles / Pondlife / Relent / 100 days and counting / Lean / Sidledown / PR exorcise / Da-a-a-ance / Short straw fate / Jamaica Street / Untitled / Neglect it / Lodged / The tens / Defence / Chestnut road / Television / Crackle song / Split up.

BRONSKI BEAT

Formed: Hackney, London . . . 1984 by Glaswegians STEVE BRONSKI and JIMMY SOMERVILLE along with LARRY STEINBACHEK. Forming their own 'Forbidden Fruit' label in conjunction with 'London' records, the trio defined their agenda with the landmark 'SMALLTOWN BOY' single in Spring of that year. The track was a heartfelt portrayal of a young gay man's exclusion from mainstream society, SOMERVILLE's piercing yet soulful and impassioned falsetto together with a haunting synth-pop backing carrying it into the Top 3. It was also accompanied by a fairly candid video, the group making their gay activist stance clear from the start.

Follow-up track, 'WHY?', meanwhile, was directed straight at the prejudices of the moral majority in the form of an uptempo Hi-NRG workout while Top 5 debut album, 'AGE OF CONSENT' (1984) left no doubt as to what its title referred to; the record came complete with a comparative chart detailing the lower age limit of consenting homosexual sex in various European countries. Needless to say, Britain didn't rank too favourably. The album itself was a wildly promising debut, rooted in Euro-disco but expansive enough to include interpretations of classic material like George Gershwin's 'IT AIN'T NECESSARILY SO'. It also turned SOMERVILLE into an 80's gay icon, his staunch left-wing political stance only adding to his appeal while no doubt further pissing off his conservative (small or large c) detractors. A faithful Top 3 rendition of Donna Summer's 'I FEEL LOVE' (a duet with SOFT CELL's MARC ALMOND) in early '85 was the first in a string of SOMERVILLE disco covers, the rest emerging after his subsequent departure from BRONSKI BEAT.

While JIMMY went off to form The COMMUNARDS, STEVE and LARRY continued with a new lead singer, JOHN JON FOSTER, releasing remix set, 'HUNDREDS AND THOUSANDS' as a stop-gap prior to late 85's 'HIT THAT PERFECT BEAT' (subsequently used on the film, 'Letter To Brezhnev'). While the track hit the Top 3 and follow-up, 'C'MON, C'MON' made the Top 20, critics and fans were generally in agreement that the forgettable 'TRUTHDARE DOUBLEDARE' (1986) album was badly in need of JIMMY's talent and charisma. A third single, 'THIS HEART', failed to chart and BRONSKI BEAT faded from view. Not even a one-off 'Arista' collaboration with the legendary EARTHA KITT ('CHA CHA HEELS') could revive their fortunes and after a couple of independently released early 90's singles they finally disbanded.

JIMMY SOMERVILLE (b.22 May'61, Glasgow) – vocals / **STEVE BRONSKI** (b. STEVE FORREST, 7 Feb'60, Glasgow) – synthesizer, piano / **LARRY STEINBACHEK** (b. 6 May'60, London) – synthesizer, keyboards

London | M.C.A.

May 84. (7"/7"sha-pic-d) *(BIT E/PD 1) <52494>* **SMALLTOWN BOY. / MEMORIES** [3] [48] Dec84
(12"+=) *(BITEX 1)* – Infatuation.
Sep 84. (7"/12") *(BITE/+X 2)* **WHY? / CADILLAC CAR** [6] [ ]
Oct 84. (lp/c)(cd) *(BIT LP/MC 1)(820171-2) <5538>* **THE AGE OF CONSENT** [4] [36] Jan85
– Why? / It ain't necessarily so / Screaming / No more war / Love and money / Smalltown boy / Heatwave / Junk / Need a man blues / I feel love – Johnny remember me. *(cd+=)* – (12"mixes of first 2 singles).
Nov 84. (7") *(BITE 3)* **IT AIN'T NECESSARILY SO. / CLOSE TO THE EDGE** [16] [ ]
(12"+=) *(BITEX 3)* – Red dance.
Apr 85. (7"; as BRONSKI BEAT & MARC ALMOND) *(BITE 4)* **I FEEL LOVE (Medley) – I FEEL LOVE / LOVE TO LOVE YOU BABY / JOHNNY REMEMBER ME. / PUIT D'AMOUR** [3] [ ]
(12+=/10"+=) *(BITE X/T 4)* – ('A'instrumental).
(12"+=) – The potato fields / Signs (and wonders).

— (May'85) **JOHN JON FOSTER** (b. Newcastle) – vocals; repl. SOMERVILLE who formed the COMMUNARDS before going solo in 1989

Sep 85. (m-lp/m-c)(m-cd) *(BIT LP/MC 2)(820291-2)* **HUNDREDS AND THOUSANDS** (remixes) [24] [ ]
– Heatwave (remix) / Why (remix) / Run from love / Hard rain / Smalltown boy (remix) / Junk / Infatuation – Memories / Close to the edge / I feel love – Love to love you baby – Johnny remember me / Cadillac car. *(re-iss. cd+c May93 on 'Spectrum')*
Nov 85. (7"/12") *(BITE/+X 6)* **HIT THAT PERFECT BEAT. / I GAVE YOU EVERYTHING** [3] [ ]
Mar 86. (7") *(BITE 7)* **C'MON, C'MON. / SOMETHING SPECIAL** [20] [-]
(12"+=) *(BITEX 7)* – Drum majors.
May 86. (lp/c)(cd) *(BIT LP/MC 3)(828010-2) <5752>* **TRUTHDARE DOUBLEDARE** [18] [ ] Jul86
– Hit that perfect beat / Truthdare doubledare / C'mon, c'mon / Punishment for love / We know how it feels / This heart / Do it / Dr. John / In my dreams. *(cd+=)* – What are you going to do about it? / I gave you everything. *(c++=)* – C'mon, c'mon (12"remix) / Hit that perfect beat (12"remix).
Aug 86. (7"/12") *(BITE 8/+X)* **THIS HEART. / WHAT ARE YOU GOING TO DO ABOUT IT?** [ ] [-]

— (Oct'88) **JONATHAN HELLYER** – vocals; repl. JOHN who left 1986

Arista | Arista

Jun 89. (7"; as EARTHA KITT & BRONSKI BEAT) *(112.331)* **CHA CHA HEELS. / MY DISCARDED MEN** [ ] [ ]
(12"+=/cd-s+=) *(612/662 331)* – ('A'version).

Zed Beat | not iss.

Nov 90. (7") **I'M GONNA RUN AWAY FROM YOU. / SWEET THING** [ ] [-]
(12"+=/cd-s+=) – ('A'extended).
Feb 91. (7"/c-s) **ONE MORE CHANCE. / BETTER TIMES** [ ] [-]
(12"+=) – I'm gonna run away from you.
(cd-s++=) – ('A'version).

— STEVE BRONSKI and his chums were no more; for more BB see Jimmy SOMERVILLE's solo career

– compilations, etc. –

Dec 00. (cd-s) *Golden Dance Classics; (GDC 21518)* **SMALLTOWN BOY** ☐ -

— in Sep'01, BRONSKI BEAT tracks were featured on the UK Top 30 album, 'THE VERY BEST OF JIMMY SOMERVILLE & BRONSKI BEAT / COMMUNARDS'

Dec 01. (cd) *ZYX; (ZYX 20340-2)* **RAINBOW NATION** ☐ -

Lorna BROOKS

Born: 1961, Glasgow. Discovered late on in her singing career (the mid-90's, to be exact!), LORNA soon found work opening for the likes of SHAWN COLVIN, MARTIN STEPHENSON and LOUDON WAINWRIGHT III. Tipped for great things in the year 2000, the raw and soulful vocalist notched up a New Orleans 'Pride' appearance and delivered her debut album, 'KOWTOW' that year; Chinese for backing down.

BROTHER CANE (see under ⇒ Hook records)

Scott BROWN (see under ⇒ Q-TEX)

BUBBLECRAFT (see under ⇒ Mint records)

BUBBLE UP (see under ⇒ Bellboy records)

David BYRNE

Born: 14 May'52, Dumbarton. Relocating to Baltimore via Canada while still a very young child (two to be exact), BYRNE grew up as an American citizen. After dropping out of a design course in Rhode Island, the teenage BYRNE concentrated on music, initially working with accordionist MARK KEHOE (calling themselves BIZADI) before hooking up with CHRIS FRANTZ and TINA WEYMOUTH in an early incarnation of TALKING HEADS.

Integral to the original NY New Wave/Punk scene, the band began making a name for themselves at the infamous CBGB's venue alongside the likes of the RAMONES, BLONDIE and TELEVISION. Featuring classic tracks such as 'PSYCHO KILLER', 'PULLED UP' and 'NEW FEELING', their debut album, 'TALKING HEADS '77', fulfilled their early promise and paved the way for a highly succesful career both artistically and commercially. As well as being the wayward visionary behind the band's left-field appeal, BYRNE's creative energies spilled over into a series of side projects, beginning with the early 80's BRIAN ENO collaboration, 'MY LIFE IN THE BUSH OF GHOSTS'. His talents even extended into the world of stage/theatre, completing a score for the production, 'The Catherine Wheel' (1981) and releasing 'MUSIC FOR THE KNEE PLAYS' (1985), a tie-in project for another stage play. BYRNE also lent his creative talents to contemporaries such as The B-52'S and the FUN BOY THREE before his interest in all things musically ethnic took hold in the mid-80's.

Following a one-off collaboration with RYUICHI SAKAMOTO (on the movie, 'The Last Emperor'), BYRNE put TALKING HEADS on the backburner as he travelled to Brazil and began his long-standing love affair with Latin-American music. The subsequent founding of his own label, 'Luaka Bop', provided the musical chameleon with an outlet for both his own solo releases (beginning with 1989's 'REI MOMO') and musical exotica from around the globe. Among the latter, the first volume of 'Beleza Tropical' deserves special mention as possibly one of the finest Brazilian compilations ever released. After years of speculation, TALKING HEADS finally split in 1991, BYRNE subsequently delivering two contrasting solo projects (the instrumental 'THE FOREST' and the more conventionally song orientated 'UH-OH') in rapid succession.

A brief return to his musical roots with 1994's 'DAVID BYRNE' was followed by yet more arty side projects including a book of his own highly acclaimed photography. Three years later, the man who once donned the baggiest suit in Rock/Pop released his solo set, 'FEELINGS' (1997), an album that was pretty weak in comparison to his later effort 'LOOK INTO THE EYEBALL', which took him four years to write and produce. The set was a collaboration with legendary 'Philly' Soul producer THOM BELL, whose string and horn arrangements helped the album glide into a genre of its own. BYRNE's vocals were still staccato and as sharp as a tack ('THE GREAT INTOXICATION' is a prime example), but the latin rhythms, chilled-out trip-hop beats and floating orchestral accompaniment were the strangest and least obvious backing tracks for his paranoid, edgy larynx. BYRNE surprised even more of his fanbase when he featured on X-PRESS 2's UK Top 10 transluscent, underground dance anthem 'LAZY'. Very lazy indeed, the song soon wormed its way into the minds of the listener who couldn't resist the "I'm wicked and I'm lazzzzy" chorus. If the dance song 'Going Back To My Roots' (by ODYSSEY, incidentally) was ever more poignant, DAVID returned to his hometown of Dumbarton in August 2002, this time to write a score – with the aid BELLE & SEBASTIAN, MOGWAI and INTERNATIONAL AIRPORT – to the soundtrack of 'Young Adam' (which will star another Scot, Ewan McGregor).

DAVID BYRNE – vocals, instruments, etc

Sire Sire

Dec 81. (7") *(SIR 4054)* **BIG BLUE PLYMOUTH (EYES WIDE OPEN). / CLOUD CHAMBER** ☐ -
(12") *(SIR 4054T)* – ('A'side) / Leg bells / Light bath.

Jan 82. (lp/c) *(SRK/SRC 3645) <3645>* **SONGS FROM 'THE CATHERINE WHEEL' (Stage score)** ☐ ☐ Dec81
– His wife refused / Two soldiers / The red house / My big hands (fall through the cracks) / Big business / Eggs in a briar patch / Poison / Cloud chamber / What a day that was / Big blue Plymouth (eyes wide open). *<US d-lp+=)* – Ade / Walking / Under the mountain / Dinosaur / Wheezing / Black flag / Combat / Leg bells / The blue flame / Danse beast / Five golden sections. *(cd-iss. Jan93; 7599 27418-2)*

Feb 82. (12"ep) *<50034>* **THREE BIG SONGS** - ☐
– Big business (remix) / My big hands (fall through the cracks) / Big blue Plymouth (eyes wide open).

E.M.I. ECM

Sep 85. (lp/c) *(EJ 240381-1/-4) <ECM 25022>* **MUSIC FOR THE KNEE PLAYS** ☐ ☐ May 85
– Tree (today is an important occasion) / In the upper room / The sound of business / Social studies / (The gift of sound) Where the sun never goes down / Theadora is

dozing / Admiral Perry / I bid you goodnight / I've tried / Winter / Jungle book / In the future.

— BYRNE recorded a collaboration set with RYUICHI SAKAMOTO on film 'THE LAST EMPEROR'.

— BYRNE (below) now used a plethora of Brazilian musicians, after compiling various artists sets 'BELEZA TROPICAL', 'O SAMBA', etc.

Luaka Bop-Sire / Luaka Bop

Oct 89. (lp/c)(cd) *(WX 319/+C)(K 925990-2) <25990>* **REI MOMO** 52 71
– Independence day / Make believe mambo / The call of the wild / Dirty old town / The rose tattoo / The dream police / Don't want to be part of your world / Marching through the wilderness / Lie to me / Women vs. men / Carnival eyes / I know sometimes a man is wrong.
Dec 89. (7"/ext.12") **MAKE BELIEVE MAMBO. / LIE TO ME**
Jun 91. (cd) *(7599 26584-2)* **THE FOREST (instrumental)**
– Ur / Kish / Dura Europus / Nineveh / Ava / Machu picchu / Teotihuaean / Asuka.
Aug 91. (m-cd) *<40177>* **FORESTRY** -
– Ava (nu wage remix) / Nineveh (industrial mix) / Ava (less space dance mix edit) / Ava (space dance mix) / Machu picchu (album version).
Mar 92. (cd)(lp/c) *(7599 26799-2)(WX 464/+C) <26799>* **UH-OH** 26
– Now I'm your mom / Girls on my mind / Something ain't right / She's mad / Hanging upside down / Twistin' in the wind / A walk in the dark / The cowboy mambo (hey lookit me now) / Tiny town / Somebody. *(re-iss. Feb95 cd/c)*
Apr 92. (7"/c-s) **GIRLS ON MY MIND. / MONKEY MAN**
(12"+=/cd-s+=) – Cantode oxum.
May 92. (7"/c-s) **HANGING UPSIDE DOWN. / TINY TOWN**
(cd-s) – ('A'side) / Dirty old town (live) / (Nothing but) Flowers (live) / Girls on my mind (live).
(cd-s) – ('A'side) / Something ain't right (live) / Who we're thinking of (live) / Rockin' in the free world (live).
Jul 92. (7"/c-s) *(W 0199/+C)* **SHE'S MAD. / SOMEBODY**
(12") *(W 0199T)* – ('A'side) / Butt naked (live) / Greenback dollar (live).
(cd-s++=) *(W 0199CD)* – Now I'm your man (live).

— with **PAUL SOCOLOW** – bass, vocals / **TODD TURKISHER** – drum, percussion / **VALERIE NARANJO** – percussion, tambourine (live: MAURO REFOSCO – percussion) / **BILL WARE** – marimba / **ARTO LINDSAY** – guitar / **JOHN MEDESKI** – organ / **BASHIRI JOHNSON** – congas, bongos / **BEBEL GILBERTO** – vocals

May 94. (cd/c) *(9362 45558-2/-4) <45558>* **DAVID BYRNE** 44
– A long time ago / Angels / Crash / A self-made man / Back in the box / Sad song / Nothing at all / My love is you / Lillies of the valley / You & eye / Strange ritual / Buck naked.
Jun 94. (7"/c-s) *(W 0253/+C)* **ANGELS. / PRINCESS** -
(12"+=/cd-s+=) *(W 0253 T/CD)* – Ready for this world.
Sep 94. (c-s/cd-s) *(W 0263 C/CD)* **BACK IN THE BOX / GYPSY WOMAN (live) / GIRLS ON MY MIND (live)** -
(US cd-ep) *<41766>* – (first 2 tracks) / Back in the box (mixes) / A woman's secret / Cool water (live).
May 97. (cd/c) *<(9362 46605-2/-4)>* **FEELINGS**
– Fuzzy freaky / Miss America / A soft seduction / Dance on vaseline / The gates of Paradise / Amnesia / You don't know me / Daddy go down / Finite = alright / Wicked little doll / Burnt by the sun / The civil wars / They are in love.
Jun 97. (cd-s) *(W 0401CD)* **MISS AMERICA (clean / album / I love America)** -
Jan 99. (cd) *<2085>* **THE VISIBLE MAN** (remixes) -
Oct 00. (m-cd) **IN SPITE OF WISHING AND WANTING** (soundtrack) -
– Horses / Sleeping up / Speech / Said & the ants / Fear / Danceonvaselinesu – Perextendedremix / Idiot music.

Virgin America / Virgin America

May 01. (cd) *(CDVUS 189) <50924>* **LOOK INTO THE EYEBALL** 58
– UB Jesus / Revolution / Great intoxication / Like humans do / Broken things / Accident / Desconocido soy / Neighbourhood / Smile / Moment of conception / Walk on water / Everyone's in love with you.
Sep 01. (cd-s) *(897529)* **LIKE HUMANS DO** -

C

CAFE JACQUES

Formed: London . . . mid-70's by fellow ex-pat Glaswegians GORDON HASTIE (ex-IMAGES), drummer MIKE OGLETREE, and a few others more or less from south of the border. Their cool, laid back approach helped them win a contract with 'Epic' records in '77, although by 1979 and two mediocre sets, 'ROUND THE BACK' and ' . . .INTERNATIONAL', all came to an abrupt end. However, OGLETREE did resurface more famously with stadium fillers, SIMPLE MINDS.

CHRISTOPHER THOMPSON – vocals, guitar / **PETER VEITCH** – keyboards / **GEOFFREY RICHARDSON** – guitar, flute / **COLIN NELSON** – bass / **MIKE OGLETREE** – drums / also augmented by **JOHN G. PERRY** – bass / **PHIL COLLINS** – percussion (of GENESIS)

Epic / Epic

Nov 77. (lp) *(EPC 82315) <35294>* **ROUND THE BACK**
– Meaningless / Ain't no love in the sands of Singapore / Farewell, my lovely / Eberehtel / Dark eyed Johnny / Sandra's a phonie / None of your business / Crime passionelle / Lifeline.
Feb 79. (lp) *(EPC 83042) <35697>* **CAFE JACQUES INTERNATIONAL**
– Boulevard of broken dreams / How easy / Waiting / Station of dreams / Chanting and raving / Can't stand still / Man in the meadow / Knife edge / This way up: the medley.

— disbanded soon after above; OGLETREE later joined SIMPLE MINDS

CAGE (see ⇒ Section 9: the 90s)

CAMERA OBSCURA

Formed: Glasgow . . . Spring '96 by TRACYANNE and fellow student JOHN, GAVIN and DAVID were found around various venues and shops although they still hadn't found a drummer. Radio station 'Beat Patrol' was the first to take note of this SIMON & GARFUNKEL-esque folk trio, 'PARK AND RIDE' and 'PORCELAIN' were played ensuring interest from local indie imprint, 'Andmoresound'.

In March '98, 'PARK AND RIDE' became their debut single, airplay this time via Steve Lamacq and John Peel. However, due to nerves and the lack of a drummer, CAMERA OBSCURA still hadn't played a worthy gig; RICHARD COLBURN of BELLE & SEBASTIAN had helped them out during an earlier outing. Towards the end of the year, a support slot to ASTRID remedied their tentative teething problems and a second single, 'YOUR SOUND', was released to healthy response. Subsequently opening for SNOW PATROL and LUNA, they duly initiated their own 'Park & Ride' monthly club at the 13th Note cafe. However, little was seen in the way of new releases (bar a part-compilation, 'RARE UK BIRD' on Japanese import!), until that is, US-based label 'Troubleman Unlimited' delivered their debut LP proper, 'TO CHANGE THE SHAPE OF AN ENVELOPE' (2000); they had now found drummer LEE THOMPSON, while DAVID went off to pursue his own dream.

TRACYANNE – vocals / **JOHN** – vocals, guitar / **GAVIN** – vocals, guitar / **DAVID** – bass

Andmoresound / not iss.

Mar 98. (7") *(AND 09 45)* **PARK AND RIDE. / SWIMMING POOL** -
Dec 98. (7"ep/cd-s) *(AND 11 45/CDS)* **YOUR SOUND. / AUTUMN TIDES / ANNAWALTZERPOSE** -

Quattro / not iss.

Dec 99. (m-cd) *(quattro-014)* **RARE UK BIRD** - - Japan
– Park and ride / Swimming pool / Your sound / Autumn tides / Annawaltzerpose / Eastwood / Railway station / Eighties fan.

— **LEE THOMPSON** – drums; repl. DAVID

Troubleman Unlimited / Troubleman Unlimited

Jul 00. (lp) *(<TMU 047>)* **TO CHANGE THE SHAPE OF AN ENVELOPE** May00
– Trigger system / Cinematheque / Theory on sex as an art form / Sarasota / Twenty five diamonds / Aeronautical / Sound / Song de la luna.

Andmoresound / not iss.

Jun 01. (7"/cd-s) *(and 16 45/cds)* **EIGHTIES FAN. / SHINE LIKE A NEW PIN / LET'S GO BOWLING** -
Nov 01. (lp/cd) *(and 17 33/cd)* **BIGGEST BLUEST HI FI** -
– Happy new year / Eighties fan / Houseboat / Pen and notebook / Swimming pool / Anti western / I don't do crowds / The sun on his back / Double feature / Arrangements of shapes and space.

CANDY STORE PROPHETS (see ⇒ Section 9: the 90s)

CANYON (see under ⇒ Bellboy records)

CAPTAIN AMERICA (see under ⇒ VASELINES)

CAPTAIN SHIFTY (see under ⇒ APPLES)

CAPTAIN STEPHANIE / PETER PERCEPT (see under ⇒ Mouthmoth records)

Andy CARRICK (see under ⇒ Glasgow Underground records)

CARTOONS (see ⇒ Section 9: wee post-punk groups)

CATERAN

Formed: Inverness . . . mid-80's by vocalist SANDY MacPHERSON, CAMERON FRASER, MURDO MacLEOD, KAI DAVIDSON and ANDY MILNE. Influenced by HUSKER DU and the DEAD KENNEDYS (SANDY was indeed a self-styled clone of GRANT HART and JELLO BIAFRA) backed by cod-Ska pop rhythm, they were one of the many Caledonian outfits to sign for a 'Fast Forward' cartel (i.e. 'D.D.T.'). With production credits going to Pete Haigh, The CATERAN delivered their first vinyl offering in 1986, the mini-set 'LITTLE CIRCLES', a record promoted by several gigs alongside the young PROCLAIMERS. Further album releases included 1988's 'BITE DEEPER', 1989's 'ACHE', while a support slot to GRANT HART (having recently split from HUSKER DU) kept up their Punky profile. When Grunge came on to the music scene in the early 90's, The CATERAN were all at sea, although MURDO (and initially KAI) plus a new gang of cohorts, JOYRIDERS, tried once again with the 'KING OF GASOLINE' EP in 1992. • **Covered:** TIRED OF WAITING FOR YOU (Kinks).

SANDY MacPHERSON – vocals / **CAMERON FRASER** – guitar / **MURDO MacLEOD** – guitar / **KAI DAVIDSON** – bass / **ANDY MILNE** – drums

D.D.T. | not iss.

Jul 86. (m-lp) *(DISPLP 005)* **LITTLE CIRCLES** ☐ -
– Belting out the truth / Who's clever now / Gracious smile / Little circles / Its your mistake, not mine / Cold comfort / Desperate planning time / Brand new refugee.

Jan 87. (7") *(DISP 006)* **LAST BIG LIE. / DIFFICULT DAYS** ☐ -

Vinyl Solution | not iss.

Mar 88. (lp) *(SOL 9)* **BITE DEEPER** ☐ -
– Don't like what I do / She doesn't say much / A bit put out / Small dark hand / Surplus to need / Mirror / Love scars / This is what becomes of the broken . . . / Knowing what I am / Strung along.

Imaginary | not iss.

Dec 88. (7"ep) *(MIRAGE 666)* **THE BLACK ALBUM EP** ☐ -
– Teach yourself / Tired of waiting for you.

What Goes On | not iss.

May 89. (lp) *(GOESON 30)* **ACHE** ☐ -
– Ache / Kitten / Early old / Tina / Hateable / Cage / Love or confusion / Someone else's sun / Traffic drone / Storm 7.

Mar 90. (7") **DIE TOMORROW. / VIRGIL'S WAY** ☐ -

— split early '91 . . .

JOYRIDERS

— **MURDO** now lead vocals, guitar / **DUNSY** (DUNSMORE) – guitar, vocals / **CRAIG SMITH** – bass; repl. DAVIDSON / **RICK HELLER** – drums

Avalanche | not iss.

1992. (12"ep) *(AVA 002)* **KING OF GASOLINE EP** ☐ -
– King of gasoline / Overboard / Here it comes / Moving on.

Incredible Shrinking | not iss.

1995. (cd-s) *(SHRINK 002)* **DON'T ASK ME / BEST FRIEND / HOME** ☐ -

— after they split, DUNSY would join Human Condition band, CHICKWEED

CATERPILLAR WORKERS (see ⇒ Section 9: the 90s)

CHAIN GANG (see under ⇒ Rational records; Supreme Int. records)

CHASAR (see under ⇒ Scotland's wee metal scene)

CHASER (see under ⇒ Soma records)

CHEEKY MONKEY

Formed: Glasgow . . . 1997 by FRANCIS MACDONALD, a seasoned campaigner via BMX BANDITS, The PASTELS, TEENAGE FANCLUB, EUGENIUS and more recently the RADIO SWEETHEARTS and SPEEDBOAT. However, one part of this unusual outfit was from across the Atlantic, New York to be exact. MICHAEL SHELLEY had just issued his POPular solo set, 'Half Empty' (1997) and was corresponding through the internet with FRANCIS. Unique – well at least for stony broke indie merchants! – the pair wrote several songs over the phone and when that got too pricy a tape was sent by MICHAEL. Making a hectic recording schedule by the skin of their teeth, but with MICHAEL still in America for the time being, FRANCIS finally delivered their efforts via his own 'Shoeshine' records. A single, 'THAT KIND OF GIRL', was almost immediately pursued by their hastily-recorded warts-n-all pop set, 'FOUR ARMS TO HOLD YOU' (1998); if you're missing BIG STAR, The BEACH BOYS and The HOLLIES, this might be for you. • **Covered:** GERRY CHEEVERS (Chixdiggit) / MONKEY MAN (Bo Diddley).

FRANCIS MACDONALD – drums, instruments, vocals (ex-see above) / **MICHAEL SHELLEY** – vocals, instruments

Shoeshine | Big Deal

Feb 98. (7") *(SHOE 010)* **THAT KIND OF GIRL. / FREE AGAIN** ☐ -

Mar 98. (cd) *(SHOECD 002)* <9049> **FOUR ARMS TO HOLD YOU** ☐ ☐ Jan98
– That kind of girl / Monkey man / Big dumb boy / Robert Lloyd / Down / Uddingston church gun terror / I wanna live with you / Gerry Cheevers / Chasin' each other around the room / All I can do is cry / Let it flow / You don't want me anymore. *(lp-iss.Jul98; SHOELP 002)*

— FRANCIS re-joined TEENAGE FANCLUB late in 2000

CHEETAHS (see under ⇒ Zoom records)

CHEMICAL PILOT (see under ⇒ McGEE, Alan)

CHERRYFIRE ASHES (see under ⇒ Starshaped records)

CHEWY RACCOON (see under ⇒ PEARLFISHERS)

CHI

Formed: Edinburgh . . . mid-90's as CHICANE by punk/pop trio of JON FU, IAN JEFFRIES, DAVEY PINNINGTON and MICHAEL BRANAGH. CHICANE were one of the fresh bunch of faces on Edinburgh's 'Human Condition' roster (along with LYD, SAWYER and METH O.D.). However, after only a couple of 45's, 'JUST NOT SORRY' and 'DRIVE' (plus one split with Irish band, GRISWOLD), they were forced to abandon/shorten the CHICANE moniker due to a dance/rave act plying their trade abroad. Benefitting slightly from knowing RODDY WOOMBLE of IDLEWILD (from his 'Human Condition' days), this HUSKER DU (or FU)-meets-CHINA DRUM sort of guitar outfit were, let's say, a little late in the Punk Rock stakes. An album, 'SINCERITY IS A BOY CALLED DEL' (1998), did little to unscramble their youthful NWOTNW renaissance.
• **Note:** Watch out for others bands with the CHICANE and CHI moniker.

CHICANE

DAVEY PINNINGTON – guitar, vocals / **IAN JEFFRIES** – guitar, vocals / **JON FU** – bass, vocals / **MICHAEL BRANAGH** – drums, vocals

Human Condition | not iss.

May 96. (7"m) *(HC 0012)* **JUST NOT SORRY. / TEN GLASS / SOMEWHERE** ☐ -

Nov 96. (7"m) *(HC 0014)* **DRIVE. / +2** ☐ -

Simpleton | not iss.

May 97. (7") *(FEEK 001)* **BUTTERCUP. / Haywire (by GRISWOLD)** ☐ -

CHI

JON FU + IAN 'FLAMEBOY' (JEFFRIES) – guitar / + a drummer/singer (unknown)

Simpleton | not iss.

Mar 98. (m-cd) *(FEEK 002)* **SINCERITY IS A BOY CALLED DEL** ☐ -
– Afterburners / Set it up / Stand fast / Pull it! / Drive / Effer-v.

CHICANE (see under ⇒ CHI)

CHICKWEED (see under ⇒ Human Condition records)

CHIMES

Formed: Edinburgh . . . 1986 as the BEAT FREAKS by rhythm men MIKE PEDAN and JAMES LOCKE, the latter also moonlighted with minor hitmakers, HEARTBEAT, and became a seasoned session man with the likes of The INDIAN GIVERS, HIPSWAY and The BATHERS.

After meeting while backing former PARLIAMENT keyboard guru BERNIE WORRELL, the BEAT FREAKS released their one and only effort in 1986 for 'Supreme Int.', entitled 'THE NATIONAL ANTHEM', before they hooked up with vocalist PAULINE HENRY through a telephone audition. Signing with 'C.B.S.', The CHIMES enlisted SOUL II SOUL's JAZZIE B as producer for their summer '89 debut single, '1-2-3'. A minor hit – as was its follow-up, 'HEAVEN' – The CHIMES never really struck a chord with the funky populace until 1990's soulful BONO-approved cover of U2's 'I STILL HAVEN'T FOUND WHAT I'M LOOKING FOR'. A huge Top 10 hit, the song's success paved the way for a relatively successful Top 20 eponymous debut album. A further trio of singles failed to consolidate their raised profile although 'HEAVEN' did make the Top 30. HENRY subsequently departed for a solo career halfway through sessions for a second album, effectively signalling the end of the band and a return to session work for the lads.

• **Note:** Not to be confused with the group who issued 'ONCE IN A WHILE' in 1987 for their own 'Chimes' label and for that matter the early 60's US outfit.

BEAT FREAKS

MIKE PEDAN – bass / **JAMES LOCKE** – drums, keyboards

Supreme Int. / not iss.

Jun 86. (12") *(EDITION86 11)* **THE NATIONAL ANTHEM. / GOVERNMENT DON'T CARE (dub)** [ ] [-]

CHIMES

— added **PAULINE HENRY** (b. England) – vocals

C.B.S. / Columbia

Aug 89. (7"/c-s) *(655166-7/-4)* *<73087>* **1-2-3. / UNDERESTIMATE** [60] [86] Jan90
(cd-s+=) *(655166-2)* – ('A'-UK raw mix) / ('B'extended).
(12"+=) *(655166-6)* – ('A'-Bodyrock mix).
(12") *(655166-8)* – ('A'side) / ('A'mixes; Silent club dub / Gospel / Philly).

Nov 89. (7"/c-s) *(655432-7/-4)* **HEAVEN. / SO MUCH LOVE (demo)** [66] [ ]
(12"/cd-s) *(655432-8/-2)* – ('A'mixes) / ('A'-Attack vocal club mix).
(12") *(655432-6)* – ('A'side) / ('A'dub) / ('A'&'B'mixes).

Apr 90. (7") *(655851-7)* **STRONGER TOGETHER. / UNDERESTIMATE** [ ] [-]
(12"+=) *(655851-6)* – ('A'mixes).

May 90. (7"/c-s) *(CHIM/+M 1)* **I STILL HAVEN'T FOUND WHAT I'M LOOKING FOR. / NO NEED TO PRETEND** [6] [ ]
(12"+=/s12"+=) *(CHIM T/QT 1)* – ('A'-Manasseh mix) / ('A'-Boom dub mix).
(cd-s+=) *(CHIMC 1)* – ('A'-Street mix).

Jun 90. (cd/c/lp) *(466481-2/-4/-1)* *<C/CK 46008>* **THE CHIMES** [17] [ ] May90
– Love so tender / Heaven / True love / 1-2-3 / Underestimate / Love comes to mind / Don't make me wait / Stronger together / I still haven't found what I'm looking for / Stay. *(cd+=)* – I still haven't found what I'm looking for (Street mix) / Heaven (Physical mix). *(cd re-iss. Oct92 +=; same)*

Jul 90. (7"/c-s) *(CHIM/+M 2)* **TRUE LOVE. /** [48] [ ]
(12"+=) *(CHIMT 2)* –
(cd-s+=) *(CHIMC 2)* –

Sep 90. (7"/c-s) *(CHIM/+M 3)* **HEAVEN. / ('A'-Saxual Healing mix)** [24] [ ]
(12"+=/cd-s+=) *(CHIM T/C 3)* – ('A'-intense mix) / ('A'-Summer breeze mix).

Nov 90. (7"/c-s) *(CHIM/+M 4)* **LOVE COMES TO MIND. /** [49] [ ]
(12"+=) *(CHIMT 4)* –
(cd-s+=) *(CHIMC 4)* –

— split up when PAULINE went solo and other concentrated on studio work for others including PAUL HAIG

CHOU PAHROT

Formed: Glasgow . . . 1978 by M. ZARB, EGGY BEARD, MAMA VOOT and THE AMPHIBIAN, the North's answer to The POP GROUP (CAPTAIN BEEFHEART also springs to mind!). Taking a wide berth from conventional punk/New Wave (unusual at the time for a Caledonian group), CHOU PAHROT became something of a catch around the West Coast of Scotland, their 'Oor Wullie'-type sense of fun and frolics going down a proverbial storm for anyone lucky enough to witness them live. However, only a few releases surfaced – the single, 'BUZGO TRAM CHORUS' and the privately pressed album, 'LIVE' (1979) – before they were free soles once more.

MAMA VOOT – guitar, vocals, saxophones / **M. ZARB** – bass, guitar, vocals / **EGGY BEARD** – violin / **THE AMPHIBIAN** – drums

Klub / not iss.

Feb 79. (7"ep) *(KEP 101)* **BUZGO TRAM CHORUS. / GWIZGWEELA GWAMPHNOO / LEMONS** [ ] [-]

Nov 79. (lp) *(KLP 19)* **LIVE** [ ] [-]
– Pantomine schrub / Syphionic diplivits / The wee thing / The random shoggy / Itchy face / Lemons / Mary submarine / Day o' the mug / The yaw yaw song.

— continued to make do with some sporadic (quite literally) gigs

Chute records (see under ⇒ SPARE SNARE)

CICERO

Born: DAVID CICERO, c.1974, Livingston, West Lothian. Signed to BOY GEORGE's 'Spaghetti' imprint in the early 90's, the Scots-Italian boy wonder failed to make the grade with his debut single, 'HEAVEN MUST HAVE SENT YOU BACK TO ME'. However, amid a fanfare of hype, the PET SHOP BOYS-sponsored sophomore single, 'LOVE IS EVERYWHERE', launched the Livvy lad into the UK Top 20. As well as being splashed all over the Scottish media, CICERO enjoyed a brief fling with the London music industry, appearing on Top Of The Pops and working his Latin charm on the Smash Hits readership. Despite the help of NEIL TENNANT and CHRIS LOWE, the boy's Hi N-R-G pop/dance failed to keep the punters' attention after the relatively poor performance of 'THAT LOVING FEELING'. Unfortunately, the release of the accompanying album coincided with the swift end of CICERO's 15 minutes of fame. After an absence of four years, an older and wiser CICERO was to be found beavering away behind his keyboard once again on a couple of singles for local label, 'Clubscene'.

CICERO – vocals, keyboards / with programmer, etc

Spaghetti / Alex

Oct 91. (7") *(CIAO 1)* **HEAVEN MUST HAVE SENT YOU BACK TO ME. / PUKKA (elevation mix)** [ ] [-]
(12"+=/cd-s+=) *(CIAO X/CD 1)* – ('A'-Melt mix).

Jan 92. (7") *(CIAO 3)* **LOVE IS EVERYWHERE. / MIND GAP** [19] [ ]
(cd-s+=) *(CIAOCD 3)* – ('A'extended).

Apr 92. (7") *(CIAO 4)* **THAT LOVING FEELING. / SPLATT** [46] [ ]
(cd-s+=) *(CIAOCD 4)* – ('A'extended).

Apr 92. (cd/c/lp) *(513428-2/-4/-1)* **FUTURE BOY** [ ] [ ]
– That loving feeling / Heaven must have sent you back to me / My middle class life / Cloud 9 / Love is everywhere / Then / As time goes by / Sonic malfunction / The butcher of Bucharest / Future generations.

Jul 92. (7") *(CIAO 5)* *<UK 1640>* **HEAVEN MUST HAVE SENT YOU BACK TO ME. / PUKKA (elevation mix)** [70] [ ]
(ext; cd-s) *(CIAOCD 5)* – Jungilism.

Nov 92. (7") *(CIAO 7)* **LIVE FOR TODAY. / LIVE FOR TODAY (gospel)** [ ] [-]
(cd-s+=) *(CIAOCD 7)* – Street life / ('A'-club mix).

Clubscene / not iss.

Jun 96. (cd-s/12") *(D+/CSRT 061)* **DON'T WORRY (3 mixes; radio / 12" Tron / Bolder) / ORESIS (pt.1 & 2)** [ ] [-]

Academy Street / not iss.

Jun 97. (cd-s/12") *(D+/ACST 006)* **SUMMERTIME (3 mixes; radio / 12" / Spanish fly) / ORERSIS (pt.3 & 4)** [ ] [-]

— CICERO has been a little quiet over the past few years

CINdYTALK

Formed: London . . . 1982 as a studio outfit by vocalist, GORDON SHARP and guitarist, DAVID CLANCY, both fresh from young Edinburgh punk outfit, The FREEZE.

After only a few independently released singles (namely 'IN COLOUR' and 'CELEBRATION'), they broke up – with SHARP subsequently lending his services to '4 a.d.' outfits the COCTEAU TWINS and THIS MORTAL COIL. Around the same time (1984), he and CLANCY (alongside JOHN BYRNE and KINNISON) resurfaced with a brand new venture, CINdYTALK, a debut album, 'CAMOUFLAGE HEART', being poorly received by critics and public alike due to its impenetrable CLOCKDVA-esque experimentation. However,

SHARP did return to the studio after a three year absence, completing the much improved follow-up double-set, 'IN THIS WORLD' (1988). ALIK and DEBBIE WRIGHT had now taken the place of CLANCY and KINNISON, the new line-up contributing to a refined ambient atmospheric sound incorporating SHARP's distinctive harsh vocal incantations.

An album in 1991, 'THE WIND IS STRONG' was another marked progression, although this in turn was surpassed with the long awaited 1996 effort, 'WAPPINSCHAW'. The album was a return to his Scottish roots and featured readings by long-time SNP affiliated novelist, Alasdair Gray, while references were made to outsider heroes like Sitting Bull and Wolfe Tone among others. Of late, GORDON has become BAMBULE (which means "dance" or "riot"), a trip acidy combo who've released two limited edition 12" EP's.

• **Songwriters:** SHARP except traditional, 'HUSH'.
• **Trivia:** SHARP (along with ROBIN GUTHRIE, DAVID ROS, JAY AHERN + NADIA LANMAN) went under the moniker of MacBETH and contributed a cover of Mary Margaret O'Hara's 'HELP ME LIFT YOU UP' to the V/A comp, 'Volume 5'.

FREEZE

GORDON SHARP – vocals / **DAVID CLANCY** – guitar, vocals / **KEITH GRANT** – bass, vocals / **GRAEME RADIN** – drums

A1 | not iss.

Aug 79. (7"ep) *(A 11)* **IN COLOUR** ☐ [-]
– Paranoia / For J.P.S. (with love & loathing) / Psychodalek nightmares.

Apr 80. (7") *(A 11 S1)* **CELEBRATION. / CROSS-OVER** ☐ [-]

— **MIKE MORAN** – bass; repl. GRANT

— **NEIL BRAIDWOOD** – drums, keyboards; repl. RADIN

— split late in 1981. A few years later, SHARPE guested for 4ad conglomerate THIS MORTAL COIL. He provided vox for the track 'KANGAROO' (a cover taken from BIG STAR) on album 'It'll End In Tears'.

CINdYTALK

GORDON SHARP – vocals, piano / **DAVID CLANCY** – guitar / **JOHN BYRNE** – bass / **KINNISON** – drums

Midnight Music | not iss.

Sep 84. (lp) *(CHIME 00.065)* **CAMOUFLAGE HEART** ☐ [-]
– It's luxury / Instinct (backtosense) / Under glass / Memories of skin and snow / The spirit behind the circus dream / The ghost never smiles / A second breath / Everybody is Christ / Disintigrate . . . *(cd-iss. 1988; CHIME 006CD) (cd re-iss. Oct96 on 'Touch'; TOUCH 3CD)*

— **SHARP** with **BYRNE** – instruments / **ALIK WRIGHT** – instruments / **DEBBIE WRIGHT** – vocals, instruments

Mar 88. (d-lp/cd) *(CHIME 027/028CD)* **IN THIS WORLD** ☐ [-]
– In this world / Janey's love / Gift of a knife / Playtime / The room of delight / Touched / Circle of shit / My sun / The beginning of wisdom / No serenade / Sight after sight / Angels of ghosts / Through water / Cherish / Homeless / Still whisper / In this world. *(cd re-iss. Oct96 on 'Touch'; TOUCH 2CD)*

Jan 91. (lp/c/cd) *(CHIME 103/+CC/CD)* **THE WIND IS STRONG** ☐ [-]
– Landing / First sight / To the room / Waiting / Through flowers / Second sight / Through the forest / Arrival / Is there a room for hire / Choked I / Choked II / Dream ritual / Fuck you Mrs. Grimace / On snow moor / Angel wings.

Jan 94. (12"/cd-s) *(DONG 76/+CD)* **SECRETS & FALLING** ☐ [-]
– Song of changes / The moon above me / In sunshine / Empty hand.

— **SHARP** now with **PAUL MIDDLETON** – drums / **PAUL JONES** – guitar / **ANDREA BROWN** – bass / **MARK STEPHENSON** – samples, keyboards, electronics

Touched | not iss.

Oct 96. (7") *(FEEL 001)* **PRINCE OF LIES. / MUSTER** ☐ [-]

Oct 96. (lp/cd) *(TOUCH/+CD 1)* **WAPPINSCHAW** ☐ ☐
– A song of changes / Empty hand / Return to pain / Wheesht / Snow kisses / Secrets and falling / Disappear / Traum lose nacht / And now in sunshine / Prince of lies / Hush. *(hidden track+=)* – Muster.

BAMBULE

GORDON SHARP + SIMON CARMICHAEL (aka CUNNING)

Praxis | not iss.

1997. (d12"ep) *(Praxis 19)* **CUNNING MEETS BAMBULE** ☐ [-]
– Signal furies / Ascent. / Disco dum dum / Descent (alone) // Lockstep part 1 / Lockstep part 2. / Spin fracture / Ubu-ma

— **SHARP** with **RICHIE YOUNG, DALE LLOYD** (of LUCID) / **STUART ARENTZEN** (of LUCID) + **TYMOTHI LOVING** (of DELAYED SHOCK REACTION)

Nov 00. (12"ep; by BAMBULE & PHOTON) *(Praxis 29)* **VERTICAL INVASION / JOY IS THE AIM. / THIRDFORCE / TRIPPED WIRE** ☐ [-]

CINEMA

Formed: Glasgow . . . mid-90's by the initially mysterious DJ duo of GREGOR REID and CRAWFORD TAIT who met while working at the Acme Recorded Music for Film and Television. Experimenting with tape loops, synths and the proverbial kitchen sink, they pieced together (quite literally!) their debut 'Domino' Series 500 platter, 'MOMENTO MORI'; rhythmic and eerie beyond description (former workmate JOHN CARPENTER would be close!), the pair went on to complete further examples of industrial waste via further singles, 'RECORDED MUSIC LIBRARY' and the extended 7" EP! film soundtrack 'THEY NICKNAMED ME EVIL'; this was rumoured to have been unearthed in a skip outside their workplace. Following a mini-set, 'YOUR INTRODUCTORY RECORD' in 2000, CINEMA finally resurfaced in August 2002 with their debut album proper, 'BEFORE THE DARK'. Atmospheric and moody with jazzy hip-hop breakbeats in the shape of DJ SHADOW, this was like a discarded 70's soundtrack given the remix treatment – nice.

GREGOR REID + CRAWFORD TAIT – electronics, etc

Series 500 | not iss.

Aug 97. (12") *(SER 505)* **MOMENTO MORI. / THE MAKER (REMADE)** ☐ [-]

Domino | not iss.

Aug 98. (12"/cd-s) *(Rug 72 t/cd)* **CINEMA RECORDED MUSIC LIBRARY** ☐ [-]
– P. Beretta (parts 1 and 2) / Astro.

Apr 99. (7"ep) *(Rug 86)* **THEY NICKNAMED ME EVIL EP** ☐ [-]
– They nicknamed me evil / The beating / Pursuit of evil / Stalk the discotheque / Electro killer / Anything with a pulse / Music box / Tone death / Dialogue.

Oct 00. (m-cd/m-lp) *(Wig cd/lp 85)* **YOUR INTRODUCTORY RECORD** ☐ [-]
– Drive by / Getting away with it / Breaks / Russian roulette / Ichiban assassin / Scimitar.

— now credited as **CINEMA RECORDED MUSIC LIBRARY** on the sleeve

Aug 02. (cd/lp) *(Wig cd/lp 113)* **BEFORE THE DARK** ☐ [-]
– Before the dark / Pendulum / Reflections / Almost there / After dark / Lost / Coming up for air / Undercurrent / Headspin / Crash and burn / The dawn.

Sep 02. (7") *(Rug 146)* **BEFORE THE DARK. / LOST** ☐ [-]

Gary CLARK (see under ⇒ DANNY WILSON)

Tom CLELLAND (see under ⇒ Shoeshine records)

CLOSE LOBSTERS

Formed: Johnstone . . . 1985 by ANDY BURNETT, his brother BOB BURNETT, TOM DONNELLY, STUART McFADYEN and GRAHAM WILKINTON. These quirky but easy-going jingle-janglers got their break via the NME C86 tape (to which they contributed 'FIRESTATION TOWERS'), subsequently netting a deal with 'Fire' and releasing 'GOING TO HEAVEN TO SEE IF IT RAINS' as their debut single in Autumn '86. Support slots to the likes of the JESUS & MARY CHAIN helped raise their profile while a follow-up single, 'NEVER SEEN BEFORE', confirmed their indie credentials and paved the way for an endearingly titled debut album, 'FOXHEADS STALK THIS LAND' (1987). Vaguely akin to a Caledonian version of The WEDDING PRESENT (especially in vocal terms), The CLOSE LOBSTERS were also – along with DAVID GEDGE & Co. – beloved of the US college circuit and even undertook a spot of transatlantic touring to promote follow-up album, 'HEADACHE RHETORIC' (1989). The strain of such a venture proved too much, however and the band fell apart at the turn of the decade, uniting briefly in 1991 for live work only. WEDDING PRESENT subsequently covered their 'LET'S MAKE SOME PLANS' on a B-side. • **Covered:** HEY HEY MY MY (INTO THE BLACK) (Neil Young) / PAPER THIN HOTEL (Leonard Cohen).

ANDY BURNETT (b.11 Feb'65) – vocals / **TOM DONNELLY** (b.29 Aug'62) – guitar / **GRAHAM WILKINTON** (b.22 Aug'65) / **BOB BURNETT** (b.11 Sep'62) – bass / **STUART McFADYEN** (b.26 Sep'65, Paisley) – drums

Fire | not iss.

Oct 86. (7") *(BLAZE 15)* **GOING TO HEAVEN TO SEE IF IT RAINS. / BOYS AND GIRLS** ☐ [-]
(12"+=) *(BLAZE 15T)* – Heaven / Pathetik trivia.

Apr 87. (7") *(BLAZE 20)* **NEVER SEEN BEFORE. / PIMPS** ☐ [-]
(12"+=) *(BLAZE 20T)* – Firestation towers / Wide waterways.

— **PAUL BENNETT** – bass; repl. BOB

Oct 87. (lp) *(FIRE 9)* **FOXHEADS STALK THIS LAND** ☐ [-]
– Just too bloody stupid / Sewer pipe dream / I kiss the flower in bloom / Pathetique / A prophecy / In spite of these times / Foxheads / I take bribes / Pimps / Mother of

God. *(cd-iss. Mar88; FIRECD 9) (re-iss. Apr89 c/cd; D4/D2 73333) (cd re-iss. Apr02 on 'Fire'; SFIRE 030CD)*

Nov 87. (7") *(BLAZE 22)* **LET'S MAKE SOME PLANS. / IN SPITE OF THESE TIMES** ☐ -
(12"+=) *(BLAZE 22T)* – Get what they deserve.

Aug 88. (7") *(BLAZE 25)* **WHAT IS THERE TO SMILE ABOUT? / FROM THIS DAY ON** ☐ -
(12"+=) *(BLAZE 25T)* – Loopholes / The skyscrapers of St. Mirin.
(cd-s++=) *(BLAZE 25CD)* – Violently pretty face.

Mar 89. (7") *(BLAZE 34)* **NATURE THING. / NEVER SEEN BEFORE (live)** ☐ -
(12"+=/cd-s+=) *(BLAZE 34 T/CD)* – Hey hey my my (into the black) / Paper thin hotel.

Mar 89. (lp/c/cd) *(FIRE LP/MC/CD 17)* **HEADACHE RHETORIC** ☐ -
– Lovely little swan / Gunpowderkeg / Nature thing / My days are numbered / Gutache / Got apprehension / Words on power / Skyscrapers / Knee trembler. *(c+=/cd+=)* – FOXHEADS STALK THIS LAND

Caff / not iss.

Dec 89. (ltd-7") *(CAFF 4)* **JUST TOO BLOODY STUPID. / ALL THE LITTLE BOYS AND GIRLS I KNEW** ☐ -

— split for two years, although a return to the live circuit was brief

- compilations, etc. -

Apr 88. (12"ep) *Night Tracks; (SFNT 008)* **THE JANICE LONG SESSIONS** (29.6.86) ☐ -
– Nothing really matters / Going to Heaven to see if it rains / Pathetic trivia / Never seen before. *(c-ep-iss.1993 on 'Dutch East India')*

CLOUDS

Formed: Glasgow . . . 1986 by brothers JOHN and BILL CHARNLEY, into acoustic psychedelia and intially boosted by some BOY HAIRDRESSERS (soon to become TEENAGE FANCLUB). Having found an outlet via the fanzine 'Sha La La Ba Ba' to issue their first recording, 'JENNY NOWHERE', the easy-going duo finally delivered their debut single proper, the appropriately-named 'TRANQUIL'. Never a massive indie hit for their Bristol-based imprint, 'Subway', the brothers left the scene as quickly as they arrived.

JOHN CHARNLEY – vocals, guitar / **BILL CHARNLEY** – vocals, guitars / with guests from the BOY HAIRDRESSERS

Sha La La Ba Ba / not iss.

1986. (7"flexi) *(001)* **JENNY NOWHERE** ☐ -
(above was actually a throwaway freebie with the fanzine)

Subway / not iss.

Jan 88. (7") *(SUBWAY 12)* **TRANQUIL. / GET OUT OF MY DREAM** ☐ -
(12"+=) *(SUBWAY 12T)* – Village green.

— quickly retired from the scene; The CLOUDS who were around in the early 90's were in fact Stockport-based

COAST

Formed: Aberdeen . . . early 90's by young upstarts DANNY YOUNG, PAUL FYFE, MARK LAWRENCE and JOHN RUSSELL. With all the usual mid-90's traits (jangly-pop with folkie harmonies with touches of KINGMAKER and THOUSAND YARD STARE), COAST found a deal with relatively fresh label, 'Sugar', a debut single 'POLLY'S DOMAIN' hitting the shops the following summer. By this time, COAST had er, moved somewhat inland and to the over-populated city that was London; STONE ROSES/VERVE producer Paul Schroeder was on hand for their third 45, 'NOW THAT YOU KNOW ME'. Always on the verge of something big, the quartet delivered a handful of singles before bowing out with their one and only full-set, 'BIG JET RISING' (1997). • **Note:** Don't get confused with the 12" dance act of early '97 who issued 'Tales From the Hard Side' on 'Sliced'.

DANNY YOUNG – vocals, guitar / **PAUL FYFE** – guitar / **MARK LAWRENCE** – bass / **JOHN RUSSELL** – drums

Fluxus / not iss.

1991. (7"m) *(FL 001)* **HEADLIGHT. / SOUNDHOLE / BLUE GREEN** ☐ -

Sugar / not iss.

Jun 95. (7") *(SUGA 3V)* **POLLY'S DOMAIN. / YOU CAN LOOK** ☐ -
(cd-s+=) *(SUGA 3CD)* – Sleepy.

Oct 95. (7") *(SUGA 5V)* **SLUGS. / PRETEND** ☐ -
(cd-s+=) *(SUGA 5CD)* – Shag wild.

Mar 96. (7") *(SUGA 8V)* **NOW THAT YOU KNOW ME. / TENDER CAGE** ☐ -
(cd-s+=) *(SUGA 8CD)* – She wears a frown.

Aug 96. (7") *(SUGA 12V)* **HEADLINES IN THE SUN. / PAINTED IN BLUE** ☐ -
(cd-s+=) *(SUGA 12CD)* – Wouldn't you like to?

Mar 97. (7") *(SUGA 15V)* **DO IT NOW. / IT'S NOT TOO LATE** ☐ -
(cd-s+=) *(SUGA 15CD1)* – Bullseye.
(cd-s) *(SUGA 15CD2)* –

Apr 97. (cd/lp) *(SUGA 13 CD/LP)* **BIG JET RISING** ☐ -
– Britannia / Now that you know me / Headlines in the sun / Entertain me / Sister we sung / Slugs / Do it now / Shag wild / You'll feel mysterious tomorrow / Eating / Oh no, something's wrong / Weekend's over.

— seemed to have disbanded

Brenda COCHRANE

Born: Glasgow. A winner of UK TV series 'Opportunity Knocks', BRENDA went on to greater things after a few releases on 'Dazzle' records including her debut set, 'THE SINGER' (1988). In 1990, 'Polydor' issued her second album, 'THE VOICE', a covers set produced by Pip Williams (Status Quo, etc) which gained her a Top 20 spot; Quo's guitarist at the time, John 'Rhino' Edwards, guested on her version of Fleetwood Mac's 'YOU MAKE LOVIN' FUN'. After another CD, 'IN DREAMS' (1991), she was named 'International Female Vocalist' of '92 and she subsequently took the lead role of Mama Morton in the West End Musical 'Chicago'. Taking time out from studio work, BRENDA returned to collaborate on a single with FRANKIE D'AGOSTINO, and on the 23rd March 2001 she guested on the Michael Barrymore Show. BRENDA has a wide-ranging, easy-listening voice and has been described as the Caledonian Celine Dion.

BRENDA COCHRANE – vocals / with session ensemble

Dazzle / not iss.

Nov 87. (7") *(DAZ 1)* **DO YOU BELIEVE IN LOVE. / YOU BELONG TO ME** ☐ -

Jun 88. (lp/c) *(DAZLP/ZCDAZ 1)* **THE SINGER** ☐ -

Nov 88. (7"/12") *(DAZ/12DAZ 4)* **AUTOMATICALLY YOURS. / ('A'-Acid remix)** ☐ -

Polydor / not iss.

Mar 90. (cd/c/lp) *(843141-2/-4/-1)* **THE VOICE** 14 -
– You're the voice / Pearl's a singer / Right here waiting for you / New York, New York / You've lost that lovin' feeling (with RAVEN KANE) / You make lovin' fun / I want to know what love is / Wind beneath my wings / Easy to love / Put the weight on my shoulders / All night long.

Apr 90. (7"/c-s) *(PO/+CS 73)* **I WANT TO KNOW WHAT LOVE IS. / NEW YORK, NEW YORK** ☐ -
(cd-s+=) *(POCD 73)* – Pearl's a singer.

Mar 91. (cd/c/lp) *(849034-2/-4/-1)* **IN DREAMS** 55 -
– Homeland / Crazy / My foolish heart / In dreams / Love has no pride / Sacrifice / Bridge over troubled water / Always on my mind / I can't let go / Desperado / Unchained melody / Flame.

— BRENDA semi-retired for a while . . .

Academy Street / not iss.

Oct 98. (cd-s/12") *(d+/acst 050)* **NATIVE NEW YORKER** ☐ -

- compilations, etc. -

May 99. (cd/c) *Telstar Premiere; (TPE CD/MC 5501)* **THE VERY BEST OF BRENDA COCHRANE** ☐ -
– New York New York / You're the voice / Bridge over troubled water / Crazy / Unchained melody / All night long / My foolish heart / Always on my mind / Sacrifice / You make lovin' fun / In dreams / Wind beneath my wings / Desperado / Homeland / Right here waiting / I want to know what love is.

COCO AND THE BEAN

Formed: Edinburgh . . . mid-90's by two musicians HODGE and McLAREN along with singer ROSANNE ERSKINE. Setting out their musical stall in a slo-core trip-hop jazz-funk fashion, the group almost immediately secured a deal with Beggars Banquet offshoot, 'Mantra'. Late in 1995, during nationwide tours alongside SUGA BULLIT, COCO AND THE BEAN released their debut EP, 'WESTERN WAYS'. However, it would be another three years and several singles later, before the trio delivered their first full-set, 'TALES FROM THE MOUSE HOUSE' (1998).

ROSANNE ERSKINE – vocals / **HODGE + McLAREN**

Mantra / not iss.

Nov 95. (12"ep) *(MNT 3T)* **WESTERN WAYS EP** ☐ -
– Fom B.mix / Nine bar blues / Stolen moments / Another bounce for yer ounce.

(cd-ep+=) *(MNT 3CD)* – V.S.L.- J.A.B.

Jul 96. (12"ep/cd-ep) *(MNT 5 T/CD)* **KILLING TIME EP** □ -
– Fah.FC (radio edit) / Chee – C funka / Qureysh – EH?1 / Shan dancer / Co – eternal beam / Last chance.

Aug 97. (12") *(MNT 14T)* **ALL-STAR. / ('A'club) / ('A'instrumental)** □ -
(cd-s+=) *(MNT 14CD)* – ('A'edit).

Nov 97. (12"/cd-s) *(MNT 25 T/CD)* **VERSUS THE 90'S (mixes; original / instrumental / Herbalizer / Herbalizer instrumental)** □ -

— added vocals by **GWEN ESTY + ZEB DICKSON**

Jul 98. (cd/c/lp) *(MNT CD/MC/LP 1003)* **TALES FROM THE MOUSE HOUSE** □ -
– Soul tones / Solid gold / Fair play / Poisoned / Weird world / Anytime / All-star / Paradise / Versus the 90's / Plain sailing / Drifting.

— COCO AND THE BEAN split

COCTEAU TWINS

Formed: Grangemouth . . . late 1981 when the (then) trio of ELIZABETH FRASER, ROBIN GUTHRIE and WILL HEGGIE visited London to hand DJ John Peel a demo tape. He booked them for sessions on his Radio One night time show and they subsequently signed to IVO WATT-RUSSELL's indie label, '4 a.d.'.

The COCTEAUS' debut offering, 'GARLANDS', was hastily recorded, hitting the shops just over a week later and giving a hint of things to come with an interesting fusion of monochromatic rhythms, textured guitar distortion and sampling technology. Resisting many offers from the majors, they were back in the studio again for 1983's 'LULLABIES' EP and 'HEAD OVER HEELS' album. A mesmerising collage of irridescent guitar soundscapes and sheets of feedback perforated with FRASER's unintelligible but highly emotive warbling, the latter record was a blueprint for the best of The COCTEAU TWINS work. After a support slot to OMD, WILL HEGGIE departed, making the long trip back north to set up his own outfit, LOWLIFE. Around the same time ROBIN and LIZ hit No.1 in the indie charts when guesting for 'IVO/4 a.d.' ensemble, THIS MORTAL COIL on 'SONG TO THE SIREN'; it was mistakenly thought by many to be a COCTEAU TWINS off-shoot, rather than IVO's project. That idea was laid to rest after the album, 'IT'LL END IN TEARS', was issued in '84. Meanwhile, The COCTEAU TWINS were back with another blissed out masterpiece, 'TREASURE', introducing newcomer, SIMON RAYMONDE on bass and seeing LIZ explore hitherto uncharted vocal territory in a fascinating, enigmatic and occasionally unsettling language that communicated everything and nothing. It also marked their first taste of Top 30 success although they surpassed this with 1986's more inscrutably minimalist Top 10 effort, 'VICTORIALAND'.

An abortive film project collaboration with HAROLD BUDD was issued at the end of the year as they headed towards an increasingly "New Age"-style sound. Two more classics, 'BLUE BELL KNOLL' and 'HEAVEN OR LAS VEGAS' were released over the next half decade, both finding a home in the US charts for 'Capitol' records.

In 1992, they finally succumbed to signing for 'Fontana' in the UK, leading to a comeback album, 'FOUR CALENDAR CAFE' in '93. Many longtime fans were disappointed with what was surely the duo's most accessible, grounded album to date yet devoid of much of the mystery that made their earlier work so alluring. The following year saw LIZ guest on FUTURE SOUND OF LONDON's ambient venture, 'Lifeforms'; she would subsequently go on to perform on MASSIVE ATTACK's 'Teardrops' single in '98.

After another 3-year hiatus, FRASER and GUTHRIE returned with 'MILK & KISSES' (1996), a typically COCTEAU-esque affair that moved some critics to suggest the band were treading water. ROBIN resurfaced towards the end of 2000 via VIOLET INDIANA. His working partner on this collaboration was former MONO diva, SIOBHAN DE MARE, a slightly less ethereal vocalist than FRASER, witnessed on their debut EP, 'CHOKE'. The material on the EP, and especially on the debut album 'ROULETTE' (2001), evoked a laid-back GALAXIE 500-esque wig-out with GUTHRIE's instrumentation quite similar to the spacey hypnotics of TRANSIENT WAVES or PIANO MAGIC. DE MARE's whispering vocals on 'ROULETTE' were awesome and she did manage to completely re-invent her voice on the stand-out track 'SUNDANCE' where she soars while GUTHRIE's guitar spirals out of control. The pair issued a single 'KILLER EYES' at the end of 2001, which featured some fantastic B-sides such as the sparse 'STORM' and the free-jazz influenced 'SAFE WORLD'.

• **Trivia:** ROBIN has produced many '4.a.d.' outfits in addition to The GUN CLUB (1987). An item for some time, LIZ and ROBIN became parents in 1989. Early in 1991, LIZ was surprisingly but not undeservedly nominated for Best Female Vocalist at the 'Brit' awards.

ELIZABETH FRASER (b.29 Aug'63) – vocals / **ROBIN GUTHRIE** (b. 4 Jan'62) – guitar, drum programming, keyboards / **WILL HEGGIE** – bass

4 a.d. not iss.

Jul 82. (lp) *(CAD 211)* **GARLANDS** □ -
– Blood bitch / Wax and wane / But I'm not / Blind dumb deaf / Grail overfloweth / Shallow than halo / The hollow men / Garlands. *(c-iss.Apr84 +=; CADC 211)* – Dear heart / Blind dumb deaf / Hearsay please / Hazel. *(cd-iss. 1986 ++=; CAD 211CD)* – Speak no evil / Perhaps some other acorn. *<US cd-iss. 1991 on 'Alliance'; 96415>*

Sep 82. (12"ep) *(BAD 213)* **LULLABIES** □ -
– It's all but an ark lark / Alas dies laughing / Feathers-Oar-Blades.

Mar 83. (7") *(AD 303)* **PEPPERMINT PIG. / LAUGH LINES** □ -
(12"+=) *(BAD 303)* – Hazel.

— Trimmed to a duo when HEGGIE left to form LOWLIFE

Oct 83. (lp) *(CAD 313)* **HEAD OVER HEELS** 51 -
– When mama was moth / Sugar hiccup / In our anglehood / Glass candle grenades / Multifoiled / In the gold dust rush / The tinderbox (of a heart) / My love paramour / Musette and drums / Five ten fiftyfold. *(c-iss.Apr84 +=; CADC 313) (cd-iss. 1986 +=; CAD 313CD)* – SUNBURST AND SNOWBLIND EP *<US cd-iss. 1991 on 'Alliance'; 96416>*

Oct 83. (12"ep) *(BAD 314)* **SUNBURST AND SNOWBLIND** □ -
– Sugar hiccup / From the flagstones / Because of whirl-Jack / Hitherto.

— added **SIMON RAYMONDE** (b. 3 Apr'62, London) – bass, keyboards, guitar (ex-DROWNING CRAZE)

Apr 84. (7") *(AD 405)* **PEARLY DEWDROPS DROP. / PEPPER-TREE** 29 -
(12"+=) *(BAD 405)* – The spangle maker.

Nov 84. (lp/c) *(CAD/+C 412)* **TREASURE** 29 -
– Ivo / Lorelei / Beatrix / Persephone / Pandora – for Cindy / Amelia / Aloysius / Cicely / Otterley / Donimo. *(cd-iss. 1986; CAD 412CD) <US cd-iss. 1991 on 'Alliance'; 96418>*

Mar 85. (7") *(AD 501)* **AIKEA-GUINEA. / KOOKABURRA** 41 -
(12"+=) *(BAD 501)* – Rococo / Quiquose.

Nov 85. (12"ep) *(BAD 510)* **TINY DYNAMITE** 52 -
– Pink orange red / Ribbed and veined / Sultitan Itan / Plain tiger.

Nov 85. (12"ep) *(BAD 511)* **ECHOES IN A SHALLOW BAY** 65 -
– Great spangled fritillary / Melonella / Pale clouded white / Eggs and their shells *(cd-iss. Oct86 +=; BAD 510/511)* – TINY DYNAMITE

— **RICHARD THOMAS** – saxophone, bass (of DIF JUZ) repl. SIMON who fell ill

Apr 86. (lp/c)(cd) *(CAD/+C 602)(CAD 602CD)* **VICTORIALAND** 10 □
– Lazy calm / Fluffy tufts / Throughout the dark months of April and May / Whales tales / Oomingmak / Little Spacey / Feet-like fins / How to bring a blush to the snow / The thinner the air. *<US cd-iss. 1991 on 'Alliance'; 96417>*

— **SIMON RAYMONDE** returned repl.temp. RICHARD (back to DIF JUZ)

Oct 86. (7") *(AD 610)* **LOVE'S EASY TEARS. / THOSE EYES, THAT MOUTH** 53 -
(12"+=) *(BAD 610)* – Sigh's smell of farewell.

— next was a one-off collaboration with label new signing **HAROLD BUDD** – piano

4 a.d. Relativity

Nov 86. (lp/c)(cd; by HAROLD BUDD, ELIZABETH FRASER, ROBIN GUTHRIE, SIMON RAYMONDE) *(CAD/+C 611)(CAD 611CD) <8143>* **THE MOON AND THE MELODIES** 46 □
– Sea, swallow me / Memory gongs / Why do you love me? / Eyes are mosaics / She will destroy you / The ghost has no home / Bloody and blunt / Ooze out and away, one how.

4 a.d. Capitol

Sep 88. (lp/c/dat)(cd) *(CAD/+C/T 807)(CAD 807CD) <90892>* **BLUE BELL KNOLL** 15 □
– Blue bell knoll / Athol-brose / Carolyn's fingers / For Phoebe still a baby / The itchy glowbo blow / Cico buff / Suckling the mender / Spooning good singing gum / A kissed out red floatboat / Ella megablast burls forever.

Oct 88. (7") **CAROLYN'S FINGERS. / BLUE BELL KNOLL** - □

— In Apr'90, LIZ was heard on Ian McCulloch's (ex-ECHO & THE BUNNYMEN) 'Candleland' single.

Aug 90. (7"/c-s) *(AD 0011/+C)* **ICEBLINK LUCK. / MIZAKE THE MIZAN** 38 -
(12"+=/cd-s+=) *(AD 0011 T/CD)* – Watchiar.

Sep 90. (cd)(lp/c) *(CAD 0012CD)(CAD/+C 0012) <C2/C1/C4 93669>* **HEAVEN OR LAS VEGAS** 7 99
– Cherry coloured funk / Pitch the baby / Iceblink luck / Fifty-fifty clown / Heaven or Las Vegas / I wear your ring / Fotzepolitic / Wolf in the breast / Road, river and rail / Frou-frou foxes in midsummer fires.

— on U.S. tour, augmented by **MITSUO TATE + BEN BLAKEMAN** – guitars

Fontana Capitol

Sep 93. (7"/c-s) *(CT/+C 1)* **EVANGELINE. / MUD AND LARK** 34 -
(12"pic-d+=/cd-s+=) *(CT X/CD 1)* – Summer-blink.

Oct 93. (cd/c/lp) *(518259-2/-4/-1) <C2/C4/C1 99375>* **FOUR CALENDAR CAFE** 13 78
– Know who you are ate every age / Evangeline / Blue beard / Theft and wandering around lost / Oil of angels / Squeeze-wax / My truth / Essence / Summerhead / Pur.

Dec 93. (cd-s) *(COCCD 1)* **WINTER WONDERLAND. / FROSTY THE SNOWMAN** [58] [-]
(above festive tracks, deleted after a week in UK Top 60)

Feb 94. (7"/c-s) *(CT/+C 2)* **BLUEBEARD. / THREE SWEPT** [33] [ ]
(12"+=) *(CTX 2)* – Ice-pulse.
(cd-s++=) *(CTCD 2)* – ('A'acoustic).

Sep 95. (7"//7"/cd-ep) *(CCT//CTT/CTCD 3)* *<30548>* **TWINLIGHTS** [59] [ ] Dec95
– Rilkean heart / Golden-vein // Pink orange red / Half-gifts.

Oct 95. (12"ep/cd-ep) *(CT X/CD 4)* *<36240>* **OTHERNESS** (An Ambient EP) [59] [ ] Dec95
– Feet like fins / Seekers who are lovers / Violaine / Cherry coloured funk.

Mar 96. (cd-ep) *(CTCD 5)* **TISHBITE / PRIMITIVE HEART / FLOCK OF SOUL** [34] [-]
(12"ep/cd-ep) *(CT X/DDD 5)* – (title track) / Round / An Elan.

Apr 96. (cd/c/lp) *(514 501-2/4/-1)* *<37049-2/-4/-1>* **MILK & KISSES** [17] [99]
– Violaine / Serpent skirt / Tishbite / Half-gifts / Calfskin smack / Rilkean heart / Ups / Eperdu / Treasure hiding / Seekers who are lovers. *(also ltd.cd; 532 363-2)*

Jul 96. (12") *(CTX 6)* **VIOLAINE. / ALICE** [56] [-]
(cd-s+=) *(CTDD 6)* – Circling girl.
(cd-s) *(CTCD 6)* – ('A'side) / Tranquil eye / Smile.

— towards the end of 2000, GUTHRIE worked as the duo VIOLET INDIANA (alongside SIOBHAN DE MARE, ex-MONO), releasing the 'CHOKE' EP for his 'Bella Union' imprint

– compilations, others, etc. –

Dec 85. (cd) *4 a.d.; (CAD 513CD) / Relativity; <ENC 8040>* **THE PINK OPAQUE** [ ] [ ] Sep85
– The spangle maker / Millimillenary / Wax and wane / Hitherto / Pearly-dewdrops' drops (12" Version) / From the flagstones / Aikea-Guinea / Lorelei / Pepper-tree / Musette and drums.

Nov 91. (10xcd-ep-box) *Capitol; (CTBOX 1)* **THE SINGLES COLLECTION** [ ] [-]
– (above featured previous 9 singles + new 1) (sold separately Mar92)

Sep 99. (d-cd) *Bella Union; (BELLACD 14)* **THE BBC SESSIONS** [ ] [ ]

Oct 00. (cd) *4 a.d.; (CAD2K 019CD) <370019>* **STARS AND TOPSOIL 1982-1990** [ ] [ ]
– Blind dumb deaf / Sugar hiccup / My love paramour / Pearly dewdrops drop / Lorelei / Pandora / Aikea guinea / Pink orange red / Pale clouded white / Lazy calm / Thinner the air / Orange appled / Cico buff / Carolyn's fingers / Fifty fifty clown / Iceblink luck / Heaven or Las Vegas / Watchiar.

VIOLET INDIANA

ROBIN GUTHRIE – guitars, etc. / **SIOBHAN DE MARE** – vocals (ex-MONO)

Bella Union / Instinct

Nov 00. (cd-ep) *(BELLACD 22)* **CHOKE EP** [ ] [-]
– Purr la perla / Busted / Silent / Torn up.

Apr 01. (cd) *(BELLACD 24)* *<571>* **ROULETTE** [ ] [ ] May01
– Air kissing / Busted / Sundance / Powder river / Little echo / Angel / Poison gorgeous / Hiding / Rage days / Liar / Feline or famine / Killer eyes.

May 01. (cd-ep) *(BELLACD 26)* **KILLER EYES EP** [ ] [-]
– Killer eyes / Storm / Safe word / Killer eyes (CD-Rom).

Oct 01. (cd-ep) *(BELLACD 28)* **SPECIAL EP** [ ] [-]
– Jailbird / Poppy / Sky / Chapter 3.

Edwyn COLLINS

Born: 23 Aug'59, Edinburgh. COLLINS formed ORANGE JUICE in Glasgow . . . 1977 initially as the NU-SONICS with JAMES KIRK, STEPHEN DALY and ALAN DUNCAN, who was subsequently replaced by DAVID McCLYMONT. In 1979, ORANGE JUICE signed to local indie label 'Postcard', the hub of the burgeoning Glasgow indie scene masterminded by ALAN HORNE.

In contrast to the post-punk miserabilism coming out of England, ORANGE JUICE were purveyors of studiedly naive, wide-eyed indie pop as best sampled on the brace of early 45's, 'FALLING AND LAUGHING', 'BLUE BOY', 'SIMPLY THRILLED HONEY' and 'POOR OLD SOUL' (later collected on 1993's retrospective, 'THE HEATHER'S ON FIRE'). They subsequently signed to 'Polydor' in 1981, releasing a debut album, 'YOU CAN'T HIDE YOUR LOVE FOREVER', early the following year. Though some of their die-hard fans inevitably accused them of selling out, the set almost made the UK Top 20, its charming guitar pop auguring well for the future. The band suffered internal ruction soon after the album's release, however, MALCOLM ROSS and ZEKE MANYIKA replacing KIRK and DALY respectively. The Nigerian-born MANYIKA injected a newfound rhythmic thrust into the follow-up album, 'RIP IT UP' (1982), the clipped funk of the title track providing the band with their only Top 40 hit, albeit a sizeable one.

Despite this belated success, further tensions reduced the band to a duo of COLLINS and MANYIKA who recorded an impressive mini-set, 'TEXAS FEVER' (1984) under the production auspices of reggae veteran, DENNIS BOVELL. Later that year saw the release of swansong set, 'THE ORANGE JUICE – THE THIRD ALBUM', a far more introspective affair which found COLLINS at a low ebb. The singer had already released a cover of The Velvet Underground's 'PALE BLUE EYES', with PAUL QUINN and subsequently embarked on a solo career which remained low key for the ensuing decade. Initially signed to ALAN McGEE's "side" label, 'Elevation', his first two solo singles flopped and as the label went belly-up, COLLINS opted for 'Demon' records. He finally issued a long-awaited album, 'HOPE AND DESPAIR' in summer '89. An eclectic, rootsy affair borne of COLLINS' troubled wilderness years, the record was hailed by the same critics who so vehemently supported ORANGE JUICE. Yet despite the praise, it seemed COLLINS was destined for cult appeal; a second 'Demon' set, 'HELLBENT ON COMPROMISE' (1990) failed to lift his profile and COLLINS went to ground. Well, not completely, the singer honing his production skills for indie outfits such as A HOUSE and The ROCKINGBIRDS.

The throaty-voxed singer finally re-emerged in 1994 with 'GORGEOUS GEORGE', the record he'd been threatening to make for years. Recorded on classic studio equipment, the record's organic feel coupled with COLLIN's mordant cynicism and razor sharp songwriting resulted in a massive worldwide hit, 'A GIRL LIKE YOU'. With its crunching, NEIL YOUNG-like riffing and infectious delivery, the record was initially released in Europe and Australia before eventually hitting the Top 5 in the UK a year on. Though 1997's 'THE MAGIC PIPER' (from the album 'I'M NOT FOLLOWING YOU') didn't quite match this commercial feat, COLLINS remains one of Scotland's most accomplished songwriters with a reliable line in caustic wit.

In 2002, his brand of humour was taken a step further via the release of 'DOCTOR SYNTAX', an album which saw COLLINS, for the first time, use beats and samples courtesy of SEBASTIAN LEWSLEY. The set comprised COLLINS' trademark guitar-led love songs, but with an edgier, personalised production. 'THE BEATLES' was obviously a direct ode to his peers, although 'SPLITTING UP' exemplified COLLINS' songwriting abilities by ten. '20 YEARS TOO LATE' employed a retro-electro-synth feel accompanied by

some strange rapping never before encountered on an EDWYN COLLINS record.

• **Songwriters:** ORANGE JUICE: most written by COLLINS, some with MANYIKA. Note that KIRK was the writer of FELICITY, and ROSS provided PUNCH DRUNK. They covered L.O.V.E. (Al Green), while COLLINS solo tried his hand at MY GIRL HAS GONE (Smokey Robinson) + TIME OF THE PREACHER (Willie Nelson) / WON'T TURN BACK (Vic Godard).

ORANGE JUICE

EDWYN COLLINS – vocals, guitar, occasional violin / **JAMES KIRK** – guitar, vocals / **DAVID McCLYMONT** – bass, synths; repl. ALAN DUNCAN / **STEPHEN DALY** – drums

Postcard — not iss.

Feb 80. (7") *(80-1)* **FALLING AND LAUGHING. / MOSCOW** [ ] [-]
(free 7"flexi) *(LYN 7609)* – FELICITY (live).

Aug 80. (7") *(80-2)* **BLUE BOY. / LOVE SICK** [ ] [-]

Dec 80. (7") *(80-6)* **SIMPLY THRILLED HONEY. / BREAKFAST TIME** [ ] [-]

Mar 81. (7") *(81-2)* **POOR OLD SOUL. / (part 2)** [ ] [-]

Jun 81. (7"; w-drawn) *(81-6)* **WAN LIGHT. / YOU OLD ECCENTRIC** [-] [-]

Polydor — Polydor

Oct 81. (7") *(POSP 357)* **L.O.V.E. LOVE. / INTUITION TOLD ME PT.2** [65] [-]
(12"+=) *(POSPX 357)* – Moscow.

Jan 82. (7") *(POSP 386)* **FELICITY. / IN A NUTSHELL** [63] [-]
(12"+=) *(POSPX 386)* – You old eccentric.

Feb 82. (lp/c) *(POLS/+C 1057)* **YOU CAN'T HIDE YOUR LOVE FOREVER** [21] [ ]
– Falling and laughing / Untitled melody / Wan light / Tender object / Dying day / L.O.V.E. love / Intuition told me (part 1) / Upwards and onwards / Satellite city / Three cheers for our side / Consolation prize / Felicity / In a nutshell.

— **MALCOLM ROSS** – guitar (ex-JOSEF K) + **ZEKE MANYIKA** (b. Nigeria) – percussion, vocals, synths; repl. KIRK DALY who subsequently formed MEMPHIS, releasing only one single for 'Swamplands', 'YOU SUPPLY THE ROSES', early 1985

Jul 82. (7"/10") *(POSP/+T 470)* **TWO HEARTS TOGETHER. / HOKOYO** [60] [-]

Oct 82. (7") *(POSP 522)* **I CAN'T HELP MYSELF. / TONGUES BEGIN TO WAG** [42] [ ]
(12"+=) *(POSPX 522)* – Barbeque.

Nov 82. (lp/c) *(POLS/+C 1076)* **RIP IT UP** [39] [ ]
– Rip it up / Breakfast time / A million pleading faces / Mud in your eye / Turn away / I can't help myself / Flesh of my flesh / Louise Louise / Hokoyo / Tenter hook. *(cd-iss. Jul89; 839768-2)*

Feb 83. (7") *(POSP 547)* **RIP IT UP (remix). / SNAKE CHARMER** [8] [ ]
(some w/ live c-s+=) – The Felicity Flexi Session: The formative years – Simply thrilled honey / Botswana / Time to develop / Blue boy.
(d7"+=) *(POSPD 547)* – Sad lament / Lovesick.
(12") *(POSPX 547)* – ('A'side) / Sad lament / ('A'long version).

May 83. (7"/7"pic-d/ext.12") *(OJ/OJP/OJX 4)* **FLESH OF MY FLESH. / LORD JOHN WHITE AND THE BOTTLENECK TRAIN** [41] [-]

— basically now a duo of **COLLINS + MANYIKA** with session people replacing ROSS (who joined AZTEC CAMERA) and McCLYMONT (to The MOODISTS)

Feb 84. (7") *(OJ 5)* **BRIDGE. / OUT FOR THE COUNT** [67] [-]
(free 7"flexi w/ above) *(JUICE 1)* – Poor old soul (live).
(12"+=) *(OJX 5)* – ('A'-Summer '83 mix).

Feb 84. (m-lp/c) *(OJM LP/MC 1)* **TEXAS FEVER** [34] [-]
– Bridge / Craziest feeling / Punch drunk / The day I went down to Texas / A place in my heart / A sad feeling. *(cd-iss. Mar98 +=; 539982-2)* – Leaner period / Out for the count / Move yourself.

Apr 84. (7") *(OJ 6)* **WHAT PRESENCE?! / A PLACE IN MY HEART (dub)** [47] [ ]
(free c-s w/ above) *(OJC 6)* – In a nutshell (live) / Simply thrilled honey (live) / Dying day (live).
(12"+=) *(OJX 6)* – ('A'extended).

Oct 84. (7") *(OJ 7)* **LEAN PERIOD. / BURY MY HEAD IN MY HANDS** [74] [-]
(free 7"flexi w/ above) *(JUICE 3)* – Rip it up / What presence?!
(12"+=) *(OJX 7)* – ('A'extended).

Nov 84. (lp/c) *(OJ LP/MC 1)* **THE ORANGE JUICE – THE THIRD ALBUM** [ ] [-]
– Get while the goings good / Salmon fishing in New York / I guess I'm just a little sensitive / Burning desire / The artisan / Lean period / What presence?! / Out for the count / All that mattered / Seacharger. *(re-iss. Aug86 lp/c; SPE LP/MC 102) (c+=remixes)* – I can't help myself / Rip it up / Love struck / Flesh of my flesh / Out for the count / What presence?! / Lean period.

— disbanded after above album; MANYIKA went solo, as did EDWYN COLLINS. He'd already (in Aug'84) hit UK No.72 with PAUL QUINN on 7"/12" 'PALE BLUES EYES' (a Velvet Underground cover) released on 'Swamplands'.

– compilations, others, etc. –

Jul 85. (lp/c) *Polydor; (OJ LP/MC 3)* **IN A NUTSHELL** [ ] [-]
– Falling and laughing / Poor old soul (live) / L.O.V.E. / In a nutshell / Felicity / I can't help myself / Hokoyo / Rip it up / Flesh of my flesh / A place in my heart / Bridge / Out for the count / The artisans / What presence?! *(w/free 7"flexi)* – Felicity.

Jan 91. (cd/c) *Polydor; (847 727-2/-4)* **THE ORANGE JUICE / YOU CAN'T HIDE YOUR LOVE FOREVER** [ ] [-]

Jul 92. (cd) *Polydor; (513618)* **THE VERY BEST OF ORANGE JUICE (THE ESTEEMED ORANGE JUICE)** [ ] [ ] Oct95
– Falling and laughing / Consolation prize (live) / Old encentric / L.O.V.E. love / Felicity / In a nutshell / Rip it up / I can't help myself / Flesh of my flesh / Tenterhook / Bridge / The day I went down to Texas / Punch drunk / A place in my heart / A sad lament / Lean period / I guess I'm just a little too sensitive / The artisans / Salmon fishing in New York / What presence?! / Out for the count. *(re-iss. cd Sep95; same)* – (extra track).

Jul 92. (lp/c/cd) *Postcard; (DUBH 922/+MC/CD)* **OSTRICH CHURCHYARD (live in Glasgow)** [ ] [-]
– Louise Louise / Three cheers for our side / To put it in a nutshell / Satellite city / Consolation prize / Holiday hymn / Intuition told me (parts 1 & 2) / Wan light / Dying day / Texas fever / Tender object. *(cd+=/c+=)* – Falling and laughing / Lovesick / Poor old soul / You old eccentric. *(cd re-iss. Oct95; DUBH 954CD)*

May 93. (7") *Postcard; (DUBH 934)* **BLUEBOY. / LOVESICK** [ ] [-]
(cd-s+=) *(DUBH 934CD)* – Poor old soul (French version) / Poor old soul (instrumental).

Jul 93. (lp/cd) *Postcard; (DUBH 932/+CD)* **THE HEATHER'S ON FIRE** [ ] [-]
– Falling and laughing / Moscow / Moscow Olympics / Blue boy / Love sick / Simply thrilled honey / Breakfast time / Poor old soul / Poor old soul pt.2 / Felicity / Upwards and onwards / Dying day / Holiday hymn. *(re-iss. cd Oct95; DUBH 955CD)*

EDWYN COLLINS

solo, with **DENNIS BOVELL, MALCOLM ROSS, ALEX GRAY + CHRIS TAYLOR**

Elevation — not iss.

May 87. (7") *(ACID 4)* **DON'T SHILLY SHALLY. / IF EVER YOU'RE READY** [ ] [-]
(12"+=) *(ACID 4T)* – Queer fish.

Elevation — not iss.

Nov 87. (7") *(ACID 6)* **MY BELOVED GIRL. / CLOUDS (FOGGING UP MY MIND)** [ ] [-]
(12"+=) *(ACID 6T)* – My (long time) beloved girl.
(7"box+=) *(ACID 6B)* – 50 shades of blue (acoustic) / What's the big idea.

— now with **BERNARD CLARKE** – keyboards / **DENNIS BOVELL** – bass / **DAVE RUFFY** – drums

Demon — not iss.

Jun 89. (lp/c/cd) *(FIEND/+C/CD 144)* **HOPE AND DESPAIR** [ ] [-]
– Coffee table song / 50 shades of blue / You're better than you know / Pushing it to the back of my mind / The wheels of love / Darling, they want it all / The beginning of the end / The measure of the man / Testing time / Let me put my arms around you / The wide eyed child in me / Ghost of a chance. *(c+=/cd+=)* – If ever you're ready. *(re-iss. cd Sep95)*

Jul 89. (7") *(D 1064)* **THE COFFEE TABLE SONG. / JUDAS IN BLUE JEANS** [ ] [-]
(12"+=) *(D 1064T)* – Out there.

Oct 89. (7") *(D 1065)* **50 SHADES OF BLUE (new mix). / IF EVER YOU'RE READY** [ ] [-]
(12") *(D 1065T)* – ('A'extended) / Kindred spirit / Just call her name / Ain't that always the way.
(cd-s) *(D 1065CD)* – ('A'side) / Judas in blue jeans / Kindred spirit / Just call her name.

Oct 90. (lp/c/cd) *(FIEND/+C/CD 195)* **HELLBENT ON COMPROMISE** [ ] [-]
– Means to an end / You poor deluded fool / It might as well be you / Take care of yourself / Graciously / Someone else besides / My girl has gone / Everything and more / What's the big idea? / Hellbent medley:- Time of the preacher – Long time gone. *(re-iss. cd Oct95; same)*

— now with **STEVEN SKINNER** – guitar / **PHIL THORNALLEY** – bass / **PAUL COOK** – drums

Setanta — Bar None

Aug 94. (cd/c/lp) *(SET CD/MC/LP 014) <058>* **GEORGEOUS GEORGE** [ ] [ ] Sep95
– The campaign for real rock / A girl like you / Low expectations / Out of this world / If you could love me / North of Heaven / Georgeous George / It's right in front of you / Make me feel again / You got it all / Subsidence / Occupy your mind. *(re-iss. Jul95, hit UK No.8)*

Oct 94. (c-ep) *(ZOP 001C)* **EXPRESSLY EP** [42] [-]
– A girl like you / A girl like you (Macrame remix by Youth).
(cd-ep+=) *(ZOP 001CD1)* – Out of this world (I hear a new world) (St.Etienne remix) / Occupy your mind.
(cd-ep) *(ZOP 001CD2)* – ('A'side) / Don't shilly shally (Spotters'86 demo) / Something's brewing / Bring it on back.

Mar 95. (12"ep) *(ZOP 002CD1)* **IF YOU COULD LOVE ME (radio edit). / IN A BROKEN DREAM / INSIDER DEALING / ('A'-MC Esher mix)** [ ] [ ]
(cd-ep) *(ZOP 002CD1)* – (first 3 tracks) / Hope and despair.
(cd-ep) *(ZOP 002CD2)* – ('A'side) / If ever you're ready / Come to your senses / A girl like you (the Victoria Spaceman mix).

Jun 95. (7") *(ZOP 0037)* **A GIRL LIKE YOU. / YOU'RE ON YOUR OWN** [4] [-]

(c-s+=) *(ZOP 003C)* – If you could love me (acoustic version).
(cd-s++=) *(ZOP 003CD)* – Don't shilly shally (Spotters '86 demo).

Oct 95. (c-s) *<58-1234>* **A GIRL LIKE YOU / IF YOU COULD LOVE ME** [-] [32]
(above used on the film 'Empire Records')

Feb 96. (c-s) *(ZOP 004C)* **KEEP ON BURNING / IF YOU COULD LOVE ME (IN TIME AND SPACE)** [45] [-]
(cd-s+=) *(ZOP 004CD1)* – Lava lamp / The campaign for real rock.
(cd-s) *(ZOP 004CD2)* – Won't turn back / You've grown a beard / A girl like you (live) / White room.

Setanta Sony

Jul 97. (12") *(SET 041T)* **THE MAGIC PIPER. / A GIRL LIKE YOU (Makrame mix) / WELWYN GARDEN CITY** [32] [-]
(cd-s) *(SETCDA 041)* – ('A'side) / More than you bargained for / Red menace / It takes a little time.
(cd-s) *(SETCDB 041)* – ('A'side) / Who is it? / Who is it? (halterbacked by the Victorian spaceman / Welwyn Garden City.

Sep 97. (cd/c/lp) *(SET CD/MC/LP 039) <68716>* **I'M NOT FOLLOWING YOU** [55] [ ] Oct97
– It's a steal / The magic piper (of love) / Seventies night / No one waved goodbye / Downer / Keep on burning / Running away with myself / Country rock / For the rest of my life / Superficial cat / Adidas world / I'm not following you.

Oct 97. (7") *(SET 045)* **ADIDAS WORLD. / HIGH FASHION** [71] [-]
(cd-s+=) *(SETCDA 045)* – Mr. Bojangles / Talking 'bout the times.
(cd-s) *(SETCDB 045)* – ('A'side) / Episode 3 / Episode 5 / Episode 10 (no, no, no Adidas – Adilated by . . .).

Nov 97. (d12") *(ZOPPR 005)* **I HEAR A NEW WORLD (mixes; Red Snapper / Deadly Avenger Supershine / Red Snapper vocal / DOWNER (James Lavelle mix) // THE MAGIC PIPER (the Wiseguys sniper mix) / ADIDAS WORLD (adilated by Sebastian Lawsely) / DOWNER (James Lavelle vocal)** [ ] [-]

— in Apr'01, EDWYN collaborated with BERNARD BUTLER on the 'Setanta' single 'MESSAGE FOR JOJO'

Apr 02. (cd) *(SETCD 098)* **DOCTOR SYNTAX** [ ] [-]
– Never felt like this / Should've done that / Mine is at / No idea / The Beathes / Back to the back room / Splitting up / Johnny Teardrop / 20 years too late / It's a funny thing / Calling on you.

COMMOTIONS

Formed: Glasgow . . . 1982 as LLOYD COLE & THE COMMOTIONS when English-born/raised frontman, LLOYD COLE, hooked up with Scots musicians NEIL CLARK (guitar), BLAIR COWAN (keyboards), STEPHEN IRVINE (drums) and LAWRENCE DONEGAN (bass) at Glasgow University. DONEGAN – son of skiffle guru LONNIE – had already cut his teeth in the music industry as an early member of cheery popsters, the BLUEBELLS. Centered around the moody musings of their leader COLE, the quintet blueprinted their unique brand of intellectual pop-rock with the 'PERFECT SKIN' single (Top 30). Although follow-up 45, 'FOREST FIRE' failed to crack the Top 40, October 1984's debut 'RATTLESNAKES' album was a landmark of sorts and paved the way for a further series of charming pop singles including 'BRAND NEW FRIEND' and 'LOST WEEKEND'. Towards the end of the decade, the band's failing fortunes resulted in an amicable split with COWAN going on to work alongside COLE as he began his solo career in the States. Meanwhile, LAWRENCE became a full-time journalist. Note that when LLOYD was interviewed by Neil Trotter prior to his debut solo album in 1990, he stated: "I'm sick of people thinking I'm Scots". Lancashire-born COLE therefore won't be disappointed to find his omission from this book.

CONDITION BLUE (see under ⇒ SPARE SNARE)

Chris CONNELLY

Born: Edinburgh. The one-time mainman of FINITRIBE and a stalwart of The REVOLTING COCKS and PIGFACE, he left the latter band for solo pastures in 1991.

Enlisting the help of friends, musicians and co-writers, MARTIN ATKINS, CHRIS BRUCE, WILLIAM TUCKER and STUART ZECHMAN, he began work on his debut UK solo outing ('WHIPLASH BOYCHILD' had already been released by 'Wax Trax!' in the States), 'PHENOBARB BAMBALAM' (1992). The record saw CONNELLY shift dramatically from his dance/industrial roots – his girlfriend had just recently committed suicide – adopting a different persona (i.e. SCOTT WALKER, BOWIE!, etc) on each track although the cover of Tom Verlaine's 'SOUVENIR FROM A DREAM', added little to the original. 'WHIPLASH BOYCHILD' was issued officially in Britain a few months later while CONNELLY moonlighted with KILLING JOKE off-shoot industrial metal-rap outfit, MURDER INC.

Now living in America, CONNELLY delivered two futher US-only albums, 'SHIPWRECK' (1994) and 'THE ULTIMATE SEASIDE COMPANION' (1997). At the beginning of the millennium, CONNELLY reunited with some of his old chums (GEORDIE WALKER, JAH WOBBLE, MARTIN ATKINS and effects man LEE FRASER) via The DAMAGE MANUAL. This heavy/industrial supergroup of sorts turned up the volume on two efforts in 2000, the mini '1' and 'THE DAMAGE MANUAL'. CONNELLY continued sailing through the sea of darkness with the release of 'BLONDE EXODUS' (2001), a startling album which featured the instrumental help of The BELLS. His swooning, bleak vocals floated through the set's lush string arrangements and acoustic guitars – a far cry from his former industrial meanderings. This eloquent delivery was followed by 2002's equally realised LP 'PRIVATE EDUCATION'.

CHRIS CONNELLY – vocals, pianoforte, keyboards, tapes / **CHRIS BRUCE** – guitars / **MARTIN ATKINS** – drums, percussion / **STUART ZECHMAN** – bass / **WILLIAM TUCKER** – guitar, tapes

Devotion Wax Trax!

Dec 90. (12"/cd-s) *<WAX/+CDS 9141>* **STOWAWAY (Downward Spiral remix) / STOWAWAY (Waking Dream mix). / DAREDEVIL (Third Eye mix)** [-] [ ]

Nov 91. (cd/c/lp) *<WAXCD 7134>* **WHIPLASH BOYCHILD** [-] [ ]
– Daredevil / Ghost of a saint / This edge of midnight / The last of joy / The amorous Humphrey Plugg / Stowaway / The hawk, the butcher, the killer of beauties / The game is all yours. *(UK-iss.Oct92; CD/T+/DVN 14)(cd+=)* – Confessions of the highest bidder / Stowaway (Daydream mix) / This edge of midnight (sparse).

Feb 92. (cd-ep) *<WAXCDS 9190>* **JULY** [-] [ ]
– July / July (version) / This edge of midnight (sparse) / The last of joy (secret mix) / Trash (live – spoken word).

Aug 92. (12") *(12DVN 108) <WAX 9190>* **COME DOWN HERE (Swollen fruit cocktail). / COME DOWN HERE (instrumental) / SOUVENIR FROM A DREAM** [ ] [ ] Jun92
(cd-s+=) *(CDDVN 108)* – ('A'version).

Sep 92. (cd/c/lp) *(CD/T+/DVN 13) <WAX 7189>* **PHENOBARB BAMBALAM** [ ] [ ]
– The whistle blower / July / Souvenir from a dream / Come down here / Too good to be true / Heartburn / No lesser of two evils / Ignition times four / Dirtbox Tennessee. *(cd+=)* – Heartburn (twister mix).

— retained **TUCKER + BRUCE**

not iss. TVT

1994. (7"blue; as CONNELLY & TUCKER) *<8710-7>* **HEARTBURN. / THE HAWK, THE BUTCHER, THE KILLER OF BEAUTIES** [-] [ ]
(cd-s+=) **SONGS FOR SWINGING JUNKIES** *<8710-2>* – July.

1994. (cd/c) *<TVT 7214-2/-4>* **SHIPWRECK** [-] [ ]
– Candyman collapse / Spoonfed celeste / What's left but solid gold? / Detestimony III / Anyone's mistake / Drench / The early nighters (for River Phoenix) / Swimming / Model murmur / Meridian afterburn / Shipwreck.

— next with his band the BELLS:- **RIEFLIN + CHRIS BRUCE + JIM O'ROURKE**

not iss. Hit It!

Oct 97. (cd) *<22>* **THE ULTIMATE SEASIDE COMPANION** [-] [ ]
– The fortune / Mississippi palisades / My east is your west / Stray / Empty Sam / No more changing of the guard / Island head / Toledo steel / Caravan / To play a slow game / The ultimate seaside companion / The fortune II. *(UK-iss.Oct00 as '. . .REVISITED' on 'Invisible'+=; INV 174CD)* – Chorus of eyes / Thunderland reel / No more changing of the guard (live) / The fortune (live).

Dream Catcher Invisible

Mar 01. (d-cd; as CHRIS CONNELLY & THE BELLS) *(CRIDE 40) <168>* **BLONDE EXODUS** [ ] [ ] Feb01
– Generique / London fields / Diamonds eat diamonds / Blonde exodus (part 1) / Twilight shiner / Blue hooray / Magnificent view / The Long weekend / Julie Delpy / Blonde exodus (part 2) / Closing titles / Blonde strings / Moonlight feels right. *(UK-iss.+=)* – THE ULTIMATE SEASIDE COMPANION

— CONNELLY was also part of cosmopolitan industrial group, MURDER INC.

Underground Inc. Underground Inc

Jun 02. (cd) *(UI 1017)* **PRIVATE EDUCATION** [ ] [ ] May02
– Harbour days / Samaritan / You versus miracle / About the beauty of Laura / Fortune strikes back / Lipstick in Labyrinth park / No one is scared / The last hit man in Heaven.

Copper records (see under ⇒ HUCKLEBERRY)

COSMIC ROUGH RIDERS

Formed: Castlemilk, Glasgow . . . 1998 by one-time THIEVES vocalist DANIEL WYLIE and his guitar-playing buddy STEPHEN FLEMING. They began by recording a skeleton bones demo of tracks in a community centre-cum-studio (on a Glasgow Council grant) and through the forthcoming months, the pair found new members, GARY CUTHBERT, MARK BROWN and JAMES CLIFFORD.

CRR also developed an important and equally compelling sound, borrowing styles from The BYRDS, NEIL YOUNG, GRAM PARSONS and even, at times, BRIAN WILSON. This was evident on their self-financed debut set, 'DELIVERANCE' (1999), which could be described as a mixed bag of neo-country TEENAGE FANCLUB fused with a Lo-Fi BEACH BOYS whispering away somewhere at the back of a spiritual surf club. 'UNGRATEFUL' was perhaps the sharpest opener on an album for some time, its steel-stringed guitar taking no prisoners; WYLIE's softly sung vocal was equal to the breezy accompaniment of his band.

The COSMIC ROUGH RIDERS released their sophomore set, 'PANORAMA' (2000), to much critical acclaim, here and across the Atlantic(!). The record might well have been a soundtrack to a great Scottish western, if, erm, Westerns were, er, shot here. Again drawing references from such luminaries as the JAYHAWKS and current alt-country meisters KNIFE IN WATER, the album was more varied via musical scope, not to mention musical talent. Neatly structured songs, awash with violin, acoustic guitar and a crisp backing melody, suggested that even if the band failed at moments (e.g. 'BROTHER GATHER ROUND' began with a tremendous pop'n'rock riff but then faded to almost nothing), their passion and country spirit finally led them to the musical promised land. ALAN McGEE, ex-honcho at 'Creation' records, seemed more than impressed with the band's development and signed the group to his 'Poptones' imprint where they issued the single 'LOSER' and its parent long-player, 'ENJOY THE MELODIC SUNSHINE' (2000). Early the following year, they paid homage to the late, great ALEX HARVEY, by covering his 'ACTION STRASSE'; it was showcased on a BBCTV tribute. In July 2001, the CRR had their first UK Top 40 hit via 'REVOLUTION (IN THE SUMMERTIME?)', it looked like the band were heading for the big time. However, by the following March, WYLIE had opted for a solo venture leaving the rest to ponder their futures.

DANIEL WYLIE (b. 2 Jan'72) – vocals (ex-THIEVES) / **STEPHEN FLEMING** – electric guitar / **GARY CUTHBERT** – acoustic guitar / **JAMES CLIFFORD** – bass / **MARK BROWN** – drums

Raft Raft

Jun 99. (cd) *(<RAFT 001>)* **DELIVERANCE** [ ] [ ]
– Ungrateful / Rape seed children / Patience / What's your sign / Country life / Still a mother's son / Baby, you're so free / Emily darling / Brand new car / Here comes my train / Lady in the lake / Glastonbury revisited / Garden of Eden / New day dawning. *(re-iss. Jul00; same)*

Mar 00. (cd) *(<RAFT 002>)* **PANORAMA** [ ] [ ]
– Revolution (in the summertime) / Have you heard the news today / Brother gather round / The gun isn't loaded / Value of life / You've got me / Afterglow / The pain inside / The charm / I call her name / The loser / Can't get any closer / To be someone / Back home again.

Poptones not iss.

Oct 00. (7") *(MC 5015 S7)* **THE LOSER. / PAIN INSIDE** [ ] [-]

Nov 00. (cd/lp) *(MC 5015 CD/LP)* **ENJOY THE MELODIC SUNSHINE** [ ] [-]
– Brother gather round / Gun isn't loaded / Glastonbury revisited / Baby, you're so free / Value of life / Revolution (in the summertime?) / Have you heard the news today / Sometime / Melanie / Pain inside / Charm / The loser / You've got me / Emily darling / Morning sun.

Feb 01. (7") *(MC 5033S)* **MELANIE. / UNIVERSAL THING** [ ] [-]
(cd-s+=) *(MC 5033SCD)* – Annie.

Apr 01. (7") *(MC 5042S)* **BABY, YOU'RE SO FREE. / NOTHING TO LOSE** [ ] [-]
(cd-s+=) *(MC 5042SCD)* – The sound of windchimes.
(cd-s) *(MC 5042SCX)* – ('A'side) / Alright / Your eyes.

Jul 01. (7") *(MC 5047S)* **REVOLUTION (IN THE SUMMERTIME?). / MOVE ALONG** [35] [-]
(cd-s+=) *(MC 5047SCD)* – The gun isn't loaded (live).
(cd-s) *(MC 5047SCX)* – ('A'side) / River runs dry / ('A'-live).

Sep 01. (7") *(MC 5052S)* **PAIN INSIDE. / I GOT OVER YOU** [36] [-]
(cd-s+=) *(MC 5052SCD)* – Camera shy.
(cd-s) *(MC 5052SCX)* – ('A'side) / Laura Nyro / Melanic acoustic.

— in Mar'02, WYLIE decided to leave; FLEMING took over vocal duties

Sep 02. (cd) *(MC 5060CD)* **PURE ESCAPISM** (compilation of B-sides) [ ] [-]
– Pain inside (remix) / Annie / Laura Nyro / I got over you / Camera shy / Universal thing / Nothing to lose / River runs dry / Sound of windchimes / Alright / Move along / Your eyes / Melanie (acoustic) / *(CD-Rom tracks)* – Melanie / Baby you're free / Revolution (in the summertime?) / Pain inside (remix).
(above was issued in Japan in December 2001)

COUNTERPLAN (see under ⇒ Soma records / SLAM)

COUNTRY TEASERS

Formed: Edinburgh . . . 1992 by singing guitarist BENEDICT R. WALLERS (the archetypal barbed bard of sorts), along with the rhythm section of SIMON STEPHENS and GEORGE MILLER. With guitarist ALAN CRICHTON borrowed from sister group THE MALE NURSE – which also featured BEN – the 4-piece CT's cut a couple of garage/punkabilly numbers including 'ONLY WHITTLIN' (which later featured on Guided Missile's 'Hits & Missiles' V/A set in 1999).

Inspired by the sounds of BILLY CHILDISH, The FALL and CAPTAIN BEEFHEART – 'BITCHES' FUCK-OFF' being a prime example, the COUNTRY TEASERS rumbled on to deliver their 'PASTORAL . . .' debut album in Spring '95. Sticksman ECK KING would subsequently supersede MARK CARR, a short-termer brought in to take the place of MILLER, who was more interested in other Beatles-esque band, The KAISERS. Towards the end of the year, just after a one-off EP was recorded (released by BEN and the group's alter-ego, ALAN COUNTRY DAVIDSON), a third guitarist RICHARD GREENAN was in place. A second album, 'SATAN IS REAL AGAIN', was issued in 1996, while their "SCOTTISH SINGLE" was another to be released by 'Guided Missile'. Keeping personnel was becoming quite a problem when STEPHENS bailed out of a second European tour late '96. ALASDAIR MacKINVEN (from THE MALE NURSE) was duly drafted in on bass, although he remained as guitarist when GREENAN departed. Early in 1998, CRICHTON was no longer a member and sadly he was to die (misadventure) the following February.

Meanwhile, WALLERS, STEPHENS, MacKINVEN had recruited yet another MALE NURSE refugee, LAWRENCE WORTHINGTON and this was the new line-up to sign for US-based 'Epitaph' records. The long-awaited third album proper, 'DESTROY ALL HUMAN LIFE' (there had been a Guided Missile compilation, 'BACK 2 THE FUTURE', in '98), finally hit the indie shops in Spring 1999 and contained fine covers of Sherill-Sutton's 'ALMOST PERSUADED' and the traditional 'GO AWAY FROM MY WINDOW'. ROBERT McNEILL was subsequently added to boost the numbers up to five again and for US tours, although STEPHENS would make them four and a half! (a quarintet, quite possibly because he became part-time) after the 'IDIOTS V SPASTICS' EP in 2000.

The group subsequently issued what was to be their oddest album ever, the sinisterly-titled 'SCIENCE HAT, ARTISTIC CUBE, MORAL NOSEBLEED EMPIRE' in 2002. Released as a 'rarities' pack, the album fused the band's jet-black humour with some interesting biblical references and a few good instumentals to boot. Amongst the highlights were the covers of Euro techno group 2 UNLIMITED's early 90's smash 'NO LIMITS' (no, I'm not kidding) and ICE CUBE's 'WE HAD TO TEAR THIS MOTHERFUCKER UP'. 'I'M A NEW PERSON, MA'AM' was a genuine heartfelt country song, whereas 'COMPRESSOR' and 'CAN'T SING' ventured into obscure territory. Great if you're a fan of The COUNTRY TEASERS, but if not, try some of their earlier stuff first.

BENEDICT R. WALLERS – vocals, guitar, keyboards / **SIMON STEPHENS** – bass / **GEORGE MILLER** – drums (also of KAISERS) / (1994) added **ALAN CRICHTON** (b.1970) – guitar

Crypt Crypt

Nov 94. (7") *(efa 11588-7)* **NUMBER 1 MAN. / ANYTIME, COWBOY** [ ] [-]
<(US + re-iss. Nov96; CRYPT 69)>

Apr 95. (cd/10"lp) *(efa 11594-2/-1)* *<CRYPT 60>* **THE PASTORAL-NOTRUSTIC WORLD OF THEIR GREATEST HITS** [ ] [ ] Jan96
– How I found Black-Brodie / Only my saviour / Bitches' fuck-off / O, nurse! / Anytime, cowboy 2 / Mosquito / Drove a truck / Been too long / Black cloud wandering / Stand by your man / Anytime, cowboy / Number 1 man.

— **ECK KING** – drums; repl. short-stay member MARK CARR who'd repl. MILLER who continued with KAISERS

— added **RICHARD GREENAN** – guitar

Jul 96. (cd/lp) *(efa 012877-2/-1)* *<CRYPT 66>* **SATAN IS REAL AGAIN** [ ] [ ] Oct96
– Wide-open beaver of Nashville / Black change / Panty shots / It is my duty / Devil on my back / Little black clouds / Lies / Thank you God for making me an angel / Cripples / Some hole / Don't like people / Country fag / Satan is real again / These things shall pass.

Guided Missile not iss.

Sep 96. (7") *(GUIDE 09)* **THE SCOTTISH SINGLE** [ ] [-]
– The last bridge of Spencer Smith / Prettiest slave on the barge.

— (late '96) **ALASDAIR MacKINVEN** – bass; repl. STEPHENS for a tour

— (1997) **STEPHENS** returned to repl. GREENAN (MacKINVEN now on guitar)

Nana / not iss.

Mar 97. (7") *(NANA 03)* **SECRETS IN WELSH. / TOUGH LUCK ON JOCK** [-] [-] welsh

— in Jun'97, the COUNTRY TEASERS were part of the 'Guided Missile' single as ALAN COUNTRY DAVIDSON; unreleased BEN stuff incl. 'Trendy Mick Fleetwood' on the 'AGAINST COUNTRY TEASERS' *(GUIDE 18)*
– After one thing / Bryson's the baker / Small shark in the tiny pool / Adam wakes up / Kenny Malcolm on smack / Henry Krinkle's theme.

— (1998) **BEN, SIMON + ALASDAIR** were joined by **LAWRENCE WORTHINGTON** – drums; repl. KING (CRICHTON also departed in 1998; he died in February '99)

Epitaph / Epitaph

Apr 99. (cd/lp) *(<8325-2/-1>)* **DESTROY ALL HUMAN LIFE** [ ] [ ] Feb99
– Reynard the fox / Golden apples / David I hope you don't mind / Hairy wine / Deliverance from misrule / Almost persuaded / Go away from my window / Broken Jews etc. / Women and children first / Come back Maggy / Song of the white feather club secretary.

Guided Missile / not iss.

May 99. (ltd-7"ep) *(GUIDE 35)* **GUIDED MISSILE SPLIT SINGLE BY COUNTRY TEASERS and AMNESIAC GODZ** [ ] [-]
– (2 by AMNESIAC GODZ) / Hairy wine / Reynard the fox.

— added **ROBERT McNEILL** – bass, guitar

Mar 00. (7"ep) *(GUIDE 40)* **THE REBEL: IDIOTS V SPASTICS EP** [ ] [-]
– The idiot / Julie's resolution / The spastic / Un Canadien errant.

— (late 2000) – STEPHENS was now only part-time (**WESLEY WILLIS**) replaced him

— **WALLERS + MILLER** recruited **KANAAN TUPPER** – bass

– compilations, etc. –

Apr 98. (cd) *Guided Missile; (GUIDE 27CD)* **BACK 2 THE FUTURE** (compilation 1992-97) [ ] [-]
– Let's have a shambles! / Good pair of hands / Kill / No limits / I get hard / Tights / Go down, mighty Devil / "The risk" / Get your hole / Milkman / I know my name is there / Women & children 1st (live) / Lies (live) / Tainted love (live) / "Axe" Greenan (live) / Drove a truck (live) / Prettiest slave on the barge (live) / Country roads (live).

Apr 02. (d-lp/cd) *In The Red; (<ITR 032/+CD>)* **SCIENCE HAT, ARTISTIC CUBE, MORAL NOSEBLEED EMPIRE** [ ] [ ]
– Compressor / Getaway / Some hole / I'm a new person, ma'am / $4.99 / Mollusc in country / Happy feet / No limits / Hat on the red / Secrets in Welsh / Adam wakes up / Loose tongues get into tight places / After one thing / Treble life No.2 / The last bridge of Spencer Smith / Can't sing / We had to tear this motherfucker up / Only whittlin' / Postman Pak and his lazy black & white cunts / Tough luck on Jock. *(d-lp+=* – (20 more!).

COWBOY MOUTH

Formed: Glasgow . . . 1994 by former LOVE AND MONEY guys PAUL McGEEGHAN and DOUGLAS McINTYRE, who teamed up with former HIPSWAY frontman GRAHAME SKINNER and ex-L&M drummer GORDON WILSON. This easy-pop/rock supergroup of sorts managed to release two albums, 'LIFE AS A DOG' (1995) and 'LOVE IS DEAD' (1995) in a short space of time, McGEECHAN and McINTYRE both moonlighted with the two-album, SUGARTOWN. • **Note:** not to be confused with the US COWBOY MOUTH.

GRAEME SKINNER – vocals, guitar (ex-HIPSWAY) / **PAUL McGEEGHAN** – keyboards (ex-LOVE AND MONEY, ex-FRIENDS AGAIN) / **DOUGLAS McINTYRE** – bass (ex-LOVE AND MONEY) / **GORDON WILSON** – drums

Marina / not iss.

Jan 95. (cd) *(MA 8 – MACD 93663)* **LIFE AS A DOG** [ ] [-]
– Headlights / My kife as a dog / Gun on the run / I won't let it happen again / Since I tasted candy / Letter from L.A. / Bad poetry / Sea shanty No.1 / Million miles / Breakdown.

May 95. (cd-ep) *(MA 10 – MACD 93963)* **MY LIFE AS A DOG E.P.** [ ] [-]
– My life as a dog / Ballad of Cowboy Mouth / Sedan delivery / Million miles (Mount Florida swamp version).

Nov 95. (cd) *(MA 17 – MACD 44642)* **LOVE IS DEAD** [ ] [-]
– Melanie / My beautiful dream / Geek love / Waiting for an echo / Sea shanty No.2 / Summer runaway / Sister Peregrine / Ballad of a Cowboy Mouth / Burning the candle / The colour of Spring / Love is dead.

Jan 96. (cd-ep) *(MA 18)* **SUGARTOWN E.P.** [ ] [-]
– Sugartown / Since I tasted candy / Melanie / A very precious time.

SUGARTOWN

— duo which also contained **McGEECHAN + McINTYRE**

Mar 95. (cd) *(MA 9 – MACD 69336)* **SWIMMING IN THE HORSEPOOL** [ ] [-]
– Secondhand / I'm set free / This is not for me / There was a time / You'll still be calling my name / The last beautiful day / Valentine / Desert bloom / Boy / John Singer blues / I'm waiting for you / Sin of pity.

Sep 97. (cd) *(MA 31 – MACD 44752)* **SLOW FLOWS THE RIVER** [ ] [-]
– I shot the albatross / The look in your eyes / Sad eyed in the city / The summer fires / The fisherman and his soul / I won't let you go again / Viaduct / State / Are you with the one you love / Soft water.

CREME DE MENTHE (see under ⇒ Oscarr records)

CROWS (see under ⇒ Scotland's wee metal scene)

CRUYFF (see under ⇒ IMPERIAL RACING CLUB)

CUBAN HEELS

Formed: Glasgow . . . late 1977 by ex-JOHNNY & THE SELF-ABUSERS (the embryonic SIMPLE MINDS) singer, JOHN MILARKY. While JIM KERR & Co. went on to explore experimental post-punk territory, The CUBAN HEELS kicked up a more straightforward blend of new-wave power-pop and 60's retro sounds.

After debuting with a charged-up cover of Petula Clark's 'DOWNTOWN' in Spring '78 on the tiny 'Housewife's Choice' label, the group underwent a shift in personnel as NICK CLARKE replaced ARMOUR and ALI McKENZIE replaced DUNCAN. A further two singles, 'LITTLE GIRL' and 'WALK ON WATER', appeared on their own 'Greville' and 'Cuba Libre' labels respectively, ushering in a major label deal with 'Virgin'. Released in Spring '81, the CUBAN HEELS' first single for the label, 'SWEET CHARITY', sounded like The B-52's FRED SCHNEIDER fronting a poppier SKIDS, a band with whom The 'HEELS were comparable in image terms as well as musical. Frantic follow-up single, 'MY COLOURS FLY', previewed the band's long awaited debut album, 'WORK OUR WAY TO HEAVEN' (1981). With a muted response from both press and punters alike, the band released a last gasp remake of 'WALK ON WATER' before calling it a day the following year. • **Covered:** MATTHEW AND SON (Cat Stevens).

JOHN MILARKY – vocals / **LAURIE CUFFE** – guitar / **PAUL ARMOUR** – bass / **DAVIE DUNCAN** – drums

Housewife's Choice / not iss.

Apr 78. (7") *(JW 1-2)* **DOWNTOWN. / DO THE SMOKE WALK** [ ] [-]

— **NICK CLARK** – bass; repl. ARMOUR

— **ALI MacKENZIE** – drums; repl. DUNCAN

Greville / not iss.

Aug 80. (7") *(GR 1)* **LITTLE GIRL. / FAST LIVING FRIEND** [ ] [-]

Cuba Libre / not iss.

Jan 81. (7") *(DRINK 1)* **WALK ON WATER. / TAKE A LOOK** [ ] [-]

Virgin / not iss.

May 81. (7") *(VS 413)* **SWEET CHARITY. / PAY AS YOU GO** [ ] [-]
Aug 81. (7") *(VS 439)* **MY COLOURS FLY. / CUBA LIBRE** [ ] [-]
Oct 81. (lp) *(V 2210)* **WORK OUR WAY TO HEAVEN** [ ] [-]
– Liberty hall / Move up a grade / A matter of time / Homes for heroes / The old school song / Walk on water / Hard times / Coming up for air / Work our way to Heaven / My colours fly.

Nov 81. (7") *(VS 440)* **WALK ON WATER. / HARD TIMES** [ ] [-]
(with free 7"flexi) – Matthew and son.

— split some time in 1982

D

DADDYLONGLEGS (see under ⇒ B, Howie)

DADDY'S FAVOURITE

Formed: Glasgow . . . mid-90's by solo DJ/producer, HARRI (aka HARRIGAN) along with co-conspirator McEWAN. HARRI's solo work from 1993 including the 'SKELPH' and 'PHUXACHE' EP's for 23rd Precinct subsidiary 'Limbo'; he was also part of 'Sativa', 'Pure', 'Sonore' and 'Mr. Egg'. Techno dance DJ HARRIGAN subsequently joined forces with a guy called McEWAN to form DADDY'S FAVOURITE; their single 'I FEEL GOOD THINGS FOR YOU' hit the Top 50 twice, in '98 and '99.

HARRI

Limbo — not iss.

Mar 93. (12") *(Limb 09)* **SKELPH. / ('A'dub) / ('A'club dub)** [ ] [-]
Jun 93. (12") *(WMR 1002)* **STRICTLY DRUM AND BASS** [ ] [-]
(above issued on 'Walking Man')
Apr 94. (12"ep) *(Limb 30T)* **PHUXACHE EP** [ ] [-]

Bomba — not iss.

Aug 94. (12"; as HARRI Vs VISNATI) *(BOMB12 007)* **VESPA** [ ] [-]

DADDY'S FAVOURITE

HARRIGAN + McEWAN

Dodgey — not iss.

Mar 97. (12") *(DS 7901)* **GOOD TIMES (mixes)** [ ] [-]

Go Beat — not iss.

Nov 98. (c-s/12"/cd-s) *(GOB MC/X/CD 12)* **I FEEL GOOD THINGS FOR YOU (mixes by ALAN BRAXE, KEVIN YOST and RESTLESS SOUL MOVEMENT)** [44] [-]
(12") *(GOBXL 12)* – ('A'mixes).
Sep 99. (12"/cd-s) *(GOB X/CD 22)* **I FEEL GOOD THINGS FOR YOU (mixes)** [50] [-]
(cd-s) *(GOLCD 22)* – ('A'mixes).

DANCE OVER DOSE (see under ⇒ Shoop records)

DANCE UNITED (see under ⇒ Limbo records)

DANNY WILSON

Formed: Dundee . . . 1986 by brothers GARY and KIT CLARK alongside friend GED GRIMES. After originally calling themselves SPENCER TRACY, they took the name DANNY WILSON after a character in a Frank Sinatra film.

Issued on 'Virgin', the band's debut single and lilting signature tune, 'MARY'S PRAYER' wasn't a hit first time round but subsequently hit the US Top 30 in summer '87; it finally cracked the British charts that August while smashing the Top 3 the following March! Peddling intelligent pop/rock influenced by STEELY DAN or an easier-going ASSOCIATES, it wasn't hard to see how the band had managed an American hit barely a year into their career. Debut album, 'MEET DANNY WILSON' (1987), followed in the traditon of creamy Scots soul/pop and wasn't all that far removed from the likes of DEACON BLUE. 1989's 'BEBOP MOPTOP' album, meanwhile, proved more successful in Britain, the band riding the luvved-up wave of the baggy generation into the Top 30 with 'THE SECOND SUMMER OF LOVE'.

Yet DANNY WILSON, like so many Scottish bands, were always nearly there but not quite. After the band's split in 1990 (and the short-lived ELEVEN project), GARY went on to release a Top 30 solo album, 'TEN SHORT SONGS ABOUT LOVE' (1993), together with a handful of minor hit singles. He subsequently formed the less popular KING L (with NEIL MacCOLL), releasing a solitary album, 'GREAT DAY FOR GRAVITY' (1995).

• **Songwriters:** GARY CLARK was main composer, except a cover of KNOWING ME KNOWING YOU (Abba). Solo, he covered SARA SMILE (Hall & Oates) / MY LOVE IS LIKE A RED RED ROSE (trad.).

• **Trivia:** On their debut album they introduced LESTER BOWLES BRASS FANTASY with DAVID PALMER, RODDY LORIMER, GEOFF DUGMORE, etc.

GARY CLARK – vocals, guitar / **KIT CLARK** – keyboards, percussion / **GED GRIMES** – bass

Virgin — Virgin

Feb 87. (7") *(VS 934)* <99465> **MARY'S PRAYER. / MONKEY'S SHINEY DAY (demo)** [ ] [23] May87
(12"+=) *(VS 934-12)* – ('A'extended).
(re-iss. Aug87) – hit No.42
(10"+=) *(VS 934-10)* – Broken china (demo) / Steamtrains to the Milky Way (demo). *(re-iss. Mar88)* – hit No.3
(cd-s+=) *(VSCD 934)* – Kooks / Mary's prairie.
Apr 87. (lp/c/cd) *(V/TCV/CDV 2419)* <90596> **MEET DANNY WILSON** [ ] [79] Jul87
– Davy / Mary's prayer / Lorraine parade / Aberdeen / Nothing ever goes to plan / Broken china / Steam trains to the milky way / Spencer-Tracey / You remain an angel / Ruby's golden wedding / A girl I used to know / Five friendly aliens / I wont be here when you get home. *(in Apr'88 the album hit UK No.65) (re-iss. Apr90 lp/c; OVED/+C 297)*
May 87. (7") *(VS 965)* **DAVY. / I WON'T FORGET** [ ] [-]
(12"+=) *(VS 965-12)* – Pleasure to pleasure.
Oct 87. (7") *(VS 1011)* **A GIRL I USED TO KNOW. / I WONT FORGET** [ ] [ ]
(12"+=) *(VST 1011)* – Pleasure to pleasure.
(cd-s++=) *(CDEP 2)* – Mary's prayer.
Jun 88. (7") *(VS 1095)* **DAVY. / LIVING TO LEARN** [ ] [ ]
(c-s+=/12"+=/cd-s+=) *(VS TC/T/CD 1095)* – Aberdeen (The way it should have been) / Kathleen.
Jun 89. (7") *(VS 1186)* **THE SECOND SUMMER OF LOVE. / I'LL BE WAITING** [23] [ ]
(12"+=/10"+=/3"cd-s+=) *(VS T/A/CD 1186)* – Growing emotional.
Jul 89. (lp/c/cd) *(V/TCV/CDV 2594)* **BEBOP MOPTOP** [24] [ ]
– Imaginary girl / The second summer of love / I can't wait / Desert hearts / If you really love me (let me go) / If everything you said was true / Loneliness / I was wrong / Charlie boy / Never gonna be the same / N.Y.C. shanty / Goodbye shanty town / The ballad of me and Shirley MacLaine. *(c re-iss. Aug91; OVEDC 387)*
Aug 89. (7") *(VS 1203)* **NEVER GONNA BE THE SAME. / NOTHING EVER GOES TO PLAN** [69] [-]
(12"+=/10"+=/cd-s+=) *(VS T/A/CD 1203)* – The lonesome road / Get happy.
Nov 89. (7") *(VS 1226)* **I CAN'T WAIT. / STEAMTRAINS TO THE MILKY WAY (live)** [ ] [ ]
(12"+=/cd-s+=) *(VS T/CD 1226)* – Knowing me knowing you.

— disbanded in February 1990, KIT would later turn up in the SWISS FAMILY ORBISON

– compilations, others, etc. –

Aug 88. (cd-ep) *Virgin; (CDEP 12)* **A GIRL I USED TO KNOW / DAVY / MARY'S PRAYER** [ ] [-]
Jul 91. (7") *Virgin* **IF YOU REALLY LOVE ME (LET ME GO) (New York mix). / THE SECOND SUMMER OF LOVE** [ ] [-]
(12"+=/cd-s+=) – I can't wait (live) / Mary's prayer (live).
Aug 91. (cd/c/lp) *Virgin; (CD/TC+/V 2669)* **SWEET DANNY WILSON** [54] [-]
– Never gonna be the same / The ballad of me and Shirley MacLaine / If you really love me (let me go) (New York mix) / Mary's prayer / A girl I used to know / Pleasure to pleasure / Davy / Ruby's golden wedding / I can't wait / I won't be here when you get home / Second summer of love / From a boy to a man. *(cd w/free cd; CDVX 2669)* – Get happy / Kathleen (house mix) / Growing emotional / I'll be waiting / Living to learn / I won't forget / Kooks / Broken China (live) / Aberdeen (live) / Steamtrains to the Milky Way (live) / Knowing me knowing you (live) / Don't know who I am (live) / I was wrong (live) / Loneliness (live).
Sep 95. (cd/c) *VIP-Virgin; (CD/TC VIP 139)* **THE BEST OF DANNY WILSON** [ ] [-]

ELEVEN

— formed by **GARY CLARK** and an ex-member of PREFAB SPROUT

Seven — not iss.

Nov 91. (12") **YOU CAN'T TURN AROUND TO ME. / A PLACE TO STAY** [ ] [-]

GARY CLARK

— with **GARY THOMPSON** – horns / **KARLOS EDWARDS** – percussion

Circa — Virgin

Jan 93. (7"/c-s) *(YR/+C 93)* **WE SAIL ON STORMY WATERS. / THE LETTER** [34] [ ]
(cd-s+=) *(YRCDX 93)* – Sara Smile. / We can love again.
(cd-s) *(YRCD 93)* – ('A'side) / My love is like a red red rose / You can't turn around to me / Now do you stop!
Mar 93. (7"/c-s) *(YR/+C 94)* **FREEFLOATING. / A RED RICKENBACKER GUITAR – WHERE I LIVE?** [50] [ ]
(cd-s+=) *(YRCDX 94)* – Jesus, do you wonder why? / House of joy.
(cd-s) *(YRCD 94)* –
Apr 93. (c/cd/lp) *(CIRC/+D/A 23)* **TEN SHORT SONGS ABOUT LOVE** [25] [ ]
– This is why J. / We sail on stormy waters / St.Jude / A short song about love / Make a family / Freefloating / Baby blue No.2 / Nancy any Sunday morning / Making people cry / Sail on! / A Jackson in your kitchen.
Jun 93. (7"/c-s) *(YR/+C 105)* **MAKE A FAMILY. / THE SECOND SUMMER OF LOVE (live)** [70] [-]
(cd-s+=) *(YRCDX 105)* – Learning to do without me (live) / Saturday night (live).
(cd-s) *(YRCD 105)* – ('A'side) / We sail on stormy waters (live) / Baby blue No.2 (live) / Mary's prayer (live).

KING L

— **GARY CLARK / NEIL MacCOLL / ERIC PRESSLEY / MATT LANG**

Aug 95. (cd-ep) **TRAGEDY GIRL / TON DRIVER / BACK TO LOVING ARMS / TWO CARS COLLIDE** [ ] [-]
Sep 95. (cd/c) *(CIRC/+D 32)* **GREAT DAY FOR GRAVITY** [ ] [ ]
– Tragedy girl / Dumbest story / Ton driver / Greedy / All hail the alien queen / Back to loving arms / Life after you / That's how it works / Hoping they'll be open / First man on the sun / Two cars collide / Don't believe in Hollywood / Lost and found and lost again / My last cigarette.
Oct 95. (c-s) *(YRC 123)* **LIFE AFTER YOU / BREAKDOWN** [ ] [-]
(cd-s+=) *(YRCD 123)* – Greedy.

(cd-s) *(YRCDX 123)* – ('A'side) / Shoe gravy / Don't believe in Hollywood / Revolution's birthday.

Jan 96. (c-s/cd-s) *(YRC/+D 124)* **FIRST MAN ON THE SUN /** [ ] [-]

DANSATAK / MASSIVE (see under ⇒ Shoop records)

DARIUS

Born: DARIUS DANESH, 1980, Glasgow. Ahhhh, yes, DARIUS DANESH was the man everybody loved to hate in 1999 following his cringe-worthy performance of Britney Spears' 'BABY, HIT ME ONE MORE TIME' on the ITV talent show 'Pop Stars' (which spawned the godawful HEAR'SAY).

Studying politics at Edinburgh, the pony-tailed DARIUS did himself no favours when he auditioned for the supergroup, with his histrionic performances (granted, the man was talented but he did go OTT), boisterous arrogance and corny speeches ("Can you feel the love in the room?", has since become a national catchphrase). After being shunted by Nasty Nigel and wanton pop guru Nicki Campbell, the 20 year-old bitterly quipped, "By the time I'm 35 I will have a multi-platinum album", and, in some respects his prophecy could still come true. Much ridicule and derisive laughter was aimed towards DARIUS after the programme had finished its run, but it was all taken in good humour by the lanky Scotsman who looked more like an apartment-sharing bohemian artist than an aspiring popstar. However, a change was on the cards for DARIUS as album deals fell through and his family were receiving some unwanted attention from the press.

He pretty much kept a low profile until a revised version of 'Pop Stars', cleverly(!) entitled 'Pop Idol', saw the return of a now clean-shaven, slightly more mature and modest DARIUS. He made the final ten but was voted out by viewers, only to be given a second chance by the coincidental demise of "big man" RIK WALLER. Proving to be the punk of 'Pop Idol', he quickly regained the public's attention due to his frequent bickering with the unsatisfied judge Simon Cowell and his smooth Sean Connery-esque appeal. DARIUS emerged as a close runner-up, coming in third, refusing a three-album deal with Cowell, instead embarking on a tour with the 'Pop Idol' bunch and signing with 'Mercury'. His self-penned, Nicky Graham (BROS and ANT & DEC) produced debut single 'COLOURBLIND' was issued to surprisingly good reviews, smashing the UK No.1 slot in August 2002. A simple, acoustic driven pop tune, DARIUS did well by reducing his arrogance factor by nil and proving to be an ambitious fellow with a lot to lose and little to gain. He was a public laughing stock for eighteen months, but like BRITNEY SPEARS said after she had watched his rendition of 'BABY . . .' on The Frank Skinner Show: "I guess that guy's got his own thing going on . . .". Indeed.

DARIUS – vocals / with various backing

Mercury | not iss.

Jul 02. (c-s) *(63965-4)* **COLOURBLIND / IT'S NOT UNUSUAL (live) / CHRYSALIS** [1] [-]
(cd-s) *(63965-2)* – (first 2 tracks) / ('A'acoustic + video).
(cd-s) *(63966-2)* – (first & third track) / ('A'-CD-Rom interview).

DAWN OF THE REPLICANTS

Formed: Galashiels . . . 1996 by Teesside-raised singer-songwriter, PAUL VICKERS along with guitarist, ROGER SIMIAN, the latter spending the bulk of his student loan on a mail-order debut EP, 'SO FAR SO SPITFIRE' (recorded as The REPLICANTS). Available from early '97, the record's R.E.M.-esque lead track, 'COCAINE ON THE CATWALK', was given airplay by both John Peel and Mark Radcliffe, selling out its initial 500 copies almost immediately.

Expanding the line-up with addition of former schoolmates, DONALD KYLE, MIKE SMALL and GRANT PRINGLE, The DAWN OF THE REPLICANTS released a second single, 'HOGWASH FARM' on their 'dumbSULK trigg-er' imprint and after interest from the likes of 'Che', 'Too Pure' and 'Chemikal Underground', they opted to sign on the dotted line for Warner Brothers subsidiary 'eastwest'.

Their major label tenure got off to a prolific start with the release of three EP's (namely 'VIOLENT SUNDAYS', 'ALL THAT CHEYENNE CABOODLE' and 'RHINO DAYS') in the latter half of '97, the lead tracks being re-recorded versions of 'COCAINE ON THE CATWALK', 'LISA BOX' and the brand new 'RADARS' respectively. With music press acclaim steadily growing, the Borders lads notched up their first chart entry with the morbidly infectious 'CANDLEFIRE', a song that invoked the ghosts of early 80's Liverpool (i.e. IAN McCULLOCH, JULIAN COPE and The ROOM's DAVE JACKSON).

The heavy release schedule continued unabated with the much anticipated Top 75 debut set, 'ONE HEAD, TWO ARMS, TWO LEGS' (1998), a pot-pourri of wilful experimentation and contrasting styles that collected together all of the aforementioned tracks side by side with fresh material such as 'WINDY MILLER' (Trumpton revisited REPLICANTS style), the U2 goes Lo-Fi 'SO SLEEPY' and the lyrically enigmatic (not for the first time) 'SGT GROWLEY'. The following April, a second set 'WRONG TOWN, WRONG PLANET, THREE HOURS LATE' (1999) was issued, although its disappointing sales returns were to lead to 'eastwest' letting them go. The group subsequently went into a sort of hibernation with only VICKERS resurfacing as spokesman for indie offshoot duo, PLUTO MONKEY. They released a couple of 45's and an album, 'LITTLE BRENDA: BLUEGRASS MISSION' (2000) for 'Shifty Disco', but what had happened to the DOTR. An answer was unveiled in September 2002, when John Peel sessions heralded new songs from their long-awaited third set, 'TOUCHING THE PROPELLER'. Released on 'Flying Sparks' records (home of GORDON HASKELL and THEA GILMORE), the record was a raw and dusty batch of rough-hewn songs, one of them 'SMOKE WITHOUT FIRE' featuring SUSI O'NIELL on theremin and other assorted instruments.

• **Covered:** BALLAD OF A THIN MAN (Bob Dylan).

PAUL VICKERS – vocals, synthesizer / **ROGER SIMIAN** – guitar, keyboards, vocals

dumbSULK trigg-er | not iss.

Jan 97. (7"ep; as The REPLICANTS) *(DST 7-1)* **SO FAR SO SPITFIRE EP** [-] [-] mail-o
– Cocaine on the catwalk / Digging bear / Lisa box / Bizarre concoction.

—— added **DONALD KYLE** – bass, guitar / **MIKE SMALL** – guitar, keyboards, vocals / **GRANT PRINGLE** – drums, keyboards, vocals

Jun 97. (10") *(SAM 2063)* **HOGWASH FARM. / CHAOS IN AN INKWELL** [ ] [-]

eastwest | not iss.

Aug 97. (d7"ep/cd-ep) *(EW 115/+CD)* **VIOLENT SUNDAYS E.P.** [ ] [-]
– Cocaine on the catwalk (re-recording) / Non capisco / Only small birds do / Beyond the nest.

Sep 97. (d7"ep/cd-ep) *(EW 125/+CD)* **ALL THAT CHEYENNE CABOODLE E.P.** [ ] [-]
– Lisa box (re-recording) / Diggin' bear (re-recording) / Will you ever phone? / Skullcrusher.

Nov 97. (d7"ep/cd-ep) *(EW 134/+CD)* **RHINO RAYS E.P.** [ ] [-]
– Radars / Bionic stardust / The wrong turnstile / Seasick odyssey.

Jan 98. (10") *(EW 147 TE/CD1)* **CANDLE FIRE. / SKULLCRUSHER (David Holmes & Tim Goldsworthy remix)** [52] [-]
(cd-s+=) *(EW 147CD1)* – Leaving so soon?
(cd-s) *(EW 147CD2)* – ('A'side) / Leaving iota / Chesty Morgan.

Feb 98. (cd/c/lp) *(0630 19600-2/-4/-1)* **ONE HEAD, TWO ARMS, TWO LEGS** [62] [-]
– Cocaine on the catwalk / Candle fire / Ten sea birds / Lisa box / Return of the board game / Windy Miller / Radars / So sleepy / Let them eat coal / Sgt Growley / Hogwash farm / Sleepy spiders / Float on a raft / Mary Louise / Fatal firework.

Mar 98. (7"ep/cd-ep) *(EW 157/+CD)* **HOGWASH FARM (THE DIESEL HANDS E.P.)** [65] [-]
– Hogwash farm (re-built) / Night train to Lichtenstein / The duchess of Surin / Crow valley.

Jun 98. (12"ep/cd-ep) *(EW 166 T/CD)* **I SMELL VOODOO E.P.** [ ] [-]
– Mary Louise / Ballad of a thin man / Myrhh tingle / Dual converter.

Aug 98. (7"/cd-s) *(NING 59/+CD)* **BORN IN BASKETS. / Inner Sleeve: Come Alive** [ ] [-]
(above 'GOING DOWN THE TUBES WITH . . . single was on 'Fierce Panda')

Apr 99. (cd/c/lp) *(3984 26474-2/-4/-1)* **WRONG TOWN, WRONG PLANET, THREE HOURS LATE.** [ ] [-]
– Gasoline vine / Love is a curse / Rule the roost / Sub erotic fields / Zulu kites / Wheelie bin drive / Cabin fever / Jack Fanny's gym / Science fiction freak / Big hefty hounds / The soil idea / Toe dog eyes / Get a bright flame / Howlin' in the dark / Hand relief / Fearless vampire hunters.

Apr 99. (12"ep/cd-ep) *(EW 197 T/CD1)* **RULE THE ROOST. / ON THE RADIO / RUNNING INTO TROUBLE** [ ] [-]
(cd-s) *(EW 197CD2)* – ('A'side) / Chaos in an inkwell (original dumb-SULK version) / Sgt Growley (Peel session version).

Jul 99. (7") *(EW 204)* **SCIENCE FICTION FREAK. / YELLOW BEATLE** [ ] [-]
(cd-s+=) *(EW 204CD)* – Buffalo ballet.

Flying Sparks | not iss.

Sep 02. (cd-s) *(TDBCDS 12)* **LEAVING TOWN / SMOKE WITHOUT FIRE / COCAINE ON THE CATWALK (original dumb/SULK trigg-er version)** [ ] [-]

Sep 02. (cd) *(TDBCD 067)* **TOUCHING THE PROPELLER** [ ] [-]
– Hollywood hills / Leaving town / Smoke without fire / Black and white rainbows / Sweet little nowhere blue / Rockefeller Center, 1932 / Trout fishing / No room at the inn / Falling down / Afraid of the ground.

PLUTO MONKEY

PAUL VICKERS + one other

		Shifty Disco	not iss.
Feb 00.	(7") *(DISCO 0002)* **JETSTREAM. / GYMNASTICS**	[ ]	[-]
Sep 00.	(cd) *(SHIFTY 0004)* **LITTLE BRENDA: BLUEGRASS MISSION** – Wild wild potion / Joe Meek / Double Dutch / Thirsty dragons / Jetstream / Ping pong sass / Forty reels / Rice cake rabbit soul / Dangerous beak / Who holds the monkey / Don't stack them with apes / Quiet life.	[ ]	[-]
Oct 00.	(7"m) *(DISCOQUICK 10)* **JOE MEEK. / MEEKSVILLE SOUND IS DEAD / DUEL AT THE RODEO**	[ ]	[-]

DAWNTREADERS (see under ⇒ Bellboy records)

D/compute (see under ⇒ Mouthmoth records)

DEACON BLUE

Formed: Glasgow . . . 1985 by former remedial teacher, RICKY ROSS, who recruited JAMES PRIME, GRAEME KELLING, EWEN VERNAL and DOUGIE VIPOND: by sheer accident/inspiration, ROSS invited girlfriend, LORRAINE to sing/accompany his vocals and she soon became the sixth member.

Subsequently signed to 'C.B.S.' by their manager, MUFF WINWOOD (ex-SPENCER DAVIS GROUP), the band released their debut single, 'DIGNITY', in Spring '87. A tale of working class pride, the song reflected DEACON BLUE's inherent politicism (although they were hardly The REDSKINS) while the slightly jazzy pop/rock dynamics of the music came as little surprise bearing in mind the group took their name from a STEELY DAN song. The debut album, 'RAINTOWN', followed a few months later, a promising set of soulful Celtic pop which suggested a more solid, less flighty PREFAB SPROUT. The melancholy ebb and flow of 'CHOCOLATE GIRL' was DEACON BLUE at their laidback best, the track a minor hit in summer '88 following similar low-key chart success for a re-issued 'DIGNITY' and 'WHEN WILL YOU (MAKE MY TELEPHONE RING)'.

It was the anthemic 'REAL GONE KID', however, which took the band from the fringes of the Scottish scene into the hearts of the mainstream pop market, the song's infectious keyboard hook and girly harmonies seeing it reach the Top 10 in October '88. Trailed by the Top 20 success of 'WAGES DAY', a second album, 'WHEN THE WORLD KNOWS YOUR NAME', topped the UK album charts the following Spring; perhaps they'd been afflicted by SIMPLE MINDS syndrome, as the cool subtletly which had characterised their first release was replaced with a heavy dose of stadium-friendly bombast. Presumably as a reaction to such critical rumblings, DEACON BLUE opted to release an EP of BACHARACH & DAVID covers in summer '90, its Top 5 success closely followed by a B-sides/rarities affair, 'OOH LAS VEGAS' (1990). A follow-up proper, 'FELLOW HOODLUMS' (1991), was another major success although it failed to convince their detractors, and roping in dance bod production duo, Paul Oakenfold/Steve Osbourne, for 'WHATEVER YOU SAY, SAY NOTHING' (1993), smacked of desperation.

A split finally came the following year, DEACON BLUE bowing out with a No.1 greatest hits set, and fittingly, with a third-time-lucky success for the superior 'DIGNITY'. While VIPOND went on to be a presenter on STV and Radio Scotland, ROSS worked with ex-STEELY DAN sessioner, JEFF 'SKUNK' BAXTER amongst others on a debut solo set, 'WHAT YOU ARE' (1996) – (ROSS also played 'T In The Park' that year). He issued his slightly disappointing solo album 'THIS IS THE LIFE' in 2002, which sounded almost exactly like DEACON's earlier works, although with a modern spin. Who would've thought such a pop icon could've been so heavily influenced by OASIS? Well, the evidence was all there; 'THREATENING RAIN' and 'RODEO BOY' all cranked up the stadium rock guitars, matched with accompanying pianos and BEATLES-esque riffs. Opener 'NORTHERN SOUL' drifted into the rest of the album, hiding like a musical chameleon behind ROSS's mournful ballads and playful pop tinkerings.

• **Songwriters:** All written by ROSS, except covers ANGELIOU (Van Morrison) / TRAMPOLENE (Julian Cope) / I'M DOWN (Beatles).

RICKY ROSS (b.22 Dec'57, Dundee) – vocals / **JAMES PRIME** (b. 3 Nov'60, Kilmarnock) – keyboards (ex-ALTERED IMAGES) / **GRAEME KELLING** (b. 4 Apr'57, Paisley) – guitar / **EWEN VERNAL** (b.27 Feb'64, Glasgow) – bass, keyboard bass / **DOUGIE VIPOND** (b.15 Oct'66, Johnstone) – drums, percussion / **LORRAINE McINTOSH** (b.13 May'64, Glasgow) – vocals

		C.B.S.	Columbia
Mar 87.	(7") *(DEAC 1) <07755>* **DIGNITY. / RICHES** (with free c-s+=) – (excerpts 'RAINTOWN' lp) (12"+=) *(DEAC T1)* – Ribbons and bows.	[ ]	[ ]
May 87.	(lp/c/cd) *(450549-1/-4/-2)* **RAINTOWN** – Born in a storm / Raintown / Ragman / He looks like Spencer Tracy now / Loaded / When will you (make my telephone ring) / Chocolate girl / Dignity / The very thing / Love's great fears / Town to be blamed. *(re-dist.Feb88; same); hit UK No.14) (re-packaged Aug88 free with above lp+c)* **RICHES** *(XPR 1361)* – Which side are you on / King of the western world * / Riches * / Angeliou / Just like boys / Raintown / Church / Suffering / Shifting sand / Ribbons and bows / Dignity. *(cd+= *) (re-iss. Jul98 cd/c; 450549-2/-4)*	[ ]	[-]
Jun 87.	(7") *(DEAC 2)* **LOADED. / LONG DISTANCE FROM ACROSS THE ROAD** (c-s+=/ext.12"+=) *(DEAC C/T 2)* – Which side of the world are you on / Kings of the western world.	[ ]	[-]
Aug 87.	(7") *(DEAC 3)* **WHEN WILL YOU (MAKE MY TELEPHONE RING). / CHURCH** (12"+=) *(DEAC T3)* – A town to be blamed (live) / Angeliou (live).	[ ]	[-]
Jan 88.	(7") *(DEAC 4)* **DIGNITY. / SUFFERING** (10"+=) *(DEAC Q4)* – Shifting sand. (cd-s++=) *(CDDEAC 4)* – Just like boys. (7"ep+=) *(DEAC EP4)* – Ronnie Spector / Raintown (piano). (ext.12"+=) *(DEAC T4)* – Ronnie Spector / Just like boys.	31	[-]
Mar 88.	(7"/7"box) *(DEAC 5)* **WHEN WILL YOU (MAKE MY TELEPHONE RING). / THAT BRILLIANT FEELING** (12"+=/cd-s+=/pic-cd-s+=) *(DEACT/CDDEAC/CPDEAC 5)* – Punch and Judy man / Disneyworld.	34	[-]
Apr 88.	(7") *<07954>* **WHEN WILL YOU (MAKE MY TELEPHONE RING). / TOWN TO BE BLAMED**	[-]	[ ]
Jul 88.	(7") *(DEAC 6)* **CHOCOLATE GIRL. / S.H.A.R.O.N.** (12"+=) *(DEAC T6)* – Love's great fears (live) / Dignity (live).	43	[-]

(7"ep+=/cd-s+=) *(DEACEP/CDDEAC 6)* – The very thing / Love's great fears.

Oct 88. (7") *(DEAC 7) <068944>* **REAL GONE KID. / LITTLE LINCOLN** [8] [ ]
(12"+=/12"w-poster+=) *(DEAC/+Q T7)* – ('A'extended).
(7"ep+=/cd-s+=) *(DEACEP/CDDEAC 7)* – Born again / It's not funny anymore.

Feb 89. (7"/s7") *(DEAC/+Q 8)* **WAGES DAY. / TAKE ME TO THE PLACE** [18] [-]
(12"+=) *(DEAC T8)* – ('A'extended).
(7"ep+=/cd-s+=) *(DEACEP/CDDEAC 8)* – Take the saints away / Trampolene.

Apr 89. (lp/c/cd) *(463321-1/-4/-2)* **WHEN THE WORLD KNOWS YOUR NAME** [1] [-]
– Queen of the New Year / Wages day / Real gone kid / Love and regret / Circus lights / This changing light / Fergus sings the blues / Sad loved girl / The world is hit by lightning / Silhouette / One hundred things / Your constant heart / Orphans. *(re-iss. Jul98 cd/c; 463321-2/-4)*

May 89. (7"/7"box) *(DEAC/+B 9)* **FERGUS SINGS THE BLUES. / LONG WINDOW TO LOVE** [14] [-]
(12"+=/12"g-f+=) *(DEAC/+G T9)* – ('A'extended).
(ext.c-ep+=) *(DEAC C9)* – London A to Z.
(10"+=/cd-ep+=) *(DEAC QT/CD DEAC 9)* – London A to Z / Back here in Beano land.

Sep 89. (7"/c-s) *(DEAC/+M 10)* **LOVE AND REGRET. / DOWN IN THE FLOOD** [28] [-]
(cd-s+=) *(CDDEAC 10)* – Undeveloped heart / ('A'extended).
(ext.12"+=) *(DEAC T10)* – Undeveloped heart.
(10"/cd-s) *(DEAC QT/CD DEAC 10)* – ('A'live) / Spanish moon – Down in the flood (live) / Dark end of the street (live) / When will you (make my telephone ring) (live).

Dec 89. (7"/c-s) *(DEAC/+M 11)* **QUEEN OF THE NEW YEAR. / MY AMERICA** [21] [-]
(12"+=) *(DEACT 11)* – ('A'extended) / Circus lights (acoustic).
(7"ep+=/cd-ep+=) *(DEAC EP/CD DEAC 11)* – Sad loved girl (extended) / Las Vegas.
(c-s/12") *(DEAC QM/DEAC QT 11)* – ('A'live) / Chocolate girl (live) / Undeveloped heart (live) / A town to be blamed (live).

Aug 90. (7"ep/12"ep/cd-ep) *(DEAC/+T/CD 12)* **FOUR BACHARACH AND DAVID SONGS** [2] [-]
– I'll never fall in love again / The look of love / Message to Michael / Are you there (with another girl).

Sep 90. (d-cd/c/d-lp) *(467 242-2/-4/-1)* **OOH LAS VEGAS** (B-sides, sessions) [3] [-]
– Disneyworld / Ronnie Spector / My America / S.H.A.R.O.N. / Undeveloped heart / Souvenirs / Born again / Down in the flood / Back here in Beanoland / Love you say / Let your hearts be troubled/ / Gentle teardrops / Little Lincoln / That country / Is it cold beneath the hill? / Circus lights / Trampolene / Las Vegas / Killing the blues / Long window to love / Christine / Take me to the place / Don't let the teardrops start.

Columbia Columbia

May 91. (7"/c-s) *(656 893-7/-4)* **YOUR SWAYING ARMS. / FOURTEEN YEARS** [23] [-]
(cd-s+=) *(656 893-2)* – Faifley.
(12"++=) *(656 893-6)* – ('A'extended).
(10") *(656 893-0)* – ('A'-12"alternative mix) / ('A'-Drumapella mix) / ('A'-7"mix) / ('A'-dub mix).

Jun 91. (cd/c/lp) *(468 550-2/-4/-1)* **FELLOW HOODLUMS** [2] [-]
– James Joyce soles / Fellow hoodlums / Your swaying arms / Cover from the sky / The day that Jackie jumped the jail / The wildness / A brighter star than you will shine / Twist and shout / Closing time / Goodnight Jamsie / I will see you tomorrow / One day I'll go walking. *(cd/md re-iss. Aug98;* **468550-2/-3)**

Jul 91. (7"/c-s) *(657 302-7/-4)* **TWIST & SHOUT. / GOOD** [10] [-]
(12"+=) *(657 302-6)* – ('A'extended) / I'm down.
(cd-s+=) *(657 302-2)* – Golden bells.

Oct 91. (7"/c-s) *(657 502-7/-4)* **CLOSING TIME. / I WAS LIKE THAT** [42] [ ]
(cd-s+=) *(657 502-2)* – Into the good night.
(12"++=) *(657 502-6)* – Friends of Billy the bear.

Dec 91. (7"/c-s) *(657 673-7/-4)* **COVER FROM THE SKY. / WHAT DO YOU WANT THE GIRL TO DO / CHRISTMAS (BABY PLEASE COME HOME)** [31] [-]
(12"+=) *(657 673-6)* – Real gone kid / Loaded / One hundred things.
(cd-s+=) *(657 673-2)* – Wild mountain thyme / Silhouette / I'll never fall in love again.

Columbia Sony

Nov 92. (7"/c-s) *(658 786-7/-4)* **YOUR TOWN. / ALMOST BEAUTIFUL** [14] [-]
(cd-s+=) *(658 786-2)* – I've been making such a fool.
(12") *(658 786-6)* – ('A'-Perfecto mix) / ('A'extended).

Feb 93. (7"/c-s) *(658 973-2/-4)* **WILL WE BE LOVERS. / SLEEPER** [31] [ ]
(cd-s+=) *(658 973-2)* – Paint it red.
(12") *(658 973-6)* – ('A'side) / (4 other A-mixes).

Mar 93. (cd/c/lp) *(473 527-2/-4/-1)* **WHATEVER YOU SAY, SAY NOTHING** [4] [-]
– Your town / Only tender love / Peace and jobs and freedom / Hang your head / Bethlehem's gate / Last night I Dreamed of Henry Thomas / Will we be lovers / Fall so freely down / Cut lip / All over the world. *(cd/md re-iss. Jan99; 473527-2/-3)*

Apr 93. (7"/c-s) *(659 184-7/-4)* **ONLY TENDER LOVE. / RICHES** [22] [-]
(cd-s+=) *(659 184-2)* – Which side are you on? / Shifting sand.
(12") *(659 184-6)* – ('A'side) / Pimp talking / Cracks you up.
(cd-s) *(659 184-5) – (above 3) / Your town (Perfecto mix).*

Jul 93. (c-ep/cd-ep) *(659 460-4/-2)* **HANG YOUR HEAD EP** [21] [-]
– Hang your head – freedom train (live) / Here on the wind / Indigo sky.
(cd-ep) *(659 460-5)* – (1st track) / Ribbons & bows / Just like boys / Church.

Mar 94. (7"/c-s) *(660 222-7/-4)* **I WAS RIGHT AND YOU WERE WRONG. / MEXICAN RAIN** [32] [-]
(cd-s+=) *(660 222-2)* – Goin' back / Wages day.
(cd-s) *(660 222-5)* – ('A'extended) / Kings of the western world / Suffering / Raintown (piano version).

Apr 94. (cd/c/d-lp) *(476 642-2/-4/-1)* **OUR TOWN – THE GREATEST HITS** (compilation) [1] [-]
– Dignity / Wages day / Real gone kid / Your swaying arms / Fergus sings the blues / I was right and you were wrong / Chocolate girl / I'll never fall in love again / When will you (make my telephone ring) / Twist and shout / Your town / Queen of the New Year / Only tender love / Cover from the sky / Love and regrets / Will we be lovers / Loaded / Bound to love / Still in the mood. *(d-lp+=)* – Beautiful stranger. *(cd/md re-iss. Aug00; 476642-2/-3)*

May 94. (7"/c-s) *(6604485-7/-4)* **DIGNITY. / BEAUTIFUL STRANGER** [20] [-]
(cd-s+=) *(660448-2)* – Waves of sorrow / Bethlehem's gate.
(cd-s) *(660448-5)* – ('A'side) / Fergus sings the blues (live) / Loaded (live) / Chocolate girl (live).

— disbanded after above release and ROSS went solo. VIPOND had already secured a regular spot on a Scottish sporty TV programme (Sportscene, etc) and joined the SWISS FAMILY ORBISON along with KIT CLARK (ex-DANNY WILSON), EWEN joined the BRIAN KELLOCK TRIO, TOMMY SMITH and the NIGEL CLARK QUINTET.

RICKY ROSS

— - vocals, guitar, piano; with **JEFF 'Skunk' BAXTER** – guitars / **MARK HARRIS** – bass / **SCOTT CRAGO** – drums / + other guests

Columbia Sony

May 96. (c-s/cd-s) *(663 135-4/-2)* **RADIO ON / DARK WEATHER / JOE / MY FRIEND TONIGHT** [35] [-]
(cd-s) *(663 135-5)* – ('A'side) / Death work song / Never always / Always alone.

Jun 96. (cd/c) *(483998-2/-4)* **WHAT YOU ARE** [36] [-]
– Good evening Philadelphia / Icarus / Cold Easter / What you are / Radio on / When sinners fall / Jack Singer / The lovers / Wake up and dream / Rosie Gordon lies so still / Promise you rain / Love isn't hard it's strong.

Jul 96. (c-s) *(663 533-4)* **GOOD EVENING PHILADELPHIA / ('A'live)** [58] [-]
(cd-s) *(663 533-5)* – ('A'side) / Radio on (live) / Icarus (live) / Rosie Gordon lies so still (demo).
(cd-s) *(663 533-2)* – ('A'side) / In the pines / The river is wide / Shake some action.

Internationalenot iss.

Oct 97. (cd) *(INTER 001)* **NEW RECORDING** [ ] [-]
– My only tie / Blue horse / The further north you go / The undeveloped heart / Cresswell Street / I love you / Earth a little lighter / I'm sure Buddy would know / Here's singer / On the line / Ash Wednesday.

Mar 98. (cd-ep) *(INTER 002)* **THE UNDEVELOPED HEART EP** [ ] [-]
– The undeveloped heart ('98 remix) / Ghost / Wake up and dream / Passing through / Only love remains.

DEACON BLUE

— re-formed with the original members

Columbia not iss.

Oct 99. (cd/c) *(496380-2/-4)* **WALKING BACK HOME** (old & new songs) [39] [-]
– Love hurts / Jesus do your hands still feel the rain / The very thing / The day that Jackie jumped the jail / Love and regret / Christmas and Glasgow / The wildness / When you are young / Love's great fears / Chocolate girl / Plastic shoes / A brighter star than you will shine / Beautiful stranger / All I want / When will you (make my telephone ring) / Walking back home / I'll never fall in love again.

Papillion not iss.

Apr 01. (cd-s) *(BTFLYS 0011)* **EVERYTIME YOU SLEEP / HEY CRAIG / WHEN YOU WERE A BOY YOU WERE A BEAUTIFUL BOY** [64] [-]
(cd-s) *(BTFLYX 0011)* – ('A'side) / Twist and shout (live) / Cover from the sky (live)

Apr 01. (cd) *(BTFLYCD 0014)* **HOMESICK** [59] [-]
– Rae / Out there / This train will take you anywhere / Everytime you sleep / Now that you're here / Silver lake / A is for astronaut / You lie so beautifully still / Homesick / Even higher ground / I am born.

Jun 01. (cd-s) *(BTFLYS 0018)* **A IS FOR ASTRONAUT / PEACE AND JOBS AND FREEDOM (live) / TOWN TO BE BLAMED (live)** [ ] [-]

– compilations, etc. –

on 'Columbia' unless mentioned otherwise

Feb 97. (cd) *(487147-2)* **RICHES AND MORE** [ ] [-]

Sep 00. (cd) *(499927-2)* **RAINTOWN / WHEN THE WORLD KNOWS YOUR NAME** [ ] [-]

Nov 01. (d-cd) *(504978-2)* **THE VERY BEST OF DEACON BLUE** [ ] [-]

RICKY ROSS

Papillion / not iss.

Apr 02. (cd) *(BTFLYCD 0021)* **THIS IS THE LIFE** [ ] [-]
– Northern soul / London comes alive / Rodeo boy / Angel and Mercedes / I sing about you / Nothing cures that / This is the life / Threatening rain / Starring love / Hippy girl / My girl going to town / Looking for my own Lone Ranger / Way to work.

DEAD END KIDS

Formed: Ayr . . . 1976 by RICKY SQUIRES, COLIN IVORY, ROBBY GRAY, ALISTAIR KERR and DAVEY JOHNSON. Initiated by producer/hitmaker, BARRY BLUE, to compete with the fellow teenybop Scots the BAY CITY ROLLERS, a group they soon supported on tour. In Spring '77, when Punk was rearing its ugly head, these DEAD END KIDS (a great Punk band name wasted!) smashed into the UK Top 10 courtesy of a watered-down pop rendition of the Honeycombs' 1964 chart-topper, 'HAVE I THE RIGHT'. However, BLUE's formulaic conveyor-belt approach didn't pay off as single after single (even a stomping version of the Dave Clark Five's 'GLAD ALL OVER') failed to woo the record buying kids; in '79, they indeed hit their proverbial dead end.

ROBBY GRAY – / **RICKY SQUIRES** – / **DAVEY JOHNSON** – / **ALISTAIR KERR** – / **COLIN IVORY** –

C.B.S. / Columbia

Mar 77. (7") *(CBS 4972)* **HAVE I THE RIGHT. / LADY PUT THE LIGHT OUT** [6] [ ]
Jul 77. (7") *(CBS 5400)* **BREAKAWAY. / I'M YOUR MUSIC MAN** [ ] [ ]
Sep 77. (7") *(CBS 5569)* **GLAD ALL OVER. / LAST NIGHT IN CHINATOWN** [ ] [-]
Nov 77. (lp) *(4082254)* **BREAKOUT** [ ] [-]
– Glad all over / All my love always / Going out the back door / Roxanne / Have I the right / Tough kids / Last night in Chinatown / C'mon let's go / I'm your music man / Breakaway.
Nov 77. (7") *(CBS 5826)* **ALL MY LOVE ALWAYS. / ROXANNE** [ ] [-]
Jan 79. (7") *(CBS 6926)* **HEART GET READY FOR LOVE. / RADANCER** [ ] [-]

— disbanded after their final flop

DEAD NEIGHBOURS (see under ⇒ LOWLIFE)

DEAF HEIGHTS CAJUN ACES

Formed: based- Glasgow . . . mid-80's by accordion-player KIM TEBBLE. Basically a Cajun-rock outfit into folk music and hoedowns, The DEAF HEIGHTS . . . delivered their first LP, 'LES FLAMMES D'ENFER', for 'Temple' records in 1987. Contemporaries of N'YA FEARTIES and TONIGHT AT NOON, these ACES took a little time to recuperate and have a further mini-set, 'HEART SONGS' (1991).

KIM TEBBLE – accordion / + quite a few others

Temple / not iss.

Jul 87. (lp/c) *(TP/CTP 025)* **LES FLAMMES D'ENFER** [ ] [-]
– Les flammes d'enfer / Madame Edourarde / New pinegrove blues / Grand mamou / Moi et mori cousin / La danse de la limonade / Bosco strip / Bayou pom pom / Colinda / La robe barree / Allons a lafayette / 'Til galop pour mamou / Hackberry zydeco. *(c-iss.Feb94; CTP 025)*

Re-Dem / not iss.

1991. (m-cd; as the DEAF HEIGHTS) **HEART SONGS** [ ] [-]
– Good lovin' / Enchantress / Lover les amants / Je suis retourne / Love's refrain / Rainfall / Colinda / Gabriel at Rosalie / Lancassine special / Green oak tree / Grand Bosco / etc

— disbanded after above

DEEP PIECE (see under ⇒ Limbo records)

DEGRASSI (see under ⇒ sl records)

DEL AMITRI

Formed: Glasgow . . . 1983 by singer/songwriter JUSTIN CURRIE and IAIN HARVIE, who recruited additional musicians BRYAN TOLLAND and PAUL TYAGI prior to recording their debut single, 'SENSE SICKNESS', for independent label, 'No Strings'.

Emerging in the golden era of Scots indie when 'Postcard' was the hippest namedrop on the block, the group's early, acoustic-orientated approach brought inevitable comparisons with ORANGE JUICE and their ilk, while CURRIE's subtly sardonic lyrics marked him out as an aspiring wordsmith. A punishing round of gigging, including a number of prestigious support slots, slowly raised DEL AMITRI's profile and subsequently attracted the interest of 'Chrysalis' records. Signed to a major label deal, the band made their album debut in Spring '85 with 'DEL AMITRI', a competent set which showcased the band's intelligent folk pop/rock. The initial press reaction was encouraging and the future looked bright prior to a subsequent dispute with the company leaving them label-less.

Lending new meaning to the term "grassroots following", DEL AMITRI's loyal band of US fans were pivotal in the success of their ensuing American tour, promoting gigs and providing an accommodation alternative to the dreaded tour van. The success of the jaunt led to another major label venture, this time around with 'A&M', who were far more successful in getting DEL AMITRI's career off the ground. Throughout the interim "wilderness" years, CURRIE had been carefully honing his writing skills, the more mature approach paying off when the 'KISS THIS THING GOODBYE' single made the UK Top 60. Released at the same time, a belated follow-up album, 'WAKING HOURS' (1989), eventually made the British Top 10 following the success of 'NOTHING EVER HAPPENS'. A world-weary diatribe on societal inertia, the track's earthy sound – if not its tone of barely concealed bitterness – was characteristic of the more accessible path DEL AMITRI were now cultivating. With his legendary sideburns and windswept good looks, CURRIE also became something of an unlikely early 90's sex symbol, the shag candidate for the more discerning female prior to EVAN DANDO cornering the market with his flowing locks.

Whatever, CURRIE was certainly the group's focal point and many fans no doubt scarcely noticed that new boys DAVID CUMMINGS (a replacement for MICK SLAVEN, who himself had succeeded TOLLAND on the previous set) and BRIAN McDERMOTT had been recruited for a third set, 'CHANGE EVERYTHING' (1992). More polished and chart-friendly than any DEL AMITRI release to date, the record narrowly missed the UK No.1 spot, its immaculately crafted (yet often verging on bland) MOR spawning another major hit in 'ALWAYS THE LAST TO KNOW' and a further trio of fairly minor chart encounters with 'BE MY DOWNFALL', 'JUST LIKE A MAN' and 'WHEN YOU WERE YOUNG'. A fourth set, 'TWISTED' (1995), hardly broke new ground, although it did spawn a US Top 10 in 'ROLL TO ME'; that DEL AMITRI appealed to the American market was hardly surprising, their reliably safe, inoffensive coffee-table roots rock ideal fodder for FM radio.

Never being the trendiest of bands, DEL AMITRI never really suffered a backlash, carving out their own little niche with relative success almost guaranteed. In 2002, the group issued the eagerly awaited set 'CAN YOU DO ME GOOD?', which featured the single 'JUST BEFORE YOU LEAVE', a light and breezy soul number that reflected the mood of the album. Tracks such as 'OUT FALLS THE PAST' and 'CASH AND PRIZES' hadn't lost 'AMITRI their melodic appeal, synonymous with the outfit's earlier works, although the album as a whole disappointed.

• **Songwriters:** CURRIE – HARVIE composed except covers; DON'T CRY NO TEARS (Neil Young) / BYE BYE PRIDE (Go-Betweens) / CINDY INCIDENTLY (Faces).

• **Trivia:** DEL AMITRI means 'from the womb' in Greek.

JUSTIN CURRIE (b.11 Dec'64) – vocals, bass, acoustic guitar / **IAIN HARVIE** (b.19 May'62) – guitar / **BRYAN TOLLAND** – guitar / **PAUL TYAGIS** – drums, percussion

No Strings / not iss.

Aug 83. (7") *(NOSP 1)* **SENSE SICKNESS. / THE DIFFERENCE IS** [ ] [-]

Chrysalis / Chrysalis

May 85. (lp/c) *(CHR/ZCHR 1499)* **DEL AMITRI** [ ] [ ]
– Heard through a wall / Hammering heart / Former owner / Sticks and stones girl / Deceive yourself (in ignorant Heaven) / I was here / Crows in a wheatfield / Keepers / Ceasefire / Breaking bread. *(cd-iss. Dec90; CCD 1499)*
Jul 85. (7") *(CHS 2859)* **STICKS AND STONES GIRL. / THIS KING IS POOR** [ ] [-]
(12"+=) *(CHS12 2859)* – The difference is.
Oct 85. (7") *(CHS 2925)* **HAMMERING HEART. / LINES RUNNING NORTH** [ ] [-]
(12"+=) *(CHS12 2925)* – Brown eyed girl.

— **MICK SLAVEN** – guitar (ex-BOURGIE BOURGIE) repl. TOLLAND / sessions from **ANDY ALSTON** – keyboards / **ROBERT CAIRNS** – violin / **BLAIR COWAN** – accordion / **STEPHEN IRVINE** – drums / **JULIAN DAWSON** – harmonica / **JAMES O'MALLEY** – bass / **CAROLINE LEVELLE** – cello / **WILL MOWAT** – seq, keyboards

A&M / A&M

Jul 89. (7") *(AM 515)* **KISS THIS THING GOODBYE. / NO HOLDING ON** [59] [ ]

(12"+=/3"cd-s+=) *(AMY/CDEE 515)* – Slowly, it's coming back.

Jul 89. (lp/c/cd) *(AMA/AMC/CDA 9006)* <5287> **WAKING HOURS** [ ] [95] Feb90
– Kiss this thing goodbye / Opposite view / Move away Jimmy Blue / Stone cold sober / You're gone / When I want you / This side of the morning / Empty / Hatful of rain / Nothing ever happens. *(re-dist.Feb90 hit UK No.6; same) (re-iss. Mar95 cd/c; same)*

Oct 89. (7") *(AM 527)* **STONE COLD SOBER. / THE RETURN OF MAGGIE BROWN** [ ] [ ]
(12"+=/3"cd-s+=) *(AMY/CDEE 527)* – Talk it to death.

Jan 90. (7"/c-s) *(AM/+MC 536)* **NOTHING EVER HAPPENS. / SO MANY SOULS TO CHANGE** [11] [ ]
(12"+=/cd-s+=) *(AMY/CDEE 536)* – Don't I look like the kind of guy you used to hate? / Evidence.

Mar 90. (7"/7"g-f/c-s) *(AM/+S/MC 551)* **KISS THIS THING GOODBYE. / NO HOLDING ON** [43] [-]
(10"+=/12"+=/cd-s+=) *(10AMX/AMY/AMCD 551)* – Slowly, it's coming back.

Apr 90. (c-s) <1485> **KISS THIS THING GOODBYE. / THE RETURN OF MAGGIE BROWN** [-] [35]

Jun 90. (7"/c-s) *(AM/+MC 555)* **MOVE AWAY JIMMY BLUE. / ANOTHER LETTER HOME** [36] [ ]
(12"+=) *(AMX 555)* – April the first / This side of the morning (live).
(12"+=/cd-s+=) *(AM Y/CD 555)* – April the first / More than you'd ever know.

Oct 90. (7"/c-s) *(AM/+MC 589)* **SPIT IN THE RAIN. / SCARED TO LIVE** [21] [ ]
(12"+=) *(AMY 589)* – The return of Maggie Brown.
(10"++=/cd-s++=) *(AM X/CD 589)* – Talk it to death.

—— **DAVID CUMMINGS** – guitar repl. SLAVEN / **BRIAN McDERMOTT** – drums (who guested on last) repl. TYGANI

Apr 92. (7"/c-s) *(AM/+MC 870)* <1604> **ALWAYS THE LAST TO KNOW. / LEARN TO CRY** [13] [-]
(cd-s+=) *(AMCD 870)* – Angel on the roof / The whole world is quiet.

Jun 92. (cd/c/lp) *(395385-2/-4/-1)* <5385> **CHANGE EVERYTHING** [2] [ ]
– Be my downfall / Just like a man / When you were young / Surface of the Moon / I won't take the blame / The first rule of love / The ones that you love lead you nowhere / Always the last to know / To last a lifetime / As soon as the tide comes in / Behind the fool / Sometimes I just have to say your name. *(re-iss. cd/c Mar95; same)*

Jun 92. (7"/c-s) *(AM/+MC 884)* **BE MY DOWNFALL. / WHISKEY REMORSE** [30] [-]
(10"+=/cd-s+=) *(AM X/CD 884)* – Lighten up the load / The heart is a bad design.

Jul 92. (c-s) <1604> **ALWAYS THE LAST TO KNOW / BE MY DOWNFALL** [-] [30]

Sep 92. (7"/c-s) *(AM/+MC 0057)* **JUST LIKE A MAN. / SPIT IN THE RAIN (remix)** [25] [ ]
(cd-s+=) *(AMCDR 0057)* – I won't to take the blame (acoustic) / Scared to live.
(cd-s) *(AMCD 0057)* – ('A'side) / Don't cry no tears / Bye bye pride / Cindy incidentally.

Jan 93. (7"/c-s) *(AM/+MC 0132)* **WHEN YOU WERE YOUNG. / LONG JOURNEY HOME THE ONES THAT YOU LOVE LEAD YOU NOWHERE** [20] [ ]
(cd-s+=) *(AMCDR 0132)* – The verb to do / Kestral road.
(cd-s) *(AMCD 0132)* – ('A'side) / The ones that you love lead you nowhere (live) / Kiss this thing goodbye (live) / Hatful of rain (live).

Feb 95. (c-s) *(580 959-4)* **HERE AND NOW / LONG WAY DOWN** [21] [ ]
(10"+=) *(580 969-1)* – Someone else will / Queen of false alarms.
(cd-s+=) *(580 959-2)* – Queen of false alarms / Crashing down.
(cd-s) *(580 969-2)* – ('A'side) / Always the last to know (live) / When I want you (live) / Stone cold sober (live).

Feb 95. (cd/c/lp) *(540 311-2/-4/-1)* <0311> **TWISTED** [3] [ ]
– Food for songs / Start with me / Here and now / One thing left to do / Tell her this / Being somebody else / Roll to me / Crashing down / It might as well be you / Never enough / It's never too late to be alone / Driving with the brakes on. *(re-iss. d-cd Aug95; 540396-2)*

Apr 95. (7"/c-s) *(581 004-7/-4)* **DRIVING WITH THE BRAKES ON. / LIFE BY MISTAKE** [18] [ ]
(cd-s+=) *(581 005-2)* – A little luck / In the meantime.
(cd-s) *(581 007-2)* – ('A'side) / Nothing ever happens / Kiss this thing goodbye / Always the last to know.

Jun 95. (c-s) *(581 128-4)* **ROLL TO ME / IN THE FRAME** [22] [-]
(cd-s+=) *(581 129-2)* – Food for songs (acoustic) / One thing left to do (acoustic).
(cd-s) *(581 131-2)* – ('A'side) / Spit in the rain / Stone cold sober (remix) / Move away Jimmy Blue.

Jun 95. (c-s) <1114> **ROLL TO ME / LONG WAY DOWN** [-] [10]

Oct 95. (c-s) *(581 214-4)* **TELL HER THIS / A BETTER MAN** [32] [-]
(cd-s+=) *(581 215-2)* – The last love song / When you were young.
(cd-s) *(518 217-2)* – ('A'side) / Whiskey remorse / Fred Partington's daughter / Learn to cry.

Jun 97. (c-s) *(582 252-4)* **NOT WHERE IT'S AT / SLEEP INSTEAD OF TEARDROPS** [21] [-]
(cd-s+=) *(582 253-2)* – Spair pair of laces / Before the evening steals the afternoon.
(cd-s+=) *(582 255-2)* – A grimace not a smile / Low friends in high places.

Jul 97. (cd/c/lp) *(540 705-2/-4/-1)* **SOME OTHER SUCKER'S PARADE** [6] [-]
– Not where it's at / Some other sucker's parade / Won't make it better / What I think she sees / Medicine / High times / Mother nature's writing / No family man / Cruel light of day / Funny way to win / Through all that nothing / Life is full / Lucky guy / Make it always be too late.

—— In Sep'97, 'MEDICINE' was due for release but withdrawn; see below single for corresponding b-sides; 582365-2/582367-2/582569-2.

Nov 97. (cd-s) *(582 433-2)* **SOME OTHER SUCKER'S PARADE / DRIVING WITH THE BRAKES ON (live) / MOVE AWAY JIMMY BLUE (live) / THE ONES THAT YOU LOVE LEAD YOU NOWHERE (live)** [46] [-]
(cd-s) *(582 435-2)* – ('A'side) / Roll to me (live) / Here & now (live) / Hatful of rain (live).
(cd-s) *(582 437-2)* – ('A'side) / ('A'live) / Always the last to know (live) / Stone cold sober (live).

Jun 98. (c-s/cd-s) *(582 705-4/-2)* **DON'T COME HOME TOO SOON / THREE LITTLE WORDS / PAPER THIN / DON'T COME HOME TOO SOON (instrumental)** [15] [-]
(cd-s) *(582 707-2)* – ('A'side) / Nothing ever happens / Kiss this thing goodbye / Always the last to know.

Aug 98. (c-s) *(566 347-4)* **CRY TO BE FOUND / CANNED LAUGHTER** [40] [-]
(cd-s+=) *(566 347-2)* – One step at a time.
(cd-s) *(566 349-2)* – ('A'side) / Being somebody else (live) / Not where it's at.

Sep 98. (cd/c) *(<540 940-2/-4>)* **HATFUL OF RAIN – THE BEST OF DEL AMITRI** (compilation) [5] [ ]
– Cry to be found / Roll to me / Kiss this thing goodbye / Not where it's at / Nothing ever happens / Always the last to know / Here & now / Just like a man / Spit in the rain / When we were young / Driving with the brakes on / Stone cold sober / Tell her this / Move away Jimmy Blue / Be my downfall / Some other sucker's parade / Don't come home too soon. *(d-cd includes* **LOUSY WITH LOVE – THE B-SIDES**; *540 941-2)* – Scared to live / The return of Maggie Brown / In the frame / Sleep instead of teardrops / Long journey home / Paper thin / The last love song / Verb to do / In the meantime / Long way down / Whiskey remorse / Before the evening steals the afternoon / So many souls to change.

Mercury — not iss.

Apr 02. (c-s) *(497696-4)* **JUST BEFORE YOU LEAVE / I'M AN UNBELIEVER** [37] [-]
(cd-s+=) *(497697-2)* – You love me.
(cd-s) *(497696-2)* – ('A'side) / Septic jubilee / Belong belong / ('A'-video).

Apr 02. (cd/c) *(493216-2/-4)* **CAN YOU DO ME GOOD?** [30] [-]
– Just before you leave / Cash and prizes / Drunk in a band / One more last hurrah / Buttons on my cloths / Baby, it's me / Wash her away / Last cheap shot at the dream / Out falls the past / She's passing this way / Jesus saves / Just getting by.

DELGADOS

Formed: Glasgow . . . late 1994 by ex-university graduates, ALUN WOODWARD, EMMA POLLOCK, STEWART HENDERSON and PAUL SAVAGE. Not only did they kickstart Scotland's flagging (nae, virtually dead) indie scene, they did it by initiating their own imprint, 'Chemikal Underground'. The label's debut, 'MONICA WEBSTER', was greatly received by the music press and of course, who else? DJ John Peel, their angular guitar reminiscent of PAVEMENT, although ALUN and EMMA's twee vocal touches called to mind BELLE & SEBASTIAN.

Single after single continued to impress until the excellent debut album, 'DOMESTIQUES', surfaced in late '96. Their "difficult" second album, 'PELOTON' (1998), managed to crack the UK Top 60, spurred on by indie hits, 'PULL THE WIRES FROM THE WALL' and 'THE WEAKER ARGUMENT DEFEATS THE STRONGER'. But perhaps it was their third and most accomplished set, 'The GREAT EASTERN' (named after a shelter in Glasgow's East end) which secured the group's ever growing reputation. For one, the album itself had not one weak point among the ten-or-so tracks, which segued like needle into thread. The DELGADOS owe much of this feat to the whistling flutes, assortment of horns and ambiguous use of orchestration which popped up throughout the set's dizzying array of songs. Stand out tracks (and, boy, did they really stand out!) included 'AMERICAN TRILOGY', 'AYE TODAY' and the frail accompaniment of closing number, 'MAKE YOUR MOVE'. Although the album failed to crack the mainstream, it did reach the minor regions of the charts, as did aforementioned single 'AMERICAN TRILOGY'. So, God bless the much dismissed DELGADOS – where would ARAB STRAP, MOGWAI and now majors-tempted BIS be without them and their seminal label?!

• **Covers:** THE DIRGE (New Bad Things) / SACRE CHARLEMAGNE (France Gall) / A VERY CELLULAR SONG (Incredible String Band) / HOW CAN WE HANG ON TO A DREAM? (Tim Hardin).

ALUN WOODWARD – vocals, guitar / **EMMA POLLOCK** – vocals, guitar / **STEWART HENDERSON** – bass / **PAUL SAVAGE** – drums

Chemikal Underground — March

Jul 95. (7") *(chem 001)* **MONICA WEBSTER. / BRAND NEW CAR** [ ] [-]

Aug 95. (7"ep/cd-ep) *(SCAN/+CS 07)* **THE LAZARWALKER EP** □ -
– Primary alternative / Lazarwalker / Buttonhole / Blackwell.
(above iss. on 'Radarscope') (below iss. on 'Boa'; B-side alter-ego)
Dec 95. (ltd-7") *(HISS 4)* **LIQUIDATION GIRL. / Van Impe: unknown** □ -
Dec 95. (7"; various artists) *<che 47>* **I've Only Just Started To Breathe** □ -
Mar 96. (7"ep/cd-ep) *(chem 004/+cd)* **CINECENTRE. / THIRTEEN GLIDING PRINCIPLES / M. EMULATOR** □ -
Aug 96. (7"ep/cd-ep) *(chem 006/+cd)* **UNDER CANVAS / EEN TELF. / BEAR CLUB / STRATHCONA** □ -
Oct 96. (7") *(100gm 18)* **BOOKER T JONES. / (other track by URUSEI YATSURA)** - - Japan
– Booker T Jones / (other track by URUSEI YATSURA).
(above on Japanese '100 Guitar Mania' via 'Stolen Ecstasy' series)
Oct 96. (7"ep/cd-ep) *(chem 008/+cd)* **SUCROSE / CHALK. / EUROSPRINT / THE DIRGE** □ -
Nov 96. (lp/cd) *(chem 009/+CD)* *<MAR 027>* **DOMESTIQUES** □ □
– Under canvas under wraps / Leaning on a cane / Strathcona slung / Tempered; not tamed / One more question / Big business in Europe / Falling & landing / Akumulator / Sucrose / Pinky / Friendly conventions / Smaller mammals / 4th channel / d'Estus morte.
Jun 97. (7") *(LISS 20)* **SACRE CHARLEMAGNE. / (other by The NEW BAD THINGS)** □ -
(above release on 'Lissys')
Mar 98. (d7"/cd-s) *(chem 022/+cd)* **EVERYTHING GOES AROUND THE WATER. / BLACKPOOL / THE DROWNED AND THE SAVED** □ -
May 98. (7") *(chem 023)* **PULL THE WIRES FROM THE WALL. / MAURON CHANSON** 69 -
(cd-s+=) *(chem 023cd)* – Mark the day.
Jun 98. (cd) *(chem 024cd)* **PELOTON** 56 -
– Everything goes around the water / The arcane model / The actress / Clarinet / Pull the wires from the wall / Repeat failure / And so the talking stopped / Don't stop / Blackpool / Russian orthodox / The weaker argument defeats the stronger.
Sep 98. (7") *(chem 029)* **THE WEAKER ARGUMENT DEFEATS THE STRONGER. / A VERY CELLULAR SONG** □ -
(cd-s+=) *(chem 029cd)* – The actress – Irian Jaya remix.

Chemikal Underground / Beggars Banquet

Apr 00. (lp/cd) *(chem 040/+cd)* *<81021>* **THE GREAT EASTERN** 72 □ May00
– The past that suits you best / Accused of stealing / American trilogy / Reasons for silence / Thirteen gliding principles / No danger / Aye today / Witness / Knowing when to run / Make your move.
May 00. (7") *(chem 039)* **AMERICAN TRILOGY. / EUPHORIA HEIGHTS** 61 -
(cd-s+=) *(chem 039cd)* – How can we hang on to a dream?
(cd-s+=) *(chem 039cdx)* – ('A'-CD rom) / Make your move.
Sep 00. (7") *(chem 044)* **NO DANGER. / THE CHOICES YOU'VE MADE** □ -
(cd-s+=) *(chem 044cd)* – Don't sleep.

Mantra / not iss.

Sep 02. (7"/cd-s) *(MNT 75/+CD)* **COMING IN FROM THE COLD. /** □ -

– compilations, etc. –

Sep 97. (cd) *Strange Fruit; (SFRSCD 037)* **BBC SESSIONS** □ -
– Primary alternative / I've only just started to breathe / Lazarwalker / Indian fables / Under canvas under wraps / Sucrose / Teen elf / Thirteen gliding principles / Friendly conventions / Tempered; not tamed / Falling and landing. *(re-iss. May00; same)*

DELMONTES (see under ⇒ Rational records)

Mick DERRICK

Born: Glaswegian "Scottish MICK" DERRICK – who apparently has a degree in Archaeology – is the rough-looking Caledonian connection with Leicester-based Punk/indie combo, PROLAPSE. Along with verbal sparring partner, LINDA STEELYARD, the brooding MICK knocks out the "odd" paranoiac rant over a barrage of uneasy, maddening riff-tastic assaults. From 1993, PROLAPSE have slipped out of place many times, but more so on their recording output. From early releases on the 'Cherry Red' imprint – mainly the 'POINTLESS WALKS TO DISMAL PLACES' set in '94 – to the more recent album for 'Cooking Vinyl', 'GHOSTS OF DEAD AEROPLANES' (1999), MICK and his PROLAPSE time team have excavated into the deepest industrial minds. With a few collaborations as CHA CHA 2000 (alongside PROLAPSE guitarist PAT MARSDEN) on the 'Tribute To Celtic F.C.' single and a guest spot on MOROCCO's 'Guided Missile' single 'New Javelins', who knows where MICK will turn up next.

DESALVO (see under ⇒ PH FAMILY)

DESC (see under ⇒ KHAYA)

DICK JOHNSON

Formed: Glasgow . . . mid-90's by three-girl PHILLIPA SMITH, TRACEY VAN DAAL and JANE EGYPT (also of LUNG LEG), the moniker either borrowed from a jazzband leader or a PUSSY GALORE track.

Finding a sympathetic home at the local 'Vesuvius' imprint, DJ erupted in a hail of scuzzy DICK DALE-style guitar, plunking bass and breathless, sassy vocals on 1997's 'FREE GIGI' EP. Later in the year, they hitched a ride with London-based Northern-ophiles 'Guided Missile' for the FALL-meets-JON SPENCER punk/rockabilly single, 'DISPOSABLE DARLING'. The BIS-founded 'teen-c! recordingz' added DICK JOHNSON to their roster in late '97 with the 'CAN'T YOU GIVE ME LOVE' single, while the group's premature finale came via 'MY LOVE LOST' on the curiously-named English label, 'Butcher's Wig'; PHILLIPA would later become part of fellow girl-group LUNG LEG.

PHILLIPA SMITH – vocals, guitar / **TRACEY VAN DAAL** – vocals, guitar / **JANE EGYPT** – drums (of LUNG LEG)

Vesuvius / not iss.

Apr 97. (7") *(POMP 009)* **FREE GIGI EP** □ -
– Dawn at death creek / Slip road blues / Glitter vs. make-up.

Guided Missile / not iss.

Aug 97. (7") *(GUIDE 20)* **DISPOSABLE DARLING. / HIP FLASK SWAGGER** □ -

teen-c! / not iss.

Dec 97. (7") *(SKETCH 004)* **CAN'T YOU GIVE ME LOVE. / BIT PART ACTRESS / DO THE TROTSKY** □ -

Butcher's Wig / not iss.

Mar 98. (7") *(SYRUP 003)* **MY LOVE LOST. / GETAWAY CAR** □ -
— disbanded after above; PHILLIPA was already part of LUNG LEG

DIGGERS

Formed: Methil, Fife . . . early 90's by ALAN MOFFAT and CHRIS MIEZITIS. After fruitlessly attempting to ply their classic indie-guitar wares around the less than sympathetic environs of Methil, Leven and surrounding Fife backwaters, the duo relocated to Glasgow where their approach was more in tune with the prevailing 'Bellshill Sound'. Completing the line-up with JOHN ESLICK and HANK ROSS, the band received encouraging support prior to a hiccup in their career as the former was laid off for six months following a car accident. Subsequently signed to 'Creation', The DIGGERS took more than three years to come up with a debut album, 'MOUNT EVEREST'. Finally surfacing in 1997, the record revealed no great surprises soundwise with an archetypal 'Creation' indie sound vaguely akin to The BLUETONES if not quite so assured, commentators drawing on the ever reliable BEATLES for comparisons; the harmony-fuelled CS&N or HALL & OATES were more accurate. • **Note:** The DIGGERS who issued an EP on 'Death Becomes Me' were not the same band.

ALAN MOFFAT – vocals, bass / **CHRIS MEIZITIS** – vocals, rhythm guitar / **JOHN ESLICK** – lead guitar / **HANK ROSS** – drums

Creation / Creation

Aug 96. (7") *(CRE 226)* **PEACE OF MIND. / TANGLED WEB** □ -
(cd-s+=) *(CRESCD 226)* – Get it.
Oct 96. (7"/c-s) *(CRE/+CS 234)* **NOBODY'S FOOL. / LIFE'S ALL WAYS** □ -
(cd-s+=) *(CRESCD 234)* – Here and there.
Feb 97. (7"/c-s) *(CRE/+CS 259)* **O.K. ALRIGHT. / ON THE LINE** □ -
(cd-s+=) *(CRESCD 259)* – Holiday Inn.
Mar 97. (cd/lp) *(<CRE CD/LP 193>)* **MOUNT EVEREST** □ □
– Circles / Peace of mind / Waking up / Nobody's fool / Come on easy / Downbeat / East coast / O.K. alright / Hormonious / Passport to Rec / They said I'd know / Up against it.
— split later in the year

D.J.EQUAZION (see under ⇒ Limbo records)

DJ KRASH SLAUGHTA
(see ⇒ Section 9: Dance/Rave)

DJ Q

Born: 1974, Glasgow. House producer, PAUL FLYNN, quit his day job hanging suspended ceilings and virtually took to spinning discs full-time. He soon became a regular DJ on the flowering underground house scene in Glasgow, recording for such aspiring labels as 'Glasgow Underground' and 'Dance Mania' with a release of the EP's 'LANDING ON A PLANET NEAR YOU' and 'PORN KING', both 1997. In the same year he issued his seminal 'WE ARE ONE' EP, which featured the voice of Scottish poet WILLIAM HALL over a minimalistic, thumping beat and a set of loosely played synths. His album, 'FACE THE MUSIC' (1997), was issued to critical acclaim on the dance scene, and catalogued the producer's previous EP's all into one sweltering mix of techno, acid jazz and hip-hop. The disappointing sophomore set, 'TWENTY FOUR 7EVEN' was delivered in early 2000 and saw DJ Q basically repeating the same formula that had before helped him rise up the ranks in the world of British Dance.

DJ Q (b. PAUL FLYNN, 1974) – turntables, etc

Go Beat — not iss.

Oct 97. (12"ep/cd-ep) *(GOB X/CD 5)* **LANDING SOON ON A PLANET NEAR YOU EP** — -
– Feelin' moody / Remembering yesterdays / 20,000hz under the bass.

Glasgow Underground — not iss.

Oct 97. (12"ep) *(GU 010)* **ORIGINAL PORN KING EP** — -
– Moody groove / Porn king / Vincent's vibe.

Filter — not iss.

Oct 97. (12"ep) *(FILT 23)* **WE ARE 1 EP** — -
Oct 97. (cd/lp) *(FILT 24 CD/LP)* **FACE THE MUSIC** — -
– We are one / Delirious / Flying home / Make your mind up / Glasgow's jazz / Paranoid impulses / Up space dance / Fila / Tracking / She'll be gone / Going forward in reverse.
Nov 97. (12"ep) *(FILT 21)* **7494 EP** — -
– Delirious / Deep thoughts / Going forward in reverse.
Jun 98. (12") *(FILT 31)* **DELIRIOUS. / GLASGOW'S JAZZ** — -
Sep 98. (12") *(FILT 33)* **ELVIS NEVER MEANT SHIT TO ME, VOL.1 EP** — -

Go Beat — not iss.

Jul 99. (12"ep) *(GOBX 16)* **THE RED ANT EP** — -
– 2 1 13 B1 Shibuya / Underground calling / Q's disco.

Filter — not iss.

Sep 99. (12") *(FILT 38)* **OPTIMUM THINKING. / THE LATIN QUARTER** — -
Jan 00. (12"ep) *(FILT 42)* **100 NOT OUT EP** — -
Feb 00. (cd/d-lp) *(FILT 43 CD/LP)* **TWENTYFOUR7EVEN** — -
– Optimum thinking / San Francisco / 100 not out / Helpline / ADTDC (A Dedication To Derek Carter) / Pressure / Hall's message / Way back then / Porn 3001 *[cd-only]* / End of the beginning.
May 00. (12"ep; as DJ Q & SILICONE SOUL) *(CON 2)* **DISCIPLINE EP** — -
(above issued on 'Consortium')
Jun 00. (12") *(FILT 48)* **SAN FRANCISCO. / MY KINDA HOUSE** — -
Oct 00. (cd/d-lp; Various Artists mixed by DJ Q) *(UTC CD/LP 04)* **COUNTER ACTION** — -
(above on 'Under The Counter')
Feb 01. (12"ep) *(FILT 47)* **HIDDEN AGENDA EP** — -

Glasgow Underground — not iss.

Aug 02. (12") *(GU 099)* **MUSIC AS WE KNOW IT** — -
– Over U now / System 600.

DJ SCOTT

Born: IAN ROBERTSON, Glasgow. Along with help from his DJ/producer brother S. ROBERTSON, DJ SCOTT managed to secure a Top 40 place for his 'Steppin' Out' debut, 'DO YOU WANNA PARTY', early in '95. Featuring LORNA B on vocals, the pairing had one further Top 40 smash, 'SWEET DREAMS'. However, an unsuccessful attempt at the Blue Nile's 'TINSELTOWN IN THE RAIN', then the Bee Gees' 'HOW DEEP IS YOUR LOVE' (produced by Stock-Aitken-Waterman) turned out to be ill-advised.
• **Note:** Not to be confused with similar German dance producer, DJ SCOT PROJECT or Englishman DJ DOC SCOTT (unsure of DJ SCOTT BELLS)

DJ SCOTT – turntables, etc

Steppin' Out — not iss.

Feb 94. (12"/cd-s) *(IAN 011 T/CD)* **DO YOU WANNA PARTY (mixes)** — -

Love This — not iss.

Jan 95. (7"/c-s; as DJ SCOTT featuring LORNA B) *(SPON/+C 2)* **DO YOU WANNA PARTY (mixes)** — 36 — -
(12"+=/cd-s+=) *(SPON T/CD 2)* – ('A'mixes).
Mar 95. (7"/c-s) *(SPON/+C 3)* **SWEET DREAMS (mixes)** — 37 — -
(12"+=/cd-s+=) *(SPON T/CD 3)* – ('A'mixes).
Mar 95. (12"/cd-s; as DJ SCOTT & OUTER RHYTHM) *(IAN 028 T/CD)* **PIANO MADNESS (mixes)** — -

Steppin' Out — not iss.

Jun 96. (c-s/12"/cd-s; as DJ SCOTT & OUTER RHYTHM) *(IAN 042 C/T/CD)* **LET'S MAKE IT HAPPEN (mixes)** — -
Nov 96. (12"/cd-s) *(IAN 050 T/CD)* **HEAVEN (mixes)** — -
Aug 97. (12"/cd-s) *(IAN 060 T/CD)* **TINSELTOWN IN THE RAIN (mixes)** — -

Perfecto — not iss.

Feb 98. (12"/cd-s) *(PERF 158 T/CD1)* **HOW DEEP IS YOUR LOVE (mixes)** — -
(cd-s) *(PERF 158CD2)* – ('A'mixes).

DOG FACED HERMANS

Formed: Edinburgh . . . 1986 by ANDY, MARION, COLIN and WILF. One of the weirdest and most experimental bands to come out of the capital, the DOG FACED HERMANS initially delivered their CHUMBAWAMBA-esque anarchist message via a single on their own 'Demon Radge' imprint. They subsequently appeared on the 'Alternative Tentacles' V/A album, 'Censorship Sucks' (a tribute set to raise funds for Jello Biafra's court case) while also releasing a trio of 45's for 'Calculus'. Towards the end of the decade, a debut LP, 'EVERYDAY TIME BOMB' finally appeared on 'Vinyl Drip', the 'HERMANS trading in the 'Burgh for the more liberal climes of Amsterdam. Finding a sympathetic Dutch recording home at 'Konkurrel' (in-house label of The EX), they released two sets, 'MENTAL BLOCKS FOR ALL AGES' (1991) and 'HUM OF LIFE' (1993), the last of which featured a cover of 8-Eyed Spy/Lydia Lunch's 'LOVE SPLIT WITH BLOOD'. Renewing their relationship with San Francisco's 'Alternative Tentacles', DOG FACED HERMANS completed a further two sets of socially aware, post-feminist avant-punk in the shape of 'BUMP & SWING' (1994) and 'THOSE DEEP BUDS' (1994); they were now at home in the Netherlands.

MARION – vocals, trumpet, cowbells / **ANDY** – guitar / **COLIN** – bass / **WILF** – drums, saxophone / **GERT-JAN** – live sound

Demon Radge — not iss.

Feb 87. (7"ep) *(RADGE 1)* **UNBEND EP** — -
– Catbrain walk / Cruelty / Incineration.

Calculus — not iss.

Mar 88. (12"ep) *(KIT 001)* **HUMANS FLY** — -
– How much vegetation have you got? / Mary Houdini / Balloon girl / Cactus.
Sep 88. (7") *(KIT 002)* **NO PARTISAN. /** — -
Sep 88. (7") *(KIT 003)* **BELLA – CIAO. / MISS O'GRADY** — -

Vinyl Drip — not iss.

Jun 89. (m-lp/m-c) *(SUK 007/+C)* **EVERY DAY TIMEBOMB** — -
– New shoots / Scottish block / Binding system / John Henry / Beautiful / Frock / Live action.

Konkurrel — A Bomb

Nov 91. (lp/cd) *(K 139/+CD)* **MENTAL BLOCKS FOR ALL AGES** — -
– Punjabi monster beat / Fortune / Supressa / Astronaut / Bhopal / The running man / Body strategic / In a row / From the top of the mountain / It's time / Incineration / Big pot / The rain it raineth / El Doggo speaks / Catbrain walk / Bella ciao. *(cd+=)* – EVERY DAY TIMEBOMB
Mar 93. (lp/cd) *(K 147/+CD)* **HUM OF LIFE** — -
– Jan 9 / Viva / Hook and the wire / How we connect / Love split with blood / Wings / White Indians / Hear the dogs / Love is the heart of everything / Madame la mer / Peace warriors.

Compulsive — not iss.

Mar 93. (7") *(CPS 2)* **PEACE WARRIORS. / (track by Jonestown)** — -

Konkurrel — Alternative Tentacles

Aug 94. (cd) *(K 153CD)* <*VIRUS 159CD*> **BUMP & SWING (live)** — Feb95
– Hear the dogs / Peace warriors / Viva / Love is the heart of everything / Transformation / Keep your laws – Off my body / Jan 9 / Human spark / Love split with blood / Fortune / The bride has feet of clay.
Oct 94. (lp/cd) *(K 155/+CD)* <*VIRUS 151/+CD*> **THOSE DEEP BUDS**
– Blessed are the follies / Volkswagen / Keep your laws – Off my body / Lie and swell / H tribe / Human spark / Les femmes et les filles vont danser / Virginia fur / Calley / Dream forever.

— disbanded some time in '95

DOMINIC WAXING LYRICAL
(see under ⇒ Bosque records)

DOPPELGANGER (see ⇒ Section 9: Dance/Rave)

DOVE (see under ⇒ ONE DOVE)

d.p. le odd
(see under ⇒ Flotsam & Jetsam records)

DRINKING ELECTRICITY

Formed: Edinburgh . . . 1980 by boy-girl pairing of ANNE-MARIE ROME and DAVID ROME, plus bassman PAUL EDGLEY. Having signed the brilliant FLOWERS and BOOTS FOR DANCING to his new 'Pop: Aural' stable, former boss of 'Fast Product' records, budding enrepreneur BOB LAST, took on this off-kilter trio. From the onset, it looked a bit dicey to say the least. With the similarly-minded SILICON TEENS fitting in quite nicely with 'Mute' and the cover-loving indie faction (there weren't that many!), the weirdly-named DRINKING ELECTRICITY generated nothing but diluted criticism. Three singles were unleashed in 1980, the first two were covers of Johnny Kidd's 'SHAKIN' ALL OVER' and the Flamin' Groovies 'SHAKE SOME ACTION', the third their own (I think!) 'CRUISE MISSILE'. The following year, the testing trio tried again, this time with 'Survival' records, although only two singles and an album, 'OVERLOAD' (1982), managed to see light of day.

ANNE-MARIE ROME – vocals / **DAVID ROME** – guitar, vocals / **PAUL EDGLEY** – bass

Pop: Aural | not iss.

May 80. (7") *(POP 004)* **SHAKIN' ALL OVER. / CHINA** [ ] [-]
Jul 80. (7") *(POP 005)* **SHAKE SOME ACTION. / (version)** [ ] [-]
Nov 80. (7") *(POP 008)* **CRUISING MISSILES. / SHAKING ALL OVER (dub)** [ ] [-]

Survival | not iss.

Jul 81. (7") *(SUR 001)* **SUBLIMAL. / RANDOM PARTICLES** [ ] [-]
Feb 82. (lp) *(SURLP 001)* **OVERLOAD** [ ] [-]
– Breakout / Discord dance / Good times / Colour coding / Fall / Breakout II / Count down / News peak / Twilight zone / Superstition / The promise.
Mar 82. (7") *(SUR 005)* **GOOD TIMES. / COLOUR CODING** [ ] [-]
(12") *(SUR12-1)* – ('A'side) / Superstition.

—— split up later in 1982

DRIVE (see ⇒ Section 9: wee post-punk groups)

DR ROBERT

Born: BRUCE ROBERT HOWARD, 2 May'61, Haddington, East Lothian; raised in the English fens of East Anglia and Sydney, Australia. In the down under city of Darwin, BRUCE cut his musical teeth with punk act, EXHIBIT A (not the British band of the same name).

After returning to Blighty at the dawn of the 80's and initially sticking a toe into the waters of both professional football (Norwich City) and music journalism, HOWARD formed the BLOW MONKEYS, a classy soul-pop outfit who made quite a splash in the middle of the decade. Going under the name of DR ROBERT (a nickname earned at boarding school . . .), the honey-voiced HOWARD made for a compelling frontman, successfully fusing his slick, sophisticated music with scathing anti-Thatcherite politics. Many artists were of course covering similar ground but none (save perhaps MATT JOHNSON) managed it with quite the same finesse as DR ROBERT and Co.

Signed to 'R.C.A.', the band hit big with the likes of 'Digging Your Scene' and 'It Doesn't Have To Be This Way', the DR even being honoured with a guest spot from his hero CURTIS MAYFIELD. '(Celebrate) The Day After You' might have been a tad optimistic as an anti-MAGGIE pre-election anthem yet it was banned by the BBC nonetheless. Surely an honorary Scotsman for nothing else if not his sterling efforts to end the scourge of the Iron Lady, ROBERT didn't hand out any prizes for guessing who 'She Was Only A Grocer's Daughter' referred to. ROBERT HOWARD's first sojourn into solo territory was a UK Top 10 duet with soul chanteuse KYM MAZELLE entitled 'WAIT' while the late 80's demise of The 'MONKEYS saw him working with fellow socialist soul crusader PAUL WELLER.

After a string of singles for 'Regal Zonophone' and 'Heavenly' in the first half of the 90's, his long awaited solo debut, 'REALMS OF GOLD' (originally scheduled for release in '92), finally arrived in 1996 on his own 'Artbus' label, an enticingly rough-around-the-edges affair not a million miles removed from the solo troubadour direction WELLER's work took in the 90's. Unsurprisingly, the ubiquitous Heavy Soul man guested on the album alongside the likes of MICK TALBOT, MARCO NELSON and even 2-tone veteran RHODA DAKAR.

ROBERTS issued covers album 'OTHER FOLK' (1997) before he began work with Alt-folk singer BETH ORTON, producing the track 'Pass In Time' for her highly-acclaimed 'Central Reservations' set. 'FLATLANDS' was issued in 1999 and was inspired by ROBERTS' move back to his childhood home of East Anglia. The scenery and traditional folk tales of the locals was a recurring theme on the set; however this was only a brief footnote to his most accomplished work yet, the excellent 'BIRDS GOTTA FLY' (2001). Combining a whole host of different instruments into the mix (harmonica, trombone, space-guitar, pedal steel giutar), ROBERTS also managed to find the time to arrange beautiful, floating strings that evoked the North Wales village in which the album was recorded. Not surprising then that he managed to pull in locals JOHN LAWRENCE (GORKY'S ZYGOTIC MYNCI) and DAVID WRENCH (BUBBLEGUN) to help him create something unique and deliciously haunting.

ROBERT HOWARD – vocals, bass, guitar / with various sessioners

Regal Zonophone | not iss.

Sep 91. (7"/c-s) *(RZ/+CS 3)* **I'VE LEARNT TO LIVE WITH LOVE. / JUST US TONIGHT** [ ] [-]
(12"+=/cd-s+=) *(RZ T/CD 3)* – ('A'dub version).
Apr 92. (7"/c-s) *(RZ/+CS 4)* **A SIMPLER PLACE AND TIME. / ('A'instrumental)** [ ] [-]
(12"+=/cd-s+=) *(RZ T/CD 4)* – ('A'original mix) / ('A'vocal mix) / (2 other 'A'mixes).

—— in Apr'92, the album 'INTO THE REALMS OF GOLD' was withdrawn/shelved

Heavenly | not iss.

Nov 94. (7") *(HVN 45)* **THE COMING OF GRACE. / LUCIFERS FRIEND** [ ] [-]
Nov 95. (7") *(HVN 49)* **CIRCULAR QUAY. / GONE FISHING** [ ] [-]
(cd-s+=/10"+=) *(HVN 49 CD/10)* – Bethesda (part 1) / Moments of madness (fearless version).

P.C.C. | not iss.

Oct 95. (cd) *(0087-2)* **BETHESDA** [-] [-] Japan
– Halfway to Heaven / Full moon fever / Footprints in the snow / This is nowhere / Bethesda / A minority of one / On the seventh day / Happy hunting ground / Deep water bound / Jamming in A / Satisfied mind – Green rocky road. *(UK-iss.May00 on 'Fen Cat'; FENCD 002)*

Permanent | Pure

Jan 96. (cd/c/lp) *(PERM CD/MC/LP 40)* <003642500-2> **REALMS OF GOLD** [ ] [ ] 1997
– Realms of gold / The coming of Grace / Comfort of the clan / Follow your path / Pond life / Sanctuary / Circular quay / Have no roots / Ode to Bacchus / Don't let it slip / So slow the rain / Moment of madness. *(cd re-iss. Sep98; same) (cd re-iss. May00 on 'Fen Cat'; FENCD 001)*
Feb 96. (10"ep/c-ep/cd-ep) *(10/CA/CD SPERM 28)* **THE COMING OF GRACE EP** [ ] [-]
– The coming of grace / Realms of gold (big demo) / Lucifers friend / Lucifers brother.
May 96. (7"/c-s) *(7/CA SPERM 29)* **POND LIFE. / SANCTUARY (original sanctuary mix)** [ ] [-]
(cd-s+=) *(CDSPERM 29)* – Don't let it slip / Deportee.

Art Bus | not iss.

May 97. (7") *(SRROOT 2)* **HALFWAY TO HEAVEN. / A MINORITY OF ONE, NOW YOU'RE GONE** [ ] [-]
(cd-s+=) *(CDROOT 2)* –
May 97. (cd/lp) *(ROOT CD/LP 1)* **OTHER FOLK . . .** [ ] [-]
– Halfway to Heaven / Sitting here / As I went out one morning / You upset the grace of living when you lie / Now you're gone / Seventh day / A little bit of rain / Badi-da / One small town / The Fen tiger / Death is not the end / Hippy gumbo. *(cd re-iss. May00 on 'Fen Cat'; FENCD 003)*

Fen Cat | import

May 99. (cd-ep) *(FEN 002)* **FULL MOON FEVER / Blow Monkeys: I'M SO GLAD / Blow Monkeys: DIGGING YOUR SCENE** [ ] [-]
Jun 99. (cd) *(FENCD 004)* **FLATLANDS** [ ] [-]
– Easy road / Hanging on to the hurt / Full moon fever / Flatlands / Further adventures of the Fen tiger / Staring down the bird / The sky is falling / Up to me / I can't remember the last time I cried / I guess this is goodbye / This one's called . . ...T.F.T.
Jun 01. (cd) *(FENCD 005)* <62910> **BIRDS GOTTA FLY** [ ] [ ] Oct01
– Birds gotta fly / A single summer / The nearly room / Blue skies / The cloud / Phantom world / Sycamore tree / Small victories / Still got a lot to learn / A little song.

Bill DRUMMOND

Born: 29 Apr'53, Butterworth, South Africa. Despite his birthplace, DRUMMOND grew up in Newton Stewart, Galloway and Clydebank, acquiring a Scottish accent and an interest in bird watching. Bizarrely enough, BILL's earliest work experience was as a fisherman off Scotland's North East coast after becoming an archetypal teenage runaway. He subsequently studied art in Liverpool where he became involved in the late 70's punk scene, forming BIG IN JAPAN with HOLLY JOHNSON and IAN BROUDIE (of FRANKIE GOES TO HOLLYWOOD and LIGHTNING SEEDS fame respectively) in 1977. The band lasted a year and a couple of singles, after which BILL co-founded the influential 'Zoo' label with future 'Food' man, DAVE BALFE.

Instrumental in the early careers of both ECHO AND THE BUNNYMEN and TEARDROP EXPLODES, DRUMMOND nevertheless parted company with both bands on acrimonious terms before taking up an A&R position at 'WEA'. As well as working with the likes of ZODIAC MINDWARP (under the pseudonym KING BOY D) and The PROCLAIMERS, DRUMMOND signed up the band BRILLIANT who boasted one JIMMY CAUTY in their ranks. After the latter act failed to break through, BILL recorded a "retiral" solo album for 'Creation' entitled 'THE MANAGER' (1986). His period of music biz retirement lasted a mere six months before he formed THE JAMMS (JUSTIFIED ANCIENTS OF MU MU) with CAUTY, an ironic pop project that used the medium of the burgeoning house craze to get across its subversive message. This subsequently metamorphosed into the infamous KLF, dance pioneers in their own right who scored massive club and chart hits with 'WHAT TIME IS LOVE', 'LAST TRAIN TO TRANSCENTRAL' and '3 A.M. ETERNAL'.

After they'd deliberately sabotaged their own success by deleting their back catalogue and performing a noise version of 'WHAT TIME IS LOVE' at the Brit awards, the dastardly duo formed The K Foundation and turned their attentions on the art world. Among their stunts was the exhibiting of a million pounds in cash and the subsequent burning of said cash on a remote Scottish island. Not your average pop star, DRUMMOND also published a book called 'Bad Wisdom' in 1996, recounting his trip to the North Pole with ZODIAC MINDWARP man, MARK MANNING.

Recent years have seen the eccentric adopted Scot continue his calling as a writer with a series of pocket book titles and short stories; his biography entitled '45' was published in 2000.

BILL DRUMMOND – vocals, etc / with backing from the TRIFFIDS and VOICE OF THE BEEHIVE

	Creation	Bar/None – Atlantic
Nov 86. (lp) *(CRELP 014)* *<781677-1>* **THE MANAGER** <US title 'BILL DRUMMOND'> – True to the trail / Ballad for a sex god / Julian Cope is dead / I want that girl / Going back / Queen of the south / I believe in rock'n'roll / Married man / I'm the king of joy / Son of a preacher man / Such a parcel of rogues in a nation. *(re-iss. Sep90 lp/c/cd; CRE LP/C/CD 14)*	☐	☐ 1989
Mar 87. (12") *(CRE 039T)* **KING OF JOY. / THE MANAGER**	☐	-

— BILL continued to work with KLF and the JUSTIFIED ANCIENTS OF MU MU

DUB COMMISSION (see under ⇒ Hubba Hubba records)

DUBREQ (see under ⇒ SPARE SNARE)

Derek DUNBAR

Born: 31 Aug'58, Aberdeen. After taking up residence in where else, London, DEREK became frontman with cosmopolitan pop band JIMMY THE HOOVER. Masterminded by BOW WOW WOW svengali, MALCOLM McLAREN (who incidentally gave them their abysmal, novelty band moniker), the quartet became a one-hit wonder for the 'Inner Vision' label, also home to WHAM. The song in question, 'TANTALISE (WO WO EE YEH YEH)', bounced into the UK Top 20 in the summer of '83, although the feelgood factor soon faded when legal problems scuppered any longer-term plans.

Pip DYLAN (see under ⇒ Fence records)

DYMENSION (see under ⇒ Clubscene records)

E

EASTMEN (see under ⇒ Soma records)

Sheena EASTON

Born: SHEENA SHIRLEY ORR, 27 Apr'59, Bellshill, Lanarkshire. A familiar tale of Glasgow girl made good, the ups and downs of SHEENA EASTON's career have always made good copy while her stormy relationship with the Scottish press is well known.

The saga began back in the late 70's after the young, fame-hungry ORR had graduated from the Royal Scottish Academy Of Music and Drama. Having begun singing in pubs and clubs while still a student, she snagged a deal with 'E.M.I.' late in '79. After gaining valuable exposure via Esther Rantzen's BBC TV talent programme, 'Big Time', EASTON (now her married name) subsequently saw her first two singles, '9 to 5' and 'MODERN GIRL' – a flop first time around – climb into the UK Top 10 in quick succession. This record-breaking feat (the first time for a female artist) was followed by an eponymous debut album in 1981 while '9 to 5' was given a US release under the title 'MORNING TRAIN'. Despite the name change (to avoid confusion with Mrs PARTON), the song was a huge hit all over again, topping the US charts and beginning a love affair with America which would come to characterise EASTON's career. A re-issued 'MODERN GIRL' followed into the US Top 20 while her theme tune to the James Bond movie, 'FOR YOUR EYES ONLY', made the Top 5. She topped off a glittering year by being awarded a Grammy for Best New Artist.

A Caledonian equivalent of OLIVIA NEWTON JOHN, EASTON consolidated her MOR standing with a further trio of albums, 'YOU COULD HAVE BEEN WITH ME' (1981), 'MADNESS, MONEY AND MUSIC' (1982) and 'BEST KEPT SECRET' (1983). Surprisingly, perhaps, she also recorded a Spanish language album from whence came Grammy winner, 'Me Gustas Tal Como Eres', a duet with LUIS MIGUEL. Shortly after in early '85, the singer's squeaky clean, homespun image was given a shake-up as she emerged with her sassiest album to date, 'A PRIVATE HEAVEN'. The infamous 'SUGAR WALLS' (written by PRINCE under the pseudonym Alexander Nevermind) was steamy enough to have the pro-censorship PMRC breathing down her neck although it still made the US Top 10 and even saw her break into the R&B market.

EASTON moved further into the realms of R&B after signing to 'M.C.A.' in the late 80's, recording 'THE LOVER IN ME' with the likes of JELLYBEAN and PRINCE, for whom she'd already returned the favour by singing on his 1987 hit, 'U Got The Look'. The album's title track narrowly missed the US top spot while the multi-talented ex-pat Bellshill lass initiated her acting career with appearances on ubiquitous 80's cop show, 'Miami Vice'. By this point, SHEENA was a fully paid-up citizen of California with a grating accent and a Real Estate portfolio (reportedly worth millions) to match. Funnily enough, this didn't endear her to music fans back in Glasgow where she was duly booed/bottled off stage at Glasgow's 'Big Day' open-air concert in 1990.

While 1991's 'WHAT COMES NATURALLY' made the chart, EASTON increasingly concentrated on thespian matters, landing roles in the movie, 'Indecent Proposal' and starring in Broadway musicals 'Man Of La Mancha' and 'Grease'. On the recording front, she offered up predictable adult contemporary fare with a more mature edge in the shape of 'MY CHERIE' (1995) and 'HOME' (1999). More interesting was SHEENA's millennial disco tribute, 'FABULOUS' (2000), blowing away the middle-aged cobwebs with a run-through of her fave glitter-ball tunes including 'DON'T LEAVE ME THIS WAY' and 'NEVER CAN SAY GOODBYE'. Despite the promotional push by her record company (appearances on the Kirsty Wark show, Richard And Judy, Graham Norton and even a BBC documentary), the album was an unequivocal flop. Things went from bad to worse in January 2001 for the post-post "Modern Girl", as her Las Vegas musical was axed amid rumours that she had fallen out with co-star DAVID CASSIDY.

SHEENA EASTON – vocals / with session people incl. PETER VAN HOOKE – drums / FRANK RICOTTI – percussion / IAN LYNN – keyboards / ANDY BOWN – bass / PHIL PALMER – guitar / etc

E.M.I. — EMI America

Feb 80. (7") *(EMI 5042)* **MODERN GIRL. / PARADOX** [56] [-]
(re-iss. Aug80; hit No.8) (re-iss. Mar84 on 'EMI Gold'; G45 3)
Jul 80. (7") *(EMI 5066)* **9 TO 5. / MOODY** [3] [-]
Oct 80. (7") *(EMI 5114)* **ONE MAN WOMAN. / SUMMER'S OVER** [14] [-]
Jan 81. (lp/c) *(EMC/TC-EMC 3354)* *<17049>* **TAKE MY TIME** <US-title 'SHEENA EASTON'> [17] [24] Mar81
– Don't send flowers / Cry / Take my time / When he shines / One man woman / Prisoner / 9 to 5 / So much in love / Voice on the radio / Calm before the storm / Modern girl / No one ever knows. *(re-iss. 1986 lp/c; ATAK/TC-ATAK 64) (cd-iss. 1988; CDP 746054-2) (cd re-iss. Jul99 as 'SHEENA EASTON' on 'One Way'; 72439986626)*
Jan 81. (7") *<8071>* **MORNING TRAIN (NINE TO FIVE). / CALM BEFORE THE STORM** [-] [1]
Feb 81. (7") *(EMI 5135)* **TAKE MY TIME. / CALM BEFORE THE STORM** [44] [-]
Apr 81. (7") *(EMI 5166)* **WHEN HE SHINES. / RIGHT OR WRONG** [12] [-]
Apr 81. (7") *<8080>* **MODERN GIRL. / SUMMER'S OVER** [-] [18]
Jun 81. (7") *(EMI 5195)* **FOR YOUR EYES ONLY. / RUNAWAY** [8] [-]
Jul 81. (7") *<1418>* **FOR YOUR EYES ONLY. / (instrumental)** [-] [4]
—— <above issued on 'Liberty' US-only>
Sep 81. (7") *(EMI 5232)* **JUST ANOTHER BROKEN HEART. / SAVIOR FAIRE** [33] [-]
Sep 81. (lp/c) *(EMC/TC-EMC 3378)* *<17061>* **YOU COULD HAVE BEEN WITH ME** [33] [47] Nov81
– A little tenderness / Savoir faire / Just another broken heart / I'm not worth the hurt / You could have been with me / A letter from Joey / Telephone lines / Johnny / Trouble in the shadows / Isn't it so. *(re-iss. Oct84 on 'MFP' lp/c; MFP 415670-1/-4) (cd-iss. May00 on 'One Way'; OW 23536)*
Nov 81. (7") *(EMI 5252)* **YOU COULD HAVE BEEN WITH ME. / FAMILY OF ONE** [54] [-]
Nov 81. (7") *<8101>* **YOU COULD HAVE BEEN WITH ME. / SAVOIR FAIRE** [-] [15]
Mar 82. (7") *<8113>* **WHEN HE SHINES. / FAMILY OF ONE** [-] [30]
Jul 82. (7") *(EMI 5326)* *<8131>* **MACHINERY. / SO WE SAY GOODBYE** [38] [57] Aug82
Sep 82. (lp/c) *(EMC/TC-EMC 3414)* *<17080>* **MADNESS, MONEY AND MUSIC** [44] [85] Oct82
– Weekend in Paris / Are you man enough / I wouldn't beg for water / Machinery / Ice out in the rain / I don't need your word / Madness, money and music / There when I needed you / Wind beneath my wings / You do it in the winter / Please don't sympathise. *(cd-iss. Jul00 on 'One Way'; 4663235372)*
Oct 82. (7") *(EMI 5349)* **ARE YOU MAN ENOUGH. / LONER** [ ] [-]
Oct 82. (7") *<8142>* **I WOULDN'T BEG FOR WATER. / SOME OF US WILL** [-] [64]
—— in Jan'83, KENNY ROGERS and SHEENA EASTON had a Top 10 hit (Top 30 UK in Feb'83) with their version of 'WE'VE GOT TONIGHT'
Sep 83. (7") *(EMI 5419)* **TELEFONE (LONG DISTANCE LOVE AFFAIR). / WISH YOU WERE HERE TONIGHT** [ ] [9] Aug83
Oct 83. (lp) *(EMC 1077951)* *<17101>* **BEST KEPT SECRET** [99] [33] Sep83
– Telefone (long distance love affair) / I like the fright / Almost over you / Devil in a fast car / Don't leave me this way / Let sleeping dogs lie / With her radio / Just one smile / Sweet talk / Best kept secret. *(cd-iss. Jul00 on 'One Way'; 4663240322)*
Nov 83. (7") *(EMI 5434)* *<8186>* **ALMOST OVER YOU. / I DON'T NEED YOUR WORD** [ ] [25]
Apr 84. (7") *<8201>* **DEVIL IN A FAST CAR. / SWEET TALK** [-] [79]
Aug 84. (7") *<8227>* **STRUT. / LETTERS FROM THE ROAD** [-] [7]
Oct 84. (7") *(EMI 5496)* **BACK IN THE CITY. / LETTER FROM THE ROAD** [ ] [ ]
Oct 84. (lp/c) *(SHEEN/TC-SHEEN 1)* *<17132>* **A PRIVATE HEAVEN** [ ] [15]
– Strut / Sugar walls / Hungry eyes / Hard to say it's over / Love and affection / Back in the city / You make me nervous / All by myself / Double standard. *(cd-iss. 1986; CDP 746054-2) (cd re-iss. May00 on 'One Way'; OW 23835)*
Nov 84. (7"/12") *(EMI/12EMI 5510)* **STRUT. / STRAIGHT TALKIN'** [ ] [-]
Dec 84. (7") *<8253>* **SUGAR WALLS. / STRAIGHT TALKING** [-] [9]
Mar 85. (7"/12") *(EMI/12EMI 5517)* **SUGAR WALLS. / DOUBLE STANDARD** [ ] [-]
Mar 85. (7") *<8263>* **SWEAR. / FALLEN ANGELS** [-] [80]
Nov 85. (7"/12") *(EMI/12EMI 5536)* *<8295>* **DO IT FOR LOVE. / CAN'T WAIT TILL TOMORROW** [ ] [29] Oct85
—— now with NILE RODGERS (ex-CHIC) / etc
Jan 86. (lp) *(EMC 3505)* *<17173>* **DO YOU** [ ] [40] Nov85
– Do it for love / Don't break my heart / Magic of love / Don't turn your back / Jimmy Mack / Can't wait till tomorrow / Young lions / Kisses / Money back guarantee / When the lightning strikes. *(cd-iss. 1986; CDP 746200-2) (cd re-iss. Jul00 on 'One Way'; 4663235382)*
Jan 86. (7") *<8309>* **JIMMY MACK. / MONEY BACK GUARANTEE** [-] [65]
Feb 86. (7"/12") *(EMI/12EMI 5547)* **MAGIC OF LOVE. / MONEY BACK GUARANTEE** [ ] [-]
Jul 86. (7") *<8332>* **SO FAR SO GOOD. / MAGIC OF LOVE** [-] [43]
Nov 86. (7") *(EA 225)* **IT'S CHRISTMAS ALL OVER THE WORLD. / THANK YOU SANTA** [ ] [-]
Jun 87. (lp/c)(cd) *(EMC/TC-EMC 3536)(CDP 746417-2)* **NO SOUND BUT A HEART** [ ] [-]
– Eternity / Still willing to try / Still in love / Wanna give my love / The last to know / No sound but a heart / What if we fall in love / No ordinary love / Floating hearts. *(cd re-iss. May99 on 'One Way'; OW 99867)*
Sep 87. (7"/7"pic-d) *(EM/+P 9)* **ETERNITY. / SHOCKWAVES** [ ] [ ]

M.C.A. — M.C.A.

Jan 89. (7") *(MCA 1289)* *<53416>* **THE LOVER IN ME. / (instrumental)** [15] [2] Oct88
(12"+=/cd-s+=) *(MCAT/DMCA 1289)* – ('A'mixes).
Feb 89. (lp/c/cd) *(MCG/MCGC/DMCG 6036)* *<42249>* **THE LOVER IN ME** [30] [44] Nov88
– No deposit, no return / The lover in me / Follow my rainbow / Without you / If it's meant to last / Days like this / One love / 101° / Cool love / Fire and rain.
Mar 89. (7") *(MCA 1325)* *<53499>* **DAYS LIKE THIS. / ('A'instrumental)** [43] [ ]
(12"+=/cd-s+=) *(MCAT/DMCA 1325)* – ('A'mixes).
Jul 89. (7") *(MCA 1348)* **101. / 101 (instrumental)** [54] [ ]
(12"+=/cd-s+=/3"cd-s+=) *(MCAT/DMCA/DMCAX 1348)* – ('A'remix).
—— in Oct'89, PRINCE and SHEENA EASTON had a Top 40 hit (Top 30 in the UK) with 'THE ARMS OF ORION'
Mar 91. (7") <53742> **WHAT COMES NATURALLY. / (no B-side)** [ ] [19]
(12"+=) *<53957>* – ('A'mixes).
Jul 91. (lp/c/cd) *(MCA/+C/D 10131)* *<10131>* **WHAT COMES NATURALLY** [ ] [90] Apr91
– What comes naturally / If you wanna keep me / You can swing it / First touch of love / Forever friends / The next time / Manic panic / Somebody / Time bomb / Half heart / To anyone.
Jul 91. (12"/c-s) *<5413 4/3>* **YOU CAN SWING IT** [-] [ ]
Aug 91. (c-s) *<54199>* **TO ANYONE** [-] [ ]
1993. (cd/c) *<10849>* **NO STRINGS** [-] [ ]
– Someone to watch over me / I'm in the mood for love / The nearness of you / How deep is the ocean / If you go away (Ne me quitte pas) / Body and soul / Little girl blue – When Sunny gets blue / The one I love (belongs to someone else) / The man that got away / I will say goodbye / Never will I marry.
Mar 95. (c-s) *<55012>* **MY CHERIE** [-] [ ]
Apr 95. (cd/c) *<11203>* **MY CHERIE** [-] [ ]
– My Cherie / 'Til death us do part / All I ask of you / Flower in the rain / Ypu've learned to live without me / Too much in love / Please don't be scared / Next to you / Dance away the blues / Crazy love.
Jan 97. (cd-s) **MODERN GIRL '97 (mixes; new / dance / instrumental)** [-] [ ]
Jul 97. (cd) *<24001>* **FREEDOM** [-] [ ]
– When you speak my name / Love me with freedom / Now that my baby's gone / One man / Misty blue / One more reason / Let me go through this alone / Love will make you wise / Foolish heart / Modern girl '97.

Universal — Universal

Mar 99. (cd-s) **CARRY A DREAM / (instrumental)** [-] [ ]
Aug 99. (cd) *<24012>* **HOME** [-] [ ]
– Our house / St. Judy's comet / Moon / Something good / Never saw a miracle / Not while I'm around / Who knows / Take me home / My treasure is you / Carry a dream.
Nov 00. (cd/c) *(<013026-2/-4>)* **FABULOUS** [ ] [ ]
– Don't leave me this way / Giving up giving in / Love is in control / That's what friends are for / Never can say goodbye / Best of my love / On my own / Can't take me eyes off you / You never gave me the chance / Get here to me.
Nov 00. (c-s) *(MCSC 40244)* **GIVING UP GIVING IN / GIVING UP GIVING IN (Sleaze Sisters mix)** [ ] [-]
(cd-s) *(MCSTD 40244)* – ('A'-Joey Negro club mix).
(12"++=) *(MCST 40244)* – ('A'-Sharp Pistol dub).

– compilations, etc. –

Mar 89. (cd/c/lp) *E.M.I.; (CD/TC+/EMC 3556)* **FOR YOUR EYES ONLY – THE BEST OF SHEENA EASTON** [ ] [ ]
– 9 to 5 / For your eyes only / Take my time / When he shines / Modern girl / Just another broken heart / Wind beneath my wings / Machinery / We've got tonight (with KENNY ROGERS) / Strut / Ice out in the rain (remix) / Telefone (long distance love affair) / Almost over you / I wouldn't beg for water / One man woman / You could have been with me / Swear / Sugar walls.
1989. (cd) *EMI America; <E2 91754>* **THE BEST OF SHEENA EASTON** [-] [ ]
1992. (cd) *EMI America; <814048>* **THE MOST OF SHEENA EASTON** [-] [ ]
Jun 93. (cd/c) *E.M.I.; (CD/TC EMS 1495)* **THE WORLD OF SHEENA EASTON – THE SINGLES COLLECTION** [ ] [-]
Mar 96. (cd/c) *EMI Gold; (CD/TC GOLD 1008)* **THE GOLD COLLECTION** [ ] [-]
Mar 97. (cd) *Ariola Express; <64732>* **BODY AND SOUL** [-] [ ]
Feb 98. (cd) *Disky; <(LS 88701-2)>* **20 GREAT LOVE SONGS** [-] [ ]
May 00. (cd) *Universal; <704343>* **BEST BALLADS** [-] [ ]
Feb 01. (cd) *EMI Plus; (529937-2)* **THE DIVINE SHEENA EASTON** [ ] [-]

EGE BAM YASI

Formed: Stirling . . . mid-80's by MR. EGG (alias JAMESY McDONALD). Leaving behind his previous incarnation as a plumber, the infamous MR. EGG took his recording alias from a CAN album and embarked upon his mission to bring egg-fried acid house to the Auld Reekie masses. One of the Scottish pioneers and most loyal adherents to the bleep and squelch of the late 80's acid house explosion, the shaven-headed one took the capital's pioneering club institution, 'Pure', as his home base. Beginning with 1987's 12", 'CIRCUMSTANCES', a string of egg-scrambling, sorry, mind-scrambling singles appeared on various labels including a split release on Glasgow's 'Soma' (where DAFT PUNK got their start) and the Gregorian chant madness of 1992's 'ACIDINDIGESTION' EP. Despite a subsequent fallout with Pure head honchos TWITCH & BRAINSTORM, MR. EGG recorded his 'EX OVO OMNIA' mini-lp (latin for 'Everything Comes From The Egg', apparently!) at the club in late '93. Featuring such memorable moments as 'THE GOOD, THE BAD AND THE ACID', the record hit the shelves in Spring '94 courtesy of FINITRIBE's 'Finiflex' label. Although originally planned as a full album, the EGG man was forced to cut it down after his label voiced concerns that DJ's might not play album tracks. Unsurprisingly, this didn't brighten Mr EGG's already fairly low opinion of DJ's, no doubt resenting the fact that he had to kow-tow to the new tastemakers.

EGE BAM YASI's association with Edinburgh's FINI crew extended to a further three 12" singles before he finally recorded a full length debut album, 'HOW TO BOIL AN EGG' (1995). The latter surfaced on the the 'UGT' label, a new venture launched by FINITRIBE stalwarts DAVID MILLER and PHILIP PINSKY. Leaving the vinyl format behind completely, the Edinburgh eggstravert released a second CD-only album, 'MOTHER GOOSE', in 1997.

MR EGG (b. JAMES McDONALD) – electronics, etc / plus various

Survival / not iss.

Jan 87. (12") *(SURT 036)* **CIRCUMSTANCES. /**

Soma / not iss.

1990's. (12"; w/ G7) *(SOMA 019)* **ACIDNATION. / GROUP OF SEVEN NATIONS**

1991. (12") **HIGHBLOW. /**

Dodgey Beast / not iss.

1990's. (12") *(SNR 9)* **EIGHT BALL (remixes)**

Groove Kissing / not iss.

Jun 92. (12"ep) *(IT 2)* **ACIDINDIGESTION EP**
– Bubble (active ingredients mix) / Bubble (acid economy mix) / Hot'n'heavy / Kinky love disco.
(d12"+=) *(IT 2D)* – ('A'original) / ('A'-Tribal Egg mix-up).

Fini Flex / not iss.

May 93. (12"/cd-s) *(FF 1003/+CD)* **I WANT MORE. / ('A'mixes)**

Mar 94. (m-lp) *(FF 1006)* **EX OVO OMNIA**
– Eight ball / Placid / Rope dope / Superclouds / The good, the bad and the acid / Acidnation.

Nov 94. (12") *(FF 1012)* **PIZZACID (Wumpa Wumpa Blare) / PIZZACID (Blarto Blart Boom). / PIZZACID (Nothing To Do With Curt Cobain) / MISS SPEEDY (You Get Up Ma Nose version)**

Jun 95. (12") *(FF 1013)* **STORE IN A COOL PLACE. / ('A'mixes)**

Sep 95. (12"/cd-s) *(FF 1014/+CD)* **REMONT. / ('A'mixes)**

U.G.T. / not iss.

Oct 95. (cd/lp) *(UGT CD/LP 001)* **HOW TO BOIL AN EGG**
– How to boil an egg (text by Mr Egg, narrated by Layanegg Spink) / The Eggsorcist (303 or 606) / Sponge (303 tribute mix) / The MacAcidreel (Sporranrash tartan eggno mix) / Basehit (Eggball pitch) / Basic – variation / I acid you (mixpop) / Rizlacid (rock'n'roll your own version) / A chronicle of rabbits / Bambi / Dome-shaped canopy (prance mix) / The early Christmas dinner of the cockroach / Bampire / Momentum and all who sail in her (duvey version) / 3 dimensional nlimited eggspanse (opus 1) / How to acid an egg.

Subversive / not iss.

Oct 97. (cd) *(SUB 40D)* **MOTHER GOOSE**
– Ovum desires eggspressed in words / 1234 beef (banned version) / Bamerica / Chickago / Acidas / Wet 'n' wild (per/version) / Eggcerpt from 'The Merchant Of Venice' narrated by Layanegg / Pimp it up / Teatroit / Acidboy / The good, the bad and the acid / Acid C.I.D. (sub/version) / Sound made through vibrations of the vocal chords when modified by the resonant eggfect of the tongue and mouth / 1234 beef (reprise).

— EGE BAM YASI split after above

18 WHEELER

Formed: Glasgow . . . early 90's by SEAN JACKSON, NEIL HALLIDAY, ALAN HAKE and DAVID KEENAN. A Glasgow band in the firmly established mould and a prime contender for Alan McGee's Creation offshoot label, 'August', 18 WHEELER emerged in 1993 with an eponymous EP prior to the cutesy indie-pop of the 'NATURE GIRL' single. This was followed by the country-ish 'SUNCRUSH', the DINOSAUR JR.-esque guitar squall of 'KUM BACK' and the TEENAGE FANCLUB impression, 'THE REVEALER', prior to the release of debut album, 'TWIN ACTION' in 1994.

A trainee TEENAGE FANCLUB wouldn't be such a bad description for this lot in fact, preoccupied as they are with airy harmonies, sugary melodies and a fixation for the classic American triple-B i.e. The BYRDS, The BEACH BOYS and BIG STAR (plus the obligatory GRAM PARSONS factor, the lads even including what is presumably a tribute track, 'GRAM'). No bad thing if you're after a pleasant listen – and 'PROCK SHAKE' really hits the mark – but hardly a contender for a Mercury music prize. With the addition of extra guitarist STEVE HADDOW, follow-up set, 'FORMANKA' (1995), was grungier and relatively more adventurous, even employing strings on the moody instrumental title track.

Still, by this point 18 WHEELER had been well and truly eclipsed at 'Creation' by a certain OASIS, the same Manc hopefuls that had supported them only a few years ago in Glasgow! Seemingly destined to forever linger in the Caledonian margins along with The PASTELS, WHITEOUT, The GYRES etc. etc., 18 WHEELER need a tank of rocket fuel if they're to have any hope of breaking through.

SEAN JACKSON – vocals, guitar, bass, piano / **ALAN HAKE** – bass, vocals, guitar, Moog / **NEIL HALLIDAY** – percussion, vocals, guitars, synth / **DAVID KEENAN** – was an early member, before he formed the TELSTAR PONIES

August-Creation / not iss.

May 93. (12"ep/cd-ep) *(caug 005 t/cd)* **18 WHEELER EP**
–

Sep 93. (12"ep/cd-ep) *(caug 006 t/cd)* **NATURE GIRL. / PILLOW FIGHT / GOLDEN CANDLES**

Dec 93. (12"ep/cd-ep) *(caug 010 t/cd)* **SUNCRUSH / YER EYES. / FALLING OUT OF LOVE / SOME THINGS LAST A LONG TIME**

Creation / not iss.

May 94. (7") *(CRE 148)* **KUM BACK. / POTS OF TEA**
(cd-s+=) *(CRESCD 148)* – Alness curls / Pond life.

Jul 94. (7") *(CRE 188)* **THE REVEALER. / HUGGY BEAR**
(cd-s+=) *(CRESCD 188)* –

Jul 94. (cd/c/lp) *(CRECD/CCRE/CRELP 164)* **TWIN ACTION**
– Sweet tooth / Nature girl / Kum back / Golden candles / The revealer / Honey mink / Gram / Prock shake / Hotel 167 / Suncrush / Frosty hands / Life is strange / I won't let you down / Wet dream.

— added **STEVEN HADDOW** – guitar (was backing vocalist on debut)

Apr 95. (7"/cd-s) *(CRE/+SCD 198)* **BODDHA. / FORMANKA**

May 95. (cd/lp) *(CRE CD/LP 181)* **FORMANKA**
– Boddha / Drought / Steel guitars / Cartoon / The bottle / Formanka / Winter grrrl / Pretty ugly / The track / John the revelator. *(free cd/lp w/ above) (CRED CD/LP 181L)* –

Jun 95. (7") *(CRE 209)* **STEEL GUITARS. / SOUNDS**
(cd-s+=) *(CRESCD 209)* – Truth drug / Zombie zombie.

Aug 96. (12") *(CRE 219T)* **THE HOURS AND THE TIMES / ('A'-Ultra Living mix). / BEYOND THE VALLEY OF THE HOURS AND THE TIMES / ('A'-the A&R guys mix – Danny Saber)**
(cd-s) *(CRESCD 219)* – ('A'side) / ('A'-William Orbit porcupine mix) / ('A'-Scissorkicks nutscape navigator mix).

Sep 96. (c-s) *(CRECD 232)* **CRABS / ('A'-Eyes on stalks mix)**
(12"+=)(cd-s+=) *(CRE 232T)(CRESCD 232)* – ('A'-Fis night fell mix) / ('A'-The Hooded claw mix).

Nov 96. (12") *(CRE 241T)* **PROZAC BEATS. / TASH**
(cd-s+=) *(CRESCD 241)* – Fuck easy listening / ('A'version).

Mar 97. (12") *(CRE 249T)* **STAY / STAY (Strange L'Escargot mix). / STAY (Big Kahuna mix) / STAY (Dr. Rockit mix)** 59
(cd-s) *(CRESCD 249)* – ('A'side) / ('A'-Radio Orbit mix) / ('A'-Strange L'escargot mix) / Grease (wide receiver aural exciter mix).
(cd-s) *(CRESCD 249X)* – ('A'side) / ('A'mixes; Stereo odessey / Big Kahuna / Dr.Rockit / album).

Mar 97. (cd/lp) *(CRE CD/LP 192)* **YEAR ZERO**
– The hours and the times / Crabs / Stay / Grease / Prozac beats / The ballad of Paul Verlaine / Everythings dead / Retard / Blue eyed son / Den dagen, den sorgen / Planesong.

Apr 97. (c-s) *(CRECS 255)* **GREASE / THE BALLAD OF PAUL VERLAINE (Bentley Rhythm Ace mix)**
(12"+=)(cd-s+=) *(CRE 255T)(CRESCD 255)* – ('A'-Wide receiver heavy goods mix) / ('A'-M.C. ARR grass in Piccadilly mix).

— split after above

ELECTRICS

Formed: Dollar, Clackmannanshire . . . early 90's by Irishman and main songwriter SAMMY HORNER, along with PAUL BAIRD, DAVIE McARTHUR, KENNY McNICHOLL, DAVID LYON and ROBIN CALLANDAR. Treading a similarly frantic folk-punk path to the POGUES (with a bit of Christian-rock thrown in for good measure), The ELECTRICS made their debut in 1991 with the 'VISIONS AND DREAMS' album.

'BIG SILENT WORLD' and 'THE WHOLE SHEBANG' (produced by Nashville bluegrass/roots man BUDDY MILLER) followed in 1993 and 1995 respectively although the band achieved more recognition abroad – especially in Germany where their records were released – than at home. 'THE ELECTRICS' (1997) was a collection of previously recorded material compiled especially for the American market where their manic Celtic jigs also went down well. Following 1998's 'LIVIN' IT UP WHEN I DIE' (its faintly ridiculous title track summing up the band's hard-partying ethos), The ELECTRICS cut their first concert set, 'DANGER LIVE' (1999), a raucous Christmas shindig recorded in Germany.

LYON subsequently left to concentrate on his solo career, having already released an album of Christian-orientated worship material entitled 'PRECIOUS LITTLE THINGS' (1997).

SAMMY HORNER – vocals, bass / **PAUL BAIRD** – guitars / **DAVID LYON** – keyboards, accordion / **KENNY McNICHOLL** – pipes, whistle / **ROBIN CALLANDAR** – fiddle / **DAVIE McARTHUR** – drums

unknown / not iss.

1991. (cd) **VISIONS AND DREAMS** [-] [-] German
– 2000 years / Mercy mercy / Disciples of disaster / Some things a young man shouldn't have seen / The turning tide / Wishing on a dream / Visions and dreams / Justify your love / Free / Stems and thorns / Hellhound on my trail / Belfast town / T-hule beannachd (The blessing).

Pilla / not iss.

1993. (cd) **BIG SILENT WORLD** [-] [-] German
– End of the world / Here's to you / Song of the least / I believe in freedom / Back of your head / Rajun Cajun / He is there / Take take take / Big important you / All that you want me to be / Irish rover / Finally over with you / I can say I tried / Sing my song.

— **JEAN-PIERRE RUDOLPH** – fiddle; repl. CALLANDAR

1995. (cd) *(27258-2)* **THE WHOLE SHEBANG** [-] [-] German
– Get to Heaven / The whole shebang / Killiecrankie / Two buns – The penny reel – Athol Highlanders / Oh my / I looked up / Benefit of hindsight / The hip shall be redeemed / Mayhem at 2013 – Dunure road – Jolly's jig / Cry for a year – My love is like a red, red rose / Leave this world behind / Pour me a pint as well / If it wassne for your wellies.

SaraBellum / 5 Minute Walk

1997. (cd) *<246691>* **THE ELECTRICS** (compilation) [-] [ ]
– Back of your head / Get to Heaven / The whole shebang / The blessing / I believe in freedom / Irish rover / 2 buns / Pour me a pint / The jig / Visions and dreams / Mercy mercy / Here's to you / Disciples of disaster / Lover of the soul. *(hidden track+)*

— added guests **PHIL MADEIRA** – producer, accordion / **ANTOINE SILVERMAN** – fiddle / **STUART ADAMSON** – guitar (of BIG COUNTRY)

Aug 98. (cd) *<25205>* **LIVIN' IT UP WHEN I DIE** [-] [ ]
– Party goin' on upstairs / Rolling home / Come back down / Livin' it up when I die / Yer man McCann can / Piping hot / Till I'm old / Hey Paddy / Have a jar on me / Raggle taggle gypsy / Face.

1998. (cd-ep) **LIVIN' IT UP WHEN I DIE** [-] [ ]
– Party goin' on upstairs / Livin' it up when I die / Come back down.

— **TIM COTTERELL** – mandolin, fiddles; repl. JEAN-PIERRE

I.C. / not iss.

1999. (cd) *(ICCD 39830)* **DANGER LIVE (live)** [ ] [-]
– Introduction / Killicrankie / Get to Heaven / Berni's wedding jig / Back of your head / Livin' it up when I die / Piping hot / Party going on upstairs / Hey Paddy / Irish rover / The blessing / Face / The welly boot song / Visions and dreams.

— DAVID LYON now departed for a solo career

ELECTROLUVS (see under ⇒ X-static records)

ELECTROSCOPE

Formed: Glasgow . . . April 1996 by radio broadcaster JOHN CAVANAGH and GAYLE, apparently in an attic room while tinkering with vintage recording equipment. Among CAVANAGH's stash of retro gear are gramophones, Farfisa organ and reel to reel tapes, all of which are utilised in creating their unique otherworldly music.

Impossible to pigeonhole, the nearest journalists have got to their sound has involved namechecking the likes of SYD BARRETT-era PINK FLOYD and others sixties-type psychedelicists. Prolific in their wilfully obscure endeavours, the pair delivered a plethora of lovingly-crafted cassettes, singles/EP's (some split), albums, etc. The pick of these came in the shape of bewitchingly diverse full-length sets, 'HOMEMADE ELECTROSCOPE' (1997) and 'JOURNEY TO THE CENTRE OF THE ELECTROSCOPE' (1999). Having already covered Pink Floyd's 'CHAPTER 24', they earmarked a handful of GEOFF GODARD songs for 2000; he apparently penned for producer JOE MEEK. The 'SCOPE also appeared on countless V/A sets alongside even more obscure acts than themselves.

GAYLE – (ex-ADVENTURES IN STEREO, ex-HEFNER, ex-DELGADOS, ex-SCREECH OWLS, ex-PLANET CLAIRE) / **JOHN CAVANAGH** – (ex-HEFNER)

Boa / not iss.

Aug 96. (c) *(HISS 8)* **WHERE THE OSCILLOSCOPE MEETS THE MAGIC EYE** [ ] [-]
– Wattle and weave / Ugaldugal / Octal starvision / Lament for the lost 70 / Pan pose / RPM overload / Soldering for beginners / Freespirit frequency / Rattle of the bees / Telephone suicide / Weave and wattle.

Wurlitzer Jukebox / not iss.

Nov 96. (7"ep) *(WJ 19)* **THE VANISHING PULSAR PLANET** [ ] [-]
– Space travel / Orion alignment / Welcome to Planet Barrett / Harmonic hiatus.

Mar 97. (7"ep) *(WJ 23)* **SOMMERZO** [ ] [-]
– Walk the plank / Storm warning / On the seventh day of May / Fisher, dogger, German bight.

Aug 97. (lp/cd) *(WJ 27/+CD)* **HOMEMADE ELECTROSCOPE** [ ] [-]
– Virtual Vega / Listen to prowlers / Fusee chain / Night flight to nowhere / Tunguska / Roter kamm / December woods / Battle lines are redrawn / Joe heard a new world / Swan song sung / Mesmeric underground / Space travel 103 / Earth loop / The trumpet from outer space / Dunwich.

Feb 98. (7",7"brown) *(WORMSS 2)* **SHAME CHANGED HIS PIGMENTATION. / (other side by Mount Vernon Arts Lab)** [ ] [-]

Tinseltones / not iss.

Apr 98. (7") *(TINT 10)* **FOLLOW THE RAINBOW. / CHAPTER 24** [ ] [-]

Lissys / not iss.

Oct 98. (7"ep; with SUZANNE RHATIGAN) *(LISS 30)* **UNHAPPY SOUL. / MAGIC LANTERN SHOW / HORACE BACHELOR'S METHOD / IF YOUR SHIP** [ ] [-]

Oggum / not iss.

Feb 99. (7"ep) *(Og 4)* **WEE BALDY / NORTH UTSHIRE, SOUTH UTSHIRE. / (other tracks by Longstone)** [ ] [-]

Boa / not iss.

Apr 99. (7") *(HISS 14)* **OUT ON THE EDGE OF TIME. / GLYCERINE GOLD** [ ] [-]

Jul 99. (7"ep) *(LYK 002)* **SPLIT SINGLE** [ ] [-]
– Where penguins are a force for good / Turbine / (other tracks by Stasola).
(above iss. on 'Lykill', below on 'Rocket Racer' – 'Airborne Virus')

Jul 99. (lp; shared with MINMAE) *(RR 006LP – AV 002LP)* **SPLIT LP** [ ] [-]
– Cloud ear / Squink / Witch's hat / Ears will spin / Kildonan / Velvet twilight / Someday soon / Toledo trio / Molten you, gamma me / (other side by MINMAE).

Sep 99. (lp/cd) *(HISS 16/+CD)* **JOURNEY TO THE CENTRE OF THE ELECTROSCOPE** [ ] [-]
– This is a box, a musical box / In the fog / Eight arms to drown you / Between two worlds / Gorse / Aradora star / Velvet shades / Friends in exile / Smile / Will morning never come? / Phase shift / Chalumeau / Lifetime flyte / Aphelion / Quartzite / Shamash / December moods / Curiously euphonic / Harbour.

May 00. (7") *(HISS 18)* **JUST LIKE GEOFF** [ ] [-]
– Sky men (with MOUNT VERNON ARTS LAB) / CASTAWAY STONES: My friend Bobby.

Jul 00. (7") *(KYLIE 056)* **CREPUSCULISNO. / (B-side by Echo Of Your Love: I Didn't Care)** [ ] [-]
(above iss.on 'Kylie Prod.', below issued on 'Octane Grammaphon')

Oct 00. (7") *(OCT 1)* **EARTH & AIR. / WARSER GATE: Fire & Water** [ ] [-]

— they have also contributed a plethora of individual cuts on various V/A compilations; they should surface one day on their own collection

ELECTROSPACE (see under ⇒ Clubscene records)

ELEVEN (see under ⇒ DANNY WILSON)

EL HOMBRE TRAJEADO

Formed: Glasgow . . . 1996 by vocalist HUBBY, STEVIE JONES and STEF SINCLAIR; BEN JONES was added after their debut 45 in the Autumn of '97, 'MOONUNIT MANUAL'. Translating the 'smart' name roughly as 'the man in the suit', this post rock outfit issued further special edition singles during '98 (some split with such indie luminaries as LUNGLEG and THE

KARELIA) before embarking on fully-fledged tours across the ocean with peers SEBADOH and The DELGADOS. Not surprisingly, DJ John Peel was impressed too. He proudly marched the band into his session studio pronto(!). This gave EL HOMBRE TRAJEADO a chance to literally hypotise the audience with their trippy, sparse but clever TORTOISE-esque angular rock. Imagine SLINT doing a spot on Blue Peter, or even a day in the life of a drug-fuelled JOHN McENTIRE – with the lights switched off of course(!).

EL HOMBRE subsequently released their long awaited debut set entitled 'SKIPAFONE' (1998), on trendy Scots label 'Guided Missile'. Tracks like 'NOFA' displayed the visual genius of EHT through soundscapes represented by staccato guitars, inane mumblings and – used to humourous effect – cowbells. 'LIKE QUICKSAND' developed minimalist strumming and lazy bass guitar to brilliant effect. Track 'NEOPRENE' found its way on to the 'GLASGOW EP', which was shared with others including MOGWAI, YUMMY FUR and the aforementioned THE KARELIA. Following after a few delays, the sophomore effort, 'SACCADE' (2000), a signing masterstroke for producer JAMIE WATSON at Edinburgh's hot-to-trot label, 'Human Condition'. EL HOMBRE TRAJEADO (pronounced EL HOM-BRAY TRA-CHEE-AH-DOH, for exotics everywhere) simply repeated the same tried and tested formula, albeit with fresh textures set to a deranged and dislocated style. Like TORTOISE, EHT didn't have an oral message per say, the music spoke for itself.

HUBBY – vocals, guitar / **STEVIE JONES** – bass / **STEF SINCLAIR** – drums

Flotsam & Jetsam | not iss.

Sep 97. (7") *(SHaG 015)* **MOONUNIT MANUAL. / LOGO** [ ] [-]
Apr 98. (7") *(SHaG 13.06)* **Club Beatroot Part Six** [ ] [-]
– Nofo / (other track by LUNG LEG)
(above released in conjunction with 'The 13th Note')

—— added **BEN JONES** – keyboards, DJ-ing

Jun 98. (7") *(SHaG 019)* **LIKE QUICKSAND. / (other track by THE KARELIA)** [ ] [-]

Guided Missile | not iss.

Sep 98. (7") *(GUIDE 28)* **SKIPAFONE. / SLEEP DEEP** [ ] [-]
Oct 98. (cd) *(GUIDE 33CD)* **SKIPAFONE** [ ] [-]
– Like quicksand / Skipafone / Nofo / Neoprene / Varispeed / Bit faster / Nearly a week nearly awake / Logo / Sleep deep.

—— also in Nov'98, EL HOMBRE TRAJEADO (with the track 'NEOPRENE') split the 'Glasgow' EP with MOGWAI, the KARELIA and YUMMY FUR; released on 'Plastic Cowboy' *(Plastic 005)*

Sep 99. (10"ep/cd-ep) *(GUIDE 32/+CD)* **SHOPLIFT EP** [ ] [-]
– Scrivener / Shopfitting / Babosa / Elhombre reworked by Auto Cade.

Jonathon Whiskey | not iss.

Aug 00. (7") *(CLYDE WHISKEY 12)* **L'AMUSIA. / (other track by IMMENSE)** [ ] [-]

Human Condition | not iss.

Oct 00. (cd) *(HCCD 0031)* **SACCADE** [ ] [-]
– i-330 / Dos / Shout out / Jetsuit / Dylar / Saccade / Double blind / Chapperon / Dig this big crux / Halo.

Sickroom Gramaphonic Collective | not iss.

Nov 01. (7") *(SGC 011)* **SARDINES. / (other track by Sputniks Down)** [ ] [-]

EMPIRE-BUILDER (see ⇒ Section 9: the 90s)

ENDGAMES

Formed: Glasgow . . . 1980 by DAVID RUDDEN, DOUGLAS MUIRDEN and former SLIK/ZONES man WILLIE GARDNER; PAUL WISHART was drafted in from the SKIDS. ENDGAMES started play via three contributions – 'WORKS', 'VISIONS OF' and 'STARE'- to a V/A compilation, 'Live Letters' (released on Polydor's 101 series and also featuring The FIX(X), HUANG CHUNG and FAY RAY); subsequent tracks 'JOY OF LIFE' and 'SIN', appeared on separate V/A sets, 'Beyond The Groove' and 'Heat From The Street' respectively.

It would be the year 1982 though, that really got the ball rolling (so to speak). 'Mercury' records were quick off the mark and they duly issued a couple of excellent easy-rock singles, 'WE FEEL GOOD (FUTURE'S LOOKING FINE)' and 'FIRST, LAST FOR EVERYTHING', although the ENDGAMES jigsaw was now complete courtesy of 5th piece, BRIAN McGEE (the original drummer of SIMPLE MINDS). No doubt encouraged by the group's celebrity find (well, JIM KERR and Co were already on their roster), 'Virgin' signed the ENDGAMES "play-boys" for a two-album deal. In the summer of '83, with the production work of Colin Campsie and George McFarlane in the can, the 6-piece were ready to take on the world. The excellent 'WAITING FOR ANOTHER CHANCE' was aptly-titled for many reasons, the ultimate reason being the band were unplugged by radio and music press alike who'd only room for bigger Scots names (i.e. SIMPLE MINDS and BIG COUNTRY).

However, ENDGAMES played on regardless and showcased their Autumn '83 debut album, 'BUILDING BEAUTY', with another fine stab at romantic electro, 'LOVE CARES'. 1984 was relatively quiet for the band, although two members MUIRDEN and WISHART had both dropped out. 'Virgin', too, were not too impressed with the demos of their follow-up set and subsequently only released 'PYRAMIDS AND TRAFFIC JAMS' (1985) in Germany. This was the death-knell for ENDGAMES and they duly blew the whistle on any future outings; only McGEE has kept in circulation as a writer for LES McKEOWN (ex-BAY CITY ROLLERS).

DAVID RUDDEN – vocals, bass / **WILLIE GARDNER** – guitar, bass, synthesizers, vocals (ex-SLIK, ex-ZONES) / **DAVID MURDOCH** – keyboards / **PAUL WISHART** – synthesizers (ex-SKIDS) / **DOUGLAS MUIRDEN** – synthesizers, saxophone

Mercury | not iss.

Apr 82. (7"/ext-12") *(GAME 1/12)* **WE FEEL GOOD (FUTURE'S LOOKING FINE). / DARKNESS** [ ] [-]
Oct 82. (7"/12") *(GAME 2/+12)* **FIRST, LAST FOR EVERYTHING. / (instrumental version)** [ ] [-]

—— (1982) added **BRIAN McGEE** – drums, percussion (ex-SIMPLE MINDS)

Virgin | M.C.A.

Jul 83. (7"/12") *(VS 605/+12)* **WAITING FOR ANOTHER CHANCE. / UNIVERSE** [ ] [-]
Sep 83. (7") *(VS 617)* **LOVE CARES. / READY OR NOT** [ ] [-]
(12"+=) *(VS 617-12)* – ('A'extended).
Oct 83. (lp/c) *(V/TCV 2287) <39013>* **BUILDING BEAUTY** [ ] [ ]
– Love cares / Universe won't mind / Ecstasy / Miracle in my heart / Love building beauty / Desire / Waiting for another chance / Searching for love / Both of us.
Nov 83. (7") *(VS 640)* **MIRACLE OF THE HEART. / (instrumental)** [ ] [-]
(12"+=) *(VS 640-12)* – Ecstasy.
Nov 84. (7"/ext-12") *(VS 651/+12)* **DESIRE. / LOOK NOW** [ ] [-]

—— reverted now to basic quartet without WISHART + MUIRDEN

Jul 85. (7"/12") *(VS 751/+12)* **SHOOTING OUT FOR LOVE. / SOMEWHERE TO RUN** [ ] [-]
Aug 85. (lp) *(206 975)* **PYRAMIDS AND TRAFFIC JAMS** [-] [-] German
– Shooting out for love / Pressure / Natural joy / Gone back baby / Keep on believing / I cried / Somewhere to run / If I fall / All my life.
(above feat. ANNE DUDLEY & MEL GAYNOR)

—— split later in the year

EQUUS (see under ⇒ Soma records)

ESKA

Formed: Strathblane, Glasgow . . . 1993 by youngsters CHRIS MACK and COLIN KEARNEY who met in their local music (instrument) shop. With drummer STUART BRAITHWAITE on board (he's now sonic guitarist with MOGWAI), the trio's early experiments were apparently too avant-garde for latecomer KENNY MacLEOD. Upon his arrival, the bass man knocked the songs into shape and the first results emerged in the form of late 1995's 'TRUCKING AND PAVING'. Released by GRAHAM KEMP (of URUSEI YATSURA) on his own 'Modern Independent' imprint, the track wore its US noise influences proudly on its sleeve . . . hardly surprising, given KEARNEY's petulant claim to dislike any music pre-1980 (with the exception of SUPERTRAMP). At least MACK had apparently been listening to his dad's record collection, his "challenging" singing sounding uncannily like LEONARD COHEN (albeit on a bender with PAVEMENT). A couple of lo-fi 7"ers followed before BRAITHWAITE went off to create sonic masterpieces with MOGWAI, replacement WILLIE MONE making his debut on 1996's 'RUNNING ON SUM SIX DEW' single. A further EP, 'LAST MAN ON THE MOON' (on London-based 'Scared Of Girls'), appeared in Autumn '97 before a gap of more than three years preceded a long awaited ESKA debut album, 'INVENT THE FORTUNE' (2000). CHRIS MACK was also leader of the JAMES ORR COMPLEX (who issued the EP, 'FIGA' for 'Rock Action') and has worked with EL HOMBRE TRAJEADO.

CHRIS MACK – vocals, guitar / **COLIN KEARNEY** – guitar, vocals / **KENNY MacLEOD** – bass / **STUART BRAITHWAITE** – drums

Modern Ind — not iss.

Nov 95. (7"m) *(MIR 003)* **TRUCKING AND PAVING. / THESE ARE THE DRY YEARS / FALSE START** [ ] [-]

Flotsam & Jetsam — not iss.

Feb 96. (7"ep) *(SHaG 002)* **SPLIT SINGLE** [ ] [-]
– In the bottle / Aristotle / (other 2 tracks by the Poison Sisters).

Love Train — not iss.

May 96. (7") *(PUBE 10)* **III PIKE. / LET'S FENCE** [ ] [-]

—— BRAITHWAITE took up his MOGWAI post full-time; new drummer **WILLIE MONE**

Oct 96. (7") *(PUBE 15)* **RUNNING ON SUM SIX DEW. / NOVA SCOTIA** [ ] [-]

Scared Of Girls — not iss.

Sep 97. (7"ep) *(GIRL 004)* **LAST MAN ON THE MOON** [ ] [-]
– Last man on the Moon / Finding it hard to do so little / Dustkicker / Ligercone.

—— now with new drummer **HOPPY** (ex-HERNANDEZ); briefly

Gringo — not iss.

Oct 00. (cd) *(WAAT 008CD)* **INVENT THE FORTUNE** [ ] [-]
– Goodbye to victories / Blast theory / From springboard to highdive / Knives, slowing / The ghosts invade / Between kings / ESP does work / The unbelievable snow of 1999.

D & C — not iss.

Feb 02. (cd-s) *(DCCD 006)* **THE CASE WRAPPED UP** [ ] [-]

JAMES ORR COMPLEX

CHRIS MACK with various

RockAction — not iss.

Nov 01. (7"ep/cd-ep) *(ROCKACT 8/+CD)* **FIGA EP** [ ] [-]
– Million men / Good prophecy / Eagle / Slip into slumber / O conde.

EUGENIUS (see under ⇒ VASELINES)

EVEREST THE HARD WAY (see under ⇒ FIRE ENGINES)

Evolution records (see under ⇒ Q-TEX)

EXCABS (see under ⇒ Bellboy records)

EX-CATHEDRA

Formed: Glasgow ... 1994 by guitarist ALEX and his motley crew of Ska-punks (MACHINE GUN ETIQUETTE drummer, PARKER, was also a member as was singer ANDI). Influenced by RANCID and G.B.H. (remember them!), EX-CATHEDRA were part of the old skool hardcore punk brigade (with Ska being top of the class). A few releases on their own 'Tartan' label, helped the band build up their profile as tours and V/A demos (alongside MACHINE GUN ETIQUETTE and Germany's NUTCASE) filled their time.

Inking a deal with 'Damaged Goods', EX-CATHEDRA released both the 'EX-CATHEDRA' (for 'Terra Nova' label) and 'TARTAN MATERIAL' sets in '96, while Scandic tours with their 'ETIQUETTE chums ensured more notoriety; both ALEX and PARKER filled in for this band while personnel changes were rife. A split EP with MGE was subsequently scheduled (with benefits going to a squat in the Czech Republic town of Ladronka), although this was postponed while a sophomore album, 'FORCED KNOWLEDGE' (2000), hit some retail shops.

• **Note:** don't get mixed up with Michael Lautenschlaeger's 'Ex-Cathedra' New Age set for 'Terra Nova' in the mid-90's and even more so, the 'Sir Christmas' festive offering around the same time.

ANDI – vocals / **ALEX** – guitar / **PARKER** – drums / + others

Tartan — not iss.

Sep 94. (7") *(TARTAN 1)* **STICK TOGETHER. /** [ ] [-]
Jun 95. (7"ep) *(TAR 002)* **WATCH OUT EP** [ ] [-]

Terra Nova — not iss.

Jan 96. (cd) **EX-CATHEDRA** [ ] [-]
– Groundheat / Desert hymn / Fire mask / Sapphire / Temple dawn / Sanctum / Ritual.

Damaged Goods — not iss.

Jul 96. (7") *(DAMGOOD 83)* **TRESPASS. /** [ ] [-]
Sep 96. (lp/cd) *(DAMGOOD 106/+CD)* **TARTAN MATERIAL** [ ] [-]
– Directions / Watch-out / Buckfast happy / Something coming down / Reasons / Dirty ol' town / Stick together / Waiting game / Stop yer running / Buckfast (reprise) / Hooligans in suits / Shock wi' surprise.

Jul 97. (7"m) *(DAMGOOD 131)* **KARMA CHAMELEON. / +2** [ ] [-]

Moon Ska — not iss.

Jul 00. (cd) *(MOONCD 048)* **FORCED KNOWLEDGE** [ ] [-]
– Breakdown / Just begun / Trapped / Truth in flight / Down to fate / Give me tomorrow / Anaesthetised / Something new / Your time / Needles / Just another war song / Geno.

– compilations, etc. –

Mar 02. (cd) *Tartan: (TART 003CD)* **2 x 4** (first two EP's) [ ] [-]

EXILE (see ⇒ Section 9: wee post-Punk groups)

EXPLOITED

Formed: East Kilbride ... 1979 by 'BIG JOHN' DUNCAN, WATTIE BUCHAN, GARY McCORMICK and DRU STIX. Subsequently moving to the capital, they issued three independently released maxi-singles in 1980, 'ARMY LIFE', 'EXPLOITED BARMY ARMY' and 'EXTRACTS FROM AN EDINBURGH NITE CLUB EP', a barrage of three-chord 100 mph punk/oi anthems with BUCHAN spitting out raging anti-establishment diatribes (Maggie Thatcher was a favourite lyrical punchbag).

In 1981, after a minor hit, 'DOGS OF WAR' (on 'Secret' records), they unleashed a whole album's worth of two-minute wonders, 'PUNK'S NOT DEAD' (a battlecry of the dyed mohawk hairdo brigade!) which incredibly hit the Top 20. It was quickly pursued by 'DEAD CITIES' (a near Top 30 hit), an abysmal live set, a shared EP with fellow oi-stars ANTI-PASTI, and a Top 50 hit single, 'ATTACK'. A second album proper, 'TROOPS OF TOMORROW' (1982) followed their debut into the Top 20, featuring their infamous tribute to punk's greatest dead hero, 'SID VICIOUS WAS INNOCENT'.

When BIG JOHN left at the end of '82 (he formed The BLOOD UNCLES before joining GOODBYE MR MACKENZIE!), the rot set in after the Falklands Conflict-inspired set, 'LET'S START A WAR (SAID MAGGIE ONE DAY)' (1983). A further series of personnel changes marred their subsequent releases, 'HORROR EPICS' in '85 relying on substandard heavy metal to get their still raging points across. WATTIE and his ever changing cast of ageing punk/metal diehards continued, if intermittently, to release predictable albums, while former member BIG JOHN found brief fame when he deputised in 1993 for an A.W.O.L. KURT COBAIN in NIRVANA.

WATTIE BUCHAN – vocals / **'BIG JOHN' DUNCAN** – guitar, vocals / **GARY McCORMICK** – bass, vocals (ex-JOSEF K) / **DRU STIX** (b. DREW CAMPBELL) – drums, vocals

Exploited — not iss.

Aug 80. (7"m) *(EXP 001)* **ARMY LIFE. / FUCK THE MODS / CRASHED OUT** [ ] [-]
(re-iss. May81 on 'Secret'; SHH 112)

Nov 80. (7"m) *(EXP 002)* **EXPLOITED BARMY ARMY. / I BELIEVE IN ANARCHY / WHAT YOU WANNA DO?** [ ] [-]
(re-iss. May81 on 'Secret'; SHH 113)

1981. (7"ep) *(EXP 003)* **EXTRACTS FROM EDINBURGH NITE CLUB (live)** [ ] [-]

Secret — not iss.

Apr 81. (7") *(SHH 110)* **DOGS OF WAR. / BLOWN TO BITS (live)** [63] [-]
May 81. (lp) *(EXP 1001)* **PUNK'S NOT DEAD** [20] [-]
– Punk's not dead / Mucky pup / Exploited barmy army / S.P.G. / Cop cars / Free flight / Army life (Pt.2) / Dole q / Out of control / Ripper / Blown to bits / Son of a copper / Sex and violence / Royalty / I believe in anarchy. *(re-iss. Feb89 on 'Link'; LINK 065) (cd-iss. Oct92 on 'Streetlink'; STRCD 006) (cd re-iss. Mar93 on 'Dojo'; DOJOCD 106) (re-iss. Mar98 on 'Harry May'; MAYLP 701) (cd re-iss. Aug98 on 'Snapper'; SMMCD 530) (pic-lp Mar01 on 'Captain Oi'; AHOYCD 521)*
(above original released on 'Exploited' records)

Oct 81. (7"m) *(SHH 120)* **DEAD CITIES. / HITLER'S IN THE CHARTS AGAIN / CLASS WAR** [31] [-]

Superville — not iss.

Nov 81. (lp) *(EXP 1002)* **EXPLOITED LIVE-ON STAGE (live)** [52] [-]
– Cop cars / Crashed out / Dole Q / Dogs of war / Army life / Out of control / Ripper / F*** the mods / Exploited barmy army / Sex & violence / Punks not dead / I believe in anarchy. *(re-iss. 1987 on 'Dojo' lp/c; DOJO LP/TC 9) <US cd-iss. Oct92 on 'Continium'; 10001-2> (UK cd-iss. Mar00 on 'Mayo-Harry May'; MAYOCD 500)*

Nov 81. (12"ep; shared with ANTI-PASTI) *(EXP 1003)* **DON'T LET 'EM GRIND YOU DOWN** [70] [-]

Secret — not iss.

Apr 82. (7") *(SHH 130)* **ATTACK. / ALTERNATIVES** [50] [-]
Jun 82. (lp) *(SEC 8)* **TROOPS OF TOMORROW** [17] [-]
– Jimmy Boyle / Daily news / Disorder / Alternatives (remix) / Germs / Rapist / UK '82 / War / Troops of tomorrow / Sid Vicious was innocent / They won't stop / So tragic. *(re-iss. Feb89 on 'Link'; LINK 066) (cd-iss. Oct92 on 'Streetlink'; STRCD 007)*

(cd re-iss. Mar93 on 'Dojo'; DOJOCD 107) (re-iss. Mar98 on 'Harry May'; MAYLP 702) (cd re-iss. Aug98 on 'Snapper'; SMMCD 529) (pic-lp Mar01 on 'Captain Oi'; AHOYPD 522)

Oct 82. (7") *(SHH 140)* **COMPUTERS DON'T BLUNDER. / ADDICTION** ☐ [-]

— **BILLY DUNN** – guitar (ex-SKROTEEZ) repl. BIG JOHN who joined the SQUARE PEG. DUNCAN subsequently formed The BLOOD UNCLES before he hooked up with GOODBYE MR MACKENZIE.

Blurg-Pax — not iss.

Oct 83. (7"m) *(PAX 15)* **RIVAL LEADERS. / ARMY STYLE / SINGALONGABUSHELL** ☐ [-]

Pax — Combat

Dec 83. (lp) *(PAX 18)* **LET'S START A WAR (SAID MAGGIE ONE DAY)** ☐ ☐
– Let's start a war / Insanity / Safe below / Eyes of the vulture / Should we can't we / Rival leaders (remix) / God save the Queen / Psycho / Kidology / False hopes / Another day to go nowhere / Wankers. *(re-iss. 1987 on 'Dojo' lp/c; DOJO LP/TC 10) (cd-iss. Mar94 on 'Dojo'; DOJOCD 010) (cd re-iss. Aug98 on 'Snapper'; SMMCD 531)*

— **DEPTFORD JOHN** repl. WAYNE / **MAD MICK** repl. EGGHEAD / also with **WATTIE, KARL, WILLIE BUCHAN** – drums / **CAPTAIN SCARLETT** – guitar

— McCORMICK formed ZULU SYNDICATE, while STIX struggled with a drug addiction and then was sentenced to seven years for armed robbery.

Konnexion — not iss.

Mar 85. (lp/c) *(KOMA/AMOK 788012)* **HORROR EPICS** ☐ [-]
– Horror epics / Don't forget the chaos / Law and order / I hate you / No more idols / Maggie / Dangerous vision / Down below / Treat you like shit / Forty odd years ago / My life. *(re-iss. Aug86 on 'Dojo' lp/c; DOJO LP/TC 37) (cd-iss. Mar94; DOJOCD 184) (cd re-iss. Aug98 on 'Snapper'; SMMCD 532)*

Rough Justice — not iss.

Apr 86. (12"ep) *(12KORE 102)* **JESUS IS DEAD / POLITICIANS. / DRUG SQUAD / PRIVACY INVASION** ☐ [-]

Nov 88. (12"ep) *(12KORE 103)* **WAR NOW. / UNITED CHAOS AND ANARCHY / SEXUAL FAVOURS** ☐ [-]

Aug 89. (lp/cd) *(JUST/+CD 6)* **DEATH BEFORE DISHONOUR** ☐ [-]
– Anti UK / Power struggle / Scaling the Derry wall / Barry Prossitt / Don't really care / No forgiveness / Death before dishonour / Adding to their fears / Police informer / Drive me insane / Pulling us down / Sexual favours. *(cd+=)* – Drug squad man / Privacy invasion / Jesus is dead / Politicians / War now / United chaos and anarchy / Sexual favours (dub version). *(cd re-iss. Jun00 on 'Dream Catcher'; CRIDE 37)*

— **WATTIE** – vocals / **SMEGS** – bass, vocals / **GOGS** – guitar / **TONY** – drums

Sep 90. (cd/c/lp) *(CD/T+/JUST 15)* **THE MASSACRE** ☐ [-]
– The massacre / Sick bastard / Porno slut / Now I'm dead / Boys in blue / Dog soldier / Don't pay the poll tax / F. . . religion / About to die / Blown out of the city / Police shit / Stop the slaughter. *(cd re-iss. Jun00 on 'Dream Catcher'; CRIDE 36)*

— new line-up mid-90's; **WATTIE** – vocals / **ARTHUR** – guitar / **BILLY** – bass / **WULLIE** – drums

Mar 96. (cd/c/lp) *(CD/T+/JUST 22)* **BEAT THE BASTARDS** ☐ [-]
– Beat the bastards / Affected by them / Law for the rich / System fucked up / They lie / If you're sad / Fightback / Massacre of innocents / Police TV / Sea of blood / Dont blame me / 15 years / Serial killer.

– compilations, etc. –

Dec 84. (lp) *Dojo; (DOJOLP 1)* **TOTALLY EXPLOITED** ☐ [-]
– Punk's not dead / Army life / F**k a mod / Barmy army / Dogs of war / Dead cities / Sex and violence / Yops / Daily news / Dole Q / Believe in anarchy / God save the Queen / Psycho / Blown to bits / Insanity / S.P.G. / Jimmy Boyle / U.S.A. / Attack / Rival leaders. *(re-iss. Apr86 lp/c/cd; DOJO LP/TC/CD 1)*

Jan 85. (c) *Chaos; (APOCA 2)* **LIVE ON THE APOCALYPSE TOUR '81 (live)** ☐ [-]
(lp-iss.Feb87; APOCA 2)

Feb 86. (lp) *Suck; (SDLP 2)* **LIVE AT THE WHITE HOUSE (live)** ☐ [-]
(cd-iss. Jul98 on 'PinHead'; PINCD 104) (cd re-iss. Jun99 on 'Snapper'; SMMCD 574)

Aug 86. (12"ep) *Archive 4; (TOF 107)* **DEAD CITIES / PUNK'S NOT DEAD. / ARMY LIFE / EXPLOITED BARMY LIFE** ☐ [-]

Mar 87. (lp) *Snow; (WAT 1)* **INNER CITY DECAY** ☐ [-]

Dec 87. (lp) *Link; (LINKLP 018)* **LIVE AND LOUD (live)** ☐ [-]
(cd-iss. Oct93; LINKCD 018) (cd re-iss. Apr96 & Apr02 on 'Anagram'; CDPUNK 18)

Jul 88. (12"ep) *Skunx; (EXPX 1)* **PUNK'S ALIVE** ☐ [-]
– Alternative / Let's start a war / Horror epics / Troops of tomorrow / Dogs of war.

1989. (d-lp) *Roadrunner; (RR 4965-1)* **PUNK'S NOT DEAD / TROOPS OF TOMORROW** ☐ ☐

1989. (lp) *Grand Slam; <SLAM 7>* **LIVE, LEWD, LUST (live)** [-] ☐
– Law and order / Let's start a war / Horror epics / Blown to bits / Hitler's in the charts again / Troops of tomorrow / Sex and violence / Alternative / Cop cars / Dole Q / Dead cities / SPG / I believe in anarchy / Warhead / Daily news / Dogs of war. *(UK cd-iss. Nov00 on 'Step 1'; STEPCD 035)*

Dec 91. (cd) *Streetlink; (STRCD 018)* **THE SINGLES COLLECTION** ☐ [-]
(re-iss. Apr93 & Jan98 on 'Dojo'; DOJOCD 118)

Feb 94. (cd) *Loma; (LOMACD 2)* **LIVE ON STAGE 1981 / LIVE AT THE WHITE HOUSE 1985** ☐ [-]

Feb 94. (cd) *Loma; (LOMACD 3)* **LET'S START A WAR . . . / HORROR EPICS** ☐ [-]

Mar 94. (cd) *Dojo; (DOJOCD 20109)* **LIVE IN JAPAN (live)** ☐ [-]

Apr 94. (cd) *Cleopatra; (CLEO 5000CD)* **THE SINGLES** ☐ [-]
(re-iss. Jun99 on 'Eagle'; EAGCD 094)

Sep 97. (d-cd) *Snapper; (SMDCD 136)* **TOTALLY EXPLOITED / LIVE IN JAPAN** ☐ [-]

May 00. (3xcd-box) *Snapper; (SMXCD 103)* **THE BOX** ☐ [-]
– (LET'S START A WAR / HORROR EPICS / LIVE AT THE WHITE HOUSE)

Jul 00. (cd) *Harry May; (CANCAN 008CD)* **DEAD CITIES** ☐ [-]
(re-iss. Jun02 on 'Harry May'; MAYOCD 131)

Mar 01. (cd) *Captain Oi; (AHOYCD 160)* **PUNK SINGLES AND RARITIES** ☐ [-]

Jun 01. (d-cd) *Snapper; (SMDCD 355)* **UNEXPLOITED** ☐ [-]

F

FAKE EYELASHES
(see under ⇒ Creeping Bent records)

FAT LIP

Formed: Glasgow . . . 1997 by quintet who quickly downgraded to a 4-piece:- HUGH McLACHLAN (ex-PLAYERS), JAMES McEWAN, TERRY TOCHEL and KENNY McEWAN. After subsequently winning the unsigned talent competition 'In The City' (which they shared with IDLEWILD) the group issued their self-financed vinyl-only EP's 'THE SOUND OF MUSIC' and 'THE SOUND OF LOVERS' in '97 and '99 respectively. Inspired by noisekins PRIMAL SCREAM and Manchester's finest The HAPPY MONDAYS, the troupe employed a scatterbrain psychedelic wall of sound, and fused it with ROXY MUSIC-esque rock'n'roll riffs c.mid-70's. They went on to deliver their debut album 'IDIOT MANTRAS' (issued on their own 'Penthouse' white label in '99) followed by a brief hiatus from the live scene, in which the band were said to be conceiving some pretty awesome material. HUGH, TERRY and JAMES are currently trading as The GHOSTS – watch this space.

HUGH McLACHLAN – vocals (ex-PLAYERS) / **JAMES McEWAN** – keyboards / **TERRY TOCHEL** – guitar / **KENNY McEWAN** – drums

U-Bahn Pro — not iss.

Oct 97. (12"ep) **THE SOUND OF MUSIC EP** ☐ [-]

Jan 99. (12"ep) **THE SOUND OF LOVERS EP** ☐ [-]

Penthouse — not iss.

Aug 99. (12"ep) *(PH 001)* **MELODIA EP** ☐ [-]
– Melodia / Mellow daydub / Bigger than better.

2000. (cd) *(PH 002)* **IDIOT MANTRAS** ☐ [-]
– Chant / Love it all / Band in a box / Kink in the noodle / Angels wish / The sound of music / Idiot mantras / Disturbance (in A minor) / Link in the chain / Melodia.

the GHOSTS

HUGO (HUGH), **T.T.** (TERRY), **JIMMY MACK** (JAMES + THE SHADOW BOXERS (a sample box)

Penthouse — not iss.

Sep 02. (10"ep) *(PH 004)* **WESTENDING E.P.** ☐ [-]
– Darlin, darlin / Westending / For the birds.

FELSONS

Formed: Edinburgh . . . 1995 by singer/songwriter DEAN OWENS and bassist KEVIN McGUIRE. Initially a part-time partnership engaged in plying country covers around the capital's pubs, The FELSONS became a more concrete proposition after a friend offered his studio for the purposes of recording an album. The end result was 'ONE STEP AHEAD OF THE POSSE' (1996), a set which never strayed far from songwriter OWENS' love of classic country while at the same time keeping a contemporary edge. The record increased their profile and in turn their gig schedule, necessitating a full-time guitarist in the shape of CALAIS BROWN as well as a drummer, KEITH BURNS.

A 1997 six-track EP/mini-set, 'LASSO THE MOON', served notice of an expanded musical palate and growing confidence, roping in various strands of American roots music to impressive effect. It was certainly enough to convince leading independent Scottish label, 'Greentrax', who signed The FELSONS up as a flagship act for their new 'G2' imprint. The band's hotly-anticipated second album proper, 'GLAD', arrived in summer '98, a CALUM MALCOLM-produced record that finally saw The FELSONS hailed as a homegrown force to be reckoned with. Running the gamut of country – in the loosest and most generous sense of the word – stylings from gritty SPRINGSTEEN/STEVE EARLE-esque roots-rock to plaintive dust-bowl laments, the album garnered encouraging reviews from a wide cross-section of the press.

Yet while OWENS' distinctive vocals attest to his band's Caledonian roots, The FELSONS continue to gain more recognition elsewhere. Although the band's profile has been boosted by recent supports slots to the likes of SUZY BOGGUS and The MAVERICKS, their relative anonymity in Edinburgh can only be put down to Scotland's perplexing failure to appreciate its own talent.

DEAN OWENS – vocals, guitar / **KEVIN McGUIRE** – bass, vocals / added **CALAIS BROWN** – lead guitar, mandolin, banjo / **KEITH BURNS** – percussion

The Music Corporation — not iss.

May 96. (cd) *(TMC 9607)* **ONE STEP AHEAD OF THE POSSE** [ ] [-]
– The arms of love / I ain't been anywhere yet / Crowded / Wishful thinking / Virginia north / One step ahead of the posse / Till the cows come home / David / Cookie's wedding / Alone in this world / I'd go anywhere / Shine like the road after / The rain / Bones.

1997. (m-cd) **LASSO THE MOON** [ ] [-]
– Spirit of us / A town called home / Rearview mirror / Sunkissed / Riverman / I ain't been anywhere yet.

— added guests **STUART NISBET** – dobro, steel guitar + **MIKE HALL** – keyboards

G2 — G2

Jul 98. (cd) *(<G2CD 7001>)* **GLAD** [ ] [ ] Mar99
– Boomerang boy / Heart is home / Missing you / Postcards / Born to lose you / Is there a dreamer here? / Joseph Black / You're everything / Wake me up / Is it yesterday yet? / What about me? / Belfast blues / On fire / Meet me after the show.

FENN

Formed: Glasgow . . . early 90's by IAN BAIRD, RICHIE DEMPSEY and original singer, MIKE SUTHERLAND, the trio taking the moniker from the 'Twin Peaks' actress, Sherilyn. However by the end of '92, the busy threesome became a foursome (without MIKE) after adding DOUGIE YOUNG and EWAN WALKER. Trips to London (Chalk Farm) and Reading in '93, promoted their debut set, 'SPANISH' (which means 'brilliant' in Scots slang), a foray into SWERVEDRIVER/FUGAZI/HUSKER DU-esque indie guitar-rock with sparse, non-lyric vox to boot.

DOUGIE YOUNG – guitar, vocals; repl. MIKE SUTHERLAND / **EWAN WALKER** – guitar / **IAN BAIRD** – bass, vocals / **RICHIE DEMPSEY** – drums (ex-STRETCHHEADS)

Mean — not iss.

Sep 93. (10") *(MEANX 003)* **NOT JELLY. / BLADDERHORN / ARIEL** [ ] [-]

Oct 93. (lp/cd) *(MEAN/+CD 004)* **SPANISH** [ ] [-]
– Quietly vegan / Not jelly / Mild mannered janitor / Anagram Stan / Numb / Pop jop / Saint's gate / Lead limb / Cosh / Head realiser.

Flotsam & Jetsam – The 13th Note — not iss.

Nov 97. (7") *(SHaG 13.01)* **Club Beatroot Part One** [ ] [-]
– (unknown) / (other by BEETROOT)

— split up after above

FICTION FACTORY

Formed: Perth . . . 1983 by KEVIN PATTERSON and CHIC MEDLEY, plus MIKE OGLETREE (ex-SIMPLE MINDS), EDDIE JORDAN and GRAHAM McGREGOR. With the help of former ASSOCIATES member, ALAN RANKINE, the quintet recorded their debut single, 'GHOST OF LOVE', for 'C.B.S.'. However, it wasn't until a tour supporting PAUL YOUNG and their follow-up single early the following year, '(FEELS LIKE) HEAVEN', that the band broke into the UK Top 10. A smoochy synthesized pop song, it nevertheless became their proverbial albatross with only a re-issue of their aforementioned debut gaining a minor chart placing. After their album, 'THROW THE WARPED WHEEL OUT' (1984), failed to sell in any significant quantity, the duo of PATTERSON and MEDLEY were left to pick up the pieces on the 'Foundry' imprint. 'ANOTHER STORY' appeared in '85, the album only making sure the outfit would remain obscure to the public.

KEVIN PATTERSON – vocals / **CHIC MEDLEY** – guitar / **EDDIE JORDAN** – keyboards / **GRAHAM McGREGOR** – bass / **MIKE OGLETREE** – drums (ex-SIMPLE MINDS, ex-CAFE JACQUES)

C.B.S. — Columbia

Oct 83. (7") *(A 3819)* **GHOST OF LOVE. / THE OTHER SIDE OF LOVE** [ ] [-]
(12"+=) *(TA 3819)* – Old game blue flame.
(re-iss. Mar84; same) – hit UK No.64

Dec 83. (7") *(A 3996)* **(FEELS LIKE) HEAVEN. / EVERYONE BUT YOU** [6] [ ]
(12"+=) *(TA 3996)* – This is.

Jun 84. (7") *(A 4453)* **ALL OR NOTHING. / DREAMING OF SOMEONE** [ ] [ ]
(12"+=) *(TA 4453)* – Who knows you.

Jul 84. (lp/c) *(CBS/40 25964)* **THROW THE WARPED WHEEL OUT** [ ] [ ]
– (Feels like) Heaven / Heart and mind / Panic / The hanging gardens / All or nothing / Hit the mark / Ghost of love / Tales of tears / The first step / The warped wheel. *(c+=)* – Rise and fall / Who knows you. *(re-iss. Apr86 lp/c; CBS/40 32778)*

— **PATTERSON + MEDLEY** recruited new session people **PIM JONES** – guitar / **PAUL WISHART** – keyboards / **GRAHAM WEIR** – brass / **JAMES LOCKE** – percussion / **MORWENNA LAIDLAW + FIONA CARLIN** – vocals

Foundry — not iss.

Mar 85. (7") *(FOUND 1)* **NOT THE ONLY ONE. / LET ME BE A PART** [ ] [-]
(12"+=) *(FOUND 1-12)* – ('A'instrumental).

Jun 85. (7"/12") *(FOUND 2/+12)* **NO TIME. / TENSION** [ ] [-]

Aug 88. (lp/c) *(FOND L/C 2)* **ANOTHER STORY** [ ] [-]
– Another story / Standing at the top of the world / Not the only one / All for you / Lose your heart in nature / No time / The powder room / Make believe / Time is right / Victoria victorious. *(re-iss. Jun88; same)*
above album was their last before their split

FIEND (see under ⇒ TELSTAR PONIES)

FIN

Born: IAN MUIR, Glasgow. From a member of The FLYING SQUAD to being catapulted into the denim and leather limelight of (Pete Way's) WAYSTED, vocalist FIN MORE contributed a good deal of the showmanship that helped promote three well-received metal albums, 'Vices', 'Waysted' and 'The Good, The Bad & The Waysted' between 1983 and '85. In this time, and probably through FIN's Scottish connections, WAYSTED played many times north of the border, a highlight being at the Scottish Rock & Pop Festival in East Kilbride in '84.

FINGER CREAMS (see under ⇒ Flotsam & Jetsam records)

FINITRIBE

Formed: Edinburgh . . . 1984 by CHRIS CONNELLY, JOHN VICK, DAVID MILLER and PHILIP PINSKY (ANDREW McGREGOR and SIMON McGLYNN made up the early sextet). Initially a conventional post-punk guitar outfit, the band released a debut EP, 'CURLING & STRETCHING' on their own 'Finiflex' label in summer '84, graduating to a John Peel session before rethinking their whole approach in the mid-80's.

Tired of the conventional drums, bass, guitar set-up, they acquired a sampler and began experimenting with electronic music. The result was 'LET THE TRIBE GROW', an EP released on the 'Cathexis' label and featuring 'DE TESTIMONY', a seminal dancefloor anthem for the original Balearic/Acid House generation. Subsequently hooking up with Chicago industrial label, 'Wax Trax', the FINI's released a further couple of 12" singles, 'I WANT MORE' and 'MAKE IT INTERNAL', raising their profile in the States but failing to advance their cause at home. A disastrous tour in early '88 led to the departure of three members – including CONNELLY, who went on to join The REVOLTING COCKS – and a parting of the ways with 'Wax Trax'. This in turn resulted in a resurrection of the 'Finiflex' label for a long-awaited debut album, 'NOISE, LUST & FUN' (1988), featuring contributions from such minor luminaries as LITTLE ANNIE, WILF PLUM (of DOG FACED HERMANS) and JESS HOPKINS.

A series of remix EP's proved their dancefloor credentials while a deal with 'One Little Indian' ran into controversy almost immediately with the 'ANIMAL FARM' EP. Subverting the nursery rhyme 'Old MacDonald', for the purposes of berating the similarly titled hamburger outlet, FINITRIBE (as they were now known) offered up a flavour of the anti-consumerist stance prevalent on new album, 'GROSSING 10K' (1989). The subsequent threat of legal action wasn't exactly helped by a "Fuck Off McDonalds" poster campaign, the group running into similar trouble in 1991 with the '101' single, released as FINITRIBE 101 and drawing the wrath of ELECTRIBE 101. The latter effort was culled from 1992's 'AN UNEXPECTED GROOVY TREAT', the FINIS' most accessible, successful album to date and home of groovy near-hit, 'FOREVERGREEN'.

The same period also the development of the 'Finiflex' label and in-house production team with releases by the likes of JUSTIN ROBERTSON, EGE BAM YASI and even SPARKS, the group co-ordinating releases from their dockside studio in Leith. A deal with 'Ffrr' gave the operation more commercial viability and even led to a Top 75 FINITRIBE hit single with 1994's 'BRAND NEW' EP. Yet by early '95, MILLER and longstanding member PINSKY were in the process of splitting from fellow founder VICK – sadly the latter died of an overdose that October. The slimmed down FINITRIBE now operated from a bedroom studio in Portobello after the pressures of running 'Finiflex' became too much.

The duo subseqently set up a new label, 'UGT', continuing to indulge in side projects such as GEKO and SOLARIZE. With rumours of a harder edged, more organic sound in the pipeline, the FINITRIBE worked on new material with the likes of PAUL HAIG, CHRIS CONNELLY and KATE MORRISON. By the late 90's, the young MORRISON was part of MILLER and PINSKY's darker version of FINI, 'SLEAZY LISTENING' in 1998 a marked breakaway from their dance roots. In the summer of 2001, the trio finally got around to delivering their first product for three years, 'BORED'.

• **Trivia:** Their group name derives from 'Finny Tribe', the collective name for the fish species known to the Rosicruscians in Ireland.

CHRIS CONNELLY – vocals, guitars, etc / **JOHN VICK** (b. 6 Nov'65) – keyboards / **DAVID MILLER** (b. 20 Jul'62, Moffat) – guitar, vocals / **PHILIP PINSKY** (b.23 Mar'65, Appleton, Wisconsin, USA) – bass, guitar, programming / **ANDREW McGREGOR** – guitar / **SIMON McGLYNN** – drums

Finiflex / not iss.

Jun 84. (12"ep) *(LT 1001)* **CURLING & STRETCHING EP** [ ] [-]
– Cathedral / Curling theme / etc.
(re-iss. 1988; FT 001)

Cathexis / not iss.

Oct 86. (12"ep) *(CRF 611)* **LET THE TRIBE GROW** [ ] [-]
– De testimony (collapsing edit) / Throttle hearts (rising mix) / Adults absolved / Monimail. *(re-iss. Oct88 on 'Finiflex')*

Wax Trax / Wax Trax

Oct 87. (12"ep) *(WAKUK 027)* **I WANT MORE / IDIOT STRENGTH. / I WANT MORE (row, row, row the mix)** [ ] [-]

— now without ANDREW

Feb 88. (12"ep) *(WAXUK 028)* **MAKE IT INTERNAL (integrity mix) / LITTLE VISITORS. / MAKE IT INTERNAL (here we go round the mulberry mix)** [ ] [ ] Nov90

— CONNELLY joined The REVOLTING COCKS before embarking on solo career

Finiflex / not iss.

Oct 88. (12"ep) *(FT 002)* **DE TESTIMONY EP** [ ] [-]
– The batter mix / Micromix / Pick'n'mix.

Nov 88. (12"ep) *(FT 003)* **ZULUS EP** [ ] [-]
– The crunchy mix / The rhythmix / Noise (pick'n'mix).

Nov 88. (lp) *(FTLP 001)* **NOISE, LUST & FUN** [ ] [-]
– Electrolux / Disturb / Swans / Finis / Throttlehearts / Zulus / Fluke / Electrolux / Swans / Disturb / Ultra. *(cd-iss. Oct89 on 'One Little Indian'; TPLP 21CD)*

Dec 88. (12"ep) *(FT 004)* **ELECT-ROLUX EP** [ ] [-]
– Electrolux (pick'n'mix) / Electrolux (minimix) / Disturb (cement mix).

One Little Indian / Rough Trade

Nov 89. (12"ep) *(31 TP12)* **ANIMAL FARM EP** [ ] [-]
Chicken mix / Ouch ya go (ouchtakes) / Monkey mix / Animal farm (meatymix).

Dec 89. (lp/c/cd) *(TPLP 24/+MC/CD)* **GROSSING 10K** [ ] [ ]
– Eyeball / Instant access / An Earth creature / Whale of a tail / Ask a silly question / Monster in the house / Asstrax / 3 AAA's / Put your trunk in it / Built in monster / Animal farm / Ouch ya go.

Mar 90. (12"ep) *(38 TP12)* **MONSTER IN THE HOUSE EP** [ ] [ ]
– Monster club / Monster in the wireless / Eyeball / Built in monsters

— trimmed to a trio of **VICK, PINSKY + MILLER** when CONNELLY took off to go solo (having already joined REVOLTING COCKS)

Jul 91. (7"/cd-s; as FINITRIBE 101) *(54 TP7/+CD)* **101. / SONIC SHUFFLE (mixed by Andy Weatherall)** [ ] [ ]
(12") *(54 TP12L)* – 101 (mixed by Graham Massey of 808 State).

Nov 91. (12"/cd-s) *(64 TP 12/7CD)* **ACE LOVE DEUCE (Steve Osbourne mix). / ('A'-Justin Robertson mix)** [ ] [-]

Jun 92. (12") *(74 TP12F)* **FOREVERGREEN (mixes)** [51] [-]
(12") *(74 TP12J)* – (2 Justin Robertson mixes)
(12") *(74 12TPY)* – ('A'-Youth mixes) / ('A'-Andy Weatherall mix).
(cd-s) *(74 TP7CD)* – (all mixes).

Sep 92. (lp/c/cd) *(TPLP 34/+C/CD) <52846>* **AN UNEXPECTED GROOVY TREAT** [ ] [ ] Feb93
– Forevergreen / 101 (sonic shuffle edit) / Come and get it / Mellowman / Yer crazy / Forevergreen (the lunar eclipse mix) / Bagomatix 2 (there can only be one) / Ace love deuce / Hypnopaedia / Glisten / An unexpected groovy treat / Forevergreen (forevermost excellent) / Ace love deuce / Forevergreen (foreverdreaming).

Ffrr-London / London

Nov 94. (12"ep/c-ep/cd-ep) *(FX/FCS/FCD 247)* **BRAND NEW EP** [69] [-]
– Tip top tune / Tip top.
(12") *(FXX 247)* – (remixes).

Mar 95. (c-s) *(FCS 258)* **LOVE ABOVE / ('A'-Sheigra 5 mix)** [ ] [ ]
(12"+=) *(FX 258)* – ('A'-Cheeky Vee half mix) / ('A'-Analogue mix).
(cd-s++=) *(FCD 258)* – ('A'-original mix).

Apr 95. (d-cd/c/d-lp) *(828 615-2/-4/-1)* **SHEIGRA** [ ] [ ]
– Dark / Sunshine / Brand new (tip-top tune) / Mushroom shaped / Sheigra 5 / Truth / Catch the whistle / We have come / Mesmerise / Off on a slow one / Love above (Analogue mix).

— JOHN VICK o.d'd in October '95 after earlier leaving the group

— next featured **JASON BEARNE**

Aura Surround Sounds / not iss.

Jun 96. (12"/cd-s) *(SUSSX/SUCD 33)* **SQUELCH 1 (remixes; Misiah / original 1 / Wreckage Inc.)** [ ] [-]
(12") *(SUSSY 33)* – Squelch 2:- (remixes; Black metal dub II / original 2 / MaC's mangattack!).

Infectious / not iss.

Aug 97. (12") *(INFECT 42T)* **FLYING PEPPERS. / WALTZER (dark hard dub) / FRANTIC (Angel Park accapella edit)** [ ] [-]
(12") *(INFECT 42TX)* – ('A'-Furnace dub) / Chiller (heartbeats for the haunted dub).

— **PINSKY + MILLER** recruited **KATE MORRISON** – vocals

Feb 98. (12") *(INFECT 51T)* **FRANTIC (mixes; Scissorkicks gets Laidback / Cut La Roc / Microspeech mix / Laidback).**
(cd-s+=) *(INFECT 51CD)* – ('A'-A1 People mix) / Witchman live jam.

Mar 98. (cd/lp) *(INFECT 43 CD/LP)* **SLEAZY LISTENING** [ ] [-]
– Sleazy rider / Mind my make-up / Frantic / Chiller / Waltzer / Flying peppers / The electrician / The bells / The shining / Oxbow incident / Theme.

Mar 98. (12"/cd-s) *(INFECT 54 T/CD)* **MIND MY MAKE-UP (mixes; original / Dust Junkys / Dope Smugglaz O.D. dub / Diminished responsibility / De-composed bass / Mind my B-cup)** [ ] [-]

— after a 3-year hiatus, FINITRIBE (**MILLER, PINSKY + MORRISON**) were back on record adding **CHRIS ROSS** – drums + **BETTY OFFERMAN** – piano

North East South West / not iss.

Jul 01. (cd-ep) *(NEWSCD 001)* **BORED** [ ] [-]
– Bored / Single skin / Ecstatic in nylon.

FIRE ENGINES

Formed: Edinburgh ... 1979 out of The DIRTY REDS by DAVEY HENDERSON, MURRAY SLADE, GRAHAM MAIN and RUSSELL BURN. Taking their name from a particularly psychotic 13th FLOOR ELEVATORS track, The FIRE ENGINES caused a minor furore at the dawn of the 80's with their trashy, discordant punk-funk din, as heard on debut single, 'GET UP AND USE ME'. The combination of the POP GROUP/GANG OF FOUR-style rhythmic guitar mangling and HENDERSON's demented vocal was enough to get the music press foaming at the mouth, a largely instrumental, self-financed mini-set, 'LUBRICATE YOUR LIVING ROOM' (1981) working out their frustrations over seven breakneck tracks.

Picked up by Bob Last's 'Pop Aural' label, the band came close to a conventional song structure with the infectious 'CANDY SKIN' single, HENDERSON's erm, "unique' vocal talents pushed centre stage. Acclaimed by the press and a sizeable indie hit, the band pushed the boat out for follow-up, 'BIG GOLD DREAM', even employing female backing vocals in a last gasp effort for pop stardom.

It wasn't to be and the FIRE ENGINES were soon parked in the station for good, RUSSELL forming the short-lived EVEREST THE HARD WAY with IAN STODDART and future ALTERED IMAGES man, STEPHEN LIRONI. He then enjoyed a further spell with The DIRTY REDS before resurfacing in the mid-80's with HENDERSON and STODDART as sophisticated soul/funk-pop outfit, WIN. Signed to Alan Horne's new 'Swamplands' label, they released two singles, 'UNAMERICAN BROADCASTING' and the anthemic 'YOU'VE GOT THE POWER' (later gaining belated exposure as the musical backdrop for a McEwan's lager TV ad), before the label was taken over by 'London' records. The major label backing led to a Top 60 placing for their debut album, 'UH! TEARS BABY (A TRASH ICON)' (1987), new members MANNY SCHONIVVA, WILLIE PERRY and SIMON SMEETON coming in as the band switched to 'Virgin'. Despite continuing critical acclaim and enthusuastic support from the press, a follow-up set, 'FREAKY TRIGGER' (1989) did nothing and WIN called it a day in 1989.

While STODDART went on to play with semi-legendary Edinburgh funksters, CAPTAIN SHIFTY, SCHONIVVA hooked up with dance act, YO YO HONEY; HENDERSON and RUSSELL recorded for 'Creation' under the PIE FINGER billing. HENDERSON went on to create quirky pop material as NECTARINE No.9, signing to the reactivated 'Postcard' label and releasing a debut album, 'A SEA WITH THREE STARS' (1993). A series of EP's followed – including a collaborative effort with PAUL QUINN and Caledonian performance poet, JOCK SCOT – prior to '95's 'SAINT JACK' album.

• **Songwriters:** All written by HENDERSON, except FASCIST GROOVE (Heaven 17). NECTARINE No.9 covered INSIDE OF YOUR HEART (Velvet Underground) / FROWNLAND (Captain Beefheart) / PULL MY DAISY (Ginsberg-Kerouac) / THESE DAYS (Jackson Browne).

DAVEY HENDERSON – vocals, guitar (ex-DIRTY REDS) / **MURRAY SLADE** – guitar / **GRAHAM MAIN** – bass / **RUSSELL BURN** – drums

Codex / not iss.

Dec 80. (7") *(CDX 1)* **GET UP AND USE ME. / EVERYTHING'S ROSES** [ ] [-]

Accessory / Fast

Jan 81. (m-lp) *(ACC 001)* *<FPA 002>* **LUBRICATE YOUR LIVING ROOM** <US title 'AUFGELADEN UND BEREIT FUR ACTION UNDER SPASS'> [ ] [ ] Aug81
– Plastic gift / Get up and use me / Hungry beat / Lubricate your living room pt.1 & 2 / New thing in the cartons / Sympathetic anaesthetic / Discord.

Pop Aural / not iss.

May 81. (7") *(POP 010)* **CANDY SKIN. / MEAT WHIPLASH** [ ] [-]

— added guests **SIMON BEST** – keyboards / **HI-RAY** (b. HILARY MORRISON) – vocals (of FLOWERS) / **KAREN BROWN** – b. vocals

Nov 81. (7") *(POP 013)* **BIG GOLD DREAM. / SYMPATHETIC ANAESTHETIC** [ ] [-]
(12"+=) *(POP 013-12)* – New thing in cartons.

— folded on the last day of '81. DAVEY and HILARY formed HEARTBEAT. (1 track on NME-c)

– compilations, etc. –

Aug 92. (lp) *Creation Rev-Ola; (CREV 001LP)* **FOND** [ ] [-]
– (contained all their work)

EVEREST THE HARD WAY

— were formed by **RUSSELL** with others **IAN STODDART** – bass / **STEPHEN LIRONI** – guitar, keyboards (later ALTERED IMAGES)

Do-It / not iss.

Apr 82. (7"/12") *(DUN 17)* **TIGHTROPE. / WHEN YOU'RE YOUNG** [ ] [-]

— split later that year. RUSSELL joined DIRTY REDS before forming below

WIN

DAVEY HENDERSON – vocals, guitar / **RUSSELL BURN** – drums / **IAN STODDART** – bass

Swamplands / not iss.

Mar 85. (7"/12") *(SW/+X 5)* **UNAMERICAN BROADCASTING (pt.1). / UNAMERICAN BROADCASTING (pt.2)** [ ] [-]

Jun 85. (7"/s7") *(SWP/+P 8)* **YOU'VE GOT THE POWER. / IN HEAVEN (LADY IN THE RADIATOR SONG)** [ ] [-]
(12"/s12") *(SWX/+X 8)* – ('A'side) / Unamerican broadcasting (pt.1 & 2).
(d7") *(SWDX 8)* – (all 4 tracks).

London / not iss.

Mar 86. (7") *(LON 85)* **SHAMPOO TEARS. / EMPTY HOLSTERS** [ ] [-]
(12"+=) *(LONX 85)* – The slider / ('A'-dub version).

Mar 87. (7") *(LON 128)* **SUPER POPOID GROVE. / BABY CUTTING** [63] [-]
(12"+=) *(LONX 128)* – You've got the power.
(d7"++=) *(LONG 128)* – In Heaven (the lady in the radiator song).

Apr 87. (lp/c)(cd) *(LON LP/C 31) (828 047-2)* **UH! TEARS BABY (A TRASH ICON)** [51] [-]
– Super popoid groove / Shampoo tears / Binding love spell / Unamerican broadcasting / Hollywood Baby too / Empty holsters / You've got the power / Charms of powerful trouble / It may be a beautiful sky tonight but it's only a shelter for a world at risk / Charms (reprise) / Baby cutting. *(c+cd+=)* – Shampoo tears (extended) / You've got the power (extended).

— added **MANNY SCHONIVVA** – guitar / **WILLIE PERRY** – keyboards / **SIMON SMEETON** – guitar (appeared on last set alongside SCHONIVVA)

Virgin / not iss.

Nov 88. (7") *(VS 1121)* **WHAT'LL YOU DO TILL SUNDAY, BABY. / TRIGGER HAPPY** [ ] [-]
(12"+=) *(VST 1121)* – ('A'-Johnson's Baby mix).
(cd-s++=) *(VSCD 1121)* – Peace on egg.

Jan 89. (7") *(VS 1157)* **LOVE UNITS. / SCARY SCARY** [ ] [-]
(12"+=) *(VST 1157)* – ('A'-12"mix).
(cd-s++=) *(VSCD 1157)* – Pull my daisy.

Mar 89. (cd/c/lp) *(CD/TC+/V 2571)* **FREAKY TRIGGER** [ ] [-]
– What'll you do til' Sunday baby / Taboo / Love units / Rainbow / Truckee river / How do you do / What's love if you can kill for chocolate / Mind the gravy / Dusty heartfelt / We can cover up the "C". *(c+=/cd+=)* – Love units (12"mix) / What's love if you can kill for chocolate (12"mix).

May 89. (7") *(VS 1178)* **DUSTY HEARTFELT. / PEACE ON EGG** [ ] [-]
(12"+=/3"cd-s+=) *(VST/VSCD 1178)* – ('A'version).

— disbanded late 1989; STODDART formed the APPLES

PIE FINGER

— **DAVEY HENDERSON + RUSSELL BURN** with **NICK PRECOTT**

Creation / not iss.

Apr 92. (lp/cd) *(CRELP/+CD 122)* **A DALI SURPRISE** [ ] [-]
– Jaggy jungle / Time will tell / Strictly planets (Jupiter) / A Dali surprise / Let them drip gold / Amazonia howl / Without a name / Re-possession mix / Jaggy pie seas.

NECTARINE No.9

— **HENDERSON, SIMON SMEETON + IAIN HOLFORD** with also poet **JOCK SCOT**

Postcard / Shake The Record Label (Canada)

Feb 93. (lp/cd) *(DUBH 931/+CD)* **A SEA WITH THREE STARS** [ ] [-]
– Pop's love thing / She's a nicer word to sing / The holes of Corpus Christi / Beautiful car / 22 blue / Peanut brain / Smiths new automatic / A sea with three stars / The No. you mean / Don't worry babe, you're not the only one awake / Trace nine / Chocolate swastika.

Oct 93. (cd-ep) *(DUBH 939CD)* **UNLOADED FOR YOU** [ ] [-]
– Pop's new thing / Chocolate swastika / Going off someone / Don't worry babe you're not the only one awake.

Apr 94. (cd) *Nighttracks-Postcard: (CDNT 004)* **GUITAR THIEVES** [ ] [-]
– Scandal / The No. you mean / American loop / Pull my daisy / Memories of a ritual / A sea with three stars / Frownland / Crazy pony / Inside of your heart / Trashslide / Don't worry babe, you're not the only one awake / Evening star thing / Going off someone / Smith snow loop No.2 / Unloaded for you / We have a rendezvous / 22 blue.

Jun 95. (cd-ep; PAUL QUINN / NECTARINE No.9 / JOCK SCOT) *(DUBH 952CD)* **PREGNANT WITH POSSIBILITIES EP** [ ] [-]
– Tiger tiger / Will I ever be inside of you / Just another fucked-up little druggy on the scene / Grunge girl groan.

Jul 95. (cd) *(DUBH 951CD)* *<SALD 223>* **SAINT JACK** [ ] [ ] Feb96
– Saint Jack / Curdled fragments / Fading memory babe / Can't scratch out / This arsehole's been burned too many times before / It's not my baby putting me down / My trapped lightning / Just another fucked-up little druggy on the scene / Couldn't phone potatoes / Dead horse arum / Firecrackers / Un-loaded for you / Clipped wings & flower stings / Tape your head on.

Jul 95. (cd) *<SALD 214>* **NIAGARA FALLS** [-] [ ]
– Un-loaded for you / The holes of Corpus Christ / Crazy pony / She's a nicer word to sing / 22 blue / Don't worry baby, you're not the only one awake / Beautiful car / Peanut brain / This arsehole's been too many times before / Going off someone / Smith snow automatic / Pop's love thing / Trace nine / Chocolate swastika / Inside of your heart / These days. *(UK-iss.Jun98; same)*

— in Apr'97, they teamed up with JOCK SCOT (once again!) on his single, 'Tape Your Head On'.

Creeping Bent / not iss.

Mar 98. (7") *(bent 033)* **THE PORT OF MARS. / Alan Vega & The Revolutionary Corps: WHO CARES WHO DIES** [ ] [-]

Apr 98. (cd) *(bent 035cd)* **FRIED FOR BLUE MATERIAL** [ ] [-]
– Stacey Keach dada message bag / Blue material / Strychnine vinaigrette / Adidas Francis Bacon / Walter Tevis / Central Deli Davis Jnr. / Boneless chops / Starthing / Friends of the cult sixties, POW / Fuzzy dice-Mahlersdog / Burnt nylon carseat cover flavour / The port of Mars / South of an imaginary line / Subtitles for the blind drunk / Soon be over, soon be over / Michelangelo.

May 98. (7") *(ST7 1879)* **ADIDAS FRANCIS BACON. / BURNT NYLON CARSEAT COVER FLAVOUR** [ ] [-]
(above issued on 'Sano')

May 98. (cd-ep) *(bent 037)* **SOUTH OF AN IMAGINARY LINE EP** [ ] [-]
– South of an imaginary line / A cold meat pie / Pregnant / Gay paean to Thierry Lacroix.

Aug 99. (7") *(bent 042)* **WALTER TEVIS (mix). / Secret Goldfish: YOU'RE FUNNY 'BOUT THAT, AREN'T YOU** [ ] [-]

Sep 99. (cd) *(bent 047cd)* **IT'S JUST THE WAY THINGS ARE JOE, IT'S JUST THE WAY THINGS ARE** (compilation) [ ] [-]

– Walter Tevis / Saint Jack / 22 blue / The port of Mars / My trapped lightning / Don't worry babe, you're not the only one awake / Unloaded for you / She's a nicer word to sing / South of an imaginary line / Going off someone / Chocolate swastika / Firecrackers / Pops love thing / Adidas Francis Bacon (unreleased version). *(re-iss. Dec00; same)*

Beggars Banquet — not iss.

Oct 00. (cd-ep) *(BBQ 348CD)* **CONSTELLATIONS OF A VANITY EP** [ ] [-]
– Constellations of a vanity / Indelible marquer / Giant haystacks / Frozen peas.

Apr 01. (cd) *(BBQCD 221)* **RECEIVED TRANSGRESSED AND TRANSMITTED** [ ] [-]
– Pong fat 6 / Susan identifier / Constellations of a vanity / Foundthings / It's raining for some cloudy reasons / Pocket radiodrops / Look at my sleeves they fall down / Sic / Lid / Fibrecane No.4 / Bongo Kong / Lazy crystal.

FISH

Born: DEREK WILLIAM DICK, 25 Apr'58, Dalkeith, Midlothian. After leaving top progsters, MARILLION, in less than agreeable circumstances in September '88, he finally released a debut single, 'STATE OF MIND', a year later. This hit the UK Top 40, as did his early 1990 follow-up, 'BIG WEDGE'.

A Top 5 album, 'VIGIL IN A WILDERNESS OF MIRRORS' was soon in the charts, FISH solo following a more commercial yet ambitiously diverse guitar-based sound while retaining the PETER GABRIEL-esque vocal theatrics. Through an ever changing cast of backing musicians, FISH recorded another two major label albums for 'Polydor, 'INTERNAL EXILE' (1991) and a covers set, 'SONGS FROM THE MIRROR' (1993), the latter of which stalled outside the Top 40.

Moving back to Scotland after living in London, the singer then set up his own label, 'Dick Bros.', proceeding to maintain a prolific recording schedule over the ensuing four years as well as producing and releasing other low-key Scottish-based projects. Much of the material consisted of concert recordings, FISH retaining a loyal live following, especially in Europe. Studio wise, he released the 'SUITS' set in 1994, another Top 20 hit despite criticisms from the usual quarters. The Caledonian maverick even recorded a duet with forgotten 80's starlet SAM BROWN although predictably it failed to make the chart. 1995 saw the release of two complementary best of/live affairs, 'YIN' and 'YANG', while the singer returned in 1997 with 'SUNSETS ON EMPIRE'. The aquatic one subsequently became an unusual signing for 'Roadrunner' after a series of legal hassles with previous labels.

The resulting Elliot Ness-produced 'RAINGODS WITH ZIPPOS' (1999) was hailed by many critics and fans as his most complete effort since splitting from MARILLION more than a decade previously. The new 'Roadrunner' deal also resulted in a veritable avalanche of live sets and oddity collections in late '98, among them 'KETTLE OF FISH 88-98', 'UNCLE FISH AND THE CRYPT CREEPERS' and 'TALES FROM THE BIG BUS'.

• **Songwriters:** FISH co-wrote most of material with MICKEY SIMMONDS. He covered; THE FAITH HEALER (Sensational Alex Harvey Band). In early 1993, he released full covers album with tracks: QUESTION (Moody Blues) / BOSTON TEA PARTY (Sensational Alex Harvey Band) / FEARLESS (Pink Floyd) / APEMAN (Kinks) / HOLD YOUR HEAD UP (Argent) / SOLD (Sandy Denny) / I KNOW WHAT I LIKE (Genesis) / JEEPSTER (T.Rex) / FIVE YEARS (David Bowie) / ROADHOUSE BLUES (Doors).

• **Trivia:** October '86, FISH was credited on TONY BANKS (Genesis) single 'Short Cut To Nowhere'.

FISH – vocals (ex-MARILLION) with guest musicians on debut album **FRANK USHER** – guitar / **HAL LINDES** – guitar / **MICKEY SIMMONDS** – keyboards / **JOHN GIBLIN** – bass / **MARK BRZEZICKI** – drums / **CAROL KENYON** – backing vocals / plus **LUIS JARDIM** – percussion / **JANICK GERS** – guitar

E.M.I. — E.M.I.

Oct 89. (c-s/7") *(TC+/EM 109)* **STATE OF MIND. / THE VOYEUR (I LIKE TO WATCH)** [32] [-]
(12"+=/cd-s+=) *(12/CD EM 109)* – ('A'-Presidential mix).

Dec 89. (7"/7"s)(c-s) *(EM/+S 125)(TC 125)* **BIG WEDGE. / JACK AND JILL** [25] [-]
(12"+=/12"pic-d)(cd-s+=) *(12EM/+PD 125)(CDEM 125)* – Faith healer (live).

Feb 90. (lp/c/cd)(pic-lp) *(CD/C+/EMD 1015)(EMPD 1015)* <2202> **VIGIL IN A WILDERNESS OF MIRRORS** [5] [ ]
– Vigil / Big wedge / State of mind / The company / A gentleman's excuse me / The voyeur (I like to watch) / Family business / View from the hill / Cliche. *(cd re-iss. Nov98 on 'Roadrunner'+=; RR 8687-2)* – Jack and Jill / Internal exile / A gentleman's excuse me / Whiplash. *(cd re-iss. Sep02 on 'Chocolate Frog – Voiceprint'; CFVP 009CD)*

Mar 90. (7"/7"red/7"sha-pic-d)(c-s) *(EM/+S/PD 135)(TCEM 135)* **A GENTLEMAN'S EXCUSE ME. / WHIPLASH** [30] [-]
(12"+=/12"pic-d+=)(cd-s+=) *(12EM/+PD 135)(CDEM 135)* – ('A'demo version).

—— retained SIMMONDS and USHER, and brought in **ROBIN BOULT** – lead guitar, vocals / **DAVID PATON** – bass / **ETHAN JOHNS** – drums, percussion / guest drummer **TED McKENNA**

Polydor — Polydor

Sep 91. (7") *(FISH Y/C 1)* **INTERNAL EXILE. / CARNIVAL MAN** [37] [-]
(12"+=) *(FISHS 1)* – ('A'-Karaoke mix).
(cd-s++=) *(FISCD 1)* – ('A'remix).

Oct 91. (cd/c/lp) *(511049-2/-4/-1)* *<513765>* **INTERNAL EXILE** [21] [ ]
– Shadowplay / Credo / Just good friends (close) / Favourite stranger / Lucky / Dear friend / Tongues / Internal exile. *(re-iss. cd Apr95; same)* *(cd re-iss. Nov98 on 'Roadrunner'+=; RR 8683-2)* – Poet's moon / Something in the air / Carnival man. *(cd re-iss. Sep02 on 'Chocolate Frog – Voiceprint'; CFVP 010CD)*

Dec 91. (7"/c-s) *(FISH Y/C 2)* **CREDO. / POET'S MOON** [38] [-]
(12"box+=/cd-s+=) *(FISHS/FISCD 2)* – ('A'mix).
(12"+=) *(FISHX 2)* – (the 2 'A'versions) / Tongues (demo).

Jun 92. (7"/c-s) *(FISH Y/C 3)* **SOMETHING IN THE AIR. / DEAR FRIEND** [51] [-]
(12"+=) *(FISHX 3)* – ('A'-Teddy bear mix).
(cd-s++=) *(FISHP 3)* – ('A'radio mix).
(cd-s) *(FISHL 3)* – ('A'side) ('A'-Christopher Robin mix) / Credo / Shadowplay.

—— **FOSTER PATTERSON** – keyboards, vocals; repl. SIMMONS / **KEVIN WILKINSON** – drums, percussion; repl. JOHNS.

Jan 93. (cd/c/lp) *(517499-2/-4/-1)* **SONGS FROM THE MIRROR** [46] [-]
– Question / Boston tea party / Fearless / Apeman / Hold your head up / Solo / I know what I like (in your wardrobe) / Jeepster / Five years. *(re-iss. cd Apr95; same)* *(cd re-iss. Nov98 on 'Roadrunner'; RR 8682-2)*

Dick Bros — Griffin

Mar 94. (d-cd) *(DDICK 002CD)* *<158>* **SUSHI (live)** [ ] [ ]
– Fearless / Big wedge / Boston tea party / Credo / Family business / View from a hill / He knows you know / She chameleon / Kayleigh / White Russian / The company / / Just good friends / Jeepster / Hold your head up / Lucky / Internal exile / Cliche / Last straw / Poet's Moon / Five years. *(re-iss. Sep96 on 'Blueprint'; DDICK 2CD)* *(re-iss. Nov98 on 'Roadrunner'; RR 8680-2)*

Apr 94. (c-s/ext-12"pic-d/cd-s) *(DDICK 3 CAS/PIC/CD1)* **LADY LET IT LIE / OUT OF MY LIFE. / BLACK CANAL** [46] [-]
(cd-s) *(DDICK 3CD2)* – ('A'extended) / ('B'live) / Emperors song (live) / Just good friends.

May 94. (cd/c/lp/pic-lp) *(DDICK 004 CD/MC/LP/PIC)* **SUITS** [18] [-]
– 1470 / Lady let it lie / Emperor's song / Fortunes of war / Somebody special / No dummy / Pipeline / Jumpsuit city / Bandwagon / Raw meat. *(cd re-iss. Sep96 on 'Blueprint'; DDICK 4CD)* *(cd re-iss. Nov98 on 'Roadrunner'; RR 8686-2)* *(cd re-iss. Sep02 on 'Chocolate Frog – Voiceprint'; CFVP 01CD)*

Sep 94. (cd-ep) *(DDICK 008CD1)* **FORTUNES OF WAR (edit) / SOMEBODY SPECIAL (live) / STATE OF MIND (live) / LUCKY (live)** [67] [-]
(cd-ep) *(DDICK 008CD2)* – ('A'live) / Warm wet circles / Jumpsuit city / The company (all live).
(cd-ep) *(DDICK 008CD3)* – ('A'acoustic) / Kayleigh (live) / Internal exile (live) / Just good friends (acoustic).
(cd-ep) *(DDICK 008CD4)* – ('A'acoustic) / Sugar mice (live) / Dear friend (live) / Lady let it lie (acoustic).

—— Above 4-cd single (nearly 90 mins.) / can be fitted in together as 1 package.

Aug 95. (c-s; FISH featuring SAM BROWN) *(DDICK 014MC)* **JUST GOOD FRIENDS / SOMEBODY SPECIAL** [63] [-]
(cd-s+=) *(DDICK 014CD1)* – State of mind.
(cd-s) *(DDICK 014CD2)* – ('A'side) / Raw meat (live) / Roadhouse blues (live).

Sep 95. (cd/c) *(DDICK 011 CD/MC)* **YIN** (THE BEST OF FISH & '95 remixes) [58] [-]
– Incommunicado / Family business / Just good friends / Pipeline / Institution waltz / Tongues / Favourite stranger / Boston tea party / Raw meat / Time & a word / Company / Incubus / Solo. *(cd re-iss. Sep96 on 'Blueprint'; DDICK 11CD)* *(cd re-iss. Sep00 & May02 on 'Chocolate Frog – Voiceprint'; CFVP 004CD)*

Sep 95. (cd/c) *(DDICK 012 CD/MC)* **YANG** (THE BEST OF FISH & '95 remixes) [52] [-]
– Lucky / Big wedge / Lady let it lie / Lavender / Credo / A gentleman's excuse me / Kayleigh / State of mind / Somebody special / Sugar mice / Punch & Judy / Internal exile / Fortunes of war. *(cd re-iss. Sep96 on 'Blueprint'; DDICK 12CD)* *(cd re-iss. Sep00 & May02 on 'Chocolate Frog – Voiceprint'; CFVP 005CD)*

Dick Bros. — Lightyear

May 97. (cd-s) *(DDICK 24CD1)* **BROTHER 52 / BROTHER 52 (Stateline mix) / DO NOT WALK OUTSIDE THIS AREA / BROTHER 52 (album version)** [ ] [-]
(cd-s) *(DDICK 24CD2)* – (first 2 tracks) / ('A'-4 am dub mix).

May 97. (cd) *(DDICK 25CD)* *<54197>* **SUNSETS ON EMPIRE** [42] [ ] Jun97
– Perception of Johnny punter / Goldfish and clowns / Change of heart / What colour is God / Tara / Jungle ride / Worm in a bottle / Brother 52 / Sunsets on empire / Say it with flowers / Do not walk outside this area. *(other cd; DDICK 26CD)* *(re-iss. Nov98 on 'Roadrunner'; RR 8679-2)*

Aug 97. (cd-s) *(DDICK 27CD)* **CHANGE OF HEART / GOLDFISH AND CLOWNS / THE PERCEPTION OF JOHNNY PUNTER** [ ] [-]

Roadrunner — Roadrunner

Apr 99. (7"pic-d/cd-s; as FISH with ELIZABETH ANTWI) *(RR 2185-7/-3)* **INCOMPLETE. / MAKE IT HAPPEN (acoustic mix) / INCOMPLETE (castle demo)** [ ] [-]

Apr 99. (cd) *(<RR 8677-2>)* **RAINGODS WITH ZIPPOS** 57
– Tumbledown / Mission statement / Incomplete / Tilted cross / Faith healer / Rites of passage / Plague of ghosts – (i) Old haunts, (ii) Digging deep, (iii) Chocolate frogs, (iv) Waving at stars, (v) Raingods dancing, (vi) Wake-up call (make it happen).

Chocolate Frog / not iss.

Aug 01. (cd) *(CFVP 007CD)* **FELLINI DAYS** -
– 3d / So Fellini / Tiki 4 / Our smile / Long cold day / Dancing in fog / Obligatory ballad / The pilgrim's address / Clock moves sideways. *(cd bonus+=)* – Hold your head up / I know what I like / Jeepster / Five years.

– compilations, others, etc. –

Sep 94. (cd) *Blueprint; (DDICK 6CD)* **ACOUSTIC SESSIONS (live)** -
– Lucky / Internal exile / Kayleigh / Fortunes of war / Dear friend / Sugar mice / Somebody special / Jumpsuit city / Lady let it lie. *(re-iss. d-cd Jan01 & May02 on 'Chocolate Frog – Voiceprint'+=; CFVP 006CD)* – KRAKOW

Sep 96. (d-cd) *Blueprint; (DDICK 16CD)* **PIGPENS BIRTHDAY** -
(re-iss. Nov98 on 'Roadrunner'; RR 8684-2)

Nov 98. (cd) *Roadrunner; (<RR 8678-2>)* **KETTLE OF FISH 88-98**
– Big wedge / Just good friends (with SAM BROWN) / Brother 52 / Chasing Miss Pretty / Credo / A gentleman's excuse me / Goldfish and clowns / Lady let it lie / Lucky / State of mind / Mr Buttons / Fortunes of war / Internal exile. *(also w/ CD-ROM; RR 8678-8)*

Nov 98. (d-cd) *Roadrunner; (RR 8681-2)* **KRAKOW (live acoustic 1995)** -
– Somebody special / Jumpsuit city / Lady let it lie / Out of my life / State of mind / Kayleigh / Solo / Company / Giz a bun / Lavender.

Nov 98. (d-cd) *Roadrunner; (RR 8685-2)* **UNCLE FISH AND THE CRYPT CREEPERS**

Nov 98. (d-cd) *Roadrunner; (RR 8688-2)* **TALES FROM THE BIG BUS (live)** -

Nov 98. (cd) *Roadrunner; (RR 8689-2)* **FORTUNES OF WAR** -

May 99. (d-cd) *Blueprint; (BP 297CD)* **THE COMPLETE BBC SESSIONS** -

Jan 01. (d-cd) *Chocolate Frog – Voiceprint; (CFVP 001CD)* **TOILING IN THE REEPERBAHN** -
(re-iss. May02; same)

Mar 01. (d-cd) *Chocolate Frog – Voiceprint; (CFVP 002CD)* **FOR WHOM THE BELL TOLLS** -
(re-iss. May02; same)

Mar 01. (d-cd) *Chocolate Frog – Voiceprint; (CFVP 003CD)* **DEREK DICK AND HIS AMAZING BEAR** -
(re-iss. May02; same)

Aug 02. (cd) *Chocolate Frog – Voiceprint; (CFVP 014CD)* **FELLINI NIGHTS** -

FIX (see under ⇒ Limbo records)

FIZZBOMBS (see under ⇒ JESSE GARON & THE DESPERADOES)

FLESH (see under ⇒ ALTERED IMAGES)

FLOWERS

Formed: Edinburgh . . . 1978 by HILARY MORRISON, SIMON BEST, ANDY COPELAND and FRASER SUTHERLAND. The quartet initially bloomed on Bob Last's 'EARCOM 1' 12"ep (a various artists collection), performing two numbers, 'CRIMINAL WASTE' and 'AFTER DARK', the second of which became a B-side of their 1979 debut single for 'Pop Aural', 'CONFESSIONS'. Lying somewhere between DELTA 5 and stablemates The FIRE ENGINES, The FLOWERS completed only one more bop-friendly indie single, 'THE BALLAD OF MISS DEMEANOR', before calling it a day in 1980.

HILARY (MORRISON) – vocals / **ANDY COPELAND** – guitar / **FRASER SUTHERLAND** – bass / **SIMON BEST** – drums

Pop Aural / not iss.

Dec 79. (7") *(POP 001)* **CONFESSIONS. / (LIFE) AFTER DARK** -

May 80. (7") *(POP 003)* **THE BALLAD OF MISS DEMEANOR. / FOOD / TEAR ALONG** -

— after their split, FRASER joined SO YOU THINK YOU'RE A COWBOY issuing one 'Cheatin' Heart' single in 1984, 'DON'T NEED YOU'; he subsequently joined the group, The SYNDICATE, while HILARY (HI RAY) joined HEARTBEAT with an ex-FIRE ENGINE (a band SIMON also made guest appearances for)

FOIL

Formed: Fauldhouse, West Lothian . . . 1995 out of guitar-rockers The NAKED SEE (who issued two singles for 'Human Condition', 'NOTHING'S LOST' and 'FACELESS') and MUTINY STRINGS by frontman/guitarist HUGH DUGGIE, guitar-man COLIN McINALLY, bassist SHUG ANDERSON and drummer JIM ANDERSON.

Spreading their word via a gig at London's Underground venue early the following year, the band were picked up by Paul Taylor, who signed them to Mute-backed imprint '13th Hour'. That summer, their debut single, 'REVIVING GENE', hit the shops and was noted for its unmistakable STEREOPHONICS-meets-SUGAR hooklines. Over the course of the next 18 months, FOIL giftwrapped a string of other, equally impressive 45's which previewed their first long-player, 'SPREAD IT ALL AROUND' (1998). Witty, barbed and exquisitely catchy, the set highlighted the aforementioned singles, 'ARE YOU ENEMY?', 'A PLACE TO HIDE' and a remixed 'REVIVER GENE', plus the comical 'ACID KEWPIE'. With new drummer ALAN LINDLAY on board, FOIL returned in 2000, although follow-up album, 'NEVER GOT HIP', did exactly as its title suggested.

NAKED SEE

PADDY – vocals, guitar / **COLIN McINALLY** – guitar / **? MOONEY** – bass / **JIM ANDERSON** – drums

Human Condition / not iss.

Aug 93. (7") *(HC 004)* **NOTHING'S LOST. / NEVER SO NEAR** -

Sep 94. (cd-ep) *(HC 006)* **FACELESS EP** -
– Faceless / Endgames / Night-town / The journey.

FOIL

— **HUGH DUGGIE** – vocals, guitar; repl. PADDY

— **SHUG ANDERSON** – bass; repl. MOONEY

13th Hour / Mute

Jul 96. (7") *(HOUR 8)* **REVIVER GENE. / SNECK** -
(cd-s+=) *(CDHOUR 8)* – In the ground.

Oct 96. (7") *(HOUR 9)* **LET IT GO BLACK. / MAN OVERBOARD** -
(cd-s+=) *(CDHOUR 9)* – Spleen / Voodoo autograph.

May 97. (7") *(HOUR 10)* **ARE YOU ENEMY? / GOIN' DOWN** -
(cd-s+=) *(CDHOUR 10)* – Denny.

Sep 97. (7"blue) *(HOUR 11)* **A PLACE TO HIDE. / DON'T COME AROUND** -
(cd-s+=) *(CDHOUR 11)* –

Nov 97. (7"green) *(HOUR 13)* **REVIVER GENE. / SEDATE ME** -
(cd-s+=) *(CDHOUR 13)* – Hey you / Play dead.

Jan 98. (cd/lp) *(13TH CD/LP 5)* *<MUS 25-2>* **SPREAD IT ALL AROUND** Mar98
– A.C. rocket / High wire / Acid kewpie / Control freak / Penicillin / A place to hide / Soup / Don't come around / Are you enemy? / Coup d'etat / Reviver gene / Carstairs.

— **ALAN LINDLAY** – drums; repl. JIM

May 00. (7") *(HOUR 14)* **I'LL TAKE MY CHANCES. / UNDERTOW** -
(cd-s+=) *(CDHOUR 14)* – Careering / Reviving gene (CD-Rom).

Jun 00. (cd/lp) *(<13TH CD/LP 6>)* **NEVER GOT HIP**
– Never got hip / Easy life and ignominy / Superhero No.1 / End of the world / Groundwork / Half life bunker / British East India Co. trafficker / Weird kid / I'll take my chances / The ghost of Vernon Howell / Claremont junction optimist.

Oct 00. (7") *(HOUR 15)* **SUPERHERO NO.1. / BAD GIRLFRIEND / HONESTY FIT** -
(cd-s) *(CDHOUR 15)* – ('A'side) / World is weird / Curse of me / Forget to breathe / Stranger's almanac.

FORKEYE

Formed: Edinburgh . . . early 90's by a mysterious guitars, bass and drums trio (including bassist DAVE BEARDS). Fusing JESUS LIZARD/BIG BLACK-like Alt-metal with nervous adrenalin, FORKEYE (a lovely play on words if ever there was one!), were producer JAMIE WATSON's first signing for 'Human Condition'. If you like your vocals squeezed through a cement mixer and your guitars grinding sludgefest, then FORKEYE are the band for you. The single, 'FRIED LIFE', opened up the proceedings early in '93, the gruesome threesome soon headlining a (quite literally!) smashing gig at Glasgow's 'King Tut's Wah Wah Hut' that September. Having already delivered a second 45, 'GRINNING SKULL' (the B-side being a cover of Chrome's 'PERFUMED METAL'), the lads unleashed their debut full-set, 'P.I.G.'. Probably too innovative for Kerrang! musos and just a tad late for anything else, FORKEYE disappeared having never really got off the ground anyway.

DAVE BEARDS + Co

Human Condition / not iss.

Jan 93. (7") *(HC 001)* **FRIED LIFE. / ATTITUDE BUTTON** [ ] [-]
May 93. (7") *(HC 005)* **GRINNING SKULL. / PERFUMED METAL** [ ] [-]
Nov 93. (cd/lp) *(HC CD/LP 001)* **P.I.G.** [ ] [-]
– Crocodile / Brutal brother / Outside now / Cursed 5th / Offski / Rantzen damage cut / Grinning skull / Tuna Turner / Little Dhal / Pig initiative / Wall again / Rocky Shaw.

— split the following year

4 AM (see under ⇒ Glasgow Underground records)

4 PAST MIDNIGHT (see ⇒ Section 9: the 90s)

Roddy FRAME (see under ⇒ AZTEC CAMERA)

FREEZE (see under ⇒ CINDYTALK)

FRESHLY SQUEEZED (see ⇒ Section 9: Dance/Rave)

Alan FREW

Born: 8 Nov'56, Glasgow. Having relocated to Canada as a young man, ALAN joined up as singer and songwriter with pop-rock outfit, GLASS TIGER. From the mid-80's onwards, the Canuck-based quintet hit the US charts on numerous occasions courtesy of three top-selling singles, 'Don't Forget Me (When I'm Gone)', 'Someday' and 'I Will Be There', all taken from Top 30 debut set, 'The Thin Red Line' (1986). However, GLASS TIGER's Stateside triumphs would be short-lived, as successive releases (all but single, 'I'm Still Searching') failed to hit the mark outside their native Canada. With the band's break-up in the early 90's, FREW found time to concentrate on some solo work. With the help of producer John Jones and session people Steve Ferrone, Mick Fleetwood, Phil Parlapiano, Jim Cregan, Anthony Vanderburgh, Lisa Dalbello and guest Mickey Dolenz (on the track, 'HEALING HANDS'), FREW recorded his solo debut, 'HOLD ON' (1994). However, even Canadian radio success of one of its tracks, 'SO BLIND', failed to generate much interest Stateside. A long-awaited sophomore set, 'WONDERLAND' was released in May 2000, this time the man was getting back to his GLASS TIGER pop roots; there was even two GT tracks included as a bonus:- 'Someday' and 'My Town' (the latter featuring a duet with another tartan lad, ROD STEWART).

ALAN FREW – vocals, guitar / with various session people

not iss. / E.M.I.

Oct 94. (cd) **HOLD ON** [-] [-] Canada
– You're the one / Healing hands / It always feels the same / Hold on / I am with you tonight / Learning to fly / So blind / Once upon a time / Cloud 9 / If only I could dream / I wonder why / Falling at your feet.
May 00. (cd) **WONDERLAND** [-] [ ]
– Open for a friend / Lipstick / Home / I could never lie to you / Mother / Wonderland / All I ever wanted / Colors of friends and places / A rose in my book / That's life / Everything must change / Everybody sing. *(bonus cd+=)* – Someday / My town / So blind / Falling at your feet.

FRIENDS AGAIN (see under ⇒ LOVE AND MONEY)

FROG POCKET (see under ⇒ Mouthmoth records)

FRUITS OF PASSION

Formed: Glasgow . . . 1984 by SHARON DUNLEAVY, GLENN GIBBONS, DAVEY FULLERTON and STEPHEN ALEXANDER. With a review in Sounds 30/03/85 – that I seemed to have mislaid – The FRUITS OF PASSION were the first band to release for a record for Virgin subsidiary 'Siren'. 'ALL I EVER WANTED' was a nice enough single, although it lacked the warmth and feeling that say, FRIENDS AGAIN and 'Postcard' outfits would stir. A year later and with newcomer, COLIN AULD (from the JAZZATEERS), the FOP were ready once again with a handful of tracks that eventually made up their one and only eponymous set in 1986 (reviewed in Record Mirror 10/05/86).

SHARON DUNLEAVY – vocals / **GLENN GIBBONS** – guitar / **DAVEY FULLERTON** – rhythm guitar / **STEPHEN ALEXANDER** – bass /

Siren / not issued

Mar 85. (7") *(SIREN 1)* **ALL I EVER WANTED. / AMBITION** [ ] [-]

— **COLIN AULD** – drums (ex-JAZZATEERS) repl. original

Mar 86. (7"/12") *(SIREN 14/+12)* **LOVE'S GLORY. / YOU BROKE MY HEART** [ ] [-]
May 86. (7"/12") *(SIREN 19/+12)* **KISS ME NOW. / A PLACE IN THE HEART** [ ] [-]
May 86. (lp/c) *(SIRENLP 3)* **FRUITS OF PASSION** [ ] [-]
– Everything (I ever wanted) / Take what you want / Devotion / Kiss me / Bring it down / Love's glory / Truthful / Don't hold your breath / No more tears / Pride. *(re-iss. Jan87 on '10-Virgin' lp/c; XID/CXID 16)*
Aug 86. (7"/12") *(SIREN 26/+12)* **EVERYTHING I EVER WANTED. / EVERYTHING I HAD** [ ] [-]
Oct 86. (7") *(SIREN 30)* **NO MORE TEARS. / NOTHING BUT A PRAYER** [ ] [-]
(12"+=) *(SIREN 30-12)* – Kissing me (extended) / ('A'version).

— disbanded after above

FUGUE (see under ⇒ Different Class records)

FUKUYAMA

Formed: based- Dunblane . . . Spring 1997 by GANGER moonlighters, guitarist CRAIG B and NATASHA NORAMLY. Naming themselves after the philosopher Francis Fukuyama, the duo followed a suitably esoteric post-Rock path on their only existing two EP's, 'GO BY SOUND' and 'WELCOME TO DISH'.

Amicably splitting with both FUKUYAMA and GANGER, CRAIG B went on to set up his own outfit, AEREOGRAMME. According to the man himself, the debut single 'TRANSLATIONS' (issued on their own 'Babi-Yaga' imprint) was an attempt to match the excellence of the RED HOUSE PAINTERS and AMERICAN MUSIC CLUB. The music took a harder turn with the arrival of drummer MARTIN SCOTT (joining CRAIG B and bassist CAMPBELL McNEIL), staking out post-Hardcore territory on further EP's, 'AEREOGRAMME' and 'HATRED'. Towards the end of 2000, after a healthy reception at both the Reading and Leeds festivals, the trio were back with a new EP, 'GLAM CRIPPLE', for the 'Chemikal Underground' fukd i.d. series.

NATASHA NORAMLY – bass, vocals, 303 synth, drums (of GANGER) / **CRAIG B** – guitar, drums, 303 synth (of GANGER)

Wurlitzer Jukebox / not iss.

Oct 97. (7"ep) *(WJ 38)* **GO BY SOUND EP** [ ] [-]
– Dog gone / Quit and walk away / Silverlining / Antidote / Alessandra and her electric fan / Magic spell / . . .For a few uncrossed miles.

Liquefaction / not iss.

Mar 98. (7"ep) *(DUSKE 2)* **WELCOME TO DISH EP** [ ] [-]
– I like you already / Argument / Into arc / Toby gets busted / Water comes too quickly / . . .So I challenge you.

— CRAIG split from FUYUYAMA and GANGER to form his own act . . .

AEREOGRAMME

CRAIG B – guitar, vocals / **CAMPBELL McNEIL** – bass

Babi-Yaga / not iss.

Jun 99. (7"ep) *(YAGA 002-7)* **TRANSLATIONS** [ ] [-]
– Salvation / The long walk home.

— added **MARTIN SCOTT** – drums

Sep 99. (7") *(YAGA 001)* **HATRED. / THE ART OF BELIEF** [ ] [-]
Nov 99. (7"ep) *(YAGA 003)* **AEREOGRAMME EP** [ ] [-]

Chemikal Underground / Matador

Oct 00. (12"ep/cd-ep) *(CHEM 046/+CD)* **fukd i.d. #1: GLAM CRIPPLE EP** [ ] [-]
– Fuel to burn / The ocean red / Fireworks / Fireworks (Gabriel's 13th dream mix).
Aug 01. (12"ep/cd-ep) *(CHEM 052/+CD)* **WHITE PAW EP** [ ] [-]
– Zionist timing / Motion / Messenger / The art of belief.
Sep 01. (cd/lp) *(CHEM 053 CD/LP)* <OLE 533> **A STORY IN WHITE** [ ] [ ] Oct01
– The question is complete / Post-tour pre-judgement / Egypt / Hatred (new version) / Zionist timing / Sunday 3:52 / Shouting for Joey / A meaningful existence / Descending / Will you still find me? *<US cd+=>* – Motion / Messenger / The art of belief.

FUNHOUSE (see under ⇒ WATERBOYS)

FUNK D'VOID (see under ⇒ Soma records)

FUTURE PILOT AKA

Formed: Glasgow . . . 1996 by ex-SOUP DRAGONS man SUSHILL K DADE, who'd also had spells with TELSTAR PONIES (also ran 'Via Satellite' records) while still being part of The BMX BANDITS.

Breaking free from all other collaborations, DADE, who was now practically a bonafide connoisseur of the Glaswegian indie scene, issued his striking debut single, 'WE SHALL OVERCOME', on 'Creeping Bent' records in 1997. Slightly misleading in places, the single displayed a very Eastern/Asian theme, with carnival drums pounding a steady beat against the voices of Indian children. However, second single 'MEDITATION RAT' (which was a collaboration with ALAN VEGA) and his early minglings with The PASTELS, were more ambient and delivered a crossover psychedelic feel. Two more singles were issued in '98/'99; one featuring BILL WELLS (appearing on the oh-so-cool 'Domino' sub-imprint 'Series 500') and the other double-A side with NATIONAL PARK and SHOMPA RAGA BHAIVAN – both just as impressive as the other. The debut album, 'FUTURE PILOT A.K.A VS A GALAXY OF SOUND' (1999), catapulted him into the indie/remixer terrain with songs fusing jazz, soul and funk – a definite change from his early 'DRAGONS days. The album brought together such independent heavyweights as CORNERSHOP, BILL WELLS, FALL guru BRIX SMITH, 60's throwback KIM FOWLEY, ALAN VEGA (of SUICIDE) and THE PASTELS, all in one sweltering, groovified brew(!).

Early 2001, SUSHIL and Co took off once again, releasing for 'Geographic' records, the difficult second set, 'TINY WAVES MIGHTY SEA'. A hybrid of Indian-style mantra-folk, MERCURY REV-esque transcendental rock and the usual indie meanderings, the set was well received by a varied cosmopolitan audience who were well aware of the inclusion of STUART DAVID (BELLE & SEBASTIAN) and others.

SUSHIL K DADE with other various singers:- A-side w/ **RANJIT NAGAR** (New Delhi schoolchildren) / B-side w/ **KIM FOWLEY**

Creeping Bent / not iss.

Jul 97. (7") *(bent 025)* **WE SHALL OVERCOME. / NIGHT FLIGHT TO MEMPHIS** ☐ -

Nov 97. (7"; by FUTURE PILOT A.K.A. & ALAN VEGA) *(bent 029)* **MEDITATION RAT. / BAD VIBRATIONS (by Mount Vernon Arts Lab & Scientific Support Dept)** ☐ -

Series 500 / not iss.

May 98. (12"; by FUTURE PILOT A.K.A. & The PASTELS) *(SER 507)* **HURRICANE FIGHTER PILOT. / THE GATES TO FILM CITY (w/ Two Lone Swordsmen)** ☐ -

— in Apr'99, the FUTURE PILOT A.K.A. teamed up with the BILL WELLS OCTET on the eponymous 'Domino' set.

Earworm / not iss.

Jan 99. (7") *(WORMSC 4)* **NATIONAL PARK VERSUS FUTURE PILOT A.K.A. / FUTURE PILOT A.K.A. VERSUS SHOMPA RAGA BHAIVAN** ☐ -

Sulphur / Beggars Banquet

Apr 99. (d-cd/d-lp) *(SUL CD/LP 001)* <85016> **FUTURE PILOT A.K.A. Vs A GALAXY OF SOUND** ☐ ☐
– The gates to film city (w/ TWO LONE SWORDSMEN) / Pink city (w/ BILL WELLS) / Indians at N.A.S.A. (w/ BRIX SMITH) / Rest and be thankful (w/ JAMES KIRK) / World wide web – We shall overcome (w/ RANJIT NAGAR) / Teri mitti bani (w/ CORNERSHOP) / Departure lounge (w/ DIGITAL COW) / Pink returns (w/ BILL WELLS) / Innocent railway (w/ JAMES KIRK) / Meditation rat (w/ ALAN VEGA) / Theme from "Buzz" (w/ 50htz) / Fresh milk! (w/ SCANNER) / Night flight to Memphis (w/ KIM FOWLEY) / Pink Money (w/ BILL WELLS) / Japan (w/ SUCKMONSTER) / Message from control tower (w/ JOWE HEAD) / Hurricane fighter pilot (w/ PASTELS) / Lee Jun fan (w/ INYO SAN) / Pink prophet (w/ BILL WELLS) / Sterling (w/ NATIONAL PARK).

Geographic / not iss.

Dec 00. (7") *(GEOGRAPHIC 9)* **DARSHAN. / OM NAMA SHIVAYA** ☐ -

Jan 01. (cd/lp) *(GEOGRAPHIC 6 CD/LP)* **TINY WAVES MIGHTY SEA** ☐ -
– Maid of the loch / Ananda is the ocean / Witchi Tai to Darshan / Beautiful dreamer / Darshan returns / Shree ram, Jai ram / Opel waters / Beat of a drum / Radhika / Om nama shivaya / Strength of the sea / Prayer for Ananda.

Apr 01. (7") *(GEOG 7)* **BEAT OF A DRUM. / MOUNT KALLASH** ☐ -
(cd-s+=) *(GEOG 7CD)* – Om namah shivaya.

G

GANGER

Formed: Glasgow . . . early 1995 by two bassists! GRAHAM GAVIN and STUART HENDERSON, plus drummer JAMES A YOUNG and guitarist LUCY McKENZIE; STEVEN CLARK (aka SCI-FI STEVEN of BIS) augmented the Krautrock-inspired instrumental combo on their 1996 debut, 'HALF NELSON.ep'. A debut of infinite, spaced-out experimentalism, its finale was the 20-minute epic 'JELLYNECK'.

Still on their FAUST, NEU! and ASH RA TEMPEL trip, GANGER walked the musical plank once more via the 'Domino' (Series 500) EP, 'THE CAT'S IN THE BAG . . . THE BAG'S IN THE RIVER', the basic 4-piece having added MARTIN ALLEN on keyboards. A further addition to the line-up came in the form of sax player CAROLINE KRAABEL, taking her place for the band's third single, the Jamie Watson-produced 'HOLLYWOOD LOAF'. After the obligatory singles compilation, GANGER re-shuffled once again, this time HENDERSON and YOUNG bringing in fresh creative blood CRAIG B and NATASHA NORAMLY. Gradually leaving behind their Germanic sprawls, they initiated their own brand of sonic architecture with the 2-minute! 'GEOCITIES' single, following it up with some fresh material for 'Domino' ('Merge' in the US) in the shape of 'WITH TONGUE TWISTING WORDS'. Shortly afterwards (in July '98), GANGER belatedly released their debut album proper, 'HAMMOCK STYLE', a Stateside jaunt alongside spiritual brethren MOGWAI increasing their street cred. However, the busy-busy CRAIG B (simultaneously a member of FUKUYAMA with NATASHA) couldn't be held down for long, subsequently lifting off with his new project, AEREOGRAMME.

1999's 'CANOPY' finally put the lid on GANGER's career, the group disbanding shortly after its release.

STUART HENDERSON – bass, effects, keyboards / **GRAHAM GAVIN** – bass, guitar / **JAMES A. YOUNG** – drums / **STEVEN CLARK** – drums, keyboards (of BIS) / **LUCY McKENZIE** – clarinet, guitar, keyboards

Vesuvius / not iss.

Apr 96. (12"ep) *(POMP 004)* **HALF NELSON.ep** ☐ -
– Guts and bravoodoo / Drummer's arms and bionic thumbs / Jellyneck.

— **MARTIN ALLEN** – keyboards; repl. SCI-FI STEVEN who continued with BIS

Planet / not iss.

Sep 96. (12"ep) *(punk 014)* **THE CAT'S IN THE BAG . . . THE BAG'S IN THE RIVER** ☐ -
– Anomovieshot / Smorgasbord / Missile that back-fired.

— added **CAROLINE KRAABEL** – saxophone

Series 500 / not iss.

Dec 96. (12"ep) *(ser 504)* **HOLLYWOOD LOAF. / PRISONER OF MY EYEBALL / SMORGASBORD (Third Eye Foundation version)** ☐ -

Domino / Merge

Apr 97. (cd/d-lp) *(WIG CD/LP 30)* **FORE** (compilation of EP's) ☐ ☐
– Hollywood loaf / Missile that back-fired / Drummer's arms and bionic thumbs / Smorgasbord / Fore / Jellyneck / Anomovieshot / Prisoner of my eyeball.

— (Sep'97) **HENDERSON + YOUNG** recruited **CRAIG B** – guitar, vocals + **NATASHA NORAMLY** – bass (ex-FUKUYAMA) to repl. others

Feb 98. (7") *(WJ 16)* **GEOCITIES. / ALESSANDRA AND HER WESTERN FAN** ☐ -
(above issued on 'Wurlitzer Jukebox')

Jun 98. (12"ep/cd-ep) *(RUG 61/+CD)* **WITH TONGUE TWISTING WORDS EP** ☐ -
– With tongue twisting words / Hammock style / Baby cats and jaws / Hope.

— (first track above was recorded with GRAHAM, MARTIN + CAROLINE)

Jul 98. (cd/lp) *(WIG CD/LP 47)* **HAMMOCK STYLE** ☐ ☐
– Cats, dogs and babies jaws / Upye / Capo (south of Caspian) / First thing in the the morning / What happened to the king happened to me / Blau / Lid of the stars.

— CRAIG B (also of FUKUYAMA with NATASHA) left to form AEREOGRAMME

Guided Missile / not iss.

Dec 99. (cd-ep) *(GUIDE 38)* **CANOPY** ☐ -
– Canopy / State conversation / Now we have you / Hai! / Standing on the shoulders of giants.

— GANGER disbanded sometime in 1999

Willie GARDNER (se under ⇒ SLIK; Zones)

GARGLEBLUD (see under ⇒ Avalanche records)

GENEVA

Formed: Aberdeen . . . late 1992 (briefly as SUNFISH) by DOUGLAS CASKIE, STEVEN DORA, STUART EVANS, KEITH GRAHAM and ex-journalist ANDREW MONTGOMERY (with The Sunday Post!). Eventually after only a few gigs, they were spotted by 'Nude' records (home to the likes of SUEDE), where they released their stunning debut, 'NO ONE SPEAKS', which bubbled under the Top 30 singles chart late '96. Around the same time, they secured a support slot on a BLUETONES' tour, exposing the angelic, high-pitched vox of MONTGOMERY, a hybrid of BILLY MacKENZIE, THOM YORKE, IAN ASTBURY or even, God forbid, an 80's style alternative rock version of MORTEN HARKET! During the first half of '97, the singles, 'INTO THE BLUE' and 'TRANQUILLIZER', both went Top 30 and featured on their soaringly spiritual Top 20 album, 'FURTHER'. • **Songwriters:** Most by DORA and MONTGOMERY, a few by MONTGOMERY, GRAHAM and one with EVANS.

ANDREW MONTGOMERY – vocals / **STEVEN DORA** – guitar / **STUART EVANS** – guitar / **KEITH GRAHAM** – bass / **DOUGLAS CASKIE** – drums

		Nude	Sony
Oct 96.	(7"/c-s) *(NUD 22 S/MC)* **NO ONE SPEAKS. / WHAT YOUR SHRINK SAYS**	32	-
	(cd-s) *(NUD 22CD)* – ('A'side) / Closer to the stars / Keep the light on.		
Jan 97.	(7"/c-s) *(NUD 25 S/MC) <78594>* **INTO THE BLUE. / AT THE CORE**	26	Jun97
	(cd-s) *(NUD 25CD)* – ('A'side) / Riverwatching / Land's End.		
May 97.	(7") *(NUD 28S)* **TRANQUILLIZER. / DRIFTWOOD**	24	-
	(cd-s) *(NUD 28CD1)* – ('A'side) / Dead giveaway / Strung out on you.		
	(cd-s) *(NUD 28CD2)* – ('A'side) / Michaelmas / Compulsive love disorder.		
Jun 97.	(cd/c/lp) *(NUDE 7 CD/MC/LP) <68156>* **FURTHER**	20	Aug97
	– Temporary wings / Into the blue / The god of sleep / Best regrets / Tranquillizer / Further / No one speaks / Worry beads / Fall apart button / Wearing off / Nature's whore / In the years remaining.		
Aug 97.	(7") *(NUD 31S)* **BEST REGRETS. / SELFBELIEF**	38	-
	(cd-s) *(NUD 31CD1)* – ('A'side) / Feel the joy / Raymond Chandler.		
	(cd-s) *(NUD 31CD2)* – ('A'side) / Last orders / The god of sleep (demo).		
Nov 99.	(7") *(NUD 46S)* **DOLLARS IN THE HEAVENS. / ECHO CHAMBER**	59	-
	(cd-s) *(NUD 46CD1)* – ('A'side) / Faintest tremor in the weakest heart / She's so familiar.		
	(cd-s) *(NUD 46CD2)* – ('A'side) / When you close your eyes / Museum mile (Dave Fridmann mix).		
Feb 00.	(cd-s) *(NUD 49CD1)* **IF YOU HAVE TO GO / HAVE YOU SEEN THE HORIZON LATELY? (Aloof mix) / VOSTOK**	69	-
	(cd-s) *(NUD 49CD2)* – ('A'side) / Mindreading / Dollars in the heavens (CD-video).		
Mar 00.	(cd/d10"lp) *(NUDE 15 CD/LP)* **WEATHER UNDERGROUND**		-
	– Dollars in the heavens / If you have to go / Killing stars / Museum mile / Amnesia valley / Morricone / Guidance system / Cassie / Rockets over California / A place in the sun / Have you seen the horizon lately?		

GENTLE WAVES (see under ⇒ BELLE AND SEBASTIAN)

GENTS

Formed: Edinburgh . . . late 90's by PETER HAWKES, RICHARD SPOONER, RICK ROMERO and his brother NICK ROMERO. Mixing a lot of humour with catchy hooks, some post-Brit pop-noodlings and tons of psychedelic overtones, The GENTS emerged on the Scottish indie scene in 1999 with the celebrated single 'YEAH TIMES NINE'. They subsequently followed that with some interesting little singles issued independently (on 'Lithium' and sister label 'Western Union') which saw the band fuse XTC-driven melodies against some pretty mean rock'n'roll. In June 2001, they released the EP 'MARVELLOUS SKIES', which featured the brilliant track 'OUT TOWARDS THE SEA'. An album is still not available, although the band plan to deliver it some time late 2002.

PETER HAWKES – vocals, lead guitar / **RICK ROMERO** – vocals, rhythm guitar / **NICK ROMERO** – bass, vocals / **RICHARD SPOONER** – drums

		Granny Smiths	not iss.
Oct 99.	(cd-s) *(none)* **YEAH TIMES NINE / JUST DESSERTS / ROMFORD**		-
		Lithium	not iss.
Feb 00.	(cd-ep) *(LITH 008CDS)* **TAMOGOTCHI**		-
	– Tamogotchi / Sore head / The world's finest rock'n'roll band / Spain.		
		Western Union	not iss.
Jun 01.	(cd-ep) *(WUCDS 101)* **MARVELLOUS SKIES**		-
	– Marvellous skies / 100 400 / Out towards the sea / Lighting out of the dark.		

GERILS (see under ⇒ WILDERNESS CHILDREN)

GHOSTS (see under ⇒ FAT LIP)

GILDED LIL

Formed: Edinburgh . . . mid-90's by GERRY HILLMAN and KERRY McDONALD, along with MALCY DUFF (ex-MONGERS, + PIZZA BOY DELIVERY), ROSS ROBERTSON and MARK BAILLIE. If you can imagine POLLY HARVEY fronting the MAGIC BAND or JON SPENCER BLUES EXPLOSION backing JANIS JOPLIN, in fact a blitzkrieg onslaught of all four, you'd be getting some way towards this quintet's abrasive sound.

Shockingly fresh-faced for such noisy youngsters, the GILDED LIL crew courted controversy from day one when they veered perilously close to the bone with their debut single, 'MOTHERFUCKER OF CALCUTTA'. Released on 'Bosque' in summer '97, the track preceded a follow-up EP entitled 'WANG', although the brilliantly titled 'LAST TANGO IN TOLLCROSS' appeared on 'Butcher's Wig'. Having trod the indie treadmill with a few Peel sessions, the group cast convention to the wind by performing in porn cinemas and young offenders institutes.

Between 1998/99, GILDED LIL issued a one-off single for 'Guided Missile' as well as making a contribution to the label's 'Hits & Missiles' V/A collection via the track, 'LANDS RIGHT'. Back to 'Bosque' for the new millennium, the ear-crushing KERRY and her pals delivered their belated debut album, 'CORPUS DELICTI' (2000).

KERRY McDONALD – vocals / **MALCY DUFF** – guitar, vocals (ex-MONGERS) / **ROSS ROBERTSON** – slide, guitar / **GERRY HILLMAN** – bass / **MARK BAILLIE** – drums

		Bosque	not iss.
Jun 97.	(7") *(bosc 023)* **MOTHERFUCKER OF CALCUTTA. /**		-
Mar 98.	(7"ep) *(bosc 026)* **WANG EP**		-
		Butcher's Wig	not iss.
Aug 98.	(7") *(SYRUP 005)* **LAST TANGO IN TOLLCROSS. /**		-
		Guided Missile	not iss.
Sep 98.	(7") *(GUIDE 31)* **WHEN I WAS YOUNG. / ROUGHIE**		-
		Stupidcat	not iss.
Apr 00.	(7") *(SCAT 05)* **DEPARTURE LOUNGE. / (other track by THE MALE NURSE)**		-
		Bosque	not iss.
Nov 00.	(cd/lp) *(bosc 028 CD/LP)* **CORPUS DELICTI**		-
	– Departure lounge / Stunt cock / Teaparty / Doctor / Klang/BingBong / Bee / Lands right / Last tango in Tollcross / Sick men.		

Mark GILLESPIE

Born: 28 Nov'66, Elgin. One of the vocalists with late 80's boy band BIG FUN, who had 4 major UK hits, 'BLAME IT ON THE BOOGIE', 'CAN'T SHAKE THE FEELING', 'HANDFUL OF PROMISES' and 'YOU'VE GOT A FRIEND', the last with Scouse hitmaker, SONIA.

GLASGOW (see under ⇒ Scotland's wee metal scene)

GLASGOW GANGSTER FUNK TRACS

Formed: Castlemilk, Glasgow . . . 1997 by minimalist house DJ, GARY GILROY. Yet again, a faceless four-to-the-floor boffin appropriates the word Funk for a dance project that effectively bears little or no resemblance to that much pimped genre. After two 12" singles, 'THE CURSE' and 'FIND ANOTHER HO!' in 1998, GGFT became unlikely labelmates of THE BETA BAND as they released two versions of 'DEEVA FEEVA' for 'Regal' recordings. More surprising still, the usually discerning 'Independiente' (home to TRAVIS), signed up GILROY for a full-length album, 'C.O.D.Y. (come on die young)'. If you bought this album thinking it had anything to do with MOGWAI's identically-titled set of a few months previous, you'd be sorely disappointed. If you thought this album had anything to do with Gangsta Rap, you'd be extremely disappointed. If you thought this album had everything to do with cliche'd dancefloor fodder, you'd be a happy punter. Incidentally, the sleevenotes attempted a kind of Dylan-esque extreme of consciousness meets Trainspotting fiasco.

GARY GILROY – electronics, turntables, etc

Quality Control — not iss.

Jul 98. (12") *(QCON 005)* **THE CURSE (mixes)** [ ] [-]

Green Light — not iss.

Sep 98. (12") *(GL 10091)* **FIND ANOTHA HO! (mixes)** [ ] [-]

Regal — Priority

Feb 99. (12") *(REG 26)* **DEEVA FEEVA (mixes)** [ ] [-]

Mar 99. (12"/cd-s) *(REG 29/+CD) <53489>* **DEEVA FEEVA (mixes; original / Plastic Avengers & 2 by PETE HELLER)** [ ] [ ] May99

Independiente — not iss.

Apr 99. (12"/cd-s) *(ISOM 25 T/CD)* **FIND ANOTHA HO! (mixes)** [ ] [-]

May 99. (cd/d-lp) *(ISOM 8 CD/LP)* **C.O.D.Y. (COME ON DIE YOUNG)** [ ] [-]
– Pirate radio / Space travellin' / West Coast bitch / Can't get hurt / Find anotha ho! / Bring back the law / The curse / The jack-off hour / Broken robots in your head.

Nov 99. (12"/cd-s) *(ISOM 36 T/CD)* **DO YOU WANNA DANCE (mixes)** [ ] [-]

Critical Mass — not iss.

May 02. (12") *(CRITICAL 024)* **HO'S FUNKIN' TONITE (mixes)** [ ] [-]

GLASS ONION (see under ⇒ TRAVIS)

GLUE (see under ⇒ Flotsam & Jetsam records)

GLUE (see under ⇒ X-static records)

GOD'S BOYFRIEND (see ⇒ Section 9: the 90s)

GOLDEN DAWN

Formed: Glasgow . . . by a mysterious quintet who signed for a time with massive twee-indie imprint 'Sarah'. After three well-received 45's, 'MY SECRET WORLD', 'GEORGE HAMILTON'S DEAD' and 'ALL OF A TREMBLE', the group tried their hand with a new moniker, The BESOTTED. However, the mood of the times was changing and NIRVANA and their ilk were already storming the charts. The GOLDEN DAWN did have one more try with 7", 'NO REASON WHY', a title never so fitting. • **Note:** not to be confused with the 60's psyche outfit.

Sarah — not iss.

Jul 88. (7"m) *(SARAH 009)* **MY SECRET WORLD. / SPRING-HEELED JACK / THE RAILWAY TRACK** [ ] [-]

Aug 89. (7"ep) *(SARAH 017)* **GEORGE HAMILTON'S DEAD EP** [ ] [-]

Feb 90. (7"ep) *(SARAH 020)* **ALL OF A TREMBLE EP** [ ] [-]

— split after above,

Blam-A-Bit — not iss.

Sep 92. (7"; as BESOTTED) *(BLAM 014)* **KALEIDOSCOPE. /** [ ] [-]

— The GOLDEN DAWN re-formed for below

Heaven — not iss.

Oct 97. (7") *(HV 10)* **NO REASON WHY. / LUMINOUS** [ ] [-]

GOODBYE MR MACKENZIE

Formed: Bathgate . . . 1984 by MARTIN METCALFE, JIMMY ANDERSON, RONA SCOBIE, SHIRLEY MANSON, FINLAY WILSON and DEREK KELLY. They recorded their first 45, 'DEATH OF A SALESMAN', via West Lothian College's 'Scruples' label before relocating to the thriving musical metropolis of Edinburgh.

The band subsequently hooked up with Elliot Davis' (WET WET WET manager) 'Precious' label for the release of their debut single, 'THE RATTLER', in Autumn '86. A limited edition 12" follow-up, 'FACE TO FACE', was subsequently issued on the 'Mack' imprint, all proceeds going to the 'Rape Crisis' charity. With the addition of ex-EXPLOITED man and local legend, BIG JOHN DUNCAN, on guitar and a signing to 'Capitol' in 1988, the group looked set to follow in the footsteps of DEACON BLUE who'd broken big earlier that year. As intelligent and subtly creative as the latter outfit with a more alternative slant, GOODBYE MR MACKENZIE's sound hinged upon METCALFE's powerful BRUCE SPRINGSTEEN / NEIL DIAMOND-esque vocals and their knack for a rousing chorus.

Continually tipped for the top, the band at last broke the Top 40 in early '89 with a re-recorded version of 'THE RATTLER', their much anticipated debut album, 'GOOD DEEDS AND DIRTY RAGS' making the Top 30 a few months later. Yet it wasn't to be, a flop set of live/rare tracks, 'FISH HEADS AND TAILS' (1989) and further clutch of minor hit singles no doubt convincing 'Capitol' to shelve a proposed follow-up album, 'HAMMER AND TONGS'. Help came in the form of M.C.A. subsidiary, 'Radioactive', who finally issued the record in Spring '91. By now, of course, much of the early buzz and momentum had been lost and the band drifted into obscurity.

While various members went on to bigger and better things – DUNCAN as a roadie and sometime touring replacement with NIRVANA (these days he's a familiar face at Edinburgh's sterling Cafe Graffiti club) and MANSON with the massively successful GARBAGE – the remnants of the original line-up recorded albums such as 'FIVE' (1993) and 'JEZEBEL' (1995) to minimal interest.

• **Songwriters:** All written by METCALFE-KELLY, except AMSTERDAM (Jaques Brel) / GREEN GREEN GRASS OF HOME (Engelbert Humperdinck) / HEROES (David Bowie) / CANDY SAYS (Velvet Underground) / FRIDAY'S CHILD (Lee Hazlewood) / THE WAY I WALK (J.Scott).

• **Trivia:** METCALFE refused to pay his poll tax (community charge) early in 1990 due to the Scots being used as its guinea-pigs for the first year.

MARTIN METCALFE – vocals, guitar / **SHIRLEY MANSON** (b. 3 Aug'66, Edinburgh) – vocals, keyboards / **JIMMY ANDERSON** – guitar / **RONA SCOBIE** – keyboards, vocals / **FINLAY WILSON** – bass / (DEREK) **KELLY** – drums

Scruples — not iss.

Nov 84. (7") *(YTS 1)* **DEATH OF A SALESMAN. / (other track by Lindy Bergman)** [ ] [-]

Precious — not iss.

Sep 86. (7") *(JEWEL 2)* **THE RATTLER. / CANDLESTICK PARK** [ ] [-]
(12"+=) *(JEWEL 2T)* – The end.

Clandestine — not iss.

Oct 87. (12"ltd) *(MACK 1)* **FACE TO FACE. / SECRETS. / GOOD DEEDS** [ ] [-]

— (above proceeds went to Rape Crisis charity)

— **BIG JOHN DUNCAN** – guitar (ex-EXPLOITED, ex-BLOOD UNCLES) repl. ANDERSON

Capitol — Capitol

Jul 88. (7") *(CL 501)* **GOODBYE MR. MACKENZIE. / GREEN TURN RED** [62] [-]
(ext.12"+=/ext.12"g-f+=)(ext.cd-s+=) *(12CL/+G 501)(CLCD 501)* – Knockin' on Joe.

Nov 88. (7"/7"g-f) *(CL/+G 513)* **OPEN YOUR ARMS. / SECRETS** [ ] [-]
(ext.12"+=/ext.12"pic-d+=) *(12CL/+P 513)* – Amsterdam.
(ext.12"g-f++=/ext.cd-s++=) *(12CLG/CLCD 513)* – Pleasure search.

Feb 89. (7"/7"g-f) *(CL/+G 52)* **THE RATTLER. / HERE COMES DEACON BRODIE** [37] [-]
(ext.12"+=) *(12CL 522)* – Calton Hill.
(12"w-poster++=/ext.cd-s++=) *(12CLG/CLCD 522)* – Drunken sailor.

Apr 89. (lp/c/cd) *(EST/TCEST/CDEST 2089) <92638>* **GOOD DEEDS AND DIRTY RAGS** [26] [ ]
– Open your arms / Wake it up / His master's voice / Goodwill city / Candlestick park / Goodbye Mr. Mackenzie / The rattler / Dust / You generous thing you / Good deeds. *(free-12"; GMM12 1) (c+=/cd+=)* – Amsterdam / Calton Hill / Secrets / Knockin' on Joe.

Jul 89. (7"/7"box/c-s) *(CL/CLX/TCCL 538)* **GOODWILL CITY. / I'M SICK OF YOU** [49] [ ]
(ext.12"+=) *(12CL 538)* – What's got into you.
(ext.12"g-f++=/cd-s++=) *(12CLG/CLCD 538)* – Insidious thing.

Oct 89. (lp/c/cd) *(CAPS/TCCAPS/CDCAPS 2001) <3357>* **FISH HEADS AND TAILS** (live & rare compilation) [ ] [ ]
– Amsterdam / Somewhere in China / Face to face / Knockin' on Joe / Sick of you / Green turn red / Pleasure search / Strangle your animal * / Mystery train / Here comes Deacon Brodie (live) *. *(cd+= *)*

Parlophone — Capitol

Apr 90. (7"/c-s) *(R/TCR 6247)* **LOVE CHILD. / HEROES** [52] [-]
(ext.12"+=) *(12R 6247)* – You generous thing you (live).
(dance.12"w-poster+=) *(12RX 6247)* – Goodwill city (Cava mix) / The rattler (live).
(cd-s) *(CDR 6247)* – ('A'side) / Goodwill city (live) / You generous thing you (live).

Jun 90. (7"/c-s) *(R/TCR 6257)* **BLACKER THAN BLACK. / GREEN GREEN GRASS OF HOME** [61] [-]
(ext.12"+=) *(12R 6257)* – Mad cow disease.
(12"pic-d++=/cd-s++=) *(12RPD/CDR 6257)* – His masters voice.

Radioactive M.C.A.

Feb 91. (7"/c-s) *(MCS/+C 1506)* **NOW WE ARE MARRIED. / FRIDAY'S CHILD** [ ] [-]
(ext.12"+=/ext.12"g-f+=/cd-s+=) *(MCST/+G/D 1506)* – Candlestick Park II/ Candy says.

Mar 91. (lp/c/cd) *(RAR/+C/D 10227)* <10174> **HAMMER AND TONGS**
<US title 'GOODBYE MR MACKENZIE'> [61] [ ]
– Blacker than black / Bold John Barleycorn / Diamonds / The burning / Now we are married / Sick baby / Down to the minimum / She's strong / Love child / Tongue-tied.

— (album was scheduled for release 1990 but dropped by 'Capitol')

May 91. (cd-ep) <54173> **THE RATTLER / OPEN YOUR ARMS / DOWN TO THE MINIMUM / FRIDAY'S CHILD / GOODBYE MR MACKENZIE** [-] [ ]

Blokshok not iss.

Apr 93. (12"ep/cd-ep) *(BLOK 001 T/CD)* **GOODWILL CITY LIVE E.P. (live)** [ ] [-]
– Goodwill city / Mystery train / Open your arms / Working on the shoe-fly.

May 93. (cd/lp) *(BLOK CD/LP 001)* **LIVE: ON THE DAY OF STORMS (live)** [ ] [-]
– Goodwill city / Blacker than black / Face to face / Diamonds / Pleasure search / Sick baby / Goodbye Mr. Mackenzie / Dust / HMV / Tongue tied / The rattler / What's got into you / Working on the shoe-fly. *(re-iss. Apr96; same)*

Sep 93. (12"ep/cd-ep) *(BLOK 002 T/CD)* **HARD / NORMAL BOY. / BAD DAY / ZOO** [ ] [-]
(re-iss. Dec95; same)

Nov 93. (cd/lp) *(BLOK CD/LP 002)* **"FIVE"** [ ] [-]
– Hard / Bam bam / The grip / Jim's killer / Niagara / Touch the bullseye / The day of storms / Yelloueze / Bugdive / Normal boy / Hands of the receiver / Titanic. *(re-iss. Mar96; same)*

— **METCALFE / WILSON / KELLY + DUNCAN** (vox on track 1)

Oct 94. (12"ep/cd-ep) *(BLOK 003 T/CD)* **THE WAY I WALK / SUPERMAN. / SICK BABY ('94) / YOU WILL** [ ] [-]

Jul 95. (m-cd) *(BLOKCD 004)* **JEZEBEL** (rare) [ ] [-]
– Jezebel / Jim's killer / Good deeds are like dirty rags / Queen Christina / Friday's child / I see no devil / Dress rehearsal rag / Niagara (live in Belgium 1991).

— now without SHIRLEY MANSON, who joined GARBAGE in 1995, after being heard in ANGELFISH (a GOODBYE MR MACKENZIE off-shoot, with her as frontperson and relegating MARTIN to guitarist). BIG JOHN had moonlighted with NIRVANA, as tour replacement for wayward KURT COBAIN.

– compilations, others, etc. –

Jul 98. (cd) *Blokshok; (BLOKCD 003)* **THE GLORY HOLE** [ ] [-]
– The ugly child / Smile trash it / She's got eggs / Troubling you / Space / Neurotic / Overboards / Concrete / Prince of Wales / Crew cut / House on fire / Neuromental.

ANGELFISH

— **MANSON, METCALFE, WILSON + KELLY**

not iss. Wasteland

Jun 93. (c-ep/cd-ep) <WSLD 9200-4/-2> **SUFFOCATE ME / YOU CAN LOVE HER / KIMBERLEY / TRASH IT** [-] [ ]

not iss. Radioactive

Feb 94. (cd) <RARD 10917> **ANGELFISH** [-] [ ]
– Dogs in a cage / Suffocate me / You can love me / King of the world / Sleep with me / Heartbreak to hate / The sun won't shine / / Mummy can't drive / Tomorrow forever / The end.

Bruce GOODING

Born: Scotland. Unfortunately, little or nothing is known about the man except he spent time with mid-90's indie-Rawkers, b.l.o.w., yes the band set up by former LITTLE ANGELS members, JIMMY and BRUCE DICKINSON (no, not that one!). The lower-cased b.l.o.w. released a couple of sets for 'Cottage Industry', namely 'Man And Goat Alike' (1995) and 'Pigs' (1996).

James GRANT (see under ⇒ LOVE AND MONEY)

Jack GREEN

Born: 12 Mar'51, Glasgow. A guitarist with T.TEX then The PRETTY THINGS in the mid 70's, JACK found a little success Stateside when his debut solo LP, 'HUMANESQUE' (1980), bubbled under the US Top 100. Three further guitar-orientated power pop sets appeared in the next few years although they were for German and Canadian consumption only.

JACK GREEN – vocals, guitar / with **IAN ELLIS** – bass / **PETER TOLSON** – guitar / **BRIAN CHATTON** – keyboards / **MAC POOLE** – drums / plus **ANDY DALBY** – guitar

R.C.A. RCA Victor

Jan 81. (7") *(RCA 26)* **THIS IS JAPAN. / CAN'T STAND IT** [ ] [ ]

Feb 81. (lp/c) *(RCA/+K 5004)* <3639> **HUMANESQUE** [ ] [ ] Oct80
– Murder / So much / Valentine / Babe / Can't stand it / I call / No answer / Life on the line / 'Bout that girl / Thought it was easy / Factory girl / This is Japan.

— **SIMON FOX** – drums; repl. MAC

Nov 81. (lp) *(PL 14122)* **REVERSE LOGIC** [-] [-] German
– One by one / Let me go / Cold modern day / When I was young / It's a hard world / Let it rock / Too many fools / Set me free / Brave Madonna / Sign of the times / Promises.

Feb 82. (7") *(RCA 194)* **ONE BY ONE. / BRAVE MADONNA** [ ] [ ]

— added **JACK CANHAM** – guitar / + others

1983. (lp) <KKL1 0512> **MYSTIQUE** [-] [-] Canada
– Look at it rain / Liar / I really love your money / Walking in my sleep / Another day, another dollar / Young blood / You're warm / Don't kick me (when I'm down) / Take it up / Storm.

— next featured SIMON KIRKE, JIM CAPALDI, SNOWY WHITE, BOZ BURRELL, KELLY GROUCUTT, JOHN 'RABBIT' BUNDRICK + JOHN CANHAM

not iss. F.M.

1986. (lp) <87> **LATEST GAME** [-] [-] Canada

GREENHOUSE (see under ⇒ McDERMOTT, Kevin)

GREEN TELESCOPE (see under ⇒ THANES)

Clare GROGAN (see under ⇒ ALTERED IMAGES)

GROOVY LITTLE NUMBERS

Formed: Bellshill, Glasgow . . . mid-80's by JOE McALINDEN, multi-instrumentalist and part-time violinist with The BOY HAIRDRESSERS (who turned into TEENAGE FANCLUB without him!) and a BMX BANDIT. However, side-projects aside, JOE re-initiated his passion with everything BEATLES and reinstated co-founder CATHERINE STEVEN and future TEENAGE FANCLUB member GERARD LOVE; minor brass musicians also took their place, COLETTE WALSH, JOHN McRORIE, KEVIN McCARTHY, JAMES WOOD and MAIRI CAMERON. During the period 1987-1988, they recorded six worthy tracks and released them over a couple of 12"er's for '53rd & 3rd', 'YOU MADE MY HEAD EXPLODE' and 'HAPPY LIKE YESTERDAY'. JOE would later surface in his own SUPERSTAR after another spell with BMX BANDITS.

JOE McALINDEN – multi-instruments / **CATHERINE STEVEN** – vocals / **GERARD LOVE** – bass, vocals / with **COLETTE WALSH** – tenor sax / **JOHN McRORIE** – alto sax / **KEVIN McCARTHY** – baritone sax / **MAIRI CAMERON + JAMES WOOD** – trumpets

53rd & 3rd not iss.

Jan 88. (12"ep) *(AGARR 013)* **YOU MADE MY HEAD EXPLODE. / HEY HEY / WINDY** [ ] [-]

Aug 88. (12"ep) *(AGARR 021)* **HAPPY LIKE YESTERDAY. / SHOOT ME DOWN / A PLACE SO HARD TO FIND** [ ] [-]

— McALINDEN would subsequently resurface with the BMX BANDITS and later formed his own outfit, SUPERSTAR

– compilations, etc. –

1998. (m-cd/m-lp) *Avalanche; (ONLY CD/LP 014)* **THE 53rd & 3rd SINGLES** [ ] [-]

GUN

Formed: Glasgow . . . 1986 by BABY STAFFORD and MARK RANKIN. Originally called HAIRSPRAY TO HEAVEN then PHOBIA, before opting simply for GUN, the band's line-up was completed by guitarist GUILIANO GIZZI, his brother DANTE on bass and SCOTT SHIELDS on drums.

In late 1987, they signed to 'A&M', soon making the UK Top 50 lists with their debut 1989 album, 'TAKING ON THE WORLD'. Along with TEXAS (whose SHARLEEN SPITERI guested on their debut) and SLIDE (anyone remember them?), the band were hailed as the saviours of the Scottish rock scene although in truth, if any group was up to that mammoth task then it was PRIMAL SCREAM, GUN essentially another bunch of workmanlike grafters in the mode of DEL AMITRI or DEACON BLUE, if a bit heavier. Their debut single, the pop/rock of 'BETTER DAYS', was a minor Top 40 hit, the album lingering on the fringes of the chart. The songwriting was competent enough and the band did have a certain cocksure swagger that caught the eye of MICK JAGGER and KEITH RICHARDS who duly invited GUN to support them on the UK leg of their 'Urban Jungle' tour.

STAFFORD quickly became disillusioned, however, departing soon after. Replacing him with ALEX DICKSON, the band began work on a new album, 'GALLUS' (1992), a more organic, harder hitting affair that almost made the Top 10 and spawned the group's first Top 30 single, 'STEAL YOUR FIRE'. By 1994's 'SWAGGER', DICKSON had left and MARK KERR had replaced SHIELDS on the drum stool. The first single from the album was a horrendous, club-footed re-hash of CAMEO's funk classic, 'WORD UP', although ironically/predictably, the song gave them a Top 10 hit at long last. Buoyed by the single's success (and to be fair, it wasn't wholly representative of the album), the album went Top 5.

In 1997, G.U.N. (as they were now called) disappointed many of their fans with their new pop/rock-orientated material, which sounded more like a poor man's INXS. Although they never officially announced their split, GUN shot off into the sunset to do other work.

• **Songwriters:** RANKIN-GIZZI-GIZZI except; LET'S GO CRAZY (Prince) / DON'T BELIEVE A WORD (Thin Lizzy) / CHILDREN OF THE REVOLUTION (T.Rex) / SUFFRAGETTE CITY (David Bowie) / PANIC (Smiths) / KILLING IN THE NAME (Rage Against The Machine) / SO LONELY (Police) / ARE YOU GONNA GO MY WAY (Lenny Kravitz).

MARK RANKIN – vocals / **BABY STAFFORD** (b. STEVE) – guitar / **GUILIANO GIZZI** – guitar / **DANTE GIZZI** – bass / **SCOTT SHIELDS** – drums

A&M A&M

May 89. (lp/c/cd) *(AMA/AMC/CDA 7007) <5285>* **TAKING ON THE WORLD** 44 □
– Better days / The feeling within / Inside out / Shame on you / Money (everybody loves her) / Taking on the world / Shame / Can't get any lower / Something to believe in / Girls in love / I will be waiting. *(re-iss. Mar95 cd/c; 397007-2/-4)*

Jun 89. (7") *(AM 505) <1482>* **BETTER DAYS. / WHEN YOU LOVE SOMEBODY** 33 □
(12"+=/cd-s+=) *(AMY/CDEE 505)* – Coming home.

Aug 89. (7") *(AM 520)* **MONEY (EVERYBODY LOVES HER). / PRIME TIME** 73 -
(12"+=/12"pic-d+=/cd-s+=) *(AMY/AMP/CDEE 520)* – Dance.

Oct 89. (7"/7"s/7"pic-d) *(AM/+S/P 531)* **INSIDE OUT. / BACK TO WHERE WE STARTED** 57 -
(12"+=/cd-s+=/d7"+=) *(AMY/CDEE/AMB 531)* – Where do we go?

Jan 90. (7"/7"s) *(AM/+S 541)* **TAKING ON THE WORLD. / DON'T BELIEVE A WORD** 50 -
(12"+=/cd-s+=) *(AMY/CDEE 541)* – Better days (extended).

Jun 90. (7"/c-s) *(AM/+MC 573)* **SHAME ON YOU. / BETTER DAYS (live)** 33 -
(12"+=/12"s+=/cd-s+=) *(AM X/T/CD 573)* – Money (everybody loves her).
(12") *(AMY 573)* – ('A'remixes).

— **ALEX DICKSON** – guitar; repl. BABY STAFFORD (to own band)

Mar 92. (7"/c-s) *(AM/+MC 851)* **STEAL YOUR FIRE. / DON'T BLAME ME** 24 -
(12"+=/cd-s+=) *(AM Y/CD 851)* – Burning down the house / Reach out for love.

Apr 92. (7"/c-s) *(AM/+MC 869)* **HIGHER GROUND. / RUN** 48 -
(12"+=/pic-cd-s+=) *(AM Y/CD 869)* – One desire.

Apr 92. (cd/c/lp) *(395383-2/-4/-1) <75021-5383-2/-4>* **GALLUS** 14 □
– Steal your fire / Money to burn / Long road / Welcome to the real world / Higher ground / Borrowed time / Freedom / Won't break down / Reach out for love / Watching the world go by. *(re-iss. Mar95 cd/c; 395383-2/-4)*

Jun 92. (7"/c-s) *(AM/+MC 885)* **WELCOME TO THE REAL WORLD. / STEAL YOUR FIRE (live)** 43 -
(12"pic-d+=) *(AMY 885)* – Standing in your shadow.
(cd-s+=) *(AMCD 885)* – Better days / Shame on you (acoustic).

— **MARK KERR** – drums; repl. SHIELDS + DICKSON

Jul 94. (7"/c-s) *(580 664-7/-4)* **WORD UP. / STAY FOREVER** 8 -
(cd-s+=) *(580 665-2)* – The man I used to be / Stranger.
(cd-s) *(580 667-2)* – ('A'mixes).
(12") *(580 665-1)* – ('A'mixes).

Aug 94. (cd/c) *(<540 254-2/-4>)* **SWAGGER** 5 □ Feb95
– Stand in line / Find my way / Word up / Don't say it's over / The only one / Something worthwhile / Seems like I'm losing you / Crying over you / One reason / Vicious heart.

Sep 94. (7") *(580 754-7)* **DON'T SAY IT'S OVER. / STEAL YOUR FIRE** 19 -
(cd-s+=) *(580 755-2)* – Shame on you.
(cd-s) *(580 757-2)* – ('A'side) / Better days / Money (everybody loves her).

Feb 95. (c-s) *(580 953-4)* **THE ONLY ONE / WORD UP (mix) / WORD UP (Tinman remix)** 29 -
(12"+=) *(580 953-1)* – Inside out – So lonely.
(cd-s++=) *(580 953-2)* – Time.
(cd-s) *(580 955-2)* – ('A'side) / Killing in the name / Panic / Are you gonna go my way.

Apr 95. (cd-ep) *(581 043-2)* **SOMETHING WORTHWHILE / SUFFRAGETTE CITY / CHILDREN OF THE REVOLUTION / WORD UP** 39 -
(cd-ep) *(581 045-2)* – ('A'side) / One reason / ('A'-Mac attack mix) / ('A'-Priory mix).
(12"pic-d-ep) *(581 043-1)* – ('A'side) / ('A'-Mac attack mix) / ('A'-King Dong mix) / ('A'-Breakdown mix).

G.U.N.

Apr 97. (cd-s) *(582 191-2)* **CRAZY YOU / SOME THINGS NEVER CHANGE / A WOMAN LIKE YOU** 21 -
(c-s/cd-s) *(582 193-4/-2)* – ('A'side) / ('A'-K.M. mix) / ('A'instrumental) / ('A'demo).

May 97. (cd/c/lp) *(540 723-2/-4/-1)* **0141 632 6326** 32 -
– Rescue you / Crazy you / Seventeen / All my love / My sweet Jane / Come a long way / All I ever wanted / I don't mind / Going down / Always friends.

Jun 97. (c-s) *(582 279-4)* **MY SWEET JANE / GOING DOWN (Mizzy Hog mix)** 51 -
(cd-s+=) *(582 279-2)* – Crazy you / Word up (Tinman mix).
(cd-s) *(582 277-2)* – ('A'side) / Don't cry / Sometimes.

— G.U.N. have since split up

Andy GUNN

Born: 1975, Inverness. Showcasing his neo-Blues style around the country with JUMPIN' THE GUNN (who fused Folk, Jazz, Funk and Blues), 17-year old ANDY found himself on the roster of Virgin Blues offshoot, 'Pointblank'. Alongside such legendary figures as JOHN LEE HOOKER, ALBERT COLLINS, JOHN HAMMOND JNR and POP STAPLES, the young GUNN and his musical compadres travelled to Memphis (where else!) to record JtG's debut album, 'SHADES OF BLUE' (1993). Subsequent sessions for Radio One & Two followed forthwith, although this heavy schedule took its toll on the band.

After their untimely split, ANDY returned to songwriting and jamming, and in 1997 his first solo set, 'STEAMROLL', was released. During the course of the next two years, ANDY delivered a few more ROBIN TROWER-inspired mp3-sets and performed with SAHB (without ALEX, of course), GARY MOORE'S MIDNIGHT BLUES BAND and MARTIN STEPHENSON.

JUMPIN' THE GUNN

ANDY GUNN – guitar

Pointblank not iss.

Apr 93. (cd/c/lp) *(VPB CD/TC/LP 14)* **SHADES OF BLUE** □ -
– Cryin' blues / Green all over / Turtle blues / Crossed wires / More and more / Tired of tryin' / Shades of blue / Mind reader / Sweet Jesus / All I say to you.

ANDY GUNN

with **KEVIN RONALDSON, NIGEL MACKENZIE, ANDY THORBURN, JO HAMILTON + GERRY COOGAN**

Provogue not iss.

Apr 97. (cd) *(PRD 7101-2)* **STEAMROLL** □ -
1999. (mp3) *(none)* **TO ALL THOSE IN THE OCEAN** □ -
2000. (mp3) *(none)* **GIVE HER DIESEL** □ -

GYPSY (see under ⇒ Limbo records)

GYRES

Formed: Blantyre, Lanarkshire . . . 1995 by brothers ANDY and PAUL McLINDEN, together with PETER LYONS, MARK McGILL and PAT FLAHERTY. Blessed with opportunities that many (more deserving) young Scottish bands would jump at, The GYRES were lucky enough to be docu-filmed during their gestation period. They were also jammy enough to land an arena support slot to BOWIE, promoting their first three singles, 'BREAK', 'POP COP' and 'ARE YOU READY', in style. Released on the 'Sugar' label, the latter two tracks hit the Top 75, although a long lay-off meant these OASIS clones failed to break through with the 'FIRST' (1997) album.

ANDY McLINDEN – vocals / **PAUL McLINDEN** – guitar, vocals / **PETER LYONS** – guitar, vocals / **MARK McGILL** – bass / **PAT FLAHERTY** – drums

		Sugar	not iss.
Jan 96.	(7") *(SUGA 7V)* **BREAK. /**		-
Apr 96.	(7"/c-s) *(SUGA 9 V/T)* **POP COP. / A FOOL TO FOLLOW**	71	-
	(cd-s+=) *(SUGA 9CD)* – Sooner or later.		
Jun 96.	(7"/c-s) *(SUGA 11/+T)* **ARE YOU READY. / A MILLION MILES**	71	-
	(cd-s+=) *(SUGA 11CD)* – Top of the tree.		
Jul 97.	(7") *(SUGA 17V)* **SLY. / CONTACT DAY**		-
	(7") *(SUGA 17VX)* – ('A'side) / Sleepless nights.		
	(cd-s++=) *(SUGA 17CD)* – (all 3 tracks).		
Aug 97.	(cd/lp) *(SUGA 16 CD/LP)* **FIRST**		-
	– Sly / Hi-fi driving / Break / A million miles / Hooligan / Are you ready? / Falling down / On a roll / I'm alright / Pop cop / Downtime.		

—— split after poor response to the above set

Paul HAIG (see under ⇒ JOSEF K)

HAMFISTED (see under ⇒ SPARE SNARE)

HANG UP

Formed: Glasgow . . . 1997 by CHARLIE JOE, RAB CORBETT and AFRIK JAHAL, as the Caledonian answer to the JERKY BOYS, so er, just hang up. Pranksters or wanksters, these three lads from the West taped their cheeky phone calls to gullable members of the public and decided to release the product on CD. The aforementioned American JERKY BOYS were masters of their t(i)rade, although this bunch of party animals were equally funny, as long as they didn't do it via a mobile on a train!

CHARLIE JOE, RAB CORBETT + AFRIK JAHAL

		God Bless	not iss.
Jun 98.	(cd) *(NOIR 008CD)* **NEVER MIND THE JERKYS HERE'S HANG UP**		-
	(re-iss. Nov01; same)		

Frank HANNAWAY & Mike BARCLAY (see under ⇒ Fast Product records)

HAPPY FAMILY (see under ⇒ MOMUS)

HARDBODY

Formed: Glasgow . . . 1996 initially as a trio of one-time death-metal fans (probably still are!) ALISTAIR COOK, his brother MICK and bassist TOBY BARBER. When former drama student, the pouting LOUISE QUINN and part-time theatrical composer RONAN BRESLIN hopped on board, the trip-pop 5-piece toned down a tad – somewhat akin to GARBAGE meeting the CARDIGANS.

After two well-received singles, 'ON YOUR OWN' and 'HAZEL'S HOB', were issued early '97 for Epic offshoot, 'Haiku', HARDBODY played that summer's 'T In The Park'. However, plans to release a debut album – recorded in voodoo country New Orleans – were shelved; the pins looked well and truly stuck in. Two years out of circulation (not counting work for RICO and the DIRTY BEATNIKS), QUINN was back to unleash her own self-named outfit, recruiting the more experienced SCOTT FRASER, CHARLIE MILNE and BAL COOKE in the process.

The Jive subsidiary, 'Lunardiscs', was behind two dance-orientated singles 'BRAND NEW LOVER' and 'THE NEXT TIME', released either side of the millennium. Changes were certainly being made when The KARELIA's ALEX HUNTLEY came in for production-bound BAL. QUINN also took the electro-pop theme to a different level on her debut album 'INBETWEEN WORLDS' (2001), which saw the indie princess mould simple house beats with sweet, mature and understated vocals.

• **Note:** not to be confused with mid-90's group who issued an eponymous set for 'P.L.R.'.

LOUISE QUINN – vocals / **MICK COOK** – guitar / **RONAN BRESLIN** – keyboards / **TOBY BARBER** – bass / **ALISTAIR COOK** – drums

		Haiku-Epic	not iss.
Jan 97.	(cd-s) **ON YOUR OWN /**		-
May 97.	(12"/cd-s) *(HAIKU 3 T/CD)* **HAZEL'S HOB / (mixes by the UNDERWOLVES)**		-

—— quickly disappeared once more

QUINN

LOUISE QUINN – vocals, guitar, sampler / **BAL COOKE** – programming, keyboards, drums / **SCOTT FRASER** – bass (ex-CRAIG ARMSTRONG, ex-MELANIE C, ex-PET SHOP BOYS) / **CHARLIE MILNE** – Wurlitzer piano (of THE KARELIA)

		Lunardiscs	not iss.
Nov 99.	(cd-s) *(LUNARCDS 001)* **BRAND NEW LOVER / ANOTHER THIN GIRL / BRAND NEW LOVER (Hi Karate vocal mix)**		-
May 00.	(12"/cd-s) *(LUNAR TS/CD 002)* **THE NEXT TIME (mixes; original / Hi Karate / Dirty Beatniks / One Eyed Boy)**		-

—— **ALEX HUNTLEY** – guitar (of THE KARELIA, ex-BLISTERS, ex-AMPHETAMEANIES, ex-GIRLS) repl. BAL

Aug 01.	(cd-s) *(LUNARCDS 004)* **NEXT TIME**		-
Sep 01.	(cd) *(LUNARCD 003)* **INBETWEEN WORLDS**		-
	– Rising star / Inbetween worlds / Came to dream / Dangerous toy / Autumn / Next time / Dreams I had / Down / Lucky sun / Colours / Somewhere to live.		
Dec 01.	(cd-s) *(LUNARCDS 005)* **INBETWEEN WORLDS /**		-

HARRI (see under ⇒ DADDY'S FAVOURITE)

HAVANA (see under ⇒ Limbo records)

Colin (James) HAY

Born: 29 Jun'53, Saltcoats, Ayrshire. Another ex-pat Scot to follow the well-worn trail to Australia, HAY emigrated with his family at the age of 14. He rose to prominence in the early 80's as the frontman of MEN AT WORK, a band he'd formed in 1979 along with RON STRYKERT, GREG HAM and JERRY SPEISER. While COLIN and RON had previously been writing and performing together as an acoustic duo, the various members were all old mates from their days at La Troube University.

Over the course of a hugely popular, year long residence at the Cricketers Arms Hotel in Melbourne, the band expanded to a five-piece with the addition of JOHN REES and more importantly, caught the attention of A&R man, Peter Karpin, who eventually signed them to 'CBS-Epic'. Their 1982 debut single, 'WHO CAN IT BE NOW?' topped the Aussie charts, as did a follow-up single and debut album. On the back of a successful Stateside support slot to FLEETWOOD MAC, the single made No.1 on the Billboard chart yet it was the unforgettable 'DOWN UNDER' that really made the band's name. Tongue-in-cheek, catchy as hell and boasting unique woodwind arrangements, the song took the world by storm in 1982/3. As well as becoming a massive selling No.1 in both Britain and America, the track was a hit on almost every continent on the planet. The accompanying album, 'BUSINESS AS USUAL' (1982), spent an unprecedented 15 weeks atop the Billboard album chart and also made No.1 in Britain albeit for a slightly shorter reign. Described as "the antipodean answer to The POLICE", the group successfully blended together amiable AOR with white reggae rhythms, HAY not sounding too dissimilar to STING.

The MEN's popularity roared on unabated in 1983 with the release of follow-up set, 'CARGO' and a massive worldwide tour which included a show at Glasgow's Apollo Theatre, HAY given a hero's welcome by Scottish fans. Although a split in the ranks led to the subsequent departure of REES and SPEISER, the band were still shifting serious amounts of albums right up until their final release, 'TWO HEARTS' (1985).

HAY went on to record a debut solo album, 'LOOKING FOR JACK' (1987), its title inspired by a meeting with film star Jack Nicholson. COLIN himself became increasingly involved in acting, appearing in top flight Australian films such as 'Raw Silk', 'Wills And Burke' and 'Heaven's Burning' (alongside Russell Crowe). His folk-influenced follow-up album, 'WAYFARING SONS' (1990) fared pretty badly in the States (British pop fans had long since lost interest) and HAY's subsequent albums were Australian only affairs, namely the acoustic 'PEAKS & VALLEYS' (1991), 'TOPANGA' (1994) and 'TRANSCENDENTAL HIGHWAY' (1998), the latter two released on HAY's own label, 'Lazy Eye'.

1996 also saw HAY and GREG HAM reform MEN AT WORK for an extensive tour of South America, releasing a live album, 'BRAZIL' (2001), complete with an intro from Rio Samba School. On the solo front, the new millennium has seen HAY return to his acoustic work on 'GOING SOMEWHERE', while his acting talents have been in demand in the new Aussie film ,'The Craic'.

COLIN JAMES HAY – vocals, guitar, etc / with session people incl. **JEREMY ALSOP** – keyboards, bass / **CHAD WACKERMAN** – drums, percussion

Epic | Columbia

Jan 87. (7") *(650297-7)* *<06580>* **HOLD ME. / HOME SWEET HOME** [ ] [99]
(12"+=) *(650297-6)* – ('A'version).

Mar 87. (lp/c/cd) *(450355-1/-4/-2)* *<40611>* **LOOKING FOR JACK** [ ] [ ] Feb87
– Hold me / Can I hold you / Looking for Jack / Master of crime / These are our finest days / Nature of the beast / Puerto Rico / Ways of the world / I don't need you anymore / Circles erratica / Fisherman's friend.

May 87. (7"/12") *(650781-7/-6)* **CAN I HOLD YOU. / NATURE OF THE BEAST** [ ] [ ]

Sep 87. (7") **LOOKING FOR JACK. / THESE ARE OUR FINEST DAYS** [-] [ ]

COLIN HAY BAND

w/ **GERRY HALE** – viola, vocals, guitar / **PAUL GADSBY** – bass, vocals / **ROBERT DILLON** – percussion, vocals

M.C.A. | M.C.A.

Feb 90. (cd/c/lp) *<MCA/+C/D 6346>* **WAYFARING SONS** [-] [ ]
– Wayfaring song / Into my life / Storm in my heart / Dream on (in the night) / Not so lonely / Don't drink the water / Help me / Dreamtime in Glasgow / Back in my loving arms / Ya (rest in peace).

Apr 90. (7"/c-s) *(MCA/+C 1408)* **INTO MY LIFE. / IF YOU WANT IT** [ ] [ ]
(cd-s+=/12"+=) *(D+/MCAT 1408)* – Wayfaring Sons.

COLIN HAY

not iss. | M.C.A.

Jan 93. (cd) **PEAKS AND VALLEYS** (acoustic) [-] [ ]
– Into the cornfields / She keeps me dreaming / Can't take this town / Walk amongst the ruins / Hold onto my hand / Keep on walking / Dream on / Boy boy / Conversation / Melbourne song / Sometimes I wish / Go ask an old man / Sea dogs. *(UK-iss.Feb97 on 'Hypertention'; HYCD 296166)* *<US-iss.1999; FMA 33>*

— now with various session people

Line | Lazy Eye

Jan 96. (cd) *(901304)* *<4950>* **TOPANGA** [ ] [ ] Jan95
– I haven't seen you in a long time / Into the cornfields / Waiting for my real life to begin / Can't take this town / I think I know / Against the tide / I don't miss you now / She put the blame on you / Woman's face / Lost generation / Road to Mandalay / Ooh, ooh, ooh, ooh baby. *<CD re-iss. 1999 on F.M.A.'; FMA 32>*

Hypertension | F.M.A.

Feb 98. (cd) *(HYCD 298174)* *<FMA 29>* **TRANSCENDENTAL HIGHWAY** [ ] [ ] Oct98
– Transcendental highway / Don't believe you anymore / My brilliant feat / Goodbye my red rose / If I go / I'm doing fine / Wash it all away / Cactus / Death row conversation / I'll leave the light on / Freedom calling / I just don't think I'll ever get over you.

Hypertension | MusicBlitz

Jun 01. (cd) *(HYP 0200)* *<30089>* **GOING SOMEWHERE** [ ] [ ] Apr01
– Beautiful world / Looking for Jack / Going somewhere / Wayfaring sons / Children on parade / My brilliant feat / Waiting for my real life to begin / Don't wait up / Lifeline / Circles erratica / Water song / Maggie / I don't know why.

HAZEY JANES (see ⇒ Section 9: the 90s)

HEADBOYS

Formed: Dundee . . . 1979 by LOU LEWIS, CALUM MALCOLM, GEORGE BOYTER and DAVY ROSS. Signed to 'R.S.O.' (home of The BEE GEES and ERIC CLAPTON), their first single, 'SHAPE OF THINGS TO COME', was a minor hit on both sides of the Atlantic. However, their brash blend of power-pop seemed a little dated at the turn of the decade, although their eponymous set (which featured the great folk fiddler, ALY BAIN) nearly scraped into the US Top 100. CALUM went on to session for The BLUE NILE.

LOU LEWIS – vocals, guitar / **GEORGE BOYTER** – vocals, bass / **CALUM MALCOLM** – vocals, keyboards / **DAVY ROSS** – vocals, drums / 5th member **BOBBY HEATTIE** – saxophone

R.S.O. | R.S.O.

Aug 79. (7") *(RSO 40)* *<RSO 1005>* **SHAPE OF THINGS TO COME. / THE MOOD I'M IN** [45] [67]

Oct 79. (lp) *(RSS 13)* *<RSO1 3608>* **THE HEADBOYS** [ ] [ ]
– Shape of things to come / Stepping stones / My favourite DJ / Kick in the cans / Changing with the times / Silver lining / Experiments / Schoolgirls / Gonna do it like this / The breakout / The ripper / Take it all down.

Nov 79. (7") *(RSO 49)* **STEPPING STONES. / TAKE IT ALL DOWN** [ ] [-]

Feb 80. (7"m) *(RSO 56)* **KICK IN THE CANS. / DOUBLE VISION / MY FAVOURITE DJ** [ ] [-]

— after their split only CALUM surfaced (with The BLUE NILE)

HEARTS & MINDS (see under ⇒ PEARLFISHERS)

HEAVY PETTIN

Formed: Glasgow . . . 1980 as WEEPER, by drummer GARY MOAT, guitarist GORDON BONNAR and bassist BRIAN WAUGH. They issued one demo single, 'NOTHIN' TO LOSE', before adding frontman HAMIE (STEVE HAYMAN) and lead guitarist PUNKY MENDOZA, subsequently becoming HEAVY PETTIN. Picked up by 'Neat' for a singles deal, the group were soon the subject of major label interest with 'Polydor' eventually securing their signatures. A BRIAN MAY-produced debut set, 'LETTIN LOOSE', eventually appeared in late '83, its fairly tepid melodic hard-rock stylings hardly setting the metal scene alight. Nevertheless, the group were encouraged by a UK rock press eager for more home-grown success and subsequent touring with big guns like OZZY OSBOURNE certainly did HEAVY PETTIN no harm.

A follow-up set, 'ROCK AIN'T DEAD' (1985), testified to their growing confidence and the band were tipped for great things. Greater than the Eurovision song contest anyhow, 'Polydor' incredibly entered new song, 'ROMEO', in a failed bid which did much to scupper the group's career. The accompanying album, 'THE BIG BANG', was duly shelved by the label and the group gave up the ghost (the record was given a belated release through 'FM Revolver' in late '89).

HAMIE (b. STEVE HAYMAN) – vocals / **PUNKY MENDOZA** – lead guitar / **GORDON BONNAR** – lead guitar / **BRIAN WAUGH** – bass / **GARY MOAT** – drums

Neat | not iss.

Aug 82. (7") *(NEAT 17)* **ROLL THE DICE. / LOVE X LOVE** [ ] [-]

Polydor | not iss.

Sep 83. (7") *(HEP 1)* **IN AND OUT OF LOVE. / LOVE ON THE RUN** [ ] [-]
(12"+=) *(HEPX 1)* – Roll the dice.

Oct 83. (lp) *(HEPLP 1)* **LETTIN LOOSE** [55] [-]
– In and out of love / Broken heart / Love on the run / Love times love / Victims of the night / Rock me / Shout it out / Devil in her eyes / Hell is beautiful.

Nov 83. (7"/ext.12") *(HEP/+X 2)* **ROCK ME. / SHADOWS OF THE NIGHT** [ ] [-]

Mar 84. (7"/7"sha-pic-d) *(HEP/+P 3)* **LOVE TIMES LOVE. / SHOUT IT OUT** [69] [-]
(12"+=) *(HEPX 3)* – Hell is beautiful.

Jul 85. (7") *(HEP 4)* **SOLE SURVIVOR. / CRAZY** [ ] [-]
(12"+=) *(HEPX 4)* – Northwinds.

Jul 85. (lp)(cd) *(HEPLP 4)(825 897-2)* **ROCK AIN'T DEAD** [81] [-]
– Rock ain't dead / Sole survivor / China boy / Lost in love / Northwinds / Angel / Heart attack / Dreamin' time / Walkin' with angels / Throw a party. *(cd+=)* – Crazy.

Apr 87. (7") *(POSP 849)* **ROMEO. / DON'T CALL IT LOVE** [ ] [-]
(12"+=) *(POSPX 849)* – City girl.

— folded early 1987, although they finally got below album released

FM Revolver | not iss.

Nov 89. (lp/c/cd) *(WFFM LP/MC/XD 130)* **THE BIG BANG** [ ] [-]
– Born to burn / Romeo / Lonely people / This is America / Looking for love / Madonna on the radio! / Don't call it love / Heaven scent / Two hearts. *(cd re-iss. Aug01; same)*

HEIRLOOM (see under ⇒ Play records)

Emily HELL

Born: Dunbar. Along with the equally sassy LOUISE PREY and Hong Kong lass MANDY WONG, the Caledonian bombshell helped form the trash-cum plastic/rubber trio the PING PONG BITCHES. Aided and abetted by the likes of MARK MOORE (ex-S'EXPRESS), DEPTH CHARGE and former punk impresario MALCOLM McLAREN, the London-based fetishists took their inspiration from ALAN VEGA (ex-SUICIDE and now The REVOLUTIONARY CORPS OF TEENAGE JESUS) and AMANDA LEAR (a transexual diva queen!), the leather-clad mistresses set to take the music world by storm in 2001. That March and signed to ALAN McGEE's newly-formed 'Poptones' imprint, the girls delivered their eponymous debut set. In the same week the trio were hounded offstage after only one song at a Bournemouth University gig! – riot grrrls, indeed!

HEXOLOGY (see under ⇒ SWAMPTRASH)

HEY! ELASTICA

Formed: Edinburgh . . . early 80's by BFJ McVICAR, SHEZ, SAMANTHA SWANSON and GILES. Described as suggestive, trashy dance-pop, it was inevitable that all the hype that surrounded HEY! ELASTICA, would result in a major contract. Winning the battle for the band's nom de plume was Richard Branson's 'Virgin' imprint, although the ever-expanding group fell short of any chart action; four singles on the trot – from 1982's 'EAT YOUR HEART OUT' to 1984's 'THIS TOWN' – all failed to spring HEY! ELASTICA into the public eye. When their debut set, 'IN ON THE OFF BEAT' (1984), reported bad sales, it was time for the band to stretch out in to other directions; SAMANTHA would later be part of indie/rave act, The APPLES. Of course, another band with ELASTICA in their name did somewhat better, but HEY! what do I know.

SAMANTHA SWANSON – vocals / **GILES** – vocals / **B.F.J. McVICAR** – guitar, vocals, maracas / **SHEZ** – guitar, synths / + session people incl. KEITH BURNS – drums / MIKE McCANN + GEORGE CATHRO – bass / etc

		Virgin	not iss.
Oct 82.	(7"/12") *(VS 547/+12)* **EAT YOUR HEART OUT. /**	☐	-
Mar 83.	(7"/12") *(VS 561/+12)* **SUCK A LITTLE HONEY. / SUCK A LITTLE MORE HONEY**	☐	-
Oct 83.	(7") *(VS 599)* **PARTY GAMES. / ELASTICAN CHANT NO.2**	☐	-
Jan 84.	(7") *(VS 650)* **THIS TOWN. / THAT TOWN** (12"+=) *(VS 650-12)* – Twist that town.	☐	-
Mar 84.	(lp/c) *(V/TCV 2273)* **IN ON THE OFF BEAT** – This town / Heaven (should've been here / Party games / Sex with your dancing partner / Cafe des bruits / My kinda guy / Perfect couple / Polaroid picture zoo / Barbarella / That town.	☐	-

— disbanded soon after above, SAMANTHA later joined The APPLES

HIBEE-NATION (see under ⇒ WELSH, Irvine)

HIGH BEES (see under ⇒ ROSS, Malcolm)

HIGH FIDELITY (see under ⇒ SOUP DRAGONS)

HIPSWAY

Formed: Glasgow . . . mid-80's by ex-ALTERED IMAGES man, JOHN McELHONE, GRAHAME SKINNER, PIM JONES and HARRY TRAVERS. Sterling Scots pop soul/funk ambassadors, HIPSWAY followed in the footsteps of ORANGE JUICE et al in proving that white boys could tackle Afro-American music with at least a modicum of style and depth.

Securing a deal with 'Mercury', the band released the stuttering funk groove of 'BROKEN YEARS' as their first single, SKINNER's smouldering vocals and chiselled good looks proving a focal point in their bid for the mainstream. Although the track wasn't an immediate hit, a follow-up, 'ASK THE LORD', met with more success and HIPSWAY finally cracked the chart early '86 with the classy 'THE HONEYTHIEF' single. The eponmyous debut album followed soon after, a strong, polished set with material to match the previous singles (all included), the overall effect not being too dissimilar to a more easy going, apolitical THE THE. A definite highlight was 'TINDER', a track Scottish readers may remember as providing the musical backdrop for an 80's lager commercial. Yet save for a further single, 'LONG WHITE CAR' later that summer, HIPSWAY subsequently disappeared for three years and lost much of their momentum in the process.

When they eventually resurfaced with 1989's 'SCRATCH THE SURFACE', the music scene had moved on, both the album and single, 'YOUR LOVE', failing to break the Top 50. A shame, as HIPSWAY promised so much with their debut, a good seller even today in its re-issued CD form. Inevitably, the band split with SKINNER and JONES going on to form WITNESS.

GRAHAME 'SKIN' SKINNER – vocals (ex-JAZZATEERS) / **PIM JONES** – guitar; repl. ALISTAIR McLEOD / **JOHNNY McALHONE** – bass (ex-ALTERED IMAGES) / **HARRY TRAVERS** (b. 2 Jan'63) – drums

		Mercury	Columbia
May 85.	(7"/12") *(MER/+X 193)* **THE BROKEN YEARS. / FORBIDDEN**	72	-
Aug 85.	(7") *(MER 195)* **ASK THE LORD. / PAIN MACHINE** (12"+=) *(MERX 195)* – ('A'extended) / The broken years. (d7"+=) *(MERXD 195)* – The broken years / Forbidden.	72	-
Feb 86.	(7") *(MER 212)* **THE HONEYTHIEF. / WILD SORROW** (12"+=) *(MERX 212)* – ('A'extended) / ('A'-Marketing mix) / The broken years (mix). (d7"+=) *(MERXD 212)* – The broken years / Forbidden.	17	-
Apr 86.	(lp/c)(cd) *(MERH/+C 85)(826821-2)* <40522> **HIPSWAY** – Tinder / Forbidden / Ask the Lord * / Upon a thread / Set this day apart / The honeythief * / Long white car / Bed thing longing / The broken years *. *(tracks – * cd versions extended mixes) (cd re-iss. Sep92; same)*	42	55 Jan87
Apr 86.	(7") *(LORD 1)* **ASK THE LORD. / ARE YOU READY TO LISTEN** (d7"+=/ext-12"+=) *(LORDX 1)* – Ask the Lord (film theme) / End titles.	50	-
Aug 86.	(7") *(MER 230)* **LONG WHITE CAR. / RING OUT THE BELL** (12"+=) *(MERX 230)* – Tinder.	55	-
Jan 87.	(7") <06579> **THE HONEYTHIEF. / FORBIDDEN**	-	19
Jul 87.	(7") <07118> **ASK THE LORD. / SET THIS DAY APART**	-	☐
Oct 87.	(7") <07330> **LONG WHITE CAR. / UPON A THREAD**	-	☐

— **P. GALDSTON** – bass; repl. McALHONE who left to form TEXAS

Mar 89.	(7") *(MAR 279)* **YOUR LOVE. / SWEET TALK** (12"+=/cd-s+=) *(MER X/CD 279)* – What makes a man (love a woman so bad).	66	☐
May 89.	(lp/c/cd) *(838249-1/-4/-2)* **SCRATCH THE SURFACE** – Show me / Keepin' it together / Your love / Emerald / I'm not perfect / Handfuls of dust / Something special / Wrong about that / Scratch the surface / Solid gone. *(re-iss. Apr93; same) (cd re-iss. Oct97 on 'Spectrum'; 554178-2)*	☐	☐

WITNESS

— were formed by **SKINNER, JONES** plus **ANDY CLARK** – bass / **JIM KIMBERLEY** – drums

		A&M	A&M
May 91.	(7") **LIGHT AT THE END OF THE TUNNEL. / WITHOUT YOU** (12"+=/cd-s+=) – Solid ground.	☐	☐
May 91.	(cd/c/lp) *(397124-2/-4/-1)* **HOUSE CALLED LOVE** – House called love / Sweet poison / Light at the end of the tunnel / Time and time again / Loverman / Sail on down / Devil's justice / Forget yesterday.	☐	☐
Jul 91.	(7") **LOVERMAN. / THE REASON IS** (cd-s+=) – She lies. (12") – ('A'side) / (2 other 'A'mixes).	☐	☐

— In May'93, they released a single, 'TAKE THE TIME', for the 'Childline' charity; *RDAKS 1)*

HIS LATEST FLAME

Formed: Glasgow . . . mid-80's out of quintet SOPHISTICATED BOOM BOOM by frontwoman TRISHA REID and three other pop-loving females. With a worldly political slant, HIS LATEST FLAME (named after an ELVIS song) were Britain's answer to the jungle-jangle BANGLES, although TRICIA vehemently protested about this awkward assessment. Disillusioned by Reagan and Thatcher's transatlantic niceties, the 'FLAME unleashed a couple of fine 45's for 'Go! Discs', entitled 'SOMEBODY'S GONNA GET HURT' and 'STOP THE TIDE'. By 1989, TRICIA and her latest flames (i.e. JACQUELINE BRADLEY and session folk BLAIR DOUGLAS, NICK CLARK and WILF GIBSON) were moved upstairs to the 'London' department of Go! Discs. With a handful of hard-biting 45's – including the excellent one-that-got-away, 'AMERICAN BLUE' – HLF delivered their only full-length platter, 'IN THE NEIGHBOURHOOD', in early 1990.

TRICIA REID – vocals, guitars / with 3 others

		Go! Discs	not iss.
May 86.	(7") *(GOD 10)* **SOMEBODY'S GONNA GET HURT. / ALL THE SAME TO ME** (12"+=) *(GODX 10)* – ('A'-instrumental).	☐	-
Sep 86.	(7") *(GOD 14)* **STOP THE TIDE. / WAKE UP (AND SMELL THE COFFEE)** (12"+=) *(GODX 14)* – ('A'-instrumental).	☐	-

— were now just **TRISHA** plus session people incl. **BLAIR DOUGLAS** – accordion (ex-RUNRIG) / **JACQUELINE BRADLEY** – synthesiser / **NICK CLARK** – bass, vocals / **WILF GIBSON** – fiddle / etc

		London	London
Jul 89.	(7"/c-s) *(LON/+CS 234)* **LONDONDERRY ROAD. / FOR THE SAKE OF** (12"+=) *(LONX 234)* – What makes you. (cd-s+=) *(LONCD 234)* – Come on, come on.	☐	-
Oct 89.	(7"/c-s) *(LON/+CS 240)* **AMERICA BLUE. / TONGUE TIED** (12"+=/cd-s+=) *(LON X/CD 240)* – Footsteps.	☐	-
Jan 90.	(cd/c/lp) *(828163-2/-4/-1)* **IN THE NEIGHBOURHOOD** – Londonderry road / Heart of the country / Finest hour / Big world / Cold, cold, cold / Love's in the neighbourhood / America blue / Crack me down / Sporting life / Take it in your stride / Old flame.	☐	☐
Apr 90.	(7"/c-s) *(LON/+CD 247)* **LOVE'S IN THE NEIGHBOURHOOD. / IT'S GETTING DARK** (12"+=/cd-s+=) *(LON X/CD 247)* – The travel song.	☐	-
Jun 90.	(7"/c-s) *(LON/+CS 268)* **AMERICA BLUE. / TONGUE TIED** (12"+=/cd-s+=) *(LON X/CD 268)* – Londonderry road.	☐	-

— disbanded after above

HOBOTALK

Formed: Dunbar . . . 1998 as the brainchild of Edinburgh hick MARC PILLEY (former writing friend of the band, CHICKWEED), who scoured the East Coast to find some musicians to complement his Americana-styled songwriting. Inspired by JIM CROCE, JIMMY WEBB or maybe even RANDY EDELMAN and dressed in suitable cowboy hat, PILLEY finally enlisted locals ROSS EDMONDS (on guitar), AL and IAN. A deal with Virgin subsidiary 'Hut', led to rave reviews for their late 1999 country-rawk debut EP, 'PICTURES OF ROMANCE'. Around six months later, 'BEAUTY IN MADNESS' (2000), was inspiring all kinds of interest, PILLEY and his crew even supporting the MAGNETIC FIELDS. • **Covered:** NEW YORK, NEW YORK (Frank Sinatra). • **Trivia:** GOMEZ appeared on one track on the album.

MARC PILLEY – vocals, guitars, keyboards / **ROSS EDMOND** – guitar, piano, backing vocals / **IAIN BRUCE** – drums / **ALLY PETRIE** – bass

Hut / not iss.

Nov 99. (12"ep/cd-ep) *(HUT T/CD 120)* **PICTURES OF ROMANCE EP** [ ] [-]
– Pictures of romance / Everything I was and I ain't now / Lately more than ever / In Mac's Ford / Love you 'till tomorrow.

Apr 00. (12"ep/cd-ep) *(HUT T/CD 132)* **I'VE SEEN SOME THINGS EP** [ ] [-]
– I've seen some things / Hymn to the boards / Kelley's heels.

May 00. (cd/lp) *(CDHUT/HUTLP 61)* **BEAUTY IN MADNESS** [ ] [-]
– Walks with me / I've seen some things / I wait for you / Letter / Dime / Motion picture scarecrow / Jackdaw / Never said when / Beauty in madness / When they call us in.

— **GREAEME FLYNN** – bass (ex-PENTHOUSE) / **CHRIS B** – drums (ex-MELVINS; offshoots); repl. rhythm section

Nov 00. (cd-s) *(HUTCD 141)* **WALKS WITH ME / STAR SURFIN' / NEW YORK, NEW YORK** [ ] [-]

HOLIDAYMAKERS
(see ⇒ Section 9: wee post-punk groups)

Danny HOLLAND
(see under ⇒ Human Condition records)

HOLOCAUST

Formed: Edinburgh . . . 1978 by GARY LETTICE, JOHN MORTIMER, ED DUDLEY, ROBIN BEGG and PAUL COLLINS. Inspired by the NWOBHM, HOLOCAUST released a few singles in 1980 on the obscure independent label, 'Phoenix'. With NICKY ARKLESS replacing COLLINS, the group released the 'GARAGE DAYS REVISITED EP', hardly a massive hit but a record which impressed a young LARS ULRICH, METALLICA later taking the title for an EP of covers (which included a run through of HOLOCAUST's 'THE SMALL HOURS'). A debut album, 'THE NIGHTCOMBERS' surfaced in 1981, an unpretentious, yet influential record that marked them out as one of the unsung heroes of their genre. They split in 1982, ED DUDLEY leaving to form the similarly titled HOLOGRAM. The one album project was short-lived however, with the guitarist returning to the HOLOCAUST fold in '84 for the 'NO MAN'S LAND' set. They split once more, only to reform for the 90's, following METALLICA's well-publicised patronage.

GARY LETTICE – vocals / **ED DUDLEY** – guitar / **JOHN MORTIMER** – guitar / **ROBIN BEGG** – bass / **PAUL COLLINS** – drums

Phoenix / not iss.

Jul 80. (7") *(PSP 1)* **HEAVY METAL MANIA. / ONLY AS YOUNG AS YOU FEEL** [ ] [-]

Dec 80. (7"ep) *(PSP 2)* **SMOKIN' VALES** [ ] [-]
– Smokin' valves / Friend or foe / Out my book.

— **NICKY ARKLESS** – drums; repl. COLLINS

Oct 81. (7") *(PSP 3)* **GARAGE DAYS REVISITED EP** [ ] [-]
– Lovin' feeling / Danger / No nonsense / Death or glory / Forcedown / Breakdown.

1981. (lp) *(PSPLP 1)* **THE NIGHTCOMBERS** [ ] [-]
– Smokin' valves / Death or glory / Come on back / Mavrock / It don't matter to me / Cryin' shame / Heavy metal mania / Push it around / The nightcombers. *(cd-iss. Jul00 on 'Edgy'+=; EDGY 106)* – Heavy metal mania / Love's power / Only as young as you feel.

Apr 82. (12"ep) *(12PSP 4)* **COMING THROUGH. / DON'T WANNA BE (A LOSER) / GOOD THING GOING** [ ] [-]

— DUDLEY left to form HOLOGRAM, who released one 'Phoenix' album, 'STEAL THE STARS' in 1982. He returned in 1983/84.

May 83. (lp) *(PSPLP 4)* **LIVE (HOT CURRY & WINE)** [ ] [-]
– No nonsense / Smokin' valves / Long the bell will toll / Jirmakenyerut / The small hours / Forcedown breakdown / Heavy metal mania – The nightcombers. *(cd-iss. Jul00 on 'Edgy'+=; EDGY 107)* – Lovin' feeling danger / Death or glory.

Apr 84. (lp) *(PSPLP 5)* **NO MAN'S LAND** [ ] [-]
– No man's land / We will rock and we will roll / No time left / Let's go / On the ropes / Satellite city / Power play / By the waterside / Missing presumed dead / Alone / Here come the good times.

Chrome / S.P.V.

Jan 90. (m-lp/m-cd) *(CROM 301/+CD)* <820974> **THE SOUND OF SOULS** [ ] [ ]
– This annihilation / I smash the void / Dance into the vortex / Curious / Three ways to die.

Taurus Moon / not iss.

Apr 93. (cd) *(TRMCD 010)* **HYPNOSIS OF BIRDS** [ ] [-]
– Hypnosis of birds / The tower / Book of seasons / Mercier and Camier / Small hours / Into Lebanon / Summer tides / Mortal mother / Cairnpapple hill / In the dark places of the earth / Caledonia.

Neat Metal / not iss.

May 96. (cd) *(NM 006CD)* **SPIRITS FLY** [ ] [-]
– Into Lebanon / The small hours / Hypnosis of birds / The tower / Book of seasons / Mercier & camier / Summer tides / Mortal mother / Cairnpapple Hill / In the dark places of the Earth / Caledonia / Heavy metal mania / Death & glory / Master of puppets. *(re-iss. Oct97; same)*

Sound Riot / not iss.

Oct 00. (cd-ep) *(SRP 004CD)* **HELLFIRE HOLOCAUST** [ ] [-]

Edgy / Edgy

Oct 00. (cd) *(<EDGY 111>)* **THE COURAGE TO BE** [ ] [ ] May01
– The collective / A gentleman's penny / Farthing / Neurosis / When Penelope dreams (part 1 & 2) / From the mine shaft to the bike shed / Fundamentalist / Spanner omelette / Home from home / The age of reason.

HOOK 'N' PULL GANG
(see ⇒ Section 9: wee post-Punk groups)

HORSE

Born: SHEENA McDONALD, 22 Nov'58, Newport-on-Tay, Fife. Growing up in Lanark from the age of one, the girl with the distinct and rare christian name found her niche in singing. HORSE first showcased her talents around the mid-80's as the androgynous-looking half of the Glasgow-based pop group ASTRAKHAN, the other half being songwriting partner ANGELA McALINDEN. In 1987, the pair took the HORSE moniker and invited seasoned session men to be part of their soulful touring act, the highlight being a spot on 'The Tube'.

A big lady with an even bigger voice in the mould of ALISON MOYET, McDONALD (or HORSE if you wished) was tipped for stardom in the early 90's as her major label ('Capitol') debut album, 'THE SAME SKY', garnered significant critical acclaim. The record's classy, soulful pop made her a hugely popular live attraction in Scotland and it seemed she was continually on the brink of a full-scale nationwide breakthrough. Singles such as 'YOU COULD BE FORGIVEN', 'THE SPEED OF THE BEAT OF MY HEART', 'SWEET THING' and the classy 'CAREFUL', all might've made it with a bit more luck (or airplay!), although support slots to TINA TURNER, NANCI GRIFFITH and BB KING, helped raise HORSE's profile. Unfortunately the breakthrough never quite arrived, despite a second major label effort, 'GOD'S HOME MOVIE' (1993), the album once again teetering tantalisingly on the edge of the UK Top 40.

Not discouraged easily, the duo embarked on one of their most ambitious projects to date, a concert ('HORSEsongs') at Glasgow's Barrowland with the Scottish Chamber Orchestra in tow – the graceful, often mesmerising results of the aforementioned 'Horsesongs' were recorded for posterity and finally made available for public consumption five years later.

In 1996, HORSE decided to split the duo and go solo; she was even invited by thespian Sir Ian McKellen to take part in the Stonewall Equity fundraiser shows. The following Spring, HORSE had her biggest chart hit to date (No.44) with remix versions – BROTHERS IN RHYTHM included – of 'CAREFUL'. In the summer of '98, having been a staunch campaigner for Gay and Women's Rights, she co-headlined a Pride Scotland gig with JIMMY SOMERVILLE; she subsequently picked up a Pink award from PHACE West. Her moonlighting work also saw her provided backing vocals for jazz-folk duo BACHUE, while the now peroxide lady of soul and jazz contributed greatly to the 'Songhunter' project with ANDY THORBURN.

Never out of the limelight at the turn of the decade and touring the States (and the UK) to promote her musical repertoire (old and new!), HORSE was once again, a hit song away from making it bigtime. Having been hounded out of Lanark by bigots in the late 80's due to her sexuality, she returned with her gay lover (Susan Kelso) and her baby daughter, Esme – the new millennium was decidedly more peaceful for SHEENA. She issued the heartfelt 'HINDSIGHT . . . IT'S A WONDERFUL THING' in 2001, to great acclaim. A beautiful record from the outset, HORSE's songs moved with a balanced grace, like a blanket of fog slowly descending on a hill top. Opener 'AND EVER I'LL BE YOURS', had her voice glide across the jazzy rumblings of the double bass and the gentle tinkering of the piano, whereas 'SHIP TO SHORE' revisited HORSE's romantic, idyllic fascination with the sea. An album to write home about.

HORSE McDONALD – vocals, acoustic / with **ANGELA McALINDEN** – acoustic guitar / with also **GEORGE HUTCHISON / BRIAN McNEILL / TONY SOAVE** – keyboards / plus **PAUL FISHMAN + ALLAN DUMBRICK**

Capitol — Capitol

Jul 89. (7") *(CL 514)* **YOU COULD BE FORGIVEN. / SOMEBODY** [ ] [ ]
(12"+=) *(12CL 514)* – Down to the dizzy heights.
(cd-s++=) *(CDCL 514)* – I close my eyes and count to ten.

Mar 90. (7") *(CL 566)* **THE SPEED OF THE BEAT OF MY HEART. / THE PICTURE COMPLETELY (live)** [ ] [ ]
(ext-12") *(12CL 566)* – Who cares enough for us.
(cd-s++=) *(CDCL 566)* – Come back.

May 90. (c-s/7") *(TC+/CL 577)* **SWEET THING. / CAT DANCING** [ ] [ ]
(12"+=/cd-s+=) *(12/CD CL 577)* – A place like today / It's all my heart could do.

Jun 90. (cd/c/lp) *(CD/TC+/EST 2123)* **THE SAME SKY** [44] [ ]
– . . .And she smiled / The speed of the beat of my heart / Never not going to / You are / Breathe me / You could be forgiven / Don't call me / Sweet thing / Stay / Careful. *(cd re-iss. Apr97 on 'E.M.I.'; CDP 748966-2)*

Nov 90. (7") *(CL 587)* **CAREFUL. / WICHITA LINEMAN** [52] [ ]
(12"+=) *(12CL 587)* – Sweet thing (acoustic).
(cd-s+=) *(CDCL 587)* – Sweet thing (live) / Time to kill (demo).

Oxygen-MCA — M.C.A.

Aug 93. (7"/c-s) *(GASP/+C 7)* **SHAKE THIS MOUNTAIN. / WILL I EVER FIND?** [52] [ ]
(cd-s+=) *(GASPD 7)* – Falling over myself (demo) / Finer (live).
(cd-s) *(GASXD 7)* – ('A'side) / Finer (orchestral) / Ebb and flow / Celebrate (demo).

Oct 93. (7"/c-s) *(GASP/+C 10)* **GOD'S HOME MOVIE. / ONE STEP AHEAD** [56] [ ]
(cd-s+=) *(GASPD 10)* – Close the door / ('A'mix).
(cd-s) *(GASXD 10)* – ('A'side) / Skin / Appetite / Won't ever leave me.

Nov 93. (cd/c/lp) *(MCD/MCC/MCA 10935)* **GOD'S HOME MOVIE** [42] [ ]
– Celebrate / Shake this mountain / God's home movie / Years from now / Natural law / Letter to Anne-Marie / Hold me now / Imitation / Sorry my dear / Finer.

Jan 94. (c-s) *(GASPC 11)* **CELEBRATE / NEVER NOT GOING TO (live)** [49] [ ]
(cd-s+=) *(GASPD 11)* – Breathe me (live) / The wild mountain thyme (live).
(12") *(GASPT 11)* – ('A'-2 mixes).
(cd-s) *(GASXD 11)* – ('A'-3 mixes).

Stress — not iss.

Mar 97. (cd-s) *(CDSTRX 79)* **CAREFUL (remixes; original / Brothers In Rhythm / Sasha / James Wiltshire)** [44] [-]

— for next HORSE was with the Scottish Chamber Orchestra plus **NIGEL CLARK** – guitar / **HILARY BROOKS** – piano / **LORNA BROOKS + ALAN HUTCHISON** – backing vocals

Randan — not iss.

Mar 00. (cd) *(ranhcda 01)* **BOTH SIDES** [ ] [-]
– Careful / Somebody / One step ahead / Finer / Close the door / Adagio for strings (op 11) / Sweet thing / The look of love / Can't break my heart / Dizzy heights / Never not going to / I close my eyes and count to ten / God's home movie.

Oct 01. (cd) *(ranhcda 02)* **HINDSIGHT . . . IT'S A WONDERFUL THING** [ ] [-]
– And ever I'll be yours / Because / Automatic / Ship to shore / Blush / Kiss my aspiration / Breathe me / Sea of love / Starfish / Dear Sophie / Guilty / Some wonderful / Hindsight . . . it's a wonderful thing.

H2O

Formed: Glasgow . . . 1980 initially as SCREW by frontman IAN DONALDSON, guitarist PETE KEAN, keyboard-player RUSS ALCOCK, drummer KENNY DORMAN and saxman COLIN GAVIGAN. After first inviting future Creation-label guru ALAN McGEE into the fold, they settled for bass player COLIN FERGUSON; oh, what might've been. With smooth pop-rock and weird fashion/haircut tastes the "in thing" for a much-maligned 80's, H2O fitted into this suit quite easily.

After a rather indifferent start via their self-financed 1981 single, 'HOLLYWOOD DREAM', the sextet subsequently signed to 'R.C.A.'. In the Spring of '83, they surprised everyone bar themselves, when their major label debut, 'DREAM TO SLEEP', hit the UK Top 20. Sophisticated, romantic and intelligent, the song lay somewhere between contemporaries like FICTION FACTORY, the CARE or The FIXX. A sophomore single, 'JUST OUTSIDE OF HEAVEN', also entered the Top 40, although a couple of flop 45's, 'ALL THAT GLITTERS' and 'WHO'LL STOP THE RAIN', made sure their much-delayed album, 'FAITH' (1984), went nowhere. Their high-brow brand of watered-down pop was drowned out by mid-80's indie icons The SMITHS and R.E.M.; H2O subsequently sunk without trace. • **Covered:** I FOUGHT THE LAW (Bobby Fuller Four).

IAN DONALDSON – vocals / **PETE KEAN** (b.12 Jan'61) – guitar / **RUSS ALCOCK** – keyboards / **COLIN FERGUSON** (b. 6 Apr'61) – bass / **COLIN GAVIGAN** – saxophone / **KENNY DORMAN** (b.27 Nov'60) – drums

Spock — not iss.

Apr 81. (7") *(PARA 2)* **HOLLYWOOD DREAM. / CHILDREN** [ ] [-]

R.C.A. — R.C.A.

Apr 83. (7"/7"pic-d/12") *(RCA/+P/T 330)* **DREAM TO SLEEP. / BORN TO WIN** [17] [ ]

Jul 83. (7"/7"pic-d/12") *(RCA/+P/T 349)* **JUST OUTSIDE OF HEAVEN. / STRANGER TO STRANGER** [38] [ ]

Oct 83. (7"/12") *(RCA/+T 367)* **ALL THAT GLITTERS. / TURN BACK IN ANGER** [ ] [-]

May 84. (7") *(RCA 406)* **WHO'LL STOP THE RAIN. / TELLING LIES** [ ] [-]
(12"+=) *(RCAT 406)* – Win.

Jun 84. (lp/c) *(PL/PK 70107)* **FAITH** [ ] [ ]
– Success / Dream to sleep / Who'll stop the rain / Just outside of Heaven / Leonard / Action / Sundays are blue / All that glitters / Another face / It's in you.

Dec 84. (7") *(RCA 468)* **YOU TAKE MY BREATH AWAY. / LEONARD** [ ] [-]
(12"+=) *(RCAT 468)* – Hollywood dream.

Legend — not iss.

Feb 87. (7") *(LM 07)* **BLUE DIAMOND. / GO ON** [ ] [-]
(12"+=) *(12LM 07)* – I fought the law.
(cd-s+=) *(CDLM 07)* – Hip cororation / ('A'version).

— split after one-off failure failed to generate any big sales

HUCKLEBERRY

Formed: Edinburgh . . . Autumn 1996 by long-time school friends VIC GALLOWAY (guitar) and JAMES WRIGHT (bass), who were raised in the village of Kingsbarns, near St.Andrews. They grew up together and bonded over their love of music – firstly ADAM & THE ANTS, then 2-Tone, Punk, Indie, Reggae, etc – and witnessed their first gig together in 1985 at the Edinburgh Playhouse watching The DAMNED.

After leaving school in 1991, the pair formed the seminal MIRACLEHEAD alongside drummer STU BASTIMAN and vocalist CLIFF SIMMS, although this popular outfit collapsed when the latter pursued a college career. WRIGHT and GALLOWAY went their separate ways and played in various combos (KHARTOUM HEROES and AGAPAPA), although they met up again in 1996 and decided to form another group with the aim of sounding like a VIOLENT FEMMES-esque Punk busking band. After auditioning and finally teaming up with DAVE SIMANDI, it became apparent that their songwriting and the latter's drumming was more rock-orientated and less acoustic so they searched for another musician to complete the line-up and sound. This came in the form of REUBAN TAYLOR, a classically trained pianist and budding Hammond organ player who defied logic with his amazing speed and dexterity on the chunky keys – he was a must and agreed to sign up! The name HUCKLEBERRY was decided upon – for its ambiguous nature (only a C&W band would call themselves that!). After a few months (and their first recording, the 'HALO JONES' EP), SIMANDI was superseded by their old pal, BASTIMAN.

Their first stroke of luck was meeting enthusiastic entrepreneur, PAUL MUSTARDE, whose vision, dedication and support to HUCKLEBERRY's cause was certainly worth its weight in gold. He set up 'Copper' records in early '97 and began promoting the band's material as best a small independent could possibly do. For the next year or two, HUCKLEBERRY and 'Copper' delivered a number of infectious but unhinged Ska-punk singles, 'THE IDIOT-LISTENING' EP, 'MOROCCO' and 'THE LIVES OF THE SAINTS', while an album, 'HARD LUCK STORIES' was issued in summer '98. PAUL eventually became disillusioned with the music business and abandoned Copper before moving to New Zealand. During this period, the weird but wonderful act that was HUCKLEBERRY – who were best described as Loungecore Garage-rock meeting JETHRO TULL/IAN ANDERSON gurning with a chainsaw – received airplay via Evening Sessions and Peelie, while the Student Radio Network and Tip Sheet were also supportive. Touring Scotland, England and France (they played 'T In The Park', 'Reading' and 'Trans Musicales' festivals), the HUCK's also supported the likes of CARTER USM, the WANNADIES, SPACE and The SUPERNATURALS.

However, the year 1999 saw the band undergoing some rigid personnel changes, CYMON ARETZ took over from BASTIMAN, while WRIGHT took

off for a more rootsy solo career under the names J WRIGHT PRESENTS and JAMES YORKSTON (the latter has supported JOHN MARTYN). It was also the year that GALLOWAY managed to secure himself a rather tasty job as a Radio One DJ co-presenting the (Evening) Session in Scotland. And thus HUCKLEBERRY were put on hold for a while. To add another weird twist, MUSTARDE's brother STEVE joined on bass in 2000, being replaced by Vic's brother ALAN GALLOWAY in 2001, and since then the band have been honing their style and sound. The songs were now heavier and even more unhinged, with a Prog-rock/psychedelic feel, although retaining their classic Hammond textures and rawk-y guitar; all witnessed during gigs at the Glasgow Green festival and subsequent support slots to NOMEANSNO, MAN OR ASTROMAN? and ZEN GUERRILLA. The band are still going strong,
are about to record new material for future release and have songs featured on various impending compilation albums.
So watch this space for continuing unpredictability and rock madness from the band!
• **Trivia:** Vic now also presents 'Air' on BBC Radio Scotland as well as the BBC Radio One show.

VIC GALLOWAY (b. MICHAEL, Muscat, Oman, 4 Aug '72) – vocals, guitars, etc / **JAMES WRIGHT** (b. Kingsbarns) – bass, vocals, acoustic guitar, concertina / **REUBEN TAYLOR** – piano / **DAVE SIMANDI** – drums

Hooj Choons | not iss.

Nov 96. (cd-ep) *(HJEP 1)* **HALO JONES ep** [ ] [-]
– Halo Jones / Pablo the donkey / Virtues / Hothead.

— **STU BASTIMAN** – drums, percussion (ex-MIRACLEHEAD) repl. DAVE

Copper | not iss.

Jun 97. (7"ep/cd-ep) *(COPP EP2 VI/CD)* **THE IDIOT-LISTENING E.P.** [ ] [-]
– Sink with me / The man who wanted a new head / Flying kites for Christ / Coffee.

Apr 98. (7"ep/cd-ep) *(COPP S5/+CD)* **MOROCCO** [ ] [-]
– Morocco / Morocco – Wreckage Inc. mix / Nervous situations / Count it over.

Jun 98. (7"m) *(COPP S6UP)* **THE LIVES OF THE SAINTS. / A MIGHTY SAINT / A MIGHTY FISH (Grove House sessions)** [ ] [-]
(cd-ep+=) *(COPP 6CD)* – Le petit Hispanic.

Jun 98. (cd) *(COPPLP 7CD)* **HARD LUCK STORIES** [ ] [-]
– Pablo the donkey / Ugly / Morocco / Marvellous sons / Flying kites for Christ / The lives of the saints / Easily led / The short Hispanic / Shake off your bones / Learning Latin / Bellyache / Paper faith.

— **CYMON ARETZ** – drums (ex-CONEY ISLAND CYCLONE) repl. BASTIMAN

— **STEVE MUSTARDE** – vocals, bass; repl. WRIGHT who went solo as JAMES YORKSTON, now signed to Domino Records and doing very well.

— (Oct'01) **ALAN MUSTARDE** – bass; repl. STEVE

— expect something soon ; as soon as Vic gets off the radio!

HUE AND CRY

Formed: Coatbridge . . . 1985 by brothers PAT and GREG KANE. Both had previously been members of local band, The WINNING LOSERS, until they formed their own UNITY EXPRESS and eventually evolved into HUE AND CRY.

After releasing a debut 45 on their own 'Stampede' records, the KANE brothers signed to Virgin subsidiary 'Circa', issuing follow-up 'I REFUSE' in Spring '86. Still, it was only a matter of time before their soulful, jazz-influenced sophisti-pop cracked the chart and the rollicking 'LABOUR OF LOVE' secured them a Top 10 hit later that year. Debut album, 'SEDUCED AND ABANDONED' (1987) made the Top 30, showcasing HUE & CRY's brassy sound coupled with PAT's thought provoking lyrics.

The late 80's proved the brothers' most successful period with sophomore album, 'REMOTE' (1988) making the Top 10 and the 'LOOKING FOR LINDA' single making the No.15 position in early '89. The same period also saw PAT elected as the rector of Glasgow University, his outspoken left-wing and nationalist views finding favour with many students. Following 1991's Top 10 set, 'STARS CRASH DOWN', the band parted company with 'Virgin', persevering into the 90's on independent labels. The brothers also recruited NEIL WEIR, GRAHAM WEIR, BOBBY HENRY and BRIAN McFIE, issuing the single 'PRFOUNDLY YOURS', after a switch to the 'Fidelity' imprint.

The LP 'TRUTH AND LOVE' was released in 1992 and displayed the group's love for jazz, taking this style a step further come 1994's 'SHOWTIME' album and its rushed follow-up, 'PIANO & VOICE' (which saw the ensemble switch labels once again, this time to 'Permanent'). The line-up was altered with the addition of classically-trained jazz musicians TOMMY SMITH, MIKE STERN, BRIAN KELLOCK, MICHAEL and RANDY BECKER, NIGEL HITCHCOCK, STEVE SIDWELL and DANNY GOTTLIEB. The troupe were to put their talents to the test with 1996's 'JAZZ NOT JAZZ', an appropriately-titled set which saw HUE & CRY at their best, mixing free-form jazz with smouldering pop sensuality – all overseen by PAT's smoothed-out vocal acrobatics. Nice. The next move was, well, erm, the 'NEXT MOVE' album, delivered in 1999 and continuing the jazz theme, that was, by this time, becoming a bit stale. However, PAT's vocals were still as sharp as ever and the music hadn't faltered one bit. PAT also wrote heavyweight newspaper articles and set up a kind of think-tank for new Scottish political development. A real asset to this fine land!

• **Songwriters:** GREG wrote the music and they also covered:- THE MAN WITH THE CHILD IN HIS EYES (Kate Bush) / IT WAS A VERY GOOD YEAR (. . . Drake) / SHIPBUILDING (Elvis Costello & Clive Langer) / A CHANGE IS GONNA COME (Sam Cooke) / SIGNED, SEALED, DELIVERED + HE'S MISSTRA KNOW IT ALL + THAT GIRL + DO I DO + VISION + TILL YOU COME BACK TO ME (Stevie Wonder) / MOTHER GLASGOW (Michael Marra) / ROUND MIDNIGHT (Davis-Monk-Hancock) / DO NOTHING (Duke Ellington) / SEND IN THE CLOWNS (Steven Sondheim) / JUTE MILL SONG (M.Brooksbank) / MARTHA (Tom Waits) / SWEET HEART OF JESUS (trad.).

PATRICK KANE (b.1964) – vocals / **GREGORY KANE** – keyboards, drum prog. with **NIGEL CLARK** – guitar / **JAME FINNIGAN** – bass / **TONY McCRACKEN** – drums

Stampede | not iss.

Feb 86. (12"m) *(STAMP 2)* **HERE COMES EVERYBODY. / FROM FIRST TO LAST / THE SUCCESS OF MONETARISM** [ ] [-]

Circa | Virgin

May 86. (7") *(YR 2)* **I REFUSE. / JOE AND JOSEPHINE** [ ] [-]
(12"+=) *(YRT 2)* – ('A'extended).
(c-s+=) *(YRC 2)* – Shipbuilding / Dangerous wreck / Tempted.

Dec 86. (7") *(YR 4)* **LABOUR OF LOVE. / WIDESCREEN** [6] [ ] May88
(10"+=) *(YRTX 4)* – Labour of love (super-bad) / I refuse (bitter suite).
(c-s+=) *(YRC 4)* – Labour of love (super-bad) / Goodbye to me.
(12"+=) *(YRT 4)* – I refuse (bitter suite) / Goodbye to me.

Sep 87. (7") *(YR 6)* **STRENGTH TO STRENGTH. / DANGEROUS WRECK** [46] [-]
(12"+=/c-s+=) *(YR T/C 6)* – Seen it all / ('A'extended).

Oct 87. (c/lp/cd) *(CIRC/+A/D 2)* **SEDUCED AND ABANDONED** [22] [ ]
– Strength to strength / History city / Goodbye to me / Human touch / Labour of love / I refuse / Something warmer * / Alligator man / Love is the master / Just one word / Truth. *(cd+= *extra tracks) (re-iss. Sep90 on 'Virgin' lp/c; OVED/+C 336) (cd re-iss. Nov96 on 'Disky'; VI 87480-2)*

Jan 88. (7") *(YR 8)* **I REFUSE. / INDIFFERENCE** [47] [ ]
(c-s+=) *(YRC 8)* – Just one word (live).
(12"+=) *(YRT 8)* – Kiss / Something warmer.
(cd-s+=) *(YRCD 8)* – History city (live) / Labour of love (super-bad).

— now with a plethora of session men incl. **WILL LEE** – bass / **TOMMY SMITH** – saxophone

Oct 88. (7") *(YR 18)* **ORDINARY ANGEL. / I AM JOHN'S HEART** [42] [ ]
(12"+=) *(YRT 18)* – Hymn to hands / ('A'version).
(cd-s++=) *(YRCD 18)* – Spending you.
(10"+=) *(YRTX 18)* – He won't smile / Remote.

Oct 88. (c/lp/cd) *(CIRC/+A/D 6)* **REMOTE** [10] [ ]
– Ordinary angel / Looking for Linda / Guy on the wall / Violently (your words hit me) / Dollar William / The only thing (more powerful than the boss) / Where we wish to remain / Sweet invisibility / Three foot blasts of fire / Remote. *(c+=/cd+=)* – Family of eyes / Under neon. *(re-iss. Dec89 d-cd+=/d-c+=/d-lp+=; CD/TC+/HUE 6)* **BITTER SUITE** – Mother Glasgow / The man with the child in his eyes / Shipbuilding / Rolling home / Peaceful face / Widescreen / O God head hid / Looking for Linda / Remote / It was a very good year / Round midnight / Truth. *(cd re-iss. Apr97 on 'VIP-Virgin'; CDVIP 187)*

Jan 89. (7") *(YR 24)* **LOOKING FOR LINDA. / HE WON'T SMILE** [15] [ ]
(12"+=) *(YRT 24)* – Under neon.
(12"+=) *(YRTX 24)* – Remote.

Apr 89. (7") *(YR 29)* **VIOLENTLY (YOUR WORDS HIT ME). / THE MAN WITH THE CHILD IN HIS EYES** [21] [ ]
(7"ep+=/12"ep+=/cd-ep+=) *(YRE/YRT/YRCD 29)* – Calamity John / Rolling home.

Sep 89. (7"/c-s) *(YR/+C 37)* **SWEET INVISIBILITY. / GREENOCK TIME** [55] [-]
(12"/cd-s) *(YRT/YRCD 37)* – ('A'side) / (2 other-'A'mixes).

Dec 89. (7"/c-s) *(YR/+C 41)* **PEACEFUL FACE. / MOTHER GLASGOW** [ ] [ ]
(10"+=/12"+=/cd-s+=) *(YRT/YRCD 41)* – A change is gonna come.

— with **NIGEL CLARK** – guitar / **EWAN VERNAL** – bass / **MARK FORSHAW** – drums / **CALUM MALCOLM** – keyboards plus other guests **EDDI READER** / **BRIAN McFIE**

May 91. (7"/c-s) *(YR/+C 64)* **MY SALT HEART. / WHITE COLLAR** [47] [-]
(12"+=) *(YRT 64)* – Poets day.
(cd-s) *(YRCD 64)* – ('A'side) / Poets day / ('A'acappella) / Signed, sealed, delivered (I'm yours) / He's mistra know it all.

Jun 91. (c/cd/lp) *(CIRC/+D/A 15)* **STARS CRASH DOWN** [10] [ ]
– My salt heart / Life as text / She makes a sound / Making strange / Remembrance and gold / Long term lovers of pain / Stars crash down / Vera drives / Woman in time / Late in the day. *(cd re-iss. Aug98 on 'VIP-Virgin'; CDVIP 207)*

Aug 91. (7"ep/12"ep/c-ep/cd-ep) *(YR/+T/C/CD 71)* **LONG TERM LOVERS OF PAIN EP** 48 -
– Long term lovers of pain / Heart of Saturday night / Rememberance and gold / Stars crash down.

— The brothers added **NEIL WEIR** – trumpet + **GRAHAM WEIR** – trombone (ex-OMD) / **BOBBY HENRY + BRIAN McFIE** – guitar

Fidelity not iss.

Jun 92. (c-s/7") *(CA+/FIDEL 1)* **PROFOUNDLY YOURS. / NEW STATE (republic of love mix)** 74 -
(cd-s+=) *(CDFIDEL 1)* – Pawn of the weekend.

Aug 92. (cd/c/lp) *(FIDEL CD/MC/LP 1)* **TRUTH AND LOVE** 33 -
– New state / Profoundly yours / Because you are nothing / Everyday chains / Mr. Bell is calling / Inbetween / That girl / Forgotten wars / Bitter bitter / Start here / Whirlwind.

Permanent not iss.

Jul 94. (c-ep/cd-ep) *(CA/CD SPERM 17)* **JUST SAY YOU LOVE ME / WRONG QUESTION, RIGHT ANSWER / SHE'S NOT THERE MARTHA** -

Aug 94. (cd/c) *(PERM CD/MC 17)* **SHOWTIME** -
– Just say you love me / Tinsel show / Bring me home / Wrong question right answer / He said, she said / Cynical / Perfect lie / Hannah and James / Shadow of a man / St. Christopher / Bright young thing. *(cd re-iss. Apr98 on 'Indelible'; INDELCD 7)*

Sep 94. (c-s) *(CASPERM 21)* **CYNICAL / ('A'mix)** -
(cd-s+=) *(CDSPERM 21)* – Vision / Do I do.

Nov 95. (cd/c) *(PERM CD/MC 39)* **PIANO & VOICE** -
– Till you come back to me / Do nothing / Send in the clowns / Jute mill song / She makes a sound (live) / Human touch / Sweet heart of Jesus / Martha / Mary Mary / I am John's heart / Violently (live).

— next featured **TOMMY SMITH** – sax / **MIKE STERN** – guitar / **BRIAN KELLOCK** – synthesizer / **MICHAEL BRECKER** – tenor sax / **NIGEL HITCHCOCK & STEVE SIDWELL** / **DANNY GOTTLIEB** – drums / **RANDY BRECKER** – trumpet

Linn Linn

Oct 96. (cd/c) *(AKD/AKC 057)* **JAZZ NOT JAZZ** -
– Free like you / Iron cage / All true man / Remember me / Virus of love / I'll be there for you / Finally / Good and evil / Makin' whoopee / Austere and beautiful / How do you repair a heart?

Jun 99. (cd) *(<AKD 102>)* **NEXT MOVE** Jun00
– She moves through the wires / I didn't know / Sign o' the times / Sonny cried / Once in a lifetime / Next move / 24-7 / Speed o' life / Pawn of the weekend.

– compilations, etc. –

Dec 90. (cd/c/lp) *Virgin; (D/C+/DATE 1)* **BITTER SUITE (live)** -

Mar 93. (7"/c-s) *Circa; (HUES/+C 1)* **LABOUR OF LOVE (Urban remix). / ('A'mix)** 25 -
(12"+=) *(HUEST 1)* – (2-'A'remixes).
(cd-s+=) *(HUESCD 1)* – Vera drives / Life as text.

Mar 93. (cd/c) *Circa; (HAC CD/MC 1)* **LABOURS OF LOVE – THE BEST OF HUE AND CRY** 27 -
– Labour of love / I refuse / Sweet invisibility / Looking for Linda / My salt heart / Violently (your words hit me) / Strength to strength / Ordinary angel / Long term lovers of pain / She makes a sound / Widescreen / Stars crash down / Peaceful face (live) / The man with the child in his eyes (live) / Truth.

May 95. (cd/c) *Virgin-VIP; (CD/TC VIP 134)* **THE BEST OF HUE AND CRY** -

HUMPFF FAMILY

Formed: Glasgow . . . 1987 by JOHN COLETTA who gathered together the extended musical family of MALKY STEVENSON, DAVY TAYLOR, STUART BROWN, KAT EVANS, KEVIN WILKINSON, PATRICIA McGOWAN, GORDON McCULLOCH and STEVEN BARKER. Born into the city's pub scene, the collective initially let rip on sets comprised largely of cover versions. The writing team of COLETTA and DAVE FITZPATRICK subsequently devised material hardy enough to survive The 'FAMILY's convulsive musical onslaught and their reputation began spreading faster than a Highland wildfire.

The independent 'Iona' label fanned the flames in October '92 with the release of a debut album, 'MOTHERS', inciting journalists to fits of verbal frenzy as they grappled to describe The HUMPFF FAMILY's frenetic roots collision. No musical genre escaped unharmed, with country, folk, cajun, blues and punkabilly all coming in for an ear-bashing. Live, the band were in their element as fans the length and breadth of the country began digging their manic hoedowns on a regular basis. A follow-up set, 'FATHERS', arrived in summer '94 as fans and critics once again fell over themselves to bless the band's unholy marriage of style(s) and fun-loving fury. Possibly the pinnacle of their career to date, a rapturously received set at the Scottish Fleadh c.mid-90's confirmed that 'FAMILY values really are safe and sound in Tony Blair's Britain. • **Songwriters:** Group except THE SKY BRIDGE SONG (trad) / etc.

JOHN COLETTA – mandolin, guitar, harp, banjo, voice / **MALKY STEVENSON** – bass, voice / **DAVY TAYLOR** – dobro electric slide guitar, voice / **STUART BROWN** – guitar, voice / **KAT EVANS** – fiddle; plus **KEVIN WILKINSON** – drums, percussion / **PATRICIA McGOWAN** – voice / **GORDON McCULLOCH** – accordion / **STEVEN BARKER** – drums

unknown not iss.

Apr 89. (7"/c-s) **IN THE FAMILY WAY** -

Dec 90. (12"ep) **FAMILY PLANNING** -
– (6 tracks).

Iona not iss.

Oct 92. (c/cd) *(IG/+CD 019)* **MOTHERS** -
– Keep it down / Brazilian blend / I'll be your baby tonight / Hoo haa / Self pity waltz / Rattle of a simple man / In that dress / Misty again / Five years and just one day / Falling apart / Shoplifting / Teach Jesus / Old film and tickets (Lordy Lordy) / Martha and Vernon / Moby Marly / Beaujolais nouveau. *(re-prom.Jun93 on 'Iona Gold'cd/c; IGCD/IGC 203)*

Jun 93. (cd-s) *(IGS 2031)* **MISTY AGAIN / BEAUJOLAIS NOUVEAU** -

Jul 94. (c/cd) *(IG/+CD 208)* **FATHERS** -
– That's what I see / Triangle / Magic journey / Can of beans / Future imperfect / The Skye Bridge song / Love, death, divorce, prison, alcohol, river & trains / Be there / Joanie's letter / Mary's luck / Rain / Henryetta / Conduct of pigeons.

Hoo Haa not iss.

Nov 95. (cd) **HOO HAA (LIVE AT THE EDINBURGH FESTIVAL)** -
– Intro / Keep it down / That's what I see / Soldier's joy / Magic journey / I'll be your baby tonight / Falling apart / Can of beans / All this fun / The self pity waltz / Rattle of a simple man / The yodle song / Louisianna Saturday night / Moby Marly / Mary's luck / Misty again / In that dress / Bootlace tie / Brazilian blend / Hoo haa / Henryetta / Beaujolais nouveau.

— disbanded some time in '96

I

I AM SCIENTIST

IDLEWILD

Formed: Edinburgh . . . late '95 by RODDY WOOMBLE, ROD JONES and COLIN NEWTON, each having a penchant for noise veterans, SONIC YOUTH and FUGAZI. Having met at a party, the erstwhile students whittled away their revision time with ramshackle rehearsals, eventually channelling their frustrations into a debut single, 'QUEEN OF THE TROUBLED TEENS'. Famously financed by a student loan (and issued on their own 'Human Condition' imprint), the track was championed by Radio One DJ Steve Lamacq, duly rescuing the band from eternal toilet gig hell and setting in motion the mechanics of A&R overload.

A follow-up single, 'CHANDELIER', appeared on 'Fierce Panda' while an acclaimed mini-album on 'Deceptive', 'CAPTAIN', kickstarted '98 and became their final fully fledged indie release prior to a deal with 'Food'. Somewhere along the way the band also picked up bassist BOB FAIRFOULL and began to coax some melancholic tunefulness from the blizzard of sound and fury that characterised their youthful approach.

'A FILM FOR THE FUTURE' announced their major label arrival in fittingly convulsive style, the first of many minor hits which have cemented the band's reputation as one of Scotland's most talked about and possibly most dedicated sonic abusers. Their highly anticipated first album proper, 'HOPE IS IMPORTANT' (late '98), made the UK Top 60 and the band's steady rise proves that noisy guitars never go out of fashion. '100 BROKEN WINDOWS' (2000) might've been the casualties of noise, perhaps. But surprisingly enough, the four-piece turned the screeching guitars down for this commercially-orientated release. The single, 'THESE WOODEN IDEAS' unveiled another side to the band that used to literally knee-cap themselves on stage. Still, with its edge intact 'LITTLE DISCOURAGE' found IDLEWILD adopting an REM-esque style (circa 1995), and 'THERE'S A GLORY IN YOUR STORY' saw them unplugging their guitars altogether. Still, this set could make ears bleed if played at the correct volume. They toned it down, however, for their next release, the bleakly entitled 'THE REMOTE PART' (2002), an album which flirted with a lot of influences; from the Top 20, AZTEC CAMERA-inspired single 'YOU HELD THE WORLD IN YOUR ARMS' to the punky R.E.M. 'Murmur'-era led 'AMERICAN ENGLISH'. The same formula (seen on the latter LP) remained with 'I NEVER WANTED', a soft, heartfelt acoustic number and even a bit of spoken-word on 'IN A REMOTE PART / SCOTTISH FICTION'. The album also crashed into the UK charts at No.3, providing one of Scotland's premier rock bands with the recognition they've been striving for since their musical birth.

RODDY WOOMBLE (b.13 Aug'76) – vocals / **ROD JONES** (b. 3 Dec'76) – guitar / **COLIN NEWTON** (b.18 Apr'77) – drums / **PAUL TIPLER** (helped out on) bass

Human Condition / not iss.

Mar 97. (7") *(HC 0017)* **QUEEN OF THE TROUBLED TEENS. / FASTER / SELF HEALER** [ ] [-]
(re-iss. Jan98; same)

— **BOB FAIRFOULL** (b. 6 Aug'76) – bass; repl. PAUL

Fierce Panda / not iss.

Dec 97. (ltd-7") *(NING 42)* **CHANDELIER. / I WANT TO BE A WRITER** [ ] [-]

Deceptive / not iss.

Jan 98. (m-cd) *(BLUFF 058CD)* **CAPTAIN** [ ] [-]
– Self healer / Annihilate now / Captain / Last night I missed all the fireworks / Satan polaroid / You just have to be who you are.

Feb 98. (7") *(BLUFF 057)* **SATAN POLAROID. / HOUSE ALONE** [ ] [-]

Food / Odeon-EMI

Apr 98. (7") *(FOOD 111)* **A FILM FOR THE FUTURE. / MINCE SHOWERCAP (part I)** [53] [-]
(cd-s+=) *(CDFOOD 111)* – What am I going to do?

Jul 98. (7") *(FOOD 113)* **EVERYONE SAYS YOU'RE SO FRAGILE. / MINCE SHOWERCAP (part II)** [47] [-]
(cd-s+=) *(CDFOOD 113)* – Theory of achievement.

Oct 98. (7") *(FOOD 114)* **I'M A MESSAGE. / MINCE SHOWERCAP (part III)** [41] [-]
(cd-s+=) *(CDFOOD 114)* – This is worse.
(cd-s) **THE SESSIONS EP** *(CDFOODS 114)* – ('A'live) / Satan polaroid (live) / You've lost your way (live).

Oct 98. (cd/c/lp) *(497132-2/-4/-1)* <9504> **HOPE IS IMPORTANT** [53] [ ]
– You've lost your way / A film for the future / Paint nothing / When I argue I see shapes / 4 people do good / I'm happy to be here tonight / Everyone says you're so fragile / I'm a message / You don't have the heart / Close the door / Safe and sound / Low light.

Feb 99. (7") *(FOOD 116)* **WHEN I ARGUE I SEE SHAPES. / (1903-70) / CHANDELIER (10.15 version)** [19] [-]
(cd-s) *(CDFOOD 116)* – (first 2 tracks) / Last night I missed all the fireworks (live).
(cd-s) *(CDFOODS 116)* – (first & third tracks) / Palace flophouse.

Sep 99. (7") *(FOOD 124)* **LITTLE DISCOURAGE. / BROKEN WINDOWS** [24] [-]
(cd-s+=) *(CDFOOD 124)* – A-Tone.
(cd-s) *(CDFOODS 124)* – ('A'side) / You don't have the heart (live) / 1990 – night-time.

Mar 00. (7") *(FOOD 127)* **ACTUALLY IT'S DARKNESS. / MEET ME AT THE HARBOUR** [23] [-]
(cd-s+=) *(CDFOODS 127)* – West Haven.
(cd-s) *(CDFOOD 127)* – ('A'side) / Forgot to follow / It'll take a long time.

Apr 00. (cd/c/lp) *(FOOD CD/TC/LP 32)* <65397> **100 BROKEN WINDOWS** [15] [ ] May00
– Little discourage / I don't have the map / These wooden ideas / Roseability / Idea track / Let me sleep (next to the mirror) / Listen to what you've got / Actually it's darkness / Rusty / Mistake pageant / Quiet crown / The bronze medal.

Jun 00. (7") *(FOOD 132)* **THESE WOODEN IDEAS. / THERE'S GLORY IN YOUR STORY** [32] [-]
(c-s) *(TCFOOD 132)* – ('A'side) / When the ship comes in.
(cd-s+=) *(CDFOODS 132)* – (three tracks above).
(cd-s) *(CDFOOD 132)* – ('A'side) / Actually it's darkness (acoustic) / Rescue.

Oct 00. (7") *(FOOD 134)* **ROSEABILITY. / RUSTY (the poop soldier mix)** [38] [-]
(cd-s+=) *(CDFOOD 134)* – A thousand.
(cd-s) *(CDFOODS 134)* – ('A'side) / I've only just begun / Self healer (live acoustic version) / ('A'-CD-Rom).

Parlophone / E.M.I.

Apr 02. (7") *(R 6575)* <55078-2> **YOU HELD THE WORLD IN YOUR ARMS. / A DISTANT HISTORY** [9] [ ] May02
(cd-s+=) *(CDR 6575)* – I was made to think it.
(cd-s) *(CDRS 6575)* – ('A'side) / All this information / No generation.

Jul 02. (7") *(R 6582)* **AMERICAN ENGLISH. / POOR THING** [15] [-]
(cd-s+=) *(CDRS 6582)* – These are just years / ('A'-CD-video).
(cd-s) *(CDR 6582)* – ('A'side) / The nothing I know / We always have to impress.

Jul 02. (cd/lp) *(540243-2/-1)* **THE REMOTE PART** [3] [-]
– You held the world in your arms / A modern way of letting go / American English / I never wanted / (I am) What I am not / Live in a hiding place / Out of routine / Century after century / Tell me ten words / Stay the same / In remote part – Scottish fiction.

IMMIGRANT (see under ⇒ Fence records)

IMPERIAL RACING CLUB

Formed: Edinburgh . . . 1995 featuring MIKE GORDON, NORD IDESSANE, DARREN ROBERTSON and DOUG JOHNSTONE. Coinciding with their long-awaited debut single, 'BIG DAY OUT', released towards the end of '98, latest IRC recruit CHRIS McARTHUR played drums and co-wrote with ROBERTSON, DAVE REID and a guy called DUGHAN for CRUYFF (named after 70's Dutch football legend, Johann Cruyff), This easier-on-the ear combo issued their one and only offering, 'DOWN YOUR LINE' (also produced by JAMIE WATSON) for 'Human Condition'. Meanwhile, the aforementioned IRC debut, 'BIG DAY OUT', was well-received in some quarters while follow-up, 'MY WORLD', was breaking indie-style courtesy of a place in the Sky One Rock Chart Top 10. IMPERIAL RACING CLUB were a throwback to the retro days of Power-pop/rock fused with a tornado of uptempo harmony-fuelled anthemic punk thrown in for good measure, as evidenced on their promising MANICS-meets-PLACEBO mini-set, 'EVERY GIRLS GOT ONE' (2000).

MIKE GORDON – vocals / **NORD IDESSANE** – guitar / **DARREN ROBERTSON** – bass / **DOUG JOHNSTONE** – drums

Oct 98. (cd-s) *(HC 0019)* **BIG DAY OUT. / WHERE SHE LIVES / IN THE PICTURE** [ ] [-]

May 99. (cd-s) *(HC 00022)* **MY WORLD / GREEN COFFEE / DELIGHT** [ ] [-]

— **CHRIS McARTHUR** – drums; repl. JOHNSTONE who became a journo

Apr 00. (m-cd) *(HCCD 0030)* **EVERY GIRLS GOT ONE** [ ] [-]
– Drama queen / And when I breathe / From a bridge / Half way girl / I want the things that people want / Submit to numb / I love you but I'm tired.

— now without ROBERTSON who left in 2001

CRUYFF

— **McARTHUR + ROBERTSON** with **DAVE REID + DUGHAN**

Oct 98. (cd-ep) *(HC 0020)* **DOWN YOUR LINE EP** [ ] [-]
– Down your line / Everywhere I go / Strength to strength.

INDIAN GIVERS

Formed: Edinburgh . . . 1988 by NIGEL SLEAFORD, SIMON FRASER and AVRIL JAMIESON (who apparently took their moniker from relevant Hoochie Coochie namesakes); in-demand session drummer JAMES LOCKE – who was also guesting for The BATHERS and The CHIMES completed the line-up. Laid back and into danceable pop, The INDIAN GIVERS signed to 'Virgin', but after only a couple of singles and an album, 'LOVE IS A LIE' (1989), the trio disintegrated. First out the door was FRASER and when JAMIESON left shortly afterwards, SLEAFORD had to sell the band's equipment to pay off an unwanted VAT bill; 'Virgin' were not impressed.

NIGEL SLEAFORD – / **SIMON FRASER** – / **AVRIL JAMIESON** –

Virgin / Virgin

Jun 89. (7") *(VS 1187)* **HATCHECK GIRL. / SOME KIND OF MOVER** [ ] [-]
(12"+=/3"cd-s+=) *(VS T/CD 1187)* – The hate song.

Jul 89. (7"/c-s) *(VS/+C 1199)* **FAKE I.D. / IT'S A WONDERFUL LIFE** [ ] [-]
(12"+=) *(VST 1199)* – Suffocate yourself.
(10"+=/cd-s+=) *(VS A/CD 1199)* –

Aug 89. (cd/c/lp) *(CD/TC+/V 2593)* **LOVE IS A LIE** [ ] [ ]
– Hatcheck girl / Fake I.D. / Unthinking of you / Under Rose / Head happy / Some kind of mover / It's a wonderful life / Love come down / Not my line / Caprice / Love is a lie / Never too late.

— disbanded after the band were served an affidavit for tax/VAT

INERTIA (see under ⇒ Bellboy records)

INTERNATIONAL AIRPORT

Formed: Glasgow . . . 1996 as the sole brainchild of TOM CROSSLEY, a part-timer with winsome indie-folkers APPENDIX OUT. For some reason, possibly because they numbered a Japanese bass player, AKI (of INCENCE), or more likely because they had a track featured on a Japanese V/A CD (see below), INTERNATIONAL AIRPORT made their vinyl debut courtesy of Eastern label, 'Osaka Lanes'; the line-up at this time was bolstered by STEPHEN, ROBBIE, CARI and JULIE. The EP in question, 'CRUNK INTO UP', was also a V/A affair and led to a one-off deal with Chicago's 'All City' imprint. The resulting 'AIRPORT SONGS' EP featured a mesmerising rendition of Ennio Morricone's 'UNA STANZA VUOTA', and even prompted one journalist to make a comparison with The RED KRAYOLA. APPENDIX OUT man, ALI ROBERTS, continued the free exchange of ideas by becoming part of INTERNATIONAL AIRPORT for the millennial 'NOTHING WE CAN CONTROL' album, a record that was also enlivened by the presence of TORTOISE's JOHN McENTIRE.

TOM CROSSLEY – guitar, vocals, keyboards, drums (of APPENDIX OUT) / **STEPHEN** – guitar, vocals / **ROBBIE** – melodica, guitar / **CARI** – keyboards / **AKI** – bass (of INCENSE) / **JULIE** – drums

— early in '98, Japanese mag 'Beikoku-Ongaku' issued the 'Dream On' CD which featured the track, 'CHORDAMOL'.

Osaka Lanes / not iss.

Apr 98. (7"ep) *(HONEY 001)* **CRUNK INTO UP** [-] [-] Japan!
– Blue wheel / (other artists are Honey Skoolmates / Disco Girl / Tirolean Tape).

— In Jan'99, another Japanese V/A compilation, 'Crunk Into Up, Volume 2', for 'LD&K' featured the 'AIRPORT track, 'MOUNTAIN MUSIC'.

All City / All City

May 99. (7"ep) <*(ac 11)*> **AIRPORT SONGS EP** [ ] [ ] Oct98
– Strident hi-fi / Una stanza vuota / Melodica 1.

— next with now full-time **ALI ROBERTS** – multi (of APPENDIX OUT)

Geographic / Overcoat

Oct 00. (cd/lp) *(geographic 2 cd/lp)* <*oc 06*> **NOTHING WE CAN CONTROL** [ ] [ ]
– Western / Moving water / Mountain music / Primo or Dutch / Vale of twisted sendal / Remnant kings / De menging van Bruin en Groen / Does chocolate live here / Gold strike / Icerink / Melodica 2 / Cyclionic lanes.

IONA (see ⇒ Section 2 : Folk)

J

Milton JACKSON (see under ⇒ Glasgow Underground records)

JAMES ORR COMPLEX (see under ⇒ ESKA)

Davie JARDINE

Born: Dumfries in the borders – he also takes walks up Ben Nevis. Complete with his broadsword and Braveheart-esque kilt, the ghostly-looking DAVIE – who's CV had been to play with the band TWISTER – was the obvious choice to join punk-metal act The JELLYS in the fall of 1999. Early the following year, the guitarist featured on two singles, 'Milk 'n' Honey' and 'Ship Goes Down', both taken from their third set, 'Doctored For Supersound'.

JASMINE MINKS

Formed: Aberdeen . . . 1983 by young lads ADAM SHEPHERD, TOM SANDERSON, JIM BALE and MARTIN ALVEY, as a 60's nostalgia outfit into BYRDS-esque jangle-pop psychedelia and influenced by the geographical proximity of Glasgow's 'Postcard' scene. Signing to Alan McGee's 'Creation' label, The JASMINE MINKS released a couple of decent 45's and an lp, '1,2,3,4,5,6,7, ALL GOOD PREACHERS GO TO HEAVEN' (1984), before the band moved down south to London; DAVE MUSKER was subsequently drafted in for one single, 'COLD HEART'.

By the release of the 'ANOTHER AGE' album in '88, The 'MINKS had sharpened up their melodies, hooklines and overall approach, as heard on the likes of 'CUT ME DEEP', also one of the standout tracks on 'Creation' V/A sampler, 'Doing It For The Kids'. Having released the very low key, 'VERITAS' (in 2000), The JASMINE MINKS returned triumphantly with McGee's newly set up 'Poptones' imprint. The comeback single in question, 'DADDY DOG', featured Scottish Socialist MSP, Tommy Sheridan and was issued in the spring of 2001 prior to their brilliant follow-up album 'POPARTGLORY'. Fresh and dazzling, the group returned to their mid-80's roots while managing to add in funky basslines, and some seriously strange head-trip psychedelica. The set seemed to impress MINKS followers, and it's certain that McGee was glad to have them back on board (for a short-time!).

ADAM SHEPHERD – guitar, vocals / **TOM SANDERSON** – vocals, guitar / **JIM BALE** – bass / **MARTIN ALVEY** – drums

Creation / not iss.

Mar 84. (7") *(CRE 004)* **THINK! / WORK FOR NOTHING** [ ] [-]

Aug 84. (7") *(CRE 008)* **WHERE THE TRAFFIC GOES. / MR. MAGIC** [ ] [-]

Dec 84. (m-lp) *(CRELP 003)* **1,2,3,4,5,6,7 ALL GOOD PREACHERS GO TO HEAVEN** [ ] [-]
– The thirty second set up / What's gone wrong / Somers town / Ghost of a young man / Mr. Magic / Where the traffic goes.

Jul 85. (7") *(CRE 018)* **WHAT'S HAPPENING. / BLACK AND BLUE** [ ] [-]

— added guest **DAVE MUSKER** – organ (ex-TV PERSONALITIES)

Apr 86. (7") *(CRE 025)* **COLD HEART. / WORLD'S NO PLACE** [ ] [-]
(12"+=) *(CRE 025T)* – Forces network (AFM version) / You got me wrong.

— MUSKER left to form SLAUGHTER JOE

Jun 86. (lp) *(CRELP 007)* **JASMINE MINKS** [ ] [-]
– I don't know / Cold heart / Choice / The ballad of Johnny Eye / Work / Forces network / Like you / Painting – Arguing / You take my freedom / Cry for a man. *(cd-iss. Oct90 +=; CRECD 007)* – The thirty second set up / What's gone wrong / Somers town / Ghost of a young man / Mr. Magic / Where the traffic goes.

Oct 86. (lp) *(CRELP 013)* **SUNSET** (compilation) [ ] [-]
– Think / Work for nothing / Where the traffic goes / Ghost of a young man / Sunset / What's happening / Black and blue / Cold heart / World's no place / Forces network / Mr. Magic.

— **ED DE FLAM** – guitar; repl. ADAM

Nov 87. (7"ep) *(PACE 1)* **PURE EP (live)** [ ] [-]
(above issued on 'Esurient Communications')

Jan 88. (lp) *(CRELP 025)* **ANOTHER AGE** [ ] [-]
– Veronica / Still waiting / Summer! where? / Follow me away / Cut me deep / Living out your dreams / Don't wait too long / Nothing can stop me / Soul station / Time for you / Another age / Sad.

Feb 89. (lp/cd) *(CRELP 044/+CD)* **SCRATCH THE SURFACE** [ ] [-]
– Lost and living / Little things / I've lost her / Marcella / Misery / Can you hear me? / Take / Reaching out / Too young (my home town) / Shiny and black / Scratch the surface / Playing for keeps.

— folded after above . . . but re-formed towards the end of the decade

— **JIM SHEPHERD** with **TOM REID** – drums / + others

Genius Move / not iss.

2000. (cd) *(GENMOVCD 1)* **VERITAS** [ ] [-]
– Easyblue / I heard 'I Wish It Would Rain' / February / Learn to suffer / Blown away / Toy story / Bloored CCR / Bad moon / Stress / Salvage / Suffer instrumental / Radio fuzz / Raving / Mother nature / On ice / Tough old birds.

Poptones / not iss.

Mar 01. (7"; JASMINE MINKS featuring TOMMY SHERIDAN) *(MC 5025S)* **DADDY DOG. /** [ ] [-]

Sep 01. (cd) *(MC 5025CD)* **POPARTGLORY** [ ] [-]
– Popartglory / 3b48 / Soul children / Daddy dog / Freefall / Midnight and I / Bloored OCR / Running ahead / On a Saturday / Ken's korubo / Keepin' hold of you / Angel / 2001 a mink odyssey / Red sky.

– compilations, etc. –

Oct 91. (cd/lp) *Creation; (CRE CD/LP 112)* **SOUL STATION** [ ] [-]
– Cold heart / Forces network / Veronica / Somers town / Think! / Where the traffic goes / The thirty second set up / Ghost of a young man / Still waiting / Cut me deep / The ballad of Johnny Eye / Soul station.

JAZZATEERS

Formed: Glasgow . . . 1981 by MATTHEW WILCOX, IAN BURGOYNE, KEITH BAND and KENNY McDONALD. Being the last act to sign for the soon-to-be defunct indie label, 'Postcard' (home of ORANGE JUICE, AZTEC CAMERA and JOSEF K), they found themselves in the unenviable position of having their debut single shelved. However, a year later the JAZZATEERS were on the books of 'Rough Trade', releasing their eponymous set and an accompanying single, 'SHOW ME THE DOOR', in the summer of '83. The album received some decent reviews with regards to the LOU REED/GORDON GANO-esque approach of lead singer, WILCOX. Unfortunately, the frontman's services were no longer required when the band metamorphosed into minor hitmakers, BOURGIE BOURGIE, their new vocalist being the crooning great, PAUL QUINN. The JAZZATEERS story was not yet over though, as WILCOX and BAND reformed the group in '85, recruiting MICK SLAVEN and COLIN AULD to record a self-financed one-off single, 'PRESSING ON'. Over a decade later – after WILCOX and BAND had spent the late 80's/early 90's in The WILD ANGELS – The JAZZATEERS released the posthumous compilation, 'I SHOT THE PRESIDENT' (1997).

MATTHEW WILCOX – vocals / **IAN BURGOYNE** – guitar / **KEITH BAND** – bass / **KENNY McDONALD** – drums

Postcard / not iss.

Jan 82. (7"; w-drawn) *(81-14)* **SINGLE. /** □ [-]

Rough Trade / not iss.

Jul 83. (7") *(RT 138)* **SHOW ME THE DOOR. / SIXTEEN REASONS** □ [-]

Jul 83. (lp) *(ROUGH 46)* **JAZZATEERS** □ [-]
– Nothing at all / Sixteen reasons / Heartbeat / Looking for a girl / Something to prove / Baby that's a no no / Once more with feeling / Texan / Show me the door / Here comes that feeling / First blood.

— all but WILCOX took off to form BOURGIE BOURGIE (⇒) with PAUL QUINN

— **WILCOX + BAND** re-formed The JAZZATEERS with **MICK SLAVEN** – guitar / **COLIN AULD** – drums

Stampede / not iss.

Jun 85. (12") *(STAMP 1)* **PRESSING ON. / SPIRAL** □ [-]

— after their demise, SLAVEN joined DEL AMITRI while AULD joined FRUITS OF PASSION

– compilations, etc. –

Apr 97. (7") *Marina; (MAR 29)* **HERE COMES THAT FEELING. / TEXAN** □ [-]

May 97. (cd) *Marina; (MA 30)* **I SHOT THE PRESIDENT** (rare & demos) □ [-]
– Nothing at all / Sixteen reasons / Heartbeat / Looking for a girl / Something to prove / Baby that's a no no / Once more with feeling / Texan / Show me the door / Here comes that feeling / Religious me / Blood is sweeter than honey / Up to my eyes / Holding court / Cowboy mouth / Pressing on / Coastline / She's black and white / Don't let your son grow up to be a cowboy.

WILD ANGELS

— were formed by **WILCOX + BAND** plus **STEPHEN LIRONI** – keyboards (ex-ALTERED IMAGES, ex-FLESH) / **DOUGLAS McINTYRE** – guitar (ex-BATHERS, ex-WHITE SAVAGES, ex-FLESH)

Supreme / not iss.

Jul 87. (12") *(EDITION 87.13)* **SHE'S BLACK AND WHITE. / DON'T LET YOUR SON GROW UP TO BE A COWBOY** □ [-]

Valentine / not iss.

Jul 88. (cd) *(VALD 8060)* **ROCKIN' ON THE RAILROAD** □ [-]
– Rockin' on the railroad / Don't leave me now / Miss Froggie / Weekend / Boogie woogie country boy / It'll be me / Old black Joe / Lights out / Blue Monday / Moonshine boogie / Ballad of a teenage queen / There's a fight going on / Little G.T.O. / Break up / Lucille / The sledgehammer strikes back.

JENNIFERS (see under ⇒ Human Condition records)

JESSE GARON & THE DESPERADOES

Formed: Edinburgh . . . 1986 by FRAN SCHOPPLER, ANGUS McPAKE and two ROTE KAPELLE members, ANDREW TULLY and MARGARITA VASQUEZ-PONTE (in fact this drummer/vocalist also moonlighted for a third "Burgh" act, The FIZZBOMBS, alongside the aforementioned ANGUS). ROTE KAPELLE – who also included CHRIS HENMAN, IAN DUNN, MALCOLM KERGAN and JONATHAN WIND – evolved a few years earlier, releasing their debut EP, 'THE BIG SMELL DINOSAUR', towards the end of '85. Signing with MARC RILEY's 'In-Tape' label, they issued a handful of other indie-pop releases, notably the JON LANGFORD-produced 'FIRE ESCAPE' single in the Spring of '88.

Meanwhile, the 'Narodnik' stable (run by part-timer, EDDY) was home for JESSE GARON & THE DESPERADOES (confusingly enough, there wasn't actually a JESSE GARON in the band!), a country-tinged, fun-loving bunch of indie-rockers who made their first break for the border late in '86 with the DOUGLAS HART-produced 45, 'SPLASHING ALONG'. They also delivered a string of 45's before finally getting around to their full-set proper (a compilation, 'A CABINET FULL OF CURIOSITIES', had already hit the shops in '88) at the turn of the decade with 'NIXON'. Released discreetly on TULLY's own 'Avalanche' records, the lp was followed by what was to be their last offering, 'HOLD ME NOW', a mini-set that featured covers of Bachman Turner Overdrive's 'YOU AIN'T SEEN NOTHING YET' and Lulu's 'LOVE LOVES TO LOVE LOVE'.

FRAN SCHOPPLER – vocals / **ANDREW TULLY** – vocals, guitar / **ANGUS McPAKE** – bass / **MARGARITA VASQUEZ-PONTE** – drums / **KEVIN + STUART** – guitars

Narodnik / not iss.

Oct 86. (7") *(NRK 001)* **SPLASHING ALONG. / PRESENCE DEAR** □ [-]

Mar 87. (7") *(NRK 002)* **THE RAIN FELL DOWN. / I'M UP HERE** □ [-]

— **BRUCE HOPKINS + JOHN ROBB** – guitars; repl. KEVIN + STUART

May 87. (12"ep) *(NRK 005T)* **THE BILLY WHIZZ EP** □ [-]
– Blacker than blue / Thursday feels fine / This town is falling down / Wealth of nations.

— **MICHAEL KERR** – lead guitar (of MEAT WHIPLASH) repl. BRUCE + JOHN

Wild Rumpus / not iss.

1987. (7"flexi) *(SHEP 001)* **HANK WILLIAMS IS DEAD. / Fizzbombs: YOU WORRY ME** □ [-]

Velocity / Fast Forward

Jan 88. (7") *(SPEED 001)* **THE ADAM FAITH EXPERIENCE. / LAUGHING AND SMILING** □ [-]
(12"+=) *(SPEEDT 001)* – Just for a while (if ever).

Jun 88. (7") *(SPEED 002)* **YOU'LL NEVER BE THAT YOUNG AGAIN. / AND IF THE SKY SHOULD FALL** □ [-]

Jan 89. (lp) *(SPEEDLP 111)* *<FFUS 3302>* **A CABINET FULL OF CURIOSITIES** (singles compilation) □ □
– Splashing along / I'm up here / The rain fell down / The Adam Faith experience / Laughing and smiling / Just for a while (if ever) / And if the sky should fall / You'll never be that young again / Blacker than blue / Thursday feels fine / This town is falling down / Wealth of nations. *(re-iss. Aug90 on 'Avalanche'; ONLYLP 004)*

— now without KERR who joined the DARLING BUDS on tour

Avalanche / not iss.

Mar 90. (cd/lp) *(ONLY CD/LP 001)* **NIXON** □ [-]
– Grand hotel / Goodbye misery / Her eyes closed / Heaven and a higher place / Love loves to love love / She falls from me / Hold me now / Bury me deep / Stand up / Eight lane freeway / Deliverance / Eden.

Oct 90. (12"ep) *(AGAP 004T)* **HOLD ME NOW (remix) / GRAND HOTEL. / YOU AIN'T SEEN NOTHING YET / HEAVEN IN YOUR HANDS / UNTITLED (gentle mix) / CALIFORNIA GIRL (live)** □ [-]

— disbanded towards the end of 1990

ROTE KAPELLE

ANDREW TULLY – vocals / **MARGARITA VASQUEZ-PONTE** – vocals / **CHRIS HENMAN** – guitar / **IAN DINN** – keyboards (also of The STAIRCASE) / **MALCOLM KERGAN** – bass / **JONATHAN WIND** – drums

Big Smell Dinosaur / not iss.

Dec 85. (7"ep) *(SMELL 1)* **THE BIG SMELL DINOSAUR** □ [-]
– King Mob / Evolution / Fergus! the sheep! / A gas fire.

In-Tape / not iss.

Oct 86. (7") *(IT 037)* **THESE ANIMALS ARE DANGEROUS. / SUNDAY** □ [-]

Aug 87. (12"ep) *(IT 044)* **IT MOVES BUT DOES IT SWING?** (John Peel Sessions) □ [-]
– Marathon man / Jellystone park / Acid face baby / Sunday / You don't know.

Apr 88. (7") *(IT 051)* **FIRE ESCAPE. /** □ [-]

Jun 88. (12"ep) *(IT 054)* **SAN FRANCISCO AGAIN EP** □ [-]
– San Francisco again / Preacher man aural / You don't know / Fire escape (non-dance version).

1990. (lp) **NO MORE BRITON** □ [-]

— they disbanded later in the year, MARGARITA having joined another indie outfit, the re-formed SHOP ASSISTANTS. TULLY became part of the short-lived BRIDGE HOPPER and ran 'Avalanche' records.

FIZZBOMBS

KATY McCULLARS – vocals / **MARGARITA + ANGUS** with **ANN DONALD** – drums (ex-SHOP ASSISTANTS)

Narodnik / not iss.

Apr 87. (7") *(NRK 003)* **SIGN ON THE LINE. / THE WORD THAT** □ [-]

— **SARAH** – vocals, bass; repl. KATY who later resurfaced (mid-90's) in The SECRET GOLDFISH along with ex-MACKENZIES

Calculus / not iss.

Mar 88. (7"ep/12"ep) *(KIT 002/+T)* **THE SURFIN' WINTER EP** □ [-]
– Surfaround / Beach party / Blue summer.

— short-lived due to other commitments (see above)

FRAN SCHOPPLER

— took her time to get back to singing; augmented by **MICK COOKE** – trumpet, flugel (of BELLE & SEBASTIAN) / double bass – **ROY HUNTER**

Dec 00. (cd) *(none)* **1 2 3 4 5 6 7 8 9** □ [-]
– Given up on love / Superman / Rain / Breathe / Snow queen / Tell him to go / Provincial town / Under your wing / Crush.

JESUS & MARY CHAIN

Formed: East Kilbride . . . 1983, by brothers WILLIAM and JIM REID, who took their name from a line in a Bing Crosby film. After local Glasgow gigs, they moved to Fulham in London, having signed for Alan McGhee's independent 'Creation' label in May'84.

Their debut SLAUGHTER JOE-produced 45, 'UPSIDE DOWN', soon topped the indie charts, leading to WEA subsidiary label, 'Blanco Y Negro', snapping them up in early 1985. They hit the UK Top 50 with their next single, 'NEVER UNDERSTAND', and they were soon antagonising new audiences, crashing gear after 20 minutes on set. Riots ensued at nearly every major gig, and more controversy arrived when the next 45's B-side 'JESUS SUCKS', was boycotted by the pressing plant. With a new B-side, the single 'YOU TRIP ME UP', hit only No.55, but was soon followed by another Top 50 hit in October, 'JUST LIKE HONEY'. A month later they unleashed their debut album, 'PSYCHOCANDY', and although this just failed to breach the UK Top 30, it was regarded by many (NME critics especially) as the album of the year. Early in '86, BOBBY GILLESPIE left to concentrate on his PRIMAL SCREAM project and soon after, JAMC hit the Top 20 with the softer single, 'SOME CANDY TALKING'.

In 1987 with new drummer JOHN MOORE, the single 'APRIL SKIES' and album 'DARKLANDS' both went Top 10. Later that year, they remixed The SUGARCUBES' classic 'Birthday' single.'BARBED WIRE KISSES' (1988) was a hotch-potch of B-sides and unreleased material, essential if only for the anarchic trashing of The Beach Boys' 'SURFIN' U.S.A.'. By the release of the 'AUTOMATIC' album in 1989, the Reid brothers had become the core of the band, enlisting additional musicians as needed. The record sounded strangely muted and uninspired although the 'ROLLERCOASTER' EP and subsequent tour (alongside MY BLOODY VALENTINE and a pre-'PARKLIFE' BLUR) were an improvement.

True to controversial style, the band returned to the singles chart in 1992 with the radio un-friendly, post-industrial mantra, 'REVERENCE'. Perhaps the last great piece of venom-spewing noise the 'MARY CHAIN produced, the follow-up album, 'HONEY'S DEAD', was tame in comparison. No surprise then, that it received mixed reviews although there were a few low key highlights, notably the melodic bubblegum grunge of 'FAR GONE AND OUT'. After 1993's 'SOUND OF SPEED' EP, the band hooked up with MAZZY STAR'S Hope Sandoval for 'STONED AND DETHRONED', a mellow set of feedback free strumming. While still echoing the brooding portent of the THE VELVETS, the style of the record was more 'PALE BLUE EYES' than 'SISTER RAY'. Predictably, the band were seen as having 'sold out' by Indie-Rock dullards and a 1995 single, 'I HATE ROCK'N'ROLL', didn't even scrape the Top 50.

1998's comeback set, 'MUNKI', peaked at only No.47 in the charts; tension had been reported from other band members as WILLIAM and JIM fought out their differences. With the latter working on something solo (and Alan McGee's label coming to a close) it was inevitable that the brothers would split the 'CHAIN late in '99. WILLIAM had already delivered his first solo outing a year earlier, 'TIRED OF FUCKING' very low key. LAZYCAME's 'SATURDAY THE FOURTEENTH' finally featured his rejected penis sleeve (from creation days) and FREEHEAT (JIM's project) comprised of BEN LURIE (guitar), ROMI MORI (bass & ex-GUN CLUB) and NICK SANDERSON (drums of EARL BRUTUS)

• **Songwriters:** All written by JIM and WILLIAM except; VEGETABLE MAN (Syd Barrett) / SURFIN' USA (Beach Boys) / WHO DO YOU LOVE (Bo Diddley) / MY GIRL (Temptations) / MUSHROOM (Can) / GUITAR MAN (Jerry Lee Hubbard) / TOWER OF SONG (Leonard Cohen) / LITTLE RED ROOSTER (Willie Dixon) / (I CAN'T GET NO) SATISFACTION (Rolling Stones) / REVERBERATION (13th Floor Elevators) / GHOST OF A SMILE (Pogues) / ALPHABET CITY (Prince) / NEW KIND OF KICK (Cramps).

• **Trivia:** Their 1986 single 'SOME CANDY TALKING' was banned by Radio 1 DJ Mike Smith, due to its drug references. The following year in the States, they were banned from a chart show due to their blasphemous name. Although yet not overwhelming, their success in the US, have made albums reach between 100 & 200. On 1994's 'STONED AND DETHRONED', they were joined by William's girlfriend HOPE SANDOVAL (of MAZZY STAR).

JIM REID (b.29 Dec'61) – vocals, guitar / **WILLIAM REID** (b.28 Oct'58) – guitar, vocals / **MURRAY DALGLISH** – drums (bass tom & snare) / **DOUGLAS HART** – bass

		Creation	not iss.
Nov 84.	(7") *(CRE 012)* **UPSIDE DOWN. / VEGETABLE MAN** (12"+=) *(CRE 012T)* – ('A' demo).		-

The Jesus and Mary Chain

— **BOBBY GILLESPIE** – drums (ex-WAKE, of PRIMAL SCREAM) repl. DALGLISH who formed BABY'S GOT A GUN

		Blanco Y Negro	Reprise
Feb 85.	(7") *(NEG 8)* **NEVER UNDERSTAND. / SUCK** (12"+=) *(NEGT 8)* – Ambition.	47	-
Jun 85.	(7") *(NEG 13)* **YOU TRIP ME UP. / JUST OUT OF REACH** (12"+=) *(NEGT 13)* – Boyfriend's dead.	55	-
Oct 85.	(7") *(NEG 017)* **JUST LIKE HONEY. / HEAD** (12"+=) *(NEGT 17)* – Just like honey (demo) / Cracked. (d7"+=) *(NEGF 17)* – ('A'demo) / Inside me.	45	-
Nov 85.	(lp/c) *(BYN/+C 11)* *<25383>* **PSYCHOCANDY** – Just like honey / The living end / Taste the floor / Hardest walk / Cut dead / In a hole / Taste of Cindy / Never understand / It's so hard / Inside me / Sowing seeds / My little underground / You trip me up / Something's wrong. *(cd-iss. Aug86 & Jan97 +=; K 242 000-2)* – Some candy talking.	31	

— **JOHN LODER** – drums (on stage when BOBBY was unavailable)

Jul 86.	(7") *(NEG 19)* **SOME CANDY TALKING. / PSYCHO CANDY / HIT** (12"+=) *(NEGT 19)* – Taste of Cindy. (d7"+=) *(NEGF 19)(SAM 291)* – Cut dead (acoustic) / You trip me up (acoustic) / Some candy talking (acoustic) / Psycho candy (acoustic).	13	-

— now basic trio of **JIM, WILLIAM** and **DOUGLAS** brought in **JOHN MOORE** (b.23

Dec'64, England) – drums repl. GILLESPIE (who was busy with PRIMAL SCREAM) / **JAMES PINKER** – drums (ex-DEAD CAN DANCE) repl. MOORE now on guitar

Apr 87. (7") *(NEG 24)* **APRIL SKIES. / KILL SURF CITY** 8 -
(12"+=) *(NEGT 24)* – Who do you love.
(d7"+=) *(NEGF 24)* – Mushroom / Bo Diddley is Jesus.

Aug 87. (7") *(NEG 25)* **HAPPY WHEN IT RAINS. / EVERYTHING IS ALRIGHT WHEN YOU'RE DOWN** 25 -
(ext.12"+=) *(NEGT 25)* – Happy place / F-Hole.
(ext.10"+=) *(NEGTE 25)* – ('A'demo) / Shake.

— trimmed to basic duo of REID brothers.

Sep 87. (lp/c)(cd) *(BYN/+C 25)(K 242 180-2) <25656>* **DARKLANDS** 5
– Darklands / Deep one perfect morning / Happy when it rains / Down on me / Nine million rainy days / April skies / Fall / Cherry came too / On the wall / About you. *(cd re-iss. Nov94; K 242 180-2)*

Oct 87. (7"/7"g-f) *(NEG/+F 29)* **DARKLANDS. / RIDER / ON THE WALL (demo)** 33 -
(12"+=/12"g-f+=) *(NEGTF 29)* – Surfin' U.S.A.
(10"+=/cd-s+=) *(NEG TE/CD 29)* – Here it comes again.

— **DAVE EVANS** – rhythm guitar repl. MOORE who formed EXPRESSWAY

Mar 88. (7") *(NEG 32)* **SIDEWALKING. / TASTE OF CINDY (live)** 30 -
(12"+=) *(NEGT 32)* – ('A'extended) / April skies (live).
(cd-s++=) *(NEGCD 32)* – Chilled to the bone.

Apr 88. (lp/c)(cd) *(BYN/+C 29)(K 242 331-2) <25729>* **BARBED WIRE KISSES** (part compilation) 9
– Kill Surf City / Head / Rider / Hit / Don't ever change / Just out of reach / Happy place / Psychocandy / Sidewalking / Who do you love / Surfin' USA / Everything's alright when you're down / Upside down / Taste of Cindy / Swing / On the wall. *(c+=/cd+=)* – Cracked / Here it comes again / Mushroom / Bo Diddley is Jesus. *(cd re-iss. Jan97; same)*

— In Nov'88, DOUGLAS HART moonlighted in The ACID ANGELS, who released 7"promo 'SPEED SPEED ECSTASY' on 'Product Inc.'; *FUEL 1)*

Nov 88. (7") *<27754>* **KILL SURF CITY. / SURFIN' USA (summer mix)** -

— Basically REID brothers, HART and EVANS. (added **RICHARD THOMAS** – drums) / **BEN LURIE** – rhythm guitar repl. EVANS

Sep 89. (7") *(NEG 41)* **BLUES FROM A GUN. / SHIMMER** 32 -
(10"+=) *(NEG 41TE)* – Break me down / Penetration.
(12"+=/c-s+=) *(NEG 41 T/C)* – Penetration / Subway.
(3"cd-s+=) *(NEG 41CD)* – Penetration / My girl.

Oct 89. (lp/c)(cd) *(BYN/+C 20)(K 246 221-2) <26015>* **AUTOMATIC** 11
– Here comes Alice / Coast to coast / Blues from a gun / Between planets / UV ray / Her way of praying / Head on / Take it / Halfway to crazy / Gimme hell. *(cd re-iss. Jan97; same)*

Nov 89. (7") *(NEG 42)* **HEAD ON. / IN THE BLACK** 57 -
(12"+=) *(NEG 42T)* – Terminal beach.
(3"cd-s++=) *(NEG 42CD)* – Drop (acoustic re-mix).
(7") *(NEG 42XB)* – ('A'side). / DEVIANT SLICE
(7") *(NEG 42Y)* – ('A'side). / I'M GLAD I NEVER
(7") *(NEG 42Z)* – ('A'side). / TERMINAL BEACH

Mar 90. (7") *<19891>* **HEAD ON. / PENETRATION** -

Aug 90. (7") *(NEG 45)* **ROLLERCOASTER. / SILVER BLADE** 46 -
(12"+=) *(NEG 45T)* – Tower of song.
(7"ep++=/cd-ep++=) *(NEG 45 D/CD)* – Low-life.

— Trimmed again, when THOMAS joined RENEGADE SOUNDWAVE on U.S.tour. HART became video director. The **REID** brothers and **BEN** recruited **MATTHEW PARKIN** – bass + **BARRY BLACKER** – drums (ex-STARLINGS)

Blanco Y Negro | American

Feb 92. (7") *(NEG 55)* **REVERENCE. / HEAT** 10 -
(12"+=/cd-s+=) *(NEG 55 T/CD)* – ('A'radio remix) / Guitar man.

Mar 92. (cd/c/lp) *(9031 76554-2/-4/-1) <26830>* **HONEY'S DEAD** 14
– Reverence / Teenage lust / Far gone and out / Almost gold / Sugar Ray / Tumbledown / Catchfire / Good for my soul / Rollercoaster / I can't get enough / Sundown / Frequency. *(cd re-iss. Jan97; same)*

Apr 92. (7") *(NEG 56)* **FAR GONE AND OUT. / WHY'D DO YOU WANT ME** 23 -
(12"+=/cd-s+=) *(NEG 56 T/CD)* – Sometimes you just can't get enough.

Jun 92. (7") *(NEG 57)* **ALMOST GOLD. / TEENAGE LUST (acoustic)** 41 -
(12"+=) *(NEG 57T)* – Honey's dead.
(gold-cd-s+=) *(NEG 57CD)* – Reverberation (doubt) / Don't come down.

Jun 93. (7"ep/c-ep/10"ep/cd-ep) *(NEG 66/+C/TE/CD)* **SOUND OF SPEED EP** 30 -
– Snakedriver / Something I can't have / White record release blues / Little red rooster.

Jul 93. (cd/c/lp) *(4509 93105-2/-4/-1)* **THE SOUND OF SPEED** (part comp '88-'93) 15 -
– Snakedriver / Reverence (radio mix) / Heat / Teenage lust (acoustic version) / Why'd you want me / Don't come down / Guitar man / Something I can't have / Sometimes / White record release blues / Shimmer / Penetration / My girl / Tower of song / Little red rooster / Break me down / Lowlife / Deviant slice / Reverberation / Sidewalking (extended version). *(cd re-iss. Jan97; same)*

— next album feat. guest vox HOPE SANDOVAL (Mazzy Star) + SHANE MacGOWAN / **STEVE MONTI** – drums repl. BLACKER

Jul 94. (7"/c-s) *(NEG 70/+C)* **SOMETIMES ALWAYS. / PERFECT CRIME** 22 -
(10"+=/cd-s+=) *(NEG 70 TE/CD)* – Little stars / Drop.

Aug 94. (cd/c/lp) *(4509 93104-2/-4/-1) <45573>* **STONED AND DETRONED** 13 98
– Dirty water / Bullet lovers / Sometimes always / Come on / Between us / Hole / Never saw it coming / She / Wish I could / Save me / Till it shines / God help me / Girlfriend / Everybody I know / You've been a friend / These days / Feeling lucky. *(cd re-iss. Jan97; same)*

Oct 94. (c-s) *<18078>* **SOMETIMES ALWAYS / DROP** - 96

Oct 94. (7"/c-s) *(NEG 73/+C)* **COME ON. / I'M IN WITH THE OUT-CROWD** 52 -
(cd-s+=) *(NEG 73CD)* – New York City / Taking it away.
(cd-s) *(NEG 73CD)* – ('A'side) / Ghost of a smile / Alphabet city / New kind of kick.

Jun 95. (c-ep/12"ep/cd-ep) *(NEG 81 C/TEX/CD)* **I HATE ROCK N ROLL / BLEED ME. / 33 1-3 / LOST STAR** 61 -

Sep 95. (cd,c) *<43043>* **HATE ROCK N ROLL** (compilation of B-sides & rarities) -
– I hate rock'n'roll / Snakedriver / Something I can't have / Bleed me / Thirty three and a third / Lost star / Penetration / New York City / Taking it away / I'm in with the out crowd / Little stars / Teenage lust / Perfect crime.

— **JIM, WILLIAM + BEN** were joined by **NICK SANDERSON** – drums / **TERRY EDWARDS** – horns / + guests vocalists **HOPE SANDOVAL + SISTER VANILLA** (PAUL KING was also a member late '97)

Creation | Sub Pop

Apr 98. (7") *(CRE 292)* **CRACKING UP. / ROCKET** 35 -
(cd-s+=) *(CRESCD 292)* – Hide myself / Commercial.

May 98. (7"/c-s) *(CRE/+CS 296)* **I LOVE ROCK N ROLL. / EASYLIFE, EASYLOVE** 38 -
(cd-s+=) *(CRESCD 296)* – 40,000k / Nineteen 666.

Jun 98. (cd/c/d-lp) *(CRECD/CCRE/CRELP 232) <SP 426>* **MUNKI** 47
– I love rock n roll / Birthday / Stardust remedy / Fizzy / Moe Tucker / Perfume / Virtually unreal / Degenerate / Cracking up / Commercial / Supertramp / Never understood / I can't find the time for times / Man on the moon / Black / Dream lover / I hate rock n roll. *(cd re-iss. Jan01; same)*

— they disbanded in October '99

– compilations, etc. –

Sep 91. (m-lp/m-c/m-cd) *Strange Fruit; (SFP MA/MC/CD 210)* **THE PEEL SESSIONS (1985-86)** -
– Inside me / The living end / Just like honey / all / Hapy place / In the rain.

Jun 94. (cd+book) *Audioglobe* **LIVE (live)** -

Jul 01. (lp) *Strange Fruit; (SFRSLP 092)* **THE COMPLETE JOHN PEEL SESSIONS** -

May 02. (cd) *Blanco Y Negro; (0927 46141-2) / Rhino; <78256>* **21 SINGLES** Jul02

LAZYCAME

WILLIAM REID – solo

Creation | not iss.

Apr 98. (cd-ep; as WILLIAM) *(CRESCD 295)* **TIRED OF FUCKING EP** -
– Tired of fucking / Lucibelle / Kissaround / Hard on.

Hot Tam | not iss.

Oct 99. (7"ep) *(HTAM 001)* **TASTER EP** -
– Muswileclouds / Stevinik / Dement / Engine8.
(cd-ep+=) *(HTAM 001CD)* – God / Complicated.

Dec 99. (cd) *(HOTTAMCD 002)* **FINBEGIN** -
– God / Complicated / Five one zero lovers / Rokit / Go get find / Fornicate / Unfinished business / Blue June / Naturallow / McIntosh lost.

May 00. (cd) *(HOTTAMCD 003)* **SATURDAY THE FOURTEENTH** -
– Drizzle / Last days of Creation / Lo Fi Li / Fuck you genius / You don't belong / Kill kool kid / Kissaround / Muswil clouds / Tired of fucking / Mayhem / Everyone knows / Dement / Unamerican.

Guided Missile | not iss.

Apr 00. (7"ep) *(GUIDE 41)* **YAWN! EP** -
– Drizzle / K to be lost.
(cd-ep+=) *(GUIDE 41CD)* – Who killed Manchester? / Male wife / Commercial.

Richard JOBSON (see under ⇒ SKIDS)

JOHNNY & THE SELF-ABUSERS (see under ⇒ SIMPLE MINDS)

JOHNSON (see under ⇒ TRASH CAN SINATRAS)

JOLT (see ⇒ Section 9: wee post-punk groups)

the JOSE (see under ⇒ Fence records)

JOSEF K

Formed: Edinburgh . . . 1979 by PAUL HAIG, MALCOLM ROSS, DAVID WEDDELL and RONNIE TORRANCE. Named after the main character from one of Franz Kafka's darkly paranoid novels and influenced by New York "No Wave" bands like TALKING HEADS, HAIG & Co. debuted in late '79 with the self-financed 'ROMANCE'. Subsequently signed to Alan Horne's ultra-hip Glasgow-based 'Postcard' label, the band were heralded as "The Sound Of Young Scotland" alongside labelmates ORANGE JUICE and AZTEC CAMERA.

A string of singles, including 'RADIO DRILL TIME' and the low-end lurch of 'SORRY FOR LAUGHING', brought fawning press acclaim with one critic moved to describe their awkward, indie-noir sound as a "cross between CAPTAIN BEEFHEART and CHIC". Problems arose, however, with a proposed debut album, 'SORRY FOR LAUGHING', the band unhappy with the production and scrapping it at the last minute; some copies did filter through, mint editions now change hands for over £100. Recorded in Belgium, 'THE ONLY FUN IN TOWN' eventually surfaced as their debut long player in summer '81. Yet no sooner was the record out than HAIG, sticking rigidly by one of punk's guiding principles, decided that they'd reached an artistic peak and had to split. After a final single, 'THE MISSIONARY', JOSEF K disbanded in early '82, TORRANCE and WEDDELL forming HAPPY FAMILY while ROSS joined ORANGE JUICE and later AZTEC CAMERA.

HAIG, meanwhile, embarked on a solo career via Belgian label, 'Crepescule', following an ill-advised, vaguely SIMPLE MINDS-ish synth-pop/rock direction with 1983's 'RHYTHM OF LIFE' album. The singer continued releasing albums throughout the 80's, never drawing more than minor cult acclaim and modest sales; while HAIG's influence was apparent in the more commercially successful material of LLOYD COLE, for instance, the man himself had to make do with recognition on the continent. • **Covered:** APPLEBUSH (Alice Cooper).

PAUL HAIG (b.1960) – vocals, guitar / **MALCOLM ROSS** (b.31 Jul'60) – guitar, keyboards / **DAVID WENDELL** – bass; repl. GARY McCORMACK who later joined The EXPLOITED / **RONNIE TORRANCE** – drums

Absolute — not iss.

Dec 79. (7") *(ABS 1)* **ROMANCE. / CHANCE MEETING** [ ] [-]

Postcard — not iss.

Aug 80. (7") *(80-3)* **RADIO DRILL TIME. / CRAZY TO EXIST (live)** [ ] [-]
Dec 80. (7") *(80-5)* **IT'S KINDA FUNNY. / FINAL REQUEST** [ ] [-]
Jan 81. (lp; w-drawn) *(81-1)* **SORRY FOR LAUGHING** [-] [-]
Feb 81. (7") *(81-4)* **SORRY FOR LAUGHING. / REVELATION** [ ] [-]
May 81. (7") *(81-5)* **CHANCE MEETING. / PICTURES (OF CINDY)** [ ] [-]
Jun 81. (lp) *(81-7)* **THE ONLY FUN IN TOWN** [ ] [-]
– Fun 'n' frenzy / Revelation / Crazy to exist / It's kinda funny / The angle / Forever drone / Heart of song / 16 years / Citizens / Sorry for laughing. *(cd-iss. Sep90 on 'Les Tempes Modernes'+=; LTMCD 2305)* – (w/ shelved album 'SORRY FOR LAUGHING')

Operation Twilight — not iss.

Feb 82. (7") *(7TWI 053)* **MISSIONARY. / ONE ANGLE / SECOND ANGLE** [ ] [-]

— split early '82 when MALCOLM joined ORANGE JUICE (later AZTEC CAMERA). TORRANCE joined BOOTS FOR DANCING and subsequently teamed up with DAVID to form The HAPPY FAMILY. In 1992, MALCOLM reunited with DAVID forming the MAGIC CLAN in the process.

– compilations, etc. –

Mar 87. (12") *Supreme; (87-7)* **HEAVEN SENT / RADIO DRILL TIME (demo). / HEADS WATCH / FUN 'N' FRENZY** [ ] [-]
Jun 87. (lp) *Supreme; (87-6)* **YOUNG AND STUPID** [ ] [-]
– Heart of song / Endless soul / Citizens / Variation of scene / It's kinda funny / Sorry for laughing / Chance meeting / Heaven sent / Drone / Sense of guilt / Revelation / Romance. *(re-iss. Mar89 as 'ENDLESS SOUL'; same) (cd-iss. Sep90 on 'Les Tempes Modernes'; LTMCD 2307)*

PAUL HAIG

— (solo) – vocals, guitar with the **RHYTHM OF LIFE** band:- **JAMES LOCKE, DAVID GRAHAM + STEPHEN HAINES** (ex-METROPAK)

1982. (c) *(none)* **DRAMA** [-] [-] gigs

Operation Twilight — not iss.

May 82. (7") *(OPT 03)* **RUNNING AWAY. / TIME** [ ] [-]

Crepescule — not iss.

Sep 82. (7") *(OPT 001)* **CHANCE. / JUSTICE** [ ] [-]
Dec 82. (12") *(TWI 106)* **BLUE FOR YOU. / BLUE FOR YOU (version)** [ ] [-]

Crepescule-Island — not iss.

May 83. (7"/ext-12") *(IS/12IS 111)* **HEAVEN SENT. / RUNNING AWAY, BACK HOME** [74] [-]
Jul 83. (7"/ext-12") *(IS/12IS 124)* **NEVER GIVE UP (PARTY, PARTY). / HEARTACHE (Party mix)** [ ] [-]
Oct 83. (lp/c) *(ILPS/ICT 9742)* **RHYTHM OF LIFE** [82] [-]
– Heaven sent / Never give up (party, party) / Adoration / Stolen love / Don't rush in / Blue for you / In the world / Justice / Work together.
Oct 83. (7") *(IS 138)* **JUSTICE. / ON THIS NIGHT OF DECISION** [ ] [-]
(12"+=) *(12IS 138)* – Justice '82.
Sep 84. (7") *(IS 198)* **THE ONLY TRUTH. / GHOST RIDER** [ ] [-]
(12"+=) *(ISX 198)* – ('A'-US remix).

— with **ALAN RANKINE** – lead guitar / **MIKE McCANN** – bass / **JAMES LOCK** – drums

Operation Twilight — not iss.

Sep 85. (7") *(OPA 2)* **HEAVEN HELP YOU NOW. / WORLD RAW** [ ] [-]
(ext-12"+=) *(12OPA 2)* – Chance.
(re-iss. Aug88; TWI 624)
Nov 85. (lp) *(OPA 3)* **THE WARP OF PURE FUN** [ ] [-]
– Silent motion / Heaven help you now / Love eternal / This dying flame / Sense of fun / Scare me / Big blue world / The only truth / One lifetime away / Love and war. *(re-iss. Feb87 on 'Crepescule' lp/cd; TWI 669/+CD)*
Feb 86. (7") *(OPA 6)* **LOVE ETERNAL. / TRUST** [ ] [-]
(12"+=) *(12OPA 6)* – Dangerous life.
(re-iss. Sep88; TWI 660)

Crepescule — not iss.

Jan 88. (lp)(cd) *(TWI 829)(IPCD 2018-36)* **EUROPEAN SUN: ARCHIVE COLLECTION 1982-1987** [ ] [-]
– Running away / Chance / Justice / Swinging for you / Shining hour / Fear and dancing / Blue for you / Ghost rider / Torchomatic / Endless song / Closer now / Dangerous life / The executioner / Psycho San Jose / On this night of indecision / World raw.
Mar 88. (12"ep) *(TWI 832)* **TORCHOMATIC. / BEAT PROGRAMME / CHASE MANHATTAN / WHITE HOTEL / SONG FOR** [ ] [-]

— now with **ALAN RANKINE** – keyboards, guitar, co-producer / **JOHN TURNER** – piano

Circa — not iss.

Mar 89. (lp/c/cd) *(CIR CA/C/CD 7)* **CHAIN** [ ] [-]
– Something good / True blue / Communication / Swinging for you / Time of her life / Faithless / Times can change / Turn the vision / Sooner or later / Chained. *(cd+=)* – Ideal of living.
Jun 89. (7") *(YR 25)* **SOMETHING GOOD. / OVER YOU** [ ] [-]
(3"cd-s+=) *(YRCD 25)* – Free to go / Outback.
(ext-12"+=) *(YRT 25)* – Free to go (technology) / ('A'radio).
(remixed-12"g-f+=) *(YTRX 25)* – The last kiss / Free to go (public).
Sep 90. (cd-s) *(YRCD 47)* **I BELIEVE IN YOU / FLIGHT X (Long Flight mix) / I BELIEVE IN YOU (Life In A Dolphinarium mix)** [ ] [-]
Feb 91. (12") *(YRTX 47)* **FLIGHT X (school mix). / FLIGHT X (Give the DJ a break mix)** [ ] [-]
(12") *(YRRR 47)* – ('A'-New school mix) / ('A'-Music School instrumental) / ('A'-Mantronik mix).

Les Tempes Modernes — not iss.

Jan 92. (cd/c/lp) *(LTMCD 2309)* **CINEMATIQUE – THEMES FOR UNKNOWN FILMS, VOLUME ONE** [-] [-] Belgian
– Black veil and gold / City of fun / Somewhere inbetween / The hunting party / Crime interlude / City of fun (slight return) / Lagondola 1 / Beauty / Highland / Deception / Intimacy / Lagondola 2 / Flashback / Eastworld / In-flight entertainment / Oil.

Crepescule — not iss.

May 93. (cd-ep) *(TWI 989-2)* **SURRENDER / HEAVEN HELP YOU NOW ('93 remix) / COINCIDENCE VS FATE** [ ] [-]
Nov 93. (cd) *(TWI 962-2)* **COINCIDENCE VS FATE** [ ] [-]
– I believe in you / Flight X / Born innocence / My kind / Si senorita / Right on line / Out of mind / Surrender / Stop and stare / The originator / 1959.

— took a hiatus until his mid-90's recording with BILLY MACKENZIE

Rhythm Of Life — not iss.

Jan 00. (cd; by PAUL HAIG & BILLY MACKENZIE) *(ROL 003)* **MEMORY PALACE** [ ] [-]
– Thunderstorm / Stone the memory palace / Beyond love / Transobsession / Trash 3 / Listen to me / Listen again / Take a chance / Give me time.
Mar 01. (cd) *(ROL 004)* **CINEMATIC VOL.2** [ ] [-]
– Paradise angel / Syncro firefly / Wild sync lair / Apple corr / Corr (part 2) / Oyster world / Looking / I.D. / Jewel divine / Spirit.

- compilations, etc. -

on 'Operation Twilight' unless mentioned otherwise

Jun 84. (7"/12") *(TWI 230/231)* **BIG BLUE WORLD. / GHOST RIDER / ENDLESS SONG** [ ] [-]

Jun 84. (7"ep) *(7TWI 240)* **HEAVEN SENT EP** (remixes) [ ] [-]
– Heaven sent / Blue for you / Never give up (party, party) / Stolen love / Justice.

Apr 85. (12"ep) *(TWI 094)* **SWING '82** [ ] [-]
– The song is you / All of you / Music and dance / Love me tender / The way you look tonight.

JOSEPHINE (see under ⇒ Lithium records)

JOYRIDERS (see under ⇒ CATERAN)

JUGGERNAUTS (see under ⇒ BOTANY 5)

JUMPIN' THE GUNN (see under ⇒ GUNN, Andy)

JX (see ⇒ Section 9: Dance/Rave)

K

KAISERS

Formed: Edinburgh . . . mid-90's by Cavern-era BEATLES tribute combo (GEORGE MILLER, MATT ARMSTRONG, JOHN GIBBS and JOHNNY MABEN) who were also into 50's/60's style/dance. With smart suits (nice waistcoats too) and quiffs to match, they delivered a plethora of 2 to 3-minute songs like some out-dated barbershop outfit (with instruments) meeting the Fab Four of The VENTURES. Taking standard R&B songs (Chuck Berry's 'I WANT TO BE YOUR DRIVER' was one of them) and matching them with their own retro-fried numbers, The KAISERS released a consistent batch of albums, the best of which was 1997's 'WISHING STREET' and the obviously BEATLES-inspired 'TWIST WITH THE KAISERS' (1998). In 2002, they delivered the Liam Watson-produced 'SHAKE ME!', with sleevenotes written by somebody called Wilhelm Wimbledon, who lambasted the group's sound. Well, it sounded pretty much like the Merseybeat scene of the early 60's, with Watson adding extra "retro" effect by the use of his vintage recording systems. The leader of this bunch, GEORGE WILSON, also played drums for The COUNTRY TEASERS and spent his spare time designing sleevework for BELLE AND SEBASTIAN, among others.

GEORGE MILLER – vocals, guitar (also drummer of COUNTRY TEASERS) / **MATT ARMSTRONG** – guitar / **JOHN GIBBS** – bass / **JOHNNY MABEN** – drums

No Hit | No Hit

Jan 94. (lp) *(NOHIT 012)* **SQUAREHEAD STOMP!** [ ] [-]
– Alligator twist / Some other guy / Soldiers of love / Uh huh oh yeah / Don't ask me / Hipshake shimmy kitten / I'm a hog for you / Valley of the Kaisers / Peanut butter / Don't believe him / Shimmy like my sister Kate / I can tell / You won't be satisfied / That's my girl / Love potion No.9 / Money (that's what I want). *<US-iss.Mar97; same as UK> (cd-iss. Jul98 on 'Get Hip'; GH 1049CD)*

Jan 94. (lp) *(NOHIT 014)* **IN STEP WITH THE KAISERS** [ ] [ ]
–
<US-iss.Feb97; same as UK>

Feb 95. (7") *(BED 004)* **BEAT SESSION NO.1. /** [ ] [-]
(above on 'No Hit' subsidiary 'Bedrock')

— **MATT CURTIS** – bass; repl. GIBBS

Apr 95. (lp/cd) *(<NOHIT 017/+CD>)* **BEAT IT UP!** [ ] [ ] Jan96
– Watcha say / Licorice twist / She's gonna two-time / Leave my kitten alone / I just don't understand / Watch your step / She's only doggin' around / Hippy hippy shake / Don't come back / Like I do / Loopy Lu / Theme from Vengeance / (Ain't that) Just like me / Don't go with him / Let's stomp / You've got to keep her underhand.

— **MARK FERRIE** – bass; repl. CURTIS

Dec 97. (lp/cd) *(TAN 001/+CD)* **WISHING STREET** [ ] [ ]
– Time to go / Little twister / Wishing Street / (She can't do) The Wiki Waki Wu / I will / Lonesome / Twist it up / Patricia Ann / I want to be your driver / Don't you worry / You're just too smart for me / Why did you lie? / Shame / The mighty atom. *(cd re-iss. Apr98; NOHITCD 025) <US-iss.Sep98; same>*

Norton | not iss.

Dec 97. (7"red) *(45 053)* **MERRY CHRISTMAS LOOPY LU. / TIPSY** [ ] [-]
(above issued on 'Norton' below on 'Ruby Smiles')

Feb 99. (7"ep) *(BEAT 62)* **BEAT IT UP EP** [ ] [-]
– Leave my kitten alone / Soldiers of love / Sugar babe / That's my girl.

not iss. | Spinout

Oct 99. (cd) *<SPIN 010>* **TWIST WITH THE KAISERS** [-] [ ]
– Come on back / Liquorice twist / Things will never be the same / Just a little bit / She's gonna two time / Shake and scream / Watch your step / Whatcha gonna do about it? / Baby Jane / That's my girl / You won't be satisfied / Tenessee waltz / I'm talking about you / Mashed potatoes / Uh huh oh yeah / She's the one / I'm a hog for you / Good, good lovin' / Dizzy Miss Lizzy / Let's stomp.

— **ANGUS McINTYRE** – rhythm guitar; repl. ARMSTRONG

Get Hip | not iss.

May 02. (cd/lp) *(GH 1103 CD/LP)* **SHAKE ME** [ ] [-]
– Take your time Caroline / Now's the time / Jenny G / Don't torture me / Paradiso twist / No other guy / Trick shot / Shake me / Foolish one / What you gonna say? / Just a little bit / Angel of love / Miserabella / Little bird.

the KARELIA

Formed: Glasgow . . . late 1996 out of rock/jazz outfit, The BLISTERS by singer ALEX HUNTLEY. Since 1994, the modest, unassuming ALEX was responsible for the '13th Note' club, which was the stamping ground for up and coming acts such as BIS, MOGWAI and URUSEI YATSURA. However, along with band members ALAN WYLIE and GLEN THOMSON (Greek drummer TASSOS BOBOS was added towards the end of '96 – the band even using the name of a Greek cigarette!), the KARELIA took off almost immediately having been signed (as The BLISTERS) to 'Roadrunner'! by Ruth Robinson after a Bucketful Of Bands contest at the Barrowlands. Prog/techno rock with IGGY-voxed overtones, their diverse jazzy film-noir Lo-fi was certainly a change from anything around at the time. Debut album, 'DIVORCE AT HIGH NOON' (1997) found some favour in the indie inkies, although live ALEX was HANNON, COCKER and even BID (the MONOCHROME SET singer to the uninitiated!) rolled into one brassy musical empire. HUNTLEY was also one of the team responsible for The AMPHETAMEANIES, a 10-piece Ska outfit into chaos and fun.

BLISTERS

ALEX HUNTLEY – vocals, guitar / **ALAN WYLIE** – trumpet, keyboards / **GLEN THOMSON** – bass

Moden Independent | not iss.

Apr 95. (7"burgundy) *(mir 001)* **A DULL THOUGHT IN ITSELF. / (other track by Urusei Yatsura)** [ ] [-]

— after the BLISTERS folded **TASSOS BOBOS** – (was on) drums

the KARELIA

Roadrunner | Roadrunner

Feb 97. (cd-ep) *(RR 2280-3)* **A SMOOTH TASTE OF THE KARELIA** [ ] [-]
– Say try / Des veaux ca taille nous une / Life in a barrat garret / Garavurghty butes.

Apr 97. (cd) *(RR 8823-3)* **DIVORCE AT HIGH NOON**
– Divorce at high noon / Love's a cliche / Say try / To his dietres / Life in a Barrat Garret / Crazy irritation / Remorse at high noon / Dancing along the nekrotaphion / Devil rides Hyndland / Infinite duration / Nostalgia / Tension / Bleach yours / Exaggeration / Garavaughty butes.

Nov 97. (cd-s) *(RR 2253-3)* **LOVE'S A CLICHE / LOVE'S A THROWAWAY CLICHE / LOVE'S A MORBID CLICHE / LOVE'S A RELENTLESS CLICHE** -

Flotsam & Jetsam | not iss.

May 98. (7") *(SHaG 13.07)* **Club Beatroot Part Seven** -
– Summer in Spain / (other track by the Poison Sisters).
(above was released in conjunction with 'The 13th Note')

Jun 98. (7") *(SHaG 019)* **VISION IN A WORLD WITHOUT SPECTACLES. / (other track by El Hombre Trajeado)** -

— Nov'98 and signed to 'Guided Missile', the band appeared on a 'Glasgow' d7"EP (with track 'NEW YEAR IN NEW YORK') alongside MOGWAI, YUMMY FUR and EL HOMBRE TRAJEADO. The KARELIA also contributed the track 'THE ONLY DIFFERENCE' to the labels' V/A comp 'Hits & Missiles'. Early in 2000, THE KARELIA shared an EP, '15 Minutes With The Smiths', alongside three Argentinian groups; GRAND PRIX, FUN PEOPLE and ULTRAMAR.

KASINO

Formed: Bellshill, nr. Glasgow . . . 1997 by Inverness-born singer/guitarist GARY MARSHALL, along with MARK CLINTON, CHRIS WARDEN and CALUM MacARTHUR; the latter from the Isle Of Lewis. Disgarding the oft too inspiring TEENAGE FANCLUB and the BMX BANDITS comparisons, KASINO showed they might be more than capable of taking the mantle from the likes of FEEDER, MANSUN or RADIOHEAD. Their one and only EP, 'YOU DON'T HAVE TO BE ALONE', was piano-led Rock although dull and uninspiring.

GARY MARSHALL – vocals, guitar / **MARK CLINTON** – guitar / **CHRIS WARDEN** – bass / **CALUM MacARTHUR** – drums

Sarcastic | not iss.

Jul 00. (cd-ep) **YOU DON'T HAVE TO BE ALONE** -
– Eyes / Catch / Turnaround / You don't have to be alone.

KETTEL (see under ⇒ Mouthmoth records)

KHARTOUM HEROES (see under ⇒ Fence records)

KHAYA

Formed: Edinburgh . . . 1996 by DAN MUTCH, GREG DODGSON, JOHN MACKIE and RICHIE ANDERSON. An early spot on local radio led to the quartet contributing a handful of tracks to 'S.L.' compilation album, 'It's A Life Sentence . . .' in 1997, the same year they released a debut single proper, 'SUMMER/WINTER SONG'. With an enthusiastic response from the likes of Steve Lamacq, John Peel and Jo Whiley, the band were spurred on to bigger and better things. These included a follow-up single, 'TWO SONGS BY KHAYA', a performance at the Edinburgh Fringe's 'Planet Pop' festival and the recruitment of a mini string section (violinist CAROLINE EVANS and cellist PETE HARVEY).

The fruits of their labour paid off with 1998's debut album, 'WE'VE GOT RHYMES 4 X LIKE THESE', a record that generated enough interest for a live performance on Radio Scotland and much airplay on Radio One's Evening Session. A subsequent Peel session was followed by abortive sessions for a second album, the band eventually knuckling down at Chamber Studios in Granton where they recorded 'AVOIDANCE' (1999). Again the record brought widespread critical acclaim with reviewers mentioning the likes of BELLE & SEBASTIAN and PAVEMENT. ARAB STRAP meets STEPS may be just a bridge too far in an attempt to describe their hook-laden sound but successive rounds of sold out gigs are testament to KHAYA's appeal. A new mini-set, 'THE LOST FEELING', was released early in 2001.

DAN MUTCH – vocals, guitar / **GREG DODGSON** – keyboards / **JOHN MACKIE** – bass / **RICHIE ANDERSON** – drums

sl | not iss.

May 97. (cd; Various Artists) *(lone 01)* **It's A Life Sentence . . .** -
– Here / It couldn't be worse / Snow song / (tracks.. other artists).

Nov 97. (7") *(lone 02)* **SUMMER/WINTER SONG. / I GET UPSET AT ALL THE RIGHT THINGS / M-MENU** -

Apr 98. (7") *(lone 04)* **TWO SONGS BY KHAYA** -
– Duet / Boy, girl dependence.

— added **CAROLINE EVENS** – violin / **PETE HARVEY** – cello

Koala Music | not iss.

Nov 98. (cd) *(KMCD 003)* **WE'VE GOT RHYMES 4 X LIKE THESE** -
– M-menu / Love and whips / Sing-a-song / Wives and lovers / We've got rhymes / Fever / Edward and Merlin / Baby, don't bother / Sportsday / Ground.

Mar 99. (10"blue-ep) *(KMVS 005)* **LOVE AND WHIPS EP** (acoustic) -
– Swap boots / It's worth trying / DAN MUTCH – Swap boots.

— now with **RUAIRIDH** – guitar (on tour)

sl | not iss.

Nov 99. (cd) *(lone 05)* **AVOIDANCE** -
– Rag / Do the thing / Avoidance / Take off / This is the most sad song / Western theme tune / Wild friends / Husbands / Music is 4 pussies Morning sounds / Baby, you terrify me.

Mar 00. (7"ep) *(lone 07)* **DO THE THING BY KHAYA** -
– Do the thing / Dan and Greg / John and Richie.

Feb 01. (m-cd) *(lone 09)* **THE LOST FEELING** -
– The vampires / I hate fucking / Death 2 numbers / More argument / The lost feeling / Acoustic guitar.

DESC

DAN MUTCH + HELENA MacGILP

sl | not iss.

Apr 02. (cd) *(lone 12)* **UP HERE IN THE HEAT** -
– I look after / Up here / City gallery / Untitled / Joy / Decision / Forgiveness.

Mary KIANI

Born: Glasgow. With her dusky latina good looks and orgasmic diva wail, KIANI helped turn techno-synth merchants THE TIME FREQUENCY into a chart topping Scottish act that also reached the UK Top 10 and very nearly made the big time. KIANI stamped her stiletto vocal all over Caledonian rave anthems such as 'REAL LOVE', 'NEW EMOTION' and 'ULTIMATE HIGH', all sizeable hits for TTF in their heyday. Following a controversial split with the group at the height of their fame, KIANI re-emerged as a solo act and hit the UK Top 20 in summer '95 with the slightly softer pop-dance of 'WHEN I CALL YOUR NAME'. Although follow-up single, 'I GIVE IT ALL TO YOU' was only a minor hit, a subsequent cover of Shannon's disco classic, 'LET THE MUSIC PLAY' saw her back in the Top 20 come spring '96. '100%' kept up the momentum in early '97 but KIANI's career began to falter as a perhaps rather unadvised cover of U2's 'WITH OR WITHOUT YOU' stalled outside the Top 40. Her long – probably too long – awaited debut album, 'LONG HARD FUNKY DREAMS' was finally released in summer '97 and its poor performance signalled the end of her 'Mercury' deal as fans were left to ponder just what might've been had TTF and KIANI stuck together.

MARY KIANI – vocals (ex-THE TIME FREQUENCY) / with various technicians

Mercury | not iss.

Jul 95. (c-s) *(MERMC 440)* **WHEN I CALL YOUR NAME** 18 -
(12"+=/cd-s+=) *(MER X/CD 440)* – ('A'mixes).

Dec 95. (c-s) *(MERMC 449)* **I GIVE IT ALL TO YOU / I IMAGINE** 35 -
(12"+=/cd-s+=) *(MER X/CD 449)* – ('B'mixes; Mister Spring or Motiv8 & EFM).

Apr 96. (c-s) *(MERMC 456)* **LET THE MUSIC PLAY / LET THE MUSIC PLAY (Perfecto radio)** 19 -
(12"+=/cd-s+=) *(MER X/CD 456)* – ('A'mixes; Motiv8 club / Mr. Spring Contrary Mary / Perfecto vocal / Argonauts Kiani Do This / Mr. Spring club).

Jan 97. (c-s) *(MERMC 469)* **100% / 100% (mixes)** 23 -
(12"+=/cd-s+=) *(MER X/CD 469)* – ('A'mixes; Lord 'n' Elliot / One World radio / Tall Paul / Dr.Ju / Qattara / Motiv8 / Eddy Fingers).

Jun 97. (c-s) *(MERC 487)* **WITH OR WITHOUT YOU (mixes)** 46 -
(12"+=/cd-s+=) *(MER X/CD 487)* – ('A'mixes).

Jun 97. (cd/c) *(534512-2/-4)* **LONG HARD FUNKY DREAMS**
– When I call your name / Till death do us disco / With or without you / Long hard funky dreams / If I see you again / Let the music play / We can be one / 100% / I imagine / Blame it on the night / I knew / Beautiful day / Memories / I give it all to you. *(d-cd+=; 534511-2)* – When I call your name (hardfloor vocal mix) / Let the music play (Perfecto vocal mix) / I imagine (Mr. Spring club mix) / 100% (Tall Paul remix) / Let the music play (Union Jack mix) / I give it all to you (Umboza mix) / When I call your name (Motiv8 special club mix). *(re-iss. Aug98; same)*
above was her last solo release for some time

ZYX | not iss.

Jan 01. (12"/cd-s) *(JAM 1004-12/8)* **WRAP YOU UP (mixes)** -

James KING

Born: Glasgow. KING first came to the attention of the public when his "hardman" persona, JIMMY LOSER, played guitar for punk combo, the REV VOLTING BACKSTABBERS. This group subsequently evolved into FUN 4 (alongside REV THOMAS, COLIN McNEIL and STEVEN DALY), finally issuing their debut EP, 'SINGING IN THE SHADOWS', at the turn of the decade. In 1981, with DALY now an ORANGE JUICE recruit, KING was signed to 'Virgin', although only two singles made it to release stage. Rumours were rife (at the time) that KING had once allegedly pulled a knife on a young EDWYN COLLINS, normal practice for an up and coming bovver boy you could say; KING's guitarist, JAMES MASON (no, not the actor!), also had a few run-ins with the law. Now competing with the likes of LLOYD COLE & THE COMMOTIONS, JAMES KING & THE LONE WOLVES embarked on their own mid-80's mission to make the charts. Unfortunately, after only a couple of singles, 'TEXAS LULLABY' and 'THE ANGELS KNOW', KING split the group up.

JAMES KING – guitar / **REV THOMAS** – vocals / **COLIN NEIL** – bass / **STEVEN DALY** – drums

N.M.C. — not iss.

Jan 80. (7"ep; as FUN 4) *(NMC 010)* **SINGING IN THE SHADOWS EP** [ ] [-]
– Singing in the shadows / Elevator crash / By products.

— **KING** – (now on vocals & guitar) + **NEIL** recruited **JAMES MASON** – guitar / **FRASER SCOTT** – drums

Virgin — not iss.

Feb 81. (7") *(VS 405)* **BACK FROM THE DEAD. / MY REWARD / AS TEARS GO BY** [ ] [-]
Oct 81. (7"; as JAMES KING & THE LONE WOLVES) *(VS 454)* **I TRIED. / SO ALONE** [ ] [-]

— **MICK + JAKE** repl. JAMES MASON (to jail) + FRASER SCOTT

Thrush — not iss.

Nov 83. (12"ep; as JAMES KING & THE LONE WOLVES) *(THRUSH 2)* **TEXAS LULLABY EP** [ ] [-]
– Texas lullaby / Sacred heart / Chance I can't deny / Until the dawn / Lost.

Swamplands — not iss.

Jan 85. (7"; as JAMES KING & THE LONE WOLVES) *(SWP 3)* **THE ANGELS KNOW. / DON'T CARE IF YOU LIVE OR DIE** [ ] [-]
(12"+=) *(SWX 3)* – Ready to fall.

Expansion — not iss.

Jun 87. (7") *(EXPAND 8)* **EASY LOVE. / HEARTBREAK, SORROW AND PAIN** [ ] [-]
Apr 88. (12") *(EXPAND 12)* **STORYTELLER (dance mix). / STORYTELER (version)** [ ] [-]

— retired from his solo career after above (a different JAMES KING released stuff on 'Rounder' in the mid-90's)

KING BISCUIT TIME (see under ⇒ BETA BAND)

KING CREOSOTE (see under ⇒ Fence records)

KING HASH

Formed: Edinburgh ... 1992 by GERRY McCUSKER and SCOTT RICHARDSON. A rootsy R&B outfit fusing The FACES, CREEDENCE CLEARWATER REVIVAL and The BLACK CROWES, KING HASH were smokin' right from the word go. After a reasonably successful tour of Caledonia between '92 and '93, the band delivered a promising debut for 'Iona Gold' (normally a folk imprint) under the glorious title, 'HUMDINGER'. Hooking the listener line'n'sinker with its cool panache and warm melodies, the album should have made KING HASH kings of British R&B. Instead, they chilled out somewhere else.

GERRY McCUSKER – vocals, guitar / **SCOTT RICHARDSON** – vocals, guitar

Iona Gold — not iss.

Jun 93. (cd-s) *(IGS 2011)* **I'M THE ONE / LEAVE A LIGHT ON / HARD AS I TRY** [ ] [-]
Jun 93. (cd/c) *(IGCD/IGC 201)* **HUMDINGER** [ ] [-]
– Hard as I try / I'm the one / Jessie May / Hey now / All I ever wanted was you / She's on the move / Deliver me from evil / What can I do / Leave a light on / Jack fell down / Jessie May (reprise).

— split after above

KING L (see under ⇒ DANNY WILSON)

KITCHEN (see under ⇒ BIS)

KITCHEN CYNICS

Formed: Aberdeen ... 1988 as the psychedelic brainchild of ALAN DAVIDSON. Possibly the only Scottish act ever to have the bulk of their records released in Germany only, the cornily-named KITCHEN CYNICS issued a series of limited cassettes and occasional vinyl on the continent over the period 1988-1995. Clearly a driven man, DAVIDSON (with part-time help from JIM WILKIE) milked his wayward muse for all it was worth, his quaint psychedelia likely to appeal to fans of SYD BARRETT's 'Madcap' era. After signing off with two EP's, 'MIMOSA' and 'WESTMINSTER CHIMES' in 1994 and '95 respectively, the Cynical ALAN's recording career seemingly went down the kitchen plughole. • **Note:** not to be confused with the COUNTRY TEASERS offshoot outfit, ALAN COUNTRY DAVIDSON.

ALAN DAVIDSON – vocals, guitar / with at times **JIM WILKIE**

Bi-Joopiter — not iss.

1988. (ltd-c) *(none)* **A GIRL EATS THE MOON** [-] [-] German

Les Enfants Du Paradiddle — not iss.

1989. (ltd-c) *(ENF 1)* **CEREBRAL SECURITY** [-] [-] German
1989. (ltd-c) *(ENF 2)* **BUZZZZZZ** [-] [-] German
1989. (ltd-c) *(ENF 3)* **LITTLE DEATHS** [-] [-] German
1990. (ltd-c) *(ENF 4)* **SCHMERZ BABIES** [-] [-] German
1991. (ltd-c) *(ENF 5)* **TRICK CYCLISTS** [-] [-] German
1991. (ltd-c) *(ENF 6)* **GHOSTS OF WASPS** [-] [-] German

Roman Cabbage — not iss.

1991. (ltd-7"ep) *(GREY 7)* **STICKLEBACKS** [-] [-] German
– My cloudy heart / I still remember your eyes / Face to face / Anyone can take your place.
1992. (ltd-lp) *(GREY 11)* **CAN YOUR HEAR THE FROG?** [-] [-] German
(re-iss. 1990's on 'Get Happy!!'; BIG 04)
1992. (ltd-lp) *(GREY 12)* **TIME OF SANDS** [-] [-] German
(re-iss. 1990's on 'Get Happy!!'; BIG 03)

Les Enfants Du Paradiddle — not iss.

1992. (ltd-c) *(ENF 8)* **THIS LITTLE HEADACHE** [-] [-] German
(re-iss. 1995 on 'Acid Tapes'; TAB 110)

Acid Tapes — not iss.

1993. (ltd-c) *(TAB 096)* **SEAGULL GIRLS** [-] [-] German

Whitey W. Davis — not iss.

1993. (ltd-lp) *(SATURN 93-II)* **FADED AND TORN** [-] [-] German
1994. (ltd-one-sided-7") *(SATURN 94-III)* **SHE WAS EVERYTHING** [-] [-] German
1994. (ltd-lp) *(test-press)* **VICE VERSES** [-] [-] German

Les Enfants Du Paradiddle — not iss.

1994. (ltd-c) *(ENF 10)* **SECRET ROOMS** [-] [-] German
1994. (ltd-c) *(ENF 11)* **KISS ME QUICK** [-] [-] German

Farce — not iss.

1994. (ltd-7") *(SENTINEL 019)* **SHE AND HER SHADOW. / FAIR TEA MAKER** [-] [-] German

Magical Jack — not iss.

1994. (ltd-7"ep) *(JACK 003)* **MIMOSA** [-] [-] German
– Mimosa / Russell Square gardens and you / What we did on our holidays / Lady under-eaves.

Hopped-Di-Hoy — not iss.

1995. (ltd-7"ep) *(006)* **WESTMINSTER CHIMES** [-] [-] German
– Westminster chimes / Dance to the music of time / The land between the bedclothes and the bed / Come little memory / This bloody cold / Seagull girl.

— ALAN retired from the music biz

KITEMONSTER (see under ⇒ ASTRID)

KITH AND KIN (see under ⇒ SWAMPTRASH)

KMC (see ⇒ Section 9: Dance/Rave)

Mark KNOPFLER (and David KNOPFLER)

Born: 12 Aug'49, Glasgow. Raised from a very early age in Newcastle (his father was an architect), MARK learned guitar and subsequently became a Rock critic with the Yorkshire Evening Post. While teaching problem students at Loughton College (early 1977), MARK and his Scottish-born (27 Dec'52) younger brother, DAVID (then a social worker and rhythm guitarist), performed a few South London pub gigs. Along with JOHN ILLSLEY and PICK WITHERS on rhythm, the group evolved into DIRE STRAITS and with the help of critic/DJ, Charlie Gillett, their demo tape was accepted by 'Warner Bros'. 'SULTANS OF SWING' – with its cool JJ CALE-meets-DYLAN style adopted by headband-wearing MARK – turned into an overnight classic . . . the rest was history.

By the time of their third album, DAVID had opted for a low-key solo career, cutting several albums including 'RELEASE' (1983), 'BEHIND THE LINES' (1985), 'CUT THE WIRE' (1987) and 'LIPS AGAINST THE STEEL' (1988). During this period, DIRE STRAITS turned into one the world's biggest bands, MARK also combining his own solo career, mainly in film soundtrack work (i.e. 'LOCAL HERO', 'CAL', 'THE PRINCESS BRIDE', 'COMFORT AND JOY' and 'LAST EXIT TO BROOKLYN'; the guitar legend also produced BOB DYLAN and AZTEC CAMERA while writing TINA TURNER's comeback hit, 'Private Dancer'.

In the early 90's and after a period away from the limelight (although MARK had moonlighted with country-folk collective The NOTTING HILLBILLIES and collaborated with CHET ATKINS), DIRE STRAITS returned to the fold once more, 'ON EVERY STREET' going platinum almost immediately.

Of late, MARK has released a couple of charting albums, 'GOLDEN HEART' (1996) and 'SAILING TO PHILADELPHIA' (2000), while his brother's last efforts were two laid back CD-albums, 'THE GIVER' and 'SMALL MERCIES', both in 1994. MARK returned to soundtrack music once again with his emotional score for the Robert Duvall-directed movie (featuring Ally McCoist playing football and acting) 'A SHOT AT GLORY' (2001). As film music went, it was pretty standard, with KNOPFLER picking guitars, backed by tinkering pianos and even rocking-out on a few tracks. The ballads were DIRE STRAITS gone lo-fi, and KNOPFLER proved, once again that he still had a keen ear for good songwriting.

MARK KNOPFLER – vocals, guitar / with various session people

Vertigo / Warners

Feb 83. (7"/12") *(DSTR 4/+12) <29725>* **GOING HOME (THEME OF 'LOCAL HERO'). / SMOOCHING** [56] [ ]

Apr 83. (lp/c) *(VERL/+C 4) <23827>* **LOCAL HERO** [14] [ ]
– The rocks and the water / Wild theme / Freeway flyer / Boomtown / The way it always starts / The rocks and the thunder / The ceilidh and the northern lights / The mist covered mountains / The ceilidh: Louis' favourite Billy's tune / Whistle theme / Smooching / The rocks and the thunder / Going home (theme from 'Local Hero'). *(cd-iss. Jul84; 811 038-2)*

Jul 83. (7") *(DSTR 5)* **THEME FROM LOCAL HERO: WILD THEME. / GOING HOME** [ ] [-]

Jul 84. (12") *(DSTR 7-12)* **JOY (FROM 'COMFORT AND JOY'). / FISTFUL OF ICE CREAM** [ ] [-]

Sep 84. (7"/ext.12") *(DSTR 8/+12)* **THE LONG ROAD (THEME FROM CAL'). / IRISH BOY** [ ] [-]

Oct 84. (lp/c)(cd) *(VERH/+C 17)(<822 769-2>)* **CAL (MUSIC FROM THE FILM)** [65] [ ]
– Irish boy / The road / Waiting for her / Irish love / A secret place / Where will you go? / Father and son / Meeting under the trees / Potato picking / in a secret place / Fear and hatred / Love and guilt / The long road.

Oct 86. (7") *(DSTR 14)* **GOING HOME. / WILD THEME** [ ] [-]
(12"+=) *(DSTR 14-12)* – Smooching.
(cd-s+=) *(DSCD 14)* – Comfort (from 'Comfort And Joy').

Nov 87. (lp/c)(cd) *(VERH/+C 53)(832 864-2) <25610>* **MUSIC FROM THE FILM SOUNDTRACK 'THE PRINCESS BRIDE'** [ ] [ ]
– Once upon a time . . . storybook love / I will never love again / Florin dance / Morning ride / The friends' song / The cliffs of insanity / The sword fight / Guide my sword / The fireswamp and the rodents of unusual size / Revenge / A happy ending / Storybook love.

Mar 88. (7"/c-s; with WILLY DeVILLE) *(VER/+MC 37)* **THEME FROM 'THE PRINCESS BRIDE': STORYBOOK LOVE. / THE FRIENDS' SONG (with GUY FLETCHER)** [ ] [-]
(cd-s+=) *(VERCD 37)* – Once upon a time . . . storybook love.

Nov 89. (lp/c/cd) *(838725-1/-4/-2) <25986>* **LAST EXIT TO BROOKLYN (Soundtrack)** [ ] [ ]
– Last exit to Brooklyn / Victims / Think fast / A love idea / Tralala / Riot / The reckoning / As low as it gets / Last exit to Brooklyn – finale.

NOTTING HILLBILLIES

MARK KNOPFLER – guitar, vocals, producer / **GUY FLETCHER** – guitar, vocals, producer / **BRENDAN CROKER** – guitar, vocals / **STEVE PHILLIPS** – guitar, vocals / with **PAUL FRANKLIN** – pedal steel guitar

Vertigo / Warners

Feb 90. (7"/c-s) *(NHB/+MC 1)* **YOUR OWN SWEET WAY. / BEWILDERED** [ ] [-]
(12"+=)(cd-s+=) *(NHB 1-12)(NHBCD 1)* – That's where I belong.

Mar 90. (cd/c/lp) *(842 671-2/-4/-1) <26147>* **MISSING . . . PRESUMED HAVING A GOOD TIME** [2] [52]
– Railroad worksong / Bewildered / Your own sweet way / Run me down / One way gal / Blues stay away from me / Will you miss me / Please baby / Weapon of prayer / That's where I belong / Feel like going home.

Apr 90. (7"/c-s) *(NHB/+MC 2)* **FEEL LIKE GOING HOME. / LONESOME WIND BLUES** [ ] [-]
(12"+=)(cd-s+=) *(NHB 2-12)(NHBCD 2)* – One way gal.

Jun 90. (7"/c-s) *(NHB/+MC 3)* **WILL YOU MISS ME. / THAT'S WHERE I BELONG** [ ] [-]
(12"+=)(cd-s+=) *(NHB 3-12)(NHBCD 3)* – Lonesome wind blues.

CHET ATKINS & MARK KNOPFLER

C.B.S. Columbia

Oct 90. (7"/c-s) *(656 373-7/-4)* **POOR BOY BLUES. / SO SOFT YOUR GOODBYE**
(cd-s+=) *(656 373-2)* – There'll be some changes made.

Nov 90. (cd/c/lp) *(467435-2/-4/-1)* <45307> **NECK AND NECK** 41 Oct90
– Poor boy blues / Sweet dreams / There'll be some changes made / Just one time / So soft / Your goodbye / Yakety axe / Tahitian skies / Tears / I'll see you in my dreams / The next time I'm in town.

MARK KNOPFLER

Vertigo Warners

Oct 93. (7"/c-s) *(VER/+MC 81)* **THEMES FROM LOCAL HERO: GOING HOME. / WILD THEME** -
(cd-s+=) *(VERCD 81)* – Comfort.
(above was obviously a re-issue. MARK also featured on HANK MARVIN's new version of 'Wonderful Land'; released Oct'93

Mar 96. (c-s/cd-s) *(VER MC/CD 88)* **DARLING PRETTY / GRAVY TRAIN** 33 -
(cd-s+=) *(VERDD 88)* – My claim to fame.

Apr 96. (cd/c) *(514732-2/-4)* <46026> **GOLDEN HEART** 9
– Darling pretty / Imelda / Golden heart / No can do / Vic and Ray / Don't you get it / A night in summer long ago / Cannibals / I'm the fool / Je suis desole / Rudiger / Nobody's got the gun / Done with Bonaparte / Are we in trouble now.

May 96. (c-s/cd-s) *(VER MC/CD 89)* **CANNIBAL / TALL ORDER** 42 -
(cd-s+=) *(VERDD 89)* – What have I got to do.

— In 1996, a collaboration cd with STEVE PHILIPS, 'JUST PICKIN' was issued by 'Buried Treasure' (TROV 2)

Jan 98. (cd) *(<536864-2>)* **WAG THE DOG** (soundtrack)
– Wag the dog / Working on it / In the heartland / Americana hero / Just instinct / Stretching out / Drooling national / We're going to war.

— in 1999, MARK released further soundtrack work, 'METROLAND', for 'Polygram' <536864>

Mercury Mercury

Sep 00. (c-s) *(562866-4)* **WHAT IT IS / LONG HIGHWAY** -
(cd-s+=) *(562866-2)* – Let's see you.

Sep 00. (cd/c) *(542981-2/-4)* <47753> **SAILING TO PHILADELPHIA** 4 60 Oct00
– What it is / Sailing to Philadelphia / Who's your baby now / Baloney again / The last laugh / Do America / Silvertown blues / El macho / Prairie wedding / Wanderlust / Speedway at Nazareth / Junkie doll / Sands of Nevada / One more matinee. *(re-iss. Aug01; same)*

Warners Warners

Oct 01. (cd) *(548127-2)* <48324> **A SHOT AT GLORY** (soundtrack) Apr02
– Sons of Scotland / Hard cases / He's the man / Training / The new laird / Say too much / Four in a row / All that I have in the world / Sons of Scotland – quiet theme / It's over / Wild mountain thyme.

– compilations, etc. –

Nov 93. (cd) *Warners; <45457-2/-4>* **SCREENPLAYING** (solo film work) -

Oct 00. (d-cd) *Universal; (E 546601-2)* **MISSING . . . PRESUMED HAVING A GOOD TIME (with the NOTTING HILLBILLIES) / SCREENPLAYING**

DAVID KNOPFLER

with various session people + guests

Peach River Passport

Sep 83. (7") *(BBPR 7)* **SOUL KISSING. / COME TO ME** -
(12"+=) *(BBPR 7-12)* – Great divide.

Sep 83. (lp/c) *(DAVID/ZCDAVID 1)* <6030> **RELEASE** 82
– Soul kissing / Come to me / Madonna's daughter / The girl and the paperboy / Roman times / Little brother / Hey Henry / Night train / The great divide. *(cd-iss. Nov93 & Nov98 on 'Paris'; CDPARIS 1)*

Fast Alley not iss.

Jun 84. (7") *(FAR 701)* **MADONNA'S DAUGHTER. / HEY HENRY** -

Making Waves not iss.

Apr 85. (lp/c/cd) *(SPRAY/CSPRAY/SPRAYCD 102)* **BEHIND THE LINES** -
– Heart to heart talk / Shockwaves / Double dealing / Missing book / I'll be there / Prophecies / Stone wall garden / Sanchez / One time. *(cd-iss. Nov93 & Nov98 on 'Paris'; CDPARIS 2)*

May 85. (7") *(SURF 105)* **HEART TO HEART. / DOUBLE DEALING** -
(12"+=) *(SURFT 105)* – Soul kissing.

Feb 86. (7"/12") *(SURF/+T 107)* **SHOCKWAVES. / THE MISSING BOOK** -

Greenhill not iss.

Jan 87. (7"/12") *(GMI/+T 9)* **WHEN WE KISS. /** -

Mar 87. (lp/c/cd) *(GMILP/GMIC/CDGM 1)* **CUT THE WIRE** -
– Freakshow / Fisherman / Hurricane / When we kiss / When granpappa sailed / Hurting / The sentenced man / Dedication / Charlie and Suzy. *(cd-iss. Nov93 & Jun99 on 'Paris'; CDPARIS 3)*

Paris Cypress

Jun 88. (7") *(DAVE 7)* **TO FEEL THAT WAY AGAIN. / SOMEONE TO BELIEVE IN** -
(12"+=) *(DAVE12 7)* – Angie and Johnny.

Jun 88. (cd/c/lp) *(CD/C+/PARIS 4)* <14166 0120-2/-4/-1> **LIPS AGAINST THE STEEL**
– Heat come down / What then must we do / To feel that way again / Someone to believe in / Sculptress / Angie and Johnny / Whispers of Gethsemane / Broken wings. *(cd re-iss. Jun99; same)*

Jul 92. (cd/c) *(CD/C PARIS 5)* **LIFELINES** -
– Rise again / Guiding star / Yeah . . . but what do men want? / Falling / Like lovers do / Lonely is the night / The bloodline / A dream so strong / I will always be.

Permanent Rhino

Jul 94. (cd/c) *(PERM CD/MC 26)* <79076> **THE GIVER**
– Mercy with the wine / Hey Jesus / Domino / Every line / How many times? / Love know / Lover's fever / Carry on / Giver of gifts / Southside tenements / Father and a son / Always.

not iss. Mesa-Atlantic

1994. (cd) <92548> **SMALL MERCIES** -
– Deptford days / The heart of it / I remember it all / A woman / All my life / The slow-mo' king / Little sun (has gotta shine) / Weeping in the wings / Rocking horse love / Papa don't you worry / I wasn't there at all / Love will find us / Forty days and nights / Going fishing.

L

LAETO

Formed: Dundee . . . mid-1998 by FRASER SIMPSON, ANDREW SMITH, KEVIN D BLACK (he left after only a week but returned to the fold in '99) and ROBBIE 'DES TROY' COOPER, one-time mucker of ALEX CHARLES in the short-lived NEUROLA; the latter also worked with the man's MAGNETIC NORTH POLE (the group that is) until he took up this hotter post full-time. A year playing the toilet circuit finally payed off when LAETO were rewarded with support slots to FUGAZI and IDLEWILD. A debut EP for 'Evol' entitled 'FIELDSETTINGS' (recorded towards the end of 1999), was a Lo-Fi part-sonic attempt at sounding somewhere between MOGWAI and FUGAZI, while the flip side 'CAR – LOW' was pure sonic. By the time their first album (for 'Guided Missile') 'MAKE US MILD' (2000) was released, their grizzly instrumental rock was finally kicking in.

FRASER SIMPSON – vocals, guitar / **ANDREW SMITH** – guitar / **KEVIN D BLACK** (b. KEVIN GILLIES, 11 Nov'82) – bass / **ROBBIE 'DES TROY' COOPER** – drums (ex-NEUROLA, of/ex-MAGNETIC NORTH POLE)

Evol not iss.

Jan 00. (7") *(evol 08)* **FIELDSETTINGS. / CAR – LOW** -

Guided Missile not iss.

Mar 00. (cd) *(GUIDE 39CD)* **MAKE US MILD** -
– Rowan guerilla / Tears on the golf course / A / Wild nature crank / B / For the driver / C / Histrography / D / El Topo.

— KEVIN GILLIES has since joined YESSA DE PASO who've now become LOKI

M.P. LANCASTER (see under ⇒ MOUNT FLORIDA)

LANTERNS

Formed: Leith, Edinburgh . . . 1997 by multi-instrumentalist and songwriter JIM SUTHERLAND (a former EMMYLOU HARRIS and VAN MORRISON musician) who enlisted the vocal help of sultry sisters GINA and SYLVIA RAE (their older sis is noneother than jazz chanteuse CATHIE RAE!), who'd both grown up in the housing estates of Livingston and Sighthill. Plying their synth-pop trade around the country like the CORRS meeting IRVINE WELSH on a sunny day, The LANTERNS found themselves almost immediately on the books of major conglomerate 'Columbia' courtesy of A&R man David Balfe. Their excellent debut single, 'HIGHRISE TOWN', dented the UK Top

50 early in 1999, its lyrically poignant anti-drugs message sung with Scots accent/attitude. However, two further attempts, 'WINTER IN MY HEART' and 'IT'S NOT THURSDAY EVERY DAY', failed to generate enough interest south of the border. The aptly-titled long-player, 'LUMINATE YER HEID' (1999), was easy-going enough but just lacked the bite necessary to be noticed; if SUZANNE VEGA had been cloned twice in Scotland she'd probably sound like this – who knows?

GINA RAE – vocals / **SYLVIA RAE** – vocals / **JIM SUTHERLAND** – multi-instruments / plus **NEIL HARLAND** – bass / **JAMES MACKINTOSH** – drums / **IAN CARR** – acoustic guitar / **PETER-JOHN VETTESE** – programming, keyboards, drums, bass / **MARK 'TUFFTY' EVANS** – programming / **SHOOGLENIFTY** – chorus

Columbia Columbia

Jan 99. (c-s) *(666571-4)* **HIGHRISE TOWN / MAYBE I DO** [50] [ ]
(cd-s+=) *(666571-2)* – ('A'-Kinky house mix).
(cd-s) *(666571-5)* – ('A'side) / ('A'-Bullet par mix) / Rolling around in the rain.
Apr 99. (12"/cd-s) *(667190-2/-6)* **WINTER IN MY HEART. / ('A'-Todd Terry remix) / LAST NIGHT** [ ] [-]
Aug 99. (cd-s) *(667578-2)* **IT'S NOT THURSDAY EVERY DAY /** [ ] [-]
Aug 99. (cd) *(494836-2)* **LUMINATE YER HEID** [ ] [ ]
– HighRise town / Winter in my heart / Big boys cry / Coriander / Sensible shoes / It's not Thursday every day / Isabel / Maybe I do / Loneliness / Infidelity / Orange crush blue / Nobody knows.

LA PAZ (see under ⇒ Scotland's wee metal scene)

LAPSUS LINGUAE

Formed: Glasgow . . . August 1999 by the ficticiously named PENELOPE COLLEGEFRIEND (or PENNY), MAGALOOF TAYLOR (or MAGGIE), RAGA WU / RAGATHA CHRISTIE (or RAGS) and GUNTHOR HUNTER (or GUNT). Taking their interesting moniker from a periodical for tutors of European languages, these Prog-rock punks – mental multi-coloured spiky tops and torn clothes, et al – were on a mission to re-invent punk/Prog through the eyes of VAN DER GRAAF and ELP – possibly.

PENELOPE COLLEGEFRIEND (PENNY) (b. 1978, Edinburgh) – piano, vocals, guitar, bass, synthesizers, etc. / **MAGALOOF TAYLOR (MAGGIE)** (b. 1980, Glasgow) – Bontempi keyboards, piano, vocals, bass, clarinet, drums / **GUNTHOR HUNTER (GUNT)** (b. 1977, Perth) – bass / **RAGA WU (RAGS)** – drums, samplers

Jonson Family not iss.

May 01. (7") *(JFR 004)* **MY NUMB LEFT HAND THE PARASITE. /** [ ] [-]

Fierce Panda not iss.

Oct 01. (cd-s) *(NUNG 05CD)* **PARADE (& THAT'S AN ORDER) / MY NUMB LEFT HAND LE PARASITE / THE STRANG MAKES EVERYTHING OK** [ ] [-]
Jan 02. (m-cd) *(NYNG 01CD)* **YOU GOT ME FRAICHE** [ ] [-]
– Sheer animal magik / The terse crimp / Cumbernauld (fragments of a great confession) / Olestra (there's only one drinking fountain in Heaven) / Tangerine torso brace – The mind vice / Are we really dancing.

LARMOUSSE

Formed: Cumbernauld . . . 1997 by the duo of CLIFF HENDERSON and SCOTT WALLACE, who set up a rehearsal studio in their garage; apparently on the same estate as the 1980 movie, Gregory's Girl, was filmed. After a few years tucked away from the rigours of normal day life, LARMOUSSE emerged with a 60-minute demo tape, which they duly sent to their favourite indie imprint, 'City Slang' (home of TO ROCOCO ROT and LAMBCHOP). Impressed with their Lo-Fi, avant-rock meanderings, the label despatched their mixing genius, GUY FIXSEN (of LAIKA), who sorted out all the loose ends, especially a 16-minute feedback piece. Early in 2000, an etched 12" of the 10-minute+ epic, 'A UNIVERSAL HELLO', was dispatched promptly to the public. TORTOISE, MOGWAI and JIM O'ROURKE were artistes thrown at them as musical references, although the subtle, tempered beauty of LARMOUSSE oozed more than just the basic and simple acoustic electronica. The eagerly-awaited eponymous debut set – released towards the end of 2000 – disappointed little or no one, from the opening soundscape 'STATIC PHASE' to the final dreamy fourth track, 'TAPE', this was sheer, uninhibited genius.

CLIFF HENDERSON + SCOTT WALLACE – instruments, vocals, etc

City Slang City Slang

Mar 00. (12"etched) *(<20155-6>)* **A UNIVERSAL HELLO** [ ] [ ]
Nov 00. (cd) *(<20162-2>)* **LARMOUSSE** [ ] [ ]
– Static phase / A universal hello / Relics & artefacts / Tape.

LAUGHING APPLE (see under ⇒ McGEE, Alan)

Carol LAULA

Born: Dec'63, Paisley. Of Romany Gypsy stock, LAULA doubtlessly had the storytelling/songwriting tradition in her blood years before she became one of Scotland's most respected if undersung female artists. After learning the guitar as a child, she graduated to her first band, PLAYING FOR TIME, in her late teens while holding down a day job. By the time she'd reached her early 20's, she decided to take the plunge and devote herself full-time to music, initially playing in the jazz-influenced THIS PERFECT HEART before striking out on her own.

In a solo capacity LAULA made her first small breakthroughs in the Scottish scene, releasing a debut single, 'GYPSY', in 1989 and following it up at the turn of the decade with 'STANDING PROUD'. The latter was subsequently adopted as the official theme tune for Glasgow's 1990 Year Of Culture and the name of CAROL LAULA was finally on the musical map.

Her next move was to surround herself by a group of crack musicians and form The CAROL LAULA BAND for a warmly received Scottish tour. With a stable fanbase secured it was but a short step into the studio to record a debut album, 'STILL'. Featuring such Scots musical alumni as DOUGIE VIPOND (DEACON BLUE) and MARK DUFF (CAPERCAILLIE), the record was released on the 'Iona' label in 1992. The critics loved it and an accompanying tour saw CAROL supported by JANE WEIDLIN, the ex-GO-GO who'd enjoyed brief solo success back in the 80's with 'RUSH HOUR'. A follow-up set, 'PRECIOUS LITTLE VICTORIES', appeared in late '93, utilising the talents of her new back-up band, GAVIN McCOMB, MARTIN HANLIN and JOHNNY CAMERON.

During a subsequent promotional tour of the States, LAULA took part in a star-studded benefit event at New York's prestigious Carnegie Hall. A spin-off CD included the song 'RESTLESS' (from CAROL's debut) alongside tracks by the likes of MARY-CHAPIN CARPENTER and NANCI GRIFFITH. Back in Glasgow, LAULA wowed home fans at the newly established Celtic Connections Festival while a couple of gigs at the city's Old Athenaeum Theatre later in the year were used to compile live album, 'NAKED' (1996).

CAROL LAULA – vocals / with various session people

Burn not iss.

1989. (7") *(7BURN 001)* **GYPSY** [ ] [-]
(12"+=; exist?) *(12BURN 001)* –
Jan 90. (7") *(7BURN 002)* **STANDING PROUD. / WITHOUT YOU** [ ] [-]
(12"+=) *(12BURN 002)* – Gypsy.
(cd-s+=) *(CDBURN 002)* – Angel.

Iona not iss.

Oct 92. (cd/c) *(IRCD/IRC 020)* **STILL** [ ] [-]
– Bad case of you / Child of mine / It's true / Gonna B.U. / Home to sister / Stay with me angel / Restless / Old brick wall / By the minute / White dress / Stars with my coffee. *(re-prom.Jun93 on 'Iona Gold' cd/c; IGCD/IGC 202)*

Iona Gold not iss.

Jun 93. (cd-s) *(IGS 202-1)* **CHILD OF MINE / RESTLESS / OLD BRICK WALL** [ ] [-]
Oct 93. (cd/c) *(IG CD/C 205)* **PRECIOUS LITTLE VICTORIES** [ ] [-]
– Raincloud court / Don't wanna B / In a dream / Lonely tonight / Flowing with the river / Ode to Bob / Silent watching daughter / Takes you all your time / Close your eyes / Little Anthony / Tragedy waltz.
Apr 94. (cd-s) *(IGS 205-1)* **MRS D & G / RESTLESS / FLOWING WITH THE RIVER** [ ] [-]
— an album 'NAKED' (early '96) was also given a low-key release?

LAWLOR (see under ⇒ STILTSKIN)

LAZYCAME (see under ⇒ JESUS & MARY CHAIN)

LEAP (see under ⇒ Lithium records)

Thomas LEER

Born: THOMAS WISHART, 1960, Port Glasgow. As a young teenager at school, the young THOMAS played and sang in a variety of local experimental pop groups, although with the advent of punk rock he moved down south to London, forming the group, PRESSURE, in the process. By late 1978, again returning to his love of electro-pop and CAN, LEER self-financed his debut single, 'PRIVATE PLANE', a machine-friendly minor classic. The following year, together with ROBERT RENTAL (former musical associate of The NORMAL), he issued a collaboration set, 'THE BRIDGE', although only one track, 'ATTACK DECAY', stood out. In the summer of '81, THOMAS resurfaced as a solo artist with the EP, '4 MOVEMENTS', his first of three promising releases for the stalwart indie imprint, 'Cherry Red'. The last of these, 'ALL ABOUT YOU' (a single and his most commercial so far), paved the way for 'Arista' to snap him up (partly reviving his 'Oblique' set-up), although their idea to release his debut's B-side, 'INTERNATIONAL', was certainly questionable. However, the mid-80's was definitely his most creative period, the long-awaited debut album proper, 'THE SCALE OF TEN', finally delivered towards the end of '85. Two years later, LEER abandoned his ineffectual solo career to help initiate the 'Z.T.T.' duo, ACT, with former PROPAGANDA chanteuse, CLAUDIA BRUCKEN. This partnership began reasonably well with a minor hit single, 'SNOBBERY AND DECAY', although their short-lived professional affair was over after their one and only long-player, 'LAUGHTER, TEARS AND RAGE' (1988), was panned by the press. • **ACT covered:** WHITE RABBIT (Jefferson Airplane) / HEAVEN KNOWS I'M MISERABLE NOW (Smiths).

THOMAS LEER – vocals, keyboards, synthesizer

		Oblique	not iss.
Nov 78.	(7") *(ER 101)* **PRIVATE PLANE. / INTERNATIONAL**	[ ]	[-]
		Industrial	not iss.
1979.	(lp; by THOMAS LEER & ROBERT RENTAL) *(IR 0007)* **THE BRIDGE** – Attack decay / Monochrome days / Day breaks, night heals / Connotations / Fade away / Interferon / 6 a.m. / The hard way & the easy way out / Perpetual. *(cd-iss. Jun92 on 'Grey Area'; BRIDGE 1CD)*	[ ]	[-]
		Cherry Red	not iss.
Jul 81.	(12"ep) *(12CHERRY 28)* **4 MOVEMENTS** – Don't / Letter from America / Light as a drum / West End.	[ ]	[-]
Jan 82.	(2x12"m-lp) *(ERED 26)* **CONTRADICTIONS** – Hear what I say / Mr. Nobody / Contradictions / Looks that kill / Soul gypsy / Choices / Gulf stream.	[ ]	[-]
Nov 82.	(7"/12") *(CHERRY/12CHERRY 52)* **ALL ABOUT YOU. / SAVING GRACE**	[ ]	[-]
		Arista	Arista
Jul 84.	(7"/12") *(LEER/+12 1)* **INTERNATIONAL. / EASY WAY**	[ ]	[-]
Feb 85.	(7"/12") *(LEER/+12 2)* **HEARTBEAT. / CONTROL YOURSELF**	[ ]	[-]
May 85.	(7") *(LEER 3)* **NO.1. / CHASING THE DRAGON** (12"+=) *(LEER 3T)* – Trust me.	[ ]	[-]
Nov 85.	(lp/c) *(207/407 208)* **THE SCALE OF TEN** –	[ ]	[ ]

ACT

— **THOMAS LEER + CLAUDIA BRUCKEN** – vocals (ex-PROPAGANDA)

		Z.T.T.	Island
May 87.	(7") *(ZTAS 28)* **SNOBBERY AND DECAY. / POISON** ('A'-That's Entertainment mix-12"+=) *(12ZTAS 28)* – I'd be surprisingly good for you. (12") *(12ZACT 28)* – ('A'-Naked Civil remix) / Strong poison / ('A'- . . .Theme from). (cd-s) *(CID 28)* – ('A'extended) / I'd be surprisingly good for you / Poison / ('A'- . . .Theme from). (c-s) *(CTIS 28)* – Snobbery and Decay Cabaret Cassette.	[60]	[ ]
Aug 87.	(7") *(IMM 1)* **ABSOLUTELY IMMUNE. / BLOODRUSH** (12"+=) *(TIMM 1)* – White rabbit. (12"+=) *(VIMM 1)* – States of logic.	[ ]	[-]
Feb 88.	(7") *(IMM 2)* **I CAN'T ESCAPE FROM YOU. / DEAR LIFE** (12"+=/cd-s+=) *(T/CD IMM 2)* – ('A'-Love And Hate) / Heaven knows I'm miserable now.	[ ]	[-]
Jun 88.	(7"; w-drawn) *(BET 1)* **CHANCE. / WINNER '88** (12"+=/cd-s+=) *(BET T/CD 1)* – Chance (we give you another chance).	[-]	[-]
Jul 88.	(lp/c/cd) *(ZQ CD/MC/LP 1)* **LAUGHTER, TEARS & RAGE** – Absolutely immune / Chance / Laughter / I can't escape from you / Poison / Under the nights of Germany / Gestures / A friendly warning / Certified / Where love lies bleeding / Snobbery and decay. *(c+=)* – Bloodrush / Poison. *(cd++=)* – Heaven knows I'm miserable now / The 3rd planet.	[ ]	[ ]

— when CLAUDIA went solo the duo split and LEER retired

– (THOMAS LEER) compilation –

Jan 94.	(cd) *Cherry Red; (CDBRED 105)* **CONTRADICTIONS – THE CHERRY RED COLLECTION** – CONTRADICTIONS (tracks) / Private plane / International / Kings of sham / Dry land / Don't / Letter from America / Tight as a drum / West end / All about you / Love and flowers / Togetherness and unity. *(re-iss. Oct00; CDMRED 105)*	[ ]	[-]

LEMONESCENT

Formed: Scotland . . . early 2002 by SARAH, SHONAGH, NIKKI and LISA. dented the UK Top 75 with debut. • **Note:** not to be confused with the LEMONESCENT who released the 'ANTICIPATION' single in 2001.

SARAH + SHONAGH + NIKKI + LISA – vocals

		Supertone–Universal	not iss.
Jun 02.	(12"/cd-s) *(SUPT/+CD 1)* **BEAUTIFUL (mixes; radio / trance radio / trance / No.1 beatmix by the Terminalheads)**	[70]	[-]
Sep 02.	(12"/cd-s) *(SUPT/+CD 2)* **SWING MY HIPS (mixes)**	[ ]	[-]

Annie LENNOX

Born: 25 Dec'54, Aberdeen. The striking face and icy vocalist of 80's superstars EURYTHMICS, ANNIE LENNOX remains one of Scotland's most highly respected musical talents. Demonstrating a precocious ability on flute and piano, the teenage LENNOX won herself a prestigious scholarship to London's Royal Academy Of Music in the late 60's. She found the rigid attitudes stifling, however, ditching her course in 1971 amid the run-up to final exams.

A more hands-on approach to music subsequently found her earning her crust in a London jazz band while working a series of day jobs. Ironically, it was a waitressing job rather than her extra-curricular musical activities which would ultimately prove more fortuitous in kick-starting her career. A chance meeting with DAVE STEWART in a restaurant led to LENNOX fronting The CATCH, a power pop trio completed by songwriter PETE COOMBES. Following an unsuccessful debut single in 1977, the group changed their name to The TOURISTS, travelling club class to the UK Top 5 in 1979 with a memorable cover of Dusty Springfield's 'I Only Want To Be With You'. At the turn of the decade, with three albums under their collective belt, the trio was trimmed to a duo following the departure of COOMBES.

LENNOX and STEWART carried on as The EURYTHMICS, formulating a distinctive spin on the New Romantic synth craze sweeping the capital. The darkly intoxicating 'Sweet Dreams (Are Made Of This)' finally broke them big in 1983, topping the US charts and narrowly missing pole position in the UK. A series of singles and albums followed in a similar vein with LENNOX ever the androgynous, unsmiling ice queen with glacial, hypnotic vocals to match. The duo's first and only UK No.1 came in 1985 as LENNOX put in a thrillingly acrobatic vocal performance on 'There Must Be An Angel (Playing With My Heart)'. As the 80's wore on, the duo pursued a more conventional pop/rock sound with ANNIE's singing increasingly taking a more accessible, soulful bent. An avid fan of classic American soul music, she teamed up with the legendary AL GREEN in 1988 on a one-off single, 'Put A Little Love In Your Heart'.

LENNOX's solo career proper got underway in the early 90's as her longtime artistic partnership with STEWART finally came to an amicable end. Now a family woman with baby in tow, she showcased a more mature, reflective direction on the multi-platinum 'DIVA' (1992). As well as outselling any single one of The EURYTHMICS' albums, the album also went down well in the States where ANNIE was nominated for three Grammy awards. 'MEDUSA' followed in 1995, a covers set which threw up some interesting interpretations including Neil Young's 'DON'T LET IT BRING YOU DOWN' and The Clash's 'TRAIN IN VAIN'. Again the record topped the UK chart and furnished her with another massive solo single in the shape of 'NO MORE I LOVE YOU'S', an obscure track originally recorded by The LOVER SPEAKS.

More recently, LENNOX was reunited with STEWART for a EURYTHMICS comeback set, 'Peace' (1999). By early 2001, she was believed to have amassed a £25,000,000 fortune, although the mum of two (Lola, 8, and Tali, 6) recently split from her movie producer hubby, Uri Fruchtmann.

ANNIE LENNOX – vocals; with various session people

		R.C.A.	Arista
Mar 92.	(7"/c-s) *(PB/PK 45317)* <12419> **WHY. / PRIMITIVE** (12"+=) *(PT 45317)* – Keep young and beautiful. (cd-s+=) *(PD 45317)* – ('A'instrumental).	[5]	[34]
Apr 92.	(cd/c/lp) *(PL/PK/PD 75326)* <18704> **ANNIE LENNOX – DIVA** – Why / Walking on broken glass / Precious / Legend in my living room / Cold / Money can't buy it / Little bird / Primitive / Stay by me / The gift. *(cd+=)* – Keep young and beautiful. *(re-iss. Feb96 cd/c; 74321 33102-2/-4)*	[1]	[27]
May 92.	(7"/c-s) *(74321 10025-7/-4)* **PRECIOUS. / ('A'version)** (cd-s+=) *(74321 10025-2)* – Step by step / Why.	[23]	[ ]

Annie Lennox

Aug 92. (7"/c-s/cd-s) *(74321 10722-7/-4/-2)* **WALKING ON BROKEN GLASS. / LEGEND IN MY OWN LIVING ROOM** [8] [-]
(12"+=/cd-s+=) *(74321 28483-1/-2)* – Don't let me down.

Aug 92. (c-s) *<12452>* **WALKING ON BROKEN GLASS / DON'T LET ME DOWN** [-] [14]

Oct 92. (7") *(74321 11688-7)* **COLD. / ('A'live)** [26] [ ]
(c-s) *(74321 11688-4)* – River deep mountain high / You have placed a chill in my heart / Why.
(cd-s) *(74321 11690-2)* – ('A'side) / River deep mountain high / Feel the need in me / Don't let me down.
(cd-s) *(74321 11689-2)* – ('A'side) / Why / The gift / Walking on broken glass.
(cd-s) *(74321 11688-2)* – ('A'side) / It's alright / Here comes the rain again / You have placed a chill in my heart.

Jan 93. (7"/c-s/12") *(74321 123383-7/-4/-1)* *<12508>* **LITTLE BIRD. / LOVE SONG FOR A VAMPIRE** [3] [49]
(cd-s+=) *(74321 12383-2)* – Feel the need (live).
(cd-s+=) *(74321 12383-5)* – River deep mountain high (live).
(cd-s+=) *(74321 12383-8)* – Don't let me down (live).

— with **STEPHEN LIPSON** – programmer, guitar, keyboards, bass

Feb 95. (7"/c-s) *(74321 25716-7/-4)* *<12804>* **NO MORE "I LOVE YOU'S". / LADIES OF THE CANYON** [2] [23]
(cd-s+=) *(74321 25551-2)* – Love song for a vampire.
(cd-s) *(74321 25716-2)* – ('A'side) / Why (acoustic) / Cold (acoustic) / Walking on broken glass (acoustic).

Mar 95. (cd/c/lp) *(<74321 25717-2/-4/-1>)* **MEDUSA** [1] [11]
– No more "I love you's" / Take me to the river / A whiter shade of pale / Don't let it bring you down / Train in vain / I can't get next to you / Downtown lights / The thin line between love and hate / Waiting in vain / Something so right. *(re-iss. d-cd Dec95; 74321 33163-2)* – w/ free 'LIVE IN CENTRAL PARK')

May 95. (c-s) *(74321 28482-4)* **A WHITER SHADE OF PALE / HEAVEN** [16] [ ]
(cd-s+=) *(74321 26482-2)* – I'm always touched by your presence dear / Love song for a vampire.
(cd-s) *(74321 28483-2)* – ('A'side) / Don't let it bring you down / You have placed a chill in my heart / Here comes the rain again.

Sep 95. (c-s) *(74321 31612-4)* **WAITING IN VAIN. / NO MORE "I LOVE YOU'S"** [31] [ ]
(cd-s+=) *(74321 31613-2)* – (interview) / ('A'-Strong body mix).
(cd-s) *(74321 31612-2)* – ('A'side) / Train in vain (3 mixes).
(12") *(74321 31612-1)* – ('A'side) / ('A'-Strong body mix) / ('A'-Howie B mix).
(below featured PAUL SIMON)

Nov 95. (cd-s) *(74321 33238-2)* **SOMETHING SO RIGHT / SWEET DREAMS (ARE MADE OF THIS) (live)** [44] [ ]
(c-s+=) *(74321 33238-4)* – Who's that girl (live) / Waiting in vain (live).
(cd-s) *(74321 33239-2)* – ('A'side) / I love you like a ball and chain / Money can't buy it.

LEOPARDS

Formed: Glasgow . . . mid-90's by veterans of the early 80's 'Postcard' scene, CAMPBELL OWENS (ex-AZTEC CAMERA), MICK SLAVEN (ex-JAZZATEERS) and SKIP REID, the former two having recently split from PAUL QUINN AND THE INDEPENDENT GROUP. The LEOPARDS fused psychobilly surf and goth (play that geetar, man!), witnessed on a legendary debut gig at Postcard records Fin de Siecle club supporting The NECTARINE No.9.

The spotted ones subsequently became one of the first signings to the 'Creeping Bent' stable and, having appeared on the inaugural 'A Leap Into The Dark' (bent 001), they unleashed their debut summer '95 single, 'BURNING'. Further support slots with the SECRET GOLDFISH, SPACEHOPPER and English punk bard VIC GODARD (all stablemates at ' . . .Bent'), earned them a higher profile around the indie circuit, while a plethora of releases in 1997 made sure they weren't about to change their proverbial spots. The album, 'THEY TRIED STAYING CALM' (1997), and split 45's with ADVENTURES IN STEREO and APPENDIX OUT, looked set to put these fiery cats back into the spotlight. However, a proposed collaboration with old mucker, GODARD, has yet to materialise; though they'd have to reform.

MICK SLAVEN – vocals, guitar (ex-JAZZATEERS, ex-PAUL QUINN) / **CAMPBELL OWENS** – bass (ex-AZTEC CAMERA, ex-PAUL QUINN) / **SKIP REID** – drums

Creeping Bent | not iss.

Jun 95. (7") *(bent 003)* **BURNING. / LITERALLY BURNING** [ ] [-]

Mar 97. (7") *(bent 007)* **SURF ON. / DERAILED BY MAD DOG** [-] [-] w-drawn

Jun 97. (7") *(bent 019)* **THEME E. / (track by Adventures In Stereo)** [ ] [-]
(cd-ep+=) *(bent 019cd)* – (tracks by the Revolutionary Corps & Spacehopper). *(re-iss. Dec00; same)*

Jun 97. (cd) *(bent 021cd)* **THEY TRIED STAYING CALM** [ ] [-]
– Ju ju girl / Surf on / Motorcycle baby / Theme E / Burning / Starlings / Always on your side / Vendetta machine / Cutting a short dog / Carried by six / Full moon light / Derailed by mad dog / Piney's prayer / Being wowed. *(re-iss. Dec00; same)*

Sep 97. (7") *(bent 027)* **CUTTING A SHORT DOG. / (other track by Appendix Out)** [ ] [-]

Mar 98. (7") *(bent 031)* **STARLINGS. / V MACHINE: BACK TO CRUISING SPEED** [ ] [-]

— the group split after above

Jackie LEVEN

Born: 18 Jun'50, Kirkcaldy, Fife. At the age of 26, JACKIE uprooted to London and formed New Wave outfit DOLL BY DOLL, although it would be a few years later that the band – which also comprised JO SHAW, ROBIN SPREAFICO and DAVID McINTOSH – would make their mark. LEVEN had previously cut his teeth as a singer/songwriter performing under the assumed name of JOHN ST. FIELD, gigging with the likes of MAN until the onset of punk rock captured his imagination and inspired him to form a band.

DOLL BY DOLL emerged in punk's wake after signing to Warner Brothers off-shoot, 'Automatic', releasing a debut album, 'REMEMBER', early in 1979. Having replaced SPEARFICO with TONY WAITE, DBD issued a second album that year, 'GYPSY BLOOD', LEVEN's Celtic fringe lyrics and stirring vocals sitting rather uneasily beside the band's elaborate rock arrangements. An unusual signing to pop label, 'Magnet', the quartet delivered two further sets, 'DOLL BY DOLL' (1981) and 'GRAND PASSION' (1982), the latter seeing LEVEN employ a new band including co-vocalist, HELEN TURNER and an array of rock establishment veterans, i.e. DAVE GILMOUR and MEL COLLINS.

The following year, LEVEN disbanded the group for a solo deal with 'Charisma', although only two flop singles were forthcoming. Things went horribly wrong as the singer found himself the victim of a street attack in London, amongst other injuries suffering damage to his larynx; it went from bad to worse as LEVEN fell into a spiral of heroin abuse. He nevertheless managed to turn things around, curing himself (with help from his wife, Carol) and setting up a support network, C.O.R.E., for fellow drug addicts. During this period in the musical wilderness, he did actually manage a few gigs with ex-SEX PISTOLS and RICH KIDS bass player, GLEN MATLOCK, as the short-lived C.B.I (CONCRETE BULLETPROOF INVISIBLE).

In 1994, LEVEN finally emerged as a fully-fledged solo artist, signed to roots label 'Cooking Vinyl'. Recorded in Scotland and released only north of the border, the mini-set, 'SONGS FROM THE ARGYLL CYCLE', re-introduced LEVEN as a folk-rock artist leaving behind all traces of his punk days amid lyrical images of windswept Highland scenes. LEVEN has since released several more sets in a similar vein while working with American poet, ROBERT BLY and fellow ex-punk Fifer, RICHARD JOBSON.

JACKIE LEVEN – vocals, guitar / with various guests

Charisma not iss.

Aug 83. (7") *(JACK 1)* **LOVE IS SHINING DOWN ON ME. / GREAT SPIRIT CALLS** [ ] [-]
Jul 84. (7") *(JACK 2)* **UPTOWN. / TROPIC OF COOL** [ ] [-]
(12"+=) *(JACK 2-12)* – Beautiful train.

— JACKIE was attacked in a London street and suffered severe larynx problems which stopped him singing for a long spell. In March '88, he and GLEN MATLOCK surfaced as CONCRETE BULLETPROOF INVISIBLE, releasing the single, 'BIG TEARS', for 'Radioactive'. JACKIE was again a solo artist in the mid 90's

Cooking Vinyl not iss.

Mar 94. (m-cd) *(COOKCD 065)* **SONGS FROM THE ARGYLL CYCLE** [-] [-] Scot
– Stranger on the square / Walking in Argyll / Honeymoon hill / Looking for love / Grievin' at the mish nish / Ballad of a simple heart / As we sailed into Skibbereen / Some ancient misty morning / History of rain / Gylen Gylen / Fly / Crazy song. *(full UK-iss.Apr96; COOKCD 101)*
Jul 94. (d-lp/c/cd) *(COOK/+C/CD 064)* **THE MYSTERY OF LOVE IS GREATER THAN THE MYSTERY OF DEATH** [ ] [-]
– Clay jugg / Shadow in my eyes / Call mother a lonely field / The crazy song / Farm boy / The garden / Snow in Central Park / Looking for love / Heartsick land / Gylen Gylen / I say a little prayer / Bars of Dundee. *(d-lp+=)* – Donna Karan / Ballad of a simple heart / Stranger on the square / Horseshoe and jug / Mary Jone's dog / So my soul can sing. *(also iss.Sep94 cd+=; COOKCDS 064)* **THE RIGHT TO REMAIN SILENT** (with ROBERT BLY & JAMES HALLAWELL)
Jan 95. (cd-ep) *(FRY 036)* **I SAY A LITTLE PRAYER / HONEYMOON HILL / AS WE SAILED INTO SKIBBEREEN / THE BONNIE EARL O' MORAY** [ ] [-]
Sep 95. (d-lp/c/cd) *(COOK/+C/CD 090)* **FORBIDDEN SONGS OF THE DYING WEST** [ ] [-]
– Young male suicide blessed by invisible woman / Some ancient misty morning / Working alone – A blessing / Leven's lament / Marble city bar / The wanderer / Exultation / Men in prison / Birds leave shadows / Stornoway girl / Silver roof / Lammermuir hills / Come back early or never of come / By the sign of the sheltered star / The scene that haunts my memory / My Lord, what a morning. *(d-lp+=)* – Exultation.
Apr 97. (d-lp/cd) *(COOK/+CD 115)* **FAIRY TALES FOR HARD MEN** [ ] [-]
– Boy trapped in a man / Desolation blues / Extremely violent man / Old West African song / Saint Judas / Poortoun / Fear of women / The walled covers of Ravenscraig / Sad Polish song / Sexual danger / Jim o' Windygates / Mad as the mist and snow / Kirkconnell flow / Listening to crows pray / Sir Patrick Spens . . . / Sunflower. *(d-lp+=)* – Torture blues / A story which could be true / Scotland the brave.
Sep 97. (cd; by JOHN ST. FIELD & JACKIE LEVEN) *(COOKCD 131)* **CONTROL** (rec.1973-5) [ ] [-]
– Soft lowland tongue / Raerona / Mansion tension / Dog star / Ruins / I'm always a Prinlaws boy / Problem / Dune voices / Sleeping in bracken. *(LP was iss.1975 by JOHN ST. FIELD on a Spanish label)*
Mar 01. (4xcd-box) *(COOKCD 212)* **GREAT SONGS FROM ETERNAL BARS** [ ] [-]
– (CONTROL / FAIRYTALES FOR HARDMEN / FORBIDDEN SONGS OF THE DYING WEST / THE WANDERER).
Aug 01. (cd; as JACKIE LEVEN & DAVID THOMAS) *(COOKCD 213)* **CREATURES OF LIGHT AND DARKNESS** [ ] [-]
– My Spanish dad / Exit wound / The sexual loneliness of Jesus Christ / Hidden world of she / Billy ate my pocket / Rainy day Bergen women / Friendship between men and women / Stopped by woods on a snowy evening / Washing by hand / Wrapped up in blue.
Jun 02. (cd) **BAREFOOT DAYS** (official bootleg) [ ] [-]

LIBERTIES

Formed: Edinburgh . . . late 80's initially as the DAN BLOCKER EXPERIENCE by ALISON McFARLANE and RICHIE HENDERSON. Taking (the) LIBERTIES moniker and shelving the old 'Bonanza'-styled billing, the duo signed a major label deal with 'Chrysalis'; it probably helped that they were friends with The PROCLAIMERS. However, this good-time Rootsy rock outfit stumbled into press apathy after the release of their one and only album, 'DISTRACTED' (1990).

ALISON McFARLANE – vocals, guitar / **RICHIE HENDERSON** – vocals, guitar

Chrysalis Chrysalis

Jul 90. (7"/c-s) *(CH S/MC 3555)* **LONELY TONIGHT. /** [ ] [-]
(12"+=/cd-s+=) *(CHS 12/CD 3555)* –
Aug 90. (cd/c/lp) *(<CCD/ZCHR/CHR 1787>)* **DISTRACTED** [ ] [ ]
– Lonely tonight / Feat for a king / Strong heart / From rags to riches / So much joy / Straight down the highway / This city's in love / The clouds just burst on you / All my doubts / I've hurt enough / Colour of my car / Man in the moon.

— disappeared after above

LIFE WITHOUT BUILDINGS

Formed: Glasgow . . . mid-1999 by English-born SUE TOMPKINS, CHRIS EVANS (no, not that one), WILL BRADLEY and lone Scotsman ROBERT JOHNSTON. The quartet were all students at the Glasgow School Of Art (like TRAVIS before them) and came together through a shared appreciation of PUBLIC IMAGE LTD and TELEVISION (probably unlike TRAVIS before them). Signed to Rough Trade outlet, 'Tugboat', on the back of their debut London gig, LIFE WITHOUT BUILDINGS (incidentally, named after a JAPAN b-side) released 'THE LEANOVER' as their first single in Spring 2000. Enjoying airplay from both Radio One and XFM, LWB went on to cut two higher profile singles, 'IS IS AND THE I.R.S.' and 'YOUNG OFFENDERS', and a full-length set, 'ANY OTHER CITY' (2001).

SUE TOMPKINS – vocals / **ROBERT JOHNSTON** (b.22 Apr'73, Scotland) – guitar / **CHRIS EVANS** – bass / **WILL BRADLEY** – drums

Tugboat not iss.

Mar 00. (7") *(TUGS 018)* **THE LEANOVER. / NEW TOWN** [ ] [-]
Jun 00. (7"/cd-s) *(TUGS/+CD 019)* **IS IS AND THE I.R.S. / LET'S GET OUT** [ ] [-]
Nov 00. (7"/cd-s) *(TUGS/+CD 026)* **YOUNG OFFENDERS. / DAYLIGHTING** [ ] [-]
Feb 01. (cd/lp) *(TUG CD/LP 023)* **ANY OTHER CITY** [ ] [-]
– PS exclusive / Let's get out / Juno / The leanover / Young offenders / Philip / Envoys / 14 days / New town / Sorrow.

LIFT (see under ⇒ Lithium records)

LIGAMENT BLUB BROTHERS (see ⇒ Section 9: wee post-Punk groups)

Craig LOGAN

Born: 22 Apr'69, Kirkcaldy, Fife. As the third member of 80's teeny-pop trio, BROS, bass player LOGAN achieved a modicum of fame via smash hits such as 'When Will I Be Famous', 'Drop The Boy', 'I Owe You Nothing', 'I Quit' and 'Cat Among The Pigeons'. As a background foil to the twin-brother visual assault that was MATT and LUKE GOSS, CRAIG was always primed to be the proverbial whipping boy for the rabid tabloid press pack. Despite their debut album, 'Push' (uncannily close to a Scots term for urination methinks . . .), selling in excess of 5 million copies, things went horribly wrong come the turn of the decade as the hits didn't keep on coming and the newspapers had a field-day amid stories of wild spending and business disaster. By this point, CRAIG was pushing his own music business career forward, subsequently ascending to the upper echelons of 'E.M.I.' records. With faded 80's pseudo icons all the sartorial rage, might we suggest a "Craig Logan" t-shirt for fun lovin' minimals, ROBBIE WILLIAMS, MADONNA and their back-slapping ilk.

LONECOP (see under ⇒ TELSTAR PONIES)

LONE PIGEON

Formed: St. Andrews, Fife . . . 1997 as the concept of GORDON ANDERSON, one-time embryonic member/songwriter of The BETA BAND. After helping conceive the aforementioned musical baby for around two years (1994 – mid'96), he had to leave the group in London (their newfound base) due to ill-health. While GORDON struggled to regain enough strength to return to the band, his songs ('Dry The Rain', 'Dogs Got A Bone' and more recently 'The Cow's Wrong') were making the grade for THE BETA BAND; it seemed fate had dealt the singer/songwriter a cruel hand. However, with a collection of songs at his command, THE LONE PIGEON secured a fresh deal with Bury St.Edmunds-based 'Bad Jazz' records (licensed through his own 'Fence' imprint). Fence had delivered the very rare 'MOSES' and '28 SECRET TRACKS' releases between 1997 and 2000. In March 2001, the first few were delivered via the EP, 'TOUCHED BY TOMOKO', a Lo-Fi/WILL OLDHAM eat-yer-heart-out, mix'n'match array of melancholy weirdness; this boy was back in town.

GORDON ANDERSON – vocals, instruments (ex-BETA BAND)

Fence / not iss.

1997. (ltd-dat) *(fnc 303)* **MOSES** [ ] [-]
– Time is a white rabbit / Heaven tree / The womblight / My distant friends on Earth / Waiting / Summertime beeswing / If I find her / Born in the light of a Sunday / Rocks / Sitting on a toadstool / The Sol / Transformers / Long way down / Various gnome tracks / I came on home / Ants.

2000. (ltd-4xc-box) *(fnc 302)* **28 SECRET TRACKS** [ ] [-]
– Maheema / I'm going down / Love will grow upon the walls / Space / Man from Nazareth / Mean old mind of man / Shadow of a distant past – Scottish heart / Smoke / She came along (big fat song) / Tootle poem deafness / Waterfall (1) / Osaka castle instrumental / Pernickity jack tar deejay / Victoria's song / Rise little baby rise – Broken face / FUKEM / T.Rex teenager / Tiger alley / Sitting on a cloud / We have walked so far / Waterfall (2) / Pernickity jack tar deejay / In the summer of '64 / Can I hold back the tears? / Who are they Iain? / All in the dark can you light me? / I'm tired and I'm happy / Roundabout.

Bad Jazz – Fence / not iss.

Mar 01. (7"ep) *(Bebop 31 – fnc 304)* **TOUCHED BY TOMOKO EP** [ ] [-]
– Summertime beeswing / Touched by Tomoko / Empty town / The mean old mind of man / Waterfall.

Nov 01. (7"ep) *(Bebop 33 – fnc 305)* **ROCKS / YOU THINK ONLY BOATS CAN SINK. / James Yorkston & The Athletes: St. Patrick** [ ] [-]

Fence / Domino

Jun 02. (m-cd) *(fnc 306)* **CONCUBINE RICE** [ ] [ ]
– Concubine rice / King Creosote's wineglass symphony / The road up to Harlow Square / Heaven come down / Beatmix chocbar wrap / Waterfall / Old Mr. Muncherman / Melonbeard / Lonely vagabond / Oh Catherine / Bona fide world / The rainking / Concubine rice. *(lp-iss.Jul01 on 'Sketch'; SKETCH 00124) (re-iss. Sep02 on 'Domino'; WIGCD 109)*

LONG FIN KILLIE (see under ⇒ BOWS)

LOOPER

Formed: Glasgow . . . by BELLE & SEBASTIAN member STUART DAVID, who made his debut with the 'Sub Pop'-endorsed single 'IMPOSSIBLE THINGS' prior to issuing the electronica-based album, 'UP A TREE' in 1999. Fusing the twee of B&S with bleeping house beats and an assortment of weird instruments, 'UP A TREE' impressed indie fans of the North on its inaugural outing.

What started as a side project, however, turned into something more full-time as DAVID departed from B&S in 2000 to concentrate on LOOPER's second full-set, 'THE GEOMETRID' (2000), a record that boasted a cleaner, polished version of 'UP A TREE'. More of a companion piece, tracks such as 'MONDO '77' and 'MY ROBOT' proved that DAVID had a keen ear for dance, house and FOUR TET-inspired folktronica. His third release, the brooding 'THE SNARE' (which also played as an imaginary soundtrack to his novel 'PEACOCK JOHNSON' – and the title of track four), divided audiences with its midnight jazz and eerie PORTISHEAD-esque drones. Appearing once again, video artist KARN DAVID, guitarist RONNIE BLACK and the sinister saxophonist EVIL BOB all contributed to the album's dark blend of slow-burning, tripped-out styles, that would've felt more at home on a TRANSCIENT WAVES album than something by a Scottish indie guru.

STUART DAVID – voice, programmer, keyboards, guitars / w/ **WEE KARN (DAVID)** + **RONNIE BLACK**

Jeepster / Sub Pop

Jul 98. (7") *<SP 446>* **IMPOSSIBLE THINGS. / SPACEBOY DREAM No.3** [-] [ ]

Feb 99. (10"ep/cd-ep) *(JPR 10/CDS 010)* **BALLAD OF RAY SUZUKI. / RAY'S GOLDEN FIST (bananahand mix) / SUZUKI'S BIG RIP-OFF (twintub remix)** [ ] [-]

Mar 99. (cd/lp) *(JPR CD/LP 005) <SP 453>* **UP A TREE** [ ] [ ]
– The treehouse / Impossible things / Burning flies / Festival '95 / Ballad of Ray Suzuki / Dave the Moon man / Quiet and small / Colombo's car / Up a tree again / Back to the treehouse.

Oct 99. (10"/cd-s) *(JPR 10/CDS 015)* **UP A TREE AGAIN. / WHO'S AFRAID OF Y2K?** [ ] [-]

—— added **SCOTT TWYNHOLM** – sampler

May 00. (10"/cd-s) *(JPR 10/CDS 017)* **MONDO '77 / (ALL OF) THESE THINGS (Are Available At Tony's Textiles mix)** [ ] [-]

May 00. (cd/col-lp) *(JPR CD/LP 009) <SP 499>* **THE GEOMETRID** [ ] [ ]
– Mondo '77 / On the flipside / Modem song / Uncle Ray / Puddle monkey / These things / Bug rain / My robot / Tomorrow's world / Money hair.

—— next featured **MICK COOKE, ISOBEL CAMPBELL, MARGARET SMITH, DEBBIE POOLE, DAVID CAMPBELL** + arranger **CHRIS LAUTERBACH**

Mute / Mute

Jun 02. (cd-s) *(CDMUTE 273)* **THE SNARE / PEACOCK'S FALL / PEACOCK'S APPEAL** [ ] [-]
(10") *(10MUTE 273)* – ('A'side) / Arrow / Peacock Johnson (original).

Jun 02. (cd/lp) *(CD+/STUMM 195) <9181>* **THE SNARE** [ ] [ ]
– The snare / Sugarcane / New York snow / Peacock Johnson / Driving myself crazy / Lover's leap / Good girls / She's a knife / This evil love / Fucking around.

LOST SOUL BAND

Formed: Penicuik, Midlothian . . . 1989 by GORDON GRAHAME, MIKE HALL, his brother BRIAN HALL and RICHARD BUCHANAN; GAVIN SMITH would soon make them a quintet. One of the most criminally overlooked outfits to come out of Scotland in the past fifteen years, The LOST SOUL BAND somehow slipped through the net – a fact all the more galling when one casts a critical eye over the surfeit of suffocatingly average dross clogging up the current music scene. In GORDON GRAHAME, the LOST SOUL BAND boasted a songwriter of breathtaking depth and ability, a man more than capable of following in the footsteps of spiritual mentors BOB DYLAN and VAN MORRISON. He also possessed a stage presence to be reckoned with, attracting a loyal following in Edinburgh, Glasgow and even London where the band gigged regularly at the The Mean Fiddler and The Borderline.

A debut single, 'COFFEE & HOPE', arrived in 1991 on their own 'Lost Oyster' label (by which time GAVIN SMITH had joined on percussion), followed later that year by 'SAVE IT'. Infamous for the STONE ROSES affair, the London-based 'Silvertone' label were savvy enough to sign the band for a third single, 'LOOKING THROUGH THE BUTCHER'S WINDOW'. As with 'TRASHSCENE' (also released in 1992) the latter track offered up a taste of the live show's rootsy sucker punch yet it took kitchen-sink mini-epic 'YOU CAN'T WIN THEM ALL MUM' to really sum up the band's world weary pathos. Memorably performed by GRAHAME on BBC2's 'Late Show', the song previewed the long awaited debut album, 'THE LAND OF DO AS YOU PLEASE'. Finally released in Autumn 1993, new fans could've been forgiven for thinking the record was a greatest hits set, including as it did no less than five singles. While GRAHAME's genius shone through on the likes of 'GOODBYE BEAUTIFUL WORLD' and existentialist masterpiece, 'GOD', the album as a whole was arguably less cohesive than the hastily-recorded "promotional" set which preceded it. Apparently recorded in six days and released as a means of raising the band's profile prior to the debut album proper (confused yet? you should be . . .), 'FRIDAY THE 13th AND EVERYTHING'S ROSIE' popped up out of the blue in April '93. Subtitled 'Excerpts From The Life Of A Scottish Cowboy' with a sleevenote outlining the band's attempts to create their own brand of spiritual country, the record was spontaneous, raw, bittersweet and at 16 tracks, surprisingly consistent. It wouldn't be going too far to say the band had captured something of the essence of GRAM PARSON's fabled 'Cosmic American Music' while GRAHAME's way with a DYLAN-esque lyric encompassed all the encrypted heartbreak, black humour and surrealist poetry which such a comparison implies.

Despite rave reviews from the likes of Select, GQ, Time Out, The Guardian etc, The LOST SOUL BAND were a band seemingly out of time, largely ignored by the Grunge-fixated likes of NME and Melody Maker. Their subsequent demise was barely even noted in the mainstream music press. Although GRAHAME went on to record a much more oblique, noisy solo internet album, 'TRAVELLED SOME WAY' (2000), and play the occasional gig (prior to the Edinburgh Oyster Bars being "stylised" in the name of "progress"), it's surely something of a tragedy that as a singer/songwriter he remains a relatively unknown entity. As does his erstwhile musical companion, The SANDYMAN, who deserves a mention here for not only his backing vocals on 'FRIDAY THE 13th..' but his overlooked talent as a singer and the many late nights of rootsy brilliance he brought Edinburgh punters back in the early-mid 90's.

GORDON GRAHAME – vocals, guitar / **MICHAEL HALL** – keyboards / **RICHARD BUCHANAN** – bass / **BRIAN HALL** – drums / **GAVIN SMITH** – percussion, vocals

Lost Oyster — not iss.

1991. (12") *(none)* **COFFEE & HOPE. / THE DEVIL CAME RIDING IN** [ ] [-]

F.T.M. — not iss.

1991. (12"ep) *(FTMS 2001)* **SAVE IT. / PROPHECY OF A DEPRESSED OLD FART / IS IT REALLY OVER DARLING / SUNDAY MORNING JUST AROUND 1.00** [ ] [-]

Silvertone — not iss.

1992. (7") *(ORE 43)* **LOOKING THROUGH THE BUTCHER'S WINDOW. / HEATHER** [ ] [-]
(12"+=/cd-s+=) *(ORE T/CD 43)* – Fungus mungus (live).

1992. (7") *(ORE 47)* **TRASHSCENE. / DATE WITH FATE (live)** [ ] [-]
(12"+=/cd-s+=) *(ORE T/CD 47)* – And the Devil came riding in (live).

Apr 93. (cd/c/lp) *(ORE CD/C/LP 529)* **FRIDAY THE 13th AND EVERYTHING'S ROSIE** [ ] [-]
– Country boy / When you're gone / Leaving / The last train / H / I don't fear (I'm not alone) / The castration song / Jane / Last time I saw you / Jeanie / Strung out sister / Half the time / If this is love it's not enough / When the dirt comes falling down / Almost here / I love you.

Jul 93. (7"/c-s) *(ORE/+C 59)* **OH YOUR EYES. / GIMME YOUR LOVE** [ ] [-]
(cd-s+=) *(ORECD 59)* – I got me down I got me real down / Johnny Eyeballs.

Sep 93. (7"/c-s) *(ORE/+C 60)* **YOU CAN'T WIN THEM ALL MUM. / I'M ALL WRONG (BUT I DO RIGHT)** [ ] [-]
(12"+=/cd-s+=) *(ORE T/CD 60)* – Never ever ever / Let's go.

Oct 93. (cd/c) *(ORE CD/C 524)* **THE LAND OF DO AS YOU PLEASE** (rec. 1992 before debut) [ ] [-]
– Looking through the butcher's window / Heather / Trashscene / You can't win them all mum / Goodbye you beautiful world / These old clothes / Oh your eyes / Everything's going to be fine / God / Stranger things have happened – I used to think (but I'm alright now) / You must have been with him / 24 hour everyday / Coffee and hope / Gorgeous George and Delilah's claws.

— disbanded sometime in '94; GORDON would later go solo (released the internet album, 'TRAVELLED SOME WAY' in 2000). MIKE HALL formed dance/beat outfit SCUBA Z while BRIAN now lives in Germany.

LOVE AND MONEY

Formed: Glasgow . . . early 80's as The CRANIUMS then FUTURE DAZE. By 1982, the band had changed name yet again, FRIENDS AGAIN comprising a line-up of JAMES GRANT, CHRIS THOMSON, PAUL McGEECHAN, NEIL CUNNINGHAM and STUART KERR. Following a self-financed debut single, 'HONEY AT THE CORE', they signed a major label deal with 'Mercury' and proceeded to release a string of singles, an eponymous EP and an album, 'TRAPPED AND UNWRAPPED' (1984).

Commercial success wasn't forthcoming, however and the project was abandoned as THOMSON went off to form The BATHERS and CUNNINGHAM became the manager of PAUL HAIG. The core of GRANT, McGEECHAN and KERR carried on where they left off, dubbing themselves LOVE AND MONEY and completing their new quartet with BOBBY PATTERSON. Sticking with 'Mercury', they almost hit the Top 40 in Spring '86 with their ANDY TAYLOR-produced debut single, 'CANDYBAR EXPRESS'. The track's similarity with HIPSWAY's 'The Honeythief' (another Glasgow band signed to 'Mercury') was striking although hardly surprising given that both bands' stock-in-trade was the white boy sophisti-soul/funk-rock sound so beloved of Scottish artists in the mid-80's. 'ALL YOU NEED IS . . . LOVE AND MONEY' (1986) fleshed out their sinewy groove over the course of a whole album, balancing the occasionally overwrought guitar dynamics with a classy ballad, 'YOU ARE BEAUTIFUL'. None of the subsequent singles made the Top 40, a frustrating and perplexing situation which would come to characterise LOVE AND MONEY's career. When sophomore set, 'STRANGE KIND OF LOVE' (1988), met a similar fate, it seemed the band were destined for perennial also-ran status. This despite a marked progression in the development of their sound, erstwhile STEELY DAN producer, GARY KATZ, providing a perfectly (sometimes too perfectly) polished sheen to complement GRANT's maturing vocals. There was something of MATT JOHNSON/THE THE's dark, politicised ruminating in 'HALLELUIAH MAN' while the release of the brooding, atmospheric title track was the closest they came to a Top 40 hit single.

The subsequent shelving of a proposed third album, 'THE MOTHER'S BOY', could hardly have consoled them yet they bounced back in fine style with 1991's 'DOGS IN THE TRAFFIC'. Flirting more openly than ever with the Americana/roots element which had always lurked in the darkest recesses of LOVE AND MONEY's dusty pockets, the likes of 'LOOKING FOR ANGELINE' and 'WINTER' seemed strangely liberating. 'LITTLEDEATH' (1994) – released on Scots label, 'Iona' – merely served to confirm this opinion; 'LAST SHIP ON THE RIVER' found GRANT sounding more convincing than ever as he finally tapped into that Celtic-gypsy ley line which runs through the best work of VAN MORRISON, MIKE SCOTT, etc. Ironically, the latter set proved to be LOVE AND MONEY's epitaph, GRANT going on to record a debut solo album, 'SAWDUST IN MY VEINS' (1998). A dark and deeply disturbing album, the set marked GRANT's arrival as a major new talent on the British independent scene. Opener 'PRAY THE DAWN' set the pace for what was to come; 'ALL HER SATURDAYS' was a haunting dirge set to plucky guitars and chamber orchestrations, while 'IS ANYBODY DREAMING' was a ballad which merely displayed GRANT's soaring vocal range. The success and critical acclaim of this set enabled GRANT to extend his songwriting talents via the follow-up 'MY THRAWN GLORY' (2001), a record that reprised his previous set with much the same effect – example the excellent 'RELIGION'. 'I SHOT THE ALBATROSS' (2002) followed a year later, and veered down a more literate, gentle and poetic path. Opening with 'TALE BEST FORGOTTEN' (featuring former THRUM vocalist MONICA QUEEN), the album relied more on GRANT's sparse orchestral arrangements than his bittersweet vocals. He was also heavily influenced by a plethora of writers, adapting E.E. CUMINGS, W.H. AUDEN and NORMAN MacCAIG's words into verse. Well read, highly-accomplished and utterly brilliant, GRANT is a poet who knows it.

• **Covered:** FAME (David Bowie), etc.

FRIENDS AGAIN

JAMES GRANT – vocals, guitar, banjo / **CHRIS THOMSON** – guitar, vocals / **PAUL McGEECHAN** – piano, synthesizers, vibes / **NEIL CUNNINGHAM** – bass / **STUART KERR** – drums percussion, vocals

Moonboot — not iss.

May 83. (7") *(MOON 1)* **HONEY AT THE CORE. / LUCKY STAR** [ ] [-]

Mercury — Mercury

Aug 83. (7"/12") *(MOON 2/+12)* **SUNKISSED. / DEALER IN SILVER** [ ] [-]

Oct 83. (7"/12") *(MOON 3/+12)* **STATE OF ART. / WINKED AT** [ ] [-]

Mar 84. (7"/12") *(MER/+X 156)* **HONEY AT THE CORE. / SNOW BOOT** [ ] [-]

Jul 84. (7"ep) *(FA 1)* **THE FRIENDS AGAIN EP** [59] [-]
– Lullaby on board / Wand you wave / Thank you for being an angel.
(12"ep+=) *(FA 1-12)* – No.2 / Sunkissed / State of art.

Oct 84. (lp/c) *(MERL/+C 43)* **TRAPPED AND UNWRAPPED** [ ] [-]
– Moon 3 / Honey at the core (reprise) / South of love. / Lucky star / Lullaby No.2 / Vaguely yours / Tomboy / State of art / Sunkissed / Skip the goldrush / Swallows in the rain / Old flame. *(re-iss. May89 on 'Fontana' lp/c/cd; 836895-1/-4/-2)*

Oct 84. (7") *(MER 177)* **SOUTH OF LOVE. / BIRD OF PARADISE** [ ] [-]
(12"+=) *(MERX 177)* – Why don't you ask someone.

— Split 1985. CHRIS formed The BATHERS. NEIL became manager of PAUL HAIG.

LOVE AND MONEY

— was formed by **JAMES GRANT, PAUL McGEECHAN** and **STUART KERR** plus **BOBBIE PATERSON** – bass

Mercury — Mercury

Apr 86. (7") *(MONEY 1)* **CANDYBAR EXPRESS. / LOVE AND MONEY (dub)** [56] [-]
(12"+=) *(MONEY 1-12)* – ('A'extended).

Jul 86. (lp/c)(cd) *(MERH/+C 89)(<830021-2>)* **ALL YOU NEED IS . . . LOVE AND MONEY** [ ] [ ]
– Candybar express / Twisted / Pain is a gun / Dear John / Love & money / Cheeseburger / River of people / You're beautiful / Temptation time.

Jul 86. (7") *(MER 228)* **DEAR JOHN. / JANE** [ ] [-]
(12"+=) *(MERX 228)* – Fame / Shape of things to come.

Jan 87. (7") *(MONEY 3)* **RIVER OF PEOPLE. / DESIRE** [ ] [-]
(12"+=) *(MONEY 3-12)* – Candybar express.
(d12"++=) *(MER 3-13)* – ('A'-acappella).

Apr 87. (7") *(MONEY 4)* **LOVE AND MONEY. / HOME IS WHERE THE HEART IS** [68] [-]
(12"+=) *(MONEY 4-12)* – ('A'mix) / ('A'dub).
(d12"+=) *(MONEY 4-13)* – ('A'mix) / Cheeseburger / You're beautiful.

— now a trio when STUART KERR left

Fontana / Mercury

Sep 88. (7") *(MONEY 5)* <870596> **HALLELUIAH MAN. / LOVE IS A MILLION MILES AWAY** [63] [75] Jan89
(12"+=) *(MONEY 5-12)* – She carved her name.
(12"+=)(cd-s+=) *(MONCD 5)(MONPK 5-12)* – Wanderlust 2.

Oct 88. (lp/c)(cd) *(SF LP/MC 7)(<836498-2>)* **STRANGE KIND OF LOVE** [71] [ ] Mar89
– Halleluiah man / Strange kind of love / Shape of things to come / Up escalator / Jocelyn Square / Inflammable. *(c+=/cd+=)* – Scapegoat.

Jan 89. (7") *(MONEY 6)* **STRANGE KIND OF LOVE. / LOOKING FOR ANGELINE** [45] [-]
(12"+=/12"s+=)(cd-s+=) *(MONEY 6-12/-22)(MONCD 6)* – Set the night on fire / Scapegoat.

Mar 89. (7") *(MONEY 7)* **JOCELYN SQUARE. / ST. HENRY** [51] [-]
(12"+=)(cd-s+=) *(MONEY 7-12)(MONCD 7)* – Candybar express (Shep Pettibone mix) / Rosemary (live).
(12") *(MONEY 7-22)* – ('A'side) / Halleluiah man (live) / Razorsedge (live).

Sep 89. (7"/c-s) *(MONEY/MONMC 8)* **UP ESCALATOR. / SOON** [ ] [-]
(12"+=)(cd-s+=) *(MONEY 8-12)(MONCD 8)* – Thistle kiss / History.

Jun 91. (7"/c-s) *(MONEY/MONMC 10)* **MY LOVE LIVES IN A DEAD HOUSE. / RUST** [ ] [-]
(12"+=)(cd-s+=) *(MONEY 10-12)(MONCD 10)* – Tomorrow never comes / Treasure and treason.

Jul 91. (cd/c/lp) *(<848993-2/-4/-1>)* **DOGS IN TRAFFIC** [41] [ ]
– Winter / Johnny's not here / My love lives in a dead house / Cheap pearls / You're not the only one / Looking for Angeline / Sometimes I want to give up / Lips like ether / Whisky dream / Pappa death.

Aug 91. (7") *(MONEY 12)* **LOOKING FOR ANGELINE. / TRUE BELIEVER** [ ] [-]
(12"+=) *(MONEY 12-12)* – Hubcap to Blue town.
(cd-s) *(MONCD 12)* – ('A'side) / Hubcap to Blue town / Who in their right mind.
(cd-ep) **WISHING WATERS** *(MONEP 12)* – ('A'side) / Wanderlust II / Halleluiah man / Candybar express.

Oct 91. (7"/c-s) *(MONEY/MONMC 9)* **WINTER. / BLUE EYED WORLD** [52] [-]
(12"+=)(cd-s+=) *(MONEY 9-12)(MONCD 9)* – Dreamscape angel / Winter '89.
(cd-s) *(MONCS 9)* – ('A'side) / Wanderlust II / Hallelujah man / Candybar express.

— **GRANT + McGEECHAN** added **DOUGLAS McINTYRE** – bass, mandolin, vocals / **GORDON WILSON** – drums

Iona Gold / not iss.

Feb 94. (cd/c) *(IG CD/C 206)* **LITTLEDEATH** [ ] [-]
– Littledeath (reprise) / The last ship on the river / I'll catch you when you fall / Keep looking for the light / Pray for love / Don't be afraid of the dark / Ugly as sin / Love is like a wave / Bitches breach / Kiss of life / Sweet black Luger / What time is the last train / Littledeath.

— after they split McGEEGHAN and McINTYRE formed COWBOY MOUTH and were also part of SUGARTOWN

– compilations, etc. –

Feb 99. (cd) *Fontana; (558 346-2)* **CHEAP THRILLS AND WHISKY DREAMS: THE BEST OF** [ ] [-]
– Halleluiah man / Winter / River of people / Who in their right mind / Walk the last mile / Last ship on the river / My love lives in a dead house / Strange kind of love / Looking for Angeline / Jocelyn Square / You are beautiful / Up escalator / Wanderlust 2 / Sometimes I want to give up / Pray for love / Candybar express / Whisky dream.

JAMES GRANT

— with **DONALD SHAW** – keyboards, accordion / **JAMES MacKINTOSH** – drums, percussion / **KAREN MATHESON** – backing vocals

Survival / Valley

Apr 98. (cd-ep) *(SURCD 56)* **PRAY THE DAWN** [ ] [-]
– Pray the dawn / Walk the last mile / Call me Slim / Comakinder.

Apr 98. (cd/c) *(SUR CD/MC 022)* <15128> **SAWDUST IN MY VEINS** [ ] [ ] Sep00
– Pray the dawn / All her Saturdays / I can't stop bleeding / Cure for life / I don't know you anymore / Is anybody dreaming / No chicane / Hide / This is the last time / Sawdust in my veins / If you love me leave me alone. *(re-iss. Jul01; same)*

— added **EWAN VERNAL** – bass / **NEIL YATES** – trumpet, flugelhorn / **HOWARD McGILL** – saxes / **WILF TAYLOR** – tambourine, shakers + the BT SCOTTISH ENSEMBLE

Vertical / not iss.

Mar 01. (cd) *(VERTCD 055)* **MY THRAWN GLORY** [ ] [-]
– Minus 10 / Belle of my burlesque / Does it all add up to nothing / Darkcountry / Jaqueline's shoes / Lodestar rising / Hey Renee / I see all of you now / Religion / Blood is sweeter than honey / My thrawn glory.

Jun 02. (cd) *(VRTCD 003)* **I SHOT THE ALBATROSS** [ ] [-]
– Tale best forgotten / Long John Brown and little Mary Bell / Tragedy of the leaves / Anyone lived in a pretty how town / Wild nights / Summer farm / Triumph of hunger / Lady weeping at the crossroads / Horses / Song.

LOVELESS (see under ⇒ APB)

Alex LOWE

Born: c.1975, Blairgowrie, Perthshire. Abandoning a career in boxing (he once landed LIAM GALLAGHER a few punches!), ALEX answered a newspaper advertisement (placed by fellow-Scot, ALAN McGEE) apparently looking for a singer to reactify the career of one-time RIDE songwriter/guitarist, ANDY BELL. In 1996, along with WILL PEPPER (ex-THEE HYPNOTICS) and GARETH 'GAZ' FARMER, the aforementioned pair became Oxford-based HURRICANE – ne HURRICANE #1. McGEE's 'Creation' imprint subsequently delivered a string of chart-hitting singles, 'Step Into My World' (twice, counting the remixed version), 'Just Another Illusion' and 'Chain Reaction', all taken from the Brit-pop band's near Top 10 eponymous set released in September 1997. However, by the time of their sophomore long-player in '99, 'Only The Strongest Will Survive', HURRICANE #1 were blowing more cold than hot.

Since yon time, ALEX was in the studio devising his next, much improved solo assault. The new millennium started out well enough after he landed a three-album deal with the Japanese outlet of 'Sony/Epic'. He'd sent them a demo of recordings he'd made in a Turiff (Aberdeenshire) studio with long-time friend and producer, STEVE RANSOME; ALEX was living in a £10,000 caravan just outside Blairgowrie. Surprisingly, his debut album 'DREAMCATCHER' (released in October 2000) rocketed up the Japanese charts, boosted by a chart-topping single, 'TAKE ME BACK' – a Hurricane #1, indeed. A sophomore set came in the form of 'BOYS UNITED NEVER DIE YOUNG', issued in September 2001. A slighty more chilled-out indie venture, opener 'FLIGHT TO NOWHERE' employed the same song structure seen on LOWE's previous work, with jangling guitars, pianos and lush orchestrations.

ALEX LOWE – vocals, guitar / with various people

not iss. / Sony/Epic

Oct 00. (cd) **DREAMCATCHER** [-] [-] Japan
– I'll be on my way / Across the waves / Sperk the truth / Think of you that way / Coming down / Take me back / Sleepless standing in the rain / I do believe / Go and tell the world / Your love / Hey bulldog.

12ft Wide / not iss.

Sep 01. (cd) *(12FTCD 2)* **BOYS UNITED NEVER DIE YOUNG** [ ] [-]
– Flight from nowhere / Between times / Just the same / Darling boy / Fields (come along) / All my life / So is it time / A new beginning ends / Now I know it's right / It's understood / End.

LOWLIFE

Formed: Grangemouth ... 1985 from the ashes of The DEAD NEIGHBOURS. Consisting of ex-COCTEAU TWINS bassist WILL HEGGIE, GRANT McDOWELL, CRAIG LORENTSON, ALEX BURNETT and DAVY STEELE and having given up on punk monikers The IDIOCS, The AVOIDED and SOCIAL SECURITY, the early to mid 80's punk outfit released a couple of LP's, 'HARMONY IN HELL' (1984) and 'STRANGE DAYS, STRANGE WAYS' (1985). GRANT, WILL and CRAIG subsequently recruited guitarist STUART EVEREST and set about forming their own 'Nightshift' label.

LOWLIFE debuted early in '86 with the mini-set, 'RAIN', following it up with first album proper, 'PERMANENT SLEEP' (1986). However, it was 1987's 'DIMINUENDO' which best captured their deep, atmospheric, vaguely gothic alt-rock sound, further albums failing to progress and leaving the band sounding increasingly dated. This was particularly evident on 1991's 'SAN ANTORIUM', recorded without the talents of EVEREST and McDOWELL (the latter is currently head of C.I.D. – not a group!). After going to ground for almost four years, LORENSTON, HEGGIE and Co resurfaced with a much-improved new album, 'GUSH' (1995), the sound lent an added edge by the presence of new secondary vocalist, JENNIFER BACHEN.

DEAD NEIGHBOURS

CRAIG LORENTSON – vocals / **WILL HEGGIE** – rhythm guitar, vocals (ex-COCTEAU TWINS) / **DAVY STEELE** – lead guitar / **ALEX BURNETT** – bass / **GRANT McDOWELL** – drums

Sharko / not iss.

Aug 84. (lp) *(BITE 1)* **HARMONY IN HELL** [ ] [-]
Mar 85. (lp) *(TUFT 2)* **STRANGE DAYS, STRANGE WAYS** [ ] [-]
1988. (lp) *(TUFT 003)* **WILD WOMAN VS. RUBBER FISH** [ ] [-]

— I think their last set just comprised DAVY, ALEX + ROBBIE BUCHANAN. They became GRIM BISCUITS; ROBBIE is now deceased.

LOWLIFE

CRAIG LORENTSON – vocals / **STUART EVEREST** – guitar, keyboards / **WILL HEGGIE** – bass, keyboards, sampling (ex-COCTEAU TWINS) / **GRANT McDOWELL** – drums

Nightshift not iss.

Jan 86. (12"ep) *(LOLIF 1)* **RAIN** [ ] [-]
– Sometime something / Gallery of shame / Reflections of 1 (for Kelly) / Sense of fondness / Hail ye / Again and again.

Oct 86. (lp/cd) *(LOLIF 2/+CD)* **PERMANENT SLEEP** [ ] [-]
– Cowards way / As it happens / Mother tongue / Wild swan / Permanent sleep / A year past July / The betting and gaming act 1964 / Do we party?.

Jan 87. (12"ep) *(LOLIF 3T)* **VAIN DELIGHTS** [ ] [-]
– Vain delights / Hollow gut / Permanent sleep (steel mix) / From side to side.

Mar 87. (lp/cd) *(LOLIF 4/+CD)* **DIMINUENDO** [ ] [-]
– Off pale yellow / Given to dreaming / A sullen sky / Big uncle ugliness / From side to side / Ragged rise to Tumbledown / Wonders will never cease / Tongue tied and twisted / Licked ones wounds.

Nov 87. (7"/12") *(LOLIF 5-7/5T)* **ETERNITY ROAD. / OFF PALE YELLOW** [ ] [-]

Jan 88. (12"ep) *(LOLIF 6T)* **SWIRL, IT SWINGS EP** [ ] [-]
– Swing / Colours blue / Ramified / Eternity road.

Feb 89. (lp/cd) *(LOLIF 7/+CD)* **FROM A SCREAM TO A WHISPER** (a retrospective 85-88) [ ] [-]
– Ramified / Sometime something / Cowards way / Big uncle ugliness / Wild swan / Hollow gut / Again and again / A sullen sky / Eternity road / Swing / From side to side.

Jul 90. (lp/cd) *(LOLIF 8/+CD)* **GODHEAD** [ ] [-]
– In thankful hands / Where I lay, I'll lie / Marjory's dream / I don't talk to me / Drowning leaves / Bittersweet / River of woe / I the cheated / Mising the kick / Forever filthy / Never ending shroud.

— **HUGH DOUGIE** – guitar / **CALUM MacLEAN** – programming, guitars, bass; repl. EVEREST + McDOWELL

Sep 91. (lp/cd) *(LOLIF 9/+CD)* **SAN ANTORIUM** [ ] [-]
– Jaw / Inside in / My mothers fatherly father / Big fat funky whale / Good as it gets / Suddenly violently random / June Wilson / Give up giving up / Bathe / As old as new.

— without CALUM but added; **JASON TAYLOR** – guitar, bass, keyboards, sampling / **JENNIFER BACHEN** – backing vocals

Nov 95. (cd) *(LOLIF 10CD)* **GUSH** [ ] [-]
– Bleach / Kiss me kick / Former comrade / Truth in needles / Tocopherol / Loaded. primal / And pulled / Wicked papa / Tantalus / Petricide / Swell.

— disbanded the following year

DEAD NEIGHBOURS

Sharko 2 not iss.

Aug 84. (lp) *(BITE 1)* **HARMONY IN HELL** [ ] [-]

Mar 85. (lp) *(TUFT 1)* **STRANGE DAYS, STRANGE WAYS** [ ] [-]
below without LORENTSON and McDOWELL

1988. (lp) *(TUFT 3)* **WILD WOMAN VS RUBBER FISH** [ ] [-]

LUCI BAINES BAND (see ⇒ Section 9: the 90s)

LUCKY PIERRE (see under ⇒ ARAB STRAP)

LUGWORM

Formed: Glasgow . . . 1994 by vocalist SUNNI CARO, guitarist DEP DOWNIE, bassist GRAHAM GAVIN and drummer/trumpeter! STEVIE DUNBAR. There was a time in the mid-90's that LUGWORM must've wondered – when they would ever manage to get a record released (apart from featuring on V/A compilations). However by Spring '97, the band had two singles in the indie shops, the first 'TE LO DIR'O!' (pronounced "Telaw a deraw") was actually recorded in May '95 for BIS' 'teen-c recordingz', the second for 'Guided Missile' was a shared affair with likeminded BIS and PINK KROSS. The latter English-based imprint was also responsible for a subsequent track, 'EL LOCO BOOGALOO' (from their V/A 'Hits & Missiles' album), by which time DUNBAR was replaced by drummer DEMPSEY. If you'd mixed the POP GROUP with the RAINCOATS you'd be close to the LUGWORM sound – short, to-the-point, quirkiness was the order of the day.

SUNNI CARO – vocals / **DEP DOWNIE** – guitar / **GRAHAM GAVIN** – bass, vocals / **STEVIE DUNBAR** – drums, trumpet

teen-c! not iss.

Mar 97. (7") *(SKETCH 002)* **TE LO DIR'O! EP** [ ] [-]
– Biodegradable disco / Toby Mangel / Sweaty says / Barmitzvah.

Guided Missile not iss.

Apr 97. (7"ep) *(GUIDE 011)* **split** [ ] [-]
– Rococ negro / Harrap ageing fast / (2 by BIS with PINK KROSS).

— **. . . DEMPSEY** – drums; repl. DUNBAR

— might've released a few more split singles before their split

LUNG LEG

Formed: Glasgow . . . early 1994 by feisty females JANE EGYPT, ANNIE SPANDEX, MO-MO and Cockney drummer JADE GREEN. Taking us back fifteen years to the end of the 70's (i.e. KLEENEX, the RAINCOATS, etc), LUNG LEG first came to light via crowd-pleasing appearances at the city's '13th Note' venue – stamping ground too for URUSEI YATSURA, The DELGADOS and the similar BIS. During this 'Riot Grrr' spell, LUNG LEG managed to please journos of the Melody Maker, who duly awarded them Singles Of The Week for both the debut EP, 'THE NEGATIVE DELINQUENT AUTOPSY' and the follow-up 'SHAGG THE TIGER'.

1996/7 saw the girls support the likes of SONIC YOUTH, MAKE UP and BIKINI KILL, all of whom were impressed by LUNG LEG's spunky array of indie 7"ers, the best of which, 'THEME PARK', was issued on 'Guided Missile'. Like SHONEN KNIFE getting their nose-wiped by YUMMY FUR, the aforementioned 'THEME PARK' was a retro-fied Riot Grrr/Punk classic. Coinciding with a support slot to 'Vesuvius' label mates YUMMY FUR, LUNG LEG (with male drummer TODD now replacing JADE) delivered their long-awaited debut set, 'MAID TO MINX', in the summer of '97. Further promotion came via top slots at T In The Park, although this would be one of their last outings with MO-MO who was superseded by ex-DICK JOHNSON guitarist PHILLIPA SMITH. However, after another fresh spate of 45's between '98 and '99, LUNG LEG croaked their last breath and high-tailed it into obscurity.

JANE EGYPT – vocals, bass / **MO-MO** (aka MONICA QUIM) – vocals, guitar / **ANNIE SPANDEX** – vocals, guitar / **JADE GREEN** – drums, vocals

Piao! not iss.

Oct 94. (7"ep) *(PIAO! 2)* **THE NEGATIVE DELINQUENT AUTOPSY EP** [ ] [-]
– Punk pop travesty / Milk & water / Eek! / Anatomy of a dolly bird / secret / Dirty plotte / Friends.

Jul 95. (7"ep) *(PIAO! 5)* **SHAGG THE TIGER EP** [ ] [-]
– Small screen queen / Edith Massey / Kung Fu on the internet / Accident / Butt sister.

Basketcase not iss.

Dec 95. (7"; shared) *(FLOP 02)* **Easter Egg-splosion** [ ] [-]

Nana not iss.

1996. (7"; shared) *(NANA 1)* **ASTRAL ANGORA. /** [ ] [-]

— (mid-1996) **TODD** – drums, percussion, theramin, vocals (ex-HECK) repl. JADE

Vesuvius not iss.

May 97. (7"m) *(POMP 010)* **RIGHT NOW BABY. / WHISKY A-GO-GO / A DIFFERENT KIND OF LOVE** [ ] [-]

May 97. (7") *(GUIDE 17)* **THEME PARK. / CHOP CHOP** [ ] [-]
(above issued on 'Guided Missile')

Jul 97. (cd/lp) *(POMP CD/LP 007)* **MAID TO MINX** [ ] [-]
– Previous condition / Theme park / Disco biscuit / The shaver / Maid to minx / Right now baby / Viva by spectacula / Lonely man / F.S.R. / Kung Fu on the internet '97 / Lust for leg. *<US-iss.& re-mast.May99 on 'Southern'; 18555>*

— (mid-97) **PHILLIPA SMITH** – guitar (ex-DICK JOHNSON) repl. MO-MO

Flotsam & Jetsam – The 13th Note not iss.

Apr 98. (7") *(SHaG 13.06)* **Club Beatroot Part Six** [ ] [-]
– Por que tevas / (other track by EL HOMBRE TRAJEADO)

Vesuvius not iss.

Jul 98. (7") *(POMP 016)* **KRAYOLA. / (other track by the MAKE-UP)** [ ] [-]

Southern Southern

Mar 99. (7") *(<18560-7>)* **MAID TO MINX. / JUANITA** [ ] [ ]

– compilations, etc. –

Nov 97. (10"m-lp/m-cd) *Kill Rock Stars; (<KRS 259/+CD>)* **HELLO SIR** (compilation of early EP's) [ ] [ ] May97

LYD (see under ⇒ Human Condition records)

LYIN' RAMPANT (see under ⇒ Scotland's wee metal scene)

Mac/Mc

McCLUSKEY BROTHERS (see under ⇒ BLUEBELLS)

Kevin McDERMOTT

Born: c.1960, Glasgow. A veteran figure on the Scottish music scene, McDERMOTT first recorded under the SUEDE CROCODILES moniker with the pop-tastic-ly catchy 'STOP THE RAIN' single in summer '83. A solo mini-set, 'SUFFOCATION BLUES', appeared in Spring '86 prior to the formation of The KEVIN McDERMOTT ORCHESTRA.

Featuring a line-up of KEVIN, his brother JIM, STEPHEN GREER, ROBBIE McINTOSH, MARCO ROSSI, BLAIR COWAN and DAVID CRICHTON, the group signed to 'Island' and made their debut in 1989 with the 'WHEELS OF WONDER' single and 'MOTHER NATURE'S KITCHEN' album. Despite encouraging reviews and a series of high profile support slots (to the likes of INXS, SIMPLE MINDS, STING and ROD STEWART), the album won only a cult following. Looking back, it's possible that their failure to win over the kids was due to the band's straightahead emotional rock style not being in tune with the 'baggy' zeitgeist.

Not that musical fashion stood in McDERMOTT's way, the man and his orchestra notching up a respectable Top 10 placing in the UK indie chart with 1991's acclaimed follow-up, 'BEDAZZLED'. The album also spawned a film which was subsequently nominated for a raft of video and drama awards in 1992. Six-track mini-set, 'THE LAST SUPPER', meanwhile, served as the band's epitaph, another well received collection of uptempo rockers and sultry ballads which had critics namechecking the likes of BOB DYLAN, The BEATLES and even BRUCE SPRINGSTEEN. In the Spring of '95, KEVIN formed the GREENHOUSE outfit for a few gigs. He eventually re-emerged in a solo capacity with 1997's 'FOR THOSE IN PERIL FROM THE SEA' album, a self-financed affair followed a year later by 'FAIR AND WHOLE'.

• **Covered:** PLEASANT VALLEY SUNDAY (Monkees) and a few others.

KEVIN McDERMOTT – vocals, guitar

No Strings / not iss.

Aug 83. (7"; by SUEDE CROCODILES) *(NOSP 2)* **STOP THE RAIN. / PLEASANT DREAMER** ☐ -

May 86. (m-lp) *(NO12 1)* **SUFFOCATION BLUES** ☐ -

KEVIN McDERMOTT ORCHESTRA

—— **KEVIN** with **JIM McDERMOTT** – drums / **STEPHEN GREER** – bass / plus **ROBBIE McINTOSH** + **MARCO ROSSI** – guitars / **BLAIR COWAN** – keyboards / **DAVID CRICHTON** – fiddle

Island / Island

Mar 89. (7") *(IS 404)* **WHEELS OF WONDER. / INDEPENDENCE DAY** ☐ ☐
(12"+=/cd-s+=) *(12IS/CID 404)* – Mother nature's kitchen.

May 89. (lp/c/cd) *(ILPS/ICT/CID 9920)* **MOTHER NATURE'S KITCHEN** ☐ ☐
– Wheels of wonder / Slow boat to something better / King of nothing / Diamond / Mother nature's kitchen / Into the blue / Where we were meant to be / Statue to a stone / What comes to pass / Suffocation blues / Angel / Healing at the harbour. *(cd re-iss. Jul91; same)*

Jul 89. (7") *(IS 423)* **WHERE WE WERE MEANT TO BE. / FAREWELL TO JENNY LYNN** ☐ ☐
(12"+=/cd-s+=) *(12IS/CID 423)* – Wheels of wonder (live).

Nov 89. (7") *(IS 437)* **HEALING AT THE HARBOUR. / YOU CAN'T DO THAT** ☐ ☐
(12"+=/cd-s+=) *(12IS/CID 437)* – To my diary.

Mar 90. (7") *(IS 456)* **WHEELS OF WONDER. / SLOW BOAT (live)** ☐ ☐
(12"+=/cd-s+=) *(12IS/CID 456)* – Pleasant valley Sunday.

Thirteen / not iss.

Aug 91. (cd/c/lp) *(KMO CD/C/LP 1)* **BEDAZZLED** ☐ -
– Hole in the ground / Bad thing / Are we having a good time yet? / Curious daylight / Somebody to believe in / Walking in the light / Is anyone alive? / Master of the man / She comes from the sun / Tell it til it's true / Every-thing is over / Til the bough breaks. *(cd re-iss. Jul01 on 'Tula'; TULAD 003)*

—— now with **JIM McDERMOTT, STEPHEN GREER, BLAIR COWAN, MARCO ROSSI, RUPERT BLACK + DAVID CRICHTON**

Iona Gold / not iss.

Jun 94. (m-cd/m-c) *(IGCDM/IGCM 207)* **THE LAST SUPPER** ☐ -
– Day in a gold mine / All that I am / Another hurricane / Can't tell that to you / Overnight sensation / Too much to dream.

KEVIN McDERMOTT

Tula / not iss.

Sep 97. (cd) *(TULAD 001)* **FOR THOSE IN PERIL FROM THE SEA** ☐ -
– For those in peril from the sea / Wandering I / Blind addiction / Icarus landing / Hayley's comet / Dealing in silver / Wandering II / Navigator / Leaving Atlantis / Windows on the world / The world's address / Seeing out loud / Wandering III / The one that got away / C.K.I.S.

Sep 98. (cd) *(TULAD 002)* **FAIR AND WHOLE** (live) ☐ -
– All that I am / Where we were meant to be / Waiting on a walking song / Hole in the ground / What comes to pass / Farewell to Jenny Lynd / Day in a goldmine / Is anyone alive? / Til the bough breaks / Tell it til it's true / Wheel of wonder / Too much to dream.

Scott MacDONALD

Born: Eaglesham, Renfrewshire. SCOTT's a much-respected singer/songwriter who has toured constantly all over the world and not the SCOTT MacDONALD who fronted I AM SCIENTIST and is now part of PILOTCAN. Described as Celtic meeting country (he's known as the Celtic NEIL YOUNG) his acoustic-driven songs went as far afield as Perth in Australia and back to Glasgow via Inverness and Wick. His much-lauded first single in '99, 'BURN BABY BURN' (released on his, and producer ANDY RIMROTH's own 'Catacol' records), was picked by the Scottish Arts Council to appear on new talent sampler, 'Seriously Scottish'. It was around this period, he took his wares to the Celtic Connections and the Highland Festival, while the young man went down a storm at Glasgow's Tron Theatre that June; SCOTT even supported The HANDSOME FAMILY – and escaped! Subsequent gigs brought him closer to home via support slots with Celtic/rootsy cousins MIKE PETERS (ex-ALARM) and Northern Ireland's guitar maestro COLIN REID. Along with a new backing band in tow, MacDONALD produced his debut solo album, 'NEW HEART' and again managed to go one better by opening for folk giant, DICK GAUGHAN, at Aberdeen's Lemon Tree venue.

SCOTT MacDONALD – vocals, guitar

Catacol / not iss.

Dec 99. (cd-ep) *(Catacol 001CD)* **BURN BABY BURN EP** ☐ -
– Burn baby burn / Beautiful world / Slow down.

—— now with **MATT HARVEY** – fiddle / **JOHNNY CAMERON** – guitar / **FRANK McGUIRE** – percussion

Dragonfly / not iss.

2000. (cd) *(DRAGONFL 001)* **NEW HEART** ☐ -
– Laydown / They can't buy you / Turning tide / Caravan song / Saturday songs / Natural mistake / New heart / Eagle Bay / Home to you / Show the world your love.

Rose McDOWELL (see under ⇒ STRAWBERRY SWITCHBLADE)

Alan McGEE

Born: 29 Sep'60, East Kilbride. Moved down south to London in 1983 to become boss of up and coming indie imprint, 'Creation'. Named after 60's cult psych-pop combo, The CREATION (who recorded a track, 'BIFF BANG POW!'), the label was to become McGEE's most successful venture into the music business after years of low-key activities on the fledgling indie scene. His first outfit had been the LAUGHING APPLE, who issued a couple of 45's in the early 80's, a trial run for BIFF BANG POW! The latter outfit's debut single, '50 YEARS OF FUN', appeared in '84, the man McGEE subsequently launching the careers of such influential acts as JESUS & MARY CHAIN, PRIMAL SCREAM and of course, OASIS. When he found the time, the flame-haired entrepreneur beavered away at BIFF BANG POW! material.

Over the course of nearly a decade, McGEE indulged his love of psychedelia, punk and NEIL YOUNG with such albums as 'PASS THE PAINTBRUSH . . . HONEY!' (1985), 'LOVE IS FOREVER' (1988) and his final studio outing 'ME' (1991). Now a multi-millionaire, McGEE has always had an uncanny ability to spot innovative "indie" rock talent, the success of outfits like RIDE, BOO RADLEYS and initially MY BLOODY VALENTINE allowing him to loyally stand by less profitable artists such as EDWARD BALL. Talking of ED, he was paid tribute by noneother than ALAN's composer-cum-panel-beater dad, JOHN, who with his orchestra released 'SLINKY' (1997) – now there's a bit of trivia. Another bit was surely his £20,000 donation to New Labour's May 1997 election campaign.

In 1999/2000 after 'Creation' were put out to pasture, McGEE opted for a new venture, 'Poptones' records; one of his first signings were Glasgow-based COSMIC ROUGH RIDERS.

LAUGHING APPLE

ALAN McGEE – vocals, guitar / with others unknown

Autonomy / not iss.

1981. (7"ep) *(AUT 001)* **HA HA HEE HEE** [ ] [-]
1981. (7") *(AUT 002)* **PARTICIPATE!. / WOULDN'T YOU** [ ] [-]

Essential / not iss.

1982. (7") *(ESS 001)* **PRECIOUS FEELING. / CELEBRATION** [ ] [-]

— in 1983, the track, 'WOULDN'T YOU' appeared on a 7"flexi given away free to buyers of the LEGEND's 7" '73 IN '83' on 'Creation' (CRE 001).

BIFF BANG POW!

— **ALAN McGEE** with **DICK GREEN** – guitar / **JOE FOSTER** – bass (aka SLAUGHTER JOE) / **KEN POPPLE** – drums

Creation / not iss.

Feb 84. (7") *(CRE 003)* **50 YEARS OF FUN. / THEN WHEN I SCREAM** [ ] [-]
Jun 84. (7") *(CRE 007)* **THERE MUST BE A BETTER LIFE. / THE CHOCOLATE ELEPHANT MAN** [ ] [-]

— **DAVE EVANS** – bass; repl. FOSTER (who continued solo)

— **ANDREW INNES** – guitar, organ (became part-timer)

Feb 85. (lp) *(CRELP 004)* **PASS THE PAINTBRUSH . . . HONEY** [ ] [-]
– There must be a better life / Lost your dreams / Love and hate / The chocolate elephant man / Water bomb / Colin Dobbins / Wouldn't you? / A day out with Jeremy Chester.

Mar 86. (7") *(CRE 024)* **LOVE'S GOING OUT OF FASHION. / IT HAPPENS ALL THE TIME** [ ] [-]
(12"+=) *(CRE 024T)* – Inside the mushroom / In the afternoon.

Nov 86. (7") *(CRE 034)* **SOMEONE STOLE MY WHEELS. / SUNNY DAYS** [ ] [-]
(12"+=) *(CRE 034T)* – It makes you scared.
below credited the artist/painter, JC BROUCHARD

Feb 87. (7") *(CRE 038)* **THE WHOLE WORLD IS TURNING BROUCHARD. / THE DEATH OF ENGLAND** [ ] [-]

Mar 87. (lp) *(CRELP 015)* **THE GIRL WHO RUNS THE BEAT HOTEL** [ ] [-]
– Someone stole my wheels / Love's going out of fashion / She never understood / He don't need that girl / She shivers inside / The beat hotel / The happiest girl in the world / If I die / Five minutes in the life of Greenwood Goulding / The whole world is turning Brouchard. *(cd/c-iss.May88 +=; CRECD/CCRE 015)* – PASS THE PAINTBRUSH . . . HONEY.

Jun 87. (lp) *(CRELP 020)* **OBLIVION** [ ] [-]
– In a mourning town / There you go again / Seven seconds to Heaven / A girl called destruction / She's got diamonds in her hair / The only colour in the world is love / Baby sister / Then when I scream / I see the sun / I'm still waiting for my time.

Feb 88. (12"ep) *(CRE 051)* **SHE HAUNTS / THE BEAT HOTEL. / SHE PAINTS / IT HAPPENS ALL THE TIME** [ ] [-]

Apr 88. (lp) *(CRELP 029)* **LOVE IS FOREVER** [ ] [-]
– Miss California Toothpaste 1972 / She haunts / Searching for the pavement / She paints / Close / Ice cream machine / Electric sugar child / Dark in mind / Startripper / She went away to love / The beat hotel / It happens all the time.

Jun 89. (lp/cd) *(CRE LP/CD 046)* **THE ACID HOUSE ALBUM** (compilation) [ ] [-]
– I'm still waiting for my time / Love and hate / Someone stole my wheels / Love's going out of fashion / She haunts / 50 years of fun / She paints / She never understood / The beat hotel / In a mourning town / Then when I scream / She's got diamonds in her hair / The girl from Well Lane / There must be a better life.

Jan 90. (cd/c/lp) *(CRECD/CCRE/CRELP 058)* **SONGS FOR THE SAD EYED GIRL** [ ] [-]
– She kills me / The girl from Well Lane / Baby you just don't care / If you don't love me now, you never ever will / Someone to share my life with / Religious / Hug me honey. *(cd+=)* – OBLIVION *(c+=)* – LOVE IS FOREVER

Nov 90. (7") *(CAFF 13)* **SLEEP. / (other by The TIMES)** [ ] [-]
(above issued on 'Caff')

Apr 91. (cd/c/lp) *(CRECD/CCRE/CRELP 071)* **ME** [ ] [-]
– My first friend / Miss you / I'm burned / Song for a nail / She saved me / You just can't buy satisfaction / Sad eyes in velvet / Guilt ridden / Lovers / Baby you just make me strong.

Nov 91. (cd/c/lp) *(CRECD/CCRE/CRELP 099)* **L'AMOUR, DEMURE, STENHOUSEMUIR** (compilation) [ ] [-]
– She haunts / Someone to share my life with / Startripper / There must be a better life / She paints / Ice cream machine / Hug me honey / Miss you / She kills me / I'm waiting for my time / Someone stole my wheels / Song for a nail / Love's going out of fashion / Girl from Well Lane / Baby you just don't care / The chocolate elephant man / Tell Laura I love her / Searching for the pavement.

Feb 92. (cd/lp) *(CRE CD/LP 125)* **DEBASEMENT TAPES** (compilation of out-takes, etc.) [ ] [-]
– Long live Neil Young and all who sail in him / In bed with Paul Weller / It makes you scared / It happens all the time / The death of England / In the afternoon / Sleep / Back to the start / Inside the mushroom / Everybody wants to divorce her.

— McGEE decided to hang up his proverbial boots and sign on OASIS

– compilations, etc. –

Apr 94. (cd) *Tristar;* **BERTULA POP** [-] [ ]

CHEMICAL PILOT

ALAN McGEE + ED BALL

Eruption / not iss.

Mar 98. (12"/cd-s) *(ERUP T/SCD 004)* **ASTRAL DOMINOES (mixes: Decoder / Matt Schwartz / Profound Noize)** [ ] [-]
Jul 98. (12") *(ERUPT 006)* **MOVE A LITTLE CLOSER. / CLASSICAL FRUIT** [ ] [-]
Oct 98. (cd/d-lp) *(ERUP CD/LP 003)* **JOURNEY TO THE CENTRE OF THE MIND** [ ] [-]
– Astral dominoes / Classical fruit / Alien abduction / Bye bye lover / Chemical gangsters / Anti-American / Move a little closer / Colours / Watch the target.

Al MACKENZIE

Born: ALAN MACKENZIE, 31 Oct'68, Edinburgh. From the early 90's, AL was one half of London-based DJ/dance duo, D:REAM, along with Derry-born co-singer PETER CUNNAH. Having made their introductory live appearance at the capital's JFK bar in February 1992, D:REAM subsequently bounced onto the mainstream dance scene via minor hit single, 'U R The Best Thing'. Now signed to pop imprint, 'Magnet', MACKENZIE and CUNNAH scored an even bigger success the following January, when 'Things Can Only Get Better' stormed the UK Top 30. Equally fruitful, further singles 'U R The Best Thing (remix)', 'Unforgiven' and 'Star / I Like It', all took the same route up the charts, although just when things looked . . . er promising, AL announced his departure in October '93. An imprudent move or just totally unhappy about D:REAM's crossover into the mainstream, AL took the decision and duly paid for it when a re-activated 'Things . . .' topped the UK chart early the following year. In fact, the remaining CUNNAH lad had several other UK hits including yet another remixed version of 'Things . . .' to tie in with New Labour's General Election campaign/win of 1997. Meanwhile, MACKENZIE carved out his own pseudonymous solo career in '94, initially as KITSCH IN SYNC, who managed to squeeze out one single, 'JAZZ MA ASS', for 'Global Grooves'.

Billy MACKENZIE (see under ⇒ ASSOCIATES)

MacKENZIES (see under ⇒ SECRET GOLDFISH)

Aileen McLAUGHLIN

Born: 1963, Linwood, Renfrewshire. Blonde-maned, pouting and a childhood fan of ABBA, AILEEN took the only step probable to her – become AGNETHA FALTSKOG (or lookalike AGNETHA FALSTART). In 1988, along with pseudonymous Australians FRIDA (LONGSTOKIN), BENNY (ANDERWEAR) and BJORN (VOLVO-US), they formed ABBA tribute band, BJORN AGAIN. For the next few years, they plied their trade from Australia to Europe and all over the world – it was like ABBA had never split.

With pop outfit, ERASURE, having already topped the charts with the 'Abba-esque' EP in July '92, BJORN AGAIN decided to hit back (UK No.25 to be exact) with their own 'Erasure-ish' single featuring 'A Little Respect' and 'Stop!'; most of ABBA were reported to have loved the about-turn concept. A couple of minor ABBA-esque UK hits followed, although BJORN AGAIN mainly concentrated on wooing large packed-out venues all over the world. Interviews, were fun also, each member forgetting their origins and adopting their tongue-in-cheek "Svedish" accent.

Having supported such pop icons as the SPICE GIRLS, CLIFF RICHARD and ROD STEWART, ABBA clones BJORN AGAIN were a surprise feature at 1999's 'T In The Park'. This was duly topped later in the year, when they sold-out (to a record 9,500 people!) at Glasgow's S.E.C.C.; AILEEN had indeed come home.

MACHINE GUN ETIQUETTE

Formed: Cumnock, Ayrshire . . . late 1995 by vocalist/bassist RAT, guitarist GEORGE and drummer PARKER. Obviously influenced by The DAMNED (well, they did have an album out by that name), MACHINE GUN ETIQUETTE showcased their wares in and around Glasgow. It would be on this short tour that they offered up a demo which interested local Ska-punk combo, EX-CATHEDRA, who invited MGE as support. However, a bit of skirmish subsequently broke out between PARKER and GEORGE, the result being that the latter was booted out. SPUCK and DAVE TOUGH were duly asked to enrol prior to the quartet entering the studio to record a German-only split LP with NUTCASE and EX-CATHEDRA. They aimed their ambitions at the European market and toured Amsterdam with the latter act, although it would be on this "trip" that mushroom-loving DAVE split from his mind and the group!

Meanwhile, 1997 looked a tad more promising – to start with at least – when they secured the services of new guitarist JIM "THE BOMBER" BROWN, although after gigs with American AUS ROTTEN and Frenchies LA FRACTION, he too departed. To fulfil their touring commitments with EX-CATHEDRA, MGE borrowed the latter band's ALEX and PARKER and luckily the gigs went without a hitch (for once!). A new drummer in the shape of TOMMY (from Glasgow punks, The DESTRUCTOS) was found early the following year and he played on the EP, 'SELF DESTRUCT' (issued on Germany's 'Campary' imprint). A heavy touring schedule on the continent was again on the cards for '99, while on the recording front, a split 45 (w/ EX-CATHEDRA) to benefit a Ladronka squat in the Czech Republic and a debut 16-track 'HATE THIS CITY' (2000) was released.

RAT – vocals, bass / **SPUCK + DAVE TOUGH** – guitars; repl. GEORGE / **PARKER** – drums

		Trapdoor Recordz	not iss.
1996.	(lp) **split w/ NUTCASE + EX-CATHEDRA**	-	- German

— now without DAVE

		Campary	not iss.
1997.	(10"m-lp) **split w/ JUGGLING JUGULARS**	-	- German

— added **JIM 'THE BOMBER' BROWN** (ex-PITYKILL) then **ALEX** (from EX-CATHEDRA)

— **TOMMY** – drums (of-DESTRUCTOS) repl. PARKER who was by now an EX-CATHEDRA member

1998.	(7"ep) **SELF RESPECT**	-	- German

— unsure if the split 7" with EX-CATHEDRA was issued?

		Problem Child	not iss.
Mar 00.	(cd) **HATE THIS CITY**	-	- German

MAC MEDA (see under ⇒ Andmoresound records)

MACROCOSMICA (see under ⇒ TELSTAR PONIES)

MAGICDRIVE

Formed: Edinburgh . . . mid-90's by Inverness-born heavy drinkers (or was that lager?) DAVE ROBERTSON and JEFF HALLAM, who flitted from the capital and found DAVID JACK, KATE GRIEVE and JANE BORDWELL. Blending a speedy mixture of Power-pop and quickfire rock, this eccentric quintet emerged from indie's darker undergrowth and into beaming sunlight with their debut single 'HAD TO BE YOU' (issued on 'Fierce Panda' in 1997). The petite ROBERTSON, supported by the New Wave elements of his fellow band members, began the strange ballad with a weird opening line and proceeded through this eclectic piece with an organic mix of oboes and flutes courtesy of talented backing singer JANE BORDWELL. The single subsequently prompted a major signing to 'Fontana', although one extremely poppy single, 'BANG 2 RIGHTS', surfaced from this transaction. Another year on and another label, Aberdeen-based 'Lithium' released 'HOTEL TRANSMISSION', but the combo's everyday ambition of appearing on Top of the Pops was wearing thin.

DAVE ROBERTSON – vocals, guitar / **DAVID JACK** – bass / **JEFF HALLAM** – drums / **KATE GRIEVE** – oboe, flute, backing vocals / **JANE BORDWELL** – oboe, flute, backing vocals

		Fierce Panda	not iss.
Feb 97.	(7") *(NING 032)* **HAD TO BE YOU. / MAMMOGRAM**		-
		Fontana	not iss.
Jun 98.	(7") *(NAD 2)* **BANG 2 RIGHTS. /** (cd-s+=) *(NADCD 2)* –		-
		Lithium	not iss.
Mar 99.	(7"ep/cd-ep) *(LITH 003/+CDS)* **HOTEL TRANSATLANTIQUE EP** – The case / Japanese school girl / Overture / Hairy girl.		-
Sep 99.	(7"ep/cd-ep) *(LITH 006/+CDS)* **GRAND HOTEL EP** – Oh Christina / Anyway you want it / Argo / Houses of the Ole.		-

— although DAVID JACK joined PILOTCAN in 2000, MAGICDRIVE had not split. In fact, the man himself released a solo trip-hop release the following July.

		Knife Fighting Monkey	not iss.
Jul 02.	(cd) *(KFM 004)* **WHAT'S THE BEEF** – Very French . . .? / I don't wanna go out / Pimento / By the balls / She's got a hold on me / What would your daddy say? / Water tirture / Do not adjust your mind / Utopia / Argonaut song / What's the beef?		-

MAGNETIC NORTH POLE

Formed: Dundee . . . summer 1998 out of the short-lived NEUROLA, by Birmingham lad ALEX CHARLES and ROBBIE 'DES TROY' COOPER (the latter became only temporary as his own band, LAETO, were taking off). ALEX was also an ex-member of 'Earworm' outfit, MAPS OF JUPITER, and played for six months with the aforementioned LAETO; he still contributes on a regular basis. However, before all of this, ALEX independently issued a handful of cassettes under the BIKESHED moniker before setting up his own N.Pole Soundlab Recordings (@ L Appleyard, Ground Left, 67 Dens Road, Dundee, DD3 7HZ); he also promotes the local 'unscene' music festival.

Enlisting the help of MIQUETTE BREITENBACH, RONNIE WALLACE (ex-NEW PANS PEOPLE, ACTOR SCREAM, MOMA, etc) and ROBBIE, MAGNETIC NORTH POLE set about trying to conquer the South. Described as SIMON AND GARFUNKEL meeting SONIC YOUTH (surely not!), MNP issued a series of split releases which included some of their own work. Newcomers to the line-up STUART GILLIES and CLAIRE THORNTON have since become YESSA DE PASO. ALEX CHARLES soon resurfaced after a spell in Canada with e-mail girlfriend DOMINIQUE; she would be part of his new project THEE MOTHS alongside old buddy RONNIE (although others such as drummer GAV, bassist KAT and guitarists HILARY and JAMES).

BIKESHED

ALEX CHARLES – vocals, guitar

		Independent	not iss.
May 95.	(c) *(none)* **BIKESHED**	-	- mail-o
Aug 95.	(c) *(none)* **SOAP STAR: HOME / AWAY**	-	- mail-o
Sep 95.	(c) *(none)* **THE ENJOYMENT OF STEREO WITH . . .**	-	- mail-o
Jul 96.	(c) *(none)* **USE WEAPONS WHERE YOU CAN**	-	- mail

MAPS OF JUPITER

ALEX CHARLES with **RICHIE** – guitar / **AIMI** – drums, vocals / **CLAIRE THORNTON** – bass, vocals

		Earworm	not iss.
Mar 98.	(7"ep) *(WORM 19)* **SIX STEREO RECORDINGS . . .** – Maybe it all came true / Wait / Angled and poised / Sleeping / My excuse / Something special.		-

— when they split, all but ALEX formed The ELECTRIC COMPANY; RICHIE moved on to TACOMA RADAR

MAGNETIC NORTH POLE

ALEX CHARLES – vocals, guitar / **MIQUETTE BREITENBACH** – guitar, drums, vocals / **RONNIE WALLACE** – bass / **ROBBIE COOPER** aka DES TROY – drums (of LAETO)

		N.Pole Soundlab	not iss.
Nov 98.	(7"ep; split) *(POLE 001)* **SOUNDS IN YOUR HEAD (VOL.1)** – Caterpillar / (tracks by other bands).		-

— in Apr'99, MNP contributed to the double-CD V/A compilation, 'The Tell Tale Signs Of Earworm' (WORM 43).

		Earworm	not iss.
Jun 99.	(lp; split w/ SOUTHALL RIOT) *(WORMSS 6)* **NOISE ROOM** – Caterpillar (pt.2) / Sleep, sleep / etc	☐	-

— **JOHN** – drums (ex-WILD HOUSE, ex-NEW PANS PEOPLE, ex-GERILS) repl. ROBBIE who continued with LAETO

— **STUART GILLIES** – guitar, vocals; repl. MIQUETTE

— **CLAIRE THORNTON** – bass, vocals; repl. RONNIE

— in March-May 2000, MNP contributed tracks to a handful of V/A cassette compilations, including 'The Eric's Trip Show' (on 'Paperhearts'), 'Nobody Lives There Anymore Vol.1' (for 'Tayside') and 'We'll Cross That Bridge When We Get There' (+ CD on 'Tangerine Tapes')

		N.Pole Soundlab	not iss.
Aug 99.	(cd-ep; by Various Artists) *(POLE 002)* EP – (SPRAYDOG / NUBIA / PHARISETS + DIRTY ROSY).	☐	-
Feb 00.	(cd-s; by MY ITALICS) *(POLE 006)* **RED IS NEXT TO GREEN. / LONGWAVE**	☐	-
May 00.	(cd-ep; split w/ LAETO, etc) *(POLE 015)* **WE STARTED WITH OVER 100 MEMBERS** – As far as here the river is deep / (other artists).	☐	-

— STUART + CLAIRE have since formed YESSA DE PASO

THEE MOTHS

ALEX CHARLES, DOMINIQUE + RONNIE with others

		Tiny Pop	not iss.
Feb 01.	(cd/c) **THE NEED**	☐	-

MAINLINE (see under ⇒ Mint records)

MALE NURSE

Formed: Edinburgh . . . 1993 by vocalist KEITH FARQUHAR and ALAN CRICHTON, along with a more settled line-up in 1994 consisting of ALASTAIR MacKINVEN, short-stay ANDREW HOBSON, PAUL CARTER on drums and RICHARD RAINEY on bass; it was at this stage KEITH decided to relocate to Baltimore and vocalist BEN WALLERS (from sister group, COUNTRY TEASERS) was drafted in to fill his shoes. A demo tape was duly recorded of this line-up, although drummer MARK DEAS deputised on this occasion. THE MALE NURSE were put on hold temporarily until 1996 when the AWOL FARQUHAR returned to duty, meanwhile WALLERS and CRICHTON were both serving time with the aforementioned COUNTRY TEASERS. After a succession of drummers, around a dozen to be exact, LAWRENCE WORTHINGTON was drafted in.

London-based "superindie" imprint, 'Guided Missile', released their first offering in 1997, 'GDR'. A rush-released sophomore 45, 'MAGIC CIRCLE IN THE SKY', was next up for grabs; imagine The FALL with IRVINE WELSH contributing lyrics and you'll be just about there. Their third single, 'MY OWN PRIVATE P. SWAYZE', saw FARQUHAR and his crew hitting a critical peak, while the band also appeared on the 'Hits & Missiles' V/A compilation; the track being the 1997 recorded 'CATWALK'. When CRICHTON left due to ill-health in October '98, THE MALE NURSE also took time off work. Sadly, CRICHTON, who was recovering from opiates addiction, died in February '99; the coroner's verdict was misadventure. However, the story was not yet over, as BEN, ALASDAIR and LAWRENCE had settled in to be a bigger part of COUNTRY TEASERS.

KEITH FARQUHAR – vocals / **BEN WALLERS** – guitar, vocals (also of COUNTRY TEASERS) / **ALAN CRICHTON** – guitar (also of COUNTRY TEASERS) / **ALASTAIR MacKINVEN** – bass / **LAWRENCE WORTHINGTON** – drums; repl. a succession of drummers incl. MARK DEAS + PAUL CARTER

		Guided Missile	not iss.
Jun 97.	(7") *(GUIDE 14)* **GDR. / I'M A MAN**	☐	-
Jul 97.	(7") *(GUIDE 19)* **MAGIC CIRCLE IN THE SKY. / WHAT DOES WOMAN WANT?**	☐	-

— **ANDREW HOBSON** – (or AM or LW above repl. CRICHTON who left then died '99)

May 98.	(7") *(GUIDE 25)* **MY OWN PRIVATE P. SWAYZE. / DEEP FRIED**	☐	-

— disbanded in October 1998; ALASDAIR and LAWRENCE had already joined BEN's group The COUNTRY TEASERS; sadly ALAN was to die in February '99. THE MALE NURSE re-formed once again after the millennium.

		Stupid Cat	not iss.
Apr 00.	(7") *(SCAT 05)* **TOWER. / (other track by Gilded Lil)**	☐	-

MANGANESE (see under ⇒ Mint records)

Mickey MANN

Born: 1965, Aberdeen. MICKEY initially came to prominence in the late 80's after advising fellow psychiatric nurses/employees COLIN ANGUS and WILL SINOTT to re-form The SHAMEN; he also became their sound engineer. In 1993, after also working as live sound engineer with ORBITAL, the rave DJ formed his own group PRESSURE OF SPEECH alongside London DK Stika and Luke Losey. POS issued a handful of self-financed, politically-motivated singles and two albums, 'Art Of The State' (1994) and 'Our Common Past Our Common Future' (1996).

Shirley MANSON

Born: 3 Aug'66, Edinburgh. From the backstreets of Bathgate to the stadiums of America, this flame-haired siren has arguably become Scotland's sexiest Alt-rock sex symbol as the frontwoman and mouthpiece of world-beating post-Grungers, GARBAGE. MANSON's career began humbly enough as she joined up with West Lothian indie-janglers GOODBYE MR MACKENZIE while still in her teens.

A sultry backing vocal counterpoint to frontman MARTIN METCALFE's husky rumblings, SHIRLEY was a crucial element to the band's sound although it wasn't until the creation of side-project ANGELFISH (in 1994) that she was given a lead role. The unit's one-off eponymous album was a US-only release and by chance a promo video caught the eye of esteemed Grunge producer BUTCH VIG. The man had recently instigated his studio-based GARBAGE operation and was on the lookout for a suitably post-modern Goth-esque lady to wield the mic. MANSON fitted the bill perfectly and, together with VIG, STEVE MARKER and DUKE ERIKSON, she was soon garnering rave reviews for singles, 'Subhuman', 'Only Happy When It Rains', 'Queer', 'Stupid Girl' and a wicked TRICKY remix of 'Milk'. Darkly sensual, subtly suggestive and brassy to boot, SHIRLEY's bad girl-next-door vocals/image was just the ticket for the brooding yet polished and commercial Grunge sound of their massive selling eponymous debut album. The record remained in the chart for over two years, still selling even when follow-up effort, 'Version 2.0', hit the shelves in Spring '98.

After another run of hit singles, 'Push It', 'I Think I'm Paranoid', 'Special', 'When I Grow Up' and 'You Look So Fine', SHIRLEY followed in SHEENA EASTON's footsteps by singing the (GARBAGE co-penned) theme tune to the most recent Bond movie, 'The World Is Not Enough'. In October 2001, GARBAGE released their third hit album, 'Beautiful', little sultry blond SHIRLEY never far from media attention during its initial promotion.

MAPS OF JUPITER (see under ⇒ MAGNETIC NORTH POLE)

Kelly MARIE

Born: JACQUELINE McKINNON, 23 Oct'57, Paisley. Another Scot to come up trumps on BBC1's 'Opportunity Knocks' talent show, KELLY made her national screen debut at the tender age of 15. Her debut album, 'WHO'S THAT LADY WITH MY MAN' (1977) went unnoticed in the UK although it did scoop a gold disc in France. KELLY's moment finally came in 1980 when her classic rendition of 'FEELS LIKE I'M IN LOVE' topped charts all over Europe. Penned by ex-MUNGO JERRY man, RAY DORSET and originally destined for ELVIS PRESLEY, KELLY turned the song into a delirious Hi-NRG/disco stormer complete with strings, trilling disco effects and a hookline to die for. Still packing out dancefloors today, the song's momentum carried MARIE on a brief wave of fame although her similarly titled album and subsequent minor hits such as 'LOVING JUST FOR FUN', 'HOT LOVE' and 'LOVE TRIAL' just couldn't live up to the high standards she'd set herself. The 90's saw KELLY make a brief return to performing, touring the gay circuit which still thrived on the Hi-NRG sound via covers of FONTELLA BASS, ROBBIE WILLIAMS, the CORRS, DIVINE and TINA TURNER songs. Away from the disco limelight, KELLY is the mother of six kids.

KELLY MARIE – vocals / + producers

Pye not iss.

Apr 76. (7") *(7N 45586)* **WHO'S THAT LADY WITH MY MAN. / GOODBYE NIGHT**
Jun 77. (7") *(7N 45696)* **RUN TO ME. / LISTEN TO THE CHILDREN** -
Jun 77. (lp) *(NSPL 18525)* **WHO'S THAT LADY WITH MY MAN** -
– Who's that lady with my man / Hush hush Maria / Sing along alone / All we need is love / Listen to the children / My blue tango / Help me / Sweet little rock'n'roller / Just a girl / Baby Belinda / Goodbye night / Goodbye, Venice Goodbye.
Feb 78. (7") *(7N 46044)* **MAKE LOVE TO ME. / SENTIMENTAL KISSES** -
Sep 78. (lp) *(NSPL 18581)* **MAKE LOVE TO ME** -
– Look what you get / Hi hi hi / Sentimental kisses / Loving just for fun / Make love to me / Run to me / Silvery moon / Take me to paradise / Goodbye night / Limelight.
Jan 79. (7") *(7N 46154)* **IF I CAN'T HAVE YOU. / TAKE ME TO PARADISE** -

Calibre not iss.

Jul 80. (7"/12") *(PLUS/+L 1)* **FEELS LIKE I'M IN LOVE. / I CAN'T GET ENOUGH** 1 -
Oct 80. (7") *(PLUS 4)* **LOVING JUST FOR FUN. / FILL ME WITH YOUR LOVE** 21 -
Nov 80. (lp) *(CABLP 1005)* **FEELS LIKE I'M IN LOVE** -
– Feels like I'm in love / Take me to paradise / I can't get enough / Get up on your feet / Make love to me / Loving just for fun / Do you like it like that / New York at night / Run to me / Fill me with your love.
Feb 81. (7") *(PLUS 5)* **HOT LOVE. / MAKE LOVE TO ME** 22 -
May 81. (7"/12") *(PLUS/+L 7)* **LOVE TRIAL. / HEAD FOR THE STARS** 51 -
Aug 81. (7"/12") *(PLUS/+L 8)* **DON'T STOP YOUR LOVE. / MAKE LOVE TO ME**
Jan 82. (7"/12") *(PLUS/+L 9)* **I NEED YOUR LOVE. / SOMEBODY** -
Jul 82. (7"/12") *(PLUS/+L 11)* **LOVE'S GOT A HOLD ON YOU. / HEARTBEAT** -
Oct 82. (7"/12") *(PLUS/+L 12)* **DON'T TAKE YOUR LOVE TO HOLLYWOOD. / NEW YORK AT NIGHT** -
Jul 83. (7"/12") *(PLUS/+L 13)* **SILENT TREATMENT. / UP ON MY STREET** -
Jul 84. (7"/12") *(PLUS/+L 14)* **BREAKOUT. / (instrumental)** -
Oct 84. (7"/12") *(PLUS/+L 15)* **I'M ON FIRE. / (instrumental)** -

Passion not iss.

Jun 85. (7"/12") *(PASH 45/+12)* **DON'T LET THE FLAME DIE OUT. / (instrumental)** -
Dec 85. (12") *(PASH12 50)* **BORN TO BE ALIVE. / ARE YOU READY FOR LOVE** -
Jun 86. (7"/12") *(PASH 56/+12)* **HANDS UP. / (instrumental)** -
Aug 87. (7"/12") *(PASH 77/+12)* **HALF WAY TO PARADISE. / THIS TIME IT'S FOR REAL** -

—— KELLY retired from the studio for around a decade

Academy Street not iss.

Nov 97. (cd-s/12") *(d+/acst 021)* **FEELS LIKE I'M IN LOVE '97 (mixes)** -
Jan 98. (cd-s/12") *(d+/acst 031)* **RESCUE ME (mixes)** -
Oct 98. (cd-s/12") *(d+/acst 052)* **I'M IN THE MOOD FOR DANCIN' (mixes)** -
Mar 99. (cd-s/12") *(d+/acst 060)* **RUNAWAY (mixes) / MILLENNIUM** -
Nov 99. (cd-s/12") *(d+/acst 069)* **I NEED A MAN (mixes) / FEELS LIKE I'M IN LOVE '99 (mixes)** -
Jun 00. (cd-s) *(dacst 075)* **RIVER DEEP, MOUNTAIN HIGH (mixes) / IF I CAN'T HAVE YOU (mixes)** -
Feb 01. (cd-s) *(dacst 084)* **HOT LOVE (2001 remix of Disco Queen)** -

– compilations, others, etc. –

Mar 86. (7") *Old Gold; (OG 9578)* **FEELS LIKE I'M IN LOVE. / HOT LOVE** -
Sep 86. (7"/12") *(7P/12P 365)* **FEELS LIKE I'M IN LOVE. / SHATTERED GLASS** -

Michael MARRA

Born: 1952, Lochee, Dundee. Expelled from Lawside Academy at the tender age of 14, MARRA made an early entry into the working world with a series of jobs including apprentice electrician and baker. In 1971 he formed his first band, HEN'S TEETH (a young DOUGIE MACLEAN figured in the line-up) before graduating to the ranks of Dundee hopefuls SKEETS BOLIVER in mid-decade (described as the best band ever to play The Four Seasons in Montrose – not the Vivaldi classic but a pub!).

Despite constant tips for the top and a couple of singles, commercial success eluded them and they split at the turn of the decade.

MICHAEL subsequently took a job as an in-house songwriter at a London publishing firm, releasing his own debut solo album, 'THE MIDAS TOUCH' on 'Polydor' in 1980. The dreaded musical differences then ensued as MARRA resisted his manager's attempts to cast him in an MOR singer-songwriter vein. 'GAELS BLUE' (1985) was the album his manager didn't want him to make (was to have been named 'DUBIETY'), a self-financed, uniquely Scottish affair released on MICHAEL's own 'Mink' label after he'd moved back to Dundee. Work at the city's Repertory Theatre followed, leading to further commissions from the likes of Communicado in Edinburgh. Although this work was purely musical, MARRA jumped at the chance to act and duly appeared in the latter company's production of 'A Wee Home From Home', subsequently broadcast by the BBC. Regular TV and film work followed, included 'Hamish MacBeth' and movies 'The Big Man' and 'Ruffian Hearts'. The talented Dundee United fan – he once recorded a 45 for their goalie Hamish McAlpine – also adding soundtrack work to his CV (John Byrne's award winnning 'Your Cheatin' Heart') and a live collaboration with poet Liz Lochhead.

On the recording front, MARRA kept up a less than prolific release schedule (early 90's sets were 'ON STOLEN STATIONERY' and 'CANDY PHILOSOPHY') although his pithy songwriting continues apace and he's forever showcasing new material in his tireless live schedule; apparently the man has even provided lyrics for Abba's BJORN ULVAEUS(!). During a lean period in his career, MARRA delivered two sets, 'PAX VOBISCUM' (1996) and 'THE MILL LAVVIES' (1998), the man only just recently settling back to good reviews courtesy of 2001's 'POSTED SOBER'; check out one of the tracks, 'REYNARD IN PARADISE', a song about the day a fox ran onto the pitch at Parkhead during a Celtic-Aberdeen game! (eat your heart out, PAUL McCARTNEY!). MARRA's blend of 50's style pop and church music, has given him the tag of Scotland's answer to RANDY NEWMAN or DR. JOHN.

SKEETS BOLIVER

MICHAEL MARRA – vocals, keyboards, bass / **CHRISTOPHER MARRA + STEWART IVINS** + others

Thunderbird not iss.

Feb 77. (7") *(THE 116)* **STREETHOUSE DOOR. / I CAN'T SEE THE LIGHT** -
Oct 77. (7") *(THE 117)* **MOONLIGHT IN JEOPARDY. / AIN'T I BEEN GOOD TO YOU** -

MICHAEL MARRA

—— with session friends

Polydor not iss.

Jan 80. (7") *(POSP 108)* **THE MIDAS TOUCH. / SLEEPWALKING** -
Jun 80. (lp) *(POLS 1016)* **THE MIDAS TOUCH** -
– The Midas touch / Pity street / Hooky's little eyes / Foolish boy / Take me out drinking tonight / Glasgow / Features / Cheese for the moondog / Benny's going home / Taking the next train home.
Jul 80. (7") *(POSP 158)* **HOOKY'S LITTLE EYES. / FOOLISH BOY** -
Aug 81. (7") *(POSP 301)* **LIKE A FRENCH MAN. / THERE'S NO SUCH THING** -

private not iss.

1983. (7") *(Pr 2AA)* **HAMISH THE GOALIE** -

Mink not iss.

Jun 85. (lp) *(SHS 2)* **GAELS BLUE** -
– Mincing wi' Chairlhi / Racing from Newburgh / The Angus man's welcome to Mary Stuart / King George III's return to sanity / General Grant's visit to Dundee / Black babies / The altar boys / Gaels blue / Happed in mist. *(re-iss. 1992 & Jan96 on 'Eclectic' cd/c; ECL CD/TC 9206)*

—— in 1986, MARRA arranged some of the music to the Dundee Rep production of 'They Fairly Mak Ye Work' by Billy Kay – on cassette.

Eclectic not iss.

1991. (cd/c) *(ECL CD/TC 9104)* **ON STOLEN STATIONERY** -
– Margaret Reilly's arrival at Craiglockhart / The wise old men of Mount Florida / Under the Ullapool moon / Rats / Hamish / Hermless / Niel Gow's apprentice / Humphy Kate's song / Like another rolling stone / Here come the weak / The Bawbee birlin' / O penitence. *(re-iss. Jan96; same)*
1993. (cd/c) *(ECL CD/TC 9309)* **CANDY PHILOSOPHY** -
– The land of golden slippers / Don't look at me / Johnny Hallyday / True love / The violin lesson / To beat the drum / Painters painting paint / King Kong's visit to Glasgow / The Guernsey kitchen porter / Australia instead of the stars / O fellow man / This evergreen bough. *(re-iss. Jan96; same)*

—— next with **CHRISTOPHER MARRA, KIT CLARK, LLOYD ANDERSON, GREGOR PHILP + CALUM McKENZIE**

Jul 96. (cd; as MICHAEL MARRA and Band) *(ECLCD 9616)* **PAX VOBISCUM** (in concert at Glasgow's Tron Theatre May '94) -
– Don't look at me / Pax vobiscum / Lieblings in the absence of love / The one and only Anne Marie / Beefhearts and bones / Chain up the swings / Moravian girls / Here come the weak / Julius / Dear Hank Williams / King Kong's visit to Glasgow / To beat the drum / Painters painting paint / The promised land.

private not iss.

1998. (cd) *(none)* **THE MILL LAVVIES** -
– Spontaneous combustion / If Dundee was Africa / Big wide world beyond the Seedlies / Oh me God (featuring ST. ANDREW) / Broom crazy / For to be or not to be / What to do / Gin eh was a gaffer for to be.

		Inner City Sounds	not iss.
Jan 01.	(cd) *(ICS 001)* **POSTED SOBER** – Albert White Feather / Letter from Perth / The butterfly flaps its wings / Botanic endgame / Reynard in Paradise / Angela Gunn / Frida Kahlo's visit to the Taybridge bar / Constable le Clock / All will be well / Pius Porteous / Bob Dylan's visit to Embra / The lonesome death of Francis Clarke / All to please Macushia / Scribbled down drunk (but posted sober). *(re-iss. Jul02; same)*	☐	-

MATTER BABIES (see under ⇒ D.D.T. records)

MEAT WHIPLASH (see under ⇒ MOTORCYCLE BOY)

MELODY DOG (see under ⇒ PASTELS)

MENTAL ERRORS (see ⇒ Section 9: wee post-Punk groups)

MERO

Formed: Glasgow . . . 1997 by teenagers TOMMY CLARK and DEREK McDONALD, the only boy band (even although there's only two of them) to emerge from north of the border. Marketed as Scotland's ander to WHAM! With the archetypal blonde one/dark one formula and amid considerable media hype, the pair signed to 'R.C.A.' and released their debut single, 'IT MUST BE LOVE'. Nine months later, a re-issued version hit the lower reaches of the UK Top 40 making them genuine one-hit wonders and apparent pin-up fodder for the SPICE GIRLS. However, although DEREK dated Atomic Kitten's NATASHA HAMILTON and TOMMY found an acting part in BBC2's 'Tinseltown', they were dropped by soon-to-be Pop Idol judge, Simon Cowell – boo! After a spell with another boyband on 'Telstar', DEREK (under the pseudonym of D MAC) signed a third deal, this time with 'E.M.I.'. A single, 'THE WORLD SHE KNOWS' (a song about celebrity and fame), was due for release in July 2001 – whatever happened to it?

TOMMY CLARK – vocals / **DEREK McDONALD** – vocals

		R.C.A.	R.C.A.
Jul 99.	(c-s/cd-s) *(74321 66476-4/-2)* **IT MUST BE LOVE / KEYS TO HEAVEN** (cd-s) *(74321 66477-2)* – ('A'mixes inc/ CD-Rom). *(re-iss. Mar00; same)* – hit No.33	☐	-

METH O.D.

Formed: Glasgow . . . 1993/4 as a punk/garage-meets sleaze outfit fronted by the bearded JIMI D'RANGE (also on lead guitar), TRIPPING ELEFANT on guitar, JOHNNY PANTHER on bass and BOB 'Kinetic' KINARDO on drums. Wired-up and with references to everyone under the sun, this combo of swamptrashers were like Tarantino, Russ Meyer and IGGY POP rolled into one huge joint (or concert hall, take your pick!). New drummer, STEFF LE BATTEUR, was in place for their first stab at a long-player, 'TEXAS GOD STARVATION', a record that was er, full of spirit – or something. The METH O.D. were back the following January on a mail-order 7" EP for North Yorkshire-based 'Induce' imprint – licensed to US fanzine Here Be Monsters entitled 'AVOID FREUD'.

JIMI D-RANGE – vocals, lead guitar / **TRIPPING ELEFANT** – guitar, vocals / **JOHNNY PANTHER** – bass, vocals / **BOB 'Kenetic' KINARDO** (b. ROBERT KINNAIRD) – drums, vocals

		Human Condition	not iss.
Sep 95.	(cd-ep) *(HCCD 0010)* **CYBERBILLY E.P.** – Elemental / Suftnazi / Storm in abcup / Yum yum girl.	☐	-
——	**STEFF LE BATTEUR** – drums, vocals; repl.		
Dec 96.	(cd) *(HCCD 002)* **TEXAS GOD STARVATION** – Long distance voyeurism / Produktiv konduktor / First zen temple of New York / Dbug now / High school high / August 22 / Goldigger / Big dipper / Kaptain Clearview / Bastard Tarantino. (below licensed to 'Here Be Monsters')	☐	-
		Induce	not iss.
Jan 97.	(7"ep) *(IND/HBM 02)* **AVOID FREUD** – dBug / Mindmaster / Bastard Tarantino / Return of the dreaded spaceship.	☐	-

—— METH O.D. are now defunct

METROPAK (see ⇒ Section 9: wee post-Punk groups)

Malcolm MIDDLETON (see under ⇒ ARAB STRAP)

John MILLER (see under ⇒ RADIO SWEETHEARTS)

MIRO

Formed: Scotland . . . but relocated to London by the late 80's. An acoustic-rock outfit led by RODDY HARRIS, who'd a slight leaning to the sound of NICK DRAKE, the band were described as 'Music For A Kensington Bedsit'. The label, 'Sacred Heart' delivered all of their output, the delightful 'ANGEL N.1' (1990) the best of all although DREAM ACADEMY were doing similar stuff in the pop field.

RODDY HARRIS – vocals / with others

		Sacred Heart	not iss.
Jan 90.	(cd/c/lp) *(SH 2008 CD/CASS/LP)* **ANGEL N.1.** – Galileo / Six stars / Mother Courage / Secret snakes / Black sky / Portsmouth the beautiful / The familiar unfamiliar / Palace of seasickness / The Devil and the Lord / Back to the start.	☐	-
Jul 90.	(ltd-7"ep) *(SH 30008)* **GREETINGS FROM THE GOLBOURNE RD**	☐	-
1990.	(ltd-7") *(SH 4008)* **THE WORLD IN MAPS. / GREAT DOMINIONS**	☐	-
May 92.	(lp/cd) *(SH 5008/+CD)* **THE GRAIN OF THE VOICE** – Belsage park / Land of God / Fishing for dreams / Urban dreaming / Bible weed / New american / Primrose hill / Scratch / Alphabet hands / Beeswax honey / Grain of the voice.	☐	-

—— disappeared after above

MIRO (see ⇒ Section 9: Dance/Rave)

MOGWAI

Formed: Glasgow . . . 1995 by DOMINIC AITCHISON, STUART BRAITHWAITE (also of ESKA) and MARTIN BULLOCH. In the Spring of '96, the band debuted with 'TUNER' / 'LOWER', a precursor to the band's double whammy NME Singles Of The Week, 'SUMMER' and 'NEW PATHS TO HELICON'. Early in 1997, they signed to the suffocatingly hip Glasgow-based 'Chemikal Underground' (home of BIS and friends, ARAB STRAP), the first outing being 'THE 4 SATIN EP'. A fine collection of their early singles was released a month later in June, although another label was responsible.

That summer, the new 5-piece MOGWAI (complete with JOHN CUMMINGS and former TEENAGE FANCLUB member, BRENDON O'HARE) alternately bludgeoned/charmed the NME tent at Scotland's premier festival 'T In The Park' with their striking hybrid of SONIC YOUTH, METALLICA and pre-'Blue Monday' NEW ORDER! The feverishly anticipated "proper" debut album, 'MOGWAI YOUNG TEAM' was released late '97 to rave reviews, also scraping into the Top 75. Stunningly dynamic, the record shifted seamlessly from tranquil, bleakly beautiful soundscapes to brain scrambling white noise and sledgehammer riffing. Prime examples were 'LIKE HEROD', 'WITH PORTFOLIO' and 'MOGWAI FEAR SATAN', while 'TRACY' was a near 10-minute collage of drifting, childlike charm segueing into a taped phone conversation. Another track, 'R U STILL IN 2 IT', featured the mumbling vocal talents of ARAB STRAP's AIDAN MOFFAT. Prior to the album's release, O'HARE was summarily dismissed, apparently for yapping his way through an ARAB STRAP gig (tsk, tsk!).

1998 was indeed a busy year for the "young team", five releases hitting the shops between March and August and nearly all making the Top 75. The first of these, ' . . ... DO THE ROCK BOOGALOO' was a split affair with fellow noisemongers MAGOO, the title not an EP but the "un"-covering of two classic BLACK SABBATH tracks, MOGWAI having a laugh with 'SWEET LEAF'. 'FEAR SATAN' was then chosen for the remix treatment (MY BLOODY VALENTINE's the highlight), while a full album, 'KICKING A DEAD PIG: MOGWAI SONGS REMIXED', was all their best tunes reworked by others including ARAB STRAP, KID LOCO and ALEC EMPIRE. 'Chemikal Underground' put their two-pennith in by issuing the 'NO EDUCATION = NO FUTURE (FUCK THE CURFEW)' ep, while 'TEN RAPID' was an early singles collection.

The following March (with newcomer pianist BARRY BURNS now a fully-fledged member) 'COME ON DIE YOUNG' was the gangland war cry they chose as the title of their more sedate second album proper. A hard album indeed, in the sense that it took time to "get into" (probably due to the slight omission of their characteristic sonic crescendos), it unearthed a softer, more delicate style which was rewarded with a Top 30 entry. Opening with 'PUNK ROCK:' (complete with IGGY POP archive interview as voiceover), the Slo-Fi 'CODY' and the sludgedelic 'HELP BOTH WAYS, the album proved the young MOGWAI were top of the class; 'EX-COWBOY' and the emotional MORRICONE-inspired finale 'PUNK ROCK / PUFF DADDY / ANtICHRISt' were also noteworthy. Towards the end of '99, they delivered a self-titled EP, attributing 'STANLEY KUBRICK' as the lead track. 'BURN GIRL PROM QUEEN', an excellent diversion from the 'WAI featured the Cowdenbeath Brass Orchestra to eerie effect.

Perhaps the best career move a band of their status could make, 'ROCK ACTION' (2001), saw MOGWAI reach new musical heights with their first release on their own 'Southpaw' label. The album, named after the band's other record label, focused its attention on the subtler side of life. It gladly took advice from the DAVID PAJO (who appears on the record) school of experimental rock, evoking his recent PAPA M meanderings. With its harmonic use of banjos, lap-steel and orchestra, the album harked back to the aforementioned 'STANLEY KUBRICK' EP. 'SINE WAVE' was briefly melodic, with hints of warped guitar static and BULLOCH's tom-toms adding an abrasive edge to the mix. '2 RIGHTS MAKE A WRONG' is quietly SLINT-ish, with the odd-kilter signature tune thrown in for good measure. But it's 'DIAL: REVENGE' with SUPER FURRY ANIMALS vocalist GRUFF RHYS which makes the album. His lingering Welsh vocals proved to be a catalyst for the overall structure of the album, and the emotions that surface during the intensified verse-chorus-verse of the song. Preceding the album by a few weeks was an unusual and unique appearance at Rothesay in the Isle Of Bute for 500 lucky fans who could afford the ferry and the entrance fee.

• **Covered:** HONEY (Spacemen 3).

pLasmatroN (b. STUART BRAITHWAITE) – guitar, vocals (also of ESKA, until Autumn '86) / **DEMONIC** (b. DOMINIC AITCHISON) – bass / **bionic** (b. MARTIN BULLOCH) – drums

Rock Action | not iss.

Feb 96. (ltd-7") *(RAR 001)* **TUNER. / LOWER** [ ] [-]

Che | not iss.

May 96. (ltd-7"green) *(che 61)* **ANGELS VERSUS ALIENS. / (other side by DWEEB)** [ ] [-]

Love Train | not iss.

Sep 96. (ltd-7"; "CAMDEN CRAWL II") *(PUBE 011)* **A PLACE FOR PARKS. / (other artists)** [ ] [-]

Oct 96. (ltd-7"; "TEN DAY WEEKEND") *(PUBE 012)* **I AM NOT BATMAN. / (other artists)** [ ] [-]

Nov 96. (ltd-7") *(PUBE 014)* **SUMMER. / ITHICA 27 o 9** [ ] [-]

Wurlitzer Jukebox | not iss.

Jan 97. (ltd-7") *(WJ 22)* **NEW PATHS TO HELICON** [ ] [-]
– Helicon 1 / Helicon 2.

— added **Cpt. Meat** (aka JOHN CUMMINGS) – guitar

Chemikal Underground | Jetset

May 97. (12"ep/cd-ep) *(chem 015/+cd)* *<TWA 14CD>* **4 SATIN EP** [ ] [ ]
– Superheroes of BMX / Now you're taken / Stereo Dee. <US++> – Guardians of space. *(re-iss. Apr99; same)*

— added **+the relic+** (aka BRENDAN O'HARE – piano (of-MACROCOSMICA, ex-TEENAGE FANCLUB, ex-TELSTAR PONIES)

Oct 97. (cd/d-lp) *(chem 018 cd/lp)* *<7>* **MOGWAI YOUNG TEAM** [75] [ ]
– Yes! I am a long way from home / Like Herod / Radar maker / Tracy / Summer (Priority version) / With portfolio / R u still in 2 it / A cheery wave from stranded youngsters / Mogwai fear Satan. *(re-iss. Apr99; same)*

Feb 98. (7") *(SHaG 13.05)* **Club Beatroot Part Four** [ ] [-]
– Stereo Dee (live) / (other side by Ph FAMILY)
(above issued on 'Flotsam & Jetsam – 13th Note')

— now without O'HARE, who was sacked (see above)

Mar 98. (7"; split w/ MAGOO) *(NING 47CD)* **. . .. DO THE ROCK BOOGALOO** [60] [-]
– Black Sabbath (by MAGOO) / Sweet leaf.
(above issued on 'Fierce Panda', below 2 for 'eye q' / US 'Jetset')

Apr 98. (cd-ep) *(eyeuk 032cd)* **FEAR SATAN remixes** [57] [-]
– Mogwai remix / U-ziq remix / Surgeon remix / My Bloody Valentine remix. *(re-iss. Apr99; same)*

May 98. (cd/d-lp) *(eyeuk cd/lp)* *<TWA 13 CD/LP>* **KICKING A DEAD PIG: MOGWAI SONGS REMIXED** [ ] [ ] Jun98
– Like Herod (Hood remix) / Helicon 2 (Max Tundra remix) / Summer (Klute's weird winter remix) / Gwai on 45 (Arab Strap remix) / A cheery wave from stranded youngsters (Third Eye Foundation tet offensive remix) / Like Herod (Alec Empire's face the future remix) / Mogwai fear Satan (Surgeon remix) / R U still in to it? (DJ Q remix) / Tracy (Kid Loco's playing with the young team remix) / Mogwai fear Satan (Mogwai remix). *(re-iss. Apr99; same) (cd re-iss. Sep01 on 'Chemikal Underground'; CHEM 057CD)*

Jun 98. (12"ep/cd-ep) *(chem 026/+cd)* *<111230>* **NO EDUCATION = NO FUTURE (FUCK THE CURFEW) e.p.** [68] [ ]
– Xmas steps / Rollerball / Small children in the background. *(re-iss. Apr99; same)*

— In Nov'98, their track 'I CAN'T REMEMBER' featured on the 'Glasgow' V/A EP along with EL HOMBRE TRAJEADO, the KARELIA and the YUMMY FUR

— added **BARRY BURNS** – piano, flute, guitar

Chemikal Underground | Matador

Mar 99. (d-lp/cd) *(chem 033/+cd)* *<OLE 365>* **COME ON DIE YOUNG** [29] [ ]
– Punk rock: / Cody / Helps both ways / Year 2000 non-compliant cardia / Kappa / Waltz for Aidan / May nothing but happiness come through your door / Oh! how the dogs stack up / Ex-cowboy / Chocky / Christmas steps / Punk rock – Puff Daddy – ANtICHRISt.

Oct 99. (12"ep/cd-ep) *(chem 036/+cd)* *<OLE 412>* **MOGWAI e.p.** [ ] [ ]
– Stanley Kubrick / Christmas song / Burn girl prom-queen / Rage: man. *(re-iss. Sep01 as 'MOGWAI+6'+=; CHEM 056CD)* – Xmas steps / Rollerball / Small children in the background / Superheroes of BMX / Now you're taken / Stereodee.

Southpaw | Matador

Apr 01. (cd/lp) *(PAW CD/LP 001)* *<OLE 490>* **ROCK ACTION** [23] [ ]
– Sine wave / Take me somewhere nice / O I sleep / Dial: revenge / You don't know Jesus / Robot chant / 2 rights make 1 wrong / Secret pint.

Rock Action | Matador

Oct 01. (cd-s) *(ROCKACTCD 10)* *<OLE 538>* **MY FATHER MY KING** [ ] [ ]

– compilations, etc. –

Aug 98. (cd) *Rock Action; (ROCKACTCD 5) / Jetset; <TWA 05LP>* **TEN RAPID (collected recordings 1996-1997)** [ ] [ ] Aug97
– Summer / Helicon 2 / Angels versus aliens / I am not Batman / Tuner / Ithica 27 o 9 / A place for parks / Helicon 1 / End.

MOMUS

Born: NICHOLAS CURRIE, 1960, Paisley. A kind of Scottish MORRISSEY with a wordy, occasionally pretentious penchant for painstakingly examining controversial subject material, especially with regards to sexual morality, CURRIE (ironically the cousin of JUSTIN CURRIE, mainman with coffee table chart-schmoozers DEL AMITRI) has courted more criticism than success (at least in Britain) over the course of his lengthy career. Initially the frontman of Scots alternative popsters The HAPPY FAMILY (who also numbered ex-JOSEF K members DAVE WENDELL and RONNIE TORRANCE), CURRIE split the group up after what he saw as "indifference" by their label, '4 a.d.', leaving behind a solitary album, 'THE MAN ON YOUR STREET' (1982).

Relocating to Sloane Square in London and adopting the MOMUS moniker (a name taken from the god who was dismissed from Heaven and who inspired the modern day poet, Peter Porter), CURRIE's debut release came in the shape of the 'BEAST WITH NO BACKS' EP, issued by the 'El' label and quickly followed by an excellent but quickly forgotten debut album, 'CIRCUS MAXIMUS' (1986). An enthusiastic fan of French legends like JACQUES BREL and SERGE GAINSBOURG – obvious influences – CURRIE relied on mood, atmosphere and lyrical expression to capture the listener's attention, setting about lyrically ridiculing everything in sight, at times transfiguring himself into the past. His episodes of infidelity and injustice were romantically delivered in a vocal vein reminiscent of a cross between the fragility of NICK DRAKE and the effete camp of NEIL TENENT.

Finding a welcoming home at 'Creation', MOMUS released 'THE POISON BOYFRIEND' album in 1987 but it was the following year's 'TENDER PERVERT' which really caused a stir. A compelling set of narratives centering on such cheery everyday topics as incest, paedophilia and bestiality, the album won him a cult following but predictably came in for flak from the usual quarters, as did 1991's 'HIPPOPOTAMOMUS', the NME famously awarding it a big round zero out of ten. In his defence, MOMUS argued that he was simply performing one of the basic functions of pop since its inception i.e. to help angst-ridden teenagers come to terms with their sexual identity. The album, which was dedicated to French pensmith SERGE GAINSBOURG, was initially removed from the record shops, due to its cover of the TV ad for the 'Michelin Man'!

Whatever, the man continued to shock and delight throughout the 90's with albums such as 'THE ULTRACONFORMIST' (1992) – a mock-live affair which featured the sleazy BRECHT-WEILL-esque gems, 'THE MOTHER-IN-LAW' and 'THE LADIES UNDERSTAND' – and 'THE PHILOSOPHY OF MOMUS' (1995). No doubt having given up on winning over the sexually repressed British public long ago, MOMUS could content himself with the fact that he was big in Japan. He was even commissioned to pen a song for a Japanese cosmetics commercial; the result was the quasi-psychedelic BEATLES via BOOKER T. strangeness of 'GOOD MORNING WORLD', a Top 5 hit in the land of saki and one of the more interesting moments on the '20 VODKA JELLIES' (1996) album. The latter set also featured a number of songs apparently written during CURRIE's grunge phase, an interesting diversion – at least musically – from the usual wistful, intellectual forays into cabaret style alternative pop.

Love him or loathe him, MOMUS should at least be given credit for having the courage to write about the stuff most people would rather sweep under the carpet.

• **Covers:** ORGASM ADDICT (Buzzcocks). In early 1997, JACQUES was understandably his new project, a half collaboration with ANTHONY REYNOLDS, they managed to excrete one badly-thought-out set, 'HOW TO MAKE LOVE (VOLUME 1)'.

• **Trivia:** MANFRED MANN'S EARTH BAND covered his 'COMPLETE HISTORY OF SEXUAL JEALOUSY' in the early 90's! He also composes for Japanese singers KAHIMI KARIE and NORIKO SEKIGUCHI, THE POISON GIRLFRIEND.

HAPPY FAMILY

NICHOLAS CURRIE – vocals, guitar / **DAVE WENDELL** – bass, vocals (ex-JOSEF K)

4 a.d. not iss.

Mar 82. (7"ep) *(AD 204)* **PURITANS. / INNERMOST THOUGHTS / THE MISTAKE** □ -

— added **RONNIE TORRANCE** – drums (ex-JOSEF K, ex-BOOTS FOR DANCING) / **NEIL MARTIN** – synthesizer / **PAUL MASON**

Nov 82. (lp) *(CAD 214)* **THE MAN ON YOUR STREET** □ -
– The salesman / Letter from Hall / The luckiest citizen / Revenge / The courier / The man on your street / A night underground / Two of a kind / March in Turin. *(cd-iss. Nov92 +=; CAD 214CD)* – Puritans / Innermost thoughts / The mistake.

— split in 1983, leaving behind last recordings below . . .

Les Tempes not iss.

Oct 84. (c) **THE BUSINESS OF LIVING** □ -

MOMUS

NICHOLAS CURRIE – vocals, guitar / with **NEIL MARTIN** / + on album only **JANE DAVIES** – vocals

El not iss.

Jul 85. (12"ep) **THE BEAST WITH 3 BACKS** □ -
– The ballad of the barrel organist / Third party fire and theft / Hotel Marquis de Sade.

Jan 86. (lp) *(ACME 2)* **CIRCUS MAXIMUS** □ -
– Lucky like St. Sebastian / The lesson of Sodom (according to Lot) / John the Baptist Jones / King Solomon's song and mine / Little Lord Obedience / The day the circus came to town / The rape of Lucretia / Paper wraps rock / Rules of the game of quoits. *(cd-iss. Jul89 & Jun97 +=; ACME 2CD)* – Nicky / Don't leave / See a friend in tears.

Jun 86. (12"m) *(GP 09T)* **NICKY. / DON'T LEAVE / SEE A FRIEND IN TEARS** □ -

— with **DEAN KLERAT** – keyboards / **FEIN O'LOCHLAINN** – bass / **TERRY NEILSON** – drums / **ARUN G. SHENDURNIKAR** – percussion

Creation not iss.

Mar 87. (12"ep) *(CRE 037T)* **MURDERERS, THE HOPE OF WOMEN. / ELEVEN EXECUTIONERS / WHAT WILL DEATH BE LIKE?** □ -

Jul 87. (lp) *(CRELP 021)* **THE POISON BOYFRIEND** □ -
– The gatecrasher / Violets / Islington John / Three wars / Flame into being / Situation comedy blues / Sex for the disabled / Closer to you. *(cd-iss. Apr88 +=; CRELP 021CD)* – Murderers, the hope of women / Eleven executioners / What will death be like?

Jul 88. (lp/cd) *(CRELP 036/+CD)* **THE TENDER PERVERT** □ -
– The angels are voyeurs / Love on ice / I was a Maoist intellectual / The homosexual / Bishonen / A complete history of sexual jealousy (parts 17-24) / Ice king / In the sanatorium / The charm of innocence / The angels are voyeurs (reprise). *(w/ free 7")*

Jan 89. (7") *(CRE 063L)* **HAIRSTYLE OF THE DEVIL. /** □ -
(12"+=) *(CRE 063LT)* –

Oct 89. (7") **LIFESTYLES OF THE RICH AND FAMOUS. /** □ -
(12"+=/3"cd-s+=) –

Nov 89. (cd)(c/lp) *(CRECD 59)(C+/CRE 59)* **DON'T STOP THE NIGHT** □ -
– Trust me, I'm a doctor / Right hand heart / Lord of the dance / Lifestyles of the rich and famous / How do you find my sister? / The hairstyle of the Devil * / Don't stop the night / Amongst women only / The guitar lesson / The cabriolet / Shaftesbury Avenue. *(cd+= *)*

Mar 90. (cd)(c/lp) *(CRECD 59)(C+/CRE 59)* **MONSTERS OF LOVE: SINGLES 85-89** (readings of my early years) □ -
– Morality is vanity / Ballad of the barrel organist / Third party, fire and theft / Hotel Marquis de Sade / Murderers, the hope of women / What will death be like? / Eleven executioners / Gilda / The hairstyle of the Devil / Monsters of love.

Jul 91. (cd)(c/lp) *(CRECD 97)(C+CRE 97)* **HIPPOPOTAMOMUS** □ -
– Hippopotamomus / I ate a girl right up / Michelin man / A dull documentary / Marquis of sadness / Bluestocking / Ventriloquists & dolls / The painter & his model / A monkey for Sallie / Pornography / Song in contravention.

May 92. (lp/cd) *(MONDE 3/+CD)* **THE ULTRACONFORMIST** (live whilst out of fashion) □ -
– Sinister themes / Last of the window cleaners / The ladies understand / Cape and stick gang / The ultraconformist / The mother-in-law / La Catrina / The cheques in the post / Spy on the moon / Forests. *(cd re-iss. Jun97; same)*
above issued on 'Richmond-Cherry Red'.

Jun 92. (cd)(lp/c) *(CRECD 113)(C+/CRE 113)* **VOYAGER** □ -
– Cibachrome blue / Virtual reality / Vocation / Conquistador / Spacewalk / Summer holiday 1999 / Afterglow / Trans Siberian express / Voyager / Momutation 3.

Sep 92. (12")(cd-s) *(CRE 134T)(CRESCD 134)* **SPACEWALK (Deja vu remix). / CONQUISTADIOR (Lovecut db remix) / MOMUTATION 3** □ -

Nov 93. (cd/lp) *(CRE CD/LP 151)* **TIMELORD** □ -
– Platinum / Enlightenment / You've changed / Landrover / Rhetoric / Suicide pact / Christmas on Earth / Breathless.

Cherry Red Cherry Red

Apr 95. (cd-s) *(CDCHERRY 137)* **THE SADENESS OF THINGS /** □ -

Jun 95. (cd) *(CDBRED 119)* **PHILOSOPHY OF MOMUS** □ -
– Toothbrushead / The madness of Lee Scratch Perry / It's important to be trendy / Quark and charm, the robot twins / Girlish boy / Yokohama Chinatown / Withinity / K's diary / Virtual Valerie / Red pyjamas / The cabinet of Kuniyoshi Kaneko / Slide projector, lie detector / Microworlds / Complicated / I had a girl / The philosophy of Momus / The loneliness of lift music / Paranoid acoustic seduction machine / The sadeness of things.

Nov 95. (cd) *(CDBRED 123)* **SLENDER SHERBET – CLASSIC SONGS REVISITED** (readings of my early years) □ -
– The complete history of sexual jealousy / The guitar lesson / Closer to you / The homosexual / Charm of innocence / Lucky like St. Sebastian / I was a Maoist intellectual / Lifestyles of the rich and famous / Angels are voyeurs / Hotel Marquis de Sade / The gatecrasher / Hairstyle of the Devil / Bi shonen / Angels (reprise).

Sep 96. (cd) *(<CDMRED 133>)* **20 VODKA JELLIES** (an assortment of curiosities and rarities) □ □ Jan97
– I am a kitten / Vogue Bambini / The poisoners / Nikon 2 / Giapponese a Roma / Paolo / The end of history / London 1888 / Streetlamp soliloquy / An inflatable doll / Saved / Someone / Howard Hughes / Three beasts / Good morning world / Germania / The girl with no body / Radiant night / Orgasm addict / Nobody.

below featured **MOMUS** with **ANTHONY REYNOLDS**

Apr 97. (cd; as JACQUES) **HOW TO MAKE LOVE (VOLUME 1)** □ -
–

Satyricon Bungalow-Setanta

Nov 97. (cd) *(SATYR 001)* <031> **PING PONG** □ □
– Ping pong with Hong Kong King Kong / His majesty the baby / My pervert doppleganger / I want you, but I don't need you / Professor Shaftenberg / Shoesize of the angel / Age of information / Sensation of orgasm / Anthem of Shibuya / Lolitapop dollhouse / Tamagotchi press officer / Space Jews / My kindly friend the censor / Animal that desires / How to get – and stay – famous / 2 p.m.

Graeme / Iain MONCRIEFF

Born: (both) late 70's, Ayrshire. GRAEME and his younger brother IAIN moved down south to Bristol with their family when they were wee laddies (so to speak). After leaving school at 17, vocalist/guitarist GRAEME taught his sibling his skills on his dad's acoustic guitar and thus the band HALO were initiated. Joined by STEVE YEOMANS on bass and keyboards plus JIM DAVEY on drums, the NIRVANA-esque/RADIOHEAD type quartet began rehearsing around the start of 2001. Winning a contract with 'Sony Soho 2', the fresh-faced combo finally delivered their Gil Norton-produced debut single, 'COLD LIGHT OF DAY' to the UK Top 50 in February 2002. This was followed by live tours, another Top 50 hit, 'SANCTIMONIOUS' and an opening day stint at Scotland's T In The Park (NME tent); an album, 'LUNATIC RIDE', would hit the shops in September.

MONGERS (see under ⇒ POLICECAT)

MONGOOSE (see under ⇒ SECRET GOLDFISH)

Mark MORRISON

Born: Springburn, Glasgow. Not exactly the Return Of The Mack (by another MARK MORRISON – the black R&B version of course), but another up and coming dance, drum'n'bass guy who'd moved down south to Bristol. Going under the pseudonym of MARKEE SUBSTANCE, he teamed up in 1999 with fellow breakbeat lover DARREN DECODER and vocalist SIAN EVANS (from Wales) to form KOSHEEN (in Japan it means old and new). MARK left Strathclyde University with a Maths and Economics degree and looked for work in the Bristol area, also spending his leisure time instigating the Ruffneck Ting club; the party had really begun. 'HIDE U' became a huge Top 10 hit in 2001 and was quickly followed by another, 'CATCH', each identifying the trio as purveyors of original funky dance/rave beats. In 2002, more success was to follow them when their debut album, 'RESIST', made it in to the UK Top 10. Given time, songwriter MARKEE SUBSTANCE could well be right up there with the dance elite.

MOST (see under ⇒ SPIREA X)

MOTORCYCLE BOY

Formed: East Kilbride . . . early 1985 as MEAT WHIPLASH (named after a FIRE ENGINES b-side!) by PAUL McDERMOTT, MICHAEL KERR (also part-time with JESSE GARON & THE DESPERADOS), EDDY CONNOLLY and STEPHEN McLEAN. They signed to Alan McGee's 'Creation' independent, supporting The JESUS & MARY CHAIN while the REID brothers produced their one and only single, 'DON'T SLIP UP'. All but STEPHEN resurfaced as MOTORCYCLE BOY (after the hero in cult film, 'Rumblefish') a few years later and, with the recruitment of female, ALEX TAYLOR (ex-SHOP ASSISTANTS) on vocals and SCOTTIE on aggressive guitar, they became a big signing for 'Rough Trade'. However, the band moved on up to 'Chrysalis', having only issued one single, 'BIG ROCK CANDY MOUNTAIN', in 1987. For a few years little was heard from ALEX's wonderful vocals until 1989 brought forth two singles, 'TRYING TO BE KIND' and 'YOU AND ME AGAINST THE WORLD', both taken from their one and only album, 'SCARLET'.

MEAT WHIPLASH

PAUL McDERMOTT – vocals, percussion / **MICHAEL KERR** – guitar / **EDDY CONNOLLY** – bass / **STEPHEN McLEAN** – drums

		Creation	not iss.
Sep 85.	(7") *(CRE 020)* **DON'T SLIP UP. / HERE IT COMES**	☐	[-]

MOTORCYCLE BOY

— added **ALEX TAYLOR** – vocals (ex-SHOP ASSISTANTS)

— **SCOTTIE** (b. DAVID SCOTT) – guitar; repl. STEPHEN

		Rough Trade	not iss.
Sep 87.	(7") *(RT 210)* **BIG ROCK CANDY MOUNTAIN. /** (12"+=) *(RTT 210)* – ('A'-Velocity dance mix) / Room at the top / His latest flame.	☐	[-]
		Chrysalis	not iss.
Jun 89.	(7") *(CHS 3310)* **TRYING TO BE KIND. / THE WORLD FALLS INTO PLACE** (12"+=) *(CHS12 3310)* – ('A'version) / Will you love me tomorrow.	☐	[-]
Sep 89.	(7") *(CHS 3398)* **YOU AND ME AGAINST THE WORLD. / UNDER THE BRIDGE** (12"+=) *(CHS12 3398)* – Some girls.	☐	[-]
Sep 89.	(lp/c/cd) *(CHR/ZCHR/CCD 1689)* **SCARLET** –	☐	[-]
		Nymphaea Pink	not iss.
Apr 90.	(12") *(NPST 001)* **THE ROAD GOES ON FOREVER. /**	☐	[-]
		Pink Sensation	not iss.
Oct 90.	(7") **HERE SHE COMES. /**	☐	[-]

— split the following year, TAYLOR became a "real" shop assistant

MOTOR LIFE CO.

Formed: Largs . . . early 1995 by SEAN GUTHRIE, MATT GILFEATHER, CHRIS GROVE and Helensburgh-raised BEN ELLIS; the 'More To Life' company was indeed a play on words. After a few grungy, noisecore 45's on their own 'Pendejo' imprint, namely 'MY MAIL ORDER THAI BRIDE' and 'BE A HERO', MOTOR LIFE CO. played some dynamic underground live gigs. In 1998, after supporting such indie luminaries as ARAB STRAP, MOGWAI and AC ACOUSTICS, the quartet finally let loose their first album, the mini-set, '(BIRDSTYLE)'. Opening with the accompanying 7", 'TROD ON YOUR HEAD-MINE', the set was both fragile and sonic courtesy of SEAN, MATT and BEN seemingly all fighting over the one mic; the BEACH BOYS they were not.

SEAN GUTHRIE – guitar, vocals / **MATT GILFEATHER** – guitar, vocals / **BEN ELLIS** – bass, vocals / **CHRIS GROVE** – drums

		Pendejo	not iss.
Nov 95.	(7") *(PEN 01)* **MY MAIL ORDER THAI BRIDE. / FELL ILL**	☐	[-]
Oct 96.	(7") *(PEN 02)* **BE A HERO. / SWERVE, THEN FREE REVERSE**	☐	[-]
		mei mei	not iss.
Jul 98.	(7") *(mei 002)* **TROD ON YOUR HEAD-MINE. / SHOW THE COSMOS**	☐	[-]
Sep 98.	(m-cd) *(mei 003CD)* **(BIRDSTYLE)** – Trod on your head-mine / In the Lee of a steeple / Airshot / Miguel the dinted / More fuel for future fires / 20k.	☐	[-]

— unsure what became of them; probably failed the M.O.T.

MOUNT FLORIDA

Formed: Mount Florida, Glasgow . . . 1996 by TWITCH (aka KEITH McIVOR) and M.P. (MIKE) LANCASTER. Both relative veterans in the music industry, LANCASTER had almost signed to 'Z.T.T.' back in the 80's before going on to compose music for art installations while TWITCH had made his name DJ'ing (with BRAINSTORM) at ambient club Sonora and Edinburgh techno institution, Pure. The pair met after M.P. played at Sonora and TWITCH & BRAINSTORM (T&B) subsequently released the man's solo album, 'STAG PIE' on his own 'Pi' label. TWITCH also organised a collaborative shindig between M.P. and Finnish label, 'Sahko', recorded for posterity as the 'Moor' EP on the obscure 'UPO' imprint. Signed to 'Matador', the eclectic duo made their debut with the 'LOST IN SATIE' 12" from the 'STEALTH' EP in Autumn '99. Two further MOUNT FLORIDA EP's – 'STORM' (opening with a re-working of Arthur Russell's 'A Little Lost' in the shape of 'ANOTHER THOUGHT' featuring Glaswegian diva MADELINE MacDONALD) and 'STRUT' – followed in the year 2000 as the lads whetted appetites for a debut album. The cryptically titled 'ARRIVED PHOENIX' finally touched down in early 2001, its livewire psychedelic ambience/Kraut-rock (using field recordings, DAT tapes, live music, samples etc) sending critics into a high voltage spasm of superlatives. In addition to his sexy MF recordings, LANCASTER also apparently has a series of his own solo recordings available on mail order. TWITCH, meanwhile, continues to rock the Glasgow club world with his much raved over Optimo Sunday night hoedown; he also set up his own electro/dance imprint, 'Oscarr' records.

TWITCH

		UK Tab	not iss.
Jan 94.	(12"; as TWITCH & BRAINSTORM) **TAB 1** – Canin' / Mr. Stumble / Zoom.	☐	[-]

M.P. LANCASTER

		T&B	not iss.
Nov 95.	(cd-s) *(TBPiCD 002)* **STAY PIE**	☐	[-]
1996.	(cd-s; V/A) *(TBPiCD 005)* **Golden Grates** – Mac addict / (+ Various Artists).	☐	[-]

— MIKE's also collaborated with Finnish outfit, 0/ for the 'Upo.2 Moor' 12"ep on 'Sahko' records. Other rare mpCD's are 'Structura', 'Space Jams' and 'Work Tape Edits' the 109 project was due in 2001.

MOUNT FLORIDA

TWITCH (b. KEVIN McIVOR) – DJ / **M.P. LANCASTER** (b. MIKE) – electronics, samples, etc

		T&B	not iss.
Apr 97.	(12") *(TBPi12 07)* **CATALYST DUBS**	☐	[-]
		Left Hand	not iss.
Apr 98.	(12"ep; with PAINKILLERS & SE-KI) *(LHR 002)* **MAJIK MOMENTS EP**	☐	[-]
		Matador	Matador
Nov 99.	(12"ep/cd-ep) *(OLE 399-1/-2)* **STEALTH EP** – Lost in Satie / Riot on Jamaica St. / Roc the Vonnegut / A tribute to Muslimgauze.	☐	[-]

— next featured **MADELINE MacDONALD** – vocals

Apr 00.	(12"ep/cd-ep) *(OLE 417-1/-2)* **STORM EP** – Another thought / Celebrate life / Flame on / Roc the Bukowski.	☐	[-]
Aug 00.	(12"ep/cd-ep) *(OLE 443-1/-2)* **STRUT EP** – Poptimo / G-twang / Last airboat to Daytona Beach / Split.	☐	[-]
Oct 00.	(cd) *(<OLE 401-2>)* **ARRIVED PHOENIX** – In there / Space echoes / Ultimo / Jamaica Street / Celebration / Yo la Kinski / Postal / Bombast / Don't do Dada / Static airwaves / Radio ocean / Out there.	☐	☐

MOUNT VERNON ARTS LAB

Formed: Glasgow . . . 1996 by the initially mysterious experimentalist, DREW MULHOLLAND. Inspired by the late, JOE MEEK, DANIEL MILLER (remember, The NORMAL) and the theremin, lab technician MULHOLLAND and his crew delivered a succession of noises and loops that would make any Kraut-rocker envious. Independent outlet, 'Via Satellite' (and at times 'Earworm') were behind MOUNT VERNON from the outset, a plethora of avant-garde/post-rock EP's being introduced to the public circa '97/'98; even Glasgow's 'Creeping Bent' got in on the act via V/A album, 'Electronic Lullabies', and track 'MV 3'. The latter also made an appearance on MVAL's first mini-set, 'GUMMY TWINKLE' (1998), a longwave/shortwave frequency collage of soundscapes that featured SONIC BOOM (aka PETE KEMBER) and NORMAN BLAKE (of TEENAGE FANCLUB).

Subsequently inking a deal with 'Ochre' records, DREW embarked on selecting all sorts of minimalistic pocket symphonics, evidenced on their 23-minute collaboration, 'WARMINSTER', with PORTISHEAD's ADRIAN UTLEY. If improvised atmospherics were God, the MOUNT VERNON ARTS LAB would be Zeus, the 21st Century had arrived via satellite and via Ochre's 'ONE MINUTE BLASTS RISING TO THREE AND THEN DIMINISHING' (2000); DREW recorded this 100 feet below ground at the abandoned nuclear bunkers at Troywood, the man was indeed, wired up to the mains!

This was followed by 2001's 'THE SEANCE AT HOBS LANE', a strange collection of songs inspired by "Victorian Skullduggery, outlaws, secret societies and subterranean experiences". The set also featured the talents of NORMAN BLAKE (TEENAGE FANCLUB), ISOBEL CAMPBELL (BELLE & SEBASTIAN), BARRY 7 (ADD N TO X) and PORTISHEAD's ADRIAN UTLEY and turned MULHOLLAND's keen sense of humour and fascination with weird subjects into one of the most interesting Scottish releases of the year.

DREW MULHOLLAND – electronics, etc

Via Satellite / not iss.

May 97. (10"ep) *(V-Sat 008)* **NOVA EP** [ ] [-]

Oct 97. (7"ep) *(WORM 007)* **split** [ ] [-]
– Window / CLOCKWORK: Exp.#1 / OMIT: Cold evolution.
(above issued on 'Earworm')

Oct 97. (7"ep) *(V-Satastra 1961)* **TALVIN STARDUST EP** [ ] [-]
– Talvin Stardust / The little velvet ladder / The mind field / Oram.

Feb 98. (7"ep) *(V-Satastra 1972)* **WILLIAM GREEN EP** [ ] [-]

Feb 98. (one-sided-7"brown) *(WORMSS 2)* **IMBER. / Electroscope: SHAME CHANGED HIS PIGMENTATION** [ ] [-]
(above issued on 'Earworm')

Sep 98. (m-cd) *(V-Sat 2525)* **GUMMY TWINKLE** [ ] [ ]
– Expo / William Green / Cabaret volt age / Live mains electricity / Mr. Astra / Shirts / Imber loop / Telek / MV 3 / Superpatch / (+ hidden track).

Ochre / not iss.

Jun 99. (m-cd; by ADRIAN UTLEY & MOUNT VERNON ARTS LAB) *(OCH 040CD)* **WARMINSTER** [ ] [-]
– Warminster.

Sep 99. (cd) *(OCH 13CD)* **E FOR EXPERIMENTAL** (compilation 1996-1999) [ ] [ ]
– Arthur Cravan / Mania / The Third Eye Centre / Frenzy / Electrolumminessense / Imps . . . I am Lubbert Das / Andromeda / Lunar three / Feldspar / Via satellite / Bedlam / Scooby don't / The mind field / Window / Imber / Talvin Stardust / Oram / The little velvet ladder / William Green / Automatic frequency control / Magic carpet ride / Broadcasting / Der lumpenrocker / Bad vibrations.

Nov 00. (m-cd) *(OCH 046)* **ONE MINUTE BLASTS RISING TO THREE AND THEN DIMINISHING** [ ] [-]
– One minute blasts rising to three and then diminishing.

Via Satellite / not iss.

Aug 01. (cd) *(ASTRA 007)* **THE SEANCE AT HOBS LANE** [ ] [-]

MUDSHARK (see under ⇒ Scotland's wee metal scene)

MUKKAA (see under ⇒ Limbo records)

MULL HISTORICAL SOCIETY

Formed: Glasgow . . . early in the year 2000 by COLIN MacINTYRE (son of KENNY MacINTYRE, the late and much missed political reporter for BBC Scotland), a man born and raised on the isle of Mull (Tobermory, to be exact). Having learned the guitar at an early age, he honed up on the music world by reading about, rather than listening to records; it was hard for him to obtain anything decent outside the Top 40. Writing a barrelload of songs (artwork complimented each one, apparently!), COLIN crossed the water to Glasgow and er, wrote some more.

Abandoning other late 90's projects such as LOVE SICK ZOMBIES, WESTERNIZED and 7/11 (good names!), COLIN met up with like-minded bassist ALAN MALLOY (also from his hometown) and formed the MULL HISTORICAL SOCIETY (is there such a thing that already exists?). Towards the end of the year, the quartet (recent additions being COLIN 'SLEEPY' MacPHERSON and TONY SOAVE) unveiled their debut single for 'Tugboat', 'BARCODE BYPASS', a fine blend of MERCURY REV, BEACH BOYS and AZTEC CAMERA – 'Mull Of MacIntyre' anyone? Indeed.

Moving on slightly and come the release of the group's debut set 'LOSS' (2001) – a universally praised homage to Glasgow (that's where most of the tracks were written) and an all-round great album – MacINTYRE's vocals did become a tad taxing on some tracks, but it was nothing that the music didn't make up for. 'PUBLIC SERVICE ANNOUNCER' opened the album with bursting, full-on guitars, heightening the pop factor to 11, whereas 'INSTEAD' offered up a quaint ballad, with a children's choir thrown in for good measure. The press had a field day over the album (and a minor hit 45, 'WATCHING XANADU'), which prompted the band to tour with the likes of The STROKES, TRAVIS and The MOLDY PEACHES, as well as being faves on the Glastonbury and T In The Park festivals.

COLIN MacINTYRE – vocals, guitar / **ALAN MALLOY** – bass / **COLIN 'SLEEPY' MacPHERSON** – keyboards / **TONY SOAVE** – drums

Tugboat / not iss.

Nov 00. (7"/cd-s) *(TUGS/+CD 28)* **BARCODE BYPASS. / MULL HISTORICAL SOCIETY** [ ] [-]

Mar 01. (7"/cd-s) *(TUGS/+CD 29)* **I TRIED. / SOME YOU WIN, SOME YOU LOSE** [ ] [-]

Rough Trade / not iss.

Jul 01. (7"/cd-s) *(RTRADES/+CD 021)* **ANIMAL CANNABUS. / UGLY BUILDINGS ARE BEAUTIFUL / INDUSTRIAL HANGERS** [53] [-]

Blanco Y Negro / Beggars XL

Oct 01. (cd/d-lp) *(0927 41307-2/-1) <85027>* **LOSS** [43] [ ]
– Public service announcer / Watching Xanadu / Instead / I tried / This is not who we were / Barcode bypass / Only I / Animal cannabus / Strangeways inside / Mull Historical Society / Paper houses.

Jan 02. (7") *(NEG 138)* **WATCHING XANADU. / PIGEON LOVESONG** [36] [-]
(cd-s) *(NEG 138CD1)* – ('A'side) / Pigeon fancier (by correspondence) / Don't suffer.
(cd-s) *(NEG 138CD2)* – ('A'side) / Naked ambition at the E.P.A. / Sad old day to be down / ('A'-CD-Rom).

Donnie MUNRO (see ⇒ Section 2: Folk)

MUPPET MULE (see under ⇒ SPARE SNARE)

MURMUR (see ⇒ Section 9 : the 90s)

MUZIQUE TROPIQUE (see under ⇒ Glasgow Underground records)

MYSTERY JUICE

Formed: Edinburgh . . . 1998 by the southern-fried dirty blues-rap fusion that was TIM on violin, JOE on bass, DONALD on drums and another DONALD on guitar (surnames of course a mystery!). Touring alongside fellow 'Burgh youngsters RANCHER to promote the 'PIGWIT' 5-song EP, their rhinestone-cum-tumbleweed zeitgeist was driven like a sparring hoedown between the FUN LOVIN' CRIMINALS and TOM WAITS! Apparently, they've gone down a storm in Russia; progress indeed. Now signed to 'Vertical' records, the band released a fresh CD-EP, 'OPEN MY MOUTH AND DO NOTHING' prior to their debut set, 'SEED' (2002).

TIM – violin / **DONALD** – guitar / **JOE** – bass / **DONALD** – drums

Human Condition / not iss.

Oct 99. (cd-ep) *(HC 00024)* **PIGWIT EP** [ ] [-]
– Pigwit / Driving man / Goin radge on holiday (live) / Ladykiller (live) / Pick it up (live).

Vertical / not iss.

Jul 01. (cd-ep) *(VERTCD 057)* **OPEN MY MOUTH AND DO NOTHING** [ ] [-]

Jun 02. (cd) *(VRTCD 004)* **SEED**
– Old man / Plastic / The butcher / Personal thing / Going radge on holiday / Open my mouth and do nothing / Push up / Ladykiller / Tricky situations / Pick it up / Black rubber bag / No.12.

N

NAKED SEE (see under ⇒ FOIL)

NAPALM STARS (see under ⇒ Stranded records)

Peter NARDINI (see ⇒ Section 2: Folk)

NATIONAL PARK

Formed: Glasgow . . . 1997 by JOHN HOGARTY (ex-BMX BANDITS and ex-TELSTAR PONIES), SIMON SHAW, MICHAEL McGAUGHRIN and SCOTT WALKER (no, not that one!). Described by some as like GALAXIE 500 meeting FAUST, NATIONAL PARK issued their first vinyl-only release via Earworm's 1998 10", 'GREAT WESTERN'. HOGARTY, meanwhile, was branching out in other directions, mainly a one-off project, PHANTOM ENGINEER, with DAVID KEENAN and jazzman BILL WELLS. Settling back with the NATIONAL PARK, he and his crew collaborated with another 'Wedgie fave The FUTURE PILOT AKA. The track in question, 'NORMAN DOLPH'S MONEY', was about the person who funded the artwork for the VELVET UNDERGROUND's debut "banana" cover. Tributes were also forthcoming towards the end of '99, when the same pairing contributed 'STERLING' – aka the recently deceased STERLING MORRISON, to the '. . .Galaxy Of Sound' set.

JOHN HOGARTY – / **SIMON SHAW** – / **SCOTT WALKER** – piano / **MICHAEL McGAUGHRIN**

Earworm / not iss.

Aug 98. (ltd-10") *(WORM 30)* **GREAT WESTERN. / SHAPES, STARS**

Jan 99. (7") *(WORMSS 4)* **NATIONAL PARK VERSUS FUTURE PILOT AKA**
– Norman Dolph's money.

— SCOTT took off to join other acts, while NP found a new live guitarist **ALI ROBERTS** (of APPENDIX OUT) / **TOM CROSSLEY** (also of APPENDIX OUT + INTERNATIONAL AIRPORT) played piano recently

David NAYLOR

Born: mid-70's, Glasgow. Drummer with London-based cosmopolitan outfit The BOHO SUB BAND, DAVID can be heard thumping his skins on their 'Mercury' EP, 'JIGGLE YOUR ROOTS', having played Glastonbury 2000 earlier that year.

NECK DOPPLER (see under ⇒ Mouthmoth records)

NECTARINE No.9 (see under ⇒ FIRE ENGINES)

NEEDLES (see under ⇒ Lithium records)

NERO (see under ⇒ Alphabetty records and Lithium records)

NERVE

Formed: Glasgow . . . early 90's by industrial-loving punks, JIM, ALI and PETE. Their debut album in '93, 'CANCER OF CHOICE', was very well-received from all portions of the press, their hookline punk rock-pop an unusual entity for the Belgian-based label 'Play It Again Sam'. However, only one further 7", 'SUBMARINE' surfaced in 1995 before contractual problems beset them the following year. Playing support slots to The TOILET BOYS, GODSMACK, etc, the NERVE were cool enough to sink their past. Their long-awaited return towards the end of 1999, the EP 'WAKE UP CALL' was trailed by their sophomore set, the mini 'SWIMMING WITH SHARKS' (2000); two others 'PSYCHO POETRY' (2001) and 'HOOKED' (2002) buried the rumours that the trio had split – watch out GREEN DAY and BLINK 182.
• **Note:** not to be confused with two other outfits of the same name who issued 'Seeds From The Electric Garden' and 'Channel 59'.

JIM – vocals, guitar / **PETE** – bass, vocals / **ALI** – drums

Play It Again Sam / not iss.

Sep 93. (cd-s) *(BIAS 156CD)* **DEDALUS / TRUST / STILL WATERS**

Oct 93. (cd) *(BIAS 261CD)* **CANCER OF CHOICE**
– Coins / Fragments / Oil / Rage / Closedown / Water / Seed / Dedalus / Trust / Waters / Thirties.

Apr 94. (12") *(BIAS 262)* **FRAGMENTS (mixes)**
(cd-s+=) *(BIAS 262CD)* – (2 'A'-mixes).

Strawberry / not iss.

Oct 95. (7") *(STRAWS 001)* **SUBMARINE. / SEEDS**

— contractual problems kept them away until below

20 Stone Blatt / not iss.

Dec 99. (cd-ep) *(BAMF 13CD)* **WAKE UP CALL**
– My least favourite things / One track mind / Uptown girl / Porno star / Take what you can get.

Jul 00. (m-cd) *(BAMF 19CD)* **SWIMMING WITH SHARKS**
– What more do you want from me / S.O.S. / My own worst enemy / Soho disco / Now or never / Going blind / Jinx.

Apr 01. (m-cd) *(BAMF 23CD)* **PSYCHO POETRY**
– Better off alone / You and me against the world / So you think / Losing streak / Cheers / All I want is you / F.O.A.D.

Sep 02. (m-cd) **HOOKED**
– Dazed and confused / Waiting room / My friend / Forget about me / Sunshine / Britcock (rehearsal) / Shallow (rehearsal).

NEW ATLANTIC (see ⇒ Section 9: Dance/Rave)

NEWTOWN GRUNTS

Formed: Glenrothes, Fife . . . 1994 by Ska-punk – or Gruntcore! – bunch ROD (DRYSDALE) on vocals, BRIAN (the second vocalist!), guitarist SKINZ (i.e. ERIC DAVIDSON), bassist DOLLY and drummer ADAM; second guitarist GAV was added for more noise! In the summer of '95 (during which, one track 'FUNDAMENTAL BASTARDS' appeared on the 'Wretch' records V/A compilation 'For A Few Crash Helmets More'), DOLLY bailed out and was replaced by the Gothic-looking PAUL, while that Xmas saw BRIAN take flight to America; two singers were in place the following year, local housewife LYNNE and Glaswegian(!) NORRI (or NORMAN to his mates).

Signing to 'Flotsam & Jetsam', the Weegie-baiting 'NO SOAP IN GLASGOW EP', was issued shortly afterwards and went down a storm – except for some reason, in the West Of Scotland! Towards the end of '97, the Glenrothes 'GRUNTS released their debut album, 'THE DAY OF THE JAKEY' (referring to down-and-outs, I think!), a Kerrang!-friendly record! that opened with 'TWO PINTS OF LAGER AND A SMACK AFF THE PUS, PLEASE' – even SPLODGENESSABOUNDS would've been offended. Winning numerous "Battle Of The Bands" competitions – they dressed as Vegas Elvis to win over the judges, no doubt – The NEWTOWN GRUNTS also released a split 45 with tour mates The AMPHETAMEANIES.

Late in 2000, the ever-evolving line-up of NG supported Boston's DROPKICK MURPHYS and later the aforementioned 'MEANIES alongside early eighties hitmakers, BAD MANNERS!

ROD (DRYSDALE) – vocals / **BRIAN** – vocals / **SKINZ** (b. ERIC DAVIDSON) – guitar / **GAV** – guitar / **PAUL** – bass; repl. DOLLY / **ADAM** – drums

— early '96; **NORRI + LYNNE** – vocals; repl. BRIAN

Flotsam & Jetsam / not iss.

Jun 96. (7"ep) *(SHaG 004)* **NO SOAP IN GLASGOW EP**
– It could be you / Me, myself & I / Dead and gone / Thrown away.

— **PEGGIE** – bass; repl. PAUL

Dec 97. (cd) *(SHaG 014D)* **DAY OF THE JAKEY**
– Two pints of lager and a smack aff the pus, please / Day of the jakey / It could be you / Mother, slave and wife / Dead and gone / The best job in town / Bleary eyed at Victoria / Angry angry angry / Adios amigo / Buckfast / In reply / They shall not pass / Super trouper.

— in 1998 (alongside a handful of V/A comps), the band split a Welsh! 12"ep 'Cheap Sweaty Fun in 200' (the track 'OUT OF THE CROWD') w/ the MISFITS, BOUNCING SOULS and SNUFF.

— **DAVE** – bass; repl. PEGGIE

Oct 99. (7") *(SHaG 026)* **TREATY AT HARTHILL** [ ] [-]
– Everywhere she goes / (other track by Amphetameanies).

Velvet Crow | not iss.

2000. (m-cd; at gigs) **LIVE IN GLASGOW (live)** [-] [-] Scot
– Solidarity / Get a life / The bottle / Everywhere she goes / Take your hand / Arsehole on the dancefloor / Dead and gone / The Newtown Grunts versus The Insidious Right Wing Conspiracy (part one) / The ballad of a New Town Grunt.

Wakusei | Speedowax

Feb 01. (7") **NOTHING TO ME / THE BOTTLE / (other two by ANN BERETTA)** [ ] [ ]

NEW YORK PIG FUNKSTERS

(see ⇒ Section 9: Dance/Rave)

NICOLETTE

Born: NICOLETTE OKOH, 1964, Glasgow. Raised by her globetrotting psychologist parents in the unlikely bases of Nigeria (Suwonton), Falkirk (yes! Falkirk, from the age of 7), France and Switzerland, the Afro-European that was NICOLETTE found it understandably difficult to find her roots. Settling in Wales for a time, the singer made her mark in dance act, CALLIOPE before hooking up with seminal hardcore/rave sample-fiends SHUT UP & DANCE. The north London collective produced NICOLETTE's debut mini-set, 'NOW IS EARLY', releasing it on their own label in 1992. Unfortunately, due to the sample-happy nature of proceedings, the record was subsequently removed from the stores (although a re-issue did appear on the 'Studio K7' label in '97).

Unfazed by the whole episode, the philosophical lass put it down to experience. She could well afford to, as MASSIVE ATTACK had been sufficiently impressed to request her exotic vocals (memorably described as "Billie Holiday On Acid") on their sophomore album, 'Protection'. Released in 1994, the record featured NICOLETTE on a couple of typically sultry, langorous tracks, 'Three' and 'Sly'.

Groove guru Gilles Peterson was another to realise her talent and soon had her signed to his prestigious 'Talkin' Loud' label. The result was 1996's highly praised 'LET NO-ONE LIVE FREE IN YOUR HEAD', an album that will definitely take up rent-free residence in your brain given half a chance, or at least a couple of spins. Kooky, off-kilter, climactic, all essential adjectives in getting to grips with NICOLETTE's unique approach to music/singing. Flirting with various strains of dance music – including soul, techno, trip-hop and jungle – and filtering them through her own wayward yet tuneful muse, she came thrillingly close to the pure essence of 90's cut and paste ideology.

NICOLETTE – vocals / with producers **SHUT UP & DANCE**

Shut Up And Dance | not iss.

1991. (12") **O SINENE** [ ] [-]
1991. (12") **SINGLE MINDED PEOPLE** [ ] [-]
1992. (12"/cd-s) **WICKED MATHEMATICS** [ ] [-]
Apr 92. (cd/c/lp) *(SUAD CD/MC/LP 1)* **NOW IS EARLY** [ ] [ ]
– No government / Dove song / Single minded vocal / I woke up / Waking up (remix) / O si nene / It's only to be expected / Wicked mathematics / A single ring. *(re-iss. Oct97 on 'Studio K7'+= d-lp/cd; K7R 016/+CD)* – School of the world / Udi egwu.

Talkin Loud

Dec 95. (12"/cd-s) *(TL X/CD 1)* **NO GOVERNMENT / (mixes)** [67] [ ]
(12") *(TLXX 1)* – ('A'mixes).
Mar 96. (c-s/12"/cd-s) *(TL MC/X/CD 6)* **WE WILL NEVER KNOW / (mixes)** [ ] [ ]
Jun 96. (c-s/12"/cd-s) *(TL MC/X/CD 8)* **BEAUTIFUL DAY / (mixes)** [ ] [ ]
Jul 96. (cd/c/lp) *(532634-2/-4/-1)* **LET NO-ONE LIVE FREE IN YOUR HEAD** [?] [ ]
– Don't be afraid / We never know / Song for Europe / Beautiful day / Always / Nervous / Where have all the flowers gone / No government (acoustic) / Nightmare / Judgement day / You are Heaven sent / Just to say peace and love / No government #2 / Don't be ashamed (don't be afraid). *(cd/c re-iss. Aug98; same)*
Nov 96. (c-s/12"/cd-s) *(TL MC/X/CD 18)* **NIGHTMARE / (mixes)** [ ] [ ]
— in Mar'97, she featured on V/A cd/d-lp & ep, 'DJ Kicks'

– compilations, others, etc. –

Mar 97. (12") *Studio K7* **ALL DAY** [ ] [-]
Mar 98. (12"ep) *Studio K7; (K7R 016EP)* **NOW IS EARLY EP** [ ] [-]
– School of the world / Udi egwu.

NIGHTCRAWLERS featuring JOHN REID

Formed: Glasgow . . . 1992 as an alias for house producer/DJ/vocalist, JOHN REID. The NIGHTCRAWLERS will always be synonymous with only one track, but what a track; 'PUSH THE FEELING ON' must go down as one of the all-time dancefloor classics. Given its strong garage/deep house slant, it's hardly surprising that the song was initially a club hit in America where it had gradually risen to No.80 on the Billboard chart by the end of 1993. Although the track failed to hit the UK chart in its initial '4th & Broadway' incarnation, a remixed version on 'ffrr' narrowly missed the Top 20 in late '94. DJ's just couldn't resist that nagging vocal hook though, and the song's mass club appeal finally saw it make the Top 3 courtesy of a MARK KINCHEN remix in Spring '95. Follow-up track 'DON'T LET THE FEELING GO' was basically a retread of the formula, hitting the Top 20 later that year. This success even spawned a Top 20 album, unashamedly titled 'LET'S PUSH IT'. A further trio of minor hits milked it till the end yet REID proved he wasn't merely a one-trick pony by penning successful material for the likes of BAD BOYS INC., ETERNAL, GEMINI and OPTIMYSTIC.

• **Note:** The NIGHTCRAWLERS who issued a CD late 2000 on 'Big Beat', were obviously not the same outfit.

JOHN REID – vocals, multi / with **GRAHAM WILSON** – keyboards / etc

4th&Broad | Great Jones

1993. (12") **LIVING INSIDE A DREAM (mixes)** [ ] [-]
Oct 92. (12") <530620> **PUSH THE FEELING ON (mixes)** [ ] [80]
1994. (7"/c-s) *(BRW/BRCA 269)* **WHENEVER YOU NEED SOMEONE. / ('A'mix)** [ ] [-]
(12"+=/cd-s+=) *(12BRW/BRCD 269)* – ('A'mixes).

ffrr | London

Oct 94. (c-s/12"/cd-s; as NIGHTCRAWLERS) *(FCS/FX/FCD 245)* **PUSH THE FEELING ON (mixes)** [22] [ ]
Feb 95. (c-s/12"/cd-s) *(FCS/FX/FCD 257)* **PUSH THE FEELING ON (mixes)** [3] [ ]

Final Vinyl – Arista | Arista

May 95. (c-s/12"/cd-s) *(74321 28398-4/-1/-2)* **SURRENDER YOUR LOVE (mixes)** [7] [ ]
Sep 95. (c-s/12"/cd-s) *(74321 29882-4/-1/-2)* **DON'T LET THE FEELING GO (mixes)** [13] [ ]
Sep 95. (cd/c) *(74321 30970-2/-4)* **LET'S PUSH IT** [14] [ ]
– Push the feeling on (MK dub of doom mix) / Surrender your love (MK club mix) / Don't let the feeling go / Should I ever (fall in love) / Just like before / Lift me up / The world turns / Let's push it / I like it / All over the world / Push the feeling on (Mk club mix) / Surrender your love (Wand's krunch nut mix) / Don't let the feeling go (Tin Tin Out mix).
Jan 96. (c-s/12"/cd-s) *(74321 32814-4/-1/-2)* **LET'S PUSH IT (mixes)** [23] [ ]
(cd-s) *(74321 32815-2)* – ('A'mixes).
Apr 96. (c-s/12"/cd-s) *(74321 35807-4/-1/-2)* **SHOULD I EVER (FALL IN LOVE) (mixes)** [34] [ ]
Jul 96. (c-s/12"/cd-s; as NIGHTCRAWLERS featuring JOHN REID and ALYSHA WARREN) *(74321 39042-4/-1/-2)* **KEEP ON PUSHING OUR LOVE (mixes)** [30] [ ]
Aug 96. (cd/c) *(74321 39043-2/-4)* **LET'S PUSH IT FURTHER: THE 12" MIXES** (compilation) [ ] [-]

Riverhorse | unknown

Jun 99. (12"/cd-s; as NIGHTCRAWLERS) *(RIVH 12/CD 1)* **NEVER KNEW LOVE (mixes; radio / Tee's freeze / Mash up Matt)** [59] [ ]
(cd-s) *(RIVHCD 1X)* – ('A'mixes).

NIGHTSHIFT

Formed: Edinburgh . . . 1978 by DAVE WILLIAMS, NEIL GAMMACK and Mr. THOMSON. Managed by Jimmy Devlin and signed to Bruce Findlay's 'Zoom' records, the melodious Power-pop outfit – somehat in the BEATLES tradition – released a couple of 45's before signing big with 'Harvest' records. Their first single for the label, 'DON'T RUSH THE GOOD THINGS' was a flop when it hit the shops initially, although many years later a certain TINA TURNER used it for a B-side. DAVE is now an arty photographer while NEIL is a taxi driver.

DAVE WILLIAMS – vocals, guitar / **NEIL GAMMACK** – bass / **Mr. THOMSON** – drums

Zoom | not iss.

Aug 78. (7") *(ZUM 7)* **LOVE IS BLIND. / SHE MAKES ME LOVE HER** [ ] [-]
Jan 79. (7") *(ZUM 9)* **JET SET. / BAD DREAMS** [ ] [-]

		Harvest	not iss.
Feb 80.	(7") *(HAR 5197)* **DON'T RUSH THE GOOD THINGS. / CHANGE IN THE WEATHER**	☐	-
Jul 80.	(7") *(HAR 5211)* **SENDING ME. / SILLY BOY**	☐	-
Sep 80.	(7") *(HAR 5214)* **DANCE IN THE MOONLIGHT. / DON'T RUSH THE GOOD THINGS (long version)**	☐	-

— split soon after above

NJ

Born: Gorbals, Glasgow. Raised from the late 60's by her Catholic mother and Sri Lankan (former sailor) dad, NJ (ANGIE), the petite, but strong-minded teenager found it difficult at times after her parents divorced. One of seven children, NJ moved with her mother to Bradford, then Leeds, before taking off to New York. Involved with drugs, in particular acid, the grown-up NJ took up singing to compensate for her disfunctional background. In 1993, her luck changed after a chance meeting with fellow glam-punks in a Camden (London) pub; they would subsequently become TINY MONROE and release their first of several singles, 'VHF 855V' (the registration of her Ford Escort car!), early the following year. She subsequently featured in a BBC TV short play, 'The Traveller' (as an android), while all the group finally delivered their debut long-player, 'VOLCANOES', in 1996; she has since taken up painting and art as more than just a hobby.

NOISE ANNOYS (see ⇒ Section 9: wee post-punk groups)

NOSTRIL (see under ⇒ Flotsam & Jetsam records)

NO WAY SIS

Formed: Glasgow . . . early '96 strictly as an OASIS tribute outfit (charging good money £8 at the door, too!). With pseudonyms such as THE FIRST NOEL, LIAM MALONE, THE COUNTERFEIT GUIGSY, ALAN SHITE and er, BONEHEAD (no change there, then!), the five-piece imposters stuck their two fingers up to the music biz just like their massive selling counterparts. What the fighting GALLAGHER brothers thought about it all was anybody's guess, especially when NO WAY SIS were tipped (by the bookies of course!) to hit the Xmas No.1 via their Manc-aye version of the New Seekers' 'I'D LIKE TO TEACH THE WORLD TO SING'. However this Coke classic (sic!) only scraped into the Top 30, the OASIS lads could breath easily again.

THE FIRST NOEL – guitar, vocals / **LIAM MALONE** – vocals / **BONEHEAD** – guitar / THE COUNTERFEIT GUIGSY – bass / **ALAN SHITE** – drums

		E.M.I.	not iss.
Dec 96.	(c-s/7") *(TC+/EM 461)* **I'D LIKE TO TEACH THE WORLD TO SING. / QUICK SAND SONG**	27	-
	(cd-s+=) *(CDEM 461)* – Good times.		

— basically still around for a few years on the tribute circuit

NT (see ⇒ Section 9: Dance/Rave)

NYAH FEARTIES

Formed: Lugton, Ayrshire . . . 1986 by the WISEMAN brothers DAVIE and STEPHEN (FEARTIE). Kicking off their musical career as street buskers in London, they fell in with fellow folk-based punk rebels The POGUES whom they subsequently supported. The band's drummer, ANDREW RANKINE, later contributed vocals to NYAH FEARTIES' debut album, 'A TASTY HEIDFU' (1986), wherein the brothers laid down their patented soundclash of screaming, bastardised acoustic folk/rockabilly and brain-clanking 'found' percussion. To promote the album, the band appeared on 80's youth TV showcase, The Tube, scaring the Sassenachs with their manic Caledonian meltdown and ensuring themselves a permanent place in the alternative scene's outer limits.

Boasting a psychedelic orange/tartan sleeve, the 'GOOD, BAD AND ALKIES' EP (1988) marked the band's return to their homeland and featured a live version of crowd favourite, 'DRUNKEN UNCLE'. 1989's 'GRAVESIDE / GRAHAMSIDE', meanwhile, was a home-produced cassette-only affair recorded for the European market where NYAH FEARTIES' crazed Celtic appeal was greatly appreciated (incredibly perhaps, they also managed to get on the bill of many a folk hoedown in Wales and Ireland).

The group's long awaited sophomore album, 'DESPERATION O' A DYIN' CULTURE' arrived in 1990, a record partly recorded at The TRASH CAN SINATRAS' 'Shabby Road' studio in Kilmarnock and featuring a version of fave live cover, 'GAMBLIN' BAR ROOM BLUES'. With the subsequent addition of ALLAN FEARTIE, FRANCIS LOPEZ and MICHAEL WOODS, the group changed their moniker to The COLLABORATORS, releasing an eponymous, initially Holland-only cassette in anticipation of a Dutch tour. The name change proved a temporary phenomenon however, the good old NYAH FEARTIES badge back in place for 1992's 'RED KOLA' EP.

Perennially more popular in Europe than back home (what they made of 1994 cassette, 'A KEECH IN A POKE!!!', I don't know), the band's final album, 'GRANPA' CRAW' was initially given a release by French label, 'Danceteria', the original sleeve featuring a painting of Kirkcaldy darts hero, Jocky Wilson while the Scottish version featured samples of Kilmarnock FC's crowd in full song. Following NYAH FEARTIES' final demise, DAVIE and MICHAEL (WOODS) continued on the folk crossover path with the wonderfully named DUB SKELPER.

DAVIE WISEMAN – bass, vocals / **STEPHEN WISEMAN** – ganjo, percussion / plus **DONALD CUTHBERTSON** – percussion

		L.Y.T.	not iss.
Mar 87.	(lp) *(DOLLP 001)* **A TASTY HEIDFU'**	☐	-
	– A tasty heidfu' / Red roller / Glen Ashdale falls / Theme fae in the barn / Lugton calling / Rantin' Robbie / Bludgeon man / Where the wind blows cold / Apathy / Hallelujah.		
		D.D.T.	not iss.
Jan 88.	(12"ep) *(DISP 14T)* **GOOD, BAD AND ALKIES**	☐	-
	– Raisin' Bible John / Recobite Grace / Theme fae in the barn / Drunken uncle (live).		

— the NYAH FEARTIES moonlighted with ANNA PALM who released two albums for 'One Little Indian', 'ARRIVING AND CAUGHT UP' (Feb'90) and 'ANNA PALM' (Sep'92).

		L.Y.T.	not iss.
1989.	(7") **BARASSIE. / MOTORWAY / PUDDOCKS IN THE MIST**	-	-
1989.	(c) **GRAVESIDE / GRAHAM SIDE**	-	- Europe
	– Barassie / Lightnin' bolt / Pagan man / Barnweil boys / Lullaby / etc		
1990.	(lp) **DESPERATION O' A DYIN' CULTURE**	☐	-
	– Trashcans / Puddocks in the mist / The railway beast waltz / Release / Life's endless grind / Flight o' the country / Hills o' new Galloway / Vexation / Lugton junction / Sair erse / Baith sides o' the bed / Desperate jig / Gamblin' bar room blues.		

— added **ALLAN FEARTIE** – bass / plus **FRANCIS LOPEZ** – guitar / **MICHAEL WOODS** – fiddle, penny whistle

1991.	(c; as the COLLABORATORS) **COLLABORATORS**	☐	-
1992.	(c-ep) **RED KOLA**	☐	-
	– Red kola / Living room rock'n'roll / Rantin' Sonsie & free / Kirk ha' jig.		
1994.	(c) **A KEECH IN A POKE!!!**	☐	-
		Danceteria	not iss.
Feb 95.	(cd) *(NYAH 942)* **GRANPA' CRAW**	☐	-
	– Jolly walkers / Bullworker jig / Slash & burn / Safe as houses – Dub housing / Granpa Craw / Good times / MOR / Lightning bolt / Away away – All the boys in Ayrshire / Wendy doon the banking / Campbelton Loch / Restless.		

— split in the summer of 1995; DAVIE and MICHAEL formed DUB SKELPER

– compilations, etc. –

1994.	(cd) *Jivaroc* **SKUD**	-	- French

O

OBABEN

Formed: Edinburgh . . . 1998 by songwriter BEN WRIGHT, who studied medieval history at Edinburgh University. Taking their moniker from the Portuguese meaning, "Hey! Ben", OBABEN (basically BEN plus DOM GIBBESON and SAM) delivered their first Mediterranean offering, 'NINETEEN', towards the end of '99. Six months on (and with DOM GOUNDAR, ROB JENKINS, GERARD McLACHAN and a handful of violinists replacing SAM), their surprisingly fresh Jamie Watson-produced debut album for 'Human Condition', 'BLUE EYE' (2000), was met with indifferent reviews – imagine 'The Wicker Man' film set in a Spanish amphitheatre topped off with NEIL HANNON (DIVINE COMEDY) on lead vox and you would be quite close to their Med/indie-Folk. Follow-up, 'MARBLEHEAD' (2001), continued in the same romantic vein and it was hard to work out why this eclectic bunch hadn't broken through. Play OBABEN to someone you meet on a foreign holiday and confuse them by saying they come from Scotland(!).

BEN WRIGHT – vocals, guitars / **DOM GIBBESON** – bass / **SAM** – drums

		Human Condition	not iss.
Nov 99.	(7") *(HC 0025)* **NINETEEN. / AUTUMN HEART**		-

— basically **BEN + DOM** with **ROB JENKINS** – lead guitar / **DOM GOUNDAR** – percussion / **GERARD McLACHAN** – drums / plus **GREG MICKELBOROUGH** – string arrangements / **JIM O'TOOLE + GAYLE SWANN + TAROT COUZYN + CARENZA HUGH-JONES** – violins / **LUCY HARDY + FRANCESCA DYMOND + JULIETTE RAWLINS + JOANNA HOWARD** – other vocals

May 00.	(cd) *(HCCD 0028)* **BLUE EYE** – Nineteen / Smash him up / Blink again / A letter / Autumn heart / Kyrie / Northern wind / Saranda / Blue eye.		-
Apr 01.	(cd) *(HCCD 32)* **MARBLEHEAD** – Intro / Beauty blinds / Sin descanso / Bar to bed / 5 a.m. / Blow up / EC4 / Blink again / Marblehead / Din-o-rush / Columbia road / Luke, who is he? / She tells tales / Sounds and signs / Outro.		-
May 01.	(cd-ep) *(HCCD 33)* **BEAUTY BLINDS / TUESDAY MORNING / PISS TALKERS**		-

OCTOPUS

Formed: Shotts, Lanarkshire . . . 1995 by frontman MARC SHEARER and guitarist ALAN McSEVENEY. Disillusioned by the Glasgow indie scene, the pair took off to London with new recruits CAMERON MILLER (an old school mate) and OLIVER GRASSEL. Having played several gigs down south, OCTOPUS were eyeballed by DAVID FRANCOLINI (ex-LEVITATION drummer), who duly despatched their demo to Andy Ross at EMI's 'Food' offshoot. Immediately impressed (as he was with The SUPERNATURALS), Ross signed the band and issued their debut single, 'MAGAZINE', early in 1996. As a live act, OCTOPUS were joined on stage by four other members (tentacles, you could say) including harmonica-player NICK REYNOLDS, son of the Great Train Robber, Bruce Reynolds; a piece for the press/media at the time. OCTOPUS' sophomore effort, 'YOUR SMILE', complete with melodic, guitar-rock appeal, certainly brightened up the Top 50. That September, the band went one better and into the Top 40 courtesy of 'SAVED', although the accompanying debut album, 'FROM A TO B', was given short-shrift on several reviews. By 1997, all four were looking for other outlets.

MARC SHEARER – vocals, guitar / ALAN McSEVENEY – guitar / **CAMERON MILLER** – bass / **OLIVER GRASSEL** – drums

		Food	not iss.
Mar 96.	(7") *(FOOD 68)* **MAGAZINE. / ADRENALINA** (cd-s+=) *(CDFOOD 68)* – (Untitled) / Unicorns and eiderdowns.		-
Jun 96.	(7") *(FOOD 78)* **YOUR SMILE. / KING FOR A DAY** (cd-s+=) *(CDFOOD 78)* – Catboy.	42	-
Sep 96.	(7") *(FOOD 84)* **SAVED. / I KNOW WHO I AM** (cd-s+=) *(CDFOODS 84)* – Guestlist. (cd-s) *(CDFOOD 84)* – ('A'side) / No answer / What did you do today? / True, true, true.	40	-
Sep 96.	(cd/c/lp) *(FOOD CD/MC/LPX 18)* **FROM A TO B** – Your smile / Everyday kiss / If you want to give me more / King for a day / Adrenalina / Instrumental 1 / Jealousy / Magazine / From A to B / Instrumental 2 / Saved / Wait & see / Theme from Joy Pop / Night song / In this world.		-
Nov 96.	(7") *(FOOD 87)* **JEALOUSY. / THIS BOOK'S FOR YOU** (cd-s+=) *CDFOODS 87)* – Neon lights. (cd-s) *(CDFOOD 87)* – ('A'side) / Everyday kiss (live) / Your smile / Theme from Yes Yes Yes.	59	-

— disbanded the following year

ODEON BEATCLUB

Formed: Glasgow . . . late 1998 by PAUL TIERNEY, his sister JOANNE and DES. This bunch of Lo-Fi punksters were proof that if you mixed BLACK SABBATH with the DIY techniques of, say, SPARE SNARE then you're left with something like ODEON BEAT CLUB. The troupe of floppy-haired songsmiths arrived on the Glasgow indie scene in early 1999, playing an eventful gig at King Tut's Wah Wah Hut, which secured their reputation and spawned more sold-out shows around the country. Adding TOMMY when JO nearly left, they delivered a self-financed debut single, 'THE PAST GONE MAD' early the following year. Scottish culture magazine, 'The List' had already championed the group in their live review section, prompting 'Play' records to give OBC their first proper single, 'I NEED MORE TIME'. A tender, melodic and simply downright brilliant slice of indie rock/pop, with PAUL's vocals shining gloriously through to the surface, Radio 1 Scotland saw the appeal and immediately played it every night on their 'Evening Session' show; Steve Lamacq subsequently playlisted the track on his programme. A nationwide tour followed, with the group (now a quartet) taking time out mid 2002 to record another homegrown CD-single, 'BEING REALISTIC'.

PAUL TIERNEY – vocals, guitar / **JOANNE TIERNEY** – bass / **DES** – drummer / added **TOMMY** – guitar

		Polyester	not iss.
Jan 01.	(cd-s) *(mail-o)* **THE PAST GONE MAD / NICKED**		-
Aug 01.	(cd-s) *(PLAY 006CD)* **I NEED MORE TIME / NICKED** *(above issued on 'Play' records)*		-
Jul 02.	(cd-s) *(mail-o)* **BEING REALISTIC / TV EMPATHY**		-

Phil 'Swill' & Jon ODGERS

Born: Best known as integral parts (guitarist and drummer respectively) of London-based indie folk outfit, The MEN THEY COULDN'T HANG. Formerly buskers, the Scottish brothers met up with their aforementioned English compadres in 1983, releasing Eric Bogle's anti-war anthem 'THE GREEN FIELDS OF FRANCE' the following year. For the next seven years, the crusty band became favourites all over the country, peaking with 1989's 'Silvertown' UK Top 40 set. After a spell with LIBERTY CAGE in the mid-90's (with the Men's PAUL SIMMONDS), SWILL helped re-form the lively band in 1996. Of late (early 2000 to be exact), SWILL recorded with that man SIMMONDS on an acoustic set, 'BABY FISHLIPS' for 'Twah!' records.

OFFHOOKS (see under ⇒ THANES)

OI POLLOI

Formed: Edinburgh . . . 1984 by DEGSY ALLAN and Co. Although their moniker might have suggested an association with the "oi" movement, OI POLLOI (which was taken from the ancient Greek meaning of "the common people") had more in common with the likes of CRASS and CONFLICT.

After building up a loyal fanbase in the capital, these politically correct anarcho-punks finally made it onto vinyl in early '86, sharing the 'UNLIMITED GENOCIDE' lp with AOA. In fact, OI POLLOI also shared their following two sets, 'MAD AS FUCK (DON'T YOU THINK?)' and 'SKINS 'N' PUNKS II', with TOXIK EPHEX and BETRAYED respectively. Lending their weight to the anti-censorship movement, OI POLLOI contributed one track, 'NO FILTHY NUCLEAR POWER', to the JELLO (BIAFRA) AID compilation album, 'Censorship Sucks', the proceeds from which went towards the cost of the DEAD KENNEDYS frontman's impending court case (cover art by the illustrious Harry Horse!).

In 1987, moving in an increasingly punk-metal hybrid direction, the band delivered their first exclusive set, 'UNITE AND WIN', a subsequent two year hiatus broken with the impassioned protest of 'IN DEFENCE OF OUR EARTH' (1990). Having earlier signed to 'Words Of Warning' (home of fellow anti-Nazis, BLAGGERS ITA), they went on to issue the EP 'OMNICIDE' in '92. Despite being largely ignored by the indie press, OI POLLOI battled on. In 1998, the quartet signed to Devon-based 'Ruptured Emotions', delivering their umpteenth 7" EP, 'GUILTY' the same year; their comeback album 'FUAIM CATHA!' (The Sound Of Battle) was issued in '99.

DEGSY ALLAN – vocals / **BOB** – guitar / **BOBBY** – bass / **MURRAY** – drums

		Children Of The Revolution	not iss.
Jan 86.	(lp; shared with AOA) *(GURT 12)* **UNLIMITED GENOCIDE** – Go green / You cough they profit / Punx or mice / Nuclear waste / The only release / Apartheid stinx / (others by AOA).		-
		Endangered Musik	**not iss.**
May 86.	(7"ep) *(EDR 5)* **RESIST THE ATOMIC MENACE EP** – Hands off Nicaragua / Scum / They shoot children don't they / Resist the atomic menace / Reach for the light. *(re-iss. 1994; same)*		-
		Green Vomit	**not iss.**
Oct 86.	(lp; shared with TOXIK EPHEX) *(PUKE 15)* **MAD AS FUCK (DON'T YOU THINK?)** – Go green / Scum / Minority authority / They shoot children, don't they? / The only release? / Foundations for a future / No filthy nuclear power / (others by TOXIC EPHEX).		-
		Oi!	**not iss.**
Jan 87.	(lp; shared with BETRAYED) *(OIR 008)* **SKINS 'N' PUNKS II**		-

– Boot down the door / Americans out / Thugs in uniform / Pigs for slaughter / Rich scumbag / Never give in / Minority authority / Skinhead / (others by the BETRAYED).

Oct 87. (lp) *(OIR 011)* **UNITE AND WIN** [ ] [-]
– Punx 'n' skins / We don't need them / Kill the bill / Lowest of the low / Nuclear waste / Commies and Nazis / Pigs for slaughter / Scum / Thrown on the scrapheap / Punx picnic in Princess Street gardens / Mindless few / Unite and win! *(cd-iss. Apr01 on 'Step 1'+=; STEPCD 132)* – SKINS'N'PUNKS lp tracks.

Words Of Warning / not iss.

Jul 90. (lp) *(WOWLP 10)* **IN DEFENCE OF OUR EARTH** [ ] [-]
– Thin green line / 23 hours / When two men kiss / Whale song / What have we done / Victims of a chemical spillage / Anarcho pie / Clachan chalanais / Free the Henge / Nazi scum / World park Antartica. *(cd-iss. May00+=; WOWCD 10)* – Dealer in death / Omnicide / Victims of a gas attack / Die for BP (time to stop the war).

Jan 92. (7"ep) *(WOW 17)* **OMNICIDE EP** [ ] [-]
– Dealer in death / Omnicide / Victims of a gas attack / Die for BP (time to stop the war).

1994. (7"ep; shared with BLOWNAPART) **BASTARDS** [ ] [-]
– Right to choose / Victims of a gas attack / (2 by other group).

Campary / not iss.

1998. (7"ep) **THC EP** [ ] [-]
– THC / Sex with strangers / Simon Weston / Meine augen.

Ruptured Ambitions / not iss.

Sep 98. (7"ep) *(RUP 1)* **GUILTY EP** [ ] [-]
– Guilty / Break the mould / John Major – fuck you / Bash the fash.

Jul 99. (7"ep) *(GRAND 1)* **LET THE BOOTS DO THE TALKING EP** [ ] [-]
– It doesn't have to be like this / Let the boots do the talking / Stay alert / Fuck the national lottery / Threshers – fuck off!

Skuld / not iss.

1999. (lp) **FUAIM CATHA!** [ ] [-]
– The Earth is our mother / Terra-Ist / Take back the land / Religious con / Don't burn the witch / The right to choose / Fuck everybody who voted Tory / Sios leis a' ghniomhachas mhoir / G.L.F. / Willie McRae / Deathcafe / Your beer is shit and your money stinks / Sell-out / No more roads / Hunt the rich / Mindrot / Anti-police aggro.

– compilations, etc. –

Jan 91. (m-lp) *Words Of Warning; (WOWLP 13)* **OUTRAGED BY THE ATOMIC MENACE** [ ] [-]
– Outrage / Thugs in uniform / Resist the atomic menace / Death by night.

Apr 92. (cd) *Released Emotions; (REM 017)* **TOTAL ANARCHOI (some live)** [ ] [-]
– Nuclear waste / Boot down the door / Pigs for slaughter / Scum / Thrown on the scrapheap / Punx picnic / Mindless few / Unite and win / Omnicide (live) / Americans out (live) / Pigs for slaughter (live) / Thugs in uniform (live) / Nazi scum (live) / Nuclear waste (live) / Free the Henge (live) / Punx picnic (live) / State violence, state control (live) * / If the kids are united *. *(re-iss. Nov97 & Mar02 on 'Step 1' cd/lp*-; STEP CD/LP 073)* – (LP w/out *).

Mar 97. (lp) *Campary; (CAMPARY 024)* **FIGHT BACK** [ ] [-]
– (split sides with the BETRAYED and AOA).

Mar 02. (cd) *Rugger Bugger; (SEEP 32CD)* **SIX OF THE BEST** [ ] [-]

Jun 02. (cd) *Step 1; (STEPCD 139)* **OUTRAGED BY THE SYSTEM** [ ] [-]

OLDSOLAR (see under ⇒ Mint records)

ONE DOVE

Formed: Glasgow ... 1991 as DOVE by Applied Biochemistry student/graduate DOROTHY 'DOT' ALLISON, along with IAN CARMICHAEL and former ALTERED IMAGES man, JIM McKINVEN. Initially released on the local 'Soma' imprint, the dreamy ambience of 'FALLEN' was subsequently remixed and re-issued by the 'Boys Own' label, an operation partly run by DJ extrordinaire, ANDREW WEATHERALL. The band's association with WEATHERALL (then a guru for the dance crossover crowd) helped create a buzz that peaked with the release of 'WHITE LOVE' (recorded with the help of JAH WOBBLE and PRIMAL SCREAM's ANDREW INNES amongst others), another slice of shimmering, crescendoing ambient dance-pop that only just missed out on a Top 40 place in summer '93.

The band's rock'n'roll credentials were assured by a headline grabbing jaunt down the Thames and with the hype machine still in overdrive, ONE DOVE's much vaunted debut album, 'MORNING DOVE WHITE' (1993), was finally released in September. Not exactly the groundbreaking opus some fans had been led to expect, the album was nevertheless a pleasant enough melange of classic pop, dub reggae, ambience and rock dynamics, all wrapped up in DOT's sensuous, JULEE CRUISE-esque vocals. The record scraped a Top 30 placing, as did subsequent singles 'BREAKDOWN' and the luscious 'WHY DON'T YOU TAKE ME', the latter featuring a groovy, chilled out cover of Dolly Parton classic, 'JOLENE'.

Very much a band of their era, ONE DOVE split acrimoniously in 1996 during the recording of their second album. DOT's fortunes went from bad to worse as she suffered a serious car crash which left her in a wheelchair for a period. However, now fighting fit, she started work in the studio on her first solo release, 'Afterglow' (1999).

• **Trivia:** IAN has produced records for The BACHELOR PAD and The ORCHIDS.

DOROTHY 'DOT' ALLISON (b.1970, Edinburgh) – vocals, keyboards, programming / **IAN CARMICHAEL** – keyboards, programming / **JIM McKINVEN** – keyboards, programming (ex-ALTERED IMAGES) with various + producer **ANDREW WEATHERALL**

Soma / not iss.

Oct 91. (12"; as DOVE) *(Soma 2)* **FALLEN. / ('A'-Farley / Heller mix)** [ ] [-]

Boys Own / London

Aug 92. (12") **TRANSIENT TRUTH. / ('A'-Sabres Of Paradise mix)** [ ] [-]
(12") – ('A'side) / ('A'vocal) / ('A'dub version).

— now with **JAH WOBBLE, ANDREW INNES, EDDIE HIGGINS, PHIL MOSSMAN, TOM BAEPPLER, GARY BURNS, JAGZ KOONER**

Jul 93. (c-s) *(BOICS 14)* **WHITE LOVE / ('A'dub mix)** [43] [ ]
(12"+=/cd-s+=) *(BOI X/CD 14)* – ('A'-Guitar mix).

Sep 93. (cd/c/lp) *(828352-2/-4/-1)* **MORNING DOVE WHITE** [30] [ ]
– Fallen / White love (guitar Paradise mix) / Breakdown (cellophane boat mix) / There goes the cure / Sirens / My friend / Transient youth / Why don't you take me / White love (piano reprise). *(cd+=/c+=)* – Breakdown (radio mix) / White love (radio mix).

Oct 93. (12"/c-s) *(BOI X/CS 15)* **BREAKDOWN. / ('A'-William Orbit mix)** [24] [ ]
(12"+=) *(BOIXR 15)* – ('A'-Squire Black Dove mix).
(cd-s++=) *(BOICD 15)* – (2 other mixes).

Jan 94. (12"/c-s) *(BOI X/CS 16)* **WHY DON'T YOU TAKE ME. / ('A'-Underworld remix)** [30] [ ]
(12"+=/cd-s+=) *(BOI XR/CD 16)* – Jolene / Skanga.

— disbanded in 1996 while recording a second set, DOT went solo in '99

1" VOLCANO (see under ⇒ Alphabetty records)

ONE O'CLOCK GANG (see under ⇒ SET THE TONE)

ORANGE JUICE (see under ⇒ COLLINS, Edwyn)

ORCHIDS

Formed: Govan, Glasgow ... by main songwriter, JAMES HACKETT, alongside MATTHEW DRUMMOND, CHRIS QUINN, JAMES MOODY and JOHN. A surprise signing to 'Sarah' records late in 1987, they released their first official debut, 'I'VE GOT A HABIT', early the following year having previously recorded a flexi-disc track for indie fanzine 'Sha La La'. A popsicle bedsit-land band with a sound similar to The BATHERS or The WEATHER PROPHETS, they released a series of singles, most of them appearing on their IAN CARMICHAEL (ONE DOVE)-produced debut set, 'UNHOLY SOUL' (1991). The ORCHIDS continued to flower over subsequent albums, namely 'EPICUREAN: A SOUNDTRACK' (1992) and 'STRIVING FOR THE LAZY PERFECTION' (1994), the latter being produced by ONE DOVE's IAN CARMICHAEL.

JAMES HACKETT – vocals / **MATTHEW DRUMMOND** – guitar / **JOHN** – guitar / **JAMES MOODY** – bass / **CHRIS QUINN** – drums

Sha La La / not iss.

Jun 87. (7"flexi) *(Sha La La Ba Ba Ba 5)* **FROM THIS DAY. / Sea Urchins:- Summertime** [ ] [-]

Sarah / not iss.

Feb 88. (7"ep) *(SARAH 002)* **I'VE GOT A HABIT EP** [ ] [-]
– I've got a habit / Apologies / Give me some peppermint freedom.

Nov 88. (7"ep) *(SARAH 011)* **UNDERNEATH THE WINDOW, UNDERNEATH THE SINK EP** [ ] [-]
– Defy the law / Underneath the window, underneath the sink / Tiny words / Walter.

Aug 89. (10"m-lp) *(SARAH 401)* **LYCEUM (live)** [ ] [-]
– It's only obvious / A place called home / Caveman / The York song / Carole-Ann / Hold on / Blue light / If you can't find love.

Sep 89. (7"m) *(SARAH 023)* **WHAT WILL WE DO NEXT. / AS TIME GOES BY / YAWN** [ ] [-]

Feb 90. (12"m) *(SARAH 029)* **SOMETHING FOR THE LONGING. / FAREWELL, DEAR BONNIE / ON A SUNDAY** [ ] [-]
(below single on 'Caff')

— DRUMMOND + MOODY were also part of The WAKE in the early 90's

Sep 90. (7"ltd) *(CAFF 11)* **AN ILL WIND THAT BLOWS. / ALL THOSE THINGS** [ ] [-]
Feb 91. (12"ep) *(SARAH 042)* **PENETRATION** [ ] [-]
– Bemused confused and bedraggled / Pelican blonde / Tropical fishbowl / How does that feel / Sigh.
May 91. (lp/cd) *(SARAH 605/+CD)* **UNHOLY SOUL** [ ] [-]
– Me and the black and white dream / Women priests and addicts / Bringing you the love / Frank De Salvo / Long drawn Sunday night / Peaches / Dirty clothing / Moon lullaby / Coloured stone / The sadness of sex (part 1) / Waiting for the storm / You know I'm fine.
Sep 92. (7"/cd-s) *(SARAH 066/+CD)* **THAUMATURGY. / I WAS JUST DREAMING / BETWEEN SLEEPING AND WAKING** [ ] [-]
Sep 92. (lp/cd) *(SARAH 611/+CD)* **EPICUREAN: A SOUNDTRACK** (compilation) [ ] [-]
– Peaches / A place called home / Tiny words / Moon lullaby / Walter / It's only obvious / Long drawn Sunday night / Blue light / Yawn / Sigh / Something for the longing / The York song / Bemused confused and bedraggled / Caveman / Underneath the window, underneath the sink / Pelican blonde / Women priests and addicts / Carole-Anne / Tropical fishbowl / The sadness of sex (part 1).
Jan 94. (lp/cd) *(SARAH 617/+CD)* **STRIVING FOR THE LAZY PERFECTION** [ ] [-]
– Obsession No.1 / Striving for the lazy perfection / The searching / Welcome to my curious heart / Avignon / A living Ken and Barbie / Beautiful liar / A kind of Eden / Prayers to St. Jude / Lovechild / Give a little honey / I've got to wake up / The perfect reprise.
— went to ground after above

– compilations, etc. –

1990's. (7"ep; split with BOUQUET + CRYSTAL GARDEN) *Bring On Bull; (BULL 007)* **STRIVING FOR LAZY PERFECTION** [ ] [-]

OSTLE BAY (see under ⇒ TRASH CAN SINATRAS)

P

PABLO (see under ⇒ Soma records)

PAINKILLERS (see under ⇒ Human Condition records)

PAINTED WORD

Formed: Glasgow ... mid-80's by ALAN McLUSKER THOMPSON, MUSHIE WESTON, ROBBIE ROSS and NIGEL HURST. Described as Baroque-rockpop, The PAINTED WORD signed a deal with U2's 'Mother' label, although only one single, 'INDEPENDENCE DAY', surfaced in '86. It looked as if the 'WORD were spreading far and wide and, when 'Elektra' came knocking the quartet looked like being on the verge of a major breakthrough. However, one of the unluckiest modern day music tales unfolded, when – just as they were about to sign with the aforementioned imprint – the US-based operation went belly-up. By 1988, only McLUSKER THOMPSON remained from the original line-up; DOUGIE VIPOND – later DEACON BLUE – had deputised in briefly. Session men were subsequently called in by PAINTED WORD's new label 'R.C.A.' (who'd picked up the proverbial pieces) but unfortunately the debut set, 'LOVELIFE' (1989), was too little too late.

ALAN McLUSKER THOMPSON – vocals, guitar / **MUSHIE WESTON** / **ROBBIE ROSS** / **NIGEL HURST** –

Mother / not iss.
Jul 86. (7") *(MUM 5)* **INDEPENDENCE DAY. / LETTER FROM JACKIE** [ ] [-]
(12"+=) *(12MUM 5)* – State of mind.
— now down to **McLUSKER THOMPSON** and session people

R.C.A. / R.C.A.
Apr 89. (7") *(PB 42703)* **WORLDWIDE. / I FOUND LOVE TODAY** [ ] [-]
(12"+=/cd-s+=) *(PT/PD 42704)* – My darkest hour.
(re-iss. May89; PB/PT 42807/42840)
Jul 89. (7") *(PB 42917)* **THAT'S THE REASON I'M ALIVE. / THIS IS GOING TO BE MY WORLD** [ ] [-]
(12"+=) *(PT 42918)* – ('A'-instrumental).
(cd-s++=) *(PD 42918)* – Perfect timing.
Sep 89. (lp/c/cd) *(PL/PK/PD 74165)* **LOVELIFE** [ ] [ ]
– That's the reason I'm alive / Lovelife / Wilderness / Frances / Joie de vivre / 24 hours / Worldwide / I want here and I want it now / '77 / The pleasure inside.
— disappeared after above

PAISLEY SHIRTS (see ⇒ Section 9: the 90s)

PALLAS

Formed: Aberdeen ... 1975 by CRAIG ANDERSON, DEREK HOLT, RONNIE BROWN, GRAEME MURRAY and DEREK FORMAN. Unable to secure a major deal, this neo-Prog rock outfit issued a self-financed EP, 'PALLAS' in 1978.

Touring constantly over the next four years, they finally delivered a follow-up single, 'ARRIVE ALIVE', EUAN LAWSON and NIALL MATHEWSON had been called in to replace CRAIG and DEREK respectively. A debut set of 1981 'Granite Wax' demos was finally released by 'Cool King' in 1983 and showed that MARILLION were not the only rock group to adopt keyboards as an overriding influence. EMI's 'Harvest' saw sufficient promise in the band to sign them, the label bringing in EDDIE OFFORD (early producer of YES) to refine their sound on the concept set, 'THE SENTINEL' (1984). The over-complex record was met with mixed reviews, although it still managed to reach No.41 in the UK charts. Shortly after, vocalist ALAN REED replaced LAWSON, a follow-up, 'THE WEDGE' (1986) disappointing all but their mothers and leading to the band being dropped by EMI.

Some band members subsequently joined ABEL GANZ, CASINO and COMEDY OF ERRORS, while also relocating to the Netherlands. With former PROMISE drummer COLIN FRASER and keyboard genius MIKE STOBBIE in tow, REED and his PALLAS returned to the fore in the mid-90's, releasing comeback set 'BEAT THE DRUM' (1999), to please their ever faithful following. The band have recorded a new set, 'THE CROSS AND THE CRUCIBLE' (2001).

CRAIG ANDERSON – vocals / **DAVID HOLT** – guitar / **RONNIE BROWN** – keyboards / **GRAEME MURRAY** – bass / **DEREK FORMAN** – drums

Sue-i-cide / not iss.
Feb 78. (7"ep) *(PAL 101)* **PALLAS** [ ] [-]
– Reds under the bed / Thought police / C.U.U.K. / Willmot Dovehouse MP.
— **EUAN LAWSON** – vocals; repl. ANDERSON
— **NIALL MATHEWSON** – guitar; repl. HOLT

Granite Wax / not iss.
Jun 81. (lp) *(GWLP 001)* **ARRIVE ALIVE** [ ] [-]
– Arrive alive / Heart attack *[not on cd]* / Queen of the deep (live) / Crown of thorns / The ripper (live). *(c-iss.Nov82; GWC 002) (re-iss. Feb83 on 'Cool King' lp/c; CKLP/CKC 002) (cd-iss. Feb99 on Germany's 'Inside Out'+=; IOMCD 38)* – 5 to 4 (live) / Flashpoint (live) / Paris is burning / The hammer falls / Stranger (on the edge of time).
May 82. (7") *(GWS 001)* **ARRIVE ALIVE. / STRANGER (ON THE EDGE OF TIME)** [ ] [-]

Cool King / not iss.
Apr 83. (7") *(CK 010)* **PARIS IS BURNING. / THE HAMMER FALLS** [ ] [-]
(12"+=) *(12CK 010)* – Stranger on the edge of time.

Harvest / Capitol
Jan 84. (7"/7"pic-d) *(PLS/+P 1)* **EYES IN THE NIGHT (ARRIVE ALIVE). / EAST WEST** [ ] [-]
(12"+=) *(12PLS 1)* – Crown of thorns.
Feb 84. (lp/c) *(SHSP/TC-SHSP 2400124)* *<ST 12350>* **THE SENTINEL** [41] [ ] Aug84
– Eyes in the night (arrive alive) / Cut and run / Rise and fall / Shock treatment / Ark of infinity / Atlantis. *(cd-iss. Oct93 on 'Centaur'; CENCD 001) (cd re-iss. Jun00 on 'S.P.V.'+=; SPV 0853199-2)* – (diff.track order & extras).
Mar 84. (7") *(PLS 2)* **SHOCK TREATMENT. / MARCH ON ATLANTIS** [ ] [-]
(12"+=) *(12PLS 2)* – Heart attack.
— **ALAN REED** – vocals; repl. LAWSON
Apr 85. (7") *(PLS 3)* **STRANGERS. / NIGHTMARE** [ ] [-]
(12"+=/12"pic-d+=) **THE KNIGHTMOVES EP** *(12PLS/+P 3)* – Sanctuary.
(12"+=) **THE KNIGHTMOVES EP** *(12PLSD 3)* – Sanctuary. *(with free 7")* – MAD MACHINE. / STITCH IN TIME
Jan 86. (7") *(PLS 4)* **THROWING STONES AT THE WIND. / CUT AND RUN (live)** [ ] [-]
(12"+=) *(12PLS 4)* – Crown of thorns (live).
Feb 86. (lp/c) *(SHVL/TC-SHVL 850)* **THE WEDGE** [70] [-]
– Dance through the fire / Throwing stones at the wind / Win or lose / Executioner (Bernie Goetz a gun) / A million miles away (imagination) / Ratracing / Just a memory. *(cd-iss. Oct93 as 'KNIGHTMOVES TO THE WEDGE' on 'Centaur'; CDNCD 002) (cd re-iss. Jun00 on 'S.P.V.'+=; SPV 0854115-2)* – (diff.track order & extras)
Apr 86. (7") *(PLS 5)* **WIN OR LOSE. / JUST A MEMORY** [ ] [-]
(12"+=) *(12PLS 5)* – ('A'version).
— folded when EMI-Harvest let them go
— re-formed in the mid-late 90's with EUAN LAWSON making a guest appearance / **MIKE STOBBIE** – on keyboards

— **COLIN FRASER** – drums (ex-PROMISE) repl. FORMAN

Pallas / not iss.

Mar 99. (cd) *(PALCD 004)* **BEAT THE DRUM** [ ] [-]
– Call to arms / Beat the drum / Hide and seek / Insomniac / All or nothing / Spirits / Man of principle / Ghosts / Blood and roses / Wilderness years / Fragments of the sun.

Jan 01. (cd) **LIVE OUR LIVES (live)** [ ] [-]
– Intro / Call to arms / Cut & run / Executioner / Hide & seek / Rat racing / Beat the drum / Insomniac / Blood & roses / Fragments. *(w/free cd+=)* – THE ATLANTIS SUITE

S.P.V. / Inside Out

Jul 01. (cd) *(SPV 0854152-2)* <2024> **THE CROSS & THE CRUCIBLE** [ ] [ ]
– The big bang / The cross & the crucible / For the greater glory / Who's to blame / The blinding darkness / Towers of Babble / Generations / Midas touch / Celebration!

Dougie PALOMPO

Born: c.1970, St. Andrews, Fife. The son of a chip-shop owner, bass player DOUGIE left his home town for the bright lights of London where he fell in with likeminded punks, The FLYING MEDALLIONS. Briefly infamous, this septet cut a series of singles and even enjoyed an ill-fated support slot to OASIS. A year on from the release of their debut album, 'We Love Everybody & Everything', the 'MEDALLIONS' short career came to a premature end after they were involved in a serious road accident while on tour in Belgium. Tragically, DOUGIE suffered head injuries and died shortly afterwards on the 16th of September 1995. The man's infectious charm and humourous left-wing opinions were sorely missed by his erstwhile bandmates; after a protracted lay-off, they were airborne once again.

PARTY ON PLASTIC (see under ⇒ Bellboy records)

PASTELS

Formed: Glasgow . . . 1982 by STEPHEN McROBBIE, who subsequently changed his surname to PASTEL. After a few indie outings, the band eventually settled for Alan McGee's 'Creation' records in late 1983 with a relatively stable line-up of PASTEL, guitarist BRIAN SUPERSTAR, bassist MARTIN HAYWARD and drummer BERNICE. An indie band in the truly classic sense of the term, The PASTELS' early mid-80's recordings such as 'SOMETHING GOING ON', 'MILLION TEARS' and 'I'M ALRIGHT WITH YOU' were endearingly amateurish jingle-jangle/VELVET UNDERGROUND swathes of melodic noise, the latter the band's final single for 'Creation' before they moved to the small 'Glass' label.

Around this time, The PASTELS, along with fellow Scottish (then) 'shamblers' PRIMAL SCREAM and a host of others, were forever immortalised via the dubious honour of having a track included on the NME's semi-legendary C86 compilation. Perhaps inspired by this modest scrape with indie stardom (though the band remain defiantly unambitious), The PASTELS soon adopted a more coherent, harmonious sound as evidenced on their trio of 'Glass' singles and the debut album 'UP FOR A BIT WITH THE PASTELS' (1987), which included a few choice moments from their earlier days.

The group label-hopped yet again for the follow-up, signing with 'Chapter 22' for 1989's 'SITTING PRETTY', arguably the band's most accomplished, if not exactly consistent work. With guest appearances by ubiquitous Glasgow scenesters like EUGENE KELLY (once of the seminal VASELINES and latterly CAPTAIN AMERICA) and TEENAGE FANCLUB's NORMAN BLAKE, the album featured some of the sweetest, juiciest moments in The PASTELS' chequered career, including the fizzing 'NOTHING TO BE DONE'. The album also saw DAVID KEEGAN contributing guitar, the ex-SHOP ASSISTANT being a partner in STEPHEN's influential '53rd & 3rd' label (which signed Scots acts The SOUP DRAGONS and BMX BANDITS amongst others).

At the turn of the decade, The PASTELS line-up was stabilised to a core of PASTEL, girlfriend AGGI WRIGHT and KATRINA MITCHELL, KEEGAN making occasional contributions. Signed to 'Paperhouse', the first release from the new-look PASTELS was a fine cover of American maverick DANIEL JOHNSTON's seminal 'SPEEDING MOTORCYCLE', the group subsequently teaming up with another respected US underground figure, JAD FAIR (HALF JAPANESE), on a collaborative album, JAD FAIR AND THE PASTELS' (1991). Working with GALAXIE 500 guru, DEAN WAREHAM (on the 1994 EP, 'OLYMPIC WORLD OF PASTELISM') further illustrated the band's cultish kudos while 'MOBILE SAFARI' (1995) was a wryly self-deprecating look at an indie band's lot.

Highly influential, if never really groundbreaking, The PASTELS remain the Grandaddies (and mammies!) of the Glasgow indie music scene.

• **Songwriters:** All written by STEPHEN and group except BOARDWALKIN' (Some Velvet Sidewalk); SVS's AL LARSEN teamed up with The PASTELS on a mid-90's side project, SANDY DIRT, releasing an eponymous EP early in '96.

STEPHEN PASTEL (b. STEPHEN McROBBIE) – vocals / **BRIAN SUPERSTAR** (b. BRIAN TAYLOR) – guitar / **MARTIN HAYWARD** – bass / **CHRIS GORDON** – drums

Whaam! / not iss.

Oct 82. (7") *(WHAAM 005)* **HEAVENS ABOVE! / TEA TIME TALES** [ ] [-]

Creation Artefact / not iss.

Apr 83. (7"flexi) *(LYN 12903)* **I WONDER WHY (live) / (other track by LAUGHING APPLES)** [ ] [-]
(above was initialy a freebie with CRE 001)

Rough Trade / not iss.

Oct 83. (7") *(RT 137)* **I WONDER WHY. / SUPPOSED TO UNDERSTAND** [ ] [-]

Creation / not iss.

Mar 84. (7") *(CRE 005)* **SOMETHING GOING ON. / STAY WITH ME TILL MORNING** [ ] [-]

Oct 84. (12"m) *(CRE 011T)* **A MILLION TEARS. / SUPRISE ME / BABY HONEY** [ ] [-]

Nov 85. (12"m) *(CRE 023T)* **I'M ALRIGHT WITH YOU. / WHAT IT'S WORTH / COULDN'T CARE LESS** [ ] [-]

Glass / Big Time

Jul 86. (7") *(GLASS 048)* **TRUCK TRAIN TRACTOR. / BREAKING LINES** [ ] [-]
(12"+=) *(GLASS12 048)* – Truck train tractor (2).

— (in '87) they added **AGGI** – keyboards (ex-BUBA & THE SHOP ASSISTANTS) + **NORMAN BLAKE** – guitar (of The BOY HAIRDRESSERS)

Feb 87. (lp) *(GLALP 022)* <6032> **UP FOR A BIT WITH THE PASTELS** [ ] [ ]
– Ride / Up for a bit / Crawl babies / Address book / I'm alright with you / Hitchin' a ride / Get round town / Baby honey / Automatically yours / If I could tell you. *(cd-iss. Oct88; GLACD 021) (re-iss. Sep91 on 'Paperhouse')*

Feb 87. (7") *(GLASS 050)* **CRAWL BABIES. / EMPTY HOUSE** [ ] [-]
(12"+=) *(GLASS12 050)* – The day I got certified.

Oct 87. (7") *(GLASS 053)* **COMING THROUGH. / SIT ON IT MOTHER** [ ] [-]
(12"+=) *(GLASS12 053)* – Lonely planet boy / Not unloved.

— guest **EUGENE KELLY** (of VASELINES) who later formed CAPTAIN AMERICA then EUGENIUS

Chapter 22 / Homestead

Apr 89. (12"m) *(12CHAP 37)* **BABY YOU'RE JUST YOU. / HOLY MOLY. / UGLY TOWN** [ ] [-]

Jun 89. (lp/c/cd) *(CHAP LP/MC/CD 43)* <HMS 1441> **SITTIN' PRETTY** [ ] [ ]
– Nothing to be done / Anne Boleyn / Sit on it mother / Holy moly / Ugly town / Zooom / Baby you're just you / Ditch the fool / Sittin' pretty / Swerve. *(also pic-lp; CHAPLP 43P) (lp re-iss. Feb95 on 'Homestead'; same as US)*

— now a trio **STEPHEN, AGGI + KATRINA MITCHELL** also with **FRANCES MACDONALD** (b.11 Sep'70) – drums (ex-TEENAGE FANCLUB)

Paperhouse / Seed

Sep 91. (7") *(PAPER 008)* **SPEEDING MOTORCYCLE. / SPEEDWAY STAR** [ ] [-]
(12"+=/cd-s+=) *(PAPER 008 T/CD)* – 4th band.

Nov 91. (7") *(PAPER 011)* **THRU YOUR HEART. / FIREBELL RINGING** [ ] [-]
(12"+=/cd-s+=) *(PAPER 011 T/CD)* – My heart's my badge / Sign across me / Thru' your heart (home recording).

— In Feb + Jun 92, they teamed up with JAD FAIR (ex-HALF JAPANESE) on his singles; THIS COULD BE THE NIGHT + HE CHOSE HIS COLOURS WELL from his 1991 album 'JAD FAIR AND THE PASTELS'. Meanwhile, KATRINA moonlighted with MELODY DOG duo alongside PAT CROOK and issued an eponymous EP for 'K' in 1991 (tracks 'Futuristic Lover', 'Tomorrow's World' and 'Sun Drenched Beach In Acapulco') and a single for 'Seminal Twang', 'CASSIE' b/w a cover of Primal Scream's 'MOVIN' ON UP' and 'LIGHT SHADE'.

Nov 92. (cd/c/lp) *(PAP CD/MC/LP 008)* <14239> **TRUCKLOAD OF TROUBLES: 1986-1993** (compilation) [ ] [ ]
– Thank you for being you / Thru' your heart / Kitted out / Comin' through / Over my shoulder / Truck train tractor / Crawl babies / Nothing to be done / Different drum / Not unloved / Baby honey / Speeding motorcycle / Speedway star / What you said / Dark side of your world / Sometimes I think of you / Sign across me. *(cd re-iss. Apr02 on 'Fire'; SFIRE 003)*

May 93. (7") *(PAPER 023)* **THANK YOU FOR BEING YOU. / KITTED OUT** [ ] [-]
(cd-s+=) *(PAPER 023CD)* – Sometimes I think about you.

— now w/ guests: **GERARD LOVE** (Teenage Fanclub) / **DEAN WAREHAM** (Galaxie 500).

May 94. (7"ep/cd-ep) *(RUG 18/+CD)* **THE PASTELS & . . . OLYMPIC WORLD OF PASTELISM** [ ] [-]
– Hot wheels / Three strip dynamite / Feedback Olympics.

— **STEPHEN, AGGI + KATRINA MITCHELL** plus various honorary PASTELS, including GERARD LOVE, NORMAN BLAKE, JONATHAN KILGOUR, DEAN WAREHAM, BILL WELLS, SARAH WARD, ISOBEL CAMPBELL, DAWN KELLY + GREGOR REID

Domino Matador

Oct 94. (12"ep/cd-ep) *(RUG 28 T/CD) <OLE 114>* **YOGA / BOARDWALKIN'. / WINTER OLYMPIC GLORY / YOGA** [ ] [ ] Apr95

Domino Domino

Feb 95. (cd/c/lp) *(<WIG CD/MC/LP 17>)* **MOBILE SAFARI** [ ] [ ]
– Exploration team / Mandarin / Yoga / Mobile deli / Exotic arcade / Classic line-up / Flightpaths to each other / Basement scam / Strategic gear / Token collecting / Coolport / Worlds of possibility. (lp w/free 7") **SAFARI COMPANION** – 1 / 2 / 3 / 4.

Apr 95. (12"ep/cd-ep) *(RUG 36 T/CD)* **WORLDS OF POSSIBILITY / PHOTOGRAM. / EVER FAR / LOVE IT'S GETTING BETTER** [ ] [-]

Dec 95. (12"ep/cd-ep; as The PASTELS & AL LARSEN) *(RUG 42/+CD)* **SANDY DIRT** [ ] [-]
– Klein international blue / Slim slow rider / Ship to shore / Matches / Moonlit lungs.

Domino Up

Jul 97. (12"ep/cd-ep) *(RUG 55 T/CD) <UP 38>* **UNFAIR KIND OF FAME / FROZEN WAVE. / CYCLE (My Bloody Valentine remix) / FROZEN WAVE (Flacco remix)** [ ] [ ] Sep97

Aug 97. (7") *(RUG 52)* **THE HITS HURT. / WINDY HILL** [ ] [-]
(cd-s+=) *(RUG 52CD)* – G12 nights.

Oct 97. (cd/lp) *(WIG CD/LP 34) <UP 41>* **ILLUMINATION** [ ] [ ]
– The hits hurt / Cycle / Thomson colour / Unfair kind of fame / Fragile gang / The viaduct / Remote climbs / Rough riders / On the way / Leaving this island / G12 nights / Attic plan / Mechanised.

— in May'98, Domino offshoot label, 'Series 500', issued a collaborative effort, 'HURRICANE FIGHTER PILOT' with FUTURE PILOT AKA

Nov 98. (cd/d-lp) *(WIG CD/LP 46)* **ILLUMINATI** [ ] [-]
– Magic nights (My Bloody Valentine remix) / The viaduct (Kid Loco remix) / Windy hill (Cornelius remix) / One wild moment (Stereolab remix) / Attic plan (Mouse on Mars remix) / Remote climbs (Cinema remix) / Remote climbs (John McEntire remix) / The viaduct (Ian Carmichael remix) / Thomson colour (To Rococo Rot remix) / Cycle (My Bloody Valentine remix) / On the way (Third Eye Foundation remix) / Rough riders (Future Pilot AKA remix) / Rough riders (Make Up remix) / Frozen wave (Flacco remix) / The viaduct (Bill Wells remix) / Leaving this island (Jim O'Rourke remix).

Dec 98. (12"ep) *(RUG 79)* **ONE WILD MOMENT (Stereolab remix). / WINDY HILL – vocal and instrumental (Cornelius remix) / THE VIADUCT – instrumental and vocal (Kid Loco remix)** [ ] [-]

– compilations, others, etc. –

Mar 85. (7"ep) *Villa 21; (VILLA 1)* **HEAVENS ABOVE! / TEA TIME TALES. / I WONDER WHY (live) / TEA TIME TALES (live)** [ ] [-]

Dec 87. (d12") *Glass; (GLASS12 048)* **TRUCK TRAIN TRACTOR. / BREAKING LINES / TRUCK TRAIN TRACTOR 2 / / CRAWL BABIES. / EMPTY HOUSE / THE DAY I GOT CERTIFIED** [ ] [-]

Jun 88. (lp/cd) *Creation; (CRE LP/CD 031)* **SUCK ON THE PASTELS** [ ] [-]
– Baby honey / I wonder why / Something going on / Million tears / Surprise me / She always cries on Sunday / Baby honey / I'm alright with you / Couldn't care less / What's it worth. *(<cd-iss. Mar94 on 'Rockville'; 6048>)*
(above to be have been issued Mar'85 as 'SHE ALWAYS CRIES ON SUNDAY')

1990. (7"colrd-ep) *Overground; (OVER 06)* **HEAVENS ABOVE! / TEA TIME TALES. / SOMETHING GOING ON (demo) / UNTIL MORNING COMES (demo)** [ ] [-]

'Big' Jim PATTERSON

Born: c.1959, Portsoy, Banff. Having studied classical music at Banff Academy (which led to a stint playing trombone with the Scottish National Brass Band!), JIM soon moved south to Leeds in 1977/78, where he found a job in a mill – he also tutored in jazz music at the local college. During this teething spell, PATTERSON spotted an ad in the Melody Maker. This was placed by a certain KEVIN ROWLAND and AL ARCHER who were looking for a brass section to augment their Punk-cum-Northern Soul sound. After an audition or two, JIM was part of the Midlands ensemble that would be known as DEXYS MIDNIGHT RUNNERS.

The DEXYS image was paramount to the initial success of ROWLAND/the band and BIG JIM PATTERSON (as he was now known) was no exception as he fitted perfectly into the "stevedore/docker" aplomb. A minor hit with 'Dance Stance' in late '79 – around the same time as support to the CLASH – paved the way for the following year's chart-topping 'Geno', the title taken from JIM's one-time idols, GENO WASHINGTON & The RAM JAM BAND. A hugely successful 1980 was put in the shade a bit the following year as the press tried to savage the uncompromising ROWLAND; the singer had also sacked the band's drummer leading to all but PATTERSON vacating the scene.

A new (Mk.II) DEXYS was underway in '82 (dungarees, hillbilly style), and, after a dodgy start with 'The Celtic Soul Brothers' single, the group scored a second No.1 with the classic sing-a-long, 'Come On Eileen'. With a string section virtually taking over the brass of BIG JIM, it was no surprise when he called it a day that June. However, the trombonist was persuaded back to the fore for 1985's 'Don't Stand Me Down' set, although it was clear that DEXYS were KEVIN ROWLAND solo in all but name. PATTERSON continued to work with the enigmatic frontman throughout the late 80's and early 90's, even featuring in a revitalised DEXYS via a Jonathan Ross 'Saturday Zoo' appearance in February '93. Remaining a resident in England, JIM apparently dreamt of returning north of the border to support his other love, Aberdeen F.C.

Owen PAUL

Born: OWEN McGEE, 1 May'62, Glasgow. From the streets of Scotland's largest city to the pin-up pages of 'Smash Hits', teenybopper OWEN found a modicum of success in the summer of '86 via his catchy, Andy Hill-produced Top 3 single, 'MY FAVOURITE WASTE OF TIME'. In fact, contrary to belief, this wasn't OWEN's first attempt at the charts as two previous 45's (on 'Epic') had actually been a waste of time. However, it wasn't long before OWEN was back down to earth courtesy of a fickle record buying public.

OWEN PAUL – vocals / w/ session people + ANDY HILL – keyboards

Epic Epic

Jun 85. (7") *(A 6395)* **PLEASED TO MEET YOU. / SONNY** [ ] [-]
(12"+=) *(TX 6395)* – Another home kind.

Jan 86. (7"/12") *(A/TX 6847)* **ONLY FOR THE YOUNG. / ANOTHER HOMELAND** [ ] [-]

May 86. (7"/12") *(A/TA 7125)* **MY FAVOURITE WASTE OF TIME. / JUST ANOTHER DAY** [3] [ ]

Sep 86. (7"/12") *(650097-7/-6)* **PLEASED TO MEET YOU. / SONNY** [ ] [-]

Oct 86. (7"/12") *(OWEN/+T 5)* **ONE WORLD. / PLEASED TO MEET YOU** [ ] [-]

Nov 86. (lp/c) *(EPC/40 57114)* **AS IT IS . . .** [ ] [-]
– Pleased to meet you / Somebody's angel / My favourite waste of time / Sonny / Just another day / One world / Only for the young / Prime time / Pharaoh / Bring me back that spark. *(cd-iss. Apr87; CD 57114)*

Apr 87. (7"/7"g-f/12") *(OWEN/+G/T 6)* **BRING BACK THAT SPARK. / A FEELING** [ ] [-]

N.B.R. not iss.

Sep 87. (7"/12") *(OWP/12OWP 1)* **MAD ABOUT THE GIRL. / GOING SOLO** [ ] [-]

— finally retired after yet another flop

PEARLFISHERS

Formed: Glasgow . . . early 90's by DAVY SCOTT and JIM GASH. SCOTT had begun music business life as the singing/songwriting brains behind Phonogram-signed act, CHEWY RACOON. Although the band were dropped after only one single, SCOTT used his 'Virgin' publishing deal to keep him afloat financially while he masterminded a new band with Aussie ex-pat GASH. Named HEARTS & MINDS and featuring a line-up of SCOTT, GASH, ROBERT McGINLAY, CHRIS KEENAN and JEANETTE BURNS, the band were snapped up by 'C.B.S.' in 1986 after winning the vocal support of DJ Mark Goodier (then at Radio Clyde). Again only one single ('Turning Turtle') surfaced amid soured relations with their label and a shelved album.

A subsequent split left SCOTT and GASH to twiddle their musical thumbs until the support of another Radio Clyde DJ, Brian Burnett, persuaded the pair to carry on where they left off. This they did with the help of new recruits MIL STRICEVIC and BRIAN McALPINE, the new look HEARTS & MINDS building up a sizeable fanbase in Glasgow. When an identically named American band signed to 'A&M' at the turn of the decade, SCOTT and Co. chose to re-christen themselves The PEARLFISHERS, a moniker more suited to their increasingly rootsy sound. With the help of the Prince's Trust, SCOTT set up his own 'My Dark Star' label to release the band's 1991 debut EP, 'SACRED'. This brought them widespread coverage in the Scottish media as well as a valuable Radio One session, setting them up for a second EP, 'HURT', later that year. A third, cassette-only EP, 'WOODENWIRE', arrived in early '92, showcasing the diversity of the band's approach with an acoustic cover of Rabbie Burns' 'CA' THE YOWES'.

A succession of high profile headline and support slots all over Scotland preceded sessions for a debut album, 'ZA ZA'S GARDEN' (1993). Previewed by the 'SAINT FRANCIS SONGS' single and released on 'Iona Gold', the record consolidated The PEARLFISHERS' melodic, rootsy pop with contributions from the likes of CAPERCAILLIE's KAREN MATHESON. Odds and sods EP, 'LIVING IN A FOREIGN COUNTY' appeared in 1994 while a belated, string quartet-enhanced follow-up set, 'THE STRANGE UNDERWORLD OF THE TALL POPPIES', surfaced in 1997. By this point, WILF TAYLOR had replaced GASH while SCOTT had taken over bass duties for the recently departed STRICEVIC. A few years later, The PEARLFISHERS (i.e. SCOTT, GASH and DEREK STAR) netted another batch of wee gems in the shape of third set, 'THE YOUNG PICNICKERS' (1999).

CHEWY RACCOON

DAVID SCOTT – vocals, guitar / **KENNY THOMPSON** – guitar / with session musicians

Shift | not iss.

Jul 85. (7"/12") *(SHIFT 3/+12)* **DON'T TOUCH ME. / IT'S LOVE** ☐ -

HEARTS & MINDS

DAVID recruited **JIM GASH** (b. Sydney, Australia) – drums, vocals, etc (ex-session HUE & CRY, etc) / **ROBERT McKINLEY** – keyboards / **CHRIS KEENAN** – bass / **JEANETTE BURNS** – backing vocals

Epic | not iss.

Sep 87. (7"/12") *(TUT/+T 1)* **TURNING TURTLE. / CHANGE** ☐ -

— early '88, the band split after featuring on a Tennent's promo cassette with the track, 'REAL MUSIC ON A REEL'.

PEARLFISHERS

DAVID SCOTT + JIM GASH recruited **MIL STRICEVIC** (b. half English/half Yugoslavian) – bass / **BRIAN McALPINE** – keyboards, guitar, accordion / with others incl. **JIM PRIME, GRAEME KELLING, DONALD SHAW + KAREN MATHESON**

My Dark Star | not iss.

Jul 91. (cd-ep) **SACRED EP** ☐ -
Nov 91. (12"ep/cd-ep) **THE HURT EP** ☐ -
Jan 92. (c-ep) **WOODENWIRE EP** ☐ -
– Ca' the yowes / Carrighdoun – my home town / etc

Iona Gold | not iss.

Aug 93. (cd-ep) *(IGS 2041)* **SAINT FRANCIS SONGS / SUNNY APRIL SKIES. / WINDOW ON THE WORLD / IT'S OVER NOW** ☐ -
Oct 93. (cd/c) *(IG CD/C 204)* **ZA ZA'S GARDEN** ☐ -
– Za Za's garden / Saint Francis song / Bottle of the best / Bedroom on the Seine / Blanket of ribbons / Living in a foreign country / Sadness of a king / Throwing it away for love / Russians punks on speed / All-round Rosie / You want love / Rhinestone in my eyes.
Apr 94. (cd-ep) *(IGS 2042)* **LIVING IN A FOREIGN COUNTRY** ☐ -
– Living in a foreign country / Blanket of ribbons / Biggest & best / Limelight.

— **SCOTT** now with **WILF TAYLOR** – drums; who repl. JIM and MIL

— added guest **CHARLIE McKERRON** – violin (2)

Marina | Portrait

Apr 97. (cd) *(MA 25)* **THE STRANGE UNDERWORLD OF THE TALL POPPIES** ☐ -
– Even on a Sunday afternoon / Cherry sky / Sugar mountain babies / Banana sandwich / Waiting on the flood / They me too late / Jelly shoes / Lord Franklin / Night breeze / In the darkest hour / Everyday storms / Away from it all. *(cd re-iss. May02; same)*
Jun 97. (cd-ep) *(MA 27)* <6484-2> **EVEN ON A SUNDAY AFTERNOON EP** ☐ ☐
– Even on a Sunday afternoon / Basking shark / Wichita lineman / Snowbird / Let's put our hearts together.
Mar 98. (cd-ep) *(MA 35)* **BANANA SANDWICH EP** - - German
– Banana sandwich / Riverrun / Sugar mountain babies (Lullaby version) / La javanaise.

— **SCOTT + JIM GASH** returned + **DEREK STAR** – on drums / plus **GABRIEL TELERMAN** – guitars / **DEEPAK BAHL** – bass / **AMY GEDDES** – fiddles / + guest **NORMAN BLAKE** – backing vox (1)

Mar 99. (cd) *(MA 43)* **THE YOUNG PICNICKERS** ☐ -
– We're gonna save the summer / An ordinary day out in the suburbs / We'll get by / Blue December / You justify my love / Battersea Bardot / The young picnickers / Once there was a man / Over & over / Every day I read your stars / Strawberries in the snow / Stella painted joy.

— added guests MICK SLAVEN, WENDY WETHERBY, ALISON LUCAS, LINDSAY COOPER, JOHNNY CAMERON, COLIN STEELE, etc

Marina | efa

Jun 01. (cd) *(MA 53)* <efa 6763> **ACROSS THE MILKY WAY** ☐ ☐
– Across the Milky Way / New stars / I was a cowboy / Steady with you / Sweet William / The vampires of Camelon / Well be the summer / Snow on the pines / Paint on a smile / Everything works out / Shine it out / When the highway ends / Is it any wonder?

PEEPS INTO FAIRYLAND

Formed: Carnoustie . . . summer 1996 by village boys MICHAEL ANGUS, PAUL HERBERT and GRAEME WILLIAMSON. Starting out as a dual songwriting team, ANGUS and HERBERT were quickly introduced to the stage-shy, but extremely talented WILLIAMSON. The quiet, brooding 4-piece (who had now added HAMISH FULFORD) recorded the 'THE WISE WITCH' 2-track EP in the summer of '98 and picked up acclaim from fellow Scottish songsmiths, IDLEWILD (who covered their grave-turning masterpiece, 'PALACE FLOPHOUSE', which takes its name from a passage in Steinbeck's 'Cannery Row').

This was followed by the exclusion of WILLIAMSON (as his stage fright overcame his ability to perform) and the drafting in of guitarist JEREMY MILLS and percussionist FERGUSON; after another single, 'MUDDY WATER' – for Bristol's 'Roisin' – MARTIN BATE would also come in as substitute for HAMISH (who had left to pursue the study of priesthood!). The 'RAIN AND WIRES' EP surfaced late in 1999, and having moved westward to Glasgow (a year earlier, in fact!), their GRANDADDY, PALACE and NICK DRAKE near impersonations were well accepted by the weep-core acoustic community. They were invited to record in Glasgow's 'Stuffhouse' studios, which resulted in their debut album, 'THE SHOT' (2000). Definitely underrated, the album continued the group's minimal/acoustic affair, with hushed and beautiful melodies; it was an album to send your children to sleep on a winter's night.

In 2000 the band went through a difficult period after their tour van bizarrely exploded; MARTIN BATE divorced himself from the group in order to concentrate on his side-project STUPID ACTING SMART. Although the band were slightly dazed by this set-back they still managed to issue the brilliant 'HAPPINESS' LP in 2002. A collection of field-recordings and ballads, the group decided to split temporarily after the music press and the music-buying public took no interest in The PEEPS' masterpiece. But, like LONE PIGEON and The RADAR BROTHERS, the group's floating melodics and lush arrangments were finding solace in the hearts of those cult record collectors who find a gem and tell their friends, who tell their friends . . . hopefully, not before long it'll have the beaming, underground reputation it deserves.

• **Trivia:** 'Take a peep into Fairyland' is the title of a pop-up children's book which the group's moniker originated from.

MICHAEL ANGUS – vocals, drums, guitar / **PAUL HERBERT** – vocals, guitar, drums / **JEREMY MILLS** – guitar / **GRAEME WILLIAMSON** – guitar / **HAMISH FULFORD** – bass

Roisin | not iss.

Jul 98. (ltd-12"ep) *(ROISIN 01)* **THE WISE WITCH EP** ☐ -
– Tales from the abbey / Wise witch of the moor slow rides backwards.

— **JEREMY MILLS** – guitar + **D. JOHN FERGUSON** – drums, accordion; repl. GRAEME who retired from music scene

Feb 99. (7") *(ROISIN 02)* **MUDDY WATER. / LAST DAY** ☐ -

— **MARTIN BATE** – bass; repl. HAMISH who went into priesthood

D & C Recordings | not iss.

Dec 99. (cd-ep) *(DC 002)* **RAIN AND WIRES EP** ☐ -
– Palace flophouse / Willow pattern / A drink to the hand / Fragment.
Sep 00. (cd) *(DCCD 004)* **THE SHOT** ☐ -
– Home / Blackspot / Go out walking / Cat / When pictures move / Cloud formation / 3 step dancing / Muddy water / Autumn / Dawnsong / Lurches and swings / Counting song / Covering the sun.

— now without MARTIN

Jan 02. (cd) *(DCCD 005)* **HAPPINESS** ☐ -
– Intro / Tremble / Deaf by hands / Passing place / Sulliven from Elphin / Death by lions / Fear of flying / I count alone / Thoughts and lines.

Marti PELLOW (see under ⇒ WET WET WET)

PEPTONE (see ⇒ Section 9: the 90s)

PERCY X (see under ⇒ Soma records)

PERSPEX WHITEOUT (see ⇒ Section 9: the 90s)

PHANTOM ENGINEER

Formed: Glasgow . . . early 1998 by the unlikely trio of DAVID KEENAN (ex-TELSTAR PONIES), JOHN HOGARTY (of NATIONAL PARK and ex-BMX BANDITS and TELSTAR PONIES) plus jazzman BILL WELLS. Described – and deservedly so – as "out there", PHANTOM ENGINEER were indeed indie improvisers of the Nth degree. A haunting, but nevertheless atmospheric eponymous debut, was delivered towards the end of 1998.

DAVID KEENAN – guitar (ex-TELSTAR PONIES) / **BILL WELLS** (b. Falkirk) – sax / **JOHN HOGARTY** – (of NATIONAL PARK, ex-BMX BANDITS, ex-TELSTAR PONIES briefly)

		Paperhouse	not iss.
Dec 98.	(cd) *(GHOST 001CD)* **PHANTOM ENGINEER**	☐	-

– Morton Bartlett's children / Sweetheart come / Western snowfall / BC52 / Arc of a jetplane / End of a holiday / Welcome home David.

PH FAMILY

Formed: Glasgow . . . mid-90's by dual vocalists FRASER LUMSDEN and ROSS McLEOD, the 5-piece line-up being completed by guitarist PAUL WITHERS, bassist ALEX GRANT and RICHIE DEMPSEY. Early in 1997, they unleashed their debut single, a shared effort with BABY ASPIRIN on 'Flotsam & Jetsam'. Described as NIRVANA at their most grimy best, with touches of UNSANE, SNUFF or LEATHERFACE, the PH FAMILY continued to assault the heavy-metal brain with 'PET NOODLE' on a 1997 V/A collection, 'Into The Kiltmakers'.

The Club Beatroot series for 'F&J' brought forth the band's next bass-tastic split effort, 'IMPORTANT INFORMATION', a record augmented by the one and only larynx-basher p6 of the STRETCHHEADS – we wondered where he was hiding. Later in '98, the 'IDEAL WEIGHT' single/EP was given short-shrift by US-obsessed Kerrang!; loud, maximum R&R, what more did you want – style? A further effort for 'F&J' came in the shape of what turned out to the band's swansong 45, 'SHILL DISPLAY'. Members of the 'FAMILY turned up in new millennium outfit, DESALVO, who released the unyielding 'DOUBLE SQUARE'.

FRASER LUMSDEN – vocals / **ROSS McLEOD** – vocals / **PAUL WITHERS** – guitar / **ALEX GRANT** – bass / **RICHIE DEMPSEY** – drums

		Flotsam & Jetsam	not iss.
Jan 97.	(7") *(SHaG 008)* **split w/ BABY ASPIRIN**	☐	-
Feb 98.	(7") *(SHaG 13.04)* **Club Beatroot Part Four**	☐	-

– I bring you important information / (other side by MOGWAI).
(above was co-issued with '13th Note')

		God Bless	not iss.
May 98.	(cd-ep) *(REX 003CD)* **IDEAL WEIGHT EP**	☐	-

– Ideal weight / Happy shoes / You don't know who I am, you don't know who I know / S(l)o / Pet noodle / Important information. *(re-iss. Apr00; same)*

		Flotsam & Jetsam	not iss.
Apr 99.	(ltd-7") *(SHaG 025)* **SHILL DISPLAY. / POLE**	☐	-

DESALVO

— with ex-Ph FAMILY members

		Sano	not iss.
Dec 00.	(cd-s) **DOUBLE SQUARE / WIDE OPEN / THIS LORRY'S OUT OF CONTROL**	☐	-

PIE FINGER (see under ⇒ FIRE ENGINES)

PIGPEN (see under ⇒ Human Condition records)

PILOTCAN

Formed: Edinburgh . . . mid-90's by leader KEIRON MELLOTTE, also subsequent founder of the capital's 'Evol' alternative nightspot every Friday. The singer/guitarist borrowed the group name from a FLAMING LIPS number, 'Pilot Can At The Queer Of God' and possibly too young to have noticed there was another 'Burgh band of a similar moniker – PILOT – who were top of the pops two decades previous.

PILOTCAN – with also JOE HERBERT, KEVIN RAE and newest member STEVE MURGATOID in their ranks – were the first act to sign for STUART BRAITHWAITE's imprint, 'Rock Action'. KEIRON and Co had been (and still are) mutual friends with the MOGWAI guitarist having witnessed their friends WORMHOLE support idols TRUMAN'S WATER. With the ethos of FLAMING LIPS, SUPER FURRY ANIMALS and melodic traditional Rock much in their blood, PILOTCAN grew up in public as the wee gigs turned into bigger ones. Two 7" singles, 'RUSTY BARKER LEARNS TO FLY' and 'FIVE MINUTES ON A TUESDAY NIGHT', were the first fruits of their short-lived musical tenure in 1996; MELLOTTE and Co ended up paying for these releases themselves.

The following year, KEIRON took PILOTCAN's US-biased indie-Rock and formed his own appropriately-billed 'Evol' label, where they were content making their PAVEMENT meets MUDHONEY meets SONIC YOUTH-styled assaults. P-CAN's 1997 single, 'LOSING MORE THAN MY FINGERS', previewed their Jamie Watson-produced parent album, 'SOCIALLY INEPT DISCO', a set that could well have fitted nicely into any American boy's CD collection. A second set, 'THE BOY WHO KNEW MAPS' (1999), fared a tad worse by comparison, although it did unearth another mighty 45, 'THE WORLD TURNS WITHOUT YOU' and the cheeky 'C(O)UNTRY SONG'. With KEIRON, JOE, STEVE, adding SCOTT MacDONALD (from I AM SCIENTIST) and new bassist DAVID JACK (of MAGICDRIVE), PILOTCAN worked as a tighter unit both live (supporting US outfit, NEW WET KOJAK) and in the studio.

In Spring/Summer 2001, the new line-up emerged from the Substation at Cowdenbeath, where they had just completed their third and best set with MOGWAI producer Michael Brennan Jr.

KEIRON MELLOTTE – vocals, guitar / **JOE HERBERT** – guitar / **KEVIN RAE** – bass / **STEVE MURGATOID** – drums

		Rock Action	not iss.
Jun 96.	(7") *(RAR 002)* **RUSTY BARKER LEARNS TO FLY. / FALLSFIRE**	☐	-
Dec 96.	(7") *(ROCKACT 04)* **FIVE MINUTES ON A TUESDAY NIGHT. / SOLID STATE (MORE SONGS ABOUT ME)**	☐	-
		Evol	**not iss.**
Oct 97.	(7") *(evol 4)* **LOSING MORE THAN MY FINGERS. / NON-TICKING CLOCKS**	☐	-
Nov 97.	(lp/cd) *(evol 2/+d)* **SOCIALLY INEPT DISCO**	☐	-

– Anakin / Greenie beanie / Spooning the grems / Losing more than my fingers / Dormouse, Sam and me / Weird sci-fi shit / Hal and Roger / Sky rocket / Non doctor / Explicit palaroids of a suicide / Decaying orbit around a dying star / Tinsel / Rainsong / 23 small trout (my hamster).

Mar 99.	(cd-s) *(evol 6)* **THE WORLD TURNS WITHOUT YOU / CUM SHOTS / JUNKIE BLOOD**	☐	-
May 99.	(cd) *(evol 7cd)* **THE BOY WHO KNEW MAPS**	☐	-

– C(o)untry song / Las Vegas monkey / A blue print for Milton / Matinee coat / Circuit breaker or catalyst? / X-wing / Non-ironie surfactant / The world turns without you / Phone machine / Lipstuck / Caitlin / Under the western approach road. *(+ hidden track)*

— added **SCOTT MacDONALD** (b. Inverness) – guitar

— (late 2000) **DAVID JACK** – bass (of MAGICDRIVE) repl. KEVIN who became a civil servant!

PINK KROSS

Formed: Glasgow . . . late 1993 by day-glo Punks, GERALDINE KANE and JUDE BOYD, the latter inviting sister VIC BOYD to the fold as drummer and vocalist! Using drums like a war cry, VIC BLUE (as she was then named) banged her way through a tidal wave of seedy glam punk, reminiscent of BLONDIE or the NEW YORK DOLLS. Sporting feather boas, knee-high boots and all the sass a female punk act could muster, the trio picked up where the RUNAWAYS had left off. Singles 'DRAG STAR RACING QUEEN' and 'ABOMINATION' really exposed the spirit of these guitar-weilding vixens who incidently – as a joke – named themselves in tribute to Brit rockers REDD KROSS.

VIC and Co later issued the single 'SCUMBAG', which, for all its glorious fuzz guitar and nihilistic lyrics, reminded a perhaps bored listener that another group could churn out trashy music from the land that was Retro. Much the same old story was evident on their low-key debut set, 'CHOPPER CHIX FROM VP HELL' (1998), which was issued by 'teen-c'. A terrible title from the Russ Meyer camp of crude, no doubt, the more discerning listener may find the head-stomping tribal drums a little too severe. On an indie/punk scale of one to ten, SHAMPOO being the worst at one and KENICKIE being ten, PINK KROSS just might be smack bang in the middle.

VIC BOYD – vocals, drums / **JUDE BOYD** – guitar / **GERALDINE KANE** – bass

		Bouvier	not iss.
1995.	(7"ep) **PUNK OR DIE EP**	☐	-

– Drag star racin' queen / No time for Bimbo / I'm gonna kill yr valentine / Pussy cat a go-go / Punk rock riot.

		Gasatanka	not iss.
1995.	(7"ep) **BIG BEAT JESUS CHEAT / CHOPPER CHIX (FROM TEENAGE HELL) / NOT COMIN BACK**	☐	-
		Modern Ind	**not iss.**
Jan 96.	(7"ep) *(MIR 004)* **THE ABOMINATION EP**	☐	-

– Abomination / Velocababy / Hot trash / Punkoutfit.

— **JANE STRAIN** – bass, vocals; repl. GERALDINE

Flotsam & Jetsam | not iss.

Oct 96. (7"ep) *(SHaG 7)* **THE ACTIVE DALMATION EP** [ ] [-]
– A-bomb prom / Wish I had a tail / Self obsessed mess.

— in Apr'97, PINK KROSS, BIS & LUGWORM all collaborated/sidelined on the 'POP SONG' single *(GUIDE 11)*

teen-c! | not iss.

Aug 97. (7"m) *(SKETCH 003)* **SCUMBAG. / HACKSAW / NOISE UP** [ ] [-]

Mar 98. (lp) *(SKETCH 005LP)* **CHOPPER CHIX FROM VP HELL** (compilation) [ ] [-]
– Tension toy / Do it Joseph / Scumbag / Slick lizard / Dinahmite / Supersucceeder / Smug / Hacksaw / Surfy pigeon / Dirty pigeon / Lobotomy bay / A-bomb prom / P.M.T. / Skinhead Pearson / Dragstar 2000 / Noise up / Egyptian / 99 star scam / Spooky dooky. *(cd-iss. Jul98; SKETCH 005CD)*

Flotsam & Jetsam | not iss.

Apr 98. (7") *(SHaG 13.05)* **Club Beatroot – Part Five (live series)** [ ] [-]
– Tension Toy / (other by the RADIO SWEETHEARTS)

Bouvier | not iss.

1998. (cd-s) **DOGZ DINNER / + 2** [ ] [-]

— split and JUDE subsequently joined LUNG LEG

— note; they've also featured on a plethora of V/A comp albums/EP's

PLUTO MONKEY (see under ⇒ DAWN OF THE REPLICANTS)

POISON SISTERS

Formed: Tighnabruaich, Argyllshire . . . 1989 by brothers, not er, sisters!, frontman SANDY and bassist PETER BLACK, the pair settling with drummer KENNY MARTIN. Also relocating their base to Glasgow in '92, the 'SISTERS eventually unleashed their debut 'CHICANE' EP a few years later. Described as a post-Grunge JOY DIVISION-meets-Goth/punk affair, that could be both deep and surreal at times with SANDY's voice somewhere between an ANDREW ELDRITCH or a MORRISSEY; the music tabloids renamed them the SISTERS OF MORRISSEY (corny, but I like it).

Signing for one of Scotland's busiest imprints, 'Flotsam & Jetsam', the POISON SISTERS delivered a few split singles (with ESKA and THE KARELIA) as well as their own long-awaited debut album, 'TARANTULA RISING' (1998). A sophomore set, 'KEELHAULING WITH . . .', was due for release late in 2000, although this seems to have been put on hold for a bit. Meanwhile, PETER bailed out for a time and numerous bass players came and went. At the turn of the millennium, JAMES A. DAVIDSON was finally chosen as a full-time member as PETER returned to the fold as a drummer(!); KENNY MARTIN having retired from music.

SANDY BLACK – vocals, guitar, keyboards / **KENNY MARTIN** – drums, percussion / **PETER BLACK** – bass, vocals

Class | not iss.

1995. (7"ep) *(SMERT 002)* **CHICANE EP** [-] [-] mail-o
– Chicane / One more time / The grind / XYY chrome (live).

Flotsam & Jetsam | not iss.

Feb 96. (7"ep) *(SHaG 002)* **split single** [ ] [-]
– Unclean / Lo-fi girlfriend / (other 2 by Eska).

Dec 96. (7"ep) *(SHaG 009)* **DIGITALIS EP** [ ] [-]
– There'll never be another who comes near / Cataract / Digitalis / Hatchet burial song.

May 98. (7") *(SHaG 13.07)* **Club Beatroot Part Seven** [ ] [-]
– Hatchet burial song (live) / (other track by the KARELIA).

Oct 98. (cd) *(SHaG 017)* **TARANTULA RISING** [ ] [-]
– 76yrs / Chicane / Up to the wagon / Cataract / Tongue-tied / Lovebug / Vagina dentate / Deep red hurt / Insect floor / 1 + 1 = 0 / The Devil's corduroy / Essential oils / Space dust.

— **JAMES A. DAVIDSON** – bass; repl. PETER

— (May 2000) **PETER BLACK** – (now on) drums; returned to repl. MARTIN who retired from music

POLICECAT

Formed: Edinburgh . . . late 1993 initially as the part-time project of the PASTELS' JONATHAN KILGOUR. Recruiting twin brother, GORDON (who was also in The MONGERS), YVONNE SLAVEN, KATRINA DIXON and JOHN HARRINGTON (who replaced original bassist NEIL MITCHARD), POLICECAT were up and running for their debut maxi-single, 'DROWN', for 'Domino' in April '94. If you could imagine the CHILLS fused with surf-legend DICK DALE, you'd be close to their unique sound.

The 'LARRY' EP, released the following year was of the indie-folk variety, The PASTELS and The VASELINES immediately come to mind. Meanwhile, POLICECAT's off-duty activities consisted of alter-ego ROYAL BRONCO – with bass players included DEKE PATTON, JEM ANDERTON and GILDED LIL's MALCY DUFF – and the Lo-Fo 'No-Fi' band, The MONGERS, who comprised RB/PC members GORDON and YVONNE with JEM and latterly JOHN. Adopting new monikers (i.e. MONSTER TRUX, leather-clad vixen JUICY DETROIT and LARD FREEWAY), the mongy cats released a couple of cheap mail-order cassettes of mainly outrageous avant-jazz; cool loungecore from the gutter it certainly wasn't.

In 1997/98, POLICECAT were back on song, delivering two split singles for 'Creeping Bent', entitled 'AUTOMOBILE' and 'DARK HOLIDAY'. Ex-OFFHOOKS/THANES man CALVIN BURT was in place for their swansong single in '99, 'GIVE US THIS DAY' but the KILGOUR's left the scene of the crime when they were invited to join the ZEPHYRS.

JONATHAN KILGOUR (b.21 Oct'68) – vocals, guitar / **GORDON KILGOUR** (b.21 Oct'68) – guitar, vocals (of The MONGERS) / **JOHN HARRINGTON** – bass, etc (of MY HUSTLER) / **YVONNE SLAVEN** – keyboards / **KATRINA DIXON** – drums

Domino | not iss.

Apr 94. (7"m) *(RUG 19)* **DROWN. / BOLDER / VOODOO HOEDOWN** [ ] [-]
<US-iss.Jun96 on 'Derby';

— an assortment of drummers **SCOTT** plus **DEKE PATTON** repl. DIXON

May 95. (10"ep) *(RUG 34T)* **LARRY EP** [ ] [-]
– Larry / Music for pleasure / Classy / Tram 22.

Creeping Bent | not iss.

Jul 97. (7") *(bent 024)* **AUTOMOBILE. / Secret Goldfish: GIVE HIM A GREAT BIG KISS** [ ] [-]

Jun 98. (7") *(bent 034)* **DARK HOLIDAY. / (other track by Appendix Out)** [ ] [-]

— **CALVIN BURT** – drums (ex-OFFHOOKS) repl. DEKE PATTON

not iss. | Fantastic

Jan 99. (7") *<010>* **GIVE US THIS DAY. /** [-] [ ]

— a release on 'No-Fi' records was shelved when GORDON and JONATHAN formed The ZEPHYRS

MONGERS

MONSTER TRUX (aka GORDON KILGOUR) + **LARD FREEWAY** (aka JEM ANDERTON) / **JUICY DETROIT** (aka YVONNE SLAVEN) – synthesizer

No-Fi | not iss.

1994. (c-ep) *(none)* **HEY HEY WE'RE THE MONGERS** [-] [-] mail-o
– Leather-look lady / Bad milk / Jesus on a motorbike.

Oct 95. (c-ep) *(none)* **TABLE FOR THREE** [-] [-] mail-o
– Broke-bottle blues / B-roq / UHT lounge.

— they had already added **JOHN HARRINGTON**

Galvani | not iss.

Jan 99. (7"ep) *(MILK 001)* **LEATHER-LOOK LADY. / (other two by APPENDIX OUT)** [ ] [-]

POLICECHIEF (see under ⇒ Electric Honey records)

POSITIVE NOISE

Formed: Glasgow . . . 1979 by the MIDDLETON brothers ROSS (who incidentally wrote for Sounds weekly under the pseudonym of MAXWELL PARK), GRAHAM and FRASER, along with RUSSELL BLACKSTOCK and LES GAFF. Appearing on V/A compilation 'Second City Statik' with 'REFUGEES' and 'THE LONG MARCH' in 1980, POSITIVE NOISE were on the 'Statik' roster (along with MODERN ENGLISH they issued a cassette). Described by many as one of the most promising anthemic indie-dance acts, the ever-evolving PN released several singles and three albums, 'HEART OF DARKNESS' (1981), 'CHANGE OF HEART' (1982) – now without ROSS – plus 'WHEN LIGHTNING STRIKES' (1985). The latter featured newcomers JOHN TELFORD and JOHN COLETTA who superseding GAFF. They also recruited producer DAVE ALLEN (of SHRIEKBACK) to boost their now dated mid-80's sound.

ROSS MIDDLETON – vocals, (some) piano / **GRAHAM MIDDLETON** – keyboards, vocals / **RUSSELL BLACKSTOCK** – guitar, vocals / **FRASER MIDDLETON** – bass, vocals / **LES GAFF** – drums

Statik / not iss.

Feb 81. (7") *(STAT 3)* **GIVE ME PASSION. / GHOSTS** [ ] [-]
(12"+=) *(STAT 3-12)* – End of a dream.
May 81. (7") *(STAT 4)* **CHARM. / . . .AND YET AGAIN** [ ] [-]
(12"+=) *(STAT 4-12)* – Moscow motion.
May 81. (lp) *(STATLP 1)* **HEART OF DARKNESS** [ ] [-]
– Darkness visible / Hypnosis / No more blood and soil / . . .And yet again / Down there / Treachery! / Warlords / Love is a many splintered thing / Refugees / Ghosts. *(w/ free 7") (STAT 5)* LOVE LIKE POVERTY

— now without ROSS; RUSSELL now frontman

Nov 81. (7") *(STAT 8)* **POSITIVE NEGATIVE. / ENERGY** [ ] [-]
(12"+=) *(STAT 8-12)* – ('A'-instrumental).
Jun 82. (7") *(STAT 15)* **WAITING FOR THE 7th MAN. / END OF TEARS** [ ] [-]
Jul 82. (lp) *(STATLP 8)* **CHANGE OF HEART** [ ] [-]
– Positive negative / Waiting for the 7th man / Out of reach / Tension / Change of heart / Feel the fear / Get up and go / Inhibitions / Obsession / Hanging on.
Sep 82. (7"/12") *(STAT 23/+12)* **GET UP AND GO. / TENSION** [ ] [-]
Sep 83. (7") *(TAK 8)* **WHEN THE LIGHTNING STRIKES. /** [ ] [-]
(12"+=) *(TAK 8-12)* –

— **JOHN TELFORD** – drums; repl. GAFF

— added **JOHN COLETTA** – guitar

Aug 84. (7") *(TAK 22)* **MILLION MILES AWAY. / SHANTY** [ ] [-]
(12"+=) *(TAK 22-12)* –
Jun 85. (7") *(TAK 32)* **DISTANT FIRES. / SWAMP** [ ] [-]
(12"+=) *(TAK 32-12)* –
Jun 85. (lp) *(STATLP 23)* **DISTANT FIRES** [ ] [-]
– When lightning strikes / I need you / Distant fires / Reckless / Embers / A million miles away / Serenade / Now is the time / Always remember / Entranced.

— disbanded after above

POTENTIAL DIFFERENCE (see ⇒ Section 9: Dance/Rave)

PRALINES (see under ⇒ Avalanche/Alva records)

PRATS

Formed: Inverness . . . late 1977 by PAUL McLAUGHLIN, DAVE MAGUIRE and his brothers JEFF and GREG. Rehearsing for a year, the punk band finally surfaced with new guitarist ELSPETH McLEOD (replacing GREG) and toured around the North of Britain. Edinburgh's up and coming 'Fast Product' label (run by BOB LAST) subsequently brought them to the attention of the punk buying public via the first of their V/A compilation 'Earcom' 12" EP's. Three fine tracks, 'INVERNESS', 'BORED' and 'PRATS 2' featured alongside others by the BLANK STUDENTS, The FLOWERS and GRAPH; note also that an 11 year-old ADAMSKI and his brother were part of the STUPID BABIES who took up space on 'Earcom 3' and not as the great Brian Hogg (writer of 'The History Of Scottish Rock & Pop') stated, part of The PRATS(!).

In 1980, McLAUGHLIN and his not so stupid babes inked a deal with 'Rough Trade', the indie giant delivering two worthy singles over the course of the next year, '1990's POP' EP and 'GENERAL DAVIS', before succumbing – like most other Scots alternative acts – to the end of their span.

• **Note:** an entirely different PRATS (possibly German!) issued the single, 'Jesus had a PA'.

PAUL McLAUGHLIN – vocals, guitar / **ELSPETH McLEOD** – guitar; repl. GREG MACGUIRE / **JEFF MAGUIRE** – bass / **DAVE MAGUIRE** – drums

Fast Product / not iss.

May 79. (12"ep; Various Artists) *(FAST 9)* **Earcom 1** [ ] [-]
– Inverness / Bored / Prats 2 / (other artists).

Rough Trade / not iss.

May 80. (7"ep) *(RT 042)* **1990'S POP EP** [ ] [-]
– Disco pope / Nothing / TV set / Nobody noticed.
Nov 81. (7") *(RT 080)* **GENERAL DAVIS. / ALLIANCE** [ ] [-]

— disbanded after above

PRAYERS (see under ⇒ Egg records)

PRESIDENT'S MEN (see under ⇒ Oily records)

PRESSURE (see under ⇒ Hubba Hubba records)

PRESSURE FUNK (see under ⇒ Soma records / SLAM)

PRIMAL SCREAM

Formed: Glasgow . . . summer 1984 by JESUS & MARY CHAIN drummer BOBBY GILLESPIE. Signing to JAMC's label, 'Creation', in 1985, they cut two singles, GILLESPIE leaving The 'MARY CHAIN after the debut, 'ALL FALL DOWN' (1985). The first album, 'SONIC FLOWER GROOVE' (1987), was recorded by the current band line-up core of ANDREW INNES, ROBERT 'THROB' YOUNG and MARTIN DUFFY (save MANI, ex-STONE ROSES, who joined up in 1996) along with an ever-changing array of additional musicians. Released on 'Creation' boss ALAN McGEE's 'WEA' subsidiary label, 'Elevation', the album saw the band pretty much live up to their name, a primitive take on raw ROLLING STONES, STOOGES etc. with a bit of BYRDS jingle jangle thrown in. This sound served the band well through their second album, PRIMAL SCREAM (1989) until the release of 'LOADED' in early 1990.

Back at 'Creation' and enamoured with the Acid House explosion, the band had enlisted the esteemed ANDREW WEATHERALL to remix 'I'M LOSING MORE THAN I'LL EVER HAVE' from the second lp. More a revolution than a remix, WEATHERALL created the stoned funk shuffle of 'LOADED', in the process bringing indie and rave kids together on the same dancefloor for the first time.

PRIMAL SCREAM were now set on pushing the parameters of rock, releasing a trio of singles that defined an era, 'COME TOGETHER' (1990) was 90's style hedonist gospel that converted even the most cynical of rock bores while 'HIGHER THAN THE SUN' (1991) was perhaps the 'SCREAM's stellar moment, a narcotic lullaby beamed from another galaxy. Combining all the aforementioned tracks with a trippy 13TH FLOOR ELEVATORS cover, a heavyweight dub workout and a clutch of STONES-like beauties, 'SCREAMADELICA' (1991) was flawless. Opening with the euphoric 'MOVIN' ON UP' (the best song the 'STONES never wrote), the album effortlessly proved that dance and rock were essentially carved out of the same soulful root source, a seam that's been mined by any artist that's ever mattered. A landmark album, 'SCREAMADELICA' was awarded the Mercury Music prize in 1992 and for sheer breadth of vision the record has yet to meet its match.

Inevitably, then, the GEORGE DRAKOULIAS-produced follow-up, 'GIVE OUT BUT DON'T GIVE UP' (1994) was a disappointment in comparison. Recorded in MEMPHIS, the record saw PRIMAL SCREAM trying far too hard to achieve a roughshod R&B grit. Where before they had made The STONES' sound their own, now they came across as mere plagiarists, and over-produced plagiarists at that. Granted, the likes of 'JAILBIRD' and 'ROCKS' were funkier than any of the insipid indie competition around at the time and GILLESPIE's epileptic handclap routine was always more endearing than the run-of-the-mill rock posturing. Rumours of severe drug abuse abounded at this point and few were shocked when, in January 1994, it emerged that DUFFY had survived a near fatal stabbing in America.

For the next couple of years, the band kept a fairly low profile, only a contribution to the 'Trainspotting' soundtrack and an unofficial Scottish 'Euro '96' single confirmed the 'SCREAM were still in existence. But while Scotland stumbled to defeat (again!!), PRIMAL SCREAM cleaned up their act and recorded the wonderful 'VANISHING POINT' (1997). Apparently cut as an alternative soundtrack to cult 70's road movie 'Kowalski', this album was the true follow-up/comedown to the psychedelic high of 'SCREAMADELICA'. 'OUT OF THE VOID' was the band's darkest moment to date while the title track and 'STUKA' were fractured, paranoid psych-outs. Only the vintage screenshow of 'GET DUFFY' and the mellow 'STAR' offered any respite. Big on dub and low on derivation, the album was a spirited return to form for one of Scotland's most enduring and groundbreaking bands.

The year of 2000 saw the 'SCREAM return with all guns blazing for the destructive release of 'EXTERMINATOR'. An aptly titled album, this was worrying music for the post Millennium tensions of anti-capitalist marches and technology protests. It shaped its own poisonous force as the listener ventured further into the set: 'KILL ALL HIPPIES' was certainly a phrase derived from the punk movement, while 'SWASTIKA EYES' had a morbid, self-asserting ring to it. GILLESPIE mixed in exuberant styles such as hip-hop ('PILLS'), trance ('ACCELERATOR') and a bit of old MY BLOODY VALENTINE tones into the devilish bru. One could only describe 'EXTERMINATOR' as a very squealing, scary disjointed affair, sort of like the soundtrack to a Jean Luc Godard horror pic, if he, er, did a horror that is.

All in all, PRIMAL SCREAM were wise to return to wigged-out psychedelia – a style they were criticised from getting out of – with the self-indulgent 'VANISHING POINT'. 'EXTERMINATOR' is a valuable lesson in the art of punk: it's loud, it has balls, it's offensive, it's not all tuneful, and most importantly, it makes sense.

This method was also applied to The 'SCREAM's seventh album proper, 'EVIL HEAT' (2002) which delved even deeper into GILLESPIE's obsession with dark, throbbing soundscapes. Possibly the musical equivalent to being repeatedly run over by a tank and then turned into a metal blob, the set curiously explored the avant-metal punk scene a little bit closer, with single 'MISS LUCIFER' spitting and bubbling like an unsteady jar of boiling acid. Basslines thrashed (especially on 'SKULL X'), keyboards sounding like they were being set on fire and GILLESPIE pumped up his frontman image by turning a piece of deadpan vocal into a plethora of screams. Apart from the SUICIDE connections, and the screeching, industrial electro-clash of it all, 'EVIL HEAT' (complete with sinister homemade, cut'n'paste album jacket) included some cringe-worthy moments: the lazy, drugged-up slur of nu-blues number 'THE LORD IS MY SHOTGUN', super-model KATE MOSS' dreary rendition of the NANCY SINATRA/LEE HAZELWOOD song 'SOME VELVET MORNING' and the re-working of 'RISE' (originally entitled 'BOMB THE PENTAGON', but shamlessly re-titled for fears of American distribution). Former MY BLOODY VALENTINE casualty KEVIN SHIELDS took on the recording duty, doing his damndest to make it sound as dirty and as translucent as possible.

PRIMAL SCREAM exist to be one of the globe's truest punk-rawk bands – a rare thing in these money spinning, 3-chord, pop-producing times. Like the BBC, They educate, entertain and inform . . . they also make one hell'uva racket too.

• **Songwriters:** GILLESPIE, YOUNG and BEATTIE, until the latter's replacement by INNES. Covered CARRY ME HOME (Dennis Wilson) / UNDERSTANDING (Small Faces) / 96 TEARS (? & The Mysterians) / KNOW YOUR RIGHTS (Clash) / MOTORHEAD (Motorhead).

BOBBY GILLESPIE (b.22 Jun'64) – vocals (ex-WAKE, also drummer of JESUS & MARY CHAIN) / **JIM BEATTIE** – guitar / **ROBERT YOUNG** – bass / **TOM McGURK** – drums / **MARTIN ST. JOHN** – tambourine

Creation / not iss.

May 85. (7") *(CRE 017)* **ALL FALL DOWN. / IT HAPPENS** [ ] [-]

— added **PAUL HARTE** – rhythm guitar (GILLESPIE left JESUS & MARY)

Apr 86. (7") *(CRE 026)* **CRYSTAL CRESCENT. / VELOCITY GIRL** [ ] [-]
(12"+=) *(CRE 026T)* – Spirea X.

— **STUART MAY** – rhythm guitar (ex-SUBMARINES) repl. HARTE (Dec'86) / **ANDREW INNES** – rhythm guitar (of REVOLVING PAINT DREAM) repl. MAY / Guest drummers **PHIL KING** (studio) + **DAVE MORGAN** (tour) repl. McGURK

Elevation / not iss.

Jun 87. (7") *(ACID 5)* **GENTLE TUESDAY. / BLACK STAR CARNIVAL** [ ] [-]
(12"+=) *(ACID 5T)* – I'm gonna make you mine.

Sep 87. (7") *(ACID 5)* **IMPERIAL. / STAR FRUIT SURF RIDER** [ ] [-]
(12"+=/s12"+=) *(ACID 5T/+W)* – So sad about us / Imperial (demo).

Oct 87. (lp/c)(cd) *(ELV 2/+C)(242-182-2)* **SONIC FLOWER GROOVE** [62] [ ]
– Gentle Tuesday / Treasure trip / May the sun shine bright for you / Sonic sister love / Silent spring / Imperial / Love you / Leaves / Aftermath / We go down slowly. *(re-iss. Jul91; same)*

— (Jun'87) **GAVIN SKINNER** – drums; repl. ST. JOHN

— (Feb'88) Now a trio **GILLESPIE, YOUNG + INNES** augmented by **JIM NAVAJO** – guitar (BEATTIE formed SPIREA X; SKINNER also left)

— (Feb'89) added **HENRY OLSEN** – bass (ex-NICO) / **PHILIP 'TOBY' TOMANOV** – drums (ex-NICO, ex-DURUTTI COLUMN, ex-BLUE ORCHIDS)

Creation / Mercenary

Jul 89. (7") *(CRE 067)* **IVY IVY IVY. / YOU'RE JUST TOO DARK TO CARE** [ ] [-]
(12"+=)(cd-s+=) *(CRE 067T)(CRESCD 067)* – I got you split wide open over me.

Sep 89. (lp/c/cd) *(CRE LP/C/CD 054) <2100>* **PRIMAL SCREAM** [ ] [ ]
– Ivy Ivy Ivy / You're just dead skin to me / She power / You're just too dark to care / I'm losing more than I'll ever have / Gimme gimme teenage head / Lone star girl / Kill the king / Sweet pretty thing / Jesus can't save me. *(free 7"ltd.)* – SPLIT WIDE OPEN (demo). / LONE STAR GIRL (demo) *(cd re-iss. Jan01; same)*

— trimmed to a trio again (**GILLESPIE, YOUNG + INNES**)

Creation / Sire

Feb 90. (7") *(CRE 070)* **LOADED. / I'M LOSING MORE THAN I'LL EVER HAVE** [16] [-]
(ext.12"+=/'A'Terry Farley remix-12"+=)(ext.cd-s+=) *(CRE 070 T/X)(CRESCD 070)* – Ramblin' Rose (live).

Jul 90. (7"/c-s)(ext.12")(ext.cd-s) *(CRE/+CS 078)(CRE 078T(CRESCD 078) <26384>* **COME TOGETHER (Terry Farley mix). / COME TOGETHER (Andrew Weatherall mix)** [26] [ ] Aug90
(12") *(CRE 078X)* – ('A'-HypnotoneBrainMachine mix) / ('A'-BBG mix).

Jun 91. (7"/ext.12") *(CRE 096/+T)* **HIGHER THAN THE SUN. / ('A' American Spring mix)** [40] [-]
(cd-s+=) *(CRESCD 096)* – Higher than the Orb.

— guest spot on above from **JAH WOBBLE** – bass

Aug 91. (7"/ext.12")(c-s) *(CRE 110/+T)(CRECS 110)* **DON'T FIGHT IT, FEEL IT. / ('A'scat mix featuring Denise Johnson)** [41] [-]
(cd-s+=) *(CRESCD 110)* – ('A'extended version).

Sep 91. (cd/c/d-lp) *(CRE CD/C/LP 076) <26714>* **SCREAMADELICA** [8] [ ]
– Movin' on up / Slip inside this house / Don't fight it, feel it / Higher than the Sun / Inner flight / Come together / Loaded / Damaged / I'm comin' down / Higher than the Sun (a dub symphony in two parts) / Shine like stars. *(cd re-iss. Jan01; same) (lp-iss.Jun01 on 'Simply Vinyl'; SVLP 344)*

Jan 92. (7"ep/c-ep) *(CRE/+CS 117) <40193>* **DIXIE-NARCO EP** [11] [ ]
– Movin' on up / Carry me home / Screamadelica.
(12"ep+=)(cd-ep+=) *(CRE 117T)(CRESCD 117)* – Stone my soul.

— In Jan'94, MARTIN DUFFY was stabbed in Memphis, although he recovered soon after.

— Line-up:- **GILLESPIE, YOUNG, INNES, DUFFY + DAVID HOOD + DENISE JOHNSON** + guest **GEORGE CLINTON** – vocals

Mar 94. (7"/c-s) *(CRE/+CS 129) <18189>* **ROCKS. / FUNKY JAM** [7] [ ] Apr94
(12")(cd-s) *(CRE 129T)(CRESCD 129)* – ('A'side) / Funky jam (hot ass mix) / Funky jam (club mix).

Apr 94. (cd/c/lp) *(CRE CD/C/LP 146) <45538>* **GIVE OUT, BUT DON'T GIVE UP** [2] [ ]
– Jailbird / Rocks / (I'm gonna) Cry myself blind / Funky jam / Big jet plane / Free / Call on me / Struttin' / Sad and blue / Give out but don't give up / I'll be there for you. *(cd re-iss. Feb00 & Jan01; same)*

Jun 94. (7"/c-s) *(CRE/+CS 145)* **JAILBIRD. / ('A'-Dust Brothers mix)** [29] [-]
(12"+=) *(CRE 145T)* – ('A'-Toxic Trio stay free mix) / ('A'-Weatherall dub chapter 3 mix).
(cd-s++=) *(CRESCD 145)* – ('A'-Sweeney 2 mix).

Nov 94. (7"/c-s) *(CRE/+CS 183)* **(I'M GONNA) CRY MYSELF BLIND (George Drakoulias mix). / ROCKS (live)** [51] [-]
(cd-s+=) *(CRESCD 183)* – I'm losing more than I'll ever have (live) / Struttin' (back in our minds) (Brendan Lynch remix).
(10") *(CRE 183X)* – ('A'side) / Struttin' (back in our minds) (Brendan Lynch remix) / Give out, but don't give up (Portishead remix) / Rockers dub (Kris Needs mix).

Jun 96. (c-s/cd-s; PRIMAL SCREAM, IRVINE WELSH AND ON-U SOUND PRESENT . . .) *(CRECS-CRESCD 194)* **THE BIG MAN AND THE SCREAM TEAM MEET THE BARMY ARMY UPTOWN (mixes:- full strength fortified dub / electric soup dub / a jake supreme)** [17] [-]

— In Oct'96, GILLESPIE, INNES, YOUNG & DUFFY were joined by **MANI MOUNFIELD** – bass (ex-STONE ROSES)

Creation / Reprise

May 97. (c-s) *(<CRECS 245>)* **KOWALSKI / 96 TEARS** [8] [ ]
(cd-s+=) *(<CRESCD 245>)* – Know your rights / ('A'-Automator mix).

Jun 97. (c-s) *CRECS 263)* **STAR / JESUS** [16] [-]
(cd-s+=) *(CRESCD 263)* – Rebel dub / How does it feel to belong.
(12"+=) *(CRE 263T)* – ('A'mixes).

Jul 97. (cd/d-lp)(c) *(CRE CD/LP 178)(CCRE 178) <46559>* **VANISHING POINT** [2] [ ]
– Burning wheel / Get Duffy / Kowalski / Star / If they move, kill 'em / Out of the void / Stuka / Medication / Motorhead / Trainspotting / Long life. *(cd re-iss. Jan01; same)*

Oct 97. (7") *(CRE 272)* **BURNING WHEEL. / HAMMOND CONNECTION** [17] [-]
(12"+=)(cd-s+=) *(CRE 272T)(CRESCD 272)* – ('A'-Chemical Brothers remix) / Higher than the sun (original).

Oct 97. (cd/7"box) *(CRE CD/L7 224)* **ECHO DEK** (remixes) [43] [-]
– Duffed up / Revolutionary / Ju-87 / First name unknown / Vanishing dub / Last train / Wise blood / Dub in vain. *(cd re-iss. Feb00 & Jan01; same)*

Feb 98. (7") *(CRE 284)* **IF THEY MOVE, KILL 'EM. / BADLANDS** [ ] [-]
(12"+=)(cd-s+=) *(CRE 284T)(CRESCD 284)* – ('A'-My Bloody Valentine Arkestra mix) / ('A'-Darklands 12"disco mix).

— added on 1998 tour **JIM HUNT** – saxophone / **DUNCAN MACKAY** – trumpet / **DARREN MOONEY** – drums

Creation / Astralwerks

Nov 99. (c-s) *(CRECS 326)* **SWASTIKA EYES / ('A'mix)** [22] [ ] May00
(12"/cd-s) *(CRE 326T)(CRESCD 326)* – ('A'-Chemical Brothers mix) / ('A'-Spectre mix) / ('A'side).

Jan 00. (cd/md/c/d-lp) *(CRECD/CREMD/CCRE/CRELP 239) <49260>* **EXTERMINATOR** [3] [ ] May00
– Kill all hippies / Accelerator / Exterminator / Swastika eyes / Pills / Blood money / Keep your dreams / Insect royalty / MBV Arkestra (if they move kill 'em) / Swastika eyes / Shoot speed – Kill light / I'm 5 years ahead of my time. *(cd re-iss. Jan01; same)*

Mar 00. (7") *(CRE 332) <8169>* **KILL ALL HIPPIES. / EXTERMINATOR (Massive Attack remix)** [24] [ ] Nov00

(cd-s+=) *(CRESCD 332)* – The revenge of the Hammond connection.
(12"+=) *(CRE 332T)* – ('A'mixes).

Sep 00. (12")(cd-s) *(CRE 333T)(CRESCD 333)* **ACCELERATOR / I'M 5 YEARS AHEAD OF MY TIME / WHEN THE KINGDOM COMES** [34] [-]

Columbia Astralwerks

Jul 02. (12"/cd-s) *(672825-6/-2)* **MISS LUCIFER / (mixes: panther / hip to hip / bone to bone)** [23] [-]

Aug 02. (cd/lp) *(508923-2/-1)* **EVIL HEAT** [9] [ ]
– Deep hit of morning sun / Miss Lucifer / Autobahn 66 / Detroit / Rise / The Lord is my shotgun / City / Some velvet morning / Skull X / A scanner darkly / Space blues number 2.

- others, etc. -

Nov 97. (12") *Creation; (PSTLS 1)* **STUKA (Two Lone Swordsmen mixes)** [ ] [-]

PRIMEVALS

Formed: Glasgow . . . 1983 by frontman MICKY ROONEY (no, not that one!), guitarist TOM RAFFERTY, bassist JOHN HONEYMAN, drummer RHOD BURNETT and last but not least, slide guitarist MALCOLM McDONALD. Having self-financed their own 'Raucous' debut single, 'WHERE ARE YOU?', in 1984, they were surprised to say the least when leading French independent, 'New Rose', gave them a call. Thinking that these PRIMEVALS were the NY version (i.e. The Real Kids' JOHN FELICE's combo), the Gauls invited the Scots lads to send in some material. Remarkably, the imprint thought their sound was suitable (well, JOHNNY THUNDERS, TAV FALCO and The CRAMPS were all on board at the time) and signed the band almost immediately.

Described as trashy, IGGY meets THUNDERS meets NY DOLLS sounding, The PRIMEVALS embarked on their own Caledonian branch of R&B sleaze. A handful of releases for New Rose, including 'ETERNAL HOTFIRE' (1985) and 'SOUND HOLE' (1986), were met with very little reaction back here in Blighty, although on the continent they became something of a cult. When GORDON GOUDIE superseded RHOD and the label no longer needed their services, The PRIMEVALS bailed out towards the send of '87.

A decade later, the members re-united for several gigs, including a great night out at the 13th Note recorded by 'Flotsam & Jetsam'.

MICKY ROONEY – vocals / **TOM RAFFERTY** – guitar / **MALCOLM McDONALD** – slide guitar / **JOHN HONEYMAN** – bass / **RHOD BURNETT** – drums

Raucous not iss.

Jun 84. (7") *(PRIME 1)* **WHERE ARE YOU? / THIS KIND OF LOVE** [ ] [-]

New Rose not iss.

Feb 85. (lp) *(ROSE 47)* **ETERNAL HOTFIRE** [ ] [-]
– She's all mine / Have some fun / Blues at my door / See the tears fall / Lucky I'm living / etc

Nov 85. (7") *(NEW 55)* **LIVING IN HELL. /** [ ] [-]

Mar 86. (lp) *(ROSE 80)* **SOUND HOLE** [ ] [-]
–

Jun 86. (10") *(NEW 73)* **ELIXIR OF LIFE. /** [ ] [-]

— **GORDON GOUDIE** – drums; repl. BURNETT

Jul 87. (7") *(NEW 93)* **HEYA. /** [ ] [-]
(12"+=) *(NEW 92)* –

— after their split, TOM formed instrumental group The BEAT POETS

— the PRIMEVALS were briefly back in 1997

Flotsam & Jetsam – The 13th Note not iss.

Dec 97. (7") *(SHaG 13.02)* **Club Beatroot Part Two** [ ] [-]
– I want / (other track by SWELLING MEG)

- compilations, etc. -

1987. (12"ep) *Strange Fruit; (SFPS 014)* **THE PEEL SESSIONS** (18.9.85) [ ] [-]
– Saint Jack / See that skin / Spiritual / Dish of fish.

Oct 87. (lp) *Greasy Pop; (GPR 127)* **CHICKEN FACTORY** [-] [-] Austra

Oct 87. (lp/c/cd) *New Rose; (NEW 123/+C/CD)* **LIVE A LITTLE** [ ] [-]
– Fertile mind / Follow her down / My dying embers / All the virtues / Bleedin' Jack / Cottonhead / Justify / Early grave / Highway / Pink catsuit (part 1) / One sweet drink / Burden of the debt / Pink catsuit (part 2) / Diamond, furcoat, champagne / Prairie skin / Spiritual / Fire and clay / Saint Jack / Primeval call.

Apr 88. (7") *New Rose; (NEW 105)* **FERTILE MIND. / CRAZY LITTLE THING** [ ] [-]

Feb 89. (lp) *D.D.T.; (DISPLP 21)* **NEON OVEN - LIVE AT THE REX, PARIS (live)** [ ] [-]

PRINTED CIRCUIT (see ⇒ Section 9: the 90s)

Eoan 'Elvis' PRITCHARD (see under ⇒ Bellboy records)

PROBE (see under ⇒ Limbo records)

PROCLAIMERS

Formed: Auchtermuchty, Fife . . . (moved to Edinburgh) 1986. Twin brothers CRAIG (vocals, tambourine, bongos, maraccas) and CHARLIE REID (acoustic guitar, 12-string bass, vocals) had progressed from local bands The HIPPIE HASSLERS (!) and REASONS FOR EMOTIONS. After a bemusing but stunning appearance on Channel 4's 'The Tube', they were signed up by 'Chrysalis' records with the help of fan/manager, Kenny McDonald.

Sales of the GERRY RAFFERTY-produced debut album, 'THIS IS THE STORY' (1987), were boosted when the anthemic 'LETTER FROM AMERICA' peaked at UK No.3, probably the first pop song ever to be graced with a heavy Fife accent. Basically a folk album (though bagpipes wern't included), 'THIS IS THE STORY', was a listenable, if slight set of acoustic strumming topped off with the REID's highly distinctive harmonies. With their boy-next door, uber-geek appeal and rousing live show, the twins built up a loyal following touring with the likes of fellow geeks, The HOUSEMARTINS.

The following year, The PROCLAIMERS went electric, recruiting a full band: JERRY DONAHUE (guitar), PETE WINGFIELD (keyboards/producer), PHIL CRANHAM (bass) and PAUL ROBINSON (drums), and almost making the Top 10 with the stompalong classic, 'I'M GONNA BE (500 MILES)'. The album, meanwhile, 'SUNSHINE ON LEITH' (1988), was an accomplished and consistent follow-up, a solid collection that made No.6 on the UK chart and put the heart back into C&W-based rock-pop.

While the twins took an extended sabbatical to record their new album and help with the campaign to save their beloved and beleaguered Hibernian football club, 'I'M GONNA BE (500 MILES)' was a massive US hit in 1993 after being featured on the soundtrack to the film 'Benny and Joon'. Always suckers for a Scottish accent, the Americans also lapped up 'SUNSHINE ON LEITH', which subsequently went double platinum. 'HIT THE HIGHWAY' eventually emerged in 1994, a more traditional country outing with equally traditional lyrics to match on songs like 'LET'S GET MARRIED' and 'I WANT TO BE A CHRISTIAN'.

After a long hiatus, the twins emerged in 2001 courtesy of their first LP in eight years, the delightful 'PERSEVERE'. Not much had changed since the whimsical 'I'M GONNA BE (500 MILES)', with the PROCLAIMERS remaining true to their original style (and original accents!). If 'THERE'S A TOUCH' was the less serious offering on the set, then 'SCOTLAND'S STORY' was the politicised 'LETTER FROM AMERICA'. They still managed to play T In The Park the same year, backed by a tent-full of avid fans. If not exactly one of Scotland's trendiest bands, they remain one of the best loved; a splendid Hogmanay show went down a treat.

• **Songwriters:** All written by REID brothers, except TWENTY FLIGHT ROCK (Eddie Cochran) / KING OF THE ROAD (Roger Miller) / THESE ARMS OF MINE (Otis Redding) / etc. • **Trivia:** The twins were proudly both activist members of the SNP (Scottish National Party).

CRAIG REID (b. 5 Mar'62, Edinburgh) – vocals, tambourine, bongos, maraccas / **CHARLIE REID** (b. 5 Mar'62) – acoustic guitar, 12-string bass, vocals / plus sessioners

Chrysalis Chrysalis

Apr 87. (lp/c/cd) *(<CHR/ZCHR/CCD 1602>)* **THIS IS THE STORY** [43] [ ]
– Throw the 'R' away / Over and done with / Misty blue / The part that really matters / (I'm gonna) Burn your Playhouse down / Letter from America (acoustic) / Sky takes the soul / It broke my heart / The first attack / Make my heart fly / Beautiful truth / The joyful Kilmarnock blues / Letter from America (band version). *(cd re-iss. Mar93; same)*

May 87. (7") *(CHS 3144)* **THROW THE 'R' AWAY. / A TRAIN WENT PAST THE WINDOW** [ ] [-]
(12"+=) *(CHS12 3144)* – Long gone lonesome (live) / I can't be myself (live).

Oct 87. (7") *(CHS 3178)* **LETTER FROM AMERICA (band version). / LETTER FROM AMERICA (acoustic version)** [3] [ ]
(12"+=) *(CHS12 3178)* – I'm lucky / Just because / 20 flight rock.

Feb 88. (7") *(CLAIM 1)* **MAKE MY HEART FLY. / WISH I COULD SAY** [63] [ ]
(12"+=) *(CLAIMX 1)* – (I'm gonna) Burn your playhouse down (live) / Throw the 'R' away.
(cd-s+=) *(CDCLAIM 1)* – Letter from America (band version).

— (1988) with **JERRY DONAHUE** – guitar / **PETE WINGFIELD** – keyboards, producer / **PHIL CRANHAM** – bass / **PAUL ROBINSON** – drums / etc.

Aug 88. (7") *(CLAIM 2)* **I'M GONNA BE (500 MILES). / BETTER DAYS** [11] [ ]
(12"+=) *(CLAIMX 2)* – Teardrops.
(cd-s++=) *(CDCLAIM 2)* – I can't be myself.
<US re-iss. May93; 24846> – hit No.3

— taken from movie, 'Benny & Joon'

Sep 88. (lp/c/cd) *(<CHR/ZCHR/CCD 1668>)* **SUNSHINE ON LEITH** [6] [ ]
– I'm gonna be (500 miles) / Cap in hand / Then I met you / My old friend the blues / Sean / Sunshine on Leith / Come on nature / I'm on my way / What do you do / It's Saturday night / Teardrops / Oh Jean. *<re-iss. Jul93; same>* – hit No.31 *(cd re-iss. Mar94; CD25CR 18)*

Oct 88. (7") *(CLAIM 3)* **SUNSHINE ON LEITH. / LEAVING HOME** [41] [ ]
(12"+=/cd-s+=) *(CLAIMX/CDCLAIM 3)* – The first attack / Letter from America (live).

Feb 89. (7") *(CLAIM 4)* **I'M ON MY WAY. / OVER AND DONE WITH** [43] [ ]
(12"+=/cd-s+=) *(CLAIMX/CDCLAIM 4)* – Throw the 'R' away / Cap in hand.

Nov 90. (7"ep/c-ep/12"ep/cd-ep) *(CLAIM/TCCLAIM/CLAIMX/CDCLAIM 5)* **KING OF THE ROAD EP** [9] [ ]
– King of the road / Long black veil / Lulu selling tea / Not ever.

Feb 94. (c-s/7") *(TC+/CLAIM 6)* **LET'S GET MARRIED. / I'M GONNA BE (500 MILES)** [21] [ ]
(cd-s+=) *(CDCLAIM 6)* – Gentle on my mind / Waiting for a train.
(cd-s) *(CDCLAIMS 6)* – ('A'side) / Invitation to the blues / Letter from America / ('A'acoustic).

Mar 94. (cd/c/lp) *(<CD/TC+/CHR 6066>)* **HIT THE HIGHWAY** [8] [ ]
– Let's get married / The more I believe / What makes you cry / Follow the money / These arms of mine / Shout shout / The light / Hit the highway / A long long long time ago / I want to be a Christian / Your childhood / Don't turn out like your mother.

Apr 94. (c-s/7") *(TC+/CLAIM 7)* **WHAT MAKES YOU CRY. / GUESS WHO WON'T BEG** [38] [ ]
(cd-s+=) *(CDCLAIM 7)* – Shout shout (acoustic) / Follow the monkey (acoustic).
(cd-s) *(CDCLAIMS 7)* – ('A'side) / Bobby / King of the road / ('A'acoustic).

Oct 94. (c-s/7") *(TC+/CLAIM 8)* **THESE ARMS OF MINE. / SUNSHINE ON LEITH** [51] [ ]
(cd-s+=) *(CDCLAIM 8)* – Joyful KIlmarnock blues / What makes you cry.
(cd-s) *(CDCLAIMS 8)* – ('A'side) / I'm on my way / Let's get married / I'm gonna be (500 miles).

— the lads took a 7-year long studio sabbatical

Persevere / Nettwerk

May 01. (cd) *(PERSRECCD 004) <30193>* **PERSEVERE** [61] [ ]
– There's a touch / Sweet little girls / A land fit for zeros / How many times / One too many / That's when he told her / Scotland's story / When you're in love / She arouses me so / Everybody's a victim / Don't give it to me / Heaven right now / Slowburner / Act of remembrance.

– compilations, etc. –

Sep 00. (3xcd-box) *E.M.I.; (528370-2)* **THIS IS THE STORY / SUNSHINE ON LEITH / HIT THE HIGHWAY** [ ] [-]

May 02. (cd) *E.M.I.; (<5 38682-2>)* **THE BEST OF THE PROCLAIMERS** [30] [ ] Jun02
– Letter from America / There's a touch / Let's get married / I'm gonna be (500 miles) / The doodle song / I'm on my way / King of the road / Ghost of love / Throw the 'R' away / What makes you cry? / Sunshine on Leith / When you're in love / Cap in hand / I want to be a christian / Act of remembrance / Lady luck / Make my heart fly / The light / The joyful Kilmarnock blues / Oh Jean.

PRO FORMA (see under ⇒ Oscarr records)

PROMISE

Formed: Aberdeen . . . 1985 as FREEBIRD then TOUR DE FORCE by GARETH DAVIES, NODS GRAHAM, COLIN CHAPMAN and DEANNE (IAN BENZIE joined in 1987). Melodic rock/AOR devotees influenced by the likes of JOURNEY, TOTO, AUTOGRAPH, THIN LIZZY and VAN HALEN, the group cut a series of demo tapes which they sold at gigs and used for promotional purposes. As well as magazine coverage and radio airplay throughout Europe and beyond, the band secured a number of high profile support slots to the likes of BIG COUNTRY and RUNRIG. In 1991 rock mag, 'Raw' even nominated them as one of the best unsigned bands in Britain yet they struggled to gain a record deal. This eventually led to the band's demise in 1992 although a subsequent offer of a deal from newly formed independent rock label, 'Now & Then', persuaded them to re-form as The PROMISE (another band were by now using the TOUR DE FORCE moniker) in 1994.

A belated eponymous debut album appeared the following year to widespread acclaim and the group performed at the London Astoria's 'Gods Of Hard Rock' festival. Personnel reshuffles and recording hitches delayed the release of a sophomore set although 'HUMAN FIRE' eventually emerged in Spring '95 featuring new members COLIN FRASER and STEVE CRAIG (although the latter has since departed). After 17 years in the music biz and a few recent gig cancellations, The PROMISE decided enough was enough in May 2002.

• **Note:** not to be confused with the mid-90's outfit on 'Station 2 Station' who issued the 'Strange Bird' set in '95 or the 2002 act who released the single, 'My True Love'.

IAN BENZIE – vocals, guitar / **GARETH DAVIES** – guitar, vocals / **COLIN CHAPMAN** – drums / **NODS GRAHAM** – guitar, vocals / **DEANNE** – bass

Now & Then / not iss.

Mar 95. (cd) *(NTHEN 014CD)* **THE PROMISE** [ ] [-]
– End of the game / You are the one / Playing dirty / Holdin' out for a miracle / Sleepin' alone / Don't keep me waiting / Holdin' on / Restless / When it rains / Silver lights. *(re-prom.Sep95) <Jap-iss.Aug95 on 'Brunette-Alfa'+=; ALCB 3080>* – Falling / All the way / The thin man.

— **COLIN FRASER** – drums, vocals; repl. CHAPMAN

— **STEVE CRAIG** – keyboards, vocals; repl. DEANNE

Frontiers / not iss.

May 99. (cd) *(FRCD 024)* **HUMAN FIRE** [ ] [-]
– Let's talk about love / Kiss me and kill me / Hold on to love / There goes my heart / When love takes a hand / Hole in my heart / Let the night go on forever / Only a woman / Looking glass / Arms of a stranger. *<Jap-iss.Aug99 on 'Nippon Crown'; CRCL 4506> (UK re-iss. Jul00; same)*

— (late '99) now without STEVE who sessioned for PALLAS

— the band official split in May 2002

PROPULSION (see under ⇒ Limbo records)

PUBLIC DOMAIN

Formed: Glasgow . . . 1997 by MARK SHERRY, ALISTAIR MacISAAC, JAMES ALLEN and vocalist MALLORCA LEE, the latter a one-time member of ULTRA-SONIC and regular DJ at Glasgow's reputable Archaos nightclub. PUBLIC DOMAIN blasted out of the city's underground house scene with the track 'OPERATION BLADE (BASS IN THE PLACE)' late in 2000, a track inspired by the vampire film 'Blade'. Originally issued on SHERRY's ultra-DIY label 'Xtravaganza', the song, with its thumping techno beats (very KLF circa 'What Time Is Love?'), Eeee-friendly crowd roars and LEE's impenetrable hollering ("Bass in the place London!") was crowned SOTW by Judge Jules on Radio 1. Its success grew, and while PUBLIC DOMAIN hurried around trying to keep up with the clubber's demands for the single, the word was already spreading. Not surprising then, it hit the UK Top 5, propelling the group into megastardom. However, the words "one hit wonder" may have sprung to mind; after a quickly released remix album the boys failed to repeat the success of 'OPERATION . . .'. Nevermind, at least they went home stars for a day.

MALLORCA LEE – vocals / **MARK SHERRY** (b.1975) + **ALISTAIR MacISAAC** + **JAMES ALLEN**

Made To Measure / not iss.

Jun 98. (cd) *(199656)* **RADIO NIGHTS** [-] [-] German
– Radio nights / No shame / If I were you / Saving grace / Immortal way / Clues / China rain / Child in my heart / Shadow of Eden / Silence of your heart / Confetti / Marching on / Crimes of passion.

Xtra Hard / Sony Int

Nov 00. (c-s/12"/cd-s) *(X2H 1 CS/12/CDS) <670670>* **OPERATION BLADE (BASS IN THE PLACE) (mixes)** [5] [ ] Apr01

Jun 01. (c-s/12"/cd-s; by PUBLIC DOMAIN featuring CHUCK D) *(X2H 3 CD/12/CDS)* **ROCK DA FUNKY BEATS (mixes; 7"version / Bumpin' Bass / original bass)** [19] [-]

Jul 01. (cd/d-lp) *(<X2H 4 CD/LP>)* **HARD HOP SUPERSTARS** [ ] [ ] Sep01
– Rock da funky beats / Pump up nation / Too many MC's / Operation blade / Let me clear my throat / Inside out (and out of control) / Just a Latin groove / No time to run / DJ's on the move / Stargate.

Oct 01. (12"/cd-s) *(X2H 7 12/CD)* **LET ME CLEAR MY THROAT (mixes)** [ ] [-]

— in Nov'01, a PUBLIC DOMAIN remix double-set, 'Hard Dance Anthems' was issued featuring various artists

Dec 01. (12"/cd-s) *(X2H 8 12/CD)* **TOO MANY MC's (mixes)** [34] [-]

PURE GREED (see under ⇒ Veesik records)

PURPLE MUNKIE (see under ⇒ Alphabetty records)

PVC2 (see under ⇒ SLIK)

Q.F.X.

Formed: Selkirk, the Borders . . . 1992 by KIRK TURNBULL, along with DAVID WALKER, BARRIE BROWN, DAVID GOONERY and female front KERRY McGREGOR. From their techno origins in the early 90's to their slightly mainstream sounds a few years later, QFX quickly established themselves as one of Scotland's top purveyors of dance. Helped by their own well-distributed ('Polygram'-backed) independent record outlet, 'Epidemic', TURNBULL and Co scored with a handful of singles. A run of chart breakers began with 1995's 'FREEDOM' (an EP) and was followed by an up-tempo massive-beat version of Moby's 'EVERYTIME YOU TOUCH ME'. However, all was a little quieter after their last Top 40 hit, 'SAY YOU'LL BE MINE', in 1999.

KIRK TURNBULL – vocals, DJ, etc / **KERRY McGREGOR** – vocals / **DAVID WALKER + BARRIE BROWN + DAVID GOONERY**

		white label	not iss.
1992.	(12") *(none)* **VIRTUAL REALITY**		-
1992.	(12") *(none)* **FEEL THE RUSH**		-
		Shoop	not iss.
May 93.	(12") *(SHOOP 002)* **PHOEBUS EP** – Robotic intro'd electronic LSD / Ocean of dreams / + 2		-
		Steppin' Out	not iss.
Aug 93.	(12") *(none)* **JUST DANCE (mixes)**		-
		Epidemic	not iss.
Apr 95.	(lp/c/cd) *(EPI/+C/D 003)* **FREEDOM** – Freedom / Energy / Virtual reality / Power of Rez / Ye ha / Feel so good / Electronic / Ocean of dreams / Just dance (Italian mix) / Feels like Heaven / Feel the rush / DE-JA-VU / Silence / Whiplash / Perfect tekno / Feel for your love / Space tripper / Kick some bass / Virtual reality (piano mix) / Freedom (instrumental). *(cd re-iss. May99; same)*		-
Apr 95.	(12"ep/cd-ep) *(EPI/+CD 004)* **FREEDOM EP** – Freedom / Metropolis / Sianora baby / The machine.	41	-
Jan 96.	(12"/cd-s) *(EPI/+CD 006)* **EVERYTIME YOU TOUCH ME (mixes; standard / house / flute / German tekno)**	22	-
Jul 96.	(12"/cd-s) *(EPI/+CD 007)* **YOU GOT THE POWER (mixes)**	33	-
Jan 97.	(12"/cd-s) *(EPI/+CD 008)* **FREEDOM 2 (remixes; radio / progressive / M.C. Braveheart radio / Happy Hardcore / 12" Clubbed up / original – new vocals / M.C. Braveheart / extended – new vocals)**	21	-
Feb 97.	(cd/c) *(EPI CD/C 009)* **ALIEN CHILD** – Everytime you touch me / Sianora baby / Teckno power / E.S.P. / Freedom 2 / Electro duck / Power house / The machine / Alien child / You got the power / Metropolis / Way oh / Happy hardcore freedom / I never feel you / Trance power / Tasman / Progression / Pizza cat / Clubbed up / The dream. *(re-iss. Dec97; same)*	62	-
Feb 98.	(cd) *(EPICD 010)* **VOYAGE – THE ALBUM**		-
		Impact	not iss.
Apr 98.	(12"; by QFX & DJ SEDUCTION) *(IMP 063)* **FREEDOM. / EVERYTIME YOU TOUCH ME**		-
		Quality	not iss.
Mar 99.	(c-s/12"/cd-s) *(QUAL 005 MC/T/CD)* **SAY YOU'LL BE MINE (mixes; radio / happy hardcore / QFX)**	34	-
Jun 99.	(cd/c/lp) *(CLASS 001 CD/MC/LP)* **HIGH ON LIFE** – Say you'll be mine / I only want you / Life and love / The beat goes on / Sunshine / Walk easy / Eternal love / Mind, body and soul / If you were mine / The way you move it / High on life / Party time people / Say you'll be mine (happy hardcore mix) / I only want you (old skool mix).		-
		Evolution	not iss.
Jun 01.	(12") *(EV 54)* **LET THE BASS GO. / FIRST PARABLE**		-
		Reign Of Sound	not iss.
Nov 01.	(12") *(RRV 2)* **TEARS OF AN ANGEL. / DEJA VU**		-
Mar 02.	(cd-s) *(RRC 3)* **FREEDOM 2002 (mixes)**		-
Jan 02.	(cd-s) *(RRC 4)* **TEARS OF AN ANGEL**		-

Q TEX

Formed: Cumbernauld, nr. Glasgow . . . 1992 by 19 year old DJ whizzkid and all round dance music maestro SCOTT BROWN along with five pals and his girlfriend (and frontwoman) GILLIAN TENNENT. After first becoming invloved in the rave scene in 1990, BROWN maintained an exhaustive work schedule of which Q TEX was only part.

The more acceptable, commercial face of BROWN's harder alter ego, DJ EQUAZION, Q TEX released their first singles (the 'EQUATOR EP's and 'NATURAL HIGH') on Glasgow's fledgling '23rd Precinct' label. Along with the more prolific 'Limbo', 'Stoatin' was a sister imprint which housed the 7-piece outfit's original version of 'THE POWER OF LOVE'. A sterling slice of anthemic rave-pop, the track was a massive Scottish club hit and even made it into the UK Top 75 in 1994. Follow-up, 'BELIEVE', went one better and almost made it into the Top 40 while Q TEX eventually became bonafide chart stars when 1996's 'LET THE LOVE' made the Top 30. Prior to this, BROWN had released another three instalments of his 'EQUAZION' series on his own 'Evolution' label, just one of the many imprints (including 'Twisted Nerve' and 'Twisted Vinyl' – see below) he set up to cater for the harder end of the rave market.

A devotee of the once very popular (in Scotland at least) Dutch "gabba" scene, BROWN's DJ set was known to include more than the odd track from labels like 'Ruffneck' and 'Terror Trax'. In fact, BROWN teamed up with PAUL ELSTAK for the 'Terror Trax' 12", 'Feel The Music', and even topped the bill over some of his European compatriots at 1994's Nightmare In Rotterdam event. He also topped the Rotterdam album charts that same year with his 'HARDCORE HELL' album while his own 'Twisted Vinyl' imprint was set up especially to cater to the ferocious bpm madness of the Dutch scene as well as homegrown product. A sample of just some of the records BROWN was involved with during the mid-90's would include the likes of KINETIK PLEASURE': 'Get The Feeling', GENASIDE: 'Fuck You', HARDWARE: 'Heavy Metal', BASS REACTION: 'Inpulse', BASS X: 'Atomic', GENETIK: 'Experiment' and LORD OF HARDCORE: 'Hellbound'. All scary stuff of course and a world away from Q TEX, who were back in the charts in 1997 with a remixed 'POWER OF LOVE' as well as a less successful accompanying album, 'INTO THE LIGHT'.

Since then, BROWN has concentrated on his EQUAZION series, consigning Q-TEX to the rave history books. Evolution's ACTIVE FORCE were DAVIE FORBES and NEIL SKINNER (also have releases on 'Freebase'), while Evolution's subsidiary, 'Dance Unite', issued THE GROOVER's 'Love Is The King'. BROWN also teamed up with MARC SMITH in June '94 to issue a collaboration set, 'VOLUME 1'. Other outfits on their labels were The DE-VIATION CREW (who feature MARTIN KAY) and SONAR ZONE were from Fife. ULTIMATE BUZZ were the duo of M.C. BEE (CALLAN BRIGHT) and DJ DEEJAY (ROBERT McCAFFERTY) plus harlequin-like dancers HYPE (PAULA RUSSELL) and BRG (KERRY WATSON) and also CYBORG (JOHN JERR).

One the Scottish rave scene's most popular P.A.'s of the period, ULTIMATE BUZZ built up a reputation for themselves as visually captivating performers with a show incorporating lasers, spectra scans and the robotic antics of CYBORG. Favourites at nights like The Source and Dance Mania as well as East Calder's Bunker, the posse released their debut single, 'CHECK DA BASS' in late '94 on SCOTT BROWN's 'Evolution Gold' imprint. The follow-up 'ENERGISE EP' featured live vocals from MC BEE while UB even ventured into the video market in conjunction with film company Double Vision.

SCOTT BROWN (b.1972) – DJ, electronics / **GILLIAN TENNANT** – vocals / + 5 others

		unknown	not iss.
Oct 92.	(12") **EQUATOR**		-
		Limbo	not iss.
Jan 93.	(12") *(Limb 006)* **NATURAL HIGH**		-
		23rd Precinct	not iss.
Mar 93.	(12") *(PREC 006)* **CELEBRATION**		-
		Stoatin'	not iss.
Mar 94.	(12"/c-s) *(STOAT 002/+MC)* **THE POWER OF LOVE (mixes)**	65	-
		23rd Precinct	not iss.
Nov 94.	(c-s/12"/cd-s) *(THIRD 2 MC/T/CD)* **BELIEVE (mixes)**	41	-
Jun 96.	(c-s/12"/cd-s) *(THIRD 4 MC/T/CD)* **LET THE LOVE (mixes)**	30	-
Nov 96.	(c-s/12"/cd-s) *(THIRD 5 MC/T/CD)* **DO YOU WANT ME (mixes)**	48	-
Jun 97.	(12"/cd-s) *(THIRD 7 T/CD)* **POWER OF LOVE 97 radio version / D.O.N.S. single punch / THE MONTINI EXPERIENCE remix / D.O.N.S. club attack / POWER OF LOVE 97 version 2 / DIGITAL BOY Italian rave remix**	49	-

Jul 97. (cd/c) *(THIRD 11 CD/MC)* **INTO THE LIGHT** ☐ -
– Do you want me / Natural high / Heart of Asia / Lies / Deliverance / Water of life / Power of love / Symphonic / Believe / Promised me / Let the love / Pressure / Tonight / Dreams / Into the light.

D.J.EQUAZION

— are SCOTT BROWN + Q-TEX

	Kore	not iss.
Mar 93. (12"ep) *(KORE 1T)* **CYBERFLUX EP**	☐	-
(above and below were actually EQUAZION PARTS I & II)		
Oct 93. (12"ep) *(KORE 3T)* **HARDCORE NATION EP**	☐	-

- Evolution (& . . .Gold) discography -

Feb 94. (12"ep) *(EV 1)* **EQUAZION – Equazion part III**
Feb 94. (12"ep) *(EV 2)* **EQUAZION – Equazion remix E.P.**
– E-creation / etc.
Apr 94. (12") *(EV 4)* **ANALOGUE – Frequencies (mixes)**
Jun 94. (12") **DE-VIATION CREW – The De-State Project**
Jun 94. (12") **SUB-SOURCE – The Sub-Source EP**
– Into euphoria / etc
Aug 94. (12") *(EVG 1)* **SONAR ZONE – Adrenalin EP**
– featuring Scott Brown mix.
Sep 94. (lp) *(EVLP 1)* **Various Artists – Hardcore Hell**
Sep 94. (12"ep) *(EVG 2)* **HARD TRANCE – Extraordinary**
Oct 94. (12"ep) *(EVG 3)* **ULTIMATE BUZZ – Check Da Bass**
Oct 94. (12"ep) *(EVG 4)* **TECHNOSIS –**
Oct 94. (12"ep) *(EVG 5)* **HARD TRANCE – 2**
Jan 95. (lp) *(EVLP 2)* **Various Artists – Hardcore Hell Vol.2**
Feb 95. (12") *(EVG 8)* **ACTIVE FORCE – Head Like A Pac Man**
Feb 95. (12"/cd-s) *(EV/+CDS 14)* **Q-TEX – Equazion pt.4**
Oct 95. (12"/cd-s) *(EV/+CDS 19)* **Q-TEX – Equazion pt.5**
Mar 96. (12"/cd-s) *(EV/+CDS 21)* **SCOTT BROWN – People Love It**
Jun 96. (12"/cd-s) *(EV/+CDS 22)* **Q-TEX – Equazion pt.6**
Jul 96. (12"/cd-s) *(EV/+CDS 23)* **SCOTT BROWN – Rock That Body**
Nov 96. (cd/lp) *(EV CD/LP 5)* **SCOTT BROWN – The Theory Of Evolution**
Jan 97. (12") *(EV 25)* **SCOTT BROWN – Andromeda / Hazardous**
Mar 97. (12") *(EV 26)* **Q-TEX – Equazion pt.7**
Apr 97. (12") *(EV 28)* **SCOTT BROWN – Dream On EP**
Jun 97. (12") *(EV 29)* **SCOTT BROWN – Wheel Of Fortune / Spaced Out**
Dec 97. (12") *(EV 31)* **Q-TEX – Equazion pt.8**
Dec 97. (12") *(EV 32)* **SCOTT BROWN – Heaven's Gate / Capricorn**
Apr 99. (12") *(EV 35)* **SCOTT BROWN – I Don't Need Anybody**
Apr 99. (12") *(EV 36)* **Q-TEX – Falling To The Earth**
May 99. (12") *(EV 37)* **SCOTT BROWN – Super Sharp Beats / Healing Mind**
Oct 99. (12") *(EV 040)* **SCOTT BROWN & GILLIAN TENNANT – Everytime I Close My Eyes**
Nov 99. (12") *(EV 41)* **SCOTT BROWN – Yeah Oh Yeah / Journey**
Jul 00. (cd) *(EVCD 7)* **SCOTT BROWN – Hardcore 2000**
Nov 00. (12") *(EV 42)* **SCOTT BROWN – Second Wave**
Aug 00. (12") *(EV 47)* **SCOTT BROWN – Love Me Too / Sensation**
Mar 01. (12") *(EV 50)* **SCOTT BROWN – Now Is The Time (remix)**
Apr 01. (12") *(EV 52)* **SCOTT BROWN – Johnny (DJ Damned mix) / Johnny (Old Skool mix)**
May 01. (12") *(EV 53)* **SCOTT BROWN – Enlightened**
Aug 01. (12") *(EV 55)* **SCOTT BROWN – Turn Up The Music**

- Dance Unite discography -

— THE GROOVER is TONY MACKLIN
Jun 94. (12") *(DUR 001)* **THE GROOVER – Love Is The King / Crazy Laces**

- Twisted Vinyl discography -

Apr 94. (12"pink) *(TV 1) GENASIDE – F**k You*
Jun 94. (12") *(TV 2)* **MR. BROWN – Jump**
Jun 94. (12") *(TV 3)* **FIRE STARTER – Burn MotherFucker**
Oct 96. (12") *(TV 26)* **SCOTT BROWN – Back With The Hardcore**
Jan 97. (12") *(TV 28)* **SCOTT BROWN & PHAZE 2 PHAZE – The Shredder EP**
Jan 97. (12") *(TV 30)* **SCOTT BROWN – Outside World / One More Chance**
Mar 97. (12") *(TV 31)* **SCOTT BROWN & DJ PLEASURE – Hallelujah**
Apr 97. (12") *(TV 33)* **Q-TEX – Classic Remixes Vol.2**
Aug 98. (12") *(TV 36)* **SCOTT BROWN & DAVIE FORBES – Rhythm On Time**
Apr 99. (12") *(TV 39)* **SCOTT BROWN – Brainbasher / Rubbernut**

SCOTT BROWN

— even more of the man on other labels

	Notorious Vinyl	not iss.
Aug 94. (12"ep) *(001)* **THE DETONATOR EP**	☐	-
	Terror Trax	not iss.
Oct 94. (12"; by SCOTT BROWN & PAUL ELSTAK) **FEEL THE MUSIC**	-	- Dutch
	Rezerection	not iss.
Jun 96. (12"ep/cd-ep) *(REZEP/REZCDEP 103)* **TECHNO REVOLUTION**	☐	-
	Screwdriver	not iss.
Aug 96. (12") *(SCREW 15)* **BURNIN' UP**	☐	-
	Inferno	not iss.
Feb 97. (12") *(INFER 014)* **HARDCORE POWER**	☐	-
	Happy Trax	not iss.
May 97. (12") *(DBM 2837)* **FEELING ALRIGHT**	☐	-
Feb 99. (12") *(DBM 3881)* **DROP THAT BEAT. / AFTERLIFE**	☐	-
	European Hardcore	not iss.
Jun 97. (12") *(EHU 008)* **FAST BEATS**	☐	-
	Mokum	not iss.
Oct 97. (12") *(MOK 81)* **ANNIHILATOR**	☐	-
	Mainframe	not iss.
Dec 97. (12"; by SCOTT BROWN & GILLIAN TENNANT) *(MF 1)* **HOLD ME**	☐	-
Nov 98. (12"; by SCOTT BROWN & GILLIAN TENNANT) *(MF 4)* **I'M THE ONLY ONE**	☐	-
Mar 99. (cd) *(MFCD 1)* **FUTURE PROGRESSION**	☐	-
	Corrode	not iss.
Mar 98. (12") *(CORRODE 6)* **LOST SOULS. / SONIC BLAST**	☐	-
	Death Becomes Me	not iss.
Jun 98. (12"ep) *(DBM 3517)* **PIANO TRAX EP**	☐	-
	Federation	not iss.
Nov 98. (12"; by SCOTT BROWN & MARC SMITH) *(FED 2)* **TAKING ME HIGHER**	☐	-
	Smokin Beats	not iss.
Mar 99. (12") *(017)* **IN MY LIFE. / TONITE**	☐	-
	Logic – Arista	not iss.
Apr 99. (d-cd/d-c; by Various Artists) *(74321 62809-2/-4)* **SCOTT BROWN & MAXIMUM NOISE PRESENT . . . ESSENTIAL HAPPY HARDCORE VOL.1**	☐	-

– DJ HAM – Your love / Q-TEX – Power of love / EUPHONY – Invader / SCOTT BROWN – Healing mind / SCOTT BROWN – Super sharp beatz / FABULOUS FABER – Better day / SCOTT BROWN & MARC SMITH – Taking me higher / BANG – Break of dawn / INTERSTATE – Get on up / SCOTT BROWN – Hardcore vibes / INTERSTATE – A.B.C. / SCOTT BROWN – Take me up / BROWN & TENNANT – I'm the only one / DJ STORM – Kickin' hard / INTERSTATE – Vitality / MARC SMITH – Your lovin' / Q-TEX – Equazion / SCOTT BROWN – Check it out now / BASS X – Horsepower / MARC SMITH – The ripper / SCOTT RAMIREZ – Push it / GOOD FELLAZ – Free your mind / FORTREZZ – Check da base / LORD RAZ & PRINCE KORDY – Hand in hand / APOLLO 1 – Force / GOOD FELLAZ – Wave ya hands in the air / MAXIMUM NOISE – Another dimension / BEATBUSTER III TILL – Future city / DJ KAREM – Daydream / BEATBUSTER II TILL – Drop zone / OLLY MAGIC – Hey rude boy / RAVE BUSTERZ – Kaos junkies / RAVE BUSTERZ – Your brotherz / DJ KILLERFACE – Sunshine / ROTTERDAM HOOLIGANS – Progressive nightmare / SCOTT RAMIREZ – Dark side of the city / TECHNOMANIA – Jump in da gym / LORD RAZ & PRINCE KORDY – Destiny / MAXIMUM NOIZE – Space da base / EL' CHAVEZ – DJ's holiday.

	Highborn	not iss.
Jul 00. (d-cd) **THE WORLD OF SCOTT BROWN**	☐	-

– Basic nature (by INTERSTATE) / Hallelujah (exclusive hardcore 2000 mix – by KINETIC PLEASURE) / Power of love (Scott Brown '98 mix – by Q-TEX) / Yeah oh yeah / Falling to the earth (by Q-TEX) / Vitality (by INTERSTATE) / Elysium / Do it hard / Everytime I close my eyes (with GILLIAN TENNANT) / Lost generation (Scott Brown remix – by INTERSTATE) / Pilgrim (by BASS-X vs SCOTT BROWN) / Turn it out (as MR.BROWN) / I don't need nobody / Check it out now / Brain basher / Falling to the earth (exclusive hardcore 200 mix – by Q-TEX) / Crushed testes (by LORDS OF HARDCORE) / You are hardcore (by the PUNISHER) / Back tracker / Pilgrim (exclusive hardcore 2000 mix – by BASS-X vs SCOTT BROWN) / Liberation / Rubbernut.

	Blatant Beats	not iss.
Nov 00. (12") *(BB 23)* **RETURN TO ELYSIUM. / IGNITION**	☐	-
	Neophyte	not iss.
Apr 01. (12") *(NEO 010)* **BUCKFAST EXPERIENCE**	☐	-

Finley QUAYE

Born: 25 Mar'74, Leith, Edinburgh . . . to a native Scots mother who died of a heroin overdose when he was still at primary school; his Ghanian jazz-playing father was absent for most of FINLEY's troubled upbringing. Subsequently living between grandparents in Edinburgh and auntie/uncle in Manchester, he also spent a lot of his youth in London. With many notable industry connections stemming from his father's side of the family (i.e. uncle ERIC QUAYE, percussionist with OSIBISA and half-brother CALEB QUAYE, a session man for the likes of ELTON JOHN), FINLEY naturally gravitated towards a career in music. Probably his most famous relative TRICKY, is rather confusingly, actually QUAYE's nephew (his sister, MAXIN QUAYE is Tricky's mother!), the pair subsequently collaborating on a couple of tracks, one of which, 'DUPPY UMBRELLA' was a lengthy ode to magic mushrooms featuring a guest spot from IGGY POP (no relation!).

One of his earliest musical endeavours was playing drums with the Rainbow Tribe hippy community in London, the reggae loving QUAYE eventually securing a deal with major 'Epic' records. In 1997, the fruits of his labour were revealed, the sun-kissed pop/reggae/hip-hop charm of his 'MAVERICK A STRIKE' album gaining him a wide cross-section of fans and a Top 3 UK chart placing. This acclaimed opus also spawned three major Top 30 hits, the biggest selling being, 'EVEN AFTER ALL'.

Afterwards, QUAYE was reluctant to issue an album until three years later when 'VANGUARD' (2000) finally surfaced. Disappointing in every aspect, the album's helmsman failed to capture the essence and soul previously heard on QUAYE's earlier albums. That is not to say all the blame should've been pinned on him; QUAYE himself tried to get away with some appalling lyrics, while the spiritual direction of the set veered off the proverbial road and came crashing to an almighty halt.

• **Songwriters:** Self-penned except; CROSSTOWN TRAFFIC (Jimi Hendrix).

FINLEY QUAYE – vocals; with session men

		Epic	Sony
Jun 97.	(c-s) *(664455-4)* **SUNDAY SHINING / MASHING UP LUCIFER: STONE THE DEVIL**	16	-
	(12"/cd-s) *(664455-6/-2)* – ('A'side) / Sunday best / I need a lover / Singing from the same hymn sheet.		
Sep 97.	(c-s/cd-s) *(664971-4/-2)* **EVEN AFTER ALL / BURNING**	10	-
	(cd-s+=) *(664971-5)* – ('A'mixes).		
Sep 97.	(cd/c/lp) *(488758-2/-4/-1)* *<68506>* **MAVERICK A STRIKE**	3	Oct97
	– Ultra stimulation / It's great when you're together / Sunday shining / Even after all / Ride on and turn the people on / The way of the explosive / Your love gets sweeter / Supreme I preme / Sweet and loving man / Red rolled and seen / Failing / I need a lover / Maverick a strike. *(cd re-iss. Jul98; same)*		
Nov 97.	(c-s) *(665338-4)* **IT'S GREAT WHEN WE'RE TOGETHER / MORNING PRACTICE**	29	-
	(cd-s+=) *(665338-5)* – ('A'mix) / Even after all (live).		
	(cd-s) *(665338-2)* – ('A'side) / ('A'mix) / Birds of one feather / Crosstown traffic.		
Feb 98.	(c-s) *(665606-4)* **YOUR LOVE GETS SWEETER / EVERYBODY KNOWS**	16	-
	(cd-s+=) *(665606-5)* – ('A'-The Abbey Road version) / Le saint des delinquents.		
	(cd-s) *(665606-2)* – ('A'side) / ('A'-The Abbey Road version) / Can't be left alone / Maverick a dub.		
Aug 98.	(cd-s) *(666079-2)* **ULTRA STIMULATION / WHITE PAPER**	51	-
	(c-s+=) *(666079-4)* – ('A'-Ultra vibration).		
	(cd-s) *(666079-5)* – ('A'side) / ('A'-Ultra vibration) / Too many guns.		
Sep 00.	(c-s) *(669803-4)* **SPIRITUALIZED / THINK FOR YOURSELF / TRIBAL WAR**	26	-
	(cd-s) *(669803-5)* – (first two tracks) / ('A'-A Guy Called Gerald remix) / ('A'-CD-rom).		
	(cd-s) *(669803-2)* – ('A'side) / ('A'-Francois Kervorkian 12" vocal mix) / The wizard.		
Oct 00.	(cd/c/lp) *(499710-2/-4/-1)* *<85143>* **VANGUARD**	35	Jan01
	– Broadcast / Spiritualized / Emperor / Burning / Everybody knows / Feeling blue / When I burn off into the distance / Chad Valley / Calendar / British air rage / White paper / Hey now.		
Dec 00.	(12") *(670566-6)* **WHEN I BURN OFF INTO THE DISTANCE. / ('A'-Primal Scream mix) / SPIRITUALIZED (Francois K vibin' vocal mix)**		-
	(cd-s) *(670566-5)* – (first 2 tracks) / First.		
	(cd-s) *(670566-2)* – ('A'side) / Spiritualized (acoustic version) / Sunday shining (acoustic version).		

Monica QUEEN (see under ⇒ THRUM)

QUESTIONS

Formed: Edinburgh . . . 1978 by Power-pop mods PAUL BARRY (only 15 at the time), STEPHEN LENNON, JOHN ROBINSON and CHRIS KOWALSKI. Their initial break came courtesy of a deal with Bruce Findlay's 'Zoom' label (soon home to SIMPLE MINDS), where they made two pleasant if not overwhelming 45's, 'SOME OTHER GUYS' and 'CAN'T GET OVER YOU'. A couple of years in the musical wilderness was all but forgotten when ex-JAM mainman PAUL WELLER asked them to join his fledgling 'Respond' imprint. Between 1983 and '84 – with a few appearances on Channel 4's 'The Tube' – the QUESTIONS had a handful of minor hit singles, including a Top 50 breaker, 'TUESDAY SUNSHINE'. Two disappointing flops, 'BUILDING ON A STRONG FOUNDATION' and 'MONTH OF SUNDAYS', preceded their patchy and mainly forgettable album, 'BELIEF' (1984). In the late 90's and now living in America, songwriter PAUL BARRY finally found fame when his song 'Believe' was taken to the top of the charts by CHER!

PAUL BARRY – vocals, bass / **STEPHEN LENNON** – lead guitar / **JOHN ROBINSON** – rhythm guitar / **CHRIS KOWALSKI** – drums

		Zoom	not iss.
Aug 78.	(7") *(ZUM 6)* **SOME OTHER GUYS. / ROCK'N'ROLL AIN'T DEAD**		-
Jan 79.	(7") *(ZUM 8)* **CAN'T GET OVER YOU. / ANSWERS**		-
		Look	not iss.
1980.	(7") *(LKSP 6095)* **SIXTY NINE. / MUMBLING MOSEY**		-
		Respond	not iss.
Oct 82.	(7") *(RESP 7)* **WORK & PLAY. / ('A'version)**		-
	(12"+=) *(RESPX 7)* – Saved by the bell.		
Apr 83.	(7"/12") *(KOB/+X 702)* **PRICE YOU PAY. / GROOVE LINE**	56	-
Aug 83.	(7"/12") *(KOB/+X 705)* **TEAR SOUP. / VITAL SPARK**	66	-
Feb 84.	(7") *(KOB 707)* **TUESDAY SUNSHINE. / NO ONE**	46	-
	(12"+=) *(KOBX 707)* – House that Jack built.		
May 84.	(7"/12") *(KOB/+X 709)* **BUILDING ON A STRONG FOUNDATION. / DREAMS COME TRUE**		-
Sep 84.	(7") *(KOB 712)* **MONTH OF SUNDAYS. / BELIEF**		-
	(12"+=) *(KOBX 712)* – Other way round.		
Oct 84.	(lp/c) *(RRL/RRC 503)* **BELIEF**		-
	– Belief / All the time in the world / The bottom line / Month of Sundays / Someone's got to lose / Body and soul / Tuesday sunshine / December / The learning tree / Everything I see.		

— disbanded after above; PAUL BARRY subsequently went to live in the US.

QUINN (see under ⇒ HARDBODY)

Paul QUINN

Born: 26 Dec'51, Glasgow. He formed BOURGIE BOURGIE in 1983 with former JAZZATEERS members (IAN BURGOYNE, KEITH BAND and KENNY McDONALD) and scraped into the Top 50 early the following year with their much lauded 'M.C.A.' debut 45, 'BREAKING POINT'. A second, 'CARELESS' flopped and the band quickly disbanded, QUINN subsequently resurfacing on a collaboration single, 'PALE BLUE EYES' (a VELVET UNDERGROUND cover) with ORANGE JUICE mainman, EDWYN COLLINS.

His first solo outing, 'AIN'T THAT ALWAYS THE WAY' was another for ALAN HORNE's (the man behind 'Postcard'; Glaswegian indie home of ORANGE JUICE, AZTEC CAMERA and JOSEF K) 'Swamplands' label, pursued by yet another top indie collaboration, this time 'ONE DAY' alongside ex-YAZOO and future ERASURE man VINCE CLARKE.

For the rest of the 80's, QUINN's unique and extremely fluid voice took a back seat until the early 90's heralded his return with a sort of "Postcard" supergroup, PAUL QUINN AND THE INDEPENDENT GROUP. This included hip musicians JAMES KIRK (Orange Juice), BLAIR COWAN (Lloyd Cole & The Commotions), CAMPBELL OWENS (Aztec Camera), ROBERT HODGENS (Bluebells) and ALAN HORNE!, who had revived the 'Postcard' stable for this new act. In 1992, an album 'THE PHANTOMS AND THE ARCHETYPES' took rave reviews, QUINN's crooning voice never better on songs such as, 'HANGING ON', 'PUNK ROCK HOTEL' and the excellent title track.

His retro film noir style (BILLY MACKENZIE or BILLY IDOL on mood pills) was again on song, when a follow-up, 'WILL I EVER BE INSIDE OF YOU' showed remarkable beauty, a re-working of 'STUPID THING' and a cover of 'MISTY BLUE' were top notch; what happened to him after their shared EP, 'PREGNANT WITH POSSIBILITIES', is anybody's guess.

BOURGIE BOURGIE

PAUL QUINN – vocals / **IAN BURGOYNE** – guitar / **KEITH BAND** – bass (ex-JAZZATEERS) / **KENNY McDONALD** – drums

M.C.A. not iss.

Feb 84. (7") *(BOU 1)* **BREAKING POINT. / APRES SKI** [48] [-]
(12"+=) *(BOUT 1)* – ('A'extended).

Apr 84. (7") *(BOU 2)* **CARELESS. / CHANGE OF ATTITUDE** [ ] [-]
(12"+=) *(BOUT 2)* – ('A'extended).

PAUL QUINN

— first single a collaboration with the ex-ORANGE JUICE frontman

Swamplands not iss.

Aug 84. (7"; PAUL QUINN & EDWYN COLLINS) *(SWP 1)* **PALE BLUE EYES. / BURROW** [ ] [-]

Mar 85. (7") *(SWP 6)* **AIN'T THAT ALWAYS THE WAY. / PUNK ROCK HOTEL** [ ] [-]
(12"+=) *(SWX 6)* – Corrina Corrina.

— In Jun'85, QUINN collaborated with VINCE CLARKE (ex-YAZOO, ex-DEPECHE MODE, now ERASURE) on 7"/12", 'ONE DAY' (Mute; TAG/12TAG 1). (this was re-issued in Apr93; same cat.no.)

PAUL QUINN AND THE INDEPENDENT GROUP

PAUL QUINN with **JAMES KIRK** – guitar (ex-ORANGE JUICE) / **ALAN HORNE** – (creator of 'Postcard' label) / **CAMPBELL OWENS** – drums (of-AZTEC CAMERA) / **BLAIR COWAN** – bass (ex-LLOYD COLE & THE COMMOTIONS) / **ROBERT HODGENS** – rhythm guitar, vocals (ex-BLUEBELLS)

Postcard Thirsty Ear

Sep 92. (lp/c/cd) *(DUBH 921/+MC/CD)* **THE PHANTOMS AND THE ARCHETYPES** [ ] [-]
– The phantoms and the archetypes / Born on the wrong side of town / What can you do to me now / Punk rock hotel / Superstar / Call my name / The damage is done / Darling / I can't fight / Hanging on.

Jul 93. (7") *(DUBH 933)* **STUPID THING. / PASSING THOUGHT** [ ] [-]
(cd-s+=) *(DUBH 933)* – Superstar.

— HODGENS replaced by **MICK SLAVEN** – (ex-JAZZATEERS) / **SKIP REID** – (ex-ASSOCIATES) / **ANDY ALSTON** – / **JANE MARIE O'BRIEN** –

Oct 94. (lp/c/cd) *(DUBH 945/+MC/CD)* <57024> **WILL I EVER BE INSIDE OF YOU** [ ] [ ] 1996
– Will I ever be inside of you / You have been seen / Lover, that's all you over / Mooreefoc (misty blue) / A passing thought / Outre / Misty blue / Stupid thing / At the end of the night.

Jun 95. (cd-ep; PAUL QUINN, The NECTARINE No.9 / JOCK SCOT) *(DUBH 952CD)* **PREGNANT WITH POSSIBILITES EP** [ ] [-]
– Tiger tiger / Will I ever be inside of you / Just another f***ed-up little druggy on the scene / Grunge girl groan.

R

RADIO CITY (see ⇒ Section 9: wee post-Punk groups)

RADIO SWEETHEARTS

Formed: Glasgow . . . 1996 by FRANCIS MACDONALD, a former drummer of BMX BANDITS, The PASTELS and The BOY HAIRDRESSERS (i.e. TEENAGE FANCLUB), along with co-writer JOHN MILLER, plus JOHN McCUSKER (ex-BATTLEFIELD BAND!) and MALCOLM McMASTER. This New Wave Alt-country band debuted with the set, 'NEW MEMORIES', recorded in Glasgow although issued on New Orleans imprint 'St. Roch' and mastered in Tennessee. It made the country Top 30 in America but failed to draw the same attention in Britain. Perhaps the flakiest part of the album was listening to a group of indie renegades try to add humour to the old country scene whilst asking to be taken seriously. However, the LP had its strong moments, 'BEER AND WHISKY' managed to get all the right nods and take a good stab at ye olde folk, while 'OUT OF THE DARKNESS' lamented MACDONALD's vocals into a transatlantic warble. During this same period, Nashville country was big business mainstream and loved by the establishment and hierarchy; where the RADIO SWEETHEARTS fitted in was anybody's guess.

Others who lapped up the combo's impressive debut were AL PERKINS, ALEX CHILTON, SID GRIFFIN and the MAVERICKS, none of them British but nevertheless revered by its citizens ye all. Listeners in the States were not disappointed when 'LONESOME BLUE' was issued in 2000, and boasted a full set of unsaturated pop/country songs. And not just that, the record, like its aforementioned predecessor recovered the main paths which led to the dreary conclusion of the first album. At times it seemed nothing more than a dull piece of trashy Nashville, only graced sometimes by pace and emotion. Who was it that once said, "the mediocre are always at their best"? JOHN MILLER, however, shied away from the new acclaim the group had reaped by issuing the lo-fi, front-porch inspired solo album, 'POPPING PILLS' (2002), which featured a whole host of songs influenced by his peers GRAM PARSONS and HANK WILLIAMS. A pretty affair, as opposed to messy, the listener was in two minds about MILLER's obvious obsession with ol' country music; was he simply taking the michael (Country Teasers please stand up), or was the man genuinely passionate about Nashville? – I think the latter. What was apparent was the charred remnants of HANK's ten-gallon hat, thrown in the fire for some slow, slow burnin'.

• **Covered:** IS ANYBODY GOING TO SAN ANTONE (hit; Charley Pride) / A HOUSE OF GOLD + I SAW THE LIGHT + RAMBLING MAN (Hank Williams) / RED CADILLAC AND A BLACK MOUSTACHE (hit; Warren Smith) / I BEEN TO GEORGIA ON A FAST TRAIN (Billy Joe Shaver).

FRANCIS MACDONALD (b.11 Sep'70, Bellshill) – drums, vocals (ex-BMX BANDITS, ex-PASTELS, ex-TEENAGE FANCLUB) / **JOHN MILLER** – vocals, guitar / **JOHN McCUSKER** – fiddle (of BATTLEFIELD BAND) / **MALCOLM McMASTER** – pedal steel guitar / with **GERARD LOVE** (of TEENAGE FANCLUB) / **BRIAN TAYLOR** (of SUPERSTAR)

Shoeshine not iss.

Oct 96. (7") *(SHOE 003)* **NEW MEMORIES. / BEER AND WHISKY** [ ] [-]

Jun 97. (7") *(SHOE 008)* **RAMBLING MAN. / FOUND A NEW LOVE** [ ] [-]

St. Roch St. Roch

Jul 97. (cd) *(<SR 1003-2>)* **NEW MEMORIES** [ ] [ ] Feb97
– Lonely footsteps / Every other song / Beer and whisky / Is anybody going to San Antone / A house of gold / I saw the light / New memories / Headin' on down the highway / Red cadillac and a black moustache / Don't make me wait / We've fallen out of love again / Out in the darkness. *(re-iss. Oct98 as 'NEW MEMORIES . . . REVISITED' +=; SHOECD 003)* – Lone star / Rambling man / Found a new love / Tossin' and turnin' / I been to Georgia on a fast train / A deeper hurt.

not iss. Swingset

1997. (7") *<006>* **HEADING ON DOWN THE HIGHWAY. / EVERY OTHER SONG / LIVING WITHOUT YOU** [-] [ ]

Flotsam & Jetsam not iss.

Apr 98. (7") *(SHaG 13.05)* **Club Beatroot – Part Five (live series)** [ ] [-]
– White freightliner blues / (other by PINK KROSS).

Spit & Polish Spit & Polish

Feb 00. (cd) *(<SPITCD 002>)* **LONESOME BLUE** [ ] [ ]
– Closing time / (Take me back to) San Francisco / Bumming around / All I see is you / Let me be your man tonight / Living without you / Heart on the line / Drinkin' about you all night / Open up your heart / Lonesome blue / Look homeward angel / Sweetheart hoedown / Love to give you / I must have been out of my mind / Forget about you.

— FRANCIS changed his style again to form SPEEDER (in 1999)

JOHN MILLER

Spit & Polish not iss.

May 02. (cd) *(SPITCD 011)* **POPPING PILLS** [ ] [-]
– One of them old country songs / Don't forget to tell him / The dream I had last night / Down Mexico way / Taking the long way to freedom / We don't care anymore / Everybody knows / This pain inside / Popping pills / I'm a loser again / We've fought once too often now.

RADIOTONES

Formed: Perth . . . 1997 by the Delta-Blues trio of singer/songwriter DAVE ARCARI, harmonica player JIM HARCUS and bassman ADRIAN PATERSON. Initiated with a modus operandi of dragging the sound of vintage acoustic blues kicking and screaming into the new millennium, the RADIOTONES made their debut in 1999 with the 'GRAVEL ROAD' album. The latter set featured renditions of JOHN LEE HOOKER's 'This Is Hip', ROBERT JOHNSON's classic 'Come On In My Kitchen' and BUKKA WHITE's 'Jitterbug Swing' alongside ARCARI-penned originals.

The group's National Steel-guitar abusing approach owed much to a punk ethos although the cover material in their live sets often featured the likes of long gone blues legends like BLIND WILLIE JOHNSON and the aforementioned WHITE. ARCARI's rough'n'ready vocals and his percussive guitar technique came in for particular critical attention, the man whipping up another hard-bitten rootsy maelstrom on sophomore set, 'WHISKEY'D UP' (2000). DAVE is also head of an A&R development at his own 'Buzz management', 14 Corsiehall Rd., Perth, PH2 0NA.

DAVE ARCARI – vocals, steel guitars / **JIM HARCUS** – harmonica / **ADRIAN PATERSON** – bass

		Buzz	not iss.
Feb 99.	(cd) *(BRS 0198)* **GRAVEL ROAD**		-

– Gravel road / Pomegranate heart / Devil got my woman / Journeytime is over / You oughta know / Where were you? / Jitterbug swing / Come on in my kitchen / Good friend blues / This is hip.

Nov 00.	(cd) *(BRSO 1200)* **WHISKEY'D UP**		-

– Don't stop / Close to the edge / She's gone / Wherever I go / Can't be satisfied / Cool it / Going to see the king / Nobody's fault but mine / No more Mr.Nice Guy / One side blind / Day job / Preachin' blues.

Cathie RAE

Born: Edinburgh. Reared in a musical family (her father RONNIE plays bass while her sisters SYLVIA and GINA are both singers), CATHIE soaked up classic jazz influences such as CHET BAKER, BOB DOROUGH, SHIRLEY HORNE and JULIE LONDON as well as the likes of RICKIE LEE JONES. She began making a name for herself in Edinburgh via her residency at The Jazz Joint, Henry's Cellar Bar, a suitably smokey, intimate environment that also played host to such native talent as NIKKI KING and SUBIE COLEMAN.

RAE subsequently teamed up with the latter two in the SISTERSOUL project, performing – both together in 3-part harmony and individually – classic songs by soul greats such as STEVIE WONDER and AL GREEN. Musical backing came from the MIDNIGHT BLUE band, CATHIE also working with band leader COLIN STEELE on the acclaimed 'A Chet Baker Tribute'. A sincere, affectionate celebration of the great trumpeter's life through both narrative and song, the show enjoyed a three week run at the now sadly defunct Cafe Graffiti Club as part of the 1999 Festival Fringe. More recently, the silky voiced chanteuse has been working with guitarist/composer SANDY WRIGHT on a set that includes both original material (by RAE herself as well as her sister GINA) and songs by such legends as JIMI HENDRIX and ELVIS COSTELLO.

Jesse RAE

Born: c.late 50's, St. Boswell's, Galashiels. From humble beginnings as a Borders farmboy, JESSE moved on and up to the unlikely environs of the USA where he joined heavy-rock combo, The BOYS, after replying to a wanted ad in Melody Maker. When their manager bolted with all the equipment, JESSE headed East to Boston where a GEORGE CLINTON/P-FUNK show changed his musical life. Bizarrely enough, RAE struck up a conversation with none other than keyboard guru, BERNIE WORRELL, the meeting leading to a brief working partnership with the likes of RUTH COPELAND.

In 1978, he briefly returned home to Scotland with the intention of securing a record deal. Disappointed, he again flew back to the States where he eventually had a debut single, 'D.E.S.I.R.E.', released by Florida label 'Bold'. He then penned the track, 'INSIDE OUT', a song originally intended for US hard-Funk act, SLAVE, although ODYSSEY were to take it into the British Top 3 in summer '82. The ever-creative JESSE subsequently cut a bi-lingual love song video promo entitled 'RUSHA'. This won him both an award at UCLA's International Music Video Festival and a thank you from the Reagan regime for improving cultural relations with the Soviet Union! Even stranger, JESSE recorded a funky collaboration with Liberal leader, David Steel, whom the big man even introduced to the nonplussed P-FUNK posse!

In 1983, RAE went back to live on his Borders farm, where he took to wearing full 13th Century Highland regalia (helmet and broadsword included) as a statement of his identity. A brief liaison with Scottish-based 'Supreme Int.' for the single, 'BE YOURSELF', was followed by a major label deal with 'Warners'. Predictably perhaps, the company saw JESSE's fervent patriotism as a lucrative novelty, and a series of disagreements ensued. Sadly, the big yin's plan to "export" his 'OVER THE SEA' single south of the border came to nothing although the song was released via his own 'Scotland The What' imprint and was accompanied by an acclaimed video (memorably aired on Channel 4's TV pop show, The Tube).

A debut album, 'THE THISTLE', was eventually completed and released in 1987, featuring his funky chums (P-FUNK, ZAPP and AWB) from over the sea in a backing capacity. The title track's video was produced by ZAPP frontman, ROGER TROUTMAN, who JESSE apparently picked up at the airport in his tractor.

Although JESSE vanished from the mainstream recording front, the irrepressible maverick went on to undertake various projects including a funk interpretation of ROBERT BURNS' 'Tam O' Shanter', an aborted film for the Scottish Rugby Union prior to the 1991 World Cup and a series of collaborations with the ON-U-SOUND people and TACKHEAD.

JESSE RAE – vocals / with session people

		Radical Choice	Bold
1981.	(7") *(TIC 7)* **D.E.S.I.R.E. / SKY DIVER**		1979
		Supreme Int.	**not iss.**
Dec 84.	(12") *(EDITION 84.5)* **BE YOURSELF. / (IT'S JUST) THE DOG IN ME**		-

— with **BERNIE WORRELL** – keyboards, bass / **ROGER + LESTER TROUTMAN** (of ZAPP) / **ONNIE McINTYRE** – bass / **JAMES LOCKE** – drums / **MICHAEL HAMPTON** – guitar / **STEVE FERRONE** – drums / etc

		Scotland The What – W.E.A.	not iss.
Apr 85.	(7"/7"pic-d; w/video) *(YZ 36/+P; w/SAM 242)* **OVER THE SEA. / PARTY CRACKERS**	65	-
	(12"+=) *(YZ 36T)* – ('A'instrumental).		
Apr 87.	(7"/12") *(YZ 116/+T)* **HOU-DI-NI. / IDIO-SYN-CRAZY**		-
Jul 87.	(7"/12") *(YZ 138/+T)* **THAT KIND O' GIRL. / FRIENDSHIP**		-
Aug 87.	(lp/c) *(WX 97/+C)* **THE THISTLE**		-

– Inside out / That kind o' girl / Hou-di-ni / Don't give up / Friendship / The thistle / Be yer self / Rusha / Over the sea / Scotland the brave – Idio-syn-crazy.

— JESSE would retire from recording soon after above, until . . .

		On-U-Sound	not iss.
Apr 93.	(10"; as JESSE RAE & STRANGE PARCELS) *(ONUDP 24)* **BODY BLASTIN'**		-
		Echo Beach	**Satellite Radio Rugby**
Sep 97.	(cd) *(EB 007)* <4101> **COMPRESSION**		

Jim RAFFERTY

Born: Paisley. If you recognise the surname of this singer/songwriter, that's because JIM is the younger brother of massive-selling solo star, GERRY. In fact, the ex-STEALER'S WHEEL frontman (alongside another name, RAB NOAKES), helped get JIM's career off the mark by guesting on his debut single, 'DON'T TALK BACK', early in 1978 – also the name of parent LP. However, with GERRY's 'Baker Street' a Top 3 hit all around the world, there wasn't much room at the time for his troubadour brother. A second set, 'SOLID LOGIC' (1979), did little to inspire a public content with the sophisticated sounds of his laid-back and arguably more talented sibling, the result being JIM retired from solo work. In 1992/3, the young RAFFERTY contributed a couple of songs to his brother's comeback set, 'On A Wing & A Prayer', while he also earned a bit cash for his backing singing.

JIM RAFFERTY – vocals, guitar / with HUGH BURNS – guitar / BJ COLE – steel guitar / FRANK BOGIE – guitar / GERRY RAFFERTY – guitar / RAB NOAKES – vocals / GRAHAM PRESKETT – fiddle, keyboards / etc

Decca London

Jan 78. (7") *(F 13747)* **DON'T TALK BACK. / BAD, BAD MOVER** [ ] [-]
Mar 78. (7";w-drawn) *(F 13696)* **GOOD DAY GO BY. / PEACE OF MIND** [-] [-]
May 78. (7") *(F 13779)* **GOOD DAY GO BY. / PEACE OF MIND** [ ] [-]
May 78. (lp) *(SKL 5291)* <722> **DON'T TALK BACK** [ ] [ ]
– Bad, bad mover / Don't talk back / Peace of mind / Brown eyed lady / Dreaming / Pills for my confusion / Bitter harvest / Good day go by / Weekend / Bishops mountain.
Sep 78. (7") *(F 13797)* **THIS TIME. / WEEKEND** [ ] [-]
Sep 79. (7") *(F 13861)* **KEEP IT IN THE FAMILY. / OH LUCY** [ ] [-]
Oct 79. (lp/c) *(SKLR/KSKCR 5314)* **SOLID LOGIC** [ ] [-]
– Keep it in the family / Look in your eyes / Stepping out / Tomorrow's another day / Oh Lucy / Home away from home / Saturday night / Get down to the rhythm / Underwood lane / Any port in a storm.
Nov 79. (7") *(F 13878)* **STEPPING OUT. / SATURDAY NIGHT** [ ] [-]

Charisma not iss.

Nov 80. (7") *(CB 377)* **THE BOGEYMAN. / SALT LAKE CITY** [ ] [-]

– others, etc. –

Jan 78. (7") *Pinnacle; (P 8453)* **SEE YOU AGAIN. / CRUISIN'** [ ] [-]

RANDOM NUMBER (see under ⇒ Mouthmoth records)

Alan RANKINE

Born: c.1957, Bridge Of Allan, Stirlingshire. As a guitarist, ALAN was the other half of cabaret outfit, CASPIAN, who became top Dundonian alt/dance outfit, The ASSOCIATES; the duo was completed by singer BILLY MACKENZIE. After a period that stretched from 1979 to 1983, in which the pair scored a handful of Top 20 hits (including 'Party Fears Two' and 'Club Country'), it was clear that MACKENZIE was holding all the aces. Following a stint of global travelling, RANKINE returned to London where he began producing for the likes of The COCTEAU TWINS, PAUL HAIG and Liverpool outfit, The PALE FOUNTAINS. In 1986, and having inked a deal with Belgian independent, 'Crepescule', RANKINE was ready to retake his place in the music business. His debut set, 'THE WORLD BEGINS TO LOOK HER AGE' (1986), was a mixture of instrumentals and his own LOU REED/DAVID SYLVIAN-esque vocal tracks, although most of them didn't quite hit the mark, especially with the critics. The pop-fuelled, 9-minute epic, 'THE BEST IN ME', with its NEW ORDER-style backing, failed to propel the man back to the limelight. However, 'Virgin' must've been impressed with most of the set as they let RANKINE remix four tracks from the debut (side by side with five new cuts) and release them under a follow-up title, 'SHE LOVES ME NOT' (1987). Towards the end of the decade and once again taking up with 'Crepescule', RANKINE delivered an ambient-style imaginary soundtrack score via the instrumental, 'THE BIG PICTURE SUCKS' (1989). This, and another under-par effort, 'DAYS AND DAYS' (1990), convinced RANKINE his strengths lay in other directions. In the mid-90's, ALAN began lecturing on music in Glasgow (he also contributed some songs to various pop/rock outfits) and helped students set-up their own indie imprint as part of a college course. Little did they know that the label in question, 'Electric Honey', would be the stamping ground for the now celebrated outfit, BELLE & SEBASTIAN, who debuted with 'Tigermilk' in May '96.

ALAN RANKINE – vocals, guitars, keyboards, etc

Crepescule not iss.

Sep 86. (7"/12") *(7+/TWI 598)* **SANDMAN. / RUMOURS OF WAR** [ ] [-]
Nov 86. (lp) *(TWI 672)* **THE WORLD BEGINS TO LOOK HER AGE** [ ] [-]
– Elephant's walk in morning glory / Mission for the Don / Your very last day / The best in me / The world begins to look her age / Last bullet / Sandman / Love in adversity.
Dec 86. (7") *(7TWI 762)* **LAST BULLET. / YOUR VERY LAST DAY** [ ] [-]

Virgin not iss.

Aug 87. (7"/12") *(VS 971/+12)* **THE WORLD BEGINS TO LOOK HER AGE. / CAN YOU BELIEVE EVERYTHING I SAY** [ ] [-]
Oct 87. (lp/c/cd) *(V/TCV/CDV 2450)* **SHE LOVES ME NOT** [ ] [-]
– Beat fit / Days and days / Loaded / Last bullet / Your very last day / The sandman / Lose control / Break for me / The world begins to look her age.
Nov 87. (7"/12") *(VS/+T 1003)* **SANDMAN. / CAN YOU BELIEVE EVERYTHING I SAY** [ ] [-]

Crepescule not iss.

1989. (cd) *(TWI 8692)* **THE BIG PICTURE SUCKS** [ ] [-]
– Shambok / Pop off / Once in a blue one / Glory to the take and the killing / Happens every minute / Lies.
1990. (cd) *(TWI 8872)* **DAYS AND DAYS** [ ] [-]
—— RANKINE retired from solo work

RAPHAELS (see under ⇒ BIG COUNTRY)

RB'S (see ⇒ Section 9: wee post-Punk groups)

REACHOUT (see ⇒ Section 9: Dance/Rave)

Eddi READER

Born: SADENIA EDNA EDDI READER, 28 Aug'59, Glasgow. She began her career after being invited to join DISC O'DELL's 'Y' records outfit, DISCONNECTION (also in their ranks, former PIGBAG guitarist JAMES JOHNSTONE and HI-TENSION bassman LEROY WILLIAMS), the quartet managing to release two singles, 'BALI HAI' in '82 and 'WE LOVE YOU' a few years later.

In 1987, the now one-time backing singer for GANG OF FOUR, WATERBOYS, etc, formed FAIRGROUND ATTRACTION with English songwriter MARC B. NEVIN. After literally busking around city centres, they subsequently progressed to gigs, recruiting guitaron player (Mexican acoustic bass) SIMON EDWARDS and drummer ROY DODDS. Soon snapped up by 'R.C.A.' records, their early '88 debut single, 'PERFECT', swooned its way to No.1, paving the way for the Top 3 album, 'FIRST OF A MILLION KISSES'. An endearingly charming folk-jazz shuffle, the song was carried with READER's dreamy, angelic Scots brogue, a voice which dominated the rootsy pop of the album. Despite winning a couple of Brit Awards the following year, the band's lifespan was brief, subsequently splitting in 1990.

While NEVIN joined MORRISSEY in '91 (later forming SWEETMOUTH), READER branched off into an acting career, scoring a major role in the acclaimed Scottish TV Country & Western comedy drama, 'Your Cheatin' Heart'. With DODDS remaining as drummer, READER hooked up with guitarists, NEIL MacCOLL and DOMINIC MILLER along with double bassist, PHIL STERIOPULOS; they were now EDDI READER & The PATRON SAINTS OF IMPERFECTION. In this guise, she recorded the 'MIRMAMA' (1992) album, a well-received set that saw contributions from JOOLS HOLLAND on piano. Shifting labels to 'Warner' subsidiary, 'Blanco Y Negro', READER found herself high in the charts once more (No.4) with an eponymous solo album in 1994, the material written by BOO HEWERDINE, former leader of The BIBLE.

HEWERDINE once again shared the writing credits on 1996's 'CANDYFLOSS AND MEDICINE', a Top 30 effort with a gentle musical ebb and hypnotic lyrical flow typical of READER's low key approach. Ironically but hardly surprisingly, the flame-haired singer's commercial pickings became progressively scarcer as her records became more exquisite. 'ANGELS AND ELECTRICITY' (1998) was another late night lullaby complete with the Ron Sexsmith-penned 'ON A WHIM' and a sterling version of HEWERDINE's BIBLE chestnut, 'BELL, BOOK AND CANDLE'. Ditto 'SIMPLE SOUL' (2001), a record that found READER musically maturing into middle age as tastefully and as temptingly as a fine red wine, hints of ethnic instrumentation and Americana flourishes enriching a reassuringly acoustic bouquet.

2002 saw the release of 'DRIFTWOOD', a Japanese import featuring a choice selection of READER's latter day solo material and a handful of live tracks (noteably another Sexsmith song 'WASTING TIME'). In May 2002,

EDDI did a fantastic rendition of 'Green Grow The Rashes O' at the new Burns festival's open-air event at Culzean Castle.

• **Songwriters:** NEVIN penned all FAIRGROUND ATTRACTION, except YOU SEND ME (Sam Cooke) / MYSTERY TRAIN (Elvis Presley) / DO YOU WANT TO KNOW A SECRET (Beatles) / WALKING AFTER MIDNIGHT (Patsy Cline) / AE FOND KISS (trad. Robert Burns) / TRYING TIMES (Donny Hathaway) / SUNDAY MORNING (Velvet Underground) / JACK O'HAZLEDEAN (trad.Walter Scott) / OLE BUTTERMILK SKY (Hoagy Carmichael). EDDI READER solo:- MY OLD FRIEND THE BLUES (Steve Earle) / WHAT YOU DO (S.W. Kahn) / SPIRIT (Waterboys) / I LOVED A LAD (trad) / WONDERBOY (Kinks) / EARLIES (Trash Can Sinatras).

EDDI READER

—— with The PATRON SAINTS OF IMPERFECTION: **ROY DODDS** – drums, percussion / **PHIL STERIOPULOS** – 5-string double bass / **NEIL MacCOLL** – guitar / **DOMINIC MILLER** – guitar / and guest **JOOLS HOLLAND** – piano

R.C.A. | Compass

Nov 91. (7"ep/12"ep/c-ep) **ALL OR NOTHING EP** [ ] [-]
– All or nothing / Sunday morning / Ole buttermilk sky / Broken vows.
(cd-ep) – (first & last track) / The blacksmith / The girl with the weight of the world in her hands.

Feb 92. (7"/c-s) **WHAT YOU DO WITH WHAT YOU'VE GOT. / I WISH YOU WERE MY BOYFRIEND** [ ] [-]
(cd-s+=) – Broken vows / Ole buttermilk sky (take 2).

Mar 92. (cd/c/lp) *(PD/PK/PL 75156) <74242>* **MIRMAMA** [34] [ ]
– What you do with what you've got / Honeychild / All or nothing / Hello in there / Dolphins / The blacksmith / That's fair / Cinderellas downfall / Pay no mind / The swimming song / My old friend the blues. *(cd re-iss. Sep94; 74321 15865-2)*

Apr 92. (7"/c-s) **HONEYCHILD. / SPIRIT (live)** [ ] [-]
(cd-s+=) – All or nothing (live).

Haven | not iss.

Mar 93. (cd-ep; as READER, GREGSON & HEWERDINE) *(HAVENT 3CD)* **WONDERFUL LIE EP** [ ] [-]
– Wonderful lie / Last night I dreamt somebody loved me / Who's your jailer now.

Blanco Y Negro | Sire

May 94. (7"/c-s) *(NEG 68/+C)* **PATIENCE OF ANGELS. / RED FACE BIG SKY** [33] [-]
(cd-s+=) *(NEG 68CD)* – Shirt & comb.

Jun 94. (cd/c) *(<4509 96177-2/-4>)* **EDDI READER** [4] [ ]
– The right place / Patience of angels / Dear John / Scarecrow / East of us / Joke (I'm laughing) / The exception / Red face big sky / Howling in Ojai / When I watch you sleeping / Wonderful lie / Siren. *(cd re-iss. Dec96 as 'HUSH'; same)*

Aug 94. (7"/c-s) *(NEG 72/+C)* **JOKE (I'M LAUGHING). / SATURDAY NIGHT** [42] [-]
(cd-s+=) *(NEG 72CD)* – Wonder boy.
(cd-s) *(NEG 72CDX)* – ('A'side) / Three crosses / Go and sit upon the grass.

Oct 94. (7"/c-s) *(NEG 75/+C)* **DEAR JOHN. / BATTERSEA MOON** [48] [-]
(cd-s+=) *(NEG 75CD)* – When I watch you sleeping / What you do with what you've got / That's fair.

Sep 95. (c-s) *(NEG 82C)* **NOBODY LIVES WITHOUT LOVE / WONDERFUL LIE** [ ] [-]
(cd-s+=) *(NEG 82CD)* – Red face, big sky.

Jun 96. (c-s) *(NEG 90C)* **TOWN WITHOUT PITY / LEAVE THE LIGHT ON** [ ] [-]
(cd-s+=) *(NEG 90CD1)* – Wonderboy / Shall I be mother.
(cd-s) *(NEG 90CD2)* – ('A'side) / Sex lives boy / If you gotta minute.

Jul 96. (cd/c) *(<0630 15129-2/-4>)* **CANDYFLOSS AND MEDICINE** [24] [ ]
– Glasgow star / Town without pity / Medicine / Rebel angel / Semi precious / Lazy heart / I loved a lad / Butterfly jar / Candyfloss / Darkhouse.

Aug 96. (c-s) *(NEG 95C)* **MEDICINE / SUGAR ON THE PILL** [ ] [-]
(cd-s) *(NEG 95CD1)* – Earlies / Nameless.
(cd-s) *(NEG 95CD2)* – ('A'side) / Green grow the rushes / John Anderson my Joe / Who knows where the time goes.

Apr 98. (cd-s) *(NEG 111CD)* **KITEFLYER'S HILL / ST. CHRISTOPHER** [ ] [-]

May 98. (cd/c) *(6398 422816-2/-4) <4265>* **ANGELS & ELECTRICITY** [49] [ ] Mar99
– Kiteflyer's hill / Prayer wheel / Postcard / Wings on my heels / On a whim / Hummingbird / Barcelona window / Bell, book and candle / California / Follow my tears / Psychic reader / Please don't ask me to dance / Clear. *(re-iss. cd+=; 1990)* – Homesick son / St. Christopher. *<US-iss.Mar99 on 'Compass'; 4265>*

Rough Trade | Compass

Jan 01. (cd) *(RTRADECD 011) <4302>* **SIMPLE SOUL** [ ] [ ]
– Wolves / The wanting kind / Lucky penny / Simple soul / Adam / Footsteps fall / Blues run the game / I felt a soul move through me / Prodigal daughter / Eden / The girl who fell in love with the Moon.

not iss. | Universal

Jan 02. (cd) *<VICE 1020>* **DRIFTWOOD** [-] [-] Japan
– Old soul / Sarasota / Meantime / Wasting time / Paper wings / Holiday / Small soul sailing / New pretender / Forgive the boy / Everything / Joke (I'm laughing) (live) / Kiteflyer's hill (live) / La vie en rose (candyfloss) (live) / Find my love (live) / The wanting kind (live).

– compilations, etc. –

Jan 02. (cd) *WEA; <10913>* **SEVENTEEN STORIES: THE BEST OF EDDI READER** [-] [-] Japan
– What do you do with what you've got / Honeychild / All or nothing / The right place / Patience of angels / Joke (I'm laughing) / Wonderful lie / Glasgow star / Town without pity / Medicine / Rebel angel / Kiteflyer's hill / Prayer wheel / On a whim / California / Wonderboy / Earlies.

REAL SHOCKS (see under ⇒ Lithium records)

RED ELLIS (see ⇒ Section 9: wee post-punk groups)

Hugh REED & THE VELVET UNDERPANTS

Formed: Maryhill, Glasgow ... late 80's by the tall, no very tall, HUGH O'HAGAN, who attributed his idols LOU REED & THE VELVET UNDERGROUND – er, sometimes. In fact, his manic Scots vernacular versions were more of the ALEX HARVEY meets the CRAMPS sort of theatrical thing; he actually wore a wedding dress on stage and ate out of a potty. 'Pants' described them better, 'SIX TO WAN' (their debut effort in 1990), was the odds offered them reaching any musical heights; it was actually about being gubbed 6-1 at football and then getting beaten up by six of the opposing team's supporters. However, witty titles such as 'WALK ON THE CLYDESIDE', 'PALE BLUE Y'S' and 'I'M GONNA SHOOT MYSELF (AND THIS TIME I WON'T MISS)', brought a few sniggers from certain audiences – HUGH hoored and toured London in 1995. Care in the community was never so rife. HUGH's broad tongue was firmly planted up his own cheek. witnessed on their 1996 set, 'TAKE A WALK ON THE CLYDESIDE' – take a walk on the wild side, indeed.

HUGH REED (O'HAGAN) – vocals / **ANGELA SMITH** – vocals / **RICHARD CAIRNEY** – guitar / **JOHNNY GRAY** – bass / **ALAN TILTSON** – drums / others incl. **MAXWELL JOHNSTON** – vocals / **JIM CREIGHTON** – guitar / **LYNDSEY WATT** – bass / **DEREK BAIRD** – keyboards / **JANEY GARVIE** – sax / **ANGELA DORAN + JEFFREY GILLESPIE** – backing vocals / **KENNY CALLEN** – guitar / **LAWSON CAMPBELL** – keyboards / **ANGELA CAIRNS** – vocals / **DES MURRAY** – guitar / **PAUL PROCTOR** – bass / **TOM DOCHERTY** – drums / **ELMO McDONALD** – guitar / **ANGELA DORAN** – backing vocals / **KEVIN MACKIE** – drums

Ball | not iss.

1990. (12") **SIX TO WAN** [ ] [-]
1992. (12") **WALK ON THE CLYDE SIDE** [ ] [-]
Oct 94. (12") **TECHNODRUG** [ ] [-]

Eclectic | not iss.

Feb 96. (cd) *(ECLCD 9615)* **TAKE A WALK ON THE CLYDESIDE** [ ] [-]
– Dog / Car nicked / Punk rocker / Stamp collecting / 10 mins 2 go / Shoot myself / Six to wan / Salt, saliva, sperm & sweat / B.A.D.D. / Satellite baby / Technodrugs / Scots 'n' proud / 621 (acid version).

—— where is he now?

REGENCY BUCK

Formed: South Glasgow ... 2000 by DUKE IRONFIST and DISCO, the fictitious? loyal order soon being joined by another convert, GODFATHER (but that was in 2001). Live shows introduced bass player THE DOC (SCOTT FRASER of the band, QUINN), SPREY GANIARD on guitar and SVEN BARTOK OLOFFSON on drums, while in the studio (or dungeon, as they described it!) SPIKE STENT took over the twiddly bits. Coming across like JESUS JONES meeting ROXETTE, this bunch of weirdo disco porn junkies, delivered their debut single, 'FREE TO CHANGE YOUR MIND', towards the end of 2000.

DUKE IRONFIST – / **DISCO** – / plus others **SCOTT FRASER** – bass (of QUINN) / **SPKIE STENT** – mixing / etc

B-Unique | not iss.

Dec 00. (cd-s) *(BUN 001CDS)* **FREE TO CHANGE YOUR MIND / FREE TO CHANGE YOUR MIND (Deliverance Ben Chapman mix) / DISCO'S DAY OUT** [ ] [-]

—— added **GODFATHER**

May 01. (cd-s) *(BUN 003CDS)* **MONKEY GIRL / RHUBARB / DEJA** [ ] [-]

REINDEER SECTION

Formed: based – Glasgow . . . by fellow Celt and full-time member of SNOW PATROL, GARY LIGHTBODY, adding to the eclectic mix militant members of the Scottish guitar army, MICHAEL BANNISTER, GARETH RUSSELL, WILLIE CAMPBELL, AIDAN MOFFAT, GILL MILLS, MICK COOKE, CHARLIE CLARK, MOGWAI's JOHN CUMMINGS, BOB KILDEA, COLIN MacINTYRE, JENNY REAVE and JONNY QUINN (also of SNOW PATROL) . . . phew!

Probably best described as GODSPEED YOU BLACK EMPEROR! for the thrift-store indie generation of the North (only a little less serious), the ensemble gathered together to record and arrange songs that LIGHTBODY had deemed too obscure for his SNOW PATROL team. Put together in a studio in Glasgow, 'Y'ALL GET SCARED NOW, YA HEAR!' (2001), displayed a whole host of interesting ideas thrown together by the eclectic members of such groups as BELLE & SEBASTIAN, ASTRID, ARAB STRAP and The MULL HISTORICAL SOCIETY. Spacy, punch-drunk love songs and slow-building instrumentals all shaped up to be the best collaboration this side of the Border. AIDAN MOFFAT's excellent lullaby 'NYTOL' told his usual narratives of lost love to brilliant effect. The gentle 'OPENING TASTE' set the scene for what was to follow; heartfelt melodics courtesy of EVA's JENNY REAVE and the floating beauty of ASTRID's own CAMPBELL and CLARKE's mellowed 'STING'. The group extended their line-up with the inclusion of RODDY WOOMBLE (IDLEWILD) and TEENAGE FANCLUB's NORMAN BLAKE come the single 'YOU ARE MY JOY'. This hit the shops just prior to their sophomore set 'SON OF EVIL REINDEER' (2002), a record that lacked the consistancy of their debut but had enough sparkle and stamina to make for some enlightened listening.

GARY LIGHTBODY (b. Ireland) – guitar, keyboards, harmonica vocals (of SNOW PATROL) / **AIDAN MOFFAT** – vocals (of ARAB STRAP) / **JOHN CUMMINGS** – guitar (of MOGWAI) / **RICHARD COLBURN** – percussion (of BELLE & SEBASTIAN) / **MICK COOKE** – trumpet, flugelhorn (of BELLE & SEBASTIAN) / **JONNY QUINN** (b. Ireland) – drums (of SNOW PATROL) / **BOB KILDEA** – guitar (of BELLE & SEBASTIAN) / **GILL MILLS** – vocals (of EVA) / **GARETH RUSSELL** – bass (of ASTRID) / **WILBUR CAMPBELL** – guitars (of ASTRID) / **CHARLIE CLARKE** – gut string guitar / **MICHAEL BANNISTER** – keyboards, organ

Bright P.I.A.S.

Aug 01. (cd/lp) *(BSR 14/+V)* <2> **Y'ALL GET SCARED NOW, YA HEAR!** ☐ ☐ Oct01
– Will you please be there for me / The opening taste / 12 hours it takes sometimes / Deviance / If there is I haven't found it yet / Fire bell / If everything fell quiet / I've never understood / Raindrop / Sting / Billed as single / Tout le monde / Nytol / The day we all died.

— added **RODDY WOOMBLE** – vocals (of IDLEWILD) / **NORMAN BLAKE** – vocals (of TEENAGE FANCLUB) / **IAIN ARCHER** (of CADET) / **NEIL PAYNE** (of ASTRID) / **MALCOLM MIDDLETON + COLIN MacPHERSON** (of ARAB STRAP) / **MARK McLELLAND** (of SNOW PATROL) / **SARAH ROBERTS** (of EVA) / **EUGENE KELLY (of VASELINES) / LEE GORTON + SAM MORRIS + BEN DUMVILLE** (of ALFIE) / **STACEY SIEVEWRIGHT + MARCUS MACKAY + PAUL FOX**

Jun 02. (7") *(BSR 22V)* **YOU ARE MY JOY. / BUDAPEST (demo)** ☐ -
(cd-s) *(BSR 22)* – You are my joy (the freelance hellraiser "birds love the 80's" remix) / ('B'side).

Jun 02. (cd/lp) *(BSR 19/+V)* <7> **SON OF EVIL REINDEER** ☐ ☐ Aug02
– Grand parade / Budapest / Strike me down / Your sweet voice / I'll be here when you wake / Where I fall / Cartwheels / Last song on the blue tape / Cold water / You are my joy / Who told you / Whodunnit?

REJUVINATION (see under ⇒ Soma records / SLAM)

RESTRICTED CODE

Formed: Glasgow . . . 1979 by frontman TOM CANAVAN, KENNY BLYTHE and their Italian connection FRANK QUADRELLI and STEPHEN LIRONI (the latter joined ALTERED IMAGES and was replaced by RAB McCORMICK). The following year, RESTRICTED CODE featured on the 'Second City Statik' EP (along with POSITIVE NOISE and The ALLEGED) with the tracks 'THE NEW MESSIAH' and 'SEEING MUCH BETTER (WITH YOUR EYES)'. 'Pop: Aural' (home to the FIRE ENGINES and the FLOWERS) unleashed two worthy indie 45's in the first half of 1981, 'FIRST NIGHT ON' and 'LOVE TO MEET YOU', although this was the last messages from the group.

TOM CANAVAN – vocals / **FRANK QUADRELLI** – guitar / **KENNY BLYTHE** – bass / **RAB McCORMICK** – drums; repl. STEPHEN LIRONI who joined ALTERED IMAGES, FLESH and The REVOLUTIONARY CORPS OF TEENAGE JESUS

Pop: Aural not iss.

Jan 81. (7") *(POP 007)* **FIRST NIGHT ON. / FROM THE TOP** ☐ -

May 81. (7") *(POP 009)* **LOVE TO MEET YOU. / MONKEY MONKEY MONKEY** ☐ -

— disbanded after above

REVILLOS (see under ⇒ REZILLOS)

REVOLUTIONARY CORPS OF TEENAGE JESUS

Formed: Glasgow . . . 1995 by former ALTERED IMAGES guitarist/drummer STEPHEN LIRONI, a veteran of numerous short-lived indie-pop outfits (RESTRICTED CODE and FLESH) as well as a co-writer and producer of both BLACK GRAPE and SARAH CRACKNELL.

REVOLUTIONARY CORPS OF TEENAGE JESUS (named after LIRONI was pipped at the post for his original choice of REVOLUTIONARY ARMY OF INFANT JESUS) was a considerably less accessible proposition than most of the above, essentially a LIRONI solo project with the added kudos of one ALAN VEGA. The former SUICIDE legend was alerted to LIRONI's activities after copping an earful of his debut single, a cover of SUICIDE classic, 'Frankie Teardrop'. The latter was released in early '96 on Glasgow's 'Creeping Bent' label while the subsequent songwriting partnership of VEGA and LIRONI bore fruit in the shape of 1997's 'PROTECTION RAT', issued as part of the 'Creeping Bent' singles club alongside the likes of ADVENTURES IN STEREO and SPACEHOPPER.

A third single, 'PAY THA WRECK, MR MUSIC KING', appeared in Spring '99, in anticipation of debut album, 'RIGHTEOUS LITE' (1999). The record sounded pretty much how you'd expect with lashings of millennial electro-minimalist angst, American evangelist samples and droning/spoken vocals courtesy of the ever deadpan VEGA. A set of remixes entitled 'A BROOKLYN NIGHTMARE', surfaced later that year, the likes of FUTURE PILOT AKA, SCIENTIFIC SUPPORT DEPT. and MONGOOSE giving 'FRANKIE TEARDROP' the once over. LIRONI is still currently married to former ALTERED IMAGES starlet CLARE GROGAN.

STEPHEN LIRONI – machines (ex-RESTRICTED CODE, ex-ALTERED IMAGES, ex-FLESH) / **ALAN VEGA** – vocals (ex-SUICIDE)

Creeping Bent not iss.

Jan 96. (12"ep; as the REVOLUTIONARY CORPS OF TEENAGE JESUS vs SUICIDE) *(bent 005)* **FRANKIE TEARDROP EP** ☐ -
– Frankie Teardrop 126bpm / USA 95 / Womb #17 / Frankie Teardrop 114bpm.

Mar 96. (12") *(bent 011)* **PROTECTION RAT. / SUPERMARKET** ☐ -

Jun 97. (cd-ep) *(bent 019cd)* **singles club #1** ☐ -
– Protection rat / (other tracks by the Leopards, Adventures In Stereo and Spacehopper).

Mar 98. (7") *(bent 033)* **WHO CARES WHO DIES. / (other side by the Nectarine No.9)** ☐ -

Apr 99. (12"/cd-s) *(bent 043/+cd)* **PAY THA WRECK, MR MUSIC KING. / SATURATION** ☐ -

May 99. (cd) *(bent 045cd)* **RIGHTEOUS LITE** ☐ -
– Righteous lite / Protection rat / Daddy died / Pay tha wreck, Mr. Music king / Money day / Puzz puzz / American / Motor cross / Who cares who dies / Sinister minister.

Nov 99. (cd-s) *(bent 051cd)* **A BROOKLYN NIGHTMARE (mixes)** ☐ -

Oct 00. (cd) *(bent 061cd)* **A BROOKLYN NIGHTMARE** (remixes) ☐ -
– Frankie Teardrop (mixes; by . . . & SUICIDE / FUTURE PILOT AKA / RADIOGRAM / SCIENTIFIC SUPPORT DEPT / MONGOOSE / QUAD 90 / etc).

REZILLOS

Formed: Edinburgh . . . March '76 by EUGENE REYNOLDS and JO CALLIS (aka LUKE WARM), alongside art school colleagues MARK 'HI-FI' HARRIS, DR. D.K. SMYTHE, ANGEL PATERSON, GAYLE WARNING and inimitable frontwoman, FAY FIFE. Early in 1977, the band signed a one-off deal with Lawrie Love's 'Sensible' records and released the semi-legendary 'CAN'T STAND MY BABY'. Three-chord dumbness in the vein of The RAMONES with the added advantage of FIFE's Scots twang, the track was followed by '(MY BABY DOES) GOOD SCULPTURES' towards the end of the year. As well as being the first fruits of their deal with 'Sire', the record marked the debut of new man, WILLIAM MYSTERIOUS, recruited as a replacement for early departees, SMYTHE, HARRIS and WARNING.

By the summer of '78, The REZILLOS were performing the tongue-in-cheek 'TOP OF THE POPS' on that self same programme as their multi-coloured freakshow crashed into the UK Top 20. A debut album, 'CAN'T STAND THE REZILLOS' also hit the Top 20 that summer, offering up for closer inspection the band's obsession with American beat/girl groups and general trash culture competing with British influences like DR. FEELGOOD. MYSTERIOUS didn't hang around long, replaced by SIMON TEMPLAR (yeah, right) as the 'DESTINATION VENUS' single carried on the sci-fi malarky but failed to crack the Top 40.

Splitting before the year was out, The REZILLOS splintered in two, with CALLIS, TEMPLAR and PATERSON forming SHAKE – CALLIS would subsequently join the more successful HUMAN LEAGUE – while FIFE and REYNOLDS remained on much the same track with The REVILLOS. Featuring a line-up completed by ROCKY RHYTHM, a returning HARRIS and a trio of female backing singers, the new-look band immersed themselves even further in retro Americana with a string of singles, 'WHERE'S THE BOY FOR ME?', 'MOTORBIKE BEAT' and 'SCUBA SCUBA'. Despite encouraging press, neither these nor an album, 'REV UP' (1980) notched up sufficient sales as the group underwent constant personnel upheaval with MYSTERIOUS and new man KID KRUPA coming and going. Over the course of the next three years, the band hopped from label to label as they continued to crank out inimitably titled material like '(SHE'S FALLEN IN LOVE WITH A) MONSTER MAN' and 'BONGO BRAIN'.

Following a final couple of singles for 'E.M.I.', the band called it a day in 1985, FIFE moving into TV acting and subsequently appearing in the likes of 'Taggart' and 'The Bill'. Like spiritual descendants BIS, the band were big in Japan, choosing the Far East as their destination for a mid-90's reunion tour.

• **Songwriters:** EUGENE and JO penned most, except; I WANNA BE YOUR MAN (Beatles) / I LIKE IT (Gerry & The Pacemakers) / GLAD ALL OVER (Dave Clark Five) / TWIST AND SHOUT (Isley Brothers) / BALLROOM BLITZ (Sweet) / TELL HIM (Exciters) / LAND OF A 1,000 DANCES (Cannibal & The Headhunters) / ON THE BEACH (hit; Cliff Richard) / THUNDERBIRDS ARE GO (Barry Gray).

FAY FIFE (b. SHEILAGH HYNDE) – vocals / **EUGENE REYNOLDS** (b. ALAN FORBES, USA) – vocals / **LUKE WARM** (b. JO CALLIS) – guitar, vocals (both ex-KNUTSFORD DOMINATORS) / **MARK 'HI-FI' HARRIS** – guitar / **Dr. D.K. SMYTHE** – bass / **ANGEL PATERSON** – drums / **GAYLE WARNING** – backing vocals

Sensible | not iss.

Aug 77. (7") *(FAB 1)* **CAN'T STAND MY BABY. / I WANNA BE YOUR MAN** [ ] [-]
(re-iss. Aug79; SAB 1) – hit No.71

— **WILLIAM MYSTERIOUS** (b.DONALDSON) – bass finally repl. SMYTHE, HARRIS & WARNING

Sire | Sire

Nov 77. (7") *(6078.612)* **(MY BABY DOES) GOOD SCULPTURES. / FLYING SAUCER ATTACK** [ ] [-]

May 78. (7";w-drawn) *(6198.215)* **COLD WARS. / WILLIAM MYSTERIOUS OVERTURE** [-] [-]

Jul 78. (7") *(SIR 4001)* **TOP OF THE POPS. / 20,000 REZILLOS UNDER THE SEA** [17] [-]
(c-s) *(SPC 3)* – ('A'side) / Destination Venus.

Jul 78. (lp/c) *(K/K4 56530) <SRK 6057>* **CAN'T STAND THE REZILLOS** [16] [ ]
– Flying saucer attack / No / Someone's gonna get their heads kicked in tonight / Top Of The Pops / 2000 AD / It gets me / Can't stand my baby / Glad all over / My baby does good sculptures / I like it / Gettin' me down / Cold wars / Bad guy reaction. *(cd-iss. Jan96; 7599 26942-2)*

— **SIMON TEMPLAR** (b. BLOOMFIELD) – bass, vocals repl. WILLIAM

Nov 78. (7") *(SIR 4008)* **DESTINATION VENUS. / MYSTERY ACTION** [43] [-]

— disbanded late '78; JO, SIMON + ANGEL formed SHAKE, who released a couple of singles, 'CULTURE SHOCK' and 'INVASION OF THE GAMMA MEN'. JO CALLIS released an EP for 'Pop Aural', 'WOAH YEAH!', in 1981. They subsequently became part of BOOTS FOR DANCING.

— The REZILLOS gave us a few more exploitation releases

Apr 79. (7"m) *(SIR 4014)* **COLD WARS. / FLYING SAUCER ATTACK (live) / TWIST AND SHOUT (live)** [ ] [-]

Apr 79. (lp/c) *(SRK/SRC 6069)* **MISSION ACCOMPLISHED . . . BUT THE BEAT GOES ON (live)** [30] [-]
– Top of the pops / Mystery action / Somebody's gonna get their head kicked in tonight / Thunderbirds are go / Cold wars / Teenbeat / Land of 10,000 dances / I need you / Gettin' me down / Culture shock / Ballroom blitz / Destination Venus / (My baby does) Good sculptures.

The REVILLOS

— (a slight change) brought together again **FAY & EUGENE** (also now on bass) / **HI-FI HARRIS** – guitar / **ROCKY RHYTHM** (b. NICKY FORBES) – drums (ex-PORK DUKES) / **JANE WHITE, JANE BROWN, TRICIA BRYCE** – backing vocals

Dindisc | not iss.

Sep 79. (7") *(DIN 1)* **WHERE'S THE BOY FOR ME?. / THE FIEND** [ ] [-]

— (Aug'79) added **KID KRUPA** – guitar (on tour) / **FELIX** – bass / **CHERIE & BABS REVETTE** – backing vocals repl. last backing trio

Jan 80. (7") *(DIN 5)* **MOTORBIKE BEAT. / NO SUCH LUCK** [45] [-]

— **WILLIAM MYSTERIOUS** – bass returned to repl. FELIX (to HEY ELASTICA)

Apr 80. (7") *(DINZ 16)* **SCUBA SCUBA. / BOY BOP** [ ] [-]

Sep 80. (lp) *(DIDX 3)* **REV UP** [ ] [-]
– Secret of the shadow / Rev up / Rock-a-boom / Voodoo / Bobby come back to me / Scuba scuba / Boy bop / Yeah yeah / Hungry for love / Jukebox sound / On the beach / Cool jerk / Hippy hippy sheik / Motorbike beat. *(re-iss. Mar84 on 'Virgin'; OVED 53) (cd-iss. Jun01 on 'Captain Oi'+=; AHOYCD 173)* – Where's the boy for me / The fiend / No such luck / Scuba scuba / Voodoo (part 2).

Sep 80. (7") *(DINZ 20)* **HUNGRY FOR LOVE. / VOODOO 2** [ ] [-]

— **KID KRUPA** (b. JON McLOUGHLIN) – guitar now totally repl. HARRIS / **DRAX** – b.vox repl. BABS / **VINCE SANTINI** – bass repl. MYSTERIOUS

Superville | not iss.

Sep 81. (7") *(SV 1001)* **(SHE'S FALLEN IN LOVE WITH A) MONSTER MAN. / MIND BENDING CUTIE DOLL** [ ] [-]

Jan 82. (lp;w-drawn) *(SV 4001)* **ATTACK** [-] [-]

Feb 82. (7"m) *(SV 2001)* **BONGO BRAIN. / HIP CITY / YOU WERE MEANT FOR ME** [ ] [-]

— **MAX ATOM** – guitar repl. KRUPA / **TERRI REVETTE** – b.vox repl. DRAX

Aura | not iss.

Nov 82. (7") *(AUS 135)* **TELL HIM. / GRAVEYARD GROOVE** [ ] [-]

— **FABIAN WONDERFUL** – guitar repl. ATOM

E.M.I. | not iss.

Oct 83. (7") *(RVL 1)* **BITTEN BY A LOVE BUG. / TRIGGER HAPPY JACK** [ ] [-]
(12"+=) *(12RVL 1)* – Cat call.

Mar 84. (7") *(RVL 2)* **MIDNIGHT. / Z-X-7** [ ] [-]
(12"+=) *(12RVL 2)* – ('A'extended).

— **BUDDY MOON** – bass; repl. SANTINI

— disbanded early 1985, FAY went into acting and later featured in 'Taggart' and 'The Bill'.

— REVILLOS re-formed with main originals (see above)

Vinyl Japan | not iss.

Dec 94. (12"ep/cd-ep) *(TASK/+CD 033)* **YEAH YEAH / CRUSH. / SCUBA SCUBA / SCUBA SCUBA (Japanese version)** [ ] [-]

May 95. (cd/lp) *(ASK CD/LP 046)* **LIVE AND ON FIRE IN JAPAN (live)** [ ] [-]
– Secret of the shadow / Bongo brain / Rockaboom / She's fallen in love with a monster man / Where's the boy for me? / Rev up! / Bitten by a lovebug / Mad from birth to death / Bobby come back to me / The fiend / Scuba scuba / My baby does good sculptures / Do the mutilation / Somebody's gonna get their head kicked in tonight / A-yeah-yeah.

Damaged Goods | not iss.

Sep 96. (7"m) *(DAMGOOD 93)* **JACK THE RIPPER. / A-YEAH-YEAH / MEET THE REVILLOS** [ ] [-]

Sep 96. (cd) *(DAMGOOD 97CD)* **FROM THE FREEZER** (demos & live tracks from 1979, 1982 & 1994) [ ] [-]
– Sputnik kiss / Superville / Jack the ripper / Motorbike beat (demo) / The last one to know / You were meant for me / Voodoo / Jukebox soul / Call me the cat / No such luck (demo) / Where's the boy for me (demo) / Snatzmobile (live) / Motorbike beat (live) / Mind bending cutie doll (live) / 1982 – make a wish / Manhunt (rehearsal) / The vampire strikes / Boys (live) / Wipeout (live) / Tango (rehearsal). *(re-iss. Jul02; same)*

– compilations, etc. (REZILLOS or REVILLOS) –

Jul 95. (cd) *Mau Mau; (MAUCD 643)* **MOTORBIKE BEAT** [ ] [-]
Aug 95. (cd) *Receiver; <RRCD 204>* **ATTACK OF THE GIANT REVILLOS** [ ] [-]
Sep 98. (cd) *Vinyl Japan; (ASKCD 80)* **THE BBC RADIO SESSIONS** [ ] [-]
Nov 01. (cd) *Captain Oi; (AHOYCD 179)* **TOTALLY ALIVE (live)** [ ] [-]

RHYTHM ECLIPSE (see under ⇒ Clubscene records)

RHYTHMIC STATE (see under ⇒ Steppin' Out records)

RHYTHM OF LIFE (see under ⇒ Rational records)

RICO

Born: ENRICO CAPUANO, 23 Jun'71, Glasgow, the son of an Italian taxi driver and a Scottish-Irish shop assistant. Having scoured his older brother's record collection on more than several occasions, the young RICO decided he'd take up drumming and played in local punk bands during the mid to late 80's. His most treasured memory was unearthing a portastudio at school. He borrowed the equipment for a while but was moved to finding his own second-hand bits and bobs when his music teacher reclaimed it. Back at his parents' house in Paisley, RICO set up his own garage studio, although some of the neighbours haven't spoken to him since.

Influenced by everyone from PiL, THE THE and NINE INCH NAILS, RICO set about creating his own homegrown one man band. From working by day at a £70 a week fast-food outlet, to working with other bands in his soundproofed studio, the greasy-haired RICO developed the self-obsessed skills needed to achieve his breakthrough. For three years between 1995 and 1998, the man pulled out all the stops to get the right mixes for his debut album. A limited-edition promo of the track, 'THIS AND THAT' (a f**ked up song, if ever there was one!), circulated around by late '98, while 'E.M.I.' produced his debut single proper, 'ATTACK ME'. The aforementioned debut set for 'Chrysalis', 'SANCTUARY MEDICINES', was finally unleashed to the public in August '99, its stark, paranoid undercurrents did indeed have all the hallmarks of NIN's TRENT REZNOR. Like mixing his favourite whiskey liquor (Jack Daniels, Jim Beam or Southern Comfort), anger and tension were always at the core of most of the album's contents.

Of late (mid-2002, to be exact), RICO teamed up with drum'n'bass experimentalist TRICKY on a one-off single, 'MIXED UP FACES'.

RICO – vocals, drums, guitar, effects

E.M.I. | not iss.

May 99. (cd-ep) *(CDEM 538)* **ATTACK ME EP** | ☐ | -
– Attack me / Burst / Millennium mutants.

Chrysalis | not iss.

Jul 99. (c-s) *(CHS 5111)* **SMOKESCREEN / THIS AND MATT** | ☐ | -
(cd-s+=) *(CDCHS 5111)* – Worst dream.

Aug 99. (cd) *(499063-2)* **SANCTUARY MEDICINES** | ☐ | -
– Shave your head / Aeroplane / Smokescreen / Black limo / Float / Overload / Sanctuary medicines / This and that / State / Attack me / Dear God.

Nov 99. (7") *(CHS 5113)* **SHAVE YOUR HEAD. / THE DOSE** | ☐ | -
(cd-s) *(CDCHSS 5113)* – ('A'side) / Next caller please / Digging the hole.
(cd-s) *(CDCHS 5113)* – ('A'side) / ('A'-Bury The Dead mix) / ('A'-Out Of Your Head mix).

Jul 00. (cd-s) *(CDCHSS 5117)* **FLOAT / AEROPLANE / SANCTUARY MEDICINES / FLOAT (video)** | ☐ | -
(cd-s) *(CDCHS 5117)* – ('A'-live in the studio) / Black limo (live in the studio) / Dear God (live in the studio).

Urban Poison | not iss.

Jul 02. (cd-s; as RICO vs TRICKY) **MIXED UP FACES / SMALL DOSES / REMIXED UP FACES** | ☐ | -

RIGHT STUFF

Formed: Glasgow . . . late 80's by former LOVE AND MONEY and (brief) DEACON BLUE member, JOHN PALMER. Having also performed with DEACON BLUE star, LORRAINE McINTOSH, in a 1984 line-up of GENE PITNEY'S BIRTHDAY (they featured on the RAB NOAKES album, 'Under The Rain'), PALMER was free to try his hand at a fresh venture, The RIGHT STUFF. Early in 1990, just prior to the launch of their debut set, 'WA WA', they were told by 'Arista' (their label) that their services would be no longer required. With brutal reviews all over the place citing them as another DEL AMITRI, the band decided enough was indeed enough; they subsequently re-united in The OCEAN, although not with PALMER.

• **Note:** not to be confused with mid-80's outfit who issued 'SIMPLE' for 'Bodybeat' in 1986.

JOHN PALMER – vocals, guitar (ex-LOVE AND MONEY, ex-DEACON BLUE) / + others unknown

Arista | not iss.

Mar 90. (cd/c/lp) *(260/410/210 460)* **WA WA** | ☐ | -
– That's right / The girl's all go / Ministry of love / The right stuff / Ghost in my life / One man band / Scissors / Sympathetic / Mission / Priceless / The girl's all go (Ipcress mix). *(cd+=)* – 24 +.

Apr 90. (7") *(113 214)* **SYMPATHETIC. /** | ☐ | -
(12"+=/cd-s+=) *(613/663 214)* –

—— split soon after above release

RISER (see under ⇒ Mint records)

RISINGSON (see under ⇒ Path records)

RIVER DETECTIVES

Formed: Ravenscraig, nr. Motherwell . . . 1987 by SAM CORRY and DAN O'NEILL. At a time when easy-listening Rock was the order of the day, this Scottish duo promised much but left with nothing. With Scots acts like DEACON BLUE, DANNY WILSON and DEL AMITRI all making it big time, The RIVER DETECTIVES worked out how to turn water into whine. Not that CORRY and O'NEILL were at all bad at their craft, they just didn't sound at all original. However, the pair did pull off a near Top 50 hit with 'CHAINS', a summer 1989 single taken from the accompanying long-player, 'SATURDAY NIGHT SUNDAY MORNING'.

SAM CORRY – vocals, guitar, harmonica / **DAN O'NEILL** – vocals, drums, percussion / with session people

WEA | not iss.

Jul 89. (7"/c-s) *(YZ 383/+C)* **CHAINS. /** | 51 | -
(12"+=/cd-s+=) *(YZ 383 T/CD)* –

Aug 89. (lp/c)(cd) *(WX 295/+C)(246169-2)* **SATURDAY NIGHT SUNDAY MORNING** | 51 | -
– Love's like a needle / Chains / The state of grace / Promises and spite / Factory / Saturday night Sunday morning / Will you spin me round / You won't listen to me / You don't know a thing about her / The ashes and the tears / A deeper love / Saturday night Sunday morning (reprise) / Train song / I go falling.

Sep 89. (7"/c-s) *(YZ 419/+C)* **SATURDAY NIGHT SUNDAY MORNING. / HE STILL NEEDS YOU** | ☐ | -
(12"+=/cd-s+=) *(YZ 419 T/CD)* – You may just be the one.

Jan 90. (7") *(YZ 451)* **YOU DON'T KNOW A THING ABOUT HER. /** | ☐ | -
(12"+=/cd-s+=) *(YZ 451 T/CD)* –

Mar 90. (7"/c-s) *(YZ 467/+C)* **WILL YOU SPIN ME ROUND (remix). / KEEPING THE SAINTS ALIVE** | ☐ | -
(12"+=/cd-s+=) *(YZ 467 T/CD)* – Who do you love.

—— disappeared into musical oblivion after above

Alasdair ROBERTS (see under ⇒ APPENDIX OUT)

B.A. ROBERTSON

Born: c.1955, BRIAN ALEXANDER ROBERTSON, Glasgow. Although B.A. (no doubt taking the abbreviation to avoid confusion with fellow Scot and future THIN LIZZY guitarist, BRIAN ROBERTSON) seems to have released an obscure US-only LP in 1973, 'WRINGING APPLAUSE', the curly-mopped Glaswegian only really kickstarted his career in the post-New Wave climate of the late 70's.

Possibly the only Scots act ever to sign to easy-AOR imprint, 'Asylum', ROBERTSON narrowly missed the UK No.1 spot with the infectious 'BANG BANG' in 1979 after failing with his first 45 a few months earlier. The man's quirky singer-songwriter persona would have fitted like a glove on the 'Stiff' roster alongside the likes of IAN DURY, JONA LEWIE and MICKY JUPP. As it was, his major label status allowed him the budget to secure further Top 20 hits including 'KNOCKED IT OFF', 'KOOL IN THE KAFTAN' and 'TO BE OR NOT TO BE'. All the singles were collected together on 1980's prophetically-titled 'INITIAL SUCCESS', a record that languished in the lower regions of the Top 40.

After B.A. suffered a mid-career commercial crisis, he hooked up with former STONE THE CROWS rasper, MAGGIE BELL, on a one-off smash hit collaboration 'HOLD ME' (previously a hit for PJ PROBY). ROBERTSON's fading career hopes were hardly bolstered by his penchant for dodgy puns, witness 1982's long-player 'R & B.A.'. Late in '83, he again teamed up with a 70's icon, this time ex-ABBA starlet, FRIDA, the resulting single, 'TIME', stalling at No.45.

Although this effectively signalled the end of the man's career, B.A. re-emerged one last time in 1986 with a specially commissioned BBC single for that year's Commonwealth Games held in Edinburgh; ROBERTSON also bequeathed to the nation the theme tune for TV show (Terry) Wogan, although sadly this was never issued on 7" . . .

B.A. ROBERTSON – vocals, keyboards

not iss. Ardent

1973. (lp) <ADS 2804> **WRINGING APPLAUSE** [-] [ ]

— now with **TERRY BRITTEN** – guitar / **BILLY LIVSEY** – keyboards / **ALAN JONES** – bass / **GRAHAM JARVIS** – drums

Asylum Asylum

Jan 79. (7") *(K 13146)* **GOOSEBUMPS. / THE B SIDE** [ ] [-]
Jun 79. (7") *(K 13152)* **BANG BANG. / B SIDE THE C SIDE** [2] [ ]
Oct 79. (7") *(K 12396)* **KNOCKED IT OFF. / SCI-FI** [8] [ ]
Feb 80. (7") *(K 12427)* **KOOL IN THE KAFTAN. / BABY I'M A BAT** [17] [ ]
Mar 80. (lp/c) *(K/K4 52216)* **INITIAL SUCCESS** [32] [ ]
– Gonzo for my girlfriend / Man or a mouse / Goosebumps / Fallin' in luv / Kool in the kaftan / Bang bang / Eat your heart out Sandy Nelson / To be or not to be / She's a beezer / England's green and pheasant land / Walking Rover / Knocked it off / Here I sit.
May 80. (7") *(K 12449)* **TO BE OR NOT TO BE. / LANGUAGE OF LOVE / HOT SHOT** [9] [ ]
Oct 80. (7") *(K 12482)* **FLIGHT 19. / ALRIGHT ON THE NIGHT** [ ] [ ]
Mar 81. (7") *(K 12523)* **SAINT SAENS. / GONZO FOR MY GIRLFRIEND** [ ] [-]
Mar 81. (lp/c) *(K/K4 52275)* **BULLY FOR YOU** [61] [ ]
– Saint Saens / Bully for you / Maggie / Growing old's unhealthy / Please miss / In the bar, at the Munich Hilton / Dart Vader / Hey presto / Flight 19 / Only one / Turn the volume down / Home sweet home.

— in Oct'81, B.A. ROBERTSON and MAGGIE BELL (ex-STONE THE CROWS) scored a UK No.11 hit with 'HOLD ME' on 'Swansong' *(BAM 1)*

Feb 82. (7"w-drawn) *(K 12595)* **ONE PLUS ONE. /** [-] [-]
Feb 82. (7") *(K 12602)* **READY OR NOT. / LES BEANS** [ ] [-]
Jul 82. (7") *(K 13183)* **DOT DOT DOT. / KEEP OFF THE GRASS** [ ] [-]
Aug 82. (lp/c) *(K/K4 52383)* **R & B.A.** [ ] [-]
– Dot dot dot / Ready or not / Moscow rules / Nothing like a great romance / Four minutes to midnight / Hold me / Legislate for love / Son of a Gunn / One plus one / Asleep with a stranger / Just like a rash.

After Hours not iss.

Mar 83. (7") *(AFT 10)* **NOW AND THEN. / PAGE 15b, SCENE 8a** [ ] [-]

— in Dec'83, FRIDA (ex-ABBA) and B.A. had a UK Top 50 breaker with 'TIME' / 'I AM A SEEKER' on 'Epic' *(A 3983)*

B.B.C. not iss.

Jul 86. (7") *(RESL 192)* **CEUD MILE FAILTE (A HUNDRED THOUSAND WELCOMES). / THE BBC TR COMMONWEALTH GAMES THEME** [ ] [-]
(12"+=) *(12RSL 192)* – See you in Auckland.

— ROBERTSON retired from music after above

- compilations, etc. -

1989. (7") *Old Gold; (OG 9914)* **BANG BANG. / TO BE OR NOT TO BE** [ ] [-]

Nick ROBERTSON & SLICE

Formed: Edinburgh. MICK ventured solo (with the band, SLICE) and signed to Virgin offshoot, 'Circa'. His one and only set for the label, 'BULLETPROOF BOY' (1990), boasted the talents of guest and backing singers, MARIA McKEE, CAROL KENYON and KATIE KISSOON, while the band were augmented by the likes of folkies ANTHONY THISTLETHWAITE, DONAL LUNNY and DAVY SPILLANE.

NICK ROBERTSON – vocals, guitar / with **RICHIE CLOSE** – keyboards / **ROBBIE BLUNT** – guitar / **SIMON EDWARDS** – bass / **KEVIN WILKINSON** – drums / **NOEL ECCLES** – percussion / + guests

Circa Charisma

Dec 90. (c/cd/lp) *(CIRC/+D/A 13) <91422-4/-2>* **BULLETPROOF BOY** [ ] [ ] 1991
– Mind reader / Show me a sign / Pride & joy / Love, life and happiness / She's looking tired / Slice of heaven / Kiss of forgiveness / Reach out and touch the Moon / Bulletproof boy / Punch a wall / The flame.

— NICK disappeared from the music scene after above

ROCKA RAGNAROCK (see under ⇒ Bosque records)

ROKOTTO

Formed: Dundee ... mid 70's by disco funksters HUGH PAUL, one of three vocalists along with CLEVELAND WALKER and SISTER B; four musicians DEREK HENDERSON, STEWART GARDEN, HOWARD LLOYD WISDON and HOWARD McLEOD made up the 7-piece line-up. Although not massive by any degree of the imagination, ROKOTTO did crack the UK singles market via two uptempo dance numbers, 'BOOGIE ON UP' and 'FUNK THEORY'. Their subsequent attempts at getting hit number three at the turn of the decade fell on deaf ears.

HUGH PAUL – vocals / **CLEVELAND WALKER** – vocals / **SISTER B** – vocals / **DEREK HENDERSON** – guitar / **STEWART GARDEN** – keyboards / **HOWARD LLOYD WISDON** – bass / **HOWARD McLEOD** – drums

State not iss.

Jun 77. (7") *(STAT 51)* **GET UP AND DANCE NOW. / ARE YOU READY** [ ] [-]
Oct 77. (7") *(STAT 62)* **BOOGIE ON UP. / JUNGLE FEVER** [40] [-]
Nov 77. (lp) *(ETAT 15)* **ROKOTTO** [ ] [-]
– Boogie on up / Tell me / Jungle fever / Shack up / Moonlight / Dancin' / For the broken hearted / Get on down / Six million dollar baby / You better / Brick house.
Jan 78. (7") *(STAT 68)* **FOR THE BROKEN HEARTED. / YOU AND I** [ ] [-]
Jun 78. (7") *(STAT 80)* **FUNK THEORY. / GET ON DOWN** [49] [-]
1979. (7") *(STAT 96)* **SOMEBODY'S BEEN SLEEPING IN MY BED. / TELL ME** [ ] [-]
Aug 81. (7") *(STAT 107)* **IF I HAD YOU. / SIX MILLION DOLLAR BABY** [ ] [-]
Dec 81. (7") *(STAT 110)* **SHE'S A WOMAN. / FOR THE BROKEN HEARTED** [ ] [-]

— disbanded the following year

Malcolm ROSS

Born: c.1960, Edinburgh. In 1979, guitarist ROSS, PAUL HAIG, RON TORRANCE and GARY McCORMACK, were part of TV ART, a band that quickly evolved into JOSEF K when their roadie DAVE WENDELL replaced EXPLOITED bound McCORMACK. With the help of ROSS's buddy STEPHEN DALY (from The NU-SONICS, the soon-to-be ORANGE JUICE), JOSEF K delivered their own self-financed 45, 'Chance Meeting', a post-punk, atonal affair. Along with the aforementioned ORANGE JUICE, JK were one of the first acts to sign for the Glasgow-based "young sound of Scotland" imprint, 'Postcard' (run by ALAN HORNE). ROSS and the boys duly rattled off several singles and an album for the label before they sadly abandoned the band in 1982.

With HAIG now a solo artist and the others in The HAPPY FAMILY, ROSS teamed up with his old pal DALY in ORANGE JUICE. Early in '84, MALCOLM became part of the third 'Postcard' outfit, AZTEC CAMERA, although this was curtailed when he and AZ's DAVE RUFFY joined forces with vocalist SUSAN BUCKLEY to form the short-lived HIGH BEES; the play on words moniker, a nickname for fans of Hibernian F.C. However, only one platter, 'SOME INDULGENCE', was released; it's seemingly very rare nowadays.

In 1992, ROSS teamed up once again with DAVE WENDELL and formed the short-lived MAGIC CLAN with new drummer PAUL MALLINEN. Finding an outlet for his solo work through the German-based 'Marina', MALCOLM ROSS delivered his solo EDWYN COLLINS-produced debut, 'LOW SHOT' (1995), a record which also featured some of his MAGIC CLAN; ROBERT VICKERS (ex-GO-BETWEENS), STEPHEN DALY and DAVY WENDELL. A second, 'HAPPY BOY', recorded in '97, marked an appearance by BARRY ADAMSON, while MALCY co-wrote a few with former ORANGE JUICE cohort, DAVID McCLYMONT. To be honest, the albums were a little disappointing, possibly in hindsight vocalist/guitarist ROSS (with a sound not too dissimilar to EDWYN C) might've been better using an up and coming trained singer.

MALCOLM ROSS – vocals, guitars / with his DELANCY ST. GROUP and the MAGIC CLAN:- **ROBERT VICKERS, STEPHEN DALY + DAVY WENDELL**

Marina Bus Stop

Sep 95. (cd) *(ma 14)* **LOW SHOT** <US-title 'MALCOLM ROSS'> [ ] [ ] May96
– Low shot / Homestreet / Another year, another town / My avenger / Tried so hard / Hiram's dead / Big woman / Frogs and grass / One more day / Scarface / Round and round.

— now with **DOMINIC MURCOTT** – drums, vibes, percussion, programming / **SEAMUS BEAGHEN** – keyboards / **DAVE CHAMBERLAIN** – bass / **GED BARRY** – sax / **ANDREA SPAIN** – bass clarinet

Jan 98. (cd) *(ma 33)* **HAPPY BOY** [ ] [-]
– Happy boy / Heavens doors / Big guitar / I really could / Traitors / Lunchbreak / Heartbroken all over again / Missing / She plays the drums / Slim Jim on the slippery slope.

Ricky ROSS (see under ⇒ DEACON BLUE)

ROTE KAPELLE (see under ⇒ JESSE GARON & THE DESPERADOES)

ROYAL BRONCO (see under ⇒ POLICECAT)

RUBY

Born: LESLEY RANKINE, 11 Apr'65, Edinburgh. Arguably, the driving vocal force behind noisy, London-based, garage Punks, SILVERFISH (who released two incredible albums, 'Fat Axl' and 'Organ Fan' in the early 90's), the outspoken LESLEY split from the band to engage in new activities across the Atlantic.

Settling first in Seattle, then moving east to New Orleans, the controversial lady of Alt-rock signed a dual deal with 'Creation' (in the UK) and 'Sony' (in the US). With computer/techno guy, MARK WALK in tow, she entered a Stateside studio. In September 1995, her new project, RUBY (named after both LESLEY and MARK's grandmothers!), surfaced with a debut single, 'PARAFFIN'. Electronic and a little mainstream, it certainly had the bite needed to succeed in the fickle world of pop/rock music, unfortunately only people in the know, knew who RUBY was. Parent album, 'SALT PETER' (1995), was well-received enough, and she did do her bit to promote the record by touring with a band. Subsequent remix packages were RUBY's only efforts during a long barren period in which Creation folded.

Then, just as you thought the wee lassie had disappeared into the swamps of Noo Orleans, RUBY popped up with some freshly cut material in 2001. Signed to 'Wichita' (home of the WEBB BROTHERS and BRAVE CAPTAIN), LESLEY/RUBY delivered her comeback single, 'GRACE', premiering the all-new 'SHORT STAFFED AT THE GENE POOL' album.

LESLEY RANKINE – vocals / with co-writer **MARK WALK**

Creation · Sony

Sep 95. (c-s) *(CRECS 165) <78188>* **PARAFFIN / THE WHOLE IS EQUAL TO THE SUM OF IT'S PARTS** ☐ ☐ Nov95
(cd-s) *(CRESCD 165)* – ('A'-Red Snapper remix) / ('A'-Wagon Christ remix) / ('A'-Dead Elvis remix) / ('A'-Mark Walk remix).
(cd-s) *(CRESCD 165X)* – ('A'-Harpie mix) / ('A'-album version) / ('A'-Wagon Christ vocal) / ('A'-Richard Fearless dub).
(above also issued as 2 x 12"singles; CTP 165/+X)

Oct 95. (cd/lp)(c) *(CRE CD/LP 166)(CCRE 166) <67458>* **SALT PETER** ☐ ☐ Nov95
– Flippin' tha bird / Salt water fish / Heidi / Tiny meat / Paraffin / Hoops / Pine / Swallow baby / The whole is equal to the sum of its parts / Bud / Carondelet. *(cd re-iss. Jan01; same)*

Feb 96. (12")(cd-s) *(CRE 173T)(CRESCD 173)* **TINY MEAT (mixes)** ☐ –
(cd-s) *(CRESCD 173X)* – ('A'remixes).

Apr 96. (cd) *(CRECD 166RL)* **REVENGE – THE SWEETEST FRUIT (SALT PETER remixed)** ☐ –
(re-iss. Jan01; same)

May 96. (12")(cd-s) *(CRE 227T)(CRESCD 227)* **HOOPS (mixes)** ☐ –
(cd-s) *(CRESCD 227X)* – ('A'remixes).

Oct 96. (m-cd) *<67883>* **STROKING THE FULL LENGTH** (remixes) – ☐
– Swallow baby / Hoops / Flippin' tha bird / Salt water fish / Tiny meat / The whole is equal to the sum of its parts.

Wichita · Thirsty Ear

Mar 01. (12"/cd-s) *(WEBB 007 T/CD) <57100>* **GRACE (mixes; Christian Vogel original / TM Schneider space / Mekon / Mira Calix warm and fragrant)** ☐ ☐

Apr 01. (cd) *(WEBB 006) <57101>* **SHORT STAFFED AT THE GENE POOL** ☐ ☐
– Beefheart / Queen of denial / Lilypad / Waterside / Lamplight / Roses / Grace / Fly / Cargo / Sweet is / Fuse again.

Jul 01. (12"/cd-s) *(WEBB 019 T/CD)* **BEEFHEART (mixes; original / Deckwreck's in the dust / Wauvenfold / Solex)** ☐ –

Aug 01. (cd) *(WEBB 016)* **ALTERED AND PROUD (THE SHORT-STAFFED REMIXES)** ☐ –

RUBY BLUE

Formed: Edinburgh ... 1986 by gorgeous American drama student REBECCA PIDGEON (also an actress on BBC2's 'Campaign' programme) and ROGER FIFE. Completing the quartet with ANTHONY COOTE and ERIKA WOODS, the group released their debut album, 'GLANCES ASKANCES' in 1987 on indie label, 'Red Flame'. A fresh, spontaneous combination of pop, folk and jazz, the record showcased PIDGEON's high, pure vocals (shades of ANNE BRIGGS and SANDY DENNY) which brought a traditional feel to proceedings. With radio support from the likes of Andy Kershaw and Nicky Campbell, the band soon became the subject of major label interest and subsequently signed to 'Fontana' at the turn of the decade.

By this point they'd bolstered their sound with drums, attracting attention for support slots to the likes of JOHN MARTYN, VAN MORRISON and MARTIN STEPHENSON. Yet despite all the media attention, the band's major label debut set, 'DOWN FROM ABOVE' (1990) failed to spawn a hit single. REBECCA's final recording with the band came at the end of the year in the shape of the 'CAN IT BE' single. Also included on the CD single was a glacial folk cover of Cyril Tawney's 'SALLY FREE AND EASY' and 'THE RAVEN', a haunting track co-written with her new husband, playwright David Mamet. Post-REBECCA, the band carried on with ERIKA as vocalist, re-signing to 'Red Flame' and releasing a couple of early 90's albums – 'BROKEN WATER' (1992) and 'ALMOST NAKED' (1993) – before splitting.

REBECCA, meanwhile, recorded a number of solo sets for American label, 'Chesky', namely 'THE RAVEN' (1994), 'THE NEW YORK GIRLS' CLUB' (1996) and 'FOUR MARYS (1998).

REBECCA PIDGEON (b. 1963, Cambridge, Massachusetts, USA) – vocals / **ROGER FIFE** (b. 1963) – guitar, bass / **ANTHONY COOTE** – bass / **ERIKA WOODS** (b. ERIKA SPOTSWOOD) – backing vocals / plus drummer **CHRIS BUCK**

Red Flame · not iss.

Jun 87. (7") *(RF7-53)* **GIVE US OUR FLAG BACK. / THE QUIET MIND** ☐ –

Sep 87. (lp) *(RF-53)* **GLANCES ASKANCES** ☐ –
– Give us our flag back / The quiet mind / Just relax / So unlike me / Walking home / The meaning of life / Wintery day / Sitting in the cafe / Bless you. *(cd-iss. Jan91; RFCD 2)*

Sep 87. (7"/12") *(RF 7/12-56)* **SO UNLIKE ME. / LIFE AND TIMES OF THE 20TH CENTURY** ☐ –

Mar 88. (7") *(RF7-57)* **BECAUSE. / THE RUBY BLUE** ☐ –
(12"+=) *(RF12-57)* – The ruby blue (extended).

Nov 88. (7") *(RF7-59)* **BLOOMSBURY BLUE. / SAVE ME** ☐ –
(12"+=) *(RF12-59)* – Childs song.

Feb 89. (7") *(RF7-62)* **STAND TOGETHER. / EASY** ☐ –
(12"+=) *(RF12-62)* – Too many suitcases.

Fontana · not iss.

Apr 90. (7") *(RB 1)* **THE QUIET MIND (FOR JOE). / POSITIVE LOVE SONG** ☐ –
(12"+=)(cd-s+=) *(RB 1-12)(RBCD 1)* – Say goodbye (live).

Apr 90. (cd/c/lp) *(842568-2/-4/-1)* **DOWN FROM ABOVE** ☐ –
– Primitive man / The quiet mind / Take your money / Can it be / Away from here / Pavan / Stand together / Betty's last letter / Bloomsbury blue / Midnight road / Not alone / Song of the mermaid / Something's gone wrong / Epitaph.

Jun 90. (7") *(RB 2)* **PRIMITIVE MAN. / THE TRAVELLER** ☐ –
(12"+=)(cd-s+=) *(RF 2-12)(RFCD 2)* – ('A'extended) / Betty's last letter.

Nov 90. (7") *(RB 3)* **CAN IT BE. / SOMETHING'S GONE WRONG (Chiltern radio session)** ☐ –
(cd-s+=) *(RBCD 3)* – Sally free and easy / The raven.

— now without COOTE and more so, REBECCA, who married and later went solo releasing three albums for 'Chesky', 'THE RAVEN' (1994), 'THE NEW YORK GIRLS' CLUB' (1996) and 'FOUR MARYS' (1998)

— **ERIKA** now lead vocals + with new drummer **KARLOS EDWARDS**

Red Flame · not iss.

Jun 91. (7") *(RF7-63)* **I FEEL GOOD NOW. / GET YOUR LIFE BACK** ☐ –
(12"+=) *(RF12-63)* – Am I turning into you?
(cd-s+=) *(RFCD-63)* – Too far / Smile slow.

Jan 92. (c; fan club) *(TAPE 2)* **PARADISE** – –
– Bless you / Strength of mind / Paradise / Elvis / Should know better / I feel good now / Beyond us / Too far / High'n'low.

Mar 93. (cd) *(RFCD 54)* **ALMOST NAKED** ☐ –
– Recreate your kiss / New way / High for a while / Goddess / You'll find out / I still love you / Done my thinking / Strength of mind / Magnificent truth / Almost naked.

Jun 93. (cd-ep) *(RFSCD 64)* **DONE MY THINKING / MAGNIFICENT TRUTH / ALMOST NAKED** ☐ –

— split for the final time after above

– compilations, etc. –

Jan 92. (cd) *Red Flame; (RFCD 5)* **BROKEN WATER** ☐ –
– Easy / Stand together / Away from here / Life and times of the twentieth century / Somebody say somethimng / Because / Shining snow / Save me / Childs song / The ruby blue / Too many suitcases / Bloomsbury blue / Betty / Stuart.

RUNRIG

Formed: North Uist . . . 1973 as The RUN-RIG DANCE BAND, by brothers RORY and CALUM McDONALD plus BLAIR DOUGLAS. Following local gigs on the islands, the band found encouraging support from the gaelic media, subsequently travelling to mainland Scotland and playing a gig at the Kelvin Hall in Glasgow. Schoolfriend DONNIE MUNRO joined the following year as a lead vocalist while DOUGLAS was replaced by ROBERT McDONALD on accordion.

This line-up remained steady through the band's debut album, 'PLAY GAELIC' (1978), released on the independent 'Neptune' label (and subsequently re-issued in 1995 on 'Lismor'). As the title suggested, this was a steadfastly indigenous release with no English language tracks although it was well received in folk circles and encouraged the group to set up their own label, 'Ridge'. Amid further line-up changes, RUNRIG released a follow-up, 'HIGHLAND CONNECTION' (1979), the record featuring a mix of Gaelic and English language tracks including 'LOCH LOMOND', a traditional song which would become a firm favourite with their growing fanbase.

It was to be a further five years before the release of 'RECOVERY' (1984), the band having toured heavily, embellishing their sound with the relative exotica of keyboards (played by, gasp, an Englishman!, RICHARD CHERNS). As a result, the album proffered a more accessible brand of Celtic-rock (described as a cross between BIG COUNTRY, The CHIEFTAINS and HORSLIPS), a sound that crystallised with 'HEARTLAND' (1986) on the likes of 'DANCE CALLED AMERICA' (dealing with the tragedy of the highland clearances).

With a growing number of admirers in both America and Europe, it seemed that the only place which failed to understand the group was, funnily enough, England. Nevertheless, the band were signed by London-based major, 'Chrysalis' in 1988, following the successful 'CUTTER AND THE CLAN' (1987) album, a collection which numbered such enduring RUNRIG favourites as 'ROCKET TO THE MOON' and 'PROTECT AND SURVIVE'. Their major label debut, the live 'ONCE IN A LIFETIME', was released the same year and dented the lower region of the UK chart. This marked the beginning of RUNRIG's most commercially successful period, the band almost making the Top 10 with the 'SEARCHLIGHT' album in 1989. An appearance on Scottish TV caused a considerable surge in interest, 'THE BIG WHEEL' (1991) making the UK Top 5. Its success caught many people off guard, and it was a testament to the support of native fans, the album once again selling negligibly south of the border. Soon after the record's release the band played an open air concert, fittingly, at Loch Lomond, before 45,000 fans.

Successive releases like 'AMAZING THINGS' (1993), a near No.1 album, and 'MARA' have consolidated the band's standing as one of Scotland's premier exports alongside whisky and PRIMAL SCREAM. While they sometimes tend to overdo the bombastic Braveheart shenanigans, they have to be applauded in their brave efforts to keep the gaelic langauge alive, often in the face of apathetic indifference or even outright hostility. However, the band's success seemed to be on hold as they searched for a replacement for the politicised DONNIE MUNRO. In 1998/99, all was revealed when Canadian (MUNRO-soundalike!) BRUCE GUTHRO filled his boots for fresh set, 'IN SEARCH OF ANGELS'. In the summer of 2001, 'THE STAMPING GROUND' was released to subdued press reviews and a brief UK Top 75 placing. • **Trivia:** Due to their religious beliefs they never play live on a Sunday.

DONNIE MUNRO (b. 2 Aug'53, Uig, Isle Of Skye) – vocals / **RORY McDONALD** (b. RODERICK, 27 Jul'49, Dornoch) – bass, vocals, acoustic guitar, accordion / **BLAIR DOUGLAS** – harmonica, organ (re-joined Jun'78) / **CALUM McDONALD** (b.MALCOLM MORRISON McDONALD, 12 Nov'53, Lochmaddy, North Uist) – drums, percussion

Neptune not iss.

Apr 78. (c) *(NA 105)* **PLAY GAELIC** [ ] [-]
– Duisg mo run / Sguaban arbhair / Tillidh mi / Criogal cridhe / Nach neonach neiad a tha E / Sunndach / Air an traigh / De ni mi – pulp / An ros / Ceolan danasa / Chi'n geamhradh / Cum 'ur n'aire. *(lp-iss.Sep84 on 'Lismor'; LILP 5182) (re-iss. Jul90 as 'RUNRIG PLAY GAELIC – THE FIRST LEGENDARY RECORDINGS' cd/c; CDLOM 9026) (c re-iss. Jul95; LICS 5182)*

— added **MALCOLM JONES** (b.12 Jul'59, Inverness) – guitar, bagpipes, mandolin to repl. BLAIR DOUGLAS (who still guested); he released a handful of albums including 1984's 'CELTOLOGY'.

Ridge not iss.

Oct 79. (lp/c) *(RR/+C 001)* **THE HIGHLAND CONNECTION** [ ] [-]
– Gamhna gealla / Mairi / What time? / Fichead bliadhna / Na luing air scoladh / Loch Lomond / Na h-vain a's t-earrach / Foghar nan Eilean / The twenty-five pounder / Going home / Morning tide / Cearcal a chuain. *(re-iss. Sep84 & Feb86; same) (cd-iss. Aug89 & Nov98; RRCD 001)*

— added on tour '81, **RICHARD CHERNS** (b.England) – keyboards

— added guests **BLAIR DOUGLAS / JOHN MARTIN** – cello / **RONNIE GERRARD** – fiddle

Dec 81. (lp/c) *(RR/+C 002)* **RECOVERY** [ ] [-]
– An toll dubh / Rubh nan cudaigean / 'Ic lain 'ic Sheimas / Recovery / Instrumental / 'S tu molceanna – Nightfall in Marsco / Breakin' the chains / Fuaim a bhlair / Tir an airna / The old boys / Dust. *(re-iss. Sep84 & Feb86; same) (cd-iss. Aug89 & Nov98; RRCD 002)*

Dec 82. (7") *(RRS 003)* **LOCH LOMOND. / TUIREADH IAIN RUAIDH** [72] [-]

Simple not iss.

Aug 84. (7") *(SIM 4)* **DANCE CALLED AMERICA. / NA H-UAIN A'S T-EARRACH** [ ] [-]
(12"+=) *(12SIM 4)* – Ribhinn.

Nov 84. (7") *(SIM 8)* **SKYE. / HEY MANDU** [ ] [-]

— **PETER WISHART** (b. 9 Mar'52, Dunfermline) – keyboards, vocals; repl. CHERNS / added **IAIN BAYNE** (b.22 Jan'60, St.Andrews) – drums, percussion (ex-NEW CELESTE)

Ridge not iss.

Feb 86. (lp/c) *(RR/+C 005)* **HEARTLAND** [ ] [-]
– O cho mealdt / This darkest winter / Life line / Air a' chuain / Dance called America / The everlasting gun / Skye / Choc na feille / The wire / An atairreachd Ard / The ferry / Tuireadh Iain ruaidh. *(cd-iss. 1989 & Nov98; same)*

Nov 86. (7") *(RRS 006)* **THE WORK SONG. / THIS TIME OF YEAR** [ ] [-]

Nov 87. (7") *(RRS 007)* **ALBA. / WORKER FOR THE WIND** [ ] [-]

Dec 87. (lp/c/cd) *(RR/+C/CD 008)* **THE CUTTER AND THE CLAN** [ ] [-]
– Alba / The cutter / Hearts of olden glory / Pride of the summer / Worker for the wind / Rocket to the Moon / The only rose / Protect and survive / Our Earth was once green / An ubhal as airde. *(re-iss. Jul88 on 'Chrysalis' lp/c/cd; CHR/ZCHR/CCD 1669) (re-iss. cd Mar94 on 'Chrysalis') (re-iss. cd May95 on 'Chrysalis' – hit No.45)*

Chrysalis Chrysalis

Aug 88. (7") *(CHS 3284)* **PROTECT AND SURVIVE. / HEARTS OF OLDEN GLORY** [ ] [-]
(12"+=/cd-s+=) *(CHS 12/CD 3284)* – ('A'live).

Nov 88. (lp/c/cd) *(<CHR/ZCHR/CCD 1695>)* **ONCE IN A LIFETIME (live)** [61] [ ]
– Dance called America / Protect and survive / Chi mi'n geamhradh / Rocket to the Moon / Going home / Choc na feille / Nightfall on Marsco / 'Stu mo Leannan / Skye / Loch Lomond / Hearts of olden glory.

Aug 89. (7"/c-s) *(CHR/+MC 3404)* **NEWS FROM HEAVEN. / CHI MI'N TIR** [ ] [-]
(12"+=/12"pic-d+=/cd-s+=) *(12/12T/CD 3404)* – The times they are a-changin'.

Sep 89. (lp/c/cd) *(<CHR/ZCHR/CCD 1713>)* **SEARCHLIGHT** [11] [ ]
– News from Heaven / Every river / City of lights / Eirinn / Tir a'mhurain / World appeal / Tear down these walls / Only the brave / Siol ghoraidh / That final mile / Smalltown / Precious years.

Nov 89. (7") *(CHS 3451)* **EVERY RIVER. / THIS TIME OF YEAR** [ ] [-]
(12"+=/cd-s+=) *(CHS 12/CD 3451)* – Once our Earth was green.

Sep 90. (10"ep/12"ep/cd-ep) *(CHS 10/12/CD 3451)* **CAPTURE THE HEART EP** [49] [-]
– Stepping down the glory road / Satellite flood / Harvest Moon / The apple came down.

Jun 91. (cd/c/lp) *(<CCD/ZCHR/CHR 1858>)* **THE BIG WHEEL** [4] [ ]
– Headlights / Healer in your heart / Abhainn an t-sluaigh – The crowded river / Always the winner / This beautiful pain / An cuibhle mor – The big wheel / Edge of the world / Hearthammer / I'll keep coming home / Flower of the West.

Aug 91. (7"ep/c-ep/12"ep/cd-ep) **HEARTHAMMER EP** [25] [-]
– Hearthammer / Pride of the summer (live) / Loch Lomond (live) / Solus na madainn (live).

Nov 91. (7"/c-s) *(CHS/+MC 3805)* **FLOWER OF THE WEST. / CHI MI'N GREAMHRADH** [43] [-]
(12"+=/cd-s+=) *(CHS12/CDCHS 3805)* – Ravenscraig / Harvest Moon (live).

Feb 93. (7"/7"blue)(c-s) *(CHS/+S 3952)(TCCHS 3952)*
WONDERFUL. / APRIL COME SHE WILL [29] [-]
(cd-s) *(CDCHS 3952)* – ('A'side) / Straidean na roinn Eorpa (Streets of Europe) / On the edge.

Mar 93. (cd/c/lp) *(<CCD/ZCHR/CHR 2000>)* **AMAZING THINGS** [2] [ ]
– Amazing things / Wonderful / The greatest flame / Move a mountain / Pog aon oidhche earraich (A kiss one evening Spring) / Dream fields / Song of the Earth / Forever eyes of blue / Straidean na roinn Eorpa (Streets of Europe) / Canada / Ard (High) / On the edge.

Apr 93. (7"/c-s) *(CHS/TCCHS 3975)* **THE GREATEST FLAME. / SUILVAN** [36] [-]
(cd-s+=) *(CDCHS 3975)* – Saints of the soil / An T-lasgair (the fisherman).
(cd-s) *(CDXCHS 3975)* – ('A'side) / The fisherman / Morning tide (re-recorded) / Chi m'in tir (I see the land).

Nov 94. (cd/c/lp) *(<CD/TC+/CHR 6090>)* **TRANSMITTING LIVE (live)** [41] [ ]
– Urlar / Ard / Edge of the world / The greatest flame / Harvest Moon / The wire / Precious years / Every river / Flower of the west / Only the brave / Alba / Pog aon oidche earraich (one kiss one Spring evening). *(cd re-iss. Mar99; same)*

Dec 94. (c-ep/12"ep/cd-ep) *(TC/12/CD CHS 5018)* **THIS TIME OF YEAR / WONDERFUL (live). / DREAM FIELDS (live) / I'LL KEEP COMING HOME (live) / THIS TIME OF YEAR (re-recorded)** [38] [-]

Apr 95. (c-s/cd-s) *(TC/CD CHS 5021)* **AN UBHAL AS AIRDE (THE HIGHEST APPLE). / ABHAINN AN T-SLUIGH / THE GREATEST FLAME** [18] [ ]
(cd-s+=) *(CDXCHS 5021)* – Flower of the west.

Chrysalis Avalanche

Oct 95. (c-s/7") *(TC+/CHS 5029)* **THINGS THAT ARE. / AN UBHAL AS AIRDE (THE HIGHEST APPLE)** [40] [-]
(cd-s+=) *(CDCHS 5029)* – Amazing things (remix) / That other landscape.

Nov 95. (cd/c/lp) *(CD/TC+/CHR 6111)* <35> **MARA** [24] [ ] Jan96
– Day in a boat / Nothing but the sun / The mighty Atlantic / Things that are / Road and the river / Meadhan Oidhche air an Acairseid / The wedding / The dancing floor / Thairis air a ghleann / Lighthouse.

Sep 96. (7") *(CHSS 5035)* **RHYTHM OF MY HEART. / THE MIGHTY ATLANTIC – MARA THEME (orchestral mix)** 24 -
(cd-s+=) *(CDCHS 5035)* – Canada (live).
(cd-s) *(CDXCHS 5035)* – ('A'side) / Cum ur N'aire (with The GLASGOW ISLAY GAELIC CHOIR) / Cadal chadian mi (demo from 1978).
Oct 96. (cd/c) *(CD/TC CHR 6116)* **THE BEST OF RUNRIG – LONG DISTANCE** (compilation) 13 -
– Glory road / Alba / Greatest flame / Rocket to the Moon / Crowded river / Protect and survive / Rhythm of my heart / Hearthammer / Highest aple / Wonderful / The mighty Atlantic / Flower of the west / Every river / Siol ghoraidh / Hearts of Olden / Skye – live / Loch Lomond – live. *(other cd w/bonus cd 'BBC SESSION – LIVE' +=; CDCHRS 6116)* – Saints of the soil / Ravenscraig / Solus na madainn (The morning light) / Chi mi'n Geamhradh / The apple came down / Chi mi 'n tir (I see the land) / Ribhinn O. *(d-cd-iss. Apr99 on 'E.M.I.'; 520218-2)*
Jan 97. (c-s) *(TCCHS 5045)* **THE GREATEST FLAME (1996 remix) / AN UBHAI AS AIRDE (THE HIGHEST APPLE)** 30 -
(cd-s) *(CDCHSS 5045)* – ('A'side) / Protect and survive / Pride of summer medley: Siol – Ghoraidh – Thains air a Ghleann (chorus).
(cd-s) *(CDCHS 5045)* – ('A'side) / The Middleton mouse medley: Hearthammer (live) / Always the winner (live) / Abhain an t-sluaigh.

— now with new singer **BRUCE GUTHRO** who replaced DONNIE (now a solo artist)

Ridge not iss.

Feb 99. (cd-s) *(RR 011)* **THE MESSAGE / THE WATER IS WIDE (live) / FEASGAR AN LA / THE MESSAGE (radio edit)** -
Mar 99. (cd) *(RR 010)* **IN SEARCH OF ANGELS** 29 -
– Maymorning / The message / Big sky / Life is / Da mhile bliadhna / Ribhinn donn / This is not a love song / A dh'innse na firinn / All things must change / Cho buidhe is a bha I riabh / Travellers / In search of angels / Brown haired girl (translation).
May 99. (cd-s) *(RR 012)* **MAYMORNING / ROCKET TO THE MOON (live in Tonder 1998) / MAYMORNING (album version)** -
Dec 99. (cd-s) *(RR 013)* **THIS IS NOT A LOVE SONG (remix for radio) / ORAN / THIS IS NOT A LOVE SONG (remix)** -
Aug 00. (cd) *(RR 014)* **LIVE AT THE CELTIC CONNECTIONS 2000 (live)** -
– Rocket to the Moon / Protect & survive / Big sky / Sio ghoraidh / The only rose / A dh'innse na firinn / Edge of the world / Hearts of Olden glory / Rubh nan cudaigean – The Middleton mouse / Maymorning / The message / Cearcal a' chuain / Pog an oidhche earraich / Skye.

— in Sep'00, MALCOLM JONES teamed up with piper DONALD BLACK on a 'MacMeanmna' label set, 'CLOSE TO HOME'

May 01. (cd) *(RR 016)* **THE STAMPING GROUND** 64 -
– The book of golden stories / The stamping ground / An sabhal aig naill / Wall of China / One man / Engine room / One thing / Ship / Summer walkers / Running to the light / Oran allein / Leaving Strathconon / Big songs of hope and cheer / Oran.
Jun 01. (cd-s) *(RR 017)* **THE BOOK OF GOLDEN STORIES / BIG SONGS OF HOPE AND CHEER** -

– compilations, etc. –

Feb 98. (cd) *EMI Gold; (493583-2)* **BEAT THE DRUM** -
May 98. (d-cd) *Ridge; (RR 009)* **THE GAELIC COLLECTION (1973-1988)** 71 -
Apr 99. (d-cd) *EMI; (520218-2)* **THE BBC SESSIONS / LIVE / THE BEST OF RUNRIG** -
Nov 99. (cd) *Connoisseur; (VSOPCD 280)* **CELTIC GLORY** -
Jan 00. (cd) *Ridge; (RV 01)* **LIVE IN BONN (live)** -
Sep 00. (3xcd-box) *EMI; (528375-2)* **THE CUTTER AND THE CLAN / THE BIG WHEEL / AMAZING THINGS** -

S

SAIDFLORENCE

Formed: Bellshill, Lanarkshire . . . early 90's by KIT CUMMINGS, his brother DES, PHIL FEENEY and KEV MURPHY, seemingly all one-time fans of ADAM & THE ANTS. Short-lived and annoyingly buoyant about their chances to make the big-time, this 4-piece indie-rock act (described as being "on the dark side of EMF") showcased their debut single, 'STUFF YOUR QUIET LIFE', before being herded off to Russia where they appeared on TV. Through manager, Bruce Findlay, A&R men from both 'Epic' and 'London' were impressed, although KIT and his crew abstained from signing – not a wise move as it turned out.

KIT CUMMINGS – vocals, bass / **PHIL FEENEY** – guitar / **KEV MURPHY** – keyboards / **DES CUMMINGS** – drums

own label not iss.

Jan 91. (7") **STUFF YOUR QUIET LIFE. /** -

unknown not iss.

1990's. (cd-s) **DEFINITELY MAYBE (seven) / DEFINITELY MAYBE (Luma-12) / DEFINITELY MAYBE (M8-12) / WRITING HISTORY** -

— disappeared after above

SALLY SKULL (see under ⇒ Vesuvius records)

Sano records (see under ⇒ Postcard records)

SATIVA DRUMMERS (see under ⇒ Bosque records)

SAWYER

Formed: Edinburgh . . . early 1994 by JOHN MACKIE, IAIN H, ANDREW HUNTER and ALAN FINDLAY. One of the many up and coming 'Human Condition' bands (remember IDLEWILD), SAWYER were all of the following: claustrophobic, uneasy and grotesque, something like MARK E SMITH sparring musically with STEVE ALBINI or even NAPALM DEATH having a bender with MARTIN HANNETT at the controls – the truth is, producer JAMIE WATSON was at the proverbial helm. Their debut, a double-pack 7" led by the bludgeoning 'GHETTY CHASUN', definitely stirred the listener into submission. However, for the latter half of the 90's, SAWYER were posted AWOL, although a few personnel changes (DEREK ANDERSON and ALAN WILSON replacing HUNTER), might have set them back slightly – who knows.

Back in circulation after six New Years, the brutal 5-piece finally delivered some (much delayed) fresh product via the debut album, 'ON THE SEVEN' (2000). The wilderness years had certainly paid off and with US groups (i.e. FUGAZI, etc) biting the dust, it was time for these Caledonian Grunge-metallers to make the grade.

JOHN MACKIE – vocals / **IAIN H.** – guitar, vocals / **ANDREW HUNTER** – bass, guitar / **ALAN FINDLAY** – drums

Human Condition not iss.

Oct 94. (d7"ep) *(HC 007)* **GHETTY CHASUN. / TORN // GUY. / G.M.** -

— **DEREK ANDERSON** – guitar + **ALAN WILSON** – bass; repl. HUNTER

Jun 00. (cd) *(HCCD 0027)* **ON THE SEVEN** -
– In the evening you could be anything in the evening / Johnny the wadd / (It's a) Dry heat / 20 etc / 20 etc version / The world is endless / Osoba / He gave what he could / No rule / In the evening reprise / Ghetty chasun / The counties.

SCAN CARRIERS (see under ⇒ Soma records)

SCARS

Formed: Edinburgh . . . late '77 by ROBERT 'BOBBY' KING, PAUL RESEARCH, JOHN MACKIE and CALUMN MacKAY. This young post-punk outfit made their vinyl debut on the local 'Fast' label with the 'Adultery' single in Spring '79, 'Charisma' sufficiently impressed to sign the band to the 'Pre' offshoot. 'THEY CAME AND TOOK HER' marked the SCARS' major label debut in early 1980, while a much anticipated debut album, 'AUTHOR! AUTHOR!' arrived in Spring the following year. Ranging from the melodic new-wave guitar pop of 'ALL ABOUT YOU' to the CURE-style reverberations of 'JE T'AIME C'EST LA MORT', the record was an encouraging debut in what was a fine year for Scots artists with releases from contemporaries like JOSEF K, ORANGE JUICE etc. Unfortunately, like most of the new young Caledonian bands, the lifespan of SCARS proved surprisingly short and the band split with only one album to their name. Perhaps this was for the best as wearing tan jodphurs wrapped with garish climbing rope (!) was surely plunging New Romantic fashion to unnecessary depths.

ROBERT 'BOBBY' KING – vocals / **PAUL RESEARCH** – guitar / **JOHN MACKIE** – bass / **CALUMN MacKAY** – drums

Fast Product not iss.

Mar 79. (7") *(FAST 8)* **HORRORSHOW. / ADULT-ERY** -

— **STEVE 'CHICK' McLAUGHLIN** – drums; repl. CALUMN

Pre Stiff

Feb 80. (7") *(PRE 002)* **THEY CAME AND TOOK HER. / ROMANCE BY MAIL** -

May 80. (7") *(PRE 005)* **LOVE SONG. / PSYCHOMODO** [ ] [-]
Apr 81. (7") *(PRE 014)* **ALL ABOUT YOU. / AUTHOR! AUTHOR!** [ ] [-]
Apr 81. (lp) *(PREX 5)* **AUTHOR! AUTHOR!** [67] [-]
– Leave me in Autumn / Fear of the dark / Aquarama / David / Obsessions / Everywhere I go / The lady in the car with glasses on and a gun / Je t'aime c'est la mort / Your attention please / All about you.
Sep 81. (7") *(PRKS 5)* **AUTHOR! AUTHOR! / SHE'S ALIVE** [ ] [-]
(12"+=) *(PRKSX 5)* – Silver dream machine.
Oct 81. (12"ep) *<TEES12 04>* **AUTHOR! AUTHOR! / SHE'S ALIVE. / ALL ABOUT YOU / LEAVE ME IN AUTUMN** [-] [ ]

— split early 1982, KING subsequently went solo releasing one single, 'PAPER HEART', in 1982 *(PRE 23)*. He later formed LIP MACHINE, who released a handful of 45's for the 'Disposable Dance' imprint.

Fran SCHOPPLER
(see under ⇒ JESSE GARON & THE DESPERADOES)

SCIENTIFIC SUPPORT DEPT.

Formed: Glasgow . . . 1997 by various electronic dubmeisters including leader and spokesman, DOHERTY. Appearing on label-samplers such as 'Bent Boutique' and 'Bentism', this loosely formed collective took their inspiration from soundtrack music and featured anonymous members from various 'Creeping Bent'-signed bands. Previous to this, two joint 45's (with MOUNT VERNON ARTS LAB and SECRET GOLDFISH respectively) surfaced on the same label. DOHERTY subsequently worked on soundtracks to theatre and film, including various Shakespearean projects; another joint single, this time with MONGOOSE, hit the indie shops in September 2000. The 'DEPT. went back into hibernation but returned with the excellent 'CABBAGENECK' in summer 2002. Brimming with eclectic sounds and weird effects (not to mention a whole host of weird instruments such as the moog, the trumpet and a set of Technic decks!), the set surprised even the hardened indie fan who thought all Scots collaborations ended with the REINDEER SECTION. A much more extreme version of this project, the group went on to tour successfully with TO ROCOCO ROT, The NECTARINE No.9 and FUTURE PILOT AKA. They/DOHERTY also took on remixing duties for ALAN VEGA, DJ HARRI, ADVENTURES IN STEREO and MOUNT VERNON ARTS LAB.

DOHERTY – electronics / + others

Creeping Bent | not iss.

Nov 97. (7") *(bent 029)* **Future Pilot aka vs. Alan Vega – Meditation Rat. / MOUNT VERNON ARTS LAB vs SCIENTIFIC SUPPORT DEPT.** [ ] [-]
Feb 98. (7") *(bent 032)* **KIPPERLYNCH. / (other track by Secret Goldfish)** [ ] [-]
Sep 00. (7"; as MONGOOSE vs. SCIENTIFIC SUPPORT DEPT.) *(bent 057)* **SUBVERT NORMALITY. / GOOSEGREEN** [ ] [-]
Jun 02. (cd) *(bent 065cd)* **CABBAGENECK** [ ] [-]
– Grammer / Shortwave / The far lows / Harpi / Kipperlynch (the afterglow) / Non-correction / J-girls / Vagrant / Horizontal bien / Peanut in dub / Enostroma.

Jock SCOT

Born: 21 Sep'52, Leith, Edinburgh. Having spent many, many, (no, many!) years as a Rock'n'roll "auxiliary", JOCK SCOT has become something of a minor legend in music business circles. Quitting his homeland during Scotland's infamous 1978 World Cup campaign, the 'Burgh's bingeing Bard made for London where he became a roadie of sorts for such Punk/New Wave luminaries as The CLASH, TALKING HEADS and RIP, RIG & PANIC. It was all grist to his stand-up poet mill, SCOT reciting his streetwise verse to any pub crowd that would listen. Having amassed reams of material, JOCK's first book, 'Where Is My Heroine?', hit the shelves in '93. Hooking up with his old chum, DAVEY HENDERSON (ex-FIRE ENGINES) and his NECTARINE No.9 project around the same time, SCOT made his recording debut via a track ('Going Off Someone') on the band's 'Unloaded For You' EP. Two years on, the same pairing worked wonders on the 'PREGNANT WITH POSSIBILITIES' EP (with PAUL QUINN also in attendance), while the loveable Leith-al patter-merchant also featured on the 'SAINT JACK' album. His first full-length solo effort was 'MY PERSONAL CULLODEN', a sort of TOM WAITS-meets-LOU REED long-player that finally appeared for 'Sano' (and 'Postcard') in '97, 'TAPE YOUR HEAD ON', indeed! • **Note:** Was the JOCK SCOT who issued the 7", 'Souvenir To Commemorate Wedding' / 'More Souvenirs' for 'Stiff' (MAX 1) c.1981 actually the man himself?

JOCK SCOT – poetry / + **NECTARINE No.9** on backing

— see under NECTARINE No.9 for even more collaborative efforts

Postcard / Sano | not iss.

May 97. (cd) *(Dubh 972cd / Sano 1877)* **MY PERSONAL CULLODEN** [ ] [-]
– Easy to write / Gay pean to Thierry / Above the volcano / Someone's yearning / Tape your head on / Just another fucked up little druggy / Farewell to FERODO / There's a hole in daddy's arm / Good God / Domestic bliss / Thunder over Kilburn / A certain beauty / Norman Vaughan's blues / The underdog / White cars passing by / All over the world, girls are dreaming / Nuts / Going off someone.

Sano | not iss.

Aug 97. (cd-s/7"; as JOCK SCOT & THE NECTARINE No.9) *(ST/+7 1876)* **TAPE YOUR HEAD ON** [-] [-] w-drawn

Scotland's wee metal scene

early 80's onwards: Bypassing the likes of bigshots HOLOCAUST, HEAVY PETTIN, PALLAS, GUN and The ALMIGHTY, Scotland also had a few other not so well-known acts around at the time.

CHASAR

were one such act. Formed in the late 70's by heavy-metal/hard-rock trio of ALEC POLLACK (vocals & guitar), PETER MARSHALL (bass & 12-string guitar) and his brother JIM (drums & percussion), this tight no-messing unit played the toilet circuit from Glasgow to Edinburgh and beyond – I'm sure only one record (below) exists.

American Phonograph | not iss.

Mar 85. (lp) *(APK 11)* **CHASAR** [ ] [-]
– Destiny / Visions of time / Deceiver / Kings / Lights / Gypsy roller / Underground.

GLASGOW

were formed 1983 in Blairdardie, Glasgow. Consisting of NEIL RUSSELL, ARCHIE DICKSON, PAUL McMANUS and MICHAEL BOYLE, they released a few hard-edged singles before branching out on their own aptly-named '041' – the Glasgow dialing code at the time.

Clydebank | not iss.

1984. (12"ep) *(CLY 001)* **GLASGOW'S MILES BETTER** [ ] [-]

Neat | not iss.

May 84. (7") *(NEAT 40)* **STRANDED. / HEAT OF THE NIGHT** [ ] [-]

041 | not iss.

Nov 87. (lp) *(041)* **ZERO FOUR ONE** [ ] [-]
– We will rock / Secrets in the dark / Back on the run / My heart is running with the night / Meet me halfway / Under the lights / No more lonely nights / Breakout. *(cd-iss. Apr88 on 'Sonet'; SNTCD 041)*
Jan 88. (7") *(041-7)* **SECRETS IN THE DARK. / MEET ME HALFWAY** [ ] [-]
1988. (7") *(041-8)* **UNDER THE LIGHTS. /** [ ] [-]
1988. (7") *(041-9)* **WILL YOU BE MINE. /** [ ] [-]

CROWS

were formed in Glasgow around the early 80's and they several hard-rock type releases.

Dingle's | not iss.

1983. (lp) *(DIN 317)* **THE CROWS** [ ] [-]

Ravin' | not iss.

Apr 86. (7"/12") *(7/12 001)* **THE SUN WENT IN. / ROUND AND ROUND** [ ] [-]
Mar 87. (12") *(RAVE 002)* **REDMAN. /** [ ] [-]

Dragon | not iss.

1987. (lp) *(DRGN 861)* **NO BONES OR GREASE** [ ] [-]

Survival | not iss.

Dec 87. (12"ep) *(SUR12 041)* **TAKAYAMA. /** [ ] [-]
Feb 88. (12"ep) *(SUR12 042)* **THE LOVE YOU RUN. / SWEPT AWAY / LEAVING YOU** [ ] [-]

LA PAZ

were another to tour Glasgow, etc around the mid-80's but I don't think there were any recordings – there were probably several more who managed to release at least a bootleg demo tape but maybe that's for another edition.

LYIN' RAMPANT

were also formed in Glasgow . . . mid-80's (unknown).

Prism | not iss.

Dec 87. (lp) *(VT 1)* **UP & CUMIN'** [ ] [-]
– Indoor games / Promises / Breakdown / Way of destiny / Don't walk away / Fantasy girl / Say goodbye (sayonara) / Time again / Crazee / Kill them all.

MUDSHARK

were a funk-rawk outfit from around the Falkirk area in the mid-90's and included drummer TOMMY (could've done with some info TOMMY!).

Pony / not iss.

Aug 95. (7") *(PONY 001)* **CUT ON THE GRAIN. / SHOWTIME** ☐ -
(cd-s+=) *(PONYCD 001)* – Jack.

Sep 95. (cd) *(PONYLPCD 001)* **MUDSHARK** ☐ -
– Wall of fame / Showtime / Cut on the grain / Cold moon rain / Natural / Gangway / Broadway bound / Put out the word / Out of my hands / It won't shine.

CAGE

were formed in Stenhousemuir around the mid-90's by unknown hard-rockers. One of the members thought I was bullshitting about the book and wouldn't give me any info, although I supplied him with a phone number – thanks!

Scratch / not iss.

Oct 95. (cd-s) *(APLCD 003)* **YOU DIRTY RAT** ☐ -

Bon SCOTT

Born: RONALD SCOTT, 9 Jul'46, Kirriemuir, Angus. Along with thousands of other Scots, his family left for the brave new world that was Australia in the early 50's. Nicknamed "Bonnie Scotland" by his school chums, RONALD subsequently shortened it to BON as he began his musical career as a pipe band drummer.

Constrained by Perth, BON ended up in Melbourne where his hell-raising ways combined more easily with successive stints in Pop/Blues acts such as The SPECTORS, The VALENTINES, The FRATERNITY and the MOUNT LOFTY RANGERS. Pre-dating the infamous Sex Pistols vs. Bill Grundy talkshow incident by a few years, BON was involved in an expletive-filled Australian TV spat that was witnessed by an impressed ANGUS YOUNG. The young ANGUS, along with his brother MALCOLM, was already treading the boards with hot-to-trot rockers, AC/DC. It wasn't long before BON was pestering the band for a crack at the drum-stool, although he ended up as frontman after original vocalist DAVE EVANS let them down. SCOTT's lascivious, woodbines 'n' whisky rasp immediately became the main ingredient in AC/DC's sleazy hard-rock soup and the band established themselves in the domestic market with two mid-70's albums, 'HIGH VOLTAGE' and 'T.N.T.'. The cream of these two sets was collected together and released in Britain, the album also confusingly titled 'HIGH VOLTAGE' (1976).

Over a series of increasingly successful albums, AC/DC showcased their defiantly un-PC (but always tongue-in-cheek!) songs with the ALEX HARVEY-inspired BON SCOTT leering over proceedings like a high priest of rock'n'roll debauchery. The likes of 'THE JACK' (a paean to VD), 'WHOLE LOTTA ROSIE' (BON apparently liked his women BIG) and 'SHE'S GOT BALLS' (he liked them with er, attitude as well . . .).

Just as the band were approaching world domination following the release of the landmark 'HIGHWAY TO HELL' album, BON's hard-boozing lifestyle finally caught up with him. On the 20th of February, 1980, after a heavy drinking session, he was found dead, having choked on his own vomit. Like KEITH MOON before him, BON was only 33 when he went to the great gig in the sky, closing the first legendary chapter in the still ongoing AC/DC story.
• **Footnote:** BON's best early work with The VALENTINES, The SPECTORS, etc, was posthumously released in '99 under 'THE LEGENDARY BON SCOTT' *(See For Miles'; SEECD 704)*

Mike SCOTT (see under ⇒ WATERBOYS)

SCROTUM POLES (see ⇒ Section 9: wee post-Punk groups)

SCUBA Z

Formed: Edinburgh . . . late 90's by the pseudonymous duo of JOHNSON WAX and BRIAN ANGER (one of them a LOST SOUL BAND refugee). Breakbeat entrepreneurs to a man, SCUBA Z set up their own label, 'Odd' records, for their acclaimed summer 2000 debut single, 'CALIFORNIAN PARANOIA'. Subsequent singles, 'HIP BOUNCE' and the recent 'INSTANT WHIP', gained support from the likes of PETE TONG, GROOVE ARMADA and even Steve Lamacq, reflecting their indie-infused dance sound.

JOHNSON WAX + BRIAN ANGER

Odd / not iss.

May 00. (12"/cd-s) *(odd 001 x/cd)* **CALIFORNIAN PARANOIA (radio edit) / SCREAMS DOWN CHIMNEYS. / CALIFORNIAN PARANOIA (ils remix)** ☐ -

Jul 00. (12"/cd-s) *(odd 002 x/cd)* **HIP BOUNCE (radio edit) / SHARON STONE'S HOUSE. / HIP BOUNCE (Blim's crazy geek mix)** ☐ -

Jun 01. (12") *(oddx 003)* **INSTANT WHIP (mixes:- radio / Terminalheads / Wax & Anger / Wax & Anger instrumental)** ☐ -

Jul 01. (cd) *(oddcd 004)* **THE VANISHING AMERICAN FAMILY** ☐ -
– Introduction / Californian paranoia / Hip bounce / The vanishing American family / Instant whip / Electrons are waves / I don't get out much / Sharon Stone's house / Sun sun sun / Super chi / This is the plastic men / King Horn (room 8, 31st floor) / Lo spontino / Screams down chimneys / A trip to Bikini Atoll.

SECOND HAND SOUL (see under ⇒ Glasgow Underground records)

SECRET GOLDFISH

Formed: Glasgow . . . mid-90's by PAUL TURNBULL and G LIRONEX (both ex-MACKENZIES), former FIZZBOMBS singer KATY McCULLARS and mysterious singer JOHN MOROSE. Like The POP GROUP fused with CAPTAIN BEEFHEART's 'Trout Mask Replica' period, The MACKENZIES released a couple of singles on the 'Ron Johnson' imprint, namely 'NEW BREED' and 'MEALY MOUTHS'. However, the short-lived act were better known for the funk-fuelled guitar-abuse of 'BIG JIM (THERE'S NO PUBS IN HEAVEN)', their contribution to the 'NME C86' cassette.

Nearly a decade later, The SECRET GOLDFISH (not the early 80's bunch who nearly issued the 11th 'Postcard' single, 'HEY MISTER' / 'POOREST BOY IN TOWN') came to the surface with indie gems, 'SEASICK' and 'COME UNDONE', before the release of their Stephen Lironi-produced debut set 'AQUA PET . . . YOU MAKE ME' (1996). Sounding much like The JESUS AND MARY CHAIN locked in a public toilet with JEFFERSON AIRPLANE and The NEW YORK DOLLS, the quartet quirkily took their name from an imaginary book credited in classic breakdown novel 'The Catcher in the Rye'. Other singles began to follow (most noteably the VIC GODARD co-penned 'SOMEWHERE IN THE WORLD' which also featured FRANCIS MACDONALD and STEVIE JACKSON), although it wasn't until summer '99 that the group returned ('JET STREAMS' was issued in 1997) with the soft and lingering third set, 'MINK RIOTS'. The album gained much attention from radio shows and music critics alike who were all baffled by the sudden change of this once indie experimental/pop collective.

The MACKENZIES (i.e. GRAHAM LIRONI and IAN BEVERIDGE) were back again in the late 90's under the guise of CABS-like, MOONGOOSE. They also were part of the 'Creeping Bent' roster, releasing a shared single in '99 before recording their 'LoLeVel' set the following year.
• **SECRET GOLDFISH covered:** THIS ARSEHOLE'S BEEN BURNED (Nectarine No.9) / SOMEWHERE IN CHINA (Shop Assistants).

MACKENZIES

G LIRONEX (b. GRAHAM LIRONI) – bass / **PAUL TURNBULL** – drums / **IAN BEVERIDGE** – keyboards

Ron Johnson / not iss.

Mar 86. (7") *(ZRON 8)* **NEW BREED. / DOG'S BREAKFAST** ☐ -

Feb 87. (12"ep) *(ZRON 18)* **MEALY MOUTHS / TROUBLE. / RADIO MEALY MOUTHS / B JIM JAM** ☐ -

— split after only two singles

SECRET GOLDFISH

— **TURNBULL + G LIRONEX** recruited **JOHN MOROSE** – guitar / **KATY McCULLARS** – vocals (ex-FIZZBOMBS)

Creeping Bent – Marina / not iss.

Jun 95. (7") *(bent 004)* **SEASICK. / VENUS BONDING (live)** ☐ -

Apr 96. (7") *(bent 008)* **COME UNDONE. / EVERYWHERE THAT YOU GO** ☐ -

Jun 96. (cd) *(bent 012cd – MA 19)* **AQUA PET . . . YOU MAKE ME** ☐ -
– Come undone / Tartan envy / The boy who left home to learn fear / Pet thang / Dandelion milk summer / Venus bonding: erotic Mars / I will see you through / I left one out, where did it go / Seasick / Glass mountain / The catalyst / Strawberry St. / Another short song about love and loss / Bandovian curve. *(re-iss. Dec00; same)*

Jul 96. (7") *(bent 016)* **DANDELION MILK SUMMER. / SNOWING IN MOUNT FLORIDA** [ ] [-]
(cd-ep) *(bent 015cd)* **E.K.O.K. EP** – – ('A'side) / Sunless / Ambulance / Afterhours – Intuition told me.
Nov 96. (7"ep) *(bent 018)* **VENUS BONDING EP** [ ] [-]
– Venus bonding / This arseholes been burned too many times before / Blue sky yesterday.

— **STEVEN SEVEN** – guitar; repl. LIRONEX who formed MONGOOSE

Mar 97. (7"m) *(bent 020)* **TARTAN ENVY. / RUDE AWAKENING / ALLEGRO** [ ] [-]
Apr 97. (cd) *(MA 26 – MACD 44712)* **JET STREAMS** [ ] [-]
– This arsehole's been burned too many times before / Casanova killer / Ambulance / Give him a great big kiss / Wasted in Carluke / Blue sky yesterday / Sunless / Tartan envy (luv'n haight version) / Allegro / Come as you are / Rude awakening / Everywhere that you go / Pink drone / Afterhours – Intuition told me.
(above issued on 'Marina')
Jul 97. (7") *(bent 024)* **GIVE HIM A GREAT BIG KISS. / (other track by Policecat)** [ ] [-]
Feb 98. (7") *(bent 032)* **PUNK DRONE. / (other track by Scientific Support Dept.)** [ ] [-]
Jul 98. (7"pink) *(ER 193)* **SOMEWHERE IN CHINA. / X-BOYFRIEND** [ ] [-]
(above issued on Spanish-based 'Elefant' through 'Creeping Bent')
Mar 99. (cd-ep) *(bent 038cd)* **SOMEWHERE IN THE WORLD / TOP OF THE WORLD / PINK WORLD** [ ] [-]
Jul 99. (cd) *(bent 044cd)* **MINK RIOTS** [ ] [-]
– Most days / All the sun / If you were me / Lashing out / World upside-down / Waterfall / 1 every 2 / Picture / Once before / Some kind of friend / Heal me. *(re-iss. Dec00; same)*
Aug 99. (7") *(bent 042)* **YOU'RE FUNNY 'BOUT THAT, AREN'T YOU. / (other track by Nectarine No.9)** [ ] [-]
Nov 99. (7") *(bent 048)* **4 EXCITED PEOPLE. / (other track by Vic Godard)** [ ] [-]

MONGOOSE

IAN BEVERIDGE + GRAHAM LIRONI – instruments, synths, etc

Oct 99. (7") *(bent 049)* **SANITISE ME. / (other track by Element)** [ ] [-]
Sep 00. (7"; as MONGOOSE Vs SCIENTIFIC SUPPORT DEPT.)
(bent 057) **SUBVERT NORMALITY. / GOOSE GREEN (extract)** [ ] [-]

Realler / not iss.

Jul 01. (cd) **LO-LEVEL** [-] [-] Danish
(above was scheduled by 'Creeping Bent' late '99; bent 052)

SET THE TONE

Formed: Glasgow . . . mid 1982 and were probably better known for including former SIMPLE MINDS drummer, KENNY HYSLOP, a New Wave veteran of also SLIK, ZONES and the SKIDS. With the latter band riding high in the charts, it no doubt helped SET THE TONE achieve a little fame of their own. A few minor UK hits came courtesy of two 'Island' singles, 'DANCE SUCKER' and 'RAP YOUR LOVE', while a mini-set, 'SHIFTIN' AIR AFFAIR' (1983), proved fruitless. In 1984, HYSLOP moved on to form the ONE O'CLOCK GANG (no, not that one!), although with song titles such as 'CLOSE YOUR EYES (AND THINK OF ENGLAND)', it was small wonder they did little up here.

KENNY HYSLOP (b.14 Feb'51, Helensburgh) – drums, etc (ex-SIMPLE MINDS, ex-SKIDS, ex-ZONES, ex-SLIK) / and others

Island / not iss.

Nov 82. (7"/12") *(WIP/12WIP 6836)* **DANCE SUCKER. / LET LOOSE** [62] [-]
Mar 83. (7"/12") *(IS/12IS 110)* **RAP YOUR LOVE. / SURPRISE** [67] [-]
Aug 83. (m-lp) *(ILPS 9736)* **SHIFTIN' AIR AFFAIR** [ ] [-]
– Rap your love / All tied up / Prove it / Skin me / Start the bus / Grind.

— split after above; HYSLOP formed . . .

ONE O'CLOCK GANG

Arista / not iss.

Aug 84. (7"/12") *(JOIN/+12 1)* **CARRY ME. / YOU ARE ON MY SIDE** [ ] [-]
Mar 85. (7"/12") *(JOIN/+12 2)* **CLOSE YOUR EYES (AND THINK OF ENGLAND). / POOR MAN'S FRIEND** [ ] [-]
May 85. (lp/c) *(207/407 121)* **ONE O'CLOCK GANG** [ ] [-]
– Close your eyes (and think of England) / Innocent / Trigger happy / Friday's child / Whipping boy / Never let you burn / Closer to the angels / Giving in / The bitter end / The drill.
May 85. (7") *(JOIN 3)* **TRIGGER HAPPY. / TESTIFY** [ ] [-]
(12"+=) *(JOIN12 3)* – Carry me.

— disbanded and unsure what HYSLOP did next

SHADOWLAND

Formed: Penicuik, Midlothian . . . 1988 by LEE VALENTINE, DAVE BLAIR, NORMAN BROWN and CHRIS COLVIN. After debut demo cassette, TONY HODGE came in for the departing COLVIN and BROWN. Prior to their debut proper the LP 'KALEIDOSCOPE' (1991) they were back as a quartet – GARY BONAR coming in for HODGE – with the addition of organist ROD SPARK, one-time member of the SECOND GENERATION.

Inspired by the "Madchester sound" fused with elements of Hammond-driven 60's outfit, The NICE, SHADOWLAND finally arrived on vinyl (after a couple of self-financed cassettes) in 1991. The aptly-titled 'KALEIDOSCOPE' set the groovy ball rolling, although accusations of ripping-off STONE ROSES clones The CHARLATANS, were indeed, questionable. After another cassette on the 'Groove Tunnel' imprint, SHADOWLAND duly switched to the German-based 'Twist', releasing the excellent 'SMOKE' single/EP early in 1993. Also featuring the terrific 'RAINBOW COLOURS' (also on that year's cassette) and a funky rendition of the Booker T's 'SOUL LIMBO', the band were truly reaching new heights. Disillusioned by the lack of interest in the southern-biased music journals, SHADOWLAND bowed out with a farewell gig early in 1994, although another great piece of psychedelia, 'SHE SELLS', was released posthumously; LEE and ROD subsequently turned up in Acid-Jazz outfit, The GROOVE TUNNEL.

• **Note:** not to be confused with the SHADOWLAND of 1990 who were on 'WEA' records, or for that matter the outfit in 1996 who released 'Mad As A Hatter'.

LEE VALENTINE – vocals, bass / **DAVE BLAIR** – guitar, vocals / **NORMAN BROWN** – bass, vocals / **CHRIS COLVIN** – drums

own label / not iss.

1989. (m-c) *(none)* **FESTIVE ROW** [ ] [-]
– Eight 'til late / Passionate expression / White lipstick / Jason dreams.

— **TONY HODGE** – drums; repl. COLVIN + BROWN

May 90. (m-c) *(none)* **ANGELA SAYS..** [ ] [-]
– A hundred years / Understand / The acid shop / The world in black and white / Throw a six (to start).

— added **ROD SPARK** – organ, vocals (ex-SECOND GENERATION)

— **GARY BONAR** – drums, percussion; repl. HODGE

Groove Tunnel / not iss.

May 91. (lp) *(GROOVELP 001)* **KALEIDOSCOPE** [ ] [-]
– The vow / City dreamers / Throw a six (to start) / Testament of hope / The love groove / Outside / Kaleidoscope / Just like Alice.
Jan 93. (c) *(GROOVELP 002)* **THE SHADOWLAND** [ ] [-]
– She sells / Rainbow colours / Yellow pink & blue / Paradise / The Sloan ranger / Vagabond / Turnaround / Introducing Mr.Sun.

Twist / not iss.

Jan 93. (7"green-ep) *(TWIST 4)* **SMOKE / SOMETHING NEW. / SOUL LIMBO / RAINBOW COLOURS** [-] [-] German
1995. (7") *(TWIST 11)* **SHE. / SHE SELLS** [-] [-] German

— had already split in 1994; LEE + ROD formed The GROOVE TUNNEL

SHAKE (see under ⇒ REZILLOS)

SHAKIN' PYRAMIDS

Formed: Glasgow . . . 1980 by frontman DAVIE DUNCAN, guitarists JAMES G CREIGHTON and RAILROAD KEN McLELLAN plus double bassist NICK CLARK. Influenced no doubt by the upsurge of Retro rockabilly outfits such as MATCHBOX, STRAY CATS and the POLECATS, Scotland's SHAKIN' PYRAMIDS took to the stage with all their colourful regalia and spiky-topped hairdos to boot. Their high-flying gigs were all the rage around the country, so up stepped CUBAN HEELS man JOHN MILARKY and ex-SUBS drummer ALI MacKENZIE of the newly formed 'Cuba Libre'. This label delivered a one-off single, 'REEFERBILLY BOOGIE' early in '81, before it – and the CUBAN HEELS – were licensed to 'Virgin' records.

Although both 'TAKE A TRIP' and 'TENNESSEE ROCK'N'ROLL' singles never made it chartwise, the 'PYRAMIDS first LP, 'SKIN 'EM UP' – another "reeference" to smoking the weed! – dented the UK Top 50 that Spring. A subsequent collaboration with 50's skiffle king, LONNIE DONEGAN, also went awry, although basically the EP was just updated, uptempo, upgrades of DONEGAN's past hits. Without CLARK, the SHAKIN' PYRAMIDS carried on for another set, 'CELTS & COBRAS' (1982) – with incidentally KIRSTY MacCOLL and JANE AIRE on backing vocals – although it was clear to everyone that their time had come and gone.

DAVIE DUNCAN – vocals, harmonica, percussion / **JAMES G. CREIGHTON** – guitar, vocals / **RAILROAD KEN McLELLAN** – guitar, vocals / **NICK CLARK** – double bass

Cuba Libre / not iss.

Jan 81. (7"m) *(DRINK 2)* **REEFERBILLY BOOGIE. / WAKE UP LITTLE SUZIE / HARMONICA LISA** [ ] [-]

Virgin / not iss.

Mar 81. (7"ep) *(VS 404)* **TAKE A TRIP / HELLBENT ON ROCKIN'. / REEFERBILLY BOOGIE / WAKE UP LITTLE SUZIE** [ ] [-]

Apr 81. (lp) *(V 2199)* **SKIN 'EM UP** [48] [-]
– Take a trip / Tennessee rock'n'roll / Let's go / Teenage boogie / Tired 'n' sleepy / Wild little Willie / Cry cry kitten / Sixteen chicks / Pretty bad blues / I got a baby / Sunset of my tears / Hellbent on rockin'. *(re-iss. Mar84; OVED 52)*

May 81. (7"ep) *(VS 415)* **TENNESSEE ROCK'N'ROLL / ALRIGHT ALRIGHT. / MUSKRAT / TOO N-NERVOUS TO ROCK** [ ] [-]

Nov 81. (7"ep; SHAKIN' PYRAMIDS & LONNIE DONEGAN) *(VS 460)* **CUMBERLAND GAP / WABASH CANNONBALL. / DON'T YOU ROCK ME DADDY-O / ONLY MY PILLOW** [ ] [-]

— now without NICK CLARK (session people took his place)

Mar 82. (7") *(VS 461)* **PHAROAH'S CHANT. / JUST ONE TIME** [ ] [-]
(above was to have been issued in Oct'81, abandoned for DONEGAN)

Jun 82. (7") *(VS 505)* **JUST A MEMORY. / WHO CARES** [ ] [-]

Jun 82. (lp) *(V 2216)* **CELTS & COBRAS** [ ] [-]
– Pharoah's chant / Like me with Noone / Pretty neat come on / Just a memory / Plain sailin' / Sugar bee / Rockin' mystique / Quit and split / It hurts to be in love / You can bet / Just rockin' / Ferocious / Who cares / Reeferbilly polka.

— split later in the year

SHAMEN

Formed: Aberdeen . . . 1984 as ALONE AGAIN OR (named after a LOVE track from '67) by COLIN ANGUS and McKENZIE brothers DEREK and KEITH. After two singles (one for 'Polydor'; DREAM COME TRUE), they became The SHAMEN, releasing the singles 'YOUNG TILL YESTERDAY' (1986) and 'SOMETHING ABOUT YOU' (1987) on their own 'Moksha' label. The debut album, 'DROP' (1987), followed soon after and at this point the band were touting a fairly derivative indie take on classic West coast psychedelia combined with overtly political/drug orientated lyrics.

As Angus became increasingly preoccupied with the nascent dance scene, however, DEREK McKENZIE split ranks and was replaced by WILL SINOTT. After the controversial single, 'JESUS LOVES AMERIKA' (1988), ANGUS and SINOTT relocated to LONDON, immersing themselves in the burgeoning acid house scene. The 'SHAMEN VS BAM BAM' (1988) moved the duo ever further into electronic territory and though the 'IN GORBACHEV WE TRUST' (1989) album fitted with the indie/dance crossover zeitgeist, The SHAMEN were one of the only acts to take the phenomenon to its ultimate conclusion.

After a last outing for 'Moksha', the band signed to the 'One Little Indian' label in 1989. Their second single for the label, 'PROGEN' (1990), finally saw The SHAMEN make their mark on the dance scene. Although it barely scraped into the charts, the track was huge on the club scene and climbed to No.4 upon its re-release (in remixed form) the following year. In addition to this pivotal track, the album 'EN-TACT' (1990), contained the liquid psychedelia of 'HYPERREAL' (featuring the velvet tones of Polish singer PLAVKA) and the dancefloor manifesto of 'MAKE IT MINE', both minor hit singles. Having initially had DJ EDDIE RICHARDS play acid house at their gigs, The SHAMEN had now developed the 'Synergy' live experience, a pioneering integration of live electronica and top flight DJ's (including the likes of MIXMASTER MORRIS and PAUL OKENFOLD) that attempted to create a cultural fusion between the excitement of live performance and the communal vibe of the party scene. Just as the band were beginning to realise their dreams, WILL SINOTT drowned while swimming off the coast of The Canary Islands in May '91.

ANGUS eventually decided to carry on and recruited RICHARD WEST aka Mr C, a veteran of the house scene, having DJ'd at the seminal RIP club. He was a natural choice, having rapped on the revamped 'PROGEN' single and collaborated on the 'Synergy' gigs, his inimitable cockney patois possessing a ragamuffin charm. He was also visually striking and along with SOUL FAMILY SENSATION singer JHELISSA ANDERSON, would become the public face of the The SHAMEN, ANGUS cannily content to communicate with the media via E-mail.

The 'L.S.I. (LOVE, SEX, INTELLIGENCE)' (1992) single introduced a more commercial sound to the new look SHAMEN, as did the unashamed pop/dance of controversial hit, 'EBENEEZER GOODE' (1992) (the question of whether Mr C did actually sing 'E's are good' was endlessly debated by those tireless moral guardians of the nation's wellbeing). Many longtime fans couldn't stomach the new sound although the band gained a whole new following of pop kids enamoured with cheeky chappy Mr C. The million selling 'BOSS DRUM' (1992) album combined the aforementioned chart fodder with typically SHAMEN-esque communiques on 'Archaic Revivals' and the like (i.e.'RE-EVOLUTION', the title track etc.). 1995 saw ex-SOUL II SOUL chanteuse VICTORIA WILSON JAMES replace ANDERSON and a new album in the shops, 'AXIS MUTATIS'. Although the record included the celebratory dance pop of single 'DESTINATION ESCHATON', overall it was more cerebral with a companion ambient album, 'ARBOR BONA/ARBOR MALA', released at the same time.

'HEMPTON MANOR' (1996) carried on The SHAMEN's overriding theme of transformation through mind altering substances and although the media profile of the band has shrunk considerably over the last couple of years, The SHAMEN have kept fans abreast of their activities with a rather fabby self-produced internet web-site, 'Nemeton'.

• **Songwriters:** All written by COLIN and DEREK, until latter's departure and replacement by the late WILL SINOTT. ANGUS & WEST took over in '91. Covered; GRIM REAPER OF LOVE (Turtles) / FIRE ENGINE + SLIP INSIDE THIS HOUSE (13th Floor Elevators) / LONG GONE (Syd Barrett) / SWEET YOUNG THING (Monkees) / PURPLE HAZE (Jimi Hendrix).

• **Trivia:** In Apr'88, they were dropped from a McEwans lager TV ad, because of their then anti-commercial approach.

ALONE AGAIN OR

COLIN ANGUS (b.24 Aug'61) – keyboards / **DEREK McKENZIE** (b.27 Feb'64) – vocals, guitar / **KEITH McKENZIE** (b.30 Aug'61) – drums

All One / not iss.

Dec 84. (7") *(ALG 1)* **DRUM THE BEAT (IN MY SOUL). / SMARTIE EDIT** [ ] [-]

All One – Polydor / not iss.

Mar 85. (7") *(ALG 2)* **DREAM COME TRUE. / SMARTER THAN THE AVERAGE BEAR** [ ] [-]
(12") *(ALGX 2)* – ('A'-Splintered version) / ('B'-Ursa Major) / Drum the beat (shall we dance?).

SHAMEN

— added **ALISON MORRISON** – bass, keyboards

One Big Guitar / not iss.

Apr 86. (12"ep) *(OBG 003T)* **THEY MAY BE RIGHT . . . BUT THEY'RE CERTAINLY WRONG** [ ] [-]
– Happy days / Velvet box / I don't like the way the world is turning.

— **PETER STEPHENSON** (b. 1 Mar,62, Ayrshire) – keyboards repl. ALISON

Moksha / not iss.

Nov 86. (7"m) *(SOMA 1)* **YOUNG TILL YESTERDAY. / WORLD THEATRE / GOLDEN HAIR** [ ] [-]
(12"m) *(SOMA 1T)* – (first 2 tracks) / It's all around / Strange days dream.

May 87. (7") *(SOMA 2)* **SOMETHING ABOUT YOU. / DO WHAT YOU WILL** [ ] [-]
(12"+=) *(SOMA 2T)* – Grim reaper of love.

Jun 87. (lp/c) *(SOMA LP/C 1)* **DROP** [ ] [-]
– Through with you / Something about you / Four letter girl / The other side / Passing away / Young till yesterday / Happy days / Where do you go / Through my window / I don't like the way the world is turning / World theatre / Velvet box. *(c+=)* – Do what you will. *(cd-iss. Nov88 ++=; SOMACD 1)* – Strange days dream. *(re-iss. Jan92 on 'Mau Mau' lp/c/cd; MAU/+MC/CD 613)*

Sep 87. (7") *(SOMA 3)* **CHRISTOPHER MAYHEW SAYS. / SHITTING ON BRITAIN** [ ] [-]
(12"+=) *(SOMA 3T)* – Fire engine / Christopher Mayhew says a lot.

— **WILL SINOTT** (b.23 Dec'60, Glasgow) – bass repl. DEREK (COLIN now vocals, guitar)

Feb 88. (7") *(SOMA 4)* **KNATURE OF A GIRL. / HAPPY DAYS** [ ] [-]
(12"+=) *(SOMA 4T)* – What's going down / Sub knature of a girl.

Ediesta / not iss.

Jun 88. (7") *(CALC 069)* **JESUS LOVES AMERIKA. / DARKNESS IN ZION** [ ] [-]
(12"+=) *(CALCT 069)* – Do what you will.
(cd-s++=) *(CALCCD 069)* – Sub knatural dub.

— now a duo of **COLIN + WILL**

Desire / not iss.

Nov 88. (12"; as SHAMEN VS BAM BAM) *(WANTX 10)* **TRANSCENDENTAL. / ('A'-housee mix)** [ ] [-]

Demon / Demon

Jan 89. (lp/c/cd) *(<FIEND/+C/CD 666>)* **IN GORBACHEV WE TRUST** [ ] [ ]
– Synergy / Sweet young thing / Raspberry infundibulum / War prayer / Adam

Strange / Jesus loves Amerika / Transcendental / Misinformation / Raptyouare / In Gorbachev we trust / (Fundamental). *(c+=)* – Resistance (once again). *(cd+=)* – Yellow cellaphane day / Mayhew speaks out.

— added **SANDRA** – percussion

		Moksha	not iss.
Apr 89.	(7") *(SOMA 6)* **YOU, ME & EVERYTHING. / RERAPTYOUARE**	[ ]	[-]

('A'-Evil edits; 12"+=/cd-s+=) *(SOMA 6 T/CD)* – Ed's bonus beats.

May 89. (10"m-lp/c/cd) *(SOMA LP/C/CD 3)* **PHORWARD** [ ] [-]
– You, me & everything (else) / Splash 2 / Negation state / Reraptyouare / SDD 89 / Phorward. *(free 7")* – (The S&N Sessions) *(c+=/cd+=)* – Happy days / Knature of a girl.

— **JOHN DELAFONS** – percussion repl. SANDRA

One Little Indian / Epic

Nov 89. (12"ep/cd-ep) *(30TP 12/7CD)* **OMEGA AMIGO / OMEGA A. / OMEGA PRE-MIX / PH 1** [ ] [-]

Mar 90. (7") *(36 TP7)* **PRO>GEN (Beatmasters mix). / ('A'dub version)** [55] [-]
(12") *(36 TP12L)* – ('A'-C-mix F+) / ('B'side) / Lightspan (Ben Chapman mix).
(c-s++=) *(36 TP7C)* – ('A'-Paul Oakenfold 'Land Of Oz' mix).
(12") *(36 TP12)* – (above mix) / Lightspan (Ben Chapman mix).
(cd-s) *(36 TP7CD)* – (above 2 mixes) / ('A'-Steve Osborne mix).

Sep 90. (7"/c-s) *(46 TP7/+C)* **MAKE IT MINE (Lenny D vox). / ('A'-Evil Ed mix)** [42] [ ] Feb92
(12"/cd-s) *(46TP 12/7CD)* *<742 36/41>* – ('A'-Lenny D mix) / ('A'-Progress mix) / ('A'-Lenny D vox) / Something wonderful.
(12") *(46 TP12L)* – ('A'-Evil Ed mix) / ('A'-Outer Limits mix) / Pro>gen (Land of Oz mix) / ('A'-Micro minimal mix).

Oct 90. (cd)(c)(2x12"lp) *(TPLP 22 CD/MC/SP)* *<48722>* **EN-TACT** [31] [ ]
– Human N.R.G. / Pro>gen (land of Oz) / Possible worlds / Omega amigo / Evil is even / Hypereal / Lightspan / Make it mine V 2.5 / Oxygen restriction / Here are my people (orbital delays expected). *(cd+=)* – (Oxygen reprise (V 2.0 mix) / Human NRG (Massey mix) / Make it mine (pirate radio mix) / (etc.) *(re-iss. Nov90 lp; TPLP 22)*

Mar 91. (7"/c-s) *(48 TP7/+C)* **HYPERREAL (William Orbit mix). / ('A'-lp version)** [29] [-]
(12") *(48 TP12)* – ('A'versions incl. Maguire + dub) / In the bag.
(cd-s) *(48 TP7CD)* – ('A'versions incl. Meatbeat Manifesto mix) / In the bag.
(12") *(48 TP12L)* – ('A'-Meatbeat Manifesto mixes) / ('A'-Maguire + Dirty dubbing mixes).
(above featured **PLAVKA** (b. Poland) – vocals)

— on the 23rd May '91, WILL drowned while on holiday abroad

Jul 91. (7"/c-s) *(52 TP7/+C)* *<74044>* **MOVE ANY MOUNTAIN – PROGEN '91 (Beatmasters edit). / ('A'-The Goat From The Well Hung Parliament mix)** [4] [38] Nov91
(12") *(52 TP12)* *<74043>* – ('A'-mixes; Landslide / Devil / Rude / R.I.P. in the Land Of Oz).
(cd-s) *(52 TP7CD)* *<74044>* – ('A'mixes; Beatmasters / Landslide / F2 Mello / Mountains in the sky).

Sep 91. (3xlp/c/cd) *(TPLP 32/+MC/CD)* **PROGENCY 2(8 versions)** [23] [-]

— New line-up **COLIN** plus **MR.C** – vocals, rhythm / + **JHELSA ANDERSON** – backing vox (ex-SOUL FAMILY SENSATION) / **BOB BREEKS** – live keyboards / **GAVIN KNIGHT** – live drums / **RICHARD SHARPE** – occasional analogue

Jun 92. (7"/12") *(68 TP 7/12)* *<74437>* **L.S.I. (LOVE SEX INTELLIGENCE). / POSSIBLE WORLDS** [6] [ ]
(c-s+=/cd-s+=) *(68 TP 7 C/CD)* – Make it mine (Moby mix).

Aug 92. (7"/c-s) *(78 TP7/+C)* **EBENEEZER GOODE. / ('A'dub)** [1] [ ]
(12"+=/cd-s+=) *(78 TP 12/7CD)* – ('A'mix) / L.S.I. (mix).

Oct 92. (lp/c/cd) *(TPLP 42/+C/CD)* *<52925>* **BOSS DRUM** [3] [ ]
– Boss drum / L.S.I.: Love Sex Intelligence / Space time / Librae solidi denari / Ebeneezer Goode (Beatmasters mix) / Comin' on / Phorever people / Fatman / Scientas / Re: evolution.

Oct 92. (7"/c-s) *(88 TP 7/+C)* *<74953>* **BOSS DRUM. / OMEGA AMIGO** [4] [ ] Apr93
(cd-s+=) *(88 TP7CD)* – (3 'A'mixes).
(12"-2 diff.) *(88 TP12)* – (5 'A'mixes either J.Robertson or Beatmasters).
(cd-s++=) *(88 TP7CDL)* – ('A'-Steve Osbourne mixes & Youth).

Dec 92. (7"ep/c-ep/12"ep/cd-ep) *(98 TP 7/7C/12/CD)* *<74898>* **PHOREVER PEOPLE. / ('A'dub + 'A'-Hyperreal orbit mix)** [5] [ ]
(cd-s++=) *(98 TP7CDL)* – ('A'mixes).

Feb 93. (c-s; as SHAMEN with TERENCE McKENNA) *(118 TP7C)* **RE:EVOLUTION / ('A'mix)** [18] [ ]
(12"+=/cd-s+=) *(118 TP 12/7CD)* – ('A'mixes).

Oct 93. (c-ep/12"ep/cd-ep) *(108 TP 7C/12/7CD)* **THE S.O.S. EP** [14] [ ]
– Comin' on / Make it mine / Possible worlds.
(cd-ep) *(108 TP7CDL)* – ('A'mixes).

— now with vocalist **VICTORIA WILSON-JAMES**

Aug 95. (c-s) *(128 TP7C)* *<78038>* **DESTINATION ESCHATON (Beatmasters mix) / ('A'-Deep melodic mix)** [15] [ ]
(cd-s) *(128 TP7CD)* – ('A'-Shamen acid: Escacid) / (2 'A'-Hardfloor mixes).
(cd-s) *(128 TP7CDL)* – (2 'A'-Basement Boys mixes) / (3 'A'-Beatmasters mixes).

Oct 95. (c-s) *(138 TP7C)* **TRANSAMAZONIA (Beatmasters mix) / ('A'-Visnadi mix) / ('A'-Watershed instrumental) / ('A'-LTJ Bukin mix)** [28] [ ]
(12"+=) *(138 TP12)* – ('A'-Deep dish mix).
(cd-s) *(138 TP7CD)* – (6 'A'mixes including; Alex Party Aguirre / Zion Train).
(cd-s+=) *(138 TP7CDL)* – ('A'-Nuv Idol mix).

Oct 95. (d-lp/c/cd) *(TPLP 52/+C/CD)* *<57796>* **AXIS MUTATIS** [27] [ ]
– Destination Eschaton / Transamazonia / Conquistador / Mauna Kea to Andromeda / Neptune / Prince of Popacatapertl / Heal the separation / Persephone's quest / Moment / Axis mundi / Eschaton omega (deep melodic techno). *(cd/c/d-lp with other cd/c/d-lp) (TPLP 52 CDL/CL/L)* **ARBOR BONA / ARBOR MALA** – Asynptotic Escaton / Sefirotic axis (a)(b)(c) Formation (d) Action / Extraterrestrial / Deneter / Beneath the underworld / Xochipilis return / Rio Negro / Above the underworld / A moment in dub / Pizarro in Paradiso / West of the underworld / Anticipation Escaton (be ready for the storm) / Out in the styx.

Feb 96. (c-s) *(158 TP7C)* **HEAL (THE SEPARATION) / ('A'mix)** [31] [ ]
(cd-s) *(158 TP7CD)* – ('A'mixes; organ / science park / PM Dawn / Steve Osborne ambient – H.E.L.P. breakfast / Beatmasters / foul play vocal).
(cd-s) *(158 TP7CDL)* – ('A'mixes; mighty organ / live '95) / Boss drum (Lionrock dub) / Phorever people (Todd Terry).

Oct 96. (3x12"lp/c/cd) *(TPLP 62/+C/CD)* **HEMPTON MANOR** [ ] [-]
– Freya / Urpflanze / Cannabeo / Khat / Bememe / Indica / Rausch / Kava / El-fin / Monoriff.

Dec 96. (c-s) *(169 TP7C)* **MOVE ANY MOUNTAIN '96 / ('A'mix)** [35] [ ]
(12"/cd-s) *(169 TP 12P/7CD)* – (mixes; Beatmasters radio / Tony De Vit edit) / Indica / L.S.I. (Beat edit).
(cd-s) *(169 TP7CDL)* – (mixes:- Tomka / Tony De Vit / Sneaker Pimps / Beatmasters 12").

Jan 97. (cd/c) *(TPLP 72 CD/C)* **THE SHAMEN COLLECTION** (compilation) [ ] [ ]

Jan 97. (cd/c) *(TPLP 72 CDR/CR)* **THE SHAMEN REMIX COLLECTION – STARS ON 45** (compilation) [ ] [ ]
(both above re-iss. Apr98 d-cd/d-c; TPLP 72 CDE/CE) – hit UK No.26

Moksha / Moksha

Oct 98. (cd-ep) *(<MOKSHA 3CD>)* **UNIVERSAL (mixes:- 1999 vocal / 187 B.P. metamix (major) / 1999 dance vocal / Sharp trade life dub / Mr.C tech house mix / 187 Lockdown dark dub)** [ ] [ ] Nov98

– compilations, others, etc. –

Aug 88. (lp/c)(cd) *Materiali Sonori; (MASO 33041/+C)(MASOCD 9008)* **STRANGE DAY DREAMS** [-] [-] Italy
(re-iss. cd Oct91 imported) (re-iss. Jan93; same)

Dec 89. (m-lp/cd) *Communion; (COMM 4 LP/CD)* **WHAT'S GOING DOWN** [-] [ ]

Nov 93. (cd/c/lp) *Band Of Joy; (BOJ CD/MC/LP 006)* **ON AIR (live BBC sessions)** [61] [-]
(cd re-iss. Mar98 on 'Strange Fruit'; SFRSCD 055)

Mar 98. (12") *Moksha; (AGC 002)* **U-NATIONS** [ ] [-]

Mar 02. (cd) *Music Club; (MCCD 484)* **HYSTERICOOL – THE BEST OF THE ALTERNATIVE MIXES** [ ] [-]

SHARP BOYS (see ⇒ Section 9: Dance/Rave)

SHATTERHAND

Formed: Bainsford, Falkirk . . . 1998 by brothers STUART and DAVE MacINTOSH, along with RAMS and BRIAN HASTINGS; a demo tape 'A MESS OF EMOTION' was issued in '99. Favourites on the Central Region punk scene, SHATTERHAND could've been pitched somewhere between the 3-chord cartoon punks GREEN DAY and the jangly melancholia of The LEMONHEADS or even The GOO GOO DOLLS. SHATTERHAND began with a small cluster of low-brow shows in Falkirk, supporting the likes of VANILLA POD and punk upstarts TURTLEHEAD. After continuous writing for a solid year, they headed into Riverside studios to cut their debut set 'WRECKAGE' (2000), issued by independent imprint 'Mythical' and featuring live faves 'ACT YOUR AGE' and the hard-edged punk anthem 'MOVING TARGETS'. Heavy touring followed, and bassist RAMS found the commitment too staggering, so he departed and was replaced by MONTY. Their sophomore set, 'PLANTING SEEDS' (2001), displayed a more mature and harmonic sound, as well as an honest ode to Scotland in the form of track 'BUCKFAST COUNTRY'. The band were kept busy writing and touring the following year, with plans of a new album and nationwide tour in the works.

STUART MacINTOSH – vocals / **DAVE MacINTOSH** – guitar / **RAMS** – bass / **BRIAN HASTINGS** – drums

Mythical not iss.

1999. (cd-ep) *(CD 001)* **A MESS OF EMOTION** [ ] [-]
– Hourglass / Miss indecision / Barfly / All been said before.

Jul 00. (cd) *(MR2K 002CD)* **WRECKAGE** [ ] [-]
– Miss indecision / Second guessing / Another broken heart / Act your age / 4th and 1 / Nation of animal lovers / Roller coaster / Don't let me be there / Devastated / Hourglass / Porno guy / All been said before / Token happy song / Barfly.

— **MONTY** – bass; repl. RAMS

Jun 01. (cd-ep) *(MR2K 003CD)* **MAKE A DIFFERENCE** [ ] [-]
– Make a difference / Planting seeds / 7 hours too late / 4th and 1 (remastered).

Jul 01. (cd) *(MR2K 004)* **PLANTING SEEDS** [ ] [-]
– Unbalanced / Smalltalk / In yr world / Make a difference / Dreams of flying / Long way home / 3am / Talk show mentality / Planting seeds / 7 hours too late / Scorched earth policy / Buckfast country / George lassoes the Moon.

Paul SHIELDS

Born: Glasgow. A relative newcomer to the world of DJ-ing and the thriving Scottish club scene, PAUL came to the attention of the public by playing the decks at Glasgow's Pivo Pivo, Loch Lomond's Duck Bay Marina and The Bar Budda in Helensburgh. Under the banner of 'Back2Roots' (the name incidentally of his double-CD collection), SHIELDS pounds his creative beats'n'rhythms onto classic FM guitar-rock tracks by such luminaries as SPRINGSTEEN, DYLAN, BLACK CROWES, LED ZEPPELIN, CSN&Y, R.E.M., OASIS and our own TEENAGE FANCLUB. Rock or dance purists beware, this man might surprise your senses.

SHOP ASSISTANTS

Formed: Edinburgh ... 1984 originally as BUBA & THE SHOP ASSISTANTS by DAVID KEEGAN, AGGI, SARAH KNEALE, ANN DONALD and LAURA McPHAIL. Following an extremely limited debut single, 'SOMETHING TO DO', on the 'Villa 21' label, the band (now without AGGI who'd been replaced by ALEX TAYLOR) released a more widely distributed follow-up, 'ALL DAY LONG' on the 'Subway Organisation' imprint. Amid increasing critical acclaim from the London-based music press, The SHOP ASSISTANTS topped the indie charts with third single, 'SAFETY NET', the first release on KEEGAN's '53rd & 3rd' label.

1986 proved to be a pivotal year as the band signed to Chrysalis offshoot 'Blue Guitar' and released their eponymous debut album, in addition contributing the delicate strum of 'IT'S UP TO YOU' to the NME's C86 tape and the noisier retro-pop of 'TRAIN FROM KANSAS CITY' to Sounds magazine's 'Showcase' sampler.

Despite their ringing, girlish charm, mainstream chart success wasn't on the cards and the band fell apart the following year with TAYLOR going off to form MOTORCYCLE BOY. A subsequent reformation in 1990 was decidedly low key, the band releasing material on the capital's 'Avalanche' label. With KEEGAN later joining The PASTELS on a full-time basis, it seems like the band have finally shut up shop for good.

• **Trivia:** In the early 90's, the 1986 line-up sued their management company, 'Globeshire', for being unforthcoming with a 5-figure royality share. Due to neglect, the band had to pay over a fee of £1,000 to the taxman as they weren't registered for VAT.

AGGI – vocals (of JUNIPER BELL BER) / **DAVID KEEGAN** – guitar / **SARAH KNEALE** – bass / **LAURA MacPHAIL** – drums / plus guests **STEPHEN PASTEL** – producer, b.vocals / **ANN DONALD** – drums (later of FIZZBOMBS)

Villa 21 not iss.

Nov 84. (7"; as BUBA & THE SHOP ASSISTANTS) *(002)*
SOMETHING TO DO. / DREAMING BACKWARDS [ ] [-]

— **ALEX(ANDRA) TAYLOR** – vocals; repl. AGGI who later joined The SUGARCUBES

Subway not iss.

Aug 85. (7"ep) *(SUBWAY 1)* **ALL DAY LONG / ALL THAT EVER MATTERED. / IT'S UP TO YOU / SWITZERLAND** [ ] [-]

53rd & 3rd not iss.

Feb 86. (7"/12") *(AGARR 001/+12)* **SAFETY NET. / SOMEWHERE IN CHINA / ALMOST MADE IT** [ ] [-]

Blue Guitar not iss.

Sep 86. (7") *(AZUR 2)* **I DON'T WANNA BE FRIENDS WITH YOU. / LOOK BACK** [ ] [-]
(12"+=) *(AZURX 2)* –

Nov 86. (lp/c) *(AZ/ZAZ LP 2)* **THE SHOP ASSISTANTS** [ ] [-]
– I don't wanna be friends with you / All day long / Before I wake / Caledonian road / All that ever mattered / Fixed grin / Somewhere in China / Train from Kansas City / Home again / Seems to be / All of the time / What a day to die / Nature lover. *(cd-iss. Jun97 as 'WILL ANYTHING HAPPEN' on 'Overground'; OVER 62CD)*

— disbanded early 1987; ALEX joined MOTORCYCLE BOY. Re-formed late '89, McPHAIL now on bass + **MARGARITA** – drums

Avalanche not iss.

Jan 90. (7"flexi-ep) *(AGAP 001C)* **HERE IT COMES / I'D RATHER BE WITH YOU / YOU TRIP ME UP / THE OTHER ONE** [ ] [-]
(7"flexi-box-ep) *(AGAP 001B)* – (first 2 tracks) / Look out / Adrenalin.

May 90. (7"/c-s) *(AGAP 003/+MC)* **BIG 'E' POWER. / SHE SAID** [ ] [-]
(12"+=/cd-s+=) *(AGAP 003 T/CD)* – One more time / ('A'version).

— split after above and KEEGAN joined The PASTELS full-time

SHRIEK

Formed: Glasgow . . . 1993 by guitar-playing singer ROZ CAIRNEY, along with her rhythm men of MARK and GORDON. Having been influenced by her piano-playing Irish mother, ROZ set about on making this band quite unique in both lyrics and deep lilting content. After an appearance (with the track 'SHAVED') on a 'Club Spangle!' V/A EP (and a collaborative effort with CLARE GROGAN in May '94), the trio's debut single for 'Deceptive', 'CALL YOURSELF A LOVER' and its B-side 'CRUSH', went down a storm at London gigs. A second 45, 'GIRL MEETS GIRL', was to become their last outing in March '95, 'Deceptive' (also home to COLLAPSED LUNG and ELASTICA) letting them go when the band wanted to release a full-set much too quickly; SHRIEK found another deal, although nothing was subsequently heard of them.

ROZ CAIRNEY – vocals, guitar / **MARK** – bass / **GORDON** – drums

Deceptive not iss.

Oct 94. (7") *(BLUFF 006)* **CALL YOURSELF A LOVER. / CRUSH** [ ] [-]
(w/free flexi) – Violent mind.

Mar 95. (7") *(BLUFF 012)* **GIRL MEETS GIRLS. / NO** [ ] [-]
(cd-s+=) *(BLUFF 012CD)* – Scared.

— sadly, this was the last we heard of SHRIEK

SILENCERS

Formed: Glasgow ... 1986 by JIMMIE O'NEIL and CHA BURNZ, who had originally played together in the 'Virgin'-signed post-punk outfit, FINGERPRINTZ (see Great Alternative & Indie Discography). Delving back even further into time, O'NEIL had briefly toyed with the stage name, JIMMY SHELTER. Following the demise of FINGERPRINTZ, JIMMY hooked up with JACQUI BROOKS in a duo called INTRO, releasing a one-off single for 'M.C.A.' in 1983, 'Lost Without Your Love'. He subsequently wrote and co-produced the bulk of BROOKS' 1984 solo set, 'Sob Stories'.

Signed to 'R.C.A.' and boasting a line-up completed by JOE DONNELLY and MARTIN HANLON, The SILENCERS emerged in 1987 with a debut single, 'PAINTED MOON' and album, 'A LETTER FROM ST. PAUL'. Under the managerial auspices of Scots svengali, BRUCE FINDLAY (who'd already masterminded the career of SIMPLE MINDS), the group gained exposure via a Stateside support slot to U2 with whom, to some extent, they shared a grand Celtic-rock vision. Like BIG COUNTRY before them, The SILENCERS initially charmed America where their debut single just nudged into the Top 100. Yet while they were warmly received back home in Scotland, their attempts to break into the UK chart were consistently frustrated. This despite another helping of fired-up, melodic pop-rock in the shape of 'A BLUES FOR BUDDHA' (1988). Granted, the final single to be lifted from the latter set, 'SCOTTISH RAIN', scraped into the Top 75 yet this hardly reflected their popularity north of the border.

A new line-up of O'NEIL, BURNS, DAVY CRIGHTON, LEWIS RANKIN, TONY SOUAVE and JAMES 'JINKY' GILMOUR took the band into the new decade with 'DANCE TO THE HOLY MAN' (1991). Heralding a folkier, more acoustic-rooted approach, the record finally broke The SILENCERS into the UK Top 40 although again the singles failed to make any headway. Perhaps the group's most realistic chance of a hit came with 1993's anthemic 'I CAN FEEL IT', yet incredibly the track stalled just outside the Top 60. The accompanying album, 'SECONDS OF PLEASURE' (1993), wound up being the band's last, and although a folkier incarnation of The SILENCERS cut a further trio of singles in 1995 (one of which, 'WILD MOUNTAIN THYME', was used on a Scottish Tourist Board TV ad), O'NEIL finally threw in the towel in 1996.

• **Songwriters:** O'NEIL + BURNS except GIMME SHELTER (Rolling Stones) / and a few trad numbers; PRETTY BOY FLOYD.

• **Trivia:** Watch out for a different (American) SILENCERS who appeared during the latter half of the 90's with the set, 'Receiving'.

JIMMIE O'NEIL – vocals, guitar / **CHA BURNZ** – guitar / **JOE DONNELLY** – bass / **MARTIN HANLON** – drums

R.C.A. R.C.A.

Apr 87. (7") *(HUSH 1) <5220>* **PAINTED MOON. / HERE COMES THE TRAIN** [ ] [82] Jul87
('A'-Blues mix-12"+=) *(HUSHT 1)* – Tickey to Disneyland.
(re-iss. Jun88; same) – hit UK No.57

May 87. (lp/c/cd) *(PL/PK/PD 71336) <6442>* **A LETTER FROM ST. PAUL** [ ] [ ] Jul87
– Painted moon / I can't cry / Bullets and blue eyes / God's gift / I see red / I ought to know / A letter from St. Paul / Possessed / Blue desire. *(cd+=)* – Painted moon (extended remix). *(cd re-iss. Sep97; same)*

Jul 87. (7") *(HUSH 2)* **I CAN'T CRY. / CRUCIFY ME** [ ] [ ]
(12"+=) *(HUSHT 2)* – Blue desire.

Jan 88. (7") *(PB 41707)* **I SEE RED (remix). / RETURN TO CENTRE** [ ] [ ]
(12"+=) *(PT 41708)* – God's gift.
(cd-s++=) *(PD 41708)* – Painted Moon (blues mix).

Oct 88. (7") *(PB 42283)* **ANSWER ME. / MY LOVE IS LIKE A WAVE – RAZOR BLADE (reprise)** [ ] [ ]
(12"+=) *(PT 42284)* – Not quite the blues / Overboard.
(cd-s+=) *(PD 42284)* – Not quite the blues / A blues for Buddha.

Nov 88. (lp/c/cd) *(PL/PK/PD 71859) <9960>* **A BLUES FOR BUDDHA** [ ] [ ] Feb90
– Answer me / Scottish rain / The real McCoy / A blues for Buddha / Walk with the night / Razor blades of love / Skin games / Wayfaring stranger / Sacred child / Sand and stars. *(cd+c+=)* – My love is like a wave – Razor blade (reprise). *(re-dist.Feb89 + Aug89 + Sep97; same)*

Dec 88. (7") **RAZOR BLADES OF LOVE. / SKIN GAMES** [ ] [-]
(12"+=/cd-s+=) – Wayfaring stranger.

Feb 89. (7") *(PB 42585)* **THE REAL McCOY. / WHITE CARNATION** [ ] [ ]
(12"+=/cd-s+=) *(PT/PD 42586)* – God's gift / Blood rosary.

May 89. (7"/c-s) *(PB/PK 42701)* **SCOTTISH RAIN. / A BLUES FOR BUDDAH** [71] [ ]
(12"+=/cd-s+=) *(PT/PD 42702)* – I can't cry / Gimme shelter.

— **O'NEILL + BURNS** plus **DAVY CRIGHTON** – electric violin, mandolin, keyboards / **LEWIS RANKINE** – bass / **TONY SOUAVE** – drums / and **JAMES 'Jinky' GILMOUR** – vocals, acoustic guitar

Mar 91. (7"/c-s) **I WANT YOU. / PAINTED MOON** [ ] [ ]
(12"+=/cd-s+=) – Rosanne / Guitar atmosphere.

Mar 91. (cd/c/lp) *(PD/PK/PL 74924) <3092>* **DANCE TO THE HOLY MAN** [39] [ ]
– Singing Ginger / Robinson Crusoe in New York / Bulletproof heart / The art of self deception / I want you / One inch in Heaven / Hey Mr. Bank manager / This is serious – John the revelation / Afraid of love / Rosanne / Electric storm / When the night comes down / Robinson rap. *(cd+=/c+=)* – Just can't be bothered / Cameras and colliseums. *(cd re-iss. Sep97; same)*

May 91. (7"/c-s) **BULLETPROOF HEART. / SLEEP SONG** [ ] [-]
(12"/cd-s) – ('A'side) / Pretty Boy Floyd / Ordinary man / Cajun jam.
(12") – ('A'side) / ('A'dub version) / ('A'-Underworld mix).

Jul 91. (7"/c-s/12"/cd-s) **THIS IS SERIOUS (long). / WALK WITH THE NIGHT (live) / ONE INCH OF HEAVEN (live)** [ ] [ ]

— **STEVE KANE** – bass, double bass + **PHIL KANE** – keyboards; repl. RANKINE + CRIGHTON

— added **HAMISH MOORE** – pipes + **IAN MUIRHEAD** – flugelhorn

May 93. (7"/c-s) *(74321 14711-7/-4)* **I CAN FEEL IT. / GOLD BARS AND CANDYBARS** [62] [-]
(ext;12"+=/cd-s+=) *(74321 14711-6/-2)* – This is serious (club).

May 93. (cd/c/lp) *(74321 14113-2/-4/-1)* **SECONDS OF PLEASURE** [52] [-]
– I can feel it / Sylvie / Cellar of dreams / Small mercy / It's only love / Misunderstood / Life can be fatal / The unhappiest man / Walkman's and magnums / Streetwalker song / My prayer / Unconscious. *(cd re-iss. Feb98; same)*

— **JIMMIE + / MILLA** fiddle, vocals, etc

Permanent not iss.

Mar 95. (c-s) *(CASPERM 23)* **WILD MOUNTAIN THYME / DARK COMMAND** [ ] [-]
(cd-s+=) *(CDSPERM 23)* – Freedom.
(above single is the theme from the Scottish Tourist Board TV ad)

Mar 95. (cd/c) *(PERM CD/MC 31)* **SO BE IT** [ ] [-]
– Something worth fighting for / Killing for God / 27 / I woke up / Number one friend / Flying / Hello stranger / Henry's black shadow / Wild mountain thyme / Listen / About the sea / I believe in you. *(cd re-iss. Mar98 on 'Indelible'; INDELCD 9)*

Aug 95. (c-s) *(CASPERM 24)* **NUMBER ONE FRIEND /** [ ] [-]
(cd-s+=) *(CDSPERM 24)* –

— disbanded the following year

– compilations, etc. –

Jul 97. (cd) *Total Energy; (NER 3011)* **BLOOD AND RAIN (THE SINGLES '86-'96)** [ ] [-]
– Painted moon (Blues mix) / I can't cry / I see red / Answer me / Scottish rain / The real McCoy / Razor blades of love / Bulletproof heart / Hey Mr Bank manager / I want you / I can feel it (extended) / Cellar of dreams / Number one friend / Wild mountain thyme / Something worth fighting for.

May 01. (cd) *Last Call; (306820-2)* **A NIGHT OF ELECTRIC SILENCE** [ ] [-]
– A Glasgow kiss / Bulletproof heart / Painted moon / Sacred child / I can feel it / 27 / Partytime in Heaven / Receiving / Cameras & collesseums / One inch of heaven / Sylvie / I want you / Wild mountain thyme / The real McCoy / La chanson de prevert. *(re-iss. Apr02 on 'Uncanny'; CANNYCD 2)*

SILICONE SOUL (see under ⇒ Soma records)

SIMPLE MINDS

Formed: Gorbals, Glasgow . . . early 1978 after four members (frontman JIM KERR, guitarists CHARLIE BURCHILL and DUNCAN BARNWELL and drummer BRIAN McGEE) had left punk band, JOHNNY & THE SELF ABUSERS. Taking the group name from a line in a BOWIE song, the band gigged constantly at Glasgow's Mars Bar, finally being signed on the strength of a demo tape by local Edinburgh music guru and record store owner, Bruce Findlay. Also becoming the band's manager, Findlay released their debut album, 'LIFE IN A DAY' (1979) on his own 'Zoom' label, the record scoring a Top 30 placing.

Its minor success led to a deal with 'Arista' who released the follow-up, 'REEL TO REEL CACOPHONY' (1979), a set of post-punk, electronic experimentation best sampled on the evocative synth spirals of 'FILM THEME'. SIMPLE MINDS took another about turn with 'EMPIRES AND DANCE' (1980), an album heavily influenced by the harder end of the Euro-disco movement, the abrasive electro pulse of the 'I TRAVEL' single becoming a cult dancefloor hit. Initially released as a double set, 'SONS AND FASCINATION' / 'SISTER FEELINGS CALL' (1981), marked the first fruits of a new deal with 'Virgin' and gave the group their first major success, peaking at No.11 in the UK chart on the back of the Top 50 single, 'LOVE SONG'.

SIMPLE MINDS were beginning to find their niche, incorporating their artier tendencies into more conventional and melodic song structures. This was fully realised with 'NEW GOLD DREAM (81-82-83-84)' (1982), a record which marked the pinnacle of their early career and one which arguably, they've since failed to better. Constructed with multiple layers of synth, the band crafted a wonderfully evocative and atmospheric series of undulating electronic soundscapes, often married to pop hooks, as with 'GLITTERING PRIZE' and 'PROMISED YOU A MIRACLE' (the group's first Top 20 hits), but more effectively allowed to veer off into dreamier territory on the likes of 'SOMEONE SOMEWHERE IN SUMMERTIME'. While SIMPLE MINDS and U2 were often compared in terms of their anthemic tendencies, a closer comparison could be made, in spirit at least, between 'NEW GOLD..' and U2's mid-80's experimental classic, 'The Unforgettable Fire'. The album reached No.3 in the UK charts, a catalyst for SIMPLE MINDS' gradual transformation from an obscure cult act to stadium candidates, this process helped along nicely by the success of 'SPARKLE IN THE RAIN' (1984), the band's first No.1 album. Though it lacked the compelling mystery of its predecessor, the record featured such memorable SIMPLE MINDS' moments as 'UP ON THE CATWALK', 'SPEED YOUR LOVE TO ME' and an inventive cover of Lou Reed's 'STREET HASSLE'. For better or worse, the album also boasted SIMPLE MINDS' first truly BIG anthem, the sonic bombast of 'WATERFRONT'. But the track that no doubt finally alienated the old faithful was 'DON'T YOU (FORGET ABOUT ME)', the theme tune for quintessentially 80's movie, 'The Breakfast Club' and surely one of the most overplayed records of that decade. The song had stadium-friendly written all over it, subsequently scaling the US charts and paving the way for the transatlantic success of 'ONCE UPON A TIME' (1985). Unashamedly going for the commmercial pop/rock jugular, the album was heady, radio orientated stuff, the likes of 'ALIVE AND KICKING', 'SANCTIFY YOURSELF' and 'OH JUNGLELAND' among the most definitive anthems of the stadium rock genre.

Predictably, the critics were unimpressed, although they didn't really stick the knife in until the release of the overblown 'BELFAST CHILD', a UK No.1 despite its snoozeworthy meandering and vague political agenda. The accompanying album, 'STREET FIGHTING YEARS' (1989) brought more of the same, although it cemented SIMPLE MINDS' position among the coffee table elite.

Down to a trio of KERR, BURCHILL and and drummer, MEL GAYNOR, the group hired a team of session players for their next album, 'REAL LIFE' (1991), the record almost spawning a Top 5 hit in the celebratory 'LET THERE BE LOVE'. Although the album narrowly missed the UK top spot, it held nothing new, nor did their next release, 'GOOD NEWS FROM THE NEXT WORLD' (1995). Although KERR and BURCHILL brought back DEREK

FORBES and signed a new deal with 'Chrysalis' for 1998's 'NEAPOLIS' set, the band only managed to scrape into the UK Top 20.

You couldn't help feeling a little sorry for JIM KERR (one-time spouse of CHRISSIE HYNDE), not only does a young pretender like LIAM GALLAGHER hook up with his then wife (PATSY KENSIT), but his band became something of an anachronism in the ever changing world of 90's music. This was realized come their 2002 release 'CRY', a leap backwards into the world of old SIMPLE MINDS. Granted, the group had started using loops and adding a little guitar playing here and there, but what remained was a keyboard-driven album that gave us little in the way of musical vision. While U2 have at least made an attempt to move with the times, SIMPLE MINDS' sound is so deeply rooted in the 80's that it seems inconceivable they could ever make any kind of relevant departure.

• **Songwriters:** All group compositions or KERR-BURCHILL. Covered BIKO (Peter Gabriel) / SIGN O' THE TIMES (Prince) / DON'T YOU FORGET ABOUT ME (Keith Forsey-Steve Chiff) / GLORIA (Them) / THE MAN WHO SOLD THE WORLD (David Bowie) / HOMOSAPIEN (Pete Shelley) / DANCING BAREFOOT (Patti Smith) / NEON LIGHTS (Kraftwerk) / HELLO I LOVE YOU (Doors) / BRING ON THE DANCING HORSES (Echo & The Bunnymen) / THE NEEDLE & THE DAMAGE DONE (Neil Young) / FOR YOUR PLEASURE (Roxy Music) / ALL TOMORROW'S PARTIES (Velvet Underground).

• **Trivia:** SIMPLE MINDS played LIVE AID and MANDELA DAY concerts in 1985 and 1988 respectively.

JOHNNY & THE SELF ABUSERS

JIM KERR (b. 9 Jul'59) – vocals / **CHARLIE BURCHILL** (b.27 Nov'59) – guitar / **BRIAN McGEE** – drums / **TONY DONALD** – bass / **JOHN MILARKY** – guitar / **ALAN McNEIL** also

Chiswick — not iss.

Nov 77. (7") *(NS 22)* **SAINTS AND SINNERS. / DEAD VANDALS** [ ] [-]

SIMPLE MINDS

— **(KERR, BURCHILL + McGEE)** recruited **MICK McNEILL** (b.20 Jul'58) – keyboards / **DEREK FORBES** (b.22 Jun'56) – bass (ex-SUBS) + **DUNCAN BARNWELL** – guitar (left before recording)

Zoom — not iss.

Apr 79. (7") *(ZUM 10)* **LIFE IN A DAY. / SPECIAL VIEW** [62] [-]

Apr 79. (lp) *(ZULP 1)* **LIFE IN A DAY** [30] [-]
– Someone / Life in a day / Sad affair / All for you / Pleasantly disurbed / No cure / Chelsea girl / Wasteland / Destiny / Murder story. *(re-iss. Oct82 on 'Virgin' lp/c; VM/+C 6) (re-iss. 1985 on 'Virgin' lp/c; OVED/+C 95) (cd-iss. Jul86; VMCD 6)*

Jun 79. (7") *(ZUM 11)* **CHELSEA GIRL. / GARDEN OF HATE** [ ] [-]

Arista — Arista

Nov 79. (lp/c) *(SPART/TC-SPART 1109)* **REAL TO REAL CACOPHONY** [ ] [ ]
– Real to real / Naked eye / Citizen (dance of youth) / Carnival (shelter in a suitcase) / Factory / Cacophony / Veldt / Premonition / Changeling / Film theme / Calling your name / Scar. *(re-iss. Oct82 on 'Virgin' lp/c; V/TCV 2246) (re-iss. 1985 on 'Virgin' lp/c; OVED/+C 124) (cd-iss. May88; CDV 2246)*

Jan 80. (7") *(ARIST 325)* **CHANGELING. / PREMONITION (live)** [ ] [-]

Sep 80. (lp/c) *(SPART/TC-SPART 1140)* **EMPIRES AND DANCE** [41] [ ]
– I travel / Today I died again / Celebrate / This fear of gods / Capital city / Constantinople line / Twist-run-repulsion / Thirty frames a seconds / Kant-kino / Room. *(re-iss. Oct82 on 'Virgin' lp/c; V/TCV 2247) (cd-iss. May88; CDV 2247)*

Oct 80. (7") *(ARIST 372)* **I TRAVEL. / NEW WARM SKIN** [ ] [ ]
(w/ free 7"blue flexi) – KALEIDOSCOPE. / FILM DUB THEME
(12") *(ARIST 12-372)* – ('A'side) / Film dub theme.

Feb 81. (7") *(ARIST 394)* **CELEBRATE. / CHANGELING (live)** [ ] [ ]
(12"+=) *(ARIST 12-394)* – I travel (live).

Virgin — A&M

May 81. (7"/remix.12") *(VS 410/+12)* **THE AMERICAN. / LEAGUE OF NATIONS** [59] [-]

— **KENNY HYSLOP** (b.14 Feb'51, Helensburgh) – drums (ex-SKIDS, ex-ZONES, ex-SLIK) repl. McGEE who joined ENDGAMES; in 1994 he became a songwriter for LES McKEOWN (ex-BAY CITY ROLLERS)

Aug 81. (7"/12") *(VS 434/+12)* **LOVE SONG. / THE EARTH THAT YOU WALK UPON (instrumental)** [47] [-]

Sep 81. (2xlp/d-c) *(V/TCV 2207)* **SONS AND FASCINATION / SISTER FEELINGS CALL** [11] [ ]
– SONS AND FASCINATION – In trance as mission / Sweat in bullet / 70 cities as love brings the fall / Boys from Brazil / Love song / This Earth that you walk upon / Sons and fascination / Seeing out the angels. SISTER FEELINGS CALL – Theme for great cities * / The American / 20th Century promised land / Wonderful in young life / League of nations / Careful in career / Sound in 70 cities. *(issued separately Oct81; V 2207 / OVED 2) (cd-iss. Apr86 + Apr90; CDV 2207)* – (omits tracks *)

Oct 81. (7") *(VS 451)* **SWEAT IN BULLET. / 20th CENTURY PROMISED LAND** [52] [-]
(d7"+=) *(VSD 451)* – League of nations (live) / Premonition (live).
(12"+=) *(VS 451-12)* – League of nations (live) / In trance as mission (live).

Apr 82. (7") *(VS 488)* **PROMISED YOU A MIRACLE. / THEME FOR GREAT CITIES** [13] [-]
(12"+=) *(VS 488-12)* – Seeing out the angel (instrumental mix).

— **MIKE OGLETREE** – drums (ex-CAFE JAQUES) repl. HYSLOP who formed SET THE TONE

Aug 82. (7"/12") *(VS 511/+12)* **GLITTERING PRIZE. / GLITTERING THEME** [16] [ ]

— **MEL GAYNOR** (b.29 May'59) – drums (ex-sessions) repl. MIKE who joined FICTION FACTORY

Sep 82. (lp/c)<gold-lp> *(V/TCV 2230) <4928>* **NEW GOLD DREAM (81-82-83-84)** [3] [69] Jan83
– Someone, somewhere in summertime / Colours fly and the Catherine wheel / Promised you a miracle / Big sleep / Somebody up there likes you / New gold dream (81-82-83-84) / Glittering prize / Hunter and the hunted / King is white and in the crowd. *(cd-iss. Jul83 & Apr92; CDV 2230) (re-iss. Apr92 lp/c; OVED/+C 393)*

Nov 82. (7"/7"pic-d) *(VS/+Y 538)* **SOMEONE, SOMEWHERE IN SUMMERTIME. / KING IS WHITE AND IN THE CROWD** [36] [ ]
(12"+=) *(VS 538-12)* – Soundtrack for every Heaven.

Nov 82. (7") **PROMISED YOU A MIRACLE. / THE AMERICAN** [-] [ ]

Nov 83. (7"/12") *(VS 636/+12)* **WATERFRONT. / HUNTER AND THE HUNTED (live)** [13] [ ]

Jan 84. (7"/7"pic-d) *(VS/+Y 649)* **SPEED YOUR LOVE TO ME. / BASS LINE** [20] [ ]
(12"+=) *(VS 649-12)* – ('A'extended).

Feb 84. (cd/c/lp,white-lp) *(CD/TC+/V 2300) <4981>* **SPARKLE IN THE RAIN** [1] [64]
– Up on the catwalk / Book of brilliant things / Speed your love to me / Waterfront / East at Easter / White hot day / Street hassle / "C" Moon cry like a baby / The kick inside of me / Shake off the ghosts. *(re-iss. cd Mar91; same)*

Mar 84. (7"/7"pic-d)(12") *(VS/+Y 661)(VS 661-12)* **UP ON THE CATWALK. / A BRASS BAND IN AFRICA** [27] [ ]

Apr 85. (7"/7"sha-pic-d)(12") *(VS/+S 749)(VS 749-12) <2703>* **DON'T YOU (FORGET ABOUT ME). / A BRASS BAND IN AFRICA** [7] [1] Feb85
(re-iss. Jun88 cd-s; CDT 2)

— **KERR, BURCHILL, McNEILL + GAYNOR** brought in new member **JOHN GIBLING** – bass (ex-PETER GABRIEL sessions) to repl. FORBES

Oct 85. (7"/12") *(VS 817/+12)* **ALIVE AND KICKING. / ('A'instrumental)** [7] [-]
(12"+=) *(VS 817-13)* – Up on the catwalk (live).

Oct 85. (cd/c/lp,pic-lp) *(CD/TC+/V 2364) <5092>* **ONCE UPON A TIME** [1] [10]
– Once upon a time / All the things she said / Ghost dancing / Alive and kicking / Oh jungleland / I wish you were here / Sanctify yourself / Come a long way. *(lp re-iss. Mar01 on 'Simple Vinyl'; SVLP 312)*

Oct 85. (7") *<2783>* **ALIVE AND KICKING. / UP ON THE CATWALK (live)** [-] [3]

Jan 86. (7") *(SM 1) <2810>* **SANCTIFY YOURSELF. / ('A'instrumental)** [10] [14]
(d7"+=) *(SMP 1)* – Love song (live) / Street hassle (live).
(12") *(SM 1-12)* – ('A'mix). / ('A'dub instrumental).

Apr 86. (7") *(VS 860) <2828>* **ALL THE THINGS SHE SAID. / DON'T YOU (FORGET ABOUT ME)** [9] [28]
(12"+=) *(VS 860-12)* – Promised you a miracle (US mix).

Nov 86. (7") *(VS 907)* **GHOSTDANCING. / JUNGLELAND (instrumental)** [13] [ ]
(12"+=/cd-s+=) *(VS/MIKE 907-12)* – ('A'instrumental) / ('B'instrumental).

May 87. (d-cd/d-c/d-lp) *(CDVSM/SMDCX/SMDLX 1) <6850>* **LIVE IN THE CITY OF LIGHT (live)** [1] [96] Jul87
– Ghostdancing / Big sleep / Waterfront / Promised you a miracle / Someone somewhere in summertime / Oh jungleland / Alive and kicking / Don't you (forget about me) / Once upon a time / Book of brilliant things / East at Easter / Sanctify yourself / Love song / Sun City – Dance to the music / New gold dream (81-82-83-84).

Jun 87. (7"/10") *(SM 2/+10)* **PROMISED YOU A MIRACLE (live). / BOOK OF BRILLIANT THINGS (live)** [19] [ ]
(12"+=/c-s+=) *(SM/+C 2-12)* – Glittering prize (live) / Celebrate (live).

— **KERR, BURCHILL + McNEILL** were basic trio, w/other 2 still sessioning.

Feb 89. (7") *(SMX 3)* **BELFAST CHILD. / MANDELA DAY** [1] [ ]
(c-s+=/12"ep+=/12"box-ep+=/cd-ep+=) **BALLAD OF THE STREETS** *(SMX C/T/C/CD 3)* – Biko.

Apr 89. (7") *(SMX 4)* **THIS IS YOUR LAND. / SATURDAY GIRL** [13] [ ]
(c-s+=/12"+=/12"g-f+=/3"cd-s+=) *(SMX C/T/TG/CD 4)* – Year of the dragon.

May 89. (cd/c/lp) *(MIND D/C/S 1) <3927>* **STREET FIGHTING YEARS** [1] [70]
– Soul crying out / Wall of love / This is your land / Take a step back / Kick it in / Let it all come down / Biko / Mandela day / Belfast child / Street fighting years. *(re-iss. Dec89 box-cd/c +=; SMBX D/C 1)* – (interview cassettes).

Jul 89. (7"/c-s) *(SMX/+C 5)* **KICK IT IN. / WATERFRONT ('89 mix)** [15] [ ]
(12"+=/cd-s+=) *(SMX T/CD 5)* – Big sleep (live).
(12"g-f+=) *(SMXTG 5)* – ('A'mix).

Dec 89. (7"ep/c-ep/12"ep/cd-ep) *(SMX/+C/T/CD 6)* **THE AMSTERDAM EP** [18] [ ]
– Let it all come down / Sign o' the times / Jerusalem.
(12"ep+=/cd-ep+=) *(SMX TR/X 6)* – Sign o' the times (mix).

— **KERR, BURCHILL + GAYNOR** brought in sessioners **MALCOLM FOSTER** – bass / **PETER JOHN VITESSE** – keyboards / **STEPHEN LIPSON** – bass, keyboards / **ANDY DUNCAN** – percussion / **GAVIN WRIGHT** – string leader / **LISA GERMANO** – violin

Mar 91. (7"/c-s) *(VS/+C 1332)* **LET THERE BE LOVE. / GOODNIGHT** [6] [ ]
(12"+=) *(VST 1332)* – Alive and kicking (live).
(cd-s++=) *(VSCD 1332)* – East at Easter (live).

Apr 91. (cd/c/lp) *(CD/TC+/V 2660) <5352>* **REAL LIFE** [2] [74]
– Real life / See the lights / Let there be love / Woman / Stand by love / African skies / Let the children speak / Ghostrider / Banging on the door / Travelling man / Rivers of ice / When two worlds collide.

May 91. (7"/c-s) *(VS/+C 1343)* **SEE THE LIGHTS. / THEME FOR GREAT CITIES ('91 edit)** [20] [–]
(12"+=/cd-s+=) *(VS T/CD 1343)* – Soul crying out (live).

May 91. (c-s,cd-s) *<1553>* **SEE THE LIGHTS / GOODNIGHT** [–] [40]

Aug 91. (7"/c-s) *(VS/+C 1358)* **STAND BY LOVE. / KING IS WHITE AND IN THE CROWD (live)** [13] [ ]
(12"+=/cd-s+=) *(VS T/CD 1358)* – Let there be love (live).

Oct 91. (7"/c-s) *(VS/+C 1382)* **REAL LIFE. / SEE THE LIGHTS** [34] [ ]
(ext.12"+=) *(VST 1382)* – Belfast child (extended).
(cd-s++=) *(VSCD 1382)* – Ghostrider.

Oct 92. (7"/c-s) *(VS/+C 1440)* **LOVE SONG. / ALIVE AND KICKING** [6] [ ]
(ext.cd-s+=) *(VSCDG 1440)* – ('B'instrumental).
(cd-s+=) *(VSCDX 1440)* – Travelling man / Oh jungleland.

Oct 92. (cd/c/lp) *(SMTV D/C/S 1)* **GLITTERING PRIZE – SIMPLE MINDS 81-92** (compilation) [1] [–]
– Waterfront / Don't you (forget about me) / Alive and kicking / Sanctify yourself / Love song / Someone somewhere in summertime / See the lights / Belfast child / The American / All the things she said / Promised you a miracle / Ghostdancing / Speed your love to me / Glittering prize / Let there be love / Mandela Day. *(lp re-iss. Oct00 on 'Simply Vinyl'; SVLP 258)*

— **KERR + BURCHILL** with guests MARK BROWNE, MALCOLM FOSTER, MARCUS MILLER + LANCE MORRISON – bass / MARK SCHULMAN, TAL BERGMAN + VINNIE COLAIUTA – drums

Virgin Virgin

Jan 95. (7"/c-s/cd-s) *(VS/+C/+DG 1509) <38467>* **SHE'S A RIVER. / E55 / ('A'mix)** [9] [52]
(cd-s) *(VSCDX 1509)* – ('A'side) / Celtic strings / ('A'mix).

Jan 95. (cd/c/lp) *(CD/TC+/V 2760) <39922>* **GOOD NEWS FROM THE NEXT WORLD** [2] [87]
– She's a river / Night music / Hypnotised / Great leap forward / 7 deadly sins / And the band played on / My life / Criminal world / This time.

Mar 95. (7"/c-s) *(VS/+C 1534)* **HYPNOTISED. / #4** [18] [–]
(cd-s+=) *(VSCDX 1534)* – ('A'-Tim Simenon extended remixes) / ('A'-Malfunction mix).
(cd-s) *(VSCDT 1534)* – ('A'side) / Up on the catwalk (live) / And the band played on (live) / She's a river (live).

— **KERR + BURCHILL** brought back **DEREK FORBES** – bass / **MEL GAYNOR** – drums / also **HAMI LEE** – additional programming

Chrysalis not iss.

Mar 98. (c-s) *(TCCHS 5078)* **GLITTERBALL / WATERFRONT (Union Jack mix)** [18] [–]
(cd-s+=) *(CDCHSS 5078)* – Love song (Philadelphia Bluntz mix).
(cd-s) *(CDCHS 5078)* – ('A'side) / Don't you forget about me (Jam & Spoon mix) / Theme for great cities (Fila Brazillia mix).

Mar 98. (cd/c) *(493712-2/-4)* **NEAPOLIS** [19] [–]
– Song for the tribes / Glitterball / War babies / Tears of a guy / Superman v supersoul / Lightning / If I had wings / Killing Andy Warhol / Androgyny.

May 98. (ext;c-s/7") *(TC+/CHS 5088)* **WAR BABIES. / I TRAVEL (Utah Saints mix)** [43] [–]
('A'-Bascombe mix;cd-s+=) *(CDCHS 5088)* – Theme for great cities '98 (Fluke's Atlantis mix) / ('A'-Johnson Somerset extended mix).

Eagle Red Ink

Sep 01. (cd-ep) *(EAGEP 198)* **DANCING BAREFOOT EP** [ ] [–]
– Dancing barefoot / Gloria / Being boiled / Love will tear us apart.

Sep 01. (cd) *(EAGCD 194) <55944>* **NEON LIGHTS** [ ] [ ] Oct01
– Gloria / The man who sold the world / Homosapien / Dancing barefoot / Neon lights / Hello I love you / Bring on the dancing horses / The needle & the damage done / For your pleasure / All tomorrow's parties.

Dec 01. (12") *(REMOTE 016)* **HOMOSAPIEN (Malcolm Duffy mix). / HOMOSAPIEN (Malcolm Duffy dub mix)** [ ] [–]
(cd-s+=) *(REMOTE 016CD)* – ('A'-Malcolm Duffy edit).
(above issued on 'Remote')

Mar 02. (cd-s) *(EAGXA 218)* **CRY / LEAD THE BLIND / HOMOSAPIEN (Vince Clarke remix)** [47] [–]
(cd-s) *(EAGXS 218)* – ('A'side) / For what it's worth / The garden.

Apr 02. (cd) *(EAGCD 196) <59145>* **CRY** [ ] [ ]
– Cry / Spaceface / New sunshine morning / One step closer / Face in the sun / Disconnected / Lazy lately / Sugar / Sleeping girl / Cry again / Slave nation / The floating world.

Jun 02. (cd-s) *(EAGXS 232)* **SPACEFACE / NEW SUNRISE** [ ] [–]

— in Jun'02, LIQUID PEOPLE vs. SIMPLE MINDS had a hit with 'Monster' which sampled 'CHANGELING'

– compilations, others, etc. –

on 'Virgin' unless otherwise mentioned

Jan 82. (7") *Arista; (ARIST 448)* **I TRAVEL. / THIRTY FRAMES A SECOND (live)** [ ] [–]
(12"+=) *(ARIST12 448)* – ('A'live).

Feb 82. (lp/c) *Arista; (SPART/TCSPART 1183)* **CELEBRATION** [45] [ ]
(re-iss. Oct82 on 'Virgin' lp/c; V/TCV 2248) (re-iss. Apr89 on 'Virgin' lp/c; OVED/+C 275) (cd-iss. Aug89; CDV 2248)

Apr 83. (12") *(VS 578-12)* **I TRAVEL (mix). / FILM THEME** [ ] [–]

Aug 90. (5xcd-box-ep) *(SMTCD 1)* **THEMES – VOLUME ONE** [ ] [–]
– (Apr79 – LIFE IN A DAY – Apr82 – PROMISED YOU A MIRACLE singles)

Sep 90. (5xcd-box-ep) *(SMTCD 2)* **THEMES – VOLUME TWO** [ ] [–]
– (Aug82 – GLITTERING PRIZE – Apr85 – DON'T YOU (FORGET ABOUT ME) singles)

Oct 90. (5xcd-box-ep) *(SMTCD 3)* **THEMES – VOLUME THREE** [ ] [–]
– (Oct85 – ALIVE AND KICKING – Jun87 – PROMISED YOU A MIRACLE (live) singles)

Nov 90. (5xcd-box-ep) *(SMTCD 4)* **THEMES – VOLUME FOUR** [ ] [–]
– (Feb89 – BELFAST CHILD, Dec89 – THE AMSTERDAM EP)

Nov 90. (3xcd-box) *(TPAK 2)* **COLLECTOR'S EDITION** [ ] [–]
– (LIFE IN A DAY / REEL TO REAL CACOPHONY / EMPIRES AND DANCE)

Nov 01. (d-cd) *(CDVD 2953)* **THE BEST OF SIMPLE MINDS** [34] [–]

SINGLESKIN (see under ⇒ Path records)

SIXTEEN SOULS (see under ⇒ Glasgow Underground records)

SKEETS BOLIVER (see under ⇒ MARRA, Michael)

SKIDS

Formed: Dunfermline . . . Spring 1977 by RICHARD JOBSON and STUART ADAMSON together with BILL SIMPSON and TOM KELLICHAN. Careering into the wreckage of the post-punk music scene with the self-financed 'CHARLES' single, the band soon found themselves with a deal courtesy of the ever eclectic 'Virgin' label. After a couple of minor hit singles, the group hit the UK Top 10 with 'INTO THE VALLEY', a shining example of The SKIDS' anthemic, new wave warriors style. In addition to JOBSON's highly distinctive, affected vocals and ADAMSON's strident axework (which he'd later perfect in BIG COUNTRY), The SKIDS were notable for their clever visual image (i.e. JOBSON's kick-dance and ultra-slick wavey hairdo).

A debut album, 'SCARED TO DANCE' (1979), made the UK Top 20 and established the group as a more tasteful Caledonian alternative to The BAY CITY ROLLERS. Later that Spring, The SKIDS scored another Top 20 hit single with 'MASQUERADE', a highlight of the BILL NELSON-produced follow-up album, 'DAYS IN EUROPA' (1979), alongside the almost militaristic clarion call of 'WORKING FOR THE YANKEE DOLLAR'.

All wasn't well within The SKIDS camp, however, personnel upheaval (leading to an all-new rhythm section of RUSSELL WEBB and MIKE BAILLIE) adding to criticisms of JOBSON's increasing lyrical complexities and the group's more schitzo pop/experimental sound. Despite all this, a third album, 'THE ABSOLUTE GAME' (1980) saw a return to form of sorts, furnishing the group with their one and only Top 10 set.

ADAMSON became increasingly disillusioned, however, and finally departed the following summer. Left to his own devices, JOBSON dominated The SKIDS' final album, 'JOY' (1981), an at times trad/folk concept effort which met with a frosty critical reception and signalled the subsequent demise of the group early in '82. While ADAMSON went on to massive success with "bagpipe"-guitar rockers, BIG COUNTRY, JOBSON concentrated on a solo career which extended to writing (and recording) poetry. He then went on to form the short-lived and critically derided ARMOURY SHOW along with ex-MAGAZINE men, JOHN McGEOGH and JOHN DOYLE, releasing a sole album, 'WAITING FOR THE FLOODS' (1985). More recently, JOBSON's recording career has taken a backseat to his more successful forays into modelling and TV journalism.

• **Songwriters:** JOBSON lyrics/group compositions, except ALL THE YOUNG DUDES (hit; Mott The Hoople) / BAND PLAYED WALTZING MATILDA (Australian trad.).

• **Trivia:** In 1981, JOBSON published book of poetry, 'A MAN FOR ALL SEASONS'.

RICHARD JOBSON (b. 6 Apr'60) – vocals, guitar / **STUART ADAMSON** (b. WILLIAM STUART ADAMSON, 11 Apr'58, Manchester) – lead guitar, vocals / **BILL SIMPSON** – bass / **TOM KELLICHAN** – drums

No-Bad / not iss.

Mar 78. (7"m) *(NB 1)* **CHARLES. / REASONS / TEST-TUBE BABIES** [ ] [-]

Virgin / not iss.

Sep 78. (7",7"white) *(VS 227)* **SWEET SUBURBIA. / OPEN SOUND** [70] [-]
Oct 78. (7"red-ep/12"red-ep) *(VS 232/+12)* **WIDE OPEN** [48] [-]
– The saints are coming / Of one skin / Confusion / Night and day.
Feb 79. (7",7"white) *(VS241)* **INTO THE VALLEY. / T.V. STARS** [10] [-]
Feb 79. (lp/c) *(V/TCV 2116)* **SCARED TO DANCE** [19] [-]
– Into the valley / Scared to dance / Of one skin / Dossier (of fallibility) / Melancholy soldiers / Hope and glory / The saints are coming / Six times / Calling the tune / Integral plot / Charles / Scale. *(re-iss. Apr84 lp/c; OVED/+C 41) (cd-iss. Jun90+=; CDV 2116)* – Sweet suburbia / Open sound / TV stars / Night and day / Contusion / Reasons / Test tube babies. *<US cd-iss. 1991 on 'Caroline'; CAROL 1817-2>*
May 79. (7") *(VS 262)* **MASQUERADE. / OUT OF TOWN** [14] [-]
(d7"+=) *(VS 262-12)* – Another emotion / Aftermath dub.

—— **RUSTY EGAN** – drums (ex-RICH KIDS) repl. KELLICHAN

Sep 79. (7") *(VS 288)* **CHARADE. / GREY PARADE** [31] [-]
Oct 79. (lp/c) *(V/TCV 2138)* **DAYS IN EUROPA** [32] [-]
– Animation * / Charade / Dulce et decorum (pro patria mor) / Pros and cons / Home of the saved / Working for the Yankee dollar / The olympian / Thanatos / Masquerade / A day in Europa / Peaceful times. *(re-dist.Mar80 += *) (re-iss. Mar84 lp/c; OVED/+C 42) (cd-iss. Jun01 on 'Captain Oi'+=; AHOYCD 172)* – Out of town / Another emotion / Aftermath dub / Grey parade / Working for the yankee dollar / Vanguard's crusade.
Nov 79. (7") *(VS 306)* **WORKING FOR THE YANKEE DOLLAR. / VANGUARD'S CRUSADE** [20] [-]
(d7"+=) *(VS 306)* – All the young dudes / Hymns from a haunted ballroom.

—— **RUSSELL WEBB** – bass, vocals (ex-ZONES, ex-SLIK) repl. SIMPSON / **MIKE BAILLIE** – drums (ex-INSECT BITES) repl. EGAN who joined VISAGE

Feb 80. (7") *(VS 323)* **ANIMATION. / PROS AND CONS** [56] [-]
Jul 80. (7") *(VS 359)* **CIRCUS GAMES. / ONE DECREE** [32] [-]
Sep 80. (lp/c) *(V/TCV 2174)* **THE ABSOLUTE GAME** [9] [-]
– Circus games / Out of town / Goodbye civilian / The children saw the shame / A woman in winter / Hurry on boys / Happy to be with you / The Devil's decade / One decree / Arena. *(free-lp w.a.) (VDJ 333)* **STRENGTH THROUGH JOY** *(re-iss. Mar84 lp/c; OVED/+C 43) (cd-iss. Oct01 on 'Track'; TRK 0006CD)*
Oct 80. (7"/7"pic-d) *(VS/+P 373)* **GOODBYE CIVILIAN. / MONKEY McGUIRE MEETS SPECKY POTTER BEHIND THE LOCHORE INSTITUTE** [52] [-]
Nov 80. (7") *(VSK 101)* **A WOMAN IN WINTER. / WORKING FOR THE YANKEE DOLLAR (live)** [49] [-]

—— **KENNY HYSLOP** (b.14 Feb'51, Helensburgh) – drums (ex-ZONES, ex-SLIK) repl. BAILLIE who joined EPSILON.

Aug 81. (7"/12") *(VS 401/+12)* **FIELDS. / BRAVE MAN** [ ] [-]

—— **JOBSON + WEBB** recruited **PAUL WISHART** – saxophone, flute to repl. ADAMSON who formed BIG COUNTRY and HYSLOP who joined SIMPLE MINDS. Session people on album incl. **J.J. JOHNSON** – drums / **The ASSOCIATES / VIRGINIA ASTLEY / MIKE OLDFIELD** – guitar / **KEN LOCKIE / TIM CROSS** – piano / **ALAN DARBY** – guitar

Oct 81. (7") *(VS 449)* **IONA. / BLOOD AND SPOIL** [ ] [-]
Nov 81. (lp/c) *(V/TCV 2217)* **JOY** [ ] [-]
– Blood and soil / A challenge, the wanderer / Men of mercy / A memory / Iona / In fear of fire / Brothers / And the band played Waltzing Matilda / The men of the fall / The sound of retreat (instrumental) / Fields. *(re-iss. 1988 lp/c; OVED/+C 200)*

—— folded early '82 with JOBSON already concentrating on poetry & solo work

– compilations, etc. –

on 'Virgin' unless mentioned otherwise

May 82. (lp/c) *(VM/+C 2)* **FANFARE** [ ] [-]
May 83. (12"ep) *(VS 591-12)* **INTO THE VALLEY / MASQUERADE. / SCARED TO DANCE / WORKING FOR THE YANKEE DOLLAR** [ ] [-]
Jul 87. (cd) *(CDVM 9022)* **DUNFERMLINE (THE SKIDS' FINEST MOMENTS)** [ ] [-]
Feb 92. (m-cd) *Windsong; (<WINCD 008>)* **BBC RADIO 1 LIVE IN CONCERT (live)** [ ] [ ]
Jan 95. (cd) *(CDOVD 457)* **SWEET SUBURBIA – THE BEST OF THE SKIDS** [ ] [-]
– Into the valley / Charles / The saints are coming / Scared to dance / Sweet suburbia / Of one skin / Night and day / Animation / Working for the Yankee dollar / Charade / Masquerade / Circus games / Out of town / Goodbye civilian / A woman in winter / Hurry on boys / Iona / Fields.

—— in May'02 – through STUART ADAMSON's death – 'Universal TV' records delivered a BIG COUNTRY 'GREATEST HITS' collection with SKIDS tracks

RICHARD JOBSON

solo with **JOHN McGEOGH** – guitar / **VIRGINIA ASTLEY** – piano, flute / **JOSEPHINE** – wind, piano

Cocteau / not iss.

Oct 81. (lp) *(JC 1)* **THE BALLAD OF ETIQUETTE** (some poetry) [ ] [-]
– India song / Don't ever tell anybody anything / Pavillion pole / Etiquette / Joy / Thomas / Anonymous / The night of crystal / Orphee / Stormy weather. *(re-iss. Jul85)*

Crepescule / not iss.

Feb 83. (lp) **10:30 ON A SUMMER NIGHT** [ ] [-]

—— with **VINI REILLY** – guitar (of DURUTTI COLUMN) / **WIM MERTENS** (of SOFT VERDICT) / **BLAINE L. REININGER** (of TUXEDO MOON) / **PAUL HAIG** – synthesizers (ex-JOSEF K) / **STEVEN BROWN** – sax

Jul 84. (lp; as THOMAS THE IMPOSTER) **AN AFTERNOON IN COMPANY** [ ] [-]
– Autumn / The return to England / Auden / The Pyrenees / Verbier / The Rhur Valley / Hollow men / Savannah / Jericho 1 / Meditation / Oran / Aragon / Jericho 2 / Dignity / Mount Fuji / The end of the era.
Feb 86. (d-lp) *(TWI 615)* **THE OTHER MAN** [ ] [-]
Jan 87. (lp) *(TWI 807)* **16 YEARS OF ALCOHOL** [ ] [-]

ARMOURY SHOW

was formed by **RICHARD JOBSON** – vocals + RUSSELL WEBB – bass / plus **JOHN McGEOGH** – guitar (ex-SIOUXSIE & THE BANSHEES, ex-MAGAZINE) / **JOHN DOYLE** – drums (ex-MAGAZINE) / **EVAN CHARLES** – keyboards (ex-COWBOYS INTERNATIONAL)

Parlophone / Capitol

Aug 84. (7") *(R 6109)* **CASTLES IN SPAIN. / INNOCENTS ABROAD** [69] [-]
(12"+=) *(12R 6109)* – Is it a wonder.
Jan 85. (7") *(R 6087)* **WE CAN BE BRAVE AGAIN. / A FEELING** [66] [-]
(12"+=) *(12R 6087)* – Catherine.
Jul 85. (7") *(R 6098)* **GLORY OF LOVE. / HIGHER THAN THE WORLD (instrumental)** [ ] [-]
(12"+=) *(12R 6098)* – ('A'part 2) / ('A'instrumental).
Sep 85. (lp/c) *(ARM/TC-ARM 1)* **WAITING FOR THE FLOODS** [57] [ ]
– Castles in Spain / Kyria / A feeling / Jungle of cities / We can be brave again / Higher than the world / Glory of love / Waiting for the floods / Sense of freedom / Sleep city sleep / Avalanche.
Oct 85. (7") *(R 6079)* **CASTLES IN SPAIN. / A GATHERING** [ ] [-]
(12"+=) *(12R 6079)* – Ring those bells.
Jan 87. (7"/12") *(R/12R 6149)* **LOVE IN ANGER. / TENDER IS THE NIGHT** [63] [-]
Apr 87. (7") *(R 6153)* **NEW YORK CITY. / WHIRLWIND** [ ] [-]
(12"+=) *(12R 6153)* – ('A'versions).

—— Crumbled around mid'87, with . . .

RICHARD JOBSON

again trying solo career augmented by co-writer RUSSELL WEBB.

Parlophone / not iss.

Aug 88. (7"/12") *(R/12R 6181)* **BADMAN. / THE HEAT IS ON** [ ] [-]
(cd-s+=) *(CDR 6181)* – Big fat city.
Nov 88. (cd/c/lp) *(CD/TC+/PCS 7321)* **BADMAN** [ ] [-]
– Badman / This thing caled love / Monkey's cry / The heat is on / Uptown – downtown / A boat called Pride / Angel / Fire. *(cd+=)* – Big fat city.

—— JOBSON, who was now a successful male model while also taking up TV work mainly interviews. Most people now know of him winning his battle against alcohol and epilepsy. In the late 80's, his marriage to TV presenter, Mariella Frostrup failed, although they remained very good friends. He subsequently went on to present late night TV shows including 'Hollywood Report'.

SKINTRADE

Formed: Aberdeen . . . early 90's by KEVIN GUNN and DAVE DUNBAR out of REJUVENATE. This techno duo were equally "at home" playing either KRAFTWERK-esque toons or Detroit house, although SKINTRADE were more at ease with the addition of DJ TITCH; a debut single 'SUBHUMAN' was issued in '93. Subsequently inking a deal with Glasgow's top dance label, 'Soma', the trio opened their musical account rather well, the 'SHAPESHIFTER / SLITHER / PSALM' single in 1994 selling out its 3,000 in the first few months; they had a large following in Germany and the Netherlands. What turned out to be the final effort, 'ANDOMRAXESS' was released the following year.

KEVIN GUNN – keyboards, etc / **DAVE DUNBAR** – keyboards, etc / **DJ TITCH** – decks

Bellboy / not iss.

1993. (12") *(BL 001)* **SUBHUMAN. / UMAN** [ ] [-]

Soma / not iss.

Sep 94. (12") *(Soma 17)* **SHAPESHIFTER / SLITHER / PSALM** [ ] [-]
Jun 95. (12") *(Soma 27)* **ANDOMRAXESS** [ ] [-]

—— not to be confused with late 90's SKINTRADE

SKROTEEZ (see ⇒ Section 9: wee post-Punk groups)

SKUOBHIE DUBH ORCHESTRA (see under ⇒ Fence records)

SLAM (see under ⇒ Soma records / SLAM)

SLIDE

Formed: Glasgow ... 1987 by GRANT RICHARDSON, KENNY PATTERSON, SCOTT FRASER and RICHARD HYND; 5th member JOHNNY McELHONE (of TEXAS) was also around for co-songwriting duties. Lazy guitar-rock in a way TEXAS without SHARLEEN might have turned out, SLIDE signed a major recording deal with 'Mercury' records. In 1989, the rocking 4-piece finally unleashed their first single, 'WHY IS IT A CRIME?', an all-too Retro affair that previewed their debut set, 'DOWN SO LONG' (1989). Unfortunately, neither these or any other singles during the following year were given much attention by the music press, although the pre-NIRVANA Kerrang! did supply the band with some hope. SLIDE were on a slippery slope when HYND took off to join the more fruitful TEXAS, while his replacement, ROSS McFARLANE, also found a little bit of fame in chart-toppers, STILTSKIN.
• **Note:** not to be confused with other act who subsequently released stuff on the 'Transient' label.

GRANT RICHARDSON – vocals, guitar / **KENNY PATTERSON** – guitar / **SCOTT FRASER** – bass / **RICHARD HYND** (b.17 May'68, Aberdeen) – drums

		Mercury	not iss.
Aug 89.	(7") *(MER 292)* **WHY IS IT A CRIME? / NEVER EVER**		-
	(12"+=/cd-s+=) *(MER X/CD 292)* – Leave your love.		
Oct 89.	(lp/c/cd) *(838964-1/-4/-2)* **DOWN SO LONG**		-
	– Why is it a crime? / Down so long / Just takes time / Make a new start / Listen / No wrong way / Everything I do / Leave your love / Only natural / I don't want to let you down / Hardest part.		
Jan 90.	(7") *(MER 312)* **DOWN SO LONG. / DON'T TURN YOUR BACK**		-
	(c-s+=/cd-s+=) *(MER MC/CD 312)* – Listen.		
	(12"+=) *(MERX 312)* – ('A'version).		
Jul 90.	(7") *(MER 324)* **WHY IS IT A CRIME? (remix). / I WANT TO BE SATISFIED**		-
	(12"+=/cd-s+=) *(MER X/CD 324)* – ('A'extended).		

— HYND joined TEXAS and was repl. by ROSS McFARLANE who after SLIDE split, went on to be part of STILTSKIN

SLIK

Formed: Glasgow ... 1972 as the initially aggressive pop combo SALVATION. Agent/manager, EDDIE TOBIN, had become a little despondent with the local rock scene and wanted a decent band to fill the local Electric Garden venue. The line-up of MIDGE URE, KENNY HYSLOP, JIM McGINLEY and original vocalist KEVIN McGINLEY (brother of JIM), saw SALVATION amass local and loyal support, although by 1974 the band were increasingly shaping into a pop band. With MIDGE taking over lead vocal duties from the departing KEVIN and keyboard player BILLY McISAAC now in tow, the all-new SLIK signed a deal at 'Bell' records through Bill Martin. A flop debut single in March '75, 'THE BOOGIEST BAND IN TOWN', saw the lads (now suited out in baseball attire) take stock for their next stab at the charts. The SLIK follow-up, 'FOREVER AND EVER', took the pop world by storm early in 1976 and raced up to the top of the UK hit parade. However, although another grandiose pop theme, 'REQUIEM', saw them back in the Top 30, two subsequent 45's, 'THE KID'S A PUNK' and 'DON'T TAKE YOUR LOVE AWAY', failed to generate any interest; it seemed only one tartan act was allowed into the hearts of teenyboppers and that was the BAY CITY ROLLERS. With the advent of Punk rock and New Wave in '76/'77, MIDGE and the boys (RUSSELL WEBB had replaced JIM) tried to get in on the act by disguising themselves as Punk badgewearers, PVC2. Bruce Findlay took the band under his wing for a one-off single, 'PUT YOU IN THE PICTURE', released on his own indie imprint, 'Zoom' (later the stamping ground for SIMPLE MINDS). In 1978, after MIDGE went south to join the RICH KIDS (with ex-SEX PISTOLS bassist, GLEN MATLOCK), the remainder of the band found WILLIE GARDNER and formed The ZONES. Like the aforementioned SIMPLE MINDS, the Power-pop outfit were duly signed from Zoom to 'Arista', although three singles and a 1979 album – 'UNDER INFLUENCE' – later, they were no more; WEBB and HYSLOP soon joined The SKIDS, while the latter also found fame in SIMPLE MINDS.

MIDGE URE (b. JAMES URE, 10 Oct'53, Cambuslang) – vocals, guitar / **BILLY McISAAC** – keyboards, vocals / **JIM McGINLEY** – bass, vocals / **KENNY HYSLOP** – drums, vocals

		Bell	Arista
Mar 75.	(7") *(BELL 1414)* **THE BOOGIEST BAND IN TOWN. / HATCHE**		-
Dec 75.	(7") *(BELL 1464)* **FOREVER AND EVER. / AGAIN MY LOVE**	1	
Apr 76.	(7") *(BELL 1478)* **REQUIEM. / EVERYDAY ANYWAY**	24	
May 76.	(lp) *(SYBEL 8004)* **SLIK**	58	-
	– Dancerama / Darlin' / Bom-bom / Better than I do / Forever and ever / Requiem / Do it again / When will I be loved / Day by day / No we won't forget you.		
Jul 76.	(7") *(BELL 1490)* **THE KID'S A PUNK. / SLIK SHUFFLE**		-
		Arista	Arista
Dec 76.	(7") *(ARIST 83)* **DON'T TAKE YOUR LOVE AWAY. / THIS SIDE UP**		

PVC2

— changed band name + **RUSSELL WEBB** – bass, vocals; repl. McGINLEY

		Zoom	not iss.
Nov 77.	(7"m) *(ZUM 2)* **PUT YOU IN THE PICTURE. / PAIN / DERANGED, DEMENTED AND FREE**		-

— MIDGE departed to help form RICH KIDS alongside GLEN MATLOCK (ex-SEX PISTOLS). In 1979 after spells with The MISFITS and THIN LIZZY, he replaced JOHN FOXX in ULTRAVOX. He of course went onto solo work and co-organized BAND AID with BOB GELDOF. The rest changed group name again . . .

ZONES

— **WILLIE GARDNER** – vocals, guitar (ex-VALVES), repl. MIDGE

		Zoom	not iss.
Apr 78.	(7") *(ZUM 4)* **STUCK WITH YOU. / NO ANGELS**		-
		Arista	not iss.
Aug 78.	(7") *(ARIST 205)* **SIGN OF THE TIMES. / AWAY FROM IT ALL**		-
May 79.	(7") *(ARIST 265)* **LOOKING TO THE FUTURE. / DO IT ALL AGAIN**		-
Jun 79.	(lp) *(SPART 1095)* **UNDER INFLUENCE**		-
	– Do it all again / Vision on / Deadle dolls / The end / Mainman / You're not folling / Anything goes / Strength to strength / Looking to the future / Mourning star.		
Aug 79.	(7") *(ARIST 286)* **MOURNING STAR. / UNDER INFLUENCE**		-

— split again late 1979 – GARDNER went solo while WEBB and later HYSLOP joined The SKIDS; in 1981, HYSLOP became a member of SIMPLE MINDS

WILLIE GARDNER

		Cuban Libre	not iss.
Feb 81.	(7") *(DRINK 3)* **GOLDEN YOUTH. / TIME TO ROT**		-
		Virgin	not iss.
Sep 81.	(7") *(VS 438)* **IMITATION. /**		-

SLIMCEA GIRL (see ⇒ Section 9: the 90s)

SLINKY (see ⇒ Section 9: the 90s)

SMALL WORLD (see ⇒ Section 9: Dance/Rave)

SMILES (see ⇒ Section 9: the 90s)

Marc SMITH

Born: c.1970, Glasgow. Years spent mastering turntable skills in his bedroom eventually led to the young breakbeat fanatic landing a residency at The Warehouse in 1989. With the rise of the indigenous Scottish rave scene in the early 90's, SMITH (Scotland's No.1 DJ of 1992) wowed the crowds at events like Technodrome, Rezerection and Earthquaker. He also began writing his own material, releasing his own debut 12", 'BREAKDOWN' on the West Lothian's 'Clubscene' label in 1992, a cut'n'paste breakbeat affair in the mould of ALTERN-8 with requisite piano breakdown and chipmunk vocals. More 'Take Me Higher'-styled rave chords were in evidence on the following year's 'TECHNO DUP'

As far as selling records went, MARC was in the handy position of actually running his own shop, 'Notorious Vinyl' (at 8 Parnie Street, Glasgow G1 5LR).

A projected in-house label of the same name was initiated with scheduled releases from the likes of SCOTT BROWN, KMC, DAVIE MURRAY, although MARC originally intended to set up two labels, one for techno and one catering to the breakbeat market. In late '93, SMITH also released a scratched and mixed compilation, 'YOU KNOW THE SCORE VOL.1 – Do Ya Luv Your Hardcore?', featuring heavy duty tracks from the likes of ULTRA-SONIC, DANCE OVER DOSE, DJ TEN, AUDIO CODE and of course, MARC himself. The 'CENTRIPITAL EP' followed in 1994 while SMITH presided over another V/A set, 'DJ'S DELITE VOL.4', in 1996. That year also saw the release of the 'LOONY TOONS' 12", a collaboration with VIBES and JIMMY J.

Other artists SMITH has been involved with include DJ TEN (with whom he cut 1997's 'AQUARIUM' for 'Clubscene'), CHRIS LEGE, SHARKEY, MARK McLAUGHLAN (the man behind Eruption records) and even MALCOLM McLAREN (!). The man has also worked with fellow rave veteran SCOTT BROWN, releasing a couple of joint 12" efforts over the course of 1998.

MARC SMITH – DJ, etc

Clubscene — not iss.

1993. (12") *(csrt 002)* **BREAKDOWN (mixes)** [ ] [-]
Apr 94. (cd-s/c-s/12") *(d/c+/csrt 020)* **TECHNO DUP** [ ] [-]
1995. (12") *(csrt 040)* **PUMP UP THE NOIZE (raid mix). / NEXUS / FORMULA** [ ] [-]

Homegrown — not iss.

Jun 94. (12"ep; by SMITH & BROWN) **VOLUME 1** [ ] [-]

Notorious Vinyl — not iss.

Sep 94. (12"; by MARC SMITH & DAVIE MURRAY) *(NVR 002)* **UNTITLED** [ ] [-]
Sep 94. (12"; by MARC SMITH & MARK McLAUGLAN) *(NVR 003)* **MARK II** [ ] [-]
Sep 94. (12"ep) *(NVR 004)* **THE CENTRIPITAL EP** [ ] [-]

DJ's Delite — not iss.

Sep 96. (cd/lp; by Various Artists) *(DBM 201-2/-1)* **DJ'S DELITE VOL.4** [ ] [-]

Most Wanted — not iss.

Nov 96. (12"; as VIBES, JIMMY J & MARC SMITH) *(2233)* **LOONY TOONS** [ ] [-]

Clubscene — not iss.

Aug 96. (12") *(CSRT 066)* **MARC SMITH & SHARKEY** [ ] [-]
Nov 96. (12") *(CSRT 072)* **BOOM 'N' POW (mixes)** [ ] [-]
Jun 97. (cd-s/12"; as MARC SMITH & DJ TEN) *(D+/CSRT 079)* **AQUARIUM (mixes)** [ ] [-]
Jun 97. (cd/c) *(D+/CSR 014)* **PAST, PRESENT AND FUTURE** [ ] [-]
– Procastinator / Taking over me / Kickstart / Oh no / Boom and pow / Pump up the noise / Nexus / Journey / Relax your mind / Do that to me / Echoplex.

Federation — not iss.

May 98. (12"; as MARC SMITH vs. SCOTT BROWN) *(FED 1)* **HITS ME LIKE THUNDER. / APOCALYPSE** [ ] [-]
Nov 98. (12"; as MARC SMITH & SCOTT BROWN) *(FED 2)* **TAKING ME HIGHER. / FIREVER** [ ] [-]

Nu Energy — not iss.

Oct 98. (12") *(003)* **ENCOUNTERS. / NOTHING MORE** [ ] [-]

Clubscene — not iss.

Oct 00. (12"; as DJ MARC SMITH) *(csrt 089)* **RELAX YOUR MIND** [ ] [-]

Bonkers — not iss.

Jan 01. (12") *(BONKERS 4)* **FUCKIN' TRIPPY. / DON'T MOVE** [ ] [-]

SNAKES OF SHAKE

Formed: Glasgow . . . 1984 by SEORI BURNETTE, SANDY BROWN, ROBERT RENFREW, TZEN VERMILLION and RHOD BURNETT. Country-tinged indie-rockers in the trademark West Of Scotland mould, the SNAKES OF SHAKE issued a mini-set, 'SOUTHERN CROSS', its title track simultaneously released in Spring '85. It wouldn't be the first time the song would surface, although by the time it revamped a year later, both VERMILLION and BURNETT had been substituted by (WILSON) NEIL SCOTT and IAIN SHEDDON respectively.

Their one and only full-length set, 'GRACELANDS AND THE NATURAL WOOD' (1987), would again feature what had now become their theme tune although the collapse of their label, 'Making Waves', put paid to any chances they might have had.

Getting a foothold once more on the music business ladder, three former SNAKES (SEORI, WILSON and IAIN, together with KEITH GILES and session man extrordinaire, BJ COLE) re-emerged in 1988 as SUMMERHILL. Following a few West Coast/BYRDS-influenced releases including the mini-set, 'LOWDOWN', the line-up was slightly amended when SHEDDON was replaced with MICHAEL STURGIS. Finally rewarded for their years of struggle, SUMMERHILL were snapped up by 'Polydor', the resulting 'WEST OF HERE' set hitting the shops early in 1990. Described (probably unfairly) as a countrified, poor man's DEACON BLUE, the band received a smattering of positive reviews but failed to make their mark on the ever fickle and evolving pop-rock scene. • **Covered:** DO RIGHT WOMAN, DO RIGHT MAN (Dan Penn – Spooner Oldham) / WILD HORSES (Rolling Stones).

SEORI BURNETTE – vocals, guitar, harmonica / **TZEN VERMILLION** – guitar / **SANDY BROWN** – piano, accordion, vocals / **ROBERT RENFREW** – bass, slide guitar, vocals / **RHOD BURNETT** – drums

Tense But Confident — not iss.

Mar 85. (m-lp) *(TBC 1)* **SOUTHERN CROSS** [ ] [-]
–
Mar 85. (12"m) *(GOBS12-1)* **SOUTHERN CROSS. / LIFE'S TOO STRONG / INDISPENSIBLE** [ ] [-]

—— **(WILSON) NEIL SCOTT** – guitar; repl. VERMILLION

—— **IAIN SHEDDON** – drums (ex-JOLT) repl. RHOD BURNETT

Making Waves — not iss.

Aug 86. (7") *(SURF 116)* **SOUTHERN CROSS. / YOU WALK** [ ] [-]
(12"+=) *(SURFT 116)* – ('A'-part 2).
Jul 87. (cd/c/lp) *(CD/C+/SPRAY 106)* **GRACELANDS AND THE NATURAL WOOD** [ ] [-]
– Southern cross / Make it shine / Gracelands / No reason / Strange affair / Man the man / Sender down / Last resort / Like no ther / Get me out of here.

SUMMERHILL

—— were formed by **SEORI, (WILSON) NEIL, IAIN / + KEITH GILES** – bass, vocals / guest **B.J. COLE** – steel guitar (session man extraordinaire)

Rocket 5 — not iss.

Jun 88. (7") *(HUCS 102)* **I WANT YOU. /** [ ] [-]

Diabolo — not iss.

Oct 88. (m-lp) *(SORCM 4)* **LOWDOWN** [ ] [-]
– Rosebud / I'll keep you in mind / Lately / Knew I would return / Hold back the heartache / It's gonna be alright / I can't stay / Say goodbye.

—— **MICHAEL STURGIS** – drums; repl. IAIN

Polydor — not iss.

Oct 89. (7"/7"g-f) *(TTRC/+G 1)* **HERE I AM. /** [ ] [-]
(12"+=) *(TTRCX 1)* –
Mar 90. (7"/c-s) *(TTRC/+S 2)* **DON'T LET IT DIE. / KEEP YOU IN MIND** [ ] [-]
(10"+=/12"+=/cd-s+=) *(TTRC T/X/D 2)* – Do right woman, do right man / It's gonna be alright.
Mar 90. (cd/c/lp) *(843130-2/-4/-1)* **WEST OF HERE** [ ] [-]
– Don't let it die / Here I am / If you hold a gun / The ballad of Summerhill / I've found a friend / If I knew you better / Somehow, somewhere / Lately / I have a reason / Last to find out. *(cd+=/c+=)* – Wild horses (live in the studio).
Apr 90. (7") *(TTRC 3)* **WILD HORSES. / RIVER BLUE** [ ] [-]
(12"+=/cd-s+=) *(TTRC X/D 3)* – Please don't go away.

—— later that year, two ex-SUMMERHILL members (they had now split) teamed up with singer, SUMISHTA BRAHM, on a one-off 13 FRIGHTENED GIRLS single, 'Lost At Sea'. The following year, WILSON SCOTT joined HORSE LATITUDES, who released a mini-set, 'SEPTEMBER SONGS'. SUMMERHILL re-formed in the mid 90's

Tupelo — unknown

Jan 95. (cd-s) *(TTRCD 4)* **NO MATTER WHAT YOU DO /** [ ] [-]

SNEAK ATTACK TIGERS (see under ⇒ Flotsam & Jetsam records)

SOCIAL LEPERS (see under ⇒ Bronx Cheer records)

SOLO (see under ⇒ Limbo records)

Jimmy SOMERVILLE

Born: 22 Jun'61, Glasgow. An 80's gay icon, the diminutive JIMMY SOMERVILLE has been a regular chart fixture through the various twists and turns of his career in addition to being a vocal proponent of gay rights and left-wing politics in general. His journey south to the bright lights of London was apparently more harrowing than most, as evidenced on the debut BRONSKI BEAT single, 'Smalltown Boy'. SOMERVILLE had formed the trio in 1984 with fellow Glaswegian STEVE BRONSKI and Londoner LARRY STEINBECK. Angst-ridden, Euro-influenced synth-pop with a nagging commercial edge, the BRONSKI sound dominated the Top 10 with a debut album, 'AGE OF CONSENT' (1984) picking up widespread critical acclaim. JIMMY's bollock-busting falsetto and gay activist manifesto was pivotal to the band's approach while a subsequent cover of 'IT AIN'T NECESSARILY SO' proved that he could easily handle more mature material.

Amid growing tension, JIMMY quit the band shortly after and, together with sometime BRONSKI keyboardist, RICHARD COLES, formed The COMMITTEE. In COLES, SOMERVILLE had found a fresh writing foil and the pair duly renamed themselves The COMMUNARDS (after objections from another band) before coming up with the piano-thumping neo-gospel of 'YOU ARE MY WORLD' as their debut single in Autumn '85. Released on 'London' and produced by Stephen Hague, the Top 30 track certainly marked a welcome break from the norm and while follow-up track, 'DISENCHANTED' sounded more familiar, the pair's eponymous 1986 debut album was characterised by swooning strings and brassy horn flourishes. A pumped-up cover of Harold Melvin's 'DON'T LEAVE ME THIS WAY' paired JIMMY's soulful scream with co-vocalist, SARAH JANE MORRIS, a thrilling combination that took the track to the top of the UK chart in summer '86. This success spurred on sales of the album, a record that explored SOMERVILLE's trademark lyrical terrain of gay alienation ('FORBIDDEN LOVE') and left wing politics ('BREADLINE BRITAIN'); earlier that year, The COMMUNARDS had played alongside BILLY BRAGG and The STYLE COUNCIL under the Labour-promoting 'Red Wedge' banner. A third single, 'SO COLD THE NIGHT', made the Top 10 a few months later while early '87 saw a remixed 'YOU ARE MY WORLD' narrowly miss the Top 20.

Following the replacement of MORRIS with ex-MODETTE, JUNE MILES-KINGSTON, the group were back with a new Top 30 single, 'TOMORROW' and album, 'RED' (1987). Yet again, the album climbed to the upper regions of the chart (Top 5) on the strength of a Hi-NRG injected disco classic; this time around, SOMERVILLE and COLES turned their hand to Gloria Gaynor's 'NEVER CAN SAY GOODBYE' and duly made the Top 5. The moving 'FOR A FRIEND' was the third single (Top 30), its lyrical concerns representative of the more direct approach taken to gay issues on the album as a whole.

Following the Top 20 success of fourth single, 'THERE'S MORE TO LOVE . . .', The COMMUNARDS unexpectedly went their separate ways in 1988. SOMERVILLE embarked on a solo career the following year, almost immediately making the Top 20 with '(COMMENT TE DIRE) ADIEU!' (an old FRANCOISE HARDY hit). A debut album, 'READ MY LIPS', followed into the Top 30 a couple of months later but as ever, it was a storming dancefloor cover that put him back in the chart spotlight. An obvious choice perhaps, but Sylvester's Hi-NRG classic, 'YOU MAKE ME FEEL (MIGHTY REAL)' was a perfect vehicle for JIMMY's vocal acrobatics. More sober but no less heartfelt was his Top 10 cover of the Bee Gees' 'TO LOVE SOMEBODY', a taster of the more romantically-inclined fare on the album.

It'd be a further five years before his next album, 'DARE TO LOVE', which saw him score with the club-friendly 'HEARTBEAT' and a cover of 'HURTS SO GOOD', originally a hit for SUSAN CADOGAN. While he's been notable for his absence from the recording front of late, SOMERVILLE continues to play live, especially abroad in more conservative cultures where he's regarded as a hero by many young gay men unable to express their sexuality.

JIMMY SOMERVILLE – vocals (ex-BRONSKI BEAT, ex-COMMUNARDS) / with **JUNE MILES-KINGSTON** – backing vocals (ex-MO-DETTES, ex-COMMUNARDS) / with numerous session people

London London

Oct 89. (7") *(LON 241)* **(COMMENT TE DIRE) ADIEU! / TELL THE WORLD** [14] [ ]
(12"+=/c-s+=/cd-s+=) *(LON X/CS/CD 241)* – Smalltown boy / Don't leave me this way / You are my world.

Dec 89. (lp/c/cd) *(828166-1/-4/-2)* **READ MY LIPS** [29] [ ]
– (Comment te dire) Adieu! / You make me feel (mighty real) / Heaven here (on Earth) with your love / Don't know what to do (without you) / My heart is in your hands / Control / And you never thought this could happen to you / Rain / Read my lips (enough is enough) *(re-iss. May93 on 'Spectrum' cd/c; 550042-2/-4)*

Jan 90. (7"/c-s) *(LON/+CS 249)* **YOU MAKE ME FEEL (MIGHTY REAL). / NOT SO GOD ALMIGHTY** [5] [ ]
(12"+=/cd-s+=) *(LON X/CD 249)* – Stranger.

Mar 90. (7"/c-s) *(LON/+CS 254)* **READ MY LIPS (ENOUGH IS ENOUGH). / AND YOU NEVER THOUGHT THIS COULD HAPPEN TO YOU** [26] [ ]
(12"/cd-s) *(LON X/CD 254)* – ('A'side) / Stranger.

Oct 90. (7"/c-s) *(LON/+CS 281)* **TO LOVE SOMEBODY. / RAIN** [8] [ ]
(12"+=/cd-s+=) *(LON X/CD 281)* – Why?

Aug 91. (7"/c-s) *(LON/+CS 301)* **RUN FROM LOVE. / DESIRE** [52] [ ]
(12"+=/cd-s+=) *(LON X/CD 301)* – To love somebody.

Jan 95. (c-s/12"/cd-s) *(LON CS/X/CD 358)* **HEARTBEAT (club mixes by E-Smoove / Armand Van Helden / Media Records)** [24] [-]

May 95. (c-s) *(LONCS 364)* **HURT SO GOOD / ('A'-Beatmasters mix)** [15] [ ]
(cd-s+=) *(LONCD 364)* – Love you forever / Been so long.
(cd-s+=) *(LONCDX 364)* – ('A'-Stevie & Clevie dub) / ('A'-2 Sly & Robbie mixes).

Jun 95. (cd/c/lp) *(828540-2/-4/-1)* **DARE TO LOVE** [38] [ ]
– Heartbeat / Hurts so good / Cry / Lovething / By your side / Dare to love / Someday we'll be together / Alright / Too much of a good thing / A dream gone wrong / Come lately / Safe in these arms / Because of him.

Oct 95. (c-s) *(LONCS 372)* **BY YOUR SIDE / NOTHING SAID, NOTHING DONE** [41] [-]
(12") *(LONX 372)* – ('A'-The shining mix) / ('A'-Miss you like crazy mix).
(cd-s) *(LONCD 372)* – (all 4 tracks above).

Sep 97. (c-s/cd-s) *(CA/CD GUT 11)* **DARK SKY / DARK SKY (Peg's study mix) / TEAR FOOL / BLAME** [66] [ ]
(cd-s) *(CXGUT 11)* – ('A'mixes; Peg's study / Dillon and Dickins / Sure is pure / Only Child / Tony De Vit).

May 99. (c-s) *(CAGUT 24)* **LAY DOWN / I BELIEVE / MOVING ON** [ ] [-]
(cd-s) *(CDGUT 24)* – ('A'mixes; radio / almighty / bonus disco).

Jun 99. (cd/c) *(GUT CD/MC 8)* **MANAGE THE DAMAGE** [ ] [-]
– Here I am / Lay down / Dark sky / My life / Something to live for / This must be love / Girl falling down / Someday soon / Eve / Stone / Rolling.

– compilations, others, etc. –

Nov 90. (cd/c/lp) *London; (828226-2/-4/-1)* **THE SINGLES COLLECTION 1984-1990** [4] [ ]
– Smalltown boy (BRONSKI BEAT) / Don't leave me this way / Ain't necessarily so (BRONSKI BEAT) / (Comment te dire) Adieu! / Never can say goodbye / Why? (BRONSKI BEAT) / You are my world / For a friend / I feel love (BRONSKI BEAT & MARC ALMOND) / So cold the night / Mighty real / To love somebody / Run

from love (remix) / There's more to love. *(cd+=)* – Tomorrow / Disenchanted. *(re-iss. Aug91; 828628-2/-4/-1)*

Jan 91. (7"/c-s; by JIMMY SOMERVILLE with BRONSKI BEAT) *London; (LON/+CS 281)* **SMALLTOWN BOY. / Communards: THERE'S MORE TO LOVE** [32] [ ]
(12"+=/cd-s+=) *(LON X/CD 281)* – To love somebody.

Sep 01. (cd) *Warner ESP; (092741258-2)* **THE VERY BEST OF JIMMY SOMERVILLE, BRONSKI BEAT & THE COMMUNARDS** [29] [-]

SOUL SURFERS (see under ⇒ Limbo records)

SOUNDMAN (see ⇒ Section 9: the 90s)

SOUP DRAGONS

Formed: Bellshill, Lanarkshire ... 1985 by SEAN DICKSON, JIM McCULLOCH, ROSS SINCLAIR and SUSHIL K DADE. Taking their name from cult kids TV show, 'The Clangers', The SOUP DRAGONS were initially signed to the 'Subway' label for whom they released the 'SUN IN THE SKY' EP and a follow-up, 'WHOLE WIDE WORLD'. The band's BUZZCOCKS/UNDERTONES three-chord flurry gained valuable exposure later that summer when the latter single's B-side, 'PLEASANTLY SURPRISED', was featured on the NME's C86 compilation.

One unlikely fan was ex-WHAM! manager, Jazz Summers, who masterminded the next phase of their career via the 'Raw TV' label and oversaw the release of a string of singles including their first Top 75 chart entry, 1987's 'CAN'T TAKE NO MORE'. Further singles, 'SOFT AS YOUR FACE' and 'THE MAJESTIC HEAD' found them dabbling with a 60's retro sound, 'Sire' trying and failing to break the band into the mainstream with a long awaited debut album, 'THIS IS OUR ART' (1988).

Moving back to 'Raw TV' and re-evaluating their approach, DICKSON & Co. emerged in the second half of 1989 with two singles, 'BACKWARDS DOG' and 'CROTCH DEEP TRASH', critics only too ready to mention the similarities with the latest STOOGES-fixated offering from fellow Glaswegians, PRIMAL SCREAM.

Following the replacement of ROSS with PAUL QUINN, detractors were furnished with further ammunition amid accusations of bandwagoneering as the 'DRAGONS released the singalong indie/dance crossover, 'MOTHER UNIVERSE', in 1990. The accompanying album, 'LOVEGOD' (1990), confirmed the transformation and The SOUP DRAGONS finally broke big time a few months later with a cover of the Rolling Stones' 'I'M FREE'. Transforming an R&B jangle into a stoned, fringe-shaking anthem for the baggy generation – complete with reggae toasting courtesy of JUNIOR REID – really didn't do the band much good in retrospect. Despite being a massive worldwide hit and an MTV stalwart, the track's success couldn't prevent The SOUP DRAGONS dying a swift commercial death when the scene came to an abrupt end in the early 90's. Granted, they spun it out with a re-issued 'MOTHER UNIVERSE' but yet another change in direction on 'HOTWIRED' (1992) made no headway with a music buying public who'd simply moved on, the band's chequered career eventually coming to a close after their short-lived tenure with 'Big Life'.

After a very disappointing US-only set in '95 bombed for DICKSON's new SOUP DRAGONS, SUSHIL – who'd moonlighted with The TELSTAR PONIES – returned a few years later with his own FUTURE PILOT A.K.A. project. Meanwhile, DICKSON made his comeback under the guise of The HIGH FIDELITY, a personal experiment into the field of psychedelic rock. After debuting on a friends' compilation CD, DICKSON managed to release the warped punk/pop single 'ADDICTED TO TV' (issued on Japanese imprint 'Plastique' due to popular demand). Since his explorations with 'THE HIGH FIDELITY' (which began as a bit of a laugh apparently), he issued a handful of delicious but disturbing singles, among them 'LOVE DUP' and '2-UP, 2-DOWN'. These borrowed heavily from the ilk of The JESUS & MARY CHAIN.

DICKSON subsequently released 'DEMONSTRATION' (1999), a full length album which boasted his craft for writing catchy but experimental pop. Songs such as 'THE NATIONAL ANTHEM' and 'LAZY B' would act as hard evidence if DICKSON was ever to be accused of dull indie imitation. However, recent single 'I'M SORRY' seemed to lack the flair and substance seen in some of his earlier work.

• **Songwriters:** DICKSON compositions, except PURPLE HAZE (Jimi Hendrix) / OUR LIPS ARE SEALED (Go-Go's) / I'M NOT YOUR STEPPING STONE (Monkees).

SEAN DICKSON (b.21 Mar'67) – vocals, guitar / **JIM McCULLOCH** (b.19 May'66) – guitar, vocals / **ROSS SINCLAIR** – drums / **SUSHIL K. DADE** (b.15 Jul'66) – bass (ex-WAKE)

Subway / not iss.

Feb 86. (ltd.7"ep) *(SUBWAY 2)* **THE SUN IN THE SKY** [ ] [-]
– Quite content / Swirling round the garden with you / Fair's fair / Not for Humbert.

May 86. (7") *(SUBWAY 4)* **WHOLE WIDE WORLD. / I KNOW EVERYTHING** [ ] [-]
(12"+=) *(SUBWAY 4T)* – Pleasantly surprised.

— May 86, SEAN (bass) & JIM (guitar) were part-time auxiliaries of BMX BANDITS who were fronted by DUGLAS and released 'SAD'. / 'E102' on '53rd & 3rd' label. JIM played on their Jan'87 follow-up 'WHAT A WONDERFUL WORLD'. / 'THE DAY BEFORE TOMORROW'.

Raw TV Products / not iss.

Sep 86. (7",7"red,7"blue) *(RTV 1)* **HANG TEN!. / SLOW THINGS DOWN** [ ] [-]
(12"+=) *(RTV 12-1)* – Just mind your step girl / Man about town with chairs.

Jan 87. (7") *(RTV 2)* **HEAD GONE ASTRAY. / GIRL IN THE WORLD** [ ] [-]
(12"+=/12"w-poster+=) *(RTV/+P 12-2)* – So sad I feel.

Jun 87. (7") *(RTV 3)* **CAN'T TAKE NO MORE. / WHITEWASH** [65] [-]
(12"+=) *(RTV 12-3)* – A-Ha! experience.
(12"ep) *(RTVL 12-3)* – ('A'&'B'live) / Hang ten! (live) / Purple haze (live).

Aug 87. (7") *(RTV 4)* **SOFT AS YOUR FACE. / IT'S ALWAYS AUTUMN** [66] [-]
(12"+=) *(RTV 12-4)* – Our lips are sealed / Soft as your face – arrangement.
(double-groove 12"+=) *(RTV 12-4D)* – Can't take no more (vocal squad version) / Whole wide world (live).

Mar 88. (7") *(RTV 5)* **THE MAJESTIC HEAD. / 4-WAY BRAIN** [ ] [-]
(12"+=) *(RTV 12-5)* – Them.
(12"pic-d+=) *(RTV 12-5P)* – Corporation headlock.

Sire / Sire

Apr 88. (lp/c)(cd) *(WX 169/+C)(K 925702-2) <25702>* **THIS IS OUR ART** [60] [ ]
– Kingdom chairs / Great empty space / The majestic head / Turning stone / Vacate my space / On overhead walkways / Passion protein / King of the castle / Another dream ticket / Soft as your face / Family ways. *(cd re-iss. Jul91; K 925702-2)*

Jun 88. (7") *(W 7820)* **KINGDOM CHAIRS. / WHITE CRUISING** [ ] [ ]
(12") *(W 7820T)* – ('A'side) / I'm not your stepping stone / All because of you.
(10") *(W 7820TE)* – ('A'&'B'live) / Family way (live) / King of the castle (live).

Raw TV / Big Life

Jul 89. (7") *(RTV 6)* **BACKWARDS DOG. / BURN OUT** [ ] [-]
(12"+=) *(RTV 6T)* – Supercherry / Kill kill kill me.

Oct 89. (7") *(RTV 7)* **CROTCH DEEP TRASH. / YOU CAN FLY** [ ] [-]
(ext.12"+=) *(RTV 7T)* – Superangel / ('A'dub version).

— **PAUL QUINN** – drums repl. ROSS. / added guest **ALEX McLAREN** – guitar

Mar 90. (7") *(RTV 8)* **MOTHER UNIVERSE. / ('A'-Solar mix)** [ ] [-]
(12"+=) *(RTV 8T)* – ('A'-Love dub mix).
(cd-s++=) *(RTV 8CD)* – 4-way brain.

May 90. (cd/c/lp) *(SOUP CD/MC/LP 2) <842985>* **LOVEGOD** [60] [88] Oct90
– Mother Universe / Backwards dog / Softly / Drive the pain / Lovegod / Dream E-forever / Sweetmeat / Kiss the gun / Love you to death / Beauty freak / Lovedog (dub) / Crotch deep trash. *(cd+=)* – (2 extra mixes) *(re-iss. Aug90 on 'Big Life'+= cd/c/lp; SOUP CD/MC/LP 2R)* – I'm free. *(hit UK No.7)*

Jul 90. (7"/c-s/ext.12") *(RTV 9/+MC/T) <877568>* **I'M FREE (featuring JUNIOR REID). / LOVEGOD (dub)** [5] [79] Sep90
(cd-s+=) *(RTV 9CD)* – ('A'-12"version).
(12") *(RTV 9R)* – ('A'-Terry Farley Boys Own mix) / Backwards dog (remix).

Big Life / Big Life

Oct 90. (7"/c-s) *(BLR/+C 30)* **MOTHER UNIVERSE. / BACKWARDS DOG** [26] [ ]
(12"+=/cd-s+=) *(BLR T/CD 30)* – ('A'dub remix) / ('A'-'89 remix).

Aug 91. (7"/c-s) *(BLR 56)* **ELECTRIC BLUES. / UNEARTHED** [ ] [ ]
(12"+=/cd-s+=) *(BLRT/BLC 56)* – Solar rise / ('A'dub version).

Apr 92. (7"/c-s) *(BLR/+C 68) <865764>* **DIVINE THING. / DRIVING** [53] [35]
(12"+=/cd-s+=) *(BLR T/CD 68)* – ('A'revisited) / American sweetmeat.

May 92. (cd/c/lp) *(BLR CD/MC/LP 15) <13178>* **HOTWIRED** [74] [97]
– Pleasure / Divine thing / Running wild / Getting down / Forever yesterday / No more / Understanding / Dream on (Solid gone) / Everlasting / Absolute heaven / Everything / Sweet layabout / Mindless.

Sep 92. (12"ep/c-ep/cd-ep) <867416> **PLEASURE / PLEASURE (revisited). / WHAT YOU WANT / DIVE-BOMBER** [ ] [69]
(cd-ep) – ('A'revisited) . . . repl. by 'Man'.
(cd-s+=) – ('A'revisited) / I'm free (original) / Mother universe / Electric blues.

— SUSHIL joined The TELSTAR PONIES

— **DICKSON** virtually solo + a plethora of session people and special guests incl. TINA WEYMOUTH, NEVILLE STAPLES, BOOTSY COLLINS

not iss. / Polygram

Jan 95. (cd,c,lp) *<522732>* **HYDROPHONIC** [-] [ ]
– One way street / Don't get down (get down) / Do you care? / May the force be with you / Contact high / All messed up / The time is now / Freeway / Rest in peace / J.F. junkie / Automatic speed queen / Out of here / Motherfunker / Black and blues / Hypersonic re-entry.

— DICKSON would later surface with outfit . . .

HIGH FIDELITY

SEAN DICKSON – vocals, guitar / with **PAUL DALLAWAY** – guitars / **ADRIAN BARRY** – bass / **ROSS McFARLANE** – drums, percussion

Vinyl Japan not iss.

Nov 96. (7") *(PAD 033)* **ADDICTED TO A TV. / PELVIC ROCK** -

Plastique not iss.

Jun 97. (7") *(FAKE 01)* **ADDICTED TO A TV. /** -
(cd-s+=) *(FAKE 1CDS)* –

Apr 98. (7") *(FAKE 02)* **COME AGAIN. / (part 2)** -
(cd-s+=) *(FAKE 02CDS)* – (part 3) / (part 4) / (part 5).
(12") *(FAKE 02TX)* – ('A'mixes).

Jul 98. (c-s) *(FAKE 03MC)* **LUV DUP /** -
(cd-s+=) *(FAKE 03CDS)* –
(cd-s) *(FAKE 03CDX)* –

Sep 99. (7") *(FAKE 101)* **2 UP – 2 DOWN. / SUGAR FREE** -
(cd-s+=) *(FAKE 101CD)* – Nothing left to fight.

Mar 00. (cd) *(FAKE 103CD)* **DEMONSTRATION** -
– Omnichord intro / Luv dup / Ithanku / Odyssey of a psychonaut / Unsorry / Lazy. B / The national anthem / A change is gonna come? / Bollywood bubblegum experiment / 2 up – 2 down / Greeneye monster / Cola-coca / Patch Granville / Never bollocks the mind. *<US-iss.Apr02 on 'Freedom In Exile'; 12>*

Jul 00. (7") *(FAKE 104)* **UNSORRY. /** -
(cd-s+=) *(FAKE 104CDS)* –
(cd-s) *(FAKE 104CDX)* –

Nov 00. (cd-s) *(FAKE 105CDS)* **A CHANGE IS GONNA COME?** -
(cd-s) *(FAKE 105CDX)* –

Mar 01. (cd-s) *(FAKE 106CD1)* **SCREAM IF YOU WANT TO GO FASTER / BASED ON A TRUE STORY / THE PLANXTY CANNON TRILOGY** -
(cd-s) *(FAKE 106CD2)* –
(12") *(FAKE 106X)* –

Apr 01. (cd) *(FAKE 107CD)* **THE OMNICHORD ALBUM** -
– Scream if you want to go faster / Electromale / Omnichord 4am / Plastiquetronica / Pig might fly / Ice cream / Commercial suicide / Paradise syndrome / Hi-fi / Nothing left to fight.

— HIGH FIDELITY (12" 'NO GOOD (TO ME)' was not the same outfit)

SOURTOOTH (see ⇒ Section 9: the 90s)

SO YOU THINK YOU'RE A COWBOY (see under ⇒ TV 21)

SPACEHOPPER (see under ⇒ Creeping Bent records)

SPACE KITTENS (see under ⇒ Flotsam & Jetsam records)

SPARE SNARE

Formed: Dundee . . . 1992 by frontman and part-time solo star (his 'A MATTER OF FACT' was played on US college radio!) JAN D. BURNETT. Along with cohorts PAUL ESPOSITO (on guitar), ALAN CORMACK (on bass) and BARRY GIBSON (on drums), they traded their early JOY DIVISION-esque meets Lo-Fi sound around the country.

Forming their own 'Chute' imprint (after JAN D released a one-off under the WHITE LEATHER CLUB pseudonym), SPARE SNARE unleashed their debut single, 'SUPER SLINKY'. After a classic second and third, 'SKATEBOARD PUNK ROCKER' and 'THORNS' in '94, they surfaced the following year with a spruced up cover of Split Enz's 'I GOT YOU'. Peel sessions followed and, after a debut set, 'LIVE AT HOME' (1995) – exactly that! – they subsequently signed to the 'Deceptive' imprint (more famous for having ELASTICA on their roster). However, after only two 45's (the first being a cover of Sir Cliff's 'WIRED FOR SOUND' in the style of WIRE!), they found themselves back on the small indie imprints again.

Second set, the US-only 'WESTFIELD LANE', was delivered early in '97 and was recorded on a home 4-track by multi-instrumentalist JAN, its sound a little sparse to say the least. The man in question brought back BARRY and ALAN for his next project/album, 'ANIMALS AND ME' (1998), and this was followed by even more 7" singles and a compilation the following year. Breaking free for their own musical trappings, SPARE SNARE were back in the Spring of 2001, first up being a Billy Connolly cover!, 'EVERYBODY KNOWS THAT' (backed by a rendition of the Destiny's Child number 'SAY MY NAME'!!!.

• **Other covers:** STRANGE AND SILENT STAIRCASE (Number One Cup) / STOOR covered REPETITION (Edwyn Collins).

JAN D. BURNETT – vocals, guitar, synthesizer

Scottish! not iss.

1993. (7"one-sided; as The WHITE LEATHER CLUB) *(SCOTTISH! 001)* **SHANDY ON THE ROCKS** -

Chute Prospective

1993. (7") *(CHUTE 001)* *<PRS 591>* **SUPER SLINKY. / AS A MATTER OF FACT**

— added **PAUL ESPOSITO** – guitar / **ALAN D. CORMACK** – bass, guitar (of MUPPET MULE) / **BARRY JAMES GIBSON** – drums (of MUPPET MULE)

Sep 94. (7") *(CHUTE 003)* **THORNS. / SKATEBOARD PUNK ROCKER** -

Jan 95. (7"flexi) *(CHUTE 004)* **WHAT IS IT** -

Mar 95. (7"clear/green) *(che 31)* **I GOT YOU. / Majesty Crush: IF JFA WERE STILL TOGETHER** -
(above issued for 'Che' records)

Chute Twin/Tone

May 95. (m-cd/10"m-lp) *(CHUTE CD/LP 005)* *<89297>* **LIVE AT HOME** Oct95
<US-title 'SPARE SNARE'>
– Thorns / Shine on now / Wired for sound / Super slinky / As a matter of fact / Skateboard punk rocker / Bugs / My better half *[cd-only]* / Call the birds / Thorns. *(cd re-iss. Apr98 & Aug99; same)*

Love Train not iss.

Sep 95. (7") *(PUBE 05)* **BUGS. / SCRABBLE** -

Anti Social not iss.

Nov 95. (7") *(ASR 002)* **SMILE, IT'S SUGAR. / Sone: FRENCH CAMPUS** -

Deceptive Prospective

Nov 95. (7"etched) *(BLUFF 021)* **WIRED FOR SOUND** -

Mar 96. (7") *<TRG 89309>* **WIRED FOR SOUND. / BUGS** -

Apr 96. (7"m) *(BLUFF 027)* **SMILE, ITS SUGAR / INDIEKIDSUCK. / HANGING AROUND** -
(c-s+=) *(BLUFF 027C)* – (30 minutes blank to send in for stuff).
(cd-s+=) *(BLUFF 027/+CD)* – Boom boom boom.

Chute not iss.

May 96. (7") *(CHUTE 006)* **HAIRCUT. / Lazerboy: AYE AYE CAPTAIN** -

100 Guitar Mania not iss.

Jun 96. (7"blue) *(100GM 14)* **BOOM BOOM BOOM (ONE). / the Summer Hits: AWAY FROM THE CITY** - - Japan

not iss. Wabana

Jan 97. (cd) *<ore 8>* **WESTFIELD LANE** -
– Action hero / James Dean poster / Let's go home and do some drugs / Before barcodes / Hit man, cha cha cha / Name with a heart / Take it, any-way / Can't you see the shit I'm in / You've got a nerve / Disturbed / Last night.

Blue Rose Blue Rose

Jun 97. (7") *(<BRRC 10095>)* **THE MONEY PIT VOLUME ONE**
– Strange and silent staircase / NUMBER ONE CUP: Smile, it's sugar.

Rebound not iss.

1997. (7"m) *(RB 001)* **T.R.E. / (other 2 by the Dakota Suite & the New Bad Things)** - - Dutch

Hummy And Joey not iss.

1997. (7"ep) *(SPAZ 03)* **LEADERS IN LIGHTCONTROL EXTENDED PLAYER EP** -
– Profile check / (other 2 by i.s.a.n. and David Wrench).

Lissys not iss.

Apr 98. (7") *(LISS 24)* **HARD OF HEARING. / Coastal Cafe: LESBIANS IN WAISTCOATS** -

— cred on the sleeve:- **BARRY GIBSON, ALAN CORMACK & JAN BURNETT**

Chute not iss.

Aug 98. (cd) *(CHUTECD 010)* **ANIMALS AND ME** -
– I'll get by / We are the Snare / Stop complaining / If I had a hi-fi / Holding on to the shore / What's going on / The lies count / Batteries gone / My kind of crazy / Here come the storms / Hit me, Satan / They airbrushed my face / Who Lee / All I want to do is touch / We grew up / I feel the sun, and it's mine. *(re-iss. Aug99; same)*

— added **ROSS MATHESON** – guitar (of STOOR)

Third Gear Third Gear

Mar 99. (7") *(<3G-19>)* **BRUISING YOU. / WHAT YOU'VE DONE** 1998

— **JAN, BARRY + ROSS** added **KEVIN DEVINE + GRAEME OGSTEN** (**ALAN CORMACK** was back in soon)

Bad Jazz not iss.

Jan 01. (7") *(Bebop 23)* **LAUNCH. / CALLING IN THE . . .** -

Chute not iss.

Apr 01. (7") *(CHUTE 013)* **EVERYBODY KNOWS THAT. / SAY MY NAME** -

May 01. (cd) *(CHUTE 015)* **CHARM** -
– No soul / Taking on the sides / Surrender / Calling in the favours / Crazy sort of hum / Shakin' and rollin' / Mod girls, mod boys / Rolled over / Heady heart / Shooting off my head / Troubles.

- compilations, etc. -

Dec 95. (m-cd) *100 Guitar Mania: (100GM 08)* **DISCO DANCING** [-] [-]
– As a matter of fact / Super slinky / Thorns / Skateboard punk rocker / Thorns (one) / Shine on now / Latin float / Skateboard punk rocker (one). *(UK-iss.Oct97 & Aug99; same)*

Oct 99. (cd) *Che; (che 83)* **LOVE YOUR EARLY STUFF** [ ] [-]
– As a matter of fact / Super slinky / Thorns / Skateboard punk rocker / Thorns (one) / Shine on now / Latin float / Skateboard punk rocker (one) / I got you / What is it / Bugs (edit) / Scrabble / Clutch me now / Bruising you / Smile, it's sugar (one) / Wired for sound / Bugs (live) / Smile it's sugar / Indiekidsuck / Hanging around / Boom boom boom / Haircut / Aftertaste / Boom boom boom (one) / Strange and silent staircase.

MUPPET MULE

ALAN CORMACK, BARRY GIBSON + ROY ANDERSON

Chute / not iss.

1994. (ltd-7"ep) *(CHUTE 002)* **TESS / FLAYLING. / (2 others by BROCCOLI)** [ ] [-]

HAMFISTED

CORMACK + GIBSON (ex-members)

Umluat / not iss.

Jun 97. (ltd-7"ep) *(UMLUAT 001)* **HAMFISTED EP** [ ] [-]
– Emma's fifteenth birthday / Bridget Riley / Get offa my bus / Class of '85.

STOOR

ROSS MATHESON – guitar / **STEPH + SCOTT**

Chute / not iss.

May 97. (7") *(CHUTE 007)* **REPETITION. / BREATHLESS** [ ] [-]

CONDITION BLUE

JAN BURNETT on production

Mar 98. (7"m) *(CHUTE 008)* **SINGLED OUT. / PRODIGAL / EVERYTHING ON** [ ] [-]

DUBREQ

JAN BURNETT + ANDY ROGERS (with stylophones)

Aug 97. (7"one-sided) *(CHUTE 011)* **DUBREQ 1** [ ] [-]

— added **BARRY GIBSON**

2000. (7"one-sided) *(CHUTE 012)* **DUBREQ 2** [-] [-] notyet

SPEEDBOAT

Formed: Glasgow ... mid-90's by former BMX BANDITS part-timer, FINLAY MACDONALD, along with like-minded SCOTT WALKER (also their producer!), ALASDAIR VANN and FRANCIS MACDONALD (also ex-BMX BANDITS, ex-PASTELS, ex-BOY HAIRDRESSERS – but no relation). Launching Glasgow's new indie-meets-country label 'Shoeshine', SPEEDBOAT's debut single, 'SATELLITE GIRL', offered up few musical surprises but pushed all the right buttons for fans of archetypal West Coast (of Scotland, that is!) melodic retro-Indie pop; well, NORMAN BLAKE (of the TEENAGE FANCLUB) did produce the record. A belated follow-up, 'LUV', was released in the summer of '97, a distinct ELVIS COSTELLO-esque edge creeping in. Sadly, SPEEDBOAT were sunk when FINLAY was given a free tranfer to, who else but TEENAGE FANCLUB; fans got a taste of what might've been with the release of posthumous retrospective, 'SATELLITE GIRL', in 1999.

FINLAY MACDONALD – vocals, guitar (ex-BMX BANDITS) / **SCOTT WALKER** – vocals, guitar / **ALASDAIR VANN** – bass, vocals / **FRANCIS MACDONALD** (b.11 Sep'70, Bellshill) – drums, vocals (ex-BMX BANDITS, ex-TEENAGE FANCLUB, ex-PASTELS)

Shoeshine / not iss.

May 95. (7") *(SHOE 001)* **SATELLITE GIRL. / SPEEDBOAT** [ ] [-]
(re-iss. Jul96; same)

Jul 97. (7") *(SHOE 007)* **LUV. / A-T-O-M-I-C** [ ] [-]

— disbanded when FINLAY was talked into joining TEENAGE FANCLUB; late in 2000, FRANCIS also re-joined TFC

- compilations, etc. -

Apr 99. (cd/lp) *(SHOE CD/LP 004)* **SATELLITE GIRL** [ ] [-]
– Speedboat / Luv / The hurtin' kind / Satellite girl / Change of habit / A-T-O-M-I-C / On the run / Tidal wave / Finding a way / Outside the band.

SPEEDER

Formed: Glasgow . . . 1997 by former TEENAGE FANCLUB, PASTELS and BMX BANDITS drummer FRANK MACDONALD (aka FRANCIS), along with his own teenage fanclub! – SCOTT McCLUSKEY, JAMES CAMERON and JAMIE CAMERON. The sound of young Scotland or even arty New York perhaps, SONIC YOUTH and DINOSAUR JR being pointers in their direction, they were even featured in the Singles pages of Kerrang! Combining dual country touches with the RADIO SWEETHEARTS and running his own label 'Shoeshine', FRANK and the boys delivered their debut single, 'EVERYTHING I DO IS WRONG', for 'Discordant' early in '98. A year and a bit later and now on 'Creeping Bent', SPEEDER released two quickfire singles, 'HEY, WHAT DO I KNOW' and 'FEELINGS', both also highlights on their much-lauded first album, 'KARMA KIDS' (2000).

FRANK MACDONALD (b.11 Sep'70, Bellshill) – drums (of RADIO SWEETHEARTS, ex-PASTELS, ex-BOY HAIRDRESSERS, ex-BMX BANDITS) / **SCOTT McCLUSKEY** – vocals, guitar / **JAMIE CAMERON** – guitar / **COLIN CAMERON** – bass

Discordant / not iss.

Jan 98. (7") *(CORDS 011)* **EVERYTHING I DO IS WRONG. / THREE FIFTEEN** [ ] [-]

Creeping Bent / not iss.

Nov 99. (ltd-7") *(bent 053)* **HEY, WHAT DO I KNOW. / D.O.A.** [ ] [-]

Mar 00. (cd-ep) *(bent 056cd)* **FEELINGS EP** [ ] [-]
– Feelings / Amhurst / Keychain.

Aug 00. (cd) *(bent 058cd)* **KARMA KIDS** [ ] [-]
– Everything I do is wrong / Take the fun out of everything / Karma kids / Feelings / On my own / Hey, what do I know / Talk about it / Underachiever / Drag me down / To remind you / Here / No: time / Speeder skull.

SPIREA X

Formed: Gourock . . . 1988 by ex-PRIMAL SCREAM member JIM BEATTIE (writer of their classic 'Velocity Girl'), who took the moniker from an old 'SCREAM b-side. Featuring a core line-up comprised of girlfriend JUDITH BOYLE and ANDY KERR, they worked on songs for well over a year before supplying a demo to a plethora of labels, eventually becoming an unlikely signing for '4 a.d.'.

In spring '91, they finally unleashed their debut disc, 'CHLORINE DREAM', inspired by the life rather than death of BRIAN JONES. In fact, the single also took its musical cue from The ROLLING STONES, BEATTIE typically arrogant in his praise for the track, although for once the critics agreed. Unfortunately the public weren't so enthusiastic, neither follow-up single, 'SPEED REACTION', nor debut album, 'FIREBLADE SKIES' (named after a volume of Arthur Rimbaud's poetry), making much of an impression outside closeknit Glasgow scene. Nevertheless, the record was a pleasant enough listen, taking in the obligatory BYRDS/LOVE influences (they covered the latter's 'SIGNED D.C.') alongside SLY STONE's style funk and soul.

Subsequently reduced to a duo of BEATTIE and BOYLE, SPIREA X were dropped by the label and later split in '93. Three years later, BEATTIE and the aforementioned BOYLE launched ADVENTURES IN STEREO, a project which would heavily reflect on the influence of 60's Americana (no surprise there!). Signing to up-and-coming label 'Creeping Bent', the determined duo released the 'AIRLINE' EP, which featured 'RUNWAY' and 'GOOD TIMES' as B-sides. They subsequently issued their self-titled debut album in 1997 to much critical acclaim, drawing comparisons from BRIAN WILSON to LOU REED. That said, the album definitely displayed a reoccurring '60's theme, although songs such as 'THE ATTIC WALK' and 'WE'LL MEET AGAIN' could safely be filed in a class of their own.

'ALTERNATIVE STEREO SOUNDS' (1999) was their follow-up, mainly concentrating on the same musical inventiveness, it dabbled in new-electronica et al, and came off better for it. 'EVERYTHING' and 'HANG ON' were stand-out tracks, proving the ADVENTURES had more to offer than Lo-fi musings from the BEACH BOYS era. However, 'MONOMANIA' (2000) was to be the group's finest achievement, seeing them swiftly moving into the left-field of psychedelia. Like a dimly remembered summer at the seaside, this album graced us with some summery pop/rock, not heard since the advent of love in 1967.

• **Covered:** NOBODY'S SCARED (Subway Sect).

JIM BEATTIE – vocals, guitar (ex-PRIMAL SCREAM) / **JUDITH BOYLE** – vocals, guitar / **ANDY KERR** – drums / with also **THOMAS McGURK** – rhythm guitar / **JAMIE O'DONNELL** – bass

4 a.d. / 4ad-Warners

Apr 91. (7") *(AD 1004)* **CHLORINE DREAM. / SPIREA RISING** [ ] [-]
(12"+=/cd-s+=) *(BAD 1004/+CD)* – Risk.

Jun 91. (7") *(AD 1006)* **SPEED REACTION. / JET PILOT** [ ] [-]
(12"+=/cd-s+=) *(BAD 1006/+CD)* – What kind of love / Re action.

Oct 91. (lp/cd)(c) *(CAD 1017/+CD)(CADC 1017)* <45001> **FIREBLADE SKIES** [ ] [ ]
– Smile / Nothing happened yesterday / Rollercoaster / Chlorine dream / Fire and light / Spirea 9 / Speed reaction / Confusion in my soul / Signed D.C. / Sisters and brothers / Sunset dawn.

— split in 1993 after being dropped by their label

ADVENTURES IN STEREO

JIM BEATTIE – vocals, guitar / with **JUDITH BOYLE** – vocals / **SIMON DINE**

Creeping Bent / not iss.

Feb 96. (blue-7"ep) *(bent 010)* **E.P. 2** [ ] [-]
– Airline / There was a time / Runaway / Good times.

Jul 96. (yellow-7"ep) *(bent 013) E.P. 3* [ ] [-]
– When we go back / Close to you / When times were young / Remain again.

Mar 97. (cd/lp) *(bent 015/+lp)* **ADVENTURES IN STEREO** [ ] [-]
– Underground sound / Cry your love away / The attic walk / Summer high / 13th floor / Airline / There was a time / Runaway / Good times / Don't you worry little one / When we go back / Flipside / When times were young / Close to you / Remain again / My buddy go / Pretty things / We'll meet again.

Jun 97. (7") *(bent 019)* **WAVES ON. / (track by the Leopards)** [ ] [-]
(cd-ep+=) *(bent 019cd)* – (tracks by the Revolutionary Corps & Spacehopper).

Aug 97. (cd-s; promo) *(bent 022)* **WAVES ON** [ ] [-]

Nov 97. (7"ep/cd-ep) *(bent 026/+cd)* **A BRAND NEW DAY** [ ] [-]
– A brand new day / Nobody's scared / Pass me by / God save us. *(re-iss. Dec97 on 'Bobsled'; BOB 1)*

— SIMON DINE formed NOONDAY UNDERGROUND

Mar 98. (7"ep/cd-ep) *(bent 028/+cd)* **DOWN IN THE TRAFFIC EP** [ ] [-]
– Down in the traffic / Down in the city / Down to the sky.

May 98. (cd) *(bent 030)* **ALTERNATIVE STEREO SOUNDS** [ ] [-]
– Silence falls / Down in the traffic / Dominique K / I once knew / When you're young / Everything / Out of sight / Brand new day / Here together / Said you said / Hang out / This time / Dream surf baby / O sister / I see / Catch my soul / Long you live / Silence is. *(lp-iss.Jul98 on 'Bobsled'; BOB 2)*

Bobsled / not iss.

Jul 00. (7") *(BOB 10)* **INTERNATIONAL. / BABY SO RICH** [ ] [-]
(cd-s+=) *(BOB 13)* – Grooves.

Aug 00. (cd/lp) *(BOB 11/+LP)* **MONOMANIA** [ ] [-]
– We will stand / International / Dust to ashes / Silence / Running / Birds / Behind the trees / Suntrips / Airkiss / Touch the rain / Ghosts / This day / When love comes in.

MOST

— were **JUDITH** and a second AIS female (they had also sidelined/guested with FUTURE PILOT AKA and MOUNT VERNON ARTS LAB

Cooler / not iss.

May 98. (7") *(COOLER 001)* **I STOLE YOUR MAN. /** [ ] [-]

SPLEEN (see ⇒ Section 9: the 90s)

SPUTNIKS DOWN (see under ⇒ Human Condition records)

the SQUARE PEG (see under ⇒ Stranded records)

SQUIBS (see under ⇒ Oily records)

STACY EFFECT (see under ⇒ Path records)

Baby STAFFORD

Born: STEVE STAFFORD, Bellshill, Lanarkshire. A founding member of Glasgow-based rawkers, GUN, guitarist BABY STAFFORD had previously made a name for himself towards the end of the 80's after said group had been 'Taking On The World'. After a support slot to The ROLLING STONES in '91, STAFFORD decided it was time for him to make a break and duly called in old pal STUART KERR, who had played drums for TEXAS. However, recording delays, etc, led to BABY STAFFORD (the band) hitting some musical blocks. When 'E.M.I.' decided to release his/their debut single, 'PAPER LOVE MAKER', in 1994, the impetus was gone. However, the BABY was not thrown out with the bath water just yet, as he returned with a new R&R venture, BREAKER. Three singles for 'Coalition' later, BABY and his gang were no more; on reflection, STEVE's decision to quit GUN while they were firing on all cylinders, proved to be the wrong one.

BABY STAFFORD – vocals, guitar (ex-GUN)

E.M.I. / not iss.

Jul 94. (c-s/12"/cd-s) *(TC/12/CD EM 334)* **PAPER LOVE MAKER. / THIS LITTLE LIFETIME / THEN? / SISTER FREEZE** [ ] [-]

BREAKER

BABY STAFFORD with various backing

Coalition / not iss.

Aug 97. (7"/c-s) *(COLA 005/+C)* **STRANGE LOVE. / UNDERWORLD** [ ] [-]
(cd-s+=) *(COLA 005CD)* – Sunburnt / ('A'extended).

Feb 98. (7"/c-s) *(COLA 033/+C)* **STEREOTYPE. / SINISTER MINISTER** [ ] [-]

Jun 98. (7") *(COLA 050)* **MODERN TIMES. / COTTON WOOL** [ ] [-]
(cd-s+=) *(COLA 050CD)* – Nicolai / ('A'-album version).

— BABY disbanded the outfit after above

STAPLETON

Formed: Glasgow . . . summer 1997 by Dumbarton lads AL PAXTON, GORDON FARQUHAR and IAN ARTHUR. Influenced by the hard/emo-core scene (FUGAZI, SUPERCHUNK and JAWBOX), the trio hit the pages of Kerrang the following year. It would take a few years and a deal with Guildford-based 'Year 3 Thousand' records and a debut album, 'REBUILD THE PIER' (2000) to get off the mark – DIY/indie rock was in full swing. Following an extensive tour of Scotland and the north of England & Wales in October 2001, STAPLETON unleashed their sophomore album, 'ON THE ENJOYMENT OF UNPLEASANT PLACES'.

AL PAXTON – vocals, guitar / **IAN ARTHUR** – bass / **GORDON FARQUHAR** – drums

Year 3 Thousand / not iss.

Nov 00. (cd) *(yr 3005)* **REBUILD THE PIER** [ ] [-]
– M is for maps / Something long and Russian / Bearhug / Learning archery / International departures / Why buildings fall down / Juneau / Shoulder length summer / Walter Brock memorial pool / Where are the alps?

2001. (7"split) **w/ Seven Storey Mountain** [ ] [-]

Subjugation / not iss.

Dec 01. (cd) *(SUB 024CD)* **ON THE ENJOYMENT OF UNPLEASANT PLACES** [ ] [-]
– Heads down, thumbs up / Esplanade / Sometimes they do but they don't tell me / Our returning champion / Now we trust the pilot / French for hi-hat / Vapour trails / Rest and be thankful.

Gravity – Dip / not iss.

Jun 02. (cd-s) *(DIP 002CD)* **ICY YOU / LIGHTS LUXEMBOURG / THE BOREDOM OF BREAD THE FUN OF CAKE** [ ] [-]

STARLETS

Formed: Glasgow . . . 1996 by female lead BIFF SMITH and four then five guys, MARK McSWIGGAN, STEPHEN McGOURTY, CRAIG LAURIE, NIGEL BAILLIE and IAIN WHITE. Downbeat and melancholy, The STARLETS ranged from a pastel VELVET UNDERGROUND to the HOUSEMARTINS, witnessed at a handful of gigs at the 13th Note. Two 45's, 'TAINTED' and 'HAPPY CAMPER', were released for different labels in 1997, while a further two, 'GIVE MY REGARDS TO BETTY FORD' and 'NEW WAVE', subsequently surfaced on fresh imprint, 'Illumiere'. They kept a low profile for a while, although a spot at Scotland's 'T In The Park' was worth noting. Towards the end of 2001, The STARLETS finally came back to life, their long-awaited debut set, 'SURELY TOMORROW YOU'LL FEEL BLUE', gathering all sorts of rave reviews.

BIFF SMITH – vocals, guitar / **MARK McSWIGGAN** – guitar, vocals / **STEPHEN McGOURTY** – bass / **CRAIG LAURIE** – drums / **NIGEL BAILLIE** – brass / **IAIN WHITE** – strings

Flotsam & Jetsam / not iss.

Feb 97. (7") *(SHaG 012)* **TAINTED. / (other track by Finger Creams)** [ ] [-]

N.G.M. / not iss.

May 97. (7") *(NGM 10)* **HAPPY CAMPER. / HOW CAN I SLEEP TONIGHT** [ ] [-]
(cd-s+=) *(NGM 009)* – Lager tops.

Illumiere / not iss.

Apr 98. (7") *(LUMIE 001)* **GIVE MY REGARDS TO BETTY FORD. / GLORIOUS TECHNICOLOR** [ ] [-]

Apr 99. (7") *(LUMIE 002)* **NEW WAVE. / WESTERN ELECTRIC** [ ] [-]

Stereotone not iss.

Oct 01. (cd) *(STEREO 1)* **SURELY TOMORROW YOU'LL FEEL BLUE** [ ] [-]
– Glorious technicolor / Rocking in a shy way / New wave / Poem on a beermat / Surely tomorrow you'll feel blue / Hypercool / We'll go diving #2 / Arcadia Square / Firestorm.

Apricot not iss.

Jul 02. (7"colrd) *(efa 27384-7)* **ROCKING IN A SHY WAY. / LITTLE THINGS CATCH ME UNAWARE / NEW WAVE** [ ] [-]

STARSTRUCK (see under ⇒ Bosque records)

STATE OF FLUX (see ⇒ Section 9: Dance/Rave)

STAYRCASE (see under ⇒ THANES)

Duglas T. STEWART (see under ⇒ BMX BANDITS)

STILETTOS (see ⇒ Section 9: wee post-Punk groups)

STILTSKIN

Formed: West Lothian . . . 1989 by songwriter PETER LAWLOR and JAMES FINNEGAN. The latter had played with HUE AND CRY, while LAWLOR had just returned from the States. They soon found ROSS McFARLANE, who had played with SLIDE, while 1993 saw them recruiting singer RAY WILSON. STILTSKIN came to the attention of the nation when their NIRVANA-esque track 'INSIDE' was aired on a Levi jeans TV commercial (the one where the quaker girls go to a lake and see what appears to be a naked man in the water, only to find he is just breaking in his new jeans). The Television company were then inundated with enquiries on who was the group/artist on its soundtrack, and where could they buy it. Unfortunately it hadn't yet been released, although due to public demand it eventually surfaced in April 1994. Now with growling lyrics, the single crashed into the UK No.5 and was soon topping the charts. However, by the end of the year, bad album reviews of their debut, 'THE MIND'S EYE', had already made them yesterday's men. LAWLOR subsequently had a brief stint as a solo artist, while WILSON stunned the rock world in 1996 by replacing PHIL COLLINS in GENESIS.

RAY WILSON – vocals / **PETER LAWLOR** – guitars, mandolin, vocals / **JAMES FINNIGAN** – bass, keyboards / **ROSS McFARLANE** – drums, percussion

Whitewater East West

May 94. (7"/c-s) *(LEV 1/+C)* **INSIDE. / AMERICA** [1] [ ]
(12"+=/cd-s+=) *(LEV 1 T/CD)* – ('A'extended).

Sep 94. (7"/c-s) *(WWR/+C 2)* **FOOTSTEPS. / SUNSHINE & BUTTERFLIES (live)** [34] [-]
(cd-s+=) *(WWRD 2)* – ('A'extended).

Oct 94. (cd/c/lp) *(WW L/M/D 1)* <61785> **THE MIND'S EYE** [17] [ ] Jan95
– Intro / Scared of ghosts / Horse / Rest in peace / Footsteps / Sunshine and butterflies / Inside / An illusion / America / When my ship comes in / Prayer before birth.

Mar 95. (7"ep/c-ep/cd-ep) *(WWR/+C/D 3)* **REST IN PEACE. / THE POLTROON / INSIDE (acoustic)** [ ] [-]

— LAWLOR has now formed his own self-named group. In 1996, WILSON took the place of PHIL COLLINS in GENESIS.

LAWLOR

PETER with his own band

Water not iss.

May 96. (c-s/cd-s) *(WAT 1 MC/CD)* **MAD ALICE LANE** [ ] [-]

STRANGE DAZE (see under ⇒ Rational records)

STRANGEWAYS

Formed: Glasgow . . . mid-80's by the sibling pairing of IAN (guitar) and DAVID STEWART (bass), the rest of the quartet being made up of vocalist TONY LIDDELL and drummer JIM DRUMMOND. Signed to 'Arista' backed 'Bonaire', this JOURNEY-meets-KANSAS hard-rock outfit released three albums from the mid to late 80's, the eponymous 'STRANGEWAYS' (1986), 'NATIVE SONS' (1987) – with new American-born singer TERRY BROCK – and 'WALK IN THE FIRE' (1989). Having had a little success in the States, the band surprisingly parted company, only to return for another stab at the AOR market in the mid 90's. • **Note:** Not to be confused with Wakefield power-pop outfit, STRANGEWAYS!

TONY LIDDELL – vocals / **IAN STEWART** – guitar / **DAVID STEWART** – bass / **JIM DRUMMOND** – drums

Bonaire – Arista Bonaire – Arista

Mar 86. (7") *(108 104)* **CLOSE TO THE EDGE. / HOLD BACK YOUR LOVE** [ ] [-]
(12"+=) *(608 104)* – Heartbeat zone.

Mar 86. (lp/c) *(207/407 648)* <207417> **STRANGEWAYS** [ ] [ ]
– The kids need love / Hold back your love / Close to the edge / Heart break zone / Cry out / Power play / Breakin' down the barriers / Now it's gone / More than promises / Hold tight. *(cd re-iss. Apr98 on 'Hangdog'; HDRCD 01001)*

— **TERRY BROCK** (b. Atlanta, USA) – vocals; repl. LIDDELL

Nov 87. (7") *(BON 6)* **ONLY A FOOL. / EMPTY STREET** [ ] [-]
(12"+=) *(BON12 6)* – Stand up & shout (live) / Breaking down the barriers (live).

Jan 88. (lp/c/cd) *(208/408/258 579)* <6569> **NATIVE SONS** [ ] [ ]
– Dance with somebody / Only a fool / So far away / Where do we go from here / Goodnight L.A. / Empty streets / Stand up and shout / Shake the seven / Never going to lose it / Face to face. *(cd re-iss. Apr98 on 'Hangdog'; HDRCD 02002)*

Dec 89. (lp/c/cd) <9662-1/-4/-2> **WALK IN THE FIRE** [-] [ ]
– Where are they now? / Danger in your eyes / Love lies dying / Everytime you cry / Talk to me / Living in the danger zone / Modern world / Into the night / Walk in the fire / After the hurt is gone.
(cd re-iss. Apr98 on 'Hangdog'; HDRCD 03003)

— BROCK left and the band folded for a while

Total not iss.

Apr 95. (cd) *(JHM 2001)* **AND THE HORSE** [ ] [-]
– Precious time / Man's maker / Out of the blue / Through the wire / The great awakening / Wonder how / Head on / Some of us lie / Over you / On. *(re-iss. Apr98 on 'Hangdog'; HDRCD 04004)*

Hangdog not iss.

Apr 98. (cd) *(HDRCD 05005)* **ANY DAY NOW** [ ] [-]
– It's alright / Come and dance / What about me? / Blue line / Northern town / Sweeter than this / Shillean / All I want / Losin' my friend / And the horse / Fallen angel / Bye bye Johnnie.

Feb 99. (cd) *(HDRCD 06006)* **GREATEST BITS** (compilation) [ ] [-]
– Love lies dying / Only a fool / It's alright / Where are they now / Face to face / Talk to me / Out of the blue / Never gonna lose it / Great awakening / Every time you cry / So far away / Fallen angel / Shake the seven / Hold back your love / Where do we go from here.

Nov 00. (cd) *(HDRCD 07007)* **GRAVITATIONAL PULL** [ ] [-]
– Five down / Electric / Gravitational pull / Afraid of flying / Southside / See what you want / Rich man's cadillac / Rap it up / Automatic / No one's perfect.

STRAWBERRY SWITCHBLADE

Formed: Glasgow . . . early 80's by JILL BRYSON and ROSE McDOWELL. This new wave female duo made their debut in 1983 with the introspective 'TREES AND FLOWERS' single, such indie scene notables as KATE ST. JOHN and RODDY FRAME lending their musical expertise. Cult acclaim turned into bonafide Top 5 success the following year when the bewitching pop atmospherics of 'SINCE YESTERDAY' gave the girls a brief period of fame. With no further major hits to support it, an eponymous debut album made a similarly brief appearance in the Top 30, the girls following in Glasgow's long C&W tradition and making a last ditch attempt to breathe some life into their career with a cover of the Dolly Parton classic, 'JOLENE'. Despite a Top 60 placing, the duo subsequently called it a day with McDOWELL going on to perform with INTO A CIRCLE and various other experimental projects like DEATH IN JUNE and PSYCHIC TV; she also delivered a solo version of Blue Oyster Cult's 'DON'T FEAR THE REAPER'.

ROSE McDOWELL – vocals, guitar / **JILL BRYSON** (b.11 Feb'61) – vocals, guitar / with guests **KATE ST. JOHN** – oboe (ex-RAVISHING BEAUTIES) / **RODDY FRAME** – acoustic guitar (of AZTEC CAMERA) / **MARK 'BEDDERS' BEDFORD** – bass (of MADNESS)

92HappyC. not iss.

Jul 83. (7") *(HAP 001)* **TREES AND FLOWERS. / GO AWAY** [ ] [-]
(12"+=) *(HAPT 001)* – Trees and flowers (just music).

— now with **GARY HITCHINS + ALAN PARK** – keyboards / **BORIS WILLIAMS** – drums / **DAVE MORRIS** – percussion / **BRUCE NOCKLES** – trumpet

Korova not iss.

Oct 84. (7") *(KOW 38)* **SINCE YESTERDAY. / BY THE SEA** [5] [-]
(12"+=) *(KOW 38T)* – Sunday morning.

Mar 85. (7") *(KOW 39)* **LET HER GO. / BEAUTIFUL END** [59] [-]
(12"+=) *(KOWT 59)* – Michael walks by night.

Apr 85. (lp/c) *(KODE/CODE 11)* **STRAWBERRY SWITCHBLADE** 25 -
– Since yesterday / Deep water / Another day / Little river / 10 James Orr Street / Let her go / Who knows what love is / Go away / Secrets / Being cold.
May 85. (7") *(KOW 41)* **WHO KNOWS WHAT LOVE IS. / POOR HEART** -
(12"+=) *(KOW 41T)* – Let her go (mix).
Sep 85. (7") *(KOW 42)* **JOLENE. / BEING COLD** 53 -
(12"+=) *(KOW 42T)* – Black taxi.
— split late '85; ROSE subsequently joined UK act, INTO A CIRCLE

ROSE McDOWELL

Rio Digital not iss.
Sep 88. (7"/12") *(7/12 RDS 3)* **DON'T FEAR THE REAPER. / CRYSTAL DAYS** -

STRETCHHEADS

Formed: Paisley . . . 1987 by ANDY and P6 ('DR. TECHNOLOGY' and 'FAT BASTARD'), adding MOFUNGO DIGGS and RICHIE DEMPSEY from their Paisley school days. Serving up a platter of fun hardcore (The EX were an early inspiration), The STRETCHHEADS were an unorthodox rock concept (they wore flashy shirts and balaclavas on stage!) in that Scots bands rarely ventured into this comic book grunge-esque genre (CHOU PAHROT eat your cage out!).

Poking fun at number one pop act at the time, BROS, was indeed their first musical mission, 'BROS ARE PISH', being the debut EP in question. Early the following year, a full-set of weird ideas was unveiled via their debut set, 'FIVE FINGERS, FOUR THINGERS, A THUMB, A FACELIFT AND A NEW IDENTITY' (1989).

Moving from Charles Cosh's 'Moshka' (once home of The SHAMEN) to top indie imprint 'Blast First' (and with MR JASON replacing DEMPSEY on drums), the zany quartet had three releases during a prolific early 90's spell. 'EYEBALL ORIGAMI AFTERMATH WIT VEGETARIAN LEG' was a fine ooh-ah! EP, while the danceable 12" '23 SKINNER (HAVE A BANG ON THIS NUMBER)' featured a sample from the American TV sitcom theme 'Rhoda', also present on their second fool-set (sic!), 'PISH IN YOUR SLEAZEBAG' (1991). However, by the time NIRVANA's 'Nevermind' had hit the shops that Autumn, the group were facing indie oblivion. In fact, it took another couple of years and a comeback 10"EP, 'BARBED ANAL EXCITER', before the band went to ground.

P6 'FAT BASTARD' – vocals / **ANDY 'DR. TECHNOLOGY'** – guitar / **MOFUNGO DIGGS** – bass / **RICHIE DEMPSEY** – drums

Moshka not iss.
Nov 88. (7"ep) *(SOMA 5)* **BROS ARE PISH EP** -
– Bros are pish / I should be so lucky / Confront / Headache / Everything's going to break in a minute / Worry.
— **MAC** – bass; repl. MOFUNGO
Jan 89. (lp) *(SOMALP 2)* **FIVE FINGERS, FOUR THINGERS, A THUMB, A FACELIFT AND A NEW IDENTITY** -
– Fans / Long faced German / Headache / Asylum suck / Skinrip / Yiddish yoddle / Shape + cleanse / Land of Ming / Rex perplexed / Semtex / I should be so lucky / Confront / Sidatorium / Spleng / Archive footage of a fish / Everything's going to brake in a minute / Illness / Cancer / Shut up. *(cd-iss. 1991; SOMACD 2)*
— **MR. JASON** – drums; repl. DEMPSEY who later surfaced with FENN and the PH FAMILY

Blast First not iss.
Nov 90. (7"ep) *(BFFP 56)* **EYEBALL ORIGAMI AFTERMATH WIT VEGETARIAN LEG EP** -
– Afghanistan bananastan / Incontinent of sex / Omnipresent octopus (Russell Grant) / New thing in Egypt (Boney M).
Jan 91. (12") *(BFFP 57T)* **23 SKINNER (HAVE A BANG ON THIS NUMBER). /** -
Feb 91. (lp/c/cd) *(BFFP 58/+C/CD)* **PISH IN YOUR SLEAZEBAG** -
– Space ape / Trippy deadzone / A freakout / Incontinent of sex / Crazy desert man / Housewife up yer fuckin' arse music / Machine in Delhi (Gary Newman's round the world trip) / Ognob / Acid Sweeney / Mao Tse Tungs meat challenge / Space jam / HMS average nostril / Pottery owls (with innuendo) / Hairy mousaka / Fly feast. *(cd+=)* – 23 skinner (the theme from 'Rhoda') / Afghanistan bananastan / Omnipresent octopus (Russell Grant) / New thing in Egypt (Boney M).
below was a posthumous release due to their demise
Jul 93. (10"ep) *(BFFP 68)* **BARBED ANAL EXCITER EP** -
— P6 subsequently turned up on a PH FAMILY release, 'Important Information' c.1997

S.T.S. (see under ⇒ Soma records)

STUDIO BLUE (see under ⇒ Glasgow Underground records)

SUBLIME (see under ⇒ Limbo records)

SUBS (see ⇒ Section 9: wee post-Punk groups)

SUBURBAN DELAY (see under ⇒ Clubscene records)

SUCKLE

Formed: Glasgow . . . 1996 by missing VASELINES frontwoman and yoga instructor, FRANCES McKEE (also ex-PAINKILLERS), who teamed up with co-vocalist and sister MARIE McKEE; JAMES SEENAN (ex-VASELINES) was also on board at some stage. Completing the line-up with fiery redhead and SYS Electronic Music graduate ELANOR TAYLOR on flute and keyboards, art school lecturer VICKY MORTON on bass, BRIAN McEWAN on guitar and his brother KENNY (ex-LONG FIN KILLIE) on drums, SUCKLE debuted in '97 on the 'Detox' label courtesy of EP, 'HORMONAL SECRETIONS'; an obscure sophomore 12" entitled 'CYBILLA', released on FRANCES' own 'LeftHand' recordings, hit the shops the following year.

Things looked increasingly brighter at the turn of the century when SUCKLE inked a deal with the much respected indie, 'Chemikal Underground' (home of The DELGADOS, etc). Their sort of comeback single, 'TO BE KING', was also the opening track on their long-awaited debut set, 'AGAINST NURTURE' (2000), a record that could be best described as a mogadon-rush retreading melodious monotone indie-pop of yesteryear.

FRANCES McKEE – vocals, guitar (ex-VASELINES, ex-PAINKILLERS) / **MARIE McKEE** – vocals / **ELANOR TAYLOR** – keyboards, flute / **BRIAN McEWAN** – guitar / **VICKY MORTON** – bass / **KENNY McEWAN** – drums (ex-LONG FIN KILLIE)

Detox not iss.
Apr 97. (7"ep/cd-ep) *(7+/DTX 9703/+CD)* **HORMONAL SECRETIONS EP** -
– Symposium / When I was dead / Boyfriend / Circle.

LeftHand not iss.
Apr 98. (12") *(LHR 001)* **CYBILLA. / SEX WITH ANIMALS** -
– Syndrome / State of mind / Cybilla.

Chemikal Underground Chemikal Underground
May 00. (7") *(chem 041)* **TO BE KING. / KISS MY FEET** -
(cd-s+=) *(chem 041cd)* – Golden hair.
May 00. (lp/cd) *(chem 042/+cd)* **AGAINST NURTURE**
– To be king / Earth without pleasures / Saturn / Honey suicide / How do you know / I tell you truly / Nothing / The colour song / Father's milk / So happy before / Symposium.
Oct 00. (12"ep/cd-ep) *(chem 045/+cd)* **THE SUN IS GOD EP** -
– Saturn / Wing / One made for me / Forever.

SUGAR BULLET / SUGA BULLIT

Formed: Edinburgh . . . late 80's by the collective of KENNY MacLEOD, SHAUN McCABE and IZZY COONAGH. SUGAR BULLET – as they were then known – first came to light after winning a Tennent's Live! talent contest in 1990. A subsequent deal with 'Virgin' records enabled this dance-orientated hip-hop and reggae-inspired outfit to get their political messages to ra people via the single, 'WORLD PEACE'. Two long years went by until their next release, 'UNREFINED' (1992), a smooth set that was split between two "positive" and "negative" sides. However, even with the aid of fellow dance buffs JAMES LOCKE and MIKE PEDEN (from The CHIMES), the record took a dive.

By the middle of the 90's, a new plan of action was needed and this came in the shape of a new moniker SUGA BULLIT, their New Jock stylee was now of the eclectic junglism variety although hip hop was always the mood. Virgin offshoot, 'Parkway', unveiled a new single, 'SUGA SHACK', a track not featured on their brief comeback mini-set, 'LIVE AND DIRECT' (1996).

KENNY MacLEOD – / **SHAUN McCABE** – / **IZZY COONAGH** –

Virgin not iss.
Jul 90. (7") *(VS 1266)* **WORLD PEACE. / WORLD PEACE (COMING TO ME)** -
(12"+=) *(VST 1266)* – ('A'-Freestyle) / ('A'-Kangabella mix).
(cd-s) *(VSCD 1266)* – ('A'-Freestyle) / ('A'-Positive Vibration) / A nation under a dope mix demonstrate in mass.

1992. (cd/c/lp) **UNREFINED** [ ] [-]

— returned much later and changed their group moniker to . . .

SUGA BULLIT

— **McCABE** + **FARMA 'C'** (b. CRAIG FARMER) – vocals

Parkway not iss.

Oct 95. (12"/cd-s) *(PARK 004/+CD)* **SUGA SHACK (mixes) / MOVE (mixes)** [ ] [-]

Apr 96. (m-lp/m-cd) *(PARK 007/+CD)* **LIVE AND DIRECT** [ ] [-]
– Sava d'flava / Soul groove / Forgotten mix / On the slope / Live and die direct / Alive in the jungle. *(m-cd+=)* – Bedways is rightways / Dubs, beats and bass.

SUGAR SUGAR
(see ⇒ Section 9: wee post-Punk groups)

SUGARTOWN (see under ⇒ COWBOY MOUTH)

SUMMERHILL (see under ⇒ SNAKES OF SHAKE)

SUNDANCE (see under ⇒ Soma records)

SUNSET GUN

Formed: Glasgow . . . 1983 by LOUISE RUTKOWSKI and ROSS CAMPBELL. Entrepreneur Elliot Davis subsequently became their manager and he duly got them signed to 'C.B.S.'. Three singles previewed their debut album, 'IN AN IDEAL WORLD' (1985), and although they all showed promise, nothing profitable came their way. When Davis founded the 'Precious Organisation' label, initial stamping ground for WET WET WET, he more or less abandoned the brighter SUNSET GUN duo. LOUISE became part of '4 ad' ensemble, THIS MORTAL COIL (and later SPIREA X), while ROSS teamed up with SHUG BRANKIN (ex-SUGAR SUGAR) to form WYOMING; they recorded one eponymous set in '87.

LOUISE RUTKOWSKI – vocals / **ROSS CAMPBELL** – instruments

C.B.S. not iss.

Jul 84. (7"/12") *(A/TA 4556)* **BE THANKFUL FOR WHAT YOU'VE GOT. / CAN'T CLOUD MY VIEW** [ ] [-]

May 85. (7") *(A 6264)* **SISTER. / NOTHING DRIES SOON THAN TEARS** [ ] [-]
(12"+=) *(TX 6264)* – Everybody loves a lover.

Jul 85. (7") *(A 6446)* **HOW DO YOU MEND A BROKEN HEART. / UNTIL YOU TIRE OF ME** [ ] [-]
(12"+=) *(TX 6446)* – Listen to me only.

Sep 85. (lp/c) *(CBS/40 26584)* **IN AN IDEAL WORLD** [ ] [-]
– Sister / Paint the town red / On the right side / Company / Stop / How can you mend a broken heart / Stay with me / Tongue tied and twisted / Life of the free man / Face up to what is true.

— they split after above

SUPERNATURALS

Formed: Glasgow . . . 1993 by JAMES McCOLL, KEN McALPINE, DEREK McMANUS, ALAN TILSTON and MARK GUTHRIE. The Scottish equivalent of HERMAN'S HERMITS, The SUPERNATURALS took the softer elements of TEENAGE FANCLUB and smiled their way WET WET WET-style into the hearts of the nation's less discerning retro-pop fans.

Early in 1995, the group's first product, the disappointing mini-CD 'SITTING IN THE SUN', was available around indie shops. 'Food' records then came a-knocking and signed them on a long-term concert; the track 'SMILE' probably convinced them. Although the aforementioned 'SMILE' failed to chart first time round in '96, the frighteningly annoying follow-up, 'LAZY LOVER' gave them their first Top 40 hit. Spookily enough, the band notched up a further series of Top 30 sub-DODGY hits the following year, all included on their debut long-player, 'IT DOESN'T MATTER ANYMORE' (you could well be right, lads!). The latter opus actually made the UK Top 10 and the Glasgow boys proved they weren't quite the runt of the Brit-pop litter with 'A TUNE A DAY' (1998), a set of tongue in cheek but well crafted slacker-pop defined by the likes of Top 30 hit, 'I WASN'T BORN TO GET UP'.

Having tried in vain to get 'SMILE' back into the charts via a TV ad, The SUPERNATURALS (JAMES, ALAN and newcomers PAUL MALCOLM and DAVE MITCHELL – KEN moved to St. Andrews) returned to the fold once again in September 2001, albeit a solitary single, 'FINISHING CREDITS', for the 'Koch' imprint. The next spring, an album 'WHAT WE DID LAST SUMMER' followed on from gigs on Mull, Orkneys and Shetlands.

• **Covered:** BOYS IN THE BAND (Leiber-Stoller) / BRONTOSAURUS (Move) / SKYWAY (Paul Westerberg) / YOU'RE MY BEST FRIEND (Queen).

JAMES McCOLL – vocals, guitar / **KEN McALPINE** – keyboards, tambourine / **DEREK McMANUS** – guitar, vocals / **ALAN TILSTON** – drums / **MARK GUTHRIE** – bass

O.F.L. not iss.

Feb 95. (m-cd) *(none)* **SITTING IN THE SUN** [ ] [-]
– Sitting in the sun / Absence / Caroline / Slab / Godfrey / I don't think it's over (yup) / Silverback.

— around the same, three other mini demos were circulating, 'BIG EP', 'DARK STAR' and 'LET IT BLEAT'

Food not iss.

Jul 96. (7") *(FOOD 79)* **SMILE. / CAN'T GET BACK TO NORMAL** [ ] [-]
(cd-s+=) *(CDFOOD 79)* – Mint choc chip.

Oct 96. (c-s/7"blue) *(TC+/FOOD 85)* **LAZY LOVER. / JOSEPHINE** [34] [-]
(cd-s) *(CDFOOD 85)* – Caterpillar song.

Jan 97. (7") *(FOOD 88)* **THE DAY BEFORE YESTERDAYS MAN. / HONK WILLIAMS** [25] [-]
(cd-s+=) *(CDFOOD 88)* – Ken's song.
(cd-s) *(CDFOODS 88)* – ('A'side) / Deep in my heart I know I'm a slob / Brontosaurus.

Apr 97. (7") *(FOOD 92)* **SMILE. / STALINGRAD** [23] [-]
(cd-s+=) *(CDFOODS 92)* – Childhood sweetheart.
(cd-s) *(CDFOOD 92)* – ('A'side) / Can't get back to normal / Mint choc chip.

May 97. (cd/c) *(FOOD CD/MC/LP 21)* **IT DOESN'T MATTER ANYMORE** [9] [-]
– Please be gentle with me / Smile / Glimpse of the light / Lazy lover / Love has passed away / Dung beetle / Stammer / I don't think so / Pie in the sky / The day before yesterday's man / Prepare to land / Trees.

Jul 97. (c-s) *(TCFOOD 99)* **LOVE HAS PASSED AWAY / THE DAY BEFORE YESTERDAY'S MAN / LAZY LOVER** [38] [-]
(cd-s) *(CDFOOD 99)* – ('A'side) / Trying too hard / Rupert the bear.
(cd-s) *(CDFOODS 99)* – ('A'side) / Scandinavian girlfriend / That's not me.

Oct 97. (7") *(FOOD 106)* **PREPARE TO LAND. / STUPID LOVE SONG** [48] [-]
(cd-s+=) *(CDFOOD 106)* – Skyway.
(cd-s) *(CDFOODS 106)* – ('A'side) / High tension at Boghead / Take some time out.

Jul 98. (c-s/cd-s) *(TCFOOD/CDFOODS 112)* **I WASN'T BUILT TO GET UP / STAR WARS / BUBBLEGUM HILL** [25] [-]
(cd-s) *(CDFOOD 112)* – ('A'side) / Robot song / I just can't go on like this.

Aug 98. (cd/c) *(856893-2/-4)* **A TUNE A DAY** [21] [-]
– You take yourself too seriously / Monday mornings / Submarine song / I wasn't built to get up / Country music / Motorcycle parts / Sheffield song (I love her more than I love you) / VW song / Idiot / Magnet / Still got that feeling / Let me know / It doesn't matter anymore / Everest.

Oct 98. (7") *(FOOD 115)* **SHEFFIELD SONG (I LOVE HER MORE THAN I LOVE YOU). / I DON'T THINK IT'S OVER** [45] [-]
(cd-s+=) *(CDFOOD 115)* – X country song.
(cd-s) *(CDFOOD 115)* – ('A'side) / Boys in the band / Hang out with you.

Mar 99. (c-s) *(TCFOOD 119)* **EVEREST / YOU'RE MY BEST FRIEND** [52] [ ]
(cd-s+=) *(CDFOOD 119)* – Smile (demo).
(cd-s) *(CDFOODS 119)* – ('A'side) / Let it bleat / Tomato man.

— **CRAIG** joined in Feb'99 but left Jul'00

Sep 00. (c-s) *(TCFOOD 131)* **SMILE / GLIMPSE OF THE LIGHT / SUBMARINE SONG** [ ] [-]
(cd-s) *(CDFOOD 79)* – ('A'side) / Can't get back to normal / Mint choc chip.
above was re-iss. due to a UK TV ad

— **JAMES, KEN + ALAN** were joined by **PAUL MALCOLM** – acoustic guitar, banjo

— **DAVE MITCHELL** – keyboards; repl. KEN

Koch not iss.

Sep 01. (cd-s) *(347956)* **FINISHING CREDITS / EASY LIFE (TV mix) / EVERYDAY THINGS CAN MAKE YOU HAPPY** [ ] [-]

Mar 02. (cd-s) *(343970)* **WHAT WE DID LAST SUMMER / MY DOOR IS OPEN / IT'S A WONDERFUL WORLD** [ ] [-]

May 02. (cd) *(343985)* **WHAT WE DID LAST SUMMER** [ ] [-]
– Elle / What we did last summer / Get myself together / Wishing you were my girlfriend / Instant healing / Life is a motorway / Late for the world / Everything / Summertime / Easy life / Why / Two songbirds / Finishing credits.

SUPERSTAR

Formed: Glasgow ... 1991 by Bellshill-born JOE McALINDEN, JIM McCULLOCH, QUENTIN McAFEE and ALAN HUTCHISON. The baby of musical maestro/trained violinist and former ex-BMX BANDITS, ex-GROOVY LITTLE NUMBERS, ex-EUGENIUS, ex-SOUP DRAGONS, JOE McALINDEN, SUPERSTAR signed to 'Creation' in '92, releasing a mini debut confusingly titled, 'GREATEST HITS VOL.1', before inking an ill-advised deal with American label, 'S.B.K.'.

A period of five years subsequently elapsed before the band re-emerged on the 'Camp Fabulous' label with the mini-set, '18 CARAT', McALINDEN famously turning down an opportunity to work with BRIAN WILSON along the way. The former BEACH BOYS genius wasn't the only famous muso bod to fall under the SUPERSTAR spell, the likes of PETER BUCK (R.E.M.) and ROD STEWART (who recorded the track 'SUPERSTAR' on his recent covers album) singing the praises of their belated debut album, 'PALM TREE' (1998). Described by one critic as a cross between QUEEN and RADIOHEAD, the Glaswegian quartet tend to draw extreme reactions (usually positive) with their alternately dramatic and heart-rending sound. Beautifully crafted and seemingly wrung from McALINDEN's tortured soul, the likes of 'EVERYDAY I FALL APART' even moved three separate Radio One DJ's to name it as their single of the week. Another admirer was novelist Alan Warner, who subsequently recorded a joint single with the band in summer '98.

JOE McALINDEN – vocals, guitar, piano, vocals (ex-EUGENIUS, ex-BMX BANDITS, ex-GROOVY LITTLE NUMBERS, ex-SOUP DRAGONS) / **JIM McCULLOCH** – guitar, vocals / **ALAN HUTCHISON** – bass, vocals, euphonium / **QUENTIN McAFEE** – drums, vocals

		Creation	Capitol
Jun 92.	(m-cd/m-lp) *(CRE CD/LP 134)* **GREATEST HITS VOL.1** – Barfly / The reason why / She's got everything I own / Let's get lost / Taste / After taste.		-
1994.	(cd) *<28819>* **SUPERSTAR** – Amouricity / Feels like forever / Barfly / Don't wanna die / The reason why / I can't help it / Noise level / Let's get lost / Will I ever see you again / Thought for today / Could it be you.	-	

—— disappeared for a while after signing a new deal with 'S.B.K.'

		Camp Fabulous	not iss.
Mar 97.	(m-cd/m-lp) *(CFAB 001 CD/LP)* **18 CARAT** – Superstar / The Ok corral / Why oh why / It feels so good to be with you / Bad hair day / Bumnote / Little picture.		-
Sep 97.	(7") *(CFAB 002)* **BREATHING SPACE. / PALM TREE** (cd-s) *(CFAB 002CD)* – ('A'side) / Blind spot / Teacher (acoustic) / Disappointed man.		-
Jan 98.	(7") *(CFAB 003S)* **EVERY DAY I FALL APART. / EVERY SECOND HURTS** (cd-s+=) *(CFAB 003CD)* – Hum / Lazy bones.	66	-
Apr 98.	(7") *(CFAB 007S)* **SUPERSTAR. / HEY MONTANA SAN** (cd-s+=) *(CFAB 007CD)* – Waiting room. (cd-s) *(CFAB 007ZCD)* – ('A'side) / Monstermind / Everyday I fall apart.	49	-
Apr 98.	(cd/c/lp) *(CFAB 005X CD/MC/LP)* **PALM TREE** – Monstermind / Superstar / Breathing space / Sparkle / Every day I fall apart / Once again / Palm tree / And when the morning comes / Two of a kind / Life is elsewhere / Teacher.		
Aug 98.	(10"ep; SUPERSTAR VS. ALAN WARNER) *(CFAB 009XS)* **SUPERSTAR VS. ALAN WARNER (SOUNDCLASH)** – Hum (whole new meaning) / One minute story / Introduction / Life is elsewhere / Every second hurts / Little picture.		-
Jun 00.	(7") *(CFAB 010S)* **I LOVE LOVE. /** (cd-s+=) *(CFAB 010CD)* –		-
Jul 00.	(cd/lp) *(CFAB 011 XCD/LP)* **PHAT DAT** – Someone's watching over me / I love love / More / Had enough / Every second hurts / The gymnast / This offering / These little things / This is my world / Phat dat.		-
Dec 00.	(2xcd-ep) *(CFAB 014XCD)* **6 MORE SONGS** – More / +5		-

SWAMPTRASH

Formed: Edinburgh ... 1986 as a sextet under the pseudonymous guise of the hillbilly (Arthur's Seat!) SCRITTON BROTHERS – i.e. HARRY HORSE, MALCOLM CROSBIE, NEIL MacARTHUR, NICK PRESCOTT, JAMES MacKINTOSH and GARRY FINLAYSON – that indicated incestual milarky, but all in good clean, er ... cowpoke-ing fun. Like WE FREE KINGS before them, SWAMPTRASH never took themselves too seriously, their folk-cum-C&W renditions of 'FOGGY MOUNTAIN BREAKDOWN' and Johnny Cash's 'RING OF FIRE', evidence, if any were needed.

Fast Forward-backed independent, 'D.D.T.' released mostly all of SWAMPTRASH's moonshine-flavoured studio output. From "thick"-vinyl'd debut LP, 'IT DON'T MAKE NO NEVER MIND' in '87 to 'THE BONE' EP the following year (recorded for the BBC's Janice Long and featuring trad number 'ROLLING IN MY SWEET BABY'S ARMS'), these bearded straw-chewers showed no signs of strain. However, only one further set, the mini 'MYSTERY GIRLS' for the 'Kissass' imprint came forth. After the sextet picked their last bale o' cotton, they splintered into two or three fragments, the CRITTERHILL VARMINTS, KITH AND KIN and HEXOLOGY; the latter two delivered eponymous sets in the early 90's (future BONGSHANG frontman JJ JAMIESON was a member of the latter). HARRY HORSE, meanwhile, became better known for his illustration work – for evidence see my own Great Rock Discography pre-5th edition.

HARRY HORSE – vocals, banjo / **MALCOLM COOLHAND CROSBIE** – guitar / **NEIL CAL MacARTHUR** – fiddle, electric guitar / **NICK DEXTOR PRESCOTT** – mandolin / **JAMES ELMORE MacKINTOSH** – drums / **GARRY DOC FINLAYSON** – electric banjo

		D.D.T.	Fast Forward
Nov 87.	(lp/c) *(DISP LP/C 12) <FFUS 3301>* **IT DON'T MAKE NO NEVER MIND** – Square as sherrifs / Foggy mountain breakdown / Fisherman's last song / Ring of fire / Pay me / Reuben's train / Mamas in the kitchen / The hex barndance / The swimmer.		1988
Oct 88.	(12"ep) *(DDTEP 002)* **THE BONE EP** – Bone / Glastnost / Cajun stomp / Ring of fire / The cuillen / Rolling in my sweet baby's arms.		-

		Kickass	not iss.
Oct 88.	(m-lp) *(KISSASS 2)* **MYSTERY GIRLS**		-

—— split into two factions (see above)

SWELLING MEG

Formed: Edinburgh ... July '94 by vocalist/cellist CORA BISSETT and acoustic guitarist SEAN KENNEDY; towards the end of the year double bassist AMY DUNCAN became their third member. Taking their extraordinary vibes all around the central belt, SWELLING MEG also recorded 'The She Whale' for the Glasgow 10-Day Weekend V/A tour/album, '12 Into 10', in October 1995.

By the time of their debut release proper, the mini-set/EP 'WELL' (1996), 'MEG's ranks were er, swelling somewhat by the guest appearance of marimba player HAZEL MORRISON and percussionist PAS. Scotland's equivalent to THROWING MUSES although with a larger sense of 'ghost tour' spookiness, SWELLING MEG were unconventional to say the least. At the fall of '97 (with newcomer GUY NICHOLSON) , they were part of the large contingent of Scots acts that appeared at the 13th Note over a series of gigs; these were subsequently released as 13 singles.

The following year, CORA, AMY, SEAN and GUY delivered their first full-set, 'ROC' (1998), pressed in small quantities on London's 'Blue Music' imprint. The inclusion of 'Baba Yaga' and 'Queen Of Tarts' (from the aforementioned 'WELL' set) plus a studio version of 'Size Of You' (their 13th note track) was a little mystifying. Of the nine fresh songs, SWELLING MEG hurtled defiantly into the avant-garde chasms of chamber-Rock without taking themselves too seriously – we await the comeback very soon.

CORA BISSETT – vocals, cello, ocarina / **AMY DUNCAN** – double bass / **SEAN KENNEDY** – acoustic guitar / plus **HAZEL MORRISON** – marimba / **PAS** – percussion

		N.G.M.	not iss.
Jun 96.	(12"ep) *(NGM 007)* **WELL e.p.** – The she whale / Baba Yaga / Queen of tarts / Bingabelly.		-
Jul 96.	(m-cd) *(NGM 007)* **WELL** – Baba Yaga / Queen of tarts / The sinking boy / Bingabelly / The she whale / The growing old song.		-

—— added **GUY NICHOLSON** – percussion, tablas, djembe, derbuka

—— HAZEL would subsequently join The BATHERS

		Flotsam & Jetsam – The 13th Note	not iss.
Nov 97.	(7") *(SHaG 13.02)* **Club Beatroot Part Two** – The size of you / (other by the PRIMEVALS)		-

		Blue Music	not iss.
Jun 98.	(cd) *(BM 1003)* **ROC** – Ostrich song / Size of you / Baba Yaga / Queen of tarts / The ice-cream van / Your kite / Hazz / Bed tourist / Treasure you / Abacus / Mad cow / Digital limbo.		-

—— they split in 1999 after contributing 'Abacus' to the d-cd V/A compilation, 'Women Of Heart And Mind' on 'Quaill' records

—— the group re-formed in 2001 for a series of 'special' gigs

SWINE FLU (see under ⇒ Stranded records)

SWISS FAMILY ORBISON

Formed: Dundee/Glasgow . . . 1997 by former DANNY WILSON man KIT CLARK, along with new writing buddy KEITH MATHESON, plus GREGOR PHILP, COLIN DAVIDSON and DOUGIE VIPOND (yes, Mr. VIPOND himself, the former DEACON BLUE drummer and later TV presenter). A classic moniker, indeed, The SWISS FAMILY ORBISON (ROY would not be amused me thinks!) delivered their debut single, 'I'M IN LOVE', a basic sounding BEACH BOYS-cum-CHILTON track backed by a version of the Human League's 'DON'T YOU WANT ME'. The song was also the opener on their 1998 eponymous CD-album for 'Haven' records (home to EDDI READER and BOO HEWERDINE of The BIBLE). VIPOND careered off into the land of TV once more, briefly taking up the post – once held by Dougie Donnelly – on BBC TV's Saturday Sportscene 2000; "cough! pardon me, I'll repeat that again" somehow comes to mind.

KIT CLARK – vocals, keyboards, harmonica (ex-DANNY WILSON) / **KEITH MATHESON** – guitar, vocals / **GREGOR PHILP** – guitar, vocals / **COLIN DAVIDSON** – bass, vocals / **DOUGIE VIPOND** – drums (ex-DEACON BLUE)

Haven not iss.

Jan 98. (cd-s) *(Havent 5CD)* **I'M IN LOVE / DON'T EVER GO / DON'T YOU WANT ME** ☐ -

Mar 98. (cd) *(HavenCD 9)* **THE SWISS FAMILY ORBISON** ☐ -
– I'm in love / Candle lane / Airline ticket / I don't know what to say / The wall of pain / Seven times / Suicide / Welcome to my heart / The luckiest man in the world / Lesley's hat / A girl I don't know / Someone different.

— the SFO were back in the studio (c.mid-2000) but as yet no records

SYMPATHY 7

Formed: Edinburgh . . . 1999 by GAVIN HENDERSON. This multi-talented, multi-instrumentalist and songwriter (mix ELLIOTT SMITH with SCOTT 4) cut some deeply moving tracks on a self-titled debut EP for 'Liquefaction'. Towards the end of 2001, GAVIN/SYMPATHY 7 unleashed his deep from "the womb" (his studio) inaugural long-player, 'WORDS AND MUSIC'; he toured with a string quartet soon afterwards.

GAVIN HENDERSON – vocals, multi

Liquefaction not iss.

Jul 98. (7"ep) *(DUSKE 007)* **SYMPATHY 7** ☐ -
– Sympathy 7 / Growing wings / Weak will / Bullet proof vest.

Starfish not iss.

Nov 01. (cd) *(SRC 001)* **WORDS AND MUSIC** ☐ -
– Fire / Black eyes / Rush / Flesh / Hypocrite / Amethyst / Starfish / Rene / Sponge / Scratch.

SYNDICATE

Formed: Edinburgh . . . 1983 by guitarist/vocalist JAMES STEWART and two others. A few years down the groove-line, The SYNDICATE signed to the capital's burgeoning dance-orientated imprint, 'Supreme Editions', run by WEA/Warners guy, Allan Campbell and already home to the HI-BEES (who included ex-'Postcard' man, MALCOLM ROSS). Entering BOB LAST's studio with producer and ex-REZILLOS/HUMAN LEAGUE twiddler, JO CALLIS, the trio created a stylish 12" single in the summer of '85, entitled 'GOLDEN KEY'. However, little or nothing was heard from STEWART and his clan for some time, until that is 'E.M.I.' gave them a tidy contract in 1988. A couple of MOTT THE HOOPLE/Glam-type singles, 'BABY'S GONE' and 'HERE COMES THE DAY', were sandwiched either side of a long-awaited debut album, 'KEEP' (1989), although this was their swansong piece. • **Note:** not to be confused with mid-60's outfit of the same name who had in their ranks DONNIE COUTTS and MIKE FRASER (see under VIKINGS). The SYNDICATE of the early 80's (also on 'E.M.I.') were not the same outfit.

JAMES STEWART – vocals, guitar / **CALLUM McNAIR** – / +1

Supreme Editions not iss.

Jun 85. (12") *(EDITION 85-9)* **GOLDEN KEY** ☐ -

Baad not iss.

May 88. (12") *(BAD 777)* **GOIN' FOR IT** ☐ -

E.M.I. not iss.

Jun 89. (7") *(EM 93)* **BABY'S GONE. / 55** ☐ -
(12"+=) *(12EM 93)* – Melting / Buildings in the sky.
(cd-s+=) *(CDEN 93)* – The winner gets the dinner.

Jul 89. (cd/c/lp) *(CD/TC+/EMC 3559)* **KEEP** ☐ -
– The name / Baby's gone / If they don't come / Underground / I love Hollywood / The word / Heaven / Here comes the day / All the people / They shine bright.

Sep 89. (7") *(EM 106)* **HERE COMES THE DAY. / NOSTALGIA LOCOMOTION** ☐ -
(ext;12"+=/cd-s+=) *(12/CD EM 196)* – I love Hollywood (the demo) / Don't let tomorrow be unkind.

— STEWART broke up the group after above; McNAIR formed the APPLES

T

TACOMA RADAR (see under ⇒ Andmoresound records)

Julienne TAYLOR

Born: Edinburgh. After following the time honoured route south at the age of only 17, JULIENNE has had more than her fair share of hard times. She's served her musical apprenticeship on both sides of the mixing desk, having cut her professional teeth in various blues/roots outfits as well as doing a stint in a studio. This despite a severe car crash and a period spent sleeping rough on the capital's streets.

Happily, it seems TAYLOR's star is finally on the rise, the blossoming songstress coming to the nation's attention via a TV ad campaign for v/a CD, 'Scottish Moods'. By putting an adult contemporary spin on Dougie MacLean's 'CALEDONIA', JULIENNE aroused considerable interest in not only the aforementioned album but also her own debut set, 'RACING THE CLOUDS HOME' (2000). Recorded at Edinburgh's 'REL' studios and featuring the co-writing talents of Gordon Campbell (the man behind the groundbreaking West Lothian College Music Business Course), the record was a classy showcase for TAYLOR's breathy, finely tuned vocals. A uillean-pipe enhanced cover of Fleetwood Mac's classic 'SECOND HAND NEWS' (subsequently released as her first single) brought obvious comparisons with The CORRS although US singer, SHANIA TWAIN has been journalists' most favoured comparative benchmark. With support from Radio Two and the promotional weight of 'Virgin' behind her, JULIENNE TAYLOR might yet become a household name in Scotland and beyond.

JULIENNE TAYLOR – vocals / with session people **GORDON CAMPBELL, RICHIE HARRISON, STUART WOOD, DOUGIE PINCOCK, RAB HOWAT, FINLAY MacDONALD, FRASER McNAUGHTON + CHRIS STOUT**

Virgin E.M.I.

Aug 00. (cd/c) *(CDV/TCV 2931)* <850356> **RACING THE CLOUDS HOME** ☐ ☐ Nov00
– Rose of Sweethay / Second hand news / Just let me be / I will protect you / Dreamworld / Land far away / I burn for you / Woolball / I would love you / Tell me where you're going / Caledonia / What am I gonna do?

Sep 00. (c-s) *(VSC 1790)* **SECOND HAND NEWS / ROSE OF SWEETHAY** ☐ -
(cd-s+=) *(VSCDT 1790)* – Woolball.

Jan 01. (c-s) *(VSC 1792)* **JUST LET ME BE (remix) / WHEN LOVE DIES** ☐ -
(cd-s+=) *(VSCDT 1792)* – Say to me.

Jun 01. (c-s) *(VSC 1804)* **CELTIC MANTRA / CELTIC MANTRA (AK remix)** ☐ -
(cd-s+=) *(VSCDT 1804)* – Husky ride (my sister and I).

TECHNOCAT (see under ⇒ WILSON, Tom)

TEENAGE FANCLUB

Formed: Glasgow . . . 1989 although earlier they had posed as The BOY HAIRDRESSERS. After a one-off single, 'GOLDEN SHOWERS' (1988), bassist GERRY LOVE was recruited and BRENDAN O'HARE replaced FRANCIS MACDONALD (who went off to join that other Glasgow institution, The PASTELS) on the drums.

As TEENAGE FANCLUB, they cut the inspired chaos of the 'EVERYTHING FLOWS' (1990) single and followed it up with the debut album, 'A CATHOLIC EDUCATION' later the same year. The term slacker rock was surely coined with this bunch of cheeky Glaswegian wide boys in mind and if it was lazy to compare their honey-in-the-dirt melodic dischord with DINOSAUR JR., that was nothing compared to the laid back, laissez faire philosophy that fuelled (if that's not too strong a word) TEENAGE FANCLUB's ramshackle racket, both on stage and in the studio. By the release of the DON FLEMING-produced 'BANDWAGONESQUE' (1991), ('THE KING' was a sub-standard effort released to fulfil contractual obligations), the band were sounding more professional, crafting an album of langourous harmonies and chiming guitar that was a thinly veiled homage to BIG STAR as well as taking in such obvious reference points as The BYRDS, The BEACH BOYS, BUFFALO SPRINGFIELD etc. Ironically, rather than propelling TEENAGE FANCLUB into the big league, the album seemed instead to merely rekindle interest in BIG STAR's back catalogue and after a honeymoon period of being indie press darlings, the backlash was sharp and swift. The fact that the self-produced 'THIRTEEN' (1993) lacked their trademark inspired sloppiness didn't help matters any. Not that the band were overly concerned, they crafted modern retro more lovingly than most and had a loyal following to lap it up.

The FANNIEs – with PAUL QUINN replacing O'HARE – further developed their niche with 'GRAND PRIX' (1995) and if it was that reliably trad, West Coast via Glasgow roots sound you were after then TEENAGE FANCLUB were your band. While they wear their influences more proudly than any other group, (O.K., so I forgot about OASIS . . .) they do it with such verve and style that it'd be churlish to write them off as mere plagiarists and they remain one of Scotland's best loved exports. Their next effort, 'SONGS FROM NORTHERN BRITAIN' (1997) was their most considered release to date, sharpening up their sound and arrangements to an unprecedented degree. But if that's what it takes to come up with something as engagingly swoonsome as 'I DON'T CARE' or 'IS THAT ENOUGH', no one's going to make much of a fuss.

Now on the roster of the mighty 'Columbia' records, TEENAGE FANCLUB (complete with former BMX BANDITS man FINLAY McDONALD) returned to the fold via album No.6 proper, 'HOWDY!' (2000). Slightly back to basics and reminiscent of BIG STAR (once again!), the album only just managed to gain a UK Top 40 placing; the appropriately-titled single from it 'I NEED DIRECTION' only just dented the Top 50. Drummer and original member, FRANCIS MACDONALD, subsequently superseded QUINN for a one-off single collaboration 'DUMB DUMB DUMB' with daisy-chain hip hop stars, DE LA SOUL, although this failed miserably with the record buying public.

The group were back to basics again (this time on STEPHEN PASTEL's 'Geographic' imprint) come their short but sweet set, 'WORDS OF WISDOM AND HOPE' (2002), a record that saw them collaborate with US-born songwriter JAD FAIR. Ditching their more commercial rock flair, TFC went for something a bit rougher – all thanks to FAIR – hammering out tracks 'I FEEL FINE', 'VAMPIRE'S CLAW' and 'NEAR TO YOU' (the single) to brilliant effect.

• **Songwriters:** BLAKE or BLAKE-McGINLEY or group compositions except; DON'T CRY NO TEARS (Neil Young) / THE BALLAD OF JOHN AND YOKO (Beatles) / LIKE A VIRGIN (Madonna) / LIFE'S A GAS (T.Rex) / FREE AGAIN + JESUS CHRIST (Alex Chilton) / CHORDS OF FAME (Phil Ochs) / BAD SEEDS (Beat Happening) / HAVE YOU EVER SEEN THE RAIN? (Creedence Clearwater Revival) / BETWEEN US (Neil Innes) / FEMME FATALE (Velvet Underground).

• **Trivia:** ALEX CHILTON (ex-BOX TOPS) guested on 1992 sessions and contributed some songs.

NORMAN BLAKE (b.20 Oct'65, Bellshill) – vocals, guitar (ex-BMX BANDITS) / **RAYMOND McGINLEY** (b. 3 Jan'64, Glasgow) – bass, vocals / **FRANCIS MACDONALD** (b.11 Sep'70, Bellshill) – drums / **JOE McALINDEN** – violin / **JIM LAMBIE** – vibraphone

53rd & 3rd — not iss.

Jan 88. (12"; as BOY HAIRDRESSERS) *(AGARR 12T)* **GOLDEN SHOWERS. / TIDAL WAVE / THE ASSUMPTION AS AN ELEVATOR** [ ] [-]

— **NORMAN + RAYMOND** – guitars, vocals plus **GERARD LOVE** (b.31 Aug'67, Motherwell) – bass, vocals / **BRENDAN O'HARE** (b.16 Jan'70, Bellshill) – drums; repl. MACDONALD who joined The PASTELS

Paperhouse — Matador

Jun 90. (7"m) *(PAPER 003)* **EVERYTHING FLOWS. / PRIMARY EDUCATION / SPEEEDER** [ ] [-]
(cd-ep+=) *(PAPER 003CD)* – Don't Cry No Tears. *(rel.Feb91)*

Jul 90. (cd/c/lp) *(PAP CD/MC/LP 004)* *<OLE 012>* **A CATHOLIC EDUCATION** [ ] [ ] Aug90
– Heavy metal / Everything flows / A catholic education / Too involved / Don't need a drum / Critical mass / Heavy metal II / A catholic education 2 / Eternal light / Every picture I paint / Everybody's fool. *(re-iss. cd Mar95; same) (cd re-iss. Apr02 on 'Fire'; SFIRE 001CD)*

Oct 90. (one-sided-7") *(PAPER 005)* **THE BALLAD OF JOHN AND YOKO** [ ] [-]

Nov 90. (7"m) *<OLE 007-7>* **EVERYBODY'S FOOL. / PRIMAL EDUCATION / SPEEDER** [-] [ ]

Nov 90. (7") *(PAPER 007)* *<OLE 023>* **GOD KNOWS IT'S TRUE. / SO FAR GONE** [ ] [ ] Jan91
(12"+=/cd-s+=) *(PAPER 007 T/CD)* – Weedbreak / Ghetto blaster.

Creation — Geffen

Aug 91. (cd/lp) *(CRE CD/LP 096)* **THE KING** (instrumental) [53] [-]
– Heavy metal 6 / Mudhoney / Interstellar overdrive / Robot love / Like a virgin / The king / Opal inquest / The ballad of Bow Evil (slow and fast) / Heavy metal 9. (above originally only meant for US ears, deleted after 24 hours)

Aug 91. (7") *(CRE 105)* **STAR SIGN. / HEAVY METAL 6** [44] [-]
(12"+=)(cd-s+=) *(CRE 105T)(CRESCD 105)* – Like a virgin / ('A'demo version).
(7"ltd) *(CRE 105L)* – ('A'side) / Like a virgin.

Oct 91. (7"/c-s) *(CRE/+CS 111)* *<4370>* **THE CONCEPT. / LONG HAIR** [51] [ ] Jan92
(12"+=)(cd-s+=) *(CRE 111T)(CRESCD 111)* – What you do to me (demo) / Robot love.

Nov 91. (cd)(c/lp) *(CRECD 106)(C+/CRE 106)* *<24461>* **BANDWAGONESQUE** [22] [ ]
– The concept / Satan / December / What you do to me / I don't know / Star sign / Metal baby / Pet rock / Sidewinder / Alcoholiday / Guiding star / Is this music?. *(cd re-iss. Jan01; same)*

Jan 92. (7"/c-s) *(CRE/+CS 115)* *<21708>* **WHAT YOU DO TO ME. / B-SIDE** [31] [ ]
(12"+=)(cd-s+=) *(CRE 115T)(CRESCD 115)* – Life's a gas / Filler.

Jun 93. (7"/c-s) *(CRE/+CS 130)* **RADIO. / DON'S GONE COLUMBIA** [31] [ ]
(12"+=)(cd-s+=) *(CRE 130T)(CRESCD 130)* – Weird horses / Chords of fame.

Sep 93. (7"/c-s) *(CRE/+CS 142)* **NORMAN 3. / OLDER GUYS** [50] [-]
(12"+=)(cd-s+=) *(CRE 142T)(CRESCD 142)* – Golden glades / Genius envy.

Oct 93. (cd)(c/lp) *(CRECD 144)(C+/CRE 144)* *<24533>* **THIRTEEN** [14] [ ] Nov93
– Hang on / The cabbage / Radio / Norman 3 / Song to the cynic / 120 minutes / Escher / Commercial alternative / Fear of flying / Tears are cool / Ret live dead / Get funky / Gene Clark. *(cd re-iss. Jan01; same)*

— also in 1993, they made a joint single with BIG STAR, 'MINE EXCLUSIVELY' b/w 'PATTI GIRL', proceeds going towards Bosnia, etc

— In Mar'94, they teamed up with DE LA SOUL on single 'FALLIN''. This was from the rock-rap album 'Judgement Day' on 'Epic' records (hit UK 59).

1994. (cd-ep) *<21887>* **AUSTRALIAN TOUR SAMPLER** [-] [ ]

— **PAUL QUINN** – drums (ex-SOUP DRAGONS) repl. O'HARE who later joined MOGWAI

Mar 95. (7"/c-s) *(CRE/+CS 175)* **MELLOW DOUBT. / SOME PEOPLE TRY TO FUCK WITH YOU** [34] [-]
(cd-s+=) *(CRESCD 175)* – Getting real / About you.
(cd-s) *(CRESCD 175X)* – ('A'side) / Have you ever seen the rain? / Between us / You're my kind.

May 95. (7"/c-s) *(CRE/+CS 201)* **SPARKY'S DREAM. / BURNED** [40] [-]
(cd-s+=) *(CRESCD 201)* – For you / Headstand.
(cd-s) *(CRESCD 201X)* – ('A'-alternative version) / Try and stop me / That's all I need to know / Who loves the sun.

May 95. (cd)(c/lp) *(CRECD 173)(C+/CRE 173)* *<24802>* **GRAND PRIX** [7] [ ] Jul95
– About you / Sparky's dream / Mellow doubt / Don't look back / Verisinilitude / Neil Jung / Tears / Discolite / Say no / Going places / I'll make it clear / I gotta know / Hardcore – ballad. *(lp w/free 7")* – DISCOLITE (demo). / I GOTTA KNOW (demo) *(cd re-iss. Jan01; same)*

Aug 95. (7"/c-s) *(CRE/+CS 210)* **NEIL JUNG. / THE SHADOWS** [62] [-]
(cd-s+=) *(CRESCD 210)* – My life / Every step is a way through love.
(cd-s) *(CRESCD 210X)* – ('A'side) / Traffic jam / Hi-fi / I heard you looking.

Dec 95. (7"ep/c-ep/cd-ep) *(CRE/+CS/SCD 216)* **TEENAGE FANCLUB HAVE LOST IT EP (acoustic)** [53] [-]
– Don't look back / Everything flows / Starsign / 120 mins.

— late in '96, LOVE and McGINLEY joined forces with The VASELINES' EUGENE KELLY to form ASTROCHIMP; one single 'DRAGGIN' for 'Shoeshine'

Creation — Sony

Jun 97. (cd-s) *(CRESCD 228)* **AIN'T THAT ENOUGH / KICKABOUT / BROKEN** [17] [-]
(cd-s) *(CRESCD 228X)* – ('A'side) / Femme fatale / Jesus Christ.

Jun 97. (cd/c/lp) *(CRECD/CCRE/CRELP 196)* *<68202>* **SONGS FROM NORTHERN BRITAIN** [3] [ ]
– Start again / Ain't that enough / Can't feel my soul / I don't want control of you / Planets / It's a bad world / Take the long way round / Winter / I don't care / Mount Everest / Your love is the place where I come from / Speed of light. *(cd re-iss. Jan01; same)*

Aug 97. (7") *(CRE 238)* **I DON'T WANT CONTROL OF YOU. / THE COUNT** [43] [-]
(cd-s+=) *(CRESCD 238)* – Middle of the road.
(cd-s) *(CRESCD 238X)* – ('A'side) / He'd be a diamond / Live my life.

Nov 97. (7") *(CRE 280)* **START AGAIN. / AIN'T THAT ENOUGH (TOTP acoustic)** [54] [-]
(cd-s+=) *(CRESCD 280)* – Take the long way round (radio).
(cd-s) *(CRESCD 280X)* – ('A'side) / How many more years / Nothing to be done.

— added **FINLAY McDONALD** – keyboards (ex-BMX BANDITS, ex-SPEEDBOAT); was p/t on tour

Jun 98. (7") *(CRE 298)* **LONG SHOT. / LOOPS AND STRINGS** [ ] [-]

Columbia Columbia

Oct 00. (7") *(669951-7)* **I NEED DIRECTION. / ON THIS GOOD NIGHT** [48] [-]
(cd-s+=) *(669951-2)* – I lied / Here comes your man.

Oct 00. (cd/lp) *(<500622-2/-1>)* **HOWDY!** [33] [ ] Nov00
– I need direction / I can't find my way home / Accidental life / Near you / Happiness / Dumb dumb dumb / Town and the city / The sun shines from you / Straight and narrow / Cul de sac / My uptight life / If I never see you again.

— **FRANCIS MACDONALD** – drums (of Shoeshine records) repl. QUINN who quit during the middle of the last set

Jun 01. (7"; as TEENAGE FANCLUB & DE LA SOUL) *(<671213-7>)* **DUMB DUMB DUMB. / STRAIGHT AND NARROW** [ ] [ ] Jan02
(cd-s+=) *(671213-2)* – Thaw me / One thousand lights.

TEENAGE FANCLUB & JAD FAIR

Geographic Alternative Tentacles

Feb 02. (7") *(GEOG 013)* **NEAR TO YOU. / ALWAYS IN MY HEART** [68] [-]
(cd-s+=) *(GEOG 013CD)* – Let's celebrate.

Mar 02. (cd/lp) *(GEOG 014 CD/LP)* <VIRUS 274> **WORDS OF WISDOM AND HOPE** [ ] [ ] Jan02
– Behold the miracle / I feel fine / Near to you / Smile / Crush on you / Cupid / The power of your tenderness / Vampire's claw / Secret heart / You rock / Love's taken over / The good thing.

– compilations, others, etc. –

May 92. (7") *K; <IPU 26>* **FREE AGAIN. / BAD SEEDS** [-] [ ]

Nov 92. (12"ep/cd-ep) *Strange Fruit; (SFPS/+CD 081)* **THE JOHN PEEL SESSION** [ ] [-]
– God knows it's true / Alcoholiday / So far gone / Long hair. *(re-iss. Dec93 & Jul95; same)*

Mar 95. (cd/c) *Fire; (FLIPCD 002)* **DEEP FRIED FANCLUB** [ ] [-]
– Everything flows / Primary education / Speeder / Critical mass (orig.) / The ballad of John and Yoko / God knows it's true / Weedbreak / So far gone / Ghetto blaster / Don't cry no tears / Free again / Bad seed.

Jul 95. (12"ep/cd-ep; as FRANK BLACK & TEENAGE FANCLUB) *Strange Fruit; (SFPS/+CD 091)* **PEEL SESSION** [ ] [-]
– Handy man / The man who was too loud / The Jacques Tati / Sister Isabel.

Apr 97. (cd) *Nectar; (NTMCD 543)* **FANDEMONIUM** [ ] [-]

Sep 97. (7"ep) *Radiation; (RARE 033)* **TEENAGE FANCLUB EP** [ ] [-]

TELSTAR PONIES

Formed: Glasgow ... mid-1994 by ex-18 WHEELER man, DAVID KEENAN and ex-TEENAGE FANCLUB japester, BRENDAN O'HARE; JOHN HOGARTY (ex-BMX BANDITS) was also an initial member before he joined NATIONAL PARK. With the intention of moving as far away as possible from the Scots-indie-by-numbers of KEENAN's former band, the pair eventually roped in GAVIN LAIRD and RACHEL DEVINE and set about creating a sound more in tune with cosmic sounds of CAN, FAUST etc. Signed to 'Fire' records, the band released the relatively hummable 'MAPS AND STARCHARTS' as their debut single that year, progressing to the more experimental 'NOT EVEN STARCROSSED' in summer '95.

The full extent of their stellar-rock experimentation was revealed later that year on the debut album, 'IN THE SPACE OF A FEW MINUTES', while the subsequent addition of organist RICHARD YOUNGS added a further dimension to the band's sound. Follow-up set, 'VOICES FROM THE NEW MUSIC' (1996), featured some of the band's most adventurous compositions to date, not least the marathon 'DOES YOUR HEART HAVE WINGS'. Yet by the end of the year, O'HARE and LAIRD (who'd gigged around the country as CAIN) had broken ranks to form their own outfit, FIEND 1 and the short-lived MACROCOSMICA, the former later enjoying a brief tenure with fellow Glaswegian sound/noise sculptors, the mighty MOGWAI. Meanwhile, KEENAN and old chum and NATIONAL PARK member, JOHN HOGARTY, teamed up with Falkirk-born jazzman BILL WELLS to form PHANTOM ENGINEER.

DAVID KEENAN – guitar, vocals (ex-18 WHEELER) / **RACHEL DEVINE** – guitar, piano, vocals / **GAVIN LAIRD** (b.18 Feb'70, Girvan, Ayrshire) – bass / **BRENDAN O'HARE** – drums (ex-TEENAGE FANCLUB)

Fire Instant Mayhem

Nov 94. (7") *(BLAZE 74)* **MAPS AND STARCHARTS. / THANKS BUT NO THANKS, MR. DULLI** [ ] [-]
(cd-s+=) *(BLAZE 74CD)* – Hang up.

Apr 95. (10"ep/cd-ep) *(BLAZE 85 T/CD)* **NOT EVEN STARCROSSED. / COLOR DELUXE / PATTY WATERS** [ ] [-]

Oct 95. (7") *(BLAZE 94)* **HER NAME. / THE BALLAD OF LIBERTY VALANCE** [ ] [-]
(cd-s+=) *(BLAZE 94CD)* – Lugengeschichte (Pylon King mix) / ('A'-Pylon King mix).

Oct 95. (cd/lp) *(FIRE CD/LP 52)* **IN THE SPACE OF A FEW MINUTES** [ ] [-]
– The Moon is not a puzzle / Lugengeschichte / Not even starcrossed / Maya / Two's insane / Moon, don't come up tonight / Monster / Side netting / Her name / Innerhalb weniger minuten / I still believe in Christmas. *(cd re-iss. Jun02 on 'Fire'; SFIRE 015CD)*

Jan 96. (cd-ep) *<IMC 9453-2>* **MORS FACTUM MUSICA** [-] [ ]
– Innerhalb weniger minuten / Lugengeschichte / I still believe in Christmas trees / Does your heart have wings? / Secret outpost.

May 96. (12"/cd-s) *(BLAZE 100 T/CD)* **DOES YOUR HEART HAVE WINGS? / GHOST CHANNELS (FLEISCH-ABGEZOGEN) / GHOST CHANNELS (FLENSE)** [ ] [-]

— added **RICHARD YOUNGS** – keyboards

Fire Velvel

Sep 96. (7") *(BLAZE 110)* **BREWERY OF EGGSHELLS. / THE FIRST KISS TAKES SO LONG** [ ] [-]
(cd-s+=) *(BLAZE 110CD)* – Wall of rock.

Oct 96. (cd/d-lp) *(FIRE CD/LP 60)* <97100> **VOICES FROM THE NEW MUSIC** [ ] [ ] Mar97
– Bells for Albert Ayler / Voices from the new music / Last outpost / Shizuka / A little cloud / Brewery of eggshells / Aegis falling / Sail her on / A feather on the breath / The fall of little summer / Does your heart have wings? / Song of Ansuz / La Vienna.

Jan 97. (cd-s) *(BLAZE 112CD)* **VOICES FROM THE NEW MUSIC** [-] [-] w-drawn

— **KEENAN + DEVINE** carried on when LAIRD + O'HARE formed MACROCOSMICA (the latter subsequently joined MOGWAI in June '97)

— KEENAN, HOGARTY and jazzman BILL WELLS became PHANTOM ENGINEER

FIEND

O'HARE – guitars, vocals + **LAIRD** – guitar, vocals

God Bless God Bless

Oct 97. (cd; as FIEND 1) *(<NOIR 001CD>)* **CALEDONIAN GOTHIC** [ ] [ ]
– Angel hair (2nd book) / Ghost kanal / Hammer into anvil empirical / Munich X / Huon pine song / Brittle horse pt.1 & 2 / Compressor / Rother / Spirit / Voyager / Origin & purpose / Rose / Traumen / Preuvial sphere (coda).

Feb 98. (cd; as FIEND 2) *(<NOIR 002CD>)* **CALEDONIAN COSMIC** [ ] [ ]
– Testimony / Paranoic timeslip / Null / Stacy / Spacedtime / Heat and soul / Blue book (1st book) / The birthplace of stars.

— with also **KENNY** (from ESKA) + **RACHEL** (ex-TELSTAR PONIES) + **DAVE TOUGH** (of ALL TOO HUMAN, etc)

Sep 98. (cd; as FIEND 3) *(<NOIR 003CD>)* **CALEDONIAN MYSTIC** [ ] [ ]
– Evermore / Kurz / Until these parallels are understood / Pharos light / Red pigment tattoo / Forgotten sea / Alliances / Continuum.

MACROCOSMICA

O'HARE + LAIRD plus **CERWYSS OWER** – bass, vocals + **RUSSELL McEWAN** – drums (of BLACK SUN MACHINE, of CYLINDER)

God Bless God Bless

Nov 97. (cd) *(<NOIR 004CD>)* **AD ASTRA** [ ] [ ] Jan98
– Rusty's arms / Orbit 48 / Ram's expo / I am the spaceship Digitalis / Lamotta / A horse can walk / Byne. *(re-iss. Nov01; same)*

May 98. (cd-ep) *(REX 002CD)* **SPACE GEEK / RA UNMOVED / WEIRD SEX DREAM #2 / LONE COP** [ ] [-]
(re-iss. Nov01; same)

— LAIRD departed mid-1998; meanwhile, **O'HARE** is part of Scot/Australian (three persons) internet link outfit, LIMINAL, who released 'aa' debut set (early '99)

LONECOP

GAVIN LAIRD + EWAN McALLAN

Static Caravan not iss.

Nov 99. (7"blue) *(VAN 10.0)* **TONE MOVIE. / HELIUM BALLOON** [ ] [-]

Obellesk not iss.

Oct 00. (cd) *(OBOE 1)* **MY PREY BETRAYS ITSELF** [ ] [-]
– Tone movie / Helium balloon / Postcard / #1 / Everything burns / I try to trap this emotion for you / #2 / Jack Christ / Towards the stars / Revenge killing / #3.

TELSTAR PONIES

— re-formed

Geographic not iss.

Jul 01. (7") *(GEOG 008)* **FAREWELL FAREWELL. / VOICE IN THE CLOUDS** [ ] [-]

TERRA DIABLO

Formed: Glasgow. . . 1999 when IAN FAIRCLOUGH and DAVE McAULAY (who'd both worked at McCormack's music shop) enlisted three others STUART MILEHAN, GORDON TURNER and PAUL WILSON. Maturing very quickly from small stints at T In The Park in 2000, to Nice'n'Sleazy's, 13th Note, King Tut's Wah Wah Hut and 2001's T In The Park (the PRS tent), TERRA DIABLO were fast becoming Scotland's hottest property. A self-financed debut EP, '(Y)OUR MUSIC' affirmed their potential, while a 10"ep, 'THE WAY THINGS ARE' late in 2001, showed off their quickfire, stripped-down and melodious songs. 2003 could be the year of the 'DIABLO.

IAN FAIRCLOUGH – vocals, guitar / **DAVE McAULAY** – guitar / **PAUL WILSON** – keyboards, guitar / **STUART MILEHAM** – bass / **GORDON TURNER** – drums

Spam not iss.

Aug 00. (ltd-cd-ep) *(SPAM 2)* **(Y)OUR MUSIC** [ ] [-]
– Must be something to do with the moon or something / Mellifluous part 1 / Mellifluous part 2 / All the bhutki.

Zuma not iss.

Oct 01. (10"ep) *(TD 1)* **THE WAY THINGS ARE** [ ] [-]
– The way things are and how they're meant to be / Must be something to do with the moon or something / Diablo style.

TEXAS

Formed: Glasgow . . .1988 by SHARLEEN SPITERI, JOHNNY McELHONE, ALLY McERLAINE and STUART KERR. Initially lumped in with the new wave of young Scottish rock bands tipped for big things (GUN, SLIDE etc.), TEXAS debuted in early '89 with the rootsy pop of 'I DON'T WANT A LOVER', its infectious slide guitar refrain infiltrating the Top 10 but subsequently becoming a millstone round the band's neck as they struggled to shake off the 'one-hit-wonder' tag. The debut album, 'SOUTHSIDE' (1989) was a Top 5 hit nevertheless, a highly listenable set of inoffensive, blues/country-tinged pop/rock which became one of the top selling albums of that year. This was without the help of any further hit singles, both 'THRILL HAS GONE' and 'EVERYDAY NOW' (very reminiscent of BOB DYLAN's 'I Shall Be Released') stalling outside the Top 40.

In fact, the group's next major hit single came more than three years later with a cover of Al Green's 'TIRED OF BEING ALONE'. There was certainly no disputing the sensuous beauty and power of SPITERI's voice, or indeed her striking looks and while TEXAS had their critics, they also boasted an extensive grassroots following, especially in their native Scotland where gigs often took on the fervour of religious gatherings.

Predictably then, the follow-up set, 'MOTHER'S HEAVEN' (1991), was well received by devotees but failed to convince many waverers. Likewise 'RICK'S ROAD' (1993), an underrated set which leant more on the country-rock side of things. With its BYRDS-esque jangle and gorgeous vocal, 'SO CALLED FRIEND' remains one of TEXAS's most affecting moments, though thousands would no doubt disagree. Many of those thousands, in fact, who probably own a copy of 'WHITE ON BLONDE', TEXAS's million selling 1997 album which must surely rank as one of the most incredible commercial turnarounds in the history of rock. Abandoning the roots trappings for a super slick soul-pop sound, TEXAS transformed themselves from yet another flagging Scottish rock band into an international phenomenon. Buoyed by the success of radio-friendly, highly infectious singles like 'SAY WHAT YOU WANT', 'HALO' and 'BLACK EYED BOY', the album was 1997's ultimate coffee table companion. Not only that, SPITERI was seemingly born again as a style mag sex symbol, her ravishing visage staring out from front cover after front cover. Bizarrely enough, among TEXAS's biggest fans were New York's hardest rap crew, The WU-TANG CLAN, surely resulting in a rather unlikely pairing (of all-time, quite possibly) on a Top 5 version of 'SAY WHAT YOU WANT (ALL DAY AND EVERY DAY)'.

Having already topped the charts with their last album, TEXAS repeated the formula with their follow-up, 'THE HUSH' (1999), a deliberately more sensual set of songs that included three massive hits, 'IN OUR LIFETIME, 'SUMMER SON' and 'WHEN WE ARE TOGETHER'.

• **Songwriters:** SPITERI lyrics / McELHONE music, except SWEET CHILD O' MINE (Guns N' Roses).

SHARLEEN SPITERI (b. 7 Nov'67) – vocals, guitar / **ALLY McERLAINE** (b. ALISTAIR, 31 Oct'68) – guitar / **JOHNNY McELHONE** (b.21 Apr'63) – bass, vocals (ex-ALTERED IMAGES, ex-HIPSWAY) / **STUART KERR** (b.16 Mar'63) – drums (ex-LOVE AND MONEY)

Mercury Mercury

Jan 89. (7") *(TEX 1) <872350>* **I DON'T WANT A LOVER. / BELIEVE ME** [8] [77]
(ext;12"+=/cd-s+=) *(TEX 1-12/CD1)* – All in vain.

Mar 89. (lp/c/cd) *(<838 171-1/-4/-2>)* **SOUTHSIDE** [3] [88]
– I don't want a lover / Tell me why / Everyday now / Southside / Prayer for you / Faith / The thrill has gone / Fight the feeling / Fool for love / One choice / Future is promises.

Apr 89. (7") *(TEX 2)* **THRILL HAS GONE. / NOWHERE LEFT TO HIDE** [60] [ ]
(12"+=/12"s+=)(cd-s+=) *(TEX/+P 2-12)(TEXCD 2)* – Dimples.

Jul 89. (7"/c-s) *(TEX/+MC 3)* **EVERYDAY NOW. / WAITING FOR THE FALL** [44] [ ]
(12"+=) *(TEX 3-12)* – Faith.
(cd-s+=) *(TEXCD 3)* – Future is promises (acoustic) / Food for love (live at Radio Clyde).
(12") *(TEXR 3-12)* – ('A'live) / Living for the city (live) / It hurts me too (live).

Nov 89. (7"/c-s) *(TEX/+MC 4)* **PRAYER FOR YOU. / RETURN** [73] [ ]
(12"+=/cd-s+=) *(TEX 4-12/CD4)* – I don't want a lover (live) / ('A'-acoustic).
(12"/cd-s) *(TEX R/CDR 4-12)* – ('A'-Southside & Northside remixes).

Aug 91. (7"/c-s) *(TEX/+MC 5)* **WHY BELIEVE IN YOU. / HOW IT FEELS** [66] [ ]
(12"+=/cd-s+=) *(TEX 5-12/CD5)* – Hold me Lord.
(cd-s) *(TEXCB 5)* – ('A'side) / Is what I do wrong / Hold me LOrd / Living for the city (live).

Sep 91. (cd/c/lp) *(<848 578-2/-4/-1>)* **MOTHER'S HEAVEN** [32] [ ]
– Mother's heaven / Why believe in you / Dream hotel / This will all be mine / Beliefs / Alone with you / In my heart / Waiting / Wrapped in clothes of blue / Return / Walk the dust.

Oct 91. (7"/c-s) *(TEX/+MC 6)* **IN MY HEART. / IS WHAT I DO WRONG** [74] [ ]
(12"+=) *(TEX 6-12)* – Alone with you.
(12"+=/cd-s+=) *(TEX 6-12/CD6)* – You gave me love / ('A'remix).

Feb 92. (7"/c-s) *(TEX/+MC 7)* **ALONE WITH YOU. / DOWN IN THE BATTLEFIELD** [32] [ ]
(cd-s) *(TEXCD 7)* – ('A'side) / Why believe in you / Everyday now / I don't want a lover.

(cd-s) *(TEXCDX 7)* – ('A'live) / Can't get next to you (live) / What goes on (live) / Sweet child o' mine (live).

Apr 92. (7"/c-s) *(TEX/+MC 8)* **TIRED OF BEING ALONE. / WRAPPED IN CLOTHES OF BLUE** 19
(cd-s) *(TEXCD 8)* – ('A'side) / Thrill has gone / In my heart (12"mix) / Prayer for you (Northside remix).
(cd-s) *(TEXCB 8)* – ('A'acoustic) / Walk the dust (acoustic) / Why believe in you (acoustic) / Return (acoustic).

— **RICHARD HYND** (b.17 May'68, Aberdeen) – drums (ex-SLIDE) repl. KERR

— added **EDDIE CAMPBELL** (b. 6 Jun'65) – keyboards

Vertigo Mercury

Aug 93. (7"/c-s) *(TEX AS/MC 9)* **SO CALLED FRIEND. / YOU'RE THE ONE I WANT IT FOR** 30
(cd-s+=) *(TEXCD 9)* – Tonight I stay with you / I've been missing you.
(box;cd-s+=) *(TEXCDP 9)* – Mother's Heaven (French mix) / Tired of being alone.

Oct 93. (7"/c-s) *(TEX AS/MC 10)* **YOU OWE IT ALL TO ME. / DON'T HELP ME THROUGH** 39
(cd-s+=) *(TEXCD 10)* – Make me want to scream / Strange that I want you.
(cd-s) *(TEXCL 10)* – ('A'side) / I don't want a lover (acoustic) / So called friend (acoustic) / Revolution (acoustic).

Nov 93. (cd/c/lp) *(<518 252-2/-4/-1>)* **RICK'S ROAD** 18
– So called friend / Fade away / Listen to me / You owe it all to me / Beautiful angel / So in love with you / You've got to live a little / I want to go to Heaven / Hear me now / Fearing these days / I've been missing you / Winter's end.

Feb 94. (7"/c-s) *(TEX AS/MC 11)* **SO IN LOVE WITH YOU. / ('A'instrumental)** 28
(cd-s) *(TEXCD 11)* – ('A'side) / So called friend / One love / You owe it all to me.
(cd-s) *(TEXCX 11)* – ('A'side) / Why believe in you (live) / Prayer for you (live) / Everyday now (live).

Mercury Mercury

Jan 97. (c-s) *(MERMC 480)* **SAY WHAT YOU WANT / COLD DAY DREAM** 3
(cd-s+=) *(MERCD 480)* – Tear it up / ('A'-Boilerhouse remix).
(cd-s) *(MERDD 480)* – ('A'side) / Good advice / ('A'-Rae & Christian mixes).

Feb 97. (cd/c) *(<534 315-2/-4>)* **WHITE ON BLONDE** 1
– Halo / Say what you want / Drawing crazy patterns / Put your arms around me / Insane / Black eyed boy / Polo mint city / White on blonde / Postcard / Ticket to lie / Good advice.

Apr 97. (c-s) *(MERMC 482)* **HALO / ASKING FOR FAVOURS** 10
(cd-s+=) *(MERCD 482)* – Coming down / ('A'-orchestral version).
(cd-s) *(MERDD 482)* – ('A'side) / ('A'-Rae & Christian mixes) / ('A'-808 mixes).

Aug 97. (c-s) *(MERMC 490)* **BLACK EYED BOY / FAITHLESS** 5
(cd-s) *(MERCD 490)* – ('A'side) / Sorry / Black eyed disco (disco boy dub mix) / Say what you want (session).
(cd-s) *(MERDD 490)* – ('A'side) / ('A'-disco/dance mixes).

Nov 97. (c-s) *(MERMC 497)* **PUT YOUR ARMS AROUND ME / NEVER NEVER** 10
(cd-s+=) *(MERCD 497)* – You're all I need to get by (session).
(cd-s) *(MERDD 497)* – ('A'mixes; Two Lone Swordsmen & Ballistic Brothers).

Mar 98. (c-s; TEXAS featuring WU-TANG) *(MERMC 499)* **SAY WHAT YOU WANT (ALL DAY EVERY DAY) / INSANE** 4
(cd-s+=) *(MERCD 499)* – Polo mint city (extended) / ('A'-Trailermen mix).
(cd-s) *(MERDD 499)* – ('A'extended) / ('B'-The econd scroll) / ('A'&'B'-RZA instrumentals & dub versions).
(12") *(MERX 499)* – ('A'-Trailermen mix) / ('A'-RZA instrumental).

Apr 99. (c-s) *(MERMC 517)* **IN OUR LIFETIME / LOVE DREAM #2** 4 -
(cd-s+=) *(MERDD 517)* – ('A'-enhanced).
(cd-s) *(MERCD 517)* – ('A'side) / ('A'-Jules disco trip mix) ('A'-Return To Tha dub mix).

May 99. (cd/c) *(<538 972-2/-4>)* **THE HUSH** 1
– In our lifetime / Tell me the answer / Summer son / Sunday afternoon / Move in / When we are together / Day after day / Zero zero / Saint / Girl / The hush / The day before I went away. *(cd hidden+=)* – Let us be thankful.

Aug 99. (c-s) *(MERMC 520)* **SUMMER SON / ('A'-Giorgio Moroder mix)** 5 -
(cd-s+=) *(MERCD 520)* – Don't you want me (live).
(cd-s+=) *(MERDD 520)* – ('A'-Tee's freeze mix).

Nov 99. (c-s) *(MERMC 525)* **WHEN WE ARE TOGETHER / SAY WHAT YOU WANT (ALL DAY AND EVERY DAY) (live)** 12 -
(cd-s+=) *(MERCD 525)* – In our lifetime (live) / ('A'-video).
(cd-s) *(MERDD 525)* – ('A'mixes) / Summer son (Euro bootleg).

Oct 00. (c-s) *(MERMC 528)* **IN DEMAND / EARLY HOURS** 6 -
(cd-s+=) *(MERCD 528)* – Like lovers (holding on) / ('A'-CD-Rom).
(cd-s) *(MERDD 528)* – ('A'-US mix) / ('A'-Sunship mix) / ('A'-Wookie remix) / ('A'-Sunshine dub).
(12") *(MERX 528)* – ('A'-US mix) / ('A'-Wookie remix).

Oct 00. (cd/c) *(548262-2/-4)* **THE GREATEST HITS** (compilation) 1 -
– I don't want a lover / In demand / Say what you want / Summer son / Inner smile / So in love with you / Black eyed boy / So called friend / Everyday now / In our lifetime / Halo / Guitar song / Prayer for you / When we are together / Insane / Tired of being alone / Put your arms around me / Say what you want (all day and every day (with METHOD MAN/RZA). *(d-cd+=; 548227-2)* – (various mixes). *(cd re-iss. Jul01; same)*

Jan 01. (c-s) *(MERMC 531)* **INNER SMILE / ('A'-Moody mix) / ('A'-Stonebridge classic house mix)** 6 -
(cd-s+=) *(MERDD 531)* – ('A'-Jule's club radio mix) / ('A'-Rae & Christian basement mix).
(cd-s) *(MERCD 531)* – ('A'-extended 12" mix) / Across the universe – Inner smile (CD-Rom mix).

Jul 01. (cd-s) *(MERDD 533)* **I DON'T WANT A LOVER (2001 mix) / SUMMER SON (live) / SUSPICIOUS MINDS (live)** 16 -
(c-s+=) *(MERCS 533)* – ('A'-Trailerman mix).
(cd-s) *(MERCD 533)* – ('A'side) / Superwrong / I don't want a lover (Stonebridge bed mix) / ('A'video) / ('A'live).

- compilations, etc. -

Sep 95. (d-cd) *Vertigo; (528604-2)* **SOUTHSIDE / RICK'S ROAD** -

THANES

Formed: Edinburgh-based . . . mid-80's as The GREEN TELESCOPE by LENNY HELSING, who had more than a slight penchant for garage/R&B of the mid-60's (i.e. PRETTY THINGS, STANDELLS and REMAINS). Along with BRUCE LYALL, DENIS BOYLE and IAN BINNS, the GT became the first act to record for the psychedelic-biased 'Imaginary' label (later home to the MOCK TURTLES and the BACHELOR PAD). Their debut single, 'TWO BY TWO', was duly followed up by 'FACE IN THE CROWD' (for the obscure 'Wump' imprint), although LENNY and his motley crew decided to change their moniker to The THANES.

These noble lords of the psychedelic indie frontier opened up their vinyl account in September '87, via a Jamie Watson-produced cracker, 'HEY GIRL (LOOK WHAT YOU'VE DONE)'. Fast Forward and 'D.D.T.' records were also behind their acclaimed Retro-fied first full-set, 'THANES OF CAWDOR' (1988), while the same partnership released a further handful of singles. Moving across the corridor to 'Nightshift' (run by Grangemouth man, BRIAN GUTHRIE, brother of Sir Robin of the COCTEAU TWINS), they showcased one last set, 'BETTER LOOK BEHIND YOU'. The multi-talented LENNY (a vocalist, guitarist, drummer, etc) had already moonlighted with other projects such as The STAYRCASE and The OFFHOOKS, both of which released a bit of vinyl in 1988.

The barren years of the 90's were put aside when The THANES re-formed in July 2000 for a prestigious US concert at the Las Vegas Grind alongside their Beat-en heroes, The STANDELLS and The REMAINS. The THANES even had time to conjure up a comeback single, 'IT'S JUST A FEAR', for Stateside-based 'Sundazed'.

• **Covered:** I CAN'T STOP THINKING ABOUT HER (Chapters) / L.S.D. (GOT A MILLION $) (Tom McGuinness) / I WANNA HEAR YOU SAY YEAH (Gray-Munroe) / etc.

GREEN TELESCOPE

BRUCE LYALL – vocals, guitar / **LENNY HELSING** – lead guitar, vocals, harmonica / **DENIS BOYLE** – bass / **IAN BINNS** – drums

Imaginary not iss.

Dec 85. (7"ep) *(MIRAGE 001)* **TWO BY TWO / A GLIMPSE. / MAKE ME STAY / THINKIN' ABOUT TODAY** -

Wump not iss.

Aug 86. (7") *(BIF 4811)* **FACE IN THE CROWD. / THOUGHTS OF A MADMAN** -

— changed their group moniker to . . .

THANES

D.D.T. not iss.

Sep 87. (7"ep) *(DISP 008)* **HEY GIRL EP** -
– Hey girl (look what you've done) / What can I do / Wish you'd stayed away / Touch.
(12"ep+=) *(DISP 008T)* –

Jan 88. (lp) *(DISPLP 011)* **THANES OF CAWDOR** -
– Keep you out / You'll be blue / Days go slowly by / She was mine / Buzz buzz yeh yeh / Where have all the good times gone / All gone now / Kicks and chicks / Won't you c'mon girl / When I love you / Girls / Cold as ice / Before I go / Some kinda fun.

Aug 88. (12"ep) *(DDTEP 001)* **HUBBLE BUBBLE** -

Jan 89. (7") *(DISP 020)* **I'LL REST. / BABY COME BACK** -

Jul 89. (10"ep) *(DDTEP 004)* **BETTER LOOK BEHIND YOU** -

Nightshift not iss.

Feb 90. (lp) *(NISHI 211)* **BETTER LOOK BEHIND YOU** -
– Can't stop thinking about her / Wonder if / Baby come back / L.S.D. (got a million $) / I'll rest / I wanna hear you say yeah / Lost or found / Don't let her dark your door.

— disbanded in the early 90's; HELSING continued with offshoots the OFFHOOKS, the NATURALS and the STAYRCASE

OFFHOOKS

LENNY HELSING with also **CALVIN BURT** – vocals, drums / **CLIVE** – guitar, harmonica, tambourine / + **ANDY** – bass

		D.D.T.	not iss.
Jun 88.	(m-lp) *(DISPLP 018)* **OFF THE HOOK** – Greed / I'm a nothing / Heartbreaking girl / No more tears / Got no lovin' / I can take it.	☐	-

— CALVIN was later the drummer for POLICECAT

STAYRCASE

IAN – vocals / **ALAN** – guitar, vocals / **DAVE** – bass, vocals / **LENNY HELSING** – drums, vocals

		Mumblin'	not iss.
Aug 88.	(m-lp) *(MR 451)* **THE STAYRCASE** – I know you lied / Who dat? / I want you / Disgust / Down around me / 1906 / Irritation / I wanna come back.	☐	-

THANES

re-formed with the same line-up

		Sundazed	Sundazed
Nov 00.	(7") *(<S 156>)* **IT'S JUST A FEAR. / SUN DIDN'T COME OUT TODAY**	☐	☐

THEE MOTHS (see under ⇒ MAGNETIC NORTH POLE)

THIS POISON! (see ⇒ Section 9: wee post-Punk groups)

Ali THOMSON

Born: 1950's, Glasgow. The younger brother of SUPERTRAMP's DOUGIE THOMPSON, the singer/songwriter signed to the aforementioned group's label, 'A&M'. ALI made an immediate impact, scoring with a few major (US!) pop hits in 1980, 'TAKE A LITTLE RHYTHM' and 'LIVE EVERY MINUTE'. Unfortunately, ALI's success was rather short-lived and after his second set, 'DECEPTION IS AN ART' (1981), he retired from solo work.

ALI THOMSON – vocals / with numerous session people incl. **TED McKENNA** – drums (ex-SENSATIONAL ALEX HARVEY BAND) / **WILLIAM C. LYALL** – synthesizer (ex-PILOT) / etc

		A&M	A&M
Jan 80.	(7") *(AMS 7505)* *<2243>* **TAKE A LITTLE RHYTHM. / JAMIE**	☐	15 May80
Feb 80.	(lp) *(AMLH 68512)* *<4803>* **TAKE A LITTLE RHYTHM** – Fools' society / Take a little rhythm / Saturday heartbreaker / We were all in love / African queen / Live every minute / Jamie / Page by page / The Hollywood role / A goodnight song.	☐	99 Jun80
Mar 80.	(7") *(AMS 7519)* *<2260>* **LIVE EVERY MINUTE. / SATURDAY HEARTBREAKER**	☐	42 Aug80
Feb 81.	(7") *(AMS 8105)* **FOOLISH CHILD. / MAN OF THE EARTH**	☐	☐
Feb 81.	(lp/c) *(AMLH 64846)* **DECEPTION IS AN ART** – Safe and warm / Foolish child / Don't hold back / Art gallery / Shells lay scattered / The one and only / Man of the earth / A simple song / Secrets hide inside / Someone in motion.	☐	☐

— ALI retired from the music scene after above

THREATS (see ⇒ Section 9: wee post-punk groups)

THREE WISE MEN (see under ⇒ Bosque records)

THRUM

Formed: Bellshill, Lanarkshire ... 1992 by JOHNNY SMILLIE, DAVE McGOWAN, GARY JOHNSTON and singer MONICA QUEEN. Following the established pedigree of homegrown indie bands (TEENAGE FANCLUB, BMX BANDITS etc.), THRUM specialised in updating the classic sounds of West Coast Americana with one ear cocked to the 90's US alternative scene.

Released as the first fruits of a deal with 'Fire' records, an eponymous debut EP surfaced in 1993 (containing a tortured version of Roy Orbison's 'CRYING') and confirmed early live evidence of potential Laurel Canyon via Bellshill greatness. Further acclaim was heaped upon singles, 'SO GLAD' and 'HERE I AM', prior to a long awaited debut album, 'RIFFERAMA' (1994). NEIL YOUNG was an obvious and oft-quoted influence with SMILLIE's rootsy guitar workouts complemented by MONICA's powerful MARIA McKEE meets DOLLY PARTON vocal. Perhaps the timing wasn't right as despite constantly being tipped for big things, THRUM seemed to be forever struggling around the toilet circuit, playing their emotive country-rock to a core of fans but failing to interest the wider music buying public.

In 1997, MONICA returned to the limelight via a special guest vocalist spot on BELLE AND SEBASTIAN's classic 'Lazy Line Painter Jane'; her terrific countrified larynx arguably the best singing indie-pop performance ever; also listen to her duets with the JAYHAWKS, GRANT LEE BUFFALO and SHANE MacGOWAN. Memories of the aforementioned John Peel favourite were still ripe in the minds of non-STEPS fans all over the country, when the girl from Bellshill released her debut solo single for 'Creeping Bent', '77X'. With SMILLIE still contributing to production, writing and guitar work on this September 2000 platter, MONICA Q was back to her old best, especially on third track 'CAMP FIRE CRACKLING'.

She subsequently followed this with her debut album 'TEN SORROWFUL MYSTERIES' in Febuary 2002. Co-written and produced by THRUM's JOHN SMILLIE, the set featured ten tracks full of blissful country melodies à la EMMYLOU HARRIS. If QUEEN was the Scottish equivalent of ALISON KRAUSS, then SMILLIE was the DAVID RAWLINGS of Scottish country/folk, with his gentle compositions fitting QUEEN's gliding field-hollers. 'TEAR BEHIND MY SMILE' was an accented folk ballad, while the hypnotic 'WHERE DO YOU SLEEP' was just one reason why this LP should've been in the record collections of many.

MONICA QUEEN – vocals, guitar / **JOHNNY SMILLIE** – guitar, vocals / **DAVE McGOWAN** – bass, vocals / **GARY JOHNSTON** – drums

		Fire	not iss.
Apr 93.	(12"ep/cd-ep) *(BLAZE 64 T/CD)* **THRUM EP** – Lullaby / Illegitimate clown (mix) / Does anybody know? / Crying (live).	☐	-
Jan 94.	(7") *(BLAZE 67)* **SO GLAD / GIVE A LITTLE** (12"+=/cd-s+=) *(BLAZE 67 T/CD)* –	☐	-
Jun 94.	(7") *(BLAZE 70)* **HERE I AM. / WAITING FOR THE SUN** (7") *(7SM 3)* – ('A'side) / Get a life. (cd-s) *(BLAZE 70CD)* – (all 3 tracks).	☐	-
Sep 94.	(cd/c/lp) *(FIRE CD/MC/LP 38)* **RIFFERAMA** – Rifferama / Purify / So glad / You wish / Lullaby II / Here I am / Hey Joe / Won't be long / Nowhere to run / Almost done.	☐	-
Dec 94.	(7") *(BLAZE 81)* **PURIFY. / IF EVERY DAY WAS LIKE CHRISTMAS DAY**	☐	-

— disbanded the following year, MONICA subsequently provided vocals for BELLE & SEBASTIAN on their classic track, 'Lazy Line Painter Jane' . . .

MONICA QUEEN

— MONICA was still augmented by co-songwriter **JOHN SMILLIE**

		Creeping Bent	not iss.
Sep 00.	(cd-ep) *(bent 060cd)* **77X e.p.** – 77X / Stay up all night / Camp fire crackling.	☐	-
Feb 02.	(cd) *(bent 063cd)* **TEN SORROWFUL MYSTERIES** – I'm sorry darling / State of grace / Do something pretty / Only love / Tear behind my smile / Broken wing / 260 / 77x / Promise for Thomas / Where do you sleep.	☐	-

THURSDAYS (see ⇒ Section 9: wee post-Punk groups)

The TIME FREQUENCY

Formed: Gallowgate, Glasgow ... early 90's by songwriter and keyboard wizard JON CAMPBELL together with PAUL INGLIS and KYLE RAMSAY. Without question, TTF were the first real heroes of the gestating Scottish suburban rave scene and their debut EP, 'FUTURAMA' – released as a white label in 1990 – set the blueprint for the likes of ULTRA-SONIC, Q-TEX, QFX and hundreds of others. With the addition of Glaswegian diva MARY KIANI, they honed a winning dancefloor formula which not only became ubiquitous on the Scottish scene but made a fair dent in the UK chart.

KIANI made her debut on 1992's 'REAL LOVE', a Top 60 hit which unleashed their trademark sound: pounding synths, Italian house-style piano breakdowns and killer choruses sharpened to a stiletto point by Miss KIANI. Headlining every rave from Saltcoats to Livingston, the group broke into the

Top 40 early the following year – largely by dint of their massive Scottish following – with the 'NEW EMOTION' EP. Summer 1993's 'THE POWER ZONE' EP went one better, entering the Top 20 and forcing the English press to sit up and take note. Finally, a re-issued 'REAL LOVE' made the Top 10 later that year, ensuring an appearance on Top Of The Pops.

Yet at the height of their fame, the combination of a controversial falling out with KIANI (who went on to an initially successful solo career) and a hefty backlash put paid to thoughts of world domination. Which didn't stop them calling their debut album 'DOMINATOR' (1994), a surprisingly listenable (even six years on!) round-up of their hits to date plus a few B-sides like their raved-up cover of Cerrone's Euro-disco classic, 'SUPERNATURE' (one to file alongside an earlier cover of 70's French electro oddity 'POPCORN'). Replacement singer MONICA REED-PRICE just didn't quite have the same lung-busting effect and 1994's 'SUCH A PHANTASY' single lingered outside the Top 20. Yet another singer, DEBBIE MILLER, was drafted in for 'DREAMSCAPE '94', a minor Top 40 hit that signalled the end of TTF's relatively brief chart career.

Left behind by the ever harder, faster demands of the increasingly hardcore Scottish rave scene, the group faded from view although they did make a belated comeback in 1998 with a single (a collaboration with renowned DJ, TOM WILSON) on the Bathgate-based 'Clubscene' imprint. The same label re-released the old chestnut 'NEW EMOTION' in 2000 with a batch of new mixes.

JON CAMPBELL – keyboards / **PAUL INGLIS** – keyboards / **KYLE RAMSAY** – keyboards

white label | not iss.

1990. (12") *(none)* **FUTURAMA** [ ] [-]

— added **MARY KIANI** – vocals

Jive | not iss.

May 92. (7") *(JIVE 307)* **REAL LOVE. / SCHIZOID** [60] [-]
(12"+=/cd-s+=) *(JIVE T/CD 307)* – ('A'mixes).

Internal Affairs-Zomba | unknown

Dec 92. (c-ep/12"ep/cd-ep) *(KGB M/T/D 009)* **THE NEW EMOTION EP** [36] [-]
– New emotion / Retribution 93 (The Prodigy meets TTF) / Higher than Heaven (remix) / U41A.

Jun 93. (c-ep) *(KGBM 010)* **THE POWER ZONE EP** [17] [ ]
– The ultimate high / The power zone / You take me away.
(12"ep/cd-ep) *(KGB T/D 010)* – ('A'side) / ('A'extended) / Popcorn / Maximum intensity (1993 remix).

Oct 93. (7") *(KGB 011)* **REAL LOVE. / REAL LOVE (Vince Clark mix)** [8] [ ]
(cd-s+=) *(KGBD 011)* – Retribution 93 (Futurama part two) / Schizoid 93 (Futurama part two).
(12") *(KGBT 011)* – ('A'side) / ('A'extended) / ('A'original) / ('A'-Dream Frequency extended).

— **MONICA REED-PRICE** – vocals; repl. KIANI who went solo

May 94. (7") *(KGB 013)* **SUCH A PHANTASY. / ('A'mix)** [25] [ ]
(12"+=/cd-s+=) *(KGB T/D 013)* – The bounce / Exosphere.
(cd-s+=) *(KGBDR 013)* – Ectoplasm / Ultrachronic (done in 30 seconds mix).

Jun 94. (cd/c/lp) *(KGB D/M/LP 500)* **DOMINATOR** [23] [ ]
– Euphoria / The ultimate high / New emotion / Jurassic Park / Supernature / Real love / Retribution / Such a phantasy / Energy rush / Smething for me / Popcorn / Maximum intensity.

— vocals now handled by **DEBBIE MILLAR**

Sep 94. (c-s) *(KGBM 015)* **DREAMSCAPE '94 / DREAMSCAPE '94 (full mix)** [32] [ ]
(12"+=/cd-s+=) *(KGB T/D 015)* – Future rhythm (live) / The hardcore bounce.
(cd-s+=) *(KGBDR 015)* – Theme for great cities ('94 remix) / Fade to grey ('94 remix).

Clubscene | not iss.

Aug 98. (cd-s/12"; as TOM WILSON & TTF) *(d+/csrt 084)* **U GOT THE PASSION (mixes)** [ ] [-]

Apr 00. (cd-s/12") *(d+/csrt 086)* **NEW EMOTION 2000 (mixes; radio / 12"extended / Steve Nelson dub)** [ ] [-]

Jive | not iss.

Aug 02. (12") *(925378-0)* **REAL LOVE 2002 (mixes; Jon Campbell / Flip'n'fill)** [43] [-]
(c-s+=/cd-s+=) *(925378-0)* – (mixes; Rob Searle / QFX).

'T' In The Park

Initiated: For years, promoters and industry people baulked at the suggestion of a bonafide major Scottish Music Festival, a two day event with camping and top flight international artists as opposed to the one-day affairs with the usual culprits (DEACON BLUE, SILENCERS etc) that had previously been the norm.

That all changed when the Tennents-lager sponsored T-In The Park was launched in 1994, the brainchild of veteran promoter STUART CLUMPUS. Held over the last weekend in July at Strathclyde Park near Glasgow, the inaugural festival featured a star-studded line-up that included the likes of BJORK, PRIMAL SCREAM, BLUR, RAGE AGAINST THE MACHINE and CYPRESS HILL alongside names to file in the "where are they now" column such as CHUMBAWAMBA, CRASH TEST DUMMIES and The LEVELLERS. As well as the more famous native talent, an obscure act called GLASS ONION were tucked away on The Caledonia Stage (subsequently renamed the Talent Tent), only to later re-emerge as superstars TRAVIS. A still relatively unknown OASIS also played an afternoon slot in one of the tents, a performance which they've previously described as one of their most memorable. Although the event wasn't a sell-out, it was an unqualified success with Scottish punters lapping up the opportunity to savour a festival in their own backyard without the annual trudge to Glastonbury, Stratford-Upon-Avon or God forbid, Reading.

The long, hot summer of 1995 saw T-In The Park go from strength to strength as the diminutive KYLIE MINOGUE had the lads and the lassies all hot and bothered. The PRODIGY put in a fearsome performance, whipping the crowd into the kind of voodoo frenzy that'd see them become perhaps the top festival headliner in Britain over the next few years. BLACK GRAPE also made the headlines as Kermit broke his ankle and proceeded to perform the rest of the set sitting on his arse.

1996 was a complete sell-out, the likes of MANIC STREET PREACHERS, RADIOHEAD and The PRODIGY (again!) seeing out the Festival's last year at Strathclyde Park in style.

1997 saw the event move to Balado, near Kinross, a wonderfully rural location where you can actually catch a glimpse of rolling hills rather than a seething mass of humanity. With the campsite expanded from humble beginnings of 2,000 to 25,000, the festival was in rude health, playing host to PAUL WELLER, The CHARLATANS, TEXAS and KULA SHAKER amongst others. If the main stage line-up wasn't as strong as previous years, native talent such as MOGWAI, The DELGADOS and URUSEI YATSURA were witnessed at the newly created Radio One Evening Session tent. On the bpm front, Glasgow's own SLAM had taken over the running of the dance tent and secured quality DJ's such as GREEN VELVET and GILLES PETERSON.

Following on from Glastonbury's horrendous mudfest in June, T In The Park 1998 saw its first real washout as the Sunday downpour detracted from an otherwise brilliant, boiler suited-up BEASTIE BOYS performance and ROBBIE WILLIAMS began his tedious rise to fame. The weather was all the more disheartening given that the previous day had witnessed a blue sky and another blistering PRODIGY show.

1999 saw the sun putting his hat back on once more as BLUR and the MANIC STREET PREACHERS hogged the main stage. More exciting fare was to be found in the Radio One tent where MOGWAI offered up a strobed-out sonic treat and DEATH IN VEGAS got all scary and moody. Sunday's highlight was undoubtedly a packed Stage 2 tent performance by a re-formed HAPPY MONDAYS; welcomed home like the prodigal sons, RYDER and Co hammed it up for a baying crowd that was almost literally hanging from the rafters. Backstage, meanwhile, Trainspotting star Robert Carlyle was the centre of attention as the papparazi checked his every move.

By the millennial T-In The Park in 2000, the festival had truly established itself on the summer calender as a major UK event given the same respect and kudos as any of the English festivals. Appropriately, TRAVIS headlined the main stage, six years after they'd originally appeared. Scottish pop Grand Dame, LULU, also appeared while the SLAM tent played host to a hotly anticipated show by LEFTFIELD. After originally being booked to headline Stage 2, MOBY ended up headlining the main stage in a triumphant year for the man that was to end with a show at Edinburgh Castle. In the King Tut's Tent were both COLDPLAY and TOPLOADER, both of whom went on to massive success regardless of their somewhat dubious merits.

Tickets sold fast and furious for T In The Park 2001, although a weaker line-up than previous years saw the likes of TEXAS, STEREOPHONICS, COLDPLAY and TOPLOADER take centre stage. Still, BECK was worth shelling out for along with blast-from-the-past STEREO MC's and US indie types GRANDADDY.

While the official 2002 programme might've been going a bit far in its claim of best international festival there was no doubt the line-up was a damn sight meatier than the previous year. OASIS might no longer be the force they once were but still a ticket-busting headliner, while The CHEMICAL BROTHERS were always a sure bet to top Sunday's bill. The indie crowd were well provided for with the likes of STARSAILOR and The HIVES playing the main stage, BLACK REBEL MOTORCYCLE CLUB roaring into the King Tut's tent and BADLY DRAWN BOY tipping a tea cosy to all things jangly and wistful. Older but not necessarily wiser, a strong line-up of SONIC YOUTH, MERCURY REV and IAN BROWN commanded the upper echelons of the King Tut's tent on the Sunday. The BETA BAND flew the freak flag for Scotland, as did PRIMAL SCREAM, returning to the fray with more venom then ever despite encroaching middle age.

In fact, the festival itself is getting on a bit, due for its 10th Birthday celebrations in 2003. Judging by another year of extremely healthy ticket sales, as yet there are no signs of an early death, something that sadly can't be said for **Glasgow's Gig On The Green** bash. Now in its 3rd year and apparently going strong, the event has played host to the likes of OASIS, TRAVIS and IGGY POP, differentiating itself from T In The Park by dint of a 2-day concert rather than festival approach. 2001 headliners EMINEM and MARILYN MANSON kicked up a storm of controversy among hardline Christian groups, something which no doubt helped ticket sales along nicely. Yet in 2002, the festival promoters – Regular Music and Mean Fiddler – were forced to halve the capacity of the event due to poor ticket sales. While Saturday saw the return of The PRODIGY to Scotland, an event presumably guaranteed to rake in the punters, the quality of the rest of the bill was debatable. Had HOWLETT and Co been backed up by some of the acts penned in for Sunday, or indeed had the line-up been more evenly spread over the two days, things may been different. Despite the downturn, the promoters maintain that they are committed to staging the event in 2003; we shall see . . .

TIPPI

Born: YVONNE TIPPING, 1977, Bellshill, Lanarkshire. Influenced by her parents' listening tastes (ELVIS, NEIL YOUNG, JONI MITCHELL, etc) and dedicating herself to learning drums, piano and guitar, YVONNE began writing her own songs at the tender age of 14.

After graduating from Strathclyde University in 1997 with an honours degree in applied music, the budding singer/songwriter concentrated on a career as a professional musician. She duly played her first gig in the homely confines of Glasgow's King Tut's Wah Wah Hut before going on to charm an 8,000-strong crowd at Edinburgh Castle as support act to LIONEL RICHIE. YVONNE subsequently topped this by playing in front of 10,000 at a BRYAN ADAMS gig. Her CV also includes solo spots at the T In The Park and Glasgow Green festivals, while the likes of BOBBY BLUEBELL and GREG KANE (of HUE AND CRY) have collaborated with the lass on material for her debut album – whatever happened to it?

YVONNE's real claim to fame, so far at least, has been a writing session with BEN TAYLOR, the son of Californian singer/songwriter legends JAMES TAYLOR and CARLY SIMON. The enthusiastic Bellshill gal flew to New York for the fruitful collaboration, the results of which should be unveiled on her scheduled debut album, 'REMEMBER MY FACE'. Meanwhile, now billed as TIPPI, her ever-growing fanbase made do with her CD-single rendition of the Blue Nile's 'TINSELTOWN IN THE RAIN'. On stage, the gutsy singer has a grungey cover of Radiohead's 'HIGH AND DRY' behind her, while another track 'PLAYING THE GAME' was inspired by a line from Garbage's 'Stupid Girl'.

TIPPI – vocals, acoustic guitar / with back-up

		Tip Top	not iss.
Jan 02.	(cd-s) *(TIPPI 001)* **TINSELTOWN IN THE RAIN / TINSELTOWN IN THE RAIN (United Rhythm mix) / REMINISCE**	☐	-
Sep 02.	(cd-s) *(TIPPI 002)* **IT'S A PHRASE**	☐	-

TIPPLE (see under ⇒ Limbo records)

TOASTER

Formed: Glasgow . . . 1996 by former Strathclyde University architecture students SINCLAIR HUTCHESON and INNES FORBES (both from The Black Isle in the north), who met up with GRANT McKEAN, PAUL MORELAND and PHILIP MUIR at the aforementioned academia. A solitary 'Fierce Panda' split 7" was all they had to show until a Dublin In The City gig led them to 'Creation' – who else! – late in '97. The boisterous lads were well up for a "battle of the bands" contest and indeed they had a "set-to" with label mates The DIGGERS whilst competing over in the Emerald Isle.

The following April, TOASTER's arty-farty PULP-meets-BLACK GRAPE sound once again popped up on their overdue EP, 'CRASKA VEGAS', described as cliched but intelligent cock-rock by the smart SINCLAIR and with a track like '60 FOOT ROCKET', who would argue. However, after only this one release for ALAN McGEE's enterprising label, TOASTER were surplus to Creation's requirements and were unceremoniously dropped. Having been all the rage only a few months previously, SINCLAIR and Co must have truly been shocked.

Taking a sabbatical to work on the film 'Mirrorball' at the Edinburgh Festival, TOASTER returned in the new millennium via a couple of singles including 'SIGNS AND WONDER'.

• **Note:** Not to be confused with punk-ska act The TOASTERS who released records around the same time.

SINCLAIR HUTCHESON – vocals / **INNES FORBES** – bass, vocals / **PHILIP MUIR** – guitar / **GRANT McKEAN** – keyboards / **PAUL MORELAND** – drums

		Fierce Panda	not iss.
Feb 97.	(7") *(NING 30)* **HUGGY. / (other track by GOD'S BOYFRIEND)**	☐	-
		Creation	not iss.
Apr 98.	(10"ep/cd-ep) *(CRE/+SCD 240)* **CRASKA VEGAS EP** – Peoples' people / 60ft rocket / Jamaican room / Phoneheads.	☐	-

—— dropped by 'Creation' and virtually dropped out themselves, until . . .

		Toaster	not iss.
2000.	(cd-ep) *(TOAST 001)* **$6,000,000 GOAT**	☐	-
		Knife Fighting Monkey	not iss.
Aug 01.	(cd-s) *(KFM 001)* **SIGNS AND WONDER**	☐	-

TONIC (see under ⇒ Flotsam & Jetsam records)

TONIGHT AT NOON

Formed: based Glasgow . . . 1987 by brothers GAVIN and PETE LIVINGSTONE. Treading a more intense, electronically enhanced path than their spiritual brethren, The PROCLAIMERS, TONIGHT AT NOON were memorably described as the HUMAN LEAGUE of folk rock. After an independently-released debut EP, the patriotic siblings signed to worthy trad bastion, 'Lismor', for what turned out to be a one-off album, 'DOWN TO THE DEVILS' (1988).

PETE LIVINGSTONE – vocals, fiddle / **GAVIN LIVINGSTONE** – guitar, etc.

		Stretch	not iss.
1988.	(12"ep) *(STR12 001)* **TONIGHT AT NOON EP**	☐	-
		Lismor	not iss.
Dec 88.	(lp/c) *(LIF L/C 7016)* **DOWN TO THE DEVILS** – The John McLean march / Hawks and eagles / The travelling song / Wire the loom / The peoples will / Run run / Hell of a man / Down to the Devils / Nae trust – The mission hall / The banks of marble / Jack the tanner / Harry Wigwams / Rolling seas. *(cd-iss. 1996; 9041)*	☐	-

—— disbanded soon after above

TOOLS (see under ⇒ Oily records)

TORQAMADA (see under ⇒ Bronx Cheer records)

TOXIK EPHEX

Formed: Powis, Aberdeenshire . . . early 80's as The ABDUCTORS by GARY 'WEE ECK' DAWSON, STEPHEN 'STEPPE' DEMPSTER, FRED 'BLAKEY' WILKINSON and KEITH THOMPSON; the latter was substituted by drummer JIMMY SIM, while the group also added bassman TROUPER.

1982 saw their first vinyl outing, courtesy of CRASS various artists double-LP, 'Bullshit Detector'. However, even more personnel changes came about when JIMMY SIM sold his drum kit and was duly booted out, CHIZ, then MIKEY SMITH in 1984 took up the vacancy. TOXIK EPHEX must've been plagued by some smell, because once again more upheaval beset the band when both WEE ECK and STEPPE were superseded by DOD COPELAND and STEVE ANDERSON respectively.

The remaining troops finally got to create a stink on the vinyl front, when they discharged their debut EP, 'PUNK AS FUCK', on their own appropriately-titled 'Green Vomit' label early in '86. Self-financed, self-made and self-sacrificing were all adjectives to describe how the band got this DIY single (sprayed glue and stick-on labels, etc) into the shops. Having sent copies to the London police constabulary, the 'EPHEX twin's duly sold the records at gigs, Edinburgh's Fast Forward distribution and anyone walking by them. All the proceeds would go into the kitty to buy petrol; who said Punk was dead.

The band swapped the northern lights of old Aberdeen for the Northern lights of Leeds, Huddersfield and Bradford, where they went down a riot, quite literally. A shared LP with Edinburgh's OI POLLOI entitled 'PUNK AS FUNK' (also the name emblazoned on their tour van) was next up for grabs, while subsequent live duties in Glasgow, Leeds and Germany – several supporting the UK SUBS – kept them in (safety)-pin money. In 1988, they split another LP, this time with Welsh punks SHRAPNEL, and a year later worked on their own for the '1 Up'-financed 'THE ADVENTURES OF NOBBY PORTHOLE, THE COCK OF THE NORTH' (1989). Listen to their barbed punk-rock rendition of the Irish folk standard, 'MAGGIE', and find out what they really thought of the Iron Lady frae No.10 Downing Street. Challenged by the onset of everything that wasn't punk (shoegazing, rave, etc), TOXIK EPHEX went out like a big thick cloud of smoke.

DOD COPELAND – vocals; repl. GARY 'WEE ECK' DAWSON / **FRED 'BLAKEY' WILKINSON** – lead guitar / **STEVE ANDERSON** – rhythm guitar; repl. STEPHEN 'STEPPE' DEMPSTER / **TROUPER** – bass / **MIKEY SMITH** – drums; repl. CHIZ who repl. JIMMY SIM who repl. KEITH THOMPSON

		Green Vomit	not iss.
Jan 86.	(7"ep) *(Puke 1 1/2)* **PUNK AS FUCK EP** – Fallout shelter / Always skint / Nothing's permissive.		-
Oct 86.	(lp; split with OI POLLOI) *(Puke 2)* **MAD AS FUCK**		-

—— **FRANK BENZIE** – rhythm guitar; repl. ANDERSON

		Words Of Warning	not iss.
1988.	(7"; split with SHRAPNEL) *(WOW 6)* **DOES SOMEONE HAVE TO DIE / LIFE'S FOR LIVING. / (other 2 by Shrapnel)**		-
		1 Up	not iss.
1989.	(lp) *(Puke 4 1/2)* **THE ADVENTURES OF NOBBY PORTHOLE, THE COCK OF THE NORTH**		-

—— split after above recording when FRED then CHIZ joined FRANTIK ZIMMER

TRASH CAN SINATRAS

Formed: Irvine, Ayrshire ... late 80's by FRANCIS READ, PAUL LIVINGSTON, GEORGE McDAID, and brothers JOHN and STEPHEN DOUGLAS. Possibly a band out of their time, TRASH CAN SINATRAS early 90's material echoed the sounds of the early 80's 'Postcard' era, particularly AZTEC CAMERA.

Signed to 'Go! Discs', the quintet released their debut EP, 'OBSCURITY KNOCKS' (chancing their arm a bit with a title that would later become a self-fulfilling prophecy!), a follow-up track, 'ONLY TONGUE CAN TELL', preceding the band's debut album, 'CAKE' (1990). As well as breaking into the UK Top 75, the record was a surprise success Stateside, eventually spending three months in the US Top 200 after gaining exposure through the influential college radio circuit.

With the pressure on to "crack America", transatlantic touring kept the 'SINATRAS' off the domestic scene for almost three years. When they did return, McDAID had been replaced by DAVID HUGHES on UK Top 50 comeback set, 'I'VE SEEN EVERYTHING' (1993), the album's relative success promoted by the preceding single, 'HAYFEVER'.

Marginalised in Britain and overtaken by the grunge scene in the States, TCS went to ground for a further three years, re-emerging with a series of singles in mid '96. An accompanying third album, 'A HAPPY POCKET', failed to win any new support while the old fans appeared to have unceremoniously dumped them, obviously preferring a bit of GARBAGE instead.

Around the same time, the TCS worked on stage with the production of Irvine Welsh's 'Marabou Stork Nightmares'. STEPHEN DOUGLAS soon resurfaced in a new outfit, JOHNSON, a gothic NICK CAVE/SCOTT WALKER-esque 5-piece featuring one-time members of The JOHNSTONE BRASS BAND, WONDER BOY BUCKLEY and SLINKY. A handful of singles (with FRANCIS as co-produder) appeared on their own 'Play' imprint around the turn of the decade. JOHNSON's talented frontman PETER ROSS continued to write songs and was the mainman behind OSTLE BAY, a collaboration with TRASH CAN SINATRAS. Their recent album, 'LOVE FROM OSTLE BAY' (2002), displayed a delicate blend of early arty 'Postcard' moods although just a tad out of time.

• **Covered:** SENSES WORKING OVERTIME (Xtc) / LITTLE THINGS (THAT KEEP US TOGETHER) (Scott Walker) / BORN FREE (hit; Matt Monro) / YOU ONLY LIVE TWICE (John Barry).

FRANCIS READ (b. 1966) – vocals / **PAUL LIVINGSTON** (b. 1970) – guitar / **JOHN DOUGLAS** (b. 1963) – guitar / **GEORGE McDAID** (b. 1966) – bass / **STEPHEN DOUGLAS** – drums

		Go! Discs	Polygram
Feb 90.	(7"ep/c-ep) *(GOD/+MC 34)* **OBSCURITY KNOCKS EP** – Obscurity knocks / Who's he? / The best man's fall. (12"ep+=/cd-ep+=) *(GOD X/CD 34)* – Drunken chorus.		-
May 90.	(7"/c-s) *(GOD/+MC 41)* **ONLY TONGUE CAN TELL. / USELESS** (12"+=/cd-s+=) *(GOD X/CD 41)* – Tonight you belong to me.		-
Jun 90.	(cd/c/lp) *(<828 201-2/-4/-1>)* **CAKE** – Obscurity knocks / Maybe I should drive / Thrupenny tears / Even the odd / The best man's fall / Circling the circumference / Funny / Only tongue can tell / You made me feel / January's little joke.	74	Jan91
Oct 90.	(7"/c-s) *(GOD/+MC 46)* **CIRCLING THE CIRCUMFERENCE. / MY MISTAKE** (12"+=/cd-s+=) *(GOD X/CD 46)* – White horses.		-
Jan 91.	(c-s) *<869 314-4>* **OBSCURITY KNOCKS / WHO'S HE**	-	

—— **DAVID HUGHES** – bass; repl. McDAID

Apr 93.	(7"/c-s) *(GOD/+MC 98)* **HAYFEVER. / SAY** (12"+=/cd-s+=) *(GOD X/CD 98)* – Kangaroo court / Skin diving.	61	-
May 93.	(cd/c/lp) *(<828 408-2/-4/-1>)* **I'VE SEEN EVERYTHING** – Easy read / Hayfever / Bloodrush / Worked a miracle / The perfect reminder / Killing the cabinet / Orange fell / I'm immortal / Send for Henny / Iceberg / One at a time / I've seen everything / The hairy years / Earlies.	50	
Jun 93.	(7"/c-s) *(GOD/+MC 100)* **I'VE SEEN EVERYTHING. / HOUSEPROUD / I'M THE ONE WHO FAINTED** (12"+=/cd-s+=) *(GOD X/CD 100)* – Ask Davy.		-
Nov 95.	(cd-ep) *(TCMCD 1)* **FIVE HUNGRY JOES E.P.** – No gasoline / Mr. Grisly / Aberration / A boy and a girl / I must fly. *(note:- this EP was a mail-order promo)*		-
Mar 96.	(7"ep/cd-ep) *(GOD/+CD 141)* **THE MAIN ATTRACTION EP** – The main attraction / Stainless Stephen / Charlie's atlas / Jane's estranged.		-
May 96.	(7"/c-s) *(GOD/+MC 147)* **TWISTED AND BENT. / MR. GRISLY** (cd-s+=) *(GODCD 147)* – No gasoline / Aberration.		
May 96.	(cd/c/lp) *(<828 696-2/-4/-1>)* **A HAPPY POCKET** – Outside / Twisted and bent / Unfortunate age / To sir with love / Make yourself at home / The main attraction / How can I apply . . .? / The pop place / The genius I was / The sleeping policeman / I must fly / I'll get them in / The safecracker / The therapist.		Sep96
Jul 96.	(7"/c-s) *(GOD/+MC 151)* **HOW CAN I APPLY. / SAVE ME** (cd-s+=) *(GODCD 151)* – A worm with a head / Little things (that keep us together).		-
Dec 96.	(7"/c-s) *(GOD/+MC 157)* **TO SIR WITH LOVE. / CLAW** (12"+=/cd-s+=) *(GOD X/CD 157)* – A boy and a girl / You only live twice.		-

—— disbanded the following year; STEPHEN turned up in JOHNSON

JOHNSON

PETER ROSE – vocals, guitar / **STEPHEN DOUGLAS** – drums, percussion, acoustic guitar, vocals / **RAFE FITZPATRICK** – violin / **CLARE HANLEY** – cornet, organ, vocals / **JOHNNY MITCHELL** – bass

Feb 99.	(7") *(PLAY 001)* **TRIPPING WITH THE MOONLIGHT. / FLIPSIDE HEAD**		-
May 99.	(7") *(PLAY 002)* **SAVOURY BODY SHOW. / SWEAR I WAS THERE**		-
Oct 99.	(7") *(PLAY 003)* **SKIN AND GOLD. / PARADISE (live)**		-
Apr 00.	(7") *(PLAY 004)* **BLONDE ON BLUE. / BARE AND BLUE**		-

—— there is a JOHNSON CD-album in the pipeline

OSTLE BAY

PETER ROSE – vocals, guitar / **STEPHEN DOUGLAS** – drums, percussion / **JOHN DOUGLAS** – guitar, keyboards / **PAUL LIVINGSTON** – guitar / **GRANT WILSON** – bass / **JODY STODDART** – guitar, harmonica (of HEIRLOOM) / with also **CLARE HANLEY** – cornet

Sep 02.	(cd) *(PLAY 008)* **LOVE FROM OSTLE BAY** – Ostle Bay / Dusting the sun / The one / Music box / Did I ever say / Wish I was with you / Wont you / Windows on the pavement / Tuesday / Farming for diamonds / Out of those eyes		-

TRAVIS

Formed: Glasgow ... 1991 as GLASS ONION by ANDY DUNLOP and NEIL PRIMROSE, who'd both been members of RUNNING RED. Songwriting singer FRAN HEALY was invited to join the fresh-faced guitar-pop quintet (with the MARTYN brothers), replacing the original female vocalist soon after. In 1993, FRAN's mother advanced the lads some cash to cut a demo and this led to a publishing contract with 'Sony'.

Winning a trip to the New Music Seminar in New York via first place in a talent contest might've given them an early break had they attended, although they did manage to squeeze out an eponymous EP the same year. With the band going nowhere fast, changes had to be made and by March '96, the MARTYN brothers had made way for FRAN's Glasgow School Of Art chum, DOUGIE PAYNE (ANDY had also been a student); TRAVIS were now in circulation. Following a self-financed debut single, 'ALL I WANT TO DO IS ROCK', the quartet were taken under the wing of (ex-Go! Discs man) Andy McDonald's 'Independiente' (still through 'Sony') early in '97.

Subsequently relocating to London, TRAVIS released their controversial follow-up single, 'U16 GIRLS', apparently a paeon to the charms of underage females. A re-vamp of their hard-to-find debut single followed it into the Top 40 and suddenly TRAVIS were one of the hippest new names on the block. Though HEALY was a charismatic frontman, the Top 10 debut album, 'GOOD FEELING', illustrated at the time the one-dimensional nature of much of their material. Nevertheless, the record did spawn two further Top 40 hits, 'TIED TO THE 90's' and 'HAPPY', indicating that there was at least some potential for the future.

After a relatively quiet '98 – although 'MORE THAN US' became their biggest hit to date at No.16 – TRAVIS were back the following March. Taking a softer, laid back approach (70's BREAD come to mind!), the quartet achieved a deserved second Top 20 spot with the beautiful ballad 'WRITING TO REACH YOU'. Further successes came in the shape of 'DRIFTWOOD', 'WHY DOES IT ALWAYS RAIN ON ME?' and 'TURN', all songwriting masterpieces from the critically acclaimed No.1 follow-up set, 'THE MAN WHO' (1999).

TRAVIS were fast becoming the United Kingdom's No.1 band and by the start of the year 2000 they were given that accolade by winning the now prestigious Brit award. OASIS (who had been tops until recently!) invited nice guy HEALY and Co to support them on a US tour, the American audiences eventually being won over by their sheer honest enthusiasm and talent. While many critics predictably put the boot in, you could bet your bottom dollar they had a secret copy of UK chart-topper 'THE INVISIBLE BAND' (2001) hidden away for furtive listening pleasure. TRAVIS simply write great songs, occasionally something more but rarely anything less. On first listen, the deceptively simple single, 'SING' may sound trite, but its subtle, banjo inflected power deepens with every spin, enveloping you in a dizzying aura of elemental truth. Similarly the lyrics of 'SIDE' were the butt of cheap jibes yet their sentiment leaks into the consciousness like a zen koan. The band's lack of image and endearing avoidance of any flirtations with the vagaries of musical fashion merely accentuates the strength of the material. While there was nothing on the album that matched the searing melancholy of say, 'WRITING TO REACH YOU', chances are you'll still be playing this album next year, and the next, and the next . . .

However, disaster struck the band on the 9th of July 2002, when drummer PRIMROSE accidently hit his upper torso on the bottom of a swimming pool in France. He underwent extensive surgery to his neck, accumulating in the cancellation of the group's entire European tour (as well as V2002). All was said to be well, though, with PRIMROSE making a slow but steady recovery, the group being set to enter the studio.

• **Covered:** BE MY BABY (Ronettes) / BABY ONE MORE TIME (Britney Spears) / ALL THE YOUNG DUDES (Mott The Hoople) / HERE COMES THE SUN (Beatles).

GLASS ONION

FRAN HEALY (b. Stafford) – vocals, guitar; repl. female / **ANDY DUNLOP** – guitar / **NEIL PRIMROSE** – drums / **. . . MARTYN** – bass / **. . . MARTYN** – keyboards

own label | not iss.

Nov 93. (cd-ep) *(GLASSCD 001)* **GLASS ONION** [ ] [ ]
– Dream on / The day before / Free soul / Whenever she comes around.

TRAVIS

—— **DOUGIE PAYNE** – bass; repl. the MARTYN brothers

Red Telephone | not iss.

Oct 96. (10"ep) *(PHONE 001)* **ALL I WANT TO DO IS ROCK. / THE LINE IS FINE / FUNNY THING** [ ] [-]

Independiente | Indep.

Mar 97. (7"pic-d/c-s) *(ISOM 1 S/CS)* **U16 GIRLS. / HAZY SHADES OF GOLD / GOOD TIME GIRLS** [40] [-]
(c-s+=/cd-s+=) *(ISOM 1MS)* – Good feeling.

Jun 97. (7") *(SOM 3S)* <6080> **ALL I WANT TO DO IS ROCK. / BLUE ON A BLACK WEEKEND** [39] [ ] Apr98
(cd-s+=) *(ISOM 3MS)* – Combing my hair.
(cd-s) *(ISOM 3SMS)* – ('A'side) / "20" / 1922.

Aug 97. (7"/cd-s) *(ISOM 5S/+MS)* <6084> **TIED TO THE 90's. / ME BESIDE YOU** [30] [ ] Apr98
(cd-s) *(ISOM 5MS)* – ('A'side) / City in the rain / Whenever she comes around / Standing on my own.

Sep 97. (cd/c/lp) *(ISOM 1 CD/MC/LP)* <68239> **GOOD FEELING** [9] [ ] Oct97
– All I want to do is rock / U16 girls / Line is fine / Good day to die / Good feeling / Midsummer nights dreamin' / Tied to the 90's / I love you anyways / Happy / More than us / Falling down / Funny thing. *(re-iss. Nov99; same) (re-dist.Jun01)* – hit No.19

Oct 97. (c-s) *(ISOM 6CS)* <6081> **HAPPY / UNBELIEVERS** [38] [ ] Apr98
(cd-s+=) *(ISOM 6MS)* – Everyday faces.
(cd-s) *(ISOM 6SMS)* – ('A'side) / When I'm feeling blue (days of the week) / Mother.

Mar 98. (7"ep/c-ep/cd-ep) *(ISOM 11 S/CS/MS)* **MORE THAN US E.P.** [16] [-]
– More than us (with Anne Dudley) / Give me some truth / All I want to do is rock (with Noel Gallagher) / Funny thing (mixed by Tim Simenon).
(cd-s) *(ISOM 11SMS)* – (lead track) / Beautiful bird (demo version) / Reason (with Susie Hug) / More than us (acoustic version).

Mar 99. (7"/c-s) *(ISOM 22 S/CS)* **WRITING TO REACH YOU. / ONLY MOLLY KNOWS** [14] [-]
(cd-s+=) *(ISOM 22MS)* – Green behind the ears.
(cd-s) *(ISOM 22SM)* – ('A'side) / Yeah yeah yeah yeah / High as a kite.

May 99. (c-s) *(ISOM 27CS)* **DRIFTWOOD / WRITING TO REACH YOU (Deadly Avenger remix)** [13] [-]
(cd-s+=) *(ISOM 27SMS)* – Wtiting to reach you (Deadly Avenger instrumental remix).
(cd-s) *(ISOM 27MS)* – ('A'side) / Be my baby / Where is the love.

May 99. (cd/c/lp) *(ISOM 9 CD/MC/LP)* <62151> **THE MAN WHO** [1] [ ] Apr00
– Writing to reach you / The fear / As you are / Driftwood / The last laugh of the laughter / Turn / Why does it always rain on me? / Luv / She's so strange / Slide show. *(lp w/free 12"; ISOM 27T)* – WRITING TO REACH YOU (Deadly Avenger mixes). *(special ltd-cd+=; ISOM 9CDX)* – Blue flashing light / Writing to reach you / Driftwood.

Aug 99. (c-s) *(ISOM 33CS)* **WHY DOES IT ALWAYS RAIN ON ME? / VILLAGE MAN** [10] [-]
(cd-s+=) *(ISOM 33MS)* – Driftwood (live).
(cd-s) *(ISOM 33SMS)* – ('A'side) / The urge for going / Slide show (live).

Nov 99. (c-s) *(ISOM 39CS)* **TURN / DAYS OF OUR LIVES** [8] [-]
(cd-s+=) *(ISOM 39MS)* – River.
(cd-s) *(ISOM 39SMS)* – ('A'side) / We are monkeys / Baby one more time.

Jun 00. (7"/c-s) *(ISOM 45 S/CS)* **COMING AROUND. / CONNECTION** [5] [ ]
(cd-s+=) *(ISOM 45MC)* – Just the faces change.
(cd-s) *(ISOM 45SMS)* – ('A'side) / Rock'n'(salad) roll / The weight.

May 01. (7"/c-s) *(ISOM 49 S/CS)* **SING. / KILLER QUEEN** [3] [ ]
(cd-s+=) *(ISOM 49MS)* – Ring out the bell.
(cd-s) *(ISOM 49SMAS)* – ('A'side) / You don't know what I'm like / Beautiful.

Jun 01. (cd/c/lp) *(ISOM 25 CD/MC/LP)* <85788> **THE INVISIBLE BAND** [1] [39]
– Sing / Dear diary / Side / Pipe dreams / Flowers in the window / The cage / Safe / Follow the light / Last train / Afterglow / Indefinitely / The Humpty Dumpty love song.

Sep 01. (7"/c-s) *(ISOM 54 S/CS)* **SIDE. / ALL THE YOUNG DUDES (live)** [14] [-]
(cd-s) *(ISOM 54MS)* – ('A'side) / Driftwood (live).
(cd-s) *(ISOM 54SMS)* – ('A'side) / You're a big girl now / Ancient train.

Mar 02. (c-s) *(ISOM 56CS)* **FLOWERS IN THE WINDOW / A LITTLE BIT OF SOUL** [18] [-]
(cd-s+=) *(ISOM 56MS)* – Here comes the sun.
(cd-s) *(ISOM 56SMS)* – ('A'side) / Central station / No cigar.
(7") *(ISOM 56S)* – ('A'side) / Here comes the sun.

TROUT (see under ⇒ Rock Action records)

TURNBULL ACS (see under ⇒ Bellboy records)

TURTLEHEAD

Formed: Falkirk . . . 1994 by GARY CUNNINGHAM, PAUL BOURNE and ROBERT FRANCIS. Roughly translated to, erm, "head of a turd", TURTLEHEAD were arguably responsible for the massive new wave of Central Region punk bands that emerged in the late 90's and early 2000. Local legends in their own right, the quartet of pogo-punks began their reign of terror after a demo tape was picked up by Swedish DIY anarchist imprint 'Bad Taste' in late '95, accumulating in a brief appearance on their 'Quality Punk Rock' label sampler. The single 'GO' was delivered in early 1996, and the troupe began work on what was to become their debut album proper, 'BACK SLAPPING PRAISE FOR BACK STABBING MEN' (autumn '96). A musical molotov cocktail of an album, the set respectively featured songs about Helen Daniels from TV soap 'Neighbours' and an aptly-titled ode to Falkirk itself: 'SMALL TOWN'. The album sold moderately well on the European indie-punk scene, prompting TURTLEHEAD to join 3 Colours Red and the Voodoo Glow Skulls on a tour of the great continent. Their sophomore effort, 'I PREFERED THEIR EARLIER STUFF' (1998), displayed the outfit's tuneful ear for melody and their abrasive passion towards the dogma of true punk. After a heavy stint of touring, guitarist GARY departed, to be quickly replaced by an old mate DAVE McINTOSH (from SHATTERHAND). PAUL was to follow, leaving the lads high and dry without a bassist in the middle of recording their third album, although RICHARD BRUCE was recruited (apparently due to his ability to play a 'high F'), and the noisesters toured Europe in 2000 with American hard-rockers Digger. A new album is said to be in the pipeline, along with a legnthy tour of the US. Lock up your daughters!

BRIAN COOPER – vocals / **ROBERT FRANCIS** – drums (or guitar) / **GARY CUNNINGHAM** – guitar / **PAUL BOURNE** – bass

Bad Taste | not iss.

Jul 96. (cd-ep) *(BTR 10)* **GO** [ ] [-]
– Go / Walltie / B movie baby / Leave / Granny.

Nov 96. (cd) *(BTR 12)* **BACK SLAPPING PRAISE FROM BACK STABBING MEN** [ ] [-]
– Flex / Thought / Go / Angel / 40 / Bellend host / Helen / Sparkle / Home / Voices / Medication time / Smalltown / Brogues.

1997. (7"ep) **BELLEND HOST / FLEX. / (other tracks by Lovejunk / Sunfactor + Mos Eisley)** [ ] [-]
(above issued on 'Speedowax')

Apr 98. (cd) *(BTR 24)* **I PREFERRED THEIR EARLIER STUFF** [ ] [-]
– Gary D / Turn away / Over you / Boyracer / Zoe Ball / Godsend / Hate him / Hot trout action / Brass arse Margaret / Another stupid song / Ruin my day / Jack the sack. *(pic lp-iss.Apr99 on 'Speedowax'; WIZZ 001)*

1998. (7"colrd-ep) **GODSEND. / (others tracks by Vanilla Pod / Jayne Doe & Raggity Anne).**

— **DAVE McINTOSH** – guitar (of SHATTERHAND); repl. GARY

— **RICH BRUCE** – bass; repl. PAUL

— TURTLEHEAD are still playing live

TV 21

Formed: Edinburgh . . . 1979 by vocalist/guitarist ALLY PALMER, guitarist NORMAN RODGERS and bassist NEAL BALDWIN; trumpeter DAVE HAMPTON and drummer IAN WALTER GREIG completed the early line-up. In April 1980, the quirky Power-pop quintet self-financed their debut 7", 'PLAYING WITH FIRE', released on their own 'Powbeat' label, while the same imprint released the follow-up, 'AMBITION'. With ex-REZILLOS man ANGEL PATERSON coming in for GREIG, TV 21 issued a one-off for 'Demon', entitled 'ON THE RUN'. Now deeply influenced by DALEK I LOVE YOU and the TEARDROP EXPLODES, with that 'Reward'-esque trumpet always prominent, the band signed a major deal with 'Deram', although after only a handful of singles and an IAN BROUDIE-produced album, 'A THIN RED LINE' (1981), their dream was over. Before the end of their all too brief musical career, TV 21 did manage to secure a support slot to The ROLLING STONES when the London R&B kings toured north of the border. If you're thinking TV21 re-formed in the late 90's, you'd be wrong, that bunch were a trio from Portsmouth.

ALLY PALMER – vocals, guitar / **NORMAN RODGERS** – guitar, vocals / **NEAL BALDWIN** – bass / **DAVE HAMPTON** – trumpet / **IAN WALTER GREIG** – drums (ex-DNV)

Powbeat | not iss.

Apr 80. (7") *(AARGH! 1)* **PLAYING WITH FIRE. / SHATTERED BY IT ALL** [ ] [-]

Aug 80. (7"m) *(AARGH! 2)* **AMBITION. / TICKING AWAY / THIS IS ZERO** [ ] [-]

— **ALISTAIR 'ANGEL' PATERSON** – drums (ex-BOOTS FOR DANCING, ex-SHAKE, ex-REZILLOS) repl. GREIG

Demon | not iss.

Mar 81. (7") *(D 1004)* **ON THE RUN (WHO'S GONNA GET ME FIRST). / END OF A DREAM** [ ] [-]

Deram | not iss.

May 81. (7") *(DM 442)* **SNAKES AND LADDERS. / ARTISTIC LICENSE** [ ] [-]
(d7"+=) *(DMF 442)* – AMBITION. / PLAYING WITH FIRE

Oct 81. (7") *(DM 447)* **SOMETHING'S WRONG. / THE HIDDEN VOICE** [ ] [-]
(12"+=) *(DMT 447)* – On the run (who's gonna get me first).

Nov 81. (lp/c) *(SML/KSCMML 1123)* **A THIN RED LINE** [ ] [-]
– Waiting for the drop / Ideal way of life / This is zero / Ticking away / It feels like it's starting to rain / Snakes and ladders / What's going on / Something's wrong / When I scream / Tomorrow / Attention span.

Feb 82. (7") *(ATV 21)* **ALL JOIN HANDS. / JOURNEY UP THE ZAMBESI AND BACK** [ ] [-]

— they split summer '82, ALLY and NORMAN subsequently formed 7-piece soul/funk outfit, SHAME (with JOHN CALDWELL; ex-ANOTHER PRETTY FACE), while NEAL joined The BLUEBELLS and ALISTAIR formed . . .

SO YOU THINK YOU'RE A COWBOY

Cheatin' Heart | not iss.

Jun 84. (7") *(AA 1)* **DON'T NEED YOU. / GOTTA LOTTA RHYTHM** [ ] [-]

TWITCH (see under ⇒ MOUNT FLORIDA)

TWO HELENS (see ⇒ Section 9: wee post-Punk groups)

U

UGLY GROOVE MOVEMENT (see ⇒ Section 9: Dance/Rave)

ULTRA-SONIC

Formed: Ayr . . . 1991 by ROGER HUGHES and MALLORCA LEE. Dedicated disciples of Saltcoats' legendary Metro club and hardcore rave enthusiasts to a man, ULTRA-SONIC made their debut on Bathgate's 'Clubscene' label in 1993 with the 'OBSESSION' single. Featuring all the essential ingredients of a classic early 90's rave track – diva vocals, chipmunk-speed samples, chunky piano breakdown and bpm madness – as well as a haunting keyboard motif, the track established the duo as Scotland's great white dance hopes.

Follow-up, 'THE PULSE' sold almost twice as many as the debut and paved the way for 1993's 'ARPEGGIO'. The track's B-side, 'ANNIHILATING RHYTHM', was a huge hit on import in Germany (and a national chart hit in Holland), where ULTRA-SONIC's heavy-duty beats went down a storm with the teutonic techno masses. Around this time, HUGHES and LEE formed their own 'Voodoo Vinyl' label, the imprint's first release by hardcore act BROOKLYN BOY also doing well in Europe.

1994 saw the release of a fourth single, 'ACID CIRCUS' as well as a re-released 'OBSESSION' (a Top 75 hit on the national UK chart), previewing the group's much anticipated debut album, 'TEKNO JUNKIES' (1994). In addition to their huge fanbase and regular DJ'ing stints on the continent, ULTRA-SONIC were also big in Australia, their international profile in contrast to a lack of coverage in England.

Yet the duo, in contrast to the likes of The PRODIGY (whom U-S supported on a tour of Japan in 1992), found it hard to make the transition from white-gloved, hands-in-the-air rave music to more serious minded techno purveyors. Although 1996's 'DO YOU BELIEVE IN LOVE' single narrowly missed the UK Top 40, susbequent releases saw their fanbase dwindling and the pair called it a day following 1998's 'THE HOUR OF CHAOS' album.

ROGER HUGHES – electronics / **MALLORCA LEE** – electronics

Clubscene | not iss.

1993. (12") *(csrt 001)* **OBSESSION (mixes)** [ ] [-]
1993. (12") *(csrt 006)* **REACT – AMNESIA (mixes)** [ ] [-]
Sep 93. (12") *(csrt 009)* **THE PULSE** [ ] [-]
Dec 93. (12") *(csrt 015)* **ARPEGGIO. / ANNIHILATING RHYTHM** [ ] [-]
May 94. (12") *(csrt 022)* **ACID CIRCUS. / BLUE SMILEYS PLAN / SUGAR FREE TEKNO** [ ] [-]
(cd-s+=) *(dcsrt 022)* – Arpeggio part two (12"mix) / Blue Smileys plan (gagged mix).
Aug 94. (cd-s/12") *(d+/csrt 027)* **OBSESSION. / CHECK YOUR HEAD / LOVE ME RIGHT** [75] [-]
Sep 94. (cd/c/d-lp) *(d/c/a csr 002)* **TEKNO JUNKIES '92-'94** [ ] [-]
– Awesome / Annihilating rhythm pt II / Ultra-sonic vs Bass Baby pt 1 / React 1994 / Check your head / Sugar free tekno (live) / Annihilating rhythm pt 1 / Blue Smileys plan / Jupiter / Obsession (12") / Beyond the clouds / The pulse (12") / Arpeggio (stomp mix) / Love me right / Eternity / What is tekno?
Apr 95. (12") *(csrt 034)* **1,2,3,4. / TIK-TOK / HEY MR. DJ** [ ] [-]
Sep 95. (12") *(csrt 047R)* **THE REMIXES** [ ] [-]
– Make that move (Let it take you higher mix) / Check your head (Insane in the brain mix).
Oct 95. (d-cd/c/t-lp) *(d/c+/csr 007)* **GLOBAL TEKNO** [ ] [-]
– 1,2,3,4 / Out of control / Hey Mr. DJ / Make that move / 180 mph / Tic tok / Total break up / Let the musik set you free / Dreamer of dreams / In the air tonight / There is no back-up / Do you believe in love / Joyriderz / We want one more / Star spangled tekno / Party people in the house / DJ ragga / US vs. bass baby pt.2 / Annihilating rhythm pt 2 / Check your head / Make that move #2 / Tekno junkies in the mix.
Apr 96. (cd-s/c-s/12") *(d/c+/csrt 058)* **PARTY NON-STOP (mixes)** [ ] [-]
Sep 96. (cd-s/c-s/12") *(d/c+/csrt 070)* **DO YOU BELIEVE IN LOVE (mixes)** [47] [-]
Sep 96. (cd) *(dcsr 010)* **LIVE AT CLUB KINETIC** [ ] [-]
– Alpha 2 Omega / We want one more / Check your head / Hey Mr. DJ / Party non-stop / Make that move / Annihilating rhythm pts 1 & 2 / Do you believe in love / 1,2,3,4 / Let the bass drum go.
Feb 97. (cd-s/12") *(d+/csrt 078)* **ASYLUM EP – I JUST CAN'T STOP (mixes)** [ ] [-]

Ultra Sonic | not iss.

Mar 98. (12"/cd-s) *(USR 293399/793394)* **GIVE ME WHAT YOU'VE GOT (12"version) / BUST THAT GROOVE. / GIVE ME WHAT YOU'VE GOT (Trevor Riley remix) / BUST THAT GROOVE (DJ Brisk remix)** [ ] [-]
May 98. (12"/cd-s) *(USR 293528/793523)* **I WANT YOUR LOVE (mixes)** [ ] [-]
May 98. (cd/c/d-lp) *(USR 693533/493539/393532)* **THE HOUR OF CHAOS** [ ] [-]
– Intro / Take me away / Where angelsa fear to tread / I want your love / 1989 / Get raw / Right about now / Music for ya / Street knowledge / Open up your mind / Give me what you've got / Outro. *(cd w/extra cd+=)* – Give me what you've got (12" version) / Bust that groove / Give me what you've got (Trevor Reilly remix) / Bust that groove (DJ Brisk mix).

UNIVERSAL PRINCIPLES
(see under ⇒ Soma records / SLAM)

Midge URE

Born: JAMES URE, 10 Oct'53, Cambuslang, nr. Glasgow. Although he's fallen out of the limelight in recent years, MIDGE URE was one of the 80's most visible Scottish pop/rock stars as the suave lead singer of synth-poppers ULTRAVOX.

Almost a decade before the band reached their commercial peak, URE was making his first mark in the music business as the lead singer of teenybop hearthrobs, SLIK. Originally formed as SALVATION, the group topped the UK chart with 'Forever And Ever' in 1974. Dissatisfied with their bubblegum pop sound, URE subsequently turned down an offer to join an early incarnation of the The SEX PISTOLS before eventually teaming up with erstwhile PISTOL, GLEN MATLOCK, to form the The RICH KIDS; during this period he was also part of the ZONES and PVC2. The aforementioned project lasted one album, 'Ghosts Of Princes In Towers' (1978) before MIDGE went on to front a revamped version of ULTRAVOX in Spring '79.

Originally led by JOHN FOXX and trading in ROXY MUSIC-style art-rock, ULTRAVOX benefitted from the injection of new creative blood and became part of the burgeoning synth-led New Romantic movement. All glacial European glamour and grandiose pretension, 1981's 'VIENNA' single made the band a household name and URE a pop star. With his talent for taking po-faced but melodic art-pop to the masses, he also had a hand in the success of VISAGE, the STEVE STRANGE-fronted act which scored with the classic 'Fade To Grey' around the same time. Ever the musical magpie, MIDGE had even found time to replace GARY MOORE as a touring guitarist with THIN LIZZY at the turn of the decade.

Hardly surprising then, that he initiated his own solo career in 1982 with the single, 'I CAN'T EVEN TOUCH YOU'. Although it flopped, a follow-up cover of The Walker Brothers' 'NO REGRETS' made the Top 10 while a link-up with MICK KARN, 'AFTER A FASHION', scraped into the Top 40 a year later. Fans would have to hold their breath for a full album as URE subsequently teamed up with BOB GELDOF to co-write and co-ordinate the BAND AID famine relief project in late '84. The resulting track, 'Do They Know It's Christmas', wiped the floor with the Xmas No.1 competition, selling millions in the process and spurring GELDOF on to initiate 'Live Aid' the following summer.

Mid '85 also marked URE's first solo No.1, 'IF I WAS', a markedly pop-hued departure from his ULTRAVOX work. With the band temporarily put on ice, the singer had also recorded a debut solo album, 'THE GIFT' (1985), from whence sprang an additional two minor hits, 'THAT CERTAIN SMILE' and 'CALL OF THE WILD'.

Following the dissolution of ULTRAVOX in 1987, URE concentrated on a full-time solo career and released sophomore set, 'ANSWERS TO NOTHING' (1988). While it made the Top 40, the album failed to spawn a Top 40 hit and for the first time in his lengthy career, MIDGE's midas touch looked to be deserting him. 'COLD COLD HEART' furnished the commercially ailing star with his first Top 20 hit in over 5 years as 'Arista' attempted to relaunch his career in 1991. Although the accompanying album, 'PURE', scraped the Top 40, it'd be a further half-decade before URE again re-emerged. Predictably, 'BREATHE' (1996), failed to resuscitate the man's domestic fortunes although after being used in a European ad campaign, the title track scaled both the German and Italian charts in 1999!

The new millennium, meanwhile, found MIDGE completing the soundtrack to acclaimed drama, 'Went To Coney Island' as well as releasing a fifth solo album, 'MOVE ME'. In summer 2000, URE was back with a new rendition of 'WE CAME TO DANCE', this time courtesy of a collaboration with TRON (aka DEJAN DJORDJEVIC). More recently (20th of March, 2001, to be exact), MIDGE was honoured via the Big Red Book on TV's 'This Is Your Life'.

MIDGE URE – vocals, guitar, keyboards, etc / debut w / ex-COCKNEY REBEL **STEVE HARLEY** – dual vocals

Chrysalis | Chrysalis

Mar 82. (7") **I CAN'T EVEN TOUCH YOU. / I CAN'T BE ANYONE** [ ] [-]
Jun 82. (7"/12") *(CHS 2618/122618)* **NO REGRETS. / MOOD MUSIC** [9] [ ]
Jul 83. (7"/12"; as MIDGE URE & MICK KARN) *(FEST/+X 1)* **AFTER A FASHION. / TEXTURES** [39] [-]
Above 45 on 'Musicfest' w / ex-JAPAN bassist

— Dec'84 saw MIDGE co-write and create BAND AID with BOB GELDOF (BOOMTOWN RATS). They hit UK No.1 with famine relief single DO THEY KNOW IT'S CHRISTMAS.

Aug 85. (7",7"clear) *(URE 1)* **IF I WAS. / PIANO** [1] [ ]
(12"+=,12"clear+=) *(UREX 1)* – The man who sold the world.
Oct 85. (lp/c/cd) *(CHR/ZCHR/CCD 1508)* **THE GIFT** [2] [ ]
– If I was / When the winds blow / Living in the past / That certain smile / The gift / Antilles / Wastelands / Edo / The chieftain / The gift (reprise). *(re-iss. cd+c Apr93)*
Nov 85. (7",7"clear/7"pic-d) *(URE/+P 2)* **THAT CERTAIN SMILE. / THE GIFT** [28] [ ]
(12"+=,d12"+=,12"clear+=) *(UREX 2)* – ('A'instrumental) / Fade to grey.
Jan 86. (7",7"clear) *(URE 3)* **WASTELANDS. / THE CHIEFTAIN** [46] [ ]
(12"+=,12"clear+=) *(UREX 3)* – Dancer.
May 86. (7",7"clear) *(URE 4)* **CALL OF THE WILD. / WHEN THE WIND BLOWS** [27] [ ]
(12"+=,12"clear+=) *(UREX 4)* – After a fashion (w/ MICK KARN).
Aug 88. (7",7"clear) *(URE 5)* **ANSWERS TO NOTHING. / HONORARE** [49] [ ]
(12"+=,12"clear+=) *(UREX 5)* – Oboe.
(cd-s++=) *(URECD 5)* – (excerpts from lp below).
Sep 88. (lp/c/cd) *(CDL/ZCHR/CCD 1649)* <41649> **ANSWERS TO NOTHING** [30] [88]

– Answers to nothing / Take me home / Sister and brother / Dear God / The leaving (so long) / Just for you / Hell to Heaven / Lied / Homeland / Remembrance day. *(<cd re-iss. Aug98 on 'E.M.I.'; 496824-2>)*

Nov 88. (7",7"clear) *(URE 6) <43319>* **DEAR GOD. / MUSIC 1** [55] [95]
(12"+=) *(UREX 6)* – All fall down (live) / Strange brew (live).
(cd-s+=) *(URECD 6)* – Remembrance day.

—— In Apr'89, SISTERS AND BROTHERS single was withdrawn.

—— **URE** now with **MARK BRZEZICKI** – drums / **STEVE BRZEZICKI + JEREMY MEEHAN** – bass / **ROBBIE KILGORE** – keys / **SIMON PHILLIPS** – drums / **STEVE WILLIAMS** – perc./ etc

Arista R.C.A.

Aug 91. (7") *(114 555)* **COLD COLD HEART. / FLOWERS** [17] [ ]
(12"+=/cd-s+=) – Supernatural *(written by GREEN; SCRITTI POLITTI)*

Sep 91. (cd/lp) *(261/211 922) <61010>* **PURE** [36] [ ]
– I see hope in the morning light / Cold, cold heart / Pure love / Sweet 'n' sensitive thing / Let it go? / Rising / Light in your eyes / Little one / Hands around my heart / Waiting days / Tumbling down.

Oct 91. (7"/c-s) **I SEE HOPE IN THE MORNING LIGHT. / THE MAN I USED TO BE** [ ] [ ]
(12"+=/cd-s+=) – Madame de Sade.

May 96. (c-s) *(74321 37117-4)* **BREATHE / COLD COLD HEART (live)** [70] [ ]
(cd-s+=) *(74321 37117-2)* – No regrets / Trail of tears (live).

Jun 96. (cd/c) *(74321 34629-2/-4)* **BREATHE** [ ] [-]
– Breathe / Fields of fire / Fallen angel / Free / Guns and arrows / Lay my body down / Sinner man / Live forever / Trail of tears / May your good Lord / Maker. *(cd re-iss. Dec97; 74321 54709-2)*

Oct 96. (c-s) *(74321 42316-4)* **GUNS & ARROWS / TRAIL OF TEARS (demo)** [ ] [-]
(cd-s+=) *(74321 42316-2)* – Tor / Man of the world (live).

not iss. Orchard

Oct 00. (cd) *<7226>* **WENT TO CONEY ISLAND** (instrumental soundtrack) [-] [ ]
– The Gabby variations / High noon on 103rd Street / Surgery / Stan's disco / Stealing candy / Arriving at Coney / Midday suite / Bumper cars – Locket stealing / Pawnshop – Jerry Mahoney / Finding Richie again / Allegra / Richie calls his mom / Wedding / Lost point / Return to Skeeball.

Curb Arista-MI5

May 01. (cd) *(CURCD 100) <03484>* **MOVE ME** [ ] [ ]
– You move me / Beneath a Spielberg sky / Words / Strong / Let me go / Alone / Monster / Absolution sometime! / The refugee song / Four / Somebody.

Jul 01. (cd-s) *(CUBC 070)* **BENEATH A SPIELBERG SKY** [ ] [-]

– compilations, etc. –

Mar 97. (cd) *Disky; (<DC 86879-2>)* **IF I WAS** [ ] [ ]
Oct 99. (cd) *Strange Fruit; (SFRSCD 086)* **LIVE IN CONCERT (live)** [ ] [-]
Sep 00. (cd) *EMI Gold; (528562-2)* **NO REGRETS** [ ] [-]
– No regrets / After a fashion / Textures / If I was / The man who sold the world / That certain smile / Wastelands / Call of the wild / Answers to nothing / Fade to grey (live) / When the winds blow (live) / After a fashion (live) / Chieftain / The dancer (live) / All fall down (live) / Strange brew (live) / Dear God (live) / Just for you (live).

– (MIDGE URE & ULTRAVOX) compilations, etc. –

on 'Chrysalis' unless mentioned otherwise

Jan 93. (7"/c-s) *(TCCHS 3936)* **VIENNA. / WASTELANDS** [13] [ ]
(cd-s+=) *(CDCHS 3936)* – Answers to nothing / The voice.
(cd-s) *(CDCHSS 3936)* – ('A'side) / Call of the wild / One small day / Hymn.

Feb 93. (cd/c/lp) *(CD/TC/+CHR 1987)* **IF I WAS: THE VERY BEST OF MIDGE URE & ULTRAVOX** [10] [ ]
– If I was / No regrets / Love's great adventure / Dear God / Cold cold heart / Vienna / Call of the wild / Dancing with tears in my eyes / All fall down / Yellow pearl / Fade to grey / Reap the wild wind / Answers to nothing / Do they know it's Christmas? (BAND AID). *(cd+=)* – After a fashion (with MICK KARN) / That certain smile.

Oct 01. (cd) *(535811-2)* **THE VERY BEST OF MIDGE URE & ULTRAVOX** [45] [ ]

URUSEI YATSURA

Formed: Glasgow . . . 1994 by FERGUS LAWRIE, GRAHAM KEMP, plus brother and sister IAN and ELAINE GRAHAM. Part of the US-influenced Glasgow indie scene, their low-key debut release was a very rare mini-lp, 'ALL HAIL URUSEI YATSURA' (1995), a follow-up single, 'PAMPERED ADOLESCENT', receiving airplay from Radio One stalwarts John Peel and Mark Radcliffe. This exposure resulted in an indie Top 30 hit, with London's 'Che' records picking them up for a long-term deal.

A handful of singles, including 'SIAMESE', 'PLASTIC ASHTRAY' and 'KEWPIES LIKE WATERMELON', preceded a debut album proper, the self-explanatory 'WE ARE URUSEI YATSURA', in the Spring of '96. Arty bubblegum noise merchants trading in a PAVEMENT meets SONIC YOUTH meets T.REX style, these colourful kitschy characters amassed further critical acclaim with another clutch of three minute gems over the course of the next two years. From 'PHASERS ON STUN' to their first Top 75 entry 'STRATEGIC HAMLETS' to summer '97's 'FAKE FUR', the band were building up to their first Top 40 hit, 'HELLO TIGER', in early '98. URUSEI YATSURA's (YATSURA only in the States!) ultra hip factor was enough to persuade 'Warners' to enter into a part deal with 'Che', the result being a collection of the aforementioned singles, 'SLAIN BY URUSEI YATSURA' (1998). The latter's title track was inspired by their finest moment to date, minor hit single 'SLAIN BY ELF'.

• **Trivia:** Their moniker roughly translates as a troublemaking female android in Japanese.

FERGUS LAWRIE (b.23 Jan'68, Marlborough, England) – vocals, guitar / **GRAHAM KEMP** (b. 3 Dec'68, Inverness) – vocals, guitar / **ELAINE GRAHAM** (b.16 Jun'70) – bass / **IAN GRAHAM** (b.19 Oct'72) – drums, percussion, programming

Hipster not iss.

Jan 95. (m-lp) *(hip 001)* **ALL HAIL URUSEI YATSURA** [ ] [-]
– It is / Death 2 everyone / Yeah / Saturn / On your mind / Teenage dream. *(m-cd iss.Mar98 on 'Tiny Superhero'; SuperCD 005)*

Modern Independent not iss.

Apr 95. (7"burgundy) *(mir 001)* **PAMPERED ADOLESCENT. / (other track by the Blisters)** [ ] [-]

Che Primary

Sep 95. (7",7"orange) *(che 38)* **SIAMESE. / LO-FI SCARY BALLOONS** [ ] [-]
Nov 95. (7") *(PUBE 08)* **KERNAL. / TEENDREAM** [ ] [-]
(above issued on 'Love Train')

Feb 96. (7",7"pink) *(che 46-7) <64338>* **PLASTIC ASHTRAY. / GOT THE SUN** [ ] [ ]
(cd-s+=) *(che 46-2)* – Miramar / Yatsura kill taster.

Apr 96. (7") *(che 53)* **KEWPIES LIKE WATERMELON. / MAJESTY** [83] [ ]
(cd-ep) **STUNRAY EP** *(che 53) <66011>* – Sucker / Burriko girl.

May 96. (cd/lp,orange-lp) *(che 54 cd/lp) <61957>* **WE ARE URUSEI YATSURA** [ ] [ ]
– Siamese / First day on a new planet / Pow R. Ball / Kewpies like watermelon / Phasers on stun – Sola kola / Black hole love / Velvy blood / Plastic ashtray / Death 2 everyone / Pachinko / Kernel / Road song. *(re-iss. Sep97; same)*

—— shared a tour freebie 7" – che 59- (via the track 'PHASERS (live)' with MOGWAI and BACKWATER

Aug 96. (d7",cd-ep) *(che 62) <66011>* **PHASERS ON STUN. / THE LOVE THAT BRINGS YOU DOWN // THE POWER OF NEGATIVE THINKING. / SID AND NANCY** [ ] [ ]

Oct 96. (7") *(100gm 18)* **SILVER KREST. / (other track by the DELGADOS)** [ ] [-]
(above iss. on '100 Guitar Mania' as part of 'Stolen Ecstasy' series)

Feb 97. (7") *(che 67)* **STRATEGIC HAMLETS. / KOZEE HEART** [64] [-]
(7") *(che 67s)* – ('A'side) / Revir.
(cd-s+=) *(che 67cd)* – Down home Kitty.

Jun 97. (7"white) *(che 70)* **FAKE FUR. / SILVER KREST** [58] [-]
(cd-s+=) *(che 73cd)* – Nova static / Secret crush.
(cd-s) *(che 73cd2)* – ('A'side) / Pampered adolescent / Bewitched / Saki & cremola.

Jun 97. (cd-s) *<62084>* **FAKE FUR / STRATEGIC HAMLETS** [-] [ ]

Aug 97. (cd; as YATSURA) *<62084>* **PULPO!** (compilation) [-] [ ]
– Strategic hamlets / Down home Kitty / Pampered adolescent / Kozee heart / Miramar / Saki & Cremola / Fake fur / Silver krest / Got the sun / Nova static / Revir / The power of negative thinking / The love that brings you down.

Feb 98. (7") *(che 75)* **HELLO TIGER. / VANILLA STARLET** [40] [ ]
(cd-s+=) *(che 75cd1)* – Vent axia.
(cd-s) *(che 75cd2)* – ('A'-Peel session version) / Nae dice nae dice (Peel session version) / Everybody hang out.

Che-Warners Sire

Mar 98. (cd) *(che 76cd – <3984-22221-2>)* **SLAIN BY URUSEI YATSURA** [64] [ ]
– Glo starz / Hello tiger / Strategic hamlets / No 1 cheesecake / Superfi / No no girl / Flaming skull / Slain by elf / King of lazy / Exidor / Fake fur / Skull in action / Amber.

May 98. (7") *(che 80)* **SLAIN BY ELF. / HAIL TO THE NEW POOR** [63] [-]
(cd-s+=) *(che 80cd2)* –
(cd-s) *(che 80cd1)* – ('A'side) / Nu style / Subatomic.

Beggars Banquet not iss.

Nov 99. (d7"white-ep/cd-ep) *(BBQ 342/+CD)* **YON KYOKU IRI EP** [ ] [-]
– Kaytronika / Still exploding / Nobody knows we're stars / Mother of the MBK.

Oni not iss.

Aug 00. (7") *(ONIV7 1)* **LOUCHE 33. / PLANET OF THE SKULLS** [ ] [-]
(cd-s+=) *(ONICDS 1)* – I'm vexed.

Sep 00. (cd/lp) *(ONI CD/LP 2)* **EVERYBODY LOVES URUSEI YATSURA** [ ] [ ]
– Louche 33 / Eastern youth / Superdeformer / Silver dragon / Uji bomb / Our shining path / Kubrick in town / Random cruise / Faking it / Thank you / Sores / Osaka white.

Mar 01. (7") *(ONIV7 2)* **EASTERN YOUTH. /** [ ] [-]

V

VALVES

Formed: Portobello, nr. Edinburgh . . . 1977 by DEE ROBOT, G. DAIR, RONNIE MacKINNON and GORDON SCOTT. This quirky fun-punk/rock act were the first band to have a record – the double A-sided 'ROBOT LOVE' & 'FOR ADOLFS ONLY' – issued on Bruce Findlay's 'Zoom' label (he subsequently signed SIMPLE MINDS). The VALVES played a number of low-key hotel/venue gigs and managed to squeeze out another 45 before the year was out, namely 'TARZAN OF THE KING'S ROAD'. However, it took all of eighteen months to deliver a third, 'DON'T MEAN NOTHIN' AT ALL', although by this time the punk/new wave scene had gone down the tubes.

DEE ROBOT (b. ROBERTSON) – vocals / **RONNIE MacKINNON** – lead guitar / **GORDON SCOTT** – bass / **G. DAIR** – drums

Zoom / not iss.

Sep 77. (7") *(ZUM 1)* **ROBOT LOVE. / FOR ADOLF'S ONLY** [ ] [-]

Dec 77. (7") *(ZUM 3)* **TARZAN OF THE KING'S ROAD. / AIN'T NO SURF IN PORTOBELLO** [ ] [-]

Albion / not iss.

Jul 79. (7") *(DEL 5)* **DON'T MEAN NOTHIN' AT ALL. / LINDA VINDALCO** [ ] [-]

— all retired from the music biz

VASELINES

Formed: Bellshill, Lanarkshire . . . 1986 by EUGENE KELLY and FRANCES McKEE. A seminal Scottish band which would've earned their place in indie folklore even without the patronage of one KURT COBAIN, The VASELINES released two influential singles in '87/'88 on the small '53rd & 3rd' label, 'SON OF A GUN' (with B-side cover of Divine's 'YOU THINK YOU'RE A MAN') and 'DYING FOR IT'. Lo-fi before lo-fi was even invented, the records sounded as if they'd been recorded in a shed; wonderful bursts of noisy guitar scree and bubblegum melody with McDONALD and McKEE harmonising over sordid, tongue-in-cheek proclamations of lust.

Enlisting a rhythm section of JAMES SHEENAN and CHARLIE KELLY, the group finally got round to recording a debut album, 'DUM-DUM' (1989). Opening with the blasphemous rock'n'roll cacophony of 'SEX SUX (AMEN)', the record boasted such tasteful vignettes as 'MONSTER PUSSY' and 'TEENAGE SUPERSTAR'. Perhaps they finally ran out of vaseline, but the group seemed to disappear almost as quickly as they'd burst onto Scotland's insular scene, splitting in 1990.

They would no doubt have faded into the annals of Bellshill musical history hadn't NIRVANA released a cover of 'MOLLY'S LIPS' in early '91 (they also covered 'SON OF A GUN' and performed a beautiful version of 'JESUS DOESN'T WANT ME FOR A SUNBEAM' on their 'MTV UNPLUGGED' set), 'Seminal Twang' subsequently re-issuing an EP compilation later that year (interested parties should seek it out, if only for the peerless 'RORY RIDES ME RAW'!).

At the Reading festival later that year, EUGENE KELLY joined NIRVANA onstage for 'MOLLY'S LIPS', his new band CAPTAIN AMERICA supporting NIRVANA on their subsequent world tour. With a line-up numbering KELLY, GORDON KEEN, RAYMOND BOYLE and ANDY ROY, CAPTAIN AMERICA released their eponymous debut EP in late '91. KELLY's trademark laconic drawl was still in evidence although, surprise, surprise, their sound was markedly more 'grunge', on lead track 'WOW!' at least. The remaining songs, meanwhile, sounded spookily close to musical cousins TEENAGE FANCLUB, only the driving 'GOD BLESS LES PAUL' retaining the wicked spirit of The VASELINES.

After another EP the following Spring (featuring a cover of the Beat Happening's 'INDIAN SUMMER'), the group changed their name to EUGENIUS following legal threats from Marvel comics. An album, 'OOMALAMA' was released later that year, yet despite the interest surrounding KELLY, the record failed to rise above cult status. A similar fate befell 'MARY QUEEN OF SCOTS' (1994), the group now residing at their natural home, 'Creation', alongside fellow under-achievers 18 WHEELER, BMX BANDITS, etc.

A freak motorcycle accident later in '94, led to the disappearance of KELLY, although he was apparently sighted in Lower Manhattan having a 2-week bender with a Lemonhead (er, EVAN DANDO, to be exact!). Crawling back from the wreckage in 1996, EUGENIUS recorded a one-off 45 for Jamie Watson's 'Human Condition'. 'WOMB BOY RETURNS', was as slick and sublime as any VASELINES recording a decade earlier, its B-sides could have been attributed to the aforementioned binge. EUGENE subsequently teamed up with the TEENAGE FANCLUB's GERRY LOVE and RAY McGINLEY to form the short-lived ASTROCHIMP, releasing one single 'DRAGGIN'' for the local 'Shoeshine' imprint (also home to the RADIO SWEETHEARTS).

EUGENE KELLY – vocals, guitars / **FRANCES McKEE** – vocals, guitar / with hired musicians

53rd & 3rd / not iss.

Sep 87. (12"ep) *(AGARR 010)* **SON OF A GUN. / RORY RIDES AWAY / YOU THINK YOU'RE A MAN** [ ] [-]

Mar 88. (7") *(AGARR 017)* **DYING FOR IT. / MOLLY'S LIPS** [ ] [-]
(12"+=/cd-s+=) *(AGARR 017 12/CD)* – Teenage superstars / Jesus wants me for a sunbeam. *(re-iss. Aug91 on 'Seminal Twang')*

— added **JAMES SEENAN** – bass / **CHARLIE KELLY** (EUGENE's brother) – drums

Jan 90. (lp) *(AGAS 007)* **DUM DUM** [ ] [-]
– Sex sux / Sloshy / Monster pussy / Teenage superstar / No hope / Oliver twisted / The day I was a horse / Dum-dum / Hairy / Lovecraft. *(cd-iss. + remastered Mar91 on 'Avalanche'; ONLYCD 009)*

— disbanded in 1990 and KELLY briefly joined The PASTELS; much later, McKEE would form his own SUCKLE outfit

– compilations, etc. –

Jun 92. (cd/lp) *Avalanche; (ONLY CD/LP 013)* **ALL THE STUFF AND MORE . . .** [ ] [-]
– Son of a gun / Rory rides me raw / You think you're a man / Dying for it / Molly's lips / Teenage superstars / Jesus wants me for a sunbeam / Sex sux (amen) / Slushy / Monsterpussy / Bitch / No hope / Oliver twisted / Day I was a horse / Dum-dum / Hairy / Lovecraft / Dying for it (the blues) / Let's get ugly. *(re-iss. Oct95; same)*

Feb 94. (lp/cd) *Sub Pop; (<SP/+CD 145>)* **THE WAY OF THE VASELINES – A COMPLETE HISTORY** (as above) [ ] [Jul92]

CAPTAIN AMERICA

— **EUGENE KELLY** – vocals, guitar / **GORDON KEEN** – lead guitar (of BMX BANDITS) / **JAMES SEENAN** – bass / **ANDY BOLLEN** – drums; repl. live guest **BRENDAN O'HARE** – drums (of TEENAGE FANCLUB)

Paperhouse / Atlantic

Nov 91. (12"ep/cd-ep) **WOW / BED-IN. / WANNA BEE / GOD BLESS LES PAUL** [ ] [-]

Apr 92. (12"ep/cd-ep) **FLAME ON. / BUTTERMILK / INDIAN SUMMER** [ ] [-]

— had to change their moniker after legal threats by Marvel comics

EUGENIUS

— **KELLY + KEEN + RAYMOND BOYLE** – bass; repl. SEENAN who formed the PAINKILLERS with FRANCES McKEE

— **ROY LAWRENCE** – drums; repl. BOLLEN + part-time O'HARE

Sep 92. (cd/c/lp) *(PAP CD/MC/LP 011) <82426>* **OOMALAMA** [ ] [ ]
– Oomalama / Breakfast / One's too many / Bed-in / Hot dog / Down on me / Flame on / Here I go / I'm the Sun / Buttermilk / Aye aye. *(cd+=)* – Wow! / Wannabee / Indian summer.

Creation-August / Atlantic

Jul 93. (7") *(caug 005)* **CAESAR'S VEIN. / GREEN BED** [ ] [ ]
(12"+=/cd-s+=) *(caug 005 t/cd)* – Mary Queen Of Scots.

Nov 93. (12"ep/cd-ep) *(caug 008 t/cd)* **EASTER BUNNY / HOMESICK. / CAESAR'S VEIN / SEX SUX** [ ] [ ]

Jan 94. (cd) *(RUST 008CD) <82562>* **MARY QUEEN OF SCOTS** [ ] [-]
– Pebble-shoe / On the breeze / Blue above the rooftops / The Moon's a balloon / Mary Queen of Scots / Easter bunny / Let's hibernate / Friendly high / River Clyde song / Tongue rock / Fake digit / Love, bread and beers.

— KELLY moonlighted on an album by Celtic outfit DE DANNAN

Human Condition / not iss.

Sep 96. (7") *(HC 0013)* **WOMB BOY RETURNS. / SEVEN OUT** [ ] [-]
(cd-s+=) *(HCCD 0013)* – Bridge / Sixty-nine minus twelve.

ASTRO CHIMP

— **EUGENE** plus **GERRY LOVE + RAY McGINLEY** (of TEENAGE FANCLUB)

Shoeshine / not iss.

Nov 96. (7") *(SHOE 006)* **DRAGGIN'. / SHE'S MY SUMMER GIRL** [ ] [-]

Champion Doug VEITCH

Born: Hawick, Borders. Dubbing himself "The King Of Caledonian Cajun Swing", this otherwise reclusive full-time painter and decorator was a bit of an oddball who fused celtic dub/reggae with country and cajun. Sporadic recordings – which were nevertheless loved by JOHN PEEL and ANDY KERSHAW – kicked off in '82 with the Greensleeves backed 'Drum'-label single, 'LUMIERE URBAN'. The man returned with two further 45's in 1985, the first 'ONE BLACK NIGHT' hitting NME's indie Top 50, while the second 'JUMPING INTO LOVE' making the NME end of year lists at No.25! His ever-patient fanbase had to wait until 1989 for a debut set, 'THE ORIGINAL', sticky reviews might've prompted DOUG to retire in the 90's. What a cult!

DOUG VEITCH – vocals, instruments / + band

		Drum – Greensleeves	not iss.
Oct 82.	(7") *(RUM 1)* **LUMIERE URBAN. / GONE TRAIN**	☐	-
May 85.	(12"ep) *(RUM 6)* **ONE BLACK NIGHT**	☐	-
		Making Waves	not iss.
Sep 85.	(7"/12") *(DOUG 1/+12)* **JUMPING INTO LOVE. / DEEP END VERSION**	☐	-
		Conga	not iss.
Aug 86.	(12") *(CON 002)* **MARGARITA (Mescales mix). / ONE BLACK NIGHT** *(re-iss. Nov88; CON 002RV)*	☐	-
		Bongo	not iss.
May 89.	(lp/c) *(CDV LP/MC 001)* **THE ORIGINAL**	☐	-

— VEITCH retired from the UK music world

VERA CRUISE

Formed: Partick, Glasgow . . . 1997 by Canadian ex-pat PAUL SMITH, along with ROGER WARD, DAVID McGOWAN, CRAIG HAMILTON and DAVE GORMLEY; their moniker was in fact the name of a friend of Andy Warhol. Having already issued a split single, 'WASTED SOUNDS' in '98 (with the AMPHETAMEANIES), VERA CRUISE were a tad silent on the recording front for a while. Returning in 2002 with an Unsigned Bands Session for Radio One's Steve Lamacq (in which they attributed 'THE LAST TIME PARTICK THISTLE WON' to their local football team), the raw and enthusiastic VERA's supported TEENAGE FANCLUB, EVAN DANDO and MARK MULCAHY. Described in some quarters as Scotland's NIRVANA, they signed a contract with 'Loose' records at Glasgow's Nice'n'Sleazy bar. A limited edition 'SEVEN – EIGHT' 45 was quickly dispatched, although it would be their most recent, 'KEEP ALL THE LIES' (a SOTW playlisted on the Phil Jupitus breakfast show) that caught the attention of the public. Hot on its heels that June was the Kerrang!-friendly debut album, 'COME ALONG AND FALL APART' (2002), reviewed in the NME as a "kind of lumberjack rock that could bring down a Scots pine with its bare hands" – excellent description.

PAUL SMITH (b. Canada) – vocals, guitar / **ROGER WARD** – guitar / **DAVID McGOWAN** – bass, vocals, steel guitar / **CRAIG HAMILTON** – keyboards / **DAVE GORMLEY** – drums, vocals

		Flotsam & Jetsam	not iss.
Jul 98.	(7") *(SHaG 13.09)* **Club Beetroot Part Nine** – Wasted sounds / AMPHETAMEANIES: Speed fever.	☐	-
		Vinyl Junkie – Loose	not iss.
Mar 02.	(7") *(VJS 1)* **SEVEN – EIGHT. / split w/ Whiskey Biscuit: Kids Hangin Out**	☐	-
Jun 02.	(7") *(VJS 2)* **KEEP ALL THE LIES. / MONOTONE** (cd-s+=) *(VJCDS 2)* – Learning to fall.	☐	-
Jun 02.	(cd) *(VJCD 130)* **COME ALONG AND FALL APART** – The last time Patrick Thistle won / Wasted sounds / Come along and fall apart / Rejecting mobile phones / Keep all the lies / The famous signs of personal collapse / Mt. Assiniboine in the fall / Seven – Eight / Measuring down / Come and goes.	☐	-

Matt VINYL & the DECORATORS (see ⇒ Section 9: wee post-Punk groups)

VIOLET INDIANA (see under ⇒ COCTEAU TWINS)

VISITORS

Formed: Dundee . . . 1978 by local lads JOHN McVAY, his brother DEREK McVAY, COLIN CRAIGIE and ALAN LAING. Like the group DRIVE before them, The VISITORS delivered their 7" debut for 'N-R-G', the record in question 'TAKE IT OR LEAVE IT', was dealt the latter rhetoric. Supported by none other than DJ, John Peel, their FALL-esque follow-up 'ELECTRIC HEAT', was given some airplay, as was the 1980 third single, 'EMPTY ROOMS'. In '81, Edinburgh's 'Rational' (run by ex-JOSEF K manager and City Lynx fanzine contributor, Allan Campbell) released their fourth and final stab at indie stardom, 'COMPATIBILITY', and on reflection it was their uncompromising 'incompatibility' that sunk the band.
• **Note:** Not to be confused with VISITORS from Australia and the USA who also released records late 70's to early 80's.

JOHN McVAY – vocals, keyboards / **DEREK McVAY** – vocals, bass / **COLIN CRAIGIE** – vocals, guitar / **ALAN LAING** – drums

		N-R-G	not iss.
1978.	(7") *(SRTS-NRG 002)* **TAKE IT OR LEAVE IT. / NO COMPROMISE**	☐	-
		Deep Cuts	not iss.
Sep 79.	(7"ep) *(DEEP 1)* **ELECTRIC HEAT. / MOTH / ONE LINE**	☐	-
		Departure	not iss.
1980.	(7") *(RAP 100)* **EMPTY ROOMS. / ORCADIAN VISITORS**	☐	-
		Rational	not iss.
1981.	(7") *(RATE 2)* **COMPATIBILITY. / POET'S END**	☐	-

— folded after above

V-TWIN

Formed: Glasgow . . . 1996 by JASON MacPHAIL and MIKE McGAUGHRIN after meeting at Art school. Lifting their name from an advanced motorcycle engine, V-TWIN became the darlings of the experimental scene in Glasgow during 1998 along with MOGWAI and BELLE AND SEBASTIAN. However, the only thing that this warped ambient pop outfit have in common with the latter is that fleeting members of B&S have graced V-TWIN's skewed, unbalanced musical landscape.

Describing themselves as "the New York Dolls playing techno", cult label 'Domino' relesed their debut single 'GIFTED' in 1998 to much critical acclaim. These two as yet unknown soldiers battled it to the death, using breakbeats, dislocated guitar sounds and warm keyboards as unthreatening weapons in a sliding vista of strangulated pop. 'IN THE LAND OF THE PHAROAHS (DARK TOURISM)' – a part of Domino's electronic offshoot 'Series 500' – followed in 1999, as did the sublime single 'THANKYOU BABY' and it's B-side 'DERAILED' (with B&S man STUART DAVID riding the faders and making the odd contribution).

After a long break, MacPHAIL and McGAUGHRIN returned in September 2000 with a further single 'DELINQUENCY', another piece of fragmented brilliance that was and is V-TWIN. • **Covered:** LUNAN (Simon Shaw) / AN AMONITE FOR BILL (Lindsay Cooper).

JASON MacPHAIL – vocals / **MIKE McGAUGHRIN** – guitar / with a plethora of guests incl. **KATRINA** – vocals (of PASTELS)

		Domino	Drag City
Jun 98.	(7") *(RUG 68)* **GIFTED. / SOUND AS EVER**	☐	-
Aug 98.	(12") *(SER 509)* **IN THE LAND OF THE PHAROAHS (DARK TOURISM). / IN THE LAND OF THE PHAROAHS (the Cinema mix)** (above issued on 'Series 500'; part of 'Domino')	☐	-
—	next with guests **CHRIS GEDDES** (of BELLE AND SEBASTIAN) plus **STUART DAVID** – producer (of BELLE AND SEBASTIAN)		
Aug 99.	(7") *(RUG 95)* **THANKYOU BABY. / DERAILED** (cd-s+=) *(RUG 95CD)* – Lunan.	☐	-
Sep 00.	(12"/cd-s) *(RUG 106 T/CD)* **DELINQUENCY (Gareth Jones mix) / DELINQUENCY (Jagz Kooner mix). / DELINQUENCY (Adam & Eve mix) / AN AMONITE FOR BILL (Adam & Eve mix)**	☐	-
Oct 00.	(cd) *(WIGCD 86)* **FREE THE TWIN** (compilation) – Delinquency / Derailed / In the land of the pharoahs (dark tourism) / Thankyou baby / Sound as ever / Lunan / Delinquency / Delinquency / An amonite for Bill / In the land of the pharoahs.	☐	☐
Sep 02.	(7") *(RUG 147)* **CALL A MEETING. /**	☐	-

VULTURES (see under ⇒ Narodnik records)

WAKE

Formed: Glasgow . . . early 80's by a mysterious bunch of gloom mongers led by singer, DUNCAN CAMERON and bass player BOBBY GILLESPIE (quite possibly!?). After a one-off self-financed 7", 'ON OUR HONEYMOON', the band joined the black-clad ranks of Tony Wilson's 'Factory' stable, where their blooding blend of NEW ORDER and The CURE fitted in perfectly. A debut LP, 'HARMONY' (1982), showcased their derivative but effective sound, although barring a few sporadic singles, it would be all of three years before a follow-up, 'HERE COMES EVERYBODY' (1985). Of these aforementioned 45's, only 'TALK ABOUT THE PAST' was of any note, featuring as it did DURUTTI COLUMN's VINI REILLY on piano.

Subsequently dropped by Factory, The WAKE were resurrected by the infamously fey 'Sarah' label, CAMERON even managing to borrow a couple of ORCHIDS (MATTHEW DRUMMOND and JAMES MOODY) for his 1990 comeback album, 'MAKE IT LOUD'. A tad brighter, if not quite opening the proverbial curtains just yet, the record was an interesting combination of effete vocals, hard-edged jangling, tinkling electric piano and of course that cheap electro drumbeat. Like fellow Glaswegians, the BLUE NILE, The WAKE took their time between albums, 1994's ironically titled 'TIDAL WAVE OF HYPE' their only other release of the decade.

DUNCAN CAMERON – vocals / + others unknown except **BOBBY GILLESPIE** (before his days with JESUS & MARY CHAIN and PRIMAL SCREAM)

		Scan	not iss.
Jan 82.	(7") *(SCN 01)* **ON OUR HONEYMOON. / GIVE UP**		-
		Factory	not iss.
Oct 82.	(lp) *(FACT 60)* **HARMONY** – Judas / Testament / Patrol / The old men / Favour / Heartburn / An immaculate conception.		-
Aug 83.	(video; Various Artists) *(FACT 71)* **A Factory Outing** – Uniform / (other 'Factory' bands)	-	-
Oct 83.	(12") *Factory Benelux; (FBN 24)* **SOMETHING OUTSIDE. / HOIST**		-
Mar 84.	(7"/ext-12") *(FAC 88/+12)* **TALK ABOUT THE PAST. / EVERYBODY WORKS SO HARD**		-
Mar 85.	(7") *(FAC 113)* **OF THE MATTER. / OF THE MATTER (version)**		-
Dec 85.	(lp) *(FACT 130)* **HERE COMES EVERYBODY** – Oh Pamela / Send them away / Sail through / Melancholy man / World of her own / Torn calendar / All I asked you to do / Here comes everybody.		-
May 87.	(12"ep) *(FAC 177T)* **SOMETHING THAT NO ONE ELSE COULD BRING EP** – Gruesome castle / Pale spectre / Furious sea / Plastic flowers.		-
		Sarah	not iss.
Dec 89.	(7") *(SARAH 021)* **CRUSH THE FLOWERS. / CARBRAIN**		-

—— now with **MATTHEW DRUMMOND + JAMES MOODY** (of the ORCHIDS)

Nov 90.	(m-lp/m-cd) *(SARAH 602/+CD)* **MAKE IT LOUD** – English rain / Glider / Firestone tyres / American grotto / Joke shop / Holy head / Henry's work / Cheer up Ferdinand.		-
Aug 91.	(7") *(SARAH 048)* **MAJOR JOHN. / LOUSY POP GROUP**		-
Mar 94.	(lp/cd) *(SARAH 618/+CD)* **TIDAL WAVE OF HYPE** – Shallow end / Obnoxious Kevin / Crasher / Selfish / Provincial disco / I told you so / Britain / Back of beyond / Solo project / Down on your knees (Brit mix) / Big noise, big deal.		-

—— split after above

- compilations, etc. -

May 02.	(cd) *Les Tempes Modernes; (LTMCD 2323)* **HARMONY AND SINGLES** (remastered)		-
May 02.	(cd) *Les Tempes Modernes; (LTMCD 2332)* **HERE COMES EVERYBODY PLUS SINGLES** (remastered)		-
Jul 02.	(cd) *Les Tempes Modernes; (LTMCD 2336)* **HOLYHEADS** – (MAKE IT LOUD / TIDAL WAVE OF HYPE).		-

WATERBOYS

Formed: London . . . 1982 by Scots-born MIKE SCOTT, Englishman ANTHONY THISTLETHWAITE and Welshman KARL WALLINGER. SCOTT had previously fronted Edinburgh new wave outfit, ANOTHER PRETTY FACE, along with old Ayr school pals, JOHN CALDWELL and JIM GEDDES. Taking their name from a track on LOU REED's sleaze-noir masterpiece, 'Berlin', The WATERBOYS soon secured a deal with the Irish-run label, 'Ensign', following the release of a self-financed debut single in Spring '83, 'A GIRL CALLED JOHNNY'. A tribute to punk priestess, PATTI SMITH (an obvious early influence), the track received a fair amount of airplay and almost broke into the lower regions of the charts. An eponymous debut album followed later that summer, an esoteric set of avant folk/rock which drew comparisons with TIM BUCKLEY's more ambitious meanderings and introduced SCOTT as a promising singing/songwriting seer. Embellished by additional instrumentation such as horns and violin, 'A PAGAN PLACE' (1984) was a confident follow-up, SCOTT venturing ever further out on his spiritual journey with the likes of 'THE BIG MUSIC' and 'CHURCH NOT MADE WITH HANDS'.

A burgeoning live reputation and gushing critical praise saw The WATERBOYS' third set, 'THIS IS THE SEA' (1985) break into the UK Top 40, its centerpiece epic, 'THE WHOLE OF THE MOON', becoming the group's first Top 30 single. Despite this overdue success, WALLINGER subsequently departed to form his own outfit, WORLD PARTY. Relocating to Galway, Ireland for an extended sabbatical at the behest of fiddler, STEVE WICKHAM (who'd played on 'THIS..'), SCOTT and THISTLETHWAITE increasingly infused their music with traditional Irish folk influences.

It was an earthier WATERBOYS, then, who eventually emerged in late '88 with the acclaimed 'FISHERMAN'S BLUES', SCOTT seemingly having at last found his true musical calling. From the strident Celtic clarion call of the title track to the soulful cover of Van Morrison's 'SWEET THING', it sounded as if The WATERBOYS had been playing this music for centuries. The record almost made the UK Top 10, an album which established The WATERBOYS as a major league act and which remains their biggest seller. 'ROOM TO ROAM' (1990) continued in the same vein, making the UK Top 5 although it lacked the depth of its predecessor. Bang on cue, 'Ensign' re-released 'THE WHOLE OF THE MOON' to massive success (Top 3), the track being played to death by radio all over again.

By this point, however, the original WATERBOYS line-up had splintered following a final UK tour (wherein the group drew criticism for their return to an all-out rock sound), THISTLETHWAITE forming The BLUE STARS while SCOTT eventually moved to New York and gathered together a new group of musicians. Now signed to 'Geffen', he recorded 'DREAM HARDER' (1993), the sixth WATERBOYS album but a SCOTT solo set in all but name. Exploring many familiar themes, the album spawned two Top 30 singles in 'THE RETURN OF PAN' and 'GLASTONBURY SONG', even boasting a brief contribution from Scots comedy legend, BILLY CONNOLLY.

Although SCOTT released two solo albums, 'BRING 'EM ALL IN' (1995) and 'STILL BURNING' (1997), the WATERBOYS had been out of action nigh on seven years. 'A ROCK IN THE WEARY LAND', put this to rights. Fusing psychedelia, folk-rock and pop, the album was a lacklustre attempt to break back into the mainstream, although it did have its moments. SCOTT harboured the current trend of rock'n'roll nihilism on opening track 'LET IT HAPPEN', while 'CROWN' remained quietly poignant. It's easy to see why SCOTT still carries on despite critical disapproval from some of the press. He at least enjoys what he does as do his dedicated fanbase who'll never forget what the man and his group have achieved. An odds'n'sods collection of outtakes and unreleased material from the band's early days, 'TOO CLOSE TO HEAVEN' (2001) was a fascinating document of MIKE SCOTT's genesis from punk beat poet to fledgling folk mystic.

• **Covered:** LOST HIGHWAY (Hank Williams) / DEATH IS NOT THE END (Bob Dylan) / WAYWARD WIND (Lebawsky-Newman) / BECAUSE THE NIGHT (Patti Smith – Bruce Springsteen) / PURPLE RAIN (Prince) / and a several traditional renditions.

ANOTHER PRETTY FACE

MIKE SCOTT (b.14 Dec'58, Edinburgh) – vocals, guitar, piano / **JOHN CALDWELL** – guitar / **JIM GEDDES** – bass / **CRIGG** (b.IAN WALTER GREIG) – drums

		New Pleasures	not iss.
May 79.	(7") *(Z1)* **ALL THE BOYS LOVE CARRIE. / THAT'S NOT ENOUGH**		-

Virgin not iss.

Feb 80. (7") *(VS 320)* **WHATEVER HAPPENED TO THE WEST?. / GODDBYE 1970's** [ ] [-]

— trimmed to basic duo of **SCOTT + CALDWELL** plus **MAIRI ROSS** – bass / added **ADRIAN JOHNSON** – drums

Chicken Jazz not iss.

Dec 80. (7") *(JAZZ 1)* **ONLY HEROES LIVE FOREVER. / HEAVEN GETS CLOSER EVERY DAY** [ ] [-]

Mar 81. (c-ep) *(JAZZ 2)* **I'M SORRY THAT I BEAT YOU, I'M SORRY THAT I SCREAMED, FOR A MOMENT THERE I REALLY LOST CONTROL(live)** [ ] [-]
– This could be Hell / My darkest hour / Lightning that strikes twice / Graduation day / Carrie. *(on most copies, studio tracks +=)* – Another kind of circus / Only heroes live forever / Out of control.

Apr 81. (7") *(JAZZ 3)* **SOUL TO SOUL. / A WOMAN'S PLACE / GOD ON THE SCREEN** [ ] [-]

FUNHOUSE

— were formed by **SCOTT + CALDWELL**

Ensign not iss.

Feb 82. (7"/ext.12") *(ENY/+T 222)* **OUT OF CONTROL. / THIS COULD BE HELL** [ ] [-]

The WATERBOYS

MIKE SCOTT plus **ANTHONY THISTLETHWAITE** (b. 8 Aug'55, Leicester) – saxophone (ex-ROBYN HITCHCOCK / of SOFT BOYS) / **KARL WALLINGER** (b.19 Oct'57, Prestatyn, Wales) – keyboards, bass

Chicken Jazz not iss.

May 83. (7") *(CJ 1)* **A GIRL CALLED JOHNNY. / THE LATE TRAIN TO HEAVEN** [ ] [-]
(12") *(CJT 1)* – ('A'side) / Ready for the monkey house / Somebody might wave back / Out of control (APF; John Peel session).

Ensign Chrysalis

Jul 83. (lp/c) *(ENC L/C 1)* **THE WATERBOYS** [ ] [-]
– December / A girl called Johnny / The three day man / Gala / I will not follow / It should have been you / The girl in the swing / Savage Earth heart. *(re-iss. Aug86 on 'Chrysalis-Ensign' lp/c; CHEN/ZCHEN 1) (cd-iss. Feb87; CCD 1541) <US cd-iss. 1987; 21541> (cd re-mast.Mar02 on 'Chrysalis'+=; 537703-2)* – (extra tracks).

Sep 83. (7") *(ENY 506)* **DECEMBER. / WHERE ARE YOU NOW WHEN I NEED YOU** [ ] [-]
(12") *(12ENY 506)* – ('A'side) / Red army blues / The three day man (Peter Powell session).

— added **KEVIN WILKINSON** – drums / **RODDY LORIMER** (b. Glasgow) – trumpet / **TIM BLANTHORN** – violin

Apr 84. (7") *(ENY 508)* **THE BIG MUSIC. / THE EARTH ONLY ENDURES** [ ] [-]
(12"+=) *(12ENY 508)* – Bury my heart.

May 84. (lp/c) *(ENC L/C 3)* **A PAGAN PLACE** [100] [-]
– Church not made with hands / All the things she gave me / The thrill is gone / Rags / Somebody might wave back / The big music / Red army blues / A pagan place. *(re-iss. Aug86 on 'Chrysalis-Ensign' lp/c; CHEN/ZCHEN 2) (cd-iss. Feb87 & Jul94; CCD 1542) <US cd-iss. 1987; 21542> (cd re-mast.Mar02 on 'Chrysalis'+=; 537704-2)* – (extra tracks).

— (Oct84) **MIKE + KARL** recruited new people for tour/lp **TERRY MANN** – bass / **CHARLIE WHITTEN** – drums / **STEVE WICKHAM** (b. Dublin) – violin / **LORIMER / DELAHAYE** – organ

Sep 85. (lp/c) *(ENC L/C 5)* **THIS IS THE SEA** [37] [-]
– Don't bang the drum / The whole of the Moon / Spirit / The pan within / Medicine bow / Old England / Be my enemy / Trumpets / This is the sea. *(re-iss. Aug86 on 'Chrysalis-Ensign' lp/c; CHEN/ZCHEN 3) (cd-iss. Feb87; CCD CCD 1543) (re-iss. cd Mar94) <US cd-iss. 1987; 21543> (lp re-iss. Aug00 on 'Simply Vinyl'; SVLP 234)*

Oct 85. (7") *(ENY 502)* **THE WHOLE OF THE MOON. / MEDICINE BOW** [26] [ ]
(ext.12"+=) *(12ENY 520)* – Spirit (extended) / The girl in the swing (live).

— **MIKE SCOTT** now only original survivor (retained THISTLETHWAITE + HUTCHISON), when KARL formed WORLD PARTY.

— additional band **STEVE WICKHAM** – violin (ex-IN TUA NUA) / **J.D. DOHERTY** – drums / **COLIN BLAKEY** (b. Falkirk) – flute (ex-WE FREE KINGS) /('88) added **SHARON SHANNON** (b. Ireland) – accordion / **NOEL BRIDGEMAN** (b. Dublin) – drums repl. DOHERTY

Nov 88. (lp/c)(cd) *(CHEN/ZCHEN 5)(CCD 1589) <41589>* **FISHERMAN'S BLUES** [13] [76]
– Fisherman's blues / We will not be lovers / Strange boat / World party / Sweet thing / And a bang on the ear / Has anybody here seen Hank? / When we will be married? / When ye go away / The stolen child. *(cd+=)* – The lost highway. *(lp re-iss. Sep00 on 'Simply Vinyl'; SVLP 245)*

Dec 88. (7"/12"/cd-s) *(ENY/+X/CD 621)* **FISHERMAN'S BLUES. / THE LOST HIGHWAY** [32] [-]

Jun 89. (7"/c-s/12"/cd-s) *(ENY/+MC/X/CD 624)* **AND A BANG ON THE EAR. / THE RAGGLE TAGGLE GYPSY** [51] [-]

— **MIKE SCOTT / THISTLETHWAITE / HUTCHISON / + KEV BLEVINS** – drums repl. last additional band members

Sep 90. (cd)(c/lp) *(CCD 1768)(Z+/CHEN 16) <21768>* **ROOM TO ROAM** [5] [ ]
– In search of a rose / Songs from the edge of the world / A man is in love / Bigger picture / Natural bridge blues / Something that is gone / The star and the sea / Life on Sundays / Island man / The raggle taggle gypsy / How long will I love you? / Upon the wind and waves / Spring rooms to Spiddal / Further up, further in / Trip to Broadford / Room to roam. *(cd+=)* – The kings of Kerry. *(re-iss. Sep94 cd/c)*

Mar 91. (7"/c-s) *(ENY/+MC 642) <Alex; 1516>* **THE WHOLE OF THE MOON. / A GOLDEN AGE** [3] [ ] Jul91
(12"+=/cd-s+=) *(ENY X/CD 642)* – Higher in time / High far soon / Soon as I get home.

Apr 91. (cd)(c/lp) *(CCD 1845)(Z+/CHEN 19) <21845>* **THE BEST OF THE WATERBOYS ('81-'90)** (compilation) [2] [ ]
– A girl called Johnny / The big music / All the things she gave me / The whole of the Moon / Spirit / Don't bang the drum / Fisherman's blues / Killing my heart / Strange boat / And a bang on the ear / Old England / A man is in love. *(cd re-iss. Aug00; same)*

May 91. (7"/c-s) *(ENY/+MC 645) <Alex; 1581>* **FISHERMAN'S BLUES. / LOST HIGHWAY** [75] [ ] Jun91
(12"+=/cd-s+=) *(ENY X/CD 645)* – Medicine bow (live).

— disbanded soon after last studio album above. In mid'91, MIKE SCOTT re-formed group and signed for US-based label 'Geffen'. THISTLETHWAITE formed The BLUE STARS.

— **MIKE SCOTT** with **CHRIS BRUCE** – guitars / **SCOTT THUNES** – bass / **CARLA AZAR** – drums / **BASHIRI JOHNSON** – percussion / **LJUBISA 'Lubi' RISTIC** – sitar / **GEORGE STATHOS** – Greek clarinet / **JAMES CAMPAGNOLA** – saxophone / **JERE PETERS** – rattles / **PAL SHAZAR + JULES SHEAR** – backing vox / **BILLY CONNOLLY**– guest 10 second voiceover

Geffen Geffen

May 93. (7"/c-s) *(GFS/+C 42)* **THE RETURN OF PAN. / KARMA** [24] [ ]
(12"+=/cd-s+=) *(GFS T/CD 42)* – Mister Powers / ('A'demo).

May 93. (cd/c/lp) *(<GED/GEC/GEF 24476>)* **DREAM HARDER** [5] [ ]
– The new life / Glastonbury song / Preparing to fly / The return of Pan / Corn circles / Suffer / Winter winter / Love and death / Spiritual city / Wonders of Lewis / The return of Jimi Hendrix / Good news. *(cd re-iss. Jul96; GFLD 19318)*

Jul 93. (7"/c-s) *(GFS/+C 49)* **GLASTONBURY SONG. / CHALICE HILL** [29] [-]
(12"+=/cd-s+=) *(GFS T/CD 49)* – Burlington Bertie – Accrington Stanley / Corn circle symphony (extended).

— MIKE SCOTT split the band after above

MIKE SCOTT

— mostly all solo with some guests

Chrysalis Chrysalis

Sep 95. (c-s/7") *(TC+/CHS 5025) <58503>* **BRING 'EM ALL IN. / CITY FULL OF GHOSTS (DUBLIN)** [56] [ ] Nov95
(cd-s+=) *(CDCHS 5025)* – Mother Cluny / Beatles reunion blues.

Sep 95. (cd/c/lp) *(<CD/TC+/CHR 6108>)* **BRING 'EM ALL IN** [23] [ ]
– Bring 'em all in / Iona song / Edinburgh Castle / What do you want me to do? / I know she's in the building / City full of ghosts (Dublin) / Wonderful disguise / Sensitive children / Learning to love him / She is so beautiful / Wonderful disguise (reprise) / Long way to the light / Building the city of light.

Nov 95. (7") *(CHS 5026)* **BUILDING THE CITY OF LIGHT. / WHERE DO YOU WANT THE BOOMBOX, BUDDY** [60] [-]
(cd-s+=) *(CDCHSS 5026)* – Goin' back to Glasters (live) / The whole of the Moon (live).
(cd-s) *(CDCHS 5026)* – ('A'side) / Two great waves / My beautiful guide / Building the city of light (Universal Hall demo).

— now with **CHRIS BRUCE** – lead guitar / **PINO PALLADINO** – bass / **JIM KELTNER** – drums / **JAMES HALLAWELL** – organ / etc

Sep 97. (c-s) *(TCCHS 5064)* **LOVE ANYWAY / KING OF STARS** [50] [-]
(cd-s) *(CDCHS 5064)* – ('A'side) / King electric (including Moonage Daydream) / Blues is my business.
(cd-s) *(CDCHSS 5064)* – ('A'side) / Big lover / Careful with the mellotron, Eugene / Since I found my school.

Oct 97. (cd/c) *(<CD/TC CHR 6122>)* **STILL BURNING** [34] [ ]
– Questions / My dark side / Open / Love anyway / Rare, precious and gone / Dark man of my dreams / Personal / Strawberry man / Sunrising / Everlasting arms.

Feb 98. (cd-ep) *(CDCHSS 5073)* **RARE, PRECIOUS AND GONE / KISS THE WIND / WHEN WILL WE BE MARRIED (live) / LOVE ANYWAY (demo)** [74] [-]
(cd-ep) *(CDCHS 5073)* – ('A'side) / All things she gave me (live) / She is so beautiful (live) / Nectar (7 days).

WATERBOYS

MIKE SCOTT re-formed the band with **LIVINGSTON BROWN + MARK SMITH** – bass / **JEREMY STACEY** – drums / **ANTHONY THISTLETHWAITE** – electric slide mandolin / + others on session

R.C.A. R.C.A.

Sep 00. (cd/c) *(<74321 78305-2/-4>)* **A ROCK IN THE WEARY LAND** [47] [ ] Nov00
– Let it happen / My love is my rock in the weary land / It's all gone / Is she conscious? / We are Jonah / Malediction / Dumbing down the world / His word is not his bond / Night falls on London / The charlatan's lament / The wind in the wires / Crown.

Oct 00. (7") *(74321 79417-7)* **MY LOVE IS MY ROCK IN THE WEARY LAND. / YOUR BABY AIN'T YOUR BABY ANYMORE (with the Half Mast Flag Country & Western Band)** [ ] [-]
(cd-s) *(74321 79417-2)* – ('A'side) / Lucky day – Bad advice / Time space and the bride's bed.
(cd-s) *(74321 79418-2)* – ('A'side) / Trouble down yonder / Send him down to Waco.

Apr 01. (7") *(74321 84870-7)* **WE ARE JONAH. / TIME, SPACE AND THE BRIDE'S BED** [ ] [-]
(cd-s) *(74321 84870-2)* – ('A'side) / Lucky day – Bad advice / Dumbing down the world (live at Glastonbury 2000).
(cd-s) *(74321 84871-2)* – ('A'side) / Martin descent / Send him down to Waco.

Sep 01. (cd) *(<74321 88152-2>)* **TOO CLOSE TO HEAVEN** (rarities) [ ] [ ] Jan02
– On my way to heaven / Higher in time / The ladder / Too close to Heaven / Good man gone / Blues for your baby / Custer's blues / A home in the meadow / Tenderfootin' / Lonesome old wind.

- compilations, etc. -

Oct 94. (cd/c) *Ensign; (CD/TC CHEN 35)* **THE SECRET LIFE OF THE WATERBOYS** (81-85 material) [ ] [ ]
(cd re-iss. Sep97; same)

Aug 98. (d-cd) *Griffin; <40>* **LIVE ADVENTURES OF THE WATERBOYS (live)** [-] [ ]
– Death is not the end / Earth only endures / Medicine bow / Fisherman's blues / This is the sea / Meet me at the station / We will not be lovers / Wayward wind / A girl called Johnny / Purple rain / Be my enemy / Old England / The thrill is gone – And the healing has begun / Pain within (including Because the night) / Whole of the moon / Spirit / Savage earth heart / Saints and angels. *(UK-iss.Jul00 on 'Burning Airlines' d-cd/t-lp; PILOT 040/+LP)*

Sep 98. (cd) *Chrysalis; (496505-2)* **THE WHOLE OF THE MOON – THE BEST OF MIKE SCOTT & THE WATERBOYS** [ ] [-]

Sep 00. (3xcd-box) *EMI; (528661-2)* **A PAGAN PLACE / THIS IS THE SEA / FISHERMAN'S BLUES** [ ] [-]

WAVELENGTH (see under ⇒ Bellboy records)

WAVE ROOM

Formed: by Scotsman HAMISH MacKINTOSH (ex-FUEL) – an atmospheric songwriter and singer in the mould of MATT JOHNSON (THE THE), PETER GABRIEL or even LLOYD COLE. Teaming up with former COCTEAU TWINS guitarist ROBIN GUTHRIE and his new label/project, 'Bella Union', The WAVE ROOM scored a hit with the ENO-esque, ambient-indie fanclub via an impressive debut, 'LOVE MEDICINE' (2000). Also present alongside the pairing was dub bass giant JAH WOBBLE (ex-PiL), vocalist MANNEY POKU and a host of other "World"ly instrumentalists.

HAMISH MacKINTOSH – vocals / with **ROBIN GUTHRIE** – guitar, bass / **JAH WOBBLE** – bass / **MITSUO TATE** – guitar / etc.

Bella Union Bella Union

Jul 00. (cd) *(<BELLACD 20>)* **LOVE MEDICINE** [ ] [ ] Jul01
– Atlas of hands / Dreaming in tongues / Anywhere here is now / One for the river / Memory one / Second box / Houdini / Manna / Oneday someday soon / Love medicine.

WEE CHERUBS (see under ⇒ BACHELOR PAD)

WE FREE KINGS

Formed: Edinburgh . . . mid-80's by lyricist/singer JOE KINGMAN and guitarist SEB HOLBROOK, raggle-taggle gypsy punks of indie-folk, who invited PAM DOBSON, GEOF PAGAN, COLIN BLAKEY, KENNY WELSH and PHIL(IPPA) BULL into the 7-piece ensemble. With more than a penchant for LOU REED and the VELVET UNDERGROUND, whom they covered – and ripped apart – on several occasions, the WE FREE KINGS unleashed their CLASH-meets-POGUES debut single, 'DEATH OF THE WILD COLONIAL BOY', in 1986; GEOF was to proclaim in a press interview that 'The Clash' was a "folk"! album.

Political, but optimistic with a capital O, WFK inked a wee deal with Fast Forward outlet, 'D.D.T.', releasing a couple of gutsy 45's ('OCEANS' and 'T-SHIRTS') and a celebrated LP, 'HELL ON EARTH AND ROSY CROSS' (1988). A rockier farewell EP, 'HOWL – AND OTHER SONGS' was issued to a mixed reception in 1991, BLAKEY having already teamed up with MIKE SCOTT in his WATERBOYS (the latter were patrons of KINGMAN and Co). BLAKEY and most of the WFK team also surfaced in the former's more traditional outfit, The CLAN, although only one cassette album, 'THE ROKE' (1990), made it to retail.

JOE KINGMAN – vocals / **SEB HOLBROOK** – guitar / **COLIN BLAKEY** (b. Falkirk) – flute, guitar, mandolin, vocals / **GEOF PAGAN** – fiddle / **PAM DOBSON** – melodeon / **PHIL(IPPA) BULL** – cello / **KENNY WELSH** – drums

Howl not iss.

Jul 86. (7") *(WOOF 1)* **DEATH OF THE WILD COLONIAL BOY. / LOVE IS IN THE AIR** [ ] [-]

D.D.T. not iss.

Mar 87. (7") *(DISP 007)* **OCEANS. / WIPE-OUT GANG** [ ] [-]
(12"+=) *(DISP 007T)* – Death of the wild colonial boy / Love is in the air.

Jan 88. (12"/cd-s) *(DISP 009T/+P)* **T-SHIRT. / STILL STANDING** [ ] [-]

Jan 88. (lp/c) *(DISP LP/PC 010)* **HELL ON EARTH AND ROSY CROSS** [ ] [-]
– Motorcycle rain / Long train / Scarecrow / Flowers / Jesus wept / Still standing / Rosy cross / Wipeout gang / Brilliant.

Avalanche not iss.

Mar 91. (12"ep) *(AGA P008T)* **HOWL AND OTHER SONGS** [ ] [-]
– Howl / She said / Firewood / Be so cruel.

— after they split, BLAKEY joined The WATERBOYS and The CLAN

the CLAN

BLAKEY with also **PHILIPPA BULL** – cello / **DAVE ROBB** – bouzouki / **GEOF PAGAN** – violin / **ROB WELSH** – digeridoo / **ROBBIE THE PICT** – guitar / **LUCY JOHNSTONE** – voice, guitar, percussion / **KENNY WELSH** – bodhran, etc / **STEVE BRADLEY** – harmonica / **WENDY BLAKEY** – drums / **MARK RITCHIE** – mandolin, guitar / **SEB HOLBROOK + KIRSTEN WEBSTER** – percussion / **JULIAN GOODACRE** – Scottish smallpipe / **MARSHALL STORMONTH** – voices / **ROB BLAKEY** – clarinet / **BILLY SMITH + PETE LIVINGSTONE** – violin / **JOE KINGMAN** – mandolin / **SHONA McMILLAN** – violin

Temple not iss.

1990. (c; as The CLAN featuring COLIN BLAKEY) *(CTP 038)* **THE ROKE** [ ] [-]
– Spiddel / The battle of Sherrifmuir / Comati (the Pictish national anthem) / Pandaemonium / Two Muneiras / Achmelvich Bay / Scarlet / The roke, the row and the wee pickle tow / Deoch slainte nan gillean / Keel row / Whelans / Ye Jacobites by name / The hermit.

WELL OILED SISTERS

Formed: Edinburgh . . . late 80's by an all-female quintet of LUCY EDWARDS, ALICS GATE-EASTLY, MISS JONES, ANGIE DYPSO and ALLEY COWAN. Like k.d. LANG gone bad, these self-styled "hooligan hillbilly honeys" were more cow grrrl than riot grrrl, aiming to inject the dusty world of C&W with a bit of low-rent glamour and tongue-in-cheek irreverence. Like all the best country artists, the 'SISTERS devoted more of their songwriting energies to the demon drink than any other subject although tear-stained heartbreak and sleazy odes to girly sex came a close second.

Despite serving their time on the London treadmill, however, the girls couldn't quite make the breakthrough. They nevertheless left many a dazed'n'confused bar-room punter in their wake, regularly gigging in London and Edinburgh as well as touring worldwide and playing the festival circuit. They also bequeathed a legacy of two albums, 'ALCOHOL & TEARS' (1994) and the self-explanatory 'MAD GIRLS DO BETTER SEX' (1999), a sentiment this writer would be inclined to agree with. When not leading her cowgirls into action, LUCY was moonlighting – along with ALICS and her partner ALICE – in her 50's-style harmony side project, THREE PEACE SWEET. Although, as the girl says, 'IT AIN'T HARD BEING EASY', financial problems were another matter and eventually contributed to the group's demise in 1999.

LUCY EDWARDS – vocals, guitar / **ALICS GATE-EASTLY** – bass, vocals / **MISS JONES** – fiddle / **ANGIE DYPSO** – accordion, vocals, guitar, percussion / **ALLEY COWAN** (aka CAROLINE) – drums

Cycle not iss.

Apr 94. (cd/c) *(CYCLE CD/C 001)* **ALCOHOL & TEARS** [ ] [-]
– Trouble / You got my heart / Alcohol & tears / Mouth / I pray for you / Strange elation / It ain't hard being easy / Your little girl / Cowboy's prayer / Scratch / Guilt / Blood turns to ice. *(cd re-iss. Nov00; same)*

own label not iss.

1999. (cd) *(unknown)* **MAD GIRLS DO BETTER SEX** [ ] [-]
– Struck dumb / E song / Ace of spades / Mad girls do better sex / Dancing in the dubs / I miss you / Amphetamine / Seven hours / Miles away / Working girl / Why am I alone / Heaven bound / Drinking song.

Bill WELLS

Born: c.1963, Falkirk. Completely self-taught, BILL WELLS began forging his idiosyncratic path through the jazz idiom in the late 80's. Learning his trade by playing in clubs, he eventually started writing his own arrangements and initially offered them to BOBBY WISHART. With the latter declining WELLS' offer, he was given the impetus to found his own band, The BILL WELLS OCTET. Comprising some of the most talented musicians on the Scottish jazz scene (PHIL and TOM BANCROFT), the group has become a regular fixture in Edinburgh and Glasgow's smokier clubs although WELLS' singular musical vision has not always enjoyed the favour of critics.

Although influenced by the melodic innovation of BRIAN WILSON and BURT BACHARACH as well as GIL EVANS and CHARLES MINGUS, WELLS has carved his own unique niche of experimental jazz – described by one critic as "structured chaos" – that doesn't lend itself to pigeonholing. Although he's yet to release his own album, the man has regularly recorded the OCTET in live performance and has subsequently sold the tapes at gigs. This has seen the message spread to cult indie artists such as STEREOLAB and BELLE & SEBASTIAN. In fact, the latter outfit's STEVIE JACKSON and ISOBEL CAMPBELL guested at a BILL WELLS gig in Stirling which also featured respected jazz improviser LOL COXHILL.

WELLS recently recorded a collaborative set with COXHILL, following on from his pairing with FUTURE PILOT AKA on 1999's 'Domino' album, 'BILL WELLS vs . . .'. Prior to this, BILL teamed up with DAVID KEENAN (ex-TELSTAR PONIES) and JOHN HOGARTY (ex-BMX BANDITS) to deliver a one-off eponymous set as PHANTOM ENGINEER, while more recently (late 2000), the jazz outcast released the solo 'INCORRECT PRACTICE' set. A brooding, but jazzy collection of songs, the album saw WELLS moving into more organic territory, with his sampled keyboard loops and staccato jazz rhythms playing over STEVIE JACKSON's (BELLE & SEBASTIAN) harmonica-driven arrangements and LINDSAY COOPER's sliding tuba. A scathing Scottish alternative to Chicago's TORTOISE (or the very similar SALLERYMAN), proving that post-rock jazz isn't just played by clever Americans in suits and ties.

In spring 2002, The Falkirk "bairn" came up with two sets, 'ALSO IN WHITE' with his TRIO and 'GHOST OF YESTERDAY' a collaborative BILLIE HOLIDAY-type album with ISOBEL CAMPBELL.

BILL WELLS – instruments

Domino not iss.

Apr 99. (cd/lp) *(Wig 58 cd/lp)* **THE BILL WELLS OCTET vs FUTURE PILOT A.K.A.** [ ] [-]
– Introduction / In your short life / Chimps / No funerals this morning / Advert / Requiem pour un con / Pink Kitty / Olympic material / Advert – Prepare for shutdown / Om namah shivaya.

BILL WELLS TRIO

Geographic not iss.

Dec 00. (cd/lp) *(GEOG 005 CD/LP)* **INCORRECT PRACTICE** [ ] [-]
– Incorrect practice / Strangers by the shore / Burmac / Four cows / Bad plumbing / Presentation piece #2.

May 02. (cd/lp) *(GEOG 015 CD/LP)* **ALSO IN WHITE** [ ] [-]
– Presentation piece 1 / Record collectors / Singleton / Jab the chemistry teacher / The last guitar lesson / New ascending staircase / Also in white / Inappropriate behaviour / Euphonia / DADE.

BILL WELLS and ISOBEL CAMPBELL

Creeping Bent not iss.

Jun 02. (cd) *(bent 067cd)* **GHOST OF YESTERDAY** [ ] [-]
– All alone / Who needs you / Please don't do it in here / Preacher boy / Tell me more and more (and then some) / Somebody's on my mind.

Irvine WELSH

Born: 1958, Leith, Edinburgh. Raised from the age of four in the capital's housing scheme of Muirhouse, the young IRVINE went on to leave school at 16 and train as a TV repair man (he was always destined for television work). With the onset of Punk rock, he moved to London where he briefly played guitar in the PUBIC LICE, lived in a squat and took liberal quantities of speed. A subsequent job with Hackney council and an entrepreneurial knack for the property market put a bit of hard cash in his pocket. The mid-80's also found IRVINE with a year-long heroin habit, the experience of which formed the basis of some short stories and a debut novel, 'Trainspotting'.

Back in Edinburgh (where he'd recently completed an MBA), WELSH rapidly became a cult hero as his hard-bitten tale of schemies, drugs and Auld Reekie's seedy underbelly caught on like wildfire. Written largely in Edinburgh council estate dialect, 'Trainspotting' found a massive cross-section readership which traversed class boundaries. A brilliant theatre production and a collection of short stories, 'The Acid House', further enhanced WELSH's critical kudos and paved the way for the Danny Boyle-directed film version of 'Trainspotting' in '96. Featuring a sterling cast of Scottish actors, namely Ewan McGregor (Mark Renton), Robert Carlyle (Begbie), Ewan Bremner (Spud) and Johnny Miller (Sick Boy), the movie was a huge international success and made superstars of many of the actors if not WELSH himself.

With "Trainspotting" mania threatening to engulf the nation, IRVINE took refuge in Amsterdam (where else!) having already published two further books, the thoroughly nasty 'Marabou Stork Nightmares' and 'Ecstasy'. A lifelong Hibernian FC fanatic (i.e. a Hibee), the shaven-headed WELSH began his recording career on the eve of Scotland's Euro '96 campaign. Collaborating with PRIMAL SCREAM (and the ON-U-SOUND), he entered the UK Top 20 via 'THE BIG MAN AND THE SCREAM TEAM MEET THE BARMY ARMY UPTOWN', a cut'n'paste WELSH monologue complete with crowd samples and dancefloor beats. It might've been Scotland's unofficial anthem but it got right up the (blue)noses of certain "weedgie" football fans who objected to the lyrics. A seasoned club campaigner, IRVINE subsequently hooked up with DJ KRIS NEEDS as the predictably titled HIBEE-NATION for a couple of techno/disco 12" singles, 'KEY TO THE HOUSE OF LOVE' and 'I SENTENCE YOU TO A LIFE OF DANCE'.

After his third novel, 'Filth' (1998) – appropriately enough about a corrupt Hearts-supporting policeman/"pig" – the reluctant working class hero stated his intention to devote his time to TV/film writing, completing the screenplay for his 'Acid House' the same year.

Of late, IRVINE has been scouring the globe for inspiration, visiting so many countries he lost track of where he'd all been. He's also made something of a literary comeback with the acclaimed 'Glue' (2001), a tale four friends over three decades.

HIBEE-NATION

IRVINE WELSH – vocals / **KRIS NEEDS** – electronics, etc

Bubbles not iss.

Nov 97. (12") *(BUB 002)* **KEY TO THE HOUSE OF LOVE. /** [ ] [-]

Eruption not iss.

Mar 98. (12"/cd-s) *(ERUPT/+CDS 002)* **I SENTENCE YOU TO A LIFE OF DANCE (mixes:- radio / Matt's Justice / original / Mad Matt / Justice instrumental / Dubstrumental)** [ ] [-]

WENDYS

Formed: Edinburgh . . . early 1990 by brothers JONATHAN and ARTHUR RENTON, alongside IAN WHITE and JOHNNY MacARTHUR. This all-male outfit were lucky enough to gain an early support slot with The HAPPY MONDAYS, encouraged by SHAUN RYDER's dad Derek to send in a demo to their label, 'Factory'. Subsequently signed to Anthony Wilson's imprint through A&R man Phil Sachs, who also became their manager, The WENDYS' short career consisted of a couple of singles and an IAN BROUDIE-produced album, 'GOBBLEDYGOOK' (1991). Manchester in approach, despite their Caledonian roots, the band were virtually clones of other 'Factory' outfits; the aforementioned HAPPY MONDAYS, JAMES or even an optimistic JOY DIVISION.

JONATHAN RENTON – vocals / **IAN WHITE** – guitars / **ARTHUR RENTON** – bass / **JOHNNY MacARTHUR** – drums

own label not iss.

1990. (c) *(none)* **WENDY'S** [ ] [-]
– Ceiling / Sickbag / Spinster / You stopped me dead.

Factory East West

Feb 91. (7"/12"/cd-s) *(FAC 289/T/CD)* **THE SUN'S GOING TO SHINE FOR ME SOON. / EVERYBODY** [ ] [-]

Apr 91. (7"/c-s) *(FAC 297)* **PULLING MY FINGERS OFF. / I FEEL SLOWLY** [ ] [-]
(12"+=/cd-s+=) *(FAC 297 T/CD)* – More than enough (instrumental).

May 91. (lp/c/cd) *(FAC 285/+C/CD)* <91754> **GOBBLEDYGOOK** [ ] [ ]
– Something's wrong somewhere / Pulling my fingers off / Half blind / Suckling / Removal / Gobbledygook / I want you and I want your friend / Soon is fine / Half pie / I feel lovely / The sun's going to shine for me soon.

Sep 91. (12"ep/cd-ep) *(FAC 337 T/CD)* **I INSTRUCT** [ ] [-]
– Enjoy the things you fear / Newspaper cows / The pop song (live) / The sun's going to shine for me soon (live).

— disappeared from the scene when Factory went bust

– compilations, etc. –

Apr 00. (cd) *Starshaped; (STARS 001)* **SIXFOOT WINGSPAN** (their shelved set from 1992) [ ] [-]

WET WET WET

Formed: Glasgow . . . 1982 by MARTI PELLOW, GRAEME CLARK, NEIL MITCHELL and TOM CUNNINGHAM. Late in '84, the group met Elliot Davis, who became their manager and co-owner of 'The Precious Organisation' label. They subsequently spent the next couple of years perfecting their blue-eyed soul-pop sound after brokering a major distribution deal with 'Phonogram' in 1985.

The group finally made their vinyl debut with the infectious 'WISHING I WAS LUCKY' in Spring '87, PELLOW's grinning good looks immediately marking him out as one of Scotland's major sex symbols. Unfortunately, PELLOW had little to grin about as the group were forced to cough up an out of court settlement to both VAN MORRISON and SQUEEZE from whom the singer had filched some lines. Nevertheless, the single gave WET WET WET their first Top 10 hit, a cocksure cover of John Martyn's 'SWEET LITTLE MYSTERY' giving them a Top 5 hit later that summer. This success ensured a No.1 placing for their debut album, 'POPPED IN SOULED OUT' (1987), an enjoyable collection of Caledonian white-boy soul that reached its zenith on the epic 'TEMPTATION'.

A mite slick for some tastes, the band nevertheless became something of a mainstream phenomenon, packing out major venues full of canoodling couples who'd just put a down payment on their joint mortgage. Obviously bruised but not battered from their earlier brush with copyright law, WET WET WET subsequently made something of a career from cover versions, taking their pop-friendly reading of The Beatles' 'WITH A LITTLE HELP FROM MY FRIENDS' to No.1 in Spring '88 (a 'Childline' charity single, it was probably the only time the group would appear on the same record as BILLY BRAGG!). Later that year the band released 'THE MEMPHIS SESSIONS', reworkings of the more soulful elements of the debut together with a couple of new tracks and a STEVIE WONDER cover, 'HEAVEN HELP US ALL'. Previewed by the sickly 'SWEET SURRENDER' single, 'HOLDING BACK THE RIVER' (1989) was the group's next album proper, narrowly missing the No.1 spot and cementing the WET WET WET's standing as coffee table soul providers par excellence.

Although the hits started to dry up, PELLOW and Co. bounced back in customarily annoying fashion with the asinine 'GOODNIGHT GIRL', their second No.1 single. The accompanying album, 'HIGH ON THE HAPPY SIDE' (1992) also topped the chart, a record which trawled new depths of blandness. It was probably only a matter of time before WET WET WET achieved BRYAN ADAMS-style chart meltdown, the group topping the UK singles list for a near record breaking fifteen weeks in the summer of '94 with the nauseous 'LOVE IS ALL AROUND', theme tune from the hugely successful 'Four Weddings And A Funeral' flick. The track might've lingered further had the group not done the nation a favour and deleted it from sale. Though their career wasn't exactly flagging, the single's success boosted WET WET WET's profile to the extent that the previous year's greatest hits set, 'END OF PART ONE', soared back to the top of the charts. Fans 'unlucky' enough to have missed out on 'LOVE IS ALL AROUND' could find it on the group's subsequent album, 'PICTURE THIS' (1995), which gave them yet another No.1 album. Strangely enough, the album's other big hit, 'JULIA SAYS', was actually the most affecting track the group had penned for years.

WET WET WET delivered album number '10' in the spring of '97, a UK Top 3 breaker which boasted two major hits, 'IF I NEVER SEE YOU AGAIN' and 'STRANGE'. They signed off from the music world with a Top 5 hit cover of the Beatles' classic standard 'YESTERDAY', their official split coming amid PELLOW's controversial admission of drug taking. However, the man cleaned up his act and re-surfaced as a Top 10 solo star. The appropriately-titled 'SMILE' album in 2001 followed his first major hit, the smoochy 'CLOSE TO YOU' (not the Carpenters track).

• **Songwriters:** PELLOW – lyrics / group compositions, except HEAVEN HELP US ALL (Stevie Wonder) / I FEEL FINE (Beatles) / MAGGIE MAY (Rod Stewart) / STONED ME (Van Morrison) / LOVE IS ALL AROUND (Troggs) / IT'S NOW OR NEVER + IN THE GHETTO (both hits; Elvis Presley) / SHARE YOUR LOVE (Malone-Braggs) / YOU'VE GOT A FRIEND (Carole King) / ATLANTIC AVENUE (Average White Band) / IF YOU ONLY KNEW (. . .Allison) / WOULDN'T HAVE MADE ANY DIFFERENCE (Todd Rundgren) / TOWN CRIER (Elvis Costello) / ANGELINE (John Martyn) / BEG YOUR PARDON DEAR (Craig-Smith) / HOURGLASS + PULLING MUSSELS FROM A SHELL (Squeeze).

• **Trivia:** Took their name from a line in a SCRITTI POLITTI song 'Gettin', Havin', Holdin''.

MARTI PELLOW (b. MARK McLOUGHLIN, 23 Mar'66, Clydebank) – vocals / **GRAEME CLARK** (b.15 Apr'66) – bass, guitar / **NEIL MITCHELL** (b. 8 Jun'67, Helensburgh) – keyboards / **TOM CUNNINGHAM** (b.22 Jun'65) – drums

Precious Uni

Mar 87. (7") *(JEWEL 3) <50000>* **WISHING I WAS LUCKY. / WORDS OF WISDOM** [6] [58] May88
(12"+=) *(JEWEL 3-12)* – Still can't remember your name.
(d12"++=) *(JWLD 3)* – ('A'-metal mix).

Jul 87. (7"/7"sha-pic-d) *(JEWEL 4/+P)* **SWEET LITTLE MYSTERY. / DON'T LET ME BE LONELY TONIGHT** [5] [ ]
(12"+=) *(JEWEL 4-12)* – World in another world.
(7"ep++=) *(JEWEL 4EP)* – ('A'different mix).

Sep 87. (lp/c)(cd) *(JWWW L/M 1)(832 726-2) <5000>* **POPPED IN SOULED OUT** [1] [ ]
– Wishing I was lucky / East of the river / I remember / Angel eyes (home and away) / Sweet little mystery / I don't believe (Sonny's letter) / Temptation / I can give you everything / The moment you left me. *(cd+=)* – Don't let me be lonely tonight / World in another world / Wishing I was lucky (live).

Nov 87. (7"/ext.12") *(JEWEL 6/+12)* **ANGEL EYES (HOME AND AWAY). / WE CAN LOVE** [5] [ ]
((c-s+=/cd-s+=) *(JWL MC/CD 6)* – ('A'extended).

Mar 88. (7"/s7") *(JEWEL 7/+77)* **TEMPTATION. / BOTTLED EMOTIONS (KEEN FOR LOVING)** [12] [ ]
(12"+=) *(JEWEL 7-12)* – I remember.
(cd-s++=) *(JEWELCD 7)* – Heaven help us all.

May 88. (7") *(CHILD 1)* **WITH A LITTLE HELP FROM MY FRIENDS. / ('B'by Billy Bragg)** [1] [ ]
(above 45 on the 'Childline' label, gave all monies to that charity).

Nov 88. (10"lp/c)(cd) *(JWWW L/M 2)(836726-2)* **THE MEMPHIS SESSIONS** [3] [ ]
– I don't believe (Sonny'e letter) / Sweet little mystery (Memphis version) / East of the river (Memphis version) / This time / Temptation (Memphis version) / I remember / For you are / Heaven help us all.

Sep 89. (7"/c-s) *(JWL/+MC 9)* **SWEET SURRENDER. / THIS TIME (live)** [6] [ ]
(12"+=)(cd-s+=) *(JEWEL 9-12)(JWKCD 9)* – H.T.H.D.T.G.T. / ('A'extended version).

Oct 89. (lp/c/cd) *(842011-1/-4/-2)* **HOLDING BACK THE RIVER** [2] [ ]
– Sweet surrender / Can't stand the night / Blue for you / Broke away / You've had it / I wish / Key to your heart / Maggie May / Hold back the river.

Wet Wet Wet

Dec 89. (7"/7"g-f/7"pic-d/c-s) *(JEWEL/JWLG/JWPD/JWLMC 10)* **BROKE AWAY. / YOU'VE HAD IT** 19
(12"+=) *(JEWEL 10-12)* – And now for something completely different.
(cd-s+=/pic-cd-s+=) *(JWLCD/JWCD 10)* – Sweet surrender (club mix).

Mar 90. (7"/c-s) *(JEWEL/JWLMC 11)* **HOLD BACK THE RIVER. / KEY TO YOUR HEART** 31
(12"+=)(cd-s+=) *(JEWEL 11-22)(JWCD 11)* – With a little help from my friends (live).
(12"+=) *(JEWEL 11-12)* – Party city / I can give you everything.

Aug 90. (7"/c-s) *(JEWEL/JWLMC 13)* **STAY WITH ME HEARTACHE. / I FEEL FINE** 30
(12"+=)(cd-s+=) *(JEWEL 13-12)(JWLCD 13)* – Hold back the river (acoustic) / ('A'-TC YOUNG & T-mix).
(10"+=) *(JEWEL 13-10)* – Stay with me heartache (stay where you are) / Stoned me.

Sep 91. (7"/c-s) *(JEWEL/JWLMC 15)* **MAKE IT TONIGHT. / ORDINARY LOVE** 37
(12"+=)(cd-s+=) *(JEWEL 15-12)(JWLCD 15)* – Big sister midnight.

Oct 91. (7"/etched-7") *(JEWEL 16)* **PUT THE LIGHT ON. / JUST LIKE ANY OTHER DAY** 56
(12"pic-d+=)(cd-s+=) *(JEWEL 16-12)(JWLCD 16)* – You've got a friend.

Dec 91. (7") *(JEWEL 17)* **GOODNIGHT GIRL. / AMBROSE WYKES** 1
(cd-s+=) *(JWLCD 17)* – With a little help from my friends / Sweet surrender / Goodnight (no strings attached).
(cd-s+=) *(JWCD 17)* – Wishing I was lucky / Temptation (Memphis version) / Angel eyes (home and away).

Jan 92. (cd/c/lp) *(510427-2/-4/-1)* **HIGH ON THE HAPPY SIDE** 1
– More than love / Lip service / Put the light on / High on the happy side / Maybe tomorrow / Goodnight girl / Celebration / Make it tonight / How long / Brand new sunrise / 2 days after midnite. *(free-7"w.a.)* – CLOAK AND DAGGER as 'MAGGIE PIE & THE IMPOSTERS")

Mar 92. (7"/c-s) *(JEWEL/JWLMC 18)* **MORE THAN LOVE. / GOODNIGHT GIRL (mix)** 19
(cd-s+=) *(JWLCD 18)* – Broke away / Sweet little mystery (Memphis session).

Jun 92. (7"ep/c-ep/cd-ep) *(JEWEL/JWLMC/JWLCD 19)* **LIP SERVICE EP** 15
– Lip service (Youth mix) / High on the happy side / Lip service (live) / More than love (live).

Apr 93. (7"/c-s) *(JEWEL/JWLMC 20)* **BLUE FOR YOU (live). / THIS TIME (live)** 38
(cd-s+=) *(JWLCD 20)* – I can give you everything.

May 93. (cd/c/lp) *(514774-2/-4/-1)* **LIVE AT THE ROYAL ALBERT HALL (live)** 10
– Angel eyes / This time / Brand new sunrise / Hold back the river / Blue for you / Goodnight girl / How long / East of the river / I can give you everything.

Oct 93. (7"/c-s) *(JEWEL/JWLMC 21)* **SHED A TEAR. / EVERYDAY** 22
(cd-s+=) *(JWLCD 21)* – Deadline.

Nov 93. (cd/c/lp) *(518477-2/-4/-1)* **END OF PART ONE (THEIR GREATEST HITS)** (compilation) 4
– Wishing I was lucky / Sweet little mystery / Angel eyes / Temptation / With a little help from my friends / Sweet surrender / Broke away / Hold back the river / Stay with me heartache / This time / Make it tonight / Put the light on / Goodnight girl / More than love / Lip service / Blue for you (live) / Shed a tear / Cold, cold heart. *(initial copies contained free cd/c/lp)*

Jan 94. (7"/c-s) *(JEWEL/JWLMC 22)* **COLD COLD HEART. / ROLL 'UM EASY** 20
(cd-s+=) *(JWLCD 22)* – (2-'A'mixes).
(cd-s) *(JWLDD 22)* – ('A'side) / Another love in me / Wishing I was lucky (2 Arthur Baker mixes).

May 94. (7"/c-s) *(JEWEL/JWLMC 23)* *<857580>* **LOVE IS ALL AROUND. / I CAN GIVE YOU EVERYTHING (Arthur Baker soul remix)** 1 41 Aug94
(cd-s+=) *(JWLCD 23)* – ('A'mix).
above track hit No.1 for a near record breaking 15 weeks. Just prior to this occurrence, it was withdrawn by the group. In Aug94, 'END OF PART ONE' compilation regained its No.1 placing.

Mar 95. (7"/c-s) *(JEWEL/JWLMC 24)* **JULIA SAYS. / IT'S NOW OR NEVER** 3
(cd-s+=) *(JWLCD 24)* – Dixie / ('A'version).
(cd-s+=) *(JWLDD 24)* – I don't want to know / ('A'-synth string version).

Apr 95. (cd/c/lp) *(526851-2/-4/-1)* **PICTURE THIS** 1
– Julia says / After the love goes / Somewhere somehow / Gypsy girl / Don't want to forgive me now / She might never know / Someone like you / Love is my shepherd / She's on my mind / Morning / Home tonight / Love is all around.

Jun 95. (c-s) *(JWLMC 25)* **DON'T WANT TO FORGIVE ME NOW / IN THE GHETTO** 7
(cd-s+=) *(JWLCD 25)* – Gypsy girl (acoustic).
(cd-s) *(JWLDD 25)* – ('A'side) / Love is all around / Angel eyes.

Sep 95. (c-s) *(JWLMC 26)* **SOMEWHERE SOMEHOW / MORNING (the Youth 1995 remix) / ('A'-synth string version)** 7
(cd-s) *(JWLCD 26)* – ('A'side) / All you need is love (live) / She might never know (live) / Somewhere somehow (live).

Nov 95. (c-s) *(JWLMC 27)* **SHE'S ALL ON MY MIND / IF YOU ONLY KNEW / WOULDN'T HAVE MADE ANY DIFFERENCE (last 2 by MAGGIE PIE & THE IMPOSTERS)** 17
(cd-s) *(JWLCD 27)* – ('A'side) / Share your love / You've got a friend / Beg your pardon dear.
(cd-s) *(JWLDD 27)* – ('A'side) / Atlantic avenue / Town crier / Angeline.

Mar 96. (c-s) *(JWLMC 28)* **MORNING ('96 mix) / JULIA SAYS** 16
(cd-s+=) *(JWLCD 28)* – Hourglass (live) / Pulling mussels from a shell (live).
(cd-s) *(JWLDD 28)* – ('A'side) / Love is my shepherd (live) / She's all on my mind (live) / Morning (live).

Mar 97. (c-s/cd-s) *(JWL MC/CD 29)* **IF I NEVER SEE YOU AGAIN / QU'EST QUE C'EST** 3
(cd-s+=) *(JWLDD 29)* – Straight from the heart.

Apr 97. (cd/c/lp) *(534585-2/-4/-1)* **10** 2
– If I never see you again / Back on my feet / Fool for your love / Only sounds / If only I could be with you / I want you / Maybe I'm in love / Beyond the sea / Lonely girl / Strange / Theme from Ten / It hurts.

Jun 97. (c-s/cd-s) *(JWLMC 30)* **STRANGE / THEME FROM GRAND PRIX** 13
(cd-s+=) *(JWLDD 30)* – Lip service / Don't want to forgive me now.

Aug 97. (c-s) *(JWLMC 31)* **YESTERDAY / MAYBE I'M IN LOVE** 4
(cd-s+=) *(JWLCD 31)* – Goodnight girl '94.
(cd-s) *(JWLDD 31)* – ('A'side) / Beyond the sea / Love is all around.

— MARTI and the boys disbanded by the late 90's

– compilations, others, etc. –

Feb 92. (7") *Old Gold* **WISHING I WAS LUCKY. / SWEET LITTLE MYSTERY** -

Oct 00. (d-cd) *Universal; (E 536491-2)* **HOLDING BACK THE RIVER / POPPED IN SOULED OUT** -

MARTI PELLOW

with session people, writers CHRIS DIFFORD, HALLAWELL, etc

Mercury Polygram

Jun 01. (c-s) *(MERCS 532)* **CLOSE TO YOU / MAYBE ONE DAY** 9 -
(cd-s+=) *(MERCD 532)* – One woman.
(cd-s) *(MERDD 532)* – ('A'side) / Rain on my parade / Coming home / ('A'-CD-Rom).

Jun 01. (cd) *(<586003-2>)* **SMILE** 7 Jul01
– Hard to cry / Close to you / Did you ever wake me / All I ever wanted / I've been around the world / The moment is OK / New York vibe / London life / Moment of truth / She can lean on me / The missing sound / Memphis moonlight.

Nov 01. (c-s) *(588777-4)* **I'VE BEEN AROUND THE WORLD / WALK AWAY** 28 -
(cd-s+=) *(588778-2)* – Universal bus.
(cd-s) *(588777-2)* – ('A'-Stargate mix) / Out of this world / The river (video).

WHITE LEATHER CLUB (see under ⇒ SPARE SNARE)

WHITEOUT

Formed: Greenock . . . early 90's by teenagers ANDREW CALDWELL and ERIC LINDSAY, along with PAUL CARROLL and STUART SMITH. Hailing squarely from the Bellshill/TEENAGE FANCLUB school of sugary harmonies and retro songwriting, WHITEOUT were nothing if not instantly recognisable as Scottish. Signed to 'Silvertone', the band released 'NOT TIME' as their debut single and, incredibly in retrospect, embarked on a co-headlining tour with OASIS.

Further prestigious support slots and festival dates followed along with a further series of singles, 'STARRCLUB', 'DETROIT' and 'JACKIE'S RACING'. The latter was their most successful release, displaying a healthy affection for 60's West Coast pop a la LOVIN' SPOONFUL and The MAMAS & THE PAPAS. B-side, 'SO CONFUSED', meanwhile, brought to mind the harmonies of 'American Beauty'-era GRATEFUL DEAD. Yet trawling the cobwebbed corridors of America's rock'n'roll hall of fame proved insufficient to elevate WHITEOUT beyond second division status, their debut album, 'BITE IT', released at the tail end of '95 to less than overwhelming reviews. When they were dropped by 'Silvertone', ERIC and PAUL (who had now taken over vocal duties from the departing ANDREW) found drummer MARK FAIRHURST, releasing an EP, 'KICKOUT', and album, 'BIG WOW' (1998) on their own 'Yoyo' label.

• **Note:** not to be confused with the WHITE OUT who issued an eponymous set or the US group on 'Ecstatic Peace' records.

ANDREW CALDWELL – vocals / **ERIC LINDSAY** – guitar / **PAUL CARROLL** – bass / **STUART SMITH** – drums

Silvertone not iss.

Apr 94. (7"/c-s) *(ORE/+C 64)* **STARRCLUB. / AND I BELIEVE** -
(12"+=/cd-s+=) *(ORE T/CD 64)* – Higher.

Sep 94. (7"/c-s) *(ORE/+C 66)* **DETROIT. /** 73 -
(12"+=/cd-s+=) *(ORE T/CD 66)* –
Feb 95. (7"/c-s) *(ORE/+C 68)* **JACKIE'S RACING. / COUSIN JANE** 72 -
(12"+=/cd-s+=) *(ORE T/CD 68)* – So confused.
May 95. (7"/c-s) *(ORE/+C 76)* **NO TIME. / GET ME THROUGH** -
(cd-s+=) *(ORECD 76)* – U drag me.
Jun 95. (cd/c/lp) *(ORE CD/C/LP 536)* **BITE IT** 71 -
– Thirty eight / No time / We should stick together / Jackie's racing / Shine on you / No more tears / Altogether / U drag me / Baby don't give up on me yet / You left me seeing stars / Everyday / Untitled / Detroit.

— **ERIC + PAUL** took over vocal duties from the departing ANDREW

— **MARK FAIRHURST** – drums (a past member) repl. STUART

Yoyo not iss.
Nov 97. (cd-ep) *(YOCD 02)* **KICKOUT EP** -
Jun 98. (cd) *(YOLP 01)* **BIG WOW** -
– Kickout / Heaven sent / Selling UP / Through all the rain / 435 / I don't wanna hear about it / Running for cover / Out on the town / Take it with ease / Get back what you give / Back where I used to be.

— **EGGY + FUDGE** repl. MARK, although WHITEOUT split soon after

WILD ANGELS (see under ⇒ JAZZATEERS)

WILDERNESS CHILDREN

Formed: Dundee . . . 1987 by urban-folkees (including PETER MOUG), who were also part of a bourgeoning folk/indie scene that included DEAF HEIGHTS CAJUN ACES, NYAH FEARTIES and TONIGHT AT NOON. Around the same time as they released a handful of singles on their own 'Doss' imprint, a number of V/A sets were released; the tracks '15 MINUTES FAME' came via 'Somethings Burning In Paradise' (on 'Subtle'), 'HAPPY BIRTHDAY' appeared on 'Are You Ready' (for 'Windmill') and 'ONE MUST DIE' was unearthed on 'Now That's Righteous'.

After the 'CHILDREN split, PETER MOUG would instigate other acts including WILDHOUSE, MOMA, NEW PAN'S PEOPLE, The GERILS and YUL-PETER. The latter two acts were around from 1999 and even shared a mail-order cassette, 'THIS IS A KILL SCIENCE NOW PRODUCT' (2000). The GERILS were like SONIC YOUTH having a fight with The FALL, while YUL-PETER took elements of free-form jazz and avant-garde experimentation to new heights. To find out more contact PETER at:- www.the-lab.zetnet.co.uk/yul-peter

PETER MOUG – guitars / + other unknown members

Doss not iss.
1988. (7"ep; flexi) *(DOSS 1)* **THERE'S A GOOD TIME A-COMIN' / ON THE WEST COAST. / (two others by Thrilled Skinny)** -
(above issued for the 'Sowing Seeds' fanzine)
1988. (7"flexi) **WE'RE A COUNCIL HOUSE PUNK ROCK BAND** -
Feb 89. (7"m) *(REID 2)* **PLASTIC BAG FROM TESCOS. / MRS SUSAN SPENCE / BAD TASTE IN MY MOUTH** -
1989. (7"m) **IF YOU LOVE HIM, LET HIM GO. / TIMELESS / CONTRACEPTIVES AND DIAMOND RINGS** -
(above issued on 'Magic Bus')
Jul 90. (12"ep) *(DOSS 012T)* **PAINT ME A PICTURE EP** -
– The red dress / A mile . . . / There's a good time a-comin' / Midsummer's night.

— went off again after above; PETER formed many outfits (see above)

YUL-PETER

PETER MOUG – everything / + at times a band!
Aug 99. (7"white-ep) *(Yulp One)* **TWO-WAY RIVER** - - mail-o
2000. (cassette; shared w/ GERILS) *(none)* **THIS IS A KILL SCIENCE NOW PRODUCT** - - mail-o
2002. (7"split; V/A) **Sounds In Your Head Volume 3** -

WILD HORSES

Formed: London . . . 1978 by two Scots-born hard-rockers BRIAN ROBERTSON (ex-THIN LIZZY) and JIMMY BAIN (ex-RAINBOW), who had met while the latter was with HARLOT; he had earlier been guitarist with THREE'S A CROWD. Taking the name from a well-known ROLLING STONES track, they recruited two more experienced players, NEIL CARTER and CLIVE EDWARDS. Signed to 'E.M.I.' on the quality of their pedigree, WILD HORSES opened the starting gate on their career in late '79 with the single, 'CRIMINAL TENDENCIES'. Criticised for their notably unoriginal hard rock sound, the 'HORSES nevertheless bolted into the UK Top 40 with their eponymous debut album, released in the Spring the following year.

CARTER was subsequently relaced by JOHN LOCKTON, and, gee'd up by the enthusiastic reception reserved for their live work, the group released an improved second set, the earthy 'STAND YOUR GROUND'. After a final single, 'EVERLASTING LOVE', however, The WILD HORSES finally trotted into the rock graveyard later that year, ROBERTSON joining MOTORHEAD while BAIN went on to play with DIO.

JIMMY BAIN (b. Edinburgh) – vocals, bass, guitar, keyboards (ex-RAINBOW, ex-HARLOT, ex-THREE'S A CROWD) / **BRIAN ROBERTSON** (b.12 Sep'56, Glasgow) – guitar, bass, vocals (ex-THIN LIZZY) / **NEIL CARTER** – guitar, keyboards (ex-GILBERT O'SULLIVAN) / **CLIVE EDWARDS** – drums (ex-PAT TRAVERS)

EMI Int. not iss.
Nov 79. (7") *(INT 599)* **CRIMINAL TENDENCIES. / THE RAPIST** -
E.M.I. not iss.
Mar 80. (7") *(EMI 5047)* **FACE DOWN. / DEALER** -
Apr 80. (lp/c) *(EMC/TC-EMC 3324)* **WILD HORSES** 38 -
– Reservation / Face down / Blackmail / Fly away / Dealer / Street girl / No strings attached / Criminal tendencies / Nights on the town / Woman.
May 80. (7"white/12"white) *(EMI/12EMI 5078)* **FLY AWAY. / BLACKMAIL** -

— **JOHN LOCKTON** – guitar; repl. CARTER who joined GARY MOORE
Apr 81. (7") *(EMI 5149)* **I'LL GIVE YOU LOVE. / ROCKY MOUNTAIN WAY** -
(free 7"w.a.) *(PSR 45)* – THE KID. / ON A SATURDAY NIGHT
May 81. (lp/c) *(EMC/TC-EMC 3368)* **STAND YOUR GROUND** -
– I'll give you love / In the city / Another lover / Back in the U.S.A. / Stand your ground / The axe / Miami justice / Precious / New York City / Stake out.

— **DIXIE LEE** – drums (ex-LONE STAR) repl. EDWARDS
Jun 81. (7") *(EMI 5199)* **EVERLASTING LOVE. / THE AXE** -

— folded in 1981, ROBERTSON joining MOTORHEAD, while BAIN sessioned for PHIL LYNOTT, KATE BUSH and went on to DIO; the latter also played bass for GARY MOORE and JOHN CALE

WILLIAM (see under ⇒ JESUS & MARY CHAIN)

Astrid WILLIAMSON

Born: c.1971, Shetlands. After attending music college in Glasgow, she took the long trip south to London where she found work playing piano in a cocktail bar. More exciting horizons beckoned as she became frontwoman for GOYA DRESS, an indie act signed to the 'Nude' label. She subsequently struck out on a solo career following the band's demise in late '96.

A subtle, sophisticated singer-songwriter as well as a classically trained pianist and multi-instrumentalist, ASTRID was compared to veteran femme confessionalists such as CAROLE KING and JONI MITCHELL although commentators found her highly original, evocative style hard to pin down. Indie lable 'Nude' were convinced of both her genius as a songwriter and her potential as an albums artist, putting up the budget for ASTRID to work on a debut album with producer Malcolm Burn (BOB DYLAN, PATTI SMITH, IGGY POP) in New Orleans. The resulting 'BOY FOR YOU' (1998) album had critics reaching for the superlatives, praising her crystalline melodies, prophetic introspection and lucid way with a pithy lyric. Neither 'I AM THE BOY FOR YOU' or the narrative 'HOZANNA' made much headway as single releases although 'Nude' MD, Saul Galpern seems to be committed to her longer term development. ASTRID's talent also came to the attention of JOHNNY MARR who recruited her earthy vocal chords for ELECTRONIC's 1999 album, 'Twisted Tenderness'.

Dropped by 'Nude' records, she found it a little difficult to get back into the mainstream. Finally, in August 2002, ASTRID WILLIAMSON (now using her full moniker) delivered an internet-only release, 'CARNATION' – available at www.astridwilliamson.net – a top set that was made for Radio 2 and possibly a proper CD release.

ASTRID

ASTRID WILLIAMSON – vocals, guitar / with session people

Nude Imprint
Jul 98. (cd-s) *(NUD 36CD1)* **I AM THE BOY FOR YOU / WORLD AT YOUR FEET (original) / SOMEONE I SHOULD LOVE (demo)** -
(cd-s) *(NUD 36CD2)* – ('A'side) / ('A'demo) / Sing for me (acoustic).
Aug 98. (cd/c) *(NUDE 10 CD/MC)* <112719> **BOY FOR YOU**
– I am the boy for you / Everyone's waiting / What do you . . . / World at your feet / Sing for me / Someone / Hozanna / If I loved you / Outside / Say what you mean.
Sep 98. (c-s) *(NUD 40C)* **HOZANNA / FAN** -
(cd-s+=) *(NUD 40CD)* – Hozanna (acoustic mix).

ASTRID WILLIAMSON

		internet	not iss.
Aug 02.	(web) **CARNATION** – Never enough / Love / To love you / Bye and bye / Blood horizon / Calling / Girlfriend / Tumbling into blue / Lucky / Call for beauty.	[ ]	[-]

Tom WILSON

Born: Edinburgh. After making his club debut at Oscars in Edinburgh's West End, the aspiring radio DJ worked with Mark Goodier (the pair had previously worked together on pirate station Radio Telstar) and subsequently secured a spot for his 'Stepping Out' show on Radio Forth in summer '85.

A champion of the Hi-NRG scene and the Stock/Aitken/Waterman pop that followed, WILSON eventually got on the rave bandwagon and became a regular fixture at many club nights around Scotland's central belt. His Sunday night show quickly became essential listening for Scottish ravers and in 1994 he sponsored V/A set, 'TOM WILSON'S BOUNCING BEATS VOL.1' on the 'Rumour' label. 'VOL.2' followed in 1995 along with 'TOM WILSON'S TARTAN TECHNO VOL.1'. Known for his selection of "pumping" tunes rather than his mixing skills, he nevertheless became a popular club draw and even remixed LOVE 4 SALE's classic 'Do You Feel So Right' in 1993.

That same year he moved into producing himself with a debut 12", 'BOUNCE YOUR BODY'. He even broke into the Top 40 in 1995 with his 'TECHNOCAT' single as the indigenous rave scene reached its zenith. A further minor (Top 60) hit followed in 1996 with 'IT'S GONNA BE ALRIGHT' on the 'Clubscene' label while a further slew of compilation albums taking his name included 'FIRED' (1996), a collection of house/garage material from Clubscene's 'Fire Island' imprint.

He even hooked up with forgotten rave heroes TTF in 1998 for 'U GOT THE PASSION' while the TECHNOCAT series (also involving BOBBY HEATLIE, IAN ROBERTSON and JOLLIE) moved into the new millennium with the 'TECHNOCAT 2000' 12". In his time as commercial dance ambassador, the man has also worked with N-TRANCE and MARY KIANI.

TOM WILSON – DJ, samples, etc

		Steppin' Out	not iss.
Dec 93.	(12") **BOUNCE YOUR BODY EP**	[ ]	[-]
		Rumour	not iss.
Oct 94.	(cd/c/d-lp; by Various Artists) *(BNC CD/MC/LP 1)* **TOM WILSON'S BOUNCING BEATS VOL.1**	[ ]	[-]
Jul 95.	(cd/c/d-lp; by Various Artists) *(BNC CD/MC/LP 2)* **TOM WILSON'S BOUNCING BEATS VOL.2**	[ ]	[-]
		Tempo Toons	not iss.
Oct 95.	(cd/c/d-lp; by Various Artists) *(TOON CD/MC/LP 101)* **TOM WILSON'S TARTAN TECHNO VOL.1**	[ ]	[-]
		Pukka	not iss.
Nov 95.	(c-s/12"/cd-s; as TECHNOCAT featuring TOM WILSON) *(CA/12/CD PUKKA 4)* **TECHNOCAT (mixes)**	[33]	[-]
		Clubscene	not iss.
Mar 96.	(12"/cd-s) *(c+/srt 050)* **LET YOUR BODY GO (mixes)**	[60]	[-]
		Rumour	not iss.
Apr 96.	(cd/c/d-lp; by Various Artists) *(BNC CD/MC/LP 3)* **TOM WILSON'S COUNCING BEATS VOL.3**	[ ]	[-]
		Steppin' Out	not iss.
May 96.	(c-s/12"/cd-s; as TECHNOCAT 3) *(IAN 044 MC/T/CD)* **IT'S GONNA BE ALRIGHT (mixes)**	[ ]	[-]
		Encore	not iss.
Aug 96.	(12"/cd-s) *(12/CD COR 020)* **IT'S GONNA BE ALRIGHT (mixes)**	[ ]	[-]
		Death Becomes Me	not iss.
Aug 96.	(d-cd/d-c; by Various Artists) *(DBM 2026/2134)* **TOM WILSON PRESENTS TONZ OF TEKNO**	[ ]	[-]
		Fire Island	not iss.
Oct 96.	(lp; by Various Artists) *(1001)* **FIRED**	[ ]	[-]
		Tempo Toons	not iss.
Feb 97.	(d-cd/d-c; by Various Artists) *(TOON CD/MC 102)* **TOM WILSON'S TARTAN TECHNO VOL.2**	[ ]	[-]
		Clubscene	not iss.
Aug 98.	(12"/cd-s; as TOM WILSON & TTF) *(c/dc srt 084)* **U GOT THE PASSION (mixes)**	[ ]	[-]
		React	not iss.
May 99.	(cd-s) *(157)* **PLAYHARD (mixes)**	[ ]	[-]
		Bass City	not iss.
Mar 00.	(12"; as TECHNOCAT) *(BCR 005T)* **TECHNOCAT 2000 (mixes)** *(re-mixed.12" Jul00 as TOM WILSON; BCR 005R)*	[ ]	[-]
		Big	not iss.
Oct 01.	(12") *(BIG 520212)* **TECHNOCAT (mixes)**	[ ]	[-]
		Z.Y.X.	not iss.
Oct 01.	(cd-s) *(ZYX 94768)* **TECHNOCAT (mixes)**	[ ]	[-]

— in Jul'02, TOM WILSON's OLD SKOOL ANTHEMS remixed the V/A double-set, 'Bouncin' Back' for 'Rumour' (CDRAID 550)

WIN (see under ⇒ FIRE ENGINES)

WITNESS (see under ⇒ HIPSWAY)

WOW CAFE (see under ⇒ Play records)

WYOMING (see under ⇒ SUNSET GUN)

Y

YELLOW CAR

Formed: Dundee . . . 1994 by JOEY CHAOS (aka BLAIR KERR), RASHID ABU-RAJAB, GRANT DICKSON and AGENT CAPER. Things looked very bright indeed for the indie-pop quartet when their demo EP, 'PUNK KISS', got them off the mark. Subsequently managed by former ASSOCIATES crooner, BILLY MACKENZIE (also a Dundonian), they inked a deal with 'Gift Of Life', who released a second EP, 'WHY DID YOU GO?' and a debut album, 'AUTO EROTICA' (1996). Sadly, just as things were looking dandy for the lads, MACKENZIE was found dead after committing suicide in his shed. It would take some time for the band to recover from this. A one-off shared EP on German label, 'Community' marked time, they even made a promo-video fitted out in kilts and featuring the ghost of Bonnie Prince Charlie. Guitarist CAPER was replaced by C.C.C. WINDMILL in time for autumn 2000's comeback single, 'BILLY SAID' (on Aberdeen's 'Lithium' imprint); the re-formed YC even supported another, let's say . . . well-known outfit, SIGUE SIGUE SPUTNIK. After eight years of struggling with all kinds of upheavals, YELLOW CAR became KATE's and released the 'ALL OVER NOW' EP in 2002.

RASHID ABU-RAJAB (b.1975) – vocals / **AGENT CAPER** – guitar / **GRANT DICKSON** (b.1976) – bass / **JOEY CHAOS** (b.1974; aka BLAIR KERR) – drums

		Cargo	not iss.
Nov 94.	(cd-ep) *(LINE 3)* **PUNK KISS EP** – Wendy O'Connor / Yellow car / Dundee high.	[ ]	[-]
		Gift Of Life	Gift Of Life
Oct 95.	(7"ep) *(<GOF 45>)* **WHY DID YOU GO? EP** – Why did you go? / Deadend life / Nothing to shout about.	[ ]	[ ] Jul96
Jul 96.	(cd/lp) *(GOF 46 CD/LP)* **AUTO EROTICA** – Why did you go? / Which way now / Drunken rock star / Hold on / Glam queen / Dead end life / Anything tonight / Born to riot / Crazy / F.R.A.D. / Student bastards / Suicide valentine / Can't stop / All over now / Bonus.	[ ]	[-]
		Three Lines	not iss.
Jul 96.	(7"ep) *(006)* **CODE OF SILENCE EP** – That's not enough / Crazy / Why did you go / Suicide valentine.	[ ]	[-]

— **C.C.C. WINDMILL** (b. 1974) – guitars; repl. CAPER

		Community	not iss.
1990's.	(cd-ep; split with BADTOWN BOYS) **split** – Badtown Boys:- Welcome to America / Friction / Little eyes / Dee Dee took the subway / YELLOW CAR: That's not enough / Wendy O'Connor.	[ ]	[-]
		Lithium	not iss.
Oct 00.	(cd-s) *(LITH 009CDS)* **BILLY SAID / SINCE YESTERDAY**	[ ]	[-]

KATE'S

— as they were now known

Jun 02.	(cd-ep) *(LITH 018CDS)* **ALL OVER NOW EP** – All over now (radio edit) / Yellow car / Hold on / All over now.	[ ]	[-]

YELLOW SUNDAYS (see under ⇒ Lithium records)

YESSA DE PASO / LOKI (see ⇒ Section 9: the 90s)

James YORKSTON (& The Athletes)

Born: Kingsbarns, Fife. YORKSTON began his musical explorations at the tender age of eight when he made his own musical entertainment with a pal named MIKE. Influenced by the songwriting talents of such eclectic artists as ANNE BRIGGS and The BHUNDU BOYS, YORKSTON flitted to Edinburgh with his girlfriend (when they were seventeen). He remained a vital part of the city's music scene supporting such acts as BERT JANSCH and JOHN MARTYN (the latter eventually invited him on a 30-date support tour) as well as joining noisekins HUCKLEBERRY.

He eventually left the group ("I was going deaf . . .", he commented) to pursue his own adventures in Hi-Fi, finally accumulating in a demo tape which was passed through industry hands until it landed on the desk of seminal radio DJ John Peel. The man played selected tracks from the tape live on air, which resulted in 'Bad Jazz' issuing the single 'MOVING UP COUNTRY / ROARING THE GOSPEL' (split with Scottish cult hero LONE PIGEON) to critical acclaim. Folky and very hushed, YORKSTON had a lot in common with fellow Scots APPENDIX OUT, with band members FAISAL, REUBEN, DOUGIE, SUN-LI and HOLLY exemplifying the WILL OLDHAM/PALACE factor.

A proper signing with 'Domino' was on the cards, with himself and The ATHLETES issuing seminal 'THE LANG TOUN' single in 2002, complete with a complementary remix by none other than KEIRAN HEBDEN (of FOUR TET). 'ST. PATRICK' was issued months later as a warm-up to his debut set 'MOVING UP COUNTRY' (2002), a placid and very emotive introduction. Contained within were the aforementioned singles as well as a few surprises that thwarted the notion that YORKSTON was just another "Scottish folk singer".

JAMES YORKSTON – vocals, acoustic guitar (ex-HUCKLEBERRY) / **DOUGIE** – bass / **FAISAL** – drums / **RUEBEN** – harmonium, piano / **SUN LI** – violin / **HOLLY** – mandolin, pipes, whistles

		Bad Jazz	not iss.
Oct 00.	(cd-s) **MOVING UP COUNTRY. / ROARING THE GOSPEL**	☐	-
—	also split a single with LONE PIGEON on 'Fence' records		
		Domino	Domino
Mar 02.	(10") *(RUG 136T)* **THE LANG TOUN. / THE LANG TOUN (Four Tet remix)**	☐	-
May 02.	(10") *(RUG 141T)* **ST. PATRICK. / ST. PATRICK (Vitus mix)** (cd-s+=) *(RUG 141CD)* – Catching eyes / Blue Madonna's.	☐	-
Jun 02.	(cd/lp) *(<WIG CD/LP 107>)* **MOVING UP COUNTRY** – In your hands / St. Patrick / Sweet Jesus / Tender to the blues / Moving up country / Cheating the game / I spy dogs / 6:30 is way too early / Patient song / I know my love.	☐	☐
Sep 02.	(10"/cd-s) *(RUG 145 T/CD)* **TENDER TO THE BLUES. /**	☐	-

Malcolm / Angus YOUNG

Born: 6 Jan'53 / 31 Mar'59, (both) Glasgow. Uprooted along with the whole YOUNG clan when they emigrated to Sydney, Australia in 1963, the brothers' rock'n'roll ambitions were fuelled by the numerous groupies hanging around their older brother GEORGE (frontman of the EASYBEATS). ANGUS took the concept of the High School band one step further by appearing on stage in shorts, blazer and school tie as the brothers laid the foundations for heavy rockers AC/DC (trivia fans will be delighted to know that the group name – far from indicating any bi-sexual tendencies – was gleaned from the family hoover!).

A year on from their formation in 1973, the brothers were joined by another ex-pat Caledonian, BON SCOTT. Intitially hired as a roadie cum driver, he quickly became the band's talismanic frontman. After a couple of Australian-only LP's (which sold well on import), AC/DC debuted in the UK with a compilation of their work to date entitled 'HIGH VOLTAGE' (1976). Going from strength to strength with each subsequent album release ('DIRTY DEEDS DONE DIRT CHEAP', 'LET THERE BE ROCK', 'POWERAGE', 'IF YOU WANT BLOOD . . .'), the increasingly unhinged wild men of hard-rock took both Britain and America by storm with 1979's Top 20 set, 'HIGHWAY TO HELL'.

However, events took a tragic turn for the worse in early 1980 as the hard-drinking SCOTT finally met his maker. On the verge of splitting up the band, the brothers and Co were amazed to find a worthy successor in the shape of the BON-fixated, gravel-throated ex-GEORDIE singer, BRIAN JOHNSON. Whether it was due to the publicity surrounding the aforementioned tragedy or the anticipation of how his replacement would perform, AC/DC were resurrected by the unprecedented interest in their "comeback" album. 'BACK IN BLACK' (1980), topped the UK chart and finally established them big time in America where they hit the Top 5.

For the next two decades, the YOUNG brothers remained an intergral part of the well-oiled AC/DC machine; most of their albums hit the Top 10/20 as the band became a headbanging institution.

Richard YOUNGS

Born: early 1970's, England. RICHARD YOUNGS is easily one of the most experimental and prolific artists to have emerged in Scotland during the 90's. His jazzy avant-garde variations of well-crafted and lengthy musical landscapes were first unearthed in 1990 on a self-distributed LP, 'ADVENT'.

From this humble beginning, the singer/songwriter, pianist, multi-instrumentalist went on to collaborate with SIMON WICKHAM-SMITH on over a dozen sets culminating with 1999's WYATT/OLDHAM meets HAMMILL/VAN DER GRAAF offering, 'METALLIC SONATAS'. Prior to this (and not including more collabs with BRIAN LAVELLE), solo RICHARD was at his most creative courtesy of the gorgeous and weepy 'SAPPHIE' (1998). Originally issued for 'Oblique' records, the 37-minute/3-song set saw light of day again in 2000 as his first release for Bloomington, Indiana label, 'Jagjaguwar'.

YOUNGS returned to his Edinburgh stamping ground for New Year 2001 and performed several gigs (on a stool) to promote his umpteenth set, 'MAKING PAPER'. Kicking off with the 19-minute 'WARRIORS' track, it was clear RICHARD's avant-meets-Prog affiliations were heralding the start of something new. This was even clearer come the songsmith's next set, 'MAY' (2002). A desolate, sparse collection of sweet folk songs, YOUNGS knew his practices well, with his NICK DRAKE/NIC JONES-esque beauty mixed in with his avant-guitar doodlings. Very much in the same vein as JIM O'ROURKE and others currently honing their skills in the obscure folk community, YOUNGS managed to add simple poetics into tracks such as 'NEON WINTER' and the, um, gliding 'GLIDING'. Hard to categorise, and hard to get into at first, the listener's lack of patience was quickly polarised by his eclectic arrangements and modest production skills.

RICHARD YOUNGS – piano, vocals, guitar, multi

		No Fans	not iss.
1990.	(lp) *<none>* **ADVENT** – Part I / Part II / Part III. *<(cd-iss. Nov97 on 'Table Of The Elements'; NIOBIUM 41)>*	-	☐
1990.	(d-lp; as RICHARD YOUNGS & SIMON WICKHAM-SMITH) *<none>* **LAKE** – Pt.1:- Lake – Anti-social behaviour – Anti-social behaviour in Iceland / Pt.2:- Let them eat records – Dance: help the ages (give them a heart) / Pt.3:- Chord / Pt.4:- Bells – Redenhall – Goat. *<(cd-iss. Oct00 on 'V.H.F.'; VHF 52)>*	-	☐
—	in 1991, RICHARD featured on A BAND's 'Any Old Records' 7" (later – 1997 – they also released an untitled CD-album). SIMON, RICHARD, A BAND and SALIVATING REGINA issued a 7"EP for 'Baby Huey'.		
		not iss.	Forced Exposure
1992.	(lp; as RICHARD YOUNGS & SIMON WICKHAM-SMITH) **CEAUCESCU**	-	☐
1993.	(lp; as NEIL / RICHARD / SIMON / STEWART) **DURIAN DURIAN**	-	☐
—	in 1993, YOUNGS featured on the ARTEX – A LOT set on 'Siltbreeze'		
1993.	(lp) *<FE 035>* **NEW ANGLOID SOUND**	-	☐
		not iss.	Insample
1994.	(7") *<001>* **ST. HELENA. / JUNIPER**	-	☐
		not iss.	Fourth Dimension
1994.	(7"; as RICHARD YOUNGS & SIMON WICKHAM-SMITH) **WORRIED ABOUT HEAVEN. / MUSCLES IN YOUR HEAD**	-	☐
1995.	(10"ep; as RICHARD YOUNGS & SIMON WICKHAM-SMITH) **444D**	-	☐
		not iss.	Majora
1994.	(lp; as RICHARD YOUNGS & SIMON WICKHAM-SMITH) **ASTHMA & DIABETES**	-	☐

1996. (lp; as RICHARD YOUNGS & SIMON WICKHAM-SMITH) **ENEDKEG** [-] [ ]

not iss. Slask

1994. (cd; as SIMON WICKHAM-SMITH & RICHARD YOUNGS) <*SLACD 008*> **KRETINMUSAK** [-] [ ]
(UK-iss.Jul00; same as US)

not iss. Crank Automotive

1995. (7"; as RICHARD YOUNGS Vs. LEATHER MOLE) **DENNY. / TWECHAR** [-] [ ]

not iss. Ignivomous

1996. (lp; as RICHARD YOUNGS & SIMON WICKHAM-SMITH) **KNISH** [-] [ ]

— next with **NEIL** – synthesizers

not iss. TableOfThe Elements

Jun 96. (cd) <*21*> **FESTIVAL** [-] [ ]
– Alban stands here / Nil a.m. / Angel Petrina Bell / Nathan Rice / The sea is madness.

V.H.F. V.H.F.

Dec 95. (lp; as RICHARD YOUNGS & MATTHEW BOWER) <*VHF 20*> **SITE – REALM** [-] [ ]

Apr 96. (cd; as STEPHEN TODD & RICHARD YOUNGS) <*VHF 22*> **GEORGIANS** [-] [ ]
– Bananas 'n' muffins / Granite eye / Sixteen OO / Higher grit / Lady of Staines / Techno won ton / Hannibal / Perranuthroe / Berry.

Mar 97. (cd; as RICHARD YOUNGS & SIMON WICKHAM-SMITH) <*(VHF 27)*> **RED AND BLUE BEAR: OPERA** [ ] [ ]
– 3 parts.

— in 1997/8, YOUNGS and WICKHAM-SMITH also issued 'VEIL (FOR GREG)' on 'Insignificant' imprint, plus a 7" 'THE ENIGMA OF ROTONS' for 'Hell's Half Halo'.

Apr 98. (cd; as RICHARD YOUNGS & SIMON WICKHAM-SMITH) <*(VHF 35)*> **PULSE OF THE ROOSTERS** [ ] [ ]
– On a bus / Shanti deva / Up a tree / My 4-sleeve hairshirt / By the sea / Learners.

— in 1998, YOUNGS featured on ILK's CD-set 'ZENITH' for 'No Fans'

1998. (cd) <*007*> **HOUSE MUSIC** [-] [ ]

— <above iss. on 'Meme'>

Feb 99. (cd; as RICHARD YOUNGS & SIMON WICKHAM-SMITH) <*(VHF 40)*> **METALLIC SONATAS** [ ] [ ]
– Metallic sonatas (nos.1-15).

Jagjaguwar Jagjaguwar

Jul 00. (cd) <*(JAG 19)*> **SAPPHIE** <rec.1998 for 'Oblique'> [ ] [ ]
– Soon it will be fire / A fullness of light in your soul / The graze of days.

Feb 01. (m-cd) <*(JAG 26)*> **MAKING PAPER** [ ] [ ]
– Warriors / The world is silence in your head / Only haligonian.

— note: too, that RICHARD appeared on a plethora of V/A sets/EP's

Mar 02. (cd) <*(JAG 43CD)*> **MAY** [ ] [ ]
– Neon winter / Bloom of all / Trees that fall / Wynding hills of Maine / Gilding / Wynd time wynd.

BRIAN LAVELLE & RICHARD YOUNGS

— **BRIAN** – guitars, keyboards

Freek Freek

Mar 96. (cd) <*FRR 018*> **RADIOS** [-] [ ]
– It and distribution . . . / Monstrously, in process . . . / Molecular field physicist . . . / Our thin processes . . . / Description level of forces that meagre alphabet B / That meagre alphabet B / Alphabet B / B.

Aug 96. (cd) <*FRR 023*> **RADIOS 2** [-] [ ]
– Beach / Coded Easter Cork completes visiting arrival / Rhymie has / Attractions: Place: Oval: Hock / Halls (0141) buildings / Meadow and price underground trails / Wedged prior every date / Monument / Protection courses / Estuary in 3190.

Jun 98. (3xcd-set) <*(FRR 028)*> **RADIOS 345** [ ] [ ]

YUL-PETER (see under ⇒ WILDERNESS CHILDREN)

YUMMY FUR

Formed: Glasgow . . . 1994 by LAWRENCE, MARK, BRIAN and JOHN McKEOWN; the sound of young Scotland a decade or so on from the 'Postcard' era. The YUMMY FUR took off in their frantic world of Sci-Fi pop (KRAFTWERK meeting ENO/ROXY MUSIC comes to mind) via the excellent Peel/Lamacq fave, 'THUS, A POLITICAL RECORD' single/EP.

Moving from Newcastle-based 'Slampt Underground' to London's 'Guided Missile', the quirky quartet issued the excellent follow-up 45, 'KODAK NANCY EUROPE' in 1995, while a third label, the Glasgow-run 'Vesuvius' also had the YUMMY's on their books. Choosing to write 1-minute bites instead of the more conventional 2-3 minute tracks, the prolific group delivered a succession of singles and a handful of albums including three for 'Guided . . .', 'NIGHT CLUB' (1996), the 60-track(!) 'KINKY CINEMA' (1997) and 'SEXY WORLD' (1998). Meanwhile, 'Vesuvius' also got into the game by releasing the mini-set, 'MALE SHADOW AT 3 O'CLOCK', arguably their best work to date under one fur-lined roof.

Towards the end of '98, they had become a bit more electronic and even shared a single with THE KARELIA, EL HOMBRE TRAJEADO and MOGWAI; one of the band is now in ska-Punks the AMPHETAMEANIES.

MARK / BRIAN / LAWRENCE / JOHN McKEOWN

Slampt Underground not iss.

Feb 95. (7"ep) *(SLAMPT 27)* **THUS, A POLITICAL RECORD** [ ] [-]
– Goosebump / + 9

Guided Missile not iss.

Jul 95. (7") *(GUIDE 003)* **KODAK NANCY EUROPE. /** [ ] [-]

Sep 96. (cd) *(GUIDE 10CD)* **NIGHT CLUB** [ ] [-]
– Plastic cowboy / Prole birthday / Kirsty Cooper / Theme from Ultrabra / Films / Chelovek / Republic of Salo / Rollerderby / Theoretically pink / Kodak Nancy Europe / Carry on nurse / I am a 'cosmetic man' / Roxy girls / Klaxxon education film / Exact copy of H. Friendly / Sergeant jumper / Chines bookie. *(lp-iss.on 'Slampt Underground'; SLAMPT 43)*

Dec 96. (7") *(GUIDE 12)* **PLASTIC COWBOY. / FLAPPY CLOWN DISCO** [ ] [-]

Jan 97. (7") *(POMP 008)* **SUPERMARKET. /** [ ] [-]
(above on 'Vesuvius')

Mar 97. (7") *(GUIDE 13)* **POLICEMAN. / 70'S CAR CRASH** [ ] [-]

Sep 97. (7") *(ROX 001)* **STEREO GIRLS. / ALWAYS CRASHING IN THE SAME CAR** [ ] [-]
(above issued on 'Roxy' label)

Sep 97. (cd) *(GUIDE 22CD)* **KINKY CINEMA** [ ] [-]
– Documentary of a kid / Amelia Scoptophilia / The replica / Xplosion / Tracy Katz / Car park / Male slut / Everything's turning to plastic / British sounds / The Candy Darling show / Goosebump / Frankenstein a go-go / Mondo coyote / Ice cream van / British children on smack / Hong Kong in stereo / Independent pop song / Popcorn / The Walt Disney murder club / 90's / Shrinky-dinc / Cosmonauts and carbonauts / Gimme cigarettes / Policemanoid / The optical meat dress / Gimmick / Pop art documentary / Found a girlfriend / Plastic cowboy (new wave) / Father Ubu repents / Vanilla Minelli / Fiery Jack / Car smash / Kodak Nancy Euro '96 / I am consumer man / The dummy / Liliput / Monophonic yum yum / Flappy clown Garry / Prostitutes / Cabaret punks / Escape from Oz / Mao Tse-Tung / Eyeball popping madness / Yummy Fur vs The Stooges / The monotony song / The yummy tummy / Bugs Bunny / Pink pop girls / Discord / Shaggy / Amphetamine education movie / Our peppermint scene / Candy Clark / Super 8 recording / Actress / Theoretically blue / Saturday night Mo-Mo / Phoning the Fundus / Brian at the gates of dawn.

Feb 98. (m-lp/m-cd) *(POMP 012/+CD)* **MALE SHADOW AT 3 O'CLOCK** [ ] [-]
– St. John of the cross / Catholic / Department / Colonel Blimp / The Canadian flag / Vacuum cleaner.
(above issued on 'Vesuvius')

Jun 98. (7") *(SHaG 13.08)* **Club Beatroot Part Eight** [ ] [-]
– ? / (other track by OLYMPIA)
(above in conjunction with 'Flotsam & Jetsam' & 'The 13th Note')

Jun 98. (ltd-7") *(GUIDE 29)* **SHOOT THE RIDICULANT. / SHOOT THE RIDICULANT (pt.2)** [ ] [-]

Nov 98. (cd/lp) *(GUIDE 32 CD/LP)* **SEXY WORLD** [ ] [-]
– Sexy world / Playboy Japan (1971) / In the company of women / British eyeballs Ltd. / Cryptdang / Analogue people / 50 million bees / Deathclub / Fantastic legs / 801 / The ballad of Piggy Wings / Young pop things / Shoot the ridiculent.

— also in Nov'98, the track 'SHIVERS' featured on the 'GLASGOW' V/A EP along with EL HOMBRE TRAJEADO, MOGWAI and the KARELIA

Z

ZEPHYRS

Formed: Edinburgh . . . late 1999 by the NICOL brothers STUART and DAVID, one-time partners in the LARRY MARSHALL FANCLUB, DOLLFUSS and INDIAN INK; DAVID was also a member of 'Narodnik' outfit, the VULTURES. With moonlighters SHALEPH O'NEILL (the PIGPEN guitarist) and drummer ROBIN JONES (from THE BETA BAND), The ZEPHYRS (taking their name from the revolutionary skateboarding team from the '70's) blew in from the East to play some local live sets. Early the following year, the brothers were joined by former POLICECAT, GORDON KILGOUR, the drummer duly augmenting the trio's studio sound for their debut set, 'IT'S OKAY NOT TO SAY ANYTHING' (2000).

A celebratory live outing at the Tron – featuring MOGWAI's STUART BRAITHWAITE as guest DJ – saw The ZEPHYRS merge with JONATHAN KILGOUR (DAVID's twin), who had also set himself free from POLICECAT. A much sought-after cassette including their best-known track, 'STARGAZER', was given away to fans at the door, while subsequent tours with 'Evol' stablemates, I AM SCIENTIST, followed on that April. The aforementioned album was mostly recorded at a substation in Cowdenbeath(!), that 4-track sound working wonders on numbers such as opener 'I CAME FOR THAT'. Further session work for BBC Scotland that same April, saw the band premiere three new songs, 'MOUNT MISERY', 'SETTING SUN' and a version of the Mongers' 'LONG'.

With new members STUART CAMPBELL and Bristol-born Edinburgh Uni student CAROLINE BARBER, the 6-piece ZEPHYRS re-surfaced on vinyl once again, this time with a new version of 'STARGAZER', recorded for MOGWAI's 'Rock Action' imprint. Largely overlooked by the British music press (if not the King-Tut's crowd), The ZEPHYRS bounded back with the astonishing 'WHEN THE SKY COMES DOWN IT COMES DOWN ON YOUR HEAD' (2001), a lush country-tinged ode to GRAM PARSONS and LOW, which featured guests ranging from MOJAVE 3, STEREOLAB and some time ARAB STRAP collaborator ADEL BETHEL (whose sweetened larynx made the track 'MODERN BEATS' even more poignant). Other standout tracks 'SETTING SUN' and 'PAINT YOUR HOUSE' redefined Scottish country, with its immaculate blend of wispy folk-electronica and laid-back, front-porch beats. Move over LAMBCHOP, GIANT SAND et al, there's a new kind of country in town.

STUART NICOL (b.1972, Currie, Edinburgh) – guitar, vocals / **DAVID NICOL** (b.1968, Currie) – bass, keyboards (ex-VULTURES) / **JONATHAN KILGOUR** (b.21 Oct'68, Glasgow) – vocals, guitar, squeezebox (ex-POLICECAT, ex-ROYAL BRONCO, ex-PASTELS) / **GORDON KILGOUR** (b.21 Oct'68, Glasgow) – drums, guitar, vocals (ex-POLICECAT, ex-ROYAL BRONCO, ex-MONGERS) / **STEWART CAMPBELL** (b.1974, Glasgow) – harmonica, keyboards / **CAROLINE BARBER** (b.1979, Bristol) – cello, keyboards

Evol / Evol

Mar 00. (cd) *(<evol 10>)* **IT'S OKAY NOT TO SAY ANYTHING** ☐ ☐
– I came for that / The most revealing hymn / In your arms / Go-go bar / Tork – Dolphin Avenue / The first guitar / Jewish hotel / ABC / Obeyesssekere / Sunglasses – Cathedral. *(re-iss. Dec00; same)*

Mar 00. (c; ltd-freebie) *(<evol 11>)* **001 TO 100** - -
– Urges / Stargazer / Carpentry.

Rock Action / not iss.

Nov 00. (7"/cd-s) *(ROCKACT/+CD 6)* **STARGAZER. / URGES** ☐ -

Southpaw / not iss.

Sep 01. (lp/cd) *(PAW/+CD 002)* **WHEN THE SKY COMES DOWN IT COMES DOWN ON YOUR HEAD** ☐ -
– The buildings aren't going anywhere / Modern beats / Mount misery / Setting sun / The green tree / Paint your house / Murder of a small man / Stargazer / Ballad of the green tree.

Acuarela / not iss.

Jul 02. (cd-ep) *(24)* **THE LOVE THAT WILL GUIDE YOU BACK HOME** ☐ -
– The love that will guide you back home / Carpentry / Obeyessekere / I came for that (Stuart Braithwaite remix).

ZIPS (see ⇒ Section 9: wee post-Punk groups)

ZONES (see under ⇒ SLIK)

record labels

Academy Street records (see under ⇒ Clubscene records)

Accessory records (see under ⇒ Fast Product records)

Alphabetty records

Founded: 192/B King Street, Aberdeen, AB24 5BH. Initiated from the unlikely environs of ADIE NUNN's local abode in early 2000, this fledgling label signed up the likes of PURPLE MUNKIE (see below), Canada's CARNATIONS, NERO (see below), EDDIE SPEED & THE GARAGE BOMBSHELLS, HEADBOARD, 1" VOLCANO and Sunderland's MAVIS. Given that Alphabetty is still in its infancy, only four singles have made it so far to the release stage and the label's self-distribution means it's easier to acquire their wares via mail order.

Stop press:– on the 27th of July 2002 the label ceased to be. RIP www.alphabetty.co.uk

– discography –

- **PURPLE MUNKIE** were formed along the road in Elgin (c.1997) by rawkers ALAN SOUTER (vocals & guitar) and CHUCK (drums), apparently in their garage. Subsequently joined by JIM (guitar) and JAMES (bass), the evolving PURPLE MUNKIE were ready to go to town (well, Aberdeen at least!). In fact it was the cities of Glasgow and London that the "punkie" quartet headed to, playing sporadic gigs while recording their debut EP, 'BALLS', in summer 2000. Followed quickly by the 'FISTY' EP, the band also delivered recordings for those lovely mp3 people and featured on a 'Fierce Panda' V/A double-7" compilation, 'Cheffing And Blinding' providing the under-a-minute ditty, 'TWO BRASS CAMELS'.

Jul 00. (7"ep) *(msf 1)* **Balls EP**
– Shut up and leave me alone / Queens of / Close enough to touch / Is it me or is it hot in here.

Nov 01. (cd-ep) *(msf 3)* **Fisty EP**
– Slightly out of reach / Never sit down with your back to the cupboard / Standoffish / Ties undone.

- **NERO** were formed by ALAN SOUTER (vocals & guitar), DAVE STEPHEN (vocals & guitar), ANDY PIRIE (vocals & bass) and STEVE LAMB (drums). If you like your Punk endearingly DIY and rough around the edges, these peppy BUZZCOCKS-esque Aberdonians are just the ticket to annoy your parents and quite possibly your dog as well. So far, their only vinyl offering has been a shared effort with Canadians, The CARNATIONS, although they've enjoyed national airplay on Radio Scotland's alternative institution, Beat Patrol.

Sep 00. (7"ep) *(msf 2) the CARNATIONS* & **NERO – split**
– the CARNATIONS – Scream & yell / Sundays / NERO – Ooh ahh ahh / Oak / Skin & bones.

- **1" VOLCANO** are from the Dundee area and in January 2001 consisted of JOHN PARKIN (vocals & guitar) – ex-SPLILINSKI, DOUG McKAY (guitar) – ex-ON NOBLE, ex-TROPICAL MEDICINES, ex-INFERNAL, GRAEME FIELD (drums) – ex-VENKMAN, ex-THROB, and LEE HAMILTON (bass). Angular, rawk-ish and loud, their inspiration came from PIXIES, QUEENS OF THE STONE AGE and SOUNDGARDEN, 1" VOLCANO – who've now performed two years running at T In The Park – displayed their wares on their split 7" with England's MAVIS. However, by this time, STUART GILLIES (from YESSA DE PASO, also ex-MAGNETIC NORTH POLE) was present replacing LEE; in May '02, newcomer MARTY had seen off STUART.

May 02. (7"ep) *(msf 4) MAVIS* / **1" VOLCANO – split**
– MAVIS – Valentine / Brighest stars in Yorkshire / 1" VOLCANO – Ants / Medicine.

Andmoresound records

Founded: Glasgow (PO Box 16103, G11 7YA) . . . spring 1997. Three bands have appeared on the imprint, MAC MEDA, CAMERA OBSCURA (see own entry) and the newest TACOMA RADAR. MAC MEDA were formed in and around Glasgow c.1996 by four indie-pop youngsters into Californian teenage surfer gangs of the 60's from which they took their unusual moniker. The following year, this initially mysterious bunch finally delivered their debut 45, 'MY FAVOURITE TRASHCAN', backed by 'HOW DELICATE', their tribute to the hard drinking actor Richard Harris. A whole year later and a long-awaited follow-up, 'THE TENTH OF ALWAYS' (a Melody Maker SOTW) was in the shops, its B-side 'MICHIGAN 400' was apparently about Indy racing cars/drivers – this was another way to be an "indie" band, me thinks. However, little was subsequently heard from the band, although one track, 'COLETTE'S CAT', did surface on an Italian V/A compilation. Newest signings, TACOMA RADAR, were also from Glasgow and sounded like a darker country cousin of LOW, YO LA TENGO or BROADCAST.

– discography –

Sep 97. (7") *(and 08 45)* **MAC MEDA – My Favourite Trashcan / How Delicate**
Mar 98. (7") *(and 09 45)* **CAMERA OBSCURA – Park And Ride**
Aug 98. (7") *(and 10 45)* **MAC MEDA – The Tenth Of Always / Michigan 400**
Dec 98. (7"/cd-s) *(and 11 45/cds)* **CAMERA OBSCURA – Your Sound**
Mar 99. (T-shirt) *(and 12t)* **Camera Obscura – girl with cine camera**
Apr 99. (T-shirt) *(and 13t)* **Andmoresound – cowboy**
Feb 00. (7"/cd-s) *(and 14 45/cds)* **TACOMA RADAR – Tuckahoe / It's getting dark / Radar Contact**
(below are due for release next months or so . . .)
Jun 01. (7"/cd-s) *(and 15 45/cds)* **TACOMA RADAR – Pilot House / Some Things Last A Long Time / Who's Gonna Hold The Line**
Jul 01. (7"/cd-s) *(and 16 45/cds)* **CAMERA OBSCURA – Eighties Fan**
Nov 01. (lp/cd) *(and 17 33/cd)* **CAMERA OBSCURA – Biggest Bluest Hi Fi**

Avalanche records (inc. Alva)

Founded: by KEVIN BUCKLE, c/o Nicolson Street, Edinburgh . . . late 80's when cult imprint '53rd & 3rd' bit the dust. Mainly a new and used independent record shop helping young local bands to get a foot up, 'Avalanche' signed the likes of The SHOP ASSISTANTS, JESSE GARON & THE DESPERADOES and even BMX BANDITS before becoming 'Alva' records (who were based at 21a Alva Street, Edinburgh, EH2 4PS). Avalanche have currently four shops in the capital and one in Glasgow. www.avalancherecords.co.uk

– discography –

Jan 90. (7"/7"s/12"/cd-s) *(AGAP 001/+B/T/CD)* **SHOP ASSISTANTS – Here She Comes**
Mar 90. (cd/lp) *(ONLY CD/LP 001)* **JESSE GARON & THE DESPERADOES – Nixon**
Apr 90. (7"/12") *(AGAP 002/+T) 13 FIRST FRIDAYS – 88 Lines About 44 Women / Things You Left Behind / ('A'-20 Line remix)* (this outfit were from California)
May 90. (7"/c-s/12"/cd-d) *(AGAP 003/+MC/T/CD)* **SHOP ASSISTANTS – Big E Power**
Aug 90. (lp) *(ONLYLP 004)* **JESSE GARON & THE DESPERADOES – A Cabinet Full Of Curiosities**
Oct 90. (12"ep) *(AGAP 004T)* **JESSE GARON & THE DESPERADOES – Hold Ne Now EP**

- **RIVERHEAD** were based in Edinburgh from the early 90's by a Scotsman from Auchtermuchty DAVID SCOTT, two Englishmen from Liverpool and Derby respectively ROD WHITE and MICHAEL DORAN, and, one from Georgia, USA, RICHARD CONTE. After one single, 'ALPHARETTA', they moved to the bargain basement offshoot, 'Alva' (their second 45 sold for 25p!) and only once more dipped their big ugly toes into the musical water.

Nov 90. (12"ep) *(AGAP 005T) RIVERHEAD – Alpharetta*
– Looking at the sky / She can / Strange / My turn.

- **GARGLEBLUD** were given their own catalogue number by the label. Influenced by The DAMNED (they even covered 'NEAT, NEAT, NEAT'), JOHN DOE on vocals, MIKIE and ARTHUR on guitars, COCO on bass and WULLIE on drums (was this the man who helped out EXTERNAL MENACE?), the 5-piece punkabilly outfit were fortunate enough to release one mini-lp.

Oct 90. (m-lp) *(BLUD 001)* **GARGLEBLUD – Howlinyowlinscreaminmess**
– Death fuck / Priest of death / Love in asylum / Jaws / Neat, neat, neat / Berserker / Souleater / Contrictor.

Dec 90. (lp) *(ONLYLP 006)* **Various Artists – 53rd & 3rd: Fun While It Lasted** *(cd-iss. later; ONLYCD 006)*
Dec 90. (cd/lp) *(ONLY CD/LP 007)* **BMX BANDITS – Totally Groovy Live Experience**
Mar 91. (12"ep) *(AGAP 008T)* **WE FREE KINGS – Howl And Other Songs**
Jun 92. (cd/lp) *(ONLY CD/LP 013)* **VASELINES – All The Stuff And More . . .**

1998. (m-cd/m-c) *(ONLY CD/LP 014)* **GROOVY LITTLE NUMBERS – The 53rd & 3rd Singles**
2000. (cd) *(ONLYCD 016)* **Various Artists – Agarr Retro: Fun While It Lasted Part II**
— others also by BMX BANDITS, VASELINES and GROOVY LITTLE NUMBERS

- Alva records -

Nov 91. (12"ep) *(AVA 001) RIVERHEAD – Haddit EP*
– Seems so real / Manhoodtrip / Thousand times blind / Simple.
1992. (12"ep) *(AVA 002)* **JOYRIDERS – King Of Gasoline EP**
Oct 92. (7";one-sided) *RIVERHEAD – Was Away*

- The **PRALINES** (pronounced "prayleens" – as it stated on their one and only recording) were NEIL BROWNLEE – vocals, guitar / CAMPBELL BRADY – guitar, vocals / COLIN SMITH – bass / JOHN LUNN – drums.

1991. (12") *(ALVA 003)* **PRALINES – pronounced "prayleens"**
– Trains Brams / Happy blue Maundy.

Bellboy records (see under ⇒ Hook records)

Bomba records (see under ⇒ Limbo records)

Bosque records

Founded: 25 Eyre Place, Edinburgh, EH3 5EX, by former GILA MONSTER (previously produced by Jamie Watson) members TOM WORTHINGTON and MARK. Having abandoned this monstrous project after only one 1994 single/EP, '165hz ALL OVER' (BET 14), the pair became STARSTRUCK alongside the so-called Big Riggers, i.e. LAWRENCE, ALEC and NICKY. After releasing a couple of long-playing cassettes (one of which stretched to 37 tracks), the experimental Glam-Punk troupers finally issued their first slice of vinyl with the 3 and a half(!) track EP, 'FONDLED ORANGE'; PHILLIPA from DICK JOHNSON guested on cheap organ. Before the band went on to scale the heights of Glasgow's 'Vesuvius', they signed off with an 8-track cartridge (effectively useless unless you've recently raided a second-hand shop); up to that point, STARSTRUCK's biggest claim to fame was having played five gigs in as many years. Also part of the Bosque posse at this time were the mysterious HEEHAW, an outfit that might well have had some connection to STARSTRUCK; the THREE WISE MEN were another obscure act of the era bearing gifts of noise and wisdom via their split effort with TROUT. Edinburgh's DOMINIC WAXING LYRICAL had been on the go since '94 and consisted of DOMINIC HARRIS (vocals, guitar), JOEY SANDERSON (bass, cello, piano, falsetto), TOM BANCROFT (drums) and RUBY WORTH (dancer). Shortly before their Bosque debut, 'CHANGE', DWL issued an eponymous LP for 'Neptunes'; (LPPIE 020). By this juncture, the label had shifted operations along the M8 to Glasgow (p.o.box 16069, Glasgow, G12 8JY, to be exact) where the bulk of the roster was based. In fact, Bosque were now on their 23rd release which arrived courtesy of new signing GILDED LIL and their charmingly titled 'Motherfucker Of Calcutta', Theresa would not be amused. Leaving the indie-rock at home for once, the label got all tribal via a split single with Edinburgh collective, The SATIVA DRUMMERS and funky rockers ROCKA RAGNAROCK. By the end of 2000, Bosque had come a long way from the days when their wilfully amateurish 7" packaging was more annoying than creative.

- discography -

1994. (12"ep) *(bosc 005)* **HEEHAW – WrigglEP**
– (5 track)
1994. (c) *(bosc 006)* **STARSTRUCK – It's Fun, It's Easy, It's You!**
– (37 track . . .)
1994. (c) *(bosc 007)* **STARSTRUCK – R Cool**
Nov 94. (c) *(bosc 008)* **Various Artists – Humpy Bosque**
– (17 track compilation)
Jan 95. (c-s) *(bosc 009)* **STARSTRUCK – R Sleepy**
Mar 95. (7"orange-ep) *(bosc 010)* **STARSTRUCK – Fondled Orange EP**
– Fondled orange / Back to yr school / Wound up boy / Give the drummer some (more).
1995. (8-track cartridge!) *(bosc 011)* **STARSTRUCK – oo (infinity)**
1995. (c) *(bosc 014)* **HEEHAW – The Death Of Heehaw**
– (A sides & grim B-sides)
Nov 96. (7"ep) *(bosc 020)* **THREE WISE MEN – Skunk Rap / UFO / (other two by TROUT and licenced from 'Rock Action' records RAR 003)**
Jan 97. (7"m) *(bosc 021)* **DOMINIC WAXING LYRICAL – Change / Colonial / Googoo Gaagaa**
Jun 97. (7"ep) *(bosc 023)* **GILDED LIL – Motherfucker Of Calcutta EP**
Feb 98. (10") *(bosc 024)* **SATIVA DRUMMERS – Project Work / ROCKA RAGNAROCK – Matchbox / Pleasure Centre Of My Mind**
Feb 98. (cd-ep) *(bosc 025)* **DOMINIC WAXING LYRICAL – Whipping Boy EP**
Mar 98. (7"ep) *(bosc 026)* **GILDED LIL – Wang EP**
Nov 00. (cd/lp) *(bosc 028 cd/lp)* **GILDED LIL – Corpus Delecti**

Bronx Cheer records

Founded: Glasgow, G12 8NS (PO Box 13) by a guy called JIM SPENCE (leader of the Grease Monkeys), who was undoubtably influenced by garage and gutter punk. Sick puppies The SOCIAL LEPERS – ie, BONER DELUXE on vocals, JONNY GASH on guitar, CLARK KUNT on base, SNOTTERS on drums, and recent addition SAWN OFF on guitar – were described as hate-core (like the DWARVES), while The GRISLY GHOSTS OF GUY were snarling 3-chord wonders. JIM subsequently sub-licensed and issued limited edition 7"s by US acts The QUADRAJETS, The DEMONICS, SPEEDEALER and MONKEYWRENCH. Back in Glasgow, TORQAMADA (featuring Jonny on base) were fusing elements of VENOM, MISFITS and BLACK FLAG and getting a high energy coup d'tat of noisy metal-punk.

- discography -

1999. (7"ep) *(1,000,001 BC)* **SOCIAL LEPERS – One For The Ladies EP**
1999. (7"ep) *(1,000,002 BC)* **GRISLY GHOSTS OF GUY – I Am The Hunted EP**
Dec 99. (7") *(1,000,003 BC) QUADRAJETS – All My Rowdy Friends Are Dead*
May 00. (7") *(1,000,004 BC) DEMONICS – She Devils On Wheels*
Apr 01. (7"ep) *(2,000,001 BC) SPEEDEALER /* **SOCIAL LEPERS – The Transatlantic Speed Trials**
– (2 by SPEEDEALER) // Drugstore Raid / Idjut Midget.
Feb 02. (7") *(3,000,001 BC)* **TORQAMADA – SHOUT WITH THE DEVIL**
– Evil possessor / Mattress mejesty.
May 02. (7") *(3,000,002 BC) MONKEYWRENCH – Levitation / IMMORTAL LEE COUNTY – Goin' Down South*
Sep 02. (cd) *(4,000,000 CD)* **GREASE MONKEYS – Grease Blast!**

Chemikal Underground records

Founded: Glasgow . . . 1994 by DELGADOS members ALUN WOODWARD, EMMA POLLOCK, STEWART HENDERSON and PAUL SAVAGE. Barely out of their teens (and university), the troupe of bonafide indie instigators decided, after many rejection letters, that it would be easier for a struggling band to issue their own records. Hence the birth of Chemikal Underground records, Scotland's rising label that boasted a bulging back catalogue of unsung talent and minor gems to boot.

Beginning in an empty kitchen somewhere in Glasgow, the DELGADOS issued their debut 1995 single, 'Monica Webster', earning the prestigious Single Of The Week in Melody Maker. BIS, a three-piece pop-punk outfit from Glasgow approached The DELGADOS that year and insisted CU put out their 'Disco Nation', a hybrid collection of skewed disco with shouty lyrics and ubiquitous guitars. Although the EP failed to generate the single-handed buzz which accompanied the DELGADOS' evolutionary release, BIS were to become the label's first big success come the eve of their 'Secret Vampire Soundtrack' release. Not only did the track 'Kandy Pop' dominate the airwaves for months on end, but the squeaky trio had a live spot on Top Of The Pops which catapulted 'Secret Vampire . . .' into the Top 30. This was perhaps beyond Chem's initial expectations; from indie meisters to indie chart-topping pioneers, the group hadn't even moved out of their kitchen(!).

Funds from the record enabled the company to sign bigger acts, while BIS, dubbed as future starlings by the press, set out on a recording crusade with 'Wiiija', finally moving onto the BEASTIE BOYS' recently established imprint 'Grand Royal'. CHEM's next two hopes were New York groovers CHA CHA COHEN and Falkirk miserablists ARAB STRAB. The latter signed a two-album deal with the prolific imprint in the Spring of 1996 and issued their introductory single, 'The First Big Weekend', the following summer. The track, which captured the essence of summer eloquently, became regarded by DJ's PEEL and LAMACQ as the decade's finest single. ARAB STRAP's queasy, dimly remembered weekend on the piss was subsequently snapped up by Guinness, who used the track for their 'Statistics' ad to much effect. AIDAN MOFFAT, lead vocalist/crooner of the outfit was scheduled to narrate the advert, but his strong Scots accent paled in comparison to the English bloke from 'Spitting Image'(!) The 'STRAP's debut album, 'THE WEEKEND NEVER STARTS AROUND HERE', followed, with some hailing it as Trainspotting on vinyl, and others dismissing it as depressing nonsense from a dying bedsit era. The DELGADOS, on the other hand, issued the light, melodic and well-received album 'DOMESTIQUES' around the same time and flitted from their humble kitchen beginnings, to a lush office building in Glasgow's West End.

Recruitment continued: MAGOO, the psychedelic pop band from Norwich issued the striking LP, 'The Soteramic Sounds Of Magoo' (1997), and MOGWAI, perhaps Chem's most pivotal signing unfetted the '4 SATIN' EP and the highly regarded album 'YOUNG TEAM'. Meanwhile ARAB STRAP were busy on their sophomore for the label, the poetic 'Philophobia' (1998), which preceded the excellent EP 'HERE WE GO' / 'TRIPPY'. The DELGADOS were also at work on their second album, 'Peloton' (1998), which spawned the singles 'Everything Goes Around The Water' and 'Pull The Wires From The Walls'. The imprint set up by an inspiring indie group was churning out some of Scotland's finest new music faster than you could say "Jimmy Krankie's Greatest Hits": MOGWAI's unflawed 'No Education = No Future (Fuck The Curfew)' earned them a support slot with Brit-rock champions The MANIC STREET PREACHERS, while ARAB STRAP had succumbed to major label temptation when they signed to 'Go Beat' at the end of '98. CHA CHA COHEN were enjoying much fetted column inches for their eponymous debut album, while Californian softcore minimalists The RADAR BROS were quickly drafted in.

MOGWAI, however, were destined to make the label's most crucial album, and unleashed their reign of terror with the uncompromising 'Come On Die Young' (1999) along with a factory-line of T-shirts plotting BLUR's demise. 'The Singing Hatchet' (1999) was the second album from troubled group The RADAR BROS, and perhaps Chem's softest. It resurrected the trio's career, reinstating them as "the best band you've never heard" – well, we think so. Along with new signings, SUCKLE, INTERPOL (from NY) and AEREOGRAMME, The DELGADOS' homegrown label has put Scottish music on the map . . . and way beyond. The founding group delivered 'The Great Eastern' in 2000, and welcomed back the prodigal ARAB STRAP, who unveiled their fourth album 'RED THREAD' in Spring 2001.

– discography –

Jul 95. (7") *(Chem 001)* **DELGADOS – Monica Webster**
Aug 95. (7") *(Chem 002)* **BIS – Disco Nation**
Mar 96. (7"ep/cd-ep) *(Chem 003/+cd)* **BIS – The Secret Vampire Soundtrack**
Mar 96. (7"ep/cd-ep) *(Chem 004/+cd)* **DELGADOS – Cinecentre**
Jul 96. (7"ep) *(Chem 005) CHA CHA COHEN – 538*
Aug 96. (7"ep/cd-ep) *(Chem 006/+cd)* **DELGADOS – Under Canvas**
Sep 96. (7") *(Chem 007)* **ARAB STRAP – The First Big Weekend**
Oct 96. (7"ep/cd-ep) *(Chem 008/+cd)* **DELGADOS – Sucrose**
Nov 96. (lp/cd) *(Chem 009/+cd)* **DELGADOS – Domestiques**
Nov 96. (lp/cd) *(Chem 010/+cd)* **ARAB STRAP – The Week Never Starts Round Here**
Mar 97. (7"ep/cd-ep) *(Chem 011/+cd) MAGOO – A To Z And Back Again*
Apr 97. (lp/cd) *(Chem 012/+cd) MAGOO – The Soateramic Sounds Of Magoo*
Mar 97. (12"/cd-s) *(Chem 013/+cd)* **ARAB STRAP – The Clearing**
May 97. (12"ep/cd-ep) *(Chem 014/+cd) CHA CHA COHEN – Spook On The High Lawn*
May 97. (12"ep/cd-ep) *(Chem 015/+cd)* **MOGWAI – 4 Satin**
Jun 97. (7"ep/cd-ep) *(Chem 016/+cd) MAGOO – Red Lines (Are Fine)*
Sep 97. (12"ep/cd-ep) *(Chem 017/+cd)* **ARAB STRAP – The Girls Of Summer**
Oct 97. (cd/d-lp) *(Chem 018 cd/lp)* **MOGWAI – Mogwai Young Team**
-. (-) *(Chem 019)* **Chemikal Underground studio**
Mar 98. (10"/cd-s) *(Chem 020/+cd)* **ARAB STRAP – Here We Go**
Apr 98. (cd) *(Chem 021cd)* **ARAB STRAP – Philophobia**
Mar 98. (7"/cd-s) *(Chem 022/+cd)* **DELGADOS – Everything Goes Around The Water**
May 98. (7"/cd-s) *(Chem 023/+cd)* **DELGADOS – Pull The Wires From The Wall**
Jun 98. (cd) *(Chem 024)* **DELGADOS – Peloton**
Jun 98. (7"ep/cd-ep) *(Chem 025/+cd) MAGOO – Holy Smoke*
Jun 98. (12"ep/cd-ep) *(Chem 026/+cd)* **MOGWAI – No Education = No Future (Fuck The Curfew)**
Sep 98. (7"/12"/cd-s) *(Chem 27/+t/cd)* **ARAB STRAP – (Afternoon) Soaps**
Sep 98. (7"ep/cd-ep) *(Chem 028/+cd) MAGOO – Swiss Border Escape*
Sep 98. (7"/cd-s) *(Chem 029/+cd)* **DELGADOS – The Weaker Argument Defeats The Stronger**
Nov 98. (cd/lp) *(Chem 030 cd/lp) MAGOO – Vote The Pacifist Ticket Today*
Oct 98. (7"/cd-s) *(Chem 031/+cd) CHA CHA COHEN – Freon Shortwave*
Jan 99. (lp/cd) *(Chem 032/+cd) CHA CHA COHEN – Cha Cha Cohen*
Mar 99. (lp/c/cd) *(Chem 033/+c/cd)* **MOGWAI – Come On Die Young**
Aug 99. (7"/cd-s) *(Chem 034/+cd) RADAR BROS. – Open Ocean Sailing*
Sep 99. (lp/cd) *(Chem 035/+cd) RADAR BROS. – The Singing Hatchet*
Oct 99. (12"ep/cd-ep) *(Chem 036/+cd)* **MOGWAI – Mogwai ep**
Nov 99. (video) *(Chem 037video) video*
Mar 00. (7"/cd-s) *(Chem 038/+cd) RADAR BROS. – Shovelling Sons*
Mar 99. (7"/cd-s) *(Chem 039/+cd)* **DELGADOS – American Trilogy**
Apr 99. (lp/cd) *(Chem 040/+cd)* **DELGADOS – The Great Eastern**
May 00. (7"/cd-s) *(Chem 041/+cd)* **SUCKLE – To Be King**
May 00. (lp/cd) *(Chem 042/+cd)* **SUCKLE – Against Nature**
-. (format) *(Chem 043) nothing*
Sep 00. (7"/cd-s) *(Chem 044/+cd)* **DELGADOS – No Danger**
- (format) *(Chem 045) [nothing]*
Nov 00. (12"ep/cd-ep) *(Chem 046/+cd)* **AEREOGRAMME – Glam Cripple**
Dec 00. (12"ep/cd-ep) *(Chem 047/+cd) INTERPOL – P.D.A.*
Nov 00. (12"/cd-s) *(Chem 048/+cd)* **ARAB STRAP – Rocket, Take Your Turn**
Jan 01. (12"/cd-s) *(Chem 049/+cd)* **ARAB STRAP – Love Detective**
Feb 01. (lp/cd) *(Chem 050/+cd)* **ARAB STRAP – The Red Thread**
May 01. (12"/cd-s) *(Chem 051/+cd)* **ARAB STRAP – Turbulence**
Aug 01. (12"ep/cd-ep) *(Chem 052/+cd)* **AEREOGRAMME – White Paw**
Sep 01. (cd/lp) *(Chem 053 cd/lp)* **AEREOGRAMME – A Story In White**
Jul 01. (12"ep/cd-ep) *(Chem 054/+cd) BRITISH MEAT SCENE – Fukd i.d. #4*
Sep 01. (cd) *(Chem 056cd)* **MOGWAI – Mogwai EP + 6** (re-iss)
Sep 01. (cd) *(Chem 057cd)* **MOGWAI – Kicking A Dead Pig** (re)
Oct 01. (12"ep/cd-ep) *(Chem 058/+cd)* **BIS – Fukd i.d. #5**
Oct 01. (12"ep/cd-ep) *(Chem 059/+cd) BEN TRAMER – Fukd i.d. #6 – Halloween (theme)*
May 02. (lp/cd) *(Chem 061/+cd) RADAR BROS. – And The Surrounding Mountains*
Sep 02. (cd) *(Chem 062cd)* **MALCOLM MIDDLETON – 5.14 Fluoxytine Seagull Alcohol**
Sep 02. (cd) *(Chem 055cd) CHA CHA COHEN – All Artists Are Criminals*

Clubscene records

Founded: 1991 . . .. by industry veteran BILL GRAINGER at 28a Academy Street, Bathgate, EH48 1DX. Beginning life as a fanzine, Clubscene quickly developed into a hardcore/techno label with self-distribution throughout the central belt.

With a readymade platform for promotion through their own Clubscene A5 mag (given away free at most record shops), the label got off the ground with ULTRA-SONIC's rave classic 'Obsession' in 1992/3. MARC SMITH, BASS BABY (i.e. OLIVER + CHONG), SUBURBAN DELAY (GILLIAN TENNANT + A.ANGUS, who had previously released 'ENERGY RUSH' for 'Internal Affairs' (KGB/+M/T/D 002) – September '92) with guest singer MICHELLE; after their short-lived spell with Clubscene on a version of Visage's 'FADE TO GREY', they released the 12" 'RE GENERATOR' – for 'Jolly Roger Lite' (JRL 6), DYMENSION (D. LIVINGSTONE + H. TAYLOR), ELECTRO SPACE (A. HALDANE) and of course ULTRA-SONIC all contributed to a frenetically prolific release schedule over the course of 1993; the cream of the label's output to date was collected together on that year's 'ESSENTIAL CLUBSCENE VOL.1'.

A new batch of signings was headed by FRISHIRO, an outfit that consisted of production duo ANDY HALDANE and NICK GEMMELL, vocals courtesy of the ubiquitous MARY KIANI. RHYTHM ECLIPSE, meanwhile, was the alias for one ARNIE MEIKLE, who in turn landed a deal with Clubscene's management branch. Number 16 in the label's catalogue was DYMENSION's 'INSIDE MY FANTASY', prior to the release of which the group added vocalist HEATHER ALLAN and dancer SCOTT FAIRLEY, expanding the line-up to a six-piece; they subsequently teamed up with veteran Hi N-R-G queen, HAZELL DEAN on the single 'Power & Passion'.

Another act in the class of '94 was Livingston's FUTURE NATION, a trio featuring the obligatory female singer KERRI. That same summer, two offshoot imprints were initiated; the JAMIE RAEBURN-headed 'Fire Island' catered to house, garage, trance, etc, while 'Annihilator' dealt in the harder side of things. The latter offshoot introduced DIGITAL GROOVE, who were MARC MACGILLIVRAY and DEN JONES. With the slow demise of the indigenous hardcore dance scene in the mid-90's, Clubscene formed the 'Academy Street' imprint, which catered for the Hi N-R-G Euro market (KELLY MARIE, etc).

– discography –

1993. (12") *(csrt 001)* **ULTRA-SONIC – Obsession**
1993. (12") *(csrt 002)* **MARC SMITH – Breakdown**
1993. (12") *(csrt 003)* **BASS BABY – Bass Mokanik**
1993. (12") *(csrt 004)* **BASS BABY – Sex-o-sexy**
1993. (12") *(csrt 005)* **DYMENSION – Phase 2 Phaze**
1993. (12") *(csrt 006)* **ULTRA-SONIC – React – Amnesia**
1993. (12") *(csrt 007)* **ELECTRO SPACE – Spatial**
1993. (12") *(csrt 008)* **SUBURBAN DELAY – Fade To Grey**
Jun 93. (12") *(csrt 009)* **ULTRA-SONIC – The Pulse**
Jun 93. (12") *(csrt 010)* **DYMENSION – Don't Stop**
Jun 93. (12") *(csrt 011)* **SUBURBAN DELAY – Got To Be There**
Jul 93. (12") *(csrt 012)* **RHYTHM ECLIPSE – Can U Feel It**
Sep 93. (cd/c/lp) *(d/c/a csr 001)* **Various Artists – Essential Clubscene (The Album)** – ULTRA-SONIC – Obsession / MARC SMITH – Breakdown / BASS BABY – Bass Mokanik / SUBURBAN DELAY – Fade To Grey / DYMENSION – Phase 2 Phaze / SUBURBAN DELAY – Energy Rush / ULTRA-SONIC – React; Amnesia / ELECTRO SPACE – Spatial / BASS BABY – Sex-o-sexy / DYMENSION – Don't Stop (Garth St. remix).
Oct 93. (12") *(csrt 013)* **FRISHIRO – Poco Loco**
Nov 93. (12") *(csrt 014)* **DYMENSION – Give In To Me**
Nov 93. (12") *(csrt 015)* **ULTRA-SONIC – Annihilating Rhythm**

Dec 93. (12") *(csrt 015x)* **ULTRA-SONIC – Arpeggio pt.2**
Nov 93. (12") *(csrt 016)* **DYMENSION – Inside My Fantasy**
Dec 93. (12") *(csrt 017)* **RHYTHM ECLIPSE – Passion**
Jan 94. (12") *(csrt 018) RIMMINI – Come Together (mixes)*
Mar 94. (12") *(csrt 019) AUDIO CODE – Where's Rotterdam*
Apr 94. (12") *(csrt 020)* **MARC SMITH – Techno Dup**
Apr 94. (12") *(csrt 021)* **FUTURE NATION – I'm For Real / High On Life / Rhythm In Rapture**
May 94. (12") *(csrt 022)* **ULTRA-SONIC – Acid Circus**
May 94. (12") *(csrt 023)* **D.J. TEN – InTENse**
Jul 94. (12") *(csrt 024)* **DANCE OVER DOSE – Mental, Mental, Mental (f**k mix) / My Dominion / Mental, Mental, Mental (cut mix) / Don't Trust Anybody**
Aug 94. (cd-s/12") *(d+/csrt 025)* **DYMENSION feat HAZELL DEAN – Power & Passion / I'm The One You Need**
Aug 94. (cd-s/12") *(d+/csrt 026)* **BOBBY DAZZLER – Believe In Yourself**
Aug 94. (cd-s/12") *(d+/csrt 027)* **ULTRA-SONIC – Obsession**
Sep 94. (cd-s/12") *(d+/csrt 028) RIMMINI – It's Got To Be Real*
Aug 94. (cd-s/12") *(d+/csrt 029)* **HEADCASE – Critical Rhythm**
Sep 94. (12") *(csrt 029R)* **HEADCASE – Critical Rhythm (original) / Berzerk**
Sep 94. (cd/c/d-lp) *(d/c/a csr 002)* **ULTRA-SONIC – Tekno Junkies '92-'94**
Oct 94. (12") *(csrt 030)* **DANCE OVER DOSE – Overdosed / Hysteric Illusion**
Oct 94. (cd/c) *(d/c csr 003)* **Various Artists – You Know The Score Vol.1**
Oct 94. (cd-s/12") *(d+/csrt 030)* **BASS BABY – King Of The Jungle**
Oct 94. (12") *(csrt 031)* **DYMENSION – I'm The One You Need**
Nov 94. (cd/lp) *(d/l csr 004)* **DYMENSION – Dymension**
Nov 94. (12") *(csrt 032)* **FRESH BEAT – Shoot Your Shot**
Nov 94. (12") *(csrt 033)* **D.J. TEN – E.F.F.E.C.T.**
Dec 94. (cd/c) *(d/c csr 005)* **Various Artists – Essential Clubscene Vol.2**
Apr 95. (12") *(csrt 034)* **ULTRA-SONIC – 1,2,3,4**
May 95. (12") *(csrt 036)* **ULTIMATE BUZZ feat. MC BEE – The Ultimate Buzz**
Jun 95. (12") *(csrt 039)* **RICKY K – untitled**
Jun 95. (12") *(csrt 040)* **MARC SMITH – Pump Up The Noize**
Jul 95. (12") *(csrt 043)* **DJ TEN – untitled**
Aug 95. (12") *(csrt 044)* **RHYTHMIC STATE – No D.S. Allowed**
Sep 95. (12") *(csrt 047R)* **ULTRA-SONIC – The Remixes**
Oct 95. (d-cd/c/t-lp) *(d/c+/csr 007)* **ULTRA-SONIC – Global Tekno**
Dec 95. (12") *(csrt 048) BANG – untitled*
Jan 96. (12") *(csrt 049)* **EUPHONY – Drum Nature (Marc Smith remix)**
Jan 96. (12") *(csrt 05?) T.R.S. – In The Music*
Mar 96. (12") *(csrt 054)* **DANCE OVER DOSE – untitled**
Mar 96. (12") *(csrt 055)* **DJ SASS – untitled**
Mar 96. (12") *(csrt 057)* **NUTJOB – untitled**
Apr 96. (c-s/cd-s/12") *(c/d+/csrt 058)* **ULTRA-SONIC – Party Non-Stop**
May 96. (cd-s/12") *(d+/csrt 060)* **ULTIMATE BUZZ – Rofo's Theme**
May 96. (cd-s/12") *(d+/csrt 062)* **EUPHONY – Time & Space**
Aug 96. (12") *(csrt 066)* **MARC SMITH & SHARKEY – untitled**
Aug 96. (12") *(csrt 067)* **THRESHOLD – Withdrawl**
Sep 96. (12") *(csrt 069)* **ULTIMATE BUZZ – People Stompin'**
Sep 96. (c-s/cd-s/12") *(c/d+/csrt 070)* **ULTRA-SONIC – Do You Believe In Love**
Sep 96. (cd) *(cdsr 010)* **ULTRA-SONIC – Live At Club Kinetic**
Nov 96. (12") *(csrt 071)* **ACTIVE FORCE – Where's The Hip Hop**
Jan 97. (12") *(csrt 072)* **MARC SMITH – Boom'n'Pow**
Jan 97. (12") *(csrt 074)* **DAVIE FORBES – The Final Cut**
Jan 97. (cd/c) *(d/c csr 011)* **Various Artists – Essential Clubscene Vol.3**
Feb 97. (12") *(csrt 075)* **TOM WILSON – The Fantasy**
Feb 97. (12") *(csrt 076)* **ULTIMATE BUZZ – In Your Dreams**
Feb 97. (12") *(csrt 077) SAN FRANCISCO PUSH – Joyriders*
Feb 97. (cd-s/12") *(d+/csrt 078)* **ULTRA-SONIC – Asylum EP – I Just Can't Stop**
Jun 97. (12") *(csrt 079)* **SMITH & DJ TEN – Aquarium**
Jun 97. (cd/c) *(d+/csr 014)* **MARC SMITH – Past, Present & Future**
Jul 97. (12") *(csrt 080)* **DAVIE FORBES & MC CYCLONE – A8 Diversion**
Aug 97. (12") *(csrt 081)* **RHYTHMIC STATE – Soap On A Rope '97**
Oct 97. (12") *(csrt 082)* **ACTIVE FORCE – Forever And A Day**
Feb 98. (12") *(csrt 083)* **ULTIMATE BUZZ – Back In Business**
Oct 00. (cd-s) *(dcsrt 086)* **TTF – New Emotion 2000**
Oct 00. (cd-s) *(dcsrt 087) LAGOS – Technocat 2000*
Oct 00. (cd-s) *(dcsrt 088) DEE JAY KEE – Loop 2000 / Fog Desire*
Oct 00. (cd-s) *(dcsrt 089)* **DJ MARC SMITH – Relax Your Mind**
Oct 00. (cd-s) *(dcsrt 090) KIRON J – Narcotic Evasion*
Nov 00. (cd-s) *(dcsrt 091) FUNKY G featuring CANDI STATON – Young Hearts Run Free*
Dec 00. (cd-ep) *(CDPAC 001)* **Various Artists – 4x12"**

– (Annihilator) discography

Aug 94. (12") *(ANN 001)* **AUDIO CODE – Alpha Express / Santa Monica'n Acid / Bullcid**
Sep 94. (12") *(ANN 002)* **DIGITAL GROOVE – Odyssey: pt.1 / pt.3**
Nov 94. (12") *(ANN 003)* **FORCE BUBBLE – Choke On This**

– (Fire Island) discography –

Oct 94. (cd-s/12") *(d+/fir 001)* **FORMIDABLE FORCE OF LOVE – Good Bassy Tone**
1999. (cd-s) *(dfir 015) FOURTEEN 14 – Everytime We Touch*
1999. (cd-s) *(dfir 016) BACON POPPER – Free*
1999. (cd-s) *(dfir 017) LUVBUG – If It Moves Funk It*
1999. (cd-s) *(dfir 018) DOUBLE VISION – Knockin' 2000*
1999. (cd-s) *(dfir 019) THUNDERCHILD – B Boys To The Dancefloor*
1999. (cd-s) *(dfir 020) LA SHANNA – Let's Start The Dance*
1999. (cd-s) *(dfir 021) PUMP SISTERS – Gotta Move On*
Mar 00. (cd-s) *(dfir 022) DJ PAGANO – Nu-Energy*
Apr 00. (cd-s) *(dfir 023) BWT ft. NINA – I've Got A Feeling*

– (Academy Street) discography –

Aug 96. (cd-s/12") *(d+/acst 001)* **A-TENSION – Angel**
Feb 97. (cd-s/12") *(d+/acst 004) UNLIMITED BEAT – Abba Medley*
Apr 97. (cd-s/12") *(d+/acst 007) JESSICA JAY – Can't Take My Eyes Off You*
Apr 97. (cd-s/12") *(d+/acst 008) UNLIMITED BEAT – Take That Medley*
Jun 97. (cd-s/12") *(d+/acst 011)* **QUEEN OF SCOTS – Stand By Your Man / Look At Me**
Jun 97. (cd-s/12") *(d+/acst 012) UNLIMITED BEAT – Spice Girls Medley*
Sep 97. (cd-s/12") *(d+/acst 015) UNLIMITED BEAT – Bee Gees Medley*
Jun 97. (cd-s/12") *(d+/acst 017)* **LAWRENCE – I Believe I Can Fly / I Believe I Can Groove**
Nov 97. (cd-s/12") *(d+/acst 020)* **KAREN DUNBAR – Halo**
Nov 97. (cd-s/12") *(d+/acst 021)* **KELLY MARIE – Feels Like I'm In Love '97**
Nov 97. (cd-s/12") *(d+/acst 022) BLUE DREAM – Heaven Is A Place On Earth*
Oct 97. (cd-s/12") *(d+/acst 023) QUEEN NADINE – This Is My Life*
Nov 97. (cd-s/12") *(d+/acst 024) JODY LEE – It's My Party*
Nov 97. (cd-s/12") *(d+/acst 026) QUEEN NADINE – Don't Stop*
Nov 97. (cd-s/12") *(d+/acst 027) ERNEST KOHL – Only You*
Dec 97. (cd-s/12") *(d+/acst 028) FRESHBEAT – Best Years Of Our Lives*
Dec 97. (cd-s/12") *(d+/acst 029) HOUSEBOYZ – Father & Son*
Jan 98. (cd-s/12") *(d+/acst 030) MASSIVE EGO – You Think You're A Man*
Jan 98. (cd-s/12") *(d+/acst 031)* **KELLY MARIE – Rescue Me**
Jan 98. (cd-s/12") *(d+/acst 032) MOONS GIRL – Material Girl*
Jan 98. (cd-s/12") *(d+/acst 033) HOUSECREAM – Knowing Me, Knowing You*
Jan 98. (cd-s/12") *(d+/acst 035) DAMIAN – Time Warp '98 / Molecular Breakdown*
Dec 97. (cd-s/12") *(d+/acst 036) BLUE DREAM – Downtown / Uptown*
Jan 98. (cd-s/12") *(d+/acst 038) BGB ft. LEX – Our Way*
Jan 98. (cd-s/12") *(d+/acst 039) JACKSON – There's No Other Way*
1998. (cd-s/12") *(d+/acst 041) WAY OUT GIRLS – I'm The Leader Of The Gang*
1998. (cd-s/12") *(d+/acst 042) KIKKA – Little Lies, How Do I Live Without You*
1998. (cd-s/12") *(d+/acst 043) BLUE DREAM – Can't Get Used To Losing You*
1998. (cd-s/12") *(d+/acst 045) WEST COAST – Daydream Believer*
Sep 98. (cd-s/12") *(d+/acst 046) BLUE DREAM & DeCAPRIO – Summer Nights*
Oct 98. (cd-s/12") *(d+/acst 047) QUEEN NADINE – Maybe This Time*
Oct 98. (cd-s/12") *(d+/acst 048)* **KAREN DUNBAR – Queen Of Hollywood**
Oct 98. (cd-s/12") *(d+/acst 049) APRIL SOMMER – Somewhere Here In My Heart*
Oct 98. (cd-s/12") *(d+/acst 050)* **BRENDA COCHRANE – Native New Yorker**
Oct 98. (cd-s/12") *(d+/acst 052)* **KELLY MARIE – I'm In The Mood For Dancin'**
Nov 98. (cd-s/12") *(d+/acst 053) KRIS MacKENZIE – Blame It On The Boogie*
Nov 98. (cd-s/12") *(d+/acst 054) BANDIDO – Wouldn't It Be Good*
Nov 98. (cd-s/12") *(d+/acst 056)* **N-R-GEES – High NRG Medley**
Mar 99. (cd-s/12") *(d+/acst 058) MORGANA – Never Gonna Make*
Jun 99. (cd-s/12") *(d+/acst 059) CHAIN GANG – You To Me Are Everything / The Full Monty*
Mar 99. (cd-s/12") *(d+/acst 060)* **KELLY MARIE – Millennium / Runaway**
Apr 99. (cd-s) *(dacst 061) MEDLEYMANIACS – Stepdance Medley*
May 99. (cd-s/12") *(d+/acst 062) 3 GIRLZ – Boogie Oogie Oogie*
Jun 99. (cd-s) *(dacst 063) CLUB-CRU – Mamma Told Me*
Aug 99. (cd-s) *(dacst 064) A-TENSION – China In Your Hands*
Oct 99. (cd-s/12") *(d+/acst 065) HAZELL DEAN – Living On A Prayer / I've Had Enough*
Oct 99. (cd-s) *(dacst 066) DOLCE VITA – Sway*
Oct 99. (cd-s) *(dacst 067) MASSIVE EGO – Planet Earth / Fight The Feeling*
Oct 99. (cd-s) *(dacst 068) DOMINO – Yes Sir I Can Boogie*
Nov 99. (cd-s/12") *(d+/acst 069)* **KELLY MARIE – I Need A Man '99 / Feels Like I'm In Love '99**
Nov 99. (cd-s) *(dacst 070) TINA CHARLES – I Love To Love*
Nov 99. (cd-s) *(dacst 071) ABBA 2000 – Thank You For The Music / Super Trouper*
Jan 00. (cd-s) *(dacst 072) ELLEN LU TRELLE – The Sun Always Shines On TV / Mad World*
Feb 00. (cd-s/12") *(d+/acst 073) TWIN SISTER – Shania Tribute*
Feb 00. (cd-s) *(dacst 074) MEDLEYMANIACS – Stepdance Medley 2*
Mar 00. (cd-s/12") *(d+/acst 075)* **KELLY MARIE – River Deep, Mountain High**
Jun 00. (cd-s/12") *(d+/acst 076) WEST COAST – Westlife Tribute*
Jul 00. (cd-s/12") *(d+/acst 077) AK & BJ – I Only Wanna Be With You / Rebel Rebel*
Oct 00. (cd-s/12") *(d+/acst 078) AMERICAN BABE – Britney Spears Tribute*
Oct 00. (cd-s/12") *(d+/acst 079) BUCKS FIZZ – Never Gonna Give You Up*
Oct 00. (cd-s/12") *(d+/acst 080) UNLIMITED BEAT – Celine Dion Tribute Medley*
Oct 00. (cd-s/12") *(d+/acst 081) KAMOUFLAGE – Shirley Bassey Tribute Medley*
Oct 00. (cd-s/12") *(d+/acst 082) SHELDON – I Turn To You*
Nov 00. (cd-s/12") *(d+/acst 084)* **KELLY MARIE – Hot Love**

Creeping Bent records

Founded: Glasgow . . . 12/12/94 by steadfastly independent entrepreneur DOUGLAS MacINTYRE (aka DOOG BENT) as a vehicle for indigenous left-field talent ignored by the corporate labels and mass media. Launched via a live event, 'A Leap Into The Void', at the city's Tramway Theatre (bent

001), the label's first bonafide release came in Spring '95 with a 10" EP by SPACEHOPPER. Since then, the operation has gone from strength to strength with neither major label nor press support, releasing acclaimed material by the likes of the LEOPARDS, SECRET GOLDFISH, The REVOLUTIONARY CORPS OF TEENAGE JESUS (Vs. whoever) and ADVENTURES IN STEREO.

Like 'Factory' records before them, Creeping Bent were wont to give catalogue numbers to everything they were involved in; thus bent 023, a monthly alternative disco night at the 13th Note club in Glassford Street. The imprint also initiated a particularly successful singles club, working largely with artists from other labels (POLICECAT, FUTURE PILOT AKA, APPENDIX OUT, MOUNT VERNON ARTS LAB, SCIENTIFIC SUPPORT DEPT and NECTARINE No.9) on a variety of split 7"ers.

Other highlights of Creeping Bent's self-styled "5-year plan" have included hosting a label night at John Peel's 1998 Meltdown Festival (bent 039) as well as a live "10-Day Weekend" which played host to veteran punk VIC GODARD amongst others. Another non-vinyl catalogue number was bent 041, actually the launch (early in '99) of a webzine entitled 'Unpopular Culture // Social Insecurity'.

More recently, the 'Bent crew have released material from SECRET GOLDFISH spin-off MONGOOSE, Francis MacDonald's SPEEDER, Burnley's ELEMENT and ex-THRUM lass MONICA QUEEN.

Contact www.13thnote.com/creepingbent for more details.

- discography -

Mar 95. (exhibition @ the Tramway, Glasgow) *(bent 001) A Leap Into The Void*

- **SPACEHOPPER** are a 4-piece from Glasgow – formed 1994 and heavily into SONIC YOUTH via their guitar assaults. After their label debut in '95, they split a single the following year with The SECRET GOLDFISH. In 1997, SPACEHOPPER shared a cd-ep alongside ADVENTURES IN STEREO, the LEOPARDS and the REVOLUTIONARY CORPS.

Apr 95. (10"ep) *(bent 002)* **SPACEHOPPER – Milkmetal EP**
– Milkmetal / Crane / Not me / Cush.

Jun 95. (7") *(bent 003)* **LEOPARDS – Burning**
Jun 95. (7") *(bent 004)* **SECRET GOLDFISH – Seasick**
Jan 96. (7") *(bent 005)* **REVOLUTIONARY CORPS OF TEENAGE JESUS Vs. SUICIDE – Frankie Teardrop**
Feb 96. (7") *(bent 006)* **SPACEHOPPER – Mars Bonding / SECRET GOLDFISH – Venus Bonding**
Mar 96. (7") *(bent 007)* **LEOPARDS – Surf On** (shelved)
Apr 96. (7") *(bent 008)* **SECRET GOLDFISH – Come Undone**
May 96. (cd) *(bent 009cd) Various Anarchists – Destructive Urges*
Feb 96. (blue-7"ep) *(bent 010)* **ADVENTURES IN STEREO – e.p.2**
May 96. (12") *(bent 011)* **REVOLUTIONARY CORPS OF TEENAGE JESUS – Protection Rat**
Jun 96. (cd) *(bent 012cd)* **SECRET GOLDFISH – Aqua Pet . . . You Make Me**
Jul 96. (yellow-7"ep) *(bent 013)* **ADVENTURES IN STEREO – e.p.3**
Jul 96. (fanzine) *(bent 014) The Erotic Urges Of Creeping Bent*
Mar 97. (cd/lp) *(bent 015/+lp)* **ADVENTURES IN STEREO – Adventures In Stereo**
Jul 96. (7") *(bent 016)* **SECRET GOLDFISH – E.K.O.K. ep**
Sep 96. (garment) *(bent 017) bentgirl / bentboy*
Nov 96. (7") *(bent 018)* **SECRET GOLDFISH – Venus Bonding**
Jun 97. (7") *(bent 019/+cd)* **ADVENTURES IN STEREO / LEOPARDS /** +cd= **SPACEHOPPER / REVOLUTIONARY CORPS OF TEENAGE JESUS**
Mar 97. (7") *(bent 020)* **SECRET GOLDFISH – Tartan Envy**
Jun 97. (cd) *(bent 021cd)* **LEOPARDS – They Tried Staying Calm**
Jun 97. (7"/cd-s) *(bent 022/+cd)* **ADVENTURES IN STEREO – Waves On**
Jul 97. (disco) *(bent 023) disco @ the 13th Note, Glassford, Glasgow (Oct 96-Oct 97)*
Jul 97. (7") *(bent 024)* **POLICECAT – Automobile / SECRET GOLDFISH – Give Him A Great Big Kiss**
Jul 97. (7") *(bent 025)* **FUTURE PILOT AKA vs RANJIT NAGAR CHORUS – We Shall Overcome /** *KIM FOWLEY – Night Flight To Memphis*
Nov 97. (7"/cd-s) *(bent 026/+cd)* **ADVENTURES IN STEREO – A Brand New Day**
Sep 97. (7") *(bent 027)* **APPENDIX OUT – Well-Lit Tonight / LEOPARDS – Cutting A Short Dog**
Mar 98. (7"ep/cd-ep) *(bent 028/+cd)* **ADVENTURES IN STEREO – Down In The Traffic**
Nov 97. (7") *(bent 029)* **FUTURE PILOT AKA vs ALAN VEGA – Meditation Rat / MOUNT VERNON ARTS LAB & SCIENTIFIC SUPPORT DEPT.**
May 98. (cd) *(bent 030cd)* **ADVENTURES IN STEREO – Alternative Stereo Sounds**
Mar 98. (7") *(bent 031)* **LEOPARDS – Starlings**
Feb 98. (7") *(bent 032)* **SCIENTIFIC SUPPORT DEPT. – Kipperlynch / SECRET GOLDFISH – Punk Drone**
Mar 98. (7") *(bent 033)* **NECTARINE No.9 – The Port Of Mars / ALAN VEGA & THE REVOLUTIONARY CORPS – Who Cares Who Dies**
Jun 98. (7") *(bent 034)* **APPENDIX OUT – Lassie, Lie Near Me / POLICECAT – Dark Holiday**
Apr 98. (cd) *(bent 035cd)* **NECTARINE No.9 – Fried For Blue Material**
May 98. (cd-ep) *(bent 036cd)* **ADVENTURES IN STEREO – Catch My Soul** (shelved)
May 98. (cd-ep) *(bent 037cd)* **NECTARINE No.9 – South Of An Imaginary Line**
Mar 99. (cd-ep) *(bent 038cd)* **SECRET GOLDFISH – Somewhere In The World**
Jun 98. (cassette freebie) *(bent 039) creeping bent @ meltdown/pin-ups*
Jun 98. (cd) *(bent 040cd) Various Artists – Bentism*
Jan 99. (web-zine) *(bent 041) Unpopular Culture / Social Insecurity*
Aug 99. (7") *(bent 042)* **NECTARINE No.9 – Walter Tevis / SECRET GOLDFISH – You're Funny 'Bout That, Aren't You**
Apr 99. (12"/cd-s) *(bent 043/+cd)* **REVOLUTIONARY CORPS OF TEENAGE JESUS – Pay Tha Wreck, Mr Music King**
Jul 99. (cd) *(bent 044cd)* **SECRET GOLDFISH – Mink Riots**
May 99. (cd) *(bent 045cd)* **REVOLUTIONARY CORPS OF TEENAGE JESUS – Righteous Lite**

- **FAKE EYELASHES** were an electronic studio outfit comprising KATY (from SECRET GOLDFISH), DAVY (from NECTARINE No.9) and other "Bent" folk

Sep 99. (m-cd; unreleased) *(bent 046cd)* **FAKE EYELASHES – Sad N' Milky**

Sep 99. (cd) *(bent 047cd)* **NECTARINE No.9 – It's Just The Way Things Are Joe**
Nov 99. (7") *(bent 048)* **SECRET GOLDFISH – 4 Excited People /** *VIC GODARD – The Place We Used To Live*
Oct 99. (7") *(bent 049)* **MONGOOSE – Sanitise Me /** *TRANSELEMENT – split*
Nov 99. (cd) *(bent 050)* **Various Artists – Electronic Lullabies**
– SCIENTIFIC SUPPORT DEPT. – Filtermouse / ALAN VEGA – King / MOUNT VERNON ARTS LAB – mv3 / MONGOOSE – Fuck off #2 / the MEASUREMENT OF SOULS – E-type Jag / ELEMENT – Tint little factories / REVOLUTIONARY CORPS OF TEENAGE JESUS – Saturation / the NECTARINE No.9 – Arabella pollen.
Nov 99. (cd-s) *(bent 051cd)* **REVOLUTIONARY CORPS OF TEENAGE JESUS – A Brooklyn Nightmare**
Nov 99. (cd; unreleased) *(bent 052)* **MONGOOSE – LoLevel**
above set will be issued late in 2001 by Danish-label, 'Realler'
Nov 99. (7") *(bent 053)* **SPEEDER – Hey, What Do I Know**
Feb 00. (cd) *(bent 054cd) TRANSELEMENT – Sour Blaster*
Mar 00. (d-cd) *(bent 055cd)* **Various Artists – Bentboutique**
Mar 00. (cd-ep) *(bent 056cd)* **SPEEDER – Feelings EP**
Oct 00. (7") *(bent 057)* **MONGOOSE Vs. SCIENTIFIC SUPPORT DEPT. – Subvert Normality**
Aug 00. (cd) *(bent 058cd)* **SPEEDER – Karma Kids**
Sep 00. (cd; unreleased) *(bent 059)* **Various Artists – Avant Bent**
Sep 00. (cd-ep) *(bent 060cd)* **MONICA QUEEN – 77X e.p.**
Oct 00. (cd) *(bent 061cd)* **REVOLUTIONARY CORPS OF TEENAGE JESUS – A Brooklyn Nightmare**
2001. (cd) *(bent 062cd)* **Various Artists – Nouvelle Vague**
Feb 02. (cd) *(bent 063cd)* **MONICA QUEEN – Ten Sorrowful Mysteries**
Jun 02. (cd) *(bent 065cd)* **SCIENTIFIC SUPPORT DEPT. – Cabbageneck**
Sep 02. (cd) *(bent 066cd) C.C. SAGER – The Last Minute Of Normal Time*
— (C.C. SAGER is in fact, GARETH SAGER, formerly of The POP GROUP)
Jun 02. (cd) *(bent 067cd)* **BILL WELLS & ISOBEL CAMPBELL – Ghost Of Yesterday**

D.D.T. records

Founded: As a base for 'Fast Forward' distributors, who were run at various times by Englishman BOB LAST and SANDY McLEAN (for further info see Fast records). Nightshift records were based at Falkirk District Business Park (Newhouse Road, Grangemouth, FK3 8LR) and it would be BRIAN GUTHRIE (brother of The COCTEAU TWINS' ROBIN) that would head the show. Although a few other releases managed to filter through, the label basically catered for BRIAN's old COCTEAU pal, WILL HEGGIE and his new outfit, LOWLIFE.

- discography -

— note:- the US catalogue no. for 'Fast Forward' <in brackets>
Jul 86. (lp) *(DISPLP 005)* **CATERAN – Little Circles**
Jan 87. (7") *(DISP 006)* **CATERAN – Last Big Lie**
Mar 87. (7"/12") *(DISP 007/+T)* **WE FREE KINGS – Oceans**
Sep 87. (7"ep/12"ep) *(DISP 008/+T)* **THANES – Hey Girl EP**
Jan 88. (12"/cd-s) *(DISP 009T/+P)* **WE FREE KINGS – T-Shirt**
Jan 88. (lp/c) *(DISP LP/C 010)* **WE FREE KINGS – Hell On Earth And Rosy Cross**
Jan 88. (lp) *(DISPLP 011)* **THANES – Thanes Of Cawdor**
Nov 87. (lp/c) *(DISP LP/C 012) <FFUS 3301/+C/CD>* **SWAMPTRASH – It Don't Make No Never Mind**
Jan 88. (12"ep) *(DISP 014T)* **NYAH FEARTIES – Good, Bad And Alkies**
Jan 88. (12"ep) *(DISP 015T)* **McCLUSKEY BROTHERS – She Said To The Driver**
Jun 88. (lp) *(DISPLP 018)* **OFFHOOKS – Off The Hook**
Aug 88. (12"ep) *(DDTEP 001)* **THANES – Hubble Bubble EP**
Oct 88. (12"ep) *(DDTEP 002)* **SWAMPTRASH – The Bone EP**
Jan 89. (lp) *<FFUS 3302>* **JESSE GARON & THE DESPERADOES – A Cabinet Full Of Curiosities**
Jan 89. (7") *(DISP 020)* **THANES – I'll Rest**
Feb 89. (lp) *(DISPLP 021)* **PRIMEVALS – Neon Oven**

Feb 89. (lp) *(DISPLP 022)* **BABY LEMONADE – One Thousand Secrets**
Jul 89. (10"ep) *(DDTEP 004)* **THANES – Better Look Behind You**

– Nightshift discography –

—— not including LOWLIFE (see own entry)
Feb 90. (m-lp) *(NISHI 211)* **THANES – Better Look Behind You**

- Based, Grangemouth, 1989 . . . by, on voices/noises ELFIN WAIFLIKE, on chainsaw guitar DOG BITE, bumble-bee bass MILLICENT and all kinds of percussion ROSE. Quite colourful really! and produced and engineered by Jamie Watson.

May 90. (m-lp) *(NISHI 212)* **MATTER BABIES – Skinny Dipping**
– Tik tik blap / Snoggin' the dog / Cul-de-sac / Confusion / Wire cutter / Loose / Happy mango / Harmo / Muffing the mule / 13 weeks.

1991. (cd) **HEXOLOGY – Hexology**

Egg records

Founded: 17 Prince Edward Street, Glasgow, G42 8LU. Egg was mainly set up to release recordings by locals The PRAYERS. They were fronted by HUGH McLACHLAN (formerly of The PRETTY FLOWERS who featured DUGLAS STEWART, later of BMX BANDITS), NORTON and SHAWN. The PLAYERS ceased to be after only two singles, 'SISTER GOODBYE' and 'FINGERDIPS', HUGH got out again and headed the band FAT LIP; there was also supposed to be a debut LP by The PRAYERS and a single by The CHURCH GRIMS. Meanwhile, The BACHELOR PAD were getting their house in order (see own entry).

– discography –

Nov 88. (7") *(EGG 001)* **PRAYERS – Sister Goodbye / Under The Deep Blue**
1989. (12"ep) *(EGG 002)* **Various Artists – A Lighthouse In The Desert EP**
– PRAYERS – Puppet clouds / REMEMBER FUN – Cold inside / CHURCH GRIMS – Mr Watt said / BACHELOR PAD – Silly girl.
Jan 90. (7"ep) *(EGG 003)* **BACHELOR PAD – Frying Tonight EP**
Aug 90. (7") *(EGG 004)* **PRAYERS – Fingerdips / Head Start**
Nov 90. (12"ep) *(EGG 005)* **PRAYERS – The Prayers EP**
– Fingerdips / Head start / Puppet clouds / Sister goodbye / Under the deep blue.
Jan 91. (7") *(EGG 006)* **BACHELOR PAD – Smoothie**
May 91. (12") *(EGG 007)* **BACHELOR PAD – Meeting The Lovely Jenny Brown**
Aug 91. (7") *(EGG 008)* **CHANGE OF SEASONS – Soft Spoken**

Electric Honey records

Founded: Stow College, 43 Shamrock Street, Glasgow, G4 9LO. Began as a course set up by ALAN RANKINE (ex-ASSOCIATES), initially to deliver one record per year. One of the first acts on the label were none other than BELLE & SEBASTIAN who released their debut LP, 'TIGERMILK' in May 1996 – who knows where B&S might've been without this foot up. The team of students subsequently signed Irish lads (based in Glasgow at Dundee University), POLARBEAR, who, after one CD-single, 'STARFIGHTER PILOT', quickly became SNOW PATROL. Latest signings, POLICECHIEF, are a Glasgow collective fronted by WIGGI and bassist GEE, the object of their ambition was to "get people dancing"; they have already supported BASEMENT JAXX and The LO-FIDELITY ALLSTARS.

– discography –

May 96. (lp) *(EHRLP 5)* **BELLE AND SEBASTIAN – Tigermilk**
Jun 97. (cd-s) *(EHRCD 007) POLARBEAR – Starfighter Pilot*
Mar 02. (cd-ep) **POLICECHIEF – Coup De Grace EP**

Evol records

Founded: Edinburgh . . . late 1996 by KEIRON MELLOTTE, leader of sonic Grunge-meisters, PILOTCAN. Initially setting up 'Evol' as a base for live gigs (he still does), the man chose to breakaway from STUART BRAITHWAITE's (MOGWAI) imprint, 'Rock Action', to fund his own. Two singles by BLIND, 'Radio Infectious' and 'Money To Burn' and PILOTCAN's own much-anticipated debut set, 'Socially Inept Disco', were up for grabs in 1997, while CHICKWEED's 'Squawk' 7", ended quite a prolific year.

MELLOTTE and his PILOTCAN delivered a sophomore single & album for Evol in 1999, although it would be new signings LAETO, I AM SCIENTIST and THE ZEPHYRS that would take pride of place. The second of these, I AM SCIENTIST, were indeed once the aforementioned BLIND and the brainchild of the mysterious carrot-top scientist, SCOTT MacDONALD, a former World BMX champion (aye, right!). Along with drummer MARCUS (from TOASTER), bassist PAUL JARVIE and guitarist NICK MUNRO (the latter two also of avant-jazzateers, JAVELIN), they set about creating their own underground sound. Early in 2000, the group's debut album, 'NO SIGNAL' (containing future single, 'GLASVEGAS'), pulled no punches and was praised in all quarters of the music industry.

– discography –

Apr 97. (cd-ep) *(evol 01)* **BLIND – Radio Infectious EP**
Nov 97. (lp/cd) *(evol 02/+d)* **PILOTCAN – Socially Inept Disco**
Sep 97. (7") *(evol 03)* **BLIND – Money To Burn / Fired Up And Burnt Out**
Oct 97. (7") *(evol 04)* **PILOTCAN – Losing More Than My Fingers**
Dec 97. (7"ep) *(evol 05)* **CHICKWEED – Squawk / Now I Realise**
Mar 99. (cd-s) *(evol 06)* **PILOTCAN – The World Turns Without You**
May 99. (cd) *(evol 07)* **PILOTCAN – The Boy Who Knew Maps**
Jan 00. (7") *(evol 08)* **LAETO – Fieldsettings**
Apr 00. (cd) *(evol 09)* **I AM SCIENTIST – No Signal**
– Glasvegas / Cancer stick / The way things are / Can't tell anyone / Map and a gun / Spring / Apes and angels / I love stars / Spirit is think / Radio infectious / Oranges.
Mar 00. (cd) *(evol 010)* **ZEPHYRS – It's Okay Not To Say Anything**
Mar 00. (c; ltd freebie) *(evol 011)* **ZEPHYRS – 001 To 100**
Feb 01. (cd-ep) *(evol 012)* **I AM SCIENTIST – Glasvegas EP**
– Glasvegas / Summer is coming / Late show (demo version) / Ineligible for chart inclusion song.

Fast Product records

Founded: 3/4 East Norton Place, Abbeyhill, Edinburgh . . . late '77 by English-born Bob Last. Influenced by the Punk revolution and the DIY ethos that gave birth to such labels as 'New Hormones', BOB set about building his Scottish-based mini-empire with bands predominantly hailing from south of the border.

Having initially no idea how to run such a project although he was bursting with tons of enthusiasm, the mild-mannered LAST found an ally in REZILLOS man JO CALLIS. The MEKONS took the honours of FAST 1 with 'Never Been In A Riot', the initially shambling Punk DIY combo residing in Leeds, also home to the more politically inclined GANG OF FOUR. Both bands got their start on 'Fast', as did Sheffield's 2.3 and The HUMAN LEAGUE. Before hitting the New Romantic bigtime, PHIL OAKEY and Co made their debut with the classic 'Being Boiled', still Fast's most memorable release.

Early '79 finally saw the release of some homegrown material in the shape of the SCARS, while more of the Scottish contingent (including the FLOWERS and the PRATS) were given an airing via three 'EARCOM' samplers. As well as claiming the kudos of releasing pre-'Unknown Pleasures'-era JOY DIVISION material, Last pulled off something of a coup with his final 'Fast Product' release, licensing the DEAD KENNEDYS 'California Uber Alles'.

The man's next project was the 'Pop: Aural' imprint, a label that catered largely for native talent. The FLOWERS, BOOTS FOR DANCING, DRINKING ELECTRICITY, RESTRICTED CODE and cult legends, The FIRE ENGINES all made 'Pop: Aural' their musical home over a brief two-year spell.

Ever ambitious, Last founded a twin label, 'Accessory', to release longer playing material; alongside The FIRE ENGINES' 'Lubricate Your Living Room' was an obscure collaborative set by pub accordionist, FRANK HANNAWAY and guitarist MIKE BARCLAY (see below for details).

Leaving the Fast enterprise behind in the 80's, Last took on the allegedly unenviable task of managing SCRITTI POLITTI (aka GREEN GARTSIDE) alongside other top pop/rock artists. Of late, Bob has been working on a new On-Line radio experience, even making a wee bid for non-exclusive internet rights to yours truly's Great Rock Discography – no thank you mate.

– discography –

(groups in italics are non-Scots)

Feb 78. (7") *(FAST 1) MEKONS – Never Been In A Riot*
Apr 78. (7") *(FAST 2) 2.3 – Where To Now*
May 78. (fanzine) *(FAST 3) The quality of life*
Jun 78. (7") *(FAST 4) HUMAN LEAGUE – Being Boiled*
Oct 78. (7") *(FAST 5) GANG OF FOUR – Damaged Goods*
Nov 78. (fanzine) *(FAST 6) Sexex*
Dec 78. (7") *(FAST 7) MEKONS – Where Were You*
Mar 79. (7") *(FAST 8)* **SCARS – Horrorshow**
May 79. (12"ep) *(FAST 9) Various Artists – Earcom 1*

– BLANK STUDENTS (2 tracks) / FLOWERS – Criminal Waste / After Dark / GRAPH (track) / PRATS – Inverness / Bored / Prats 2.
May 79. (12"ep) *(FAST 9b) Various Artists – Earcom 2*
– JOY DIVISION (2 tracks) / THURSDAYS – Perfection / Dock Of The Bay / BASCZAX – (2 tracks).
May 79. (d7"ep) *(FAST 9c) Various Artists – Earcom 3*
– D.A.F. (track) / MIDDLE CLASS (2 tracks) / NOH MERCY (2 tracks) / STUPID BABIES (2 tracks) / FROM CHORLEY (track).
May 79. (12"ep) *(FAST 10) HUMAN LEAGUE – The Dignity Of Labour*
Dec 79. (lp) *(EMC 3312)* **Various Artists – The First Year Plan**
(above was issued on 'E.M.I.' in the UK and 'Fast' <F 11> in US
Oct 79. (7") *(FAST 12) DEAD KENNEDYS – California Uber Alles*

– (Pop: Aural) discography –

Dec 79. (7") *(POP 001)* **FLOWERS – Confessions**
Apr 80. (12"ep) *(POP 002)* **BOOTS FOR DANCING – Boots For Dancing**
May 80. (7") *(POP 003)* **FLOWERS – The Ballad Of Miss Demeanor**
May 80. (7") *(POP 004)* **DRINKING ELECTRICITY – Shakin' All Over**
Jul 80. (7") *(POP 005)* **DRINKING ELECTRICITY – Shake Some Action**
Mar 81. (7") *(POP 006)* **BOOTS FOR DANCING – Rain Song**
Jan 81. (7") *(POP 007)* **RESTRICTED CODE – First Night On**
Nov 80. (7") *(POP 008)* **DRINKING ELECTRICITY – Cruising Missiles**
May 81. (7") *(POP 009)* **RESTRICTED CODE – Love To Meet You**
May 81. (7") *(POP 010)* **FIRE ENGINES – Candy Skin**
Jun 81. (7") *(POP 011) MARCHING GIRLS – True Love* (these "lads" were originally from the UK but moved to Australia c.1978; this was originally issued in May'80 for 'Anda'; *ANDA 8)*
Nov 81. (7") *(POP 012)* **JO CALLIS – Woah Yeah! / Sinistrale / Dodo Boys**
Nov 81. (7") *(POP 013)* **FIRE ENGINES – Big Gold Dream**

– (Accessory) discography –

Jan 81. (m-lp) *(ACC 001)* **FIRE ENGINES – Lubricate Your Living Room** *<US-title 'AUFGELADEN UND BEREIT FUR ACTION UNDER SPASS' on 'Fast Product'; FPA 002>*
Mar 82. (m-lp) *(ACC 002)* **FRANK HANNAWAY & MIKE BARCLAY – At Home (Background Music For Housework)**

— Bob Last's final release was a bizarre instrumental set (including a cover of an ABBA song!) by pub accordionist FRANK HANNAWAY and Rock guitarist MIKE BARCLAY (ex-Punk bands, etc); the latter became a tutor in furniture design at St. Andrews Uni – so there!

Fence records

Founded: Crail, Fife . . . 1994 by KENNY ANDERSON, one-time member of The SKUOBHIE DUBH ORCHESTRA, an energetic traditional/rock outfit who had folk purists up in arms with their thrashy-indie type songs; actually they released one album, 'SPIKE'S 23 COLLECTION', for 'Lochshore' records in July '94. With EEN ANDERSON his brother, KENNY and another Edinburgh-based bunch of cajun folkabillies, The KHARTOUM HEROES, also delivered one eponymous set for the same label. Back over to 'Fence', St. Andrews-born KENNY chose a completely original approach by releasing only records by people who worked or were connected to the label. PIP DYLAN (aka, the aforementioned EEN ANDERSON) is a talented busker-type singer-songwriter and guitarist whose inspiration comes from commuting back and forth to Spain and France (flamenco and bluegrass were two styles PIP utilised). KING CREOSOTE, meanwhile, is in fact KENNY himself on a return to his beloved bluegrass technique. His old mucker, JAMES WRIGHT (now JAMES YORKSTON), augmented him on his/KC's '12 O'CLOCK ON THE DOT' set, the same guy also co-licensing 'Fence' stuff on his own London-based imprint, 'Bad Jazz'.

The JOSE were swanky lounge lizards, ALAN COUTTS, JAMES GOURLAY and JOHN McCULLOCH, The ABRAHAMS are Edinburgh students/pilgrims (MARTIN NOBLE from Leeds, RICK LYONS and JOANNA) who fused folk and country, IMMIGRANT (aka LINGUS GORDON) was also about to be unleashed via his home in Clackmannanshire; the album was er, 'UNTITLED' (2002). ON THE FLY (who've played nearly every week at the Rialto Bar in Falkirk!) and GUMMI BAKO were also on the 'Fence' roster, while (ex-BETA BAND songwriter) LONE PIGEON . . . well, we know all about the man, don't we? (see under own entry).

SKUOBHIE DUBH ORCHESTRA

KENNY ANDERSON – guitar, accordion, vocals / **EEN ANDERSON** – double bass, banjo, vocals / **ANDY ROBINSON** – drums, vocals / **DONNA VINCENT + JASON BRASS** – fiddle / **ERIC BAEKEROOT** – banjo, guitar, mandolin / **ATHOLL FRASER** – bass, guitar

Lochshore not iss.

Jul 94. (cd) *(CDLDL 121)* **SPIKE'S 23 COLLECTION**
– The seminar / Baby pink / Old Lloyd / Say something / Long pockets, short arms / Graeme hallelujah Gaeme Wilson / Swinging on a gate / Please yourself / Unseen / Bloody red / Clown / Fisticuffs / Stupid world of rails / Spike's 23 collection.

KHARTOUM HEROES

KENNY ANDERSON – guitar, bouzouki, bass, keyboards, banjo, accordion, etc / **EEN ANDERSON** – banjo, bass, mouth-organ, vocals, etc / **ERIC BAECHEROOT** – guitars, mandolin, banjo, etc / **JASON BRASS** – fiddle, bass, vocals / **ANDY ROBINSON** – drums / with also **BUCK KINNEAR** – keyboards / **DOUGI McMILLAN** – samples, keyboards + **OLIVIA** – cello

Lochshore not iss.

Sep 95. (cd) *(CDLDL 1222)* **KHARTOUM HEROES**
– Cat-gut / St Swithin / Mother Hubbard / Space hopper / Charles and die laughing / Interference / Heaven / Bitter honey / Colossal angel / Song for a flower / Leaves out of bounds / Saints within / Moon barking.

– Fence discography –

1997. (cd) *(fnc 301)* **PIP DYLAN – Ain't A Classical Piece, Not By A Long Shot**
– Withered tree / Flamenco bar / Sweet angel / Nomanian polka / Eagle / Lavender moon / This'll bring a smile to your face / Stan the Nissan / All walks lost / Orr my dawg / Somewhat unknown / Trip / Where I once belonged / Lazy boy.
1997. (ltd-dat) *(fnc 303)* **LONE PIGEON – Moses**
1998. (cd) *(fnc 12)* **KING CREOSOTE – 12 O'clock On The Dot**
– Someting beginning with d . . . / Teapot / Abacus / Tumble dry / Greasy railroad / All the 3's / Margarita red / Hunger / Harper's dough / Hans Waddesh / Just after eleven she left / Goodbye Mrs. Hyde.
1999. (cd) *(fnc 13)* **KING CREOSOTE – Stinks**
– Tongue in groove / Little grown ups / Punchbag / Sulphur breeze / X-reg bartender / For pity's sake / Handful of 78's / Hellen / Short & sweet / Ten posts nine gaps / Heaven colour dyes / Happily never after / Small child . . . . cries / La dc di dah / Silence no more / All over Caroline / Marie Celeste / Lost again Billy.
1999. (cd-ep) *(fnc 1ep)* **KING CREOSOTE – Chalks EP**
– Monotony / Space / Homeboy / King of the fairies.
1999. (cd-ep) *(fnc 2ep)* **The JOSE – Beginners Fluke**
– Mail sunshine / The lounge bit / Whooee! whooee! / Catapult.
1999. (cd) *(fnc s1)* **various artists – Who's Afraid Of.. Fence**
– ST. ANDREWS CITIZENS – Jane Birkin / LONE PIGEON – Fall in thee / PIP DYLAN & LONE PIGEON – Ricketty road / MC QUAKE & DUBH SHOES – Flagstaff / KING CREOSOTE – Wonder woman / LONE PIGEON – Sun is down / ST. ANDREWS CITIZENS – Hector / KING CREOSOTE & LONE PIGEON – Marcel's parcel.
2000. (cd) *(fnc s2)* **various artists – Fence Go Fishin'**
– LONE PIGEON – Hello / MUNDO JAZZ – Quincy / PIP DYLAN – Splinter / BILLY PILGRIM – Never trust the ju-ju bird / ARMANDO LACERDA – Chillin' / HAIRY BOB'S GRANNY MAGNET – Feel the niceness / LONE PIGEON – Waiting for the wide open space / GUMMI BAKO – Mantra-k / KING CREOSOTE – Happy never after / DINKI KAIJU – Kingu kongu tai gojira / BILLY PILGRIM – In memorium.
2000. (cd) *(fnc 14)* **KING CREOSOTE – G**
– Your face / Two of a kind / Missionary / Russian sailor shirts / S.E.P. / Once was lost / Now who'd believe it? / A prairie tale / Walk tall / All I ask / Once was broken / Breaking up . . .
2001. (cd) *(fnc 15)* **KING CREOSOTE – Radge Weekend Starts Here**
– Laid if I'm lucky / With hindsight blues / No daddy / Handwashed / Creos'medleyote: Kir(kc)aldy – Fun(kc)rap – Fol(kc)ough / High wire / Heaven come down tonight / Life of lows / Far from saving grace / Mantra-rap / What's with this frown? / Were I not so tired Xhosa.
2001. (cd) *(fnc 16)* **KING CREOSOTE – King Creosote says "Buy The Bazouki Hair Oil"**
– Whine glasses / Conscience / Sunny-side up / Moral tenderhooks / Bubble / It's boredom alright / Fine / Sunshine / Crybaby / You want to walk / I'll fly by the seat of my pants / It's all very well Lester Flatt / How brave am I?
2001. (ltd-4xc-box) *(fnc 302)* **LONE PIGEON – 28 Secret Tracks**
Mar 01. (7"ep) *(fnc 304 – Bebop 31)* **LONE PIGEON – Touched By Tomoko EP**
2001. (cd) *(fnc s3)* **various artists – Fence Sampler #3**
– LONE PIGEON – Blue mantle / GUMMI BAKO – Dope on a rope / KING CREOSOTE – Little heart / BILLY PILGRIM – Walter De La Mare / The JOSE – Three mile trip / DWAYNE'S DOG SPARKY – / JO FOSTER & LONE PIGEON – Hold on Gordon / CHEEHI – Easy on the head / GUMMI BAKO, KING CREOSOTE & LONE PIGEON – Nova / U.N.P.O.C. – Amsterdam / BILLY PILGRIM & LONE PIGEON – Looks like a sunrise / JAMES YORKSTON – The lang toun.
2001. (cd) *(fnc mbf)* **various artists – Missing Behind Fence**
– KING CREOSOTE – Space / JAMES YORKSTON – Tender to the blues / LONE PIGEON – Won't you take me back / BILLY PILGRIM – Sssh . . . / LONE PIGEON – Hill upon the tower / PIP DYLAN – Wind in the trees / LONE PIGEON & KING CREOSOTE – Lonely vagabond / GUMMI BAKO – Little man / BILLY PILGRIM – Waiting for a lifetime / KING CREOSOTE – Monotony / JAMES YORKSTON – St. Patrick / LONE PIGEON – Jesus and me.
(above was an exclusive sampler for Missing records shop in Glasgow)
Nov 01. (7") *(fnc 305 – Bebop 33)* **LONE PIGEON – Rocks / You Think Only Boats Can Sink. / JAMES YORKSTON & THE ATHLETES – St. Patrick**
(below was an exclusive sampler for Avalanche records shops)
2002. (cd) *(fnc basf)* **various artists – Big Avalanche Small Fence**
– LONE PIGEON – Lone Pigeon's wineglass symphony / KING CREOSOTE – Worldly wiser / PIP DYLAN – A-ring-ting-ting / The ABRAHAMS – Gone in the

city / AERODYNAMICO – Burt's magical hands / MC QUAKE – A million bikes / CHEEHI – Said and done / The JOSE – Shockwave / PAPA BOOMHAUER & KING CREOSOTE – Back in the day / AMINO PEOPLE – Piano loop / IMMIGRANT – Stone heart / GUMMI BAKO & KING CREOSOTE – Going . . . gone / LONE PIGEON – Ride around in the sun.

Apr 02. (cd) *(fnc 901)* **IMMIGRANT – Untitled**
– Last hurrah / Five pound bomb / So close / A fall from grace / You / Two words three lies / Fare the winter well / Hellvelyn / Lost letters / Don't take it away from me / Stone heart.

Jun 02. (7") *(fnc 1v – Bebop 35)* **KING CREOSOTE – So Forlorn. / Mantra Rap / And So For Lorna**

Jun 02. (m-cd) *(fnc 306)* **LONE PIGEON – Concubine Rice**

2002. (cd) *(fnc 307)* **PIP DYLAN – Of All The Things I Can Eat, I'm Always Pleased With A Piece Of Cheese**
– Walk away / Lemon belly / Splinter / 8-ball chalkhouse / Pianomad / Moon man / Loft creek / So I wonder / The morning sun / Shoes / Bumbling blues / Spooked and on the run / Barony damp / No longer my forever / Senorita.

Fenetik Music records
(see under ⇒ Soma records / SLAM)

53rd & 3rd records

Founded: Bellshill, Lanarkshire . . . 1985 and set up by DAVID KEEGAN (of The SHOP ASSISTANTS) and STEPHEN PASTEL (of The PASTELS). Both disillusioned by the lack of independent support throughout Scotland, the pair were happy to form their own imprint when asked by 'Fast Forward' distributor, SANDY McLEAN. Having already delivered one 45 for the Bristol-based 'Subway' the previous year, The SHOP ASSISTANTS – KEEGAN being the only lad among four spiky-topped females! – launched 53rd & 3rd via the single, 'Safety Net'.

Not content with signing Scots acts, the label snapped up former SWELL MAPS frontman JOWE HEAD in his new project, The HOUSEHUNTERS. Their single, 'Cuticles', was a huge disappointment to all concerned – if you can imagine Buddy Holly's 'Heartbeat' ripped to shreds in a blender you'd have a fair idea of the content.

However, single No.3, a double A-sided 'Sad?' & 'E102' by the BMX BANDITS, was a different kettle of fish. This evolving local band led by DUGLAS STEWART, released a further couple of 45's over the course of the next two years. Oxford's TALULAH GOSH were next to spring up, the dual November '86 release of 'Beatnik Boy' and 'Steaming Train', being the first two of many twee-pop singles they delivered for the 53rd & 3rd.

Scottish talent was also on show for #'s 9 and 10, the BEAT POETS (with former PRIMEVALS guitarist TOM RAFFERTY) and The VASELINES (fronted by EUGENE KELLY and FRANCES McKEE), delivering two excellent EP's. The VASELINES' 'Son Of A Gun' and their follow-up's B-side, 'Molly's Lips', subsequently became live standards for Washington-based Grunge giants, NIRVANA; it seemed the music was somehow getting across to the States(!). An American friend of STEPHEN's was CALVIN JOHNSON, whose outfit, The BEAT HAPPENING, had already issued a handful of cassettes/LP's before becoming a surprise signing to 53rd & 3rd. Their 'Crashing Through' and 'Polly Peregrin' EP's in early '88, established a new fanbase in Britain, alongside the likes of homegrown new Scots acts, The BOY HAIRDRESSERS (soon to become TEENAGE FANCLUB) and The GROOVY LITTLE NUMBERS (who included JOE McALINDEN, later behind SUPERSTAR).

Around the same time, the label dug out their first long-player, a mini-set by CHIN CHIN ('Stop! Your Crying'), which became a bit of a curiosity in that no one at the time knew anything about them. Further albums by the BEAT POETS, Welsh indie-poppers the POOH STICKS and the VASELINES' farewell offering, 'Dum Dum', were the last remnants of what was to be Scotland's last indie outpost of the 80's.

– discography – *(italics are non-Scots)*

singles

Feb 86. (7"/12") *(AGARR 1/+T)* **SHOP ASSISTANTS – Safety Net**
Jul 86. (12") *(AGARR 2T) HOUSEHUNTERS – Cuticles*
Jul 86. (7"/12") *(AGARR 3/+T)* **BMX BANDITS – Sad? / E102**
Nov 86. (7"/12") *(AGARR 4/+T) TALULAH GOSH – Beatnik Boy*
Nov 86. (7"/12") *(AGARR 5/+T) TALULAH GOSH – Steaming Train*
Jan 87. (7"/12") *(AGARR 6/+T)* **BMX BANDITS – What A Wonderful World / The Day Before Tomorrow**
May 87. (7") *(AGARR 7) BEN VAUGHN COMBO – My First Band*
May 87. (7"/12") *(AGARR 8/+T) TALULAH GOSH – Talulah Gosh*

• The **BEAT POETS** were from Glasgow and comprised ex-PRIMEVALS guitarist TOM RAFFERTY, plus other musicians-only KEITH BRUCE, STEWART A NICOL, ROBERT RENFREW and JOHN CURRIE who (in no particular order) played drums, sax, bass and second guitar. Harking back to the days of DUANE EDDY and LINK WRAY (they covered the latter's 'I'M BRANDED') the band were suited up with smart tartan teddy-boy jackets.

May 87. (12"ep) *(AGARR 9T)* **BEAT POETS – Glasgow, Howard, Missouri EP**

Sep 87. (12"ep) *(AGARR 10)* **VASELINES – Son Of A Gun**
Jan 88. (12"ep) *(AGARR 11) HOUSEHUNTERS – Cooler Than Thou*
Jan 88. (12"ep) *(AGARR 12)* **BOY HAIRDRESSERS – Golden Showers**
Jan 88. (12"ep) *(AGARR 13)* **GROOVY LITTLE NUMBERS – You Made My Head Explode**
Jan 88. (7"/12") *(AGARR 14) TALULAH GOSH – Bringing Up Baby*
Jan 88. (12"ep) *(AGARR 15) BEAT HAPPENING – Crashing Through*
Feb 88. (7") *(AGARR 16) TALULAH GOSH – Testcard Girl*
Mar 88. (7"/12") *(AGARR 17)* **VASELINES – Dying For It**
Jun 88. (7"/12") *(AGARR 18)* **BMX BANDITS – Figure 4**
Jul 88. (7") *(AGARR 19)* **BEAT POETS – Rebel Surf / I'm Branded**
Aug 88. (12"ep) *(AGARR 20) BEAT HAPPENING – Polly Peregrin / SCREAMING TREES*
Aug 88. (12"ep) *(AGARR 21)* **GROOVY LITTLE NUMBERS – Happy Like Yesterday**

albums

Aug 88. (m-lp) *(AGAS 001)* **CHIN CHIN – Stop! Your Crying**
– Stop! your crying / Dark days / Never surrender / Cry in vain / Revolution / Stay with me / My guy / Jungle of fear.

Aug 88. (lp) *(AGAS 002) BEAT HAPPENING – Jamboree*
Sep 88. (lp) *(AGAS 003) Various Artists – Good Feeling*
Oct 88. (clear-lp) *(AGAS 004) TALULAH GOSH – Rock Legends Vol.69*
Jan 89. (pink-m-lp) *(AGAMC 5) POOH STICKS – Orgasm*
Aug 89. (lp) *(AGAS 006)* **BEAT POETS – Totally Radio** (shelved & later issued by Imaginary)
Jan 90. (lp) *(AGAS 007)* **VASELINES – Dum Dum**

— see also Avalanche/Alva records

Fire Island records (see under ⇒ Clubscene records)

Flotsam & Jetsam (F&J) records

Founded: by GORDON DAVIDSON, B2, 185 Kent Road, Charing Cross, Glasgow, G3 7HD. Apparently more interested in making records than money, this label came into existence amid the environs of the Kazoo club held at The 13th Note (based at 80 Glassford Street, Glasgow, G1 1UR).

A 10" mini-set by unknowns, TONIC, initiated the catalogue in early '96, closely followed by a ESKA (featuring a pre-MOGWAI STUART BRAITHWAITE) / POISON SISTERS split single. Subsequent obscurities from the Flotsam & Jetsam vaults included D.P. LE ODD, GLUE, FINGER CREAMS, NOSTRIL, BABY ASPIRIN, SPACE KITTENS, OLYMPIA, COMMERCIALS and VERA CRUISE, while the relatively more famous/infamous NEWTOWN GRUNTS, PINK KROSS, LUNG LEG, EL HOMBRE TRAJEADO, YUMMY FUR, The AMPHETAMEANIES and even MOGWAI occasionally spruced up the release schedule. Definitely worth a mention was the Club Beatroot series of split singles featuring live acts recorded at the 13th Note (with whom the release duties – all 13 of them – were shared) from December 1997 onwards.

– discography –

Feb 96. (10"m-lp) *(SHaG 001)* **TONIC – Window Shopping**
Feb 96. (7"ep) *(SHaG 002)* **ESKA + POISON SISTERS – split**
Jun 96. (7"ep) *(SHaG 003)* **D.P. LE ODD + GLUE – split – Prehumous**
Jun 96. (7"ep) *(SHaG 004)* **NEWTOWN GRUNTS – No Soap In Glasgow**
Jul 96. (7"ep) *(SHaG 005)* **FINGER CREAMS – Stars**
Aug 96. (7"ep) *(SHaG 006)* **NOSTRIL – Long Division Souffle**
Oct 96. (7"ep) *(SHaG 007)* **PINK KROSS – Active Dalmation**
Jan 97. (7"ep) *(SHaG 008)* **BABY ASPIRIN + Ph FAMILY – split**
Dec 96. (7"ep) *(SHaG 009)* **POISON SISTERS – Digitalis**
Feb 97. (7") *(SHaG 010)* **SPACE KITTENS – Felix**
Apr 97. (7") *(SHaG 011)* **BANGTWISTER – Agony Aunt**
Apr 97. (7") *(SHaG 012)* **FINGER CREAMS – Rich Girlfriend**
(split 45's below were shared w/ '13th Note' as CLUB BEATROOT series)
Nov 97. (7") *(SHaG 13.01)* **FENN + BEATROOT**
Dec 97. (7") *(SHaG 13.02)* **the PRIMEVALS + SWELLING MEG**
Jan 98. (7") *(SHaG 13.03)* **SPACE KITTENS + TROUT**
Feb 98. (7") *(SHaG 13.04)* **Ph FAMILY + MOGWAI**
Mar 98. (7") *(SHaG 13.05)* **?**
Apr 98. (7") *(SHaG 13.06)* **LUNGLEG + EL HOMBRE TREJEADO**
May 98. (7") *(SHaG 13.07)* **POISON SISTERS + THE KARELIA**
Jun 98. (7") *(SHaG 13.08)* **YUMMY FUR + OLYMPIA**
Jul 98. (7") *(SHaG 13.09)* **AMPHETAMEANIES + VERA CRUISE**

— I think there were some more to 13.13

Dec 97. (cd) *(SHaG 014D)* **NEWTOWN GRUNTS – The Day Of The Jakey**
Sep 97. (7") *(SHaG 015)* **EL HOMBRE TRAJEADO – Moonunit Manual**
1998. (cd) *(SHaG 016)* **COMMERCIALS – When I Saw Her Face**
1998. (cd) *(SHaG 017D)* **POISON GIRLS – Tarantula Rising**
1998. ? *(ShaG 018)* **?**
Jun 98. (7") *(SHaG 019)* **EL HOMBRE TRAJEADO + THE KARELIA**
1998. (cd) *(SHaG 020D)* **COMMERCIALS – Backstabbing**
Dec 98. (7") *(SHaG 021)* **AMPHETAMEANIES – Around The World In 5 And A Half Minutes**
Apr 99. (cd-s) *(SHaG 022)* **COMMERCIALS – Power Of Love**

- **SNEAK ATTACK TIGERS** were formed in Glasgow around 1998. They were of the harmony guitar-rock ilk and consisted of PAUL McLAUGHLIN (vocals & guitar), JIM LANG (guitar & vocals), GEORGE McINTYRE (bass & vocals) and CHRIS BLACK (percussion).

Apr 99. (7") *(SHaG 023)* **SNEAK ATTACK TIGERS – You Should Stick Around / Getting Out**

Apr 99. (7"/cd-s) *(SHaG 024)* **AMPHETAMEANIES – Last Night**
Apr 99. (7") *(SHaG 025)* **Ph FAMILY – Shill Display**
Oct 99. (7") *(SHaG 026)* **AMPHETAMEANIES + NEWTOWN GRUNTS – Treaty At Harthill**
Jul 00. (cd) *(SHaG 027)* **AMPHETAMEANIES – Right Line In Nylons**

Geographic records

Founded: by STEPHEN PASTEL, PO Box 549, Glasgow, G12 9NQ. The PASTELS man's first signing was the Japanese MAHER SHALAL HASH BAZ (an outfit fronted by classically-trained composer and jazz musician TORI KUDO (and his wife REIKO) who abandoned that claustrophobic musical environment for a more open-minded avant-garde fusion; future Geographic artist NAGISA NI TE was also Japanese. Third on the roster, EMPRESS were in fact a slowcore act from Leeds, while others INTERNATIONAL AIRPORT, BILL WELLS TRIO, FUTURE PILOT AKA, TELSTAR PONIES and TEENAGE FANCLUB (with American indie legend JAD FAIR) were all major Scottish-based acts in their own right. Latest signings, SISTER VANILLA, have a sound not too dissimilar to The JESUS & MARY CHAIN. I suppose that's because it has the backing of WILLIAM and JIM REID (plus BEN LURIE) for their sister LINDA REID's vocals. A track, 'PASTEL BLUE' (on the Geographic sampler 'YOU DON'T NEED DARKNESS . . .' showed off her/their VELVET UNDERGROUND leanings.

– discography –

Jun 00. (cd/d-lp) *(geog 1 cd/lp) MAHER SHALAL HASH BAZ – From A Summer To Another Summer (An Egypt To Another Egypt)*
Oct 00. (cd/lp) *(geog 2 cd/lp)* **INTERNATIONAL AIRPORT – Nothing We Can Control**
Sep 00. (cd/lp) *(geog 3 cd/lp) EMPRESS – Empress*
Nov 00. (7") *(geog 4) MAHER SHALAL HASH BAZ – Unknown Happiness*
Dec 00. (cd/lp) *(geog 5 cd/lp)* **BILL WELLS TRIO – Incorrect Practice**
Jan 01. (cd/lp) *(geog 6 cd/lp)* **FUTURE PILOT AKA – Tiny Waves Mighty Sea**
Apr 01. (7"/cd-s) *(geog 7/+cd)* **FUTURE PILOT AKA – Beat Of A Drum**
Jul 01. (7") *(geog 8)* **TELSTAR PONIES – Farewell Farewell**
Dec 00. (7") *(geog 9)* **FUTURE PILOT AKA – Darshan**
Oct 01. (7") *(geog 10) NAGISA NI TE – They / Me, On A Beach*
Nov 01. (cd/lp) *(geog 11 cd/lp) NAGISA NI TE – Songs For A Simple Moment*
Apr 02. (cd) *(geog 12cd)* **Various Artists – You Don't Need Darkness To Do What You Think Is Right**
– PASTELS – Introduction – Everybody is a star / INTERNATIONAL AIRPORT – Cordial arrest / FUTURE PILOT AKA – Remember fun (like we was young) / BILL WELLS OCTET – Wiltz / MAHER SHALAL HASH BAZ – Stone in the river / NAGISA NI TE – Me, on the beach / SISTER VANILLA – Pastel blue / PEDRO – Amber / BARBARA MORGENSTERN – Kleiner ausschnitt / EMPRESS – Known for years / APPENDIX OUT – The language in things / TELSTAR PONIES – Farewell, farewell / DIRECTORSOUND – Theme from Hythe hill / NATIONAL PARK – No more rides / PLINTH – Bracken / KEVIN SHIELDS – Outro.
Feb 02. (7"/cd-s) *(geog 13/+cd)* **TEENAGE FANCLUB & JAD FAIR – Near To You**
Mar 02. (cd/lp) *(geog 14 cd/lp)* **TEENAGE FANCLUB & JAD FAIR – Words Of Wisdom And Hope**
May 02. (cd/lp) *(geog 15 cd/lp)* **BILL WELLS TRIO – Also In White**
Aug 02. (cd) *(geog 16cd) MAHER SHALAL HASH BAZ – Maher On Water*

Glasgow Underground records

Founded: Glasgow (funnily enough) . . . 1997 by dance producers/DJ's KEVIN McKAY and ANDY CARRICK. The pair had originally released a series of acclaimed 12"ers on their own 'Muzique Tropique' label in the mid-90's, using a variety of aliases – 4AM, MYSTIC SOUL, WEST COAST CONNECTION etc. – for their inimitable brand of sultry deep house. 'Glasgow Underground' was subsequently set up to release tracks by MUZIQUE TROPIQUE (confusingly perhaps as artist rather than label) along with a raft of local and more exotic talent.

GU001 came courtesy of STUDIO BLUE – a duo of McKAY and KENNY INGLIS – and 'Just A Mood', an alias used a further twice during the label's infancy with 'Cantina Scene' (GU002) and 'Lost In Edinburgh' (GU004). CARRICK then released a couple of tracks under his own name, 'Funk The Police' and 'Golden Monkey Theme'. The ever distinctive MUZIQUE TROPIQUE weighed in with the label's 7th and 8th releases (and double debut set), namely 'Kingston' (remixed by ANDREW WEATHERALL's TWO LONE SWORDSMEN) and 'Shipwrecked'.

New Yorkers MATEO & MATOS were the first foreigners to be signed up with their 'Release The Rhythm' while Glasgow's own DJQ graced GU010 with his filter classic, 'The Original Porn King'.

McKAY was never far from the release schedule himself, making up one half of both SIXTEEN SOULS (alongside OMID NOURIZADEH) and SECOND HAND SOUL (with MILES WILSON), releasing 'On My Mind' and 'Bar Blues' respectively. More top notch American gear arrived in the shape of ROMANTHONY (& DJ PREDATOR), 'Do U Wanna Dance' and 'It's On 2Nite (Parts 1&2)', the latter featuring NAIDA. English-born Glasgow School of Art graduate DANIEL IBBOTSON made his GU debut with 'Celebrate' followed by the Nottingham-based NEON HEIGHTS and 'Cherry Trees'.

Local lads AIRFIX (a collective of Glasgow producers) took time off from creating theme music for 'Taggart' with their 'STORIES' 12" and even the Portuguese got a look in via LOVE REC's 'The Scene'. Album wise, the first long player to hit the racks was MUZIQUE TROPIQUE's 'Collection', gathering together all the pseudonymous treats from McKAY and CARRICK's early days. Big Apple producers MATEO & MATOS released a couple of volumes of their 'New York Rhythms' while the aforementioned IBBOTSON, ROMANTHONY, NEON HEIGHTS, London deep house dons IDJUT BOYS (& QUAKERMAN) and Greek MIKAEL DELTA all released large slabs of vinyl.

The label also issued an obligatory sampler, 'Glasgow Underground Volume 1' in May '98, while a further two volumes were testament to GU's unrelentingly prolific output. Counting both albums and singles, the label are well on their way to the 100 mark, supported all the way by quality DJ's such as ROGER SANCHEZ, FRANCOIS KEVORKIAN, DJ SNEAK and DERRICK CARTER. Recent addition, MILTON JACKSON (aka BARRY CHRISTIE), is a 20 year-old from Edinburgh who moved to Glasgow for a course on sound engineering. Taking his name from 70's vives man, MILTON JACKS, BARRY released his first long-playing record, 'THE BIONIC BOY' (2002), having previously released the 'SUNLIGHT' 12". His sounds are strictly wigged-out funky electronics with dark and moody dancefloor beats.

4 AM

CARRICK + McKAY

Pure White — not iss.
Mar 95. (12") *(STU 6T)* **4 AM (remixes)**

Musique Tropique — not iss.
Mar 96. (12"ep) *(MTR12 002)* **UNDERWATER BLUES EP**
– 4 am theme / Underwater blues / Return of the sea turtle.

– discography –

Mar 97. (12") *(GU 001)* **STUDIO BLUE – Just A Mood / Shona's Song**
Apr 97. (12") *(GU 002)* **STUDIO BLUE – Cantina Scene / Aquaman**
May 97. (12") *(GU 003)* **SIXTEEN SOULS – Late Night Jam / On My Mind**
Jun 97. (12") *(GU 004)* **STUDIO BLUE – Lost In Edinburgh / Dub 4 Marc**
Jun 97. (12") *(GU 005)* **ANDY CARRICK – Funk The Police / Freak Vibrations**
Jul 97. (12") *(GU 006)* **ANDY CARRICK – Golden Monkey Theme / Surprise Reprise**
Aug 97. (12") *(GU 007)* **MUZIQUE TROPIQUE – Kingston (2 Lone Swordsmen & 16B mixes) / Jazz The Street**
Aug 97. (12") *(GU 008)* **MUZIQUE TROPIQUE – Shipwrecked 1+2**
Sep 97. (d-cd/q-lp) *(GU CD/LP 001)* **MUZIQUE TROPIQUE – Collection**
– Siesta / Stella Sunday (Idjut Boys string-a-pella) / Jazz the sea turtle (16B remix) / Back to black (House of 909 remix) / 90 in the shade (DIY & Toka Project remix) / Voodoo rhythm (Abacus remix) / Kingston (Two Lone Swordsmen remix) / Shipwrecked (Swag's primnitive remix) / Gospel song (Dubtribe's gospel dub) / Stella Sunday (Idjut Bots Sarbeni remix) / Kingston / Ice spinner / Stella Sunday / Return of the sea turtle / 4am theme / Montego Bay (sea turtle remix) / Jazz the sea turtle / 90 in the shade / Dub attraction.
Sep 97. (12") *(GU 009) MATEO & MATOS – Release The Rhythm*
Oct 97. (cd/lp) *(GU CD/LP 002) MATEO & MATOS – New York Rhythms*
Oct 97. (12") *(GU 010)* **DJ Q – Original Porn King EP**
– Moody groove / Porn king / Vincent's vibe.
Oct 97. (12") *(GU 011)* **MUZIQUE TROPIQUE – Soul Cruising**
– Black America / Desert Moon / Soul Cruising

Dec 97. (12") *(GU 012)* **SIXTEEN SOULS – On My Mind (2 mixes) / Late Night Jam (2 Idjut Boys remixes)**
Jan 98. (12") *(GU 013) MATEO & MATOS – Keep On Dancin'*
Feb 98. (12") *(GU 014) RICK PRESTON – Chasing The Sun*
Mar 98. (12") *(GU 015) ROMANTHONY & NAIDA – Do You Think You Can Love Me*
Apr 98. (12") *(GU 016)* **SECOND HAND SOUL – Summer Nights EP**
– Bar blues / Swing it / Summer nights.
Apr 98. (12") *(GU 017)* **MUZIQUE TROPIQUE – Phazers Set To Funk / Midnight In Atlantis**
May 98. (12") *(GU 018) ALEX MORAN – Vibes From The Dark Side*
– Room 9 / Vibes from the dark side / Don't fancy yours much.
May 98. (12") *(GU 019) ROMANTHONY PRESENTS NAIDA – Do You Think You Can Move Me*
May 98. (12") *(GU 020) ROMATT PRODUCTIONS featuring NEDELKA – I Wanna Ride*
Jun 98. (cd/d-lp) *(GU CD/LP 003)* **Various Artists – Glasgow Underground Volume 1**
– STUDIO BLUE – Just a mood (Andy Carrick's just a remix) / RICK PRESTON – Two fisted smoke / MATEO & MATOS – Keep on dancin' (Kevin's DJ groove) / ANDY CARRICK – Freak vibrations (Kevin's freaky groove) / CASSIO – Baby love (Muzique Tropique's love the bass remix) / MUZIQUE TROPIQUE – Black America / DJ Q – The original porn king / SIXTEEN SOULS – Late night jam / ROMANTHONY PRESENTS NAIDA – Do you think you can love me.
Jun 98. (12") *(GU 021) LHK PRODUCTIONS – Danger Zone EP*
Jun 98. (12") *(GU 022) MATEO & MATOS – Release The Rhythm*
Jul 98. (12") *(GU 023) ROMANTHONY & DJ PREDATOR – Do U Wanna Dance*
Jul 98. (12") *(GU 024) CASSIO WIRE – Baby Love (remixes)*
Jul 98. (12") *(GU 025) POWDER PRODUCTIONS – El Loco*
Aug 98. (12") *(GU 026) MATEO & MATOS – Remixes EP*
Aug 98. (12") *(GU 027) MATEO & MATOS – Swing Solution*
Sep 98. (12") *(GU 028) CHARLES SILENCE TRIO – Winter Sadness*
Sep 98. (12") *(GU 029) LHK PRODUCTIONS – Changes EP*
Sep 98. (cd/d-lp) *(GU CD/LP 004) MATEO & MATOS –*
Oct 98. (12") *(GU 030) FREEFORM FIVE – Hustling EP*
Oct 98. (12") *(GU 031) RICK PRESTON – Future Paradise EP*
Nov 98. (cd/d-lp) *(GU CD/LP 005) POWDER PRODUCTIONS – Pipe Dreams*
Nov 98. (12") *(GU 032) ROMANTHONY presents NAIDA – It's On Tonite (part 1)*
Nov 98. (12") *(GU 033) ROMANTHONY presents NAIDA – It's On Tonite (part 2)*
Nov 98. (cd/d-lp) *(GU CD/LP 006) DANIEL IBBOTSON – Streamlines*
Feb 99. (cd/lp) *(GU CD/LP 007) ROMANTHONY & DJ PREDATOR – Instinctual*
Feb 99. (12") *(GU 034) RICK PRESTON – Soul Searchin'*
Feb 99. (12") *(GU 035) ROMANTHONY & DJ PREDATOR – Clap Ya Handz*
Feb 99. (12") *(GU 036) MATEO & MATOS – Just A Dab (remixes)*
Mar 99. (12") *(GU 037) LHK PRODUCTIONS – Just Groovin' EP*
Mar 99. (cd/d-lp) *(GU CD/LP 008) Idjut Boys & Quakerman – The Shoeing You Deserve*
Apr 99. (12") *(GU 038) SLAM MODE – Outre-mer*
Apr 99. (cd/d-lp) *(GU CD/LP 009) SLAM MODE – La Colecion*
Apr 99. (12") *(GU 039) DANIEL IBBOTSON – Celebrate*
Jun 99. (12") *(GU 040) DANIEL IBBOTSON – Things Change*
Jul 99. (12") *(GU 041) NEON HEIGHTS – Cherry Trees*
Jun 99. (cd/d-lp) *(GU CD/LP 010) Various Artists – Glasgow Underground Volume 2 (re-mixed by Kevin McKay; GUCD 010X)*
Jun 99. (12") *(GU 042) MATEO & MATOS – The Real Thing*
Aug 99. (12") *(GU 043) DJ PREDATOR & ROMANTHONY – Findamusic*
Sep 99. (12") *(GU 044) POWDER PRODUCTIONS – Chile Sauce*
Sep 99. (12") *(GU 045) AIRFIX – Stories*
Sep 99. (cd/lp) *(GU CD/LP 011) MIKAEL DELTA – Blue Emotions*
Oct 99. (12") *(GU 046) CASSIO WARE – Baby Love*
Oct 99. (12") *(GU 047) JERSEY STREET – Vaya A Vivir*
Oct 99. (cd/d-lp) *(GU CD/LP 012) MATEO & MATOS – The Many Shades Of Mateo & Matos*
Nov 99. (12") *(GU 048) ROMANTHONY – Countdown 2000*
Nov 99. (12") *(GU 050) IDJUT BOYS & QUAKERMAN – Radio Rage*
Nov 99. (cd/d-lp) *(GU CD/LP 013) DANIEL IBBOTSON – Frequency And Phase*
Apr 01. (12"/12"remix) *(GU 50/+R) Various Artists – Glasgow Underground Allstars*
Dec 99. (12") *(GU 051) LHK PRODUCTIONS – Body Works EP*
Feb 00. (12") *(GU 052) MATEO & MATOS – Got A Message*
Mar 00. (12") *(GU 053)* **LHK PRODUCTIONS – Under Your Skin EP**
Mar 00. (12") *(GU 054) JERSEY STREET – How Could I Be Loved*
Mar 00. (cd/d-lp) *(GU CD/LP 015) ROMANTHONY – R.Hide In Plain Site*
Apr 00. (cd/d-lp) *(GU CD/LP 016) NEON HEIGHTS – A View From The Heights*
May 00. (12"/cd-s) *(GU 055/+CD) ROMANTHONY – Bring U Up*
Feb 00. (12") *(GU 056) POWDER PRODUCTIONS – Future*
Apr 00. (12") *(GU 057) MATEO & MATOS – Stomp Your Feet*
May 00. (12") *(GU 058) PHATT PUSSYCAT – Find A Way*
May 00. (cd/d-lp) *(GU CD/LP 017) Various Artists – Glasgow Underground Volume 3*
Jun 00. (12") *(GU 059) LOVE REC – The Scene (revisited)*
Sep 00. (12") *(GU 060) DANIEL IBBOTSON – Comin' 2 Get You*
Jul 00. (12") *(GU 061) MATEO & MATOS – Don't Ever Stop Lovin'*
Jul 00. (12") *(GU 062) POWDER PRODUCTIONS – Nutonic*
Sep 00. (cd/d-lp) *(GU CD/LP 014) Various Artists – Slow Burning*
Sep 00. (12") *(GU 063) ALEX MORAN – Earth Women Are Easy*
Oct 00. (12") *(GU 064) PASCAL & MR. DAY – It's A Disco Night*
Oct 00. (12") *(GU 065) NEON HEIGHTS – 16 Again*
Nov 00. (cd/d-lp) *(GU CD/LP 019) PASCAL & TEDDY G – High Flying*
Nov 00. (12") *(GU 066) LHK PRODUCTIONS – Nothing Is Sacred EP*
Dec 00. (12"/cd-s) *(GU 067/+CD) JERSEY STREET – Disappear*
Jan 01. (cd/-d-lp) *(GU CD/LP 020) PHATT PUSSYCAT – Phatt Life*
Feb 01. (12"ep) *(GU 068) POWDER PRODUCTIONS – Powder Beats EP*
Feb 01. (12") *(GU 069) LHK PRODUCTIONS – Ican / Candy*
Mar 01. (12") *(GU 070) JERSEY STREET – Step Into The Light*
Mar 01. (cd/d-lp) *(GUCD/GULP 021) POWDER PRODUCTIONS – Cuban Fire*
Apr 01. (12") *(GU 071) JERSEY STREET – Brand New Day*
Apr 01. (12") *(GU 072) JERSEY STREET – Brand New Day (remix)*
May 01. (12") *(GU 073) SPANISH FLY – Gringo*
May 01. (12") *(GU 074) PASCAL & MR.DAY – Visions (Rollercone*
May 01. (12") *(GU 075) PASCAL & MR.DAY – Visions (Brothers Of*
May 01. (cd/d-lp) *(GU CD/LP 022) MATEO & MATMOS – Inspirations: mixed by John Mateo & Eddie Matmos*
Jun 01. (cd/d-lp) *(GUCD/GULP 023) Various Artists – Glasgow Underground Volume 4*
Jun 01. (12") *(GU 076) TEDDY G – Open Sound*
Jun 01. (12") *(GU 077) NEON HEIGHTS & ZOE JOHNSON – Are We Thru (Bent's mixes)*
Jun 01. (12") *(GU 078) NEON HEIGHTS & ZOE JOHNSON – Are We Thru (club mixes)*
Jul 01. (12") *(GU 079) PASCAL & MR. DAY – The Lure Of Melody*
Jul 01. (12") *(GU 080)* **MILTON JACKSON – Sunlight**
Jul 01. (cd/lp) *(GUCD/GULP 024) PASCAL & MR. DAY – The Lure Of Melody*
Jul 01. (12"ep) *(GU 081) POWDER PRODUCTIONS – Powder Beats Volume 2*
Aug 01. (12") *(GU 082) TEDDY G – Brazilia City mix*
Aug 01. (12") *(GU 083)* **ANDY CARRICK – Needin' You**
Sep 01. (12") *(GU 084) LINUS LOVES – Body And Soul*
Sep 01. (cd/d-lp) *(GUCD/GULP 025) C.PEN – Freestyle Mechanic*
Sep 01. (12") *(GU 085) MATEO & MATMOS – Body 'N' Soul*
Oct 01. (cd) *(GUCD 026) Various Artists mixed by G-HA – Skansen Music*
Nov 01. (12") *(GU 086) LHK – Easy*
Nov 01. (12") *(GU 087) JERSEY STREET – Born Again*
Nov 01. (12") *(GU 088) JERSEY STREET – Born Again (remixes)*
Dec 01. (12") *(GU 089) GROOVE ASSASSINS – Dancin' Warrior*
Jan 02. (12") *(GU 090) LINUS LOVES – Body And Soul (Powder Productions remix)*
Jan 02. (cd/d-lp) *(GUCD/GULP 028)* **MILTON JACKSON – The Bionic Boy**
– Who needs forever / In the mood / Beat my beat / Shock me all nite / I see you / All new / Bionic boy / Dimensional / Double trouble / Old styles / Sunlight.
Feb 02. (12") *(GU 091) PASCAL & MR. DAY – Shelter (Milton Jackson EQ mixes)*
Feb 02. (12") *(GU 092) PASCAL & MR. DAY – Shelter (Milton Jackson M-A-D dub mixes)*
Mar 02. (cd/d-lp) *(GUCD/GULP 029) JERSEY STREET – After The Rain*
Mar 02. (12") *(GU 093) GROOVE ASSASSINS & DJ RAW – DJ's Preachin' Machine*
Apr 02. (12") *(GU 094) TEDDY G – Zis A Not A Rap Song*
Apr 02. (cd/d-lp) *(GUCD/GULP 030) GROOVE ASSASSINS & DJ RAW – Street Level Jams*
Apr 02. (12") *(GU 095)* **MILTON JACKSON – Dimensional**
May 02. (12") *(GU 096) ROSE SMITH – Life Changes (2 Banks 4)*
May 02. (12") *(GU 097) PASCAL & MISTER DAY – The Lure Of Melody*
May 02. (cd/d-lp) *(GUCD/GULP 031) ROSE SMITH – Rose Smith*
Jul 02. (cd/d-lp) *(GUCD/GULP 032) Various Artists – Glasgow Underground Volume 5*
Jul 02. (12") *(GU 098) PHATT PUSSYCAT – 2 B Near U*
Aug 02. (12") *(GU 099)* **DJ Q – Over U Now / System 600**
Aug 02. (12"ep) *(GU 100/+R) Various Artists – Glasgow Underground All Stars Volume 2*
Sep 02. (12") *(GU 101) MATEO & MATOS – Feelin' Sexy*
Sep 02. (12") *(GU 102)* **MODEM – Do It Right**

— MODEM are KEVIN McKAY & MILTON JACKSON

Hook records

Founded: Aberdeen . . . 1993 by EOAN 'ELVIS' PRITCHARD and CHRIS COWIE. Both relative veterans of the local music scene (COWIE had worked as an engineer while PRITCHARD had played in a couple of early 80's indie bands), the pair found their true vocation in the DIY ethos of the late 80's house explosion. After recording some material with a collective of local musicians and DJ's, the duo failed to attract any label interest and subsequently decided to release their own records.

With an independent distribution deal through 'Great Asset', Hook enjoyed their first two 12"ers, 'Give Myself To You' by PARTY ON PLASTIC (an alias for PRITCHARD and COWIE themselves) and 'Barimba' by BUBBLE UP. Unfortunately, the distributor went bankrupt shortly after and Hook was left in limbo for almost a year. HK 003 eventually emerged in 1994 in the shape of 'Keep On Pumping It Up' by BROTHER SLEDGE, the same year PRITCHARD and COWIE initiated their left-field sister imprint, 'Bellboy'. The latter's first release was 'Uman/Subuman', a track by experimental techno-heads, SKINTRADE. A duo of KEV GUNN and DAVE DUNBAR, SKINTRADE started life at the dawn of the 90's as REJUVENATE, having an early track featured on a CD free with Future Music Magazine. The aforementioned 'Uman/Subuman' piqued the interest of Glasgow's hip 'Soma' label, with whom the pair went on to record the acclaimed 'Shape Shifter' and 'Andomraxess' 12"ers. Studio boffins of the highest order, SKINTRADE's renowned collection of modern and vintage recording equipment was at least partly displayed to the public in 1995 when they brought their synths and computers to the live arena on a British/European tour.

Hook, meanwhile, kept on reeling in the club punters with 1994 singles by The TURNBULL ACS ('Bring It On Down') and BROTHER SLEDGE ('The Trade Marks') while Bellboy catered to the likes of CANYON ('Tumbleweed'), WAVELENGTH ('Morpheus') and INERTIA ('Inertia'). 1995 saw a further slew of releases including tracks by future 'Lithium' act, SCAN CARRIERS ('Ezascumby'), EXCABS ('Neuro') and even EOAN 'ELVIS' PRITCHARD himself with 'Zed's Ded Baby'. From the mid-90's through to the new millennium, both Hook and Bellboy notched up a fairly impressive 50+ releases each, casting their net wider with foreign talent such as CHRISTOPHER LAWRENCE (from the States). During this productive period, COWIE and his crew also founded another couple of sister imprints: trance label 'U.G.' was initiated with ACID FUNK (late '96) and has since become a favourite with DJ's like PAUL OAKENFOLD and JUDGE JULES, 'Panther', meanwhile, was set up in early 1998 and aimed at the funky house/soulful garage market. The latter label's first release was a track by the DISCO KINGS entitled 'Black Fudge'.

- (Hook) discography

1993. (12") *(HK 001)* **PARTY ON PLASTIC - Give Myself To You**
1993. (12") *(HK 002)* **BUBBLE UP - Barimba**
1994. (12") *(HK 003)* **BROTHER SLEDGE - Keep On Pumping It Up**
1994. (12") *(HK 004)* **the TURNBULL ACS - Bring It On Down**
1994. (12"ep) *(HK 005)* **BROTHER SLEDGE - The Trade Marks**
1995. (12") *(HK 006)* **CANYON - Planet Source**
Dec 95. (12") *(HK 007T)* **X CABS - Avalon / Adena**
Jan 96. (12") *(HK 008T)* **CANYON - Planet 10 / Move**
Mar 96. (12") *(HK 009T) TRANSA – Prophase*
Mar 96. (12") *(HK 010T) TRANSA – Prophase remix (re-iss. May00 on Hook: silver series; HK 010SIL)*
Apr 96. (12") *(HK 011T)* **DE NIRO - Evolver / mix**
May 96. (12") *(HK 012T)* **CANYON - Universe / remix**
May 96. (12") *(HK 013T) THIRD MAN – Blood Music / Neutral Nervous*

— **DAWNTREADER** discography up until they were on 'Hook'
1993. (7") *(DTV 001)* **Today / Time**
1994. (cd-ep) *(DTCD 002)* **Talk EP**
– Close your eyes / Save / John says.
1996. (cd/c) *(DT CD/MC 003)* **Puppy**
(above releases on their own 'Cannonball' imprint)

Jun 96. (12") *(HK 014T)* **DAWNTREADER - Dominion / red room mix**
Aug 96. (12") *(HK 015T) THIRD MAN – Planet Hunters / Solar Cycle*
Sep 96. (12") *(HK 016T)* **DE NIRO - Mind Of Man / remix**
Sep 96. (12") *(HK 017T)* **LIQUID ART - Liquid Art / Liquid Art mix / Xplorer / Recoil**
Nov 96. (12") *(HK 018T)* **DE NIRO - Elan Vital / Tried And True**
Jan 97. (12") *(HK 020T)* **DAWNTREADER - Overland / Evans Tide**
Mar 97. (12") *(HK 021T)* **CANYON - Purple Haze / Agitator**
Apr 97. (12") *(HK 022T)* **CANYON - Forbidden Channel / mix**
May 97. (12") *(HK 023T) TRANSA – Enervate*
May 97. (12") *(HK 024T) CHRISTOPHER LAWRENCE – Navigator / Neodog (re-iss. May00 on Hook: silver series; HK 024SIL)*
Jun 97. (12") *(HK 025T)* **X CABS - Engage / System**
— note: TRANSA + X-CABS had a single on 'Perfecto'; *PERF 147)*
Aug 97. (12") *(HK 026)* **HAVANA - Discorder**
Nov 97. (12") *(HK 027) CHRISTOPHER LAWRENCE – Interceptor / Geoscape (re-iss. May00 on Hook: silver series; HK 027SIL)*
Nov 97. (12") *(HK 028)* **MIKE FIX - Steeldrum**
Mar 98. (12") *(HK 030)* **X CABS - Infectious**
(above also on 12"remix; *HK 030R)* cd-s; *HKCD 030)*
(re-iss. May00 on Hook: silver series; HK 030SIL)
Mar 98. (12") *(HK 031)* **CANYON - Blackout**
Mar 98. (12"/cd-s) *(HK 032/+CDS) TAYLOR – Slide*
Aug 98. (12") *(HK 033)* **LIQUID ART - Magnetic North**
Sep 98. (cd/d-lp) *(HK/+CDXY/XY 003)* **X CABS - Chemistry**
– Neuro / Pinball / Cut to zero / Innocent rush / System / Hold the day / Disco X3 / Rhythm of life / Infectious / Engage.
Sep 98. (12") *(HK 034)* **X CABS - Cut To Zero** *(re-iss. May00 on Hook: silver series; HK 034SIL)*
Oct 98. (12") *(HK 035) CHRISTOPHER LAWRENCE – Shredder (re-iss. Aug00 on Hook: silver series; HK 035SIL)*
Dec 98. (12"/cd-s) *(HK 036/+CDS) TRANSA – Behind The Sun*
Mar 99. (12") *(HK 037) CASCADE – Transcend (re-iss. May00 on Hook: silver series; HK 037SIL)*
Apr 99. (12") *(HK 038)* **DAWNTREADER - Mission / Relay**
May 99. (12") *(HK 039)* **DE NIRO - State Of Mind / Deepsky** *(re-iss. May00 on Hook: silver series; HK 039SIL)*
May 99. (12") *(HK 041) CHRISTOPHER LAWRENCE – Renegade (re-iss. Aug00 on Hook: silver series; HK 041SIL)*
Jul 99. (12") *(HK 042) SANDRA COLLINS – Flutterby*
Jul 99. (12") *(HK 043) TRANSA – Carla's Theme (re-iss. May00 on Hook: silver series; HK 043SIL)*
Nov 99. (d12"/cd-ep) *(HK/+CDS 044)* **X CABS - Neuro 99 (9 mixes)**
Nov 99. (12") *(HK 045)* **X CABS - Neuro 99 Vol.2**
Nov 99. (12") *(HK 046)* **LIQUID ART - Liquid Groove**
Jan 00. (12") *(HK 047) CHRISTOPHER LAWRENCE – Rush Hour*
Mar 00. (12") *(HK 049) TRANSA – Astro Dawn*
Jul 00. (12"remox/cd-s) *(HK/+CDS 050)* **X CABS - Infectious**
Jun 00. (d-cd) *(HKCDXY 050)* **Various Artists mixed by X CABS - Exposure**
– CHRISTOPHER LAWRENCE – Shredder / UNKNOWN – Don't look back / LIQUID ART – Liquidgroove / DAWNTREADER – Missions / TRANSA – Transtar / CANYON – Twighlight / DeNIRO – Deepsky / CHRISTOPHER LAWRENCE – Renegade / MIKE FIX – Steeldrum / CASCADE – Transcend (Transa remix).
Sep 00. (12") *(HK 051) SPX – Straight To The Point*
(orig.rel.Oct99 on 'Smash Trax'; ST 006)
(re-iss. Oct00 on 'Inversus'; INV 05)
Dec 00. (d-cd) *(HKCDXY 051)* **Various Artists mixed by CHRIS COWIE - Exposure Vol.2**
Oct 00. (12") *(HK 052) CHRISTOPHER LAWRENCE – Cruise Control*
Nov 00. (12") *(HK 053) KODANSHA – The Longer Now*
Jan 01. (12") *(HK 054)* **CHRIS COWIE - Habana**
May 01. (12") *(HK 055) TRANSA – Rotation / Escada*

- (Bellboy) discography -

1993. (12") *(BL 001)* **SKINTRADE - Subhuman**
— SKINTRADE went on to 'Soma' records
1994. (12"ep) *(BL 002)* **CANYON - Tumbleweed**
1994. (12"ep) *(BL 003)* **WAVELENGTH - Morpheus**
1994. (12"ep) *(BL 004)* **INERTIA - Inertia**
— note:- two other INERTIA's issued the 'Infiltrator' CD on 'Celtic Circle' in Nov'95 and the 'Inertia' EP for 'Regal' in Apr'96.
Sep 95. (12") *(BL 006)* **SCAN CARRIERS - Eza Scumby / Refunction**
Oct 95. (12") *(BL 007)* **X CABS - Neuro / Outcast**
Nov 95. (12") *(BL 008)* **EOAN 'ELVIS' PRITCHARD - Zeds Ded Baby / Pricks**
Dec 95. (12") *(BL 009)* **VEGAS SOUL - Vegas / Diffusion**
Jan 96. (12") *(BL 010)* **BULKHEAD - The Fever / House Cruise**
Jan 96. (12") *(BL 011)* **SCAN CARRIERS - Hubcap / Lemon / Calok**
— the SCAN CARRIERS would later surface on 'Lithium' records
Mar 96. (12") *(BL 012)* **BULKHEAD - Mr Jones / Mrs Jones**
Apr 96. (12") *(BL 013)* **EOAN 'ELVIS' PRITCHARD - Dark Chronicles Vol.1:- Lust / Revenge**
May 96. (12") *(BL 014)* **VEGAS SOUL - Connection**
Jun 96. (12") *(BL 015)* **MARK FINNIE - Blunted Vision / Fire Cooler**
Aug 96. (12") *(BL 016)* **LYNX - Structures / remix**
— (an earlier LYNX single was 'BLASFEMA' on 'ACV' *(ACV 1059)*
Aug 96. (12") *(BL 017)* **SCAN CARRIERS - Re Entry / Datum / Nautilus**
Sep 96. (12") *(BL 018)* **VEGAS SOUL - My Life / Fine Funk / Beyond The Belt**
Nov 96. (12") *(BL 019) STONEMAKER – 9000 Miles / remix*
Dec 96. (cd) *(BLCD 01)* **Various Artists - State Of Play**
– VEGAS SOUL – Connection / SCAN CARRIERS – Hubcap / LYNX – Structures / SCAN CARRIERS – Refunktion / VEGAS SOUL – My life / SCAN CARRIERS – 3M5 / STONEMAKER – 9000 miles / MARK FINNIE – Sunless / VEGAS SOUL – Diffusion / VEGAS SOUL – Charged / EOAN ELVIS PRITCHARD – Pricks / EOAN ELVIS PRITCHARD – Zed's dead baby.
Jan 97. (12") *(BL 021)* **BULKHEAD - Easy Rider / Easy Rider Blues**
Feb 97. (12") *(BL 022)* **ANALOGUE WAX - Morphology / Process**
Mar 97. (12") *(BL 024)* **SCAN CARRIERS - Citizen X / Auto Kick**
Apr 97. (12"ep) *(BL 025)* **MARK FINNIE - Sunless / Forcefield**
Jun 97. (12") *(BL 026)* **LANDLORD - +1 / - 1**
Jul 97. (12") *(BL 027)* **SCAN CARRIERS - Jamba / Finally The Shadows**
Oct 97. (12") *(BL 028)* **LANDLORD - Magnitude 1 / 2**
Nov 97. (12") *(BL 029)* **MARK FINNIE - Blackjack EP**
Dec 97. (12") *(BL 030)* **SCAN CARRIERS - 30 Seconds**
Jan 98. (12") *(BL 031)* **VEGAS SOUL - Optic / Flat Response**
Mar 98. (12") *(BL 032)* **MARK FINNIE - Stark**
Mar 98. (12") *(BL 033) STONEMAKER – Empire State / Tangent*
Mar 98. (cd) *(BLCDXY 02)* **Various Artists - State Of Play 2**
– VEGAS SOUL – t4 / SCAN CARRIERS – Jamba / EOAN ELVIS – Halley / BULKHEAD – Easy rider / SCAN CARRIERS – Datum / MARK FINNIE – Blunted vision / LANDLORD – Magnitude 1 / SCAN CARRIERS – Citizen X / MARK FINNIE – Blackjack / VEGAS SOUL – Club Class / EOAN ELVIS – Saigon.
Jun 98. (12") *(BL 034)* **LANDLORD - The Shift / Nymphomation**
— (a few months earlier, LANDLORD "let out", the 'CRASH' 12" for 'Aquatrax'; *AQT 008)*
Jul 98. (12") *(BL 035)* **VEGAS SOUL - Mute / SCAN CARRIERS - Kick Start**
Oct 98. (12") *(BL 036)* **LYNX - Freeforms / Ramada**
Nov 98. (12") *(BL 037) STONEMAKER – Flashfunk / Re-mission*
Dec 98. (12") *(BL 038) RICHARD BECK – Faith / Memory Dance*
Jan 99. (12") *(BL 039) KENICHI – Room On / Vegas Soul mix*
Mar 99. (12") *(BL 040)* **VEGAS SOUL - Retrograde / Freeze**
Jun 99. (cd) *(BLVSCD 02)* **VEGAS SOUL - Day By Day**
– Milano / Optic / Retrograde / Junk funk / Air / Mute / Day by day / Sub-mission / Late nighter / Century / Deep south. *(lp-iss.Oct00; BLVS 02)*
Aug 99. (12") *(BL 041) FRANKIE BONES – The Way U Like It*
Dec 99. (12") *(BL 043) 808 STATE – Invader*
Jun 00. (12") *(BL 044)* **F2 - Dominica (mixes)**

Jul 00. (12") *(BL 045) NYGEL REISS – Move On*
Oct 00. (12") *(BL 046)* **CHRIS COWIE – Therapy One**
Oct 00. (12") *(BL 047)* **DE NIRO – Mind Of Man (Binary Finary mix)**
Nov 00. (cd) *(BL 047) unknown (Frankie Bones) – Try To Make Sense / It's Good For America / Black And White (2 mixes)*
Mar 01. (12") *(BL 048) NYGEL REISS – Rochetta*
2001. (cd; ?) *(BLCD 03)* **VEGAS SOUL – Pure**
– Time flies (prelude) / Swan pressure / Mortal measure / T4 / Self control / Time flies / Connection / Beyond the belt / Diffusion / My life / Liquid light.

– (U.G.) discography –

Dec 96. (12") *(UG 001) ACID FUNK – Acid Funk / Acid Reign*
Jan 97. (12") *(UG 002) DJ SEVY – Trancemutation*
Jan 97. (12") *(UG 003)* **X-CABS – Trance Mutation**
Mar 97. (12") *(UG 004) TWISTER – The Fix*
May 97. (12") *(UG 005)* **CANYON – Enigma / Exile**
Jul 97. (12") *(UG 006) LITTLE BIG MAN – Dawn Chorus*
Nov 97. (12") *(UG 008) SUB ONE – Never Change Me / Control*
Nov 97. (12") *(UG 010) ICON & DJ OBERON – Slowburn*
Jan 98. (12") *(UG 011) LITTLE BIG MAN – Moving Mars*
Mar 98. (12") *(UG 011) Q – Eminence / Angel*
Mar 98. (12") *(UG 012) MINDSTAR – Soundtrack*
Jun 98. (12") *(UG 013) WILDLIFE – Wildlife / Lifespan*
Oct 98. (12") *(UG 014) WILDLIFE – Delicate Future / Crystal Rush*
Dec 98. (12") *(UG 015) SUB ONE – Deja Vu / Reload / Porcupine*
Feb 99. (12") *(UG 016) ATLANTIS – Drifting / Out Of The Blue*
Apr 99. (12") *(UG 018) EXOGENESIS – Squelch / Into The Fire*
May 99. (cd) *(UGCD 001) Various Artists – Danny Howells Presents U.G.*
Jun 99. (12") *(UG 019) CASCADE – Somewhere Out There*
Aug 99. (12") *(UG 020) CASCADE – Transcend (mixes)*
Jan 00. (12") *(UG 021) TRANSA – Supernova / Transtar*
Feb 00. (12") *(UG 022) ASCENTION – Stasis*
May 00. (12") *(UG 024) FREON – Heaven's Gate*
Jul 00. (12") *(UG 025) JON THE DENTIST & OLLIE JAYE – Music Takes You High*
Aug 00. (12") *(UG 026) JACOB & MENDEZ – One Breath*
Sep 00. (12") *(UG 027) CASCADE – Electronique*
Nov 00. (12") *(UG 029) C.L. McSPADDEN – Barracuda*
Apr 01. (12") *(UG 030)* **X-CABS – Strider / Breaker**

– (Panther) discography –

Apr 98. (12") *(PANTH 001) DISCO KINGS – Black Fudge / Kings Are Groovin'*
Aug 98. (12") *(PANTH 003) DISCO KINGS – Give You Up*
Nov 98. (12") *(PANTH 003)* **FRANK LE FEVER – Deep Within / Bluegroove / Mirage**
Apr 99. (12") *(PANTH 004) POPE PAUL – Smoove Moova*
Jul 00. (12") *(PANTH 005) SONS OF DAVID – Crusader*
Aug 00. (12") *(PANTH 006) SONS OF DAVID – Can't Wait / Your Love*
May 01. (12") *(PANTH 007) SONS OF DAVID – For Those Who Like To Groove Too*

Hubba Hubba records

Founded: Falkirk, Stirlingshire ... early 90's. The Hubba Hubba label immediately established itself as a purveyor of quality dancefloor sounds along the lines of Glasgow imprints such as 'Bomba' and 'Limbo'. Run by UTAH SAINTS manager John MacLennan, the label maintained an eclectic release schedule with the likes of OHM's 'Tribal Zone' and The FORGEMASTERS' 'Quababa' EP alongside native 12"ers by The DUB COMMISSION and BAMBOO (aka STEVE DONALDSON with backing from Glasgow funk act, GAZELLE). A mark of the label's quality A&R policy was the interest from Miami's trendy house/garage label, 'Murk' and the subsequent licensing of material to that label's 'Vibe' subsidiary. Hubba Hubba also licensed stuff in from the States (Chicago's HARRISON CRUMP), releasing records from house pioneer Roy Davies Jnr's 'Megatrend' imprint.

– discography –

Apr 93. (12"/cd-s) *(HUB 006/+CD)* **PRESSURE – Amour**
May 93. (12") *(HUB 008) OHM – Why Don't Cha*
Jun 93. (12") *(HUB 009) BBR STREET GANG – Loyal To You*
Jul 93. (12") *(HUB 010)* **DUB COMMISSION – Concorde**
— also done above's Lost In House
Oct 93. (12") *(HUB 011) OHM – Tribal Tone*
Nov 93. (12") *(HUB 012) ZERO B – Dat Funky Thing*
Nov 93. (12"ep) *(HUB 013) COTILLION – Soft Drinks EP*
Nov 93. (12"ep) *(HUB 014) BBR STREET GANG – United House EP*
Feb 94. (12"ep) *(HUB 017) HARRISON CRUMP – Sounds Of Life EP*
May 94. (12"ep) *(HUB 018) SANTURI – The Truth EP*
— FORGEMASTERS – Quababa EP
May 94. (12") **BAMBOO – Coney Island**

Human Condition records

Founded: 34 Westfield Road, Edinburgh, EH11 2QB. By summer 2002, the East of Scotland's favourite indie bastion had over a decade of sonic experimentation under its belt; 2001's 10th Anniversary celebrations witnessed performances by such HC faves as EUGENE KELLY, OBABEN and IMPERIAL RACING CLUB as well as well as DJ sets from VIC GALLOWAY (of HUCKLEBERRY and Radio One fame), ANDREW TULLY (of 'Avalanche' records), EDWARD PYBUS (of 'sl' records) and JOHN HUTCHISON (of the 'Path' imprint). Masterminded initially by PAUL KIRK before guitarist/singer-cum-producer JAMIE WATSON took over the reins, Human Condition first spluttered into existence early in 1993 with the FORKEYE single, 'FRIED LIFE'. After a productive couple of years that saw releases from the likes of The NAKED SEE (who became FOIL), SAWYER, PAINKILLERS (aka FRANCES McKEE and JAMES SEENAN) and LYD, the HC HQ relocated to the coastal climes of 120a West Granton Road.

The new Chambers Studios played host to the fresh, and not so fresh faces of METH O.D., CHICANE (now CHI), EUGENIUS, CHICKWEED, The JENNIFERS, IDLEWILD ('Queen Of The Troubled Teens'), IMPERIAL RACING CLUB, CRUYFF, PIGPEN, MYSTERY JUICE, OBABEN, DANNY HOLLAND (who!), SPUTNIKS DOWN and their biggest signing to date, Glasgow veterans EL HOMBRE TRAJEADO. Lifelong Hibs fan JAMIE WATSON (and fellow-producer GRANT MACNAMARA) also opened Chambers' doors to various non-HC artists; for details see the prolific Mr. WATSON's own A-Z of bands/production/work.

– discography –

Jan 93. (7") *(HC 001)* **FORKEYE – Fried Life**

- **BIGSHOT** were basically PAUL KIRK and FORKEYE's DAVE BEARDS with the assistance of JAMIE as engineer. A sampletastic industrial effort that utilizes feedback, overdubs, narratives and similarities to early BUTTHOLES/KILLING JOKE. Subject matter on each side was the homeless and anti-religion – deep very deep, but also meaningful.

Mar 93. (12") *(HC 002T)* **BIGSHOT – Intentional / Glory Bus**

- **BRIDGE HOPPER** were JAMIE WATSON on guitar, bass & keys along with one-time JESSE GARON & THE DESPERADOES singer/guitarist ANDREW TULLY. Augmented by drummer ROY LAWRENCE (borrowed from EUGENIUS) and harmony vocalist JOANNE (of DOG FACED HERMANS), this makeshift band released their one and only piece of 12" vinyl, 'ANNALONG'. Their sound was a bit derivative to be taken too seriously. If you can imagine PRIMAL SCREAM playing Seattle you'd be close to the mark.

Mar 93. (12"ep) *(HC 003T)* **BRIDGE HOPPER – Annalong EP**
– Annalong / Galveston / Break my hands / Tasted Heaven.

Aug 93. (7") *(HC 004)* **NAKED SEE – Nothing's Lost**
May 93. (7") *(HC 005)* **FORKEYE – Grinning Skull**
Nov 93. (cd/lp) *(HC CD/LP 001)* **FORKEYE – P.I.G.**
Sep 94. (cd-ep) *(HC 006)* **NAKED SEE – Faceless**
Oct 94. (d7") *(HC 007)* **SAWYER – Ghetty Chasun**

- **PAINKILLERS** were a short-lived Glasgow-based pairing of former VASELINES members FRANCES McKEE and JAMES SEENAN

Apr 94. (7") *(HC 008)* **PAINKILLERS – Tropical Zodiac / Doin' The Same / Five Signs**

- **LYD** were psychedelic rockers from Portobello, 3 miles from the heart of Edinburgh. The line-up featuring vocalist RAJAN SHARMA, guitarist DYLAN MITCHELL, guitarist/sleeve artist GAVIN HENDERSON, drummer JAMES ALEXANDER and bassist DAVID BIDDULPH, were unfairly pigeonholed under the CORNERSHOP tag due to their singer's exotic ancestry.

Jan 95. (7") *(HC 009)* **Lids / Shopping For Girls**
(cd-s+=) *(HCCD 009)* – Don't Like You / Ostrich on a bike.
May 95. (cd-ep) *(HCCD 0011)* **White Telephone EP**
– White telephone / Parachute / Biscuit tin / Aim.

Sep 95. (cd-ep) *(HCCD 0010)* **METH O.D. – Cyberbilly E.P.**
May 96. (7") *(HC 0012)* **CHICANE – Just Not Sorry**
Sep 96. (7"/cd-s) *(HC/+CD 0013)* **EUGENIUS – Womb Boy Returns**
Nov 96. (7") *(HC 0014)* **CHICANE – Drive**
Dec 96. (cd) *(HCCD 002)* **METH O.D. – Texas God Starvation**

- **CHICKWEED** were from the 'Burgh, and consisted of JENNI (vocals), ex-JOYRIDERS guy 'DUNSY' DUNSMORE (guitar & vocals), VELDA (bass) and ANDY (drums). Power-pop/punk with BYRDS-esque style harmonies, this two-girl/two-boy combo harked back to the 80's for inspiration via The PRIMITIVES or The DARLING BUDS. Their debut 45, 'PERFECT DAY', hit the indie shops early 1997, as did 'SQUAWK' for Human Condition's sub-label, 'Evol'. The latter song was co-written by non-member MARC PILLEY and introduced new singer/guitarist/co-writer DONNA McDOUGALL to replace the outgoing JENNI. First album, 'TODAY IS A GOOD DAY' was a nice and easy start to the band's musical campaign, songsmith DUNSY augmented on a few this time by the co-writing of ALI DENHOLM and the aforementioned PILLEY, who was now thinking about his own HOBOTALK.

Jan 97. (7") *(HC 0015)* **Perfect Day / Wannabe**
Mar 98. (m-cd) *(HCCD 004)* **Today Is A Good Day**
– Ghost behind the sun / Imitation sun / Here today / Squawk / You think not / Thinking / Harbour bar / Piece of laughter.

• The **JENNIFERS** were formed in and around Bridge Of Earn and Perthshire district. The line-up of MICHAEL RATTRAY (vocals & guitar), GAVIN KELLY (bass) and CHRIS FINDLAY (drums), took the moniker formerly abandoned by another well-known trio, SUPERGRASS! The JENS' debut 45, 'YESTERDAY' (not the Beatles song!), was released to very little or muted response, the pop-Grunge number a fine start to the threesome's musical career. A long wait ensued before their much improved follow-up in the Spring of '98, 'JELLY BELLY'. It was also one of 15 tracks on their debut set, 'DRESSED FOR A DOGS LIFE', which also found its way into a few Japanese houses via a deal with 'NoizeWorks'. If you can imagine NIRVANA's power-pop fused with the harmonies of TALK TALK, you'd be quite close to their sonic sound.

Feb 97. (7") *(HC 0016)* **Yesterday / Little World / Numb**
Mar 98. (7") *(HC 0018)* **Jelly Belly / Sleek / 100 Strangers**
Apr 98. (cd) *(HCCD 0003)* **Dressed For A Dogs Life**
– Wembley / King of queens / Honey / Jelly belly / 1000 of you / Yesterday / Mugwump / Budgie / Hamlet & I / Break glass to open / Fred's broken arm / Stink like a man / Out stone cold / After all / Kisho.

Mar 97. (7") *(HC 0017)* **IDLEWILD – Queen Of The Troubled Teens**
Oct 98. (cd-ep) *(HC 0019)* **IMPERIAL RACING CLUB – Big Day Out**
Oct 98. (cd-ep) *(HC 0020)* **CRUYFF – Down Your Line**

• **PIGPEN** were formed in the 'Burgh 1998 by local faves EWAN JOHN (guitar & vocals), SHALEPH O'NEILL (guitar, vocals), ROCCO LIEUALLEN (bass & vocals) and JOHN HALL (drums & vocals). Obviously inspired by either GRATEFUL DEAD's deadhead 'RON 'PIGPEN' McKERNAN or jazz avant-gardist WAYNE HORVITZ's moonlighting project, the band PIGPEN (not the band on 'Tim/Kerr' either!) were underway. The quartet were voted 'Band Of The Month' in Grapevine and have been playlisted on Scotland's Beat Patrol radio programme – The BETA BAND they were not. PIGPEN's sound was certainly a little off-kilter in a way PAVEMENT might've turned out had they gone into the studio with BRIAN WILSON.

Mar 99. (cd-ep) *(HC 00021)* **Stay Low**
– Stay low / Waiting for the day / Happy.
Jun 99. (cd-ep) *(HC 00023)* **So Good**
– So good (I'm sorry) / Head / Baby.

May 99. (cd-s) *(HC 00022)* **IMPERIAL RACING CLUB – My World**
Oct 99. (cd-ep) *(HC 00024)* **MYSTERY JUICE – Pigwit EP**
Nov 99. (7") *(HC 0025)* **OBABEN – Nineteen**

• **DANNY HOLLAND** was the label's first solo singer/songwriter – a chance taken if ever there was one. Coming from across the Forth in Kirkcaldy, DANNY released his one and only single (B-side featured backing vocals by RICH DAVIES) in conjunction with 'Path' records.

Nov 99. (7") *(HC 0026)* **DANNY HOLLAND – Hey! Halloween / Lifetime And A Day**

Jun 00. (cd) *(HCCD 0027)* **SAWYER – On The Seven**
May 00. (cd) *(HCCD 0028)* **OBABEN – Blue Eye**

• **SPUTNIKS DOWN** were formed early in '99 and another young (21-ish!) band/trio, this time signed from the other side of Scotland, Bishopbriggs, near Glasgow; they all attended Turnbull High School. A qualified sound engineer, a physics graduate and chemistry graduate respectively, instru-mental-ists DAVID ROY (guitar & programming), ANDREW BLUE (bass) and MARTYN HEALEY (keyboards & xylophone!) were no doubt inspired by the YOUNG MARBLE GIANTS and/or GODSPEED YOU BLACK EMPEROR. SPUTNIKS DOWN (now what song does this come from?) delivered their debut EP, 'THE MONOTONE MOUNTAIN', receiving (for once in the NME!), a rave review – oh, and one in Select.

Apr 00. (cd-ep) *(HCCD 0029)* **SPUTNIKS DOWN – The Monotone Mountain**
– MM / ME / Songs for the tiny radio children.

Apr 00. (m-cd) *(HCCD 0030)* **IMPERIAL RACING CLUB – Every Girls Got One**
Oct 00. (cd) *(HCCD 0031)* **EL HOMBRE TRAJEADO – Saccade**
Apr 01. (cd) *(HCCD 0032)* **OBABEN – Marblehead**
May 01. (cd-ep) *(HCCD 33)* **OBABEN – Beauty Blinds**
Oct 01. (cd) *(HCCD 0034)* **Various Artists – Handbags At Dawn**
– CRUISER – McCoy / EL HOMBRE TRAJEADO – Saccade / FRIDGEHOPPER – I've got a knife / GO COMMANDO – Wow, progress / I AM SCIENTIST – Generation galactica / IMPERIAL RACING CLUB – I love you but I'm tired / KHAYA – Husbands / OBABEN – Blink again / PILOTCAN – Ratcatcher / RISINGSON – Thousand mile stare / SAWYER – Osoba / SINGLESKIN – 79 electroscock treatments / SPUTNIKS DOWN – MM / STACY EFFECT – Buzzkill / TOASTER – 13th floor / ZEPHYRS – The most revealing hymn.
Oct 01. (cd) *(HCCD 0035)* **SPUTNIKS DOWN – Much Was Decided Before You Were Born**
– Ralph M / Golden era of respectability / Atonement / Champion of the last handclappers / Pixielated / Mie scattering / PK.
— in Nov'01, SPUTNIKS DOWN split a single, 'PIXIELATED' with EL HOMBRE TRAJEADO

Iona Gold records

Founded: Glasgow – this is the pop/rock offshoot.
(see biography under parent label 'Lismor' records)

– Iona Gold discography –

Jun 93. (cd-s) *(IGS 201-1)* **KING HASH – I'm The One**
Jun 93. (cd/c) *(IG CD/C 201)* **KING HASH – Humdinger**
Jun 93. (cd-s) *(IGS 202-1)* **CAROL LAULA – Child Of Mine**
Jun 93. (cd/c) *(IG CD/C 202)* **CAROL LAULA – Still**
Jun 93. (cd/c; re-) *(IG CD/C 203)* **HUMPFF FAMILY – Mothers**
Jun 93. (cd-s) *(IGS 203-1)* **HUMPFF FAMILY – Misty Again**
Aug 93. (cd-s) *(IGS 204-1)* **PEARLFISHERS – Saint Francis Songs**
Oct 93. (cd/c) *(IG CD/C 204)* **PEARLFISHERS – Za Za's Garden**
Apr 94. (cd-s) *(IGS 204-2)* **PEARLFISHERS – Living In A Foreign Country**
Oct 93. (cd/c) *(IG CD/C 205)* **CAROL LAULA – Precious Little Victories**
Apr 94. (cd-s) *(IGS 205-1)* **CAROL LAULA – Mr D & G**
Feb 94. (cd/c) *(IG CD/C 206)* **LOVE AND MONEY – Littledeath**
Jun 94. (m-cd/m-c) *(IG CDM/CM 207)* **KEVIN McDERMOTT ORCHESTRA – The Last Supper**
Jul 94. (c/cd) *(IG/+CD 208)* **HUMPFF FAMILY – Fathers**
— Iona Gold was re-activated for World Music release below
Feb 01. (cd) *(IGCD 210) ZUBA – Chameleon*

Kore records (see under ⇒ Limbo records)

Limbo records

Founded: 23 Bath Street, Glasgow (G2 1HW) . . . 1992 by BILLY KILTIE, veteran DJ and owner of premier dance music emporium '23rd Precinct'. After taking over the store in August 1989, BILLY doubled its turnover in the space of two years before setting up Limbo as the shop's in-house label. A pivotal player in the development of progressive house through its halcyon early 90's period, Limbo carved out a distinctive identity with a series of classic club tracks.

First off the racks was HAVANA (RICHARD MILLER, TONY SCOTT and GRAHAM 'GYPSY' DRINNAN) with the seminal 'SCHTOOM' (LIMB 001) and 'SHIFT' singles (LIMB 002) while LIMB 003 came in the shape of GYPSY's 'I TRANCE YOU'. 1993 saw a stream of compelling singles by the likes of SUBLIME (aka GYPSY), HARRI, RITMO DE VIDA, STEALTH SONIC SOUL, DEEP PIECE (MICHAEL KILKIE and STUART CRICHTON) and the brilliant CRICHTON-masterminded MUKKAA, whose throbbing 'YER CHUCKED' surely ranks as one of the label's finest moments.

KILTIE's incredibly tight quality control was evident on summer 93's sampler, 'HOUSE OF LIMBO VOL. 1', a near flawless collection of hypnotic, squelchy, compulsive, often cheeky and always funky dance music. Other key tracks during Limbo's formative years were DEEP PIECE's mighty 'TORWART', KILTIE and CRICHTON hailed as the MORODER and JARRE of house music. 1994 saw the release of 'HOUSE OF LIMBO VOL.2' as the label went from strength to strength while retaining the readily identifiable core of DJ's that made up the vast majority of Limbo aliases. Having already branched out with 'Marimba', that year also saw the formation of subsidiary imprint, 'Out On A Limb', catering to the more left-field sounds of SPACEBUGGY (TONY SCOTT) and REMOULD (TONY SCOTT and CHRIS COWIE) amongst others.

As mentioned above, the 23rd Precinct empire also took an interest in the more commercial end of the dance market, initiating the 'Stoatin' imprint to release material by Q-TEX, DANCE UNITED and SOLO (STUART CHRICHTON, again!); the man had previously had a relatively close shave with the charts via 'RAINBOW (SAMPLE FREE)' for 'Reverb' (rvbt 003) – in July '91 and 'COME ON!' (rvbt 008) – in January '92. Not to be confused with the US group of the same name, the Scottish SOLO subsequently worked with former TTF frontwoman MARY KIANI.

The short-lived 'Kore' subsidiary, meanwhile, dealt in the harder end of the rave/techno scene with much in demand 12"ers from DJ EQUAZION (aka the ubiquitous SCOTT BROWN) and ACTIVE FORCE over the course of 1993.

The '23rd Precinct' label was again used for Q-TEX material in 1996 as 'LET THE LOVE' made the UK Top 30. The following year saw the re-release of their former rave nugget, 'POWER OF LOVE' as well as an album, 'INTO THE LIGHT'.

Towards the end of the decade and into the new millennium, Limbo has increasingly looked further afield for talent, releasing tracks by English producers such as FLYTRAP and PRISM and even casting their net across the Atlantic for material by CHRIS McSPADDEN (CLM), SEAFIELD and FADE (aka CHRIS FORTIER). The likes of PROPULSION (aka DAVIE FORBES), meanwhile, have maintained Limbo's reputation as curators of some of the finest dance grooves Scotland has to offer.

- (Limbo) discography -

Aug 92. (12") *(Limb 001)* **HAVANA - Schtoom / kuba mix**
Sep 92. (12") *(Limb 002)* **HAVANA - Shift / High & Dry**
Oct 92. (12") *(Limb 003)* **GYPSY - I Trance You**
Nov 92. (12") *(Limb 004)* **DEEP PIECE - Bup Bup Biri Biri**
Jan 93. (12") *(Limb 005)* **SUBLIME - Sublime Theme**
Jan 93. (12") *(Limb 006)* **Q-TEX - Natural High EP**
Feb 93. (12"/cd-s) *(Limb 007/+CD)* **HAVANA - Ethnic Prayer (reached 71)**
Feb 93. (12") *(Limb 008)* **MUKKAA - Buruchacca (mixes) (reached 74)**
Mar 93. (12") *(Limb 009)* **HARRI - Skelph**
Apr 93. (12") *(Limb 010)* **RITMO DE VIDA - Taboo (mixes)**
Apr 93. (12") *(Limb 011) STEALTH-SONIC-SOUL – Stealth Sonic Soul (mixes)*
May 93. (12") *(Limb 12T)* **SUBLIME - Transamerican (mixes)**
May 93. (12"/cd-s) *(Limb 13 T/CD)* **MUKKAA - Neebro (mixes)**
May 93. (12") *(Limb 14T)* **READY FOR DEAD - Ready For Dead**
Jun 93. (12") *(Limb 15T)* **STRAWBERRY BAZAAR - Bingo Specs Boogie**
Jul 93. (12") *(Limb 16T) P.G.I. – Jazz Energy*
Jul 93. (12") *(Limb 17T)* **DEEP PIECE - Who Gotcha Car / Panoramic Shuffle**
Jul 93. (cd/c/lp) *(Limb 18 CD/MC/LP)* **Various Artists - House Of Limbo Vol.1**
Jul 93. (12") *(Limb 19T) SANDMAN – Temple Drum*
Aug 93. (12"/cd-s) *(Limb 20 T/CD)* **GYPSY - Skinny Bumble Bee**
Sep 93. (12") *(Limb 21T) WHITEBOY – Aura (mixes)*
Oct 93. (12"/cd-s) *(Limb 22 T/CD)* **MUKKAA - Yer Chucked (mixes)**
Nov 93. (12") *(Limb 23T)* **BABROO - Trak-A-Laka**
Nov 93. (12"ep) *(Limb 24T)* **PROBE - Edible Tracks Vol.1**
– Hulabaloo / Orca / Rapid 'R'.
Jan 94. (12") *(Limb 25T)* **STRAWBERRY BAZAAR - Bazaar Club Grooves**
Jan 94. (12"ep/cd-ep) *(Limb 26 LP/CD)* **HAVANA - Condensed EP**
– Skyhat part I / Skyhat part IV / Skyhat part V / Disorder / Nymph / Discorder. *(orig.12"-Dec93; Limb 26P)*
Feb 94. (12"/cd-s) *(Limb 27 T/CD)* **SUBLIME - TGV**
– TGV (Paris – Marseille) / TGV (Paris – Lyon) / Gipsy love mix.
Mar 94. (12") *(Limb 28T)* **REMOULD - Soular - VS1 / VS2**
Apr 94. (12"ep) *(Limb 30T)* **HARRI - Phuxache EP**
May 94. (12"/cd-s) *(Limb 31 T/CD)* **GYPSY - Funk De Fino / Varisuvia**
Jun 94. (12") *(Limb 32T)* **DEEP PIECE - Torwart**
Jul 94. (12"/cd-s) *(Limb 33 T/CD) WINC – Thoughts Of A Tranced Love*
Aug 94. (12"/cd-s) *(Limb 34 T/CD)* **MUKKAA - Blinder (mixes)**
Sep 94. (12"/cd-s) *(Limb 35 T/CD)* **FIX - In Gods House**
Sep 94. (cd/c) *(Limb 36CDX)* **Various Artists - House Of Limbo Vol.II**
Oct 94. (lp/c/cd) *(Limb 37/+MC/CD)* **GYPSY - Soundtracks**
Oct 94. (12"/cd-s) *(Limb 38 T/CD)* **HAVANA - Outland / Blanc / Winc Disorder remix**
Nov 94. (12"/cd-s) *(Limb 39 T/CD) AFFECTION – Morning*
Nov 94. (12") *(Limb 40T) MELONHAUS – Dopamine*
Dec 94. (12"/cd-s) *(Limb 41 T/CD) FLANGE SQUAD – Justine Juice*
Mar 95. (12"/cd-s) *(Limb 43 T/CD) TOCAYO – Live In Peace*
Apr 95. (12") *(Limb 44T) EEG – The Virgo EP*
Jul 95. (12"/cd-s) *(Limb 46 T/CD) YOSH – It's What's Upfront That Counts (reached 69)*
Sep 95. (12"/cd-s) *(Limb 47 T/CD)* **RITMO DE VIDA - Havara**
Sep 95. (12"/cd-s) *(Limb 48 T/CD) TOCAYO – All Night*
Nov 95. (12"/cd-s) *(Limb 49 T/CD)* **MUKKAA - Kiss My Acid / Madness Goes To Kilmarnock**
Nov 95. (12"/cd-s) *(Limb 50 T/CD) YOSH – It's What's Upfront That Counts (reached 31)*
Jan 96. (12"/cd-s) *(Limb 51 T/CD) CULTHOUSE – Pro-active*
Feb 96. (12"/cd-s) *(Limb 52 T/CD)* **GYPSY - I Trance You**
Apr 96. (12"/cd-s) *(Limb 54 T/CD) YOSH – The Screamer (reached 38)*
Jun 96. (12"/cd-s) *(Limb 55 T/CD) DARK SESSIONS – . . . Vol.1*
May 96. (3xcd-box/3xc-box) *(Limb 56 CD/MC) Various Artists – The Tunnel Mixes: Paul Oakenfold / Michael Kilkie*
Jul 96. (12"/cd-s) *(Limb 57 T/CD) FADE – So Good*
Jul 96. (12"/cd-s) *(Limb 58 T/CD)* **RITMO DE VIDA - The Spirit Is Justified**
Oct 96. (12"/cd-s) *(Limb 59 T/CD) PLANET '95 – Talk To Me*
Nov 96. (12"/cd-s) *(Limb 60 T/CD) CHUPHER – The Chupher EP*
Nov 96. (3xcd-box) *(Limb 61CDX)* **Various Artists - House Of Limbo Trilogy (mixed by Mark Moore**
Nov 96. (12") *(Limb 62T) SOUL SURFERS – Slip*
Mar 97. (12") *(Limb 63T) FADE – Heaven To Heaven remix*
Feb 97. (12") *(Limb 64T) DEFACTO – Glove*
May 97. (12") *(Limb 65T)* **TIPPLE - Discoveries**
May 97. (12") *(Limb 67T) VICTOR CALDERONE – Give It Up*
Jun 97. (12") *(Limb 68T)* **TIPPLE - The Drift**
Oct 97. (cd) *(Limb 69CD) Various Artists – Dubs In Limbo Vol.1*
Sep 97. (12") *(Limb 70T) FREESPIRIT – Twilight / I Need It*
Dec 97. (12") *(Limb 71T)* **PROPULSION - Readers Demo**
Dec 97. (12") *(Limb 72T) CHUPHER – Funk 2 Nite*
Nov 97. (12") *(Limb 73T) SEAFIELD – Feel Free / Ice Cream . . .*
Dec 97. (12") *(Limb 74T)* **TIPPLE - Summation EP**
(re-mixed re-iss. Jun98 +=; Limb 74TG) – The Drift
Dec 97. (12") *(Limb 75T) FADE – No Resolve*
Feb 98. (12") *(Limb 76T) TERRY FARLEY & PETE HELLER – Colours The Full Spectrum*
Jan 98. (12") *(Limb 77T)* **FLYTRAP - Crystalise / Vivid**
Mar 98. (12") *(Limb 79T) SOUND OF SIN – Future Funk*
Apr 98. (12") *(Limb 80T) ALLENBY – Nobody's In The House..*
Apr 98. (12") *(Limb 81T) M31 – Galactic*
May 98. (12") *(Limb 82T)* **PROPULSION - Liberty / Pressure**
Jul 98. (12") *(Limb 83T) SEAFIELD – Twisted / Spin-off*
Sep 98. (12") *(Limb 84T) OPTIMUS – Delete The Weak*
Aug 98. (12") *(Limb 85T) SENSE OF SOLITAIRE – Meteor*
Oct 98. (12") *(Limb 86T) EQUATE – Sanctuary*
Sep 98. (12") *(Limb 87T) PRISM – Slant / Rising Calm*
Nov 98. (12") *(Limb 88T) CLM – Centrode / Luminous*
Dec 98. (12") *(Limb 89T) NOEL SANGER – Subterfuge / Voice*
May 99. (12") *(Limb 90T) FLYTRAP – Tundra*
Dec 98. (12") *(Limb 91T)* **TIPPLE - Concave / Hope**
Feb 99. (cd) *(Limb 92CD)* **Various Artists - Limbo Live @ The Tunnel**
Jul 99. (12") *(Limb 93T) FADE – The Love Dubs*
Mar 99. (12") *(Limb 94T) PRISM – Innerscape / Obsessive*
Jun 99. (12") *(Limb 95T)* **PROPULSION - Innocence / Pressure**
Sep 99. (12"0 *(Limb 97T) CLM – Fireball / Teleport*
Oct 99. (12") *(Limb 98T) PRISM – Aura / Salvation*
Nov 99. (12") *(Limb 99T) FLYTRAP – Neon / Protocol*
Mar 00. (12") *(Limb 101T) TECRA – Excavations / Stay Press*
May 00. (12") *(Limb 102T) INKFISH – Lost (Transa mix) / Agony Aunt*
Jul 00. (12") *(Limb23 02T1)* **HAVANA - Ethnic Prayer (remixes)**
Aug 00. (12") *(Limb23 02T2)* **HAVANA - Ethnic Prayer (remixes)**
— HAVANA had also released the 'ORANGE' EP in January'00 for 'Bitter Lemon'; *BLR 335)*
May 01. (12") *(Limb23 03) FLEXIK – Cosway*

- Kore discography -

Mar 93. (12"ep) *(KORE 1T)* **D.J.EQUAZION - Cyberflux EP**
(above and below were actually EQUAZION PARTS I & II)
Oct 93. (12"ep) *(KORE 3T)* **D.J.EQUAZION - Hardcore Nation EP**
Nov 93. (12"ep) *(KORE 4T)* **ACTIVE FORCE - The Hanger EP**

- Stoatin' discography -

— note: SOLO had issued for 'Reverb' two hits (see above) + 'So Beautiful' *(rvb t/cds 15)*
Apr 93. (12"/c-s/cd-s) *(STOAT 001/+MC/CD)* **SOLO - Love Can't Turn Around**
Mar 94. (12"/c-s/cd-s) *(STOAT 002/+MC/CD)* **Q-TEX - The Power Of Love**
Sep 93. (12"/c-s/cd-s) *(STOAT 003/+MC/CD)* **SOLO - Come On! (remix) (reached 63)**
Feb 94. (12"/c-s/cd-s) *(STOAT 004/+MC/CD)* **DANCE UNITED - Freedom Of Life**

- 23rd Precinct discography -

Mar 93. (12") *(PREC 006T)* **Q-TEX - Celebration**
Jun 93. (12") *(PREC 009T) HOBO – Freedom / Vibe*
Jun 93. (12") *(PREC 010T) SKONK – Banjo'd*
Oct 94. (c-s/12"/cd-s) *(THIRD 1 MC/T/CD) SOUL SURFERS – Slip*
Nov 94. (c-s/12"/cd-s) *(THIRD 2 MC/T/CD)* **Q-TEX - Believe**
Jun 96. (c-s/12"/cd-s) *(THIRD 4 MC/T/CD)* **Q-TEX - Let The Love**
Nov 96. (c-s/12"/cd-s) *(THIRD 5 MC/T/CD)* **Q-TEX - Do You Want Me**
Jun 97. (12"/cd-s) *(THIRD 7 T/CD)* **Q-TEX - Power Of Love '97**
Jul 97. (12") *(THIRD 8T) TOCAYO – Show Me*
May 97. (12"/cd-s) *(THIRD 9 T/CD) DEFACTO – Glove*
Jul 97. (12") *(THIRD 10T)* **CHUPHER - The Chupher EP (re-issue)**
Jul 97. (cd/c) *(THIRD 11 CD/MC)* **Q-TEX - Into The Light**
Sep 97. (12") *(THIRD 13T)* **JOX - Out Of Control**

- Out On A Limb records -

Jun 94. (12") *(SOOL 1T)* **MANUAL - XYZ**
Jul 94. (12") *(SOOL 2T)* **SPACEBUGGY - Spacebuggy EP**
Aug 94. (12") *(SOOL 3T)* **READY FOR DEAD - Diffusion**
Sep 94. (12") *(SOOL 4T)* **REMOULD - Upbeat / Stringthing**
Oct 94. (12") *(SOOL 5T)* **F2 - Dominica**
Nov 94. (12") *(SOOL 6T)* **MANUAL - In Sense**
Dec 94. (12") *(SOOL 7T)* **HALF QUE - Warehouse EP - Night Visit**
Jan 95. (12") *(SOOL 8T)* **CHUBBA VS SPIRALHEAD - Carabou Pink / El Corazon**
Feb 95. (12") *(SOOL 9T)* **SPACES - Freeflow / 8.14**
Mar 95. (12") *(SOOL 10T)* **DISTANT DRUMS - Work That Body**

Mar 95. (12") *(SOOL 11T)* **STALLIN – Dragon Drums 1 + 2**
Apr 95. (12") *(SOOL 12T)* **REMOULD – A.C.T. / Rear Entry**
May 95. (12") *(SOOL 13T)* **MANUAL – Baby / Disjoint / Disent**
Jun 95. (12") *(SOOL 14T)* **SPACES – Look / Sends**
Jul 95. (12") *(SOOL 15T)* **F2 – Zephyr / Atlantis**
Aug 95. (12") *(SOOL 16T)* **HAWKY – Rock And Roll**
Oct 95. (12") *(SOOL 18T)* **DISTANT DRUMS – Junk Funk / Acid Test**
Nov 95. (12") *(SOOL 19T)* **QORG – Factor**
Dec 95. (12") *(SOOL 21T)* **AFFECTION – Motor City / Spice / Scubaman**
Jan 96. (12") *(SOOL 22T)* **SPACE BUGGY – Space Buggy 3**
Feb 96. (12") *(SOOL 23T)* **RECYCLE – Rama / The Heart Of**
Mar 96. (12") *(SOOL 24T)* **ASTRAL – Astral EP – Fluid / Echo**
Apr 96. (12") *(SOOL 25T)* **CHUBBA – Chubblegum / Baxach**
May 96. (12") *(SOOL 26T) REMOULD – Remould 4*
Sep 96. (12") *(SOOL 29T)* **ASTRAL – Astral Project EP**
Oct 96. (12") *(SOOL 30T)* **MANUAL – Tuneage**
May 97. (12") *(SOOL 35T)* **SPACE BUGGY – On This Planet / Minimal Force / Butt Splice / Rim / Wilt / Mackanik**
Jun 97. (12") *(SOOL 36T)* **MANUAL – Beef Situation EP – Lonic / Sims / Rotary**
Jul 97. (12") *(SOOL 37T)* **RECYCLE – Switch Channels / Cycle 3**
Sep 97. (12") *(SOOL 39T)* **AFFECTION – Surfing The Net / Rack Em Up / Reborn**

— (unsure of some of the above dates – could go back to mid 1995)

– Bomba records –

Sep 93. (12") *(Bomb12 001) STATE OF HOUSE – Pacific Dance*
Nov 93. (12"ep) *(Bomb12 003) OHM – Discouse EP*
May 94. (12") *(Bomb12 005P) PEPPERMINT LOUNGE – Lemon Project*
Jun 94. (12") *(Bomb12 006) PEPPERMINT LOUNGE – Lemon Project (remixes)*
Aug 94. (12") *(Bomb12 007)* **HARRI Vs VISNATI – Vespa**
Jul 94. (12"ep) *(Bomb12 008) SHINDIG – Timeless EP Part 1*
Aug 94. (12"ep) *(Bomb12 009) SHINDIG – Timeless EP Part 2*
1995. (12") *(Bomb12 016) FRESH AND LOW – Interact / Get Up*
1996. (12") *(Bomb12 019) AQUATHERIUM – The Struggle EP*
1996. (12") *(Bomb12 020) SMOOTH & SIMMONDS – Vertigo*
Nov 96. (12") *(Bomb12 021) PATTERSON & PRICE – Eric The Red*
Jan 97. (d12"ep) *(Bomb12 022) MELONHAUS & ROTARY TEN – House Of Melon EP*
Sep 97. (12") *(Bomb12 023) MELONHAUS – Screwbass Drive*
Nov 97. (12") *(Bomb12 024) ROTARY TEN – Esperanto*

— In Jun'99, ROTARY TEN released 'KINGMAKER' for 'Haus Of Melon'

– others, etc. –

Jun 97. (12") *(TSOLE 008) SOUL ONLY – Come Together*

Lithium records

Founded: Aberdeen . . . early '98 by songwriter MARK NICOL, musician CRAIG PERT and fanzine editor ADIE NUNN. Formed with the raison d'etre of shining a much needed light into dark shadowy corners of the North Eastern music scene, Lithium first lit the fuse in summer '98 with the NEEDLES' 'Teenage Bomb'. The single received a launch at London's Barfly club, the sharp-edged noisesters supported by Granite City compadres, The LIFT and CLOCKER. Having made many useful contacts down south, the Lithium trio set to work on a V/A sampler album which featured a raft of up and coming Grampian talent including Aberdeen Rawkers DEADLOSS SUPERSTAR (now into 'LIVING THE LIFESTYLE' on mp3), Peterhead's YELLOW SUNDAYS and Ellon-based CHICAGO DEFENDER alongside more experienced Aberdonian faves MAPLE and ATOM FLASK (with frontman NEIL ROBERTSON). The CD-album was even lent something of a cosmopolitan slant with the inclusion of a track by Aberdeen-based singer/songwriter DANE STEWART.

1999 saw a flood of single releases by the Lithium posse, launching the recording career of The LIFT, while taking in the homeless MAGICDRIVE, the SCAN CARRIERS, the GENTS and YELLOW CAR (now named KATE'S). The label cast its A&R net further afield in the new millennium, releasing material by Cornish juveniles, QUINCY, and straight outta ABBA-land (that's Sweden, to younger readers), AMBULANCE.

Of late, the label's success has prompted the founding of a subsidiary imprint, 'Revol', which basically caters to the ever-growing mp3 market. To date, the operation has posted up one track from DOORS/TEARDROP EXPLODES-esque locals The LEAP. The label can be contacted at www.lithiumrecords.co.uk or PO Box 10259, Aberdeen, AB11 6WR – Revol's PO Box No is 10259. Offshoot imprint, 'Western union', can also be found there.

– Lithium discography –

- **the NEEDLES** were formed in the North East capital around spring 1996 and included vocalist/guitarist DAVE DIXON, plus keyboards man PAUL CURTISS, drummer JOHNNY WOLFE and bassist RICHEY WOLFE. The group finally emerged with the 1998 EP 'TEENAGE BOMB', a typical JON SPENCER-meets-Motown effort.

Jun 98. (cd-ep) *(LITH 001CDS)* **NEEDLES – Teenage Bomb EP**
– Teenage bomb / Stop messin' me around / Hey mister (Northsound One session version) / Now it's time (live version).

Aug 98. (cd) *(LITH 011CDA)* **Lithium Records Volume 1**
– CLOCKER – Erase / LIFT – Caught up in myself / the NEEDLES – Any other girl / DANE STEWART – Dry erase board life / SPACEBOY – Pamela Smith / MAPLE – Dangerous boy / ATOM FLASK – Planet girl (biological washer whiter remix) / JO McCAFFERTY – Unsung hero / YELLOW SUNDAYS – Yellow Sunday / the LEAP – Experiment #6 / SPIRAL – I'm dead / DEFORM – Crush / CHICAGO DEFENDER – Slip inside / FRISBEE – Paying the price / CLOUDBURST – Going back to go / DEADLOSS SUPERSTAR – Rising sun / VERGE – Millionaire / ELEMENT – Changing rain / ERIC EUAN – Happy go lucky.

- **LIFT** were also formed in the Granite City early in 1997 by frontman MARK COATES, and four others including DAVE (bass) and DONALD (drums). Shades of RADIOHEAD . . .

Jan 99. (cd-s) *(LITH 002CDS)* **LIFT – Bleeding You Dry**
– Bleeding you dry / Don't forget / Inside.

— note:- another outfit of the same name issued a 12" for 'Mighty High Music', 'Lessons In Funky Tracks'.

Mar 99. (7"ep/cd-ep) *(LITH 003/+CDS)* **MAGICDRIVE – Hotel Transatlantique EP**
Aug 99. (cd-ep) *(LITH 004CDS)* **NEEDLES – We Got The Soul EP**
– We got the soul / Hang on to yourself / Only if U want me 2 / Teenage bomb (Star'n'Garta remix).
Sep 99. (cd-ep) *(LITH 005CDS)* **SCAN CARRIERS – Mindfield**
– Mindfield (radio) / Last train / Marshall X / Mindfield.
Sep 99. (7"ep/cd-ep) *(LITH 006/+CDS)* **MAGICDRIVE – Grand Hotel EP**
Jan 00. (cd-ep) *(LITH 007CDS)* **NEEDLES – Beat Of The City EP**
– Beat of the city / In her arms again / Cryin' in the rain / Because I can dream.
Feb 00. (cd-ep) *(LITH 008CDS)* **GENTS – Tamogotchi EP**
Apr 00. (cd) *(LITH 012CDA)* **Lithium Records Vol.2**
– MAGICDRIVE – Baby's alright / LIFT – Take my hand / the NEEDLES – Richie's magic hammond / THEE EXCERPTS – Spencer / STORM PETRELS – This only happens / PHONEFREAK – Breathe / KING LOUIE – Blush / the TIGER LILLIES – Julie / DANNY YOUNG – Bagley St. / AERIAL – Sounds good / FAMILIAR – Come into the real world / KELEBECK BUTTERFLY – Flying time / PHEONIX – Smiling back / ORANGE PEEL – Calling / HAULLER – Exposed / VERANO – Something higher / FUZ – In theory / (+ 2 hidden tracks).
Oct 00. (cd-s) *(LITH 009CDS)* **YELLOW CAR – Billy Said**

— *LITH 010CDS* was scheduled for Swedish band, AMBULANCE

Jul 00. (cd-s) *(LITH 011CDS) QUINCY – After Dark* (this group come from Cornwall)

- **JOSEPHINE** are the new TALKING HEADS with a hint of the WEDDING PRESENT. Headed by KEITH GERRARD (vocals), with backing from female ROZ DAVIES (bass & flute) and others, they were another act to be tipped for greater things.

Sep 01. (7") *(LITH 012)* **JOSEPHINE – Vinyl Hit. / This Is Not An Exit**

- **REAL SHOCKS** were five big fans of the SWELL MAPS (they took their moniker from one of their songs) and even covered 'VERTICAL SLUM'. Fronted by STEPHEN REVERSE and others of his ilk, they were signed to 'Lithium' without even playing a gig.

Apr 02. (cd-ep) *(LITH 013CDS)* **REAL SHOCKS – Curly wurly / Boring / Vertical slum / Curly wurly (disco version).**

Feb 02. (7") *(LITH 014)* **NEEDLES – Let U Down. / I Don't Wanna Go To Skool**
Mar 02. (7") *(LITH 015)* **JOSEPHINE – Lipstick Circus. / Cuban Heel**
Sep 02. (cd) *(LITH 014CDA)* **JOSEPHINE – This Is Not An Advertisement**
– Picture book Jesus / Vinyl hit / Movie flix / Flute song #2 / Hit the youth / Lipstick circus / Bad actor / Fortunately gone / Respiridol / This is not an exit / Idea No.5 / Kings cross / Cut it up / Wide open / Punka tu-tu.
Aug 02. (cd-ep) *(LITH 016CDS)* **NEEDLES – The King And Queen Of Style EP**
– The king and queen of style / Treatin' me bad / Everything I want in the world / Ritchie and the magic hammond.
Apr 02. (cd-ep) *(LITH 017CDS)* **NERO – A Good Smack In The Mouth EP**
– This is not science / Monkey song / Norman Petty / Girls with cellos.
Jun 02. (cd-ep) *(LITH 018CDS)* **KATE'S – All Over Now**

- Revol discography -

2000. (mp3) *(LOVER 1)* **The LEAP – Experiment #6**

- Western Union records discography -

Jun 01. (cd-ep) *(WUCDS 101)* **GENTS – Marvellous Skies EP**
Feb 02. (cd-s) *(WUCDS 102) QUINCY – Alien*
Mar 02. (m-cd) *(WU 103CDMA)* **YELLOW SUNDAYS – Systems**
– I came home / Chocolate kneecaps / Black block / Freckles / Clay experiment / Counterfeit coinage / Sunny day / Green.

Marimba records (see under ⇒ Limbo records)

Mint records

Founded: Kilsyth, nr. Glasgow . . . January 1999 by DAMIAN BEATTIE and (JOHN) PAUL RENNIE. With freedom of artistic control the starting point for this very small mail-order outlet, Mint signed up young 'Wedgie outfits, the grungy MANGANESE and MAINLINE (the latter were to issue a 12", 'INNERSPACE' / 'NARCOTIC') in June 2000 for 'Bedrock'; BED 6). Kilsyth's synthier MAINLINE (a fusion between AIR and MOGWAI) moved on to Mint's www.music33.com parent mp3 label, issuing on-line 'THE SPY' track in April 2001. That year, also saw two more combos inking a deal, young rockers RISER (like 10,000 MANIACS) and OLDSOLAR (comprising Glaswegians MARK RUSSELL and ANDREW HOWIE) delivering their eclectic, BETH ORTON-meets-SIGUR ROS or BOARDS OF CANADA debut CD (see below); the label was now billed as 'Mint Blue' due to a label in Canada. Glasgow outfit, BUBBLECRAFT, are a quartet who mix COLDPLAY with RADIOHEAD or MUSE style; they've just managed to get a deal with Sky training for recruitment training!

- discography -

1999. (cd) *(Mint 001)* **(Glasgow) Sampler**
1999. (cd-ep) *(Mint 002)* **MANGANESE – Headcase EP**
– Backbone / DIY / Headcase / Theme from Manganese / Backbone (Andy G mix).
2000. (cd-s) *(Mint 003B)* **RISER – Midget Gems**
2000. (8"clear/square) *(Mint 004s)* **RISER – Just Get By**
2000. (8"clear/square) *(Mint 005s)* **MANGANESE – Glimmer / Your Domain**
2000. (c) *(Mint 006)* **Various – The Horror Years**
(above featured the 'worst' demos ever sent to 'Mint')
Apr 01. (mp3) *(Mint 007)* **MAINLINE – The Spy / 12.D**
Dec 01. (cd) *(Mint 008)* **OLDSOLAR – Many Visitors Have Been Gored By Buffalo**
– Arousal / This golden mile / Cut / I feel it more than I can explain it / Great Dane dying / Endangered / The vessel / Out of it (part 2) / Recycle / Out of it (part 1).
Jul 02. (cd-s) *(Mint 009B)* **BUBBLECRAFT – Technophobe / The Cynic**
Jul 02. (cd) *(Mint 10)* **MANGANESE – Lo-Fi Fo Fum**

Mouthmoth records

Founded: Ayrshire . . . 1998 by JOHN C. WILSON, mainly as an outlet to put out titles (limited to 100 copies) by his own one-man bands, FROG POCKET and AYR UNIT. Atmospheric electronica and ambient musings were two descriptions of sampler WILSON and his soundtrack-esque projects. Complete with a guitarist, harmonica-player and dancer/artist, FROG POCKET performed the odd (very odd!) night at Glasgow's 13th Note, initially premiering his debut set, 'YOU'RE THE ONE FOR ME' (1999). AYR UNIT, meanwhile, also played their minimalistic set at the venue, 45 minutes culminating with a crescendo.

Recordings were also sprouting out thick and fast, newcomers ASTERISK (aka GREG DAVIS) and SNOTRA featuring on V/A 7" EP's, 'Mothballs (vol.1)' and 'Mothballs (vol.3)'; 'Mothballs (vol.2)' featured FROG POCKET alongside the equally abstract and reverb-friendly VOLTERGEIST (albeit 43 seconds of), PARALLEL and LIPS VAGO. 'Mothballs (vol.3)' – released in October 2000 – saw the arrival of D/compute (aka ALISTAIR CROSBIE – ex-INVERSION), again atmospheric and experimental, he subsequently delivered the EP, 'IWILLPUSHMYSELF. . .' the following month. FROG POCKET too had been busy in the studio, releasing sophomore set, 'MY FAVOURITE' in May 2000, with further CD's, 'CARIC KILS' and 'BARAL ORGEN' (correct spelling) delivered a few years later.

Other signings STRAIGHT OUTTA MONGOLIA (aka JEREMY SMITH), KETTEL, RANDOM NUMBER, NECK DOPPLER, EYE MAN and CAPTAIN STEPHANIE (aka PETER PERCEPT) also emerged from the Mouthmoth studio with ambient-type noodlings.

- discography -

Feb 99. (cd) *(moth 1cd)* **FROG POCKET – You're the One For Me**
– Golgi / Shun bem / Celtic humour / The jolly lominade / Face chew / East coast moshers / Carpus narwhal / Big beater Borg / Bovine boy / Alfa rock / Nautilus eye brother / I've been listening to motorbikes.
May 99. (c) *(moth 2mc)* **AYR UNIT – Summer Album**
– Bod / Ayr Unit theme / Gorilla boy / Orb/eye / Grind the core / State of the glottis / And / I am the flanger / Bagpuss / Zero zzyzz / I am the filter.
Nov 99. (7"ep) *(moth 3)* **Mothballs (vol.1)**
– FROG POCKET – Egg hoek / AYR UNIT – Quaorthon (ii) / ASTERISK – 13/8b, version 2 / SNOTRA – Robins.
Apr 00. (7"ep) *(moth 4)* **Mothballs (vol.2)**
– FROG POCKET – Drosophila my brother / VOLTERGEIST – Binn pooka (edit) / PARALLEL – E 3.2 / LIPS VAGO – Freak lobbies.
May 00. (cd) *(moth 5cd)* **FROG POCKET – My Favourite**
– Woocky / 8 glothad / Ran / Buffalo skateboard / Bovis / Chib / Flahwy doo / Rub it to the ducks / New borg weeper / West Coast ravers / Green Carrick dub.
Jun 00. (cd-ep) *(moth 6cd)* **AYR UNIT – The Moving Finger..** – The moving finger writes and having writ moves on / Nor all thy piety or wit can lure it back / Nor all thy tears will wash out a word of it.
Oct 00. (7"ep) *(moth 7A/B)* **Mothballs. Volume 3**
– STRAIGHT OUTTA MONGOLIA – Don't be so crass / SNOTRA – Song for breaking stuff / D/compute – In breach / ASTERISK – Sea green and Cyan / PULSAR – The people with computers in their head.
Nov 00. (cd-ep) *(moth 8cd)* **FROG POCKET – Illustrated By Carol Meldrum**
– Vader / Henry Healy / Mats & rice / My favourite / The benevolent lobster.
Nov 00. (cd-ep) *(moth 9cd)* **D/compute – Iwillpushmyselfintotheforestandiwillbedeadthere**
– This is a driving accident / M-fire / To move the sun / Spine of the forest / . . .Drewtheirswordsandshoteachother.
Jun 01. (7") *(moth 10)* **KETTEL – Brother Max**
– These birds around meadows / Embolaze (remixed by Max).
Jun 01. (m-lp; split) *(moth 11)* **RANDOM NUMBER / FROG POCKET**
– RANDOM NUMBER: Best regards (part two) / Some level playing field / Rakes / These streets and sadness / FROG POCKET: Lorax / The man with 2 eyes / Erra balloon.
Oct 01. (7"; split) *(moth 12)* **NECK DOPPLER – Sit Down. / STRAIGHT OUTTA MONGOLIA – Complications**
Feb 02. (cd) *(moth 13cd)* **FROG POCKET – Caric Kils**
– Fir faas / Underwood Ladykirk / Ersweet / My little friend / Felix Kubin / Syml fetlar / Come on the archies! / Eye beby y Ben II.
May 02. (cd-s) *(moth 14cd)* **EYE MAN – Fucker (original) / RANDOM NUMBER remix / PETER PERCEPT remix / NECK DOPPLER remix.**
Sep 02. (cd) *(moth 15cd)* **FROG POCKET – Baral Orgen**
– Jupiter lady mountain village / Caril cyls / Eyewarm / Oh, the places you'll go! / The stare / Omulad / My mettle ass / Foghair.
Sep 02. (cd) *(moth 16cd)* **CAPTAIN STEPHANIE – Caca Poussiere**

Narodnik records

Founded: Edinburgh . . . 1986 by EDDY CONNELLY, one-time bassist of MEAT WHIPLASH, an indie outfit who went on to become MOTORCYCLE BOY. The label was basically set up to cater for recordings by locals JESSE GARON AND THE DESPERADOES and the group's offshoot outfit The FIZZBOMBS. However, by 1988 and last signing The VULTURES, EDDY and his team of assistants moved to pastures new.

- discography -

Oct 86. (7") *(NRK 001)* **JESSE GARON & THE DESPERADOES – Splashing Along**
Mar 87. (7") *(NRK 002)* **JESSE GARON & THE DESPERADOES – The Rain Fell Down**
Apr 87. (7") *(NRK 003)* **FIZZBOMBS – Sign On the Line**
May 87. (7") *(NRK 004)* **BABY LEMONADE – Secret Goldfish**
May 87. (12"ep) *(NRK 005T)* **JESSE GARON & THE DESPERADOES – The Billy Whizz EP**

- The **VULTURES** were from Edinburgh and consisted of JANIE (vocals), ANNA (guitar), ALLISON (bass) and IAN (drums).

May 88. (12"ep) *(NRK 006T)* **VULTURES – Good Thing e.p.**
– Good thing / You're not scared / Whay I say / Jack the ripper.

Nightshift records (see under ⇒ D.D.T. records)

Oily records

Founded: Aberdeen . . . 1978 by Edinburgh native JIM ALLARDICE alongside HOWARD GEMMELL and MIKE CRAIG. With a brief to create a platform for the marginalised North East music scene independent of the London-centric media, 'Oily' became fully operational with the release of 'On The Line' by flagship act, The SQUIBS. Featuring a line-up of DAVE BAIRD,

GORDON LEMON, MURRAY HADDEN, COLIN GARDEN and DAVE CATTENACH, the latter act had previously won through to the quarter finals of a Kid Jensen/Radio One Battle Of The Bands contest, their reggae-tinged debut single (SLICK 1) eventually selling out of its 1000-copy pressing. The label's second release, a single by hotly tipped Dingwall band, The TOOLS, wasn't to go so smoothly. An ambitious initial pressing of 5,000 (their manager had apparently asked for 15,000) for 'Gotta Make Some Money Somehow' resulted in financial headaches for 'Oily' as the band suddenly stopped gigging and the single died on its feet. More successful was The SQUIBS' follow-up, 'Parades', released in 1980 as SLICK 3 and selling out of its 1500 pressing. Yet despite their local popularity and staunch support for the single from John Peel, The SQUIBS failed to make a national breakthrough and split up shortly after.

With the help of OILY's erstwhile manager (and future director of Aberdeen's Alternative Music Festival), Duncan Hendry, the label moved on to a new act, The PRESIDENT'S MEN (formerly The SPLITTING HEADACHES and The ESCORTS). Consisting of JEREMY THOMS, ROY INGRAM, DONALD McDONALD and JOHN WATSON, the group cut 'Out In The Open' to critical acclaim in 1980. As well as coverage from the NME, the group also enjoyed a playlisting on a college radio station across the Atlantic in Philadelphia. With increased support from Edinburgh-based indie distributor, 'Fast Product', Oily was at last getting its records into all the right shops although The PM's second single, 'Reasons For Leaving' was a disappointment sales wise.

Presumably, the Transatlantic success of Ellon-based post-punk funkers APB more than made up for it. The band's first single for Oily, 'Shoot You Down', was a surprise club hit in New York and subsequently led to an East Coast tour. A follow-up single, 1982's 'Palace Filled With Love', became the label's fastest selling release to date and prompted an upsurge in interest from major record companies, agents etc. Fresh from supporting none other than JAMES BROWN himself, APB and Oily geared up for the big time with the 'One Day' single, released with high hopes in 1983. Although the track made the UK Indie Top 10, the demise of Bob Last's 'Fast Product' hit Oily hard given that they'd been promised financial sponsorship from the man. Cutting their losses and licking their wounds, Oily transferred the rights for the single to Sandy McLean and his newly established 'Fast Forward' company, set up in the wake of Fast's demise. In the end, the track was to shift a respectable number of copies although Oily's financial constraints and APB's ever broadening horizons led to a parting of the ways after a final single, 'Danceability'. Licensed to the 'Albion' label and released on 12", the track was another US dancefloor smash.

While APB continued to work in the USA throughout the 80's, Oily wound up their operation shortly after due to a number of factors including family commitments and the spiralling cost of recording. While they never broke a band on a large scale, Oily's success with APB – and to a lesser extent The PM – proved it was possible to both promote quality music without a major label budget and bypass the London-based music industry completely.

- discography -

1978. (7") *(Slick 1)* **SQUIBS – On The Line / Satisfy Me**
1979. (7") *(Slick 2)* **TOOLS – Gotta Make Some Money Somehow / TV Eyes**
1980. (7") *(Slick 3)* **SQUIBS – Parades / Out On The Town**
Jan 81. (7"m) *(Slick 4)* **PRESIDENT'S MEN – Out In The Open / State Of Mind / When Someone Says No**
Mar 81. (7"m) *(Slick 5)* **PRESIDENT'S MEN – Reasons For Living / Cry / I've Got My Best Suit On Today**
Jul 81. (7") *(Slick 6)* **APB – Chain Reaction**
Oct 81. (7") *(Slick 7)* **APB – (I'd Like To) Shoot You Down**
Apr 82. (7") *(Slick 8)* **APB – Palace Filled With Love**
Oct 82. (7") *(Slick 9)* **APB – Rainy Day**
Aug 83. (7"/12") *(Slick/+12 10)* **APB – One Day**
— when APB signed to 'Albion', the label dissolved

Oscarr records

Founded: Glasgow . . . early 2001 by KEITH McIVOR (aka DJ TWITCH of MOUNT FLORIDA fame). CREME DE MENTHE were their first Scottish signings, while PRO FORMA were a Glaswegian trio fusing JOY DIVISION with CHICKS ON SPEED! The most interesting of their releases was arguably BIS doing cover version of famous 'Factory' labels outfits.

- discography -

— unsure of first two 12"ers; probably imports from the States – LOOSE JOINTS – It Is All Over My Face
May 02. (12"ep) *(OSC 003)* **CREME DE MENTHE – Plastique EP**
– Plastique / Hot / We are living in the night / Destroy the human race. *(re-iss. May02 on 'Disko B' Germany; efa 27906-6)*
May 02. (12"ep) *(OSC 004)* **BIS – Fact 2002 EP**
Aug 02. (lp) *(OSC 005)* **Various Artists – Fake Matador Bulletin Board**
Aug 02. (12"ep) *(OSC 008)* **PRO FORMA – Human Error EP**
Jul 02. (12"ep) *(OSC 009)* **Various Artists – Betty Botox EP**
Aug 02. (12"split) *(OSC 010)* **SECRETS / DL BUCKET**

Out On A Limb records (see under ⇒ Limbo records)

Panther records (see under ⇒ Hook records)

Path records

Founded: January 1999 by JOHN HUTCHISON then owner of the music venue The Path Tavern in Kirkcaldy which in that year won Scottish Licensed Trade News Music Pub of The Year. His first protégés, RISINGSON were another youthful band from Edinburgh to emerge from the Chamber Studios. Originally named COFFEE, the 5-piece of RICH DAVIES (vocals, guitar), ROSS KILGOUR (lead guitar, keyboards, vocals), DAVE BRUNTON (drums, vocals), Fifer BRETT ALLAN (bass, vocals) and DONNA MACIOCIA (keyboards), played trip-hop punk rock and released the 'SUBWAY WALL' EP in early 1999; HUTCHISON was also their DJ/sampler at this stage. In April 2001, RISINGSON issued a second EP, 'EVIL TV'.

While all this excitement was going on, newcomers to the scene, Dunfermline's SINGLESKIN – i.e. PAUL BUNNING (vocals & guitar), DAVE BERNTHAL (guitar & vocals), COLIN SMITH (bass & vocals) and DARRELL ANTHONY (drums) – were busy cutting their teeth supporting the likes of SUPERSTAR and COSMIC ROUGH RIDERS. Taking elements of dEUS, SPARKLEHORSE and TEENAGE FANCLUB, the quartet were beginning to breach the local Edinburgh scene, selling copies of their debut EP, '79 ELECTROSHOCK TREATMENTS' at gigs from April 2001.

After a quiet 2002 (which saw John move on from the Path Tavern) the label is soon to have a major re-launch in January 2003 with singles and albums by Singleskin and new signings Amateur Guitar Anti-Heroes. The label also co-organised the Handbags at Dawn compilation with Human Condition and has licensed tracks onto several compilations.

- discography -

Apr 99. (cd-ep) *Path 6901* **RISINGSON - Subway Wall** (Self Distribution)
Nov 99. (cd-ep) *Path 6902 / HC0026* **DANNY HOLLAND – A Lifetime And A Day** (in conjunction with Human Condition)
Apr 00. (cd-ep) *Path 6903* **RISINGSON – Evil TV** (Self Distribution)
Oct 00. (cd-ep) *Path 6904* **The STACEY EFFECT – Buzzkill** (Prime Distribution)
Oct 00. (cd-ep) *Path 6905* **RISINGSON – Mind Control EP** (Prime Distribution)
May 01. (cd-ep) *Path 6906* **SINGLESKIN – 79 Electroshock Treatments** (Mac Distribution)

Play records

Founded: 9 Hampden Terrace, Mount Florida, Glasgow, G42 9XQ, the brainchild of JOHNSON members, PETER ROSS and former TRASH CAN SINATRAS drummer STEPHEN DOUGLAS. Their motive was to release limited edition singles and possibly sign a few local outfits and this they finally achieved post-millennium:- HEIRLOOM are JOHNNY DILLON (vocals & guitar), JODY STODDART (guitar & vocals), NEIL HUGHES (bass) and JAMES MOIR (drums & vocals); JOHN DOUGLAS (ex-TRASH CAN SINATRAS) makes a guest appearance on their B-side; The WOW CAFE are RAY MOLLER + BILL WRIGHT – guitars, MATTHEW LOWE – bass + STEF LE BATTEUR – drums; have issued one 7" (3-track) so far, 'NIGHT APPLES OVER KANSAS'. ODEON BEATCLUB were also on the roster, while OSTLE BAY were a combination of ROSS and defunct TRASH CAN SINATRAS members.

- discography -

Feb 99. (7") *(PLAY 001)* **JOHNSON – Tripping With The Moonlight**
May 99. (7") *(PLAY 002)* **JOHNSON – Savoury Body Show**
Oct 99. (7") *(PLAY 003)* **JOHNSON – Skin And Gold**

Apr 00. (7") *(PLAY 004)* **JOHNSON – Blonde On Blue**
Aug 01. (7") *(PLAY 005)* **WOW CAFE – Night Apples Over Kansas**
Aug 01. (7") *(PLAY 006)* **ODEON BEATCLUB – I Need More time**
Apr 02. (7") *(PLAY 007)* **HEIRLOOM – He Is In Jail / Without A Station**
Sep 02. (cd) *(PLAY 008)* **OSTLE BAY – Love From Ostle Bay**

Pop: Aural records (see under ⇒ Fast Product records)

Postcard Records

Founded: 185 West Princes Street, Glasgow . . . late 70's by ALAN HORNE, a young man inspired by the ethos of New Wave and the 7" 45. Having just discovered local alternative outfit ORANGE JUICE (formerly known as the NU-SONICS), HORNE set about creating his own perfect Postcard. With the tag, "the young sound of Scotland", emblazoned on its brown DIY (drumming cat!) sleevework, HORNE and his new EDWYN COLLINS-led signings delivered the debut 'Postcard' release in February 1980. 'Falling And Laughing' was well-received by both the public and critics alike (even south of the border!) and led to a second ORANGE JUICE single 'Blue Boy' hitting the indie shops that August. Meticulously hand-crafted designs led to both singles almost immediately being collectable, and, when HORNE signed a second band – Edinburgh's JOSEF K (led by PAUL HAIG) – the small label looked to be taking off.

Although ALAN lost out to 'Pop: Aural' for the FIRE ENGINES' nom de plumes, JOSEF K's 'Radio Drill Time' became their third class single in a row. Going further afield (although the band had been touring in Britain!), the man inked a deal with Australia's GO-BETWEENS, who delivered Postcard No.4, 'I Need Two Heads'. Towards the end of a glorious year for HORNE and Co, two further gems were unleashed, JOSEF K's second 'It's Kinda Funny' and ORANGE JUICE's third 'Simply Thrilled Honey'. However, 1981 began on a sour note, when HAIG and Co objected to the sound quality of their subsequent debut album, 'Sorry For Laughing'. It was immediately shelved, although later in the year, two JOSEF K singles 'Sorry For Laughing' and 'Chance Meeting' (a re-recording of their 1979 non-Postcard debut!) were issued prior to the all-new debut LP, 'The Only Fun In Town'.

Meanwhile, the label's third Scots-based signings, AZTEC CAMERA (led by 16-year old RODDY FRAME), were unveiled that March. 'Just Like Gold' was a lighter pastel-pop tune compared to the work of the aforementioned OJ's and AC's, and this certainly marked a poppier direction. That same month of March, saw ORANGE JUICE bow out with the single, 'Poor Old Soul', another clever three-minute track that led to major 'Polydor' records enrolling the group; another 7", 'Wan Light', was subsequently shelved. July '81 was a better month for Postcard when AZTEC CAMERA and the GO-BETWEENS both released singles, the former with another fine jangly acoustic-led number, 'Mattress Of Wire'.

However, with JOSEF K now on the roster of a Belgian label, it seemed only AZTEC CAMERA could be the saviour of HORNE's ailing label. This was not to be and when RODDY and Co were tempted south to London's 'Rough Trade' (shelving their debut LP, 'Green Jacket Grey', in the process!), Postcard looked all washed up. Newcomers the SECRET GOLFISH, the BLUEBELLS and the JAZZATEERS were hardly given a chance as HORNE shelved their subsequent singles to formulate new projects. POSTCARD was no more.

HORNE remained a photographer and re-surfaced with the 'Swamplands' imprint in 1984. The first release for the label, 'Pale Blue Eyes', teamed up EDWYN COLLINS with former BOURGIE BOURGIE singer PAUL QUINN. Further recordings included WIN, led by DAVEY HENDERSON, whom he'd tried to sign when he was leader of The FIRE ENGINES. Like most of HORNE's protegees, WIN finally succumbed to the wiles of the English music pop industry by signing to 'London' then 'Virgin'.

In the early 90's, Postcard were back in operation, mainly to re-actify old ORANGE JUICE material, although fresh new signings included PAUL QUINN & THE INDEPENDENT GROUP, NECTARINE No.9 (who included HENDERSON) and Londoner VIC GODARD (who's now living in Scotland!). Meanwhile, sister label, Sano records (based at Unit 14, Firhill Business Centre, 76 Firhill Road, Glasgow, G20 7BA) were also in operation, combining releases by JOCK SCOT & NECTARINE No.9, among others.

— to find out more, see under the artists' own entries

– early label discography –

Feb 80. (7") *(80-1)* **ORANGE JUICE – Falling And Laughing**
Aug 80. (7") *(80-2)* **ORANGE JUICE – Blue Boy**
Aug 80. (7") *(80-3)* **JOSEF K – Radio Drill Time**
Nov 80. (7") *(80-4) GO-BETWEENS – I Need Two Heads*
Dec 80. (7") *(80-5)* **JOSEF K – It's Kinda Funny**
Dec 80. (7") *(80-6)* **ORANGE JUICE – Simply Thrilled Honey**
Jan 81. (lp) *(81-1)* **JOSEF K – Sorry For Laughing** (shelved)
Mar 81. (7") *(81-2)* **ORANGE JUICE – Poor Old Soul**
Mar 81. (7") *(81-3)* **AZTEC CAMERA – Just Like Gold**
Mar 81. (7") *(81-4)* **JOSEF K – Sorry For Laughing**
May 81. (7") *(81-5)* **JOSEF K – Chance Meeting**
Jun 81. (7") *(81-6)* **ORANGE JUICE – Wan Light** (shelved)
Jun 81. (lp) *(81-7)* **JOSEF K – The Only Fun In Town**
Jul 81. (7") *(81-8)* **AZTEC CAMERA – Mattress Of Wire**
Jul 81. (7") *(81-9) GO-BETWEENS – Your Turn, My Turn*
— (81-10 was also shelved, as was all 4 below)
Sep 81. (7") *(81-11)* **SECRET GOLDFISH – Hey Mister / Poorest Boy In Town**
Sep 81. (7") *(81-12)* **BLUEBELLS – Everybody's Somebody's Fool**
Sep 81. (lp) *(81-13)* **AZTEC CAMERA – Green Jacket Grey**
Jan 82. (7") *(81-14)* **JAZZATEERS –** (withdrawn single)

– Swamplands records –

Aug 84. (7") *(SWP 1)* **PAUL QUINN & EDWYN COLLINS – Pale Blue Eyes**
Jan 85. (7"/12") *(SWP/SWX 3)* **JAMES KING & THE LONE WOLVES – The Angels Know**
Mar 95. (7"/12") *(SWP/SWX 5)* **WIN – Unamerican Broadcasting**
Mar 85. (7"/12") *(SWP/SWX 6)* **PAUL QUINN – Ain't That Always The Way**
Jun 85. (7"/12") *(SWP/SWX 8)* **WIN – You've Got The Power**

– Postcard (re-activated) –

Sep 92. (lp/c/cd) *(DUBH 921/+MC/CD)* **PAUL QUINN & THE INDEPENDENT GROUP – The Phantoms And The Archetypes**
Jul 92. (lp/c/cd) *(DUBH 922/+MC/CD)* **ORANGE JUICE – Ostrich Churchyard (live in Glasgow)**
Feb 93. (lp/cd) *(DUBH 931/+CD)* **NECTARINE No.9 – A Sea With Three Stars**
Jul 93. (lp/cd) *(DUBH 932/+CD)* **ORANGE JUICE – The Heather's On Fire**
Jul 93. (7"/cd-s) *(DUBH 933/+CD)* **PAUL QUINN & THE INDEPENDENT GROUP – Stupid Thing**
May 93. (7"/cd-s) *(DUBH 934/+CD)* **ORANGE JUICE – Blueboy**
Oct 93. (cd-ep) *(DUBH 935CD)* **NECTARINE No.9 – Unloaded For You EP**
Jun 93. (lp/cd) *(DUBH 936/+CD) VIC GODARD – End Of The Surrey People*
May 93. (7"/cd-s) *(DUBH 937/+CD) VIC GODARD – Won't Turn Back*
Oct 93. (cd-ep) *(DUBH 939)* **NECTARINE No.9 – Unloaded For You**
Oct 94. (lp/c/cd) *(DUBH 945/+MC/CD)* **PAUL QUINN & THE INDEPENDENT GROUP – Will I Ever Be Inside Of You**
Jul 95. (cd) *(DUBH 951CD)* **NECTARINE No.9 – Saint Jack**
Jun 95. (cd-ep) *(DUBH 952CD)* **PAUL QUINN, NECTARINE No.9 + JOCK SCOT – Pregnant With Possibilities EP**
May 97. (cd) *(DUBH 972 – SANO 1877)* **JOCK SCOT – My Personal Culloden**

Rational records

Founded: c/o Gutter Music (a shop run by actor ANDRE THORNTON-GRIMES) at 19 Henderson Row, Edinburgh . . . 1980 by former JOSEF K manager, ALLAN CAMPBELL, who also supplied material for City Lynx around the late 70's. An entrepreneur of sorts, the man also arranged benefit gigs to support the aforementioned soon-to-be defunct magazine (described by many as Scotland's answer to Time Out). These early gigs featured the likes of SIMPLE MINDS, the ONLY ONES and The DIRTY DOSSERS, the latter an ad hoc outfit comprising STUART NISBET (later a guitarist with the PROCLAIMERS), a very young EDDI READER and most of The VALVES.

In 1980, CAMPBELL unveiled his new adventurous Aquarius Club (situated in Grindlay Street) and it was there he introduced bands such as The SCARS, METROPAK and of course, The DELMONTES. Out of STRANGE DAZE – well four of them at least – the punky riff-tastic combo consisted of mainly JULIE HEPBURN (on vocals), BERNICE (on drums), another female and two local lads; they were actually supported by the FIRE ENGINES at Valentino's (Edinburgh) April 27, 1980. Touring with The TEARDROP EXPLODES, the 5-piece band completed their debut single, 'TOUS LES SOIRS', which was said to have borrowed a riff from the 13th FLOOR ELEVATORS 'You're Gonna Miss Me'. A sophomore 45, 'DON'T CRY YOUR TEARS', was released a few months later in May '81, although things soon went belly-up when 'WEA' shelved a proposed ALAN RANKINE-produced set; BERNICE would turn up with The PASTELS.

The second 'Rational' signing was Dundee's the VISITORS, who had been on the go for a few years now. Their contribution was 'COMPATIBILITY'. Early in 1982, solo star PAUL HAIG (formerly of JOSEF K) took a backseat for a short while, letting his new backing band, RHYTHM OF LIFE (i.e. JAMES LOCKE and ex-METROPAK guy STEVEN HAINES) take the reins on two solid 45's, 'SOON' and 'UNCLE SAM'. The latter featured a local sculptor-cum-singer, SEBASTIAN HORSLEY, although this was the briefest of liaisons as the man hooked up with 'Sense Of Freedom' ex-con JIMMY BOYLE at the Gateway Exchange. 'Rational' suffered the same fate as 'Postcard' and 'Fast Product' records when CAMPBELL decided to wind things down later in 1982.

A few years later, the never say die AC was back running the 'Supreme Int.' imprint after previously working with one of its first signings, JESSE RAE. Other signings at the time were the JUGGERNAUTS (featuring JAMES LOCKE, GORDON KERR and PAUL and NIGEL SLEVOR), the HIGH BEES (featuring MALCOLM ROSS, DAVE RUFFY and SUSAN BUCKLEY) and The SYNDICATE (run by JAMES STEWART), all delivering their take on upbeat indie/dance music. In 1986, several more outfits were to be on the Supreme roster. They included the BEAT FREAKS (LOCKE and MIKE PEDAN, later of The CHIMES), BOTANY 500 (aka GORDON KERR and DAVE GALBRAITH) and the CHAIN GANG, the latter a conglomerate of famous musos, namely PAT KANE, JAMES GRANT, STEPHEN PASTEL and CLARE GROGAN, who wanted to raise funds for the workers occupying their Uddingston factory.

After a few archival releases by the legendary JOSEF K, Supreme Int was wound up by CAMPBELL who found solace in his own established monthly music rag, Cut. Its first edition in October 1986, featured Derby-born LLOYD COLE, DAVID BYRNE, GOODBYE MR MACKENZIE, SHOP ASSISTANTS, JAMES GRANT, BING HITLER and IVOR CUTLER, while later publications were graced with the presence of writers STEPHEN DALY (ex-ORANGE JUICE) and ALASTAIR MacKAY. In 1989, disillusioned by the paper's growing need to please its southern masters (the New Statesman Distribution), CAMPBELL left the building as they say; the last Cut was published that September.

– Rational discography –

Jan 81. (7") *(RATE 1)* **DELMONTES – Tous Les Soirs / Gaga Infectious Smile**
Mar 81. (7") *(RATE 2)* **VISITORS – Compatibility**
May 81. (7") *(RATE 3)* **DELMONTES – Don't Cry Your Tears / So It's Not To Be**
— STRANGE DAZE released a posthumous 7" in Jan'84 on 'Aura' (AUS 141), 'THROUGH THE DOORS' / 'COME OUT TONIGHT'.
Jan 82. (7") *(RATE 6 – RHYTHM 1)* **RHYTHM OF LIFE – Soon / Summertime**
Apr 82. (7") *(RATE 7 – RHYTHM 2)* **RHYTHM OF LIFE – Uncle Sam / Portrait Of The Heart**

– Supreme Int. discography –

Nov 84. (12") *(EDITION84 2)* **JUGGERNAUTS – Come Throw Yourself Under The Monstrous Wheels Of The Rock'n'Roll Industry As It Approaches Destruction**
Dec 84. (12") *(EDITION84 5)* **JESSE RAE – Be Yourself**
Apr 85. (12") *(EDITION85 8)* **HIGH BEES – She's Killing Time / Some Indulgence**
Jun 85. (12") *(EDITION85 9)* **SYNDICATE – Golden Key**
Jun 86. (12") *(EDITION86 11)* **BEAT FREAKS – The National Anthem**
Jul 86. (12") *(EDITION86 12)* **BOTANY 500 – Bully Beef**
Feb 87. (12") *(EDITION87 14)* **CHAIN GANG – Makin' Tracks / Creepy Crawlies**
Mar 87. (12") *(EDITION87 7)* **JOSEF K – Heaven Sent**
Jun 87. (lp) *(EDITION87 6)* **JOSEF K – Young And Stupid**

– other CHAIN GANG discography –

May 87. (12") *Idea; (IDT 002)* **Long Time Gone**
1987. (12"ep) *Troll Kitchen; (WORKS 002)* **More Than A Dream**
– More than a dream / Ridin' down the line / Long time gone / Fight for your life.

Revol records (see under ⇒ Lithium records)

Rock Action records

Founded: 9 Manse Brae, Dalserf, Lanarkshire, M19 3BN – by MOGWAI and ESKA guitar man STUART BRAITHWAITE. Mainly to issue MOGWAI's debut release, 'Tuner', the Rock Action imprint was duly underway by early '96. Sophomore release, 'Rusty Barker Learns To Fly', by much-feted Edinburgh indie outfit, PILOTCAN, secured fans among the rising Glasgwegian alt-rock fraternity. Squeezed in between a second PILOTCAN 7", 'Five Minutes On A Tuesday Night', was the third Rock Action delivery, a split affair between TROUT and the THREE WISE MEN.

Commitments with other labels – including a debut album for 'Chemikal Underground' – meant BRAITHWAITE's Rock Action psyche was out of commission for a lengthy period. During this sort of hiatus, STUART and MOGWAI took the opportunity to issue singles compilation, 'Ten Rapid' (1998), which arguably remains the pièce de resistance of all the label's output to date.

Four years on from Rock Action's last proper release, the label acquired three new prospects, The ZEPHYRS, the JAMES ORR COMPLEX and former Yankie Post-Rock pioneer and guitar-wielder DAVID PAJO (ex-SLINT, ex-TORTOISE, ex-AERIAL-M, etc), under the pseudonymous guise of PAPA M. From late 2000 onwards, all three groups released much in-demand records, The ZEPHYRS single, 'Stargazer', selling its limited copies almost immediately. Meanwhile, PAJO and PAPA M received renewed interest via the label's 7th release, ' . . . Sings', a record which focused on the more sublime nature of modern-day mello-dramatics. Recent signings, RANDOM NUMBER, were in fact, a one-man (MATT ROBSON) from Leeds, while CEX (pronounced 'sex') is American RJYAN KIDWELL.

– discography –

Feb 96. (7") *(RAR 001)* **MOGWAI – Tuner**
Jun 96. (7") *(RAR 002)* **PILOTCAN – Rusty Barker Learns To Fly**

- **TROUT** were formed in Glasgow around the mid-90's by vocalist WILLIAM 'TROUT' ROFAN and three mates. TROUT the band dipped their proverbial fins into the musical pond with a debut 45, a split affair with the THREE WISE MEN' jointly issued by 'Rock Action' and 'Bosque' records; a tour with PILOTCAN followed. Another split 7", this time with the SPACE KITTENS was released on 'Flotsam & Jetsam' (as part of the Club Beatroot series; *SHaG 13.03*) the following year. October '97, saw the fishy ones turn up on a 'Tribute To Celtic F.C.' single along with CHA CHA 2000 (aka MICK DERRICK of PROLAPSE) for 'Guided Missile offshoot, 'Flighted Miskick'; *FLICK 002)*

Nov 96. (7"ep) *(RAR 003)* **TROUT – Livin In An Oven / Plasma / (+ two by THREE WISE MEN licenced to 'Bosque' records;** *bosc 020)*

Dec 96. (7") *(ROCKACT 4)* **PILOTCAN – Five Minutes On A Tuesday Night**
Aug 98. (cd) *(ROCKACT 5cd)* **MOGWAI – Ten Rapid**
Nov 00. (7"/cd-s) *(ROCKACT/+CD 6)* **ZEPHYRS – Stargazer**
Mar 01. (cd-ep) *(ROCKACTCD 7) PAPA M – Papa M Sings*
Nov 01. (7"ep/cd-ep) *(ROCKACT 8/+CD)* **JAMES ORR COMPLEX – Figa**
Jan 02. (12"ep/cd-ep) *(ROCKACT/+CD 9) RANDOM NUMBER – The Fact That I Dis EP*
Oct 01. (cd-s) *(ROCKACTCD 10)* **MOGWAI – My Father My King**
Apr 02. (cd) *(ROCKACT 11CD) CEX – Oops, I Did It Again*

Shoeshine records

Founded: Glasgow . . . 1995 by former BMX BANDITS member FRANCIS MACDONALD (b.11 September 1970), who'd previously served his time with Bellshill minor legends The PASTELS and TEENAGE FANCLUB. Launching the label with the SPEEDBOAT project (which whom he played drums), MACDONALD subsequently developed Shoeshine as a bastion of rootsy retro rock via releases from the likes of BMX BANDITS (who else!), RADIO SWEETHEARTS (with whom he was also involved), FRANK BLAKE (FRANCIS and NORMAN in disguise), American "Big Star" ALEX CHILTON, ASTRO CHIMP (more of his mates from EUGENIUS and the 'FANNIES), CHEEKY MONKEY (FRANCIS and American Shoeshine solo artist, MICHAEL SHELLEY) and BEN VAUGHN.

Far less incestuous was Country/Americana sub-division, 'Spit & Polish', boasting relatively unsung Stateside talents such as LAURA CANTRELL, JOHN HERALD, STEVE YOUNG, PAUL BURCH, TIM CARROLL, JASON RINGENBERG and SHE-HAW. A recent addition in 2002 was TOM CLELLAND, an acoustic country/folk singer-songwriter from East Lothian. The former Gram Parsons tribute performer delivered his debut set, 'LITTLE STORIES' at the age of 50!; Americana was taking over Caledonia. Meanwhile, back at the Shoeshine ranch, new signings were Cork-based group BOA MORTE and Champaign-Urbana (Illinois) combo The BEAUTY SHOP; MAJOR MATT MASON USA was indeed an anti-folk hero from NYC. If you like your rock with a large dose of country, then look no further than this oasis in the West (of Glasgow, that is). You can peruse their wares online at:- www.shoeshine.co.uk

– discography –

singles
May 95. (7") *(SHOE 001)* **SPEEDBOAT – Satellite Girl**
Oct 96. (7") *(SHOE 002)* **BMX BANDITS – Help Me, Somebody**
Oct 96. (7") *(SHOE 003)* **RADIO SWEETHEARTS – New Memories**
Oct 96. (7") *(SHOE 004)* **FRANK BLAKE – Plastic Bag / Don't Let Love Pass You By**
Oct 96. (7") *(SHOE 005) ALEX CHILTON – Margie*
Nov 96. (7") *(SHOE 006)* **ASTRO CHIMP – Draggin'**
Jul 97. (7") *(SHOE 007)* **SPEEDBOAT – Luv**
Jun 97. (7") *(SHOE 008)* **RADIO SWEETHEARTS – Rambling Man**
Jul 97. (7") *(SHOE 009) MICHAEL SHELLEY – Think With Your Heart*
Feb 98. (7") *(SHOE 010)* **CHEEKY MONKEY – That Kind Of Girl**
Nov 00. (7") *(SHOE 011) MICHAEL SHELLEY – Baby's In A Bad Mood*

Jan 02. (7") *(SHOE 012) MAJOR MATT MASON USA – Mr. Softie*
Jul 02. (7") *(SHOE 013) BEAUTY SHOP – Death March*
Jul 02. (7") *(SHOE 014) BOA MORTE – Clarence White*
albums
Feb 98. (cd/lp) *(SHOE CD/LP 001) Shoeshine Chartbusters*
Mar 98. (cd/lp) *(SHOE CD/LP 002)* **CHEEKY MONKEY – Four Arms To Hold You**
Oct 98. (cd) *(SHOECD 003)* **RADIO SWEETHEARTS – New Memories . . . Revisited** (re-issue)
Apr 99. (cd/lp) *(SHOE CD/LP 004)* **SPEEDBOAT – Satellite Girl**
Jul 99. (cd) *(SHOECD 005) BEN VAUGHN – A Date With Ben Vaughn*
Feb 00. (cd) *(SHOECD 006) MICHAEL SHELLEY – Half Empty* (re-issue)
Feb 00. (cd) *(SHOECD 007) MICHAEL SHELLEY – Too Many Movies* (re-issue)
Jan 02. (cd) *(SHOECD 008) MAJOR MATT MASON USA – Me Me Me*
Feb 02. (cd) *(SHOECD 009) Various Artists – Shoeshine Sampler*
May 02. (cd) *(SHOECD 010) BEAUTY SHOP – Yr Money Or Yr Life*
Jun 02. (cd) *(SHOECD 011) BOA MORTE – Soon It Will Come Time To Face The World Outside*
Sep 02. (cd) *(SHOECD 012) BEN VAUGHN – Glasgow Time*

– Spit & Polish UK discography –

Feb 00. (cd) *(SPITCD 001) LAURA CANTRELL – Not The Tremblin Kind*
Feb 00. (cd) *(SPITCD 002)* **RADIO SWEETHEARTS – Lonesome Blue**
Jun 00. (cd) *(SPITCD 003) JOHN HERALD – Roll On John*
Jun 00. (cd) *(SPITCD 004) STEVE YOUNG – Primal Young*
May 01. (cd) *(SPITCD 005) PAUL BURCH & THE WPA BALLCLUB – Blue Notes*
Nov 01. (cd) *(SPITCD 006) PAUL BURCH – Last Of My Kind*
Sep 01. (cd) *(SPITCD 007) TIM CARROLL – If I Could*
Jan 02. (cd) *(SPITCD 008)* **TOM CLELLAND – Little Stories**
– I wish I could write like old Guy Clark / Slowdown / The Devil & the hangman / Getaway / Country music once again / Nevada / Still a friend of mine / The number song / Somewhere in a better place / Old cars / Lock me on fat forward / I will bring you home / Let it snow.
Apr 02. (cd) *(SPITCD 009) JASON RINGENBERG – All Over Creation*
Jun 02. (cd) *(SPITCD 010) SHE-HAW – Splinter*
May 02. (cd) *(SPITCD 011)* **JOHN MILLER – Popping Pills**

Shoop records

Founded: 01592 number, Fife . . . early 1993 by DJ ZBD, who also writes for Clubscene fanzine. ZBD, aka GORDON TENNANT, also has his own AURAL 4 PLAY (with MC SIMMY), their debut a bit like the 'Dinosaurs' (puppets) theme tune. BASS X, meanwhile, were STEWART BROWN and SCOTT BROWN, MASSIVE are DJ MONTANA (BARRY McLEAN) and SCOTT BROWN; they had to change their name to DANSATAK (added female singer) to distinguish from Bristol's MASSIVE ATTACK – 'Equator Arctic' re-released 'HEAVEN IN MIND' a major dancefloor smash. TECHNOSIS were made up of VINCE WATSON (also of TECHNOTRIBE), DECKY BROGAN, RICKY RANKINE and MICK McFADYEN, D-TOX = the aforementioned GORDON TENNANT and HARDWARE = SCOTT BROWN; the latter was also HYPERACT with ALEC MULLEN. MASS ENERGY comprised C. WILSON and KENNETH HANNAH, while another duo on the label were LENNY DEE (DIDESIDARIO) and DARRIEN KELLY.

– discography –

Apr 93. (12") *(SHOOP 1)* **Q.F.X. – Phoebus EP**
Apr 93. (12") *(SHOOP 2)* **BASS X – Hardcore Disco**
Jul 93. (12") *(SHOOP 3)* **DANCE OVER DOSE – Chemically Insane**
Aug 93. (12") *(SHOOP 4)* **AURAL 4 PLAY – Gotta Love Me**
Nov 93. (12") *(SHOOP 5)* **DANCE OVER DOSE – Overdose Stomp**
Sep 93. (12") *(SHOOP 6)* **MASSIVE – Heaven In Mind**
Jan 94. (d12") *(SHOOP 7)* **BASS X – Atomic EP – Bounce**
Dec 93. (12") *(SHOOP 8)* **BASS X – Bass Xmas**
Jan 94. (12") *(SHOOP 9)* **MASSIVE featuring TRACY B – Key Of Life / Street Knowledge**
1994. (12") *(SHOOP 10)* **AURAL 4 PLAY – Barracuda**
1994. (12") *(SHOOP 11)* **TECHNOSIS – Holocaust / Rush Bins. / Infiltrator / Pro 2 Type**
1994. (12") *(SHOOP 12)* **D-TOX – Sex / Simply A Question. / Bass Drum / Thrash**
1994. (12") *(SHOOP 14)* **HARDWARE – Heavy Metal. / Heavy metal (doing mix) / Bass Shake**
1994. (12"ep) *(SHOOP 15)* **DANCE OVER DOSE – Nausea EP**
1994. (12") *(SHOOP 16)* **BASS X – Exterminate / Don't Get That. / Mother Fucker / Psychopath**
1994. (12") *(SHOOP 17)* **HYPERACT – Monster Sound (technotrance mix). / That Sample (Mr Crazy remix) / Technotrance vs MC XXX (G.T. sampler mix)**
1994. (12") *(SHOOP 18)* **TECHNOTRIBE – Technotribe EP: Aural Assault. / Ecstatica / Neurotica**
1994. (12") *(SHOOP 20)* **LENNY DEE & DARRIEN KELLY – Hardcore Trax Vol.1: Speedbump / Schoom! / Move It**
1995. (12") *(SHOOP 21)* **MASS ENERGY – Futurizer. / Destruction Day / 090**
1995. (12") *(SHOOP 22)* **HYPERHYTHM – Can't Fight This Feeling. / Hyperhythmic / What's Happening**
1995. (12") *(SHOOP 23)* **TECHNOSIS featuring THE MANIAC – State Of Flux. / Pulsar**
1995. (12") *(SHOOP 24)* **UNKNOWN SOURCE – Nuclear Anarchy. / Urban Terrorist / Indistrial Revolution**
1995.(12") *(SHOOP 29)* **PETER PIPER – Peter Piper**
— the label folded after above

sl records

Founded: 70 Arden Street, Edinburgh, EH9 1BN . . . 1996 by ED PYBUS, MERLIN and BRIDGET as a vehicle for promoting their own radio show on the capital's student station, 'Fresh Air FM'. The promotional tool in question was a sampler entitled 'It's a Life Sentence . . .', featuring tracks by BALLBOY, The SELFISH GENE, MY PVC DREAM, LIFE WITH NIXON and KHAYA. The latter act then graced sl's first ever 7", 'SUMMER/WINTER SONG', a track much beloved of Steve Lamacq, John Peel and Jo Whiley amongst others.

A subsequent release from BALLBOY was cancelled after a "big band from Glasgow released a song that sounded exactly the same". Instead, the label released a second single by KHAYA and, with the financial muscle of fellow Edinburgh indie, 'Koala', a debut album. Another two albums by the ever prolific KHAYA ensued as did a series of limited edition EP's by BALLBOY, all of which sold out amid considerable press acclaim.

The burgeoning indie is currently in buoyant health with an upcoming collection of videos – produced by local company 'Brainhole' – on the cards and a number of worldwide distribution deals in the bag.

– discography –

May 97. (cd) *(lone 01)* **Various Artists – It's A Life Sentence . . .**
– BALLBOY – Cra crashes / I could eat you up / Photographers / the SELFISH GENE – Transporter / How's your head / Strange these days / KHAYA – Here / It couldn't be worse / Snow song / MY PVC DREAM – Coma / The big issue / Messages / LIFE WITH NIXON – Being young / Charlie / Bubblehead / the SUBSTITUTE – Retro.
Nov 97. (7") *(lone 02)* **KHAYA – Summer/Winter Song**
Dec 97. (7") *(lone 03)* **BALLBOY – A Day In Space / Car Crashes / Postcards From The Beach** (this was never released)
Apr 98. (7") *(lone 04)* **KHAYA – Two Songs By Khaya**
Nov 99. (cd) *(lone 05)* **KHAYA – Avoidance**
Nov 99. (cd-ep) *(lone 06)* **BALLBOY – Silver Suits For Astronauts**
Mar 00. (7"ep) *(lone 07)* **KHAYA – Do The Thing . . .**
Jul 00. (cd-ep) *(lone 08)* **BALLBOY – I Hate Scotland**
Feb 01. (m-cd) *(lone 09)* **KHAYA – The Lost Feeling**
Mar 01. (cd-ep) *(lone 10)* **BALLBOY – Girls Are Better Than Boys**
Jul 01. (cd) *(lone 11)* **BALLBOY – A Europewide Search For Love**
Apr 02. (cd) *(lone 12)* **DESC – Up Here In The Heat**

• **DEGRASSI** underwent major personnel surgery before they finally made it through to the recording studio, incidentally funded by the Scottish Arts Council. Comprising of CHRIS BATHGATE (guitars & vocals), SCOTT SMITH (guitars & vocals), MICHAEL BRANAGH (drums & vocals), TOM NICOL (bass & noise) – who replaced singer/guitarist STUART TURNER – and PAUL PHILLIPS (keyboards & synths), the post-punk rawk quintet smashed onto the Scottish underground scene courtesy of some storming gigs around the country. Recruiting MOGWAI's JOHN CUMMINGS as a sound engineer, DEGRASSI (not the South London pop quintet) played sessions for John Peel, Steve Lamacq, etc, ensuring interest in their debut single/EP, 'TERMINAL OCEAN'; FAUST meets BLACK FLAG or FUGAZI, quite possibly.

Jun 02. (cd-s) *(lone 16)* **DeGRASSI – Terminal Ocean**
– No tracks in the snow / Terminal ocean / Emerald city / Air force one.

• BARRICHELLO were in fact from south of the border, although they did settle in Edinburgh post-millennium. DYLAN (vocals & guitar), ALUN (drums & vocals), DEAN (bass & guitar) and MATT (bass & keyboards) were actually from Harlow, Llanelli and Wrexham; their debut EP in August 2001, 'BONDIES HOLLOW' was partly financed by 'sl'.

Jul 02. (cd-ep) *(lone 17) BARRICHELLO – Down Soft EP*
– Down soft / Sometimes the voices make me do bad things / The glockenspiel song / Catherine The Great.

Soma records / SLAM

Founded: Scotland's premier independent dance label not to mention one of the most respected labels in Britain and indeed Europe, Soma has now been kicking out the dancefloor jams for nigh on a decade. The label was founded in Glasgow (Otago Street) back in the summer of 1991 by Oxford-born ORDE

MEIKLE, STUART McMILLAN, DAVE CLARKE, GLEN GIBBONS and JIM MOUTUNE, initially as an outlet for their own music. All had been involved in the city's club scene since the mid-80's, McMILLAN and MEIKLE credited as being the first to expose Glasgow clubbers to acid house via their DJ partnership SLAM. The pair can also lay claim to both organising and playing at the UK's first run of licensed all-nighters prior to establishing their famous Friday night residency at The Arches.

The obvious next step was to produce their own tracks and in 1991, SLAM's 'Eterna' (one half of a double-A side along with 'IBO' by REJUVINATION) became Soma's first release. Although now regarded as a classic, it was the legendary 'Positive Education' that really put both SLAM and Soma on the international clubland map. Released in 1993, the track was feted by DJ's, critics and producers from Detroit to London to Amsterdam, paving the way for the boys' debut album, 'HEADSTATES' (1996). SLAM's lovingly crafted meltdown of funky house and techno has since seen them in demand in such far flung corners of the globe as Japan and Brazil. They've also set up their very own tent at Scotland's 'T In The Park' Festival in recent years, playing host to the likes of PLASTIKMAN (aka RICHIE HAWTIN) and CARL COX.

On the recording front, STUART and ORDE have been working under the new moniker PRESSURE FUNK, releasing the harder-edged 'Twisted Funk' album in 1999, while promising a second SLAM album very soon as well as a one-off single collaboration with James Lavelle's UNKLE which will mark Soma's 100th release. Going way back to the label's first release, the other featured artists, REJUVINATION, consisted of fellow founders GIBBONS and MOUTUNE, a more short-lived partnership but one which threw up such notable Soma moments as 'Work In Progress' and 'Requiem'. GIBBONS continues to record under the guise of UNIVERSAL PRINCIPLES along with SLAM man STUART McMILLAN and veteran Glasgow DJ NICK PEACOCK, 1998's 'Inspiration and Light' album a jazzier counterpoint to Soma's raft of techno meisters. Among these are FUNK D'VOID (named after GEORGE CLINTON's P-Funk character, Sir Nose D'Void Of Funk) aka LARS SANDBERG, a native Glaswegian now resident in Barcelona who was responsible for the memorable 'Jack Me Off' and 1997's 'Technoir' album. He's also released jazzier material for Soma as one half of CHASE (alongside Londoner NIGEL HAYES), charming the more selective beatz connoisseur with 1995's 'Sides Of Iron'.

PERCY X is another Glaswegian (actually Paisley-born TONY SCOTT) on the Soma books, one half of the team behind HAVANA (a classic progressive house operation that recorded for Glasgow's 'Limbo' label back in the early 90's) and current purveyor of pulsating electro-techno. On a housier trip, SILICONE SOUL (the brainchild of CRAIG MORRISON and GRAEME REEDIE) caused quite a stir with singles 'Right On 4 Tha Darkness' and 'Nosferatu' and album, 'A Soul Thing'.

In addition to their wealth of Scottish talent, Soma released one of the first singles by French stars DAFT PUNK ('Alive') as well as material by the likes of MAAS and EQUUS. The people behind Soma have also launched Fenetik, a sub label aiming to cater for more left-field club music and currently home to the likes of PABLO + SUNDANCE (aka MICHAEL HUNTER), SIDEWINDER (aka non-Scots ALAN BRYDEN), STS (aka Paisley Hip-Hop producer) and Nottingham-born DANIEL IBBOTSON, now residing in Glasgow.

– discography –

Aug 91. (12") *(Soma 1)* **SLAM / REJUVINATION – Eterna**
Oct 91. (12") *(Soma 2)* **DOVE – Fallen**
Mar 92. (12") *(Soma 3)* **G7 – Seduced**
Jul 92. (12") *(Soma 4)* **REJUVINATION – Work In Progress**
Nov 92. (12") *(Soma 5) PIECE & JAMMIN' – Kettle On The Pan*
Mar 93. (12") *(Soma 6) OTAKU – Percussion Obsession*
Mar 93. (12") *(Soma 7)* **REJUVINATION – Requiem**
Aug 93. (12") *(Soma 8)* **SLAM – Chronologie 6**
Oct 93. (12") *(Soma 9) SIDETRAX – Off Track*
Dec 93. (12") *(Soma 10) LIEBEZEIT – Something Wonderful*
Jan 94. (12") *(Soma 11)* **EASTMEN – U Dig / U Dub**
Feb 94. (12") *(Soma 12)* **HOLMES & McMILLAN – Total Toxic Overload**
Mar 94. (12") *(Soma 13) DESERT STORM – Desert Storm*
Apr 94. (12") *(Soma 14) DAFT PUNK – Alive*
Jun 94. (12") *(Soma 15) SHARKIMAXX – Clashback*
Jul 94. (12") *(Soma 16)* **REJUVINATION – Sychophantasy / Psychophenetic**
Sep 94. (12") *(Soma 17)* **SKINTRADE – Shapeshifter**
Nov 94. (12"/cd-s) *(Soma 18/+CD)* **REJUVINATION – Dr. Peter**
Nov 94. (cd/d-lp) *(Soma CD/LP 1) Soma Compilation 1*
Dec 94. (12") *(Soma 19)* **EGE BAM YASI – Acid Nation**
Jan 95. (12") *(Soma 20)* **PERCY X – X-Tracks**
Feb 95. (d12"ep/cd-ep) *(Soma 21/+CDS)* **SLAM – Snapshots E.P.**
Mar 95. (12") *(Soma 22) MAAS – San Narcisco*
Apr 95. (12") *(Soma 23) MODE 4 – Eurobliss*
May 95. (12") *(Soma 24)* **REJUVINATION – Don't Forget Who You Are**
May 95. (12") *(Soma 25) DAFT PUNK – Da Funk*
May 95. (12") *(Soma 26)* **PERCY X – Odyssey**
Jun 95. (cd/d-lp) *(Soma CD/LP 2)* **REJUVINATION – Introduction**
– Introduction / Subtle indoctination / Life is / Dr. Peter / Till death us do part / The conflict / All that glitters / Don't forget who you are / Phaze transition / Sychophantasy / Requiem.

— In Sep'96, REJUVINATION released the 12" for 'Music Man' (MM 022), 'presents PHAZE II'; tracks:- Vertigo / Dida. *(re-iss. Dec97; MM 039)*

Jun 95. (12") *(Soma 27)* **SKINTRADE – Andomraxess**
Jul 95. (12"ep) *(Soma 28) ENVOY – Solitary Mission EP*
Aug 95. (12") *(Soma 29)* **FUNK D'VOID – Jack Me Off**
Sep 95. (d12"ep/cd-ep) *(Soma 30/+CDS)* **SLAM – Positive Education (mixes; Slam / Carl Cox / Josh Wink deep 2)**
Oct 95. (12"ep) *(Soma 31) ENVOY – Heart Of The Soul EP*
Oct 95. (cd/d-lp) *(Soma CD/LP 3) Soma Compilation 2*
Nov 95. (12"/cd-s) *(Soma 32/+CDS)* **PERCY X vs BLOODSUGAR – 3**
Nov 95. (12") *(Soma 33)* **CHASER – Sides Of Iron**
Dec 95. (12") *(Soma 34) MODE 4 – Blip*
Jan 96. (12") *(Soma 35) INDO SILVER CLUB – Part 1*
Feb 96. (cd/d-lp) *(Soma CD/LP 4)* **PERCY X – Spyx**
Mar 96. (12"ep) *(Soma 36) RUSS GABRIEL'S AUDIO SPECTRUM – Pilgrimage EP*
Mar 96. (12") *(Soma 37) THE SURGEON – Muggerscum Out*
Apr 96. (12"ep) *(Soma 38) MASS – Suture Self EP*
Apr 96. (ltd-12") *(Soma 39)* **SLAM – Dark Forces**
May 96. (cd/c/d-lp) *(Soma CD/MC/LP 5)* **SLAM – Headstates**
– Emotive / Life between life / White shadows / Low life / Beneath / Hybrid / First bass / Alaska / Free fall / Dark forces.
Jul 96. (12") *(Soma 40)* **EQUUS – Lava Flow**
Jul 96. (12") *(Soma 41) OTAKU – Emelia*
Aug 96. (12"ep) *(Soma 42) ENVOY – Coalition EP*
Aug 96. (12"ep) *(Soma 43) BUSHFUNK – Tales From The Bush EP*
Sep 96. (12") *(Soma 44)* **FUNK D'VOID – Soul Man**
Sep 96. (12"/cd-s) *(Soma 45/+CDS)* **SLAM – Dark Forces**
Oct 96. (12") *(Soma 45) SPACE DJZ – Lights*
Nov 96. (cd/d-lp) *(Soma CD/LP 6) Soma Compilation 3*
Dec 96. (12") *(Soma 47) NEW SOUL FUSION – Prelude*
Dec 96. (12"ep) *(Soma 48)* **PERCY X – Day 3 EP**
Jan 97. (12"ep) *(Soma 49)* **PRESSURE FUNK – Raw Spirit EP**
– Raw spirit / Linear phase / Pressure funk / Nemesis cycle.
Mar 97. (cd/d-lp) *(Soma CD/LP 50) Soma 50* (Various)
Apr 97. (cd/d-lp) *(Soma CD/LP 7) MAAS – Latitude*
May 97. (12") *(Soma 51) HUTTON DRIVE – Escapades From The End Of The World*
May 97. (12") *(Soma 52)* **FUNK D'VOID – Bad Coffee**
Jun 97. (cd/d-lp) *(Soma CD/LP 8)* **FUNK D'VOID – Technoir**
– Light / Martian love dance / Herbie on rhodes / Fewshun / Bad coffee / Dop lullaby / Angelic upstart / Lucky strike / Soundtrack / Snakebite / V ger / Thank you (reprise).
Jul 97. (12"ep) *(Soma 53) 20:20 VISION – The Future Remembrance EP*
Jul 97. (12"/cd-s) *(Soma 54/+CDS) MAAS – Look At Me Now Falling*
Aug 97. (12") *(Soma 55) HUMAN ARTS – Big Sur Highway*
Sep 97. (12"ep) *(Soma 56) ALLERGY – Intuition EP*
Oct 97. (cd/d-lp) *(Soma CD/LP 9) Soma Compilation 4*
Oct 97. (12") *(Soma 57) GENE FARRIS – A place 4 Me*
Nov 97. (12") *(Soma 58) SCOTT GROOVES – A New Day*
Nov 97. (12"ep) *(Soma 59) ENVOY – Emotional EP*
Jan 98. (12"ep) *(Soma 60)* **SILICONE SOUL – The Strip EP**
– The strip / Candy love / Climbing walls.
Feb 98. (12") *(Soma 61) MAAS – Another Saturday Night*
Feb 98. (ltd-12") *(Soma 62)* **PRESSURE FUNK – Twisted Funk / Voices**
Mar 98. (12") *(Soma 63)* **PERCY X – New Ground**
Mar 98. (12") *(Soma 64)* **CHASER – Life In Loisaida**
May 98. (12"/cd-s/12"remix) *(Soma 65/+CDS/R) SCOTT GROOVES feat. ROY AYERS – Expansions*
Apr 98. (12") *(Soma 66)* **FUNK D'VOID – Herbie On Rhodes**
May 98. (cd/d-lp) *(Soma CD/LP 10) SCOTT GROOVES – Pieces Of A Dream*
Jun 98. (12"ep) *(Soma 67)* **COUNTERPLAN – 90 Degrees**
– 90 degrees / The day after / Peoples groove.
Jul 98. (12") *(Soma 68)* **UNIVERSAL PRINCIPLES – Inspiration & Light**
Aug 98. (12") *(Soma 69)* **FUNK D'VOID – Lucky Strike / Bossa bitch**

— note:- FUNK D'VOID's next 12", 'TONE OF TONE', was for 'Fierce'; *(DBM 4095)*

Aug 98. (12"ep) *(Soma 70)* **SILICONE SOUL – All Night Long EP**
– All nite long / Sly guy / Midnight rambler.
Oct 98. (cd/d-lp) *(Soma CD/LP 11) ENVOY – Where There's Life*
Nov 98. (12") *(Soma 71) SCOTT GROOVES – Scott Grooves feat. Parliament/Funkadelic*
Sep 98. (12") *(Soma 72) MFON – Ron Hardy*
Oct 98. (12") *(Soma 73) ALLERGY – No Boundaries*
Nov 98. (12") *(Soma 74) GENE FARRIS – Mainline Disco*
Nov 98. (cd/d-lp) *(Soma CD/LP 12) Soma Compilation 5*
Dec 98. (12") *(Soma 75) RETROFLEX – Variations In Conciousness Pt.1*
Dec 98. (12"ep) *(Soma 76)* **PERCY X – User Friendly EP**

Feb 99. (12") *(Soma 77) ENVOY – Beautiful World*
Feb 99. (12") *(Soma 78) ENVOY – Rundown*
Feb 99. (cd/d-lp) *(Soma CD/LP 13)* **CHASER – Game On**
– Sleazy listening / Friend like you / Blue planet / Changing minds / Everything must change / Tall stories / F train / Life in Loisaida / Chaser (theme) / Assassin / Sides of iron.
Mar 99. (12") *(Soma 79) RETROFLEX – Variations In Conciousness Pt.2*
Mar 99. (12") *(Soma 80)* **CHASER – Tall Stories**
Mar 99. (cd/d-lp) *(Soma CD/LP 14)* **PRESSURE FUNK – Twisted Funk**
– Darkest hour / Pressure theme / Raw spirit / Sound 011 / Quick fix / Ghetto Jack / Nemesis cycle / Menace / Twisted funk / Full force / LG3 / Night zone / Interpose / Round up / Outro.
Mar 99. (12") *(Soma 81) EBE – Synaptic Flow*
Apr 99. (12") *(Soma 82) SPACE DJS – Solaris*
May 99. (12"ep) *(Soma 83)* **SILICONE SOUL – Right On 4 Tha Darkness EP**
– Right on 4 tha darkness / Feelin' / Ride tha groove / Sundance.
May 99. (12") *(Soma 84) MFON – Dance Of The Drunk Mantis*
Jun 99. (12"ep) *(Soma 85) CRATESAVERS – Cratesavers EP*
Jun 99. (cd/d-lp) *(Soma CD/LP 15) SPACE DJS – On Patrol*
Jul 99. (12") *(Soma 86)* **PRESSURE FUNK – Ghetto Jack**
Sep 99. (12") *(Soma 87) HUTTON DRIVE – Push It*
Sep 99. (12"/cd-s/12"remix) *(Soma 88/+CDS/R)* **CHASER – Blue Planet**
Oct 99. (cd) *(SomaCD 16) Fenetik Music: The Word In The Sound*
Oct 99. (12") *(Soma 89)* **PRESSURE FUNK – Pressure Theme / Full Force (mixes)**
Oct 99. (cd/d-lp) *(Soma CD/LP 17) Soma Compilation 6*
Nov 99. (12") *(Soma 90) MAAS – Powers Of Ten*
Dec 99. (12"ep) *(Soma 91)* **PERCY X – Worklike EP**
– Worklike / Worklike groove lock / By night / Salsa break No.2.
Jan 00. (12"ep) *(Soma 92) EBE – Neural Response EP*
Feb 00. (12"ep) *(Soma 93)* **SILICONE SOUL – Nosferatu EP**
– Nosferatu / Gimme danger / In your own sweet time.
Mar 00. (cd/d-lp) *(Soma CD/LP 18)* **SILICONE SOUL – A Soul Thing**
– Chic-o-laa / The all nite dub / This is the sound! *[cd-only]* / Have U seen my baby? / Mong the merciless / The answer / Nosferatu / I need an angel / Sundance *[cd-only]* / The strip / Understanding / Right on 4 tha darkness.
May 00. (12") *(Soma 94) GENE FARRIS – Come On Home*
May 00. (cd/d-lp) *(Soma CD/LP 19)* **UNIVERSAL PRINCIPLES – Inspiration & Light**
– Inspiration & light / Inspirational breaks / Afro-zen-trick / Latin stroll / Future manifesto / Flyin' high / Ignite the night / Don's different ducks / Voodoo sun / Guyana.
Jun 00. (12") *(Soma 95) HIPP-E & TONY – Soul Interactive*
Jun 00. (12") *(Soma 96)* **UNIVERSAL PRINCIPLES – Flyin' High**
Jul 00. (cd/d-lp) *(Soma CD/LP 20) GENE FARRIS – This Is My Religion*
Aug 00. (12"ep/cd-ep) *(Soma 97/+CDS)* **SILICONE SOUL – The Answer (Miguel Migs remixes) / Right On Right On**
Sep 00. (12"ep) *(Soma 98) RETROFLEX – Spanning Time EP*
Sep 00. (12") *(Soma 99)* **PERCY X – Break It Down EP (mixes: Carl Lekebusch / Percy X / original).**
Oct 00. (cd/d-lp) *(Soma CD/LP 21)* **PERCY X – Gain**
– Interlink / Break it down / Maintain / Gain / Whatever whenever / Quok / U know what it is / By right / Seven heroes / Track 2.
— in Oct'00, SLAM were responsible for a Various (dance) Artists double-CD/triple-LP, 'PAST LESSONS / FUTURE THEORIES', released on 'Distinctive Breaks' (DISN CD/LP 65)
Mar 01. (12"/cd-s; as SLAM vs. UNKLE) *(Soma 100/+CDS)* **NARCO TOURIST (mixes; original / Slam / Unkle)** 66 -
Oct 00. (12") *(Soma 101) MASTER H – Mayflower*
Nov 00. (12") *(Soma 102)* **FUNK D'VOID – Move Ya Waistline / Barnabeats**
Nov 00. (cd/d-lp) *(Soma CD/LP 22) Soma Compilation 7*
Dec 00. (12") *(Soma 103) FRAME – Fase 2*
Dec 00. (12"ep) *(Soma 104)* **SILICONE SOUL – The Seven Day Weekend EP**
– Chic-O-Laa (H Foundation mix) / Minted / Chic-O-Laa (original mix).
Feb 01. (12") *(Soma 105)* **PERCY X – Maintain / Maintain (Steve Bicknell mix) / Where's The Music?**
Feb 01. (12") *(Soma 106)* **FUNK D'VOID – Desperado / Barnabeats (Octave One mix)**
Mar 01. (cd/d-lp) *(Soma CD/LP 23)* **FUNK D'VOID – Dos**
– Blue planet (Chaser abacus remix) / Serenity (E.B.E. remix) / Flyin' high (Universal Principles Sidewinder remix) / Rubberlegs (Mfon studio 54 remix) / Right on, right on (Silicone Soul remix) / Push it (Hutton Drive remix) / Powers of ten (Maas remix) / Confession (Gene Farris remix) / Riddem control (Hipp-E & Tony present soul interactive remix) / Break it down (Percy X Carl Lekebusch remix) / Pressure theme (Pressure Funk Marco Carola remix).
Jan 01. (cd) *(SomaCD 24) EWAN PEARSON – Small Change*
May 01. (12"/cd-s) *(Soma 107/+cds)* **SLAM featuring TYRONE PALMER – Lifetimes** 61
May 01. (12") *(Soma 108)* **FUNK D'VOID & PERCY X – Voyager / Let's Go Back / Breaking Out**
Jun 01. (cd/d-lp) *(Soma CD/LP 25)* **SLAM – Alien Radio**
– This is *[cd-only]* / Lifetimes / Alien radio / Narco tourists (album remix) / Visions / Eyes of your soul / Positive education (Slam remix) / Bass addiction / Virtuoso.
Jun 01. (12"/12"/cd-s) *(Soma 107/+R/CDS)* **SLAM & TYRONE – Lifetimes (mixes)**
Aug 01. (12") *(Soma 110) TONY THOMAS – Beginnings EP*
Sep 01. (12"/12"/cd-s) *(Soma 112/+R/CDS)* **FUNK D'VOID – Diabla** 70
Nov 01. (12") *(Soma 113)* **SLAM – Alien Radio (mixes; original / Paul Daley "Leftfield" / Tony Thomas)**
Nov 01. (12") *(Soma 113R)* **SLAM – Alien Radio (Darren Emerson mix) / Alien Radio (Tony Thomas mix)**
Feb 02. (d-cd/d-lp) *(Soma CD/LP 26)* **Various Artists – Fenetik Music Volume 2; The Sounds Of Music**
Feb 02. (12") *(Soma 116) H-FOUNDATION – Passage Of Time*
Mar 02. (12") *(Soma 117) TONY THOMAS – Get High*
Mar 02. (d-cd/d-lp) *(Soma CD/LP 27)* **Various Artists – Soma 10th Anthology**
Apr 02. (12") *(Soma 118R)* **SLAM – Virtuoso (Rolando remix) / Virtuoso (The Youngsters remix)**
Jun 02. (12") *(Soma 119) ENVOY – Sex Drive*
Jun 02. (d-lp) *(SomaLP 28)* **PERCY X – Where's The Music**
– Afterplan / Club X / Casiotone / Afterplan / Where's the music / Vox digital / Inbox / Dark n' sharp.
Jul 02. (12") *(Soma 120) MASTER H – Magic K*
Jun 02. (12") *(Soma 121)* **PERCY X – Afterplan EP**
– Afterplan / Feel it / No Su.
Aug 02. (12") *(Soma 122)* **PERCY X – Time To Jack (Radioactive Man mix) / Time To Jack (original) / Club x**
Aug 02. (cd) *(SomaCD 29)* **SLAM – Alien Radio (remixed)**

– Fenetik Music discography

(TIK 001) was the label launch cat.no.
Oct 98. (12"ep) *(TIK 002)* **SUNDANCE – Here Comes The Funk EP**
Jan 99. (12"ep) *(TIK 003) SIDEWINDER – Troubled Times EP*
Mar 99. (12"ep) *(TIK 004)* **S.T.S. – Rainy City Blues EP**
May 99. (12"ep) *(TIK 005) DANIEL IBBOTSON – Inversions EP*
May 00. (12"ep) *(TIK 006)* **PABLO – The Supersweet EP**
May 00. (12"ep) *(TIK 007) SIDEWINDER – Flight EP*
Sep 00. (12") *(TIK 008) SIDEWINDER – Sundance EP*

– FUNK D'VOID others

Nov 00. (12") *Blue; (BLUE 008)* **No Witness**

– other SLAM stuff –

Oct 00. (d-cd/t-lp; by Various Artists) *Distinct'ive; (DISN CD/LP 65)* **Past Lessons / Future Theories**
Feb 01. (12") *VC; (VCRT 84)* **POSITIVE EDUCATION (Carl Cox n' tec mix). / POSITIVE EDUCATION (Slam remix)** 44 -
(cd-s+=) *(VSRD 84)* – ('A'edit) / ('A'-Josh Wink mix).
(cd-s) *(VSRTX 84)* – ('A'-Josh Wink mixes).

SILICONE SOUL

— more of . . .

V.C. not iss.
Sep 01. (c-s) *(VCRC 96)* **RIGHT ON / (instrumental)** 15 -
(12"+=/cd-s+=) *(VC RT/RD 96)* – ('A'-Steve Lawlor mixes).

Spit & Polish records (see under ⇒ Shoeshine records)

Starshaped records

Founded: PO Box 28424, Edinburgh, EH4 5YH (www.starshaped.co.uk). Initially activated in early 2000 to bring about the release of the long-lost WENDYS album, 'SIXFOOT WINGSPAN' (this outfit were a latterday 'Factory' quartet), the label progressed to signing a new band for the millennium, the CHERRYFIRE ASHES. Comprising of NEWTON HARPER (vocals & guitar), CAROLYN CUTTER (guitar) and GREGOR DOUGLAS (PAUL RENNIE was 4th member on drums), the young trio ventured into JAMIE WATSON at Human Condition's studio. That June, the 'WIREWORKS' EP, hit the wee shops around the country, the 'ASHES sound quite punky, gothy and NEW MODEL ARMY-esque. The start of 2001, saw the label sign another 'Burgh outfit, BENDY TOY, which was noneother than freakbeat synth-and-samples guy, STEPHEN EVANS. So far, only one EP, 'FANTASTIC CHICKEN' (a Steve Lamacq fave) and several gigs have been forthcoming – now known as the "Scottish Fatboy Slim".

– discography –

Apr 00. (cd) *(STARS 001)* **WENDYS – Sixfoot Wingspan**
Jun 00. (cd-ep) *(STARS 002)* **the CHERRYFIRE ASHES – Wireworks EP**
– Sparks and spooks / The furnace / Kiowa / The Lord ship.
Feb 02. (cd-ep) *(STARS 003)* **BENDY TOY – Fantastic Chicken EP**
– Fantasic chicken / Dirty disco / Thin ice / Walken.

Steppin' Out records

Founded: by DJ SCOTT (aka IAN ROBERTSON), 6 Whitehart Street, Dalkeith, Midlothian, EH22 1AE; allegedly he borrowed some Italian rave tunes and made them his own! One of the first signings were two local DJs, MC MARINER & ROSS KEDDIE; MARINER was A. STENTIFORD who also wrote/worked with TOM WILSON.

Meanwhile, M.R.X. was A. JOHNSTON; the first single on the label in early '93 was by DJ CARTOONS (on 'BEEP BEEP') and they comprised M. MARCOLIN, V. GARRURINI + R. SIGNORELLI, who also worked with ALISON PRICE (alias W. CREMONINI) on her 'IT'S GONNA BE ALRIGHT'.

One of their biggest acts were arguably THE RHYTHMIC STATE. They formed in Glasgow in the early 90's by NICK WILLIAMS, ANDY COCOZZA, along with AMANDA GENT and IAN PATERSON, the moniker so called because apparently they're always in the right rhythmic state (quite possibly because they listen to the likes of JOEY BELTRAM and DIGITAL BOY). After their debut gig at Ayr's infamous Hanger 13 club, TRS quickly established themselves as a top draw on the Scottish rave circuit. Initially signing with 'Steppin' Out', the group released the controversial 'SOAP ON A ROPE' single which not only featured drug references in the lyrics but also included a Liberace sample! After their record deal ended acrimoniousy, The RHYTHMIC STATE switched to the 'Massive Respect' label for 'ANOTHER WORLD', a combination of Euro techno and happy hardcore that epitomised the group's "bouncy" sound.

• **More Trivia:** SUNSET REGIME's 'I GOT THE REAL FEEL' was written by RHYTHM, LOVE and GRASSIE. TECHNO TOO ('HI-E-NA') were STEWART + DRUMMOND. A-TENSION ('TRUE FEELINGS') were THOMPSON, JACK + WILLIAMS. LOVE 4 SALE and BEE BUZZ were basically L. STANGE, I. GECHELE + G. LODA. TERRORIZE (aka JOHNNY O'HALLORAN) had three 12" singles out, 'FEEL THE RHYTHM' in Aug'92 for 'Hamster' (12STER 2), 'NATURAL HIGH' in Jun'93 for 'Devil' (12DEVIL 3) and 'IT'S JUST A FEELING' in Aug'95 for 'Escapade' (JAPE 11). DJ DADO the Italian producer/hitmaker also started here.

– discography –

Jan 93. (12") *(IAN 001T)* **DJ CARTOONS – Beep Beep**
Jan 93. (12") *(IAN 002T)* **MC MARINER & ROSS KEDDIE – Freebase EP**
Jun 93. (12"/cd-s) *(IAN 003 T/CD)* **LOVE 4 SALE – Do You Feel So Right**
Aug 93. (12"/cd-s) **RHYTHMIC STATE – Power People / The Creator**
Mar 94. (12"/cd-s) *(IAN 010 T/CD)* **LOVE 4 SALE – Dream**
Feb 94. (12"/cd-s) *(IAN 011 T/CD)* **DJ SCOTT – Do You Wanna Party**
Jun 94. (12"/cd-s) *(IAN 014 T/CD) MRX – Temptation*
Oct 94. (12"/cd-s) *(IAN 015 T/CD)* **BRENDA – All The Things I Like**
Oct 94. (12"/cd-s) *(IAN 016 T/CD)* **OUTER RHYTHM – Energy**
Oct 94. (12"/cd-s) *(IAN 018 T/CD)* **2 EXAMPLES – Let It Come Into Your Heart**
Dec 94. (12") *(IAN 019T) LUXOR – Big Bang*
Feb 95. (12"/cd-s) *(IAN 023 T/CD) PCP – That Whitney Song*
Apr 95. (c-s/12"/cd-s) *(IAN 025 MC/T/CD)* **DATURA – El Sueno**
Jun 95. (12"/cd-s) *(IAN 027 T/CD) PIANOMAN & NILS BOOPH – Revelation*
Jun 95. (12"/cd-s) *(IAN 028 T/CD)* **DJ SCOTT & OUTER RHYTHM – Piano Madness**
Jul 95. (c-s/12"/cd-s) *(IAN 031 MC/T/CD) UNITED COLOURS – Missing You*
Jun 95. (c-s/12"/cd-s) *(IAN 032 MC/T/CD) NIDO – Asilo*
Mar 96. (12"/cd-s) *(IAN 037 T/CD) DJ DADO – The Same*
May 96. (12"/cd-s) *(IAN 044 T/CD)* **TECHNOCAT – It's Gonna Be Alright**
Jul 96. (12"/cd-s) *(IAN 045 T/CD) DJ DADO – Face It*
Sep 96. (cd/c/lp) *(STEP 001 CD/MC/LP)* **Various Artists – Steppin' Out Records 1: The Album – 16 Essential Dance Tracks**
Sep 96. (cd/c/lp) *(STEP 002 CD/MC/LP)* **Various Artists – Steppin' Out Records 2: The Album**
Sep 96. (cd/c/lp) *(STEP 003 CD/MC/LP)* **Various Artists – Steppin' Out Records 3: The Album**
Sep 96. (cd/c/lp) *(STEP 004 CD/MC/LP)* **Various Artists – Steppin' Out Records 4: The Album**
Oct 96. (12"/cd-s) *(IAN 046 T/CD)* **DJ DAVE – Gangsta's Paradise**
Dec 96. (12"/cd-s) *(IAN 057 T/CD)* **STEPPIN' OUT ALL-STARS – Christmas Jollies**
Dec 96. (12"/cd-s) *(IAN 058 T/CD) RED RHYTHM – Jungle Bells*

Stoatin' records (see under ⇒ Limbo records)

Stranded records

Founded: by LARRY NICOL, 6 Iona Street, Edinburgh, EH6 8QJ . . . early 1984. The label was initially instigated to release the debut single, 'ECHOES OF WAR', by NICOL's own Punk-rock outfit, The SQUARE PEG. Also present on the single were EXPLOITED guitarists BIG JOHN DUNCAN and GARY McCORMICK, although the latter was absent from their 1985 follow-up, 'CAN'T SAY NO'. Squeezed in between the aforementioned platters was a lonesome Punk offering by NAPALM STARS, 'FICTION', while Stranded release No.4 came via Power-poppers BOHN LEGION (aka BILL – guitar, vocals / KIT – bass, vocals / IAIN – drums).

Re-emerging in 1994 from a new base at 45 Lorne Street, Edinburgh, EH6 8QJ, the indie imprint's 5th single, 'KILLING TIME' by SWINE FLU (with the line-up of WELSHY – vocals / CRAIG – lead guitar / BILLY – bass / KEV – rhythm guitar / STU – drums) was produced by 'Human Condition' man JAMIE WATSON at his Chambers studio. WELSHY and BILLY would subsequently form EXTERNAL MENACE, while LARRY resumed his day job as a painter/decorator/joiner/etc.

– discography –

Jun 84. (7") *(XLNT 1)* **the SQUARE PEG – Echoes Of War / Bad Connection / No Explanation**
Jun 85. (7") *(XLNT 2)* **NAPALM STARS – Fiction / Workhard**
Apr 86. (7") *(XLNT 3)* **the SQUARE PEG – Can't Say No / Nuclear Attack**
? (7") *(XLNT 4)* **BOHN LEGION – May In Berlin / Heaven Knows**
Jul 94. (7") *(XLNT 5)* **SWINE FLU – Killing Time / Lost Innocence**
— unsure if there were any more releases

Supreme Int. records (see under ⇒ Rational records)

Swamplands records (see under ⇒ Postcard records)

teen-c! recordingz (see under ⇒ BIS)

23rd Precinct records/shop (see under ⇒ Limbo records)

Twisted Nerve records (see under ⇒ Q-TEX)

U.G. records (see under ⇒ Hook records)

Veesik records

Formed: Lerwick, Shetland . . . 1996 by ALAN LONGMUIR. Complete with a new digital studio, the man set about signing local rock/folk acts, including COLIN REED (from N. Ireland) and PURE GREED. The latter consist of songwriter JOHN BOYD (vocals, bass & acoustic guitar), STEVE YARRINGTON (guitars), JOHN PETTIGREW (guitars, etc) and BOB PARKER (drums); JOANNE GIBSON was added on harmony vocals. They play rock'n'roll boogie. Other recordings on the label were Shetland dialect.

2001. (cd) **HAND SIGNALS ONLY**
– Wherever you go / I'll go along for the ride / Long distance lover / I don't wanna be / Too many friends / There's love / What ya gonna do / Get it on down the road / Out of my misery / Hand signals only / I'll turn to tears.

Vesuvius records

Founded: Glasgow (Vesuvius, Wowsville, PO Box 15096, Glasgow, G4 9YZ) . . . 1995 by PAT ('Laureate') CROOK and designer MARC BAINES. The former was also part of MELODY DOG with part-time PASTELS drummer, KATRINA MITCHELL, while the PASTELS connection extended to the latter in his capacity as guitarist.

Inspired by the self-starting DIY ethic of American Lo-Fi legends such as HALF JAPANESE, Vesuvius put their shoestring budget where their mouth was by making HJ mainman JAD FAIR one of their earliest signings. However, the label's first release came in the shape of a Various Artists 10" mini-set previewing their roster of raw, unsigned talent. This included the aforementioned MELODY DOG (who'd already released a couple of acclaimed 45's for 'Seminal Twang' and 'K'), the fanzine-friendly MANXISH BOYS (possibly from the Isle Of Man, perhaps?) and the cosmopolitan HELLO SKINNY.

Flying the flag for the Glaswegian contingent were the future cottage indie-stry faves LUNG LEG and The YUMMY FUR, while the short-lived COTTON GUM was a partial amalgamation of the two featuring AMANDA, JOHN and Vesuvius' own MARC BAINES. Recognising that there was actually musical life at the other end of the M8, the label took on a couple of Edinburgh outfits: STARSTRUCK were relative veterans having previously issued a number of cassettes, etc for the 'Bosque' label, while SALLY SKULL (apparently named after an infamous Wild West female pioneer) were hellbent on trashing the legacy of 60's girl groups; weird of sound rather than Wall Of Sound. In fact, SS were the first Vesuvius act to release a single in their own right, 'THE TANTIVY TRACKS' EP, although it took them all of a year and a half to realise their 'Slampt Underground' follow-up, 'FRACTURED'.

Further eruptions from the Vesuvius canon came via releases by the aforementioned LUNG LEG and YUMMY FUR plus Glaswegian all-girl newcomers DICK JOHNSON (featuring LUNG LEG's JANE) and New York duo DYMAXION.

- discography -

Aug 95. (10"m-lp) *(POMP 001)* **Various Artists – In Spelunca**
– MELODY DOG / MANXISH BOYS / SALLY SKULL / HELLO SKINNY / LUNG LEG / COTTON GUM / YUMMY FUR / STARSTRUCK
Aug 95. (7"ep) *(POMP 002)* **SALLY SKULL – The Tantivy Tracks EP**
Apr 96. (12"ep) *(POMP 004)* **GANGER – Half Nelson.ep**
1997. (cd) *(POMP 006CD) JAD FAIR – Best Friends*
Jul 97. (cd/lp) *(POMP 007 CD/LP)* **LUNG LEG – Maid To Minx**
Jan 97. (7") *(POMP 008)* **YUMMY FUR – Supermarket**
Dec 96. (7"ep) *(POMP 009)* **DICK JOHNSON – Free Gigi EP**
May 97. (7"ep) *(POMP 010)* **LUNG LEG – Right Now Baby**
Mar 98. (7") *(POMP 011) DYMAXION – Verfremdungseffekt*
Feb 98. (m-lp/m-cd) *(POMP 012/+CD)* **YUMMY FUR – Male Shadow At 3 O'Clock**
Jul 98. (7"split) *(POMP 016)* **LUNG LEG – Krayola** / *the MAKE-UP – Pow! To The People*

X-static records

Founded: 12 Busbie Holdings, Crosshouse, Kilmarnock, KA2 0DJ . . . late 1998 by BILLY SAMSON, a member of Power-Pop Punk combo GLUE (nothing to do with 'Flotsam & Jetsam' band of the mid-90's). The label stated they're "dedicated to releasing only the most innovative and life-affirming of modern music". Another Killie outfit, the ELECTROLUVS (led by SAMSON) took us back to the time of SOFT CELL and HUMAN LEAGUE played with synths.

- discography -

• **GLUE** were vocalist/guitarist GORDON BERRY (b.14 Sep'76) – from GROWLER – plus BILLY SAMSON, SUSAN VENNARD, BARRY LEWIS, and other ex-GROWLERS, BRENDON McGILL and PAUL STEVENSON.

Sep 98. (m-cd) *(EXT 001)* **Various Artists – The Great Unknown**
– ELECTROLUVS – Digging your grave / GLUE / GROWLER / LYM / TOPPLERS + DUFFER.
Oct 98. (m-cd) *(EXT 002)* **GROWLER – Glue**
Jun 99. (cd-ep) *(EXT 003)* **GLUE – Monsterland**
– Monsterland / B one son / Growing up.
Jan 01. (mp3) *(EXT 011)* **GLUE – Funk Dancing**
– Funk dancing for self defence / Grover's return / Reminiscing applejacks / We want solvent abuse.

• the **ELECTROLUVS** are vocalist/guitarist BILLY SAMSON (b. 1 Jun'76) and vocalist/melodica/keyboard-player SUSAN VENNARD (b.12 Dec'76).

Nov 00. (mp3) *(EXT 010)* **the ELECTROLUVS – Balti e.p.**
– Balti FC / Love in the kitchen sink / A question of temperature / Do me some damage.
Jul 02. (mp3) **the ELECTROLUVS – Nu Nightmare e.p.**
– He's a nightmare / Amstrad / Back on the small screen.

Zoom records

Founded: 45 Shandwick Place, Edinburgh . . . by BRUCE FINDLAY, a one-time employee at the Bungys club before he took off to run an outdoor bar in Majorca (c. 1966). By the late 60's, he and his brother BRIAN had hooked up to open a 'hippie-rock' record store (today it's still going, but by the name Sleeves!).

Inspired by other homebased DIY/indie outlets such as Edinburgh's 'Sensible' records, BRUCE decided to instigate his own, Zoom records. With the help of Radio Edinburgh (REL) and engineer, Neil Ross, local punks The VALVES recorded their debut single, the double A-sided 'Robot Love' / 'For Adolfs Only', on the 11th August, 1977; a second 45, 'Tarzan Of The King's Road' was issued a little later although the quartet would subsequently move briefly to 'Albion' records. Slight Punk credibility was lost however, when the label's sophomore effort ('Put You In The Picture') by PVC2, was unmasked to be noneother than former teen-pop stars, SLIK (featuring MIDGE URE). With another slight change of line-up, the group became The ZONES, releasing another piece of Power-Pop vinyl before joining the 'Arista' stable. In fact – in between releasing a one-off 45 for his old buddy MIKE HERON (ex-INCREDIBLE STRING BAND) – BRUCE secured a marketing deal with the major, although this did little to boost the sales of his new protegees, the QUESTIONS and NIGHTSHIFT.

SIMPLE MINDS, however, were just different class. Having supported ULTRAVOX around parts of Britain (even the Grangemouth town hall!), they released the classiest Zoom product so far, 'Life In A Day' , which also hit No.62 in the Spring of '79 single. This previewed the UK Top 30 album of the same name, while a second single, 'Chelsea Girl', won even more recruits. SIMPLE MINDS also moved to 'Arista', this time taking manager BRUCE with them – the 'Zoom' label was now defunct. Throughout the 80's, the man enjoyed a great period as a manager (also with other acts!) and even augmented his activities with DJ work at Radio Forth.

- discography -

Sep 77. (7") *(ZUM 1)* **VALVES – Robot Love**
Nov 77. (7") *(ZUM 2)* **PVC2 – Put You In The Picture**
Dec 77. (7") *(ZUM 3)* **VALVES – Tarzan Of The King's Road**
Mar 78. (7") *(ZUM 4)* **ZONES – Stuck With You**
Aug 78. (7") *(ZUM 5)* **MIKE HERON – Sold On Your Love**
Aug 78. (7") *(ZUM 6)* **QUESTIONS – Some Other Guy**
Aug 78. (7") *(ZUM 7)* **NIGHTSHIFT – Love Is Blind**
Jan 79. (7") *(ZUM 8)* **QUESTIONS – Can't Get Over You**
Jan 79. (7") *(ZUM 9)* **NIGHTSHIFT – Jet Set**
Apr 79. (7") *(ZUM 10)* **SIMPLE MINDS – Life In A Day**
Apr 79. (lp) *(ZULP 1)* **SIMPLE MINDS – Life In A Day**
Jun 79. (7") *(ZUM 11)* **SIMPLE MINDS – Chelsea Girl**
Feb 80. (7") *(ZUM 12) LONDON ZOO – Receiving End*

— LONDON ZOO were actually from that wee place down south but the drummer DAVE SINCLAIR was from Edinburgh

— (ZUM 13) was scheduled for TONY PILLEY producer of The REZILLOS

• **CHEETAHS** were managed by Lenny Love, one-time manager of The REZILLOS. They consisted Newcastle-born JOE DONKIN (vocals), JOHN ROBERTS DOBSON (guitar), ANDREW ALLAN (bass), DROO FARMER (drums) and not forgetting NASTY PHIL (harmonica).

Apr 80. (7") *(ZUM 14)* **CHEETAHS – Radio Active (I Don't Wanna Be) / The Only One / Minefield**

9

Wee post-Punk groups • Jamie Watson • The 90s • Dance/Rave •

The following sub-sections are dedicated to groups/singers that didn't quite make the A-list due to bad luck, bad karma or bad playing. The **post-Punk section** is an A-Z of wee bands who started out after 1977 and who released a record or two, mostly on small independent record labels. Squeezed in between this and **The 90s section** of wee outfits is a special bit on producer **JAMIE WATSON** who has dedicated his time in Chambers Studios in Edinburgh to producing up-and-coming bands; he also runs 'Human Condition' records. After this we have a small **Dance/Rave section** of various groups who've come and gone. Although I don't know everything about them, some information might be useful to you the reader. If you have extra material on anything in these sections – or indeed any sections – please don't hesitate to contact me through my publishers Mercat Press.

* * * * *

Wee post-Punk groups

(post-'77 out-takes, etc.) These are the bands that didn't quite make the A-list due to bad luck, bad karma or bad playing . . .

– A – Z discography –

ADULTERY

- Clydebank punks who appeared on a V/A compilation set, 'Bland-Out In Britain', in 1980.

BREAD POULTICE & THE RUNNING SORES

- Dundee punks whose imaginative lyrics (found on the back of their set list) inspired another of Tayside's finest The SCROTUM POLES.

CARTOONS

- were virtually BOOKLESS and McCANN (the songwriters) and were not the CARTOONS as the one in the early 80's; produced by JAMES KING

Another Fabulous Product — not iss.

Jun 84. (7") *(CAGE 002)* **ONCE THE VICTOR. / (instrumental)**

DRIVE

- were formed in Dundee . . . late 1977 by an unknown bunch of punks who released only one pubescent, pub-rock single, 'JERKIN', from the city's 17 Union Street base of 'N-R-G'; the track was also included on 'Beggars Banquet' V/A compilation, 'Streets'.

N-R-G — not iss.

Jul 78. (7") *(NE 46)* **JERKIN'. / PUSH 'N' SHOVE**

EXILE

- were formed in Bishopbriggs, near Glasgow . . . 1977 by unknown bunch into lightweight punk/New Wave (DAVE SCOTT could have been a member). They featured on the 'Streets' V/A comp (late '77) with track 'DISASTER MOVIE' and were one of first (alongside The REZILLOS and The DRIVE) to release a home-made single; these 45's are now worth over £25 each! • **Note:** they were obviously not the EXILE who had hits with 'Kiss You All Over' and 'Heart And Soul'.

Boring — not iss.

1977. (7"ep) *(BO 1)* **DON'T TAX ME EP**
– Jubilee 77 / Hooked on you / Fascist DJ / Windmill.

Charly — not iss.

1978. (7"m) *(CYS 1033)* **THE REAL PEOPLE. / TOMORROW TODAY / DISASTER MOVIE**

HOLIDAYMAKERS

- were from Edinburgh (Fowler Terrace, E11) and consisted of ADRIAN SMITH on vocals & 12-string guitar, fellow songwriter NEIL CRAIG on 6-string guitar, MARK CUNNINGHAM on bass and RICHARD GUY on drums. Inspired by The PALE SAINTS and The SMITHS, these lads left behind a couple singles (the second for the 'Gay Cowboy' recording organisation in England!) before they took a permanent vacation.

Woosh — not iss.

Jan 89. (7") *(WOOSH 4)* **CINCINNATI. / SEVENTH VALLEY GIRL**

Gay Cowboy — not iss.

1989. (12") *(maker 001t)* **SKYRIDER. / CROSS RIVER STATE / BEGINNING AT THE END**

HOOK 'N' PULL GANG

- were formed in Edinburgh . . . mid-80's by bassist ALAN McDADE and drumming singer EILEEN McMULLAN, who invited guitarist/vocalist RITA BLAZYCA into the fold. Scatty and noisy outfit, they were the Texas Chainsaw Massacre of music (as depicted on their on their only single, 'POUR IT DOWN YER THROAT').

Bitch Hog — not iss.

Mar 87. (7") *(BITCH 1)* **POUR IT DOWN YER THROAT. / GASOLINE**

— split up later in the year; EILEEN joined another unknown band

JOLT

- were formed in Glasgow . . . 1977 by the power-pop trio of ROBERT COLLINS (vocals & guitar), JIM DOAK (bass & vocals) and IAIN SHEDDON (drums). After signing to 'Polydor' records, they were one of the first batch of Scots Punk/New Wave acts to release a single. 'YOU'RE COLD' did nothing to raise the temperature, although a subsequent eponymous album in '78 was quirky but a little out of its depth. The JOLT were never heard of again, except SHEDDON who resurfaced in mid-80's country-tinged outfit, The SNAKES OF SHAKE.

Oct 77. (7") *(2058 936)* **YOU'RE COLD. / ALL I CAN DO**
Jun 78. (7") *(2059 039)* **I CAN'T WAIT. / ROUTE 66**
Jul 78. (lp) *(2383 504)* **THE JOLT**
– Mr. Radio man / I can't wait / Whatcha gonna do about it / Chains / No excuses / Decoyed / I'm leaving / In my time / Everybody's the same / Hard lines / It's over / All I can do.

Aug 78. (7") *(2059 008)* **WHATCHA GONNA DO ABOUT YOU. / AGAIN AND AGAIN**
May 79. (7"ep) *(2229 215)* **MAYBE TONIGHT / I'M IN TEARS. / SEE SAW / STOP, LOOK**

LIGAMENT BLUB BROTHERS

- consisted of KENNY HUTTON (vocals), fellow songwriter STUART CUMMINGS (guitars), DAVID GIBSON (bass) and SCOTT RULE (drums). Recorded at the Evenload Auldhouse, 'BIG SHOE BOY' had a sleeve depicting a large Doc Marten! – enough said.

Scrundlepatch not iss.

Aug 86. (7") *(Blub 01)* **BIG SHOE BOY. / A STEP BEHIND / PULLOVER AND PULL ME**

MENTAL ERRORS

- were punks from Paisley . . . but no records!

METROPAK

- were formed in Edinburgh . . . late 70's by punk lads who included future RHYTHM OF LIFE (PAUL HAIG) stalwart, STEVEN HAINES. METROPAK delivered three 45's at the dawn of the 80's, all bouyant but uninspiring although quite collectable now.

Barclay Towers not iss.

Jan 80. (7"m) *(PAK 1)* **YOU'RE A REBEL. / OK LET'S GO / RUN RUN RUN**
1980. (7") *(PAK 2)* **HERE'S LOOKING AT YOU. / WALKING**
1981. (7") *(PAK 3)* **BALINESE DANCE. / SEX CULT THING**

— unsure that the final single ever made it out; they split and HAINES joined RHYTHM OF LIFE (PAUL HAIG's outfit)

NOISE ANNOYS

- were formed in the Western Isles of Scotland . . . late 70's (band members unknown) taking their punk moniker from a recent BUZZCOCKS number. However, only one self-financed 45 surfaced (December 1980) on the 'Adult Entertainment' (ARS 1) imprint, 'TOMORROW' / 'CHEAP LOCAL TALENT'.

RB'S

- unknown outfit who played Ska-pop beat, the missing link between BAD MANNERS, The POLICE and The BEAT. Their debut was a Double-A side.

Phoenix not iss.

Nov 80. (7") *(PSP 21)* **EXPLAIN. / LET ME FEEL IT**

Hansa not iss.

Apr 82. (7"/12") *(HANSA/+12 14)* **URUGUAY. / TIME**

RADIO CITY

- were formed in the nothern town of Thurso . . . late 70's by unknowns.

Media Wave not iss.

1980. (7") *(MW 001)* **SHE'S A RADIO. / LOVE AND A PICTURE**

RED ELLIS

- were formed in Uddingston . . . late 70's by songwriter CHIC McSHERRY (guitar & vocals), JOE COCHRANE (vocals), DAVY SWEET (bass) and JOE JAMES (drums). Power-pop sliding into RUSH-like rock, RED ELLIS managed only one single ('PRETTY POLLY') – given away at gigs – before their demise. Produced by HENRY GORMAN, known throughout the East Of Scotland for his er, knob-twiddling, the man also starred in his own band imaginatively-titled The HENRY GORMAN BAND.

R.E.P. not iss.

1980. (7") *(EJSP 9537)* **PRETTY POLLY. / URBAN LIFE**

SCROTUM POLES

- were formed in Dundee . . . 1978 by punky fun-chasers COLIN SMITH (guitar) and CRAIG METHVEN (vocals), the students – who'd borrowed a battered out-of-tune guitar – adding STEVE GRIMMOND (bass) and Carnoustie-born GLEN CONNELL (drums). They might just have giggled all the way to the social with this play-on-words moniker (another local outfit who didn't quite make it, was the aforementioned BREAD POULTICE & THE RUNNING SORES!). The SCROTs from Tayside only managed to squeeze out one EP ('REVELATION') and an equally hard to find cassette – we are puzzled why?

Scrotum Poles not iss.

1980. (7"ep) *(ERECT 1)* **REVELATION EP**
– Why don't you come out tonight / Night train / Pick the cat's eyes out / Helicopter honeymoon / Radio Tay. *(cd-ep-iss.1999 on own label)*

One-Tone not iss.

1980. (c) *(ERECT 1)* **AUCHMITHIE CALLING**
– It just ain't fuckin' funny / Just another number / You can't say anything nowadays / Thank Christ for the bomb / Be N more / Swing baby / Pick the cat's eyes out / Laughing policeman / Blair Peach dead / I don't like the way you talk down to me / I go wrong / This is love / Cocaine / Fast changes.

— the SCROTUM POLES split in 1980's summer and a few were in the PIGS ARE CUTE and AAGA; CRAIG went on to work for Amnesty International, GLEN is the manager of the El Bar in Edinburgh, STEVE works for his local housing department and COLIN has disappeared – get in touch with CRAIG through the e-mail Net (thanks to the www.jockrock site)
(address at http://hp1.switchboard.com/FetchPage/20752/)

SKROTEEZ

- were formed in Livingston, West Lothian . . . early 80's by the "new town" punk lads (unknown). However, only a solitary single surfaced, the 'NEW TOWN' EP boasted the appropriately-named title track; where are the SKROTEEZ now?

Overspill not iss.

May 82. (7"ep) *(SPILL 1)* **NEW TOWN EP**
– New town / Who's law / Livi punkz.

STILETTOS

- were formed in East Kilbride . . . late 70's by unknown guys into pop. Only managed to stamp out one 45, 'THIS IS THE WAY', before they were shown the door by 'Ariola' (their German-based label); the single is now worth £10 and I don't know why.

Ariola not iss.

Jan 80. (7") *(ARO 200)* **THIS IS THE WAY. / WHO CAN IT BE**

SUBS

- were formed by Glasgow . . . late 1977 by unknown punks including drummer ALI MacKENZIE and future SIMPLE MINDS bassist, DEREK FORBES. Early the following year, saw the band get a little press coverage in the Highlands after saving the life of an English couple trapped under a snow drift on the A835 (and apparently writing their last will and testament!) outside Aultguish Inn. This just might have led to a 'One-off' single, 'GIMME YOUR HEART' for the appropriately-named 'Stiff' subsidiary that Spring. However, the band gave up shortly afterwards. ALI was the first to bail out, his replacement (for a brief time) being JOHNNY & THE SELF-ABUSERS (later SIMPLE MINDS) sticksman, BRIAN McGEE, DEREK also became connected with JIM KERR's stadium fillers.

One-Off not iss.

Apr 78. (7") *(OFF 1)* **GIMME YOUR HEART. / PARTY CLOTHES**

SUGAR SUGAR

- were formed in Glasgow . . . 1983 by SHUG BRANKIN and basically they were not new wave or punk but they had to go somewhere. They disbanded after their sophomore 45; SHUG formed WYOMING with ex-SUNSET GUN member ROSS CAMPBELL.

C.B.S. not iss.

Sep 84. (7") *(A 4663)* **NOT IN FRONT OF THE CHILDREN. / OUT OF THE FRYING PAN**
(12"+=) *(TA 4663)* – Call it nature.
Apr 85. (7"/12") *(A/TX 6095)* **BOUNCING UP. / DON'T DON'T DON'T**

THIS POISON!

- were formed in Perth . . . 1986 by unknown quartet. They signed to Leeds imprint 'Reception' (home to WEDDING PRESENT, etc); late goths.

Reception not iss.

Mar 87. (7") *(REC 004)* **ENGINE FAILURE. / YOU;- THINK!!**
Nov 87. (7") *(REC 008)* **POISED OVER THE PAUSE BUTTON. / I'M NOT ASKING**
(12"+=) *(REC 008-12)* – THE FIERCE CRACK EP – Engine failure / You;- think!!

— disappeared after a mid-'89 appearance (the track 'THE GREAT DIVIDE') on the V/A compilation, 'Airspace'

THREATS

- were formed in Dalkeith, Midlothian . . . early 80's by unknowns (there's a CD that has their single on it!).

Playlist not iss.

Sep 81. (7"ep) *(PLAY 2)* **BACKLASH EP**
– End result / Significant zeros / Factory poems / Victims of what.

— unsure that the single above was released and if was them

Rondelet not iss.

Jun 82. (7"ep) *(ROUND 22)* **GO TO HELL EP**
– Go to hell / Afghanistan / Wasted.

Nov 82. (12"ep/7"ep) *(12+/ROUND 29)* **POLITICIANS & MINISTERS EP**
– Politicians & ministers / Writing's on the wall / Deep end depression.

THURSDAYS

• formed in Glenrothes, Fife . . . 1978 by alternative punksters (unknown). One of several New Wave outfits to appear on the seminal 'Earcom' V/A compilation EP's released in mid-'79 on Bob Last's 'Fast Product' records. The THURSDAYS tracks in question, 'PERFECTION' and 'DOCK OF THE BAY', would fit nicely into Earcom's second batch along with BASCZAX and JOY DIVISION(!)

TWO HELENS

• were formed in Falkirk . . . 1985 by lead singer, IAN MURRAY, bassist ALAN WHITE and two others (possibly BOB GREENAWAY was one). The leather-clad goth-punks played the toilet circuit but for various reasons the band fell apart.

Sharko not iss.

Oct 86. (lp) *(SHARKO 1 – TUFT 4)* **REFLECTIONS IN RED**

Jan 88. (7") *(SHARKO 2 – TUFT 57)* **SILVER AND GOLD. / XV RHYTHM / GUN**

Matt VINYL & THE DECORATORS

• were formed in Edinburgh . . . 1977 by MATTHEW BLACK and his unknown gang of messed up punks. Although they never quite painted the town red – so to speak – MATT brushed his way past the establishment with a rare piece of er, vinyl, 'USELESS TASKS'. Released on 'Housewife's Choice', it was much too silky for the more discerning punk/New Wave palette.

Housewife's Choice not iss.

1977. (7"flexi) *(none)* **USELESS TASKS**

ZIPS

• were formed out of ROAD ANGEL in February 1978 and from Glasgow. Consisting of youngsters JOHN McNEILL (vocals/guitar), BRIAN JACKSON (lead guitar), PHIL MULLEN (bass/vocals) and JOE JACONELLI (drums/vocals), The ZIPS played their first gig at a pub called The Peel. Made their own DIY EP's and covered Dr. Feelgood's 'BACK IN THE NIGHT'. They re-formed in 2001 with a new guy JOHN McMAHON taking over from JACKSON who was now living somewhere in New Zealand.

Black Gold not iss.

Apr 79. (7"ep) *(none)* **THE ZIPS**
– Take me down / Don't be pushed around / I'm in love / Over and over.

Tenement Toons not iss.

Apr 80. (7") *(none)* **RADIOACTIVITY. / I'M NOT IMPRESSED**

Jamie WATSON

Born: 3 Jun'54, Hamilton, Ontario, Canada, but raised by his Scots parents in Colinton, Edinburgh from the age of one. Surprisingly enough perhaps, JAMIE's first musical experience came via a 1959 seven-inch of 'Pink Shoe Laces / The Universe' by ALMA COGAN, kindly gifted by his parents. Thankfully this wasn't to have a great bearing on his future career as a Punk/Indie production guru.

After leaving school he studied at Edinburgh Art College, where he formed his first band, LYSANDER, a combo that numbered future REZILLOS drummer ANGEL PATTERSON in their ranks. A short-lived stint with Punk outfit ARMAGEDDON (just one of many acts around at the time taking this over-subscribed moniker) was followed by a more serious position as guitarist with The MONOS. Once again the name proved a problem (a group by the same name were already signed to 'R.C.A.') and the group subsequently billed themselves as The SOLOS. Towards the end of '79, the quintet released their one and only single, 'TALKING PICTURES', through EMI subsididiary 'Cobra'.

JAMIE's next studio venture came with PERSIAN RUGS, a trio that included SOLOS/MONOS drummer BRIAN O'DONNELL and ex-FREEZE bassist KEITH GRANT with the man himself on lead vocals and guitar. Trivia fans might be interested to know that the B-side of their first single ('BURNING PASSION PAIN'), 'POISON IN THE AIRWAVES' (originally released in '82) was later adapted by none other than late eighties shoegazing types, The PALE SAINTS. Follow-up mini-set, 'DROWNING POOL' (1983), employed the production/session skills of a still relatively unknown BLUE NILE. However, after the addition of new vocalist PAUL and one further platter, the 'RUGS cut their losses as JAMIE found his niche behind the production desk.

Over the course of the mid to late 80's, the unassuming punk veteran could be found twiddling the knobs at 'Narodnik', where he worked with the likes of JESSE GARON & THE DESPERADOES, offshoot ROTE KAPELLE, BABY LEMONADE and The VULTURES. With 'Fast Forward' ('D.D.T.', 'Avalanche/Alva' and 'Nightshift' imprints) productions, he oversaw records by The THANES (also LENNY HELSING projects The STAYRCASE and The OFFHOOKS), WE FREE KINGS, etc, etc, etc (see below discography).

The 90's were even more prolific as JAMIE (together with PAUL KIRK) helped form the Human Condition label from his working homebase of Chambers Studios. Since then the company has gone from strength to strength, releasing records by local heroes such as FORKEYE, EL HOMBRE TRAJEADO and OBABEN. Unfortunately, the label has unashamedly been by and large dismissed by the London-centric music press, who would have you think 'Queen Of The Troubled Teens' by IDLEWILD was their only release. Widely regarded as one of the most respected producers on the Scottish indie scene (ask anyone who's worked with the man!), it's hardly surprising that JAMIE also has a busy extracurricular schedule that has seen him work with 'Jeepster' outfit, SNOW PATROL (Irish boys living in Glasgow) as well as up and coming act The CHERRYFIRE ASHES. But who is that man KEN McGINTY? . . .

SOLOS

JAMIE WATSON – guitar, vocals / **FREDDIE KING** – vocals / **DAVE BUCHANAN** – guitar / **WINSTON ODDIYE** – bass / **BRIAN O'DONNELL** – drums

Cobra-EMI not iss.

Oct 79. (7"m) *(COB 8)* **TALKING PICTURES. / ONE WAY LOVE / PSYCHIC ERIC**

PERSIAN RUGS

JAMIE – vocals, guitar, keyboards / **KEITH GRANT** – bass (ex-FREEZE) / **BRIAN O'DONNELL** – drums

Phoenix not iss.

Mar 82. (7") *(PSP 11)* **BURNING PASSION PAIN. / POISON IN THE AIRWAVES**

— now with the **BLUE NILE** on session/production

May 83. (m-lp) *(PSPLP 3)* **DROWNING POOL**
– Drowning pool / Mirrors / Perfectly still / Home / War machine / Party lines.

— added **PAUL** – lead vocals

Plus One not iss.

Jan 84. (7"/12") *(RUG 1/+12)* **SHE SAID. / HOME**

— when the group split, JAMIE went into production (see above biog).
(he's now the boss at 'Human Condition' records – for more see under)

– JAMIE's wee production credits (A – Z) –

A = *AIR FRESHENER* were from Zagreb c.1998 'Hang Above Your Head' CD-EP was like a bloody air-freshener! / **Avalanche & Alva records** (see ⇒)

B = **BABY LEMONADE** (see ⇒) / **BIGSHOT** (see ⇒ Human Condition) / **BLIND** (see ⇒ Human Condition + Evol) / **BRIDGE HOPPER** (see ⇒ Human Condition)

• **BLUEFINGER** were from Prestonpans; N. JOHNSON was frontman as they covered Smiley Lewis' 'I HEAR YOU KNOCKIN' ans Chris Isaak's 'WICKED GAME'.

1990's. (ep) **MAXIMUM ROCK'N'ROLL**
– There's this girl / Leave my kitten alone / I hear you knockin' / Wicked game.

C = **CHERRYFIRE ASHES** (see ⇒ Starshaped records) / **CHICANE** (see ⇒ CHI) / **CHICKWEED** (see ⇒ Human Condition) / **CRUYFF** (see ⇒ IMPERIAL RACING CLUB)

• **CINNAMON SKIN** were from Edinburgh and issued 2 EP's.

• **COMEDIANS** were from Springhills in Edinburgh and released at least one folk cassette in the early 80's. They comprised ALI McINNES (vocals & guitar), LINZI BLACK (accordion & vocals), ADY POWERS (electric guitar & vocals), TIM MARTIN (electric violin), GUS McINNES (bass) and RICK CONTE (drums).

• **CRITIKILL** self-financed their one and only EP on 'Negative'.

1990's. (7"ep) *(none)* **Our Way EP**
– Our way / Sick and tired / See it through / Some people.

• **CUPID MOUNT ETNA** were formed in Dumfries (the Borders) around the mid-90's by MALCOLM IRVING (vocals, lead guitar & keyboards) and his musicial chums KEITH McRAE (rhythm guitar), ROBIN FOWLER (bass) and the KEITH COOPER (drums). CME self-financed their own imprint under the 'Colon Blast Records' billing and recorded most of their material at JAMIE WATSON's Chamber studio; very WIRE meets the early GO-BETWEENS or JOY DIVISION.

1995. (7") *(CB 1)* **Float / Clones '92**
1995. (7") *(CB 2)*
1996. (cd) *(CB 3)* **SuperGling**
– Carnival / Satellites / Intonarumori / Holiday / Cosmo girl – Cosmo man / French kiss / Baby / Rush hour.

D = **D.D.T. . .** (see ⇒) / **DOG FACED HERMANS** (see ⇒)

• **DECEIVERS** were Mods from Dalkeith (issued on their own 'Adrenalin' records); MEYNALL or BAXTER were the songwriters; the label was run by NEIL MORGAN of East Calder in West Lothian.
1995. (7") *(ADR 001)* **It's A Mod Mod world / Something Out Or Nothing**
1996. (7") *(ADR 003)* **Can You Hold On (To What You Believe)**

E = **EL HOMBRE TRAJEADO** (see under ⇒) / **EUGENIUS** (see ⇒ VASELINES)

• **EXTERNAL MENACE** were formed in Livingston (Deans South, to be exact) around mid-90's out of the ashes of SWINE FLU by punks WELSHY (vocals) and BILLY (bass), along with others BOBE (lead guitar), SNEDDY (rhythm guitar & vocals) and WULLIE (drums). / what happened to WULLIE / 195 Deans South, Livingston, West Lothian, EH54 8DZ.
1996. (7") *(none)* **I'd Rather Be Dead / Detonate Your Hate**
1996. (7"ep) *(none)* **Seize The Day EP**
– Naked prey / Shocktrooper / Seize the day / No mean feat.
(above was dedicated to WULLIE HAMILL + TYLER STEVENS + MACKAY)
Nov 97. (lp) *(EPI 022)* **External Menace**
– This country / Standin' on the U.K. / These pricks are wrong / Watch you drown / Rude awakening / Don't conform / Bullet of persuasion / the process of elimination / In this time / Killin' me asylum / we wanna know / Seize the day / Don't call it livin' / Sort it out.
1997. (7") *Suspect Device; (SDR 007)* **This Country / RECTIFY: Virtual Reality / Their Demise**
Feb 98. (cd) *Negative; (NCD 014)* **Process Of Elimination**
Nov 00. (cd) *Captain Oi; (AHOYCD 052)* **Pure Punk** (compilation)

F = **FINITRIBE** (see ⇒) / **FOIL** (see ⇒) / **FORKEYE** (see ⇒ Human Condition)

• **FLAMIN' GURUS** were a 4-piece who released 2 cassettes.

• **FROG** were from the 'Burgh and consisted of LENNY and others.
1990's. (12"ep) *(none)* **Stay Calm EP**
– Stay / Marshmallow kid / Calm / Stay (instrumental) / Marshmallow kid (Love dip mallow mix).

G = **GANGER** (see ⇒) / **GARGLEBLUD** (see ⇒ Avalanche records) / **GENTS** (see ⇒ Lithium records) / **GILA MONSTER** (see ⇒ Bosque records)

• **GIROS** from Dunbar featured the line-up of BARRIE HOOD (bass & vocals), JASON JAMES (guitars & vocals), STEVEN BAILLIE (guitars) and JAMIE WILSON (drums). They released one CD-EP on their own 'Shanky' imprint.
1990's. (cd-ep) *(Shankycd 1)* **Better Sticky e.p.**
– The blisters / Baby goes down / Things I say.

H = **HEEHAW** (see ⇒ Bosque) / **Danny HOLLAND** (see ⇒ Human Condition) / *HOOTON 3 CAR* / **HUCKLEBERRY** (see ⇒) / **Human Condition** (90%)

• **HAZE** were formed towards the end of the 90's by co-songwriters ANDY NAGLE (vocals & guitar) and RAYMOND KACZMAREK (vocals & bass), along with RYAN SHERIDAN (keyboards) and JAMES McKAY (drums); er, JAMIE told me recently that GRANT produced this one! ach well.
1999. (cd-ep) *(none)* **The Haze EP**
– Don't take my love away / Taste the thrill / Excuse me / Standing on 3rd Street.

I = **I AM SCIENTIST** (see ⇒ Human Condition) / **IDLEWILD** (see ⇒) / **IMPERIAL RACING CLUB** (see ⇒)

• **INFORMERS** were from Tranent, while INNER CITY CRAWL produced a LONG FIN KILLIE member.

J = **JENNIFERS** (see ⇒ Human Condition) / **JESSE GARON & THE DESPERADOES** (see ⇒)
K = **KAISERS** (see ⇒) / **KHAYA** (see ⇒)
L = **LONG FIN KILLIE** (see ⇒ BOWS) / **LYD** (see ⇒ Human Condition)
M = **MATTER BABIES** (see ⇒ D.D.T. records) / **Ken McGINTY** (see ⇒ folk/trad section) / **METH O.D.** (see ⇒ Human Condition) / **MONOS** (see above) / **MYSTERY JUICE** (see ⇒ Human Condition)
N = **NAKED SEE** (see ⇒ FOIL)
O = **OBABEN** (see ⇒) / **OFFHOOKS** (see ⇒ THANES)
P = **PAINKILLERS** (see ⇒ Human Condition) / **PERSIAN RUGS** (see above) / **PIGPEN** (see ⇒ Human Condition) / **PILOTCAN** (see ⇒) / *POLARBEAR* / **PRALINES** (see ⇒ Avalanche records)

• **PROI** were from East Lothian and consisted of the shy and retiring MG (vocals & Rickenbacker guitar) – self-proclaimed best songwriter in the world, GRAHAM (keyboards) – self-proclaimed maddest . . ., MARKIE MANNERS (bass) – er, Mr.Basstastic; close! and BILLY STEEL (drums) – self-proclaimed best . . . and he also plays the bagpipes; GRANT also produced them.
1990's. (cd-ep) *(none)* **She'll Be Back EP**
– She'll be back / As good as you / I'm always happy / One more night.

Q = 'Queen Of The Troubled Teens' by IDLEWILD which is now worth £50.
R = **RIVERHEAD** (see ⇒ Avalanche records) / **RISINGSON** (see ⇒ Path records) / **ROTE KAPELLE** (see ⇒ JESSE GARON . . .)

• **RADIUM CATS** were formed in Edinburgh . . . 1987 by Munster-loving PAUL PATERSON (vocals & guitar), his brother LES PATERSON (vocals & bass) and JOHNNY MABEN (drums). Obviously overdosing on TV show, The Munsters, as well as musically The METEORS and The CRAMPS, The RADIUM CATS unleashed their "Little Eddie" for 'Mental Decay'. Moving to 'Rumble' records in the early 90's, the trio released a second set.
Jun 88. (m-lp) *(FLATOP 002)* **Munster Madness**
– Munsters theme / (I hear it) Howling in the swamp / Go, go, go / Screaming from the grave / Froggy / Long black train / Thump, thump, thump / Jungle drums.
1990's. (cd/lp) *(Rumble 016 cd/lp)* **Other Worlds**
– Martian hop / Six foot down / The freak / My girl is like uranium / Idol with the golden head / Pink hearse / Great shakin' fever / Return of the mystery train / Strange, baby strange / Eraserhead / Zurembi stroll / Surfin' D.O.A. *(cd re-iss. May92 on 'Nervous'; NERCD 068)*

• **RAINKINGS** were from Edinburgh and formed by Glasgow-born RAB HOWATT who was once a member of North of England punk outfit, PENETRATION. They only managed to release one single for 'Playtime'.
Apr 90. (7"/12"/cd-s) *(AMUSE 008/+T/CD)* **Get Ready**

S = **SAWYER** (see ⇒) / **SHADOWLAND** (see ⇒) / *SNOW PATROL (ex-POLARBEAR)* / **SOLOS** (see above) / **SPUTNIKS DOWN** (see ⇒ Human Condition) / **STACEY EFFECT** (ex-LYD) / **STAYRCASE** (see ⇒ THANES) / **SWAMPTRASH** (see ⇒) / **SWINE FLU** (see ⇒ Stranded records)

• **SCATTER!** were also from the capital, the line-up for their one and only 'Manatee' released recording being JAMES LEAR (vocals & guitar), NELSON WRIGHT (guitar & harmonica), ANDREW KERR (bass) and AL ROSS (drums, trumpet and backing vocals).
Mar 92. (12"ep) *(MANATEE 1)* **Burn A Hole In Me EP**
– Burn a hole in me / Time in a banquet / Wear mine in / Ascension of Johnny.

• **SECOND GENERATION** were Edinburgh mods ROD SPARK (vocals & guitar), GARRY LYNCH (bass), NICK KENNEDY (organ & keyboards) and STEVE MASON (drums). They were signed to East Calder label, 'Unicorn'. ROD SPARK later joined SHADOWLAND and others.
Oct 88. (lp) *(PHZA 22)* **SPY-CATCHER**
– Kick in the teeth / Standard life / Threw it all away / Fade / Day of the triffids / You're all mine / Spy-catcher / Changing faces / Thinking of you / Pictures on my wall / The way you were / Look who's coming.

• **SOLARIS** were from Edinburgh and consisted of ANDREW McINTOSH (vocals & guitars), ANDY KELLY (guitars & keyboards), SIMON RITSON (bass) and STEVE SMART (drums & percussion).
1999. (cd-ep) *(none)* **Treasure EP**
– Treasure / Your time will come / Blue (demo).
1999. (cd-ep) *(sol.ep.2)* **The Story Of My Life EP**
– The story of my life / White lies and dishonesty / My world is getting smaller.

• **SUBSTATE** are PAUL BRADLEY (vocals & bass), JONNY HALL (guitar), GEORGE NISBET (guitar) and MATT HOLLAND (drums).
1999. (cd-ep) *(none)* **Final Indulgence EP**
– Final indulgence / Fake / Lost / Crushing the soul.

T = **THANES** (see ⇒)

• **THIGHSMOKE** from Dunfermline were EWAN CLARK (vocals & guitar), PHIL CONKEY (guitar), STEVEN TAYLOR (bass) and ROBBIE (drums) – self-financed a cassette-EP's
Apr 94. (c-ep) *(none)* **Thighsmoke EP**
– 15 minutes / Her scarlet hair / Mrs Brown / Trace for a trier.

• **TIN COMIC** were from Edinburgh; SEAN BELL (vocals & guitar), GARRY ELLARD (bass), GREG MacVEAN (drums) and JACKIE CABLE (vox & synths). They released one eponymous cassette which featured the tracks, 'Look both ways', 'Electric shock walk' and 'Two Fifty Eight'.

U = **UGLY GROOVE MOVEMENT** (see ⇒ Dance section)
V = **VASELINES** (see ⇒) / **VULTURES** (see ⇒ Narodnik . . .)

• **VARIKOSE VEINS** were from Edinburgh (EH12, to be exact!) – surnames being BEARDS, BINNS, CAMPBELL and er, LUGOSI – aye right. They only managed to sneak out one noisy, CHROME-esque long-player on 'Chrome' records (which included a cover of the aforemention's 'YOU'VE BEEN DUPLICATED') before they returned to their proverbial crypts.

Sep 89. (lp) *(CROM 303)* **Beirut Everywhere**
– Beirut everywhere / Waster / You've been duplicated / Stinking world / Twisted loose / We will bury you / Dog killer / Out of words. – -
W = **WATSON, Jamie** (of course!) / **WENDY'S** (see ⇒)
X = X is how much money you need to survive when (see below)!
Y = Y the Southern journals have dismissed this Edinburgh label?
Z = **ZEPHYRS** (see ⇒)

The 90s . . .

(wee out-takes from recent times)

– A – Z discography –

AERIAL

• were formed in Aberdeen . . . 1999 by the young 5-piece of COLIN (vocals, guitar), SCOTT (guitar, vocals), PAUL (bass, vocals), NEIL (keyboards) and DALE (drums). Having built up a wee following north of the border, AERIAL found a home at London's 'Plastic Fantastic' label (also stable of other Scots band, ASTRID). By the following summer, this Americanised, BEACH BOYS-meets-SUPERGRASS combo delivered their debut EP, 'SIGNAL'. Harmonious, catchy and infectious was also the description of their September sophomore EP, 'STAR OF THE SHOW', the blistering closing track 'MACKIE'S OPUS' was certainly a star in its own right.

Fantastic Plastic — not iss.

May 00. (ltd-cd-ep) *(FPS 019)* **SIGNAL E.P.**
– Signal / In with you / Sign of the times / One track mind.

Sep 00. (ltd-cd-ep) *(FPS 022)* **STAR OF THE SHOW E.P.**
– Star of the show / Don't feel bad / I believe I can McFly / Mackie's opus.

ALASKA

• were actually featured on the 'Zeroes And Ones' V/A set.

Tim ALLON

• was born in Glasgow. He was described as a weird/funny little singer/guitarist who sent a make-shift demo to 'Fierce Panda' just before Xmas 1999. Rewarded with a one-off limited edition single, 'TEN THOUSAND YEARS FROM NOW' was released the following spring. The track was a lovelorn indie-pop tune while its B-side, 'I CAN HEAR A NEW WORLD', was a little more whimsical and upbeat and featured the flute-player from MONSOON BASSOON. TIM has no backing band and has never promoted the 45 live.

Fierce Panda — not iss.

Apr 00. (7") *(NING 91)* **TEN THOUSAND YEARS FROM NOW. / I CAN HEAR A NEW WORLD**

the BLIMP

• are soulful, BLACK CROWES-esque rawk'n'roll from Glasgow. Kerrang! said of the single "a rambling Rab C Nesbitt type spluttering about his pet pooch. Next." – at least they love our accents down south!

Stuntman — not iss.

Nov 01. (7") *(MAJORS 002)* **BAD DOG BITCH DON'T BITE. / THOUSAND BEARS**

CALAMATEUR

• were formed in Glasgow but basically unknown and on the newly-formed 'Timshell'; their glorious gentle-pop, GALAXIE 500-inspired 45 was a favourite of many DJ's including John Peel.

Timshell — not iss.

Oct 00. (7") **WHITE LIGHT UNKNOWN. / INHABIT**

CANDY STORE PROPHETS

• were formed in Dundee . . . late 90's by unknown 5-piece (a.J.WOOD, was one) exacting out their ARAB STRAP meets indie-pop C-86 revenge; spoken word ditties interspersed with meaningful dark music. However, only one EP surfaced from this promising bunch entitled 'SONGS FOR ANGELS'. Airplay from Beat Patrol and gigs opening for SPARE SNARE, The DELGADOS and The PASTELS might've found them a few more friends – who knows?

Pioneer — not iss.

Aug 99. (7"ep) *(PISS ONE)* **SONGS FOR ANGELS**
– Cindy's on fire / Life flies away / The shortness of life does not stop us entertaining long hopes.

CARSON

• are from Fort William and currently very hot on the Northern Exposure circuit (Oban, etc). Their semi-acoustic selection of half covers/half originals are highlighted by their own heavy instrumental, 'GET IT UP YOU' – all together now!

CATERPILLAR WORKERS

• 'THE CHAIN GANG' appeared on a V/A set, 'Making Tracks' (other groups included The CRACK)

EMPIRE-BUILDER

• were formed in Glasgow . . . summer '97 by STEVEN WARD (vocals, guitar & samples), ROBERT JAPP (bass) and COLIN KEARNEY (drums & occasional guitar). A band heavily inspired by SLINT, MOGWAI, etc – slow, melodic and moody sad-core New-wave – they signed to Essex (Clacton on Sea) label, 'Gringo'. However, they received some bad press and lost touch.

Gringo — not iss.

Jul 99. (7"ep) *(WAAT 006)* **WATERS OF THE ORIENT EP**
– Waters of the Orient / Trade in fiction / I am Vasco da Gama.

4 PAST MIDNIGHT

• were a mysterious political hardcore punk/retro-Oi band from Scotland similar to STIFF LITTLE FINGERS. Among many others, they covered the Partisans 'POLICE STORY'. Their manic record sleeves (issued only in France!) were certainly of note.

Weird — not iss.

1993. (12"ep) *(WEIRD 007)* **THE FEARS WE HIDE**
– This is Bosnia / Jimmy is a junkie / My feelings / Nowhere to go.

One By One — not iss.

1995. (12"ep) *(OBO 006)* **GET A LIFE OR FUCK OFF!**
– See the light / Get a life or fuck off / Abused.

Smokin' Troll — not iss.

Sep 99. (cd) *(ST 21)* **JESUS CHRIST IT'S 4PM (AGAIN!)** (compilation)
– Nobody listens anymore / I love her so / UK (a) / Wasted life (the story of little Jimmy) / The answer is still no / Police story / Senseless murder / Hands off / Little Sid 10 – Jimmy is a junkie / Party political bullshit / No reason / Majors on the street / As your world turns / Join the army / This is Bosnia / See the light / Same old policies / Nowhere to go / Get a little or fuck off / My feelings / The war goes on / Outro / Pipers lament.

GOD'S BOYFRIEND

• were formed in Glasgow in the mid-90's by a largely unknown 1-boy/3-girl (including singer LAURA DONNELLY) combination. Much like the SHOP ASSISTANTS of old and other twee/indie outfits, their second 45 (for 'Fierce Panda') was a shared effort with TOASTER: 'I DON'T WASH'.

Flux — not iss.

Oct 96. (7") *(GOD 001)* **WITCH**

Fierce Panda — not iss.

Feb 97. (7") *(NING 30)* **I DON'T WASH. / (other track by TOASTER)**

Trade 2 — not iss.

Nov 97. (7"ep/cd-ep) *(TRDSC/+CD 011)* **POND / SLEEP. / WASHERS / INVERSE ARACHNOPHOBIA**

HAZEY JANES

• were formed in Dundee, 1999 by a 5-piece comprising ANDREW MITCHELL (vocals & guitar), MARTIN DEMPSTER (guitar), ALICE MARRA (vocals), MATTHEW MARRA (bass) and MICHAEL BENBOW (drums & vocals). Drawing their rootsy traditions from seminal folk/West Coast acts like FAIRPORT CONVENTION, BIG STAR and BUFFALO SPRINGFIELD, The HAZEY JANES (named after a song by NICK DRAKE), completed support tours with COSMIC ROUGH RIDERS, CAST, GENEVA, GORKY'S ZYGOTIC MYNCI and ASTRID; a debut set is due any any time, although they have already issued a single, 'SAY IT AGAIN', on their own 'Hot Cup' records late in 2000 (re-iss. March 2001).

LUCI BAINES BAND

• were formed in Greenock . . . summer '95 and again 4 years later! They comprised SAMI CUSHNAGHAN, a Motown/Northern Soul fan along with conspirators

ROBERT McGOVERN, WILL GALLAGHER, GERRY STEVENSON and ANDREW KERR. Taking the group name from an ARTHUR LEE (ex-LOVE) recording when he was with The AMERICAN FOUR, The LUCI BAINES BAND released a one-off for 'YoYo' records, 'FIND A L'IL LOVE' in 1996; one of their re-formed gigs was at the 13th Nore during Glasgow's 10-Day Weekend.

YoYo not iss.

Jun 96. (7") *(YO 1)* **FIND A L'IL LOVE**

MURMUR

• were formed in Glasgow in the late 80's by RICK CRAWFORD (vocals, bass, piano), TONEYE "T-ISAAM" BROWN (percussion, drums) and STIRLING GORMAN (vocals, harmonica, bass, guitar & piano). Taking their moniker from a classic R.E.M. album, the band managed to release only one set. • **Note:** the MURMUR on 'Warners' was not the same band.

Cloudland not iss.

Apr 95. (cd) *(RAIN 013CD)* **SEXPOWDER 2000 VOLTS**
– Myriapod / Heard somewhere (people kill themselves) / Fall / Imagined cup of tea / L O U D! / Bullcalf / Enjoy / Lulababe / Why do they? / Why do they? / Such a waste of me / Able.

PAISLEY SHIRTS

• were formed in Leven, Fife . . . 1993 by JED LIVINGSTONE (vocals & keyboards) and RON SMITH (guitar, keyboards & effects), the latter was a member of PATROL, an early 80's punk outfit. Their one and only German EP covered Leonard Cohen's 'SUZANNE', the TV Personalities 'SAD MONA LISA', Kaleidoscope's '(LOVE SONG) FOR ANNIE' and Pink Floyd's 'JULIA DREAM'.

Roman Cabbage not iss.

1995. (ltd-7"ep) *(GREY 5)* **FOR ALL THE GIRLS WE'VE LOVED BEFORE**
– Suzanne / (Love song) For Annie / Sad Mona Lisa / Julia dream.

PEPTONE

• were formed in Glasgow . . . 1995 by KEITH (vocals), JAMIE (drummer) and JUSTIN (bass). Basically a punkoid pop outfit, they played the Ten Day Weekend gig and subsequently performed around the country from Inverness to Camden. PEPTONE were to have featured on a split 45 with touring mates DAWN OF THE REPLICANTS until the latter signed to a major. In their last days in early '98, the quartet (with recent addition/guitarist KERR in tow) were looking for a synth man.

Peptone not iss.

Feb 96. (7") *(SID 001)* **SMASHING. / MALCOLM / LOOP THE LOOP**
May 96. (7") *(SID 002)* **AMAZING GRACE. / DON'T ASK DEREK**

PERSPEX WHITE OUT

• were formed in Glasgow . . . 1990 by the youthful TEENAGE FANCLUB-inspired lads CALUM WALKER (vocals, guitar), WARRICK MALCOLM (bass), RICHARD (vocals & guitar) and drummer ANN. Having opened for the aforementioned 'FANNIES, the fun-filled grunge/shoegazer quartet delivered their debut for 'Sunflower', via the 12" 'YOU TURN ON MY WORLD'. With a dual vocal harmony of CALUM and RICHARD (who incidentally was a white-collar worker, i.e. Doctor Of Science!), it was surprising that the band didn't last the pace.

Sunflower not iss.

Nov 91. (12") **YOU TURN ON MY WORLD**

Imaginary not iss.

Jun 92. (12"ep) **PERSPEX WHITEOUT EP**
– Cool to be afraid / + 2
Oct 92. (12"ep) **TRIPLEALBUM EP**
– Hey girl / etc.

PRINTED CIRCUIT

• is apparently the brainchild of CLAIRE, who puts her Moogs into gear on the Japanese gameboy-inspired one-off for Spanish 'Elefant' imprint.

Sep 00. (7"red) *(ER 223)* **GIMME AIBO**

SLIMCEA GIRL

• were formed somewhere in Scotland . . . mid-90's by a mysterious indie-pop outfit who liked to pull the heartstrings a bit. Signed to 'Royal Mint' (Bob Stanley's – ST. ETIENNE – label) for their debut, they went through a rather er, lean period.

Royal Mint not iss.

Oct 95. (7") *(MINT 002)* **MILLION MILES. / MARIANNE**

SLINKY

• are known because one member – I'm not sure which – joined JOHNSON who included one-time TRASH CAN SINATRAS drummer STEPHEN DOUGLAS.

Kinglake not iss.

Feb 95. (cd-s) *(KLR 004CD)* **SHOOT ME DOWN**

SMILES

• were formed in Glasgow . . . 1998 as a blues-tinged, indie 5-piece (including future group ASTRID drummer, NEIL PAYNE) inspired by the SMALL FACES and OCEAN COLOUR SCENE. Signed to 'A&M' before they went bust. • **Note:** not sure if below is by the same group.

not iss. Resurgence

Jul 00. (d-cd) **WORLD OF BRIGHT FUTURES**
– World of bright futures / Dreaming of Babylon / (Watching) Over me / Sorry looking soldier / Two hands / Red eye removal / Something of you / Lisa – Ophelia / Small / Smaller // Come to me / Never lose control / Something of you / Sweet kiss / Brightest blue.

SOUNDMAN

• were formed in Glasgow . . . mid-90's; a catchy-pop band loved by Peely.

Image not iss.

Mar 97. (7"/cd-s) *(IM/+CD 10002)* **SHATTERPROOF. / NINE STONE ELVIS**

SOURTOOTH

• were formed in Glasgow 1998 by MARTIN WILSON (guitar & vocals), VICTORIA HENDERSON (bass & vocals), FIONA DAVIDSON (guitar) and ANDREW FRIENDLY (drums). ADRIANNE are AMY and ROSE with ANDREW FRIENDLY on drums, all very BIS-meets-SLITS-meets-C-86.

own label not iss.

1999. (7"split) *(none)* **INVISIBLE INK / DIG A DITCH. / ADRIANNE: The pink lady / Mapped Out**

SPLEEN

• were formed in Scotland . . . 1997 by PAUL BOYD, his brother SCOTT BOYD and BRIAN DILLON, all veterans of the toilet circuit scene and a plethora of bands. Like BEN HARPER on a stage with PEARL JAM, SPLEEN only managed one single – I think? • **Note:** not to be confused with English band who released records on 'Swarf Finger'.

PAUL BOYD – vocals, guitar (ex-FLOOD, ex-INJUN JOE)/ **BRIAN DILLON** – bass (ex-ALBANACHIE, ex-LaVELLE, ex-GROUND CONTROL, ex-13th TRIBE, ex-FELON BRUN, ex-CURTIS, ex-CHONG, ex-ELIAS) / **SCOTT BOYD** – drums (ex-loads of bands)

Rocket Girl not iss.

Nov 99. (7") *(LAUNCH 007)* **L'IL LENNY CUTS OUT. / Hacker: RAW SCENT OF MAIL**

TAM!

• were formed in London by Edinburgh-born vocalist TAM (or THOMAS, to you) TREANOR. He "popped" in and out of the music scene in mid'96 and appeared (alongside FURBALL and COADE) on a 'Dedicated' V/A EP, 'BEST KEPT SECRET 2'; a little like BOWIE or the LO-FIDELITY ALLSTARS.

Things To Come not iss.

Aug 98. (7"/cd-s) *(IPL 01)* **ALIENS. / FE FI LO FI**
Nov 99. (7") *(IPL 07)* **SWALLOW ME WHOLE. / (mix)**
(cd-s+=) *(IPLCD 07)* – (mixes).

J.V.C. Japan not iss.

2000. (cd) **HELLO MY FRIENDS DO YOU READ ME**
– Punctured brain / Aliens / Level 10 baby / Liquid love / Swallow me whole / Jealousy free / Machines / Sting / Let go get low / Ultramontane / Blam blam / The sky is falling in.

YESSA DE PASO

• were a 4-piece from Carnoustie . . . 2000. Two members (guitarist STUART GILLIES and bassist/voice CLAIRE THORNTON) had served their time in Dundee outfit, MAGNETIC NORTH POLE, while KEVIN GILLIES had been in LAETO; 4th member CHRIS MARR had also worked with various bands. Lo-fi and compared to SMOG, LOW or The HOOD, YESSA DE PASO played a number of gigs (including a T In The Park stint) before they decided to call it a day. However, KEVIN and CHRIS bounced back in 2002 with Sunderland-born drummer IAN CAVANAGH and a new billing, LOKI (they had always moonlighted as LOKI TRANSPORT); STUART joined up with 1" VOLCANO until summer 2002.

Dance / Rave

(a wee nightclubbing . . .)

— the faceless outfits who've nevertheless stirred up some people to dance their socks off well into the night when mere mortals (like me!) are just taking in the milk – before it gets nicked.

– A – Z discography –

I needed a lot of help with this section, so instead of omitting them altogether I'm asking any people out there to fill in the gaps . . .

ANGELHEART

- was an unknown Scottish female dance producer who enlisted the outside help of various singers (see below) to augment her on two minor hits.

Hi-Life – Polydor | not iss.

Apr 96. (12"/cd-s; as ANGELHEART featuring ROCHELLE HARRIS) *(577631-1/-2)* **FANTASY (COME BACK TO ME) – mixes** 68 -

Mar 97. (12"/cd-s; as ANGELHEART featuring ALETIA BOURNE) *(573545-1/-2)* **I'M STILL WAITING – mixes** 74 -

BE-ING

- were formed in Edinburgh . . . 1995 by DAVE BEING, exponent of the trance-dance electroid techno (nothing to do with similar Detroit guy CLAUDE YOUNG).

Leaf | not iss.

Jul 95. (lp; Various Artists) *(REEL 1)* **INVISIBLE SOUNDTRACK VOLUME 1**

Special Emissions | not iss.

Sep 95. (12") *(SE 002)* **BE-ING TWO**
– Foottball / Fotts / Footpeel / Mavebeep part three.

Oct 95. (12") *(SE 003)* **BE-ING THREE**

Spacefrog | not iss.

Nov 95. (cd/lp) *(efa 290009-2/-1)* **THE TIDES**

Special Emissions | not iss.

Feb 96. (d-cd) *(SE 006)* **SELECTED TRANSMISSIONS**
– Mune / McLaren / Fotts / Mavebeep part 3 / Flee / Ayemooth / Foamy / Ryam / Toobit / Aquapan / Eeeshab / Toyled / Quickie.

Leaf | not iss.

Jul 96. (lp; Various Artists) *(REEL 2)* **INVISIBLE SOUNDTRACKS VOLUME 2**

Push | not iss.

Nov 96. (12"/cd-s) *(556450 430/220)* **TIDES (remixes)**

BIOS

- were formed in Edinburgh . . . mid-90's by electronic obsessed youngsters. Late in '95, the minimalist BIOS people were featured on a free 7" given away with a ANDREW WEATHERALL compilation, their one and only UK effort coming in the shape of the 'DOUBLE SEVEN EP' the following Spring.

Special Emissions | not iss.

Apr 96. (d7"ep) *(SE 009)* **THE DOUBLE SEVEN EP**
– Neutral / Live / Shift.

BLACKA'NIZED

- were formed in Edinburgh . . . 1994 by JOSEPH MALIK and CALVIN NUTTAL. Signed to London imprint 'Response', they stylised themselves on P-FUNK or CURTIS MAYFIELD/MILES DAVIS-ish trip-hop. The line up was:-

JOSEPH MALIK – vocals, turntable / **CALVIN NUTTAL** – keyboards / with others from other outfits; **COLIN STEELE** – trumpet / **MISTA MATICK** (b. HENDRY) – vocals / **DYNAMIC DUO:- JONES + DAILLY** (mainly on 1998 release)

Response | not iss.

Nov 94. (m-cd) **360°**

Dec 94. (12"ep) **VIB'RATIONS**

Sep 98. (12"ep/cd-ep) *(RESP 009/+CD)* **THE ALL-NEW ADVENTURES OF BLACKA'NIZED EP – Vol One**
– Crack pipe / Vertical forms / Crack pipe – instrumental / UFO beats / Livin ina' jungle / DYNAMIC DUO – The soldier monk skit.
(above featured FRESHLY SQUEEZED)

Yush | Yush

Oct 98. (12"ep) *(YUSH 003)* **YUSH EP VOL.3**

Apr 99. (12"ep) *(YUSH 004)* **BLACKA'NIZED**

May 99. (12"ep) *(YUSH 005)* **CHOICES EP**

Oct 99. (d-lp/cd) *(YUSH 006/007)* **FUTURE GENERATIONS**

Jul 00. (12") *(YUSH 009)* **YUSH VS THE BEATFREEKZ**
– Sesame beats / Soun' check: Beat Freekz / La la means laterz: Beat Freekz / Dept S: Yush & Blacka'nized.

David CALIKES

- was born in Dundee 1958 and played the decks at the city's Fat Sam's Club from the mid-80's. In the late 80's, the highly-rated techno DJ was resident at the Metropolis in Saltcoats, inviting a lot of top dance acts such as ADAMSKI and PAUL OAKENFOLD to headline the shows. CALIKES subsequently worked in journalism (mainly for dance mag M8). Sadly, he was to die on the 31st of January 1996; complications from his diabetes was said to be the cause of death.

Stevie CHRISTIE 'Experience'

- producer/keyboard-man STEVIE was another from Edinburgh and around in the mid-90's. A fan fave was the track 'REVOLUTION' (from V/A set, 'Blunted: The Edinburgh Project'), while the man guested for SUGA BULLIT and 3 BAG CREW (BARNEY STRACHAN's band). Along with DAVID DEMUS DONNELLY (on bass, guitar, trumpet) he was part of The OUTA' NATIONALS, an ensemble boasting JAMES McKINTOSH (drums), GUY NICHOLSON (percussion), plus vocalists ROSANNE ERSKINE (from COCO AND THE BEAN) and DONALD GORGAN.

DJ KRASH SLAUGHTA

- was based in Scotland. He and his breakbeat crew were into rap, jazz and er, nursery rhymes; mixed a lot of other Scottish dance artists.

unknown | not iss.

Jun 95. (12") *(X 001)* **ALWAYS REMAIN HARDCORE**

DOPPELGANGER

Groove Attack – Mind The Gap | not iss.

Oct 96. (12") *(GAP 0023-1)* **DAYS GONE (mixes)**

Dec 98. (12") *(GAP 0037-1)* **DAYS GONE REMEMBERED (mixes)**

FRESHLY SQUEEZED

- were formed in Edinburgh . . . mid-90's by San Francisco-type DJ, AONE, plus FROSTY J on vocals, ANDREW AKIN + TEWE on drums, plus others GEORGE MACDONALD on tenor sax, MARTIN KERSHAW on alto, BRIAN SHIELS on double bass and DAVIS 'DEMUS' DONNELLY on guitar.

Freshly Squeezed | not iss.

May 95. (12"ep) **HERBS AND SPICES EP**
– Rok da house / Spice / Herb.

JX

- were formed Scotland . . . 1993 by unknown dance DJ

Internal | not iss.

Mar 94. (7") *(IDS 5)* **SON OF A GUN**
(12"+=/cd-s+=) *(IDX/IDC 5)* – ('A'mixes).

Hooj Choons | not iss.

Feb 95. (12") **YOU BELONG TO ME (mixes)**

Ffrr | not iss.

Mar 96. (c-s/12"/cd-s) *(TAB MC/X/CD 241)* **NOTHING I WON'T DO (mixes)**

Feb 97. (c-s/12"/cd-s) *(TAB MC/X/CD 245)* **CLOSE TO YOUR HEART (mixes)**

KMC

- were formed in Edinburgh . . . mid-90's as a breakbeat dance outfit.

Champion | not iss.

Sep 95. (c-s/12"/cd-s; KMC featuring DHANY) *(CHAMP K/12/CD 320)* **SOMEBODY TO TOUCH ME (mixes)**

MIRO

- were formed in Scotland I think . . . 1997 by dance unknowns

Effective | not iss.

Jun 97. (12") *(EFFS 029)* **PURE SILK (mixes)**

Red Alert | not iss.

Dec 97. (12") *(RED 090)* **PURPLE MOON (mixes)**
(re-iss. Feb98 on 'Mindstar'; MS 14)

Hooj Choons not iss.

May 98. (12"/cd-s) *(JOOJ 061/+CD)* **PARADISE (mixes)**
(12") *(HOOJ 061R)* – ('A'remixes).

Sonic Soul not iss.

1998. (12") **MOVING ON (mixes)**

Red Alert not iss.

Mar 99. (12") *(RED 151)* **SHINING. / IT'S LIKE XTC**

Varunee not iss.

Jun 01. (cd) *(VARUNEE 003)* **SUBTIDAL**
– Beso / Msc / Fuzzy matters / Industry, indiscreet / Not so clear after all / Truck south / C-matic / Libertine / Deejay D.K.

Lost Language not iss.

Jan 02. (12"/12"remix) *(LOST 011/+R)* **BY YOUR SIDE (Ian Wilkie & Markus Schulz mix)** [ ] [-]

NEW ATLANTIC

• were formed by a teenage male production duo of QUAKE and LOVE DECADE. Recruiting singer BERRI (aka BEVERLEY SLEIGHT), they had a monster hit with their debut, 'I KNOW'; two versions of a subsequent single, 'SUNSHINE AFTER THE RAIN', also reached high in the charts.

3 Beat not iss.

Feb 92. (7") *(3BT 1)* **I KNOW. / ('A'-Flute mix)** [12] [-]
(12"+=/cd-s+=) *(3BT T/CD 1)* – ('A'-Love Decade remix) / Yes to Satan (bonus techno mix).
(below featured LINDA WRIGHT)
Sep 92. (7") *(3BT 2)* **INTO THE FUTURE. / ('A'-PA mix)** [70] [-]
(12"+=/cd-s+=) *(3BT T/CD 2)* – Kinetic synthesis / Kinetic origin.
Feb 93. (c-s) *(3BTCA 14)* **TAKE OFF SOME TIME** [64] [-]
(12"+=/cd-s+=) *(3BT T/CD 14)* – ('A'mixes).
Nov 93. (12") *(3BTT 24)* **FIORE (mixes)** [ ] [-]
Nov 94. (7"; as NEW ATLANTIC / U4EA featuring BERRI) *(TAB 223)* **THE SUNSHINE AFTER THE RAIN. / (New Atlantic version)** [26] [-]
(12"+=/cd-s+=) *(TAB 12/CD 223)* – ('A'-original U4EA breakbeat mix) / ('A'-Two cowboys 12" mix) / ('A'-Tall Paul remix).
(above issued on 'Ffrreedom')
Jul 95. (cd/c/lp) *(3BTT CD/MC/LP)* **GLOBAL** [ ] [-]
– I know (Love Decade remix) / San Andreas / Song of the earth / Rude / Into the future / Water / Fiore / Bandito mix) / Bass (one little bit) / Solaris / Take off some time (Love Decade remix) / Sunshine creed / Life spirit.

— BERRI went on to have two further UK Top 20 hits towards the end of '95, a re-mix of the aforementioned 'The Sunshine After The Rain' and 'Shine Like A Star'

Feb 99. (12"; as NEW ATLANTIC & QUAKE) *(3BTT 41)* **I KNOW (1999 remixes)** [ ] [-]

NEW YORK PIG FUNKSTERS

• were formed in Edinburgh . . . mid-80's by an unknown crew of dance orientated trotters into biting chunks out the Big Apple. However, only one 12" single, 'HOTHOUSE ORGAN', was to surface before they tried some other work to bring home the bacon.

Pasta Spectacular not iss.

1987. (12") *(PASTA 001T)* **HOTHOUSE ORGAN. / TOMATO GROSSO**

NT

• were formed in Glasgow . . . mid-90's as part of the growing Groove-merchant scene. Signed to 'Natural Response' (owned by the STEREO MC's and licensed to 'R.C.A.'), the outfit issued the single, 'RESPONSIBILITIES'.

Natural Response not iss.

Jun 96. (7"/c-s) *(74321 30086-7/-4)* **RESPONSIBILITIES (mixes)**
(12"+=/cd-s+=) *(74321 30086-1/-2)* – ('A'mixes).
1990's. (cd-s) **POSITIVE Pt.1 (album version – Underdog remix – Syze-Up remix)**

POTENTIAL DIFFERENCE

• were formed in Edinburgh . . . mid-90's, the brainchild of DJ STEVE BROWN, a scuzzy technoid producer/sampler.

Subjective not iss.

Mar 96. (12") **POTENTIAL DIFFERENCE EP**

Drought not iss.

Mar 97. (12"ep) *(DROUGHT 002)* **FULL DAT EP**

— unsure what happened to STEVE, could have went solo (checking)

REACHOUT

• are Colinton's (Edinburgh) answer to hip hop from the US; ROOTS MANUVA they weren't. Their album, 'ROKS'N'ROLL' was released in May 2001, you'll sample it before you buy it.

SHARP BOYS

• were unknowns formed in Scotland and soon showcased their wares on V/A artists double-CD set in 1999. Their re-mixing work with ALL SAINTS, M-PEOPLE, BACKSTREET BOYS, etc. was combined with white label singles 'SHARP GO BOOM' and 'I BREATHE AGAIN'.

Sharp not iss.

May 95. (12"; as SHARP TOOLS) *(TOOLS 001)* **SHARP TOOLS VOL.1**
Jul 97. (12") *(SHARP 009)* **SHARP TOOLS VOL.3**

— in May'99, they released a V/A set, 'SHARP VS SHARP', of all their remix work

May 99. (12"; as SHARP BOYS Vs. ADAM) **I BREATHE AGAIN**

Azuli not iss.

Nov 99. (12"/cd-s; as SHARP BOYS & KENNY C) *(AZNY/+CDX 108)* **RAISE THE ALARM (mixes)**
(12") *(AZNY 111)* – ('A'mixes).

Sharp not iss.

May 00. (12") *(SHARP 017)* **SHARP TOOLS VOL.4**

SMALL WORLD

• were formed in Glasgow . . . mid-90's by breakbeat, avant-garde electronics man PAUL HUNTER.

Hard Hands not iss.

Mar 95. (12"ep) *(HAND 17T)* **OLD SKOOL PLASMA BLASTER EP**
– Dual tone / Pause.
Jan 96. (12"ep/cd-ep) *(HAND 025 T/CD)* **LIVIN' FREE EP**

STATE OF FLUX

• were formed in Glasgow . . . late 1992 by an unknown duo.

Sony not iss.

Jul 93. (12") *(TB 1004)* **MIND WEEDS**
Aug 93. (12") *(TB 1005)* **GROW MORE POT**

Finiflex not iss.

May 94. (12") *(FF 1009)* **MERCURY EP**
Nov 94. (12") *(FF 1010)* **GREAT BALANCING ACT**

UGLY GROOVE MOVEMENT

• were formed in Edinburgh . . . mid-90's by a dozen-strong funk ensemble with the fascinating names BILLY DADDY LOVE, DIZZY-JO SOUL and SMOOTH MAMA GROOVE (feat. GROOVE JAR) all taking the mic, MS. FELICIA FEATHER-LIPS on vocals and flute (don't even think it!), BLAZIN' DAVE on trumpet, HIS EXCELLENCY JIM (AMBASSADOR FOR FUNKATIVITY) on sax, DR DOUBLE-WAH on guitars, CAPTAIN FUNK on bass/vocals, MR UP THE-COUNTRY THUMPIN' on keyboards, HERMETO BOMBA on percussion and not forgetting 2nd TECHNICIAN A-JUNGLE BOOGIEBABY on drums.

1995. (cd) *(none)* **ULTRA-GROOVED**
– Funky fantastic / Fat vibration / Big steamroller / Chill / Glad to see you / Love train / Move closer / Lifestyle / Funky town / Dance / Ugly people.

10

mp3 bytes

Mainly artists/records that haven't found a home on the conventional label set-up, but have been snapped up by internet companies.

* * * * *

AETHER FLUX

- were a Cumbernauld noise trio comprising MATTHEW McVEY (guitars), LEE KIRK (bass) and SCOTT KELSO (drums & guitars), although from their formation in 1999, they've underwent a series of personnel changes. They are an experimental fusion of samples, loops and trips; featured on the V/A 2001 cd-album, 'Smoke' and you can download an EP, 'DON'T DO KIDS DRUGS' from their website.

AIERIS

- the phonetic spelling of "Iris". Comprising ANDY DORRAT (vocals & rhythm guitar), ALAN BELL (guitar & vocals), JOHN RONALDSON (bass & vocals) and GRAEME SUTHERLAND (drums), the melodious rock band from Dundee (who studied in Inverness, Perth, etc) all got together in summer 1999. Around a year later, several successful gigs had yielded airplay on BBC Radio Scotland, while a demo EP, 'MEET YOUR MAKER' was doing well. The appropriately-titled 'SOPHOMORE' EP also carried off minor awards (with top website Jockrock). Stints at King Tuts, The Venue and Dundee Rock City Festival are highlights so far.

May 00. (mp3-ep) **MEET YOUR MAKER**
– Down here and waiting / Meet your maker / Up and dreaming / Whatever man.
May 02. (mp3-ep) **SOPHOMORE**
– Better still / Blind / One of these days / Static.

AKIRA

- fuse SLEATHER-KINNEY and SONIC YOUTH and you have AKIRA; supported POST DILUVIAN, BELLATRIX, MOGWAI, . . .TRAIL OF DEAD. They were scheduled for one single, 'I DIZZY YOU' on 'Fierce Panda' in summer 2001 – must have been cancelled due to the circulation of another AKIRA.

ANGULUS

- were formed early 1999 in Leith, Edinburgh by CAIREEN HARRISON (guitar, vocals & keyboards), JAMIE THOMPSON (bass) and JOHN (guitar & vocals); drummer ALEX was added at this time. Touring regularly since that July, the strange beats'n'pop ANGULUS recorded an EP (which included 'EMOTIONLESS') at Granton's Chamber Studios in early 2000; the band have since split – CAIREEN and JAMIE are now with SLOWLORIS featuring ex-CHICANE man IAN JEFFRIES.

ASHTON LANE

- a youthful Glasgow-based 5-piece unit – consisting of three guys and two gals including teenager vocalist ESTHER DUFFIN, daughter of WET WET WET's GRAEME DUFFIN – who opened at King Tut's Wah Wah Hut in 2002's T In The Park. Described as Boho soul (folk, country + rock), their single, 'YESTERDAY'S TOO LATE', featured the classy singer who's recently been tipped for stardom.

BABACOOL

- are/were CALLUM MAGUIRE (vocals), SEAN HALLIDAY (guitar), WILLIE STARK (beatz & programming) and PAUL GILBODY (bass); dreamy additional vox stemming from NICOLA RODGER. She featured alongside new bassist STEVE VANTSIS on their mind-blowing EP, 'THE SPACE IN BETWEEN', late in 2000. Opening with the hard-driving PRIMAL SCREAM-esque beat of 'ONE IN A MILLION', and going through the downbeat 'PITY PAINT ME WITH CURLY TOES' and uptempo 'SATURATION', the Edinburgh breakbeat-rock act should have received greater recognition.

Milton BALGONI & THE BALGONI BOYZ

- actually began way back in 1986 to play a one-off Xmas gig at their local Cuinzie Neuk in Kinghorn, Fife. Out of the ashes of BLAZING APOSTLES, METAL FATIGUE and LIQUMAPIQUIE, MILTON BALGONI (vocals & guitar), WES WEMYSS (bass) and JOHN F KENNOWAY (drums) performed colourful punk'd-up versions of 'WHAT A DIFFERENCE A DAY MAKES' and 'GREEN GREEN GRASS OF HOME', while also adding their own er, compositions 'YIRERSE!', 'MARY MARQUIS (KENS MA FAITHER)' and 'BAD BAD BUGGER'. Described as "punkateers of anarcho-cabaret aural terrorism", all of their repertoire is available on their CD, 'MAIR LIVE THAN A JAKEY'S KEKS' (recorded live at Cupar Corn Exchange).

Dicky BILLS & THE COUNTERFEITTERS

- are from the Highlands and comprise NEIL KINGHORN (vocals & samples) and SLIMEY TOAD (bass). They have released one reggae/dub mp3, 'SUBURBAN RASTAMAN' in 2000; KELLY SILVER sings atmospheric vocals on the track, 'LIVIN'.

Stuart BLANCE

- is from Perth and has been compared to DAVID GRAY, BECK, PETER GABRIEL and FRAN HEALY (TRAVIS). Since 1998, STUART has spent over 100 hours in the studio coming up with internet album, 'UTOPIA' in 2002 – available through www.resemblancerecords.com. He has travelled to Glasgow, London and New York to get his acoustic songs across to the public; his track 'SLOWER THAN THE FLOW' was an internet hit.

BLOCO VOMIT

- were formed in Edinburgh . . . (also known as BLOCO V) 1995 by JOHN HICKS (vocals & guitar), CLAIRE HEWSON (bass) and SAM HICKS (percussion). These samba punk rockers, yes(!) punk classics served up their music in a Brazilian fashion. 40-something cross-dressing accountants/estate agents who should know better. They toured Portugal, Brazil, wrote a couple of songs themselves and covered such punk ditties as Alternative TV's 'LOVE LIES LIMP', Sex Pistols' 'PRETTY VACANT' and X-Ray Spex's 'OH! BONDAGE UP YOURS', on their debut for 'X Creature' records in '98.

Jul 98. (cd) **NEVER MIND THE BOSSA NOVA HERE'S BLOCO VOMIT**
– Do they owe us a living / Jilted John / Teenage kicks / Police and thieves / Pretty vacant / Metal postcard / Oh bondage, up yours! / Love lies limp / Gambinda nova / Should I stay or should I go / Roadrunner / D.T.'s in Droichead.
Jan 00. (cd) **PLAY THIS YA BASTARD**

BONE MACHINE

- deliver the goods heavy style. Hailing from Glasgow (1997) their line-up only just recently fragmented when bassman ALLAN COPE departed in February 2001; his replacement was GARY CRAIG, whoi they say added a new dimension to their sound. So far The BONE MACHINE have issued two demo EP's; self-financed of course.

BORIS YELTSIN LOVE XI

- formed in Edinburgh . . . 1997 by the pairing of electronics guy GASH ANDERSON and er, the other Boris's. An industrial dance outfit like NINE INCH NAILS meeting DEPECHE MODE, John Peel has even played their songs; 'IT GETS BETTER' sampled Crushzone's 'Tribal Dancing'.

Aug 98. (mp3-ep) **THE DRIVEN EP**
– Under your skin / Loveless / It gets better / Nutty love fingers / How would you like it to be?
Jan 99. (mp3-ep) **THE JUDY EP**
– Judy / Under your skin / Loveless / It gets better / Celebratory.
Oct 99. (mp3-ep) **DRACULA'S TEABAGS EP**
– Intro / This is the loveless / Fade away / Crawling / Tuan's day / Outro.
Aug 00. (cd-s) **THE DARLEY DANCE / THE DARLEY DANCE (instrumental) / MRS MAD MEETS THE LOVE XI IN A NAKED STATE (instrumental)**

BOTHAN

• comprise STEVEN LENNIE and ANDREW KELLY (the latter originally from Liverpool) and both live on the Isle of Scalpay in the Western Isles. They play an unusual blend of trance/techno, witnessed on a few TV appearances (mainly on BBC's Tacsi) and one self-financed CD, 'TAKE THREE TIMES' (2000).

BOVINE

• were formed in October 1998 in Stenhousemuir and Falkirk. A melodic pop-punk outfit, they comprise DAVID KING (vocals & guitar), ANDY HILL (guitar & vocals), CRAIG HAYWORTH (bass) and STEVEN TOSH (drums & vocals). So far they have only managed to sell/distribute one 3-track ('Tell A Lie', 'Angry Red Member' & 'Go!') EP at gigs, but they are promising to release an CD-album soon (it was recorded early 2002).

BOY CARTOGRAPHER

• are a trio based in Glasgow comprising ex-NOVA EXPRESS man ROWAN (drums & vocals), NEIL McDERMOTT (guitar & vocals) and DUNCAN ROBERTSON (bass & vocals); the latter two were 2/3rd's of late 90's trio PENTOTHAL (alongside MARTIN GILLON) who issued the 'WEST COAST' EP and sold it at gigs for £1. The BOY CARTOGRAPHER have now supported the likes of BALLBOY, SPARE SNARE, The STARLETS and MACROCOSMICA at all sorts of venues including The 13th Note, Nice'n'Sleazy's and the weekender in Leeds. Airtime has been allocated by Vic Galloway and John Peel, the latter having played their first demo which featured 'THRENODY', 'THE TEETH OF WIND AND WEATHER', 'SKETCH' and 'PACIFIC COAST NOWHERE', in 2002; all very honest, wistful but played with complex instrumentation.

BRESCHNEV

• are from Perth . . . 1999 and have played at their local . . . Friarton Prison, that is, T Break at T In The Park (2001). Comprising CRAIG MENZIES (vocals & guitar), RAB FAY (rhythm guitar), MARK PIRIE (keyboards & sampler), NEIL DEWAR (bass), RUSSELL STEWART (drums & percussion) and PAUL McGLASHAN (moog & percussion), BRESCHNEV have a sort of SPIRITUALIZED-meets-MOGWAI feel about them, although they play slightly differently . . . with their backs to the audience!

CAL

• was born MICHAEL CALLAGHAN, 27 Mar'63, Redding; raised in Slamannan, Stirlingshire. Always ambitious of becoming a singer, CAL (as he was nicknamed) left school to work in a foundry, although it was while toiling at his trade that he suffered a serious back injury which nearly paralysed him. That was around 1991. Recovering with a new guitar (and electric bagpipes) in hand and finally getting his first proper gig at the Dockers Club in Grangemouth in '95, CAL subsequently auditioned for the post of RUNRIG frontman (left by DONNIE MUNRO). Unfortunately, that place was filled by a Canadian. MICHAEL made up for the disappointment by releasing a few home-made cassettes (mid-late 90's). The new millennium began with a bang. He recorded his own Celtic-inspired songs alongside a couple of trad-folk ballads, including 'GREEN GROW THE RASHES, O' and 'COME BY THE HILLS'. The CD-album, '(SCOTLAND) A PART OF ME' (2000), almost immediately sold its first batch of 1000, prompting distributor 'Highlander' to package more albums for the overseas market; his success in 2001 could lead to RUNRIG thinking yet again.

own label

1996. (c) *(CAL 001C)* **ONE OF ONE**
– Breakfast at Tiffanys / Disco 2000 / Forever in blue jeans / White lightning / Wild mountain thyme / Alright / Gonna be a breeze / Don't want to forgive me now / Caledonia / Jessie / Circle of life / Everything I do (I do it fo you).

1998. (c) *(CAL 002C)* **VINTAGE YEARS**
– Sea of heartbreak / Gypsy woman / Stand by me / Medley: What do you want to make those eyes at me for? – I never felt more like singing the blues – King of the road / Rhinestone cowboy / You're my best friend / Your cheatin' heart / Mary Lou / Blanket on the ground / Only make believe / Please stay / Medley: Let's dance – No partucular place to go – The wanderer – OI hear you knockin' / Lucille – Great balls of fire / True love.

Dec 00. (cd) *(CAL 003CD)* **(SCOTLAND) A PART OF ME**
– Distant pipers / In her mother tongue / The lost days / Dochas naomha / In a new light / Green grow the rashes, O / (Scotland) A part of me / Rest and be thankful / Passion for the homelands / Old young boy / Come by the hills / Heaven to me.

CARTEL

• are a metal band from Dundee formed in January 2001. They comprise former POTENTIAL FOR INJURY members DAVE KERR (guitar) and BOB DONNACHIE (vocals); they subsequently found NEILL BIRSE (guitars), ECK ARCHIBALD (bass) – who replaced GAV BURTON and MIKE LINDSAY – and KEIR MURDOCH (drums). Insprired by 90's metal brigade of SLIPKNOT, RAGE AGAINST THE MACHINE, etc, they delivered two mp3 EP's 'WITH INTENT' and 'PARADIGM SHIFT' between mid 2001 to spring 2002.

CAYTO

• are a metal band from Glasgow comprising PAUL HENRY (vocals), GORDON 'NOBBY' NELSON (lead guitar), NEIL HENRY (bass), PAT McKENNA (drums) and ANDREW McLEAN (keyboards); the latter departed in 2001 after the recording two demos. Later that year, they surfaced from the studio with 'A SIN OF ADULT SWIMMING', a weird retro post-Grunge CD that opened with the 7-minute epic, 'EVIL COMES FROM THE NORTH'.

CINEPHILE

• are Scotland's newest experimental/dance/electronic wizzkids comprising producer ROBERT MORETTI and vocalist BEAUJEST. They have released their eerie, movie-centric mp3 debut in 2002, 'BEING HUMAN'.

CLAUDE INSECTE

• are from the Highlands and are WINSTON E. (vocals, guitar, drums & samples) and VON STREHLER (bass). Two mp3 sets have been released, 'FISH PRESIDENT' and 'HEON AGERR', basically alternative electro-funk.

CLOSER

• are from Glasgow and consist of childhood buddies DAVID WASON, (guitar & vocals), JOHN McCRACKEN (bass & vocals) and ANDREW MILLS (drums). From 1997's first gig at Qudos (in Glasgow's Queen Margaret Union), the CLOSER trio have been steadily rising up the proverbial ladder culminating in a prestigious Gig On The Green appearance in August 25th, 2002; INDY having replaced JOHN in summer 2002. A demo CD, 'LOVELIFE' was taken from post-millennium recordings, while CD-ep 'PRACTICE BEING HAPPY' (recorded in 1999) was frenetic and menacing buzzsaw rawk in the mould of FOO FIGHTERS or SMASHING PUMPKINS.

Wastingeeks not iss.

Nov 99. (cd-s) **GAY DISCO**

2000. (cd) **LOVELIFE**
– Olympus mans / Practice being happy / Anderson / Going / Another canvas day / Disco-necked / Sit astride the blame / Sweet / [Shy] / Vanity / Buttons / For you all / In case of the geek / Last night's mistake / [intermission . . .].

2000. (cd-ep) **PUBLIC DISPLAY OF AFFECTION**
– Chapter 7 / Come back to life / For you all / Vanity.

Low Profile not iss.

Jul 01. (cd-ep) *(LPR 01)* **PRACTICE BEING HAPPY EP**
– Practice being happy / Eleven / Blue piece / Post anxiety call.

DAMN QUAILS

• are a trio from Dundee (out of PIT O' SHARKS) comprising DAVE, JIMI and bassist BOB; the latter was replaced by another DAVE and then HAMISH (from PEEPS INTO FAIRYLAND). Formed in the mid-90's the guitar-based punk swing combo borrowed their slightly altered moniker from a certain American Vice President and the rest was history – although they haven't quite managed to give us any recordings bar a few V/A compilation appearances.

DEADLOSS SUPERSTAR

• from Aberdeen started out as SCUFF U.K. in 1996. By summer '98, BRIAN YOUNGSON (vocals), CRAIG MACNISH (guitar), MARTIN HILL (guitar), IAIN PATERSON (bass) and NICK TAYLOR (drums) all thought about a more rawkish moniker and came up with DEADLOSS SUPERSTAR. Having featured on two Aberdeen-label V/A compilations by 'Lithium' and 'Alphabetty', DEADLOSS SUPERSTAR signed a deal with internet imprint Peoplesound. A mini-debut, 'LIVING THE LIFESTYLE' (2000), was subsequently licenced to the 'Southside' label, as the band received constant airplay for their BLACK GRAPE-meets-FUN LOVIN' CRIMINALS approach.

Southside

2000. (mp3) **LIVING THE LIFESTYLE**
– Laughing gas (rock mix) / Springfield U.S.A. / Kiss / C'mon tiger! / Spit / Rising sun / Mainline 757 / Houston / In training / . . . Mors.

DEBASER

• were formed in August 1999 by ROSS THORBURN (guitar/vocals), ANDY MacLEOD (bass), MICHAEL LAMBERT (guitar) and EUAN DOUGLAS (drums/vocals); see below for further personnel changes. However, after an EP, 'MOODSWINGS . . .', one proper gig and a very limited pressing of an album, 'ANOTHER WEEKEND INDOORS', the band went off to university land (ANDY, MIKEE and ROSS to Edinburgh, EUAN to Strathclyde). The latter twosome started a group in the capital but by spring 2001, the pair re-formed DEBASER; commuting between Edinburgh, Perth and Dundee for education and gigs.

Apr 00. (mp3-ep) *(peoplesound)*
MOODSWINGSANDROUNDABOUTS EP
– Dream 29 / She died from cigarettes / Killing time / Coffee and cocaine.

munkee

Sep 00. (mp3-lpcd) *(munk 001cd)* **ANOTHER WEEKEND INDOORS**
– Track one / She died from cigarettes / Like the stars / Killing time / Wasted / Bouncy song / Hell and high water / Sell out / Curse of life / 11:21 / Coffee and cocaine / Adios / All she wants for Christmas.

—— (Apr'01) **JASON LOYD-ELWYN BLYTH** – drums, vocals; repl. EUAN

May 01. (mp3-ep) **IT'S FAR TOO EASY TO GET THINGS RIGHT**
– This is not clever / Fuck you / Shutdown / Love song / Where did the time go? / Acoustic song.

—— now without MICHAEL/MIKEE who set up SGT. ROCK

Gazpacho

Jan 02. (cd-ep) *(none)* **THIRTY FINGERS**
– This is / Slow suicide / Scarlet fever / She / I'm sorry / Swing.

—— (Aug'02) added **HELLEN MacLEOD** (ANDY's sis) – guitar (of FLAUZE)

—— (Sep'02) **GRANT** – drums; repl. JASON; he was also solo as DJ FLOAF

—— now go to POLICE CONTROL for ROSS's extra activities

DOLPHIN BOY

• is from Edinburgh and into leftfield types of music – 'TRACK 1' being his own; www.blokshok.com stated that he was raised by dolphins after his parents were killed in a plane crash – what's this all about, man?

DYING SUN

• were formed in Newton Mearns, Glasgow . . . mid-90's initially as a 5-piece, although when the singer dropped out, leader GRAEME DUFF (vocals & guitar), SCOTT MILLER (vocals & guitar), KEVIN BURGES (bass & noises) and MALKY T (drums), carried on regardless. 1997 saw their demo 'COLD BLACK EMPTY FEELINGS' being circulated, while support slots to KARMA TO BURN and ORANGE GOBLIN followed on. Stoner-rock crossing PANTERA and ANATHEMA best described this noisy metal crew, witnessed on their first MP3 release, 'PRIME ORDEAL' (1998). However, after the follow-up, 'NONDESCRIPT?' (1999), the quartet decided a change of moniker was needed. They came up with the er, nondescript? MARSHAN and toured England when they could get some ready cash.

1997. (demo) **COLD BLACK EMPTY FEELINGS**

May 98. (mp3) **PRIME ORDEAL EP**
– The bitter memory / As the snow falls / Faithless / Sorrow's smile / Betrayal / Cold blood (acoustic).

Jan 99. (mp3) **NONDESCRIPT? EP**
– Half mast / F.E.A.R. / Slagwaste.

FIGHTING RED CHAIR

• have been around since mid 2000 and are based in Lanarkshire. They comprise JAMES D (bass), MARV (guitar) and KENNY (drums) and sound a little like FUGAZI and JESUS LIZARD; a 7-track mini-set 'AURAL EXCITER' was issued in 2002.

FUSE

• got into gear in the summer of '97. Carnoustie and Edinburgh lads ROB DOIG (guitar), KIRK KETTLES (vocals), MIKE CRANSTON (bass) and DAVE 'MIXU' McCLORY (drums) – nicknamed after a local football striker, no doubt – were only getting under way in rehearsals when members duly bailed out; a new rhythm section of GARTH COATES and CRAIG STARK were subsequently found, although they were duly SPINAL TAP'd many times over. The FUSE have released a few bluesy/indie-rock demos and have had interest from 'V2' and 'Roundhouse' records.

GODS' MONKEY

• were formed in Edinburgh . . . 1994 when thirty-somethings FRASER WOOD (rhythm guitar), STUART KENNEDY (lead guitar) and KEN CAMPBELL (vocals & rhythm guitar) decided to form a band. The former's better half GILL then introduced the loud rock trio to rhythm and ex-UNREAL guys, PETER JOHNSTONE (bass) and JAMES JAFFERY (drums). Totally independent, their policy is to raise money to buy better PA systems, etc. This cash would be generated from sales of the CD's (see below).

own label not iss.

1995. (c-ep) *(none)* **A BURNING AMBITION**
– Here comes the rain (Jaff's jam) / Running man / Seafarer / Trusting you / Food and champagne / (Everything starts with a) F.

—— (1996) added **LYNNE MITCHELL** – keyboards, vocals

—— in 1997, they contributed three tracks, 'FANTASTIC LIES', 'WATCHING PAINT DRY' and 'SKOWHEGAN', to the V/A compilation, 'The Pentland Files'

—— now without KENNEDY who left after contributing to the former track

1998. (cd) *(none)* **HOLDING COURT**
– Gravity well / King Cane / Falling down / Fantastic lies / Lost / Second bends / Skowhegan / Watching paint dry / Tall houses / Touch of an angel / Borderland / Metalhead.

Aug 00. (cd) *(none)* **MILTONS ANGEL**
– Rubberman / All said and done / Breathe / Carrion for breakfast / Stickman / Talisman / Engines of God / Still life / Melt down / Strange world / Empty vessels.

GRAPEFRUIT

• are from Dundee and play indie-pop much like that of idols HURRICANE #1 and OASIS. Guitarist RIKKI's claim to fame is that his old band The FRASERS nearly signed to 'Virgin'; things might've been different if a certain 'Creation' boss ALAN McGEE hadn't snapped up lead singer ALEX LOWE to join ex-RIDE man ANDY BELL with his new pop venture. GRAPEFRUIT (with JIM - vocals, BOB - bass, and GARY - drums), meanwhile, left it a bit late to get the attention they seeked, although mp3's are available; seek out 'ORANGES AND LEMONS', 'THIS IS EASY' and 'SUNBURN'.

GREEBO

• were formed in 1999 having abandoned the name CADMUS and their lead singer. After settling with the line-up of songwriter MICHAEL COLL (vocals & guitar), MARK CAIRNS (drums & vocals), MICHAEL KING (bass) and NEIL DAWSON (guitars), the band from Glasgow played their first gig at their local Strawberry Fields; they have since featured on V/A compilation, 'Smoke'.

INDIGOECHO

• started out in Edinburgh . . . May '98. CLIVE PARNELL, along with ANDY, GARY and RIK, performed the odd gig around the capital and beyond; England's Greenbelt Festival was one such concert. A type of 90's Christian rock in the mould of DELIRIOUS, U2, RADIOHEAD or TRAVIS, the quartet began filling halls such as the Traverse Theatre. Early in 2000, 'Room3' records delivered their debut set, 'ONE' to the internet, while the band continued to entertain audiences nationwide. • **Note:** There is also a 5-track CD-EP by CLIVE PARNELL & BAND (3-piece) entitled 'LISTEN'; it was recorded 1997/98 before guitarist RIK came on board.

ITALIAN ELECTRO

• were a mysterious boy/girl duo based in Glasgow. Wearing shades to disguise their electro-pop antics, ITALIAN ELECTRO and Japanese crew KUMARI split their debut single for 'Catmobile' (PO Box 3726, Glasgow G42 9YR); it received a few airplays on the John Peel radio show.

Mar 00. (7") *(CMOB 01)* **ITALIAN ELECTRO – Don't Come Back Alone /** *KUMARI – Candy Tears*

KASINO

• are a 4-piece from Glasgow . . . 1998 comprising vocalist/guitarist GARY MARSHALL, guitarist MARK CLINTON, bassist CHRIS WARDEN and drummer CALUM MacARTHUR (from the Isle of Lewis); their 'FEARLESS' album in 2002 featured new bassist JOHN CLARKE and guitarist DAVID MARSHALL (from Inverness). KASINO mix catchy anthemic MANICS, U2, RADIOHEAD hooks with rawking guitar witnessed on their mp3-ep, 'YOU DON'T HAVE TO BE ALONE'; over 40,000 got it for free on the internet. Young, loud and shouty, KASINO were described as epic and should surely have went on to bigger and better things, although they did appear on Grampian TV's 'Nochd Gun Chadal' programme; DJ Jim Gellatly played a few of their songs on his Beat 106 radio show.

Sarcastic

Jul 00. (cd-ep) **YOU DON'T HAVE TO BE ALONE**
– Eyes / Catch / Turnaround / You don't have to be alone.

2000. (cd) **FEARLESS**
– Turn the skies grey / Who set you up? / Never see / Shy / Microcelebrity / Pigfear / See you fall / The state we're in / Not enough / Bonnie & Clyde.

KNIGHTRIDER

• were a Scottish retro-psychedelic outfit that sounded a tad too 60's and well over-produced.

own label not iss.

Apr 01. (7") **ONE NIGHT STANDS. / ELECTRIFY ME**
(cd-s+=) – Get me out.

John LEE

• is a singer/songwriter/poet from Inverness (b. 1968). Accompanied by guitarist ROBIN ABBOT, the acoustic JOHN LEE has delivered two self-financed CD's 'SWIM' and 'THROUGH THE DRIVING RAIN'.

LIGHTS OUT BY NINE

• formed in 1987 and are a hard-grafting 9-piece R&B outfit from all over Scotland who have played numerous gigs around the world including Germany, Russia, Scandinavia and Edinburgh's Princes Street Gardens. Featuring AL HUGHES (vocals, slide guitar & harmonica), ALAN KYLE (guitar & vocals), DOUGIE HUNTER (bass), GRAHAM KEY (keyboards), PETER MEANEY (sax), RICHARD MUSZYNSKI (trumpet), PAUL HADDOW (trombone), IAIN DOUGLAS (drums) and ALAN (CONNY) McCONNACHER (percussion), the band have self-financed one CD, 'MOVING ON' and a single 'ON A NIGHT LIKE THIS'. AL, DOUGIE and ALAN had played with the band SIDE EFFECTS from 1980-1984. Veteran AL HUGHES has also released a few CD's, the eponymous 'AL HUGHES' and 'SITTING ON SUPERBAD'S HAT'.

LIQUID LUNCH

• were formed in Edinburgh . . . 1997 by the lads McCUSKER, McGREGOR, ROBERTSON, ROGERS and SUTHERLAND (surnames supplied on record). Vanity publishing struck once again when their own 'Bourbon Sunday Records', released 'RED SIX' EP in '98.

Bourbon Sunday — not iss.

1998. (cd-ep) *(none)* **RED SIX E.P.**
– One stage to another / Red six / Satellites / All eyes on us.

MADMAN IS ABSOLUTE

• are one of the newest kids on the metal block. Comprising TONY NEWALL (vocals), DAVID SANDFORD (guitar), JIM RAFFERTY (bass) and MARTIN DOYLE (drums), the Glasgow hardcore noiseniks – fuse DILLINGER ESCAPE PLAN with MESHUGGAH – delivered their first 7-track EP, 'COMPLIANCE IS COMPULSORY' in September 2002. Two years previously, they had one MP3 demo track available, 'BLUEPRINT FOR NIHILISM'.

MAN MOUNTAIN

• from the Highlands released the CD, 'THE EDGE' in 2000, an electronic Celtic/World fusion attempt lying somewhere between AFRO CELT SOUND SYSTEM, DEEP FOREST and SHOOGLENIFTY.

MERCURY TILT SWITCH

• from Dundee, had been around for some time before they finally got around to releasing their own records; they just could be one of the small bands to make it big. Comprising ANTHONY BRACHI (guitar), MARTIN ROBISON, LES OGILVIE, CHRIS BRIDHES and singer ANDY McGARRY (ex-guitarist ANDY TEMPLE now plays with the DAMN QUAILS), MTS – who were being compared to IDLEWILD, the PIXIES and HUNDRED REASONS – were getting all sorts of attention from the likes of 'Fierce Panda'. In 2002, they delivered a split mail-order single with YAKUSA courtesy of '1970 Recordings' through their own 'Pet Piranha' imprint; the same set up had already delivered debut mini-CD 'BRUNDLE KID' that October.

— they released 2 EP's in 2000:- 'CHRONIC' and 'HEAVEN LEFT ME WHERE I'M STANDING UP'

Pet Piranha

Mar 01. (cd-ep) *(PP 001)* **KNOW WHERE YOUR EXITS ARE**

2002. (cd) *(PP 002)* **BRUNDLE KID**
– Caffeine avalanche / Radar response / Tall trees / There is no such thing as a freak wave / Edge of the swimming pool / Half time Shankly / Where is Charlie Brown? / Carter 78 / Firefly strike / Casualties in the global village.

2002. (7"ep) *(PP 003V)* **split with YAKUSA**
– There is no such thing as a freak wave / Caffeine avalanche / + 2 by YAKUSA.

— they are about to release a split 7" with SPYAMP

MIRACLE PILLS

• consist of Eastwood High School mates GRAEME 'DEV' DEVLIN (on bass), LAURIE MacKINTOSH (on drums) and CHRIS FULLERTON (the latter a one-time guitarist of LATE NIGHT FOREIGN RADIO). Hailing from Dundee, CHRIS soon took his guitar to Glasgow and met Belfast-born MARTY McCOMB, another guitarist; The MIRACLE PILLS were now a quartet. So far, they have made no records.

MY LEGENDARY GIRLFRIEND

• were formed in Glasgow . . . 1996 by clean-cut vocalist PAUL McGAZZ (with a student loan apparently!), who invited the boyish ENZO MENONI (bass), the serious NEIL DAWSON (guitar) and the Oriental JENNY WAN (keyboards) to join his musical club. Taking their group moniker from a PULP track, MLG plied their alt-pop, cod-reggae/ska style-ee like The BEAT meeting The POLICE. After a few demos/mp3's, etc, they inked a deal with Nottingham-based label 'Short Fuse'.

Short Fuse — not iss.

Nov 99. (7"ep) *(SFUSE 02)* **CREOSOUND EP**
– A kidnapper's lament / Superior / Staying in / Winter sun.

Dec 00. (7"ep) *(SFUSE 05)* **UNFASHIONABLY HI-FI EP**
– Operation London / When the music stops / Big white haircut / Hey! Adric.

2002. (mp3-ep) **FAMILY FOUR TUNES**

ANDI NEATE

• A stylish singer-songwriter from Scoraig in Wester Ross; a charismatic lady of the Northern pop and rock world.

own label — not iss.

Jun 00. (cd) *(PL 001)* **ICARUS**
– Want to believe / Inside / Six week itch / Feeling guilty / I'm undone / Crazy girl / See what I'm missing / Wanted it all / My life / No sense / In the city / Icarus.

NIBUSHI SHANG HONG

• comprise SIMON ALEXANDER, ALAN BROGAN, RONNIE BROWN and 19-year-old ANGI MOORE. In 2001, the Glasgow pop/rock band (perm any x The WONDER STUFF, KINGMAKER and SUPERGRASS), receives 'Single Of The Fortnight' in The List mag for their 'EVERYTHING YOU NEED TO SURVIVE' EP. Having been picked to support a re-formed WONDER STUFF and JESUS JONES gig at Glasgow's Barrowlands and playing regularly at King Tut's, NIBUSHI delivered a sophomore EP, 'DESPERATE TO PAYOUT' in 2002.

Hong — not iss.

Sep 01. (cd-ep) *(HONGCD 01)* **EVERYTHING YOU NEED TO SURVIVE**
– Leading to little street / Aqualung / Before tomorrow / Song in 3 parts.

Apr 02. (cd-ep) *(HONGCD 02)* **DESPERATE TO PAYOUT**
– Every picture / Jim'll fix it / Classic in the key of g / Howzitmakeufeel?

Noisewave productions

• is a fanzine/webpage label run by Pete Syme and based in Glasgow (28 Mary Gardens, to be exact!) since the early 90's. They mainly cater for Scottish bands like Stirling's TEMPTING KATE, The NEARLYS and PARKER. TEMPTING KATE consist of two Fifers vocalists/guitarists PETE – vocals & guitar and TAM – guitar; the two fellow punk-hating ABBA-lovers from south of the border were rhythm section CRAIG and PAUL; 'WAITING FOR NOTHING' is their mp3 EP. The NEARLYS (aka MARTIN – drums, WOODY – bass, DAVID – vox and BRYAN – guitar) were on the go in the early 90's and play a type of PROCLAIMERS meets R.E.M. style thing. PARKER have been going under various monikers including MEDIA FALLS and The TONGS. The pop-rock sextet have issued one EP, 'BIZARRE AND DIVINE'.

Graeme E. PEARSON & THE MUTINEERS

• are folkies (probably should have been in Folk section) featuring GRAEME himself on vocals and guitar, DAVID VERNON (accordion), STEVE RHIND (drums) and ROY WATERSON (bass). They formed in Edinburgh 1993 and have self-financed a couple of CD albums, 'THE FIRST ALBUM' (1999) and 'THE SECOND ALBUM: HALF ALIVE IN EDINBURGH' (2000).

PENTOTHAL

• see the BOY CARTOGRAPHER above

POLICE CONTROL

• were a band started by DEBASER man ROSS THORBURN

Munkee

Jan 01. (mp3-ep) *(munk 004cds)* **CHOKE BY LO-FI**
– End again / My wee cloud / Waves (demo).

Aug 01. (mp3-ep) *(munk 007cds)* **NOT IMPRESSING ANYONE**
– Falling into the sea / Green flash trainers / Going nowhere nice / 2:38 to save the world . . .

POMEGRANATE

• appeared in the late 90's after VANESSA RIGG (vocals & viola) teamed up with STEF McGLINCHEY after the formed returned from Portugal to Glasgow. He and VANESSA set up their own home studio and planned to release a debut album in 2001, 'THIS ILLUSION SOUND', on 'Integral' records. The edgy but cool 'STARING AT THE SKIES' was one of their better known tracks and it received a few plays on Radio Scotland's 'Air'.

POST DILUVIAN

• are a punk-rock trio from Edinburgh who are undoubtably inspired by STEVE ALBINI and SONIC YOUTH. They self-financed their debut demo CD-ep,

'MEANS OF DESTRUCTION' (on '1970 Recordings') in November 2001; it contained 'Warsaw Pact', 'Singles Disco', 'All Present And Correct' and 'Naked Like Valentine'.

PULSAR

• is CRAIG WELDON, a former submarine pilot who was equally at home with ABBA (and who wouldn't be with at least two of them), IRON MAIDEN, classical (J.S. BACH) and Scottish folk music. Armed with a new synthesizer and a mic, WELDON recorded 11 tracks for 'SPLENDID!' (2000) in his Glasgow tenement flat. Also that year, the man (originally from Buxtehude and Rotterdam) featured on a 'Mothmouth' 7"ep V/A compilation, 'Mothballs volume 3', the track in question being the messy KRAFTWERK-meets-cyberpunk track, 'THE PEOPLE WITH COMPUTERS IN THEIR HEAD' (I think he has!). The following summer, PULSAR was one of nineteen unsigned Glasgow-based acts to feature on the 'Smoke' compilation; the track 'WANT YOU TO KNOW' – with guest vox from ROB HARLAND – was also on the CD-album's 13th Note launch set list. Sadly for WELDON, he had to put PULSAR (and his sophomore CD, 'NOIR') in the backburner for a bit while he took a "proper" day-time job in Birmingham.

Jan 00. (cd) *(Boss records)* **SPLENDID!**
– History of dance pt.1 / My eyes / Jenny is a full time flirt / Where did she come from? / Perfect song / When I fall in love / Craigieburn Wood / The things we do / Buttshaker / Splendid / Ten to 2.

QUEELUM

• are a mysterious experimental noise outfit based in and around Inverness. Influenced by classical, avant-garde and er, ZAPPA and ENO, QUEELUM unleashed three mp3 sets, 'GEM-STAR' (1996), 'COPENHAGEN' (1998) and 'OBERON TALES' (2000).

QUICKSAND

• were formed in Edinburgh . . . 1998 by 4-piece (unknown). They played The Venue and attracted a good following and were nearly picked up by 'Mother' (U2's label); QUICKSAND were voted Top 5 act in the city by George Duffin (Venue man).

RANGE#ELEVEN

• are ALAN YUILL (vocals), STEVE DICKSON (keyboards/vocals), GREGG MILLER (lead guitar), LEE NOON (drums) and DOUGIE MURRAY (bass); the latter the grandson of comic genius CHIC MURRAY; one on-line album, 'KEEP IT RIGHT' has sold over 6,000 copies from 2001.

SINGLE POINT OF LIGHT

• were formed in the 00's by STEVEN, ROSS, PAUL and ROGER, a witty, fun-poking outfit from Glasgow (if there website is anything to go by); yes, "SINGLE POINT OF LIGHT are a rock band" but DAVE (their artist) thinks they're arty punks. Their most recent EP, 'THE ABSOLUTE', was available on their website or to buy at gigs; in September 2002 they performed at the Bull & Gate in London.

2001. (cd-ep) **ALWAYS UPWARDS**
– The same sky / Counting / For let read make.

2001. (cd-ep) **THERE IS HOPE**
– Island of the city / Sandgate / Pilot dog / Shikse.

Think Like This

2002. (cd-ep) **THE ABSOLUTE**

SKELTER

• have been based in Glasgow since 1998 and have become virtually resident at King Tut's. The line-up is ALI McMILLAN (vocals & guitar), PETER McCLURG (guitars) – both ex-RHYMES and HARMONICA JONES – with more recent additions ALAN DEANS and RICHIE and HEWITT on rhythm; they've so far released a couple of Lo-tech, pop/rock demos which they say.

SMACKVAN

• had waited 7 years to finally come up with an album of material. Mixing female & male vocals, 'Swimming Pool' released 'THE COMPANY OF WOLVES' set in early 2001. Hailing from Glasgow and Edinburgh, the moody and intense group also delivered a debut single in 1998, 'GENERATING' / 'COAST TO COAST' for 'Sano' records.

SNIBGLIDER

• are one of Scotland's hopefuls and from Cumbernauld (out of SUBROC and EXIT) . . . 1997. Comprising guitarist/songwriter TOM McCREERY, singer SCOTT WYLIE, bassist ANTS and drummer CHA(RLOS) TAGGART, this commercial indie quartet were hitting all the right notes when reviewed by the Daily Record way back on 3rd November, 2000. Having been courted by several major record labels, SNIBGLIDER – what does it mean? – entered manager Billy's studio to record their first album. Subsequent EP's, 'YESTERDAY TODAY', 'TECHNOPOSEUR' and 'HONEST' all surfaced via the internet and preceded an mp3 album in 2002.

SPEED RACER

• comprise JAMES QUINNEY (on guitar & vocals), MATTHEW (bass & cello) and DEL SPRINGER (drums, keyboards & backing vocals). Resurfacing from a summer 2000 studio campaign at Jamie Watson's Chamber Street Studios, the folk-pop SPEED RACER finally released their debut single, 'FOUNTAIN', for Irish-based imprint 'NEPtunes'. Supporting QUICKSPACE and TUNIC, the Edinburgh outfit, who now include former remix man DUNCAN REDDISH (on keyboards) and LAURA (on drums) and not DEL, played several gigs down south.

SQUANDER PILOTS

• are Glasgow's LAIKA, an eclectic, sample/dub-friendly trip-hop breakbeat outfit consisting of COLIN BAILEY (bass & toy keyboards), JOSEPH REEVES (programming & effects), ALUN WALLACE (guitar & piano) and DONNA SWABEY (smoky vocals, brass & keyboards). A dance group for the new millennium quite possibly, the SQUANDER PILOTS received some positive vibes from some of the music journos after playing local gigs at The 13th Note; a few singles have since appeared the last on Birmingham's small 'Neptune' records. The band were looking for a new bass player when COLIN departed in August 2002.

Sep 00. (cd-ep) **HOME & SAFE**
– Game over / Condiment / Say goodbye / Mustard / Condiment (reopened).

Neptune

Jul 01. (cd-s) **GIVEN / LUNAN / LUNAN (Maikeru remix)**

SUNDOWNS

• were Americana from the state of Edinburgh, a 5-piece alt-country outfit that released 'THE MERCHANT HOUSE TAPES' (for mp3) in July 2002.

TENESEE KAIT

• were based in Perthshire and formed in 1998 by CRAIG ROSS (vocals/guitar), CHRIS WARD (guitar), alongside the slightly younger GORDON DONALD (bass) and MARK McCABE (drums). Two high-energy alt-rock demos, 'THE ILLUSTRIOUS LIFE' and 'PRETTY PLEASE' showcased their brash early sound, support slots to fellow Scots BIFFY CLYRO and ANNIE CHRISTIAN preceded their web single, 'CHERRIES' in June 2002.

TOURIST INFORMATION

• sprung out from border town of Galashiels and comprised SHAQULIE CAFFEINE (drums), STIQUE FIN, GO-VAN and JENNYFOO. In the year 2000, they played the Green Fair festival but were disappointed when their T In The Park debut failed to materialise. PeopleSound, the dot.com imprint offered them a wee slice of money, but personnel changes (SHAQ moving to Ibiza to DJ) and GO-VAN's glandular fever became a little problematic.

TRANSAUDIO

• formed early in 1998 somewhere in Glasgow. Formerly of Dunfermline rock act The DREAM DISCIPLES, vocalist SCOTT PRENTICE and bassist STEPHEN/STEVIE McKEAN decided to change their direction into the big noise, techno-rock that was TRANSAUDIO; one single 'BLACK AND WHITE' was duly issued. Recruiting guitarist IAN COYLE and drummer STEPHEN DARROCH, the group played numerous gigs at King Tut's supporting such acts as COSMIC ROUGH RIDERS, CAMPAG VELOCET and ED HARCOURT. A couple of EP's were turned out for their growing fanbase and they opened for FISH on his 'Fellini Days' tour in April 2001. Still going strong over a year later, the band released their third EP 'AT-XS', while they also did a guest spot on the FRANKIE MILLER benefit concert in September 2002.

own label

May 98. (cd-s) **BLACK AND WHITE / REFLECTING ANGELS**

Aug 98. (cd-ep) **UNIQUE EP**
– Unique / Memory lies / Faithless.

Arcana

Oct 00. (cd-ep) **UNCUT EP**
– Stansted / Uncut / Unique / Open.

Mar 02. (cd-ep) **AT-XS EP**
– Another time / Excess / Comedown.

TRENT

• originate from Coatbridge and comprise of young 20-somethings PETE EVANS (vocals), STEPHEN 'SEEBY' LLEWELLYN (guitar), CRAIG MONTEITH (bass) and ROBERT TOAL (drums). They came to light after TEXAS invited the Daily

Record to help them find a support group for their 2000 tour; TRENT won and played in front of 10,000 on consecutive nights at the SECC. A five-track CD was subsequently issued while the band's 'CAN YOU HEAR ME?' was featured on a TV ad for the Original Shoe Co. TRENT were looking to be the Next Big Thing after this presitigious introduction but a single, 'TOP OF THE WORLD', never hit the shops; their www.trent.uk.com has since bit the dust.

TROIKA

• first appeared in 1999 and comprised NEIL MILTON (guitar & vocals), IAIN MURNIN (bass & vocals) and PAUL AGNEW (drums), although it wouldn't be until ANDY BONAR (vocals & guitar) moved in that TROIKA really got underway. Travelling to nearby Chem 19 studios in Hamilton and recorded by ANDY MILLER, the schizoid part melancholy/part noise-pop quartet finally released their first EP, 'MISSING PASSPORT', on NEIL's own 'Too Many Fireworks' imprint.

Too Many Fireworks

Jan 02. (cd-ep) *(2mfcd 001)* **MISSING PASSPORT e.p.**
– Are we? / Winter hair / Rip up the last words / Are we swimming (codeine effect mix).

UMBAH

• comprise ANT RYAN (vocals & bass), CAL SCOTT (guitar) and FINLAY LIGHT (drums). Out of Inverness thrash-metal outfit, NECROSANCT, who incidentally released two gory thrash-metal sets, 'INCARNATE' (1992) and 'DESOLATE' (1994); the latter adding rhythm guitarist CHRIS COOPER; as MICROCOSM they issued the 1996 CD, 'THE UMBAH EXPERIENCE'. With a complete overhaul in sound (ambient and synthesized with guitars), UMBAH have sorted out two mp3 sets so far, 'CONTINUUM' (1998) and 'SOLARIS' (2000).

Black Mark

Apr 92. (cd/c; as NECROSANCT) *(BMCD/BMCT 21)* **INCARNATE**
– Ritual acts / Inevitable demise / Undeath dead dying / Abhorence / Necronomicon / incarnate / Exiternity / Restless dead / Solace / Ominous despair / Oblivion seed.

Feb 94. (cd/c; as NECROSANCT) *(BMCD/BMCT 35)* **DESOLATE**
– Bleed / Reprisal / Plagued mind / Epitaph / Darkest fears / Chaotic vein / Black dawn / Manifest / Desolate / Dirge.

1996. (cd; as MICROCOSM) **THE UMBAH EXPERIENCE**

1998. (mp3) **CONTINUUM**

2000. (mp3) **SOLARIS**

VEER

• were formed in Edinburgh . . . 1997 by main writer PAUL BLACKWOOD, along with DOUG ANTHONEY, GORDON ANTHONEY, RICHARD CRAWFORD + SHANE GORMAN.

Veer not iss.

1998. (cd) **http://www.cheerfulhouse.ndirect.co.uk**
– Stingy puppy / Wrong angle / Basically D / Another astronaut / Loosehead / Something just / If I think I am / Foodtravelcompetition / Victoria comes undone / Silverman.

VENETIAN LOVE TRIANGLE

• were formed by STEF and GAZZ as a school band SOUR RED way back in 1993; they split in 1997. In September 1999, VENETIAN LOVE TRIANGLE were born when the pair recruited LEE. An EP was delivered early in 2000 and more V/A work followed on after it was sold out. With an album, AT BIRTH I DIDN'T HAVE A NAME', available on the net in September 2002, the trio of post-grunge noise were on their way to London and beyond; GAZZ subsequently moonlighted with 4-piece SERVO and STEF joined TENESEE KAIT.

VINYLREVERB

• formed in Motherwell . . . 2000. "JAMIE plays the drums, PAUL MARTIN sings, SIMON strums the guitar and on-one knows what DOC does!!" is how their webpage reads; it must be the bass? (GRANTY was once their part-time keyboard player). Although they managed to get a place on the V/A compilation set, 'Smoke', the fiery rock group have released only two EP's, 'ACT THE FOOL' (JJRCD 001) and 'MAD ROCKETS: EMPTY POCKETS' (JJRCD 002) both on 'JamJar' records.

VIVA STEREO

• are now based in Glasgow having arrived from the outskirts of the city. Stow College student STUART GRAY (vocals & synths), ROB McKINLAY (vocals & guitar), Larbert-born DOUG HENDRY (guitar), Stirling-raised TIM TROUP (bass & vocals) and Falkirk bairn JAMES ARCHIBALD (drums) formed in June 2001. They have delivered two EP's so far and have been compared to SPIRITUALIZED, HAPPY MONDAYS and THE BETA BAND.

Much Better

Feb 02. (cd-ep) **TRY HARDER EP**

Sep 02. (cd-ep) **LAST SCENE EP**

WHITEROOM

• were a baggy Edinburgh boy/girl outfit who'd forgotten the Madchester scene was a decade prior to their 2001 mp3 single, 'MUSIC IN MY HEAD'; bring back The FARM.

WONDERING-I

• are another mp3 outfit to emerge from Inverness. Technotroniq, jungle and breakbeat were all adjectives to describe 'I, listen to the 'SNUFFfICTION' (2000) set to indulge in their original fusions.

X-TIGERS

• are from Edinburgh and played their first gig In Edinburgh in September 2001. SEAN (vocals & guitar), ANNMARIE (drums), MAL (guitar) and DARREN (vocals & bass) subsequently played a live session for BBC Radio Scotland and turned out at T In The Park. Fuse ZIGGY-period BOWIE with an offbeat PIXIES and you might be close to their sound.

ZOIDBERG

• have released two records so far, the 8-track EP, 'DISCRIMINATION FOR FUN' a split 7" with MOTORMARK, 'OUR MONKEY SONG'. MATT and MARTIN (originally hailing from Scarborough and Peterhead respectively) formed the rocking VAN HALEN-meets-CARTER-like outfit (2 guys and a beatbox) in 2000.

• I should also give a mention to other hopefuls (who didn't/haven't quite managed to make it):- AFTER THE WAVES (punks from Denny fronted by JOHNNY GORDON), ALKAHOUNDS (indie-guitar band from Glasgow), BASH STREET KIDS (comedy rock from Aberdeen), BIG GEORGE & THE BUSINESS (blues outfit from the late 70's; leader George Watt), BIGGER THAN BOB (from Glasgow), Andy CHUNG (Oriental/Scots trad-folk performer with 2 CD's), CONEY ISLAND CYCLONE (Edinburgh noise-trio; drummer later to HUCKLEBERRY), COPS AND ROBBERS (with Falkirk guitarist Colin Green), CRUZER (indies from Dundee), DAZES (from Motherwell), DEFT JERKS (from Falkirk . . . late 70's by DOUGIE AITKEN, GRANT, STUART CUTHELL, CHARLIE HAY and GEORGE FALCONER; IAN 'HARRY' HARRISON, BILLY TAYLOR and ROY JACK were in Mk.II), DOOLAH (post-millennium punk-grungers from Edinburgh), DRIFT (from Glasgow), ELIUS, ELEMENTAL (Edinburgh funk), FEed! (from Falkirk who've got a recording contract), FIRBALL (connections to TAM! and COADE), GAELS BLUE, HONEY (from Glasgow), HUCKSTERS, IGNATZ, IVES (on the 'Smoke' V/A set), LATE NIGHT FOREIGN RADIO (from 'Smoke'), LIES DAMNED LIES, ONEROOT (late 90's Kerrang!-friendly metal quartet from the 01236 area – about to sign to Glasgow's 'Silent Music' label), MAGNIFICENTS (from Edinburgh and fronted by TOMMY STUART), MENTAL ERRORS (punks from Paisley), MEROCAINE (5-piece punks from Dundee), METHYL ORANGE (metal from Fife), MOODY (are alt-rock from Glasgow consisting of vocalist DEREK SEMPLE, guitarist DAVID SWEENEY, guitarist J.P. PAYNE, bassist ANDY LEAMAN and drummer NIALL RUSSELL), MOONDIALS (from Glasgow), MOUSE ORGAN (who covered Simon & Garfunkel's '53rd Street Bridge Song'), OFF THE WALL (from Shieldhill near Falkirk; MARION, GLENNY and BIG TAM), PLASTIC MERINGUE, SAZ (from Dundee), REVERBAPHON (aka PAUL SMITH), SILVER PILLS (featuring PAUL WHITELAW on EP, 'The Martian Chronicles'), SINISTER TURKEYS, SPYAMP (from Dundee), SWELLBELLYS (from Falkirk), TANTARA BLADE, 3D SCREAM (from Glasgow), THIRDWAY (4-piece like Feeder & Nirvana; released an mp3 in October '99, 'COMFORT DON'T WAKE ME' EP), THRUSH (70's/80's country-folk act from Falkirk with DAVIE WAUGH, DICKIE DOW, NORRIE STURROT and DEREK LENAHAN), TISSUM (from Glasgow), TRIBE (a 6-piece from Fife), UNDERWATER GEORGE (from Arbroath), UNSKILLED LABOUR (from Dundee), VINYL JUSTICE (millennium Perth College punks with PETE, JOHN, HARRIS and KEGS), WILD RIVER APPLES, YOUNG GIRLS WANTED (from Dundee area).

Index

Artists / Bands / Record-labels

A

B

C

D

E

F

G

W

X

Y

Z